W9-ACW-377

ENCYCLOPEDIA OF

ARCHITECTURE

DESIGN, ENGINEERING & CONSTRUCTION

EDITORIAL BOARD

ENCYCLOPEDIA OF ARCHITECTURE
DESIGN, ENGINEERING & CONSTRUCTION

JOSEPH A. WILKES, FAIA
Editor-in-Chief

ROBERT T. PACKARD, AIA
Associate Editor

VOLUME 3
Industrialized Construction
to
Polyesters

A WILEY-INTERSCIENCE PUBLICATION

JOHN WILEY & SONS

New York • Chichester • Brisbane • Toronto • Singapore

*For her help in so many ways,
this encyclopedia is dedicated to
my wife Margaret.*

Library of Congress Cataloging in Publication Data:

Encyclopedia of architecture.

"A Wiley-Interscience publication."
Includes bibliographies.
Contents: v. 3. Industrialized Construction to Polyesters
1. Architecture—Dictionaries. I. Wilkes, Joseph A. II. Packard, Robert T.

NA31.E59 1988 720′.3 87–25222
ISBN 0–471–63244–9 (v. 3)
ISBN 0–471–63351–8 (set)

Printed in the United States of America

10 9 8 7 6 5 4 3 2 1

EDITORIAL STAFF

Editor-in-chief: Joseph A. Wilkes, FAIA
Associate Editor: Robert T. Packard, AIA
Managing Editor: Stephen A. Kliment, FAIA
Editorial Supervisor: Karen M. Trost

Production Manager: Jenet McIver
Production Supervisor: Jean Spranger
Designer: Jean Morley

CONTRIBUTORS

Nezar Alsayyad, *Albany, Calif.,* Mosques
Blair Anthony, *GE Plastics, Pittsfield, Mass.,* Polyesters
Francis Baden-Powell, *R M J M, London, U.K.,* International Practice
Samuel T. Balen, FAIA, *National Council of Architectural Registration Boards, Washington, D.C.,* National Council of Architectural Registration Boards (NCARB)
Eric Balinski, *GE Plastics, Pittsfield, Mass.,* Polyesters
Abel Banov, *Greenvale, N.Y.,* Paints and Coatings
Steven Bedford, *Middlebury, Conn.,* Noyes, Eliot
Mitchell Benjamin, *Montreal, Canada,* Music Halls
Guita Boostani, *Albany, Calif.,* Mosques
Susan Braybrooke, *London, U.K.,* Laboratories
Paul Broches, AIA, *Mitchell/Giurgola Architects, New York, N.Y.,* Mitchell/Giurgola Architects
Brent C. Brolin, *New York, N.Y.,* Ornament in Architecture
John Bukowski, *The Asphalt Institute, College Park, Md.,* Paving Systems, Asphalt
Juan Carlos Calderon, *Florida A & M University, Tallahassee, Fla.,* Latin American Architecture
Donald Carter, *CT-Plus, Inc., Kensington, Md.,* Plumbing Systems
Barbara Chabrowe, *Washington, D.C.,* Piano, Renzo
Donald Coe, *Borg-Warner Chemicals, Washington, W.V.,* Plastics, ABS
Michael Cohn, *The American Institute of Architects, Washington, D.C.,* Justice Buildings—Law Enforcement, Courts, and Corrections
Michael J. Crosbie, PhD, *Branford, Conn.,* Pattern-book Architecture
Manuel Cuadra, *Technische Hochschule Darmstadt, Darmstadt, FRG,* Kraemer, Friedrich W.; Neufert, Ernst
Sarah A. Cuniff, *Berkeley, Calif.,* Mediation in Architectural and Construction Disputes
Charles M. Custin, *Tech-Aerofoam Products, Inc.,* Miami, Fla., Plastic Laminates
Peter Dalrymple, *GE Plastics, Pittsfield, Mass.,* Polycarbonates
Mary Dean, *New Haven, Conn.,* Literature of Architecture
Alphonse J. Dell'Isola, *Smith Hinchman & Grylls, Washington, D.C.,* Life-cycle Costing
Albert G. H. Dietz, PhD, *Winchester, Mass.,* Plastics
Karen J. Dominguez, *Pennsylvania State University, State College, Pa.,* Industrialized Construction (Engineered Buildings—Prefabrication); Morgan, Julia; National Architectural Accrediting Board (NAAB); Paxton, Joseph
M. David Dubin, FAIA, *Dubin Dubin & Moutoussamy, Chicago, Ill.,* Inspection, Observation, and Supervision
Edward G. Echeverria, *Washington, D.C.,* Planned Communities (New Towns)
Paula Echeverria, *Washington, D.C.,* Planned Communities (New Towns)
Joyce Elliott, *National Building Museum, Washington, D.C.,* National Building Museum
Benjamin H. Evans, FAIA, *Virginia Polytechnic Institute & State University, Blacksburg, Va.,* Lighting—Day Lighting; Lighting—Electric
Edwin Feldman, PE, *Service Engineering Associates, Inc., Atlanta, Ga.,* Maintenance, Building
David P. Fogle, AICP, *University of Maryland, College Park, Md.,* Jefferson, Thomas; Latrobe, Benjamin; L'Enfant, Pierre; Niemeyer, Oscar; Palladio, Andrea
Eric O. Forster, PhD, *Scotch Plains, N.J.,* Insulation, Electrical

Patrick J. Galvin, *Galvin Publications, East Windsor, N.J.,* Kitchens, Residential

David Geiger, Phd, *Geiger KKBNA, New York, N.Y.,* Membrane Structures

Lewis S. Goodfriend, *Lewis S. Goodfriend and Associates, Cedar Knolls, N.J.,* Noise Control in Buildings

Nora Greer, *The American Institute of Architects, Washington, D.C.,* Mixed-use Buildings

Besim Hakim, Islamic Architecture and Urbanism

Mark A. Hewitt, *Columbia University, New York, N.Y.,* Jones, Inigo; Lutyens, Edwin L.

William Hooper, Jr., AIA, *The American Institute of Architects, Washington, D.C.,* Joint Ventures

Edward Howell, *K & H Communications, Monterey, Calif.,* Liability Insurance

Gregory K. Hunt, *Virginia Polytechnic Institute & State University, Alexandria, Va.,* Lescaze, William; Neutra, Richard J.

Mark Isaacs, *Alexandria, Va.,* Isaacs, Reginald; Olmsted, Frederick Law

Reginald Isaacs (†), *Cambridge, Mass.,* Le Corbusier (Charles-Edouard Jeanneret); Mies van der Rohe, Ludwig

John M. Johansen, FAIA, *Johansen & Bhavnani Architects, New York, N.Y.,* Johansen, John M.

Jeh V. Johnson, FAIA, *Wappingers Falls, N.Y.,* Multifamily Housing

Y. Bertram Kinzey, Jr., AIA, *University of Florida, Gainesville, Fla.,* Mechanical Systems

Robert B. Klug, AIA, *The American Institute of Architects, Washington, D.C.,* Justice Buildings—Law Enforcement, Courts, and Corrections

Richard Krutenat, *Lowell, Mass.,* Metallic Coatings

Robert C. Lautman, *Washington, D.C.,* Photography, Architectural

Clark Lundell, AIA, *Auburn University, Auburn, Ala.,* Isozaki, Arata; Oriental Architecture

Louis R. Lundgren, FAIA, *St. Paul, Minn.,* Ownership of Buildings

Victor A. Lundy, FAIA, *Houston, Texas,* Lundy, Victor A.

Ruth Lusher, PhD, *Vienna, Va.,* Physical and Mental Disability, Design for

Ronald Mace, FAIA, *Barrier-Free Environments, Inc., Raleigh, N.C.,* Physical and Mental Disability, Design for

John McGough, FAIA, *The American Institute of Architects, Washington, D.C.,* Justice Buildings—Law Enforcement, Courts, and Corrections

Richard Meier, FAIA, *Richard Meier & Partners, New York, N.Y.,* Meier, Richard

Francisco J. Menendez, *Washington, D.C.,* Nervi, Pier Luigi

Frederic Moyer, AIA, *The American Institute of Architects, Washington, D.C.,* Justice Buildings—Law Enforcement, Courts, and Corrections

National Institute of Standards and Technology, *Gaithersburg, Md.,* National Bureau of Standards (NBS)

Robert T. Packard, AIA, *Reston, Va.,* Kahn, Albert; Kiesler, Frederich; Maekawa, Kunio; Maki, Fumihiko; Nelson, George; Nowicki, Matthew; Olbrich, Joseph Maria; Pevsner, Nikolaus

Allen Patrick, FAIA, *The American Institute of Architects, Washington, D.C.,* Justice Buildings—Law Enforcement, Courts, and Corrections

Jake Pauls, *Hughes Associates Inc., Wheaton, Md.,* Movement of People

Labelle Prussin, *The City University of New York, New York, N.Y.,* Nomadic Architecture

Richard E. Putscher, *E.I. du Pont de Nemours & Co., Inc., Wilmington, Del.,* Polyamides (Nylon)

George Rambo, *National Pest Control Association, Dun Loring, Va.,* Pest Control

Jerry P. Re, *Eugene, Oreg.,* Phenolic Resins

Peter Reed, *Philadelphia, Pa.,* Kahn, Louis I.

Raymond P. Rhinehart, *The American Institute of Architects, Washington, D.C.,* Media Criticism

Barry Riccio, *University of Illinois, Urbana, Ill.,* McKim, Mead & White

J. D. Richards, *Robert Matthew, Johnson-Marshall and Partners, Whitekirk, U.K.,* Matthew, Robert

Robert Rosenfeld, *National Council of Architectural Registration Boards, Washington, D.C.,* Intern Programs

J. Walter Roth, AIA, *Alexandria, Va.,* National Park Service

David W. Scott, PhD, *Washington, D.C.,* Museums

John P. Sheehy, AIA, *The Architects Collaborative, Cambridge, Mass.,* Office Buildings

Maree Simmons-Forbes, PhD, *The Forbes Group, Ltd., Washington, D.C.,* Office Facility Planning

Maeve Slavin, *New York, N.Y.,* Knoll, Florence

Steven Smith, *JHK & Associates, Orlando, Fla.,* Parking and Traffic Circulation

Walter Sobel, FAIA, *The American Institute of Architects, Washington, D.C.,* Justice Buildings—Law Enforcement, Courts, and Corrections

Alfred Steele, PE, *Chicago, Ill.,* Plumbing Systems

Charles Szoradi, *Washington, D.C.,* Mumford, Lewis

Danforth W. Toan, FAIA, *Warner Burns Toan Lunde, New York, N.Y.,* Libraries

George B. Tobey, *Carrollton, Texas,* Landscape Architecture

Jack Verschoor, *Bailey, Colo.,* Insulation, Thermal

Anne Vytlacil, *Chilmark, Mass.,* Ketchum, Morris; Markelius, Sven G.

Barbara L. Wadkins, *Chula Vista, Calif.,* Loos, Adolf

Ravi S. Waldon, AIA, *Bignell & Watkins, Annapolis, Md.,* Otto, Frei

Ralph Warburton, FAIA, *University of Miami, Coral Gables, Fla.,* Maybeck, Bernard

Gerald G. Weisbach, FAIA, *Natkin & Weisbach, San Francisco, Calif.,* Mediation in Architectural and Construction Disputes

Robert Woertendyke, *Owen & Mandolfo, Interior Design, New York, N.Y.,* Interior Design

Jeremy S. Wood, *The Architects Collaborative, Cambridge, Mass.,* Office Buildings

Robert Zwirn, *Miami University, Oxford, Ohio,* Johnson, Philip; Pei, Ieoh M.

† deceased

CONTENTS

CONVERSION FACTORS, ABBREVIATIONS, AND UNIT SYMBOLS

Selected SI Units (Adopted 1960)

Quantity	*Unit*	*Symbol*	*Acceptable equivalent*
BASE UNITS			
length	meter[†]	m	
mass[‡]	kilogram	kg	
time	second	s	
electric current	ampere	A	
thermodynamic temperature[§]	kelvin	K	
DERIVED UNITS AND OTHER ACCEPTABLE UNITS			
* absorbed dose	gray	Gy	J/kg
acceleration	meter per second squared	m/s^2	
* activity (of ionizing radiation source)	becquerel	Bq	1/s
area	square kilometer	km^2	
	square hectometer	hm^2	ha (hectare)
	square meter	m^2	
density, mass density	kilogram per cubic meter	kg/m^3	g/L; mg/cm^3
* electric potential, potential difference, electromotive force	volt	V	W/A
* electric resistance	ohm	Ω	V/A
* energy, work, quantity of heat	megajoule	MJ	
	kilojoule	kJ	
	joule	J	N·m
	electron volt[x]	eV[x]	
	kilowatt hour[x]	kW·h[x]	
* force	kilonewton	kN	
	newton	N	$kg \cdot m/s^2$
* frequency	megahertz	MHz	
	hertz	Hz	1/s
heat capacity, entropy	joule per kelvin	J/K	
heat capacity (specific), specific entropy	joule per kilogram kelvin	J/(kg·K)	
heat transfer coefficient	watt per square meter kelvin	$W/(m^2 \cdot K)$	
linear density	kilogram per meter	kg/m	
magnetic field strength	ampere per meter	A/m	
moment of force, torque	newton meter	N·m	
momentum	kilogram meter per second	kg·m/s	
* power, heat flow rate, radiant flux	kilowatt	kW	
	watt	W	J/s
power density, heat flux density, irradiance	watt per square meter	W/m^2	
* pressure, stress	megapascal	MPa	
	kilopascal	kPa	
	pascal	Pa	
sound level	decibel	dB	
specific energy	joule per kilogram	J/kg	
specific volume	cubic meter per kilogram	m^3/kg	

Quantity	*Unit*	*Symbol*	*Acceptable equivalent*
surface tension	newton per meter	N/m	
thermal conductivity	watt per meter kelvin	W/(m·K)	
velocity	meter per second	m/s	
	kilometer per hour	km/h	
viscosity, dynamic	pascal second	Pa·s	
	millipascal second	mPa·s	
volume	cubic meter	m^3	
	cubic decimeter	dm^3	L (liter)
	cubic centimeter	cm^3	mL

[*] The asterisk denotes those units having special names and symbols.
[†] The spellings "metre" and "litre" are preferred by ASTM; however "er-" is used in the Encyclopedia.
[‡] "Weight" is the commonly used term for "mass."
[§] Wide use is made of "Celsius temperature" (t) defined by

$$t = T - T_0$$

where t is the thermodynamic temperature, expressed in kelvins, and T_0 = 273.15 by definition. A temperature interval may be expressed in degrees Celsius as well as in kelvins.
[x] This non-SI unit is recognized by the CIPM as having to be retained because of practical importance or use in specialized fields.

In addition, there are 16 prefixes used to indicate order of magnitude, as follows:

Multiplication factor	*Prefix*	*Symbol*
10^{18}	exa	E
10^{15}	peta	P
10^{12}	tera	T
10^{9}	giga	G
10^{6}	mega	M
10^{3}	kilo	k
10^{2}	hecto	h[a]
10	deka	da[a]
10^{-1}	deci	d[a]
10^{-2}	centi	c[a]
10^{-3}	milli	m
10^{-6}	micro	μ
10^{-9}	nano	n
10^{-12}	pico	p
10^{-15}	femto	f
10^{-18}	atto	a

[a] Although hecto, deka, deci, and centi are SI prefixes, their use should be avoided except for SI unit-multiples for area and volume and nontechnical use of centimeter, as for body and clothing measurement.

Conversion Factors to SI Units

To convert from	*To*	*Multiply by*
acre	square meter (m^2)	4.047×10^{3}
angstrom	meter (m)	1.0×10^{-10}[†]
atmosphere	pascal (Pa)	1.013×10^{5}
bar	pascal (Pa)	1.0×10^{5}[†]
barn	square meter (m^2)	1.0×10^{-28}[†]
barrel (42 U.S. liquid gallons)	cubic meter (m^3)	0.1590
Btu (thermochemical)	joule (J)	1.054×10^{3}
bushel	cubic meter (m^3)	3.524×10^{-2}
calorie (thermochemical)	joule (J)	4.184[†]
centipoise	pascal second (Pa·s)	1.0×10^{-3}[†]
cfm (cubic foot per minute)	cubic meter per second (m^3/s)	4.72×10^{-4}
cubic inch	cubic meter (m^3)	1.639×10^{-5}
cubic foot	cubic meter (m^3)	2.832×10^{-2}
cubic yard	cubic meter (m^3)	0.7646

To convert from	*To*	*Multiply by*
dram (apothecaries')	kilogram (kg)	3.888×10^{-3}
dram (avoirdupois)	kilogram (kg)	1.772×10^{-3}
dram (U.S. fluid)	cubic meter (m^3)	3.697×10^{-6}
dyne	newton (N)	$1.0 \times 10^{-5\dagger}$
dyne/cm	newton per meter (N/m)	$1.0 \times 10^{-3\dagger}$
fluid ounce (U.S.)	cubic meter (m^3)	2.957×10^{-5}
foot	meter (m)	$0.3048^{\dagger}$
gallon (U.S. dry)	cubic meter (m^3)	4.405×10^{-3}
gallon (U.S. liquid)	cubic meter (m^3)	3.785×10^{-3}
gallon per minute (gpm)	cubic meter per second (m^3/s)	6.308×10^{-5}
	cubic meter per hour (m^3/h)	0.2271
grain	kilogram (kg)	6.480×10^{-5}
horsepower (550 ft·lbf/s)	watt (W)	7.457×10^{2}
inch	meter (m)	$2.54 \times 10^{-2\dagger}$
inch of mercury (32°F)	pascal (Pa)	3.386×10^{3}
inch of water (39.2°F)	pascal (Pa)	2.491×10^{2}
kilogram-force	newton (N)	9.807
kilowatt hour	megajoule (MJ)	$3.6^{\dagger}$
liter (for fluids only)	cubic meter (m^3)	$1.0 \times 10^{-3\dagger}$
micron	meter (m)	$1.0 \times 10^{-6\dagger}$
mil	meter (m)	$2.54 \times 10^{-5\dagger}$
mile (statute)	meter (m)	1.609×10^{3}
mile per hour	meter per second (m/s)	0.4470
millimeter of mercury (0°C)	pascal (Pa)	$1.333 \times 10^{2\dagger}$
ounce (avoirdupois)	kilogram (kg)	2.835×10^{-2}
ounce (troy)	kilogram (kg)	3.110×10^{-2}
ounce (U.S. fluid)	cubic meter (m^3)	2.957×10^{-5}
ounce-force	newton (N)	0.2780
peck (U.S.)	cubic meter (m^3)	8.810×10^{-3}
pennyweight	kilogram (kg)	1.555×10^{-3}
pint (U.S. dry)	cubic meter (m^3)	5.506×10^{-4}
pint (U.S. liquid)	cubic meter (m^3)	4.732×10^{-4}
poise (absolute viscosity)	pascal second (Pa·s)	$0.10^{\dagger}$
pound (avoirdupois)	kilogram (kg)	0.4536
pound (troy)	kilogram (kg)	0.3732
pound-force	newton (N)	4.448
pound-force per square inch (psi)	pascal (Pa)	6.895×10^{3}
quart (U.S. dry)	cubic meter (m^3)	1.101×10^{-3}
quart (U.S. liquid)	cubic meter (m^3)	9.464×10^{-4}
quintal	kilogram (kg)	$1.0 \times 10^{2\dagger}$
rad	gray (Gy)	$1.0 \times 10^{-2\dagger}$
square inch	square meter (m^2)	6.452×10^{-4}
square foot	square meter (m^2)	9.290×10^{-2}
square mile	square meter (m^2)	2.590×10^{6}
square yard	square meter (m^2)	0.8361
ton (long, 2240 pounds)	kilogram (kg)	1.016×10^{3}
ton (metric)	kilogram (kg)	$1.0 \times 10^{3\dagger}$
ton (short, 2000 pounds)	kilogram (kg)	9.072×10^{2}
torr	pascal (Pa)	1.333×10^{2}
yard	meter (m)	$0.9144^{\dagger}$

† Exact.

Acronyms and Abbreviations

AA	Archigram Architects
AAA	American Arbitration Association
AACA	Architects Accreditation Council of Australia
AAL	Association of Architectural Librarians
AAMA	American Architectural Manufacturers Association
AASHO	American Association of State Highway Officials
AASHTO	American Association of State Highway and Transportation Officials
AAT	Art and Architecture Thesaurus
ABA	Architectural Barriers Act
ABC	Alternate birthing center; Associate Builders and Contractors
ABNT	Associacao Brasileira de Normas Tecnicas

ABPMA	Acoustical and Board Products Manufacturers Association
ABS	Acrylonitrile–butadiene–styrene
AC	Alternating current
ACA	American Correction Association; Ammoniacal copper arsenate
ACEC	American Consulting Engineers Council
ACI	American Concrete Institute
ACS	Acrylonitrile–chlorinated polyethylene–styrene
ACSA	Association of Collegiate Schools of Architecture
ADC	Air Diffusion Council
ADL	Activities of daily living
ADPI	Air Distribution Performance Index
ADR	Alternative dispute resolution
AEC	Atomic Energy Commission
AEG	Allgemeine Elektricitats-Geselschaft
AEIC	Association of Edison Illuminating Companies
AEPIC	Architecture and Engineering Performance Information Center
AFD	Air filtration devices
AFL/CIO	American Federation of Labor and Congress of Industrial Organizations
AFNOR	Association Francaise de Normalisation
AFUE	Annual fuel utilization efficiency
AGA	American Gas Association
AGC	Associated General Contractors of America
AGIC	Architectural Group for Industry and Commerce
AGTS	Automated guideway transit systems
AHA	American Hardboard Association
AHAM	Association of Home Appliance Manufacturers
AHU	Air handler unit
AI	Articulation Index; Artificial Intelligence
AIA	American Institute of Architects
AIA/F	American Institute of Architects Foundation
AIAS	American Institute of Architecture Students
AIA/SC	American Institute of Architects Service Corporation
AICP	American Institute of Certified Planners
AID	Agency for International Development
AIKD	American Institute of Kitchen Dealers
AIREA	American Institute of Real Estate Appraisers
AISC	American Institute of Steel Construction
AISI	American Iron and Steel Institute
AITC	American Institute of Timber Construction
ALS	American Lumber Standards
AMA	Acoustical Materials Association
AMCA	Air Moving and Conditioning Association
ANSI	American National Standards Institute
APA	American Planning Association; American Plywood Association
APR	Air purifying respirators; Architectural program report
APS	Arrival point of sight
ARCC	Architectural Research Centers Consortium
ARCUK	Architects Registration Council of the United Kingdom
ARE	Architect Registration Examination
ARI	Air-Conditioning and Refrigeration Institute
ARLIS/N	Art Libraries Society of North America
ARMA	Asphalt Roofing Manufacturers Association
ARP	Air raid precaution
ASA	Acoustical Society of America; American Subcontractors Association
ASCE	American Society of Civil Engineers
ASET	Available safe egress time
ASHRAE	American Society of Heating, Refrigerating, and Air Conditioning Engineers
ASHVE	American Society of Heating and Ventilating Engineers
ASID	American Society of Interior Designers
ASLA	American Society of Landscape Architects
ASM	American Society for Metals
ASME	American Society of Mechanical Engineers
ASTM	American Society for Testing and Materials
ATA	Air Transportation Association of America
AtBat	l'Atelier des Batisseurs
ATBCB	Architectural and Transportation Barriers Compliance Board
ATC	Air Transport Command
ATM	Automatic teller machine
ATMA	American Textile Machinery Association
A/V	Audio/video
AWG	American wire gauge
AWI	Architectural Woodwork Institute
AWPA	American Wood Preservers Association
AWPB	American Wood Preservers Bureau
AWT	Advanced wastewater treatment
BBC	British Broadcasting Company
BBN	Bolt Beranek and Newman
BBP	Butylbenzyl phthalate
BCMC	Board for the Coordination of the Model Codes
BDA	Bund Deutscher Architekten
BEEP	Black Executive Exchange Program
BEL	*Bauentwerfslehre*
BEPS	Building Energy Performance Standard
BFE	Base flood elevation
BFSM	Building Fire Simulation Model
BH	Boxed heart
BIA	Brick Institute of America

BJS	Bureau of Justice Statistics
BOCA	Building Officials and Code Administrators International
BOD	Biological oxygen demand
BOMA	Building Owners and Managers Association International
BOSTI	Buffalo Organization for Social and Technological Innovation
BPST	British portable skid tester
BRA	Boston Redevelopment Authority
BRAB	Building Research Advisory Board
BRB	Building Research Board
BRI	Building related illness
BS	Building standards
BSR	Board of Standards Review
BSSC	Building Seismic Safety Council
Btu	British thermal unit
BUR	Built-up roofing
BV	Bolt value
CA	Cellulose acetate
CAA	Clean Air Act
CABO	Council of American Building Officials
CACE	Council of Architectural Component Executives
CAD	Computer-aided Design
CADD	Computer-aided Design and Drafting
CAGI	Compressed Air and Gas Institute
CAJ	Committee on Architecture for Justice
CARF	Committee on Accreditation of Rehabilitation Facilities
CB	Cellulose butyrate
CBD	Central business district
CBR	California bearing ratio
CCA	Chromated copper arsenate
CCC	Civilian Conservation Corps
CCR	Ceiling cavity ratio
CCTV	Closed-circuit television
cd	candela
CDA	Copper Development Association
CDC	Community design center
CEC	Canadian Electrical Code; Consulting Engineers Council
cfm	cubic feet per minute
CFR	Airport Crash, Fire and Rescue Service; Code of Federal Regulations
CIAM	Les Congres Internationaux d'Architecture Moderne
CIB	International Council for Building Research, Studies, and Documentation
CIMA	Construction Industry Manufacturers Association
CKD	Certified kitchen designer
CLARB	National Council of Landscape Architectural Registration Boards
CLEP	College-level Examination Program
CLTD	Cooling load temperature difference
CM	Construction management; Construction manager
CMAA	Construction Management Association of America
CMU	Concrete masonry unit(s)
CN	Cellulose nitrate
COD	Chemical oxygen demand
COF	Coefficient of friction

CON	Certificate of need
CP	Cellulose propionate
CPD	Continuing professional development
CPE	Chlorinated polyethylene
CPM	Critical path method
cps	cycles per second
CPSC	Consumer Product Safety Commission
CPU	Central processing unit; Computer processing unit
CPVC	Chlorinated poly(vinyl chloride); Critical pigment volume concentration
CR	Cavity ratio; Condensation resistance
CRI	Color Rendering Index
CRREL	Cold Regions Research and Engineering Laboratory
CRS	Caudill Rowlett Scott
CRSI	Concrete Reinforcing Steel Institute
CRSS	Caudill Rowlett Scott Sirrine
CRT	Cathode ray tube; Computer relay terminal
CSI	Construction Specifications Institute
CSPE	Chlorosulfonated polyethylene
CSRF	Construction Science Research Foundation
CU	Coefficient of utilization
CUA	The Catholic University of America
CVS	Certified value specialist
DAL	Federation of Danish Architects
dB	decibel
DC	Direct current
DEW	Distant Early Warning
DHHS	Department of Health and Human Services
DOD	Department of Defense
DOE	Department of Energy
DOL	Department of Labor
DOP	Dioctyl phthalate
DOT	Department of Transportation
DP	Data processing; Degree of polymerization
DPIC	Design Professionals Insurance Company
DPLG	Diplome par le gouvernmente
DPU	Data processing unit
DWV	Drain–waste–vent
DX	Direct-expansion
EDRA	Environmental Design Research Association
EENT	Eye, ear, nose, and throat
EER	Energy efficiency ratio
EERI	Earthquake Engineering Research Institute
EESA	Education Evaluation Services for Architects
EIP	Ethylene interpolymers
EJCDC	Engineers Joint Contract Documents Committee
ELR	Equivalent length of run
EMT	Electrical metallic tubing
ENT	Ear, nose, and throat
EP	Epoxies
EPA	Environmental Protection Agency

EPCOT	Experimental Prototype Community of Tomorrow
EPDM	Ethylene propylene diene monomer
EPI	Emulsion polymer/isocyanate
EPS	Expandable polystyrene
ERM	Escape and rescue model
ESD	Electrostatic discharge
ESI	Equivalent sphere illumination
ESP	Education Services for the Professions
ET	Evapotranspiration
ETP	Electrolytic tough pitch
ETS	Environmental tobacco smoke
E&B	*Environment and Behavior* (journal)
f	Fiber(s)
FAA	Federal Aviation Administration
FAIA	Fellow of the American Institute of Architects
FAR	Floor area ratio
FBI	Federal Bureau of Investigation
FBO	Foreign Building Operations
fc	footcandle(s)
FCARM	Federation of Colleges of Architects of the Mexican Republic
FCR	Floor cavity ratio
FEMA	Federal Emergency Management Agency
FG	Flat grain
FHA	Federal Housing Administration
FHWA	Federal Highway Administration
FIDCR	Federal Interagency Day Care Requirements
FIDIC	Federation Internationale des Ingenieurs-conseils (Federation of Consulting Engineers)
FIDS	Flight Information Display Systems
FIRM	Flood insurance rate map
FM	Fineness modulus
FmHA	Farmers Home Administration
FMRL	Factory Mutual Research Laboratories
FOHC	Free-of-heart center
fpm	feet per minute
fps	feet per second
FR	Flame retardant
FRP	Fiber glass-reinforced plastic
FRT	Fire retardant treated
FS	Factor of safety
FSES	Fire Safety Evaluation System
ft	foot (feet)
FU	Fixture units
GA	Gypsum Association
GAO	General Accounting Office
GATT	General Agreement on Tariffs and Trade
GDP	Gross domestic product
GFCI	Ground fault circuit interrupter
Glulam	Glued laminated wood
GMAW	Gas metal arc welding
GMP	Guaranteed maximum price
gpm	gallons per minute
GRP	Glass reinforced plastic
GSA	General Services Administration
GSIS	Government Service Insurance System
GTAW	Gas tungsten arc welding
h	hour(s)
HABS	Historic American Buildings Survey
HDO	High density overlay
HDPE	High density polyethylene
HEGIS	Higher Education General Information Survey
HEPA	High-efficiency particulate absolute
HGSD	Harvard Graduate School of Design
HHS	Department of Health & Human Services
HID	High-intensity discharge
HOK	Hellmuth Obata and Kassabaum
HPL	High-pressure laminate
HPS	High-pressure sodium
HUD	Department of Housing & Urban Development
HVAC	Heating, ventilating, and air conditioning
Hz	Hertz
I	Candlepower
IACC	International Association of Conference Centers
IALD	International Association of Lighting Designers
IAPS	International Association for the Study of People and their Physical Surroundings
IATA	International Air Transport Association
IBD	Institute of Business Designers
ICAO	International Civil Aviation Organization
ICBO	International Conference of Building Officials
ICEA	Insulated Cable Engineers Association
ICOR	Interprofessional Council on Registration
IDP	Intern–Architect Development Program
IDSA	Industrial Designers Society of America
IEC	International Electrotechnical Commission
IEEE	Institute of Electrical and Electronics Engineers
IES	Illuminating Engineering Society of North America
IF	Industrialization Forum
IG	International Group
IIC	Impact insulation class
IIT	Illinois Institute of Technology
ILS	Instrument landing system
in.	inch(es)
INCRA	International Copper Research Association
IP	Image processing
ir	infrared
IRA	Initial rate of water absorption
ISO	International Organization for Standardization

IUA	Institute Universitario di Architettura; International Union of Architects
JAE	*Journal of Architectural Education*
JAPR	*Journal of Architectural and Planning Research*
JCAH	Joint Commission on Accreditation of Hospitals
JEP	*Journal of Environmental Psychology*
JIS	Japanese industry standards
JIT	Just in time
JSAH	*Journal of the Society of Architectural Historians*
KCPI	Knife cuts per inch
KD	Kiln-dried
kg	kilogram
kip	1000 pounds
km	kilometer
kPa	kilopascal
ksi	kips per square inch
kW	kilowatt(s)
L	liter
lb	pound
LCC	London County Council
LDPE	Low density polyethylene
LDR	Luminaire dirt replacement; Labor/delivery/recovery
LDRP	Labor/delivery/recovery/postpartum
LFT	Laminated floor tile
LLDPE	Linear low density polyethylene
LLF	Light loss factor
LOF	Large ordering framework
LPS	Low-pressure sodium
LRI	Lighting Research Institute
LSC	Life Safety Code
m	meter
MAAT	Mean average air temperature
MAI	Member of the Appraisers Institute
MARTA	Metropolitan Atlanta Rapid Transit Authority
MBMA	Metal Building Manufacturers Association
MC	Moisture content
MDF	Medium density fiberboard
MDI	Methylene diisocyanate
MDO	Medium density overlay
MDP	Main distribution panelboard
MDPE	Medium density polyethylene
MERA	Man and Environment Research Association
MG	Motor generator
MGRAD	Minimum Guidelines and Requirements for Accessible Design
MH	Metal halide
MIA	Marble Institute of America
min	minute(s)
MIT	Massachusetts Institute of Technology
MLS	Master of Library Science
mm	millimeter
MOE	Modulus of elasticity
MOR	Modulus of rupture
MPa	Megapascal
MPS	Minimum property standards
mpy	mils per year
msec	millisecond(s)
MSHA	Mine Safety and Health Administration
MSR	Machine stress-rated
MV	Mercury vapor
μm	micrometer
NAAB	National Architectural Accrediting Board
NACA	National Advisory Council on Aging
NAEC	National Association of Elevator Contractors
NAHB	National Association of Home Builders of the United States
NAPF	National Association of Plastic Fabricators
NASA	National Aeronautics and Space Administration
NASFCA	National Automatic Sprinkler and Fire Control Association
NAVFAC	Naval Facilities Engineering Command
NBC	National Building Code
NBCC	National Building Code of Canada
NBFU	National Board of Fire Underwriters
NBM	National Building Museum
NBS	National Bureau of Standards
NC	Network communications; Noise criteria
NCA	National Constructors Association
NCAR	National Council of Architectural Registration
NCARB	National Council of Architectural Registration Boards
NCEE	National Council of Engineering Examiners
NCIDQ	National Council of Interior Design Qualification
NCMA	National Concrete Masonry Association
NCS	Natural color system
NCSBCS	National Conference of States on Building Codes and Standards
NDS	National design specifications
NEA	National Endowment for the Arts
NEC	National Electrical Code
NECA	National Electrical Contractors Association
NEH	National Endowment for the Humanities
NEISS	National Electronic Injury Surveillance System
NEMA	National Electrical Manufacturers Association
NFIP	National Flood Insurance Program
NFPA	National Fire Protection Association; National Forest Products Association
NGR	National grading rule
NIBS	National Institute of Building Sciences
NIC	Noise insulation class
NIOSH	National Institute for Occupational Safety and Health

NKCA	National Kitchen Cabinet Association
nm	nanometers
NMS	Nonmetallic sheathed
NMTB	National Machine Tool Builders Association
NPS	National Park Service
NR	Noise reduction
NRC	Noise reduction coefficient
NRCA	National Roofing Contractors Association
NSF	National Science Foundation; National Sanitation Foundation
NSPE	National Society of Professional Engineers
NSSEA	National School Supply and Equipment Association
oc	on center
OEM	Original equipment manufacturer
OPLR	Office for Professional Liability Research
ORBIT-2	Organizations, Buildings and Information Technology (study)
OSA	Olefin–styrene–acrylonitrile
OSB	Oriented strand board
OSHA	Occupational Safety and Health Administration
PA	Polyamide
P/A	*Progressive Architecture* (journal)
PACO	Probing Alternate Career Opportunities
PADC	Pennsylvania Avenue Development Corporation
PAPER	People and the Physical Environment Research
PAT	Proficiency analytical testing
PB	Polybutylene
PBS	Public Building Service
PBT	Polybutylene terephthalate
PC	Personal computer; Polycarbonate; Polymer concrete
PCA	Portland Cement Association
PCB	Pentachlorobiphenyl
PCC	Polymer cement concrete
PCD	Planned community development
PCEH	President's Committee for the Employment of Handicapped
PCI	Prestressed Concrete Institute
PE	Polyethylene
PEPP	Professional Engineers in Private Practice
PERT	Program evaluation and review technique
PET	Polyethylene terephthalate
PIB	Polyisobutylene
PIC	Polymer-impregnated concrete
PMMA	Polymethyl methacrylate
PMR	Protected membrane roof
PMS	Pavement management system
POE	Post-occupancy evaluation
PP	Period payment; Polypropylene
ppm	parts per million
PRF	Phenol–resorcinol–formaldehyde
PS	Polystyrene
PSAE	Production Systems for Architects and Engineers
psf	pounds per square foot
PSFS	Philadelphia Savings Fund Society
psi	pounds per square inch
PTFE	Polytetrafluoroethylene
PTO	Power take-off
PTV	Passenger transfer vehicle
PUD	Planned unit development
PVA	Paralyzed Veterans of America; Poly(vinyl acrylic)
PVAC	Polyvinyl acetate
PVAL	Polyvinyl alcohol
PVB	Polyvinyl butyral
PVC	Poly(vinyl chloride); Pigment volume concentration
PVDC	Polyvinylidene chloride
PVDF	Polyvinylidene fluoride
PVF	Polyvinyl fluoride; Polyvinyl formal
PW	Present worth
PWA	Present worth of annuity
PWF	Permanent wood foundation
RAIC	Royal Architectural Institute of Canada
RBM	Reinforced brick masonry
RCR	Room cavity ratio
REA	Rural Electrification Administration
REI	Relative exposure index
REIT	Real estate investment trust
RF	Resorcinol–formaldehyde
RFC	Reconstruction Finance Corporation
RFP	Request for proposal
rh	Relative humidity
RIBA	Royal Institute of British Architects
RIM	Reaction injection molding
RL, R/L	Random length
ROI	Return on investment
rpm	revolutions per minute
R/UDAT	Regional/Urban Design Assistance Team(s)
SAC	Sound absorption coefficient
SAE	Society of Automotive Engineers, Inc.
SAN	Styrene–acrylonitrile
SAR	Stichting Architekten Research
SAVE	Society of American Value Engineers
SBCC	Standard Building Construction Code
SBCCI	Southern Building Code Congress International, Inc.
SBR	Styrene butadiene rubber
SBS	Sick building syndrome
SCFF	Silicone-coated fiber glass fabrics
SCS	Soil Conservation Service
SCSD	School Construction System Development
SE	Service entrance
sec	second(s)
SERI	Solar Energy Research Institute
SG	Slash grain
SHHA	Self-help Housing Agency
SIC	Standard Industrial Classification
SIR	Society of Industrial Realtors
SJI	Steel Joist Institute
SLA	Special Libraries Association
SMACNA	Sheet Metal and Air Conditioning Contractors National Association
SMH	Super metal halide

SMPS	Society for Marketing Professional Services
SMU	Southern Methodist University
SOCOTEC	Societe de Controle Technique
SOM	Skidmore Owings and Merrill
SPD	Supply, processing, and distribution
SPI	Society of the Plastics Industry
SPP	Speech privacy potential
SPRI	Single Ply Roofing Institute
SSPB	South Side Planning Board (Chicago)
ST	Structural tubing
STC	Sound transmission class
STD	Standard
STL	Sound transmission loss
TAC	The Architects Collaborative
TAS	Technical Assistance Series
TCFF	Teflon-coated fiber glass fabrics
TDD	Telecommunication devices for deaf persons
TDI	Toluene diisocyanate
TEM	Transmission electron microscopy
TH	Technische Hochschule
THB	Technische Hochschule Braunschweig
TIMA	Thermal Insulation Manufacturers Association
TL	Transmission loss
T-PV	Temperature–pressure relief valve
TV	Television
TVA	Tennessee Valley Authority
TWA	Time-weighted average
T & G	Tongue and groove
T & P	Temperature and pressure
UBC	Uniform Building Code
UCC	Uniform Commercial Code
UCI	Uniform Construction Index
UDDC	Urban Design and Development Corporation
UF	Urea–formaldehyde
UFAS	Uniform Federal Accessibility Standards
UFI	Urea–formaldehyde foam insulation
UHMWPE	Ultra-high molecular weight polyethylene
UIA	Union Internationale des Architects
UIDC	Urban Investment Development Company
UL	Underwriters Laboratories
ULI	Urban Land Institute
UNESCO	United Nations Educational, Scientific, and Cultural Organization
UNS	Unified numbering systems
UPS	Uninterruptible power supply
USCOLD	United States Committee on Large Dams
USDA	United States Department of Agriculture
USIA	United States Information Agency
USPS	United States Postal Service
uv	ultraviolet
VA	Veterans Administration
VAT	Vinyl asbestos tile
VCP	Visual Comfort Probability Factor
VCT	Vinyl composition tile
VDT	Video display terminal
VG	Vertical grain
VISTA	Volunteers in Service to America
VLH	Very low heat
VMA	Voids in the mineral aggregate
VOC	Volatile organic compound
VU	Value unit(s)
WAA	War Assets Administration; Western Association of Architects
WHO	World Health Organization
WMMA	Woodworking Machinery Manufacturers Association
WP	Word processing; Word processor
WPA	Work Progress Administration; Work Projects Administration

INCINERATORS. See MAINTENANCE, BUILDING

INDUSTRIALIZED CONSTRUCTION (ENGINEERED BUILDINGS—PREFABRICATION)

This classification of building is also commonly referenced as industrialized building and housing, preengineered building, manufactured building and housing, and prefabrication. In each of the identifying names, there is an intent to define the difference between this type of building construction and its conventional counterpart, on-site building construction. As a broad definition, industrialized construction is generally described as off-site construction where complete buildings or building parts are constructed within a factory setting and thereafter transported to, and assembled or erected on, a building site. An exception to this definition would be where a temporary on-site factory is set up to prefabricate its building parts. From the basis of this definition, a vast industry significant in its own history has evolved, so that today, every form of building engages, to a degree, in industrialized construction. Large-scale buildings employing prefabricated steel or precast concrete structural members with curtain-wall cladding, mid-size preengineered metal commercial structures, residential multifamily units composed of modular or panel systems, single-family sectional dwellings, mobile homes, kit-of-parts packages, and small-scale home improvements, such as the addition of a window or a door, all utilize some form of industrialized building.

To the reader unfamiliar with this specialized area of building, some of the terms mentioned above such as "modular" or "system" have particular reference within the nomenclature of industrialized construction; for this reason discussion of the subject invites definition and explanation of its terminology. For example, industrialized construction, in its more formal working definition, is considerably more complex than initially rendered. Industrialization of building can be defined as a process that utilizes technology and mass production techniques to effect an increase in productivity, efficiencies in cost and production time, and quality control, where the intent is that the manufacture of its product supersede traditional, craft-oriented methods previously employed in producing the same product. For further clarification, in common parlance, both inside and outside the building industry, industrialization and prefabrication are often used interchangeably and understood to have the same meaning. They do, however, have separate definitions. Industrialization refers to a process of building, whereas prefabrication is associated with the product of the process. Prefabrication identifies the fabrication or assembly of standardized parts for a building, usually in a factory setting. It is also important to note that the degree of assembly of the prefabricated product is variable; that is, both a mobile home and a window unit are prefabricated products. Prefabrication is more restricted in its meaning than the term industrialization.

Industrialized construction encompasses numerous functional building types: office, retail, manufacturing, warehousing, services, sport and educational facilities, as well as residential buildings, both multiple- and single-unit types. For the purpose of simple classification, they can be categorized into five groups: residential, institutional, recreational, industrial, and commercial, as presented in Figure 1. From this point of departure, further classification can be made of the two types of prefabricated products produced by the process of industrialized construction. They are components and unit systems, as illustrated in Figure 1. The first classification, components, makes reference to all and any parts of a building that are factory produced. Under this category, there are two other categories: subsystems and unit elements. A subsystem is a minor system of the larger building. Subsystems are smaller, but complete entities in and of themselves. As secondary systems, they function as serviceable parts of the overall building. Structural systems, wetcore modules (ie, one-piece molded bathroom units, combination kitchen sink and cabinet units), volumetric cores (combination kitchen and bath units), exterior cladding systems (curtain walls, etc), interior partitioning systems, and mechanical cores are various common types of subsystems. Elements, the other category of components, are understood to be and are identified more as smaller, single-unit component pieces. These include structural framing members such as floor and roof trusses, post and beam elements, window units, doors, stair units, skylights, and so on. The range of items in this category is quite extensive and is continually expanding as the building industry discovers new manufacturing components that can substitute for more costly conventional methods of construction.

The second classification, unit systems, refers to the total building. There are various types of whole complete building systems that are identified within this category. They include modular, mobile, panel, metal, sectional, precut, geodesic, and log. Other unit systems types (ie, glazed, earth-sheltered, etc) are produced, although in less significant production numbers. All of the building systems are similar in that they can be identified as a set of mass-produced interrelated and coordinated building parts that, when either factory or site assembled, function as a total building. Beyond this their similarities end, as physically and compositionally they vary considerably from one another. Figure 2 provides a graphic description of the various unit systems discussed in Table 1. Aside from these general definitions and summaries of characteristics representative of the products of industrialized construction, there are additional terms that require elaboration.

The term system, for example, has common usage in the realm of industrialized construction. The term system as defined in Ref. 1 is a "coherent set of physical entities

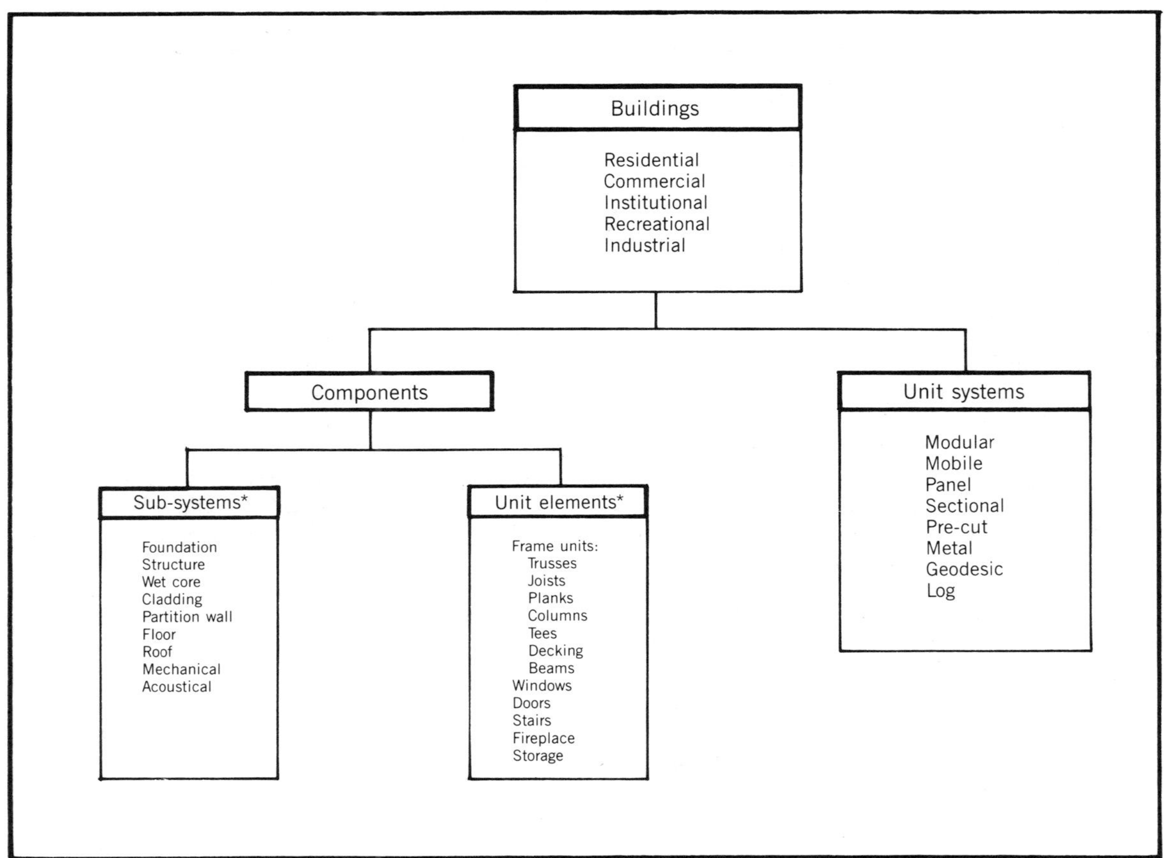

Figure 1. Industrialized construction classification. The asterisks represent an extensible item listing.

organized for a particular purpose." Another definition, from Ref. 2, defines a system as a kit of parts designed to be combined into a unified whole to accomplish a desired objective. In a general sense, it refers to a group of interrelated parts that combine to make a whole unit. Within the context of industrialized construction, a system is typed in one of two ways: open or closed. Each system's name refers to its operational flexibilities. An open building system can accommodate interchangeability of its own component parts (subsystems and elements) with other systems' or other producers' components within its own principal system. Conversely, a closed system is where interchangeability of components is internal. Modular and mobile home units are two examples of closed systems. In addition to unit systems, subsystems, and open and closed systems, the term systems has yet another descriptive meaning, which refers to the nature of a system's preprogrammed design intent. Specifically, an industrialized building system can be designed as either a hardware or software system package. Hardware relates to physical products, such as those building systems presented in Figure 2. A software system design package is descriptively nonphysical and generally marketed as a program or procedure for producing and marketing industrialized building products. It is also important to note that some systems are designed as combination hardware/software packages.

The term conventional construction, as previously identified, is generally understood to be construction that occurs on site. In the past, conventional construction meant that all building parts were site fabricated. For the past few decades, conventional construction, in its purest sense, has been all but nonexistent. The more appropriate descriptive term, and one which is commonly used in industrialized construction nomenclature, is rationalized building. It is defined as conventional building with the adaptation of some of the principles, techniques, and component products of systems building. All building today is either rationalized or industrialized; however, the term conventional remains the more commonly used and is favored over rationalized.

Because of its specialized language of technical terms and operational procedures, industrialized building is viewed by many as a somewhat segregated or ancillary part of the building industry as a whole. This is a paradoxical view, given the reality of its prevalence within the building industry today. The component products of this industry sector, subsystems and especially building unit elements, continuously and increasingly over time have been integrated into the mainstream of building activity, as it was realized that such items facilitated ease of construction, enabled greater economies in time and construction cost, and provided a higher standard of quality over that which they replaced.

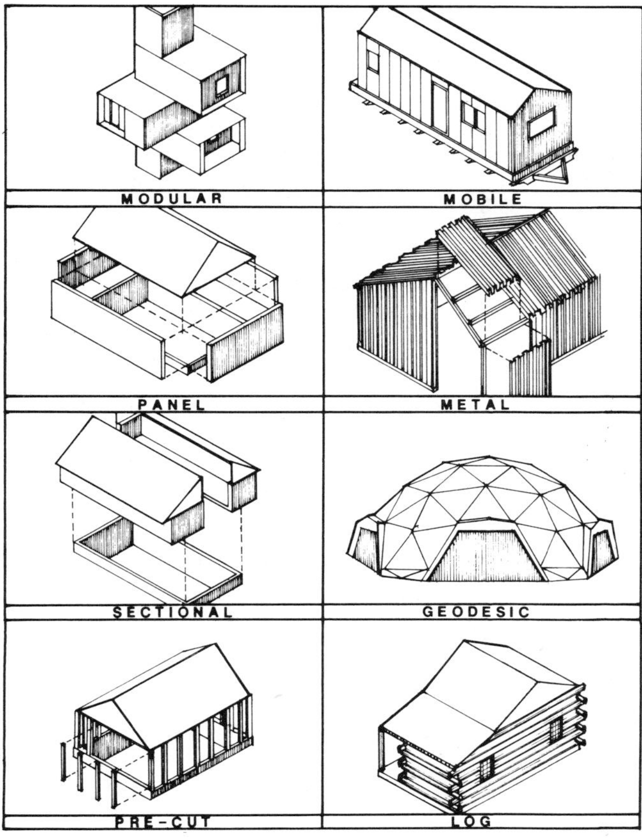

Figure 2. Unit system building types.

Industrialized building does tend to be viewed as a separate subarea of building within the unit systems category. Its specialized production processes make its operational activities subsidiary to the general building industry. Given their size, cost, production, transportation, erection, and zoning prerequisites, unit systems cannot be assimilated as easily into the regular mainstream across-the-board building industry as the smaller industrialized construction components. Although the manufacture of unit systems has maintained a representative market share of building industry revenues, particularly in the mobile home and metal building industries (see State of the Industry), by and large, unit systems manufacturing has functioned as an associated subindustry of the whole building industry. Another factor inhibiting growth of unit systems is building specification codes, which vary distinctly according to region, country, municipality, and so on, and, as such, lack a general uniformity of standards necessary to standardize the manufacture and eventual marketability of unit systems.

Another reason why unit systems construction has been slow to penetrate the greater building industry, particularly in the area of single-family and low-rise multiunit residential housing, is that conventional or stick-built construction has proved itself in its own right as a viable, cost-effective, and efficient form of construction for this sector of the marketplace. In a sense, this method of construction, which utilizes predimensioned lumber and other standard-dimensioned material units such as brick and concrete block, by its earlier definition straddles a fine line between conventional and industrialized construction. This common building process has been further served over the years by the availability of portable hand power tools, which speed up the process of cutting and assembly. In addition, with the integration of industrialized component construction, particularly of prefabricated elements such as windows, doors, stairs, trim, wallboard, fireplaces, rails, and so on, these commonplace components have acted as a competitive counterforce. They have held at bay unit systems growth, since components contribute to minimizing the construction period, which has served the tradesperson and the consumer in realizing overall cost economies.

This further explains why builders and tradespersons and their unions have been slow to favor unit systems construction. Not only have conventional construction methods continued to improve over time, but also there are those among industry personnel who identify a large-scale proliferation of unit systems in the marketplace with a risk of undoing the working operational status quo of the existing building industry. An expanded market of industrialized unit systems has in the past been viewed as an economic threat by the rank-and-file members of the construction trades as well as their unions. Builders and developers have also voiced similar reservations concerning a dominant market in unit systems, recognizing the potential elimination of their role and consequent economic base, given that direct transactions between manufacturer and consumer could be facilitated. Today, these concerns about unit systems are more relaxed. As they are progressively assimilated into the marketplace, the builder/developer has, in effect, become the intermediary between the factory and the consumer, and the tradesperson has not experienced employment displacement, but rather has remained a necessary participant within a continually expanding industry.

Architects and other design professionals have also expressed skepticism about unit systems. Their disenchantment has focused primarily on the viability of industrialization as a design-worthy concept impacting the environment. For example, industrialized building has been dominant in the USSR over the past few decades. In a recently related interview, an architect in the USSR's government employ for many years identified his envy of a U.S. architect visitor because, during his long tenure with the Soviet government, he had built many buildings, but they were always the same building executed repeatedly from the same plans and working drawings. Inasmuch as industrialization depends on a process of mass production to ensure economic viability, the conclusion is drawn that aesthetics must ultimately be sacrificed in some way for the sake of economy. Unit systems construction, for some architects and designers, conjures visualizations of living complexes that are aesthetic impositions upon the environment, forwarding the concern that, as products of manufacture, they are incapable of responding to site and environmental dictates, the latter being pertinent to effecting favorable design. Such a concern is mindful of and further supports the notion of enlisting professional design input prior to manufacture, as well as throughout

Table 1. Various Unit Systems

Type	Description	Features	Constraints
Modular	Complete prefabricated three-dimensional volume-enclosed units generally erected in multiples.	Construction superior to mobile, as its design can blend with traditional housing. Code compliance and mortgage financing generally favorable. It has design flexibility and capital value appreciation over time.	Comparably more expensive than mobile and measurably equal to conventional, so interim (financing) advantages are realized in construction/erection. Truck transport cumbersome, subject to size restrictions, which similarly lead to design constraints. Volume production required to support economic viability. Erection requires crane-operated equipment.
Mobile	Basic rectilinear wood or metal-framed structure, built on a steel transportable chassis and sheathed in metal or wood.	Low-cost relative to alternative housing types, transport, taxes, and maintenance. Immediacy of occupancy, and financing obtainable.	Zoning is restrictive. Value of purchase depreciates over time, given limited life span. Transport limitations lead to design constraints. Chassis base and exterior material quality selection impede blend with environmental context.
Panel	Panelized wall, floor, and roof components preengineered for rapid site assembly of a whole unit system.	Design flexibility exceeds mobile and modular, as does ease of transport, the latter affording a broader shipping radius. Consumer can engage in a participatory role in the design process as well as assembly or finishing, thereby reducing costs. Compliance with codes and zoning restrictions easily facilitated.	Site work preparation and erection more extensive and costly than modular and mobile; quality control is consequently lessened. Requires site storage of materials and components.
Metal	Prefabricated metal panel system and components technically specified to facilitate rapid site assembly. Typically used for nonresidential construction.	Markedly lower in overall cost compared to conventional counterpart. Minimized construction erection period enables immediacy of occupancy, thus lower construction financing costs. Design affords spatial expansion.	Not contextually compatible with traditional environmental fabric. Climatically more suitable to certain regions.
Sectional	Double-section, three-dimensional volume units, site-connected together to form a complete unit system.	Similar, can be combined with mobile and modular.	Same as modular/mobile.
Precut	Components and elements presized, cut and coded in fabrication, and packaged in ordered bundles for transport, to be site assembled into a complete unit system (wood frame or post and beam structure).	Similar to panel systems.	Constraints similar to panel systems; site assembly is more complex and time consuming, often necessitating services of a building contractor.
Geodesic	Panels and component parts assemble into a dome structure with functional application for both residential and nonresidential.	Cost-worthy investment over conventional construction, quick erection, ease of transport, unique interior spatial quality.	Subject to zoning and code restrictions. This structural form does not easily integrate with the existing built environment, and structure weakens with fenestration. Interior space organizations restrictive within domical form.
Log	Log component elements factory cut to interlock in site assembly producing a bearing wall unit system.	Interior spatial design flexibility, ease of transport.	Similar to precut systems with the added constraint that assimilation within the environmental fabric is limited to country more than urban areas.

the various process phases, to effect an outcome that satisfies site, function, aesthetic, and economic requirements. Architecture has similarly played a contributory role in the history of industrialization. Throughout its historical course, many noted architects and designers have identified and been intrigued with this design concept, seeing the subject area as a creative challenge and its inherent constraints not as hindrances, but rather as design directives.

HISTORICAL OVERVIEW

Industrialized construction has an historical legacy in its own right. Its roots reach back to the beginning of the Industrial Revolution in the middle and later nineteenth century to the advent of new fabrication processes in iron and steel. Prior to this period, prefabricated buildings had been documented as far back as the seventeenth century, when the English brought a demountable panelized house to Cape Ann, Massachusetts (3). Similarly, settlers moving from the United Kingdom to Australia carried along portable cottages as well as larger hospital structures, which were assembled without tools. The Gold Rush of 1848 also claimed imports of prefabricated housing from Europe and from distant places such as China and New Zealand. Some shelter units arrived complete with wallpaper, carpets, and furnishings. During the early years, prefabricated building was generally enlisted as an alternative method of building to serve immediate shelter needs. A cluster of these types of activities began to spawn an embryonic industry in prefabrication, as more and more businesses engaged in producing packaged buildings. It marked the beginning of mass production, whereby multiples could be produced in large quantities, as contrasted to the historical single-unit production.

Simultaneously, a new building material, cast iron, was making its appearance, and marked the beginning of the coming age of industrialized construction. During the era of the mid-1700s to the mid-1800s, Western civilization was in the process of changing from an agrarian-based society to an industrial economy. The Industrial Revolution was emerging as new technologies, new materials, and new commercial and manufacturing enterprises developed. Within the building industry, new materials led to new methods of construction. With the development of coke and its use in smelting iron, the commercial use of steel as a cheap and readily available material became widespread. Simultaneous breakthroughs such as the invention of the steam engine resulted in the powering of production operations that previously depended on waterways for energy sources. Railway networks were prominent, and all industries seemed to be working cooperatively, each engaged in a positive growth circle leading to the eventual mass production of iron and steel; a new integrated industrial complex with these materials served as its base. The earliest implementation of these materials in construction occurred in bridge and railway construction. Thomas Telford, master engineer, in building the Menai Bridge in 1826, had shown the world a new building form had emerged, a form dictated by the materials and technology of the day. It was the first major structure to exploit the tensile strength of iron, spanning an unheard-of distance of 570 ft and eclipsing the earlier span limits of 350 ft.

Cast iron's structural attributes and its malleable design properties were soon recognized and applied in building construction. Its early uses were as structural replacements for cumbersome wooden structural posts in textile mills. In addition to its nonflammable properties, iron framework trusses accommodated more open space, and less material was needed compared to the heavy, limited span timber trusses it replaced. It was also timely that cast-iron structural elements became available given that new, larger machinery was replacing former methods in textile production. As an example, the newly invented cotton-spinning machine needed a housing that was not only ample, but which could support its weight. This is exemplary of the origin of the Industrial Revolution; one product need was accommodated by another product designed to meet that need, and soon an entire interdependent network of new products and materials became a part of everyday commerce.

For decades to follow, cast-iron components played a primary role in building. Architects and builders of the time soon realized the new freedoms in design that this material afforded them. It was visually and structurally a much lighter material than previously available. Cast iron formed in columns exhibited very long and slender properties, and also enabled new dimensioning and proportioning opportunities for the use of spaces. In addition to its functional structural value, because of this material's malleable properties, it could be manipulated for aesthetic interest, which led to some rather fantastic ornamentation of these building elements. By 1823, cast iron was being used for the principal supports in churches, theaters, and manufacturing buildings. Siegfried Giedion stated that the reign of cast iron in the nineteenth century was founded on its fire-resistant qualities, economy, simplicity of manufacture, and resistance to heavy loads (4). These material attributes enabled it to dominate building until the 1880s, when the steel frame was developed. The industry had grown to such proportions that it was actually producing whole building systems in cast iron. Cast-iron component production had reached a level of usage that would garner the respect of many modern systems builders today. Catalogs existed that listed pages upon pages of building elements, all available through mail order. Factories in Europe and North America produced, packaged, and shipped cast-iron buildings and component parts all over the world.

James Bogardus was among those identified with cast-iron architecture. An inventor by trade, his work led him to obtain patents for constructing prefabricated iron buildings of mass-produced parts, and his activities as a contractor in erecting these cast-iron-faced structures brought him architectural recognition. He contacted various foundries and blacksmiths for the fabrication of the building components and would then supervise their assembly. He constructed several buildings in large East Coast cities from New York to as far south as Havana. His own factory, constructed in New York City in 1849, was the first all-iron building in the United States (Fig. 3).

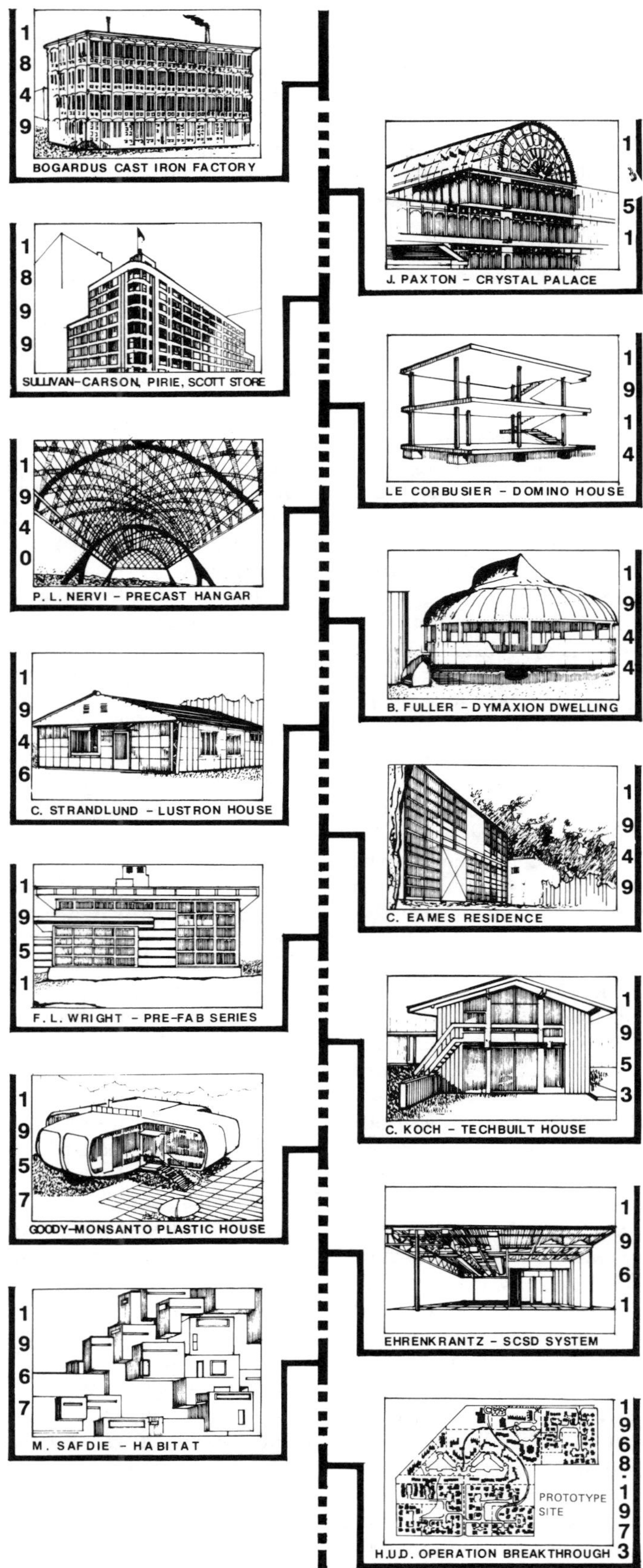

Figure 3. Industrialized architecture timeline.

Another important name in cast-iron production and manufacturing of that period is Daniel Badger. Operating out of New York, he produced parts for more than 300 buildings, many in the city of New York, and throughout the United States. Badger stands out among iron producers of his time because, unlike others, he sold his products as whole building concepts, systems of frame and skin. All components were standardized and manufactured in one place, then shipped, and assembled on site, having been ordered from his finely illustrated catalog.

The most widely known building using cast iron as a principal material was the famous Crystal Palace, as shown in Figure 3. The Crystal Palace was designed by Joseph Paxton, a former landscape gardener, for the 1851 World Exhibition in London. It was the first large building to utilize materials and methods of industrialized construction. Its architectural form and design were quite different for this period in time, and it stood as a representative aesthetic expression of the materials of which it was formed. Selected from among numerous competition entries for its promised expedience in construction, as the exposition was only months from its scheduled opening, it fulfilled that aim to the extent that even in this day of high industrialization and technology it reigns as a prominent example of industrialized building. From the signing of the contract agreement between Paxton, the Royal Commission, and the key contractors on July 16, 1850, a facility of almost 1 million ft^2 was completed and ready for occupancy in 39 weeks. The structural and mechanical innovations that emerged from Paxton's earlier, although smaller, glass buildings came together in the Crystal Palace, and it is considered today one of the foundation stones in the modern movement. For building system proponents, it was a powerful example of industrialized building since it embodied all of the attributes that they believed supersede conventional forms of building.

The Crystal Palace was designed on a dimensioned structural and cladding module lending itself to the repetitive use of building elements. The components were standardized and mass produced. They were interchangeable, and the assembly process was dry, facilitating and speeding fieldwork. This made possible the phenomenally rapid erection, in less than 39 weeks, of an enclosed 989,884 ft^2 of floor space. The frame was dual purpose, serving first as its own scaffolding during erection, and finally, its main purpose, as the building's structure, supporting a lightweight glass curtain wall. Paxton also introduced some innovative mechanized erection techniques, among them a roof-glazing wagon and sash bar finishing machine. In addition to these features, the building was demountable. After the Exposition terminated, it was disassembled and moved to another site in Sydenham, some distance from London's center. The Palace's standardized components were of three materials: iron and wood for structure, the latter also for casings, and sheet glass for the skin of the structure. When all was done, the building covered almost 18 acres. It used 4,500 tons of iron, 900,000 ft^2 of glass, and 600,000 ft^3 of timber. The significance of Paxton's Crystal Palace in this history of industrialized architecture is manifold: the innovative methods he employed in manufacturing the elements, the rate at which they were produced, the minimal time for erection, the assembly line methods devised, and the repetitive use of building elements resulted in an aesthetically pleasing solution. Destroyed by fire in 1936, it remains to this day a memorable example of industrialized building.

In 1856, Henry Bessemer patented a method of decarbonizing iron to make steel. With the Bessemer process of iron–steel conversion, steel could be made available at a reasonable cost. Soon after this material refinement, the technology of rolling and forming steel was developed, making available a newer, stronger construction material. It came to revolutionize building form, both in function and aesthetics. The impact of the development of this new building material and the range of structural components made possible the multistory office tower with its steel-frame structural form. Building design in the latter 1800s embarked on a new, forward, and vertical direction. Chicago, Illinois, led in the development of steel-frame buildings, displaying early evidence of a new machine design aesthetic that was to come to full bloom in Europe and the Bauhaus.

One of the first important all-steel structures was the Second Lieter Building (Chicago, 1889) by architect William le Baron Jenney. The first to introduce an all-steel skeleton construction, it was also the first to use what was to become known as the "Chicago window," story-height glazing that completely filled the grid of the frame. In addition to the building being a visual expression of its material structural form, its frame, from a functional standpoint, offered the advantages of more usable space within the interior, allowing for more spatial flexibilities in planning than previous masonry construction. In addition, it proved a much faster method of construction.

One of the most celebrated steel structures of this period was Louis Sullivan's Carson Pirie Scott department store in Chicago, built between 1899 and 1904. Illustrated in Figure 3, its style is clear, and it is visually relevant to the machine. The repetition of its machine-fabricated structural members and industrially produced glass "curtains" exhibits a systematized design approach that reflects a definite architectural response to a new machine technology.

In Europe, during the early 1900s, similar architectural responses were addressing another new industrialized construction material: reinforced concrete. Although others before him had worked with this material in a utilitarian fashion, Pier Luigi Nervi, an architectural engineer, utilized the material to its fullest advantage through his experiments with prefabrication, standardization, and systematization of building. With prefabricated steel reinforcement, Nervi gave concrete a richness of aesthetic expression as he exploited its plasticizing potential for architectural form. His pioneering work with reinforced concrete, which led to his eventual use of precast concrete, brought him international attention. His airplane hangars of the late 1930s and early 1940s, as shown in Figure 3, are monumental latticelike structural compositions networking concrete in a fashion never seen before. In the years following, he developed ferro concrete, which is similar to the thin-shell concrete used today. Compositionally, it was a thin, elastic, durable, strong, flexible material constructed of a number of layers of steel mesh sprayed with concrete and laid up without formwork. With this technique, Nervi was able to execute great spanned structures that not only were economical in time, cost, and material, but also artistically addressed the material's inherent potential. With Nervi's early efforts and, notably, since the 1950s, precast, prestressed concrete has assumed a dominant role in industrialized construction. Its uses extend from component elements to structural subsystems to complete unit systems. Nervi designed several large-span structures employing precast diamond-shaped components known as lamella to roof large areas for sports buildings in both Italy and the United States in the post-war period.

With the introduction of these new industrialized materials serving the building process more efficiently in terms of material cost and construction ease, it was inevitable that they would come to replace previous methods and materials; for architecture, that inevitability encompassed a whole new stylistic direction in philosophy, design, and execution.

Perhaps the two most recognized vanguards in architecture who identified with and embraced this new stylistic direction in industrialized architecture were Le Corbusier and Walter Gropius. In Europe, shortly after World War I, a transition was taking place in architecture. Le Corbusier, Gropius, and the Bauhaus School Gropius directed, were at the forefront of this change. The design philosophy expounded by them was focused on making a break with historical precedent by creating a new style that more accurately reflected the social, economic, and technical reality of the twentieth century. It was similarly a recognition of the undiscovered industrial capabilities of the new technology that provided new freedoms in spatial design and a means of standardizing components and systems for mass production and building. The conditions of the time reflected a need for a design type that would best demonstrate the principles of mass production; the house form appeared to best serve this purpose. With this in mind, Gropius and Le Corbusier set out to give meaning to the concept of industrialized design and building through their professional expressions in writing and by way of their proposed and built examples.

Le Corbusier undertook a number of projects that experimented with the concept of mass-produced housing and utilized standardized components. Among his earliest proposals was the 1914 Domino House design, as represented in Figure 3. It became both a physical and philosophical symbol of the new machine age. The Domino House was more simply a conception of a system of standardized building components that were meant to be extensible as units. Its construction was basically a structural slab carrying the load of columns positioned to form bays, which together created visions of extensibility in both vertical and horizontal directions. In this, the Domino House told the future of industrialized construction. Although the Domino House, as well as Le Corbusier's later projects, including the factory housing complex at Pessac, France, were in actuality realized with somewhat modified, although essentially traditional, site-built methods, it was the visual statement that stood as a symbolic representation of the "new machine for living," as Le Corbusier himself stated. Another reinforcement of his design philosophy of mass production was attempted with the Citrohan House, a namesake of the Swiss-produced car. The houses in this 1920 proposal were to be produced in the same standardized assembly-line fashion as automobiles. Le Corbusier's preoccupation with the human condition in an industrialized society led to other developments in the area of standardization, including extensive research and writing about a dimensioning system he devised and defined as a harmonious measure to the human scale applicable to architecture and mechanics, known as "Le Modular," which he then carried forth and implemented in his later work (5).

Gropius and the Bauhaus became identified as the institutional school of thought practicing a philosophy of design that embraced the new machine age. Whereas most other schools remained ensconced in the beaux-arts dictum, Gropius, the Bauhaus curriculum, and its architects, designers, and educators were all influential in directing this stylistic expression, which spread from Europe across and throughout the United States. Its architecture was distinctly different from all previous work. It intently displayed its skeletal machine-fabricated structure. Its expressed fenestration with machine-repetitive ribbon windows and barrier-free visibility, made possible by glass-skinned curtain walls, emphasized a visual union between the exterior and interior environments. These new materials of the industrial age were boldly displayed in their barren simplicity, economy of form, and yielding flat roofs; identifying that form was a function of the structure that the machine-produced material took on. The architectural aesthetic identified as "modern" stood as a vivid expression of mass production in its repetitive presentation of industrialized building components.

Gropius, in addition to his treatises on the subject, generated several of his own architectural proposals furthering the concept of standardization and mass production. Most noteworthy among them were his Serial Houses of 1921, which addressed maximum variability in form and space with maximum standardization. Another of his buildings, which stands as an early visual statement about the machine age, is the Fagus Factory at Alfeld, FRG. Its repetitions of machine elements, structure visible through transparent "screen" walls, and overall lightness, distinct from the earlier massive bearing-wall construction, were all design solutions that projected a building facade openly displaying the capabilities, potentialities, and economies of mass production. The modern machine aesthetic, which came to be recognized as the international style, emigrated to the United States when the Bauhaus in Germany was forcibly closed in the 1930s. The Bauhaus faculty dispersed to educational institutions throughout the United States and redirected the course of architectural education to focus on the "new machine architecture." Prior to the Bauhaus movement taking hold in the United States, industrialized building and its inherent style were already strongly represented in the United States. The work of Louis Sullivan and other architects of the Chicago School of the industrialized high-rise was having an impact in defining a future course of the form of cityscapes, as architects throughout the country undertook the design challenge to produce a new architecture expressive of modern-day materials.

Buckminster Fuller was one example of a true visionary of industrialized architecture. A number of present-day concepts about the uses of machine technology came from some of his early contributions, dating back to 1920. One of the first involvements with building technology was a dual effort with his father-in-law, the architect James Monroe Hewlett. Together they invented the Stockade Block System. The blocks, fibrous material infused and bonded with cement, were lightweight, moisture proof, and noncorrosible. In these features, their advantages extended beyond those of common heavy block construction. The system, used in a few building projects, was ultimately sold to the Celotex Corporation. Today this company uses the material as a base in its manufacture of acoustical wall and ceiling treatments.

Another widely recognized contribution to industrialized building was Fuller's design for the Dymaxion house. First proposed in 1927, it was well beyond its time in that many of the building materials he specified had not yet been manufactured. The Dymaxion Dwelling was identified as the "true machine for living" that Corbusier had envisioned. In this structure, Fuller's design elicited a multitude of innovative design ideas and philosophical and pragmatic intentions in all aspects of production, construction, and function for present and future human occupancy. The structure was supported in tension from a central mast, the latter also containing the power unit to distribute light, heat, and air. Sheathed in vacuum pane plates, its form and design manipulated the natural elements of wind and sun. To serve its functional efficiencies, a "catch up with life" function zone contained utility units hung radially about the mast; together, they defined and divided the interior spaces. Fuller's design considered their eventual obsolescence in designing them to be replaceable as more advanced technologically refined units were developed. One-piece bathroom units with atomizer baths and waterless toilets provided self-sufficiency and energy conservation. A grill utility contained conveniences such as a dishwashing machine that, in addition to washing and drying the dishes, returned them to their shelves after cleaning. Vertical and horizontal moving shelves and hangers were pneumatically operative to the convenience of such work functions. To balance Dymaxion living, Fuller's "go ahead with life" functional zone was designed to enhance the mind with its built-in revolving educational equipment and materials to facilitate the learning process. Adding to this, the Dymaxion was designed to be in reach of every consumer's pocketbook. Priced by the pound, 6000 lb to be exact, a completely equipped package was estimated by Fuller to have a market value of $1500 in 1928, at 25¢/lb. The Dymaxion came to its fullest realization in 1944, in the Wichita House, so named for its construction location. This experimental project, as seen in Figure 3, produced two structures that were modifications of the original. Although it stirred widespread attention, the Dymaxion Dwelling never became a mass-produced realization.

Another of Fuller's revolutionary sheltering design concepts did, however, become realized in mass production. Known as the father of the geodesic dome, Fuller devised a mathematical means for executing an enclosure that was simple and easily adaptable to prefabrication methods. Its spherical surface, as seen in Figure 2, is constructed of a three-way triangulated grid and is capable of enclosing vast spaces. The structure's space-spanning attributes facilitate large-scale building functions of all types. In their residential applications, geodesic domes as form givers deliver unique interior space configurations.

Fuller was the consummate inventor–designer whose life span coincided with the age of industrialization. In addition to these architectural triumphs, he contributed numerous other ideas and inventions related to building technology (6).

Unlike abroad, and until the post-World War I period, industrialized construction in the United States developed largely without government commitment, either in programs or subsidies. Its progress was aligned with the flow of cultural changes and lifestyles of the U.S. people. Component elements of industrialized building were being produced, and in this activity a kind of vernacular in U.S. industrialized building began to appear that was germane to the United States and could be readily distinguished from that of Europe. This was particularly true with respect to housing and governmental support programs. In contrast to the United States, European governments were actively committed to underwriting and commissioning a number of building programs in industrialized building, which generated an architectural concentration in multiunit housing far exceeding anything witnessed in the United States. After World War II, however, the U.S. government position did change. At that time, it moved to address a nationwide housing shortage. In 1947, President Harry S. Truman appointed Wilson Wyatt by executive order to head the "Veteran's Emergency Housing Program," which set a national goal of producing 2.7 million housing units by year end. Prefabrication was the identifiable means cited to meet this governmental objective.

The plan called for government assistance in providing war factories for conversion to housing production, where the government itself would serve as a market base. Supportive financing, from subsidies on building materials to interim financing, was also made available. In addition, numerous other accommodations were established up to and including compensation for losses. It would appear that such up-front commitment would have ensured a successful program. In fact, the opposite was true. Reasons forwarded ranged from a lack of operative interest by other dependent government agencies from the Federal Housing Authority to the War Assets Administration (WAA), which refused to release surplus war plants, to the building industry's lack of attending any price controls. The program failed after two years of operation. One of the most publicized prefabricated products that emerged as a result of this program was the Lustron House, as seen in Figure 3. It was designed and manufactured by Carl Strandlund. In time, it also failed, and symbolically carried the badge of failure for the entire program.

Developed in 1946, the Lustron House was a steel and porcelain enamel prefabrication. Produced in an aircraft factory like Fuller's prototype, it was a panel construction with rubber gasket fittings on a steel-stud structure. All interior walls, built-ins, storage, and so on were of steel fabrication. The production process employed automotive assembly techniques, yielding four 1022-ft^2 houses per hour. Lustron's main operational problems were field related. Local building regulators and owner financing posed continuing difficulties. Customers had to pay the $6000 total amount up front, which forced a limited cash market. The houses proved durable and reasonably maintenance free; however, the material composition had its drawbacks. For example, magnets were needed to hang up pictures on the metal wall surfaces. Overall, 5000 units were produced before the company entered into bankruptcy. Contrasted with Fuller's two constructed Dymaxion structures, its showing in terms of numbers was respectable, but hardly sustaining. The Lustron project was viewed by many observers with mixed feelings. Proponents of industrialized housing felt it was a step forward in the learning and growing process of this industry. Others held it up as an exemplary failure and felt that future ideas to further similar projects be quelled before they start.

Another notable contributor to industrialized architecture was designer–architect Charles Eames, whose design and construction of his personal residence demonstrated both in function and aesthetics the potential of building with industrialized components. The Eames House, as illustrated in Figure 3, characterized an open system, as contrasted with Fuller's closed system, utilizing standard off-the-shelf prefabricated components. Its visual presence was a poignant icon of the machine age concept and caused professional critics to take a closer look at mass production. With materials of light metal structure and colored panels and glass, its exterior surfaces recalled modernist painter Piet Mondrian's canvas compositions; it was a stunning artistic organization of machine-produced components. Its built form, simple rectangular units, was also an expression of the modern style, at the same time giving the impression that it had been "clipped off" a production assembly line. It was also significant for its flexibilities in spatial organization. Recounted information about its preconstruction phase indicates that materials ordered from an earlier design were the same used for a later revised design. Another important feature of this structure was that a maximum of space enclosed an open plan that allowed for a continuum of lifestyle changes over time. It also proved to realize the economic attributes of industrialized construction. The structure, with 4-in steel columns and open-web steel joists, was erected in 16 hours by a five-man crew, reducing labor costs from 50 to 33%. The Eames House, in its meticulous detail, was admired by design professionals. It is recalled as a clear example of the successful communion between design and production.

Frank Lloyd Wright was another architect who exercised an interest in industrialized design and building. It appeared to him to have the potential capability of serving a long-harbored interest, which was to provide low-income housing to the masses, given that its machine-produced materials allowed for mass production and economies of scale. In addition to penning his own thoughts about it in "Art and Craft of the Machine," at several points in his career he became involved in projects that were undertaken to address his preoccupation to "solve the small house problem" because, as he said, "it is not only America's major architectural problem, but the problem most difficult for her major architects" (7). Among the earliest of these projects was the American System Ready Cut, a timber-frame system sheathed in plaster, which he developed between 1910 and 1915. Wright was also fascinated with the standardized machine-produced concrete blocks, which he believed held great promise in their undiscovered aesthetic potential. He enlisted significant design attention to this material, deriving some striking textured surfaces, which were put to use in his textile block houses built in the 1920s in Los Angeles.

These interests converged in a residence he built in 1953, identified as the Usonian Automatic. Wright thought that its basic construction, of prefabricated lightweight inexpensive concrete blocks, would allow production of low-cost residences ranging in value from $5000 to $6000. The actual cost, however, reached $25,000, and the adjunct commentary was that it was too stark and mechanical in appearance.

A few years later, Wright collaborated with a building firm, Marshall Erdman, to design and produce four types of prefabricated model homes. Two were built, Pre Fab I and Pre Fab II; the latter is pictured in Figure 3. Both were more rationalized constructions in comparison with today's prefabrication, although by intent they stand as examples instrumental in defining future directions in industrialized construction. Although Wright's desire to solve the housing problem was not realized as he would have liked, he did introduce ideas and building methods to residential construction that remain in use today, from the flat slab foundation, eliminating basement or crawlspace construction, to the car port concept, bypassing the construction of a complete garage enclosure. Such cost-saving economic measures strongly impacted the U.S. house. It, in effect, fostered a systematization that made housing more affordable to the general public. This circumstance subsequently aided the proliferation of subdivisions nationwide. Although their actualizations were far removed from Wright's concept of Broad Acre City, an early subdivision proposal by Wright, his idea appears to have provided the seed for these later suburban enclave communities. The typical repeated house-form design, a single-level, low-slung hip roof, ranch-type dwelling, in its strained representational appearance, recalls an expression from familiar Wrightian design devices. Thus, in a curious way, Wright's goals for housing the many have been served, even though the translation is far removed from the vision.

Among the illustrative works presented in the timeline of industrialized architecture in Figure 3, the architects and designers were involved with a single principal industrialized building material, with the exception of architect Carl Koch. His Techbuilt House of 1953 is one example of his numerous efforts to engage all principal materials of industrialized construction. His career is reflective of a continuous design interest and involvement in industrialized architecture. Prior to the market success of the Techbuilt House, his previous experience dates back to work he had done with Strandlund on the metal-fabricated Lustron House. His design efforts in wood included a prestressed skin paneled expandable fold-out residential structure. From there he went on to design the Techbuilt House, and his later work in prefabrication concentrated on precast concrete, identified as the Techcrete system. Its structural and component package consisted of precast wall panels and supporting, precast, pretensioned, extruded, sawed-off floor slabs.

The Techbuilt House design intention began with securing spatial economy. It was a two-story proposal that combined both the basement and attic spaces into the first and second floors, respectively, thereby addressing the climatic requirements of the former without separate construction and resolving the commonplace waste of the latter with the complement of an architectural cathedral ceiling to the living area. This brought a new look to prefabrication. The shell of house, walls, roof, and second floor was constructed of panels made on a 4-ft module. The panel construction was stressed skin, plywood sheets bonded to wood framing members. Window elements were constructed on the same module as the panels to facilitate variations in planning. The basic exterior frame erection was accomplished in a two-day time period with two to four workers. In this, it allowed for owner assembly; an instruction manual was provided for this purpose. The prototype residence, as seen in Figure 3, attracted publicity and attention when it was first introduced, and consequently, orders for the production of more were significant. As it grew, it was franchised, and its market stretched across the nation and abroad. The initial design concept was later expanded to include vacation houses and Techbuilt space-making furniture. It was competitive in price as well as design, both functionally, in its facility of assembly, and aesthetically, as it blended contextually with existing architecture. These features explain its success in the marketplace.

One of the first examples of industrialized housing to utilize plastic as its principal structural and component material was the Monsanto House, as seen in Figure 3. Designed by architect Marvin Goody, it was prefabricated and erected in 1957. Its construction of honeycomb form-molded core panels of glass-reinforced plastic were fitted together in a crisscross, extended wing configuration set on a central core pedestal. Its built form suggested the futuristic, while retaining expression of its inherent material. It was, in fact, planned and built to be a prototypical representation of the house of the future, where in its location within the confines of the "Land of Tomorrow" in Disneyland Park in Buena Park, California, it was on display for public viewing. A guided tour through the structure at the time of its opening disclosed that in the next two decades the typical household would include such accoutrements as a microwave oven and a household computer. These mechanical and electronic marvels of yesteryear are current-day commonplace realizations, and although the space-age-designed, prototypical unit system structure still has a remote likelihood of being marketed as a product of the immediate future, its plastic material base has assumed a prominent role in the fabrication of industrialized building components, as both subsystem and elemental marketplace items.

In 1961, an industrialized system building concept for school facilities was proposed by Ezra Ehrenkrantz. The School Construction System Development (SCSD) system, as shown in Figure 3, was identifiably an "open system," as contrasted with most of the "closed system" structures represented in the timeline of architecture. Aside from Le Corbusier's Domino dwelling concept and the Eames House's suggestion of extended multiples, an actual full-scale demonstration of the open system concept was first realized in the SCSD system. The SCSD project was researched and developed with the intent of creating a school building system for the construction of 22 schools throughout 13 California public school districts. The program began in 1961 and was assisted by the Ford Foundation Educational Facility Research Funds. It was planned in interrelational phases, beginning with a user analysis requirement phase, a performance specification preparation phase, industry market surveys, invitational bidding by subsystem producers, selected subsystem design integration, architect selection, and design implementation. In addition to its categorical identification as an open system, the SCSD system, in its various planned phases, is also descriptively aligned with the earlier definition of a combination hardware/software system package.

The complete school facility was operationally dependent on four primary subsystem producers, including structure, lighting and ceiling, partition, and mechanical producers. Together, these subsystems composed a final integrated building system. The SCSD system afforded planning flexibilities and design variability. The four subsystems compositionally provided the building's functional basics. Beyond these system components, which comprised 50% of the value of the building, the rest of the project was considered "nonsystem," and the task responsibility was completed by the local project architect. In addressing the system's flexibility features, the architect could then carry forth the building design to address site dictates; the building cladding was open to utilize a wide range of exterior materials and finishes, which, in turn, would allow for a wide range of architectural expression. An added advantage was the minimized time required in planning and erection of the structure. In the reevaluation of the system, the problems most prominent were acoustical inefficiencies and the user's lack of understanding and/or nonutilization of the system's internal functioning flexibilities. Aside from this, it did serve as an example for later school projects, which built upon the SCSD project's initial innovative building concepts.

In 1967, when Moshe Safdie's Habitat was constructed for the Montreal World's Fair, it generated a great deal of international attention. Habitat was constructed just prior to the U.S. government's Operation Breakthrough program, which was then in the planning stage. Together, they marked a point in history when more attention than ever was being given to the concept of industrialized mass-produced housing. Habitat displays a provocative organization of precast concrete modules in a multistoried structure of varied and unique configurations. This can be seen in Figure 3. It breaks away from the monolithic apartment block look that often characterizes modular building. It was Safdie's intention to create a multilevel neighborhood of individual apartment villas, which would incorporate a variety of community facilities. The basic system of Habitat used single repetitive modules to form a variety of house types with varying plans and sizes of living units. The complex organization within identified terraced groupings of the modules, each with its own roof garden, pedestrian and mechanical circulation skyway, streets covered with acrylic sheet networked about the rear of the dwelling complex, and parking and plaza levels at the ground and subfloor. The entire assemblage of parts, 2700 of them, were an integral part of the structure. The beams and walkways acted as horizontal ties, and the modular boxes were under high torsional stress. The modules were constructed of precast concrete near the building site. Much specialized equipment was required to produce them, and some new construction techniques had to be employed. Each module weighed approximately 75 tons. The completed units were hoisted into place by two overhead cranes, one built especially for lifting the weighted modules. One hundred and fifty-eight of the 900 units initially planned were constructed with the cost per unit averaging between $80,000 and $100,000, costly by 1968 standards.

Given the specialized erection expense and other cost factors experienced in the fabrication stages, it was not an economically viable example of modular building. However, because it was a prototypical model, it was bound by the schedule and cost overruns commonly experienced in introducing a building system to the marketplace. In assessing its architectural design and aesthetics, it stands as a pioneering example of what can be done with modular prefabricated housing.

In addition to the innovative aesthetic concept of Habitat, other features included a fiber glass bathroom subsystem unit placed in the module prior to erection. The adjoining street network was also an inventive solution that was multipurpose in function. Two precast members, when joined in the structure, formed box girders facilitating the pedestrian street above and a mechanical distribution system tunnel beneath that carried all the services. After the Habitat experience, Safdie went on to develop further and refine his design concepts in more complex proposals in Puerto Rico and Israel. They were both physically distinct from his first effort, although similar in their cluster organization and design intent.

Two decades after its previous effort, the U.S. government once again initiated an even more ambitious program to establish industrialized housing as a viable vehicle for augmenting housing. As previously cited in the earlier Wyatt program under the Truman administration, it too was a bootstraps effort to alleviate finally the upsurge in housing shortages that was fast approaching crisis proportions.

Operation Breakthrough was the name of the program, and George Romney, former Chief Executive of American Motors, was its administrator. As Secretary of the Department of Housing and Urban Development (HUD), Romney moved to apply his knowledge of mass production and the assembly line methods of automotive industrialization to housing. The program's objective was simply stated "to improve the process of providing housing," which meant far more than just building houses. In 1969, Romney predicted that by 1980, nearly 75% of all U.S. housing would either be factory built or utilize prefabricated components. To this end, proposals were solicited by HUD from a total of 5000 companies throughout the nation. The requests for proposals, Operation Breakthrough—Application of Improved Housing Systems Concepts for Large Volume Production (RFP #H-55-69), were of two types: Type A for design and Type B for research and development of advanced concepts and components. Six hundred one proposals were submitted. By a three-stage review process, the number selected was reduced to 136 and then 37, and finally, on February 26, 1970, Romney announced the 22 housing systems producers that had been selected for contract negotiation.

The Breakthrough program, in seeking better ways to build houses, was oriented toward adding new dimensions to industrialized housing, testing fresh ideas in materials, fabrication and production, erection, labor standards, financing, and marketing. To emphasize this, the Breakthrough program directed particular attention to the innovative aspects of the selected proposals.

The actual selection criteria identified 21 evaluation factors in three groups: concepts, capacity, and plans. Concept factors determined the physical housing system qualities of flexibility, efficiency in use of labor, materials, and schedule forecasts. Capacity was reviewed for strength of the proposed built form and its proposer's financial profile. Plans revealed the proposer's view of the program and anticipated goals for marketing and production.

Overall, the systems represented a rich diversity of building types and construction methods. In terms of basic structural content, ten of the systems were volumetric (or modular), nine were panel systems, and three were component subassemblies. There were variations in principal materials; six systems were of concrete, one of metal, eight of wood, two of plastic, and five of a composite material. Variety was anticipated in the price range, although the market was directed toward low to medium price levels. Multivariate prototype units, including single-family detached, single-family attached (townhouses), and multifamily apartment units in low- to mid- to high-rise buildings, further profiled the 22 selected housing system producers. A physical information description of each system's principal characteristics is presented in Figure 4.

There was a significant representation of members of the architectural profession throughout the Breakthrough experience. Architects participated in the initial call, proposing their own system designs and others worked in tandem with existing companies designing and developing systems proposals. Their involvement in the Breakthrough program was especially pertinent in light of an essential program objective, innovation. In compliance with the stipulated proposal criteria, each proposer was directed to produce and forward his or her system's principal innovative features. The design and development of many of

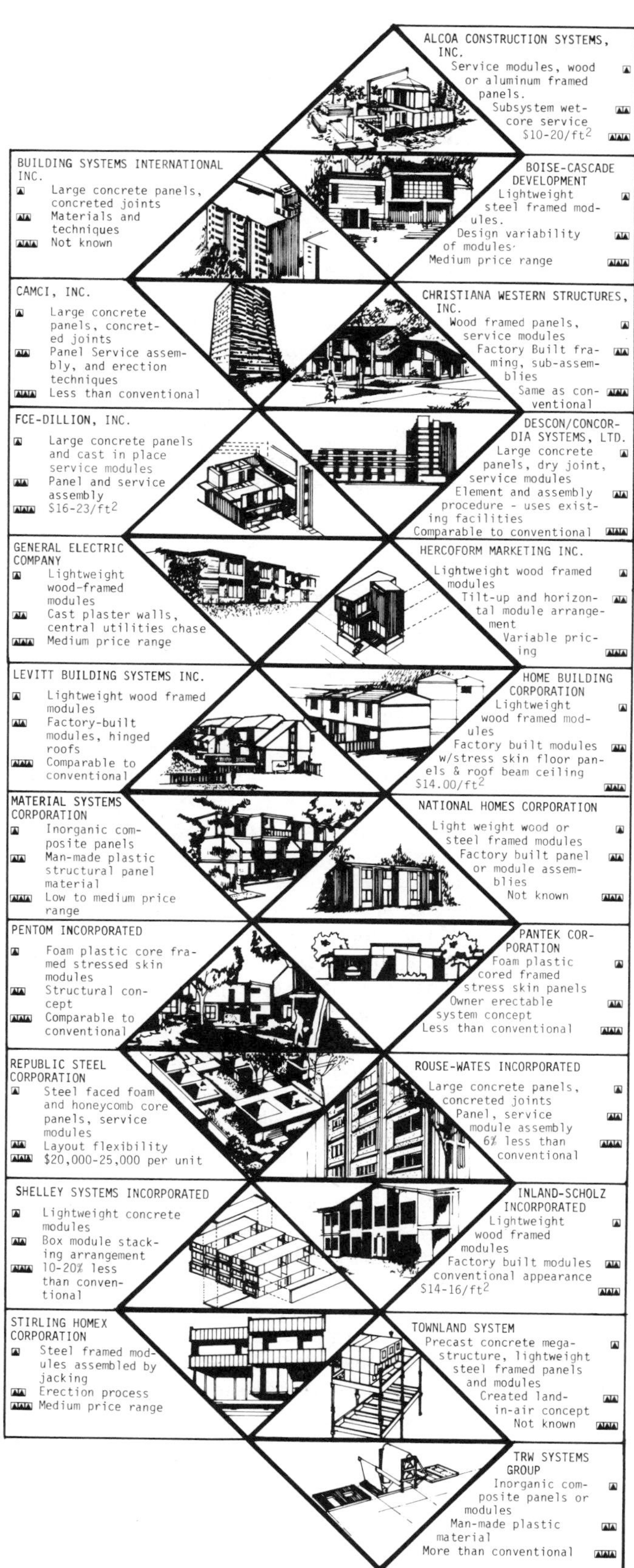

ALCOA CONSTRUCTION SYSTEMS, INC.
Service modules, wood or aluminum framed panels.
Subsystem wet-core service
$10-20/ft²
BUILDING SYSTEMS INTERNATIONAL INC.
Large concrete panels, concreted joints
Materials and techniques
Not known
BOISE-CASCADE DEVELOPMENT
Lightweight steel framed modules.
Design variability of modules·
Medium price range
CAMCI, INC.
Large concrete panels, concreted joints
Panel Service assembly, and erection techniques
Less than conventional
CHRISTIANA WESTERN STRUCTURES, INC.
Wood framed panels, service modules
Factory Built framing, sub-assemblies
Same as conventional
FCE-DILLION, INC.
Large concrete panels and cast in place service modules
Panel and service assembly
$16-23/ft²
DESCON/CONCORDIA SYSTEMS, LTD.
Large concrete panels, dry joint, service modules
Element and assembly procedure - uses existing facilities
Comparable to conventional
GENERAL ELECTRIC COMPANY
Lightweight wood-framed modules
Cast plaster walls, central utilities chase
Medium price range
HERCOFORM MARKETING INC.
Lightweight wood framed modules
Tilt-up and horizontal module arrangement
Variable pricing
LEVITT BUILDING SYSTEMS INC.
Lightweight wood framed modules
Factory-built modules, hinged roofs
Comparable to conventional
HOME BUILDING CORPORATION
Lightweight wood framed modules
Factory built modules w/stress skin floor panels & roof beam ceiling
$14.00/ft²
MATERIAL SYSTEMS CORPORATION
Inorganic composite panels
Man-made plastic structural panel material
Low to medium price range
NATIONAL HOMES CORPORATION
Light weight wood or steel framed modules
Factory built panel or module assemblies
Not known
PENTOM INCORPORATED
Foam plastic core framed stressed skin modules
Structural concept
Comparable to conventional
PANTEK CORPORATION
Foam plastic cored framed stress skin panels
Owner erectable system concept
Less than conventional
REPUBLIC STEEL CORPORATION
Steel faced foam and honeycomb core panels, service modules
Layout flexibility
$20,000-25,000 per unit
ROUSE-WATES INCORPORATED
Large concrete panels, concreted joints
Panel, service module assembly
6% less than conventional
SHELLEY SYSTEMS INCORPORATED
Lightweight concrete modules
Box module stacking arrangement
10-20% less than conventional
INLAND-SCHOLZ INCORPORATED
Lightweight wood framed modules
Factory built modules conventional appearance
$14-16/ft²
STIRLING HOMEX CORPORATION
Steel framed modules assembled by jacking
Erection process
Medium price range
TOWNLAND SYSTEM
Precast concrete megastructure, lightweight steel framed panels and modules
Created land-in-air concept
Not known
TRW SYSTEMS GROUP
Inorganic composite panels or modules
Man-made plastic material
More than conventional

Figure 4. Operation Breakthrough. Selected housing systems producers. Key: ▲, system; ▲▲, principal innovation; ▲▲▲, economics (8).

the proposed systems innovations represented the efforts of numerous professionally trained and experienced creative designers and thinkers. Another of HUD's criteria for selection of the housing systems producers was financial solvency, which ultimately resulted in relying on companies that could show that the selected proposals would be realized. Many small architectural firms would not have been able to qualify as principals under the HUD solvency test. Thus, their professional participatory roles were usually in the nature of consultancy, or as employees of selected housing system producers and/or by service contractual affiliation.

Operation Breakthrough was established as a three-phase program: Phase I—Design and Development; Phase II—Prototype Construction; and Phase III—Production. In Phase I, the housing system producers were charged with the completion of a series of tasks, which included the development of the systems design, housing design, construction drawings, specifications, cost quotations, prototype site planning, codes and regulations, system feasibility studies, program planning for management, construction, production, testing, quality control, community participation, marketing, and financing. The list was extensive, but sufficed for this phase's purpose to complete the development and testing of the 22 systems. The latter was of particular importance because these prototypical and innovative systems, with their new materials, construction methods, and so on, could not be evaluated using existing criteria, although evaluation was needed to ensure that the systems designs met the standards for adequate housing. To this end, HUD commissioned the U.S. Department of Commerce's National Bureau of Standards (NBS) to develop criteria to evaluate the housing systems and to ensure that the systems met government standards for adequate housing. NBS was asked to develop "Guide Criteria for the Evaluation of Operation Breakthrough Systems." The Breakthrough systems were then evaluated against the guide criteria, which included design analysis and physical testing of selected building components to ensure their safety and performance. These evaluation and performance criteria proved worthy beyond the Breakthrough program because they established a point of departure for various factions across the nation to reorient their own codes and standards to allow for the inspection and approval of unit systems buildings.

The purpose of Phase II—Prototype Construction was to facilitate visual demonstration of the capabilities of industrialized housing construction. This was to be accomplished through the construction of prototype housing system units at various sites throughout the country. Several system producers would be represented at each site to include sufficient numbers of units such that land use patterns and housing system variety could be demonstrated.

Following a nationwide proposal invitation and a subsequent review process to determine the most feasible locations for the prototype sites, nine sites were selected. They were viewed to be representative of various climatic and market characteristics and to address a typical portion of the U.S. housing market. The carry-through responsibilities of this phase were left to the eight selected prototype site developers. With the selection of the housing system producers, prototype site developers had been contracted to manage site construction, to administer and supervise arrangements with various producers during the demonstration and management period, and, after construction completion, to market the housing. Prototype site planners included teams of architects, landscape architects, site planners, and engineers. They were selected by competition to develop and execute innovative land-use designs on the prototype sites. Their tasks included data collection and analysis, conceptual design for HUD review and approval, coordination of the various housing systems assigned to each site, and finally, preparation of construction documents for site development.

The Breakthrough Phase III—Production was essentially identified as a transfer of responsibility. Given HUD's main program objective, which was to provide an operational place for industrialized housing within the existing building industry, its goal would be served with the culmination of this phase. It was planned that, upon completion of the preceding two phases, the new housing systems would be ready for both the market and volume production to the degree that private enterprise could assume the leadership from HUD; in so doing, HUD's mission would be accomplished. Although this three-phase program was thorough and involved extensive planning, it did not achieve fruition at the level it had hoped.

The success of the Operation Breakthrough program was evaluated by most on a "measure of immediacy" rather than on its merits over a reasonable length of time. Because of this, it has commonly been referred to as a project failure. However, if its effect on the building industry is studied retrospectively over the past one and a half decades since its inception, the assessment of its merits becomes more favorable. Because of an overstated campaign to herald Operation Breakthrough as changing overnight the whole method and industry of building houses, an oversimplified basis for review was established early. That the program's conclusion forced immediate evaluation was a further limitation to judging fairly its pioneering accomplishments. Since these proposals were innovative and the program experimental, it was inevitable that organizational and operational problems would develop. This expectation that assimilation of the housing system producers into the larger market system would occur immediately after the conclusion of Phase III was unrealistic. In retrospect, program planning aspects did not address long-term goals and objectives beyond the three-phase program calendar, and it was therefore judged on the basis of its performance and failure to impact the industry within the confines of the program's active operational dates. The broader question, which was to be answered eventually in the affirmative, was whether this great-scaled demonstration of industrialized housing brought forth courses of action that have encouraged expansion and viable economic growth within the overall building industry.

STATE OF THE INDUSTRY

The preceding section's discussion and timeline focused on architecture's temporal relationship to industrialized construction over the course of history. An overview of this information tends to suggest that industrialized construction's role in the industry of building has been ancillary and its potential economic viability unproven. In the real picture, it is true that architecture's role has been peripheral to the larger whole of a vast, successful industry that has developed over time its own historical ground.

The metal building, precast concrete, and manufactured housing and mobile home industries are the compositional entities that constitute the larger whole of the industrialized building industry. Over the past five decades, each, as an independent industry, has been engaged in the development and utilization of industrialized processes and products. To that extent, these operations have resulted in a gradual usurping of conventional site building activity, whereby the state of today's building industry, as identified at the onset, is far more industrialized than it had been. The commonly cited percentage for the proportionate representation of industrialized construction is 95%. This includes all categories of industrialized building, as presented in Figure 1, with the larger representation being component production.

At the base of industrialized building industry operations are the same principal materials utilized in conventional building. They are steel, aluminum and its alloys, concrete, and wood. These materials also serve categorically to reference the specific industry market-segmented types of industrialized construction mentioned above. Steel and other metals are predominantly used in the metal building industry. Concrete is the base material of the precast, prestressed building industry. Wood is ostensibly utilized in the manufactured housing and mobile home industry. These three industry types function as giant autonomous units in their own right, although they can all be classified under industrialized building. What further distinguishes the operational nature of each of these industries, and stems from their basic material differences, is their respective manufacturing processes. The processes of producing unit systems and component products are distinctly different for each material; tooling, machinery, and operational procedures unique to the inherent properties of each industry's particular base material are utilized. Figure 5 presents a summary view of the processes of industrialization. Differences in each are identifiable, particularly insofar as the fabrication processes are accomplished. The similarities of these three industries are addressed overall in the phasing stages. Each industry engages in a three-phase process to bring the product from a raw material stage to the final building site as either a component or unit system. These three phases include the fabrication of the product, its transportation to the site, and the erection of the product on the site. The transportation and erection phases are generally more complex

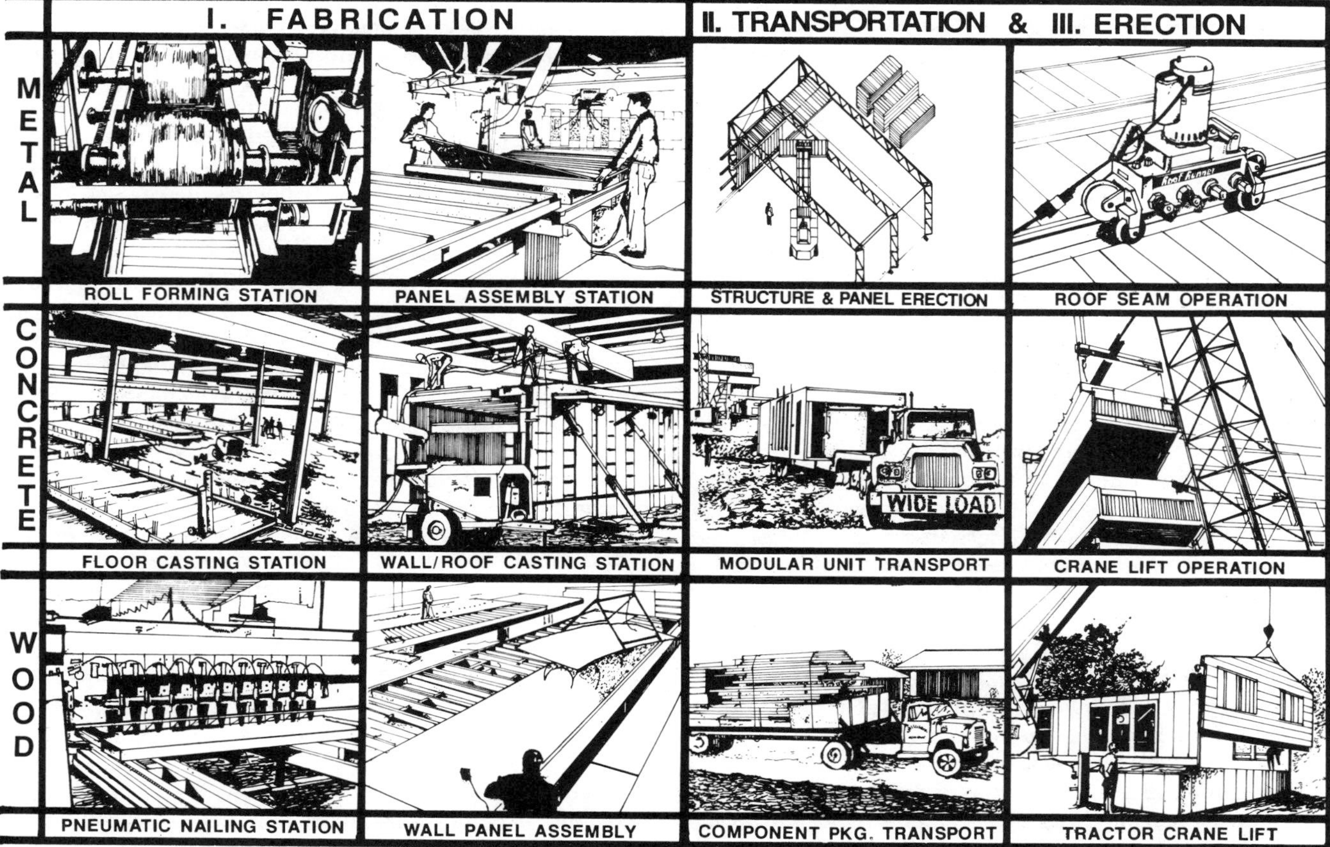

Figure 5. Industrialized construction processes. Fabrication processes represented are exemplary activities of unit system and component production. Total processes engage additional sequential steps for fabrication.

for the handling of unit systems, although, as is implied in the term industrialization, step-by-step procedures for all process phases are planned in detail, ensuring ultimately the time, quality, and economic advantage of the product over nonfactory methods of fabrication.

A further circumstance that dictates a separation of these specific branches within an industry is their variable market differences. Each essentially serves a different market. Notably, manufactured housing, as its name implies, serves the residential building market. The metal building industry focuses on the small- and mid-scale commercial, industrial, and institutional operations, whereas the products of both the precast industry and the structural steel industry predominantly serve mid- to high-rise building market areas. Although crossover in these industry markets is common, the bulk production of each industry supplies the needs of its identified market.

Of these industrialized entities, architecture's primary interface occurs with the precast and structural steel industry because its professional involvement in this area is more directly focused on large-scale building, and similarly, smaller-scale industrialized structures are routinely erected by engineering personnel, builders, developers, or contractors without an architect's involvement.

The current economic state of these separate industry units indicates a continued pattern of upward growth over decade spans, where time and expanding markets have fostered the development of complex business operations. Today they function with the latest state-of-the-art technology, production management procedures, and systematized communication networks in place to accommodate and enhance further their market positions within the overall building industry.

The metal building industry is one example. Its roots are aligned with the technological development of iron and steel, as refinements in the technology of alloying, sheet metal and roll forming, and structural components occurred. The standardized metal unit made its appearance as early as 1915 and was manufactured by the Truscon Steel Company (9). Economical, portable, and quickly assembled, it appealed to both government and commerce. The U.S. military provided a market for these structures during both world wars. The most noteworthy of the metal structures were the familiar quonset huts, used to the extent that they are credited with having helped establish the metal building industry. The design of the ribbed steel, semicircular cross section building is credited to British army colonel P.N. Nissen, who introduced his concept in the 1930s (9). The commercial sector of the metal building market at that time included mainly warehousing, factories, and gasoline service stations, the latter utilizing wall and roof panel components of porcelainized steel, a conceptual forerunner of the later metal curtain-wall system.

The longevity of many metal building manufacturers is notable. Several that began their operations during the war period are flourishing enterprises today. This continuity of operation and maintenance of marketability over many decades has similarly facilitated technological and operational development. Since 1956, the metal building manufacturers have been organized as a national association, so formed to engage in research of building materials and methods and address issues such as safety codes and construction practices, toward a unified goal of market expansion. Today, upward of 25% of all nonresidential, low-rise buildings are constructed from metal building systems (10). Their growth pattern in nonresidential construction is unparalleled. As one brochure states, "people work, shop, bank, pray, and play" in these industrialized structures (10). Their prevalence has so significantly impacted numerous urban scapes that they stand in some places as dominant physical icons of today's building environment.

This circumstance stirs the aesthetic sensibilities of architects and other design professionals. Despite faulted attempts to lend many of them architectural character by panel coloring, fascia, and facade additions of other materials, these metal structures remain undisguisedly utilitarian and visually incompatible within an existing traditional built environment or natural setting. Where architects have had input in applying their professional design skill to organizing these systems' structures and other components, the result warrants a closer look at this industry product's aesthetic potential.

In practice, very large projects contract the services of an architect or engineer, although the majority of structures erected utilize in-house dealer representatives to carry through the project. This cost-saving benefit, together with a cost-effective building system that can be quickly erected, thus minimizing interim finance construction costs, provides for an enticing consumer package. What is more, they are engineered to provide for expansion capabilities. End walls are removable and reusable. Frames can be extended, and add-on sections are easily accommodated. These are design options that further this product's economic factors, which site-built architecturally designed structures cannot offer. The bottom line is that metal building systems serve to shelter utilitarian functions economically and so, resolutely, are sought for such purposes. When aesthetic additives and/or professional services threaten to escalate tight building budgets, they are minimized or dismissed for the sake of economy.

The metal building system design is a straightforward expression of its structural function. The rigid frame, tapered beam, post and beam, and truss beam are the four basic types produced today. Beyond these basic differences, variations are found in panel finishing and contouring configurations, joint detailing, component durability, system flexibility, and ease of assembly. Most systems manufacturers offer complete design–build or "turn-key" packages.

The process of mass producing these various types of components employs a variety of industrial techniques. Rolled sections and steel plate are used in the fabrication of beams and columns. Siding and roofing panel members are formed from large coils of 20 gauge steel, which is coated with synthetic polymers or resins and painted. The coils are fed into a multistation roll former, where the different-shaped rollers cold-form sheet metal into sculptured contours. These are then cut into panels, which have been insulated on the assembly line using an injection process; alternatively, the insulation may be field applied. Automated equipment is used in the production process, where machinery controls, inventory, and flow of materials are handled by computers. Computers are also utilized for design, engineering, and field erection. The primary market goal of the metal building industry is to produce structures rapidly, at a very competitive price, with precision-detailed design to facilitate rapid field erection. The whole process is systematized from production to erection. Components are systematically loaded, carried to the site, and placed strategically around the site perimeter to speed erection. A portable truck crane is used for positioning large structural members. Field personnel utilize scaffolds and ladders to attach smaller components.

A more recent focus on product refinement and new product development has expanded the market to include interior systems in addition to structural enclosure systems. Interior systems comprise panels, partitions, and ceiling systems. Additionally, the metal building industry's market has expanded internationally. Export of these systems' products, technology, and production facilities has brought industrialization to some foreign countries.

Within this material focus on steel and alloy metals, another product of industrialization, with which architects have had more direct contact, is space frames. Its advantages serve both function and aesthetics in architectural design. Compositionally, space frames are three-dimensional frameworks of two basic structural members, rods and connectors. They can span large spaces using a minimum of material. What is more, there is a high visual appeal in seeing these lattice grid geometries of tetrahedral and octahedral combinations stretched either vertically or horizontally across grand expanses of space. Over the last two decades, as sheltered atrium spaces have become a fashionable design solution for public gathering spaces in hotels, shopping centers, museums, and so on, space frame structures have been used frequently in architecturally designed structures. In addition to their basic architectural attributes of function and aesthetics, they are ideal products of industrialization because of their essential simplicity of manufacturing, transport ease, and quick erection.

Concrete, comparatively speaking, as an industrialized building material, has had wider international usage over the history of industrialization than either of the other two principal materials discussed here. Since the last war period, in European countries, in particular Eastern Europe, concrete has been used extensively in major buildings for several reasons. There were great shortages of housing due to war demolition as well as increasing numbers of new households. Also, there was an inadequate pool of skilled labor and building material shortages. Concrete, with its systems building potential, offered an expedient solution for new building construction.

Governments were also committed to furthering precast system building to varying degrees ranging from funding programs to assuming control of the construction industry. In France, the Ministry of Housing sponsored the Camus system to produce several thousand housing units. This was typical of circumstances in the United Kingdom, Sweden, and other Western European countries, although most precast system building was done in the Eastern European countries, especially in the USSR. Under state programs, the government produced thousands of housing units per year. These Soviet programs serve as a clear example of realized economies of scale in precast systems building. Having been operationally active over many decades, the industry has evolved technologically to where computers control the on-line component production process. The facilities' layouts utilize a series of assembly lines of component products, that is, interior and exterior wall panels and floor and ceiling roof slabs. Each line consists of several workstations, where a component passes through from start to finish and each station performs a progressive level of refinement of that component. This includes reinforcing with steel bars, casting, steam curing, and finishing. Other station processes may include pretensioning or posttensioning operations on the steel reinforcement of the concrete structural components. This industrialized process for precast unit systems, although its functions are on a grander scale in the USSR, bears operational similarities to those in the United States and other countries. Figure 5 provides a representational example of two of the production stages in the fabrication of a precast modular unit.

Precasting, by the material's nature, is cumbersome and requires heavy machinery throughout the process from production to erection. It is a costly process that realizes economic returns only when its market is consistent and large. Generally, in countries where this industry operates under government control or support, a guaranteed market exists. In free enterprise, market-oriented systems, such as that of the United States, the process and product must compete with other industrialized counterparts where supplies of the other are comfortably available. The precast industry in the United States has, however, maintained a growth position over time and, as cited, focuses primarily on the larger nonresidential construction markets. Of the three industry types, metal, modular, and precast, the architectural profession's design involvement with industrialized building has been largely concentrated on the last. Precast concrete's material properties enable a wide latitude in design expression. As a moldable material, it may render architectural form with a strong sense of plasticity or, contrastingly, a distinct planar expression.

The design flexibilities of precast concrete have played a prominent role in contemporary Japanese architecture in all aspects of building, and in modular housing in particular. With precast concrete as their frequent material base, Japanese metabolist architects have executed innovative designs that reflect, aesthetically, a highly industrialized dynamic society and functionally, mass-produced living systems with open-exchange components (11). These realized concepts of clip-on capsules and plug-in modules, in fact, utilize all available industrialized materials and technologies. Plastics, as an example of industrialized materials that have yet to find their fullest expression in the building arts, have served as multipurpose building materials; their use in Japan has not yet been surpassed.

In the industrialization of wood building products, the principal market concentration is in housing. Under the encompassing heading of manufactured housing, the production of industrialized unit systems—mobile, modular, panel, sectional, and other precut component packages—

identifies these as broad-based industries within the larger-scoped industry. Historically, and aside from the replacement of conventional site fabrication by factory-produced building components (ie, doors, windows, structural units, etc), industrialized housing has produced a distinct growth pattern.

Among the system types identified above, the mobile home industry has shown a record of growth and expansion similar to that of the metal building industry. Its success is explained by the fact that its product has also found market acceptance as a cost-worthy substitute for conventional construction. This industry's history spans more than a half century. Its market concept initially began with the notion of mobility coupled with economy. "Travel trailers" had found their market in World War II as a condition of the time; the rapid development of war industries spawned dispersion and mobility of the labor force. An immediate need for low-cost housing was the result, and trailer home manufacturers could deliver it. Trailer housing, from this point on, became a solution to shelter that was both immediate and within economic reach of the masses. In the ensuing years, the housing shortage continued to rise and, consequently, so did the growth of the mobile home industry.

Industry forces soon recognized that the bottom line of market interest in mobile over conventional housing was economy rather than mobility. This resulted in a redirected focus by the industry toward providing a product that was more comparable to site-built housing in its interior and exterior amenities. The mobility feature of the structure was becoming of incidental value. This industry response led to an array of physical size and material alterations about what remained a basic rectilinear unit set on a steel travel chassis. Long, extra-long, double-wide, multilevel, fold-out, pop-up, and expandable units enabled spatial configurations akin to those of site-built housing. Similarly, interior and exterior finishes and pitched or other house-form roof configurations moved this industry into a market position such that, by the late 1970s, figures showed that mobile home manufacturers were producing one-fifth of all housing stock in the United States.

From an aesthetic perspective, mobile home structures have been held in disfavor by many designers. Limitations of their structural forms by transportation ordinances, and the use of low-quality construction materials in their manufacture to maintain low market prices, tend to make them merely synthetic realizations of residences. As such, they do not blend well with existing built or natural environments. Design attention by the architectural profession to the mobile home concept has occurred occasionally and sporadically. Architectural professionals such as Frank Lloyd Wright and Paul Rudolph have submitted interesting proposals for mobile unit housing (12,13). Also, a significant body of research on the subject by Arthur D. Bernhardt, entitled *Building Tomorrow: The Mobile/Manufactured Housing Industry,* presents an in-depth treatment of the industry's past, present, and forecasted future from a designer's perspective (14).

The process of manufacturing mobile housing occurs within a multistation assembly line, which begins with constructing a wood floor on a prefabricated 10-in. steel beam frame. From there it is structured and pneumatically tool finished in a manner similar to today's site construction, which also uses pneumatic fastening tools; the principal difference is that the factory-dimensioned unit moves along the line for each layered construction task. This factory fabrication process bears a close operational resemblance to that of nonmobile, wood modular, and sectional unit systems industrialized construction. Essentially, the process produces modules in the same organizational manner with similar machinery without the steel frame chassis. The total market package for a single house or apartment living unit comprises multiple modules. Although this industry has yet to realize the market success of the mobile housing industry, it has, in recent years, along with wood panel and precut system manufacturers, experienced an increased market focus for its products. In this way, mobile unit manufacturers have also revamped their fabrication operations and are producing modular and sectional units materially compatible with site-built housing. In this same vein, they have altered erection processes to accommodate in-ground foundation settings for these units to maintain an identity closer to that of conventional structures.

With wood module, sectional, panel, and precut unit system designs that are integrable within traditional built settings, coupled with conditions of construction labor shortages, builders and developers are increasingly opting for erecting manufactured housing systems and realizing time and cost efficiencies in the long run. Previously, industry housing manufacturers interfaced more directly with the consumers, and builders and developers only involved themselves with site stick-built housing. Now they have come to realize the advantages of unit systems over stick-built, where site work and labor are minimized, and inventories of materials and security measures involved in housing or safeguarding them from pilferage do not exist. Further, material waste is no longer an issue of concern, and thus, in consideration of all of these issues, including a shortening of the construction time schedule and consequent reduction in interim financing costs, the overall overhead costs are reduced. What is more, earlier income revenues can be realized. Of further import is that with the profit potential afforded by selecting industrialized housing systems over conventional methods, financial gains are possible, even though factory-fabricated units may be priced slightly above similarly sized conventionally constructed units.

This increasing market trend of builders and developers replacing traditional stick-built housing with factory-produced unit systems has attracted international interest. The Scandinavian countries of Sweden, Denmark, and Finland have entered the U.S. market with their energy-efficient panel system imports (15). Similarly, Japan, in assessing the positive directional market of manufactured housing in the United States, has set up factory modular unit operations in both East and West Coast locations. These state-of-the-industry trends in nonmobile manufactured housing are informationally revealing from both yesteryear and future-year perspectives. Previously held public assumptions about the inferiority of this industry's product seem to have waned. The turnaround has come about from the marked improvements in material quality and the attempts at aesthetic compatibility with the site-built counterpart. The benefits of its economic attributes in time and cost savings are also being realized. This circumstance, coupled with the current growth and expansion trends by U.S. and foreign markets, forecasts a substantial growth direction for the future.

Contemplating the future of industrialized housing from an architectural perspective directs the summary treatment of this subject area to design research and expression. Theoretical and practical concerns that address design issues in an industrialized housing aesthetic or how the process of industrialization can serve the process of life continue to be studied by both architectural practitioners and academicians.

The work of the Japanese metabolist architects, cited earlier, is exemplary of a concentrated focus in this direction. Design proposals and built examples examine and render solutions that address human functioning in a society of high industry and technology. Their presentations of built form appear as an indigenous expression of industrialized architecture.

Another celebrated effort is that of architect N. J. Habraken. His "Supports" system of housing redresses earlier built examples of mass-produced housing insensitive to fundamental humanistic values of need and accommodation. The Supports concept emphasizes that future building and, in particular, industrialized building address the importance of providing for the user/dweller to engage in the process of place-making his or her own personal environment. The complete planning proposal envelops the larger societal community or municipality base and the neighborhood strata, as well as the individual user and user groups. The physical system consists of a support structure and system-integrable, although detachable, component units. The Supports concept, beyond its social base, is physically congruous with industrialized design and construction. Although its realization has been limited to scale demonstration in the Netherlands, its example proposes a sound working interface between architecture, industrialized construction, and the users of built form.

In the past, architecture and its role in the design process of industrialized construction, although contributory, as stated here, have been peripheral to the construction industry. As master interpreters of the design building process, the profession could purposefully support the continuum of change in the interrelational cycle of processes, where the design process serves the industrialized building process, which ultimately contributes to the quality of life within the built environment.

BIBLIOGRAPHY

1. American Institute of Architects, *The Building Systems Integration Handbook,* John Wiley & Sons, Inc., New York, 1985, p. 4.
2. R. Sluzas and A. Ryan, *A Graphic Guide to Industrialized Building Elements,* CBI Publishing Co., Inc., Boston, Mass., 1977.
3. L. S. Cutler and S. S. Cutler, *Handbook of Housing Systems for Designers and Developers,* Van Nostrand Reinhold Co., New York, 1984, p. 19.
4. S. Giedion, *Space, Time, and Architecture,* Harvard University Press, Cambridge, Mass., 1949, p. 123.
5. Le Corbusier, *The Modular: A Harmonious Measure to the Human Scale Universally Applicable to Architecture and Mechanics,* MIT Press, Cambridge, Mass., 1977.
6. R. Marks, *The Dymaxion World of Buckminster Fuller,* Anchor Books, Garden City, New York, 1973.
7. R. C. Twombly, *Frank Lloyd Wright, His Life and His Architecture,* John Wiley & Sons, Inc., New York, 1979, p. 237.
8. U.S. Department of Housing and Urban Development, *Phase I—Design and Development of Housing Systems for Operation Breakthrough,* U.S. Government Printing Office, Washington, D.C., 1973.
9. B. J. Sullivan, *Industrialization in the Building Industry,* Van Nostrand Reinhold Co., New York, 1980, p. 125.
10. *Ibid.,* p. 128.
11. M. F. Ross, *Beyond Metabolism, The New Japanese Architecture,* McGraw-Hill Inc., New York, 1978.
12. Taliesin Associated Architects of the Frank Lloyd Wright Foundations, *Production Dwellings,* Wisconsin Department of Natural Resources, Madison, Wis., 1970.
13. J. Carreiro and co-workers, *The New Building Block: A Report on the Factory-produced Dwelling Module,* Res. Rep. No. 8, Center for Housing and Environmental Studies, Cornell University, Ithaca, N.Y., 1969, pp. 98–105.
14. A. D. Bernhardt, *Building Tomorrow: The Mobile/Manufactured Housing Industry,* MIT Press, Cambridge, Mass., 1980.
15. "Scandinavians Introduce New Closed-panel Building System," *Automation in Housing and Manufactured Home Dealer* **22** (6), 16 (June 1985).

General References

References 2–7, 9, and 11–14 are good general references.

K. M. Ford and T. H. Creighton, *The American House Today,* Reinhold Publishing Corp., New York, 1951.

B. Kelly, *The Prefabrication of Houses,* MIT Technology Press, Cambridge, Mass., and John Wiley & Sons, Inc., New York, 1951.

A. Q. Jones and F. E. Emmons, *Builders' Homes for Better Living,* Reinhold Publishing Corp., New York, 1957.

C. Koch and A. Lewis, *At Home with Tomorrow,* Rinehart and Co., Inc., New York, 1958.

A. L. Huxtable, *Pier Luigi Nervi,* George Braziller, Inc., New York, 1960.

Preassembled Building Components, Proceedings of the 1960 Conference of Building Research Institute, National Academy of Sciences, National Research Council, Washington, D.C., 1961.

T. Schmid and C. Testa, *Systems Building, An International Survey of Methods,* Frederick A. Praeger Publishers, New York, 1969.

P. Beaver, *The Crystal Palace 1851–1936, A Portrait of Victorian Enterprise,* Hugh Evelyn Limited, London, 1970.

M. Safdie, *Beyond Habitat,* MIT Press, Cambridge, Mass., 1970.

R. J. Lytle, *Industrialized Builders Handbook,* Structures Publishing Co., Farmington, Mich., 1971.

J. A. Reidelback, *Modular Housing—1971 Facts and Concepts,* Cahner Publishing Co., Inc., Boston, Mass., 1971.

R. Bender, *A Crack in the Rear View Mirror, A View of Industrialized Building,* Van Nostrand Reinhold Co., New York, 1973.

M. Gayle and E. Gillon, Jr., *Cast-iron Architecture in New York,* Dover Publications, New York, 1974.

U.S. Department of Housing and Urban Development, *Phase II—Prototype Construction and Demonstration,* Vol. 4, U.S. Government Printing Office, Washington, D.C., 1975.

N. J. Habraken and co-workers, *Variations, The Systematic Design of Supports,* MIT Laboratory of Architecture and Planning, MIT Press, Cambridge, Mass., 1976.

G. Herbert, *Pioneers of Prefabrication, The British Contribution in the Nineteenth Century,* Johns Hopkins University Press, Baltimore, Md., 1978.

F. Coffee, *The Complete Kit House Catalog,* Wallaby Pocket Books, New York, 1979.

K. J. Dominguez, *Production Dwellings: A Design Proposal for Multi-resident Housing and Its Market and Cost Feasibility,* Department of Architecture, MIT, Cambridge, Mass., 1979.

A. M. Watkins, *The Complete Guide to Factory Made Houses,* E. P. Dutton, New York, 1980.

B. Russell, *Building Systems Industrialization and Architecture,* John Wiley & Sons, Inc., London, 1981.

A. Brooks, *Cladding of Buildings,* Construction Press, Longman Group Limited, Essex, UK, 1983.

Professional Builder, Apartment Business (Oct. 1984); (Dec. 1984); (Feb. 1985); (July 1985).

Automation in Housing and Manufactured Home Dealer, **22** (1) (Jan. 1985); **22** (6) (June 1985); **22** (9) (Sept. 1985); **22** (11) (Nov. 1985).

See also CONSTRUCTION INDUSTRY; PAXTON, JOSEPH; RESIDENTIAL BUILDINGS

KAREN J. DOMINGUEZ
Penn State University
State College, Pennsylvania

INSPECTION, OBSERVATION, AND SUPERVISION

CONSTRUCTION RESPONSIBILITIES: ARCHITECT–ENGINEER, OWNER, CONTRACTOR

Modifications have evolved over the past 25 years in the design professional's usage of the terms inspection, observation, and supervision during construction administration. Unless the design professional has contracted to provide full-time comprehensive contract administration during the construction period, architect–engineers avoid the term supervision in concert with construction administration. Supervision tends to imply a broader authority over a contractor's work than design professionals assume in standard owner–architect agreements.

The term inspection has also tended to be avoided by design professionals except when full-time comprehensive contract administration has been contracted for by them. Inspection tends to imply more minute focus on the details of construction than is assumed by design professionals in standard owner–architect agreements.

The term observation is currently included in standard owner–architect documents. It describes the actions of design professionals reviewing construction work during performance of construction administration.

A construction project will normally be successful if the following measures are expeditiously and harmoniously undertaken (1).

1. The owner selects a qualified architect–engineer and explains to him or her the parameters of the project.
2. The architect–engineer transforms these parameters into a complete set of working drawings and specifications.
3. These drawings are reviewed by one or more contractors for a favorable construction proposal.
4. The owner, after consulting the architect–engineer on these proposals, selects and engages the most qualified contractor to perform the construction of the project.
5. The contractor completes the project according to the terms of the contract, within the agreed period of time.

Construction industry progress over the past 25 years has done little to diminish the appropriateness of this traditional method of construction commencement. However, the high costs of real property financing in combination with inflation trends have tended to stress a design professional's need to adhere to an owner's budgetary constraints as well as to the design program the property requires.

Further, a newer driving factor in the construction environment is litigation (2). It tends to involve approximately one-third of all design professionals on a yearly basis. It creates pressures that, in turn, factor into construction administration techniques.

This traditional procedure for construction commencement remains prevalent during periods of stable and reasonable interest rates and when cost escalations are modest because of limited inflation. It is particularly germane for real property developments where the need for initial economy of replacement cost outweighs a need for early occupancy and accelerated completion.

To counter the deleterious effects on construction costs of high interest rates and significant inflation, the industry has augmented its traditional methods of construction commencement. New techniques include construction management, fast-tracking, and design–build. The last-named has been excluded from discussion as it has limited application.

Construction initiation and contractor selection using either traditional or newer techniques employ two basic forms of owner–contractor contracts. They are competitively bid lump-sum contracts and negotiated contracts. In application of any technique, fair and ethical procedures employed by all principals are essential.

Lump-sum, private sector, construction contracts often cause some owners to resort to unfair and unwise practices in their zeal for getting the greatest construction volume per dollar. After competitive bids have been tabulated, these owners will suggest that their favorite contractor be permitted to match the low bid. Even worse is their attempt to play off low bidders against one another to produce even lower bids. These practices are, of course, unethical. They are shortsighted as well, and owners or their agents who engage in them will eventually encounter a shortage of competent contractors willing to associate with them on construction projects. When projects are bid higher than the allowed budget, cooperative negotiations can be conducted to effect substitutions and bring the project to fruition without offensive shopping.

Negotiated owner–contractor contracts may be cost-plus contracts, those based on the reimbursement of a contractor for all expenses incurred in the performance of a project plus an established fixed fee or cost percentage profit. Negotiated contracts may also be for a lump-sum upset price with possible inclusion of designated sharing of potential savings—as between the owner and contractor.

The cost-plus contract generally provides higher unit-cost construction than the competitively bid lump-sum contract. Nevertheless, the cost-plus contract may be of greater service to an owner in projects of unusual complexity, or in those in which construction cannot await completion of the working drawings and specifications.

Although the general contract work is to be performed on a time and material expenditure basis, as many subcontractors as possible should be contracted on a competitively bid lump-sum basis if this can be accomplished without defeating the time-saving element.

Equipment rental rates for the construction work should be established in the contract of a negotiated construction contract. These rates require cautious examination before contract execution as standard book value rental rates may yield a high secondary profit compared with competitive market rental rates.

Construction management is a contemporary technique for initiating construction. It has evolved from numerous complexities in the construction industry. Particular influence on this technique relates to construction cost escalation, which has been manifest during periods of inflation. Another factor has been high-interest construction loans and mortgages. Accordingly, methods have been sought to accelerate the construction process in order to save time and cost.

Owners always require accurate construction capital budget projections during the period when the owner and the design professionals formulate the development's prerequisites and as the program transforms into a set of working drawings and specifications. Construction managers' usage augments the construction knowledge of the design professionals as an additional agent for the owner. A construction manager can enhance many aspects of the construction process, but must help to generate successful cost and completion control in order to attain the objective.

Because construction managers are reimbursed on a fee basis, their employment, in theory, may combine the desired objectives that owners separately seek from both competitively bid lump-sum construction contracts and negotiated construction contracts.

The construction manager's role consists of assisting the owners and their design professionals to establish and maintain a cogent capital program budget. The manager assists in developing the shortest and most efficient time of construction, from the commencement of the design to the completion of the development. All aspects of the construction procedure, including some overview of contractors' safety programs, are coordinated by the construction manager.

Unlike a contractor, the construction manager is not reimbursed from profits on the construction work. Construction managers are not direct or indirect implementers of contractor's means, methods, or procedural techniques. Accordingly, there is no established conflict of interest between an owner and the construction manager as may exist between owner and contractor. Therefore, construction management lends itself to construction work in both the private and the public sector. It does not supersede obtaining competitive bids as may occur in certain negotiated contract awards.

Construction initiation by fast-tracking segments a development into timely sequential bid packages established by a construction manager. As the design professional completes the early-stage contract documents, the construction manager obtains a contractor for this work segment and the construction commences. In successful fast-tracking, the time for completing the capital program has thus been reduced by that increment of time that is required for the design professional to complete the entire design and all contract documents.

Adroit construction fast-tracking has been accomplished in circumstances where the owner, architect–engineer, construction manager, and contractors for the sequential bid packages have worked appropriately and harmoniously. It can be an effective procedure. Targeted costs and accelerated completions may result.

Conversely, when improperly accomplished, this procedure may fail, with dire consequences, in instances where the spirit of cooperation and harmony of the major contributors part company. Two damaging consequences may result. First, the project may rapidly proceed without control of both its allowable budget and completion date and with damages accumulating. Second, although this technique may include a general contractor, it is likely that no general contractor is present in this process. If there is no general contractor and the procedure fails, there occurs a lack of single-party responsibility for problems. The remedy is complex, costly, and difficult.

Regardless of the technique chosen to implement and initiate construction, there are sources that assist in the determination of contractors' prequalifications. A contractor's qualifications generally are known to architect–engineers in the same area. References on out-of-town contractors can be obtained by checking with their banking facilities. Owners, architect–engineers, and construction managers having past dealings with a particular contractor can also supply information. The architect–engineer, the construction manager, and the owner have a common responsibility to determine a prospective contractor's competence before qualifying the firm as a bidder or before beginning contract negotiations.

When prequalifying contractors and making a contractors' bidding list, the person responsible for selection should consider several factors. The prospective bidders should appear competent—neither too large nor too small for the type of job—and they should be financially acceptable. The low bidder should usually be awarded the job.

Generally speaking, large contracting organizations, with sizable office and equipment facilities, operate on a higher overhead basis than do small companies. For this reason, small projects of a simple nature rarely will prove economically feasible for large contractors if they must bid competitively against small organizations. Conversely, a large, complex project might literally overwhelm a small contractor not equipped to handle work of such magnitude. Therefore, the selector should obtain logical competitive bids from experienced, successful contractors with organizations of the appropriate size.

Credit ratings and bonding capacity from financial organizations, material suppliers, and other allied firms can also assist in evaluating the contractor. Finally, the contractor's current work volume should be checked as this can greatly affect both the contractor's current credit and ability to perform within the designated time period.

The contractor's responsibility is to complete all construction according to plans and specifications, within the agreed time period, not including time losses from changes ordered by others. Additional factors that may be considered as a legal basis for delay are excessive bad weather, labor disputes, fire or mishaps, and other causes beyond the contractor's control. The architect–engineer's responsibility during the construction phase is to monitor construction in a manner that will reasonably safeguard the owner from defective or nonconforming work. However, the architect–engineer does not guarantee the performance of the contractor (3). The task of contract administration for the architect–engineer consists of interpreting plans and specifications when these are questioned, assisting the contractor during the initial stages of each trade to establish quality levels, and rendering assistance in coordinating construction period responsibilities for which the architect–engineer has contracted.

The architect–engineer is not directly or indirectly involved with contractor's techniques, means, methods, or procedures for construction (3). He or she has a basic interest in a result that may be accomplished by diverse techniques. However, when the architect–engineer is aware that a contractor's procedure will generate an improper building characteristic, he or she must try to counter that undesirable result. The art of initiating and maintaining superior architect–engineer construction administration involves understanding how to effectively employ a basically passive role. Work stoppage and work rejection are active procedures and contractor's responsibilities (4). The architect–engineer also checks contractor payment requests and appropriately issues payment certificates in accordance with the contract.

The owner's responsibilities during the construction phase are to make prompt payments to the contractor, to make any necessary changes in the project with as little disruption as possible, and to bear the cost of all such changes. Owners traditionally provide resources for furnishing soils and materials testing, surveys, and legal, accounting, and insurance counseling, as required, to conduct the work. Generally, an owner must furnish expeditious information to allow an orderly progression of the work. Interference by the owner with the contractor's business can have the effect of suspending the contractor's responsibility.

Construction management responsibilities are those as an owner's agent, which have many characteristics that simulate an owner's responsibilities. Construction manager's responsibilities closely replicate many of the traditional responsibilities associated with a general contractor—having a fee stipulated cost plus negotiated general contract in which that contractor performs construction administration only and is reimbursed solely on a fee basis for such administration.

The architect–engineer, the owner, and the contractor must all help promote a harmonious working atmosphere. The benefits of such an atmosphere cannot be overemphasized. In today's litigious society, the construction procedure grows ever more complex. When the process fails and troubles arise, responsibilities become blurred. Then the principals tend to blame one another for failures, and the legal system becomes the master builder.

ORGANIZATION OF THE PROJECT

The first step in getting a construction project underway after the construction contract has been awarded is a meeting of the representatives of the owner, the architect–engineer, the construction manager, if applicable, and the contractor to establish necessary liaison channels.

The policies of the owner may emanate from a single person, in the simplest situation, or from an entire board of directors acting for a corporate body (5). For the sake of expediency during construction, however, one or perhaps two persons should be designated as the owner's representative(s) with authority to act on the owner's behalf.

The policies of the architect–engineer at all stages of the project, from initial development to completion, are in the hands of a project manager. In the design stage, control is exercised by the principal architectural designer. Working drawings and specifications formulation are controlled by the project architect or architectural job captain who additionally coordinates the structural, mechanical, electrical, and civil engineers, and various consultants engaged in the work. But in all of this design professional work, the project manager is usually the chief liaison with the owner; he or she is the development's final authority within the office of the architect–engineer.

The architect–engineer's responsibility during the construction stage is delegated to a representative, who was formerly designated as the architect–engineer's superintendent, project engineer, or supervising architect but is now most aptly termed architect's representative, architect–engineer's representative, or project representative. The representative reports to the project manager within the office of the architect–engineer. In accordance with the owner–architect–engineer agreement, the architect–engineer's representative is responsible for construction-phase administration related to the project, for the architect–engineer.

The contractor's personnel organization is larger and more complex than are those of the representatives for either the owner or the architect–engineer. Most contracting firms place control of the entire project with their own project manager, usually an executive in the contractor's organization. The contractor's project manager is his or her chief representative, operating on a level comparable to the architect–engineer's project manager and the owner's representative.

On the construction site, the ranking contractor official is the project superintendent, who actuates and is in charge of the work. He or she must ensure that the work conforms to contract requirements and is responsible for progress toward completion. The project superintendent's proximity to the project and decisions underlie all work production and coordination of construction. The project superintendent controls job safety and all ancillary work aspects. One might accurately state that a construction firm's ability to produce a successful project directly depends on the personal decisions and capabilities of its project superintendent.

Beneath the superintendent, the contractor's work responsibility is divided between the field office and field production. The field office hires labor, purchases materials, and provides job accounting services. On occasion, subcontracts are negotiated from the field office, although more often these subcontracts are awarded in the contractor's main office. Standard specified architect–engineer's general conditions of the contract indicate that general condition contractual requirements to be borne by the contractor shall be borne by subcontractors in their subcontracts and so designated in contractor–subcontractor agreements. Field production is performed by a hierarchy of assistants to the superintendent who control construction engineering, coordination of subcontractors, and direction of trade labor foremen.

Progress meetings are an excellent method of maintaining a smooth flow of construction because they provide a forum where representatives of the owner, the architect–engineer, the contractor, subcontractors, and material suppliers can discuss various aspects of the project. A collateral benefit of these meetings is the business-oriented familiarity that develops among these principals of authority. This forum should have a cogent agenda and prompt, accurate minutes.

On a large project, progress meetings should be held with some regularity, probably every week, with appropriate parties in attendance. These meetings often will reveal problems known to one group but not known to the others. Meetings should be frequent enough to solve all problems that arise.

Correspondence and reports should be discussed at the earliest project meetings so that adequate records of job programs will be kept and so that all parties will receive copies of pertinent communications. It is very important that the architect–engineer furnish the project representative with copies of all cogent correspondence relating to the project and of all letters to the owner and the contractor.

Internal architect–engineer communications are important to the architect's representative, for they can give a thorough understanding of the reasoning behind the design elements of the project and therefore a more intelligent approach to the construction. In the construction stage, appropriate correspondence and letters to the contractor from the architect–engineer may emanate from the architect's representative, to give added strength to his or her position. Oral instructions should be avoided. Copies of all correspondence between the architect–engineer and the contractor, except routine transmittals, should normally be furnished to the owner's representative. This is an excellent way to keep the owner apprised of progress.

Weekly progress reports prepared by the architect–engineer's project representative are invaluable for recording job progress and setting forth any problems to be resolved. This report should include data such as weather conditions, lost production time, average number of workers for the various trades on site, description of work performed, percentage of work completed, progress or special meetings held, problems existing, and any unusual items of interest.

Change orders of work authorization should be processed by the architect–engineer, contractor, and owner on appropriate forms, in an established routine so that the owner will be aware of all changes and their cost ramifications, and so that the contractor will feel free to perform work in connection with modified plans and specifications and to incorporate the new costs into the billing.

Changes generally arise out of unforeseen field conditions, or from requests to meet a specific program change requirement of the owner. Architects do not have authority to stop work, nor should they want this authority, as it could generate undesired responsibility—particularly in the area of safety. Standard contracts between the architect–engineer and the owner and between the owner and contractor usually stipulate that the architect–engineer is not empowered to authorize contract extras or changes without the owner's authorization. It is essential to observe this stipulation lest the owner refuse to accept a changed scope of work or cost obligations that arise from unauthorized changes.

When the owner wants a work change, or if the architect–engineer considers one to be appropriate during the construction period, the potential change should be documented on a supplementary drawing or in a descriptive letter, which is then sent to the contractor for a cost proposal.

After the cost proposal has been received and analyzed by the architect–engineer, he or she should transmit it with recommendations to the owner for action. When the owner's written authorization has been received, a change-order number should be assigned to the work. The change order is then issued to the contractor for incorporation into the contract. All such correspondence should be issued in sufficient copies so that the principal representatives of all parties can keep current and accurate files of the project contract cost and the scope of work.

Proper coordination of shop drawings and related review of samples is essential to the maintenance of a construction schedule. This coordination is a responsibility of both the architect–engineer and the contractor. These documents have prior reviews by subcontractors, the contractor, the construction manager, if applicable, and, lastly, the architect–engineer.

Notification to adjacent property owners of impending construction is the responsibility of the owner or the contractor. The legal aspects of construction work relating to a common property line and its effect on the adjuncts are complex and vary from one jurisdiction to another.

Adjacent property owners must be advised when new construction work will begin so that they can protect their property if they are required to do so. Alternatively, they must allow the contractor onto their property if the contractor is obligated to protect it. This notification is required almost universally, and if it is not given in the correct manner, the new construction may violate laws and ordinances of the area. Furthermore, an absence of such notification unquestionably places liability for damage to adjacent property on those initiating the new work.

The impending construction work notification to adjacent property owners should be issued by certified letter at least 30 days before construction begins. It must give the date construction is to begin, the general extent of work on the site, and the depth below the established grade to which the foundations will extend. The new foundation depth is important because most building codes fix the responsibility for lateral support maintenance of adjacent foundations according to whether the new excavation depth falls below a standard excavation depth, as defined by code.

The architect–engineer is not expected to be a competent attorney. When matters of law are in question with regard to adjacent properties or any other cogent matter, the advice of an attorney should be solicited and followed. Therefore, an attorney should prepare the impending construction notices. These may be reviewed by the architect–engineer before they are served. Similarly, architect–engineers should require that owners provide external expertise in matters pertaining to legal matters, audits and accounting, surveys, materials testing, and insurance.

Obtaining municipal permits and clearances so that project construction may begin is usually done by the contractor, and the costs of such permits are included in the contractor's contract. The architect–engineer's project representative should make sure that these documents are obtained and are posted so that the development and the owner will not be at variance with the applicable codes and ordinances.

While the contractor is having the contract plans and specifications processed through the municipal reviewing institution, the architect–engineer frequently will confer directly with the reviewing group to give supplementary design information about the project. When such supplementary information is needed, the architect–engineer should offer services immediately to prevent possible construction delays.

An architect's contract documents specify insurance programs to be borne by contractors. These programs should be developed by insurance experts. Insurance certificates for policies of the contractor and all subcontractors should be reviewed by the contractor and then forwarded by the contractor to the construction manager, if applicable, and finally to the architect–engineer for review before work is started. The architect–engineer assists in determining if the coverage in these policies meets the requirements set forth in the owner–contractor contract. Copies of the certificates are then filed in the architect–engineer's field office. No subcontractor should be allowed by the contractor to work on the project unless that contractor's insurance is in good order.

The construction safety program is controlled by the contractor (6). It is the contractor's responsibility to maintain the construction site in compliance with all applicable safety requirements for that jurisdiction. The architect's representative should not attend safety meetings or progress meetings where safety is discussed in order to prevent the responsibility for construction safety from accruing to the architect–engineer.

Although contractors are responsible for construction safety, plaintiffs aim claims at all related parties. In particular, current legal techniques seek claimed damage remuneration from the wealthiest parties or those most available, including owners, architect–engineers, construction managers, and others who are identified with a real property development. Design professionals who have traditionally not been responsible for construction job safety are current targets for claims of culpability in this regard predicated on actions pursuant to safety that they may have performed or failed to perform.

Although liability insurance grows scarce and dear, appropriate coverage should be in force as a job cost. Mishaps do remain an integral aspect of construction work, although actuarial improvements have been effected in this regard.

MOBILIZATION OF ARCHITECT–ENGINEER'S FIELD OFFICE

The composition of the architect–engineer's field office and its personnel depends to a great extent on the location, type, and size of the construction project as well as on pertinent provisions of the contracts between the owner and architect–engineer and between the owner and contractor. Whether or not the owner has engaged a construction manager is an additional determinant.

The expense of providing and maintaining the physical field office and all facilities customarily is included in the cost of construction. Therefore, the contractor provides these facilities and the owner pays for them, as provided in their contract.

The architect–engineer project representative's field office should contain a plan table of at least 32 ft^2 and a plan rack sufficiently large to hold in separate sections the sets of architectural, structural, mechanical, and electrical contract drawings, as well as the various shop drawings that will be needed during construction.

Enough filing cabinets should be provided to hold all correspondence. For easy reference, correspondence should be indexed and placed by date or category in index-tabbed manila folders. Adequate shelving is needed for holding approved material samples and samples of soil, construction tests, and so on, as well as the architect–engineer's field library. Bulletin boards are an excellent place to post construction schedules, bulletins, and progress photographs. Besides offering this ready reference, they help speed the completion of priority items.

Each member of the permanent field organization will require a desk and telephone extension. If the field staff exceeds three persons, the project representative should have a private office where he or she can confer and be secluded from noise and confusion. A facility is required for job progress meetings.

The architect–engineer staff usually provides its own reference library, any portable equipment, and all necessary clothing or other gear. A comprehensive library should be available to the field staff so that technical information can be readily obtained.

Architect–engineer on-site observation is desirable on a continuous basis on every project, whether large or small, but on smaller projects, cost considerations will not permit this optimum level of observation (7). As most architectural–engineering reimbursement depends on the total project construction cost, continuous site observation usually becomes feasible only when the project cost produces design professional fees that allow such a continuum of representation.

Some projects may be sufficiently complex to require a comprehensive staff, or they may prove so simple and repetitive as to require only periodic representation. The relative complexity of the development must be considered when negotiating architect–engineer fees so that there will be an adequate budget for construction administration.

Every development should receive proper design professional attention during the construction stage, for it is then that the owner gets or does not get the building structure designed by the architect–engineer. An appropriately designed building can be harmed by improper construction, and the good working relationship between owner and architect–engineer can quickly be damaged.

With a cost-plus or upset fee owner–contractor contract, the owner may want a complete checking analysis of the contractor's cost accounting program. In this case, additional specialized personnel are required. It is not feasible for the architect–engineer to attempt both on-site design professional representation and the special requirements of continuous cost accounting with a staff geared for usual construction administration.

A proper checking of the contractor's cost accounting requires that all material deliveries be logged in when they reach the site and that all billings be checked against delivery tickets. Labor on the site must also be checked daily, and all weekly payroll vouchers must be checked for accuracy by comparing them to the daily payroll checklists. When owners want this service, they should retain a construction manager or hire their own clerk of the works. Alternatively, for provision of this service, the owners can contract for assignment of additional qualified personnel from the architect–engineer for the work to augment the usual duties of the architect's representative.

Maintaining adequate records of construction progress is an important part of the job of the architect–engineer's project representative. The project representative should maintain them with the understanding that they may serve as documentary evidence in the event of future dispute or litigation arising in connection with the job. Records form the complete history of the construction project and can also be used for projecting work completion.

Proper documentation of a construction project requires several procedures. The exacting architect's representative will record, in a pocket notebook, notes about various project activities observed during project rounds. Later, the architect's representative will record the salient facts from this notebook in the architect–engineer's diary or log, a bound volume containing job records and a daily accounting of job progress. This diary should be locked in the representative's desk or private filing cabinet.

For comprehensive construction administration, or where otherwise required, the architect–engineer's project manager should receive daily progress reports from the project representative. Standard daily report forms should be printed in quantity for each project to save repetitious typing. They should always list the following information:

1. Name of the project, owner, architect–engineer, and contractor.
2. Name of the architect–engineer project representative.
3. The day and date.
4. Weather, including high and low temperature.
5. A listing and description of all subcontractors.
6. Number of workers for contractor and all subcontractors.
7. A description of the work performed.
8. A description of any special meetings, tests, accidents, or visitors.
9. A section for remarks.

The daily reports are synopsized to form the weekly report. This weekly report is frequently given to the owner's representative to help him or her keep abreast of events. The architect–engineer's main office personnel and contractor's personnel also will find this report helpful for monitoring the construction work.

On certain occasions, specific incidents such as fires or accidents must be reported. The contractor should immediately develop this report, while the facts are fresh and evidence and witnesses (if required) are still available. Photographs of serious incidents should supplement the written report if possible. Again, these reports should be written with the understanding that they may be used as evidence at some future time in the event of a dispute or possible litigation.

Progress photographs specified to be furnished by the contractor are an excellent way for recording the construction history of a development. They should be taken at appropriate intervals.

PREPARATION OF CONSTRUCTION SCHEDULES

Construction schedules contribute to project completion in three essential ways:

1. They outline construction progress and predict a completion date. The data let the owner know when to expect final project acceptance for occupancy.
2. They program projected construction stages so that at each stage the estimated percentage of completion is known. From the data the owner can predict the necessary construction progress payments and related capital resources that may be needed at any stage of development.
3. They reveal whether or not a project is proceeding on time and indicate the coordination needed for processing shop drawings, providing supplementary details, expediting material deliveries, and increasing labor forces to meet the completion date.

If a construction manager has been employed, he or she develops the construction schedule. If there is no construction manager, the contractor works up the construction schedule before the project is begun. The schedule is based on the length of time required for construction as defined by terms of the owner–contractor contract. Copies of the schedule are sent to the architect–engineer and to the owner for review and subsequent incorporation in their records.

Weather Factors. Several important factors must be considered in planning the construction schedule. First is the climate. Some phases of construction cannot be performed under certain weather conditions, and others can be performed only at a substantial increase in cost. Therefore, a well-planned construction schedule should relate to the climate and the seasons. Construction protection resources must be provided as the work continues throughout the year.

Interdependency of Trades. A second factor to be considered in construction scheduling is the interdependency of the various construction trades, which follow one another in an interlocking sequence. Trades must be coordinated so that they neither complicate nor damage others. Care must be taken to expedite the flow of materials to the project site to prevent work stoppages due to shortages. Stoppage in one trade affects other trades and, therefore, the overall progress. In recent years, computerized scheduling of construction developments has become a useful tool for helping to obtain expeditious completions.

Scheduling Costs. Financing methods available to the owner vary. Sometimes the owner will meet cost obligations to pay for a construction contract with funds placed in reserve for the project, but supplemental capital is usually obtained from outside sources. This mortgaged capital, together with the owner's required equity capital, provides monies for the total cost of the project.

When construction is lengthy, interest on this capital becomes significant. Interest accumulations often exceed the fees paid for architectural–engineering services and the profits earned by contractors. For this reason, a good construction schedule will program projected financing charges at every construction stage so the owner may know what proportion of the total cost must be appropriated at any stage. Obviously, construction delays hurt owners, design professionals, and contractors.

Relations with Subcontractors. Every project, whether large or small, even one with an outstanding contractor managing the work, will have at least one subcontractor or materials supplier who will not maintain the established pace. No set method exists for coping with this situation, but methods exist for applying pressure that may prevent such delinquency.

A contractor should be as careful in selecting subcontractors and suppliers as the owner and architect–engineer were in selecting the contractor. Contractors exercise substantial control over subcontractors and suppliers because they can withhold future associations if contractual relations prove unsatisfactory. This relationship is significant, and if emphasized when required, it usually will avoid trouble. A delinquent subcontractor should be made to understand the damage potential of such behavior.

Conversely, contractors can maintain good relations with their subcontractors by making proper and timely payments, allowing them sufficient time to do their work, and providing ample work space and satisfactory working conditions. A good relationship between the contractor and subcontractors can result in more rapid construction and cost savings for both.

Scheduling Assistance of the Design Professional. The contractor must obtain, review, and transmit shop drawings to the architect–engineer for review sufficiently in advance of construction to allow adequate time for processing of this material by the architect–engineer, and for material fabrication and delivery after processed shop drawings are returned to fabricators. The architect–engineer can help by promptly reviewing shop drawings, especially when this action is critical to the construction schedule. A diligent architect–engineer's project representative will aid the contractor in obtaining reviewed shop drawings by the design professionals when these documents are critical to the construction process.

Strict adherence to this schedule is required if the project is to avoid delay. It is virtually impossible to hold a contractor to a fixed completion time if the contractor can show that critical deliveries of material to the construction site were delayed by untimely shop drawing reviews caused by the designers. Such occurrences awkwardly position the architect–engineer and the owner regarding responsibility for delays. This situation may generate compensation claims by the contractor toward the owner.

Construction schedules and progress meetings will help the architect–engineer's project representative follow the contractor's projected dates for materials deliveries and new work phases. Certain construction items serve as "keystones" to the completion of various work phases. These so-called construction keystones must be maintained on schedule. The diligent architect–engineer's project representative will keep a trained eye on these construction keystones even though actuating their expeditious construction rhythm is the contractor's responsibility.

Although architect–engineers do not expedite a contractor's schedule or meddle in contractor's responsibilities, owners always require that the architect's representative be informed about schedule and completion. Accordingly, the architect's representative should be well informed in this regard.

Occasionally, a contractor's communication with a subcontractor or supplier will reveal that necessary materials may not be ready for the planned delivery sequence. Where these materials merit special attention, the contractor should send a representative to the fabricator to ascertain what is causing the delay and what the ramifications are. Direct contact of this sort may prevent delays or initiate appropriate alternatives.

PREPARATION OF THE CONSTRUCTION SITE

After the contractor takes possession of the construction site, he or she prepares the area for the building construction. Because modern construction methods require temporary fuel, power, and light utilities, the contractor must make these arrangements.

Meetings with Utility Companies. While the contractor is arranging temporary services, it is useful for the architect–engineer's representative to meet with representatives of the utility companies to double-check their requirements. Most of this work will have been completed during the design. Utility connections form a costly portion of the related subcontracts and usually are included in the contract documents. Nevertheless, construction commencement is an excellent time to review utility connections and for the architect–engineer's representative to become acquainted with the utility company representatives. He or she most likely will have further contact with them during the course of construction. The meeting with utility representatives should be held as a project progress meeting, and the owner's and contractor's representatives should be present.

Protection of Existing Utilities. Construction sites in congested areas are surrounded by existing utilities. The contractor may find it necessary to shore up, brace, or otherwise protect these utilities from possible damage that may arise from the construction process. Such precautions can substantially reduce the possibility of claims for damages involving this work.

Underground electric lines can be dangerous during excavation, whereas overhead electric lines become a hazard during superstructure work. Such lines should be rendered harmless before any work near them is begun. If the possibility of fouling by cranes or towers exists, overhead lines should be removed.

Underground gas lines can explode if severed. Sewer and water lines can also cause trouble. Inflowing water from a severed water line can make subgrade work slow and costly. Washouts and floodings can cause adjacent property to subside, as well as harm the construction.

If a contractor disrupts utilities in a congested location with resultant business interruption, damage claims can be significant. A comprehensive line and grade survey by the contractor in such a location is an appropriate method of checking whether the adjacent infrastructure is shifting or subsiding; then, appropriate actions can be taken.

Deliveries and Removals. At the outset of construction, the contractor plans the layout of field facilities and the organization of the construction work. He or she must determine methods for transporting materials to the work area and select access points for deliveries. This planning becomes extremely complex when the construction site is in a crowded downtown area.

The positioning of construction tower hoisting apparatus will have several effects. It will establish the point of personnel access flow to the project superstructure levels and the route of materials deliveries and rubbish removal. The building exterior and related interior work adjacent to the hoist area will usually be one of the last areas of the structure to be completed. Precautions should be taken to protect the completed sections adjacent to these locations.

Barricades and Bridges. Project barricades must be erected to protect adjacent property, screen off and protect passersby, and prevent unauthorized persons from entering the site and injuring themselves or damaging work or equipment. When the structure rises above a sidewalk—introducing the possibility that material may fall on people below—a sidewalk bridge should be constructed over the area. Often this bridge becomes a base for placement of construction shanties, toolsheds, or construction towers that are used for hoisting materials and personnel.

Shanties. Shanties are required so workers can store clothing, lunches, and personally owned tools, and so that they can find shelter for a break or lunch. Shanties should also be provided for the contractor's tools, supplies, and heavier equipment. Facilities are required for every subcontractor.

Contractor's Field Office. The contractor's field office is similar to that of the architect–engineer's representative and is often under the same roof or in an adjacent building. The contractor's office is larger, however, because of the larger staff. Although the contractor's field office varies with the size and complexity of the job, it must always have a secluded area for the contractor's superintendent and an area for those associates who aid in the construction engineering, work layout, labor instructions, and subcontractors' coordination. Another area is set aside for project accounting, materials purchasing, and personnel hiring. Finally, there must be a general area for plan tables and for storage of plans, specifications, and materials samples. This last area is normally made available to materials suppliers, union officials, subcontractors, and any other interested parties. Progress meetings may be held in this facility.

CONSTRUCTION PAYMENTS

A major function of the architect–engineer's project representative during the construction process is to certify as acceptable the contractor's monthly progress payment requests. Because these requests transfer the owner's funds to the contractor, the architect–engineer's project representative must be certain that they are correct and properly documented.

Establishing a Routine for Payment. At an early progress meeting, representatives of the owner, the architect–engineer, and the contractor should establish a satisfactory routine for progress payments (3). A standard owner–contractor contract will stipulate the exact steps for issuing construction funds. Usually the contractor will submit payment requests to the architect–engineer approximately 10 days before the beginning of each month. These requests, if proper, should be certified by the architect–engineer within 1 week and subsequently honored by the owner as quickly as is reasonable.

Requests for Early Work Phases. At this early progress meeting the contractor should submit a schedule of values, also known as a trade cost breakdown (8). This breakdown of the construction contract should be examined carefully. Contractors have shown a tendency to place high cost values on the early work phases. This premature loading of the trade breakdown, if not corrected, permits the contractor to draw funds in advance of completing the work.

Serious problems can occur if a contractor draws funds in excess of those actually due. An owner using outside financing is forced to pay additional interest on those funds not backed by work accomplished; with self-financing, the owner loses the use of funds from his or her reserve and, of course, the interest they would have yielded if invested elsewhere.

Probably an even more serious consequence of premature payment occurs in the event that the contractor defaults on the project. Such a default can cause the owner a serious loss, particularly if the contractor is unable to pay subsequent damages awarded by a court judgment. Currently, bonding agencies, which furnish contractors' completion bonds, tend to seek redress from design professionals if payments to defaulting contractors are shown to have been improperly certified.

Standard owner–contractor contracts contain a retainage clause as a device to prevent overpayment on progress billings. This clause stipulates that a certain percentage of funds due—usually 10%—be withheld until the project is substantially completed. In recent years there has been a tendency to reduce the retainage at the midpoint of a satisfactorily progressing construction development. The contractor deducts this retainage before submitting each payment request so that the funds paid are in the order of 90% of the value of the already completed construction work.

The retainage is a factor in aiding the owner to pay for less than the actual completion value, and it also usually ensures that all items uncompleted at the end of construction will be completed promptly. The cost to complete construction when the project has reached substantial completion should be far less than the amount of retainage that has been withheld. At any construction stage, the unpaid payment balance to the contractor's contract should be sufficient to "buy" completion of the development's construction.

Contents of Requests. The progress payment request at any given time consists of (*1*) the contractor's monthly progress billing, (*2*) the affidavit identifying the project and itemizing a schedule of values or a trade breakdown of construction costs, and (*3*) partial waivers of lien by each subcontractor and materials supplier. Listed as extensions from each trade heading on the affidavit will be the previous payments, the value of the amount completed to date, and the balance. The amount completed as of any billing date minus the retainage and minus the previous payments becomes the current billing. The affidavit must have been executed by an officer of the contracting firm. Falsification of an affidavit so endorsed constitutes fraud. All subcontractors and materials suppliers' partial waivers will be in the amount shown for each on the affidavit. All documents should be prepared in sufficient copies for all principal parties.

Accompanying Documents. The contractor's payment request always is accompanied by documents intended to protect the owner against possible claims by unpaid subcontractors or materials suppliers. These documents are submitted in the form of partial waivers and the affidavit executed by an officer of the contracting firm. The affidavit presents an assertion by the contractor of right to payment. The partial waivers of lien from all materials suppliers and subcontractors are evidence that the contractor has paid them for the payment period.

Billing for Materials Stored on Site. Whether or not the contractor bills the owner for materials stored on site but not yet used in the construction will depend on the terms of their contract. It is current usual practice for contractors to include such billings in their payment requests, although some owners refuse to contract to pay for materials not incorporated in the structure. Storing materials on the site generally is necessary because they are available when needed. The owner benefits from this practice, and it is not unreasonable that the owner should reimburse the contractor for such materials if their bills of sale indicate that they have been paid for and if they are protected and appropriately insured.

Processing Requests. The architect–engineer should process the contractor's payment request in the following way (3). A few days before the request is expected, he or she should review the project completion to that date by checking all trades and determining the percentage of completion of each as evidenced by work in place. The method of establishing the percentage of completion of each trade is to ascertain the number of work stages required to install each trade or subcontract and then to evaluate each work stage to determine what percent of one completed trade or subcontract it represents. The architect–engineer should also ascertain the value of materials stored on the site but not yet incorporated in the project and then withhold from this appraisal a retainage as is done for work in place. If the contract precludes payment on stored materials, this step is omitted.

By referring to the contractor's schedule of values or trade cost breakdown, which lists the values of all trades or subcontracts, the architect–engineer can compute funds due at any given progress payment by simply correlating the percentage of trade completion with the trade cost breakdown.

After the architect–engineer has approved the payment

request with regard to its technical aspects and its proper correlation to the development's completion, he or she should send it to the owner's attorney to determine legal indemnification and related aspects of the data. Actually, the contractor can save payment collection time by sending copies of the payment request, assuming that it is correct, to the owner's attorney and to the agents of the outside lending institutions if there are any, when sending the request to the architect–engineer.

When all reviewing parties have notified the architect–engineer of their approval, he or she should execute a progress payment certificate and send it to the contractor. Endorsed copies will be required by the owner, the owner's attorney, and any lending institutions. The contractor presents this certificate and all accompanying data to the owner for payment.

Withholding Payment. In certain situations the architect–engineer will be justified in withholding payment certificates (3). The most significant of these is where there is a reasonable doubt that the contract can be completed for the unpaid balance. When such a situation seems to be developing, the architect–engineer must be unusually careful in approving progress payments because the usual retainage leverage on the contractor may be absent. This situation clearly illustrates why certain bids are rejected as too low in the original bid analysis. If a proposal is unreasonably low, it should be discarded. Obviously such a contract could be unsatisfactory, as there would be little control over an irresponsible contractor whose contract remuneration is insufficient to sustain his or her responsibilities before that contractor begins work.

Payments may also be withheld (*1*) if claims exist or may be filed against the project by unpaid materials suppliers or subcontractors, (*2*) if defective work is unremedied, or (*3*) if damages caused by the contractor arising out of his or her contract may produce claims against the project.

Final Payments. The final progress payment for the project is not paid until the contractor has submitted final waivers of lien from all materials suppliers and subcontractors as well as his or her own organization.

Standard owner–contractor's contracts stipulate that progress payments do not constitute acceptance of work not conforming to contract requirements. The final payment may act as such a waiver except for stipulated guarantees applying to the construction work, for owner's claims arising from unsettled liens, and for faulty work appearing after final payment has been made.

THE CONTRACTOR'S CONSTRUCTION SAFEGUARDS

The Safety Program. Safety programs have been established by builders, unions, insurance companies, municipalities, states, the federal government, and the industry at large to help in attaining this hard-sought goal. Safety programs consist of safeguards that are put into force in the construction's early phases and are then adhered to rigidly throughout the project.

The safety program is not the responsibility of the architect–engineer (6). The discussion of these matters is herein included primarily for the education of younger design professionals and for noting an overview of the contractor's responsibilities pursuant to safety.

The first step in a safety program is for the contractor to name a chief safety inspector from his or her staff. The safety inspector establishes first-aid facilities, ensures medical examination and hospital care for more serious injuries, keeps a record of all injuries for examination by insurance companies processing claims arising from such injuries, and regularly inspects the site for any hazards.

Every tradesperson can help the safety program by observing its rules. Contractors' construction executives should both observe and enforce these rules, or else little things—a frayed scaffold rope not inspected, a loose plank left near the building's edge, an unprotected shaft—can put human life in jeopardy. In many jurisdictions an injured worker is rarely considered legally responsible for his or her injury. Accordingly, claims by the injured worker will be made against others.

The safety program should extend to the adjacent sidewalks, streets, and buildings. The structure must not become a nuisance to the community. Dirt, dust, water, and paint must be kept from dropping on neighboring properties or passing pedestrians. Construction barricades should fence off the project. A sidewalk bridge barricade, which provides overhead protection, is required where building construction is conducted above and proximate to public sidewalks.

A watchman service should supplement the use of site barricades in congested locations. On major projects, security guards are used 24 hours a day. They keep out unauthorized persons, thus preventing pilferage, vandalism, and injuries to trespassers.

Another common safeguard in modern construction is the mandatory wearing of hard hats. This safeguard should be instituted on all construction projects. Many workers owe their well-being and even their lives to hard hats and other protective gear and clothing.

Current, comprehensive national and local regulatory bodies have precise codes that specify all aspects of health and safety regulations to be accomplished in the work place. Contractors and subcontractors must maintain these programs.

Most codes and ordinances prescribe that for buildings in which the construction of the superstructure proceeds without the installation of permanent flooring, a substantial temporary floor must be put down that will prevent more than a two-story open interval between levels where work is in progress. All interior shaft openings must be either boarded over or protected by temporary handrails.

Particularly hazardous is work done from scaffolds. Scaffolds must be made safe for those working on them. Such work should be assigned only to experienced persons. The stairs, ladders, and other means of vertical circulation are danger areas. Keeping them safe on a multistory project is an important task. Ladders must be sturdy, well-braced in position, and equipped with railings. Satisfactory illumination must be provided and lights must be inspected frequently.

Sanitary temporary toilet facilities and garbage disposal arrangements are important to the health of the workers as well as the neighborhood in general.

All construction equipment should be kept in top working order by regular maintenance schedules as an important phase of the safety program. Large pieces of machinery can be particularly dangerous if not kept in proper working order or if handled improperly. Construction hoists, towers, and rigs should always be operated by qualified persons and only within the machine's normal capacities. Temporary hoists used for transporting personnel require extraordinary care.

During construction it is important that the building's structure not be subjected to stresses exceeding its elastic limits and structural capability. Many buildings may have imposed higher loadings during construction than after completion; at least local areas may be subjected to such loadings. The contractor must exercise great care in this regard.

Where overloading has happened, there have sometimes been dire results. It is frequently difficult to avoid loading areas in slight excess of their designed loading, but this loading must be done in a manner that will minimize stresses, and the areas affected must be braced and shored so as to preclude nonelastic deformations.

Another consideration is the safe storage of construction materials on the superstructure. These materials should always be properly secured. Wind forces at upper story levels are higher than might be expected. Improperly secured heavy planking, metal decking, and other materials of large surface have been blown off superstructures.

A construction project should make provisions for both fire prevention and fire fighting. Good housekeeping is one of the best preventatives; a project littered with debris is a ready target for fire damage or for injury to personnel. A second preventive measure is to establish a fire watch. The regular watchmen can act as fire watchers during their tours; they can prevent serious fires from developing by prompt reporting of fires to municipal facilities and direct extinguishing. Additional personnel should be assigned to fire watch duty while welding, burning, and temporary heating work are being done. No burning or welding should be permitted unless fire extinguishers and sand are nearby. Also, fire extinguishers of the proper types should be posted conveniently around the entire project. Some buildings may require comprehensive standpipe or other fire protection systems during construction.

Contractors General Liability Insurance. Adequate insurance coverage is required to augment a proper safety program on any construction project. Much confusion regarding insurance programs exists among many construction executives. This is attributable, in part, to the complexity of the subject. A knowledgeable insurance consultant is as beneficial to the owner, architect–engineer, and contractor, as is proper legal counsel. The contractor's and the owner's insurance programs must be comprehensively coordinated. As partial contractor's payments transfer work ownership from the contractor to the owner, the work must be permanently and appropriately protected by insurance.

Determining proper construction insurance coverage is a function of the size, location, and complexity of the project. Furthermore, time rapidly changes requirements for limits of coverage. The contractor must adequately insure a project while indemnifying the owner, the architect–engineer, and other agents from liability for claims that might arise. This coverage should include many forms of liability coverage and property damage coverage (including automobiles and other vehicles) and workmen's compensation coverage, as required by maximum statutory limits or as deemed necessary by experts.

Certificates of insurance should be filed by the contractor with the owner and the architect–engineer's field office before any work is begun. All such policies must carry a stipulation that the owner and the architect–engineer will receive written notification 10 days before the policies expire or are canceled.

A "hold-harmless" clause and contractor's related contractual liability insurance may be helpful for indemnifying the owner, the architect–engineer, and other agents from liability claims arising from construction mishaps. However, the effectiveness of such instruments appears to be diminishing where owners and architects are claimed to be negligent pursuant to such claims (9).

An owner's protective policy, whether borne by the owner or the contractor, is an essential indemnification implement for owners, architect–engineers, and their agents. These parties should be named insureds on such policies. The contractor's liability insurance certificate should stipulate that it incorporates the hold-harmless clause described in the specifications and should identify the clause by specification page and paragraph. It should also specifically name all parties to be indemnified. Cases have arisen where, despite such indemnification, the contractor's insurance companies have not held the owners or architect–engineers harmless, and litigation had to be instituted to force them to do so. Accordingly, it is wise to have an owner's protective policy in force. It will directly initiate a defense of its insureds in the event of a claim.

Where unusually hazardous work, such as underpinning, is done and where collapse through either improper construction or mishap is possible, it may be required that the contractor carry special collapse policies on that part of the structure under his or her care, custody, and control. The adjacent properties may be protected by the standard property damage coverage if the contractor's program includes explosion, collapse, and underground clauses.

Fire and Extended Coverage Insurance. This insurance for finished parts of the project has traditionally been carried by the owner. There is considerable current tendency to have this builder's risk insurance carried by the contractor so that deductible sums are borne by the contractor and to have a single responsible insurer. Other fire insurance is carried by the contractor on tools and equipment stored on the site, field office facilities, and other items not incorporated into the permanent structure.

When the owner's and contractor's insurance programs are carefully coordinated, there should be no gaps in coverage or divided responsibilities should a mishap occur when a development is partially completed. Then it may be difficult, in hindsight, to determine whether the development was under control of the owner or the contractor.

INSPECTION, OBSERVATION, SUPERVISION, AND PROJECT SPIRIT

The architect–engineer's project representative must gain the respect of the principal parties connected with the project. He or she must prove technical competence by rendering correct decisions promptly and behaving in a manner beneficial to the project. In addition, the decisions must be just. The project representative must learn to be firm when required and yielding, too, when the occasion arises. The fewer emotional actions and the more rational ones, the better. He or she must learn when to be active and when to be appropriately passive.

The easiest but least satisfactory course of professional conduct for the architect–engineer's project representative to follow is a strictly literal interpretation of the "boilerplate" contained in the specifications. A wiser and more understanding representative would show a better understanding of adroit observation by distinguishing between varying degrees of importance. Also, appropriate design professional representation should assist the owner to obtain a superior structure because it demands results little short of perfection on the critical aspects of the project. It tends to relax restrictive requirements of routine or relatively unimportant phases of the work. Of paramount importance is knowing which is which. This wisdom comes with experience supplemented by integrity.

Another area where the architect–engineer's representative enhances respect is to effect an appropriate personal appearance. This is difficult because of limited office facilities, construction dirt, exposure to weather, and certain dangerous aspects of the work that necessitate wearing proper gear. Nevertheless, he or she should dress neatly in business attire but have supplementary construction equipment available so that, for example, he or she can observe footings in a muddy excavation one minute and attend a conference with the owner's representative or even the owner's board of directors the next.

Orderly projects encourage a higher caliber of workmanship than slovenly, poorly maintained ones. Public notice of an orderly project is given by attractively painted barricades, signs, and sidewalk bridges.

The architect–engineer's project representative will be employing sound human relations with the builders by appropriately praising work well done. This positive attitude will intensify the project spirit and enthusiasm. It will motivate builders to work with continued high standards of quality.

An architect–engineer's representative learns that the more friends he or she has on the project, the better the job will be. His or her satisfaction with a job well done will increase, too, by the pleasant business relationships developed during construction. However, the architect–engineer's representative must never issue instructions directly to contractor's personnel, only to the contractor's superintendent. It is axiomatic that personal relationships must never interfere with or compromise the rendering of the highest quality of professional service.

The project representative's approach to the subject of approving or rejecting finished work will directly affect the spirit of the project. At the very beginning of the project, he or she must help to establish the acceptable standards of workmanship asserted by the owner–contractor contract. Upgrading below-standard work is difficult. It is wiser to press for reasonably above-standard workmanship at the project's start so that when completion pressures are felt, and if work quality falls, it will not fall below the required standard but only to the level of basic expectation.

The architect–engineer's representative who approves slipshod work is not only unfair to the owner, but also to him- or herself because the respect of the builders will be lost. On the other hand, unreasonable rejection of completed work is no better, for it can cause a severe financial hardship on the contractor and result in a sagging project spirit. In fact, unwarranted rejections may result in project delays and even legal action to determine whether the rejections may be cause for damage allegations.

The owner–contractor contract usually stipulates that reexamination of questioned work may be ordered by the architect–engineer (3). If the work uncovered is determined to be not in accordance with the plans or specifications, the contractor must then remove and replace it at his or her own expense. If the work conforms to the contract, the owner must bear the costs of examination and replacement.

Because reexamination of covered work entails possible financial burden for the owner or the contractor, the procedure is considered a last resort. This is why appropriate architectural–engineering representation attempts, at the outset, to have the contractor exert responsibility to establish production quality and to properly initiate and continue each stage of work. Difficulties and flaws that occur after a considerable lapse of time invariably are embarrassing to all parties, even when the work is repaired by the contractor within the contract or the guarantee period.

One way that the contractor can keep the project on schedule and maintain costs at an anticipated level is for the architect–engineer's project representative to be readily available for making timely decisions on construction quality and for interpreting and clarifying ambiguities in the plans and specifications. Architect–engineer construction administration must provide to both the owner and the contractor the security of their belief that the project representative's decisions will be fair, competent, authoritative, and timely.

Written correspondence to the contractor by the architect–engineer or his or her representative with copies provided for the owner will create a good record. This procedure assists harmony among all principal parties by removing the cause of many misunderstandings that attend oral instructions. Oral communication may be appropriate for routine work function, but where special instructions are required or where the contractor's methods seem questionable, the project representative should follow up any oral communication with cogent letters.

Written instructions are not only less ambiguous, they also can be referred to and studied at leisure, and they indicate the project representative's competence and willingness to take a position. Clearly written communications of this nature lend weight to the project representative's record of conducting actions to protect the development.

If they indicate otherwise, a new representative must be substituted.

The spirit of harmonious construction relies heavily on the relationship between the owner and the contractor. The importance of prompt progress payments to the contractor cannot be overstressed. Extra work orders and the contractor's charges for them are also an important part of the financial relationship between the owner and the contractor.

The owner may and should alter the scope of a project to meet his or her needs more fully. The contractor is obligated to conform with the owner's desires in this respect, provided that the remuneration and completion date are also reasonably changed.

When the owner, construction manager, or architect–engineer solicits a proposal for extra work during the course of construction, it usually is issued by the contractor with a breakdown of labor, material, overhead, and profit. The parties can then review this breakdown to see that charges are reasonable.

Friction frequently develops over what is considered a reasonable charge for these changes, as it cannot be corroborated by competitive bidding. New contractors generally are not interested in entering a job already under way, nor would it be desirable, from a standpoint of divisions of responsibility or general relationship, for an owner to want them to do so. The owner thus has little choice but to award the extra work to the existing contractor at a price that can be negotiated, or else do without the work.

Both the owner and the contractor should adopt reasonable attitudes when negotiating the price of changes. The owner must remember that extra work is not bid competitively, and therefore its unit price may be higher than work that is. The owner should recognize that changes may disrupt a contractor's procedures to such a degree that what may seem costly may be rather reasonable. The contractor must keep in mind the benefits of having the owner's goodwill and a good project spirit. The contractor should avoid price gouging.

An unpleasant scenario may occur when an owner needs a change order for which a contractor's extra proposal appears out of line, and the owner's actions grow dilatory on decisions regarding related work on the project while he or she determines a course of action regarding the change proposal. This delay affects the contractor's time schedule, increases overhead, and may trigger claims by subcontractors. Meanwhile, the owner may have impeded the project's completion, thus causing additional financing charges and loss of project utilization.

The foregoing situation is fraught with the possibility of impending litigation, loss of harmonious job spirit, and the wasting of resources and emotions. All parties should exercise reasonable attitudes to avoid this breakdown of an orderly construction process. Conversely, reasonable owners and builders may conduct fruitful and harmonious relationships to their mutual benefit on numerous developments for many years.

FINAL ACCEPTANCE OF THE PROJECT

The final acceptance of a building project places responsibilities on the architect–engineer's representative in several areas. Among these requirements are compiling and transmitting to the contractor a punchlist or a series of punchlists. These documents are comprehensive enumerations of incomplete or unacceptable construction. The project representative should make sure that punchlist items are promptly completed by the contractor and that no new faults have arisen. The final payment certificate should be issued to the contractor only when the project representative believes that all contract requirements have been met.

After the project is completed and for a reasonable duration, it is desirable for the architect–engineer's representative to continue to make periodic observations of the project for determination of any new problems or flaws, which should be remedied within the contractor's guarantee period. These periodic observations not only will satisfy the architect–engineer that his or her work has been completed successfully, but they contribute toward informing the owner that he or she has received diligent design professional service.

Compilation of completion punchlists for a building project by the architect–engineer's project representative is a comprehensive task that requires a lengthy observation of the entire development. Completion of the work is simplified when construction work strictly conforms to the contract requirements, but even under favorable conditions, punchlist compilation is a lengthy job requiring formulation of detailed and exacting documents.

Two procedures can assist in preparing punchlists for complex building projects. One is use of printed forms specifically developed for each project; these list its repetitive areas. Using these forms, the architect–engineer's project representative can "punch out" an area by circling or checking typical items on the form. This check-off, together with some additional remarks, can greatly reduce the amount of description needed. A second aid is better used with projects that are limited in the number of repetitive areas. This is simply the use of an accompanying stenographer or portable dictation machine during examination of the project. These aids expedite the documenting of the punchlist requirements into a written report that can then be sent to the contractor for his or her use and to the owner for his or her information and record. Punch lists should be dated at issuance.

The architect–engineer's project representative reexamines all construction after being notified by the contractor that all prior punchlist work has been reviewed and completed. New punchlists may have to be issued on reexamination by the project representative to show either new defects or old ones that have not been satisfactorily remedied.

A diligent architect–engineer's project representative makes a thorough compilation of the initial punchlist before its issuance. It is not in the best interests of rapid project completion for a second issuance punchlist to contain new items that existed at the time of the first examination but that were not noted. This disrupts the contractor's systematic effort to complete the building area by area. It disturbs the occupants unduly when the building is occupied.

The architect–engineer's project representative and the contractor's representatives who are assigned to punchlist completion can create either a favorable or an unfavorable relationship with project occupants and the owner at this early stage of occupancy. Tempers are often short in this period, which may be fraught with many last-minute changes, completion deadlines, noise, dirt, general inconveniences caused by continuing construction, and complications arising from the moving in of equipment, occupants, and furnishings. Further, the building may not yet be functioning smoothly because final adjustment of systems and equipment takes several months.

If early occupancy takes place while construction still is under way, disputes may arise between the owner and the contractor over the cause and responsibility for possible damage in the building. When such damage occurs, it should be quickly investigated and documented while the facts are available.

Issuance to the owner by the contractor of keys, guarantees, instructions, plans, and descriptive data covering the completed project as required by the contract agreements constitutes a last stage of completion before the architect–engineer issues the final payment certificate to the contractor. Actually, much of this material can be given to the owner or his or her custodians when the owner assumes partial use and operation of the building. Owners should understand requirements and obligations of the building's operation and maintenance before they assume that responsibility, or else the project may suffer from improper care. During a period when the contractor is still on the job, or subsequently, disputes may arise between the owner and the contractor over who is responsible for possible remedial work.

The final payment certificate is executed by the architect–engineer after the project representative has determined that the work is complete and the quality of the project appears to conform to the owner–contractor contract documents. Final certification never should be made when the architect–engineer's project representative is aware of faulty or nonconforming work. However, the architect–engineer's final certificate and its issuance do not represent to an owner that all work has been performed in detail according to contract documents; this should be clearly understood by the owner. Even the most diligent full-time architect–engineer's project representative could never be in a position to make such a certification. Also, the architect–engineer is never responsible for guaranteeing the performance of a contractor.

Before executing the final certificate, the architect–engineer's project representative should review for correctness the contractor's supporting affidavit and waivers of lien with regard for their design professional and construction characteristics only. This material then must be reviewed by the owner's attorneys for legal conformity, since this legal aspect is beyond the architect–engineer's professional scope.

Final payment by the owner to the contractor does not constitute a release from responsibility for the contractor toward the project for the guarantee period specified in the contract. From a practical standpoint, however, final payment means that the owner must depend on the contractor's integrity to remedy defective work or that he or she must look to costly and tedious litigation to force such remedy unless there exists the possibility of redress against a bonding company for the duration of the guarantee period. When a project is protected by a completion or performance bond, the protection exists through the guarantee period. However, even a bonded project may involve litigation to force a successful completion in the event of a contractor's default. Furthermore, bond companies may then attempt to recover their costs from the design professionals, with or without merit. It is obvious that diligent observation of the work to ascertain its completion should be performed by the architect–engineer's project representative before executing certification of the contractor's final payment.

At this closing point, it seems appropriate to once more discuss the words inspection, observation, and supervision. Design professionals often attempt to vary the semantic description of their responsibility during construction administration (10). This is defensively done to counter those who would burden them with responsibilities beyond their traditions and contracts (11).

It is a sad fact that diligent design professionals face increasing risks in a litigious society. Furthermore, one may presume that whatever words or other nomenclature are ascribed to the professional service, somewhere in the legal system a future adversarial interpreter of words and the law will attempt to assign greater risk and more responsibility to the design professional. Liability turns not on the simplistic substitution of one word for another, but rather on the importance of the items in question to the integrity of the design (12).

Courts have, in fact, decided that "inspect" and "supervise" mean superintend, oversee, control, manage, direct, restrict, regulate, govern, administer, and conduct. It should be obvious that "inspect" and "supervise" are dangerous words, even if defined in the documents. Describing the process as "periodic observation of work in progress" is more precise (13).

The contemporary building construction process is a complex assemblage of materials brought from remote areas to a specific construction site where they are installed in a process once described by a capable builder as resembling peacetime warfare. The luxuries of today's buildings become the necessities of tomorrow's, so that general building technology is constantly changing. As buildings become complex, they may grow bolder in an effort to shed the superfluous in the face of rising costs. Boldness without risk and competence despite complexity are the outstanding characteristics sought in contemporary buildings. These characteristics will be accented by tomorrow's buildings (14).

The role of the architect–engineer in contemporary building construction requires understanding of that process, combined with great expertise in the practice of architecture and engineering. Today's role requires greater design professional ability than when buildings were less complicated. Tomorrow's buildings will require honorable and courageous men and women of even greater comprehension who are willing to fulfill this role.

BIBLIOGRAPHY

1. M. D. Dubin, *Architectural Supervision of Modern Buildings*, Reinhold Publishing Corporation, New York, 1963.

2. *DPIC Companies' Guide to Better Contracts,* Design Professionals Insurance Company, Monterey, Calif., 1987, Foreword.
3. AIA Document B141, *Standard Form of Agreement Between Owner and Architect,* current ed., and AIA Document A201, *General Conditions of the Contract for Construction,* current ed., The American Institute of Architects, Washington, D.C.
4. Ref. 2, p. 79.
5. Ref. 2, p. 72.
6. Ref. 2, p. 58.
7. J. R. Groves, Jr., "Contract Administration: Friend or Foe?" *The Construction Specifier,* 76 (April 1985).
8. The Construction Contractor Guide Committee, American Institute of Certified Public Accountants, *Audit and Accounting Guide, Construction Contractors,* American Institute of Certified Public Accountants, New York, 1981, p. 9.
9. B. B. LePatner, "The Expanding Scope of Liability," *Architecture,* 92 (Aug. 1987).
10. "Inspection and acceptance of the work," *Construction Claims Monthly* **8**(8), 1 (Aug. 1986).
11. K. E. Roberts, *Obligations of On-Site Observations,* Victor O. Schinner & Company, Inc. in cooperation with the American Institute of Architects, the National Society of Professional Engineers/Professional Engineers in Private Practice, and CNA/Insurance, 1972, Volume II, No. 9, pp. 1–6.
12. S. G. M. Stein, M. T. Callahan, I. P. Gould, H. P. Kamin, P. M. Lurie, R. E. Martell, M. J. McElroy, J. A. McManus, Jr., and S. P. Sklar, *Construction Law,* Vol. 2, Mathew Bender, New York, 1986, p. 8-7, paragraph 8.01.
13. DPIC Companies, *Lessons in Professional Liability,* 1988, Formerly titled *Untangling the Web,* 1980, by Design Professionals Insurance Company, Monterey, Calif., p. 10.
14. Ref. 1, p. 280.

See also Construction Documents; Construction Law; Construction Management; Contract Administration

M. David Dubin, FAIA
Dubin, Dubin & Moutoussamy
Chicago, Illinois

INSULATION, ACOUSTICAL. See Acoustical Insulation and Materials

INSULATION, ELECTRICAL

Today's society depends extensively on electrical energy. To transport this form of energy from the generating plant to the ultimate consumer requires elaborate transmission and distribution systems. In all of these systems the main goal is to accomplish this transfer of power safely and efficiently. To achieve this goal, use is made of copper or aluminum conductors protected by a variety of insulating systems such as gases (or vacuum), liquids, and solids. These insulating materials have one feature in common: they have very high resistivities; that is, they prevent electric current, electrons, from flowing between the metallic conductors, cables, or wires that act as the transport medium for the electric energy.

The power requirements as well as the environment in which these cables must operate dictate the choice of wire size and insulating material to be used. To appreciate the power requirements it should be recalled here that the power level is determined by both the operating voltage and the current. The voltage used in most buildings is either a nominal 120 or 240 V or, in some special cases, 480 V ac (60 Hz). Since the voltage is more or less fixed, it is the current that determines the electric power available. It is within the discretion of the engineer to design the various electrical circuits so that sufficient power is available at all locations within the building. In the following paragraphs the types and sizes of electrical conductors, their manufacture, and the methods by which they are installed are described. This is followed by a discussion of the physical and electrical characteristics of these conductors and the appropriate test methods.

CLASSIFICATION OF ELECTRICAL CONDUCTORS

There may exist in a given building a spectrum of power requirements. To ensure the proper use of wires and cables to provide reliability of the system, the National Electrical Manufacturers Association (NEMA), the Institute of Electrical and Electronics Engineers (IEEE), the Association of Edison Illuminating Companies (AEIC), the Insulated Cables Engineers Association (ICEA), and the Rural Electrification Administration (REA) have developed various standards and guidelines to define the types and sizes of these wires as well as methods by which they are to be installed in buildings. In the United States these standards are contained in the *National Electrical Code* (NEC) and in Canada in the *Canadian Electrical Code* (CEC). There exist also, on the local level, specific codes that usually follow the national standards. A detailed knowledge of these local codes is imperative since they represent the law that is enforced by building inspectors. Two private organizations need to be mentioned here, Underwriters Laboratories (UL) and the Factory Mutual Research Laboratories (FMRL). As will be seen later, UL and FMRL have developed performance standards and tests to assure the quality and performance level of the finished wires and cables. The purpose of all of these codes is to assure safe operation of the electrical systems by preventing overheating that could lead to combustion, the generation of sparks that could lead to electrical failure, or shock hazards (1). Mention should also be made of the American Society for Testing and Materials (ASTM), an industry-wide group that develops testing procedures for the evaluation of materials (2).

To understand why so many different types and sizes of wires and cables exist, it is necessary to understand how electrical power is supplied by an electrical utility to individual structures and eventually to the consumer. The point at which the electric power enters a building is called the service entrance. This entrance can be located either below ground or high on one side of the structure. In the case of commercial and industrial buildings in urban areas, an underground service entrance is commonly used. In many suburban developments this form of service entrance is also prevalent because local building codes prohibit the use of poles to support overhead wiring. If the power cables are buried, they enter the structure through a pipe or conduit. Otherwise, the utility runs a cable from one of its poles to the service head on the nearest side of the building. At the service head the transition is made from utility to house wires. The latter then lead to a meter and eventually into the house to a service panel containing the various circuits with their respective breakers. The number and size of the circuit breakers determines the number of house circuits and their respective loads. To avoid errors in connecting circuit wires to the appropriate terminals, the wire insulation is color coded. The hot wire is almost always covered with black insulation, the neutral wire is covered with white or gray insulation, and the ground wire is left bare, wrapped in paper, or covered with green insulation. If there are other hot wires, they are coded red or blue. For many applications, particularly in residential structures, it is convenient to have these three wires (hot, neutral, and ground) grouped together and covered by a single jacket. Such an arrangement is usually referred to as a cable; its use greatly facilitates installation, particularly in existing structures.

A special type of wire is needed for the plenum, the space between the ceiling and the roof that is usually found in commercial buildings. For safety reasons, all power-limited wire, that is, wire designed for 600 V or less, to be installed in the plenum is required by the NEC to be encased in metal sheathing or conduit unless it is classified as having adequate fire resistance and low smoke-producing tendencies.

CLASSIFICATION OF INSULATED WIRES

The wires referred to in the preceding section consist of a metallic conductor and a nonmetallic insulating jacket. The current-carrying conductors are usually made of copper or aluminum. These conductors can be made either as one single solid conductor or as a bundle of thin wires twisted together into a strand to give greater flexibility to the ultimate structure. The insulating jacket acts to prevent the flow of electricity from one conductor to another of different potential. Materials commonly used for insulation purposes include synthetic rubber, plastics, or occasionally paper. The thickness of the insulation layer depends on both the diameter of the wire and the voltage rating. The voltage rating at which typical building wires are designed to operate is indicated on the wire's surface. Standard voltage ratings are 250 and 600 V, depending on the voltage requirements dictated by the end use. Also indicated on the wire surface is the type of insulating material used and the type of service condition for which the insulated wire is designed. These service conditions include information on the environment in which the wires can be operated safely, wet, dry, or hot. For example, type RHW refers to a rubber-covered wire that may be used in both wet and dry environments, whereas types RH and RHH refer to rubber insulation that can withstand more heat and thus can be used at higher current levels (higher ampacity), particularly in larger wire sizes. However, these two types must be used only under dry conditions. Type

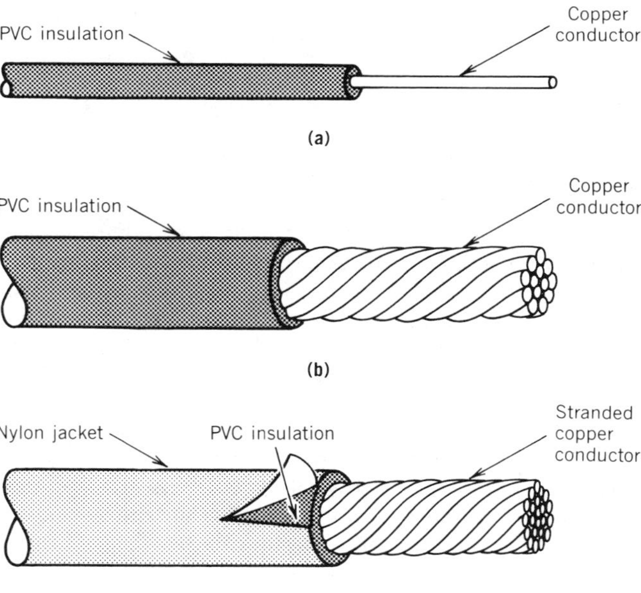

Figure 1. Examples of three types of building wire. **(a)** Type TW wire; **(b)** type THW wire; **(c)** type THHN-THWN wire (3). Courtesy of the Wire Association International, Inc.

TW building wire uses poly (vinyl chloride) (PVC) insulation on a solid center conductor. It is designed to operate at temperatures below 60°C in both dry and wet environments. Type THW wire uses a flame-retardant PVC compound and may operate at temperatures up to 75°C in wet or dry locations, whereas type THH is restricted to use under dry conditions only up to the same temperature limit. In either case the center conductor is of the stranded type. Types THHN and THWN refer to a more complex insulation system consisting of, in addition to a thinner PVC insulation, a nylon jacket. The latter gives greater electrical and mechanical strength to the finished wire and thus permits reduction of the overall thickness of the insulation. These two types of wire are preferred when conduits, ducts, or other raceways are used in dry (THHN) or wet (THWN) environments. Finally, there has come into existence in recent years type XHHW. This type resembles the ones above, but its thinner layer of insulation is made up of a cross-linked synthetic polymer, polyethylene (PE). This material, because of its cross-linking, resembles rubber in its good moisture and heat resistance, but has better insulating properties. Examples of three types of building wire are shown in Figure 1.

CLASSIFICATION OF MULTICONDUCTOR CABLES

The preceding discussion has dealt with wires having a single conductor, made of either one solid piece or many strands of thin metal pieces twisted together, and its insulation. A few words need to be said about cable structures involving two or more insulated wires combined into a single structure. It is obvious that such structures are easier to install, particularly in existing buildings. These cables can be classified, in terms of the sheathing used to cover the wires, into nonmetallic and metallic cables.

The Nonmetallic Sheathed Cable

This is the most common form of building wire used in residential housing. It is identified by the NEC and UL code symbol NM. This type is known by several proprietary names. As shown in Figure 2, this type of cable consists of insulated hot and neutral wires as well as a bare ground wire surrounded by a paper separator. These three wires and the paper separator are enclosed in a protective sheath, which generally is made of a thermoplastic material such as PVC. This type of cable is rated for 600-V continuous operation at 60°C.

Cables with conductors rated for operation up to 75 and 90°C are identified by the suffixes A and B, respectively, on the cable surface after the type letters. Also indicated on the surface of the cable is the type of conductor. The symbol AL imprinted on the cable surface indicates that the conductors are made of aluminum, whereas the symbols AL (Cu-CLAD) or Cu-CLAD AL indicate copper-clad aluminum conductors. These cables are approved for single- and multiple-family dwellings and structures not exceeding three floors above grade. According to Article 336 of the NEC, Type NM cables should not be embedded in masonry, concrete, and covered with plaster or similar finish. They should not be exposed to corrosive fumes or used as service entrance cables either. In a corrosive environment, type NMC cable should be used. The construction of this type is similar to that of the regular type NM cable except that its jacket is made of a material that is resistant to both corrosion and fungus growth. It can be used wherever type NM cables are acceptable, and it is also cleared for use under wet conditions.

For use in cable trays, raceways, and hazardous locations, type SNM is recommended. This is a shielded nonmetallic sheathed cable rated for 600-V service. In this structure the individual conductors are of the THHN or THWN type, and they are embedded in an extruded core of insulation, usually consisting of a PVC compound. This core is covered with an overlapping spiral metal tape and wire shield. Then another nonmetallic jacket is applied, which is made of a material that is moisture, flame, oil, corrosion, fungus, and sunlight resistant. Another common type of cable is the armored cable, type AC. The individual conductors in this cable are protected by a paper wrapping in addition to a PVC layer. The ground wire, if any, is bare.

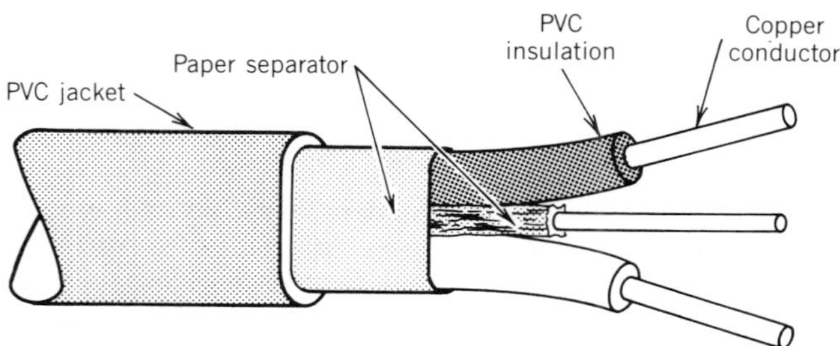

Figure 2. Type NM building wire. Courtesy of the Wire Association International, Inc.

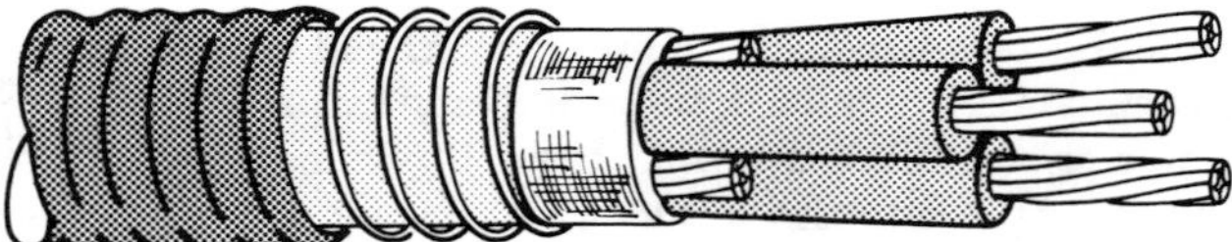

Figure 3. Type MC interlocking armor power and control cable with overall outer black PVC jacket compound. Courtesy of the Wire Association International, Inc.

The wires are protected by a jacket of galvanized steel, wound spirally for greater flexibility. Type AC cables may be used only indoors in dry locations because the steel jacket is subject to corrosion. In wet or damp environments, lead-covered armored cables of type ACL must be used.

Metal-clad Cables

These cables are designated by the NEC as type MC. They consist of one or more insulated wires that are held together by a binder tape and covered by a metallic sheath. Various types of fillers are used to occupy the empty spaces between the conductors and the circular sheath. An example of such a structure is shown in Figure 3.

This type comes in three distinct designs: interlocked metal type (Fig. 3), corrugated tube, and smooth tube. It can be rated for use up to 5000 V and can be installed above or below ground. In the latter case it has an outer jacket similar to the one shown in Figure 3 to protect the armor from corrosion. It comes in sizes #18 AWG and larger for copper-clad aluminum conductor designs. It is installed usually in racks, trays, troughs, or baskets or is suspended from poles. Armored cables find extensive use as service entrance, aerial feeder, and branch circuit cables.

OUTDOOR CABLES

The various types of cable mentioned in the preceding paragraphs were all designed for use within buildings. Often it is necessary to install cables outdoors to interconnect various structures or to provide electrical power for outdoor lighting purposes. Although basic indoor and outdoor wiring techniques are the same, the material requirements are different. Outdoor cables are designed for either underground or overhead use. Their constructions are quite different.

Underground Cables

These cables must be able to withstand fluctuations in the moisture level as well as attacks by rodents and fungi. In addition, the NEC requires all outdoor installations utilizing receptacles to be protected by a ground fault interrupter to prevent serious shock from an outdoor appliance. To withstand years of burial, these cables are sheathed in tough plastics or enclosed in conduits. There are great variations in local electrical codes regarding the use of conduits in outdoor installations. In areas requiring conduits, type TW cables are employed. In locations where direct burial of the cable is permitted, type UF cables are used. This type of cable is similar to the NM type, except that no paper separator is used and the PVC jacket is extruded directly over the conductors, two of which have color-coded insulation. Also, the PVC compound used for the jacket is formulated to withstand sunlight. These UF cables are rated for continuous operation at 60°C and 600 V. The metallic conductors are made either of solid copper (sizes #14 to 4/0 AWG) or of aluminum as well as copper-clad aluminum (sizes #12 to 4/0 AWG).

Overhead Cables

Occasionally, wires are run overhead between buildings. In these cases they are suspended at a considerable distance above the ground and are not close to each other. Since there is little chance of anyone touching them, there is no need for the same kind of insulation required for indoor wiring. However, it is advisable to protect the metal conductor from exposure to the deleterious effects of weather. In this case one or more layers of nonconducting materials that are not recognized as electrical insulation materials may be extruded on the conductor to weatherproof it. The wire then resembles the type T wire, but it can never be used for any other purpose.

SERVICE ENTRANCE CABLES

There are several types of cable available for use as service entrance cables, either overhead or underground. Type SE cables are suitable for direct earth burial to complete the circuit from the utility source to the consumer's meter. This type of cable comes in single- and multiple-conductor structures. The most commonly used service entrance cables are type SE-U. This type of cable consists of two or three insulated conductors with a bare concentric neutral conductor surrounded by a reinforcement tape and an extruded PVC jacket, as shown in Figure 4. It can also be used to connect the customer's meter to the service panel.

The type SE-SER service entrance cable differs from the SE-U type in that the neutral conductor is also insulated and cabled together with the other two conductors into a bundle. In this configuration it is referred to as a three-conductor cable. If a bare grounding wire is included, it is called a four-conductor cable (Fig. 5). In either case the conductors are protected by a reinforcement tape, and an extruded PVC jacket is applied.

These type SE cables are also approved for use in certain interior circuits. They find use particularly in apartment buildings to connect many distribution panels and branch

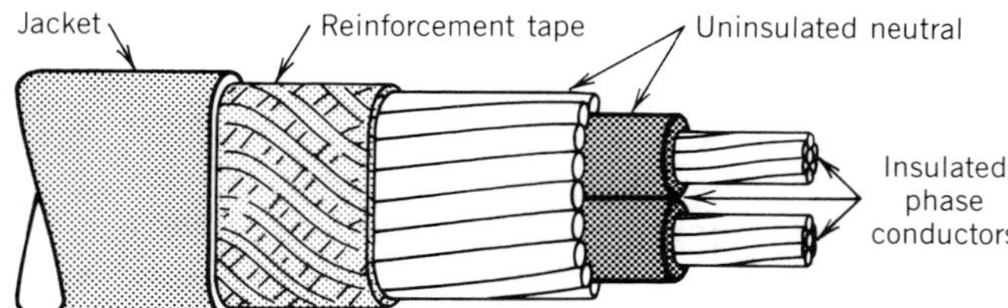

Figure 4. Type SE-U service entrance cable structure. Courtesy of the Wire Association International, Inc.

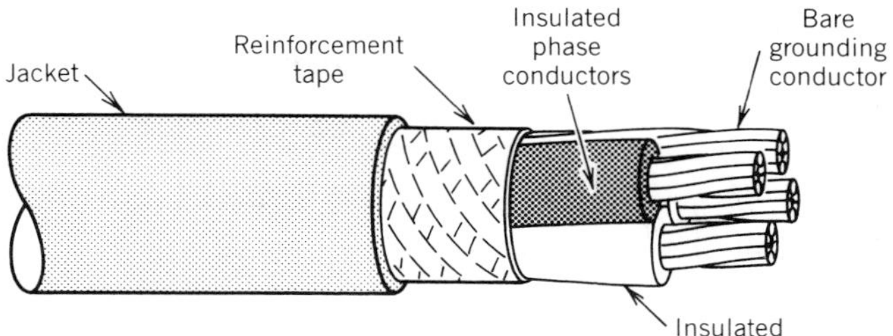

Figure 5. Type SE-SER 4 conductor service entrance cable. Courtesy of the Wire Association International, Inc.

meters as well as equipment requiring three-conductor service, such as laundry room appliances and electric ranges.

CONTROL AND SIGNAL CABLES

The term control cable covers a broad range of applications, which, in general, involve the activation of some equipment remotely located from the source of control. It can be as simple as a two-wire cable running from a push button on the wall to the motor activator on a garage door, or as complex as a multifunctional TV camera cable containing video, audio, and power elements along with control functions for pan, tilt, and zoom. Other applications include the use of these cables in automatic alarm and security systems to provide protection of industrial, commercial, and private residential property. Control cables usually operate in a range from 6 to 150 V (dc or ac, peak to peak). The individual conductors range in size from #22 to #12 AWG, depending on the current and voltage requirements. All control cables are required to be rugged, capable of withstanding thousands of cycles of repeated flexing without failure. They may be directly buried in concrete or soil, and their outer covering or jacket may have to withstand prolonged exposure to harsh chemicals, solvents, abrasion, and crushing. Year-round exposure to extreme weather conditions must also be considered. One type of signal cable not mentioned explicitly in this section is coaxial cable. Its unique structure is discussed separately.

Coaxial Cables

Coaxial cable is used for the transmission of high-frequency signals covering a range from about 1 MHz (1 million HZ) to 10 GHz (10 billion Hz). The lower end of this frequency range covers TV and video channels, and the upper range involves telecommunication systems and microwave applications in general. In general, a coaxial cable is composed of a metallic center conductor surrounded concentrically by an insulating dielectric, an outer conductor, and a jacket, as shown in Figure 6. In principle, it resembles a two-wire transmission line designed to operate at much lower voltages. The design of the coaxial cable produces a drastically reduced external field and thus reduces electromagnetic losses to the environment. This arrangement is necessary to preserve the signal and prevent

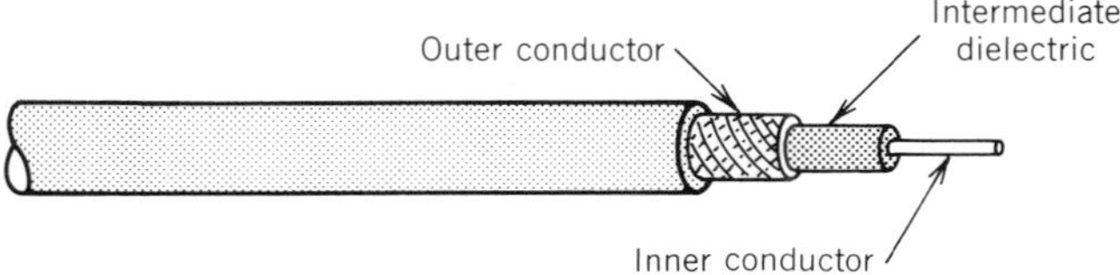

Figure 6. A typical coaxial cable design. Courtesy of the Wire Association International, Inc.

its interaction with the environment as well as to shield it from external electromagnetic interferences.

The choice of cable depends on the contemplated application, which includes considerations of the combined physical and electronic requirements. The physical requirements include the temperature rating of the materials used and the flex and breaking strength of the finished cable. The electronic requirements are determined by the nature and the strength of the signal to be transmitted as well as by the cable's electrical characteristics, which are controlled by the choice of dielectric insulation and overall design parameters.

A large part of the coaxial cables produced is used by the military, and these cables are designed to meet standards set by the Department of Defense or military procurement agencies. These types of coaxial cable are readily recognized by the RG/U number assigned to them. To qualify for these military designations, the cables must be subjected to rigorous testing, which is rather expensive. The additional cost is reflected in the price tag these military cables carry. Commercial users do not require such extensive, costly testing, and for this reason industry provides commercial coaxial cables. These nonmilitary cables may show only minor design changes to provide special handling capabilities such as higher power and lower attenuation.

Copper is used generally as the inner conductor in military cables because of its superior electrical characteristics. The inner conductor is usually made of stranded copper for increased flexibility and enhanced break resistance. In many cases the copper surface is coated with a very thin layer of tin or silver to prevent oxidation and enhance solderability.

Solid PE is the most commonly used dielectric because of its many desirable properties. For high-temperature applications, use is often made of perfluorinated polymers because they can be operated up to 200°C and are flame retardant. In commercial cables and some special military cables, one also finds foamed PE or fluoropolymers as dielectrics. These materials, because of the minute gas bubbles they contain, have a lower dielectric constant than solid polymers and therefore provide a lower signal attenuation.

The outer conductor, surrounding the dielectric, is usually made from woven strands of copper. The latter may be bare or covered with a thin layer of tin or silver. In commercial cables this braided structure may be replaced or supplemented by a metal foil tape to provide better insulation of the signal from the outside environment.

The jacket material used most often on coaxial cables is PVC, which can be made flexible and resistant to sunlight and year-round weather conditions. It can operate in temperatures ranging from 0 to 80°C. If higher operating temperatures are anticipated, use is made of fluorinated ethylene–propylene copolymers or similar materials.

The electrical characteristics of coaxial cables can be readily specified in terms of their characteristic impedance as 50-, 75-, and 93-Ω cables. The 50-Ω cables are used broadly for many applications such as two-way radio installations. The 75-Ω cables are used mainly in telecommunications and community antenna television systems, whereas the 93-Ω cables are used in those cases requiring very low capacitance, such as in data transmission applications. In principle, the impedance and capacitance of a cable are interrelated, and for cables using the same dielectric material it can be stated that the higher the impedance, the lower the capacitance.

Flexible Cables

Usually, wires and cables are installed permanently in a structure and then need only be sufficiently flexible to allow a certain ease in handling. There exist, however, many movable pieces of electrical equipment that need to be connected to the fixed wiring system in a building. For this purpose a flexible cord or cable is required. The many different types of flexible cords or cables on the market today must meet the specifications of Article 400 of the NEC. This type of cord or cable may not be used as a replacement for a building's fixed wiring unless specially permitted by Article 400–7 of the NEC. The conductors in these cables are always made of copper, and the ratings are divided into those operating below 600 V and those rated for use above 600 V.

One special type of flexible cable is designed for low-voltage applications such as doorbells, chimes, and thermostats. These are electrical systems that operate at less than 120 V. These systems usually require in the neighborhood of 24 V, and their installation therefore requires the use of a transformer to reduce the voltage from 120 V to the required level. Small wires having #18 or #29 AWG conductors connect the transformer to the chimes or the push button. Naturally, the transformer is connected to the building's electrical system at a regular outlet box. The small wires used here are also referred to as "bell wires," and they consist of, in addition to the solid copper conductor, a plastic insulation and/or jacket. For use as thermostat cables, two or more of the bell wires are twisted together into one cable. These cables are used in connection with heating or cooling systems in homes and commercial and industrial buildings. They also find use in wiring intercom and burglar alarm systems.

ELECTRICAL INSULATION REQUIREMENTS

The preceding discussion presents a general overview of the various types of electrical wires and cables needed to provide private, commercial, or industrial buildings with electric power and all functional services connected with it. The various types of electrical systems use a variety of insulation materials to assure the reliability of the system. It is appropriate at this time to identify these materials in terms of their physical properties to provide the reader with a knowledge of their relative merits. Such a knowledge is particularly useful when making decisions as to which electrical system should be used. A general overview of the materials and properties can be found in Refs. 4–10. It must be kept in mind that their physical properties are determined using small samples of the material that are usually molded rather than extruded for this purpose. In other words, many physical tests are not conducted on the finished wire, but on specially prepared samples. For example, it is impossible to evaluate the elongation of a wire covering once it is applied to the metallic conductor because the latter is considerably stiffer than the cover material. Similarly, it is difficult to determine the volume resistivity of a cable insulation once it is extruded onto the wire. It is much easier to determine in the laboratory under controlled physical conditions. Naturally, there exist several performance tests designed to test the actual finished product (2,5,8). With these tests, as with all others, it is difficult to obtain statistically meaningful information about the material characteristics unless a large number of tests are conducted.

The insulating materials commonly used in the aforementioned wire systems can be classified into thermoplastic and thermosetting materials, all being synthetic polymers. PVC and PE are found in the first group, and in the latter, synthetic rubbers such as EPR (ethylene–propylene rubber) and EPDM (ethylene–propylene–diene terpolymer rubber), and XLPE (cross-linked PE). Each of these materials possesses some advantages and some disadvantages that must be weighed in deciding what material to use where. This is illustrated in Tables 1–4 which list the compositions of typical wire compounds as well as their physical characteristics and costs. These data have been assembled from various sales brochures and advertisements of products supplied by several manufacturers. No mention is made of the individual suppliers to avoid the implications associated with such disclosure as an endorsement of the various products in favor of others. This information is produced in good faith, and it is believed to be accurate.

Table 1 lists four examples of building wires based on PVC. The physical properties of these four wires are quite similar, whereas the electrical ones of the first two are somewhat different from the others. This difference is caused by variations in their compositions, as shown in Table 2. The reduced amount of filler and plasticizer is responsible for the lower dielectric constant and the lower breakdown strength. At the same time the price per unit mass increases substantially since the filler is less expensive than the PVC resin. Two formulations based on PE are shown in Table 3. They are somewhat softer than the PVC compounds, and their electrical properties are similar to the more resin-rich formulations in Tables 1 and 2. The advantage of the PE compounds is their price, which is slightly below that of the cheapest PVC formulations.

The synthetic rubber formulation shown in Table 4 is comparable in electrical properties and price with the best PVC compounds.

Table 1. Typical Physical and Electrical Properties of Insulating Compounds[a] for Building Wires

	UL Designation			
Property	T/TL	THV/THWN	THHN	NM-B
Tensile strength, psi	2450	2600	3000	3000
Elongation, %	310	200	270	270
Low-temperature flex, °C	−20	−25	−10	−15
Volume resistivity[b]	2	5	2	3
Dielectric constant[c]	6.5	5.0	4.1	4.7
Breakdown voltage[d]	700	700	400	450

[a] Base material: PVC.
[b] TΩ·cm at 70°C and 500 V dc (for a pad sample).
[c] At 1000 Hz and 23°C.
[d] V/mil at 60 Hz ac and 25°C.

The examples shown above illustrate the variety of properties available from the various materials. No mention has been made so far about thermal limitations of these materials. To evaluate them, the basic characteristics associated with the various classes of compounds must be understood. For this purpose, both thermoplastic and thermoset systems are subdivided into filled and unfilled systems. The compounds listed in Tables 1 and 2 belong to the group of filled thermoplastic materials, whereas the PE sample in Table 3 belongs to the unfilled thermoplastic one. The EPDM sample in Table 4 is representative of the filled thermosetting compounds, whereas XLPE would be classified as an unfilled thermoset material. In general, the thermal limitations of the thermoplastic materials are more severe than those for the thermoset ones. The maximum temperature at which these materials can be used ranges from a low 70°C for low-density PE to about 130°C for some of the filled PVC formulations. The thermoset ones can exceed these values by 20–30°C and are usually capable of operating much longer at these elevated temperatures. The basic difference between the two principal types of polymers is their molecular structure. The thermoplastic materials consist of many polymer molecules that are entangled, and the thermoset material

Table 2. Typical Formulations and Cost Figures for Building Wire[a]

	UL Designation			NM-B	
Material	TTW	TH/THW	THHN	Primary	Jacket
PVC, phr[b]	100	100	100	100	100
Plasticizer, phr	60	50	50	47	50
Filler, phr	30	30	15	12	20
Additives, phr	5	5	8	8	6
Stearic acid, phr	0.3	0.3	0.3	0.3	0.3
Cost, ¢/lb volume[c]	42	45	56	56	44

[a] Base material: PVC.
[b] phr = parts per hundred parts of polymer.
[c] Based on 1984 raw material prices. This figure takes into consideration the density and quantity of each ingredient used.

Table 3. Typical Composition and Physical Properties of Insulation for Building Wires[a]

Composition, phr[b]		
LDPE[c]	100	90
Vinyl acetate		10
Antioxidant	0.1	0.1
Physical properties		
Tensile strength, psi	2,200	2,150
Elongation, %	600	350
Low-temperature flex, °C	−100	−80
Volume resistivity[d]	10,000	10,000
Dielectric constant[e]	2.5	5.2
Power factor[f]	3.0	60
Breakdown voltage[g]	480	350
Cost, ¢/lb volume[h]	39	39

[a] Base material: PE.
[b] phr = parts per hundred parts of polymer.
[c] LDPE = low-density PE.
[d] TΩ·cm at 25°C and 500 V dc (for a pad sample).
[e] At 1000 Hz and 25°C.
[f] At 60 Hz times 10,000.
[g] V/mil at 60 Hz ac and 25°C.
[h] Based on 1984 raw material prices.

is made up of a three-dimensional network of polymer strands that are chemically linked together (hence the word "set," implying that once the network is formed, it is very difficult to undo). Recently, a new type of material has gained recognition as a viable insulating material, thermoplastic rubber (11). This material represents a compromise between the desirable features of thermoset rubber and the processing ease of thermoplastics. The three-dimensional network is created by physical rather than chemical bonds. This means that it can be undone by heating the material to temperatures in excess of 180°C. The base materials for these thermoplastic rubbers are generically called ionomers to indicate the presence of ionic groups in the polymer system. The alignment of these ionic groups belonging to different polymer chains leads to the creation of the three-dimensional network.

Table 4. Typical Composition and Physical Properties of Insulation for Building Wire[a]

Composition, phr[b]	
EPDM (ethylene–propylene–diene terpolymer)	100
Filler (clay)	300
Extender oil	130
Additive package	4.5
Cross-linking agent (organic peroxide)	8.5
Physical properties	
Tensile strength, psi	425
Elongation, %	285
Volume resistivity[c]	1000
Dielectric constant[d]	3.1
Power factor[e]	54
Breakdown voltage[f]	400
Cost, ¢/lb volume[g]	56

[a] Base material: synthetic rubber.
[b] phr = parts per hundred parts of polymer.
[c] TΩ·cm at 25°C and 500 V dc (for a pad sample).
[d] At 1000 Hz and 25°C.
[e] At 60 Hz times 10,000.
[f] V/mil at 60 Hz ac and 25°C.
[g] Based on 1984 raw material prices.

In addition to the physical and electrical properties mentioned above, the electrical insulation of today's wiring systems must meet an environmental requirement that is particularly important to the building trade. The insulation should not represent a fire and smoke hazard. For the evaluation of the flammability of an insulation compound, numerous tests have been developed (1,2,12–15). They are all empirical tests that attempt to simulate actual conditions occurring in building structures. The satisfactory passing of these tests assures merely that the particular compounds meet minimum standards under the prevailing test conditions. To assure the successful passage of a given insulation compound, the manufacturers usually add some inorganic flame-retardant compounds, which can occasionally cause more damage than an actual fire because they can generate hazardous fumes prior to actual combustion of the insulation. Recently, a new family of polymers has become available that has much-improved fire-retardant properties. These are the fluoropolymers and the mixed chlorofluoropolymers such as blends of PE and polychlorotrifluoroethylene, fluorinated ethylene–propylene, and poly(perfluoroalkoxy tetrafluoroethylene). These products have been classified by UL as having "adequate fire-retardant and low smoke-producing characteristics" (16). Of particular interest for communications and control cable insulation are some of the foamed versions of these materials. These foamed perfluoropolymers provide not only the desired fire retardancy, but they also have a dielectric constant of less than 2, thus permitting the construction of low-capacitance coaxial cables without sacrificing other important properties. Cables insulated with these polymers can be installed directly in buildings without metal sheathing or conduits, thus compensating somewhat for the inherently higher cost of the polymer itself.

In most cases, the physical and electrical properties of the wires and cables to be used in a given application are determined by wiring codes such as those published by NEC, UL, and local governments. These codes and ordinances also define the manner of installation, including information as to the number of cables allowed in the same conduit. There are obviously many factors involved in the selection of the ideal wire or cable. Invariably, compromises and tradeoffs must be made in arriving at a satisfactory practical solution.

BIBLIOGRAPHY

1. *Reference Standard for Electrical Wires, Cables, and Flexible Cords,* UL 1581, Underwriters Laboratories, Inc., Melville, N.Y., August 1983.
2. *ASTM Procedures,* Vols. 39 and 40, American Society for Testing and Materials, Philadelphia, Pa., 1985.
3. J. K. Gillette and M. H. Suba, eds., *Electrical Wire Handbook,* Wire Association International, Inc., Guilford, Conn., 1983.
4. R. N. Sampson, "Insulation, Electric: Properties and Materials," in *Kirk-Othmer Encyclopedia of Chemical Technology,* 3rd ed., Vol. 13, John Wiley & Sons, Inc., New York, 1981, pp. 534–563.
5. J. E. Hogan, "Insulation, Electric: Wire and Cable Covers," in *Kirk-Othmer Encyclopedia of Chemical Technology,* 3rd

ed., Vol. 13, John Wiley & Sons, Inc., New York, 1981, pp. 564–590.

6. A. R. von Hippel, *Dielectric Materials and Applications,* MIT Technology Press, Cambridge, Mass., and John Wiley & Sons, Inc., New York, 1954.
7. R. W. Sillars, *Electrical Insulating Materials and their Application,* Peter Peregrinus Ltd., Publisher for the Institute of Electrical Engineers, Stevenage, UK, 1973.
8. A. R. Blythe, *Electrical Properties of Polymers,* Cambridge University Press, Cambridge, UK, 1979.
9. R. Bartnikas and R. M. Eichhorn, eds., *Electrical Properties of Solid Insulating Materials: Molecular Structure and Electrical Behavior,* Vol. IIA of *Engineering Dielectrics,* ASTM Special Technical Publication 783, American Society for Testing and Materials, Philadelphia, Pa., 1982.
10. C. A. Harper, "Fundamentals of Electrical Insulating Materials," *Industrial Research & Development* **20**(12) (1978).
11. "Dynamically Vulcanized Thermoplastic Rubber—The Mean Between Extremes," *Wire Tech* **13**(6), 24 (1985).
12. "Flammability of Solid Polymer Cables," EPRI #EL-1263, Electric Power Research Institute, Palo Alto, Calif.
13. "Study of Damageability of Electrical Cables in Simulated Fire Environments," EPRI #NP-1767, Electric Power Research Institute, Palo Alto, Calif.
14. "Categorization of Cable Flammability: Detection of Smoldering and Flaming Cable Fire," EPRI #NP-1630, Electric Power Research Institute, Palo Alto, Calif.
15. "Categorization of Cable Flammability, Part 1," EPRI #1200, Electric Power Research Institute, Palo Alto, Calif.
16. D. Chung and H. Finelli, "Fluoropolymers Boost Communication Line Quality," *Research & Development,* 79–82 (Mar. 1986).

ERIC O. FORSTER
Scotch Plains, New Jersey

INSULATION, THERMAL

PURPOSE OF THERMAL INSULATION

The primary purpose of installing thermal insulation is to retard the transmission of heat resulting from an imposed temperature difference. In a building application, thermal insulation may perform a variety of functions:

1. Conservation of energy by reducing the heat loss or gain through the building exterior envelope or interior piping, ducts, and equipment.
2. Reduction of equipment size and building cost by reducing the peak demands for heating or cooling, and thus the equipment size and space required for it.
3. Improvement in comfort by increasing (or reducing) the surface temperature to which occupants are exposed and thereby improving the average or mean radiant temperature, and by minimizing the rate of temperature swings.
4. Provision of safety by reducing the temperature of exposed surfaces where possible personnel contact exists.
5. Reduction of damage by reducing the rate of temperature rise of structural components and building separation elements during a fire.
6. Prevention of surface condensation by raising the exposed surface temperature above that of the dew point.
7. Retardation of freezing by slowing loss of heat from exposed piping and equipment.

INSULATION MATERIALS, TYPES, AND FORMS

Thermal insulations suitable for building applications are available in a variety of materials, types, and forms. Materials and types include:

1. Inorganic (fibrous—glass, asbestos, rock, or slag wool; cellular—glass, vermiculite, perlite).
2. Organic (fibrous—wood, paper; cellular—cork, foamed rubber, polystyrene, polyurethane, and other polymers).
3. Metallic—reflective metals or metallized surfaces.

Forms of building insulation available include:

1. Loose fill—fibers, powders, granules, or nodules designed to be poured or blown into enclosed wall cavities or attic spaces.
2. Flexible and semirigid—blankets, batts, and felts available in sheet and roll form. These may have an integral surface covering such as a finish, air/vapor retarder, or reflective surface.
3. Rigid—preformed blocks, boards, sheets, and pipe covering. These may also have an integral surface treatment.
4. Reflective—single or preformed multiple reflective surfaces available in sheet or roll form.
5. Formed-in-place—liquid components that when mixed and poured, sprayed, or frothed on a surface or in a cavity react to expand and form rigid or semirigid foam insulation.
6. Cement—loose material designed to be mixed with water or a binder and sprayed or troweled in place.

INSULATION AND HEAT TRANSFER NOMENCLATURE

Symbols and Terms

Following are some of the more common terms and symbols relating to heat transfer and insulations, along with their definitions, metric (SI) units, and comparable U.S. customary (IP) units. For a more complete listing, refer to ASTM C-168, Standard Definitions of Terms Relating to Thermal Insulating Materials (1).

Q is the total thermal transmission or rate of heat flow, the total quantity of heat flowing in unit time through an area (A) normal to the flow; W (SI unit), Btu/h (IP unit).

q is the unit thermal transmission, the quantity of heat

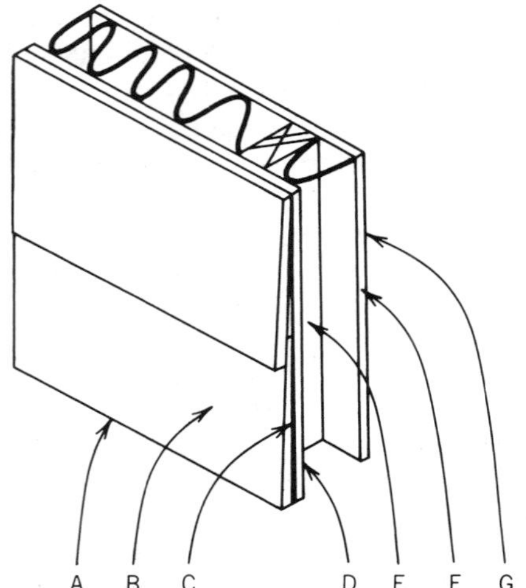

Figure 1. Example of thermal transmittance (U-factor) calculation for an insulated wood frame wall. A, outside surface (winter, 6.7 m/s); B, siding (13 × 203 mm wood); C, sheathing (13 mm vegetable fiber); D, insulation (89 mm/R 1.94 mineral fiber batt); E, stud (nominal 2 × 4, 38 × 39 mm wood); F, wallboard (13 mm gypsum); G, inside surface (still air).

Element	R_i (insulation), $m^2 \cdot K/W$	R_f (framing), $m^2 \cdot K/W$
A. Outside surface	0.03	0.03
B. Siding	0.14	0.14
C. Sheathing	0.23	0.23
D. Insulation	1.94	
E. Stud		0.75
F. Wallboard	0.08	0.08
G. Inside surface	0.12	0.12
Total	*2.54*	*1.35*

$$U_i = 1/R_i = 1/2.54 = 0.39\ W/m^2 \cdot K$$

$$U_f = 1/R_f = 1/1.35 = 0.74\ W/m^2 \cdot K$$

$$U_{avg} = 1/R_{avg} = 0.85/2.54 + 0.15/1.35 = 0.45\ W/m^2 \cdot K$$

(from Eq. 8, assuming 15% of wall area is framing) (2). Courtesy of the American Society of Heating, Refrigerating and Air-Conditioning Engineers, Inc.

flowing in unit time through unit area; W/m^2 (SI unit), $Btu/h \cdot ft^2$ (IP unit).

k is the thermal conductivity, the time rate of heat flow in a direction perpendicular to the surface, through unit area of an infinite slab of a homogeneous material of unit thickness, induced by a unit temperature difference; $W/m \cdot K$ (SI unit), $Btu \cdot in./h \cdot ft^2 \cdot °F$ (IP unit).

r is the thermal resistivity, the reciprocal of thermal conductivity; $m \cdot K/W$ (SI unit), $h \cdot ft^2 \cdot °F/Btu \cdot in.$ (IP unit).

C is the thermal conductance, the time rate of heat flow through unit area of a particular body or assembly, induced by a unit temperature difference between the body or assembly surfaces; $W/m^2 \cdot K$ (SI unit), $Btu/h \cdot ft^2 \cdot °F$ (IP unit).

h is the surface conductance, the time rate of heat flow to or from a surface in contact with its surroundings, through unit area, induced by a unit temperature difference; $W/m^2 \cdot K$ (SI unit), $Btu/h \cdot ft^2 \cdot °F$ (IP unit).

R is the thermal resistance, the reciprocal of thermal conductance; $m^2 \cdot K/W$ (SI unit), $h \cdot ft^2 \cdot °F/Btu$ (IP unit).

U is the thermal transmittance (often referred to as the overall coefficient of heat transfer and commonly known as the U-factor), the thermal transmission in unit time through a unit area of a particular body or assembly, including its boundary films, divided by the difference between the environmental temperatures on either side of the body or assembly. C and U are similar; U includes the effects of the surface film resistances, whereas C applies only to the material or assembly of materials. See Figure 1 for an example of a thermal transmittance calculation; $W/m^2 \cdot K$ (SI unit), $Btu/h \cdot ft^2 \cdot °F$ (IP unit).

Conversion Factors (to IP Units)

The units in this article are given in metric (SI) units. Refer to ASTM E-380, Standard for Metric Practice (1) and Chapter 37 of the *1985 ASHRAE Handbook of Fundamentals* (2) for standard metric conversion factors.

INSULATION PROPERTIES

Insulation Testing

The performance of a particular building insulation material in an application depends in part on how well suited its properties are to the requirements of that installation. Over the years, ASTM Committee C-16 has promulgated many standard test procedures related to determining the physical properties of insulating and related materials, including thermal transmission, strength, density, specific heat, emittance, and water vapor transmission (1).

Thermal Insulation Properties

The thermal transmission properties of insulation generally increase with temperature; however, the amount of increase is small for the temperature range typically encountered in building applications. Therefore, it is customary to quote the thermal conductivity or k of building insulations at a single mean temperature of 24 °C (75 °F). Under winter conditions the actual thermal transmission will be somewhat less than that calculated using a 24 °C mean, and somewhat higher under summer conditions (see Heat Transfer for a discussion of thermal transmission equations).

Table 1, taken from the *1985 ASHRAE Handbook of Fundamentals* (2), lists the density, conductivity, specific heat, resistivity, and resistance of many common building insulation and construction materials. Table 2, also from ASHRAE, lists the density and lists the conductivity as a function of mean temperature for industrial insulations used on piping, ducts, and equipment in building applications. Reference 3 contains a more complete listing of insulation properties.

Table 1. Typical Thermal Properties of Building Insulations and Materials[a,b]

Description	Density, kg/m³	Conductivity (*k*), W/m · K	Conductance (*C*), W/m² · K	Resistance (*R*): Per Meter Thickness (1/*k*), m · K/W	Resistance (*R*): For Thickness Listed (1/*C*), m² · K/W	Specific Heat, kJ/kg · K
Building board						
Asbestos–cement board	1920	0.576		1.74		1.01
3.18 mm (0.12 in.)	1920		187.4		0.005	
6.35 mm (0.25 in.)	1920		93.72		0.011	
Gypsum or plaster board						
9.53 mm (0.38 in.)	800		17.61		0.056	1.09
12.70 mm (0.50 in.)	800		12.61		0.079	
15.88 mm (0.62 in.)	800		10.11		0.099	
Plywood (Douglas Fir)	544	0.115		8.68		1.22
6.35 mm (0.25 in.)	544		18.18		0.055	
9.53 mm (0.38 in.)	544		12.10		0.083	
12.70 mm (0.50 in.)	544		9.09		0.11	
15.88 mm (0.62 in.)	544		7.33		0.14	
Plywood or wood panels, 19.05 mm (0.75 in.)	544		6.08		0.16	1.22
Vegetable fiberboard						
sheathing, regular density						
12.70 mm (0.50 in.)	288		4.32		0.23	1.30
19.84 mm (0.78 in.)	288		2.78		0.36	
sheathing, intermediate density, 12.70 mm (0.50 in.)	352		4.66		0.21	1.30
nail-base sheathing, 12.70 mm (0.50 in.)	400		5.00		0.20	1.30
shingle backer, 9.53 mm (0.38 in.)	288		6.02		0.17	1.30
shingle backer, 7.94 mm (0.31 in.)	288		7.27		0.14	
sound-deadening board, 12.70 mm (0.50 in.)	240		4.20		0.24	1.26
tile and lay-in panels, plain or acoustic	288	0.058		17.35		0.59
12.70 mm (0.50 in.)	288		4.54		0.22	
19.05 mm (0.75 in.)	288		3.01		0.33	
laminated paperboard	480	0.072		13.88		1.38
homogeneous board from repulped paper	480	0.072		13.88		1.17
Hardboard						
medium density	800	0.105		9.51		1.30
high density, service tempered service underlay	880	0.118		8.47		1.34
high density, standard tempered	1008	0.144		6.94		1.34
Particleboard						
low density	592	0.078		12.84		1.30
medium density	800	0.135		7.36		1.30
high density	1000	0.170		5.90		1.30
underlayment, 15.88 mm (0.62 in.)	640		6.93		0.14	1.22
Wood subfloor, 19.05 mm (0.75 in.)			6.02		0.17	1.38
Building membrane						
Vapor—permeable felt			94.86		0.011	
Vapor—seal, 2 layers of mopped 0.73 kg/m² felt			47.43		0.021	
Vapor—seal, plastic film					negligible	
Finish flooring materials						
Carpet and fibrous pad			2.73		0.37	1.42
Carpet and rubber pad			4.60		0.22	1.38
Cork tile, 3.18 mm (0.12 in.)			20.45		0.049	2.01
Terrazzo, 25.40 mm (1.00 in.)			71.00		0.014	0.80
Tile—asphalt, linoleum, vinyl, rubber			113.6		0.009	1.26
vinyl asbestos						1.01
ceramic						0.80
Wood, hardwood finish 19.05 mm (0.75 in.)			8.35		0.12	

Table 1. *(continued)*

Description	Density, kg/m³	Conductivity (*k*), W/m · K	Conductance (*C*), W/m² · K	Resistance (*R*) Per meter thickness (1/*k*), m · K/W	For thickness listed (1/*C*), m² · K/W	Specific Heat, kJ/kg · K
Insulating materials						
Blanket and batt						
Mineral fiber, fibrous form processed from rock, slag, or glass						
approximately 76.2–101.6 mm (3.0–4.0 in.)	4.8–32.0		0.52		1.94	
approximately 88.9 mm (3.5 in.)	4.8–32.0		0.44		2.29	
approximately 139.7–165.1 mm (5.5–6.5 in.)	4.8–32.0		0.30		3.34	
approximately 152.4–177.8 mm (6.0–7.0 in.)	4.8–32.0		0.26		3.87	
approximately 215.9–228.6 mm (8.5–9.0 in.)	4.8–32.0		0.19		5.28	
approximately 304.8 mm (12.0 in)	4.8–32.0		0.15		6.69	
Board and slabs						
Cellular glass	136	0.050		19.85		0.75
Glass fiber, organic bonded	64–144	0.036		27.76		0.96
Expanded perlite, organic bonded	16.0	0.052		19.29		1.26
Expanded rubber (rigid)	72.0	0.032		31.58		1.68
Expanded polystyrene extruded						
cut cell surface	28.8	0.036		27.76		1.22
smooth skin surface	28.8–56.0	0.029		34.70		1.22
Expanded polystyrene, molded beads	16.0	0.037		23.25		
	20.0	0.036		27.76		
	24.0	0.035		28.94		
	28.0	0.035		28.94		
	32.0	0.033		30.19		
Cellular polyurethane[c], R–1.94 (*R*–11) (unfaced)	24.0	0.023		43.38		1.59
Foil-faced, glass fiber-reinforced cellular polyisocyanurate, *R*–1.94 (*R*–11)[d]	32.0	0.020		49.97		0.92
nominal 12.70 mm (0.50 in.)			1.58		0.63	
nominal 25.40 mm (1.0 in.)			0.79		1.27	
nominal 50.80 mm (2.0 in.)			0.39		2.53	
Mineral fiber with resin binder	240	0.042		23.94		0.71
Mineral fiberboard, wet felted						
core or roof insulation	256–272	0.049		20.40		
acoustical tile	288	0.050		19.85		0.80
	336	0.053		18.74		
Mineral fiberboard, wet molded						
acoustical tile	368	0.060		16.52		0.59
Wood or cane fiberboard						
acoustical tile, 12.70 mm (0.50 in.)			4.54		0.22	1.30
19.05 mm (0.75 in.)			3.01		0.33	
Interior finish (plank, tile)	240	0.050		19.85		1.34
Cement fiber slabs (shredded wood with Portland cement binder	400–432	0.072–0.070		13.88–13.12		
Cement fiber slabs (shredded wood with magnesia oxysulfide binder)	352	0.082		12.15		1.30
Loose fill						
Cellulosic insulation (milled paper or wood pulp)	36.8–51.2	0.039–0.046		25.68–21.72		1.38
Sawdust or shavings	128–240	0.065		15.41		1.38
Wood fiber, softwoods	32.0–56.0	0.043		23.11		1.38

Table 1. *(continued)*

Description	Density, kg/m³	Conductivity (k), W/m · K	Conductance (C), W/m² · K	Resistance (R) Per meter thickness (1/k), m · K/W	For thickness listed (1/C), m² · K/W	Specific Heat, kJ/kg · K
Perlite, expanded	32.0–65.6	0.039–0.045		25.68–22.90		
	65–118	0.045–0.052		22.90–19.43		
	118–176	0.052–0.060		19.43–16.66		
Mineral fiber (rock, slag, or glass)						
approximately 95.3–127.0 mm (3.75–5.0 in.)	9.6–32.0				1.94	0.71
approximately 165.1–222.3 mm (6.5–8.75 in.)	9.6–32.0				3.34	
approximately 190.5–254.0 mm (7.5–10.0 in.)	9.6–32.0				3.87	
approximately 260.4–349.3 mm (10.25–13.75 in.)	9.6–32.0				5.28	
Mineral fiber (rock, slag, or glass)						
approximately 88.9 mm (3.5 in.) (closed sidewall application)	32.0–56.0				2.46	
Vermiculite, exfoliated	112–131	0.068		14.78		1.34
	64.0–96.0	0.063		15.75		
Field Applied						
Polyurethane foam	24.0–40.0	0.023–0.026		43.38–36.50		
Ureaformaldehyde foam	11.2–25.6	0.032–0.040		24.78–31.58		
Spray cellulosic fiber base	32.0–96.0	0.035–0.043		23.11–28.94		
Plastering materials						
Cement plaster, sand aggregate	1865	0.720		1.39		0.84
sand aggregate, 9.53 mm (0.38 in.)			75.54		0.014	0.84
19.05 mm (0.75 in.)			37.83		0.026	0.84
Gypsum plaster						
lightweight aggregate, 12.70 mm (0.50 in.)	720		17.72		0.056	
15.88 mm (0.62 in.)	720		15.17		0.069	
lightweight aggregate on metal lath, 19.05 mm (0.75 in.)			12.10		0.083	
Perlite aggregate	720	0.216		4.65		1.34
sand aggregate	1680	0.806		1.25		0.84
12.70 mm (0.50 in.)	1680		63.05		0.016	
15.88 mm (0.62 in.)	1680		51.69		0.019	
sand aggregate on metal lath, 19.05 mm (0.75 in.)			43.74		0.023	
vermiculite aggregate	720	0.245		4.09		
Masonry materials						
Concretes						
Cement mortar	1856	0.720		1.39		
Gypsum-fiber concrete, 87.5% gypsum, 12.5% wood chips	816	0.239		4.16		0.88
Lightweight aggregates including expanded shale, clay, or slate; expanded slags; cinders; pumice; vermiculite; and also cellular concretes	1920	0.749		1.32		
	1600	0.518		1.94		
	1280	0.360		2.78		
	960	0.245		4.09		
	640	0.166		5.97		
	480	0.130		7.70		
	320	0.101		9.92		
Perlite, expanded	640	0.134		7.50		
	480	0.102		9.76		
	320	0.072		13.88		1.34

Table 1. *(continued)*

Description	Density, kg/m^3	Conductivity (k), W/m · K	Conductance (C), W/m^2 · K	Resistance (R) Per meter thickness ($1/k$), m · K/W	Resistance (R) For thickness listed ($1/C$), m^2 · K/W	Specific Heat, kJ/kg · K
Sand and gravel or stone aggregate (oven dried	2240	1.296		0.76		0.92
Sand and gravel or stone aggregate (not dried)	2240	1.728		0.56		
Stucco	1856	0.720		1.39		
Masonry units						
Brick, common[e]	1920	0.720		1.39		0.80
Brick, face[e]	2080	1.296		0.76		
Clay tile, hollow						
1 cell deep, 76.2 mm (3.0 in.)			7.10		0.14	0.88
1 cell deep, 101.6 mm (4.0 in.)			5.11		0.20	
2 cells deep, 152.4 mm (6.0 in.)			3.75		0.27	
2 cells deep, 203.2 mm (8.0 in.)			3.07		0.33	
2 cells deep, 254.0 mm (10.0 in.)			2.56		0.39	
3 cells deep, 304.8 mm (12.0 in.)			2.27		0.44	
Concrete blocks, three oval core						
sand and gravel aggregate						
101.6 mm (4.0 in.)			7.95		0.12	0.92
203.2 mm (8.0 in.)			5.11		0.20	
304.8 mm (12.0 in.)			4.43		0.23	
cinder aggregate						
76.2 mm (3.0 in.)			6.59		0.15	0.88
101.6 mm (4.0 in.)			5.11		0.20	
203.2 mm (8.0 in.)			3.29		0.30	
304.8 mm (12.0 in.)			3.01		0.33	
lightweight aggregate (expanded shale, clay, slate or slag; pumice)						
76.2 mm (3.0 in.)			4.49		0.22	0.88
101.6 mm (4.0 in.)			3.81		0.26	
203.2 mm (8.0 in.)			2.84		0.35	
304.8 mm (12.0 in.)			2.50		0.40	
Concrete blocks, rectangular core						
sand and gravel aggregate						
2-core, 203.2 mm, 16.3 kg (8.0 in.)			5.45		0.18	0.92
same with filled cores[f]			2.95		0.34	0.92
lightweight aggregate (expanded shale, clay, slate or slag, pumice)						
3-core 152.4 mm, 8.6 kg (6.0 in.)			3.46		0.29	0.88
same with filled cores[f]			1.87		0.53	
2-core, 203.2 mm, 10.9 kg (8.0 in.)			2.61		0.38	
same with filled cores[f]			1.14		0.89	
3-core, 304.8 mm, 17.3 kg (12.0 in.)			2.27		0.44	
same with filled cores[f]			0.97		1.02	
Stone, lime, or sand		1.800		0.56		0.80
Gypsum partition tile						
76.2 × 304.8 × 762.0 mm, solid (3 × 12 × 30 in.)			4.49		0.22	0.80
76.2 × 304.8 × 762.0 mm, 4-cell (3 × 12 × 30 in.)			4.20		0.24	
101.6 × 304.8 × 762.0 mm, 3-cell (4 × 12 × 30 in.)			3.41		0.29	
Roofing						
Asbestos–cement shingles	1920		27.04		0.037	1.01
Asphalt roll roofing	1120		36.92		0.026	1.51
Asphalt shingles	1120		12.89		0.077	1.26

Table 1. *(continued)*

Description	Density, kg/m^3	Conductivity (k), $W/m \cdot K$	Conductance (C), $W/m^2 \cdot K$	Resistance (R) Per meter thickness ($1/k$), $m \cdot K/W$	Resistance (R) For thickness listed ($1/C$), $m^2 \cdot K/W$	Specific Heat, $kJ/kg \cdot K$
Built up, 9.53 mm (0.38 in.)	1120		17.04		0.058	1.47
Slate, 12.70 mm (0.50 in.)			113.6		0.009	1.26
Wood shingles, plain and plastic film faced			6.02		0.17	1.30
Siding materials (on flat surface)						
Shingles						
asbestos–cement	1920		26.98		0.037	
wood, 406.4 mm, 190.5 mm exposure (16 in., 7.5 in. exposure)			6.53		0.15	1.30
wood, double, 406.4 mm, 304.8 mm exposure (16 in., 12 in. exposure)			4.77		0.21	1.17
wood, plus insul. backer board, 7.94 mm (0.31 in.)			4.03		0.25	1.30
siding						
asbestos–cement, 6.35 mm, (0.25 in.), lapped			27.04		0.037	1.01
asphalt roll siding			36.92		0.026	1.47
asphalt insulating siding, 12.70 mm (0.50 in.)			3.92		0.26	1.47
hardboard siding, 11.1 mm (0.44 in.)	640	0.215		4.65		1.17
wood, drop, 25.4 × 203.2 mm (1 × 8 in.)			7.21		0.14	1.17
wood, bevel, 12.7 × 203.2 mm (0.5 × 8 in.), lapped			6.99		0.14	1.17
wood, bevel, 19.1 × 254.0 mm (0.75 × 10 in.), lapped			5.40		0.18	1.17
wood, plywood, 9.53 mm (0.38 in.), lapped			9.03		0.10	1.22
Aluminum or steel, over sheathing						
hollow-backed			9.14		0.11	1.22
insulating-board-backed nominal 9.53 mm (0.38 in.)			3.12		0.32	1.34
insulating-board-backed nominal 9.53 mm (0.38 in.), foil backed			1.93		0.52	
Architectural glass			56.80		0.018	0.84
Woods (12% moisture content)						
Hardwoods						1.63
oak	659–749	0.161–0.180		6.18–5.55		
birch	682–726	0.167–0.176		6.04–5.69		
maple	637–704	0.157–0.171		6.52–6.11		
ash	614–670	0.153–0.164		6.52–6.11		
Softwoods						1.63
southern pine	570–659	0.144–0.161		6.94–6.18		
Douglas fir–larch	536–581	0.137–0.145		7.36–6.87		
southern cypress	502–514	0.130–0.132		7.70–7.56		
hem fir, spruce pine fir	392–502	0.107–0.130		9.37–7.70		
West Coast woods, cedars	347–502	0.098–0.130		10.27–7.70		
California redwood	392–448	0.107–0.118		9.37–8.47		

[a] Ref. 2. Courtesy of the American Society of Heating, Refrigerating and Air-Conditioning Engineers, Inc.
[b] Representative values for typical dry materials at a mean temperature of 24 °C (75 °F). For specific properties of a particular product, use manufacturer's or unbiased test data.
[c] Values for aged, unfaced board stock.
[d] Time-aged values for board stock with gas barrier quality aluminum foil facers on two major surfaces.
[e] Face brick and common brick do not always have these specific densities. When the density differs from that shown, there is a change in the thermal conductivity.
[f] Vermiculite, perlite, or mineral wool insulation.

Table 2. Typical Thermal Properties of Industrial Insulations[a,b]

Form Material Composition	Accepted Maximum Temperature for Use, °C	Typical density, kg/m³	Typical Conductivity λ at Mean Temperature (°C), W/m · K													
			−73.3	−59.4	−45.6	−31.7	−17.8	−3.9	10.0	23.9	37.8	93.3	148.9	260.0	371.1	482.2
Blankets and felts																
Mineral fiber																
Rock, slag, or glass																
Blanket, metal reinforced	650	96–192									0.037	0.046	0.056	0.078		
	540	40.0–96.0									0.035	0.045	0.058	0.088		
Mineral fiber, glass	180	less														
Blanket, flexible, fine-fiber		than				0.036	0.037	0.040	0.043	0.048	0.052	0.076				
organic bonded		12.0				0.035	0.036	0.039	0.042	0.046	0.049	0.069				
		16.0				0.033	0.035	0.036	0.039	0.042	0.046	0.062				
		24.0				0.030	0.032	0.033	0.036	0.039	0.040	0.053				
		32.0				0.029	0.030	0.032	0.033	0.036	0.037	0.048				
		48.0				0.027	0.029	0.030	0.032	0.033	0.035	0.045				
Blanket, flexible, textile-fiber	180	10.4				0.039	0.040	0.042	0.043	0.045	0.046	0.072	0.098			
organic bonded		12.0				0.037	0.039	0.040	0.042	0.045	0.046	0.069	0.095			
		16.0				0.035	0.036	0.037	0.039	0.042	0.045	0.065	0.086			
		24.0				0.032	0.033	0.035	0.036	0.039	0.042	0.056	0.073			
		48.0				0.029	0.030	0.032	0.033	0.035	0.036	0.046	0.059			
Felt, semirigid organic bonded	200	48–128						0.035	0.036	0.037	0.039	0.050	0.063			
	450	48.0	0.023	0.024	0.026	0.027	0.029	0.030	0.032	0.033	0.035	0.050	0.079			
Laminated and felted without binder	650	120											0.050	0.065	0.086	
Vegetable and animal fiber																
Hair felt or hair felt plus jute	80	160						0.037	0.040	0.042	0.043					
Blocks, boards and pipe insulation																
Asbestos																
Laminated asbestos paper	370	480									0.058	0.065	0.072	0.086		
Corrugated and laminated asbestos paper																
4-ply	150	176–208								0.078	0.082	0.098				
6-ply	150	240–272								0.071	0.073	0.085				
8-ply	150	288–320								0.068	0.071	0.082				
Molded amosite and binder	820	240–288									0.046	0.053	0.060	0.075	0.089	0.104
85% Magnesia	320	176–192									0.050	0.055	0.060			
Calcium silicate	650	176–240									0.055	0.059	0.063	0.075	0.089	0.104
	980	192–240												0.091	0.107	0.137
Cellular glass	480	136	0.039	0.040	0.042	0.043	0.045	0.046	0.048	0.050	0.052	0.060	0.071	0.101	0.148	
Diatomaceous silica	870	336–352												0.092	0.098	0.104
	1040	368–400												0.101	0.108	0.115

Mineral fiber																
Glass																
Organic bonded, block and boards	200	48–160	0.023	0.024	0.026	0.027	0.029	0.032	0.035	0.036	0.037	0.048	0.058			
Nonpunking binder	540	48–160									0.037	0.045	0.055	0.075		
Pipe insulation, slag or glass	180	48.0–64.0					0.029	0.030	0.032	0.033	0.035	0.042				
	260	48–160					0.029	0.032	0.035	0.036	0.037	0.048	0.058			
Inorganic bonded, block	540	160–240									0.048	0.055	0.065	0.079		
	980	240–384									0.046	0.053	0.060	0.075	0.089	0.107
Pipe insulation, slag or glass	540	160–240									0.048	0.055	0.065	0.079		
Mineral fiber																
Resin binder		240			0.033	0.035	0.036	0.037	0.040	0.042						
Rigid polystyrene																
Extruded, refrigerant 12 expanded smooth skin surface	80	35.2	0.023	0.023	0.024	0.023	0.024	0.026	0.027	0.029						
Extruded cut cell surface	80	28.8	0.024	0.026	0.027	0.029	0.030	0.033	0.035	0.036	0.039					
Molded beads	80	16.0	0.024	0.027	0.029	0.030	0.032	0.035	0.036	0.037	0.040					
		20.0	0.024	0.026	0.027	0.029	0.032	0.033	0.035	0.036	0.039					
		24.0	0.023	0.024	0.027	0.029	0.030	0.032	0.033	0.035	0.037					
		28.0	0.023	0.024	0.026	0.027	0.029	0.032	0.033	0.035	0.036					
		32.0	0.022	0.023	0.026	0.027	0.029	0.030	0.032	0.033	0.035					
Rigid polyisocyanurate[c]																
Cellular, foil-faced glass fiber reinforced, refrigerant 11 expanded	120	32.0						0.017	0.019	0.020	0.022					
Polyurethane[d]																
Refrigerant 11 expanded (unfaced)	100	24.0–40.0	0.023	0.024	0.026	0.026	0.026	0.024	0.023	0.023	0.024					
Rubber																
Rigid foamed	70	72						0.029	0.030	0.032	0.033					
Vegetable and animal fiber																
Wood felt (pipe insulation)	80	320						0.040	0.043	0.045	0.048					
Insulating cements																
Mineral fiber																
Rock, slag, or glass																
With colloidal clay binder	980	384–480									0.071	0.079	0.088	0.105	0.122	
With hydraulic setting binder	650	480–640									0.108	0.115	0.122	0.137		
Loose fill																
Cellulose insulation (milled pulverized paper or wood pulp)		40.0–48.0							0.037	0.039	0.042					
Mineral fiber, slag, rock, or glass		32.0–80.0			0.027	0.030	0.033	0.036	0.037	0.040	0.045					
Perlite (expanded)		48.0–80.0	0.032	0.035	0.036	0.039	0.040	0.043	0.045	0.048	0.050					
Silica aerogel		122			0.019	0.020	0.022	0.022	0.023	0.024	0.026					
Vermiculite (expanded)		112–131			0.056	0.058	0.060	0.063	0.065	0.068	0.071					
		64–96			0.049	0.050	0.055	0.058	0.060	0.063	0.066					

[a] Ref. 2. Courtesy of the American Society of Heating, Refrigerating and Air-Conditioning Engineers, Inc.

[b] Representative values for typical dry materials; use manufacturer's recommendations and specifications for specific products, including maximum use temperature.

[c] Time-aged values for board stock with gas barrier quality aluminum foil facers on two major surfaces.

[d] Values are for aged, unfaced board stock. Some polyurethane foams are formed by means that produce a stable product with respect to thermal conductivity, but most are blown with refrigerant and will change with time.

Building Insulation Specifications

ASTM Committee C-16 has also promulgated specifications for many building insulations. Generally, these include a product description including types available, applicable test methods, physical properties, and packaging and marking. Reference 1 contains current ASTM specifications for building insulations.

INSULATION SELECTION CRITERIA

The selection of an insulating material for a particular building application involves consideration of many factors. The initial concern is low thermal transfer. However, many secondary factors are also important. These include applied cost, available space, installation ease, strength, rigidity, fire hazard and fire resistance, water vapor permeance, and air flow resistance.

Thermal Recommendations

For many buildings, such as residential structures, the annual energy requirement for space conditioning is strongly dependent on the design of the building envelope. For many commercial buildings, because of large internal heat gains, the thermal resistance of the envelope is of secondary concern. Industrial buildings usually have large roof areas, where the thermal resistance is a consideration.

Thermal resistance values recommended by the U.S. Department of Energy (DOE) for residential structures are given in Table 3 (4). The values given refer to barriers of conditioned space from unconditioned space. These recommendations must be considered as minimum values. Greater insulation levels are usually desirable from the standpoints of occupant comfort and future energy costs.

Recently, the concept of a "super-insulated" house, with much higher thermal resistances than those recommended in Table 3, has enjoyed increased popularity. Greatly increased thermal resistance in the walls is achieved by the use of nominal 2 × 6-in. (140-mm wide) studs rather than the usual nominal 2 × 4 in. (89-mm wide), low-thermal-conductivity foam board sheathing or double exterior walls. The advantages achieved are its very low space heating and cooling energy requirements, smaller heating, ventilating, and air-conditioning (HVAC) equipment size, and improved occupant comfort.

Moisture Considerations

Water vapor is universally present in the air. It tends to migrate by a process of diffusion. The direction of migration is toward reduced water vapor partial pressure; the rate is proportional to the water vapor pressure gradient. Condensation occurs when the temperature of a surface is below that of the dew point of the surrounding humid air. Internal condensation can be very damaging to a structure when it causes corrosion or decay. In insulation, condensation causes a marked increase in the heat transfer rate.

In a building structure component such as a wall, internal condensation can be prevented by retarding the rate of water vapor entering the component on one side and doing nothing to hinder the egress of water vapor on the other side. In a cold climate this means installing a vapor retarder element (also known as a vapor barrier) on the warm side of the insulation, where the water vapor pressure is greatest. In buildings, experience has shown that a vapor retarder with a permeance of not more than one Perm (a unit of permeance: 57 ng/s · m^2 · Pa or 1 gr/h · ft^2 · in. Hg in IP units) will generally prevent internal condensation. The cold side of the component should have a water vapor permeance five times that of the warm side.

In cold climates the vapor retarder is installed on the inside surface of the building envelope. In very warm, humid climates, where minimum winter heating is required, the vapor retarder is installed on the outside. Climates with both significant winter heating and summer cooling require careful consideration with regard to the placement of the vapor retarder for least condensation hazard.

Table 3. Recommended Residential Insulation Levels[a]

Heating Degree Days	Minimum Thermal Resistance[b]		
18.3 °C (65 °F) base	Walls[c]	Ceiling	Floors
0–560 (0–1000)		3.3 (19)	
560–1390 (1000–2500)	1.9–2.3 (11–13)	3.3 (19)	
1390–1940 (2500–3500)	1.9–2.3 (11–13)	3.9 (22)	
1940–3890 (3500–7000)	1.9–2.3 (11–13)	5.3 (30)	1.9 (11)
>3890 (>7000)	1.9–2.3 (11–13)	6.7 (38)	3.3 (19)

[a] Ref 4.
[b] m^2 · K/W (h · ft^2 · °F/Btu); higher values recommended for electric resistance heating.
[c] Assumes 89 mm (3.5 in.) wall studs.

Pipes and ducts carrying chilled fluids present a similar condensation hazard. Using eq. 14 (see Heat Transfer), sufficient insulation should be installed so that the surface temperature is above that of the dew point of the surrounding air. A vapor retarder of as low a permeance as possible is needed on the outside surface to prevent water vapor from entering the insulation and condensing on the cold pipe or duct surface.

Condensation can also be a problem in cold weather on glazed sections, and through metal sash and mullion window members. The use of double and triple glazing, and incorporation of insulation in the form of "thermal breaks" in the through metal members, can increase the surface temperature to the point that occupant comfort is improved and the condensation potential is reduced.

The water vapor transmission (WVT) properties of materials are determined by ASTM E-96, Standard Test Methods for Water Vapor Transmission of Materials (1). Various test conditions are provided for, including wet and dry test cups in order to simulate a variety of exposures. Tables 4 and 5, from the *1985 ASHRAE Handbook of Fundamentals* (2), list the WVT of many building construction, insulation, and vapor retarder materials. Also refer to ASTM C-755, Standard Recommended Practice for Selection of Vapor Barriers for Thermal Insulations (1).

Closely related to the problem of condensation caused by water vapor diffusion is that caused by air leakage in a building. Air leakage results from small pressure differences across the building envelope caused by wind and temperature or buoyancy effects since it is impossible to construct a building without some unintentional openings. It is the outward leakage or exfiltration of humid air through the unintentional openings that causes condensation problems. In Canada, with severe winter conditions, it has been observed that excessive air leakage in a structure can be a more important cause of internal condensation problems than an inadequate vapor retarder (5). Also, excessive air leakage is both a waste of energy and a cause of uncomfortable drafts. Fortunately, a carefully installed polyethylene film can function as both an air leakage and water vapor retarder.

In summary, control of moisture condensation in a structure requires a combination of considerations: adequate and properly installed vapor retarder, reduction of excessive air leakage, control of excessive moisture generation within the structure, and sufficient building ventilation to remove excess water vapor. Refer to Chapter 21 of the *1985 ASHRAE Handbook of Fundamentals* (2) for a more detailed discussion of moisture in buildings and to Chapter 22 for ventilation and infiltration.

Economic Considerations

The thicker the insulation installed, the less the heat loss, but the greater the first cost of the insulation. Therefore, the proper economic thickness of insulation can be treated as the minimization of the sum of two costs: the installed cost of the insulation and the lost energy cost, both on an annual basis. Although the concept is simple, applications are usually not. One difficulty is insulation thickness, which is not always a continuously variable function because of space and other considerations. For example, residential walls can be insulated up to the width of the stud without incurring other than insulation material costs. Greater insulation thicknesses can require substantial ancillary installation costs.

The Thermal Insulation Manufacturers Association (TIMA) has a computational program to calculate economic insulation thickness (6). The economic thickness of roof insulation is considered in Ref. 7.

Health and Safety Considerations

At one time asbestos fiber was a common constituent of many insulating cements and spray-applied insulations used under flat roofs and for fire protection of the structural steel of high-rise buildings. With the recognition of the health hazards associated with respirable asbestos fiber in the 1970s, asbestos has been removed from the composition of current insulations. Removal of previously installed asbestos-containing insulation should be undertaken with great care. The U.S. Environmental Protection Agency (EPA) has detailed procedures to be followed. Health questions have also been raised concerning the handling of other mineral fibers (glass, slag, and rock wool). They can be irritating, but no health hazards similar to those of asbestos fibers have been demonstrated.

Urea–formaldehyde foam insulation (UFI) was commonly used as a residential insulation. However, problems developed with people sensitive to formaldehyde. In 1979 Massachusetts banned the further use of UFI because of gas release. Relative to the use of UFI, the U.S. Consumer Products Safety Commission (CPSC) has proposed a warning concerning the possible release of formaldehyde gas, which may cause eye, nose, and throat irritation, coughing, shortness of breath, skin irritation, nausea, headaches, and dizziness or more serious reactions (4).

Flammable insulations, such as plastic foams and insulations with a flammable vapor retarder, should be covered with gypsum wallboard or other approved fire-retardant surfacing material. Combustible insulations designed for use in exposed installations such as attics should have a flame retardant incorporated. As an example, refer to ASTM C-739, Standard Specification for Cellulosic Fiber (Wood-base) Loose-fill Thermal Insulation for a description of surface burning characteristics and flame-resistance permanency requirements to be met by this material (1).

Code Considerations

At one time the DOE attempted to promote a comprehensive Building Energy Performance Standard (BEPS). However, the attempt met with much opposition and was never adopted. ASHRAE has developed a single energy conservation standard for new buildings, Standard 90 (8), and a series of energy standards for existing buildings, Standard 100.2—High Rise Residential (9), Standard 100.5—Institutional (10), and Standard 100.6—Public Assembly (11).

Standard 90 has been incorporated in all 50 state energy codes and various regional building codes. Since originally published in 1975, it has been updated. A number of revi-

Table 4. Typical WVT Properties of Building Insulation, Construction, and Vapor Retarder Materials[a]

Material	Thickness, mm	Permeance ng/s · m^2 · Pa	Resistance, Tpa · m^2 · s/kg	Permeability, ng/s · m · Pa	Resistance Per Meter, (TPa · m^2 · s/kg)/m
Materials used in construction					
Concrete 1:2:4 mix)				4.7	0.21
Brick masonry	102	46	0.022		
Concrete block (cored, limestone aggregate)	203	137	0.0073		
Tile masonry, glazed	102	6.9	0.14		
Asbestos–cement board	3	229–458[b]	0.0017–0.0035		
With oil base finishes		17–29[b]	0.0035–0.052		
Plaster on metal lath	19	860	0.0012		
Plaster on wood lath		630[c]	0.0016		
Plaster on plain gypsum lath (with studs)		1140	0.00088		
Gypsum wallboard (plain)	9.5	2860	0.00035		
Gypsum sheathing (asphalt impregnated)	13			29[b]	0.038
Structural insulating board (sheathing quality)				29–73	0.038–0.014
Structural insulating board (interior, uncoated)	13	2860–5150	0.00035–0.00019		
Hardboard (standard)	3.2	630	0.0016		
Hardboard (tempered)	3.2	290	0.0034		
Built-up roofing (hot mopped)		0.0	∞		
Wood, sugar pine				0.58–7.8	172.0–131
Plywood (Douglas fir, exterior glue)	6.4	40	0.025		
Plywood (Douglas fir, interior glue)	6.4	109	0.0092		
Acrylic, glass fiber reinforced sheet	1.4	6.9[b]	0.145		
Polyester, glass fiber reinforced sheet	1.2	2.9[b]	0.345		
Thermal insulations					
Air (still)				174	0.0057
Cellular glass				0.0[b]	∞
Corkboard				3.0–3.8[b]	0.33–0.26
				14[c]	0.076
Mineral wool (unprotected)				245[c]	0.0059
Expanded polyurethane (R-11 blown) board stock				0.58–2.3[b]	1.72–0.43
Expanded polystyrene (extruded)				1.7[b]	0.57
Expanded polystyrene (bead)				2.9–8.4[b]	0.34–0.12
Phenolic foam (covering removed)				38	0.026
Unicellular synthetic flexible rubber foam				0.029[c]	34–4.61
Plastic and metal foils and films					
Aluminum foil	0.025	0.0[b]	∞		
	0.009	2.9[b]	0.345		
Polyethylene	0.051	9.1[b]	0.110		2133
	0.1	4.6[b]	0.217		2133
	0.15	3.4[b]	0.294		2133
	0.2	2.3[b]	0.435		2133
	0.25	1.7[b]	0.588		2133
Polyvinylchloride, unplasticized	0.051	39 [b]	0.026		
Polyvinylchloride, plasticized	0.1	46–80[b]	0.032		
Polyester	0.025	42 [b]	0.042		
	0.09	13 [b]	0.075		
	0.19	4.6[b]	0.22		
Cellulose acetate	0.25	263 [b]	0.0035		
	3.2	18 [b]	0.054		

[a] Ref. 2. Courtesy of the American Society of Heating, Refrigerating and Air-Conditioning Engineers, Inc.
[b] Dry cup method.
[c] Wet cup method.

sions are currently underway, including development of a separate residential standard, to be designated Standard 90.2. A Standard 100.1 for existing low-rise residential buildings was attempted, but after extensive efforts was abandoned. Standards 100.3 (existing commercial buildings) and 100.4 (existing industrial) were also attempted, but have not yet been formally adopted.

Installation Considerations

In low-rise residential construction it is current practice in new construction to use batt-type insulation in enclosed areas such as the walls and floors over unheated areas and to use blown-type insulation in open exposed areas such as attics. For retrofitting it is common practice to

Table 5. Typical WVT Properties of Building Insulation, Construction, and Vapor Retarder Materials[a]

Material	Mass, kg/m^2	Thickness, mm	Permeance[b]			Resistance[c]		
			Dry Cup	Wet Cup	Other	Dry Cup	Wet Cup	Other
Building paper, felts, roofing papers								
Duplex sheet, asphalt laminated, aluminum foil one side	0.42		0.1	10		10	0.1	
Saturated and coated roll roofing	3.18		2.9	14		0.34	0.071	
Kraft paper and asphalt laminated, reinforced 30–120–30	0.33		17	103		0.059	0.0097	
Blanket thermal insulation back-up paper, asphalt coated	0.30		23	34–240		0.043	0.029–0.0042	
Asphalt-saturated and coated vapor retarder paper	0.42		11–17	34		0.091–0.059	0.029	
Asphalt-saturated but not coated sheathing paper	0.21		190	1160		0.0053	0.00086	
6.8 kg asphalt felt	0.68		57	320		0.017	0.0031	
6.8 kg tar felt	0.68		230	1040		0.0043	0.0096	
Single-kraft, double	0.16		1170	2400		0.00056	0.00042	
Liquid-applied coating materials								
Commercial latex paints (dry film thickness)								
Vapor retarder paint		0.070			26			0.038
Primer–sealer		0.031			360			0.0028
Vinyl acetate/ acrylic primer		0.051			424			0.0024
Vinyl–acrylic primer		0.040			491			0.0020
Semigloss vinyl–acrylic enamel		0.060			378			0.0026
Exterior acrylic house and trim		0.042			313			0.0032
Paint, 2 coats								
Asphalt paint on plywood				23			0.043	
Aluminum varnish on wood			17–29			0.059–0.034		
Enamels on smooth plaster					29–86			0.034–0.012
Primers and sealers on interior insulation board					51–20			0.020–0.0083
Various primers plus 1 coat flat oil paint on plaster					91–172			0.011–0.0058

Table 5 (*continued*)

Material	Mass, kg/m²	Thickness, mm	Permeance[b]			Resistance[c]		
			Dry Cup	Wet Cup	Other	Dry Cup	Wet Cup	Other
Flat paint on interior insulation board					229			0.0044
Water emulsion on interior insulation board					1716–4863			0.00058–0.00021
Paint, 3 coats								
Exterior paint, white lead and oil on wood siding			17–57			0.0059–0.017		
Exterior paint, white lead–zinc oxide and oil on wood			51			0.020		
Styrene–butadiene latex coating	0.6		629			0.0016		
Polyvinyl acetate latex coating	1.2		315			0.0032		
Chlorosulfonated polyethylene mastic	1.1		97			0.010		
	2.2							
Asphalt cut-back mastic								
1.6 mm, dry			8.0			0.125		
4.8 mm, dry			0.0			∞		
Hot melt asphalt	0.6		29			0.034		
	1.1		5.7			0.175		

[a] Ref. 2. Courtesy of the American Society of Heating, Refrigerating and Air-Conditioning Engineers, Inc.
[b] ng/s · m² · Pa.
[c] TPa · m² · s/kg.

use blown insulation in the walls and ceilings, except for owner applications in a ceiling, where a pourable insulation might be used.

With blown insulations it is important to install the material at sufficient density that appreciable settling will not occur in the future. Settling can produce voids in a wall and reduce the thickness in a ceiling. Both of these effects reduce the thermal effectiveness of the insulation (see eq. 2). Most batt insulations are shipped in compressed form. When installing this type of material, it is important that the installed thickness of the batt be at least equal to that shown on the label. If the batt does not recover to the label thickness, the thermal resistance is reduced proportionately.

Reflective accordion-type insulation must be opened up to form air spaces. For this type of insulation to be effective the manufacturer's recommendations must be followed exactly to provide the proper reflective air spaces and avoid air convection currents.

It is important that care be taken in installing any type of insulation to ensure that there are no void or uninsulated areas. Void areas can impair seriously the overall effectiveness of the installation. Likewise, in installing a water vapor retarder, the retarder must be installed on the warm side of the insulation with no gaps present. Similarly, to be effective, an air barrier must be installed without any breaks in its continuity.

HEAT TRANSFER

Principles

Within an insulating material, heat is transferred from one surface to the other under the pressure of a thermal gradient. The greater the difference in temperature per unit of insulation thickness, the greater the quantity of heat transferred. The amount of heat transferred under a given exposure condition can be reduced by reducing the thermal gradient (increasing the insulation thickness) or using an insulating material of lower unit thermal conductance.

The mechanisms of heat transfer within an insulation include a combination of radiation, gas conduction, gas convection, and solid conduction (12). Each operates under its own laws. The relative importance of each mechanism depends on environmental conditions as well as the physical properties of the insulation. For example, radiation becomes more important at higher temperatures. However, even at the moderate temperatures encountered by building insulations, the radiation component of heat transfer is important in low-density insulating materials (13).

Heat Transfer Equations

Below are equations useful in calculating heat transfer. Except as noted, terms and units are as defined under Insulation and Heat Transfer Nomenclature. For a more complete discussion refer to Chapters 3 and 23 in the *1985 ASHRAE Handbook of Fundamentals* (2) and Chapter 1 in the *Thermal Insulation Handbook* (3).

The basic steady-state heat conduction equation for one-dimensional heat flow is that by Fourier:

$$Q = -k \cdot A \cdot (dt/dx) \quad (1)$$

where k is the thermal conductivity of the material, (dt/dx) is the temperature gradient, and A is the area normal to the heat flow.

Conductance. Thermal conductance (C) is the thermal transmission through unit area of a body or assembly under unit surface to surface temperature difference. It is also the reciprocal of thermal resistance:

$$C = Q/A \cdot (t_2 - t_1) = 1/R_o \quad (2)$$

Resistance (Homogeneous Material). The thermal resistance (R) of a homogeneous material is defined as

$$R = L/k \quad (3)$$

where L is the thickness of the material, measured parallel to the heat flow path. Equation 1 may then be rewritten as

$$Q = k \cdot A \cdot (t_2 - t_1) \cdot 1/L = A \cdot (t_2 - t_1) \cdot 1/R \quad (4)$$

where $(t_2 - t_1)$ is the temperature difference. Or

$$R = A \cdot (t_2 - t_1)/Q \quad (5)$$

Resistance (Composite Material). Thermal resistance is the reciprocal of thermal conductance and may also be used for the total or average thermal resistance of a composite structure or assembly (see below).

$$R = 1/C \quad (6)$$

Resistances in Series. When (n) materials are combined in such a manner that heat flows through them in series, the thermal resistance of the combination is

$$R_o = R_1 + R_2 + R_3 + \cdots + R_n \quad (7)$$

where R_o is the overall thermal resistance of the assembly.

Resistances in Parallel. When (n) materials are combined in such a manner that heat flows through them in parallel, the average thermal resistance of the combination is

$$1/R_o = A_1/R_1 + A_2/R_2 + \cdots A_n/R_n \quad (8)$$

where R_o is the average thermal resistance of the combination and A_n is the area fraction of R_n.

Surface Resistance. Surface resistance (R_s) is the reciprocal of the surface or film conductance:

$$R_s = 1/h_s \quad (9)$$

where h_n is the surface or film conductance.

Total Resistance. The total resistance (R_t) is the sum of all the thermal resistances from the environmental temperature on one side of an assembly to that on the other side, including surface resistances:

$$R_t = 1/h_2 + R_o + 1/h_1 \quad (10)$$

where h_n is the surface or film conductance.

Thermal Transmittance. Thermal transmittance (also referred to as the overall coefficient of heat transfer and commonly known as the U-factor) is the reciprocal of the total thermal resistances, including surface resistances. See Figure 1 for an example of a U-factor calculation:

$$U = 1/R_T = 1/[1/h_2 + R_1 + R_2 + \cdots + R_n + 1/h_1] \quad (11)$$

Overall Thermal Transmittance. The area-weighted thermal transmittance (U_o) is useful in describing the average overall thermal performance of a building element such as a wall:

$$U_o = (U_1 \cdot A_1 + U_2 \cdot A_2 + U_3 \cdot A_3)/A_o \quad (12)$$

where the subscripts 1, 2, and 3 refer to the wall, window, and door transmittance and area, respectively, and A_o is the total area of the wall, $A_1 + A_2 + A_3$.

Pipe Insulation. Because of the cylindrical form of pipe insulation, the resistance term in eq. 3 must be modified. The heat flow from an insulated pipe (Q_p) is

$$Q_p = A_p \cdot (t_2 - t_1) \cdot 1/[r_p \cdot \ln(r_s/r_p) \cdot 1/k + (r_p/r_s) \cdot R_s] \quad (13)$$

where A_p is the outside pipe surface area, r_s is the outside surface radius of the insulation, r_p is the outside radius of the pipe, and R_s is the surface resistance (see also ASTM C-680 (1)).

Surface Temperature. The temperature distribution through an insulated assembly is proportional to the thermal resistances. Equations 9 and 10 may be used to calculate surface temperature (t_s):

$$t_s = t_2 - (t_2 - t_1) \cdot R_s/R_T \quad (14)$$

Building Heat Loss Calculations

Equation 11 may be used to calculate the thermal transmittance of a unit area of a particular construction. Use eq. 7 to calculate the total thermal resistance of a building component with a number of elements in series thermally. Select the proper surface conductance from Table 6. Use eqs. 10 and 11 to calculate the thermal transmittance of the component.

When the building component contains framing or other through-conduction members, the thermal transmittance should be calculated separately for the area between the framing members and that through the framing. An area-weighted average thermal transmittance should then be calculated, similarly to the procedure used for parallel heat flow in eq. 8.

The coefficient of thermal transmittance (U) of a number of common building constructions has been calculated in Tables 4A–4L in Chapter 23 of the *1981 ASHRAE Handbook of Fundamentals* (14). Because of their complexity, the thermal transmittance of some construction assemblies cannot readily be calculated with much reliability. The transmittance may be determined experimentally by following the test procedures in ASTM C-236, Standard Test Method for Steady-state Thermal Performance of Building Assemblies by Means of a Guarded Hot Box (1) or ASTM C-976, Standard Test Method for Thermal Performance of Building Assemblies by Means of a Calibrated Hot Box (1).

Multiplying the thermal transmittance of the building component by its area and the temperature difference across it yields the total heat transmitted through the component under those conditions:

$$Q = U \cdot A \cdot (t_2 - t_1) \tag{15}$$

The total heat loss from a building is the sum of the heat losses of all components composing the building envelope.

The maximum building heat loss, upon which the heating equipment requirements are designed, is calculated on the basis of a typical inside temperature, such as 20 °C, and an extreme outside temperature. For the outside temperature it is customary to use a winter "design day." Tables 1, 2, and 3 in Chapter 24 in the *1985 ASHRAE Handbook of Fundamentals* (2) show climatic data for a number of locations in the United States, Canada, and other countries, respectively. The winter columns show 99% and 97.5% design dry-bulb temperatures, that is, the percentage of time that the outside temperature is above the listed temperature during the three-month period of December through February.

Table 6. Building Surface Conductances (*h*) (High-emissivity/Nonreflective Surfaces)[a]

Position of Surface	Heat Flow Direction	Conductance, $W/m^2 \cdot K$	Resistance, $m^2 \cdot K/W$
Still air			
Horizontal	Upward	9.3	0.11
Vertical	Horizontal	8.3	0.12
Horizontal	Downward	6.1	0.16
Moving air			
Winter (average 6.7 m/s)	Any	34	0.03
Summer (average 3.4 m/s)	Any	23	0.04

[a] Ref. 2. Courtesy of the American Society of Heating, Refrigerating and Air-Conditioning Engineers, Inc.

Chapter 25 of the *1985 ASHRAE Handbook of Fundamentals* (2) gives a detailed discussion of procedures to be used in calculating building heating load. Similarly, Chapter 26 of the *1985 ASHRAE Handbook of Fundamentals* (2) discusses procedures to be used in calculating the air-conditioning cooling load of a building, including heat transmitted through the building components. Reference 15 also describes a detailed procedure for calculating building and cooling loads.

Annual Energy Requirements

The average annual heating energy requirements (E) of a building may be estimated by use of the equation

$$E = C_D \cdot [H_L \cdot DD \cdot 24]/(t_2 - t_1) \tag{16}$$

where C_D is an empirical correction factor, DD is the number of heating degree days for a particular location, H_L is the design heat loss for the building, and $(t_2 - t_1)$ is the design temperature difference.

The heating degree days (DD) for a number of locations in the United States and Canada are given in Table 4, Chapter 24 of the *1981 ASHRAE Handbook of Fundamentals* (14). These tables utilize the traditional base temperature of 18.3 °C (65 °F). Below the base outside temperature, some heating energy is required to maintain comfort in a building. The empirical correction factor (C_D) takes into account improvements in the typical level of insulation, greater internal heat gains (as from increased use of appliances), and more utilization of solar gains in today's building, compared with the building of 1930–1932, when the concept of degree days and the 18.3 °C base were originally proposed.

The annual fuel requirements may be estimated by dividing the heating energy requirements by the average seasonal efficiency of the heating system. Similarly, annual cooling energy requirements may be estimated by utilizing cooling degree days (CDD). Chapter 28 of the *1985 ASHRAE Handbook of Fundamentals* (2) gives a detailed discussion of building energy calculations (see also Ref. 16).

The ready availability of large computer systems has permitted the development of very sophisticated annual energy estimation programs, utilizing hour-by-hour weather data. Some of the more popular programs are AXCESS, BLAST, BLDSIM, DOE-2, E-CUBE, ESAS, and TRACE. Reference 17 gives a detailed description of the various computer programs available.

Dynamic Thermal Performance

The above discussion has been based largely on a steady-state concept of thermal performance. However, real buildings experience an ever-changing thermal environment. The effect of a building's mass can have a marked effect on the instantaneous heat transmission during transient temperature conditions.

An early investigation of dynamic thermal performance at the National Bureau of Standards (NBS) compared the measured dynamic heat transfer and temperature of a small masonry building with that calculated using "thermal response factors" (18). More recently, an NBS study investigated the thermal performance of six small residential-type structures with various degrees of thermal insulation and thermal mass. It was concluded that thermal mass in a structure can conserve energy during the summer and intermediate heating seasons, as representative of fall or spring in a moderate climate. At the same time, no mass effect was observed during the winter heating season (19).

BIBLIOGRAPHY

1. *ASTM Standards, Volume 04.06: Thermal Insulation, and Environmental Acoustics,* American Society for Testing and Materials, Philadelphia, Pa., 1985.
2. *1985 ASHRAE Handbook of Fundamentals,* American Society of Heating, Refrigerating and Air-Conditioning Engineers, Inc., Atlanta, Ga., 1985.
3. W. C. Turner and J. F. Malloy, *Thermal Insulation Handbook,* McGraw-Hill Inc., New York, and Robert E. Krieger Publishing, Malabar, Fla., 1981.
4. *Insulation,* DOE/CS-0192, U.S. Department of Energy, Washington, D.C., 1980.
5. J. K. Latta, *Vapour Barriers: What Are They? Are They Effective?,* CBD 175, Canadian Building Digest, National Research Council of Canada, Ottawa, Ont., Canada, 1976.
6. *ECON-I, How to Determine Economic Thickness of Thermal Insulation,* Thermal Insulation Manufacturers Association, Mt. Kisco, N.Y., 1973.
7. W. K. Hesse, "An Approach to Establishing the Most Economical Amount of Roof Insulation," *ASHRAE Journal* **24**(3) (Mar. 1982).
8. *Energy Conservation in New Building Design,* Standard 90, American Society of Heating, Refrigerating and Air-Conditioning Engineers, Inc., Atlanta, Ga., 1980.
9. *Energy Conservation in Existing Buildings—High Rise Residential,* Standard 100.2, American Society of Heating, Refrigerating and Air-Conditioning Engineers, Inc., Atlanta, Ga., 1981.
10. *Energy Conservation in Existing Buildings—Institutional,* Standard 100.5, American Society of Heating, Refrigerating and Air-Conditioning Engineers, Inc., Atlanta, Ga., 1981.
11. *Energy Conservation in Existing Buildings—Public Assembly,* Standard 100.6, American Society of Heating, Refrigerating and Air-Conditioning Engineers, Inc., Atlanta, Ga., 1981.
12. J. D. Verschoor and P. Greebler, "Heat Transfer by Gas Conduction and Radiation in Fibrous Insulation," *ASME Transactions* **74,** 961 (1952).
13. C. M. Pelanne, "Heat Flow Principles in Thermal Insulations," *Journal of Thermal Insulation* **1,** 48 (July 1977).
14. *1981 ASHRAE Handbook of Fundamentals,* American Society of Heating, Refrigerating and Air-Conditioning Engineers, Inc., Atlanta, Ga., 1981.
15. *Cooling and Heating Load Calculation Manual,* Code: SPLCM, American Society of Heating, Refrigerating and Air-Conditioning Engineers, Inc., Atlanta, Ga., 1979.
16. D. E. Knebel, *Simplified Energy Analysis Using the Modified Bin Method,* Code: SEAP, American Society of Heating, Refrigerating and Air-Conditioning Engineers, Inc., Atlanta, Ga., 1984.
17. R. H. Howell and H. J. Sauer, Jr., *Bibliography on Available Computer Programs in the General Area of Heating, Refrigerating, Air-Conditioning and Ventilating,* Code: SPSP22, American Society of Heating, Refrigerating and Air-Conditioning Engineers, Inc., Atlanta, Ga., 1980.
18. B. A. Peavy, F. J. Powell, and D. M. Burch, *Dynamic Thermal Performance of an Experimental Masonry Building,* National Bureau of Standards Building Science Series #45, National Bureau of Standards, Washington, D.C., 1973.
19. "Thermal Mass Effect of Energy Conservation in Residential Buildings," *ASHRAE Journal* **25**(2) (Feb. 1983).

See also Hazardous Materials—Asbestos; Mechanical Systems; Roofing Materials; Solar Design

Jack Verschoor
Bailey, Colorado

INSURANCE. See Liability Insurance

INTERIOR DESIGN

Before the beginning of recorded history mankind sought shelter. Historically, this enclosure, whether a rocky overhang, cave, trullo, or palatial villa, was a place to hide from the elements; a place to go for protection and comfort; a place in which one's family could await his or her return—a home. Despite early man's inability to intellectualize or verbalize this concept, the occupation of one's private space was made known to others. Home possessed a distinctive character, a distinctive scent. Perhaps there were drawings on the walls, the signs of bedding, fireplace recently used. Early man may have instinctively marked his territory like any other animal, or he may have felt a primordial need for the expression and communication of that which belonged to him and to his family. The basic concept of "home," of personalized interior space, represents only one aspect of the interior. Interior design is an elusive pursuit, falling between art and science, psychology and anthropology, ergonomics and engineering. Not only does it impact homes, but also places of worship and work.

Interior design has been motivated by the same forces throughout history. Each design is a reflection of a desire for comfort and the personal fantasy of the occupant. It is the projection of one's sense of self to others and visual response to the pragmatic problems inherent in space. Variations from one period to another, whether organizational/planning issues or matters of aesthetics, are understandable in terms of political climate, religious issues, the environment, and the creativity which infuses these styles with new energy and direction. Additionally, each has added to the vocabulary of space through construction techniques and materials applications which directly impact possibilities for styles to come. The interior's importance throughout history is reflected in the renown of those who have directed others in the task of making interiors beautiful. From pharaohs and emperors to clergy and politicians, there has been a search for spaces that reflect the desired image of the philosophy and power of their patron(s). Of equal renown, in many instances, is the artist and/or builder responsible for the creation of these spaces—from Leonardo da Vinci and Michelangelo to Frank Lloyd Wright and Mies van der Rohe.

Beyond the fantasy and functionalism of interior space are actual structural and material elements inherent in its manipulation and embellishment that give it form and character. A floor plan can evoke a sense of order or it can make a space seem disjointed. Each partition, soffit, beam, and raised or sunken floor affects the way in which space makes one feel. Windows and skylights can transform an amorphous space into an interior that is alive with light and shadow. The introduction of light can dramatize sill, jamb, and head details and instill a sense of three dimensionality and depth, emphasizing the interior as an outcropping of the architecture. The column, which has persisted throughout antiquity into the twentieth century with the modern movement, has (despite its modifications and varying contexts) remained steadfast in its effect. Its structural function is matched by its ability to interrupt a space with its circumference and presence; to sculpturally fuse ceiling and floor; and to express scale. The door, frequently miscast as a solely functional entry, endows entrances and exits with theatrics, as in the entries to Gothic cathedrals, or the more unassuming entry into the Roman domus which saves its dramatics for the inner peristyle.

Historically, surface ornamentation is probably the most consistently used form of interior decoration. Surface treatments change interior shells from culturally void and unassuming spaces to rich and resplendent spaces that tell a story about the people, and their symbols, fears, and philosophies. From simple cave paintings to the opulent ornamentation of the early Egyptian home, to the spectacular baroque or rococo interior, paint has been a vital element in surface decoration. Discussion of this ornamentation would not be complete without including the tilework of the Roman and Byzantine craftsmen, the art glass of the Gothic cathedrals, Victorian interiors, and the Prairie school homes of the twentieth century.

EGYPTIAN

Order and tradition provided the basis for the tenets of Egyptian culture and hence the foundation for Egyptian

Figure 1. Temple of Aman at Karnak (Thebes), a restoration. Courtesy of The Bettmann Archive.

design. In examining the extent of these influences, a better understanding of the impact of Egyptian interiors can be achieved. The pyramids are lasting symbols of this order. The shafts leading to their internal burial chambers are at an angle conforming to that of the polar star Alpha Draconis. The angles of the sides of the pyramid of Cheops correspond to Sothis, known today as Sirius, the brightest star in the heavens; the perimeter of the pyramid has been found to coincide with the solar year. Evidence of this symbolic need for order can additionally be found in the simple symmetrical Egyptian floor plan, and in the highly integrated decoration of columns and walls. The early Egyptians were less inclined toward surface decoration, paying closer attention to details such as the refined cut and polish of columns and capitals. Later Egyptians embellished every surface. Interiors were decorated with symbolic images of nature. Ceilings were painted a deep blue to suggest the heavens. Exquisitely painted flocks of birds and butterflies increased the sensation that one was out-of-doors. Walls and tile floors came alive with marsh scenes of animal life, foliage, and water.

These artistic depictions were more than simple recreations of nature. The lotus blossom and papyrus symbolized nourishment for the body. The feathers of rare birds reflected sovereignty. These are just examples of common symbols used in the decoration of the interior.

Aesthetically, the infiltration of light became increasingly more important for the Egyptian interior. Temples, for example, frequently had central rows of columns higher than their flanking columns (Fig. 1). This structural modification provided a break in the plane of the roof for the inclusion of clerestories which flooded the interior with natural light, revealing perfect diagrammatic ornamentation. Each of these painted surfaces was designed to form patterns by the equal division of similar lines in a symmetrical arrangement over the wall. The geometric arrangements were polychromatic: red, blue, and yellow outlined in black or white were the most commonly used colors.

GREEK

Little remains to help understand how Early and Middle Greek architecture developed and functioned. Ruins reveal square rooms with centralized hearths. Space was evidently not planned, as rooms along corridors appear to have been appended as needed. The purpose of the home during this period was functional. It was unpretentious, unlike the highly decorative Roman domus, and was used primarily for eating and sleeping purposes. Despite this simplicity, some evidence of decoration has been discovered, such as fresco fragments of chariot scenes and a frieze of blown lilies in the house of an oil merchant. Unlike Roman architecture (which actually derived its aesthetic sensibility from the Greeks), and unlike the Egyptian compulsion for lavish interiors, Greek design was externally focused; interiors never truly attained great importance. Greek temples were designed to house statues of gods and were not built on a human scale (Fig. 2). These temples soon became the focal point of Greek heritage. More attention to the expansion and development of interiors occurred during the later Hellenistic period, as exemplified by the Temple of Apollo at Dydydma. Within this temple is a large sanctuary enclosed by a shrine. This burgeoning interest in interiors eventually culminated in the development of the basilica, an enclosed meeting place with the stature of a Greek temple. As the focus of the Greek interior became people-oriented, the need for lighting became a concern. Clerestories, introduced well into the Hellenistic period, solved this problem and, with this new emphasis on a "humanizing" interior, ornamentation flourished. Because decorative themes were not restricted by religious law, they were more readily accepted in subsequent cultures without modification. The depiction of the acanthus leaf, for example, was developed during this period and used again by the Romans. Since these motifs were purely secular in content, the Greeks were able to pursue a higher degree of abstraction and aesthetic perfection. This differs greatly from the philosophy of Egyptian ornamentation, which is strongly rooted in symbolism.

Figure 2. Rendering of Greek temple in Olimpia. Courtesy of The Bettmann Archive.

ROMAN

The sophistication of Roman civilization is evident in the union of aesthetics and philosophy in designing private and public spaces. Their utilization of architectural and artistic design elements—elaborate floor plans; vibrant mosaics; the creative and varied use of paint in the embellishment of walls and ceilings; and the use of closed and open space as a means of functional and structural differentiation—are testimony to a culture strongly embedded in personal pleasures and visual stimulation.

The typical Roman home had an inward orientation. Small shops facing the street lined the outside while the building's entry was generally centered on the street elevation. This entry was functional, in addition to being an expression of the owner's status and wealth, and was spatially designed as a "viewing platform" for scrutinizing guests. Beyond the entry was the vestibule, which served as a transitory space. Within this area one would still be under close scrutiny and yet visually without a true sense of the interior. At the heart of the Roman home was the peristyle, a central court from which the house radiated and the place in which interior design motifs were generally established (Fig. 3). The court allowed for the greatest amount of architectural expression, functioning as a well for natural light and as a garden. It was replete with plant life, fountains, pools, and brilliantly colored mosaics. Courtyard themes consistently maintained specific design elements with varying degrees of dominance in a given motif. Some courtyards were paved entirely with mosaics, placing emphasis on the architecture and minimizing any extraneous decorative impact. Fountains were frequently included; water and vegetation were always considered complementary to the primary design. In some cases, the courtyard functioned as a large pool. The peristyle was a multi-functioning space used for intimate activities and social occasions. It was the space from which all other rooms emanated, including bedrooms, offices, libraries, and dining rooms. Some homes even had rooms designated specifically for reading and writing. The dining room, known as the triclinia, was second in importance to the peristyle. The triclinia was used for family, business, and social events. Its importance in family life was emphasized by its size and sumptuous decoration in the form of painted walls or mosaics. The dinner ceremony was a means of displaying the host's wealth, occupation, and philosophical outlook. Walls were frequently tiled with mosaics of animals, fish, or acanthus leaves. The depiction of marine life was believed to stave off disease and to protect the Roman home and its occupants from harm.

Figure 3. Rendering of Roman house. Reconstruction of the house of Cornelius Rufus in Pompeii. Courtesy of The Bettmann Archive.

As evidenced by its many functions, the rich decoration of the Roman interior was laden with symbolism. It was aesthetically pleasing to the eye, a gauge of social status, and a form of protection for the home and its occupants. In Pompeii and Herculaneum, however, the use of elaborate decorative schemes, particularly painting, served a physical and illusory purpose, utilizing large unbroken wall elevations and extending interior space. The walls were initially prepared with a combination of plaster and marble dust compressed and carefully finished, which caused the wall to take on a marble-like finish. Mock finishes were but one of the Romans' innovative surface treatments. Four distinct categories of wall painting techniques evolved. The Encrustation style involved the creation of a series of solid, brightly colored wall panels combined with a textured surface, and was first discovered in the Greek period. The Architectural style was achieved by painting walls with details such as columns and windows in concise perspective. The "view" through these "windows" was often a distant and meticulously painted landscape. The architectural details themselves were quite deceptive, giving a flat wall a sense of dimension and depth. The Ornate style, unlike the Architectural, was purely decorative. This style entailed the painting of slender, highly detailed columns. The scenes between these columns were simple but colorful. Lastly, the Intricate style returned to a simpler depiction of painted columns. This style was a culmination of the three aforementioned approaches, designed to create optical illusions.

BYZANTINE

Byzantium, once the focal point for many cultures, greatly influenced the development of the interior. With the relocation of the Roman Empire's capital to Constantinople in 324 A.D., a new decorative style with an eastern flavor emerged. The impact on the interiors of this period's grand basilicas was profound. Metallic gold, Moorish arches, and detailed mosaics were but a few of the East's contributions to this style. With Constantine's declaration of Christianity as the state religion came the construction of several churches by oriental artists and craftsmen. A decor both colorful and joyous developed for the first time. Paintings and mosaics designed with brilliantly colored glass were commissioned. The glass was irregularly set and the color often arbitrarily applied. The effect of light washing over the interior surfaces created exquisite patterns (Fig. 4).

ROMANESQUE

The ninth through the twelfth centuries were politically unsettling for all of Europe. The anarchy inherent in the feudal system was disruptive and contributed to an interior style devoid of any influence from antiquity and considered to be the first true Western style. This was a tremendous

Figure 4. Apse of Saint Apollinare in Classe, Ravenna (533–549 A.D.). Courtesy of The Bettmann Archive.

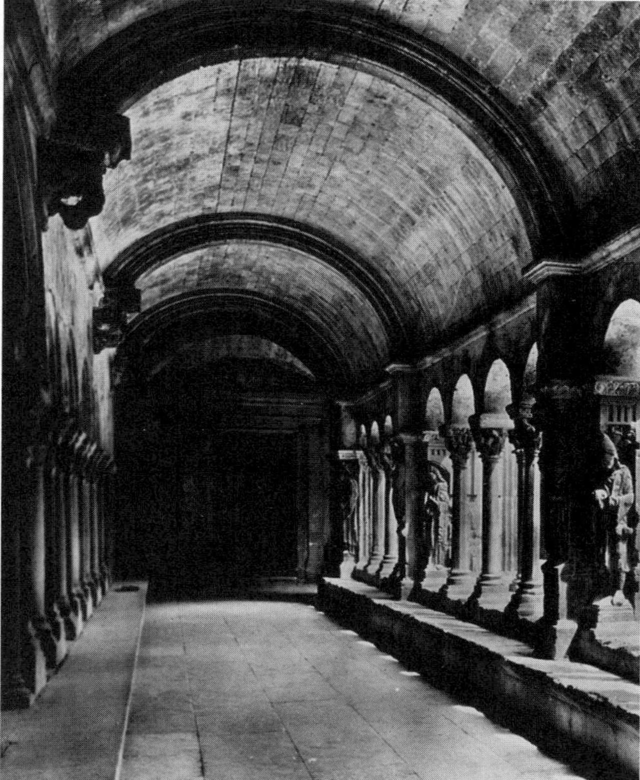

Figure 5. Outer hall to the cloisters of Saint Trophisme, France, eleventh century. Courtesy of The Bettmann Archive.

departure from the preceding styles and affected both church and domestic architecture. The Middle Ages had none of the sophistication present in the Roman home.

The typical Romanesque dwelling was scantily furnished and contained items that could be easily moved. A large room used for dining, entertaining, and receiving visitors was the primary space and functioned as a parlor. The salle, as this room was called, became the bedroom when night fell and lack of light left little else to do but sleep.

There were political as well as religious implications affecting the development of the Romanesque interior. Monastic orders flourished, and the role of the church in monastic and civic life had a tremendous effect on the history of interiors. The Crusades and extensive pilgrimages to these churches caused a new influx of people to churches throughout Europe. This increased the need for circulation, which prompted the modification of the church interior. In addition to the spatial augmentations necessary to accommodate the increase in the population of churchgoers, there was now a strong fear of fire in the monasteries, which created pressure to exchange wooden roofs for stone vaults. These vaults, repeated throughout the nave and transept of the Romanesque church, were perhaps the most dramatic feature of this style. Massive walls and substructures were imperative for the support of these vaults. Only small, sparsely spaced windows were permitted to interrupt the dense walls. The cold, stone interior remained dark. This darkness left scant reason for the development of details which would not be seen. Despite this seemingly cold void there was a strength in the rhythm of the columns and the vaults that made these foreboding churches of stone rather austere.

Although minimal light did not invite extensive surface treatment, stone carving and painting were implemented in the decoration of the Romanesque church. Sculptors carved delightful figures and patterns in the stone capitals of columns. Stone carving, which was revived during the Romanesque period, was used on the interiors only to decorate column capitals. Liturgical furniture, mostly pulpits and sarcophagi, were the only other carved surfaces. Religious scenes were painted on walls and vaults, the latter of which were difficult surfaces to navigate with a paintbrush. Figures were often distorted to accommodate the odd shape of the vault (Fig. 5).

GOTHIC

Although many factors caused the development of a distinct style, one of the earliest examples of the Gothic interior emerged from the efforts of Abbot Suger of France, charged with the rebuilding of his monastery at St. Denis.

Figure 6. Interior of nave, Cathedral of Notre Dame. Courtesy of The Bettmann Archive.

This style represented the antithesis of the massive, dark Romanesque style. Gothic architecture was installed with a sense of order, self-confidence, and etherealness, effectively expressing renewed hope and negating the chaotic state of the preceding, rather grim Medieval era which was punctuated with political and civil strife. This uplifting of the spirit initiated the union between architectural exterior and interior, unmatched until the twentieth century (Fig. 6). The sole interior decorative element of this style was the exterior wall, which was divided by columns with varying degrees of tracery, and windows with the magnificent stained glass that made the Gothic cathedral famous. The tracery was integrated with rib and barrel vaults creating a union between the vertical surfaces and the ceiling overhead. This detailing was not lost in darkness as it would have been in a Romanesque church, but was instead bathed in light, considered the essence of Gothic design. The stained glass was so magnificent that the architecture continued to be modified to accommodate more and more glass.

RENAISSANCE

In 1453, the Sultan Muhammad II invaded the city of Constantinople. The Greeks fled to Rome, Florence, and Bologna. The philosophy of Humanism, brought to Italy by the Greeks, borne of a search for independent thought and the cultivation of the intellect, revived an interest in antiquity. This renewed spirit and confidence in the power of mankind, in conjunction with the sophistication of the interiors which these Humanists were exposed to during their stay in Constantinople, ushered in a new sensitivity toward the interior. The cruciform floor plan was the spring board for emerging Renaissance design which was based on proportionate, mathematical formulas. Toward this end of perfect symmetry, the Golden Section, dating from Euclid, was applied to all forms of architectural and artistic pursuits. This rigid basis for design was to become both a strength and a weakness for the Renaissance interior. Although the approach posed creative limitations, the humanization of interiors was long overdue, and has left mankind some of the most beautiful and well-thought-out interiors possible. The Humanist philosophy was responsible for creating an architecture which related to man on his own scale. Spatial layouts opened up. Light played a more decisive role in design. Columns were now graceful in stature, and not quite so imposing. An entirely new order of architecture governed by human scale created an atmosphere of comfort and an elegance not achieved (and more importantly, not strived for) previously (Fig. 7).

Architecture and interior design were not the only art forms experiencing a renaissance. The impact of the visual arts on interior design has been significant throughout history. The Renaissance artist was also the architect, and the passion for perfection permeated all materials

Figure 7. Central hall of Saint Lorenzo, Florence (1421–1428). Courtesy of The Bettmann Archive.

from stone and mortar to marble and paint. The sculptor could refine the edges of a marble bas-relief and design interior ornamentation. The painter could create the subtle tonal qualities of a portrait or select the appropriate colors for reliefs or frescoes. In his notes, Leonardo da Vinci gives some sense of the rules governing design. He wrote, for example, that the abacus or plinth should be as broad as the thickness of the wall to which it is attached and that the height of the wall of the courtyard should be half its breadth. In other words, architectural elements should relate to each other proportionately. If da Vinci is representative of the quintessential Renaissance artist and thinker, Michelangelo would be the essence of Late Renaissance and Mannerism. If balance and harmony are the goals of da Vinci and the Renaissance in which his work flourished, then Michelangelo is looking to disrupt this harmony for the sake of drama. Michelangelo turned the interior into a medium for individual expression, a philosophy which has since been the key to the development of interiors. This progression toward individual expression inevitably led to excess, which in its late stages gave way to the baroque style.

BAROQUE AND ROCOCO

The baroque style existed primarily for the self-indulgence of the church and the wealthiest of monarchs. The restrained and elegant individual expression of the Mannerist period in the last phase of the Renaissance paved the way for the excessive sensuality of the baroque period to follow.

Michelangelo's St. Peter's set the stage; it is Michelangelo who has been credited as the father of the baroque style. Bernini located a massive bronze canopy supported by four massive, twisted columns under St. Peter's dome. The motif surrounding the columns was so excessive and sensual that it left no place for the eye to rest. Detail upon detail had been designed without restraint.

Baroque interiors were symptomatic of the break from the absolutism displayed by the Catholic countries to rebuff the Reformation. The costs were as extravagant as the motifs (Fig. 8). At the same time, the results were joyous and rich. The rococo style developed during the last stages of the baroque period. Evolved from Regence, so named for the period of the regency of Philippe d'Orleans, Louis

Figure 8. Altar of abbey church, Germany. Courtesy of The Bettmann Archive.

Quinze (named after Louis XV), and Louis Seize (after Louis XVI), rococo was a purely French style.

Rococo was the first style which recognized the difference in scale between external and interior architectural details. Through this recognition, details became smaller in scale, prettier to the eye and economically feasible for a wider audience. Thus, the rococo style has been described as the first entirely interior style.

NEOCLASSICISM

The rediscovery and incorporation of elements from antiquity is a theme which recurs in the development of Neoclassicism. The Neoclassic style rediscovered and revived Greek and Roman architectural elements in order to form the basis for new interior motifs. Innovation, evaluation, and reevaluation occur in order to arrive at solutions appropriate for the economic, political, and aesthetic climate of the time.

Robert Adams, the father of the Classical Revival in Britain, traveled extensively throughout Rome and Greece. Professionally, he applied classical elements of Roman and Grecian architecture, but was inclined toward a delicate adaptation of these motifs. They were frequently adapted from external architectural details and implemented as interior elements. Greek entablature, for example, was modified for the head detail of doorways. Interiors were delicate and exquisitely designed (Fig. 9). The light, airy feel to the space is similar in elegance to that of the Renaissance, but there is more sensitivity to scale. No sooner did this style reach its peak than it began to evolve into a more general and less controlled revivalism, ultimately becoming "historicism." This evolution was largely due to the beginning of the middle class and its access to mass-produced revival furniture and furnishings now available because of the industrial revolution. Not only did historicism utilize elements from many periods (Egyptian, Greek, Roman, Gothic, and Renaissance), it also combined diverse elements of these styles.

This era of historicism, known as the Victorian era, is marked by an unprecedented focus on interior decoration. It was a period of great economic development and the middle class and nouveau riche needed a suitable means to display their newly acquired wealth. The home became the perfect solution. Homes were rich in details: carved woodwork and fireplaces, plaster moldings, brass hardware, and beveled and stained glass. To this shell the Victorians added lavish draperies, carved wooden furniture often incised and gilded, silk upholstery, brocades, velvets, oriental carpets layered on parquet floors, and elaborate gas-lit chandeliers. Paintings and prints covered wallpapered walls, and objets d'art and personal treasures were displayed everywhere. Barely a surface escaped ornamentation (Fig. 10).

Toward the middle of the nineteenth century the excesses of historicism and the apparent lack of influence that artists and designers bore on manufacturers could be seen at the Great Exhibition of 1851. The reaction from the design community would be the catalyst for an awakened sensitivity that would culminate in the arts and crafts and art nouveau movements.

Figure 9. Lower Hall of the Vyne, Bastingstoke, Hampshire, England (1760). Courtesy of The Bettmann Archive.

Figure 10. Edwardian era study, nineteenth century. Courtesy of The Bettmann Archive.

ARTS AND CRAFTS

The arts and crafts movement developed as a reaction to the ineptitude of early furniture manufacturers whose main clientele was the middle class. William Morris and John Ruskin argued for reuniting the design with the manufacturer, the artist, and the craftsperson. The designers and architects identified with this ideology, based on a purity and simplicity akin to fundamentalism. It is clear in Frank Lloyd Wright's writing that he had been greatly influenced by oriental, particularly Japanese, design. Although this influence is not as easily discernible in earlier arts and crafts design, it does appear likely that the structural integrity and expression of the fundamental purpose of each design may have been influenced by Japan. Gustav Stickley expressed this fundamentalism succinctly when he said, "the structural lines should not be subjected to the 'indignity' of applied ornament" (1).

Frank Lloyd Wright extended the discipline encompassed by the arts and crafts movement and revolutionized the whole concept of interior space within the home. His domestic architecture is called Prairie School architecture. His house plans spread out loosely into a play of geometric shapes held together by horizontal moldings, dropped soffits, and door and window headers. This conglomerate of rooms was balanced and tightly composed, but informal. The low, spacious interiors had subtle boundaries separating the interior space from the surrounding terraces. Although Wright had a penchant for highly angular spaces and forms, his designs remain very inviting. This is partly due to the spatial arrangements, the low and comfortable scale, and to the commitment to natural materials of the region in which he was designing (Figs. 11–14).

ART NOUVEAU

Concurrently, painters, illustrators, and craftspersons of the art nouveau style, reacting against historicism and the crude beginnings of the machine age, developed a sensuous but elegant style free of any period referenced and returned to the craftsmanship identified with the Middle Ages. Art nouveau's basic characteristic was the curve. This curve had a natural, almost plant-like quality playing on contrast and tension of the inclination of the curve to counterbalance itself with a secondary curve. Invention and fantasy drove the artists and designers toward this new decorative motif. While art nouveau developed in the United Kingdom, this same style developed simultaneously in other countries and was known as the modern

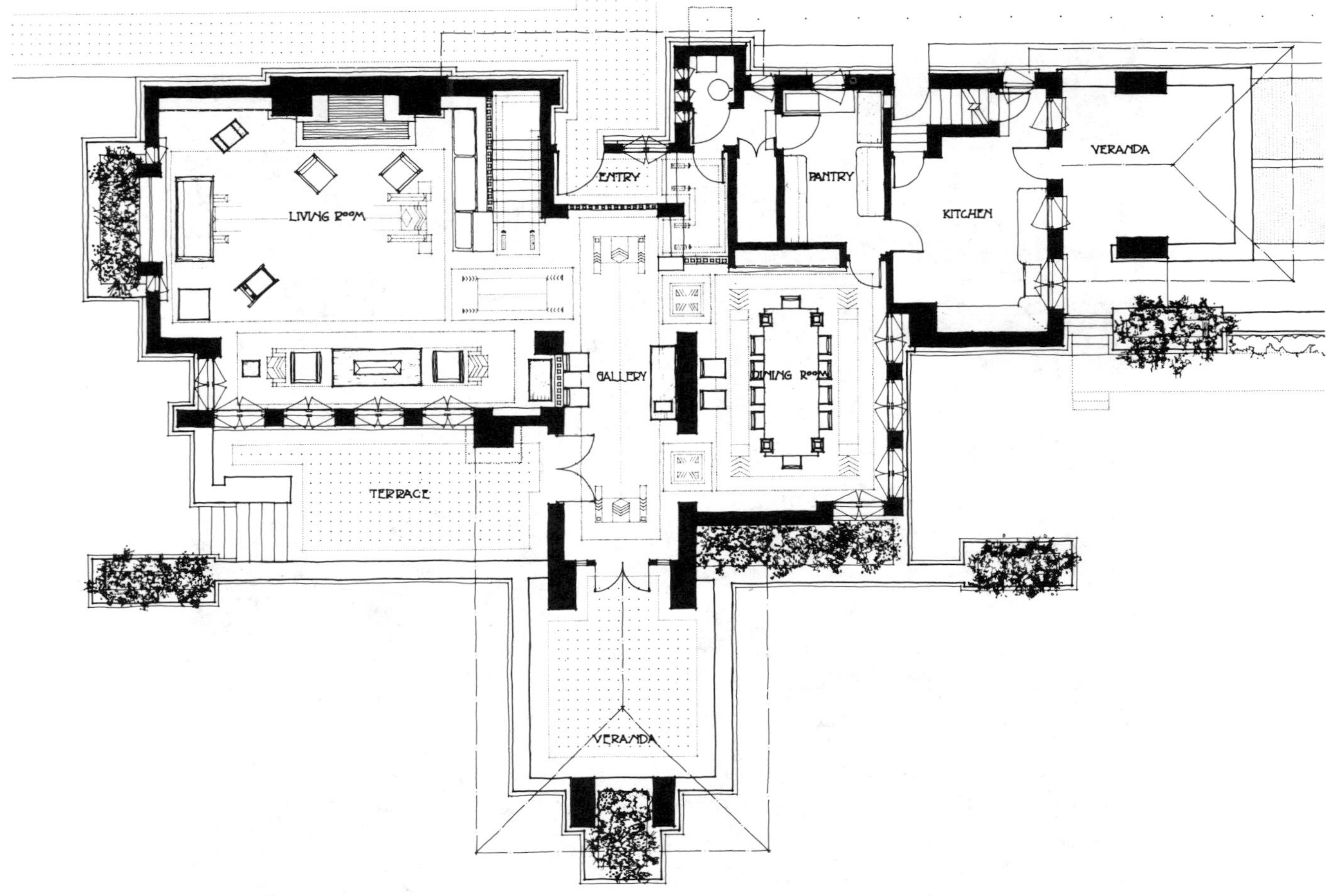

Figure 11. Meyer May House (1909 ff) restoration by Tilton + Lewis Associates, for Steelcase. Courtesy of Tilton + Lewis Associates.

style in France, the Jugendstil in Germany, and Secessionstil in Austria. Interior design was limited primarily by the brevity of this period. Louis Sullivan in Chicago and Charles Rennie Mackintosh in Glasgow were perhaps the most significant practitioners of art nouveau.

There is a dichotomy in the work of both Sullivan and Mackintosh. Sullivan stated in his book *Ornament in Architecture* that "ornament is mentally a luxury," and that "we should refrain entirely from the use of ornament for a period of years, in order that our thought might concentrate acutely upon the production of buildings well formed and comely in the nude" (2), and yet his ornamentation in the interiors of his Auditorium Building in Chicago was an organic tangle of tracery, cabbage-like vegetation, scalloped leaves, and coral growths which could be found on the ceilings, walls, and columns. What is even more dramatic is the way Sullivan contrasted this ornamentation with the austerity of the main lines and blocks of his skyscrapers. The skyscraper, or high-rise, foreshadows the true beginnings of interior design as a distinct profession, for this marks the advent of generic undefined space for multitenant use. As the high-rise became larger and more complex, the architect focused his attention on the exterior shell while designers began to understand and specialize on interior needs.

Mackintosh also seemed to recognize and practice the general tenets of the arts and crafts movement with his structurally expressive interiors for the School of Art in Glasgow, and yet his interior would not be complete without the final touches of artistry which in his case were art nouveau in style. Many of the spatial arrangements, vistas, and layerings of space foreshadowed the modern movement.

ART DECO

Art deco derives its name from the famous Exposition des Arts Decoratifs et Industriels in Paris in 1925. Its greatest and most prolific practitioner was Jacques-Emile Ruhlmann. Ruhlmann designed and built superb cabinets, bureaus, and other furniture pieces using rare woods, and exquisite ornamentation with ivory, tortoise shell, lacquer, mirrors, silk, and tooled metals. Art deco was a style for the elite. The notion of fundamentalism so important during the arts and crafts movement was set aside. Craftsmanship and unquestionable beauty were achieved by the designers of the art deco. They were masters of their craft with absolute self-confidence, producing furniture and interiors with a new modern opulence using geometric abstractions in both surface ornamentation and form.

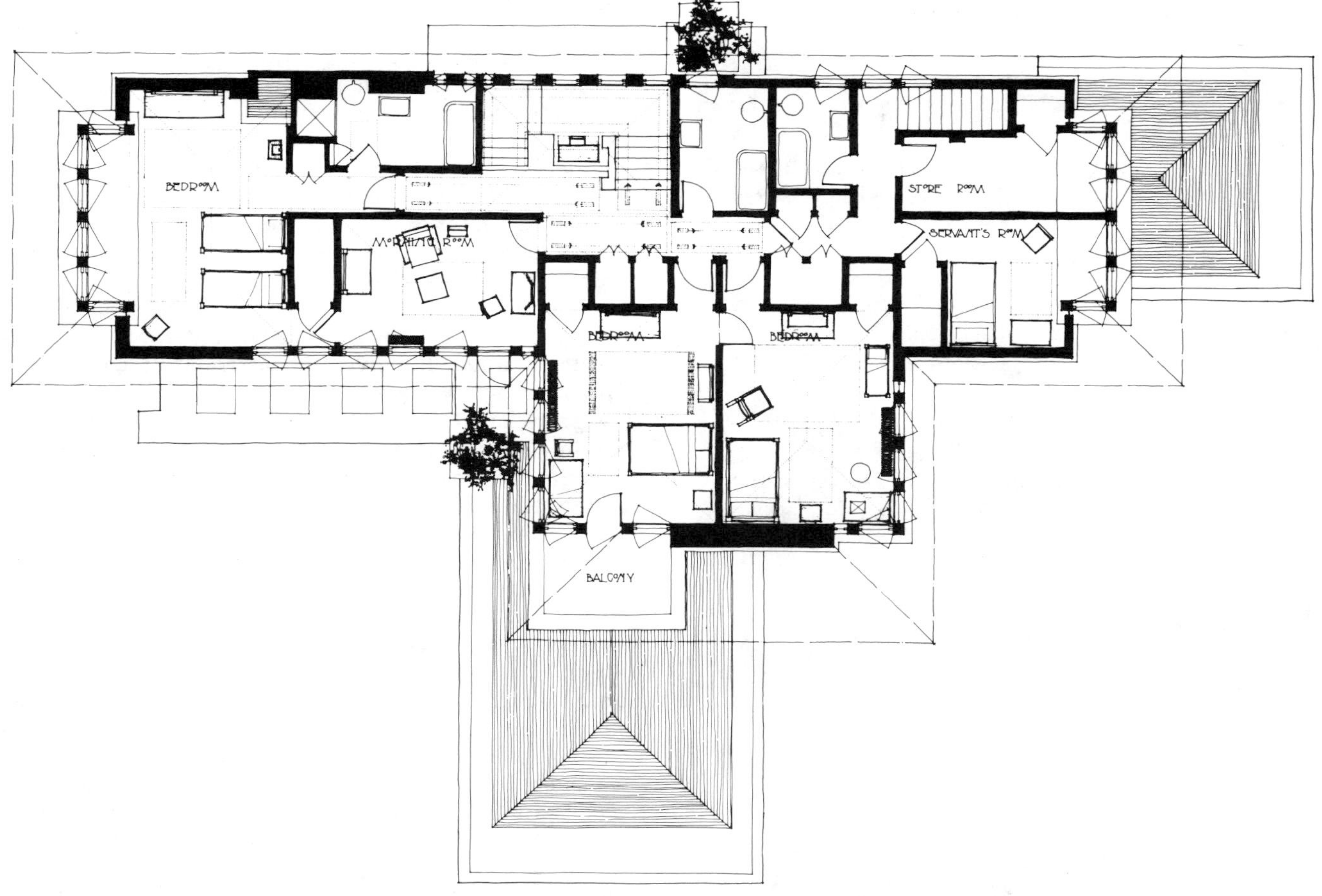

Figure 12. Meyer May House (1909 ff) restoration by Tilton + Lewis Associates, for Steelcase. Courtesy of Tilton + Lewis Associates.

MODERN MOVEMENT

Twentieth-century domestic architecture was influenced by many architectural and design practitioners. Experimentation with new materials and forms gave rise to distinctive and expressive spaces varying in character from the cubist buildings of Le Corbusier and the Prairie School homes of Frank Lloyd Wright to Mies van der Rohe's constructions of steel and glass. In all of its diversity, this new age of architecture managed to retain consistency in its starkness (ornamentation was forbidden), thereby placing the emphasis of interior decoration on artwork, furniture, and furnishings. This new focus (in conjunction with a dramatic growth of the middle class) became the catalyst for the diverse development of domestic interior styles. Although there was extensive experimentation during and after the arts and crafts movement, its significance was not felt in interior design until a synthesis of two disparate concepts was fused during the early Bauhaus years. The Bauhaus was a German school of fine and applied arts, design, and architecture created by Walter Gropius. Bauhaus made significant strides in many disciplines; however, the Bauhaus had a very specific bearing on the interior. Mies van de Rohe, one of the School's instructors, outlined a philosophy to be applied to the interior space. This philosophy fused the "spatial unity" so important to Frank Lloyd Wright's work and Sullivan's work on high-rise design. Mies described the space enclosed by the steel and glass buildings of the twentieth century as "universal space." This was not so much an oversimplification of interiors as an ideal in a time of tremendous idealism. The elimination of ornamentation, the simplification of forms, the study of proportions, the experimentation with new materials, and the perfection of detail were all components of interior design development during the modern movement. This style was called the International style. In order to fully express the essence of the modern movement, designers had to develop a faith in and an understanding of the machine, science, and technology. They had to be willing to utilize diverse materials regardless of their lack of standardization. With Gropius's and Mies's development of the glass and steel building, the exterior and interior became one (Fig. 15). This symbiosis, combined with greater structural spans, allowed for more uninterrupted, enclosed space, and set the stage for the tremendous potential of interior space, which up until this time had not been fully realized. The twentieth century saw a predominantly agricultural work force transfer its skills to industrialism and manufacturing. By the third quarter of the century, over 50% of the work

Figure 13. Meyer May House (1909 ff) restoration by Tilton + Lewis Associates, for Steelcase. Courtesy of Tilton + Lewis Associates.

Figure 14. Meyer May House (1909 ff) restoration by Tilton + Lewis Associates, for Steelcase. Courtesy of Tilton + Lewis Associates.

force was comprised of office workers. The rapidity of this growth, along with the development of high-rise buildings designed for multitenant speculative space, acted as a catalyst for the establishment of interior design. Early International style interior design concentrated on the refinement of planning. In attempting to achieve an "ideal" solution, the designer would strive for the integration of ceiling plan, elevation, and details into the floor plan in order to create an interior with a sense of unity. The challenge facing designers of the modern movement was to create unity out of chaos. No longer were designers directing craftspersons in the custom creation of independent design elements which together established order. The challenge was to coordinate hundreds of nonstandardized materials. The desired outcome was a sense of order. Additionally, designers found it difficult to integrate the materials and details of the "skin" of high-rise buildings with the interior modules, as was successfully accomplished with Gothic architecture, certain "Wrightian" Prairie School homes, and in single-use International style buildings such as the Barcelona Pavilion. The Barcelona Pavilion, designed by Mies van der Rohe, embodied the aesthetic which International style design consistently sought to achieve. Its sense of twentieth-century classicism has permeated every aspect of the design process. The plan has the spatial unity Wright insisted upon in his designs, but greater subtlety and elegance. Separation of exterior and interior is eliminated. There is a sense of the interior being an extension of the outside world. This "etherealization" of architecture (described by Wright) was achieved by Gropius, Wright, and Sullivan, but the Barcelona Pavilion captured the concept of etherealization without diminishing the whole. This interior was conceived from the plan and through thoughtful resolution of many details achieved the unity so important to a successful design statement. No detail diminishes the whole. Each has been studied in relation to its position within the interior, down to the stitching on the chairs designed for the Pavilion. This building represents what each practitioner of International style interior design has sought to achieve. Mies's often quoted statement, "God is in the details," is symbolic of the degree of commitment and idealism which pervaded the attitudes and goals of the time. During the first 20 years of the development of modern interior space, designers worked toward a classic plan that would successfully embody a sense of spatial unity and would be identified with the International style. In the process of accomplishing this, the designer worked with elevations, details, and non-standardized industrial materials. The goal was a challenge. Ultimately, the designer was working to maximize the potential of these nonstandardized materials and to make them functional as well as attractive within the interior.

The client played a passive role in the development of early International style interior spaces. As clients' needs evolved and the interior products industry began to grow, the selection process for product coordination became more complex. There were now more potential solutions for compounded and changing problems. Additionally, as the industries related to interiors grew, more research and development began to occur, eventually leading to the introduction of new solutions to the problems of interiors.

Figure 15. Armstrong Central Engineering Building by Skidmore Owings & Merrill for Armstrong. Courtesy of Lawrence S. Williams, Inc.

The importance of communication within the office and the habits of the office worker were examined in studies conducted in Europe and the United States. From this research came conceptual ideas about design as it related to communications between workers and their work styles. The partial height movable partition with componentry (modular furniture elements), such as work surfaces and storage units, hanging from the partitions, was developed as a result of this research. Two elements which have revolutionized interior design were introduced simultaneously. The partial height partition marks the beginning of the open space plan, and the componentry hanging from the partition marks the beginning of the systems furniture industry. The essence of interior space was now on the verge of becoming a machine for the implementation of business transactions rather than a place away from home to house people while they worked. With these changing values and growing economic pressures, the design profession was finding the aesthetics as only a part of the planning and designing of interiors. As clients continued to grow larger and more complex, and competition and economic restraints increased, all of the "systems" at work in the interior were forced to respond. "Systems" has become a term used to describe a series of components which, when used together, were necessary in the performance of a task. For example: a ceiling is often made by hanging a metal "T" from an unfinished structural slab and supporting acoustical tile from that "T." Various systems were developed through the efforts of designers to create a means for solving aesthetic and functional problems with diverse industrial products (Figs. 16 and 17).

The original goal of the early International style gave

Figure 16. Arco Tower interior mock-up by Neville Lewis Associates for Arco (1982). Courtesy of Neville Lewis Associates and Arco. Photograph by Louis Reens.

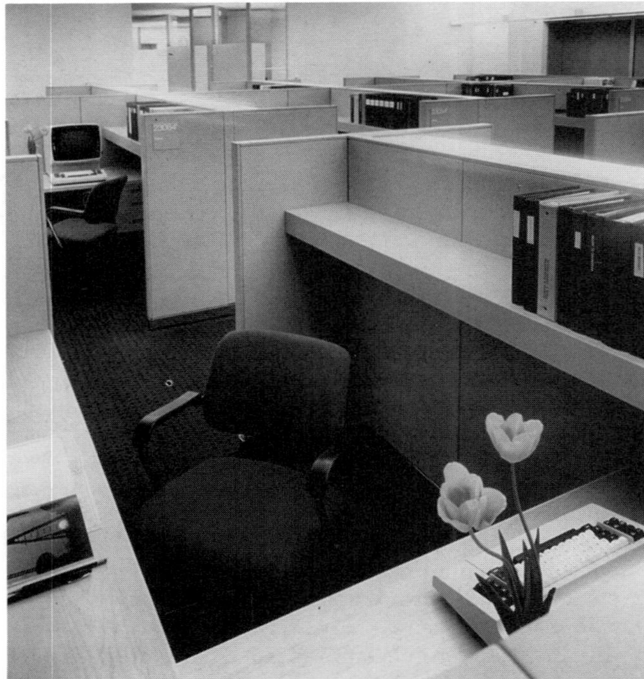

Figure 17. Arco Tower interior mock-up by Neville Lewis Associates for Arco (1982). Courtesy of Neville Lewis Associates and Arco. Photograph by Louis Reens.

way to more complex interior design problems. The issue of technology such as electronic data processing, video switching, and innumerable voice and communications systems emerged. To ensure the proper performance of business systems, environmental systems grew proportionately. These included HVAC, electrical power supply, distribution, lighting, emergency generation, and uninterruptible power supply systems. These systems were developed to ensure the maintenance of a working environment conducive to productivity and comfort and included new developments in flooring, walls, furniture, and acoustics as well as ergonomically designed seating and workstation componentry.

The issue was no longer only aesthetic mastery, although aesthetics would continue to play a major role in the design of the interior; the psychology of space for personal and group identification has become essential for pride in one's place, work, and person. International style idealism could not accommodate the needs of the new and more sophisticated client. Interiors without ornamentation would always leave a majority of the occupants dissatisfied and wanting more texture and surface treatment. It was inevitable that experimentation in decorative motifs would cautiously reappear, along with a return to historical references not seen in 80 years.

POSTMODERNISM

Robert Venturi, in his book *Complexity and Contradiction in Architecture,* written in 1966, foreshadowed the inevitable break with the austerity and purity of orthodox modern

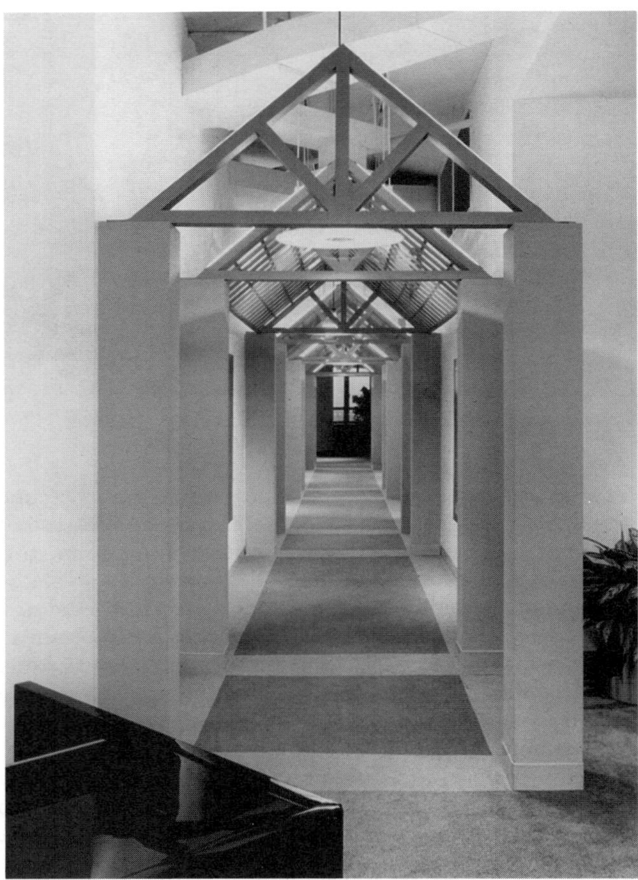

Figure 18. ERT&K transition corridor by Neville Lewis Associates (1987). Courtesy of Elliott Kaufman.

architecture (3). This break began as an abstracted and noncontextual use of historical motifs. Techniques such as wall murals (i.e. Encrustation style of the Romans) and caricatures of columns and colonnades were introduced. Pitched pyramidal open canopies were used to dramatize the colonnade or to create a focal point or transition space (Fig. 18). The work of Michael Graves, devoted to both the continued abstraction of historic references and a formal geometry, represents the essence of the postmodern genre. Charles Jencks, on the other hand, in his book *Symbolic Architecture* (4), searches for meaning beyond that of abstract beauty. Jencks argues for a symbolic program giving meaning to design.

THE FUTURE

Domestic interiors have had minimal stylistic guidance in the twentieth century and will probably never again have a single direction as was common in the past. The fashion industry has successfully begun to market styles for the home and sell these concepts to a growing middle class. The development of mass production/marketing of a style may be effectively used in developing a style or styles readily available at retail outlets for the home. Clothing and fabric designer Ralph Lauren designed a collection of home accessory styles called "Log Cabin," "Thoroughbred," "New England," and "Jamaica," which cater to the middle and upper middle classes. This new direction represents an "image option" for the people who can afford its implementation. A style can be chosen for the home much as one selects a china or silver service.

Institutional interior design has the potential for simultaneous development in diverse directions. Certain current trends can be projected to develop in the last quarter of the twentieth century and into the twenty-first. The experimentation in surface ornamentation developed in the postmodern movement will expand, and selective spaces as ornate as those which developed in the Egyptian, Roman, rococo, and Victorian periods may become common. These styles will perhaps be revived because of their sophisticated applications of paint, paper, and other inexpensive surface textures and symbolic possibilities. This allows tremendous expression and is not restricted by manufacturers, codes, colors, or construction schedules. Color theorists are experimenting with color, pattern, and texture to understand their potential. These will be the decorative techniques of tomorrow.

As the number of mega-interiors increases, an interior may take on the characteristics of a small town. Interior images and functional considerations may eventually expand to include streets and street lights with utilities (i.e. voice, data, power) accessible from the street for each work unit. The interior image for a town may be standard lot sizes for workspaces along the street with zoning regulations for the location of centralized community computers, photocopiers, and conference centers. An interior code may emerge which would define the parameters for the construction of particular workstation types within a given block or community, seeking homogeneity of style while recognizing the individual need for marking one's work environment within the contextual setting.

Within major cities where size has institutionalized life, there is a need to personalize institutions. This personalization expresses corporate recognition that people are the most important asset in the office environment. Focus on the productivity issue and the impact of automation in the workplace as well as on the quality of the total environment is increasing. Design has come full circle, from the simple markings on the cave walls to the highly sophisticated "caves and commons" research of the 1980s which studies the ratio of individual and group needs to develop spatial design. The design profession will require a greater understanding of the social sciences and group dynamics. Classes on environmental psychology will begin to appear in design programs along with tools for understanding human behavior such as the Myers–Briggs Type Indicator which distinguishes sixteen patterns of human behavior. An interior code will evolve which will delineate acceptable qualities of light and ambient sound levels. The individual workplace will be studied in greater detail to understand the impact of productivity and group interaction. Design has yet to address color in a fashion appropriate to its impact on the people in their environment. With a growing number of white collar workers spending a third of their lives in the workplace, pressure will increase for a comprehensive understanding of works such as Faber Birren's *Color Psychology and Color Therapy* (5).

With all of this, a systematic method for keeping current information on technology and its impact on people and the environment will be necessary, for the most dramatic source of change will be technology. Technology's thrust has been to process faster, to communicate faster and more completely, and to minimize wasted movement. This "high-tech" will require "high-touch," as John Naisbitt suggests in his book *Megatrends* (6). The postmodern movement has recognized this need for more texture and uniqueness, but this is just the beginning. Not only will spaces become more unique, casual, homey, and comfortable, but they will also require spaces for intellectual and physical refreshment. The collapse of the information float will overload the office worker, who will require parks for relief, and distractions in the form of the performing arts and the fine arts. The small town referred to above may need the equivalent of the tree-lined street and town center for social interaction and a breath of humanity in a world increasingly dictated by machines.

BIBLIOGRAPHY

1. G. Stickley, *The Best of Crafsman Homes,* Peregrine Smith, Inc., Salt Lake City, Utah, 1979.
2. L. Sullivan, *Ornament in Architecture,* Chicago, 1892. Reprinted in N. Pevsner, *Pioneers of Modern Design,* Pelican Books, Ltd., Harmondsworth, 1960.
3. R. Venturi, *Complexity and Contradiction in Architecture,* Museum of Modern Art, New York, 1966.
4. C. Jencks, *Symbolic Architecture,* Rizzoli International Publications, Inc., New York, 1985.
5. F. Birren, *Color Psychology and Color Therapy,* Citadel Press, Secaucus, N.J., 1950.
6. J. Naisbitt, *Megatrends,* Warner Books, Inc., New York, 1982.

See also BAUHAUS; ECOLE DES BEAUX ARTS; FURNITURE; GROPIUS, WALTER; LE CORBUSIER (CHARLES-EDOUARD JEANNERET); OFFICE FACILITY PLANNING; WRIGHT, FRANK LLOYD

ROBERT WOERTENDYKE
Brooklyn, New York

INTERNATIONAL PRACTICE

DESIGN

The international practice of architecture is defined as practice that extends beyond the boundaries of the home country of the firm to one or more foreign countries. The essential nature of the international practice of architecture derives from an understanding of local people, their culture, and their politics; the climate of their country; and the state of development of their building technology. In a sense this is inherent in the practice of architecture at home, but it requires dedication, flexibility, hard work, and a great degree of humility to practice internationally.

Architects work abroad for a number of reasons: to make an international reputation; lack of work in their home country; the desire to serve the needs of the developing world; or to follow a specialist market abroad. However attractive the idea of working abroad may be, it is radically different from working at home. A much higher proportion of time (and money) must be devoted to dealing with staff, including their families, and to administration, covering a multitude of office and accounting functions. It is not an enterprise to be undertaken lightly. Success requires long-term involvement, time, money, and staying power. The right attitude of mind, commitment to overseas work, speed, and flexibility are essential to success.

This article concentrates on aspects that go beyond usual practice in the home country; these are taken for granted as continuing in addition to the special characteristics of practice abroad.

Clients for Work Abroad

Clients may be the home government (eg, embassies, military installations, bilateral aid projects overseas); multinational corporations (eg, banks, pharmaceutical manufacturers); resource-rich countries (eg, producers of oil, gas, and other minerals; timber or other agricultural cash crops); or multinational aid agencies lending to developing countries (eg, World Bank, European Development Fund, Inter-American, Asian and African Development Banks, United Nations Development Program).

Countries fall broadly into three main categories: developed countries, with a GNP (gross national product) per capita of $1000 to $1500 or more, mainly Europe, North America, Japan, Australia, New Zealand and South Africa; oil-rich countries, the Middle East, North Africa; and developing countries, with a GNP per capita below $1000 to $1500, mainly Africa, Central and South America, and Asia. The dividing lines vary according to definitions adopted by organizations such as the World Bank or national aid agencies.

Most developed countries have established architectural professions that compete strongly with foreign firms, so in the oil-rich and developing countries there are more opportunities for foreign firms, as local architectural practices are less well-established. Projects cover the whole range, with emphasis on planning, infrastructure (energy, water, transportation), housing, health, education, tourism and leisure, and defense. Many are package-deal or turnkey projects (often preferred by less experienced user-clients), so the architect's immediate client is a contractor or equipment manufacturer and not the ultimate user. There is often an emphasis on project or program management rather than design, and there are opportunities for architects with a specialty (such as hospitals, universities, airports, or conservation of historic buildings).

Executive or Consultant

The architect may operate in an executive capacity overseas in the same way as at home, undertaking every stage in a project from design to construction supervision. Alternatively, he or she may have a consultant appointment as an adviser to the user, for example, in the preparation of the brief (program), in the selection of the building team, in the appointment of executive architects, or in supervision of construction.

Relationship with Local Architects

Possibly as a consultant, and probably as an executive architect, an association is needed with a local architect. This is essential for an understanding of local professional practice, the building industry, conformity to local codes and procedures, and for interpretation of local language, culture, and politics. Such an association is normally required in developing countries in accordance with national indigenization decrees.

Appropriate Design

Much has been written and said about the appropriateness of style in which buildings overseas are designed. Buildings may be designed in an international idiom in the house style of their architects or in a local style responsive to the climate and culture of the country in which they are built. The first may be appropriate as a symbol of the international standing of the country or as a mark of respect for a distinguished architect: the second is becoming more prominent as developing countries seek national identity and search for a recognizable regional style (eg, Islamic architecture, Malaysian architecture).

In addition to an understanding of the local culture and national history, architects working overseas must appreciate sociological aspects: religious observance (eg, abstinence from alcohol), dietary restrictions, Feng Shui (the Chinese art of geomancy), Koranic symbolism, social status and grouping, attitudes toward women, etc.

Perhaps the most critical local influence on design is climate. Much of a building's character, especially in tropical countries, comes from its function in modifying climate to provide shelter and comfort for human activities. The designer must understand the local range of solar radiation, temperature, humidity, rainfall, wind speed, and wind direction. These climatic characteristics tend to group into main climatic zones, as illustrated for hot climates in Figure 1. The majority of oil-rich and developing countries (and therefore those with opportunities for international practice) lie in the tropical belt in this figure.

To achieve the comfort zone illustrated in Figure 2, special consideration should be given to the local microclimate, topography (eg, proximity of sea or lakes), seasonal changes (eg, monsoon, dust storms), and diurnal changes. The importance of orientation (to encourage or exclude sun penetration) and landscaping must be grasped and an examination must be made of the likelihood of natural hazards (eg, earthquakes, volcanoes, hurricanes, sand storms, or insect infestation).

Given this analysis, characteristic types of building design tend to emerge in similar climatic zones: for example, heavy walls and roofs, small external openings, and courtyard houses in hot, dry zones (eg, in Egypt); and lightly constructed buildings raised off the ground, with pitched roofs and large overhangs, and large external openings

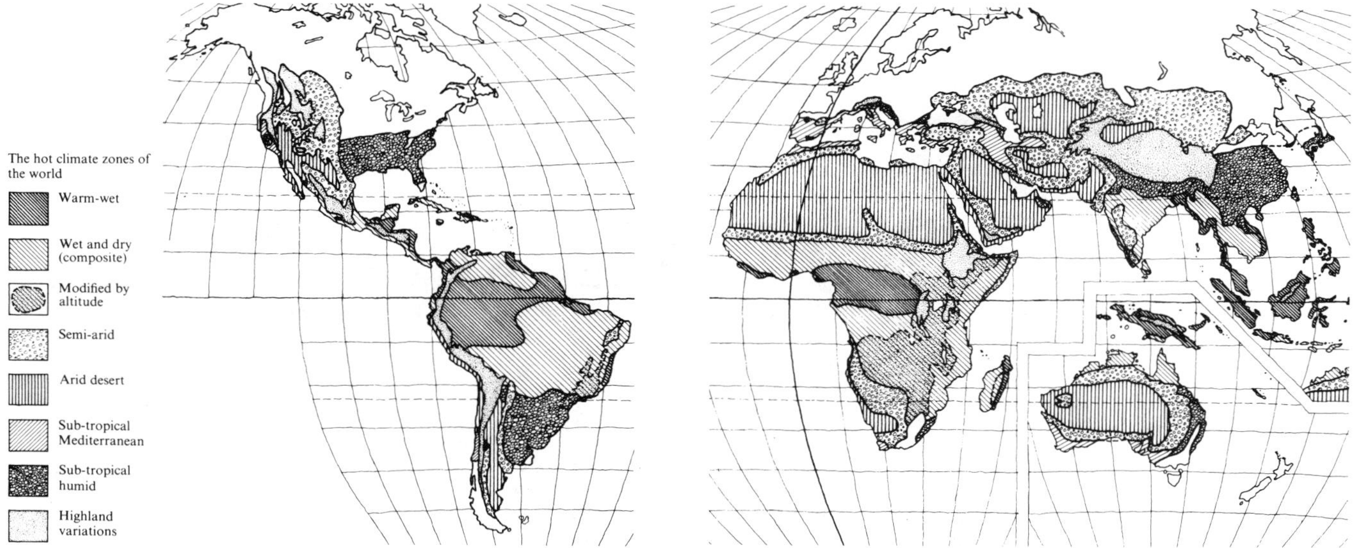

Figure 1. The hot climates of the world. An understanding of the characteristics of each of these is essential to design appropriate buildings to provide comfort and shelter (1). Courtesy of A. Konya.

in hot, humid zones (eg, in Indonesia). Although air conditioning has revolutionized building design (and made it more international), it is preferable to design for optimum modification of climatic conditions by the building itself, both to conserve energy and to "fail-safe" during power interruptions (particularly in developing countries). It also produces more interesting architecture that fits in better. Examples of these characteristic types are shown in Figures 3 and 4.

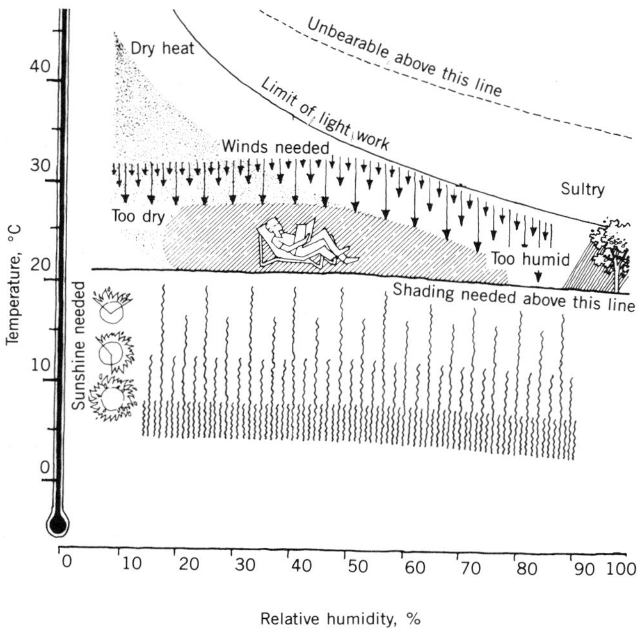

Figure 2. Schematic diagram of Victor Olgyay's bioclimate chart indicating the shaded comfort zone (between 22 and 27°C, and 15 to 80% relative humidity) and the climatic modification required if the temperature or humidity deviates from this zone (2). Courtesy of A. Konya.

Appropriate Technology

At the start of a job, experienced architects are needed to make a careful analysis of the availability of local craftspeople and labor and of building materials and components. It is necessary to decide whether the building should be labor- or capital-intensive; for example, a project funded by a multinational funding agency might require a high level of local employment of labor (eg, in India), or speed and remoteness might require a highly prefabricated building with imported skilled erectors (eg, in the Falkland Islands). The capacity and skills of local craftspeople must be evaluated and then used and encouraged if a truly indigenous character is to be achieved.

In addition, the availability and quality of local building materials needs assessing to minimize imports; similarly, locally produced components should be assessed, such as roof sheeting, doors, windows, fittings, and equipment. Conformity to recognized standards and warranties from manufacturers or contractors are necessary in case of later failures. Import and transport problems such as programming, customs clearance, and replacement of defective or stolen items can cause serious delays in building operations.

Standards of maintenance vary greatly from country to country and should be taken into account at an early stage; inoperative elevators, uncleared roof gutters, or sudden failures of power supply can make a building unusable. Soil investigation can be critical to building design, particularly when allied to local natural hazards such as sinking ground coupled with floods in Bangkok or salt-rich sand in Egypt.

Figure 3. Head office for Saudi–British Bank, Riyadh, Saudi Arabia, by Robert Matthew, Johnson–Marshall & Partners. A typical building in a hot, dry climate, with heavy structure and small, well-shaded external openings. Courtesy of the author.

Appropriate Standards and Procedures

It is vital at the outset to identify the building regulations that apply locally. In former colonial countries these may be based on the standards of European countries [eg, British Standards (BS) in the United Kingdom or Association Française de Normalisation (AFNOR) in France]; in countries within a particular economic sphere of influence they may reflect the standards of the dominant country concerned [eg, American National Standards Institute (ANSI) or American Society for Testing and Materials (ASTM) in the United States or Japanese Industry Standards (JIS) in Japan]. The application of building ordinance laws and procedures with which a design must comply to obtain local building consent may be fundamental to design (eg, when set against the measurement of rentable areas for office buildings in Hong Kong). Rules concerning fire fighting and means of escape may be crucial to the building design.

PRACTICE

Marketing

The first step is to collect background information on the country in question. Sources include home governmental departments for trade, aid, and construction; foreign embassies; chambers of commerce; professional institutes; special supplements and economic digests in newspapers (eg, Financial Times, Wall Street Journal); bank economic reviews; and publications by United Nations agencies (eg, World Bank, United Nations Development Program). From this information an initial appraisal should be made of a number of factors: political and financial stability, strength of economy, national development planning priorities, opportunities for architectural work in the private and public sectors, strength of trading links between home and foreign countries, exchange control regulations, local taxes, strength of the local architectural profession, the necessity for indigenous architectural partners, freedom for expatriates to practice, living conditions for expatriates, and ability to remit local earnings.

Having decided to investigate further, an exploratory visit (possibly as part of a trade mission) is made to follow up as many of the specific leads by direct contact as possible, including with the home embassy in the country concerned. Local national and school holidays should be avoided (including Ramadan and the Hadj in Muslim countries and the Chinese New Year in Southeast Asia).

It is also advisable to visit the World Bank, the relevant regional development banks, and the European Economic Community if applicable, and to get the firm registered

Figure 4. World Bank School in eastern Nigeria by Robert Matthew, Johnson–Marshall & Partners. A typical building in a hot, humid climate with lightweight structure, large overhanging roof to discharge rainwater, and large windows to take advantage of cooling breezes. Courtesy of the author.

(by completing the lengthy Data on Consultants (DACON) or other form). This is a necessary prerequisite for being considered for aid-funded projects, although not of itself enough to become short-listed. It is essential to identify and visit the executing agency or user-client in the country concerned.

A supply of prospectuses and brochures describing the firm's capacity and experience should be taken on all visits to give to interested parties. The firm should be registered with local governmental agencies.

Once a project has been identified, a statement of interest or capability statement is sent, followed by a competitive submission once the firm has been added to the short-list. This submission contains a technical proposal (even an outline design), a list of associated consultants and staff to be allocated to the job with curriculum vitae, a statement on how the work will be carried out, and a separate estimate of costs (quoted in home currency for home costs and local currency for local costs).

Competitions are an important source of work internationally. Although conditions may vary, the generally accepted ones are those issued by the International Union of Architects.

Professional Service

The understanding of professional service varies greatly in different countries. In Arab countries, for example, the concept of professional service is not understood and architects are regarded more as contractors or suppliers of commodities; furthermore, there is no separate word for architect as distinct from engineer.

It is preferable for selection to be made on the basis of the services to be provided, with the price for these services negotiated once the services are established. In this respect the "two-envelope system" (that is, one for services opened before a separate one for price) practiced by international lending agencies is recommended.

It is important to describe the scope of services and code of conduct as fully as possible in the agreement with the client, by reference to published national documents. In addition to normal clauses, the agreement needs to state stage payment of fees (and where paid and in what currency); procedures for late payment; payment for staff housing, office, transport, travel for people and families, if appropriate; and the country of law and arbitration. The International Model Form of Agreement between Client and Consulting Engineer published by the International Federation of Consulting Engineers (FIDIC) provides a useful reference to similar practice by consulting engineers.

Corporate Structure

Once the decision has been made to work in another country, the form of corporate structure there must be established. The work may be done through the home country or another country "offshore" to the country concerned (either for convenient location of the design team or for reasons of tax or remittance of fees).

An agent or sponsor is sometimes required by law, usually a sensible and necessary appointment. It is important to have an agreement defining such factors as scope of services, appropriate ethical rules to be followed, public acknowledgment of agency/sponsorship, payment of fees (after securing jobs if possible), and review period.

Alternatively, a local branch office of the head office or a subsidiary, dependent on local rules (eg, on minimum equity held locally), may be established. Another alternative is a joint venture with a similar firm, preferably matching in character, size, standing, and architectural objectives. An agreement should be drawn up (usually job by job) showing professional inputs by each firm, location of work at each stage, fee and expenses division and payment, payment of commissions, allocation of overheads, and time span. Guidelines published by FIDIC for ad-hoc collaboration agreements between consulting firms are a useful reference.

Design Team

The selection of the design team is of critical importance. It will usually be composed of home and local staff, possibly with engineering and construction cost consultants from other countries; however, the fewer countries of origin the better, for compatibility of professional attitudes and skills.

The team leader is a key person. He or she must be experienced in overseas work, flexible, and equable in personality and technically competent. The team leader must be able to deal with the client, local professional advisers, the bank manager, staff and their families, and be ready to cope with emergencies (eg, accidents, critical illness, personnel problems, coups, natural catastrophes).

An experienced administrator is useful in the setting-up stage: finding domestic and office accommodations, furniture and equipment, transport, local advisers, local staff; obtaining work permits; and organizing accounting, tax advice, and insurance.

Work Location

The decision on the appropriate location for different stages of work on a project depends on factors that vary in importance for the main stages. A critical common factor is the location of the offices of the main members of the design team (architects, engineers, and construction cost consultants). The greatest speed and efficiency is achieved by setting up a single office for the team in which all members work.

At feasibility or design stage, this single office is best located overseas close to the client, local authorities, and the site, for ease of communication during the critical development of design and to ensure rapid decisions.

At the proposal and contract documentation stages the location of the office depends on balancing the efficiency of the home office (where, eg, computer-aided drafting facilities may be available) against the availability of information on appropriate documentation for the local country and the location of construction cost consultants when bills of quantities form part of the proposal information. The right balance must be found between local and international contractors, depending on the size of the project and strength of the local building industry.

After the contract is awarded, a local office is established on site as a base for inspection or observation of the work, by the construction manager and/or the resident architect. It is important to set up a local office early in the development of work in a particular country overseas of suitable location and character to represent the practice (eg, in the office of a local joint venture partner). This facilitates contact with actual and potential clients and is an efficient base for the stages of work already described.

Personnel

In an overseas operation, the architectural practice will be known more by its representatives than by its architecture. For this reason, and because going overseas is a major and traumatic experience for most people, choosing expatriate staff to represent the practice locally is of paramount importance; age, motivation, health, marital status, ages of children, and attitude of spouse are all as important as design or technical skills. A balance needs to be found between the respect clients may give to an older and more senior staff member (often at least 15 years of professional experience is demanded) and the adaptability of a younger, more fit, and more flexible person. Suitable nomenclature and status for staff and considerable delegation of authority are important to give confidence in the person's ability to represent the practice decisively, without frequent reference to the home office. The tendency is to locate more senior people overseas, as junior staff are readily provided by local associated practices.

Social life is important in relation to both other expatriates and the local community. People need opportunities for relaxation and sport and to get away from office colleagues out of working hours. Much depends on the character and personal qualities of spouses and their ability to adapt to an unfamiliar environment and culture. In tropical countries, heat and humidity require a high degree of adaptability and tolerance. Special care is needed to respect local customs, eg, consumption of alcohol, dress, physical gestures, segregation of the sexes.

Good local administrative backup is essential. Appropriate housing, schools for children, medical care, registration with local embassy or consulate in case of emergency, immigration procedures, employment permits, office and personal transport, and availability of cash in countries where credit cards and traveler's checks are not accepted, are some examples.

Strong matching administrative backup is also required at the head office, eg, logistical support, travel arrangements, home news, and emergency arrangements for repatriation. Curriculum vitae for alternative people are maintained to help rapid substitution in the event of accident, illness, or leave. Clients are often very particular on the choice and remuneration of individual team members based on their experience and seniority, and are thus very sensitive to substitution.

Language and Communications

It is important that staff who reside long-term in a foreign country speak the local language and write reports fluently in it. Multilingual local secretaries have an essential role in communicating with clients, local partners, or contractors in their own language. Whether speaking in the home language or that of the foreign country, the ability to communicate easily in nontechnical language to clients and local associates is an advantage. Technical jargon is best avoided in speaking to people abroad.

Good communication between headquarters and the local office is essential, with awareness of time differences and agreed contact points out of office hours at either end. Effective use of different modes of communication should be considered (eg, telephone, telex, facsimile transmission, electronic mail, courier), as should customs clearance of drawings and models and the compatibility of computer programs and floppy disks.

Plentiful nontechnical communications contribute greatly to good morale overseas (eg, personal mail, newspapers, professional magazines, and videos).

Feedback and Transfer of Technology

Overseas practice must be aimed at a developing and changing target. In any project there is a large element of transfer of technology, which for architects is in essence an exchange of experience. Local associates and joint-venture partners learn from working on the project and are progressively more able to execute future projects unaided. In most internationally funded projects an identified objective is that counterpart staff should learn new techniques by working with more experienced expatriates. Equal experience is gained in the opposite direction and can be applied to future projects in other less-developed countries.

Ultimately, overseas practice depends on the home firm's ability to have up-to-date and relevant experience that the foreign country needs and wishes to buy; alternatively, the firm's reputation must be so good that this in itself is an internationally desirable commodity.

ADMINISTRATION

Exporting exerts greater strains than does working at home. This stress affects people and their way of life, the finances of the firm, and the administrative and logistic support services. Communication takes on a greater importance, as does mutual trust and understanding between people making decisions, often in isolation.

Two of the chief constraints to growth of overseas business are the financing of work-search activities and finding working capital. More working capital is needed because of large or protracted projects overseas, inflation, exchange variations, on-demand bonds, and higher turnover for each unit of technical input. Consulting architects experience severe financial problems when new to overseas work, as do architects practicing as partnerships (which cannot attract as much financial backing as corporate entities) or operating in certain difficult countries.

Financial Information

Thus, a clear view of finances is a fundamental need when exporting, with strong management, systems, and controls. Techniques need to be developed for surviving liquidity problems arising from longer credit periods, political risks, currency variations, harsher taxation regimes, and proliferating documentation. Financial and legal information is needed not only by the home office management for policy-making and control, but also by prospective clients, funding agencies, and banks or institutions lending funds, both at home and overseas. Hence the firm's personal, financial, and management track records must be well demonstrated.

Management techniques are required for dealing with a multiplicity of banks, accountants, lawyers, other expert advisers (eg, insurance brokers), and perhaps a mixture of partnerships, companies, branches, and offices in different locations. For the balance sheet, the usual bankers' touchstones loom even larger as projects enter areas of greater risk and uncertainty and become more difficult to control. The equity base/capital gearing is critical, as few banks want to put more into a firm than the owners themselves are prepared to risk. Security or collateral for borrowing needs to be first class and interest cover needs to be sufficient to repay funds and meet interest charges. Tax affairs need to be up to date.

For financial planning and the requirements of the banks, clarity is needed on the amount, purpose, and timing of finance required and the financial position and prospects of the firm. The firm needs to show that it can apply and manage funds effectively.

Audited accounts are analyzed for profitability by geographic areas over a five-year period. The balance sheet is carefully analyzed and annotated, and trading and cash flow are projected for a reasonable period ahead, certainly for the length of the next project being undertaken. Assumptions need to be realistic and clearly stated. Lenders impose conditions that have professional as well as financial implications, eg, the danger of loss of independence, of overtrading (of people, money, or time), or undercapitalization. Before making a project submission, the costing and reimbursement methods, financial sequences, cash flow, and banking or other financial support available (including export insurance) need to be worked out carefully.

Banking

The key is to find a banker willing to lend against overseas fees debtors; there are plenty of funds available, but the snag is the criterion for lending. The banker asks about bonds (such as bid bonds, performance bonds, guarantees against advance payments) for clients or for overseas bankers as a counterindemnity, about the overdrafts needed overseas, and any guarantees in that connection. The banker may ask for a confirmed, irrevocable letter of credit from the client. He or she may look critically at facilities with other bankers for particular areas or projects. Some banks overseas are nationalized and not permitted to grant overdraft facilities. Only the firm is able to coordinate relationships and facilities with the various banks used.

Accounting

Accounting, auditing, and bookkeeping methods; project costing, budgeting, monitoring, and financial statements (including frequency and detail); and integration into a home or worldwide system are all affected by where the project team is set up, whether at home, in an overseas office, or on site, and whether by itself or with other teams.

Accountants are needed at home who know about exporting, the tax reliefs available, techniques for dealing with exchange variations, and so on. Accountants overseas are needed who have knowledge of local tax for expatriate staff, custom duties, remittances laws, and tax clearance procedures. It helps if they have links with a home firm. They advise on what audit methods are acceptable locally, and whether the audit of time, costs, and overheads are acceptable to the overseas regime. Accounting timetables are adjusted to maintain a grip on the firm as a whole, a branch, a joint venture, or a project. Partners, bankers, home tax authorities, and insurers all need up-to-date financial information. Advice is needed from the tax-planning consultant on dual residence and the antiavoidance sections of relevant legislation.

Exchange Control

Advice may be needed on home exchange control regulations, such as consent to open an account overseas, to receive or spend foreign currency, to make payments to nonresidents, to incorporate overseas or establish a nonresident subsidiary, to own property overseas, and to grant guarantees in favor of nonresidents. Procedures are carried out either by the home bank or, if applicable, by direct application to the national central bank of the country in which the project is located. Advice on overseas exchange control regulations is needed from local accountants and lawyers.

Export Insurance

Particular care is needed in understanding and implementing export insurance coverage for nonpayment and nonremittance of funds to the home office and for other risks.

Taxation

Tax planning advice is needed on the effect of tax on the legal trading entity used, where the work is done, accounting methods and timetables, profitability, and cash flow. The more countries operated in, the more complex the position becomes, especially for partnerships, because of the interaction of capital allowances, advance payments subject to varying exchange rates, withholding taxes, double/unilateral tax relief incidence, and timing. To solve these equations with more than a few variables requires a computer. Speedily produced accounts leading to prompt tax filing overseas have a direct effect on cash flow at final account stage, release of bonds, and remittances to the home office. The way different authorities view trading figures is vital because sometimes they ignore losses and impose a tax on a notional or deemed profit, say, related to turnover. No relief against tax may be given for tax paid overseas on a loss as defined by the home tax authorities. The various ways in which the same information is presented to different authorities, how exchange gains or losses are dealt with, and how home indirect overheads are allocated to various projects and branches are key subjects involving the design and workings of the home office costing system.

It is advisable as well to understand clearly the home and overseas tax effects on short- and long-term contracts, direct pay, and other emoluments and allowances (spouses' fares, school fees, and so on). Taxation considerations radically change first thoughts when it comes to a partner residing overseas, leading perhaps to the setting up of an overseas partnership that can also yield relief for its partners at home. Overall return and control over financial affairs is more important than minimizing the tax paid.

Legal Matters

The legal adviser takes into account decisions made on financial, technical, and administrative matters. He or she also looks at the operation and requirements of local laws, codes, and customs, including immigration, labor, and insurance. Commercial and professional registration involving long documents and lead times is needed. The simplest, most tax-effective legal entity should be chosen for practicing; the costs of setting up and maintaining different forms vary greatly, as do their tax holiday effects. Local agents, consultants, or representatives are involved, either at arm's length or as participants. A decision about whether to form a partnership, a joint venture, or a consortium must be made respecting indigenization laws stipulating the degree of local participation and the commission or share payable. Advice is obtained at home from international lawyers, or locally, from lawyers and accountants (with advice from embassies on the advisers' track record). Owning or leasing property is dependent on special local prohibitions or conditions. A notarized power of attorney is needed for the most senior person on the spot. Apart from notarized deeds and accounts of the firm and professional qualifications to prepare, there is the primary agreement with the client to draw up; subconsultancy agreements with other firms on the team and local consultants; and interfirm, joint venture, or consortium agreements.

Fundamentally, the concern is for equity with the client and avoiding joint liability with other consultants or contractors. Legal systems and concepts vary widely: the Napoleonic code may demand physical retribution for professional negligence, the Islamic strict liability code may impose 10 to 20 years of legal liability, sometimes jointly with all others involved. In the United States, exemplary and punitive damages are a criminal award and are not insurable, unlike their equivalent, aggravated damages, in the United Kingdom.

CONCLUSION

The international practice of architecture requires a new attitude toward the environment, a sense of humility in understanding the needs of clients overseas, and a new dimension of involvement with staff and their families. Increased demands are made on administration, both in the home office and overseas, and financial and legal implications need careful attention. However, the rewards, both in imaginative architectural responses to wider climatic and social demands and in financial terms, can more than compensate for the logistical problems involved.

BIBLIOGRAPHY

1. A. Konya, *Design Primer for Hot Climates,* The Architectural Press, London, 1980, pp. 18, 19.
2. *Ibid.,* p. 28.

General References

J. Arkell, *Overseas Contracts Seminar: Paper on Finance, Insurance, Tax and Law,* The Institution of Civil Engineers, London, 1979.

R. Bidgood, *Future Markets for Consultancy,* Northwood Publications, London, 1980.

R. Cunliffe, "The lessons from working abroad," *Architects Journal* **171**(7), 351–356 (February 13, 1980).

M. Evans, *Housing, Climate and Comfort,* Architectural Press, London, 1980.

M. Fry and J. Drew, *Tropical Architecture in the Dry and Humid Zones,* Krieger, New York, 1975.

Guidelines for Ad-hoc Collaboration Agreements between Consulting Firms, FIDIC, Lausanne, 1977.

Guidelines for the Use of Consultants by World Bank Borrowers and by the World Bank as Executing Agency, World Bank, Washington, D.C., 1981.

International Model Form of Agreement between Client and Consulting Engineer and International General Rules of Agreement between Client and Consulting Engineer for Design and Supervision of Construction of Works, FIDIC, Lausanne, 1979.

International Model Form of Agreement between Client and Consulting Engineer and International General Rules of Agreement between Client and Consulting Engineer for Pre-Investment Studies, FIDIC, Lausanne, 1979.

International Model Form of Agreement between Client and Consulting Engineer and International General Rules of Agreement between Client and Consulting Engineer for Project Management, FIDIC, Lausanne, 1980.

O. H. Koenigsberger, et al., *Manual of Tropical Housing, Part 1 Climatic Design,* Longmans, London, 1974.

A. Konya, "Architecture for Export, Climate," *Architects Journal* **168**(34), 340–351 (August 23, 1978).

A. Konya, "Architecture for Export, Design Factors," *Architects Journal* **168**(35), 391–403 (August 30, 1978).

A. Konya, "Architecture for Export, How to go about it," *Architects Journal* **168**(34), 318–339 (August 23, 1978).

R. Matthew, S. Johnson-Marshall, et al., *Standards Guide for Universities,* National Universities Commission, Lagos, 1978.

V. Olgyay, *Design with Climate: Bioclimatic Approach to Architectural Regionalism,* Princeton University Press, Princeton, N.J., 1963.

Revised Recommendations Concerning International Competitions in Architecture and Town Planning, UIA/UNESCO, Paris, 1978.

See also Islamic Architecture; Latin American Architecture; Oriental Architecture; Southeast Asian Architecture; Soviet Union Architecture; West African Vernacular Architecture

Francis Baden-Powell
RMJM
London, United Kingdom

INTERN PROGRAMS

In today's complex world, competent architectural practice depends on competent practitioners—men and women whose education and experience provides them with the knowledge, skills, and judgment to provide quality professional services. The typical path leading to architectural registration begins with education in a professional-degree program accredited by the National Architectural Accrediting Board (NAAB), followed by a prescribed period of practical training, or internship, in the office of a registered architect. After the successful completion of the architectural registration examination, the process of refining knowledge and skills, and keeping abreast of emerging trends continues throughout an architect's career.

Internship serves as a bridge between formal education and practice as a registered architect. It is an important period when the intern begins to understand the mechanics of professional practice and apply knowledge and skills acquired in school to the daily problems an architect encounters. Many architectural schools encourage—some even require—students to gain internship experience prior to graduation. In addition to exposing the student to life in an architect's office and thereby serving a strictly educational purpose, certain pregraduation internships are credited by many state registration boards against the experience required to sit for the registration examination.

Architectural internship, if effectively undertaken, serves to instill a strong interest in lifelong professional development. Some architectural firms assist interns as they prepare to take the registration examination. Many firms provide opportunities for staff members to attend continuing education programs designed to explore contemporary issues and inform practitioners about relevant new developments both within and outside of the profession.

Historically, an internship meant a young aspirant learning from an experienced mentor, and gradually acquiring greater responsibilities over time. Today, however, there is no clear framework for this element of continuous professional development. Schools provide basic knowledge and practical skills, but graduates are then left to expand on their abilities in relatively unstructured office environments. Many interns lack a solid understanding of the kinds of experience they should be acquiring. The increased demands of the marketplace and the impact of new technologies have altered priorities and created nontraditional approaches to personnel management. Factors such as office workload and compensation may lead to rapid job turnover, which results in piecemeal learning.

Interns often must acquire practical knowledge through continued formal education, rather than through a more effective process of experience-based learning.

The profession has attempted to address these problems through the development of a comprehensive internship program designed to provide a smooth transition between formal education and registration: the Intern–Architect Development Program (IDP).

INTERN–ARCHITECT DEVELOPMENT PROGRAM

The purpose of the IDP is the development of competent architects—young men and women who can provide exemplary architectural services. The program is designed to make the purpose of internship years more understandable and to make them more productive. It helps intern–architects sharpen their skills and gain the knowledge needed to enter the profession at the highest level of competence. A comprehensive internship is essential to acquire and reinforce the education, discipline, integrity, judgment, skills, knowledge, and quest for learning that must serve the registered architect for a lifetime.

The objectives of the IDP are (*1*) to provide information and advice of the highest quality on educational, internship, and professional issues and opportunities; (*2*) to define and encourage activity in critical areas of architectural practice in which intern–architects are expected to acquire basic levels of knowledge and skill, and to encourage additional activity in the broad aspects of architectural practice; (*3*) to provide a uniform system for documentation and periodic assessment of individual internship activity; and (*4*) to provide greater access to supplementary educational opportunities designed to augment training.

The program was created in 1974 and since 1978 a growing number of states have implemented the IDP. Its policies are established by a national IDP Coordinating Committee, composed of representatives of the American Institute of Architects (AIA), the National Council of Architectural Registration Boards (NCARB), the Association of Collegiate Schools of Architecture (ACSA), and the American Institute of Architecture Students (AIAS).

The AIA is a professional society that deals with all aspects of architectural practice and, in particular, pursues the important goal of raising the level of professional competence. The AIA's primary role in the IDP is to develop and provide supplementary education resources and to organize and maintain an advisory system for intern–architects.

As a federation of all registration boards in the United States, the NCARB sets national standards for training, examination, and registration. The NCARB interprets these standards, maintains records, and acts as the central clearinghouse and contact point for all intern–architects, architects, and registration boards in matters dealing with the registration and professional conduct of architects. The NCARB is responsible for detailing, interpreting, and enforcing the IDP training requirements.

The ACSA and AIAS both function in a review and advisory role within the IDP Coordinating Committee. Their assistance ensures input from the educational community.

Advisory System

At the state level, the IDP involves two important participants: the sponsor and the advisor. They function as elements of an advisory system designed to provide both daily and long-term guidance to the intern–architect.

The sponsor is typically a registered architect in the intern's firm who assumes the traditional responsibility of providing opportunities to the intern for acquiring experience in various areas of architectural practice. The sponsor also reviews the quality of work performed and periodically certifies the intern's experiences. Professional engineers, landscape architects, interior designers, planners, or contractors may serve as sponsors. To satisfy the program's training requirements, however, the intern–architect must work at least 1½ years under the direct supervision of a registered architect.

The advisor is a registered architect, usually outside the intern's firm, with whom the intern meets periodically for evaluation of progress and assistance in developing long-term career goals. Advisors conduct individual meetings and group discussion sessions for sharing experiences and resolving common problems. When conditions warrant, the sponsor and advisor may meet to review the intern's progress.

Training Requirements

Participants in the IDP are expected to meet specific levels of exposure in 14 areas of architectural practice grouped into three major categories: design and construction documents, construction administration, and office management. A fourth category, related special activities, includes areas beyond the traditional scope of architectural practice. Interns must acquire a total of 700 value units (VUs) to satisfy the program's training standard; one value unit equals eight hours of acceptable internship activity. The NCARB has established specific conditions for acceptable ways of acquiring value units in the various categories and training areas. Table 1 lists the value unit requirements for each category and area.

Each architectural registration board has the authority to establish requirements necessary for admission to examination and for registration. Several registration boards have adopted the IDP training requirements as their training standard, while other boards have endorsed the requirements as acceptable.

Candidates for NCARB certification may satisfy that council's training standard by completing the IDP training requirements. Certification is a vehicle through which reciprocal registration may be obtained in other states.

Record–keeping System

Interns participating in the IDP are expected to assess their progress continuously. They must maintain ongoing

Table 1. Value Unit Requirements[a]

Category A: Design and Construction Documents
Minimum total VUs required: 360

Training Areas	Minimum VUs Required
1. Programming–client contact	10
2. Site and environmental analysis	10
3. Schematic design	15
4. Building cost analysis	10
5. Code research	15
6. Design development	40
7. Construction documents	155
8. Specifications and materials research	15
9. Documents checking and coordination	15

The required minimum in category A totals 285 VUs, allowing for 75 additional VUs to be acquired in training areas 1–9. All of the 75 VUs may be acquired in one area or spread throughout the nine areas.

Category B: Construction Administration
Minimum total VUs required: 70

Training Areas	Minimum VUs Required
10. Bidding and contract negotiation	10
11. Construction phase (office)	15
12. Construction phase (observation)	15

The required minimum in category B totals 40 VUs, allowing for 30 additional VUs to be acquired in training areas 10–12. All of the 30 VUs may be acquired in one area or spread throughout the three areas.

Category C: Office Management
Minimum total VUs required: 35

Training Areas	Minimum VUs Required
13. Office procedures	15
14. Professional activities	10

The required minimum in category C totals 25 VUs, allowing for 10 additional VUs to be acquired in training areas 13–14. All of the 10 VUs may be acquired in one area or spread between the two areas.

Category D: Related Special Activities
No minimum VUs required: 0
Training Areas
- Energy conservation
- Computer applications
- Construction management
- Planning
- Interior design
- Landscape architecture
- Environmental engineering
- Structural engineering
- Applied research
- Teaching
- Historic restoration
- Professional delineation
- Other

The required minimum in categories A, B, and C totals 465 VUs. The remaining 235 VUs may be acquired in any of the listed training categories, including category D. All 235 VUs may be acquired in one category or spread throughout the categories.

[a] Ref. 1.

records of training and supplementary education, however gained, in fulfillment of the program's training requirements.

This record-keeping system helps interns monitor their experience and plan future activities, and at the same time allows the sponsor to assess the quality and range of tasks the intern performs and to manage staff assignments more effectively. It also provides state registration boards with comprehensive information on the training received by individuals applying for examination.

On entering the IDP, the intern–architect prepares an initial assessment of experience already gained. While moving through the program, the intern keeps a record of experiences and adds these to the initial assessment. All experience is verified periodically by the sponsor. The advisor also reviews the general character of the intern's training and provides long-range guidance. When the IDP training requirements have been fulfilled, a final assessment report is prepared by the intern, certified by the sponsor, and acknowledged by the advisor.

This important documentation can be maintained in an NCARB/IDP Council record. Although it is not required for participation in the program, this record-keeping service is recognized by most registration boards and assists the intern in documenting and monitoring experience. After an intern has passed the examination and acquired registration, the Council record can be considered for NCARB certification.

Supplementary Education System

The IDP recognizes the importance of a rich and varied exposure to all aspects of professional practice during the internship period, while it also recognizes that not all employers can provide this kind of exposure. Although experience gained in each IDP training category and area will not be the same for every intern–architect, every participant is encouraged to gain meaningful training in all areas by participation and observation.

The intern acquires knowledge and skills by direct involvement in the work. This can include working on the drafting board, attending meetings, visiting construction sites, writing reports, researching products, and other such activities. Exposure by observation also occurs, when the intern does not have the opportunity to participate in a given area of practice, but can observe other professionals who are.

Although a significant portion of the IDP training requirements must be achieved through either participation or observation, some requirements may be satisfied through supplementary education.

A series of learning components in the AIA *Architect's Handbook of Professional Practice* forms the foundation of the IDP's supplementary education system. These components are keyed to the program's 14 required areas of training and focus on topics pertinent to today's expanded practice of architecture. They identify important issues and suggest both individual and group learning approaches. Other acceptable supplementary resources provided through the AIA include correspondence courses;

architectural training labs; and approved local, regional, and national professional development programs.

IDP and Architectural Registration

The IDP training requirements are more flexible than traditional durational training standards, and thus allow IDP participants to proceed at a self-directed pace. The IDP system recognizes overtime work and supplementary education, while durational standards do not. Many interns satisfy the IDP requirements in less time than the traditional three-year training period.

IDP participants receive full value unit credit for work performed under the direct supervision of a professional engineer, landscape architect, planner, interior designer, or general contractor, although, as noted earlier, at least 1½ years in an architect's office are required to satisfy the IDP training standard. Most state registration boards only award partial credit for experience outside an architect's office; some boards require that all experience be acquired in the office of a registered architect.

Intern–architects may also receive value unit credit for experience in such nontraditional areas as applied research, teaching, energy conservation, computer applications, and historic preservation. These experiences must be reviewed on an individual basis before credit is granted.

Since intern–architects began participating in the IDP in the late 1970s, it has been asked if the program has helped interns pass the registration examination. Although success on the examination is caused by a number of variable factors, a well-rounded internship plays an important role in examination performance. A major portion of the examination tests for knowledge, skills, and judgmental ability in situations directly related to the IDP training areas.

The principal objective of the IDP is not, however, to ensure that all interns pass the examination. The objective is to serve the public interest by providing the best start to a lifelong professional career. Interns will be better prepared to make a more immediate and lasting contribution to a firm, the profession, and to society.

BIBLIOGRAPHY

1. *IDP Training Guidelines,* The American Institute of Architects and the National Council of Architectural Registration Boards, Washington, D.C., 1987–1988, pp. 2–3.

General References

Circular of Information No. 1, National Council of Architectural Registration Boards, Washington, D.C., annual.

Architect's Handbook of Professional Practice, The American Institute of Architects, Washington, D.C., 1988.

Professional Development Resource Catalog, The American Institute of Architects, Washington, D.C., annual.

Facts About IDP, The American Institute of Architects and National Council of Architectural Registration Boards, Washington, D.C., 1981.

The IDP, vols. 1–8, The American Institute of Architects and National Council of Architectural Registration Boards, Washington, D.C., 1981–1988.

IDP Guidelines, The American Institute of Architects and National Council of Architectural Registration Boards, Washington, D.C., annual.

W. Wiese II, "Architectural Education: Who Needs IDP?," *Architectural Record* **172**, 57–61 (May 1984).

See also American Institute of Architects (AIA); Association of Collegiate Schools of Architecture (ACSA); National Architectural Accrediting Board (NAAB); National Council of Architectural Registration Boards (NCARB); Registration Examination Process—Architects

Robert A. Rosenfeld
National Council of Architectural Registration Boards
Washington, D.C.

IRON, CAST. See Industrialized Construction (Engineered Buildings—Prefabrication)

ISAACS, REGINALD

Born in 1911 in Winnipeg, Manitoba, Canada, of Sophia Rau and Mark Isaacs, Reginald Isaacs was the second oldest of six siblings: Aurel (businessman), Charles (writer, producer), Alvin (engineer), Kenneth (psychologist), and Leone Blooston (artist). He became a U.S. citizen before 1920 when his parents became naturalized. He attended grade school in both Winnipeg and Minneapolis, Minnesota, and began his architectural career in Minneapolis as an office boy at age 14 for Jack J. Liebenberg, a 1917 graduate architect of Harvard University, Cambridge, Massachusetts, who set Isaacs on the then usual path of The University of Minnesota, Minneapolis (Bachelor of Architecture, 1935), and Harvard (Master of Architecture, 1939). In this he came under the influence of beaux-arts diplomes Leon Arnal (Minnesota) and Jean-Jacques Haffner (Harvard). He quit Harvard because of its repetition of Minnesota's beaux-arts orientation, but returned there to study under Walter Gropius and was encouraged by him toward his already chosen fields of social housing, planning, and ultimately education. Following World War II (1947–1952), Isaacs studied sociology and planning at the University of Chicago, Chicago, Illinois, under sociologist Louis Wirth and New Dealer Professor Rexford Guy Tugwell.

As an urban and regional planner, Isaacs was best known for his pioneering work in urban renewal, in community facilities planning, and health facilities and health services delivery planning. Through his planning and architectural work, he made important contributions in citizen participation and as an advocate for human rights.

Isaacs was one of the leaders of the reform movement in the housing and planning professions in the mid-twentieth century. Paramount in this movement was the concept that the planner's true client is the public that would be affected by the planner's recommendations. The previous orientation of the planner's role was parochial; it was serving the specific interest of the direct client.

By the 1930s Isaacs was interested in social housing. His interest in planning stemmed from his determination that a framework was needed to locate and program housing for moderate-income families.

Early on, Isaacs found that planning involved an educational process: educating the public as to what it should expect from the government, assisting clientele government agencies to explore how they can constructively make use of both the concerns and recommendations of the general public, and training professionals to develop individual approaches to reconciling the needs of the client and those of the public. Much of Isaacs's career as a consultant and as a teacher involved educating professionals about their responsibilities.

Isaacs started his formal career in teaching in 1950–1951 as a Visiting Critic and Lecturer in the Planning Department at Harvard's Graduate School of Design (HGSD), where he also served a two-year term as a member of the Board of Overseers Committee to HGSD (1951–1953). Then in 1953, based on Gropius's recommendation, he was named Chairman of the Department of City and Regional Planning (1953–1964) as well as Chairman of the Department of Landscape Architecture (1953–1958)(1). He became the Charles Dyer Norton Professor of Regional Planning at Harvard University (1953–1978). Isaacs's involvement with HGSD spanned nearly the entire 50 years of the school. He was named Professor Emeritus in 1978. Many of his former students remember him as a popular teacher who cared about his colleagues and students as individuals and was an advocate of citizen involvement.

Isaacs and Dean José Luis Sert brought in new staff, replacing those who left as Dean Hudnut and Gropius retired in the spring of 1953. Isaacs took the opportunity to restructure both programs and had an important role in developing the Urban Design Program with Sert.

In restructuring the Planning Department, Isaacs welded the Graduate School of Design to other Harvard graduate schools, such as the Graduate School of Public Administration and the Harvard Schools of Law and Business, by utilizing courses, professors such as John Merriam Gaus and Arthur Maas, and some of the students from these other faculties to serve the growing needs of the rapidly emerging academic field of planning. Furthermore, Isaacs also brought the land planner–landscape architect Charles Eliot, 2nd, to Harvard, strengthening both the planning program and the role of landscape architects and architects on the planning team at a time when many believed that the field was predominantly an extension of economics, sociology, or municipal finance. Isaacs's concept of planning was that a plan, by definition, included an implementable physical plan that reflected the goals and objectives of the people.

Isaacs emphasized landscape architecture as a physical planning field in which a physical plan is based on the social needs and cultural orientation of the community as well as on the physical constraints of the site. This approach was built on the unbroken heritage provided by the Olmsteds and Eliots, among others. Based on this perspective, Isaacs first recommended Walter Chambers and then Hideo Sasaki to succeed him as chairmen of the Department of Landscape Architecture. He had recommended and brought Sasaki to Harvard in 1953, and for several years they were in professional partnership with Chester Nagel in Cambridge; earlier, Isaacs and Sasaki had collaborated in Chicago.

Isaacs encouraged students from other nations and from depressed areas to make use of their short years at HGSD to concentrate on preparing to help their communities. Even in the 1980s his earlier insistence that individuals must be appropriately trained specifically to help their home community has provoked controversy. Isaacs's approach to educating those who were to return to their native lands was to emphasize their personal educational needs, which were not necessarily identical to the needs of U.S. students. Their studies were to be developed with procedures and solutions that met their legal, economic, and cultural systems.

Isaacs was also known for his pioneering work for an integrated society. Planner Francois Vigier once stated to Ann Leroyer that (2)

> Isaacs's career was distinguished by a profound commitment to social justice and the highest professional ethic. As a consultant to government as well as to medical and educational institutions, he believed that his role went beyond that of giving technical advice to including raising the conscience of his clients.

Isaacs's articles in the *Journal of Housing* in the spring of 1948 were instrumental in exposing the role that the Federal Housing Administration had in instructing developers in writing restrictive covenants (3,4).

Isaacs was Director of Planning and Development for Michael Reese Hospital (MRH) in Chicago (1945–1953) (Fig. 1), where Gropius, planner Walter Blucher, and Wirth collaborated with him as consultants. In 1944 MRH found it needed professional planning assistance to determine whether it was feasible for the hospital to stay in Chicago. Isaacs was selected for this job based on Blucher's recommendation, his experience with the Syracuse and Onondaga County, New York, Post War Planning Board under Sergei Grimm, his previous work in Chicago, and his experiences in hospital architecture in Minneapolis. His work in Syracuse was crucial in his being hired because it centered on community facilities and citizen participation (6). Grimm stated that Isaacs "practically single-handedly (did) the work on, [the] community facilities plan" for Syracuse (7).

Isaacs quickly found that the urban blight and problems that confronted MRH were too massive for the hospital alone to reconcile: the whole diverse community on the Chicago south side, an area of seven square miles, had to work together. He conceptualized and urged the creation of the South Side Planning Board (SSPB), whose executive committee was under the joint leadership of blacks and whites, public housers and real estate people, industrialists and labor leaders, and Catholic and Protestant clergy. The SSPB became the key to proper planning in Chicago's south side since it provided the forum with which to garner public input and support. Today, the continuing success

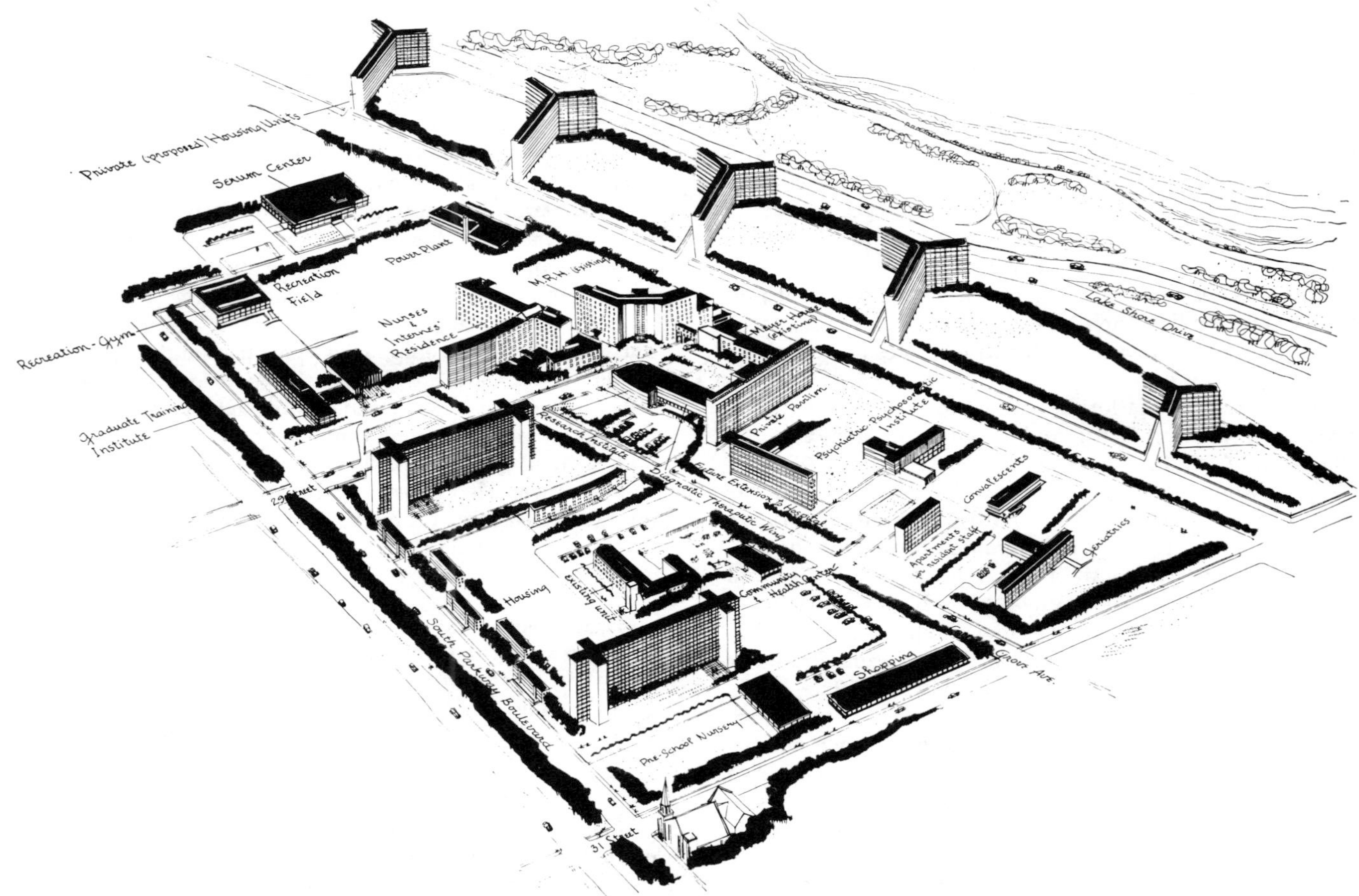

Figure 1. Perspective view of campus plan for Michael Reese Hospital (5). Courtesy of Michael Reese Hospital.

of the 1940–1950s redevelopment of the south side is contingent on the integration of its diverse population and certainly on the integrity of the SSPB (Figs. 2 and 3) (8). Originally only the energetic drive of Isaacs and the full support of MRH could encourage the participation of these diverse groups. He achieved this by assisting the individual groups to see the advantage they would have in being part of the renewal of the area. With each group's reputation riding on the success of the joint venture, the ongoing cooperation of previously diverse and separate entities became institutionalized. Many institutions and individuals were involved, including MRH, Elizabeth Woods (then Executive Director of the Chicago Housing Authority), the Illinois Institute of Technology, the New York Life Insurance Company, and Blucher (then Executive Director of the American Society of Planning officials (5).

Isaacs's colleagues and closest friends included Blucher, Wirth, Gropius, Gaus, artist Jackson Pollock, Vigier, and his siblings. Additionally, he cherished his colleagues and friends in the Caribbean and Latin America, such as planner Raphael Pico, historian Isidor Paiewonsky, and the Peruvian President, architect Fernando Belunde-Terry. Many of his students went on to succeed in furthering the goals of humankind. Their successes were Isaacs's success. He strove to further the growth of HGSD by stressing the same general goals as Gropius for teamwork.

Isaacs was an NCARB-licensed architect in several states. He lectured in universities throughout the United States, in almost every country of Central and South America, and in the Caribbean; he was Miembro Académico at the Universidad Católica in Santiago, Chile, and Visiting Professor at the University of Puerto Rico. Isaacs served on the staffs of the planning commissions of Minneapolis, Syracuse, and Chicago and in the federal government in the National Youth Agency, the Public Housing Authority, and the Housing and Home Finance Agency. His architectural practices in Minneapolis, Washington, D.C., Chicago, and other cities included the design of housing, colleges, and hospitals. He has been a United Nations expert on regional planning in South America and a consultant for the Ford Foundation; the U.S. State Department; CINVA in Bogota, Colombia; the Universidad Central in Caracas, Venezuela; and the Instituto de Planeacion, Medellin, Colombia. Isaacs consulted in Puerto Rico (1956–1971), in the U.S. Virgin Islands (1960–1972), and for

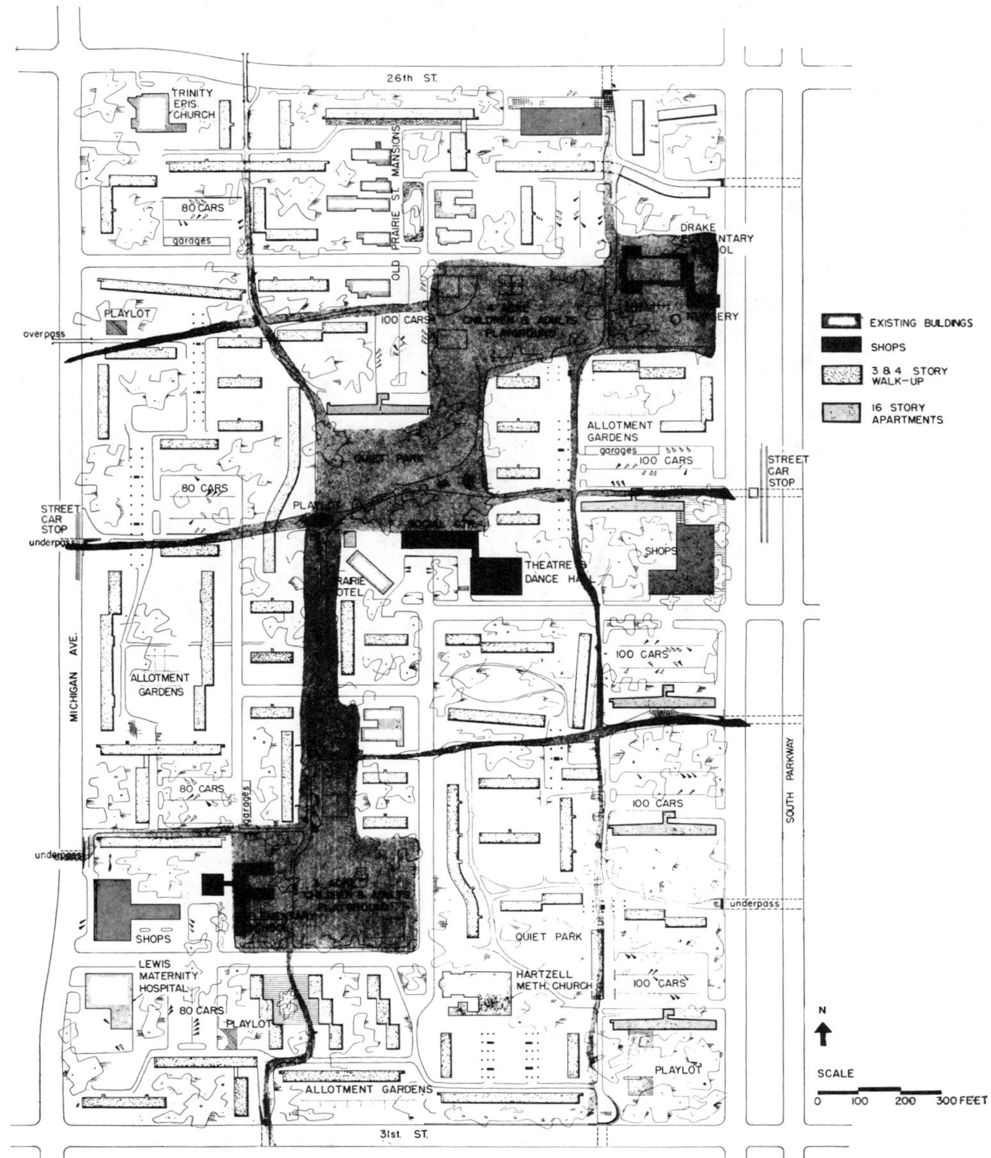

Figure 2. Bird's eye view of plan for Michael Reese Hospital contrasting existing buildings and new construction (5). Courtesy of Michael Reese Hospital.

the Gulfport Regional Planning Commission, Mississippi (1965–1976).

Isaacs's awards included Mencion Honorífica: VII Congress de Pan-Americano Arquitectos (given for Chicago South Side Redevelopment Plan); Academica de Artes y Ciencias, Honorary Member; Fellow, Royal Society of Arts (UK); Service Award, Society of American Registered Architects; Miembro Academico, Universidad Católica, Santiago; 25-year service award, Harvard; Citation, MRH; and Citation, SSPB.

Isaacs is the author or publisher of many works on planning, housing, and education and sociology published in North America, South America, and Europe. These include *Planning Primer: Children and the City* (9); *Urban Renewal Research Program, A Program of Research in Urban Renewal for the American Council to Improve Our Neighborhoods,* (10); *Comprehensive Program for the Planning of the Medical Center of Mayaquez* for the Puerto Rican Department of Health (11); and encyclopedia pieces. Isaacs also was known as the chief biographer of Gropius; two volumes of *Gropius, Der Mensch und Sein Verk* (12) were published before Isaacs's death in 1986.

Isaacs married an art student, C. Charlotte Aldes, in 1937 in Saint Paul, Minnesota. The Isaacs had three children: Merry White, Mark Aldes Isaacs, and Henry Aldes Isaacs.

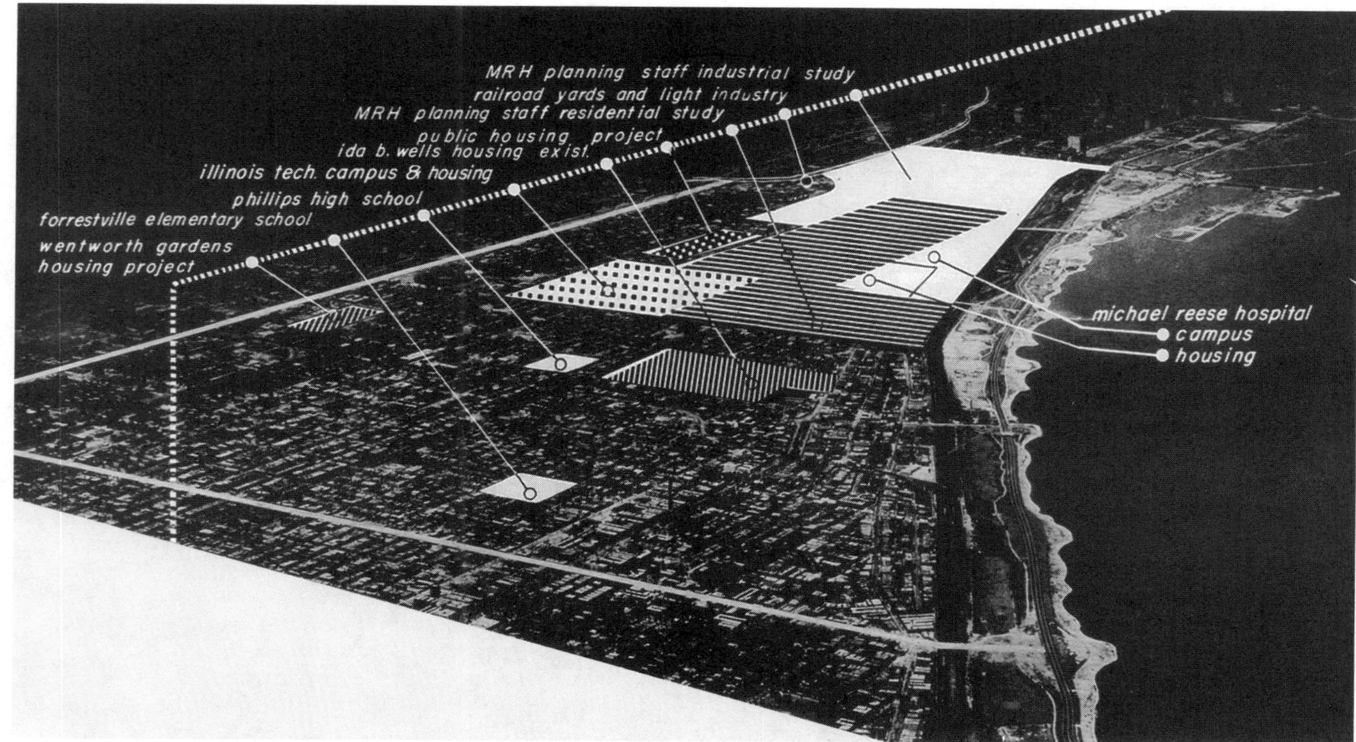

Figure 3. Redevelopment of Chicago's South Side (5). Courtesy of Michael Reese Hospital.

BIBLIOGRAPHY

1. A. Leroyer, "Reginald R. Isaacs Remembered," *GSD News* (Aug. 1986).
2. F. Vigier, private communication, Washington, D.C., Nov. 1986.
3. R. R. Isaacs, "Are Neighborhoods Possible?" *Journal of Housing* **5**(7) (July 1948).
4. R. R. Isaacs, "The 'Neighborhood Unit' Is an Instrument for Segregation," *Journal of Housing* **5**(8) (Aug. 1948).
5. Staff, Michael Reese Hospital Housing Project, "Michael Reese Hospital, Seven Square Miles of Chicago Slums Are Scheduled for Redevelopment Under a Unique Planning Program Sponsored by Michael Reese Hospital," *Architectural Forum* (Sept. 1946).
6. W. H. Blucher, private communication, Washington, D.C., 1984.
7. S. Grimm, G. Greer, and co-workers, "Syracuse Plans Its Future," in *Planning, 1944,* American Society of Planning Officials, Chicago, Ill., 1944.
8. R. Isaacs, W. Blucher, and co-workers, *An Opportunity for Private and Public Investment in Rebuilding Chicago,* Michael Reese Hospital; Illinois Institute of Technology; South Side Planning Board; Metropolitan Housing Council; Pace Associates, Architects; and Chicago Housing Authority, Chicago, Ill., 1947.
9. O. Adams, *Planning Primer: Children and the City,* Reginald R. Isaacs, Chicago, Ill., 1952.
10. R. R. Isaacs, W. H. Blucher, J. M. Ducey, M. Meyerson, and J. M. Siegel, *Urban Renewal Research Program, A Program of Research in Urban Renewal for the American Council to Improve Our Neighborhoods,* ACTION, Inc., New York, Nov. 1954.
11. R. R. Isaacs, C. Lavandero, H. Sasaki, and co-workers, *Comprehensive Program for the Planning of the Medical Center of Mayaquez, Puerto Rico,* 4 vols., Associated Consultants, Cambridge, Mass., and San Juan, Puerto Rico, Apr. 1961.
12. R. R. Isaacs, *Gropius, Der Mensch und Sein Verk,* 2 vols., Gebr. Mann Verlag GmbH & Co. Kg, Berlin, 1983 and 1984.

General References

L. Freeman, *Hospital in Action: The Story of the Michael Reese Medical Center,* Rand McNally and Co., New York, 1956, pp. 207–219.

J. Dyckman and R. R. Isaacs, *Capital Requirements for Urban Development and Renewal,* McGraw-Hill Inc., New York, 1961.

R. R. Isaacs, *Metropolitan Area Planning for Northeastern Illinois and Northwestern Indiana,* Metropolitan Housing and Planning Council, Chicago, Ill., 1965.

Mark Isaacs
Alexandria, Virginia

ISLAMIC ARCHITECTURE AND URBANISM

Many people have preconceived ideas about Islamic architecture as consisting of a distinctive style. Much has been written on the development, spread, and qualities of this style, and it is suggested that the reader refer to the bibliography for information of that kind. It is more appropriate in this encyclopedic context to discuss the essential underlying factors that have shaped the traditional built environment in Islamic culture. Therefore, this article is not about style, nor about buildings in isolation. It is, instead, about the interaction of societal values—which in Islamic culture are directly rooted in religion—with decision making, the production process, and the resulting built form. The context of the discussion is holistic, beyond the building scale, to produce a clear understanding of the relationship of the part to the whole, the building to its immediate surroundings and to the urban scale. An understanding of the reciprocal effects of the overall built environment and the various levels of the environment, down to single buildings and their design, is crucial to a comprehension of architecture in the context of Islamic culture.

The levels of the environment to be stressed are the city, neighborhood, clusters of buildings, and the single building. That order is not always critical to the following discussions, but the relationship between levels should be kept in mind, particularly when trying to interrelate the impact of values underlying decision making and the nature of the production and construction processes. Thus, a clear understanding of the overall system that prevailed in traditional Islamic societies, as well as the changes that have occurred in contemporary times, is fundamental.

The first part of the article is a discussion of the traditional system that produced the built environment, and is followed by a survey of the changes that have occurred in contemporary times, using the case of Saudi Arabia as a focus for discussion to illuminate why most contemporary urbanism and architecture produced in the Islamic countries cannot be described as Islamic. The third part discusses ways of learning from the past and recycling the traditional experience toward the goal of reestablishing authenticity and identity for contemporary and future architecture in Islamic countries.

THE TRADITIONAL SETTING

Pre-Islamic settlement patterns, building typologies, construction techniques, and related decision-making processes influenced the emergent pattern of built form in Islamic cultures. One of the verses in the *Quran,* the holy book of Islam, is interpreted by some Muslim scholars as an instruction to accept local traditions and conventions, provided they do not contravene Islamic values, ethics, or codes. The *Quran* is considered by Muslims to be the word of God as revealed to the Prophet Mohammed. The applicable verse (from Surah, or chapter, 7 titled Al-A'raf, verse number 199) uses the Arabic term *urf* to refer to an established local tradition for how something is to be done.

From the sketchy evidence available, the predominant pattern of settlement in Medina, the city in Arabia where the Prophet Mohammed chose to settle during the last decade of his life, was similar to the ancient Mesopotamian model of clustered courtyard buildings (1). Evidence of this tradition dates back to about 2500 B.C. in towns such as Ur, an ancient city in Southern Mesopotamia, (now contemporary Iraq). Archaeological digs in Ur were undertaken by the architect–archaeologist Leonard Woolley in the late 1920s; his findings were published in the early 1930s (2). Part of Woolley's discovery was the *Omen Text,* which contains various omens, some relating to building design; these may reflect some of the values of the people of that ancient time. Consider the following examples.

> If a house blocks the main street in its building, the owners of the house will die; if a home overshadows or obstructs the side of the main street, the heart of the dweller in that house will not be glad.
>
> If the water in the court runs to the back, expense will be continual; if the water in the court runs to the middle of the court, that man will have wealth.

Woolley published portions of the plan of Ur. Figure 1 reproduces a segment, along with, for comparative purposes, part of the plan of Tunis Medina as documented in the 1960s. Contemplation of the complex plan pattern raises the question of how the common wall problems were addressed and resolved. Later it will be shown how this and other problems related to this pattern and type of construction were addressed by Islamic law. Pre-Islamic legal precedents seem to have existed, as evidenced by the work of some scholars (3,4).

After these brief notes on the pre-Islamic pattern, consider now the system of building and urbanism as it evolved in Islamic culture. Islam was proclaimed by the Prophet Mohammed soon after 610 A.D. in Makkah, 450 km (280 mi) south of Medina, where the Prophet finally settled in 622 A.D. That date represents year 1 of the Islamic calendar.

The next decade in Medina, which came under the guidance and leadership of the Prophet, is considered very important as a source of example and precedent for all aspects of Islamic community living, including building. A number of cases are recorded of the Prophet's attitude to specific problems related to building activity. This is also true of the caliphs who succeeded him, including Omar bin Al-Khattab, the second caliph, who ruled during the period 634 to 644 A.D. This guidance concerning building proved to be particularly crucial for the Maliki School of Law, which evolved under Malik ben Anas (712–795 A.D.), who lived all his life in Medina and whose followers live to this day in the maghreb countries of Libya, Tunisia, Algeria, Morocco, and also in Andalusia on the Iberian peninsula until the early 1500s.

During the first three centuries of Islam, a number of schools of thought and approaches to law were formulated. Under the Sunni branch of Islam, the survivors today are grouped into four schools: Hanafi, Maliki, Shafi'i, and Hanbali. Followers of Sunni Islam constitute the majority in the Muslim world, although in Iran, parts of Iraq, and some communites in Syria and Lebanon, the people are followers of Shi'ism and have their own school of law. It is important to note that the legal differences about building are minor, and result from different interpretations by the various schools of law. Thus, the discussion based on the Maliki School in North Africa would largely hold true for other regions of the Muslim world.

Eighty-three years after the Prophet's death on June 8, 632, Islam already encompassed a vast territory stretch-

Figure 1. Portions from the cities of **(a)** Ur (2000 B.C.) in southern Mesopotamia, now Iraq (2); and **(b)** Tunis Medina in Tunisia in 1960s A.D., reproduced to the same scale and compass orientation (3). The predominant use in these plans is housing. The plan from Tunis Medina is based on sources dating from the mid-1920s to the mid-1960s, as compiled by the author.

ing from the shores of the Atlantic Ocean and the Pyrenees to the borders of China—an area greater than Rome's at its zenith. This was achieved under the leadership of Abd al-Malik (685–705 A.D.) from his seat in Damascus, and his four sons who succeeded him.

Across this vast geographic area, three factors influenced the nature of building and planning as it evolved within the framework of Islamic civilization. First, the urban models of pre-Islamic cultures and civilizations in territories converted to Islam influenced the evolution of the structure and form of subsequent Islamic cities. This was particularly true in the region known as the Fertile Crescent and in Iran. Second, the camel was the primary means of transportation, predominating in the Middle East between the fourth and sixth centuries A.D. (5). This important and often forgotten factor had a major impact on the street system and urban form of the Islamic city. Finally, the location of most territories of the Islamic world between latitudes 10 and 40°, and the resulting similarity in macroclimatic conditions, contributed toward certain unifying influences in building practice.

Some historians agree that three discernible urban models evolved within the framework of Islamic civilization. These are the renewed or remodeled pre-Islamic city; the planned and designed city; and the spontaneously created and incrementally grown city.

The renewed city is found most often in previously held Roman territories, and is exemplified by Damascus and Aleppo. Earlier structures and configurations were altered to suit the social requirements of the Muslim community. The pre-Islamic Southwest Arabian model of isolated multistory structures, such as Sana'a and particularly prevalent in Yemen, is also classified under this model grouping. Research is required to determine why this type did not spread beyond the few localities in which it arose.

The second type of city was preplanned and designed by Muslim rulers to be the capital of a dynasty or, more typically, as the seat of a palace complex and its related facilities. A prime example of a city constructed as a complete entity was the original round city of Baghdad, while Al-Abbasiyah, south of present Kairouan, was a palace complex; neither survives today. The model influencing the plan and design of this second type of city can generally be identified by the geographic location. In the case of the *mashreq* (eastern regions), pre-Islamic models had a distinct influence, whereas in the *maghreb* (western regions), the influences on the ruler and his experiences determined the model and approach followed. After the collapse of a dynasty, the tradition was to abandon this type of city or palace complex, with the result that today they remain as ruins or are completely obliterated and require restoration by archaeologists.

The third model of the Islamic city proved to be the most enduring and pervasive, and today most of the older areas of capitals and major towns in the Muslim world evolved out of this model (Figs. 2 and 3). The best examples of the old quarters or *medina* survive in the maghreb countries, but in some instances are severely threatened today by the automobile.

Although the organizational principles of this model predate Islam by at least 2500 years and were particularly common in southern Mesopotamia, the strength, characteristics, and longevity of this city type reflect the manner in which building activity was pursued in Islamic society. The initial model for this building process occurred in Medina since the Prophet's arrival there in 622 A.D. Note

Figure 2. Oblique air photo of the central portion of Fez in Morocco. The main mosque of the city and the adjacent *suq* (market) is on the upper right. Photograph by Papini, M. H. A. T., Rabat.

that this article focuses on this predominant model, found most often in the maghreb countries, and built under the guidance of the Maliki school of law.

Viewing the city as a process and a product is an effective analytical–evaluation and planning tool, and is indispensable for the study of the Islamic city. The process encompasses the decision making in building activity as guided by Islamic values. Looking at the city as a product clarifies how a complex, heterogeneous, and sophisticated built form is achievable with a simple set of physical organizational components, and a related mechanism of verbal communication used in building decisions. The essential urban elements are the courtyard building, the street system, and the elements above the street.

The Courtyard Building. This is the basic module used for housing and public buildings. The ratio of building area to plot is 1:1 (Fig. 1). In housing, the courtyard takes up approximately 24% of the ground coverage, and the building is one, two, or occasionally three stories in height. Public buildings differ in their ratio of courtyard size to ground coverage, and the height is one story, as in mosques, but frequently is two stories, as in a *funduk* or *khan* (hostels for merchants). It should be noted that the Prophet affirmed the use of this plan type by building his mosque–residence soon after his arrival in Medina in the form of a square courtyard structure.

The Street System. Street systems are primarily of two types: the through, open-ended street, which was considered a public right of way and had to be wide enough for two packed camels to pass; and the cul-de-sac which, according to Islamic law, is considered to be the private property of the people living on it.

Figure 3. Vertical air photo of a portion of old Unayzah, located in the north central region of Saudi Arabia. The large building is one of the mosques in the city, surrounded by housing. Courtesy of Ministry of Petroleum and Mineral Resources, Saudi Arabia.

Elements Above the Street. The elements usually found above the street were a *sabat,* a room actually bridging the street, and the buttressing arches spanning between walls on either side of the street to provide structural strength and support (Fig. 4).

In addition to this basically simple set of organizational elements, the Islamic city evolved a sophisticated communication system in the form of a language or vocabulary of building design that operated at all scales of the built environment. At the scale of the city, it identified urban elements such as building types, public squares, and other uses. At the building scale, it identified spatial configurations and related uses, as well as details of construction, decoration, and symbolic motifs. An important attribute of this language was that it integrated a physical component's form and function into its name. This vocabulary was known and popular among most segments of society involved in building activity, and it was an effective communication device between users and builders. Regional variations in the design vocabulary existed, but the language was unified by the similarity of the built form and its constituents.

The process can best be appreciated by viewing the dynamics of building decision making as affecting two scales of the city: citywide and neighborhood. Decisions about the citywide scale were usually made by the ruler or government; they concerned the birth, growth, and revitalization of a city, and would include the location of the

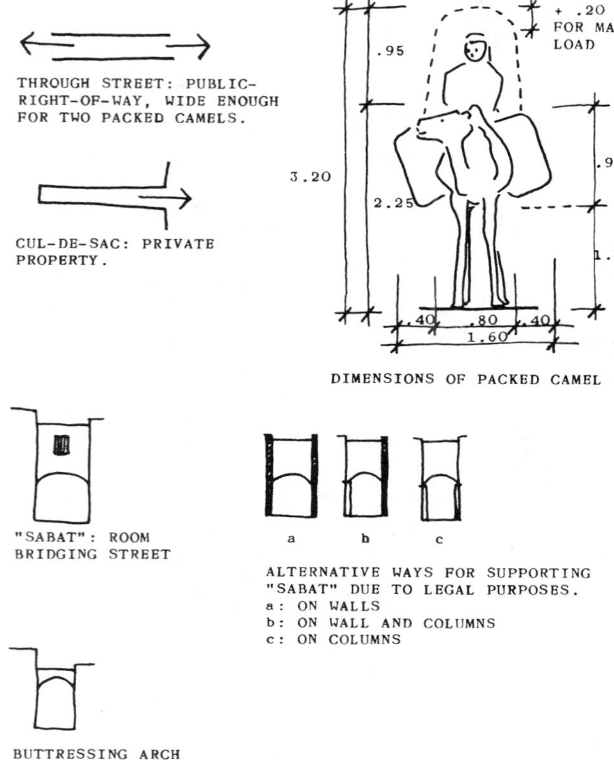

Figure 4. The street and its primary elements (3,6).

primary mosque; the distribution of the land in the projected boundaries of the city to various ethnic, familial, or tribal affiliations; and the location and configuration of the city's gates and walls. All of these are the result of decisions taken in the first few years of a city's founding.

Other typical primary decisions occurring during a city's growth involved the building of major public buildings such as mosques and public baths, or the location of new cemeteries. Revitalization activity often took place under the leadership of ambitious rulers and governments during eras marked by security and prosperity. Site conditions and the location of determining factors, such as water and natural features useful for defensive purposes, had an impact on macro decision making and, hence, the resulting urban form.

The dynamics of decisions made at the neighborhood scale tended to be of a different nature and the results were of immediate significance. The effect on urban form of numerous micro decisions by citizens of a neighborhood was indirect and usually obvious only on an aggregate basis, whereas the results of the larger decisions by rulers—such as the location of major mosques, the *suq* (market) and its configurations, and important industries—tended to be individually discernible.

Building decisions at the neighborhood scale had an impact on both the initiator and on immediate neighbors. Building activity and decisions involve the relationships and interdependence of people, and more specifically neighbors; such activity was therefore the concern of Islamic law. The development of guidelines for neighborhood building activity became the concern of the science of *fiqh* from its very early development.

Fiqh is the Arabic term for jurisprudence, or the science of religious law in Islam. It concerns itself with two spheres of activity: *ibadat,* dealing with matters concerning ritual observances; and *muamalat,* the legal questions that arise in social life (e.g., family law, law of inheritance, of property, of contracts, criminal law, etc.), and problems arising from building activity and related procedures. The latter were viewed by the fiqh in the same light as other problems resulting from human activities and interaction. In essence, therefore, fiqh is the science of laws based on religion and is concerned with all aspects of public and private life and business.

The bulk of the knowledge developed by the fiqh for most aspects of human relationships, including those of building activity, appeared in the first 300 years of Islam, although subsequent generations developed and refined it. The source of most guidelines stemmed from Quranic values and from the *Hadith* which are the sayings and tradition of the Prophet particularly during the decade of his leadership and rule in Medina. (The term *sunnah* is more commonly used to mean the total traditions of the Prophet, including his deeds and life-style, as well as his sayings). Note that the recorded nature of most guidelines in the fiqh literature is implicit in the numerous cases also recorded which include the judgments of local *kadis* (judges), and the opinions of *muftis* (specialists on the law who can give authoritative opinions on points of doctrine).

A set of guidelines documented in the literature of the Maliki school of law are identified and discussed elsewhere (6). Examples follow.

- Avoid harm to others and oneself.
- Accept the concept of interdependence.
- Respect the privacy of the private domain of others, particularly avoiding the creation of direct visual corridors.
- Respect the rights of original or earlier usage.
- Respect the rights of building higher within one's air space.
- Respect property of others.
- The rights of preemption by adjacent neighbors.
- Seven cubits as the minimum width of public through-streets (to allow two fully loaded camels to pass).
- Avoid locating the sources of unpleasant smells and noisy activities adjacent or near to mosques.

In addition, other guidelines operate as a self-regulating mechanism on the behavior of the individual and community. A prime example is the concept of beauty without arrogance, which strongly influenced the manner in which exterior facades and elevations were regarded and treated. This concept is attributed directly to the Prophet Mohammed in the form of the saying, "No person with an atom of arrogance in his heart will enter paradise." According to Muslim, the renowned Hadith scholar, a man said: "A person likes to wear good clothes and shoes." The Prophet answered: "God is beautiful and He loves beauty" (Fig.

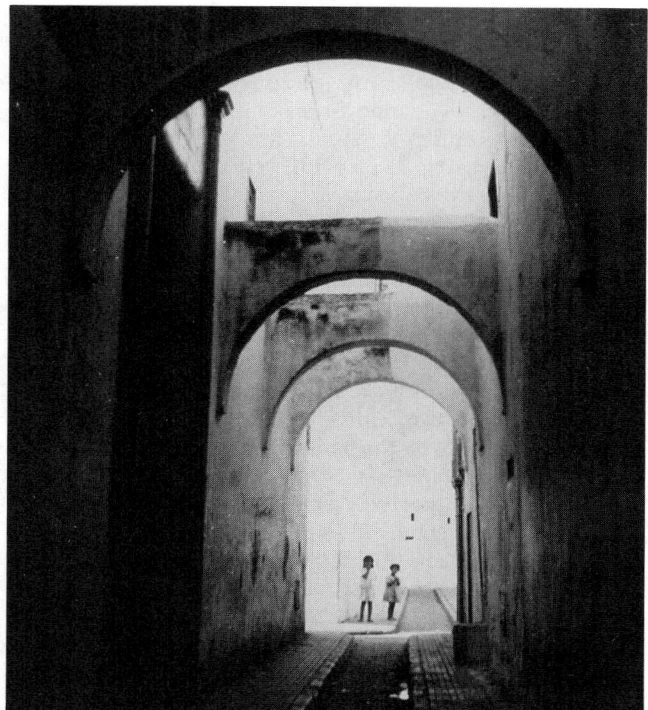

Figure 5. A residential street in the city of Rabat, Morocco, showing blank exterior walls and buttressing arches. Photograph by Papini, M. H. A. T., Rabat.

5). By tradition, and allowing for beauty without arrogance, an owner was permitted to decorate only the front door of a building, to express his attitudes and identity (Fig. 6). In contrast, the interiors of buildings were decorated, particularly the facades of the courtyard. The sophistication or level of such decoration depended on the financial ability and taste of the owner (Fig. 7).

Quranic verses and sayings of the Prophet used as the source for building guidelines can be found elsewhere (6). In most cases these verses and sayings were specifically pointed out by the author of a fiqh manuscript to back up or elaborate on the reasons and rationale behind a kadi's decision or an opinion of a mufti. A mufti is a specialist on law who can give an authoritative opinion on points of doctrine; his considered legal opinion is called *fatwa*.

To appreciate the interaction between the mechanisms of the building process, consider the following simulation, which includes one example for each component of a five-part framework devised here to represent the physical factors that shaped the traditional Islamic city, particularly at its neighborhood scale. (This framework encompasses all building activity issues touched on in the fiqh literature of the Maliki school of law.) The components are: (*1*) streets, including through streets and cul-de-sacs, and related elements; (*2*) locational restrictions of uses causing harm, such as smoke, offensive odor, and noise; (*3*) overlooking elements, including visual corridors generated by doors, window openings, and heights; (*4*) walls between neighbors, and their rights of ownership and usage; and (*5*) drainage of rain and waste water.

Imagine that a man wants to build on a vacant lot or

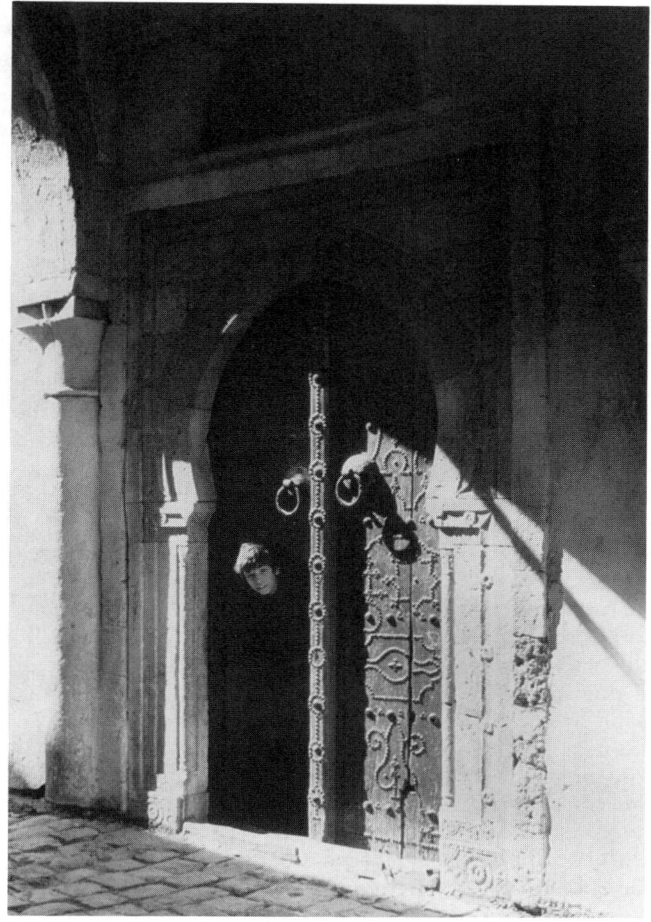

Figure 6. A typical front door to a medium-size, middle-class house in Tunis. Note the studded decoration, knockers, and small inset door for daily and frequent use. Photograph by the author, 1977.

Figure 7. Typical decorated courtyard of a palace in Tunis. Taken in the main courtyard of the restored Dar Lasram palace. Photograph by Wisam Hakim, 1975.

to reuse a site on which a dilapidated house stands. If the intention is to rebuild a structure for the same use, then he can proceed with no objections; if the plan is to build a public bath or bakery, however, then he will more than likely be faced with objections from the neighbors. The reasons given are that such new public uses will create harm in three ways; (*1*) by generating additional traffic on the street(s) providing access to the facility, thus causing the people living nearby to have to adjust to this new condition; (*2*) by the nuisance of the smoke generated; and (*3*) by diminishing the value of the adjacent houses because of the impending adjacent public uses and the nuisances that will result.

Two frequently cited sources supporting these complaints are used by the *fuqaha* (plural of *feqih,* a jurisprudence scholar), for preventing the change in use. The Quran says: "And diminish not the goods of the people, and do not mischief in the earth working corruption" (26:183). From the sayings of the Prophet comes: "Do not harm others or yourself, and others should not harm you or themselves" (cited by Ahmad and Ibn Majah).

After exploring other uses of the site, the owner decides to build a house. He asks a local builder to construct it; the two will communicate with each other about the design requirements by using the local design language. This is done by identifying each part according to its name in the design language. To illustrate, examples from the local language in the Tunis region are used: the owner requires one *skifa* (entrance lobby with entry doors placed so that no one can see directly into the courtyard from the outside), with two *dukkana* facing each other (built-in benches provided in the skifa, traditionally used by the male owner or occupant to receive casual visitors or salesmen). He specifies that the *wust al-dar* (open courtyard in the center of the house) should have under it a *majin* (cistern for the collection of rainwater from the roofs), and one *burtal* (a colonnaded gallery off the courtyard giving importance and sometimes sun protection to the room behind) off the main room. Around the courtyard he asks the builder for three *bit trida* (simple rooms) and one *bit bel-kbu u mkasar* (a primary room common in middle- and upper-middle-class houses), which is usually located opposite the entrance to the court. This primary room is divided into (*1*) a central alcove called a *kbu,* usually containing built-in seating and elaborate wall and ceiling decorations, and used to receive close relatives and friends; (*2*) two small rooms symmetrically located on each side of the kbu called *maqsura,* and used as bedrooms; and (*3*) two alcoves, constructed opposite each other, with built-in beds and/or storage. The built-in beds could be placed on one or both sides of the alcove, and are usually framed with a decorative wooden structure called *hanut hajjam.* This listing could continue on to the smallest details of decoration and finishes (Fig. 8).

If the house is relatively complex, then the builder will more than likely sketch out the plan and any other details, but for his own use and not to communicate with the owner. When the design language is not adequate for both owner and builder to clarify a point, then either one, but more commonly the owner, takes the other to see a house to indicate what he has in mind.

The builder is expected to know about the customs and traditions of building practice and the principles to be followed and respected. Surprisingly, the detailed implications of the building guidelines were not common knowledge among the lower ranks of builders. Often, references are made in ancient manuscripts to implemented building decisions that were violations and were later ordered by the local kadi to be demolished or corrected in response to a neighbor's complaints. It seems, however, that the more established and older builders with many years of experience, who were often hired by affluent clients, had detailed insights.

Having determined the usage of the site and using the

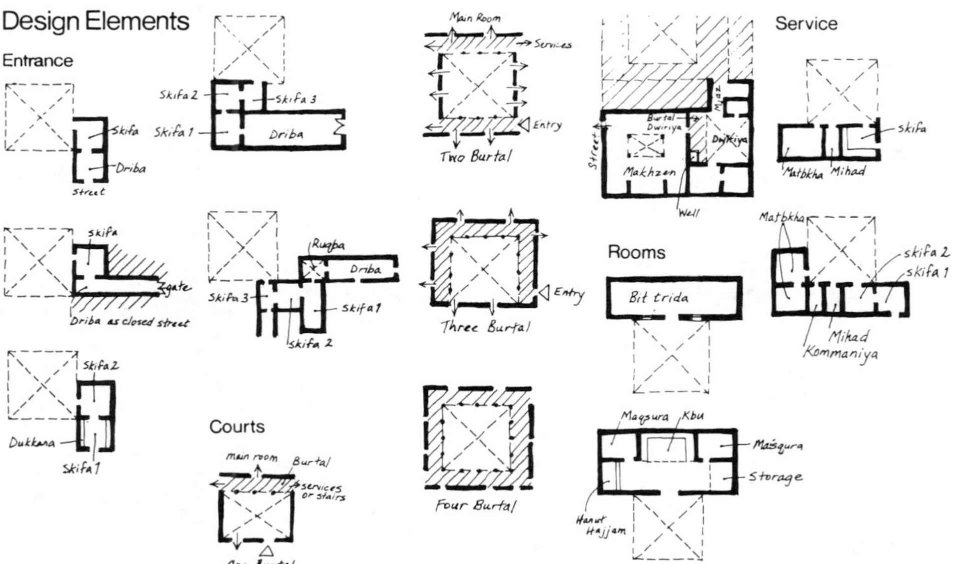

Figure 8. Examples of traditional housing design elements and their associated vocabulary, or design language, from the Tunis region (7).

design language for planning purposes, the builder and owner examine the likely effects on their requirements and decisions of existing surrounding buildings. If a window exists on one of the neighbor's walls, for example, then its location had to be considered out of the respect due to the principle of the earlier rights of usage. The new house had to avoid creating a direct visual corridor from the existing window into its private domain; in effect it had to block potential overlooking problems.

A neighbor's wall could be used, however, to insert beams for support, rather than building another, adjacent wall. This practice was specifically encouraged by the Prophet: "A neighbor should not forbid his neighbor to insert wooden beams in his wall" (cited by Abu Hurairah). Nonetheless, there were elaborate guidelines to be respected in using a neighbor's wall, and the associated problems of subsequent maintenance rights. For example, the ratio of the wall to be used depended on its ownership. In the case of rebuilding a dilapidated house, correct identification of the ownership of adjacent walls was therefore crucial. Careful examination of the wall was guided by criteria that determined whether ownership was single or joint. The most common of these criteria was to discover the nature of the *akd* or wall bond at the corners or junction of two walls, by examining the materials and mortar to resolve whether the two walls were built together. This practice, which was sanctioned by the Prophet, is traceable to the decade of 622–632 A.D. in Medina, and is still followed today in the older parts of Islamic cities under the local customary law, or urf.

The question of drainage of rain and waste water also had to follow certain rules and guidelines. Drainage of rainwater was a particularly delicate problem because excess water was not to be barred from others. This principle is directly attributed to two sayings of the Prophet: "If you deny excess water, you will deny the benefits of pasture" (cited by Abu Hurairah), and "Muslims are partners in three things: water, pasture, and fire" (cited by Abu Dawood and Ibn Majah via Ibn Abbas).

As to the relationship of houses to streets, assume that one side of a house adjoins a through street, and the owner wants more space. One option is to build a sabat (room bridging the street). To support the structure on the opposite side the owner could acquire permission from the owner of the facing building, but the granting of such permission was not totally irrevocable and thus this alternative depended on the owner's perception of his future relationship with his opposite neighbor. More than likely the owner would choose to use columns for support, keeping the owner totally independent of his neighbor. Another option would be to use columns for supporting both sides, opening up the future possibility of being able to sell the sabat to the owner of the opposite building, and generally upgrading the marketability of the house (Fig. 4).

The preceding illustrations provide only an overview of the issues involved in the typical building process. Many other cases, some of them extremely involved, may be found elsewhere (6). This discussion is adequate, however, to illuminate the fact that the built form was a direct outcome of the dynamics of decision making, using specific mechanisms, and as governed by fiqh guidelines derived from the Islamic values embodied in the *Quran* and the *Hadith*.

THE CONTEMPORARY SITUATION

In most Islamic countries major changes have resulted in a shift from the traditional system of construction and design to a contemporary, so-called modern system. Background, forces of change, and motivation differed from country to country, but in most instances change was the direct result of the intervention and influence of non-Muslim colonial powers, primarily the British, French, and Italians. This coincided with the introduction of contemporary technology in transportation and construction, and new building materials. Planning patterns and architectural styles introduced by these colonial powers came to be models to be emulated. The notion was that the use of modern technologies and materials meant also employing the colonials' system of planning and design. Western ideas and techniques for dealing with land subdivision, the distribution of buildings, and their design were synonymous with modernism and progress.

Unfortunately, well-documented cases of the architectural transformations of various Islamic countries is scarce, but it is very clear that, despite the differences and discrepancies in the processes of change, remarkable similarities are manifest in the end result, the contemporary built environment. To understand this phenomenon, a brief description follows of the changes that have occurred in Saudi Arabia over the last three decades.

Saudi Arabia is a mashreq country, historically considered to be part of the eastern region of the Islamic world, as opposed to the maghreb countries, those in the western region whose traditional system was the basis of the discussion above. Although the Islamic schools of law in effect in the two regions are distinct (the Maliki in North Africa, and the Hanbali in Saudi Arabia), these and other schools of law traditionally shared more similarities than differences in matters related to cities and building. The regions' historical continuity in legal matters is supported by a comparison of the traditional morphology in North Africa with that found in central and eastern Saudi Arabia.

The case of Saudi Arabia is interesting for a number of reasons (1,8,9):

1. The country was not under colonial rule by non-Muslims. Parts of the country, primarily the Hijaz (the western region bordering on the Red Sea) and for shorter periods Al-Hasa (in the east, bordering the Arabian Gulf), were under Islamic Ottoman Turkish rule, during which time the traditional Islamic system of building and planning continued without change.
2. The changes that occurred later were primarily instigated by the Saudis themselves, with the clear objective of creating a modern built environment, as a result of a rapid shift in the perception of what a new, good, built environment should be and how it should look. This perception was diametrically op-

posed to that produced by traditional settlements and their architecture.

3. Reliable information, including three valuable doctoral dissertations, is available on the changes in Saudi Arabia. The information in the second part of this article relies, to a large extent, on these sources.

Underlying the changes in Saudi Arabia's built environment was the introduction of the grid as a street pattern and of the villa as a dwelling type. Following is a brief description of how they were introduced in Saudi Arabia and the process by which they were developed and institutionalized.

The Introduction of the Grid Pattern

In the Eastern Province of Saudi Arabia, the development of the cities of Dammam and Al-Khobar resulted from the expansion and growth of the oil industry. The Arabian–American Oil Company (ARAMCO) played a major role in the planning and development of these two cities, as well as other communities (1,8,9).

The initial growth of Dammam and Al-Khobar in the late 1930s and early 1940s was not planned in an orderly fashion. As the population grew, people took over any available land and erected basic shelters and fences from local materials. Following the traditional pattern, streets were narrow and irregular. When the physical development of the two towns increased substantially in the mid 1940s, the government felt they needed to be laid out in a controlled way. In 1947, the governor of the Eastern Province therefore requested assistance from the oil company in producing layouts for both Dammam and Al-Khobar. In response, ARAMCO's surveyors prepared land subdivision plans and actually staked out the streets and blocks. Original plans, covering only limited areas, were laid out in a gridiron pattern. For information on historical developments, see Ref. 10 (Fig. 9).

When Dammam was made the provincial capital of the Eastern Province, the pressure for development increased. Government offices moved from the old capital

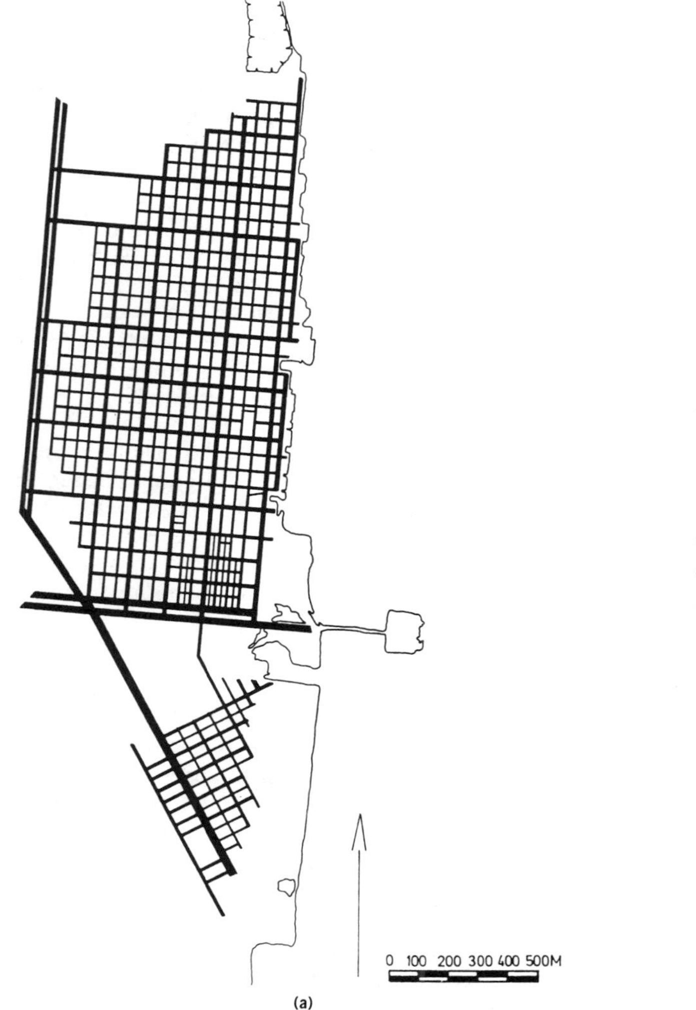

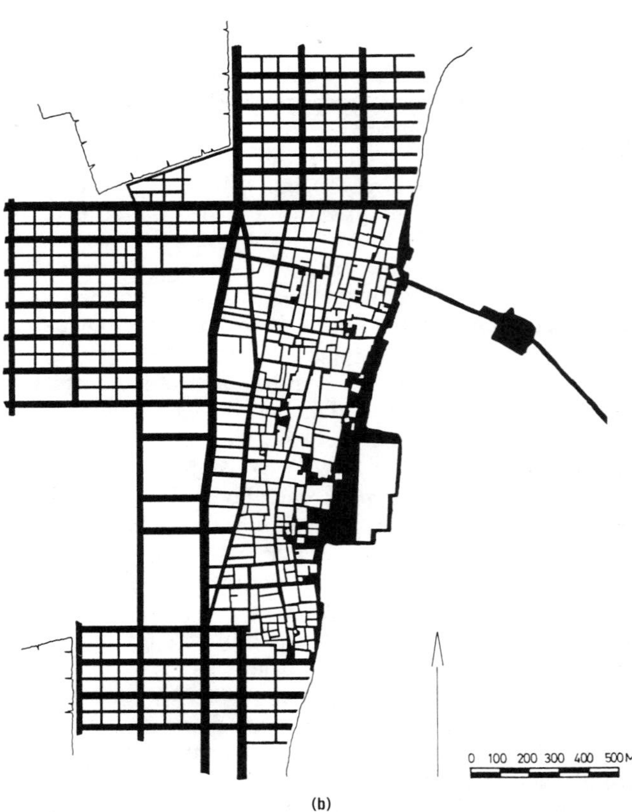

Figure 9. Road network of Al-Khobar (left) and Dammam (right) on the eastern coast of Saudi Arabia. The sketches are based on information from the decade 1956–1966 (8).

of Hofuf in 1952; by the end of that year, Dammam comprised 525 acres, plus the 400 acres of ARAMCO's subdivided plan, and its population was 25,000 (10). Engineers then engaged by ARAMCO to develop their own communities were made available to local government agencies. These engineers, in cooperation with the municipality of Dammam, developed a major street plan for the city that is still being followed today. They also developed a layout scheme for another 1000 acres, which were subdivided and sold off by the municipality of Dammam. Subsequent subdivided areas were laid out by the municipality following the earlier gridiron layout—in some areas only roughly, but in others with precisely the same dimensions (10).

Similar techniques were used in ARAMCO's planning and layout of Al-Khobar; the city was taken as a model of modern planning for many years, and its planning established numerous unfortunate precedents. Al-Khobar was the first Saudi Arabian community to be wholly planned, and to use an overall grid plan. It was also the first to start the demolition process of the traditional fabric within its boundaries. For other reasons as well (8), it led the way as a model that other Saudi cities followed from the 1950s through the 1970s (Fig. 9).

Riyadh, the capital of Saudi Arabia, was founded on the ruins of several communities around 1740, but assumed little prominence until Abdul-Aziz Al-Saud took over as its independent governor in 1902 and began his campaign for the consolidation of modern Saudi Arabia. From that time, Riyadh was the permanent residence of the king and it also eventually became the capital of the kingdom, although Makkah, the religious capital, continued to house most government agencies until the 1950s (11).

Riyadh preserved its size during the first 30 years of Abdul-Aziz's reign. Only after the consolidation of the kingdom, however, did the king himself in the 1930s take first steps toward developing the city, which involved the construction of a number of projects outside the city core. One of the prominent later developments that had profound impact on the city is a housing complex known as Al-Malaz built in the late 1950s.

When the government decided in 1953 to move its agencies from Makkah to Riyadh and, subsequently, to build ministries along the road to the city airport, housing for the transferred government employees became necessary. The site of Al-Malaz, 4.5 km northeast of the city center, was chosen and the housing project was initiated by the Ministry of Finance. The ministry was assisted by the U.S. Corps of Engineers in the planning and design of Al-Malaz (9). In 1957, when the transfer of the agencies actually took place, the project was under way and some parts had been completed. The project consisted of 754 detached dwelling units, or villas, and 180 apartment units in three apartment buildings; the houses were sold to employees under a long-term payment plan, while the apartments were rented on a permanent basis.

Al-Malaz contained a public garden, a municipal hall, and a public library. It also housed the buildings, originally planned as schools, for the newly founded university. It also had a race course, a football field, and a public zoo; supporting facilities such as schools, markets, and clinics were planned, although they were built by agencies other than the finance ministry.

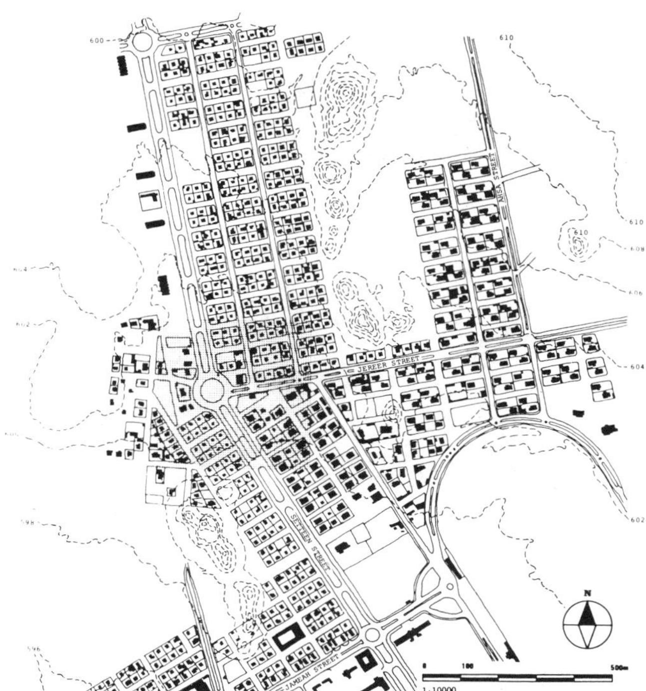

Figure 10. The layout of Al-Malaz, Riyadh. Located approximately three kilometers northeast of the CBD. The grid pattern predominates. Most blocks are 100 × 50 m and lot sizes have a standard depth of 25 m and a variety of widths: 25, 37, 40, and 50 m (14).

The physical organization of Al-Malaz follows a gridiron plan with a hierarchy of streets, rectangular blocks, and large lots, which in most cases take a square shape. Thoroughfares are 30 m wide, main streets 20 m, and secondary or access streets 10 and 15 m. A 60-m boulevard divided the project into two parts. Most blocks are 100 × 50 m. The typical lot size is 25 × 25 m, but within some blocks there are a variety of widths, such as 25 m, 37.5 m, and 50 m. The depth of 25 m, however, remains constant in almost all blocks.

Comparing the new and traditional patterns, reproduced to the same scale in Figures 10 and 11, it is clear that new values in the concept of space and land use were introduced at Al-Malaz. The new pattern has a low density, one-fifth the traditional density; areas assigned to streets are three times as great, and only half of the area of the development is reserved for private lots, as compared to more than 75% in the traditional pattern.

Al-Malaz covers an area of 500 hectares and its impact on Riyadh was enormous: it was seen as a city by itself, a new town in town, and thus named New Riyadh. The project's introduction of new patterns and typologies meant the grid as a street pattern and the villa as the new house type became powerful models for the developments of the 1960s and 1970s in every Saudi Arabian city and town.

Al-Malaz became a model reproduced in later developments for three main reasons. First, the project was sponsored by the government, and was a governmental state-

Figure 11. Al-Dira, a portion of the old city of Riyadh, Saudi Arabia. Note the traditional pattern of urbanism and recent vehicular roads cutting through the traditional urban tissue (14).

ment on how a modern neighborhood should be planned. It was taken for granted by others that what is good and suitable for Riyadh must be good for other cities in the country. Second, Al-Malaz was seen as a symbol of modernity, in sharp contrast to the traditional. It was the only project at that time to use new materials and techniques, hence its subsequent imitation. Finally, in contrast to royal residences built shortly before it, Al-Malaz was constructed for government employees who were part of the public. In the 1950s and early 1960s, these employees were highly regarded by other segments of society, and their life-style admired. Almost everyone dreamed of settling into a new and similarly planned neighborhood. Riyadh now covers an area of more than 300 km^2 with an estimated density of 50 persons per hectare. Almost all of this area follows the grid pattern and has the villa as its dominant building type.

Land Subdivision: Lots and Villas

The ARAMCO Home Ownership Plan, a loan program initiated in 1951 (12,15), played a major role in spreading the concept of the dwelling as a detached building, and determining the subdivision of land. Under the program, the government provided the land, either as a grant or for a nominal price passed on to the employees, and ARAMCO undertook the planning and subdivision. ARAMCO also gave employees interest-free loans, the terms of which stated that the employees could choose their own designs and contractors.

To qualify for the loan, an employee had to submit a design for the house, that was to be implemented precisely, without any major changes. Due to a lack of Saudi architects at that time, employees had to rely on foreign ARAMCO architects. Employees could choose from a catalog of designs, which reflected the alien cultures and tastes of the designers. According to statistics gathered in the early 1970s, 15–25% of the houses in most Eastern Province cities are of this catalog type (13,16). Subdivision of land, whether in Dammam, Al-Khobar, or other communities, consisted of lot sizes ranging from 400 to 900 m^2, which is very large compared to traditional lot sizes. These lots tended to be roughly square in shape, and the villas planted in the middle of each (Fig. 12).

Again, the Al-Malaz project and the ARAMCO Home Ownership Plan set up the pattern and shape of lots, introduced the villa as the favored house type, and became models for other developments. In fact, as early as 1938 in some cases, these models were institutionalized by the government: the square lot through decrees, directives, and circulars, and the villa through zoning regulations and related setback requirements, all of which were legitimized later by master plans that incorporated these implementation devices.

The Process of Psychological Institutionalization

Government media played an important promotional role in influencing attitudes toward the models of planning and design being introduced. This promotion occurred primarily through the press, various other publications, and broadcasting, although television was not operational nationally as an effective medium until the early 1970s. Dialogue in the media was not possible, however, because of

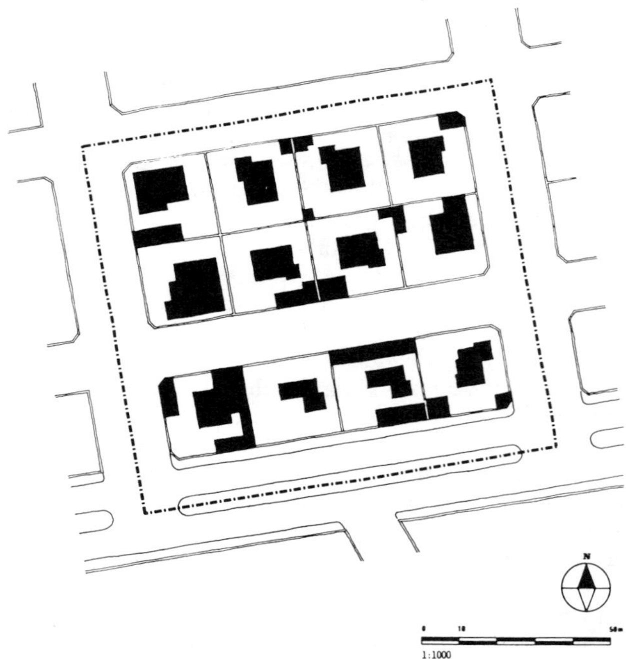

Figure 12. Two typical blocks from the Al-Malaz district in Riyadh, Saudi Arabia. The square lot 25 × 25 m; later 20 × 20 m became predominant in Saudi Arabia due to its institutionalization by the government through decrees, directives, and circulars. The villa is planted in its midst through setback requirements (14).

an unwritten code forbidding criticism of the government (9).

Implementation then followed with the adoption of the system of land subdivision and related building regulations. An important note regarding cultural conditioning: It could not be expected that a conservative government and system such as that of Saudi Arabia would openly express enthusiasm for practices of Western civilization. In fact, almost all official statements for major projects or development policies stressed the conformity of the goals and policies to Islamic law and the society's cultural heritage. On the other hand, terms such as *tammadon* (civilization), *al-tatawr al-mimmari* (architectural progress), *al-imarah al-muaasirah* (contemporary architecture), and *al-taqaddom* (modernization and progress) are among the many terms used to raise the general level of aspiration and to provide a climate for national development. By associating such terms with the actual architecture and planning built and practiced in the country, there is no doubt as to the Western models to which such terms refer.

It is not surprising that Saudi Arabia, a culture that strongly adheres to Islamic traditions, has in fact, through certain events and processes, rejected the established, traditional, building and planning conventions that had strong ties to Islamic law. As a result of the prototypes initiated by the government (with the assistance of ARAMCO in the Eastern Province, the U.S. Corps of Engineers in Riyadh, and reinforced by a concerted media campaign), traditional building practices, associated forms and configurations, and traditional materials such as adobe were soon viewed by most people as substandard, and the new building conventions implemented by new technologies as superstandard (17). A rejection of tradition resulted. Accordingly, a questionable side effect was that a concern with tradition was posited firmly against opportunities in all-or-nothing terms, without selective consideration of how new technology, building materials, and patterns of land use might be adjusted and molded to suit established conventions rooted in the society's religion and values (18).

The scale of contemporary developments coupled with the centralization of authority and decision-making processes also had a major impact on the abandonment of the traditional system. Traditional environments had grown incrementally, over relatively adequate periods of time; the decision-making processes were decentralized. That is, the owners of property and their project builders were directly involved in the day-to-day decision making and monitoring of the building as it took shape. Another factor in the eyes of contemporary government officials and their Western consultants was the apparent inadequacy of traditional practices in coping with large-scale modern building projects, which were to be built in very short periods of time. (The experience of Turkey in the nineteenth and early twentieth centuries is illuminating for an understanding of similar changes and attitudes (19).) This was certainly not true for housing projects, yet housing also did not benefit from traditional practices, as these projects followed similar processes of implementation.

Centralization of decision making in almost all contemporary projects in Saudi Arabia meant that determinations about the configurations of large-scale developments were made by a very small group on behalf of many, and in the absence of a known user group (20). In housing projects, this contrasted with the traditional system, in which decisions were made by owners and builders, in which neighbors were considered, and in which modifications took place through an incremental, decentralized system.

Two studies document in detail the implementation devices and procedures used by the government in Saudi Arabia to institutionalize the contemporary Western system using the grid pattern, villas, apartment and other building types, and the distribution of these citywide (1,9). Among the devices was the drawing up of master plans, notably the plan undertaken by Doxiadis Associates for Riyadh. Statutes and other regulations are other devices that have had an impact: these include the statutes of the Makkah municipality, the Roads and Buildings Statutes, regulations pertaining to apartment buildings, and the specific zoning regulation introduced by the Doxiadis master plan of Riyadh in the 1970s. This was followed by zoning regulations proposed by the new master plan for Riyadh by SCET International in the 1980s. These proposed regulations, particularly those related to the protection of visual privacy in housing areas, are specifically worked out to suit the cultural requirements of an Arab–Islamic city (21). An evaluation of their effectiveness, assuming that they have been adopted and implemented, should stress that specific legal and implementation devices must be compatible with the values of the people for whom they are intended.

LEARNING FROM THE PAST

It has now been seen how the traditional system produced environments compatible with people's values and culture, so that the resulting built environment could be described as directly influenced and molded by Islamic culture. In contrast, contemporary events, such as those in Saudi Arabia, have created a situation that precludes a linkage between people's values and design and the resulting built form.

An attempt will be made now to indicate ways in which it might be possible to recycle and reintroduce traditional experiences into contemporary building and planning activities in many Islamic countries. The goal is to re-establish cultural aspirations and identity in the built environment produced today and in the future. The lessons and experiences to examine for possible recycling and emulation are grouped in two areas: those related to procedure, and those directly related to the organizational system of planning, design, and morphology.

Lessons Derived from the Procedures of Building

These lessons can be grouped into the following categories: impact of decisions by the governing authority; how Islamic a traditional city is, as was made possible by the role of the *fiqh* and its special attributes; and the principles that governed the building production process.

The Impact of Decisions by Governing Authorities. Traditionally, the decisions of the governing authority always had an important effect on the location of important buildings and the alignment of primary streets, thus establishing the overall framework of the city. It should be noted, however, that these decisions were made within an established framework of design norms and planning–organizational relationships. Historically, these were influenced by cultural values and unified by similar approaches arising from the exchange of knowledge among Islamic regions.

Decisions by today's governments in the Islamic countries have even more impact, but are usually based on proposals and recommendations developed by foreign consultants. The input from these consultants for the most part ignores or is insensitive to local traditions and trends; foreign prototypes are usually imposed without consideration of cultural norms and values. In some cases this has been due to specific instructions from a client or his representative to ignore traditional architecture. The problem of outside influence is compounded by the fact that various regions of the Islamic world today are aligned to different foreign countries or systems, thus complicating city planning and building. For example, in Tunisia, Algeria, and Morocco, the French approach is followed; in Libya and, until recently, Egypt, the Soviet approach; and in Saudi Arabia the influence comes from the United States. In Iraq and the gulf states, the British approach seems to be predominant.

As has been seen in the focus on housing, the traditional experience and its decentralized decision-making processes offered many positives. Yet most contemporary housing is produced as a result of decisions from the top, as opposed to grass roots decisions, and requirements drawn up without apparent consideration of the culture's Islamic values and its deep-rooted intentions. Even the design requirements that are linked to loans and mortgages preclude design preferences and significant alterations by users. Thus, the role of the individual in shaping his house and immediate environment in cooperation with neighbors is virtually eliminated—a situation diametrically opposed to that of the Islamic past.

The findings by many researchers and housing specialists in many countries concerning the significance and positive attributes of grass roots housing decisions support the urgency of changing implementation strategies in this area.

The Traditional Islamic City and the Role of the Fiqh. The nature of the fiqh guidelines and their application depended on intent and/or performance, and not on prescriptive standards. Thus people in the traditional setting involved in building decision-making operated within a flexible framework of performance criteria. Each design situation could be resolved according to the conditions in the specific locality and the requirements of the people concerned. As long as the intent of the guidelines was met, the peculiar configurations of the solution would be acceptable. This approach directly influenced the three-dimensional outcome and quality of the built environment.

The earlier, brief discussion of the fiqh influence on traditional settlements raises a central question: how can the link be made between the fiqh and contemporary activities of building and urbanization? In many Islamic countries today, particularly since the introduction of the automobile and Western techniques of city planning, urbanization activities have gradually become detached from the traditional umbrella of the fiqh and the urf. The ignorance of foreign consultants and even government officials in Islamic countries about the deep-rootedness of Islamic values in the traditional processes of building activities is compounded by the quasi-technical nature of master planning and architectural design packaging. In short, what has happened, and is continuing, is the implantation of an alien approach, the generally gradual, but occasionally sudden, displacement of traditional practices legitimized by the policies of modernization.

This displacement occurred at various times in different places during the nineteenth and twentieth centuries, depending on when European influence or colonization occurred. Design decisions based on quasi-technical regulations came into conflict with traditional law. In certain cases, the municipal technical code allowed a situation that the *sharia* (religious) court later rejected (1). The dislocation of the fiqh from building and urbanization activities in the name of modernization is now gradually being recognized as inappropriate. The challenge and task for the future is to reintegrate the fiqh into building and planning, which can be accelerated when adequate new approaches are developed by interdisciplinary teams of fuqaha and those involved in urbanization and building. It is encouraging to see the recent interest in building topics by fiqh graduate students in Saudi Arabia (22,23). It should be possible to externalize Islamic values in contemporary and future architecture; the results would be exciting and unpredictable, with potential for unique models and approaches.

The Production Process. The traditional building and urban production process in Islamic cultures is markedly different from that followed today, as the example of Saudi Arabia illustrates. Effectively, what has occurred in Saudi Arabia and most other Islamic countries is the abandonment of principles and practices of production that ensured quality in the built environment and the adoption of processes that render it impossible to achieve what Christopher Alexander describes as the "quality without a name" (24). Alexander has pointed out that (25):

> The production system which we have at present defines a pattern of control which makes it almost impossible for things to be done carefully or appropriately because, almost without exception, decisions are in the wrong hands, decisions are being made at levels far removed from the immediate concrete places where they have impact . . . and, all in all, there is a colossal mismatch between the organization of the decision and control and the needs for appropriateness and good adaptation which the biological reality of the housing system actually requires.

Alexander goes on to identify seven principles that "are essential to the production of houses under all circumstances, and must be followed, whether other necessary social changes are made or not" (26).

Indeed, the traditional production process followed in most Islamic cultures over a period of more than 1000 years in large part embodied these principles. They can be reintroduced effectively in the contemporary production of houses. The initiative in the centralized and autocratic systems of government operational in most Islamic countries today must come from the responsible government agencies and their local representatives. Essentially, they must create situations in which it will be possible to recycle and reintroduce an age-old and successful tradition of production.

Lessons Derived from the Organizational System and Built Form

These lessons can be grouped under three categories: compatibility with ecology and climate; organizational system and planning; and architectural design, style, and decoration.

Compatibility with Ecology and Climate. Much has been written about the traditional use of natural building materials, cooling and heating devices, and the environmental attributes of compact courtyard housing (27–29). These historically were used extensively in the Middle East, as were specialized facilities such as the natural ice-maker. These all provide excellent precedents and impetus for contemporary designers in an approach to building and community design that is passive, that relies minimally on mechanical devices for cooling and heating and uses the least possible energy and other resources for manufacturing materials and production.

Contemporary literature on the Islamic tradition of landscaping, its approach and foundations in the culture's value system can help lead landscape designers to a sensitive understanding and appreciation of the deep-rooted Islamic structure, its rationale, and ultimate manifestation in built form that is essential for intelligent recycling (30).

Organizational System and Planning. A study of aerial photographs of traditional towns and villages reveals the astonishing similarity in organization and clustering across the vast territory of the Islamic world. Although security and defense were major determinants in maintaining the compactness of towns and in surrounding them with walls, it is in the use of land and the three-dimensional distribution of space that the interesting lessons lie for architects and planners. The residential and commercial sectors contain the most relevant lessons.

Design and configuration are essential features of the typical unit in the residential sector. Rooms surround a courtyard open to the sky, with almost all windows open onto this interior court. The structure has one or two stories, and sometimes a basement for summer use in regions such as Iraq and Iran. In other regions, such as Tunisia, a cistern is built under the court to collect winter rainwater for year-round household use.

Clusters of houses are created by adjoining homes; at least three external walls of each house abut other houses. Access to these clusters is by narrow cul-de-sacs that branch off from a network of through streets. The cul-de-sacs are owned and maintained by the people who use them and are regarded as private property. Occasionally, rooms bridge the public through streets, usually to create extra space in a dwelling. Often, these rooms link two properties owned by the same family, but that are across the street from each other.

There are many benefits to this form of residential design and organization. The courtyard floor and earth beneath it act as a combined radiating and storage unit. The walls on four sides shade the court and protect it from direct sunlight during the greater part of the day, particularly if the height of the walls is greater than the width of the courtyard in the direction of the sun. The courtyard floor, however, is left open to the sky (the zenith) for heat radiation during the day and particularly during the night. The earth beneath the court acts as a radiating heat sink, which in turn attracts more heat from surrounding areas in contact with it (27).

In addition, this form of housing provides high standards of privacy and security within a physical setting, which can promote neighborly social interaction among the occupants. The clustering of housing is economical because most external walls are shared. There are, of course, alternative technical solutions to these party walls that can solve problems of ownership, maintenance, acoustics, and fire. This housing form provides medium densities of between 11 and 14 units per acre, yet provides large living areas in each unit: from 1345 to 1840 ft^2 for a single-story house, to 2690 and up to 3680 ft^2 for a two-story house. These figures were based on a prototype design the author developed. On average, the courtyard house creates 45% more living area than that provided in the typical tract-built single family house in the United States, yet achieves three times the density.

As for the commercial sector, the central market or shopping center of each traditional Islamic city is composed of a web of covered pedestrian malls called *suq* in Arabic, *bazar* in Farsi, and *carsi* in Turkish. Each mall is composed of repetitive cells opposite each other and separated by a 10–20-ft walkway covered by vaults with skylights at intervals, creating pleasant and cool environments for shopping. Security during nights and holidays is easily maintained by locking gates strategically located at entry points to the mall system. Typically, various other facilities adjoining the web of market malls are all linked together by an overall access system. The mosque is usually in this area, as are the public bath, hotels, individual workshops, and storage facilities for the various shop owners (Fig. 13).

Architectural Design, Style, and Decoration. Much has been published in the West about Islamic architecture and decoration. For the purpose of this article, the issue to be addressed is how traditional building design, including its technologies, can prove to be of relevance to contemporary and future building activities. Since the early 1970s, a growing interest in tradition and historical precedents has been evident among architects in many countries, particularly in the United States. Clients have also been sympathetic and receptive. In some Islamic countries, particu-

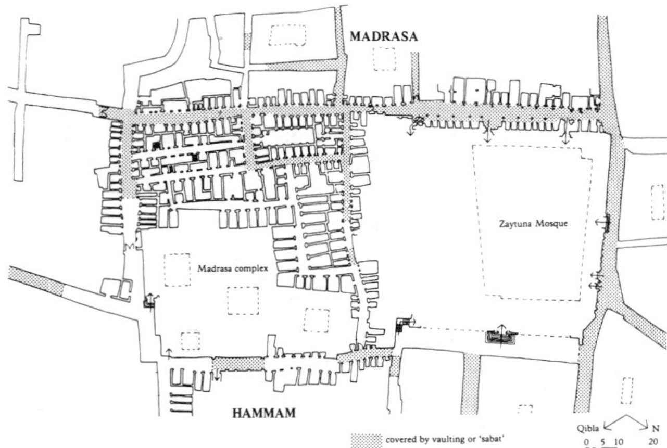

Figure 13. The area of the *suq* south of the main Zaytuna Mosque in Tunis. Note the manner in which the shops are inset on the west and south sides of the mosque, and on the north and west sides of the Madrasa complex. The tinted areas of the access system represent covering by vaulting or *sabat,* a room bridging over the street (6).

larly in Iraq, this was certainly evident a decade earlier. A number of Iraqi architects experimented by using traditional motifs in contemporary design and architecture. Mohammed Makiya, Kahtan Madfai, Rifaat Chadirji, and the late Kahtan Awni, all of Baghdad, Iraq, were probably the most serious in the pursuit of this approach since the early 1960s (Fig. 14).

Departure from the strict doctrines of the modern movement in architecture faced much opposition and criticism; nevertheless, the trend toward linkages with the past continues to fill a vacuum that contemporary architectural design, following the ideology of the modern movement, is unable to fill. In the Islamic countries, as well as in other cultures, the need for expressing local cultural identity through architecture is growing stronger. The question of how this ought to be done without creating superficial results remains paramount. Moreover, the problem of contemporary and future building types without historical precedents, such as office buildings, airports, and bus terminals, requires careful study in terms of recycling traditional architectonic and decorative elements.

Figure 14. An early example of the work of Dr. M. Makiya of Baghdad, Iraq. This building is the Rafidain Branch Bank in Kufa, Iraq. Designed in the late 1950s and completed in 1968. The historic city of Kufa contains some of the finest brick buildings in Iraq, which has provided a source of inspiration. The walls appear as massive units emphasizing solidity and security, with the windows deeply recessed for shade. The recessed arch treatment is reminiscent of dome squinches found in early Islamic architecture. They provide a powerful formal element in the facade enhancing the solidity of the walls. Courtesy of Makiya Associates Consultants, Ltd., London.

Once again, the impact of decisions by governing authorities, which is the first issue related to building procedures, requires serious consideration at the policy level both by national governments and in local-level jurisdictions. Also an important issue is whether or not to reapply the fiqh in planning and building activities. There is today much discussion and awareness of the government's role, but less of the fiqh's, primarily due to the lack of knowledge of traditional practice. Both issues, however, will continue to grow in importance.

The question of decision making within a framework of performance criteria, addressed in the discussion of the second issue, is the responsibility of government agencies and the architect. The implementation of performance regulations in lieu of Western-style prescriptive standards will require, in some instances, sophistication that might not be available in certain countries or localities. It is, however, the responsibility of government, as the primary client in most Islamic countries today, to instruct local or foreign consultants who are retained to develop such mechanisms of control. This is true despite the fact that most contemporary structures and sectors of the city were built using the typical mechanisms of zoning and other prescriptive types of regulations. It is not too late to convert the system to performance-based mechanisms of control.

The third issue concerning the production process might be more difficult to implement, as centralized authorities are reluctant to create situations in which their influence is reduced. It is, however, possible for a government to help initiate an appropriate process on an experimental basis.

The scale of the first project(s) might be small, in order to monitor the results and ensure success. Hope of success rests in the time when powerful individuals in some Islamic countries realize that decentralization will enhance the chances of achieving a contemporary equivalent of genuine Islamic architecture and urbanism.

These three issues encompass most of the deep-rooted programmatic, production modes and ideologically based sources for recycling tradition in contemporary and future Islamic environments. The traditional organizational system and built form offer lessons on ecological and climatic compatibility, the nature of planning and physical organization, and architectural design and decoration. Broken down further, the lessons cover planning, function, space, technology, building materials, problems of style, image making, and the meaning of the architecture produced, which are the concerns that are most difficult to handle. Yet, these are not ungraspable if intelligently approached from the careful understanding of traditional experience.

History and tradition do provide a fertile base from which to learn and, when necessary, from which to recycle experiences of process and built form. The matrix of experiences are numerous and at different levels, however. Some cannot be recycled without a total commitment at the policy level by government; others are recyclable at the cluster or building scale with few participants and decision makers involved. Contemporary examples of the latter can be found that use partial aspects of traditional experience. In other words, only a very small segment of the wide spectrum provided by history has so far been used, most of it unsuccessfully. Much must yet be accomplished.

CONCLUSION

The case of the traditional Islamic city as discussed in the first part of this article provides numerous critical lessons (6). Obviously the fields of architecture and urban planning would be the ones most concerned with this knowledge, particularly as it relates to their respective values and theories. In addition, those involved in the creation and delivery of housing will also find these lessons important.

The traditional system of building and urban activities was an incremental and constantly rebalanced process of development involving the synthesis of religious and sociocultural conventions. The system was self-regulating, so that any significant departure or contravention of the principles and conventions created a situation where corrective action had to be undertaken; in the absence of such action, the intervention of the Kadi (local judge) provided the prescription for normalizing the conflict within the system, in line with the established norms and principles operational in the community.

Specifically, three experiences are valuable to the contemporary context. The first is the importance of the legal framework as the prime shaper of the urban environment, particularly environments at the scale of the neighborhood. Certainly this is also true today with zoning ordinances, subdivision regulations, and building codes. However, the nature of the legal framework is where the Islamic city can provide new experience and insight. The fiqh building guidelines were derived from societal values based on religious beliefs and were supported by adequate elaboration of the intent of each principle. Specific numerical prescriptions were not indicated and only rarely cited as an example of how a specific problem ought to be resolved. In essence, the guidelines functioned as performance criteria, as opposed to contemporary building and planning laws, which are based on standards. The former is qualitative, intent oriented, and responsive to changes in requirements or site conditions, whereas the latter is quantitative, numerically oriented, and not suitable to changes in requirements or location. Not only is the performance criteria approach more sophisticated in terms of addressing each building problem within its own context, but the aggregate results it helps to create as built environment are various and complex. Laws based on standards address all problems uniformly, with results of monotony and sameness in the built environment. The best examples are the thousands of suburbs which were developed in the West during the twentieth century and particularly since World War II.

The second lesson is the use of a building "design language" as a communication and design decision-making aid. The components of the language integrate the three-dimensional form and function of the design element being communicated. This mechanism helps the user and builder to communicate with each other. It also preserves and perpetuates design configurations and forms which have proved their durability through experience without hindering diversity in the individual design solution. Recent research in architecture is rediscovering this attribute.

The third primary lesson is in the nature of the physical organization. As mentioned earlier, the system of courtyard buildings serviced by cul-de-sacs and through streets pre-date Islam; however, Islamic civilization developed and refined this system and spread it across a vast geographic area, aided by the simultaneous development and acquisition of fiqh knowledge.

Some highlights of the attributes of this organizational system follow. The courtyard plan form is able to accommodate diverse uses. The densities created in housing are efficient without sacrificing the privacy of the individual unit. Streets as an access network are maximally utilized, as in the central portion of Tunis Medina. All streets take up 12.5% of the gross built up area and only 13.3% of those are cul-de-sacs serving 28.5% of all buildings, i.e. a relatively low proportion of cul-de-sacs serving a high proportion of buildings. Sabats (rooms over streets) are used to create extra space for private users, simultaneously providing cover to the public in the streets. In the central portion of Tunis Medina, 8% of all streets are covered by sabats, in addition to 7.5% covered by vaulting, providing coverage to a total of 15.5% of the city's streets.

There are numerous attributes in addition to those mentioned above, such as the use and details of decoration and ornament in the realm of art. Another important attribute which has received some attention before is the energy saving attributes of the built form within an arid region context, aided by energy saving practices and devices such as the wind tower, air vent, cisterns for storing water and keeping it cool, and the ice maker (28). Other practices were the collection and storage of rain water in cisterns under the courtyard of buildings, the effective use of basements as living quarters during the hot season, and the recycling of building materials.

In the second part of the article it is shown that a new, foreign system was introduced and adopted under the notion and aspiration of modernism. This modern system is based on preconceived prescriptive standards conceived and based on experiences of other cultures whose values are different from the local culture importing the system. The organizational nature of the system is legitimized by master plans and related zoning regulations. These regulations prescribe street widths, setback requirements, densities, building heights, lot sizes, and so on. They are designed to tell people what to do, thus inhibiting flexibility, responsiveness, and sometimes innovation in response to specific local constraints and conditions. In contrast, the traditional system allows for variety and innovation in response to specific local conditions of the built environment. The contemporary prescriptive system allows only for what is prescribed regardless of the unique requirements of the locality and site, thus promoting sameness, repetitiveness, and monotony. This explains the contrast in quality between traditional and contemporary sectors of Islamic cities, particularly those found in North Africa where the modern European sector was built adjacent to the medinas or traditional towns, such as in Tunis, Rabat and others.

In Learning from the Past, the possibilities of recycling aspects of the traditional experience for improving contemporary and future architecture and urbanism were examined. Although the discussion addressed Islamic environments, there are universal benefits; it is hoped that the value of this information will be of interest and use to peoples of other cultures today and in the future (31).

Amos Rapoport clearly points out the relevance and importance of this information, when he says (31):

> The broader our sample in space and time, the more likely we are to see regularities in apparent chaos, as well as to understand better those differences that are significant. Thus, the more likely we are to see patterns and relationships, and these are the most significant things for which to look. Being able to establish the presence of such patterns may help us deal with the problem of constancy and change. . . . It is very important to understand constancies as well as change, since our culture stresses change to an inordinate degree. Also, if apparent change and variability are an expression of invariant processes, this is extremely important because the reasons for doing apparently different things remain the same.

BIBLIOGRAPHY

1. S. A. Al-Hathloul, *Tradition, Continuity and Change in the Physical Environment: The Arab-Muslim City,* Ph.D. dissertation, Massachusetts Institute of Technology, Cambridge, Mass., 1981.
2. *The Antiquaries Journal* **XI** (4) (October 1931).
3. G. R. Driver and J. C. Miles, eds., *Babylonian Laws, Vol. 1: Legal Commentary,* Oxford University Press, London, 1952.
4. B. S. Hakim, "Arab-Islamic Urban Structure," *The Arabian Journal for Science and Engineering* **7**(2), 72 (April 1982).
5. R. W. Bulliet, *The Camel and the Wheel,* Harvard University Press, Cambridge, Mass., 1975.
6. B. S. Hakim, *Arabic-Islamic Cities: Building and Planning Principles,* KPI/Routledge and Kegan Paul, London, 1986.
7. B. S. Hakim, ed., *Sidi Bou Sa'id-Tunisia: A Study in Structure and Form,* Technical University of Nova Scotia, Halifax, Canada, 1978. Reprints available from University Microfilm International, Ann Arbor, Mich., and London, United Kingdom.
8. C. P. Winterhalter, *Indigenous Housing Patterns and Design Principles in the Eastern Province of Saudi Arabia,* dissertation for D. Tech. Sci., Swiss Federal Institute of Technology, Zurich, 1981.
9. Y. M. O. Fadan, *The Development of Contemporary Housing in Saudi Arabia [1950–1983]: A Study in Cross-Cultural Influence Under Conditions of Rapid Change,* Ph.D. Dissertation, Massachusetts Institute of Technology, Cambridge, Mass., 1983.
10. S. G. Shiber, "Report on City Growth in the Eastern Province, Saudi Arabia," *Recent Arab City Growth,* Kuwait Government Printing Press, Kuwait, 1970.
11. H. al-Jasir, *Madinat al-Riyadh Abr Atwar al-Tarikh,* Dar al-Yamamah, Riyadh, 1966.
12. *ARAMCO Handbook,* Oil and the Middle East, Arabian-American Oil Company, Dhahran, 1968.
13. *Eastern Region Plan, Existing Conditions,* Candilis, Metra Int., Dammam, June 1974.
14. S. al-Hathloul, M. al-Hussayen, and A. Shuaibi, *Urban Land Utilization, Case Study: Riyadh, Saudi Arabia,* Urban Settlement Design Program, Massachusetts Institute of Technology, 1975.
15. Ref. 1, p. 166.
16. Ref. 1, p. 167.
17. B. S. Hakim and P. G. Rowe, two articles, "The Representation of Values in Traditional and Contemporary Islamic Cities," *Journal of Architectural Education* **36** (4), 26 (Summer 1983). (The reference is to Rowe's article subtitled "Contemporary Developments in Saudi Arabia.")
18. *Ibid.,* p. 26.
19. Y. Yavus and S. Ozkan, "The Final Years of the Ottoman Empire," Chapter 2 in R. Holod and A. Evin, eds., *Modern Turkish Architecture,* University of Pennsylvania Press, 1984.
20. Ref. 17, p. 27.
21. "Technical Report No. 9 of SCET International/SEDES," in *Riyadh Action Master Plans,* Technical Reports Nos. 1–17, May 1977–March 1980.
22. S. al-Tuwaijri, *Haqq al-Irtifag,* Ph.D. dissertation, Um al-Qura University, Makkah, 1982. Deals with traditional building practices.
23. I. al-Fayez, *Al-Bina wa Ahkamahu fi al-Fiqh al-Islami,* Ph.D. dissertation, Higher Institute for Law, University of Ibn Saud al-Islamiyah, Riyadh, 1986. Deals with laws of building in Islamic fiqh.
24. C. Alexander, *The Timeless Way of Building,* Oxford University Press, New York, 1979.
25. C. Alexander et al, *The Production of Houses,* Oxford University Press, New York, 1985, p. 40.
26. *Ibid.,* pp. 48–49.
27. D. Dunham, "The Courtyard House as a Temperature Regulator," *The New Scientist,* 663–666 (September 1960).
28. M. N. Bahadori, "Passive Cooling Systems in Iranian Architecture," *Scientific American,* 144–154 (February 1978).
29. M. Danby, F. Moore, and S. Roaf in A. Germen, ed., *Islamic Architecture and Urbanism,* College of Architecture and Planning, King Faisal University, Dammam, Saudi Arabia, 1983.
30. O. Llewellyn, "Shari'ah Values Pertaining to Landscape Planning and Design," and S. Lesiuk, "Landscape Planning for Energy Conservation Design in the Middle East," in A. Germen, ed., *Islamic Architecture and Urbanism,* College of Architecture and Planning, King Faisal University, Dammam, Saudi Arabia, 1983.
31. A. Rapoport, "Cultural Origins of Architecture," in J. C. Snyder and A. J. Catanese, eds., *Introduction to Architecture,* McGraw-Hill Book Co., New York, 1979, Chapt. 1, p. 18.

General References

R. Holod and D. Rastorfer, eds., *Architecture & Community: Building in the Islamic World Today,* Aperture, Millerton, New York, 1983.

I. Serageldin and S. el-Sadek, eds., *The Arab City: Its Character and Islamic Cultural Heritage,* a collection of papers from a symposium held in Medina, Saudi Arabia, March 1981, Arab Urban Development Institute, Riyadh, Saudi Arabia, 1982.

E. Beazley and M. Harverson, *Living with the Desert: Working Buildings of the Iranian Plateau,* Aris & Phillips Ltd., Warminster, Wilts, UK, 1982.

C. L. Brown, ed., *From Medina to Metropolis: Heritage and Change in the Near Eastern City,* The Darwin Press, Princeton, 1973.

N. J. Coulson, *A History of Islamic Law,* Edinburgh University Press, Edinburgh, 1964.

K. A. C. Creswell, *Early Muslim Architecture: Umayyads, early Abbasids and Tulunids,* 2 vols., The Clarendon Press, Oxford, 1932–1940.

B. S. Hakim, "Recycling a Traditional Housing Process: A Case in Abiquiu, New Mexico," paper published in the proceedings of the 74th Annual Meeting, held in New Orleans, Louisiana, March 1986, of the Association of Collegiate Schools of Architecture, based in Washington, D.C.

J. D. Hoag, *Islamic Architecture,* History of World Architecture Series, edited by Pier Luigi Nervi, Harry N. Abrams, Inc., New York, 1977.

A. H. Hourani and S. M. Stern, eds., *The Islamic City,* Bruno Cassirer, Oxford, 1970.

I. M. Lapidus, ed., *Middle Eastern Cities,* University of California Press, Berkeley, California, 1969.

E. B. Macdougall and R. Ettinghausen, eds., *The Islamic Garden,* Dumbarton Oaks Colloquium on the History of Landscape Architecture IV, Trustees for Harvard University, Washington, D.C., 1976.

G. Michell, ed., *Architecture of the Islamic World: Its History & Social Meaning,* Thames & Hudson Ltd., London, and William Morrow & Co., Inc., New York, 1978.

A. L. M. T. Nijst, H. Priemus, H. L. Swets, and J. J. Van Ijzeren, *Living on the Edge of the Sahara: A Study of Traditional Forms of Habitation and Types of Settlement in Morocco,* Government Publishing Office, The Hague, 1973.

P. Oliver, ed., *Shelter and Society,* Barrie and Rockliff, London, 1969.

J. M. Richards, et al, *Hassan Fathy*, Concept Media Pte Ltd., Singapore and the Architectural Press, London, 1985.

J. Schacht, *An Introduction to Islamic Law,* the Clarendon Press, Oxford, 1964.

B. Ünsal, *Turkish Islamic Architecture: In Seljuk and Ottoman Times 1071–1923,* Alec Tiranti, London, 1959.

J. L. Abu-Lughod, "The Islamic City—Historic Myth, Islamic Essence, and Contemporary Relevance," *International Journal of Middle East Studies* **19**(2) (May 1987).

J. Akbar, *Crisis in the Built Environment, The Case of the Muslim City,* Concept Media Pte Ltd., Singapore, 1988.

A. Rapoport, *House Form and Culture,* Prentice-Hall, Inc., Englewood Cliffs, N.J., 1969.

A. Rapoport, "Environmental Quality, Metropolitan Areas and Traditional Settlements," *Habitat International* **7**(3/4) (1983).

A. Rapoport, "Development, Culture Change and Supportive Design," *Habitat International* **7**(5/6) (1983).

J. F. C. Turner, *Housing By People, Towards Autonomy in Building Environments,* Pantheon Books, New York, 1976.

See also MOSQUES

BESIM S. HAKIM, AIA, AICP

ISOZAKI, ARATA

Arata Isozaki (b. 1931) is a late twentieth-century Japanese architect who inherited the tradition of Corbusian Modernism through Kenzo Tange. Isozaki is one of the principal architects of his time and was responsible for the shift from functionalism to formalism–mannerism. Isozaki's work represents a developmental, thematic search for self-realization. Considered by critics to be enigmatic in his use of architectural elements, his work is more readily understood when viewed in the context of the Japanese culture, and particularly the rigorous methodology applied in the mastery of Zen Buddhism. In most of his work, Isozaki is seeking an altered state of perception through changes in scale, alignment, perspective, or cultural context. This altered state of perception may be likened to the Zen concept of *satori,* or enlightenment. This condition is achieved by Isozaki through creating an oppositional relationship either within his work, or between it and the supporting context. Isozaki forces a confrontation between rationalism and intuition. He often uses cultural historicism as a vehicle to demonstrate and create opposition in his work. Rarely are these oppositional devices intended to be threatening; they more accurately are the outcome of sophisticated whimsy. Arata Isozaki's architectural intention is to provide the observer with the opportunity to see the forest by looking at the trees.

Arata Isozaki was born on July 23, 1931 in the city of Oita. This small provincial center is located on the north shore of Kyushu, the southernmost island in the Japanese archipelago. To date, most of the architectural work produced by Isozaki is located on Kyushu, even though most of his professional career has been spent in Tokyo, 500 mi to the north.

Throughout history, Kyushu has served as a cultural gateway to Japan. Almost all Chinese influences have entered the Japanese island chain through Korea across the Sea of Japan to Kyushu. Western influence has also entered Japan through this portal. The Portuguese navigators used Kyushu as the eastern terminus for their trading routes in the sixteenth century. They traded for silk with the Japanese and brought Christian missionaries to Japan.

Although politically isolated from the central power structure of Japan located in Tokyo, Kyushu has played an important role in the introduction of foreign culture and technology to Japanese society. The broad and receptive cultural posture of Kyushu is reflected in Isozaki's capacity for absorbing and applying Western architectural notions to conditions that exist in a Japanese cultural context.

Isozaki is a prolific writer and essayist. He applies his skill to his own architecture to justify, and thereby become self-conscious of, his work. He exemplifies the mannerist tradition of self-awareness. His reflective nature and the internal mechanics of his architecture are most likely interrelated with his father's position as a leading figure in the Amano-Gawa (Milky Way) group of Haiku poets. It is probable that Isozaki's father was exercising both his poetic and prophetic nature when he named the eldest of his four children Arata, which means newness. Today, Arata Isozaki is considered by many to be the father of the Japanese New Wave.

Arata Isozaki graduated from Oita Ueno-Go-Oka high school in 1950. That same year, at the age of 19, he commenced study at the University of Tokyo. In 1953, Isozaki entered a Tokyo University seminar offered by Kenzo Tange, an architect who dominated postwar Japanese architecture and was considered by many to be the Japanese Walter Gropius. Through Tange, Isozaki was exposed to the Japanese modernist tradition: Kunio Maekawa, Antonin Raymond, and Le Corbusier. Isozaki submitted a diploma thesis entitled "Development of Skyscraper Designs in the USA, 1875–1935" and was graduated in 1956.

Isozaki worked in Tange's office from 1954 to 1963 and participated in the development of almost all work produced in the office during this time. Projects of note include the Kagawa Prefectural Hall, the Imbari City Hall, and the Tokyo Plan. Isozaki's City in the Air proposal is reflected in Tange's solution for the Yamanashi Communication Center.

The tutelage of Kenzo Tange exposed Isozaki to a great architect, educator, and gifted organizer, but in 1963 Isozaki left Tange and opened his own office in Tokyo. In their relationship, Isozaki realized that his own personality as a designer was distinctly different from that of Tange, who was a modernist in the classical tradition. Isozaki was a mannerist and independent individualist. The schism between Tange and Isozaki was implied in Isozaki's 1962 essay "City Demolition Industry Inc.," a veiled attack on the homogeneous Tokyo plan in which the urban designer is presented as a hit man (1). From his experience with Tange, however, Isozaki has developed two consistent traits: a clear developmental methodology and a commitment to the mastery of form.

Much of Arata Isozaki's work is developed around thematic explorations of various types. Certainly one of the earliest and most powerful was the heavenly column, a theme linked to Japanese mythology and the traditional creation myth. The heavenly column in Japanese mythology acts as a vehicle through which heaven and earth are connected; the depth of its symbolism is not understood by most Westerners. This theme is expressed in most of the work Isozaki did in the 1960s.

The Oita Prefectural Library (1962–1966) is the culmination of a number of other works of this period. The Oita library illustrates the application of a traditional mythology to a mannerist expression of structure in architecture. The structural elements are exaggerated to the point that they begin to enclose and define space. This level of manneristic expression is unique to the work of Isozaki. The only other architect developing a similar approach to structure at this time was Paul Rudolph in the United States. The Headquarters Building, Fukuoka Mutual Bank, Fukuoka (1963–1971) is also a good example of this thematic type (Fig. 1).

The Kitakyushi City Museum of Art (1972–1974) is the last building expressing this approach to exaggerated structural form. At the same time, it begins to introduce Isozaki's next phase of thematic exploration. The exaggerated structural configuration of the Kitakyushi Museum begins to express a subjugation to an internal grid. The internal orthogonal skeleton becomes clearly apparent in the external membrane of the building.

In this second period of thematic expression, Isozaki began to subdivide the powerful structural geometry of his designs. The Gunman Prefectural Museum of Fine

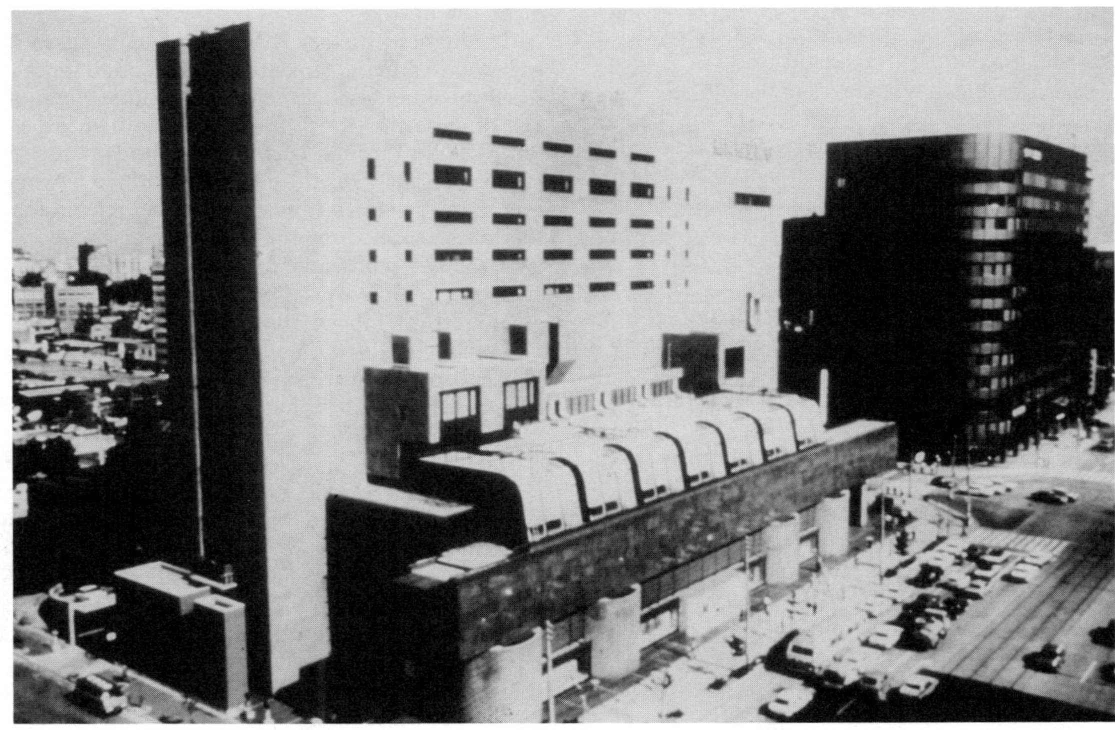

Figure 1. Fukuoka Mutual Bank Headquarters Building, Fukuoka, Japan (1971). Photograph by Michael Franklin Ross.

Arts (1971–1974) demonstrates the subjugation of the mass by the interior orthogonal grid, and the geometries in the building are manipulated and juxtaposed. The building conveys a sense of late modernism, similar to the work of Richard Meier, but when tested the mannerism of Isozaki is revealed. Internal spaces contrast, one with the other, to reveal their real condition; no attempt is made at creating a harmonious and coherent whole. Continuity is established through a very selective use of materials that helps to express the discontinuity of the mass and space.

The manipulation of the orthogonal grid evolved through a number of buildings, including the Shukosha Building, Fukuoka (1974–1975), to a point where the grid itself combined with another geometry, the circle or cylinder. The exploration of combined geometries is exemplified by Isozaki's work on the Kamioka Town Hall, Kamioka (1978), a curious and highly complex demonstration of Isozaki's high mannerist style that reveals an emerging overtone in Isozaki's work. His manipulation of the cube follows the work of Claude–Nicolas Ledoux in the expression of spatial discontinuities through discontinuous geometry.

If Ledoux is the precedent for Isozaki's discontinuous geometry, then it is Etienne–Louis Boullee who set the precedent for Isozaki's work using the continuous barrel vault. This thematic exploration is exemplified by the Central Library of Kitakyushu City (1972–1975), of which Boullee's Royal Library design is clearly the progenitor. The slow curving perpendicular alignment of the Central Library's two continuous vaults implies graceful, organic movement through the landscape.

The historical references made in the Shukosha Building and the Kitakyushu Library imply the evolution of a new thematic exploration that applied neoclassicism to Isozaki's latest work. The Tsukuba Civic Center (1979–82) exemplifies this theme. It introduces a surreal interpretation of Michelangelo's piazza of the Campidoglio as the central organizing device for the Civic Center. Although the historical illusion is overt, there is still a strong sense of manneristic interpretation.

Arata Isozaki has established himself as an important international figure in the second half of the twentieth century. His work, considered phenomenological in its approach, traces its evolutionary thematic development to traditional devices of aesthetic perception. It is Arata Isozaki's deeply rooted cultural foundation that allows his ethereal exploration of the phenomenon of perception and reality.

BIBLIOGRAPHY

1. A. Isozaki, "City Demolition Industry Inc.," in *A New Wave of Japanese Architecture; Catalogue 10,* The Institute for Architecture and Urban Studies, New York, 1978, pp. 49–51.

General References

P. Drew, *The Architecture of Arata Isozaki,* Harper & Row, New York, 1982.

B. Chaitkin, "Zen and the Art of Arata Isozaki," *Architectural Design* (47), 19–20 (January 1977).

Clark Lundell, AIA
Auburn University
Auburn, Alabama

J

JACOBS, JANE. See Media Criticism

JAILS. See Justice Buildings—Law Enforcement, Courts, and Corrections

JEFFERSON, THOMAS

Thomas Jefferson, lawyer, statesman, farmer, architect, and third president of the United States, was born in Shadwell, in Goochland (later Albemarle) County, Virginia, on April 13, 1743, the son of Peter and Jane Randolph Jefferson. His father, a farmer and surveyor, undoubtedly stimulated his interest in architecture. Thomas was drawing plats and house plans at an early age.

Peter Jefferson died when his son was 14, leaving him to a rather unguided adolescence and desultory school career. In 1760, Thomas enrolled at the College of William and Mary in Williamsburg, where his interest in architecture took shape. He studied the buildings of the Virginia colonial capital as well as those of Maryland's capital city, Annapolis, which he preferred. He made study sketches of Annapolis's Hammond–Harwood house, redesigned Williamsburg's governor's palace and college building, and, at age 24, embarked on designs for his home, Monticello (Fig. 1). Jefferson devoted his thoughts and efforts to this project the rest of his life, during his extraordinarily accomplished career. Monticello has been referred to as an "autobiographical house," embodying Jefferson's social and political philosophies. It became his laboratory for creative design and construction over a period of 40 years.

From his earliest years, Jefferson was familiar with the great eighteenth-century Virginia houses—Rosewell, Westover, Carter's Grove, Mt. Airy, Stratford—as well as with the palace in Williamsburg, in which he would eventually reside as governor of Virginia. He was connected either by social or family ties to almost all of the owner–builders of these great houses. In addition to the early, primarily Georgian, building tradition in Virginia, the writings and drawings of Italian architect Andrea Palladio (1508–1580) influenced Jefferson. As his architectural interests developed, Jefferson would reject the plainer architecture of early Virginia in favor of the more monumental Greco–Roman classicism, a style he thought more befitting the needs of the new republic. This belief is one of the reasons for his moving the capital from Williamsburg to Richmond.

Figure 1. General view of facade of Monticello, Charlottesville, Va. Courtesy of the University of Maryland School of Architecture slide collection.

At William and Mary, Jefferson studied mathematics and classics, which provided the basis for his professional career in the law and in politics. Architecture was not taught in schools of the time, and his successes in the field were achieved by his own initiative, study, and self-discipline. He had one of the outstanding architectural libraries of his day, and referred to Palladio's *The Four Books of Architecture* as his bible. The major influence of Palladio on Jeffersonian architecture is notable in the work at Monticello and the University of Virginia at Charlottesville, as well as in various designs for public buildings and private residences. Among these were studies for remodeling the Palace at Williamsburg (1772), the new state capitol at Richmond (1785), and residences at Bremo, Farmington, Barboursville, and Poplar Forest.

In 1772, Jefferson married Martha Wayles. They had six children before Martha Wayles Jefferson died in 1782, only two of whom reached adulthood. A daughter, Martha, who married Thomas Randolph, Jr., was the only one to survive her father.

In addition to architectural studies, Jefferson also pursued the art of city planning. In 1780, he prepared a plan, based on a gridiron, for expanding the city of Richmond, and in 1791 he made studies, paralleling the work of Pierre L'Enfant, for the new federal city of Washington, D.C. Alternate squares were to be devoted to open space and to building lots, four lots to a square. Jefferson believed that the grid plan was ideal for health, efficiency, and ease of development.

He was also a designer of gardens, preferring the naturalistic or romantic English style to the formal, geometric French and Italian gardens. He made a detailed record of plant materials and agricultural procedures that he favored at his Monticello plantation.

Jefferson's political career follows a steady progression of increasing responsibility in state and federal affairs, culminating in his election to the presidency of the United States in 1800. He was not a good public speaker, but was an accomplished writer, authoring many of the important documents of the new Republic, notably the Declaration of Independence (1776). Jefferson's first elected office was to the Virginia House of Burgesses. He served in the Continental Congress at Philadelphia (1775–1776), and in 1779 succeeded Patrick Henry as governor of Virginia. In 1783 he was again in Congress, where he drafted a national monetary proposal based on the dollar decimal system. He succeeded Benjamin Franklin as minister to France in 1785, where he remained as a sympathetic witness to the French Revolution. Jefferson returned to the

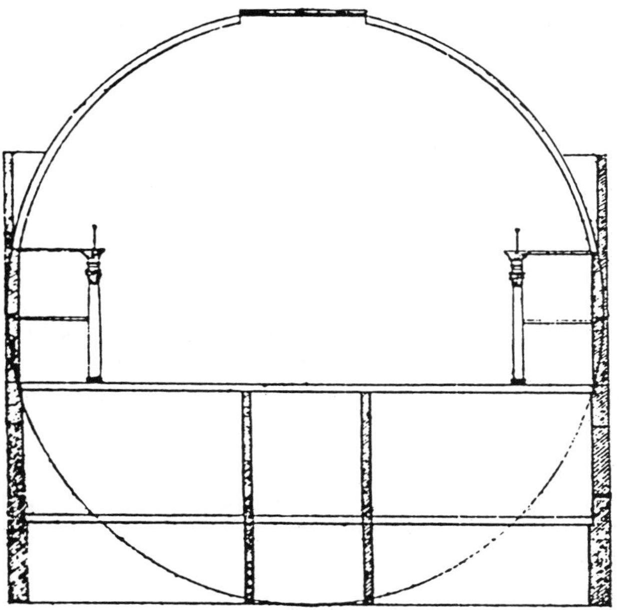

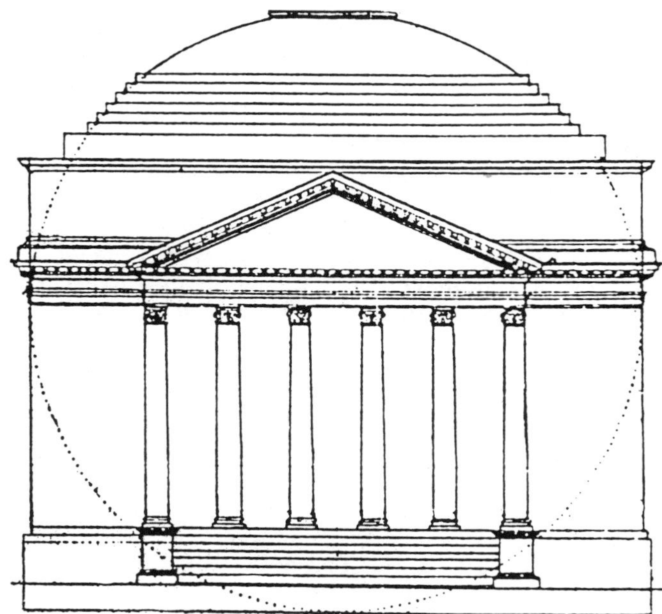

Figure 2. University of Virginia: Rotunda, section, and elevation.

United States in 1790 to become President George Washington's Secretary of State.

Jefferson was elected vice-president under John Adams in 1796; in this office, he presided over the Senate, and concerned himself with parliamentary practice for Congress. In 1800, Jefferson and Aaron Burr tied in the race for the presidency; the decision went to the House of Representatives and Jefferson was elected. The first president to be inaugurated in the new capital city of Washington, he served for two terms. He left the presidency in 1808 and retired to Monticello, where he spent the rest of his life pursuing architectural and agricultural interests. It was here that he completed designs for Monticello as well as a number of houses and public buildings, and that he made one of the great contributions to planning and design in the United States, the campus and buildings of the University of Virginia at Charlottesville (Fig. 2).

BIBLIOGRAPHY

General References

F. Kimball, *Thomas Jefferson, Architect,* Boston, 1916.

F. Nichols, *Thomas Jefferson's Architectural Drawings,* Massachusetts Historical Society, Boston, 1960.

D. Malone, *Jefferson the Virginian,* Little Brown and Co., Boston, 1948.

P. F. Norton, *Latrobe, Jefferson, and the Capitol,* Garland Publishing, Inc., New York and London, 1977.

David P. Fogle, AICP
University of Maryland
College Park, Maryland

JOHANSEN, JOHN M.

John M. Johansen, architect and educator, was born in 1916 in New York City. He attended Harvard University where he received a degree in architecture and a master's degree in 1943. He was awarded an Honorary Doctorate of Fine Arts from the University of Maryland in 1965 and from Clark University in 1970.

After graduating from Harvard, he worked for Marcel Breuer and Skidmore, Owings & Merrill in New York City. In 1950 Johansen opened an independent practice in New Canaan, Conn.

Among his more famous buildings are the U.S. Embassy in Dublin (1963), Clowes Hall in Indianapolis, Ind. (1964), the Morris Mechanic Theater in Baltimore, Md, (1967), and the Mummers Theater in Oklahoma City, Okla. (1970). His studies in expressing the component functions of the buildings in the exterior design brought wide attention to his theater work, culminating with the Mummers Theater. He is also known for his residential design, of which the Taylor house (1966) is an example. Many articles concerning his work have appeared in magazines and books in the United States and abroad. Twenty major national publications have featured his work, including *Time, Life, Newsweek, Fortune, Holiday,* and *The New York Times.*

Johansen holds the title of distinguished Professor at Pratt Institute. He was formerly a professor of architecture at Yale University, the University of Pennsylvania, and Columbia University, as well as visiting critic at Massachusetts Institute of Technology, Harvard University, Carnegie Tech, Rhode Island School of Design, and other schools of architecture.

He has lectured extensively at universities in the United States and abroad. His work has been published and his articles have appeared in many magazines. Johansen has been a frequent speaker at AIA regional conventions, has spoken at AIA national conventions, and has addressed the General Services Administration in Washington, D.C. In 1974 he conducted a lecture tour of Italy for the Cultural Institute of Italy. Photographs of his work were exhibited at the Museum of Modern Art (*Built in U.S.A.* and *Transformations in Modern Architecture*), at an International Exhibit in Berlin, at Expo '70 in Osaka, and in Poland and Yugoslavia. A recent exhibit of his work from 1953 to 1987 was sponsored by the National Institute of Architectural Education (NIAE). He has appeared on television on several occasions, including a program entitled, "John M. Johansen, Portrait of an Architect."

Johansen is also a painter, and his work has been exhibited on many occasions. One of his paintings is in the collection of the Corcoran Gallery of Art in Washington, D.C.

Included among the awards bestowed on Johansen are AIA national and chapter design awards, and the Brunner Award of the National Institute of Arts and Letters. He has been honored by the U.S. Department of Health, Education, and Welfare and the Royal Institute of Architects of Ireland among others. He was made a fellow of the American Institute of Architects in 1969.

John M. Johansen, FAIA
Johansen & Bhavnani Architects
New York, New York

Edited by Robert T. Packard, AIA

JOHNSON, PHILIP C.

Philip Cortelyou Johnson was born in Cleveland, Ohio in 1906. The son of a wealthy corporate attorney, Johnson was raised in a privileged environment that included servants, a 2500-acre farm, education at the Hackley School in Tarrytown, New York, and both undergraduate and graduate degrees from Harvard. Philip Johnson went to Harvard as an undergraduate to study philosophy and the classics. His interests ranged, however, and he thought of music, art, and art history as possible careers. Through family connections he met Alfred Barr, Jr., then a professor of art history at Wellesley. When a group of wealthy New Yorkers, led by Mrs. John D. Rockefeller II, formed the Museum of Modern Art, it was Alfred Barr, Jr. they hired to be its director. Barr brought with him a group of bright young advisors, including Johnson, whose task it was to run the architectural section of the museum. Thus, at age 24 Philip Johnson found himself in the center of a group which would be one of the major cultural forces for art and architecture in the twentieth century.

As part of his work at the Museum of Modern Art Johnson traveled to Europe with his friend, the architectural historian Henry Russell Hitchcock, to see the work of the several modern movements, including Germany's Bauhaus, Holland's de Stijl, and the CIAM group. The results of the trip included a museum show and a book entitled *The International Style* (1). The exhibit was the basic introduction for the American public and the architectural community to the work of the modernists in Europe. The book, which was based on the exhibit, was both a pictorial review and a written manual with dos and don'ts for the "modern" architect. The book was published in 1932 and would prove to be the most influential architectural document of the prewar era.

Two years later the ever-restless Johnson abruptly dropped his work in New York and went to work for Louisiana politician and self-styled populist Huey Long for one year. Johnson then journeyed to Europe where he fell under the spell of Hitler's Nazi movement. In later years Johnson would alternately be called to task and forgiven for his dalliance with Fascism, depending largely on whether he and his work were in or out of favor with the intelligentsia. Through it all Johnson retained the image of the aloof, wealthy iconoclast.

On his return to the United States Johnson moved to Cambridge, Massachusetts, to study architecture at Harvard, which was the educational center for the promulgation of modernism in the United States. For his thesis project he built a walled courtyard house in Cambridge. After service in the Army for two years, Johnson settled in New York and New Canaan, Connecticut, where he designed the celebrated Glass House. At this point in his architectural career Johnson was a self-proclaimed Miesian and had seen drawings for Mies' Farnsworth House, to be built outside of Chicago in Plano, Illinois.

While there are obvious similarities between the two buildings, their differences are more striking. Johnson's Glass House sits rather solidly on the ground, its transparent walls freely allowing the interior and exterior spaces to become one. Much of the living area of the house is, in fact, outside on terraces at grade level. By contrast, the Farnsworth House floats above the ground, its outdoor spaces carefully proscribed by the limits of the building perimeter. This marked distinction in how these two architects view the relationship of building and landscape is probably traceable to Johnson's early fascination with the work of Frank Lloyd Wright.

The Glass House received an astonishing amount of publicity, getting eight pages in *House and Garden* (2) (a feat Johnson would later repeat when he himself appeared on the cover of *Time* (3), cradling a model of the A.T.&T. building). The house and the publicity catapulted Johnson into the vanguard of U.S. architecture and for the next 15 years he maintained a practice designing houses and small institutional buildings.

Not since Sullivan or Wright has a practicing U.S. architect written as extensively as Johnson. As his practice was small, he was able to spend a good deal of his time in the pursuit of comment and criticism. A knowledgeable historian with a penchant for the provocative phrase, Johnson nurtured modernism and the International style. His own work ranged from the highly articulated and delicate houses of the 1950s to the almost brutalist Kline Biology Center built for Yale University in 1965.

It was in those early houses that Johnson both established his reputation and learned his craft. Relying on a combination of long years of observation of the modernists and unerring good taste, Johnson was able to create what are arguably many of the most elegant small buildings in the United States. The Glass House of 1949 was followed by a series of even smaller buildings on his own New Canaan estate. These include a guest house, a painting gallery, and a diminutive pavilion sitting in a small pond. Later he would add a skylit sculpture gallery to the collection.

In the early 1950s he collaborated with Ludwig Mies van der Rohe on the Seagrams Building. Johnson's most important contribution to that effort was the design of the Four Seasons restaurant. The large space had originally been conceived as an automobile showroom. Johnson's design for the restaurant remains a bastion of restrained modernism in an era where the theme restaurant and post-modernism have all but obliterated the crisp, clear ideals of projects such as the Four Seasons.

Johnson's association with the Rockefeller family and the Museum of Modern Art led to the Rockefeller Guest House commission (1950). A narrow building of brick, steel and glass, it sits among the townhouses of midtown Manhattan in the most anonymous manner. Only those privileged to enter may be treated to the extraordinary restraint and repose Johnson achieves. With only three spaces arranged in a row he manages to exploit the narrow lot to create a spaciousness largely unanticipated from the street facade. The living room in the front and the bedroom at the rear flank an unroofed court; white, concrete, reflecting pool; and ivy-draped, white-painted brick walls. A respite in the city, it anticipates Zion and Breen's Paley Park by more than 12 years.

Two houses in 1956 again illustrate Johnson's dedication to the crisp and elegant solution. In the Eric Boissonnas House in New Canaan, a grouping of brick-cornered, slab-roofed, two-story, glass pavilions utilizing square plans sit serenely on a grass-covered knoll. By contrast, the Robert Leonhardt House in Lloyd's Neck, Long Island, is a steel and glass box raised high above the ground, thrusting a cantilevered prow over Long Island Sound. This house is reminiscent of the earlier (1953) Robert Wiley House in New Canaan, where a glass living box is perched and cantilevered from a solid stone plinth.

The Wiley House's relation to the landscape is, like Johnson's own house, a clue to his roots in U.S. architecture. Despite the extraordinary homage paid to the European modernists in both buildings, there is in them a sense of the land which is clearly rooted in Wright's domestic work and Jefferson's Monticello. The spreading silhouette, the use of brick and/or stone plinths, and the elegant yet solid connections to the earth are all lessons Johnson could not have learned from Mies.

With the exception of a few institutional buildings—most notably the Museum for Pre-Columbian Art at Dumbarton Oaks in Washington, D.C. (1963), the Munson-Williams-Proctor Museum in Utica, New York (1960), and the Amos Carter Museum of Western Art in Fort Worth (1961)—Johnson's practice was small. He has acknowledged that up until the mid-1960s it was often an unprofitable endeavor which he kept afloat only by infusions from his personal assets.

In the late 1960s Johnson formed a partnership with John Burgee and from that association came a series of large-scale corporate buildings which would move Johnson away from both the small scale and elegance of his International style roots, and from the unprofitable practice of total involvement with small buildings. Johnson could see the impending changes. Already restless with the constraints of the International style he had helped promulgate, Johnson began to make the first tentative steps away from it. In the Dumbarton Oaks project he created an eight-domed, nine-circled composition reminiscent of mid-Eastern architecture. At Lincoln Center in New York, his project for the New York State Theatre and his old college friend Lincoln Kirstein, Director of the New York City Ballet, is another attempt to break from the constraints of modernism.

While the former follows Johnson's early style of elegant creations, the State Theatre, like a number of his larger projects in the sixties—the Sheldon Memorial Art Gallery at the University of Nebraska (1963) and the New York State Pavilion at the New York World's Fair (1964)—is without restraint and comes perilously close to the bad taste Johnson had so judiciously eschewed. This movement away from modernism, particularly in larger buildings, was to prove problematic for many architects in the 1960s and 1970s. Johnson, in retrospect, seems to have been of two minds during this period, moving from the classical modernity of a building such as the East Wing and Garden of the Museum of Modern Art in New York (1964) to the excesses and unresolved spaces of the New York State Theatre (1964). In between there appear to be brief forays into the styles of some of his former Harvard classmates. Both the Kreeger House in Washington, D.C. (1968), with its series of vaulted, concrete pavilions and the List Art Building at Brown University (1971) with its massive upper level supported on thin columns and complex volumetrics seem to have their essential ideas taken from the work of Paul Rudolph. The Bielefeld Art Gallery in Germany (1968) and the Neuberger Museum at Purchase, New York (1972), might be, on cursory examination, early sketches from I.M. Pei. Finally, in the Boston Public Library project of 1974, Johnson and Burgee, working next to the neoclassical monument of McKim, Mead and White, manage to overwhelm the old building with a series of white stone solids and arched voids which Johnson defends as contextual.

Johnson's work of the late 1960s and early 1970s is in many ways a microcosm of the struggle which all serious architects faced, how to break from the banalities of modernism and to build elegantly at scales which, by their very nature, would seem to obviate elegance. Ironically, Johnson's modernistic works were, in the 1950s at least, rarely banal; as the scale of projects increased, Johnson seems to have had a particularly difficult time translating that excitement of elegance from small to large buildings.

In the mid-1970s, the Johnson-Burgee partnership made a series of breakthroughs which would end the period of transition and give several U.S. cities buildings with an urbanity which Johnson had previously only been able to achieve at much smaller scale. If one building were to be selected as the fulcrum for this change, it would have to be the I.D.S. Center in Minneapolis (1973). Here Johnson and Burgee conquer both the issues of scale and elegance in a composition of glass curtain wall towers and low-rise pavilions, which combine to create a shopping, working, and gathering area that is welcoming and urbane. The aesthetic vocabulary is still Miesian, but the low-key disposition of the buildings is a fitting backdrop for the activities contained within and around the complex. Seen by millions of television viewers, as it was prominently featured in the long-running *Mary Tyler Moore Show,* the I.D.S. Center came to be a symbol for the rebirth of the U.S. downtown and the return of the young professional to the city.

A similar kind of excitement is created by two projects in Houston in 1976. In Pennzoil Place and Post Oak Center, Johnson and Burgee, still relying largely on the International style, are able to create two projects of fascinating sculptural elegance. To be sure, both lack the vitality of I.D.S. and its sustaining interest, but in Pennzoil, particularly, there appear to be the first steps in moving modernism away, once and for all, from the banalities of the box.

The period since 1976 has been astonishingly prolific. Johnson and Burgee produced corporate and institutional projects across the country in styles ranging from medieval Dutch at the Republic Bank Center in Houston (1983) to neo-Gothic at the corporate headquarters for PPG Industries in Pittsburgh (1984) to Spanish Colonial at a cultural complex in Fort Lauderdale (1984).

Each new project seems to bring a new form of expression. Certainly no architect has exploited the liberating forces of postmodernism more than Johnson. The very acceptability of postmodernism by corporate America may well be traced to Johnson and Burgee's AT&T Building on Madison Avenue in New York City (1982). While this work, clad in massive, granite blocks and slabs, with its arcaded base and split, pedimented top seems tame in retrospect, it was, at its inception in the late 1970s, viewed by many as a heresy. Johnson's appearance on the cover of *Time* magazine (3) signaled many things. It gave the stamp of approval of the United States' most avowed modernist to the freewheeling style which has come to be known as postmodernism; it signaled the shift of corporate America away from the glass box; it reaffirmed the use of stone as a viable material for tall buildings; it repudiated the band windows of the Bauhaus in favor of the punched holes of commercial architecture of the earlier part of the twentieth century; and it established Johnson as the most recognizable public figure in U.S. architecture. His subsequent receipt of the A.I.A.'s Gold Medal (1978) and the Pritzker Prize (1980) only confirmed what was already common knowledge. In his seventh decade Philip Johnson had become the most influential architect in the United States. His continued association with the Museum of Modern Art, as well as the most important developers of the time, has allowed him to maneuver a number of younger architects into important positions in U.S. business and culture, Michael Graves and Robert A. M. Stern among them.

This power and prestige has not gone uncriticized. Much of the work of the late 1970s and 1980s has been sharply questioned by the foremost U.S. critics and architectural educators. Ada Louise Huxtable, writing in *The New York Times,* called the AT&T Building "[s]tolid, shapeless, expensively dressed (good materials, bad cut)," with "inflated and simplistic references to history" (4). Writing about the Boylston Street Tower project in Boston, Paul Goldberger, also in *The New York Times,* refers to Johnson and Burgee, "flipping through the history books," and finds the design "crude" (5). Carter Wiseman, in *New York Magazine,* said that the so-called "Lipstick" building at 53rd Street and Third Avenue, which Johnson and Burgee designed for developer Gerald Hines, was "not just plug-ugly, but dangerous" (6).

The record of work in the 1980s seems to more closely resemble the spotty production of Johnson's projects of the 1960s than it does the more assured and elegant pieces which he and Burgee brought forth in the 1970s. The restraint and thoughtfulness of I.D.S. or Pennzoil have given way to turretted towers and buildings in which miles of "trim" are clipped to the surface. The previously mentioned "Lipstick" building for developer Gerald Hines on New York's Third Avenue is such a work. Sheathed in pink granite and girdled in shiny metal stripes, it rises like an oval wedding cake. Many have seen such architectural events as whimsical and long overdue in a profession whose work, for so long, has been so stultifyingly serious. Johnson himself seems to relish the attention, both positive and negative.

In Johnson's 1954 talk to Harvard architecture students entitled, "The Seven Crutches of Modern Architecture" (6), he takes to task, among others, the crutch of history and the crutch of the pretty drawing. He concludes that neither of these crutches was operative in 1954. How ironic that 30 years later these would be the issues for which Johnson and his followers would be criticized.

More telling is Johnson's discussion of two other crutches, the crutch of serving the client and the crutch of utility. In the former he notes that "It's got to be clear, back in your own mind, that serving the client is one thing and the art of architecture is another" (7). Thirty years later Johnson was fond of saying, "[t]his is a service profession. The architect is a prostitute. We do the job we are told. Like the Supreme Court we follow the ballot boxes" (8).

As to the crutch of utility, Johnson said in 1954, "If the business of getting the house to run well takes precedence over your artistic invention the result won't be architecture at all, merely an assemblage of useful parts" (9). To that polemic Philip Johnson has been much more true. His work has never allowed artistic invention anything but the leading role.

Never one to accept his own dogma for long, Johnson, in his eighty-first year, returned to the Museum of Modern Art to curate a show on "Deconstructivism in Architecture." As with his embrace of modernism in the 1940s and post-modernism in the 1970s, it is likely that the Johnson seal will mark deconstructivism as the next wave in architecture's continuing, but problematic, relationship to U.S. culture.

BIBLIOGRAPHY

1. H.-R. Hitchcock and P. Johnson, *The International Style: Architecture since 1922,* W. W. Norton, New York, 1932.

2. "A glass house in Connecticut," *House and Garden,* 168–173, 215 (October 1949).

3. R. Hughes, "Architecture: Doing Their Own Thing," *Time,* 52–59 (January 8, 1979).

4. A. L. Huxtable, "Creeping Gigantism in Manhattan," *The New York Times,* 36 (March 22, 1987).

5. P. Goldberger, "A Tale of Two Towers on Boston's Boylston Street," *The New York Times,* 31 (January 24, 1988).

6. C. Wiseman, "Tarted Up," *New York Magazine,* 72 (April 20, 1987).

7. P. Johnson, "The Seven Crutches of Modern Architecture," *Philip Johnson, Writings,* Oxford University Press, New York, 1979, pp. 136–140.

8. *Ibid.,* p. 139.

9. Ref. 7, pp. 137–138.

General References

"Philip Johnson," *A + U—Architecture and Urbanism* (June 1979).

P. Johnson, *Philip Johnson 1949–1965,* Holt, Rinehart, and Winston, New York, 1965.

P. Johnson, *Writings,* Oxford University Press, New York, 1979.

J. M. Jacobus, Jr., *Philip Johnson,* George Braziller, New York, 1962.

W. Salisbury, "Philip Johnson," *Cleveland Plain Dealer Magazine* (October 5, 1986).

ROBERT ZWIRN
Miami University
Oxford, Ohio

JOINT VENTURES

A joint venture is a legal entity formed by two or more independent firms, usually in an effort to be awarded the design of a project. Although most firms are structured as sole proprietorships, partnerships, professional associations, or corporations, there may be opportunities where the services of one firm can be merged with another with the express intent to find work, for which either firm individually may not have been qualified.

Joint ventures are partnerships between firms and, like partnerships between principals in a firm, are presumed to have a termination, unlike a corporation that is presumed to continue *ad infinitum.* There is no prohibition on the legal structure of the joint venturers and often it will be between firms of different legal organizations, such as a partnership working with a corporation. The joint venture parties practice together for the purposes of the joint venture, but continue to operate legally as independent entities for work outside of the venture. Joint ventures still retain the capability to hire consultants directly.

A successful joint venture is predicated on a clear understanding of the scope of the work, the duration of the venture, the process for termination of the venture, and the levels of contribution to be made by each party. All of the above should be negotiated prior to the signing of any agreements with a client as a joint venture.

The levels of contribution of each firm should be documented so that anticipated levels of compensation can be equitably apportioned and to set the expectation of each party at the beginning of the project, so that significant deviations can be discussed and negotiated if they arise. Contributions can be described specifically, highlighting which firm will perform which services and the anticipated length of time it will take, or generally, stating that one firm will contribute a percentage of necessary hours to produce the project.

Remuneration is based on two alternative methods for equitably dividing the proceeds of the project. If two architectural firms are to joint venture and there is an overlap of services or the potential of conflict in the work performed, a profit–loss approach may be preferred. This method calls for all monies collected to be pooled in a single joint venture account, which is distributed to the venture parties based on their completion of phases of the work, not on the hours expended. The risk of this approach is that efficient firms may be profitable while their inefficient venture partner may lose money.

The alternative approach is based on compensation. It rewards both parties based on their expenses for the project and does not involve pooling of money, as the venture parties are paid directly from revenues received. The advantage of this method is that the inefficient firm will not harm the efficient one. This approach is preferred if the joint venture is comprised of different disciplines, where overlap of services is unlikely.

Because the joint venture is presumed to end, the terms for dissolving the relationship need to be stipulated. Which firm will retain the marketing rights to the client in the future? Which firm is responsible for maintenance and follow-on inquiries from the client? What are the terms for continuing professional liability coverage? What should happen if one firm dissolves for financial or personal reasons before the project is completed? If staff has been contributed to a pool for the project, what are their rights? These subjects should be addressed by written agreement.

The term of the agreement is critical. It can stipulate that marketing work required to bring the project to the joint venture may or may not be recognized for compensation because it occurred before an agreement was signed. It should be consistent with the anticipated length of the project and usually is based, not on time, but on the requirements to perform services related to the project, regardless of the length of time.

To monitor the agreement and to manage the joint venture's efforts, a policy committee should be established by the agreement. The committee meets to review progress and the marketing direction of the joint venture, to settle disputes between the firms regarding responsibilities, and to act as a single conduit for dealings with the client.

For the client, a joint venture offers a customized team approach, a unique meshing of talent for a single project. The firms can joint venture because they complement each other, perhaps because one is a generalist firm and the other a specialist. The venturers can be two architectural firms with one more locally based, thus providing better contract administration, or they can be an architect and an engineer, providing total design services. Joint ventures may include very large firms responding to major governmental projects, or two small firms seeking work available only to medium or large firms. The alternatives and reasons are many.

Joint ventures usually respond to the specific demands of a client. Rarely are joint ventures set up in a speculative fashion without a particular project in mind. However, some firms do keep an ongoing joint venture agreement in force should they have the need to prepare a very quick response to a request for proposals. To this end, the AIA developed document C801, *Joint Venture Agreement for Professional Services,* which is a valuable guideline for beginning negotiations.

Joint ventures have proven to be a useful tool for firms looking to enter the international marketplace, especially as they can tie design strength, technology, and other resources of one firm with the local experience of another. This becomes particularly useful in working with local building code and government officials, and locally available materials and construction techniques.

The joint venture must be identified to the client; many states have prohibitions against the use of a fictitious name. Jones Architects and Smith Design may be precluded from referring to themselves contractually as Conglomerate Associates by state architectural registration boards. There are legal limitations on nonprofessionals entering into joint ventures with licensed practitioners and offering services under the label of architect. Under such circumstances, further investigation is warranted.

In a partnership, either partner is usually liable for the actions of the other. In joint ventures, care should be taken in the structuring of the initial agreement so that neither party is left unduly liable.

Because joint ventures usually entail the merging of personnel, available space, support equipment, and supplies, the agreement should stipulate how these contributions will be accounted. Further thought should go to the tax implications for each firm. If the fiscal years of the firms are not synchronized, planning is needed to provide an accounting of the performance of the joint venture as each firm requires. Members of the venture need to investigate whether separate offices or a joint office are needed, and the respective, as well as incidental, costs involved.

Independent record keeping is necessary to document expenditures as long as the relationship exists. It is highly desirable for each firm to keep separate records detailing their expenditures. In each firm, personnel costs will also vary, so each party must be ready to share information on direct labor costs and overhead, so that a balanced sharing of costs can be reached.

Joint ventures appear to be creatures of more difficult economic times, thus allowing a firm the flexibility to pursue many different project types. The number of joint ventures is hard to pinpoint at any time, but most firms enter into this form of partnership at some point in the life of the practice. Many firms, finding success with one venture partner, may enter into subsequent agreements, but each of these agreements should be independent of the ones preceding.

Insurance creates special obstacles for joint ventures. If the firms have established an independent office for the particular project, then a general liability coverage needs to be placed. The larger issue is professional liability insurance. If both parties are insured by the same company, then protection can easily be negotiated. If the firms are insured through different companies, a negotiated policy can be structured, but the costs and the length of time to come to an agreement between the insurers may be considerable. If one of the parties is not insured, there is a great likelihood that coverage will not be available, unless the levels of compensation and contribution are skewed heavily in favor of the insured firm. If neither firm is insured at the time of the agreement, the present economic climate in the insurance industry practically guarantees that coverage will not be found.

The resultant products of the joint venture, the contract documents, are usually presumed to be jointly owned unless one firm is clearly the producer of documents that will carry the seal of that architect. In either case, the ownership and the ensuing copyright protection should be a part of the agreement.

The venturer's proportion of the compensation is usually used as the guideline to determine the level of risk. If the project loses money, the participants, unless otherwise indicated, will share that level of loss. Furthermore, if a project is held liable, courts will assess the contribution, level of negligence, and damages in the same proportion.

If a joint venture fails before the project is completed, perhaps due to the insolvency of one of the parties, the remaining parties must be equipped to absorb the unfinished work, either internally or through consultants. In either case, rights to the remaining proceeds that are outstanding and due to the insolvent partner need to be negotiated.

As more firms use computers to develop contract documents, there is a greater need to make sure that equipment is compatible and that interfacing between systems is planned before the joint venture work gets underway. If one firm uses a system that does not interface with the other firm's, additional costs will be incurred and the delivery of the project may be affected.

In conclusion, joint ventures are a hybrid form of practice for design firms and allow for great flexibility with a comparable need to plan and build in contingencies. The advice of an attorney and the firm's accountant will be indispensable.

See also Construction Documents; Construction Law; Contract Administration; International Practice; Remuneration

William Hooper, Jr., AIA
The American Institute of Architects
Washington, D.C.

JONES, INIGO

Inigo Jones (1573–1652) was England's first classical architect of the Renaissance and can be counted as one of a handful of truly revolutionary figures in the history of western architecture. Although represented today by only seven extant buildings, his talent, imagination, and intellect left a legacy in his country's architecture that lasted into the eighteenth century and beyond.

Born the son of a cloth worker in 1573, he emerged as a professional painter, or "picture maker," in the early seventeenth century; no record exists of his youth, training, or education. His first significant contribution to the art of Jacobean England came after he traveled to Italy as a connoisseur (probably between 1597 and 1603) for the king of Denmark, where he saw Venice and studied the works of Italian artists firsthand. Because England was just emerging from a kind of cold war with Rome after Henry VIII's break with the Catholic church, Jones was one of the first of his countrymen to fully appreciate the achievements of Renaissance art. An extraordinarily quick study, the young artist returned to England with a mastery of Italian draftsmanship that immediately served him well as a designer of stage decorations and sets. With Ben Jonson and the leading composers and literati of the Stuart court, he helped to create a series of masques (modeled after the Italian *intermedio* and considered to be precursors of the modern opera and ballet) that would themselves have assured him lasting fame. His visually dazzling and mechanically clever sets and costumes for these courtly entertainments attracted the attention of aristocratic patrons, among them the Earl of Arundel, Anne of Denmark, and Prince Henry. He quickly rose to prominence in royal circles, so much so as to incur the ire and envy of Jonson, who satirized him savagely (in *An Expostulation* and *Tale of a Tub,* among other works).

Jones made his first foray into architecture as an amateur when he was appointed Surveyor to the Prince of Wales, heir to the throne, in 1610. More important to his education as an architect was his second journey to Italy, as adviser to Thomas Howard, Earl of Arundel, during 1614–1615. At that time he not only acquired art works and drawings, but was able to study the buildings of Andrea Palladio firsthand; he annotated a copy of the famous *Quattro Libri* and kept a magnificent sketchbook, both now in the library at Chatsworth. The secret of Jones's success as a self-taught classical architect lay in his superb drawing ability combined with a keen analytical mind, capable of discovering the secrets of proportioning, construction, and ornament in Renaissance buildings through painstaking study. He measured many of Palladio's buildings, noted problems and discrepancies in his copy of the treatise, and attempted to follow the master's precepts in his own designs. There is evidence in the set of drawings he left to his pupil John Webb that he intended to publish a treatise of his own.

Jones advanced to the Surveyorship of the King's Works in 1615, the highest architectural post in England, with only his reputation as an inventor of stage designs as a credential. In his first buildings, he attempted nothing less than the complete conversion of medieval, Jacobean prototypes to the rigorous classical models of Palladio. The Queen's House, Greenwich (1616–1635) (Fig. 1), would have been a nine-square plan villa after the master's works in the Veneto, as an original design has suggested, were the exigencies of a program not brought to bear on it. The Prince's Lodging at Newmarket (1619, destroyed) further advanced the English country house into Palladianism, employing a tripartite, pedimental elevation, complete with rusticated base and *piano nobile*. Finally, his

(a)

(b)

Figure 1. (a) Plan (from *Vitruvius Brittanicus*) and **(b)** photograph of the Queen's House in Greenwich (1616–1635). Courtesy of the author.

best-known work, the Banqueting House at Whitehall (1622, to have been part of a larger palace), adapted the Vicentine urban palazzo elevation to a new spatial conception—a great double-cube room used for masques, banquets, and royal entertainments. Here Jones employed two equal rusticated stories, articulated by Ionic and Corinithian trabeation and elegant aedicular windows, to create one of the most serene and harmonious facade compositions in English architecture. It is astounding that at age 40, with little or no experience in building, working in a highly closed medieval masonic system, he could have so convincingly assimilated the Italian system and erected several masterpieces in the process.

As royal architect, Jones was able to design projects that changed the face of the London of his day. He executed a new, quasi-classical double tower west front for old Saint Paul's (1634–1642) and planned a monumental, multicourted new palace at Whitehall for Charles I in 1638 that rivaled French palaces in scale. His most important urbanistic contribution to the city was the great piazza at Covent Garden, with the rustic, Tuscan-porticoed St. Paul's church (1631), designed for the Earl of Bedford. With this square and its uniform rows of arcaded buildings, Jones established a prototype that the great London terraces and squares subdividing the estates in the Georgian period would follow.

Other extant buildings include the Queen's Chapel at St. James Palace (1623–1627) and the great double-cube room at Wilton House in Wiltshire (1633–1640), really the design of Isaac de Caus after Jones's recommendations. However, it is not Jones's buildings so much as his intellectual and artistic ideas that left their mark in seventeenth-century British culture. As England's first architect–artist, Jones left his imprint on such figures as Roger Pratt, the builder of Coleshill (a Jonesian country house); John Webb, his pupil and successor as Surveyor; and even Christopher Wren. His influence never entirely waned, awaiting the great resurgence of Palladianism under Burlington in the early eighteenth century, when Jones became an architectural hero, a *nonpareil* in British architecture.

With the British Civil War and fall of his patron Charles I, Jones's architectural career came to an abrupt end. Captured in 1644 by Cromwell's forces, he was stripped of his position and estate, and passed his final years quietly, leaving to Webb his mantle, a great number of his own drawings, and his collection of Palladio drawings. These would later find their way into the hands of Lord Burlington, becoming the core of the great Burlington–Devonshire collection. He died in London on June 21, 1652.

BIBLIOGRAPHY

R. T. Blomfield, *A History of Renaissance Architecture in England, 1500–1800,* 2 vols., G. Bell and Sons, London, 1897.

J. A. Gotch, *Inigo Jones,* Methuen & Co., Inc., London, 1928.

S. Orgel and R. Strong, *Inigo Jones and the Theatre of the Stuart Court,* 2 vols., University of California Press, Berkeley, Calif., 1973.

J. Harris, *Catalogue of the Drawings Collection in the Royal Institute of British Architects: Inigo Jones & John Webb,* Gregg International, Farnborough, UK, 1972.

J. Summerson, *Inigo Jones,* Penguin Books, Harmondsworth, 1966.

J. Summerson, *Architecture in Britain, 1530–1830,* 4th ed., Chaps. 7–9, Penguin Books, Harmondsworth, 1966.

R. Wittkower in *Palladio & English Palladianism,* George Braziller, New York, 1974, pp. 50–64.

MARK A. HEWITT
Columbia University
New York, New York

JOURNAL OF ARCHITECTURAL EDUCATION. See ASSOCIATION OF COLLEGIATE SCHOOLS OF ARCHITECTURE (ACSA)

JUDICIAL BUILDINGS. See JUSTICE BUILDINGS—LAW ENFORCEMENT, COURTS, AND CORRECTIONS

JUSTICE BUILDINGS—LAW ENFORCEMENT, COURTS, AND CORRECTIONS

The justice system is the U.S. government's means of maintaining order in society. As a result, citizens see the government as symbolized by justice institutions and their buildings. As the justice system and its individual components have become a differentiated, specialized segment of government activity, special facilities have been created to support them. The history of U.S. justice buildings reflects a judicial system that was brought to the United States from Great Britain, but which was subsequently changed to adapt to the new democratic system of government and the new freedoms that government created. This article describes the planning and design of modern U.S. justice facilities, including law enforcement, judicial, and correctional facilities, with special emphasis on facilities for juvenile offenders. Each section provides appropriate historical background as it affects the current thinking of architects and justice professionals.

THE JUSTICE SYSTEM

The planning and design of justice facilities have as their first requirement recognition of the context in which architecture will be applied. The traditional three components of the justice system—law enforcement, the courts, and corrections—bring needs that are unique to each, but develop out of their interaction with one another. This establishes additional requirements for architecture.

Within this spectrum of justice facilities is included the primary focus of law enforcement on the delivery of public safety services. Law enforcement facilities are most frequently called on to provide a base of support for services delivered in the field by law enforcement officers, for communications and public safety services, for criminal investigations, and for the processing and possible short-term detention of arrested individuals.

The courts system requires facilities that will provide an appropriate environment for the adjudication process; that is, the determination of probable cause for court proceedings, the determination of guilt or innocence, and the imposition of sanctions. A wide variety of facility settings is required to meet the needs within this area, depending on the level of jurisdiction and the judicial system involved.

The corrections component includes a broad range of subsystem components. There are two basic categories: (*1*) facilities for the safe and secure detention of individuals charged with crime but not yet convicted (jails) and (*2*) facilities for the incarceration of individuals who have been found guilty and sentenced (prisons). There are a variety of alternative facilities such as those that support work programs or other activities that call for intermittent confinement as part of a sentence. Special facilities must also be provided for juveniles in the justice system.

It is significant for justice facility planning to be aware of the synergism of the system components and the fact that the level of activity in one component affects the service demands in another component. This is critical to the volume of activity that a facility will be required to handle, the level of staffing, the space requirements, and other facility needs.

Yet another dimension of the interaction that occurs between components is the flow of people, and information between them. In addition to the movement of system clients through the judicial process and the facility components that serve it, line staff and administrative personnel as well as the public have the need to access various components as a part of their respective involvement in the process.

As a result, facility planning for any one component should be conducted with a sensitivity to the larger system context and the dynamics of its operations. The facilities may be independent structures on separate sites, coordinated on a single site, or incorporated in a single building (Fig. 1).

Not surprisingly, in recent years there has been an increasing number of instances of the development of justice or public safety complexes in which more than one justice system component is housed within the same facility. Quite frequently, such complexes are developed out of an awareness of the high volume of movement that occurs between components and the operational economies and functional efficiencies that can be attained through their co-location. They may also be developed out of a recognition that the facilities that serve each of the justice system components in that jurisdiction may be equally outdated, overloaded, or otherwise in need of improvement or replacement.

Another phenomenon is the consolidation of service delivery. Examples include combined communications and dispatch for city and county jurisdictions, combined judicial facilities for city and district courts, and the developments emanating out of unified state court systems.

In larger urban areas, the development of metrogovernments that administer public services on a centralized basis over a large geographic and multijurisdictional area has had an effect on the type and location of justice facilities in such areas. In some instances this has created unique facility types such as satellite intake centers, which reduce travel time for law enforcement personnel with arraignment courts for the initial appearances of arrested individuals.

In more rural areas, recent attention has been focused on the development of regional correctional facilities that meet certain needs generated by a population that is dispersed over a large geographic area. In creating regional facilities, a balance is sought between the requirements of local law enforcement and court systems, and the efficiencies of operating combined detention facilities to serve larger numbers of individuals. One form that this may take is the evolution of a local intake service center in which initial booking and processing occurs, complemented by a regional correctional facility where longer term confinement occurs while the individuals await trial or serve sentences.

Another form of jurisdictional cooperation has emerged that has implications for facilities. This involves a transfer of responsibilities between state and local units of government accompanied by funding arrangements that make such realignment possible. In the corrections arena, there has been an increased reliance on county facilities by state government as state facilities have become overloaded. Various models can be observed, including one from New Jersey, where capital funding has been made available to counties to enlarge local facilities for state prisoners, and one from Minnesota, where a program involving standards for both operations and facilities is tied to a state subsidy program. In either instance, and many others that might be cited, implications for facility requirements are manifest.

Accordingly, the justice system presents an area for architectural response that defies reduction to a few standardized models or statements of building types. To the contrary, it suggests the need for a keen awareness of the system dynamics occurring within a particular service jurisdiction. It also suggests a methodical and systematic approach to planning and design.

Role of the Architect

Planning for justice facilities presents a challenge that is perhaps more complex than for any other building type. Considering the widely accepted maxim that form follows function, the architect is faced with the need to respond to extremely diverse, and sometimes apparently conflicting, functional requirements.

The most immediate task presented is the need to clearly comprehend the particular functional requirements that accompany an individual project. These may be determined by the involvement of the user agencies, funding agencies, legislative bodies, professionally recommended standards, court orders, citizens' groups, previous consultant reports, or any combination of these or other party involvements.

Without doubt, any previous experience that the architect may have had in developing a justice facility will be invaluable. However, it is not unusual for the architect to have no such prior experience. Local justice facilities are built at infrequent intervals, and once constructed, are expected to serve for a long time.

Consequently, it has been most common for local architects to bring together a team of specialists to deal with this kind of planning and design challenge when it is presented. The team will often include a programming consultant who has experience in data analysis, population projections, staffing, and operations assessment. This consultant will also have experience with a variety of design concepts, necessary functional relationships, applicable facility standards, construction technologies, specialized equipment applications, and facility cost histories.

The team, normally referred to as the "architect," is only one entity within the planning environment out of which justice facilities are typically developed. The complexity of the justice system combined with the plurality of participants that accompany most public facility procurement processes establish a milieu that calls for the utmost in professional skill and experience.

Depending on the level of definition that a project may have at the time that the architect is retained, the architect may be assigned the role of assisting the client agency in determining the range of functions that a proposed facility should have; the anticipated future growth, which should be planned and designed for; the site selection criteria and site selection process; the assessment of staffing requirements and associated operating costs; and life-cycle facility option cost analyses, in addition to the delivery of basic architectural and engineering design services. It is also not uncommon for the architect to be an integral part of the building procurement process through partici-

(a)

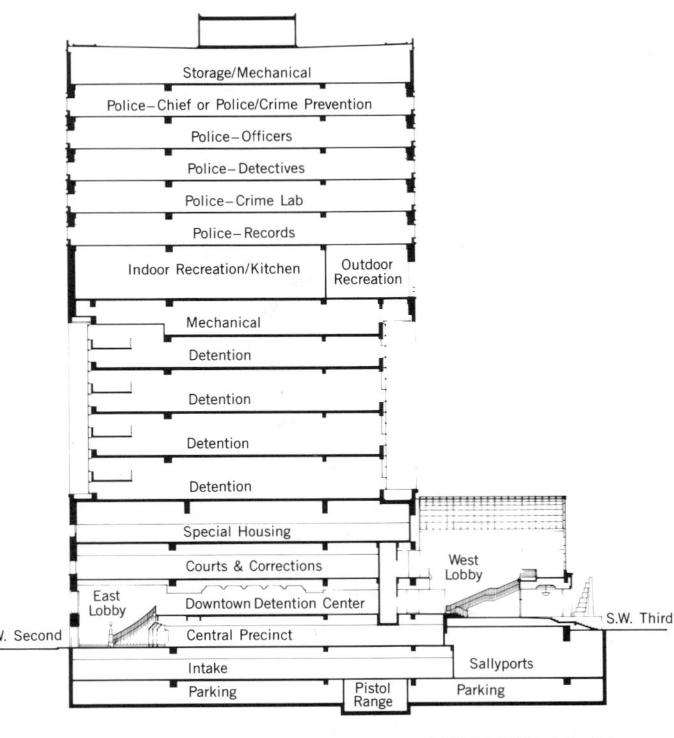

(b)

(c)

Figure 1. Portland Justice Center, Portland, Oregon. Architects: Zimmer, Gunsul, Frasca Partnership. Illustrates all aspects of the justice system in one building, combining police, courts, and detention facilities. The "high-rise" solution is appropriate to the urban site. (**a**) Exterior, SW Third Street entrance; (**b**) section; (**c**) interior of SW Third Street lobby. Courtesy of Zimmer Gunsul Frasca Partnership. Photograph by Timothy Hursley.

pation in legislative testimony relative to statutory change or funding commitments, presentations to county board meetings concerned with funding requirements, and design approvals and appearances at public hearings or other public presentations intended to inform and involve the general citizenry with developments that are contemplated.

Unsatisfactory justice facility conditions may become the focus of proceedings requiring the architect's testimony concerning the improvements that are being proposed in a new project and their adequacy in relation to nationally recognized standards or already mandated court orders.

The AIA has recognized the importance and critical nature of justice system architecture by establishing the Committee on Architecture for Justice (CAJ). The mission of this committee is to maintain a network for the exchange of information among architects and between architects and justice professionals. The CAJ has developed a policy for the AIA, which supports the use of a rational planning process and the development and application of national standards for justice facility design and operation.

LAW ENFORCEMENT FACILITIES

The design of police facilities must satisfy and balance the needs of five basic groups.

1. *The Justice System.* Those other agencies outside of law enforcement that interface with the law enforcement activity, eg, courts, probation, and corrections. There should also be an awareness of nonjustice system public safety relations that impact the law enforcement facility, such as civil defense or emergency preparedness.
2. *The Community.* The interaction with the citizens of a community, the public relations of the agency, and the access to services in time of need.
3. *The Law Enforcement Officer.* The facility must nurture the development of the individual as well as provide space that facilitates law enforcement activity in an efficient, safe, and secure environment.
4. *The Technology of Law Enforcement.* Special equipment and procedures must be considered in terms of their inherent needs and the people that use them.
5. *The Administration.* The needs required to coordinate the complex activity and maintain accountability to the laws that are to be enforced.

The complexity of the law enforcement facility will vary with the number and extent to which these five groups must be accommodated in a single structure. Depending on the size of the law enforcement agency and the community that it serves, there may be a network of facilities with specific purposes or a single structure that serves them all. The components may be organized in various configurations to fit the needs of the system, whether a community-based or precinct facility, an independent freestanding facility that incorporates all activities for a small town, a regional center, or a specialized activity such as a forensic laboratory or an intake and booking facility (Fig. 2).

Programming and Design

Regardless of the size or complexity of the law enforcement facility, there are basic factors that must be accommodated by the design. These factors are inherent in most institutional buildings, especially justice facilities. There are five categories worth repeating.

1. *Economy.* The design must fit the current needs of the agency, yet be flexible or large enough to allow for projected growth and unexpected change over a period of ten years. Alternatives to new facilities should be considered, along with the possibilities for sharing facilities with other agencies. Economies should be considered on a first-cost and life-cycle basis.
2. *Security.* The facility should contribute to the physical security of all occupants. The possibilities for sabotage or vandalism can be reduced through proper separation of public and secure circulation areas, stationing personnel at key points, providing clear lines of sight, and providing adequate lighting inside and out. Special attention must be paid to critical areas, such as the armory, evidence storage, and arrestee holding areas. As public buildings, law enforcement facilities must achieve a secure environment while maintaining an open public feeling.
3. *Safety and Accessibility.* The role of the police in society requires that facilities be entirely accessible to handicapped persons in the public and staff areas. The 24-hour nature of the police function requires special attention to life safety considerations for protection of personnel and equipment. The critical nature of the police function may also require special seismic consideration and provision of auxiliary power to ensure continued operation in times of emergency.
4. *Attractiveness.* Police law enforcement facilities need to provide for the people who work and visit the facility. They should convey a feeling of efficiency and strength, while nurturing the feelings of human caring. Decorative arts should be included in the attention to details of the building design.
5. *Operational Efficiency.* The planning and design process should include a detailed analysis of the work flow and procedures of the agency, which are then reflected in the adjacencies and circulation of the building and the site. Special equipment such as computers, laboratories, and communications must be accommodated as well as attention to lighting and acoustics in critical areas such as the firing range. The administrative areas should include the most up-to-date features to enhance performance of tasks and storage of records and equipment.

Each law enforcement system has its own specific configuration to satisfy its needs. Although all law enforce-

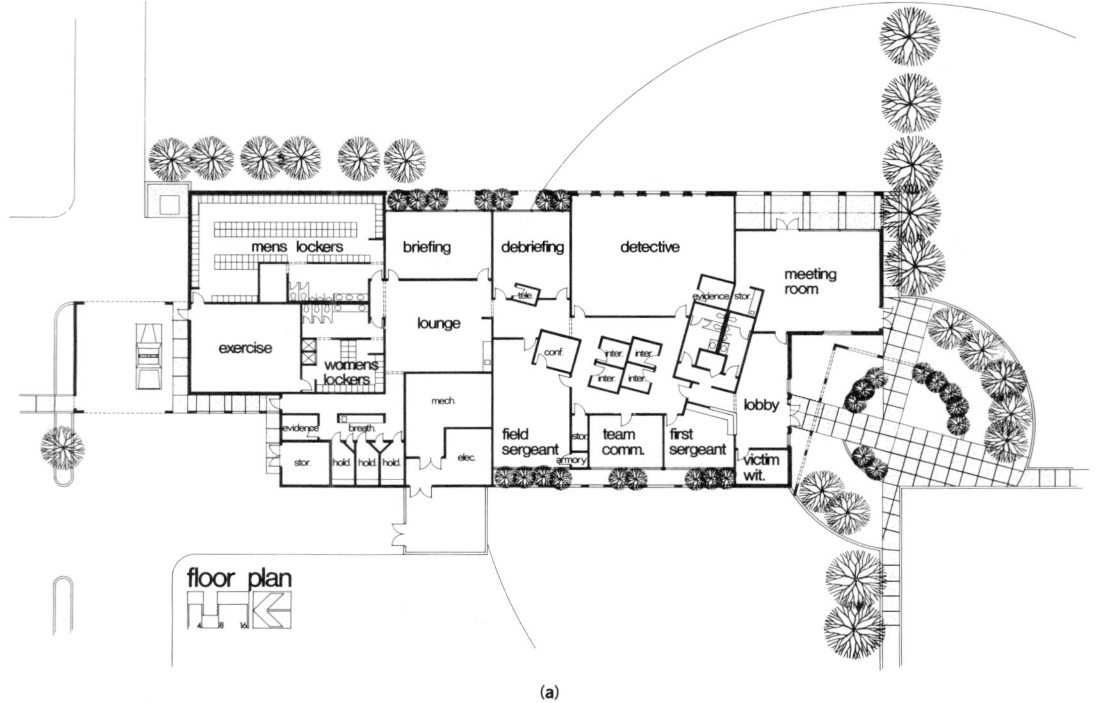

(a)

(b)

Figure 2. Santa Cruz Police Substation, Tucson, Arizona. Architects: Architecture One, Ltd. A typical neighborhood police station in plan, designed to fit into the context of its neighborhood. (**a**) Floor plan, courtesy of Architecture One Ltd; (**b**) exterior of entrance courtyards, courtesy of James Prett Photo.

ment agencies are similar enough to discuss the programmatic elements that make up the facility, the size and shape should be based on an in-depth programmatic analysis of the agency's goals and how these goals will be achieved. The facility can then be created to support the agency's methods and procedures, containing the elements listed below.

1. *Public Areas*. The public entrance provides access to the facility reception area. It should provide a comfortable waiting area, rest rooms, and a convenient place for private consultation. If the facility contains a classroom or auditorium, the space should have public access for meetings or press conferences. The staff library or reading room may also be accessible to the public, as well as a cafeteria in larger facilities. The public areas should be visible by staff at all times. Access to the other areas of the facility should be tightly controlled.
2. *Staff Area*. The shift commander's office is the operational center for police activities. It should be centrally located with access to all electronic information and communication activity. A secure storage area with lockers should also be conveniently located. The briefing room, or squad room, should be large enough to accommodate all officers on a shift. A space should be provided for preparation of routine paperwork. This space should be convenient to the locker rooms and staff entrance. Locker rooms should be provided for both men and women with showers and shared exercise equipment. Weapons storage needs to be secure and conveniently placed to the briefing area.

   The detectives' work area should utilize open office planning with a comfortable waiting area and private interview rooms. The interview area should be secure, as it may be used as a short-term holding area for a prisoner. Provisions should be made for electronic listening and audio and video recording.

   A separate area for juvenile activities, including waiting area, office space, and interview rooms, should be created in a softer environment, recognizing the status of juveniles under the law. A conference room for small meetings of approximately 12 people should be accessible to the detective area as well as the administrative area.

   The administrative area of the law enforcement facility contains all activities that support the individual officer and the organization of the agency. Functions such as planning, personnel, accounting, public relations, legal offices, and records storage are located in this area. A combination of contemporary open office planning and private space should be utilized. The staff training area is related to the administrative function, public areas, and line staff areas and should contain storage space for materials and equipment.

   The technical support areas have the critical requirement for accommodation of specialized equipment and activities. The communications center must be arranged to facilitate the orderly exchange of information from various specialized areas for complaint reception, dispatch, information retrieval, incident–personnel status, and visitor viewing area.

   The forensic laboratory can vary widely in its use of scientific equipment. The ballistics section will require a bullet retrieval system. A photographic facility should be convenient, and the evidence storage area should be accessible. The weapons area and firing range require special attention to safety and procedure. Elements of this area include the bullet trap, firing line, target mechanisms, rangemaster's station, and weapons storage. Attention to the acoustical properties of this area is also required.
3. *Prisoner Area*. Access to the prisoner processing and holding area should be through separate and secure sally ports. Direct vehicular access through a vehicle sally port is often used. There should be lockers outside the processing area for temporary storage of officers' weapons. The processing area requires space for fingerprinting and photographing arrestees and separate areas for interviewing or interrogating and testing for alcohol or drugs. Arrestees must have access to a telephone, and property and evidence storage should be secure and convenient.

   The prisoner processing area should contain facilities for short-term holding of prisoners for up to four hours. The cells should be constructed of maximum security materials and fixtures. A special padded cell for extreme prisoner behavior should also be provided. Sight line and procedure are critical to security in this sensitive area.
4. *Vehicle Storage and Maintenance*. In most areas, the planning and development of the site will be dominated by the vehicular traffic and should be coordinated with the overall security plan for the facility.

COURT FACILITIES

Near to the heart of most U.S. communities stands the symbol of their system of justice—the courthouse. It has been argued that each courthouse must be a symbol of the U.S. dream of justice, which assures citizens that justice is a functioning reality of the American way of life.

Although the symbolic nature of the courthouse is common to all of its buildings, justice in the United States is organized into trial and appellate levels each addressing specific aspects of the legal code. The U.S. legal system is a multilevel structure of federal, state, county, and municipal courts, each developed to service different jurisdictions. Within each of these structures are several components that identify the types of courts and their hierarchical relationships. The particular level of court being housed has both functional and design implications with greater similarity across federal and state jurisdictions than across hierarchical systems within those jurisdictions.

Historically, the courthouse achieved its identity through its size, siting, and specific architectural elements such as columns, domes, clock towers, grand entrances, and massiveness. This special identity has remained re-

Figure 3. Monroe County/City of Bloomington Public Safety Building, Bloomington, Indiana. Architects: Odle & Burke Architects. Typical interior of a criminal court. Courtesy of Moyer Associates Inc.

markably consistent since colonial times, regardless of architectural idiom. The openness and free spirit of design contributes to the distinctly American character of the courthouse (Fig. 3).

Programming and Design

In developing the courthouse identity, the architect must (*1*) communicate the meaning and spirit of justice and the special significance of the particular court to be housed; (*2*) complement and enhance the architectural and environmental character and importance of the site and often respond as well to particular urban development goals and objectives; (*3*) respond to programmed spaces, adjacencies, hierarchical relationships, and security needs; (*4*) provide a cost-effective solution that promotes efficiency of planning, function, operations, maintenance, and structure as well as economical energy consumption; and (*5*) be sufficiently flexible to accommodate change and growth of the justice system and its support facilities and to respond to rapidly changing technologies.

Programming activities must document historic growth in personnel and space in each case, and identify those factors influencing past, present, and future change. From these data, projected space need is developed to identify time-phased space needs for the courts and their support offices. Particular skills required for these tasks include in-depth knowledge of the organization of the judicial system, statistical analyses of large data bases (eg, court caseload activities), flexible interview and presentation techniques, and architectural and engineering building analyses. The programming results will be used by a variety of professionals who have different questions and needs, for example, architects to design the building, government officials to decide if the building is needed, and the public to decide whether or not to fund the construction. Relevant consultants include planners, demographers, and environmental psychologists. The process should also include users, judges, court administrators, clerks of court, other departmental representatives, and practicing attorneys.

Courthouse planning requires consideration of several design criteria, materials, and building arrangements. The meaning and spirit of the courthouse can be communicated through conscious use of analogy, context, metaphor, and symbolism (Fig. 4). The order of authority in courtrooms and hearing rooms establishes requirements for visual, acoustical, and security elements as seen in the placement and elevation of the bench, clerk, witness stand, and jury box. As a rule, daylight should be provided wherever possible. Priority should be given to high use, high status areas. Light sources must be controlled to provide energy effi-

(a)

(b)

Figure 4. Western District Missouri Court of Appeals, Kansas City, Missouri, architects: Abend Singleton Associates, Inc. A design that supports the dignity and function of the court. (**a**) Court interior; (**b**) floor plan. Courtesy of Paul Kivett Architectural Foto Graphics.

ciency and privacy. These same high use, high status spaces must also have individual controls and acoustically isolated ducting for supply–return air.

The relationship of net assignable space to gross building area is a measure of building efficiency. Court-related spaces should obtain a 70% net-to-gross efficiency. This level of efficiency is the result of the need for three separated circulation systems—public, private, and prisoner. Judicial support and constitutional offices should obtain 75% net-to-gross efficiency, and shared facilities should develop an 80% net-to-gross efficiency. To promote greater use of space, courtrooms, hearing rooms, chambers, and jury deliberation rooms should be designed for flexible, rather than specific, use and assignment. Yet, their construction and environmental systems should be designed as permanent spaces to insure acoustical isolation.

Courthouse planning should emphasize prevention of problems and the safety of individuals. Proper sectoring and circulation systems contribute to security and reduce the personnel required to maintain security. Technological advances should be considered to allow for monitoring. Detection systems and space should be designed to coordinate all security personnel and staff members who function as a "first-level" security force.

Proper courtroom sight lines are critical. They must be checked painstakingly during the design planning phases. Courtrooms must be designed to allow all participants within the bar to see each other's faces during proceedings. Courtrooms must be designed to allow all participants to hear and understand each other during proceedings, preferably without the use of sound amplification systems. Generally, a combination of hard (reflective) and soft (absorptive) materials are used to provide good acoustical quality in courtrooms. Acoustical isolation is requisite for chambers, hearing rooms, conference spaces, and jury deliberation rooms. Acoustical control must be provided in spaces that are more flexible in character.

Federal and state standards for barrier-free access to and within the courthouse must be met for all facilities including parking, grading, walks, entrances, elevators, toilets, phones, and drinking fountains. Reference to ANSI A117.1–1986 is suggested, if not mandatory. In addition, courtrooms should have barrier-free access to the bench, bar, clerk's and reporter's stations, witness stand, jury box, and spectator areas.

Master planning should consider specific space needs for at least a 20-year period, regardless of how much is built during the current building program. In addition, master planning should recognize that the courthouse will serve the community for at least 100 years. Expansion after the initial 20-year period should be considered. Generally, horizontal expansion causes minimum disruption for users.

The courthouse must accommodate an ever changing use of technology. Staff who require work stations with access to computer terminals should be identified. At a minimum, wiring conduit should be roughed-in for future technology. Courtrooms and hearing rooms need a variety of technological access and systems such as multitrack audiovisual recording with control from the clerk's station; sound-reinforcement systems and facilities for the hearing impaired; computer terminals; slide projectors; x rays; and overhead projectors, to name the most important.

A well-planned court facility is organized into a four-sectored system. This system groups the participants according to functional needs and separates them until they meet in the courtroom. By separating participants in this way, security, dignity, efficiency, flexibility, and privacy are increased. The four sectors are as follows.

1. The public sector, which contains offices and support spaces serving the public.
2. The interface sector, which contains those spaces in which the attorneys and public meet judges, jurors, and those in custody. It is the core of the judicial process. This sector also houses offices that require access from two different kinds of circulation patterns. Optimally, all users should enter courtrooms from only one of the circulation systems without crossing into another sector.
3. The private sector, which includes those spaces that separate judges, jurors, staff, and identified users from the public and prisoners. This separation, which prevents possible prejudicial observations and actions, enhances the judicial process.
4. The prisoner sector, which provides for the movement of persons in custody between detention and courtrooms. Absolute security is requisite. When sectoring is combined with multiple circulation systems to serve the sectors, security is increased, manpower costs are decreased, confidentiality is enhanced, and courthouse facilities are used more efficiently.

Codes and Standards

Although standards have been adopted by almost all states for hospitals, schools, and jails, a relatively small number of states have adopted statewide criteria, guidelines, or standards for courthouses: New Hampshire (the first to do so), Colorado, Illinois, Georgia, Maine, Minnesota, and Wisconsin. The number of state standards is growing at a slow rate. These guidelines have had varying degrees of effectiveness depending on means of monitoring, available resources, and the political environment.

The American Courthouse, published in 1972 under the direction of a joint task force of the American Bar Association and the American Institute of Architects, remains the only systematic and documented guide for courthouse architecture in all of its forms. At the federal level, the *U.S. Design Guide* is available to architects serving the General Services Administration (GSA) in projects involving the federal courts.

New Concepts and Technologies

The courts can look forward to many areas of innovation and development. Organizationally, court unification is already being implemented in some states as a means of achieving a more efficient use of judicial resources. Technological advances are well underway in some courts (eg, Michigan Recorder's Court), with extensive use and integration of computerized systems in courtrooms, clerk's offices, prosecuting attorney's offices, sheriff's departments, and related agencies. The use of closed-circuit television (CCTV) to connect jail and court for first appearance and arraignments has been a major advancement, saving manpower and minimizing security risks.

In the law library, advances are being made by providing access to research materials through computer indexing. Future advances will come from the ability to access information by optical scanning of disks.

Functional changes in the courts are being seen in the area of caseload management, which focuses on improved record-keeping procedures, case flow organization, and transfer of specific case types to administrative disposition. Finally, the role of the Court Planner is gaining formal recognition as seen in the involvement of an architect as a member of the staff of the Administrative Office of the Court of Colorado. His role is to guide and assist counties in the planning of facilities using the state guidelines. Furthermore, the Conference of Chief Justices, Conference of State Court Administrators, and the National Association of Court Managers have passed resolutions urging all states to adopt statewide criteria for effective and efficient facilities. In so doing, the standard of the delivery of justice will be raised to the level the courts deserve and the court's symbolic image will be preserved for the public it serves.

CORRECTIONS FACILITIES

Buildings and building complexes identified today as detention and correctional facilities shared a common development until a certain point in history. At that point, the unique attributes of the separate facility types gave recognition and relatively clear understanding of their respective missions. Even with the difference in goals between detention and corrections, the two building types continue to share common aspects of uses of space, plan configurations, building materials, security barriers, staffing concerns, application of building codes, etc.

It should be noted that "correctional architecture" is often used generically to refer to both detention and correctional facilities. Both detention and correctional facilities respond to the requirements for security confinement environments; however, a distinction is necessary when addressing certain design requirements for each.

Detention facilities are commonly identified as jails. Their primary mission is to detain adults accused of a crime until their guilt or innocence is determined by a court of law. Jails are also used to hold individuals under protective custody, to prevent others from doing them physical harm, or to prevent the detained from doing harm to others. In some legal jurisdictions, jails are used to confine persons found to be guilty by a court of law for shorter periods of sentencing, usually one year or less. Jails are administered by local governments (city and county) and by the federal government.

New detention facilities are most often multipurpose facilities, with all degrees of security and support services. They are usually single-building schemes on urban sites with a loose relationship to other justice services. Larger populated counties and municipalities tend to develop detention systems including special-purpose facilities and dedicated buildings for inmate classifications.

Correctional facilities are commonly identified as prisons. Their mission is to provide a supervised living environment for persons who are sentenced by the court. Prisons are intended to provide support and rehabilitation services and programs for felony offenders with sentences longer than a year. Correctional systems serve adult males and females, generally defined as persons who are 18 years and older.

Correctional facilities also respond to a number of needs beyond the basic requirements for security, including all degrees of special-purpose institutions such as those used for diagnosis–evaluation and treatment, special inmate training programs, a variety of security levels, and work furlough and community-based prerelease centers.

Prison facilities are administered by the state, or by the federal government through the Bureau of Prisons. New prison facilities are generally removed from, or on the fringe of, urban areas. Common sizes for correctional facilities range from 300 to 600 beds; 500 beds is the recommended limit in current corrections standards. In states with extremely large corrections populations, such as New York and California, new institutions have been designed for several thousand beds. The juvenile corrections system, which is independently administered in the majority of state governments, is addressed in a separate section.

History

The history and evolution of modern confinement facilities have been, for the most part, the reaction to change in social trends and development, religious beliefs, penal or punishment codes, judicial system development, prison development, and mental health development. Since the first recognition of the so-called jail, as distinguished from a prison, the changes that occurred were a result of deliberate change in other directly (and sometimes indirectly) related areas. Only recently has there been deliberate focus on and direct change of facility operational philosophies and physical facilities for detention and corrections.

Prior to the emergence of correctional facilities, social wrongdoings were punished directly by individuals, families, or clans. Punishment was in the form of blood for blood or some type of payment. The punished was not always the actual offender. As the question of innocence or guilt became more vague, the idea of providing a place for holding the accused, until innocence or guilt was decided or until punishment by a person, a tribunal, or groups of persons, evolved.

Some of the earliest recognized corrections facilities appeared during the Roman Empire, approximately 64 B.C. During that time, cages or dungeons located under the main sewer system of Rome were used. Death was most often the punishment sentence; therefore, the Roman dungeons essentially held persons awaiting tribunal or execution. As the need for mass labor for the construction of public buildings arose, the lower classes were largely sentenced to penal servitude or, in essence, a civil death in lieu of actual death.

The church exerted influence and control during the Middle Ages. Criminals were deemed to owe payment or penance to society for wrongdoing and also to God. During this period, dungeons were again used until guilt or innocence was determined. Guilt or innocence was established in the form of an "ordeal," which more often than not resulted in the death of the accused or offender. The science and development of torture and death was advanced significantly during this era.

Under the rule of Henry II, the construction of gaols was authorized by the Assize of Clarendon in 1166 A.D. Gaols were used from this period until the late 1600s to house the poor, mentally disabled, vagrants, those awaiting trial, and those sentenced to death or some form of corporal punishment. Henry II placed the gaols under the control of local sheriffs, but did not provide any money to operate them. Prisoners or their families paid for their upkeep including food, bedding, release from irons, and release from the gaol. No standards for the care of the gaol population or for classification and separation of the inmates existed.

Gaols became crowded, then overcrowded in the mid-1500s and in the early 1700s; with the first facility at the Royal Palace of Bridewell, the concept of workhouses evolved. Workhouses were to provide training for the poor; Bridewell houses were an answer to overcrowding by removing many of the misdemeanants and compelling the inmates to work under strict discipline. Operationally, little distinction could be made between Bridewell houses and goals. During this period, serious crimes such as thievery were punished with some advanced form of capital punishment, torture, mutilation, or branding. During the reign of Henry VIII, 72,000 people were executed. Continued overcrowding and social conditions led to the use of banishment and "hulks," or prison ships anchored in harbors. Banishment led to some of the early colonization of America.

Early American colonies such as Jamestown, Williamsburg, and the New England colonies constructed gaols in much the same manner as the British gaols of the time. However, the use of capital punishment was significantly reduced and reserved only for the most serious crimes. The use of corporal punishment such as stocks, pillars, dunkings, and brandings became more prevalent. Still, gaol populations were not segregated or separated, nor was the public particularly concerned about conditions in them.

Similar to the system conceived by Henry II, gaols in America were placed under the control of the local sheriff. By the late 1600s, both the Virginia and Massachusetts colonies had legislatively placed these facilities under the control of the County Shire Sheriff.

During the early development of the United States, the fact that jails or prisons were used for punishment evolved from the philosophy that they should be used as a place for the guilty to do penance. William Penn, when establishing the first American penal code in 1682, included such items as prisoners being eligible for bail and the provision of free food and lodging. He also wrote that counties were to provide houses of detention (jails). During these eras there was no clear distinction between holding for trial and holding as a sentence or punishment; the facilities were, for the most part, mixed in their use.

In 1777, in Great Britain, John Howard wrote about the deplorable state in which he found prison conditions. Howard suggested changes such as the use of single cells, ventilation, separation of offenders, separation of young from old, separation of males from females, and provisions for bathing and laundry. Many of those concerns were not seriously dealt with in some jurisdictions until the late 1960s and 1970s. A significant result of Howard's writings was the emergence of the distinction between jails and prisons.

From the late 1700s until recently, changes focusing directly on jails and prisons have been few. Most deliberate changes have focused on the convicted population—developing prisons and continual concerns and changes in prison philosophy.

Leading the effort in Pennsylvania was a group of concerned individuals who ultimately became known as the Pennsylvania Prison Society. The legislation effected renovation of Philadelphia's Walnut Street Jail, which is reputed to be the first true correctional institution in America. Eastern State Penitentiary, designed by John Haviland, was completed in Philadelphia in 1829, and with it came a system of corrections known as the Pennsylvania System.

This system involved confinement of the prisoners in their cells at all times. The prisoners were given crafts or semiskilled activities to perform in their cells. It was thought that this total confinement would make the convicts introspective and facilitate their rehabilitation. It did not succeed.

The Auburn System in New York State was developed in parallel as a variation of the Pennsylvania model, and in 1816, New York began constructing the new prison at Auburn (Fig. 5). The Auburn System removed the prisoners from their cells for meals and to perform work in prison industries. The inmates were confined in their cell only for sleeping or emergency conditions. The Pennsylvania and Auburn approaches provided models for prisons throughout the United States and Europe, including extensions of the Pennsylvania System into Canada. Other significant examples of these very large early penitentiaries in the United States include Sing Sing Prison, Ossining, New York, 1825; Western State Penitentiary, Pittsburgh, Pennsylvania, 1826 (Fig. 6); Wethersfield Penitentiary, Connecticut, 1827; and Jefferson Prison, Indiana, 1847.

As the justice system of the United States categorized the types and locations of court trials, the task of holding the accused followed suit. With the layering of court hearings corresponding with the layering of state and federal government jurisdictions and law, provision for and operation of jails were relegated to county governments whereas prisons become the responsibility of the state. The federal government maintained responsibility for both.

Jails evolved to an operational level of holding those accused awaiting trial, sentenced misdemeanants, and sentenced felons returned for further court hearings. By this time, jail was the name generally used to identify

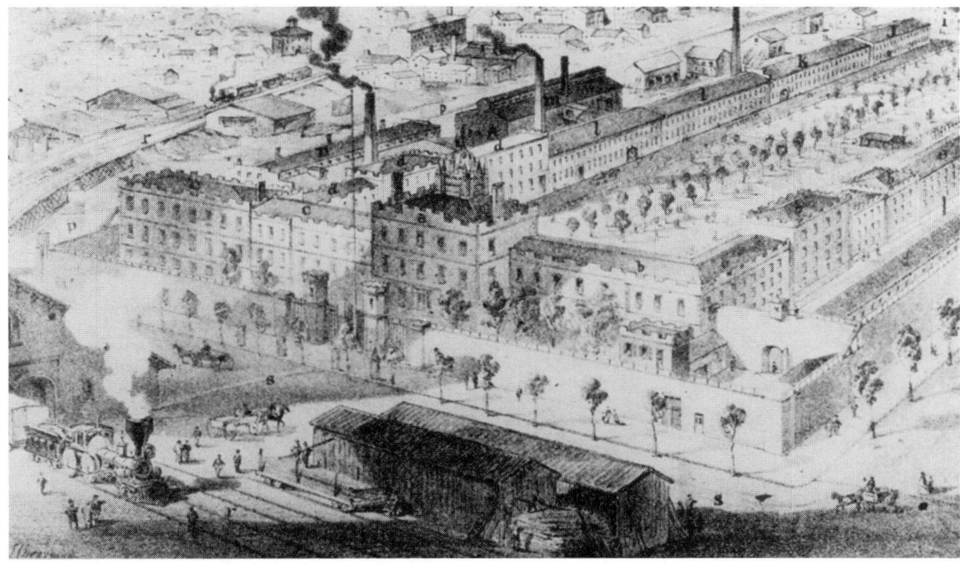

Figure 5. Auburn Prison, New York, 1868. Courtesy of American Correctional Association.

the county holding facility. However, some states, such as Pennsylvania, commonly refer to their county jail as a county prison. Jails are for the most part controlled and operated by a county or municipality; however, in the 1970s the U.S. government developed detention (holding) facilities housing those accused of violating federal offenses and awaiting federal adjudication. As facilities were built in counties across the nation, the makeup, conditions, and financing of jails represented the needs, financing, and philosophy of the particular counties establishing them.

The emergence of the "medical model" and the changed concept of treatment of mental illness during the 1920s removed many of the mentally ill from jails. During this period, much of society viewed the convict as being sick instead of a sinner. Again, during the 1950s the criminal was viewed by penologists and professionals of the industry as having a deficiency of some nature—medical, social, intellectual, or emotional. These attitudes influenced the jails and prisons in that a public consciousness surfaced relative to the fact that these facilities did exist and were costly to operate.

As the prison system developed, particularly after 1900, so did the development of extensive prison industries and farm programs (Fig. 7). From 1932 into the 1950s, a new prison design system evolved, commonly called the telephone pole plan. The first facility was the Federal Penitentiary in Lewisburg, Pennsylvania, designed by Alfred Hopkins and built in 1932. Similar designs followed in a number of states, California having three large units at Soledad, Tracy, and Vacaville.

Overcrowding, prison disturbances, and riots in the 1960s and 1970s raised philosophical and legal questions regarding conditions of confinement, police activities, and attitudes of the judiciary. These problems became the focus of public and political attention of unprecedented heights and led to court intervention. There was also a broad federal legislative effort including the Omnibus Crime Control and Safe Streets Act of 1968 (reinforced by its 1971 amendments), which brought significant reform to the approach

Figure 6. Western Pennsylvania Penitentiary, Pittsburgh, Pennsylvania, 1892. Auburn style prison. Courtesy of American Correctional Association.

Figure 7. Typical multitiered cell block, Joliet, Illinois, circa 1900. Courtesy of American Correctional Association.

of programming and planning criminal justice facilities.

As of June 30, 1985, over 100 adult institutions in the United States were under court order. While significant new correctional facility construction took place in the 1950s and early 1960s, the 1970s saw the beginnings of new and more humane prison designs. The construction programs have continued at an accelerated rate into the 1980s in response to continued crowding and escalating jail and prison populations. The number of inmates in state and federal prisons reached the half-million mark in 1985, an all-time high, as announced by the Bureau of Justice Statistics (BJS). The prison population grew by 39,000 during 1985, and at year's end stood at 504,000 inmates.

During the evolution of the legal era (1980–present), prisoners' rights movements, standards' evolution, court decisions, and federal and state controls have had the most dramatic effect on jails and prisons since their beginning. Evolution in concepts from civil death to innocent until proven guilty, the establishment of basic human and prisoners' rights, and the corresponding requirements for conditions of confinement have had the most direct effect on jail and prison operation and architecture.

The most significant single activity having effect during the first half of the 1980s was the development, refinement, and enforcement of standards for operation and construction of jails and prisons. During this period the realization of costs for staffing, operating, and constructing jails as part of the overall system of justice, including law enforcement, adjudication, and detention, caused an awakening of concern by elected officials and the public. This awakening has in turn led to the generation of more focused efforts in the planning, development, and operation of existing and new jail and prison facilities. During this period a new professionalism in operating, staff training, planning, and designing has occurred. Physical facilities have progressively evolved from the linear configurations of predominance in the pre-1970s to the podular, from the barrier intense to the more barrier-free, from the remote control, indirect supervision to the direct control, direct supervision models of the 1980s.

Programming and Design

Jail and prison facilities differ from most conventional building types in that they are asked to house individuals, usually against their desire. Security in terms of containment is required. Freedom of movement within a facility is usually controlled while movement from inside the facility to the outside is strictly controlled through physical security barriers and operation by staff. Elements such as fire exiting, fire identification and suppression, smoke identification and control, and policies and procedures in correctional facilities are restricted and carefully controlled and, therefore, contrary to similar regulations for nonsecurity type facilities. For example, inmates being housed in a jail cannot be given free and easy access to open public areas in the event of a fire emergency. A jail is a very sophisticated building type requiring a high level of detail in drawings and specifications for construction.

In terms of physical barriers and security by physical barriers, the goal of the correctional facility is to keep individuals contained and prevent the entrance of contraband. (Contraband is materials or devices not allowed inside a jail facility and includes items such as narcotics, weapons, and materials that can be fashioned and used as weapons.) Spaces between materials and junctions of different materials must be dealt with very carefully to prevent the hiding of contraband. Details and specifications should be created to provide materials and assemblies with adequate strength for the appropriate security barriers required.

Levels of security are generally defined as minimum, medium, and maximum. Minimum security spaces are, in many cases, dormitory-like spaces with less restrictive physical barriers provided by items such as locks on doors and windows. Medium security spaces provide more staff supervision and more restriction and control of inmates' activities, but permitting movement of inmates within the facility for such purposes as physical exercise, educational programs, etc. Physical barriers such as locking devices on doors and windows are more restrictive and resistive to attack. Maximum security spaces provide the most staff-intensive observation and the most restricted areas in terms of inmate movement. The most restrictive and attack-resistant physical barriers and fixtures are used for this level.

The creation of clear lines of sight are important to enable staff to appropriately observe as required by the designed level of security. Spaces designed not to facilitate appropriate observation will increase staff requirements of a facility.

Materials used for interior spaces and graphics in modern facilities can provide surfaces that will resist abuse and are easily cleaned and maintained. Similarly, many conventional materials such as painted reinforced masonry walls, plaster ceilings, and carpeting are used to provide a more normal living environment.

During the period of emergence of concern about the civil rights of inmates during the 1960s, construction of several new facilities was planned and executed. During this period, corrections philosophies, operational techniques, and facilities design underwent an evolutionary change. These philosophies and facilities have been identified in terms of their generations of development. Facilities identified as first generation are linear in concept and are made up of dormitory, multi-occupancy, and single-cell configurations. Dayroom areas are usually adjacent to the sleeping areas utilizing perimeter inspection corridors. Custodial staff is separated from the inmates. Prisoner observation and supervision is intermittent. First-generation facilities provided security barriers primarily through bar grating walls, steel plate walls, sliding bar grating doors, and remote control locking systems.

In the late 1970s and 1980s, the attitudes of supervision of inmates as well as types of security barrier began to change. The type of facility identified as second generation provides for direct observation, intermittent supervision, and remote control locking systems. With the second-generation facilities, a podular concept was developed and the bar grating on cell fronts was replaced by vision panels of glass and plastic. Cell walls constructed of reinforced masonry and hollow metal or wooden doors used in either swinging or sliding configurations depending on the level of security are prevalent in the second-generation jail facility.

In the second-generation facilities, sleeping areas, whether cells or dormitories, were designed at an exterior wall to allow direct sunlight into them as well as direct observation of the inmate from the interior. Podular designs were used to control the number of inmates in any one area. Physical separation between custodial staff and the inmate was thought to be necessary for the safety of the staff.

The third-generation facility is based on an operational policy of direct communication between the custodial staff and the inmate. It allows direct observation, direct supervision, and direct control of cell locking systems. The configuration of space tends to be podular. Materials used in third-generation facilities are glass, plastics, or combinations of glass and plastics as laminated vision panels, hollow metal or wooden doors usually in a swinging con-

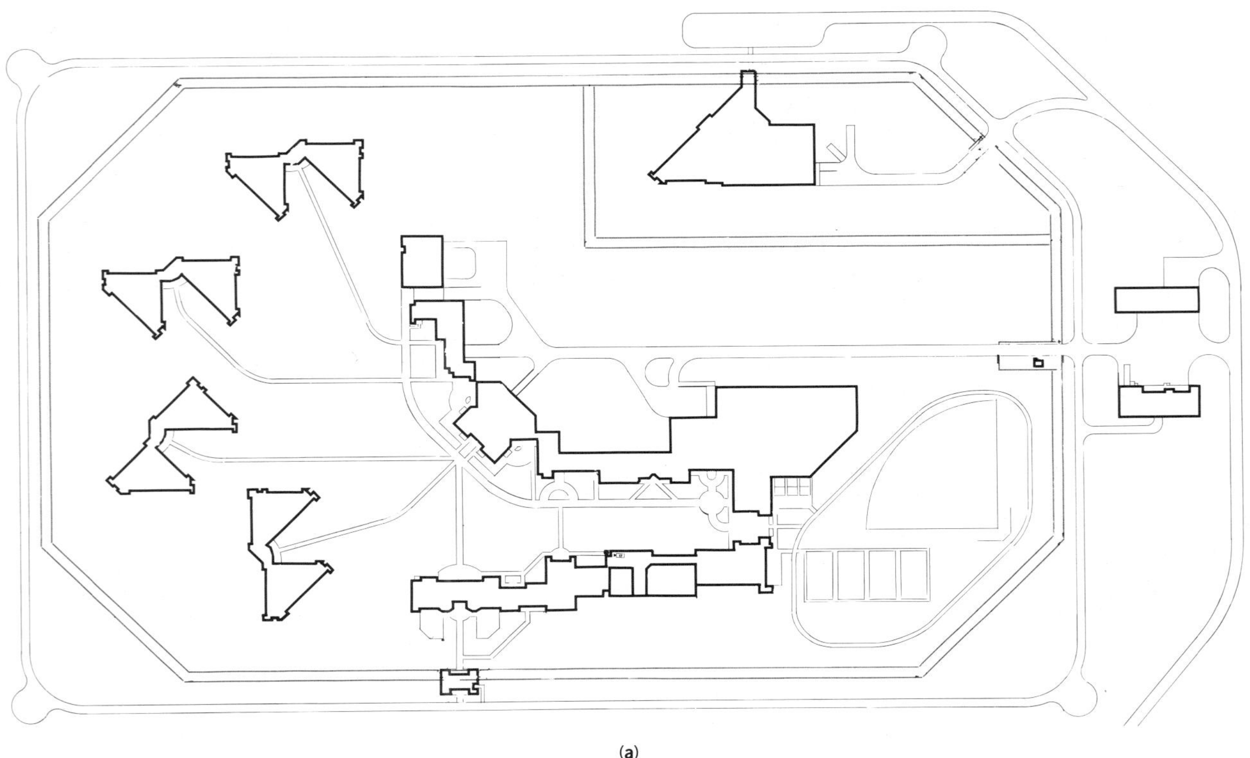

(a)

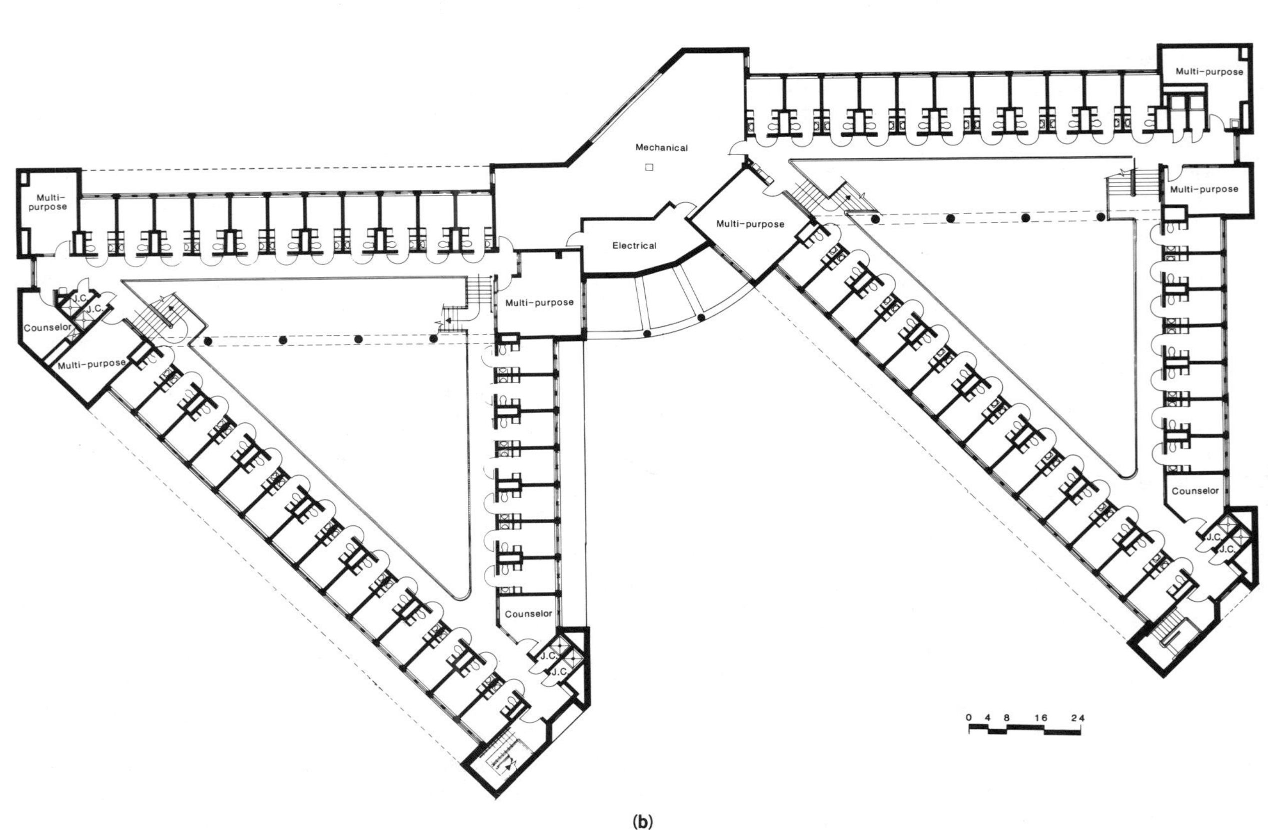

Multi-purpose
Mechanical
Multi-purpose
Electrical
Multi-purpose
Multi-purpose
J.C.
J.C.
Counselor
Multi-purpose
Counselor
J.C.
J.C.
Counselor
J.C.
J.C.
0 4 8 16 24

(b)

(c)

Figure 8. U.S. Department of Justice, Federal Bureau of Prisons, Marianna, Florida. Architects: Hansen Lind Meyer, Inc. State-of-the-art campus plan prison with podular housing and secure perimeter. (**a**) Site plan; (**b**) plan of podular housing unit; (**c**) model of housing unit. Courtesy of Hansen Lind Meyer Inc.

figuration, and concrete or reinforced masonry partition walls. Custodial staff is stationed in the dayroom or common area of a cell pod with controls for the doors also located within the dayroom area; therefore, in the third-generation facility custodial personnel have direct communications with the inmates with no separation from them other than at times when the inmate may be locked in his or her cell (Fig. 8).

Correctional professionals involved in the operation of facilities are not unanimous in acceptance of any one of these approaches as the universal solution to correctional management and facility design problems. A conclusion could be reached that the use of any of these schemes depends on the attitude of the community that the facility serves and operational philosophies relative to the mission and goals of the facility.

The programmatic requirements of jails and prisons are basically similar. They differ in the level or levels of security. The jail is required to accommodate all levels of security, while prisons are often segregated into uniform security levels. In addition, it is more difficult to maintain appropriate security in jails and recognize the rights of persons accused of, but not convicted of, a crime. Jails also differ from prisons in the level of support facilities required. Because of the longer period of confinement, prisons require more extensive support facilities, including industries and educational spaces. Prisons also tend to be farther from metropolitan areas, requiring more self-contained support such as laundry, power supply, and sewage disposal. The operational differences and the staff requirements maintain the separate and unique character of prisons and jails.

The majority of space in a corrections facility is for inmate housing. Current correctional practice suggests that inmates should be provided with single sleeping rooms; however, limited resources and limitation for prison capacity result in two or three people in a room intended for one. Sleeping rooms are usually between 60 and 80 ft^2 and contain a bed, writing surface, storage for clothing and books, a toilet, and a sink. Sleeping is arranged around a common space or dayroom, forming pods of 45–65 rooms. The dayroom contains space and equipment for passive and active recreation. In institutions where meals are brought to the pod, food preparation and serving space is provided. The pod also contains showers, telephones, storage, maintenance, and correctional staff space. Pods are often combined so that some support spaces and staff duties are combined, while maintaining the separate identity and security of each pod.

The pods are designed for specific security level or types of inmate with special units for administrative and disciplinary segregation providing the most secure environment. The housing pods of prisons are commonly planned in a campus setting with the primary security barrier on the perimeter. This allows for more normalized movement within the facility. This can also be achieved with the building configuration in more urban settings (Fig. 9).

Entrances to the pods and facility are made secure through the use of sally ports. Sally ports are created with two secure doors with a space between them. Movement is allowed through only one door at a time, so there is always a locked barrier.

Jails and prisons will vary in the extent and completeness of inmate services and support spaces. The nature

(a)

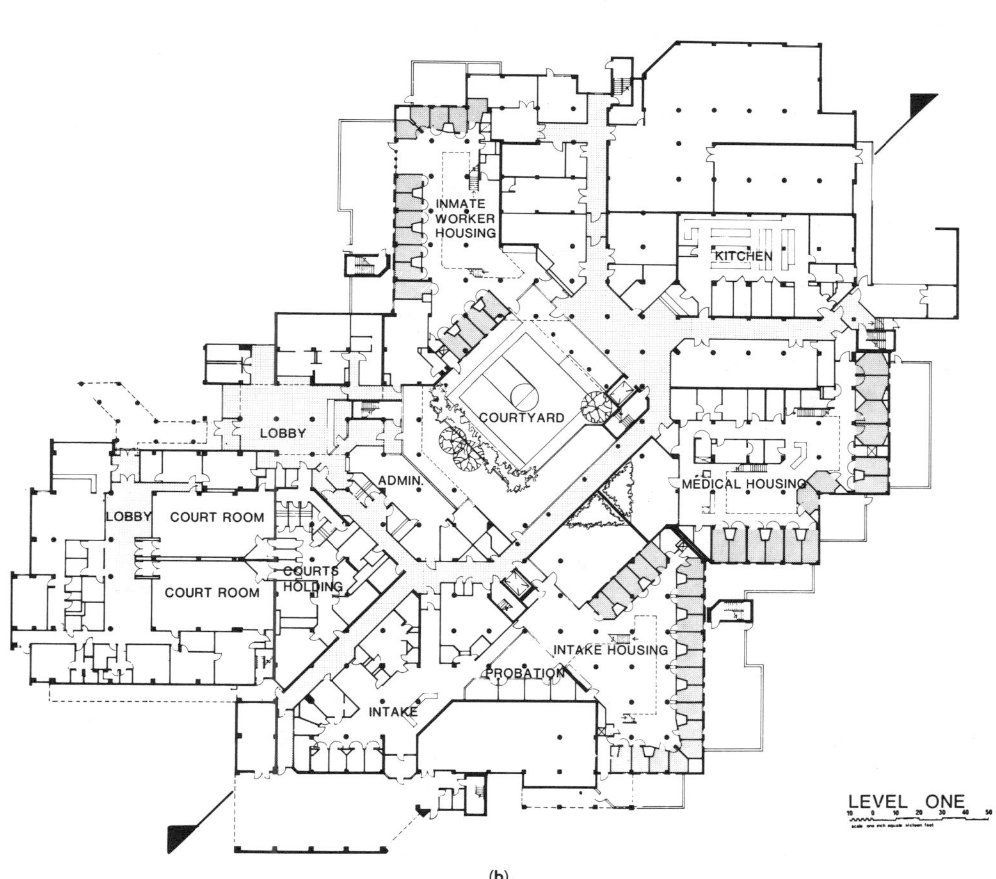
INMATE WORKER HOUSING
KITCHEN
LOBBY
COURTYARD
ADMIN
MEDICAL HOUSING
LOBBY
COURT ROOM
COURTS HOLDING
COURT ROOM
INTAKE HOUSING
PROBATION
INTAKE
LEVEL ONE
(b)

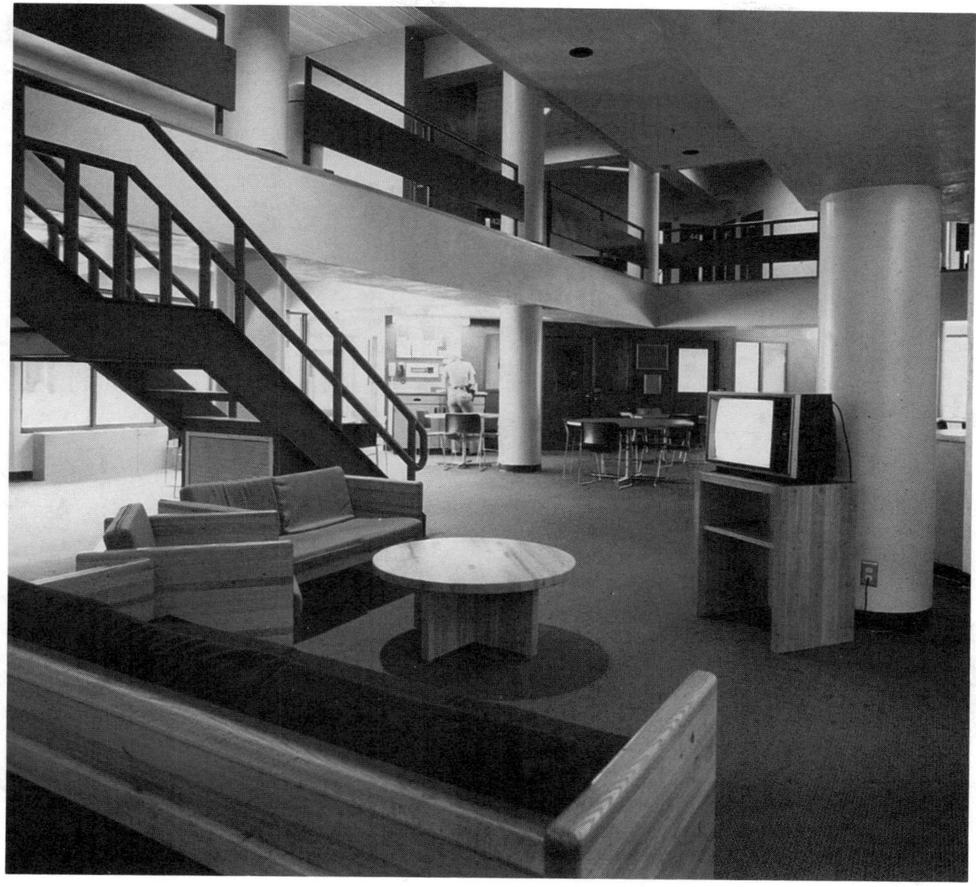

(c)

Figure 9. Contra Costa Detention Facility, Martinez, California. Architects: Kaplan, McLaughlin, Diaz. An example of a podular direct supervision jail that creates a humane environment for pretrial detention. (**a**) Public entrance, courtesy of Douglas Symes; (**b**) first-floor plan, courtesy of Kaplan McLaughlin Diaz; (**c**) interior of housing unit with security officer at his post, courtesy of Douglas Symes.

of confinement requires that jails and prisons become miniature self-contained communities. (In jails, because there is less movement of inmates, the services are brought to the housing pod.) In prisons, the secure perimeter allows for controlled movement within the facility. The service areas typically found in correctional facilities are medical and dental clinics and units for emergency treatment and outpatient services; mail distribution; a canteen or shop for inmates to purchase small items such as candy or cigarettes; laundry; and food preparation and food service areas that create a normalized atmosphere with dining at tables of four or six persons (fixed seating similar to fast-food restaurants is commonly used). Other program areas include spaces for classroom, individual, or vocational learning; recreation and physical fitness; general library and law library services; religious activities; and secure spaces for visiting activities, which include noncontact visiting, contact visiting, and, in some facilities, conjugal visiting.

The intake and discharge area is more critical in a jail than in prison because of the unknown and at times violent behavior of persons being detained. In prisons the activity is more routine to assure proper processing and elimination of contraband. The intake area is accessed through a sally port, often at the vehicle entrance. Space is provided for temporary holding, search and shower, processing, and medical storage. In jails, this area will include a padded cell to detain violent persons.

The administrative areas of correctional facilities include normal office space for support services and executive offices. Staff support spaces such as locker rooms, meeting rooms, exercise equipment, and staff cafeteria will also be found in this area.

Service and maintenance of correctional facilities are accomplished with inmate labor requiring special attention to security and the storage and flow of materials and equipment. For this reason, systems should be laid out to facilitate service by less experienced persons.

Security is the most important aspect of most correctional facilities (the exception being facilities such as an honor farm with no perimeter confinement). Security is constantly monitored from the facility's control center. Information from electronic surveillance, lock monitors, and communications with staff funnel through the control cen-

Figure 10. Pretrial Detention Facility—Main Jail, Ventura, California. Architects: Daniel L. Dworsky, FAIA & Associates, Inc. From the enclosed control booth the unit manager can see all the living space, cell fronts, and showers of the 4- to 12-cell units in this 48-cell pod. Courtesy of Dworsky Associates.

ter. Other critical security functions such as the armory or locksmith shop are also located in this area (Fig. 10).

It is to the ultimate benefit of society to provide humane and secure corrections facilities. It is the responsibility of the corrections institution to return people to society in no worse, and preferably better, condition than when they entered confinement. The nature of the facility plays a large role in the creation of an environment that can nurture personal growth.

Codes and Standards

Sensitivity to elements of life safety including fire suppression and smoke control, security, operational philosophies, food preparation and distribution, laundry requirements, lighting, closed-circuit television, and communications are not usually within the capabilities of the normal architectural and engineering services and require input from specialists. The extent to which specialists are used depends on the size, complexity, and operational philosophies of the facility.

Prior to the reemergence of interest and activities of correctional facilities in the 1960s, very few standards existed in regard to barrier security and operations of facilities for confinement. Most building codes addressed the issues of all other building types but exempted confinement facilities from the requirements, leaving applicable codes to the discretion and interpretation of local code officials. With the volume of activity in correctional construction, as well as the influence of civil rights court cases focusing on the rights of inmates and their confinement environment, a proliferation of activities relative to codes and standards has taken place since the mid-1960s. Through funding from the Omnibus Crime Bill of 1968, the University of Illinois was awarded a grant to develop guidelines for the programming and design of facilities. The resulting document established certain suggestions for types and sizes of spaces to be used in the development of new facilities. During the mid- to late 1970s, the American Correctional Association (ACA), funded by grants from the National Institute of Corrections of the U.S. Attorney General's Office, developed standards establishing guidelines for physical facilities and operational procedures. Those standards are used as a basis for auditing and determining whether candidate facilities meet the minimum requirements and if they should be certified or accredited as having met those minimum requirements. Concurrently, standards for physical facilities and operations have been developed by other agencies and organizations such as the National Sheriff's Association, the American Bar Association, and individual state agencies as being applicable and endorsed by those respective organizations. Observation of the various standards reveals that the majority of the states and organizations and their respective standards are similar to the ACA minimum standards.

Building codes organizations and officials have been addressing the problem to bring consistent and enforceable requirements codes for corrections facilities. The Uniform Building Code (UBC), Building Officials and Code Administrators International (BOCA), and the National Fire Protection Agency (NFPA) have revised their codes to address requirements for confinement facilities. A number of state code agencies have also addressed the requirements of jails and have incorporated them in their documents. There is sufficient variation between the various codes and standards that no single standard or code document is universally accepted. Architects, contractors, and operators of facilities are, therefore, faced with resolving the issue of determining which standards and codes are applicable to their building project.

A limited number of standards for construction and materials in terms of performance have been developed by the American Society for Testing and Materials (ASTM). An expanded number of standards for assemblies of materials is currently being developed by that organization.

New Concepts and Technologies

Materials and their assembly may vary depending on the level of security required. The success in the use of any material or product depends greatly on how and where it is used, how appropriately it is used, and how it works in support of staff of the facility. A variety of products and materials has been manufactured and marketed as specialty items for use in jail facilities. Items such as bullet-resistant vision panels made of glass, plastic, or composite; doors and frames; plumbing fixtures; hardware and locks; CCTV; communications; perimeter security fencing; wall partitioning systems; food service; and furnishings are included in this category. In many instances, security levels and the physical barriers required to support them can be accomplished through logical utilization of more conventional materials such as the use of reinforced masonry walls.

The use of any material in a correctional facility, whether specialized or conventional, must be carefully analyzed and used in a manner in which it has been intended. The incorporation of any specialized material or assembly in a jail or prison must be appropriately detailed and installed to provide continuity of its intended purpose. For example, the installation of a maximum security door and hardware should be in a wall constructed of similar barrier strength so there is continuity of the barrier value of the door, its frame, hardware, and wall. Designers and corrections practitioners are many times led to believe that the installation of specialized equipment solves the security barrier problem and are not aware that a security barrier is a combination of the physical barrier working in concert with the human staff. The purpose of the physical security barrier is to withstand attack for a time sufficient to allow identification of an attack and to withstand the attack until the attack situation has been stopped or controlled.

There has also been the misconception that certain materials are bulletproof or escape-proof. History has proven that material or assemblies used in corrections facilities are not escape-proof, bulletproof, or vandal-proof. Physical materials and assemblies provide resistance to such activities—given appropriate tools and time any physical barrier will fail and be breached; therefore, it is the combination of physical barrier and human element that provides appropriate security and security barriers.

Security assemblies may also have aesthetic value. Appropriate and tasteful use of graphics and lighting brighten and create a living environment that is humane to the inmates and palatable to the community. In appropriate settings, furnishings of heavy commercial grade use, durable wood, plastics, etc, in lieu of heavy metal institutional items, can soften and provide a more normal living environment without jeopardizing security. The use of a variety of furnishings, materials, and equipment should be in harmony with the security levels and philosophies of the building project and its mission.

Durable vandal-resistant surfaces, such as certain paints that can be easily cleaned, are utilized in many facilities. Any material, if subjected to abuse over a period of time, will fail and will require replacement or repair. An evaluation as to the cost and maintenance value of room finishes and specialized equipment such as stainless steel toilet fixtures, must be balanced against the amount of abuse they will be subjected to and their anticipated life. After such an evaluation, a determination can be made as to the level of maintenance required and life-cycle cost of the equipment or fixtures.

Correctional philosophies and the functions of facilities are in a continual state of change with the exception of the basic mission of confinement. Civil rights of inmates has brought a consciousness to the public and to the agencies that have the task of providing and operating facilities. Philosophies differ with attitudes of the public, geographic regions, and the size of facilities. Within these philosophies, the physical facilities change in terms of living environment, level of security, and physical appearance. Ranging from the harder living environment and appearance of the linear first-generation jail or prison, to the softer living environment and appearance of the podular second generation, to the even more open and more normal living environment and appearance of the third-generation facility, there has been a common goal of development of a more staff-effective, efficient, cost-effective facility. The use of more sophisticated electronics aids such as CCTV, personal (staff) alarm systems, and perimeter security systems will allow the general appearance of the physical facility to be softened. The advancement of technology and reliance on, but balance between, staff requirements, the physical facility, and supplemental assistance of electronic and mechanical technology will allow the architect to provide environments that will be perceived as more normal in residential character. Electronic technology brings confinement and safety alarm capabilities to enhance security of facilities, yet allows more contact and communication between staff and inmate populations. Perimeter security in terms of identification capabilities and barrier lines may in the future be in the form of laser fields that will replace more conventional methods of fencing seen in the facilities in the 1980s. The continuing development of vision panels composed of plastics and glass are reducing the hard physical barriers of steel grating that were commonplace ten years ago.

Development of new materials and technology will provide further softening of the secure institutional living environment. Technology of locking systems and the control of locking systems using metal keys, plastic keys, and a variety of puzzle systems such as fingerprint identification will be used more extensively as time goes on.

Identification and location of inmates via electronic methods such as ankle or wrist band sensors may, in the future, allow certain inmate classifications to reside in their home settings, avoiding detention or holding in a jail facility. In the future, the correctional facilities in the United States will be used to confine more sophisticated inmates and higher levels of security risks. Activities of terrorists will bring another generation of security requirements and philosophies to the jail–detention facility. The terrorist inmate will affect security by increasing security requirements compared to those provided historically. With the concerns of intrusion security coupled with containment security, philosophies regarding operations, staff, materials, and aesthetic palatability will undoubtedly undergo extensive revision.

JUVENILE CORRECTIONS FACILITIES

The Hospice of San Michele in Rome, Italy, built in 1704 by Pope Clement XI, was one of the earliest institutions designed exclusively for the reform of delinquent boys. More than a century passed before special facilities for juvenile offenders were established in the United States. In 1825, the New York City House of Refuge was opened. In the 1850s, "Cottage Housing" systems were begun in a few states, but courts were usually still free to send juvenile delinquents to adult prisons. Separation of juveniles and adults in facilities has been a fundamental goal of juvenile corrections since the first juvenile court was established in 1899 in Chicago, Illinois. State legislation passed prior to World War I established juvenile courts and corrections and correctional programs, usually "detention homes" that were private residences, converted jails, or other public buildings such as workhouses and hospitals. Between 1920 and 1940, there was significant progress in keeping juveniles out of adult jails and prisons.

After World War II, facilities specially designed for juveniles were constructed. It should be noted, however, that until the 1950s dependent and neglected children were often in the care of the same agency responsible for the reform of delinquent juveniles. Facilities were designed to group children by age, sex, similarity of problems, and offense history. Campus style planning, small separate dormitories or cottages with common support facilities, academic, recreational, food service, and administration became the archetype for present-day juvenile correctional facilities.

Most youths that enter the juvenile justice system usually go no further than the local jurisdictional level. The majority of juveniles are released to the custody of their families soon after police apprehension. The few that are held by law enforcement must be housed in facilities that are completely separate from any adult detention building. Juvenile courts try to return children adjudicated of delinquent behavior to the home community and their own families. This is accomplished through extensive use of probation and placement in local youth facilities and programs. Youths committing serious or violent crimes and those who cannot be reasonably treated at the local level are committed to the state agency responsible for juvenile corrections.

The mandate of juvenile corrections is to (*1*) control unruly and wayward behavior, (*2*) rehabilitate the child, and (*3*) protect the public. Although many of the youth that enter the juvenile justice system are indeed "hardened kids," most are the products of poor family structure, broken homes, and are in need of education, proper care, shelter, and counseling.

There are two general classifications of children in the juvenile justice and correctional system: (*1*) juvenile delinquent and (*2*) status offender. Because of variations in statutes, juveniles still enter the correctional system for committing offenses that would not be crimes if the offender was not a minor. The term "status offender" applies to a minor who has been adjudicated of committing an act that would otherwise be legal if committed by an adult. Status offenders have not been adjudicated of violation of criminal statutes. Juvenile delinquents are minors who have been adjudicated of committing an offense that would be a criminal violation if committed by an adult. It is necessary to remember that whether status offender or delinquent, the user of a juvenile correctional facility is a child. The design of such facilities should respond to the needs of children separated from the familial environment. Juvenile facilities are not intended to be prisons.

Programming and Design

The local juvenile detention center is a facility for the temporary custody and care of juveniles awaiting disposition of their case. Juveniles accused of an offense and awaiting a court hearing and those awaiting post-adjudication placement in a program or facility are usually housed without separation. Many existing detention centers are little more than jails. Detention centers should be thought of as shelters, because a child taken into custody is usually frightened and confused. The environment should be nonintimidating and reassuring where staff can interact directly with juveniles and have visual contact with all parts of the facility. Children in custody do need privacy; however, suicide prevention must be a designed-in feature. Detention generally means physically restrictive, whereas shelter implies unrestrictive. Group size should not exceed 12, with 8 preferred. Eighty percent of the beds should be in individual sleeping rooms with a minimum of 60 ft^2 per room.

Community-based juvenile correctional facilities include halfway houses and group homes that are small nonsecure residential facilities located in communities where local school attendance, employment opportunities, and public services are available to the youth. Halfway houses typically serve 12 to 25 residents, whereas larger programs may serve as many as 40. The age range in community-based facilities is generally 14 to 18. Group homes may serve as few as 4, but usually not more than

12 residents. Children in group homes are as young as 10, but generally are ages 13 to 16.

Full-time staff, preferably a married couple, actually live in group homes with the residents, whereas most halfway house programs are operated by shifts of houseparents or social workers providing 24-hour coverage. Juvenile sleeping quarters should be well lighted and ventilated, have a minimum of 60 ft^2 of floor space per resident, and provide some degree of privacy.

The facility should have a minimum of one toilet for each 10 residents, one washbasin for each 6, and one shower with temperature controls (hot water not to exceed 110°F, 43°C) for each 8. Every facility should provide living and recreation space and be able to accommodate group meetings of all residents. If a facility serves male and female juveniles, separate sleeping rooms are required for each sex. Separate toilet and bath facilities are recommended. If adult staff live or sleep at the facility, no children should be allowed to share a sleeping room with an adult.

Although community programs are preferred for juveniles, there are individuals who must be placed in a secure or highly structured program, which can only be offered at a training school. Youth in need of intensive supervision, counseling, and basic educational, social, and job skills are committed to training schools in hope that the programs offered can assist them in a successful return to the community in the shortest possible time. Juveniles at training schools may be as young as 8 years, but in no case should they be older than 18, except where statute extends juvenile status to age 21. Under no circumstances should adult offenders be mixed or housed with juveniles. Status offenders should not be committed to training schools.

The maximum population of a training school usually numbers 100 juveniles; however, budgetary constraints often make it difficult to keep facilities small. If a training school is large, it should be designed and operated to create small population groups within the school. The ideal training school will be designed as an open campus with low, residential scale buildings, separated by conservatively landscaped yards. In many ways, a juvenile training school is not unlike a campus style junior–senior high school with on-site student housing. Again, it is worth mentioning that juvenile residents, although adjudicated for committing a criminal offense, are still children and are there for rehabilitation, not punishment. The environment should be as normal as possible and reflect an attitude of caring, fairness, and humanity. A facility can be open or secure. Most juvenile residents are not a serious threat to the public and are generally not escape risks; therefore, an open, unfenced perimeter is possible. If a state or agency operates several training schools, it may only be necessary to fence or secure the perimeter of the school(s) housing violent offenders and juveniles prone to running away.

Training school residents are housed in small cottages or houses that are durable and easily supervised, but are not prisonlike. The maximum size of a cottage should not exceed 25 juveniles and should be subdivided into groups of approximately 12 or less. Individual sleeping rooms should be a minimum of 70 ft^2 each, with 100 ft^2 preferred, although up to 5 suitably screened juveniles can safely share the same sleeping room. Each juvenile must be provided with a bed, desk, chair or stool, natural light, and closet space. Toilet facilities must be available for use, without staff assistance, 24 hours a day. One toilet and shower should be available for every 8 residents and one lavatory for every 5.

Each housing unit should include a dayroom space for leisure time activities and should have a separate quiet room for reading, group counseling, or other activities. Supervisory staff should be stationed within, or immediately adjacent to, the resident living area so observation of most or all areas and activities is possible. If a desk or work counter is provided for staff, it should not be enclosed or be of such a design that it will separate staff from juveniles.

Food service at the living unit, while homelike, is not desirable because of high operational costs and because it tends to keep residents housebound. A central dining room and kitchen (with adjacent warehouse) is the most desirable method with regard to dietary control and food quality assurance. The dining area should permit residents to sit in groups of four to six, in an atmosphere of minimal regimentation. It is desirable to provide wider than normal circulation and avoid opposing juvenile traffic altogether.

Academic classrooms at training schools should meet the local or state educational requirements. The classroom building will differ from its public school counterpart in that student observation and control are important design factors that influence toilet room, corridor, and classroom configuration. Materials will generally be similar to those used in public school buildings. Vocational education programs, if offered, need facilities similar to high-school vocational educational or technical-school instruction areas and shops.

Gymnasiums, pools or natatoriums, and outdoor recreational fields will normally not require accommodation for many spectators. Daily sport and physical activity is limited to small group participation. A small infirmary or dispensary is required, but a local hospital can be used for inpatient care, if nursing care is not provided at the facility.

For administrators and other staff, typical buildings normally require no special features. Record storage and security is important, because juvenile records are not a matter of public record.

A flexible, multi-use center is desirable for family visitation, a place where religious services can be conducted, or where large gatherings can be held; small, private meeting rooms are desirable for family visitation. Adjacent to this area should be an outdoor area conducive to family visitation with social worker offices nearby.

If a security section, apart from the living quarters, is required, complete toilet and shower facilities with detention type furnishings are appropriate. Continuous staff observation and supervision are required whenever a juvenile is placed in a temporary security room.

Juvenile living quarters should be durably constructed, but should be as homelike as possible. Prison type construction is usually not necessary or desirable (Fig. 11).

Ceilings in common areas should be kept high, over 12 ft, whereas 9-ft ceilings in individual rooms generally eliminate easy access and routine vandalism. Ceilings of

Figure 11. Johnson County Juvenile Detention Center, Olathe, Kansas. Architects: Abend Singleton Associates, Inc. Day space with recreational facilities helps create a therapeutic environment. Courtesy of Paul Kivett Architectural Foto Graphics.

⅝-in. gypsum board applied over ¾-in.-thick backer board (fire resistive) often can replace plaster. Similar construction can be used for walls and partitions, although reinforced concrete masonry construction is preferred where security and vandalism are major concerns.

Doors and hardware should be heavy duty, especially exit and exterior units. Generally, the maximum window protection required will be either security screens or high impact glazing.

BIBLIOGRAPHY

General References

The American Courthouse, American Bar Association and the American Institute of Architects, Washington, D.C., 1972.

The American Prison: From the Beginning . . . a Pictorial History, American Correctional Association, College Park, Md., 1983.

Design Guide for Secure Adult Correctional Facilities, American Correctional Association, College Park, Md., 1983.

National Institute for Corrections, *Design for Contemporary Correctional Facilities,* Capitol Publishing, Crofton, Md., 1985.

W. G. Nagel, *The New Red Barn: A Critical Look at the Modern American Prison,* Walker & Company, New York, 1973.

J. Farbstein, *Correctional Facility Planning and Design,* 2d ed., Van Nostrand Reinhold Co., Inc., New York, 1986.

R. Pare, *Courthouse: A Photographic Document,* Horizon Press, New York, 1978.

Architecture for Justice Exhibition, American Institute of Architects, Committee on Architecture for Justice, Washington, D.C., 1979–1988.

F. D. Moyer, *Architecture and Corrections: Interdisciplinary Strategies in Planning and Design,* University of Illinois Press, Chicago, 1972.

MICHAEL COHN
ROBERT B. KLUG, AIA
JOHN MCGOUGH, FAIA
FREDERIC MOYER, AIA
ALLEN PATRICK, FAIA
WALTER SOBEL, FAIA
The American Institute of Architects
Washington, D.C.

K

KAHN, ALBERT

Albert Kahn (1869–1942) was born in Rhaunen, Germany, the oldest son of a rabbi. The Kahns and their six children emigrated to the United States in 1880. Albert Kahn received his professional training as an apprentice to an architect with the firm of Mason and Rice in Detroit. In 1891, he was awarded a scholarship for a year's travel in Europe. During his travels he met the young architect Henry Bacon, and the two of them traveled together in Italy, France, Germany, and Belgium. In 1896, he married Ernestine Krolik and formed a partnership with George W. Nettleton and Alexander B. Trowbridge. Trowbridge left to become dean of the Cornell University School of Architecture in 1897, Nettleton died in 1900, and by 1902, Kahn was in practice alone. Kahn's practice is internationally known for industrial work; his more traditional designs are less well known.

Because he practiced in Detroit, Kahn's career closely followed the growth of the automotive industry. Kahn was introduced to Henry B. Joy in 1902. Joy was instrumental in Kahn's selection for projects at the University of Michigan, and when Joy became manager of the Packard Motor Car Co. in 1903, Kahn was named architect for the company. That same year, Henry Ford founded the Ford Motor Co.

Kahn's early industrial work was conservative in nature. Nine factories were designed between 1903 and 1905 for the Packard Motor Car Co. The first concrete-framed building dated from 1905. This advanced structural system depended on the manufacture of appropriate reinforcing rods. Although Kahn's brother was an engineer and manufacturer of reinforcing, the Kahn bar did not succeed in the market. However, the experience with the concrete structure put Kahn's office in the forefront of industrial design.

Many industrial commissions followed. Rather than relegating the design to junior staff, Kahn carefully designed the factories, using such designers as his associate Ernest Wilby to assist him. Kahn's factories were the first to use steel sash in concrete-framed structures. He helped develop buildings for continuously moving assembly lines. His factories were known for the maximum use of natural lighting and ventilation, using continuous strip windows, roof monitors, or skylights. He pioneered the use of long-span steel trusses, resulting in large floor areas free of columns.

There were a number of famous factories. Among the early ones was the Ford Motor Co. in Highland Park, Michigan (1909), which was under one roof. Among later buildings for Ford was a 1918 building with cantilevered balconies inside the factory, allowing easier handling of materials and parts. Plants for the Burroughs Adding Machine Co. in Detroit (1919) and for the Fisher Body Co. in Cleveland, Ohio (1921), were other early works.

In 1917, Kahn began the design of the Ford River Rouge Plant in Detroit. The first of the buildings (Building B) was 0.5 mi long, housing the entire assembly line for automobiles. In 1936, he designed the Chrysler Corp. plant in Detroit using large trusses and glass curtain walls. In 1938, he designed another Chrysler Corp. plant at Warren, Michigan, for the Half-Ton Truck Plant of the Dodge Division. It featured long-span trusses and roof monitors as well as glass curtain walls. This series of buildings was elegant in design, using advanced construction technology.

Kahn's office designed many other buildings in addition to the industrial work. These included several buildings for the University of Michigan, office buildings such as the General Motors Building in Detroit, and luxury residential projects, particularly for the homes of automotive executives.

Kahn's World War II buildings included the Glen Martin bomber plant at Baltimore and the Willow Run Bomber plant for Ford, later used for automobile manufacture and assembly. Because of wartime blackout regulations, the latter building was windowless and electrically lit.

Kahn worked continuously up to 1942, completing 57 years of practice as an architect, and the firm continues under the name of Albert Kahn Associates, Inc. A high point of Kahn's fame was his influence on European work. In 1929, a Soviet commission touring Detroit asked him to design a tractor plant in Stalingrad. This turned out so well that the firm built over 500 factories in the USSR in two years and trained many Soviet engineers and technicians to assist in the building program.

The comparison of Kahn's work with Peter Behrens's monumental work in Germany for the A.E.G. or Walter Gropius's and Adolph Meyers's 1911 Fagus Shoe-last Factory at Alfeld an der Liene clarifies the differences between European and American approaches. The European examples were more designed, with the use of brick, neoclassic forms, and delight in the technology that allowed such details as wrapping glass around corners. The spirit of that work differs from Kahn, who evolved industrial buildings without prototypes or use of traditional design concepts. The industrial building was of continued aesthetic interest as reflected in Gropius's design of the Bauhaus at Dessau, Germany, in 1926. The best of Kahn's work implies a different aesthetic based on simple construction, standard materials, and ease of construction. In this sense it was more like the manufactured product than a symbolic interpretation.

BIBLIOGRAPHY

General References

G. Hilebrand, *The Architecture of Albert Kahn,* M.I.T. Press, Cambridge, Mass., 1974.

"The Legacy of Albert Kahn," exhibition catalog, The Detroit Institute of Arts, Detroit, Mich., 1970.

Robert T. Packard, AIA
Reston, Virginia

KAHN, LOUIS I.

Louis Isadore Kahn (1901–1974), U.S. architect, educator, and philosopher, is one of the foremost twentieth-century architects. He evolved an original theoretical and formal language that revitalized modern architecture. His best known works, located in the United States, India, and Bangladesh, were produced in the last two decades of his life. They reveal an integration of structure, a reverence for materials and light, a devotion to archetypal geometry, and a profound concern for humanistic values.

Born in 1901 on the Baltic island of Osel, Kahn's family emigrated to Philadelphia, Pennsylvania, in 1905, where he lived the rest of his life. Trained in the manner of the Ecole des Beaux Arts under Paul Philippe Cret, he graduated from the University of Pennsylvania School of Fine Arts in 1924. Among his first professional experiences was the 1926 Philadelphia Sesquicentennial Exhibition. In the following years he worked in the offices of Philadelphia's leading architects, Paul Cret (1929–1930) and Zantzinger, Borie and Medary (1930–1932). During the lean years of the 1930s, Kahn was devoted to the study of modern architecture and housing in particular. He undertook housing studies for the Architectural Research Group (1932–1933), a short-lived organization he helped to establish, and for the Philadelphia City Planning Commission. In the later 1930s he served as a consultant to the Philadelphia Housing Authority and the United States Housing Authority. His familiarity with modern architecture was broadened when he worked with European émigrés Alfred Kastner and Oskar Stonorov. In the early 1940s Kahn associated with Stonorov and George Howe, with whom he designed several wartime housing projects such as Carver Court in Coatesville, Pennsylvania (1941–1944) and Pennypack Woods in Philadelphia (1941–1943). His interest in public housing culminated in Philadelphia's Mill Creek Housing project (1951–1963). From these experiences, Kahn developed a deep sense of social responsibility reflected in his later philosophy of the "institutions" of man.

The year 1947 was a turning point in Kahn's career. He established an independent practice and began a distinguished teaching career, first at Yale University as Chief Critic in Architectural Design and Professor of Architecture (1947–1957) and then at the University of Pennsylvania as Cret Professor of Architecture (1957–1974). During those years, his ideas about architecture and the city took shape. Eschewing the international style modernism that characterized his earlier work, Kahn sought to redefine the bases of architecture through a reexamination of structure, form, space, and light. Kahn described his quest for meaningful form as a search for "beginnings," a spiritual resource from which modern man could draw inspiration. The powerful and evocative forms of ancient brick and stone ruins in Italy, Greece, and Egypt where Kahn traveled in 1950–1951 while serving as Resident Architect at the American Academy in Rome were an inspiration in his search for what is timeless and essential. The effects of this European odyssey, the honest display of structure, a desire to create a sense of place, and a vocabulary of abstract forms rooted in Platonic geometry resonate in his later masterpieces of brick and concrete, his preferred materials. Kahn reintroduced geometric, axial plans, centralized spaces, and a sense of solid mural strength, reflective of his beaux-arts training and eschewed by modern architects.

Kahn's first mature work, the addition to the Yale University Art Gallery (New Haven, Connecticut, 1951–1953), indicates his interest in experimental structural systems. The floor slabs of poured-in-place concrete were inspired by tetrahedral space frames. The raw texture of the concrete reveals his belief that the method of construction should not be concealed. The hollow, pyramidal spaces in the ceiling, which accommodate lighting and mechanical systems, anticipate his later idea of "served and servant spaces"—the hierarchical definition of a building's functions. The expression of served and servant spaces is clearly enunciated in two later works, the Richards Medical Research Building at the University of Pennsylvania (1957–1965) and the Salk Institute for Biological Studies (La Jolla, California, 1959–1965). In the design of the Richards Building (Figs. 1 and 2), Kahn gave form to a brilliant structural system devised with the engineer August E. Komendant, with whom he collaborated on numerous projects. The laboratories were constructed of precast, post-tensioned reinforced concrete, a system that permitted large flexible laboratory spaces. The servant spaces containing stairs and exhaust chimneys become monumental brick towers attached to the perimeter of the cellular laboratory spaces. The towers form a silhouette complementing the chimneys and towers of the neighboring collegiate Gothic dormitories, and in an abstract guise they suggest the towers of medieval Italian towns that Kahn admired. In the design of the Salk Institute, Kahn gives further expression to servant spaces with a 9-ft-high mechanical floor sandwiched between laboratory floors. Much more than the demonstration of service spaces, the Salk Institute is an example of Kahn's desire to give form to the institutions of man. In a spectacular setting overlooking the Pacific Ocean, two long laboratory wings flank a stone-paved plaza bisected by a narrow rill. In accord with the

Figure 1. Richards Medical Research Building and Goddard Laboratories at the University of Pennsylvania, Philadelphia. Photograph by George E. Thomas.

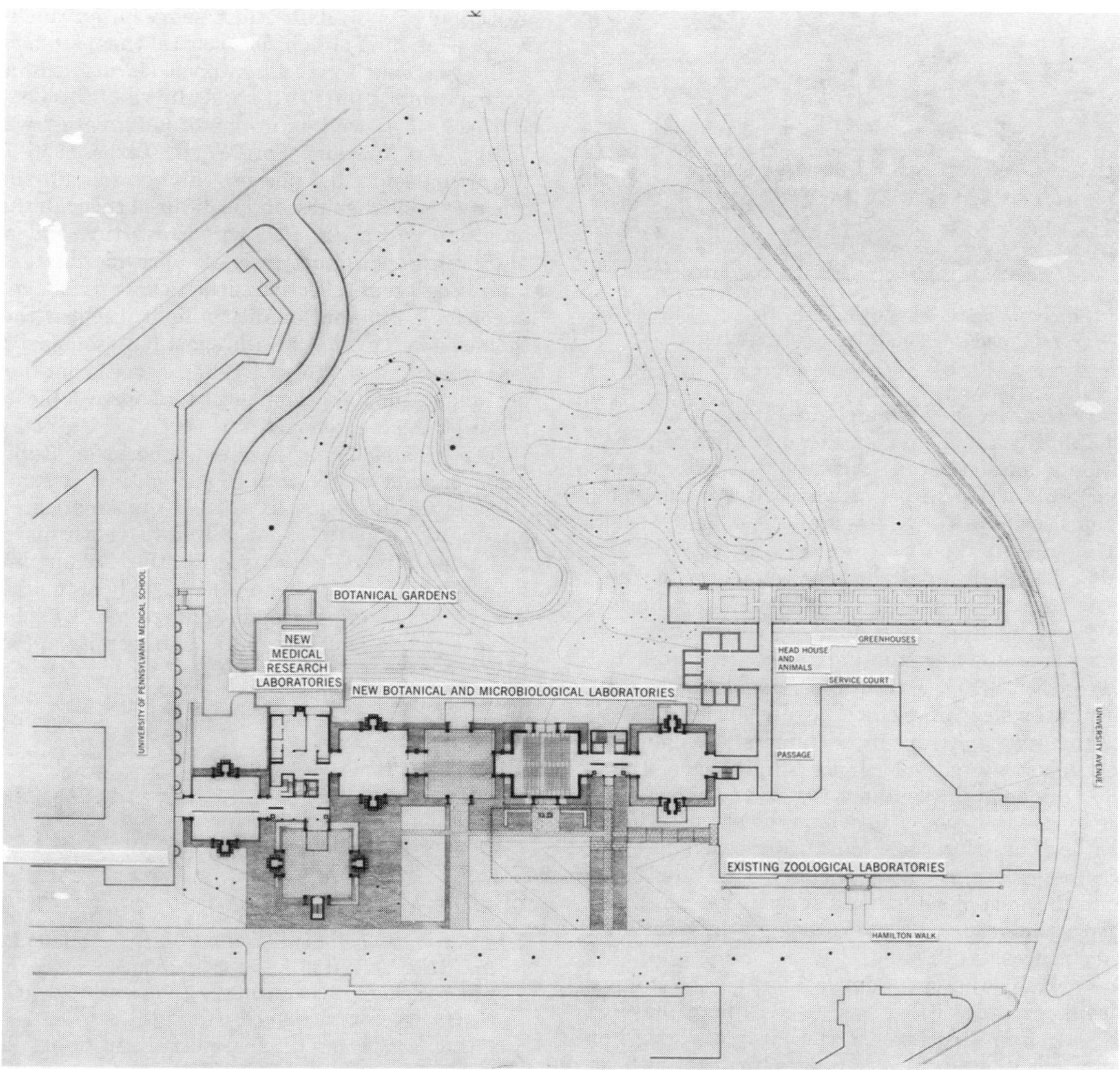

Figure 2. Plan (c. 1958) of the Richards Medical Research Building and Goddard Laboratories at the University of Pennsylvania, Philadelphia. Courtesy of the Louis I. Kahn Collection, University of Pennsylvania, Philadelphia, and the Pennsylvania Historical and Museum Commission.

wishes of the patron and founder, Dr. Jonas Salk, Kahn created an environment where the interdependency of scientific and humanistic disciplines could be realized.

While Kahn exhibited a compelling concern for structure, he sought to infuse his buildings with the symbolic meaning of the institutions they housed. Composed of austere geometries, his spaces are intended to evoke an emotional, empathetic response. "Architecture," Kahn said, "is the thoughtful making of spaces" (1). Beyond its functional role, Kahn believed architecture must also evoke the feeling and symbolism of timeless human values. Kahn attempted to explain the relationship between the rational and romantic dichotomy in his "form–design" thesis, a theory of composition articulated in 1959. In his personal philosophy, form is conceived as formless and unmeasurable, a spiritual power common to all mankind. It transcends individual thoughts, feelings, and conventions. Form characterizes the conceptual essence of one project from another, and thus it is the initial step in the creative process. Design, however, is measurable and takes into consideration the specific circumstances of the program. Practical and functional concerns are contained in design. The union of form and design is realized in the final product, and the building's symbolic meaning is once again unmeasurable.

In his search for a formal vocabulary symbolic of man's institutions, Kahn consistently based his compositions on a centralized enclosed space surrounded by secondary spaces. He created a cloistered, contemplative atmosphere within the walls. This is seen most clearly in the design of the Jewish Community Center Bath House (Trenton, New Jersey, 1954–1959), the First Unitarian Church (Rochester, New York, 1959–1969), Erdman Hall (Bryn Mawr, Pennsylvania, 1960–1965), Phillips Exeter Acad-

Figure 3. National Capital of Bangladesh, Dacca. Courtesy of Henry N. Wilcots, David Wisdom & Associates Architects.

emy Library (Exeter, New Hampshire, 1965–1972), and in one of Kahn's most monumental works, the National Capital of Bangladesh (Dacca, 1962–1983). Kahn's preference for the enclosed core is pervasive in his work, appearing at various scales. As a "hollow stone," it was the basic structural element in the City Tower project (1952–1957), a triangulated space frame structure designed with Anne G. Tyng. At Dacca, the concrete diamond-shaped Parliament Building rises from the head of the capital complex. Its center contains the assembly hall, which is surrounded by secondary rooms (Fig. 3). Using universal abstract geometry, Kahn evoked an archaic, awe-inspiring past to symbolize the unity inherent in his understanding of the institution of assembly. On a much larger scale, Kahn envisioned Philadelphia's center city surrounded by a wall of parking towers that serves to defend the symbolic institutions in the pedestrian core from the encroaching automobile. By means of the central enclosed core, often integrated with the idea of served and servant spaces, Kahn established a sense of order that synthesizes differentiated and specific spaces.

Integral to Kahn's notion of timeless form in the making of significant architectural spaces is the role of natural light. He described structure as the giver of light. For several projects located in hot sunny climates, such as the U.S. Consulate in Luanda, Angola (1959–1962), the meeting houses of the Salk Institute, the Indian Institute of Management (Ahmadabad, India, 1962–1974), and the National Capital at Dacca, Kahn developed visually dynamic sunscreens. Great walls with variously shaped openings shield inner rooms from the harsh light (Fig. 3). The evocation of a wall in ruins suggests an ancient past. Kahn's handling of light is a central theme in two unrealized synagogue projects, Mikveh Israel (Philadelphia, Pennsylvania, 1961–1972) and Hurva (Jerusalem, Israel, 1967–1974) as well as in one of his greatest works, the Kimbell Art Museum (Fort Worth, Texas, 1966–1972). In the art museum, light enters through narrow slits in the concrete cycloid vaults and is diffused through the gallery interiors, which are rich with travertine and oak (Fig. 4). Several open courtyards also provide light, each containing different reflective surfaces such as foliage or water to convey a different quality of light. Light is the central theme as well in one of Kahn's last philosophical concepts, "silence and light." Silence represents the darkness of the beginning, and light symbolizes the source of life, the inspiration of the creative act.

Figure 4. Kimbell Art Museum, Fort Worth, Texas. Photograph by James Dart.

The greatest honors were bestowed on Kahn for his achievements in architecture and education. Among them he received the Gold Medal from the American Institute of Architects in 1971. After Kahn's death his drawings and papers were purchased by the Commonwealth of Pennsylvania and placed in the custody of the Pennsylvania Historical and Museum Commission. They have been given a permanent home at the University of Pennsylvania.

BIBLIOGRAPHY

1. L. I. Kahn, "Architecture is the Thoughtful Making of Spaces," *Perspecta* **4,** 2 (1957).

General References

J. P. Brown, *Louis I. Kahn. A Bibliography,* Garland Publishing, Inc., New York, 1987. The most complete bibliography published to date with references to Kahn's writings and hundreds of secondary articles and books.

C. Chang, ed., "Louis I. Kahn: Silence and Light," *A+U* **3,** 5–222 (1973).

R. Giurgola and J. Mehta, *Louis I. Kahn,* Westview Press, Boulder, Colo., 1975.

W. Jordy, "What the Building 'Wants to Be': Louis I. Kahn's Richards Medical Research Building at the University of Pennsylvania," in *American Buildings and Their Architects,* Vol. 4, Doubleday & Company, Inc., New York, 1972.

The Louis I. Kahn Archive: Personal Drawings, 7 Vols., Garland Publishing, Inc., New York, 1987. The publication of over 6000 drawings by Kahn contained in the Louis I. Kahn Collection, University of Pennsylvania.

"Louis I. Kahn: Conception and Meaning," *A+U* **11,** Extra ed., 4–240 (1983).

A. E. Komendant, *18 Years with Architect Louis I. Kahn,* Aloray Publisher, Englewood, N.J., 1975. Account by the structural engineer for many of Kahn's most important works and projects.

A. Latour, ed., *Louis I. Kahn. l'uomo, il maestro,* Edizioni Kappa, Rome, 1986. Interviews with people who knew Kahn.

J. Lobell, *Between Silence and Light,* Shambhala Publications, Inc., Boulder, Colo., 1979.

H. Ronner, S. Jhaveri, and A. Vasella, eds., *Louis I. Kahn Complete Works 1935–1974,* Westview Press, Boulder, Colo., 1977. The most complete publication of drawings, models, and photographs of buildings illustrating the design development of each project.

M. Sabini, ed., "Louis I. Kahn 1901/1971," *Rassegna* **21**, 4–88 (1985).

V. Scully, Jr., *Louis I. Kahn,* George Braziller, Inc., New York, 1962.

The Travel Sketches of Louis I. Kahn, Pennsylvania Academy of the Fine Arts, Philadelphia, 1978. Contains an excellent introductory essay by V. Scully.

A. Tyng, *Beginnings: Louis I. Kahn's Philosophy of Architecture,* John Wiley & Sons, Inc., New York, 1984.

R. S. Wurman, *What Will Be Has Always Been. The Words of Louis I. Kahn,* Access Press Ltd. and Rizzoli International Publications, Inc., New York, 1986. Contains nearly all of Kahn's published writings, transcriptions of his speeches and interviews, excerpts from his notebooks, and interviews with people who knew him.

R. S. Wurman and E. Feldman, eds., *The Notebooks and Drawings of Louis I. Kahn,* Falcon Press, Philadelphia, 1962.

PETER REED
Philadelphia, Pennsylvania

KETCHUM, MORRIS

Morris Ketchum, Jr. (1904–1984), practiced architecture in his native New York City for more than 40 years as principal of his own firm of architects and planners. In that time a large number of educational, commercial, institutional, and zoological projects were completed both in the United States and abroad. Despite the varied nature of his practice, Ketchum is probably best known for his commercial work, ranging in scale from individual specialty shops and department stores to regional shopping centers. He was an innovative retail designer, and his conceptual theories and planning principles have become prototypical of contemporary mercantile design. Also, as an early advocate of the modern movement in architecture, Ketchum believed that consistent use of good design and rational planning is the most effective method of expanding the scope of the architect's contribution to the visual environment. His professional service as director, vice president, and president (1965–1966) of the American Institute of Architects supported this aim through a focus on the inspiration of public interest in architecture and architectural services.

Morris Ketchum was a student in the late 1920s, a time when discontent with the then current eclectic style in building was growing in the United States. In Europe, architectural theory was changing radically, offering new ideas with special appeal for young architects. Modernism was being widely explored as a visual expression of the new social consciousness developing in the aftermath of World War I. On graduation from Columbia University in 1928 with a Bachelor of Architecture degree, he went to France where in the same year he received a diploma from the School of Fine Arts at Fontainebleau. The eight months of travel that followed, principally in Germany and the Netherlands, served to convince him that the contemporary design approach of the modern movement was the appropriate direction to pursue (1).

On returning to the United States in 1929 and after working in several New York offices, Ketchum, in 1934, was forced by the Depression to open his own office and attempt to build an independent practice. It was in commercial work that he found the best opportunity for expression of the new modernist design principles. In this area, creative design ideas could be integrated with careful planning and market analysis to develop successful merchandising spaces. From this thinking arose the concept that the customer could be attracted through visual integration of the exterior storefront with interior sales areas. A series of innovative designs for storefronts and interiors based on this idea brought attention to the young architect's work. Particularly distinctive is the three-dimensional approach to the Lederer de Paris Store (1934; in collaboration with Victor Gruen) that created an outdoor shopping lobby with wall-hung and freestanding display cases by recessing the storefront from the building line (Fig. 1).

Many commissions for similar projects followed, at first in New York, and later, as his reputation grew, in other parts of the United States. When the volume of commercial work declined due to World War II and Ketchum's active participation in the conflict was prevented by a hearing defect, he turned to research and product development as a consultant to several organizations including the Kawneer Co. and the U.S. Gypsum Co. The postwar development boom brought commissions for larger commercial projects, including the award-winning Davison–Paxon Co. department store in Augusta, Georgia (1948). Here, open flexible merchandising space was provided on all four sales floors by means of a single bay, reinforced concrete structural system with cantilevered floors. In keeping with Ketchum's design theory, the first-floor facade acts as a show window open to the interior sales area. The primary

Figure 1. Lederer de Paris Store, Fifth Avenue, New York, 1934. Courtesy of The American Institute of Architects Archives.

portion of the remaining facade is closed, forming a distinctive background for the store's signature. Ketchum was also instrumental in developing the early planning concepts that would become typical for regional suburban shopping centers. At Shoppers' World center in Framingham, Massachusetts (1952), the parking areas surround a building complex of arcaded shops that in turn enclose an open-air landscaped pedestrian mall. Smaller store locations are carefully interrelated with the large department stores placed in anchor positions at each end of the mall. Thus, automobile, pedestrian, and service traffic could be completely separated. In 1948 and again in the revised edition of 1957, Ketchum documented the results of all of his research and experience in retail design in the building-type textbook, *Shops and Stores* (2).

Between 1941 and 1943, Francis X. Gina and J. Stanley Sharp joined the growing firm as partners. By 1955, Ketchum, Giná and Sharp, Architects had a staff of 30 and a successful practice primarily in commercial and educational projects. After the departure of first Giná (1958) and later Sharp (1961), the firm continued in practice as Morris Ketchum, Jr., and Associates. Innovative conceptual thinking continued to mark the firm's approach to the more varied work of later years. The contextually responsive design for the U.S. Embassy in Rabat, Morocco (1961), blends traditional materials and native craftsmanship with the contemporary precast concrete elements of the building's structural framework. In P.S. 45, an experimental public school for the City of New York (1965), classrooms are oriented toward interior courts while turning a windowless facade to the urban problems of vandalism and street noise. Particularly innovative are Ketchum's solutions to zoological projects, which recognize the importance of appropriate natural habitats to the physical and mental health of zoo animals. In the World of Darkness at the Bronx Zoo (1969), the daily cycle of nocturnal animals was adjusted to allow public viewing in a natural setting during their active periods. The World of Birds, also at the Bronx Zoo (1972), displays a worldwide collection of birds in skylit forest settings connected by viewing ramps between ground and treetop levels.

Always conscious of the importance of students to the future of architecture, Ketchum found time throughout his career to combine teaching with practice and other professional activities. At various times he served on the architectural faculties of New York University (1936–1938), Yale University (1943–1946), The Cooper Union (1947–1948), and Pratt Institute (1954–1957) (3). Also believing in the architect's responsibility to contribute to the community and the profession through public service, he served as president of the Architectural League of New York (1958–1960) and president of the Municipal Art Society of New York (1962–1963). In 1966, he was awarded a medal of honor for design, professional practice, and public service by the New York Chapter of the AIA. On retirement from active practice in 1974, he became vice-chairman of the Landmarks Preservation Commission of New York City where his work was recognized in 1979 by a certificate of appreciation presented by Mayor Edward Koch. In addition to numerous national and local awards for architectural projects, other significant honors include fellowship in the American Institute of Architects (1953), honorary membership in the architectural societies of Argentina (1965), Venezuela (1965), and Mexico (1966), and honorary fellowship in the Royal Architectural Institute of Canada (1966). He received the honorary order of Chevalier des Arts et Lettres of France in 1966 (4).

Morris Ketchum's personal philosophy on his eventful career is well expressed in his own words from the foreword to a recollection and commentary published in 1982 (5):

> Blazing a trail to mark the way to a clearly seen objective will create a path for others.
>
> They then enlarge that path first to a paved roadway and next to a six-lane highway.
>
> At that point the original objective has become an accepted rule of the game and the discoverer has been forgotten.
>
> This is the story of my life but I am content to have led the way and inspired others to follow.

BIBLIOGRAPHY

1. K. Reid, "Perspectives," *Pencil Points* **XXV,** 65–66 (Aug. 1944).
2. M. Ketchum, Jr., *Shops and Stores,* Reinhold Publishing Corp., New York, 1948, Rev. ed. 1957, pp. 124–127.
3. M. Ketchum, Jr., *Selected Projects,* privately printed, 1962.
4. J. F. Gane, ed., *American Architects Directory,* 3rd ed., R. R. Bowker Co., New York, 1970, pp. 485–486.
5. M. Ketchum, Jr., *Blazing a Trail,* Vantage Press, Inc., New York, 1982, p. ix.

ANNE VYTLACIL, AIA
Washington, D.C.

KIESLER, FREDERICK

Frederick Kiesler, the visionary U.S. architect and stage designer, was born in Vienna, Austria, in 1890. Educated in Vienna, he worked with Adolf Loos in 1920 on a slum clearance and rehousing project. In 1922, he designed the sets for Karel Capek's play *R.U.R.*

In 1923, Kiesler designed the first version of his "endless house" and, in 1924, was architect and director of the Music and Theater Festival in Vienna. In 1923–1924, he was identified with the Dutch de Stijl group and designed "The City in Space" exhibited in the Austrian Pavilion at the 1925 Paris Exposition des Arts Decoratifs. This daring ceiling-supported structure consisted of extended coordinates of planar surfaces within a Cartesian grid. This was identified by Theo van Doesburg as a product of the de Stijl movement.

In 1926, Kiesler emigrated from Austria to New York, where he was appointed director of the International Theater Exhibition that year. In 1936, he was named director of the Laboratory for Design Correlation at the School of Architecture, Columbia University, and designed the exhibition hall for the School of Architecture (1937–1939).

Kiesler designed the Art of This Century gallery for

Peggy Guggenheim in 1942. This famous gallery was a center for surrealist art and was where much of Jackson Pollock's early work was exhibited.

He formed a partnership with Armand Bartos in 1957, which survived until Kiesler's death in 1965. As designer for the office, he designed a number of noteworthy projects, including the World House Gallery (1957), Albert Einstein Medical Center Hospital, the Ullman Research Center, and the Shrine of the Book for the Hebrew University of Jerusalem, completed in 1965.

Although Kiesler built few permanent buildings, he created a number of theater and exhibition designs in New York for the Metropolitan Opera and Juilliard School productions. A later version of the "endless house" was commissioned by the Museum of Modern Art, in 1960, for possible construction in the garden of the museum and is recorded in drawings and model form.

BIBLIOGRAPHY

General References

T. Creighton, "Kiesler's Pursuit of an Idea," *Progressive Architecture* **42**(7), 104–123 (July 1961).

M. Emanuel, ed., *Contemporary Architects,* St. Martins Press, New York, 1980.

F. Kiesler, "Kiesler by Kiesler," *Architectural Forum* **123**(2), 64–71 (Sept. 1965).

F. St. Florian, "Frederick Kiesler," exhibition catalog, Galerie Nachst St. Stephan, Vienna, 1975.

ROBERT T. PACKARD, AIA
Reston, Virginia

KITCHENS, RESIDENTIAL

Residential kitchens in the United States in design, conformation, and placement in the house, are as various as the population itself. Some are buried deep in the interior with no outside windows; others are glass-walled "greenhouse" extensions of the house. Some are well-planned for function and efficiency; others are assembled almost at random. Some are spacious, but most are small. Some are tightly enclosed rooms, others are so open as to be part of the living or family room. Some come entirely from factories; others are built laboriously on-site by carpenters or woodworkers. Some are inexpensive, even cheap, whereas others cost as much as an entire "average" house.

These differences arise from several geographic, climatic, cultural, social, and economic considerations. U.S. geography ranges from ocean shores to mountains, lush tropics to deserts. Climate ranges from year-round summer in the south to ten-month winters in northern states, and differences are even more extreme when the detached states of Alaska and Hawaii are considered. There are population segments segregated culturally and socially by "old-country" backgrounds, by language barriers, by the camaraderie of a shared workplace, and by residence in huge tract-built communities or apartment complexes.

Economically, low-income and high-income communities have a direct bearing on the nature of kitchens, although sometimes in contradictory ways. For example, a wealthy suburban home might have a beautiful, spacious, well-planned and designed kitchen, whereas a wealthier apartment area a few miles away in New York City might have atrocious kitchens simply because they are seldom seen except by the hired help.

HISTORY

Mankind discovered early that some foods tasted better and were easier to eat when cooked. Early humans mastered fire and eventually learned to use rocks and to work clay and metals to fashion cooking surfaces and vessels.

Hearths were developed to raise the fire and prevent its being extinguished by rain. The vagaries of weather, even in warm climates, drove kitchens indoors. Drawings from the early Middle Ages show what probably always has been the indoor ventilation system of the poor: holes fashioned in the roofs to let the smoke out (Fig. 1).

The first planned kitchens in medieval Europe were in monasteries (Fig. 2) dating from around 1000 A.D. There might be several such rooms: one for baking, one for cooking meats, and one for preparing medicines (1). In early New England, the kitchen was not a discrete entity. It was, instead, a "keeping room" in which the fireplace was used for cooking, for heating water for bathing, and for general warmth in the house, as in Figure 3. Cooking equipment was kept near the fireplace or, in some cases, stored nearby in a pantry along with foods.

In Britain, the kitchen included the scullery, a room for cleaning and storing dishes (tableware). In colonial

Figure 1. Peasant kitchens of the early Middle Ages had an open hearth for cooking, a brick oven for baking, and a hole in the roof for smoke to escape. Courtesy of *Kitchen & Bath Business.*

Figure 2. The upscale kitchens of the thirteenth century were found in castles, monasteries, and convents. Here, spits for cooking are mounted on a hood. The plate racks on the wall are too high for convenient use. Courtesy of *Kitchen & Bath Business*.

America, particularly in the South, because of the smoke and heat of cooking, the kitchen often was in a building separate from the main house. Even today, in the older part of Charleston, S.C., the primary job in kitchen remodeling is to move the kitchen into the house.

Figure 3. In the early American home the kitchen was part of the living area. A kettle was always suspended from the fireplace for hot water. The fireplace was the source of warmth for the house as well as of heat for cooking. Courtesy of *Kitchen & Bath Business*.

Modern kitchen history in the United States started after the 1850s with the invention of the cast-iron stove fueled by wood or coal and, in the 1880s, also by either gas or oil. The electric range was developed in 1910. By this time there were many multipurpose cabinets for storing pots, pans, utensils, and foods, the more advanced of which had built-in flour sifters, bins for sugar, and drawers for linens.

Electric dishwashers, patented in 1914, and garbage disposers, patented in 1928, did not come into general use until steel again became plentiful after World War II. In the building booms of the postwar years, several factors came together that led to the modern built-in kitchen as it is known today. These factors included the development of built-in cooktops and wall ovens, and of a fasten-down rim that enabled recessing of a sink in a countertop without the rotting effects of water leakage; popularizing of decorative high-pressure laminate as a countertop surface; and development of integrated complete kitchens with both cabinets and appliances of steel.

Also of key importance was the formation of several industry associations to promote the concept of modern kitchens. These included the National Kitchen Cabinet Association (NKCA); the National Association of Plastic Fabricators (NAPF), now the Decorative Laminated Products Association; and, in 1963, the American Institute of Kitchen Dealers (AIKD), now the National Kitchen and Bath Association. These associations worked together to improve product development and to further dealer and manufacturer education, developing what is now a sophisticated and communicative kitchen industry.

When the NKCA was organized in 1955 to promote factory-built wood cabinets, half the kitchen cabinets sold in the United States were made of steel. Half of the other 50% were built on site. In the next 15 years, the handful of wood-cabinet plants grew to hundreds, and the market share of steel residential kitchen cabinets dwindled to almost nothing. People preferred the look and warmth of wood.

The NAPF formed in 1954 when "sinktop" manufacturers organized to fight a patent on the plastic laminating process held by North American Aviation. They succeeded a few years later, opening the gates for a flood of decorative melamine laminate tops that have become standard in U.S. kitchens. The material also serves now as surfacing on 25% of U.S. cabinets. However, in the early 1950s, laminate surfacing on countertops actually was almost legislated out of existence in some states because of the fear of bacteria growth around the sink cutout, a problem that was solved by invention of the fasten-down sink rim.

Built-in ranges made necessary the kitchen designer who could both plan and install these new appliances. Appliance stores had neither the personnel nor the inclination to do this kind of work. Kitchen designers, which numbered in the dozens before, quickly grew to thousands, and the kitchen field took form as an industry. The process was aided by studies and publications of the Small Homes Council–Building Research Council of the University of Illinois and by product and time–motion studies at Cornell University.

The AIKD role was of paramount importance, giving

all new designers a forum for communication and providing schools where they could learn more. AIKD also became a certifying agency, issuing the Certified Kitchen Designer (CKD) designation to those who qualified.

American cabinet manufacturers started very small, for the most part, and for 20 years were occupied with repeated expansions to keep up with an expanding market. European cabinet manufacturers quickly outgrew their markets and concentrated on making their plants more sophisticated. This opened the way for European expansion to the United States and Canada in the mid-1970s, which had a very beneficial effect on the U.S. market because of the new and different product line. It stimulated consumer interest, and it also moved U.S. manufacturers to improve their plants with modern, computerized machinery and with "Euro-style" copies of European cabinets.

The primary difference was that U.S. cabinets were made with face frames, which in turn called for lipped doors. European cabinets were simply boxes with doors attached, so the doors fit flush for a contemporary look. Framed cabinets had greater rigidity, so they were less subject to racking when attached to uneven walls. Frameless cabinets made up for this with more sophisticated, six-way adjustable hinges that could correct minor racking. U.S. manufacturers, who still favor framed construction, achieve a more contemporary look with doors that look flush by butting, overlaying the face frame with apparent narrowing of the horizontal rails and vertical stiles of the face frame. But many now offer both framed and frameless cabinets, with the framed usually in the higher-end lines.

There were two other very visible differences. European cabinets were introduced in the United States with decorative laminate surfaces in solid colors and with the interiors fully fitted and accessorized. They also were much more expensive than U.S. cabinets. This promptly upgraded the image of "plastic" cabinets among U.S. consumers, triggering greater use of the material in the United States. The interior accessories were always available in U.S. cabinets, but had never been promoted to builders or consumers, so these also experienced a boost in popularity, leading to a general upgrading of U.S. kitchens.

Built-in appliances gained through the postwar building booms of the 1950s and early 1960s, largely because of the great growth in numbers of kitchen dealer–designers, who favored them because they required design and installation service, and because appliance manufacturers offered "package prices" that were very attractive to builders. The invention of pyrolytic self-cleaning ovens was one of the main factors that reversed this trend in ranges, because the popular feature was offered initially only in freestanding models. By the mid-1980s, freestanding ranges outsold built-ins by about four to one, according to the Association of Home Appliance Manufacturers (AHAM). Dishwashers, on the other hand, were almost all built in, outselling freestanding models, or "portables," by about 16 to 1, according to AHAM figures. Built-in refrigeration never achieved significant market share and is not counted separately by AHAM, although there are several brands, both domestic and imported, on the market. Garbage disposers now are installed in about 75% of new U.S. housing, trash compactors in less than 5%.

BASIC DIMENSIONS

Measurements in U.S. kitchens and kitchen equipment differ from those of other countries because the United States continues on the "foot and inch" system and consumers have resisted metrication. Some foreign cabinet and appliance manufacturers have converted their metric measurements to inches for the U.S. market, but in many cases they have not, and U.S. designers have had to make their own conversions.

This usually makes no substantive difference in the way kitchen equipment fits. The differences work out to only a few centimeters at most, and any gaps are corrected by use of fillers at the ends of cabinet runs or on either side of the sink cabinet or range. However, it does make a difference in floor-plan drawings, because U.S. practice is to use a scale of ½ in. to 1 ft (1.27 cm to 30.48 cm) whereas European drawings use a scale of 1:20 cm. The difference is demonstrated in Figure 4 of a U.S. kitchen, and Figure 5 of the same kitchen using West German cabinets, both of which are reduced from those scales. To avoid confusion, on U.S. drawings measurements are in inches, not combinations of feet and inches.

In some instances European manufacturers must make special-size cabinets. For example, the most common range size in the U.S. is 30 in. (76.2 cm) wide, which is an odd size in Europe for a wall cabinet to fit over the range hood. Changes such as this, however, are few.

Standard ceiling height in U.S. kitchens is 8 ft (2.44 m), and standard door framing height is 7 ft (2.13 m). Standard cabinet height from the floor to the tops of the wall cabinets is 7 ft, about even with door framing, leaving 1 ft (0.3 m) above the wall cabinets for furring, which is (inaccurately) referred to as the soffit.

Standard base cabinets are 30–31 in. (76–79 cm) high, but they sit on a toekick 4 in. (10 cm) high and 2–3 in. (5.1–7.6 cm) deep, known as a plinth in Europe. They are topped by the countertop, 1.5 in. (3.8 cm) thick, the surface of which is 36 in. (91.4 cm) above the floor. This height is unvarying, because the dishwasher must fit under the counter and the range is sized to fit that height. Some slip-in ranges actually hang from flanges that fit over the countertop. Base cabinets are 24 in. (60.96 cm) deep. Wall cabinets are 12 in. (30.5 cm) deep, and usually are 30–33 in. (76–84 cm) high. Cabinets made to order might be as much as 48 in. (122 cm) high, but this is rare. In such cases, they go all the way to the ceiling. The standard measurements are shown in Figure 6. The space between the countertop and the bottoms of the wall cabinets will normally be about 18 in. (45.7 cm).

Standard dishwasher width is 24 in. (60.96 cm), although some are available at 18 in. (45.7 cm) wide. Common range width is 30 in. (76.2 cm), although some are as little as 20 in. (50.8 cm) or as much as 42 in. (106.68 cm). Widths of refrigerators vary greatly, but usually 36 in. (91.4 cm) is allowed in any designs done in advance.

CONFORMATIONS

There are four basic conformations for residential kitchen cabinets and equipment. These are the one-wall, the corri-

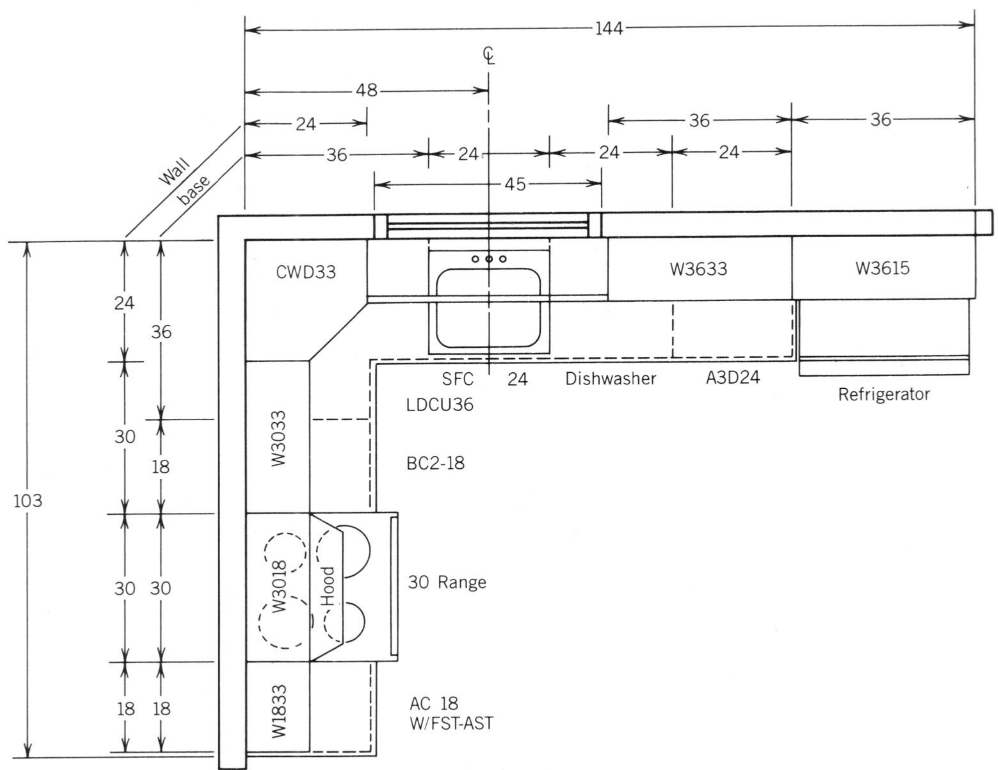

Figure 4. Kitchen drawn in inches, in scale of ½ in. to 1 ft, with Wood-Mode Kitchens nomenclature. Drawing by R.A. Cuccaro, CKD.

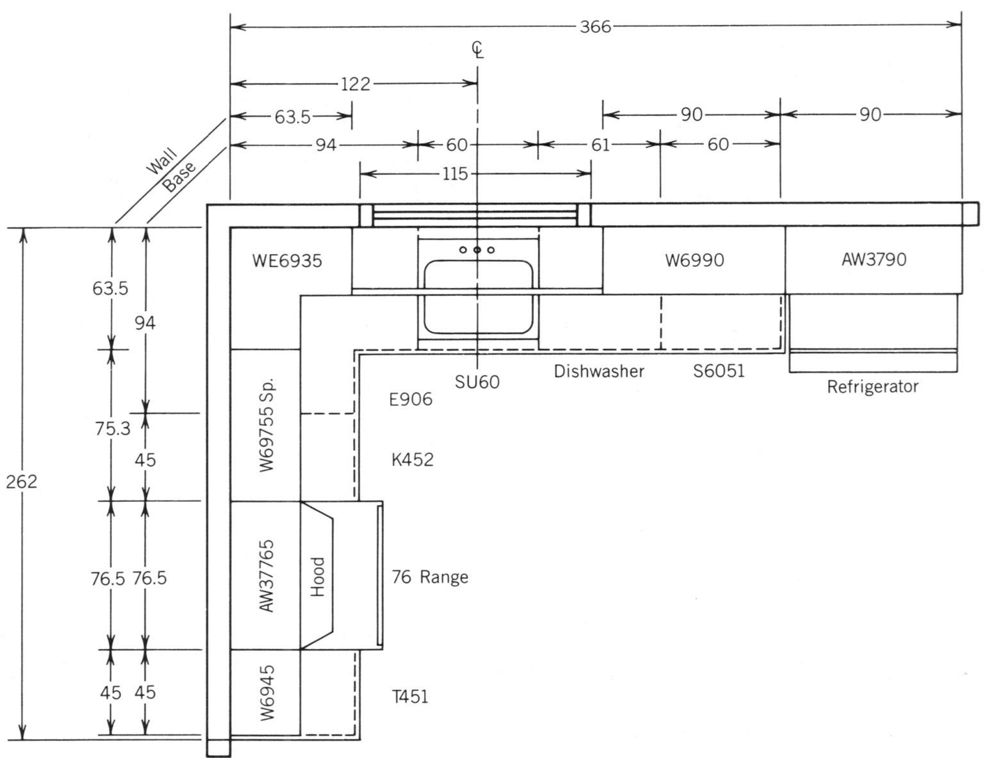

Figure 5. Same kitchen as in Figure 4, but 1:20 cm, with Allmilmo nomenclature. Drawing by R. A. Cuccaro, CKD.

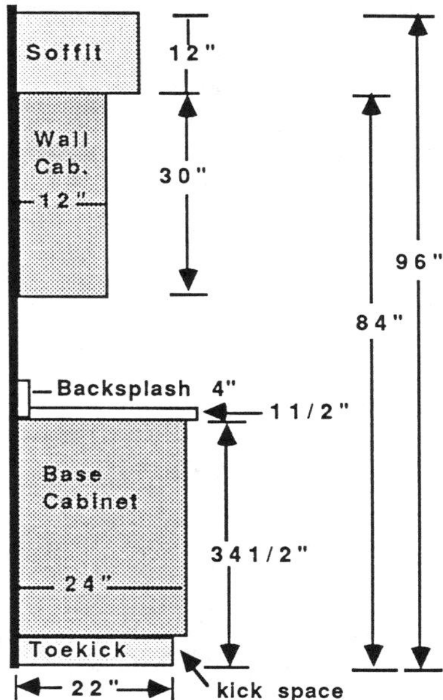

Figure 6. The standard U.S. kitchen is fitted to the standard 96 in. (2.44 m) high room. Measurements are standardized to fit with appliances.

dor or galley, the L, and the U. Choice of one of these floor plans will depend on available space and budget.

One-wall kitchens have all cabinets, counters, and appliances arranged in line along one wall. This is the minimal arrangement requiring the least space and the least expense. It can be very efficient, but it usually is hampered by a paucity of counter space and cabinet storage. It requires a minimum depth of 5 ft (1.5 m), of which 2 ft (0.6 m) is taken up by the depth of the base cabinets, plus 3 ft (0.9 m) for movement and space for doors to open. This one-wall kitchen is illustrated in Figure 7, which in this case also includes a dishwasher.

The corridor, or galley, kitchen usually provides more cabinet and counter space with equipment arranged on two walls, as shown in Figure 8. Each side of this kitchen requires at least 2 ft (0.6 m) of depth for the base cabinets, and the refrigerator usually protrudes another 4–5 in. (10–12.7 cm) beyond that. Minimum space for movement between the two sides is 3 ft (0.9 m), but this often is not acceptable to a consumer buying a house. Space of 4 ft (1.2 m) is more realistic, and 5 ft (1.5 m) would be desirable. This can be very efficient, providing family traffic patterns do not go through the kitchen.

An L conformation uses two adjacent walls and, if not spread out too much, can be very efficient. With it tucked

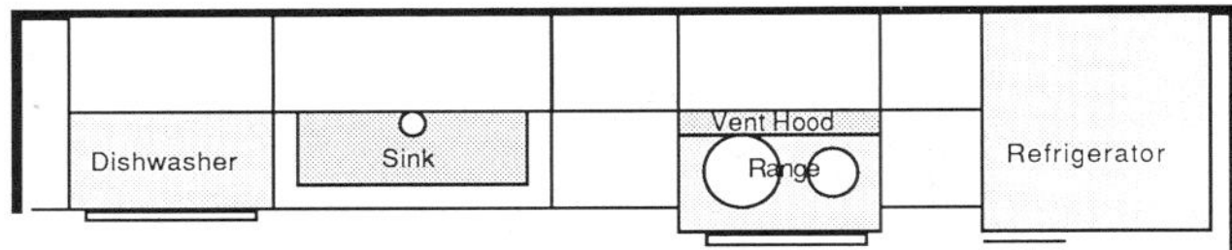

Figure 7. The one-wall kitchen needs the least space and is the most inexpensive. The dishwasher is under the counter, which allows work space beside the sink. Drawing by the author.

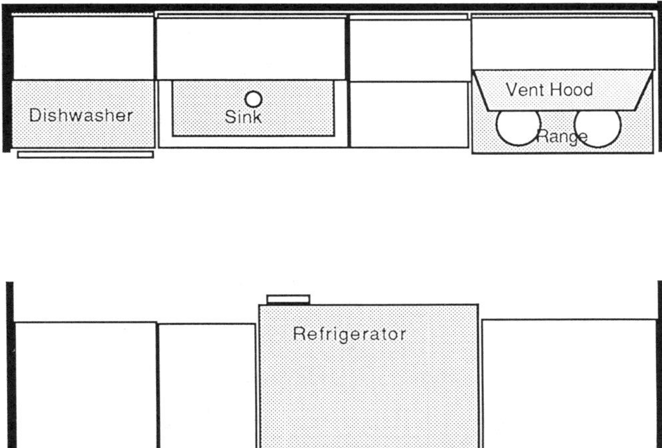

Figure 8. The corridor kitchen adds counter space, but it might be subject to interference from through traffic. Drawing by the author.

away in a corner location as it is, family traffic patterns are not a problem and no one gets in the way of the person doing the cooking. It is illustrated in Figure 9, along with the work triangle, which will be discussed later.

The U kitchen, illustrated in Figure 10, usually is considered to be the most desirable and most efficient, the only potential problem being that the legs of the U might be stretched out too far in larger rooms. There are no interfering traffic patterns in this kind of layout.

The question of a kitchen being too large is one that relates to the work triangle, an imaginary line running between the center lines of the sink, the range, the refrigerator, and back to the sink. The work triangle is a formula resulting from many years of time–motion studies. According to this formula, maximum efficiency with plenty of

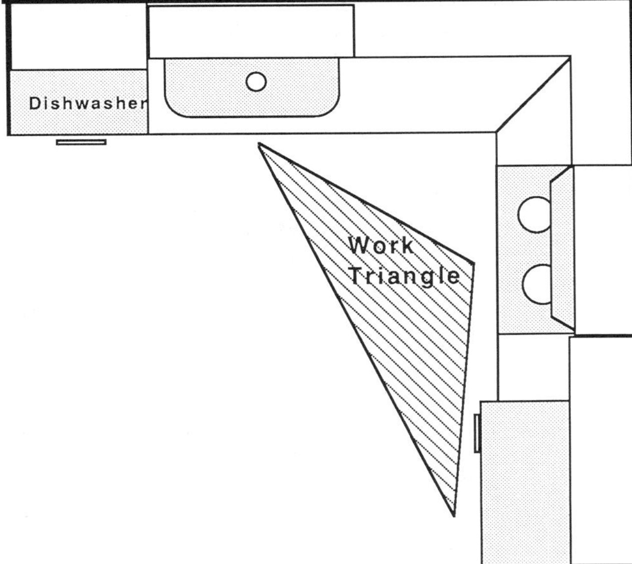

Figure 9. L-shaped kitchens usually are in a corner area, so there is room for through traffic without interference. Drawing by the author.

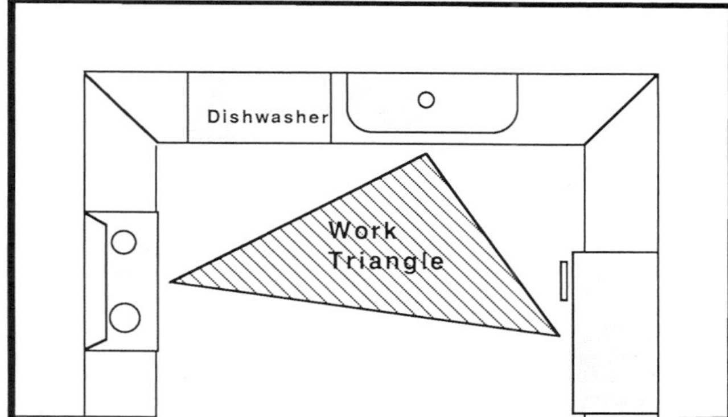

Figure 10. The U-shaped kitchen usually is the most desired. It offers the best efficiency with no through traffic. Drawing by the author.

room to work and with the fewest wasted steps is gained by holding the sum of the three legs of the work triangle to not less than 13 ft (3.96 m) and not more than 23 ft (7 m). When the room is too large for that formula, the designer will create an island or peninsula to form one leg of the L or U or one side of a corridor kitchen. Ideally, no leg of the triangle will be less than 4 ft (1.2 m). Ideally, the sink and range will be closest together, up to 6 ft (1.8 m); the sink and the refrigerator up to 8 ft (2.44 m), and the refrigerator and range up to 9 ft (2.74 m).

There are kitchens in which a doorway breaks an L or U shape, permitting traffic flow through the work triangle. The objective in remodeling such a broken L or U, or in remodeling a corridor kitchen that invites traffic flow, is to reroute the traffic by moving the doorway to maintain the integrity of the L or U work triangle or by creating a route around the triangle in the corridor kitchen. At least 65% of the kitchens created each year in the United States are in the remodeling sector of the industry and, according to many consumer surveys, correcting such a functional problem ranks third as the reason for remodeling, behind shortage of storage space and shortage of counter space (2).

Islands and Peninsulas

Inclusion of an island or peninsula in a kitchen design does not change the basic conformation. It facilitates use by shortening the work triangle and making possible an L or U. It also can add function. An island or peninsula usually will include the sink or range within the kitchen space and, if space permits, a breakfast bar on the side that is outside the kitchen space. Base and wall cabinets for a peninsula might open both ways for easier access from either side. When there is a sink or range on one side and an eating counter on the other, a barrier is advisable to prevent splash or spatter. This sometimes is accomplished by raising the eating counter 6 in. (15 cm), more or less, and equipping it with high stools.

For such an eating counter, recommended lateral space for persons seated side by side is 24 in. (60.9 cm) per person. Distance from the counter to the wall behind it should be at least 26 in. (66 cm) for movement to get in and out of the seating, but 36 in. (91 cm) is desirable. To allow this movement and also space for others to walk behind the seats, 36 in. (91 cm) is the minimum requirement and 44 in. (112 cm) is desirable. Counter space in front of each person should be at least 15 in. (38 cm) deep.

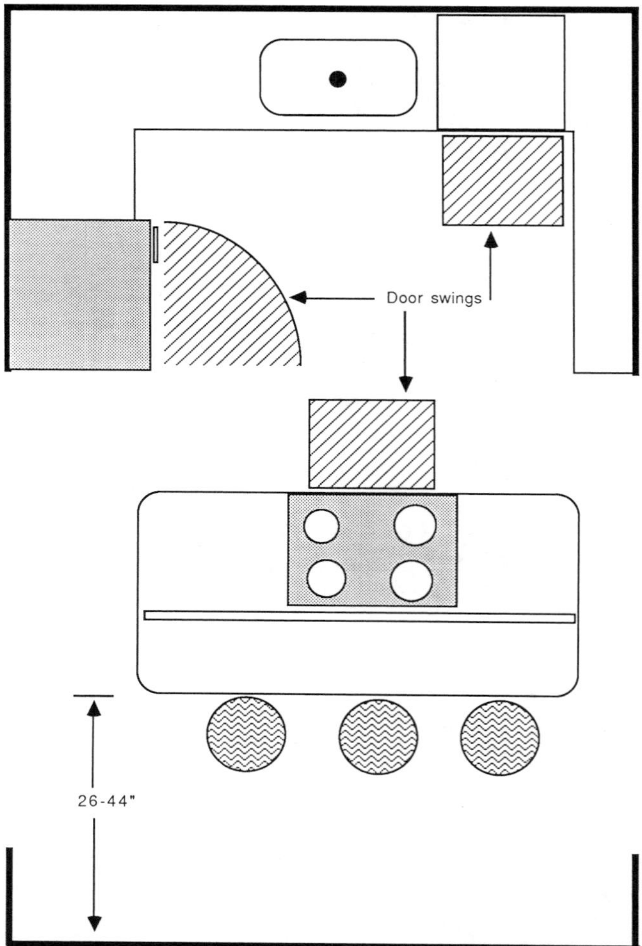

Figure 11. An island often is added to help form a U kitchen. Appliance door swings must be checked to be sure they clear. Drawing by the author.

The most frequent problem in designing islands and peninsulas is failure to allow space for opening of the appliance doors. It is safest to include drawings of door swings for refrigerator, oven, and dishwasher in the floor plan to avoid this problem. Also, it is best to round the corners of island and peninsula countertops to avoid injuries to hips. A representative island with breakfast bar is shown in Figure 11.

KITCHEN COMPONENTS

Cabinets

Kitchen cabinets are classified generally in two ways: by material—wood, plastic, or steel—and by whether they are stock or custom.

Figure 12. The traditional look of U.S. framed cabinets shows the face frame against which lipped doors rest. Courtesy of Merillat Industries.

Figure 13. Euro-style is gained in this kitchen, showing the same cabinets as in Figure 12 by the same manufacturer but with laminate-surfaced doors overlaying the face frame for a contemporary look. Courtesy of Merillat Industries.

Wood cabinets are the most popular, by far. Some are solid lumber, some are plywood or particleboard with a wood-grain finish printed on their surfaces, and some have a wood veneer on particleboard or plywood. Of the solid woods, oak accounts for about 80% of production, followed by cherry, maple, ash, and birch. Most of the printed and veneered surfaces are also oak.

Plastic, as it is called, refers to decorative laminate on substrates of particleboard or plywood. Traditionally, this has been high-pressure decorative laminate, but the recent trend has been to low-pressure laminated board because it comes laminated by the board manufacturer, eliminating the laying-up of sheet laminate to the substrate. Other choices include vinyl and polyester. Polyester generally is a lower-grade material except for the expensive, high-gloss material from Europe.

Steel cabinets, which once dominated the market, now are made by only a handful of companies and mostly for the low-priced apartment market, although one manufacturer continues to make high-end steel cabinets for the luxury market.

Stock cabinets are those made in quantity to be warehoused by manufacturers and/or distributors. Custom cabinets are made in similar factories, but have more special sizes and types and are not made until a kitchen has been designed and sold at retail.

A newer classification, since the mid-1970s, has been European or Euro-style. "European" designates cabinets imported from Europe, Canada, Israel, or the Far East, characterized by frameless construction, decorative laminate finish, and a contemporary look. "Euro-style" refers to U.S. copies or derivatives of that appearance, in some cases frameless and in other cases framed. Figure 12 shows the traditional framed cabinet with lipped doors, and Figure 13 shows a Euro-style cabinet made by the same manufacturer with the same framed box, but with overlay doors and the strong horizontal lines that characterize Euro-style.

A stock-cabinet manufacturer might offer a half-dozen styles in a choice of two or three wood species. However, the distributor for that manufacturer, in any area, will seldom stock all of these in inventory. It is more customary for any distributor to stock only two or three of the lines of any manufacturer, limiting the selections at the point of sale.

Stock cabinets are made in 3-in. (7.6-cm) increments, so for a perfect fit between walls in a house the measurement would have to be divisible by three. If, for example, a wall is 98 in. (248.9 cm) long, a run of stock cabinets could total 96 in. (243.8 cm). To fill the remaining 2 in. (5 cm), a matching 2-in. filler would be provided. This could be cut to fit symmetrically with 1 in. (2.54 cm) at each end of the run or on either side of the sink or range cabinet.

Custom manufacturers usually offer many more styles in many more wood species. Theoretically, the choices are almost unlimited, because the cabinets are not made until they are bought by the homeowner or builder and ordered from the factory. In practice, however, many custom manufacturers limit styles, species, finishes, and construction methods as well as hardware selections to conform with their own buying power and practices and with what is available from their suppliers. If, for example, a customer wants pecan wood with dowel joints and a particular drawer slide, the custom plant might insist on hickory (which looks the same), miter joints because that is the way it is done at this plant, and the drawer slide that the plant customarily uses and has stocked in considerable quantity. But in the case of the 98-in. (248.9-cm) wall, above, the custom plant will size the cabinets to fit or will put extended stiles on the end cabinets that can be scribed to the walls and cut to fit.

Most European cabinets available in the United States are called custom, but they are not. They are made on highly sophisticated production lines, and there can be no deviation from the specific items in the catalogs. In general, they are not shipped from overseas until sold to the customer, but delivery schedules are about the same as those for U.S. custom cabinets, about 4 to 8 weeks. Stock cabinets usually are available almost immediately from regional or local warehouses.

Countertops

The standard U.S. countertop consists of a high-pressure decorative laminate surface glued to a particleboard or plywood substrate to a thickness of 1.5 in. (3.8 cm). This surface laminate consists of up to 12 sheets of decorative paper on which is printed the design and a backer sheet, all of which are impregnated with transparent melamine resin under heat and high pressure to form a rigid sheet of laminate 1/16 in. (1.58 mm) thick. It provides extreme durability for high-wear kitchen use. (A vertical-grade laminate, used as a cabinet surface, is made to half that thickness by leaving out several sheets of paper.) The laminates are manufactured in 4 × 8-ft (1.2 × 2.4-m) and 5 × 12-ft (1.5 × 3.7-m) sheets and sold through independent distributors to local fabricators, who make counters and other products in their shops, and to kitchen dealers who often fabricate the tops in the kitchen after cabinets have been installed. Some major countertop fabricators sell countertop "blanks" to home centers. These are tops in specific sizes that can be bought by consumers and cut to fit in their own kitchens.

Laminate tops are designated according to construction as "self-edged" or "postformed." A self-edged top has square edges all around, with 1.5-in. (3.8-cm) strips of edge banding that usually match the material on top. Postformed tops are all one piece from the lower edge of the front to the back edge of the backsplash. For postforming, the laminate is bendable when heated, and once bent it retains the bent shape. Under the laminate at the front, the substrate is shaped into a "bullnose" or grooved for plastic T-molding that is inserted to shape the laminate. When the laminate comes up and over straight, it is a "waterfall" edge. When it bulges slightly over the front of the top (over the T-molding) it is called a "no-drip" edge. At the back it is bent upward and then back to form the backsplash. Usually the backsplash is 5 in. (12.7 cm) high, but many prefer to run the backsplash laminate all the way up to the bottoms of the wall cabinets.

Postformed tops (Fig. 14) have no sharp edges and no interior corners to catch dirt. However, because of the postforming in one dimension, they cannot be curved in the other dimension, so they cannot be used for horizontally curved counters and tables that are popular for today's kitchens. Self-edged countertops continue to be popular because the substrate can be shaped for any desired curves, and the edge banding can be applied with contact adhesive around any such curves.

High-pressure decorative laminates are excellent as a counter material because of their durability and cleanability. Their only problem is that they are not repairable. They can pick up small cuts from kitchen knives, and they can be scorched by excessive heat. A laminate top will withstand the heat from a pot of boiling water, but not the heat from a very hot empty pot. For this reason, kitchen designers often will design inserts in the tops, near the range, of ceramic tile, stainless steel, or tempered glass. Wood inserts are often included for use as cutting boards.

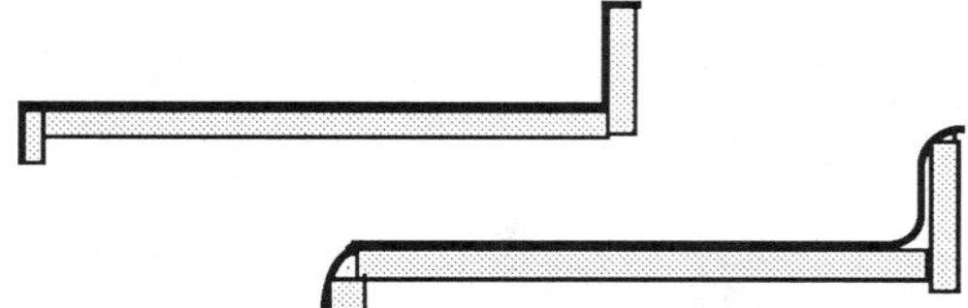

Figure 14. Heavy lines denote laminate on self-edged countertop, above, and postformed top, below. The self-edged countertop has four pieces of laminate glued to the substrate. The postformed countertop has one continuous sheet bent over front and coved upward at back. Drawing by the author.

Other materials for kitchen countertops include ceramic tile, which is popular in western states; solid wood, usually maple, which is more often used as an insert for cutting and chopping of meats and vegetables; granite, which is very expensive and was introduced as a fashion material with European cabinets; and an acrylic monomer, which actually is a form of cultured marble but differs in that it is homogeneous and therefore machinable with woodworking tools. Only one type of this acrylic monomer was available for nearly 20 years until competing brands and other polyester-based materials were developed in the late 1980s.

The acrylic monomer and other new materials, being homogeneous, can be routed for fancy ogee edges, or for insertion of strips of wood veneer or decorative laminate. Solid wood edges also are used to upgrade decorative laminate tops. Such fabrication adds greatly to the expense.

Standard cultured marbles so popular in bathrooms are not considered durable enough for kitchen use because of their gel-coat finish, although methods were introduced in the 1980s for repairing gel coats and, with new equipment and fillers, even eliminating them.

Cooking Ranges

Standard cooking ranges, for the most part, are fueled by electricity or natural gas in urban areas, often by propane gas in rural areas. They are 30 in. (76 cm) wide with four burners and one oven, which also serves as a broiler. Most are freestanding and rest on the floor. Many are "slip-ins" that are suspended by their flanges, which rest on the countertop on either side and might or might not extend to the floor. Upgraded versions have convertible cooktops with cartridge elements that are interchangeable, with options that include standard burners, European-style solid burners, burners embedded in tempered ceramic tops, barbecue grill units, deep fryers, and rotisseries. One type even offers a magnetic induction cartridge (Fig. 15).

Built-in cooktops offer all of these options. They also are available with two, four, or six burners in widths ranging up to 42 in. (106.7 cm). Built-in ovens can be multipurpose single or double with separate cavities for baking and broiling. Some also offer convection cooking in which a fan circulates air around the cooking food, which speeds cooking at lower temperatures. Some offer microwave cooking in one unit. Some offer conventional, convection, and

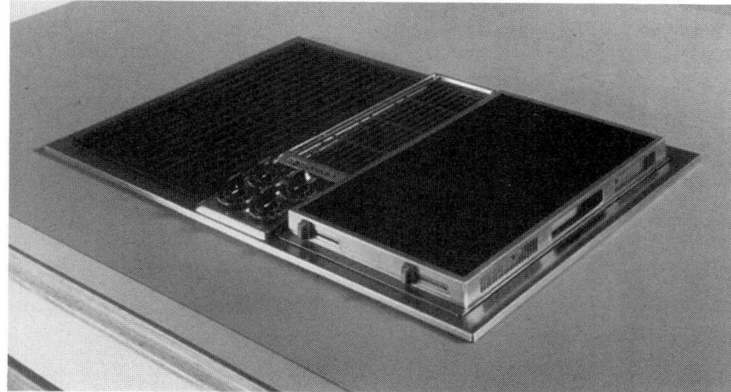

Figure 15. This built-in cooktop has a magnetic induction cartridge and a barbecue grill, but these are interchangeable with other cartridges. The original down-draft venting cooktop, it vents through the center grill. Courtesy of Jenn-Air.

microwave cooking in a single cavity (Fig. 16). Many are programmable for a full day of cooking activity at preset times with a "keep-warm" feature, so the cook can put the food in in the morning, leave for a day's work, then return home to find this part of the dinner ready to eat. This is in keeping with changing life-styles in the United States, which find more households in which both adults

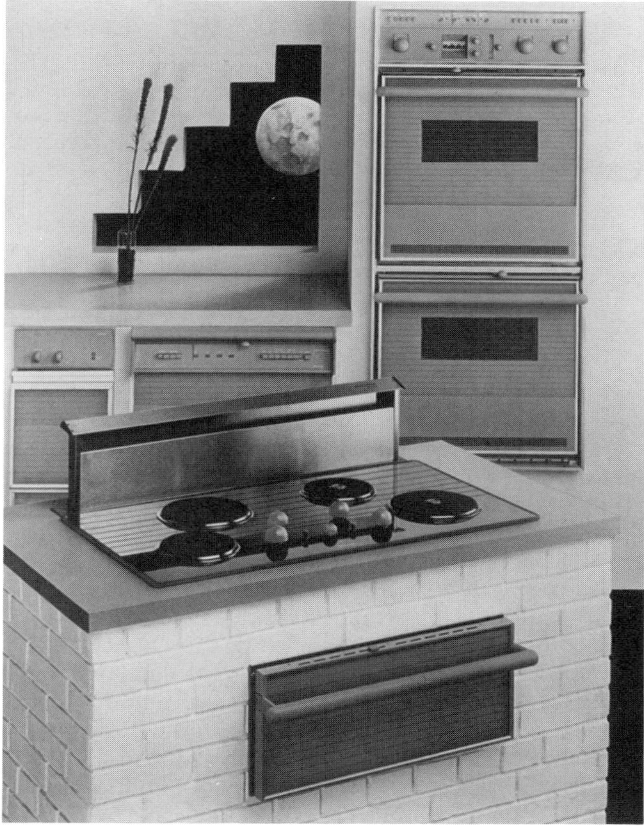

Figure 16. A double oven that combines microwave and conventional cooking in one cavity and that has a built-in vent. The cooktop vents downward from a raised duct in the back; a warming drawer is added below. The dishwasher and compactor match. Courtesy of Thermador.

work. Upgraded freestanding and slip-in ranges are also fully programmable.

Magnetic induction is the newest method for surface cooking. It uses a magnetic current that emanates from a glass ceramic surface and causes instant heat when it contacts a ferrous pot or pan, cooking the food more quickly. It also is safer because the range surface does not get hot except by conduction from the cooking vessel. This makes possible such interesting kitchen tricks as boiling a pot of water while it rests on a paper napkin that does not ignite. A disadvantage is that induction will not work with aluminum, copper, glass, or ceramic cookware, all of which are widely used.

Imported European ranges offer other options. Some cook with halogen light, for example, which, like gas or magnetic induction, is instantly hot. These have been slow to get the approval of Underwriters Laboratories, commonly considered to be necessary for sale in the United States. However, there are competing laboratories that are legally acceptable through which at least one European brand has gained approval. More interesting to designers is a European technique of mounting cooking controls remote from the range, on a wall or even on the front of a wall cabinet, for example, which keeps them spatter-free and out of reach of young children.

Many kitchen counters are cluttered with plug-in cooking appliances that are more generally called housewares, such as coffee makers, roasters, broilers, convection cookers, microwave units, toasters, hot plates, and mixers. In homes of many elderly people, these tend to become the primary cooking appliances despite the presence of adequate ranges, simply because they are considered more convenient. These, and the ever-present TV, pose a counter-space problem unless cabinet storage space is provided in the design stage.

Refrigerators/Freezers

There are no standard sizes for refrigerators, freezers, or combinations of the two. Freestanding and undercounter models are measured by cubic feet of capacity, whereas full-size built-ins are measured by width. Builders usually leave vacant a space 36 in. (91.4 cm) wide and topped by a wall cabinet 15 in. (38 cm) high for the refrigerator, assuming it will be a combination with 17–24 ft^3 (0.48–0.67 m^3) capacity, although the space will accept larger than that.

Single-door refrigerators have one exterior door and a small inner door that partitions off the area for ice cubes and frozen-food storage. Most must be defrosted manually. Most units sold, however, are combination refrigerator/freezers with two exterior doors, either over–under or side by side, maintaining a temperature of about 41°F (5°C) in the refrigerator compartment and lower than 8°F (−13°C) in the freezer compartment (Fig. 17). A sustained temperature of less than 8°F is needed to freeze foods. Defrosting is partially or totally automatic. When it is partially automatic, the freezer must be defrosted manually. When the freezer is on top, it is called top-mount. Only a few models are bottom-mount. In side-by-sides, the smaller compartment on the left is the freezer.

Figure 17. A typical modern upscale free-standing refrigerator–freezer, with ice and drinks through the door and an electronic monitor at the upper right that can warn of malfunctions. Courtesy of Whirlpool.

Some side-by-sides have three doors, including a smaller one upper left for an ice maker and flash freezing. Some have a convenience door in the larger door that opens for high-traffic foods without opening the larger door. Some have dispensers that deliver ice water, juices, and ice through the freezer door without opening the door. Some have accessories that make ice cream or yogurt in the freezer compartment.

The main difference in built-in units is that they are only 24 in. (61 cm) deep, matching the depth of base cabinets, so a built-in becomes part of the kitchen design rather than a hole in it. There are only four U.S. brands of full-size built-ins, although another company imports models from Italy, and there are a few foreign brand names. One manufacturer has an innovative "power module" that sits on top and jets refrigerated air down into the box, eliminating refrigerant coils, and is detachable. This eliminates the problem of moving a large built-in into the house through existing doors, since the power unit ships separately. This manufacturer also offers units as small as 18 in. (45.7 cm) wide, which can be all refrigerator, all freezer, or two-door combinations (Fig. 18). This adds to design freedom, as separate units can be placed in different areas of the kitchen. In one side-by-side model the refrigerator box is open to the freezer at the bottom, and a movable shelf in the freezer can be moved up and down to vary freezer capacity by 60%, changing refrigerator volume proportionately. Most of these units, freestanding or built-in, are equipped with "decorator kits" that accept paneling to match the cabinets or decorative laminate sheets or other materials.

Separate freezers are of two types, upright or chest. These are for families that do large-quantity buying, particularly of meats that can be purchased in bulk, then butchered and packaged to specification. Chest freezers range in capacity from 4.7 to 28 ft^3 (0.13–0.79 m^3), uprights from 1.3 to 31 ft^3 (0.04–0.87 m^3). Smaller sizes might go in the kitchen, but the larger ones more commonly go in a basement, utility room, or garage. All chest-type freezers and most uprights must be defrosted manually.

Figure 18. The advantage of 18-in. wide refrigerator/freezer units is shown here. The kitchen had columns that had to stay, so an all-freezer unit was mounted in the column at left, a two-door refrigerator in the wall at the rear. Courtesy of Defiance International.

Clean-up Appliances

Clean-up appliances in the kitchen are dishwashers, garbage disposers, and trash compactors. Of these, dishwashers and disposers are accepted as basic and are installed in about half of all new and remodeled kitchens each year. Compactors have never been popular and have been in decline through the 1980s despite great growth in disposable cartoning that adds to trash bulk.

Dishwashers are made to fit under the counter, a standard 24 in. (60.9 cm) wide except for two space-saving models that are 18 in. (45.7 cm) wide. The bottom of the countertop is 34.5 in. (87.6 cm) above the floor, and dishwashers have adjustable feet to get them into this space and then raise them so they can be screwed to the counter. They always should be mounted adjacent to the sink cabinet for ease of use, and they are provided with hose and piping to work off the sink hot water supply and to exhaust water directly or through the disposer to the sink drain.

Incoming hot water should be 140°F (60°C). Safety and cost factors make this too hot a setting at the water heater for most homes, so most upgraded dishwashers now have a booster heater to raise supply water to that temperature from about 110°F (43°C). One West German dishwasher sold in the United States has a booster heater so powerful it can be supplied from the cold water line. Dishwashers also are capable of disposing of minor food particles from the dishes.

Better dishwashers are equipped with trim kits to accept panels to match the cabinets, countertops, or other decorative surfaces. They have electronic controls to provide several choices of short or long cycles, including a delayed start so they can be activated in periods of low electricity consumption.

Portable dishwashers, as the freestanding models are called, are still available for kitchens too small for built-in installation. They must be wheeled into place where a supply hose can be attached to the sink faucet and a waste hose can be fed into the sink. They usually have wood butcher block or decorative laminate tops to provide an added work surface in the kitchen.

Disposers are mounted in the sink drain line directly under the sink. They are available in two types, batch or continuous feed. For batch feed, waste foods are loaded into the disposer, a top is affixed, and then the switch is thrown. For continuous feed, the switch is thrown and foods are continuously fed in through the sink drain. The switch for either usually is mounted on the backsplash wall. Both need a good flow of cold water to carry the liquefied garbage out through the waste line and house drain. Neither type has any advantage over the other. It is a matter of personal preference.

Some local building codes prohibit disposers because it is thought that they can overload the sewer lines. Others require them to lighten the burden of garbage collection. Testing over the years tends to support the codes that require them, but local codes should always be checked before disposers are designed into the kitchen.

Compactors vary in width, so specifications must be checked before they are designed into the kitchen. They range from 12 in. (30.4 cm) to 18 in. (45.7 cm) wide. They compact solid trash into a bag, reducing volume but not weight. When kitchen space is limited, there is no reason why these must be in the kitchen if other handy space is available. Many use freestanding models that are placed in a garage, utility room, or other space enroute to the trash container.

Sinks, Faucets

The kitchen sink, once no more than a utility tub in the kitchen, has become somewhat glamorous in many of its forms in the last 20 years. Today it might have a single bowl, two equal bowls, a deep and shallow bowl, a special minibowl for mounting a disposer, even three bowls. It can be of stainless steel, porcelain on steel, or porcelain on cast iron, or it can be vitreous china, even plastic. It can come in any color, bright or subdued in the various materials, or shiny or satin gray in stainless steel.

Sizes that have been standard for many years are no longer so because of the many foreign lines now being imported. Standard U.S. sizes have been 43 in. (109 cm) wide for the deluxe three-bowl models, 33 in. (83.8 cm) for two-bowl models, and 25 in. (63.5 cm) for single bowls. These measurements refer to the size from the outer edges of the flanges, not the bowls themselves, which can vary. Front-to-back depth is 22 in. (55.8 cm).

Stainless steel sinks have been most popular in kitchen remodeling. These might be 18- or 20-gauge steel. The 18-gauge is heavier and more satisfactory. They sometimes are designated by two other numbers, which refer to the mixture of alloys. For example, 18–8 refers to 18% chrome content and 8% nickel content. Chrome enhances the sink's ability to stand up over the years and keep its finish. Nickel gives it the ability to withstand corrosion.

For corner installations, designers can put any sink in a diagonal corner base cabinet or choose a special two-bowl sink with a pie-cut configuration to wrap around the corner. Corner installations command a lot of space on each adjacent wall, so kitchen space must be plentiful.

Sinks come with one, two, three, or four holes punched for faucets and/or accessories. One hole is for the cold water supply, one for the hot water supply, and one for the faucet spout, if needed. It is not always needed because the spout might be mounted on a raised deck. An extra hole might be used for a pull-out spray, an instant hot water accessory, or to vent the waste line of a too-distant dishwasher. Single-lever faucets, which are popular, need only one hole. Some come with detergent and lotion pumps to take advantage of the other two holes. Others have escutcheon plates to cover those holes.

The choice of faucets has become complicated with, literally, dozens of brands available from around the world. They come in all colors and are made of various materials, including glass, brass, silver, gold, many different plastics, even wood. They also have several different valve constructions. One U.S. manufacturer introduced an interior cartridge that could be guaranteed drip-proof for as long as the purchaser owned it. The same manufacturer also introduced such innovations as the "riser," which pulls up several inches to make room for large pots, and another that rotates to form a drinking fountain. Another manufacturer offers faucets for kitchen or bathroom that have light-powered temperature read-outs on the stalk. Still another makes a faucet with two infrared sensors that turn the water on and off automatically, at any preset temperature, when hands or other objects are placed in position under the spout. With the many different shapes and materials available, it becomes important for the kitchen designer to be aware of faucet choice before selecting the sink to be used.

KITCHEN LIGHTING

Lighting in the kitchen is a function of available natural light, installed light, and the surfaces that will reflect light. A kitchen with dark cabinets and a dark floor can need twice as much installed light as one with light surfaces. Age of the users is also a factor. Persons 60 years old need twice as much light for seeing and for general well-being as persons of 40.

Lighting needs vary also with the size of the kitchen, and there are big differences in the output of fluorescent and incandescent lamps. Fluorescent tubes are much more efficient in light output per watt, but incandescent bulbs are pinpoints that are better at showing textures in the kitchen. Fluorescent tubes tend toward the blue end of the spectrum, whereas incandescent bulbs are red-oriented. If the cabinets or walls are red, incandescence will show much richer colors. If tubes are used in a red environment, "grow" lights will show the reds much better than other tubes. These differences in color balance have a profound effect on all apparent colors in the kitchen, making it imperative that a client see all products in the same kind of light as that installed in the home.

The kitchen designer must be concerned with both general light and task light in a kitchen. Small kitchens of 75 ft^2 (6.97 m^2) or less will need at least 60 W of fluorescent lighting for general illumination. For incandescence, there should be at least 150 W in one to three sockets. But if these units are recessed in the ceiling with enclosed bottoms, the panels should be at least 12 in. (30.48 cm) wide and the small kitchen would need 80 W fluorescence or 300 W incandescence.

An average kitchen of 75–150 ft^2 (6.9–13.93 m^2) will need 60–80 W fluorescent or 150–200 W incandescent. For recessed fixtures, minimums would be 80 W fluorescent or four 100 W incandescent bulbs.

Large kitchens with more than 120 ft^2 (11.1 m^2) can be calculated. Figure 0.75 W/ft^2 (8.3 W/m^2) fluorescent or 2 W/ft^2 incandescent; if recessed, 80–120 W per 60 ft^2 (per 5.6 m^2) fluorescent or 150 W/40 ft^2 (per 3.7 m^2) incandescent.

However, task lighting that applies light to specific work areas also is needed. This includes counter surfaces and the sink and range areas, although the range normally has its own light or a light in the ventilating hood above it.

Counter surfaces are best lighted with under-cabinet lighting, which is easiest to add under framed cabinets. Euro-style cabinets without face frames have no lower front rail to shield the eyes, so some form of shield must be added or the lights must be recessed in the cabinet bottoms. With these cabinets, surface-mounted down lights, track lighting (which is essentially the same thing), or wall brackets might be the easiest answer to the need for task lighting (Fig. 19). The down lights, or track lights, should be 20 in. (51 cm) apart, centered over the countertop with 75-W reflector flood bulbs.

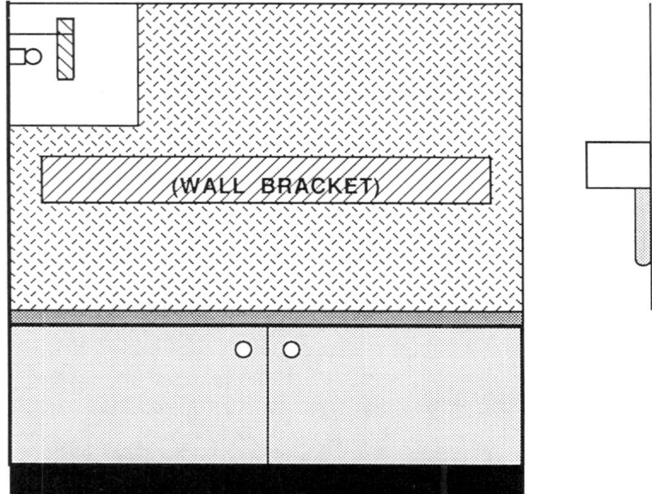

Figure 19. A wall bracket can be constructed to provide task lighting. It goes 24 in. (60.9 cm) above the counter and has a front board to shield the eyes (see inset). Fixture brackets also can be bought to mount on either side. Drawing by the author.

With down lights, a person must often work in his or her own shadow. Wall brackets, as an alternative, should be mounted 24–27 in. (61–69 cm) higher than the work surface, either with 75-W reflector floods, 36-in. (91.4-cm) 30-W, or 48-in. (122-cm) 40-W tubes.

KITCHEN VENTILATION

The by-products of cooking are smoke, odors, moisture, and heat. These create the need for a mechanical ventilation system in the kitchen. The usual system consists of a hood over the cooking surface, acting as a collector from which a fan or blower removes those contaminants to the outside of the house.

It is important to realize that the fan does not draw the smoke, odors, moisture, and heat from the cooking surface. These, being hot, rise naturally into the hood and then can be drawn out by the fan. The exception is downdraft ventilation, now available in many ranges, in which the fan, because it is very close, can draw the pollutants directly into the ductwork. A ventilating fan in a wall can be useful if it is directly over the range, but it loses all value when installed on a remote wall because the moisture and vaporized grease can cool and condense on other surfaces in the kitchen before they circulate to the fan. Air currents in a kitchen will move independently of a remote fan.

Built-in ovens need their own ventilation. Venting systems are built into many models, serving both cavities in a double-oven model. These should be ducted to the outside. In the absence of a built-in vent system a hood should be added, but an added hood will not serve the lower cavity of a double oven. Microwave units generate a lot of moisture and odors, so they also should be vented, preferably with a ventilating hood, but at least with a wall fan.

Ventilating performance is measured in cubic feet per minute (cfm) of air movement, and in sones, which measures relative noise. Most units in the U.S. are rated in cfm and sones by the Home Ventilating Institute. The cfm is also a function of duct length, depth of the hood, and its height above the cooking surface.

Duct length should be the shortest possible, and the straightest. Each 10 ft (3 m) of duct length will cost about 50 cfm (1.41 m^3/min) of the fan's capacity, and each 90° elbow is the equivalent of an added 10 ft of duct length.

A hood 17 in. (43 cm) deep (front to back) should be no more than 21 in. (53.3 cm) above the cooking surface. If it is 18 to 21 in. (45.7 to 53.3 cm) deep, it should be 24 in. (60.9 cm) from the surface. If it is 24 in. (60.9 cm) deep, it can be 30 in. (76 cm) off the surface. Maximum distance off the surface is 30 in. A ventilating hood over an island or peninsula will need about twice the cfm capacity of one installed against a wall because of air movement in the room.

Sone level for a hood or kitchen fan should be no more than 9 sones. This compares with a level of 1 sone for a refrigerator operating in a quiet kitchen. Sound level in the kitchen can be reduced by installing a remote fan or blower at the end of the ductwork where it leaves the house, and by using a higher-powered unit that can operate at medium speed rather than a low-powered unit that must operate at high speed.

DESIGN CONCEPTS

The "open" kitchen—open to the family room or living room—has been the guiding design concept of the late 1980s. Carried to the extreme, this concept extends to open shelving in the kitchen and even racks from which the pots and pans hang. There is considerable resistance to this concept because it means that everything must always be clean and neat because it is constantly in view, and also because many persons find they would much rather concentrate on what they are doing in the kitchen than be participants in the noise and activity of the adjacent areas. This is at least part of the reason why 14% of the homes built between 1980 and 1984 underwent alterations or remodeling, according to a U.S. Department of Commerce report (3).

This emphasizes the point that kitchens cannot be designed by kitchen designers alone. To be successful, they must be designed in the interaction between a kitchen designer and the persons who will live in and use the kitchen. Kitchens, in speculative new houses—and these comprise the overwhelming majority of U.S. houses built each year—are designed by builders and their architects for the average buyer. Any idea in kitchen design that is different might lose customers for the house; so, when the homeowners can afford it, they must adapt the house to themselves, their families, and the way they live. That is why there are more than twice as many remodeled kitchens as new home kitchens in any given year (3).

In planning a kitchen, one potential problem that can be overlooked easily is that of counter work space around the appliances. Appliances should be considered not as objects, but as the hubs of work centers, and that means there must be space for the work around them. There also must be proper storage for what is used and what is done in these centers, in accordance with the step-saving principle of storing at the point of first use or the point of last use.

The refrigerator is the hub of the food preparation center, sometimes called the mixing center. The cold and frozen foods are handy here at the point of first use. As a food preparation or mixing center, it also is good to have a pantry cabinet near. This center also works in concert with the sink, which is the hub of the clean-up center. As shown in Figure 20, with both centers in mind, the minimum counter space needed at the opening side of the refrigerator is 18 in. (45.7 cm), assuming that more preparation space is nearby, at the sink. This is also the

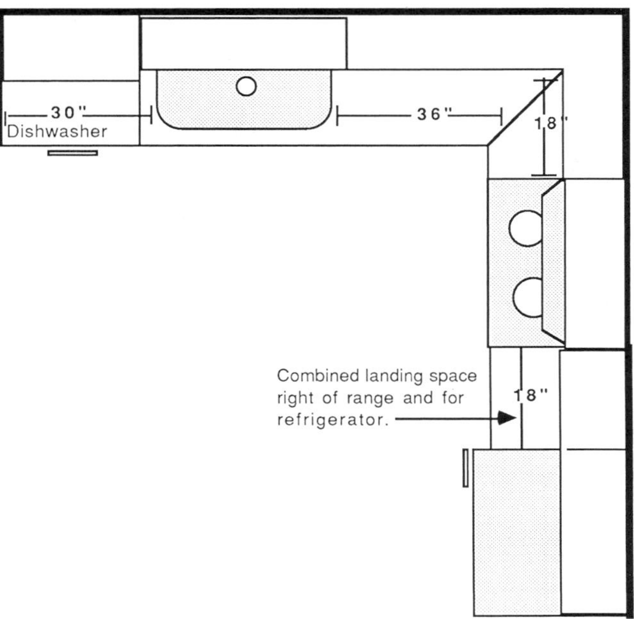

Figure 20. Many motion studies have established minimum work space near various kitchen centers. This includes 30 in. (76.2 cm) to the left of the sink; 36 in. (91.4 cm) to the right of the sink; 18 in. (45.7 m) to the left and right of the cooktop, and 18-in. (45.7 m) landing space at the opening side of the refrigerator. These spaces can be combined, as shown here for the refrigerator and right of the range. Drawing by the author.

area where space should be provided for storage of such food preparation appliances as a mixer or food processor.

The range is the hub of the cooking and serving center. As such, it should be the nearest appliance to a dining area or to a passthrough to a dining area. Serving dishes should be near it (point of first use), or near the sink and dishwasher (point of last use). The range needs 18 in. (45.7 cm) of countertop working space on either side. If the range is a built-in cooktop and the oven is remote, also a built-in, the cooktop needs that space. The remote oven needs 24 in. (61 cm) of landing space. In built-in installations the oven can be remote, because it is seldom used on a daily basis.

The sink is the hub of the clean-up center. The dishwasher should be adjacent to it, the disposer under it, and storage should be nearby for clean-up supplies (usually in the sink cabinet), for saucepans, coffeepot, fruits and vegetables that do not require refrigeration, and for foods that require soaking and washing. Counter space minimums for the sink are 36 in. (91.4 cm) to the right and 30 in. (76 cm) to the left. All of these measurements are for a right-handed person.

If all of these measurements seem insignificant, one should note a study by Cornell University that found that a cook preparing two meals a day for a family might walk a distance of 120 miles each year. Observance of the design requirements here can cut that distance by 40 miles (4).

The designer, in concert with the homeowner, should plan floor and wall coverings with an eye to color and texture as well as cleanability and serviceablilty. Flooring options include ceramic tile, wood, resilient sheet or squares, and kitchen carpeting. Ceramic tile should be glazed to withstand spills and stains. Wood, usually in the form of squares or random planks, has become a very suitable material for kitchen floors because it is impregnated with acrylics and resists spills. With the addition of rugs, it can provide for interesting texture relief. Resilient floor covering is by far the most popular in U.S. kitchens, particularly the no-wax and cushioned lines. Carpet provides texture and a pleasant feel to bare feet in the morning, but the designer should be sure to specify carpeting that is made to repel kitchen spills (and does so very effectively). Kitchen carpet is made with a nylon nap separated from a foam or sponge rubber base by an impermeable membrane that protects floors from liquids. This often is confused, even by flooring salespersons, with "indoor-outdoor" carpet, which is made so water will pass through it easily.

In any kitchen remodeling work the existing floor should be checked carefully by the flooring subcontractor, as many houses that are sold with wall-to-wall carpeting installed have subfloors but no underlayment. Underlayment, usually particleboard or plywood, is essential for a smooth floor-covering installation, and the underlayment must go in before the base cabinets.

For color, ceramic tile and resilients offer many choices. Wood is limited to light, medium, or dark, and kitchen carpet is made in only a few colors.

For kitchen walls the choice usually is paint. However, there are many other options, including wood paneling, ceramic tile, cultured marble or onyx, decorative laminates, fabrics, wallpapers, even carpet.

A wall area of particular concern is the backsplash between the countertop and the bottoms of the wall cabinets. This is a high-splash high-spatter zone, and many appreciate a decorative laminate here because it is easy to clean and is very durable. This can be the same piece as the countertop, coved at the wall and extended up to the cabinets, or it can be a separate matching or harmonizing sheet adhered to the wall. It also is a good place for cultured marble or onyx, available in ¼-in. (0.635-cm) sheets for wall applications. Ceramic tile can be excellent for design purposes, although the grout can pose a cleaning problem.

When carpet is used on a kitchen floor, designers sometimes run it partially up one wall as a wainscoting topped by a decorative wood molding. This is especially effective in an eating area where it can protect walls from chairs and help set off the area. Wood paneling, half-way or all the way up the wall, also is used in such areas.

Wallpaper, a misnomer in these days of foils, vinyls, and fabrics, is often favored on the "off-walls," the one or two walls that are part of the room but not actually within an L or U kitchen. It must be remembered that in a kitchen area these materials can be kept clean only with adequate ventilation over the range that exhausts greases and other cooking by-products to the outside. Foils appear cleanable, but the surface pattern often will rub off easily. Fabrics can be very difficult to clean. Vinyl surfaces clean easily.

The Barrier-free Kitchen

The term "barrier-free" is relatively new in the designer's lexicon, referring to design that is hospitable to any persons who are impaired physically. Federal guidelines were enacted in 1973 to make public facilities more accessible to the impaired, but no standards have been set for private homes. Designers, therefore, often resort to institutional standards for home kitchens for the impaired, resulting in an institutional look where it is not desirable. Unfortunately, impairment comes in many forms, so the only real answer is continuous consultation in both the design and installation stages with the user of the kitchen and others, such as relatives, who will be in frequent attendance.

General practices for doors, electrical outlets, and such are detailed elsewhere. Other practices pertaining specifically to the kitchen for a person in a wheelchair might include the following:

- Consider various heights for countertops, remembering that lowering all of them might be very uncomfortable for others working in the kitchen. Counter surfaces a few inches lower might be helpful at the range and some other work space and at an eating area.
- Wall cabinets often should be lowered several inches.
- Switches should be accessible. A disposer switch, for example, can be in a sink cabinet; light switches should be low; electric range controls should be on a front panel, and the hood switch low on a wall.
- Allow plenty of kick space, possibly up to 7 in. (17.8 cm).
- Select and place appliances with an eye to door swings and easy controls, and include single-lever faucets.

BIBLIOGRAPHY

1. V. Habeeb, *Thousands of Creative Kitchen Ideas,* Funk & Wagnalls, New York, 1976.
2. *Consumer Kitchen Remodeling Report,* survey of consumer buying, Kitchen & Bath Business, New York, September 1984.
3. *U.S. Industrial Outlook 1986—Construction,* U.S. Department of Commerce, Washington, D.C., 1986.
4. Experiment Bulletin 971, *Trips Between Centers in Kitchens for 100 Meals,* Cornell University, Ithaca, N.Y., 1961.

General References

E. Cheever, *Beyond the Basics, Advanced Kitchen Design,* National Kitchen & Bath Association, Hackettstown, N.J., 1978.

S. Clark, *The Motion-Minded Kitchen,* Houghton Mifflin, Boston, Mass., 1983.

P. J. Galvin, *Kitchen Planning Guide for Builders, Designers & Architects,* Structures Publishing, Farmingham, Mich., 1978.

P. J. Galvin, *Kitchen Planning & Remodeling,* Ideals Publishing, Milwaukee, Wis., 1981.

K. Paradies, *The Kitchen Book,* Wyden, New York, 1973.

R. Steidl, *Using Kitchen Storage,* Research Report 5, Cornell University, Ithaca, N.Y., 1961. Also various Steidl Cornell Extension Bulletins.

R. Steidl and E. Bratton, *Work in the Home,* John Wiley & Sons, New York, 1968.

University of Illinois Small Homes Council/Building Research Council, *Kitchen Industry Technical Manuals,* National Kitchen & Bath Association, Hackettstown, N.J., 1972–1975.

See also Restaurant and Service Kitchens

Patrick J. Galvin
Galvin Publications
East Windsor, New Jersey

KNOLL, FLORENCE

Florence Knoll was born Florence Schust on May 24, 1917, in Saginaw, Michigan. Although her active career was short (1941–1965), she left an indelible impression on the design profession and is still considered its doyenne. She is chiefly remembered as the founder, with Hans Knoll (1914–1955), and design director of one of the most prestigious furniture companies of this century, Knoll Associates, Inc., now Knoll International Inc. Her pioneering work in the evolution of the interior design profession is often overlooked since her early retirement in 1965.

As an architect trained at Kingswood School and Cranbrook Academy of Art by Eliel Saarinen, the Architectural Association in London, and the Illinois Institute of Technology under Mies van der Rohe, Florence Knoll brought impeccable credentials to interior architecture and furniture design. Her architectural eye focused on the totally integrated environment, applying architectonic order and logic to the planning and design of interior space and furniture. Her Knoll Planning Unit, an integral interior design service of Knoll Associates and later of Knoll International, served prestigious corporate clients, creating a contemporary, fresh aesthetic in the modern vocabulary. The span of her professional career marched with the gradual acceptance of that idiom as the expression of U.S. corporate identity. As U.S. corporations became international, the Knoll Company also grew internationally and reached such levels of renown that when the "Knoll au Louvre" retrospective was held in Paris in 1972, the French press predicted that "Knoll" would come to symbolize its era as Regency and Empire had epitomized theirs.

Hans and Florence Knoll met and married as a new chapter in history opened with the end of World War II. A "better world" was to be shaped by "good design" and the Knolls were in the vanguard of that excitement. Hans Knoll emigrated from Germany to New York in 1937 to start a company dedicated to the production of modern furniture, at that time a virtually nonexistent commodity. When in 1946 his entrepreneurial genius was allied to the design intelligence of Florence Schust, the combination was unstoppable. Their first significant project, considered shockingly modern, was the design of the Rockefeller family offices at 30 Rockefeller Plaza. This was truly starting at the top, and Nelson Rockefeller's influential reference opened many doors to the young Knolls.

Through its international connections, the Knoll company commissioned furniture from architects and designers from many countries, including Franco Albini of Italy, Hans Bellman of Switzerland, Pierre Jeanneret of France, and Ilmari Tapiovaara of Finland. In the United States, they turned to Eero Saarinen, Harry Bertoia, Isamu Noguchi, Mies van der Rohe, Jens Risom, Ralph Rapson, and many others. Florence Knoll herself designed tables, desks, credenzas, and seating not otherwise available for ongoing Knoll Planning Unit projects, and which subsequently became part of the Knoll collection. Her innovative Structural T and parallel bar and rivet construction systems won two awards from the American Institute of Decorators in 1954, and six of her designs won "good design" accreditation from the Museum of Modern Art (1950–1954). Another landmark was her boat-shaped conference table that facilitated boardroom eye contact and communication (Fig. 1). Her universal desk, which adapted to secretarial or executive use, was designed on architectural principles with structural components engineered into the frame. This desk was widely copied and is still a standard for function and economy. Florence Knoll's belief in total design, influenced by Eliel Saarinen, led to the development at Knoll of a seamless package of design, manufacturing, interior design, textiles, graphics, advertising, and presentation.

But it was as an interior architect, designer, and planner that her total design made its most lasting imprint on following generations. The application of design principles to solving the space problems of business and industry became her special sphere. The Knoll Planning Unit's scope of services, defined in the early 1950s, is still used in current practice, representing a radical departure from interior decoration services then in vogue. Client operations were studied and analyzed in graphic and written form. Personnel and equipment were surveyed. Interdepartmental relations, work, and traffic flow were studied through a process of interviews with executives and department supervisors. A preliminary space plan was developed, and the character of the interiors was established

Figure 1. Florence Knoll's boat-shaped conference table shown at Connecticut General Life Insurance Company, Bloomfield, Connecticut. Courtesy of Florence Knoll.

Figure 2. The president's office, CBS Building, New York. Courtesy of Florence Knoll.

in consultation with the client and the building architect. Study models were constructed and materials were studied; interior and exterior materials were coordinated with the architect. Mechanical and communications elements were evaluated and integrated into the plan. Engineering drawings and shop drawings were checked. All finishes and furnishings were selected, and recommendations were made for the functional and unobtrusive placement and design of all special equipment. Construction observation services were provided as was installation of all furniture and furnishings. Maintenance manuals were also provided. Florence Knoll is credited with originating client presentation techniques using three-dimensional models with actual fabric swatches applied to furniture layout plans. Her consummate professionalism, resulting in a remarkable ability to lead and influence clients to accept her ideas, has become legendary. Fastidious attention to detail allied to a totally visualized functional space scaled to the building module was her signature on a pristine environment which was efficient, comfortable, and beautiful.

The Knoll Planning Unit, under Florence Knoll, worked for clients in the corporate, financial, and banking sectors; for hospitals, colleges, and universities; for hotels and restaurants; and for U.S. government agencies including the State and Defense Departments. Outstanding projects among them were CBS executive offices, Center for Advanced Study in Behavioral Sciences, Connecticut General Life Insurance Co., Look Magazine, H.J. Heinz Co., Alcoa,

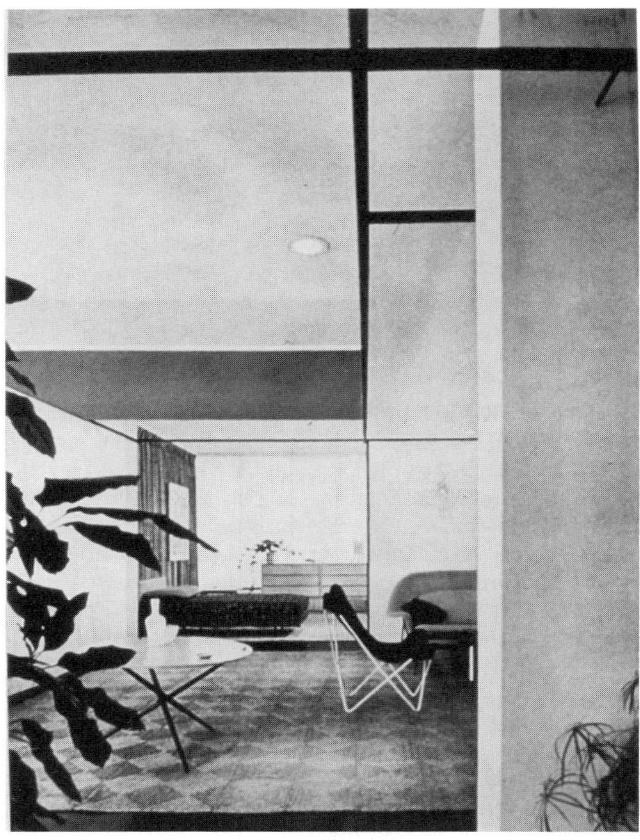

Figure 3. Knoll showroom at 575 Madison Avenue, New York. Courtesy of Florence Knoll.

The Rockefeller Institute, and CBS headquarters (Fig. 2). Florence Knoll's design of Knoll showrooms in the United States (Fig. 3) and abroad (Fig. 4) spoke to the quality of the company, its products, and its philosophy. After

Figure 4. Knoll showroom in Milan, Italy. Courtesy of Florence Knoll.

Hans Knoll's death, the company continued to grow under the leadership of Florence Knoll, and there was no interior design firm more distinguished than the Knoll Planning Unit. In 1959, the year after her marriage to H. Hood Bassett, a leading Florida banker, she sold the company but remained design director until her final retirement in 1965.

Florence Knoll, who now divides her time between homes in Florida and Vermont, continues to receive honors and accolades including the American Institute of Interior Designers International Design award (1962), Illinois Institute of Technology Professional Achievement award (1969), Parsons School of Design honorary doctorate of Fine Arts (1979), Illinois Institute of Technology Hall of Fame award (1983), Rhode Island School of Design Aethena medallion (1983), honorary membership in the Industrial Designers Society of America (1983), Interior Design Magazine Hall of Fame (1985), and the Norwood Institute Distinguished Woman award (1987). As an architect, her most treasured award is the Gold Medal for Industrial Design from the American Institute of Architects (1961). Her citation, noting that she had "abundantly justified [her] training as an architect," concluded with the ringing praise: "Your training, skill and unfailing good judgement have written your name high on the roll of masters of our contemporary design."

See also Electrical Equipment; Furniture; Interior Design; Office Facility Planning

Maeve Slavin
New York, New York

KRAEMER, FRIEDRICH W.

Friedrich Wilhelm Kraemer, German architect, was born in 1907 in Halberstadt, a town in what is today the German Democratic Republic, the youngest of four children of a businessman. He married in 1947 and has four children, one of them an architect.

He went to school in Halberstadt, and there received his Abitur (baccalaureate) in 1925. In the same year he moved to Brunswick and studied architecture at the Technische Hochschule Braunschweig, THB, today Technische Universität, until 1929, with an interval at the Technische Hochschule in Vienna in 1927. From 1929 to 1934 he taught as an assistant of C. Mühlenpfordt at the THB. He left the school because of his disagreements with the Nazis, and opened his own office in 1936. In 1943 Kraemer was recruited and sent to the front. In 1944 he was wounded, and spent the convalescence in Brunswick. At this time he wrote a dissertation on the theater architecture of P. J. Krahe and K. T. Ottmer, and obtained the title of Dr.-Ing. of the THB in 1945.

After the war he stayed in Brunswick, today in the Federal Republic of Germany, was appointed Oberbaurat (head of the city planning department) in 1945, and Professor für Gebäudelehre und Entwerfen (professor of theory of building types and design) at the THB in 1946. He reopened his private office and worked on his own until 1960. In this year he entered a partnership with his former assistants, Günter Pfennig and Ernst Sieverts, KPS, which lasted until 1974. Since 1975 he headed the partnership KSP, Kraemer, Sieverts & Partner, with offices in Brunswick and Cologne. Kraemer retired from his professorship at the THB in 1974, and as the head of KSP in 1985.

Friedrich Wilhelm Kraemer's importance for German postwar developments in architecture is founded both in his role as an intellectual and leading figure of the Brunswick architectural school, and as one of the architects heading the Modern mainstream of the 1950s and 1960s. In addition to teaching his students, in his articles and books he revealed a clear, sharp, systematic, and logical intellect.

In his research, Kraemer emphasized functional aspects as a factor of architecture. He sought to go further than understanding and explaining the objective aspects of architecture. His first aim was to comprehend the formal implications of function and construction, ie, the gestalt resulting from the synthesis of form and content. His second aim was to develop—departing from the consideration of the actual evolution of functional needs and constructive possibilities—new building types at first, and then new forms in accordance with them. The aim was, thus, to discover, logically, a new gestalt. He achieved this through the development of the concept of *Bürolandschaft* and its realization in several buildings.

Kraemer's professional development began in the 1930s. His buildings of this period, mainly private homes, such as the house for Wolff-Limper in Brunswick, show him to be influenced by conservative architects such as Paul Bonatz and Paul Schmitthenner. He preferred, just as they did, regionalistic formal languages, artisan construction methods with natural materials, and traditional building types. The war interrupted this initial development. However, it gave him the opportunity to dedicate himself to architectural thought, and to sharpen his mind through scientific work while writing his dissertation.

After the war, Kraemer belonged to the group of middle-aged architects who, in the absence of the great prewar personalities, occupied the most important public positions. Like Egon Eiermann in Karlsruhe and Ernst Neufert in Darmstadt, he became a professor and leader of the architectural school of his hometown. His aim as a teacher to impart an objective, rational, and logical view of architecture was based in the nature of his personality and in the *Zeitgeist* of the postwar period. After the ideological and political excesses of the Nazis and the postwar depression, modesty, self-control, reserve, and temperance became values which characterized public life in the early years of the FRG. The very first phase after 1945 was marked by misery and hopeless emergency. Changes took place only after the monetary reform of 1948, the founding of the FRG in 1949, and the beginning of the reconstruction period, the *Wiederaufbau,* in the 1950s.

The work of Kraemer around 1950 shows, in the very few projects of this time, a continuation of his architecture of the early 1930s, exemplified by his own house in Brunswick. Then, a general reorientation toward a modernization of architectural language took place.

The models for such a modernization now came from foreign areas such as the United States and Scandinavia. This constituted a kind of reimport of modern architecture to Germany, after having been, in the Weimar Republic, one of its main focuses. The new models had in common their reduction to the essential, the minimum, and the simplest language. All of their elements were derived from what was functionally necessary to realize the desired building type, and the construction necessary to realize the required structural system. Their character was always cool, without emotion, apparently free from any personal expression, in the spirit of Ludwig Mies van der Rohe. The models themselves came from Skidmore, Owings & Merrill (SOM) (the Lever House in New York City, 1955; the U.S. Consulate in Bremen, 1953–1954), from Eero Saarinen (the General Motors Technical Center in Detroit, 1949–1956), from Arne Jacobsen (the Townhall Rødovre, Denmark, 1954– 1956), and others.

Examples of this phase are, among many others, the Handelsschule in Heidelberg, a commercial college (1952–1954), many administration and office buildings, banks, such as the Stadtsparkasse in Düsseldorf (1958), industrial buildings, private houses, and cultural buildings, such as the Jahrhunderthalle Hoechst in Frankfurt (1960–1963). They all show good and correct design from a functional, constructive, and formal point of view, and accurate realization. But they did not provide anything original, and had no room for speculation of any kind; they all constituted variations of internationally accepted solutions. This was no obstacle to their success. On the contrary, possibly it was the certainty of general international acceptance which satisfied a profound social need and won the acclaim of the local public.

In fact, with these buildings Kraemer became one of the most important figures in the German architectural scene. Architecturally, the secret of his success resided in his truly coherent re-creation of common types, in accordance with their principles. This demanded a high degree of comprehension of the international developments in architecture, which he achieved as a by-product of his teaching and research work. He concentrated mainly on the study of office buildings. His main early article on this subject was *Bauten der Wirtschaft und Verwaltung,* written in 1957. It demonstrates a clear understanding of the historical origins and the background of the office building types. And it shows Kraemer's ability to touch with his reasoning the limits of knowledge, the limits of the state of the art, reaching the point where the creative jump is the only possible next step.

Kraemer's buildings of the above phase illustrate his typological understanding of architecture. The Handelsschule in Heidelberg, for example, corresponds basically to a courtyard type, with the main entrance into a closed courtyard with the administration rooms and a special classroom tract, a courtyard, open on one side, in the back, and an additional pavilion with normal classrooms. The construction corresponds to a skeleton type, a regular orthogonal grid with the same span between all axes. The formal language corresponds directly to the functional type, and is based on the orthogonal order of the ensemble, shaping all of the elements in a linear, rectangular, or prismatic fashion. It corresponds to the constructive type because of its reduction to the elements of the construction and their order, differentiating the supporting elements—stays, beams, plates, and slabs—from the enclosing ones, and shaping each one in a constructively correct manner.

The Stadtsparkasse in Düsseldorf, a representative administration building with a bank hall, corresponds to one of the main international types of the 1950s, the high-rise on a pedestal platform. It consists of an office tower and a lower tract with the public rooms, and was realized with a skeleton construction and a curtain wall facade. It corresponds to the type set by SOM's Lever House.

The Jahrhunderthalle Hoechst constitutes a more original building because of its less common functional and constructive solutions. It corresponds, nevertheless, as clearly as the other examples to a simple typological solution. It consists of a flexible auditorium under a cupola on the top of a one-story platform with halls and service rooms. Geometrically it is a spherical segment on the top of a wide, flat prism. The construction of the platform is a regular, orthogonal, reinforced concrete skeleton. The construction of the cupola is more sophisticated: it is a shell construction supported only on six points connected by arches. The enormous stress concentration of such a solution for a shell makes it unusual for its time. It was only possible using prestressed concrete. The advantages of this solution are striking: the cupola seems to float, both from the outside and from the inside. It combines the traditional introverted and closed character with the opening to the exterior allowing the entrance of light and a visual contact, and it permits the desired geometricality and typologically clear solution (Fig. 1).

Kraemer's jump from re-creation to originality took place in the late 1960s, with the *Wirtschaftswunder,* the West German "economic miracle." It was the time of the successfully seasoned reconstruction phase, a time of confidence in the future and in one's own way. It was also a time of searching—socially, politically, technologically, in the culture and the sciences. It was also a time of discoveries and of the development of new perspectives, including the perception of one's limits. For German architecture it was the time of abandoning the limits of the last decade, of seeking new ways, personified by the elder Hans Scharoun and Egon Eiermann, and the younger Frei Otto, Günter Behnisch, and Gottfried Böhm, with their formal, constructive, and ideological innovations. It was also the time of Kraemer, with his innovations in the field of office building.

Transformations in office work were the point of departure for the development of innovations in the field of office building. In the U.S., there had already been a change from the historical type for small companies, ie, the addition of single office rooms, to the type for larger companies with a more complex and hierarchical organization of work, such as the addition of office rooms of different sizes, from individual ones to large offices for several people, the state of the art in the 1950s. Some key buildings of the modern history of architecture, such as Mies's Seagram Building and SOM's Lever House, are directly based on this type. The logic of this type resides in its concept of flexibility through standardization, with grid formation taking into

Figure 1. Jahrhunderthalle Hoechst, Frankfurt, FRG (1960–1963). Courtesy of the author.

consideration the requirements of an individual work unit and the arrangement of units in rooms of different sizes. The construction consists of a regular, orthogonal skeleton closed by a curtain wall facade.

In the 1960s, and mainly in the FRG, office work grew more and more complex in its organization, particularly in the administration of enterprises largely tied to office work, such as insurance companies. In many cases, office work lost its linear character and became much more a group activity. The traditional rectangular office room with its rows of single desks proved to be inappropriate for a more complex arrangement of working places in groups of differing sizes and configurations. On the other side, the growing divergences from the old building type led to incongruences, thereby making the need for the development of an integrally new type evident. The answer was in a functional sense the *Grossraumbüro,* the open plan office of large dimensions. The typological concept behind it was that of the *Bürolandschaft.*

The term *Bürolandschaft* (office landscape) alludes to the intention to create for office work a completely artificial scenery within a building. It includes its own climate, light, acoustics, views, paths, and places, able to satisfy human needs in their material and psychological aspects in all parts of the building in a uniform way. This had to be achieved through a thorough design and with the help of sophisticated technical installations, thus requiring years of research and experience. The aims now were to satisfy these functional conditions, and then to develop an architecture akin to them. Kraemer achieved this in the 1960s with the DKV Insurance Headquarters (1966–1970) in Cologne.

The DKV Insurance Headquarters was conceived as a tall building with open plan office rooms. It represents a special solution which combines the characteristics of both types. The working rooms were divided into pure office rooms and service rooms, and then located in stories containing only office rooms according to the open plan system, and others containing only service rooms. The communication between these two types of stories was through central staircases specially situated for this purpose, in addition to the main vertical communications system placed peripherally. The floor plans were dimensioned in accordance with the minimum necessary to avoid acoustic problems (an area of 500 m^2, and a distance of 20 m between parallel panels), to permit a flexible arrangement of groups of at least 50–60 persons, and to maximize distance from the windows and the staircases. The floor plans were shaped in accordance with the initially hexagonal geometrical module, and then with the triangular grid of the construction system. The open plan offices were shaped to avoid too many parallel panels, thus eliminating echoes (Fig. 2).

In order to create similar conditions for all working places, office spaces needed to be completely independent of the external climate and light. The climatization differentiates outer and inner zones, in accordance with the dependence on the facade and in order to allow the installation of individual rooms if desired. The use of artificial light is permanent, the entrance of natural light reduced to a minimum through dark glass.

The design of the facade is based on a module obtained by coordinating the dimensions of the ceiling elements and the window panes, and the power of the lighting elements. The facade is a curtain wall with glass and light metal elements of a similar bronze color for the open plan office stories. The facade of the service stories is retracted behind the curtain wall. The shadows obtained in this way help to articulate the facade as a whole. The design of the masses is based on the triangular grid of the construction system with concave and convex 120° angles, and on the different heights of the tracts composing the whole (Fig. 3).

The DKV building shows a high degree of inner coherence of all aspects of design. It is, therefore, an example of a conceptual way of understanding architecture, here strongly based on typological considerations. It shows the architectural qualities that can be achieved by this way of working, and the aspects of design that can be inte-

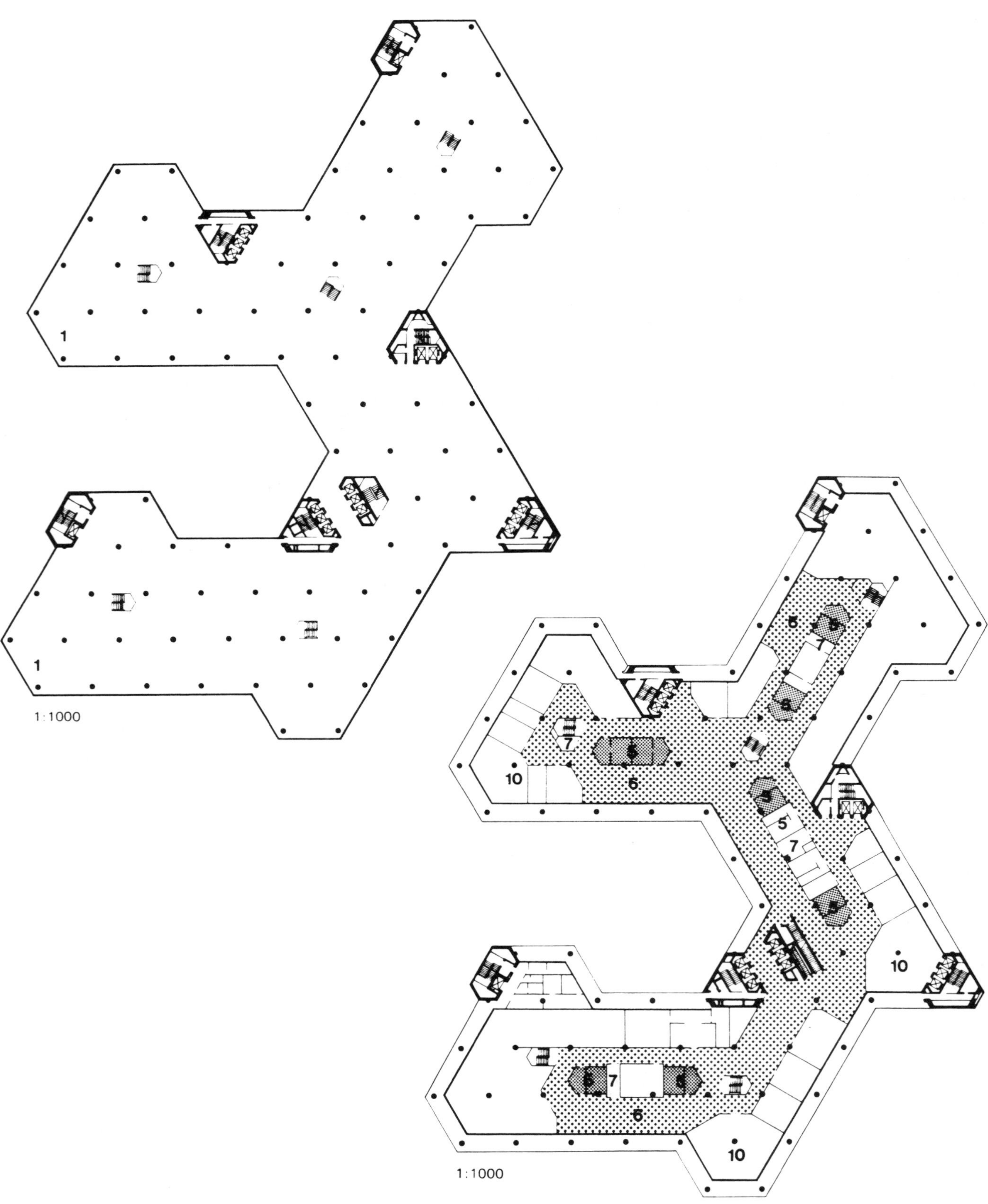

Figure 2. DKV Insurance Headquarters, Cologne, FRG (1966–1970). Typical plans for the *Buro-landschaft* stories (left), and the service stories (right). Courtesy of Friedrich Wilhelm Kraemer.

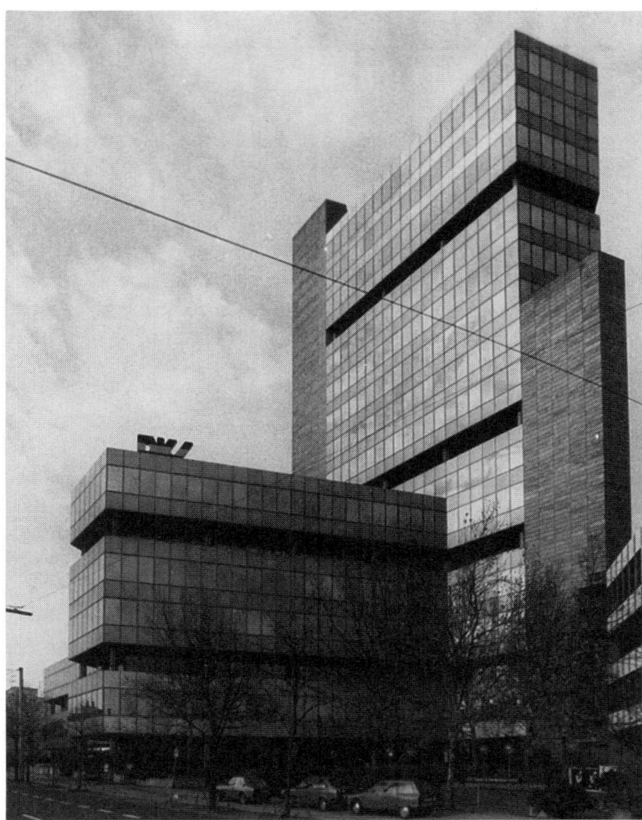

Figure 3. DKV Insurance Headquarters, Cologne (1966–1970). Courtesy of the author.

grated. Kraemer's innovation in office building design continues in the GEW Headquarters Building in Cologne (1976–1980). The aims realized in this project are, as in earlier ones, not only perfecting functional aspects, achieved with reversible plans, or economic ones, through energy-saving solutions, but synthesizing these into a new architecture.

Kraemer's awards include the Peter Josef Krahe Preis 1955, the Laves-Medaille 1957, the Kunstpreis des Landes Hessen 1965, the Kölner Architekturpreis 1980, the Preis Bund Deutscher Architekten Nordrhein-Westfalen 1965, Bremen 1974, Cologne 1975, Niedersachsen 1976, 1982, and 1985, and the Mies van der Rohe Anerkennung 1981.

BIBLIOGRAPHY

General References

F. W. Kraemer, "Bauten der Wirtschaft und Verwaltung," in *Handbuch moderner Architektur,* Safari, West Berlin, 1957, pp. 309–443.

F. W. Kraemer, E. Sieverts, and H. Huth, *Grossraumbüros—Dargestellt am Beispiel der DKV Köln,* Karl Krämer, Stuttgart, 1968.

F. W. Kraemer, "Die Gestalt von Bürohäusern," in *Bauen + Wohnen* (1), 1–4 (1968).

F. W. Kraemer and D. Meyer, *Bürohaus-Grundrisse,* Alexander Koch, Stuttgart, 1974.

F. W. Kraemer, E. Sieverts, & Partner, *Grossraumbüros,* Moderne Industrie, Munich, 1975.

F. W. Kraemer, E. Sieverts, & Partner, *KSP, Bauten und Projekte,* Karl Krämer, Stuttgart, 1983.

Manuel Cuadra
Technische Hochschule Darmstadt
Darmstadt, Federal Republic of Germany

L

LABORATORIES

The essential challenge in the design of the research laboratory is to provide a high quality and extremely flexible working environment that meets exacting safety standards and highly sophisticated technical criteria. Not only is the laboratory the forum for the advancement of many areas of knowledge, it is also the repository of enormously valuable equipment and of significant government, institutional, and corporate investment. Whether for pure or specifically applied research, the laboratory must provide the scientist with adequate bench space, engineered to bring to each work station such mechanical or electrical systems as steam, distilled water, compressed air, vacuum, and possible other specialized services. Desk space, various kinds of storage, fume hoods to exhaust toxic gases, alternative means of egress in the event of fire, chemical spills, or explosion, are also prime program requirements. In addition, the entire laboratory may require an environment in which such factors as humidity, air purity, and temperature can be carefully controlled; it may be necessary to provide vibration-free settings for special equipment such as the electron microscope, containment laboratories for genetic research, and structurally reinforced areas where potentially explosive experiments are carried out. The overall planning must ensure sufficient physical separation between such high risk facilities (some of which may need their own dedicated mechanical systems) and conventional laboratory and administrative areas. It is also essential for the building to be planned, engineered, and oriented to ensure safe evacuation of toxic fumes into the atmosphere away from any neighboring residential communities.

In addition to the laboratories themselves, a range of support spaces may be required, tailored to the specific discipline involved. Some of these are shown in Table 1.

In general, biology and biochemistry laboratories require the most bench services, chemistry laboratories the most fume hoods (possibly with cabinets vented to the hoods), whereas physics laboratories are the least complicated to service. Glass washing and sterilizing may be provided within the laboratory areas or as a centralized service for the building as a whole.

Some degree of computerization can be assumed in every area of research endeavor and in many cases electronic equipment is outmoding the conventional laboratory bench approach. In some facilities, central computer rooms may be required; in educational institutions where audiovisual instruction is carried out in the laboratories themselves, the planner must take account of sight lines, viewing angles, distances, and methods of darkening the room. Teaching laboratories will also require seminar rooms and auditoriums, while in industrial laboratories, pilot plants for testing materials and manufacture of sample products may be part of the building program. In corporate installations, the laboratory wings may be attached to quite elaborate administrative operations with which they share such amenities as lounges, cafeterias, and recreation and health centers. In other cases, some provision for all of these will be part of the building program.

In the planning of the laboratories themselves, the relationship of desk to bench space becomes increasingly important in an era when much of the scientist's time is spent in front of a video display unit, performing or recording complicated calculations. Office areas must be provided either within the laboratories themselves or closely adjacent to them (Fig. 1). In some cases, both are needed: a length of bench perhaps dropped to 30 in. from 36 in. to become a desk, and more formal, enclosed offices across the corridor. When offices are contained within the laboratories themselves, this may complicate the planner's task in relation to access, emergency egress, and positioning of fume hoods.

The question of open or enclosed laboratory units is a function of the scientific discipline involved, the kinds and risk factors of experiments performed, and the individual preferences of the scientists. Many laboratory buildings are designed to provide a range of options within the essential planning module (Fig. 2). Laboratory furniture and equipment manufacturers have managed to build considerable flexibility into their furniture systems, which can be demounted and reassembled in a variety of configura-

Table 1. Support Spaces Required for Various Laboratory Types[a]

Type of Laboratory	Support Spaces
Biology	Live animals Herbarium Greenhouse Sterile transfer Growth chambers Electron microscope Darkroom Instrument rooms constant temp. + humidity Storage
Chemistry	Stockrooms (near laboratories) Balance rooms Instrumentation Spectrometry Chromatography Storage (remote)
Physics	Optics darkrooms Metal–woodworking shop Nuclear procedures Isotope storage–transfer Equipment storage
Geology, Earth Sciences, Astrogeology	Instrumentation Rock storage, thin section, polishing Observatory

[a] Ref. 1.

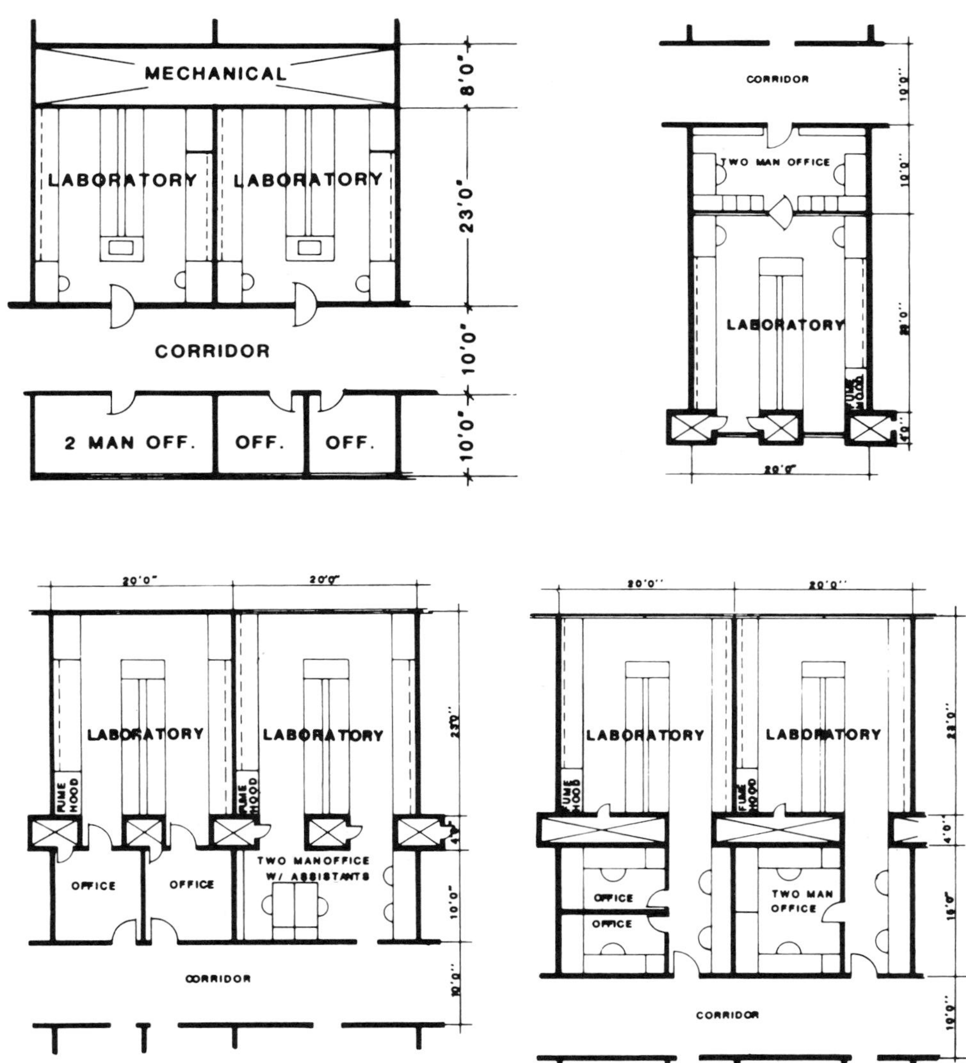

Figure 1. Some possible arrangements of laboratories and offices. Courtesy of Bryant Gould.

tions. In some cases, the planning of laboratory units with separately defined preparation rooms to take up most of the "messy" work is a successful device in leaving bench areas relatively uncluttered.

Specification of laboratory floor, wall, and counter surfaces is something to be handled with special care, because solvents and chemicals spilled on and absorbed into these surfaces can be released into the laboratory atmosphere over a considerable period, causing low level contamination as the surface slowly dries out.

Among the other stringent technical requirements of the laboratory environment is the need for expert attention to lighting, because many tasks require a high level of illumination; in the case of medical research, lamps of sufficient color quality are required to prevent any color distortion of materials under examination. While a general task illuminance of 300 to 500 lux across the working plane is a reasonable norm in laboratory design, some tasks may require an illuminance level as high as 1500 lux. If this is provided by local supplementary lighting, care must be taken to avoid the visual discomfort associated with too extreme a contrast between the highly illuminated task areas and the general laboratory lighting. Some lighting of the vertical elements will generally improve the visual comfort of the laboratory environment. Generally such lighting is in the range of 0.5 to 0.8 of the task illuminance (1).

An important event in the evolution of laboratory design was the publication in 1961 of *The Design of Research Laboratories,* a volume whose nucleus was a report of research into key aspects of laboratory design conducted by the Nuffield Division for Architectural Studies in the UK (under the direction of the late Richard Llewelyn-Davies) (2). This research, thought to be the first serious attempt to study laboratory design from the behavioral point of view, and an early investigation of the interaction of users and buildings, produced some anthropometrically derived measurements that are still valid today. British

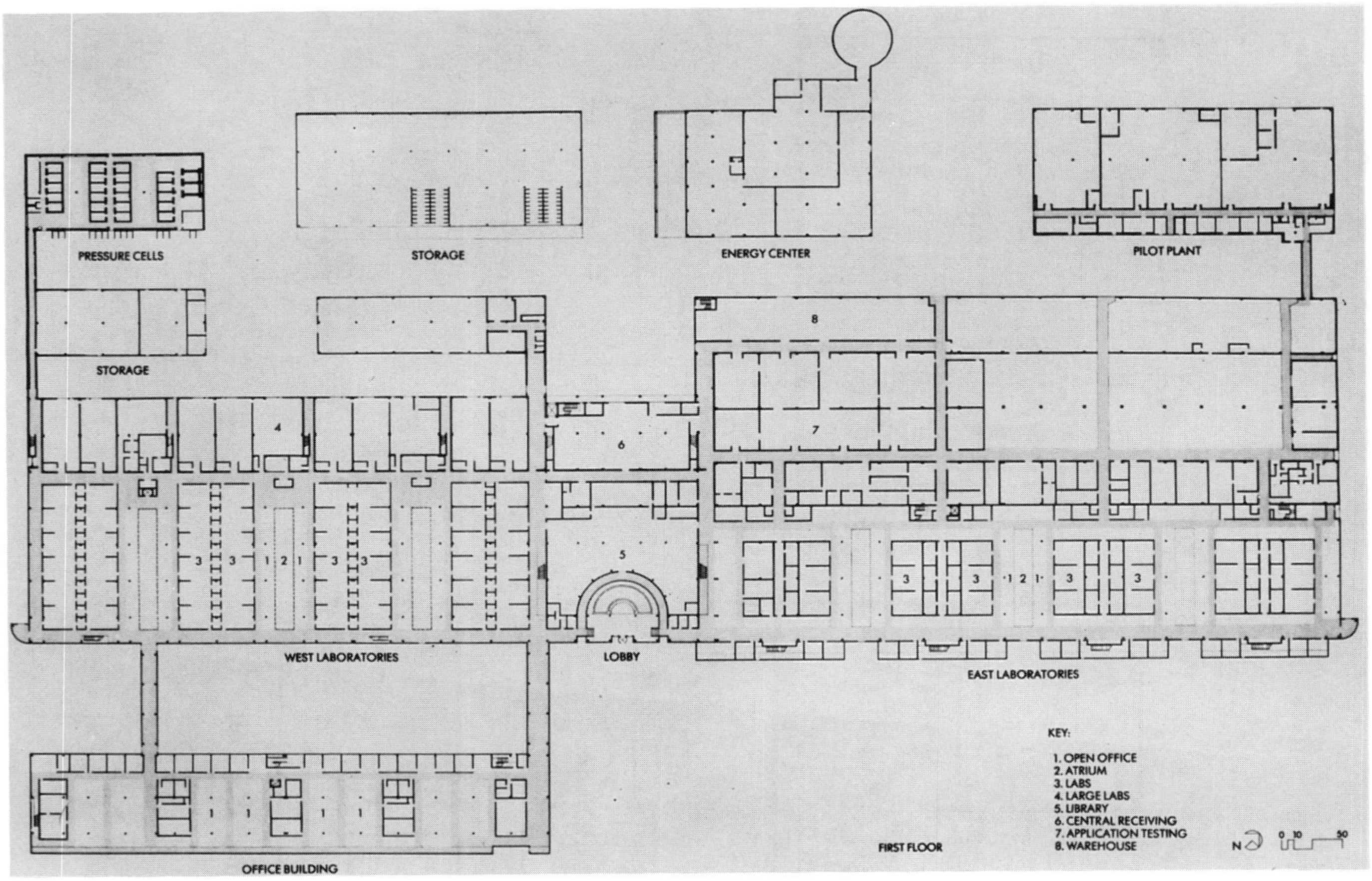

(a)

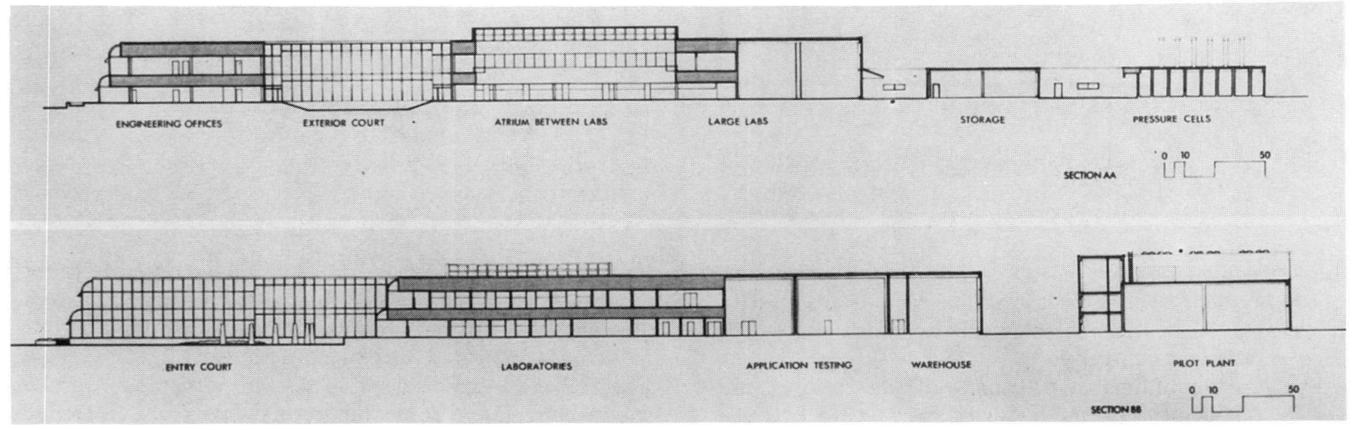

(b)

Figure 2. (a), Plan and **(b),** sections of the Arco Chemical Company Research and Engineering Center in Pennsylvania, showing open and closed laboratories. Laboratories in the east wing have separately defined preparation areas. Paved atria separate groups of laboratories. Architects: Davis, Brody & Associates; Llewelyn-Davies Associates.

architect John Weeks, who was part of the Nuffield research effort, quotes the following dimensions (3):

> Laboratory tasks typically involve two elements, equipment and somebody to operate it. Sometimes two tasks occur with operators back to back. Work tops (generally 914 mm (36 in.) high) are conveniently about 600 mm (23.6 in.) deep with 150 mm (5.9 in.) behind them for wall-mounted services; an operator occupies a similar space. When these dimensions are added together, and circulation space is added as well, a working dimension is derived that is a measure of most laboratory tasks. An interval of about 3.6 meters (11.811 ft) between the center line of laboratory partitions will allow space in which two people may work back to back at equipment and

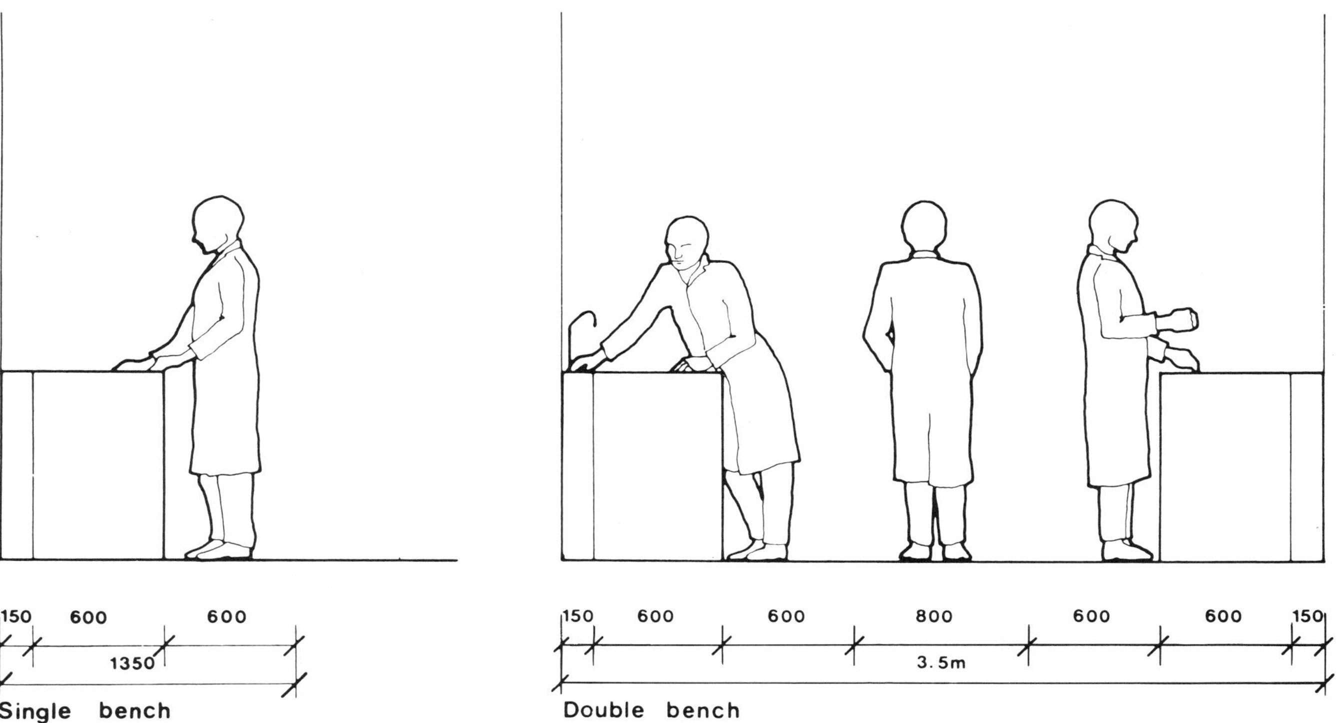

Figure 3. Ergonomic dimensions for laboratory work. Courtesy of John Weeks.

a third person may pass between them (Fig. 3). This is an ergonomic measure, and is as true for the different sorts of equipment which nowadays make up the armamentary of the laboratory worker as it has always been. The fact that wall and floor space, once used for benches, is now used for electronic equipment makes no difference. A planning module of 3.6 meters (11.811 ft) × 7.2 meters (23.622 ft) is available within the same plan discipline and a room may be increased further in 3.6 meter steps.

The way in which services are introduced and distributed throughout the building directly affects layout (Fig. 4). While there are many possible arrangements (and spe-

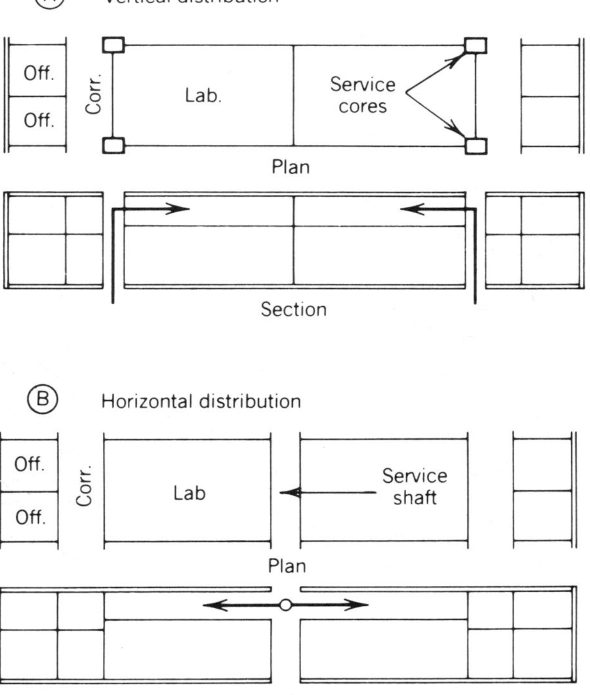

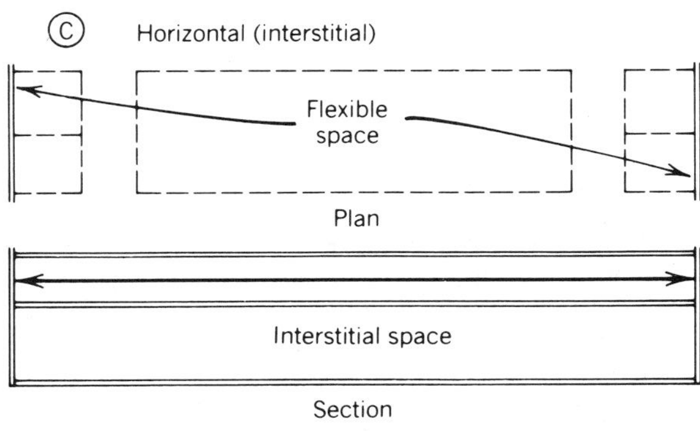

Figure 4. Alternative methods of service distribution. Courtesy of Bryant Gould.

Table 2. Typical Laboratory Layouts, Their Mechanical and Electrical Distributions, and the Implications of Each[a]

Laboratory Layout	Mechanical and Electrical Distribution	Implications
Single-loaded corridor Continuous service core	Vertical mains and horizontal subdistribution along core walls	Perimeter circulation corridor Reduced floor-to-floor heights Easy maintenance Allows service rearrangement and modification with little interruption of laboratory operation
Double-loaded public corridor	Vertical utility zones near laboratories with horizontal runouts above or below the floor slab from risers to remote equipment	Minimum total building volume occupied by services Lower first cost of installation Minimum floor-to-floor height requirements Relatively inflexible unless service risers are closely spaced Costly to maintain and modify Central mechanical room from which risers are tapped Individual floors cannot be shutdown
Double-loaded service corridor	Horizontal distribution along ceiling of service corridor	Easy to modify and rearrange or expand laboratory floors Higher first cost but lower life-cycle costs for laboratories where change is frequent Hoods can be grouped for energy conservation purposes Laboratories can be controlled on a floor-by-floor basis
Interstitial service floors	Horizontal distribution	Ultimate flexibility and tolerance of service modifications without affecting the operation of other laboratories Significant increase in "cube" of structure and, therefore, of its cost

[a] Ref. 4.

cial requirements for such specialized facilities as electronic, nuclear, and containment laboratories, animal rooms, and pilot plants), Table 2 sets out the relationship between typical laboratory layouts and electrical and mechanical distribution and some of the implications of each.

Although the absentminded scientist has been traditionally associated with an unattractively cluttered, even smelly environment to which he is rendered indifferent by his dedication to the higher pursuits of knowledge, the quality of the research environment is in fact a major design challenge and preoccupation today and one to which much enlightened attention has been paid in recent years. Of particular concern is the need for communication, because scientific research can be a rather solitary, isolating endeavor, and scientists apparently find it difficult to engage in the kind of informal, cross-disciplinary conversation known to be a fertile avenue for progress. For this reason, and in order to introduce color, change of pace, and access to natural light and views of the outdoors in

Figure 5. Laboratories in the Rowland Institute for Science in Cambridge, Massachusetts, were designed around a serene, landscaped atrium to give scientists a change of pace and opportunities for informal communication. Architects: The Stubbins Associates. Photograph by Edward Jacoby.

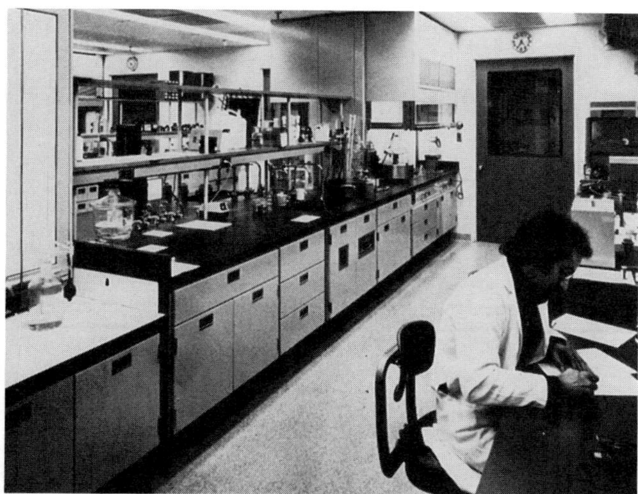

Figure 6. Organic chemistry laboratory in E. R. Squibb and Son's Headquarters in Princeton, New Jersey, symbolizes contemporary concern for a pleasant, flexible laboratory environment. Architects: Hellmuth, Obata & Kassabaum.

what is otherwise a carefully controlled environment, modern laboratories are often designed around landscaped, skylit atria (Fig. 5), or with a perimeter corridor system that includes informal seating and seminar alcoves—perhaps equipped with a blackboard—and enlivened by views out over the complex and its surroundings. In some cases, color is introduced into the laboratories themselves, and some have their own windows—often with the desk areas beneath them. Thus, the laboratory environment today, although almost always cluttered to the eye of the layperson or office worker, is a great deal more pleasant than scientists have been accustomed to or perhaps even traditionally thought themselves worthy of receiving (Figs. 6 and 7). Scientists introduced to modern facilities designed around their stated needs have been heard to comment that the surroundings are really "too good" for them. The scientist in the past may have been able to rise above his environment, and genius, it seems, can flourish anywhere, but there is no longer any reason why such powers of endurance should be required.

The architectural design of the laboratory, which began with the alchemist's cell and progressed through a series of specialized rooms with ever more elaborate furniture and services, has always been more directly tied into the organization of mechanical and electrical systems than any other building type; this is even more true today (Fig. 8). Changing scientific methods depend on the "universal" availability of services throughout the laboratory areas; built-in benches have largely given way to movable furniture and a minimum of fixed equipment. Indeed, as John Weeks has put it (3):

> The interior environment of a laboratory is not in fact controllable by architectural means; the essential requirement of the

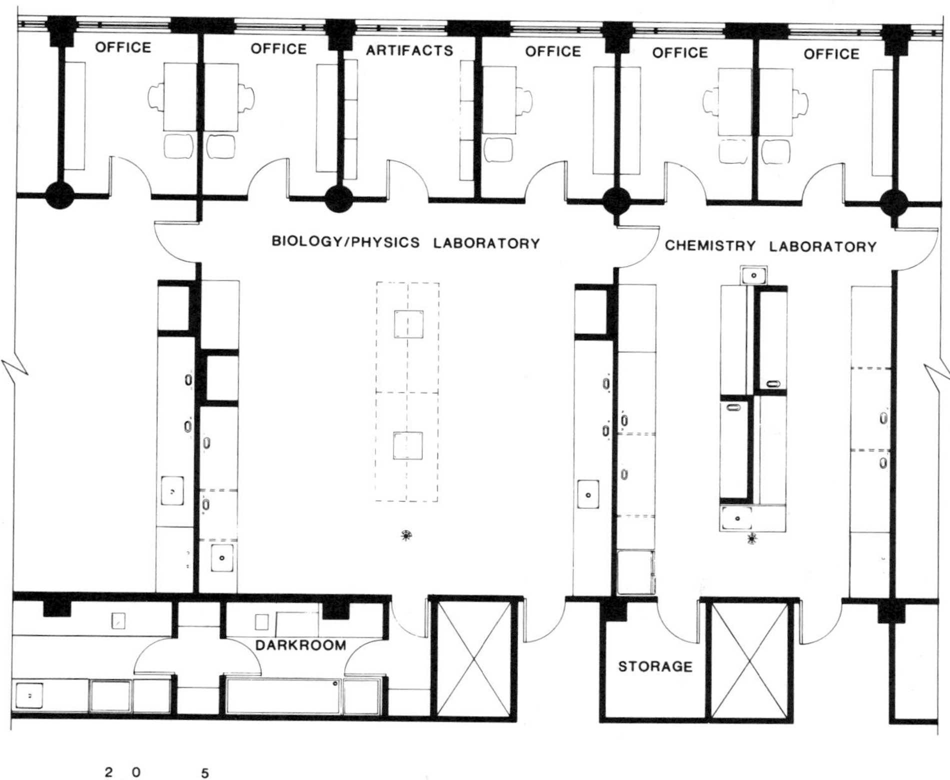

Figure 7. Plan of two laboratories at the Rowland Institute for Science can be used interchangeably for different research disciplines. Offices are placed beneath windows and doors lead out to an atrium. Architects: The Stubbins Associates.

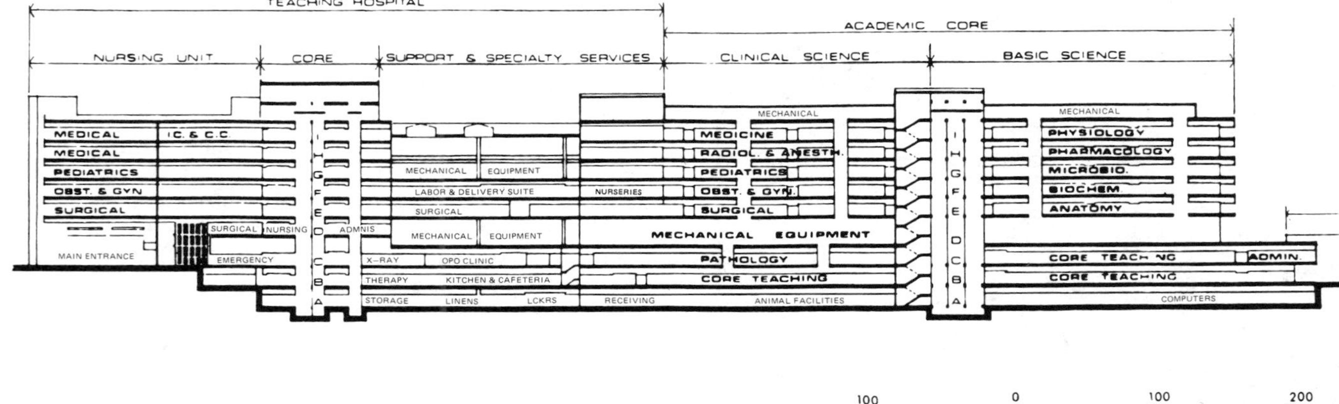

Figure 8. Section of the University of Medicine and Dentistry of New Jersey shows the pivotal role of mechanical services in determining the organization of the laboratory floors, which are carefully linked to floors in the nursing unit. Architects: The Eggers Group, PC; The Grad Partnership; Gilbert L. Seltzer Associates.

> users is that, since their requirements inevitably will change, everything in sight should be movable. The architect is required to design and put into the hands of the client the means of transforming the environment himself; the architect is judged a success in direct proportion to the ease with which his client can alter his building.

Weeks further suggests that this lack of architectural control has tended to deter "star architects" from undertaking laboratory design; in cases where such architects have taken on laboratory work, they have tended to articulate function into separate zones (Fig. 9), putting some limits on total flexibility. Most useful laboratories, therefore, may be said to be competent buildings rather than architectural masterpieces while labs that are beautiful may have limits to their usefulness.

A positive corollary to this observation is that if laboratories have been architectural monuments less often than other building types, they have usually been much freer of fads and fashion. Perhaps the rigorous technical requirements of the laboratory have forced the architects of this genre to direct their most serious efforts to the solution of functional and environmental questions in close and creative collaboration with the engineers and other consultants on the building team.

Figure 9. Louis Kahn's Salk Institute in California, a recognized architectural masterpiece, contains flexible workshop areas and articulated spaces for specifically defined activities. Courtesy of the Salk Institute.

BIBLIOGRAPHY

1. N. Watson, E. Rowlands, and D. Loe in S. Braybrooke, ed., *Design for Research: Principles of Laboratory Architecture,* John Wiley & Sons, Inc., New York, 1986, Chapt. 5.
2. *The Design of Research Laboratories,* Oxford University Press, New York, 1961.
3. J. Weeks in Ref. 1, Chapt. 1.
4. J. R. Loring and H. Goodman in Ref. 1, Chapt. 4.

SUSAN BRAYBROOKE
London, United Kingdom

LAMINATES.

See GLASS FILMS; GLASS IN CONSTRUCTION; PLASTICS; WOOD IN CONSTRUCTION

LANDMARK COMMISSIONS.

See PRESERVATION, HISTORIC

LANDSCAPE ARCHITECTURE

HISTORY

The terms architecture and landscape architecture include the concept of structured environments. Examination of the controlled environments of societies throughout history shows two kinds of patterns appearing consistently: (*1*) those based on strict geometry, turning away from the apparent disorder of natural systems; and (*2*) those recognizing man-made control near buildings, but exercising less and less control over the landscape as one moves away from structures, until man-controlled space blends imperceptibly into natural patterns.

Since the advent of civilization in China, the Middle East, and Egypt, one or the other of these patterns has dominated the landscape. For most of that time geometry proved the dominant choice of planners. Strongly influenced by the irrigation-inspired square geometry of the Nile River valley, the layout of an Egyptian estate (Fig. 1) illustrates the principle of strict organization of immediate environment. The estate is walled for protection against marauders and from the harsh desert outside. Structures within the walls are ordered for convenience. Fish ponds create coolness while supplying protein from fish and ducks. Trees supply either food or shade. The central grape arbor creates a shaded walk to the house, as well as supplying food and drink.

The Sumerians and Babylonians of the Tigris–Euphrates river valley developed city–states to a high art. Assyria and Persia followed by extending control over kingdoms and empires.

The high culture of the Greeks provided form and proportion, while Rome supplied superb administrative skills, as well as engineering lore that introduced highway communication, concrete, municipal drainage, and water supply systems, as well as the arch. Along the way, the Plinys, Elder and Younger, expanded knowledge of the natural world, and how to adapt nature's principles to the immediate environment. Pliny the Younger knew what kinds of plants would grow around his seaside villa, while he oriented rooms of his Tuscan house to take advantage of sun, views, and cooling breezes (1).

The decline of the Roman Empire, culminating in its collapse in the fifth century A.D., brought a return to more primitive lifestyles. People were more concerned with defense against outside forces than in expanding control over land, or in widening knowledge of the world. Living–working spaces became confined, while cities, if they grew at all, became walled bastions, leaving little room for outdoor pleasure gardens.

Yet, even during those dangerous times, man was slowly gaining knowledge and skills. City planning functions became a necessity as cities grew more crowded. People moved to urban areas for economic reasons. The crowds demanded improved means of communication, better municipal services, and more efficient distribution of goods.

Street systems improved, public sewer and water supplies were introduced, industry began, and international trade fairs brought knowledge of the world. Europe made its way out of the Dark Ages in the thirteenth and fourteenth centuries. Institutions of public welfare and increased economic power led to the Renaissance, or rebirth of self-awareness and knowledge of the world.

At this juncture, the Persian–Arabic culture made its major contribution to landscape architecture, the poetic use of water. Both Persia (Iran) and the Arabic peninsula are largely desert. To the people of these regions, water was a scarce and precious commodity. In the Koran, paradise is pictured as a place of cool shade, tinkling fountains, and restful pools. Paradise to the Arab was a walled garden filled with moving water and fragrant flowers, cooled by trees, which provided shade and offered delectable fruits. To the Arab, from the time of Mohammed, the idea "garden" contained at least two of these elements. Thus, as the Moors (North African Arabs) penetrated north into Spain and ultimately southern France, they carried with them the characteristics of the desert oasis.

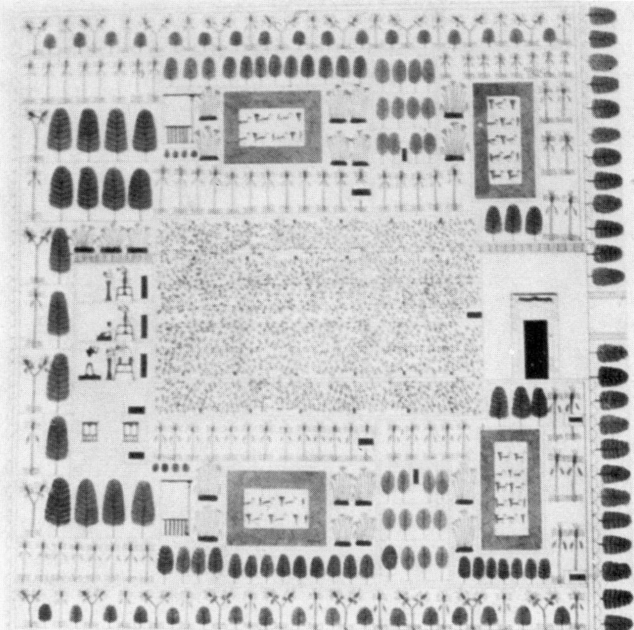

Figure 1. Plan, Egyptian estate, 1400 B.C. Courtesy of Faber & Faber Ltd.

The principal exemplar of the Moorish influence in Europe is the Alhambra and Generalife at Granada, in southern Spain. The Alhambra was the last stronghold of Islam in Spain; it was captured in 1492 by Ferdinand and Isabella, the monarchs who financed Columbus's discovery of the New World.

The Alhambra was a medieval fort, located on the crest of a steep hill. Garden spaces are architectonic, as one would expect, given the defensive situation. In contrast to the utilitarian exterior, interior courts at Granada express a sophisticated delicacy of forms, suggesting the ephemeral character of the tents of desert nomads.

Water, in the Court of the Myrtles (Fig. 2), takes form as a broad, mirrorlike pool, telling visitors that their host has spared no expense to delight guests. In contrast, the Court of the Lions (Fig. 3) shows Moorish skill at making maximum aesthetic use of limited water, channeling the streams outward from the center of the court, in the four cardinal directions, representing the four rivers of paradise, which flowed out of the Garden of Eden. The visitor also takes note of the way in which the channels tie exterior and interior spaces together. A sense of coolness is engendered by the sound of splashing fountains, and a clever system for natural cooling enhances the flow of air throughout the courts.

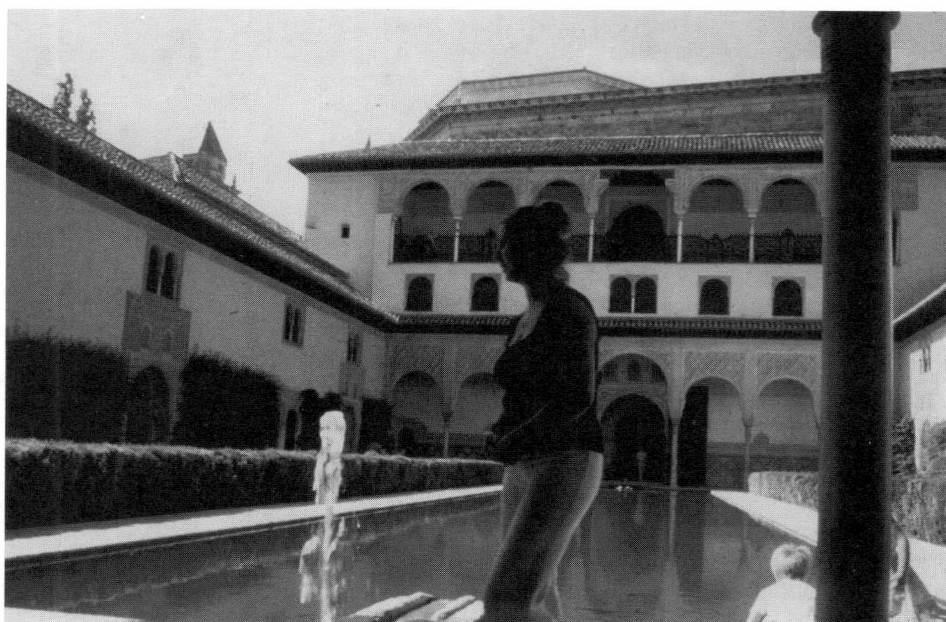

Figure 2. Court of the Myrtles, the Alhambra, Granada, Spain.

In the sixteenth and seventeenth centuries, this skill in the aesthetic and functional use of water was adopted in Italy, where it became a vital part of the Italian Renaissance. No one fully understands why a surge of brainpower occurred in northern Italy during this time. Galileo, da Vinci, Dante, Boccaccio, de Medici, and many others were part of an awakening of knowledge, both of man and his world.

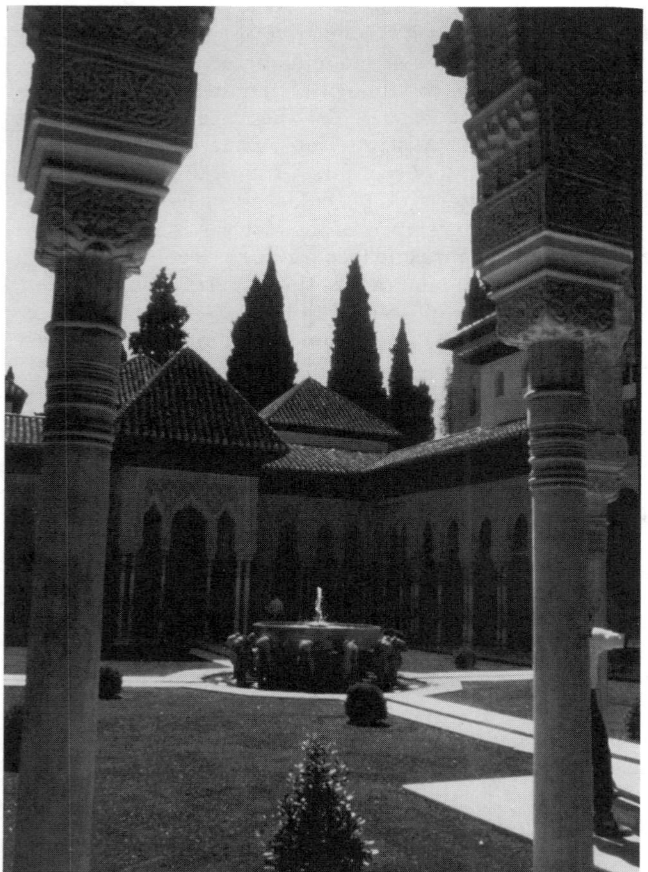

Figure 3. Court of the Lions, the Alhambra, Granada, Spain.

Geographic and political factors in the Renaissance are easier to grasp. Italy extends deep into the Mediterranean, and its indented coastline made trade advantageous. Independent city–states developed, each dominated by a powerful family. The existing economic system led to great wealth, which, coupled with a favorable intellectual climate, led to an explosion of artistic expression.

Wealthy sponsors collected both contemporary and antique art works, and built extensive libraries of art, literature, philosophy, and science. The power brokers also collected people.

Cosimo de Medici, leader of Florence, kept a magnificent library and art collection that had few rivals. He wrote poetry himself and also supported a number of artists.

Summer in Florence was hot, humid, and often subject to air pollution. De Medici owned land near Fiesole, a hilside suburb of the city. He knew that Pliny the Younger had, in Roman times, owned a villa in Tuscany, sited to utilize the coolness of the hills, but providing delightful views over the countryside (2).

In 1450, de Medici commissioned Michelozzo Michelozzi, a prominent architect, to design for grandson Lorenzo de Medici, a small villa in those hills. This casino with its adjacent gardens, designed as a unit, began a garden design revolution. Being a "magnificent and honored palace, founded in the steepness of the slope at huge expense but not without utility," as described by Giorgio Vasari (3), contemporary art critic, Villa Medici proved man's dominance over nature, but also expressed man's awareness of the surrounding world.

Subsequent examples, such as the Villa d'Este at Tivoli, and the Villa Lante at Bagnaia, followed the de Medici pattern, but on a larger scale and with increasing intricacy. Villa d'Este especially, partly because of its steep site over-

Figure 4. Water Organ, Villa d'Este, Tivoli, 1550. Courtesy of Harvard University Press. Photograph by Norman T. Newton.

looking the falls of the Tiber, became known for its lavish water displays (Fig. 4). Here, water, by diversion of the river through pipes and channels, is displayed in a myriad of ways. Small jets fall into stairway balustrade rills, while roaring waterfalls make powerful sounds, all to proclaim the owner's control over his surroundings. The Dragon Fountain, a central feature of the gardens, shoots a wrist-sized jet thirty feet in the air. Today these gardens are public property, exemplifying the splendor created by private capital at the height of the renaissance.

By the seventeenth century, competition among owners led to excessive elaboration. Isola Bella, a tour de force, was begun in 1632. Count Vitalione bought a low, rocky island in Lago Maggiore, near the Alps. He transformed it into a casino and gardens that people likened to the Hanging Gardens of Babylon. The villa might be taken for a mid-nineteenth century river steamer. Isola Bella's five terraces rise into the air like decks, as ornate in stone as the decks of the river steamer in wood. The selection of a difficult site, and on it erecting an island paradise showed the arrogance of man, and his power to transform his environment.

Meanwhile France experienced a modified Renaissance. Despite 100 years of interior and exterior turmoil, France developed a strong monarchy. Defensive limits were the kingdom's borders, not castle walls. Yet Italy's influence was strong in France as she emerged as a world power. Catherine and Marie de Medici, both queens of France, brought from Italy their own ideas and Italian gardeners to execute their dreams.

Fontainebleau and Château Neuf showed strong Italian influence in their designs. They were villas, greatly enlarged in scale, and adapted to the French climate and terrain, but not yet châteaux.

In the late seventeenth century, two people had a strong impact on garden design. Louis XIV, the self-styled Sun King, became king of France in 1643. Louis's mother, Anne of Austria, acted as regent, advised by her chief minister, Cardinal Mazarin. After Mazarin's death, Louis declared himself chief of state.

Andrè le Nôtre, son of Louis XIV's chief gardener, had been trained as artist, architect, and gardener under his father's influence. André le Nôtre's prominence came through the completion, in collaboration with the architect Le Vau and the sculptor Le Brun, of a palatial garden in the modified Italianate geometric style for Nicholas Fouquet, Louis XIV's finance minister.

Vaux-le-Vicomte, at Melun, near Paris was designed to be seen as a unit, with strictly geometric forms. The terrain, however, lacked the steep slopes favored by Italian designers, so, at Vaux-le-Vicomte, the waters were gathered together in mirrorlike sheets, as huge canals and lagoons (Figs. 5 and 6).

Le Nôtre's innovations extended to design in vast scale, accommodating crowds of pleasure seekers. Wide paths and many ramps replacing steps eased circulation. For the first time, le Nôtre was able to design completely anew. The results established le Nôtre's reputation.

In 1661, Louis XIV brought Le Nôtre, Le Vau, and Le Brun together again to transform Louis XIII's hunting lodge, near Versailles. The three artists, along with Louis XIV himself, were in Versailles to create the most spectacular palace and gardens the world had seen. The palace itself, with over 2000 rooms, spanned 2700 ft, overlooking gardens covering 5 mi^2.

Versailles drew the admiration and envy of the European world. From the late seventeenth century and into the first quarter of the eighteenth century, residences of European rulers emulated Versailles. Schönbrunn and the Nymphenburg in Austria, and Karlsruhe in Germany bloomed as copies of the French king's court. In England, Hampton Court, long a residence of kings, was greatly expanded in an obviously French manner. Near Naples, Caserta, a virtual replica of Versailles, spread over the countryside.

French Renaissance influence may be seen today in the axial pattern of the city of Williamsburg, Virginia. The plan of the capital city, Washington, D.C., originally was laid out, in 1777, by the French engineer Major Pierre L'Enfant in the grand manner and with the geometry of Versailles.

While the French built grandiloquent, elaborate gardens, England was quietly becoming a world power. Under Elizabeth I, England began her rise to prominence, but seemed to remain a follower in terms of fanciful land patterns. Gardens remained relatively small and simple. Personal independence and the pragmatism of landowners kept things simple, while the British maritime climate permitted superb lawns and fostered the use of a wide variety of plants. Seventeenth-century estates such as Haddon Hall were unassuming country places rather than royal palaces (Fig. 7).

The eighteenth century brought changes in attitudes and land-use patterns. The Age of Exploration was drawing to a close. Industrial technology increased production

Figure 5. Château from gardens, Vaux-le-Vicomte, France.

of goods, and made travel easier; society youth made the grand tour on the continent part of their education. Fear of the unknown, so prevalent in the Middle Ages, gave way to complacency and to virtual delight in raw nature.

These changes are exemplified in the estate called Stowe, in Buckinghamshire. Lord Cobham gained fame and fortune under Marlborough (4). In recognition of his new prominence, Cobham hired the architect Van Brugh to build a palace overlooking the town. Charles Bridgeman, gardener to Queen Anne, laid out the grounds in a manner reminiscent of Versailles.

When Bridgeman retired in 1733, William Kent became the garden designer. He had traveled extensively and had seen Italian villas as they appeared after 200 years of neglect. Kent therefore saw classic landscapes in romantic ruin. Kent modified Bridgeman's scheme into an idyllic retrospect of the sixteenth century. Gone was plane geometry, and in its place appeared glimpses of ruined buildings and sculptures from half-forgotten mythology.

During Kent's tenure at Stowe, Lancelot Brown became kitchen gardener. One of Brown's tasks was to conduct tours of the estate. A glib student of human nature, Brown made easy acquaintance with visitors, many of whom later became Brown's clients.

After Kent's death, Brown carried Kent's theories to their logical extreme at Stowe. His design palette held

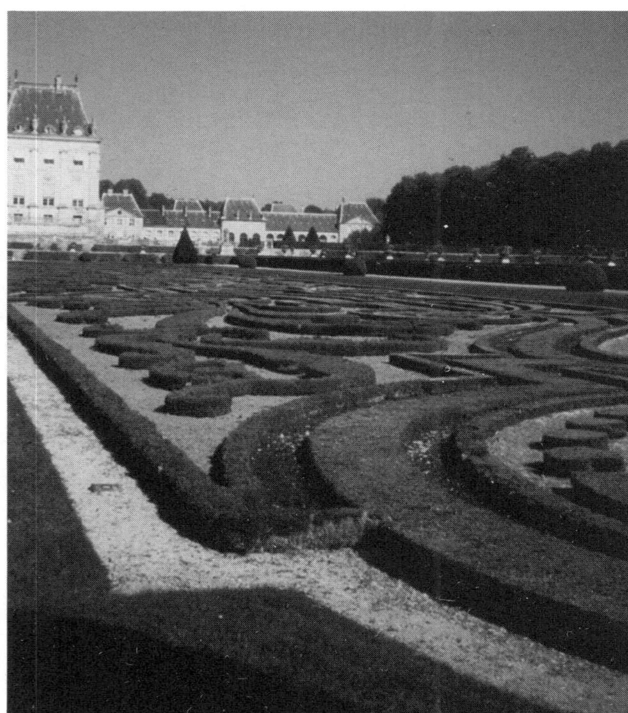

Figure 6. Parterre de Broiderie, Vaux-le-Vicomte, France.

Figure 7. Lower garden, Haddon Hall, England.

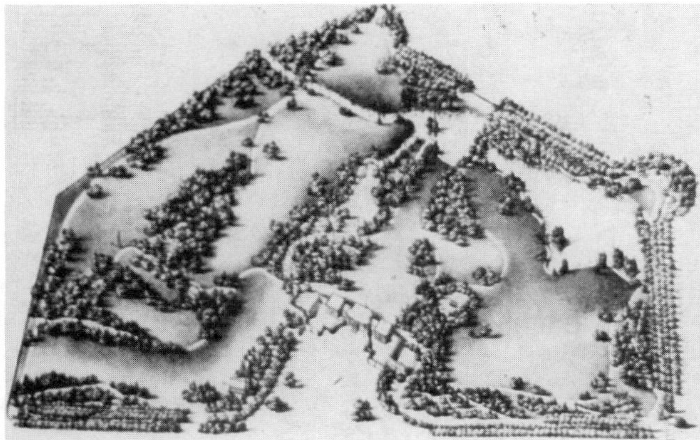

Figure 8. Stowe as modified by Lancelot Brown. Courtesy of Faber & Faber Ltd.

rolling, grassy slopes; clumps of trees, creating shadow patterns; and "naturalized" streams and lakes, establishing picturesque settings as foci for landscape paintings (Fig. 8).

Brown became the best known landscape gardener in England, reworking most of its country estates, to the regret of those who mourned the loss of geometric gardens. Several factors influenced those who followed Brown's dictates, thus establishing what came to be called the English Landscape school. One was a romanticized vision of classic gardens and architecture pervading Europe in this period. Country places frequently included replicas of classic temples and sculptures (Fig. 9).

The other compelling fact was an awakened interest in and travel to China. William Chambers, influential designer of Kew Gardens, visited the Orient and translated what he had seen into architectural details of his designs. Bridges, teahouses, and pagodas became usual adornments of landscape gardens. At Kew Gardens, Chambers erected a 10-story pagoda that today identifies Kew Gardens from the air (Fig. 10).

Figure 9. Temple of Bellona, Kew Gardens, by William Chambers, 1760.

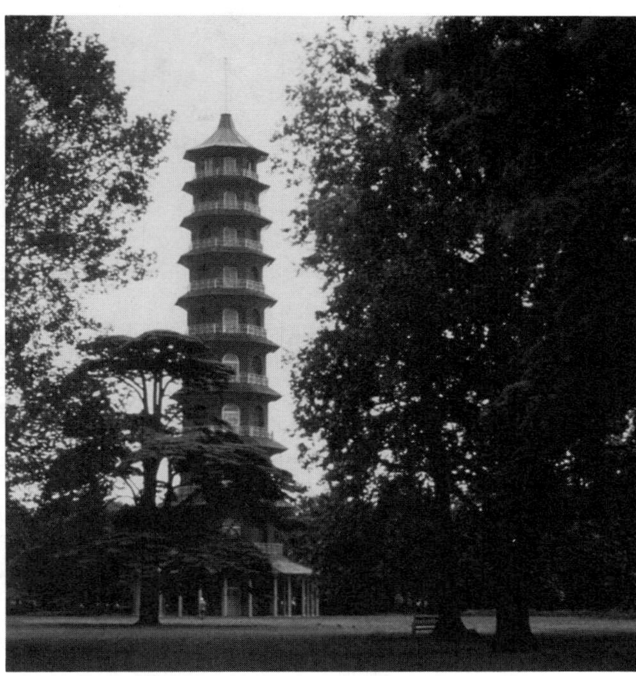

Figure 10. Chinese Pagoda, Kew Gardens, by William Chambers, 1761.

While Sir Humphry Repton and J. C. Loudon kept the English Landscape school alive in England well into the nineteenth century, its influence quickly spread across Europe. Marie Antoinette, consort of Louis XVI, developed her own "Jardin Anglais" at Versailles, its layout following Brown's style.

It seemed natural for the British to accept nature as a domesticated pet, because England had for centuries been under human control; here there were no more wildernesses. In contrast, colonial North America was a savage wilderness, perhaps to be conquered eventually, but at first to be endured if not defied. Consequently, early settlements built gardens in the geometric style, as preserved in Williamsburg, Virginia, and New Berne, North Carolina (Figs. 11 and 12).

As the new nation of the United States expanded westward, feelings of security grew, enabling the English Landscape school's influence to be felt. George Washington, completing Mt. Vernon after the Revolution, followed Brown's ideas, as modified by U.S. conditions. The kitchen and flower gardens, in their symmetry, reflect the seventeenth century, while the lawn overlooking the Potomac shows the English Landscape school's influence.

Thomas Jefferson was an accomplished architect, inventor, and gardener. Monticello, his home near Charlottesville, Virginia, reflects Jefferson's delight in the romanticism of the period. The classic house, with its dome modeled on the Roman Pantheon, sat on its "little mountain" so that Jefferson could regard the design complex of which he was most proud, the buildings and grounds of the University of Virginia. Jefferson's skill as a site planner is evident in the way "the Lawn" progresses gently down the spine of the campus ridge. The elements of Brown's British landscape are here: classic structures, set

Figure 11. Formal garden, Governor's Palace, Williamsburg, Virginia.

on a picturesque meadow, shaded by majestic trees (Figs. 13 and 14).

The early nineteenth century brought together the classicism of the past with the results of the Industrial Revolution. The dominant figure in landscape architecture at this time was Andrew Jackson Downing. Born the son of a nurseryman in 1815, in Newburgh, New York, Downing was strongly influenced by Hudson River valley culture. Near neighbor of Washington Irving, he was exposed to the Hudson River school of painters. Its leader, Thomas Cole, strongly imposed his romanticized views of nature on the region.

Downing, through his book *Treatise on the Theory and Practice of Landscape Gardening, Adapted to North America, With a View to the Improvement of Country Residences,* became the principal authority on landscape art in the

Figure 12. Green garden, Governor's Palace, New Berne, North Carolina.

Figure 13. Library at head of "The Lawn," University of Virginia, Charlottesville.

mid-nineteenth century United States. From 1841 to his tragic drowning in a steamboat accident on the Hudson River in 1852, Downing edited the magazine *The Horticulturist,* which was devoted to plant culture and garden art. Its wide circulation further extended Downing's influence. His most important works include the grounds of the Smithsonian Institution in Washington, D.C., and the layout of Vassar College, Poughkeepsie, New York.

Downing's contributions to the art–science of landscape architecture are profound. Although imbued with Kent's and Brown's dicta that the natural landscape was man's to control and within it man could create landscape "pictures," Downing developed a new, sound hypothesis. He believed every situation to have its own inherent and unique quality that he called the genius loci. Downing knew that each site possessed unique topography, climate, and vegetation. The quality of design, he wrote, depends on using indigenous plant material, or plants adaptable to the specific environment (5).

Downing dominated the first half of the nineteenth century. At the same time, a young New Englander was gaining practical experience that would enable him to create a new profession and to name that profession. Frederick Law Olmsted, Sr., started life as a farmer on a New York state farm; later he purchased acreage on Staten Island. Here he had considerable success propagating and selling fruit trees. Restless in the pursuit of a single career, Olmsted for a time became a publisher, which gave him contacts at *The New York Times*. In 1850, the *Times* commissioned Olmsted to travel in the South. He sent daily

Figure 14. Pavilion I, University of Virginia, Charlottesville.

dispatches, describing social and economic conditions. The summation resulted in a book, *The Cotton Kingdom,* published in 1861. This treatise on the pre-Civil War South remains an important reference.

Olmsted's managerial skills enabled him to serve with distinction as Secretary of the U.S. Sanitary Commission, predecessor of the American Red Cross. Failing health and work pressures forced Olmsted to resign his post. He accepted a position as manager of a gold mine in California. While there, Olmsted involved himself in preserving park lands. Some of these lands eventually became Yosemite National Park. Thus Olmsted, long before preservation became a popular cause, worked to save national landscapes of unique value to the nation.

On his return to New York in 1858, Olmsted became superintendent of works for the recently purchased Central Park. Olmsted was to manage earthwork, drainage, development of play areas, paths, roads, and plantings on a huge rectangle of raw land given over to swamps, rocky outcrops, and trash dumps. He quickly proved his skill as he soon had the 2000-man work force operating smoothly. While engaged in this work, Olmsted was asked by Calvert Vaux, architect, to collaborate on a plan for Central Park to be entered in the 1858 design competition. At first reluctant to enter the competition, Olmsted finally agreed. On April 1, 1858, Olmsted and Vaux submitted their entry, titled "Greensward" to the judges. Plans included comprehensive specifications justifying their proposals. The "Greensward" entry won first prize, and the firm of Olmsted and Vaux was hired to supervise realization of the plans. Thus began a long and fruitful partnership, the first to call themselves landscape architects (6).

Their commissions included numerous urban park systems in the United States and Canada. The partners produced plans for Riverside, near Chicago, one of the first suburban "bedroom communities" in 1869. In all of their work, they carefully studied land form and the surroundings of the site, as well as the needs and wants of their clients. They thus produced functional works, with long useful lives.

Central Park illustrates this philosophy of planning. When completed in 1869, the park was already a popular recreational area. Today the park remains, with few changes, the principal open space of New York City.

In 1886 Olmsted, in concert with a Boston firm of architects, laid out Stanford University in Palo Alto, California. While imposing in form, the campus fits its locale well, is admirably sited on the eastern slope of the coastal range, and reflects the Spanish cultural history of the region.

Another of Olmsted's major projects occurred in collaboration with William Morris Hunt, then president of the American Institute of Architects. George Washington Vanderbilt had purchased 100,000 acres of forested land in the Blue Ridge Mountains near Asheville, North Carolina. The extent of the baronial estate was more than twice as large as Louis XIV's Versailles.

Hunt designed the four-acre mansion in the beaux-arts tradition, which espoused the belief that all great architecture had already been created, and thus the style that best suited the client's interests must be chosen. The French château was chosen as a model. The site selected permitted wide views across the Appalachians.

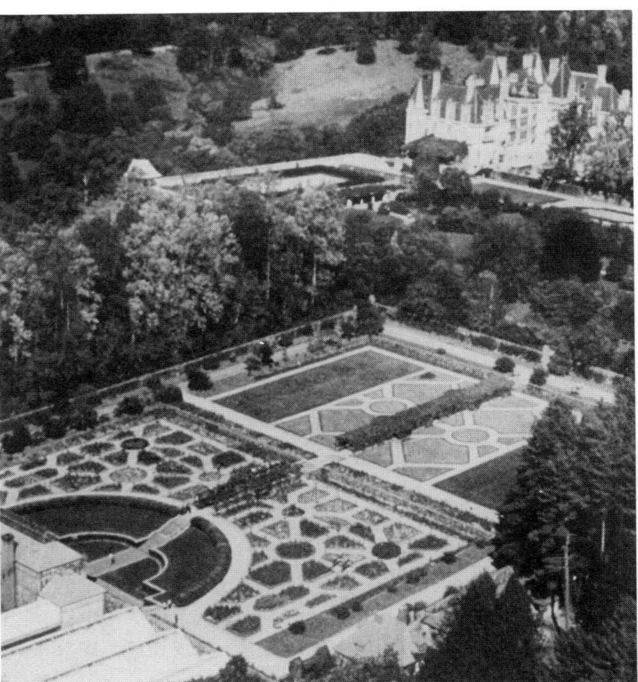

Figure 15. Biltmore House and gardens, Asheville, North Carolina. Courtesy of the Biltmore Company.

Olmsted also chose eclectically for the grounds around the château. The forecourt is pure French Renaissance. Adjacent is an Italianate terrace, scaled to the French manor. Beyond, Olmsted designed a Reptonian shrub garden, a horticulturist's delight. The walled cutting garden on a lower terrace reminds one of an enlarged British kitchen garden.

Beyond the close environs of the house, however, lay 100,000 acres of forest. What purpose, other than seclusion, could these lands serve? Olmsted considered them a legacy. He suggested to Vanderbilt that he experiment with forestry practices. Thus was established the first U.S. forestry school, which produced some of the early leaders in the field of forest conservation. Much of the original acreage now is part of the National Forest System (Fig. 15).

Frederick Law Olmsted did not survive to see the founding of the American Society of Landscape Architects, but his two sons, John and Frederick Law Jr., became charter members of the professional society, founded in 1899. One of the best known charter members was Beatrix Jones (later Mrs. Max Farrand). Most of her early work was in New York City. Later she practiced in both Maine and California.

An extant example of Farrand's work is Dumbarton Oaks, Washington, D.C. Beginning in 1922, Farrand devoted some 20 years to developing this diplomat's home. The plan is eclectic, as was customary in its time. Her periodic return was proof of her professional skill and

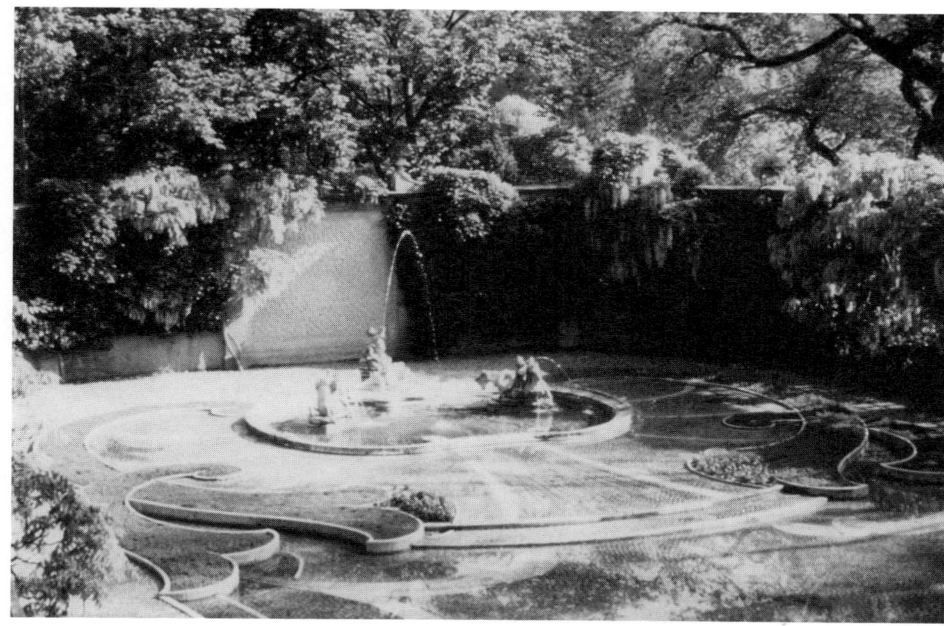

Figure 16. Water garden, Dumbarton Oaks, Washington, D.C.

her understanding of the changing nature of garden design (Fig. 16).

There were no training schools in the early twentieth century; practitioners entered landscape architecture from various professions. Ossian Cole Simonds was originally a civil engineer and was for a time partner in the architectural firm Holabird, Simonds & Roche of Chicago. "He then became superintendent and landscape architect of Chicago's Graceland Cemetery, which he developed into one of the most remarkable park-like cemeteries of the Western World. After 1888 he branched out into an extensive private practice, starting with the layout of Fort Sheridan, Illinois; but Graceland continues to be regarded as his masterpiece" (7).

H. W. S. Cleveland was another well-known figure of the early twentieth century. Cleveland came from a background of farming, civil engineering, and surveying. His most widely recognized works included the park system of Minneapolis, Minnesota, one of the earliest connected rings of parks and parkways, later popularized in Cleveland's "Emerald Necklace," and the Cook County, Illinois, park district.

Warren Manning came to landscape architecture from the nursery profession. He collaborated frequently in the 1920s with Charles Platt, well-known architect of the period. On a bluff on the south shore of Lake Erie, in Bratenahl, Ohio, Manning and Platt combined their talents to produce an Italianate villa for the Mathers, iron ore shippers. The estate, called Gwinn, has remained a mecca for landscape design students (Fig. 17).

The 1929 stock market crash brought on the Great Depression, which caused the end of the country estate era and changed the character of the landscape architecture profession. Federal works programs, designed to stimulate the economy, opened new areas for landscape architects. Since that time, approximately half of the practitioners in the field have been engaged in national, state, and local park and forestry programs. In the 1930s and 1940s the National Park Service was the largest employer of landscape architects.

National Park Service holdings greatly increased in the depression years. Shenandoah, Great Smoky Mountains, and Everglades National Parks were established in the eastern United States in those years.

Opportunities also opened in transportation. Skyline Drive, the Blue Ridge Parkway, and the Natchez Trace Parkway owe their design excellence to landscape architects teamed with civil engineers (Fig. 18).

Public housing also opened up for landscape architects in the period prior to World War II, as defense preparations generated needs for new housing. Greenbelt, Maryland, was the first of these government projects, designed as communities that provided housing, recreation, education,

Figure 17. Entrance of Gwinn, Mather Estate, Bratenahl, Ohio.

Figure 18. Blue Ridge Parkway, North Carolina.

and pleasure spaces often not found in conventional subdivisions. Greenhills, Ohio, and Greendale, Wisconsin, were two other such projects.

World War II naturally disrupted the profession, but after the war, landscape architecture prospered as never before. Landscape architects began to achieve national recognition. Thomas Church of California first became known for residential design in the San Francisco Bay area. Through magazine articles and other publications, Church's style became widely known and imitated in the United States. His designs derived from two sources. The International school of architecture, made famous through works of Gropius, Le Corbusier, and van der Rohe, established a trend toward crisp line, a Puritan aversion to decoration, and strict adherence to Frank Lloyd Wright's dictum: Form follows function.

The second source of Church's inspiration was the garden art of Japan (Fig. 19). The oriental philosophy abjures bilateral symmetry, as found in Europe and the United States. Japanese culture is based on the yin and yang, the theory of opposites. Church and others translated the oriental concepts into a form of balance they named occult, because, although the geometry used is as strict as that of le Nôtre, the symmetry is hidden, and therefore occult.

Others followed Church's lead. Garrett Eckbo, also in California, published *Landscape For Living,* outlining the principles of the new landscapes. This he followed with *The Art of Home Landscaping,* which became a popular design text (Fig. 20).

Other name firms of landscape architects provided widely known quality design services. Simonds and Simonds of Pittsburgh, and Sasaki, Dawson & DeMay Associates in Boston accepted widely known commissions.

Shopping malls, subdivisions, and commercial and in-

Figure 19. Japanese garden, Cheekwood, Nashville, Tennessee.

Figure 20. Wohlstetter garden, California, by Garrett Eckbo, landscape architect.

Figure 21. Freeway Park, Seattle, Washington, by Lawrence Halprin, landscape architect.

dustrial complexes received careful design attention, often combining interior with exterior landscapes. Oakbrook Center, near Chicago, designed by Lawrence Halprin, was an early typical project. The interior atrium of the Ford Foundation in New York City became the prototype for what is now known as "interior scape."

Halprin was responsible for completely renovating an abandoned chocolate factory in San Francisco, turning it into a tourist shopping mecca overlooking the Golden Gate Bridge. Mellon Square, Pittsburgh, by Simonds and Simonds, was one of the first urban plazas built with underground parking. Constitution Plaza, Hartford, Connecticut, by Sasaki, Dawson & DeMay combined high-rise office buildings, underground parking, and outdoor seating into one harmonious whole. Their redesign of Copley Square, Boston, achieved national recognition.

In Cincinnati, Ohio, the river theme fountain in the center of a downtown thoroughfare was becoming dilapidated. George Patton, landscape architect of Philadelphia, was hired to relocate the fountain and create a civic plaza. Fountain Square, with the rehabilitated Victorian fountain as the focus, became one of the world's successful urban plazas, rivaling San Marco in Venice in activity if not in size.

The latter third of the twentieth century has seen a movement toward preservation and conservation. With the publication of Ian McHarg's *Design With Nature,* attention has turned to preserving not only culture, but the environment as well.

Woodlands, near Houston, Texas (McHarg, Roberts & Todd, Landscape Architects), demonstrated that it is possible to provide useful living space, while preserving existing nature in an exurban community. Sea Ranch, on the Pacific Ocean north of San Francisco, combines architecture adapted to environment with landscape design calculated to preserve the fragile seacoast environment.

In recent years, urban sprawl has aroused concern about superhighways chopping up city neighborhoods. While citizen groups successfully stymied interstate throughways in New Orleans and San Francisco, Seattle, Washington, took a different approach. Halprin's Freeway Parks have proved a successful effort to allow public use of freeway airspace while still permitting large volumes of traffic through the city (Figs. 21 and 22).

Figure 22. Freeway Park, Seattle, Washington, by Lawrence Halprin, landscape architect.

GENERAL PRINCIPLES

Landscape architecture is the art–science of arranging land, and objects on it, for the use and enjoyment of people. Competence at this task requires the landscape architect to play a number of different roles. He or she must be a successful businessperson to get jobs and money management skills are essential in order to make a living. The landscape architect accepts the role of planner in relating a project site to social, economic, and political factors impinging on it.

Once hired for a project, the landscape architect becomes an engineer. He or she uses surveying techniques to study and lay out the work site, calculates earthwork necessary for site preparation, lays out, both horizontally and vertically, roads, parking lots, and floor levels of buildings, designs drainage systems and utility networks for site functions, and knows the strengths of materials and their physical limitations.

The professional becomes an architect in organizing interior or exterior spaces for people, as well as organizing comfortable circulation patterns for them. The landscape architect is an artist who modulates forms, colors, and textures in three-dimensional space. Artfully, mass and volume are molded into well-proportioned use spaces, balanced within themselves and with adjacent spaces.

As a horticulturist, the landscape architect is knowledgeable of plant materials, their propagation, their use, and their maintenance. He ascertains the appropriate plant materials for the cultural needs of specific situations. Finally, he selects plant materials on the basis of their growth characteristics, so that their ultimate size will be adequate yet not overwhelm the site.

As an ecologist, the landscape architect studies the inherent stability of the local soils, climate, flora, and fauna before determining how project land uses will affect the natural health and ongoing vigor of the existing habitat. He or she also works out systems that make the site suitable for its intended use with minimal disturbance of the ecosystem.

The landscape architect becomes a hydrologist in determining natural and manmade water supply requirements of the project. As a meteorologist, he or she establishes the orientation of site functions based on daily, monthly, and yearly movement of the earth in relation to the sun, and studies climate and weather variations as they affect land uses.

The landscape architect as an economist calculates budgets for material and labor costs that will determine the viability of the project. Relationships to clients and jobs often involve legal aspects. Thus the skills of an attorney are needed in preparing contracts and handling legal questions involving local, regional, and national laws, especially as they touch on zoning and building codes.

No single project requires exercise of all of these skills, and no single landscape architect has equal ability in all of these fields. Consequently, most projects of any size and complexity require the combined efforts of a compatible team of professionals, whose specific talents complement each other, to produce an aesthetically pleasing, cost-effective project.

COLLABORATION

> It is doubtful that any other single event in the history of the arts in America served as notably as the Fair [1893 Chicago Columbian Exposition] in stimulating the practice of interprofessional collaboration. . . .
>
> The teamwork involving architects, landscape architects, sculptors and painters, all striving—not separately, but together—toward an agreed goal, proved its own value in the visual harmony and wholeness of the Fair itself (8).

The roster of those who created the most spectacular and widely known cooperative venture the United States has experienced reads like a who's who of architecture and the arts.

- Daniel Burnham—Chief of construction
- Frederick Law Olmsted, Sr.—Landscape architect–site planner
- Richard Morris Hunt—Administration Building
- Peabody & Stearns—Machinery Hall
- McKim, Mead & White—Agriculture
- G. B. Post—Manufactures and Liberal Arts
- Van Brunt & Howe—Electricity
- S. S. Beman—Mines and Mining
- Adler & Sullivan—Transportation
- H. I. Cobb—Fisheries
- Burling & Whitehouse—Venetian Village
- Jenney & Mundie—Horticulture
- Augustus Saint-Gaudens—Coordinator of sculpture
- Daniel Chester French—"Republic" Statue, Court of Honor, east end
- Frederick MacMonnies—Fountain, Court of Honor, west end
- Francis D. Millet—Director of color
- Edwin Blashfield, Kenyon Cox, Gary Melchers—Murals

Despite the neoclassic theme, the 1893 Fair entranced the world and influenced civic design for decades afterwards. One of its most remarkable accomplishments was the spatial conformation of the Court of Honor, integrating the variety of building facades surrounding it (Fig. 23).

A second influential example of a cooperative venture followed in 1901. A century after George Washington commissioned Major L'Enfant to plan the capital city, the Mall, central to L'Enfant's scheme, was in almost total disarray. For example, when the railroad came to the city in 1853, tracks were laid across the vista below the Capitol. The Smithsonian Institution encroached on the Mall in 1850, and the Washington Monument, completed in 1884, stood 400 ft off of its planned focal site.

In 1901 Congress authorized the Senate Park Commission to establish parks in the capital city. It soon got the name McMillan Commission, for Senator James McMillan, chairman of the Senate Committee on the District of Columbia.

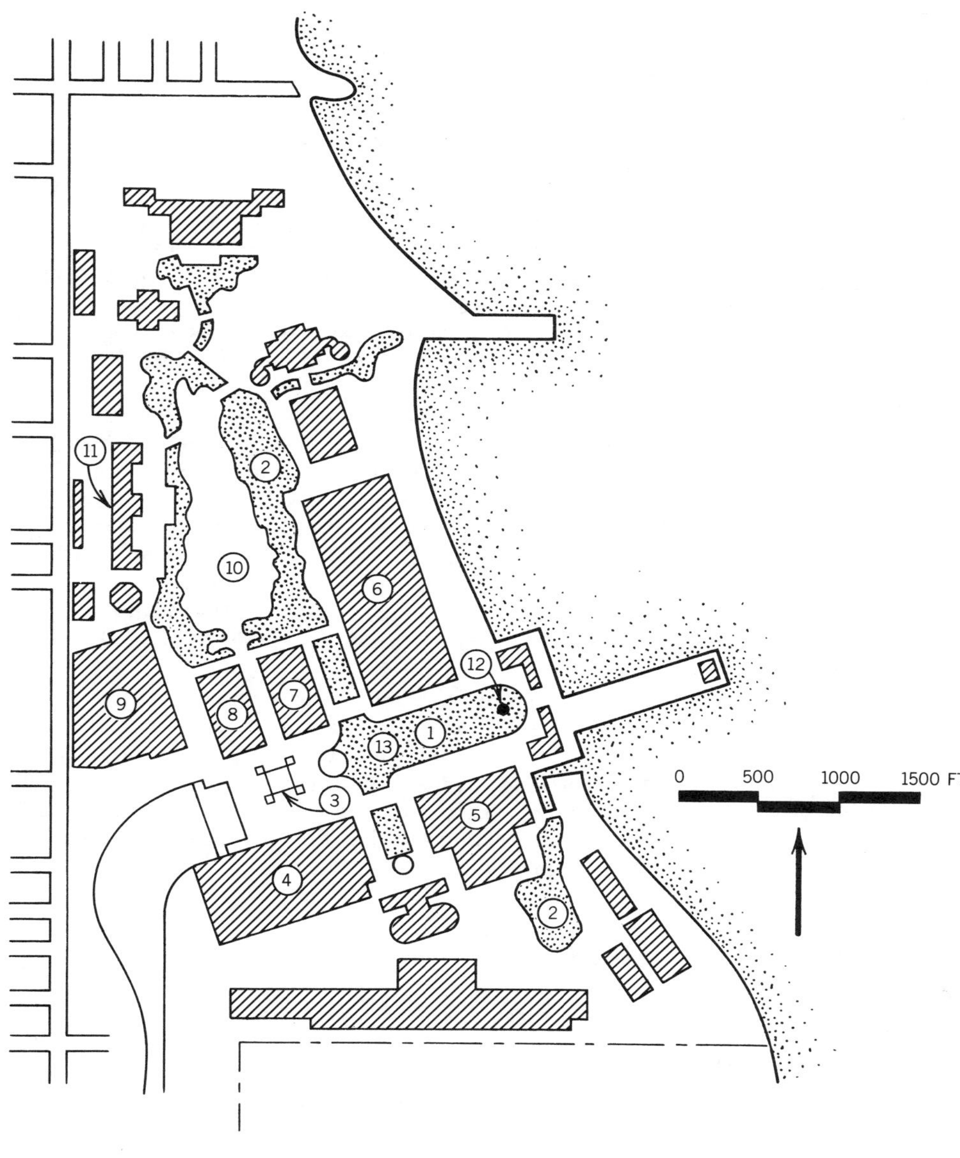

Figure 23. Sketch plan of 1893 Columbian Exposition, Chicago, Illinois, by F. L. Olmsted, Sr., landscape architect. 1: Court of Honor; 2: Lagoons; 3: Administration; 4: Machinery; 5: Agriculture; 6: Manufacturing & Liberal Arts; 7: Electricity; 8: Mines; 9: Transportation; 10: Venetian Village; 11: Horticulture; 12: "Republic"; 13: Fountain.

Because of their national recognition as designers of the Chicago Columbian Exposition, four men were appointed to the Commission. Frederick Law Olmsted, Jr. (Olmsted, Sr., had by now retired) was chosen as landscape architect. Daniel Burnham, Chicago architect, persuaded the Boston architect Charles F. McKim to join him. Augustus Saint-Gaudens, sculptor, rounded out the committee.

It became apparent that the two major axes, one from the Capitol to the Potomac River and the other, crossing the first, centered on the White House, were keys to restoring L'Enfant's plan. The railroad problem was solved by tunneling beneath Capitol Hill. Burnham, commissioned to design a union rail station for the city, agreed to a site that avoided intrusion on the major axes. Olmsted planted double rows of trees on both sides of the Mall, thus unifying the many disparate building facades flanking the greensward. The Lincoln Memorial furnished a terminus opposite the Capitol, while the Jefferson Memorial later terminated the White House axis. By 1940, L'Enfant's inspired plan had been restored, as the result of collaborative effort.

In 1910, President Taft and Congress, as a follow-up to the McMillan Commission's work, established a national Commission of Fine Arts. The commission consisted of three architects, a landscape architect, a painter, a sculptor, and an art historian or critic. Both Burnham and Olmsted were charter members of the commission. Landscape architect members since Olmsted have been selected from lists presented by the American Society of Landscape Architects. The commission remains a vital force in resolving design conflicts as they arise in the nation's capital. Most recently, Hideo Sasaki has been involved with the Franklin Delano Roosevelt Memorial and the Vietnam War Memorial, both near the Mall.

Other projects requiring cooperative effort on the part of a multidisciplinary team include

1928 Reconstruction of Williamsburg, Va.
Perry, Shaw & Hepburn, architects
Arthur A. Shurcliff, landscape architect
Project: historic preservation

1932 Chatham Village, Pittsburgh, Pa.
Wright & Stein, architects
Ingham & Boyd, architects
Ralph E. Griswold, landscape architect
Theodore M. Kohankie, landscape architect
Project: Row house community designed for pedestrian living

1933 Tennessee Valley Authority, Norris, Tenn.
Roland A. Wank, architect
Tracy B. Augur, landscape architect
Carroll A. Towne, landscape architect
Project: new town for workers, Norris Dam

1935 Greenbelt, Md.
Douglas D. Ellington, architect
Reginald J. Wadsworth, architect
Harold B. Bursley, landscape architect
Hale J. Walker, landscape architect
Project: new town for defense employees

1960 Foothills College, Los Altos, Calif.
Ernest J. Kemp, architect
Master & Hurd Associates, architects
Sasaki, Walker & Associates, landscape architects
Project: pedestrian-oriented campus

TRAINING

The landscape architect's training enhances and reinforces the many concerns and capacities of the practitioner. First, a landscape architect needs a well-rounded education. Ideally, the practitioner should have a liberal arts undergraduate degree, followed by intense concentration on technical subjects. Practically, however, most students are unable, or unwilling, to invest that amount of time in academics. Commonly, students receive an undergraduate education in mathematics, social sciences and humanities, natural science, and elective subjects.

Second, the major requirements in a landscape architecture curriculum place heavy emphasis on design. Design is an all-inclusive term but means that the student is asked to produce solutions to given problems involving relations of people and activities to specific environments. Because design involves individual thought processes, it is best learned through close rapport between student and instructor. Other skills are enhanced through courses in construction. Here the student learns how to use materials; the structural limitations of steel, wood, and concrete; and how materials go together to produce useful structures. In addition, students learn graphic skills, needed to communicate ideas clearly and concisely. A study of the history of landscape architecture rounds out the essentials.

Courses in allied subjects include botany, horticulture, architecture, city and regional planning, geology, and civil engineering. The percentage of time spent in these three broad categories varies from school to school. A four-year curriculum usually contains 30–40% basic education; 40–60% design, construction, and graphics; and 10–20% pertaining to the allied professions.

A large proportion of those completing an undergraduate program enter the profession directly. Some choose to enhance their skills through graduate programs. Most students prefer to attend schools whose landscape architecture curricula are accredited by the American Society of Landscape Architects. The Society has accredited 46 programs in 31 states and Canada. Thirty-two of these offer undergraduate programs only; eight offer only graduate programs; six offer both undergraduate and graduate programs.

Growing awareness of major problems inherent to mankind's survival forces landscape architecture and its allied professions to seek a wider variety of technical skills. The science component of training becomes of increasing importance. Many enter the field with skills in meteorology, geology, hydrology, soil science, anthropology, and, frequently, the social sciences. Computer programming abilities are increasingly in demand. Thus, the Master's degree in landscape architecture becomes the first professional degree.

Because practice of the profession requires both technical skills and professional judgment, most states require landscape architects to be licensed. Entrants normally enter a period of internship prior to taking the state examination. On passing the registration test, a registered landscape architect may affix his seal to drawings and specifications as proof of competence.

BIBLIOGRAPHY

1. G. B. Tobey, *A History of Landscape Architecture: The Relationship of People to Environment,* Elsevier Science Publishing Co., Inc., New York, 1973, pp. 67–68.
2. H. Tanzer, *The Villas of Pliny The Younger,* Columbia University Press, New York, 1924.
3. Ref. 1, p. 100.
4. Ref. 1, p. 131.
5. Ref. 1, pp. 156, 157.
6. N. T. Newton, *Design on the Land; The Devlopment of Landscape Architecture,* Belknap Press, Cambridge, Mass., 1971, p. 273.
7. Ref. 6, pp. 390–391.
8. Ref. 6, p. 365.

General References

Refs. 1 and 6 are good general references.

T. Church, *Gardens Are For People,* Reinhold, New York, 1955.

D. Clifford, *A History of Garden Design,* Praeger, New York, 1963.

A. J. Downing, *A Treatise on the Theory and Practice of Landscape Gardening Adapted to North America,* Wiley and Putnam, New York, 1841.

G. Eckbo, *Landscape For Living,* F. W. Dodge Corp., New York, 1950.

G. Eckbo, *The Art of Home Landscaping,* McGraw-Hill Inc., New York, 1956.

P. H. Elwood, ed., *American Landscape Architecture,* Architectural Book Publishing Co., New York, 1924.

M. L. Gothein, *A History of Garden Art,* 2 vols., E. P. Dutton, New York, 1928.

H. V. Hubbard and T. Kimball, *An Introduction to the Study of Landscape Design,* MIT Press, Cambridge, Mass., 1959.

T. Ishimoto, *The Art of the Japanese Garden,* Crown, New York, 1958.

A. G. B. Lockwood, *Gardens of Colony and State,* The Scribner Book Companies, Inc., New York, 1934.

J. C. Loudon, *The Suburban Garden and Villa Companion,* Longman, Orne, Brown, Green and Longmans, London, 1838.

I. McHarg, *Design With Nature,* Natural History Press, Garden City, New York, 1969.

F. L. Olmsted, Sr. in F. L. Olmsted, Jr. and T. K. Kimball, eds., *Forty Years of Landscape Architecture, vol. I and II,* Putnam, New York, 1928.

H. Repton in J. Nolen, ed., *The Art of Landscape Gardening,* Houghton Mifflin, Boston, 1907.

J. C. Shepherd and G. A Jellicoe, *Gardens and Design,* Ernest Benn, London, 1927.

J. O. Simonds, *Landscape Architecture: The Shaping of Man's Environment,* F. W. Dodge Corp., New York, 1961.

O. Siren, *China and the Gardens of Europe of the Eighteenth Century,* Ronald, New York, 1950.

W. B. Snow, ed., *The Highway and the Landscape,* Rutgers University Press, New Brunswick, N.J., 1959.

F. Steele, *Design in the Little Garden,* The Atlantic Monthly Press, Boston, 1924.

C. Tunnard, *Gardens in the Modern Landscape,* The Architectural Press, London, 1938.

E. Wharton, *The Italian Villas and Their Gardens,* The Century Co., New York, 1910.

D. N. Wilbur, *Persian Gardens and Pavilions,* Tuttle, Rutland Vt., 1962.

See also Cluster Development and Land Subdivision; Fine Arts Commission; Olmsted, Frederick Law; Planned Communities (New Towns); Sasaki, Hideo; Shrubs and Trees; Stormwater Systems; Urban Design—Creation of Livable Cities

George B. Tobey
Carrollton, Texas

LATIN AMERICAN ARCHITECTURE

The vast subject of architecture in Latin America can be grasped in full only within the parameters of two basic determinants: the large extension of the territory in which it was produced, encompassing large parts of North America and nearly all of Central and South America, and the span of time elapsed from the flourishing of the first pre-Columbian civilizations, through the conquest and colonization of the continent by the Spanish and Portuguese empires, the creation of independent republics at the beginning of the nineteenth century, and up to the surge of the energetic architectural activity of the twentieth century. Over a time span of some 3000 years, the imposing structures of indigenous cultures were developed, followed by the adaptable Iberian architecture of the colonial period, the adoption of French canons by the young nations, and the important contribution to contemporary architecture in the twentieth century.

PRE-COLUMBIAN ARCHITECTURE

Almost all of the information on the architecture of pre-Columbian America is based on archaeological studies and, consequently, lacks the precision and certainty of the chronicles of later architectural periods. The main areas of development of pre-Columbian architecture are located in what today are the territories of Mexico and Central America in the north, and in the coastal valleys and highlands of Peru and Bolivia in the south. Definite architectural styles mark chronological and territorial divisions corresponding to the various civilizations known to have existed in those areas from approximately 1500 B.C. to the Spanish Conquest in the sixteenth century. In Mesoamerica, three periods have been established: Preclassic, from 1500 B.C. to A.D. 100; Classic, from A.D. 100 to approximately A.D. 900, and Postclassic, from A.D. 900 to A.D. 1500. The central valley of Mexico, southern Mexico, the eastern Gulf Coast, the Yucatán Peninsula, and the Pacific highlands of Mexico, Guatemala, and western Honduras were the main cultural areas.

In the Andes of Peru and Bolivia, although chronological divisions have not been unanimously formulated, six periods have been established with some variations: Initial, from 2000 B.C. to 900 B.C.; Early Horizon, from 900 to 200 B.C.; Early Intermediate, from 200 B.C. to 600 A.D.; Middle Horizon, from 600 to 1000 A.D.; Late Intermediate, from 1000 to 1476 A.D.; and Late Horizon, from 1476 to 1534 A.D.

Mesoamerica

The inhabitants of pre-Columbian Mesoamerica were, in general, mound builders. Such structures started as earth accumulations and developed through the centuries into highly sophisticated stone pyramids and edifices, exquisitely ornamented and designed as elements of broader concepts of urban design.

The first important work of this type is the Pyramid of Cuicuilco in central Mexico, dating from 500 B.C. Five hundred years later, at the onset of the Classic Period, Teotihuacán, the biggest of all pre-Columbian complexes, emerged first as a theocratic center, eventually taken over by a cast of warrior priests through four stages of development up to its sudden collapse by invasion and fire before 700 A.D. Teotihuacán's urban plan is organized along a wide esplanade, 130 ft wide and 1.5 mi long; La Calzada de los Muertos, limited by hundreds of small platforms, is flanked to the east by the imposing Pirámide del Sol, 720 × 740 ft at the base, and terminated to the north by the Pirámide de la Luna with a base measuring 460 × 490 ft, and rising 151 ft.

To the south, built before 300 A.D., is the Templo de Quetzalcóatl. The typical pyramid configuration followed by many other cultures in Mesoamerica consists of an alternate arrangement of inclined planes called *talus,* in between vertical bands of *tableros*. Most structures were covered with painted stucco and decorated with large stone sculptures. Palaces and courtyards were built on top of platforms and ornamented with stone carvings and color.

Teotihuacán, the most accessible of pre-Columbian ceremonial centers, 30 mi from Mexico City, is perhaps the most impressive because of its size, design lucidity, and comparatively good condition of preservation and restoration.

Two other important centers of the Classic Period in central Mexico are Cholula and Xochicalco. In Cholula there are structures built before 900 A.D. Xochicalco, south of Cuernavaca, was active after the fall of Teotihuacán and is related to the Classic Maya period of which it probably was an outpost. It influenced Toltec architecture in the ninth and tenth centuries. Its main structure is the platform temple in which the *tableros* remain relatively plain, whereas the steep *talus* display elaborate stone carvings with some traces of color. Protruding, slanting cornices give the design a concave silhouette at each level. The temple on top is a continuation of the system.

After 800 A.D., the Toltec culture prevailed in central Mexico from the ninth to the thirteenth century. The Toltecs were elite warriors, aggressive, bent on conquering their neighbors, and adept at human sacrifices. Their capital was Tula, on Cerro del Tesoro, northeast of Teotihuacán, from which some influence is evident as well as from Chichén Itzá of the Mayas, after 1000 A.D.

The complex was not fortified, and colonnades placed at right angles are used for the first time in Mesoamerica to define a courtyard. The Main Pyramid, to the east, has a square base of about 215 ft. A northern platform forms the base for a five-tier pyramid with a colonnaded entrance. Farther north there is a ball court duplicating the one at Xochicalco, and a freestanding stone wall, the Muro de las Serpientes, with carvings depicting snakes on a continuous band over a double *talud*. Four huge monolithic figures of awesome, stylized warriors, towering 15 ft, typical of Toltec art, are now placed on top of the Main Pyramid, once the site of a temple. The whole complex was painted red, blue, and white. Tula fell prey to the Chichimecs between the twelfth and thirteenth centuries A.D. They were a group of nomadic tribes warring with each other, and eventually establishing their power in central Mexico until the rise of the Aztecs. The Chichimec history is well known through their detailed drawings on paper depicting their dynastic stories. Teyanuca and Texcoco, now in the suburbs of Mexico City, were the main religious centers. The pyramid at Teyanuca shows to best advantage the typical Mesoamerican custom of building one structure to cover the previous one, as it goes from an original edifice of 102 × 39 ft at the base and 25 ft high, to final measurements of 204 × 164 ft, rising 52 ft and topped by twin temples in a process spanning three centuries and eight consecutive pyramids.

A tribe of Chichimec origin, the Tenochka or Mexica, settled in 1350 on an island they named Tenochtitlán. Allying themselves with the Tacuba and Texcoco tribes, they formed the Aztec Confederacy and eventually they conquered a vast territory reaching to southern Mexico and parts of Central America. Tenochtitlán flourished until 1521, when it was destroyed by the Spanish conquistadores and transformed into what today is Mexico City. The lake has long dried up, and the present metropolis of 17 million people is built on it. Eyewitnesses of Tenochtitlán described it as surrounded by water and connected to the mainland by three roads directed to the north, south, and west. The main ceremonial space was enclosed by a high wall, or *coatepantli,* pierced by three main gates entering into a symmetrically designed complex in which the Gran Templo, a pyramid topped by the temples to Tlaloc and Huitzilopochtli, was the central element in the back part. At the center of the great plaza stood the pyramid and round Templo de Quetzalcóatl. The scheme was completed with colonnaded buildings, a ball court, and smaller pyramids and temples. A large model of the complex is on permanent display in the Museo Nacional de Antropología in Mexico City, depicting the Aztec capital at the height of its splendor. Outside the walls, the ruling class lived in private dwellings, amid gardens and orchards. Montezuma, the last emperor, had a palace to the south, now the site of the National Palace. Between it and the Spanish Colonial Cathedral only a few ruins remain of what once was the awesome Tenochtitlán.

Along the Gulf Coast of Mexico there are three definite areas of cultural development: the river deltas of the states of Tabasco and Veracruz, occupied by the Olmec people; the region of central Veracruz from Misquetilla to the south up to the Panuco River, home of the Totonac tribes; and north of that river, the territory occupied by the Huastecs.

The Olmecs, an ancient culture, prevailed during Preclassic times and went through three phases of development until their decline around 100 B.C. They anticipated, with their architecture and urban planning, forms and concepts of later generations. Before 1200 B.C., they built platforms and worshipped the jaguar at San Lorenzo. From 1200 B.C. to 600 B.C. they built massive clay buildings and sculpture, including the enormous monolithic stone heads, 9–10 ft high, for which they are best known. La Venta, an island on the Tonala River, seems to have been their main cultural center. It was a complex built on a north–south axis with a northern pyramid rising 115 ft, as a focal point of a system of platforms and sunken courts with clay mosaic paving. The concept of *talus* and *tableros* in pyramid design seems to have originated with the Olmecs.

It is thought that the Totonacs, who settled between the Antigua and Tuxpan rivers at the time of the Spanish Conquest, were the builders of a culture that, from the first to the eleventh centuries A.D., concentrated at El Tajín, near Papantla, considered to be as important a center as Monte Albán, Uxmal, or Copán. Through twelve building phases, the complex developed into two distinct zones: the southern section, oriented toward the cardinal points and including the famous Pirámide de los Nichos, a seven-tier structure built before 500 A.D., with low *talus, tableros* pierced by square, framed niches, and cantilevered, sloping cornices; and the Late Classic section to the north, called El Tajín Chico, with more complex buildings probably dating from 600 A.D. and after, with strong ties to Mitla and Yucatán. A poured concretelike roofing material was used here in some of the structures.

The Huastecs, established between the Mexican highlands and eastern Texas, influenced their contemporaries in the region. They were builders of pyramids and platforms of circular bases, some of which, like the one at El Ebano, may be older than the round pyramid at Cuicuilco and thus the oldest in Mesoamerica.

In southern Mexico, two civilizations occupied the region now encompassed by the states of Tehuantepec, Oaxaca and Puebla: the Zapotecs in the eastern valleys and the Mixtecs in the western highlands. Monte Albán, the capital of the Zapotecs, dates from the Formative Period. It flourished during the Classic Phase and continued along five stages through the domination of the Mixtecs and the Aztecs. Considered to be one of the greatest works of urban planning of all time, Monte Albán is organized around a great rectangular central space defined by two platforms to the north and south, three separate temples flanking the east, and a continuous row of stairs and temples to the west. At the center of the esplanade there is a rectangular platform with side stairs and temples on top, and an arrow-shaped structure pointing southwest. The Palacio de los Danzantes is so named for its stone slabs carved to depict groups of dancers in contorted positions.

Typical of Monte Albán are the wide building entrances flanked by circular columns within the span and the many stairs within wide ramplike planes topped by massive vertical *tableros* shaped like upside-down battlements. Underground tombs were developed through the centuries from simple stone cubicles to cruciform, vaulted chambers and elaborate rooms with painted walls.

Mitla, dating from about 800 A.D., was the main religious center of the Mixtecs. In contrast to Monte Albán, Mitla has no coherent master plan. It is rather a cluster of five separate complexes, each one a group of rectangular buildings around a central space. Round columns forming colonnades supporting flat roofs are typical, as are the elaborate stone mosaics covering the walls in intricate zigzag patterns. Underground tombs and the upside-down battlement motif are also characteristic of Mitla.

The Mayas, one of the most remarkable civilizations the world has ever known, expressed in their architecture a strong commitment to urban planning, a sophisticated use of external spaces, and a highly sensitive treatment of architectural elements in an impressive and prolific array of religious centers. They built their complexes, many of which are still being discovered, in three main geographical regions: the central Petén area of today's Guatemala, the river valleys of southeastern Mexico, and the plains of central and northern Yucatán.

Mayan architecture in central Petén is the oldest. Ceremonial centers were built as islands connected by causeways surrounded by lagoons. Pyramids, with inset corners, were part of a total urban concept, and temples were topped with "roof combs," slablike elements ornamented in various ways and generally resembling the back of a high chair. No columnar structures are found in the region, and the structures are built of stone cores faced with stucco. Important sites are Uaxactún, Nakún, and Tikal.

Uaxactún is known for its biaxial, symmetric pyramid dating from 100 A.D., in which the four wide stairs with large intermediate masks become the main feature of a structure that was entirely finished in stucco. At Tikal, one of the best known and best restored of Maya complexes, the scheme is composed of nine groups of plazas and courtyards. Of the Classic phase, the steep pyramid is accessible by only one set of stairs. The ball court is the only one in the Petén area, amid several temples, atop pyramids, displaying large roof combs directly over elegant square entryways. Nakum is arranged around two plazas connected by an 80 ft wide esplanade oriented on a north–south axis.

Within the surrounding valleys of the Usumacinta and Motagua rivers, the main centers of Mayan architecture are Copán, Seibal, Altar de Sacrificios, Yaxchilán, Piedras Negras, Comalcalco, and Palenque. Copán, a veritable acropolis on western Honduras, is basically a great platform on which other platforms and temples are built. Started in 465 A.D., it developed from a construction system of river boulders and mud faced with stucco in Preclassic and early Classic times, through its Classic and late Classic periods to become a sensitive arrangement of open spaces. Multileveled plazas and platforms with heavily ornamented stairs display a vast array of sculpture. The comparatively few buildings date from 600 A.D. and are built of tufa, a greenish volcanic rock, giving the site its particular coloration. The temples have carved friezes with portraiture and are devoid of roof combs.

Yaxchilán and Piedras Negras are 37 mi apart on the Usumacinta River. Yaxchilán maintains the Petén style, with platforms and pyramids with inset corners. In one structure, ca. 750 A.D., a long, corbelled vault supports a roof comb, and in unique fashion it is buttressed from the inside by transversal room divisions. Piedras Negras partakes of the Petén style as well, but it has some reminiscent features of Palenque such as Siamese twin parallel vaulting, galleried rooms, and mansardlike roof combs. Several baths with steam and dry heat conveniences have been found within the complex built in two defined sections, the Acrópolis Grande and the Acrópolis Pequeña.

Palenque, located above the floodplain of the Usumacinta River in Tabasco, was developed between 600 and 800 A.D., in frank contrast to the conservative Petén style. Typical are its temples with Siamese twin corbelled vaults, colonnaded facades, mansardlike roof combs, and wooden lintels. From Early Classic to Late Classic, Palenque became one of the most fascinating and original complexes in Mayan architecture. Remarkable buildings are El Palacio, a series of rooms for an elite and his servants, with baths and latrines with running water, and above it La Torre, a four-story square tower with an interior stair topped by a mansardlike roof. El Templo de Inscripciones, a nine-tier platform, has a temple at the summit in which 65 steps lead to an underground tomb. El Templo del Sol, ca. 692 A.D., is a beautifully proportioned temple with three doorways atop a four-tier platform terminated with a latticed roof comb.

Comalcalco shares the Palenque features. A Mayan outpost, not far from Olmec territory, it has within its site ruins of a palace with stucco reliefs and unusual corbelled vaults, typically Mayan, but built of fired brick.

In the central and northern plains, two substyles developed in what today are the states of Campeche and Yucatán: Rio Bec and Puuc. Rio Bec is characterized by temples combined with chambered palaces built on low platforms. A symmetrical treatment of lateral volumes—or avant corps—are reminiscent of the towers of a Christian church in such characteristic sites as Calakmul, Bekan, Xpuhil, and Rio Bec, all of them within 60 mi of each other in northern Campeche.

The Puuc style breaks away from the traditional Mayan forms and building techniques to almost become an independent current. Rubble structures faced with cut stone and mosaics replace the usual stucco-faced stone. Square and round columns take the place of heavy piers, and mansard roofs give way to "flying facades," centrally located, slablike roof combs.

Edzna, Uxmal, and Sayil are outstanding examples of Puuc architecture. Edzna, built over Petén type structures, partakes from both styles. Uxmal trascends its primarily Puuc style and, in such buildings as El Palacio del Gobernador, it achieves one of the architectural masterpieces of mankind. Founded in 600 A.D., it reached its peak during the ninth and tenth centuries. It is composed of clusters of pyramids forming quadrangles and temples reminiscent of Mitla for their open corners and plain facades broken only by doorways and crowned by elaborate carved stone friezes running the length of the building. Important structures are El Cuadrángulo de las Monjas, El Palomar, so called for its dovecote appearance, and La Pirámide del Adivino, an eclectic oval pyramid, 125 ft high, built from the sixth to the tenth centuries A.D.

At Sayil, corbelled chambers surround the platforms, and stone building facades are carved to simulate continuous, slender semicircular columns. Heavy round piers, capped by square capitals, support the stone door lintels.

Chichén Itzá is one of the most important archaeological sites in pre-Columbian architecture. Probably already in existence by the fifth century A.D., it was a center of the Mayan civilization in central Yucatán through three periods of development: Late Classic to A.D. 1000, Toltec Mayan to the thirteenth century, and Mayan reoccupation to the sixteenth century. These changes are expressed in several building clusters distributed in an area of about 2.25 mi^2. To the south, the Edificio de las Monjas is of Puuc style, whereas the Casa Colorada and the Casa del Venado are classic buildings. El Caracol, an astronomic observatory, is a round building on a square platform with an interior winding staircase, showing a combination of central highland and classic Mayan features. To the north, the site is entirely given to the Toltec Mayan style in such buildings as the Templo de los Guerreros with its twin serpent entrance, flanked by a colonnade; the Grupo de las Mil Columnas, with El Mercado, a peristyle atrium, defines a vast courtyard. El Castillo, a nine-tier pyramid 190 ft^2 and biaxial in its symmetry, has rounded corners, four stairs, and stone reliefs at each level in the shape of the merlons and crenels of an upside-down battlement. There is a temple at the top. All construction ceased at Chichén Itzá A.D. 1200 and the capital was moved to Mayapán, a smaller stucco reproduction of the old city in existence until about 1400 A.D.

The inexplicable collapse of the Mayas cut short an architectural style increasingly occupied with interior spaces. The use of corbelled, Siamese twin vaulting and of poured concretelike materials pointed to new structural solutions unrealized in the wake of an untimely end.

The Andes

Pre-Columbian architecture in South America developed along the Andes from Venezuela to northern Chile between the western flank of the highest mountain ranges and the Pacific coast. A practical approach toward harnessing natural forces and a willingness to achieve political unity were strong determinants differentiating Andean from Mesoamerican architecture.

The main focus of cultural activity took place in Peru along the coastal river valleys and their corresponding mountain sites, within three definite northern, middle, and southern areas, including the Bolivian highlands. In northern Peru, three important cultures developed at different times: Chavín, in today's department of Ancash, from Early Horizon times; Moche—or Mochica—near Trujillo, contemporary with Classic Mayan; and Chimú, after 1000 A.D., also near Trujillo and extending as far as Piura.

The Chavín culture built grand religious centers with walled terraced platforms of vast proportions crowned by groups of temples. Chavín de Huántar, on the Mosna River, is the best-known site, with its walled group of steep rubble platforms, temples, passages, and a sunken plaza. El Lanzón, the famed lance-shaped monolith, was found in El Castillo, the main building of the complex. Other Chavín sites are Cerro Blanco and Punkuri in the Nepeña Valley, Moxeque in the Casma Valley, and Kunturwasi in the highlands.

The Mochica developed in the region of the Nepeña valley and beyond, from approximately 350 B.C. to 900 A.D. An expansionist culture, they produced enormous pyramidal platforms, aqueducts, canals, and country residences before they were conquered by the Huari Tiahuanacu invaders. Moche, near Trujillo, is a pyramid cluster, unmodified by subsequent occupants and with the largest pyramid in South America: La Pirámide del Sol, an adobe structure 135 ft high. Arch construction, exceptional in pre-Columbian architecture, has been found in Mochica tomb vaulting and irrigation systems.

Some sites in the Lambayeque, Leche, and Trujillo river valleys seem to date after Mochica times and before the Chimú period. Examples include El Purgatorio, with some pre-Huari Tiahuanacu features, and Huaca Dragón, a walled pyramid surrounded by rooms, and with a ramp decorated with moulded mud bands.

The Chimú culture developed in the thirteenth century A.D., and eventually spread northward to Tumbes until it was absorbed by the Inca empire in 1460. The ruins of Chan Chan, their main city, occupy an area of 11 mi^2 in an accumulative building process of several generations. The urban scheme consists of 10 rectangular complexes of adobe houses arranged around courtyards and protected by high walls with very few openings. The Incas assimilated from the Chimú many of their commercial, political, and cultural systems.

In central Peru, some structures of the Preceramic Period are the earliest religious edifices in America, dating as far back as 2000 B.C. Later developments share the canons of cultures to the north and south as in Playa Grande and Cerro Culebra, where a 65-ft-long fresco depicts geometric and animal subjects.

Pachacamac was a large ceremonial center comprising colonnaded pyramids, esplanades, and platforms still intact at the time of the Spanish Conquest. Within 8 mi on the Lurín River, a rectangular scheme oriented toward the cardinal points features important structures such as the Templo del Sol, an earth mound painted in red; the Templo de Pachacamac, an older temple; and El Convento, a rose-colored stone building of Inca times.

In southern Peru, earlier settlements occurred in the Inca River Valley from 1400 B.C. to 600 A.D. From this culture, named Paracas, bottle-shaped, underground tombs remain as well as adjoining, rectangular surface burials. Beyond the mouths of the Ingenio and Palpa rivers, the famous Nazca figures, drawn on a plain 60 mi long and depicting birds and animals, constitute a gigantic unexplained effort in landscape architecture.

In the Lake Titicaca region, between Peru and Bolivia, two cultures, Pucara and Tiahuanacu, developed beginning in 500 B.C. Round floor plans are characteristic of the Pucara style. Only red stone foundations remain of their large funerary chambers. Two massive, kneeling stone figures, now at the entrance of the church of Tiahuanacu, are considered to be the oldest and most important of Pucara art.

Tiahuanacu, at an altitude of 12,500 ft above sea level, on a barren plain near the southern coast of Lake Titicaca in Bolivia, is a site that has inflamed the imagination of later cultures, but it has also fallen prey to their greed for stone. Somewhat modified through a controversial restoration scheme, it is dominated by an earthen mound, La Pirámide de Akapana, rising 50 ft and showing only traces of its original stone phasing. Next to it, a rectangular raised platform, Kalasasaya, with cut stone retaining walls, has an eastern set of monolithic stairs in front of which a smaller depressed quadrangle displays carved, gargoylelike heads protruding from their stone walls; square monoliths, some as high as 21 ft, carved with anthropomorphic motifs, have been found at the site. The Puerta del Sol, a 10 × 12 ft piece of stone carved as a gate with a frieze depicting the Sun King and 48 attendants, is one of the important pieces of pre-Columbian architecture (Fig. 1). Puma Puncu, another group to the southwest, shows ruins of a structure built with megalithic slabs, superbly carved and fitted together with bronze ties and interlocking corners. The whole complex, axial in concept and oriented toward the cardinal points, was developed between 600 B.C. and 1200 A.D.

Among the separate states formed after the fall of the Tiahuanacu culture, the Collas, in the Bolivian altiplano, created interesting funerary structures such as the perfectly shaped stone cylinders at Sillustani. One of these groups, the Incas, achieved greatness and eventually developed the largest empire in America. Masters of the larger vision, the Incas developed a practical society in which great works of engineering took priority over the purely aesthetic works of Mesoamerica. Agricultural terracing, suspension bridges, inaccessible fortresses, and admirable road systems were built in a territory extending

Figure 1. The central element of the Puerta del Sol in the ruins of Tiahuanacu, Bolivia, 600 B.C. to A.D. 1200, is inscribed in stone directly above a doorway. It is part of a frieze designed within a square grid formed by 48 secondary figures topping a plain, monolithic slab. Drawing by Juan Carlos Calderón after A. Posnanzky.

from Ecuador to the north of Chile, in an effort spanning merely 90 years from the time of their expanding drive to the arrival of the Spaniards. Cuzco, the capital, was the home of the Inca emperor and the nobility. Each monarch built his own palace and preserved the dwellings of his ancestors.

The Templo del Sol, or Coricancha, was the main religious center and although no sculpture was allowed, it was covered inside with large decorated panels of gold. Trapezoidal openings and niches, typical of Inca architecture, were the only relief in otherwise plain, sometimes circular stone walls built with incredible precision and roofed with wood and straw. Architectural excellence was achieved by means of a harmonious handling of volumes in the construction of buildings and terraces, complemented by bathing nooks; open-water ducts and falls; and monolithic solar clocks or Intihuatanas, treated in an intimate, humanistic way. Cuzco was leveled by the conquistadores, and only some walls and parts of temples remain today. Sacsahuamán, a magnificent fortress up on the hills, protected the capital with its triple-tier, megalithic zigzag

Figure 2. Machu Picchu, the lost city of the Incas, was not discovered by the Spanish conquerors and was left intact under jungle growth until Hiram Bingham set foot on it in 1911. Its breathtaking mountain setting, the natural treatment of its human-scaled spaces on a series of escalating platforms, and the contrast of its gray stone walls with the vivid green grass surrounding them, produce in the visitor an unforgettable metaphysical experience. Photograph by Juan Carlos Calderón.

bastions. Other important centers are Ollantaytambo, a walled city on the Urbamba River; Pisac on the Vilcanota River; El Kenko, a semicircular sanctuary near Cuzco; and Machu Picchu (Fig. 2), the best known and best preserved of Inca cities, discovered by Hiram Bingham in 1911. High up on a vertical cliff at the winding of the Vilcanota River, the complex constitutes the most organic scheme in pre-Columbian architecture. Its terraces, narrow stone steps, and buildings hug the mountain and play among themselves and with nature to create what is perhaps the world's most metaphysical setting.

On Lake Titicaca two islands, the Isla del Sol and the Isla de la Luna, are the sites of important religious centers. Here, the Tiahuanacu style influences the architecture of the empire with its treatment of light and shadow and its geometric designs.

SPANISH COLONIAL ARCHITECTURE

Spanish colonial architecture occurs in America as the expression of an expanding political and religious process starting from Columbus's point of landing, on to the Caribbean litoral; continuing into Mexico and Central America and some parts of the United States; and finally reaching the entirety of South America with the exception of Brazil. From 1492 to the Wars of Independence at the beginning of the nineteenth century, it responded to the constraints imposed by Catholic Spain on its colonies, to European currents of those times, to the various geographic characteristics of the vast territory, and to the still-vibrant creative energy of the indigenous cultures.

The Caribbean Region

As early as 1510, the city of Santo Domingo was laid out along the typical Spanish gridiron, which later would be the typical pattern of most cities founded elsewhere. The architecture of the Caribbean seacoast is influenced by the work of Sevillian and Castilian architects in the plateresque style, so called for its silversmithlike ornament. The cathedral in Santo Domingo, completed in 1541, is still of late Spanish Gothic style. The cathedral of Mérida, with coffered vaults and aisled plan, influenced the schemes of other churches in Cuba, Cartagena, and Caracas.

By the beginning of the seventeenth century, the vulnerability of ports such as Santo Domingo, plundered by Sir Francis Drake in 1586, forced Spain to start an era of fortress building that lasted for a century and a half, from 1600 to 1760. Architects were replaced by engineers who produced impressive structures in Panama, Cartagena de Indias, Veracruz, Portobello, and Campeche.

After 1760, and as a result of Cádiz becoming Spain's most important port, the influence of the architecture of that region was felt in the Caribbean, reaching full development in Cuba with such typical features as Arabian styled ceilings, called *Mudejar,* and scrolled brackets under transverse beams. Churches were roofed by means of crisscross arches, or *artesonado,* roofing each bay, a system invented by Alejandro Hernandez in the church of Guanabacoa, started in 1714. Pyramidal spires with dormer windows are typical of Cuban architecture of that period. The cathedral of Havana, started in 1748, with rococo influences in its interior, displays on its facade a mixture of Borrominesque and Vignolan features. Also in Havana, public buildings such as the Casa de Correos and the Casa de Gobierno, both finished in 1792, have mezzanines placed between the ground floor and the second level. In general, the Cádiz facade with its typical doorway pervades public and private buildings in the city. The influence is felt in other coastal points down to Colombia and Venezuela where some currents from the Canary Islands are recognizable.

Mexico

In Mexico and Central America, city building along with religious indoctrination followed quickly after the Conquest. In less than a century after contact, the entire Indian population had converted to Catholicism. Cities were laid out in the typical gridiron pattern around a main square, the Plaza Mayor, around which the main cathedral and, often, other churches were placed along with buildings for the government. However, at the beginning of the Conquest, plain, temporary churches were built facing a walled open space for outside worship, with open corner chapels.

Three mendicant orders took the first missionary inroads into Mexican territory. The Franciscans occupied the central and western regions on their arrival in 1542. Influenced by Sir Thomas More's *Utopia,* they concentrated mostly at the edges of the spreading culture and usually among poorer living conditions. The Dominicans were given the territory to the south of the capital, where they settled in 1526 and advanced to Oaxaca, which they eventually controlled. Their architecture tended to be massive, the result of solid construction. Finally, the Augustinians reached the region to the north and west of Mexico City in 1533, sharing some areas with the Franciscans in Michoacán. The Augustinian Order favored an ornate church style with facades along plateresque currents and didactic panels.

By 1550, local craftsmen were fully in control of Spanish building techniques. The facade of the church at Cuitzeo, for example, is signed by Juan Metl, a native artisan. Churches adopted more sophisticated features; rib vaulting, naves with aisles, choir lofts, and polygonal endings became more frequent. Cloisters acquired finely carved arched corridors and the architecture in general showed a variety of ornaments freely chosen from several styles.

By the last quarter of the sixteenth century, the influence of the mendicant orders had waned, their missionary task accomplished, and a full colonial approach to building took place in the form of cathedral design. Three great structures are typical of the period: the cathedral of Guadalajara, ca. 1618, built according to original plans, and the sister cathedrals of Puebla, ca. 1649, and Mexico City, ca. 1667, both modified sixteenth-century plans to adapt them to the basilican scheme used by Herrera in El Escorial and the cathedral of Valladolid. The dome occurs for the first time in Mexico at Mérida and most abundantly in Puebla where, by the end of the seventeenth century, 36 church domes could be counted, some of them covered with glazed tile.

From the mid-seventeenth century to 1730, styles adhered closely to Spanish canons, but differed in character between the regions to the north and south of the capital. To the north, churches displayed retables on their facades, with didactic features and polylobulated arches as in Santa Monica in Guadalajara, ca. 1733; La Profesa in Mexico City, ca. 1720; the cathedral of Chihuahua, ca. 1741; and the cathedral of Zacatecas, ca. 1752. The integrity of entablatures, cornices, and supporting members was broken, and there was an emphasis on flat foliated decoration, reminiscent of the facades of the Peruvian Andes.

To the south in Puebla, Oaxaca, and Guatemala ornament was reticulated, influenced by the stucco craftsmen of Andalusia. There was a plastic treatment of the facades and a prevalence of multicolored glazed surfaces. The church of Santo Domingo in Oaxaca shows an indigenous undercurrent despite its obvious ties to La Cartuja in Granada. In Guatemala, the influence of colored surfaces was translated to pigmented plaster techniques.

In the first third of the eighteenth century, Mexico adopted a new dynamic architectural pattern to replace the static architecture of the previous century. In this ultrabaroque period all elements were directed upward to create a moving, ascending whole (Fig. 3). The *estípite,* a supporting member of blurred outline, replaced the column and is the trademark of the period along with

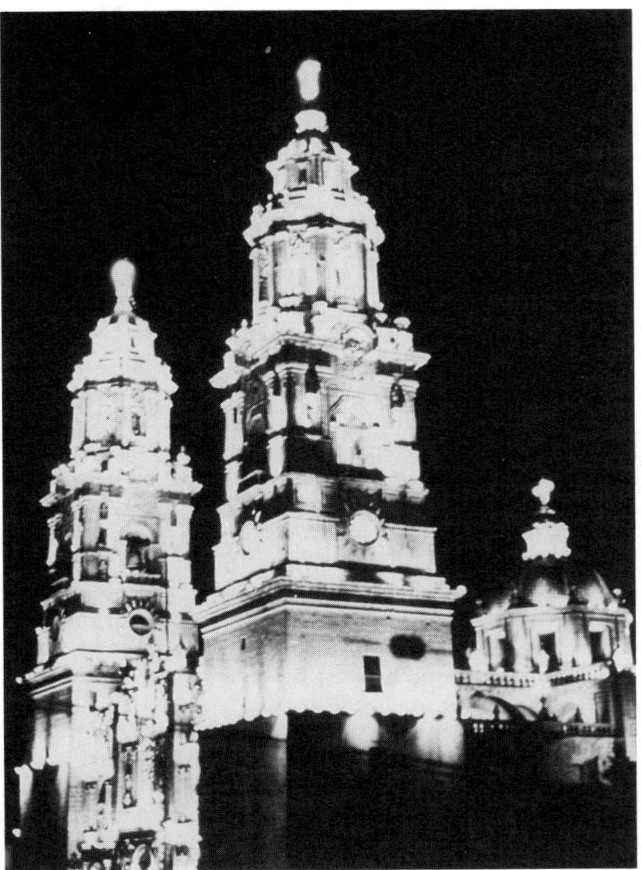

Figure 3. The Cathedral of Morelia, Mexico, 1640–1744, resplendent on the eve of a religious festivity, is still, typically, very much the center of the city's social, cultural, and spiritual activities. Its yellow buff stone carvings are modeled along a system of rectangular panels within which some biblical scenes are depicted in the didactic substyle of the baroque period. Photograph by Juan Carlos Calderón.

multicolored surfaces and massive scale. A celebration of the ultrabaroque style is the church of Santa Prisca in Taxco, ca. 1748, influencing La Valenciana in Guanajuato and the Santuario of Ocotlán in Tlaxcala with its combination of Mexican and Andalusian features. The Sagrario of the cathedral in Mexico City by Lorenzo Rodriguez is a triumph of the *estípite.*

The Mexican architect Francisco Antonio Guerrero y Torres introduced new forms in 1780, thus ending the ultrabaroque period. His Casa Valparaiso with strong intersecting arches and arched sills predicted art nouveau elements and influenced residential architecture all of the way to the pseudo-Spanish chalets of the twentieth century.

The convents of Santa Rosa and Santa Clara, built in the last years of the eighteenth century, are examples of the Querétaro school. Ornament is abstract and textured, plans are traditional and the *estípite* disappears. At the turn of the century, Mexican architects such as Francisco Tresgueras and José Ortiz de Castro adopted the neoclassic style in vogue in Europe. The Spaniard Manuel Tolsá produced the Escuela de Minería in Mexico City, considered to be the most impressive late colonial structure in Latin America; the style reached as far north as California.

Central America

The most important Spanish colonial architecture of the region exists in Guatemala but, because of the severity of earthquakes, only a few truncated examples survive from the sixteenth century. After 1650, Antigua embraced the Spanish mannerist architecture of Granada, and soon building proportions became lower and construction more massive to overcome the seismic threat.

Ornament was used profusely to cover the awkward proportions, such as on the facade of the cathedral, ca. 1690, and the church of Santa Teresa, ca. 1687. In the first decades of the seventeenth century the emphasis was on a play of volumes and massive construction. Examples are the churches of El Carmen, ca. 1728, and Santa Cruz, ca. 1731, and the Santuario at Esquipulas, the most successful structure of the period, ca. 1785. It is placed on an elevated base with four tall corner towers ending in octagons and a central dome on an octagonal drum. Jośe Manuel de Ramirez, the most influential member of a family of mestizo architects, designed the University of Antigua, rebuilt after 1763.

In 1773, the capital was moved to Guatemala City, less prone to seismic movements; it was designed in the typical gridiron pattern by the Mexican Luis Diez de Navarro. Its architecture is a return to more orthodox Spanish currents as in the church of La Merced.

Spanish South America

Spanish colonial architecture is concentrated mainly along the Andes, and generally developed in the principal centers of the vanquished Inca empire. Civil wars among feuding Spanish factions prevented the Renaissance spirit to fully develop during the sixteenth century. In the seventeenth century, architectural expressions received from Spain were already in accordance with the Counter Reformation. After 1650, a duality of styles occurred between the coast and the highlands, apparent through baroque formats on one hand, and the use of ornamented, flat surfaces on the other.

In the northern Andes, Quito, as an important center of the Vice Royalty of Nueva Granada, shared with Mexico, the capital of the Vice Royalty of Nueva España, the humanistic ideas of Charles V of Spain. The church of San Francisco in Quito, built on the ruins of the palace of the Inca Huayna Capac and completed in 1575, is the most influential church of the sixteenth century in South America. Its Italianate facade, with arched doorway flanked by double columns supporting a flat, arched entablature on brackets, and its rigidly symmetrical design constitute an image repeatedly used in colonial South American architecture. Quito, in general, followed orthodox European canons with craftsmanship equal to European standards. Elsewhere, as in Cuenca and Bogotá, these influences were quickly assimilated, and they spread throughout Nueva Granada. The Capilla del Sagrario in Bogotá, ca. 1689, features what may be the first spiral or Solomonic columns in South America. By the eighteenth century, Quito gave way to Popoyán as the focus of colonial architecture in Nueva Granada.

Lima, the capital of the Vice Royalty of Peru, has vestiges of sixteenth-century buildings such as the cloisters of Santo Domingo and San Francisco. Some late gothic arches exist in Chiclayo, and in the highlands some adobe chapels of that time are built with balconied facades, simple wooden roofs, and a walled space, sometimes with open corner chapels. In Alto Peru, now Bolivia, Sucre and Potosí were the main colonial centers, the latter a populous mining emporium of great importance for the Spanish empire. Several sixteenth-century churches exist in both places with aisleless naves, geometric Mudejar ceilings, and walled front courtyards. In Sucre, the churches of San Lázaro (ca. 1585), San Agustín (ca. 1581), and San Francisco are typical examples.

Roughly contemporary with Mexico, three cathedrals are the most important structures of the period in Sucre, Cuzco, and Lima. The cathedral of Sucre, started in 1561, with an aisled scheme and rib vaulting over the transept and sanctuary, was completed in 1692 by José Gonzales Merguete. Francisco Becerra designed the cathedrals of Cuzco and Lima, in 1598, following the Spanish scheme of nave and aisles of equal height and the unornamented style typical of pre-Escorial architecture.

The plain, almost timid style of colonial architecture in Peru before 1650 gave way to two strong coexisting currents: the mestizo style in Arequipa and Potosí; and the Cuzco–Lima axis, a movement of mutual feedback lasting until 1800. The mestizo style developed as a result of the mixture of American and Americanized races, their distance from the cultural sources, regional idiosyncracies, and, above all, a remnant of creative pre-Columbian energy forcefully expressing itself through Spanish forms and ornamentation, and transcending them. In Arequipa, church facades are treated as embroidery, the pebblelike ornamentation catching the light and producing a bubbly effect. The monastery of Santo Domingo, ca. 1677, is the first example of the style, followed by La Compañía, San Agustín, and La Casa Ugarteche. Outside Arequipa, churches in Caima, Chihuata, Paukarpata, and Yanahuari carry the style into the middle of the eighteenth century. In Potosí, the facade treatment is equally intricate, but the emphasis is on the deep incising of the stone, thus relying more on the shadow effect as in wood carving. The most accomplished facade is the one of the church of San Lorenzo, ca. 1728, with a portal set back under a plain stone arch in frank contrast to the totally carved surface. Solomonic columns flank the entrance and end in semicircular lunettes, typical of many churches in Potosí. Elsewhere, on the high plateau around Lake Titicaca, the mestizo style is somewhat influenced by Cuzco as in the churches of San Juan de July, Pomata, and San Francisco in La Paz, ca. 1722, where the Indian influence is very much in evidence in the isolated interior rectangles of the dome and the carved faces at the base possessing all of the telluric energy of pre-Columbian cultures.

The cathedral of Cajamarca in Peru is the best example of the mestizo style, though combined with Cuzco elements. The portal of San Martín in Vilque, completed in 1793, formally ends it.

The Cuzco style, started after the earthquake of 1651,

Figure 4. The Jesuit church of La Compañía, 1668, in Cuzco, Peru, is one of the finest examples of Latin American baroque architecture. Many of its features were later used in Europe in such religious structures as the church of Santa María del Popolo in Rome, 1658; the cathedrals of Granada, 1667, and Jaén, and the church of El Salvador in Seville, 1711. Photograph by Juan Carlos Calderón.

creates a true metropolitan look and starts the exchange of influences between this city and Lima. In the retable entrance of the cathedral, lateral pilasters emphasize an upward motion accentuated by broken pediments and interlocking arches and segments of arches. The Jesuit church of La Compañía, 1651–1658 (Fig. 4), one of the glories of Spanish colonial architecture, influences the Lima style and antecedes Bernini's Santa Maria del Popolo in Rome with its trilobulated retable, and the facade of Granada's cathedral with its upward dynamism. It also influences church architecture in Europe with such features as the square towers ending in octagonal forms with turrets at the resulting corners, and with the most original flattened ovals of the belfry, which frame the bells and make them appear suspended in space.

Lima's dialogue with Cuzco starts with the church of San Francisco, rebuilt and finished in 1674, showing the influence of La Compañía. The elegance of the capital reflects itself in such buildings as the cloister of San Francisco, completed in 1674, and in turn the second Cuzco style, an intense wave of church building from 1673 to 1699, nurtures itself from the coastal currents in buildings such as San Sebastián (1673–1678), Belén (ca. 1688), and San Pedro (ca. 1696). In the first years of the eighteenth century, Lima once again absorbed the style of the highlands with its flat facades and broken pediments in the churches of La Merced (ca. 1704), and San Agustín (ca. 1720). This is in frank opposition to a new current in which protruding elements are extended perpendicularly to the facade, and in residential architecture, retablelike entrances with curved cantilevered features and screened balconies become the typical elements of eighteenth-century Spanish colonial domestic design.

After 1750, Italian concepts of stage design influenced churches such as Las Nazarenas, designed by the Viceroy Manuel Amat. Curved forms appear as well as rococo features and some influence from current Andalusian concepts. In the highlands and along Catalán patterns, Fray Miguel de Sanahuja designed in Potosí the last cathedral of Spanish colonial America. The construction began in 1809, coinciding with the first serious demand for independence from Spain. By its completion in 1830, the South American republics were no longer part of the Spanish empire. In Argentina, the most important structures were built along the route from Lima to Buenos Aires. The work of Jesuit architects is evident in the churches of La Compañía in Córdoba, ca. 1645; San Francisco in Santa Fe, ca. 1680; and San Ignacio in Buenos Aires, ca. 1712. However, the most significant building of the region is the cathedral of Córdoba, started at the end of the seventeenth century by José Gonzales Merguete, with vaults and main entrance by Andres Blanqui and turreted dome by Vicente Muñoz. Residential architecture in Buenos Aires and Córdoba was at the time an extension of the stuccoed entrances of single-story houses in Cádiz, with their vertical elements extending beyond the roof edge.

The Missions

One of the most extraordinary and self-sufficient schemes the Western world has ever known was conducted in Argentina, Brazil, Paraguay, and Bolivia by the Jesuit Order from 1609 to 1767. Created by Diego de Torres for the education of the Guaraní Indians within the context of their own tribal lives, it reached admirable levels of social, cultural, and religious interaction. Responding to communal life, its architecture went from clusters of wooden sheds supported by posts with nonbearing adobe walls, to elaborate churches with vaulted stone structures.

This remarkable social experiment was eventually abolished by the crowns of Spain and Portugal but, although all the mission activities have long disappeared, several buildings still remain along with some of the cultural traits assimilated centuries ago.

Brazilian Colonial Architecture

Brazil, colonized by Portugal, maintained a close tie with the architecture of the mother country. Church designs before 1740 followed an elongated octagonal form in nave schemes. At the church of Nossa Senhora da Gloria de Onteiro, for example, the long octagonal nave has a double wall system allowing for private passages leading to pulpits. Similar designs occur at San Pedro dos Clerigos in

Recife, 1782, and at the Pilar at Ouro Preto, 1772. At the Conceicao da Praia in São Salvador, by Manuel Cardoso de Saldanha, the diagonally placed towers antecede Portuguese churches in expressing the octagonal space externally. After 1750, Minas Gerais became the focus of Brazilian architecture as curved, deceivingly wide facades cover narrower naves with undulating walls. Such is the concept for the Bon Jesus de Matozinhos at Congonas do Campo, 1770; San Francisco at Ouro Preto, 1776; San Pedros dos Clerigos at Mariana, 1771; and the Rosario Chapel at Ouro Preto, 1776, by Francisco Lisboa, called Aleijadinho, who is also the architect of São Jao d'el Rei, 1774, a church with a flat facade and towers wrapping around its flanks.

THE NINETEENTH AND TWENTIETH CENTURIES

The French Influence

The reaction against Spanish rule, which culminated in the independence of Spain's American colonies in the early 1800s, created a rejection among the budding Latin American republics of all that was Iberian. Looking elsewhere for architectural canons, they found them in France, which had already inspired them politically throughout their long and bloody wars with Spain.

Although neoclassicism remained a dominant current until midcentury, the First French Empire, and especially the Second, had great influence in Latin America. As early as 1816, Brazil, untouched by revolution and enjoying the presence in Rio de Janeiro of the Portuguese court (established there to escape from Napoleon's conquests), imported a group of French architects, Victor Grandjean de Montigny among them. De Montigny eventually became the author of such important projects as the Imperial Academy of Fine Arts, dating from 1825; the Market; and the Custom House. Later in the century, Brazilian architects following the French tradition produced several significant buildings, among them the Itamaraty Palace designed by J. M. Rebelo in 1851, and the National Library, the National Senate, and the Municipal Theater by Pereira Passos, veritable monuments placed along Rio's haussmanian boulevards. In Chile, C. F. Brunet Debaines and other French architects employed by the government had great influence on the architecture of that country. In Mexico City, the Paseo de la Reforma, the central avenue of the metropolis, was traced by the Emperor Maximilian's architects as a great 200-ft-wide European boulevard. It was flanked by private mansions more Parisian than their contemporaries in Boston or Newport. In Peru, La Colmena, a commercial complex with pavilions and mansard roofs, compared favorably with the Sotorvet in Copenhagen or the Galerij in Amsterdam. Elsewhere, and especially in cities where Spanish architecture had never been fully developed, as in Montevideo, Uruguay, intense urban growth closely followed the concepts of the Second French Empire. By the end of the nineteenth century, some religious architecture went through the paces of a pseudo neo-Gothic exercise totally alien to Latin American architecture, and generally showed no attempt to revive the Gothic style's structural integrity.

From 1900, and well into the first three decades of the twentieth century, an eclectic approach to architectural design was heavily influenced, first by art nouveau and eventually by art deco ornamentation. The Palacio de Bellas Artes in Mexico City, designed by Adam Boari in 1903 and finished in 1934 by Federico Mariscal, constitutes a curious combination of these currents with its Tiffany-glass stage curtain and ceiling in the auditorium, its Aztecoid art deco motifs in the great foyer, and its impressive eclectic facade.

MODERN ARCHITECTURE

Several Latin American architects had adopted the grammar of modern architecture by early in the twentieth century. In 1930, Juan O'Gorman designed the Diego Rivera House–Studio in Mexico City along functionalist, Bauhaus-like lines; Gregorio Warchavchic's house in São Paolo, Brazil, also dates from that year, foreshadowing the architecture of Luis Barragán. Julio Villamajo's unique architecture influenced younger professionals beyond Uruguay's frontiers, and is just now being appreciated fully. In Colombia, Leopoldo Rother designed the campus of the Ciudad Universitaria in 1936 using rationalistic principles. In Bolivia, Emilio Villanueva, departing from his previous eclectic designs, experimented with pre-Columbian themes and modern structures in the Hernando Siles Stadium and the master plan for the Universidad de San Andres, both in La Paz, somewhat preceding postmodernistic forms.

The Influence of Le Corbusier

Le Corbusier visited Argentina in 1929, and in 1936 he was invited to intervene as a consultant in the design of the Ministry of Education and Health Building in Rio de Janeiro. By 1948, when he produced an urban scheme for Bogotá, Colombia, he had already influenced the work of most young Latin American architects. Some of the most talented adopted his theories and went on to formulate the basis for what they hoped could become a truly Latin American architecture. In Brazil, Oscar Niemeyer achieved international recognition through his imaginative use of reinforced concrete, his handling of curvilinear forms, and his brilliant structural solutions. These qualities are expressed in buildings such as the church of Sao Francisco at Pampulha, 1939; the Palacio de la Industria, built in Rio de Janeiro in 1953; the Yacht Club in Pampulha, 1961; in his designs for Brasília (Fig. 5), and the various projects he executed for Israel, France, Algiers, and Italy during the 1970s. Niemeyer was awarded the 1988 Pritzker prize with Gordon Bunshaft of the United States.

Lucio Costa designed Brasília, the new capital, in 1957 in a daring attempt to achieve a total concept in the urban organization of a new city. Built at once along two intersecting main spines, and with the Plaza de los Tres Poderes as its focal point, the city is too dispersed over vast expanses of grassy flatlands; as a result, it lacks the scale essential to create a sense of human interaction. It is

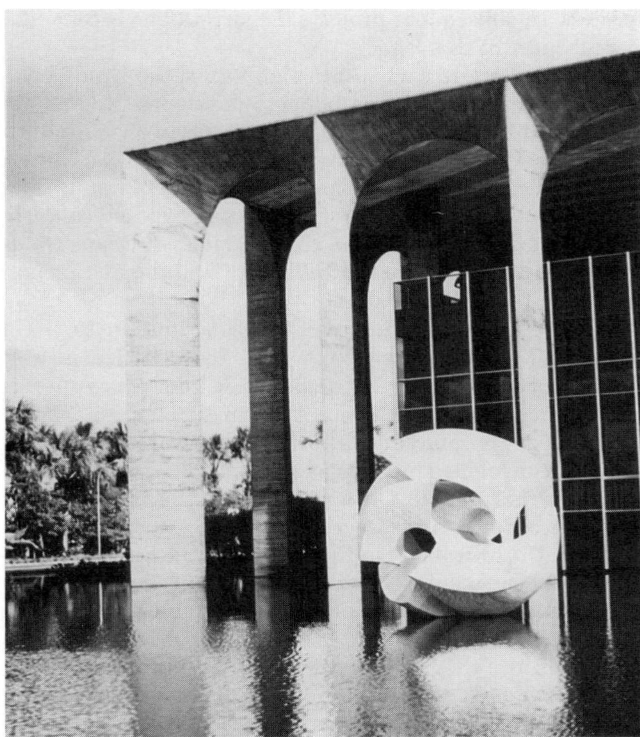

Figure 5. The Foreign Office Building in Brasília, the new capital of Brazil, was designed by Oscar Niemeyer. The exposed concrete structure is a series of arches developing from a surrounding shallow pool and reaching the full height of the building. The interior spaces are subdivided independently of the structural system. Photograph by Juan Carlos Calderón.

nevertheless an impressive architectural experiment, and one that consolidated Brazil's reputation for being at the vanguard of world architecture.

Roberto Burle Marx, considered to be one of the most important landscape architects of the twentieth century, participated actively from 1939 in almost all significant projects in Brazil. Through the use of undulating shapes, he created a highly original language of landscape design, strongly influencing the work of architects in Brazil and elsewhere and relaxing the rigidity of many rationalistic schemes. Le Corbusier's concepts are also evident in the buildings of E. A. Reidy, in particular in the serpentine scheme for El Pedregulho, an apartment complex built in Rio de Janeiro in 1952, and in the Museum of Modern Art, also in Rio.

In Argentina, the Austral Group was formed in the early 1940s by a group of architects, disciples of Le Corbusier, who, although loyal to the master's ideas, deplored the dehumanizing aspects of abstract rationalism, and rejected the idea of a building considered as a machine for living. Their intent not to fall into aesthetic prejudices and skin-deep cliches was realized in significant projects: Antonio Bonet designed La Solana del Mar, a hotel–restaurant in Uruguay; Jorge Ferrari Hardoy and Juan Kurchan were the authors of Virrey del Pino, an apartment building built in Buenos Aires in 1943; Amancio Williams supervised the construction of the Curruchet House by Le Corbusier in La Plata in 1943, and in 1945 he built his famed Bridge House in Mar del Plata.

The influence of Le Corbusier in Mexico was somewhat modified by the strong currents of its indigenous culture, and by the intense search for national expression. The overwhelming presence of the great muralists, Orozco, Rivera, and Siqueiros, produced around 1950 an architecture in which, typically, great mosaic designs, or stone and metal bas reliefs, covered entire facades of otherwise rationalistic structures. Criticized at the time for lacking the purist character of contemporary buildings elsewhere, this utterly Mexican answer to the desire for a national style has survived the test of time remarkably well.

The master plan for the Ciudad Universitaria in Mexico City was designed in 1953 by Mario Pani, Enrique del Moral, and Carlos Lazo. Within it some of the best examples of the muralist tradition can be found, in such buildings as the Biblioteca Central, by Juan O'Gorman, Gustavo Saavedra, and Juan Martinez de Velasco and the Escuela de Medicina and the Estadio Olímpico by Augusto Perez Palacios, Raul Salinas, and Jorge Bravo Jimenez, with murals by Rivera. The synthesis of mural and building occurs in these structures with varying degrees of success, but it produces nevertheless a powerful architectural statement.

Apart from Le Corbusier's enveloping influence, Felix Candela stands out as one of Mexico's most lucid architectural thinkers. His work, rather than being shaped by the currents of his time, reflects the logic and imagination of an architect–engineer. The concrete shell structures he designed for the Cosmic Rays Pavilion at the University of Mexico in 1952, and the Produce Market in Coyoacán in 1954, are but two of many such buildings. As did Pier Lugi Nervi in Italy, Candela led the way in the field of geometric forms in which aesthetics and engineering are inseparable elements.

Carlos Raul Villanueva is Venezuela's most outstanding architect. His work, spanning from 1928 to 1975, ranks among the best of the century. Although influenced by Le Corbusier, Villanueva displayed such a variety of ideas and forms in the solution of every one of his projects that his architecture eventually transcended its origins. His design for El Silencio, an urban renewal complex built in Caracas in 1941, had a total of 33,000 units and was the first of its kind in Latin America. Similar projects ensued at El Paraiso in 1952, Cerro Piloto in 1954, and Veintitrés de Enero in 1955. The Ciudad Universitaria in Caracas is Villanueva's best-known work. Developed from the late 1940s to 1965, it covers five hundred acres, has over 1 mi of covered walks, and displays a great number of outstanding works of art by such artists as Leger and Vasarely. Acoustic panels designed by Alexander Calder are integrated into the great space of the Aula Magna, an auditorium seating 2600 persons. In the Escuela de Arquitectura, the use of vibrant colors and textures are typical of Villanueva's architecture.

Chile's Emilio Duhart studied at Harvard with Gropius, worked with I. M. Pei, and in 1952 worked with Le Corbusier. In 1960, he won a competition for the ONU–CEPAL Building. Completed in 1966, the complex is the successful culmination of a Chilean rationalistic trend that started in 1943 with the architecture of Mauricio Despouy, Enrique Gebhard, and Juan Martinez. It is also one of the last buildings designed under a strong Corbusian influence in Latin America.

Le Corbusier's urban plan for Bogotá, Colombia, was completed in 1951. It proved to be inadequate, as it tried to impose a linear scheme on a basically radial city. The influence first of his rationalism, and later of his sculptural brutalism is evident in the Sala de Conciertos of the Biblioteca Luis Arango in Bogotá, designed by German Semper in 1963; in the apartment complex of El Polo, Bogotá, 1965, by Rogelio Salmona and Guillermo Bermudez; and in the early work of Fernando Martinez.

Other Latin American countries were no less influenced by rationalist architecture. In Cuba, for example, Aquilo Capablanca's building for the Office of the Comptroller, completed in Havana in 1954, closely followed the concepts of the Ministry of Education Building in Rio de Janeiro. In general, at least the adoption of the *brise soleil,* the modulated facades, and the long rectangular building on pilotis were very much apparent throughout the continent. From the second half of the 1960s on, Latin American architecture has been influenced by different currents of thought. The concepts of Mies van der Rohe are particularly apparent in high-rise buildings which, unfortunately, seldom approach the purity of their source. A lack of urban planning and an emphasis on the profit motive have blighted most major cities, destroying their once harmonious fabric, and, for the most part, wasting the opportunities that arose during the building boom of the 1970s. In places such as Havana, Cuba, where the center of town was left intact, new housing developments on the outskirts are generally unattractive and dehumanizing. Serious attempts to produce significant architecture have not been lacking in the last two decades, however, and many important projects have been completed during this time.

Brutalism

Brutalism seems to permeate contemporary Latin American architecture: its harsh treatment of volumes and its predilection for exposed concrete are a logical sequel to Le Corbusier's late manner of design, embracing some of the architectural language of Paul Rudolph and Louis Kahn.

In Mexico, Pedro Ramirez Vasquez designed in 1965 the Museo Antropológico in Mexico City, an impressive building housing the country's priceless pre-Columbian pieces, and surrounding a large, open rectangular courtyard partially covered by a gigantic umbrellalike cantilevered fountain. His project for the Palacio Legislativo, also in the capital, dates from 1982. Abraham Zabludovsky and Teodoro Gonzales de Leon have developed a grammar of design based on great open atriums and diagonal spaces defined by oversized concrete trellises and lintels. Their most well known buildings are the Colegio de Mexico, 1977; the Museo Rufino Tamayo, 1982; and the Universidad Pedagógica, 1984. Jorge Legorreta's Hotel Camino Real, 1968, reflects in its morphology and colors the architecture of Luis Barragán, who was a consultant for the project. In subsequent projects, Legorreta has become the torchbearer of this legacy.

A throwback to early Corbusian forms, the Unidad Nonoalco–Tlatelolco, a large housing development, was designed by Mario Pani in 1960, and progressively built until 1978. The Centro Cultural Universitario by Oscar Nuñez, Arcadio Ortiz Esprín, Manuel Medina, and Antonio Treviño is a cultural center in which strong exposed concrete volumes are balanced by a rolling, casual landscape treatment. Outstanding are the Biblioteca and the auditorium building, the Sala Nezahualcoyotl.

In Argentina, Clorindo Testa's contribution to Latin American architecture spans four decades. He is best known for his building for the Banco de Londres y America del Sur, completed in Buenos Aires in 1966, a remarkable exercise in the play and interaction of large spaces and volumes enveloped by a perforated facade of exposed concrete. In his Centro Cultural, and in the buildings for the Banco Nacional de Desarollo, all done in Buenos Aires in 1985, the brutalistic individualism of the Banco de Londres has been subdued to conform to a strong shift toward contextualism. His ambitious project for the Biblioteca Nacional is still to be completed. Justo Solsona treats his buildings as if they were contained by an outer skin, giving few clues about their interior spaces, as can be seen in the Fate Building in Buenos Aires, 1966. In association with a group of younger architects, the MGSSV cooperative, Solsona has produced some of the most refreshing contemporary work in Argentina. Bank buildings such as the Banco Municipal de Préstamo; the Banco de la Ciudad, 1968; and Condor Branch, 1973 as well as residences such as the grass-covered La Lucila, 1973, testify to the group's versatility.

Venezuela's capital city, Caracas, has experienced an impressive, if not well-planned, rate of growth since the 1960s. Proliferation of high-rise living has resulted in apartment buildings housing over 35% of the population. Vega and Galia, Jose Sanabria, and Dick Bornhorst have used a new rationalistic–brutalistic approach, as well as drawing from previous Latin American sources for their designs. Miguel Galia, whose architectural practice goes back to the 1950s, is the author of the Banco de Caracas and the building for Seguros del Orinoco, 1971, in which there is a successful interplay of voids and solid brick surfaces. Sisso Shaw and Associates produced the master plan for Parque Central, an ambitious 16-h project that includes two 56-story office high-rises, four 49-story apartment buildings, a hotel, shopping centers, banks, plazas, and cultural facilities. The landscape scheme is by Roberto Burle Marx. The Teatro Teresa Carreño, a multipurpose cultural conglomerate by Tomás Lugo Marcano and J. Sandoval Parra, was completed in 1983. Its hexagonal grid, within which spaces and volumes are successfully handled, permits an architectural unity that makes the building one of the most completely integrated performing arts complexes anywhere.

The leading role of Brazilian architecture during the 1950s and 1960s, which culminated in the construction of Brasília, produced as its aftermath a tendency toward diminishing the importance of the master architect in favor of responding to the many different local conditions of such a large and varied country. Villanova Artigas, whose long career trajectory started with organic residential schemes in the 1930s, and who later based his architecture on functionalism and brutalism, designed the School of Architecture Building in São Paolo in 1969 and the bus terminal at Jau in 1973. In Recife, Acacio Gil Borso has formed young architects along vernacular parameters and trained them in local mud wall construction techniques. In Fortaleza, Jose Liberal de Castro and Neudsen Braga founded the School of Architecture. In Manaos, Severino Mario Porto received the Brazilian Architect's Award in 1978 for a country house emphasizing climate control. Several buildings were completed in Brasília after 1966; outstanding among them are the Sports Center Building by Icaro Castro Melo, the large Public Servants Building by Pedro Meilo Saravia, and the Taguatinga Hospital by Jao Figueiras Lima.

In Colombia, Rogelio Salmona took advantage of local craftsmanship to build exposed-brick structures for residential complexes such as El Parque, 1972, and San Cristóbal, 1976, both in Bogotá. His Museo de Arte Moderno, also in the capital, dates from 1975. The National Prize of Architecture was given in 1973 to the Auditorium of the Universidad Nacional by Eugenia Cardozo. Reminiscent of the Berlin Philharmonic Concert Hall, it houses 1600 people in a large space fully paneled in wood.

In Peru, brutalism strongly dominated the architecture of the 1970s, mainly in such government buildings as Petro Peru, the Ministerio de Minería by Rodrigo, Cruchaga, and Soyer; the Ministerio de Industria y Turismo by P. Arana; and the Ministerio de Guerra by Ibérico y Tanaca, all based on schemes in which a play of heavy, exposed concrete volumes tends to emphasize the tops of the structures in contrast to the large expanses of plain, darkly tinted glass below. In the 1980s, softer forms are evident in the high-rises housing banking and financial institutions such as the Financiera Peruinvest by F. Vella, the Banco Continental de Lima, the Banco de Crédito del Peru by J. Crouse and J. Paez, and the Centro Commercial Las Americas by W. Weberhofer, with its slender, curvilinear tower totally clad in mirrored glass.

In Bolivia, a period of intense building construction took place between 1972 and 1980, which, although it totally changed the scale of the city of La Paz, produced only a few buildings of architectural value. Typically brutalistic with some local undertones are the Escuela Normal Superior Simón Bolivar in La Paz by Rodolfo Alborta and Ricardo Perez Alcalá; the campus for the Universidad Tecnica de Oruro by Franklin Anaya and Gustavo Medeiros, not completed; and the Biblioteca Central and the Escuela de Agronomia at the University of San Simón in Cochabamba by Jorge Aramburu and Oscar Gonzales Tellez, 1973. Following international canons, Luis Zúñiga designed the building for the Banco de Brazil and the Progreso Apartments, both in La Paz, and the Escuela Enrique Finot in Santa Cruz. Also in Santa Cruz, Sergio Antelo is the author of the powerful exposed concrete structure for the Estación de Autobuses.

In Ecuador, also within a brutalist frame, the church of La Dolorosa in Quito, by Milton Barragán, 1978, cuts a bold silhouette against the sky with its arrangement of strong, irregular, diagonal planes. The condominium building in Quito Tenis by Lodono, Uribe, and Swarkoff, 1984, is reminiscent of Louis Kahn's architecture in the treatment of its rectangular brick volumes. The building for the Comision de Valores by Jacome and Wappenstein, 1980, also in Quito, is a reticulated high-rise of assertive, almost foreboding solidity.

Organicism

The concepts of organic architecture have appealed to a number of Latin American architects throughout the years as a reaction against the dehumanizing effects of rationalism, although in some cases, as with Villanova Artigas in Brazil, the change in design philosophy took place in reverse, from organicism to functionalism. In 1951, Bruno Zevi visited Latin America and gave a series of lectures on organicism, and as early as 1956 Juan O'Gorman disowned his previous work and built his own house at El Pedregal in Mexico City using an utterly naturalistic approach. Constantin Nechodoma introduced the concept of the prairie house in Puerto Rico, and Henry Klumb, disciple of Frank Lloyd Wright, based his practice on his Taliesin experience. In 1961, Sergio Bernardes built a house for himself, perched on a hill overlooking the ocean in Gavea, Rio de Janeiro, using stone and wood, with a dynamic cantilevered deck and a pool. In Argentina, Horacio Baliero designed a residence in 1961 in San Isidro, Buenos Aires, reminiscent of Wright's Robie House. Rubén Pesci, author of many residences, used the concepts of a centralized hearth generating the outward-going spaces, long, horizontal planes, and built-in furniture. Eladio Dieste, an engineer by training, designed the acclaimed church of La Atlántida in Montevideo, Uruguay, in 1958, using brick and concrete to produce a curvilinear building in which the marriage of whimsical form and logical structure places it alongside the intuitive work of Gaudi and creates a fascinating organic space, rich in texture and feeling. Fernando Martinez, a functionalist turned organicist, designed the first truly organic project in Colombia, the Escuela Emilio Cifuentes at Facatativa, which was the winner of the Colombian Architectural Bienal of 1962. Later, Martinez went back to more geometrical solutions. Anibal Moreno's Escuela de Enfermería at the Universidad Javeriana in Bogotá, 1967, is a lucid, organic brick building reaching out to the landscape, and well integrated with it. His Instituto Colombiano de Educación, done in the 1970s, is both organic and contextual. Rogelio Salmona's latest buildings evoke the organic forms of Wright and Aalto.

At the onset of the Cuban revolution, Ricardo Porro designed the buildings for the Escuela de Danza Moderna and the Escuela de Artes Plasticas. Completed in Havana in 1965, they are a fascinating complex in which brick domes are organized along meandering brick, vaulted, open corridors. Its totally Caribbean character and the wholesomeness of its structure could have started an architectural language symbolic of the new order, but, as

Figure 6. The Hansa Building, in La Paz, Bolivia, designed in 1975 by Juan Carlos Calderón, exemplifies the intense architectural activity that took place in Latin America during the building boom of the 1970s. Photograph by Enrique Jaúregui.

happened with the constructivists in Russia, Porro was publicly denounced; he left Cuba in 1965.

In Bolivia, Juan Carlos Calderón was awarded the grand prize of the first Bienal of Architecture in 1987 for the totality of his work. His concepts on time and motion as elements of design are expressed in projects such as the Hansa Building, 1980 (Fig. 6); the Illimani Building, 1981; the Contextual Jesuit Residence, 1982; and the Ministry of Communications Building, 1988, all in La Paz. His disciples formed the S4D Society, and they have produced some important structures, outstanding among them the La Salle School in La Paz, 1982, by Carlos Adriazola, Fernando Montes, and Carlos Ramirez.

In Mexico, Agustin Hernandez produced some of his country's most original contemporary architecture. The building for the Escuela Del Ballet Folklorico, 1968, and several residences testify to his highly imaginative use of organic concepts. His office, built in 1978 on a very steep hill bordered by a hairpin road in a suburb of Mexico City, cantilevers daringly into space from the top of a tree-trunklike vertical element in an impressive play of geometric volumes.

Postmodern Architecture

Postmodernism, as known in Europe and the United States, is a movement that has not strongly influenced the architecture of Latin America. Perhaps because eclecticism has been a prevalent attitude in much that has been built since the Spanish Conquest and because the notion of integrity of structure has very seldom been a strong determinant (even during the functionalist period), watered-down versions of by now overused postmodernistic clichés are being used only sporadically. If they produce in the observer an overdue sense of place, they fail to evoke, however, the sense of soul that previous similar exercises have so whimsically achieved. Within this current, but with a more profound sense of architecture, are some younger professionals, such as Miguel Angel Roca and Jose I. Diaz in Argentina; Larrain, Murtinho and Associates, Luhrs, Muzard and Associates, and Vergaro, Bravo in Chile; Celina Bentata, Helene de Garay, Gorka Dorrosonro, and Jesus Teneiro in Venezuela; and Juvenal Baraco in Peru.

Luis Barragán

The quest for a true Latin American architecture in general, and for national expressions in particular, has occupied the attention of many Latin American architects in this century, but even though architects in Brazil and Mexico achieved widespread recognition for their energetic creativity in the 1950s and 1960s, their design concepts clearly originated abroad. Luis Barragán, on the contrary, is the exceptional artist–architect who has singlehandedly produced architectural forms that are both indigenous to his native Mexico and universal, at once utterly contemporary and timeless. His brilliant colors, his metaphysical spaces, and his serene originality, expressed in works such as the stables at Las Arboledas and the Capilla de las Capuchinas, make him one of the most important architects of this century. Winner of the Pritzker Prize in 1980, Barragán has achieved international acclaim and has had an enormous influence among the younger generation of architects in Mexico. He has fired their imagination and has shown to them, and indeed to all, that the architectural heritage of Latin America is anchored far deeper than the theatrics of the Second French Empire, the strong influence of the modern masters, or the pastiche of the postmodern style. It shares, rather, metaphysical spaces with the severity of the Spanish cloisters, and transcendental mysteries with pre-Columbian America. The future of Latin American architecture seems to point to Barragán's vibrancy, but also to the unmovable solidity of his timeless volumes.

BIBLIOGRAPHY

General References

G. Ekholm, *Ancient Mexico and Central America,* New York, 1970.

G. Gasparini and L. Margolies, *Inca Architecture,* Bloomington, 1980.

G. Kubler, *The art and architecture of ancient America,* Harmondsworth, Penguin Books, 1962.

D. Heyden and P. Gendrop, *Pre-Columbian Architecture of Mesoamerica,* New York, 1975.

J. G. Lumbreras, *The Peoples and Cultures of Ancient Peru,* Washington, D.C., 1974.

I. Marquina, *Arquitectura prehispanica,* Mexico, 1951.

J. A. Mason, *The Ancient Civilizations of Peru,* Harmondsworth, 1957.

P. A. Means, *Ancient Civilizations of the Andes,* New York, 1931.

H. J. Spinden, *Ancient Civilizations of Mexico and Central America,* New York, 1928.

D. Angulo Iniguez, E. Marco Dorta, and M. J. Buschiazzo, *Historia del arte hispano-americano,* 3 Vols., Barcelona, 1945–1956.

M. J. Buschiazzo, *Historia de la arquitectura colonial en Iberoamerica,* Buenos Aires, 1961.

P. Kelemen, *Baroque and Rococo in Latin America,* New York, 1951.

G. Kubler and M. Soria, *Art and Architecture in Spain and Portugal and Their American Dominions: 1500–1800,* Baltimore, 1959.

R. C. Smith in H. V. Livermore, ed., *Portugal and Brazil, an Introduction,* Oxford, 1953.

M. Toussaint, *Arte colonial en Mexico,* 2d ed., Mexico, 1962.

H. Wethey, *Colonial Architecture and Sculpture in Peru,* Cambridge, Mass., 1949.

F. Bullrich, *Nuevos caminos de la arquitectura Latinoamerica,* Blume, Barcelona, 1969.

F. Bullrich, *Arquitectura Latinoamericana, 1930–1970,* Sudamericana, Buenos Aires, 1969.

L. Castedo, *A History of Latin American Art and Architecture, from pre-Columbian Times to the Present,* Praeger, New York, 1969.

P. E. Damaz, *Art in Latin American Architecture,* Reinhold, New York, 1956.

A. Garcia, "Colombia: Medio Siglo de Historia Contemporanea," in *America Latina: Historia de Medio Siglo,* Siglo XXI, Mexico, 1979.

R. Gutierrez, *Arquitectura y urbanismo en Iberoamerica,* Catedra, Madrid, 1983.

H. R. Hitchcock, *Latin American Architecture since 1945,* New York, 1955.

W. Sanderson, *International Handbook of Contemporary Developments in Architecture,* Greenwood Press, Westport, Conn., 1981.

See also Barragán, Luís

Juan Carlos Calderón
La Paz, Bolivia

LATROBE, BENJAMIN H.

Benjamin Henry Latrobe was born in Fulneck, Yorkshire, England in May 1764, and died of yellow fever in New Orleans, Louisiana in 1820. His parents, both Moravians, were noted educators. His Irish father, Benjamin, a school headmaster, was well known as an educator, scholar, and musician; his mother, born Margaret Antes in Pennsylvania, was a teacher of music and later headmistress of a girls' school at Fulneck. Latrobe was educated at Moravian schools in England and in Germany, and attended the University of Leipzig. After extensive travels through Europe, which may have included a brief period of enlistment in the German army, Latrobe returned to England in 1784. His career path toward the Moravian ministry was changed to architecture in about 1783, with the influence of his German mentor, Baron Karl von Schachmann.

Latrobe remained in London for the next 11 years in a routine job at the Stamp Office. His broad educational background, which had given him proficiency in Latin and Greek as well as German, French, and Italian, combined with a sensitive, inquiring mind, ill fitted him for a stolid civil service career. His charm and wit, however, made him a social success in London. In 1790 he married Lydia Sellon, a well-placed lady three years older than he. Latrobe was now working in the architectural office of Sam Cockerell, and in 1791 he opened his own office. Two of Latrobe's works, Ashdown House and Hammerwood Lodge, still stand in England. His London career was cut short by the death of his wife in 1793 and a decline in work occasioned by the war in France. In November 1795, he left England for America to take possession of lands in Pennsylvania left him by his mother. After a difficult sea voyage he left the boat when it docked at Norfolk, Virginia, where he remained.

In a month's time Latrobe had gained entry into Virginia society, and began to practice architecture. His personal charm and letters of introduction provided him with immediate connections which included a visit to George Washington at Mount Vernon. His first work in the United States, the Pennock House in Norfolk (1796), led to other residential commissions, now preserved as a collection of drawings in the Library of Congress entitled "Design of Buildings in Virginia." In 1798, he completed his last Virginia design, the state penitentiary at Richmond, and moved to Philadelphia where he had received the commission for the Bank of Pennsylvania and the city water system. As his professional abilities quickly established his reputation as an accomplished architect and engineer, so his personal qualities put him into the inner circle of Philadelphia's best families. However, his professional and social successes were accompanied by the business and financial difficulties which plagued him throughout his lifetime.

In 1800, Latrobe married Mary Hazelhurst of Philadelphia and continued for the next few years to develop his practice there. Significant works were alterations of Chestnut Street Theatre, Philadelphia, Nassau Hall at Princeton, and new buildings for the University of Pennsylvania Medical School and Dickinson College, as well as notable residential work.

In 1802, Latrobe was appointed by President Thomas Jefferson, whom he had met in Virginia in 1798, to be Surveyor of Public Buildings of the United States. He moved for a short time to Newcastle, Delaware, in order to work on plans for the Chesapeake and Delaware Canal. After numbers of trips to Washington, he decided to move to the new capital in 1807.

Except for extended design work for the Roman Catholic Cathedral at Baltimore, a major achievement, most of his professional work until 1813 was in Washington for the U.S. government. His first job was the completion of the

Figure 1. One of six "corncob" columns in the first floor vestibule of the Capitol at the entrance to the Old Supreme Court Chamber. Courtesy of the Architect of the Capitol.

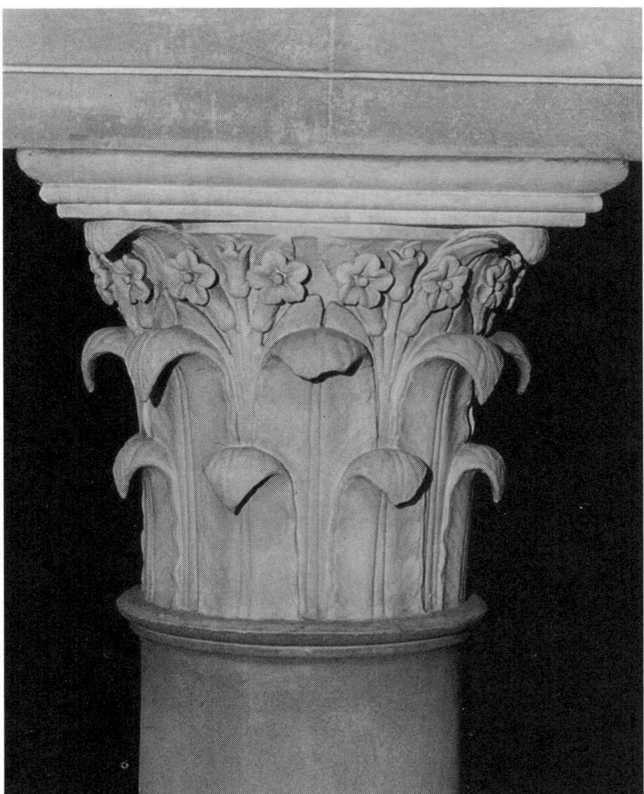

Figure 2. Tobacco leaf column capital recalling the classic acanthus leaf, also designed by Latrobe for the U.S. Capitol. Courtesy of the Architect of the Capitol.

U.S. Capitol (Figs. 1, 2). Subsequent work included completion of the President's house, buildings for the Washington Navy Yard, a fireproof addition to the Treasury building, a lighthouse at the mouth of the Mississippi River, and a plan for the Brooklyn Navy Yard. He also undertook some private work—the Markoe House in Philadelphia, Christ Church, and Kalorama, the Barlow estate, in Washington.

In 1813 the family moved to Pittsburgh where Latrobe engaged in an unsuccessful venture to build an Ohio River steamboat. While there he did drawings for buildings at the Pittsburgh Arsenal.

Latrobe returned to Washington in 1815 to embark on the most successful part of his career. For the next five years he was busy with plans for rebuilding the Capitol, burned by the British a year earlier, and a multitude of design projects including St. John's Church, Blodgett's Hotel, fine city houses for Decatur, Van Ness, and Casenove, and plans for a National University. By 1918 Latrobe's ongoing work consisted of the Cathedral and the Exchange in Baltimore and the New Orleans Waterworks. The Exchange was a large project done in cooperation with Baltimore architect Maximilian Godefoy and included a customs house, warehouses, insurance company and brokers' offices, and a central domed exchange hall. The Latrobes moved to Baltimore, where they were received again by Baltimoreans of wealth and influence. However, no further work appeared, and in 1819 the Latrobes moved to New Orleans where prospects were brighter for architectural commissions. Further work on the Mississippi River Lighthouse, the New Orleans Waterworks, Louisiana State Bank, and an addition to the New Orleans Cathedral gave promise of a much needed financial recovery. Overworked and exhausted by problems with the Waterworks, Latrobe contracted yellow fever and died on September 30, 1820.

BIBLIOGRAPHY

General References

T. Hamlin, *Benjamin Henry Latrobe,* Oxford University Press, New York, 1955.

P. Norton, *Latrobe, Jefferson and the National Capital,* Garland Publishing, Inc., New York and London, 1977.

G. Brown, *A History of the United States Capitol,* Vol. 1, U.S. Government Printing Office, Washington, D.C., 1900.

National Capital Planning Commission, *Worthy of a Nation,* Smithsonian Press, Washington, D.C., 1977.

David P. Fogle, AICP
University of Maryland
College Park, Maryland

LE CORBUSIER (CHARLES-EDOUARD JEANNERET)

Le Corbusier, architect and artist, was responsible for much of the direction and philosophy of modern architecture. He was born Charles-Edouard Jeanneret in La Chaux-de-Fonds, Switzerland, on October 6, 1887. His father was employed in the local watchmaking industry and his mother was an accomplished teacher of piano. At the age of 13 he entered a local school of art where he studied for four years under Charles L'Eplattenier, an admirer of French Art Nouveau and Naturalism. Thereafter, Le Corbusier supervised the construction of his professor's house, and with his wages, he traveled in Italy examining and sketching medieval art and architecture. In the winter of 1907–1908, he visited Vienna, declined an invitation to join Josef Hoffmann's studio, and departed for Paris where he worked beginning in 1908 for Auguste Perret. In 1910, he worked for a brief period in the office of Peter Behrens. In that year and in 1911, Le Corbusier became involved in the Deutsche Werkbund discussion of standardization and industrial production. By 1914–1915, his interest in such housing was manifest in his plans for the Domino construction system. In 1916, he designed a house for La Chaux-de-Fonds that was innovative in its open plan and fluid use of space. Through the war years he continued his research on civic planning, and evolved the ferroconcrete abattoirs near Bordeaux (1917).

Settling in Paris in 1917, he founded the journal *L'Esprit Nouveau* in collaboration with the architect–artist Amédée Ozenfant, which was published until 1925. It was in 1921 that he adopted his maternal grandfather's name, Le Corbusier, as his architectural pseudonym, reserving the name Jeanneret for his Purism paintings, a movement that he cofounded in 1918. A most active part of his career began after World War I when he designed his Citrohan houses. Subsequently, in addition to developing his theory of aesthetics and its publication, in 1922 he designed a city project for three million inhabitants, and actual houses for Ozenfant, his cousin Pierre Jeanneret, and others. Invited by Walter Gropius to display his works in the Weimar Bauhaus exhibition of 1923, Le Corbusier responded by sending four drawings detailing the manner of wall mounting he desired. That year, Gropius journeyed to Paris to meet Le Corbusier and to discuss their mutual interest in housing. This was the beginning of their lifetime friendship. For the Deutsche Werkbund's 1927 housing exhibition in Stuttgart, the Wiesenhof, Le Corbusier designed two houses with Pierre Jeanneret that displayed his several requirements for the new architecture. These included the pilotis or freestanding columns at ground level, glass walls, continuous strip windows, flat roofs with gardens, and functional flowing interior spaces.

The Villa de Monzie–Stein at Garches (1926–1927) was commissioned by Gabrielle De Monzie; Michael and Sarah Stein were also clients for a jointly shared house. The structure is based on a regular grid (ABABA). The problem was to design a house for four people not in a family group. Features included outdoor terraces with curved walls within the controlling structure. Strip windows and smooth white walls are typical of this luxurious house. The design vocabulary has the elements that came to be described as the international style.

The Villa Savoie at Poissy (1929) (Fig. 1) was Le Corbusier's most typical house of the 1920s. The Villa is a complex sculpture that needs to be visited to be completely comprehended. Set in an open field and raised on columns, ramps lead to the living floor, with its terrace, and above to the famous roof garden. The villa was in poor condition after World War II, but has since been restored. It has been compared to a sun-filled health camp or an ocean liner, and it has been described to be as carefully approached as the Acropolis in Athens (the strip windows representing the Parthenon's frieze) as well as an analogue of the automobile.

The Swiss dormitory in the Cité Universitaire, Paris (1930–1932) has a residential block set on massive pilotis of curved concrete supported on deep foundations, contrasted with a curved stone-faced, single-story form and stairway above. The famous photographs were carefully cropped to give only glimpses of the building. The visual strength of the pilotis reflect Le Corbusier's growing interest in simple materials that culminated in his later brutalist buildings.

Le Corbusier planned several buildings for construction in Moscow (1928–1931; not built) and the City of Refuge for the Salvation Army in Paris (1930–1931). Mme. la Princesse Singer-de-Polignac was instrumental in commissioning Le Corbusier for the Salvation Army refuge. Complex in composition, the all-glass south wall created an uncomfortable interior because the original innovative intent of two walls of glass with cooled or heated air between them was not installed. The later addition of *brises soleil* and operable windows on this wall changed the appearance of the building. This project was the largest by Le Corbusier until after World War II.

During the 1930s, the acceptance of Le Corbusier's city planning theories led to his appointment as consultant on various projects for the redevelopment of cities, among these Algiers, Nemours (Algeria), Antwerp, Barcelona, Buenos Aires, Stockholm, Montevideo, and Sao Paulo, and for the rebuilding of the Sixth Arrondissement of Paris.

Figure 1. The Villa Savoie at Poissy. Courtesy of the University of Maryland.

Le Corbusier's many city plans and proposals were not built. Most work was done in the 1930s and through the war years, when architectural commissions were hard to get. They were often not paid for and were grandiose in concept.

Under Nazi Germany the modern movement, and particularly Le Corbusier, was attacked. Declared ineligible by the Vichy Government for its architectural society, Le Corbusier undertook research on urbanism and was appointed by the Vichy Government for urban studies. His proposal for Algiers included a skyscraper project. Throughout the war years he did not compromise his architectural ideals.

In 1928 Le Corbusier was a cofounder of the Congres Internationaux d'Architecture Moderne (CIAM) and remained active in its deliberations and publications. Beginning in 1934, he was associated with a group of sociologists and engineers absorbed in a study of social problems. During the war years he produced modular studies for ASCORAL and the Union of French Architects, a resistance group, in order to formulate a practical and aesthetic basis for reconstruction. In 1945, he founded another cooperative concern, l'Atelier des Batisseurs (AtBat). Also in that year he was chief of a cultural relations mission to the United States. The French Ministry of Reconstruction appointed him technical consultant to the supreme council of city planning with the responsibility of rebuilding areas in the La Rochelle-Palisse region, the Algerian city of Nemours, and the town of Saint Die.

Soon after the war, Le Corbusier was commissioned to design a large apartment block for Marseilles that would include all of the community facilities required by the residents. This was the first of his *unités d'habitation*. Based on a series of modular dimensions, the modular system produced a powerful rough concrete building. The facades are complex and three-dimensional within a rhythmic organization. The apartments have two-story living spaces, but suffer from very narrow children's bedrooms. The apartments adapt to a variety of living styles, with 23 apartment types. The communal spaces have been criti-

Figure 2. The Chapel at Ronchamp. Courtesy of the University of Maryland.

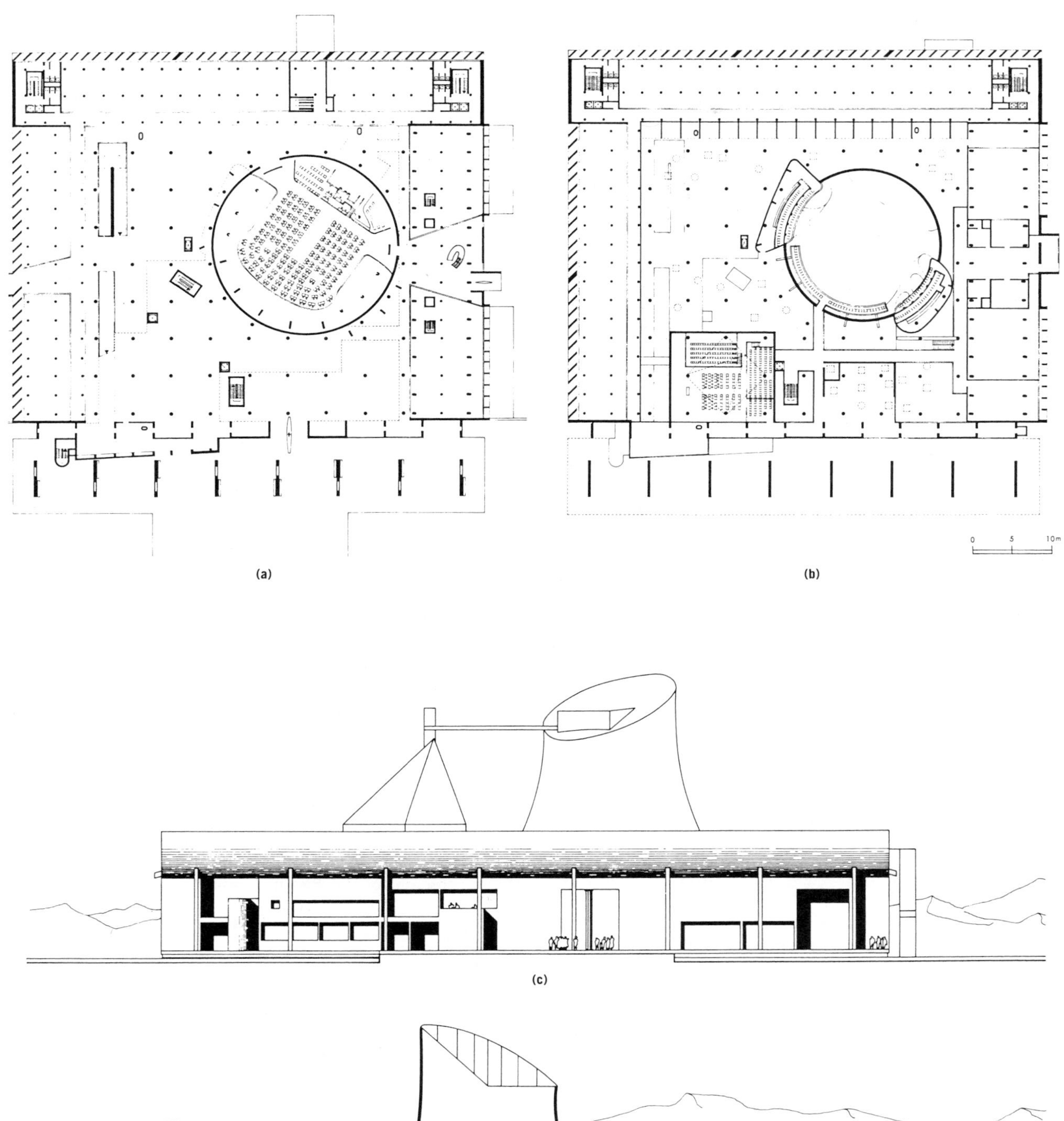

Figure 3. The Palace of Assembly, Chandigarh, India. (**a**) Ground floor plan; (**b**) Second floor plan; (**c**) Southeast elevation; (**d**) Section. Courtesy of Fondation Le Corbusier, Paris, France.

cized because the shop spaces remained vacant for a long time before they were sold to merchants. The sense of shopping seven and eight floors above the ground has been compared to shopping on an ocean liner. It does provide an option of leaving the building. Despite maintenance problems, the roof play-spaces are reported to be well used, and safely away from the streets. Although the building has had a history of criticism, it would appear to operate successfully and remains a strong design.

The facades of the unité d'habitation were designed on a proportional system based on the human figure that Le Corbusier called the Modulor. This system was described in his books *Le Modulor 1* and *Le Modulor 2,* published in 1948 and 1955 (1). The "modular man" was inscribed in concrete at the entrance to the Unité d'habitation at Marseilles, and in a late example incorporated in a mural at the Baghdad Sportshall completed in the 1980s. The use of the Modulor system in Le Corbusier's work gave order to the complexity of the wide range of his designs and has been used by other designers.

The Chapel at Ronchamp (1950–1955) (Fig. 2) was controversial to the architectural community and the public, seeming to turn against all of Le Corbusier's earlier work. It is a work of sculpture, full of allusion to all sorts of images. It has been interpreted as possibly the most convincing religious building of this century. Situated in a rolling landscape, its white form is visible for miles. Because of the chapel's remote location, concrete sprayed on reinforcing steel was the selected construction material. The roof appears slung from walls, but is separated from them by a light slot, and the curved walls are penetrated with small stained glass windows set in deep recesses in irregular patterns. A curved and perforated bell tower identifies the entrance to this pilgrimage chapel. In this building, Le Corbusier constructed a new world of forms that appear to have evolved over a long time, fully visually integrated.

The monastery at La Tourette (1957–1960) is placed on a sloping site. The compact, complex raw concrete structure is one of Le Corbusier's masterpieces. The requirements of the program for a teaching monastery were met in inventive and appropriate organization of spaces. The rough concrete finishes were accepted by the monks, although not admired by some critics. The richness of forms and simplicity of spaces are remarkable achievements.

In the 1950s, Le Corbusier planned his largest commission, the capitol complex on the north side of Chandigarh, India. The complex is interesting for its individual buildings, but they are spaced so far apart that it is difficult to comprehend the total plan; it is not suitable for pedestrians. The most successful of the buildings is the General Assembly (Fig. 3), with its upturned roof penetrated by the pyramid and hyperbola of the two legislative halls. The public Forum is an amazing composition of immense concrete forms controlled by the use of the Modulor system of dimensions. Work continued at Chandigarh after Le Corbusier's death in 1965.

Although a good number of his 200 disciples (former employees) were in the United States, Le Corbusier is represented in that country by only the Carpenter Center for the Visual Arts at Harvard University (1964). The pleasure that Le Corbusier had in his significant accomplishments was irreparably diminished in 1957 by the death of his wife of 27 years, Yvonne Victorine Gallis, a loss not to be compensated for by new commissions, new honors, or friends.

Among his honors were degrees from several universities: Zurich, Cambridge, Florence, Geneva, Columbia, and from the Swiss Federal Institute of Technology. He was in succession a Chevalier, Commandeur, and grand officer of the Legion d'Honneur. He received the medals of the American Institute of Architects and the Royal Institute of British Architects. He was also a member of the Royal Academy of Fine Arts of Sweden and of the Russian Academy of Architecture.

Perhaps the greatest disappointments suffered by Le Corbusier in architectural practice resulted from the politics that denied him the commission to build the League of Nations building in Geneva (despite his first prize in the 1927 competition), and thereafter the opportunities to design the United Nations building in New York or the UNESCO permanent headquarters building in Paris. Technically, as a member of an international five-man guidance committee with Walter Gropius, Sven Markelius, Lucio Costa, and Ernesto Rogers, Le Corbusier was not eligible for the later project, awarded to Marcel Breuer, Bernard Zehrfuss, and Pier Luigi Nervi.

In his later years, a small cabin on the beach at Roque-Cap-Martin afforded him time to recreate and think. It was there, on August 27, 1965, that he died while swimming. In a final tribute to Le Corbusier, Gropius wrote to Sigfried Giedion (2):

> The full impact and weight of his great personality came to one's consciousness with a flash in the moment he disappeared beyond recall from our limited field of vision. Yes, it is most tragic that he could not live out his immeasurable potentialities, that he had to break off in a state of bitterness and loneliness. Now his glorification will start all over the world, the echo of which cannot reach him anymore, and how much he would have needed it.

BIBLIOGRAPHY

1. Le Corbusier, *The Modulor 1 and 2,* Harvard University Press, Cambridge, Mass., 1980.
2. W. Gropius, letter to Sigfried Giedion, Cambridge, Mass., September 3, 1965.

General References

N. Evenson, *Chandigarh,* University of California Press, Berkeley, 1966.

R. Fishman, *Urban Utopias in the Twentieth Century, Ebenezer Howard, Frank Lloyd Wright and Le Corbusier,* Basic Books, Inc., Publishers, New York, 1977.

M. Girsberger, *Im Umgang mit Le Corbusier; Mes contacts avec Le Corbusier,* Artemis, Zurich, 1981.

Le Corbusier, *Vers une architecture,* 1923. Translation: *Towards a New Architecture,* Praeger, New York, 1927; and Dover Publications, Inc., New York, 1986.

Le Corbusier, *Urbanisme,* 1925. Translation: *The City of Tomorrow and its Planning,* MIT Press, Cambridge, Mass., 1971.

Le Corbusier, *La ville radieuse,* 1935. Translation: *The Radiant City,* Orion, New York, 1967.

Le Corbusier, *Quand les cathédrales étaient blanches,* 1937. Translation: *When the Cathedrals were White,* McGraw-Hill, Inc., New York, 1964.

Le Corbusier, *La charte d'athenes avec un discours liminaire de Jean Giraudoux,* 1943. Translation: *The Athens Charter,* Grossman, New York, 1973.

A. Ozenfant and C. E. Jeanneret, *La peinture moderne,* Cres, Paris, 1927.

S. Papadaki, ed., *Le Corbusier; Architect, Painter, Writer,* Macmillan Publishing Co., New York, 1948.

M. Sekler, ed., *The Early Drawings of Charles-Edouard Jeanneret (Le Corbusier), 1902–1908,* Garland Publishing Inc., New York, 1977.

B. Taylor, *Le Corbusier at Pessac: The Search for Systems and Standards in the Design of Low Cost Housing,* Carpenter Center for Visual Arts, Harvard University Press, Cambridge, Mass., 1973.

S. von Moos, *Le Corbusier: Elements of a Synthesis,* MIT Press, Cambridge, Mass., 1979.

REGINALD ISAACS
Cambridge, Massachusetts

LEGITIMATE THEATERS. See THEATERS AND OPERA HOUSES

L'ENFANT, PIERRE

Major Pierre Charles L'Enfant, urban designer and creator of the original plan for Washington, D.C., was born in Paris, France on August 2, 1754 to Pierre and Marie Leullier L'Enfant. His father, a painter and member of the Royal Academy, was in the service of the king. His work served as the basis for design of Gobelin's tapestries and generally depicted scenes of battle victories. The young L'Enfant grew up in this artistic environment and studied the fine arts.

In 1777 at age 23, being a political idealist, L'Enfant came to the United States to join the American Revolution. He was commissioned as lieutenant in the U.S. Army and was with George Washington at Valley Forge. There he utilized his artistic talent to sketch Washington and fellow officers. He was wounded in battle at Savannah and fled to Charleston, where he was later captured. He was freed in a prisoner exchange, and in 1782 was commended for his military activities by General George Washington, who wrote to say, ". . . your zeal and active services are such as reflect the highest honor. . . ." He was promoted to the rank of major by the U.S. Congress in 1783.

L'Enfant's exceptional design talents were utilized during and after the war for a variety of projects from fortifications, to jewelry, banquet halls, and celebrations. He designed a festival hall located in Philadelphia for the French ambassador that was described by a French official as a beautiful, tasteful building in which "simplicity is united with an air of dignity."

Having spent five years in the service of the American army engineers, L'Enfant returned to France in 1783. After visiting his aged father and performing commissions for the Society of the Cincinnati, the organization of French and American military officers of which he was a founding member, he returned to the United States in 1784 to practice as an architect in New York. His first major work was the old New York City Hall. The building was remodeled to serve as a meeting place for Congress, which moved to New York from Philadelphia in 1789. At the time, L'Enfant's building (demolished in 1812) was considered the most beautiful in the country. It was there that George Washington was inaugurated as the first president of the United States.

In September 1789, L'Enfant wrote to President Washington and offered his services for the design of the new capital on the Potomac. Washington hired him as principal architect and planner of the new Federal City, and later wrote, "he [L'Enfant] was better qualified than any one who had come within my knowledge in the country."

By March of 1791 L'Enfant was in Georgetown, long an established Maryland river port and soon to become part of the federal district, at work on a general plan for the new city. He turned to his native France as the basis for his design, and adapted the baroque plan of Versailles prepared in 1661 by French landscape architect Andre Le Nôtre. The Versailles scheme is combined with features of the eighteenth-century redesign of Paris, as well as L'Enfant's original ideas based on a careful site analysis. It has been referred to by Professor Alexander Butler of Michigan State University as expressing the "Imperial-Roman-Versailles-American supercolossal aesthetic." The plan created two focal points on which radial avenues converged: the legislative center, the "Federal House," now the Capitol; and the executive center, the Palace of the President, now the White House. Minor points of convergence for radials were squares or circles for the location of monuments. Overlaying and extending the radial plan was a grid street system. The rationale for the design, its utilization of river and hill configurations, the grand scale of plan elements, buildings, avenues, and vistas, would make the plan an enduring document.

Between March and September of 1791, L'Enfant made several reports to President Washington, the last of which contained the plan in its final form and studies for the Capitol, the White House, a market, bridges, and other features. L'Enfant had applied his exceptional talents in this short amount of time, encompassing periods of stress and conflict, to produce a timeless landmark.

Although L'Enfant's work received the enthusiastic support of President Washington, Secretary of State Jefferson, and others, his insistence on literal execution of the plan and a volatile temper, combined with an imperfect command of the English language, led him into conflict with the three commissioners appointed to oversee the building of the new capital. The beginning of a series of events that led to his dismissal was his demolition of a house being built by Daniel Carroll, one of the city's commissioners. In March of 1792, L'Enfant was notified that his services were terminated. He refused to accept payment for his work.

L'Enfant spent his remaining years in the United States

in private practice and doing work for the army engineers, but was not financially successful. A project to design and build a grand mansion in Philadelphia for Robert Morris, the richest man in America, failed with the collapse of Morris's financial empire. (L'Enfant was never paid for his work and, in fact, lent money to Morris.) His last years were spent in Washington where he watched his plan develop and lived as a guest of the Digges family on their country estate in Prince George's County, Md. He died in 1825 and was buried there. His estate was valued at $46.

Long overdue recognition of his achievements came in 1909. L'Enfant's remains were removed, with much ceremony, to Arlington National Cemetery. A monument marking his burial place is inscribed with his greatest work, the plan of the City of Washington.

BIBLIOGRAPHY

General References

E. S. Kite, *The Rise of Urban America, L'Enfant and Washington,* Arno Press, New York, 1970 (Johns Hopkins Press, Baltimore, Md., 1929).

National Capital Planning Commission, *Worthy of the Nation,* Smithsonian Institute Press, Washington, D.C., 1970.

H. P. Caemmerer, *The Life of Pierre Charles L'Enfant, Planner of the City Beautiful, The City of Washington,* National Republic, Washington, D.C., 1950.

J. W. Reps, *Monumental Washington: The Planning and Development of the Capital Center,* Princeton University Press, Princeton, N.J., 1967.

DAVID P. FOGLE
Washington, D.C.

LESCAZE, WILLIAM

William Lescaze's principal contribution to the development of modern architecture was the introduction of the international style to the United States. Considered by Henry-Russell Hitchcock to be one of the "New Pioneers in America" during the 1920s, Lescaze, along with emigrés Richard Neutra and Richard Schindler, served to enunciate and promote the major tenets of the modern movement.

Lescaze was born in Geneva in 1896 and studied architecture under Professor Karl Moser at the Eidgenossiche Technische Hochschule in Zurich. After graduating in 1919, he worked for a short time on the reconstruction of devastated areas in France, then moved to Paris and joined the office of Henri Sauvage, one of the major proponents of the modern movement in France. In time, Lescaze sought opportunities to engage in more monumental work and on the advice of Moser he left Europe for the United States in 1920. Unable to obtain a position in New York City, he traveled to Cleveland where he was employed by the firm of Hubbell and Benes and later by the office of Walter R. MacCormack, chief of the design bureau for the Cleveland Board of Education. Lescaze returned to New York City in 1923 to establish his own architectural practice.

The commissions that followed included a number of residential and commercial interiors done mainly in the Moderne mode. With their reflective surfaces and use of contrasting geometric patterns, these apartments and department store interiors exhibited an exploratory mixture of art deco and purist motifs. Several unbuilt projects of this period illustrate his search for a controlled and cohesive modernist architectural language. His Country House for a Young Couple, commissioned by *Architectural Forum* magazine in 1927, and his Future American Country House—An American House in 1938, a project commissioned by *Architectural Record* magazine in 1928, both display the modernist vocabulary of flat roofs, freestanding columns (*pilotis*), cantilevered overhangs, and freely composed elevations, but without an assured compositional order.

The opportunity for Lescaze's mature development as an architect of the modern movement came with his partnership with George Howe in 1929. Howe, an architect trained at Harvard (1904) and at the Ecole des Beaux Arts (1907), wished to end his traditional practice and become a "thoroughly modern" architect. Lescaze, on the other hand, was very familiar with the achievements of modern European art and architecture and sought a much larger scale of building in which to incorporate the principles of a valid contemporary architecture. The partnership agreement stipulated that Howe was to have primary responsibility for business connections and meetings, while Lescaze was to be responsible for architectural design and supervision of building construction. The first executed work of the firm was the Oak Lane Country Day School, completed in 1929 near Philadelphia. This progressive nursery school, designed by Lescaze, was the first international style school building built in the United States. Its asymmetrical massing, articulated and interlocked volumes, and white stuccoed surfaces (except for the blue east elevation) reflected the principal characteristics of the international style as they were soon to be outlined by Henry-Russell Hitchcock and Philip Johnson in their polemical "Modern Architecture: International Exhibition" held at the Museum of Modern Art in New York in 1932, as well as in their accompanying publication *The International Style: Architecture since 1922* (1). A number of projects for country houses followed the widely published Oak Lane School and these provided the opportunity for Lescaze to further develop his modernist architectural syntax. As with many other architects practicing in the 1930s, his work was indebted to Le Corbusier's seminal "Five Points of the New Architecture" of 1926: (*1*) use of ordered column supports instead of bearing walls, (*2*) use of the free and open plan, (*3*) incorporation of the roof terrace, (*4*) employment of the strip window, and (*5*) development of the freely organized facade. Although Lescaze's designs

Figure 1. Philadelphia Savings Fund Society Building, Philadelphia, Pa. Courtesy of the PSFS/Meritor Corporate Archives, Meritor Financial Group, Philadelphia, Pa.

referenced Le Corbusier's architectural vocabulary, they never really pursued the same conceptual and formal logic (as in the potentials of the free plan), and the acknowledgments were primarily visual. The design *parti* of the Oak Lane School was again employed in the Frederick Field House of 1930–1931 in New Hartford, Conn., his first modern house to be realized and one of the first international style houses to be built on the East Coast. In 1930 the firm was asked to prepare designs for a new museum for the trustees of the Museum of Modern Art in New York. Over a two-year period, Lescaze prepared a succession of intriguing schemes for a museum located on a hypothetical, but typical, city lot. Each scheme was for an 11-story tower building that attempted to achieve maximum natural light for each display gallery. Collectively, the designs illustrate his ingenuity in spatial planning, building massing, and experimentation with glazing and lighting systems.

Howe and Lescaze's major achievement was the design of the headquarters building in Philadelphia for the Philadelphia Savings Fund Society (PSFS) of 1929–1932. It was to be the first realized skyscraper in the international style and one of the major monuments of the modern movement (Fig. 1). The commission for the PSFS building had originally led Howe to search for a new design partner, and the building's design is based on the talents of both architects. At 32 stories, PSFS was a truly modern skyscraper—one that deftly displayed the contemporary architectural possibilites derived from functional and structural expression—and its position as a modern architectural icon was immediate. The building consisted of ground floor retail space, a raised two-story banking floor with three stories of banking operations above, and an off-centered tower positioned and proportioned for optimum light for all offices. A thin service core adjacent to the adjoining property on the south side acted as a windowless vertical spine to contrast with the composition of horizontal window banding and projecting columns that characterized the main office tower. Executive meeting and dining facilities, a solarium, and an observation deck were located on the top floor, as was the large neon PSFS sign that masked the cooling towers and still remains as the building's signature graphic along Philadelphia's skyline. With its charcoal-colored granite base and cantilevered banking hall above, sand-colored limestone banking floors, gray brick spandrels with aluminum framed windows and limestone-faced columns projecting along the long dimension of the dominating tower, PSFS possessed an austere but rich material and color palette. The interiors, all of which were designed by the architects, featured acoustical ceiling tiles in a metal frame (the forerunner of today's acoustical tile hung ceiling), rich and contrasting marble finishes in the banking hall, Lescaze-designed lamps, clocks, desk sets, and tubular steel furniture, and stainless steel window sills and radiator covers. One of the earliest buildings to make large-scale use of aluminum in its interiors, PSFS was also the second air-conditioned office building in the United States. Completed in 1932, PSFS was a unique accomplishment, and, as historian William Jordy has noted, "in the development of the bare-bones aesthetic of modern skyscraper design, PSFS is the most important tall building erected between the Chicago School of the eighteen eighties and nineties and the metal-and-glass revival beginning around 1950" (2).

The Howe and Lescaze partnership lasted until 1935. Prior to the firm's dissolution, Lescaze, apparently without the collaboration of his partner, had undertaken several other noteworthy projects. A major building program for Dartington Hall Estate in Devon, England, for example, provided him with the opportunity to pursue a project for a Progressive Junior High School in 1931. Although unrealized, the project's rectangular residential blocks raised on *pilotis* and interconnected with a glazed circulation link outwardly recall the Bauhaus complex at Dessau. The William Curry House ("High Cross"), designed with English collaborator Robert Hening and built at Dartington Hall in 1932, was one of the first houses in the "new style" to be constructed in England. These were followed by a series of school buildings designed and built at Dartington between 1932 and 1935 with Hening, all of which clearly showed Lecaze's awareness of the Bauhaus architectural aesthetic. Also commissioned by the trustees at Dartington Hall was the Churston Housing Estate of 1932–1935, a housing development for a 200-acre coastal site at Churston, England. With an overall site plan designed by Henry Wright, the scheme consisted of small clusters of flat-roofed, stuccoed units set around cul-de-sacs and large open green spaces. Intended for the retired middle class, this vision of social housing was not met with great enthusiasm by potential buyers and only a small number of units was completed.

Lescaze's interest in large-scale urban housing reflected his allegiance to the social concerns of the modern movement and is best exemplified in his 1931–1933 proposal for the Chrystie-Forsyth Street Housing Development in New York City (done with Albert Frey). Projected for a site on the Lower East Side of Manhattan, his proposal was for a dense complex of 24 L-shaped buildings raised on columns, extending for seven city blocks. By raising the apartment slabs on *pilotis* and carrying them directly across the street grid, Lescaze freed the ground plane and achieved a nearly continuous park and recreation space, a *parti* that undoubtedly had its origins in Le Corbusier's Ville Radieuse project of the late 1920s. The apartment buildings were laid out with single-loaded corridors, had steel frame structural systems allowing for maximum flexibility of interior partitioning, and their L-shaped configurations were sited to achieve maximum light and air for all units. Later housing schemes, including the Ten Eyck Houses of 1933–1938 (with others) and the Manhattanville Houses of 1960, both built in New York City, were far more conventional solutions to the urban housing problem and failed to equal the vision of the earlier Chrystie-Forsyth scheme. Lescaze's own New York City townhouse, which he remodeled in 1934, served as his residence and studio–office until his death in 1969. Described by contemporary journals as being the "house of an uncompromising modernist," it is considered to be the first townhouse in the "new style" built in the United States (Fig. 2). Between 1935 and 1939 a series of commissions from a major American corporation, the Columbia Broadcasting System (CBS), challenged Lescaze's interest in interior and product design. He completed designs for studio and office interiors and furnishings, a mobile broadcasting facility, a CBS graphic system, and a major new broadcasting facility in Hollywood, Calif. His work was highly effective in promoting the national visual identity of CBS, and it reaffirmed his strong belief in the communicative function of contemporary design.

Figure 2. William Lescaze Townhouse, New York, N.Y. Courtesy of William Lescaze Papers, George Arents Research Library for Special Collections at Syracuse University, Syracuse, N.Y.

Two buildings erected at the 1939 New York World's Fair, the Aviation Building (with J. Gordon Carr) and the Swiss Pavilion (with John R. Weber) displayed his continuing design virtuosity and technical experimentation, but by the end of the 1930s Lescaze's major contributions to the development of contemporary architecture had been achieved. Various commissions for corporate, municipal, and speculative office buildings formed the bulk of his architectural practice through the mid-1960s and presented him with additional large-scale projects, but these would not yield the architectural inventiveness and accomplishment of his early work. The Longfellow Building (1941) located in Washington, D.C. was one of the city's first modern office buildings. It introduced a continuous strip window aesthetic with projecting concrete sunshades. Subsequent designs for urban office buildings attempted to incorporate the base-and-tower *parti* and elevation elements of the PSFS project, but by no means did they achieve the complex massing and consummate grace of PSFS. His last high-rise office structures share the anonymous and prosaic aesthetic of the ubiquitous curtain-walled speculative buildings of the 1960s.

In 1942, Lescaze published an autobiography entitled, *On Being an Architect,* which presented his views on architecture and its relationship to society. He wrote movingly of the need for what he termed a "vital architecture," that is, one emerging from a clear understanding of the needs of the American, for, in his words, "such an American deserves, and is capable of an architecture built for his use, expressive of himself, his ideas, his ideals, his own time" (3). Newly arrived in America, his early work had brought the principles of European avant-garde architecture and design to the tradition-bound. But by the end of the 1930s, the international style aesthetic was no longer provocatively experimental and new, and its innovative pre-World War II phase faced its inevitable demise. The latter half of the 1930s also witnessed the arrival of a new wave of European artists and architects, including Walter Gropius, Marcel Breuer, and Mies van der Rohe. William Lescaze's position as a leading theorist and influential practitioner in America was thus eclipsed. His most lasting architectural achievements were confined to his first two decades of practice.

BIBLIOGRAPHY

1. H. R. Hitchcock and P. Johnson, *The International Style: Architecture since 1922,"* Museum of Modern Art, New York, 1932; revised edition 1966 (*The International Style*).
2. W. H. Jordy, "The American Acceptance of the International Style: George Howe and William Lescaze's Philadelphia Saving Fund Society Building" in W. H. Jordy, *American Buildings and Their Architects: The Impact of European Modernism in the Mid-Twentieth Century,* Anchor Press/Doubleday, Garden City, N.Y., 1976, p. 88.
3. W. Lescaze, *On Being an Architect,* G. P. Putnam's Sons, New York, 1942, p. XI.

General References

M. Emanuel, ed., "William Lescaze" in *Contemporary Architects,* St. Martin's Press, New York, 1980, pp. 466–467 (Complete list of works included).

K. Frampton and S. Kolbowski, eds., *William Lescaze IAUS Catalogue 16,* Institute for Architecture and Urban Studies and Rizzoli International Publications, Inc., New York, 1982 (includes essays by C. Hubert and L. Stamm Shapiro and a complete bibliography compiled by L. Lanmon).

H. Hitchcock, "Howe and Lescaze" in H. R. Hitchcock et al., *Modern Architecture: International Exhibition* (exhibition catalogue), Museum of Modern Art, New York, 1932.

G. Robinson, ed., *William Lescaze: The Rise of Modern Design in America (Syracuse University Library Associates Courier),* Volume XIX, Number One, Syracuse University Library Associates, Syracuse, N.Y., Spring 1984.

GREGORY K. HUNT
Virginia Polytechnic Institute and State University
Blacksburg, Virginia

LIABILITY INSURANCE

Professional liability is a universal problem facing professional people in the United States. Claims made by clients, patients, or third parties allege that professionals' performance has not been up to the standard of care usual in their communities and further allege that this failure has caused damages. The rampant nature of these claims reached crisis proportions in the mid-1970s, causing doctors, lawyers, accountants, and design professionals to wonder whether their career choices had been wise. Since that time, many professional people have left their chosen fields in direct response to this onslaught of claims.

Architects and other design professionals have been horrified by the professional liability phenomenon and are constantly on the lookout for means of reducing their claims' frequency and severity. In fact, finding a solution is imperative because the cost of dealing with the problem has made the economic feasibility of architectural practice dubious.

Perhaps even greater than the financial cost to a design firm are the hidden costs that these claims stimulate: loss of productive time spent in seemingly endless deposition, the enormous psychological burden that is triggered by accusations of failed profession, and the warping of creativity that is hampered by the reluctance to adopt new techniques for fear that claims will result.

One good gauge of the seriousness of this problem for architects is the cost of their professional liability insurance. Next to payroll and rent, many design professionals' largest expense is the cost of this coverage. In recent years the cost has soared to such an extent that many design firms are practicing without its protection; in today's lingo, going bare.

The insurers, for their part, insist that the steep cost of this insurance is a direct result of high claims frequency and severity. To substantiate this position they cite the insurance industry trade journals' reports of some six underwriters withdrawing from the line in 1986 and 1987 or curbing their writings in the face of adverse underwriting results.

The following text is aimed toward giving historical insight into this nagging problem, as well as providing information on available professional liability insurance and alternative means of coping with the exposure so that designers are better equipped to deal with it as one cost of practicing their professions.

HISTORY

Claims of designer error are as old as civilization. Much of what mankind has learned about construction has come about through trial and error. Obviously, this approach to establishing an art will have quite a bit of error. In ancient times, errors in design were treated at the whim of local authority. It is known that Xerxes, seeking to march his army across the Hellespont, had a bridge designed and constructed for that purpose. When the bridge was destroyed by a storm, Xerxes had the designers beheaded and appointed others who, on learning what had happened to their predecessors, took a decidedly conservative approach. It is recorded that the flax cable that kept the floating bridge in place weighed 50 pounds a foot (1). The second bridge held, and Xerxes's armies crossed without incident, only to be decimated by the lack of food and other provisions during their campaign to conquer Hellas (Greece and its environs).

There are many mentions of design flaws in the Bible. Perhaps the ones most quoted are Matthew 7:25, "[The house] fell not: for it was founded on rock," and Matthew 7:26, "A foolish man which built his house upon the sand." In the absence of gross incompetence, mankind throughout history seemed to be fairly tolerant of design errors. For their part, architects had such a high sense of identity with their work that allegations of failure simply devastated them.

A building of stunning architectural achievement is the Vienna Opera House (2). Even so, one of its architects, Eduard van der Null, committed suicide following a wave of criticism about its design. The other architect, August von Siccardsburg, died shortly thereafter, presumably from a broken heart because of the rampant spiteful commentary about his design sense (3).

English, and then U.S., common law held that an architect was liable for his negligence only to his client, and to no one else (4). Shortly before the turn of the century, architects were not found to be liable to third parties even if they acted with malicious intent (5). Even more astounding by today's standards is that in the nineteenth century architects in the United States were free of any potential liability while acting in their judicial capacity, that is, making decisions of an interpretive nature at the job site (6).

Professional liability claims based on simple negligence against design professionals in private practice are of fairly recent origin and have reached crisis proportions only in the last 30 years. Until recently, these troublesome claims were peculiarly prevalent in the United States. Now they are emerging in the United Kingdom as well. Although it would be too much to expect designs to be completely free of errors, something has happened since World War II that has triggered staggering demands of design professionals.

How this all came about must be a matter for speculation. U.S. common law underwent a dramatic evolution during the 1920s, 1930s, and 1940s that may have contributed to the problem. A case frequently cited by jurists typifying the change was MacPherson v. Buick Motor Co. (7). In that case the court found that a buyer of an automobile (MacPherson) need not be in privity of contract with the manufacturer (Buick Motor Co.) in order to bring action against them for negligence in the manufacture of a vehicle.

The precedent set in MacPherson has been adopted in virtually all jurisdictions of the United States. Its importance to design professionals can be readily appreciated, because its holding opened the way for parties other than the client to bring action against an architect or consulting engineer based on allegations of professional negligence. The impact of this finding on the design professions has been enormous, as it is logical to assume that it has had a contributory effect on the professional liability claims explosion.

Added to the changes of U.S. common law was the attitudinal shift in the public's perception of all professions. Whereas at one time it would take a dramatic showing of culpability for a client (or a patient) to bring action against their hired professional, the situation changed in the 1940s. The public's perception of the once-revered professional deteriorated. "Good Old Doc" became a target of claims along with other business people. It did not matter that the professional person against whom claims were made had done his work to the best of his ability, nor did it matter that his performance was up to the standard of care within his community. Suits were brought all the same. Disappointed expectations served as the common denominator for bringing suit or claim.

Victor O. Schinnerer & Company and the AIA

Suits against architects mounted in frequency and severity so rapidly in the late 1940s and early 1950s that the American Institute of Architects (AIA) became alarmed. In 1955, Victor O. Schinnerer & Company (Schinnerer) became involved with the AIA through discussions with Leon Chatelain, Jr., then treasurer of the national association and also a member of the AIA Committee on Professional Liability Insurance. Schinnerer, which had been in business since 1938, was a well-established insurance firm located in Washington, D.C.

As a result of these discussions Schinnerer undertook an independent study of the problem without obligation on the part of the AIA. The study was conducted during 1955. As a result, a trial policy form was developed and a great deal of exploration was done to review existing markets to ascertain the feasibility of establishing a permanent and stable market for this class of insurance. The suggested policy form, as well as recommendations based on the findings of the studies, were presented to Chatelain for his review.

In March 1956, Schinnerer met with the Committee on Professional Liability of the AIA at the association offices. After a review of the proposed policy form and the findings of the independent studies done by Schinnerer, the committee agreed that a questionnaire should be sent to members of the AIA surveying the demand for coverage. A copy of this questionnaire was also supplied to Paul Robbins of the National Society of Professional Engineers (NSPE) for his study.

The results of the survey were tabulated and proved a very strong demand for a broad-form architects' professional liability policy. In July 1956, results of the survey and additional study results were presented to a joint meeting of the professional liability committee of the AIA and representatives of the NSPE and The American Society of Civil Engineers (ASCE).

This meeting culminated in the authorization by the AIA committee to proceed to a final policy form and rates to be submitted for their consideration. During final formalization of the policy form and rate structure, Schinnerer approached a number of insurance companies about writing the coverage for the new program. Because there was very little historical data about this class of insurance, some insurance companies were hesitant to enter this market. Continental Casualty Company (CNA) expressed its interest in pursuing the program in cooperation with Schinnerer and the AIA. The final policy form and rate structure as well as the carrier, CNA, were submitted to the AIA committee in a meeting in November 1956. During this meeting the committee made further requirements and suggested a number of provisions with which both Schinnerer and CNA agreed.

During this same period of time, preliminary details of the program were presented to the Task Force for Professional Liability of the NSPE at the annual board of directors meeting. A survey of the NSPE membership was authorized to determine demand for coverage. After tabulation of the survey results and additional correspondence with the task force, a written report was submitted by Schinnerer to NSPE in November 1956.

On November 28, 1956, the AIA Board of Directors approved the report of the committee on professional liability and commended the CNA/Schinnerer policy to its members. By January 1957, CNA had completed its filing of the new policy form with the then-existing 48 state insurance departments.

In February 1957, the functional section of the NSPE recommended the CNA/Schinnerer policy to the board of directors at a meeting in Charleston, South Carolina. The board approved the report of the committee and commended the policy to its members. This was the beginning of a cooperative effort between the American Institute of Architects, the National Society of Professional Engineers/Professional Engineers in Private Practice (PEPP), Continental Casualty Company, and Victor O. Schinnerer & Company, Inc., which continues to this day.

Active participation by the AIA in the direction of the program was ensured from the beginning when, as a condition of commendation, the minutes of the board meeting of the AIA contained the following excerpt: "Resolved, that the committee on professional liability review the procedures of the handling of this insurance on behalf of the Institute."

In 1958, Schinnerer began conducting loss-prevention meetings and workshops at the local, state, and national levels for groups of AIA and NSPE chapter members (see Professional Liability Loss Prevention). These meetings have grown into full-day quality control seminars and are now conducted in some 20 locations across the country every year. Some 2000 architects and engineers attend these seminars annually. In 1959, Schinnerer began its continuing service as insurance adviser to the insurance committee and the contract documents board of the AIA and NSPE/PEPP.

Since the early years, legislation affecting architects and engineers has been monitored and supported or opposed by Schinnerer and the national societies. A prime example of this activity was the first model legislation developed and supported by AIA, NSPE, and Schinnerer calling for statutes of limitation for the construction industry. Since that model legislation was introduced, most states have adopted statutes of limitations.

In 1961, a series of loss-prevention bulletins was begun by Schinnerer for AIA and NSPE/PEPP members. This series of articles, which has been continuously published since that time, is based on actual and claims data collected through the operation of the program. It is then analyzed and disseminated as loss-prevention and quality control information for design professionals. These continuing loss-prevention articles, known as "Guidelines for Improving Practice," now constitute one of the most comprehensive single sources of loss prevention, legislative, and quality control information available to design professionals.

In 1962, Schinnerer organized the first annual meeting of lawyers involved in defending professional liability claims against architects and engineers. The purpose of these meetings is to bring specialists together to exchange experiences and successful techniques to improve legal defense capabilities. The meetings are held every year and are jointly sponsored by AIA, NSPE/PEPP, Schinnerer, and CNA. Several hundred lawyers from across the country attend the meetings each year. Regional meetings are held at various times when new legal trends develop in specific areas of the country.

Operations of the program by Schinnerer and CNA have been open at all times to the scrutiny of the committees representing both national societies. However, in 1969, during an overall restructuring of the program to respond to a serious loss picture, an annual joint meeting was set up between AIA, NSPE, Schinnerer, and CNA. At these meetings the actuarial operation of the program is reviewed by the committees in detail. This meeting takes place every year for the purpose of reviewing the results of the past year, the actuarial rate recommendations for the coming year, any changes or revisions in coverage that might be proposed, and all other items pertaining to the program.

To further improve the gathering and dissemination of technical, insurance, and legal information, the Office for Professional Liability Research (OPLR) was established in 1972. The analysis of the data and causes of thousands of claims lodged against design professionals since 1957 has been included in the seminar program by OPLR. Additionally, a subscription service for defense attorneys called the "A/E Legal Newsletter" was started in the early 1970s.

Through the years of the CNA/Schinnerer program of Professional Liability Insurance for Architects and Engineers, a close and meaningful working relationship has been maintained with both the American Institute of Architects and the National Society of Professional Engineers/PEPP. Joint efforts on behalf of the national societies and the carrier and underwriting manager of this program have resulted in a stable national program of coverage for design professionals. Great strides have been made in legislation affecting these professionals and in the education of architects and engineers in the knowledge of professional liability, loss prevention, and quality control. Efforts to address all important problems faced by design professionals in these areas continue, and effective solutions to the problems continue to be developed through the efforts of this unique long-term program.

Design Professionals Insurance Company

In 1962, soil and foundation engineers in California found it difficult to purchase professional liability insurance. They approached Alexander & Alexander, Inc., national insurance brokers, with their plight. They worked with the San Francisco office of that company, which advised them that historical precedent suggested the answer to their problem lay in effective loss-prevention measures.

The problem was that very little effort had ever been applied to the concept of loss prevention for professional liability claims situations.

All the same, the Consulting Engineers Association of California made a determination to try to do something about the rising cost of professional liability insurance through a unique plan of professional liability loss prevention—one that focused on the business and communications aspects of the practice as opposed to quality control, coupled with a new insurance program. The Alexander & Alexander people, relying on tenets of the social sciences, pieced together a pilot loss-prevention program and began talking with potential insurance markets. It was only after lengthy negotiations and the promise of other lines of insurance that they were able to convince the American Motorists Insurance Company, one of the Kemper Group, to underwrite the program.

The program was an instant success, and a significant number of consulting engineers were insured the first year. By 1964, other chapters of the Consulting Engineers Council (CEC)—today called The American Consulting Engineers Council—began to show a keen interest in this new approach to the growing professional liability problem. By March 1965, the concept was adopted by the CEC of Washington; Oregon, Maryland, Washington, D.C., and Colorado quickly followed suit. In 1967, 10 state organizations had subscribed to the concept of controlling professional liability losses through education, seminars, and home study. In the interim, the soil and foundation engineers lost their insurability due to mounting claims, largely from work done in connection with residential subdivisions.

In 1968, the CEC evinced interest in making the program available in all states. Toward that end, they commissioned the production of a professional liability loss-prevention manual that could be used by their members nationwide.

A phenomenon similar to that of 1987 had struck the insurance industry: capacity shortage. The cyclical nature of the insurance industry spelled doom to expanding the program. Kemper said they were in no position to expand their writings. They did offer to lend assistance should the CEC decide to do something on their own.

With guidance from an Alexander & Alexander, Inc. subsidiary, Risk Analysis & Research Corporation, the concept of an industry-owned insurance company was conceived. After all, almost every insurance company ever founded was set up to meet the special needs of insurance-distressed business groups. Thus, the Lumbermans Mutual Insurance Company was founded by lumbermen who were unable to purchase needed workers compensation coverage on terms they could afford. Employers Mutuals of Wausau was formed by companies in the pulp, paper, and forest industries to meet their insurance needs. And the Fireman's Fund Insurance Company was organized by West Coast business leaders who were uninsurable in the eyes of the eastern insurance establishment. This same approach was used by the CEC, which led to the idea of a new company to write insurance for their professional liability exposure.

In 1969, the Design Professionals Insurance Company (DPIC) was incorporated with California as its domicile. Then the arduous task of capitalization was commenced. While $1 million may not seem like much money in today's megabuck world, in 1969 it was a respectable sum, not easy to raise. Sales of common stock were commenced in about 30 states. The other states had restrictions that made it too expensive or impossible to sell stock in their jurisdictions. Another factor militating against raising capital was the fact that design professionals in private practice did not have the financial resources to invest in a somewhat speculative venture.

Money dribbled in through 1970. By January 1971, it appeared that the necessary funds would not be forthcoming. The board of directors of the struggling company set April 1, 1971, as the deadline. If the capital and surplus was not raised by that time, they would cancel the issue and fold the company. During the last 10 days left for investment the subscription was met, and by the first of April it was oversubscribed by a whopping 25%. The new company was born.

THE CLAIMS

Just what are the areas of practice that seem to trigger claims? Although this question begs for a simple answer, a simple answer is not possible. In today's litigation-prone world, the plaintiffs' attorneys are lavish with their imaginations and seem to concoct theories for liability that at times seem incomprehensible. For example, in Arizona an architect was sued by a restaurant patron who was showered by shards of glass. It seems that the restaurant was run in connection with a race track where a disgruntled bettor was so incensed by his loss that he threw a rock through the restaurant window, injuring the patron. The patron then sued the restaurant owner and the architect with the allegation that the glass should have been safety glass, because the architect should have reasonably foreseen the possibility that someone would throw a rock through it. Although this claim may seem inane, it is not that atypical of the use of imaginative powers by plaintiff attorneys in their quest for damages.

An excellent monograph, entitled *Liability of Architects and Engineers,* has been produced by the Defense Research Institute in Chicago. It makes a thorough examination of professional liability law and its impact on the design professions. It should be read by design professionals in private practice interested in the legal aspects of professional liability claims.

In general, claims grow out of two areas of professional practice: (*1*) errors, omissions, or negligent professional acts in the preparation of plans and specifications (including feasibility reports); (*2*) negligent professional acts in performing construction review. It seems obvious that if there are errors in the plans and specifications that cause someone damages, the damaged party will be justified in making a claim against the person who produced them. The trouble is that determining whether something is an error or a negligent professional act is not always that easy. The law recognizes this difficulty by setting up a standard of care. In one case it was expressed as follows (8):

> An architect is not a guarantor or an insurer, but as a member of a learned and skilled profession, he is under a duty to exercise the ordinary, reasonable technical skill, ability and competence that is required of an architect in a similar situation, and if by reason of a failure to use due care under the circumstances a foreseeable injury results, liability accrues.

Even with a clearly stated standard of care, a problem still exists because, inevitably it seems, there are differing opinions as to what the "ability, skill and care" are in the community where the loss occurred. Most usually this is a question of fact that a jury may have to decide. They will make their decision based on testimony that is given by expert witnesses as to what the standard of care is in their particular community. Because the expert witnesses most usually have divergent views, this leaves the decision to a coin toss, whim, or even prejudice of the jury, a legal crapshoot that can often be devastating (9).

PROFESSIONAL LIABILITY INSURANCE

With the threat of claims ever-present in private practice, seemingly without regard for due care, architects must do all that they can to protect themselves from loss. Most choose to purchase professional liability insurance to provide defense and indemnity in the event a claim is made. At this writing, the state of the professional liability insurance market may best be described as "stormy." It seems that in the recent past underwriters, in their zeal to garner more premiums, cut their rates below a prudent level. Thereafter, as claims materialized, they found themselves without the necessary claims reserves to pay losses and defense costs on a profitable basis. So, in 1986–1987 they either restricted their writings or increased their rates to try to catch up with the losses they suffered and show a current profit. This reaction has had a prodigious effect on the cost of professional liability insurance. Many practitioners have felt the cost is too great and have dropped coverage. In early 1987, nearly 25% of licensed architects were estimated to be going bare.

Professional liability insurance is one of the most enigmatic of all insurance coverages. Some of the differences that should be highlighted are as follows:

1. Coverage is written on a claims made basis. This means that, unlike most liability insurance, coverage is in effect at the time that a claim is made, not when the tortious act that caused the loss was committed. This makes dropping coverage very difficult because once coverage is discontinued, all past acts that give rise to a claim are left uncovered. It poses a special problem for those architects who decide to retire and are unsure when or whether to discontinue coverage.
2. Another peculiarity that should be noted is that most underwriters have a clause that causes the cost of defense to deplete the limit of indemnity. This is of special importance because defense costs can be astronomical. To demonstrate the enormity of this fact, it is interesting to note that, according to one underwriter, nearly 70% of loss dollars goes to feed the legal system. It is not uncommon for the defense costs to soar to six figures. This fact may have devastating impact on the indemnity limit.
3. One attribute of professional liability insurance that requires special consideration is that all policies issued are subject to a deductible. Although the amount of the deductible may vary, most companies have their minimum set at $5000 (CNA offers coverage with a $2000 deductible for an increase in premium). The policy requires the policyholder to reimburse the deductible when called to do so. The deductible is applicable to costs of defense as well as indemnity. Very often the deductible is used up by legal fees.

The Coverage

It is not possible to cover all the intricacies of the various underwriters' policies here. An insurance agent or broker should be consulted to make such a comparison, preferably one who specializes in architects' professional liability insurance. Some important general features follow.

The Insuring Agreement. All policies of professional liability insurance will have a clause stipulating what the insurance is intending to cover. In the case of professional liability insurance, the clause will usually say that the policy intends to pay for damages arising out of errors, omissions, or negligent professional acts. It is clearly the underwriter's intent to cover for liability that is strictly professional in nature, ie, they have no intention of insuring for liability resulting from operational negligence and not the result of the exercise of professional expertise. This may create problems, because it is not always clear what is and what is not a professional act. This confusion may lead an underwriter to deny liability or, at least, reserve its rights (meaning that it will defend the action, but reserve its rights to deny liability at a later date if it establishes that the claim was based on ordinary negligence as opposed to professional negligence). To provide protection from this potential situation, some insurance agents may recommend that professional liability insurance and comprehensive general liability insurance (for operational negligence) be placed with the same underwriter.

Supplementary Payments. A further section of the policy worth noting deals with the supplemental payments that an underwriter will make in the event of a claim. Supplemental payments will include premiums for appeal bonds, costs of emergency medical aid, expenses incurred at the specific request of the underwriter, judgment interest, allocated claim expense, costs of defense for counsel, and expert witness fees (most expenses for defense not including the underwriter's paid staff). In this latter regard, keep in mind that as costs of defense mount, the limit of liability is being depleted. If the limit of liability is reduced significantly by costs of defense, it may be necessary to look into purchasing limit-reinstatement coverage from the underwriter. The cost should approximate the original cost of the professional liability coverage.

Exclusions. There is an axiom in the insurance industry that says, "With the insuring agreement you give coverage and with the exclusions you take it away." Although this may seem like a cynical statement, it is partly correct. The exclusions limit coverage in such a way that the underwriter does not provide coverage for an exposure they do not intend to insure. Again, it is not possible to cover all the ramifications of the exclusions here.

There are a few exclusions that should be kept constantly in mind. The first of these is the exclusion which stipulates that the policy of insurance will not apply to liability assumed in a contract or an agreement. Its purpose is to make certain that the underwriter is providing coverage only for liability for professional negligence and not for liability that should be someone else's burden. Thus, they will not cover liability assumed in a hold harmless and indemnity clause (unless they would have been liable even in its absence), nor will they cover liability imposed by any warranty, guaranty, or certification clause that expands an architect's liability beyond that imposed by common law. Because today's attorneys consider it *de rigueur* to include all sorts of exculpatory language in contracts of hire, practitioners should take special precautions so that they do not assume liability that will not be covered by insurance.

Another exclusion requiring caution is related to claims arising out of property in which the insured has an ownership interest. Underwriters feel there is a conflict of interest if an architect owns all or a portion of a building on which he or she has performed design. In this regard, they are especially concerned about condominiums or other structures that are constructed on a speculative basis. As a consequence, there are exclusions in virtually all underwriters' policies related to ownership interest exposure.

There are two other exclusions of note. These are related to claims arising out of pollutants (asbestos and waste pollutants). The fact that there may not be any coverage for these exposures places an onerous burden on architects, because it is too hard to conceive of a structure that will not produce some waste (eg, smoke, vapor, soot, fumes). Then, too, owners are anxious to avoid potential liability for these contaminants and have, in recent years, sought to shift responsibility for the exposure by putting the task of asbestos removal under the duties and responsibilities of the architect. If that is permitted to become a service, it is not likely that there will be coverage in effect for the risk.

There are several other exclusions in all policies issued that should be reviewed with the insurance agent or broker, because the coverage purchased will be limited by them. In general, they will be related to the following subjects:

1. Underwriters do not intend to insure against claims arising out of negligence in connection with property of others that may be in the care, custody, and control of the architect.
2. They will exclude claims arising out of claims by employees under the Employee Retirement Income Security Act (ERISA).
3. The policies will disclaim liability for any claim based on job-connected injury by employees of the architect; thus Workers Compensation claims and Employers Liability claims will be excluded.
4. Liability arising from the use of real and personal property will not be covered.
5. Cost estimates and quantity surveys will usually be excluded, but some underwriters may cover these exposures as long as they are done in connection with the architect's work.
6. Punitive and exemplary damages will not be covered. Although these damages are rarely awarded, they are requested by many plaintiffs. The underwriter may then put the architect on notice of an uncovered exposure if such damages are sought.
7. Claims alleging fraud or dishonesty will not be covered. These claims fall in a group of potential allegations called "intentional torts," ie, acts that are intentionally done by or at the direction of the insured. These acts are usually not, but sometimes are, insured.
8. Computer and electronic data-processing claims will frequently be excluded. This is particularly true if the claim arises out of providing data-processing services for others. Coverage is usually afforded if the services that cause the loss are in connection with the architect's own design work.
9. Failure to maintain or effect insurance claims will be excluded, such as failing to effect coverage for a client's construction project. The contract of hire must be made clear in this regard.
10. Derivative liability (ie, liability from the negligent act of a coventuree) in a joint venture will not be covered. Entering a joint venture in effect creates a partnership. Underwriters are reluctant to incur liability that is derived from entities that they have not had the opportunity to underwrite, particularly if the claim is based on the negligent act of one whom they do not insure. This might be one of the coventurees whose professional liability coverage is placed elsewhere. Therefore, special coverage may be required for joint ventures.
11. A catchall clause excluding claims from activities not usual and customary to the architect's practice is found in most policies. Some underwriters also exclude anything in connection with doing construction. This effectively eliminates coverage for design/build jobs or turnkey work of any type.
12. Nuclear energy liability claims are inevitably excluded, but this is frequently done by a special endorsement.

There may be others. Each policy from each underwriter needs to be thoroughly analyzed by someone skilled in policy evaluation. Although it may seem like the exclusions remove a tremendous amount of coverage, in reality the coverage offered by today's insurance markets is relatively good (10).

Limits and Deductibles. Two questions are almost always raised by architects about their professional liability insurance. One is, "What should my limit of liability be?" The other is, "What should my deductible be?" Being pragmatic, architects would like a formula or a plan that gives them the best answers to these questions. The trouble is that not even the most learned expert on the subject of insurance is able to come up with a logical answer to the first question, and the second is subject to debate. It goes without saying that the higher the limit carried, the greater the cost. Conversely, the higher the deductible, the lower the cost. Although $1 million claims were once a rarity, today they are fairly common. Thus carrying a limit of $1 million or more would seem to be prudent in today's litigious climate, particularly as the cost of defense reduces the indemnity available in the event of a claim. The only solid rule that bears up under any argument for a limit of liability is: Buy as high a limit as can be afforded. Although affordability may seem like it is begging the question, there is no other good measure, particularly when the wild nature of some of the claims being made against architects is considered.

Deductibility is another story. It should be set at an affordable amount, preferably without having to borrow any money. Most underwriters will give close scrutiny to any deductible that they feel is beyond the architect's financial resource capability. The last thing that they want is to have to sue to collect the deductible. They can ill afford to alienate a policyholder, particularly if there is a large claim involved. Therefore, they may require proof of financial capability to pay a large deductible if called on to do so. In making an assessment of whether the capacity for paying the deductible exists, the underwriter will hypothesize that the architect may be called on to pay more than one deductible in a policy period.

The deductible is usually a sum that is paid by the company in the insured's behalf for the lower sums of indemnity and costs of defense. The insured is required to reimburse the full amount advanced by the company within a stated period of time. Failure to pay the sum to the company within the prescribed period of time entitles the underwriter to recover reasonable costs, expenses, and legal fees incurred in the collection of the advanced sum. This amount will include interest at the rate permitted in the jurisdiction applying to judgments.

One further point that should be noted as respects the limit of liability is that the limit is an aggregate amount, not available per claim but available per policy period (usually 1 year). Two or more claims in any one policy year may deplete the limit and require the purchase of a reinstatement of limit. Although the limit is aggregate, the deductible applies per claim or, as a practical matter, per reported error, omission, or negligent professional act. Again, this is a matter to be determined by each underwriter under the circumstance of the claim, but most of them treat multiple claims from a single error as one claim for deductible purposes.

Time and Territory. Most underwriters give full retroactive coverage in their professional liability policies for architects. This means that they will cover the exposure for errors, omissions, or negligent professional acts as long as the insured had no knowledge about the claim before the inception of the policy, or any knowledge about the claim before the inception of the policy, or any knowledge of any circumstances or situations that might reasonably be expected to give rise to a claim. This gives rise to another professional liability insurance axiom: Do not change underwriters if you have knowledge of any circumstance that might reasonably be expected to give rise to a claim.

Whereas at one time underwriters were fairly restrictive about the territory in which they would provide coverage, they are fairly liberal today. Most will provide coverage for work done in the United States, including its territories and possessions, Puerto Rico, Canada, and anywhere else in the world as long as claim is made or suit is brought in the United States. This point should be verified with the agent or broker if plans are made to provide services outside the United States.

Duties in the Event of Claim. As with any insurance policy, there are certain things that the architect must do as an insured in the event claim is made. Notification of the company is the first duty, and with sufficient information so that they may conduct an investigation. This will normally include the four "W's," ie, What? Where? When? Who? The underwriter is interested in finding out what the nature of the claim might be, the location of the property damage or bodily injury, when the injury or damage took place and its extent, and who the claimants or potential claimants might be. They will also require the names and addresses of any witnesses and persons who may have been injured. They require this information in writing. It must also be done promptly, and failure to do so may result in their denying liability. Even if a claim appears to be entirely specious, the underwriter should be notified in order to preserve coverage rights.

Settlement. Most policies issued to architects stipulate that the underwriter will not settle a claim against the architect without securing his or her prior written consent. If the insured architect refuses to give consent, the underwriter will not be liable beyond a certain amount. Most professional liability policies stipulate that this will be the amount they could have settled the claim for at the time they sought written request and were refused. Sometimes righteous indignation stimulates the architect to take a position based on principle. This can be dangerous in professional liability claims situations because taking the position to "fight to the bitter end" may impair coverage. It is an area that sometimes gives rise to acrimonious feelings between architects and their insurers; it is where pragmatism and morality clash head-on.

Once claim has been made, the insured has a contractual duty to cooperate with the company in its defense. This means that the insured must attend hearings, depositions, and trials without reimbursement for time. Then too, the loss of time can be enormous, and it will have an adverse effect on the insured's willingness to continue defending. Nonetheless, the insured must give of his or her time at the request of the company until the claim has been resolved.

Who is Insured by Professional Liability Policies? In general, coverage is intended for the business owners, their officers, and employees while acting within the scope of their duties for the named insured. This normally includes former officers and employees, but only for activities that were conducted during their term of employment with the named insured. Coverage is not intended for employees when they moonlight or perform services that are outside the scope of their employment.

Arbitration. The various underwriters providing professional liability coverage for architects differ on how to treat clauses that make arbitration the sole and exclusive remedy between the insured and the client. Some stipulate that the insured will not sign such an agreement without prior written consent from the underwriter, and then will grant to the underwriter all rights of the insured for choice of arbitrators and to conduct the arbitration proceedings. Others are more liberal and permit the insured to enter into such agreements, but preserve the company's right to choose the arbitrator and conduct the arbitration proceedings. Guidance regarding the best course of action to pursue should be sought from competent legal counsel in a particular jurisdiction.

PROFESSIONAL LIABILITY LOSS PREVENTION

At least two underwriters provide professional liability loss-prevention programs: DPIC and CNA. DPIC offers rate credits for completion of a home-study course based on their loss prevention manual *Untangling the Web of Professional Liability* and its successor, *Lessons In Professional Liability* (11). They also offer rate credits for diligent use of a limitation of liability clause in their insureds' contracts of hire (see Limitation of Liability).

The CNA program centers on a publication produced by Victor O. Schinnerer & Company, Inc., Office for Professional Liability Research, entitled *Guidelines for Improving Practice, Architects and Engineers Professional Liability* (12). It contains not only researched information, but empirical advice from architects as well. The data contained in it is in loose-leaf form so that it may be replaced as information becomes available or is outdated. The *Guidelines for Improving Practice* is published in cooperation with the American Institute of Architects, the National Society of Professional Engineers/Professional Engineers in Private Practice, and CNA Insurance. The content is color-coded under the following headings: Type of Structure, Phase of Professional Service, Special Studies, General Information, Insurance, Legal Highlights. There is also a legal newsletter published for attorneys who serve architects and engineers. The information has a bias toward legal considerations of practice.

For its part, DPIC's *Untangling the Web of Professional Liability* heads its subject matter with the following titles: Professionalism, Interpersonal Relationships, Business Procedures, Technical Procedures, and Insurance. This reflects DPIC's conviction that a large percentage of professional liability claims are a result of breakdowns in communication and human relations rather than errors in design.

Both programs have much to offer the practitioner who is interested in reducing exposure. The DPIC program is made available only to policyholders; the CNA material may be purchased from the Office of Professional Liability Research, Victor O. Schinnerer & Company, Inc., Chevy Chase, Md.

INSURANCE MARKETS

As mentioned above, the insurance marketplace is in a state of disarray at this time. Most underwriters have raised their rates for design professionals dramatically since the mid-1980s, and many have curbed their writing or withdrawn from the field entirely. This has created a seller's market in which the buyer should be cautious about putting too much credence in cost, particularly because buying professional liability insurance is not unlike buying design professionals' services. Price should be a consideration only after many other attributes have been explored. These attributes in an insurance carrier are as follows:

1. *Stability*. How long they have been in business; do they have staying power in years of adversity?
2. *Financial strength*. Does the underwriter have the financial capability of meeting its financial commitment to pay claims now and in the future? One guide in this regard is A. M. Best's *Property and Casualty Insurance Co. Guide* (13). Their book rates property and casualty insurance companies based on financial strength and other considerations. It should be used only as a guide, because their evaluations are sometimes skewed by the fact that their ratings are done annually.
3. *Coverage*. Is there as much coverage for the premium dollar as might reasonably be expected? This is a question that should be answered by a trained insurance agent or broker in cooperation with the architect. The architect should ask questions and provide information about any unique aspects of the firm's operation. For example, if a financial position in design jobs is taken by the architect, the agent or broker should be advised, because some underwriters exclude such jobs from coverage.
4. *Claims-handling capability*. Does the underwriter have a claims staff to do investigation, get statements, and perform the four W's described under "Duties in the Event of Claim"? If not, they may be handing the case directly to an attorney whose charges will go into effect just to do legwork, an expensive way to manage claims.

The carriers that may be available to architects for coverage are as follows:

CNA Insurance Companies
Victor O. Schinnerer & Company, Inc.
2 Wisconsin Circle
Chevy Chase, MD 20815-7003

DPIC Companies
P.O. Box DPIC
Monterey, CA 93942

Imperial Casualty & Indemnity Co.
c/o Thomas F. Sheehan Inc.
801 North Plaza Drive
Schaumburg, IL 60195

Evanston Insurance Group
Shand, Morahan & Co., Inc.
Shand Morahan Plaza
Evanston, IL 60201

Lexington Insurance Co.
c/o Professional Managers, Inc.
2 North Riverside Plaza
Suite 1460
Chicago, IL 60606

Lloyd's
c/o Illinois R. B. Jones
175 West Jackson Blvd.
Chicago, IL 60604

William B. Turner & Associates
33 East Wacker Drive
Chicago, IL 60601

IMI Insurance Co.
2600 River Rd.
Des Plaines, IL 60018

A number of the available markets are located in the Chicago area. This may be because the principals of some of those firms were once employees of the Kemper Group and were involved in their programs of insurance for architects and engineers. The American Institute of Architects published a monograph titled "1986 Professional Liability Insurance Survey" that should be studied while making an evaluation of potential underwriters. It may be of some interest that the AIA still commends only one underwriter, CNA, as managed by Victor O. Schinnerer & Company, Inc.

CAPTIVE INSURANCE AND SELF-INSURANCE

In the early 1970s it became popular to set up captive insurance companies to insure difficult-to-place risks. The soil and foundation engineers did this by forming a company in Bermuda—Terra Insurance, Ltd.—that is ostensibly successful. DPIC was formed under a similar set of circumstances and, although not technically speaking a captive, it was, until 1984, an industry-owned insurance company serving the needs of a special group—consulting engineers in private practice—many of whom owned stock in the company.

Much has changed that militates against architects trying to form their own insurance facility today. The impediments to this approach are as follows:

1. Capital and surplus requirements have increased exponentially with the growth of claims frequency and severity. These factors have swelled so much since 1970 that capital demands to start a company are almost out of sight. One former employee of the Department of Insurance of the State of New York opined that $25 million would be needed to form a company to provide coverage for architects. Although this sum is on the conservative side, it does give a ballpark figure for the capital needs of a new company in a difficult line.
2. Today's reinsurance markets are extremely tight and would not show a keen interest in a start-up professional liability insurance company for architects. It continues to be a seller's market in the reinsurance business, and the reinsurance companies are prone to charge what the traffic will bear. In the case of all types of professional liability insurance (including medical malpractice), it will bear a lot. Reinsurance is a necessity for a new, small company. Such a company must insure against losses exceeding the number and amount of claims they predicted at the start (aggregate excess reinsurance). It must also reinsure against losses exceeding that portion of the risk (excess of loss reinsurance) that it retains as its share of the risk on any one policy (the company might issue a policy of insurance with a policy limit of $1 million; it might retain as its share $250,000 of any one loss and reinsure the remaining $750,000).

   Reinsurance may be purchased in other ways. One is for the primary insurer (the captive) to hold varying (horizontal) layers of loss as its retention. Another would be to take a quota (vertical) share of the $1 million of the limit equivalent to 25% of the total limit (ie, $250,000) and reinsure the balance (quota share reinsurance). The high cost of reinsurance coverage in today's reinsurance marketplace might doom a new company before it got started.
3. Architects in private practice run businesses where their cash flow demands are such that gathering resources to make a major nonproductive investment is difficult. Nor is there a likelihood that there are venture capitalists that would look on investment in a start-up insurance company with much favor, because the recent track record of the "experts in the field," the current underwriters, does not look all that attractive from an investment point of view.

This does not mean that architects in private practice have no method for fighting the rising costs of professional liability insurance. One method that might be employed is to use the Risk Retention Act of 1986. It has two provisions that bear on this issue. One makes it possible for groups of businesses with a common exposure to join in a self-insurance pool. For the reasons stated above, this may not be a good choice. The other aspect of the Act that shows promise makes it possible for groups of businesses to join together in a single body to purchase their insurance. This ploy has been illegal in most states until the passage of this Act. It may have some attractive attributes for architects.

LIMITATION OF LIABILITY

In the time of the Phoenicians (circa 1200 B.C.), a concept was given birth that may have applicability in today's litigation-prone business environment. The Phoenicians were master mariners. They were some of the first people able to construct ships that could withstand the rigors of the open sea. They used this technological advantage to develop a profitable business in the transportation of trade goods. For a fee they would carry cargo to the ports of the Mediterranean Sea. The trouble was that when the ship and cargo were lost owing to factors beyond the control of the shipowner, the cargo owner would seek redress in an amount equivalent to the value of the lost cargo, often many times the value of the hull of the ship and beyond the financial resources of the shipowner. This liability was impeding the development of trade and commerce, making the risk greater than the potential reward to the ship owner.

It was in this environment that some clever person conceived of limitation of liability. It was a doctrine which said that the ship owner would do his best to deliver the goods of the cargo owner, but if he should fail owing to the vagaries of weather and navigation, his liability would be limited to the value of the hull of the ship. When this doctrine was introduced, trade resumed and both shippers and shipowners prospered.

In 1601, the British Parliament recognized the equitable need for limitation of liability on the sea and passed legislation incorporating limitation of liability into admiralty law. Today it is recognized throughout the world as a fair and equitable means of apportioning risk. It is used in dozens of business relationships where there is some doubt about the worth of the consideration for performing a service when measured against the risk of loss. These include airline travel, interstate trucking, financial planning, hotel management, patent law, and others where the risk/reward quotients are out of balance.

In 1972 the members of the Association of Soil and Foundation Engineers were beset by professional liability claims. Usually their fees were infinitesimal when compared with the value of the job. So in the face of their desperate situation, they determined to start using limitation of liability clauses in their contracts of hire. Almost immediately, these contractual clauses worked like a claims-reducing vaccine. Why is difficult to say, but their claims frequency and severity fell so dramatically that they became one of the least claims-troubled groups of the design professions.

Some analysts have felt that for design professionals to use these defensive measures is somehow unprofessional. These same people feel it is proper to hold harmless and indemnity clauses forgiving all liability in connection with hazardous waste and asbestos removal jobs. How they reconcile their feelings is difficult to discern. The point is that having an agreement with the client and the contractors on the job as to what the amount of liability will be in the event errors and omissions damage them may be a way to reduce exposure (14).

THE BURDEN OF BEING THE PRIME DESIGN PROFESSIONAL

As the prime design professional, architects are responsible for the errors, omissions, and professional negligence of the consultants they hire and over whom they have the right of control. This doctrine, *respondeat superior,* holds that a master is responsible for the damages occasioned by the tortious conduct of his servants committed in the course of his business. This means, then, that an architect will usually be in the chain of liability should the consultants he or she hires and directs commit an error, omission, or negligent professional act that causes other damages. Many architects feel that their greatest exposure to claims comes from their consultants and not from their own work. This may be so simply because the law of large numbers dictates that the addition of four or five design professionals to the architect's exposure increases his or her potential liability.

Faced with this obvious area of increased exposure during an era when professional liability claims are seriously threatening many architects' ability to practice, some architects, with the help of their attorneys, are removing themselves from the chain of potential liability. They are doing this by foregoing their role as prime design professional by surrendering the responsibility for the consultants to the owner. This is accomplished by contractually agreeing with the owner that the owner will hire the consultants and that the architect will neither have control nor the right of control over the consultants' execution of their work. This does not mean that the architect will not be the governing force over the important aspects of work, only that he will not have the consultants reporting to him. They will report directly to the owner, and the architect's wants will be transmitted to the consultants via the owner.

This technique is highly controversial. Some attorneys and architects believe that to use it would cause greater claims than now exist, because they would lose control of the job and compound the chance of errors through a lack of coordination of the various elements of the job. It certainly is a methodology that should be studied thoroughly by a firm, with competent legal advice, before being adopted.

Even so, in many larger urban areas the practice of having the owner assume the task of job administration has become a reality. Some architects continue to rebel at this concept. Others say they now are comfortable with the arrangement and contend they have found the following benefits:

1. *Increased profitability.* This is brought about by staff considerations, ie, fewer people required to coordinate the activities of consultants.

2. *Lower insurance cost.* Under the traditional method, all gross receipts earned by an architect are reported to the professional liability underwriter, including those receipts that are then paid to the consultants. With the fees no longer flowing through the architect's books, premiums are lessened.
3. *Less time lost in litigation.* When plaintiffs learn that the architect is not the prime design professional, they are less apt to name him or her in claims that are the result of the consultants' work.
4. *Exposure to budget considerations is largely eliminated.* Because much of the work in a structure is engineering in nature, questions of cost of completed work are left to the structural, mechanical, electrical, acoustical, or other consultants. The architect is freed from their budgetary considerations. This approach runs counter to the traditional role of an architect in practice, but it is worth exploring with an attorney as a means of reducing exposure.

CONCLUSION

For reasons that remain obscure, it appears that today's architect in private practice will be faced with a continuing onslaught of professional liability claims. The best response to this situation is to improve practice procedures to minimize exposure, continue to strive for technical excellence, and use those legal remedies that will place the burden of this exposure in proper perspective. Insurance against this risk is not likely to get much cheaper in the foreseeable future, nor is there apt to be any salvation in the form of a new type of insurance entity. Examination of the possibilities available under the Risk Retention Act of 1986 should be made. Group purchasing may be in order. Serious consideration should be given to either limiting liability by contractual means or changing the contracting techniques so that consultants are solely responsible for their portion of the work.

BIBLIOGRAPHY

1. L. Sprague de Camp, *The Ancient Engineers,* Ballantine Books, New York, 1960, p. 480.
2. M. Prawy, *The Vienna Opera,* Praeger Publishers, New York, 1970, plate III/3.
3. *Ibid.,* p. 26.
4. *Feltus v. Swan,* 62 Miss 415 (1884); *Downer v. Davis,* 19 Pick. 72; *Mayor v. Cunliff,* 2 N.Y. 165.
5. *Tharsis S. & C. Co. v. Loftus,* L.R. 8 C.P.1 (1872).
6. *Pappa v. Rose,* L.R. 7 C.P.32, 525.
7. *Macpherson v. Buick Motor Co.,* 111 N.E. 1050 (1916).
8. *Aetna Insurance Co. v. Hellmuth, Obata & Kassabaum, Inc.,* 392F 2d 472 (1968), 8th Circuit.
9. *Laukkanen v. Jewel Tea Co.,* 222 NE 2d 584. (Ill. Appeals, 1966).
10. "1986 Professional Liability Insurance Survey," the AIA Liability Task Group, The American Institute of Architects, Washington, D.C., Dec. 1986.
11. *Lessons in Professional Liability,* Design Professionals Insurance Company, Monterey, Calif., 1988.
12. *Guidelines for Improving Practice, Architects and Engineers Professional Liability,* Victor O. Schinner & Company, Inc., Chevy Chase, Md., continually updated.
13. *Property and Casualty Insurance Co. Guide,* A. M. Best Company, Oldwick, N.J., published yearly.
14. E. B. Howell and R. P. Howell, *Untangling the Web of Professional Liability,* Design Professionals Insurance Company, San Francisco, Calif., 1976, p. 81.

General References

Courtesy of the Defense Research Institute.

Acret, *Architects and Engineers: Their Professional Responsibilities,* Shepard's Inc., Colorado Springs, Colo., 1977, Supp. 1981.

Sweet, *Legal Aspects of Architecture, Engineering and the Construction Process,* West Publishing, Inc., St. Paul, Minn., 1977.

"Admissibility of Codes or Standards of Safety Issued or Sponsored by Governmental Body or Voluntary Association," 58 *ALR3d* 148 (1974).

"Architect's Liability for Personal Injury or Death Allegedly Caused by Improper or Defective Plans or Design," 97 *ALR3d* 455 (1980).

"Architect's Liability for Personal Injury or Death From Improper Plans or Design," 59 *ALR2d* 1081 (1958).

"Construction and Application of Liability or Indemnity Policy on Civil Engineer, Architect or the Like," 83 *ALR3d* 539 (1978).

"Liability to One Injured in Course of Construction, Based upon Architect's Alleged Failure to Carry Out Supervisory Responsibilities," 59 *ALR3d* 869 (1974).

"Necessity of Expert Testimony to Show Malpractice of Architect," 3 *ALR4th* 1023 (1981).

"Tort Liability of Project Architect for Economic Damages Suffered by Contractor," 65 *ALR3d* 249 (1975).

"Validity and Construction, As to Claim Alleging Design Defects, of Statute Imposing Time Limitations Upon Action Against Architect or Engineer for Injury or Death Arising Out of Defective or Unsafe Condition of Improvement to Real Property," 93 *ALR3d* 1242 (1979).

"When Statute of Limitations Begins to Run on Negligent Design Claim Against Architect," 90 *ALR3d* 507 (1979).

"Architectural Malpractice Litigation," 19 Am. Jur. Trials 231.

Kaskell, "Architect's Negligence," 26 *Proof of Facts* 2d 325 (1981).

"Accrual of Cause of Action in Products Liability and Other Tort Actions," 42 *Tenn. L. Rev.* 593 (1975).

Andrews, "Surety Recovery From Architect or Engineer—Why Not?" 8 *Forum* 571 (1973).

"Architectural Malpractice: a Contract-Based Approach," 92 *Harvard L. Rev.* 1075 (1979).

Carey, "Assessing Liability of Architects and Engineers for Construction Supervision," *Ins. L. J.* 147 (1979).

Collins, "Limitation of Action Statutes for Architects and Builders—An Examination of Constitutionality," 29 *Federation Ins. Coun. Q.* 41 (1978).

Collins and Livingston, "Aspects of Conclusive Evidence Clauses," 1974 *J. Bus. L.* 212 (1974).

"Construction Law Symposium," 23 *St. Louis U. L. Rev.* 1–222 (1979).

Crishham, "Liability of Architects and Engineers to Third Parties," 26 *Federation Ins. Coun. Q.* 177 (1976).

Davidson, "Liability of Architects," 13 *Trial* 20 (1977).

"Defective Design—Wisconsin's Limitation of Action Statute for Architects, Contractors and Others Involved in Design and Improvement to Real Property," 63 *Marq. L. Rev.* 87 (1979).

"Defense Catalog for the Design Professional," 45 *UM-KC L Rev.* 75 (1976).

"Design Professionals—Recognizing a Duty to Inform," 30 *Hastings L. J.* 729 (1979).

Easton and Koeppl, "Some Other Engineering Defenses," 63 *Ill. B. J.* 90 (Sept.–Oct. 1974).

Goldberg, "Liability of Architects and Engineers for Construction Site Accidents in Maryland—Krieger v. J. E. Greiner Co.: Background and Unanswered Questions," 39 *Md. L. Rev.* 475 (1980).

Hart, "Representing the Architect in Dealing with the Owner and Contractor," 7 *Forum* 197 (July 1972).

Jenswold, "How to Best Handle Litigation Involving Architects and Engineers," 45 *Insurance Coun. J.* 316 (1978).

"Jones v. Continental Casualty Company: the Dilemma of Architects' Malpractice Insurance Contracts," 9 *New England L. Rev.* 357 (1974).

Kaskell, "Possible Avenues of Liability of the Architect and Engineer to Contractors and Subcontractors or How Claimants Will Try to Anticipate and Overcome the A-E's Favorite Defenses," 47 *Ins. Coun. J.* 353 (1980).

Kaskell, "Representing the Contractor in Dealing with Architect, Owner and Sub-Contractors," 7 *Forum* 215 (July 1972).

Kaskell, "The Bidding Process," 1 *Construction Lawyer* No. 4 at 1 (1981).

L'Abbate, "Who's In Charge Here?" 11 *Forum* 925 (Spring 1976).

"Legislation: Oklahoma's Statute Limiting Actions Against Designers and Builders," 27 *Okla. L. Rev.* 723 (1974).

"Liability of Design Architects and Engineers to Third Parties: a New Approach," 53 *Notre Dame Law* 306 (1977).

"Liability of Design Professionals—the Necessity of Fault," 59 *Ia. L. Rev.* 1221 (1973).

"Malpractice: the Design Professional's Dilemma," 10 *John Marshall J.* 287 (1977).

Marshall, "When the Architect is Not a Quasi-Arbitrator," 37 *Modern L. Rev.* 566 (1974).

Maurer, "Architects, Engineers and Hold Harmless Clauses," *Ins. L. J.* 725 (1976).

McGovern, "Status of Statutes of Limitations and Statutes of Repose in Product Liability Actions," 16 *Forum* 416 (1981) (includes tables and lists of statutes applicable to architects and engineers).

Murphy, "Impact of the 1976 Edition of the AIA Document A201 on the Liability of Architects and Engineers to the Construction Surety for Negligent Certification of Payments," 45 *Ins. Counsel J.* 200 (1978).

Neeson, "Current Status of Professional Architects' and Engineers' Malpractice Liability Insurance," 45 *Ins. Counsel J.* 39 (1978).

Philips, "Judgment and Discretion in Architects' and Engineers' Professional Decisionmaking," 16 *Forum* 332 (1980).

"Recent Statutory Developments Concerning the Limitations of Actions Against Architects, Engineers and Builders," 60 *Ky. L. J.* 462 (1971–1972).

Rogers, "Constitutionality of Alabama's Statute of Limitations for Construction Litigation," 11 *Cumberland L. Rev.* 1 (1980).

"Roles of Architect and Contractor in Construction Management," 6 *U. Mich. J.L.* Ref 447 (1973).

Sanbar and Pataki, "Professional Liability: Malpractice of Attorneys, Accountants, Architects and Engineers," 3 *Okla. City U.L. Rev.* 689 (1979).

"Selected Materials on Architects, Engineers and Contractors," 34 *Record* 247 (1979).

Shea, "Architect-Engineer Liability Suits by the Government, a Case for Expanding Jurisdiction of the A.S.B.C.A.," 19 *AF. L. R.* 250 (1977).

Stanton and Dugdale, "Design Responsibility in Civil Engineering Work, (building law—Great Britain)," 131 *New L.J.* 583 (1981).

"Supervisory Duties of an Architect," 3 *Memphis St. U. L. Rev.* 139 (1972).

Sweet, "Site Architects and Construction Workers: Brothers and Keepers or Strangers?" 28 *Emory L.J.* 291 (1979).

Vandall, "Architects' Liability in Georgia: A Special Statute of Limitations," 14 *Ga. SB. J.* 164 (1978).

See also Arbitration in Construction; Architecture and Engineering Performance Information Center (AEPIC); Construction Law; Inspection, Observation, and Supervision; Mediation in Architectural and Construction Disputes; Reasonable Care, Standard of; Specifications

Edward B. Howell
K&H Communications
Monterey, California

LIBRARIES

As human societies began to commit the spoken word to a graphic form, the need for storing, preserving, and retrieving this material became vital to its owner and, as collections grew beyond manageable size, the need for architectural solutions became critical.

HISTORY

The Invention of Writing

From the beginning of civilization, humans have felt compelled to record their deeds and thoughts in order to perpetuate their wealth, fame, and knowledge. Indeed, every form of art was employed in this task: architecture, painting, and sculpture, as well as various forms of calligraphic representation.

The need to preserve these records led to one of the most remarkable of human inventions: writing. In Egypt, written language began around 3000 B.C. as hieroglyphics, developing by 1200 B.C. into a more phonographic form using syllables and letters. The development of phonetics, whereby the sounds of speech are recorded in written symbols, gave language its enormous capacity to record and transmit complex ideas precisely in ways hieroglyphics never could. In its various forms, Egyptian writing with its links to Semitic languages spans some 38 centuries to about 400 A.D.; it is history's longest continuous linguistic tradition. As written languages emerged in other cultures, each developed its own increasingly sophisticated vocabulary, grammar, and syntax to serve administration and commerce as well as science and religion. Buildings were soon required to house these earliest collections. Traces of libraries are still evident at Karnak and Edfu, where catalogs were incised into the walls.

The Technology of Writing. Although tens of thousands remain, the clay tablets of cuneiform writing from 2000 B.C. and earlier were unwieldy and difficult to store. The extraordinary expansion of writing required a technical means of recording texts simply and economically. By 1000 B.C., the preferred medium became ink writing on papyrus (Egyptian paperlike sheets made of Nile sedge that had been woven into mats and glued together). It was exported through Alexandria to much of the known Western world, in scrolls from 12 to 18 in. wide and as much as 100 ft long. Coincidentally, Alexandria also became a center for reproduction of texts and the seat of the world's first great library.

But papyrus, like clay tablets, had its limitations. A more readily available material was employed in the East for record keeping: parchment made from the skin of goats, sheep, or pigs. Its polished surface, bleached with lime, was far more durable and from 190 B.C. until the fifteenth century parchment was the preferred medium for writing. Limited by the size of the hides, the book format evolved to replace the scrolls of earlier times.

Chinese legend credits a court attendant, Ts'ai Lun, with the invention of paper around 100 A.D., but it took about eight centuries to reach Europe. Not until the invention of printing in the fifteenth century did its use become widespread.

Ancient Libraries

The first and, by reputation, the greatest of the early libraries was in Hellenic Alexandria, where Alexander himself wished to build a library like that of his teacher, Aristotle, with store rooms, study halls, lecture rooms, cloisters, garden, and even dining rooms. Ptolemy I (323–285 B.C.) brought together Egyptian and Greek scholarship to generate a collection said to consist eventually of 700,000 scrolls cataloged in book form in 120 volumes. The rolls, tagged at their ends and kept in boxes, were arranged by five subjects: history, oratory, poetry, philosophy, and miscellany, as proposed by Aristotle. Built within the palace grounds, it was inadvertently partly destroyed by Caesar's troops when the harbor was fired upon in 47 B.C. In 391 A.D., the library met its total demise, engineered by the Archbishop of Alexandria, who was intent on destroying its heathen material.

A second great collection, that of Pergamum, a Greek city in Asia Minor, is said to have alarmed the jealous Ptolemy V (203–181 B.C.) by its size. He decreed an embargo on the shipment of papyrus. The unforeseen consequence was to stimulate the development of parchment as the superior medium of writing and to supplant papyrus completely some 700 years later.

Aristotle (384–322 B.C.) is credited with founding the first great library in Greece. There were innumerable private and official collections, which eventually made their way to Rome centuries later. Tragically, most of these buildings and their vast collections fell victim to the barbarian invaders during the decline of the Empire.

The Medieval Period

Historian Daniel J. Boorstin writes (1):

> The Latin culture of medieval Europe could hardly have prospered without the enthusiasm, the passion, and the good sense of Saint Benedict of Nursia [480?–543?]. The father of Christian monasticism in Europe, he was also the godfather of libraries. The preservation of the literary treasures of antiquity and of Christianity through the Middle Ages was a Benedictine achievement.

The Rule (Regula) of Saint Benedict prescribed a reading schedule of about two hours a day for the monks. Three centuries later, with the appointment of Alcium (732–804), an English monk, Charlemagne's splendid palace library became renowned as a cultural center of Western Europe.

By the twelfth century the revival of learning spurred further rapid demand for and growth of collections fostered by social and commercial changes and the rise of universities throughout Europe. Latin religious texts were supplemented by vernacular languages presaging the humanistic nationalism of the Renaissance.

The Renaissance

By the twelfth century, Renaissance Italy became the center of a rapidly expanding book trade as decaying monasteries made their collections in Greek and Latin literature available. Michelangelo, commissioned by Lorenzo the Magnificent, created a truly magnificent suite of rooms in the cloister of San Lorenzo, which comprise the Biblioteca Laurenziana (1525–1559). Steeply sloped carrel desks and benches line the main reading room (Fig. 1). Chains were used to prevent the removal of the heavy incunabula so that the reader simply had to move to the appropriate desk (Fig. 2). Typically, collections were shelved by size of subject and cataloged accordingly with labels on the spines.

Great collections thrived. The spatial grandeur of the library of the Escorial by Juan Herrera set a precedent. Pope Nicholas V (1447–1455) revitalized the 1000-year-

Figure 1. Biblioteca Laurenziana, San Lorenzo, Florence, Michelangelo (1525–1559).

Figure 2. Carrels at Biblioteca Laurenziana, San Lorenzo, Florence.

old Vatican Library, while the beginnings of great national and university libraries were evident everywhere, including the Bibliotheque du Roi, later to become France's Bibliotheque Nationale, Canterbury, the Sorbonne, and Oxford. For Trinity College at Cambridge, Sir Christopher Wren placed the library on the piano nobile, leaving the ground level open to the view (Fig. 3). Eleven pairs of arched windows lighted the book-lined alcoves (Fig. 4).

Throughout Europe, Renaissance scholarship flourished, but the ravages of centuries of wars and neglect had taken their toll. Much of the extraordinary production of 1000 years from the monastic scriptoria was lost forever.

The Gutenberg Bible and the Printed Word

Excepting gunpowder and the miracles of twentieth-century science, it is difficult to imagine an invention which so profoundly affected Western civilization as the printing press.

So long as the written word was held hostage by kings and clergy through the media of their libraries, their scriptoria, and the use of Latin to the exclusion of the vernacular languages, intellectual change was obstructed.

Gutenberg's Bible was an extraordinary technological breakthrough. First printed in 1455 (or perhaps 2 years earlier), it introduced innovations that still persist in the printing industry. Of Gutenberg's master work, Boorstin writes, "Bibliophiles agree that the very first printed book in Europe was one of its most beautiful. The technical efficiency of Gutenberg's work, the clarity of impression and the durability of the product, were not substantially improved until the nineteenth century" (2).

Figure 3. Trinity College Library, Cambridge, Sir Christopher Wren (1676–1684).

Figure 4. Interior, Trinity College Library, Cambridge.

The industrial revolution changed all of that with remarkable swiftness. During its first 400 years, the printed word, with all of its technical refinements, released into the collective mind ideas previously limited either to scholarly preoccupation or to languish in mysticism, as the dispersion of scientific and philosophical knowledge changed the nature of Western civilization. With it came the great collections and the need to house them in buildings appropriate to their use, in effect the need for the modern library. It is the nineteenth-century development of these library buildings that anticipated the forms and technology of today.

The American Library Movement

The Emersonian philosophy of the early nineteenth century, with its faith in the common man and democratic ideals of perfectibility, reinforced by the rapid rise in industrialization, awakened a need to make libraries available to a wider and increasingly educated public. That need received its initial expression in the library convention of 1853, which brought together many leading librarians, including William F. Poole of the Boston Atheneum, perhaps the premier public library of the day; Justin Winsor, later librarian of Harvard College, and Charles Coffin Jewitt, president of the Smithsonian Institution. A number of farsighted recommendations emerged from the proceedings, including support for the concept of a national library and a uniform method of cataloging.

Two decades later (1876), three important institutions emerged to strengthen the country's library movement: the American Library Association, a powerful professional voice; the *Library Journal,* the principal professional publication; and the Library Bureau, a service organization

Figure 5. Exterior, Redwood Library, Newport, R. I., Peter Harrison (1749–1750). Photograph by Charles Blomberg.

devoted to planning and supply of appropriately designed equipment and furniture. Most prominent among the founders of all three institutions was a young Amherst graduate, Melvin Dewey. While at Amherst, he developed a system of classification which became known as the Dewey Decimal System; it was widely adopted and became the principal method of cataloging until superseded by the Library of Congress system. Dewey went on to found the first Library School at Columbia University in 1886. When the trustees took exception to the enrollment of women (there were 7 men and 18 women in the first class), the resourceful Dewey moved the school to Albany, where he later served also as chief librarian of the New York State Library, and eventually as secretary and executive officer of the University of the State of New York, leaving there in 1906 amid rumors of scandal. A controversial figure, he was nevertheless the catalyst behind the profession.

American Library Building to 1900

The Redwood Library of Newport, R.I. (1749–1750) (Figs. 5,6) is the first U.S. example of its type worthy of the name. The work of Peter Harrison, widely recognized as the nation's first professional architect, the building is Palladian in concept and duplicates in remarkable fashion the "Headpiece to Fourth Book of Palladio (1736)" as it appeared in an English translation. With remarkable care, the exterior has rendered Palladio's concept in wood down to the rustication of the facades with pine planking.

In Jefferson's remarkable composition for the University of Virginia, the library (1820) was adroitly placed where its symbolic meaning could not be misconstrued. Two symmetrical wings of pavilions and dormitories con-

Figure 6. Reading room, Redwood Library, Newport, R. I. Photograph by Charles Blomberg.

nected by classical colonnades form two sides of the quadrangle of roughly 200 × 600 ft. At its head, the library assumes a dominant presence. Its cylindrical form, 80 ft in diameter, is taken directly from the Roman Pantheon, a building of twice the diameter with its rotunda capped by a dome. The powerful classical form unmistakably identifies the library as the core of Jefferson's "academical village," in contrast to the loosely structured arrangements of single-purpose buildings to be found at Harvard, Yale, the college of New Jersey (Princeton), and Brown, or the earlier tight, monastic cloisters typical of Oxford and Cambridge, where the chapel was the dominant element. The library additionally contained a lecture room, gymnasium, and other facilities, including the first U.S. planetarium. Its stark, soaring interior volume was an impressive image not lost on later designers. It is hardly a coincidence that McKim, Mead, and White, who were called upon to reconstruct Jefferson's rotunda after it was seriously damaged by fire in the early 1900s, should use the theme of the Pantheon for the design of Low Memorial Library at Columbia University in 1907. The classic placement of both buildings with their formal symmetrical axes was to be adopted widely to reinforce the centrality of the library as the repository of knowledge.

The rotunda of the University of Virginia library follows a pattern of principal libraries of the Renaissance, the concept of the "Great Hall," which continued to be the basic plan through the nineteenth century and well into the twentieth. In essence, it consisted of a large square or rectangular high-ceilinged space lined with bookcases. By midcentury, two dynamic factors became increasingly influential:

1. The liberalization of access to higher education brought an increasing number of users into the libraries and an unprecedented increase in the production of books resulted from both the technological improvement in printing and the enormous intellectual output of the times. The former proved to be a less demanding problem than the latter.
2. The need to accommodate the increasing collections required new patterns beyond typical wall shelving. As the hall grew in width, columns were introduced to reduce spans to more manageable lengths. The column spacing, often 15–18 ft on center, became the basis of alcove arrangements of shelving allowing for additional low shelving or a study table with chairs in the alcove itself.

The Boston Atheneum (1855) used two tiers of alcoved stacks, while the Boston Public Library, in its Boylston Street Building (1858), employed three tiers to house a collection that grew to an unprecedented 100,000 volumes in its first 10 years. The trend culminated in such multitiered gallery libraries as the Public Library of Detroit, (1858), the Peabody Library of Baltimore (1861), and the Cincinnati Public Libary (1874). Reading and exhibit areas were generally located in the center of the hall, lit by skylights and/or clerestories.

The Boston Public Library, however, very quickly proved to be too successful, crowded, and noisy, unable to serve its growing public. Librarian Justin Winsor, in criticizing the building, took particular exception to the alcove stacks in the main reading room which were impossible to operate as a closed stack; he proposed a new stack with a "compact storage to save space and short distances to save time" (3).

Nineteenth-century European Influences

The rise of the great national libraries throughout Europe led in the nineteenth century to two remarkable buildings which widely influenced American concepts: the Bibliotheque Ste. Genevieve and the Bibliotheque Nationale, both in Paris.

The Bibliotheque Ste. Genevieve (Fig. 7), created by Le Duc de La Rochefoucauld (1624), was rebuilt (1843–1850) by Henri Labrouste, a remarkable achievement, both in concept and as a response to specific library problems of the day. Its elegant neo-Renaissance astylar exterior encloses a long rectangle 263 × 75 ft, while an independent cast-iron frame within supports its main floor. The lofty metal of two parallel longitudinal barrel vaults springs from filigreed cast-iron vaulting ribs supported by a center row of columns placed at 4-m (13.3 ft) centers (Fig. 8). In its completely rational architectural organization, the exterior became a paradigm for McKim, Mead, and White's design for the Boston Public Library. The collection was shelved along the line of the center columns and separated from the readers' tables by a low railing with two tiers of stacks along the outer wall. Since 1930, the library has become part of the University of Paris.

The French Revolution gave enormous impetus to the development of the Bibliotheque Nationale when all ecclesiastical collections (1789) and those of the nobility (1792) were seized by the government and added to those of the former Bibliotheque Royale. From 1862 to 1868 Labrouste ingeniously added to the library housed in an undistinguished seventeenth-century Paris mansion. By filling in courtyards, he was able to develop an extraordinarily handsome reading room covered by nine pendentive terracotta domes, each with a center oculus carried on 124-ft-high slender cast-iron columns (Fig. 9). The elliptical plan is ringed with three tiers of wall cases served by slender stepped galleries for paging books; the long central tables can seat 500 readers. A second room for periodicals is covered by a single, oval dome with a great double-layered skylight in its center with a perimeter ring of 16 oculi (Fig. 10). The dome itself springs from 16 pairs of columns, which carry shallow arches above four tiers of wall shelving. There is spacious seating for 300 readers at long tables. These two superb mid-nineteenth-century reading rooms offer a far more sophisticated solution than his earlier Bibliotheque St. Genevieve, and are perhaps the finest library rooms of all time.

Equally impressive is Labrouste's handling of the rapidly growing collection by adding an adjacent stack room (Fig. 11). Visible from the reading room, its four tiers of skylit stacks and strap steel walkways flank a central gallery area with connecting bridges. Although anticipated in the British Museum a few years earlier, this extraordi-

Figure 7. Exterior, Bibliotheque Ste. Genevieve, Paris, Henri Labrouste (1843–1850).

Figure 8. Reading room, Bibliotheque Ste. Genevieve, Paris.

Figure 9. Reading room, Bibliotheque Nationale, Paris, Henri Labrouste (1868).

nary construction became the prototype for the great self-supporting stacks which were to become the pattern in American libraries from 1890 to 1940.

While contemporary with Paxton's remarkable Crystal Palace (1850–1851) and many other technically sophisticated structures exploiting the potential of cast iron and steel, Labrouste's two great works are exemplary. They dealt sensitively with the needs of the collection through a rigorous and rational organization and gave the reader "great hall" reading rooms which were well lit, ventilated, and modulated to their scale and purpose. Among the many great nineteenth-century wrought-iron framing structures in France, culminating in the work of Gustave Eiffel (1832–1923), Labrouste's work emerges as brilliant in its synthesis of structural rationalism, neoclassical scale and restraint, and a "modernist" attention to the func-

Figure 10. Periodicals reading room, Bibliotheque Nationale, Paris, Henri Labrouste (1868).

Figure 11. Multistory stacks, Bibliotheque Nationale, Paris.

tional. Perhaps the greatest library buildings ever designed, these two works influenced U.S. contemporaries, although none dared adopt these innovations wholeheartedly.

H. H. Richardson and the Romanesque Style

Returning from Paris in 1865 after seven years of study at the Ecole des Beaux Arts, H. H. Richardson promptly launched his extraordinarily successful practice, won two competitions in 1870 (Brattle Square Church in Boston's Back Bay and the Buffalo, N.Y., State Hospital) and followed this in 1872 by winning the competition for Trinity Church in Boston, which firmly established him as the leading U.S. architect of the day. Its massive masonry walls, pierced with freely adapted Romanesque arches, enclose a squarish plan with an extended semicircular chancel, which is crowned with a great turreted lantern at the crossing. The parts receive a variety of pitched roofs, beginning with the octagon at the center. Its bold, almost brutal, forms and banded rusticated masonry details greatly influenced contemporary architects, who accepted its spirit as an appropriate aesthetic expression of the times and the nation.

Several years after the completion of Trinity, Richardson received commissions to design a series of public libraries; first, the Winn Memorial Library (1877–1878) (Fig. 12) of Woburn, Mass. While modest in scale, it exhibits

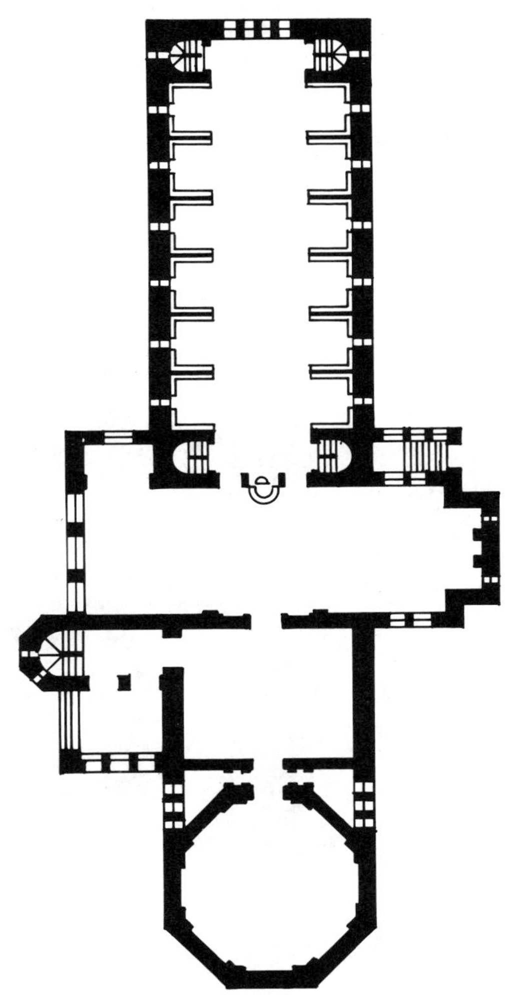

Figure 12. Plan and elevation, Winn Memorial Library, Woburn, Mass., H. H. Richardson (1877–1878).

Figure 13. Exterior, Crane Memorial Library, Quincy, Mass., H. H. Richardson (1880–1883). Photograph by Charles Blomberg.

his characteristic vigorous massing of heavily textured masonry, pierced with clusters of arched windows and surmounted by his typical pitched roofs. The plan, a powerful example of Richardson's mastery in defining spaces, provides for an octagonal "museum" and a two-tiered, alcoved "library" room spanned by a wooden vaulted ceiling. A band of clerestory windows admits light above the upper tier, while a narrow slot window allows a view from the lower level, a detail repeated in his later libraries. For all its virtuosity, the building is architecturally overstated, most notably in the oddly jointed octagonal museum room.

The Ames Museum Library of North Easton, Mass. (1877–1879) repeats many of the Woburn elements in a simpler form with the main library room repeating the alcoved, wood barrel vaulted window pattern of the former. These elements are most successfully synthesized in the

Figure 14. Front facade, Boston Public Library, McKim, Mead & White (1887–1893). Courtesy of the Boston Public Library.

Figure 15. Bates Hall, Boston Public Library. Photograph by Charles Blomberg.

Crane Memorial Public Library in Quincy, Mass. (1880–1883) (Fig. 13). The simple pitched roof runs the length of the linear plan, interrupted with a gable at the arched entrance. Bands of high clerestory windows illuminate the library alcoves while groups of tall windows divided by stone mullions admit light to the reading room.

Unfortunately, these eloquent architectural statements failed to address the questions which were becoming of increasing concern to librarians: how to deal with rapidly expanding book collections and a growing number of users. Nevertheless they did provide the visual image which was to recur in numerous college and Carnegie libraries over the next 30 years.

McKim, Mead, and White and the Boston Public Library

The Boston Public Library Building of 1887 (Figs. 14–16) was 30 years late in coming, according to the criticism of its early librarian, Justin Winsor. Among the inadequacies of the original building were listed awkward alcoves lining the reading room, poor lighting, ventilation and heating, and, principally, the lack of adequate shelving.

Actually, the original 1857 structure was, to a degree, the victim of its time. No one then could have foreseen its enormous success and the consequent demands placed on its facilities. The leading advocate of the long-sought expansion was Samuel A. B. Abbott, a prominent lawyer and later president of the board of trustees. Earlier studies by various local architects, including Henry Van Brunt (1882) and several city architects, and a competition (1884) proved inconclusive. Pile driving began at virtually the last minute—the afternoon of the final day on which it was legal to do so, when Abbott took matters into his own hands.

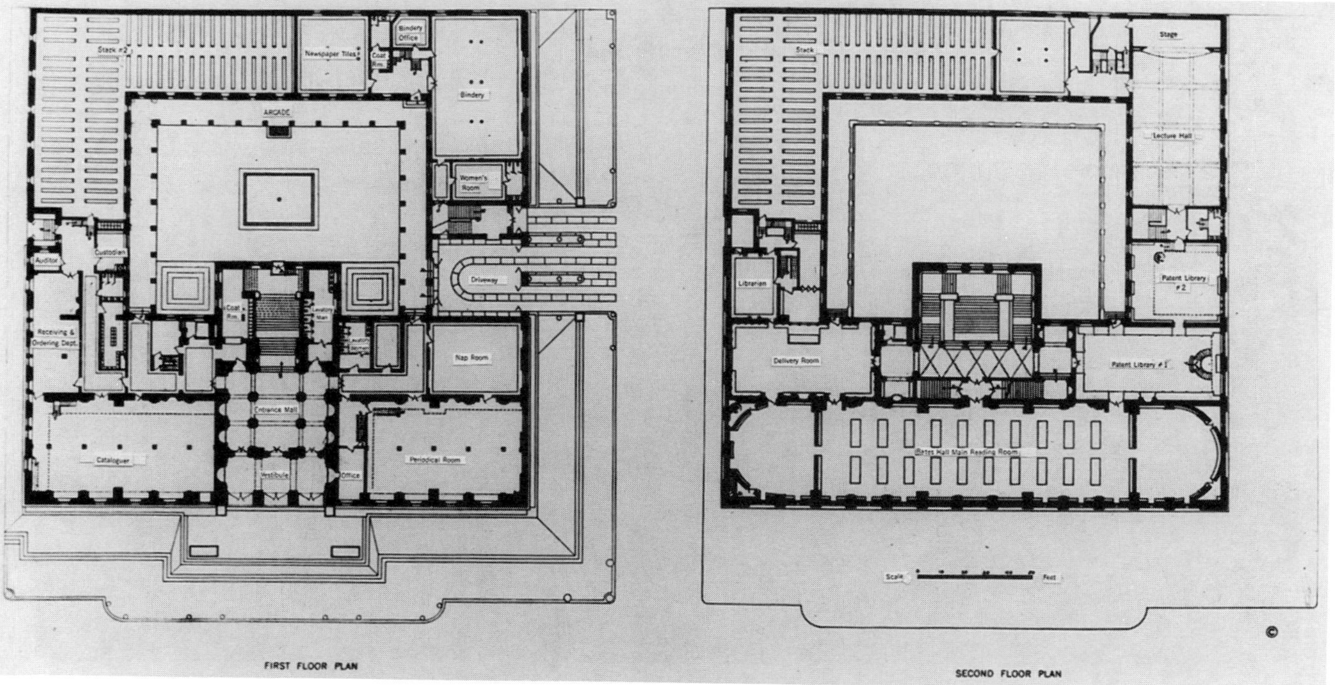

Figure 16. Plans, Boston Public Library.

An enthusiastic admirer of McKim, Mead, and White's Villard Houses (1883) in New York, Abbott convinced the Board to abandon the inadequate, vaguely Richardsonian proposal of one of the city architects and select the New York firm. It did not appear to matter that their austere classical approach would undoubtedly contrast strongly to Richardson's boldly Romanesque pile, Trinity Church, directly across Copley Square. Contextualism was not the order of the day. Nor did the architects' refined tastes, which caused the budget to escalate from $400,000 to more than $2.5 million, appear to have lessened Abbott's and the board's enthusiasm; however, there was considerable public outcry.

McKim's planning followed directly from his strongly held beaux-arts convictions: a perfect square, entered through three arches on the center of its main (south) facade, leading directly by the grand staircase to the piano nobile with the great main reading room (Bates Hall) behind the 13 arches of the main facade. In the center of the plan, the garden courtyard, based on the Palazzo della Cancelleria, Rome (1486–1496) with its cloistered walk, is surrounded by a U-shaped six-story closed stack (and, in the altered version of McKim's plan, assorted workrooms). The exedra at the southwest end of the main reading room originally contained the catalog. Books paged from the closed stacks were brought by conveyor and track to the adjoining Delway Room (which, since 1961, has housed the catalog). Within the classic formalism, the location of special collections, workrooms, lecture rooms, and service areas suffer functionally from their limited rooms, and service areas suffer functionally from their limited freedom of placement and much of McKim's original U-shaped stack, originally designed to house 2 million volumes, was co-opted for additional service areas. The miscellaneous incursions are further reflected in the diffuse fenestration of the side elevations.

But it is in the bold beaux-arts classicism of its main facade facing Trinity Church across Copley Square that McKim made his statement, designing the building with a precision, elegance, and refinement that fixed its neo-Renaissance image on U.S. academic architecture for the next 50 years (4).

Chicago's Newberry Library (1888–1893) demonstrated another attempt to develop a rational architectural form for a great public library. Conceived by the brilliant librarian, William Frederick Poole, the scheme proposed a multistory structure providing a series of subject reading rooms with nearby freestanding stacks for the related collection. While only a part of the total building (architect, Henry Ives Cobb) was realized because of its inherent duplication of facilities, its flexibility and the immediate accessibility of reader to books offered an attractive alternative to the closed stacks then generally in use. It, also, is a concept to which the mid-twentieth century turned.

Figure 17. Exterior, Library of Congress, Washington D.C., Smithmeyer and Pelz (1885–1895). Courtesy of the Library of Congress.

The Library of Congress

Created by President John Adams and Congress in 1800, the Library of Congress was intended to be a resource of information vital to the government. Its initial collection of 740 volumes dealt mostly with law and government. Burned in 1814 by the British, the collection was replenished by President James Madison, who authorized the purchase of former President Thomas Jefferson's extraordinary personal collection of 6000 volumes (for which the somewhat impoverished owner received $23,950). Given Jefferson's breadth of interest, his collection forever established the library's perspective and set it on its present course of serving the entire country. In 1851, the library's third fire destroyed 35,000 volumes, leading Thomas U. Walters, the Capitol Architect, to construct the so-called "Iron Room" against further catastrophe.

Although it was the Library of Congress, the president had the prerogative of appointing the Librarian, and in 1864, Abraham Lincoln made an excellent choice: Ainsworth Rand Spofford. Under his 40 years of leadership, two transcendent goals were accomplished: first, the Copyright Act of 1870 made the library the repository of all copyrighted materials, greatly expanding the collection, and second, there was the construction of the library building itself.

Responding to Spofford's entreaties, Congress authorized a design competition in 1873. Spofford specified a building of 270 × 340 ft, a capacity for 2 million books, and a central domed reading room. Of the 28 entries, an Italianate design of John L. Smithmeyer and his partner, Paul J. Pelz, was declared the winner.

Fate did not treat the winners kindly. A new competition specified Victorian Gothic and it received 41 submissions, including that of Smithmeyer and Pelz. Subsequently they submitted Romanesque, French, German, and Modern Renaissance proposals, as well as variations of their first design. The 1885 version of the latter was approved, and construction began two years later (Figs. 17, 18).

As Chief Army Engineer, Brig. Gen. Thomas Lincoln Casey was placed in charge, ably assisted by civil engineer Bernard R. Green as superintendent of construction. Smithmeyer was soon dismissed in a dispute about the

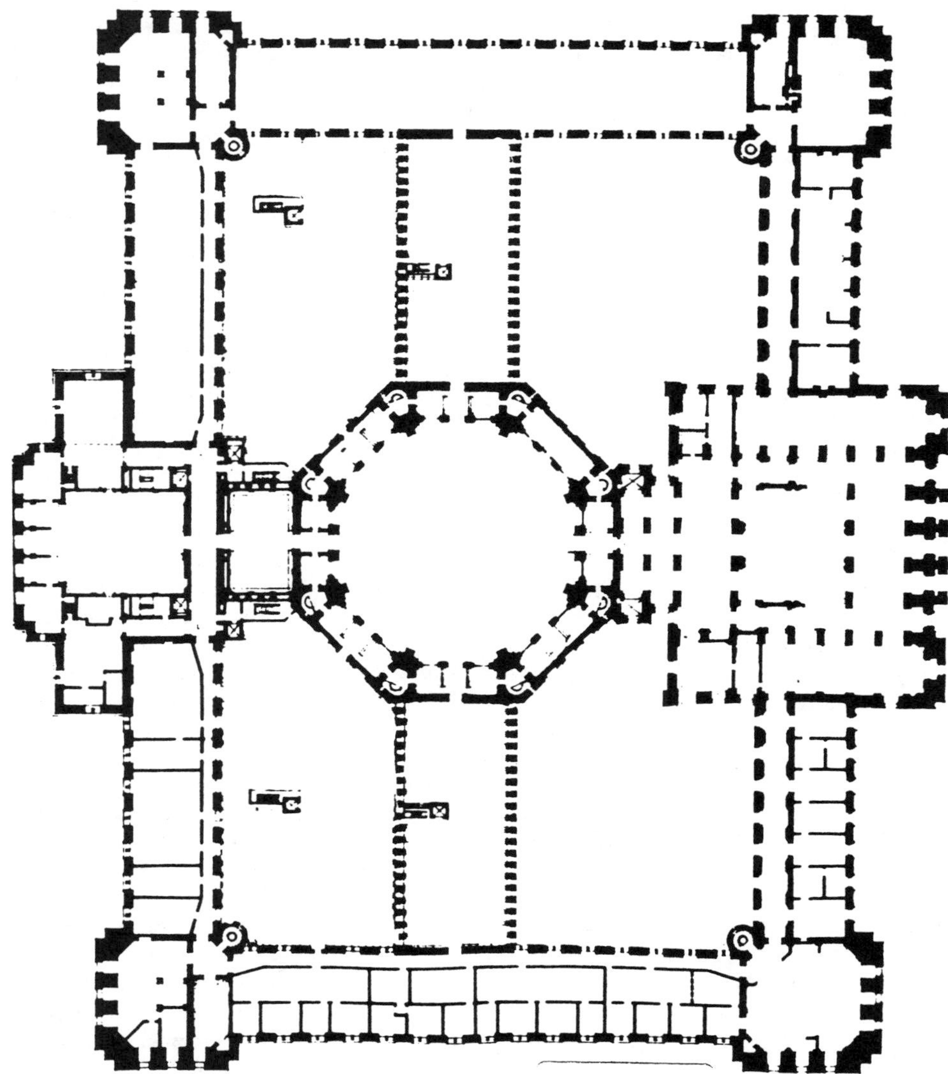

Figure 18. Main floor plan, Library of Congress, Washington, D.C.

Figure 19. Domed reading room, Library of Congress, Washington, D.C. Courtesy of the Library of Congress.

quality of the concrete, and Pelz replaced him. He in turn was forced out in 1892 by Green, in favor of General Casey's 28-year-old son, Edward, a recent graduate of the Ecole des Beaux Arts, who proceeded to redesign much of the interior. Fortunately, the results do not reflect the somewhat sordid history of the library's construction.

The Smithmeyer–Pelz design was quite splendid. Spofford's proposal for a circular (100-ft diameter) domed main reading room (Fig. 19) provided the opportunity for a splendid central space recalling Sydney Smirke's design (with a 140-ft dome) for the British Museum (1854–1856) and its librarian, Sir Anthony Panizzi. Panizzi's greater innovation was a completely cast-iron, multilevel stack room, emulated in the Bibliotheque Nationale and the Library of Congress. Spofford's program was increased from a $4 million to a $6 million project with an exterior expanded to 470 × 338 ft and capacity more than doubled to 4.5 million volumes. The project, in an outstanding demonstration of fiscal responsibility, came in at $6,090,153.28 including works of art—1.015% over the budget.

The building has served the nation well. To provide for the burgeoning collection, two courtyards were later filled in with stacks in 1910 and 1926, and renovations, including air-conditioning, were instituted during the 1960s. In 1934, the first of the two annexes, the John Adams, was constructed and, in 1980, the James Madison Memorial Building was ready for occupancy. The original building was named for Thomas Jefferson.

THE GROWTH OF COLLECTIONS

The dictionary describes stacks as "a set of bookshelves ranged compactly one above the other in a library," as well as "an area or part of a library in which books are stored or kept" (5).

With the dramatic growth of book collections, the massive, multitiered stack appeared to be the ultimate solution: efficient use of space, easily controlled and easily paged. To carry the heavy book loads (roughly 150 lb/ft^2 on each level) the uprights, either in column or panel form, were designed to carry the accumulated loads of all tiers.

The Multitiered Stack

It was 1877 before the first U.S. example of the multitiered stack appeared, a six-tiered installation added to Harvard's Gothic revival Gore Library, designed by Justin Winsor, then its librarian, Professor William R. Ware of MIT, and his partner, Henry Von Brunt. In 1866, Ware had traveled to London and Paris and he was undoubtedly aware of the earlier installations. While lacking the sensitive detailing and sophistication of Labrouste, the Ware–Winsor design nevertheless clearly defined the nature of the self-supporting stack—a multitiered assemblage of uniform uprights 7 ft high and set in long rows (ranges) 4 ft apart with 28-in. aisles of steel grating. As in Labrouste's design, the shelves were of wood. In the Harvard installation and in many subsequent installations, the stack often carried its own roof or, in the case of the New York Public Library, a reading room. "By the eighties," writes Jordy, "the stack problem dominated any discussion of library architecture" (6).

The rise in collection growth was most evident in the government area. The Army Corps of Engineers was responsible for much federal construction during the late nineteenth century and a young engineer, Bernard Richardson Green, was given the responsibility of designing the stack system for both the Army Medical Museum and Library (1887) and the State, War, and Navy Department building (1888). Both employed a system similar to the Gore stack, except that metal bar shelving replaced the wood and some of the cast-iron castings became more ornate. Snead and Company, a manufacturer of miscellaneous iron products (among others, the 980 iron steps in the Washington Monument), appears to have experienced delays in the installation, quite understandable, considering the complexity involved in the prefabrication of such a system, and the end product was apparently "very heavy and awkward to use" (7). In 1890, Green was assigned the design of the stack for the Library of Congress, a project already three years into construction. He set 18 criteria for the stack, including great strength, good lighting and ventilation, freedom from dust, fire, and vermin, a book retrieval system, and a stack that could house 2 million volumes.

The concern with fire was spurred by the growing list of cast-iron structures destroyed by fire. Since, for purposes of ventilation and light, the stack was designed with unprotected metal in a grid system of flooring and a 5-in. ventila-

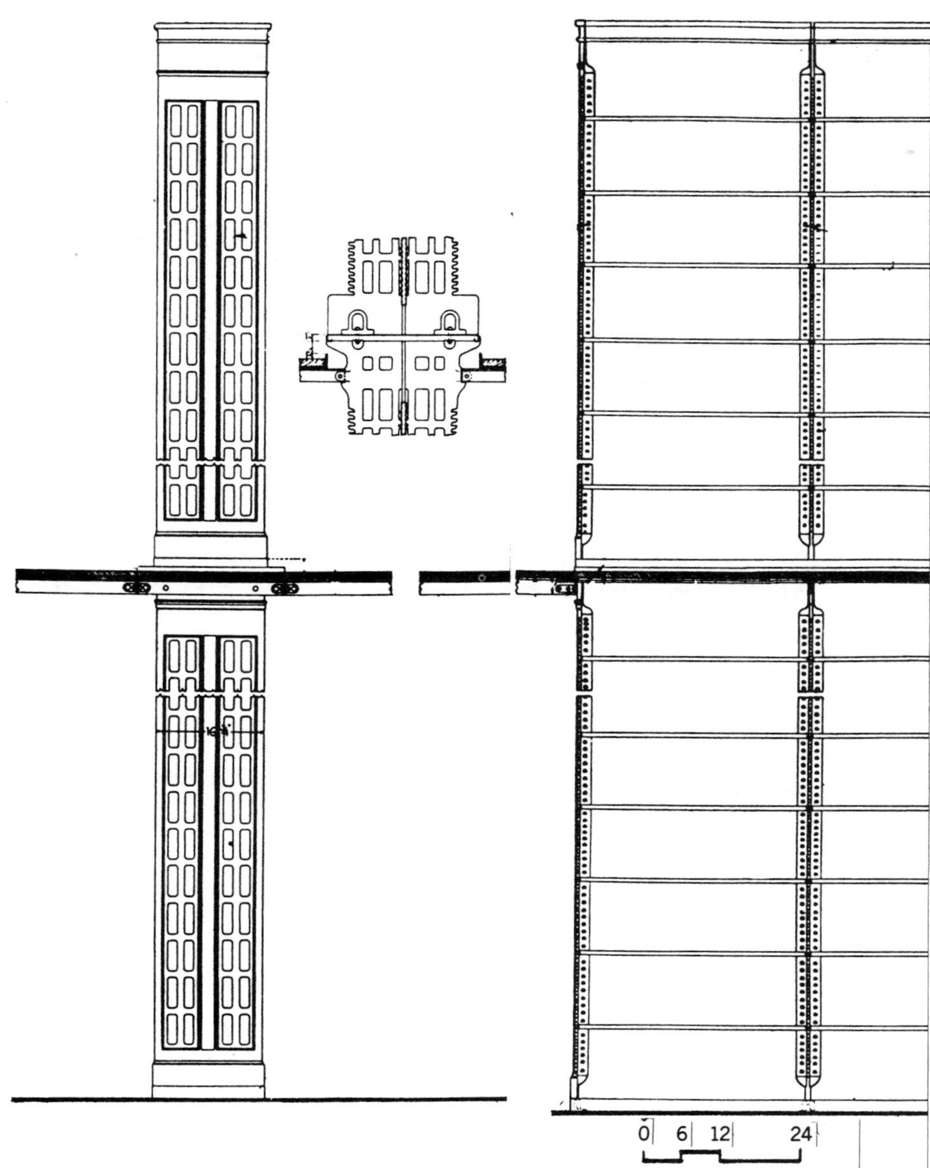

Figure 20. Multistory stack system, elevation, Snead and Company Iron Works.

tion slot below the lowest shelf, it provided a vast flue for its combustible contents. Surprisingly, over the years there have been very few serious fires in multitiered stacks.

The Snead Company and Angus Snead Macdonald

Green's design, patented in 1890, required a multitiered steel structure using 2-in. stone panel flooring in aisles with electric lighting centered in the aisles. A pneumatic tube and conveyor system reduced retrieval time to a matter of minutes. Green built a full-sized mock-up and requested bids. Snead and Company emerged as the winner and, in what now appears to have been a rather unorthodox move, paid royalties to Green. Construction began in 1891. Green's multitiered stack design overcame many of the earlier objections. A system of electrically powered fans forced tempered outside air into the lowest level, from which it rose by gravity to the top, permitting exterior windows to be sealed. The steel structural columns far exceeded the limitations of the earlier cast iron and made possible, as Green himself predicted, "stacks of twenty or more stories or tiers in height—and of almost any dimensions" (7). The multitiered stack had arrived and Snead and Company became the instrument of its success (Fig. 20). In turn, the Snead firm began to concentrate its manufacturing effort on this product.

In a series of highly contested bids, Snead won out over Library Bureau, Art Metal, and others to build the stacks for a great new project, the New York Public Library (Figs. 21–23). The firm was selected on the basis of its experience and the quality of mock-up, although Snead was not the lowest bidder. The six-tiered, 3-million-volume stack was designed so that alternate levels lined up with the building floors while the stack columns also supported the main reading room.

Snead's cast-iron shelf supports remained the standard for the industry until the 1930s, being used for the great academic stacks of the Widener Library at Harvard, the

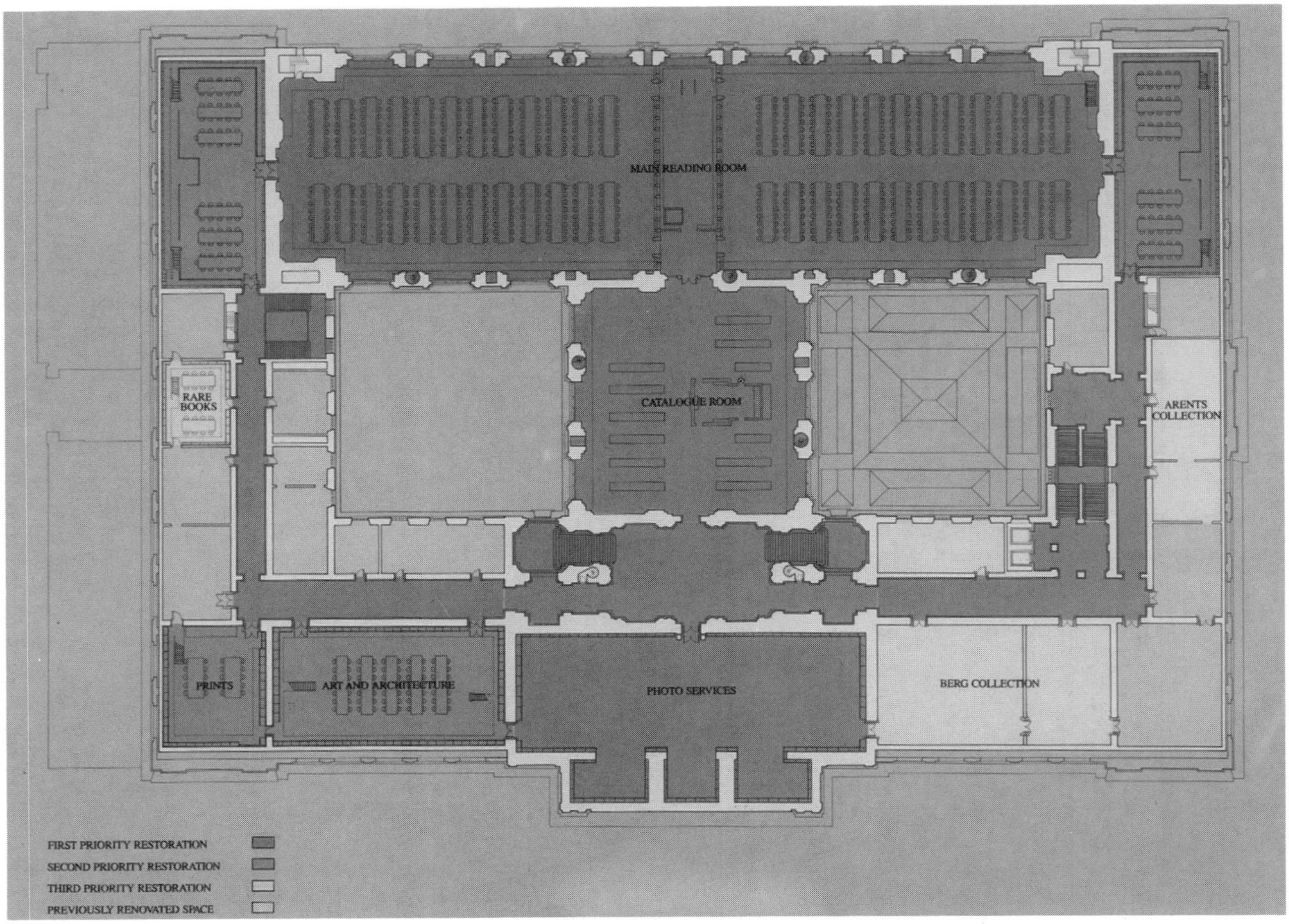

Figure 21. Third floor (main floor) plan, New York Public Library, New York City. Courtesy of Davis/Brody and Associates.

Stanford University Library, the Sterling Library at Yale, the University of Illinois Library, and Columbia University's Butler Library, each with capacities of millions of volumes. By 1940, Snead had provided stacks for a total of almost 500 institutions throughout the United States and abroad, from Manchuria to the Vatican.

Much of the Snead firm's success can be attributed to a nephew of the founders, Angus Snead Macdonald, who in 1905 joined the 50-year-old firm and in 1916 became its president and driving force. Macdonald was a recent graduate of the School of Architecture of Columbia University.

Over the next half-century, Macdonald put his considerable talents to work on the problems of stacks and related

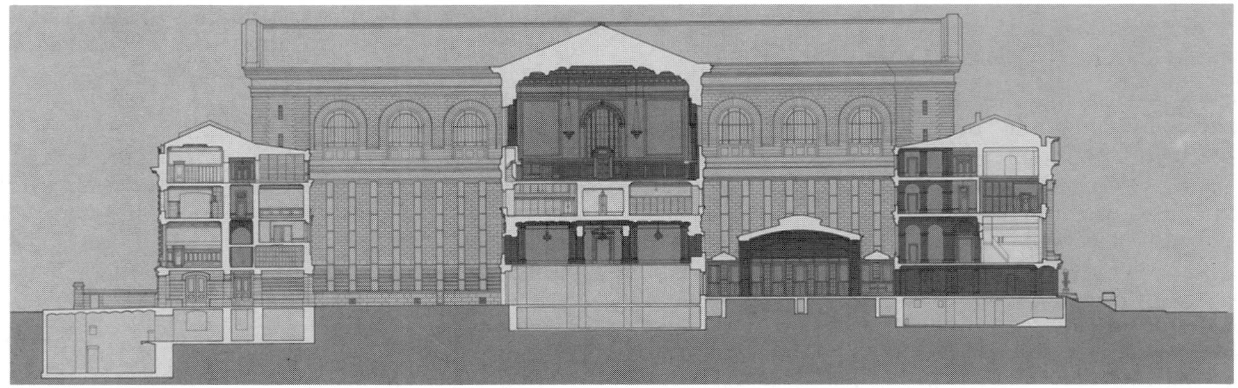

Figure 22. Section, New York Public Library, New York City. Courtesy of Davis/Brody and Associates.

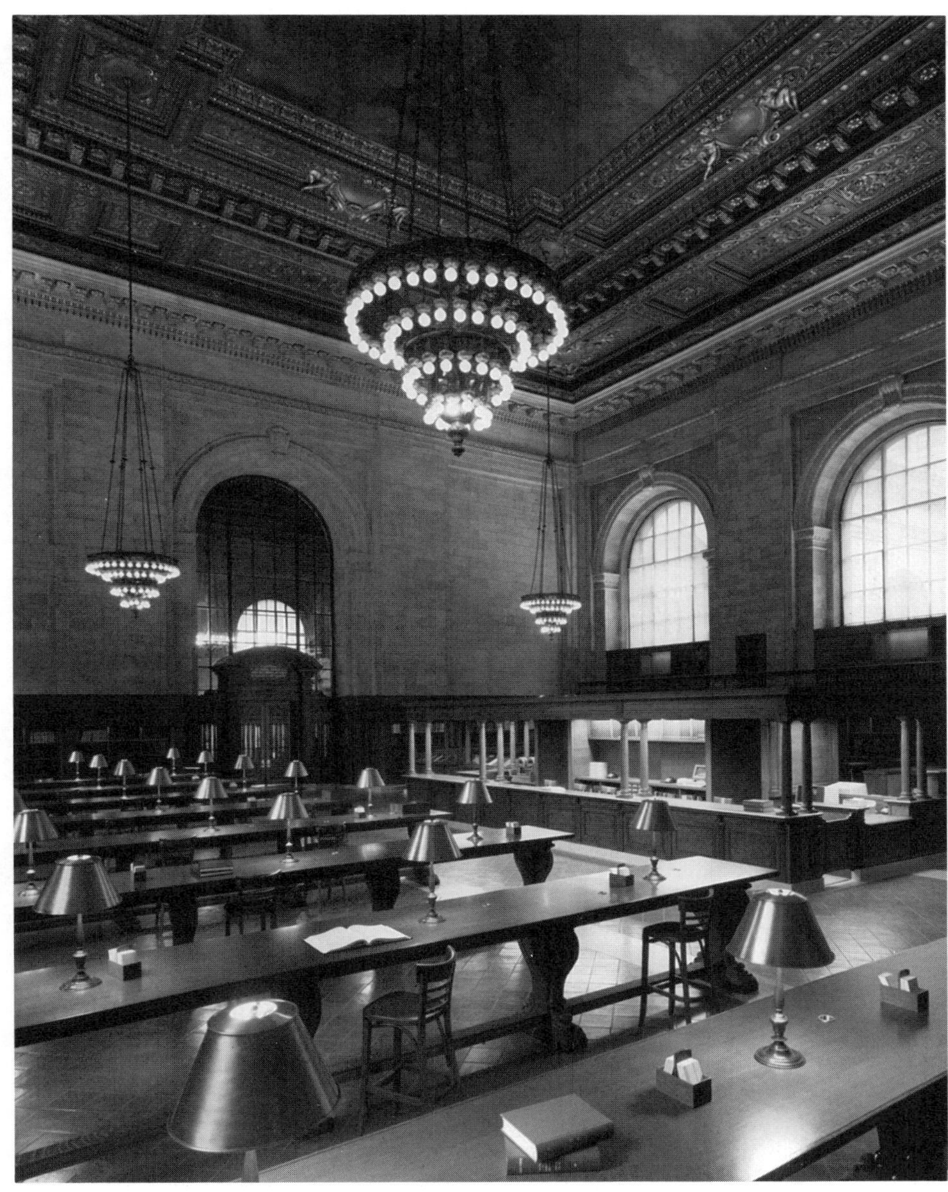

Figure 23. Catalog room, New York Public Library, Carrere and Hastings (1897–1911). Restoration by Davis Brody and Associates and Giorgio Cavagliere (1986). Photograph by Peter Aaron, ESTO.

design problems; these included lighting, book conveyor systems, concrete slab floors, and new methods of stack ventilation.

Macdonald and Snead designed the Snead tubular steel bracket stack in 1915, which finally received its first major installation in the Butler Library at Columbia (1934) and proved its superior strength, flexibility of shelf depth, and lower cost. Whether tiered or freestanding, it became the basic stack system and remains so today. In 1913 Macdonald addressed himself to another troubling detail of stack design—optimal shelf length. Varying lengths had been common, but if architectural design could conform with a standard shelf length, say 3 ft, the standardization in manufacture and interchangeability in usage would provide great advantages. Three feet soon became the industry standard.

While Macdonald's innovations in stack design were considerable, his major contribution was in the concept of the modern library building. Oddly enough, his proposal ran against the best interests of Snead's stack business: the idea that the multitiered stack failed to provide the kind of flexibility a library should have in bringing users into closer contact with the books they were using.

Macdonald and "The Library of The Future"

In 1933, Macdonald was invited to contribute an article to a volume commemorating the fiftieth year of service of the director of the University of Oslo Library, Wilhelm Munthe. Macdonald described the library of the future, ie, 25 years ahead, in an article later described as a turning point in library architecture. In it Macdonald sought to define the library in terms of its role in society, its architectural character and interior arrangement, and its advanced technology. In retrospect, one would have to credit him with remarkable judgment and prescience.

First, Macdonald envisioned a library as a "resource center" (8), a term much in vogue some 30 years later. As such it would appeal to the broadest possible public to enrich the life of the community and encourage a better informed citizenry. Situated in a parklike setting with reading terraces and perhaps a restaurant, 50 subject departments with expert staffs would be available to assist the user. By providing equipment and nonbook material, the library would provide service to all, including businesses and professionals.

Secondly, Macdonald roundly criticized the monumentality and formal beaux-arts planning then in vogue. Readers, he posited, would be more comfortable in low-ceilinged alcoves, homelike settings at small tables or with lounge chairs. For serious users, clusters of seating or carrels would be scattered throughout the library near the collection being used. Except for stair and elevator enclosures, toilets and similar functions, interior walls would be eliminated. He found that some ceiling heights of two stories with adjacent mezzanines in about 25% of the area were necessary to relieve the monotony of the low ceilings, but generally he accepted the standard of 8-ft floor to floor with 4-in. slabs throughout. The resulting floor would thereby provide total flexibility for use by readers and staff or for the collection.

To support these floors, a building column system would be required, based, obviously, on the spacings of the stacks themselves—stack shelving 3 ft long in ranges 4.5 ft apart. Over time, Macdonald experimented with virtually every multiple of these dimensions, beginning with 9 × 9 ft. Over time and with experimentation, the limitations of the 9 × 9 became all too apparent, and later recommendations were for 18 × 27 ft bays and larger. The importance of this approach, however, was in its concentration on dimensional consistency, a concept which by 1945 Macdonald had begun to refer to as "modular" and the 3 × 4.5 ft dimensions and their multiples (which also served for reader tables) as "modules." If one recalls the libraries of Sansavino, Wren, Labrouste, and a host of others, with their orderly and repetitive bays of alcoves and windows, it is apparent that architectural regularity based on the library's essential components—bookcases and reader tables—is inherent in its typology. Nevertheless, it was Macdonald who articulated this relationship at a time when modern architecture had not yet grasped the modularity which even today is its fundamental character. And it is doubtful if any libraries designed after 1950 ignored the tenets of the module.

Thirdly, as an enthusiast for new technology, Macdonald saw the library as having a nuclear power department and a mathematics department equipped with "calculating machines." For illumination he advocated fluorescent tubes, which had been introduced that year and which went into commercial production two years later (1935). These would make possible the elimination of interior courtyards and minimize the dependence on natural lighting and large windows. Acoustic treatment would absorb excessive sound in the open planned areas. To provide ventilation, air of the quality of "a fine autumn day," he proposed air-conditioning, invented by William Carrier for industrial processing at the beginning of the century but not installed in public buildings (theaters) until the mid-1920s. Despite his advocacy of these technologies, fluorescent lighting, acoustical treatment, and air-conditioning did not become standard in libraries until well into the 1950s. The only problem ignored was that of fireproofing, a serious oversight.

Always striving to integrate all aspects of library construction into one cohesive model, Macdonald gradually realized that the column module itself became the key because it limited all aspects of planning, both horizontally and vertically. With cost as an incentive, low ceiling heights in stack and adjacent areas seemed critical, although this did seriously inhibit proper ventilation since there was insufficient headroom for horizontal ducts. In 1934, Macdonald hit upon the notion of integrating a hollow steel structural column into his stack system and using that as a means of distributing air-conditioning. With HVAC technology in its infancy, the difficulties in such an air distribution method were not immediately apparent, but after years of experimentation including a full-sized stack mock-up built by Snead (1945) and several libraries, notably Hardin–Simmons College (1947) and the University of Georgia (1953), the hollow column passed into history, beset by cost, patents, unions, systems integration, and fireproofing considerations.

During the balance of the 1930s and into the 1940s, Macdonald continued to develop "The Library of the Future" in meetings and in library journals, gradually winning over many to his theories. Dr. Ralph Ellsworth, a longtime supporter and later a distinguished library consultant, corresponded with Macdonald extensively during this period, in particular while he was planning his own library for the University of Iowa. Dr. Keyes Metcalf (head of the Reference Department of the New York Public Library and later director of libraries at Harvard as well as a distinguished library consultant) advocated many of Macdonald's theories. "He made us think," Metcalf said of Macdonald.

While many librarians and architects contributed to the so-called modern library of the decades after World War II, it is fair to say that Macdonald was probably the first and certainly the most articulate and persistent advocate of a more rational design approach which responded to the needs and wishes of vast new waves of library users and the flood of printed materials. The result: an unprecedented tide of new library construction combining new and changing technologies much as Macdonald had forecast.

THE POSTWAR EDUCATION EXPLOSION

The postwar era witnessed an unprecedented increase in students in the colleges and universities of the United States. Backed by the G.I. Bill, veterans flocked to every conceivable academic program and professional school with zeal. Their demands began to break down classic departmental divisions, forcing a greater range of electives, interdisciplinary survey courses, and independent study options, all of which had an impact on library use.

In addition, the explosion in the publishing of works in both the physical sciences and humanities responded to the two decades of enormous cultural change in the country brought on by depression, wars, recovery, and world leadership. Collections expanded exponentially.

As enrollment and collections soared, the pressure on academic libraries was great since most had been built prior to the Depression of 1929 and lacked space for either the expanding collections or the influx of readers. Federal and state support of investment in construction added funds to those from private donors. Nevertheless, the funding and planning of new facilities lasted for many years, and it was not until the 1960s that the construction reached the pace which carried it into the 1970s before reaching a hiatus.

The Academic Library Redefined: 1945–1955

By 1945, it was apparent to many forward-thinking librarians that drastic change in the nature of library service was inevitable, necessitated by the escalation in numbers of books and readers and a corresponding increase in service which had become neither adequate nor affordable. For them, and for the architects involved, Macdonald's proposal for a modular library building seemed the ready-made answer, although it appears that few had a very clear idea of just what it meant.

The new building, it was determined, should have a modular structure designed to house the bookstacks with optimal efficiency; no monumentality; a single entrance controlled by the circulation desk; the catalog located on the main level where it could most conveniently serve both the public and the technical staff; the largest possible floor without interruptions; uniform, low loft ceiling heights of 8 ft, 4 in., except in double-height reading rooms with mezzanines; and open stacks with readers dispersed throughout. Theory would be put into practice.

In 1944, President Harold W. Dodds of Princeton convened a group of librarians representing Harvard (Metcalf), Iowa (Ellsworth), MIT (Burchard), Princeton (Boyd), the universities of North Carolina, Pennsylvania, Rutgers, and Missouri, and others, all of which were contemplating building after the end of the war. The group, which also included architects Robert O'Connor, Walter Killam, Alfred Githens, and Angus Snead Macdonald, was called the "Cooperative Committee on Library Building Plans" (9). The spectrum of U.S. research libraries was personified by two members of this group: Keyes Metcalf, director of libraries for Harvard, who had a New Englander's dry, scholarly intensity with special concern for the perpetual growth of collections; and Ralph Ellsworth, director of libraries at the University of Colorado and the University of Iowa from 1937 to 1972, who held a Midwestern populist view in which the library's mission focused on service to an ever-expanding readership for the state universities

Figure 24. Exterior, Firestone Library, Princeton, N.J., O'Connor and Killam (1955). Photograph by Clem Fiori.

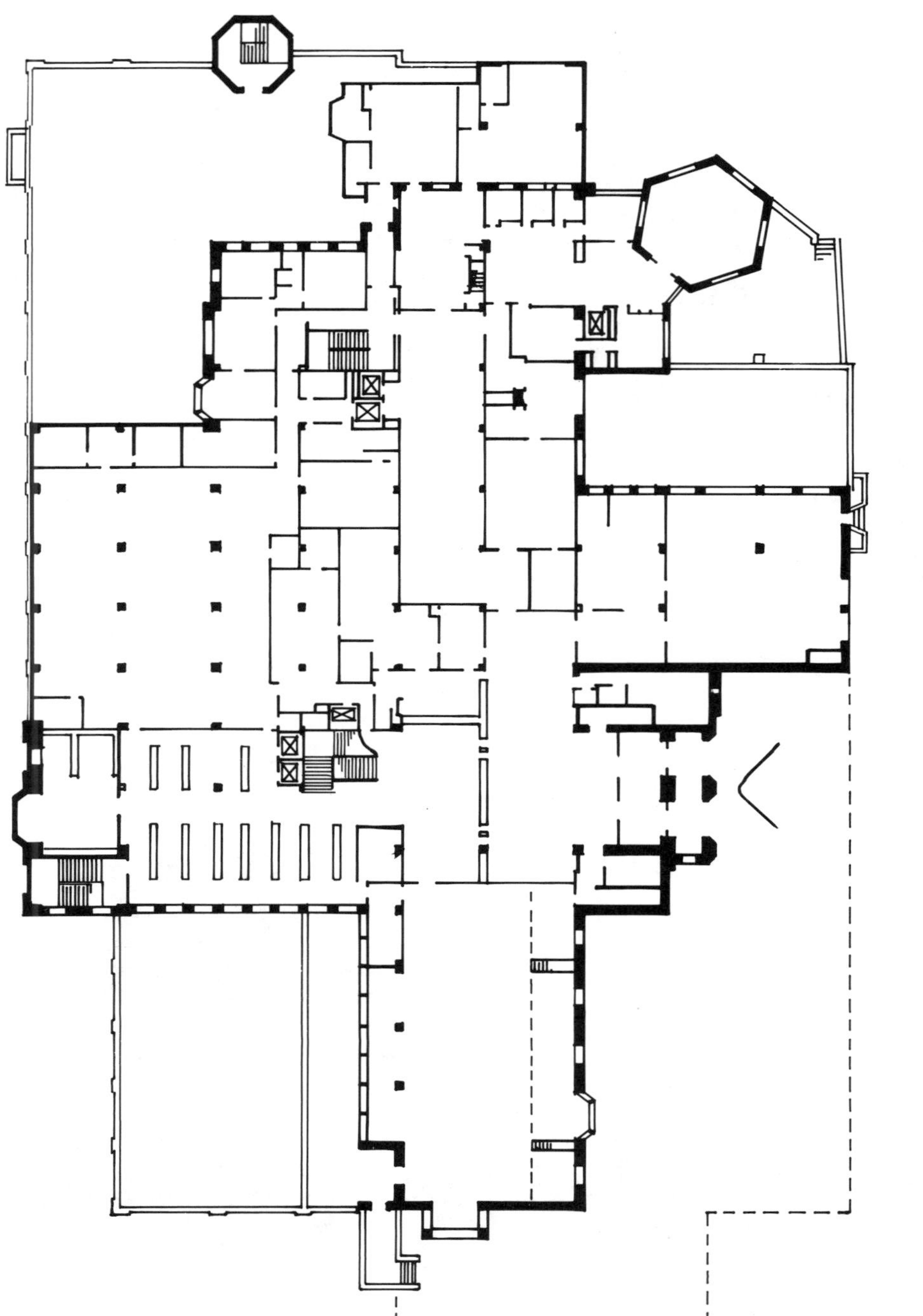

Figure 25. Plan, Firestone Library, Princeton, N.J.

with their large enrollments. While their emphasis may have diverged, their objectives converged: the development of a new, more functional library incorporating many of the modular concepts enunciated by Macdonald.

In the Princeton's Firestone Library (Figs. 24, 25), Ralph Ellsworth teamed with the architects O'Connor and Killam, in applying the "Macdonald doctrine": a modular structural layout of 18 × 27 ft bays, each column split to allow for an air conditioning duct in the middle, free-standing stacks on structural floors, and fluorescent lighting. The building's irregular massing of terraced roofs and matching exterior stone veneer reflected in scale, materials, and details the neighboring gothic chapel. A main reading room adjoining the entrance recalled the earlier "great hall" tradition. The open stacks, accessed by stairs, are largely below the entry level, interspersed with study "oases" and rimmed with studies and special reading areas adjoining the windows. The result neither confirmed nor refuted the Macdonald hypothesis. The "library of the future" had arrived, with its advantages and limitations illustrated.

Early Prototypes: 1955–1960

Two projects, named for their principal donor, John M. Olin, adapted the modular concept more successfully. Mur-

Figure 26. John M. Olin Library, Cornell University, Ithaca, N.Y., Warner Burns Toan Lunde Architects (1961). Photograph by Peter M. Warner.

phy and Mackey's admired design for Washington University in St. Louis and the John M. Olin graduate library at Cornell University by Warner Burns Toan Lunde (Fig. 26), with Metcalf as a consultant, illustrated that a single function of library operations, access to the public card catalog, which made a large main floor mandatory, would ultimately highly influence the form of libraries for the next decades with respect to its area and shape. Stacks and studies occupy upper levels.

Unprecedented Proliferation: 1960–1972

With variations, this pattern recurred in numerous large research libraries—a simple rectangular, multistoried, modular building of 25,000–50,000 ft^2 per floor was entered at grade level on the main floor where the major public areas and technical services clustered around the card catalog.

Beginning in 1967, Jerold Orne annually inventoried current academic library projects in the December issue of the *Library Journal*. In 1971, his review of the previous five-year period produced some amazing statistics (10): Almost $1 billion in construction in the United States and Canada had produced 23 million ft^2 of space accommodating 127 million volumes and 338,000 readers. The university of Chicago's 584,000 ft^2 library, designed by Walter Netsch, Indiana University's 582,000 ft^2 library, and the Bobst Library for New York University by Philip Johnson were among the 14 having more than 200,000 ft^2. The University of Toronto's massive Robarts Library of 1 million ft^2 by Warner Burns Toan Lunde, providing for 4,500 readers and a collection of 5 million, was completed in 1972.

As Orne wrote prophetically, this period "represents the greatest flowering of academic library building experience this country has ever known or is likely to see" (11).

Illustrative works of this period are the following:

1. Marcel Breuer's library at St. John's University, Collegeville, Minn. (Fig. 27), avoids the "forest of columns" effect often associated with a large open plan by planting two huge concrete trees at its center to support the roof above. The plan looks inward to central space, allowing staff areas and studies to line the exterior.
2. The Stanford Undergraduate Library by John Carl Warnecke (Fig. 28) uses a powerful symmetrical plan which can be entered on all sides through an undercut ground floor. The plan centers on a multistory central atrium on the piano nobile.
3. Skidmore, Owings, and Merrill's hegemonic megalith at the University of Chicago (Fig. 29) successfully articulates its mass through innumerable crenellations, both at a small and larger scale and in both plan and elevation. The functional organization of the plan responds to the library program in an organic matrix of forms.
4. The Goddard Library by John Johansen (Fig. 30) clearly defines the central mass of stacks, ringed by reader spaces which spin off the solid mass. The two functions are separated by open slots, bridged only by hanging stairs.

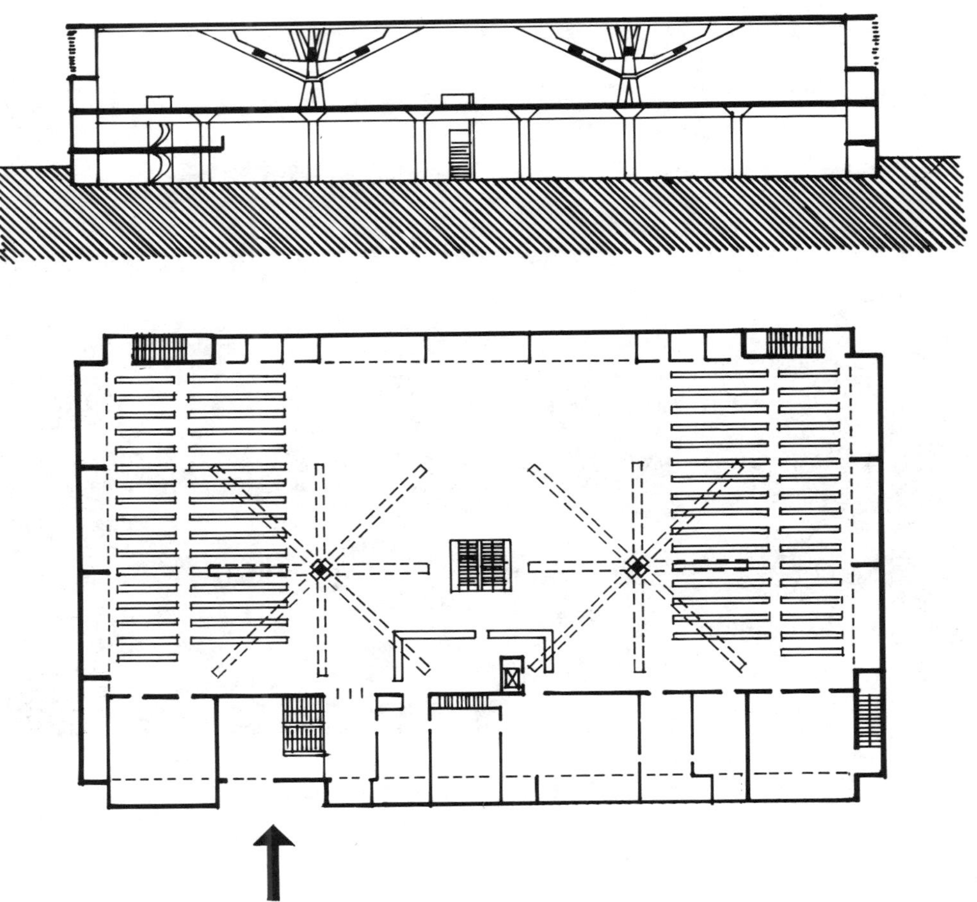

Figure 27. Plan and section, St. John's University Library, at Collegeville, Minn., Marcel Breuer and Hamilton Smith (1968).

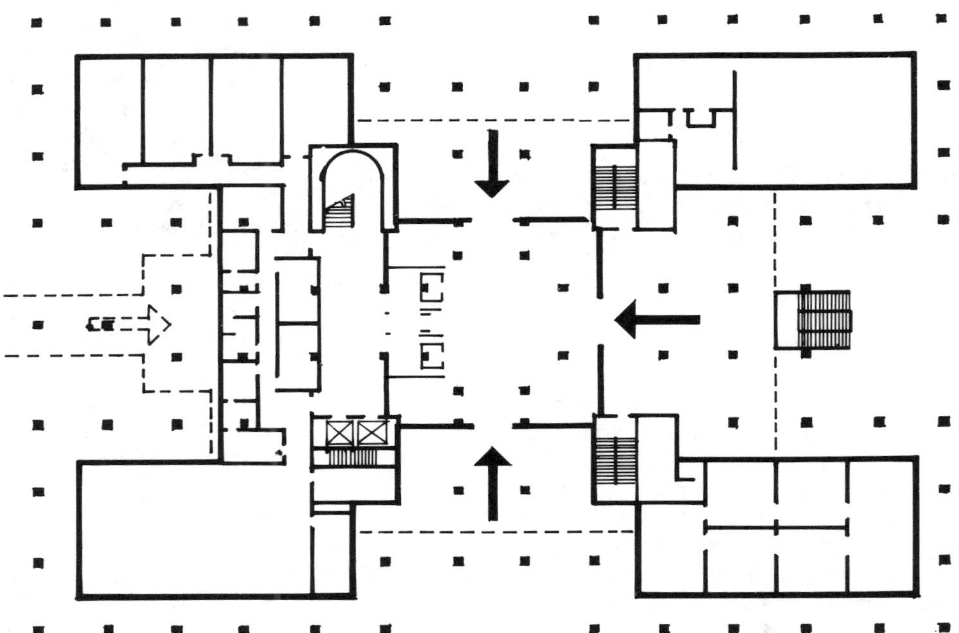

Figure 28. Plan, Stanford Undergraduate Library, Palo Alto, Calif., John Carl Warnecke and Associates (1967).

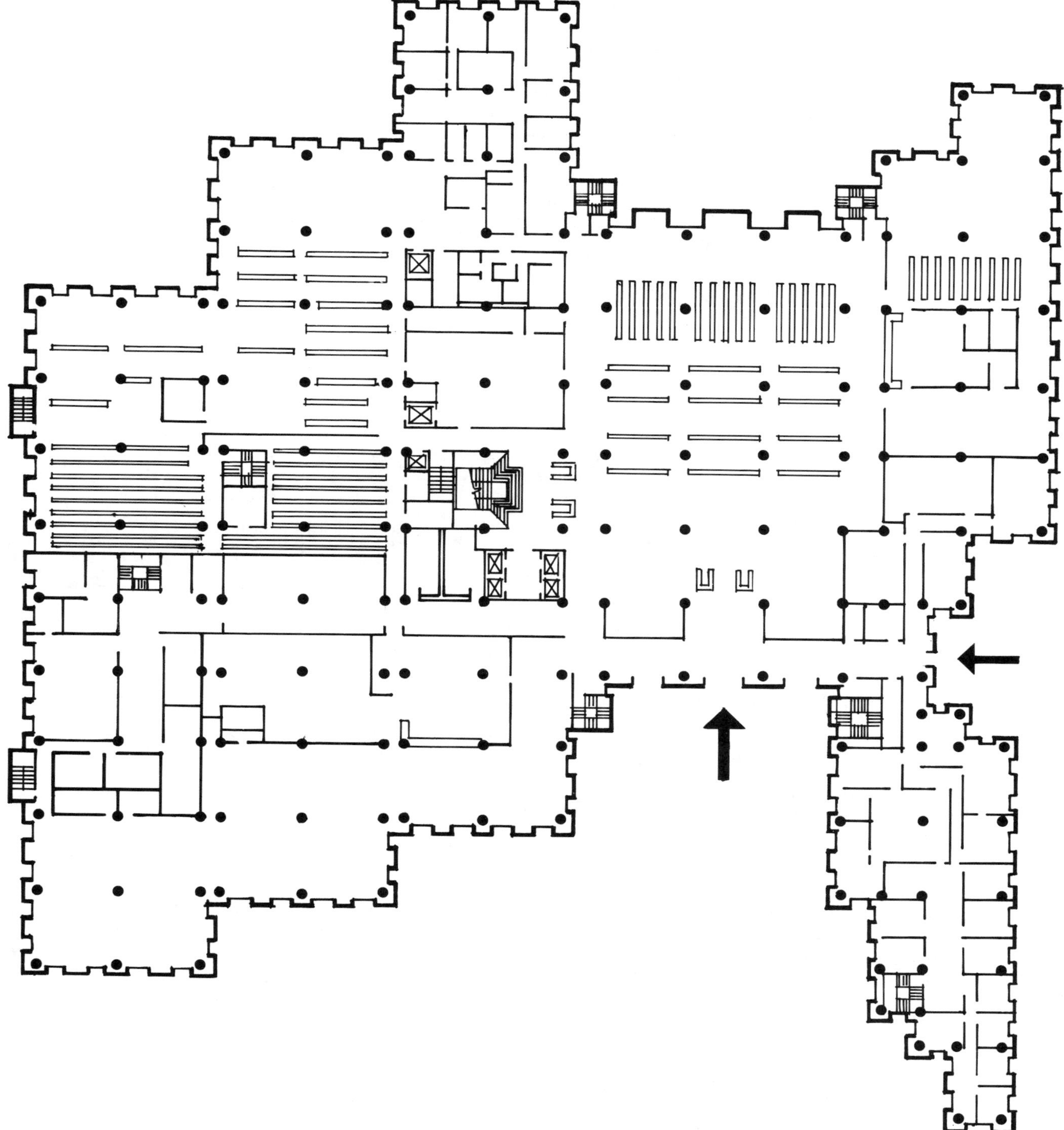

Figure 29. Plan, Joseph Regenstein Library, University of Chicago, Skidmore, Owings, and Merrill (1971).

5. Unmistakably, Alvar Aalto's Mount Saint Angel Seminary Library (Figs. 31, 32) radiates in multilevels from the central desk, opening outward toward the landscape.
6. The Exeter Academy Library by Louis Kahn (Figs. 33, 34) embraces an entry atrium on two sides with stack and reader spaces. The perfect circles cut in the sides of the atrium reveal the library beyond.

Academic Libraries: 1973–1988

The impact of the energy crisis of 1973 and the long-expected decline in college enrollment had a devastating

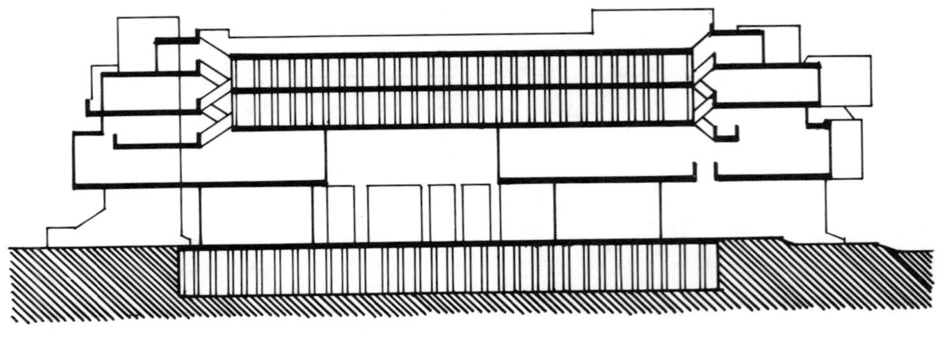

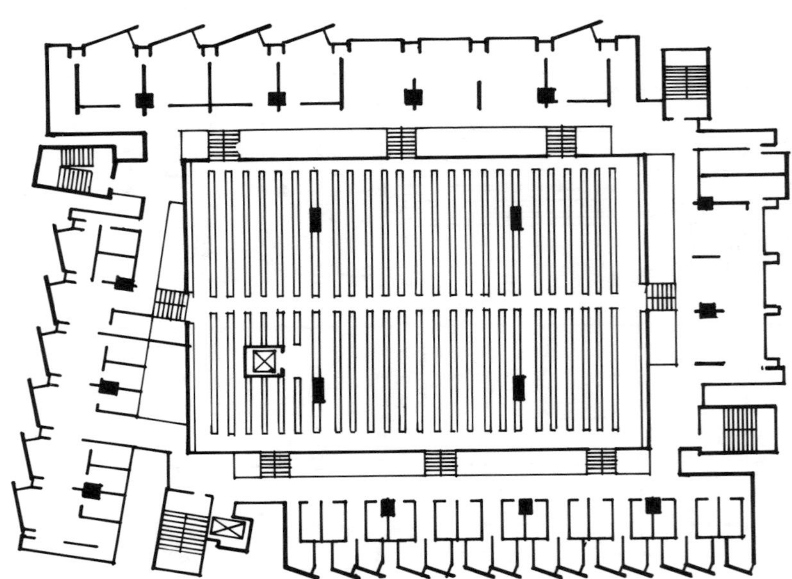

Figure 30. Plan and section, Robert Hutchings Goddard Library, Clark University, Worcester, Mass., John M. Johansen and Associates (1966).

effect on the quantity of library construction. For colleges and universities, declining acquisition budgets, costs relating to the automation of catalogs and uncertainties about the library's future role were accompanied by overcrowding of reader and stack areas. This led to a re-examination of the collection itself, and a systematic weeding of irrelevant material. Regional networks of interlibrary lending grew more extensive. The concurrent interest in historic preservation focused on attention on the possibilities of restoration, renovation, and addition to existing libraries, thereby prolonging their useful life. This led to a remarkable set of restorations and additions which has produced some of the finest library designs of the past 40 years.

Examples of the work of this period include the following:

1. The Esther Rauchenburg Library of Sarah Lawrence College (Fig. 35), Warner Burns Toan Lunde architects (1975). The forms and scale relate to the character of the adjoining neighborhood.
2. The underground addition to Cornell University's Uris Library in Ithaca, N.Y. (Figs. 36, 37) by Gunnar Birkerts and Associates (1985) wraps the vase of the 1891 Richardsonian original.
3. Perry, Dean, Rogers, and Partners's (1985) addition to McKim, Mead and White's 1928 colonial design (Figs. 38, 39) respectfully emulates the original.
4. For the Walter Royal Davis Library at the University of North Carolina, Chapel Hill, N.C., Mitchel Giurgola, with Boney Architects, (1985) placed a two-story gallery beneath the six-story stack block (Figs. 40, 41). The paired longitudinal barrel vaults of the main reading room allude to Labrouste's Ste. Genevieve.

THE ACADEMIC LIBRARY PROGRAM

In order to develop an academic library program, it is first necessary to determine the long-range goals of the

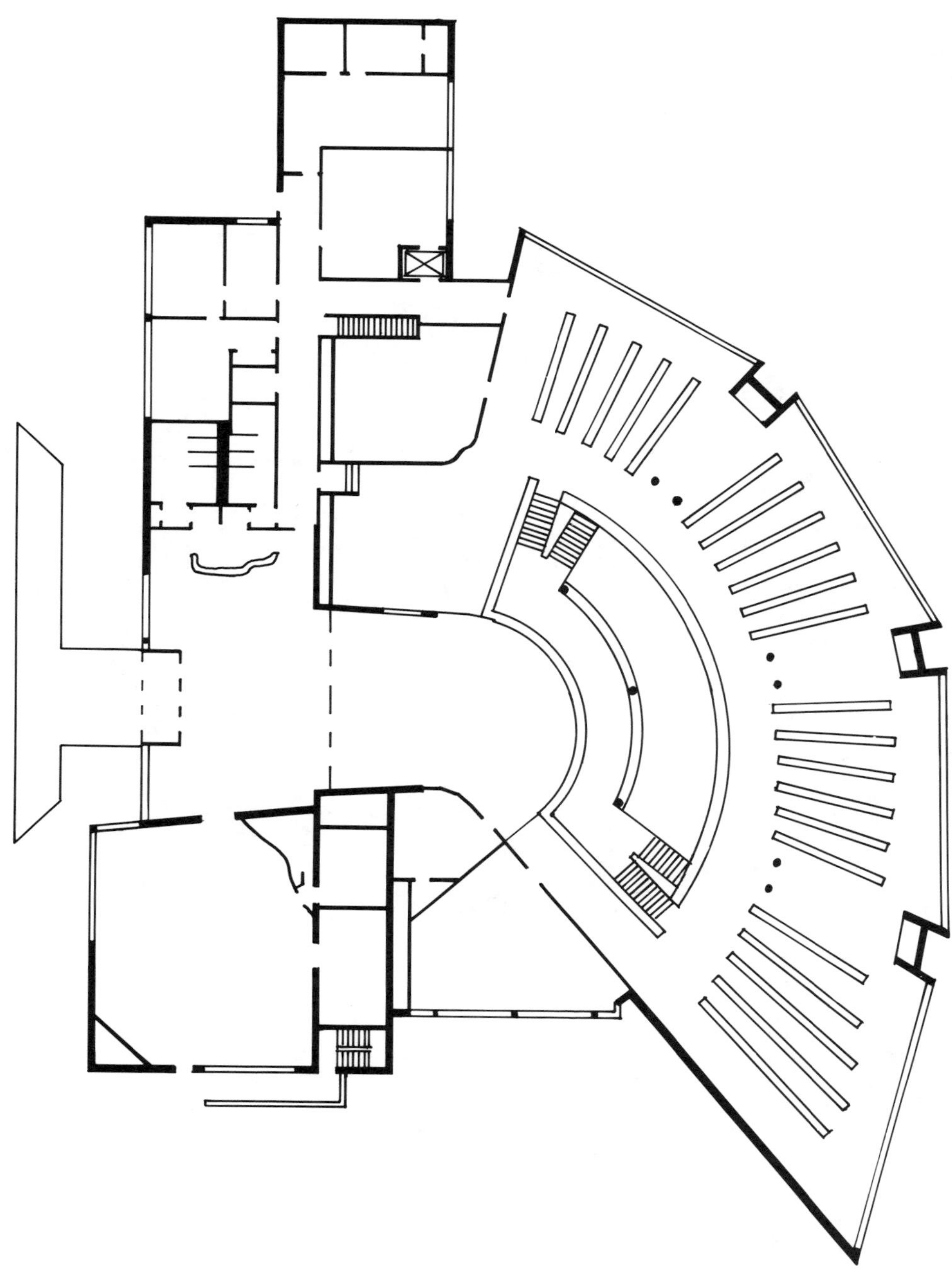

Figure 31. Plan, Mount Angel Seminary Library.

institution as a whole, regarding its educational mission and intellectual objectives, its position in the academic world, its financial support, and its ability to attract and retain faculty and students.

Next, an analysis of the academic program, including both the liberal arts and the professional schools, existing or anticipated, is required. Enrollment, present and future, forms the basis for estimating the required seating while the institution's curriculum and research program indicates the size and depth of the collection required to support it. Then it is essential to determine how best to provide library service—in smaller departmental or professional libraries with their attendant costs in duplication of books and staff or in a central facility with its comprehensive but less convenient collection. More often than not, both approaches are used.

A library is defined by three distinct categories: users, the collections, and staff. Each building seeks to respond to the requirements in these categories.

The Library Users

A library's constituency is broadly based and is determined by courses of study, levels of scholarship, and work habits.

The forecast seating requirements are complicated by considerable variation in the nature of the institutions

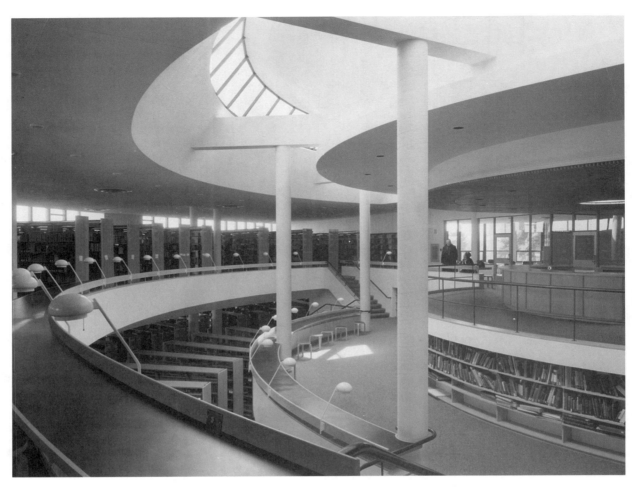

Figure 32. Mount Angel Seminary Library, St. Benedict, Oreg., Alvar Aalto (1970). Work spaces overlook a sweeping skylit gallery and circulation desk. Courtesy of Mt. Angel Abbey. Photograph by William H. Grand.

Figure 33. Exterior, Exeter Library, Phillips Exeter Academy, New Hampshire, Louis I. Kahn (1971). Courtesy of the Library, Phillips Exeter Academy. Photograph by Peter Randall.

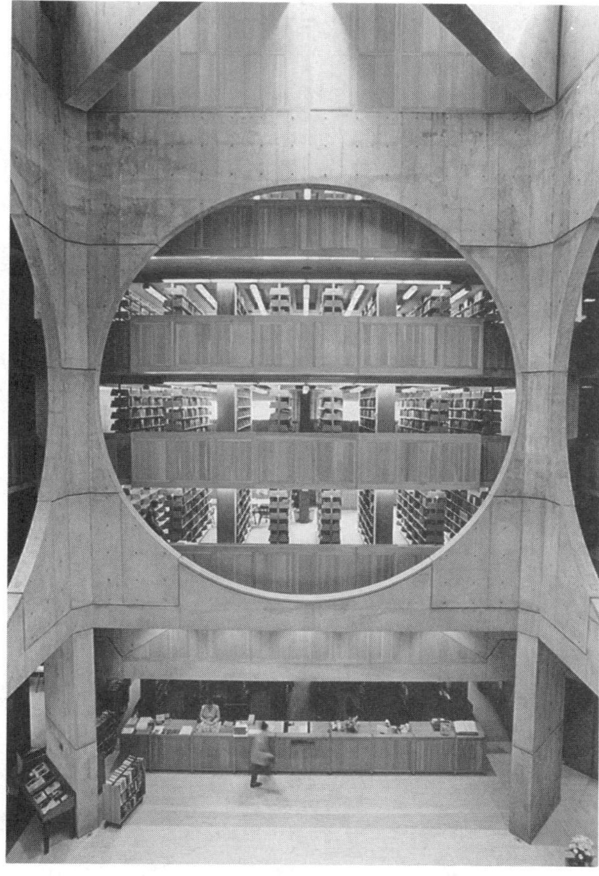

Figure 34. Interior, Exeter Library. Kahn's seminal interior surrounds a monumental skylit cube with small, quiet study spaces. The success of the architecture overrides the well-founded concerns over volumes that interrupt continuous stack areas, decreasing efficiency and flexibility. Photograph by Peter Randall. Courtesy of the Library, Phillips Exeter Academy.

themselves; key characteristics are academic or public, residential or commuting students, urban or nonurban, and level of research materials. Past experience is not necessarily the best guide, since an increase of 50% in use of a new facility is quite normal. Normal standards of seating for academic libraries are

Residential undergraduates	20% Full-time equivalent (15–25%)
Masters	20–25% FTE
Doctorate	30–40% FTE
Nonresidential colleges	10% FTE
Faculty (with social sciences and humanities)	15% FTE (10–25%)

The library program will adjudicate these averages and propose final totals in appropriate categories. User patterns vary widely, according to a number of factors which will strongly influence both the program and the solution, including location and proximity (residential/commuter) user demographics (age, number, subject interest), and use patterns (hour, day, month, and assignment), usually with peak periods at the end of a semester.

A hypothetical pattern of the use of a collection by student researchers preparing a thesis at various levels of scholarship might be as follows:

Thesis	Use of collection (volumes)			
	Scan	Consult	Read	Time
Undergraduate	50	20	5–10	1–2 mo
Graduate MA	200	80	40–60	1½ yr
PhD	1000	400	100–200	3 yr

Normal user seating allowances have traditionally been as follows:

1. 25 net ft^2/seat—normal study carrels (50–70%), tables (25–15%), and lounge seating (25–15%) all require the same area.
2. 35 net ft^2/seat for so-called "wet" carrels, ie, supplied with electricity and/or other electronic connections. These include microcomputer, CRT stations, microform readers, and audiovisual setups. Additional allowance for printers must be considered. Carrels are much preferred by the user because of their privacy and particularly if they are located at the perimeter and near a window. Tables are efficient and allow one to spread out. Lounge chairs offer a welcome variety and are of particular use in current periodicals, new book areas, browsing areas and, of course, in lounges.
3. 60 net ft^2 to 50–75 net ft^2 for faculty or graduate studies (closed).

The Library Staff—Public and Technical Services

The staff is typically organized in three areas of responsibility. Reader services includes those activities which assist the reader in using the library's total resources and control the collections, while technical services select, acquire, and catalog the collections.

Public Services. Primary among the reader services are the circulation department, which has the responsibility of controlling the collection, the reference department, whose staff guides the user through the intricacies of a bibliographical search, and various other points of reader contact which include the catalog, interlibrary loan, current periodicals, and reserve, among others.

The circulation department controls the collection by charging out books lent from the library, charging them in on their return, sorting, and reshelving them in the stacks. The staff is principally clerical and is under the direction of a librarian. The stack supervisor is responsible for maintaining order in the general stacks. The charge-out desk incorporates a security system controlling the exits, so the preferred location is next to the main entrance, usually to the right as one exits. Specific requirements include:

Checkout equipment (frequently bar code read by laser or light pen) with sufficient positions to handle anticipated traffic.

Figure 35. Esther Raushenburg Library, Sarah Lawrence College, Bronxville, N.Y., Warner Burns Toan Lunde (1975). Photograph by Louis Reens.

Computer terminals for computerized circulation control replacing the time-honored card system.

Security gate with magnetic tape detector.

Return book drop, frequently from the exterior as well as in the desk itself.

In the circulation workroom, returned books are sorted onto shelves or directly into book trucks for reshelving in the stacks. The service elevator should be nearby. The circulation librarian is provided with an office of 150 to 180 ft^2.

The interlibrary loan department provides for the lending or borrowing from other libraries, usually affiliated through a regional association, which may include university and college as well as public libraries. A local interlibrary delivery service facilitates movement of material. The extent of this activity is highly dependent on local factors, but it can be expected to expand.

The catalog provides an index to the library's holdings. In its computerized form, it is easy to use and can be made available in locations throughout the building. However, its major concentration will be near the reference desk so that assistance is always at hand. Despite the inevitable transition to the computerized catalog, many libraries must retain some of their card catalog to cover their older holdings which they may elect not to computerize immediately for reasons of cost. The catalog is generally placed in plain view from the entrance.

The reference department provides assistance in searching the library's resources by the use of the catalog and the reference collection. As one of the most frequently used and prestigious areas, the reference department is

Figure 36. Uris Library addition, Cornell University, Ithaca, N.Y., Gunnar Birkerts and Associates (1985). Underground addition wraps the base of Cornell's 1891 Richardsonian library with a sweeping curve. Photograph by Tim Hursley.

generally located in a prominent position near the entrance.

The reference desk is staffed by one or several librarians to answer patrons' requests. Choice of desks or counters is a matter of library policy. Nearby is a small collection of ready reference material and computer terminals and the reference office itself.

Figure 37. Interior, Uris Library addition, Cornell University, Ithaca, N.Y. The curvilinear form adds 200 much-needed seats. Photograph by Tim Hursley.

The staff also renders assistance in computer searches of data bases for materials held in other library collections. The number of available networks is constantly growing with access generally limited only by cost. Regional networks usually develop an on-line catalog with dial-up access.

The bibliographical instruction room houses programs on instruction of the use of the library's facilities and particularly the use of the catalog and the reference and bibliographical collection. Instruction is provided by the reference staff. It is often located near the reference department for easy access to resources, and is mostly applicable to academic libraries. Increasingly, the instruction will be provided by interactive video.

Technical Services. Technical services include all the activities in the selection, purchasing, cataloging, and preparing of all materials received by the library. The requirements include pleasant work stations for the professional and nonprofessional staff and work areas for labeling and preparing materials for shelving.

Acquisitions. Book dealers, jobbers and publishers are frequently selected to send material on the basis of a carefully prescribed profile of desired subjects on an approval basis. Acquisition librarians and departmental readers examine the material and return whatever is not wanted. If returns exceed 3%, the selection profile is usually care-

Figure 38. Olin Memorial Library addition, Wesleyan University, Middletown, Conn., Perry, Dean, Rogers, and Partners, Architects (1985). Photograph by Steve Rosenthal.

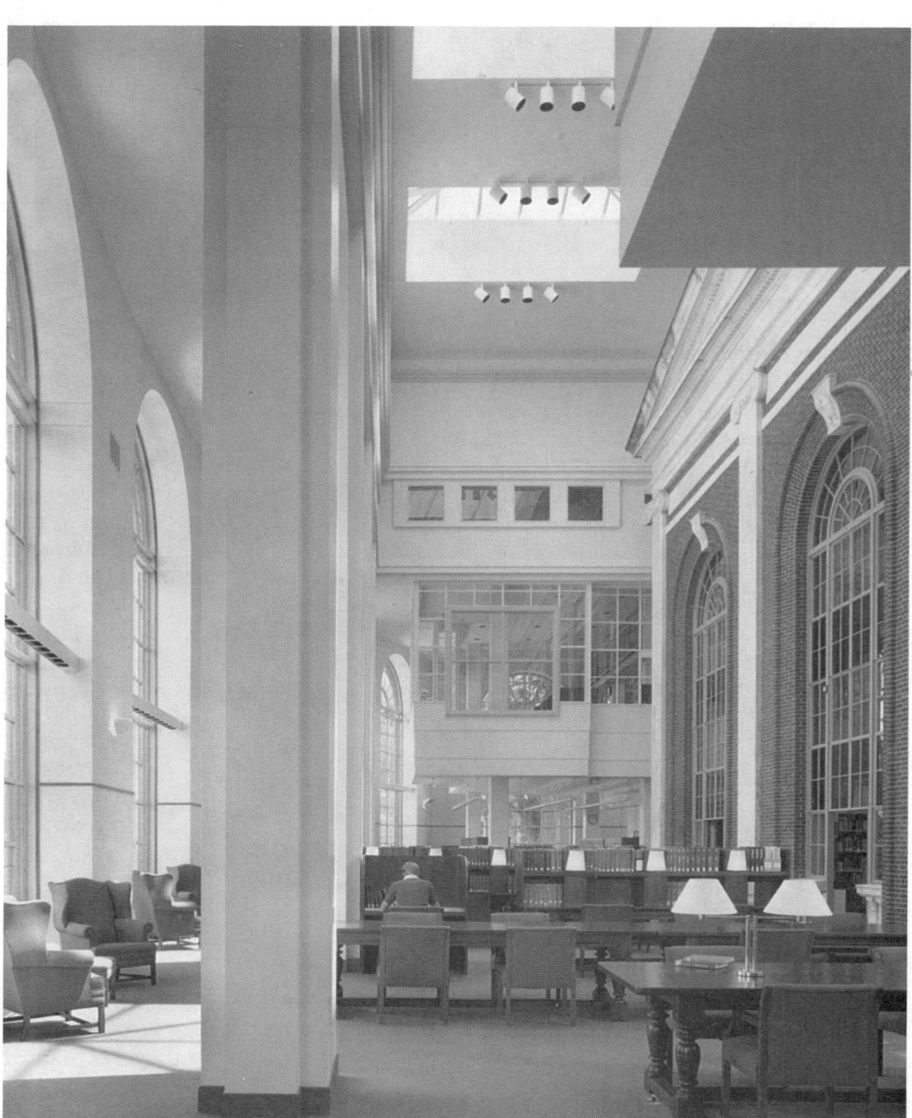

Figure 39. Interior, Olin Memorial Library, Wesleyan University, Middletown, Conn. Photograph by Steve Rosenthal.

Figure 40. Walter Royal Davis Library, University of North Carolina, Chapel Hill, N.C., Mitchell/Giurgola Architects with Boney Architects (1985). Photograph by Tim Hursley.

Figure 41. Interior, Walter Royal Davis Library, University of North Carolina. Mitchell/Giurgola Architects with Boney Architects (1985). Photograph by Tim Hursley.

fully reviewed. New books can now appear on the shelves shortly after their publication and the library, as a major customer, benefits from substantial price reductions by purchasing in volume.

For the large research library there may be several designated sources: foreign, scientific, and professional.

The acquisition budget is established each year and is shaped by curriculum, academic policy, and/or specially allocated funds.

Cataloging. As with many aspects of automation, application of the computer has taken longer than expected, with new problems developing along the way and without the enormous savings in personnel originally envisioned. In general, the result is greater accuracy, uniformity, and speed.

Periodicals. Periodicals are usually the responsibility of a special serials staff. The material is usually bound annually or preserved on microfilm.

Administration. Regardless of the library's size, the administrative suite seems to constitute a relatively small area with a relatively consistent number of positions.

The director of the library has an office with conference area of 250 to 350 ft^2. At most colleges or universities, the position also carries a deanship and faculty status.

Assistant director(s) offices, responsible for library operations, personnel, finance, etc.	80–240 ft^2
Administrative assistant(s) offices responsible for communications, building operations, etc.	120–150 ft^2

Secretaries.	100–120 ft^2
Reception area.	
Friends of the library (2–3 persons)	75–100 ft^2
Conference room large enough for meetings of senior staff, trustees, donors, senior adviser, etc.	400–500 ft^2
Files, copy, storage, and pantry.	

The Collection

Categories of collection include general, reference, periodicals, government documents, special or rare, multimedia, and reserve.

General Collection. The general collection varies with each institution, and is highly dependent on the goals, programs, and funding within each subject field. They may be characterized as follows:

1. *Comprehensive.* Including original sources (roughly 1–5 million volumes).
2. *Extensive research.* All related published material (roughly 500,000 to 1 million volumes).
3. *Teaching/research.* Broad coverage, fundamental (roughly 250,000–500,000 volumes).
4. *Undergraduate research.* Supportive, reference, including major journals (roughly 150,000–300,000 volumes).
5. *Minimal.* Community college (roughly 30,000–150,000 volumes).

It is a widely held axiom of library planning that 90% of the readers use 10% of the collection and vice versa.

Comprehensive collections generally refer to the great university collections as well as the equally great national or public libraries. For obvious reasons, these institutions will wish to restrict user access to the collection on a basis of need. Hence the largest collections are generally of greatest value to scholars and researchers, while undergraduate libraries provide the study environment and more modest collections suitable to their users' needs.

The organization of the stack requires that the first-time user be able to find the desired material without assistance. Stack ranges on each floor should automatically impart a natural sequence. Lighting and carefully conceived graphics contribute substantially in this respect.

The typical stack consists of a double section (DS), 3 ft long and 7 shelves high. Each shelf is assumed for planning purposes to hold 6 volumes/lin ft or 18 volumes/shelf. Each DS is assumed to hold 250 volumes, which is 85% of its capacity, with the balance allowing for growth. However, with the reduction in new acquisitions due to funding restrictions, more extensive "weeding" of the collection, the willingness to put less active parts of the collection in storage, and with regional networks, the growth factor of the 1960s no longer appears justified. Growth varies within subject headings (business vs religion), and in physical size of volumes (literature vs law). Since the program for new construction undoubtedly includes stack expansion, a larger average capacity/DS seems appropriate. An actual audit of a collection is always enlightening. By simply counting the volumes in representative sections throughout the stack, the capacity of stacks may be determined accurately.

The traditional standard is as follows: 250 volumes per double-faced section (DS) of 7 shelves at 85% capacity = 15 volumes/ft^2, based on 3 ft DS with ranges 4.5 ft oc of at least 9 DS and allowing for cross-aisles.

The stack ranges are usually set 4.5 ft apart. If the standard 20-in. base is used, the resulting stack aisle is 34 in., or 2 in. less than present handicap requirements for wheelchairs. While this requirement is not universally applied to stack areas, manufacturers are prepared to supply 18-in. bases and prudence would dictate adoption of the narrower base. Because of the resultant reduction in stability, top bracing of the stacks at about 6-ft centers is essential. Stack uprights are typically 90 in. Without significant additional cost, a 96-in. upright can be provided, which raises the height of the stack light normally attached to the bottom of the cross-tie and permits the addition of an eighth shelf should the collection outgrow the normal seven shelves. This 14% additional capacity can prove to be excellent low-cost insurance (Fig. 42).

Where ceiling height permits, additional stack capacity may be achieved by addition of a second level, either in the original construction or at a later date. A normal stack post has the capacity to support one or two levels with no structural change. It should be at least 8 ft tall in clear height to allow for lighting and air-conditioning. Stacks used in this way must be detailed to avoid having to reinstall lighting or ducts with the addition of the second level. Here, then, technological history can repeat itself looking back 100 years for a reapplication of the multi-tiered stack. Certainly the most glamorous and arresting application of this idea is the Rare Books Library at Yale by SOM's Gordon Bunshaft, where the glass-enclosed, tiered, self-supporting stack is the centerpiece of a walled exhibit room.

The bookstack contract is usually bid separately and based on a separate set of stack drawings and specifications. The drawings will indicate all specific types, number and depth of shelves above the base, end panels, top bracing, canopies, and other details, such as timer or light switching, if any. Shop drawings should be required with gauges of metals indicated. The bidder should provide experience and references in the normal fashion and, if the project is sizable, be required to construct a mock-up of two double sections demonstrating the product before receiving bids.

Collection growth is inevitably constrained by availability of funds. Stack areas in new construction are designed to absorb the projected growth while accommodating existing overcrowded stacks or adjustments in collections. The growth factor normally anticipates 10 years' growth, or at best 20 years.

Reference Collection. The reference collection consists of encyclopedias and bibliographies—preliminary searching tools with which much research begins.

The reference collection is shelved on typical or custom stacks usually with a somewhat wider aisle spacing and with consulting surfaces nearby in the form of 4.5-ft-high

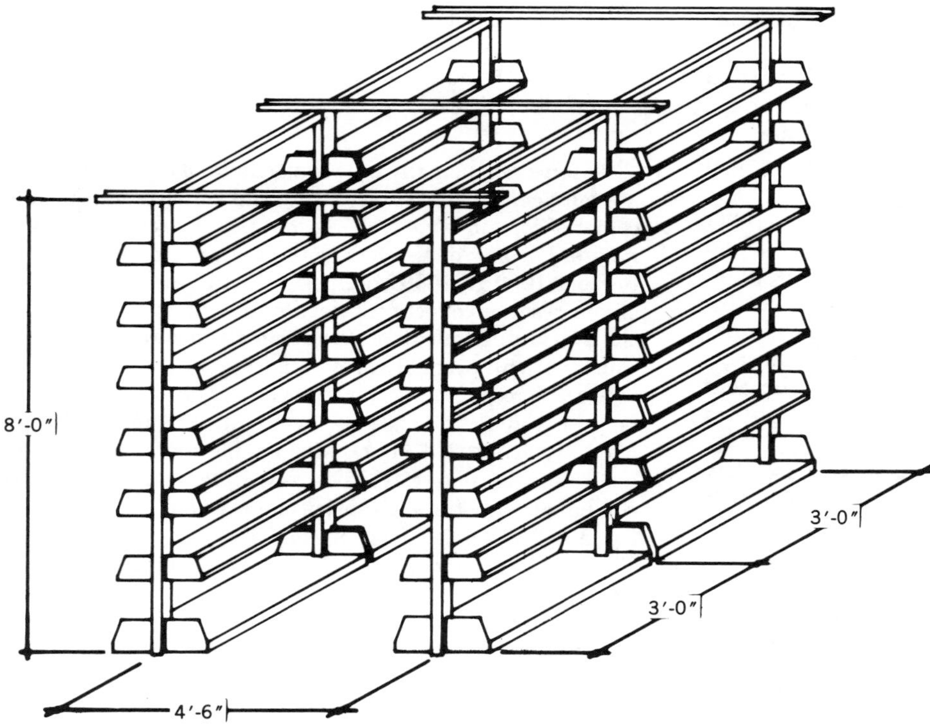

Figure 42. Standard stacks.

stack sections, tables, or pullout shelves. This collection may total between 5000 and 35,000 volumes.

A third essential component of the reference collection is the indexes (the *Readers' Guide to Periodicals, Books in Print,* etc), which, because of their bulk and weight, are usually accorded their own tables with two levels of shelving and with fixed stools to discourage other than specific use. While these indexes are likely targets for commercial computerization (as some already are), for the near term a considerable amount of linear footage of shelf and table is required for this function, in the order of 100 to 250 lineal ft of table to accommodate on two tiers as many as 1200 to 3000 volumes.

Ideally, the reference collection should be close to the catalog, current periodicals, government documents, the microform collection, and interlibrary loan, and even the map collection.

Periodicals/Serials. Because of their specific character, periodicals have a unique and invaluable position in the scheme of information and enjoyment. Along with scholarly journals on esoteric subjects in a dozen languages, the academic library may subscribe, at considerable cost, to from 1000 to 15,000 periodicals; public libraries, with their more broadly based clientele in mind, might take a similar number, although of wider appeal.

The serials department normally oversees the use of the collection (usually one year) before it is bound and shelved in the general collection. The current periodicals reading area is often treated partly as a lounge space and is easily accessible.

Popular titles should be displayed face-out on hinged shelves which normally hold about a year's back issues on a normal shelf directly behind. While there may be only about 15 titles per section, the high visibility attracts the browser. More specialized publications which attract the informed user can be displayed on clearly labeled horizontal shelves.

Newspapers such as the *New York Times* are eventually replaced with microfilm reprints.

Government Documents. As official depositories, designated libraries, both public and private, receive copies selected from lists of everything published by the Federal Superintendent of Documents, which must then be made available to all citizens on request. Because of its diversity of subject matter and format, varying from books and pamphlets to microfilm and CD ROM, the government document collection is somewhat difficult to use and assistance is normally provided. The government documents collection is frequently enclosed, and is located near the reference department whenever practical.

Rare Books and Special Collections. To both the bibliophile and the scholar, these collections enjoy a special importance by virtue of their origin, age, and/or uniqueness. As source material they bring scholarly prestige to the library and attract those collectors who may one day elect to add their own holdings to those of the library. The rare book suite thereby becomes both an enhancement and an added expense to the institution which, in times of reduced funds, must exercise caution in undertaking the obligation. It is becoming less common for libraries to accept even valuable collections unless the gift is endowed with funds to house and staff it properly. All rare books or special collections suites require similar facilities and are virtually libraries unto themselves.

An exhibition area for representative selections from the collection is usually on display for the benefit of the casual visitor. Since these exhibits require detailed research and coordination to prepare, they are not changed frequently.

Materials are predominantly in printed form and must be exhibited behind glass. Perhaps the most popular and least satisfactory method is the flat table with a glass top about 6 in. above the display surface. To be effective this glass should be lit from within with no overhead light to reflect from the glass but this is not usually the case. If a fixture is placed within the contained area, the heat buildup will adversely affect the displayed material unless the case is adequately air-conditioned.

Vertical wall cases are more successful because they offer greater depth (18–24 in.), an internal top lighting system, and opportunities to ventilate adequately. However, the lighting may not work uniformly for the entire height of the case. For this reason, permanent built-in show windows of considerable depth (36–48 in.) have proven to be the most satisfactory, since the light can be distributed more evenly and proper air-conditioning provisions can be made to prevent damage from overheating.

After credentials have been authenticated, the scholar examines the rare books catalog and requests the required material. The paged material will be brought to the reading room where the reader is free to examine it under the watchful eye of the attendant.

Curator/librarian's office and workrooms and the appropriate work areas may be located to allow the staff to survey the readers through adjoining windows.

The closed stack is environmentally controlled with preservation foremost in mind. If it includes a halon gas fire-suppression system, some risk is posed to humans. Stack capacity depends on the nature of the collection. Wider shelves may very well be required at wider spacings, because of the size and weight of some of the material.

Multimedia. Without supplanting the book, the multimedia collection, including microform, video, records, and tapes, is steadily assuming a larger role. Multimedia services house collections of all nonbook material under a single control with its own expert staff. Both software and equipment require special assistance. This area may be adjacent to other special functions, such as reference, current periodicals, or government documents. Reels of film in standard shelving nine shelves high will hold approximately:

800 reels/DSS
5 reels/lin ft
50 reels/ft^2
20,000 fiche/ft^2
2,200 fiche/ft^2

With the advent of digitized computer readout, it seems inevitable that microform will eventually give way to computerization. Since the medium of storage and presentation is changing so rapidly, measuring of any specific collection is the best clue to the shelf space required. Provisions for computers, microform readers, and audio or video equipment all require adequate electrical power and local control of light levels.

Reserve. Principally the requirement of an undergraduate curriculum, the reserve material consists of multiple copies of certain texts relating specifically to course assignments. For any one semester the material might amount to from 1000 to 2500 volumes with the inactive balance of the reserve collection relegated to the stacks. Despite the continuing growth of paperbacks and xerography, this collection will probably grow.

Occasionally a limited set of heavily used material will be reserved to increase its availability. Time limits on loans, typically 2–4 hours, also enable many students to use the same material. The reserve department may be combined with the circulation department, or, if the reserve collection is large, it may have a separate desk. The reserve area includes a checkout counter, and shelving for the currently active reserve collection.

If the readers are restricted in the use of the reserve material in a reserve reading room, it must be sized accordingly. In any event, some seating near the desk is necessary.

If it has a separate entry and is highly visible, this area can also serve as an all-night study. Toilets are required, and a food-vending area is desirable. A security staff is mandatory on most campuses, regardless of the number of outside patrols.

Although most libraries do not allow food in any area, it is a lively subject of debate among planners. The overriding concerns are protection of the books and reduction of litter. On the other hand, provision for some refreshment is an amenity for the users, especially when they are in the library for long periods of time. If vending is included, it is usually separate, sometimes in a late-night study area.

The Program and Planning Efficiency

Because it is subject to individual interpretation and confusion, the question of the ratio between the net assignable or program area of a library and the gross building area must be clarified at the beginning of the project.

The gross building area includes all construction (walls, columns, etc), entrances, circulation, stairs, elevators, toilets, shafts, loading docks, custodial areas, and mechanical/electrical areas; in effect, everything except the programmed spaces. The recommended standard is a net assignable area of 67% of the gross area or a net-to-gross ratio of 1.5. Some agencies (and some consultants) have been known to advocate greater efficiency but to do so is to invite crowded entranceways, narrow circulation, cramped reading rooms, and longer stack ranges, and to preclude any latitude in the design of the interior.

Table 1 presents a summary of a typical midsized academic library program. Table 2 illustrates a prototypical total project budget. Table 3 is a summary for a public library.

Table 1. Summary—Typical Academic Library Program for College or Small University[a]

	Users[b]	Collection[c]	Staff[d]	Area, net ft^2
General				
General study	300 seats at 25 ft^2			7,500
	200 seats at 30 ft^2			6,000
Faculty offices	40 at 50 ft^2			2,000
General stacks		480,000 volumes[c] at 15 V/ft^2		32,000
Catalog reference				1,000
Study collection	100 seats at 30 ft^2			3,000
		20,000 volumes at 10 V/ft^2		2,000
Staff			8 at 150 ft^2	1,200
Reserve				
Study collection	40 seats at 25 ft^2			1,000
		3,000 volumes at 15 V/ft^2		200
Current periodicals				
Study collection	40 seats at 25 ft^2			1,000
		6,000 periodicals at 3 P/ft^2		2,000
Multimedia		2,000 ft^2		2,000
Circulation/Sorting			12 at 150 ft^2	1,800
Interlibrary loan		100 ft^2	6 at 150 ft^2	1,000
Technical services			40 at 150 ft^2	6,000
Administration			15 at 200 ft^2	3,000
Special collections				2,300
Total	680 seats	465,000 V	81 persons	
	40 offices	6,000 Per.		
	20,500 n ft^2	33,000 n ft^2	13,000 n ft^2	
Net program area				66,500
+ 50% (circulation, structure, building services)				33,500
Gross program area				100,000

[a] User population 3200 FTE (full-time equivalent); 800 graduate FTE; 200 faculty.
[b] 3,200 undergraduate FTE × 15% = 480 seats
800 graduade FTE × 25% = 200 seats
680 seats
[c] Allows collection growth of 2 to 3%/year for 10 years.
[d] Includes student positions.
[e] Computer positions.

PUBLIC LIBRARIES

While academic building declined, public libraries came to the fore. Because they are tax-based, new town libraries developed to serve growing populations. For example, in December, 1987, *Library Journal* listed more than 500 public projects under way, while academic projects declined to around 80. These new public and regional libraries have emphasized the input of the community in determining the type of service that they require. Rather than prescribing specific standards as it has in the past, the American Library Association now fosters local prerogatives in specifying size, location, and quality of their libraries.

Many recent designs seek a contextual or historical relevance through a humanist approach. They tend to avoid the free-flowing flexible space so prevalent in modern libraries, focusing on smaller, more intimate spaces.

Many popularly labeled "postmodern" libraries have taken their cue from local historical landmarks and metaphorical relationships. Ignoring the modern, "international" architecture which filled the intervening years, architects have attempted to relate their work to local architectural character through recall of its traditional forms and details.

The Public Library Program

> Knowledge will forever govern ignorance. . . . A popular government without popular information or the means of acquiring it, is but a prologue to a farce or a tragedy, or perhaps both.
>
> *James Madison*

Since its beginning in the mid-nineteenth century, the public library has been the principal informational and cultural resource of most communities in the United States. Today, from converted frame houses or suburban storefronts to the great marble palaces of the New York Public or Boston Public libraries; from collections of several thousand to NYPL's 10 million volumes, they serve a population as varied as the country itself. Although they gener-

Table 2. Prototypical Total Project Budget[a]

1. Building construction		70%
A. Program area	100% net ft^2	
B. Construction area	+50%	
	150% gross ft^2	
C. Construction cost area gross ft^2 × estimated cost/ft^2 The estimated cost/sq ft should be an informed opinion and include the following: • Cost of similar library facilities adjusted for date and location. • Degree of sophistication and finish. • Allowance for escalation to the bid date.		
2. Architectural and engineering fees and expenses 0.5% allowance for reimbursable expenses (printing, hard, telephone, etc)	(7.5% of No. 1)	5.25%
3. Interior (furnishings, furniture, and equipment—FFE) Includes carpet, stacks, window treatment, decorative lighting, graphics, interior design; fee of 10%	(15% of No. 1)	10.5%
4. Library expenses Includes consultant, security system, miscellaneous electronics, moving		3%
5. Owner's expenses • Legal • Surveys • Supervising clerk-of-works • Testing and inspections		2.25%
6. Contingency Including allowances for variations in construction cost, design development, programmatic requirements and other unanticipated costs	(10% of 1, 2, 3)	9%
Total		100%

[a] Cost of site and its development is not included.

ally receive public tax support, they nevertheless withstand occasional efforts at censorship to emerge as symbols of civic pride while serving the community much as Madison would have wished.

Since the patrons of public libraries are far more diverse than the more prescribed users of college and university libraries, there are distinct differences in emphasis and requirements to be considered concerning size, site, and interior programming.

Size. What is an appropriate size for a public library? To establish a reasonable measure (12), Joseph Wheeler, formerly librarian for the State of New York, began in the 1930s to examine a cross-section of existing libraries and developed a series of standards for the size of collections, seating, staffing, and total building area. These guidelines, frequently amended over time, have been adopted by a number of states as a guide to public policy. Recently, the ALA has promoted the concept of local determination and autonomy and avoids promulgating any standards.

Site. High visibility in a prime location near shopping and local business with good public transportation is of great advantage in assuring maximum accessibility for the entire community. While a parklike suburban site is undoubtedly appealing, it requires an extra stop for those with cars; without a car it may be inaccessible.

Children's Department. The children's department is a unique characteristic of the public library, including at least four categories of library patrons, each of which requires distinctly different provisions. Children's skill levels and interests vary widely, necessitating a graduated collection spanning from preschool to high school. The children's service desk should provide for easy supervision of the areas with its workroom nearby so that other staff members can assist during busy periods.

Four groups can be categorized:

1. Preschoolers (2 to 5 years old) include prereading children. Their books will probably be read to them, the child commenting on pictures while learning letters and words. Their collection will include records and video cassettes, a story-telling area, and/or provisions to present video programs. A studio room to accommodate various arts projects is desirable. Realia are popular.
2. Early readers (5 to 10) include a collection of progressively advanced reading matter. Provisions to display art, perhaps the work of the young patrons, adds interest for both the children and their parents.
3. Advanced readers (8 to 12) have begun to develop keen interests in selected areas such as history, nature, geography, astronomy, or other sciences, as well as adventure tales. Appropriate reading and

Table 3. Summary—Typical Public Library Program: Central or Regional[a]

	Users	Collection	Staff	Area (net ft²)
Children				
Users	120 seats at 20 ft²			2,400
Collection		37,500 volumes at 15 V/ft²		2,500
Staff			10 at 150 ft²	1,500
Adult				
Users	200 seats at 25 ft²			5,000
Collection		300,000 volumes at 15 V/ft²		20,000
Reference				
Users	50 seats at 25 ft²			1,250
Collection		5,000 volumes at 10 V/ft²		500
Staff			8 at 150 ft²	1,200
Current periodicals				
Users	50 seats at 25 ft²			1,250
Collection		2,250 periodicals at 3 P /ft²		750
Multimedia				
Users	20 seats at 30 ft²			600
Collection		1,500 ft²		1,500
Staff			2 at 150 ft²	300
Community auditorium	300 seats at 12 ft²			3,600
Circulation			10 at 150 ft²	1,500
Sorting				
Interlibrary loan				
Technical services			25 at 150 ft²	3,750
Administration			12 at 200 ft²	2,400
Total	740 seats	342,500 V 2,250 Per.	70 persons	
Net program area	14,100 n ft²	25,250 n ft²	10,650 n ft²	50,000
+ 50% (circulation, structure, building services)				25,000
Gross building area				75,000

[a] User population: 200,000. See Table 2 for prototypical budget.

study areas are needed. More and more of these children are arriving unaccompanied by their parents.

4. Young adults (10 to 16) exhibit the teen-ager's wide-ranging curiosity about oneself and his or her world. Ambitious school research projects require a reference collection and adequate provisions for study.

For obvious reasons, the children's area must be well supervised and is generally placed very near the front entrance. Low bookcases 3–3.5 ft high favor the youngest users. The books tend to be thin (so that they can be read aloud in 10–15 min) and hence shelf capacity in terms of volumes is very great. Bookcases can become progressively higher, consistent with the age group as long as supervision can be maintained. Upper shelves on the wall cases can be used for display with storage behind. Seating is graduated in size with appropriately informal lounging mixed with study tables.

The adult department also responds to the varied interests of its patrons.

Browsing/New Books. A reading room with a display of the current "best sellers," both fiction and nonfiction, should be near the entry, as this is always a major attraction.

Current Periodicals. From the *Wall Street Journal* to *Cosmopolitan* and *Consumers Reports* to *Car and Driver,* readers invariably seek out these up-to-the-minute sources of their own personal interest. A variety of comfortable seating should be provided close to the display shelving.

Public Catalog and Reference Department. As in academic libraries, these are the principal reader service locations. The traditional card catalogs are rapidly giving way to computer terminals. In fact, since their collections are modest, their automation is less complicated and expensive and in many cases has taken place while colleges and universities, with their large collections and diminished funds, are lagging behind. Increasingly, high school, college, postgraduate, and continuing education students, professional writers and researchers, and the local business community are using the library's reference staff, collection, and study areas to aid them in their work. Local area networks (LAN), with interlibrary loans, greatly expand the library's resources.

The Collection

With an emphasis on current fiction and nonfiction, the public library provides material of immediate interest to

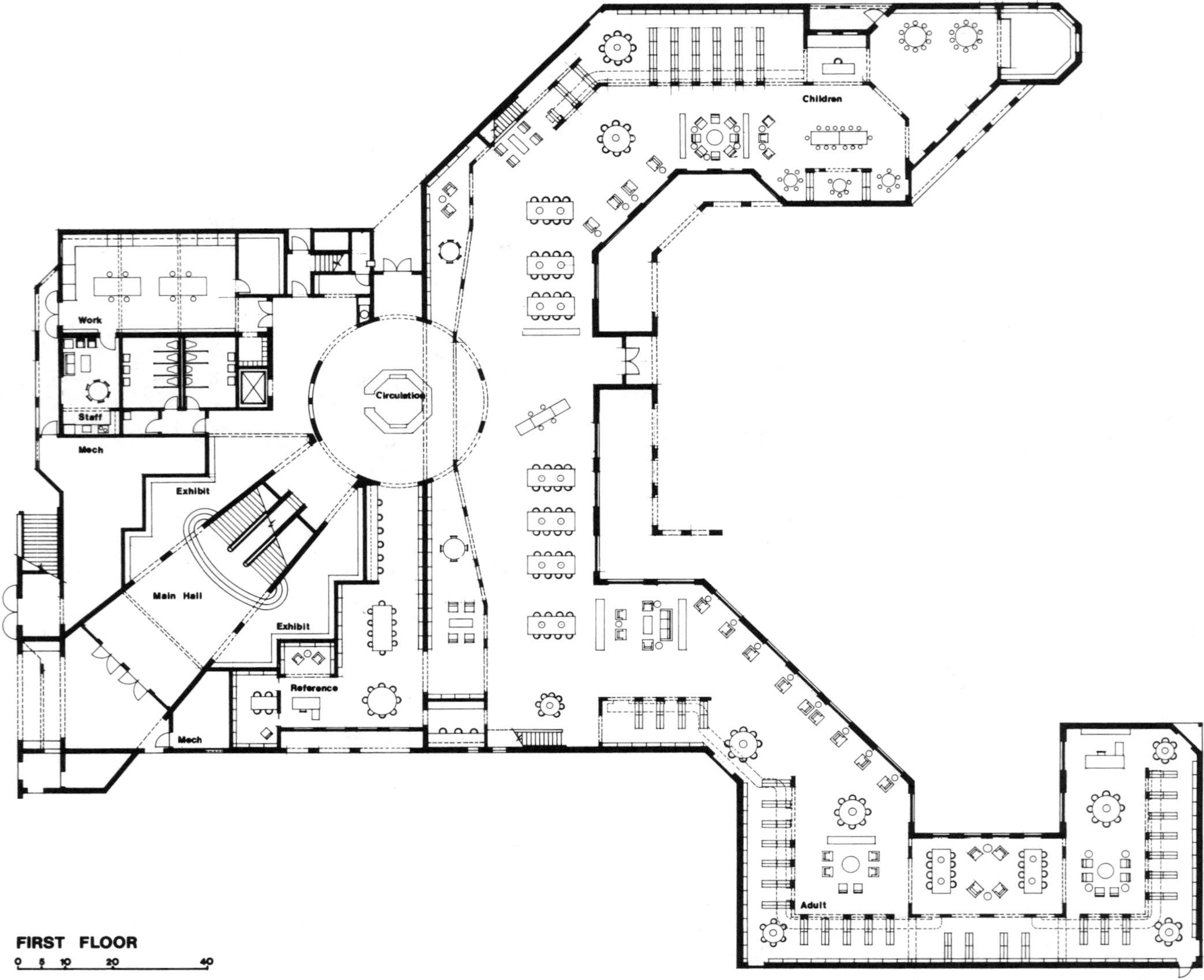

Figure 43. Plan, Biloxi Library and Cultural Center, Biloxi, Miss.

its patrons while maintaining a well-balanced general collection. Information on career choices, career changes, hobbies, computers, investments, travel, health, retirement, and the plethora of "how to" books, are much sought. Special collections of local history, genealogy, etc, are of particular interest to patrons. An avid reader, at the rate of one book a week for 60 years, would only read 3000 books in a lifetime. Through diversity, the collection seeks to cater to various interests.

Nonprint Media. Collections of video cassettes, records, and tapes are in considerable demand. Microform collections provide access to back issues of the newspapers, periodicals, etc, for research in depth. Additionally, microcomputers and software, microform collections, etc, are becoming available for patron use.

Auditorium

Consistent with their traditional mandate as a cultural resource to an informed citizenry, public libraries usually include an auditorium as a public forum for discussion and entertainment. Without stage paraphernalia of a theater or fixed seating, the auditorium usually holds audiences in the 100- to 400-seat range or provides an area for such events as art shows or book fairs.

A simple stage, projection booth, and adequate storage are required as well as a separate outside entrance if possible. Academic libraries gave up the auditorium half a century ago as being an unnecessary intrusion, but public libraries continue to find it a stimulating means of fostering community involvement. For a summary of a typical public library program, see Table 3.

Figure 44. Exterior, Biloxi Library and Cultural Center, Charles Moore/William Turnbull Associates (1976). Photograph by Morley Baer.

Public Libraries: 1976–1985

Examples of recent public library buildings include the following:

1. In the Biloxi Library and Cultural Center, Biloxi, Miss., by Charles Moore/William Turnbull Associates (1976) (Figs. 43, 44), the plan eschews library modularity and flexibility in creating a unique community place and symbol.
2. In the Conrad Sulzer Regional Library, Chicago, by Hammond, Beeby, and Babka, with Joseph Casserly (1985) (Figs. 45, 46), the compact efficiency of the plan within a monumentally expressed enclosure allows for sectionally rich skylit spaces.
3. In the Broward County Main Library, Fort Lauderdale, Fla., Gatje, Papachristou, Smith/Miller, & Meier, and Associates (1985) (Figs. 47, 48), two glassy facades terracing toward the protected entry plaza are solidly backed by limestone on the two street sides. The central atrium provides a dynamic focus to the large open floors.
4. Sited within view of the famed mission church, Michael Graves's (1984) San Juan Capistrano Regional Library (Figs. 49–51) emulates without imitating its historic paradigm with ochre stuccoed walls, red tiled roofs, discrete rooms, and incised window openings. The plan avoids motions of open, flexible, modular planning, preferring a complex of richly varied, self-contained spaces and forms.

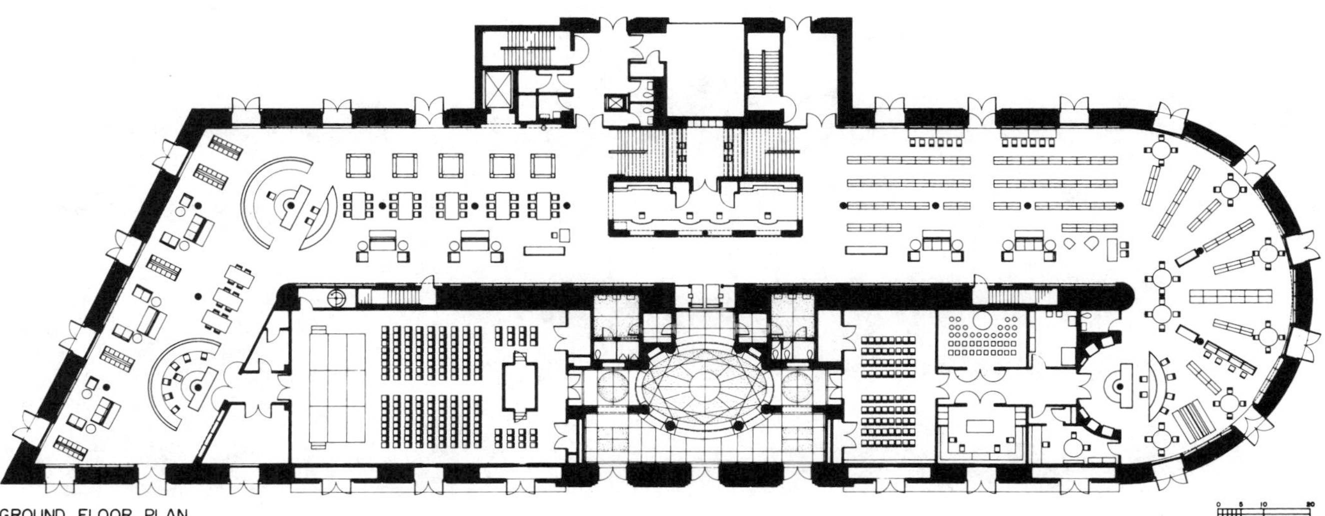

Figure 45. Ground floor plan, Conrad Sulzer Regional Library, Chicago.

Figure 46. Exterior, Conrad Sulzer Regional Library, Hammond, Beeby, and Babka, with Joseph Casserly (1985). Photograph by Tim Hursley.

Figure 47. Exterior, Broward County Main Library, Fort Lauderdale, Fla., Gatje, Papachristou, Smith/Miller, and Meier and Associates (1985). Two glassy facades terracing toward the protected entry plaza are solidly backed by limestone on the two street sides. Photograph by Steven Brooke.

Figure 48. Interior, Broward County Main Library. A dynamic central atrium gives a focus to the large open floors. Photograph by Steven Brooke.

TECHNICAL INFORMATION

Structure

The unique requirements of a library impose significant demands on its structure. A concrete structure is often preferred because of the heavy 150 lb/ft^2 live load for the bookstacks. (This live load would be increased to 300 lb/ft^2 to accommodate compact stacks.) To allow for flexibility and future alterations, the live load should be maintained throughout the building. The necessary strength could, of course, be achieved in steel, but only with a deeper structural section, which would add to the overall height of the building without an increase in clear interior height. Stack loading has proportionally less impact on the overall efficiency of a concrete structure, with its intrinsically high dead load, while the natural continuity of concrete with its ability to cantilever where required makes it the preferred structural medium. Since a concrete structure is naturally fireproof, it allows the underside of the slab to be left exposed in certain areas, particularly over the stacks. This increases the height of the interior space and is an additional economy over steel which, with its metal deck, subframing, and fireproofing, usually requires a ceiling to achieve an acceptable level of finish.

A key factor in the consideration of column bay sizes is the modularity of bookstack spacing. With a concrete structure, square bays are preferable in order to achieve a flat slab.

Various column spacings have been used, from 22.5 to 36 ft, generally following the 3 × 4.5 ft module of the stacks. A square bay of 27 ft is quite usual and allows for desirable stack and table spacing. A number of architects have employed precast double tees or similar structures to achieve spans of 54 ft while accepting the added floor to floor height required. The overriding factors in establishing bay sizes, however, should be structural costs, the scale of the project and the desired architectural effect. In large floor areas, a wide bay size may be preferable to avoid the effect of a forest of columns, although structure in varying patterns may be well used in some situations to define spaces. An orderly modularity adds immeasurably to the efficiency, economy, and aesthetics of library structures.

Lighting

Eye comfort, visual acuity and interior appearance are critically influenced by lighting.

It is generally agreed that 50 fc of light are required on the work surface, which is easily achieved using fluorescent fixtures. Because of their efficiency and long life, fluorescent luminaires are the preferred source. One popular form employs parabolic, specular alzak reflectors on a modular spacing. Typically, a two-tube fixture placed at 8 × 10 ft on center at a ceiling height of 10 to 12 ft will produce the desired glare-free illumination at about 50 fc, an expenditure of about 1.25 W/ft^2 with an energy-saving ballast of 1.125 W/ft^2.

In stack areas, however, the pattern changes to adapt to the spacing of the stack ranges. Despite their flexibility, stacks are rarely moved and for lighting efficiency a continuous fluorescent strip of a single tube mounted from the stack bracing directly between the stacks is the most effective means of illuminating the spines of the books. Frequently, two range aisles will be controlled by a low voltage time switch at either end of one of the ranges set to provide a prescribed illumination period such as 10–15 minutes. The advantage of this arrangement, obviously, is to save both the electric consumption of about 3.4 W/ft^2 throughout the stacks which would result if they were burning constantly. Time switches only make sense in larger, less frequently used stack areas and certainly not in reference rooms or similar high use areas. It is probable that motion-activated light switches or similar devices will be in common use in the future. The conclusion is obvious: concentrate reader areas and, where practical, consider putting stack lighting on timers.

With the current reintroduction of high bay spaces in principal reading areas, other means of lighting should be considered. High output luminaires such as halide offer high foot candles at low wattage. A popular indirect lighting form conceals the halide lighting element within a hanging disk. This produces uplight on the ceiling but may not generate enough light at the task level. A custom-designed version of this fixture includes a lensed downlight component which adds some much-needed sparkle and additional foot candles on the work surface. The contrast in color is important: halide with a Kelvin of 4000 K gives off a cool light with a color rendering index (R) of 65 while

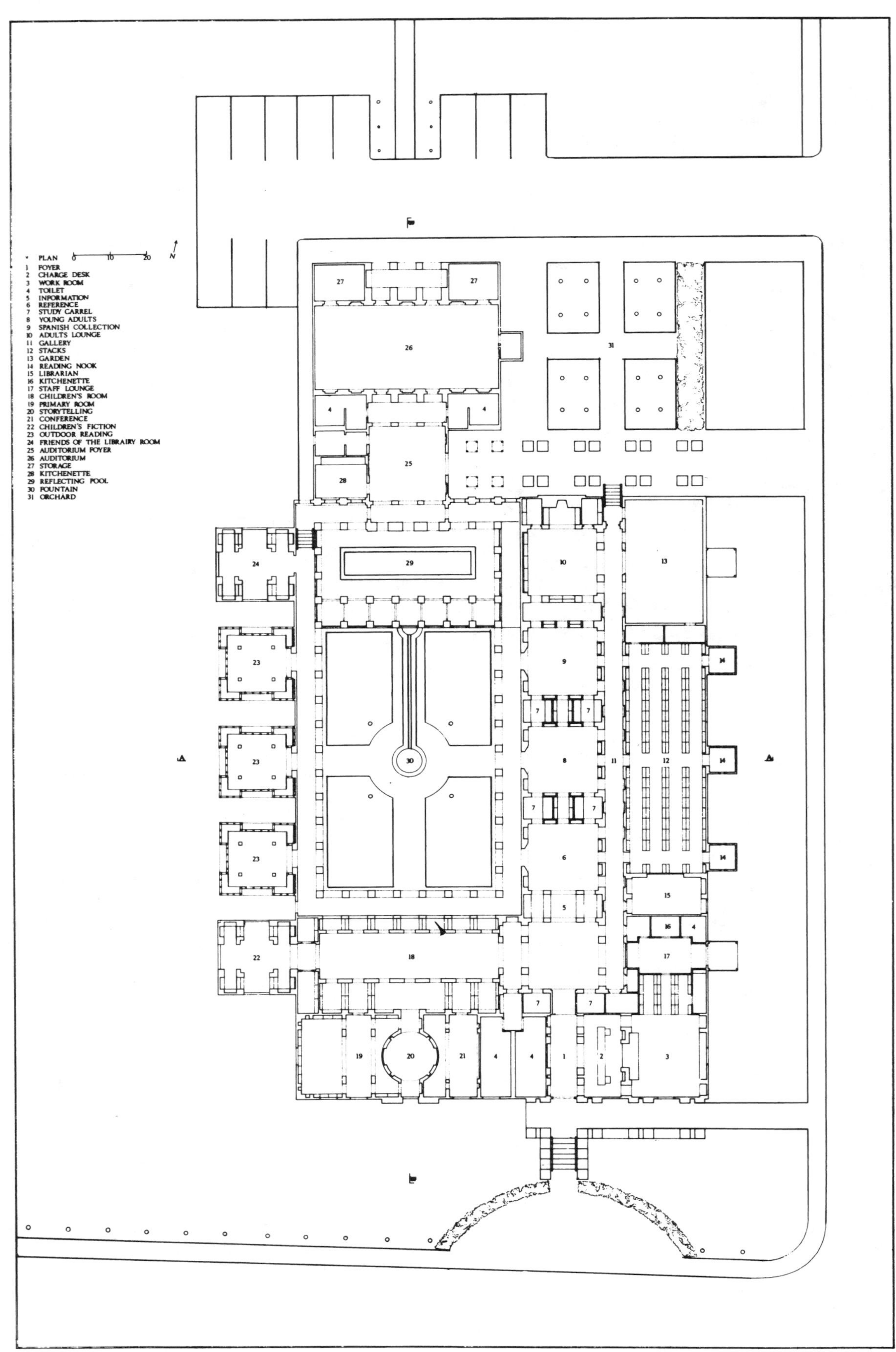

Figure 49. Plan, San Juan Capistrano Regional Library, San Juan Capistrano, Calif. The plan eschews modernist notions of open planning and flexibility, preferring a complex of richly varied self-contained spaces and forms. Courtesy of the architect.

Figure 50. San Juan Capistrano Regional Library, Michael Graves, Architect (1984). View from the mission landmark. Photograph by Paschall/Taylor.

warm white fluorescent with its 2950 K has an R of 73 and on the warm side, a welcome visual contrast. Furthermore, halide has an expected life of 15,000 h vs 10,000 h for fluorescent tubes twice the average annual hours of operation for a university library. Although incandescent bulbs have a pleasant warm color (R = 97), they require far more watts for the equivalent light and a life of only 700 to 1000 hr. (Extended service 2500 w.)

Although the optimal humidity level for books is much higher than that for people, it is impossible to vary humidity levels within a simple, contiguous area, so usually a compromise is reached. Fresh air and air changes in reader areas directly affect the quality of environment. As the supply of air enhances comfort and concentration, codes typically require 8–12 air changes/h.

Requirements were lowered significantly during the energy crisis of the 1970s, and are perhaps lower than many consultants recommend. Studying is a sedentary activity but one which requires concentration and hard work. The "sick building syndrome" is a widely recognized phenomenon in sealed buildings, where the occupants become sluggish and doze off for lack of fresh air. Air movement in basement spaces is a particular problem. Libraries tend to have extensive basements, often with inactive storage areas. In the mid-1980s these spaces came under particular scrutiny because of concern with radon gas. Radon contains a cancer-causing agent which results from decay of radioactive particles in the earth and tends to collect in stagnant basement areas. The cure is air circulation and eliminating any pockets of stale air in remote corners. While the code specifies 5 ft^3/min (cfm) of fresh air per person, there is a body of opinion which prefers a level of fresh air of 15 cfm per person for the above reasons.

Since libraries are heavily used in the evening both on campus and in the community, exterior lighting is of prime importance to ensure a feeling of welcome, safety, and shared activity. Light pouring out from the inside windows should be offset by light on the building and surrounding areas and especially around landscaping and parking. If staff offices occupy substantial parts of the entrance level, thought should be given to maintaining sufficient lighting in those areas to convey the impression that the building is "open for business" as usual. At night, the library should be a beacon of light, both physically and intellectually.

Heating and Air-Conditioning Systems (HVAC)

Since the 1960s, as a consequence of the contemporary planning concepts of universal space and total flexibility, libraries tend to have extensive open floor areas, made practical by the advent of air-conditioning during the 1950s. Often the entire building, aside from staff and service areas, is one continuous space, containing both reader and stack areas. This poses a special problem to the mechanical engineer designing the air-handling system. Because the heat load of reader areas is much greater than that of stack areas, the area must be zoned accordingly. For efficiency, prudence dictates that stack and reader areas be differentiated early in the design. Variable air volume systems are often recommended, as they more easily accommodate this differentiation.

Relative humidity (RH) is another matter. Unfortunately books do enjoy a more humid environment: 40–55% RH, while people can be quite happy with a winter RH of 30–40%. The 1987 HVAC handbook recommends 40–55% RH for libraries year-round, a level which seems excessively high for northern low winter temperatures and imposes risks of condensation, especially on glass areas. For example, with a 40% RH in a building with double glazing, condensation will occur on the glass when the outside temperature drops to 0°F; 35% and 30% RH will produce condensation at −15°F and −25°F respectively. The thermal break now standard in metal mullion design should reduce the potential for condensation on them. Since the general collection is not so sensitive to the RH,

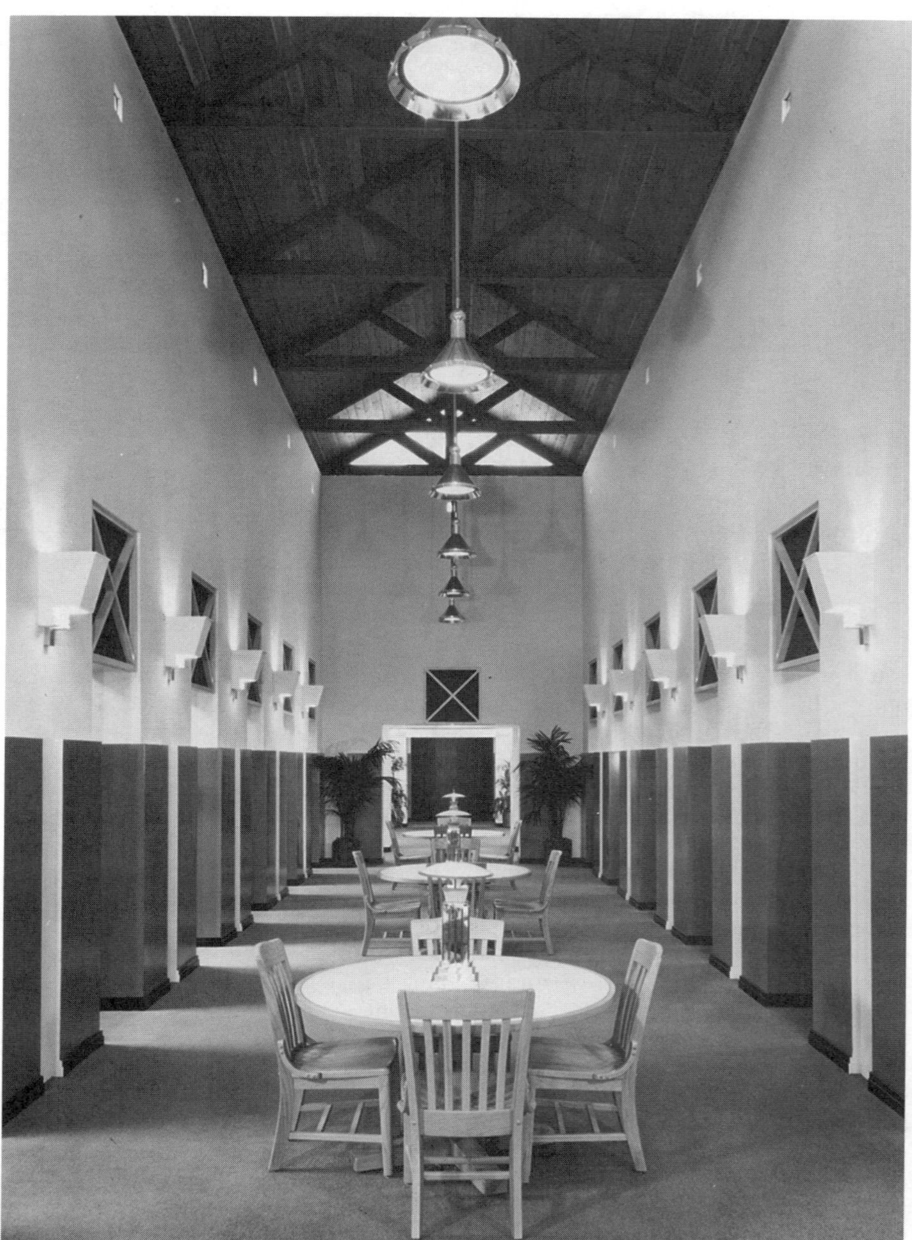

Figure 51. Interior, San Juan Capistrano Regional Library. Photograph by Paschall/Taylor.

general practice is to lower the interior moisture level where climate dictates while maintaining the higher recommended levels only in those areas where rare or special material is stored. By reducing the RH generally throughout the building in cold weather, less stress is imposed on the vapor barrier throughout the walls and roof, which is frequently less than perfect.

For both environmental quality and aesthetics, it is important to maintain as high a ceiling as possible in reader areas. To accomplish this, ductwork can be carried above stacks or channeled into limited dropped ceiling areas bordering reading spaces, rather than be allowed to spread out above them in a continuous flat hung ceiling. This allows for welcome breaks in an otherwise monotonous horizontal ceiling plane, but requires early and thoughtful attention by the architect and careful coordination with the mechanical engineer.

In the early postwar period, vertical ducts were often run alongside columns. This technique was found to be inadvisable, because of the complications it introduced in concrete reinforcing and the cost and efficiency of the ductwork itself. The tendency now is to locate shafts near stair and elevator cores, and to distribute the air horizontally from these points. Air-conditioning loads are determined on the basis of three sources: sun, readers, and lighting. Since the sun load is periodic and dependent on orientation, windows, and insulation, it is project-specific and will not be addressed here.

A reader studying and occasionally walking generates an average of 550 BTUH (British thermal units per hour). Fluorescent lighting, the typical system since the 1950s and for the foreseeable future, requires about one watt per square ft (W/ft^2) to produce the desired 50 fc in reader areas. Each reader is assumed to occupy 25 ft^2 and generate 22 BTUH/ft^2. The lighting load of one W/ft^2 amounts to 3.4 BTUH/ft^2. The combined load, therefore, is 25.4 BTUH/ft^2. Since a ton of air-conditioning is 12,000 BTUH, the resultant load would require 1 ton for every 472 ft^2 of readers' areas (12,000 ÷ 25.4 = 472). This area would be expected to seat about 18 readers.

Stacks, on the other hand, have virtually no human occupancy and the lighting load is considerably higher (100 W for every 36 ft (4.5 ft × 8 ft) or 2.77 w/ft^2 requiring a ton of air-conditioning approximately every 1200 square ft (2.77 × 3.516 BTUH = 9.74 BTUH/ft^2) (12,000 divided by 9.74 = 1,232 ft^2), or lighting of about 72 DS, including cross-aisles.

Because of their extremely long hours of operation, libraries require especially efficient energy systems to keep these costs within reasonable bounds. New energy codes concern themselves with the building shell. A study undertaken by the architect and mechanical engineer should establish a target energy budget to include all heating and air-conditioning loads as well as electrical consumption including both lighting and motors (fans, pumps, elevators, etc). Combined with hours of operation, these loads would generate an annual requirement of BTUs per square ft. Comparisons with facilities of like characteristics and standards would indicate the overall efficiency of the total energy design. Often, this study offers clues as to where savings can be made (energy cycles on consumption of power by motors, for example, or the aforementioned time switches).

Windows

Studies of libraries have repeatedly shown that the users are highly phototropic; whenever possible, the majority will gravitate toward windows. Alternating between focusing on the printed page and a longer view to the outside is both restful and pleasant to the eyes. Nevertheless, solar glare and heat gain can be a problem for both readers and books and architects must resort to means of reducing the consequent effects. Experience indicates that a light mirroring (±20% transmittance) and tinting of glass in the upper stories minimizes both glare and solar gain while still avoiding the image of a sealed and empty building to the outside observer. On the main floor of the library and in areas where bypassers can look in, clear glass is of great importance in giving assurance that the library is welcoming, attractive, busy, and full of interesting material. Hence, shading devices may prove necessary.

Interior glare control is still best managed by the ubiquitous venetian blind because of its high degree of adjustability and low cost. As the blinds have become thinner they have become more attractive. Vertical blind shades and curtains have proven to be more easily mistreated and consequently less durable in the average library situation but do have their appropriate uses.

Acoustics

The question of ambient noise is important to the study environment, where concentration is of concern. Many librarians prefer a quite "dead" space, that is, where the noise created is muffled by extensive sound-absorptive materials. Experience, however, tends to say that for the generation who has grown up studying in front of the television set and wearing personal stereos, a certain liveliness is acceptable. In fact, some ambient noise level is often found to promote concentration. The HVAC system is frequently designed to create a certain amount of noninformation-bearing "white noise," which will mask much of the random assorted noises. The generally accepted standard is a noise coefficient (NC) of 35 dB.

Footfalls, the noise of people walking can be annoying to readers; it is generally best attenuated by carpeting.

Additional sound absorption may be necessary in reader areas, where noise levels are the highest. The stack areas are not a major problem, as the books themselves absorb a considerable amount of sound, and noise generation is low. Since conversation between patrons and staff is probably the most annoying intrusion, location of public service desks—circulation, reference, serials, etc—should be somewhat removed from areas of concentrated study. A noise level of 40 dB is quite acceptable.

Ceilings

Spatial configurations are largely defined by the ceiling plane. Because of the blocks of stacks and the plane of tables and chairs it is the ceiling which illuminates the perimeter and contour of the plan. As previously suggested, requirements of acoustics, lighting, and air-conditioning must be accommodated, but if the ceiling is allowed to extend uninterrupted from wall to wall the effect will be boring at best.

Below a roof, the ceiling can follow the roof forms or incorporate skylights or clerestories allowing natural light to penetrate into the interior with dramatic effect. Floor penetrations, while reducing flexibility, introduce new volumetric relationships. Within the normal ceiling heights, coffers of plaster board relieve the flatness and provide a chance to break the sameness of the ubiquitous exposed spline acoustic ceiling. With its low cost and accessibility to the mechanical and electrical systems, the basic suspended ceiling will undoubtedly prevail for years to come but that only increases the importance of offsetting its sameness with lighting and intelligent detailing.

Safety and Security for Persons and Property

Theft, vandalism, drugs, verbal abuse, assault (including rape), indecent exposure, and arson (13) threaten property and persons in urban and suburban as well as the collegiate settings more often than is generally realized. Actually, considering the freedom of access, the hours of operation, and the almost unsupervisable character of the large floor areas usually obstructed by stacks, the opportunities for aberrant behavior are ineluctable. However, because of the tranquil nature of the library environment, any misconduct becomes doubly shocking, destroying the fabric of trust and serenity. Can design reduce the probability of these unsettling events? In combination with library management policies, the answer appears to be a qualified "yes," although sometimes the cost is considerable.

Tragically, there have been sufficient numbers of incidents of assault and harassment to warrant taking precautions for the patrons and staff, particularly in the more remote parts of the floor and during less populous hours. Open spaces between floors aid in supervision and appear to discourage misconduct. Dispersement of staff areas throughout the floors may add security during working hours. Use of fire stairs for circulation should be discouraged. While the restriction of patron use is anathema to U.S. librarianship it is becoming an issue in the protection of person and collection. To some degree, the thoughtful design of the traffic pattern can produce a kind of self-surveillance where the users themselves, by moving through the floors, discourage the occasional miscreant.

Theft is a major problem. Prior to the installation of a magnetic detection system book thefts of 10% of the collection and higher in a single year have been reported. Today, detection installations at the checkout station are virtually universal. Not only rare books are subject to theft. Reference material, genealogies, yearbooks, and local histories offer backgrounds to writers. Pages are torn from bound periodicals or newspapers, maps and etchings from rare books. Putting some of this type of material on reserve can help, especially if an identifying card with the user's picture is required for checkout, as the staff can scan the material quickly when it is returned. Personal property must also be guarded. Refundable coin lockers may be an answer. Fire exits must be guarded with alarms and loading docks supervised.

In rare books or special collections suites, strict procedures are followed to prevent misappropriation. Unfortunately, experience indicates that even these precautions may not be adequate. In 1987 a notorious case came to light in which a man posing as a scholar, Charles Merrill Mount, was accused of extensive thefts of hundreds of historic American documents and manuscripts from the Library of Congress and the National Archives, including presidential letters and Civil War material discovered in his possession. His thefts were extraordinary but unfortunately not without precedent.

Mischief, damage, and even assault occurs when the perpetrator feels unobserved. Planning should begin with the need for the natural circulation of staff and users throughout all floor areas. In large libraries, staff positions arranged in pairs may be located in supervisory locations with one on each floor. Seating should be grouped. Circulation should be designed with no dead ends. Talk and seminar rooms should have partly glazed walls and doors and open off high traffic areas. Since nighttime use is usually heavy, the building perimeter and paths to parking or transportation should be well lit with no landscaping for concealment. As use declines in the late hours or on weekends, access to some floors may be restricted. As a last resort, television cameras have been installed; to be effective they must be monitored. A roving uniformed guard is a far better deterrent, and may be the best able to recognize the telltale behavior patterns, such as those associated with drug use or transactions or in discouraging excessive loitering.

Elevators are particularly vulnerable. Glazed cars are more safe and less prone to graffiti; mirrored walls of the car seem to distract the miscreants by fascination with their own image.

Building technology can be of the greatest help in protection against fire and arson. Although librarians and architects were long opposed to sprinkler systems because of potential damage to books, the widely publicized and devastating fires set by an arsonist in the Los Angeles Public Library offered sufficient evidence of their necessity. With rate-of-rise and smoke detection sensors, call boxes at staff desk, and fire stairs, all hard-wired to the firehouse, fire damage can now be restricted, if not prevented. Upholstery materials and other fabrics should be fire-resistant to minimize fire and smoke.

Interiors

Libraries present special interior design problems because of the extensive undivided floor areas needed for flexibility and growth. In this setting, finishes and furnishings are especially crucial in providing a sense of distinction, spatial definition, and an inviting study environment.

Flooring. Undoubtedly, carpet as the preferred floor covering has a number of important advantages. With its enormous range of colors and textures it provides a quality of warmth and well-being and even appears to heighten the standards of respect and comportment. Carpet tends to collect dust, which is then easily removed with a vacuum cleaner. Acoustically, it mutes footfalls and absorbs ambient noise.

Since library traffic, particularly book trucks, will cause carpet with an underlayment to wear more quickly, carpet should be glued directly to the slab. Wiring under the carpet may require by code the use of carpet tiles for accessibility, although in some cases, unglued, roll carpeting has been used successfully over wiring. Replacement of worn carpet should be carefully considered. Wear occurs most rapidly in areas of heaviest traffic, particularly at doorways, counters, and other locations involving changes of direction or waiting area where feet are shuffled. In some libraries, contrasting carpets have been used to accentuate the major paths of circulation and to allow the carpet in these areas to be more easily replaced without disturbing the less worn areas in the reading rooms and stacks. In computer areas, special antistatic carpeting should be used to ground the terminals.

Entrances generally call for durable masonry surfaces which can withstand the wear and dirt from constant use, especially during inclement weather. These materials may be recalled in the main stairs and related lobby areas on other levels. Other floor treatments, such as wood flooring in strips or parquet, may be appropriate in a special collection or conference room, while a stone or wood border may set off a distinctive carpeted area. Oriental rugs lend distinction to special-use areas.

Wall Treatments. As in any public building, heavy-wear areas must be protected. Particularly around elevators and stairwells, hard durable materials should be considered. Corners are especially vulnerable to damage by book trucks, wainscots, and chair rails should be used to protect the lower partitions of walls in high traffic zones.

Wood or masonry paneling in limited areas lends great distinction without significant total cost. Colors add definition, a distinctive image and sense of space. Where appropriate, walls can be lined with books, in metal stacks or wood bookcases.

Furniture. As a dominant element in the interior, furniture creates much of the character of the library (Fig. 52); most successful interiors have used the furniture to complement and enhance the aesthetics of the building. Custom-designed tables and carrels, for instance, designed by the architect or interior designer, can often be purchased inexpensively in quantity. This allows coordination of colors, similarity of molding and trim details, matching of woods to the interior woodwork, and incorporation of selected local lighting and power, in a consistent design concept throughout the building. Experience has shown that the furniture industry is gratifyingly responsive and competitive to this approach. Although the tendency in furnishings has been to concentrate the best furniture in the most public area of the library, every effort should be made to maintain a consistent quality and character throughout the stack areas where most of the intense research and study is done.

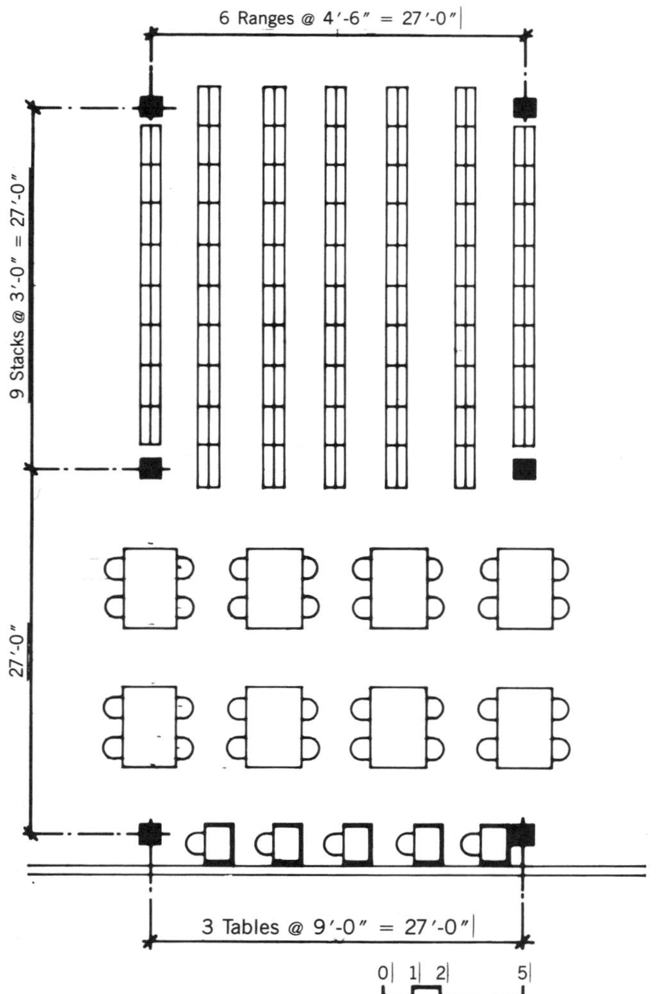

Figure 52. Stack and seating layout.

Light-colored tops on tables and carrels reduce eye strain because they more closely approximate the reflectivity of the paper on which the words are printed. Research has shown that it is more fatiguing to read and work on a dark-topped wood table than a lighter, noncontrasting surface. For this reason, matte-finished plastic laminate is often preferred as a working surface with wood nosings and details. But wood is easily vandalized, so it should be used with care.

Different chairs are required for a variety of uses in the library. Reader chairs with and without arms are needed for tables and carrels. Chairs for computer terminals should be of the adjustable stenographic type, which avoid back strain when using a keyboard over a period of time. Lounge chairs provide an excellent opportunity to express the character of the building. Overstuffed wing chairs, rockers, and "bean bag" chairs can provide a welcome contrast to the more predictable alternatives. In waiting areas, benches are highly successful; however, sofas invite sleeping and should be avoided.

ADDITIONS AND RENOVATIONS

Economics alone do not totally explain why, since the early 1970s and for the foreseeable future, many libraries will elect to add and renovate rather than build anew. The reasons are many. First, there is the scarcity of good, well-located sites on the campus or in the community. Second, sensitivity to the preservation of historic architecture has saved many fine libraries from the wrecker's ball. As architects and their engineers have become more skilled in preservation methods, alteration design by structural and mechanical engineers and architectural restoration have become an area of special expertise. Third, the capacity of the existing building in stacks, reader and/or staff space is hard to give up. Fourth, the architectural results are frequently more interesting than either the original or a totally new structure. There is one theory which holds that postmodern architecture, with its concern for contextual relationships and analogous historic detail, was one consequence of the strength of the preservation movement. In any event, a number of extremely successful mergings of images and functions has been produced. Finally, are those factors reflecting library use? Access to information by computers at home or office may reduce the need for seating. Despite the continued growth in published books each year, television, for many, has replaced reading as a source of both information and entertainment. Limited funds and rising costs have restricted the growth of collections, accelerating the development of lending networks and the intelligent and increasing trend to weed collections of obsolete and unused material.

The renovation process must begin with a complete survey of the existing facility. Is the structure adequate for modern floor loadings? Can proper air-conditioning be accommodated? How about exits, sprinklers, and other fire protection questions? Do the windows need to be replaced or saved? Must a self-supporting stack be replaced with fireproof structural floors? The functional potential of the building should next be evaluated by librarians and architect. What are the most valuable assets—the large self-supporting stack, the impressive main reading room, or the colonial facade with its entrance portico dear to alumni and patrons? Obviously, the intent is to restore the best, renovate the rest, and add new areas and facilities where most needed.

The nature of the problem is so unique that generalization is difficult. However, certain patterns have emerged. It has been observed that a library tends to outgrow itself every 30 years and must wait 15 more before anything is done about it. By then, the collection has usually spilled over into reading areas, reducing seating, the staff is in the process of automating its catalog, and satellite libraries have sprung up to relieve the pressure. In older buildings, the stacks were usually closed and devoid of (or had extremely limited) study areas. Changes in library operations offer opportunities to revise staffing positions, and the computerized catalog can be dispersed throughout the floors.

If architecturally distinguished, preservation of the facades, entrance, and principal reading areas are universally applauded by users and the general public. Expanded specialized areas become even more appreciated for the enhanced services provided. On the other hand, some highly successful additions have simply engulfed the previous structure, providing new environmental and service facilities and amenities sorely lacking in the original while saving its stack capacity. Each approach has merit. Interestingly, the challenge of additions and renovations to existing buildings has produced many of the finest recent designs. Preserving and continuing the architectural context and the essence of the building is in the basic tradition of the institution for which preservation and continuity are fundamental.

AUTOMATION AND THE FUTURE OF LIBRARIES

The approach of the year 2000 finds libraries facing a series of alternative futures, each with its advocates and detractors. For the architect each scenario reflects attitudes which may affect, subtly or substantially, the nature of the solution. How has the computer influenced the design of library buildings? Will it replace the book? Will users stay home and search out information on their microcomputer making the building itself obsolete? A brief discussion of these matters may provide a basic understanding of the factors increasingly affecting the architectural design of libraries.

In the 1950s, dire predictions of the demise of the book were widespread. Microforms and the computer spelled its doom. Three decades later the death of the book, as with Mark Twain's rumored passing, has proven to be "highly exaggerated." In fact, more books are being published each year, reaching 800,000 in 1988.

Despite the growth of computer technology and its promise for the future, it is unlikely that the book is doomed to extinction. Certainly, heavily used scientific and technical data, such as chemical abstracts or pharmacological information, are naturally suited for computerization and have been rapidly assimilated into electronic form. With the advent of digitization and optical character recognition, microprint may eventually be replaced by compact disks or tape. Despite the costs of production and distribution and its physical bulk, the book remains a marvel of convenience for storage of knowledge and art: highly compressed, easily searched, extremely portable, and fun to read in a plane or in bed.

Early on, it became apparent that the computerized evolution would progress through automating tasks of increasing complexity and density: the public catalog, circulation records, bibliographical records and indexes, encyclopedias, and, finally, text.

While it appeared that its computerization would be relatively simple, the catalog has proven to be a formidable undertaking and far more complex than expected. That is why the astonishing success of OCLC and its inventor and resident genius, Frederick Kilgour, is so impressive.

After an unsuccessful effort to computerize the medical catalogs of Columbia, Yale, and Harvard, Kilgour became a consultant to the Ohio College Library Center (OCLC), and in 1967 its first executive director with the stated purpose of carrying forward the automation project forming "a computerized regional library center for the academic libraries of Ohio (both State and Private) and designed so as to become part of a national network. . ." (14). The first objectives were shared cataloging, bibliographical information retrieval system, automated circulation control, serials control, and technical cataloging system, all based on computer technology. The operative word is shared and its success over its first two decades surprised the library world while encouraging other more specialized (Research Libraries Information Network, RLIN), regional (New England Library Information Network, NEUNET; Washington Library Network, WLN); commercial (DIALOG, BRS), and full text (VU/text) undertakings.

Underlying OCLC's success has been the Library of Congress's machine-readable cataloging effort (MARC) which, beginning in 1961, transferred the LC card catalog into a computerized format and onto tape, largely replacing its comprehensive book catalog and providing the basis for the national on-line catalog. The speed and broad acceptance of OCLC and other networks soon became evident as they began to outperform LC even in the production of its catalog cards. Between 1971 and 1980, the demand for LC cards dropped from 74 million to 19 million. Working in accordance with MARC II, the Anglo-American Cataloging Rules (AACR2-1974), a standardized basis for a national bibliographical network, was established, and it was responsive to the precision required of computerization.

By the mid-1980s, a plethora of public, private, and

commercial networks covering scientific, business, and professional fields in far greater depth than LC's traditional area of copyrighted trade books and international publications made information available to a broader constituency than ever before possible. And "Boolean logic," "key-word" search expanded upon a system formerly limited to writer-author-subject-title classification.

OCLC's success as a self-sustaining business venture has enabled it to expand and refine its operations beyond its initial program. By the mid-1980s, with about 7000 member libraries, an on-line catalog of more than 25 million records and its myriad of services and revenues which will exceed $100 million a year by 1990, it has radically changed the art of librarianship. It has its detractors, who see its standards as less comprehensive and/or rigorous than their needs (such as the Research Library Network) or too expensive for use by many local area networks (LAN).

Furthermore, with the expansion of on-line retrieval systems (DIALOG, BRS, ORBIT, etc) the cost of searches raises complex questions as to who pays the price. By the late 1980s there were perhaps as many as 2000 data bases, promising more thorough and accurate bibliographical information for academic, professional, public library, or home users. To what extent or how soon will traditional printed indexes be replaced? The interdependency of vendors and users raises complex contractual issues involving hardware, software, performance, termination, and fees that will complicate library policy for many years to come.

As yet, the computer has not generated the expected cost savings in library operations; rather it has saved somewhat in personnel, only to expend the funds on technology. Additionally, the benefits of the computer's enormous potential accrues mainly to the researcher while its cost is borne by the general public.

As these costs increase, the possibility of user fees arises, but this is hotly contested and antithetical to the U.S. tradition of free access to information to the populace at large.

Microcomputers are obviously rapidly gaining in speed and capacity while decreasing in cost. Through digitization of information and retention of visual images in full color in a video format, microprocessor potential has been enlarged far beyond its previous alphanumerical limitations. Direct access to bibliographical data bases will gradually expand to include information and as transmission speeds increase it will appreciably decline in cost. Beyond chips, plastic diskettes, disks, and bubble memory technology lies laser/video disk. Video disks capable of storing 54,000 separate images or electronically scanned text were in limited but expanding use by 1985 at the Library of Congress, and other extraordinary potentials envisioned by information technologists bring with each progressive step profound changes in the nature of libraries and information.

By the mid 1980s the frequent inability of libraries to provide requested information was becoming less acceptable, inasmuch as society had become increasingly dependent on information. Frederick Kilgour cites a study by James R. Beniger indicating that the information sector of the U.S. civilian labor force had grown from 0.2% in 1800 to 24.5% by 1930 to 46.6% by 1980. Commenting on this trend, he states (15):

> It has been apparent for some time that libraries are a failure. First, because the titles that patrons need have not been acquired; second, because materials that have been acquired are unavailable on the shelf 40 percent of the time; third, when a requested item is available it may not contain the information the user is seeking; and fourth, reference librarians answer questions correctly only half the time.

His solution is EIDOS, Electronic Information Delivery On-line System, whereby text is digitally stored on a video disk in an extremely compact form. Kilgour's proposal, which OCLC began to develop in 1983, will make possible simultaneous access to this on-line information by means of the user's own microcomputer in his or her home or office, with a very high success rate guaranteed. Kilgour envisions that this process will be enhanced by direct transference electronically of all forms of books and journals directly to a video disk from which copies can be made xerographically.

Simultaneously, the Library of Congress began to consider a similar path in order to solve three aggravating problems: a very high percentage of "not-on-shelf" replies to requests for a title, the rapid deterioration of paper, and the increasing demand for shelf space. The library has been experimenting with this type of technology since 1970 for its Congressional Research Service, converting it to video disk in the early 1980s with success. LC envisions this technique for print material, maps, even art works, but not for the heavily used 350,000 copyrighted volumes acquired each year. Present technology would record this information in an almost indestructible format and permit the contents of 10,000 volumes to be stored in one linear foot of shelving.

Libraries have discovered that after a 20-year period only about 20% of that collection is used. The question is, which 20%? The video disk, by providing greater access, may increase that utilization while simultaneously indicating those titles which might eventually be weeded.

Automation notwithstanding, the greatest threat to the book is the book itself, most specifically the paper on which it has been printed. Since the late nineteenth century wood pulp, treated with powerful acids, has provided an economical alternative to rag fibers (16). Unfortunately, the chemical action of the residue acids is relentless. About 50 years after publication, the rate of deterioration appears to accelerate, causing the paper to become brittle and break from its bindings. Despite deacidification attempts, the Library of Congress estimates that approximately 25% of its massive collection is already in a brittle state and continuing at a rate of almost 100,000 volumes each year. Similar experience with the great university collections reinforces concern over the enormity of the problem. It is paradoxical that the very medium of the book, its paper, may become the inevitable instrument of its demise.

For researchers and scholars, the power and convenience of the new technologies will more than justify their cost but will not supplant the book for the average user as a source of general information and enjoyment.

BIBLIOGRAPHY

1. D. J. Boorstin, *The Discoverers,* Random House, New York, 1983, p. 491.
2. *Ibid.,* pp. 514–515.
3. J. Winsor, "Library Buildings," *Public Libraries in the U.S.A.,* U.S. Bureau of Education Special report Part 1, U.S. Government Printing Office, Washington, D.C., 1876, pp. 465–466.
4. W. H. Jordy, *American Buildings and Their Architects—Progressive and Academic Ideals at the Turn of the Twentieth Century,* Doubleday & Co., Inc., New York, 1972, p. 318.
5. *The Random House Dictionary of the English Language,* unabridged edition, Random House, New York, 1966.
6. Ref. 4, p. 327.
7. C. Bauman, *The Influence of Angus Snead Macdonald and the Snead Bookstack on Library Architecture,* The Scarecrow Press Inc., Metuchen, N.J., 1972, p. 65.
8. *Ibid.,* p. 70.
9. The Cooperative Committee on Library Building Plans, *Planning the University Library Building,* Princeton University Press, Princeton, N.J., 1949.
10. J. Orne, "The Renaissance of Academic Library 1967–1971," *Library Journal* (Dec. 1, 1971).
11. *Ibid.,* p. 3947.
12. J. L. Wheeler, *The American Public Library Building: Planning and Design with Special Reference to its Administration and Service,* Scribner, New York, 1941.
13. A. J. Lincoln, *Crime in the Library. A Study of Patterns, Impact and Security,* R. R. Bowker Co., New York and London, 1984.
14. K. L. Marcuszko, *OCLC A Decade of Development 1967–1977,* Libraries Unlimited Inc., Littleton, Colo., 1984.
15. F. Kilgour, "EIDOS and the Transformation of Libraries," *Library Journal* (Oct. 1, 1987).
16. B. L. Mount, "Save the Paper," *Columbia, the Magazine of Columbia University* **13**(3) (Dec. 1987).

Danforth W. Toan, FAIA
Warner Burns Toan Lunde
New York, New York

LIEN LAWS. See Liability Insurance

LIFE CYCLE COSTING

Life cycle costing (LCC) is the process of making an economic assessment of an item, area, system, or facility by considering all significant costs of ownership over an economic life, expressed in terms of equivalent costs. The essence of life cycle costing is the analysis of equivalent costs of various alternative proposals.

In order to ensure that costs are compared on an equivalent basis, the baselines used for initial costs must be the same as those used for all other costs associated with each proposal, including maintenance and operating costs.

Life cycle costing is used to compare various proposals by identifying and assessing economic impacts over the whole life of each alternative. In making decisions, both present and future costs are taken into account and related to one another. Today's dollar is not equal to tomorrow's dollar. Money invested in any form earns, or has the capacity to earn, interest. For example, $100 invested at 10% annual interest, compounded annually, will grow to $673 in 20 years. In other words, it can be said that $100 today is equivalent to $673 in twenty years' time providing that the money is invested at the rate of 10% per year. A current dollar is worth more than the prospect of a dollar at some future time. The exact amount depends on the investment rate (cost of money) and the length of time. Inflation also changes the value of money over time, but constant dollars are used in life cycle cost analysis.

Figure 1 demonstrates that total owning and operating costs of buildings have been rising at a steadily increasing rate for many years. Consequently, owners are becoming more concerned about their cost of ownership.

Life cycle costing techniques should also be used when undertaking cost effectiveness studies and benefit–cost analysis. The lack of such formal procedures has resulted in many poor decisions.

LCC techniques were introduced as a direct consequence of the energy crisis. The Office of the President of the United States has issued directives to government agencies to reduce energy consumption and has allowed investment tax credits and incentives under The Energy Recovery Act of 1982 for everyone who reduces energy use. Since energy is an annual cost, LCC principles are required to equate its impact against initial costs.

A number of government agencies have already introduced mandatory LCC requirements. Foremost of these is the Environmental Protection Agency (EPA), which requires a cost effectiveness analysis of alternative processes for the early planning and design of waste water treatment plants. The U.S. Air Force was one of the first government agencies to use LCC for its housing schemes. The U.S. Naval Facilities Engineering Command has published a guide (2), and the Corps of Engineers has issued a manual (3).

Several years ago, Alaska was the first state to have mandatory LCC passed by its legislature. It was followed closely by Florida. By 1985, the states of Colorado, Idaho, Maryland, Massachusetts, Missouri, Nebraska, New Mexico, North Carolina, Texas, Washington, Wisconsin, Wyoming, and New York had passed mandatory provisions, and the states of Florida, Wyoming, and New York had issued formal guidance manuals for LCC requirements (1).

DECISION-MAKERS' IMPACT ON LIFE CYCLE COSTS

Figure 2 illustrates the impact decisions made at the design stage have on building costs. It portrays the design process as a team involvement in which there are various disciplines making decisions in a discipline-oriented environment. Decisions made by one discipline will affect the cost of the work covered by the other disciplines.

One of the principal reasons for unnecessary costs has been the uni-discipline approach used by most designers.

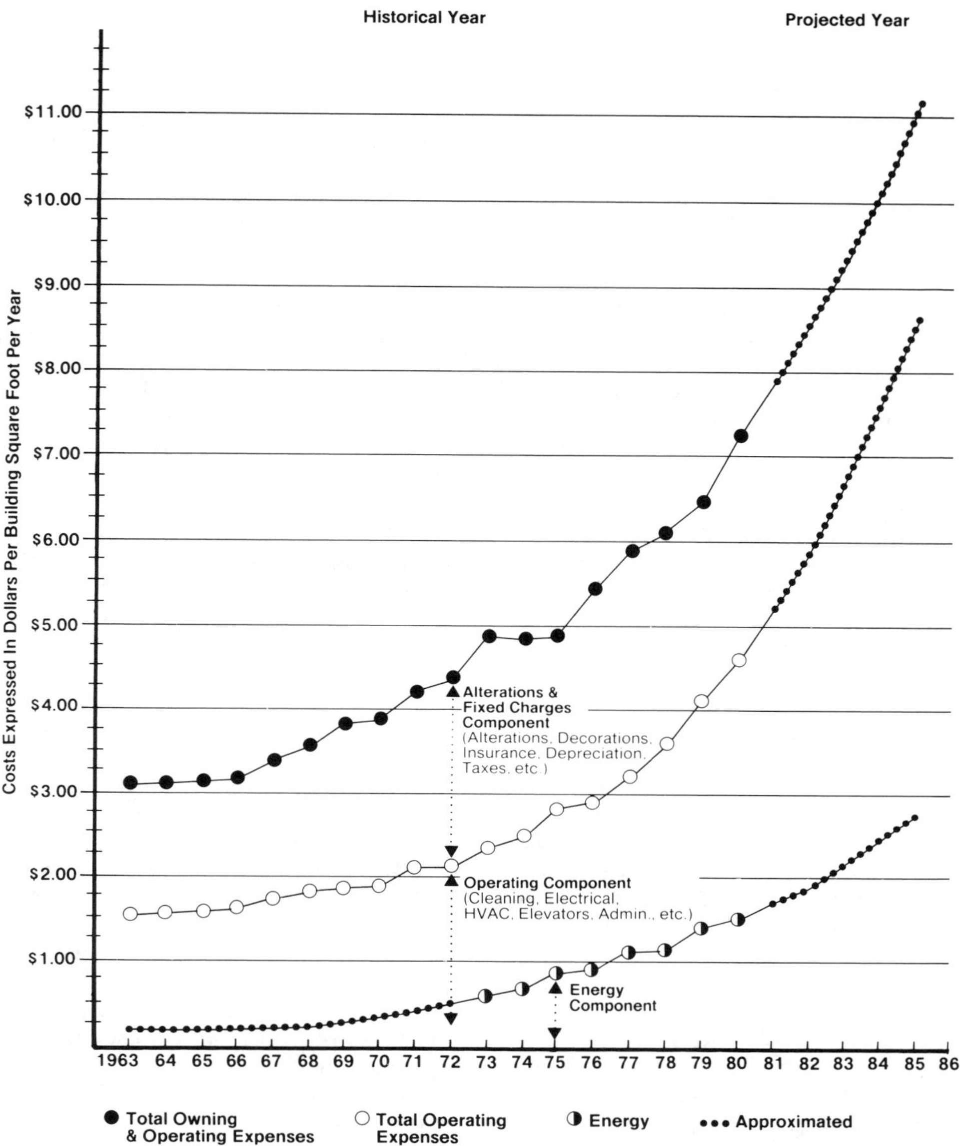

Figure 1. Historical life cycle costs (1).

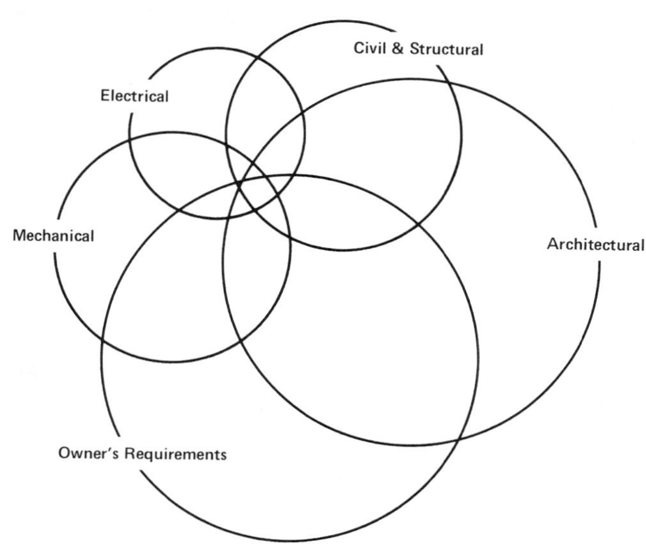

Figure 2. Decision maker's impact on total building costs (1). Chart based on typical office building. Impact will vary by type of structure.

Unnecessary costs particularly occur where decision areas overlap. Traditionally, the design has been dictated by the architect; other disciplines merely responded to the architect's direction. A multi-disciplinary approach to optimize building as a system has produced significant results in terms of reducing unnecessary costs. Unfortunately, the uni-disciplinary approach has flowed over into life cycle costing and discipline-oriented solutions to energy problems. In some cases, such as highly automated office facilities and high-tech laboratories, the design of mechanical–electrical systems is taking precedence over architectural design. In many cases, it seems that the basic function of a facility, to house people, has been superseded by the concerns of conserving energy. The best solutions are developed when all participants cooperate to solve the total problem.

Timing of LCC procedures is important. In order to take maximum advantage of LCC, the techniques should be applied at the earliest stages of the design concept, particularly during planning and budgeting, preliminary design, and design development phases. The cost of changing a design increases significantly with time. LCC exercises that are undertaken during the construction phase or owning and operating phases are only beneficial in providing data for future projects.

TOTAL BUILDING COSTS

LCC is concerned with total building costs over the economic life of a facility. Figure 3 shows how these total costs of buildings are incurred. The model has been used as a basis for an automated approach, for example, a template available for IBM-compatible equipment. Blocks C-1 (initial costs), C-2 (financing costs), C-3 (operating costs), and C-4 (maintenance costs) are self-explanatory. Block C-5 (alteration and replacement costs) identifies those costs involved with changing the function of a space. A replacement cost would be a one-time cost incurred at some time in the future to maintain the original function of the facility or item. Block C-6 (tax elements) deals with the cost impact of the tax laws, and each case must be analyzed on an individual basis. These costs must be continually reviewed as tax laws change; for example, investment tax credits are given for energy conservation, different depreciation rates can be used, and different depreciation periods are allowed. Block C-7 (associated costs), is concerned with those costs, such as staffing, that are related to functional use, denial of use, security, insurance, and any other annual cost impact not covered elsewhere. As an example of staffing and personnel costs related to functional use, suppose an LCC analysis is required for a branch bank. The function of the bank is to "service customers." Now, suppose there are two banks that have exactly the same initial costs. One bank can process 200 clients per day with a total staff of 10 people; the other bank requires a staff of 12 to process the same number of clients per day. Clearly, the one that uses less staff is more cost effective. This block of staffing–personnel costs represents those requirements related to the building function. So, functional use costs for a branch bank would have to do with servicing customers. In life cycle analysis a cost difference or some other weighting would have to be considered for the difference in staffing of these two banks to provide the basic function of the facility.

As an example of denial of use costs, suppose that in doing building alterations there are two approaches, the construction costs of which are the same. One alternative would require moving people out of a space for six months; the other alternative could be accomplished during non-working hours. In LCC, the cost difference of not being able to use the space would have to be taken into account.

The cost impact of insurance was illustrated by a recent study of a food-distribution warehouse. In comparing different fire-protection systems, all costs were comparable, except one system had a lower annual insurance premium. In this case, the estimated cost equal to the present worth of the annual rates was used for each system in the LCC.

Block C-8 (salvage value) is the value of competing alternates at the end of the life cycle period. The value

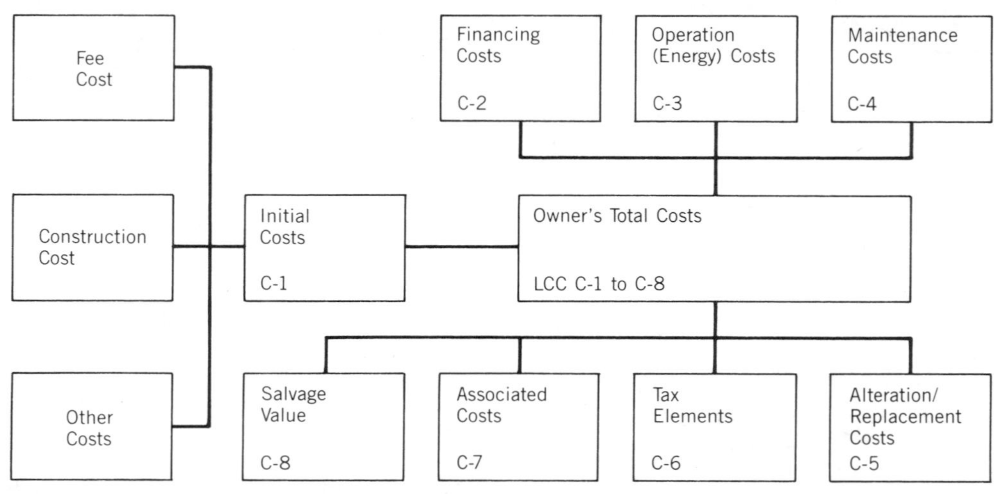

Figure 3. Life cycle cost elements (1).

is positive if it has residual economic value and negative if additional costs are required, such as demolition.

TERMINOLOGY AND EXAMPLES

In order to compare design alternatives, both present and future costs for each alternative must be brought to a common point in time. One of two methods is used. Costs may be converted to today's cost by the present worth method, or they may be converted to an annual series of payments by the annualized method. Either will properly allow comparison between design alternatives. Procedures, conversion tables, and examples for both methods are discussed.

Present Worth Method

The present worth method requires conversion of all present and future expenditures to a baseline of today's cost. Initial (present) costs are automatically expressed in present worth. The following formulas are used to convert recurring and nonrecurring costs to present day values. Recurring costs (when A = \$1.00) are as follows (3):

$$P = A\,\frac{(1+i)^n - 1}{i\,(1+i)^n} = PWA \qquad (1)$$

where i is the interest rate per interest period (in decimals); minimum attractive rate of return; n is the number of interest periods; P is the present sum of money (present worth); A is the end-of-period payment or receipt in a uniform series continuing for the coming n periods, entire series equivalent to p at interest rate i; and PWA is the present worth of an annuity factor.

Nonrecurring costs (when F = \$1.00) are as follows:

$$P = F\,\frac{1}{(1+i)^n} = PW \qquad (2)$$

where F is the sum of money at the end of n from the present date that is equivalent to P with interest rate i; and PW is the present worth factor.

To use these formulas the owner or designer must determine the rate of return. This interest rate is discussed later. The federal government, through OMB Circular A-94 has established 10% as the interest rate to be used in studies of this type, excluding the lease or purchase of real property. The number of interest periods, n, or the life cycle period of the study is usually expressed in years. Normally, a life cycle between 25 and 40 years is considered adequate for estimating future expenses. Differential escalation (that rate of inflation above the general economy) is taken into account for recurring costs, such as energy, by the following formula (1):

$$P = A \cdot \frac{[(1+e)/(1+i)] \times [((1+e)/(1+i))^n - 1]}{[(1+e)/(1+i)] - 1} \qquad (3)$$

$$= PWA \text{ esc}$$

where e is the escalation rate; and A equals \$1.00. Where $e = 1$, $P = An$.

Economic tables exist for the many combinations of interest rates, interest periods, and discount rates. However, escalation tables are not available. Some calculators, such as the Texas Instruments Business Analyst and the Hewlett-Packard HP-22 Business Management calculators, have economic equations built in for quick calculation, but they do not deal with escalation. For reader convenience, Table 1, a series of escalating values at a base interest rate of 10%, is included.

Annualized Method

The second method converts initial, recurring, and nonrecurring costs to an annual series of payments. It may be used to express all life cycle costs as an annual expenditure. Home payments are an example of this procedure; that is, a buyer opts to purchase a home for \$349 per month (360 equal monthly payments at 10% yearly interest) rather than pay \$50,000 all at once. Recurring costs, as previously discussed, are already expressed as annual costs; therefore no adjustment is necessary. Initial and nonrecurring costs, however, require equivalent cost conversion. The following formulas are used for this conversion:
Initial costs (1):

$$A = P\,\frac{i\,(1+i)^n}{(1+i)^n - 1} = PP \qquad (4)$$

where A is the annualized cost; P equals \$1.00; and PP is the period payment factor. For nonrecurring costs, use equation 2 to convert future expenditure to current cost (present worth), then use equation 4 to convert today's cost (present worth) to an annual expenditure (annualized cost). Since all costs are expressed in equivalent dollars, for both the present worth and the annualized methods, the life cycle cost is the sum of the initial, recurring, and nonrecurring costs, all expressed in equivalent dollars.

Discount or Interest Rate

Calculation of present worth is often referred to as discounting by writers on economics who frequently refer to an interest rate used in present worth calculations as a discount rate. Any reference to the discount rate here means either the minimum acceptable rate of return for the client for investment purposes, or the current prime or borrowing rate of interest. In establishing this rate, several factors must be considered, including the source of finance (borrowed money or capital assets), the client (government agency or private industry), and the rate of return for the industry (before or after income taxes).

At times the owner may establish the minimum attractive rate of return based only on the cost of borrowed money. Although this approach is particularly common in government projects and in personal economic studies, the same approach may not be applicable to projects in competitive industry.

Escalation

Escalation has a significant impact on life cycle costs and is accommodated in LCC by expressing all costs in terms of constant dollars. For example, if the LCC is being conducted in 1990 dollars, then the purchasing power of a 1990 dollar should be used throughout the analysis. That is, in a comparative analysis it is not correct to mix 1990, 1995, 2000, and 2010 year dollars, as they will differ in terms of buying power.

When the comparative analysis includes items with equal escalation rates, the effect of escalation will be canceled out. However, when cost elements having varying escalation rates are included, account must be taken of the differences. For example, the rates of escalation for certain items such as energy have been increasing above the average devaluation of the dollar. In order to accommodate these differences, those elements that are differentially escalating or devaluating (at a different rate than the inflation of all other costs) need to be moderated. It is recommended that a differential escalation be applied. Equation 3 is the formula used to determine present worth

Table 1. Present Worth of an Escalating Annual Amount, 10% Discount Rate[a]

	Escalation Rate, %														
Year	0	1	2	3	4	5	6	7	8	9	10	11	12	13	14	Year
1	0.909	0.918	0.927	0.936	0.945	0.955	1.964	1.973	0.982	0.991	1.000	1.009	1.018	1.027	1.036	1
2	1.736	1.761	1.787	1.813	1.839	1.866	1.892	1.919	1.946	1.973	2.000	2.027	2.055	2.083	2.110	2
3	2.487	2.535	2.584	2.634	2.684	2.735	2.787	2.839	2.892	2.946	3.000	3.055	3.110	3.167	3.224	3
4	3.170	3.246	3.324	3.403	3.483	3.566	3.649	3.735	3.821	3.910	4.000	4.092	4.185	4.280	4.377	4
5	3.791	3.899	4.009	4.123	4.239	4.358	4.480	4.605	4.734	4.865	5.000	5.138	5.279	5.424	5.573	5
6	4.355	4.498	4.645	4.797	4.953	5.115	5.281	5.453	5.630	5.812	6.000	6.194	6.394	6.599	6.812	6
7	4.868	5.048	5.234	5.428	5.628	5.837	6.053	6.277	6.509	6.750	7.000	7.259	7.528	7.807	8.096	7
8	5.335	5.553	5.781	6.019	6.267	6.526	6.796	7.078	7.372	7.680	8.000	8.334	8.683	9.047	9.426	8
9	5.759	6.017	6.288	6.572	6.871	7.184	7.513	7.858	8.220	8.601	9.000	9.419	9.859	10.321	10.806	9
10	6.145	6.443	6.758	7.090	7.441	7.812	8.203	8.616	9.053	9.513	10.000	10.514	11.057	11.630	12.235	10
11	6.495	6.834	7.194	7.575	7.981	8.411	8.868	9.354	9.870	10.418	11.000	11.619	12.276	12.974	13.716	11
12	6.814	7.193	7.598	8.030	8.491	8.983	9.510	10.072	10.672	11.314	12.000	12.733	13.517	14.355	15.251	12
13	7.103	7.523	7.972	8.455	8.973	9.530	10.127	10.770	11.460	12.202	13.000	13.858	14.781	15.774	16.842	13
14	7.367	7.825	8.320	8.853	9.429	10.051	10.723	11.449	12.233	13.082	14.000	14.993	16.068	17.231	18.491	14
15	7.606	8.103	8.642	9.226	9.860	10.549	11.296	12.109	12.993	13.954	15.000	16.139	17.378	18.729	20.200	15
16	7.824	8.358	8.941	9.576	10.268	11.024	11.849	12.752	13.739	14.818	16.000	17.294	18.713	20.267	21.971	16
17	8.022	8.593	9.218	9.903	10.653	11.477	12.382	13.377	14.470	15.674	17.000	18.461	20.071	21.847	23.806	17
18	8.201	8.808	9.475	10.209	11.018	11.910	12.895	13.985	15.189	16.523	18.000	19.638	21.454	23.470	25.708	18
19	8.365	9.005	9.713	10.496	11.362	12.323	13.390	14.576	15.895	17.363	19.000	20.825	22.862	25.137	27.679	19
20	8.514	9.187	9.934	10.764	11.688	12.718	13.867	15.151	16.588	18.196	20.000	22.024	24.296	26.850	29.722	20
21	8.649	9.353	10.139	11.015	11.996	13.094	14.326	15.711	17.268	19.022	21.000	23.233	25.756	28.610	31.839	21
22	8.772	9.506	10.329	11.251	12.287	13.454	14.769	16.255	17.936	19.840	22.000	24.453	27.243	30.417	34.033	22
23	8.883	9.647	10.505	11.471	12.562	13.797	15.196	16.784	18.591	20.650	23.000	25.685	28.756	32.274	36.307	23
24	8.985	9.776	10.668	11.678	12.822	14.124	15.607	17.299	19.235	21.454	24.000	26.927	30.297	34.181	38.664	24
25	9.077	9.894	10.819	11.871	13.069	14.437	16.003	17.800	19.867	22.250	25.000	28.181	31.866	36.141	41.106	25
26	9.161	10.003	10.960	12.052	13.301	14.735	16.384	18.287	20.488	23.038	26.000	29.446	33.464	38.154	43.638	26
27	9.237	10.102	11.090	12.221	13.521	15.020	16.752	18.761	21.097	23.820	27.000	30.723	35.090	40.222	46.261	27
28	9.307	10.194	11.211	12.380	13.729	15.291	17.107	19.222	21.695	24.594	28.000	32.012	36.746	42.346	48.979	28
29	9.370	10.278	11.323	12.528	13.926	15.551	17.448	19.671	22.283	25.361	29.000	33.312	38.433	44.528	51.797	29
30	9.427	10.355	11.426	12.667	14.112	15.799	17.777	20.107	22.859	26.122	30.000	34.624	40.150	46.770	54.717	30
31	9.479	10.426	11.523	12.798	14.287	16.035	18.095	20.532	23.426	26.875	31.000	35.947	41.898	49.073	57.743	31
32	9.526	10.491	11.612	12.920	14.453	16.261	18.400	20.944	23.982	27.622	32.000	37.283	43.678	51.438	60.879	32
33	9.569	10.551	11.695	13.034	14.610	16.476	18.695	21.346	24.527	28.362	33.000	38.631	45.490	53.868	64.129	33
34	9.609	10.606	11.771	13.141	14.759	16.682	18.979	21.736	25.063	29.095	34.000	39.992	47.335	56.365	67.497	34
35	9.644	10.657	11.843	13.241	14.899	16.878	19.252	22.116	25.589	29.821	35.000	41.364	49.214	58.929	70.988	35
36	9.677	10.703	11.909	13.335	15.032	17.065	19.516	22.486	26.106	30.541	36.000	42.749	51.127	61.564	74.606	36
37	9.706	10.745	11.970	13.423	15.158	17.244	19.770	22.845	26.613	31.254	37.000	44.147	53.075	64.270	78.355	37
38	9.733	10.784	12.027	13.505	15.276	17.415	20.014	23.195	27.111	31.961	38.000	45.558	55.058	67.050	82.241	38
39	9.757	10.820	12.079	13.582	15.389	17.578	20.250	23.535	27.600	32.661	39.000	46.981	57.077	69.906	86.268	39
40	9.779	10.853	12.128	13.654	15.495	17.733	20.478	23.866	28.080	33.355	40.000	48.417	59.133	72.840	90.441	40

[a] $P = A\left[\frac{1+e}{1+i}\right]\cdot\left[\left(\frac{1+e}{1+i}\right)^n - 1\right]\Big/\left(\frac{1+e}{1+i}\right) - 1$ where e represents the escalation rate. Note: where $e = i$, $P = An$.

of annuity factors. Table 1 gives the present-day value of an escalating annual amount starting at $1.00 per year at a 10% interest rate.

Depreciation Period

The depreciation period usually corresponds with the estimated useful life of an asset, during which time the capital cost of the asset is written off. This period becomes the basis for a deduction against income in calculating income taxes. There are several ways commonly used to distribute the initial cost over time, for example, straight line, sum of the year's digits, and double declining balance. The Internal Revenue Service has established and made available certain guidelines for various system components. Tax accountants have ready access to these changes in rates.

Amortization Period

The amortization period is the time over which periodic payments are made to discharge a debt. The period used is often arbitrary and is selected to meet the needs of the project. Financing costs are assessed during this period.

Salvage (Residual) Value

When evaluating alternatives with unequal useful lives during the economic life cycle period, a salvage or residual value must be established. The salvage value is the estimated value of the system or component at the end of the economic life cycle or study period. The value of a system at the end of its useful life is normally equal to its salvage value less the cost incurred for its removal or disposal.

Time Frames

Several time frames are used in an LCC analysis. First is the economic or study period used in comparing design alternatives. The owner, not the designer, must establish this time frame. If the building life is considered as being forever, 25–40 years is long enough to predict future costs for economic purposes to capture the most significant costs. This is illustrated in Figure 4 where an annual cost for 100 years discounted to present worth at a 10% interest rate is plotted. The area under the curve is the cumulative total present-worth equivalent cost of the system. Note that 80% of the total equivalent cost is consumed in the first 25 years.

A time frame must also be used for each system under analysis. The useful life of each system, component, or item under study may be the physical, technological, or economic life. The useful life of any item depends on such things as the frequency with which it is used, its age when acquired, the policy for repairs and replacements, whether preventive maintenance procedures are followed as recommended by the manufacturer, the climate in which it is used, the state of the art, economic changes, inventions, and other developments within the industry.

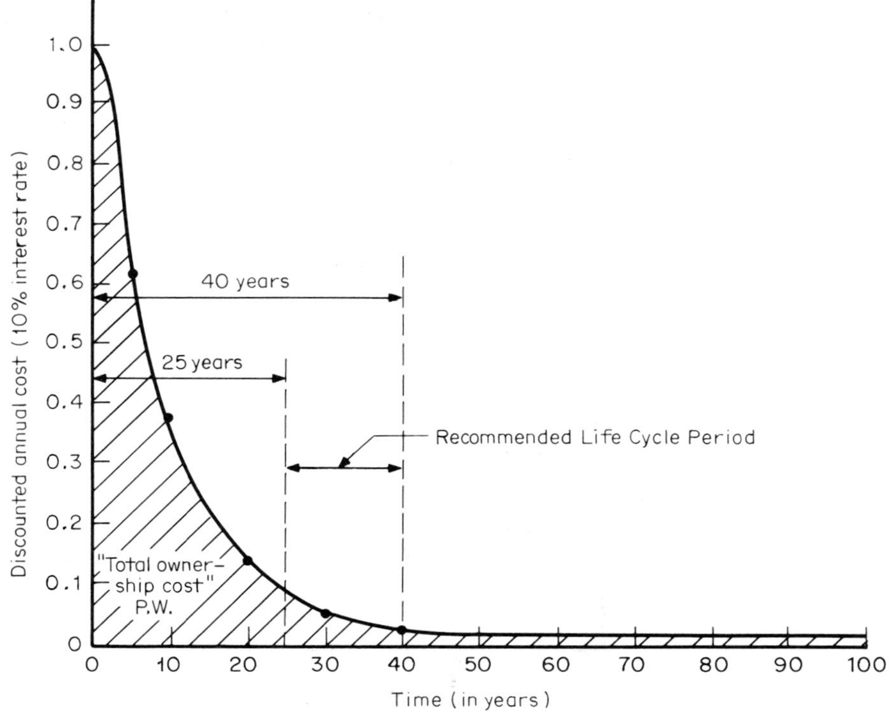

Figure 4. Recommended economic life cycle period.

Other Methods of Economic Analysis

Other methods of economic analysis can be used in a life cycle study, depending on the client's requirements and special needs. With additional rules and mechanics, it is possible to perform a sensitivity analysis, to determine the payback period, to establish a break-even point between alternatives, to determine rates of return and extra-investment, rate-of-return alternatives, to perform a cash flow analysis, and to review the benefits and costs.

LIFE CYCLE COSTING METHODOLOGY

Figure 5 illustrates a recommended logic flow when applying LCC to a project. The first requirement is the input data. With this data, the generation of alternatives can occur that is followed by the life cycle predictions. From these predictions a noneconomic comparison is made together with a forecast output of the lowest optimum cost alternative. Of the input data required, specific project information and site data are usually available, but it is unusual for facility components' data to be available, especially information regarding useful life, maintenance, and operations. Such input is needed to calculate roughly 25% of total costs. Yet few designers have access to comprehensive data in these areas in a format facilitating LCC analysis. There is no system retrieval format for LCC data readily available to designers, which presents a serious problem. Reference 4 is the first attempt to publish such data.

The following example illustrates LCC methodology. A hospital staff and its design team are considering two alternative nursing-station designs for each bed wing. One will cost far more to construct than the other because it relies more heavily on automated devices for patient monitoring and record keeping. Will the savings in nursing salaries justify the increased facility cost? Several steps are required to obtain the answer to this question, using the LCC methodology.

First, those facility elements that will be the same in any of the options being reviewed should be identified. Then, those elements should be fixed or removed from consideration in order to reduce the time and complexity of the comparative analysis. Next, the decision-making team isolates the significant varying costs associated with each alternative. The hypothetical automated solution in the above example has higher capital investment costs but lower functional use (nursing salary) costs. The costs isolated for each alternative must be grouped by year over a number of years equal to the economic life of the facility or, if more appropriate, by time spans equal to the mode of user operation. In either case, probable replacement and alteration costs should be considered. Salvage value, if relevant, is also considered for the end of the life cycle period.

All costs are converted to current dollar value by present worth techniques using a reasonable discount factor. A 10% interest rate is used by some federal agencies, but many private owners use a higher rate. Finally, the discounted costs are totaled and the lowest cost alternative

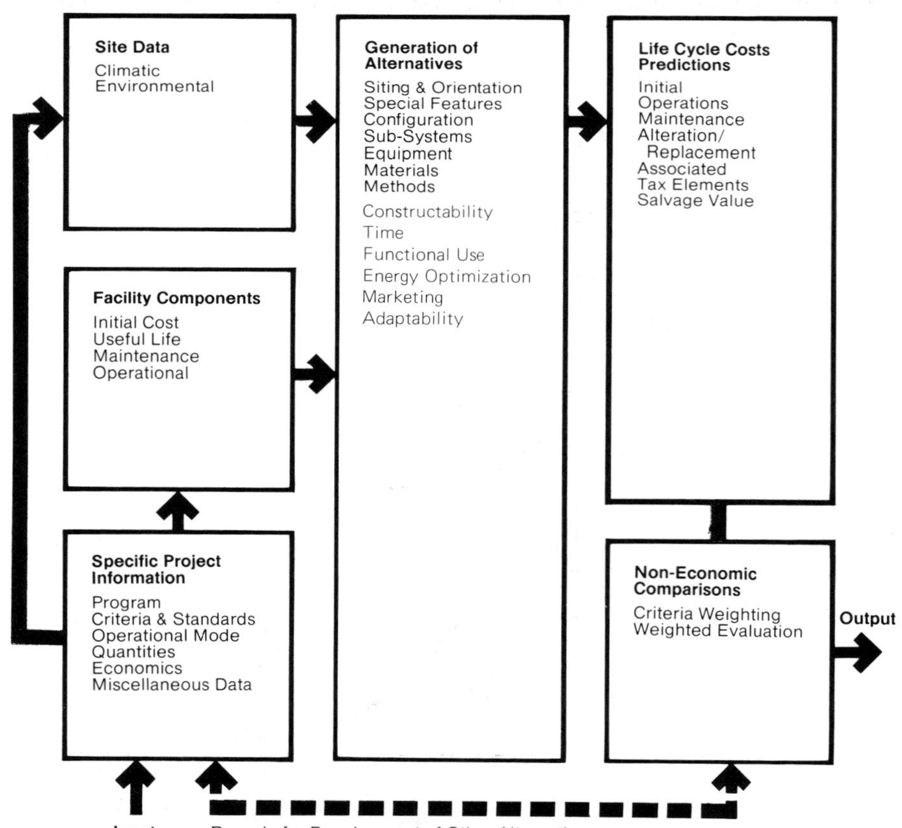

Figure 5. Life cycle costing logic (1).

is identified. It may be necessary to make a sensitivity analysis of each of the assumptions to see if a reasonable change in any of the cost assumptions would change the conclusions. If this happens, the probability of such an occurrence must be carefully weighed. If it seems probable that two or more events have roughly the same likelihood of occurrence, then the option selected must reflect this. The final selection of an option should be tempered with noneconomic factors. The impact on total cost of any noneconomic factors will be factored in by the decision-maker at the time of decision using a weighted evaluation procedure. See Ref. 1 for further details of the weighted evaluation process.

Formats for LCC

Formats for manual techniques and for computerized spread sheets are given as examples. The short manual form procedure is primarily used in comparing specific facility components such as the type of exterior siding, various roofing materials, piping, and so forth. The long, more detailed manual procedure allows a more comprehensive total system or facility to be analyzed based on life cycle costing. The manual procedures will provide the user with additional LCC information from which decisions can be made.

When the annualized method of LCC is being used,

Table 2. Present Worth (PW). What $1.00 Due in the Future is Worth Today (Present Worth) Single Payment[a]

Yrs.	6% PW	7% PW	8% PW	9% PW	10% PW	12% PW	14% PW	16% PW	18% PW	20% PW	Yrs.
1	0.943396	0.934579	0.925926	0.917431	0.909091	0.892857	0.877193	0.862069	0.847458	0.833333	1
2	0.889996	0.873439	0.857339	0.841680	0.826446	0.797194	0.769468	0.743163	0.718184	0.694444	2
3	0.839169	0.816298	0.793832	0.772183	0.751315	0.711780	0.674972	0.640658	0.608631	0.578704	3
4	0.792094	0.762895	0.735030	0.708425	0.683013	0.635518	0.592080	0.552291	0.515789	0.482253	4
5	0.747258	0.712986	0.680583	0.649931	0.620921	0.567427	0.519369	0.476113	0.437109	0.401878	5
6	0.704961	0.666342	0.630170	0.596267	0.564474	0.506631	0.455587	0.410442	0.370432	0.334898	6
7	0.665057	0.622750	0.583490	0.547034	0.513158	0.452349	0.399637	0.353830	0.313925	0.279082	7
8	0.627412	0.582009	0.540269	0.501866	0.466507	0.403883	0.350559	0.305025	0.266038	0.232568	8
9	0.591898	0.543934	0.500249	0.460428	0.424098	0.360610	0.307508	0.262953	0.225456	0.193807	9
10	0.558395	0.508349	0.463193	0.422411	0.385543	0.321973	0.269744	0.226684	0.191064	0.161506	10
11	0.526788	0.475093	0.428883	0.387533	0.350494	0.287476	0.236617	0.195417	0.161919	0.134588	11
12	0.496969	0.444012	0.397114	0.355535	0.318631	0.256675	0.207559	0.168463	0.137220	0.112157	12
13	0.468839	0.414964	0.367698	0.326170	0.289664	0.229174	0.182069	0.145227	0.116288	0.093464	13
14	0.442301	0.387817	0.340461	0.299246	0.263331	0.204620	0.159710	0.125195	0.098549	0.077887	14
15	0.417265	0.362446	0.315242	0.274538	0.239392	0.182696	0.140096	0.107927	0.083516	0.064905	15
16	0.393646	0.338735	0.291890	0.251870	0.217629	0.163122	0.122892				16
17	0.371364	0.316574	0.270269	0.231073	0.197845	0.145644	0.107800				17
18	0.350344	0.295864	0.250249	0.211994	0.179859	0.130040	0.094561				18
19	0.330513	0.276508	0.231712	0.194490	0.163508	0.116107	0.082948				19
20	0.311805	0.258419	0.214548	0.178431	0.148644	0.103667	0.072762	0.051385	0.036506	0.026084	20
21	0.294155	0.241513	0.198656	0.163698	0.135131	0.092560	0.063826				21
22	0.277505	0.225713	0.183941	0.150182	0.122846	0.082643	0.055988				22
23	0.261797	0.210947	0.170315	0.137781	0.111678	0.073788	0.049112				23
24	0.246979	0.197147	0.157699	0.126405	0.101526	0.065882	0.043081				24
25	0.232999	0.184249	0.146018	0.115968	0.092296	0.058823	0.037790	0.024465	0.015957	0.010482	25
26	0.210810	0.172195	0.135202	0.106393	0.083905	0.052521	0.033149				26
27	0.207368	0.160930	0.125187	0.097608	0.076278	0.046894	0.029078				27
28	0.195630	0.150102	0.115914	0.089548	0.069343	0.041869	0.025507				28
29	0.184557	0.140563	0.107328	0.082155	0.063039	0.037383	0.022375				29
30	0.174110	0.131367	0.099377	0.075371	0.057309	0.033378	0.019627	0.011648	0.006975	0.004212	30
31	0.164255	0.122773	0.092016	0.069148	0.052090	0.029802	0.017217				31
32	0.154957	0.114741	0.085200	0.063438	0.017362	0.026609	0.015102				32
33	0.146186	0.107235	0.078889	0.058200	0.043057	0.023758	0.013248				33
34	0.137912	0.100219	0.073045	0.053395	0.039143	0.021212	0.011621				34
35	0.130105	0.093663	0.067635	0.048986	0.035584	0.018940	0.010194	0.005546	0.0030488	0.001693	35
36	0.122741	0.087535	0.062625	0.044941	0.032349	0.016910	0.008942				36
37	0.115793	0.081809	0.057986	0.041231	0.029408	0.015098	0.007844				37
38	0.109239	0.076457	0.053690	0.037826	0.026735	0.013481	0.006880				38
39	0.103056	0.071455	0.049713	0.034703	0.024304	0.012036	0.006035				39
40	0.097222	0.066780	0.046031	0.031838	0.022095	0.010747	0.005294	0.002640	0.001333	0.000680	40

[a] Formula $P = F[1/(1 + i)^n]$ where
i represents an interest rate per interest period;
n represents a number of interest periods;
P represents a present sum of money;
F represents a sum of money at the end of n periods from the present; date that is equivalent to P with interest i.

the equivalent cost base line is annual costs. Initial cost and present worth of future costs are reduced to annual series. For example, assume that the mortgage payment on a house is a monthly series that can be converted to an annualized series. Annual costs of operations, maintenance, taxes, and so forth, are added to yield the total annual costs.

For the present worth method, the equivalent cost baseline is present day values. All initial capital expenditures are in present-day values and require no conversion. All follow-on costs are recalculated to present-day values (discounted for the cost of money).

Either procedure will result in the same economic recommendation. The present worth method allows easier consideration of differential escalation; therefore, it is more commonly used. Both formats are used for comparison in this article. Referenced economic tables are contained in Tables 1–4, and blank worksheets are contained in the text as figures.

Format Using the Annualized Method. Figure 6 shows a model form for predicting annualized life cycle cost. The form is divided into three parts as follows:

1. Initial project costs or other capital investment costs.
2. All major single future costs of replacement expenditures and salvage values taken back to present worth (discounted), using data from Table 2.

Table 3. Compound Interest Factors. Present Worth of Annuity (PWA): What $1.00 Payable Periodically is Worth Today[a]

Yrs.	6% PW	7% PW	8% PW	9% PW	10% PW	12% PW	14% PW	16% PW	18% PW	20% PW	Yrs.
1	0.943396	0.934570	0.925926	0.917431	0.909001	0.89286	0.877193	0.862089	0.847458	0.833333	1
2	1.833393	1.808018	1.783265	1.759111	1.735537	1.69005	1.646661	1.605232	1.565642	1.527778	2
3	2.673012	2.624316	2.577097	2.531295	2.486852	2.40183	2.321632	2.245890	2.174273	2.106481	3
4	3.465106	3.387211	3.312127	3.329720	3.169865	3.03735	2.913712	2.798181	2.690062	2.588735	4
5	4.212364	4.100197	3.992710	3.889651	3.790787	3.60477	3.433081	3.274294	3.127171	2.990612	5
6	4.917324	4.766540	4.622880	4.485919	4.355261	4.11140	3.888668	3.684736	3.497603	3.325510	6
7	5.582381	5.389289	5.206370	5.032953	4.868419	4.56375	4.288305	4.038565	3.811528	3.604592	7
8	6.209794	5.971299	5.746639	5.534819	5.334926	4.96764	4.638864	4.343591	4.077566	3.837160	8
9	6.801602	6.515232	6.246888	5.995247	5.759024	5.32825	4.946372	4.606544	4.303022	4.030967	9
10	7.360087	7.023582	6.710081	6.417658	6.144567	5.65023	5.216116	4.833227	4.494086	4.192472	10
11	7.886875	7.498674	7.138964	6.805191	6.495061	5.93771	5.452733	5.028644	4.656005	4.327060	11
12	8.383844	7.942686	7.536078	7.160725	6.813692	6.19437	5.660292	5.197107	4.793225	4.439217	12
13	8.852683	8.357651	7.903776	7.486904	7.103356	6.42356	5.842362	5.342334	4.909513	4.532681	13
14	9.294984	8.745468	8.244237	7.786150	7.366687	6.62818	6.002072	5.467529	5.008062	4.610567	14
15	10.712249	9.107914	8.559479	8.060688	7.606080	6.81088	6.142168	5.575456	5.091578	4.675473	15
16	10.105895	9.446649	8.851369	8.312558	7.823709	6.97399	6.265060				16
17	10.477260	9.763223	9.121638	8.543631	8.021553	7.11962	6.372859				17
18	10.827603	10.059087	9.371887	8.755625	8.201412	7.24969	6.467420				18
19	11.158116	10.335595	9.603599	8.950115	8.364920	7.36578	6.550369				19
20	11.409921	10.594014	9.818147	9.128546	8.513564	7.46943	6.623131	5.928844	5.352744	4.869580	20
21	11.764077	10.835527	10.016803	9.292244	8.648694	7.56201	6.686957				21
22	12.041582	11.061240	10.200744	9.442425	8.771540	7.64462	6.742944				22
23	12.303379	11.272187	10.371059	9.580207	8.883218	7.71843	6.792056				23
24	12.550358	11.469334	10.528758	9.706612	8.984744	7.78434	6.835137				24
25	12.783356	11.653583	10.674776	9.822580	9.077040	7.84314	6.872927	6.097094	5.466905	4.947590	25
26	13.003186	11.825779	10.809978	9.928972	9.160945	7.89565	6.906077				26
27	13.210536	11.986709	10.935165	10.026580	9.237223	7.94256	6.935155				27
28	13.406166	12.137111	11.051078	10.116128	9.306567	7.98441	6.960662				28
29	13.590721	12.277674	11.158406	10.198283	9.369606	8.02182	6.983037				29
30	13.764831	12.409041	11.257783	10.273654	9.426914	8.05516	7.002664	6.177200	5.516805	4.978940	30
31	13.929086	12.531814	11.349799	10.342802	9.479013	8.08499	7.019881				31
32	14.084013	12.646555	11.434999	10.406240	9.526376	8.11162	7.034983				32
33	14.230230	12.753790	11.513888	10.464441	9.569432	8.13537	7.048231				33
34	14.368141	12.854009	11.586934	10.517835	9.608575	8.15654	7.059852				34
35	14.498246	12.947672	11.654568	10.566821	9.644159	8.17548	7.070045	6.215337	5.538618	4.991535	35
36	14.620987	13.035208	11.717193	10.611763	9.676508	8.19242	7.078987				36
37	14.736780	13.117017	11.775179	10.652993	9.705917	8.20749	7.086831				37
38	14.846019	13.193473	11.828869	10.690820	9.732651	8.22098	7.093711				38
39	14.949073	13.264928	11.878582	10.722523	9.756956	8.23303	7.099747				39
40	15.046297	13.331700	11.924613	10.757360	9.779051	8.24375	7.105041	6.233500	5.548150	4.996600	40

[a] Formula $P = A\,[(1 + i)^n - 1/i(1 + i)^n]$ where A represents the end-of-period payment or receipt in a uniform series continuing for the coming n periods, the entire series equivalent to P at interest rate i.

3. The output data which takes all present worth equivalent costs and equates them to a common baseline of annual costs using the capital recovery factor or period payment (PP) necessary to pay off a loan of $1 from Table 4. These costs are totaled, all annual costs are added, and the annual differences are calculated. These can then be converted to present worth costs.

Example. The following is an example (Fig. 7) of a life cycle costing study for a proposed car purchase. A consulting engineer needs to purchase a new car. It will be a company car and as such will be eligible for investment tax credits and depreciation allowances. He has selected three cars for an in-depth LCC analysis: Car A is a large, moderately-priced luxury import; Car B is a large-size American model; and Car C is a top-of-the-line import. The data he collected are shown in Table 5.

First, the initial costs of getting the car on the road are calculated. The intended purchaser has friends in the local dealerships and can purchase these cars slightly above dealer cost. The investment tax credit is calculated at 10% of each car's base cost. For example, Car A's credit is 10% of $16,500, or $1,650. The next step is to calculate

Table 4. Compound Interest Factors. Periodic Payment (PP): Periodic Payment Necessary to Pay Off a Loan of $1.00; (Capital Recovery) Annuities (Uniform Series Payments)[a]

Yrs.	6% Capital Recovery	7% Capital Recovery	8% Capital Recovery	9% Capital Recovery	10% Capital Recovery	12% Capital Recovery	14% Capital Recovery	16% Capital Recovery	18% Capital Recovery	20% Capital Recovery	Yrs.
1	1.060000	1.070000	1.080000	1.090000	1.100000	1.120000	1.14000000	1.16000000	1.18000000	1.20000000	1
2	0.545437	0.553092	0.560769	0.568469	0.576190	0.591698	0.60728972	0.62296296	0.63871560	0.65454545	2
3	0.374110	0.381052	0.388034	0.395055	0.402115	0.416349	0.43073148	0.44525787	0.45992386	0.47472527	3
4	0.288591	0.295228	0.301921	0.308669	0.315471	0.329234	0.34320478	0.35737507	0.37173867	0.38628912	4
5	0.237396	0.243891	0.250156	0.257092	0.263797	0.277410	0.29128355	0.30540938	0.31977784	0.33437970	5
6	0.203363	0.209796	0.216315	0.222920	0.229607	0.243226	0.25715750	0.27138987	0.28591013	0.30070575	6
7	0.179135	0.185553	0.192072	0.198691	0.205405	0.219118	0.23319238	0.24761268	0.26236200	0.27742393	7
8	0.161036	0.167468	0.174015	0.180674	0.187444	0.201303	0.21557002	0.23022426	0.24524436	0.26060942	8
9	0.147022	0.153486	0.160080	0.166799	0.173641	0.187679	0.20216838	0.21708249	0.23239482	0.24807946	9
10	0.135868	0.142378	0.149029	0.155820	0.162745	0.176984	0.19171354	0.20690108	0.22251464	0.23852276	10
11	0.126793	0.133357	0.140076	0.146947	0.153963	0.168415	0.18339427	0.19886075	0.21477639	0.23110379	11
12	0.119277	0.125902	0.132695	0.139651	0.146763	0.161437	0.17666933	0.19241473	0.20862781	0.22526496	12
13	0.112960	0.119651	0.126522	0.133567	0.140779	0.155677	0.17116366	0.18718411	0.20368621	0.22062000	13
14	0.107585	0.114345	0.211297	0.128433	0.135746	0.150871	0.16660914	0.18289797	0.19967806	0.21689306	14
15	0.102963	0.109795	0.116830	0.124059	0.131474	0.146824	0.16280896	0.17935752	0.19640278	0.21388212	15
16	0.098952	0.105858	0.112977	0.120300	0.127817	0.143390	0.15961540				16
17	0.095445	0.102425	0.109629	0.117046	0.124664	0.140457	0.15691544				17
18	0.092357	0.099413	0.106702	0.114212	0.121930	0.137937	0.15462115				18
19	0.089621	0.096753	0.104128	0.111730	0.119547	0.135763	0.15266316				19
20	0.087185	0.094393	0.101852	0.109546	0.117460	0.133879	0.15098600	0.168667	0.186820	0.205356	20
21	0.085005	0.092289	0.099832	0.107617	0.115624	0.132240	0.14954486				21
22	0.083016	0.090106	0.098032	0.105905	0.114005	0.130811	0.14830317				22
23	0.081278	0.088714	0.096422	0.104382	0.112572	0.129560	0.14723081				23
24	0.079679	0.087189	0.094978	0.103023	0.111300	0.128463	0.14630284				24
25	0.078227	0.085811	0.093679	0.101806	0.110168	0.127500	0.14549841	0.164012	0.182919	0.202119	25
26	0.076904	0.081561	0.092507	0.100715	0.109159	0.126652	0.14480001				26
27	0.075697	0.083426	0.091448	0.099735	0.108258	0.125904	0.14419288				27
28	0.074593	0.082392	0.090489	0.098852	0.107451	0.125244	0.14366449				28
29	0.073580	0.081449	0.089619	0.098056	0.106728	0.124660	0.14320417				29
30	0.072649	0.089586	0.088827	0.097336	0.106079	0.124144	0.14280279	0.161886	0.181264	0.200846	30
31	0.071792	0.079797	0.088107	0.096686	0.105496	0.123686	0.14245256				31
32	0.071002	0.079073	0.087451	0.096096	0.104972	0.123280	0.14214675				32
33	0.070273	0.078408	0.086852	0.095562	0.101499	0.122920	0.14187958				33
34	0.069598	0.077797	0.086304	0.095077	0.104074	0.122601	0.14164604				34
35	0.068974	0.077234	0.085803	0.094636	0.103690	0.122317	0.14144181	0.160892	0.180550	0.200339	35
36	0.068395	0.076715	0.085345	0.094235	0.103343	0.122064	0.14126315				36
37	0.067857	0.076237	0.084924	0.093870	0.103030	0.121840	0.14110680				37
38	0.067358	0.075795	0.084539	0.093538	0.102747	0.121640	0.14096993				38
39	0.066894	0.075387	0.084185	0.093236	0.102491	0.121462	0.14085010				39
40	0.066462	0.075009	0.083860	0.092960	0.102259	0.121304	0.14074514	0.160423	0.180240	0.200136	40

[a] Formula $A = P\,[i(1+i)^n/\{(1+i)^n - 1\}]$.

Item ________________ Date ________________

Section		Original	Alt. No.1	Alt No.2
Input Data — Collateral & Instant Contract Costs	**Initial Costs**			
	Base Costs			
	Interface Costs			
	a. ________			
	b. ________			
	c. ________			
	Other Initial Costs			
	a. ________			
	b. ________			
	c. ________			
	Total Initial Cost Impact (IC)			
	Initial Cost Savings			
Input Data — Salvage & Replacement Costs	**Single Expenditures** @ ________ **Interest**			
	Present Worth			
	1. Year ________ Amount			
	PW= Amount × (PW Factor ________) =			
	2. Year ________ Amount			
	Amount × (PW Factor ________) =			
	3. Year ________ Amount			
	Amount × (PW Factor ________) =			
	4. Year ________ Amount			
	Amount × (PW Factor ________) =			
	5. Year ________ Amount			
	Amount × (PW Factor ________) =			
	Salvage Amount × (PW Factor ________)=			
Output — Life Cycle Costs (Annualized)	**Annual Owning & Operating Costs**			
	1. Capital IC × (PP ________) =			
	Recovery ____ Years@ ________ %			
	Replacement Cost: PP × PW			
	a. Year ________			
	b. Year ________			
	c. Year ________			
	d. Year ________			
	e. Year ________			
	Salvage:			
	2. Annual Costs			
	a. Maintenance			
	b. Operations			
	c. ________			
	d. ________			
	e.			
	3. Total Annual Cost			
	Annual Difference (AD)			
	4. Present Worth of Annual Difference			
	(PWA Factor ________) × AD			

Figure 6. Format, life cycle cost analysis—using annual owning and operating costs (1). PP = periodic payment to pay off loan of \$1; PWA = present worth of annuity (what \$1 payable periodically is worth today); PW = present worth (what \$1 due in the future is worth today).

the present worth of replacement–salvage costs. The replacement costs are listed and the present worth factor (Table 2) for each year determined. The present worth of the future costs are then calculated. All costs should be in constant dollars; that is, the LCC analysis baseline is normally current dollar so all costs listed should be the equivalent to the purchasing power of the current dollar. It is only when there is differential escalation that the use of differentially escalated dollars should be considered. For example, assume that tires are replaced in two and four years. For Car A, the cost is estimated at \$225 each cycle. In terms of constant dollars, the costs of the tires in terms of current dollars (a loaf of bread) is constant. The present worth factors for two and four years are 0.826 and 0.683 (Table 2), respectively, so the present worth of the tire replacement at two years is \$186 (\$225 × 0.826) and at four years is \$154 (\$225 × 0.683).

The salvage value should be taken into account. When dollars are realized from the trade-in, a credit results, the salvage or residual value. For example, the trade in of Car A equates to a credit of \$3900 in the fifth year, a present worth credit of \$3900 × 0.62, or \$2418.

Part 3 of Figure 7 summarizes the annual owning and operating costs. The periodic payment (PP) necessary to pay off a loan of \$1 at 10% interest over five years (Table 4) is \$0.2638, or \$4,135/year for five years. The same calculation is made for salvage and replacement costs. The present worth of each cost is amortized using the periodic payment (PP) factor. For example, for the salvage of Car A, the equivalent annual cost at 10% interest over five years would be a credit of \$2418 (present worth of salvage) × 0.2638, or \$638/year for five years.

In terms of equivalent costs, \$3900 five years from now has the same buying power as \$2418 today as has \$638/year for five years. They all are equivalent costs.

After determining the annualized equivalent cost for

Item CAR PURCHASE Date N/A

Input Data — Collateral & Instant Contract Costs; Salvage & Replacement Costs

	Original	Alt. No. 1	Alt. No. 2
Initial Costs	A	B	C
Base Cost	16,500	15,000	30,000
Interface Costs			
a. Sales Tax	825	750	1,500
b.			
c.			
Other Initial Costs			
a. Investment Tax Credit	(1,650)	(1,500)	(3,000)
b.			
c.			
Total Initial Cost Impact (IC)	15,675	14,250	28,500
Initial Cost Savings			
Single Expenditures @ 10% Interest Present Worth			
1. Year 2 (Tires) Amount	225	300	350
PW = Amount x (PW Factor (0.826) =	186	248	289
2. Year 2.5 (Major Replac). Amount	500	750	400
Amount x (PW Factor (0.789) =	395	592	316
3. Year 4 (Tires) Amount	225	300	350
Amount x (PW Factor (0.683) =	154	205	239
4. Year 5 Trade-In Amount	(3,900)	(3,500)	(15,000)
Amount x (PW Factor (0.62) =	(2,418)	(2,170)	(9,300)
5. Year Amount		-	
Amount x (PW Factor) =			
Salvage Amount x (PW Factor) =			

Output — Life Cycle Costs (Annualized)

	A	B	C
Annual Owning & Operating Costs			
1. Capital IC x (PP (0.2638) = Recovery Years @ %	4,135	3,759	7,518
Replacement Cost: PP x PW			
a. Year 2 Tires	49	65	76
b. Year 2.5 Major Replac.	104	156	83
c. Year 4 Tires	41	54	63
d. Year 5 Trade-In	(638)	(572)	(2,453)
e. Year			
Salvage:			
2. Annual Costs			
a. Maintenance & Operation	2,200	2,800	2,000
b. Licenses & Insurance	750	1,000	1,500
c. Depreciation Credits*	(990)	(900)	(1,800)
d.			
e.			
3. Total Annual Costs	5,651	6,362	6,987
Annual Difference (AD)	1,336	625	
4. Present Worth of Annual Difference	21,403	24,118	26,488
(PWA Factor 3.791) x AD	5,065	2,367	

Figure 7. Life cycle cost analysis—annualized cost—car purchase. PP = periodic payment to pay off loan of $1; PWA = present worth of annuity (what $1 payable periodically is worth today); PW = present worth (what $1 due in the future is worth today). The investment tax credit column assumes a 30% tax bracket, five-year straight line depreciation.

Table 5. Car Purchase Input Data, $

Cost Element	Car A	Car B	Car C
Initial cost	$16,500	$15,000	$30,000
Sales tax	5%	5%	5%
Trade-in value (5 years)	3,900	3,500	15,000
License and insurance cost/yr	750	1,000	1,500
Maintenance and operating cost/yr	2,200	2,800	2,000
Tire costs at 2 and 4 years	225	300	350
Major replacement at 2½ years	500	750	400
Depreciation 5 years straight line			
Investment tax credit 10%			
Tax bracket of consultant 30% tax rate			

the initial and replacement costs, the annual costs are entered. Car A has $2,200/year for maintenance and operations costs, $750/year for licenses and insurance, and a depreciation credit of $990/year.

$$16{,}500 \text{ (initial cost)} \div \text{five years (straight line depreciation)} = \$3{,}300/\text{yr} \times 30\% \text{ tax bracket or } \$990/\text{year credit.}$$

The same result is obtained when the present worth concept is used, as demonstrated in Figure 8. In Part 1, the initial costs are listed and are already in present worth terms. Next, the present worth of the replacement–salvage costs are calculated. Again, salvage values are negative.

Project Life Cycle Costing Example	LCC No	
Item Car Purchase	Sheet 1	Of 3
	Discount Rate = 10 %	Economic Rate = 5 years

	Year	PWF	Original (describe) A Est. Costs	A PW	Alternative 1 (describe) B Est. Costs	B PW	Alternative 2 (describe) C Est. Costs	C PW
1. Initial/Collateral Costs								
A. Base Costs on Road.			16,500	16,500	15,000	15,000	30,000	30,000
B. Sales Tax			825	825	750	750	1,500	1,500
C. Investment Tax Credits			(1,650)	(1,650)	(1,500)	(1,500)	(3,000)	(3,000)
D.								
E.								
F.								
G.								
Total Initial/Collateral Costs (PW)				15,675		14,250		28,500
Total Initial/Collateral Cost Savings								
2. Replacement/Salvage Costs	Year	PWF						
A. Tires	2	0.826	225	186	300	248	350	289
B. Major Replacement	2.5	0.789	500	395	750	592	400	316
C. Tires	4	0.683	225	154	300	205	350	239
D.								
E. Salvage	5	0.62	(3,900)	(2,418)	(3,500)	(2,170)	(15,000)	(9,300)
F.								
G.								
H.								
Total Replacement/Salvage Costs (PW)				(1683)		(1125)		(8956)
3. Annual Costs	Esc Rate	PWA						
A. Operating Costs	0	3.791	2,200	9,340	2,800	10,615	2,000	7,532
B.								
C. Licenses & Insurance	0	3.791	650	2,843	1,000	3,791	1,500	5,687
D.								
E. Depreciation Credits	0	3.791	(990)	(3,753)	(900)	(3,412)	(1,800)	(6,824)
F.								
G.								
Total Annual Costs								
Total Annual Costs (PW)				7,430		10,994		6,445
Grand Total Present Worth Costs				21,422		24,119		26,488
Life Cycle Present Worth Savings				5,066		2,369		
Savings %				24%		10%		

Figure 8. Life cycle cost analysis—present worth costs—car purchase. PWF = present worth factor (what \$1 due in the future is worth today); PWA = present worth of annuity factor (what \$1 payable periodically is worth today) or present worth of an escalating amount. The depreciation credits column is based on 30% tax rate, straight line five-year depreciation rate 95%.

For example, the present worth of salvage of Car A is \$3,100 × 0.62, or a credit of \$2,418.

Finally, the annual costs are converted to present worth. For example, the annual operating cost of Car A is \$2,200/yr, equivalent to \$2,200/yr × (present worth of annuity) 3.791 (Table 3), or \$9,340 present worth. The present worth amounts are then totaled and differences calculated.

APPLICATION OF LCC TO BUILDINGS

The application of the life cycle costing concept to buildings is graphically illustrated by Figure 9, which shows cost of ownership (hypothetical) of a building using present worth concepts. The figure indicates that for the building type and data used, approximately 40% of the total cost of ownership is in initial cost, 28% of the cost of ownership is in financing (cost of money), and 22.5% is in annual maintenance and operation charges. The remaining amounts are for design, indirect costs, and alterations and replacement costs.

The data on which the figure is based are as follows:

Bases of cost data:	
Initial cost of building	\$80/ft^2 (\$861/m^2)
Building size	100,000 ft^2 (9290 m^2)
Cost of real estate—not included	
Interest rate	12%
Life cycle	20 years
Maintenance, operations, etc, costs	Average \$6.00/ft^2 (\$64.58/m^2)

Design costs	4.5%
Indirect construction costs	10%
Alteration and replacement costs	$1,500,000 every 10 years

Cost of Ownership Calculations:

1. Present worth of initial costs equals cost per unit area times building size. Initial Costs = $80/ft^2 \times 100,000 ft^2 = $8,000,000 ($861/m^2 \times 9290 m^2 = approximately $8,000,000).
2. Present worth of annual costs equals annual cost times the present worth of $1.00 payable periodically (Table 3). Annual cost = 100,000 ft^2 × $6.00 × 7.47 (PWA) or approximately $4,482,000 (9290 m^2 × $64.58 × 7.47 PWA).
3. Present worth of financing costs equals present worth of financing for estimated initial costs and annual costs.
   - Present worth of the interest costs for the estimated costs equals the present worth of annual difference of payoff with interest, less the payoff without interest. Annual change with interest equals initial costs times periodic payment necessary to pay off a loan of $1.00 (Table 4). $8,000,000 × 0.134 = $1,072,000/year. Annual charge without interest equals initial costs divided by number of years: $8,000,000/20 = $400,000/year. Difference = $1,072,000 − $400,000 = $672,000/year, which is the annual value of interest. Present worth interest = $672,000 × 7.47 (Table 3) = $5,019,840, approx. $5,020,000.
   - Present worth of interest (financing) of annual costs equals annual financing costs times present worth of $1.00 payable periodically (Table 3).
   - Annual financing charge = 12% × $600,000 = $120,000. Present worth = $120,000 × 7.47 (Table 3) = $537,840 (approximately $540,000). (Total present worth of financing costs = $540,000 + $5,020,000 = $5,560,000.)
4. Other costs.
   - Design costs = design percentage times initial costs = 4.5% × $8,000,000 = $360,000.
   - Indirect cost = indirect cost percentage times initial costs = 10% × $8,000,000 = $800,000.
   - Present worth of alteration and replacement costs = cost in future year(s) times present worth of $1.00 due in the future (Table 2).

     Present worth of alteration and replacement costs = $1,500,000 × 0.322 (tenth year) = $483,000 $1,500,000 × 0.104 (twentieth year) = $156,000 $483,000 + $156,000 = $639,000.

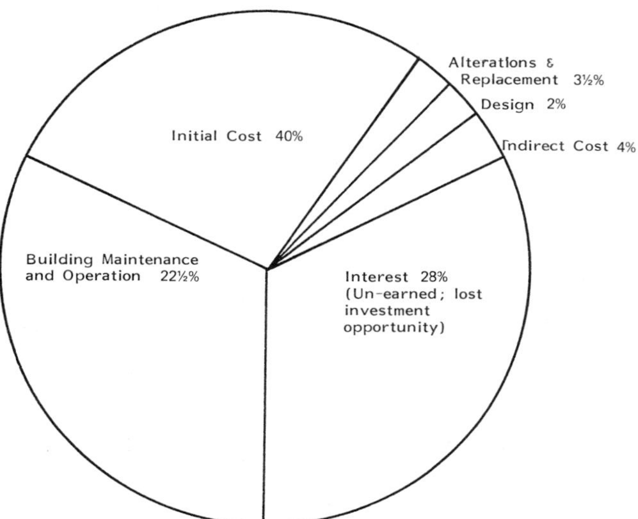

Figure 9. Cost of ownership using present worth concepts for a typical office building.

Summary of costs:

	Present Worth	Approx. Percent of Total
1. Initial costs	$ 8,000,000	40
2. Annual costs	4,482,000	22.5
3. Financing costs:		
Initial	5,020,000	
Annual	540,000	28
4. Other costs:		
Design	360,000	2
Indirect	800,000	4
Alteration and replacement	639,000	3.5
Present worth—Total cost of ownership	*$19,841,000*	

Application of LCC to HVAC Systems

A hypothetical example of a building system follows in which a heating, ventilation, air conditioning system (HVAC) system will be used. It is assumed that the study group considered the original design and developed two alternatives for comparison. Figure 10 shows the LCC analysis of this example using the annualized method.

The original design initial base bid cost is estimated at $49,150, alternative system no. 1 is estimated at $70,000, and alternative system no. 2 is estimated at $62,000. These figures are shown under "base costs." The interface costs for electrical total $10,000 for the original design, $4,835 for alternative no. 1, and $7,200 for alternative no. 2. Owner-supplied equipment costs $48,450 for the original design, $25,000 for alternative no. 1, and $27,000 for alternative no. 2.

Next, replacement and salvage costs are considered. The original design results in substantial replacement costs of $35,000 at the tenth and twentieth year. For alternative no. 1, replacement costs of $30,000 will be incurred in the twentieth year. For alternative no. 2, costs of $35,000 are estimated for the twentieth year. Finally, the salvage value of each alternative at the end of the life cycle period is estimated. These amounts are then discounted to deter-

Item ENLISTED MENS QUARTERS, HVAC SYSTEM Date N/A

			Original	Alt. No. 1	Alt. No. 2
Input Data	Collateral & Instant Contract Costs	**Initial Costs**			
		Base Cost	49,150	70,000	62,000
		Interface Costs			
		a. Electrical Installation	10,000	4,835	7,200
		b.			
		c.			
		Other Initial Costs			
		a. Owner Supplied Equipment	48,450	25,000	27,000
		b.			
		c.			
		Total Initial Cost Impact (IC)	107,600	99,035	96,200
		Initial Cost Savings		8,565	11,400
	Salvage & Replacement Costs	**Single Expenditures @ 10% Interest**			
		Present Worth			
		1. Year 10-Equip. Replac. Amount	35,000		
		PW = Amount x (PW Factor (0.3855) =	13,494		
		2. Year 20 Equip. Replac. Amount	35,000	30,000	35,000
		Amount x (PW Factor 0.1486 =	5,203	4,459	5,203
		3. Year Amount			
		Amount x (PW Factor) =			
		4. Year Amount			
		Amount x (PW Factor) =			
		5. Year Amount			
		Amount x (PW Factor 0.0923) =	(18,000)	(22,500)	(26,250)
		Salvage Amount x (PW Factor) =	(1,661)	(2,077)	(2,423)
Output	Life Cycle Costs (Annualized)	**Annual Owning & Operating Costs**			
		1. Capital IC x (PP 0.1102) =	11,858	10,914	10,601
		Recovery 25 Years @ 10 %			
		Replacement Cost: PP x PW			
		a. Year 10	1,487		
		b. Year 20	573	491	573
		c. Year			
		d. Year			
		e. Year 25	(183)	(229)	(267)
		Salvage:			
		2. Annual Costs			
		a. Maintenance	2,900	2,200	2,000
		b. Operations			
		c. Cooling Energy	13,650	13,950	16,025
		d. Heating Energy	1,060	2,425	2,425
		e. Domestic HW Energy	7,500	3,667	3,667
		3. Total Annual Costs	38,845	33,418	35,024
		Annual Difference (AD)		5,427	3,821
		4. Present Worth of Annual Difference (PWA Factor 9.077) x AD		49,261	34,683

Figure 10. Life cycle cost analysis—annualized—enlisted men's quarters, HVAC system. PP = periodic payment to pay off loan of $1; PWA = present worth of annuity (what $1 payable periodically is worth today); PW = present worth (what $1 due in the future is worth today).

mine the present worth using Table 2. For example, the present worth of $35,000 due 10 years in the future is 0.3855 × $35,000, or $13,494. Replacement costs used must be those costs (using current dollars) estimated for the year indicated. In some cases, this will require using present-day costs escalated for future price increases. However, the escalation should be limited to only the amounts of differential escalation over and above dollar devaluation. This must be done to keep all amounts in terms of a constant present-day dollar purchasing power. For example, replacement of a chiller was estimated to occur at 20 years. A market study indicated that the cost of that particular type of chiller was estimated to escalate at 12% per year and dollar devaluation was averaging 10% per year. A 2% differential escalation would be applied to the 20-year cost estimate. The formula for calculating escalation is

$$F = (1 + i)^y$$

where F is the factor to be used, i is the differential interest rate in decimals, and y is the number of years. In this instance $F = (1 + .02)^{20} = 1.49$.

Next, the annualized costs are determined. The initial costs must be amortized by determining the annual payment costs necessary to pay off a loan equaling the total initial cost impact. For the exercise, a span of 25 years at 10% interest is used. Table 4 is entered under the interest rate across the 25-year line to find the periodic payment necessary to pay off a loan of $1, in this case $0.1102 per year. Each total initial cost is multiplied by this factor to determine the annual capital recovery costs. For example, the annual cost required to recover the original cost of $107,600 over 25 years at 10% would be $107,600 × 0.1102, or $11,858 per year.

The next step is to convert the replacement and salvage costs to a uniform series of payments. To do this, the present worth (discounted future costs) is amortized over the projected life. In the case of salvage value, the costs are negative, as indicated by the parentheses. For example, alternative no. 1 has replacement costs of $35,000 at year 10 which has a present worth of $13,494. The periodic payment necessary to pay off a loan of this amount is $13,494 × 0.1102 (Table 4), or $1,487 per year.

After determining the annual amount of initial and replacement costs, other annual costs, such as operation, maintenance, and taxes, are added. The total represents a uniform baseline comparison for the alternatives over a projected life at a selected interest rate. The annual differences are then determined and used for recommendations. In this example, alternative no. 2, which has the lowest annual owning and operating costs savings (annual difference), $5,427/year, would be recommended.

The present worth of the annual difference (constant from Table 3 × the annual difference) can also be determined. In this example, the present worth of the annual difference indicated for alternative no. 2 is the annual difference of $5,427 × the present worth of $1.00 payable annually for 25 years, or $5,427 × 9.077, which equals $49,261.

As previously stated, life cycle analysis can be accomplished using either the annualized method or the present worth method. In the case of the present worth method, the base line of comparison is the present-day value. Figure 11 shows the application of the present worth method

LIFE CYCLE COST ANALYSIS USING PRESENT WORTH COSTS			ORIGINAL CLOSED LOOP HEAT PUMP SYSTEM ______		ALTERNATIVE 1 4-PIPE SYSTEM W/ WATER-CLD CHILLER & HEAT RECOVERY		ALTERNATIVE 2 4-PIPE SYSTEM W/ AIR CLD CHILLER & HEAT RECOVERY		ALTERNATIVE 3 ______ ______ ______	
DISCOUNT RATE =	10 %		ESTIM	PW	ESTIM	PW	ESTIM	PW	ESTIM	PW
ECONOMIC LIFE =	25 YEARS		COSTS	COSTS	COSTS	COSTS	COSTS	COSTS	COSTS	COSTS
1. INITIAL/COLLATERAL COSTS										
A. REFRIGERATION EQUIPMENT			48450	48450	25000	25000	27000	27000	______	0
B. PIPING, DUCTWORK AND SUPPORT EQUIP			49150	49150	70000	70000	62000	62000	______	0
C. ELECTRICAL INSTALLATION			10000	10000	4035	4035	7200	7200	______	0
D. ______			______	0	______	0	______	0	______	0
E. ______			______	0	______	0	______	0	______	0
F. ______			______	0	______	0	______	0	______	0
G. ______			______	0	______	0	______	0	______	0
TOTAL INITIAL/COLLATERAL COSTS (PW)				107600		99035		96200		0
TOTAL INITIAL/COLLATERAL COSTS SAVINGS						8565		11400		0
2. REPLACEMENT/SALVAGE COSTS	YEAR	FACTOR								
A. EQUIPMENT REPLACEMENT	10	.3855	35000	13494	______	0	______	0	______	0
B. EQUIPMENT REPLACEMENT	20	.1486	35000	5203	30000	4459	35000	5203	______	0
C. SALVAGE VALUE	25	.0923	-18000	-1661	-22500	-2077	-26250	-2423	______	0
D. ______	--	1	______	0	______	0	______	0	______	0
E. ______	--	1	______	0	______	0	______	0	______	0
F. ______	--	1	______	0	______	0	______	0	______	0
G. ______	--	1	______	0	______	0	______	0	______	0
H. ______	--	1	______	0	______	0	______	0	______	0
I. ______	--	1	______	0	______	0	______	0	______	0
TOTAL REPLACEMENT/SALVAGE COSTS (PW)				17035		2383		2780		0
3. ANNUAL COSTS	ESCAL RATE	PWA								
A. MAINTENANCE	--	9.077	2900	26323	2200	19969	2000	18154	______	0
B. COOLING ENERGY	--	9.077	13650	123902	13950	126625	16025	145459	______	0
C. HEATING ENERGY	--	9.077	1060	9622	2425	22012	2425	22012	______	0
D. DOMESTIC HOT WATER ENERGY	--	9.077	7500	68078	3667	33285	3667	33285	______	0
E. ______	--	9.077	______	0	______	0	______	0	______	0
F. ______	--	9.077	______	0	______	0	______	0	______	0
G. ______	--	9.077	______	0	______	0	______	0	______	0
H. ______	--	9.077	______	0	______	0	______	0	______	0
I. ______	--	9.077	______	0	______	0	______	0	______	0
TOTAL ANNUAL COSTS (PW)				227924		201891		218911		0
GRAND TOTAL PRESENT WORTH COSTS				352560		303309		317891		0
LIFE CYCLE PRESENT WORTH SAVINGS						49250		34669		0
(SAVINGS %)						14		10		0

Figure 11. Life cycle cost analysis—present worth—enlisted men's quarters, HVAC system.

LIFE CYCLE COST ANALYSIS USING PRESENT WORTH COSTS			ORIGINAL CLOSED LOOP HEAT PUMP SYSTEM		ALTERNATIVE 1 4-PIPE SYSTEM W/ WATER-CLD CHILLER & HEAT RECOVERY		ALTERNATIVE 2 4-PIPE SYSTEM W/ AIR CLD CHILLER & HEAT RECOVERY		ALTERNATIVE 3 ______	
DISCOUNT RATE =	10 %			PW		PW		PW		PW
ECONOMIC LIFE =	25 YEARS		COST	COSTS	COST	COSTS	COST	COSTS	COST	COSTS
1. INITIAL/COLLATERAL COSTS										
A. REFRIGERATION EQUIPMENT			48450	48450	25000	25000	27000	27000	______	0
B. PIPING, DUCTWORK AND SUPPORT EQUIP			49150	49150	70000	70000	62000	62000	______	0
C. ELECTRICAL INTERFACE			10000	10000	4035	4035	7200	7200	______	0
D. ______			______	0	______	0	______	0	______	0
E. ______			______	0	______	0	______	0	______	0
F. ______			______	0	______	0	______	0	______	0
G. ______			______	0	______	0	______	0	______	0
TOTAL INITIAL/COLLATERAL COSTS (PW)				107600		99035		96200		0
TOTAL INITIAL/COLLATERAL COSTS SAVINGS						8565		11400		0
2. REPLACEMENT/SALVAGE COSTS	YEAR	FACTOR								
A. EQUIPMENT REPLACEMENT	10	.3855	35000	13494	______	0	______	0	______	0
B. EQUIPMENT REPLACEMENT	20	.1486	35000	5203	30000	4459	35000	5203	______	0
C. SALVAGE VALUE	25	.0923	-18000	-1661	-22500	-2077	-26250	-2423	______	0
D.	__	1	______	0	______	0	______	0	______	0
E. ______	__	1	______	0	______	0	______	0	______	0
F. ______	__	1	______	0	______	0	______	0	______	0
G. ______	__	1	______	0	______	0	______	0	______	0
H. ______	__	1	______	0	______	0	______	0	______	0
I. ______	__	1	______	0	______	0	______	0	______	0
TOTAL REPLACEMENT/SALVAGE COSTS (PW)				17035		2383		2780		0
3. ANNUAL COSTS	ESCAL RATE	PWA								
A. MAINTENANCE	2	10.82	2900	31376	2200	23803	2000	21639	______	0
B. COOLING ENERGY	5	14.44	13650	197058	13950	201389	16025	231345	______	0
C. HEATING ENERGY	5	14.44	1060	15303	2425	35009	2425	35009	______	0
D. DOMESTIC HOT WATER ENERGY	5	14.44	7500	108274	3667	52939	3667	52939	______	0
E. ______	__	9.077	______	0	______	0	______	0	______	0
F. ______	__	9.077	______	0	______	0	______	0	______	0
G. ______	__	9.077	______	0	______	0	______	0	______	0
H. ______	__	9.077	______	0	______	0	______	0	______	0
I. ______	__	9.077	______	0	______	0	______	0	______	0
TOTAL ANNUAL COSTS				352011		313139		340931		0
GRAND TOTAL PRESENT WORTH COSTS				476646		414557		439911		0
LIFE CYCLE PRESENT WORTH SAVINGS						62089		36735		0
(SAVINGS %)						13		8		0

Figure 12. Life cycle cost analysis—present worth escalated—enlisted men's quarters, HVAC system.

and uses the information from the previous example. In using the present worth concept, collateral and initial costs are in present-day values and are entered directly. Single costs in the future (salvage and replacement) are discounted using present worth factors from Table 2.

Annual costs are entered and multiplied by present worth of annuity (PWA) factors from Table 3. For example, for the original design the present worth of the annual costs for maintenance equals \$2,900/yr × 9.077 (PWA), or \$26,323.

All present worth amounts are added and the comparison is made for recommendations. The results validate conclusions developed using the annualized cost base line.

Figure 12 shows the same example but uses differentially escalating rates using a discount rate of 10% for operation and maintenance costs. As previously explained, these escalating rates were calculated as the differential rates these costs will rise from the inflation rate. Operation costs are differentially escalated at 5% [14.44 (Table 1) versus 9.077] per year while maintenance costs are differentially escalated at 2% [10.82 (Table 1) versus 9.077] per year.

If the annualized method is used, the annual sum for operations and maintenance may also be increased by a factor to account for differential escalation. Table 1 provides the required data. For example, the factor for 2% differentially escalating maintenance cost would be 10.82/9.077, or 1.19. The operation cost factor for 5% would be 14.44/9.077, or 1.59. These factors would be used to adjust the annual costs per year accordingly. For example, the

Study Title ______________________________

____

Discount Rate ______________ Economic Life ______________

				Original Describe:		Alternative 1 Describe:		Alternative 2 Describe:		Alternative 3 Describe:	
				Estimated Costs	Present Worth	Estimated Costs	Present Worth	Estimated Costs	Present Worth	Estimated Costs	Present Worth
Initial Costs	**Initial Costs**										
	A.										
	B.										
	C.										
	D.										
	E.										
	F.										
	G.										
	H.										
	I.										
	J. Contingencies %										
	K. Escalation %										
	Total Initial Costs										
Owning Costs	**Operations (Annual)**	Diff.Escal.Rate	PWA w/Escal								
	A.										
	B.										
	C.										
	D.										
	E.										
	F.										
	Total Annual Operations Costs										
	Maintenance (Annual)	Diff.Escal.Rate	PWA w/Escal								
	A.										
	B.										
	C.										
	D.										
	E.										
	F.										
	G.										
	Total Annual Maintenance Costs										
	Replacement/Alterations (Single Expenditure)	Year	PW Factor								
	A.										
	B.										
	C.										
	D.										
	E.										
	F.										
	G.										
	H.										
	I.										
	J.										
	Total Replacement/Alterations Costs										
	Tax Elements	Diff.Escal.Rate	PWA w/Escal								
	A.										
	B.										
	C.										
	D.										
	E.										
	F.										
	G.										
	Total Tax Elements										
	Associated (Annual)	Diff.Escal.Rate	PWA w/Escal								
	A.										
	B.										
	C.										
	Total Annual Associated Costs										
	Total Owning Present Worth Costs										
Salvage	**Salvage at End of Economic Life**	Year	PW Factor								
	Building (Struc., Arch., Mech., Elec., Equip.)										
	Other										
	Sitework										
	Total Salvage										
LCC	**Total Present Worth Life Cycle Costs**										
	Life Cycle Present Worth Dollar Savings										

Figure 13. Format, life cycle costing estimate—general purpose worksheet. PW = present worth; PWA = present worth of annuity.

adjustment for the annual maintenance costs of the original design would be \$2,900/yr × 1.19, or \$3,541/yr.

General Purpose Worksheet Using Escalation

Figure 13 shows a general purpose LCC worksheet that can be utilized for a more detailed system analysis using present worth. This form is also useful as a summary sheet for individual items or component analysis.

Figure 14 shows a life cycle cost analysis conducted for the selection of the emergency power systems of a large computer complex. The original concept was validated as the optimum choice. As for process type facilities, a similar LCC analysis of a conveying system was con-

Study Title: STANDBY GENERATORS

Discount Rate: 10% Economic Life: 40 YRS.

Section	Item	Diff. Escal. Rate / Year	PWA w/Escal / PW Factor	Original — Describe: 8-1000 KW RECIP. DIESEL ENGINES — Estimated Costs	Original — Present Worth	Alternative 1 — Describe: 4-2000 KW RECIP. DIESEL ENGINES — Estimated Costs	Alternative 1 — Present Worth	Alternative 2 — Describe: 8-1000 KW GAS TURBINES — Estimated Costs	Alternative 2 — Present Worth	Alternative 3 — Describe: 4-2000 KW GAS TURBINES — Estimated Costs	Alternative 3 — Present Worth
Initial Costs	**Initial Costs**										
	A. GENERATORS				1,400,000		1,800,000		2,000,000		2,000,000
	B. SWITCHGEAR				128,000		126,000		128,000		126,000
	C. MECHANICAL				157,000		175,000		151,000		175,000
	D.										
	E.										
	F.										
	G.										
	H.										
	I.										
	J. Contingencies %										
	K. Escalation %										
	Total Initial Costs				1,685,000		2,101,000		2,279,000		2,301,000
Owning Costs	**Operations (Annual)**	Diff. Escal. Rate	PWA w/Escal								
	A. 1-MW RECIP. 70GAL/HR×8	0%	9.779	89,600	876,200						
	B. 2-MW RECIP. 140GAL/HR×4	0%	9.779			89,600	876,200				
	C. 1-MW TURBINE 161 GAL/HR×8	0%	9.779					154,600	1,511,800		
	D. 2-MW TURBINE 268GAL/HR×4	0%	9.779							128,600	1,258,000
	E.										
	F.										
	Total Annual Operations Costs				876,200		876,200		1,511,800		1,258,000
	Maintenance (Annual)	Diff. Escal. Rate	PWA w/Escal								
	A. LUBRICATE, CHANGE FILTERS	0%	9.779	10,200	99,700	9,000	88,000	10,200	99,700	9,000	88,000
	B. CHECK & ADJUST IGNITION										
	C. INSPECT WINDING RINGS										
	D. BELTS, ETC. CHECK FUEL										
	E. COOLANT, ELECTROLYTE, ETC.	0%	9.779								
	F. REPLACE FAILED COMPONENTS	0%	9.779	800	7,800	400	3,900	2,000	19,600	1,000	9,800
	G. AS REQUIRED										
	Total Annual Maintenance Costs				107,500		91,900		119,300		97,800
	Replacement/Alterations (Single Expenditure)	Year	PW Factor								
	A. 1-MW TURBINE	25	.0923					500,000	46,100		
	B. 2-MW TURBINE	25	.0923							500,000	46,100
	C. 1-MW DIESEL	25	.0923	350,000	36,300						
	D. 2-MW DIESEL	25	.0923			450,000	41,500				
	E.										
	F.										
	G. (FAILURE RATE ONE IN FOUR)										
	H.										
	I.										
	J.										
	Total Replacement/Alterations Costs				32,300		41,500		46,100		46,100
	Tax Elements	Diff. Escal. Rate	PWA w/Escal								
	A.										
	B.										
	C.										
	D.										
	E.										
	F.										
	G.										
	Total Tax Elements										
	Associated (Annual)	Diff. Escal. Rate	PWA w/Escal								
	A. DENIAL OF USE SPACE	–	–	6000 SF	270,000	3500 SF	157,500	1000 SF	45,000	–	–
	B. COST $ 45.00/SF										
	C.										
	Total Annual Associated Costs				270,000		157,500		45,000		–
	Total Owning Present Worth Costs				1,286,000		1,167,100		1,722,200		1,401,900
Salvage	**Salvage at End of Economic Life @ 10%**	Year	PW Factor								
	Building (Struc., Arch., Mech., Elec., Equip.)	40	.022	(140,000)	(3,100)	(180,000)	(4,000)	(224,000)	(4,900)	(200,000)	(4,400)
	Other										
	Sitework										
	Total Salvage				(3,100)		(4,000)		(4,900)		(4,400)
LCC	**Total Present Worth Life Cycle Costs**				2,967,900		3,264,100		3,996,300		3,698,500
	Life Cycle Present Worth Dollar Savings				–		(296,200)		(1,028,600)		(730,600)

Figure 14. Life cycle costing estimate—standby generators. PW = present worth; PWA = present worth of annuity.

ducted during a plant study. The study results were implemented, resulting in significant savings.

Life Cycle Cost Analysis—Equipment Procurement

Table 6 outlines a formal procedure for equipment procurement (freezer). For this procurement, bidder D was awarded the contract even though the initial unit cost was $309.50 versus $231.53 for bidder B. The impact of recurring costs, $357.42 for D versus $464.91 for B, more than offset (on the basis of present worth analysis) the difference in initial cost.

The procurement in Table 6, based on anticipated demand quantities, provided a projected cost savings over

Table 6. Summary of Life Cycle Costs—Top Mounted Freezer[a]

Zone	Type Cost	Bidders A	B	C	D	E	F
	A[b]	242.21	231.53	263.45	309.50	252.90	248.36
1	R[c]	518.01	464.91	431.24	357.42	486.96	493.40
	LCC[d]	760.22	696.44	694.69	666.92	739.86	741.76
	A	243.33	230.37	263.45	309.50	244.95	248.38
2	R	518.01	464.91	431.24	357.42	486.96	493.40
	LCC	761.34	695.28	694.69	666.92	731.91	741.76
	A	250.84	232.98	263.45	309.50	251.69	248.36
3	R	518.01	464.91	431.24	357.42	486.96	493.40
	LCC	768.85	697.89	694.69	666.92	738.65	741.76
	A	272.09	245.04	257.45	309.50	267.25	248.36
4	R	518.01	464.91	431.24	357.42	486.96	493.40
	LCC	790.10	709.95	688.69	666.92	754.21	741.76

[a] Ref. 5.
[b] A = Acquisition.
[c] R = Recurring.
[d] LCC = Life cycle costs—present worth.

the useful life (15 years) of some $260,000. The LCC formula used in this procurement is LCC = $A + R$, where LCC is the life cycle cost in present value dollars, A is the acquisition cost (bid price), and R is the present value sum of the cost of the electrical energy required by the refrigerator–freezer during its useful life. $R = P \times C \times T \times D$, where P is the computed electrical energy, T is the annual operating time in days, and D is the total discount factor, which will convert the stream of operating costs over the life of the equipment to present value form (Table 3), and C is the cost of one kilowatt hour of electricity.

The discounted cash flow or present value methodology was used as a decision-making tool to allow direct comparison between different expenditure patterns of alternative investment opportunities. The present value sum represents the amount of money that would be required to be invested today, at a given rate of interest, in order to pay the expected future costs associated with a particular investment alternative. For purposes of this procurement a discount rate of 8% and a product life of 15 years were used, resulting in a total discount factor, D, of 8.56 (Table 3).

The value for P in the energy cost equation is a function of the net refrigerated volume, V, of the product being offered and the energy factor, EF, which relates refrigerated volume and the electrical energy consumed to maintain the refrigerated volume. Stated in mathematical notation, the value of P is determined as $P = V/EF$, where

$$EF = \frac{\text{(Volume of frozen food compartment)} \times \text{(Correction factor)} + \text{Food compartment}}{\text{Kilowatt-hours of electric energy consumed in 24 hours of operation}}$$

and the correction factor is a constant of 1.63. Thus, the life cycle cost evaluation formula LCC = $A + R = A + (P \times C \times T \times D)$ can be written as follows:

$$\text{LCC} = V + \frac{V}{EF} \times \$.04 \times 365 \times 8.56$$

$$= A + \frac{V}{EF} \times 124.976.$$

It must be pointed out that certain liberties have been taken in the above discussion to simplify the LCC process. One such liberty was assuming all initial and collateral costs were at the same base line. In some cases, these costs could vary a few years in a construction project, but the complications involved did not warrant incorporation of additional refinement. Also, follow-on costs, for example, annual, replacement, would vary from the beginning of the year to the end of the year. Tables for annuity factors, and so forth, have been developed for beginning of the year, middle of the year, and end of the year values. In this article, all costs were end of the year values; the tables reflect that assumption.

CONCLUSION

With the advent of increasing interest rates and escalating energy and labor rates, the concept of life cycle costing for decision-making has become increasingly important. No major decision in the areas of buildings that involve large follow-on costs should be made without using the life cycle costing technique. This technique must be based on bringing all costs to a common base line—the concept of equivalent costs for comparison before selection.

Escalation factors based on differential factors should be applied if the evaluation group feels they are appropriate. It is recommended that when the evaluation group feels the data available are too variable, a sensitivity analysis should be conducted using the best available estimated escalation factors. Where savings are augmented by escalation, a stronger recommendation can be made. Where savings are compromised by escalation, a conditional recommendation should be made. Life cycle analysis techniques using the equivalent cost concept provide vital tools that should be used by all designers.

BIBLIOGRAPHY

1. A. J. Dell'Isola and S. J. Kirk, *Life Cycle Costing for Design Professionals,* McGraw-Hill, Inc., New York, 1981.
2. *Economic Analysis Handbook,* P-442, U.S. Naval Facilities Engineering Command, Washington, D.C., July 1980.
3. *Economic Studies for Military Construction Design Applications,* TM-5–802–1, U.S. Army Corps of Engineers.
4. A. Dell'Isola and S. J. Kirk, *Life Cycle Cost Data,* McGraw-Hill, Inc., New York, 1983.
5. NBS-GCR-ETIP 76–10, *Life Cycle Costing in the Procurement of Refrigerator–Freezers,* National Technical Information Service, Springfield, Va.

General References

Engineering Economy, 3rd ed., McGraw-Hill, Inc., N.Y., 1977.

E. L. Grant and W. Grant Ireson, *Principles of Engineering Economy,* The Ronald Press Company, New York, 1970.

D. S. Haviland, *Life Cycle Cost Analysis 2: Using It in Practice,* The American Institute of Architects, Washington, D.C., 1978.

LCC-1, Life Cycle Costing Procurement Guide, U.S. Department of Defense, Washington, D.C., July 1970.

LCC-2, Casebook—Life Cycle Costing in Equipment Procurement, U.S. Department of Defense, Washington, D.C., July 1970.

LCC-3, Life Cycle Costing Guide For System Acquisition, U.S. Department of Defense, Washington, D.C., January 1973.

Life Cycle Budgeting as an Aid to Decision Making, Building Information Circular, U.S. Department of Health, Education, and Welfare, Office of Facilities Engineering and Property Management, Washington, D.C., 1973.

Life Cycle Cost Analysis, A Guide for Architects, The American Institute of Architects, Washington, D.C., 1977.

Office Building Experience Exchange Report, The Building Owners and Managers Association International, Washington, D.C., published annually. Report includes data and analyses of office building costs. Over 1000 buildings and data are also broken down by age, height, size, and location of buildings.

Life Cycle Costing Template, Reston Microcomputer Consultants Inc., Herndon, Va., June 1988.

Alphonse J. Dell'Isola
Smith, Hinchman and Grylls
Washington, D.C.

LIFE SAFETY.

See Fire Safety—Life Safety; Movement of People

LIGHTING—DAYLIGHTING

Until the turn of the twentieth century and the invention of the electric light, daylight was considered a necessary component of all buildings. Since then, daylight's use has diminished until, with the introduction of the fluorescent lamp in the 1950s, the need for daylighting was all but dismissed except for what might be termed aesthetic and psychological purposes.

With the energy crisis of the 1970s, however, daylighting was seen as a potential technique for conserving energy in buildings. Electric lighting in commercial buildings, a significant portion of total enclosed space in the United States, typically consumed up to 40 and even 60% of a building's entire annual energy consumption. A renewed emphasis on the design of buildings to properly take advantage of daylight indicated that 20–50% of current energy consumption for lighting could be eliminated. Savings has been shown to be possible in other types of buildings also, but unless a building consumes a significant quantity of electric light energy, the percent of savings will be small. In the typical residence, for instance, the percent of total household energy devoted to electric lighting is very small and the use of daylight would probably not introduce a significant savings.

In any case, the introduction of daylight does not automatically conserve energy. Buildings must be properly designed to control and use the available daylight, and the electric lighting system must be of such a nature that lights can be turned off or dimmed (preferably automatically) where and when they are not needed. It is paradoxical that in a building that uses daylighting entirely, with no electric light use, there would be no creditable energy savings.

There are many other advantages to the use of daylight in buildings. Among them are the following:

1. *Aesthetic.* The play of light from apertures on surfaces and textures casting interesting and beautiful shadows and creating areas of light and dark; the endless variety of architectural moods and appearances due to the movement of the sun and the changing of the skies.
2. *Psychological.* The sense of well being associated with "natural" light rather than "artificial" light; the sense of orientation associated with the view to the exterior and a knowledge of current weather conditions; the sense of security associated with being able to see to the exterior and knowing how to exit if circumstances demand it for survival; the variation in lighting patterns and intensity that provide variety and visual stimulus.
3. *Health-related.* The bodily production of necessary vitamin D due to the presence of daylight and associated reduction in bone breakage, particularly in the elderly; improved resistance to infections, cardiovascular impairment, and some types of skin disorders; reduction of severe stress and time-lag problems associated with jet lag.
4. *Energy/cost related.* The reduction in use of electric lighting and associated energy consumption for both lighting and air conditioning; the use of sunlight in buildings to heat spaces during cold weather.

The achievement of all of these advantages is possible, but some understanding is required of the process for achieving good daylighting. That process includes the establishment of design objectives, determination of the daylight that is available for use in particular locales, determination of the amount of electric lighting that can be reduced, some guidelines for effective design, and techniques for analysis and quantification of daylighted building designs.

DESIGN OBJECTIVES

How people will wish to be able to see inside a building is a key factor in that building's design, operation, energy consumption, and cost. How well occupants will be able to see once they are in the finished building will be a key factor in productivity, satisfaction, and long-term costs. Thus, concerns for an economical, energy-conserving, and productive building must start with the issue of the quality of lighting to be provided, then move to the most appropriate techniques for accomplishing that end.

Any attempt to establish goals for building systems, components, or materials must consider the relationship of those goals to the overall goals of the design for the total building. Sometimes, specific subsystem goals must give way to the broader aims for the total environment.

In the context of energy, it is the conservation of energy consumed by the total building that is more important than what is consumed or conserved by any subsystem such as lighting. Building energy performance standards that have been adopted by many states and municipalities form the foundation for establishing targeted building energy use for specific types of buildings and site conditions.

Specific goals related to daylighting of buildings may be stated in simple terms: (*1*) get the daylight into all feasible areas of the building in significant, useful quantities; (*2*) distribute the daylight reasonably uniformly through all floor areas, with no significant dark spots; (*3*) avoid allowing direct sunshine into the building interior where visual tasks are critical; (*4*) avoid bringing daylight into the interior in such a way that it may cause visual discomfort (excessive brightness differences) or visual disability (glare); and (*5*) provide controls for the electric lighting so that it will be diminished or eliminated when not needed.

Each of these goals must be evaluated against some standard where such standards exist. For instance, necessary interior quantities of light for various visual tasks as well as criteria for judging other goals related to good visual acuity and quality lighting are put forth in the Illuminating Engineering Society (IES) *Lighting Handbook, Applications Volume* (1).

In terms of energy consumption, enough new buildings have been designed and built in recent years to indicate that with the introduction of daylighting, about 2 W/ft^2 of floor space for electric lighting is sufficient to provide good quality visual conditions. With good design, even greater savings can be achieved, but 2 W/ft^2 has emerged as a reasonable goal for the present.

DAYLIGHT AVAILABILITY

Three types of skies are generally associated with the daylighting of buildings; each provides different opportunities and problems.

1. The clear blue sky provides a relatively steady source of low-intensity light (eg, 2000–3000 fc on the ground), penetrated by direct sun of high intensity (eg, 6000–7000 fc, or 5000–10,000 fc of total light on the ground). (Note: One fc (footcandle) = 10.76 lx (lux), the metric equivalent. For practical purposes, 1 fc translates to 10 lx (eg, 10 fc = 100 lx).)
2. The overcast sky may be very dark, providing only a few hundred footcandles on the ground, or it may be extremely bright, producing several thousand footcandles. It can be excessively bright as viewed from inside a building, or it can be relatively dark in appearance.
3. The third type of sky is partly cloudy and is characterized by a blue background with bright, white clouds (often passing and changing shape very rapidly) with direct sunshine penetrating off and on. Intensities on the ground can change rapidly from 2000–3000 to 8000–10,000 fc. These clouds, when viewed from the interior of a building, can be exceedingly bright, causing excessive contrasts and visual discomfort (Fig. 1).

Throughout the United States, during the principal daylight hours, there is almost always enough light available from the sun and sky to provide illumination (several thousand footcandles) for most human visual tasks. Because the amount of daylight available from the sun and sky

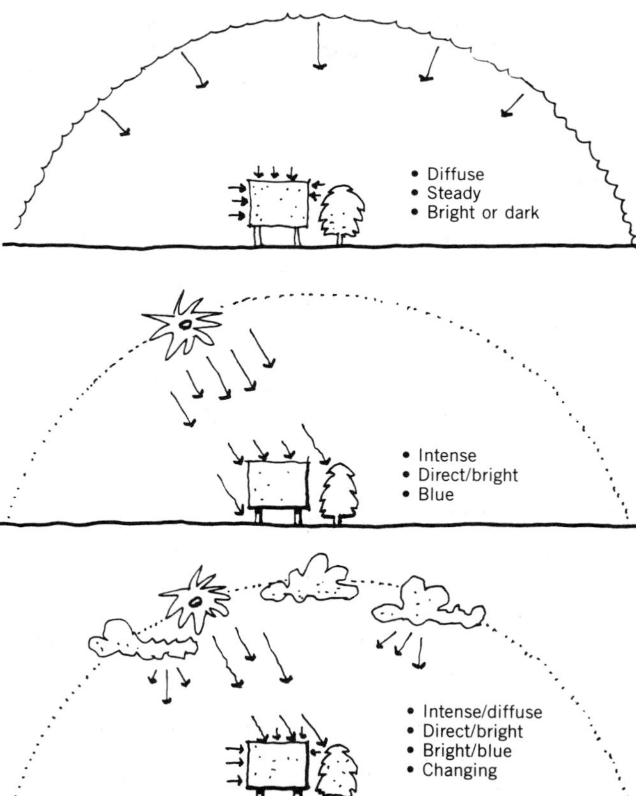

Figure 1. The three types of skies used in quantification of daylighting and electric lighting energy savings are overcast, clear with sun, and partly cloudy.

tends to change almost momentarily, it is impossible to predict with any precision what will be the interior daylighting conditions in any building at any moment, although excellent data are available on which to base an estimate of typical quantities of available exterior illumination.

However, it is not necessary that conditions be precisely predictable. The building designer will establish a set of goals to be achieved within a reasonable range of expected exterior daylight conditions and then will attempt to make the most of that available daylight, while providing a supplemental or alternative electric lighting system to contribute the necessary lighting when sky conditions are inadequate.

Decisions regarding the design of buildings and apertures will, of course, be somewhat based on the quantity and frequency of available daylight in a particular locale. Resources are available that provide data on anticipated daylight at particular locations based on time of the year, time of day, type of sky, and building orientation (2). These data are reasonably accurate and empirically quantified. However, they must be modified by localized data on historical cloud cover, which is generally not as predictable.

The process of designing for good daylighting is not critically dependent on the predictability of available daylight, but the justification for introducing daylight as an electric lighting energy-conserving agent is dependent on critical analysis and, therefore, on daylight predictability. Thus, data on availability is of significant importance in determining what periods of time in the life and operations of a building the electric lights must burn because daylight is not available in sufficient quantity. The process for analyzing electric lighting energy consumption is detailed later.

ENERGY USE

Energy-efficient design requires that the designer be concerned with three major aspects of the lighting system: (*1*) the heat gains and losses associated with the glazing used for daylighting; (*2*) the amount of electrical energy needed to operate the lights; and (*3*) the energy given off as heat in the electric lighting process, which must be considered in terms of its effect on the mechanical system operation (Fig. 2).

Solar and Conductive Losses/Gains

Solar heat gain results when isolation (direct and diffuse solar radiation) is converted into heat after passing through, in this case, an aperture. Heat gain can be of a relatively large magnitude, but it can be controlled through proper design such that gains are minimized during periods of net heat gain and maximized during peaks of net heat loss. Proper control may be achieved through geometric design or through the use of architectural controls (eg, overhangs, louvers, light shelves, blinds, screens) and/or light-controlling glazing (eg, selectively transmitting glass).

Although total heat gain from direct and diffuse solar radiation depends on the total fenestration design (including exterior overhangs and louvers), there may be times when only the glazing is involved. To determine the amount of solar heat that reaches the interior of a building through the glazing, three variables must be taken into consideration: (*1*) the amount of insolation available at the aperture; (*2*) the area (glass) exposed to radiation; and (*3*) the proportion of incident heat transmitted (available/transmitted).

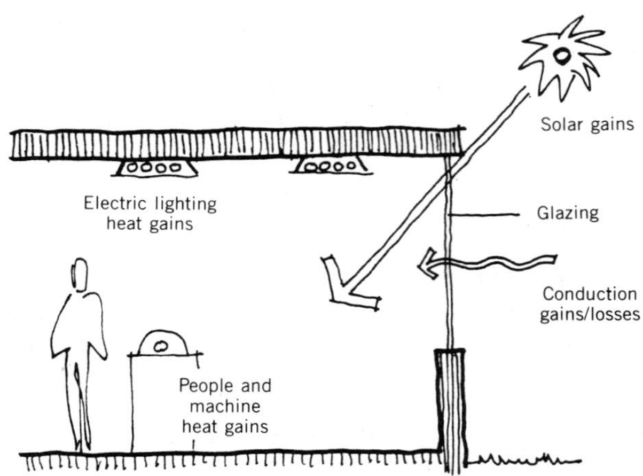

Figure 2. There are several means of heat exchange in daylighted buildings that are important to energy efficient and cost effective designs.

Available insolation can be taken from weather charts such as those available in the *ASHRAE Handbook of Fundamentals* (3), by hour and orientation of the building fenestration.

The area exposed to insolation is the number of square feet in a particular orientation and is a function of the building's geometry. The amount of insolation exposure can be partially optimized with building orientation.

Transmission of conductive heat between the exterior and interior depends on the U-value and transmissivity of the glazing (see manufacturer's literature). These thermal heat gains/losses depend on the differential between average outdoor temperature (t_0) and planned indoor temperature (t_i). The following formula may be used to calculate these thermal gains/losses:

$$\text{Annual thermal heat gains/losses} = \text{U-value} \times (t_0 - t_i) \times \text{exposed area} \times \text{days per year} \times \text{operating hours per day} = \text{Btu/yr}$$

Operating days may be used for a more general analysis. Annual solar heat gain through glazing can be calculated (for each different orientation) by using the following formula:

$$\text{Annual solar heat gain} = \text{insolation} \times \text{exposed area of glazing} \times \text{transmissivity of glazing or ``shading coefficient''} \times \text{days per year} \times \text{hours per day} = \text{Btu/yr}$$

(Note: Insolation is in Btu/h/ft^2.) Hours per year can be substituted for a more sophisticated analysis.

Thermal Effects

Calculation of the energy needed to operate a lighting system must include the energy consumption of the luminaires in a given space (total watts), multiplied by the hours per day of operation, multiplied by the days per year of operation, multiplied by the utilization factor (percent of total period lights will be on). The following equation can be used to compute the heat gain from lights:

$$\text{Heat gain} = \text{fc/ft}^2 \times \text{area} \times 0.06 \text{ W/fc} \times 3.41 \text{ Btu/h/W} = \text{Btu/h}$$

(Note: 1 W = 3.41 Btu/h.)

From the use profile developed for the building, the annual heat gain from the lighting system can be found by the following formula:

$$\text{Annual lighting heat gain} = \text{total watts} \times \text{lighted hours/day} \times \text{lighted days per year} \times \text{utilization factor} \times 3.41 \text{ Btu/W} \times \text{cooling load factor} = \text{Btu/yr}$$

Utilization is the ratio of wattage in use to the total installed wattage (in commercial buildings this ratio is usually one).

The cooling load factor (based on the number of hours per day that the lights are on) can be applied to achieve a more accurate calculation. The cooling load factor equals 1.0 if the cooling system is operated only when the lights are on, or if the lights are on more than 16 h/day. Cooling load tables are available in the *ASHRAE Handbook* (3). For fluorescent lamps, use a cooling load factor of 1.25.

Determining Electric Lighting Savings

In determining the amount of electric lighting energy to be saved with the use of daylighting, the following must be determined:

1. The amount of daylight incident on the aperture (vertical fenestration) at various times of the day and year. Usually these will be grouped into several typical periods.
2. The levels of daylight that will occur in various interior zones at the critical periods established in (1).
3. The periods of time during the year (occupied time) when various electric lights (usually by zone) can be turned off or dimmed.

Incident Daylight. The amount of available daylight to be expected on the aperture can be determined using the Solar Energy Research Institute (SERI) reference mentioned earlier (2). Usually these values will be grouped into average periods such as 12 typical periods, corresponding to months of the year, and further divided into expected hours of daylight for each day, usually corresponding to occupied times such as 8:00 A.M. to 5:00 P.M. For example, this suggested grouping will result in 2160 hourly periods over the year (12 months × 4 weeks × 5 days × 9 hours).

The expected incident daylight levels must be modified according to the percentages of time the sky will be overcast, partly cloudly, or clear, according to local weather data. The expected available daylight can be determined from the SERI reference as if the sky were to be clear 100% of the daylight hours per year, then multiplied by the expected percent of clear skies for the local area. The overcast sky can be treated in a similar manner. However, there are no data on daylight availability for partly cloudy skies, as these skies are so variable. Thus, the partly cloudy sky can be treated as an average between clear and overcast.

The result will be an approximation of available daylight for an average year. For a more detailed description of this process, see Refs. 4 and 5.

Interior Daylighting. Having derived the amount of incident daylight available for various periods of the year, it is next necessary to determine the expected daylighting levels in various interior areas of the building design. This is best accomplished through the testing of physical scale models or by calculation using the IES *Recommended Practice of Daylighting* (6), or one of several computer programs available for this purpose.

Electric Light Energy Saved. Having determined the probable daylight available to enter the aperture and knowing with a given amount of incident light what the interior daylight levels will be, it is then possible to calculate the number of hours per day, month, and year that various electric lights may be turned off or left burning and to determine the watts saved or consumed as follows:

$$\text{Annual lighting energy consumed} = \text{total watts/square foot} \times \text{floor area} \times \text{lighted hours/day} \times \text{lighted days/year} = \text{watts/year}$$

If the electric lighting system has not yet been designed when this analysis is needed, often an assumption is made that the electric lights will approximate 2 W/ft^2 of lighted floor space.

DESIGN GUIDELINES

Keeping in mind the specific goals for good daylighting discussed under Design Objectives, there are certain concerns associated with the design process.

Site Selection

In any kind of design for daylighting, some consideration should be given to conditions of the site. The selection of the site might be significantly influenced by daylighting considerations. Several features that should be considered follow:

1. The new building must be located on the site so that daylight can reach the apertures without significant interference from nearby obstacles. Is the property surrounded by tall buildings, mountains, trees, or other obstructions to daylight?

2. Highly reflective surfaces near the site, such as glass-covered buildings, could cause excessive glare on the interior.
3. Trees and shrubs on the site might be an asset to reduce the possibility of interior discomfort glare caused by a view from the interior of the bright sky or other nearby bright surfaces.

None of these features prohibit the use of daylight in a new building, but their implications for the design should be considered carefully.

Ground surfaces can be excessively bright (eg, white concrete illuminated by sunlight), so they must be shielded from view inside the new building. However, they also can contribute considerable daylight to the interior by reflection. As much as 40% of interior daylighting can be reflected from ground surfaces.

Building Configuration

If daylight is to be a consideration, multistory buildings will be most effective if they are long and narrow so that daylight will have an opportunity to penetrate to the deep interior from both sides. A rule of thumb is that useful daylighting with reasonably sized fenestration openings can be achieved to a depth of about 20 ft from the aperture. In a single-story building, skylights can be used, thus permitting the building to assume a more square shape.

Courtyards, light wells, and atria can be used effectively to admit some daylight, not only into the well opening, but into interior spaces in the building adjacent to the well. However, the effectiveness of such wells cannot be equated with the effectiveness of apertures exposed to the unobstructed outdoors.

The effectiveness of light wells can be improved by using high-reflecting finishes (white paint, concrete) on the well surfaces; if any direct sun illuminates these surfaces, they may be excessively bright if they can be viewed from the building interior (Fig. 3).

Building Orientation

Walls of any orientation may be used for effective daylighting, although the amount of daylight available will differ with each orientation. The essential difference in the quality and quantity of daylighting received from different orientations has to do with the direct sun. For instance, the south fenestration will receive direct sun, but the north will not, except, possibly, in the early morning or late afternoon. There is some difference in the brightness of the sky in different sky quadrants, but this difference is only of minor importance to the designer.

Apertures to the north will probably require larger glass areas than other orientations to achieve similar results. There can be certain advantages to the north orientation (eg, no sun control is necessary; illumination tends to be soft and diffuse), but sky glare control may still be required and heat losses in the winter may be a concern.

East and west fenestrations require treatment to avoid excessive brightness and overheating from the early morning and late afternoon low-altitude sun, which tends to move across the sky in relatively rapid fashion. This low-altitude sun, moving rapidly from east to south to west, is best controlled on the east and west facades by some type of vertical louver. Horizontal louvers provide no essential control until the sun is relatively high in the sky and often, by the time the sun reaches this point in its movement, its direct component switches to the south facade. To the east and west, vertical louvers that can be operated (preferably automatically) will best respond to the sun's changing location. If movable vertical louvers are not feasible, static louvers can still be used effectively, but with some limitation to vision to the exterior. Also, a combination of vertical and horizontal louvers can sometimes provide satisfactory control. In any case, the use of these orientations for daylighting should not be dismissed arbitrarily (Fig. 4).

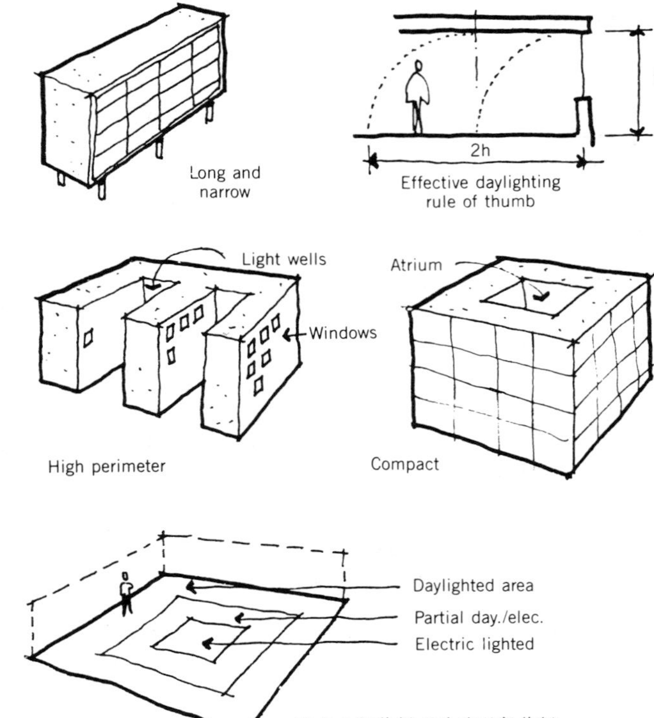

Figure 3. Optimum use of daylight in buildings suggests that the building shape provides a maximum of interior space adjacent to window walls. This must be balanced against the opportunities for use of compact building shapes for other energy conservation means.

The south-facing facade provides the best opportunity for daylighting because this orientation receives the maximum quantity and duration of daylight. Horizontal controls (eg, overhangs, louvers, venetian blinds) will provide control when the sun is in the southern quadrant. There is also the advantage with the south orientation that the sun, being high in the sky in the summer, can easily be shaded by a horizontal shading device that can be so designed to allow some low-altitude sun penetration during cold winter conditions (Fig. 5).

If this winter sun is allowed into the interior, care

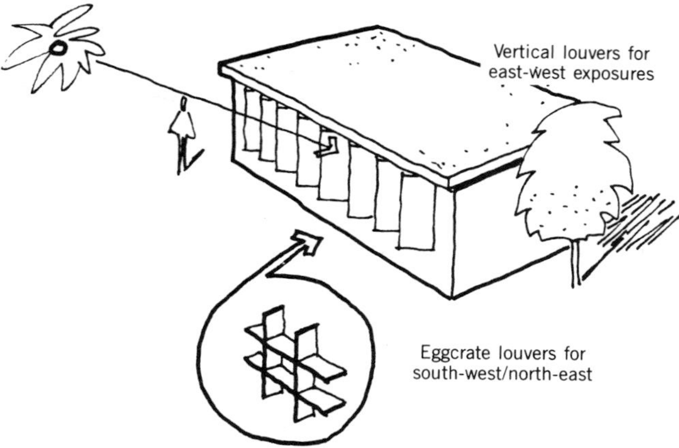

Figure 4. Vertical solar controls are most effective for easterly and westerly building orientations. Eggcrate type louvers can be effective for northeast and southwest orientations.

should be exercised to ensure that it will not result in excessive brightness in the occupant's field of view, thereby causing visual discomfort or disability.

Apertures

The amount of daylight that enters apertures is directly proportional to the site of the glazing and, of course, the daylight available to enter. The amount of daylight that reaches any point in the interior is related to the area and brightness of both the exterior sources of daylight and interior daylighted surfaces that are "seen" from that particular point. Thus, a point close to the aperture "sees" a larger portion of the sky and has a higher footcandle level than a point farther away from the aperture. Interior surfaces also contribute daylight and are influenced by light reflected from other surfaces, particularly the ground surface. Overhangs help to pick up ground-reflected daylight and direct it into interior spaces.

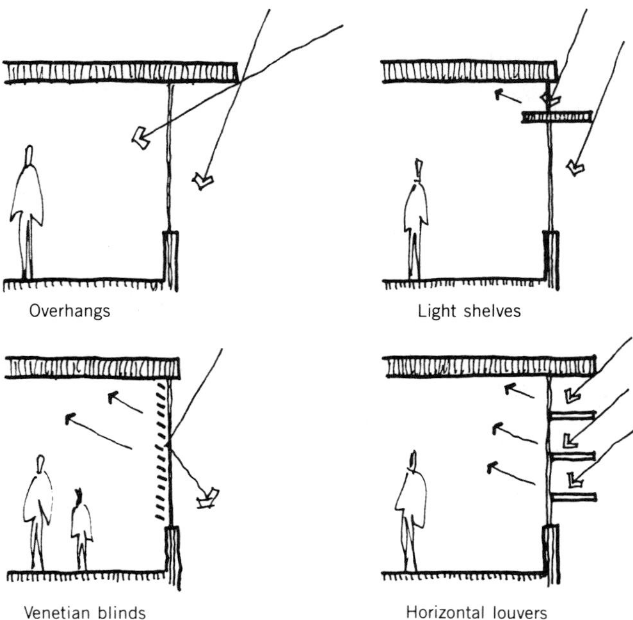

Figure 5. Southerly exposures are best shaded from direct sun by overhangs, horizontal louvers, light shelves, louvered screens, or venetian blinds.

To maximize daylighting results, interior surfaces should be kept light in color (high reflectivity), particularly the ceiling, which is the most important light-reflecting surface.

Clerestories in single-story buildings are useful apertures for introducing and distributing daylight deep into interiors and, being high in the ceiling, offer some advantage in being out of the normal field of vision so that sky brightness may not be a concern. Clerestories oriented to the east, west, and south will probably need some kind of control for direct sun, but controls are not needed when clerestories are oriented to the north. Light-colored roof materials such as white rock can be helpful in reflecting daylight into the interior, thereby increasing the effectiveness of the clerestory.

Skylights can also be used to allow daylight into the interior, but some type of control is usually necessary for handling direct sun, excessive thermal gains and losses, and interior visual brightness. Shading devices outside the skylight (above the roof) are the most effective in keeping out excess solar radiation, because light from the sky and reflected sunlight carry less heat (infrared) than does direct sun. Such controls can be located inside the building, but with less effective heat control, and can be used to prevent the skylight from producing excessive brightness as viewed from below. Diffusing ceiling panels of translucent glazing material, when illuminated by daylight, particularly direct sun, can create glare and veiling reflections on work tasks below (Fig. 6).

Skylights in the roof can collect solar energy, which may be helpful for heating as well as lighting in the winter, but can be detrimental in warm weather when the building is in the cooling mode. They can lose considerable energy day or night by exfiltration through cracks and by nighttime radiation to the exterior. Thus, shades and movable insulation should be considered. Double glazing is recommended in skylights for colder climates and triple glazing for severely cold climates.

Although the location of the aperture is an important element in the quantity and distribution of daylight to the interior, for purposes of preliminary thermal analysis associated with daylight, the amount of heat exchange between exterior and interior is essentially a function of the aperture size and glazing transmissivity. The aperture's location is relatively unimportant to this thermal exchange.

The size of the aperture is the principal factor in admitting daylight, but the character of the glazing used can also be a major factor. Common clear glass has a transmission factor of about 80–90%, depending on dirt accumulation. If a glazing material with a lower transmissivity is used (eg, tinted glass or high-performance glass), the size of the aperture must be increased to allow the same quantity of daylight to enter. For this reason, the use of low-transmission glazing materials tends to negate the opportunities for cost-effective daylighting.

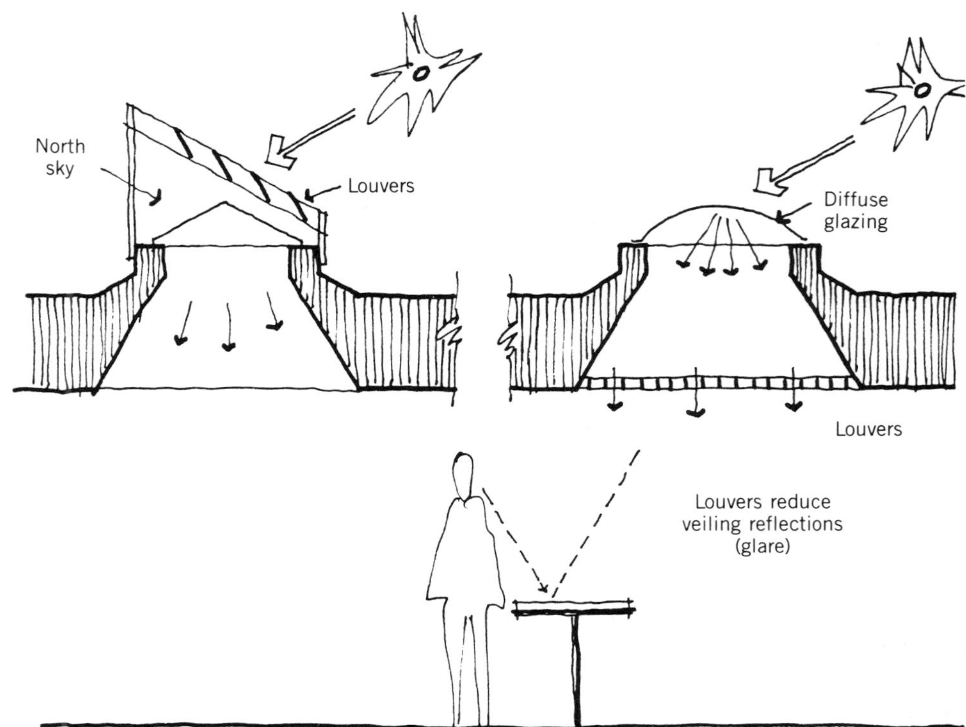

Figure 6. Skylights can be shielded from direct sun by exterior louvers. The inside view of skylights should be screened from view so as not to cause direct glare or veiling reflections in interior spaces.

Glare Control

Glare is potentially a problem with any source of light. With daylighting apertures, exterior surfaces illuminated by the sun become excessively bright as compared to interior surfaces illuminated by reflected daylight. The human eye has difficulty adjusting to distinguish detail when there is such a wide range of brightnesses. An occupant attempting a visual task when bright clouds are within the field of view will have difficulty distinguishing details. The glare may be a minor factor causing discomfort (causing the occupant to tire unnecessarily), or it may be a major factor preventing the occupant from seeing the task properly (causing visual errors) (Fig. 7).

The elimination of the effects of exterior glare (it can be interior glare if direct sun enters into the interior space)

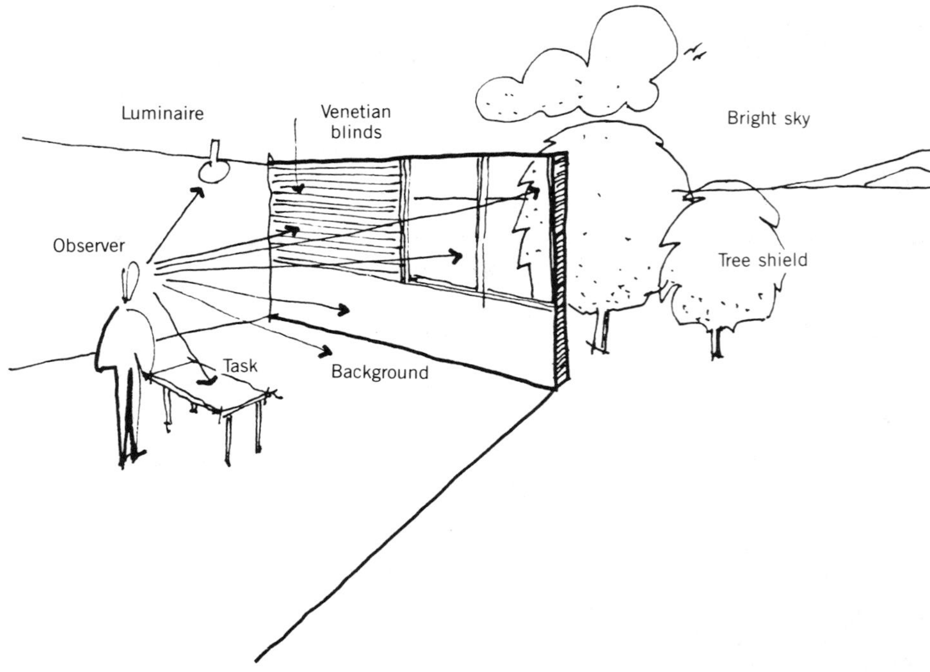

Figure 7. Brightness of various surfaces in the field of view of observers should be controlled to provide acceptable brightness ratios.

can be accomplished by preventing visual contact from the inside. One way to do this is to orient workstations so that occupants do not face toward the apertures while performing visual tasks. Of course, this is not always feasible. Trees planted outside the aperture to block the occupant's direct view of the bright sky and other outside surfaces can also be effective. Overhangs and louvers (on the exterior or interior) can likewise be effective. Venetian blinds, for instance, are excellent glare controls and have the advantage of being movable to accommodate different sky conditions and user needs. Drapes and curtains can also be effective, but care should be exercised in the selection of materials. Sheer curtains that restrict the view out to bright surfaces may themselves become excessively bright if illuminated by direct sun. Tinted glazing can also be used to reduce the apparent brightness of exterior surfaces. However, all of these techniques for reducing glare also reduce the amount of daylighting reaching the interior. Achieving a balance between glare control, aperture size, and glazing transmittance is a key element in daylighting design.

Glazing Materials

Glazing materials commonly used in buildings include clear glass (single or multiple layers), heat-absorbing glass, heat-reflecting glass, selectively transmitting glass, glare-control glass, and plastic sheets and panels that have good light transmittance. Each of these types of glazing has heat/light characteristics that are usually described by the manufacturer in current literature.

Heat-absorbing and heat-reflecting glasses are intended to eliminate the transmission of significant amounts of solar radiation heat. Selectively transmitting glasses reduce infrared (heat) transmission by a slightly greater percentage than they reduce visible light transmission and are thus somewhat useful in allowing daylight to enter while restricting heat entry. Apertures with selectively transmitting glass generally do not have as high a shading coefficient as apertures with exterior shading devices that totally shade the aperture from direct sun. The use of exterior shading devices is often overlooked as a cost-effective and energy-effective control.

DAYLIGHTING ANALYSIS PROCESSES

The creative design of a well-daylighted building will be based on a fundamental understanding of how daylight behaves and of the principles concerning its interaction with buildings. Analysis by physical or mathematical modeling may be used for checking a design or for refining details of the design, but analysis is not the design process itself. Design is the synthesis, or putting together, of many concerns into a workable and beautiful whole. Analysis is taking a whole apart to look at the separate parts. Nevertheless, there are many reasons why analysis may prove valuable.

Physical Scale Modeling

Physical scale models behave such that a scale model of a building will react to daylight (produce the same interior light distribution) as the full-scale building, assuming that the model is identical with the full-scale building and that they are both exposed to identical skies. Although these assumptions can never be completely achieved, scale models come closer to simulating the daylighting of real buildings than any other simulation technique now known (Fig. 8).

However, precise simulation is seldom the goal of the building designer. The designer's need is for a process that will be helpful in making decisions about the daylighting design—whether one scheme or detail is more productive than another. Scale-model studies can be used for determining the approximate illuminance levels to be achieved, for comparing design schemes, and for visually and photographically observing the daylighting results inside the model.

Scale-model studies may be conducted using simple and inexpensive materials and can provide answers regarding design alternatives with a minimum of time and energy. Scale models for daylighting studies are not unlike those often used by architects for conventional purposes. Some attention must be given to detailing, materials, and glazing and to an appropriate light meter.

Generally, it is not necessary to perform measurements for an entire building design, as there will usually be repetitive spaces (eg, classrooms in a school) or several special areas (eg, atrium, gym) that raise questions. Models of partial building areas will generally suffice and will be easier and less costly to build and test.

Models can be at any scale, but generally if they are built at less than ½ in. = 1 ft, reproduction of details and measurements will be more difficult. Surfaces can be of any material that is opaque (foam-core board is not opaque and must be covered or painted) and painted to approximate surface reflectances of the real building. Avoid using white board for all interior surfaces because this will indicate higher light levels than will actually be present in the real building where surfaces are usually darker and often dirty. Major obstructions such as partitions and dark furniture should be modeled. A transparent plastic material such as acetate can be used in glazed openings to approximate glass. It is often expedient when comparing two or more design details (skylights, clerestories, or fenestration alternatives, for instance) to construct

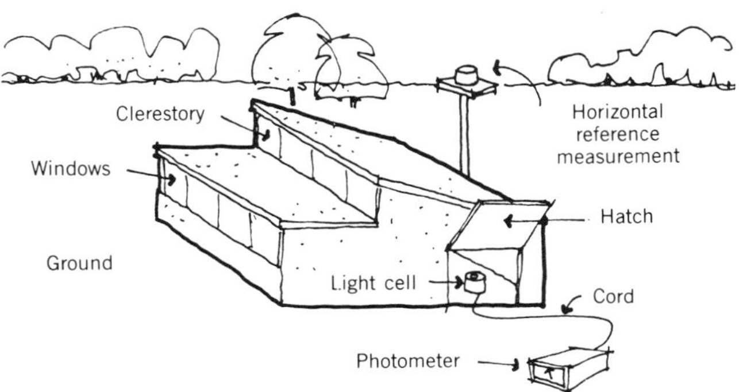

Figure 8. Daylighting studies can be performed on scale models outdoors with the use of a good photometer and with proper measurement techniques.

two or more model fenestrations or panels that can be easily and quickly exchanged during measurements.

The model should be tested outdoors under an overcast sky or under a totally clear sky where illuminances will generally remain reasonably constant for 30 min to 1 h. Partly cloudy skies should be avoided because of the generally rapidly changing conditions. An exterior measurement of the uninterrupted illumination on the horizontal plane (eg, ground or flat roof of model) will provide an indication of changeability in sky illuminances and provide a basis for comparing measurements made at different times. If this exterior illuminance changes as much as about 5% over a 30-min period (eg, 300 fc), two or more design schemes cannot be directly compared.

Photometers (light meters) should be color- and cosine-corrected and should have a remote sensor (photocell) so that the photocell can be placed inside the model and the illumination read from the photometer outside the model. The model should be constructed so that the cord connecting the photocell and the photometer can pass through the model shell. Usually some type of swinging access panel will facilitate moving the cell from one location to another inside the model.

The model should be set up outdoors where no nearby buildings or trees will obstruct the daylight reaching the model. Sometimes working from the top edge of a card table is convenient. Ground conditions should approximate the real ground conditions, although for comparing one design scheme to another, the type of ground may not be important. Several series of measurements should be made to help ensure that errors are not made or that the sky conditions have not changed significantly. For a complete explanation of the scale-modeling process see Ref. 4.

The Lumen Method

The first comprehensive daylight calculation technique was published by the Libby-Owens-Ford Company and has been referred to as the Lumen Method because of its similarity to the lumen method of calculating light levels from electric lights. This method was adopted by the IES in 1979 and is published in *Recommended Practice of Daylighting* (6), as well as in the *IES Handbook* (1).

It is an empiric method based on measurements of daylighting in a variety of scale models and actual buildings. The technique began with the measured daylighting results and worked back toward establishing a process by which those answers could be reached. Thus, it is a system of matching the characteristics of a proposed daylighting design with those represented in the method and then deriving the illuminance levels to be expected.

The Lumen Method of daylighting analysis involves the use of a number of coefficients of utilization and a formula for relating the size, shape, and materials of a building design to the available daylight. The daylight levels at three points in a rectangular room from both the sky and the ground can be determined for each point through the use of the following generalized formula:

Illumination on the work plane = available daylight on the vertical surface of the window × net area of glazing × transmission factor of glazing × K coefficient × C coefficient = footcandles

(Note: The interior illuminance levels from sky and sun are calculated separately from illuminance levels from ground-reflected light.) The method allows consideration for variances in room height, width, and length dimensions; room reflectances; glazing transmission; the use of overhangs, venetian blinds, and shades; and several other details in design. For a building whose characteristics fit the simulation circumstances of the Lumen Method, the resulting daylighting levels can be considered to be quite accurate. However, there are many building designs whose characteristics do not fit into the Lumen Method (eg, round rooms, sloping glass windows, atria, sloping ceilings, skylights) and, although some interpolation is possible, there are building designs for which the Lumen Method is not appropriate.

Computerized Methods

Several programs are available for calculating daylight illuminance levels through the use of programmable calculators, microcomputers, and mainframe computers. Each of these programs requires special input data and each is based on certain assumptions regarding how buildings respond to daylight. Each has some limitations as to the building configurations that can be simulated. Thus, it is the responsibility of the user to know something of the particular computer and computer program to be used and any limitations regarding the application of the results.

One programmable calculator program is *Quicklite I* (7). The program is relatively fast and simple and applicable to typical building shapes and materials. It will not simulate the contributions to interior spaces from direct sun or from skylights. An enhanced version of Quicklite is available for use with some personal computers.

A similar program, called *Energy* (8), for use with some personal computers, can provide daylighting results as well as annual energy savings due to daylighting.

Daylite (9) calculates daylight factors for a room for overcast and clear sky conditions (including direct sun) and includes a routine for dealing with certain complementary electric lighting schemes and performing an energy analysis.

Mainframe computer programs including *Superlite* (10), *DOE-2.1B* (10), *Lumen III* (8), *Uwlight* (11), and others are capable of sophisticated computations involving building configurations of all but the most complex geometries and materials. Several combine daylight and electric lighting calculations, and most include the resulting energy analysis.

BIBLIOGRAPHY

1. *IES Lighting Handbook, Applications Volume,* Illuminating Engineering Society of North America, New York, 1981.
2. C. L. Robbins and K. C. Hunter, *Daylight Availability Data for Selected Cities in the United States,* Solar Energy Research Institute, Golden, Colo., 1982.

3. *ASHRAE Handbook 1985 Fundamentals,* American Society of Heating, Refrigerating and Air-Conditioning Engineers, Atlanta, Ga., 1985.
4. B. H. Evans, *Daylight in Architecture,* Architectural Record Books, McGraw–Hill, New York, 1981, Chapt. 5.
5. C. L. Robbins and K. C. Hunter, *A Method of Predicting Energy Savings Attributed to Daylighting,* Solar Energy Research Institute, Golden, Colo., 1982.
6. *Recommended Practice of Daylighting,* RP-5, Illuminating Engineering Society of North America, New York, 1979.
7. H. Bryan, R. Clear, J. Rosen, and S. Selkowitz, "Quicklite I. New Procedure for Daylighting Design," *Solar Age* (1982).
8. *Energy,* Lighting Technologies, Inc., Boulder, Colo.
9. *Daylite,* SolarSoft, Inc., Snowmass, Colo.
10. S. Selkowitz, "The DOE-2 and Superlite Daylighting Programs," *Proceedings, Seventh National Passive Solar Conference,* American Solar Energy Society, New York, 1982.
11. J. R. Bedrick, M. S. Millet, G. S. Spencer, D. R. Heerwagen, and G. B. Varey, "The Development and Use of the Computer Program Uwlight for the Simulation of Natural and Artificial Illumination in Buildings," *Proceedings, Second National Passive Solar Conference,* American Solar Energy Society, New York.

General References

F. Birren, *Light, Color, and Environment,* Reinhold, New York, 1969.

P. R. Boyce, *Human Factors in Lighting,* Macmillan, New York, 1981.

M. D. Egan, *Concepts in Architectural Lighting,* McGraw–Hill, New York, 1983.

B. H. Evans, *Daylighting in Architecture,* Architectural Record Books, McGraw–Hill, New York, 1981.

J. K. Holton, *Daylighting of Buildings: A Compendium and Study of Its Introduction and Control,* National Bureau of Standards, Washington, D.C., 1976.

R. G. Hopkinson and J. D. Kay, *The Lighting of Buildings,* Praeger, New York, 1969.

How to Predict Interior Daylight Illumination, Libbey-Owens-Ford Co., 1976.

IES Lighting Handbook, Illuminating Engineering Society, New York, 1972.

W. C. M. Lam, *Perception and Lighting as Formgivers for Architecture,* McGraw–Hill, New York, 1977.

W. C. M. Lam, *Sunlighting as a Formgiver for Architecture,* Van Nostrand Reinhold Company, Inc., New York, 1986.

L. Larson, *Lighting and Its Design,* Whitney Library of Design, New York, 1964.

W. J. McGuiness, B. Stein, and J. S. Reynolds, *Mechanical and Electrical Equipment for Buildings,* John Wiley & Sons, Inc., New York, 1986.

F. Moore, *Concepts and Practices of Architectural Daylighting,* Van Nostrand Reinhold, New York, 1985.

D. Phillips, *Lighting in Architectural Design,* McGraw–Hill, New York, 1964.

Recommended Practice of Daylighting, Illuminating Engineering Society, New York, 1979.

See also LIGHTING—ELECTRIC; MECHANICAL SYSTEMS; SOLAR DESIGN

BENJAMIN EVANS, FAIA
Virginia Polytechnic Institute and State University
Blacksburg, Virginia

LIGHTING—ELECTRIC

Light, and its impact on the human eye, is one of the principal ways through which people interact with their surroundings. The other human senses are also important, but none is quite so important to so many as the ability to see. Thus, interaction of a person with the environment depends principally on the lighting environment. That interaction is usually related to both the perception of beauty (eg, architecture) and productivity (ie, performing visual tasks).

There are two basic sources of light for buildings: daylight and electric (or manufactured) light. In most cases they must function both separately and together to produce a satisfactory lighting environment.

Energy consumption is an important issue in the lighting of buildings. It takes energy to produce lighting; along with that, heat is produced. When the building is being cooled, that heat must be taken away by the air conditioning system, which requires the use of additional energy. Since energy is becoming increasingly scarce and its cost is constantly escalating, the use of energy-efficient and cost-effective lighting systems is an important concern to building developers, owners, and operators and, therefore, must be one of the designer's primary concerns.

Thus, the design of lighting systems for buildings is critically important for the majority of people who will occupy those buildings; any successful lighting design should encompass both the aesthetic and the functional aspects associated with seeing, and do it with optimal use of energy.

The process of designing for lighting is no different from any other design process except for the basic elements involved. The designer must: establish goals and objectives based on a fundamental understanding of the behavior of light and the way occupants are expected to interact with the building and the lighting system; set criteria for the performance of the lighting system against which success can be measured; and select and specify the hardware that will fill the criteria and accomplish the goals and objectives established.

There are no mathematical formulas to produce a good lighting design. There are techniques for analyzing a proposed system which is intended to produce a particular design, but these techniques will not of themselves produce a design. That must come from a creative designer who is sensitive to and knowledgeable of the possibilities and who can integrate lighting concerns with all of the other concerns related to a comprehensive and holistic architectural design. The subject of lighting is complex and cannot be covered entirely here. This article is intended to provide a brief guide for developing a lighting design, insofar as the lighting of interiors of buildings is concerned, and to supply data and/or references concerning principal factors involved.

DEFINITIONS

Some understanding of basic and frequently used concepts and terms is necessary for lighting design. For further definitions see the Illuminating Engineering Society (IES) Lighting Handbook (1).

Light. Radiant energy that is capable of exciting the retina and producing a visual sensation. The visible portion of the electromagnetic spectrum extends from about 380 to 770 nanometers (nm = unit of wavelength equal to 10^{-9} m).

Lumen (lm). SI unit of luminous flux.

Luminous flux. Time rate of flow of light (unit: lumen). *Note:* Since light is almost instantaneous, time is usually ignored. Therefore, flux becomes a unit of instant "quantity."

Illuminance (E). The density of luminous flux incident upon a surface (unit: lumens per unit area, footcandle, or lux).

Footcandle (fc). A unit of illuminance, (fc = lumens per square foot). One footcandle is the illuminance produced on a surface, all points of which are at a distance of one foot from a directionally uniform point source of one candela (one footcandle = 10.76 lux).

Lux (lx). SI unit of illuminance (lx = lumens/square meter).

Illumination. The act of illuminating or being illuminated.

Luminous intensity (l). The luminous flux of a point source per solid angle in the direction in question (unit: candela or lumens per steradian).

Candlepower. Luminous intensity expressed in candelas; a source of one cd produces an illuminance of one footcandle on the inside surface of a surrounding sphere of one-foot radius.

Candela (cd). The SI unit of luminous intensity.

Luminance (formerly, photometric brightness). For practical purposes, the unit of luminance is the footlambert; a surface reflecting, transmitting, or emitting one lumen of illumination per square foot of area in the direction being viewed has an illuminance of one footlambert (In general, luminance = illuminance × reflectance).

Brightness. Strength of sensation which results from viewing surfaces from which light comes to the eye. (This is a subjective term for which there are no units.)

Transmission. General term for the process by which incident flux passes through a medium, leaving the other side without a change in frequency.

Transmittance. The ratio of the transmitted flux to the incident flux (unit: %).

Reflectance. The ratio of the reflected flux to the incident flux (unit: %).

Absorptance. The ratio of the flux absorbed by a medium to the incident flux (unit: %). All of the incident flux is accounted for by the process of reflection, transmission, and absorption.

Visual acuity. The ability to distinguish fine detail.

Visibility. The quality or state of being perceivable by the eye.

Luminous contrast. The relationship between the luminances of an object and its immediate background.

Veiling reflection. Regular reflections superimposed upon diffuse reflections from an object (eg, book) that partially or totally obscure the details to be seen (eg, writing) by reducing the contrast. This is sometimes called reflected glare. It occurs at a particular angle between the light source, the task, and the observer, often referred to as the "mirror" angle.

Equivalent sphere illumination (ESI). The level of sphere illumination which would produce task visibility equivalent to that produced by a specific lighting environment. Sphere illumination is the illumination on a task from a source providing equal luminance in all directions about that task, such as an illuminated sphere with the task located at the center.

Luminaire. A complete lighting unit consisting of a lamp or lamps, together with the parts provided to distribute the light, to position, operate, and protect the lamps, and to connect the lamps to the power supply.

Lamp. A generic term for a human-made source of light.

Inverse square law. The light from a point source striking a surface decreases as that surface gets farther away from the source. This is defined by the Inverse Square Law, which states that the illuminance at a point on a surface varies directly with the intensity of a point source, and inversely as the square of the distance between the source and the point.

This principle is often used in the calculation of illuminance on a surface from a luminaire. Single incandescent lamps are considered point sources and illuminance produced by that lamp on a surface (eg, table or floor) can be calculated using the luminous intensity (l) or candlepower of the lamp (in candelas) with the following formula based on the Inverse Square Law:

$$\text{Footcandles} = \frac{1}{D^2} \text{Cos } \theta$$

LIGHTING DESIGN GOALS

There are many aspects of lighting design that may be encompassed in a set of goals for the designer. It sometimes is difficult to achieve, simultaneously, all of the potential elements of what may be considered good design. Indeed, it is difficult just to delineate all such elements for they are often as much a matter of taste as they are technology.

Some of the elements that go to make up a good lighting design are considered more or less concrete in nature, that is, they can be technically quantified (eg, reflected glare); and some (eg, aesthetics) are much more subjective and depend on taste, cultural background, and so forth. The following discussion is intended to suggest some of those elements that might be considered significant.

Aesthetics

A good lighting design should help to make clear the intent of the designer in any particular space. That is, the lighting

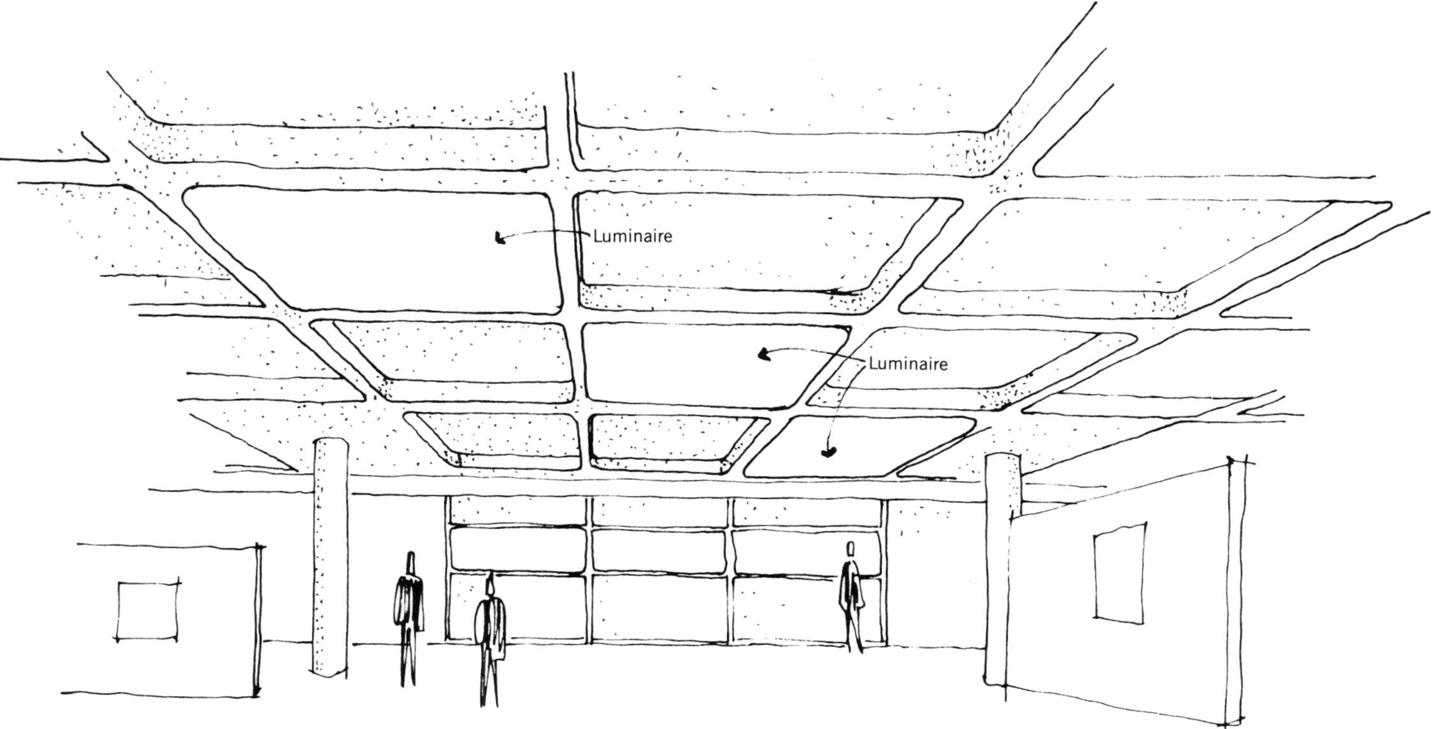

Figure 1. Lighting systems should complement rather than confuse a strong structural expression.

should emphasize those things that the designer considers significant and should not detract from his intent. A lighting design which attempts to redirect that intent (perhaps done by a separate designer) will result in confusion and failure of the original goals. For instance, if the building structural system is obvious and dominant, the lighting should emphasize the structure's continuity and not obscure it (2) (Fig. 1).

Large surfaces such as walls, ceilings, and floors are generally expected to be flat, and vertical or horizontal. Thus, they tend to be perceived that way unless the lighting confuses the issue and makes them appear uneven or unnatural. Viewers will instinctively feel uncomfortable under these conditions (Fig. 2).

A good lighting system design should place emphasis on lighting the objects and surfaces that are to be seen, rather than on the appearance of the lighting fixtures themselves. It is important to avoid the issues of excessive brightness and brightness distribution patterns associated with lamps and/or luminaires that can be viewed directly. Of course, in the case where the sparkle or appearance of a lamp or luminaire is intentionally part of the design, exposed low-brightness lamps can be visually acceptable.

The lighting system should appear to be part of the total building design and not cause or add to any visual confusion or ambiguity. Often, too many visible fixtures or patterns of light can cause an observer to focus visually on the wrong things or to be unable to focus on any single thing without a struggle. The lighting system can be used to focus that attention on one area or to provide for a selection among several focal points, provided that the system does not cause confusion.

Relationships between visual focuses and background is another point of concern. Sometimes lighting the background evenly, such as a wall, will emphasize an object in the foreground more appropriately than lighting the foreground object itself. Conversely, if the background brightness is excessive, view of the foreground may be obscured because of the eye's tendency to adapt to the brightest area in view.

Lighting for social environments presents special kinds of situations where the appearance of faces and the mood of the surroundings are critical to social intercourse. Low levels of illumination, especially reflected from table tops and floor surfaces, help to eliminate harsh shadow patterns on human faces and warm light, tending toward the red end of the spectrum (eg, incandescent, candle) helps create the illusion of a desirable soft, ruddy complexion. Bright areas tend to stimulate people, low brightness to soothe.

The above are only a few of the objective concerns that should be a part of the designer's goals. Several resources for more detailed discussions are included in the General References. A discussion of some of the more objective elements of good lighting and seeing follows.

Good Seeing

Quantity of Light. Light is necessary to the visual process. Just how much light is needed for any visual task

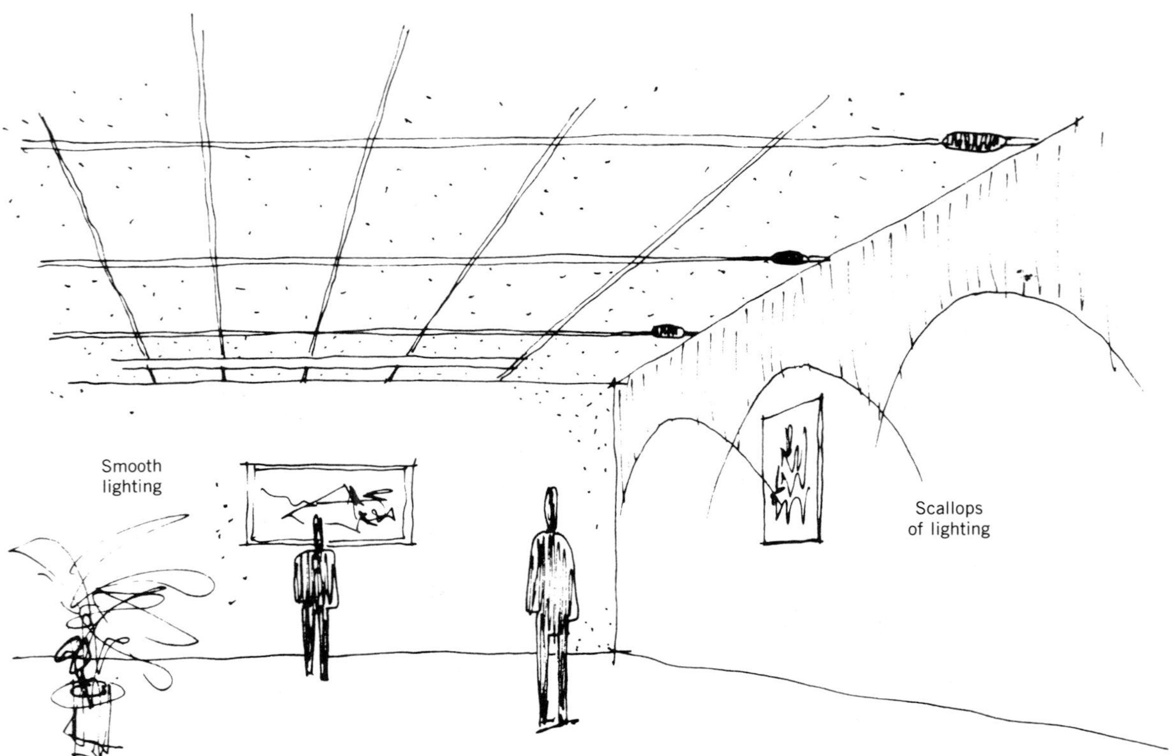

Figure 2. Uncomfortable visual conditions may result when lighting makes smooth walls and surfaces appear uneven.

depends on the physical characteristics of the viewer (eg, older people generally require more light), the nature of the task, and the circumstances under which the task is to be viewed. While the quantities recommended for various tasks have been debated in recent years, the IES recommends illuminance levels for various tasks, reached by consensus, on the basis of empirical and scientific research (1). The IES-recommended light levels were developed in response to the energy-related need to avoid unnecessarily high overall levels. The IES procedure for selecting light levels is based on specific tasks to be performed, weighted for differences in viewer age, the type of task, and the task background brightness. This prompts a critical analysis of any area to be lighted according to specific task, not by whole rooms. Providing levels of light suitable for specific tasks can save energy (Table 1).

Luminance (Brightness). Luminance (brightness as the eye perceives it) is also critical to the seeing process. The eye does not see light; rather, it sees surfaces that have brightness because they are lighted. Luminance is a function of the light striking a surface and the reflectivity of that surface. A dark surface has lower brightness, a light surface higher brightness, even though both receive the same quantity of light. Thus, surfaces must have brightness to be seen, regardless of the quantity of light striking them. Light sources such as electric lamps, the sun, and the sky also emit irradiance which appears to the eye as brightness (Fig. 3).

Further, for the eye to distinguish between surfaces, those surfaces must have different brightnesses. That is, there must be brightness contrast. For instance, it is difficult to distinguish between two green walls. Black lettering on black paper cannot be seen. Maximum contrast between specific task (eg, printed letters) and immediate background (eg, white paper) increases visibility (the eye's ability to distinguish fine detail), and reduces the amount of light needed.

However, excessive contrasts in brightness between immediate task background (eg, paper) and surrounding background (eg, clouds seen through the window) can produce eye-adaptability problems, or glare, which should be kept to a minimum (Fig. 4). An example of excessive brightness contrast (eg, auto headlights in the field of view, surrounded by darkness) can prevent the driver from seeing the road.

Glare. Glare is perhaps the most common cause of lighting complaints from building occupants. It may be discomfort glare, which is not generally discernible, but which can lead to annoyance, irritation, fatigue, and/or headaches. Alternately, it may be disability glare which actually interferes with ability to see a task. Discomfort glare may be caused by bright lights in the periphery of one's view or by direct light reflected off a task surface (book page).

Disability glare is perhaps the most critical criterion for a good quality lighting system. It may be caused by the reflection of a light off the specular surface of a task (veiling reflection) that reduces contrast and prevents discrimination of detail, or it may be caused by a very bright

Table 1. Illuminance Categories and Illuminance Values for Generic Types of Activities in Interiors[a]

Type of Activity	Illuminance Category	Ranges of Illuminances		Reference Work Plane
		Lux	Footcandles	
Public spaces with dark surroundings	A	20–30–50	2–3–5	
Simple orientation for short temporary visits	B	50–75–100	5–7.5–10	General lighting throughout spaces
Working spaces where visual tasks are only occasionally performed	C	100–150–200	10–15–20	
Performance of visual tasks of high contrast or large size	D	200–300–500	20–30–50	
Performance of visual tasks of medium contrast or small size	E	500–750–1000	50–75–100	Illuminance on task
Performance of visual tasks of low contrast or very small size	F	1000–1500–2000	100–150–200	
Performance of visual tasks of low contrast and very small size over a prolonged period	G	2000–3000–5000	200–300–500	
Performance of very prolonged and exacting visual tasks	H	5,000–7,500–10,000	500–750–1000	Illuminance on task, obtained by a combination of general and local (supplementary lighting)
Performance of very special visual tasks of extremely low contrast and small size	I	10,000–15,000–20,000	1000–1500–2000	

[a] Ref. 2. Courtesy of the Illuminating Engineering Society of North America.

light source in the field of view that prevents discrimination of detail beyond the light source (eg, book held in front of a window where bright clouds may be seen). Disability glare can also be caused by incorrectly screened light sources, large or small bright surfaces near the task, or by light reflected off the task into the eye. All of the recommended illuminance levels from the IES are based on the assumption that there will be no disability glare on the task (Fig. 5).

Providing a lighting system that avoids glare is much more important than simply producing a recommended footcandle level. A lighting system that produces glare will require much higher levels of light to achieve similar visibility. Conversely, a lighting system that does not create disability glare will require the production of less light. One way to avoid disability glare altogether is with the use of indirect lighting. That is, illuminating the ceiling with light sources hidden from view where that light is then reflected diffusely to the work area below. In many cases, an indirect lighting system may provide better lighting with less energy consumption than direct lighting that produces glare.

Methods of reducing disability and discomfort glare include the following:

Watts
(energy consumed)
Candlepower (cd)
(intensity)
Lumens
(lamp output—quantity)
Luminance (lumens/ft^2)
(brightness of source or surface)
Illuminance
(foot candles or lux)
Reflectance (%)
(ratio of reflected to incident light)
Absorptance (%)
(ratio of absorbed to incident light)
Transmittance (%)
(ratio of transmitted to incident light)

Figure 3. A graphic expression of lighting terms.

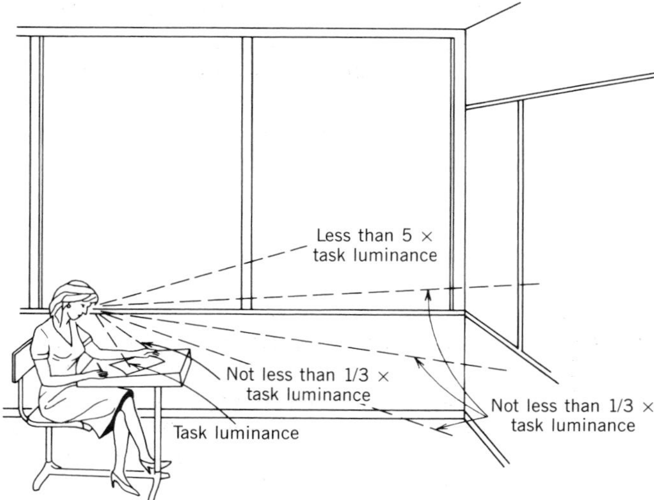

Figure 4. Recommended luminance ratios for a classroom. In a classroom the luminance of significant surfaces should not differ greatly from the visual task. The luminance of the surface immediately surrounding the task should be less than the task but not less than one-third the task luminance. The lowest acceptable luminance of any significant surface should not be less than one-third the task luminance. The highest acceptable luminance should not be greater than five times the task luminance (2). Courtesy of the Illuminating Engineering Society of North America.

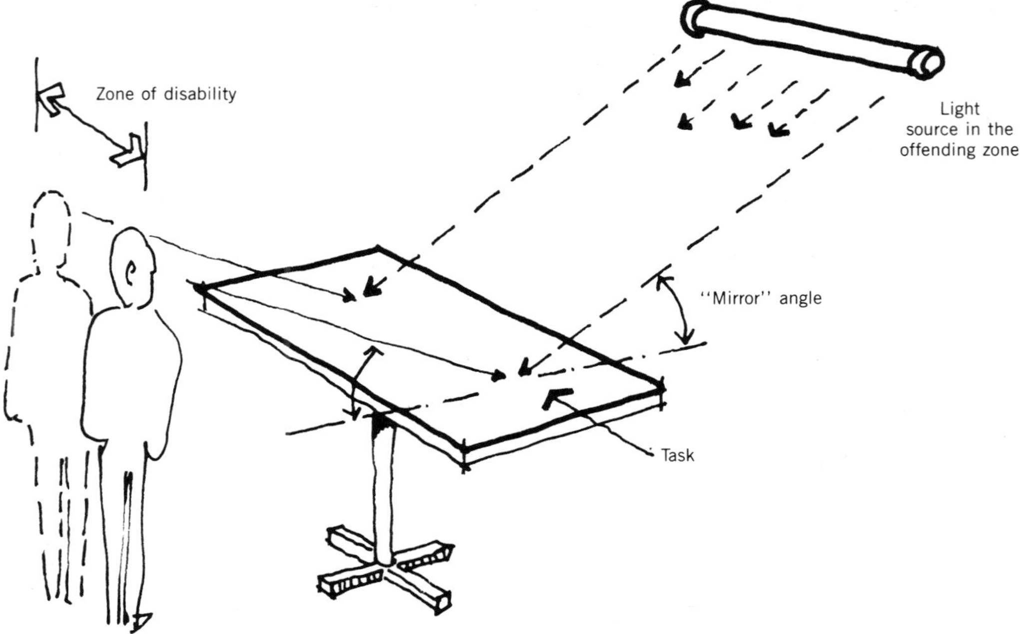

Figure 5. Veiling reflections (which occur at the "mirror angle") cause loss of contrast, requiring increased levels of illuminance, and should be avoided.

- Locating the light source so that it is not in the field of view.
- Raising luminaires above eye level (disability glare is rapidly reduced until, at an angular displacement of 40°, it is almost negligible).
- Shielding the light source from view with louvers.
- Reducing the brightness of the light source (translucent diffuser), although this also reduces lumen output.
- Increasing the brightness of areas surrounding the light source (eg, ceiling).
- Increasing the brightness of the task.

Color

The color of a surface represents the ability of the surface to modify the color of the light incident upon it. Thus, what the human eye sees as "color" is affected by the color of the light and by the nature of the surface being viewed. It does this by a process called selective absorption. Through this process, the surface absorbs some of the light incident upon it, reflecting or transmitting that light which is rich in a single hue. The hue is that attribute by which colors such as red, green, and blue are recognized. The color reflected or transmitted is perceived by the eye as the color of the surface. A surface is colorless when it does not exhibit selective absorption. Thus, white, black, and shades of gray are colorless.

The difference between colors of the same hue is called value. The value of a coloration is related to its reflectance of white (total spectrum) light. The higher the value, the higher the reflectance factor.

Colors of the same hue and value may still differ in saturation, which is an indication of the color's variation in gray, or the purity of the color. Pure gray has no hue. As color is added, the saturation is changed without changing the value. Spectral colors have 100% purity and therefore maximum saturation.

All three of these characteristics, hue, value, and saturation, are used to describe a coloration. A dab of yellow water color on paper produces the hue, or color, of yellow. If more yellow is added to the same dab, the saturation of yellow is increased. If a dab of gray (colorless) is added to the same mixture, the hue is still yellow, but the value, or brightness, of the spot is reduced.

Pigments produce color on a surface by the subtractive process. That is, each pigment subtracts or absorbs certain portions of white light and leaves only that color that finally constitutes the hue, value, and saturation of the pigment. Conversely, when light sources which include the three primary colors of red, green, and blue are combined, they form white by an additive process.

Light of a particular hue, other than white, is not often used in general illumination. However, the many different types of lamps used in building illumination each produce light with somewhat different spectral or color qualities. Their color qualities should be matched to the needs for a particular environment. In general, those which are nearest to white light, or sunlight, tend to be more desirable but also expensive to operate. One of the least expensive lamps to operate is the sodium lamp. It produces a monochromatic light almost entirely limited to the yellow or yellow–orange range, which is generally not suitable for most interior activities. When a space is lighted with "colored" light, the eye tends to adapt by a phenomenon known as color constancy so that it can, to a degree, recognize colors of surfaces in spite of the spectral quality of the light. However, the use of such monochromatic light would not be appropriate where proper rendition of colors is important.

Light sources (lamps) can be categorized by color temperature in Kelvin. When a "black body" is heated, it will first glow deep red, then cherry red, then orange until it finally becomes blue-white hot. The color of the light radiated is thus related to the temperature at which the black body must be heated to produce that color. The color of light emitted by all lamps can then be related to the temperature, in Kelvin, of the black body which produces that color. Of course, the color temperature of a light source is an indication only of the color of light produced and not of the lamp temperature. Incandescent lamps tend to produce a yellow-orange light (said to be a "warm" light), sodium a very yellow light. Fluorescent lamps are available which produce light from bluish-white (similar to daylight) to deluxe white warm (red end of the spectrum). A variety of mercury and metal halide lamps are available which produce light rich in yellow, blue, and/or green.

Color-rendering properties of various lamps are denoted by their Color Rendering Index (CRI). The CRI provides a method of comparing the color rendering properties of a lamp with those of a standard "all spectrum" lamp. Thus, the CRI provides a method for determining the relative abilities of light sources to render color as they might appear under daylight (standard).

LIGHT DISTRIBUTION SYSTEMS

There are three basic methods for delivering light generally to building interiors. The selection of the method will be a significant factor in the quality, efficiency, and cost of the lighting produced. There are many special lighting needs in buildings which require particular kinds of light for particular tasks which will not be covered here.

Direct Lighting

Direct lighting is delivering the light from a source in a direct route to the task. This often implies luminaires mounted in, on, or suspended from the ceiling. However, direct lighting is also supplied by task lights, such as floor or table lamps. Where direct lighting is used, all of the light leaving the luminaire is directed to the work plane. In direct systems, distribution of light from the luminaire may be modified, or controlled, through the use of reflectors, lenses, and/or baffles. Direct lighting is most commonly used in general lighting where the level of illuminance produced on the work plane is relatively uniform throughout a particular area. However, sometimes direct lighting in the ceiling can be used to provide a high level of task lighting in a particular area and low-level general lighting in another area as needed, optimizing the use of electric energy. Systems that are designed to illuminate several specific tasks in a building interior may not serve needs properly when the furniture or visual tasks are changed with time. Thus, flexibility in relocating luminaires should be a consideration in any design.

Advantages of a direct lighting system include:

- The production of quantities of light on the work plane with maximum efficacy (watts per lumen delivered).
- Simplicity of design and installation.
- Ease of maintenance.
- Low first costs.

The disadvantages are that the potential for the creation of disability and discomfort glare is high and, unless safeguards are taken, the quality of the lighting produced may be poor for critical tasks, thus losing the benefits outlined above (Fig. 6).

Indirect Lighting

Indirect lighting means reflecting light from a luminaire off a ceiling or other surface to illuminate tasks on the work plane where the luminaire delivers no light directly. Indirect lighting can be produced by luminaires suspended from the ceiling, but directed toward the ceiling, hidden in wall coffers, or mounted in furniture or freestanding units directed toward the ceiling and/or walls. Indirect lighting greatly reduces the probability of disability or discomfort glare, but depends largely on the proximity and surface treatment of the ceiling and wall surfaces in the space to be lighted. In effect, the room surfaces become part of the lighting system where location of the light sources and treatment of surfaces are important factors.

While indirect lighting can be used for critical task lighting and provide excellent quality seeing conditions, the quantities of light required to be produced may be much higher than with direct lighting and, hence, increase energy consumption. However, indirect lighting often provides the opportunity for use of efficient, high intensity discharge lamps which can be more energy-efficient than other types. More often, indirect lighting is used to provide general illumination of relatively low intensity (Fig. 7).

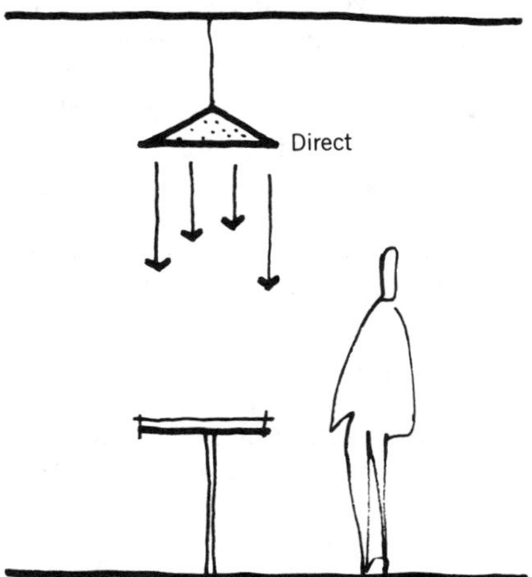

Figure 6. With direct lighting the luminaire distributes its light to the area directly below.

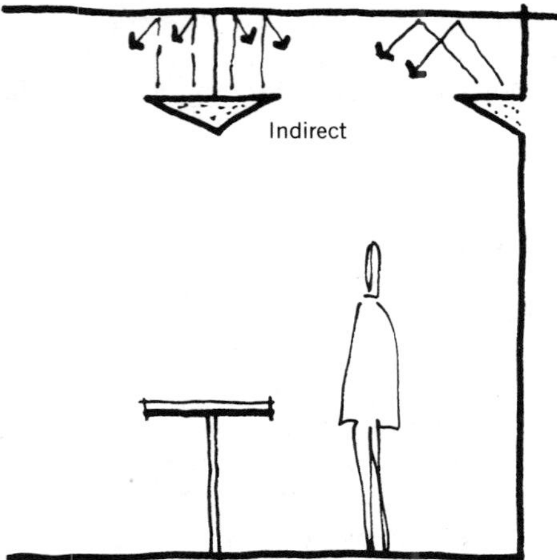

Figure 7. With indirect lighting the luminaire cannot be seen and distributes its light to the area above, reflecting from ceilings and upper walls.

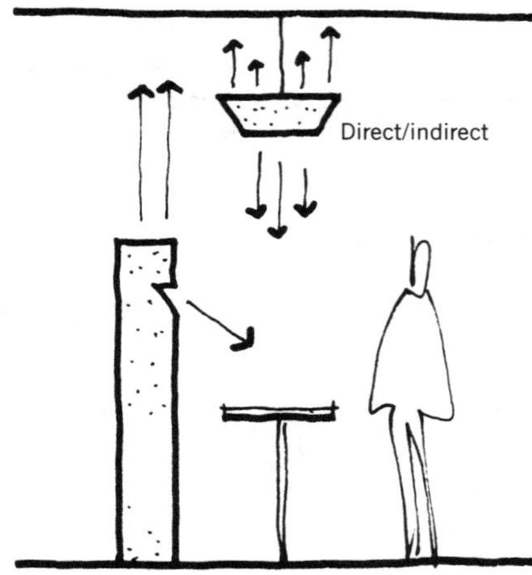

Figure 8. With direct/indirect lighting the luminaire distributes part of its light above and part below.

Direct/Indirect Lighting

Direct/indirect implies the use of both direct and indirect lighting to provide both general lighting and task lighting. One way this can be accomplished is through the use of luminaires (eg, suspended from the ceiling) that direct part of their output toward the ceiling and part to the work plane below. Another way is with luminaires that direct all light toward the ceiling (indirect) and, in addition, desk lamps which direct all light (direct) to the immediate task (Fig. 8).

The popular term "task-ambient" is often applied to direct/indirect systems which theoretically deliver the light only where it is needed and only in the various quantities needed, ambient referring to the general lighting of a space, usually where the needed illumination is low, compared with that needed for task lighting. General lighting levels may be 30 footcandles, for instance, while lighting on a critical task (eg, drafting table) might be 200 footcandles. General lighting systems are often indirect, but may also be direct, while task systems are usually direct. Task lights are located close to workstations, frequently mounted in or on the furniture, usually for an individual, and are supplemented with general lighting for the surrounding areas. Such systems are often integrated into the furniture and a single light source may provide both task lighting (down to the desk) and general indirect lighting (up to the ceiling).

To prevent problems with eye adaptation, ambient lighting levels should be at least 20–30% of the task lighting level. Also, the relationship of the task luminaire relative to the task itself (eg, book) must be such that excessive direct or reflected glare is not created. Generally, this implies locating the task light to the side of the occupant or using luminaires with lenses or other controls to prevent light from coming from the offending zone, where light is directed at the task at the "mirror" angle.

The advantages of task-ambient lighting systems include the ability to adapt to changes in the location of tasks, as in open plan offices, by changing the location of task lights, and the potential for a minimum of energy consumption per square foot of floor space. One disadvantage is that most task lights operate from 120V electrical outlets, whereas general lighting located in the ceiling often allows the use of a 277V system, resulting in potential economies.

LIGHT-PRODUCING HARDWARE

The essential elements of light-producing hardware (ie, luminaire) include a lamp or lamps, reflector, lens, often a ballast, connecting wiring, and a switching mechanism (possibly including dimming). Each has its own effect on the production, effectiveness, and cost of the light that reaches important areas of a building interior.

Lamps

There is a variety of types of lamps normally used in building design. Each type has a limited life and each has a deterioration rate (lumen depreciation). Lumen depreciation is related not only to the lamp design and the type of luminaire it is used in, but also to operation (eg, voltage; number of times it is switched on or off) and to the collection of dirt. A regular program of maintenance for cleaning and relamping is necessary if any lighting system is to maintain the designed light level production. Lamps are generally of two basic classifications: incandescent filament and gaseous discharge. Gaseous discharge lamps are usually thought of as either fluorescent lamps or high intensity discharge (HID) lamps.

The incandescent category includes two primary types of lamps for general use in buildings: the common tungsten filament and the tungsten–halogen lamp. Tungsten filament lamps come in a multitude of sizes, shapes, and bases, but the primary one of concern is the standard incandescent tungsten-filament lamp with the standard base, in the conventional glass bulb, in indoor reflector lamps (R), outdoor (hard glass) (PAR) (both in spots and floods), or the elliptical (E) lamp for special focusing.

Incandescent lamps have an efficacy (lumens per watt) of only about 8 to 13. Most of the energy used to operate this type of lamp is dissipated in the form of heat. The lamp's color is generally considered white, with a strong yellow-red component. Varieties include lamps designed for extended service, that is, long life and relatively low output (lumens), and lamps for short life and higher output. Tungsten filaments can be operated at less than rated voltage, giving extended life, or at above the rate voltage, providing greater output and shorter life. Extended service lamps are intended for use where lamp replacement is inconvenient or might be hazardous, and maintenance irregular.

The advantages of the incandescent lamp include low initial cost, simplicity, instant start, inexpensive dimming, ability to focus as a point source, and adaptability to inexpensive fixtures. The disadvantages include low efficacy, relatively short life, and high heat production. The incandescent lamp can be advantageous when used where its color will enhance the appearance of objects, such as skin tone, or disadvantageous where good color rendering of products or materials is important.

Tungsten–halogen lamps are a special class of incandescent filament lamps. They are designed for higher operating temperatures, longer life, and better light control, and are, therefore, enclosed in stronger (quartz) glass. They are used when their improved color rendition, compactness, and focusing characteristics are advantageous. They have a higher color temperature than regular incandescent (more blue light) and lower lamp depreciation qualities. They emit higher levels of ultraviolet radiation which is sometimes not advantageous. They have a higher efficacy than incandescent lamps and that efficacy can be improved even further (to 28 or 30) with the addition of a multilayer interference film (dichroic).

Gaseous discharge lamps include fluorescent lamps, high intensity discharge (HID) lamps (mercury, metal halide, and high pressure sodium), and low pressure sodium lamps.

The fluorescent is perhaps the most widely used of all lamps for general lighting in commercial buildings. The typical fluorescent lamp comprises a cylindrical glass tube sealed at both ends containing a mixture of an inert gas, generally argon, and low-pressure mercury vapor. At each end of the tube is a cathode that supplies the electrons to start and maintain the mercury arc, or gaseous discharge. The mercury arc produces ultraviolet light which is absorbed by the phosphor coating on the inside of the glass tube and reradiated as visible light.

Virtually any spectral energy distribution can be obtained with fluorescent lamps by altering the mixture of phosphors on the inside coating and the enclosed gas. Higher efficacies are achieved by producing emitted light that will be in the center of the visible spectrum where the eye is most responsive. If, however, good color rendering is desirable, there must be more energy at the red and blue ends of the spectrum where the eye is less responsive. As a result, the efficacy will be lower. Thus, there are a range of "whites" available for various purposes. The new triphosphor fluorescents have significantly improved color rendering characteristics and efficacies, but at considerable increased cost. Also, there are a number of fluorescent lower wattage lamps available, which conserve energy with only small reductions in lumen output.

Fluorescent lamps require the use of a ballast to supply sufficient voltage to start lamp operation and maintain appropriate current levels.

High intensity discharge (HID) lamps include the lamps commonly referred to as mercury, metal halide, and high pressure sodium. These lamps include a stabilized arc discharge contained within an arc tube under significant pressure. The arc tube is generally enclosed in another glass housing or outer bulb.

Mercury lamps are so distinguished because of the mercury gas used in the bulb which is vaporized by an electric current to produce light. Most mercury lamps are constructed with two envelopes: an inner (arc tube) one which contains the mercury gas and the arc; and an outer one which shields the arc tube, providing an inner surface for coating of phosphors, and which normally acts as a filter to remove certain wavelengths, notably the ultraviolet. Since a significant part of the energy radiated by the mercury arc is in the ultraviolet region and could be dangerous if exposed, special types are available for those applications where it is desirable to extinguish the arc if the outer bulb is punctured.

Mercury lamps require some type of ballast. Two-level operation can be accomplished by switching capacitors on lead circuit ballasts which will allow the operation of a lamp at two levels (eg, a 400-watt lamp can be operated at either 400 or 300 watts).

Generally, mercury lamps must be operated in the designated vertical or horizontal position or sustain serious loss in life and light output. When operating current is cut off, they require 3–7 minutes for restrike. The pressure at which the lamp operates is principally responsible for its characteristic spectral power distribution, resulting in a greenish-blue light at efficacies of 30 to 65 lumens per watt (without ballast losses). There is generally an absence of red radiation so that blue, green, and yellow colors of objects appear overemphasized, while orange and red colors appear brownish. "Color improved" mercury lamps are available which provide a more balanced spectral distribution.

Mercury lamps can be dimmed with proper dimming devices, but will sustain color changes, below about 25% of full lumen output.

Metal halide lamps are similar in construction to mercury lamps except that the metal halide arc tube contains various metal halides in addition to mercury and argon.

The efficacy of metal halide lamps is from 75 to 125 and, generally, their color-rendering abilities are superior to mercury vapor lamps.

Metal halide lamps require a special type of ballast for operation, but certain types of metal halide lamps can be operated on mercury lamp-type ballasts. Generally, metal halide lamps must be operated in their designated position or suffer losses in color output and life. If extinguished, they must cool for as long as 15 minutes before restrike. Metal halide lamps can be dimmed, but at about 60% lumen output their color begins to change to a blue-green color.

High pressure sodium (HPS) lamps produce light by passing current through sodium vapor. High pressure sodium lamps can be dimmed and generally will produce their full output color quality down to about 50% lumen output, when a strong yellow color begins to prevail. High pressure sodium lamps radiate energy across the visible spectrum producing a golden-white color and have efficacies from 60 to 140, depending on their size. Increasing the sodium pressure can increase the amount of radiation in the red range, thus improving color rendition, but life and efficacy are reduced. HPS lamps are available which provide increased color rendition and are sometimes used in inhabited areas where accurate visual rendition of colors is not critical. Restrike time after arc extinguishment for HPS lamps is significantly shorter than for other types of HID lamps and, in addition, they can be equipped with an instant restrike feature when needed.

Low pressure sodium (LPS) lamps fall in the "miscellaneous discharge" category; they are not HID, but neither are they incandescent. The light produced by passing an arc through vaporized sodium is almost monochromatic yellow and is not recommended where color rendition of objects is considered important.

Low pressure sodium lamps require some type of ballast and, when ignited, burn with a red appearance until, in 7 to 15 minutes, they reach full light output and their characteristic yellow color. Efficacies can be as much as 180 lumens per watt.

Ballasts

All gaseous discharge and HID lamps require some form of ballast or control equipment to provide adequate starting voltage, and to limit the current after the lamp has started.

Luminaire manufacturers select the appropriate combination of ballast, lamps, wiring, and frame for effective operation. However, there are differences in efficiency, noise production, and cost. For instance, ballast hum is a natural result of any electromagnetic device, but some ballasts are more noisy than others.

The average life of a fluorescent ballast at a 50% duty cycle and at proper ballast operating temperature is estimated to be about 12 years. Life expectancy is decreased at high operating temperatures. Low temperature ballasts should be used for fluorescent lamps where ambient temperatures are below 10°C (50° F).

Ballasts consume some energy. Those used with fluorescent lamps can turn as much as 12% of the luminaire's energy consumption into heat. Reduced wattage ballasts are available which operate standard lamps at 50–80% of their rated wattage, thus conserving energy with reduced lumen output. Energy-saving lamps should not be used in combination with these ballasts.

Low wattage ballasts compatible with 34-watt fluorescent lamps are available that consume 3 to 5 watts less than the conventional ballast. Very low heat (VLH) ballasts operate at lower ambient temperatures, thereby increasing ballast life and reducing maintenance. The use of single-lamp ballasts should be minimized since this scheme may consume as much as 17% more energy than a scheme with multilamp ballasts. Solid-state electronic ballasts now available allow dimming of fluorescent lamps; they have higher efficiencies in operating fluorescent lamps and consume less energy than the conventional core and coil magnetic ballasts. The combination of reduced ballast energy consumption and lower wattage use by the lamps decreases the heat buildup, thus reducing thermal lamp lumen depreciation. Also, the electronic ballast increases the output of fluorescent lamps by operating them at high frequency, 20–30 kilohertz. It also reduces visible flicker as it cycles the lamps off and on 44,000 times per second, or more, as opposed to 120 times per second for conventional ballasts.

Luminaires

A luminaire is that part of the lighting system consisting of a housing unit (possibly including a reflector, lens, louver, one or more lamps, a ballast, and/or lamp brackets), and appropriate wiring for the function (Fig. 9).

The efficiency of a luminaire depends on materials and finishes used and the design of the reflector and housing (used in conjunction with lamps made by lamp manufacturers). Efficiency can be determined by calculating the coefficient of utilization (CU) for the various generic types of luminaire (see Ref. 1) or from data supplied by the manufacturer. The CU provides an indication of the effectiveness of a particular type of luminaire in a particular type of space. The CU can be multiplied by the lamp lumen output for the luminaire and divided by the area to be illuminated to determine the footcandle level expected at the work plane. Low efficiency luminaires contribute less light and more heat than do more efficient ones.

Reflectors are used in luminaires to redirect lamp light in a generally useful direction. Their shape or curvature is usually designed for a particular lamp or lamps and to avoid light absorption, which increases heat and detracts from the luminaire's efficiency.

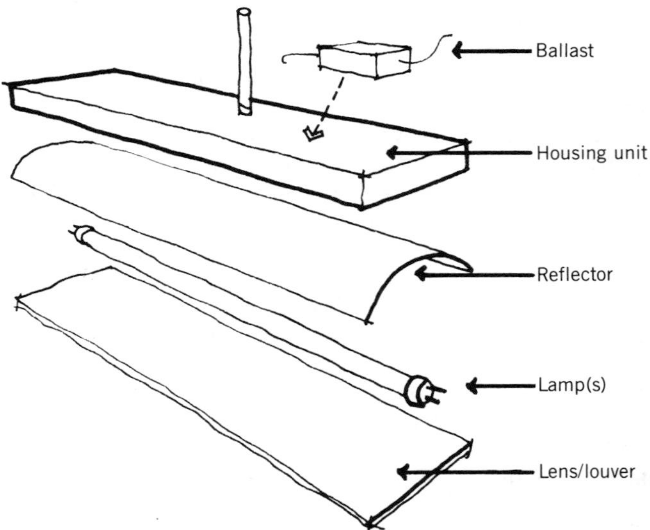

Figure 9. The composition of a luminaire.

Covering glass or plastic panels with patterned or prismatic surfaces are used with luminaires to inhibit lamp dirt accumulation, to protect lamps from breakage, and to redirect lamp light above to the ceiling and/or below to the work area to avoid the glare zone. Some covering panels merely diffuse lamp light and generally reduce luminance, or brightness, and/or lumen output. Some types of luminaires employ louvers below and/or on the sides of the lamps to redistribute light and to prevent direct visual contact with the lamp's brightness from below.

The CU of the luminaire provides an indication of the luminaire's total efficiency in producing usable light. An indication of a luminaire's candlepower distribution is usually provided by the manufacturer. Distribution patterns for generic luminaire types are provided in Ref. 1.

Visual discomfort can be caused by luminaires which produce excessively high luminances in the field of view of observers. This is referred to as direct glare and can be evaluated through the use of the visual comfort probability (VCP) factor. VCP is an estimator of the fraction of the observer population which will accept a lighting system and its environment as being comfortable, using the perception of glare due to direct light from luminaires to the observer as a criterion. While in principle VCP is based on a variety of factors in the environment in addition to the luminaire, these factors have been standardized so as to provide a basis for comparison of various luminaires. These data are provided by the luminaire manufacturer based on standard testing procedures. The VCP provides a rating of the luminaire (in this standard setting) expressed as a percentage of people viewing along a specified line of sight who will be expected to find it acceptable.

By consensus, direct glare will not be a problem in lighting installations if all three of the following conditions are satisfied (2):

1. The VCP is 70 or more.
2. The ratio of maximum-to-average luminaire luminance does not exceed five to one at 45, 55, 65, 75, and 85° from nadir crosswise and lengthwise.
3. Maximum luminaire luminances crosswise and lengthwise do not exceed the values in Figure 4.

Lighting Controls

The two principal types of lighting system control are selective switching (on/off) and dimming, although there are a number of variations of these.

Selective Switching. The simple switching of lamps on and off, either manually or automatically, is referred to as selective switching. The concept allows for the elimination or reduction of work plane footcandles from electric lights by level and/or by zone. This technique can be effective in discouraging the use of lighting energy when it is not needed and, thus, reduce waste. It also allows for the reduction of electric lighting energy use when daylight is available.

Switches can be controlled manually, by photosensors that switch lamps on or off, depending on the levels of daylighting available on the task, by timers that switch lights according to some preselected times (eg, on at 8 A.M. and off at 6 P.M.), or by an occupancy sensor that switches lamps on or off based on the proximity of persons to the controlled area.

Selective switching can be categorized as two-, three-, four-, or five-step. The two-step system is a simple on/off of all lamps on the circuit. The three-step system is used with luminaires with two lamps, or multiples of two. The three steps are: (*1*) all lamps on, (*2*) half of the lamps on, (*3*) all of the lamps off. The four-step system is applied to luminaires with three lamps, or multiples of three, and the four steps are: (*1*) all lamps on, (*2*) one third of the lamps on, (*3*) two thirds of the lamps on, and (*4*) all lamps off. The five-step system is applied to luminaires with four lamps, or multiples of four, and the steps are: (*1*) all lamps on, (*2*) one fourth on, (*3*) one half on, (*4*) three quarters on, and (*5*) all lamps off.

Dimming. Almost all types of lamps can now be dimmed. Lamps that require ballasts can be dimmed if they are equipped with a proper dimming ballast. Dimmers allow control of electric lights to provide only the additional footcandles needed to supplement daylighting and maintain the targeted footcandle level. Dimmers can be activated manually or with photosensors.

ILLUMINANCE CALCULATION METHODS

A lighting system should provide sufficient, but not excessive, illuminance on a visual task. Thus it is important that it be possible to calculate the illumination from a given lighting system, or to determine what type of lighting system will be needed to produce the targeted light quantity.

Point Illuminance Calculations

In many cases targeted illuminance values may need to be provided at specific tasks rather than for large areas of various tasks. In these cases, a point method of illuminance calculation can be used. The Isofootcandle Method described in Ref. 1 for calculating illuminance at a point makes use of predetermined plots of lines of equal illuminance on surfaces.

By locating a point on the Isofootcandle chart for a particular luminaire with reference to the ratio of distance/mounting height, the direct illuminance at the task point can be read. If a number of luminaires are involved, the various contributions from each can be read from the Isofootcandle charts and added together to obtain the direct illuminance at the given point.

Average Illuminance Calculations

Where the targeted illuminance values are "average maintained values," the Zonal-Cavity Method can be used. It can be used to determine the number of luminaires required for a given situation and targeted footcandle level, or to determine the area of floor that can be effectively covered by a given system of luminaires.

Number of Luminaires for a Space. The number of luminaires required for a given space is a product of the illumination desired and the task area to be covered, divided by the light (in lumens) provided by each luminaire. In this calculation, this latter quantity is adjusted to account for both the amount of light produced by the luminaire that does not reach the work surface (the luminaire's Coefficient of Utilization, or CU) and the degradation of the luminaire's efficiency caused by temperature and voltage variations, dirt accumulation on luminaires and room surfaces, output depreciation of the luminaires, and maintenance conditions (the luminaire's Light Loss Factor, or LLF). The formula is as follows:

$$\text{Number of luminaires} = \frac{(\text{fc}) \times (\text{ft}^2)}{(\text{lumens/luminaire}) \times \text{CU} \times \text{LLF}}$$

Lumens per luminaire, for this calculation, is determined by multiplying the number of lamps per luminaire times the lumens produced by each lamp. The CU is determined from manufacturer's data or from Ref. 1.

The light loss factor is determined by multiplying values for room surface dirt, lamp lumen depreciation, lamp burnout rate, and luminaire dirt depreciation, as well as adjustment factor. The values for these five factors are:

- *Room Surface Dirt.* Clean room, frequent maintenance, 0.95; medium conditions and medium frequency of cleaning, 0.9; dirty room, infrequent maintenance, 0.85.
- *Lamp Lumen Depreciation.* See Ref. 1.
- *Burnout Rate.* Group-replacement, 1.0; individual replacement on burnout, 0.95.
- *Luminaire Dirt Replacement.* LDR depends on luminaire design and maintenance schedule. The maintenance category can be obtained from the manufacturer's data or from Ref. 1.
- *Adjustment Factor.* A factor of 0.9 accounts for voltage variations, ballast differences, luminaire ambient temperature, and luminaire deterioration not caused by dirt.

These five factors are multiplied and used in the original equation for the LLF.

Area of Space Covered by Luminaire. Determining the area of floor which each luminaire covers effectively can be a more useful procedure for large spaces. The values in the preceding procedure are used in a different equation:

$$\text{floor area per luminaire} = \frac{(\text{lumens/luminaire}) \times \text{CU} \times \text{LLF}}{\text{fc}}$$

Zonal Cavity Calculation. The zonal cavity calculation can be used to adjust the luminaire's CU in the foregoing equations to account for the effective (as opposed to nominal) reflectances of walls, ceilings, and floors.

The room is divided into three cavities: the ceiling cavity is the space between the luminaire and the ceiling; the floor cavity is the space between the work plane and the floor; the room cavity is the space between the work plane and the luminaire. The "h" in Figure 10 refers to the various heights of the cavities.

$$\text{Cavity Ratio} = 2.5 \times \frac{\text{area of cavity wall}}{\text{area of workplane}}$$

In a rectangular space, the area of the cavity wall is: $h \times (2L + 2W)$, or $2h(L + W)$; from the following:

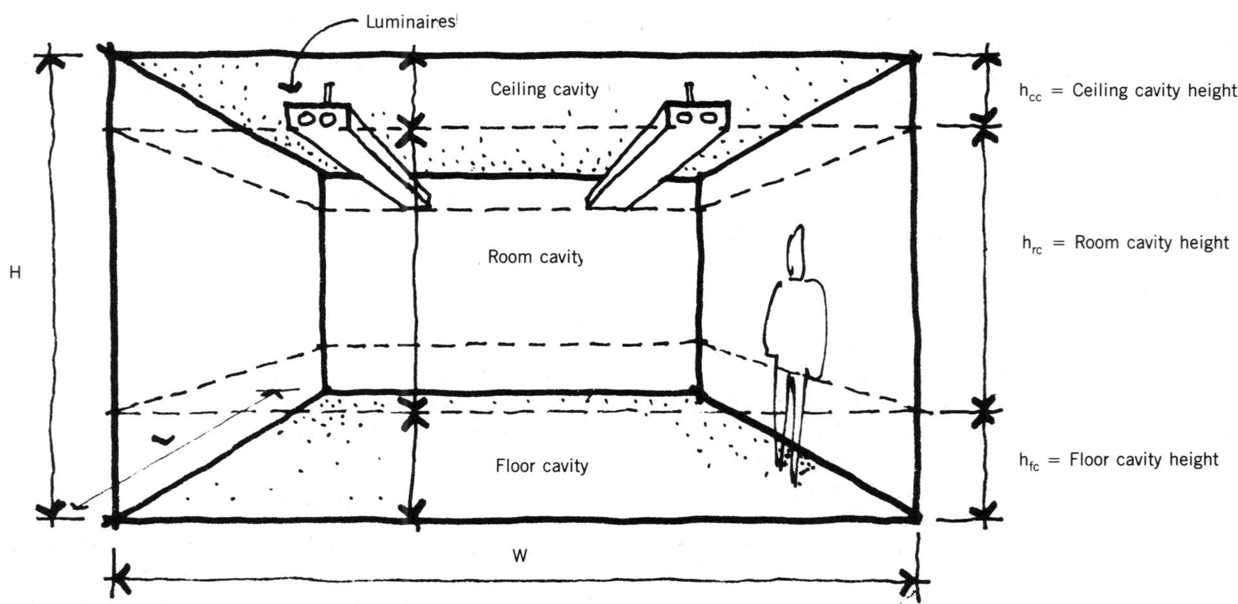

Figure 10. The zonal cavity areas.

$$CR = \frac{2.5 \times 2h \times (L + W)}{\text{area of workplane}}$$

$$CR = 5h \times \frac{(L + W)}{(L \times W)}$$

$$\text{Ceiling Cavity Ratio, CCR} = 5h \times \frac{L + W}{L \times W}$$

$$\text{Room Cavity Ratio, RCR} = 5h \times \frac{L + W}{L \times W}$$

$$\text{Floor Cavity Ratio, FCR} = \frac{L + W}{L \times W}$$

Cavity ratios can be obtained from Ref. 1.

Effective ceiling and floor reflectances can be determined on the basis of known or assumed values. If luminaires are surface-mounted or recessed, then CCR = 0 and P = known or assumed ceiling reflectance. If the floor is the work plane, FCR = 0, and P = known or assumed floor reflectance.

Computer Calculations

There are a number of computer programs that will carry out these lighting calculations. Programs range from algorithms for hand-held calculators that perform simple footcandle calculations for simple lighting systems, to the more complex personal computers, and to mainframe computers that are capable of calculating illuminances, luminances, and equivalent sphere illumination. Some will combine these with daylight calculations and some will provide shaded and even colored perspectives of the interior building space.

BIBLIOGRAPHY

1. *IES Lighting Handbook,* reference volume, Illuminating Engineering Society of North America, New York, 1984.
2. *IES Lighting Handbook,* applications volume, Illuminating Engineering Society of North America, New York, 1987.

General References

Refs. 1 and 2 are good general references.

F. Birren, *Light, Color, and Environment,* Van Nostrand Reinhold, New York, 1969.

P. R. Boyce, *Human Factors in Lighting,* Macmillan, New York, 1981.

M. D. Egan, *Concepts in Architectural Lighting,* McGraw-Hill Inc., New York, 1983.

J. E. Flynn and S. M. Mills, *Architectural Lighting Graphics,* Van Nostrand Reinhold Co., New York, 1962.

R. N. Helms, *Illuminating Engineering for Energy Efficient Luminous Environments,* Prentice-Hall, Englewood Cliffs, N.J., 1980.

R. G. Hopkinson and J. D. Kay, *The Lighting of Buildings,* Praeger, New York, 1969.

W. C. M. Lam, *Perception and Lighting as Formgivers for Architecture,* McGraw-Hill Inc., New York, 1977.

L. Larson, *Lighting and Its Design,* Whitney Library of Design, New York, 1964.

W. J. McGuiness, B. Stein, and J. S. Reynolds, *Mechanical and Electrical Equipment for Buildings,* John Wiley & Sons, Inc., New York, 1986.

J. L. Nuckolls, *Interior Lighting for Environmental Designers,* John Wiley & Sons, Inc., New York, 1976.

D. Phillips, *Lighting in Architectural Design,* McGraw-Hill Inc., New York, 1964.

See also Behavior and Architecture; Electrical Principles; Interior Design; Lighting—Daylighting; Office Facility Planning

Benjamin Evans, FAIA, FIES
Virginia Polytechnic Institute and State University
Blacksburg, Virginia

LIGHT MEASUREMENT. See Lighting—Day Lighting; Lighting—Electric

LITERATURE OF ARCHITECTURE

Books and periodicals have become a necessary adjunct to the profession of architecture for teaching, daily reference, and transmitting ideas and developments quickly and accurately to practitioners throughout the world. Today's "information explosion" is a reflection of contemporary society and the character of contemporary architecture, as architecture and its literature have always reflected their place and time. Architectural literature has grown along with the idea that architecture has meaning and that the architect is a professional; in the Middle Ages very little was written on the subject. Even in the nineteenth and twentieth centuries condemnations of the importance of architectural writing are found along with a call for the return to craft traditions, or for more emphasis on the role of the eye or the intuition of the artist. Nevertheless, such comments did more to acknowledge the potent force of writing in the profession than to suppress architectural writing.

A definition of architectural literature would ideally encompass all architecture-related material recorded on paper: drawings, manuscripts, catalogs, magazines, and books. Among books are included works by and for architects along with fictional representations and guidebooks. Speaking practically and more critically, a literature of architecture might be considered to include only those publications that have affected the history of architectural theory and design or that reflect current ideas in a special or representative way. There are many of these, and it is impossible to understand the history of architecture since the year 1400 without reference to written works. At times books have even stood in lieu of buildings in the development or transmission of architectural ideas. Palladio's *Four Books on Architecture* may be the best example of this, but it holds true in any case where personal contacts are inhibited by war, politics, or distance. In Protestant England books were needed to learn about the Italian Renaissance; Fischer von Erlach was otherwise cut off from developments in France; modern architects depend on critics and reporters to keep them abreast of today's simultaneous, worldwide developments. Books have also served to keep the flow of ideas moving when building was inhibited by war, economic depression, or other stress.

It must be understood that the above definition has exceptions. It assumes the existence of a developed architectural literature; however, before the fifteenth century architectural ideas were not so commonly conveyed by writing, and few early written records on architecture were demonstrably influential—few even existed in multiple copies. Nevertheless, it is essential that these works be considered, at least as background to the development of a proper literature of architecture. Even after the invention of the printing press there were a number of unpublished manuscripts written that are important historically such as the early treatises of Filarete and Francesco di Giorgio or the writings of Boulée, and some that were demonstrably influential, such as Serlio's Book IV on houses.

Unusual or uninfluential books cannot be ignored because they may be significant in other ways. John Shute's *First and Chief Groundes of Architecture* (1563) is an example. There is only one known building that shows a knowledge of Shute, but the book is important as the first on architecture to be written in England. Martino Bassi's pamphlet condemning work on Milan Cathedral, *Dispareri in materia d'architettura, et perspettiva . . .* (Brescia, 1572), is an early case of an architect using print to argue a position. Architects' biographies and studies of the profession are also important, as are reference books such as encyclopedias and dictionaries.

A third exception would be publications that have influenced the history of architecture in a notable but indirect way, such as popular *vedute* or the works of archaeologists such as Winckelmann and Schliemann in the eighteenth century. The writings of reformers, from medieval churchmen to modern social and political polemicists, have always been noteworthy. However, because of the size of this group of writings they cannot be included here unless they are specifically addressed to architects or patrons.

It would also be useful to consider the nonarchitectural books that architects read. Since Roman times architects have been admonished to be learned and to read widely in order to add authority and information to natural skill. In the first century B.C. Vitruvius recommended the study of geometry, history, philosophy, music, medicine, law, and astronomy. Even in the mid-eighteenth century, when Lord Chesterfield was telling his son in Vicenza to "employ three or four days in learning the Five Orders of Architecture and you may know all that you need to know" (1) the great teacher Jacques-François Blondel was publishing a book list for students, *Discours sur la necessité de l'étude de l'architecture* (2). Architects such as Balthasar Neumann are known to have consulted book collections and were heavily influenced by books on architecture. Neumann's own library covered many of the subjects recommended by Vitruvius and also poetry, fiction, natural science, theology, and mathematics, as well as a large number of architecture books. In 1924 a magazine article quoted famous architects again calling for those in the profession to be well-read; among them Louis Sullivan, decrying the "present isolation" of architecture, recommended the study of literature (with reference to Victor Hugo), and Cass Gilbert spoke in favor of history, Greek literature, and the lives of Italian Renaissance artists (3).

The types of publications that make up architectural literature vary considerably over time as the profession developed as to format, subject, and audience. In the West, continuous development began in Italy in the fifteenth and sixteenth centuries with the publication of a series of architectural treatises that were ultimately based on the only treatise to survive from antiquity, Vitruvius's *De Architectura*. Like Vitruvius, they surveyed many aspects of the subject in an attempt to summarize knowledge. By introducing the classical Orders and offering instruction on the use of perspective, they dealt with architectural theory and design techniques. They addressed the practical needs of the patron and builder by discussing construction issues and giving plans and elevations. Again following Vitruvius, questions of engineering and military designs were also sometimes found in these books.

The early books were scholarly; many were editions or interpretations of Vitruvius itself and many were by humanists rather than architects, without illustrations and written in Latin. However, by 1530 the first treatises on modern architecture began being produced. Many of these were still learned in tone, but tended to be written by architects and were addressed to architects, with a more practical choice of subject matter and organization. They also spoke in the vernacular, with an emphasis on illustration. Serlio was the first such author; others included Palladio and Scamozzi.

Sixteenth-century books in Spain, France, England, and other European countries included not only translations of the major Italian treatises but native contributions as well, and by the seventeenth century an architectural literature of great variety had developed throughout Europe. Many types of books appeared: some served new and more specific purposes while some were encyclopedic; some were exercises in abstract architectural theory while some were builders' handbooks; and some attempted new formats to reach nonprofessional audiences. They were written not only by scholars and architects but by craftspersons, patrons, amateurs, mathematicians, and artists. By the end of the eighteenth century all major classes of architectural books were established. From its beginning in Vitruvius's comprehensive treatise, architectural literature had come to separate major issues into categories, each represented in the literature: theory, including speculative writings and texts; practical building matters; portfolios, for example, designs of a geographic area, a style, an architect, or a building type; engineering or military architecture; history; design techniques, for example perspective, drafting; and landscape design. Books were produced for and used by all types of readers from amateur and dilettante to patron and practitioner. The maturity of the architectural book business was also to be seen in the appearance of specialized publishing houses and in the ability of authors not only to make money on their books but to make a living by writing.

The nineteenth and twentieth centuries have been distinguished by a general profusion of architectural writing, including the appearance of architectural periodicals and trade publications, bringing with them the appearance of businesspeople and professional journalists as important writers on architecture. The categorization of architectural literature continued and featured construction, urban planning, and architectural history. Architects themselves have more commonly used print as a medium to advertise and explain their work and their theories, including published manifestos on art and politics. Perhaps the most recent development has been that of architectural criticism and didactic writing as a regular feature of daily newspapers and even as subjects for television programs. Thus, architectural "literature" is now directed at the widest possible audience, not only the practitioner, patron, scholar, or critic, but everyone inhabiting the environments created by these professionals. The literature of architecture is accepted not only as an adjunct to the building of buildings but as a vital, alternate arena, to use for influencing the course of developments in the industry itself. More than ever before there is a balance between writing and building, *ars* and *scientia,* and theory and practice.

This survey is of necessity restricted to European and American architectural literature, although Eastern cultures also have architectural literature. The *Ying-tsao fa-shih* (4), for example, was originally a Chinese government study of the cost of labor and materials for different types of construction; it was compiled in 1103. Seventeenth-century Ottoman literature includes the *Risāle-i Mi^{c} mariyye* by Ca fer Efendi (5), with a biography of the architect Mehmed Aga, an account of his work and a trilingual glossary of technical terms in Turkish, Arabic, and Persian. Such writings existed in comparative isolation, however; the world literature of architecture of the late twentieth century is a recent development, the result of the spread of western concepts about writing and building reviewed herein.

ARCHITECTURAL WRITING IN ANTIQUITY

Architectural writing began in antiquity. In addition to Vitruvius, there were many Roman and Greek writers who wrote of building and buildings. Vitruvius himself acknowledged a debt to previous writers and named over 60 other books. The Greek authors he named wrote architectural works of at least three types. Some early Ionic architects wrote accounts of the buildings they designed, including Ictinus and Carpion on the Parthenon (ca 430 B.C.), and Satyros and Pytheos on the Mausoleum of Halicarnassus (ca 353 B.C.). Some of the same men and, as Vitruvius said, "many less celebrated," also wrote treatises on the proportions of temples, on the proportions of the Doric order, and on the Corinthian order. Symmetry was a favorite subject and commentaries on scenographic perspective were also available.

Finally, there were treatises on machinery, especially useful to Vitruvius, who complained that there were few books by his own countrymen on that subject but many by Greeks. He named 12 Greek authors but only three Roman authors, Fuficius, Marcus Terentius Varro, and Publius Septimius.

Little is known about later Latin architectural literature. The only surviving accounts or discussions are those incorporated in histories such as Tacitus's *Historiae,* Pliny's *Historia Naturalis,* or Varro's *Lingua Latina,* and in travel accounts and biographies such as Pausanias's *Description of Greece* written in the second century A.D. or Eusebius's *Vita Constantini* (*Life of Constantine*) written in the fourth century A.D. The most important of such books is the separate volume by Procopius of Caesaria, Justinian's Court Historian, on the emperor's buildings, *De aedificiis conditiis vel restoratis Auspicio Justiniani Libra VI,* in which he not only describes the imperial building program but includes such information as the problems encountered during construction of the Hagia Sophia. An exceptional monograph is the volume by Sextus Julius Frontinus on the aqueducts of Rome, *De Aquis Urbis Romae,* written in the first century A.D.

None of these books influenced architecture or architects, but there was one Latin writer whose letters were a source of inspiration in the Renaissance: Pliny the Younger (first century A.D.). Among other remarks relating to architecture, the author described his two villas (6). This was a Roman building type about which Vitruvius provided little information, and Raphael, for one, studied Pliny's descriptions with care when he attempted to revive that building type at the Villa Madama. Later publications describing and reconstructing Pliny's villas included Scamozzi's *Idea* (7), Jean-François Félibien des Avaux's *Les plans et les descriptions de deux plus belles maisons de campagne de pline le consul . . .* (8), and Robert Castell's *The Villas of the Ancients Illustrated* (9).

The only book on the practice of architecture to survive from antiquity is *De Architectura* (*The Ten Books on Architecture*) by Vitruvius (ca 90–ca 20 B.C.), an architect and military engineer who served Julius Caesar and Octavian, to whom (as Caesar Augustus) the book is dedicated (10). The manual was apparently the work of many decades. In its final form it was divided into 10 books, each with an introductory preface. It is the seminal document for western architectural literature, the foundation for what was to come. It defined the scope of the subject and inaugurated many basic themes, including the definition of an architect and of architecture. Thus, its contents must be reviewed in detail.

The author begins by discussing the education of the architect (Book I, Chapter 1) and only then reviews the principles and categories of architecture (I, 2–3). Vitruvius divided architecture into three "departments," the art of building, the making of time-pieces, and the construction of machinery. Building was divided into public architecture, including defensive, religious, and utilitarian buildings, and houses. The rest of Book I is devoted to a description of the siting, fortifications, and layout of a town.

After a digression to the origins of building and a survey of building materials, Books III and IV deal with temples. Book III discusses symmetry and proportion as compared to the human body, an idea that has enjoyed a long history. The most profoundly influential part of this section, however, has been the chapters describing the Ionic, Corinthian, and Doric Orders, the classical language of architecture first systematically presented by Vitruvius (III, 5; IV, 1–3).

The next two books deal with secular building: public structures of various kinds (V) and houses (VI). These chapters also include the consideration of harmonics (V, 4), symmetry and proportion (VI, 2–3), and the roles of owner, workman, and architect (VI, 8–10).

Book VII considers finishing materials such as stucco and concrete for vaults and floors, and fresco painting. Water is discussed in Book VIII, the tapping and conducting of it, along with the construction of aqueducts.

Vitruvius's other two "departments" of architecture are covered in Book IX, on instruments for measuring time (including surveying and astronomy), and Book X, on mechanics and military engineering. Book X is the longest, no doubt because Vitruvius had been a successful military architect. He describes not only battering rams, catapults, and other war engines, but the technology of peace, including pulleys, waterwheels, a water-organ, and odometers.

The original manuscript offered clarification of professional jargon in the form of diagrams at the end of at least six of the books, including drawings of the entasis of a column and the Archimedean screw. However, these drawings have not survived, and the interpretation of Vitruvius has occupied philologists (present-day linguists) ever since the fifteenth century.

Vitruvius's text survived into the Middle Ages in only one manuscript, but after about 850 A.D. it was copied and selections were extracted many times. As was the case with Bishop Isidore of Seville in the seventh century, medieval men used the text for its information on pigments, acoustics, mechanics, and other nonarchitectural subjects. The history of its influence on architectural style begins only in 1414 or 1416, when the humanist Poggio Bracciolini saw a copy at the monastery of St. Gall in Switzerland. As the only surviving treatise on classical architecture, it was prized by architects anxious to revive the forms of Roman buildings, and it was read by or to many leading architects even before it became widely accessible through the first printed edition in 1486, the first illustrated, critical edition by Fra Giocondo in 1511, or the first translation into a modern language by Cesare Cesariano in 1521. Cesariano's edition also included the first commentary and an important set of new illustrations.

The influence exerted by the book on the architects of the Renaissance was far-reaching and profound. Not only was its form and content reflected in their work, but Vitruvius's definition of the profession must have contributed to their changing self-image. For Vitruvius, the architect was distinguished from the master workman by his liberal education. The architect was presented as a person with technical skill, who was also informed concerning the high ideals of symmetry and proportion, capable of investing his buildings with not only beauty (*venustas*), but with convenience (*utilitas*) and propriety (*firmitas*), as well (10).

Among the many editions of Vitruvius several are noteworthy, including the annotated version of 1544 by Guillaume Philander (who claimed that he had solved most of the difficulties presented by the original Latin and Greek text, arcane and corrupted, "except for a few places not even Apollo could have deciphered"), and the translation with commentary by Daniele Barbaro in 1556, which was illustrated by Palladio. Vitruvius also heralded the Renaissance in northern countries, with editions in French, German, and English by 1550. Claude Perrault's French edition (1673) was distinguished as the work of a man who was both architect and classical scholar and was standard until the mid-nineteenth century. The first full English edition was by William Newton in 1791.

THE MIDDLE AGES

In the Middle Ages architecture was produced by men working within the craft tradition; Vitruvius's professional architect as a man of comprehensive learning and as a writer of treatises had disappeared. The literary sources on medieval architecture are confined primarily to the same sorts of writings that survive from antiquity: inscriptions, letters, histories, and guides. Among the more interesting of these are the twelfth-century writings of Abbot Suger on the rebuilding of St. Denis, the first Gothic church in *On the abbey church of St. Denis and its art treasures* (11) and the *Gesta Abbatum* by Gervase of Canterbury (12) that records the destruction and rebuilding of Canterbury Cathedral.

Although they usually do not qualify as literature, architectural drawings were used at this time as records and methods of instruction. The oldest architectural plan on parchment, the plan of St. Gall, was apparently a summary of a synod on monastic planning sent to an abbot around 820 A.D. who was going to rebuild his monastery (13). The number of surviving drawings increased dramatically in the early thirteenth century, when masons became concerned with particular details, such as tracery windows. Even when drawings did not survive, scholars sometimes suggested their use, as when identical forms appeared in related but distant buildings.

The early thirteenth-century sketchbook of Villard de Honnecourt may be claimed to be not only a collection of architectural drawings but a book in manuscript form. Thirty-three leaves survive with drawings of plans, elevations, sculpture, and stained-glass windows, as well as miscellanies such as a lion "drawn from life." The illustrations are accompanied by an explanatory text and commentary. It has been called a lodge-book, and Villard suggests it was compiled to instruct; but, in fact, scholars do not know the purpose it served or indeed whether Villard was an architect at all. A later hand contributed some of the illustrations and their captions.

Editions of the manuscript include Robert Willis's *Facsimile of the Sketch-book of Wilars de Honecort* (14) and, in paperback, *The Sketchbook of Villard de Honnecourt,* Theodore Bowie, editor (15). The original is in the Bibliothèque Nationale, Paris.

At the end of the Middle Ages northern masons began to record and publish their design techniques and two Germans, Hans Schmuttermayer and Mathes Roriczer, did so even before the influence of Italian treatises could be felt. Roriczer was a member of a family of masons in southern Germany who became a master mason in Nuremburg in 1463.

His first booklet, 16 pages on *Correct Finials,* described their design using proven geometric principles. His second work, now known as *Geometria Deutsch,* demonstrated in eight pages how to solve geometric problems common to medieval building design using a compass and a straightedge (16). Following the publication of an essay on the design of finials and gables by Hans Schmuttermayer, a goldsmith (ca 1488), Roriczer produced another short booklet on the subject around the year 1490. These four tracts provide important evidence concerning the geometric techniques of medieval masons, including the way an elevation could be generated from a ground plan and the mechanical, rather than mathematical, way masons solved geometrical problems.

THE FIFTEENTH CENTURY IN ITALY

The first book on architecture to go from pen to press was Leon Battista Alberti's treatise, *De re Aedificatoria* (17). It appeared in 1485, 25 years after the first book was printed in Italy. Most of the other early architectural books were editions of Vitruvius: the first from Rome in 1486, and others from Florence in 1496 and Venice in 1497. E. A. Connolly points out that all of these books resembled manuscripts in their appearance and intended audience, especially because they were written in Latin and used "Roman" type, as did the classics. The obvious difference was that they were produced in editions of two to three hundred copies, assuring much wider dissemination and influence (18).

As indicated by its title and its division into 10 books, Alberti's treatise was based on Vitruvius's work. Indeed, it is often considered that the humanist scholar originally intended only to translate *De Architectura,* but found it so difficult to understand that he was moved to produce a treatise of his own instead. It may have been 10 years or more between the time he conceived of the project and the formal presentation of a manuscript to Pope Nicholas V in 1452.

Alberti encountered two problems with Vitruvius's work. The first was the text. It was loosely organized and full of Greek and Latin architectural terminology that could no longer be deciphered except by referring to the buildings, most of which had been replaced by Imperial monuments of entirely different character. Therein lay the second problem. It was those later buildings that Alberti and the men of his time saw, admired, and wanted to emulate. Vitruvius alone could not provide the key to understanding them.

De re Aedificatoria was the first book to summarize and clarify classical architecture and building techniques in a way useful to men in the fifteenth century. First, as Richard Krautheimer has demonstrated (19), Alberti reorganized Vitruvius, treating the subject matter in a reasoned, thematic way, which made it much more accessible. Second, he augmented the information in Vitruvius through his knowledge of other classical authors, particularly classical philosophy, and through the study of surviving Roman monuments and contemporary building practice. The result was a book of architectural theory, one that was of profound importance.

Alberti approached architecture as a humanist, emphasizing the importance of the architect and the role of architecture in human society. He begins his work with an introductory book in which he defines the architect as a man of special talents and wide learning. In this, as in so much of his book, he follows themes in Vitruvius but clarifies and updates them, transmitting them to modern practitioners in a new and more potent form.

Vitruvius had mentioned (10) that one of the distinctions between the architect and layperson was that the former did not need to see a work complete in order to recognize its merits, but could, "as soon as he has formed the conception, and before he begins the work, [have] a definite idea of the beauty, the convenience and the propriety that will distinguish it" (20). Alberti took these aspects of good design and organized the book around them: *firmitas* (propriety), the rational basis of architecture, is covered in Books two and three; *utilitas* (convenience), the way it serves men in society, is covered in Books four and five; and *venustas* (beauty), handling building materials and techniques, is covered in Books six through nine. Book ten treats the mechanical issue of water supply and the modern problem of building restoration.

Among the concepts in architectural theory that are traced specifically to Alberti is that of city planning as a social issue, not only as a military one. Another is the importance of proportion in architecture; it was Alberti who first discussed classical concepts of harmonic proportion as a basis for beautiful design.

Although immensely important, Alberti's erudite treatise was not transformed into popular editions as quickly as that of Vitruvius. It was not translated into Italian until 1546, or equipped with illustrations before 1550. The first English-language edition was prepared in 1726.

Even before the publication of Vitruvius and Alberti, other fifteenth-century treatises on architecture were written, specifically Il Filarete's *Treatise on Architecture* (21) and Francesco di Giorgio Martini's *Trattati di architettura, ingengneria e arte militare* (22). Neither was printed until the twentieth century, but both are of great historical importance. Filarete's work was written by 1465 and it has the distinctions of being the first Italian treatise to be composed in the vernacular and the first to be illustrated. It is also remarkably original in concept and form. It is presented (in 24 books) as a series of dialogues in which an architect instructs a Renaissance prince in the planning of a new city. Filarete was a Florentine working in Milan, and the book was a means of communicating the new Renaissance style to the North. The concepts and rules he proposes are also remarkably novel, but this was due in part to Filarete's comparative ignorance of original classical material and to his need to tailor the subject to Milanese taste.

Francesco di Giorgio wrote two treatises, an earlier and more primitive one completed around 1476, and the final treatise, more polished and theoretical, probably done in the 1480s (23). They covered the scope of contemporary architecture, relating it to the architecture of the ancients. The earlier treatise already showed the influence of Vitruvius, and Francesco also depended on his own studies of ancient ruins.

His work is distinguished from others of the time by its more practical approach and by an abundance of illustrations. An accomplished architect and engineer himself, he was concerned with the production of useful modern buildings and he demonstrated the application of such things as rules of symmetry and proportion or mathematical formulas. For example, while Vitruvius introduced the idea of an analogy between the proportions of the human body and a building, Francesco was the first to attempt a practical application of the idea: among his illustrations the figure of a man is used to determine the dimensions of a cruciform church plan.

Francesco di Giorgio's treatises were influential. Leonardo da Vinci, who knew the author, had a copy and made notes in it. Francesco also influenced his student Peruzzi (whose records were the basis for Serlio's later treatise) as well as many readers including Palladio, Philibert de l'Orme, and Vincenzo Scamozzi.

THE SIXTEENTH CENTURY

In the first quarter of the sixteenth century the only new developments in architectural literature centered around editions of Vitruvius: Fra Giocondo's edition of 1511 was the first architectural book to be illustrated (with 136 woodcuts), and in 1521 Cesare Cesariano produced the first translation of Vitruvius into a modern language. Illustration, translation, and Cesariano's commentary encouraged a wide use.

This hiatus in book production did not, however, indicate a lack of interest in writing about architecture. A number of artists, including Leonardo da Vinci, are known to have worked on treatises they never finished, and by the late 1540s important new volumes were appearing in countries other than Italy.

One of the most important sixteenth-century developments in architectural literature was the production of books in Spain, France, England, the Low Countries, and Germany, an indication of the spread of Renaissance ideas and of the new maturity of schools outside Italy. Their presses brought out not only treatises in the Italian vein but new subjects and approaches as well, such as the magnificent topographic survey of Du Cerceau and the overtly fantastic approach to the Orders found in Wendel Dietterlin's *Architectura . . . der Funff Seulen* (24).

In Italy, too, the sixteenth century brought new types of books on architecture. Treatises began to emphasize practical utility and many became handbooks on specific topics. Dora Weibenson has observed that this began from the division of Vitruvius into discrete subjects and that the Orders, the foundation of classical style, were the first and most popular of these to be treated independently. Giacomo Barozzi da Vignola's *Regola delli cinque ordini* [Rome, (1562)] has been published and republished more often than any other architectural book (25). The first separate study of the Orders was, in fact, Spanish, *Medidas del Romano* by Diego da Sagredo (26), and was also distinguished as the first Renaissance book on architecture published in a vernacular language.

Weibenson has also identified two additional topics that inspired separate literatures: geometry and perspective, and technology. Geometry had always been a subject of importance to builders. Juan de Herrera, an example of the Renaissance scholar–architect, collected treatises on mathematics as well as architecture and wrote a geometrical treatise of his own. Perspective rendering and the related subjects of stereotomy and scenography were also very important to architects until the eighteenth century when one of the most important works, Ferdinando Galli Bibiena's *L'architectura civile . . .* (27) appeared. A thorough introduction can be found in *Architectural Theory and Practice* (28).

A new emphasis on improving technical skills is seen in books that not only encouraged good drawing through example, but actually demonstrated drafting techniques. Vignola's "treatise," *Regola delli cinque ordini,* is at its heart a simplified, technical presentation of the way to calculate the parts of the various Orders, all clearly illustrated in large, precise, copper-engraved plates suitable for use as patterns. Vignola's northern counterpart was Hans Blum, whose book on the proportions of the Orders and how to draw them, *Quinque columnarum exacta discritio atque delineatio* (Zurich, 1550), was also immensely popular, with 30 editions before 1690 (29).

Unlike the Orders and perspective and geometry, there were not many sixteenth-century books specifically on technology. Vitruvius and the Italian treatises considered building materials and techniques, but separate emphasis on the subject came first from northern architects with their traditional responsibility for construction as well as design. Philibert Delorme's *Nouvelles Inventions pour bien bastir et à petit frais* (Paris, 1561), on carpentry, was one of the earliest examples.

Other important architectural subjects that first appeared as separate book types in the sixteenth century included military architecture and engineering (Pietro Cataneo's *I Quattro Primi Libri di Architettura,* Venice, 1554, was the last treatise to cover both civil and military architecture (30)), domestic architecture, and books that concentrated on examining the architecture of a specific building, site, patron, or country. Writings about architects became more common: this reflection on the rise of the profession had already begun with Manetti's late fifteenth-century biography of Brunelleschi, and for the sixteenth century Vasari's *Lives of the Most Eminent Painters, Sculptors and Architects* (*Le vite de piu eccelenti architetti,* Florence, 1550) is the paramount example. There were also commentaries on architecture and its role, the most interesting of which may be *Instructionum Fabricae et Supellectilis Ecclesiasticae* (1577) by Archbishop Carlo Borromeo (St. Charles Borromeo), a set of rules for the design and decoration of churches that heavily influenced the Jesuits and other counter-Reformation Orders.

Serlio's treatise, *Tutte l'opere d'architectura* (31), has a complicated history for it was written and published piecemeal. Book IV on the Orders appeared in Venice (1537), followed by Book III on Roman antiquities (1540). In 1541, Serlio went to France, and Books I and II on geometry and perspective (1545) and Book V on temples (1547) were published in Paris. He also wrote a book (VI) on houses, one (VII) on palazzi and restorations, and one (VIII) on military architecture. In addition, there was a separate publication, *Estraordinario libro di architettura . . .* (Lyons, 1551). After his death Book VII was published in Frankfurt. In 1584, a collected edition of seven books appeared in Venice as *Tutte l'opere d'architettura,* with the *libro estraordinario* substituted for Book VI. Books VI and VIII remained in manuscript.

This was the first architectural treatise in which illustration dominated text, and the book was enriched not only by the learning Serlio derived from his teacher, Peruzzi, but by drawings, some from Bramante, he had presumably inherited from the same source. These include the plan of Bramante's Tempietto (Book V) and elevations of the Belvedere Courtyard, both now altered. His volume on the Orders offered a practical application of Vitruvius's theory both through clear illustration of the column Orders themselves and through demonstrations of their use in other, modern, contexts such as doors and gates. It was the most popular and influential of the volumes, often republished, translated, and emulated.

Although Book VI on houses was not published, it was influential, and was known in France through an incomplete manuscript. It is also historically important as the first book devoted to the study of domestic architecture. Like Vitruvius's Book VI it considers both country and city dwellings; however, Serlio develops a hierarchy of building types within these categories, an approach that was to be followed by many subsequent authors.

Palladio's treatise, *I quattro libri dell'architettura* (32), differs in many ways from its predecessors. He begins with a book on general principles and the classical Orders but the rest of the treatise is primarily a visual survey, with commentary, of ancient buildings and those buildings he had designed. Palladio had studied Roman ruins and his knowledge of Vitruvius was perfected when he worked on the illustrations to Daniele Barbaro's edition of that book (1556). Among the notable plates on ancient architecture in the treatise are the Egyptian Hall (from Vitruvius, used by Lord Burlington for the York Assembly Rooms) and the Tempietto by Bramante, the only modern work included under ancient architecture.

Many of the plates in the book are of Palladio's own designs for country and city houses, and the treatise is in this sense an early example of the published portfolio. It is also distinguished for its emphasis on correct proportion, including the use of harmonic proportions. The clarity of his system for achieving an ideal ratio between the parts of the Orders or the shapes and sizes of rooms, together with the symmetry and regularity of his designs overall (with the illustrations sometimes in fact "correcting" the buildings themselves in these respects) recommended the treatise as a guide and source for later architects.

Bernini was among those who studied Palladio, but his most important influence was on the English-speaking world in the early eighteenth century. Following the lead of Inigo Jones and reacting to the "excesses" of Baroque design, Lord Burlington and his circle revived Palladian principles and lionized his designs. Their Palladian Revival was, in fact, largely a phenomenon of architectural book publishing because it was inaugurated and stimulated by publications, including the first English translation of the *Quattro libri* (1715) and Isaac Ware's *The Four Books of A. Palladio's Architecture* (1738), and most of its proponents, for example Thomas Jefferson, knew Palladio's work only from the books.

Dell'idea dell'architettura universale, by Vincenzo Scamozzi (33) was originally projected for 12 books; this was later reduced to 10 and only six were published: architectural history and theory; town planning; civic and domestic architecture; the Orders; building materials; and construction. It represents a compendium of sixteenth-century ideas on architecture and not new ones. Its importance was further limited by a difficult prose style that could not always be clarified by its few illustrations. Book VI on the Orders was, however, often reproduced as one of the classic approaches to their design.

The first book on architecture published in English was *The First and Chief Groundes of Architecture* (34). Shute claimed it was based on studies in Italy, but its obvious debt was to Flemish and other northern architectural books, as was true of sixteenth-century English architecture in general. Such books, for example, Vredeman de Vries's *Architectura Oder Bauung der Antiquen* (Antwerp, 1577–1581), offered a type of non-Roman ornamentation that continued to influence England and central Europe into the seventeenth century.

Le premier tome de l'architecture (35) was the most comprehensive early study produced in the North and one of the most important treatises of its time. It contained 600 pages, organized in nine books covering the following roles : mason; architect and patron; materials and foundations; geometry; stonecutting and stereotomy (Books I–IV); the Orders (Books V–VIII); and chimneys (Book IX). It has over 200 woodcut illustrations. A second volume on divine proportions was announced but never produced.

Delorme was the son of a master mason who spent three years in Rome and perceived himself to be an architect in the Renaissance mode. His intention was to proclaim the new French architecture based on classical principles and models and his treatise, like those from Italy, was founded on a knowledge of Vitruvius, Alberti, Serlio, and other writers, and the study of Roman monuments. It also emphasized the special education of the architect, making a clear distinction between him and the master mason. The section on the Orders included new, French versions.

Delorme's northern background is also much in evidence. The book is addressed specifically to architects and their needs, with an orientation more professional and pragmatic than abstract or ideal. It recalls medieval attitudes in its use of allegory and its emphasis on God. Most significant, it assumes the important knowledge of vaulting and carpentry. Books III and IV constitute the first-known writing on stereotomy, and Delorme's solutions to stonecutting problems were long considered fundamental.

Thus, *Le premier tome de l'architecture* was a combination of medieval traditions and techniques with Renaissance classicism, analogous to the career and architecture of its author.

Du Cerceau was an architect and founder of a dynasty of architects, but his reputation is primarily based on the books he produced to transmit and promote the Renaissance style. The more important of these were the *Premier livre d'architecture,* a practical handbook with plans and elevations of fifty townhouses, the *Second livre,* with architectural details, the *Troisième livre,* with plans for country houses (36); and his *Les plus excellents bastiments de France* (37) in two volumes. As was Serlio's unpublished book on houses, the *Livres d'architecture* divides its subject by social class. This approach was to have a long subsequent history in French and English literature. The *Bastiments,* with engraved illustrations of 15 French châteaus, has been called a masterpiece of printing. It is not just a visual survey, however; the text is brief but considers a full range of architectural matters including building materials, history and condition, and site and function. It was the first of the great French topographic folios.

THE SEVENTEENTH CENTURY

The seventeenth century was a period of transformation. The older treatises were still fundamental and many were republished together with some original contributions to the genre—Henry Aldrich even published his treatise in Latin. Vitruvius and the Orders also continued to hold places of central importance. As in the sixteenth century there were new books built on the foundation of the treatises that were more specific in subject or approach, and the architectural press outside of Italy continued to grow. In quality and originality the seventeenth century was dominated by the French, and for quantity the career of Leonard Christoph Sturm (1669–1719) might be noted. He wrote, edited, and translated an extraordinary number of architecture books in German.

New users and uses for architectural literature inspired new book types and forms. Changes in the profession of architecture made separate audiences of designers, students, and workers and patrons, and books were produced to address the distinct needs of each group. New approaches to subject matter may have been inspired when authors and publishers observed the ways professionals actually used the treatises—as learning tools, as pattern books, as canons—and produced books to serve specific needs. There were also volumes only for amateurs, which reflected architecture's increased social status.

Among the most remarkable developments of the seventeenth century was the specific discussion of appropriate form in architecture. The most famous example of contemporary architectural theory was the debate between Blondel and Perrault on the correct way to determine the dimensions of the classical Orders; however, it was at least equally important that writers were for the first time seriously working to enlarge their discussion of architecture beyond the range of sixteenth-century styles and issues. They produced material as fresh as a reconsideration of the Gothic style, and they used archaeology and mathematics to supply new authority. By 1800, time, distance, and maturity had combined to liberate architectural literature as well as architectural design from the strict forms and rules of the fifteenth and sixteenth centuries.

A variety of new works on Vitruvius and on the Orders appeared, including Dutch handbooks such as Simon Bosboom's *Cort onderwys van de Vyf Colmmen* (Amsterdam. n.d.) and Barnardino Baldi's much-reprinted study, *De verborum Vitruvianorum significatione Siue. . .* (Augsburg, 1612). Perrault's annotated translation of Vitruvius was the most important of these (38); the folio became the standard edition of *De Architectura* and a condensed version for the amateur reader, *Abrégé des dix livres d'architecture de Vitruve* (Paris, 1674), was widely published and read.

Perrault's ideas about classical design were first published in a preface to his translation of Vitruvius and later formed the basis for his important treatise on the Orders, *Ordonnance des cinq espèces de colonnes selon la méthod des anciens* (39). Rejecting the strict authority of the ancients and the theory that there were ideal proportions that arose from reason or nature, he held that beauty was derived arbitrarily. To paraphrase Wolfgang Herrmann, Perrault believed that custom played a greater role in the determination of beauty than did the cosmic order. Thus he emphasized the architect's freedom to choose according to his own taste, although he offered only a limited range of acceptable choices.

These ideas inspired the most important of contemporary debates on architectural theory. The newly founded Royal Academy of Architecture took the opposite position, affirming the authority of Vitruvius and the importance of ratio and proportion to architectural beauty. Its strict classical doctrine was published in the *Cours d'architecture enseigné dans l'Académie royale d'Architecture* by Blondel (40), first director of the Academy. The book was a text in that it was based on his lectures and it sought to acquaint the reader with basic principles of design. These, according to Blondel, were largely concerned with proportions. In it he studied the Orders in detail with an emphasis on the proportional relationships of, for example, capital to shaft and column to space. There was some discussion of vaulting, bridges, and other architectural topics in Parts IV (arches) and V (construction) of special interest because Blondel was an engineer and he looked at these subjects with some originality. For example, the *Cours* included an early study of Gothic construction. However, it was important as an authoritative text on classicism.

Seventeenth-century authors worked in a number of ways to critically reconsider architectural style. Fréart's position was absolute orthodoxy. He compared the Orders according to Renaissance authors and the Orders of the ancients and criticized modern useage in *Parallèle de l'architecture antique et de la moderne* (41). His ideal was, in fact, not Roman architecture but Greek, and he inaugurated the Academy debates with his arguments for the authority of the ancients and a rational basis for beauty.

Desgodets's *Les edifices antiques de Rome dessinés et*

mesurés tres exactement (42) was the result of a royal commission to provide measured drawings of ancient Roman buildings. As many later archaeological works would do, it provided new, more accurate information about classical architecture that forced the reconsideration of older publications. Desgodets himself corrected errors in Serlio, Palladio, and Fréart de Chambray. The influence of *Edifices antiques de Rome* was limited by the strength of the academic establishment, but the value and importance of the work was recognized and the French tradition of learning by drawing measured plans, sections, elevations, and details began with Desgodets (43).

By the end of the century the beginnings of the rehabilitation of the Gothic style can even be found. Caramuel de Lobkowitz illustrates another, highly original avenue, *Architecture civil, recta y obliqua* (44). He followed the earlier writer Villalpando in discussing the Temple of Solomon, not classical architecture, as the basis for divinely inspired architectural principles. His treatise also emphasizes historical considerations, includes the building techniques of nomadic peoples and others, and offers some new Orders, for example, Gothic and "atlantic" as well as one from the Temple of Solomon. The book was not influential but is of interest as an early example of a highly intellectual sort of architectural writing, not practical, but fantastic.

Some architectural treatises emphasized practicality because they were comprehensive and handy. Large numbers of pocket-sized manuals began to appear, among them Wotton's distinguished *Elements of Architecture* (45), the first architectural treatise in English, which transmitted the result of his first-hand experience of Italian architecture to generations of northern architects. In Italy, Giovanni Branca's *Manuale d'architettura* . . . (Ascoli, 1629) was standard, summarizing in one volume basic information including the Orders, building materials, and mathematics.

In Germany, a series of treatises, *Architectura Civilis, Architectura Universalis, Architectura Privata,* and *Architura Recreationis* (46–49) written by the Italian-trained city architect of Ulm, Josef Furttenbach, were practical guides to the construction of all types of buildings. They were illustrated heavily with views, plans, sections, and details.

Daviler (or d'Aviler) produced the most important of the comprehensive architectural treatises, "a systematic topical exploration of the entire field of architecture" (50,51), full of practical advice, with an emphasis on houses. Its second volume, *Explication des termes d'architecture* (52) was a new sort of book, the architectural dictionary. The audience for books on architecture was expanding in all directions and the increasingly large number of nonprofessional writers and readers needed guides to terminology and principles. A significant early example was written not by an architect for architects but by the historiographer of the French king's buildings, André Félibien des Avaux, as part of his *Des principes de l'architecture, de la sculpture, de la peinture et des autres Arts* . . . (53). Following Daviler, an illustrated word list with terms in several languages formed part of *Nicolai Goldmann's Vollst ändige Anweisung zu der Civil-Bau-Kunst* (Leipzig, 1696; facs. ed. Baden-Baden, 1962).

Practical building handbooks with guides to building trades and practices also began to appear at this time. Although most would be produced to serve the industry, an early manual *L'architecture françoise des bâstiments particuliers* by Louis Savot (54), a physician, was written to provide patrons with basic information on house building. He instructed them on principles of siting and design and on practical matters such as costs, regulations, and building materials. His was the forerunner of a long line of architectural books specifically for the consumer.

Other books provided similar information, as is shown by the title of Sir Balthasar Gerbier's *Counsel and Advice to all Builders; for the Choice of their Surveyors . . . and Other Workmen. As also in Respect to Their Works, Materials, and Rates thereof. . . .* (London, 1663; facs. ed. Farnborough, 1969). At that time even the Académie Royale d'Architecture began to concern itself with the more practical aspects of the trade and take part in the publication of books on building procedures (55): the Director, Blondel, published editions of Savot in 1673 and 1685, and it was the establishment architect Pierre Bullet who wrote the most important of the trade's handbooks, *L'Architecture pratique* . . . (56).

Seventeenth-century authors appreciated the importance of illustrations in the dissemination of architectural knowledge, and the book of plates or the portfolio began to come into its own at this time. In France, this development was prefigured by the books of J. A. du Cerceau, and the most important of his successors was another architect best known for his engravings, Jean Marot. Like *Les plus excellent bastiments,* the "Petit Marot" (57) and the "Grand Marot" (58) illustrated contemporary buildings and provided an important record of the architecture of the time. Unlike the earlier book there was no accompanying text; these were purely sets of images without explanation or discussion.

Le Pautre published his own designs, as had du Cerceau in his first three books on architecture. Originally presented without a text in *Dessens de plusieurs palais* (59), the plates were republished in 1681 after the death of the author with an extensive commentary on their style by Daviler.

Several of the best-known architects of the time also prepared plates or texts for publication, although in several cases the books themselves were edited by others and appeared long after the authors' deaths. This was true of titles by Borromini and Wren, and it was the case with Guarino Guarini's treatise on architecture, *Architettura civile.* Guarini had published books on suveying and mathematics and on fortifications, but his architectural treatise did not appear until 1737, when it was prepared by Bernardo Vittone from unfinished manuscripts. However, a volume of the illustrations had been published in *Desegni di architettura civile ed ecclesiastica* (60) and that plate volume made Guarini's architectural work widely known. Independent of the text, the images served to spread interest in his designs, especially in Germany and Eastern Europe.

THE EIGHTEENTH CENTURY

With treatises and theory, portfolios and trade books, volumes on house building, and studies of ancient architecture, eighteenth-century books continued to develop many of the subjects introduced earlier. They also continued to serve an increasingly diverse audience from workmen to connoisseurs and to include many titles directed toward specific types of readers. Another point of continuity was the expansion of the architectural press into new geographic areas such as Russia and the United States as the influence of Western Europe spread.

There were also noticeable differences in the architectural press at this time, including the sheer number of books produced and purchased. Not only was writing acknowledged to be a legitimate branch of architectural activity and a mark of achievement for designers, as it had been in the seventeenth century, but the publication of books on architecture became a profitable business. By 1800 there were authors whose primary occupation was writing books on architecture. Some, such as the drawing teacher George Richardson, were otherwise undistinguished, but there were others such as Pierre Patte, "writer, editor, compiler and technical critic" (61), the man who finished J. F. Blondel's great treatise. Book sellers and publishers, notably Taylor and Taylor in London, also began to be able to advertise a specialty in architectural books.

A second important difference was an increased consciousness of purpose. Authors clearly understood the role publications had assumed; that is, architectural publications had never been simply records of developments, ideas, and designs, but always had promoted, even if unintentionally, their contents. Architects now more commonly published books to promote themselves as designers, and not only to promote their ideas about architecture. Entire movements, such as Neo-Palladianism in England, owed much of their influence to the power of the press.

Architects more commonly used words to launch criticism and to discuss theoretical issues perhaps, as had been suggested, because criticism and theory now had a real effect on built architecture. They began to speak out on matters of social concern. For instance, John Wood the Younger anticipated the nineteenth-century architect's involvement in social planning when he wrote *A Series of Plans for Cottages or Habitations of the Labourer* (62), which advocated decent housing for the rural poor. An architect who was not a writer, such as Paul Decker, could still present his thesis in the form of published designs, and architects such as Piranesi or Boulée could develop their theories on paper when circumstances prevented them from building.

There was also more exploitation of books as vehicles to broadcast architectural information. Many offered the text in more than one language; for example, Piranesi's last treatise, *Diverse maniere d'adornare* (Rome, 1769), reached out to his international audience with texts in French and English as well as Italian. An undistinguished London architect, Charles Cameron, succeeded dramatically in the use of a book to advertise himself: he was invited to Russia because Catherine II saw *The Baths of the Romans* (London, 1772); as a result he became her court architect.

In fact, the profession became dependent on the printed page to transport information. The geographic extent of western architecture, including established colonies and countryside patrons now ready for the latest styles, was enlarging at a rapid rate. One of the major developments in eighteenth-century architectural literature is the plethora of model books, pattern books, manuals and other books produced for the instruction of craftspersons and amateurs. The preface to James Gibbs' *A Book of Architecture* deplores the "abuses and absurdities" to be seen in "remote parts of the country," and recommends its "draughts of useful and convenient buildings and proper ornaments" to patrons who want buildings worthy of their expense (63). One of Batty Langley's many handbooks had a title that served as its own advertisement: *The Builder's Director, or Bench-mate: Being a Pocket-Treasury of the Grecian, Roman and Gothic Orders of Architecture, made easy to the Meanest Capacity by near 500 Examples* (64).

The most interesting of the new developments of this period was the expanded scope of ideas and styles under discussion. There was a general spirit of inquiry about origins and fundamental principles that had a profound effect on architecture. In the second half of the century archaeology and antiquarianism became potent forces for change. The search began for appropriate national styles and for exotica such as Chinese and Egyptian motifs. Many new kinds of theoretical and conceptual works were encouraged, from the rationalist theories of Cordemoy, Frézier, and Laugier to unbuildable "visionary" projects by Boulée. Architects embraced entire new areas of interest such as garden design and urban planning. In terms of publishing, this climate of wide-ranging inquiry was seen in the numbers of new translations (for example, the first translations of Palladio and Alberti into English), new editions, first editions of old manuscripts such as Guarini's *Architectura civilis* (1737) or Henry Aldrich's *Elementa architecturae civilis* (1789), and the publication of theories or writings by others, most notably those of Carlo Lodoli but also including Christopher Wren's *Parentalia* (65), edited by his son.

Eighteenth-century architecture was influenced not only by the content of contemporary books, but by the character of the illustrations that had begun to be provided. Surely the most important architectural illustrator of the century was Giovanni Battista Piranesi, who inspired romantic concepts of Roman classicism and encouraged its revival. Even his most abstract work in the *Carceri d'invenzione* was echoed in designs by architects such as Ledoux and George Dance the Younger. On a less elevated but wider plane there was the impact of the illustrations in English Palladian publications. These were comparatively simple line drawings with little sense of depth, such as the woodcuts in Palladio's treatise. This method of representation was copied by many popular pattern books and handbooks, and it transmitted the chaste, anti-baroque Palladian taste as effectively as any theoretical explanation. A very contrasting style, that of the picturesque movement, was later promoted by the more subtle printing technique of aquatint and by the style of illustrating elevations in landscape settings.

There were also two entirely new types of publication that dealt with architecture: the encyclopedia and the periodical. The most important of these was the *Encyclopédie, ou Dictionnaire raissonné des sciences, des arts et des métiers* published by Denis Didenot (Paris, 1751–1765) which covered the subject in articles written principally by Jacques-François Blondel (66). By the end of the century other encyclopedias had followed, including the *Encyclopédie Méthodique* (Paris, 1788–1820), with articles on architecture by the critic Quatremère de Quincy and articles on construction by J. B. Rondelet. Early periodicals such as the *Gentleman's Magazine* also began to include important letters, comments, and reports about building. For example, many reviews by A.-F. Frézier appeared in the *Mercure de France*.

Early encyclopedias or periodicals treated architecture simply as part of their general discussion of culture, which was typical of a certain fluidity between publications for architects and those of the society at large. For example, any discussion of eighteenth-century architectural literature should note the importance of Winckelmann and Goethe, whose focus was not specifically on architects or building design but whose work had a profound impact on contemporary culture, including architecture. Architects themselves were writing books on archaeology, history, social comment, and garden planning. "Architectural literature" started to become a broad term.

Colin Campbell's *Vitruvius Britannicus* (67) is now considered to be the first of the many books associated with neo-Palladianism in England. Its original intention was to publicize the work of its young author in a portfolio of 100 designs chosen to illustrate great English building in the classic style, but its preface heralded the anti-baroque sentiment and nationalist theme of the movement (68). It was a very influential volume and inspired imitations and responses in other countries as well, including *Vitruvius Scoticus* by William Adam (Edinburgh, 1750), *Den Danske Vitruvius* by Laurids Lauridsen de Thurah (Copenhagen, 1746), and J.-F. Blondel's *Architecture Françoise* (Paris, 1752–1755).

From the first, neo-Palladianism was associated with publishing (69): with Campbell, with the first English edition of Palladio's treatise (by Leoni; London, 1716), and with the multitude of pattern books that later popularized the movement. Lord Burlington supported the publication of a number of expensive volumes. These included a corrected edition of Palladio by Isaac Ware (London, 1737), William Kent's *Designs of Inigo Jones* (London, 1727), Burlington's own book on Palladio's drawings, *Fabbriche antiche* (London, 1730), and Robert Chastell's *Villas of the Ancients* (London, 1728).

The theory of neo-Palladianism was published in Robert Morris' books *An Essay in Defense of Ancient Architecture* (70) and *Lectures on Architecture* (71). Morris also produced books of designs consistent with these theories that encouraged the use of classical styles at a time when Gothic and Chinese were popular in England. As other Palladian books, the illustrations emphasized simple-to-follow geometric proportions and this encouraged their popularity, especially in America.

Other influential pattern books with designs in the Palladian manner included William Salmon's popular manual *Palladio Londonensis* (72) and the first architecture book to be printed in America, Abraham Swan's *The British Architect* (73).

Batty Langley and William Halfpenny inaugurated and were the most important authors of classic English pattern books, that is, handbooks with derivative collections of designs intended for the use of builders and craftspersons, often slapdash in appearance and pocket sized for ready reference. Langley began as a gardener and author of books on gardening but quickly shifted to the larger architecture market. He produced over 20 books on architecture not only for profit but also to educate fellow craftspersons, for he was closely associated with the Masonic Order, which emphasized fraternal bonds and improvement through instruction (74). His titles often suggest this intention, for example, *The Builder's Jewel: or the Youth's Instructor, and Workman's Remembrancer,* of which there were 14 editions after 1741. Eventually he came to advertise himself as a builder and teacher of architecture, apparently on the strength of his publishing experience alone (75).

Langley's books incorporated a wide variety of material including garden planning and the Gothic style. *Ancient Masonry* (76) was his most ambitious publication, the last word in pattern books and the largest English architectural book (77). Its text covered the Orders, mathematics and construction, and some 500 plates gave designs culled from English, French, and German sources, including rococo designs distinctly at odds with reigning Palladian taste.

William Halfpenny, also insignificant as an architect, produced a comparable number of titles between 1724 and his death in 1755. The later volumes were written with his brother John. *Practical Architecture* (78) covered the Orders and gave designs for architectural features based on Campbell's illustrations and on buildings by Inigo Jones. Seven editions were published during the life of its author. Halfpenny also wrote books on drawing the five Orders, building construction, and arithmetic and mensuration; then, in 1749, he began a series of design books most notable for "Chinese" buildings. He also published "Gothic" designs and an early volume on farmhouses.

Other pattern-book authors included the Palladian Robert Morris, and in the second half of the eighteenth century William Paine continued the tradition with eight handbooks of instruction and example. His earliest was *The Builder's Companion, and Workman's General Assistant* (London, 1758), a later version of which claimed to put the workman's "whole Trade in his Pocket." The wide popularity of the Adam style was due in part to his books. The first American pattern-book author was Asher Benjamin, a housewright, who published *The Country Builder's Assistant* in 1797.

Von Erlach's *Entwurff einer historischen Architectur*

(79), Langley's *Ancient Architecture Restored* (80), Chambers's *Designs of Chinese Buildings* (81), Stuart and Revett's *The Antiquities of Athens* (82), and Piranesi's *Della magnificenza ed architettura de'Romani* (83) were among the books that took part in a newly sympathetic discussion of non-Roman styles. Nicholas Pevsner has claimed for Fischer von Erlach's book the distinction of being the first general and pictorial history of architecture (84). It was a picture book of a different sort; it began with a broad survey of world architecture that included Stonehenge, a Chinese suspension bridge, the Hagia Sophia, and reconstructions of the Seven Wonders of the World, as well as Greek and Roman material, and it ended with a fifth book of his own designs. The use of a locational atlas and an attempt to verify, not merely copy, illustrations has given the book an historical perspective. Fischer's survey is also remarkably disinterested; he rejects the Gothic style but suggests no necessary superiority among the things he illustrates. "Artists will here see, that Nations dissent no less in their Taste for Architecture, than in Food and Raiment, and, by comparing one with the other they themselves make a judicious Choice" (85).

Fischer's book remained unique but not particularly influential. Other authors studied new styles specifically to expand their repertoire. Gothic was among the first to attract attention. Batty Langley's book on the subject, which attempted to systematize the style by suggesting five Gothic orders as counterpart to the classical ones, was original but ludicrous. The French rationalists were already seriously studying Gothic architecture, and in 1741 Soufflot lectured on its validity as a style.

Chinese architecture became popular for its exotic decorative vocabulary as well as its garden design. In England, Chinese influence was particularly strong in the 1740s, and several of the Halfpenny books promoted *chinoiserie* borrowed from France. William Chambers had actually been to China and he was the first English author to publish authentic examples. His book was particularly influential abroad; the section on gardens even had a Russian edition.

Like Gothic, Greek architecture inspired a more profound investigation and a significant architectural response. Antiquarians and archaeologists drew attention to the primacy of Greek classicism and Winckelmann argued for it as the better model (86). Stuart and Revett, Robert Adam, and Piranesi were among the architects who responded, studying and recording Greek buildings in an effort to expand knowledge about the origins of the classical style. These books, which began with J. D. Le Roy's *Les Ruines des plus beaux monuments de la Grèce* (Paris?, 1758), were presentation folios, sponsored by and intended for gentlemen amateurs as well as professional architects.

The Antiquities of Athens is a distinguished example of the group and it was the first to be undertaken. Stuart and Revett sailed for Greece in 1751 with the stated intention of producing very careful descriptions and measured drawings of its monuments and instructing "Artists, who aim at Perfection . . ." with "Examples, from the Fountain-head" of antiquity and the arts (87). The first volume of their book, sponsored by the London Society of Dilettanti, did not appear until 1762 and, in fact, concentrated on exceptional Hellenistic monuments that served as models only for garden ornaments; the immediate influence of Stuart and Revett was exerted through their advertised prospectus and their example as architect–archaeologists, which inspired many other expeditions and publications in the 1750s and 1760s (88). The second volume of *The Antiquities of Athens* was delayed until 1788, the year of Stuart's death, and subsequent volumes were associated with the Greek Revival of the early nineteenth century.

Piranesi was the champion of Roman architecture. Beginning in 1743, the architect had been producing books of etchings based on Roman buildings and ruins, both reconstructions and fantasies informed by archaeological inquiry and his own imaginative approach to design. There was a long tradition of Roman scenic views and of exercises in archaeological reconstruction, but Piranesi's intention was always different: he wanted to demonstrate the way ancient buildings could inspire a creative response in the modern designer. He answered the notion of Greek superiority with his first polemical treatise, *Della magnificenza,* which supplied an enormous amount of information about Roman architecture as evidence of its greatness. His position subsequently changed to a recommendation that artists seek inspiration through eclecticism, studying not only Roman, Tuscan, and Greek art, but Egyptian as well.

In the eighteenth century, France continued its great tradition of folios celebrating national architecture with the publication of *L'architecture Françoise* by Jean Mariette (89) and *Architecture Françoise* by Jacques-François Blondel (90); both authors reused material from their precursor Marot. Most other collections of illustrations aimed to demonstrate the architecture or architectural ideas of their authors. Two important types should be noted: the model book of designs, particularly of different types of houses, and the presentation folio of an architect's oeuvre.

The most important of the design books was James Gibbs' *A Book of Architecture* (91), which John Summerson has called "probably the most widely used architectural book of the century, not only throughout Britain but in the American colonies and the West Indies" (92). Gibbs was an architect with affinities to the Italian baroque style, which put him at odds with the neo-Palladian establishment of his time, and *A Book of Architecture* was his published response. It contains designs for buildings and ornaments; some were works he had already built, others were based on sources in Italy and France as well as England. Its excellent, practical illustrations contributed to its utility. Among other design books the Belgian Jean-François de Neufforge's *Receuil elémentaire d'architecture* (93) is remarkable for the range of designs presented, including lighthouses and prisons, and Paul Decker's books, *Ausführliche Anleitung zur Civilbaukunst* (94) and *Fürstlicher Baumeister . . .* (95), transmitted his architectural theory entirely through illustration.

Fürstlicher Baumeister gives designs for the house of a noble, as did J.-F. Blondel's important first book, *De la distribution de maisons de plaisance* (96). Of greater historical interest, however, are the many books that addressed the design of houses for all classes of people, such as

Charles-Etienne Briseux in *L'Art de bâtir des maisons de campagne* (2 vols., Paris, 1743), which expanded on Blondel's work, or the six editions of *Convenient and Ornamental Architecture* by John Crunden (London, 1767). It was in the eighteenth century that architects began to concern themselves with housing for the rural worker. The first volume exclusively on the subject was *Designs and Estimates of Farm-houses* by Daniel Garrett, which appeared in 1747 and was intended to instruct landowners. Its format was influential on later house publications: each farmhouse was illustated in plan and elevation, the dimensions and purposes of each room were given and estimates of price were included. John Plaw was the most important author of books on cottage design. Between 1785 and 1800 he produced three popular and influential volumes that used farmhouses as a model for middle-class homes and emphasized their picturesque aspects, including the integration of building and landscape. It was he and James Malton (*An Essay on British Cottage Architecture* (97)) who introduced asymmetrical design and advocated the use of vernacular materials such as half-timber and thatch, did much to idealize and romanticize the cottage.

Portfolios, which served to advertise an architect–author, were an important book type. As before, many of these had other stated purposes, such as the *Vitruvius Britannicus, The Antiquities of Athens,* or Ledoux's grandly titled *L'Architecture considérée sous le rapport de l'art, des moeurs, et de la législation* (98). However, pure demonstration volumes became increasingly common. Among the architects who published them were the otherwise undistinguished Marie-Joseph Peyre, whose *Oeuvres d'Architecture* (99) influenced the development of French neo-Classicism, and the young John Soane (*Designs in Architecture* (100), *Plans . . . of Buildings executed in Several Counties* (101), and *Sketches in Architecture* (102)). The most remarkable example from the period was *The Works in Architecture of Robert and James Adam,* which was exceptionally brash and exceptionally important. Its authors claimed to have succeeded in making "a remarkable improvement in the form, convenience, arrangement, and relief of apartments; a greater movement and variety, in the outside composition, and in the decoration of the inside, an almost total change" (103). Their book showed a mature architectural style and a free mix of influences from Palladianism to Piranesi, and it offered a brilliant display of plans and elevations and fixtures and furniture for churches and houses of all types. "Nothing like it had been known in the history of architectural publications," observed R. Wittkower (104). The Adam style of interior planning and decoration, which was codified, transmitted, and popularized by their books, became widely influential.

Boulée's manuscript *Essai sur l'art* (105) should be mentioned, although it was not published until the twentieth century. This is a treatise, but it is the character of the designs that is of particular importance. They have been called "visionary": the designs feature imaginary sites and ideal designs unconcerned with buildability. They are musings on architecture to accompany a text of a highly theoretical and intellectual nature.

The French and the Italians led the way in architectural theory at this time, particularly in the development of rationalist or functionalist doctrines. In 1702, Michel de Frémin wrote *Mémoires critiques de l'architecture, contenans l'idée de la vraye et de la fausse architecture,* an unusual pocket-book directed at laymen, architectural clients, which opposed ornament and orders in favor of practical building design based on function. The Abbé de Cordemoy's book *Nouveau traité de toute l'architecture ou l'art de bâtir* (106) took up this idea and applied it to an appreciation of the clarity and honesty of Greek and Gothic architecture, a theme traceable to Claude Perrault and Félibien in the seventeenth century. Among other things, Cordemoy proposed that the column be a support feature again, as it was in those styles. All of these emphases made Cordemoy, as Campbell, a benchmark for the end of the baroque style.

They were also among the ideas Laugier took from Cordemoy. Laugier was a Jesuit and a critic of architecture, painting, and music. His *Essai sur l'architecture* (107) attempted to establish a set of first principles for architecture, seeking, as did Rousseau, a basis in primitive culture. Thus arose the image of a "rustic cabin" and the proposal that its column, architrave, and pediment were the basic elements of all architecture. Any additional ornaments, such as the classical Orders, were to be kept as simple and logical as possible, with proportion and geometric shapes substituted as the basis for design when no Order was appropriate. His discussion of the logic of Greek temple design contributed to the rise of interest in Greek architecture, and his description of the ideal church was realized in Soufflot's Ste. Geneviève. The book also discussed garden design and urban planning, an unusual subject. The *Essai* was translated into both English and German by 1755 and it has had a considerable history of influence extending to the twentieth-century champions of rationalism and the Greek temple, Perret and Le Corbusier.

In Italy the Venetian teacher Fra Carlo Lodoli had preceded Laugier with an even bolder and more novel doctrine of functionalism. According to Lodoli, "It is essential that the structure of the building should be closely related to the static working of the whole building but that this should be visible to the spectator." He said, "materials should be used demonstratively, according to their proper nature and the proposed end" (108). Lodoli published nothing himself. His ideas were recorded first by Algarotti in Refs. 109, 110 and then by Memmo in Ref. 111, who sought to correct misrepresentations by Algarotti, among them the idea that Lodoli had advocated the rejection of all architectural ornament (112).

Palladian literature was still being produced as late as 1756 in *A Complete Body of Architecture* by Isaac Ware (113), but this was a mid-century treatise with a more comprehensive scope. Ware even included material from Laugier's recent *Essai.* The author's stated intention is particularly interesting in the context of architectural literature for, acknowledging the importance of books as sources of knowledge about architectural "discoveries and rules," he proposes to provide his readers with essential information by gathering "all that is useful in the work of others, at whatever time they have been written, or in whatsoever language," thus "supplying the place of all other books" (114).

Chambers's *A Treatise on Civil Architecture* (115) also reflected mid-century independence from the Palladians and was exceptionally important. It discusses the use of the orders—a second volume on construction and economics was never completed (116)—and for the third edition (1791) it was finally renamed *A Treatise on the Decorative Part of Civil Architecture.* As did Ware, Chambers sought to gather into one volume "sound precepts and good designs" from many sources. However, his book was informed by both learning and exceptionally wide personal experience, including travels in the Far East and five years in Rome. It reflected a more cultivated taste and encouraged personal judgment. It also introduced contemporary French architectural ideas and brought to the attention of English architects an enlarged range of Italian Renaissance buildings (117). Chambers' *Treatise* was one of the most influential books of its time.

Jacques-François Blondel was the most important author of architectural literature in the eighteenth century. In addition to *Maisons de Plaisance, Architecture françoise,* and his articles for the *Encyclopédie,* his ideas were presented in many books and pamphlets—even in a romance novel (118). He was also the most important teacher of architecture in the eighteenth century, whose students included many distinguished architects from England, Germany, and Russia, as well as France. The *Cours d'architecture* (119), his lectures as professor at the Royal Academy of Architecture, exhibits his doctrine most comprehensively. As he presents his ideas here and elsewhere, particularly in the *Architecture françoise,* Blondel was a consummate academic, a classicist grounded in the orders and the texts of the early treatises, and a teacher concerned with attention to detail. He divided the study of architecture into "Decoration," "Distribution and Arrangement of Buildings" (planning and details), "Construction," and "Materials and Methods," the last part finished after his death by his student Pierre Patte. His approach was not narrow or prejudiced (he considered the virtues of Gothic and baroque architecture and included what was perhaps the first published illustration of the Erechtheum (120), but aimed at the development of taste and the rational analysis of problems.

Blondel's *Cours* was similar to a number of other volumes from that time, a sort of textbook. In the eighteenth century many people were learning from books: craftspersons and carpenters, patrons and draughtsmen, and now formal students of architecture as well. Architectural textbooks aimed to be comprehensive introductions to architecture and in that respect they were the descendants of the original treatises. Among those who worked in the Vitruvian tradition was the architect Bernardo Vittone from Turin, whose treatises, *Instruzioni elementari per indirizzo de' giovani allo studio dell' architettura civile,* (2 vols., Lugano, 1760) and its supplement, *Instruzione diverse* . . . (2 vols., Lugano, 1766), covered mathematics, measurement, the orders, and ornament, as well as illustrating buildings and features. Francesco Milizia, one of the new breed of professional writers, even borrowed Vitruvius's classifications as the structure for his *Principj di architettura civile* (121), with one volume on beauty, one on commodiousness, and a third on materials and methods of building. Milizia's work was a text in the best sense, a source book of information gathered from great writers on architecture—although he rarely credited them. It offers a foundation in ancient and Renaissance sources and a summary and interpretation of many of the great architectural writers of his century, including Algarotti, Laugier, Blondel, the *Encyclopédie,* and Chambers.

THE NINETEENTH CENTURY

With the development of efficient printing methods as well as a truly diverse building industry, the literature on architecture grew exponentially. Many of the classic book types continued to be important, including design portfolios, books on domestic architecture, and theoretical works. Others, such as builders' guides, followed established lines for only a short time. Some subjects quickly became the domain of a specialized literature. Architectural history was one of these, but it is appropriate to survey at least some of the major works here because not only was the subject vital to nineteenth-century designers, but many of the histories were written by major architects.

The two most important new developments of the time were the appearance of architectural magazines and the proliferation of reference works, particularly encyclopedias, on architecture. The architectural encyclopedia was the modern version of the treatise, with information and instruction on all aspects of the subject. Tony Vidler has called the *Dictionnaire historique d'Architecture* (by A. C. Quatremère de Quincy, 3 vols, from the *Encyclopédie Méthodique,* Paris, 1788–1823) "the first truly systematic work of theory and criticism," a discussion of metaphysical and theoretical concepts as well as practical, historical, archaeological, and didactic material (122). By the nineteenth century predictably this required many volumes. It is interesting to note that the only author to attempt an "encyclopedia" in one volume, Joseph Gwilt, was an editor of Vitruvius, and his book (*Encyclopedia of Architecture, Historical, Theoretical and Practical,* London, 1842) is, in fact, more like an old treatise in form and in its emphasis on subjects such as geometry and the Orders. The most extensive early reference work was the *Handbuch der Architektur* (orig. ed. Josef Durm, Darmstadt, 1883–1943), a series of 79 monographs on all aspects of architectural types.

An important type of portfolio was the book of ornamental details. Ornament was a central issue for architects of the period, who first desired to understand with accuracy and to replicate the decorative features of Gothic and other styles and later attempted to develop a wholly modern decorative vocabulary. The most important of the books was by Owen Jones, the *Grammar of Ornament* (London, 1856), an album of color plates with a brief text on the character and principles of ornament. Jones's book was primarily devoted to exotic styles from Egypt to the Far East; others were more limited in scope. The literature of architecture had also begun to feature discussions about ornament, such as Sullivan's "Ornament in Architecture" (123).

Topographic surveys were still important and among the many picture books that inspired architects, those by John Britton and Paul Marie Letarouilly were most significant. Each produced exceptionally fine engraved work and each stimulated appreciation for the style he illustrated: English medieval for Britton, Italian Renaissance for Letarouilly. Britton published over 12 works on English architecture including *The Architectural Antiquities of Great Britain* (London, 1807–1826). Letarouilly's *Edifices de Rome moderne* (3 vols., Paris, 1840–1857) instructed generations of academic architects and served some of them as a model book: the drawings for the Boston Public Library are even said to imitate their style of draftsmanship (124).

However, there was also an important variation of the topographic survey, in which the author reported and commented on the most recent developments abroad. There were many examples of this internationalism after about 1880, including Paul Sédille, *L'Architecture moderne en Angleterre* (Paris, 1890) and the periodical *Academy Architecture,* which was founded in 1888 by a German architect specifically to bring to the attention of European designers information about contemporary English production. In 1896, the German government sent Hermann Muthesius to England to study housing, and his books illuminated late-nineteenth-century English achievements in a way that would not be traced in English for a long time. The same can be seen a short time later in the case of Frank Lloyd Wright. In 1929 it was noted his work could be studied in two German books, one Dutch book, and one in French, but in English there were only articles and parts of general histories of U.S. architecture (125).

This was just one of many manifestations of the now constantly acknowledged importance of publishing to contemporary architecture. When the Royal Institute of British Architects was founded in 1834 it had as one of its original objectives "the publication of such communications as may be curious and interesting to the Public and the Profession" (126). Fifteen years later the architects Sidney Smirke, C. R. Cockerell, and Sir Charles Barry were among the board members of the new Architectural Publication Society, a forerunner of other ventures, the goals of which were to publish and republish standard architectural material. More recent examples are the *Bauwelt Fundamente* series and the Architectural History Foundation.

Another encouragement to architectural writing was the rise in the number of teachers of architecture. From John Soane and J.-N.-L. Durand at the beginning of the century to Lethaby and Gaudet at its end, many ideas originally formulated for lectures naturally found their way into print. Karl Friedrich Schinkel, author of *Sammlung Architektonischer Entwerfe* (Berlin, 1819–1840), even sketched the contents for an architectural textbook (127).

This was also the time of the first architectural critics writing for the public. Ruskin is thought of immediately, but by the end of the century architectural criticism was already a part of the much less-elevated literature of popular magazines. The first American example of this may have been A. J. Downing's editorials in *The Horticulturist* about 1850. Later, *Harper's* and *Scribner's* published articles by Montgomery Schuyler and Russell Sturgis.

With the advent of the modern novel, the nonprofessional books that influenced architects in this age of romanticism began to include literature. The best example is perhaps the profound effect of Victor Hugo's *Notre Dame de Paris* (1831) on his contemporaries, an important foundation for the popularity of the Gothic style in France and the work of Viollet-le-Duc. The influence of architecture on literature may also be noted because as architectural writings developed a consistent vocabulary and propagated attitudes about building types, they started to be used as evocative settings. *Jane Eyre,* for example, features the innocent, rustic cottage and the forbidding castellated manor, among other architectural backdrops.

Since 1800 there have been so many new materials and new building techniques that technical literature can only be introduced here with a few examples that continue earlier book types. For books such as William Fairbairn's *On the Application of Cast and Wrought Iron to Building Purposes,* New York, 1854, or J. K. Freitag's, *Architectural Engineering with Special Reference to High Building Construction,* New York, 1895 (both published by John Wiley & Sons), reference should be made to specialized books such as Peter Collins's *Concrete: Vision of a New Architecture* (London, [1959]).

Rondelet's, *Traité theorique et pratique de l'art de bâtir* (128) was the major study of building construction in the early nineteenth century, and as such was widely read and imitated by other authors. Rondelet had been a pupil of Blondel and one of those who finished Soufflot's Panthéon. He was professor at the Ecole Centrale des Travaux Publics and later at the Ecole Spéciale d'Architecture. His book advocated the point of view that "the essential purpose of architecture was to construct solid edifices by employing exact quantities of selected materials, and setting them in position with skill and economy . . . its essential aim was . . . to build edifices which combined in the most beautiful form all the parts necessary for its destination" (129). In other words, it was rationalist, and one of its interesting features (appropriate for a disciple of Soufflot) was a discussion of the principles of Gothic building construction.

Most early nineteenth-century building manuals were intended for craftspersons and were more strictly pragmatic, as were their predecessors. They continued to be produced in large numbers and to be very influential. One of the most important of these authors was Peter Nicholson, an Englishman whose books such as *The New Carpenter's Guide* (London, 1792; 16th ed., Philadelphia, 1867) were the major source of information for American technical writers such as Asher Benjamin (130), a prolific author of handbooks for the American market such as *The Architect* (formerly *Practical House Carpenter,* Boston, 1830, in its 6th edition by 1839).

Neither Nicholson nor Benjamin was original in his writing, but at least one major new idea did appear in the craft handbooks: the first description of balloon-frame construction, found in Bell's *Carpentry Made Easy* (131). A few of the technical books of the time also remained in print long enough to be very significant; for example,

Thomas Tredgold's *Elementary Principles of Carpentry* was first published in 1820 and its eighth edition was recommended as standard in 1893 (132). Ira O. Baker's *A Treatise on Masonry Construction* is another example; it entered a ninth edition in 1903 (133).

Durand's treatise, *Précis des leçons de' architecture données à l'école de Polytechnique* (134), was the most important one published in the early nineteenth century. A major source of instruction and advice for classical architects, and a synthesis of late eighteenth-century French theory and practice, it was published and republished until 1840 (135).

These were his lectures at the Ecole Polytechnique, where he became professor of architecture in 1795. The first section covers general information and principles, including the use of materials, and the second section offers eclectic designs derived from the combination of structural elements. The second volume contains his influential designs for various building types, both public and private, ancient (temples) and modern (hospitals; museums), "all the individual structures of the model Napoleonic city, of which . . . the next decades . . . were to see so many executed by Durand's pupils and other emulators of his ideals" (136).

Durand's approach to composition was especially practical, with an emphasis on functionalism, economy, and formal clarity. For drawing plans he used the elementary technique of gridded paper with the square as a repeated module. The utility and accessibility of Durand's designs made the *Précis* widely popular. It was used, for example, by Maximilian Godefoy in America. Its most important heritage was, however, among the great Neoclassical buildings of Germany by Klenze, Görtner, and Schinkel.

Pugin was a polemicist with decided and brilliantly projected opinions concerning appropriate form in architecture. They were largely inspired by a parochial concern, religious reform, and sprang from his perception that modern society and modern architecture as well as modern religion should rid itself of base and muddled post-Reformation influences. Pugin championed Gothic architecture—the subtitle of *Contrasts* (137) is *A Parallel Between the Noble Edifices of the Fourteenth and Fifteenth Centuries, and Similar Buildings of the Present Day, Shewing the Present Decay of Taste*—and his defense of that style is one of the foundations of the Gothic revival.

Not only was Pugin's effect on his contemporaries profound, but his influence has also extended well beyond the period of the Gothic revival. Many basic principles of modern architectural design have been traced to him, and he also anticipated architects' involvement in the decorative arts. Not only did he design church furniture, liturgical clothing, and instruments, but he argued the importance of excellence in the minor arts, and thus lay both the practical and theoretical foundation for the later arts and crafts movement (138).

John Ruskin and Viollet-le-Duc were the two most influential architectural writers of their day. Ruskin began writing about architecture for J. C. Loudon's *Architectural Magazine;* the subject was "the poetry of architecture," prefiguring his high-minded and rhetorical approach to the subject. Fired by his conviction and by his brilliant use of language, Ruskin's criticism was especially effective. While identifying the seven lamps of architecture (Sacrifice, Truth, Power, Beauty, Life, Memory, and Obedience) (139), Ruskin discusses the morality of architecture, the sublime, the basis of architectural beauty in nature, craftsmanship, the preservation and restoration of buildings, and appropriate styles for the time. Ruskin did not believe that a new, modern style was necessary; he advocated the use of some of the medieval styles of Italy, including Venetian Gothic, or the early English decorated style.

Among the aspects of his work that had a visible impact the promotion of Italian medieval architecture, with its brick and polychromatic traditions as a model, should be mentioned. In addition, Ruskin was a primary source for the ideal of a return-to-craft tradition developed by subsequent arts and crafts movements. The lamp of life proclaimed the joy of craftsmanship, and Ruskin's *Stones of Venice* (2 vols., London, 1851 and 1853) contained an essay on "The Nature of Gothic," which contrasted the free artisans of the Middle Ages with the slave artists of classical times. William Morris was one of Ruskin's most important followers and he helped found not only the first modern crafts studio, but the Society for the Protection of Ancient Monuments (1877).

Viollet-le-Duc was an architect best known for his restoration of French medieval buildings and for his writings. Among these, *Entretiens sur l'architecture* (140) carried his ideas as far as the USSR (141), and in the U.S. it was recommended by Frank Lloyd Wright as the only other source of instruction his son needed to be an architect (142).

Viollet-le-Duc's theoretical position was structural rationalism. He sought in the architecture of the Middle Ages a model for his own time and he credited the Gothic style with achieving "truth" in architecture, in which all the features, from ribs and buttresses to pinnacles and gargoyles, were, he believed, dictated by functional or structural necessity.

These ideas were most fully worked out in the 10 volumes of his great *Dictionnaire raisonné de l'architecture française du XIe au XVIe siècle* (10 vols., Paris, 1854–1868); the *Entretiens,* which he began in 1857 when he began teaching, was more didactic and broader in scope. It is divided into 16 discourses. The first 10 covered art and society and the history of architecture; the remainder lectured on architectural education, decoration, and sculpture. The eleventh and twelfth discourses are famous for advocating the use of modern materials in contemporary design, with examples of exposed iron supports.

Gottfried Semper began writing architectural theory after he was forced to leave Dresden, where he had been director of the Bauschule of the Royal Academy, and interrupt his design practice. *Der Stil in den technischen und tektonischen Kunsten oder praktische Aesthetik* (143) was his major work but it contained comparatively little on architecture; inspired by a stay in England he considered the evolution of industrial arts such as textiles and masonry. This was, presumably, background for a study of comparable evolutionary changes in architecture, but in the end he did not provide a separate section on building.

His ideas about architectural form were recorded in

other essays, however, including his early work *Die Vier Elemente der Baukunst* (Braunsweig, 1851), in which it is suggested all architecture is based on four elements including the hearth, symbol of civilization, a prefiguration of Frank Lloyd Wright's emphasis on the fireplace as symbolic heart of a house. Semper was, in fact, known to the Chicago School, especially to Louis Sullivan, and a translation by John Root of his essay "Uber Baustile" appeared in the *Inland Architect* for 1890–1891. European architects such as Berlage and Wagner also cited his influence, although in many cases his ideas were simplified or misinterpreted to conform to their own.

Americans were contributing to the discussion as well. Books by Louis Sullivan, notably *The Autobiography of an Idea* (144), did not appear until the twentieth century, but he had already written a great deal in magazines. His essay on "The Tall Office Building Artistically Considered" (145) is an example, one in which the author grapples with the problem of appropriate form for an entirely new type of building and suggests the aphoristic principle "form follows function."

With the rise of the middle class, housing design had become a matter of concern for increased numbers of architects and consumers. At the beginning of the century J. C. Krafft provided books of French designs including the *Plans, coupes et élévations des plus belles maisons et des hôtels construits à Paris . . .* (146). In England the period was dominated by a taste for cottages and villas in the picturesque manner promoted in many design collections by P. F. Robinson or Francis Goodwin, for example, or in "the culminating anthology of the Picturesque" (147), J. C. Loudon's *An Encyclopedia of Cottage, Farm, and Villa Architecture* (148).

In the U.S. the most important volumes on the smaller detached house were by Alexander Jackson Downing, the horticulturalist, landscape gardener, and self-styled "rural architect." His books, prepared in collaboration with A. J. Davis, were the first in the United States to promote picturesque asymmetry and other aspects of the cottage and villa mode, and they were extremely popular (*The Architecture of Country Houses* (149)). It has been said they have altered forever the look of the countryside. *Cottage Residences* (150) appeared in subsequent editions until 1887, and untold numbers of Gothic or Italianate houses in the United States were based on its designs.

By the start of the Civil War the popularity of such houses was being challenged by a new taste for the French Second Empire style, transmitted largely by books such as César Daly's *L'architecture privée du XIXe Siècle . . . sous Napoleon III* (151). In America the style was much less restrained than in France, and surely this is partially due to the mode of transmission.

In the late nineteenth century, books on domestic architecture were produced by many of the important figures of the time, including Viollet-le-Duc (*Histoire de l'habitation humaine . . .*, Paris, n.d.; trans. as *Habitations of Man in All Ages,* London, 1875/6) and Richard Norman Shaw (*Sketches for Cottages and Other Buildings,* London, 1878). However, the most significant group of books is probably that of the "indefatigable" house design publishers A. J. Bicknell, George Woodward, and Palliser, Palliser & Co. They made the late nineteenth century a period of great importance for pattern books in the United States.

A growth of interest in architectural history was, as before, largely due to architects' desires to emulate past styles or to investigate principles of design. These needs produced many specialized books, some of which have profoundly influenced architects. A sample might include Thomas Rickman's *An Attempt to Discriminate the Styles of English Architecture from the Conquest to the Reformation* (London, 1819), the first successful attempt to categorize English medieval styles, which suggested terminology still in use. Seven editions appeared by 1881. Reginald Blomfield furthered the neoclassical revival with his *History of Renaissance Architecture in England: 1500 to 1800* (2 vols., London, 1897), and many other architects also wrote on the topic of ancient buildings. The Grand Prix winners also produced historical studies of sorts in the drawings and restorations of monuments each was required to send to Paris, selections of which have been published; for example, H. d'Espouy, *Fragments d'architecture antique d'après les relevés et restaurations des anciens pensionnaires de l'Académie de France à Rome* (152) and *Fragments d'architecture du Môyen Age et de la Renaissance . . .* (153) and the exhibition *Roma antiqua: envoies des architectes français (1788–1924)* (154).

At this time surveys of the history of architecture were also produced with increasing frequency and skill. David Watkin discusses them in his book *The Rise of Architectural History*. This will serve to introduce only the more important of the general histories and biographies.

James Fergusson, a Scot, wrote the first history of architecture that was comprehensive in the modern sense, *History of Architecture in all Countries, from the Earliest Times to the Present Day* (155). While making a fortune in India as a businessman he developed an interest in the architecture of the East, and began his long writing career with a volume on the temples of India. In its final form Fergusson's *History of Architecture in All Countries* had four volumes, two on ancient and medieval architecture, and separate volumes on Indian and Eastern architecture and modern styles. It was useful to architects not only because of its scope, but also because of its wood engravings. It was kept current until 1893 with a third revised edition.

German histories were distinguished. Karl Schnaase was a pupil of Hegel and an early proponent of the idea of architecture as an expression of *Zeitgeist* or the spirit of an age (*Geschichte der Bildenden Kunst* (156)). Franz Kugler's *Geschichte der Baukunst* (157) was less theoretical. Kugler was a professor of art history in Berlin and for the first time a modern book of architectural history did not emphasize medieval architecture. In fact, the Renaissance in Italy was surveyed in an essay entitled by Jacob Burckhardt himself (158). The most important nineteenth-century history of architecture was written by Choisy, a civil engineer and a professor of architecture at the Ecole des Ponts et Chaussées in Paris. Unlike previous French histories, he approached the subject from a rigorously rationalist point of view: architectural form derived exclusively from the circumstances of building construction. Thus style was not a function of taste but was the result of geographical and social circumstances, including materials, tools, and machinery and the organization of labor and transport. Thus, his book was a history of construction, as were his many other volumes on "The Art of Building" such as *L'art de bâtir chez les Egyptiens* (159). All were notable for their engravings (more than 1700 in the *Histoire de l'architecture* (160) alone), primarily the simplified axonometric diagrams that proved to be one of the most memorable and influential aspects of the work. As Reynar Banham pointed out, their homogeneity of style reinforced the notion of continuity in architectural practice and their abstract, elegant appearance would appeal to men such as Le Corbusier, one of many who have reprinted them (161).

As histories, Choisy's books have become dated, but they will always be important for the role they played in history. Choisy was an important link between the rationalism of Viollet-le-Duc and that of modern architects, especially Perret and Le Corbusier (162), and his influence on the perception of architectural history has been profound.

The study of architects themselves is a special point of view that also gained momentum in the nineteenth century. Collections of architects' biographies began with Vasari, of course, and in the eighteenth century Milizia wrote *Le vite de' celebri architetti d'ogni nazione e d'ogni tempo* (Rome, 1768, trans. as *The Lives of Celebrated Architects Ancient and Modern,* London, 1826). Three types of books on the subject were written in the nineteenth century: the general survey, such as Quatremére de Quincy's *Histoire de la vie et des ouvrages des plus célèbres architectes du XIe siècle . . . à . . . XVIIIe* (2 vols., Paris, 1830), or Elie Brault, *Les Architects par leurs oeuvres* (3 vols., Paris, 1893); biographical entries in dictionaries and encyclopedias, particularly that of the Architectural Publication Society; and individual biographies such as Luigi Vanvitelli the Younger's *Vita dell'architectto Luigi Vanvitelli* (Naples, 1825), or *The Life of Thomas Telford, Civil Engineer, written by himself* (London 1838)). There were also books on Barry, Lefuel, Görtner, Pugin, and Charles Garnier, among others, and Marianna Van Rensselaer's distinguished early study of *Henry Hobson Richardson and His Works* (163).

The single most important development in architectural literature since 1800 has been the appearance and rise of magazines devoted to the profession. Architectural magazines are directed primarily at architects, offering information concerning current designs, techniques, materials, and ideas. They are distinguished from books particularly by their emphasis on timeliness; indeed, their worth has sometimes been measured by their ability to be avant-garde. New journals have challenged established ones whose points of view have become dated. This was already true by the mid-nineteenth century, and it is one of the reasons there have been so many journal titles.

The spectrum of architectural periodicals, in fact, reflected that of architectural books: some were synoptic (especially the earlier examples); some were directed primarily at builders (for Liverpool tradespersons of the 1830's *The Pioneer;* in America *Manufacturer & Builder,* fd. 1869; and some at engineers (*The Surveyor, Engineer and Architect,* London 1840–1843; *Zeitschrift für architektur und ingenieurwesen,* Hannover, 1855–1921); some were portfolios (*Croquis d'architecture,* Paris, 1866–1888/1895–1898; *Architectural Record Great American Artist Series,* 1895–1899); and some had a more theoretical or critical character.

In addition there were the journals of architectural societies, trade magazines such as *The Brickbuilder* (Boston, fd. 1892) or the Hennebec house publication *Le béton armée* (Paris, fd. 1898), along with many nonarchitectural magazines. Of these last, a large number were associated with the applied-art movement, such as The *Studio* in England (1893–1964), the *Jahrbuch des Deutschen Werkbundes* in Germany (1912–5/20), or *The Craftsman* in America (1901–1916). At one end of the spectrum *Godey's Lady's Book* was an important indicator of popular taste in building (164); at the other were magazines such as *Harper's* that published professional architectural criticism. Of all the nonprofessional magazines the most influential was *The Ecclesiologist,* a small publication begun in 1841 by Cambridge undergraduates to promote a reform of church architecture as part of a more general religious reform. One of the original polemical architectural magazines, it played a central role in the Gothic revival and has been called "the most powerful journal ever influencing people in [England]" (165).

Among true architectural periodicals the earliest examples are in German; early English titles such as *The Builder's Magazine* (London, 1774–1786), or the *London Architectural Society Publications* (1808–1810) were serial books or antiquarian publications rather than architectural journals. The first major architectural periodical has been said to be the *Allgemeine bauzeitung,* founded in Vienna in 1836 and published until World War I. However it was preceded by a number of shorter-lived journals including the *Journal für Baukunst* (Berlin, 1829–1851) and the *Sammlung nützlicher aufsütze und nachrichten, die baukunst betreffend* (Berlin, 1797–1806), edited by David Gilly, which may be the earliest example of an architects' magazine.

In England the most important periodical of the century was *The Builder* (London, 1843–1966). It had the great advantage of frequent publication—it was, in fact a newspaper—and of brilliant leadership, especially in George Godwin, who was editor from 1844 to 1883. *The Builder* was a center for architectural discussion as well as news, with potent editorials, articles, and correspondence on all subjects from historic restorations to civil engineering. Earlier English periodicals included J. C. Loudon's *Architectural Magazine* (1834–1839) and the Anglo-American *The Civil Engineer and Architect's Journal* (1837–1868), not to mention the publications of the Royal Institute of British Architects (*Proceedings* and *Transactions*), which began in 1834. English magazines soon exhibited important changes in the technology of printing illustrations, changes that affected contemporary architecture; for example, *The Building News and Engineering Journal* (1854–1926) distinguished itself by using photo-litho and pen and ink sketch illustrations rather than wood engravings; *The Architect and Contract Reporter* (fd. 1869) used two-color lithography (166). Only the *Architectural Review, for the artist and Craftsman* (fd. 1896) survived as a major force in the twentieth century, at first as one of the beautifully designed and produced magazines associated with the arts and crafts and art nouveau movements, and later as a potent advocate for the modern movement.

France and the United States were also active centers of periodical publishing in the nineteenth century. The *Revue général de l'architecture et des traveaux publics* appeared in Paris in 1840, the same year the Société Centrale des Architectes Français was founded. (Its journal, *L'Architecture,* began in 1888.) The *Revue,* edited by César Daly, used precise, steel-engraved illustrations. *Encyclopédie d'Architecture* (1851–1931) and *Le Moniteur des architectes* (1866–1869) followed. In 1885, Paul Planat founded one of the most important of the French journals, *La Construction Moderne,* which emphasized practical considerations.

The first American architectural periodical was *The Architects' and Mechanics' Journal* (1859–1861), followed by *The American Builder and Journal of Art* (1868–1895) and other, shorter-lived magazines. It was not until the last quarter of the century that magazines of long and significant history appeared: *The American Architect and Building News* (1876–1938), the *Architectural Record* (fd. 1891), and *The Architectural Review* (1891–1921). Important journals also began to be produced in regional centers at that time, such as the *Inland Architect* in Chicago and the *California Architect and Building News.*

Other early periodicals included *Bouwkundige bijdragen* (Amsterdam, fd. 1842) and *Boletin español de arquitectura* (Madrid, fd. 1846), but, in general, the appearance of architectural periodicals in European countries such as Holland and Russia was an indication of the modern movement of the twentieth century.

THE TWENTIETH CENTURY

By the end of the nineteenth century architectural literature had not only expanded in terms of the number of books and the range of building types and styles covered, but it had begun to respond to new demands from both the profession and the public. For example, with changes in the training of architects, books came to be used to supplement or supply some of the education offered at academies and universities. Books and articles also helped the builder keep abreast of industrial and professional developments. The publishing industry itself has sought to produce useful and hence profitable new types of books, for example, *Sweet's Catalog Files.*

In this century more information and news on architecture has been recorded than ever before. This is because of continued expansion along earlier lines, and also because architects and members of the public by now have come to expect that information will be made available in print. Also, the number of voices to be heard keeps rising. Modern architects are expected to be not only artists but advocates: to exhort and interpret as well as create, to demonstrate ideas with words as well as with buildings. Many factors have contributed to this development, including the increased importance of theory to architecture—especially the idea of certain styles or ways of building being more "honest" or "appropriate" than others, which has encouraged debate. Another contributing factor has been the rise of the idea of an architect's social responsibility, culminating in the notion of the modern movement that architecture could and should play a decisive role in the creation of an ideal society. The result has been that a large number of better-educated twentieth-century architects have written books and articles; indeed, architects such as Mies van der Rohe who do not write are exceptions.

Some of the more important of these authors were teachers whose writings were extensions of their teaching and whose influence was due to a combination of personal contacts and published ideas. W. R. Lethaby was an early example, a man whose influence has waxed and waned since his own time, when his romantic notions of medieval architecture, a combination of arts and crafts ideals and Viollet-le-Duc, underlay the antiformalism of *Architecture, an Introduction to the History and Theory of the Art of Building* (167). Walter Gropius is perhaps the most famous teacher–writer of the century, with a long and important bibliography (168) which includes editing volumes of the "Bauhausbucher," the series of books produced by the Bauhaus on subjects related to its activity. He summarized his principles in *The Scope of Total Architecture* (169).

The proliferation of architectural literature, especially architectural journalism, has itself contributed to the situation. The literature now virtually guarantees a forum for any important architect. Architectural journalism also pursues new ideas more actively, publishing projects as well as buildings, generating comment and explanation even before they are volunteered; this branch of the literature has expanded rapidly into popular magazines, newspapers, and television. To publish and to be published is now an important (if regrettable) measure of success for U.S. architects.

As in the nineteenth century, there was a continued separation of technical and practical writing from the main body of architectural literature. Architectural history developed as a separate discipline, especially after 1930 under the influence of German and Swiss art historians. Urban studies presented a special case because, although it too was expanding rapidly as an independent subject, it occupied the minds of many important architects. In 1904, Tony Garnier had already exhibited his comprehensive design for a *Cité industrielle* (published with revisions 1918), and subsequent architects have often applied themselves to the grand design problems inherent in urban planning. Le Corbusier is the most important of these. Among books on urban design, those by the philosopher and historian Lewis Mumford are especially noteworthy (170).

Classic forms of architectural literature such as the design portfolio and books on houses continue to be important, with an international perspective now the norm. The most famous portfolio of the twentieth century may be the 1910 Wasmuth volume on Frank Lloyd Wright, *Ausgeführte Bauten und Entwerfe von Frank Lloyd Wright* (171), also a major example of international influences. The *Ouevre complete* of Le Corbusier (172) doubtless is the most extensive. Among the innumerable books and exhibitions that have transported news from other countries, a few important examples are *Die englische Baukunst der Gegenwart* by Hermann Muthesius (173), *Amerikaansche Reiserinneringen* by H. P. Berlage (174), *Wie baut Amerika?* by Richard Neutra (175), and the RIBA Centenary Exhibition, "International Architecture 1924–34."

Books on houses assumed all forms. Among the volumes of designs, one of the most important was *Das fenglische Haus* by Hermann Muthesius (176). From 1896 to 1903 Muthesius was a diplomatic attaché in London, there to study developments in English architecture and design, and *Das englische Haus* was one of the surveys he produced. It had both superficial influence (an "English style" for German houses) and a more basic one in promoting functionalism. Some studies have addressed current interests in mass housing or prefabricated units, R. Buckminster Fuller's "Dymaxion House" (177), for example, while others have recalled book types established centuries before such as the book of advice for patrons or the pattern book.

The literature has also been expanded by the fact that because they have been better aware of the sequence of architectural developments in the past, twentieth-century writers have been quick to attempt a definition of the architecture of their own time. The number of prewar books that addressed "modern architecture" is impressive, beginning perhaps in 1896 with Otto Wagner's *Moderne Architektur* (Vienna). In 1901, the Wasmuth series *Die Architektur des XX. Jahrhunderts: Zeitschrift für moderne Baukunst* began, with commentary in three languages. Other such titles, some with large, international audiences, included Gustav Platz's *Die Baukunst der neuesesten Zeit* (178), Bruno Taut's *Die neue Baukunst in Europa und Amerika* (trans. as *Modern Architecture,* London and New York, 1929) (179), J. M. Richards', *An Introduction to Modern Architecture* (180), and Alfred Roth's, *La nouvelle architecture. Die neue architektur. The New Architecture* (181). Charles Jencks is among those now writing books that define and interpret current movements.

As for new varieties of architectural literature, at least two, the manifesto and the exhibition catalog, deserve special mention. The idea of a published manifesto, a terse public statement of philosophical position and design intention, was an end result of the nineteenth-century emphasis on theory crystallized by the close relationship between radical politics and the arts in early twentieth-century Europe. Often the manifesto was an opening shot for a movement such as futurism, for example, *Manifesto dell'architettura futurista* (182), or a group such as de Stijl, " 'De Stijl' Manifesto I," *De Stijl* (183). Other important early manifestos included that of constructivism by Naum Gabo and Antoine Pevsner, *Realist Manifesto* (184), and of suprematism by Kasimir Malevich, *Suprematist manifesto Unovis* (185). A manifesto has some irresistible connotations and in spite of a tendency to become empty declamation it outlived the revolutionary 1920s; *Acceptera* by Uno Åhren, Gunnar Asplund and co-workers (186) and " 'Situationists': International Manifesto" (187) are two subsequent examples.

Architectural exhibitions have come of age in the twentieth century and have spawned many publications, most obviously their catalogs, which make an important contribution simply just by gathering material together in a particular way. The best example of this may be *The International Style* by Henry-Russell Hitchcock and Philip Johnson (188), from the first architectural exhibition at the New York Museum of Modern Art. The book surveyed, defined, and for better or worse gave a name to the architecture of the preceding decade. Venice's Biennales have also been particularly important exhibition places for architecture, and its first International Exhibition of Architecture produced *The Presence of the Past* (189).

Modern architects have been affected by nonprofessional literature to a degree even greater than their predecessors. There are a number of suggested explanations, including not only their level of education and a Vitruvian self-image but also the concept of a close relationship between architecture, art, and society. All sorts of books have been cited as influences, such as the philosophy of the mathematician Schoenmaekers on the de Stijl movement and the poet Scheerbart on German architects of the same period. It was Ralph Adams Cram who brought about the publication of Henry Adams' *Mont St. Michel and Chartres* in 1913. Even more interesting is the influence exerted by the world of architecture on modern popular literature; the image of architecture and of architects projected to a wide public. *The Fountainhead* (190) and the 1949 movie made from it showed an architect as Master Builder, hero, and genius. *House* (191), by contrast, chronicles the everyday business of small-scale design and construction. *Inside the Third Reich* by Albert Speer (192) and *From Bauhaus to Our House* (193) by Tom Wolfe have offered more complex versions of the motives of designers, and they, too, have been bestsellers. Although Wolfe protested that his real target was not modern architecture itself (194), the satirist found himself the center of an uproar—and an expert on the subject of literature's power over the profession.

In this century many new sorts of ambitious and useful reference works have appeared, not only new dictionaries and encyclopedias such as Wasmuth's *Lexikon der Baukunst* (195) or the *Macmillan Encyclopedia of Architects* (196), but periodical indexes, published catalogs, and bibliographies, some of which are available online as well as in printed form. These guides to architectural literature are a direct result of its dramatic growth and an indication of the fact that no one any longer can expect to command a personal knowledge of the subject. Their purpose is to order the material and provide access to it; they have become an essential key to information. Now there is even at least one bibliography of relevant bibliographies. Although these reference tools seem to be somewhat removed from the literature of architecture itself, they are increasingly indispensable gateways to it. Thus, those who want to know more about architectural writing should begin by using this newest variety of "architectural literature."

Although Julien Gaudet's *Eléments et théorie de l'architecture* (197) was published in the twentieth century, its importance is as a summary of beaux-arts academic theory. Gaudet was at the Ecole des Beaux Arts from 1871 until his death in 1908, and the *Elements* represents the lectures he gave in 1901–1904 on designing or composing buildings. Reynar Banham describes them as a great and basic source of information on "functional matters": "instruments and techniques of draughtsmanship, systems of proportion, walls and their openings; porticoes . . . ; roofs, vaults, ceilings and stairs: type plans and schedules of accommodation for all conceivable sorts of public and semi-public buildings. . . ." Add axial planning and historical styling, two academic principles that he does not bother to discuss, and Gaudet "formed the mental climate in which perhaps half the architects of the twentieth century grew up." Thus, although its size and cost prevented much direct influence, it is a fundamental piece of architectural literature (198).

Adolf Loos was a prolific writer of occasional pieces whose most influential ideas were found in the essay "Ornament and Crime." A diatribe against art nouveau, the *Wiener Sezession,* and the *Wiener Werkstatte,* it was couched in terms as striking as a manifesto: "I have therefore evolved the following maxim, and pronounce it to the world: the evolution of culture marches with the elimination of ornament from useful objects" (199). He was alone among the architects of his generation in this attitude, but his work was an important source of inspiration to radical European architects after World War I, and "Ornament and Crime" was reprinted in the magazine *L'Esprit Nouveau* in 1920.

The Architecture of Humanism by Geoffrey Scott (200) is about Renaissance architecture, but it is a book of pure theory. Scott, opposing the "fallacies" of Ruskin and other nineteenth-century writers, defended classicism and gave the appreciation of Renaissance and baroque architecture a new intellectual basis. However, his influence reaches well beyond the confines of discussions of style: he was a brilliant writer and made memorable contributions to architectural theory not only with his aesthetic approach to architecture, but also with his response to fundamental questions such as honesty in architecture or the relation of architecture to society (201).

Le Corbusier's *Vers une Architecture* (202) is probably the single most important book from this period. The first of his more than 40 books, it consisted almost entirely of essays that appeared in *L'Esprit Nouveau,* rhetorical essays here juxtaposed to suggest some continuity of theme. This unusual structure has encouraged a variety of interpretations, and Reynar Banham has called it "one of the most influential, widely read and least understood of all the architectural writings of the twentieth century" (203).

It was a comprehensive statement of the architect's ideas about design, especially remarkable considering that at the time Le Corbusier had very few actual buildings to his credit. The book illustrated a variety of sources of inspiration for the new architecture, especially works of engineering and modern machines: U.S. grain elevators, ocean liners, cars, and airplanes. At the same time, Le Corbusier followed the long line of architectural theorists who championed Greek architecture and its essential, geometric laws of design. The new architecture was to be a combination of modern technology and classical order.

Vers une architecture also emphasized the design of mass-produced houses, using concrete. Le Corbusier referred to the house as "une machine à habiter," an irresistible image from one of the great documents on engineering and architectural design.

The number of books on theory or architectural criticism published in the last 50 years is vast; many would agree with Kenneth Frampton that "the history of modern architecture is for me as much about consciousness and polemical intent as it is about buildings themselves" (204). Robert Venturi's first book will stand as representative, and it is notable that Vincent Scully considers it "probably the most important writing on architecture since Le Corbusier's *Vers une Architecture of* 1923, its first and natural complement across time" (205).

Complexity and Contradiction was one of the more memorable books that criticized postwar modern architecture, no doubt in part because it offered a new perspective and some new language for architecture in place of the pure and abstracted world of the international style (206). It also tempered its polemicism with witty remarks ("less is a bore," paraphrasing Mies van der Rohe), catchy new categories for architecture (the "duck" or shaped building and the "decorated shed") and illustrations. Venturi wanted architects to accept existing contexts and to reconsider the value of even "honky-tonk elements" in architecture. Their buildings had to move in the real world of popular culture (not to mention that of economics) and Venturi argues for the study of signs and symbols and history and language, as the key to satisfying a universal need "for variety and communication."

At the turn of the century the history most familiar to English-speaking architects appeared: "Banister Fletcher." It was first published in 1896, in London, as *History of Architecture for the Student, Craftsman and Amateur, being a comparative view of the historical styles from the earliest period,* a small book with an unusual, nonchronological arrangement of material by classes and the remarkable feature of a section on comparisons. This approach appealed to architectural students and the book was soon revised and enlarged in collaboration with Banister F. Fletcher, his son and fellow teacher at King's College, London, who throughout his life continued to revise and enlarge it as *A History of Architecture on the Comparative Method* (207). It may be considered to be a twentieth-century book because it was only in 1901 (the fourth edition) that it acquired the memorable line drawings that have characterized it for generations of architects. These additions brought the number of its illustrations to 1300. By 1931 there were over 1000 pages and over 4000 illustrations. Its emphasis was on the description of buildings and it was the most successful history text of its time. The current, 19th, edition was reorganized and a team of scholars was employed to modernize the text along the old lines (208).

In the early twentieth century much work was done to enlarge the scope of architectural histories to include sympathetic analyses of baroque and rococo, U.S. architectural history (Fiske Kimball, *American Architecture* (209)), and eighteenth- and nineteenth-century architecture (Peter Meyer, *Moderne Architektur und Tradition* (210), and

Henry-Russell Hitchcock, *Modern Architecture: Romanticism and Reintegration* (211)). Regions such as Latin America began to be chronicled in, for example, *Contribución a la Historia de la Arquitectura Hispano-Americana* by Martin Noel (212) and western-trained architectural historians such as Liang Ssu-Ch'eng began to study the architecture of the East.

This period also saw the transformation of architectural history into an independent academic discipline. Nikolaus Pevsner was one of those who brought German and Swiss methodologies west. His *An Outline of European Architecture* (213) is the most important of the twentieth-century histories, having been translated into at least seven languages, including Japanese. It reflects its author's German background in its emphasis on space in architecture and reveals his lifelong bias toward the principles and architecture of the modern movement, for which he had already done much to place in an historic context with *Pioneers of the Modern Movement from William Morris to Walter Gropius* (214). These positions were remarkable for London in 1942 but were becoming outdated by 1963 when the 7th and last edition was produced.

Siegfried Giedion's most famous book was also a history, of sorts, and it also has been widely disseminated in six languages. *Space, Time, and Architecture* perhaps is best described as a critical commentary on history; Giedion's stated purpose was to trace in history the "moving process of life," which resulted in modern architecture, and his stated method was to depend not on "a compilation of facts" but on being "permeated by the spirit of his own time [so] he [is] prepared to detect those tracts of the past which previous generations have overlooked" (215). In those terms Giedion was a historian singly well prepared, for as secretary of CIAM (Congrès International d'Architecture Moderne) throughout its history he was a key player in the definition and discussion of modern architecture. The book has been criticized for its errors of fact and interpretation, but praised for making modern architecture more understandable by connecting its themes and ideas with history. It was also important for expressing the opinions and attitudes of the so-called pioneers of modernism, and Gropius called it "the standard work on the development of modern architecture" (216).

Rudolf Wittkower's *Architectural Principles in the Age of Humanism* (217), a book of essays on Renaissance architecture, was an unusual case of direct influence exerted by a work of history on contemporary theory and design. His subject was the classical tradition and as Reynar Banham puts it, "The effect . . . was galvanic" (218). A general interest in classical architecture was revived among post-war London critics and designers, and there was specific emphasis on the tradition of classical proportions: see also his student Colin Rowe's "The Mathematics of the Ideal Villa" (originally published in Ref. 219).

Architects' biographies are now commonplace. Many architects write of their own lives and work, most notably, perhaps, Frank Lloyd Wright. Histories of the profession, however, are still uncommon. In English, only Martin Briggs, *The Architect in History* (London, 1927) appeared before Spiro Kostof edited *The Architect: Chapters in the History of the Profession* (New York, 1977). Most recently, Andrew Saint's *The Image of the Architect* (New Haven and London, 1983) has studied public perceptions of the designer.

Magazines have continued to develop as the most active and influential branch of architectural publishing. They have also continued to reflect general developments in all of architectural literature, including specific titles for separate trade, engineering, design (and house design), theory, and craft audiences, among others. Many have been overtly polemical. Society's general interest in architecture is reflected in the magazines, too, with a rise in the amount of important commentary found in nonprofessional journals such as *Country Life* or *Hound and Horn: a Harvard Miscellany* (where Henry-Russell Hitchcock and Philip Johnson published early articles on modern architecture); even *Vogue* has carried an article by Ada Louise Huxtable.

There has been increased participation by practicing architects. Already in the nineteenth century they had often edited journals, for example, Viollet-le-Duc and later J.-E.-A. de Baudot at the *Gazette des Architects et du Bâtiment* (Paris, fd. 1863) or M. H. Baillie Scott at *The Studio* from 1895 to 1914. In the twentieth century it became much more common for an architect to be associated with a journal as part of his professional activity, rather as book production had been for earlier generations of architects. Ralph Adams Cram founded or edited four journals: *Knight Errant, Christian Art, Speculum,* and *Commonweal.* On the continent, Victor and Pierre Bourgeois brought out *Au volant* (1919), *Le Geste* (1920), and *7 Arts* (1922–1928), and Ernest May published *Das neue Frankfurt* (fd. 1926) and *Das neue Berlin,* among other journals. It was a trend that began early (for example, Adolf Loos's *Das Andere,* 1903) and became more common in the 1920s when, for example, Le Corbusier founded *L'Esprit Nouveau* (1919–1925), Albert Sartoris founded *La città futurista* (1929), Bruno Taut founded *Frülicht* (1920–1922), and El Lissitzky founded *Veshch/Gegenstand/Object* (1922). Architects' groups and movements also had their journals, among them *G* (for *Gestaltung* or "Form," 1923–1925), *ABC* (1923–1925), *Sovremennaya Arkhitektura* (Moscow, 1925–1930), *Wendigen* (1919–1925), and of course *de Stijl* (1917–1931).

Most of these journals were organs for the ideas of those involved in the redefinition of the arts, but artists and architects were not the only ones involved. There were now professional architectural journalists and critics—Jean Badovici, for example, who edited the progressive revue of modern art and architecture *L'Architecture Vivante* (1923–1933). Art historians also began to make important contributions. As early as the 1920s Siegfried Giedeon was architectural editor for *Cahiers d'Art* and Henry-Russell Hitchcock was briefly a contributing editor of *The Architectural Record.* Christopher Hussey, author of *The Picturesque* (London, 1927), began his long and important association with *Country Life* in 1933. The critic J. M. Richards and the art historian Nikolaus Pevsner were editors of *The Architectural Review* and were responsible for its early espousal of the modern movement in England.

The production of a journal was an important part of giving twentieth-century art or architectural movements reality and validity. Now important centers of the profession are expected to produce architectural periodicals, and in fact, the ability to mount and sustain a publication is one indication of vitality. Many journals expired with changes in ideals, economics, and society in the 1930s. Others were founded or transformed to serve new needs and audiences. A few good examples are *Architectural Forum, Progressive Architecture,* and *Oppositions.* When a publication of international importance is produced it indicates not only vitality but leadership. Japan may be the best present-day example; it has at least two titles of the first importance, *GA* (*Global Architecture*) *Document* (Tokyo, fd. 1980) and the international edition of *Japan Architect* (fd. 1956), of the first importance. These things are true from the most prestigious publications to the architectural schools, some of which (such as the London Architectural Association's *AA Journal* (fd. 1887), Yale's *Perspecta* (fd. 1952), or *Oppositions* (fd. 1973) from the Institute for Architecture and Urban Studies, New York have made important contributions to architectural literature.

The experience of Frank Lloyd Wright provides a good summary of the many types of contemporary architectural literature and the roles publishing plays in the career of an architect. After his first critical review in the *Architectural Record* in 1900, the publication of his work encouraged his ideas (including the "House in a Prairie Town" for *Ladies Home Journal* (220)) and the development of his practice. Following the appearance of the Wasmuth volumes in 1910 and 1911 his status in Europe was similarly secured, and he was the subject of other European publications including seven issues of *Wendigen,* collected as *The Life Work of the American Architect, Frank Lloyd Wright* (221).

His own writing did not begin until the late 1920s during the lull in his practice; during that time he wrote *An Autobiography* (London, New York, and Toronto, 1932) and published some of his lectures, including *Modern Architecture* (Princeton, 1931). Publishing again played a role when he re-emerged as a major architect in the late 1930s. In 1938, he wrote and designed an issue of *Architectural Forum,* "Frank Lloyd Wright," and in 1940 a show at the Museum of Modern Art and its associated publications helped fuel the revival still further. One of these was an anthology of his writings to date. In lieu of the catalog, Henry-Russell Hitchcock's great interpretive study, *In the Nature of Materials,* appeared in 1942, and the exhaustive publication of Wright's work and words began in earnest: among the bibliographies see Ref. 222.

BIBLIOGRAPHY

1. A. Laurence Kocher, "The Library of an Architect," *Architectural Review* **56,** 316 (1924).
2. Jacques-François Blondel, *Discours sur la necessité de l'étude de l'architecture* Paris, 1754; facs. ed. Minkoff, Geneva, 1973.
3. Ref. 1, p. 124.
4. Li Chieh, ed. *Ying-tsao fa-shih,* Building Standards, reprinted Peking, 1925.
5. Ca fer Efendi, *Risāle-i Mi^c mariyye,* facs. transl. and ed. Howard Crane, E. J. Brill, Leiden and New York, 1987.
6. Pliny the Younger, *Letters,* V, in many editions including *Pliny: A Selection of His Letters,* trans. C. Greig, University Press, Cambridge Mass. 1978, pp. 50–53.
7. Vincenzo Scamozzi, *Idea,* 1615.
8. Jean-François Félibien des Avaux, *Les plans et les descriptions de deux plus belles maisons de campagne de pline le consul. . . . ,* Paris, 1699.
9. Robert Castell, *The Villas of the Ancients Illustrated,* London, 1728.
10. Marcus Vitruvius Pollio, *De Architectura, The Ten Books on Architecture,* transl. Morris Hicky Morgan, Cambridge, Mass., 1914; reprinted New York, 1960.
11. Abbot Suger, *On the abbey church of St. Denis and its art treasures,* ed. and trans. Erwin Panofsky, Princeton University Press, Princeton, N.J., 1946.
12. Gervase of Canterbury, *Gesta Abbatum,* trans. Robert Willis in "Canterbury Cathedral," reprinted in *Architectural History of Some English Cathedrals,* Chicheley, 1979.
13. W. Horn, *The Plan of St. Gall,* University of California Press, Berkeley, Calif. 1979, I, pp. 20–25.
14. Robert Willis, *Facisimile of the Sketch-book of Wilars de Honecort,* J. and H. Parker, London, 1859.
15. T. Bowie, ed., *The Sketchbook of Villard de Honnecourt,* University of Indiana Press, Bloomington and London, 1959.
16. Mathes Roriczer, *Das Büchlein von der fialen Gerechtigkeit,* Regensburg, 1486; and *Geometria Deutsch,* Regensburg, 1487/8; together ed. Ferdinand Geldner, Wiesbaden, 1965.
17. Leone Battista Alberti, *Leonis Baptiste Alberti de re Aedificatoria,* Florence, 1485; crit. ed. Milan, 1966; facs. 1755 Engl. ed., Toronto and London, 1986.
18. E. A. Connolly, *Printed Books on Architecture 1485–1805,* (no publisher given), Urbana, Ill., 1960, p. 192.
19. Richard Krautheimer, "Alberti and Vitruvius," in *Studies in Early Christian, Medieval and Renaissance Art,* University Press, New York, 1969, p. 327, first printed in *Acts of the XX Congress of the History of Art, II,* Princeton University Press, Princeton, N.J., pp. 42–52.
20. *Vitruvius: The Ten Books on Architecture,* transl. Morris Hicky Morgan, Dover, New York, 1960, p. 192.
21. J. R. Spencer, ed., "Il Filarete (Antonio di Pietro Averlino)," *Treatise on architecture,* Yale University Press, New Haven, Conn., 1965.
22. C. Maltese, ed., Francesco di Giorgio Martini, *Trattati di architettura, ingengneria e arte militare,* Milan, Italy, 1967.
23. G. Hersey and S. Ryan in D. Wiebenson, ed., *Architectural Theory and Practice from Alberti to Ledoux,* Architectural Publications and University of Chicago Press, Chicago, Ill., 1983, I-4.
24. Wendel Dietterlin, *Architectura . . . der Funff Seulen,* 1593, 1594; enlarged 2nd ed, Nurenberg 1598; facs. ed. Dover Publications, New York, 1968.
25. D. Wiebenson, Ref. 23, Introduction, p. 6.
26. Diego da Sagredo, *Medidas del Romano,* Toledo, 1526.
27. Ferdinando Galli Bibiena, *L'architectura civile. . . ,* Parma, 1711; facs. ed. Dover Publications, New York, 1971.
28. D. Wiebenson, ed., *Architectural Theory and Practice from Alberti to Ledoux,* Architectural Publications, Inc., 1982. Second Revised edition 1983.
29. D. Thomson, Ref. 23, III-A-3.
30. N. Adams, Ref. 23, I-22.
31. Sebastiano Serlio, *Tutte l'opere d'architectura,* facs. 1584

ed., Ridgewood, 1964; facs. 1611 English ed. B. Blom, New York, 1970.

32. Andrea Palladio, *I quattro libri dell'architettura,* Venice, 1570; facs. ed. Milan, 1968; facs. 1748 English ed. Dover Publications, New York, 1965.
33. Vincenzo Scamozzi, *Dell'idea dell'architettura universale,* Venice, 1615; facs. ed. Gregg Press, Farnborough, 1964.
34. John Shute, *The First and Chief Groundes of Architecture,* London, 1563; facs. ed. Gregg Press, London, 1964.
35. Philibert Delorme, *Le premier tome de l'architecture,* Paris, 1567; facs. ed. Ridgewood, 1964.
36. Jacques Androuet Du Cerceau the Elder, *Les trois livres d'architecture,* Paris, 1559, 1561, 1572; facs. ed., Gregg Press, Ridgewood, 1965.
37. Jacques Androuet Du Cerceau the Elder, *Les plus excellents bastiments de France,* Paris, 1576–9; facs. ed., Gregg Press, Farnborough, 1972.
38. Charles Perrault, *Les dix livres d'architecture de Vitruve corrigez et traduits nouvellement en François,* Paris, 1673; facs. ed. Paris, 1979.
39. Charles Perrault, *Ordonnance des cinq espèces de colonnes selon la mèthod des anciens,* Paris, 1683.
40. Nicolas-François Blondel, *Cours d'architecture enseigné dans l'Académie royale d'Architecture,* Part 1, Paris, 1675; Parts 2–3, 4–5, 1683; 2nd ed. 1698.
41. Roland Fréart de Chambray, *Parallèle de l'architecture antique et de la moderne,* Paris, 1650.
42. Antoine Desgodets, *Les Edifices antiques de Rome dessinés et mesurés trés exactement,* Paris, 1682; facs. ed. London, 1969.
43. S. Frear, Ref. 23, II-10.
44. Jean Caramuel de Lobkowitz, *Architectura civil, recta y obliqua,* Vigevano, 1678–1681.
45. Sir Henry Wotton, *The Elements of Architecture,* London, 1624; facs. ed. Charlottesville, 1968.
46. Josef Furttenbach, *Architectura Civilis,* Ulm, 1628.
47. Josef Furttenbach, *Architectura Universalis,* Ulm, 1635.
48. Josef Furttenbach, *Architectura Privata,* Augsburg, 1641.
49. Josepf Furttenbach, *Architectura Recreationis,* Augsburg, 1640.
50. D. Wiebenson, Ref. 25, Introduction, p. 4.
51. Charles Augustin Daviler, *Cours d'architecture qui comprend les ordres de Vignole,* Paris, 1691; facs. ed. Geneva, 1973.
52. Charles Augustin Daviler, *Explication des termes d'architecture,* Paris, 1691; facs. ed. Geneva, 1973.
53. André Félibien des Avaux, *Des principes de l'architecture, de la sculpture, de la peinture et des autres arts. . . ,* Paris, 1676, facs. ed., Gregg Press, Farnborough, 1966.
54. Louis Savot, *L'architecture françoise des bâtiments particuliers,* Paris, 1624; facs. ed. Geneva, 1973.
55. H. Ballon, Ref. 23, III-C-14.
56. Pierre Bullet, *L'architecture pratique. . . ,* Paris, 1691; facs. ed. Geneva, 1973.
57. Jean Marot, *Recueil des plans, profils et elévations des plusiers palais, chateaux, eglises, sepultres, grotes et hostels bâtis dans Paris* ("Petit Marot"), Paris, ca. 1660; facs. ed. Gregg Press, Farnborough, 1969.
58. Jean Marot, *Le grand ouevre d'architecture de Jean Marot* ("Grand Marot"), Paris, c. 1665; facs. ed. Paris, 1967.
59. Antoine Le Pautre, *Dessins de plusieurs palais,* Paris, 1652 or 1653; facs. of 1681 ed., Gregg Press, Farnborough, 1966.
60. Guarino Guarini, *Disegni di architettura civile ed ecclesiastica,* Torino, 1686.
61. K. Harrington, "Pierre Patte," A. K. Placzek, ed., *Macmillan Encyclopedia of Architects;* Free Press, New York; Collier Macmillan, London; c. 1982, III, p. 676.
62. John Wood the Younger, *A Series of Plans for Cottages or Habitations of the Labourer,* London, 1781; facs. ed. Gregg Press, Farnborough, 1972.
63. J. Gibbs, *A Book of Architecture,* facs. ed. Arno Press, New York, 1980, pp. i-ii.
64. Batty Langley, *The Builder's Director, or Bench-mate: Being a Pocket-Treasury of the Grecian, Roman and Gothic Orders of Architecture, Made Easy to the Meanest Capacity by near 500 Examples,* London, 1747, facs. ed of 2nd ed., 1751; New York, 1970.
65. Christopher Wren, *Parentalia,* London, 1750; facs. ed. Gregg Press, Farnborough, 1965.
66. K. Harrington, *Changing Ideas on Architecture in the Encyclopédie, 1750–1776,* UMI Research Press, Ann Arbor, Mich., 1985.
67. Colin Campbell, *Vitruvius Britannicus,* London, 1716 (continued by Campbell and others to 5 volumes, 171[5]–1771).
68. T. P. Conner, "The Making of Vitruvius Britannicus," *Art History* **20,** 18 (1977).
69. J. Summerson, *Architecture in Britain 1530–1830,* 7th ed., Penguin Books Ltd., Harmondsworth, 1983, pp. 365–368.
70. Robert Morris, *An Essay in Defense of Ancient Architecture,* London, 1728.
71. Robert Morris, *Lectures on Architecture,* London, 1734–1736.
72. William Salmon, *Palladio Londonensis,* London, 1734; facs. ed. Gregg Press, Farnborough, 1969.
73. Abraham Swan, *The British Architect,* London, 1745; Philadelphia, 1775.
74. E. Harris, "Batty Langley: Tutor to Freemasons," *Burlington Magazine* **119,** 329–330 (May 1977).
75. *Ibid.,* p. 328.
76. Batty Langley, *Ancient Masonry,* 2 vols., London, 1734–1736.
77. Ref. 74, p. 329.
78. William Halfpenny, *Practical Architecture,* London, 1724.
79. Johann Fischer von Erlach, *Entwurff einer historischen Architektur,* Vienna, 1721.
80. Batty Langley, *Ancient Architecture Restored,* London, 1742; republished 1747 as *Gothic Architecture Improved by Rules and Proportions. . . ,* facs. 1747 ed. Gregg Press, Farnborough, 1967.
81. William Chambers, *Designs of Chinese Buildings,* London, 1757.
82. James Stuart and Nicholas Revett, *The Antiquities of Athens,* 5 Vols., London, 1762–1830; facs. ed. New York, 1968.
83. Giovanni Battista Piranesi, *Della magnificenza ed architettura de'Romani,* Rome, 1761.
84. N. Pevsner, "Fischer von Erlach, 1656–1723" *Architectural Review* **120,** 216 (1956).
85. T. Lediard, trans., *A Plan of Civil and Historical Architecture,* London, 1730, p. ii.
86. "Gedanken ber die Nachahmung der greichischen Werke," in F. Forschepiepe, ed., *J. J. Wincklemann: Ewiges griechentum,* A. Kroner, Stuttgart, 1944.
87. L. Lawrence, "Stuart and Revett: Their Literary and Archi-

tectural Careers," *J. the Warburg and Courtauld Institutes* **2,** 128 (1938).

88. D. Wiebenson, *Sources of Greek Revival Architecture,* A. Zwemmer, London, 1968, pp. 34–35.
89. Jean Mariette, *L'Architecture Françoise,* 5 vols., Paris, 1727; facs. ed. Paris, 1927.
90. Jacques-François Blondel, *Architecture Françoise,* Paris, 1752–1756.
91. James Gibbs, *A Book of Architecture,* London, 1728.
92. Ref. 69, p. 359.
93. Jean-François de Neufforge, *Receuil elémentaire d'architecture,* Paris, 1757–1768; suppl. 1772–1780; facs. ed. Gregg Press, Farnborough, 1968.
94. Paul Decker, *Ausführliche Anleitung zur Civilbaukunst,* Nuremberg, no date.
95. Paul Decker, *Fürstlicher Baumeister. . . . ,* 3 vols., Augsburg, 1711, 1713, 1716; facs. ed. Hildesheim, 1978.
96. J.-F. Blondel, *De la distribution de maisons de plaisance,* Paris, 1737; facs. ed. Gregg Press, Farnborough, 1967.
97. John Plaw and James Malton, *An Essay on British Cottage Architecture,* London, 1798; facs. ed. Gregg Press, Farnborough, 1972.
98. C. N. Ledoux, *L'architecture considérée sous le rapport de l'art, des moeurs, et de la législation,* Paris, 1804; facs. ed. Paris, 1961; Hildesheim, 1980.
99. Marie-Joseph Peyre, *Oeuvres d'Architecture,* Paris, 1765; 2nd ed., 1795; facs. ed. Gregg Press, Farnborough, 1967.
100. John Soane, *Designs in Architecture,* London, 1778.
101. John Soane, *Plans . . . of Buildings executed in Several Counties,* London, 1788.
102. John Soane, *Sketches in Architecture,* 1793; 2nd ed., 1798; facs. ed. Gregg Press, Farnborough, 1971.
103. Robert Adam, *The Works of Architecture of Robert and James Adam,* 2 vols., London, 1773–1778 and 1779; facs. ed. Dover, New York, 1981.
104. R. Wittkower, *English Literature on Architecture, Palladio and English Palladianism,* G. Braziller, New York, 1974, p. 112.
105. Etienne-Louis Boulée, *Essai sur l'art,* trans. and ed. Helen Rosenau, *Boulée's Treatise on Architecture. . . . ,* London, 1953.
106. Jean Louis de Cordemoy, *Nouveau traité de toute l'architecture ou l'art de bâtir. . . . ,* Paris, 1706; 2nd ed. 1714; facs. ed. Gregg Press, Farnborough, 1966.
107. Marc-Antoine Laugier, *Essai sur l'architecture,* Paris, 1753, 2nd ed. enlarged 1755.
108. J. Rykwert, *The First Moderns: the Architects of the Eighteenth Century,* MIT Press, Cambridge, Mass., 1980, p. 324.
109. Francesco Algarotti, *Letter sopra l'architettura* (Pisa, 1753?).
110. Francesco Algarotti, *Saggio sopra l'architettura,* Pisa, 1756.
111. Andra Memmo, *Elementi d'architettura Lodoliana. . . . ,* Venice, 1786; complete ed. Zara (Zadar), 1833–1834; facs. ed. Milan, 1973.
112. Ref. 108, p. 311.
113. Isaac Ware, *A Complete Body of Architecture,* London, 1756.
114. *Ibid.,* Preface, p. 1.
115. William Chambers, *A Treatise on Civil Architecture,* London, 1759; facs. 1791 ed. New York, 1968.
116. E. Lambert, Ref. 23, II-30.
117. Ref. 69, p. 418.
118. Ref. 23, II-35.
119. Jacques-François Blondel, *Cours d'architecture,* 9 vols., Paris, 1771–1777.
120. E. R. Smith, "Architectural Books—Architectural Classics," *Architectural Review* **7,** 140 (1900).
121. Francesco Milizia, *Principi di architettura civile,* 3 vols., Finale, 1781; 4th ed. and atlas 1800.
122. A. Vidler, "Type: Quatremère de Quincy," *Oppositions* **8,** 148 (1977).
123. L. Sullivan, "Ornament in Architecture," *Engineering Magazines* **III,** 633 (1892); reprinted in Benton, *Architecture and Design,* pp. 2–4.
124. H. R. Hitchcock, *Architecture: Nineteenth and Twentieth Centuries,* 4th ed., Penguin Books, Harmondsworth, 1977, p. 323.
125. H. R. Hitchcock, *Modern Architecture, Romanticism and Reintegration,* Payson and Clarke Ltd., New York, 1929, p. 240.
126. F. Jenkins, "Nineteenth-Century Architectural Periodicals," in J. Summerson, ed., *Concerning Architecture,* Allen Lane, London, 1968, p. 156.
127. G. Peschken, *Das Architektonischen Lehrbuch,* in P. Rave and M. Kuhn, eds., *Schinkels lebenswerk,* 14 vols., Deutscher Kunstverlag, Berlin, 1939 ff.
128. J. B. Rondelet, *Traité théorique et pratique de l'art de bâtir,* 4 vols., Paris, 1802–1817.
129. P. Collins, *Changing Ideals in Modern Architecture, 1750–1950,* McGill University Press, Montreal, 1965, p. 204.
130. H. R. Hitchcock, *American Architectural Books,* expanded ed., Da Capo, New York, 1976, pp. vi and vii.
131. William E. Bell, *Carpentry Made Easy,* Philadelphia, Pa., 1858.
132. T. R. Smith, "An Architect's Library," *The American Architect and Building News* **42,** 100 (1893).
133. I. O. Baker, *A Treatise on Masonry Construction,* 9th ed., John Wiley and Sons, New York, 1903.
134. Jean Nicolas Louis Durand, *Précis des leçons d'architecture données à l'Ecole Polytechnique,* Paris, 1802–1805.
135. Ref. 124, p. 47 ("The Doctrine of J.-N.-L. Durand and Its Application in Northern Europe").
136. Ref. 124, pp. 48–49.
137. A. W. N. Pugin, *Contrasts,* London, 1836; 2nd ed. expanded, 1841.
138. M. Belcher, *A. W. N. Pugin: An Annotated Critical Bibliography,* Mansell Pub. Ltd., London and New York, 1987.
139. John Ruskin, *Seven Lamps of Architecture,* London, 1849.
140. Eugene Emmanuel Viollet-le-Duc, *Entretiens sur l'architecture,* 2 vols., Paris, 1863, 1872; trans. as *Discourses on Architecture,* 2 vols., Boston, 1875, 1881 and *Lectures on Architecture,* 2 vols., London, 1877, 1881; reprinted New York, 1959.
141. R. Middleton, "Viollet-le-Duc's Academic Ventures and the Entretiens sur l'architecture," in A. M. Vogt, C. Reble, and M. Frohlich, eds., *Gottfried Semper und die Mitte des 19. Jahrhunderts,* Birkhäuser, Basel, 1976, pp. 239–254.
142. D. Hoffmann, "Frank Lloyd Wright and Viollet-le-Duc," *J. Society of Architectural Historians* **28,** 173 (1969).
143. Gottfried Semper, *Der Stil in den technischen und tektonischen Kunsten oder praktische Aesthetik,* Frankfurt, 1860–1863.
144. L. Sullivan, *The Autobiography of an Idea,* The AIA Press, New York, 1924.
145. Louis Sullivan, "The Tall Office Building Artistically Consid-

ered," *Lippincott's Magazine* **LVII,** 403 (1896); reprinted in T. and C. Benton, *Architecture and Design,* pp. 11–14.

146. Jean-Charles Krafft, *Plans, coupes et élévations des plus belles maisons et des hôtels construits à Paris . . .* Paris, 1801–1803.
147. Ref. 124, p. 600, nt. (6) 12.
148. J. C. Loudon, *An Encyclopedia of Cottage, Farm, and Villa Architecture,* London, 1833, 2nd ed. with supplement, 1842.
149. A. J. Downing, *The Architecture of Country Houses,* New York, 1850.
150. A. J. Downing, *Cottage Residences,* New York, 1842.
151. Cesar Daly, *L'architecture privée du XIXe Siècle . . . sous Napoléon III,* 3 vols., Paris, 1864.
152. H. d'Espouy, *Fragments d'architecture antique d'après les relevés et restaurations des anciens pensionnaires de l'Académie de France à Rome,* 2 vols., Paris, 1890–1905.
153. H. d'Espouy, *Fragments d'architecture du Môyen Age et de la Renaissance. . . . ,* Paris, 1897.
154. H. d'Espouy, *Roma antiqua: envoies des architectes français 1788–1924,* exhibition catalogue, Rome, c. 1985.
155. James Fergusson, *History of Architecture in all Countries, from the Earliest Times to the Present Day,* 4 vols., London, 2nd ed. 1873, 3rd ed., revised 1891–1893.
156. Karl Julius Ferdinand Schnaase, *Geschichte der Bildenden Kunst,* 7 vols., Düsseldorf, 1843–1864.
157. Franz Theodor Kugler, *Geschichte der Baukunst,* 4 vols., Stuttgart, 1856–1872.
158. Jacob Burckhardt, Ref. 157, Part I, Volume 4.
159. François-Auguste Choisy, *L'art de bâtir chez les Egyptiens,* Paris, 1904.
160. François-Auguste Choisy, *Histoire de l'Architecture,* 2 vols., Paris, 1899.
161. R. Banham, *Theory and Design in the First Machine Age,* Praeger, New York, pp. 24–25.
162. Ref. 161, p. 31.
163. Marianna Van Rensselaer, *Henry Hobson Richardson and His Works,* Boston and New York, 1888, facs. ed. Park Forest, Ill., 1967.
164. G. L. Hersey, "Godey's Choice," *J. Society of Architectural Historians* **18,** 104 (1959).
165. G. Rendel in discussion of H. Casson, "100 Years of Architectural Journalism," *The Builder* **174,** 707 (1948).
166. H. Casson, Ref. 126, p. 707.
167. W. R. Lethaby, *Architecture, An Introduction to the History and Theory of the Art of Building,* London, 1911 and subsequent editions.
168. R. A. Cook, *A Bibliography: Walter Gropius, 1919–1950,* American Institute of Architects, Chicago, Ill., 1951.
169. Walter Gropius, *The Scope of Total Architecture,* New York, 1955.
170. D. L. Miller, ed., *The Lewis Mumford Reader,* Random House, New York, 1986.
171. *Ausgefürte Bauten und Entwerfe von Frank Lloyd Wright,* Wasmuth, Berlin, 1910; new ed. *Buildings, Plans and Designs,* New York, 1963.
172. Le Corbusier, *Ouevre complète,* 8 vols., Zurich, 1930–1970.
173. Hermann Muthesius, *Die englische Baukunst der Gegenwart,* 2 vols., Berlin, 1900, 1901.
174. H. P. Berlage, *Amerikaansche Reiserinneringen,* Rotterdam, 1913.
175. R. Neutra, *Wie baut Amerika?,* Stuttgart, 1929.
176. H. Muthesius, *Das englische Haus,* 3 vols., Berlin, 1903.
177. R. Buckminster Fuller, "Dymaxion House," *Architectural Forum* **LVI,** 285 (1932).
178. G. Platz, *Die Baukunst der neuesesten Zeit,* Berlin, 1927.
179. B. Taut, *Die neue Baukunst in Europa und Amerika,* Stuttgart, 1929; trans. as *Modern Architecture,* London and New York, 1929.
180. J. M. Richards, *An Introduction to Modern Architecture,* Penguin, Harmondsworth, 1940.
181. A. Roth, *La nouvelle architecture. Die neue architektur. The New Architecture,* Zurich, 1940.
182. A. Sant'Elia, *Manifesto dell'architettura futurista,* 1914.
183. "De Stijl' Manifesto I," *De Stijl* **II,** (November 1918).
184. N. Gabo and A. Pevsner, *Realist Manifesto,* Moscow, 1920.
185. K. Malevich, *Suprematist manifesto Unovis,* 1924.
186. Uno Åhren, Gunnar Asplund and co-workers, *Acceptera,* Stockholm, 1931.
187. "Situationists: International Manifesto," *Internationale Situationniste* **4,** 36 (1960).
188. H. R. Hitchcock and P. Johnson, *The International Style,* First Architectural Exhibition at the New York Museum of Modern Art, New York, 1932; 2nd ed., MOMA, New York, 1966.
189. *The Presence of the Past,* First International Exhibition of Architecture, in Venice, New York, 1980.
190. A. Rand, *The Fountainhead,* New York, 1943.
191. T. Kidder, *House,* Houghton Mifflin Co., Boston, Mass., 1985.
192. A. Speer, *Inside the Third Reich.*
193. T. Wolfe, *From Bauhaus to Our House.*
194. R. Kimball, "Booking architecture: a symposium on architectural publishing at Columbia," *Architectural Record* **174,** 55 (1986).
195. *Lexikon der Baukunst,* 5 vols., Wasmuth, Berlin, c. 1929–1937.
196. *Macmillan Encyclopedia of Architects,* Macmillan, New York.
197. J. Gaudet, *Eléments et théorie de l'architecture,* 5 vols., Paris, 1902.
198. Ref. 161, pp. 16–17.
199. A. Loos, "Ornament und Verbrechen," *Der Sturm* (1912).
200. G. Scott, *The Architecture of Humanism,* Boston and London, 1914; 2nd ed., revised, 1924 with introduction by D. Watkin, London, 1980.
201. *Ibid.,* Introduction to 1980 ed.
202. Le Corbusier, *Vers une Architecture,* Paris, 1923; transl. into English as *Towards a New Architecture,* 1927.
203. Ref. 161, p. 220.
204. K. Frampton, *Modern Architecture: A Critical History,* Oxford University Press, New York and Toronto, 1980, p. 9.
205. V. Scully, Introduction to *Complexity and Contradiction in Architecture,* Museum of Modern Art, New York, 1966, p. 11.
206. R. Venturi, *Complexity and Contradiction in Architecture,* New York, 1966.
207. B. Fletcher, *A History of Architecture on the Comparative Method,* London, various eds.
208. John Musgrove, ed., *A History of Architecture,* Butterworth's, London and Boston, 1987, Introduction.
209. F. Kimball, *American Architecture,* Indianapolis, Ind., 1928.

210. P. Meyer, *Moderne Architektur und Tradition,* Zurich, 1928.
211. H. R. Hitchcock, *Modern Architecture: Romanticism and Reintegration,* Payson and Clarke, Ltd., New York, 1929.
212. M. Noel, *Contribución a la Historia de la Arquitectura Hispano-Americana,* Buenos Aires, 1921.
213. N. Pevsner, *An Outline of European Architecture,* Penguin, Harmondsworth and New York, 1942.
214. N. Pevsner, *Pioneers of the Modern Movement from William Morris to Walter Gropius,* Faber and Faber, London, 1936.
215. S. Giedion, *Space, Time, and Architecture,* Harvard University Press, Cambridge, Mass., 1941, Introduction, pp. 5–6.
216. D. Watkin, *Morality and Architecture,* Oxford University Press, Oxford, pp. 53–59.
217. R. Wittkower, *Architectural Principles in the Age of Humanism,* Studies of the Warburg Institute, XIX, London, 1949; 4th ed. London, 1973.
218. R. Banham, "The Revenge of the Picturesque, Concerning Architecture," in Ref. 126, p. 268.
219. C. Rowe, "The Mathematics of the Ideal Villa," *Architectural Review* **CI,** 101 (1947).
220. F. L. Wright, "House in a Prairie Town," *Ladies Home Journal* **XVIII,** 17 (1901).
221. H. T. Wijdeveld, ed., *The Life Work of the American Architect, Frank Lloyd Wright,* Santpoort, Holland, 1925.
222. E. Kauffmann and B. Raeburn, *Frank Lloyd Wright: Writings and Buildings,* New York, 1960.

General References

D. B. Alexander, *The Sources of Classicism: five centuries of architecture books from the collections of the Humanities Research Center,* (University of Texas) The Center, Austin, Tex., 1975.

R. Banham, *Theory and Design in the First Machine Age,* Praeger, New York, 1960.

T. and C. Benton, *Architecture and Design, 1890–1930: an international anthology,* Whitney Library of Design, New York, 1975.

E. A. Connally, *Printed Books on Architecture 1485–1805,* Urbana, Ill., 1960.

U. Conrads, *Programs and Manifestoes on 20th century architecture,* MIT Press, Cambridge, Mass., 1970.

D. L. Ehresmann, *Architecture, A Bibliographic Guide to Basic Reference Works, Histories, and Handbooks,* Libraries Unlimited, Littleton, Colo., 1984.

P. Frankl, *The Gothic: Literary Sources and Interpretations through Eight Centuries,* Princeton University Press, Princeton, N.J., 1960.

D. C. Gifford, *The Literature of Architecture: The Evolution of Architectural Theory and Practice in Nineteenth-Century America,* E. P. Dutton and Co., New York, 1966.

H. R. Hitchcock, *American Architectural Books: a list of books, portfolios, and pamphlets on architecture and related subjects published in America before 1895,* new expanded ed., Da Capo Press, New York, 1976.

C. L. W. Meeks, "Books and Buildings 1449–1949: One Hundred Great Architectural Books Most Influential in Shaping the Architecture of the World," *Journal of the Society of Architectural Historians* **8,** 55–67 (1949).

N. Pevsner, *Some Architectural Writers of the Nineteenth Century,* Clarendon Press, Oxford, 1972.

A. K. Placzek, ed., *Macmillan Encyclopedia of Architects,* Free Press, New York; Collier Macmillan, London; ca. 1982.

J. Schlosser Magnino, *La Letteratura Artistica,* Firenze and Wien, 3rd ed., 1964.

D. Sharp, *Sources of Modern Architecture. A Bibliography,* Architectural Association Paper #2, Wittenborn, New York, 1967.

E. R. Smith, "Architectural Books; Architectural Classics, dictionaries, periodicals, manuals and histories," *Architectural Review* **7,** 113–117, 137–142 (1900); **8,** 39–43, 99–102 (1901).

E. R. Smith, "A List of Standard Architectural Books for Offices and Public Libraries," *The Brickbuilder* **17,** 149–150, 167–168, 215–216 (1908); **18,** 35–36, 55–56, 167–168 (1909).

J. Summerson, ed., *Concerning Architecture: essays on architectural writers and writing presented to Nicholas Pevsner,* Allen Lane, London, 1968.

D. Watkin, *The Rise of Architectural History,* Architectural Press, London, 1980.

D. Wiebenson, ed., *Architectural Theory and Practice from Alberti to Ledoux,* Architectural Publications and the University of Chicago Press, Chicago, 1983.

C. B. Wood, III, "A Survey and Bibliography of Writings on English and American Architectural Books Published Before 1895," *Winterthur Portfolio* **2,** 127–137 (1965).

See also ALBERTI, LEON BATTISTA; ARCHITECTURAL PRESS, U.S.; BACON, EDMUND N.; BANHAM, REYNAR; BLAKE, PETER; CRITICISM, ARCHITECTURAL; FLETCHER, BANISTER; GROPIUS, WALTER; JOHNSON, PHILIP; LE CORBUSIER (CHARLES-EDOUARD JEANNERET); LOOS, ADOLF; MEDIA CRITICISM; MUMFORD, LEWIS; NELSON, GEORGE; PALLADIO, ANDREA; PATTERN-BOOK ARCHITECTURE; SAARINEN, ELIEL; VENTURI RAUCH AND SCOTT BROWN; WRIGHT, FRANK LLOYD

MARY DEAN
New Haven, Connecticut

LITIGATION. See CONSTRUCTION LAW; MEDIATION IN ARCHITECTURAL AND CONSTRUCTION DISPUTES

LOOS, ADOLF

Adolf Loos (1870–1933) ranks as one of the most important pioneers of the modern movement in architecture. Ironically, his influence was based largely on a few interior designs and a body of controversial essays. Loos's buildings were rigorous examples of austere beauty, ranging from conventional country cottages to planar compositions for storefronts and residences. His built compositions were little known outside his native Austria during his early years of practice.

Loos was born in Brno (Bruenn), Moravia, now Czechoslovakia, on December 10, 1870. He was introduced to the craft of building at an early age while working in his father's stone masonry shop. At the age of seventeen, he attended the Royal and Imperial State College at Reichenberg in Bohemia. In 1889 he was drafted for one year of service in the Austrian army. From 1890 to 1893, Loos studied architecture at the Technical College in Dresden. As a student, he was particularly interested in the works of the classicist Schinkel and, above all, the works of Vitruvius. Loos's developing tastes were considerably broadened during a three-year stay in the United States, which began in 1893. The 23-year-old architect was particularly impressed by what he regarded as the innovative efficiency of U.S. industrial buildings, clothing, and household furnishings. In 1896, Loos returned to Vienna where he began working in the building firm of Carl Mayreder.

In 1897, in the pages of *The Neue Freie Presse* of Vienna, Loos initiated a series of polemic articles that later established his international reputation. He did not directly address architecture in his writings. Instead, he examined a wide range of social ills, which he identified as the motivating factors behind the struggle for a transformation of everyday life. Loos's writings focused increasingly on what he regarded as the excess of decoration in both traditional Viennese design and in the more recent products of the Vienna Secession and the Wiener Werkstatte. In 1898, in the pages of the review Ver Sacrum, which was an organ of the Wiener Secession, Loos published an essay that marked the beginning of a long theoretical opposition to the then popular art noveau movement. His theories culminated in a short essay entitled, "Ornament And Crime," published in 1908. To Loos, the lack of ornament in architecture was a sign of spiritual strength. He referred to the opposite, excessive ornamentation, as criminal—not for abstract moral reasons, but because of the economics of labor and wasted materials in modern industrial civilization. He argued that because ornament was no longer an important manifestation of culture, the worker dedicated to its production could not be paid a fair price for his labor. The essay rapidly became a theoretical manifesto and a key document in modernist literature and was widely circulated abroad. Le Corbusier later attributed "an Homeric cleansing" of architecture to the work.

Another point of contention decried by Loos was the masking of the true nature and beauty of materials by useless and indecent ornament. In his 1898 essay entitled "Principles of Building," Loos wrote that the true vocabulary of architecture lies in the materials themselves, and that a building should remain "dumb" on the outside. In his own work, he contrasted austere facades with lavish interiors. Much like Mies van der Rohe, Loos arrived at the reduction of architecture to a purely technical tautology that emphasized the simple assemblage of materials. This article was followed by the 1910 essay entitled "Architecture," in which Loos explained important contradictions in design: between the interior and the exterior, the monument and the house, and art works and objects of function. To Loos, the house did not belong to art because the house must please everyone, unlike a work of art, which does not need to please anyone. The only exception, that is, the only constructions that belong both to art and architecture, were the monument and the tombstone. He felt that the rest of architecture, which by necessity must serve a specific end, must be excluded from the realm of art.

In 1899, Loos designed the Cafe Museum, which proved to be one of the most notable projects of his early work. The austere interior was a mature architectural embodiment of his theorized renunciation of stylish ornamentation. The starkness of the "untattooed" facade that inspired the popular name Cafe Nihilismus asserted Loos's developing theory of the predominance of technique over decoration. The cafe also affirms his aesthetic equation of beauty and utility by bringing every object back to its purely utilitarian value. To Loos, that which is beautiful must also be useful. Thus, the only elements he used to pattern the vaulted ceiling of the cafe interior were strips of brass, which also served as electrical conductors. A more refined work, the tiny Karntner Bar Vienna (1907), reveals in microcosm the architect's great sensitivity to spatial manipulation. Once again, Loos showed his fondness for the expressive use of natural materials as he skillfully manipulated classical materials including marble, onyx, wood, and mirror, into a careful composition of visual patterns.

Between 1909 and 1911, Loos designed and constructed one of his best known works, the controversial Looshaus in the Michaelerplatz, in the heart of old Vienna. This complex design enunciated theorems on the relationship between the memory of the historic past of a great city and the invention of the new city based on the modern work of architecture. The design was characterized by a mute facade from which all ornamental plastic shapes were absent. For Loos, the language of the environment of the metropolis was centered in the absence of all ornament. In 1910, a public furor spawned by the simplicity of the modernistic design resulted in a municipal order to suspend work; construction ceased and building permits were denied. Loos responded to the attacks in a public meeting attended by more than 2000 angry residents. The controversy ended with an agreement to add window boxes in an attempt to countrify and familiarize the unpopular design.

Loos's private residential works were characterized by unembellished white facades. As a result, these buildings have routinely been associated with the work of Le Corbusier, J. J. Oud, and others. Among the more famous were the much published Steiner House (1910) and Scheu House (1912), both in Vienna. One of Loos's best known projects was the entry for the Chicago Tribune Tower competition of 1922. Loos's surprising combination of Doric columns at ground level with modern skyscraper technology indicated that he was less doctrinaire about ornament than his modernist colleagues believed. To Loos, the polished black granite columns, durable classical symbols in a building, were altogether useful and therefore beautiful.

Also in 1922, Loos was appointed to the post of Chief Architect of the Housing Department of the Commune of Vienna. His projects during this time were primarily constructions modulated around simply-composed layouts, utilizing basic construction technology. Flexible interior arrangements were achieved through the use of movable partitions. Exteriors were typical of suburban housing. Vegetable gardens, which were considered essential extensions of the dwellings, were assigned high priorities. Loos soon grew disillusioned with his work as chief architect. As a result of his opposition to the then current ideology of Austrian Marxism, he resigned from his post the same year he was appointed.

Loos moved to France in 1922. He lived there until 1927, dividing his time between Paris and the Riviera with frequent journeys to Austria, Germany, and Czechoslovakia. Loos was received enthusiastically by the French avant-garde. His work entitled "Ornament and Crime" was translated in 1920 in *Esprit Nouveau,* a publication edited by Le Corbusier, Paul Dermee, and Ozenfant. Loos also exhibited regularly at d'Automne, and became the first foreigner to be elected to its jury. Loos built some of his most significant works during this period. These included The Tzara House in Paris (1926–1927), Villa Moller in Vienna (1928), Villa Muller (1930), Villa Winternitz in Prague (1931–1932) and the Khuner Country House at Payerbach in lower Austria. Monolithic in nature, these works contrasted greatly with the glass architecture that dominated rationalist styles of the 1920s. Once again, Loos was in a posture of contentious indifference to fluctuations in current taste.

In 1930, on his sixtieth birthday, Loos was officially recognized as a master of architecture. He was bestowed with an annual honorific income by the president of the Czechoslovakian Republic. His collected essays were published the following year. Adolf Loos died on August 23, 1933 and was buried beneath a simple tombstone of his own design. His most significant contribution to architecture remains his literary discourse.

BIBLIOGRAPHY

General References

A. Loos, *Spoken into the void: collected essays, 1897–1900,* MIT Press, Cambridge, Mass., 1982.

B. Gravagnuolo, *Adolf Loos,* Rizzoli, New York, 1982.

L. Münz, *Adolf Loos,* Praeger, New York, 1966.

Barbara L. Wadkins
Chula Vista, Calif.

LUNDY, VICTOR A.

Victor A. Lundy, U.S. architect, was born in New York City in 1923. Educated there, he studied at New York University with its beaux-arts curriculum before World War II. After military service as an infantry squad leader in General Patton's Third Army, he attended Harvard University where he received his Bachelor of Architecture and Master in Architecture degrees in 1947 and 1948. In addition to his career in architecture, Victor Lundy is an active artist in painting and sculpture. During his school years, he won a number of student competitions, and was awarded the Rotch Travelling Scholarship in Architecture by the Boston Society of Architects (the oldest in the U.S.), allowing him to study and travel in Europe, the Middle East, and North Africa during 1949 and 1950.

Receiving a commission for a house in Florida, Lundy established his practice of architecture in Sarasota, Florida in 1951, where he practiced for eight years. During this period he received design awards for a number of churches and other projects in Florida, and wide notice in the architectural press.

In 1960 he opened his office in New York City, and was responsible for the design of many notable commercial, religious, and government projects in the United States and overseas. He practiced in New York, with a one-year teaching sabbatical (1975), until 1976, when he established his office in Houston, Texas, where he now resides and practices. During his time in Houston, he formed a partnership with Harwood Taylor/HKS for five years. He is a Fellow of the American Institute of Architects for Design.

His architecture has been recognized nationally and internationally by publications and numerous awards, including Honor Awards from the American Institute of Architects.

Throughout his career, Lundy has also been an educator as well as a design theorist, serving as visiting professor, critic, and lecturer at architectural schools throughout the U.S. He was an Adjunct Professor of Architecture at the University of Houston for four years.

Among Lundy's work, the following are noteworthy:

1. St. Paul's Lutheran Church, Sarasota, 1960 and 1969 (Fig. 1). The roof over the sanctuary is framed of heavy wood decking supported on steel cables that hang in catenary curves from the central steel and cable truss system. The sweeping tent-like form recalls one of the most ancient of enclosures. It is a place of shade in contrast to the brightness outside. Natural light is kept out purposefully, except at the concrete end wall, which is washed with sunlight through a narrow band of skylight.

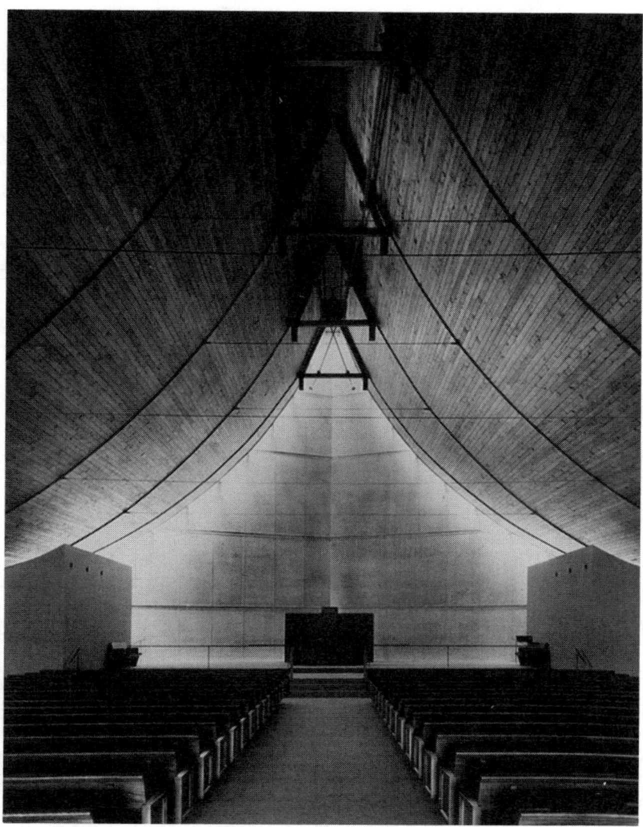

Figure 1. New Sanctuary for St. Paul's Lutheran Church, Sarasota, Florida, 1969. Photograph by George Cserna.

Figure 2. United States Tax Court Building, Washington, D.C., 1975. Photograph by Robert Lautman.

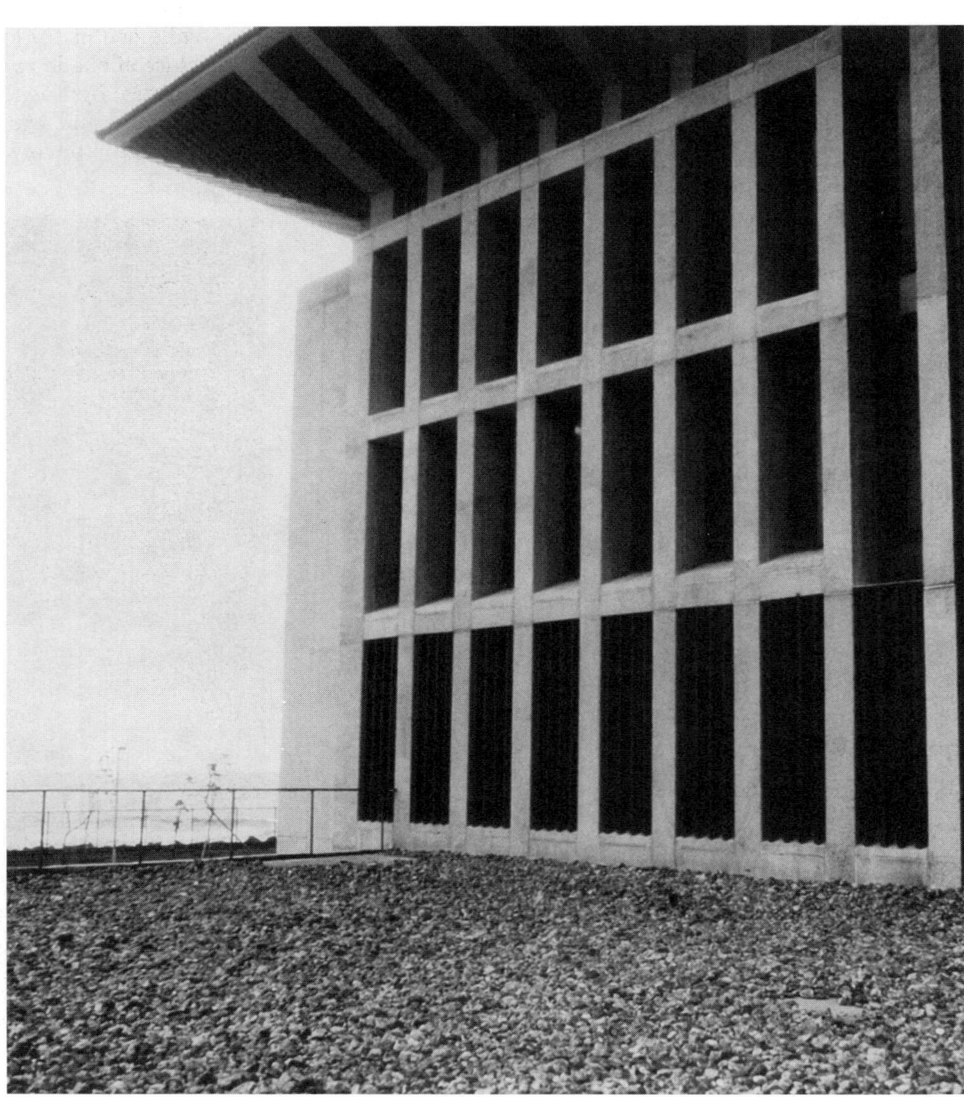

Figure 3. The United States Embassy for Sri Lanka (Ceylon), Colombo, 1984. Photograph by Victor A. Lundy, FAIA.

2. The United States Tax Court Building in Washington, D.C. (Fig. 2), was completed in 1975. This government building is notable for its presence in the city. Arthur Drexler, in the Museum of Modern Art's 1979 publication "Transformations in Modern Architecture" had this to say (1):

> Occasionally the expressive content of a building that is conceived as a minimalist sculpture, like Victor Lundy's in Washington, D.C. bears some plausible relationship to its program. Thus, the blank, format symmetry and the threatening mass cantilevered 55 feet seem appropriate enough when one learns that the building is the United States Tax Court.

Ada Louise Huxtable wrote (2):

> The Tax Court Building deals in the generalized and timeless sense of balance, order, and serenity that is genuine classicism, not in substitutes of vestigial ornament or stylized recall. It meets the challenge of today's expression and technology as a prime creative objective.

3. The United States Embassy for Sri Lanka (Ceylon) was completed in 1984 (Fig. 3). The commission for this project was awarded to Victor A. Lundy in 1961, but construction was delayed during the Viet Nam War. The site is on the Indian Ocean at Colombo. The steeply pitched, wide-overhanging roof provides sun and rain protection for the building, and is surfaced with local traditional clay tiles. The use of Burma teak grilles provides shade, security and visual screening of the offices in the four-story block. Views of the ocean are preserved across the site by placing the long axis of the building at right angles to the sea and main road. The exterior is sheathed with hand-tooled granite slabs from India.

In the 1988 Presidential Design Awards program, Lundy's U.S. Embassy for Sri Lanka was selected for a Federal Design Achievement Award, the National Endowment for the Arts' highest honor in design.

BIBLIOGRAPHY

1. A. Drexler, *Transformations in Modern Architecture,* Museum of Modern Art, New York, 1979.
2. A. L. Huxtable, "Architecture: Full Speed Forward," *The New York Times* (October 1, 1967).

General References

W. McQuade, "Lundy's Personal Architecture," *Architectural Forum* (Dec. 1959).

"Four Churches by Victor Lundy," *Architectural Record* (Dec. 1959).

"Victor A. Lundy and the Development of the American Architectural Tradition," H. F. Lenning, P. Simond, 1964.

"U.S. Embassy Building, After 23 Years," *Architecture,* 64–71 (July 1984).

"U.S. Embassy Office Building," *Architectural Record,* 104–105 (Dec. 1980).

S. Abercrombie, "Tax Court," *Progressive Architecture,* 52–59 (July 1976).

Victor A. Lundy, FAIA
Houston, Texas

LUTYENS, EDWIN L.

Sir Edwin Landseer Lutyens was the greatest "traditional" architect of the twentieth century. His prolific achievements rank him with the giants of architecture in the UK: the building of dozens of large country houses, the design of monuments, major public buildings and commercial structures all over the British empire, and the masterful planning and architectural design of Imperial Delhi in India. So close was this "architect laureate" of the UK to the heart of his country's modern history and politics, that his work has often been criticized for its regal, imperialist, and aristocratic associations. His genius has transcended such criticism, and his buildings continue to speak with a clear, powerful voice about "Englishness," classicism, and romantic domesticity, among other things.

Lutyens's youth portended nothing of the stature he was to achieve in his mature years. He was born in London on March 29, 1869 to Captain Charles Lutyens and Mary Gallwey. After serving in Canada (where he met his wife) and the Crimean War, Lutyens's father retired to become a painter of race horses and hunting scenes. He named his ninth son after the noted animal painter Sir Edwin Landseer, who was the child's godfather. "Ned," as he was called, was a quiet, sickly boy whose fragile health forced him to be tutored at home. Learning to imagine vividly as a child to compensate for play, "to use my eyes instead of my feet," as he recalled, contributed to his extraordinary visual inventiveness. A lover of mental games, Lutyens's shyness did not prevent him from being clever, both verbally and with architectural forms. As he often said, "Architecture is building with wit."

Lutyens attended the South Kensington School of Art from 1885 to 1887, architecture being his intended career, and spent only one year as an apprentice with Ernest George and Peto, the Edwardian advocates of romantic classicism, before striking out on his own at the age of 20. With one country house commission under his belt, he met Gertrude Jekyll, the noted garden writer and designer, in the family's home county of Surrey. Their collaboration, initially on Jekyll's own house, Munstead Wood (extending from 1894 to 1897), would not only launch the young man's practice as a country house architect, but would produce a brilliant series of house and garden ensembles. Such works as Deanery Garden (1899–1902), Hestercombe (1906), and Little Thakeham (1902) (Fig. 1) are marked by spectacular axial and geometric relationships in plan, tempered by Jekyll's soft and rustic feeling for planting textures and impressionistic color mixing.

Lutyens's domestic works during the 1890s fall into a somewhat romantic, arts and crafts style influenced by

Figure 1. Little Thakeham, Sussex, 1902. Courtesy of the author.

Richard Norman Shaw and Philip Webb; this has been called his Surrey Vernacular period. However, this association can be deceiving. The Queen Anne and Old English models of Shaw merely provided fodder for young Lutyens, who transformed butterfly plans, medievalizing massing, picturesque assemblages of gables, traditional material craftsmanship, and interlocking room planning into wholly unorthodox juxtapositions of architectural forms, patterns, and motifs. Underlying all of his more overtly rustic early houses was a rigorous formal armature which eventually led to flirtations with classicism. The watershed years of the Surrey period were 1898–1901, during which Orchards, Goddards, Tigbourne Court, Deanery Garden, and Homewood were produced; all were small country houses with big ideas. Of this distinguished five, the germ of the Lutyens house is contained best in Homewood (for the Dowager, Countess of Lytton, the architect's mother-in-law), and the tricks of the Lutyens–Jekyll garden is best exemplified by Deanery (the first of several commissions for Edward Hudson, the influential publisher of *Country Life*). At Homewood the center is voided by a crossing staircase, the massing is deceptively masked by four different elevations, and the plan has a latent nine-square classical grid. The site plan at Deanery Garden is a *tour de force* of axial vistas and interpenetrations in which the house clearly plays a secondary role to larger design ideas in the landscape.

By 1902, Lutyens's reputation as a country house architect was established, and he had underway his first large estate plan, Marshcourt (1901–1904), near Stockbridge and Winchester. In the next ten years he would build a group of masterful and grand country houses for the Edwardian smart set, most of which were in one way or another classically inspired.

Heathcote (1906) in Yorkshire was the most elaborate and mannered of these great houses, with its echoes of Sanmicheli and Vanbrugh, and what is surely the most wittily tortuous classical plan ever conceived by an English architect. Equally excessive by its grand banality was Great Maytham (1907–1909), the Kentish "Whig Seat," with its endless Georgian facades fairly packed with double hung windows. But the finest of Lutyens's classical houses was The Salutation at Sandwich, built for Gaspard and Henry Farrer in 1911. Here, by looking to the beginnings of the formal block Georgian house in the seventeenth century and to Hugh May's Eltham Lodge, Lutyens produced a subtly proportioned classical plan and elevations which bespoke the graceful essence of the English country house.

This prewar period also brought Lutyens into the patronage of government and large businesses, among them the Midland Bank, for which he executed several branch offices and finally a major headquarters building in London. His public work included housing, St. Jude's church, and planning for Hampstead Garden Suburb (1908–1909). Castle Drogo, Devon, designed for the wealthy grocer Julius Drewe (1910–1930) would have been his largest domestic commission, had it been built according to the original plans. It remains, even in a truncated state, the most powerful modern example of the English castle, another genre in which Lutyens worked extensively.

In 1912, Lutyens was appointed to the coveted position of architect to the Delhi Town Planning Committee charged with planning the new capital of the British Raj, a city which would at once sum up British Imperial domination and India's own history. In this commission of a lifetime, Lutyens designed what must be among the largest and most elaborate government buildings of the century, the Viceroy's House (completed in April 1929), and was largely responsible for the layout of the entire city of New Delhi.

The Lutyens plan, influenced by topography, history, and politics, recalled the principles of English garden city planning, French axial gardens, Wren's 1666 plan for London, and even the plan of Washington, D.C. Its centerpiece, the Kingsway, ran east–west, linking the new seat of power, the Viceroy's house and its great dome, with the old fort of Purana Kila; a second ceremonial axis, at 60° to the first, linked the Secretariat buildings (by Herbert Baker) to the old walled city of Delhi and the Friday Mosque or Jumma Masjid. Thus both the traditional Indian way and the English were fused, as they would be in the architecture of the Viceroy's house. Here Lutyens looked both to the design of great European palaces and to traditional Indian architecture, with its use of water, garden courts, the Mogul *chujja* or projecting cornice, and the *chattris* or hat-like turrets which adorn palaces and forts. Lutyens even designed a new order, the quasi-Ionic bell capital, utilizing a powerful native symbol. In the final synthesis, the Viceroy's house represented the best aspects of monumental classicism in the Western tradition while evoking an austere and exotic Eastern one.

The architect spent almost twenty years seeing his vision for New Delhi realized, to the exclusion of other major projects, only to be confronted with the reality of the end of British rule at the approach of World War II. His finest later projects included a moving and brilliant set of war memorials, among them the Whitehall Cenotaph (1919) and Thiepval Arch at the Somme (1927–1932), as well as the impressive project for the Roman Catholic Cathedral of Christ the King at Liverpool (1929–1958). Few architects of this century have understood the problems of monumental design as well; none have seen so many fine monumental works built.

Lutyens was amply recognized for his achievements during his time. He received the RIBA Gold Medal in 1921 and knighthood in 1918, as well as membership and later presidency of the Royal Academy (1920, 1938). However, his stature had already dimmed by the date of the posthumous publication of his complete works in the *Memorial Volumes* in 1950; modernism had become firmly entrenched following the war. Lutyens died on January 1, 1944. His ashes are interred in St. Paul's.

BIBLIOGRAPHY

General References

Lutyens, The Work of the English Architect Sir Edwin Lutyens (1869–1944), Arts Council of Great Britain, London, 1981.

J. Brown, *Gardens of a Golden Afternoon,* Van Nostrand Reinhold, New York, 1982.

A. S. G. Butler, *The Architecture of Sir Edwin Lutyens,* 3 vols., Country Life Limited, London, 1950.

D. Dunster and P. Inskip, eds., *Edwin Lutyens,* Architectural Monographs 6, Academy Editions, New York and London, 1979.

R. Gradidge, *Edwin Lutyens: Architect Laureate,* G. Allen and Unwin, London, 1981.

A. Greenberg, "Lutyens' Architecture Restudied," *Perspecta* **12,** 129–152 (1969).

C. Hussey, *The Life of Sir Edwin Lutyens,* Country Life Limited, London, 1950.

R. G. Irving, *Indian Summer: Lutyens, Baker and Imperial Delhi,* Yale University Press, New Haven, 1981.

M. Lutyens, *Edwin Lutyens, a Memoir by his Daughter,* Murray, London, 1980.

D. O'Neil, *Lutyens Country Houses,* Lund Humphries, London, 1980.

Mark A. Hewitt
Columbia University
New York, New York

M

McKIM, MEAD, AND WHITE

Some 60 years ago, Sir Charles Reilly, head of the Liverpool School of Architecture, declared that the architectural firm of McKim, Mead, and White was "one of the great determining forces in the history of the architecture of our own time" (1). Perhaps Reilly went a bit too far when he likened the founding father of the firm, Charles Follen McKim, to Sir Christopher Wren. But the influence of McKim, Mead, and White could hardly be overstated. That influence was expressed in the work of Reilly's contemporary, Sir Aston Webb. And in the United States of the Gilded Age, according to cultural historian Henry Steele Commager, this particular trio "came to exercise such a monopoly as might have called for the application of a new Sherman Antitrust Law" (2).

Commager may have exaggerated, but only slightly. The firm of McKim, Mead, and White was in operation from 1879 until McKim's death in 1909 (the enterprise lasted nominally until 1961, for the younger architects in the firm understandably did not want to give up the prestigious name). The firm employed more than 100 persons at its apogee. It received at least 800 commissions, nearly half of which were major ones. Although headquartered in New York City, there were branch offices in Boston and Kansas City. The architectural style with which McKim, Mead, and White were most intimately associated dominated public architecture in the United States until right before World War II. Even today, the handiwork of Charles McKim and the flamboyant Stanford White command respect and attention. Architectural critic Paul Goldberger reports having encountered townhouses built around 1840 which some realtors have attributed to White, even though White was not born until 1853 (3).

In the case of McKim, Mead, and White, the whole may have been greater than the sum of the parts, but the parts are important in their own right. The austere and Pennsylvania-born McKim was of abolitionist and Quaker roots. After studying mining engineering at Harvard, McKim attended the Ecole des Beaux Arts in Paris. He then worked for the noted architect Henry Hobson Richardson and assisted in the design of Boston's Trinity Church. McKim was generally regarded as the scholar of the firm. He was largely responsible for the acquisition of some 25,000 books for the firm's library. William Rutherford Mead was the most obscure of the three partners. A native of Vermont and a relative (through marriage) of novelist William Dean Howells, Mead studied in Florence before signing up with McKim. While the Rhode Island State House was largely his brainchild, Mead is remembered today more for his managerial and diplomatic skills than for his architectural genius.

To the nonarchitect, the name of Stanford White stands out the most. Paul Goldberger, for one, believes that White is "better known to the public than any other American architect except Frank Lloyd Wright" (3). The son of Shakespeare scholar Richard Grant White, Stanford White was, in addition to being a talented architect, an imaginative interior decorator and a designer of yachts, Pullman cars, and magazine covers. (*Scribner's* and *Century* bore his mark.) He distinguished himself as much by his style of living, so it seems, as by his style of architecture. In the words of architect Norval White, Stanford White was "gourmand, gourmet, lover, and bon vivant" (4). Some Americans recall more how he died than how he lived. In 1906 the jealous husband of actress Evelyn Nesbit shot the colorful architect to death on the roof of Madison Square Garden, which White himself had designed some 15 years earlier.

In the larger scheme of things the accomplishments of McKim, Mead, and White matter more than their personalities. The following are but a few of their achievements: the Boston Public Library, Columbia University's Low Library in New York City (Fig. 1), the Army War College in Washington (under the administration of Theodore Roosevelt), Manhattan's Century Club, the Robert Gould Shaw Memorial in Boston, the Bowdoin College Art Gallery, two of the gates at Harvard College, and an addition to the University of Virginia. Stanford White was the guiding force behind the Newport Casino; White and McKim also designed the base of a work done by their friend, Augustus Saint-Gaudens, the William Tecumseh Sherman monument at the edge of Central Park in New York City. And McKim put up four pavilions at the 1893 Columbian Exposition in Chicago. According to Richard Guy Wilson, McKim served as "the artistic conscience for Daniel Burnham, the grand master of the undertaking" (5). Finally, McKim and his associates were central figures in the City Beautiful movement, the distinguishing feature of which was the self-conscious, emulation of classical Renaissance forms.

There were several distinctive McKim, Mead, and White styles. Their earliest work was done largely in the shingle style that Vincent Scully has celebrated in his writings (6). Partly due to the influence of Joseph Wells, the firm gravitated to the Italian Renaissance style in the mid-1880s. This was not as abrupt a change as it appears, however, for McKim had always favored Greco-Roman motifs. In fact, he had traveled extensively throughout Italy before setting up his own shop. Admittedly, many of the early works of McKim, Mead, and White reflected the lingering influence of Richardson (with whom White had also worked) more than they did a devotion to the classical revival. But the penchant for the latter was present from the start of McKim's travels. As his firm expanded, McKim would demonstrate his indebtedness to Italian architectural forms in no uncertain terms. The *New York Herald* building designed for James Gordon Bennett, for instance, owed something to the Palazzo del Consiglio in Verona, and the old Pennsylvania Station in New York City was deliberately modeled after the baths of the Roman emperor Caracalla. As Italy influenced McKim, so did McKim also—to a far lesser extent—influence Italy: he was instrumental in establishing the American Academy in Rome.

Figure 1. Front view of Low Library at Columbia University in New York City. In front, on the steps, is Daniel Chester French's *Alma Mater.* At left are the School of Mines and Earl Hall. Courtesy of the Library of Congress.

Leland Roth contends that McKim, Mead, and White utilized several different styles at the same time. In Roth's view, the firm tended to use a High Renaissance or Augustan Roman classicism for government buildings and libraries, a Georgian or Federal style for colleges, and a North Italian or Spanish Renaissance style for buildings that were meant to convey a playful or festive attitude (7). One can even suggest that decidedly different architectural styles were sometimes expressed by McKim, Mead, and White in one and the same house. The Tilton house is a good example, with its blending of Tudor, Colonial, Queen Anne, and Japanese motifs. Sir Charles Reilly concluded that McKim, Mead, and White composed "an architecture of conscious eclecticism" (8). Such eclecticism may offend the sensibilities of purists, but it is instructive that the first professional journal of architecture in this country, the *American Architect and Building News,* made a pitch for eclecticism in its inaugural issue, more than a century ago (9). According to one critic, the eclecticism of Stanford White is not far removed from the postmodern efforts of Robert Venturi and Charles Moore (10).

McKim, Mead, and White were architects of and for the Gilded Age. Although offended by the rank materialism that pervaded the "age of enterprise," these three men did some of their most memorable work for the so-called Robber Barons. The J. Pierpont Morgan Library in New York City comes to mind, not to mention the many summer resorts at Newport, R.I., or the homes of railroad magnate Henry Villard. McKim's biographer tells us that the firm's "list of clients reads like a social directory" (11). Wealthy industrialists living in the urban or semirural Northeast craved status as much as they did wealth. Hence they sought to ape the European aristocracy, an ambitious aim inasmuch as the United States lacked an aristocratic tradition of its own. McKim, Mead, and White, sedulously attentive to "user needs," gave their clients what they wanted. As historian Edward Kirkland has shown in his *Dream and Thought in the Business Community,* this was the age of the big house (12). It was not uncommon in the era of the Crockers, Palmers, and Vanderbilts to have homes which included libraries, chapels, art galleries, and theaters. In 1884, the *New York World* described with awe the Tiffany home in mid-Manhattan as "the largest private residence in the city" (13).

McKim, Mead, and White were hardly unusual in serving the needs of the elite. Richard Morris Hunt, among many others, had distinguished himself for doing essentially the same thing, although in a different architectural style. It should also be noted that "conspicuous consumption" (to use Thorstein Veblen's term) was endorsed not only by the power elite and custodians of high culture. Ministers and editorial writers, as well as schoolteachers, found the architectural tastes of the wealthy both understandable and desirable. Economists justified the construction of mansions and country "cottages" because of the jobs provided for laborers. Even a few social critics could be found defending ostentatiousness, albeit in a backhanded way. On one ocasion, in fact, muckraker Ida Tarbell assailed John D. Rockefeller for not being pretentious enough in his architectural tastes (14).

In another respect, the architecture of McKim, Mead, and White was very much the product of the Gilded Age. This was a period, after all, when what philosopher George Santayana dubbed the "genteel tradition" held sway. To Santayana, "The American Will inhabits the skyscraper, the American Intellect inhabits the colonial mansion. The one is the sphere of the American man; the other, at least predominantly, of the American woman. The one is all aggressive enterprise; the other is all genteel tradition" (15). The American, in short, was a split personality. One was practical and tough-minded; the other was elegant and refined. High culture chose not to mimic the raw reality of the industrial United States but rather to stand apart from it, hence the appeal of a Carroll Beckwith or Will Low in painting, an Edward MacDowell in music, a William Dean Howells in literature, and of the neoclassical in not a few aspects of culture.

McKim, Mead, and White certainly have had their share of criticism. The architecture of Louis Sullivan and his protégé Frank Lloyd Wright was in large part a self-conscious rejection of virtually all that the indefatigable trio represented. For one, Wright was not as enamored of the city as were McKim and company. For another, both Wright and Sullivan resented the seeming hegemony of the Eastern architectural firms. More importantly, the founding fathers of U.S. modernism believed that McKim's firm subordinated function to form (a not wholly unjustifiable charge). Finally, Sullivan and Wright held that U.S. architecture was too obsessed with European models and not sufficiently sensitive to the U.S. landscape. Not unlike Ralph Waldo Emerson in his famous "American Scholar" address, they declared it high time for the United States to emancipate itself, culturally and artistically, from its European fetters (16). Needless to say, this amounted to a frontal assault on the philosophy and practice of McKim, Mead, and White.

Many cultural commentators have concurred with Wright and Sullivan. Writing in the 1920s, critic Suzanne La Follette blasted McKim, Mead, and White. During the Gilded Age, LaFollette wrote in *Art in America,* "American architecture was still plundering the past." As if this did not make the point strongly enough, she went on to say "Europe was pillaged for designs to be adapted to American uses" (17). Lewis Mumford would proffer a similar indictment a few years later in *The Brown Decades* (18). In *The Course of American Democratic Thought,* written just before America's entry into World War II, intellectual historian Ralph Gabriel acidly noted that "In the 1870's American architecture broke out with a rash of jig-saw ornament" (19). In 1950, echoing the sentiments of the jaundiced Henry Adams, historian Henry Commager had this to say about the Columbian Exposition in which McKim and his associates figured so prominently: "The whole Exposition proclaimed in unmistakable terms that there had been little advance since Rome and that it was the first duty of architects to copy." Moreover, the exposition "condemned American architecture to the imitative and the derivative for another generation" (20). Commager did manage to acknowledge at least one bright spot on the otherwise dreary architectural horizon—the Transportation Building of Louis Sullivan at the Chicago World's Fair.

Since the 1960s, McKim, Mead, and White have been treated more generously. It is true that their neoclassicism is derivative, but to leave the matter at that hardly does justice to the precision, scholarliness, and versatility of their efforts. In any event, it is one thing to recognize the value of Sullivan and Wright; it is quite another to give the back of the hand to other and less "original" styles.

The last word is left to a part-time architect and full-time liberal theorist, Herbert Croly. Writing in the *Architectural Record* around the turn of the century, just a few years before he would launch the influential *New Republic,* and on the eve of what he and many others regarded as a cultural and political renascence, Croly asserted, "Of all modern peoples we are most completely the children of the Renaissance, and it would be fatal for us to deny our parentage" (21).

BIBLIOGRAPHY

1. C. H. Reilly, *McKim, Mead, and White,* Charles Scribner's Sons, New York, 1924, p. 7.
2. H. S. Commager, *The American Mind,* Yale University Press, New Haven, Conn., 1950, p. 396.
3. P. Goldberger in C. C. Baldwin, *Stanford White,* DaCapo Press, New York, 1976, p. iii.
4. N. White, *The Architecture Book,* Alfred A. Knopf, New York, 1976, p. 334.
5. R. G. Wilson, *McKim, Mead, & White,* Rizzoli International Publications, Inc., New York, 1983, p. 30.
6. V. Scully, *The Shingle Style,* Yale University Press, New Haven, Conn., 1955.
7. L. M. Roth, "McKim, Mead, and White," in J. M. Richards, ed., *Who's Who in Architecture,* Holt, Rinehart & Winston, New York, 1977, p. 207.
8. Ref. 1, p. 15.
9. Ref. 5, p. 56.
10. Ref. 3, p. iv.
11. C. Moore, *The Life and Time of Charles Follen McKim,* Houghton Mifflin Co., Boston, 1929, p. 47.
12. E. C. Kirkland, *Dream and Thought in the Business Community, 1860–1900,* Quadrangle Books, Chicago, 1964, pp. 29–49.
13. Ref. 3, p. 122.
14. Ref. 12, p. 38.
15. D. Wilson, ed., *The Genteel Tradition: Nine Essays by George Santayana,* Harvard University Press, Cambridge, Mass., 1967, p. 40.
16. D. W. Noble, *The Progressive Mind, 1890–1917,* Rand McNally & Co., Chicago, 1971, pp. 117–127.
17. S. LaFollette, *Art in America,* Harper & Brothers, New York, 1929, pp. 259–273.
18. L. Mumford, *The Brown Decades,* Dover Publications, Inc., New York, 1955, p. 127.
19. R. H. Gabriel, *The Course of American Democratic Thought,* Ronald Press Co., New York, 1940, p. 188.
20. Ref. 2, pp. 394–395.
21. Ref. 5, p. 98.

Barry D. Riccio
University of Illinois
Urbana, Illinois

MAEKAWA, KUNIO

Kunio Maekawa, born in 1905, was among the first to introduce modern architecture to Japan. After graduating from Tokyo University, he joined the atelier of Le Corbusier in Paris, where he worked on the Villa Savoye and the Swiss Pavilion. Another well-known Japanese architect, Junzo Sakakura, was also in Le Corbusier's atelier during the late 1930s.

On returning to Tokyo, he worked in the office of Antonin Raymond. Maekawa left there in 1935 to open his own practice. During the 1930s he entered several competitions in international style design. Although he did not win in the conservative Japanese society of the time, his work was published. This publicity drew the attention of the younger Kenzo Tange (b. 1913), who worked in Maekawa's office from 1938 to 1941.

Although no buildings were erected by him until after World War II, Maekawa did design a number of buildings in the immediate postwar period. He has been recognized as a positive influence on Japanese design by the postwar generation, even though they have moved away from the influence of CIAM and Le Corbusier.

Examples of Maekawa's work in Japan are the Nippon Sogo Bank (1952), the first use of curtain walls in Japan, and the concrete Harumi Apartments of 1958, which can be compared to Le Corbusier's Unité d'Habitation at Marseilles. His Metropolitan Festival Hall in Tokyo (1961) is another example of the high quality work inspired by Le Corbusier.

Maekawa and Sakakura collaborated with Le Corbusier on the National Museum of Western Art in Toyko completed in 1959, with a later addition by Maekawa (1979). The museum is one in a series of three based on the concept of the Museum of Unlimited Growth developed by Le Corbusier. Other museums by Maekawa include the Perfectual museums in Ohmiya (1971) and Fukoaka (1979). All are set in landscaped surroundings.

Maekawa has become the most influential Japanese architect of his generation. Throughout his career he has encouraged efforts to promote the social status of the architect in Japan, as well as to establish the profession there.

BIBLIOGRAPHY

General References

A. Drexler, *The Architecture of Japan,* Museum of Modern Art, New York, 1955.

D. Gans, *The Le Corbusier Guide,* Princeton Architectural Press, Princeton, N.J., 1987.

H. R. Hitchcock, *Architecture: Nineteenth and Twentieth Centuries,* 4th ed., The Pelican History of Art, Penguin Books Ltd., Harmondsworth, UK, 1977.

M.F. Ross, *Beyond Metabolism: The New Japanese Architecture,* Architectural Record Books, McGraw-Hill Book Company, New York, 1978.

See also Oriental Architecture

Robert T. Packard, AIA
Reston, Virginia

MAINTENANCE, BUILDING

Design for maintenance can provide major savings for the owner and users of a building. A definition of maintainability would be a design that permits repair, adjustment, and cleaning at a reasonable cost. Maintenance costs over 2 or 3 decades equal the original cost of construction for most buildings. Even a minor reduction in maintenance costs can provide major economic benefits.

A maintenance program needs planning. Client personnel, the architect, engineers, and interior designers should jointly consider the selection of materials and surfaces. The owner needs to want such a plan, and it is the duty of the architect, engineer, maintenance managers, and other consultants to awaken and sustain the owner's interest.

The appearance of a building depends on proper design and maintenance. Signs of an effective exterior program include a well-drained pavement outside the building entrance, inclusion of ice-melting systems in northern climates, a grating to remove moisture and dirt, matting or a runner and possibly a rough-surfaced stone floor before stepping onto carpet.

Factors working against maintainability include inadequate funds and unexpected costs, which may preclude the added expense of easily maintained surfaces. Early occupancy before the trades have completed their work can add to the maintenance problems, as does the need to add such items as additional cables for communication and electronic equipment in an already finished interior.

The use of post-occupancy evaluations to assess actual operations can be an important tool for both the designers and users of a building. Maintenance considerations will vary depending on the site of the building (urban/suburban or rual), climate variations, utilities available, and the use of the building.

DURING CONSTRUCTION

The maintenance manager should be identified during the construction process, so that he or she may become familiar with the building construction.

The control of dirt and dust during construction or renovation is a major maintenance concern. The maintenance personnel will benefit from a contractor's willingness to keep the job-site free of dust using dust-reduction procedures. Temporary protection of existing finished surfaces is important.

The building specifications will indicate systems and finish materials used in a building. Problems can occur with new materials that do not have a maintenance record.

Specification of a limited number of finish materials will simplify maintenance, as will the use of standardized items where possible. This is of particular help in large projects or complexes of buildings such as collage campuses.

Proper preparation of surfaces to receive coatings and other finishes will simplify later maintenance. Frequent problems occur with incorrectly installed resilient or ceramic-tile flooring, and damaged acoustical tile. Another item to check is floor drains. They must be free from construction debris and function properly. A common problem is that drains may be set too high, causing back up and water damage.

Custodial maintenance is needed at the end of construction in preparation for move-in. In buildings undergoing renovation or additions, further custodial work is required. Use of dust barriers, adequate trash removal, and protection of floors are important. For major installations, separate contracts for supervision of move-in may be needed.

Site Considerations

What happens below ground is a major concern. In most areas of the country, termite-control treatment of the soil in the area of construction is a maintenance factor.

Access to underground drainage and utility lines, and provision of extra capacity for possible future utility lines will be needed to permit proper maintenance.

Landscaping

Landscaping is also a major issue. The owner should be informed of the inherent costs involved in maintaining landscaped areas. Costs of replanting, watering, mowing, fertilizing, litter removal, and insect control are all part of the cost of lawn maintenance. Avoid over-planting, protect plants from damage by keeping mowers away from trees, and do not allow planting too close to parking surfaces. For interior landscaped courtyards, consider access and equipment storage.

Paving

Maintenance of paved areas suggests that materials other than concrete or asphalt may complicate use of snowplows, shovels, and brooms. The use of brick, stone, or wood should be carefully detailed to prevent slippage, freezing water from damaging materials, or encouraging plants to take root in the paving joints. Unless grade differences are excessive, ramps are preferred to steps. Access to buildings by the handicapped is an issue for public buildings.

External Features

Building exterior concerns include truck access to loading docks and for trash removal. Fencing is an issue because it tends to collect wind-blown debris and is difficult to keep free of weeds. One procedure would be to place the fencing on a 4 ft-wide concrete strip to allow power mowing without the need for hand trimming.

Exterior lighting improves site security. Minimum exterior light levels for walks, roads and parking is 2 fc.

Exterior Building Surfaces

Vandalism should be considered in the design of the building. Exterior surfaces should be durable and easily cleaned. A building with an irregular configuration provides concealment for vandals and is thus apt to require much more money for repairs than a building with simpler lines. This is a consideration for public schools, certain industries, and shopping centers.

Roofs

Design for roof maintenance can reduce costs. Provide walkways or tread boards for roof inspection and maintenance, particularly around elevator penthouses and stairway entrances. Roof penetrations require special attention since they are a frequent location of leaks. Proper edge details are essential to reduce water problems on the walls below.

Bird Control

Try to keep to a minimum surfaces where birds may alight. Consider nonferrous- or sheet-metal wire netting installed at a 45° angle. A less sightly solution is a spiked contrivance used in small areas, for example, over doors. In some installations, an electrically charged-wire system may be used which will not kill the birds, but keeps them away.

INTERIOR MAINTENANCE

The following checklists serve as useful guides to control interior maintenance.

Floors

Experience has shown that 40–60% of interior maintenance entails floor care.

- Avoid asphalt tile, which is a poor investment although initial cost is low.
- Consider ceramic tile, which is highly durable and has a generally trouble-free surface. (Use dark grout.)
- Try concrete for industrial and other uses where appearance is not a prime factor, but remember that it should be densified or sealed.
- Remember that cork's acoustical qualities are better provided by carpet.
- Be cautious with homogeneous vinyl, which is both expensive and tends to show subfloor irregularities.
- Be cautious with impregnated wood, which has some of the same drawbacks as natural wood although it is more durable.
- Avoid linoleum, as after a time it develops a poor, irregular appearance.
- Be cautious with marble, as its porous structure is eaily stained, and it is easily damaged by harsh chemicals.
- Consider plastic laminates, which are good for some problem situations, but can give irregular performance based on installation.
- Consider plastic tile, which is expensive but is generally maintenance-free.
- Also consider rubber tile, which is also expensive.

- Remember that stone is durable if well set; grout must be sealed; but appearance may deteriorate.
- Try terrazzo, one of the most durable and attractive of all surfaces, but avoid white terrazzo; terrazzo must be sealed.
- Avoid travertine except where crevices are filled with epoxy resin.
- Remember that wood is susceptible to damage by water and mechanical scratching, and should be sealed.

Stairs

- Avoid resilient tile, bluestone, slate or marble for stair treads and landings.
- Use good surfaces—precast terrazzo, stone, and formed synthetic materials.
- Use carpeted landings, which are beneficial as a soil trap.
- Stairwell walls should be durable and not easily marked, such as natural brick.
- Handrails should be simply designed, continuous, and well attached.
- Do not locate lights over stairs; also, they should be replaceable.
- Landings should contain a wall-mounted cigarette urn/waste-receptacle unit.
- Provide for an electric receptacle on each stair landing.
- Use a ramp rather than a stairway of three or less risers.

Walls

- Use glazed tile for problem areas such as those for food processing, health care, etc.
- If wood is to be used, specify plastic-protected varieties.
- For plastered walls, locate casing beads where cracking would otherwise occur.
- Finish plastered corners to a quarter-round metal.
- For gypsum wallboard, use two $\frac{3}{8}$-in. laminated panels for best results.
- Avoid wood bases for walls; use vinyl or rubber cove bases.
- Give special attention to lobby walls.

Windows

- Consider fixed rather than operating windows.
- Remember that pivoting windows can be washed from inside a room.
- Avoid any internal treatment that will make pivoting windows inoperable.
- Flat glass is preferable to corrugated, embossed, or ribbed glass.
- Prevent damage to large panes of vertical glass by using adequate bars or marking.
- Do not design window ledges that are near floor level in such a way that they can be sat or stood on.
- Consider glazing with plastic panes rather than glass where breakage is a problem.
- In industrial-type situations, use corrugated fiber glass for roof lighting.
- Rabbet design should provide handling and setting of glass without damage to the rabbet or the glass.
- Use mullions of stainless steel for long life and little maintenance.
- Consider using the mullions as guide tracks for an automatic window-washing system.
- Design a fixed track around the perimeter of the roof for supporting window washing and other maintenance staging.
- If vertical blinds are used, specify heavy-duty hardware.
- Consider using double-pane windows with a Venetian blind between.
- Use fiber glass draperies or curtains.
- Avoid setting exterior louvers or decorative masonry that will interfere with window washing.
- If windows are to be washed manually, provide suitable hooks.
- If windows are flush with exterior walls, provide a means of conducting water around the window.
- Consider tinted, heat-reducing, glare-reducing glass.

Doors

Exterior doors

- In severe-weather areas, protect doors with vestibules or canopies.
- Design door pulls to avoid a lever action.
- Avoid center posts, or make them removable.
- Frame glass doors in aluminum or stainless steel.
- Provide a slope away from the door to prevent water backup and icy spots.
- For best economy, use heavy-duty hardware throughout.
- Where through bolts are used, provide spacer sleeves to prevent door collapsing.
- Use door closers on the hinged side, thus avoiding a bracket.
- Avoid floor-type closers.
- Standardize hardware types throughout.
- Do not use floor-mounted door stops.
- For push plates and kick plates, use plastic laminates.
- Use a hardware system that resists tampering and loosening through shock or vibration.
- Provide protection or warning for full-length glass doors.
- Use rubber swinging doors in industrial warehouse areas.
- Equip doors to rooms containing mechanical equip-

ment with self-locking locks and free knobs on the inside.

Ceilings

- Do not use soft, blown-on mineral materials; they simply cannot be cleaned.
- Do not glue or nail acoustic tile to ceiling surfaces; use lift-out tiles.
- If mineral acoustic tile is to be used, remember that the plastic-faced variety is washable.
- Provide air relief for lay-in tiles in foyers and entranceways.
- Remember that aluminum metal-pan ceilings are the most durable acoustic materials.
- Where diffusors are used, be sure the adjacent surface is smooth tile or metal to provide for easier cleaning.
- Try to avoid the installation of equipment in overhead areas.
- Avoid the problems associated with skylights by using artificial lighting.

Furniture

- Wall-mount as much furniture as possible.
- Require that furniture surfaces be cleanable and that they resist marking and scratching.
- Use plastic laminates for desk and table surfaces.
- Require a toe space under counters, displays, cabinets, and other fixtures.
- Minimize the number of legs.
- Avoid the use of grilles and screens.
- Avoid unprotected wood.
- Provide deep undercuts for finger pulls in cabinets and drawers.
- Use anodized aluminum or wooden bases for lamps that are susceptible to rusting.
- Use recessed ceiling tracks for cubicle curtains.
- For files, use recessed cabinets or floor-to-ceiling cabinets.

Fixtures and Equipment

- Protect fixtures by locating them in recessed areas or by using curbs and rails.
- Use only large, heavy-duty casters on mobile equipment.
- Wall-mount drinking fountains; recess them as far as possible.
- Avoid painted metal fountains; use ceramic or fiber glass.
- In wet areas, place fixtures on elevated bases to avoid rust.
- Where fixtures may flood or discharge water, avoid locating them overhead.
- Provide adequate ventilation for refrigeration equipment.
- In designing food-handling or food-processing equipment, consult the National Sanitation Foundation.
- Provide slanting rather than horizontal tops on such items as sills, lockers, radiator covers, baseboards.

Plumbing

- Permanent drawings should show location of all plumbing systems, including underground.
- Standardize fixtures as much as possible.
- Provide adequate space for working on plumbing and piping.
- Locate piping so it does not obstruct openings.
- Protect maintenance workers from hot piping or dripping liquids.
- Use plugged tees rather than elbows to provide cleanout points.
- Provide enough valving so that systems can be closed down in sections.
- In cold-weather areas, protect outside faucets and bibbs.
- Specify corrosion-resistant drip pans where leakage is a problem.
- Equip laundry chutes and waste chutes with floor drain and cleaning spray head.
- Use a metal saddle to protect pipe supported by rollers.
- Avoid damage to pipes by using antifriction piping supports on long runs.
- Where pipes or valves are subjected to temperatures over 190° use a heat-resisting paint.

Mechanical

- Be sure that drawings show mechanical equipment in open, or extended, positions to assure clarity and accessibility.
- Provide separate space secured from the occupants of a building for major mechanical and electrical equipment.
- Provide sufficient illumination for machine maintenance.
- See that the correct information is available initially for future maintenance.
- Use self-cleaning filtration units for air-handling systems where possible.
- Grade pipelines for drains with the low point in the direction of flow.
- Use floor drains in areas for mechanical maintenance where spillages may be expected.
- Provide drip pans to catch coolants, lubricants, process chemicals, and other fluids.
- Locate shutoff valves for convenient maintenance.

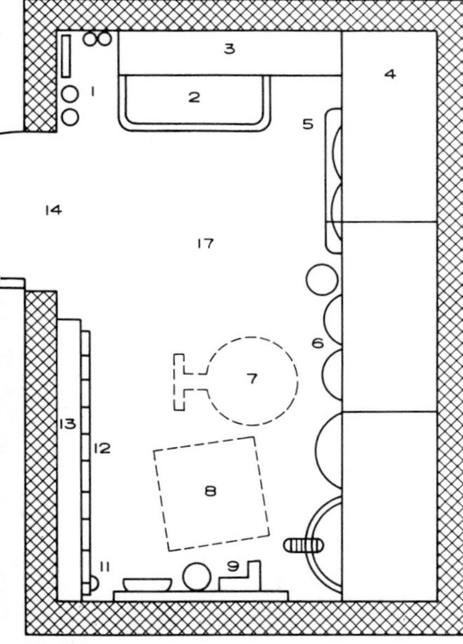

PLAN

SECTION

NOTE

Housekeeping and maintenance facilities are an important program item in practically every building. Provide adequate space for all standard custodial functions, and add space for special equipment if required.

KEY—OPTIMUM CUSTODIAL CLOSET

1. Storage area for hoses, extension wands, pipes, etc.
2. Built in ceramic tile floor sink with drain (second choice: wall mounted utility sink).
3. Shelves over utility sink 9 in. deep, 12 in. spacing.
4. Storage shelving over floor stock, 18 in. deep, 12 in. spacing.
5. Mopping outfit in stored position.
6. Floor stock (drums, cans, etc.).
7. Floor machine in stored position.
8. Vacuum in stored position.
9. Accessories, fittings, and tools mounted on pegboard.
10. Aluminum or ceramic drip tray.
11. Mop in stored position.
12. Trigrip tool holders.
13. 4-in. spacer to keep mops away from wall.
14. Bulletin board containing instructions, schedules, etc.
15. 30 in. wide door with louver—location of door interchangeable with accessories pegboard if necessary because of orientation of area.
16. Ceiling light providing minimum 40 ft-c; light should be shielded to prevent damage.
17. Floor of ceramic tile or concrete with floor drain if possible.
18. Bibb (threaded) faucet with brace.
19. Length of hose for washing equipment. A custodial cabinet should be used where there is insufficient space to install a custodial closet.

OPTIMUM CUSTODIAL CLOSET (6' × 9' INSIDE)

PLAN

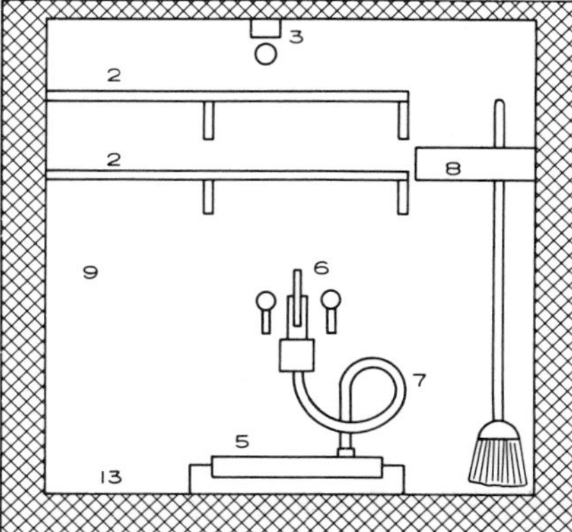

SECTION

KEY—MINIMUM CUSTODIAL CLOSET

1. Dimensions: 8 ft long, $4^1/_2$ ft deep (36 ft^2).
2. Shelving 10 in. deep with bracket supports.
3. 75 W lamp with door hinge switch.
4. Two 30 in. doors pierced for ventilation.
5. Utility floor sink with stainless steel lip cover; note off center.
6. Bibb faucet with support hanger.
7. 4-ft length of hose.
8. Tool holder.
9. Walls ceramic to 4 ft, painted enamel (including ceiling) above 4 ft.
10. Location for custodial cart or waste hamper.
11. Location for two bucket (or three bucket) mopping outfit.
12. Location for floor machine or vacuum.
13. Floor—concrete, ceramic, or terrazzo (not resilient).

MINIMUM CLOSET ($4^1/_2$' × 8')

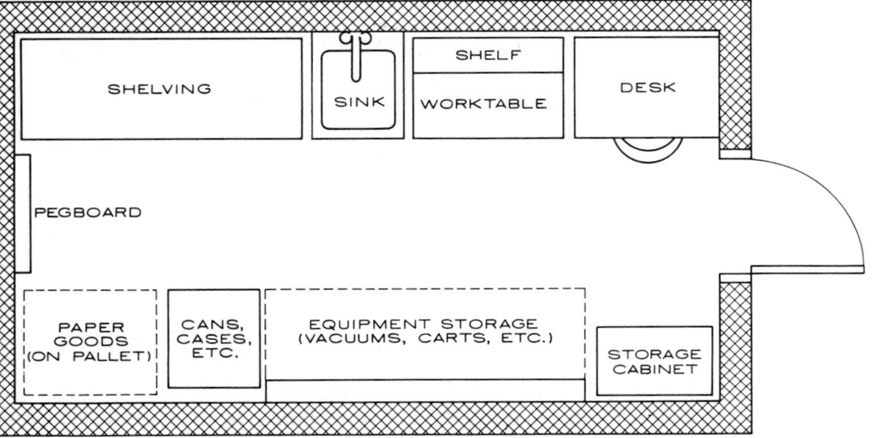

SMALL CENTRAL STORAGE AREA (8' × 15' INSIDE)

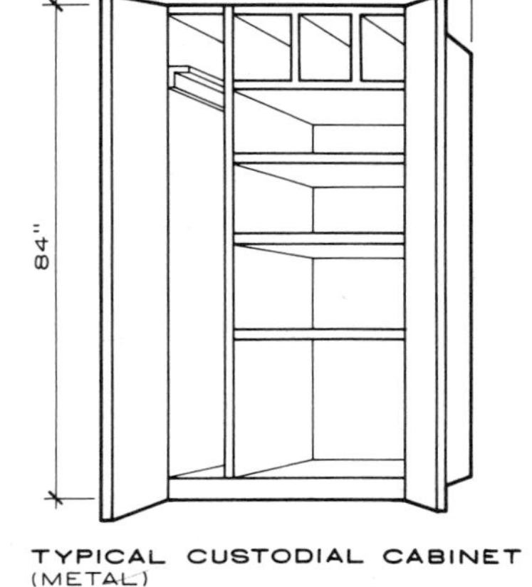

TYPICAL CUSTODIAL CABINET (METAL)

Figure 1. Custodial Facilities (1). Courtesy of Edwin B. Feldman.

Electrical

- Install empty conduit in some situations to handle future requirements.
- Consider the likelihood that building areas will be upgraded and provide sufficient electrical requirements initially.
- In changing situations, use rack, tray, or channel construction for wire supports.
- Space electrical outlets at reasonable intervals.
- Avoid canopy switches, pull-chain operation, and light-fixture outlets.
- Avoid many problems by eliminating floor-mounted receptacles.
- Do not permit running water and drain lines to pass through electrical equipment areas.
- Provide work room around electrical equipment for easy, safe maintenance.
- Protect electric gear from physical damage.
- Provide specific enclosure for high-voltage equipment.
- See that electric gear areas are well ventilated.
- Be sure that adequate insulation is provided to protect maintenance workers.
- Be sure that electric vaults are accessible from building exteriors.
- See that indoor electric vaults contain a floor drain.

Lighting

- Be sure that lighting fixtures are accessible.
- Place lighting fixtures over landings, not over stairs.
- Use rough-service lamps in problem areas.
- Provide central lighting controls for each floor.
- Where possible, use standard voltage for lighting.
- In areas normally dimly lit, provide alternative lighting for maintenance.
- Do not locate accent lights in hard-to-reach areas.
- Consider exterior floodlighting to minimize vandalism.
- Where a number of long fluorescent tubes are used, provide a tube crusher.
- Select fixture designs that do not collect dirt.
- Use low-temperature lamps where conditions warrant.
- Use high-impact plastic rather than glass globes.
- Where dust is a problem, consider ventilated fixtures.

MAINTENANCE FACILITIES

Maintenance facilities should be convenient to areas served. Their size is dependent on the building type and complexity of operation. Typical spaces might include manager's office, secretarial office, staff lounge, training room, locker rooms, rest rooms, showers, and first-aid office. Repairs for larger facilities may require special shops and storage space. Ladder storage is frequently overlooked.

Loading dock operations, and facilities for storing vehicles, ground maintenance equipment, fuels and combustible cleaning materials, and rooms for waste storage and waste compactors are typical of spaces required for maintenance. Typical custodial spaces of various sizes are shown in Figure 1(1).

BIBLIOGRAPHY

1. R. T. Packard, ed., *Ramsey/Sleeper Architectural Graphic Standards*, 7th ed., John Wiley & Sons, Inc. New York, 1981, p. 24.

General References

H. S. Conover, *Grounds Maintenance Handbook,* 3rd ed., McGraw-Hill Book Company, New York, 1976.

E. B. Feldman, *Building Design for Maintainability,* Service Engineering Associates, Inc., Atlanta, Ga., 1983.

L. R. Higgins and L. C. Morrow, *Maintenance Engineering Handbook,* 3rd ed., McGraw-Hill Book Company, New York, 1977.

R. E. Billow, technical coordinator, *Facilities Management: A Manual for Physical Plant Administration,* Association of Physical Plant Administrators of Universities and Colleges, Alexandria, Va., 1986.

EDWIN B. FELDMAN
Service Engineering Associates, Inc.
Atlanta, Georgia

This article was in large part derived from E. B. Feldman, *Building Design for Maintainability* with permission of the author.

MAKI, FUMIHIKO

Fumihiko Maki has been identified with the beginning of the Metabolism group of Japanese architects in 1960, having collaborated with Kisho Kirokawa and others in authoring the book entitled *Metabolism 1960—A Proposal for a New Urbanism*. However, the theories expressed in that publication are not evident in Maki's later work. In his writings Maki has emphasized urban design, the use of new technology, and order in the built environment.

Maki was born in 1928. After receiving a degree in architecture from Tokyo University in 1952, he studied in the United States at Cranbrook Academy, and at Harvard University under José Luis Sert. In 1965 he opened his own practice, Maki & Associates, in Tokyo.

Maki has lectured and taught at Washington University, and has been a visiting critic at Harvard University, the University of California at Berkeley and at Los Angeles, and Columbia University. He has been a professor of architecture at Tokyo University since 1979.

The simplicity and formality of Maki's work are shown in the Hillside Terrace Housing in Tokyo (1969–1979).

He was the architect of the National Museum of Modern Art in Kyoto (1978) and its later addition (1986), and of the New Library at Keio University Tokyo (1981).

One of Maki's projects, the Central Building for Tsukuba University at Tsukuba Newtown, Japan (1973–1974), is faced with prefabricated glass block panels in steel frames and clear window panels resulting in an effective, low cost enclosure. In 1979 his design for the University was exhibited in the *Transformations in Modern Architecture* exhibit at New York's Museum of Modern Art (1).

Bibliography

1. A. Drexler, *Transformations in Modern Architecture,* The Museum of Modern Art, New York, 1979, p. 74.

General References

The Japan Architect **54,** 265 (1979).

K. Kurokawa, *Metabolism in Architecture,* Westview Press, Boulder, Colo., 1977.

A New Wave of Japanese Architecture, Exhibition Catalogue 10, The Institute for Architecture and Urban Studies, New York, 1978.

M. F. Ross, *Beyond Metabolism, The New Japanese Architecture,* Architectural Books, McGraw-Hill Book Company, New York, 1978.

See also ORIENTAL ARCHITECTURE

ROBERT T. PACKARD, AIA
Reston, Virginia

MALLS, SHOPPING. See SHOPPING CENTERS

MARKELIUS, SVEN G.

Throughout his long career, Sven Gottfrid Markelius (1889–1972) combined mastery of a personal yet traditionally Swedish design aesthetic with a responsive acceptance of contemporary trends in international architectural design and building technology. His work as both architect and urban planner demonstrates the best of the idealistic Swedish approach to modern design principles in which the relationship between architecture and social planning is stressed. In 1964, he wrote of his beliefs (1):

> Our aim must be towards a structure of society, and of cities, that promotes the health and happiness of the citizen. Here our major task should be to find new and better ways of planning our cities, as well as of replanning those existing ones which are no longer workable as instruments for good life.

Born and educated in Stockholm, Markelius graduated first from the Institute of Technology (1913) and later from the Academy of Fine Arts (1915). Architecture in Sweden at that time was under the influence of the nineteenth-century *nationalromantik* movement, which encouraged appreciation of traditional Swedish culture through craftsmanship, use of native materials and decorative detailing, and sympathetic relationships between building and landscape (2).

Through his early professional experience in the office of Ragnar Ostberg, Markelius absorbed lessons in the older romantic style, which would be reinterpreted and reexpressed in his own work in a contemporary manner. At the same period, travel through Europe served to introduce him to the new functional logic and simplicity of the modern movement. Although the building was not completed until 1934, his first important commission, the Concert Hall at Hälsingborg, was the result of taking first prize in a 1925 competition. Here Markelius's admiration for Le Corbusier is reflected in the functional juxtaposition of geometric shapes as determined by acoustic design requirements for musical performance.

In contrast with other European countries, modernism in Sweden was directly related to a new awareness of social conditions as generators of architectural form. Through the Stockholm Exhibition of 1930, created by Gunnar Asplund with Markelius and others, the new architecture was established in Sweden as a popular movement; modernism and the concept of functionalism were directly associated with a new life, which would develop through socially conscious design processes as well as progressive social planning. This approach is well expressed in Markelius's work in the Stockholm Kollektivhus (1935) where well-planned apartment unit housing for working parents includes restaurant, service facilities, and provision for collective child care located within the building on a communal ground floor. Each apartment on the upper floors is organized to provide both privacy and open space with access to sunlight and exterior views. Many of the advantages usually associated with luxury apartment hotel living are thus provided for middle-income working families.

It was this social orientation that led many Swedish architects including Markelius to combine the careers of architect and town planner. During years of service as Director of the Planning Department, Stockholm Building Institute (1938–1944) and Director of the Stockholm Planning Regulation Office (1944–1954), his important contributions to land-use policy include development and implementation of the satellite new town concept, which provides for orderly urban growth by controlling the timing and placement of new development. At Vallingby (begun 1953), the best known of these "town sections," housing areas of varying residential types are organized around transportation lines and planned to include a range of cultural and social community facilities. At Ör (Sundyberg) (ca. 1965), large apartment blocks enclosing open space and communal facilities are surrounded by single-family housing units in higher than usual densities through use of an innovative interlocking pattern built over connecting streets and walkways. Each separate community is surrounded by parkland containing children's playgrounds and other recreational areas. Circulation systems are designed to separate pedestrians and vehicles to the greatest extent possible (3). Markelius is probably best known internationally for his work in the evolution of these particularly Swedish planning concepts. Most significantly, two of these new towns, Vallingby and Farsta, received the Reynolds Memorial Award for Community Architecture in 1967.

Despite his continuing concern for the planning process, in his architecture Markelius remained sensitive to the scale of the individual building and its importance as part of the urban whole. The Swedish Pavilion at the New York World's Fair (1939), through careful integration of all systems and components into the basic simplicity of the building concept, demonstrates that particular elegance of detail associated with Swedish design. In his own villa at Kevinge, Stockholm (1945), Markelius best expresses the synthesis of traditional Swedish and innovative modernist directions that serve to distinguish his personal approach to architecture. Here, response to the specific site and sympathy with the environment are of prime importance to the successful integration of the building into its natural garden setting. In contrast with the traditionally Swedish concern with native materials, however, the house itself is experimental, composed entirely of standardized and prefabricated building elements.

In the course of his long career, Markelius was the recipient of many architectural design competitions and personal awards. Among the most significant of these are the Award of the Federation of Swedish Architects (1961), of which he served as President (1953–1956), the Patrick Abercrombie Prize of the International Union of Architects (1961), and the Gold Medal of the Royal Institute of British Architects (1962). He became an Honorary Corresponding Member of the American Institute of Architects in 1945 and from 1947 to 1952 served as a member of an international group of consultants for the United Nations Building in New York with Le Corbusier, Oscar Niemeyer, and Wallace K. Harrison (4).

Reflecting on the context of architecture in 1964 in the preface to a review of his own work, Markelius described his perspective on contemporary architecture (1):

> There was once a belief that architecture had to carry certain external attributes to be regarded as "modern." We do not need a "modern style." We need an architecture which is faithful to its purpose and which is true to its own time: to its needs, its inherent forces and its possibilities.

BIBLIOGRAPHY

1. S. Markelius, "Architecture in a Social Context,"*Architectural Record* **135,** 153 (1964).
2. N. Ahrbom, "New Swedish Architecture," in T. P. Jacobson and S. Silow, eds., *Ten Lectures on Swedish Architecture,* Svenska Arkitekters Riksforbund, Stockholm, 1949, pp. 6–7.
3. S. Markelius, "Swedish Land Policy," in G. E. Kidder Smith, *Sweden Builds,* 1st ed., Albert Bonnier, New York, 1950, pp. 27–29.
4. A. K. Placzek, ed., *Macmillan Encyclopedia of Architects,* Vol. 3, Macmillan Publishing Co., New York, 1982, pp. 107–108.

Anne Vytlacil, AIA
Washington, D.C.

MARKETING, ARCHITECTURAL.

See Communications in Architecture

MASONRY.

See Brick Masonry; Concrete Masonry

MATTHEW, ROBERT

Robert Matthew, eldest son of John Matthew, himself an architect and partner of Robert Lorimer, was born in 1906 and was educated at Melville College, Edinburgh, Scotland. He spent one year studying geology, then entered Edinburgh College of Art to study architecture. Upon graduating in 1930, he joined the firm of Lorimer and Matthew. Despite the advantages of Robert Lorimer's reputation as a leading arts and crafts architect, the partnership was seriously short of work during the economic depression of the 1930s. Matthew stayed with the firm for six years, during which he spent his energy winning scholarships to keep himself going financially. For one entire year he received no salary; however, his prizes allowed him to travel to Germany, Holland, and Scandinavia. In 1933, he met Patrick Abercrombie who later introduced him to the world of planning and international collaboration. After this meeting, Matthew was awarded a further scholarship with a planning project for Edinburgh, which could have taken him to the United States for two years, but he had recently married and his wife Lorna was expecting her first child. Therefore, when the opportunity of obtaining a government job at the Scottish Office arose, Matthew took it. He stayed at the Scottish Office as a civil servant for the next nine years, and devoted much of the rest of his career to housing and urban issues.

During the war years Matthew had planning and advisory responsibilities for hostels and emergency hospitals. Toward the end of the war, Patrick Abercrombie recruited Matthew to head a technical team to assist Abercrombie in preparing the Clyde Valley Report, published in 1946. The plan put forth policies that have become the basis of Glasgow's redevelopment to this day. By this time Matthew was Chief Architect and Planning Officer at the Scottish Office. At a meeting of the Royal Institute of British Architects post-war planning committee, he learned that the London County Council (LCC) was looking for a chief architect. This was a post with even greater responsibilities than those he had been carrying, and the challenge of helping to replan and rebuild London after the Blitz was one he was glad to take up.

When Robert Matthew arrived at the LCC, its Architect's Department had wide duties but a weak internal structure and a reputation for dull work. Four years after Matthew's arrival all responsibilities for housing, which had been designed in the Valuer's Department, were transferred to the Architect's Department. Matthew's main administrative move was the creation of a group structure that gave responsibility for projects to small teams from start to finish, many of which were comprised of progressive young architects who had arrived directly from architecture schools. The housing program was one of the largest of any city authority in the world. The Housing

Division had over 350 professionals, the Planning Division 250, and there were large schools and maintenance divisions.

During Matthew's time there, the LCC replaced the advisory County of London Plan with a new statutory development plan which included eight comprehensive development areas. Among the best-known of the housing plans were those produced in 1952 for a group of sites in the Putney-Roehampton area, including the Ackroydon Estate and the Portsmouth Road Estate. In both schemes, development was a medium-density mixture of flats, maisonettes and houses, with clubrooms, laundries, workshops, and playgrounds. Most of the flats were in 8- or 11-story point blocks on the Swedish model, and the housing layouts in landscaped parkland became the prototypes for numerous British housing schemes that followed.

One of the first tasks of the rejuvenated department was to prepare for London's contributions to the Festival of Britain in 1951, which were to include a new concert hall on the south bank of the Thames and a demonstration neighborhood at Poplar in the East End. The Royal Festival Hall, as the new concert hall came to be called, was a highly influential building, not so much because it broke new ground stylistically (it drew for its sources on prewar Scandinavian models), but because it demonstrated new management processes. Its design incorporated advanced building technology, particularly in the new science of acoustics, and it was designed by a team that included not only architects but also engineers and scientists. The basic conception of the building's form, in which the auditorium appears suspended between circulation and ancillary spaces, is practical in that it isolates the auditorium from the surrounding air-borne and structure-borne noise of adjacent trains, and is satisfying in that it resolves the flow of space and movement around the mass of the main concert chamber. The layout provides a series of dramatic vistas up and down constantly changing levels and through glass screens. Matthew's hand can be seen in the original exterior. He had an unusual sense of scale and said that he found that a feeling of excitement and lightness was given to a building if there were sharp contrasts between the size of its features. The elevations of the Festival Hall in their original form had huge central windows on each facade with stacks of small windows and contrasting materials in the staircase cores at each corner. Leslie Martin, Deputy Chief Architect at the LCC when the Festival Hall was built, had special responsibilities for leading the design team. The building was later extended and altered by Martin, who succeeded Matthew as chief architect.

Robert Matthew was still young, at age 44, when the Festival Hall opened, and thought it was time for a change. His department had become famous, and was to remain so for many years. However, he doubted his capacity to indefinitely sustain a job such as the one he had held at the LCC, and he had a strong interest in education. He had served on the Royal Institute of British Architects (RIBA) Council and its Board of Education. It was obvious to him that even though the role of the architect was changing, the schools of architecture remained geared to prewar thinking. Like several of his contemporaries, he decided that the real need lay in education. Two events combined: an offer to design a new airport building near Edinburgh that would allow him to begin a practice in Scotland, and the opportunity to become the first Professor of Architecture at Edinburgh University and to head the School of Architecture in the Edinburgh College of Art.

The sketches for a new passenger terminal at the wartime aerodrome at Turnhouse (Fig. 1) were done very quickly by Matthew in William Holford's house in London. As soon as they were approved he opened an office in Edinburgh and assembled a small team led by Tom Spaven, who was later to become the managing partner of Matthew's very large Scottish practice.

The building, clad and lined internally in neatly detailed timber boarding, was instantly popular and was given an architectural award. The play with volumes, especially the penetration of the customs block with the main concourse to provide a balcony outside the restaurant, and the idea of an entrance through a low door leading into a double-story space with low areas opening from it, the

Figure 1. Turnhouse Airport, Edinburgh.

whole sequence linked by routes, were modern ideas that Matthew used again at New Zealand House three years later and in a number of other buildings.

Other projects followed: two small hydroelectric generating stations, a coal-fired power station, a shop, a group of residential buildings and common rooms for students at Aberdeen University, and a teaching building for Queen's College at Dundee. In all of these early buildings there was an emphasis on the use of natural, local materials: random rubble masonry, stained timber weatherboarding, and pantiles, to give a familiar and Scottish character. Matthew was a collage-ist by temperament. Contrasts in color, scale, and texture gave him pleasure, and just as some post-cubist painters introduced scraps of familiar material into their paintings, Matthew brought materials such as natural stone into his designs to intensify a sense of reality and directness, sometimes without regard for structural purity or economy: the Dundee building is a slender tower in which thick, coursed, rubble masonry is hung onto a concrete frame. The buildings spoke in the vernacular of the everyday world, their plans emerged pragmatically from the brief, and spaces were arranged according to function and practical relationships. In the larger building groups, different functions were separated into buildings of contrasting scale; these were then loosely and informally dispersed around the site to take advantage of site features.

A commission in 1954 to design New Zealand House in London (Fig. 2) was not only Matthew's biggest project to date but it led him into partnership with Stirrat Johnson-Marshall. The practice of Robert Matthew Johnson-Marshall and Partners was later to become one of the largest firms of architects and engineers in the UK. Stirrat Johnson-Marshall had been chief architect to the Ministry of Education, and he brought with him several good young architects from public sector offices. The New Zealand House project was a joint effort. Matthew did the first sketch designs in Scotland, and the execution of the scheme lay with the London office. Matthew's proposals for the interpenetration of volumes in the lower floors was carried through in the final designs, which were developed by Maurice Lee, the London partner in charge of the project, who was responsible for the generous scale and good materials throughout.

Figure 2. New Zealand House, London. Photograph by Henk Snoek.

In the meantime, Robert Matthew had taken up his Chair at Edinburgh. After a brief interregnum he had withdrawn from the Headship at the College of Art to an environment where he could think out the future for a new kind of architectural education based on a broad university curriculum and on what he saw as an improved scale of architectural practice. He attracted two old colleagues to Edinburgh, Frank Clark and Percy Johnson-Marshall, and within a few years the team had established a post-graduate course in landscape design, the Department of Urban Design and Regional Planning, the Planning Research Unit, the Architecture Research Unit, a Chair in Architectural Science, and courses in hospital design and public health. The concept was of a faculty for environmental studies, which in time might include departments of architectural structures, services, and building economics.

As the pressures of practice and professional affairs began to consume most of his time, Matthew's contact with his university department became less continuous and personal. By the late 1950s the Edinburgh office was busy with several university projects, schools, housing, and two teaching hospitals. Nearly all senior appointments at both of the firm's locations had some public sector background. It was this depth of experience, linked to Matthew's and Johnson-Marshall's connections in central and local government, together with the wave of public spending from the mid-1950s to the mid-1970s, that fueled the firm's rapid growth. As the effects of the post-war baby boom moved through primary, secondary, and tertiary education, and as the hospital program got under way, the practice flourished on primary and secondary schools and development plans for universities (including four, at York, Bath, Stirling, and Ulster, for which it built virtually all the buildings) and several hospitals. The practice became a training ground for many people who were later to make their names in the architectural profession.

Matthew's sympathy for newly emerging nations and his sense of the injustice of poverty, together with a passionate love of travel and fresh experiences, drew him toward an involvement in international affairs. He became vice-president of the International Union of Architects (IUA) in 1957, and president in 1961, the year of the sixth International Union of Architects Congress in London. He was commissioned in 1962 to work out in detail the plan for the administrative sector of Doxiadis's master plan for Islamabad, the new capital of Pakistan. Here his job was to coordinate the work of a number of internationally-known architects. He was also to design several civic buildings; these were never executed. The firm also had several educational projects in Nigeria at this time. Matthew believed strongly in the value of the IUA as an agency for international understanding, and despite pressure on the European members from Africa, the Far East, and South America, and despite the effects of the Hungarian uprising and the Cuban Missile Crisis on U.S.-Soviet relations, he managed to hold the IUA together as an effective and businesslike organization during his presidency.

In the year after taking on the IUA, Robert Matthew was knighted. In the same year he became president of the Royal Institute of British Architects. Under his predecessor, the RIBA had commissioned a survey of the way British architects worked. This report, entitled "The Architect and His Office," directed by Andrew Derbyshire (later a partner in the firm's London office) (1) was a landmark in the history of the profession in the UK. It also set the tone for much of Matthew's presidency, during which he was active in introducing a range of sweeping reforms in administration, architectural education, and consulting. From 1965 to 1969 Matthew was president of the Commonwealth Association of Architects. In this role also he quickly acquired a reputation for tact combined with firmness, and for getting things done.

In his home country a string of appointments followed. Matthew served on the Royal Fine Art Commission for Scotland for 22 years. He also served on the Historic Buildings Council for Scotland. From 1963 to 1967 he was a member of the British Broadcasting Corporation's General Advisory Council. He was an associate of the Royal Scottish Academy. Matthew's interest in the Saltire Society, a body promoting Scottish culture, had been a long one: a true Scot, he had been chairman of its London branch. He later became its president and helped it to establish its housing awards scheme. He was a founder trustee of the Scottish Civic Trust. At its inauguration in 1967 Matthew set in motion a survey of the New Town of Edinburgh, which had been built in the eighteenth century and was now threatened with decay. The survey led to a conference in 1970, which set out the conservation problems involved, and gave an indication of the likely cost of repairs. The result was that the New Town was saved.

All of this was done while Matthew's office was expanding rapidly. By the end of the 1960s it included structural engineers, services engineers, quantity surveyors, landscape architects, and industrial designers. There were partners in most of these disciplines, and staff members numbered almost 300. Like his department at the LCC, the office was organized on a group system. Each partner had responsibility for particular projects, and some partners were responsible for aspects of administration. In this way Matthew was able to delegate work widely. Individual initiative was encouraged, but quixotic and self-indulgent decisions were not tolerated if they stood in the way of the firm's social responsibilities. Matthew was a master at chairing meetings. Always serious and courteous, he asked blunt, shrewd questions that showed a keenly analytical mind at work and the ability to separate the main issues in any argument from subsidiary matters. He trusted his colleagues' intentions and their commitment; in return he received passionate loyalty.

During this period Matthew retained personal responsibility for the planning work of the Edinburgh office (overlapping with the London office's work on the Central Lancashire New Town) and a number of building projects. The Matthew Plan for the Belfast Region of 1963 had led to an appointment in 1968 to draw up a program of development for Northern Ireland for 1970–1975, and, in turn, to an appointment for the planning of the New University of Ulster and certain buildings there, and for a local Area Plan. These Ulster projects were Matthew's personal responsibility. Other projects were almost entirely delegated to his partners. By the end of the decade the Edinburgh office of Robert Matthew Johnson-Marshall and Partners had completed a large number of award-winning buildings designed by Matthew's partners, including several housing schemes by Kenneth Graham, Ninewells Hospital at Dundee by Alan Wightman (succeeded by Tom Spaven), the Royal Commonwealth Pool in Edinburgh by John Richards, a power station at Cockenzie by Chris Carter, and Stirling University by John Richards.

In 1970 Robert Matthew received the RIBA's Gold Medal. In the same year he became conservation advisor to the Secretary of State for Scotland. He had retired from the Chair of Architecture in 1968, although he was made chairman of Edinburgh University School of the Built Environment; this allowed him to continue the process he had begun. Later, he was appointed Professor Emeritus. In 1972 he was commissioned by the government, together with W. D. Skillington, to report on the promotion of good design in government buildings.

By this time Matthew was past normal retirement age, but continued working. The firm had become involved in a large housing project in Libya, in which he took an active part, and in 1974 it was appointed to design a new opera house in Edinburgh, for which Matthew was the coordinating partner. In 1975 he was again very active in the IUA. Although by this time very ill, he went first to Venice and then to Madrid, where he spoke, but did most of his work behind the scenes and was glad to see that the commonwealth was playing a powerful part in the IUA's affairs. One of his tasks was to draw up the text of a general statement from the IUA to the United Nations Conference on Human Settlements to be held in Vancouver, encouraging governments across the world to adopt a Charter of Human Rights in relation to housing. He was working on the text of a film to support this statement up to the day he died in 1975.

BIBLIOGRAPHY

1. A. Derbyshire, *The Architect and His Office,* Royal Institute of British Architects, London, 1962.

General References

R. Matthew, "The Future of Town Planning," *The Architects' Journal* (June 4, 1959).

K. Wharton, "Talking to Sir Robert Matthew," *The Architect and Building News* (Feb. 5, 1970).

D. Sharp, "The Architecture of Robert Matthew," *Country Life* (June 25, 1970).

R. Matthew, "Robert Matthew: Royal Gold Medallist 1970," *RIBA Journal* (Aug. 1970).

JOHN D. RICHARDS
Robert Matthew Johnson-Marshall and Partners
Edinburgh, United Kingdom

MAYBECK, BERNARD

Bernard Maybeck was born in Greenwich Village, New York City, on February 7, 1862. He was the son of a professional woodcarver, a German immigrant who furnished his son with art lessons and apprenticed him to a cabinetmaker. "Ben" also worked in his father's furniture workshops and attended the City College of New York in 1879. In 1881, he went to Paris to work in a furniture firm and also developed a design for a reversible Pullman car seat, which he later refined and patented. He entered the Ecole des Beaux Arts atelier of Jules-Louis André in 1882. André carried on the traditions of Henri Labrouste's "free classic" atelier and was a teacher of Henry Hobson Richardson; Maybeck was also influenced at the Ecole by the teachings of Viollet-le-Duc (1,2).

Maybeck returned to the United States in 1886 and joined the New York City firm of Carrere and Hastings. There he worked on the designs and oversaw construction of the Ponce de Leon and Alcazar hotels in St. Augustine, Fla. In an endeavor to start an independent practice, he went to Kansas City, Mo. in 1888, where he married Annie White, whose brother, Mark, later served as Maybeck's partner and engineer. By 1890 he had patented a design for a lady's folding fan and moved to San Francisco, where he worked in the architectural office of A. Page Brown with Willis Polk, and A. C. Schweinfurth. He supervised the California Building at the Chicago World's Fair in 1893.

In 1894, Maybeck was appointed instructor of drawing in the Civil Engineering College of the University of California at Berkeley, and also became director of the Architectural section of the San Francisco Art Association in 1895. In 1896, he began to organize the successful international competition for the Master Plan of the University of California campus. From 1898 to 1903 his title at Berkeley was Instructor in Architecture. This was the first time the University of California recognized architecture as a professional field and was the beginning of its architecture curriculum.

Maybeck's major architectural works at the university include: Hearst Hall for Women (1899), the first use of the laminated wood arch, destroyed by fire in 1922; the Men's Faculty Club (1900); and the Hearst Memorial Gymnasium (1927). The gymnasium was designed in collaboration with Julia Morgan, who had been one of Maybeck's students.

From 1910 to 1912, Maybeck was occupied with the design of his most important work, the First Church of Christ, Scientist, in Berkeley, California, to which he added a Sunday school and office wing in 1927–1929 in collaboration with Henry Gutterson. He designed the Palace of Fine Arts for the Panama-Pacific Exposition in San Francisco (c. 1913). During this period he explored the nature of materials, experimenting with new concrete techniques to produce low-cost single-family housing, and also designed several significant expensive redwood residences in the area. These included the 1916 Bingham House in Santa Barbara. From this grew the San Francisco Bay Region residential design tradition.

In 1917, Maybeck said: "An architectural plan is not primarily made for the glorification of the architect. Neither is it a matter of elaborating buildings senselessly as a tribute to the vanity of human nature. If this were all, modern democracy would not hesitate to eliminate such an art by the simple expedient of neglect." And, in 1923, he added: "There is an undiscovered beauty, a divine excellence, just beyond us. Let us stand on tiptoe, forgetting the nearer things and grasp what we may" (1).

From 1923 to 1938, Maybeck was largely occupied with the Master Plan and the design of many buildings of the new campus of The Principia in Elsah, Ill., his last major work. Among the notable buildings at this college for Christian Scientists are its residence halls and the chapel; the latter was designed in 1931 in collaboration with others.

Maybeck's beliefs are best embodied in First Church of Christ, Scientist, Berkeley, which wisely enjoins the ingredients of economical craftsmanship and technology. There he combined cast concrete, heavy timber, industrial steel sash, and stenciled and hand-painted decoration in lovely symbolic coordination with a classical individualistic romanticism that, seen from the perspective of the 1980s, appears somewhat timelessly "post-modernistic" (3).

Maybeck's achievements earned him an honorary doctorate from the University of California at Berkeley in 1930 and the Gold Medal of the American Institute of Architects in 1951. These were among other tributes he received before his death in 1957.

BIBLIOGRAPHY

1. K. Cardwell, *Bernard Maybeck, Artisan, Architect, Artist,* Peregrine Smith, Inc., Salt Lake City, Utah, 1977.
2. K. Cardwell, in A. K. Placzek, ed., *MacMillan Encyclopedia of Architects,* The Free Press, New York, 1982, Vol. 3, pp. 127–129.
3. E. McCoy, *Five California Architects,* Reinhold Publishing Company, New York, 1960, p. 31.

General References

K. Cardwell, in R. G. Wilson, *The AIA Gold Medal,* McGraw-Hill Book Co., New York, 1984.

P. W. Goetz, ed., *The New Encyclopedia Britannica,* Encyclopedia Britannica, Inc., Chicago, Ill., 1980, Vol. VI, p. 721.

C. Hosmer, Jr., "Principia's Chapel," in H. S. Hamlin, ed., *The Principia Alumni Purpose,* The Principia, St. Louis, Mo., Spring 1986, pp. 10–15.

E. S. Leonard, Jr., *As the Sowing,* The Lakeside Press, R. R. Donnelley & Sons Company, Chicago, Ill., 1948; condensed and reprinted in 1951, 1958.

R. Longstreth, *On the Edge of the World: Four Architects in San Francisco at the Turn of the Century,* The Architecture History Foundation and the M.I.T. Press, Cambridge, Mass., 1985.

J. Maybeck, *Maybeck the Family View,* Berkeley Architectural Heritage Association, Berkeley, Calif., 1980.

J. M. Richards, ed., *Who's Who in Architecture,* Weidenfeld and Nicholson, Ltd., London, UK, 1977.

S. Woodbridge, ed., *Bay Area Houses,* Peregrine Smith Books, Salt Lake City, Utah, 1988.

RALPH WARBURTON, FAIA
University of Miami
Coral Gables, Florida

MECHANICAL SYSTEMS

HISTORY

Building design has been influenced by a concern for thermal comfort from the earliest efforts to construct shelter. Vitruvius in his *Ten Books on Architecture* refers to appropriate orientation to the sun and prevailing winds. Indigenous architecture, from the igloos of the Eskimos to the heavy masonry of the arid, sunny Middle East, with their narrow openings in deep reveals, illustrates the use of passive techniques to moderate climatic influences on internal thermal conditions.

Efforts to devise and include building systems to accomplish comfort control far better than that achieved by the passive building envelope alone dates back to ancient times. Vitruvius describes the well-known practice of the Romans of directing flue gases through passages under the floor to heat baths.

In 1660 Sir Christopher Wren attempted to ventilate the Houses of Parliament by placing large, square openings at the corners of rooms with funnels containing dampers which led to rooms above. But he did not provide for a fresh air supply, ventilation was not good, and there were complaints about downdrafts.

Schemes to have better space heating included improved fireplace design. A notable example was Ben Franklin's invention of 1744 that provided a passage for heating room air which circulated heat by convection to the room to augment the highly directional radiant heat from a fire. This invention was soon replaced by the freestanding cast-iron stove. Air movement in early ventilation schemes was accomplished by warming the air to activate convection currents or by large fans. In 1811, Sir Humphrey Davy introduced an arrangement of floor and ceiling openings in the House of Lords around which heat could be added to increase airflow. Deterioration of air and flue passages permitted flue gases to enter the hall so that in 1834, when a large quantity of waste paper was burned, woodwork was ignited, and both Houses of Parliament were burned. For the new houses, Dr. David B. Reid introduced an improved design in which outside air was heated by steam coils, and movement of exhaust air was induced by fire (1) (Fig. 1).

In 1855–1861 new House and Senate wings were added to the U.S. Capitol. Captain Montgomery C. Meigs, superintendent of construction, proceeded to devise chambers for debate which were lighted, ventilated, and heated by mechanical means. "It seems to me," he said, "that members, occupied in the business of legislation, did not need, and would not have time to enjoy, any external prospect" (3). But the reaction of legislators was not altogether warm. Meigs' heating and ventilating system consisted of low-pressure steam coils to heat air which was moved by huge, steam-driven fans as large as 4.9 m (16 ft) in diameter.

It is interesting to note nineteenth-century arguments for introducing outside ventilating air. The main advantages cited were replacement of oxygen depleted by breathing and expulsion of bacteria that caused infectious diseases. A ventilation rate of 2 l/second per person (4 cfm per person) was recommended.

In the early 1800s, central hot air, steam, and water systems began to make their appearance. Jacob Perkins of Philadelphia, who emigrated to England, devised high pressure steam and water systems. His high temperature hot water system was installed in the White House about 1840. In the latter half of the century, numerous configurations of tube and cast-iron radiators were made and used with low pressure steam and two-pipe gravity hot water

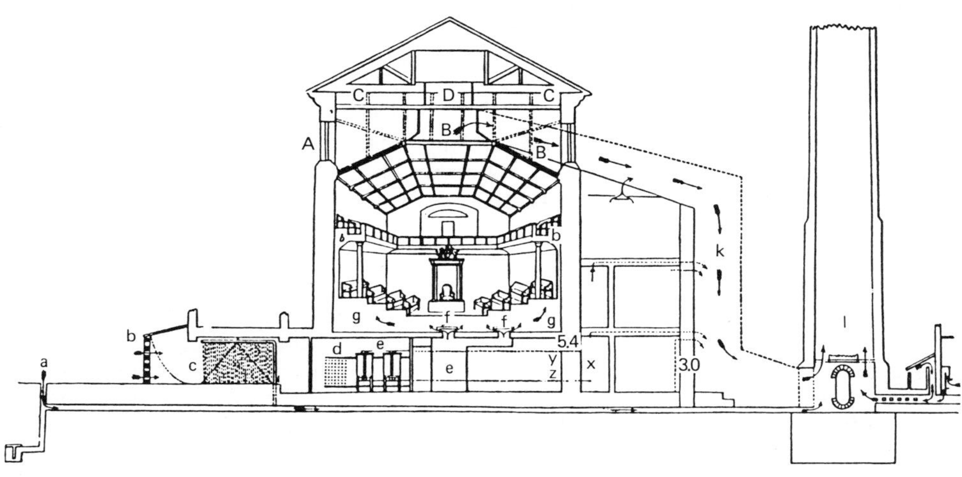

Figure 1. Heating and ventilating system. House of Commons, 1836. Outside air entered at B and was filtered by screen C. Coil D heated air as it passed to floor plenums b, f, and g. Air entered the room through small holes in the floor. A fire at chimney 1 moved exhaust air out of vent B (2).

systems. Standard heating medium temperatures for rating radiation were 102°C (215°F) for steam and 77°C (170°F) for water systems when room air was 21°C (70°F).

Cooling by mechanical means had rudimentary beginnings in 1833 when Dr. John Gorie, a physician, had air blown over ice to cool rooms for malaria and yellow fever patients. Dr. Reid suggested in 1848 that the Houses of Parliament could be cooled if artesian well water was circulated through steam pipes in summer.

Significant progress in summer cooling required development of mechanical refrigeration. In 1851, Dr. Gorie, then working in Apalachicola, Fla., received a patent for an ice-making machine. Patents for systems using ammonia, sulfuric ether, or carbon dioxide as refrigerants were numerous for more than three decades. The refrigeration systems were designed primarily for the production of ice used until about 1930 for home iceboxes for storage of perishable foods. As early as 1871, Andrew Muhl of Waco, Texas, invented a system in which air was passed over refrigerated coils, but passing air over ice remained the usual practice for room cooling. However, the cooling of buildings for human comfort did not become a common practice until well into the twentieth century.

Real progress in room air conditioning, the control of temperature and humidity of an enclosed environment, was motivated initially by the need for rather precise conditions for industrial processes, including printing, film manufacture, and weaving mills. Willis H. Carrier, who is referred to as the father of air conditioning (4), tackled the problem of precise humidity control in 1902 when Sackett-Wilhems Lithographing and Publishing Co., of Brooklyn, N.Y., decided that the problems associated with printing in color on paper needed to be solved. Expansion and contraction of a hydroscopic material such as paper caused poor indexing of separate color runs. A brine solution was tested briefly as a dehumidification agent, but was quickly abandoned because the salty air rusted machinery. Cold water was passed through heating coils in order to establish the psychometric data required for close humidity control. Carrier was then able to set the airflow rates and coil temperatures required to achieve both the sensible heating and water evaporation in winter and cooling and dehumidification in summer, meeting the present criteria of 26.7°C (80°F) and 21.1°C (70°F) for indoor temperatures for summer and winter, respectively, and a year-round humidity of 55%. An artesian well and ammonia refrigeration machine were used to obtain 54 tons of cooling.

Carrier's significant contribution was the concept of controlling the dew point of an airstream as a means of obtaining a specified moisture content. The early scheme for accomplishing this was refrigerated water sprays through which the airstream was passed.

Carrier did his early work as an employee of the Buffalo Forge Co. In 1907, The Carrier Air Conditioning Co. was set up as a subsidiary, with Carrier as a vice-president. In 1915, The Carrier Engineering Corp. became an independent company. It progressed from an engineering firm designing systems for industry using equipment manufactured by others to a manufacturing firm in 1922. This change came about in order to market a significant Carrier invention, the first centrifugal compressor using a refrigerant requiring lower pressures and having less toxicity than ammonia or carbon dioxide.

Improved refrigeration machines provided the impetus to raise air conditioning from the industrial level to comfort conditioning. Carrier's first installation was for the J. L. Hudson Co. department store in Detroit, but the prime market was movie houses, for which a simple ventilating system was not adequate in coping with the body heat of audiences.

By the 1930s, mechanical home refrigeration replaced the icebox for keeping food, but it was not until the 1960s that the cooling of all enclosed environments, including residences and cars, became a relatively uniform practice. Cheap energy made year-round thermal and atmospheric control of buildings economical.

However, the oil embargo of 1972 sent energy costs soaring; as a consequence, higher values of building insulation have become mandatory, inordinately high lighting levels have been questioned, and new attention has been given to the use of passive systems in place of, or integrated with, mechanical systems to reduce operating costs. Equipment has been redesigned with improved efficiencies. Additional features include heat recovery and conservation practices described below. Energy codes have been promulgated and adopted which mandate these and other practices. Most are patterned on the initial ASHRAE Standard 90–75 adopted in 1975.

Engineering practices have been improved through research sponsored since 1919 by the American Society of Heating and Ventilating Engineers. The society was founded in 1895. In 1954, it became the American Society of Heating and Air-conditioning Engineers and merged in 1959 with the American Society of Refrigerating Engineers to become the American Society of Heating, Refrigerating, and Air-conditioning Engineers (ASHRAE).

COMFORT AND OTHER SYSTEM OBJECTIVES

The object of building climate control is usually human thermal and atmospheric comfort. Therefore, one must determine the proper environmental parameters that establish comfort for a given activity in a building.

From the physiological standpoint, the body produces heat at a rate which is a function of physical activity, clothing, state of health, age, and sex. A climate control system and building envelope must establish room conditions which permit the body to lose heat at the same rate it is produced. Body heat is exchanged with the environment by convection, radiation, and evaporation. Therefore, a complete statement of comfort parameters must include air temperature and rate of its movement, mean surface temperature of an enclosure, and the relative humidity or wet-bulb temperature. As surrounding surface temperatures are increased, as, for example, by adding double glazing in winter, loss of body heat by radiation is reduced. As a consequence, the air temperature can be reduced to permit more body heat loss by convection to re-establish the equality between body heat production and its dissipation. Thus, thermal design parameters vary in different situations to provide the necessary quantitative relationship for thermal comfort. In addition, the parameters must meet psychological considerations.

The thermodynamic description of the ambient environment is given by the psychometric chart which plots the dry-bulb temperature of the air against its moisture content. From the point on the chart established by these two parameters one can also read the relative humidity, and the dew point (Fig. 2).

Figure 2 represents a portion of the psychometric chart. It contains two shaded areas which research has determined to represent the range of operating temperatures and humidity in which 80% or more persons engaging in sedentary activity and typically clothed say they are comfortable during winter or summer. The operating temperature is approximately the average of the room air temperature and the mean radiant temperature of all surrounding surfaces (3). Thus, large, cold glass areas causing a low mean radiant temperature require a corresponding elevation in the air temperature to obtain an equal degree of comfort. The parameters within the shaded areas are valid for air movement not over 0.15 m/s (30 ft per min) in winter or 0.25 m/s (50 ft per min) in summer within the occupied zone, ie, to 180 cm (6 ft) above the floor.

From the practical standpoint, it is easier to maintain a higher air temperature than to raise humidity in winter and to cool air in summer than lower the humidity any more than necessary to acquire comfort. In addition, energy codes recently promulgated dictate those inside conditions that are deemed to require minimum energy consumption to maintain. ANSI/ASHRAE/IES Standard 90A–1981, Energy Conservation in New Building Design, lists 22°C (72°F) air temperature and 30% relative humidity for winter and 25.5°C (78°F) air temperature and a relative humidity within the shaded envelope in Fig. 2 in summer. Practically speaking, summer humidities are maintained at 50% to 60%, except in arid regions. Thus, humidities are set near the lower and upper limits of acceptability for winter and summer.

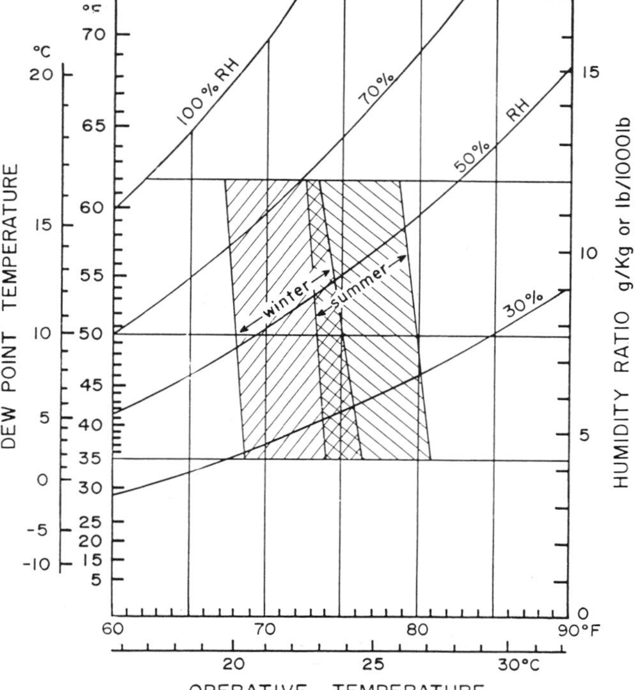

Figure 2. Acceptable ranges of operative temperature and humidity for persons in typical summer clothing and winter clothing, at light, mainly sedentary activity (3). Courtesy of the American Society of Heating, Refrigerating and Air-Conditioning Engineers, Inc.

Upward adjustments of temperatures must be made for conditions where light or no clothing may be worn or where persons are ill. Conversely, air temperatures would be set lower than Fig. 2 or codes indicate where occupants are physically active and/or heavily clothed.

The quality of indoor air is also a factor that must be controlled if a satisfactory enclosed thermal and atmospheric environment is to be realized. Air contaminants include gases, particulate matter, microorganisms, and odors. The traditional method of maintaining air quality is through dilution by the introduction of outside ventilating air and the use of filters, air washers, desiccants, or other cleaning equipment.

ASHRAE Standard 62–1981, Ventilation for Acceptable Indoor Air Quality, describes acceptable concentrations of air contaminants (5). It lists outdoor air requirements for various types of occupancies. Currently, 2.5 l/s (5 cfm) per person is considered the minimum rate for diluting CO_2 and the body odor produced by rather sedentary, nonsmoking occupants. If occupants are smoking, the recommended ventilation rate is 3–5 times higher. Sparsely occupied buildings may receive adequate ventilation through natural infiltration and exfiltration through door and window cracks and other openings that cannot be sealed tightly. The denser occupancies encountered in public and commercial buildings, especially places of assembly, require introduction of outside air. A system with an exhaust flow rate about equal to the inflow of ventilating air is called for. In spaces where odor control is a primary concern, such as bathrooms, 100% exhaust of air is customary.

THE BUILDING ENVELOPE AND CLIMATE CONTROL

The building envelope is an inescapable element in a system of thermal and atmospheric control. If the building fabric could be devised to lose heat to its exterior environment at the same rate that it takes on heat from occupants, other heat-producing items in the structure, and external sources, then no mechanical assistance would be needed to maintain constant internal design conditions.

Since complete passive control is not typically a viable option, one must consider how much thermal insulation, solar shading of glass, etc., should be included in building design in order to lower equipment size, cost, and operating expense. ASHRAE Standard 90A–1981 (6) and other energy codes patterned after it that have been adopted by local governmental bodies mandate minimal thermal properties for building construction. Code provisions are not so restrictive as to inhibit design options. For example, glass areas can be increased if they and opaque walls are made correspondingly more insulative to keep heat losses within reason and shading and/or orientation is used to avoid excessive solar gain through glazing.

The same features that lessen building heating and cooling loads also assist in creating comfortable conditions. Added insulation to walls and glazing raise inside surface temperatures in winter, thereby reducing excessive body heat loss by radiation to establish a sensation of comfort. No amount of warmer circulating air offsets the chill caused by a large loss of body heat to nearby, very cold glass. Therefore, addition of insulation to raise the inside surface temperature and in turn reduce body heat loss by radiation is a better option. Similarly, hot glass and lightweight exterior wall and roof construction can have high internal surface temperatures which cause high rates of radiation to occupants. Shaded and reflective glazing and ventilated passages behind outer surfaces of light opaque construction conveying solar heat back to the outdoors are far more effective than increased insulation in reducing cooling loads; the resulting lower interior surface temperatures promote comfort conditions.

Heavyweight walls and roofs can be effective in lowering cooling loads. They can store a considerable quantity of solar energy during the daylight hours before any significant rate of heat flow will occur to the interior. The cooler nighttime conditions promote heat flow from storage to the outside rather than to the building interior. Older buildings with their massive, load-bearing walls are often comfortable in hot weather, even without thermal insulation. The mass alone prevents high peaks of heat gain to the outer surface from reaching the interior. Thermal insulation must be included in construction in temperate and arctic zones to lessen winter heat loads, and a very heavy construction adds excessively to structural loads that must be supported. Therefore, reducing cooling loads through opaque construction is a matter of using both insulation and mass to lower the values of peak loads.

SOURCES OF HEATING AND COOLING

Energy

All mechanical building systems require energy inputs to function. For climate control systems the energy may come from a combination of fossil fuels, electricity, and solar energy.

Traditionally, heat energy has been supplied through the combustion of hydrocarbon fuels, coal, oil, and gas. The utilization of these fossil fuels requires a combustion chamber into which an appropriate fuel–air mixture is introduced. When the mixture is ignited, oxidation of the carbon ensues with an accompanying release of heat. The heat of combustion is produced as long as the fuel–air mixture is supplied (7,8).

Coal as an unrefined mined substance ranges from anthracite, which is hard, high in carbon content, and clean burning, to bituminous and lignite coals, which contain water and constituents such as sulfur, mineral matter, and inert gases, in addition to carbon. The water must be vaporized, and heat for this purpose goes up the chimney as vapor passes out of the flue with flue gases. Oxidation of sulfur adds to pollution. Therefore, use of low grade coal entails the addition of flue gas treatment to lower levels of carbon, nitrogen, sulfur oxides, and particulates that are discharged into the atmosphere.

The usable heat content of coals ranges from about 33,000 kJ/kg (14,000 Btu/lb) for anthracites and low volatile bituminous grades to 16,000 kJ/kg (6,900 Btu/lb) for lignites.

When coal is selected as a fuel for heating a building, storage must be provided at a rate of 1.13 m^3/ton (40 ft^3/ton), and the problem of ash disposal must be solved. These two requirements and the necessity of maintaining an idling fire during periods of no demand on a heating system militate against the choice of coal for heating buildings. Use of high sulfur content coals has generally become unacceptable because of the high cost of pollution control equipment mandated by law.

Coals are supplied automatically to boilers and furnaces by stokers which feed in coal appropriately graded as to size for the equipment along with air for combustion at the rate required to produce the output of the boiler or furnace. The coal–air mixture is introduced either from below a fire in upfed stokers, which are common for smaller applications, or overfed above a fire in larger installations where industrial power from boilers may be needed on a continuing basis in addition to building heat. Handling of coal from a bin and removal of ash is manual rather than automatic for most smaller stokers in buildings.

Fuel oils are liquid fuels obtained from varying degrees of refinement of crude oil. The lighter, more refined oils, termed distillate fuel oils, are those most commonly used for building heating. No. 1 is easily vaporized by applying a little heat. Therefore, it is used in small, vaporizing pot type burners where a continuous flame generates the oil–air mixture by vaporizing the fuel in the presence of the natural air draft through the heater and the flue. The flame is also the pilot, providing continuous ignition. No. 1 oil is used only for very small heating loads, and it is not suitable for intermittent operation requiring automatic ignition. Instead, the less expensive No. 2 oil is generally selected for building heating. It is atomized by mechanical means in a burner using nozzles or rotating cups in the fan-induced draft. An electric arc ignites the oil–air mixture. The heating value of No. 1 and 2 oils ranges from 37,040 kJ/l (132,900 Btu/gal) to 39,520 kJ/l (141,800 Btu/gal).

Heavier oils, called residual fuel oils, are grades No. 4, 5, and 6 (the higher the grade, the less viscous the oil). Heat must be applied to No. 5 and 6 oils to enable them to flow and be pumped and atomized. Consequently, they are applicable to larger industrial power applications requiring continuous operation which also may supply building heating and cooling needs.

On-site storage tanks must be provided for oil-fired systems. Most building codes allow up to two tanks, neither exceeding 1040-l (275-gal) capacity, to be installed in basements or mechanical rooms. Larger indoor tanks require an enclosing structure with a fire resistance of 2 or 3 hours. Underground installations are generally used for larger tanks. Tank connections include a fill line, measuring line, vent, and suction and return lines to the burner. The fill and measuring line can be the same if it is straight down to accept a measuring rod. Tanks above a burner do not need a return line from the burner.

Current gases in use as energy sources for buildings are natural gas obtained from wells or liquefied petroleum. Natural gases have a heat content around 37,300 kJ/m^3 (1000–1050 Btu/ft^3). Petroleum gases contain primarily butane or propane. Under moderate pressure they can be liquefied for transport and storage. They vaporize (boil) upon release of pressure so that at burner jets a gas–air mixture is fed to the continuing flame. Propanes have a heating value about 50,150 kJ/kg (21,560 Btu/lb) or 93,150 kJ/m^3 (2,500 Btu/ft^3) of gas. The heating value of butanes is about 30% higher than that of propane.

Gas burners are typically integral parts of the boilers and furnaces with which they are associated.

Burners for larger commercial applications may be designed to burn either oil or gas, thereby allowing changes from one fuel to the other for reasons of economics and availability.

Electric energy input may be used solely to operate motors, control devices, or other auxiliary items in climate systems. For resistance heating and most refrigeration systems it is the only energy input.

Lately, conservation of depletable energy sources has stimulated interest in harnessing solar energy. The result has been the development of systems which make use of solar energy as an alternate or augmentation of another energy input (eg, the solar-assisted heat pump). Since the maximum radiation of a collector surface normal to the sun's rays is only about 945 W/hr m^2 (300 Btu/hr ft^2), it is obvious that solar energy cannot be obtained at a rate sufficient to supply the large maximum inputs needed by the typical building climate control system, which can easily range up to 100,000 kJ/hr (94,780 Btu/hr) for even a modest-sized building. Another energy supply must be available for use as both a backup when solar energy is reduced by weather conditions and to make up the difference between the maximum solar input and the maximum building requirement.

Boilers and Furnaces

Utilization of heat from the combustion process is accomplished by passing flue gases through passages in a furnace around which air can circulate and be heated, or through passages in a boiler, around which water can move and be elevated in temperature and, if desired, be converted to steam (9).

A typical furnace consists of an insulated casing through which air passes in order the filters, a centrifugal fan, around the combustion chamber, flue passages, and out to the supply system. Components may be arranged so that airflow is down from above, through the unit, and up to supply ducts; up from below, vertically through the unit, and up to supply ducts above; down from above, vertically down through the unit to supply ducts below; or in one end, horizontally through the unit, and out the other end. The arrangements are called low-boy, upflow, counterflow or downflow, and horizontal furnaces, respectively. They are packaged units containing a combustion chamber and burner for the fuel to be used or electrical coils for a unit using electric energy. Gross outputs generally range from 17.2 kW (60,000 Btu/hr) to 86 kW (300,000 Btu/hr), although larger sizes are made for commercial use. Furnaces are also designed to be a part of rooftop air-conditioning units and unit heaters where gas or electricity is the source of heat energy.

Furnaces require a control which senses the temperature of the heated air at the supply bonnet, which will cut off the energy supply when the temperature reaches an unsafe level. The common temperature limit is 93°C (200°F). Some furnaces are made for zero clearance installation, which permits them to be installed on and against combustible material. However, flue pipes to the chimney should be at least 150 mm (6 in.) from any combustible material.

Furnace ratings are given in terms of the heat output at the bonnet. Correct selection of a unit must include a summation of the estimated building heat loss, losses from the duct system, heat for humidification if a humidifier is included in the installation, and an allowance for pickup heat required to bring a building up to temperature after a setback to a lower temperature. Ratings on the fuel efficiency of units are now federally mandated. The annual fuel utilization efficiency (AFUE) takes into account drops in efficiency that occur in milder weather and which result from the operation of continuous gas pilots. The AFUE varies from 60% to 90% for various types of gas and oil furnaces.

Boilers are made of assembled cast-iron vertical sections or of welded steel. Smaller steel boilers are factory-assembled units that have tubes through which flue gases pass to heat water and are termed fire tube boilers. Large boilers may be the water tube type, in which flue gases flow around the tubes. Boilers are available with gross outputs ranging from about 21.5 kW (75,000 Btu/hr) to about 14,000 kW (50,000 MBtu/hr). Most are low-pressure boilers rated for 103 kPa (15 psi) steam or 1103 kPa (160 psi) hot water. Higher pressure boilers are available for systems requiring their use (Fig. 3).

A safe low-pressure boiler installation includes limit controls to cut off the energy supply when a steam boiler attains a pressure of 103 kPa (15 psi) or a water boiler temperature of 121°C (250°F). In case of limit control failure, every boiler must have a pressure relief valve which will discharge steam or hot water at a rate sufficient to limit boiler steam pressure to 103 kPa (15 psi) or water boiler pressure to 206 kPa (30 psi). Steam boilers also have low water cutoffs to shut down the energy supply when the water level falls below a safe point. Low water cutoffs are sometimes installed in water boiler supply header piping so that a loss of water from the system will cut off the energy supply before the water level drops to a point within the boiler.

Ratings for boilers are given as gross or net. Gross ratings are outputs at the boiler header, and net loads are gross loads, less allowances for system pipe heat losses and pickup allowances to permit the system to raise its rate of output. Standard codes set the differences between

(a)

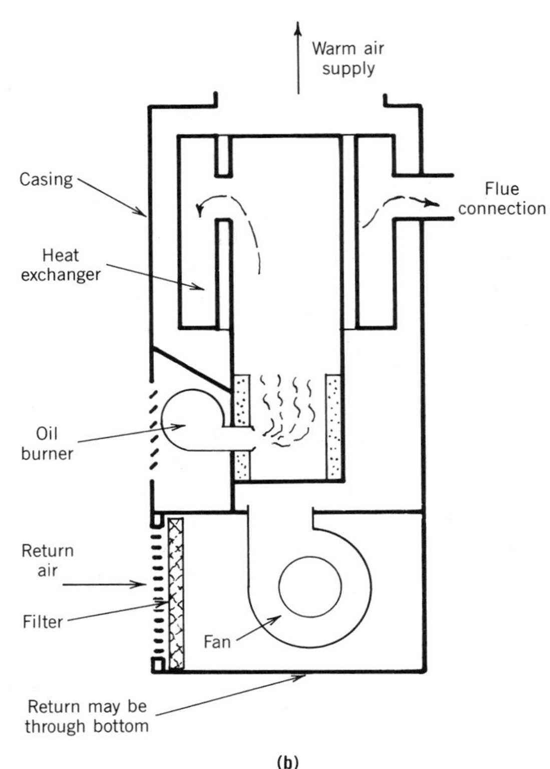

(b)

Figure 3. **(a)** Cast-iron boiler. Courtesy of the Hydronics Division of the Burnham Corporation, Lancaster, Pa.; **(b)** Furnace.

gross and net outputs. Unusual installations which have a large length of piping in unheated areas or are subject to large temperature setbacks during intermittent operation will require that the designer estimate the pipe losses and pickup loads which must be added to the net load, ie, the building heat loss, to determine the gross output required.

Boiler rooms must be large enough to accommodate the boilers, all piping around and over them, access to them, all appurtenances for maintenance, and clearance for cleaning internal flue passages or removing tubes.

Flues of adequate size and height are needed to establish draft requirements. Where chimney height cannot be provided, forced draft equipment can be installed, which uses a fan to establish the necessary air flow.

Refrigeration

A refrigeration system is one in which heat is taken into the system at one point and discharged from it at another point (10). If cooling is desired, heat can be extracted from water, air, or other source substance and moved through the system to the point of rejection where it flows to a substance called a heat sink. Alternatively, the process can be reversed where heat is withdrawn from a source, moved through the system, and delivered to water or air used to heat a building. When the system is arranged to both heat and cool, it is called a heat pump.

The common unit of capacity for refrigeration in the United States is the ton. It is the heat necessary to melt one ton of ice in one day. Since the latent heat required to melt ice is 144 Btu/lb, a ton of cooling is 2,000(144)/24 = 12,000 Btu/hr.

The most common refrigeration system is the mechanical type in which a compressor applies a pressure to a refrigerant. The boiling point is raised, and when it passes through a condenser, which is a heat transfer surface permitting heat transfer to air or water, the refrigerant rejects latent heat to the air or water as it changes from a high-pressure gas to a high-pressure liquid. The refrigerant then passes at a controlled rate through an expansion valve, which lets it flow into an evaporator coil at a lower pressure so that it turns into a vapor. In order to vaporize, it must draw its latent heat of vaporization from its surroundings. Hence, it cools the water or other substance around the coil. Then, the compressor draws the low pressure gas for reapplication of pressure to repeat the cycle. Figure 4 illustrates the mechanical refrigeration process.

Typical refrigeration equipment packages include a reciprocating, rotary, centrifugal, or screw compressor, coupled with an air or water-cooled condenser serving an evaporator coil located in an air-handling unit. Since the coil cools air directly, it is known as the direct expansion (DX) coil. For smaller loads to about 50 tons, the compressor–condenser package is usually placed outdoors so that the condenser can be air-cooled. Water-cooled units are available, but generally water is not the economical cooling agent. A complete refrigeration system to chill water for circulation to cooling coils in various air-handling units is generally a unitary package containing evaporator, com-

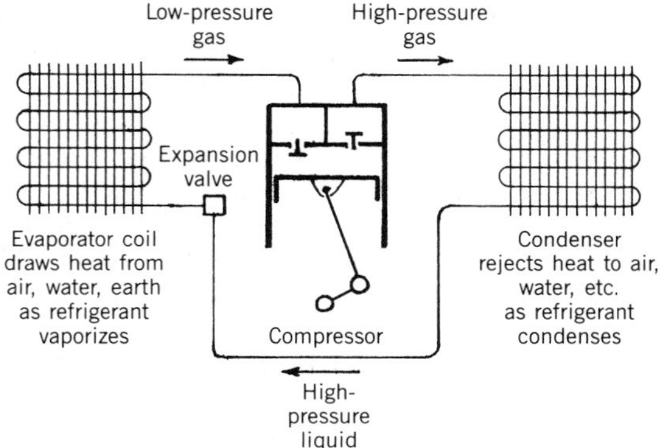

Figure 4. The mechanical refrigeration process.

pressor, and condenser which, again, is air-cooled for smaller applications and water-cooled for larger installations.

Since water-cooled condensers will require a source of cooling water at the rate of about 12 l/min/ton (3 gal/min/ton), economic considerations do not permit discharge of spent water to a sewer. Instead, it must be conserved by passing it through a cooling tower where it is brought into intimate contact with outdoor air. Evaporation of some water cools the remaining water for reuse in the condenser. The utilization of the latent heat rather than the sensible heat property of water for cooling greatly reduces the rate of water consumption needed for cooling.

Heat pumps are commonly arranged for air-to-air operation. That is, outside air is the heat source in winter. The heat is drawn into the system by an outside evaporator coil. Inside air is heated as it passes over the condenser. In summer, the direction of refrigerant flow is reversed so that the coils switch functions. Thus, the inside coil becomes the evaporator, cooling room air, and the outside coil becomes the condenser, rejecting heat to outside air.

A recent development is the water source heat pump. Many of these units are served by water loops from which heat can be extracted or to which it can be rejected, depending on whether room heating or cooling is required. These systems are described under unitary equipment systems.

Solar energy or ground water are sometimes used as supplemental heat sources for heat pumps.

Absorption refrigeration systems are utilized in lieu of mechanical systems when heat is available to reconcentrate the absorbent solution as shown in Figure 5. Large lithium bromide–water machines are available in sizes from 176 to 5280 kW (50–1500 tons) and find use in cogeneration plants. Smaller-tonnage gas-fired units have been produced for residential and small commercial use, and solar energy has been tried as an alternative source to drive them. Smaller units may use ammonia rather than lithium bromide as the refrigerant.

Refrigeration equipment is rated for its energy efficiency as well as its cooling capacity. The energy efficiency ratio (EER) is defined as the capacity in watts (Btu/h) divided by the energy input in watts. As equipment capacity increases, the EER tends to increase. Oversized equipment for smaller installations will result in long off cycles and poor humidity control as well as inefficient energy usage.

Evaporative Cooling

Refrigeration equipment is needed when air is to be cooled below its dew point in order to lower humidity (11). In dry climates, where the humidity is below 25%, evaporative cooling of air can be considered. Air is passed through a wetted mat. Some heat is extracted from the air to evaporate some water. Thus, sensible heat in the air has been reduced with an accompanying lowering of air temperature. The sensible heat has become latent heat in the

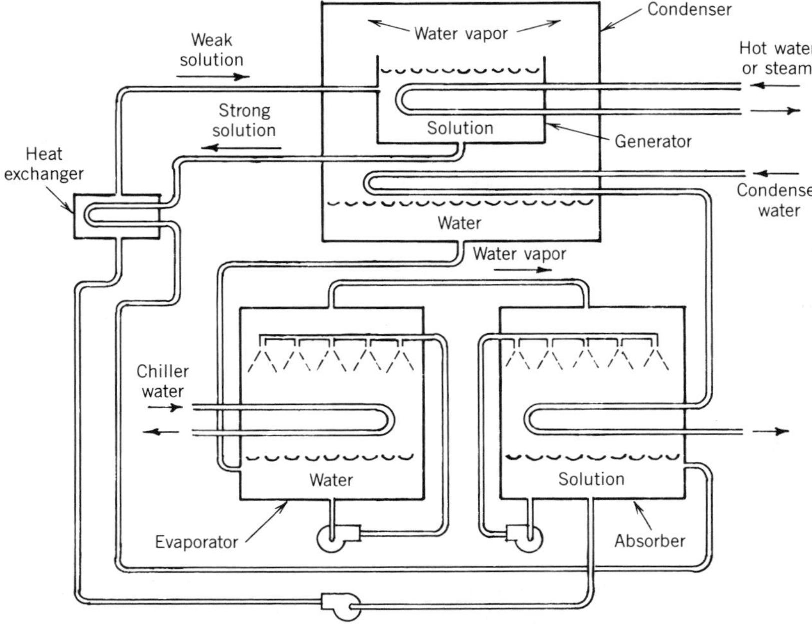

Figure 5. The lithium bromide absorption refrigeration system. Water vapor passes through the absorber where a salt solution spray makes it give up heat when it condenses to water. The solution becomes more dilute, and the heat of condensation is rejected to a water-cooled condenser coil. The weak solution is reconcentrated in the generator, where heat is applied to drive off water vapor which is condensed by a condenser coil to carry off the heat. The water passes to the evaporator where it is sprayed over a coil to chill water within it as evaporation of spray water occurs. The attraction of the water spray to the absorber salt spray adds to the cooling effect. The warm strong solution from the generator preheats the weak solution in the heat exchanger on its way to the generator.

water vapor in the air. Of course, the increased vapor content in the air causes an increase in its relative humidity, which can be 50–60% without causing discomfort.

Cogeneration Systems

For larger buildings or groups of buildings under single management, it may be economical to employ a system which will supply all required forms of energy (12). In this so-called cogeneration system, fuel as a primary energy source produces shaft energy, which sequentially produces the needed mechanical, heat, and electrical energy. Prime movers are reciprocating engines using oil or gas, or gas turbines. They drive generators to produce electric power. Exhaust heat from prime movers is recovered to produce steam and/or hot water for process and building heating and for driving absorption water chillers. It is this recovery of heat from prime movers for other purposes that results in greater efficiency in energy usage to meet all needs that makes a cogeneration system more economical than separate plants for heating, cooling, and electrical power, each with its own energy source.

ROOM DISTRIBUTION OF THERMAL AND ATMOSPHERIC CONDITIONING

Radiative Equipment

Hot water or steam from a central source can be circulated to radiation equipment located low on exposed walls of rooms (13). The heating medium transfers its heat through the surface of the radiation, where it is distributed to the room by direct radiation to room surfaces, furnishings, and occupants. Room air also circulates by convection over radiators to raise room air temperature to design conditions at, for example, 1.5 m (5 ft) above the floor. Air temperature will vary from a low value at the floor to a high value at the top of the occupied zone, but comfort conditions require that the range be kept to no more than 2°C (3.6°F).

The common type of radiator is the tubular cast-iron unit. Convectors have cast-iron or nonferrous heating elements set low in a cabinet to promote heat circulation by convection. Baseboard cast-iron or finned tube units are linear versions of radiators and convectors. The exposed cast-iron or sheet steel cabinets and enclosures of radiation can be painted with all except metallic paints without significant loss of heat output over that of the unpainted surfaces. Baseboard radiation is for hot water heating only.

Room surfaces can become radiators when tubes for hot water, electric resistance wire, or warm air plenums are behind floors or ceilings. Panel radiant heating in concrete floor slabs must be operated at surface temperatures not over 30°C (86°F) to avoid discomfort. Consequently, heat output is limited and will not be adequate to cope with loads in poorly insulated buildings. Concrete slabs possess considerable inertia against prompt change to a higher or lower rate of output. This makes them unsuitable for use in such spaces as auditoriums, where an entering audience may actually change the system demand quite quickly from a heating to a cooling mode. Lighter weight metal or plastered ceiling panels are more responsive to load changes.

When spot heating is required and raising the air temperature is not practical, infrared heaters using gas, oil, or electricity provide a solution. They radiate under marquees, on loading docks, etc, keeping people warm without heating the air.

When space heat losses are large and/or ventilation is to be introduced, gravity radiation using natural convection is inadequate. For this application a fan is used to pass air over a steam, water, electric coil, or fuel-fired combustion chamber. The device is called a unit heater. If it also has an outside air inlet and damper to proportion the quantities of outside and inside air entering the cabinet, the equipment is called a unit ventilator. It has the capacity to do some cooling when outside temperature is below design room temperature and the room is experiencing internal heat gains in excess of losses in room heat to the exterior (Fig. 6).

Air Diffusion

Ventilating and air-conditioning systems and heating systems utilizing air as the heat-carrying medium must have supply outlets and return and exhaust inlets properly sized and arranged to introduce air in such a way that a relatively uniform temperature exists in the occupied zone or to about 2 m (6 ft) above the floor. Air motion in the zone must be at or somewhat below limits noted under comfort criteria. Since supply air must be introduced at

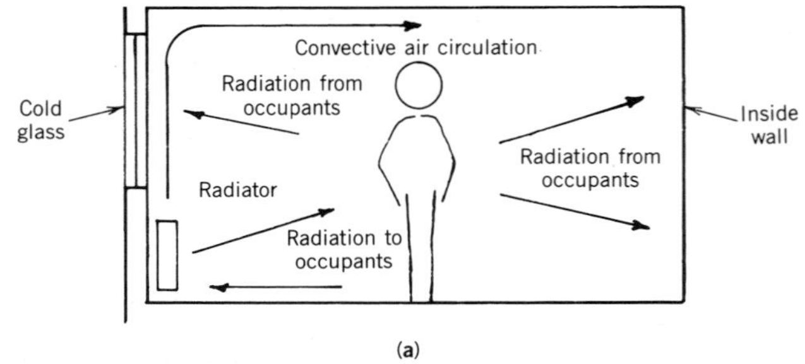

(a)

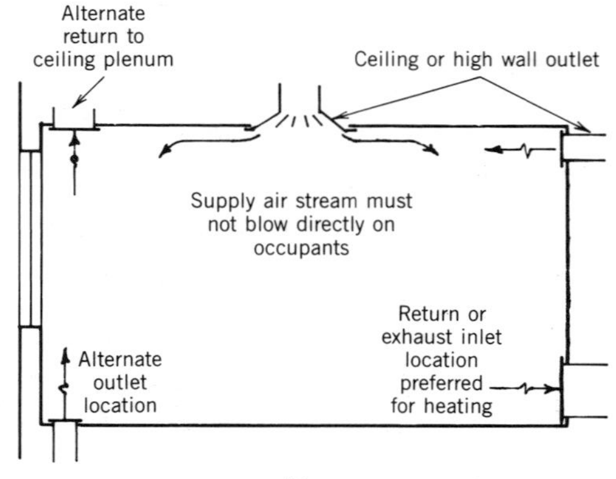

(b)

Figure 6. (a) Room heating by radiation; **(b)** Arrangement of air inlets and outlets for room heating and cooling.

temperatures some 11–19°C (20–35°F) above or below room temperature in order to heat or cool a space, outlets must be able to discharge air above the occupied zone or up or down wall surfaces where it can become entrained in room air. During a process of diffusion, its temperature and velocity assume the appropriate values by the time the airstream reaches the occupied zone (14).

Ceiling diffusers, which are round, square, rectangular, or slots, typically have vanes to direct air out parallel to the ceiling which, because of a plate effect, helps extend the horizontal throw of the airstream. Wall registers or diffusers have horizontal and/or vertical vanes to adjust the spread and throw of the airstream to suit the space.

Air supply can be through a perforated ceiling or acoustical tiles with slots from an overhead supply plenum. Slot diffusers at the edges of troffer lighting are common.

Air return and exhaust is generally through grilles with fixed vanes. For cooling only or for exhaust purposes they can be high on the wall or in the ceiling. When the system also heats the building, return inlets should be set low to collect the cooler air at the floor.

MEDIA FOR HEATING AND AIR-CONDITIONING TRANSPORT

A fluid or combination of fluids must be selected for transporting heating or cooling from a source of supply to spaces. Consideration of several factors leads to logical choices for given applications.

Steam

When water is boiled under low pressure, it takes on latent heat at an approximate rate of 2300 kJ/kg (1000 Btu/lb). It also increases in volume about 1600 times. Therefore, while a small quantity of water can as vapor carry to and give up a sizable amount of heat when it condenses at radiation, it is bulky. Steam piping must be large enough to carry steam and the condensate produced by pipe losses to ambient conditions. Pipe slope must permit condensate return by gravity to a boiler or to a condensate return pump which delivers it to the boiler. Each time steam is generated, air in the system must be driven out to permit steam circulation. Air in systems under elevated temperatures in which moisture is present promotes equipment corrosion. System pressure changes are too small to vary the latent heat of steam significantly; thus, modulation of heat output is more a function of varying the time of the intermittent firing cycle. Since steam is not a cooling medium or one that can be used for humidity transfer, it cannot be used for year-round heating–cooling systems. There are several reasons why steam is not as common for building systems as it once was. However, it can be appropriate for delivering heat in tall buildings without problems of static head change present in water systems or of the space requirements of ducts in air systems.

Water

Water as a heat transporting medium can be circulated to heat transfer surfaces where it can go through a temperature drop to deliver heat or a temperature rise to absorb heat from air or water that flows over the surface. Water transfers heat by using its sensible heat properties in which a flow rate of 1 kg/hr (1 lb/hr) gives up or absorbs 1 cal/hr (1 Btu/hr) for each °C (°F) it drops or rises. It is, therefore, both a heating and cooling medium, and its rate of transferring heat can be modulated to meet the varying system load by controlling its delivery temperature and the temperature drop or rise at the heat transfer surface. Furthermore, if chilled water cools a coil over which air flows below the dew point of the air–water vapor mixture, condensation occurs and lowers the humidity. Water is a compact medium, so the pipes occupy little space. In tall buildings, the large change in static pressure with height requires large internal pressures at the bottom of a system to maintain positive pressures throughout the system which are necessary to obtain air removal from the system and to avoid cavitation in suction lines to pumps. Water systems are closed vessels which need provision for the volumetric change of the fluid with temperature change without causing widely varying pressure changes. Expansion tanks with a cushion of air in them solve the problem. Since systems are closed, air removal occurs only at the initial filling of the system, and pipes are full of water, which is continually recirculated. This reuse of water in a system purged of air greatly reduces the corrosion problems experienced when steam is the heating medium.

Air

Air can transfer heating or cooling to spaces by being introduced above or below design room temperature in the amount necessary to give up or absorb heat at rates required to maintain the design conditions. Thus, air and water use the sensible property of a medium to transfer heat. Air transfers 1 kJ/kg (0.24 Btu/lb) for each °C (°F) temperature change. And 1 kg (lb) of air occupies 0.84 m^3 (13.3 ft^3) at 22°C (70°F). Air is therefore a bulky medium requiring large ducts to transfer heating or cooling at the same rate as a much smaller water pipe. When air is the medium, one can introduce humidity control, ventilation, and filtration, or other conditioning of air at a central point. These capabilities make it popular, if not essential, as the choice for a building system, or its ultimate subsystem, serving rooms where the required parameters for air temperature, humidity, cleanliness, and distribution are to be controlled. An air system does provide air circulation among rooms that can spread contagious organisms, but disinfection of air can be accomplished if this is a critical matter, as in hospitals. If a system is to remain off during freezing temperatures, the use of air avoids the risk of damage that might occur if steam or water were selected as the system medium.

TYPES OF HEATING AND AIR-CONDITIONING SYSTEMS

Zoning

The configuration of a logical air-conditioning system for a given application is influenced profoundly by decisions regarding the degree to which separate rooms or groups of spaces require separate air temperature control. The decisions are determined by considering the patterns of variability of heating and cooling loads in various spaces as influenced by geographic orientation and varying times of occupancy. Physical problems in equipment size and layout also have an impact on zoning decisions.

The typical floor of a multistory office building will experience a lessened heat loss in winter and a maximum cooling load in summer when solar gains on glass are significant. As the sun moves to the west, this load condition moves in turn from the east to the south and west exposures. While the loads on the different exterior exposures are continually changing, the building core experiences a cooling load year-round from lights and people. In winter the perimeter requires heating when the core requires cooling. Maintenance of a constant interior design air temperature throughout all office space under such load variations obviously requires a system layout that permits separate thermostatic control of each of the separate patterns of building heating and cooling loads. For example, separate thermostatic control of offices on each compass exposure and for the core would be a minimum satisfactory degree of zoning.

Time of occupancy frequently sets zoning decisions. An auditorium heat load varies considerably and generally in an irregular pattern, according to the number of people in it and the scheduling of events. During a rehearsal or periods of no occupancy, heating loads would be high and cooling loads small relative to those experienced during full occupancy. Meanwhile, other parts of the building may have offices and service spaces that are occupied during a typical eight-hour workday. Here, separate patterns of heating and cooling load variation demand individual temperature control to maintain interior design temperatures.

The maintenance of different interior temperatures does not necessarily require separate thermostatic control. As long as the temperature differences between spaces are constant with time, a thermostat in, for example an office set at 22°C (72°F), can control a zone having some storage spaces where a lower temperature is desired. The zone can be balanced to distribute the heating medium to the spaces, maintaining the fixed differential between room temperatures.

Finally, large system layouts can require equipment components of such inordinate size that they are either unavailable and/or take up too much valuable building volume to accommodate them. Zoning solves the problem. Air systems are often divided into separate layouts on each floor of buildings to avoid the large vertical duct shafts required if they were combined in a single layout to serve several floors. A sports arena, although it is a large, single space, will be divided into zones because a single unit large enough to handle the air is not available and/or ducts near it would be extremely large and would have to extend over very long distances.

All-Air Systems

When air is the heat-carrying medium, the central equipment to supply conditioned air will vary considerably, depending on the degree of conditioning required, physical accommodation of the equipment in the building, and whether or not the prime energy input occurs at the equipment or is supplied remotely through steam, water, or refrigerant systems (15).

The coal, oil, gas-fired, or electric furnace with its filters, blower, and evaporator coil in its bonnet is a simple arrangement of central equipment for smaller air-heating and -cooling systems not requiring close humidity control. An outdoor compressor-condenser unit completes the supply equipment. All of these components are often contained in a single package for rooftop installation. This package may include an outside inlet for ventilating air, dampering to permit separate zones from a common conditioning unit, and arrangements to utilize condenser heat for reheating as an energy-saving scheme when possible in lieu of using fuel or electricity.

Air-handling units in public and commercial buildings usually contain the following items in order of the direction of airflow. A mixing box with linkage-connected dampers at two openings proportions the amounts of room return and outside air entering the unit. Filters consisting of 20–40-cm (1–2-in.) -thick mats to intercept particulate matter are mounted in a frame covering the cross-section where air enters. Various filter media are available. Some are intended to be thrown away and others are washed when loaded. Electrostatic filters are used when high efficiency is needed and/or fine particulate matter must be retained. Heating and cooling coils are finned tube transfer surfaces through which steam, hot or chilled water, or a vaporizing refrigerant flows to heat or cool air. If a centrifugal fan discharges air from the unit, it is termed a draw-through unit. When multiple zones are to be supplied, the fan precedes the heating and cooling coils which are arranged one above the other to form hot and cold decks which terminate in dampers capable of proportioning air from each deck as needed to maintain separate zone indoor temperature conditions. Some units have a third bypass deck. The unit with two decks but without discharge dampers is needed for air systems with separate hot and cold supply ducts from which air is extracted and mixed at remote points for temperature control, as described later (Fig. 7).

Strictly speaking, air conditioning cannot be said to have been supplied by the above units. In winter, they heat and clean the air but do not add a controlled amount of moisture to obtain a specific humidity. In summer, the cooling coil establishes the supply air temperature necessary to extract sensible heat in order to maintain room temperatures, and moisture varies according to the relation of coil temperature to the varying dew point of the incoming airstream. Precise humidity control is not attempted. Fortunately, for most comfort conditions the lack of sophisticated humidity control does not result in unacceptable thermal room environments.

If the central equipment must control both the temperature and moisture content of the airstream rather precisely, certain added components are required. Figure 8 illustrates an arrangement in which outside and return air are mixed and filtered as described above. In winter it passes through a preheat coil, which adds a quantity of sensible heat determined by the amount of heat required

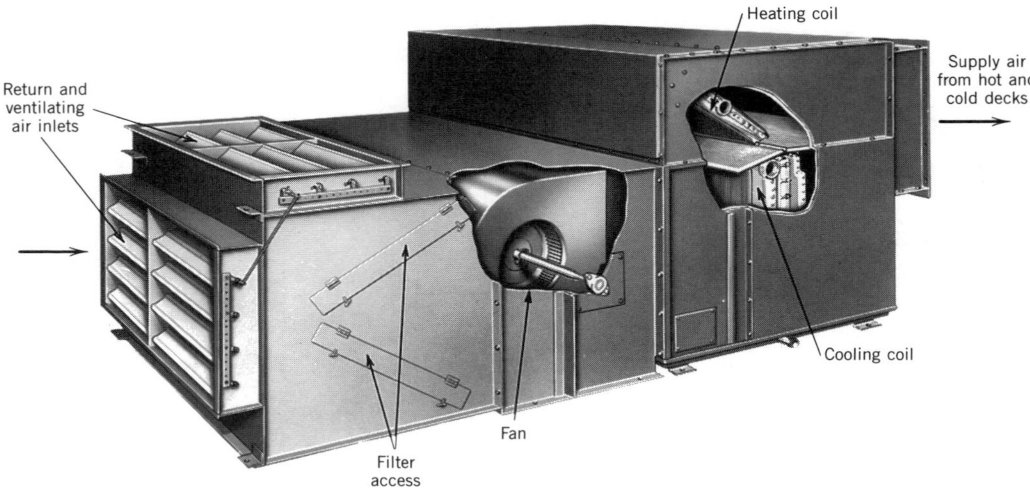

Figure 7. Air-handling unit for multizone and dual-duct systems. Courtesy of the Trane Company, La Crosse, Wis.

to vaporize the proper quantity of water to add the humidity. The heated airstream passes through an air washer. Here the intimate contact between air and water causes the air to be cooled down to its dew point. That is, sensible heat has been extracted from the air and has become latent heat to vaporize enough water to saturate the air–water vapor mixture. Air from the washer contains the concentration of moisture ultimately desired in occupied spaces, but it is too cold, and is at 100% relative humidity. Reheating the air is needed to raise its temperature to that required for heating rooms, and the relative humidity is simultaneously lowered to the proper value. Variations on the above scheme include heating the spray water or spraying heated coils. Where close humidity control is not needed, pan humidifiers are sometimes used, which have heating coils in pans of water to create the vapor.

The air washer can be used for close control of summer dehumidification if it is supplied with refrigerated water. The spray cools the incoming airstream below its dew point, as necessary to reach design moisture content. Since the dew point temperature is often lower than that needed for sensible cooling, the air temperature must be raised

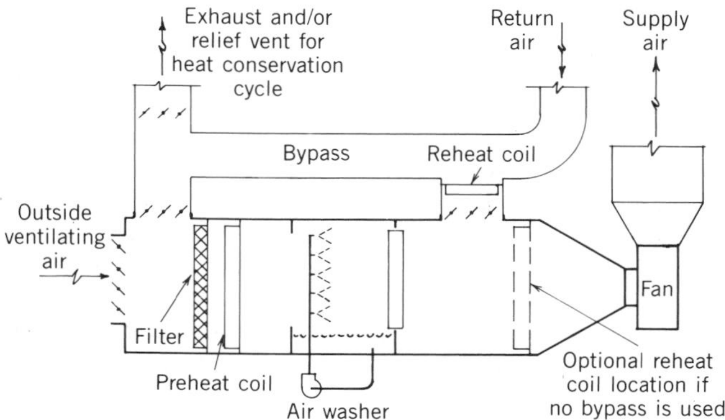

Figure 8. Central air-conditioning unit for year-round temperature and humidity control.

by reheating. Refrigerant or chilled water cooling coils of sufficient depth can also be used to cool the air stream and extract a controlled amount of moisture from it.

In the schemes for humidity control, excess cooling to use the dew point property for regulating moisture content dictates the use of reheating. When energy was inexpensive, reheat using fossil fuels was widespread. Today, in addition to the bypass of air around the washer or cooling coil to reduce reheat, it is economically advisable to devise ways of capturing such sources for reheating as refrigeration condenser heat and exhaust air heat which were once rejected and wasted.

When all rooms served by a central unit are to be controlled by a single thermostat, the scheme is called a single-duct, single-zone, all-air system. This is typically applicable to smaller layouts where load variation between rooms is small enough that zoning is not necessary. A main supply duct supplies branches to outlets strategically placed to provide a constant volume of air in a pattern to obtain good air distribution. Return of air to the unit occurs through larger, more central grilles. Return duct layouts are kept to a minimum by placing grilles close to the central unit and by using ceiling voids as return plenums. These systems are typically low-pressure, low-velocity systems in which the initial main duct velocity will be 5–8 m/s (1000–1575 ft/min) (Fig. 9).

Zoning can be added to the above system through the introduction of reheat. The main duct is divided to create separate duct distribution to each zone. A reheat coil is introduced at the point of origin of each zone. Instead of the reheat coil in the central unit as shown in Figure 8, this single-duct, constant volume system has the capability of bringing air up to temperature independently for each zone through separate control of each zone reheat coil. Since reheating with fuels is not energy-efficient, current energy codes place restrictions on the use of reheat. Thus, either some energy-conserving scheme such as the use of refrigeration condenser heat is included in a reheat scheme, or some other system of zoning is adopted.

Separate temperature control of various groups of

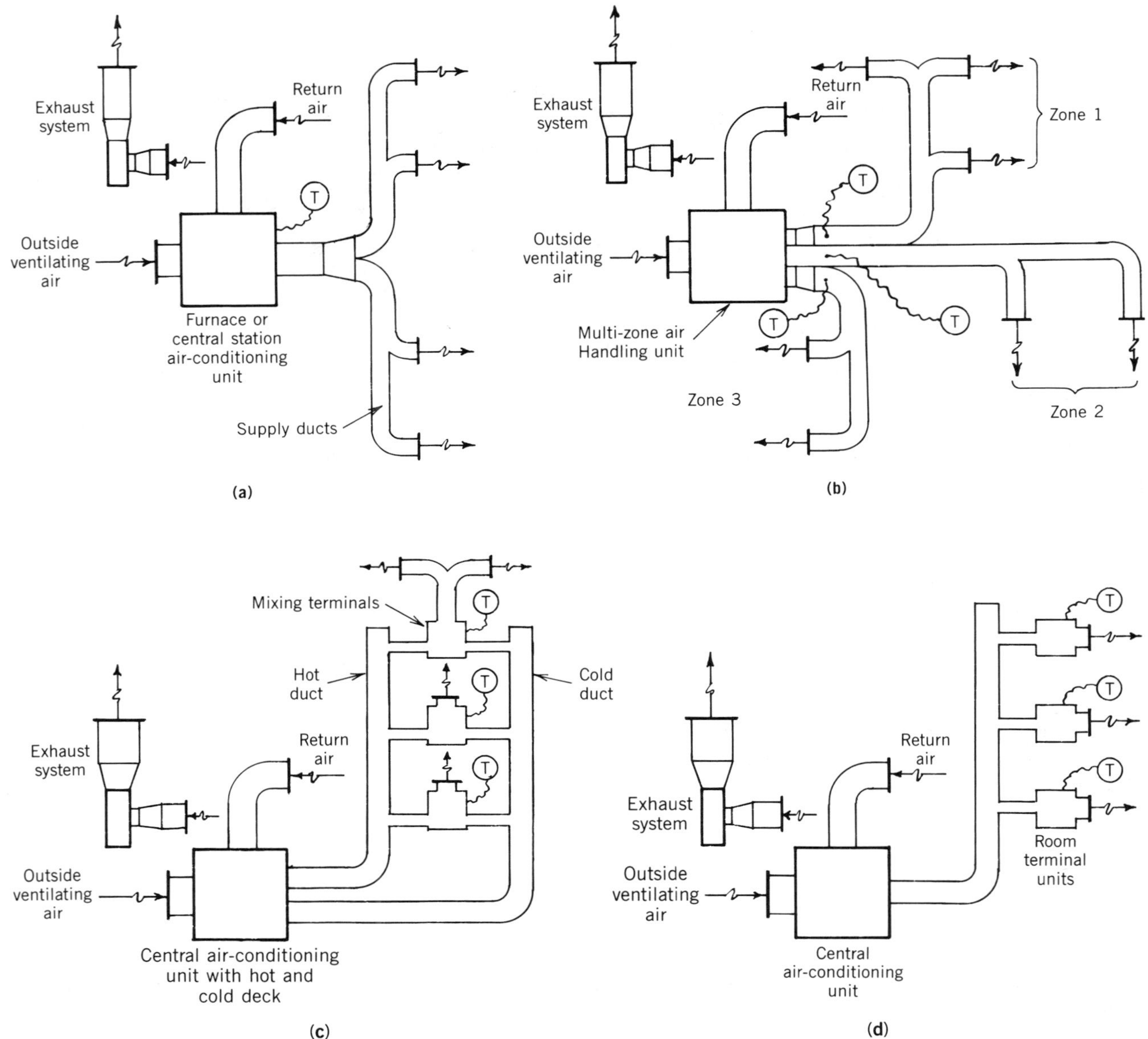

Figure 9. (a) Single-duct, single-zone, all-air system; **(b)** Multizone all-air system; **(c)** Dual-duct constant volume system; **(d)** Variable volume air system.

spaces using a constant volume system can be accomplished by using a multizone central unit with a hot and cold deck. For each zone, dampers change the proportion of air flowing through each deck as needed to maintain the temperature of each zone. In winter only the heating coil will be in use, and the cold deck is a bypass through which a mixture of outside and return air passes in an amount necessary to bring the air from the heating coil down to the desired temperature. In summer, the outside-return air mixture through the hot deck reheats air from the cooling coil. Most available multizone central air-handling units do not have components for adding humidity or for close control of dehumidification; thus, they are heating and cooling units which also supply ventilation rather than true air-conditioning equipment. They can handle up to about 12 zones per unit. Each zone has its own single-duct, constant volume system. All zones share a common return and exhaust system.

If separate room temperature control is desired, it becomes more convenient to mix hot and cold supply airstreams at each room to deliver air at constant volume and the appropriate temperature. By eliminating the zone dampers at a multizone unit and extending supply ducts from the hot and cold decks so that they are available at all rooms, one can install a mixing box at each room which has a connection to each duct. Two dampers, one at the hot inlet and the other at the cold inlet, which are linkage connected, can be moved by thermostatic control to vary the ratio of hot to cold air to maintain the room temperature. The scheme is called a dual-duct, constant volume system. It is particularly applicable to larger layouts where a great deal of individual temperature control is desired. Any room can be heated or cooled independently of other room requirements at any time.

The above systems deliver constant rates of airflow to room outlets. Therefore, air distribution patterns are constant. Room air temperature can be varied by controlling the rate of flow of air from a supply duct at a common temperature rather than by mixing hot and cold air streams. But too much reduction in airflow can result in inadequate air distribution for maintenance of reasonably uniform room conditions. Variable volume can be used within flow limits that ensure adequate air distribution. In recent years variable volume air systems have become quite popular; they provide an economic alternative to a dual-duct, constant volume system for a large layout with individual temperature control of all rooms or areas of modest size.

The variable volume system is typically a single supply duct system with branches containing volume control units which throttle the rates of airflow to an outlet or group of outlets as the heating or cooling load drops. Since a single duct cannot serve heating and cooling simultaneously, its layout must recognize the need for zoning external building perimeters that can require heating from interior areas that at the same time need cooling to cope with internal heat gains. Interconnection between these zones permits the transfer of internal heat to the perimeter for heating, an energy conservation advantage. In colder climates the variable volume system in this application can supply cooling air only, and radiation can be installed for heating the perimeter. The air system provides only summer cooling and year-round ventilation for the perimeter.

Throttling of supply air changes the load on fans. Maintenance of a constant system pressure as air volume changes demands a method of control of fan output. Shutters can be installed on fan inlets to add resistance to airflow as throttling increases. But the energy consumption to drive the fan remains constant. A preferable means of control is the use of a variable speed drive which reduces fan output by slowing it down. At the same time, the load on the motor is reduced, resulting in significant savings in electrical energy.

A constant volume can be maintained on the fan and duct system if return plenum dumping is used. In this scheme, the supply airflow to a control terminal is constant. As the volume to the room is reduced for smaller heating or cooling loads, the terminal dumps more and more excess air into the ceiling plenum. Since it is not energy-efficient to waste treated air, overcool or overheat the plenums, or move larger air quantities than necessary, this arrangement is limited to small systems where the simplicity might be considered more of an advantage than the energy-efficient variable flow in the main supply duct.

The variation in supply airflow requires careful selection of outlet devices so that adequate room air distribution occurs throughout the range from maximum to minimum flow conditions. Air-entrainment-type devices are preferred. A popular type is the slot diffuser at the side of light troffers or incorporated in the bars of a ceiling suspension system.

Variable airflow at outlets causes variable background noise levels in occupied spaces. Room-to-room privacy depends on a minimum background noise level, usually supplied by selection of proper outlet devices for air-conditioning systems. Since variable volume systems at minimum rates of flow may fail to provide the necessary level of background noise, their selection can entail the need for an electronic masking system to provide the noise.

A variation on the variable volume system is the variable volume induction system. It supplies primary air at a terminal unit in a ceiling plenum or within the room. The unit is dampered to permit varying amounts of room or plenum return air to be mixed with the primary air by induction. It is possible with this scheme to have either constant or variable room supply air flow.

Variable volume control terminals will sometimes require a reheat coil when internal heat gains may at times be expected to drop to a low level during periods of building occupancy, when cooling of air in excess of the sensible load requirement is needed to meet dehumidification criteria, or when minimum flow rate from the terminal creates overcooling during a period of very low space cooling load.

The dual-duct and variable volume features can be combined into a dual-duct, variable volume system. Hot and cold ducts from separate fans and coils supply room mixing terminals as in the constant volume scheme. A volume damper is also included in the terminal to vary the rate of flow of mixed air to the room. It combines some of the advantages of its parent systems. Some rooms can be heated while others are cooled. The ability to reduce airflow means less energy consumption than a dual-duct system, but more than for the variable volume system.

The problem of limiting the size of supply ducts for dual-duct and variable volume systems is usually solved by increasing duct velocities to two to four times that in the smaller, low velocity systems. Consequently, system pressures are higher which cause corresponding increases in system noise and energy use. The cost of the building volume to contain ducts must be compared with the initial and operating costs of higher and lower velocity options so that the economical choice can be made.

Air ducts can be routes through which fire and smoke can travel. Where ducts pass through construction with fire resistance ratings, fire dampers are required to preserve the integrity of the rating of the construction. Control systems are arranged to put a zone at a fire under negative pressure relative to surrounding areas to prevent smoke migration away from the fire.

Air-and-Water Systems

Space required to accommodate hot and chilled water in pipes is much less than that needed for ductwork. In order to save space yet retain the ability to introduce ventilating air and centrally controlled humidity and air cleanliness, systems using both air and water have been devised (16).

An air–water induction system (Fig. 10) conditions ventilating air at a central point and distributes it through a high velocity system to rooms where induction units are installed. The conditioned air is discharged through nozzles in a cabinet so that room air is drawn into the unit, and the mixture is distributed to the room. A water

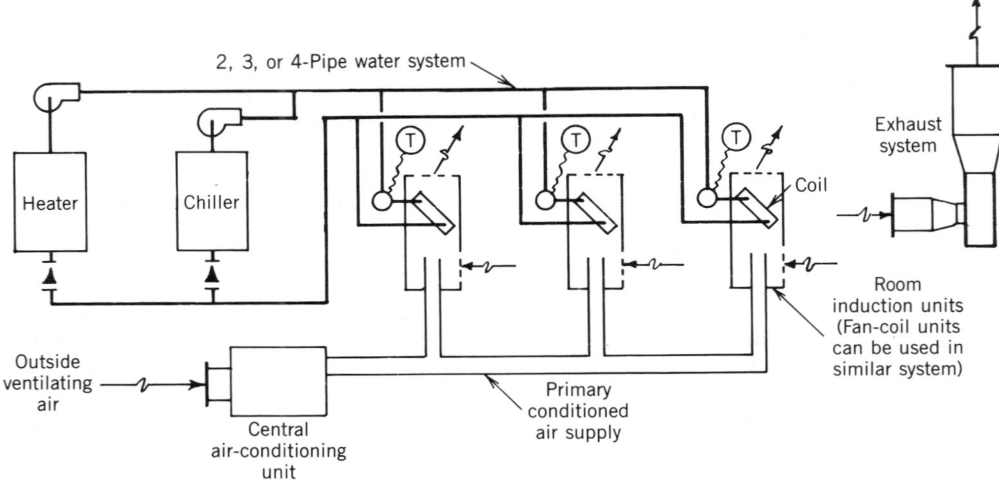

Figure 10. Air–water induction system.

coil in the unit supplied by a two-, three-, or four-pipe system, as described below for all-water systems, modifies the temperature of the air entering the room as required to maintain the room air temperature. The induction units are generally installed under windows where they intercept perimeter heating and cooling loads. They can act as convectors to provide heating only when ventilation is not needed during building warm-up.

The induction system affords individual room temperature control with reduced ductwork to the units and reduced or no return air ducts to the central unit. The reduction in the quantities of air handled over an all-air alternative represents an energy savings. Four-pipe water distribution to coils permits heating in some rooms simultaneous with cooling in others. The system is primarily used for perimeter conditioning and is not easily adapted for use in core areas. Where ventilation rates are high and approach the supply air quantities to spaces, induction systems cannot be used to advantage, since there would be little or no induction of room air to units.

Instead of an induction unit in each room, an air–water system can have room fan-coil units. In each unit, circulation of air to the room is provided by a fan, and the air temperature is adjusted by a single or separate coils for heating and cooling. Ventilating air is conditioned centrally and distributed to rooms in similar manner to the induction scheme. Since air is not needed for induction, it can be introduced either at the fan-coil unit or separately into a room. Fan-coil air–water systems cost more to install and room fans consume energy, but the presence of the fan permits both heating and cooling with or without the operation of the ventilating air equipment. The result can be energy savings during building warm-up or cool-down before periods of building occupancy.

Radiant ceiling panels are used in another variation of the air–water system. Conditioned primary air is distributed to plenums above the ceiling of each room. Ceiling coils are installed above and clipped to a metal ceiling surface which is perforated for admitting air to the room. A water distribution system to the coils is used to regulate the ultimate air temperature in each room. At the same time the radiant temperature of the room varies to contribute to comfort conditions. This scheme creates a virtually draftless distribution and separates rooms atmospherically if the primary air is limited to ventilating air which is discharged through an exhaust system. These features make it attractive for hospitals, despite its high cost.

All-Water Systems

The most rudimentary water systems are for heating only. A piping system circulates water to room radiation by gravity or by pumping. Where cooling, ventilation above normal building infiltration, and humidity control are not needed, a water system is an appropriate choice. Pipes occupy little space. Pumping energy for water is significantly less than for moving air in a comparable air heating system, and warm radiator surfaces in a room add to comfort conditions, especially when they are placed below cold glazed surfaces (17).

Small heating systems using baseboard radiation can be arranged on series loops (Fig. 11). Water passes from the boiler around a circuit composed of piping and radiators in series. Hence, the same rate of water flow passes through both mains and radiators. Circuit length is limited by

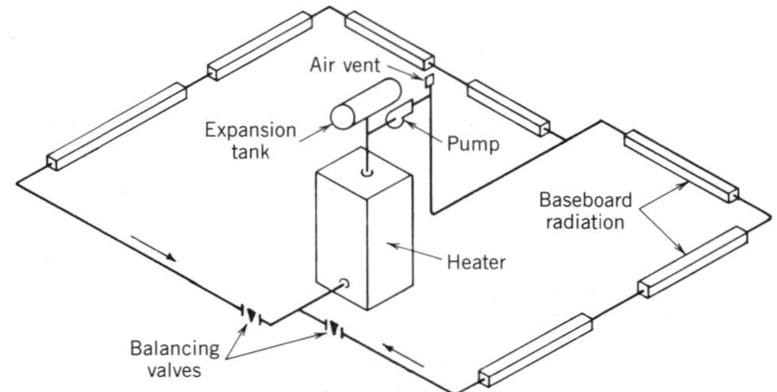

Figure 11. Series-loop hot water heating system.

considerations of pressure and temperature drop. Hence, most systems have a number of these loops of series-connected radiation. They must have provision for balancing the pressure drops of the loops to ensure proper heat distribution to each loop. Successive radiators on a loop receive cooler and cooler water, which causes a corresponding drop in heat output per unit of radiation. Therefore, radiators must be increased in size per unit of load along the loop in order to compensate for the lowering emission rate. Individual valving of room radiators is not possible unless the item has a one-pipe connection to the series loop. Series-loop systems are limited to use with gravity radiation. Unit heaters, etc, with fans would cool water too much.

A one-pipe hot water system (Fig. 12) is one in which radiation is supplied water by a main, and the cooled water from the radiator is returned to the same main. Successive cooling of water occurs around the main, but the radiation temperature drop is now more than the main temperature drop between the supply and return branches to the radiator, rather than being equal as it was for the series-loop. Most systems will employ more than one one-pipe loop from a boiler in order to limit pressure and temperature drops. Individual radiator valving is possible. Proprietary diverting tees are commonly used to encourage water flow through branches to radiators.

If water is to be used to supply large systems containing gravity radiation, any system with forced convection radiation, or where both heating and cooling are to be included, a two-pipe water distribution system is the minimum usable type (Fig. 13). Supply mains extend from boilers and chillers to serve the terminal units, and separate return mains collect water from units to carry it back to the central point for reheating or recooling. Proper distribution of water to the units is achieved when the friction offered to flow to each unit is equal to that to every other unit. This can be realized with less problem in establishing the balance to each unit and less total pressure required from a pump by returning the units in reverse order to that used to supply them.

A two-pipe arrangement can be used for heating and cooling if fan-coil units are used in rooms. The units can have an outside air inlet through the wall to admit ventilating air. This and the entering room air can be proportioned by fixed or automatically controlled dampers. The air then passes through a filter, the coil, and the fan. It can be discharged directly through a grille in the cabinet of the unit, or a short run of duct with air outlets can be used when necessary to solve some air distribution problems. The unit must have a condensate drip pan to receive moisture from the coil when air is cooled below its dew point. A two-pipe system is limited to applications where all fan-coil units are either heating or cooling. Frequent change-over from heating to cooling and vice versa that can occur during spring and fall is not easily accommodated by a two-pipe system.

When some spaces must be cooled when others are heated, a two-pipe system must be zoned or a three or four-pipe distribution system must be used to supply fan-coil units. In the three-pipe scheme, separate hot and chilled water mains are available to each unit. There is one return main for routing water back to the boiler and chiller. The four-pipe system consists of contiguous two-pipe heating and two-pipe cooling system (Figs. 14 and 15). Fan-coil room units and air-handling units serving

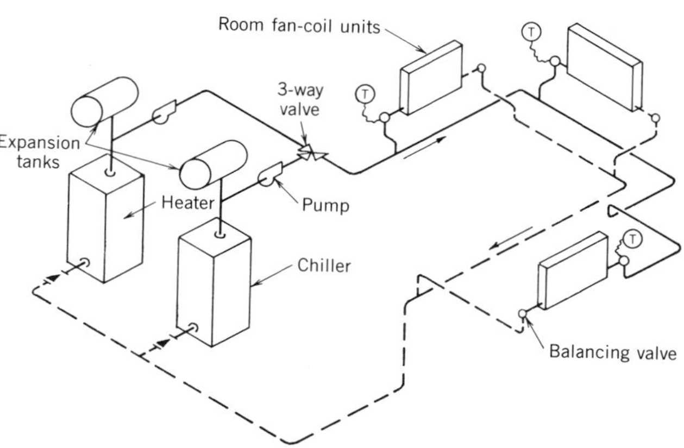

Figure 13. Two-pipe hot–chilled water system with reversed return.

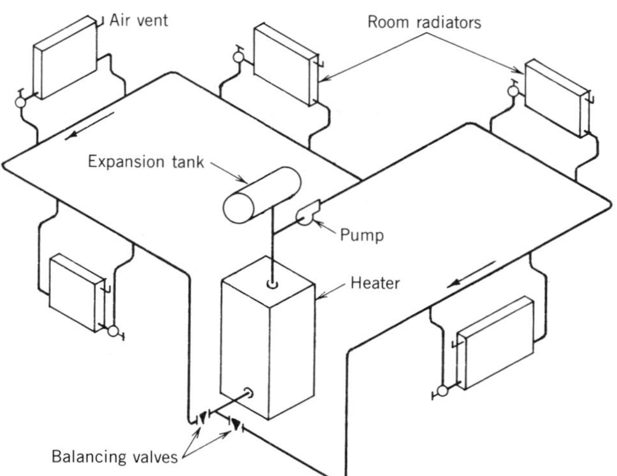

Figure 12. One-pipe hot water heating system.

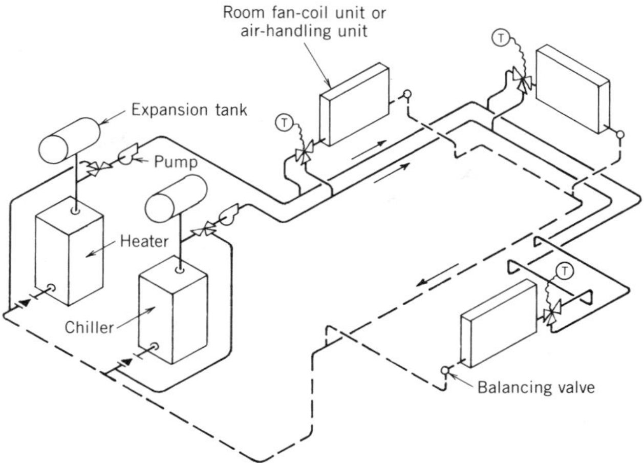

Figure 14. Three-pipe hot–chilled water system.

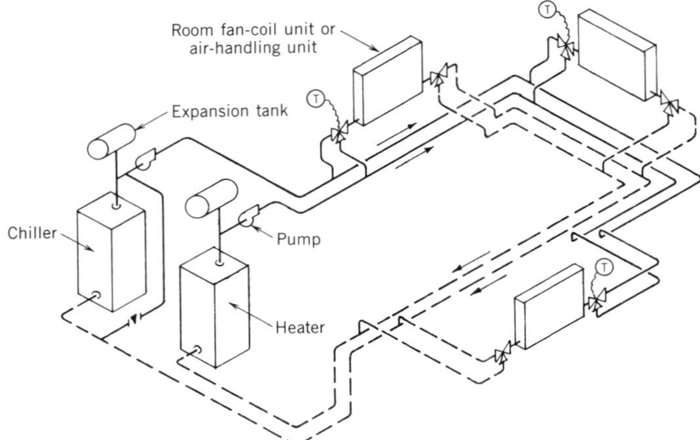

Figure 15. Four-pipe hot–chilled water system.

air systems supplied by the four-pipe arrangement can cool or heat independently of one another by drawing on hot or chilled water as required. Coils of units are individually supplied through the use of thermostatically controlled three-way valves which modulate coil temperatures in proportion to the heating or cooling load.

All-water heating and cooling systems provide individual room temperatures at a much reduced space requirement than ducts and central conditioning apparatus of air systems need, and rooms can be atmospherically isolated from one another. The multiplicity of fans, filters, and drains present in room units is a maintenance concern. Fan-coil units do not supply moisture to raise humidity in winter nor do they control dehumidification closely in summer. To be effective, ventilation using outside air into fan-coil units must have an associated exhaust system.

Instead of using fan-coil units, some all-water systems have valance units located up against the ceiling at outside walls. They consist of coils above insulated condensate pans. In summer the coil cools air which drops down the wall by natural convection, and condensate is drained from the pan. In winter, air is heated at the ceiling and falls to the floor as it cools. The absence of a fan results in less energy cost and quiet operation, but ventilating air is not furnished, and cold glazing in northern locations is not effectively covered.

Water systems can be a mixture of the types described above. It has already been noted that one-pipe radiator connections can be made to a series-loop heating system. Or a system may have a series-loop in one area such as a living room, dining room, and kitchen, and a one-pipe arrangement in the bedroom to permit cutting back radiators for sleeping, according to individual preference. A large, primary two-pipe heating system can be used to supply individual series-loop systems which have their own pumps and thermostatic controls. This scheme would be especially suited to apartment buildings.

Unitary Equipment Systems

Central air or water distributing systems are eliminated when packaged unitary equipment with integral refrigeration components is used (18). A common unit is that made for a through-the-wall installation. A single casing has two compartments. The inside compartment is essentially a fan-coil unit. The outside compartment contains a compressor and an air-cooled condenser. Cooling is accomplished by a direct expansion coil in the inside compartment. If the unit must also heat, an electric or water coil could be added, in which case a substantial investment in an electrical or water distribution system must be made. When the unit must heat and cool, a more likely choice is a package arranged to be a heat pump where the inside and outside coils trade functions as evaporator and condenser as the unit switches between heating and cooling. Since for good humidity control the refrigeration system must be sized for the cooling load and the reverse cycle often does not have adequate capacity to meet the maximum heat loads for most locations in the United States and buildings with sparse occupancy densities, electric coils are required to supplement the heat output in winter (Fig. 16).

These units provide the same quality of individual room conditioning as fan-coil units on water systems. Their initial cost is less, but maintenance and replacement costs are higher than for central systems. Their use is profitable in applications where a room or two would have long-term or frequent occupancy in a building which otherwise experiences intermittent occupancy. This might be true of many auditoriums where certain offices and service facilities are used during usual working hours, but the auditorium and some of its auxiliary spaces need central system operation intermittently.

Since these units contain two fans and a compressor, they are usually rather noisy and cannot be used where an especially quiet ambient condition must be maintained.

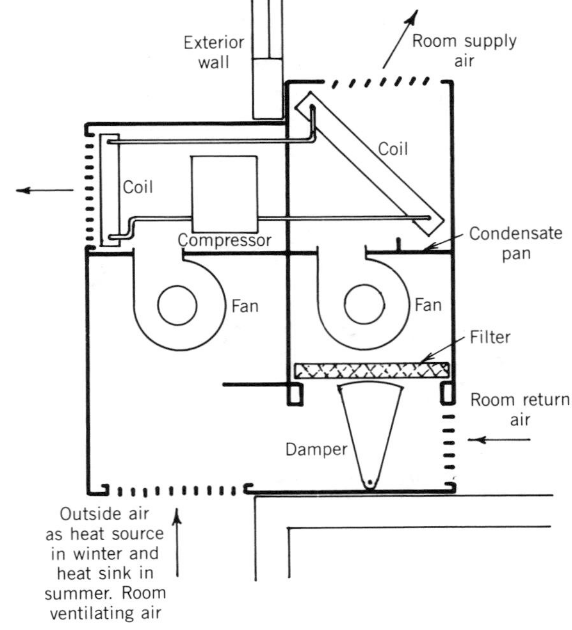

Figure 16. Unitary through-the-wall heat pump.

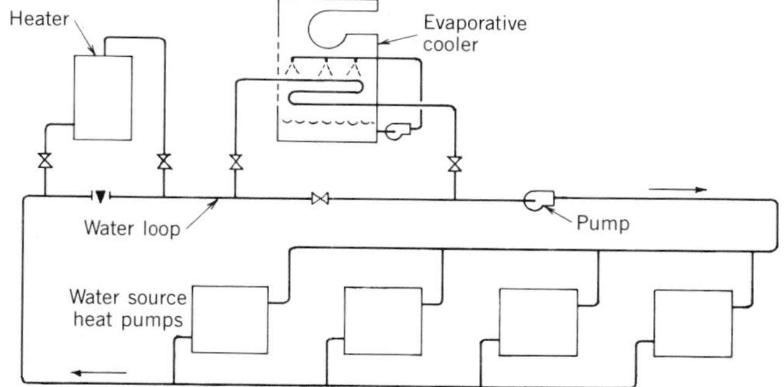

Figure 17. Water source heat pump system.

Recently, water source heat pump systems (Fig.17) have become popular because of their energy conservation. Water is circulated to and from all heat pump units in a closed loop. The water temperature ranges from 16 to 35°C (60 to 95°F). Each heat pump can use the water as a heat source, in which case its coil acts as an evaporator to cool the water, or the water can be a heat sink into which the coil acts as a condenser to reject heat to the loop. The other coil in the heat pump will heat or cool the air flowing through it for distribution to the rooms. In order to maintain the temperature range of the water loop, an evaporative cooler extracts heat from a coil over which it sprays water. Evaporation of water from the external coil surface is accomplished by extracting heat from the water flowing through the loop. Conversely, when the water temperature in the loop drops because most pumps are in the heating cycle, a water heater operates to maintain the required temperature. Systems can be arranged to have heat extraction and rejection to separate loops. Since the temperature is low, solar collectors can be an effective alternate heat source.

The heat pump units are available as cabinets suitable for room installation in the same manner as fan-coil units. Concealed units ranging in size from a single-room unit to one serving a cooling load of several tons which supplies a single zone ducted air system are manufactured.

When some units are cooling and others are heating, the water loop is a path where the former can transfer their heat to the latter, thereby saving energy that might otherwise be used to heat and chill water simultaneously in a four-pipe fan-coil system or to operate unitary air-to-air heat pumps. Water source heat pumps do not require wall openings to outside air which are necessary for air-to-air heat pumps, and water source heat pumps have a longer life expectancy, but the water source heat pumps do require central space for the heating and evaporative cooling equipment.

District Heating and Cooling

When a group of buildings are under a single ownership, such as on college campuses and in certain commercial and industrial complexes, there are compelling reasons for supplying heating and cooling from a central plant in lieu of separate heating and refrigeration equipment for each building (19). Individual systems would have to be sized to meet the maximum loads for each building. Since these maximum loads do not occur simultaneously, the greater diversity of loading on a central plant serving them would have a maximum load less than the sum of the separate maximum building loads. Larger plants with multiple units of equipment paralleled can supply partial loads much more efficiently by operating one or more units at capacity. A smaller, single unit in a building would, under partial loading, experience a drop in efficiency of energy use. Central plants reduce the space requirements for central equipment in the buildings they serve. The electrical distribution system to the buildings requires much less capacity when refrigeration equipment is centralized. Large central systems generally have full-time personnel to ensure good performance and maintenance.

For some years steam systems from central plants have been used for district heating. System siting must include consideration for gravity movement of condensate from buildings and steam mains back to the boiler plant or to a point where it can be pumped back to the boilers. Steam tunnels, trenches, and manholes are necessary for access to the system for maintenance. If the tunnel runs can be under sidewalks, heat losses from piping are useful for snow melting.

Through use of heat exchangers at each building, the district steam system heats water for the building system, or it could heat air directly with steam coils in air-handling units. The former practice of lowering steam pressure for use in a building steam-heating system is now very rare. Control of heat output by varying the temperature of air or water in proportion to load variation is more successful than a scheme using steam in off and on cycles.

High temperature, high pressure water central systems have been used since World War II as an alternative to steam district systems. Water in closed systems under pressures as high as 2000 kPa (290 psi) permit water to be heated to a corresponding temperature of 200°C (392° F) without boiling. As a result, water can be circulated at low flow rates through large temperature drops to transfer heat at high rates to heat transfer surfaces in each building; this will heat water for low-pressure heating systems or will heat air passing over coils made to withstand the high-pressure water.

Water system piping is always full of water. It does not require the continuous air venting or the dripping of condensate from low points needed in steam systems. Hence, water systems experience less problems with pipe corrosion and system maintenance. Steam plants must be sized to meet their largest instantaneous load; water can store heat for future use. Therefore, hot water generator capacity in a water system can be less than boiler capacity if water is heated during off-peak periods and stored so that maximum generator capacity plus stored heat equals the maximum instantaneous heating load.

Central chilled water plants are suitable for use where distribution distances are limited, as dictated by capacity losses through the piping and the high cost of large, insulated lines. The operating temperature rise is generally higher than for individual building system practice, 9–11°C (16–20°F). Chilled water temperatures delivered to building coils are generally higher than if the building had an individual system. Therefore, coil size is larger to handle the same load. But the higher efficiency of larger central plants over smaller building water chillers and the reduction in overall capacity, due to diversity of loading, often makes the central system the proper alternative.

APPLICATIONS OF SYSTEMS TO BUILDING TYPES

Some buildings will be served by a system of one of the generic types that have been described. Others, especially larger ones, will typically have a primary system of one type as a source of supply to subsystems of another type. Various factors that influence decisions regarding appropriate total systems are noted below as they relate to various kinds of building occupancies (20).

Residences

For the single-family detached residence, initial commitments must be made regarding the appropriate heat-carrying medium, whether or not any zoning is anticipated, and whether heating only or heating and cooling are to be provided.

There is increasing acceptance of year-round heating and cooling for residences in most temperate locations. In far northern regions or higher elevations with low night temperatures and locations where a separate evaporative cooling system might be installed, heating only can be an appropriate decision.

Most residences are operated as a single zone. A thermostat at a given position maintains the temperature setting in its space while the temperature in others will vary somewhat in accord with solar gains as the sun moves from one exposure to another or other influences change individual room heating and cooling loads. Certain residential configurations will require zoning to keep temperature swings within reason. Rooms with extensive south glass will collect considerable solar energy from a low sun in winter even if eaves shade glass from a higher sun in summer. North rooms would not receive this advantage. Therefore, a thermostat in a south room will be satisfied in part by the sun. As a result the system output will be lowered, and northern rooms will be too cold. Placing the thermostat in a northern room will have the opposite effect. A decision to utilize some solar energy demands zoning as a consequence.

Warm air systems are the most common systems for residences. A low-pressure supply duct overhead or under the floor serves branches to the room registers either high up on inside walls or, better still, in the ceiling or in the floor or lower wall at the exterior wall where air can counteract building losses occurring there. Return air typically moves back to the furnace through doors to halls and central grilles with little or no ductwork between the grille and the furnace. The popularity of the air system is due to its low cost and its ability to be designed to anticipate the addition of refrigeration equipment for summer cooling at a later date. This prospect means that ducts must be insulated to keep them from sweating and be larger than required for heating alone.

In cooler climates where below-freezing temperatures are typically experienced during the middle of the day, air systems do not help overcome discomfort from increased body radiant heat loss due to the rather low inside surface temperatures of exterior surfaces, especially glass. Elevation of room air temperatures to offset this discomfort is not successful when radiant temperatures of large surfaces are well below the air temperature. The hot surfaces of radiators in water or steam systems provide the higher mean radiant temperature for spaces. Air systems have been laid out so that warm air passes through ducts embedded in a concrete floor slab or under-floor plenums before it is discharged into the room at perimeter outlets. This is an effort to obtain radiant surfaces from an air system.

If system operation is desired whether or not doors are closed, then return ducts with return grilles in each room must be installed.

Residential heating is easily accomplished with series-loop or one-pipe hot water systems or even a combination of these types as noted elsewhere. The supply of both convective and radiant heat is especially conducive to comfort conditions because of the gentle air movement and the warm radiant surfaces which offset cold room surfaces as noted above. Integrating piping into the building structure is easier than solving the problem of accommodating ductwork. Zoning for a hot water system is easily added by installing a separate pump to serve the mains to each zone. Energy for pumping water is much less than for moving air. A pump motor would typically be 1/12 horsepower whereas an equivalent fan motor for an air system would be 1/3 horsepower. But gravity radiation cannot be used to cool, for circulation of chilled water through the system would cause its surface to sweat.

Furnaces and heaters for air or water systems are selected for the appropriate fuel or electricity as the result of a study of relative costs of the alternatives for system operation over a typical season of the system.

Radiant panel heating for residences can be water coils or electric resistance wires in concrete floor slabs or plaster ceilings. Air can be used to heat ceiling or floor plenums to form radiant surfaces. Proprietary surface-applied electrical panels are also available for radiant ceiling use.

Electrical baseboard radiation can be used in lieu of water radiation where electric power is economical. Electrical radiation is installed using individual room thermostatic control in order to keep electrical circuit size within reason.

When both heating and cooling of a residence is contemplated, the air system is virtually no different in configuration than that described for heating only. The cooling is often provided by an evaporator coil in the furnace bonnet which is connected to an outside compressor–condenser unit. In rare cases where water is economically available for condenser cooling, an indoor compressor with a water-cooled condenser is an alternative.

For air heating and cooling applications, the air-to-air heat pump is a possible alternative to a furnace with separate refrigeration equipment. On the reverse cycle the heat pump makes efficient use of electrical energy for heating in mild weather as it draws heat from the outside air. In the typical residence in temperate and colder zones, the heat pump, which must be sized for cooling, will not have an output on the reverse cycle adequate to heat the building during cooler weather. Thus, supplemental heat must be available below a certain outdoor temperature, and it is usually supplied by electric coils. If there is much cold weather, this higher cost utilization of electrical energy will suggest the fuel-fired furnace with separate summer refrigeration equipment as the better alternative.

The heat pump may be a through-the-wall unit containing all refrigeration components, filters, and system fan. Most often an inside blower unit with coil and filters and separate outside unit with compressor, coil, and fan are installed.

Residential heating and cooling can be accomplished with hot–chilled water systems which would be two-pipe layouts for single zone application or three- or four-pipe systems for larger zone installations. Small residential fan-coil units are placed in each room. A fuel-fired heater and an outdoor liquid chiller which has an air-cooled condenser are typical choices for supplying hot and chilled water. Chillers with water-cooled condensers are available. These water systems are more costly to install and maintain than the air system alternatives. The manual choice of fan speeds in each room affords a modicum of individual room temperature control.

If one wants the advantage of winter radiant heating and summer cooling, an appropriate residential scheme can be a water-heating system with radiators or convectors completely separate from an air-cooling system, which has the same inside and outside units as the air-to-air heat pump; however, the outside coil is always a condenser and the inside coil an evaporator, for no provision is made for reversing the cycle. This alternative costs more than an all-air system, but it can be more economical than an all-water system.

In the installation of all systems, location of units containing oil burners, compressors, and central system and condenser fans must be determined with regard for considerations of fire safety and airborne and structurally transmitted noise. Units next to bedrooms should be avoided. Enclosure of inside units requires that code provisions for clearance between units and combustible construction be observed. Surrounding construction needs to be heavy enough to have adequate airborne sound insulation. The insulation rating requirement can be lowered significantly by selecting quiet equipment. Sound-level ratings are often given by manufacturers. Access doors to equipment spaces should have gasketed perimeters, and openings through which pipes and ducts pass need to be sealed airtight. Units installed on or suspended from lightweight frame structures need to have effective vibration isolation mountings. Internally insulated ductwork extending from the central unit attenuates fan noise if it is given sufficient length and/or passes through some turns. The insulation also helps to prevent sound transmission between rooms via ducts. Boiler and furnace rooms will need outside inlets for introducing combustion air.

Outdoor compressor units near windows or patios will be an annoyance to building owners and nearby neighbors.

Systems for town houses and walk-up apartments are typically separate for each unit, and thus may be any of those noted for detached residences. With separate systems, each tenant is responsible for his or her own energy bill, which tends to result in less energy consumption than in a scheme in which a central plant distributes hot and chilled water through a primary system to individual unit systems.

High-rise apartments may have a secondary baseboard heating system for each unit supplied by a primary central two-pipe water system with its heater in a basement location. For heating and cooling, the primary three- or four-pipe system supplies hot and chilled water from a central heater and liquid chiller to fan-coil units. A fan-coil unit is placed at a central point above the ceiling of each apartment, from which a short length of ductwork extends to room registers. A central ceiling grille returns air to the unit. Alternatively, fan-coil units under windows could be used.

Through-the-wall heat pumps are also commonly used for high-rise apartments. They increase the electrical equipment size and investment but eliminate central water systems and usually ductwork as well.

Hotels and Motels

Guest accommodations for travelers require a system with individual temperature control for each guest unit. Each unit in a sense is a very small apartment; therefore, either fan-coil units in each room supplied by a central hot and chilled water system or self-contained through-the-wall heat pumps are generally utilized. Care must be exercised in the selection of these units to ensure that they will not produce an average sound level more than 40 dBA in the room. Bath exhaust systems receive their air from the ventilating air introduced at room air-conditioning units.

Dining, meeting rooms, etc, which are a part of these establishments will generally be served by all-air systems which originate at air-handling units. They will be separate single zone systems and/or dual-duct or variable volume systems as zoning for the application may dictate. Public spaces are rooms where smoking will be prevalent, and will require higher than average ventilation rates.

Central heating and refrigeration equipment including cooling towers must be located away from guest units and meeting rooms where noise levels must be relatively low.

Office Buildings

Office buildings range in size from small, single-occupancy structures to the world's largest multistory buildings. Therefore, no common practice for heating and air conditioning can be cited.

The smaller building of one or two stories with a number of rather permanently defined suites is similar to a walk-up apartment. Climate control systems are the same as described for apartments.

The larger multistory office building usually involves the problem of laying out a perimeter system to deal with heat losses and cooling loads occurring at the perimeter and a central core system to handle year-round heat gains.

The use of variable-volume systems for each floor is common practice with the possible addition of perimeter radiation for winter in northern climates. System zoning can be arranged to transfer heat from internal cooling zones to perimeter zones when the latter experience heat losses. All-air systems can be used for a core with the perimeter served by fan-coil or induction units. On each floor a room for central air-handling equipment must be provided. These rooms are preferably one above the other so that they may be served by a four-pipe water system which extends vertically up from a basement or down from penthouse water heating and chilling equipment. Vent shafts, often contiguous, are needed for introducing outside ventilating air to the air-handling units on each floor and to extract the exhaust air. Fans to move this air would be in the penthouse. Since penthouses usually contain large refrigeration compressors, control system compressors, water pumps, fans, and sometimes air-handling equipment and standby generators, high noise levels will exist directly above the top floor where prime office space is located. Floating floor slabs in the penthouse and very careful vibration isolation of machinery and lines to it is essential if sufficiently low noise levels are to be maintained in the offices below.

In very tall buildings, intermediate floors devoted to central water-heating and -cooling equipment are needed in addition to the penthouse.

Cooling towers are large components requiring access to outside air; hence, they are usually set on roofs, or in less crowded sites on the ground to one side of a building. Siting must take into consideration the noise levels and vibration potential at rooms.

Water source heat pumps on each floor can be used to serve perimeter and core air systems on each floor, in which case the vertical water loop extends to a heater inside and an evaporative cooler outside. As noted earlier, this is an excellent system for transferring internal heat gains to the perimeter to offset heat losses in winter.

If the building is intended for office use for a number of separate tenants or one under one owner whose needs are subject to change, office arrangements may be varied from time to time. Demountable partitions, under-floor raceways, and suspended modular ceilings permit the change. It is also necessary that air-conditioning systems and lighting be amenable to change. Troffer lighting with slot diffusers which can be moved as needed or ceiling suspension systems with diffuser slots accommodate new room configurations. Connections to these slots are through flexible ducts. Air return is through the ceiling plenum.

Stores

A great deal of retail merchandising now takes place in adjacent one-story stores forming a shopping mall. For these buildings a rooftop air-conditioning unit serving a single, multizone, or variable-volume air distribution system in the ceiling below is common practice. High internal gains from lights and people cause high cooling loads which are likely to be higher than winter heat losses. In such cases an air-to-air heat pump could be an economical choice for the rooftop unit. Instead of a heat pump, a unit with gas or electric heating and the direct expansion cooling coil with its compressor and air-cooled condenser can be the choice.

Large department stores are usually multistory structures with a minimum amount of exterior wall surface and little or no glass relative to the volume. Large cooling loads from people and lighting are present. Customer density and movement varies considerably, and a system must be zoned to keep up with this variability. These stores can be served by systems as described for larger, multistory office buildings except that the concern for perimeter loads is generally less.

Smaller department stores of one or two stories generally have systems as noted for one-story stores.

Restaurants and Nightclubs

Dining and nightclub establishments experience wide fluctuations in building loads. These are caused by large variations in the density and degree of activity of patrons, loads from cooking and hot foods, and infiltration at entries. In addition, substantial ventilation rates are required to cope with tobacco and body odor. Kitchens must have hoods over heat-producing appliances in order to exhaust much of the high sensible and latent heat gains of cooking from the building so that the cooling load on the air-conditioning system can be kept to a minimum. Kitchens must be under negative pressure and have a ventilating requirement flowing to them at a rate adequate to enable hoods to pick up warm air and its moisture and odors. Kitchen exhaust systems are subject to grease collection on the interior surfaces of ducts. Local codes will dictate the fire-fighting equipment that must be installed to protect against grease fires. The system could be built to contain the fire until depletion of the grease results in extinguishment.

Area zoning is important for coping with load variations, even within a single dining space. It must be coordinated with any scheme of closing off areas with folding doors for private dining. Smaller establishments will usually have rooftop units serving air systems in rather similar fashion to one-story stores. Very large dining or entertainment centers will use chillers and heaters to produce hot and chilled water for air-handling units which in turn serve single duct, multizone, or variable volume systems.

Auditoriums

Spaces for events for which a large assembly of spectators or participants are present are rooms in which there is a dense occupancy on the floor. Major cooling loads when audiences are present are the sensible and latent heat gains from people and that attributable to the ventilation they require. Since the latent gains are high, relative to the total load, cooling coils cannot condense out the requisite quantity of moisture without cooling the supply air below the temperature needed to absorb the sensible heat load in the auditorium. This problem can be minimized by setting the ventilation rate as low as possible, not over 2.5 l/s (5 cfm) per person for nonsmoking audiences, and by cooling the room a little below design conditions before occupancy. During an hour or two of occupancy the audience adds heat and humidity to the room, bringing it up to and somewhat above design conditions; for higher ventilation rates over extended periods of occupancy, some means of reheating the overcooled, dehumidified air must be employed. Recovery of condenser heat from the refrigeration equipment for this purpose is a method of keeping the additional system energy input needed for reheating to a minimum.

Most auditoriums are served by single zone, single duct, low velocity all-air systems. Ceiling or sidewall outlets must be arranged to distribute air over the entire area. This can be a problem in tall spaces such as some churches. Sidewall outlets can provide cooling in the lower occupied part of the volume and let the upper portion remain at elevated temperatures. Low sidewall outlets cannot throw air very far without using high velocities, which create excessive noise levels for concert halls, theaters, and churches. They must have very low to low background noise levels (noise criteria (NC) 20–30). Wide spaces, say more than 20 m (65 ft) wide, must use overhead ceiling outlets in lieu of sidewall outlets to cover at least the central seating areas. However, for convenience of duct layout in this case, all air supply would generally be from the ceiling rather than from a combination of sidewall and ceiling outlets. Returns are best located low on walls and/or may be numerous small inlets under seating into a return plenum. A very large return grille or two on a short duct to the air-handling unit will transmit excessive fan noise to nearby seating even if the duct has internal insulation to attenuate sound. The use of more smaller returns distribute the fan sound power, thereby lowering the level at each inlet. Small ducts attenuate better than larger ones. Substituting air-foil fans for the more common forward curved-blade type helps lower the level of low-frequency fan rumble.

Balancing dampers at faces of outlets creates noise levels which are elevated significantly as they are closed down to achieve desired airflow rates. Outlet devices chosen for their proper airflow rates and appropriate noise levels can, after system balance, prove to be much too noisy. The problem must be avoided by placing dampers about 2.5 m (8.2 ft) upstream in the branch from the outlet. Main and branch duct velocities should not exceed 5 m/s and 3 m/s (1000 fpm and 600 fpm, respectively) for concert halls, theaters, etc, where very good listening conditions are required.

Air-handling units must not be above auditorium ceilings or within stage houses. These and other machine items must be in rooms beside the auditorium and stage with intervening construction of adequate sound insulation value or in rooms at a sufficient distance to maintain background noise levels in the auditorium at or below the design noise criterion. Vibration isolation must be installed to keep structurally transmitted vibrations from reaching the auditorium. Equipment components on an auditorium roof should be avoided.

Air distribution to stages presents the problems of dealing with scenery and variable lighting heat loads that can be large. A common solution is to throw air out at rather low velocity from the back wall at a high position where good coverage across the depth is possible. The cool air drops until it is picked up by returns lower down. If returns can be placed near lighting, they can help remove the heat that lighting generates before it makes a big impact on the cooling load of the space.

Support spaces, such as lobbies, dressing rooms, shops, storage, and rest rooms, should be on separate zones from the auditorium. When the house is occupied for short periods by a full audience and service facilities are used throughout full working days, energy savings can be achieved if there is separate refrigeration and heat source equipment.

Sports arenas may require zoning of a system for one space in order to keep air-handling equipment and ducts within reasonable physical size. The system noise level will be a function of the variety of events anticipated. For sports events only a NC of 40–45 would be acceptable. Maximum use of these structures for realizing a good financial return often leads to scheduling of a wide variety of entertainment attractions, many of which must have low background noise levels.

Schools

Selection of an appropriate climate control system for a school building with typical classrooms and offices involves a basic decision as to whether or not summer cooling is to be provided in addition to winter heating and ventilation. It is now generally accepted that schools in southern climates with short winter seasons will have air conditioning. Those in northern climates that are not used during the summer months may have heating and ventilating systems only. People and lights will create net cooling loads, even though outside temperatures are several degrees below inside temperatures. In this circumstance, the outside air can be used as a source of cooling rather than as a refrigeration system. Energy codes now generally require that such an outdoor air economizer cycle be a feature of any ventilating system. When outside temperatures are close to or even exceed indoor design temperatures during the school session, summer air conditioning will be needed. Use of school facilities for summer and evening classes throughout the year in addition to the traditional schoolyear occupancy dictates that a system supply heating and air conditioning.

A minimum building volume is used to house a system, and individual room temperature control is provided to cope with room-to-room load variation due to variable patterns of occupancy, solar exposure, etc, if a two-pipe hot water system supplies room unit ventilators for heating and ventilation or a four-pipe hot–chilled water system is used with room fan-coil units for year-round control. Room units draw outside air directly through the wall and mix it with room air. Provision must be made for exhaust of a quantity of air equal to the ventilating air brought in. Where cloak rooms are in classrooms, exhausting air through these hanging spaces helps to remove odors and moisture from the clothes kept there.

The dual-duct system can be used in lieu of all-water systems if individual room temperature control is to be accomplished. Its central air-conditioning unit permits close humidity control if needed. Corridor ceilings must have plenum space for hot and cold supply ducts. The ceiling plenum can act as a return. The practice of returning classroom air through door grilles and down corridors to mechanical rooms has been discontinued. Noise through the grilles can be a problem, and the openings are outlawed because they would allow a fire to travel easily from rooms. Ducts passing through corridor walls require fire dampers.

If individual room temperature control is not thought to be necessary, zoning could be according to load variations because of building exposure. A multizone air-handling unit could supply a separate zone duct to rooms facing each compass exposure. Instead, each exposure can be a variable volume system so that cooling of a southern exposure is possible when a northern one needs heating. Variable volume permits individual room temperature control. Schools can use unitary heat pump packages for classrooms and eliminate the need for central equipment and duct and piping systems.

Schools will have any number of rooms that have special problems to be solved. These include labs that generate fumes to be exhausted, music suites where excellent noise control and perhaps humidity control are musts, and shops where dust is created. For large spaces, such as auditoriums and gymnasiums, refer to the discussion under auditoriums.

Water systems will be supplied by central heater and water chiller plants for the building or group of buildings. Air-handling units supplying air systems can be supplied by a water system from a central plant. Alternately, the air system can be one or more zones supplied by a rooftop unit. Care must be exercised in placing rooftop units to avoid noise and vibration problems. They must not be over classrooms, music rooms, and other spaces where low background noise levels are essential. Lightweight roof structures over long spans are especially sensitive to vibration, and spring isolators are necessary.

Electric energy can be used for resistance heating coils in lieu of water if an economic study justifies the choice.

Hospitals

The design of air-conditioning systems for hospitals and health care structures providing similar services involves a number of characteristic problems. These include the concern for maintaining aseptic conditions, controlling odors, providing various temperatures and humidities necessary for patients in various conditions of health and dress, and provision for standby operation in the event of normal energy source or equipment item failure. Governmental regulation of hospitals has produced standards, some of whose provisions relate to system design.

Systems will need to be zoned for all of the usual reasons for any building and to separate areas for contagion control. In addition, certain spaces will need to have a positive or negative pressure relative to surrounding rooms. Toilets, most laboratories, soiled linen storage, and other rooms generating odors need to be negative, to encourage airflow to them so that odors are contained. Most of these spaces will require exhausting of all air entering them. Conversely, positive pressure in delivery, operating, and intensive-care rooms, relative to surrounding rooms, inhibits the incoming flow of air that may be less aseptic than desirable.

Filter equipment that is highly efficient in removing particulate matter also does well in removing bacteria. Sterilizing or disinfecting the airstream effectively is difficult to achieve and maintain and, hence, not generally attempted.

Since hospitals are in continuous operation, a central mechanical room will generally house heaters and chillers that supply hot and chilled water to air-handling units for the all-air systems, air–water systems, or to room fan-coil units on all-water systems. The central installation should consist of more than one heater and chiller operating in parallel. During lighter loads, one unit operating near its capacity is more efficient than a single, larger idling unit, and the others are available on a standby basis.

Interior systems will be the all-air type, but perimeter systems for patient rooms may be any of those described under Types of Heating and Air-conditioning Systems which are suitable for public and commercial buildings. Those which can provide individual room temperature control will generally be preferred.

A summary of interior conditions for various kinds of spaces requiring functions other than comfort for healthy adults is as follows.

Fluoroscopic, radiographic, and deep therapy rooms: 25–27°C (75–80°F), relative humidity 40–50%.

Hydrotherapy: 27°C (80°F).

Nurseries: 24°C (75°F), relative humidity 30–60%.

Treatment and patient rooms: 24°C (75°F), relative humidity 30–50%.

Operating rooms: Adjustable 20–24°C (68–76°F), relative humidity 50–60%.

Intensive care: Adjustable 24–27°C (75–80°F), relative humidity 30–60%.

Libraries and Museums

Depositories for books and artifacts must have conditions that preserve these items and protect them from gradual deterioration which exposure to changing and deleterious atmospheres causes. The longevity of the paper of books, microfilms, and tapes requires that libraries maintain constant conditions favorable to all these items. Modern acid papers fare best in low temperatures and humidities. For films and tapes the relative humidity must not drop below 40% and it cannot be more than 65% without risk of mildew. These factors generally lead to internal conditions all year of 18°C (65°F) and 35% relative humidity for book stacks or archival material and 21°C (70°F) and 40–50% relative humidity for film collections. In the usual community or local public school library 22°C (72°F) and 40–50% relative humidity is typical for all areas.

Museums have collections of such a wide range of materials that optimal conditions for their display and storage vary considerably, and design criteria need to be determined from the advice of museum directors and the kind of collections planned.

It is apparent that libraries and museums need all-air systems with central apparatus capable of maintaining close humidity control. They will also need to filter chemical pollutants from outside ventilating air. Sulfur dioxide from the burning of fuels is a common contaminant which can be removed in an air washer or canister filter. Water systems to terminal room units should be avoided to prevent risk of water damage to irreplaceable building contents.

Computer and Clean Rooms

Installation of computer equipment poses special problems of climatic environmental control (21). Small electronic items and other products, such as delicate instruments and sterile supplies for medical uses adversely affected by various contaminants, demand clean rooms for their manufacture.

Computer equipment generates heat, and its reliable operation requires that room temperature and humidity stay within defined limits. Manufacturers should be consulted regarding this data. Usually environmental recommendations coincide with comfort requirements, eg, 22 ± 1°C (72 ± 2°F) dry-bulb temperature and a relative humidity of 50% ± 5%. Most equipment is cooled by drawing room air into it and discharging the warmer air back to the room. Some computer units are made to be supplied directly with cooling air, and the entering condition is generally at a lower temperature and higher humidity than room air. Dust in the air is detrimental to computer operations; reliable particulate filters need to be a part of any conditioning equipment.

Precision in maintaining given criteria is not so important as the avoidance of fluctuations in environmental conditions. Wide variations in humidity cause dimensional changes in cards and paper that interfere with reliability of machine handling. Very high humidities can produce condensation on equipment, and very low values generate static electricity detrimental to the functioning of electronic equipment.

Ventilation air requirements for computer installations are limited to that needed for the personnel. Since occupancies are low, the quantity required is quite small. As a consequence, latent loads are very low, and most of the cooling load is sensible heat from the equipment and lighting. For this condition, the required air supply per unit of cooling load is higher than for typical comfort systems with a larger proportion of latent load.

Reliable, uninterrupted operation of air-conditioning equipment suggests self-contained unitary equipment, often in the computer room, capable of being powered by emergency generator systems which also ensures continuous power for the computers. Packaged units designed for computer rooms are made which contain the fan, filters, heating and cooling coils, and refrigeration components, except the outside air-cooled condenser or a water-cooling tower. Typical central station air-handling units supplying the computer installation only are an option and are generally selected for larger systems. They and the heating and refrigeration equipment for them will require a space accommodation close to the computer area.

Distribution of air to computer rooms must be accomplished to maintain the close range of conditions in spite of concentrations of heat from machines occurring in a varying pattern during operation. The high rate of supply airflow required for the sensible loads, if well distributed, helps ensure uniform conditions. Computer installations have raised floors for access to cables. The floor cavity can be an air supply plenum through the use of perforated floor panels or floor registers placed so that conditioned and room air become well mixed at the outlets before flowing to machines. Floor plenums need to be clean and sealed airtight; this includes access panels to ensure airflow only through outlets. Plenum depth must be adequate for both cables and the rate of supply airflow. The ceiling plenum can be an effective return for a floor supply. It picks up heat from lighting and keeps it from becoming a space load.

Overhead air distribution can be through a ceiling plenum with perforated panels or acoustical tile, or through a ducted system. The plenum is profitable because it permits very easy arrangement and alteration of outlets to cope with various distributions of loads from computer equipment.

Return air enters self-contained units in computer rooms directly. Returns to central stations should be devised so that inlets can be moved as necessary to place them near concentrations of heat loads as an aid to minimizing room condition variation.

Reliability of computer air-conditioning systems is paramount. Standby or redundancy features in design are justifiable. Monitoring instruments are advisable to track system performance. Alarms should be installed to alert maintenance personnel to any malfunction that will affect air quality.

Clean rooms are spaces designated for applications of unique control to ensure freedom from particulate, and possibly, other contaminants, such as bacteria or gases. Temperature and humidity control may be for comfort only, but some clean room processes may require conditions to be within given values. As in computer rooms, high humidities in clean rooms can cause condensation on surfaces, and low humidities can create static electricity.

For most clean rooms, elimination of particles in the air and on surfaces is the primary goal. Airborne particles come in with ventilating air and by infiltration through openings and cracks in a room. These are excluded through selection of the appropriate filtration equipment, the sealing of all cracks, room pressurization, and air locks. Particulate contamination is also internal. Room occupants shed particles from the skin and by respiration and are the significant source of direct room contamination. In addition, the room processes can generate particulate matter. Rubbing of one material on another creates fine, loose particles. For example, fibers from paper or cloth are dislodged if anything moves across the material's surface. Air movement in the room induced by air conditioning and by people moving about or other objects in the room causes the dislodged particles to move about in air currents. This particle movement creates cross-contamination in a room which can foul the location of the operation requiring extremely clean conditions.

Some operations may generate gases that are toxic, explosive, or corrosive. Others may create odors. Processes involving medical products will demand a germ-free room. Determination of the proper climate control system requires a complete, accurate assessment of the tolerable level of contaminants that can be permitted without adverse effects on the processes or the workers in the controlled clean environment.

Cleanliness in the room is aided by the selection of smooth, joint-free room surfaces not subject to particle shedding through rubbing contact. Openings in surface for room electrical and mechanical services should be sealed. Provisions for personnel to wash and put on lint-free clothing will be necessary for some applications.

The air distribution pattern in a clean room is crucial to the success of controlling particulate contamination. Generally, air should move directly to the work. From this critical point it can move with any contaminants picked up at the work or around personnel and move to return or exhaust inlets. Air can be introduced through large ceiling outlets at low velocities and returned near the floor. Sometimes laminar flow is used which makes contamination that is picked up flow along a predicted path. In this scheme, air supply is introduced through the entire ceiling surface or through an entire wall surface at a velocity of 0.46 m/s ± 0.1 m/s (90 fpm ± 20 fpm). Filters are installed behind the outlet surface. The return or exhaust air is removed through a floor grating or opposite grille wall.

Central air-handling equipment for clean rooms include all components typically used for year-round air conditioning. In addition, final filtering is added at points of air entry to rooms. Systems need to be tested for leaks, especially in filters and around their frames, before being put into service. Also, their capacity to maintain design cleanliness needs to be verified during operating conditions. Failure to perform up to standards can mean defective goods or dangerous conditions, either of which can prove costly.

ENERGY CONSERVATION AND MANAGEMENT

For more than a decade, efforts have been directed at designing and operating heating and air-conditioning systems so that desired thermal and atmospheric conditions are obtained with reduced rates of energy consumption.

Certain recent developments in system design have lessened energy requirements. These improvements include the ability to transfer excess heat from one area of the building to another requiring heat to offset its heat losses or reheat needs, heat recovery techniques, and the use of the heat conservation cycle.

Descriptions of all-air systems and water source heat pump systems have explained how these capture heat from interior areas which always need cooling and move it to building perimeters when heat losses occur there.

When outside air is brought into a building for ventilation, it imposes a rather significant cooling and dehumidification load on the system in summer or a heating and, perhaps, humidification load in winter, as air is brought to room conditions. An exhaust system must discharge air to the outside at the same rate of flow as the incoming air. But the exhaust air at room conditions has the capacity to cool incoming warmer ventilating air in summer or heat it during winter. Equipment is needed to transfer heat from one airstream to the other. This use of the heating or cooling capacity of exhaust airstreams instead of using external energy for the purpose is one example of heat recovery.

A water coil in each airstream with a pump circulating water between them can extract heat from an incoming ventilating airstream and lessen the load on refrigerating equipment provided the cooler exhausting air has cooled the water in the exhaust air coil. Another heat recovery scheme uses a slowly moving wheel containing a heat transfer medium which moves through the airstreams in adjacent ducts. The medium becomes alternately warmer and cooler as it moves heat from one airstream to the other. Some devices transfer only sensible heat, but transfer of both sensible and latent heat is preferred for comfort systems.

Use of condenser heat from refrigeration systems for reheat of air or heating domestic hot water is another heat recovery practice.

There are times when outside air is cooler than inside design conditions at the same time that cooling loads exist in a space because of internal heat sources such as people or lights, or because a building has stored solar energy in its construction that is continuing to impose a cooling load. It is logical to consider using the outside air for cooling rather than the energy-consuming alternative of operating the refrigeration system. Alternately, outside air can heat up to a point where it is above room temperature and could be used to bring the building up to that temperature after a cool night. This technique of using outside air as the total supply quantity for heating and cooling is called the heat conservation or economizer cycle, and many codes require it for all but residential buildings when energy consumption will be reduced through its use. The system must be arranged to permit the introduction of 100% outside air when an enthalpy controller senses that outside temperature and humidity are at appropriate values for operation of the heat conservation cycle. Dampers move to introduce all outside and no return air to the air-conditioning unit. Relief vents must be installed to exhaust air at an equal rate.

Optimal energy utilization in the operation of heating and air-conditioning systems is only possible with a properly designed and functioning automatic control system (22).

Since World War II there has been a progression from electrical and pneumatic control systems to those which now include centralized computer management systems. Computers can be programmed to start up components and stop them according to times of building use, and optimal selection of various sequences of operations in terms of a set of measured temperatures (as for selection between cooling or a heating cycle), etc. A central console is often installed to enable one to monitor temperatures at numerous points in the building system as an aid in determining system performance at any time.

It must be noted that the more complex the control system, the greater is the need for personnel who know how to monitor it and ensure that it is in good operating order. Malfunction of a single item in a system can create uncomfortable conditions everywhere and increased energy consumption. For large buildings, at least one full-time person should be responsible for the operation and maintenance of systems. He or she must understand both controls and energy management of computer systems.

The role of energy codes in reducing energy use by building climate control systems has been discussed. Codes set limits regarding thermal properties of construction, design conditions to be maintained by climate control systems, etc. However, the ultimate goal for energy conservation would be to limit the energy budget for a given building type in a given location for all its energy needs to a specified unit of energy per unit floor area per year. The means of meeting the criterion would be the prerogative of the persons involved in the design of the building fabric, its climate control systems, lighting system, etc. The simplicity of the statement of a criterion in this form is in sharp contrast to the complexity involved in proving that a proposed building will meet a specified energy budget.

The variables involved in predicting energy consumption are numerous and difficult to quantify. They include simulation of yearly weather patterns and of equipment operation sequences of all kinds, variations of building occupancy, machinery efficiency, etc. Habits of tenants vary, so that one occupant could have significantly lower energy costs than another using the building for the same purpose. It is evident that implementation of a simple budget criterion demands the adoption of a mutually agreeable means of estimating energy consumption for proposed buildings. Many computer programs have been promulgated for energy estimation. For code purposes, a consensus is needed regarding a given program and acceptable data that will be used to determine whether or not a proposed building meets a required energy budget.

BIBLIOGRAPHY

1. J. S. Billings, "Ventilation and Heating," *Engineering Record* (1893).
2. D. B. Reid, *Illustrations of the Theory and Practice of Ventilation,* London, 1844.
3. *Thermal Environmental Conditions for Human Occupancy,* ANSI/ASHRAE Standard 55–1981, American National Standards Institute and American Society of Heating, Refrigerating, and Air-conditioning Engineers, New York and Atlanta, Ga., 1981.
4. M. Ingels, *Willis Haviland Carrier, Father of Air Conditioning,* Doubleday and Company, New York, 1952.
5. *Ventilation for Acceptable Indoor Air Quality,* ASHRAE Standard 62–1981, American Society of Heating, Refrigerating, and Air-conditioning Engineers, Atlanta, Ga., 1981.
6. *ASHRAE Standard 90A–1981,* American Society of Heating, Refrigerating, and Air-conditioning Engineers, Atlanta, Ga., 1981.
7. *ASHRAE Handbook of Fundamentals,* American Society of Heating, Refrigerating, and Air-conditioning Engineers, Atlanta, Ga., 1981, Chapt. 15.
8. *ASHRAE Handbook, Equipment,* American Society of Heating, Refrigerating, and Air-conditioning Engineers, Atlanta, Ga., 1983, Chapt. 23.
9. *Ibid.*, Chapts. 24, 25.
10. A. R. Trott, *Refrigeration and Air Conditioning,* McGraw–Hill Book Company, New York, 1981, Chapt. 2.
11. Ref. 8, Chapt. 4, Parts I and II.
12. *ASHRAE Handbook, Systems,* American Society of Heating, Refrigerating, and Air-conditioning Engineers, Atlanta, 1984, Chapt. 9.
13. Ref. 8, Chapts. 28–30.
14. F. C. McQuiston and J. D. Parker, *Heating, Ventilating, and Air Conditioning,* John Wiley & Sons, New York, 1982, Chapt. 10.
15. Ref. 12, Chapts. 3 and 11.
16. Ref. 12., Chapt. 4.
17. Ref. 12., Chapts. 5 and 15.
18. Ref. 12., Chapt. 6.
19. Ref. 12., Chapts. 13 and 16.
20. *ASHRAE Handbook, Applications,* American Society of Heating, Refrigerating, and Air-conditioning Engineers, Atlanta, 1982, Chapts. 1–7.
21. *Ibid.*, Chapts. 16 and 17.
22. Ref. 12, Chapt. 31.

See also Apartment Buildings, High-Rise; Diagnostics, Building; Envelopes, Building; Insulation, Thermal; Office Buildings; Systems Integration; Value Engineering

Bertram Y. Kinzey, Jr.
Gainesville, Florida

MEDIA CRITICISM

Meeting the pent-up demand for new buildings after World War II spurred not only a construction boom in the U.S., it sparked spirited debate in the second half of the twentieth century about the direction of change in the built environment. While much of this debate occurred in academic publications and the trade press that serves members of the construction industry, U.S. newspapers emerged as an increasingly visible forum for community discussion of design issues. Led by informed commentators who helped identify and focus critical issues, U.S. cities saw the rise of a public constituency concerned about the quality of community growth.

Newspapers, the academic press, and the trade or professional media all address the stages of the creative act that leads to architecture: idea, process, and product. However, since the audience for each differs, the particular stage being emphasized likewise differs from one to the next. Of the three, no audience has been more unpredictable or more potentially influential than the general public.

THE ACADEMIC PRESS

From the standpoint of budget, circulation, and often size, the academic press tends to be the smallest of the three types of media, yet at times it has been the most influential. The magazines, newsletters, and monographs that make up this medium participate in and help create the climate of ideas in which the science and art of architecture receive their theoretical base. At its best, the academic press defines important design issues, identifies new horizons, and paves the way for major aesthetic breakthroughs.

The academic press tends to be less visual than verbal. Content tends to theory rather than practice. Marxist dialectics, for example, are a more likely focus than more practical considerations such as cost per square foot (a professional matter) or zoning variances (a more public concern). If architects are, as is often alleged, non-readers, this would explain why practicing architects are not usually the primary audience for the academic press. The appeal of this medium to the general public is likewise limited, and the same may be said of those who pay for the architect's services—the client. The academic press is most at home within the academy itself, and exerts its strongest influence in the university design studio on student and professor alike, as opposed to the practicing architect, who must factor into the design process the economic and regulatory exigencies of the real world.

Since the academic press is not so dependent on advertising revenue as both the trade and mass media, it can be and often is the most combative of the three. But combat is waged far more around the ideologies and design theories that generate architecture than individual projects. In the pages of the University of Pennsylvania's *VIA,* for example, or *The Harvard Architecture Review,* buildings tend to be regarded as signs or symbols of a larger theory or design philosophy, which is the real object of academic scrutiny. Whereas the ideology of the trade or mass media critic is typically for the reader to infer, it is usually the banner under which academic critics write.

THE TRADE OR PROFESSIONAL PRESS

Whereas the word is the dominant vehicle for communication within the academic press, the trade press communicates through images, not only within the individual stories or features themselves, but also through the medium's many advertisements. The latter is a covert form of criticism in that advertisements inevitably carry a message as to what is and is not mainstream or fashionable.

The architectural trade press and the art directors who serve this medium recognize the power of imagery. They recognize, too, that in an era in which eyes have been trained by movies, television, and videos, they must have budgets large enough to gain access to the best imagery money can buy. Thus, since the end of World War II, a key chapter in the evolution of the trade press has been the increasing sophistication and power of photography, both in the editorial copy and the advertisements. It has been argued that these images, often created by photographers of international stature, go far beyond mere documentation, that they are a powerful advocate of a particular style or movement. To choose one well-known example, the striking photography of Ezra Stoller in the 1950s clearly had much to do with the popularity of the International style in corporate America. Often overlooked is the fact that Stoller's medium of choice was a black and white format. It is perhaps no coincidence that the reaction in the late 1970s and early 1980s against the minimalism of the International style in favor of the more colorful palette of postmodernism coincided with the perfection of a cost-effective technology for the mass production of four-color separations.

The point to be made is that any discussion of the way architectural criticism works in the latter half of the twentieth century, at least in its impact on the schools of architecture, the profession itself, and corporate decision makers, must consider the decisive impact of photojournalism. In this arena, the trade press has played a preeminent role among the other architectural media, and in conjunction with the so-called "wish books" (*Architectural Digest,* for example) and the shelter magazines (*Better Homes and Gardens,* etc.) of the mass media may have done as much to shape the look of the twentieth-century U.S. built environment as any theory, ideology, or design curriculum.

While the picturebook quality of the trade press is one of its most obvious distinguishing characteristics, there are other important traits that set it apart from the academic and mass media. Once again, audience is key: since readers are largely architects and, to a lesser extent, other members of the construction industry, the process of architecture (projects, business practice, education, and so forth) dominates. Not surprisingly, the information contained within its pages tends to be pragmatic. Information can be found on a range of professional concerns from office practice to technology. The trade press may thus be thought of and certainly advertises itself to be a practice aid for the profession, although the medium's reason for being is very much promotional as well as educational. It is the professional press that typically gives the most coverage to honors and awards programs. This is how the trade press recognizes the fact that its existence depends not only on the interest but also on the good will of its readers. It seldom engages in the sort of no-holds-barred critiques common in the academic press or even in the mass media. In the 1980s, the big three magazines of nationwide distribution serving architects are *Architecture, Architectural Record,* and *Progressive Architecture.*

All three publications share a commitment to promote and nourish the architectural profession. They sponsor or carry news about significant awards programs. All of them go farther afield than U.S. architecture to weigh the innovative or significant around the world, and are accessible at libraries and to a limited extent at newsstands where the public can overhear, as it were, what architects are saying about architecture and one another. By their inclusion of interior design sections, all three move to varying degrees toward a characteristic trait of the mass media, which treats architecture as a consumable product.

Whereas *Architecture, Architectural Record,* and *Progressive Architecture* serve a national professional audience, professional publications with a decidedly regional or local cast also exist, many of which are published by the larger AIA state societies. *Texas Architect* and *Architecture Minnesota* are two of the best known and most widely honored regional AIA publications for the quality of their content and layout. For-profit publications such as *Metropolis,* which comes out of New York City and tends to have an almost mass media orientation toward both the professional and non-professional as consumers of the latest design trends, and *Inland Architect,* based in Chicago and in format as well as content resembling the academic press, illustrate how wide a range is covered by this medium. Their availability to a national public and the public's support once again demonstrate the broad market that exists for intelligent and creative coverage of what has been called the most public of the arts.

Those related professional publications that serve disciplines that have more consumer or public policy implications (*Landscape Architecture, Interiors,* and the *ULI Journal*) are by definition more accessible to a general audience. Their contribution toward developing a demand for quality throughout the designed environment is pervasive to the degree that such publications are available to the public at newsstands and in bookstores nationally. Those that carry advertising are likely to feature products that are either directly available to the public or indirectly, like the fabrics and furnishings available at metropolitan design centers through a professional intermediary.

U.S. NEWSPAPERS AND THE MASS MEDIA

Whereas both academic and trade publications have always been in one way or another available to a well-educated public willing to go out of its way to read about architects and their work, a regular diet of timely architectural criticism in U.S. newspapers and magazines aimed at a mass audience is a relatively recent phenomenon. Whereas the academic and trade media have, for all of their diversity, an identity as well as a tradition, architectural criticism in the mass media almost defies description, much less analysis. But it is distinguished by its emphasis on the user or consumer of architecture. Its appearance in the news media tends to dictate a point of view that emphasizes current events as opposed to the past or distant future. Architecture, therefore, is typically approached from the standpoint of its direct effect on the public. *Philadelphia Inquirer* critic Tom Hine illustrates the point being made through an analogy: a newspaper column on dental hygiene would not be called "Dentistry," but "Your Teeth"; similarly, Hine argues, a column on architecture directed at a mass audience would not be called "Architecture"; it would be called, as it is in the *Inquirer,* "Surroundings."

Montgomery Schuyler's critique in the *New York World* of a Fifth Avenue synagogue shows that architectural criticism in U.S. newspapers goes at least as far back as 1868 (1). In the years following the Civil War, when the U.S. experienced a great building boom and new building technologies as well as new design aesthetics were transforming the look of the nation's older cities, occasional critiques appeared in newspapers and magazines, particularly when an important civic or national project was at issue, such as the design of New York's Central Park or the recommitment in the early years of the twentieth century to L'Enfant's plan for Washington, D.C. The clear assumption by these pioneering writers was that public projects paid for and intended to serve the entire community were a legitimate subject for community understanding if not debate.

The wide dissemination in the nineteenth century of the Englishman John Ruskin's writings on architecture, and in the twentieth of the more popular work of the American Lewis Mumford (available in the 1930s to *New Yorker* readers), played an important role in accelerating the development of a mass audience for architectural criticism. The rise of an educated public interested in and participating increasingly in critical discussions was helped greatly by the growing visual sophistication of trade publications. Non-professionals who were fascinated by architects, their work, and the rapid succession of various period revivals struggling for stylistic supremacy in the nineteenth and twentieth centuries had access to these publications either through subscription or through the growing network of public libraries. Venerable women's magazines like *Ladies' Home Journal* developed a design vocabulary for the general public, which was used to discuss residential design and landscaping, as well as the larger issues of the City Beautiful movement. Photography made these publications uniquely effective communicators of the latest fashions in residential design.

By the second half of the twentieth century, after the construction hiatus imposed first by the Depression and then by World War II, hardly a single U.S. city of any size as well as the surrounding countryside escaped the changes wrought by the unprecedented postwar expansion of the economy and the newfound mobility of most segments of the population. The commitment by planners and public officials to shelter a new society and the clearly visible changes transforming what had once been familiar provided the impetus for a growing public awareness of the designed environment. Mass global communication and a rise in the number of college graduates transformed this awareness into an expanded audience for architectural criticism.

Surprisingly, however, the first newspaper columns that scrutinized in a critical way how U.S. communities were changing did not appear in the largest metropolitan areas on either coast. Two inland cities, Louisville, Kentucky, and St. Louis, Missouri, led the way. In 1949 Grady Clay assumed editorial control of the Sunday real estate section of the *Louisville Courier* and transformed that department from the then typical bulletin board style of real estate reporting to a broad critical interpretation of the changing urban environment. Clay's influence extended beyond Louisville when his byline began to appear regularly in the pages of *The New York Times, House Beautiful,* and *Fortune,* and when he became editor of *Landscape Architecture Quarterly,* the professional publication of The American Society of Landscape Architects. In St. Louis, George McCue became the art and urban design critic when in 1956 the *St. Louis Post-Dispatch* created a Sunday Music and Arts page. In this position, which he held for two decades, McCue approached the streets, parks, buildings, and monuments of St. Louis as objects for critical comment and public discussion. Together, Clay and McCue demonstrated that there was a mass audience in the U.S. heartland for insightful and well-written commentary about the relationship between design and a community's quality of life.

In 1961 there appeared first in Washington and then in New York and San Francisco other reporters whose chief responsibility was, like that of Clay and McCue, to write regular columns about architecture and urban design for their papers: Wolf Von Eckardt for *The Washington Post,* Ada Louise Huxtable for *The New York Times,* and Allan Temko for *The San Francisco Chronicle.* In response to the pioneering efforts of first Clay and McCue, and then Von Eckardt, Huxtable, and Temko, as well as well-respected commentators such as Peter Blake (*God's Own Junkyard*) and Mumford, The American Institute of Architects called a conference of 30 reporters from large dailies to encourage U.S. newspapers to scrutinize urban-renewal plans and other design issues so that the forces transforming U.S. communities would be more accessible to public comment and discussion.

By the late 1980s, the number of U.S. reporters whose time was spent largely or even totally writing about architecture, urban design, or design in general had grown to between 25 and 30 (2). The national syndication of many of these columns has carried the phenomenon of architectural criticism into communities that would otherwise have no other media forum for this type of intellectual inquiry. That architectural criticism in the mass media had become a recognized and respected contribution to journalism by the last decades of the twentieth century was demonstrated when *New York Times* critic Ada Louise Huxtable (1970), Paul Gapp of the *Chicago Tribune* (1981), and Paul Goldberger, again of the *Times* (1984), were awarded Pulitzer Prizes for their work. In the 1980s both *Time* magazine and *Newsweek* inaugurated departments entitled "Design," which provided national and world coverage of trends, events, and personalities shaping the built environment.

During this time, there also appeared a growing number of freelance writers whose reputations for clear and informed writing about architecture earned them bylines in a wide range of publications from airline magazines to prestigious periodicals such as *Atlantic* and *The New Yorker,* which carries a column, "Skyline," written by Brendan Gill. The rise of influential regional magazines in the 1970s and 1980s such as *Southern Living* and *New York Magazine* provided a public forum for increased scrutiny of regional design.

If the legitimacy of a phenomenon in U.S. society is finally measured by its being the subject of academic conferences and seminars, architectural criticism in the mass media has arrived in the 1980s. In 1981, the national AIA funded the first of a series of media advisory committees, whose first members included Douglas Davis (*Newsweek*), Paul Gapp (*Chicago Tribune*), John Dreyfuss (*Los Angeles Times*), and Robert Campbell (*Boston Globe*). Its charge was to make recommendations to the AIA as to how the Institute could be a resource to the media in developing stories about architecture and architects. In 1985, Virginia Polytechnic Institute sponsored a conference on "The Architectural Press: Forming an Architectural Culture" at its Alexandria, Virginia, Center for Architecture and Urban Studies (3). The following year, at its national convention in San Antonio, Texas, the AIA's Committee on Design organized a program titled "Meet the Press. American Architectural Journalism: Criticism and Critical Independence," which, to quote the committee's promotional material, featured "five architectural critics from prominent daily newspapers and the editors of the three leading architectural magazines" (4). Attendees and invited guests were to consider such questions as: "How do critics and journalists select their subjects?" "What is the process of writing a critical piece?" and "What purpose does architectural criticism serve?" *Boston Globe* critic Robert Campbell answered the latter question by saying: "One of the major purposes of art and architectural critics in our society is to create heroes and monuments, to make out of trivial gestures such as a work of art or architecture, something monumental in the contemporary sense of having a presence in the media culture in which we live" (5).

Yet despite individual recognition, those reporters who write critically about architecture do not, by and large, have the type of recognition among editors and publishers enjoyed by their colleagues in real estate or home furnishings. This is one reason why it is difficult to identify with any certitude the number of architectural writers in the mass media at any one time. Some of those who write about architecture wear several hats, including music, home furnishings, and even religion. Editors tend to see their papers as a predictable aggregate of distinct sections that must be filled each day with content appropriate to these sections: hard news, editorial, sports, business, real estate, and so forth. Each has its own department with its own staff. Despite its obvious economic and policy implications, architecture is usually segregated in the arts or style sections. While less rigidly structured, magazines are laid out in similar fashion, as a quick glance at the table of contents of *Time* or *House Beautiful* makes clear.

Finding the right slot for architectural criticism is not easy. The scope and impact of architecture cut across the business, editorial, hard news, real estate, and so-called lifestyle pages. Indeed, the scope of the subject is so large that a number of newspapers, such as *The New York Times, The Washington Post,* and *The Los Angeles Times,* now employ the services of several reporters who have divided the subject among themselves. Unlike film, television, dance, or even music, architecture is the one art form that can be ignored but not escaped. Yet more often than not criticism of architecture and the related issues of urban design are exiled to what editors call the back of the book.

Complicating the editor's decision where to place the architectural reporter/critic is the economic impact of design decisions. Given the millions of dollars involved in major projects, the jobs generated by such projects, and the prestige or self-image of the community, how much latitude does an editor give the reporter to go beyond the quantitative to the qualitative issues of any particular construction project? Does an editor risk alienating the business community not to mention important elements of the general public by having on his or her staff a reporter whose column calls into question an expressway, a mass transit system, a shopping center, or sports complex? This is not an idle question, considering that during the building boom of the 1970s and early 1980s, when, as *New York Times* architecture writer Paul Goldberger argued, Houston was defining the look of U.S. skylines, neither of the two major Houston dailies committed a full-time reporter or assigned a regular column to what was by all accounts one of that city's most significant ongoing stories.

That there are risks was made clear in 1985, when New York developer Donald Trump sued the *Chicago Tribune* for damages allegedly brought on by a negative critique that derided a proposal to build the world's tallest building on Manhattan's West Side (6). Although the suit ultimately failed (at no small cost to the *Tribune*), it revealed just how nervously some developers as well as public officials take the prospect of the potential impact of a mass public forum for architectural criticism.

Major architectural critics in both magazines and newspapers have resisted being tied to reporting about architecture as fashion, yet many acknowledge strong editorial pressure to do so. That pressure is compounded by those architects who show a keen media sensibility and develop intellectual or aesthetic positions, not to mention personas, that are carefully calculated to have the maximum public impact. Whether the movement is the Russian constructivism of the 1920s or the deconstructivist architecture of the 1980s, their proponents know the value of staged scandal and passionate controversy in the media.

Writing about architecture in the mass media courts a related trait of feature writing in the 1980s—the cult of personality. Again, a number of architects are eager to oblige a public taste for the portrait of the architect as super star (7). Stardom can be a lucrative marketing tool for the architect, especially for those members of the profession who have developed a wide range of consumer products from fabrics to teakettles. The very accessibility of such products to a public that often feels the architect's services are beyond their financial grasp ensures wide media coverage. Those readers who are interested in consuming personalities as much as high-priced "designer" products can find both well covered in the pages of such publications as *USA Today, People, Interview,* or *Vanity Fair*.

There is also the question of purpose or intent. If some academic writers seem deliberately to aim for a scholarly jargon accessible to initiates alone, rendering even the most transparently obvious painfully complex, newspaper reporters must make their subject understandable to an audience that, unlike the readers of the academic and trade press, has little or no background in the subject under discussion.

There is a further difference that distinguishes the architectural reporter from his or her colleagues in the mass media. Movie critics, for example, write for a public looking for advice on how to spend time and money. An enthusiastic review means a sold-out house; a negative commentary can spell disaster at the box office. Reporters who choose architecture and urban design for their subject operate under different assumptions and have the potential to affect public policy. To begin with, unless the writer is covering an architectural exhibition or working for a consumer-oriented publication that specifically showcases personalities (e.g., *People* or *Interview*), the architectural or urban design critic is not dealing with an ephemeral event, which is available to the public for a limited time only. A building is not likely to close or be avoided as a consequence of bad press, although increasingly marketing professionals are quoting from favorable reviews of their clients' projects as a way of adding prestige and luring potential tenants.

Architectural critics can, however, affect the outcome of proposed projects. Negative criticism in *The New York Times* or *The Washington Post,* for example, can and has been instrumental in halting or significantly modifying projects on the drawing board whose impact ranges in scale from a threatened early twentieth-century theater to massive highway construction schemes. The restaurant or movie critic, by contrast, is not likely to have any effect whatsoever on a project still in the planning stage.

The fact that architectural criticism in the mass media appeals directly to the public suggests a characteristic that further distinguishes this individual from writers in the academic and architectural trade press: he or she serves as a mediator between the public interest and that complex interplay of economic, commercial, and aesthetic forces that shapes the environment. Architectural criticism in the mass media may therefore be seen as yet another manifestation of the contemporary consumer movement that seeks to ensure a voice for the public in determining the quality of their lives. The rise of the consumer movement in the 1960s and the simultaneous appearance of architectural critics in the newspapers of New York, Washington, and San Francisco, with their large well-educated, upscale audiences, may not be unrelated phenomena. If so, it would follow that at its most effective, architectural criticism in the mass media is ultimately political in its consequences. It helps the public take charge of its own destiny, whether it be the mandating of height and density limitations (as enacted in San Francisco in 1985), the decision to exceed a previously agreed-upon height limitation (Philadelphia, 1986), or the scuttling of a vast highway scheme in favor of regional mass transit (as was the outcome of a fiercely fought battle in the Washington D.C. metropolitan area in the 1960s). In all three instances, the media played a key role in providing a forum for community debate while at the same time shaping and informing that debate. And in all three instances, the architectural writers of the *San Francisco Chronicle,* the *Philadelphia Inquirer,* and the *Washington Post* played no small role in the outcome through their persuasive critiques.

No doubt architects, developers, chambers of commerce, public officials, and sometimes editors would prefer the architectural critic to be an uncritical advocate of new construction. The architectural critic who acts as a kind of design ombudsman for the public can be a nuisance if not an expensive threat. In the spring of 1986, architect Robert A. M. Stern, the creater and host of the eight-part public television series "Pride of Place," came to Charlotte, North Carolina, and in an interview in the *Charlotte*

Observer with local critic Richard Maschal pronounced the "new" Charlotte inferior to the old (8). The ensuing citizen uproar in both the printed and electronic media suggested that boom towns like Charlotte do not take urban design reviews lightly. The Charlotte episode, besides revealing that the public can be ill-prepared for commentary that falls short of unmitigated promotion, also demonstrated the importance of editorial support for the reporter prepared to touch sensitive community nerves.

The importance of supportive editors and publishers cannot be stressed enough. It is an issue as well as a concern uniquely urgent for the mass media. Whereas critics in the academic and trade media must constantly demonstrate their intellectual and professional credentials, newspaper reporters must justify the craft itself. Former *Washington Post* and *Time* magazine architecture critic Wolf Von Eckardt attributes this state of affairs to the inability of editors and publishers as a group to understand the importance of urban design issues for an increasing number of the general public: "The only people who don't see the growing sophistication of the American public are newspaper and magazine editors. They still only want to cover politics and football. We're having a cultural revolution in this country and editors generally ignore it. If someone threw a rotten orange at the mayor while he visited South Street Seaport (New York City), there would be a big story about who threw the orange, where it hit the mayor exactly, when had other mayors been hit by oranges, why he didn't use a banana—and not a word about South Street Seaport and what it does to the city. Editors have tunnel vision" (9). Von Eckardt's assessment suggests that for the U.S. mass media it is not really the "new" that is newsworthy, but what is broadly accepted as newsworthy that wins space and comment. If this is so, it would explain why, despite debate over such design issues as historic preservation, land use, and infrastructure, there is not more architectural criticism in the mass media and why the criticism that does exist tends to be placed in the back pages. An interesting contrast is provided by the growing number of community or neighborhood weeklies that place writing about the environment, as well as the arts, up toward the front and often as lead stories.

The exceptions to the above argue that it is editorial support as much as the intrinsic newsworthiness of the subject itself which ensures a place for architectural criticism in U.S. newspapers and magazines. *Time* magnate Henry Luce's fascination with architecture not only guaranteed the publication in the decades after World War II of the widely influential although not too profitable trade publication, *Architectural Forum,* but also prompted *Time* cover stories that featured prominent designers from Frank Lloyd Wright to Minoru Yamasaki. No other national magazine has accorded architects a similar honor, including the trade press, which in fact never features an architect on their covers. The architectural critic of the *Tucson Citizen,* Larry Cheek, makes the same point when he says: "The most important thing for an architecture critic is 100 percent support from the publisher." He goes on to add that such support is not only necessary for visibility, but also for protection "because the clients for architecture are invariably wealthy and powerful people" (10). *Dallas Morning News* critic David Dillon has said: "I've never been told to avoid offending someone or had a story killed. But it is a hazard of the trade: architecture critics are in a very political, powerful position, and a newspaper has to know what it's getting into when it hires a critic. There are inevitably going to be pressures created from interested parties, and it can cost people a lot of money" (11).

It is not just the developer or public official who may be made uneasy by broad public dissemination of architectural critiques. Art and architecture critic for the *Kansas City Star,* Donald Hoffmann, recalls that when in the early 1960s he began to write architecture pieces for the *Star,* representatives from the local AIA chapter told his editors they would not support a local architectural column if it were critical of their work. In the late 1970s, the *Star* was sold to an owner who, according to Hoffmann, had no ties to the city's business establishment. Hoffmann was at last free, in his own words, "to get away with holy murder" (12).

The editorial decision to locate architectural criticism in the company of film and restaurant reviews opens the door not only to a view of architecture as a consumable product, but also an expectation that the writer is a performer. Whereas straight news reporters are often credible to the degree that they are able to transcend or mask their opinions, the critic is often encouraged to be colorful and highly subjective. Architectural criticism in the pages of the *San Francisco Chronicle,* the *Village Voice,* and magazines like *New York* or *Washingtonian* is distinguished to no small extent for its urbane iconoclastic wit as well as its critical insight. Readers may love or hate the persona that meets them in such columns, but few can resist the urge to discover who or what is being sent up. The writers of these columns would be quick to make the obvious point that their performance does compel what might otherwise be an indifferent reader to think about architects and architecture.

It has also been suggested that the rhetorical approach of an architectural critic is not only a consequence of that writer's personality and the direction of management, but is also subtly influenced by site and audience. Philadelphia *Inquirer* critic Tom Hine directly addresses this issue (13):

> There is a saying in journalism that journalists reflect the people they cover, so the guy who covers the police station dresses like a cop and talks like a cop, and the fellow who covers the state legislature starts to dress like a state legislator. Well, I am a fairly decent mirror of the Philadelphia architect—kind of rumpled and thoughtful and not too aggressive, and very nice.

The clear implication is that in another context of different subjects and audience, the critic will develop, somewhat chameleon-like, the voice of his or her locale.

THE FUTURE OF ARCHITECTURAL CRITICISM IN THE MASS MEDIA

It has become a commonplace to say, along with Herbert Muschamp, that the U.S. has witnessed a "dramatic surge of popular interest in architecture and design" (14). Writing in *Metropolis,* David Dillon observes: "The reason I was hired was not that the editors (of the *Dallas Morning News*) have any compelling interest in architecture or art. Rather, they recognized that architecture is one of the biggest ongoing stories" (11).

One consequence of the broad exposure of architecture in the media has been the rise of a profitable new industry that can boast a wide line of money-making products ranging from Tom Wolfe's best seller *From Bauhaus to Our House* (1982), which cleverly tapped the reaction against modernism, to a growing line of expensive boutique consumables from postmodern teapots to the truncated classical columns that are directly attributable to the architect's emerging status. The deepening public interest in interior and exterior design has also provided something of a livelihood to the communicators, reporters, and freelance writers who cater to this need in wish books and shelter magazines such as *HG* and *Architectural Digest.*

Critics themselves can become discouraged over what they perceive is their lack of influence on the process that shapes the built environment (15):

> Public criticism has little effect. We're in a discouraging atmosphere, where real estate is king, the developer a decision maker of incredible power, and government an expediter, not regulator. Too many wrongheaded projects are unchanged, immovable, and unstoppable.

Former *New York Post* architecture critic Roberta Brandes Gratz lays at least part of the blame at the critic's feet (15):

> Critics could have a lot more impact with a larger dose of investigative journalism. There's not enough skeptical reporting or follow-up, and there's too much concern about the establishment's reaction. Most criticism is a one-time review.

Developers, public officials, architects, and to a lesser extent business writers take the potential if not the actual influence of the critic seriously—not the critic in the academic or even the trade press, but those who write in the mass media, for the simple reason that the stakes are much higher and the potential consequences far greater. If the twin engines that drive U.S. society are money and votes, it is clear that architectural critics in the mass media have their fingers on both pulses in a way quite unlike the dance reviewer or film critic. A newspaper or magazine that carries an architectural column accessible to the general public provides that public with a forum and a focus to develop a constituency which, if large enough, can delay, alter, or even stop a multimillion dollar project. Legal action against *Chicago Tribune* critic Paul Gapp serves notice on editors and their publishers that there may be a critical line too expensive for their reporters to cross. There are as yet no documented cases where such a line has in fact been drawn, but the chilling effect can manifest itself in many other ways ranging from the space and placement of the critic's commentary to deciding whether or not to cover a controversial design issue in the first place. If lively construction markets such as New York City, Chicago, and Washington, D.C., become nervous over bad press, those communities eager to lure new investment into their tax districts can be expected to be wary at least over the prospect of a design watchdog who, moreover, may have a social agenda.

On the other hand, the concern of developers, the local business community, and public officials cannot be dismissed out of hand as being basely self-serving; the critic and the public can be wrong. The most casual research into library archives can uncover devastating critiques of acknowledged masterworks such as the Chrysler Building and Rockefeller Center, as well as lavish praise of urban renewal and subsidized housing schemes that today are textbook cases of misguided design and planning. This no doubt is one explanation for James Marston Fitch's impatience with more public participation in the design process: "Their critical interventions are counterproductive because of their fundamentally superficial understanding of the environmental physics of architecture" (16).

Yet neither the charge that architectural criticism in the mass media is ineffective nor the argument that it is bound to be wrong-headed can obscure the fact that communities such as San Francisco, Dallas, Miami, Philadelphia, and Boston, which have a public forum for critical public comment, have seen those forums become instrumental in developing an informed and, of equal importance, an active constituency for a broader involvement of the community in managing change. The newspaper reporter can be an effective ally not only of the public, but also of the architect who in the final analysis has much less power than America's real estate and banking interests in shaping U.S. towns and cities. They can help create a climate or culture for informed debate about a community's or even the nation's future. They can articulate a social agenda on matters ranging from affordable housing to open space that can be mandated formally by elected public officials or informally by the weight of public opinion. As *New York Times* critic Paul Goldberger has said (17):

> Ada Louise Huxtable, my predecessor in this position, has been very committed to historic preservation, and her influence has helped make that movement as important as it is today and has become in this country. She didn't create it; she couldn't have created it alone, but on the other hand, it probably wouldn't have happened in quite that way without her prestige and influence behind it.

There is no lack of evidence to demonstrate that the public as well as the profession of architecture has been well served by the men and women in the mass media who have taken as their subject the how, what, and why of the U.S. built environment. It can be argued that they, more than their colleagues in the academic and trade media, have had a visible impact on setting the social and political agendas that are shaping the environment, even though they typically have far less academic training in the subject than those who write for scholarly journals and the professional press. Indeed, most architectural writers in the mass media have not come to their profession directly, but by way of a number of oblique routes ranging from arts and entertainment reporters and real estate writers to the architectural profession itself.

If architectural criticism in the mass media continues to grow and if critics successfully avoid becoming preoccupied with personalities and the fashions of a moneyed elite, the potential for developing within the general public a sense of ownership and responsibility for their communities will increase. That increase will be amplified by a continued growth of coverage in the electronic media, which has already seen two major series, "Pride of Place" and "America By Design," that have demonstrated a broad-based national interest in an educated analysis of what is after all a visual medium.

The rising visibility and effectiveness of a media forum for architectural criticism is likely to be accompanied by increased conflict between the critic and local economic interests. Developers as well as community leaders may try to frame debates about growth or change as conflicts between the privileged few and economic benefits for the entire community. This has already occurred in the business press as well as in the council chambers of city hall. In addition, increased public participation does have the potential to water down design integrity and complicate the already complex design process by politicizing it. The controversy in Washington over the design of a national memorial for the veterans of the Viet Nam War is an extreme example of how abrasive the process can be when the public and its representatives are no longer passive spectators but featured players.

However, there may not be any choice. As *Boston Globe* critic Robert Campbell has said: ". . . people have a terrible yearning for buildings that can create a sense of being together again in a community, something lost in the dispersion of our population after World War II" (18). If the evolution of the United States has been the story of the struggle for political enfranchisement, there now seems to be a growing concern not only over what goes on in city hall, but what city hall looks like and how it fits into a well designed, humane context. However difficult it has been to reach a political consensus, evolving a design consensus that heals and nurtures the community is bound to be far more difficult since the ground rules remain to be discovered and accepted by decision makers.

The connection between effective government and citizen involvement was one of western culture's greatest contributions to the growth of civilization; a similar insight concerning the quality of life of U.S. communities may be evolving with architectural writers in the mass media taking a strategic leadership role.

BIBLIOGRAPHY

1. J. Temple, unpublished paper, Northwestern University, Evanston, Ill., July 1984, p. 1.
2. *The Observer Observed,* The American Institute of Architects, Washington, D.C., published annually.
3. *The Architectural Press: Forming an Architectural Culture,* Virginia Polytechnic Institute, Center for Architecture and Urban Studies, Alexandria, Va., Nov. 15–17, 1985.
4. "Meet the Press. American Architectural Journalism: Criticism and Critical Independence," *Proceedings of the Annual Convention of the American Institute of Architects,* San Antonio, Texas, 1986.
5. *Ibid.,* p. 2, appendix B.
6. N. Hentoff, "Citizen Trump," *The Washington Post,* editorial page (Oct. 20, 1985).
7. *Time,* cover (Jan. 8, 1979).
8. *Charlotte Observer,* Sec. 6B, 1 (May 17, 1986).
9. *Metropolis,* 39 (Nov. 1985).
10. Ref. 1, p. 8.
11. Ref. 9, p. 39.
12. Ref. 1, pp. 6–7.
13. T. Hine, "Philadelphia Architect, Philadelphia Chapter/AIA," *Philadelphia Chapter/AIA Newsletter,* 5 (Dec. 1985–Jan. 1986).
14. H. Muschamp, *Interiors,* 17 (Mar. 1986).
15. Ref. 9, p. 41.
16. Ref. 9, p. 28.
17. K. Dietsch, *Crit/ASJ,* 16 (Spring 1981).
18. G. Clack, *Cultural Post,* 33 (Jan.–Feb. 1981).

See also Architectural Press, U.S.; Criticism, Architectural; Literature of Architecture

Raymond P. Rhinehart
The American Architectural Foundation
Washington, D.C.

MEDIATION IN ARCHITECTURAL AND CONSTRUCTION DISPUTES

This article outlines the basic sources of conflict in the construction industry and the manner in which disputes arise. It presents a general overview of applications of mediation and a comparison with other standard means of resolving disputes. It then discusses in greater detail how mediation functions, its applications to the construction industry, advantages and disadvantages, and suggestions for further developing mediation as a tool for the efficient and effective resolution of construction disputes.

The design process and the construction of buildings are by nature prone to dispute. The parties involved are multiple and their work is highly interdependent, yet they have little control over each other's performance. Large sums of money are at stake. The highly complex construction documents are imprecise at best, and are usually assembled under the pressure of time and budget constraints. The documents' complexity hinders their users from anticipating such problems. Furthermore, the standards of the industry are in many respects unclear and may vary from place to place. What constitutes an acceptable standard of performance is often difficult to write into a contract, and compliance may be equally difficult to ascertain. The design process continues through construction as unanticipated situations always arise; many decisions are made on the site, too often with no written record, so that the job as actually performed varies to some degree from the performance contracted for.

The same factors which give rise to construction disputes make them difficult to resolve. Even the simplest construction project involves multiple parties who may or may not be in direct contractual relations with each other. In addition to the owner, architect, and contractor, there are subcontractors and material and equipment suppliers. The architect has employees and consultants, including engineers and cost estimators. Nonparties to the construction agreement, including lenders and other holders of security interests, and tenants of preleased commercial buildings, also may have interests in the project and, consequently, in any disputes which may arise. Workers' interests are often represented by trade unions. The interests of these parties often conflict. The owner is concerned with budget, time, and quality of the product. Design professionals and contractors wish to make a profit on their services while performing satisfactory work. The contractor's interest in making a profit on his or her work may conflict with the owner's need to stay on budget when unexpected difficulties arise in construction. Design professionals are often caught between their role as the agent of the owner, and their role as an impartial decision maker during construction.

The construction contract itself is composed of numerous documents, not one of which binds all of the participants or fully describes the requirements of the project. The owner contracts separately with the architect and contractor who, in turn, enter into independent agreements with their consultants and subcontractors. The contract documents typically include not only written agreements but also working drawings, specifications, addenda, field clarifications, shop drawings, bid advertisements, and any number of professional service agreements. Increasingly complex and possibly conflicting government codes may also be referred to explicitly or implicitly.

The factual basis of a construction dispute is likely to be similarly complex. The work of both design professionals and contractors requires technical expertise; thus, anyone attempting to understand or resolve a dispute must also be schooled in the facts. Because delays of projects are costly, any dispute which arises is exacerbated by the time required to resolve it.

These complexities and conflicts have become even more exaggerated in recent years. Competitive bidding rewards the low bidder, who may later feel obliged to supplement his or her fees with change orders. The emphasis of price over quality may lead to substandard workmanship and result in defects. Contractors under fixed-price contracts are vulnerable to market fluctuations: changes in interest rates and inflation can wreak havoc with projections. In an uncertain economy, contractors may attempt to recoup their losses through change orders or with later claims for delay damages.

New ways of doing business, largely intended to reduce costs to institutional owners, have also exposed design professionals and builders to greater liability. In "design-build," the owner contracts with a single entity rather than separately with the architect and the contractor. The design–build entity (either a joint venture or a single firm providing both design and construction services) delivers a completed project to the owner. This alters the traditional arrangement, where the owner is involved in the project from beginning to end. The architect and contractor are also in a relationship; no longer separate entities, they do not act as checks on each other. "Fast-track" construction, often combined with design–build, allows design and construction to be performed simultaneously; the building is designed in phases, with each phase being constructed while the next is being designed. While this method can save time, it also entails greater cost, due to problems of coordination. Both design–build and fast-tracking present serious problems of quality control.

A general trend toward increased expectations on the part of consumers of all kinds of products and services has affected the design profession and construction industry. Higher expectations are more frequently disappointed; when the gap between expectations and reality is too wide, legal claims may follow. In addition, design professionals and contractors are under greater pressure of both time and money. Such pressure may adversely affect the quality of the work, further opening the way for claims. Changes in substantive law, including the development of product liability and its extension to providers of services, and the doctrine of implied warranties, have had the effect of increasing the liability of all professionals associated with the construction industry. Procedural law has also facilitated access to courts, especially where, as in construction, multiple parties are involved. The development of professional liability insurance, itself a result of expanded liability, has made awards more collectible, making the parties insured more ready targets for claims. A less cohesive society has begun looking more to external means of dealing with controversy (i.e., courts of law), than using personal and informal approaches.

ADVERSARIAL APPROACHES: LITIGATION AND ARBITRATION

Litigation and arbitration, the conventional means of resolving disputes, have often proved less than satisfactory in dealing with problems arising out of the construction process. This is due in part to limitations inherent in these procedures and, in part, to the particular types of problems encountered in construction disputes.

Litigation is usually the most costly and time-consuming of the solutions to construction disputes. Both state and federal courts have in recent years had increasing difficulty in keeping up with an ever-growing caseload; several years may elapse between the time a problem arises and its resolution in court. Discovery, the means by which each side assembles the documents and information on which it bases its case, can be used as an expensive tactic of abuse and delay. Attorneys' fees and court costs, as well as diversion of human resources from more productive uses, can make the expense of litigation crippling even to the nominal winner of a lawsuit. Litigation can rarely be limited to its original scope: once a party makes a claim, the suit will typically expand to include counterclaims and cross-claims among all the parties, each trying to ensure that it has the greatest possible chance of recovery or of defense.

The complex and specialized nature of the facts in construction and architectural disputes also limit the courtroom's effectiveness in resolving them. The parties' attorneys, whose decisions greatly influence the course of litigation, often lack the training to understand the technical facts and the issues involved. This may lead not only to an inefficient prosecution or defense, but also to the filing of nonmeritorious claims. The judge and, in some cases, the jury, to whom the attorneys must present the case, are also usually untrained in design and construction. Both judge and jury must be "educated" in complex facts; the jury must also learn the applicable law. This places a heavy burden on the litigants in presenting their case. They must establish the significance of the contract documents, which are in a specialized language readily understood only by those trained in its conventions. They must establish complex and technical facts, as well as their significance to the issues in question. Perhaps the most difficult task for litigants is to establish the standards of the industry which, ultimately, are the deciding factor in allocating responsibility for construction defects, delays, and cost overruns. This generally requires expert witnesses, often leading to a "battle of the experts." Lack of expertise may result in inequitable judgments as well as inefficiency.

Arbitration, both compulsory (by statute) and consensual (by agreement) is now generally recognized as a valid alternative to litigation in the courts. The construction industry has accepted arbitration as its primary forum since 1966. The American Institute of Architects and the Engineers Joint Contract Documents Committee (representing the three major U.S. engineering societies) provide in their standard contracts for arbitration as a first forum for disputes arising out of construction projects. Arbitration is preferred to litigation by these professional societies because the setting is more informal, the technical rules of evidence and fact finding are relaxed, and the arbitrator is likely to have a more specialized knowledge of construction procedures and practices. Arbitration, however, shares many of the drawbacks of litigation. It can be expensive: filing fees for commencing arbitration can be quite costly, indeed more so than the cost of initiating litigation. While not usually as time consuming as litigation, arbitration may be protracted if the issues are technically complex. As in litigation, the parties are in adversarial positions, which structurally encourages them to polarize their positions and often rewards delay rather than expedited solutions.

In both litigation and arbitration, many months can elapse between the first occurrence of the problem and its resolution, making it more difficult to establish the factual basis of the claim. Some contend that arbitration is itself becoming so technical as to be merely a modified form of litigation. The number of cases submitted to arbitration is approaching current capacity. Between 1970 and 1980, the number of construction claims submitted to the American Arbitration Society increased 181% (1).

Arbitration also has its own disadvantages. It does not provide for discovery, the process by which the parties assemble the factual materials on which they base their case, including inspection of opposing parties' documents and depositions of witnesses. Unless the parties agree to discovery or it is required by the arbitrator, the parties may be forced to conduct the case without an adequate factual base. Costs may be increased because the presentation of evidence is often not limited. Arbitration also does not provide, as does litigation, for the joinder of other concerned parties in a single proceeding. Thus, the parties risk the added costs and inconsistent results of multiple proceedings. The award in arbitration, as in litigation, is final, but the scope of judicial review is far more limited. Erroneous determinations of fact or law, or clearly inequitable awards, are not subject to appeal. Insurers may not accept arbitration as establishing a party's legal liability; in some jurisdictions, insurers may successfully claim that arbitration violates a policy and, therefore, voids coverage.

MEDIATION

While litigation and arbitration will remain a central means of resolving disputes, the need for alternatives to these traditional approaches is widely recognized. Former Chief Justice Warren E. Burger stated in 1982: "We must now use the inventiveness, the ingenuity, and the resourcefulness that have long characterized the American business and legal community to shape new tools. . . . We need to consider moving some cases from the adversary system to administrative processes . . . or to mediation" (1).

While they are not appropriate under all circumstances, mediation and mediation-related processes are an important addition to the choices available to individuals and businesses seeking the most effective means of resolving disputes arising out of construction projects. Mediation is a voluntary process, whereby a neutral third party aids the disputants in seeking a resolution to their conflict. Mediation thus differs from adversary proceedings in two major respects: the parties participate by choice rather than duress, and the third party, the mediator, is not empowered to impose a resolution on them.

Mediation is also to be distinguished from negotiation and settlement of legal claims. In negotiation, a common means of resolving conflicts in design and construction, the parties attempt to solve their own differences without the aid of a neutral third party. Mediation is like settlement in that it may be a reaction to a pending lawsuit and can result in an agreement which ends the suit but, whereas settlement is conducted by the parties' representatives either alone or in conjunction with a judge, mediation employs a third party whose sole concern is to assist the parties themselves in reaching an agreement.

The mediator's role is to encourage communication among the parties, assist them in identifying areas of agreement as well as disagreement, and then work to bring the parties to a mutually acceptable solution. Unlike adversary procedures, in which the judge remains aloof from the parties' agreements before rendering a verdict, the mediator may take an active role in evaluating facts and contentions and proposing solutions. The disputants also take a more active role in mediation than in adversary proceedings; rather than relinquish the process to attorneys and accept a judgment rendered by a judge, jury, or arbitrator, they are free to decide whether or not to agree to a proposal, and may be directly involved in the presentation of facts and arguments at the mediation sessions. Since mediation is entirely voluntary, the participants may object to any aspect of the proceedings, and may terminate them at any time.

While still far from being a common practice in the construction industry, mediation is a long-standing means of reconciling differences. Forms of mediation are still the preferred method of resolving disputes in many cultures. In the tribal moot, which is common to many African cultures, village elders are routinely called upon to hear disputes, propose solutions, and induce the disputants to agree to them. While the disputants are not bound by the results, social pressure aids in ensuring compliance. In societies where the official legal system is perceived as inadequate or is felt not to reflect the mores of the community, mediation often coexists with formal courts. This is the case in more remote areas of modern countries such as Mexico, and in religious subcultures, exemplified in this country by the Puritans, Quakers, and Mormons, and historically by the Jews in ancient Rome. In the People's Republic of China, about 80% of civil disputes are currently resolved by mediation, which draws on traditional cultural precepts of concern for the harmony of society over individual rights.

Members of the construction industry may be most familiar with the use of mediation in the labor field where, in the form of collective bargaining, it has been a central means of resolving disputes for many years. Family and community disputes are often diverted from the courts to mediation, which can frequently address aspects of such problems which adversary proceedings cannot. As of 1982, about 200 programs in the United States provided for mediation of domestic disputes, notably divorce and custody, landlord–tenant problems, and minor criminal charges. Mediation of environmental disputes and medical malpractice claims is also being tested. State legislative and administrative practices relative to mediation vary widely, with about one-half employing regular mediators of some kind. The 1980s have seen the beginning of a more widespread use of mediation in commercial and construction matters. The American Arbitration Association established Mediation Rules for the Construction Industry in 1980, and began training mediators in the same year.

Mediation presents several distinct advantages over adversary proceedings. It is usually quite rapid: in some cases the process can be complete within a few days or even hours. It is thus particularly attractive in construction, where maintaining the contract schedule is a primary concern. While adversary procedures by their nature often lead to a focus on minutiae, mediation is more likely to follow general principles of fairness, regardless of their technical legal validity. Because of its concern with reconciliation rather than fault, there may be less need to trace causal connections which may be obscure or multiple. Since there is less emphasis on researching legal precedents and factual events, parties spend less time preparing for the proceedings. The process itself is expedited, since the primary focus is on the relevant facts and a speedy resolution to which the parties can agree, rather than on mounting elaborate legal arguments. The informality of the proceedings encourages both sides to limit inquiry and dispute to the most essential issues. Attorneys, should they be involved, are forced by the compressed schedule of mediation to grasp the factual and legal aspects of the case quickly and thoroughly. Time as well as money are saved by keeping few written records. Since the mediator is usually selected in advance by the parties, mediation is not subject to delay while a suitable individual or panel are identified and agreed upon, as may occur in arbitration. The parties are able to control the timing of the proceedings, rather than being at the mercy of the court's docket.

Mediation is also less expensive than arbitration and litigation, largely because of its compressed schedule and the absence of costly discovery procedures. While in arbitration the absence of discovery may impede the parties' preparation of their arguments, mediation does not depend on legal arguments, and has less need of discovery procedures. The mediator may request the production of documents or other evidence; the parties need not comply, but they must accept the consequences of their decision. The parties may or may not be represented by attorneys, but the informality of the proceedings, the de-emphasis of legal precedent, and the premise that the parties are genuinely seeking a solution mean that less time is spent on technical minutiae and in tactics of delay. Fact finding is intended to find the essentials rather than pose a burden to the opposing party. While the parties bear the cost of the mediator's services and of the site of the mediation (whereas the taxpayer provides the judge and courtroom), this expense is easily offset by the reduction in legal fees. Indirect costs of disputes may also be saved: lengthy adversarial proceedings divert the disputants' time and resources, whereas a quick resolution allows them to return to more productive work. Funds which would otherwise be held up pending the outcome of arbitration or litigation may be released for other purposes.

The mediator in a construction dispute normally has some expertise in construction practices and preferably also in construction law. The mediator's knowledge and experience help to expedite the proceedings and may lead to more equitable results. Establishing a standard of care—a major part of a construction lawsuit—can be bypassed if the mediator is familiar with current practices. The mediator may be able to limit the number and scope of participation of expert witnesses. The flexible format of mediation allows a knowledgeable mediator to separate those parties actually affected by the problem from those brought in by the exigencies of litigation. The mediator's knowledge helps to promote a resolution based on the merits of the case rather than either technical legal claims, as in litigation, or a simple "split-the-difference" compromise, as often happens in arbitration. The expert mediator may make factual findings which, while not binding, may aid in forging a compromise; for example, when a specification is ambiguous, which interpretation is the more reasonable one. A mediator who has the respect of the participants may be able to convince a party to accept an adverse finding of fact.

An experienced mediator may provide the parties with a valuable neutral assessment of the merits of the case. Because of their limited knowledge and their role as advocates, adversary attorneys are often not in a position to provide their clients with a balanced view of the strengths and weaknesses of their claims. This can hinder settlement attempts, or cause parties to bring suits of dubious merit. The mediator's impartial evaluation of the case, which includes pointing out to each side its own weaknesses, may make compromise more acceptable to the parties.

Lack of provisions for multiple-party joinder, which can limit the effectiveness of arbitration, is less of an impediment in mediation, where parties participate voluntarily or not at all. Thus, mediation has a lower risk of multiple proceedings and inconsistent results. (The voluntary nature of mediation may pose other problems, however, as discussed below.) While adversary proceedings may tend to obscure factual truth in order to emphasize fault finding, mediation, ideally, encourages fuller disclosure of the facts. In litigation and arbitration, parties typically are seeking compensation for pecuniary loss already incurred. Mediation, since it is often used while a project is still being built, may allow parties to achieve solutions to long-term controversies and to forestall others, thereby reducing the cost of impact of unresolved problems. Mediation may also be of use when no "solution" is sought, other than the airing of certain grievances. The parties are not limited to the remedies offered by the courts, but may use any solution that they are able to invent and agree to. If an attempt at mediation is unsuccessful, the parties have lost little time before turning to more conventional means of resolving their problems. In addition, an attempted mediation often results in a reduced number of issues should they then go before a judge or arbitration, or may clarify the issues which remain. Because the parties themselves create the agreement resulting from a mediation, they may be more inclined to abide by it than by the decision of a judge or arbitrator.

Mediation is considered particularly appropriate where the disputants have ongoing, interdependent relationships which require them to live or work together over extended periods of time. While this most typically describes the areas of family, community, and employer–employee relations, it may also be true of construction, where performance of contractual duties takes place over a period of many months or years. The design professional and construction industries are quite ingrown even in large cities, and relationships are based to a large degree on reputation and personal connections. Designing and successfully constructing a building depend greatly on mutual respect and cooperation. Architects, contractors, and others in the industry are accustomed to resolving their many points of contention among themselves, by similar processes of proposal, counterproposal, and compromise, motivated to do so in part by reluctance to invoke full-scale adversarial proceedings. Mediation may be seen as an extension of such person-to-person negotiation in the case of disputes which are beyond the parties' abilities to resolve without outside aid.

Disputants may arrive at mediation in several different ways. The most desirable is for the parties to provide in their initial design or construction contract for mediation of disputes which arise during the project. In this way the parties address the risk of claims at a time when they are well disposed toward each other, ie, at the beginning of their contractual relationship. When the parties are unable to resolve a dispute arising in the course of the job, one or more will initiate mediation.

The advantages of a contractual provision are several. Naming the mediator in advance (usually done by each party presenting a list of acceptable candidates, the mediator being selected from those on whom the parties agree) prevents disputes over who is to preside. Having a prior agreement allows the procedure to be set into motion on short notice, which may improve the chance of a resolution; mediation is most effective while a dispute is still fresh. Once the parties' positions have polarized, they have invested time and energy in preparing their claim, and the number of affected parties has multiplied, it is more difficult to bring about an agreement.

Since it is less cumbersome than adversary proceedings, the parties may be more likely to use the contractual provision for mediation of disputes which are considered too minor for litigation and arbitration. This may prevent small disputes from expanding. Some mediation agreements designate a mediator who is paid a sufficient fee in advance to become familiar with the contract documents and to follow the construction from the beginning. This further minimizes the time necessary for the mediator to understand the project and the source of conflict, and encourages the use of the mediator's services as problems arise. The mediator in such a case could also oversee the implementation of the agreement.

A provision for mediation in a contract reduces the perception of an offer to mediate (or the fear of such a perception) as an admission of weakness in the party's case. The American Arbitration Association Rules for mediation in the construction industry include the following sample mediation clause for contracts (2):

> If a dispute arises out of or relating to this contract, or the breach thereof, and if said dispute cannot be settled through direct discussions, the parties agree to first endeavor to settle the dispute in an amicable manner by mediation under the Construction Industry Mediation Rules of the American Arbitration Association, before having recourse to arbitration or a judicial forum.

The parties may also make the agreement self-executing, by setting forth procedures in the contract, thus exercising control over the manner of resolving disputes before they arise. The AAA Rules provide for the form of the request for mediation, the appointment of the mediator and his or her qualifications, the time and place, and confidentiality. The rules require a filing fee which is a percentage of the amount in controversy. The parties are permitted representatives of their choice. At present, the various industry documents do not include mediation as a forum for dispute resolution.

A second path to mediation is for parties to an existing dispute to try mediation prior to resorting to adversary proceedings. This may occur at the initiative of one of the parties, or, in the case of a dispute already slated for adversary proceedings, may be decided upon in the course of prehearing or procedural meetings. In the event that the parties do not reach a successful agreement, they may still proceed with arbitration or litigation. The AAA encourages this path to dispute resolution, and provides a sample agreement for submission of an existing dispute to mediation in its Construction Industry Rules. If the parties have already filed for arbitration under the rules of the AAA, they pay no further fee to initiate mediation. Regardless of how the disputants arrive at mediation, they usually bear the cost of the procedure equally.

While the format which mediation follows is flexible, certain procedures are typical. Once a mediator has been chosen and the initial request filed, there is usually an informal meeting to establish procedures. The meetings usually take place in neutral surroundings. The mediator serves two functions: first, finding facts and allowing each party to present its view of the situation and, secondly, aiding the parties in finding solutions. In the fact-finding phase, the parties submit the pertinent documents to the mediator and make a brief summary of their positions, either orally or in a short written form. Often several problems are submitted at once. The mediator meets briefly with each party, both together and separately, possibly several times over a period of a few days. In a construction dispute, where multiple parties are concerned with the outcome, these meetings might take place with various combinations of the interested parties. The mediator may prepare findings of fact, either generally or for each of the parties separately. If appropriate, the mediator may visit the construction site in order to assess the facts as they exist.

The mediator's role in both fact finding and proposing solutions may be more or less active. At one extreme, where the issues are well defined, the mediator's role is limited to that of "confidential listener": each side tells the mediator its high and low compromise offers, with a prior agreement that they will settle their claims and split the difference if the numbers overlap. If the numbers do not cross, the mediator reports this and may aid the parties in another attempt. More typically, the mediator will actively propose solutions, which the parties are free to accept, reject, or counter with a new proposal. For example, the mediator may suggest that one party agree to absorb certain costs or do corrective work. The mediator may attempt to induce one side to accept a proposed solution, although he or she has no power to compel compliance. It is recommended that mediation take place on a compressed schedule, possibly with each party allocating several days for the procedure, in order to maintain the momentum of the discussions.

A successful mediation typically results in an agreement drawn up by the mediator and signed by the parties. If the parties are not represented by counsel, independent legal review of the agreement is recommended at this point. The agreement is enforceable as is any contract, but is not a legally binding judgment. Breaches of the agreement arrived at through mediation may result in further mediation, or the parties may resort at that point to adversary proceedings.

Effective mediation can only take place when a pool of skilled mediators is available. Various programs offer training to mediators, including the American Arbitration Association. Most mediators are attorneys, often drawn from the lists of arbitrators in the same field. Training includes discussions of the goals and procedures of mediation, focusing on developing the skills necessary to make the procedure work. These include the ability to listen to each side's grievances, to keep the parties communicating with each other, and to synthesize the facts in order to present them again to the parties. Mediators must be able to think on their feet in order to find solutions not proposed by either party. Training often includes role playing, which gives the new mediator a chance to apply the theoretical skills in a practical context. A new mediator is usually teamed with more experienced mediators for the first few actual mediation sessions. Mediators, in order to command the necessary respect of the participants, must be recognized in their field of expertise. Most procedural rules require that they reveal any potential conflict of interest that they might have. Mediation may some day evolve into a legal specialty of its own.

Mediation-related Processes

Mediation is the leading form of alternative dispute resolution, but variations on the process also exist which may be well adapted for use in the architectural and construction fields. The "minitrial," as the name suggests, is a private, scaled-down trial, outside of both the official court system and formal arbitration. The parties agree on the presiding individual or panel; procedural and evidentiary rules follow the courtroom pattern but are relaxed and expedited. Similar "rent-a-judge" programs often use the resource of retired judges or other experts. In both minitrials and rent-a-judge, the parties choose to what extent they will be bound by the final decision.

Mediation–arbitration is a recent refinement of mediation which has found success in resolving construction disputes. Under this procedure, which combines elements of both processes, the third party chosen in advance acts first as a mediator, attempting to bring the parties to a voluntary agreement. If the parties are unable to arrive at a solution which is acceptable to all, the mediator becomes an arbitrator and has the power to bind the parties to a decision. In this situation, the factual information has already been assembled and the mediator–arbitrator has heard and considered the parties' positions. The parties have an incentive to reach a settlement voluntarily when faced with the alternative of a binding judgment. This approach may be hindered, however, by greater reluctance on the disputants' part to reveal facts which may later be used against them if the proceedings turn to arbitration. While mediator–arbitrators disagree as to whether such facts revealed in the course of mediation should be recognized when the dispute is under arbitration, the facts undoubtedly affect a later decision.

Other multitiered procedures for dispute resolution include one provisionally adopted by the Associated General Contractors of California, which combines mediation, minitrials, and arbitration. Parties to controversies below a certain dollar amount are required to try mediation first and, if this is unsuccessful, go to a minitrial, and finally arbitration. Larger disputes begin at either the minitrial or arbitration level. "Structured" mediation, borrowed from family dispute resolution, differs from more informal mediation in that it sets in advance a number of sessions and specific goals to be accomplished, including defining issues, presenting each party's side, and discussing proposals. This structure may expedite the process, although it risks being too confining. Fact finding is a process which isolates one of the functions of mediation: an impartial individual or panel is appointed to make findings of fact in order to clarify the issues and promote settlement. The parties decide in advance whether the findings are to be binding or merely advisory in future proceedings. This step is somewhat useful in construction, where the facts can be so complex and so much time and money are spent on discovery. Similarly, "early neutral evaluation" of cases slated for litigation gives the parties an incentive to prepare the facts in their case early and receive an impartial assessment of its probable legal consequences. Telephone mediation has been used successfully in construction disputes where the problem is well defined and the mediator is well versed in the issues. These procedures indicate the flexibility of mediation, and its adaptability to a variety of settings and needs. Many of them may also be useful in expediting later adversarial proceedings, should they become necessary.

Current Practice of Mediation

Information on mediation in construction and architectural disputes is not readily available. This is due, in part, to the extrajudicial nature of the proceedings and thus, their absence from official legal reporting; furthermore, the participants keep few records, in order to maintain expediency and confidentiality. While mediation is often practiced informally, its use as a legitimate forum for construction disputes is not widespread. However, at least two organizations involved in construction are currently committed to the use of mediation in disputes. One is the Metropolitan Atlanta Rapid Transit Authority (MARTA), which built and operates a bus/rail system in Atlanta. MARTA offers mediation in its initial letters of acknowledgment to all contractors on its projects. MARTA has used mediation successfully on a number of claims, both large and small. The roofing industry (represented by the National Roofing Contractors Association and the Asphalt Roofing Manufacturers Association) has adopted rules and procedures for mediation under the auspices of the American Arbitration Association, which are similar to the general rules for the construction industry.

Current Problems and Constraints

Lack of information is a major obstacle to the broader use of mediation in the construction industry. Design professionals and contractors typically are unfamiliar with the process, and are unlikely to initiate it. The legal profession as a whole is not fully informed about mediation, and thus does not consider it an alternative to litigation and arbitration. Despite some recent changes, most law schools do not acknowledge mediation as an alternative to traditional dispute resolution and, therefore, offer no training in the requisite skills. Even those attorneys who are aware of mediation often lack the skills required for a process which focuses on bringing the parties to an understanding rather than competing from opposite sides of an issue. Some members of the legal profession resist alternatives to standard dispute resolution. To date, none of the standard contracts used in construction projects provide for mediation of future disputes; when problems arise the parties look first to more conventional means of resolving them.

In some contexts, such as family or community disputes, mediation, more than adversary proceedings, may not adequately protect individuals in weaker bargaining positions. Those with less knowledge or experience may sign away rights to which they are legally entitled. This is of lesser concern in construction mediation, however, where the parties tend to be fairly sophisticated with regard to their rights, and are usually represented by counsel. Mediation, like arbitration, may suffer from the same reluctance on the part of insurers to cover liability established in the course of such proceedings. It is, therefore, essential that parties ascertain the position of insurers and sureties prior to entering mediation agreements.

Questions of confidentiality may hinder the use of mediation in construction disputes. Confidentiality promotes the open exchange which is necessary for successful mediation. Parties may be reluctant to make admissions to a mediator which may be detrimental to their claim if they later go to court. Mediators must use considerable skill to achieve an agreement without providing other parties with potentially damaging information should the dispute end up being litigated. In addition, the parties may resist making admissions to mediators who may themselves be subpoenaed as witnesses in a later action; it is uncertain whether mediators themselves enjoy a quasijudicial privilege. However, courts will usually honor an agreement of confidentiality. Federal Rule of Evidence 408, also codified by many states, rules that conduct or statements made in compromise negotiations is inadmissible evidence. The rule is intended to encourage out-of-court settlement. If mediation is considered an offer to compromise, this affords strong protection against misuse of the facts revealed during the proceedings.

Mediation, like arbitration, does not benefit from the rules of party joinder which facilitate bringing all the interested parties together in a single lawsuit. No one can be forced to mediate. As mentioned above, the voluntary nature of the proceeding may compensate for this drawback, but this is only true where all interested parties in fact are willing to mediate. The multiplicity and interdependence of parties which make mediation an attractive choice for construction-related disputes also require that all those concerned participate in the process. An agreement resulting from mediation, no matter how amicable, cannot be effective when key parties are not represented. In general, mediation is subject to the limitations inherent in any voluntary undertaking. It is only effective if each of the parties is actively willing to seek a solution to the problem. Even when all of the parties have agreed to mediate, it may be difficult to arrive at a settlement which is acceptable to everyone. Not the least of the problems of multiplicity of parties is logistical: simply assembling all the parties in the same place at the same time. Parties are known to use mediation as a prelude to adversary proceedings merely in order to demonstrate a good faith attempt to reconcile differences. Some question whether parties are likely to perceive the advantages of mediation while the threat of litigation is still far off.

Other factors which may impede the use of mediation include unresolved enforceability and subject matter of the dispute. It is uncertain whether an agreement to mediate is enforceable. While the courts maintain a pro-arbitration policy and enforce arbitration contract clauses wherever possible, they do not recognize mediation. Enforcement of mediation clauses may be impracticable in any event, since the process must be voluntary to be effective. A second enforceability issue pertains to the agreement resulting from a successful mediation. Just as with any contract, if one side fails to comply with its terms, the dispute may ultimately end up in court. Some matters by their nature do not lend themselves to mediation. The procedure is probably not appropriate in cases of death or serious injury, nor where one party has clearly engaged in egregious conduct of any kind. When the relationship among the disputants has deteriorated beyond a certain point, it may be impossible to bring them to a mutually acceptable resolution.

DIRECTIONS FOR THE FUTURE

Lack of awareness is perhaps the greatest obstacle to the effective use of mediation; education is an obvious solution. Law schools and bar associations should expand their focus to include mediation as a legitimate means of bringing disputes to effective resolution. They should provide training for mediators and encourage attorneys to present mediation, where appropriate, as an alternative to their clients. Members of the construction industry must also lead in encouraging the inclusion of mediation clauses in construction contracts, and the submission of existing disputes to mediation. Referral services to make preliminary evaluations of the problem and match disputants with qualified mediators would facilitate the use of available resources.

Some writers have suggested court-annexed (mandatory) mediation, on the model of similar procedures of arbitration, with which several states have had some success. Under this program, certain kinds of cases (usually with a limited monetary amount at stake) would be required to attempt mediation before using more conventional means of dispute resolution. This has the advantage of diverting cases from the courts; however, some find mandatory mediation to be in conflict with the basic premise of voluntary participation. Compulsory mediation may also deny participants due process protections. The agreement itself may establish or avoid legally enforceable rights. To reduce the danger that less powerful persons unwittingly will give up important legal adversary rights, they must be informed of the likely result of an adversary procedure. A mediator with legal training may be able to inform the parties of the legal merits of their claims. In an extreme case, the mediator may refuse to draft an agreement which he or she believes is unacceptable.

The courts have the authority to encourage the use of mediation, either as a mandatory prerequisite to other procedures, or by such means as stays or delays of court proceedings pending mediation. In this way, mediation would enjoy the same official support as arbitration does currently. Resolution of the current ambiguity with regard to mediator privilege in favor of immunity to subpoena (possibly by legislation) would help foster mediation. Negotiation for construction contracts might provide for all parties with an interest above a certain percentage (eg, subcontractors and suppliers) to agree to mediate future disputes, in order to ensure the presence of all those necessary for resolution.

Mediation will never entirely replace litigation as a means of resolving architectural and construction conflicts, but it may well become one of several options for parties who are seeking an efficient and effective resolution to their disputes.

BIBLIOGRAPHY

1. Former Chief Justice Warren E. Burger, *Annual Report on the State of the Judiciary,* Washington, D.C., January, 1982.
2. *Construction Industry Mediation Rules,* American Arbitration Association, New York, 1982.

General References

Construction Industry Mediation Rules, effective May 1, 1985, American Arbitration Association, New York, 1985.

Roofing Industry Mediation Rules, effective Feb. 2, 1980, American Arbitration Association, New York, 1980.

J. S. Auerbach, *Justice Without Law?,* Oxford University Press, New York, 1983. Historical perspective on the struggle between the American legal system and alternative forms of dispute resolution which have coexisted throughout American history.

H. G. Block, "As the Walls Came Tumbling Down: Architects' Expanded Liability under Design-Build Construction Contracts," *John Marshall Law Review* **17**(1), 1–48 (Winter 1984). Traces the history of the new relationship between owner, designer, and contractor and its effect on the design profession.

L. H. Cook, "Mediation, A Boon or A Bust?," *New York Law School Law Review* **28**(1), 3–29 (1983). A judge's assessment of current problems of the legal system, and of the success of various mediation programs, both civil and criminal, supported by statistics. A definite "boon," he concludes.

R. Coulson, *How to Stay out of Court,* 2nd ed., American Arbitration Association, New York, 1984. Presents the many alternatives to litigation, including prevention and avoidance as well as mediation, arbitration, and negotiation, and describes bargaining techniques.

Donald J. Duck, "Negotiating Construction Claims," *Journal of American Waterworks Association,* **76**(2), 39–41 (February 1984).

J. Folberg, and A. Taylor, *Mediation: A Comprehensive Guide to Resolving Conflict without Litigation,* Jossey–Bass, San Francisco, 1984. A sociological analysis of conflict resolution; discusses training and techniques; history of mediation. General.

C. A. Foster, ed., "Construction Management and Design-Build/Fast-Track Construction," *Law & Contemporary Problems,* **46** (1) (Winter 1983). An issue of 10 articles exploring the legal consequences of new trends in design and construction techniques from the perspective of various industry participants. Especially relevant is "Dispute Management under Modern

Construction Systems," which describes alternative dispute resolution techniques which have emerged out of the "void created by the absence of the architect as first level decision-maker."

G. H. Friedman, "When is Mediation an Alternative to Litigation?" *National Law Journal* **7**(25) (Mar. 4, 1985). Most comprehensive general discussion of commercial mediation in short article form, with several examples from the construction industry.

L. L. Fuller, "Mediation—Its Forms and Functions," *Southern California Law Review* **44**(2), 305–339 (Winter 1971). Much-cited article analyzing mediation in sociological terms as producing and restoring order in society. Little practical or factual material.

M. Hoellering, "Construction Arbitration and Mediation," *Journal of American Waterworks Association* **76**(2), 34–38 (February 1984). Brief, general discussion focusing mainly on arbitration.

C. W. Ibbs, Jr., "Key Elements of Construction Specifications," *Journal of American Waterworks Association* **76**(2), 48–55 (February 1984).

J. K. Lieberman, *The Litigious Society,* Basic Books, New York, 1981. Critique of the current "litigation explosion" for the general reader; social changes and changes in procedural and substantive law. Focuses on the problem rather than solutions.

D. D. Meisel and W. M. Stein, "Mediation, the Possible Resolution of 'Impossible' Situations," *Construction Specifier,* 22–25 (June 1982). Brief, general discussion of the advantages of mediation and how it works in construction.

F. Muller, "Mediation, an Alternative to Litigation," *Journal of American Waterworks Association* **76**(2), 42 (February 1984). Brief, general discussion of mediation as it relates to construction projects.

L. Nader and H. F. Todd, Jr., eds., *The Disputing Process in Ten Societies,* Columbia University Press, New York, 1978. Anthropologists' view; discusses many traditional approaches to dispute resolution.

J. Pearson, "An Evaluation of Alternatives to Court Adjudication," *Justice System Journal* **7**(1), 420–450 (1982). Survey of available information on existing alternative dispute resolution programs, including summaries of several studies of their efficacy, participant satisfaction, etc.

L. Ray, ed., *Alternative Dispute Resolution: Mediation and the Law: Will Reason Prevail?,* American Bar Association, Washington, D.C., 1983. Transcript compiled by the ABA Special Committee on Dispute Resolution, Public Services Division, of panel discussion, emphasizing neighborhood and family disputes. Includes article on confidentiality.

L. L. Riskin, "Mediation and Lawyers," *Ohio State Law Journal* **43**(1), 29–60 (1982). General overview of mediation in the United States and in relation to the legal profession. Ethical and practical considerations.

R. A. Rubin et al., *Construction Claims Analysis: Presentation, Defenses,* Van Nostrand Reinhold, New York, 1983. Nature of claims, how to anticipate and deal with them in court and out. Outlines risks and responsibilities of each party.

F. E. A. Sander and F. E. Snyder, *Alternative Methods of Dispute Settlement: A Selected Bibliography,* American Bar Association, Division of Public Services Activities, Washington, D.C., 1982.

See also Arbitration in Construction; Construction Documents; Construction Industry; Construction Law; Contract Administration; Inspection, Observation, and Supervision

Gerald Weisbach, FAIA
Natkin & Weisbach
San Francisco, California

Sarah Cuniff
Heller, Ehrman, White & McAuliffe
San Francisco, California

MEIER, RICHARD

Richard Alan Meier was the 1984 winner of the Pritzker Architecture Prize. Carleton Smith, Secretary to the Jury and Chairman of the International Awards Foundation quoted the jury's citation as follows:

> We honor Richard Meier for his single-minded pursuit of new directions in contemporary architecture. In his search for clarity and his experiments in balancing light, form, and space, he has created works which are personal, vigorous, original. His houses, seminary, museums, and public buildings have stretched and enriched our imaging, our thinking, our wanting, and perhaps our doing. They are intended not to overwhelm but to celebrate.

Born in Newark, New Jersey, on October 12, 1934 to Jerome and Carolyn (Kaltenbacher) Meier, he received his bachelor of architecture degree in 1957. He apprenticed in New York at Davis, Brody and Wisnieweski and later at Skidmore, Owings and Merrill, as well as with Marcel Breuer. After graduating from Cornell University, Ithaca, New York, he vacationed in Europe and met Le Corbusier. This event, together with a visit in 1963 to an opening of an exhibition of models and drawings by Le Corbusier at the Museum of Modern Art, New York, had a vivid impact on his life. According to Meier, "The Le Corbusier exhibition marked a turning point in my life. To me, he was the greatest architect of the century. Every architect practicing today is affected by his work. I'm quite often labeled a disciple of Le Corbusier, but like most people, I dislike being labeled by anything."

Working out of his New York City apartment, Meier established his private practice in 1963 with a commission for his parents, a residence in Essex Fells, New Jersey, under the acknowledged influence of Frank Lloyd Wright. Meier said "Frank Lloyd Wright was a great architect, and I could not have done my parents' house the way I did, without being overwhelmed by Falling Water. It doesn't come close to Falling Water, but it was still an influence. . . . With Wright, there is more concern with the horizontal extension of space. . . . Le Corbusier's designs emphasize vertical penetration of space, and much of my work has this vertical interest, more so than the horizontal, at least in the Wrightian sense. . . . We are all affected by Frank Lloyd Wright, Alvar Aalto, and Mies van der Rohe. But no less than by Bramante, Borromini, and Bernini. Architecture is a tradition, a long continuum. Whether we break with tradition or enhance it, we are still connected to that past. We evolve."

In addition to the residence of his parents, he redesigned the studio and apartment of Frank Stella in New York

City (1965). In fact, for a few years after college, Meier worked in Stella's studio painting large expressionist canvases and making collages. "Making collages keeps the eye and hand in training," said Meier, "it is in effect, my workout."

His private practice has included residences, housing, medical facilities, museums, and commercial buildings.

The project that first brought Meier to national prominence was the Smith House in Darien, Connecticut (1967). In retrospect, Meier spoke of "the clarity of the building, the openness, the direct articulation of private and public spaces, how it relates to the land and water." He continued, "It's been over 17 years, and what was innovative and captured a great many people's imagination and admiration then, is already a part of our language, and somewhat taken for granted today."

With regard to the Smith House, it was written that (1)

> It was already clear that something else beside the standard modernist impulse was at work—a kind of picturesque compositional design sense, as sure and fine an intuitive design ability as had been seen in years. The Smith House was lighter than most modernist houses of the 1960s, more a kind of frame; it was very beautiful as an object, and nothing about it said "This is an awkward form, but you will like it when you get used to it." One became used to it instantly, and this alone set it apart from all sorts of buildings that were going up at the same time.

Subsequent private residences designed by Meier included the Saltzman House in East Hampton, New York, the Douglas House in Harbor Springs, Michigan, and the Maidman House in Sands Point, New York.

In 1967 a commission followed for Westbeth Artists' Housing. Meier began work on the transformation of the Old Bell Telephone Laboratories buildings in Manhattan's Greenwich Village into 383 loft-type studio residences for artists, the largest existing housing facility for artists and the first of its kind in this country. "The phrase 'adaptive re-use' wasn't even in the language then. We were really pioneering a new area," said Meier.

In 1969 the New York State Urban Development Corporation commissioned Meier for Twin Parks Northeast Housing in the Bronx. The design approach was to integrate the new buildings into the existing urban context in such a way as to revitalize that context and to provide a maximum of usable private and public space for the needs of both the residents and the community at large. The project was described as "an exemplary piece of housing, and few are the projects, in America or elsewhere, in which the modulation of form and surface has such rhythmic authority, or in which acknowledgment of the existing context has in no way inhibited the creation of a new situation" (2).

The Villa Strozzi in Florence, Italy, was modified by Meier in 1973 to serve as the enclosure for a new museum, and several facilities for the New York State Department of Mental Hygiene were designed in the 1970s, the largest of which is the Bronx Developmental Center; it has been called one of the most significant architectural accomplishments of the decade. Originally planned as a total-care residential facility for 750 physically disabled and mentally retarded children, the project, as built, accommodates 380 residents, as well as serving as an outpatient facility. The design of this facility is an attempt to create a sense of place that responds to the special feelings and needs of the residents.

The building known as the Atheneum, a visitor orientation center in the restored historic town of New Harmony, Indiana, was completed in 1979 (Fig. 1). According to Meier,

> This is a totally public building; with the obvious exception of the mechanical spaces, there isn't a corner that isn't experienced. . . . The design of the Atheneum reflects one's sense of permanence of places, the sense of volume of space is at the heart of things. Preoccupation with space, not abstract space, not scaleless space, but space whose order and definition is related to light. . . . Fundamentally, my meditations are on space, form, light, and how to make them. My goal is presence not illusion, I pursue it with unrelenting vigor. I believe that it is the heart and soul of architecture.

The building advances "conventional modernist practice provocatively beyond established limits" (3). In addition, the Atheneum is (4)

> [A]n assertion of quintessential modernity, without flourishes, rhetoric, or gimmickry. It is consequently an object for the future as much as for our time, a building that puts forward the claim of the architecture of this century before centuries

Figure 1. Two views of The Atheneum of New Harmony, Indiana, completed in 1979. Photograph by Ezra Stoller.

Figure 2. The High Museum of Art, Atlanta, Georgia. View from Peachtree Street, showing the ramp leading to the main entrance. Photograph by Ezra Stoller.

to come. . . . There is no doubt now that the Atheneum of Richard Meier is a work of genius.

The High Museum of Art in Atlanta, Georgia (1983), attempts to resolve the best of the old and modern notions of the art museum (Fig. 2). The intent is to encourage discovery of aesthetic values and to convey a sense of the museum as a contemplative place. The structure consists of white porcelain panels, glass, some granite, and pipe rails.

As an architecture critic has written (1), "It is no accident, then, that Richard Meier is becoming one of the preeminent architects of museums. In addition to the High Museum, he has designed a major museum for Frankfurt, West Germany . . . and an addition to the Des Moines Art Center in Iowa."

All of the above projects have won National Honor Awards from the American Institute of Architects. Meier has received many other awards for his work, including the Arnold Brunner Memorial Prize from the National Institute of Arts and Letters in 1972, the R. S. Reynolds Memorial Award in 1977, and awards from *Progressive Architecture* and the *Architectural Record.* In the spring of 1980 he won an international competition for the new Museum for Decorative Arts (Museum für Kunsthandwerk) in Frankfurt, Federal Republic of Germany, which opened in the spring of 1985. Among the numerous projects presently under design are the new People's Bank headquarters, to be known as Bridgeport Center, in Bridgeport, Connecticut, and the new City Hall and Central Library in The Hague, Netherlands.

In October, 1984, Meier was awarded the commission to design the J. Paul Getty Center in Los Angeles. Scheduled completion date of that prestigious $100 million-plus project is 1993.

In addition to his building projects, Meier also designs tableware and furniture. The furniture collection for Knoll International has already received critical praise.

Whenever time permits, Meier enjoys lecturing and teaching. From 1964 to 1973, he was an Adjunct Professor of Architecture at Cooper Union, New York. In 1975 and 1977 he was the William Henry Bishop Visiting Professor at Yale University, New Haven, Connecticut, and the Eliot Noyes Visiting Design Critic in Architecture at Harvard University, Cambridge, Massachusetts, in 1980. He has guest lectured at universities and museums around the world.

Mr. Meier became a Fellow of the American Institute of Architects in 1976, and received a Medal of Honor from the New York Chapter of that organization in 1980. In 1983, he was elected to the American Academy and the Institute of Arts and Letters, and in 1984 the French Government honored him as an Officer of Arts and Letters. In 1986 he was elected a member of the International Academy of Architecture, and in 1988, he was awarded the Royal Gold Medal from the Royal Institute of British Architects.

BIBLIOGRAPHY

1. P. Golberger, "Ad-Meier-ing," *Vogue,* 196–203 (June 1983).
2. K. Frampton, "Introduction" *Richard Meier Architect: Buildings and Projects 1966–76,* New York, Oxford University Press, 1976.
3. A. L. Huxtable, "A Radical New Addition for Mid-America," The New York Times (September 30, 1979).
4. A. Cohen, "Richard Meier: An American Architect," *GA Document,* Issue 1 (Summer 1980).

Richard Meier, FAIA
Richard Meier and Partners
New York, New York

MEMBRANE STRUCTURES

Tent structures, made of woven natural fibers, have been used since antiquity to provide portable shelters, originally for armies and nomads, and more recently for circuses. The development in the last 20 years of noncombustible fabric membranes woven from glass filament fibers has ushered in the era of architectural fabric structures, where translucency, economy, and architectural expression are the driving forces behind the ever-expanding market for this new method of construction.

Pneumatic structures are similarly constructed of fabrics; the hot air balloon, used extensively during the Civil War, may be considered to be an early version of an air-inflated structure. With the advent of electrically driven blowers, Frederick William Lanchester in a 1917 patent proposed an air-supported building for use as a portable field hospital whereby one entered the pressurized space through means of an airlock. It was not, however, until 1946 that the concepts first proposed by Lanchester were put into practice by Walter Bird in the construction of an air-inflated structure 15 m in diameter built to protect military radomes from the weather while allowing for the transmission of radar waves through the fabric (Fig. **1a**) (1). These structures were designed, manufactured, and

Figure 1. Air-supported structures. **(a)** Radomes. **(b)** Sports bubble. **(c)** Interior during construction of U.S. Pavilion, Expo '70, Osaka, Japan. **(d)** University of Santa Clara Student Activities Center, Santa Clara, California. **(e)** UNI Dome, University of Northern Iowa, Cedar Falls, Iowa, showing the partial acoustic liner. **(f)** Silverdome, Pontiac, Mich. **(g)** The acoustic banner of the Silverdome. **(a)** and **(b)** Courtesy of Birdair Structures, Inc. **(c)–(g)** Courtesy of Geiger Associates.

erected to very high engineering standards and gave rise to an industry that produced high-grade industrial fabrics constructed of strong synthetic fibers covered by a synthetic coating of vinyl, neoprene, or Hypalon.

In 1956, Walter Bird and his colleagues formed Birdair Structures, Inc. to promote, design, and manufacture pneumatic structures. Shortly thereafter, there were about 50 manufacturers in the business producing air-supported buildings for sports facilities (Fig. 1**b**), exhibition halls, storage facilities, light industry, and military applications. Not all engineers or manufacturers exercised the required sophistication in design or construction, nor did owners exercise the required care in maintenance and operations; consequently a number of disasters occurred, and the number of manufacturers greatly diminished as it became recognized that air structures were a sophisticated building type requiring unusual care in engineering, manufacturing, maintenance, and operations.

In the early 1960s, Frei Otto, through the Institute of Light Weight Structures at Stuttgart University in West Germany, began a comprehensive, systematic evaluation of membrane structures. This work was summarized in two volumes published in 1962 and 1965 (2,3). Frei Otto worked extensively with soap-film models. Frei Otto's work in the 1950s and 1960s consisted of a number of tension structures manufactured from synthetic yarns by the tent manufacturer Stromeyer in Konstantz, Germany and a number of cable-supported structures made up of a cable net supporting in turn either a fabric membrane or other cladding such as wood. The most notable of these later structures was the West German Pavilion at Expo '67 in Montreal.

In 1968, Davis Brody Associates of New York, along with David Geiger as engineer, submitted a design based on an air-supported structure in the competition to design the United States pavilion at Expo '70 in Osaka, Japan. After winning the competition, as the budget was cut from $25 million to $2.5 million, the building design changed form from a super sphere 300 ft high "floating" above the site, to a super elliptical low profile air structure 23 ft high covering a 100,000 ft^2 exhibit area (4) (Fig. 1**c**). It is this latter form that gave rise to the changes that marked air structures from 1968 to 1987 (5).

Now that the air structure could no longer be considered only temporary or portable, there was a need for a membrane material that would allow for the construction of a "permanent" structure. The opportunity arose to develop such a membrane when the Educational Facilities Laboratory funded Geiger Associates to develop this material. Working with Dupont, Owens Corning Fiberglas, Birdair Structures, and Chemical Fabrics Corporation, fiber-glass fabric coated with Teflon was modified by the inclusion of 10-μ glass beads into the Teflon dispersion to improve abrasion resistance and by precoating the fabric with silicone to prevent wicking of water (5). It was now possible to apply membrane structures made of fabric to permanent noncombustible construction as defined by building codes within the United States. The first structures so built were the La Verne College Student Center, a tensile structure by the architect John Shaver, and the University of Santa Clara Student Activities Center (Fig. 1**d**), a low profile air-supported roof by the architect Paul Kennon of CRSS, both of which were completed by 1973.

The structural design of the low-profile air-supported roof required the development of new computer techniques of analysis as well. The nonlinear cable net program was developed by David Geiger and John M. McCormick at Columbia University in 1968. It was later refined by McCormick and Joseph P. Wright to permit the analysis of cable nets where horizontal displacements were of the same order of magnitude as vertical displacements. Until 1974, it was not possible to establish the initial configuration by computer when the cable net did not project in plan as straight lines. The modeling techniques of Frei

(a)

(b)

Figure 2. Tensile structures. **(a)** Queeny Park, St. Louis, Missouri. **(b)** Florida Festival, Orlando. **(c)** Good Shepherd Lutheran Church, Fresno, California. **(d)** Haj Terminal, Jeddah, Saudi Arabia. **(e)** Bullock's Department Store, San Mateo, California. **(f)** Cross-arch system: Bullock's Department Store, San Jose, California. **(g)** Stephan C. O'Connell Center, University of Florida, Gainesville. **(h)** Tennessee State Amphitheatre, Expo 82, Knoxville. **(a)**, **(b)**, **(d–h)**, Courtesy of Geiger Associates. **(c)** Courtesy of Birdair Structures, Inc.

(c)

(d)

(e)

(f)

(g)

(h)

Otto could not be used because the low extensibility of glass fabric required much more precise methods of determining cutting shapes; consequently, the ability to analyze tensile structures was limited to classic shapes for which the initial configuration could be established by specific formula. Finally, for the design of the tensile structures of Expo '76 in Philadelphia, Geiger Associates, based on the force density method proposed by Schek (6), were able to modify the analysis program to allow for the initial form finding of membrane structures of general configuration. This now permitted the patterning of membrane structures by computer. The first significant structures using this technique were developed by Horst Berger of Geiger Associates (at that time Geiger Berger Associates); these included the tensile structures for Expo '76 in Philadelphia, Queeny Park in St. Louis (Fig. 2**a**), and Florida Festival in Orlando, Florida (Fig. 2**b**).

During the period from 1974 to 1987, fabric structures were firmly established as an architectural form. Todd Dolland and Nicholas Goldsmith of Future Tents Limited

(FTL) extended the work of Frei Otto and computer-modeling techniques developed by the office of Burro Happold into the precise design of party tents and camping tents. Gene Zellmer introduced the use of tension structures to religious architecture (Fig. **2c**), an application that surprisingly has not found wider use. The late Fazlar Kahn of SOM brought the encapsulation concept into reality in the 105 acres of the Haj Terminal in Jeddah, Saudi Arabia (Fig. **2d**). Geiger Associates, working with various architects, designed more than nine domed stadia, six of which covered approximately 10 acres (Figs. **1e, f,** and **g**).

New tensile systems were developed by Geiger Associates during this period. The radial tent was developed first for the Sea World picnic pavilion in San Diego; it was further developed for the Bullock's Department Store in San Mateo (Fig. **2e**) and ultimately in the 945-ft diameter cantilever shade structure for Riyadh Stadium in Saudi Arabia. The cross-arch system was first introduced in the Bullock's Department Store in San Jose (Fig. **2f**). This system, extended to the Miami Mall, became the standard of this building type. The parallel arch system introduced in the skirt of the Stephan C. O'Connell Center in Gainesville, Florida (Fig. **2g**) has also found wide applications. The wave form used successfully as an outdoor pavilion at Eakins Oval at Expo '76 in Philadelphia was extended to a closed form for the Canadian Pavilion at Expo '86 in Vancouver. The conical form with exterior mast support introduced at Queeny Park was extended to a multiconical form for Tennessee State Amphitheatre at Expo '82 in Knoxville (Fig. **2h**).

Technologic developments required for acoustical and thermal control advanced as well during this period. Ranger Farrell, the acoustic consultant on the U.S. Pavilion in Osaka, Japan, suggested after the success of that project that a liner could be developed that would be acoustically absorptive if the porosity of the coated fabric could be controlled. Working with John Cook, president of Chemical Fabrics Corp., Farrell developed the Teflon-coated fiber-glass acoustic liner with a noise reduction coefficient (NRC) of 0.65. It was first applied in the UNI Dome at Cedar Falls, Iowa in 1974 (Fig. **1e**). Parallel to this development, the acoustical consultant, Bob Coffeen, developed acoustic banners that were used in the Silverdome (Fig. **1g**). The acoustic liner provided some slight thermal benefit by increasing the R value from 1 to approximately 2. However, a way of delivering a much higher R value, on the order of 12 to 22, while maintaining a minimum translucency of 4% was needed. This was considered to be the minimum translucency required to avoid the use of daytime artificial lighting and allow significant plant growth. The solution was not found until 1981. It was applied to the design of the Lindsay Park Sports Centre in Calgary, Alberta, Canada. Here, the roof construction consists of many layers (7) (Fig. 3).

Below the outer layer are multiple layers of 4-in. thick translucent insulation, each layer of which has an R value of approximately 3.5. Below the insulation is a 2-mil transparent Tedlar vapor barrier supported on a polyester scrim at 1-in. spacing. The vapor barrier has a mass low enough that, with the insulation above, the ceiling construction provides a noise reduction coefficient (NRC) of 0.80. With

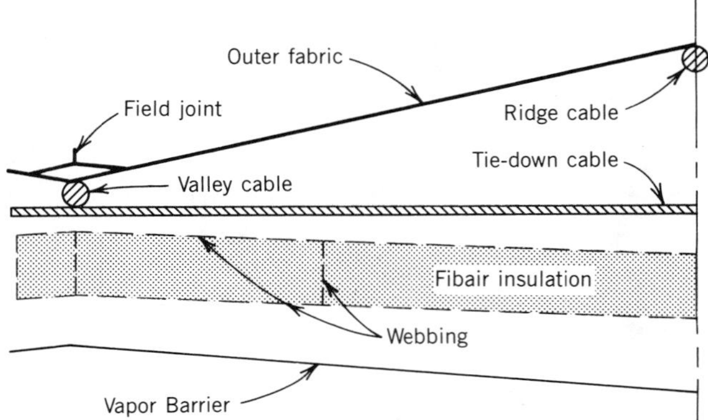

Figure 3. Cross section through insulated translucent roof, Lindsay Park Sports Centre, Calgary, Alberta, Canada.

this construction, an R value of 12 can be obtained when Teflon-coated fiber glass is used and if silicone-coated fiber glass is used, the R value can be increased to 22 with a minimum translucency of 4% being maintained.

For the design of structures in hot climates, Teflon-coated fiber-glass fabric offered new opportunities as well. The high reflectivity of the roof surface (75%), along with the low thermal mass (10%), results in the roof membrane getting no hotter than the ambient air temperature. It is even possible because of the low emissivity of the fabric that when there is low humidity the membrane temperature will be less than the ambient air temperature. In 1972, Karl Beitin of Geiger Associates received a research grant to study this phenomenon from the Educational Facilities Laboratories. He proved that in a desert climate it would be possible to reduce the interior space temperature to 20° below the night ambient air temperature. Thus, with a daytime temperature of 115°F and a night temperature of 85°F, the temperature within the facility during the beginning of the day would begin at 65°F and the increase would be limited owing to the high reflectivity, the low thermal mass and the low translucency of the roof membrane, all without air conditioning. The lack of need for daytime lighting would further reduce the thermal load, and if the occupancy requirements and/or the volume of the space were such that the ventilation requirements could be limited, then the temperature buildup would be further moderated. The large volume with large thermal mass of the interior construction would further limit the temperature swings. The practical consequence of this study was that in the design of the mechanical systems for the nine stadia built by Geiger Associates in the period from 1974 to 1987, only three of them needed air conditioning. For the others, satisfactory performance was achieved without air conditioning even though for the largest of these, the Silverdome, the seating capacity was for more than 80,000 spectators.

In the design, construction, and operation of the low-profile air-supported roofs in the period from 1978 to 1986, problems arose that needed to be addressed. As the energy crisis deepened during this period, it became clear that it would be desirable to insulate the air-supported roofs while still preserving translucency. The requirements of snow melt and the existence of internal pressure have prevented a reasonable solution to this problem. Construction experiences indicated a vulnerability of the air structure in that roofs were often inflated and occupancy initiated even though mechanical systems were incomplete and operators were inexperienced. On a number of occasions, this resulted in roof deflations under snow conditions while the building was under construction. These problems disappeared after punch-list items were corrected and operators gained more experience. This problem was prevented in the Tokyo Korakuen Stadium completed in 1987 in that the Takenaka company functioned both as designers and general contractors. Moreover, they developed an automated snow melt system that significantly reduced the need for operator intervention (8). Finally, operators of air structures must provide proper maintenance so that the system will perform as designed. Failure to provide such maintenance increases the risk of deflation as time goes on.

To overcome the problems with air structures enumerated above, a new structural system was required that would offer the advantages of the air structures while not requiring the need for pressurization or snow melt and allowing for the possibility of insulation while maintaining translucency. The cable dome developed by David Geiger (9) and realized in two structures designed with Kim Swoo Guen of Space Group of Korea for the 1988 Korean Olympics offered the solution to this problem (Fig. **4a**). The domes in Korea, having diameters of 393 ft and 295 ft, are translucent and insulated to R10 (10). Other cable domes under construction include the 256 × 304 ft super-elliptical cable dome for the Illinois State University Arena, and the 680 ft diameter circular cable dome for St. Petersburg Stadium (Fig. 4**b**).

DESCRIPTION OF STRUCTURAL SYSTEMS

For suspension-cable-supported structures, the cables carry the gravity loads while stability and resistance to wind uplift is provided by the weight of the roof-deck system. For pneumatic structures and tension structures, the weight of the membrane that serves as both weather barrier and structural deck is so small that stability and resistance to wind uplift is either provided by the roof membrane acting alone or the roof membrane acting in conjunction with arching cables. If the membrane is constructed of synthetic yarns or fiber-glass filament yarns, it can be considered weightless. As a consequence, for tension structures, the membrane and cable system must, in the absence of applied loads, be prestressed. That is to say, fabric and cables arching in one direction apply load to fabric and cables sagging in the other direction. The resultant surface is anticlastic, one where the principal curvatures are of opposite sign. Under the application of gravity loads, the sagging cables or sagging membrane increase their stress, while the arching cables or arching membrane decrease their stress. On the other hand, under wind uplift, the stresses on the arching cables and membrane increase while the stresses on the sagging cables and membrane decrease. Prestressing is considered adequate if under maximum gravity load the residual prestress in the arching members has not quite gone to zero and if under maximum wind suction the residual prestress in the sagging members has not quite gone to zero. For the purpose of analysis and discussion, the continuous membrane may be represented by discreet cables at a finite spacing so that in the diagrams that follow cables and fabric need not be distinguished. One should bear in mind, though, that in the actual tension structure it is usual to have cables acting in one direction and fabric in the other, for if fabric is supported on a two-way cable net, special care is required to control the prestress in the fabric. The anticlastic prestressed membrane is represented in Figure 5**a,** while its distortion under gravity load is represented in Figure 5**b,** and its distortion under wind suction is represented in Figure 5**c,** thus illustrating the principles discussed above.

For pneumatic structures, the membrane and cable system is prestressed by the internal pressure acting outward on the membrane, thus forming a synclastic surface. The membrane may act alone or together with a cable system to resist the internal pressure and environmental forces. External forces acting in the same direction as the internal pressure, such as wind suction, will cause the membrane and/or cable forces to increase, whereas forces acting opposite to but less than the internal pressure will cause the membrane and cable forces to decrease. If the external forces are greater than the internal pressure, the membrane surface will reverse curvature near the point of application of load and membrane forces will increase as the loads increase. As a consequence, the capacity of pneumatic structures to carry local loading well in excess of the internal pressure is significant. It is limited, though, by considerations of ponding in those parts of the roof where the resultant dimple may attract water or sliding snow. These principles are illustrated in Figure 6. This figure illustrates the fact that an air structure forms a synclastic surface, ie, one where the principal curvatures are of the same sign. It is possible for an air structure to form a cylindrical surface, ie, a surface having zero curvature in one direction.

Pneumatic structures may be further classified as being either air inflated or air supported, where the latter is distinguished by the pressurized space being occupied. If it is occupied, then air locks are required for entering or exiting. For people, revolving doors function as air locks, and for vehicles, pairs of garage-type doors serve this purpose. For emergency exiting, revolving doors are not permitted by code, so pressure-balanced doors are used. These, once opened, will close against the internal pressure, but while open there is risk of deflation of the roof if the blower capacity is not sufficient to handle the air loss through the open doors. This air loss is typically reduced by the space occupied by the exiting people. The pressure within the occupied space is limited through consideration of leakage and safe operation of doors. This results in a maximum positive pressure of less than 2.4-in. water gauge and a normal operating pressure of 0.8 in. for low-profile air structures and 1.0 to 1.5 in. water pressure for high-rise bubbles. Considerations of leakage also require that great care and attention to detail apply to all aspects of the

(a)

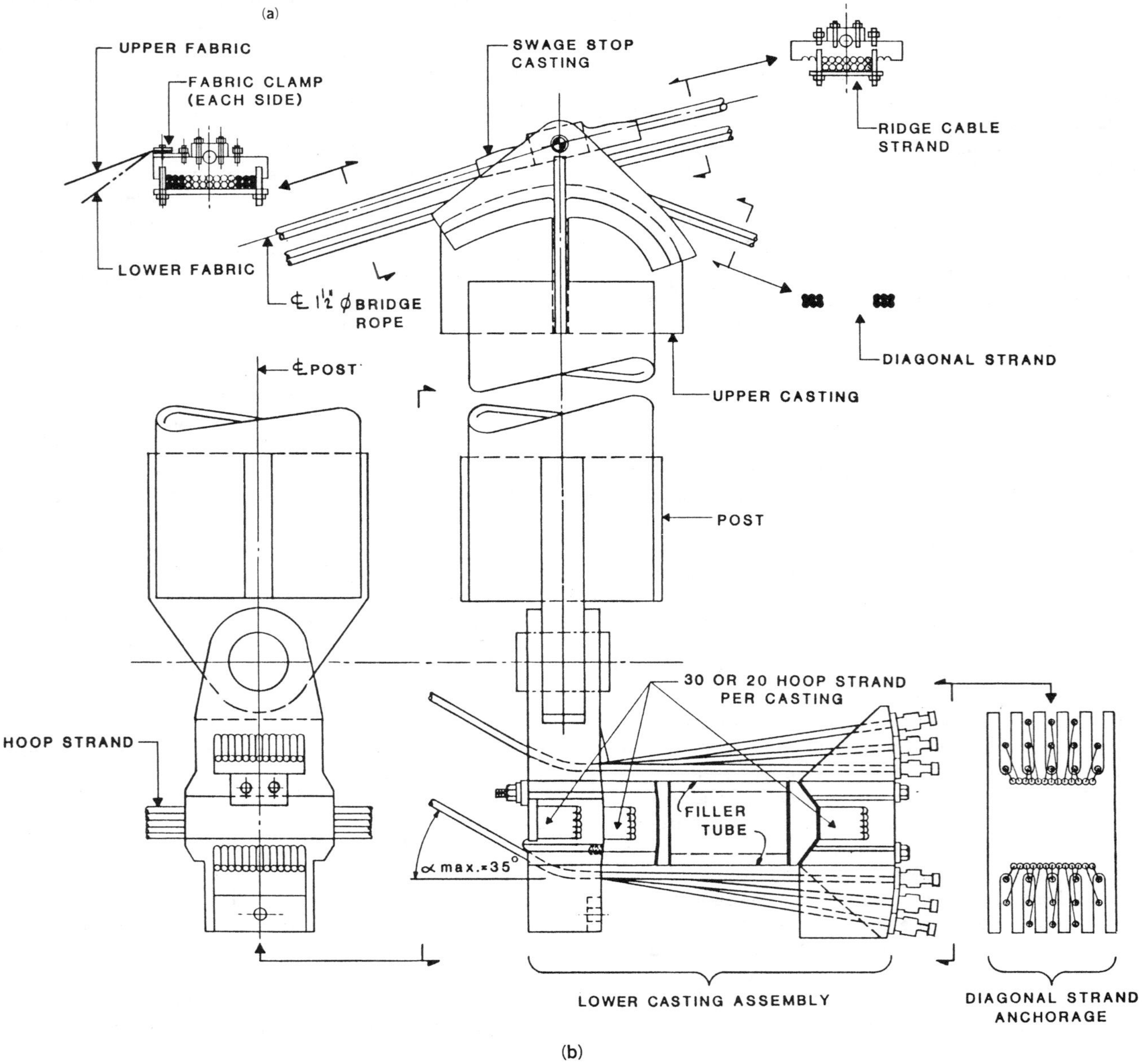

Figure 4. Cable domes. **(a)** Gymnastics arena for the 1988 Olympics under construction in Seoul, Korea. **(b)** Casting, post, and strand assembly for the Florida Sun Coast Dome, St. Petersburg.

UPPER FABRIC
FABRIC CLAMP (EACH SIDE)
LOWER FABRIC
SWAGE STOP CASTING
RIDGE CABLE STRAND
℄ 1½" ϕ BRIDGE ROPE
DIAGONAL STRAND
UPPER CASTING
℄ POST
POST
HOOP STRAND
30 OR 20 HOOP STRAND PER CASTING
FILLER TUBE
α max.=35°
LOWER CASTING ASSEMBLY
DIAGONAL STRAND ANCHORAGE

(b)

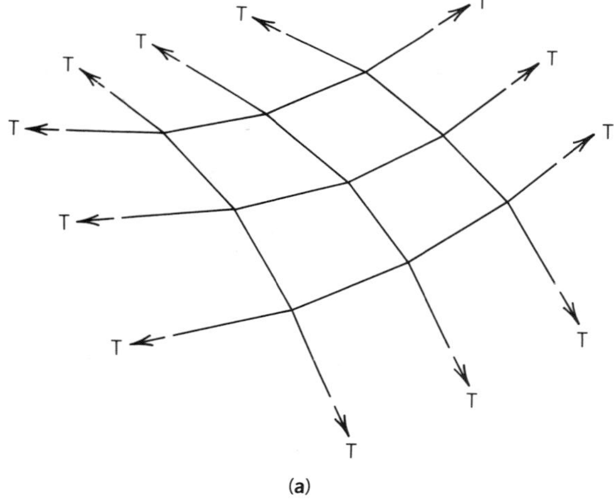

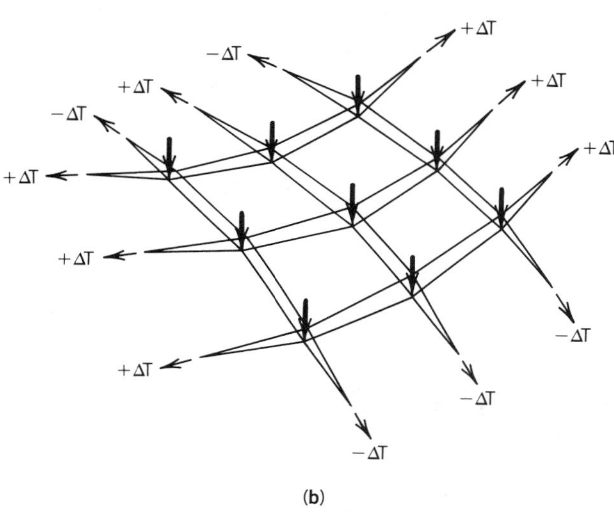

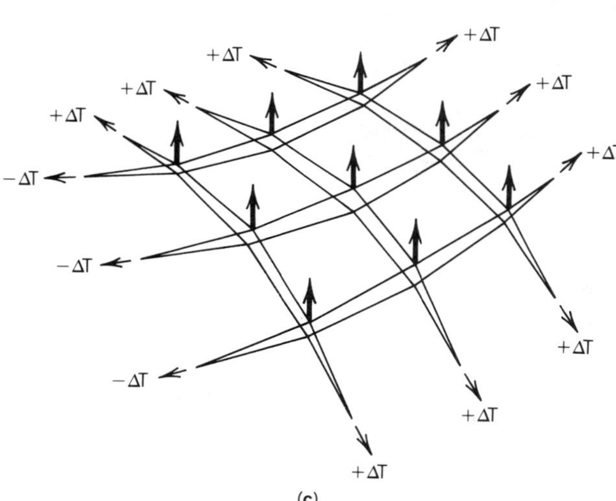

Figure 5. Anticlastic net behavior under load. **(a)** Prestressed load. **(b)** Under gravity. **(c)** Under wind suction.

enclosure so as to reduce leakage and the possibilities of local failure of elements that could result in pressure loss. The limitation on maximum pressure requires that snow-melt systems be installed and manual removal of snow be considered since the maximum pressure allowed may carry less than the code snow loading. Since the functioning of an air-supported structure is highly dependent upon considerations of power supply, maintenance, and operations, the possibility of deflation must be a consideration in the design. For low occupancy air structures such as tennis structures, this may be accounted for by use of light stanchions and the like that can be quickly lowered so that they will not pierce the roof in the event of deflation. For high-occupancy air structures such as stadia, the roof must be designed so that it hangs free over the occupied space in the event of deflation. The low-profile air structure is quite suitable in meeting this design criterion.

When used for buildings, air-inflated structures use internal pressure to prestress a multicelled structure so that the structure can resist the environmental forces. As such, the structure exists above and quite possibly around the occupied space, but the occupied space is not pressurized; consequently the internal pressure is not limited and full snow loading can be carried by the pressure. Air-inflated structures typically operate at much higher pressures than do air-supported structures. Often the material strength requirements are much greater and the practical span limitations are much less than for the air-inflated structure. As a consequence, the air-inflated structure is most typically used as a portable structure for the military or for exhibit purposes (Figs. 7 and 8).

THE DETERMINATION OF MEMBRANE SHAPES

Pneumatic and tensile structures have been described earlier in terms of the signs of the principal curvatures. When for a pneumatic structure the principal curvatures have the same value, a minimal surface is described; such is the case for a soap film. In this case, not only are the principal stresses equal but the surface area is a minimum for the given boundary conditions. This is the same problem that is approximately defined in standard courses in partial differential equations by the expression:

$$\frac{\partial^2 Z}{\partial X^2} + \frac{\partial^2 Z}{\partial^2 Y} = \frac{P}{h} \qquad (1)$$

where z represents the vertical ordinate from the x, y plane, h is the uniform biaxial state of stress in the membrane projected on the x, y plane, and P is the pressure normal to the x, y plane. It is important to realize, though, that in this formulation the boundary is assumed to be infinitely stiff, that is, it is capable of carrying the stresses being transmitted to it by the membrane without the boundary distorting. Such is the actual case in soap-film membranes because of the very low stress levels in the soap film. For a very high pneumatic structure where the membrane nearly approaches the ground at right angles, it is possible that this condition may be realized by the anchorage system. On the other hand, for the low-profile

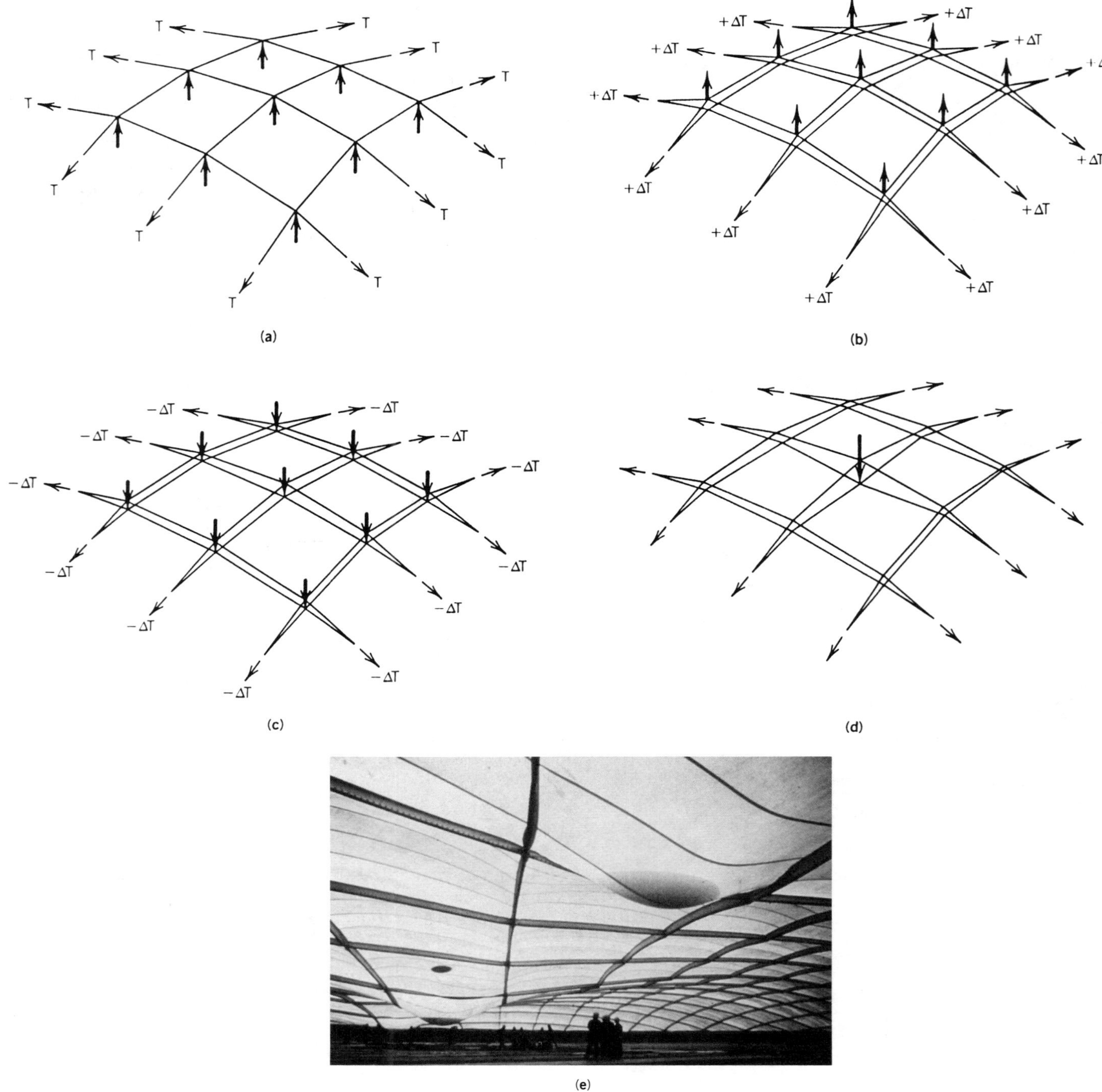

Figure 6. Synclastic net behavior under load. **(a)** Net prestressed by internal pressure. **(b)** Under wind suction. **(c)** Under gravity load. **(d)** Under gravity load in excess of pressure (the stress change is indeterminate). **(e)** Bending during inflation of the U.S. Pavilion, Expo' 70, Osaka, Japan.

air-supported roofs, it is likely that a boundary ring could not carry the tensile forces from the membrane without significant distortion, unless, by coincidence, the distribution of the forces from the minimal surface was identical to that required for the funicular loading of a boundary ring. This would be the case, for example, for a minimal surface attached to a circular boundary shape. It would not be the case if it were attached to an elliptical or a super elliptical boundary shape.

With Cables Projecting in Plan as Straight Lines

When it is desired that the membrane forces be in horizontal equilibrium with the perimeter ring and the ring have

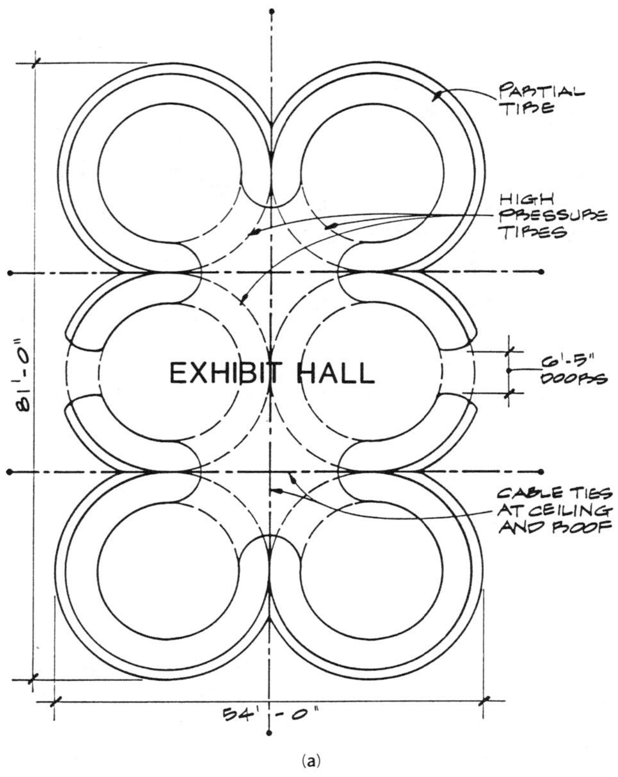

(a)

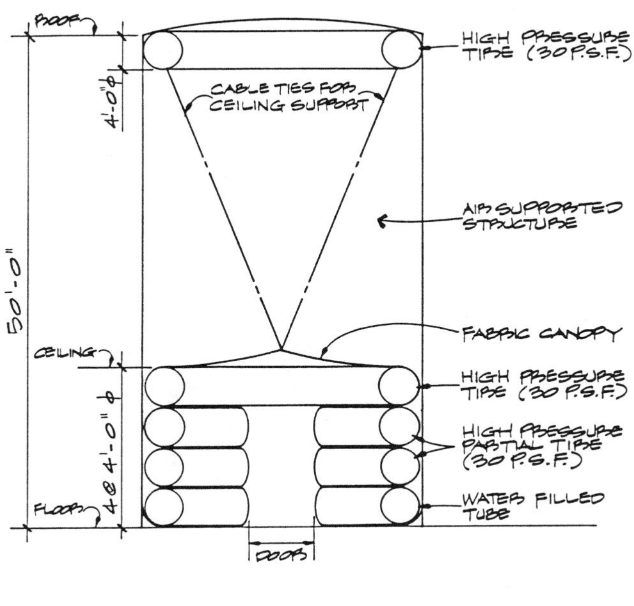

(b)

(c)

(d)

Figure 7. An inflatable six-pack exhibit hall. **(a)** Plain view. **(b)** Section through a can. **(c)** Exterior view. **(d)** Interior view. **(c)** and **(d)** Courtesy of Geiger Associates.

zero bending moments, the membrane shape is determined by the ring configuration. From equations of statics, the horizontal component of the membrane forces H_i and H_j are then determined so that there is no bending in the ring. These can be determined in terms of the internal compressive force in the ring (Fig. 9**b**). From these forces and the applied loads, the membrane shape, ordinates $Z_{i,j}$, is determined through consideration of equilibrium in the Z direction (Fig. 10**a**) which yields the equation:

$$P_{i,j} + H_j\left[\frac{Z_{i+1,j} - Z_{i,j}}{S_{i+1,j}} - \frac{Z_{i,j} - Z_{i-1,j}}{S_{i-1,j}}\right] + H_i\left[\frac{Z_{i,j+1} - Z_{i,j}}{S_{i,j+1}} - \frac{Z_{i,j} - Z_{i,j-1}}{S_{i,j-1}}\right] = 0 \qquad (2)$$

Since for each point *i,j*, there is one unknown $Z_{i,j}$ and one equation of statics, there are for roofs, as illustrated

Figure 8. King Kong, an air-inflated structure on the Empire State Building. Courtesy of Geiger Associates.

in Figure 9**c** and **d,** as many unknowns as equations of statics and $Z_{i,j}$ can be determined.

Note that if in equation 2 these substitutions are made

$$S_i = S_{i,j+1} = S_{i,j-1}$$
$$S_j = S_{i-1,j} = S_{i+1,j}$$
$$h_j = H_j/S_j \text{ and } h_i = H_i/S_i$$
$$h_j = h_i = h$$
$$P = \frac{P_{i,j}}{S_i S_j}$$
$$\text{and } S = S_i = S_j$$

Then equation 2 reduces to:

$$-Z_{i+1,j} - Z_{i-1,j} + 4Z_{i,j} - Z_{i,j+1} - Z_{i,j-1} = \frac{p \cdot S^2}{h} \quad (3)$$

which is the finite difference expression for the minimal surface as defined by equation 1.

Figure 9**a** shows a family of super elliptical curves, all of which could function as funicular rings for an air or tension structure (11). For these there are many possible cable directions: cables parallel to either the cartesian x, y axis or the skewed symmetries ξ, η axis would be suitable for an air structure (Fig. 9**c**). For either of these, equation 2 could be used to find this roof shape which, if $m \neq 2$, would be different for each of the cable directions chosen. With $m = 2$, the cables would be parabolic. A radial cable pattern would also be possible. This would be most suitable to cable domes or tents. For a radial tent with a rectangular base, horizontal sections from the crown to the rectangular base would be super-ellipses of exponent 2 to exponent infinity (Fig. 11).

If the exponent M is less than 1, the "ring" is actually a catenary restrained by four anchorages along the major and minor axes. For a radial cable system, symmetry around the major and minor axes need not be maintained (Fig. 2**a**). Other funicular rings and cable patterns are possible. One used extensively for low-profile air supported roofs is the minimal roof defined as the cable grid having the minimum number of cables all carrying the same force (12). These lead to the most economical roof (Fig. 9**d**). A variation on these allows for equal ring segments by distorting the cable pattern from the center diamond pattern where the cables cross the ring (Fig. 9**e**). This causes some bending in the ring. The resultant bending moments can be reduced by providing a horizontal spring support to the ring (Fig. 9**f**). The horizontal springs carry the non-funicular component of the cable force (13).

It is not necessary that this funicular ring lie in a plane. For an air structure, a planner ring is preferred since then the cable pattern will deliver funicular loading to the ring with the roof either inflated or deflated. For a tensile structure the funicular ring may warp as with a saddle roof. For superimposed loads, the horizontal bending can be significant since cables in one direction have their loads increase significantly while in the other direction they may go to zero. This bending can be minimized by prestressing the ring with horizontal cables (Fig. 12**a**) (14).

For a tensile structure, stretch fabric models are often used in preliminary design (Fig. 12**d**). When the membrane is a minimal surface, the principal curvatures are not only equal and opposite but they are also 90° to each other (Fig. 12**c**). The minimal surface may also be represented by a soap-film model (Fig. 12**b**).

When the membrane is not a minimal surface, the principal curvatures are not equal, nor are they 90° to each other. They are, though, on the angle bisection of the lines of zero curvature. Since the lines of zero curvature are easy to establish, the fabric stretch model gives a means of establishing the radii of curvature for the membrane. This information is essential to preliminary design.

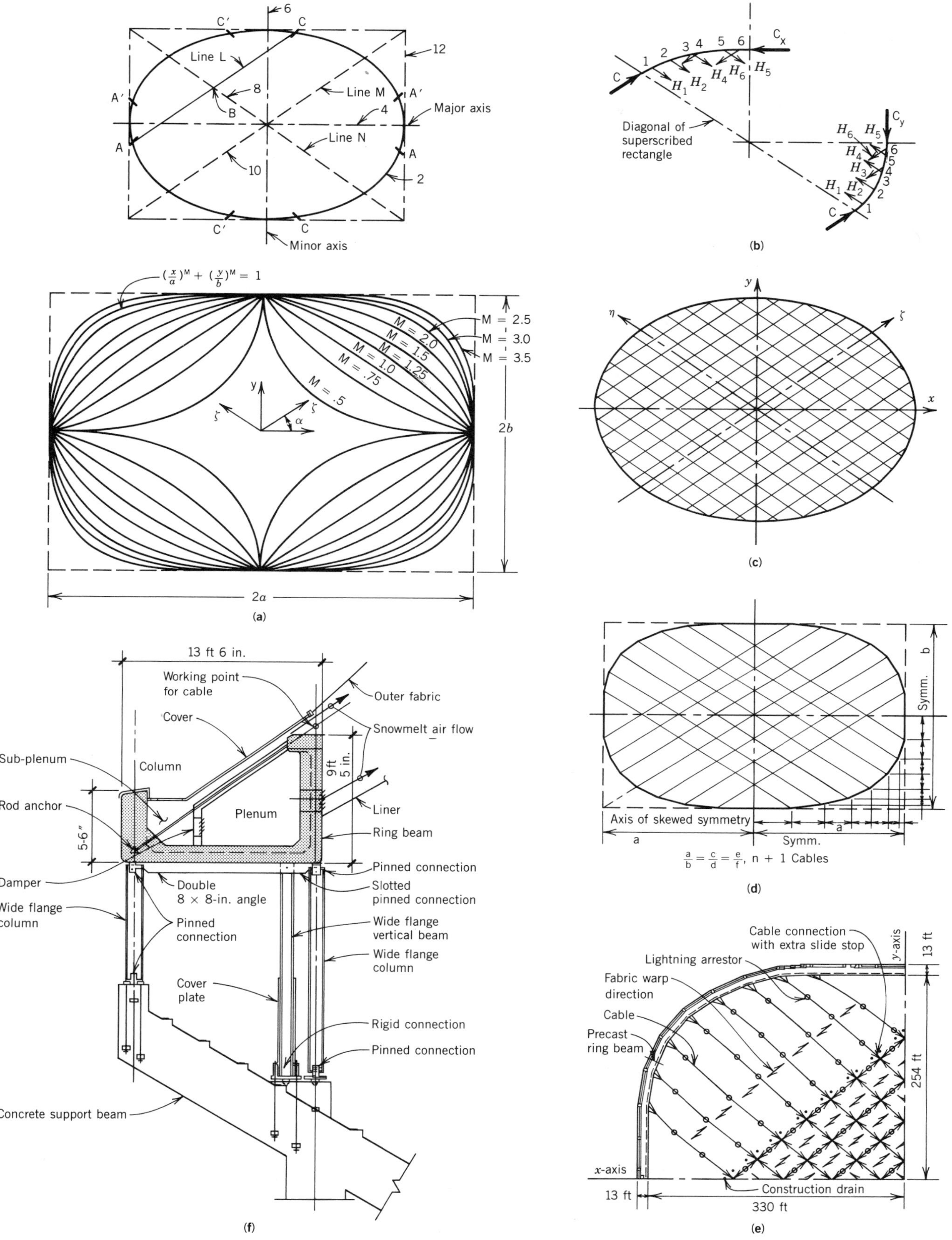

Figure 9. Funicular rings. **(a)** Illustrations from U.S. Pat. 3,835,599 (11). **(b)** Free body of funicular ring. **(c)** Cable pattern super elliptical ring. **(d)** Cable pattern, minimal roof. **(e)** Minimal roof with equal ring segments. **(f)** Ring beam with horizontal spring supports.

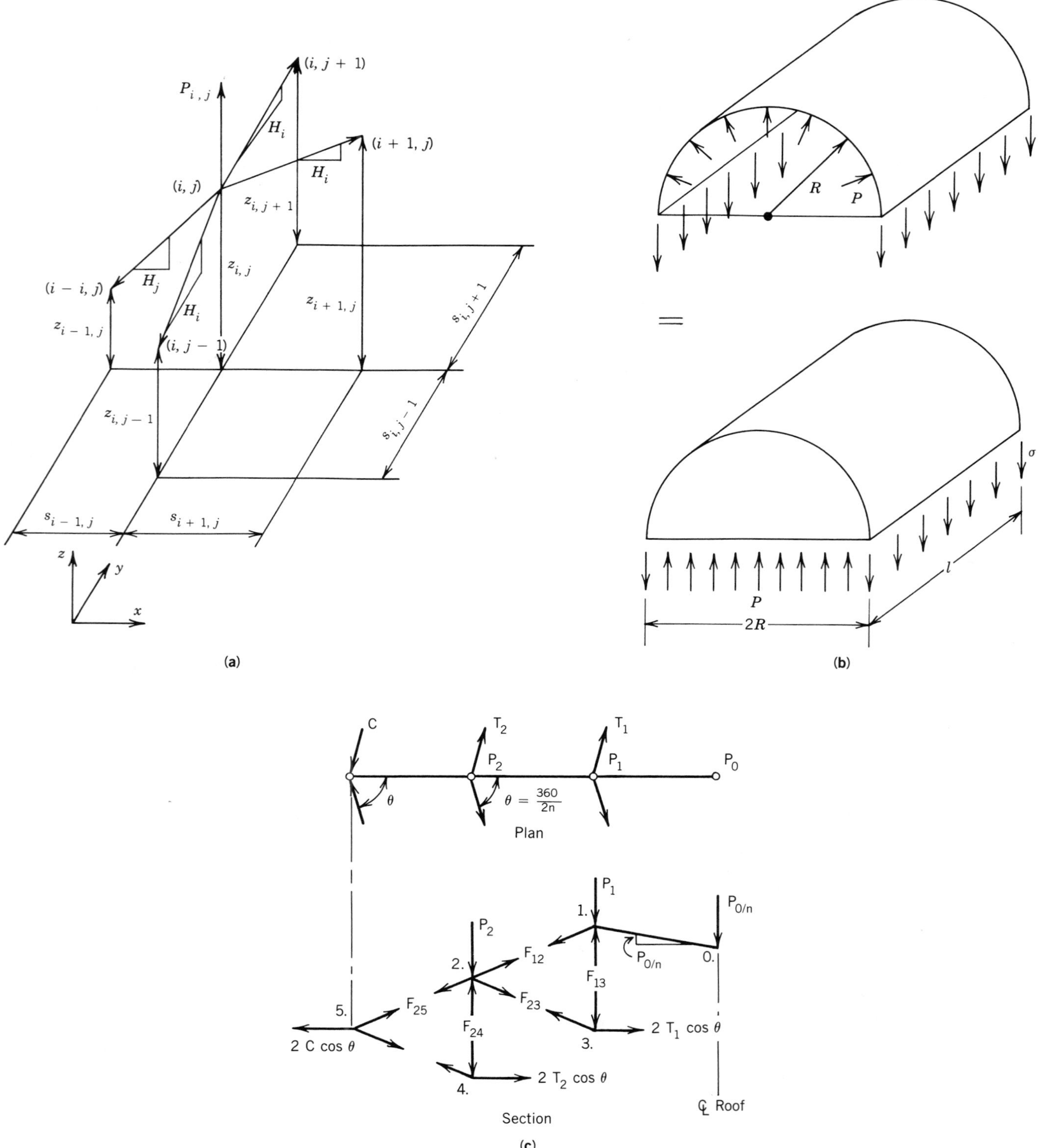

Figure 10. Static equilibrium of membrane structures. **(a)** Free body of node. **(b)** Free body of cylindrical-shaped air-supported roof. **(c)** Cable dome—statically determinate analysis.

Figure 11. **(a)** Great Adventure Tent. **(b)** The computer plots show the funicular rings as elevation contours of the square-based tent. **(c)** Flexible boundary supports allow for redistribution of stress.

(b)

(a)

Key:

Original position of tent

Final position of tent

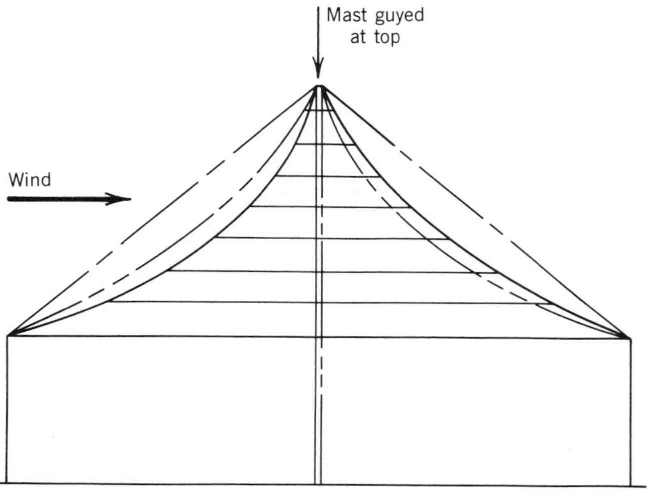

Guyed mast

Radial stress on windward side increases, on lee side decreases, circumferential stresses vary.

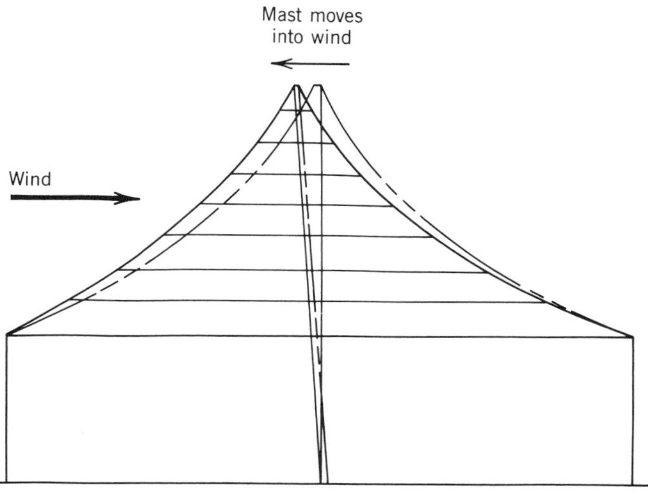

Mast free to move

Sag on windward side increases, on lee side decreases, stresses are nearly constant.

(c)

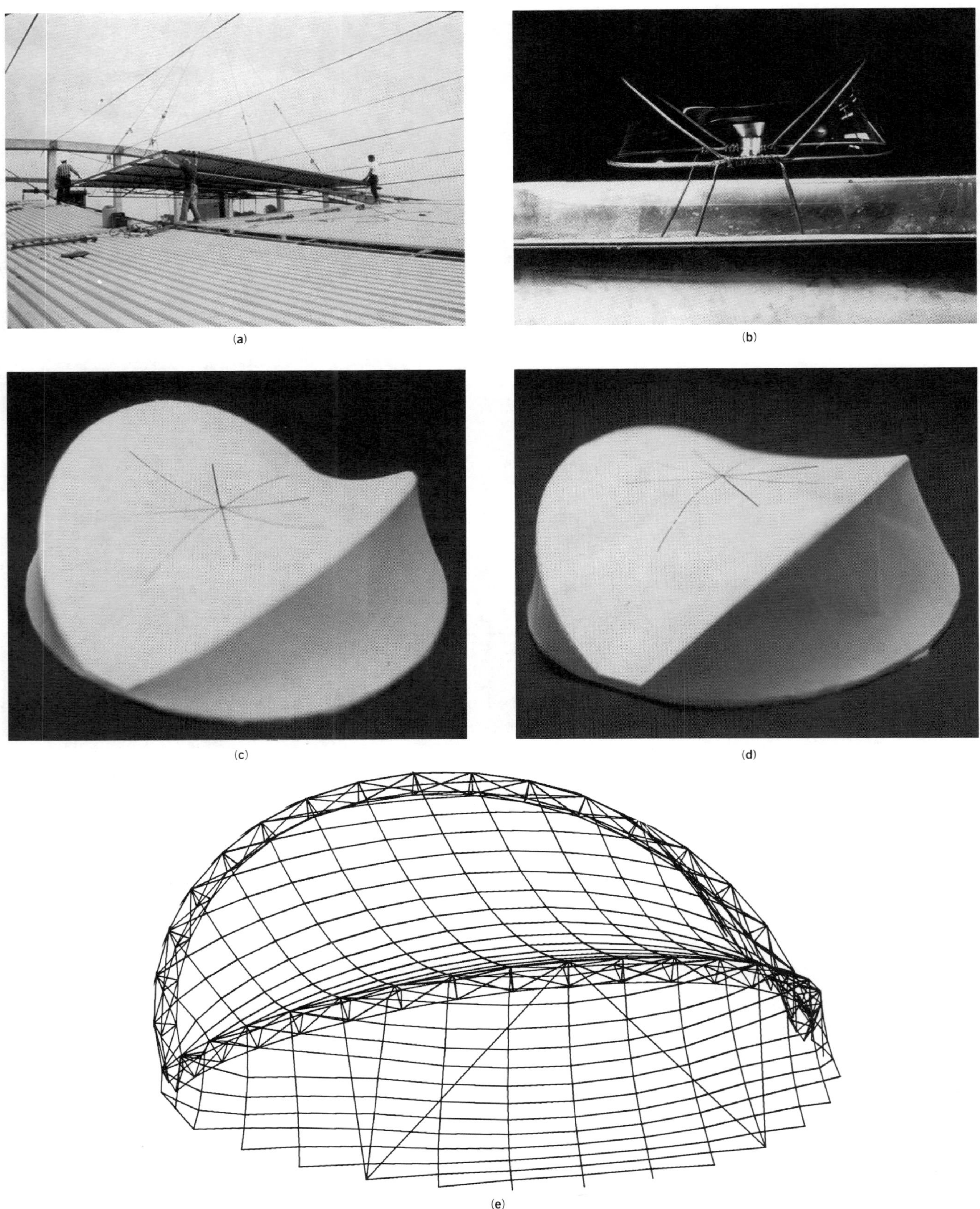

Figure 12. Tensile membranes as a saddle surface. **(a)** Saddle roof during construction, Capitol Centre, Largo, Maryland. **(b)** Soap-film model. **(c)** Fabric stretch model of minimal surface. **(d)** Fabric stretch model of fabric, not a minimal surface. **(e)** Saddle surface represented by computer model showing fabric strip. **(a)** and **(b)** Courtesy of Geiger Associates.

When Cables Do Not Project as Straight Lines

An iterative computer approach used to determine the prestressed membrane shape may be derived from free bodies similar to Figure 10**a,** except that now cables do not project in plan as straight lines and equilibrium in the x, y as well as the z directions must be considered at each node. This yields three equations in terms of the three coordinates x_i, y_i, and z_i at each node. If cable forces and cable lengths framing to node i, j is represented by $T_{i+1,j}$; $T_{i-1,j}$; $T_{i,j+1}$; $T_{i,j-1}$ and $l_{i+1,j}$; $l_{i-1,j}$; $l_{i,j+1}$; and $l_{i,j-1}$ respectively; equilibrium in the z direction yields the equation:

$$Pz_{i,j} + \frac{T_{i+1,j}}{l_{i+1,j}} \Delta Z_{i+1,j} - \frac{T_{i-1,j}}{l_{i-1,j}} \Delta Z_{i-1,j} + \frac{T_{i,j+1}}{l_{i,j+1}} \Delta Z_{i,j+1} - \frac{T_{i,j-1}}{l_{i,j-1}} \Delta Z_{i,j-1} = 0 \tag{4}$$

where $Pz_{i,j}$ = the Z component of load $P_{i,j}$ and $\Delta Z_{i+1,j} = Z_{i+1,j} - Z_{i,j}$, $\Delta Z_{i-1,j} = Z_{i,j} - Z_{i-1,j}$, $\Delta Z_{i,j+1} = Z_{i,j+1} - Z_{i,j}$, $\Delta Z_{i,j-1} = Z_{i,j} - Z_{i,j-1}$, where $Z_{i,j}$ = the Z coordinate of node i,j.

Similar equations in terms of $Px_{i,j}$ and $Py_{i,j}$ are found for equilibrium in the x direction and similarly for equilibrium in the y direction.

The actual lengths $l_{i+1,j}$ are related to the coordinates $x_{i,j}$, $y_{i,j}$, and $z_{i,j}$ through equation:

$$l_{i,j+1} = \sqrt{(\Delta X_{i,j+1})^2 + (\Delta Y_{i,j+1})^2 + (\Delta Z_{i,j+1})^2} \tag{5}$$

For the prestress case where $P_{i,j} = 0$, the system of equations is homogeneous and a unique solution does not exist. A particular solution can be obtained through iteration if one begins with an approximate solution. If the membrane is of a fairly regular configuration, the input can be obtained through a best-guess mathematical model. If the form is quite sculptural or defies formulation through a mathematical model, the input coordinates can be measured off of a stretch fabric model. With the input coordinates given and prestress forces $T_{i+1,j}$ for each link assumed, the resultant system of equations can be solved by calculating the link lengths $l_{i+1,j}$ from the input coordinates; calculating the "rubberband spring constant" $T_{i+1,j}/l_{i+1,j}$ and from the system of equations calculating new coordinates $x_{i,y}$, $y_{i,j}$ and $z_{i,j}$. The process is repeated until the lengths $l_{i,j}$ converge. Convergence will occur if the original coordinate input is not grossly out of line with the final results.

If the mathematical model is meant to represent fabric as well as cables, it is imperative that the fabric directions approximately represent the warp and fill direction of the fabric. This is required because the shape program is the input geometry for the analysis program and in the analysis program the fabric stiffness in the warp and fill direction will be required. Moreover, because the shape program and prestress level may be used to establish the cutting patterns for the fabric, it is best to space the elements representing the fabric in the warp direction, the direction along the length of the fabric roll, so that they are spaced not less than the fabric width. In this manner, if the grid on the fabric model is triangulated, it can be laid flat and it may then be used to represent the uncompensated shape of the fabric cutting pattern (Fig. 12**e**).

Fabric Utilization and Surface Area Aspect Ratios

Since for permanent member structures the cost of the fabricated membrane material is the largest component of the total cost, often as much as 60%, keeping the surface area–plan area ratio to a minimum results in the lowest roof cost. On the other hand, interior clearance requirements or the unique opportunities for architectural expressions may result in sculptural forms having large surface area–plan area ratios and this resultant high costs are an accepted consequence of these decisions. Figure 13 shows how the surface area/plan area varies for different types of membrane structures. Fabric utilization per square foot of surface area is also a function of membrane shape.

ROOF LOADS

Since the gravity loads of membrane structures is minimal, the proper evaluation of superimposed loads is of particular importance. Stresses due to wind, snow, and temperature change govern their design.

Wind

The equivalent wind pressure acting perpendicular to a membrane surface is obtained in accordance with the following expressions:

$$P_W = c_p q$$

where C_p = wind pressure coefficient

q = dynamic wind pressure = $\frac{1}{2}\rho V^2$

ρ = air density

v = wind velocity

with v in miles/h and q in lb/ft^2: $q = 0.00256\ v^2$

The value of the wind pressure coefficient is a function of shape, scale, surface condition surroundings, wind velocity and wind direction, and for air structures, internal pressure. For tent structures that are open or have large openings, the effect of wind forces from below the membrane must also be taken into account. Because of the complexity of these many factors, wind tunnel tests must be performed to evaluate the wind pressure coefficient. For high profile air structures or tent structures lightly stressed or on flexible frameworks, the wind tunnel tests should be performed on aeroelastic models that allow for the change in the structural shape under the action of wind.

Results for a cylindrical form showing the variation in wind pressure coefficient as a function of internal pressure is shown in Figure 14**a** (15). For a low-profile air

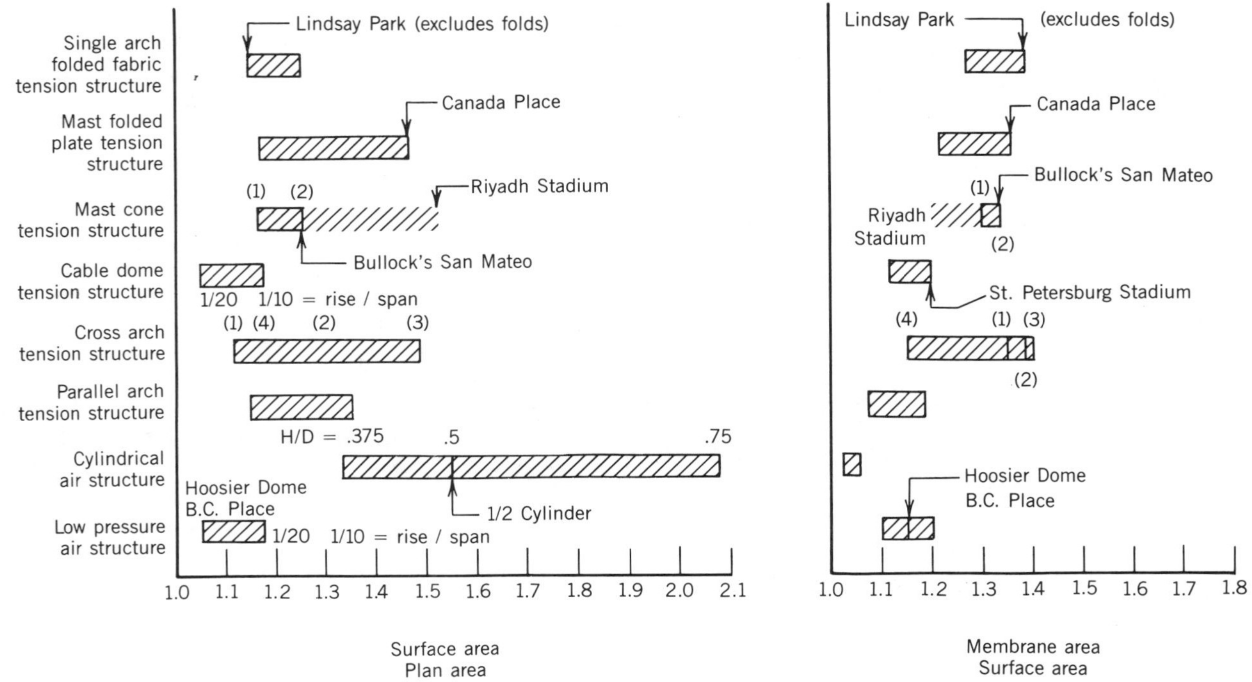

Figure 13. Fabric utilization. Fabric–surface ratio. Courtesy of Birdair Structures, Inc.

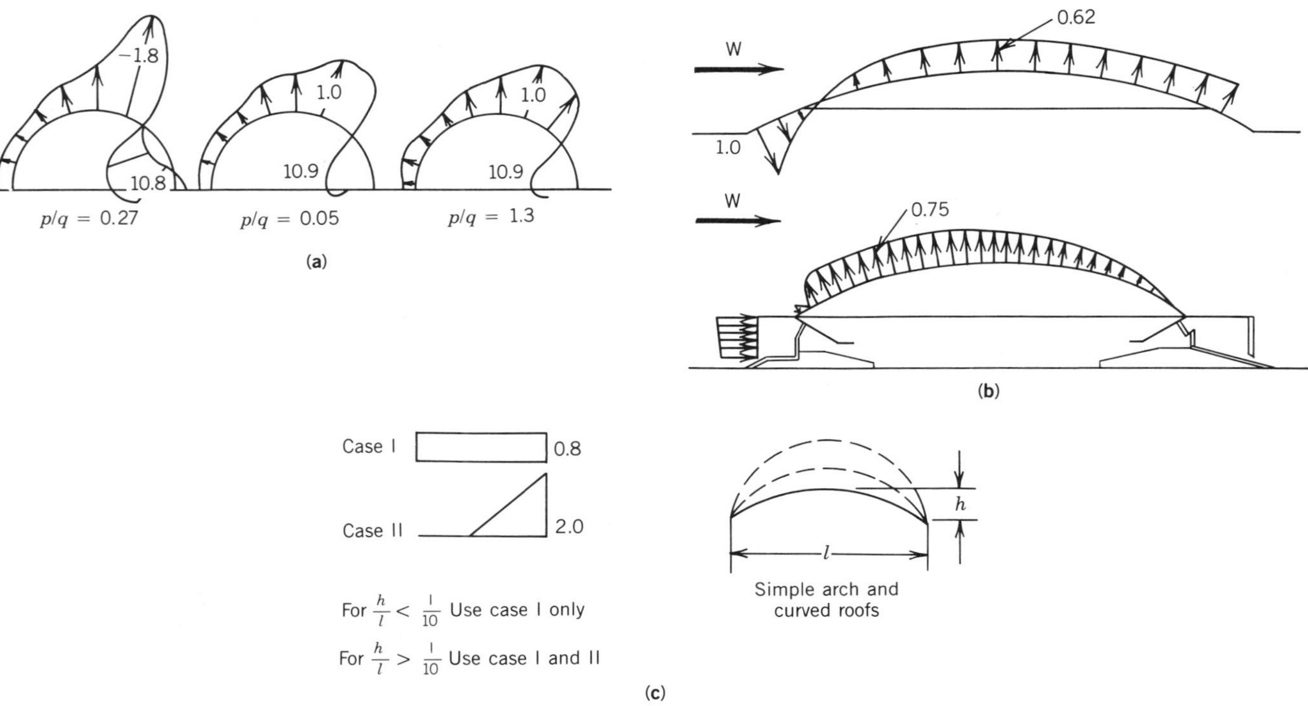

Figure 14. Considerations of wind and snow loading. **(a)** Wind tunnel tests on sectional cylindrical forms (11). **(b)** Wind tunnel tests on low-profile air structures. Courtesy of Geiger Associates. **(c)** Snow-load distribution as a function of rise (12). Courtesy of ANSI. **(d)** Roof displacements as function of snow load divided by pressure (9). **(e)** Formation of snow sacks (9). **(f)** Lindsay Park Sports Centre snow-drift studies. Courtesy of RWD1. **(g)** Silverdome snow-drift model. Courtesy of CDP. **(h)** Canada Place snow-drift studies. Courtesy of CDP. **(i)** Canada Place, actual structure. Courtesy of Geiger Associates.

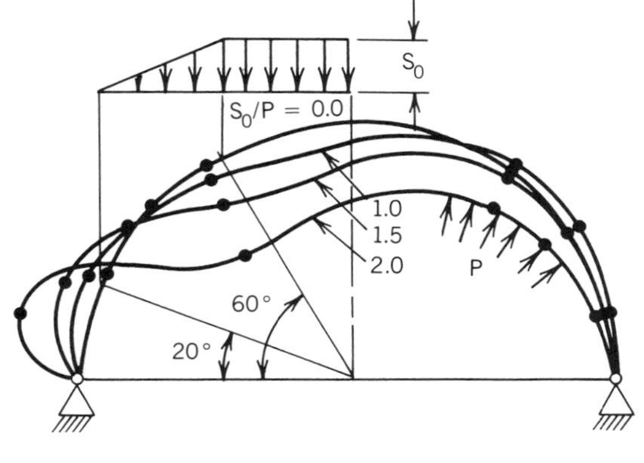

S_0
$S_0/P = 0.0$
1.0
1.5
2.0
P
60°
20°

(f)

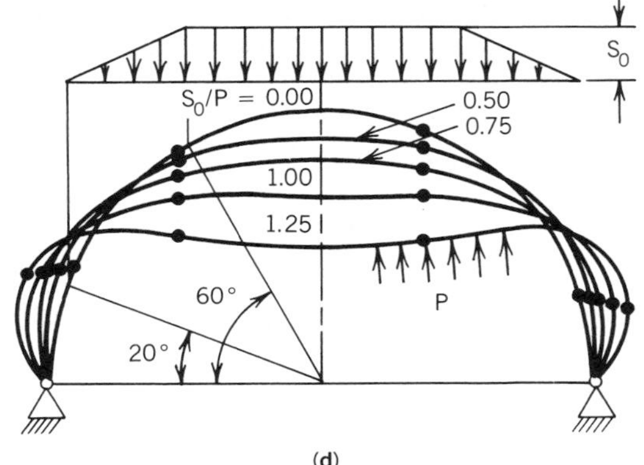

S_0
$S_0/P = 0.00$
0.50
0.75
1.00
1.25
P
60°
20°

(d)

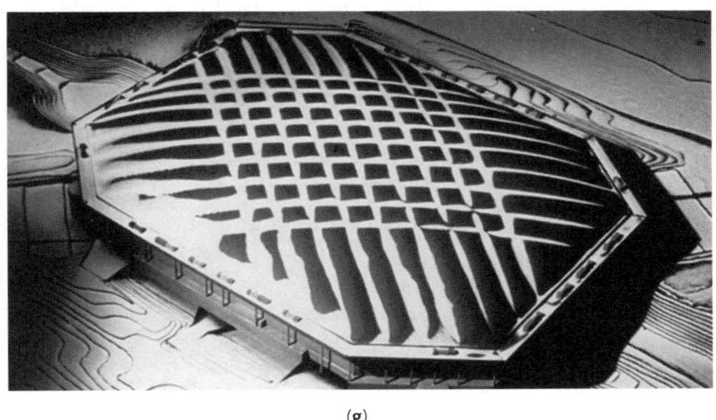

(g)

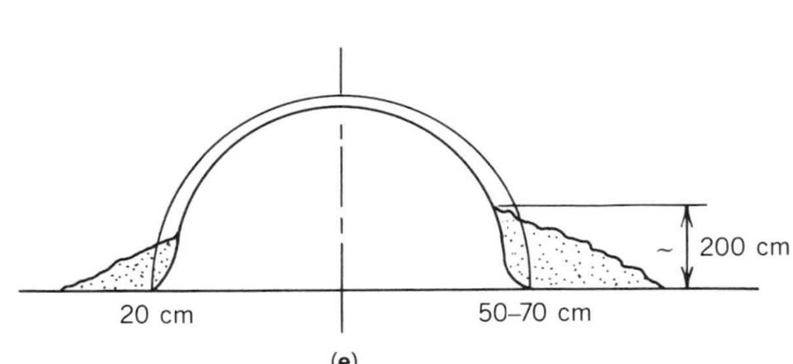

~ 200 cm
20 cm
50–70 cm

(e)

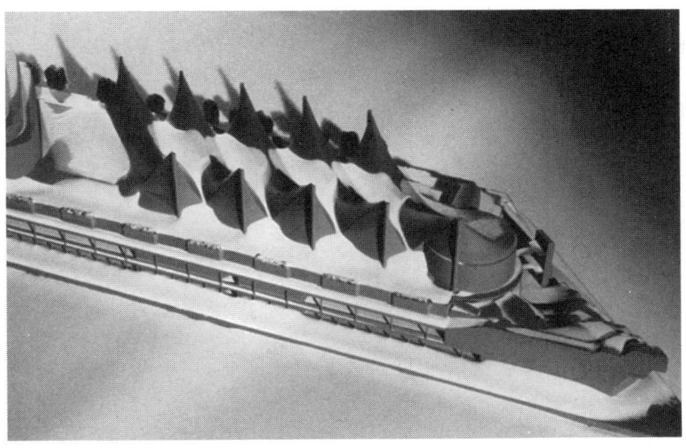

(h)

(i)

structure, variation with internal pressure is negligible. Results for berm-mounted and wall-mounted air structures are shown in Figure 14**b.** For preliminary design, the above results may be applied to low-profile membrane structures such as cable domes and saddle roofs. For tent-type membrane structures, since the forms are quite varied, there is more need for wind tunnel tests for each specific case.

Snow

Tension structures may be designed to carry the full snow load as dictated by building codes. Their flexibility requires consideration of ponding in flat areas of the roof or for particularly heavy snow loads. Although codes such as ANSI A58.1 (16) make significant provisions for drifting, unusual shapes that result from the sculptural forms that membrane structures take may require wind tunnel or water flume based snow-drift studies. Such studies have been done for the Convention Center in Vancouver, British Columbia, Canada, the Lindsay Park Sports Centre in Calgary, Canada, and the Silverdome in Pontiac, Michigan (Figs. 14**f**, **g** and **h**).

Because most membranes have low coefficients of friction and may be uninsulated, particular attention should be given to snow sliding and the formation of snow sacks at the base (17) (Fig. 14**e**).

The large deformation of air structures makes them particularly sensitive to ponding, the risk of which increases as the ratio of snow load divided by pressure increases (Fig. 14**d**). Low-profile air structures are particularly susceptible to ponding instability. If internal pressure is low, the ponding from snow or water will result in inversion of a panel due to the load of the accumulated ponding medium. Consequently, it may be necessary to resort to various methods of snow removal. These include snow melt through the application of heat, snow shoveling, and the use of water jets. If the snow is dry and accompanied by winds, it is usually best not to apply heat, which would cause the snow to stick but rather to allow the snow to blow off the roof. When snow melt systems are being used, it is essential to allow uninterrupted flow of water along the drainage paths.

Low-profile membrane structures, either air or tension, have the advantage that snow tends to blow off the roof rather than accumulate on the leeward side of the roof. This is most graphically represented by the provision from the ANSI code shown in Figure 14**c.** Allowance must additionally be made for drifting in the valleys of the roof. For air structures, provision is usually made to increase the pressure up to 2.4 in. of water gauge (12 psf) to deal with snow emergencies. For low-profile air structures, standard practice provides for designing the roof in the deflated position for 60% of the ground snow load or 12 psf or the maximum snow fall in 24 hours, whichever is greater.

Recurrence Interval

In determining the design wind velocity or snow load, the recurrence interval is taken into account. For structures having a short life span such as temporary buildings, a lower recurrence interval can be used. Recurrence interval (*RI*), life span (*LS*) and factor of safety (*SF*) are related by the formula (17):

$$RI = 1/[1-(SF)^{1/LS}] \tag{7}$$

In Japan, where pneumatic structures have a life span of 6 months, a recurrence interval of 10 years may be used, ie, the structure is designed for a 10-year storm. Equation 7 indicates that the factor of safety is then 95%, which indicates that the probability of the wind velocity not exceeding the design wind velocity is approximately 95%.

In the United States, the recurrence interval used in the design of temporary buildings is typically 25 years, whereas, for permanent construction, 50 or 100 years is used depending on occupancy (16).

Internal Pressure Load

For air structures, minimum internal pressure is required to prevent excessive deformation under external load. In the case of snow load, the internal pressure should be larger than the design snow load plus the dead weight of the roof.

Wind load on a high-rise air structure will cause significant distortion of the roof unless the internal pressure exceeds the positive pressure from the wind. The necessary internal pressure under wind load is given in Table 1.

Table 1. Operating Pressures for Air Structures[a,b]

	H/S			
	0.75	0.50	0.30	0.10
Minimum operating pressure				
psf	6.7	5.0	5.0	3.5
kg/m²	30.6	22.7	22.7	15.9
Minimum pressure wind load				
Spherical shape	1.0 q	0.70 q	0.6 q	0.5 q
Cylindrical shape	0.8 q	0.60 q	0.5 q	0.4 q
Minimum pressure snow load				
Spherical shape	1.3 s	1.0 s	1.0 s	1.0 s
Cylindrical shape	1.6 s	1.3 s	1.1 s	1.1 s

[a] *H*, height of structure; *S*, span of structure; q, velocity pressure, psf or (kg/m²); s, snow load, psf or (kg/m²).
[b] Ref. 17.

The minimum operating pressure given in Table 1 will be considered as the long-term loading.

DEFORMATION OF THE STRUCTURE

Because pneumatic structures can undergo large deformations, they must in particular be designed to clear objects stored within the structure. In certain codes, clearances are prescribed. Often, provisions are made that even allow for deflation of the roof. This is particularly the case for low-profile air-supported roofs that are allowed to hang free in the deflated state. In this position they may require special padding if clearance to all objects can not be realized. All details in pneumatic and tension structures must accommodate the large movements these structures undergo. These provisions do not normally make allowances for ponding due to operator error. Structural movements should be considered with a factor of safety of two (17).

MEMBRANE STRESSES

Preliminary Design

The determination of membrane stresses for the purpose of preliminary design is quite readily accomplished for both pneumatic and tension structures.

For pneumatic structures, the total external force, P (lb/ft^2) is the sum of the internal pressure plus the maximum wind suction. For a semi-cylindrical pneumatic membrane of radius R (ft), the free body (Fig. 10**b**) yields the membrane stress:

$$\sigma = P\,R \text{ (lb/ft)} \qquad (8)$$

This formula applies to partial cylinders as well.

For hemispherical membranes, the free body yields the membrane stress σ as

$$\sigma \cdot 2\pi R = P \cdot \pi R^2$$

or

$$\sigma = \frac{P \cdot R}{2} \text{ (lb/ft)} \qquad (9)$$

This formula applies as well for spherical caps.

If, for cylindrical shells or spherical caps, cables at a spacing S carry the membrane stresses, then the cable forces are $S \cdot \sigma$, with σ determined by equation 9. If, on the other hand, the cables are designed to carry the funicular loads to a funicular ring, as with an air-supported roof, then the roof geometry is established from the formulas discussed previously. The fabric membrane is then considered as an in-fill panel. When the fabric is much stiffer in one direction than the other, equation 8 gives an upper bound for the fabric membrane stress even though the fabric spans to cables that form a cable net.

Tension structures may similarly be analyzed. From a fabric stretch model, the principal curvatures may be determined. With R the radius of curvature of the fabric—concave upward, and p the snow load, the membrane stress can be determined from $\sigma s = pR$ (lb/ft) on the assumption that the arching fabric has lost its prestress under full snow load. Similarly, the same formula is used with R the radius of curvature of the fabric—concave downward, and p the maximum wind suction. If there exists residual prestress in either case, an allowance must be made by allowing for some increase in these stresses.

For both pneumatic and tension structures, the radii of curvature will be less than the initial radii of curvature because of the stretch in the fabric under load; consequently, actual stresses will be less than that given by these formulas.

Final Design

Membrane stresses for final design and roof geometry for fabrication will generally require nonlinear analysis using digital computers.

For low-profile air-supported roofs, the initial configuration is typically the uniform maximum snow load on the deflated roof. Wind suction plus pressure is applied; this is a nonuniform load, and the bending moments in the ring are determined. If the ring is restrained by horizontal springs, the nonfunicular component of load may be largely carried by the springs and the moments are then small. If, on the other hand, the ring is free to move, the ring movement results in a redistribution of cable forces that also cause a reduction in ring movements and ring moments. For bubbles, ie, high-rise air structures of limited span with fixed anchorages, the approximate methods equation is generally adequate for final design.

For tension structures, with boundary conditions established and a membrane prestress level assumed, the initial prestressed configuration of the membrane is established by equation 4. Superimposed loads are applied. If membrane elements go slack, prestress levels are normally increased. Flexible boundary supports tend to allow for redistribution of stresses and more uniform stress levels under superimposed loads (Fig. 11**c**). A flexible element such as an arch may be assumed as a given shape under prestress, but if the assumed prestress levels deliver forces to the arch that are not funicular, the arch will distort and prestress distribution and arch shape will have to be modified to bring these into equilibrium.

For cable domes, one begins with the maximum snow load and assumes that the radial fabric stress and the valley cables have gone slack. The circumferential fabric stresses have then delivered the snow load to the ridge cables, which in turn deliver the load to the top of the posts based on tributory area. Given radial symmetry, the forces in the cable truss can be determined by simple equations of statics (Fig. 10**c**). This then gives the initial configuration and stress levels from which the nonlinear analysis can proceed. The valley cable is sized on the assumption that the fabric spans circumferentially under wind suction to the valley cable. With member stiffnesses determined from the above preliminary analysis, the nonlinear analysis proceeds, removing the snow load from the membrane. As this is done, the fabric tries to move upward; it is restrained by the valley cable and, with the snow load removed, the fabric prestress case is determined. To allow for a more uniform level of prestress, there will likely be iteration on this load case.

Nonlinear Analysis

Final member forces and roof diplacements are determined through use of nonlinear analysis. This analysis should yield the change in shape and change in stress of the membrane under change in load. As in the shape program, equation 4 is used excepting now the load $P_{i,j}$ is not equal to zero. The member forces $T_{i,j+1}$, $T_{i,j-1}$ etc, are not held constant, and member lengths $l_{i,j+1}$, $l_{i,j-1}$, etc, undergo change in length due to their elasticity. Load increments are chosen sufficiently small so that the coordinates from the previous equilibrium position are used as input to find the new equilibrium position. The iteration process proceeds as before, except now $T_{i+1,j}$ is allowed to change, and changes in $l_{i+1,j}$ are calculated from changes in load $T_{i+1,j}$ and elastic properties of the cables. The procedural steps are as follows:

1. Apply the increment load $P_{i,j}$.
2. Use $T_{i,j+1}$ and $l_{i,j+1}$ from the previous run, initially from the shape run.
3. Calculate new X_i, Y_i, Z_i.
4. Calculate new $l_{i,j+1}$ from the X_i, Y_i, Z_i.
5. From the elastic properties, calculate the new $T_{i,j+1}$ to cause this change in length.
6. Repeat steps 2 through 5 until convergence occurs.
7. With a new load increment, repeat steps 1 through 6.

As will be discussed under material properties, the elastic properties of fabric are quite complicated. Practice has shown, though, that final results are not very sensitive to these properties as load changes are carried more by prestress level and distortion of the net rather than changes in length of the members of the net. For this reason, the elastic properties typically used are the tangent modulus for the biaxial stress–strain curve for the given prestress level.

MEMBRANE MATERIALS

The choice of materials for pneumatic structures and tension structures is quite varied and as a consequence only an overview differentiating between the most common representative materials can be the subject of this text. These results are summarized in Table 2.

Films

Films without reinforcing are used in low-cost pneumatic structures. They require reinforcing by aircraft cables varying in diameter from ⅛ to ⅜ in. These are embedded in seams at the edge of the film roll, approximately 50 in. on center. The cost of these cables, which depends on span, is not considered in the material cost data of Table 2. Films offer the possibility of transparency as with window glass, but in this case, special care must be taken to prevent condensation on the membrane, as the dirt pickup will tend to result in a translucent appearance. Sixteen-mil thick poly(vinyl chloride) (PVC) film with a Tedlar film laminate on the outer surface is the most common construction. The Tedlar film retards the tendency of the PVC film to pick up dirt and retards the ultraviolet degradation of the PVC film.

If a more permanent noncombustible film with good self-cleaning characteristics and higher strengths is desired, Tefzel film may be considered. Through the use of many layers, transparent roofs with high R values can be achieved. Films may be assembled by induction heat sealing, where a metal-impregnated tape is placed between films and passed over induction coils.

Films with Scrim

The low strength of unreinforced films has resulted in lamination of a fibrous scrim, typically polyester between two PVC film layers or a layer of Tedlar and PVC film. Higher strengths may be achieved by laminating twin scrim layers between three films. The rather remarkable tear resistance of the resultant construction is due to the fact that the scrim construction allows the fibers to bunch up at the edge of the tear and thus inhibit its further propagation.

Other films with scrim construction are possible. A single 2-mil clear Tedlar film with a polyester scrim at 1-in. spacing glued on one side has been used effectively as a liner of insulated roof construction so as to maximize translucency and sound absorption of the roof membrane. When vapor barriers are sewn, an excellent sealing system should be provided.

When scrims are used, the most common method of fabrication is sewn construction where a webbing is sewn into the joint. In this manner, the reinforced film primarily spans to the webbing while the webbing spans to the supporting cable or structural framework. Scrim-reinforced films are used extensively in pneumatic structures spanning to 150 ft without cables but with webbing.

Coated Fabrics

With coated fabrics there are many choices possible for the filament fiber. The most common material in use is either polyester or fiber glass. Kevlar, the material from which bulletproof vests are made, has found use in one major application, the Montreal Stadium retractable roof. A fixed roof of this size would normally utilize a lower strength fabric spanning to a cable grid. Other filament fibers used in air or tension structures are rayon and nylon, although their application is most commonly found in small tents and parachutes.

The filament fibers are spun into yarn, and the yarn is either laid up into an overlay scrim or woven into a fabric. The three kinds of weaving methods in use are plain weave, twill weave, and sateen weave. Basket weave and rib weave are variations of plain weave.

Various materials are used for coating. PVC resin is the most common coating, although urethane rubber and Hypalon are also used. PVC-coated fabric with Tedlar film laminated to the upper surface has a life expectancy in excess of 10 years and has excellent self-cleaning properties. Urethane finds use in military applications where folding and unfolding at low temperatures require considerations of cold cracking. Neoprene and Hypalon find use where opaqueness and recoating in the field are considerations, as with reservoir covers or radomes.

Silicone rubber and ethylene tetrafluoride resin (Teflon) are the only coatings that can be used for "permanent" noncombustible fabric structures. Permanency refers to membrane life in excess of 25 years. Noncombustibility is primarily a characteristic of the base yarn and requires

Table 2. Comparison of Membrane Materials

	Filament Fiber	Weave or Scrim	Coating and/or Film (Laminate)	Strip Tensile Strength, PLI	Trapezoidal Tear, lb	1987 Material Costs—\$/ft² Unfabricated	Fabricated (Minimum)	Membrane Life, yr	Maximum Translucency, %	Maximum Reflection, %
Films Only			PVC Film	0	0	0	0	0	100	0
			w/Tedlar	100	20	1.00	2.00			
			(20 mil.)	200	40	2.00	4.00	5	90	10
									80	20
Film with Scrim				300	60	3.00	6.00			
			PVC Film	400	80	4.00	8.00		70	30
	Polyester	Scrim	w/Tedlar					10		
			(1999 TCN)							
			(2213 TCN)	500	100	5.00	10.00		60	40
				600	120	6.00	12.00			
								15	50	50
Coated Fabrics				700	140	7.00	14.00			
	Polyester	Overlay	PVC Coat						40	60
			w/Tedlar	800	180	8.00	16.00			
			(8128)					20		
				900	200	9.00	18.00	?		
			Teflon	1000	300	10.00	20.00		30	70
	Fiber glass	Plain	(Sheerfill IIA)					25	20	80
			(Sheerfill I)	2000	400	11.00	22.00			
									10	90
			PVC Coat	3000	500	12.00	24.00	30	0	? 100
	Kevlar	Panima	w/urethane	4000	600	13.00	26.00			

the use of either fiber glass or Kevlar fibers. Kevlar is highly susceptible to ultraviolet degradation and consequently the Kevlar fibers must be shielded with an opaque carbon black protective coat. This would not preclude the possibility of laminating a clear Teflon or Tefzel film to a Kevlar open weave fabric precoated with a material that would act as the glue in the heat sealing of the film to the laminate (18). Such a construction would allow for sewing as the method of construction and could find application in ultralight large-span low-profile air-supported roofs spanning thousands of feet (19).

For the permanent applications considered to date, Teflon coated fiber glass has found the broadest use. Its ability to shed dirt and contaminants, accompanied by high reflectivity, and the reliability of its heat sealed joints are its major attributes whereas its low tear strength is its most critical drawback. Teflon-coated fiber glass is most appropriately used in those applications where the material can be shipped as rolls on pipe sleeves. When the fabric is folded and packed in crates, the possible damage that may occur during unfolding can not be readily discerned by field investigation (Fig. 15**a**). The possible damage coupled with the low tear strength of the material requires higher factors of safety for the material when used in this manner and special care in the handling of the material.

Silicone-coated fiber glass has significantly improved tear resistance over that of Teflon-coated fiber glass; how-

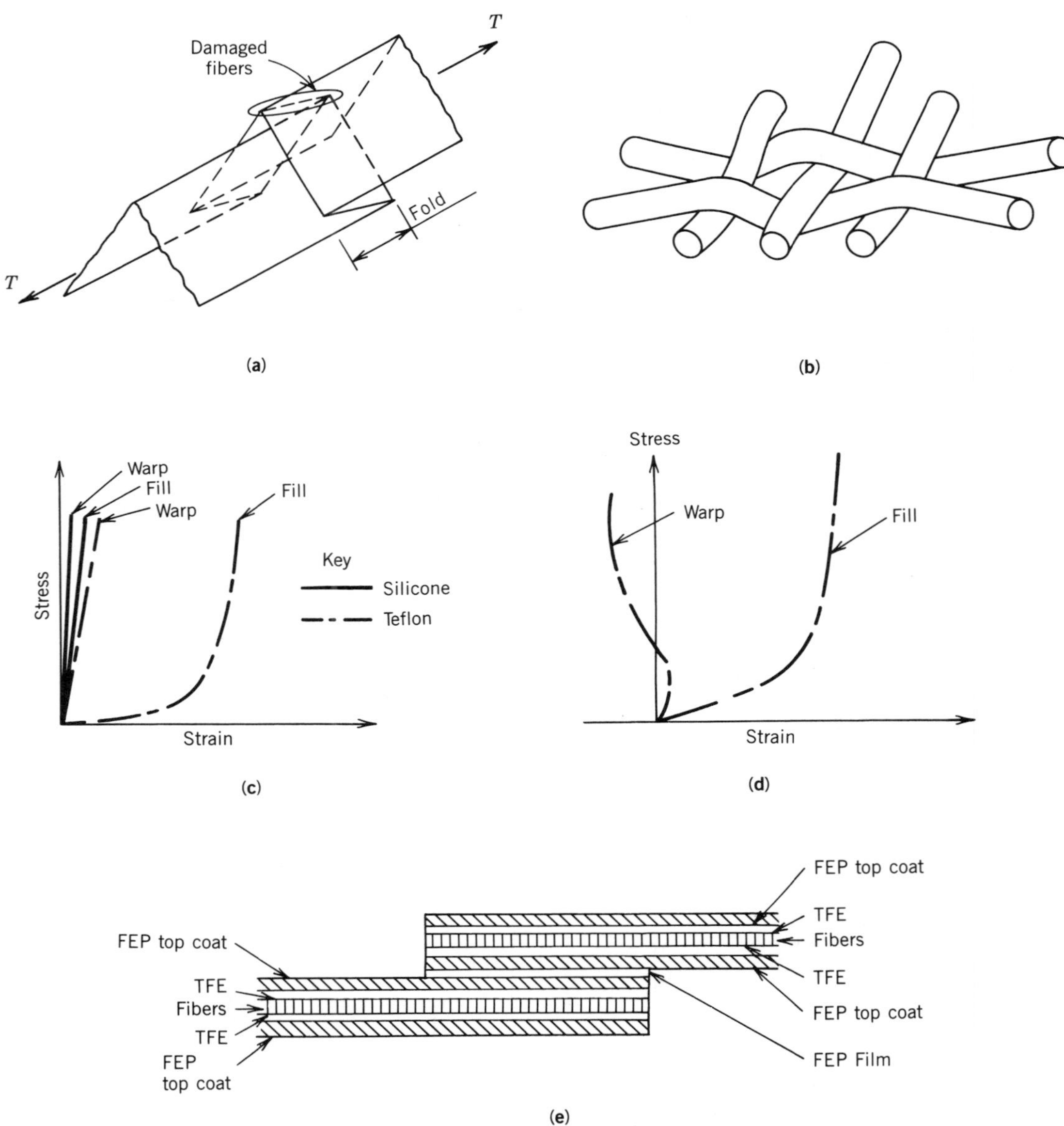

Figure 15. Considerations in use of fiber-glass fabric. **(a)** Damage of fiber-glass fabric fibers during unfolding. **(b)** Coated fiber glass—differences in stress–strain characteristics. **(c)** Crimp in yarns of woven fabric. **(d)** Biaxial behavior of woven fabric. **(e)** Heat-sealed joint with Teflon-coated fiber glass.

ever, this is offset by much more brittle stress–strain characteristics (Fig. 15**c**). For the same weave this difference will still occur as the consequence of the high temperatures at which the Teflon is applied, 620°F (327°C), which causes the fabric to shrink on cooling. In shrinking, the fibers in the fill direction crimp (Fig. 15**b**), while those in the warp direction (the direction of the roll) remain straight as they are held in tension. The resultant crimp interchange results in biaxial stress–strain characteristics much different than the stress–strain characteristics of the individual yarn (Fig. 15**d**). This results in the Teflon-coated fiber glass having more "forgiveness" and assists in compensating for local overstress due to stress concentrations. Weave characteristics can also cause a "brittle yarn" to behave more elastic as a fabric.

The use of fiber glass and the brittle characteristics of the yarn preclude the use of sewing of fiber-glass membranes. The fact that Teflon comes in two forms, PTFE and FEP, which have different melt points, 500°F (260°C) and 392°F (200°C), respectively, has resulted in a method of construction that facilitates the heat sealing of joints (Fig. 15**c**). The resultant membrane cost has been kept low in that the fabric width is typically 12 ft wide and may be as wide as 16 ft, thus minimizing the amount of heat sealing required.

Silicone-coated fiber-glass joints must be glued. The reliability of these joints under sustained load and at elevated temperatures must be investigated. Failure of joints at stresses as low as 100 pli are possible. It is possible, though, in those tension structures where the primary stresses are carried in one direction to avoid dependence on the reliability of glued joints by having the fabric span from clamped end to clamped end in the warp direction and to have the stresses through the glued joint in the fill direction to be lower and less significant. This was the basis of the design of the Lindsay Park Sports Centre, the Ontario Pavilion, and the cable domes of Korea, all designed originally for the use of silicone-coated fiber glass.

Vinyl-coated Kevlar must be sewn. The base material is so strong it is impossible to develop the full strength of the fabric through the joints.

Translucency with Multilayers

The "self-cleaning" characteristic of silicone-coated fiber glass is unproven. At this moment one should assume that manual cleaning of the roof will generally be required at least at 1-year intervals. The very high translucency that is possible with silicone-coated fiber glass makes the "self-cleaning" characteristics not as critical.

It is important to note that when more than one layer of membrane is used, the net translucency t is governed by the formula:

$$t = \frac{t_1 \cdot t_2}{1 - r_1 \cdot r_2} \qquad (10)$$

where t_1, t_2, and r_1, r_2, are the translucencies and reflectivities of surfaces 1 and 2 respectively. As a consequence of the high reflectivity of the Teflon-coated fiber glass and the fibrous insulation used in insulated roofs, the net translucency is almost double what it would be if the surfaces were nonreflective:

$$\frac{t_1 \cdot t_2}{1 - 0.7 \cdot 0.7} = 2t_1 \cdot t_2 \qquad (11)$$

If higher R values and maintaining translucency are required, one would need to consider the use of silicone-coated fiber glass as the outer fabric.

Fabric Strengths

Various methods are used to measure fabric strengths. The uniaxial strip tensile strength (cut-strip method) measures strength in either the warp or fill direction. Strength is given in pounds per linear inch (pli) width.

The tear strength of the membrane is also very important. The tearing force acts directly on a flaw or cut in the fabric and cuts out the weaving yarns one by one, causing the tear to propagate gradually or instantaneously. Tear resistance of a material is usually measured by the trapezoidal method. Strength is given in pounds.

Other Considerations

Other factors that must be taken into account are temperature conditions, fatigue to repeated loads, and deterioration of base yarn owing to water absorption. Synthetic yarns are most susceptible to deterioration at high temperatures. On the other hand, fiber glass is most susceptible to deterioration by water absorption. For this reason, Teflon-coated or vinyl-coated fiber glass is precoated with silicone. Fiber glass is also subject to deterioration in strength under long term loadings. These various considerations are taken into account in the factors of safety assigned to different fabrics under conditions of use (Table 3).

Table 3. Factors of Safety for Building Applications (Normal Temperature Ranges, U.S.)

	Factor of Safety		
	Prestress	Wind	Snow
Polyester	4	4	4
Fiber glass	10	4	5

These factors of safety apply against the dry-strip tensile strength. As such they do not represent the actual factor of safety given the biaxial state of stress and the deterioration of fabric with time.

Other standards have more complicated and more reli- a ble methods of establishing factors of safety methods that take into account the many variables that affect fabric structure performance (17).

Membrane Costs

Material costs for unfabricated sheet goods and the minimum fabricated cost are given in Table 2. For a given shape, the actual fabricated cost per unit of surface area

Table 4. Properties of Various Types of Cable

Type of Cable	Modulus, ksi	Ultimate Strength, ksi	Specific Gravity	Size–Diameter Variation	Cost $/ft Kip
Wire rope	20,000	200	7.80	3/8 to 4 in.	
Structural strand	24,000	200	7.80	1/2 to 4 in.	Fig. 16
Prestressing strand	28,000	270	7.80	3/8, 1/2, 0.6 in.	Fig. 16
Kevlar 49-rope	19,000	400	1.45	1/4 in. and 1/2 in.	0.03[a]
S-Glass rope	12,500	450	2.48		0.03[a]

[a] Excludes cost of end fittings.

is obtained by multiplying the minimum fabricated cost by the utilization factor. To obtain the cost per square foot of plan area, the result is multiplied by the surface area aspect ratio. By taking into account the difference in cost between unfabricated and minimum fabricated costs with adjustments of current material costs and local labor costs, these figures can be appropriately adjusted for other locations and times (20).

CABLES

Cables may be part of the membrane envelope. Various cables are indicated in Table 4.

Costs of cables and end fittings and swaged stops for various cable types are given in Figure 16.

Factors of safety for cables used in structural design vary depending on load case (21); normally 2 to 2.2 may be used.

STRUCTURAL DETAILS

Cable-to-cable clamp details are shown in Figure 17**a.** Fabric clamps to cables are shown in Figure 17**b.** Fabric clamps to rigid supports are shown in Figure 17**c.** Membrane structures may also terminate at an edge catenary, as shown in Figure 17**d.**

Tensile membranes functioning as canopies may be bounded by catenary cables. For smaller tents, cables may be heat sealed into the fabric, whereas for larger tents the cables will be external and the fabric will be clamped to the cable (Fig. 17**e**).

With polyester fabrics, catenaries with cables built in are the common method of transfer of load from the membrane to the surrounding cables, arches, frame, or ground support. In considering the use of unclamped catenaries, careful consideration must be given to the tendency of the fabric to slide up the catenary, away from the cusp or anchor point of the catenary.

Cables may be used in conjunction with fabrics either above or below the fabric without the fabric being clamped to the cables. Provisions must be made for wear strips between the fabric and the cable and to prevent the cable from sliding off the wear strip. Since methods of analysis may not model the sliding forces between the fabric and the cable, special care must be given to this case. If the sliding force under prestress is zero, then the prestress level in the warp and fill directions must be equal. For all other cases, a sliding force will exist.

If one considers the mast of a tent with radial cables below the fabric, there will be radial forces in the fabric if the fabric is clamped at the top of the mast. If the fabric is not clamped at the top, then hoop stresses will exist in the fabric as the fabric tries to slide down the cables. In either case, if there are few radial cables and/or a brittle fabric such as fiberglass is used, these forces may be significant and could cause membrane failure.

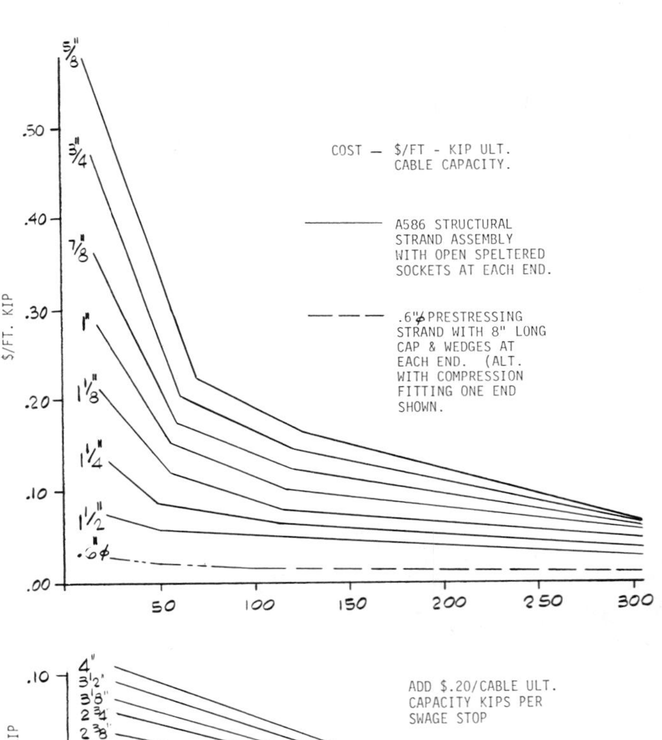

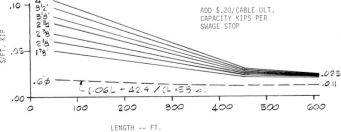

Figure 16. Cost characteristics of cables, with cost of end fittings and swaged stops.

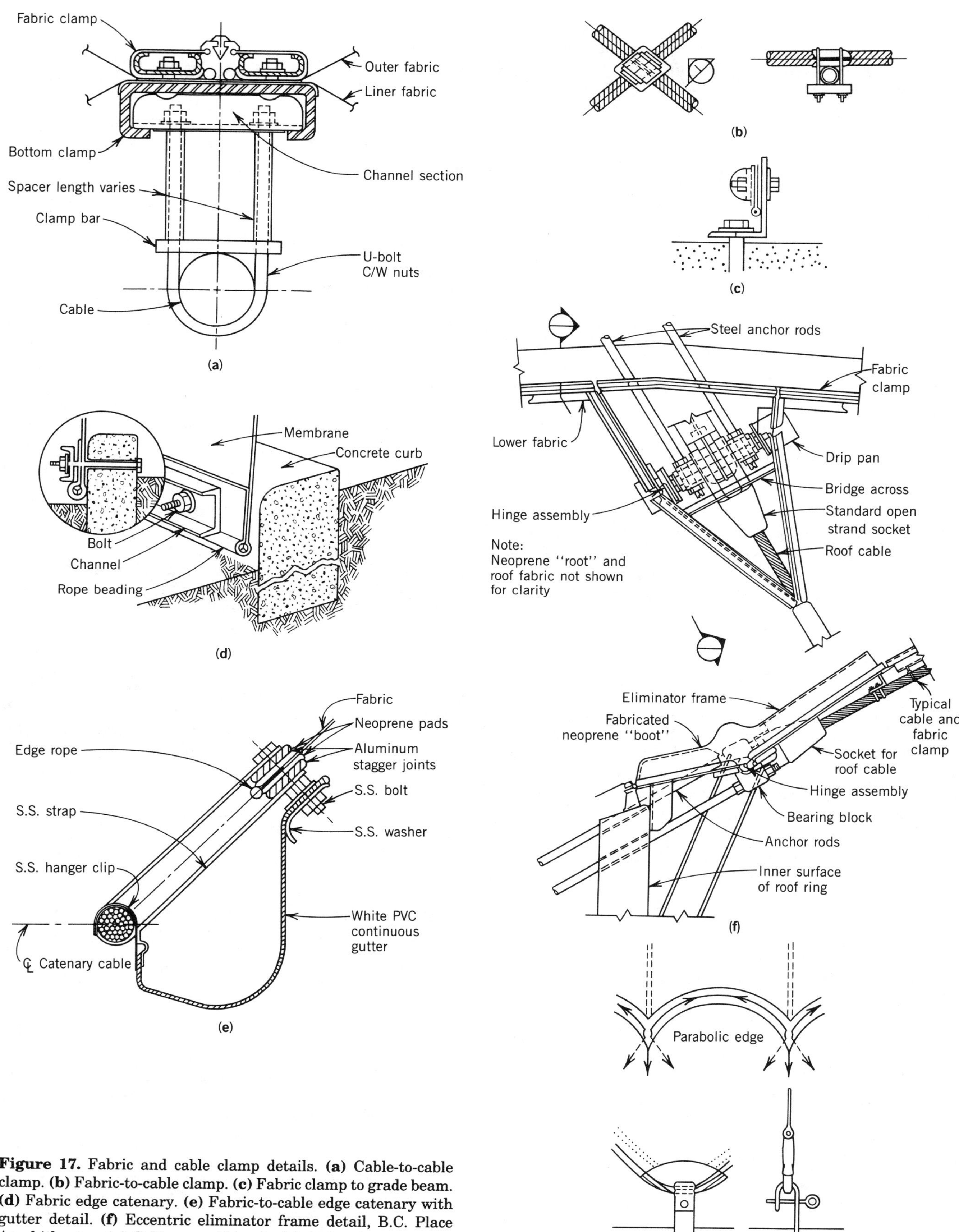

Figure 17. Fabric and cable clamp details. **(a)** Cable-to-cable clamp. **(b)** Fabric-to-cable clamp. **(c)** Fabric clamp to grade beam. **(d)** Fabric edge catenary. **(e)** Fabric-to-cable edge catenary with gutter detail. **(f)** Eccentric eliminator frame detail, B.C. Place Amphitheatre. **(g)** Cable or webbing in fabric forming catenary.

Similar considerations should be given to fabric over arches. Transverse sliding forces due to unbalanced loads may be considerable. Allowing this sliding to occur usually results in a favorable redistribution of fabric stress, but may cause undesirable lateral bending on the arch elements.

For air structures and tension structures, all structural details must allow for large scale local displacements and rotations (Figs. **4b** and **17f**). Failure to accommodate these motions may result in premature failure of elements.

Approximate costs of various structural details are given in Table 5.

Table 5. Cost of Structural Details

Type	Figure	Cost
Edge clamp	17**c**	$20/ft
Fabric to cable	17**b**	$40/ft
Cable clamp[a]	17**a**	$1000 each
Eccentric eliminator frame[a]	17**f**	$1500 each
Edge catenary	17**d**	$2/ft

[a] Applicable for 2.5- to 4-in. diameter cables.

Patterning Costs

It is preferable for the design to allow for maximum repetition in patterning of fabric panels. Each new pattern costs about $5000 with one-half of this cost reflecting engineering costs at $40/h including computer costs and the balance reflecting shop costs at $10/h.

STRUCTURAL DESIGN PHILOSOPHY: ALLOWABLE STRESS DESIGN VERSUS LIMIT STATE DESIGN

The structural design of membrane structures is, according to common practice, based on allowable stresses. The appropriate factor of safety—based on material and load considerations—is divided into the ultimate strength of the material. The resultant allowable stress is not exceeded under the particular conditions of load.

Because of the large displacements that are possible with air and tension structures, it is possible that allowable stress design may not result in the anticipated factors of safety remaining at ultimate load. This may occur because of nonlinear behavior of the structure. This phenomenon became particularly apparent in the design of the Ontario Pavilion of Expo '86 in Vancouver (Fig. 18**a**) (9). Figure 18**b** summarizes these results and shows the reason for concern.

In summary, for unusual structures, particularly tension structures, that are indeterminate and combine compression struts and cables, consider analysis by limit state design as well as by allowable stress design.

ERECTION CONSIDERATIONS

Maximum fabric panel size plays a major role in erection considerations. If the fabric is to be shipped to the site in a single pallet or a truck bed, lifted to a horizontal surface, and pulled out by human labor using rollers or air cushions to facilitate horizontal movement, the largest single panel so moved is the 100,000-ft^2 single membrane weighing about 20,000 lb (Fig. 19**a**). Most typically for ground mounted air structures, the largest panel size handled is about 50,000 ft^2 of roof surface area.

For aerial erection of low-profile air structures where fabric is shipped on rolls, either single or double layer, the largest size rolls are typically rectangular, about 45 ft by 240 ft, weighing approximately 50 oz/yd^2 or 4000 lb (Fig. 19**b**). Aerial erection of triangular panels from the compression ring slide over a rope grid stretched between cables is typically limited to triangular panels having a maximum base of 240 ft and altitude of 120 ft, weighing about 60 oz/yd^2 or 6000 lb. Diamond-shaped panels typically measure 45 ft on a side and are easily erected (Fig. 19**c**).

The largest planned aerial erection of triangular panels (double layer) is for St. Petersburg cable dome. These will be approximately 90 ft wide at the base and 330 ft long, weighing 50 oz/yd^2 or 5000 lb.

Tent structures may be crated and erected in panels weighing up to 10,000 lb. The tension ring at the top of the posts facilitates the lifting of the membranes out of the crate (Fig. 19**d**). If a larger roof area than approximately 25,000 ft^2 is required, field joints will be needed. For tension structures, if these field joints are not made at grade they may require scaffolding along cable lines and consequently may be somewhat awkward in execution (Fig. 19**e**).

The time required for erection of membrane structures is indicated in Figure 20. When compared with conventional construction covering the same plan area or surface area, and considering that with erection completed a waterproof enclosure is the result, these erection periods are unbelievably short. This is made possible because the fabrication of all membrane components, excluding the compression ring and/or anchorages, is done off-site and the actual field erection is done with large scale prefabricated components. Figure 20 shows how brief the time frame from beginning of erection to full enclosure can be.

The rapid time required for roof erection will result in overall cost savings as the total construction period will be much shorter. A 65,000-seat domed stadium using convention construction will take approximately three years; with an air-supported roof, it will take approximately 24 months. A cable dome roof would require about 28 months.

The erection costs must be considered on a case-by-case basis. For permanent membrane structures where the fabric is panelized and there are more clamp lines, the erection cost varies between $5 and $10/ft^2. Seventy percent of the erection cost is labor which will vary from $13–35/h, which largely accounts for the spread in erection costs. For temporary air structures or tent structures of a small enough scale as to be brought to the site in one piece, or that only have catenaries at field joints, these erection costs may be reduced to $2.50–5/ft^2 for air structures and $4–7/ft^2 for tension structures.

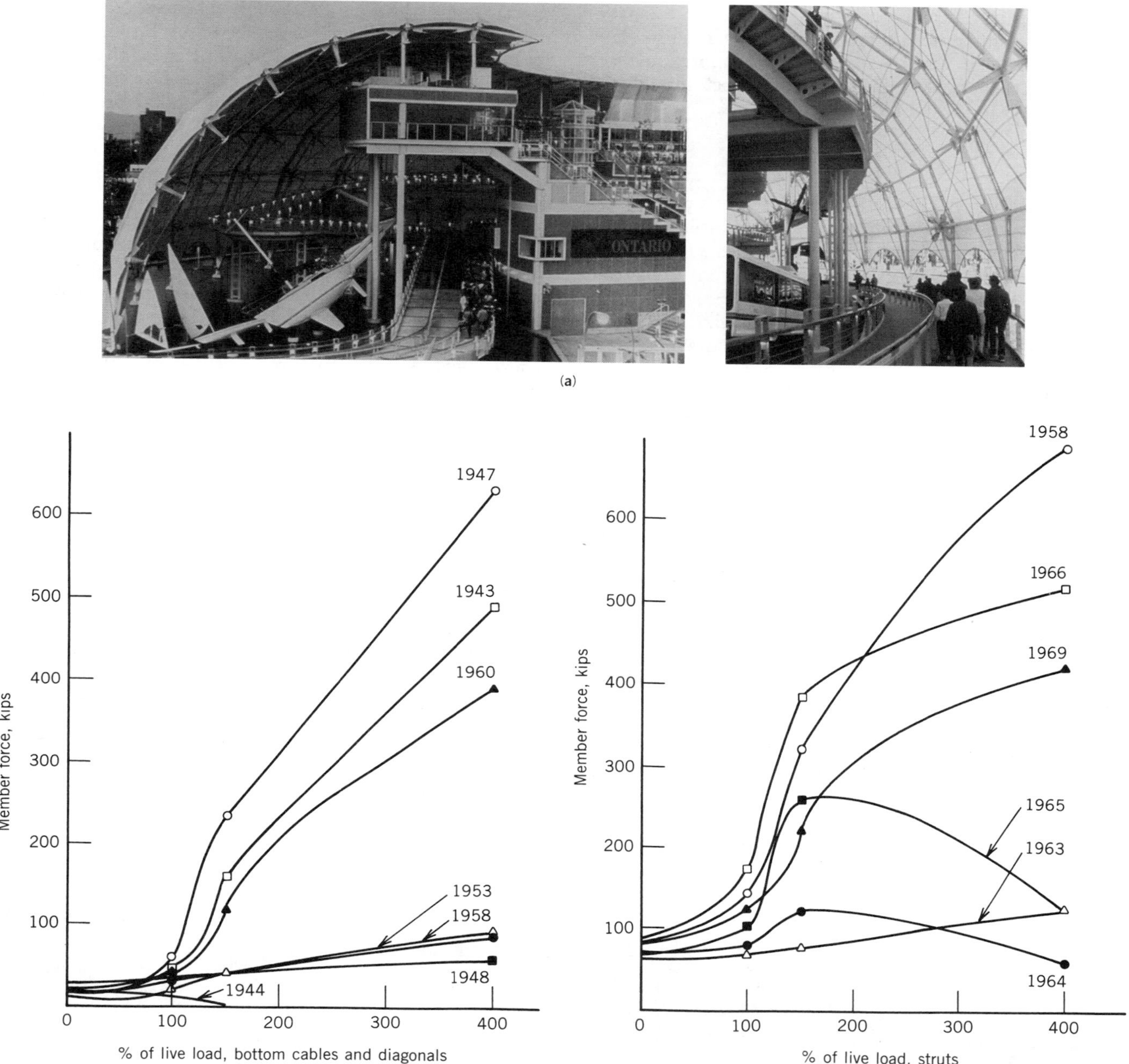

Figure 18. Post cable truss. Considerations of allowable stress vs. limit state design methods of Ontario Pavilion, Expo '86. Courtesy of Geiger Associates.

MECHANICAL DESIGN CONSIDERATIONS

Fabric properties of membrane roofs as they relate to mechanical design are shown in Figure 21**a** for single membrane, dual membrane and insulated roofs. Membrane properties required for mechanical design are given in Table 6.

For air-supported roofs, pressurization results in leakage and a requirement for makeup air that affects the design of mechanical equipment. When ventilation is required, the capacity of the blowers must also exceed the air loss due to ventilation. This air loss will be higher than that which exists for conventional construction because of the higher internal pressure. For large air structures having significant occupancy, the blower capacity is that required for ventilation and not that required because of leakage. For stadia an arena approximately 150,000 cfm capacity is required per 5000 spectators. Typical air losses are given in Table 7.

Blowers

Blowers used in pneumatic air-supported structures are typically electrically driven centrifugal multiblade-type fans with characteristic curves as shown in Figure 21**b.** These performance characteristics will prevent overpressurization of the building.

For large scale air structures such as stadia, axial flow fans have been used. Overpressurization is prevented by control systems that relieve excess pressure. Since controls may malfunction or be overridden, there is a risk of overpressurization that is less likely with centrifugal blowers.

Snow Melt Systems

Air structures in cold climates will require snow-melt systems. With a single membrane, heating the incoming air is a simple way of doing this. If this is done by means of direct fired units, there is a risk of condensation on the underskin if there is inadequate ventilation. Condensation gutters along cable lines may be used to collect this condensation.

With dual-walled air structures, the air must be introduced between the two skins. Figure 9**f** illustrates this approach for large-scale air structures. Note the provision for snow melt along this compression ring and at the fabric clamp along the compression ring. When the lower of the two fabric layers is a porous acoustic liner, this liner also serves to collect condensate that will drip from the upper surface onto the liner. Although the liner is porous for moisture vapor, it is not porous for water. Provisions must be made to collect the condensate water along the compression ring. Similar provisions for condensate control must be made for tension structure roofs, either dual wall or insulated.

Power Sources

It is necessary to provide the blowers of an air structure with more than one power source. Both sources must have a device that activates the other when one of the two stops functioning. Usually one of these power sources is a diesel-powered generator with sufficient power to operate the fans required to carry the maximum pressure under snow loads. Major structures can use two independent power grids as sources with generator backup.

Spare Inflation Equipment

Because the inflation equipment is essential for structural support, all aspects of it must be designed with redundancy, ie, a factor of safety of two.

Lightning Arrestors

Lightning arrestors must normally be used in conjunction with membrane structures. Figure 21**c** shows the lightning arrestor attachment at the crown of air structures. For cable restrained air structures or tension structures with ridge cables, the cable structural elements, if large enough, may be used as the ground. Typically, lightning arrestors are attached to these cables. It has been shown that if the cable grid is close enough, the lightning arrestors can be eliminated.

(a)

Figure 19. Fabric handling during erection. **(a)** Handling of 100,000 ft^2 of fabric, U.S. Pavilion, Expo '70, Osaka, Japan. **(b)** The unveiling of a rectangular fabric for the Silverdome, Pontiac, Mich. **(c)** Aerial erection of diamond-shaped panels for an air-supported roof, Silverdome. **(d)** Erection of tent structuring, lifting out of crate by the tension ring. **(e)** Scaffolding to make a joint along a valley cable, Florida Festival, St. Petersburg. **(a)–(c)** and **(e)** Courtesy of Geiger Associates. **(d)** Courtesy of O. C. Birdair.

(b)

(c)

(d)

(e)

AUG. 13/82

SEPT. 14/82

OCT. 12/82

NOV. 15/82

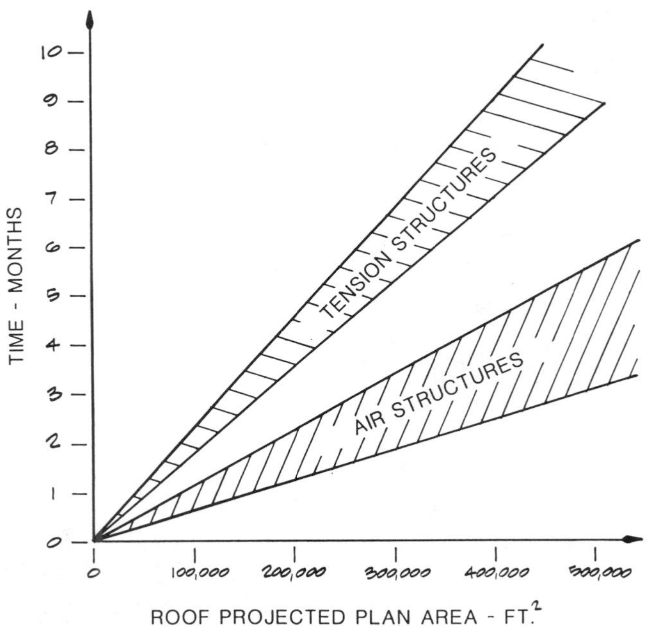

Figure 20. Required time for erection of membrane structures, Lindsay Park Sports Centre. Courtesy of Geiger Associates.

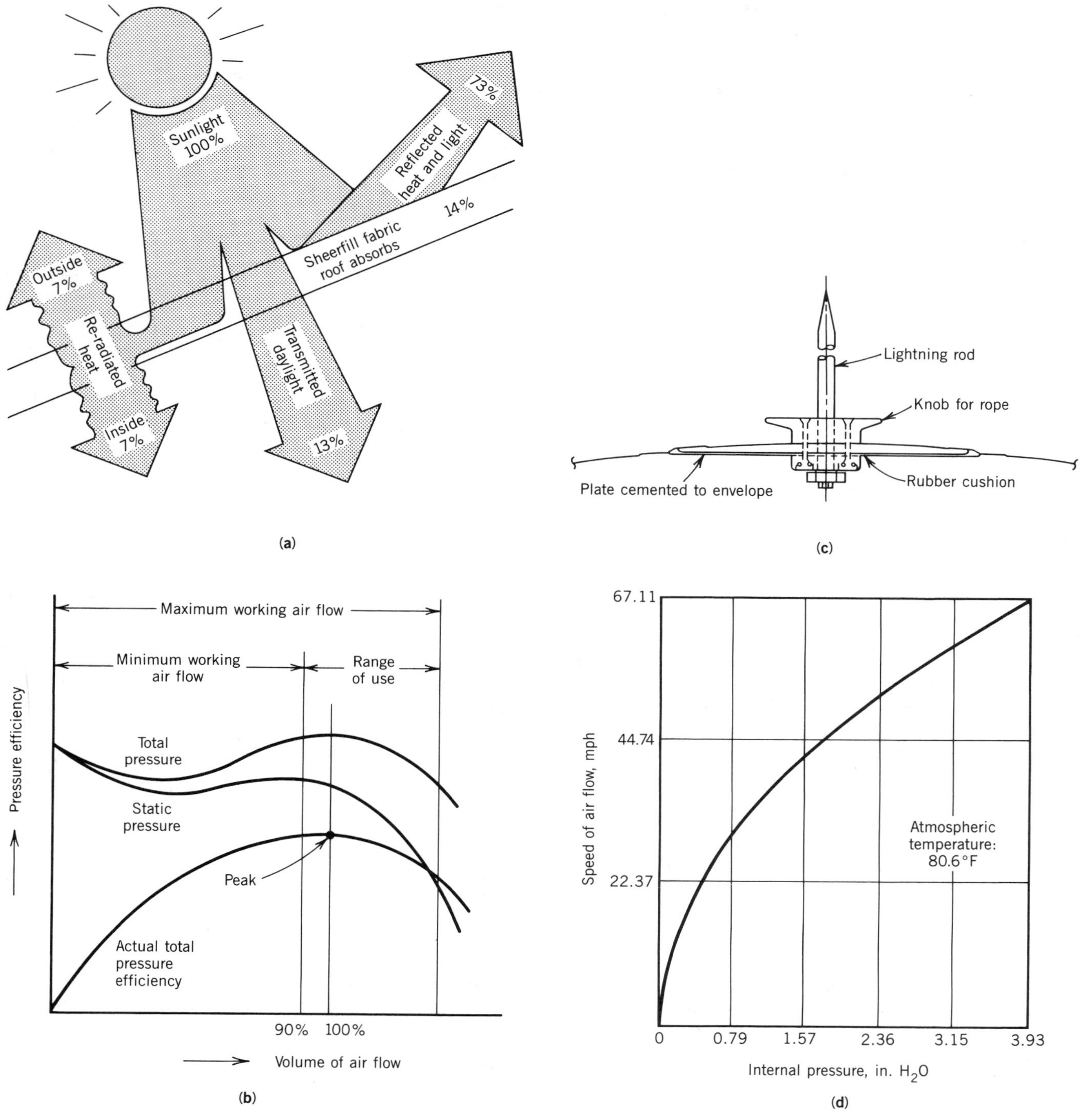

Figure 21. Mechanical design considerations. **(a)** Fabric properties as they relate to mechanical design. **(b)** Characteristic curves of a centrifugal multiblade-type fan. **(c)** Lightning arrestor and crown plate attached to the top of a radome. **(d)** Instantaneous speed of air outflow from opening.

ARCHITECTURAL CONSIDERATIONS

As permanent construction, membrane structures find their primary applications where one or more of the following considerations predominate: sculptural form, translucency, and economy of long spans. Membrane structures allow for quickly erected sculptural forms similar to the more ponderously erected thin shell concrete forms of decades ago.

The translucency of the membrane forms are of impor-

Table 6. Thermal/Optical Properties of Membrane Structures

Roof Configuration	Sheerfill No.	Transmission, % T	Reflectance, % R	Absorption, % A	Visable Trans., % T_{vis}	Summer Shading Coefficient	System R Value ft²·H·°F/Btu
Single Membrane	No. I: High T	9	73	18	7	0.15	Winter = 0.85
	Low T	7	75	18	5	0.12	
	No. II: High T	13	73	14	11	0.18	Summer = 0.10
	Low T	9	75	16	8	0.14	
	No. II A	18	68	14	15	0.24	
Double Membrane	No. I, High T	4	74	22	3	0.08	Winter = 1.65
	No. II, High T	6	75	19	4	0.10	
	No. II A	8	72	20	5	0.13	Summer = 1.95
Insulated No. 11A with:	4 in. Fibair and Herculite (T = .67%)	8	73	19	4	0.08	Winter = 7.8 Summer = 9.8
	8 in. Fibair and Herculite	6	73	21	3	0.06	Winter = 5.4 Summer = 6.5
	12 in. Fibair and Herculite[a]	4	73	23	3	0.06	Winter ≈ 10.2 Summer ≈ 13.1
	16 in. Fibair and Orcon (T = .90%)[a]	4	73	23	3	0.06	Winter ≈ 13.6 Summer ≈ 16.6

[a] Approximate, calculated, not supported by test data. Balance of data courtesy of O. C. Birdair.

tance both day and night. During the daytime, the translucency allows for a feeling of being outdoors in a controlled environment. Sunrise, sunset, clouds, and rain, although occurring outside, have their effect on the light levels, and in the case of rain, on the acoustics of the interior environment. This may be true for insulated as well as single- and dual-wall membranes (Fig. 1**d**). Tension structures, if of a sculptural form, may offer a sky that is too busy, that detracts from the feeling of being outdoors. At night, the translucent roof forms a large-scale illuminated landmark that will attract visitors (Fig. 2**b**).

The economy of large-span membrane roofs results in their application irrespective of sculptural form or translucency. These features are then no cost bonuses in the consideration of membrane structures.

Doors

Revolving Doors. Revolving doors allow for the continuous ingress and egress of people with minimum leakage of air and no loss in pressure. The U.S.A. standard (17) requires the use of revolving doors where more than 100 people per hour enter and leave a structure. With continuous flow of people, 50 people per minute may be considered as a reasonable rate of flow. Revolving doors are normally not considered for emergency exiting.

Pressure Balanced Doors. Pressure-balanced doors opening outward without access handles on the outside are usually considered for emergency exiting from air structures. If properly balanced, they will close against operating pressures up to about 1.2 in. water gauge. At higher pressures, they will only partly close.

Butt-Hinge Doors. Butt-hinge doors opening outward are typically not used. They run the risk of opening suddenly owing to the pressure acting on the door.

Table 7. Typical Air Losses[a,b]

Item	cfm	Unit
Base Perimeter		
Clamped hem	3	Linear foot
Buried skirt	4	Linear foot
Skirt on concrete	6	Linear foot
Skirt on earth	12	Linear foot
Field Junctions		
Clamped	3	Linear foot
Roped	6	Linear foot
Toggled	6	Linear foot
Seams		
Sewn	0.1	Linear foot
Welded or cemented	0	Linear foot
Doors (Closed)		
Hatch	100	Each
Emergency exit	300	Each
Revolving door	300	Each
Personnel air lock	200	Each
Vehicle air lock (8 × 8 ft)	200	Each
Vehicle air lock (12 × 12 ft)	400	Each
Vehicle air lock (16 × 16 ft)	600	Each
Mechanical Equipment		
Blower duct	100	Each
Heater duct	150	Each
Air conditioning duct	150	Each
Vents (Closed)		
Diameter 4 in.	200	Each
Diameter 6 in.	450	Each
Diameter 12 in.	1700	Each
Diameter 16 in.	3100	Each

[a] From Ref. 17.
[b] These values are based on cfm at 1.00 IWG. Multiply these values by a factor of 1.12 to obtain values for an operating pressure of 1.25 IWG.

Table 8. Pneumatic Structure Personnel Required for Operations[a,b]

Application	A		B		C	
Floor Area	Full-Time Operator	Operator Holding Another Post Concurrently	Full-Time Operator	Operator Holding Another Post Concurrently	Full-Time Operator	Operator Holding Another Post Concurrently
Less than 500 m^2		2				
500 m^2 or more		3				
1000 m^2 or more	1	5				
No. of Persons to Be Accommodated						
Less than 30 persons	1	2	1	1	1	2
30 persons or more	1	2	1	1	1	3
100 persons or more	1	2	1	2	1	4
300 persons or more	1	2	1	3	1	5
500 persons or more	1	2	1	4	1	6
1000 persons or more	1	2	1	6	2	8

[a] Ref. 17.
[b] Besides above, one full time operator is usually added for each doorway.

Vehicular Doors. Garage-type doors in pairs are typically used for vehicular access to air structures.

Velocity of Air

The velocity of air through open exiting doors may create discomfort to people in the doorway. Velocity is related to pressure per Figure 21**d**. For vehicular entrances when the air lock is open to allow the ingress or egress of large trucks, the velocity of air may affect goods on the truck or in the passageway.

Windows

In air structures, large windows must be shatterproof glass, as the loss of a large glassed area could result in deflation of a roof.

Nonfabric Enclosure

Standard construction abutting or part of air structure construction must make special allowances for the internal pressure in the air structure: toilet traps, operation of elevators, flashing around convention roofs, interior doors that may create pressurized areas, reliability, low air leakage of building elements, and support of suspended ceilings may all be affected by the pressurization of the building.

MAINTENANCE, INSPECTION, AND OPERATION OF PNEUMATIC STRUCTURES

For pneumatic structures, it is necessary periodically to inspect the membrane material, the rope and/or cable materials, the anchorage systems, the inflation systems, emergency power systems, and the balance of the elements that provide the pressurized enclosure, eg, doors, glazing, and siding. Inspection should be carried out with scrupulous care when strong wind or heavy snowfall are forecast, and after such an event. Repairs as required must be made immediately. The roof contractor should provide a checklist for inspection, with the frequency of inspection of relevant items noted.

As the size of the pneumatic structure increases, the number of personnel required for operations increases. This is represented in Table 8. If heavy snowfall is possible, trained personnel must be on standby for emergency operations.

MAINTENANCE AND INSPECTION OF TENSION STRUCTURES

For tension structures, it is necessary to inspect periodically the membrane material, the rope and/or cable materials, and the anchorage systems. If the membrane material is constructed of synthetic yarn, it will be necessary periodically to prestress the structure. This is not required of membranes constructed of fiber glass. The schedule of inspection and restressing should be provided by the roof contractor.

COST COMPARISON OF TOTAL SYSTEMS

In a detailed study presented to the IASS Symposium in Beijing in 1987, there was presented a cost comparison of three structural systems used extensively for long span

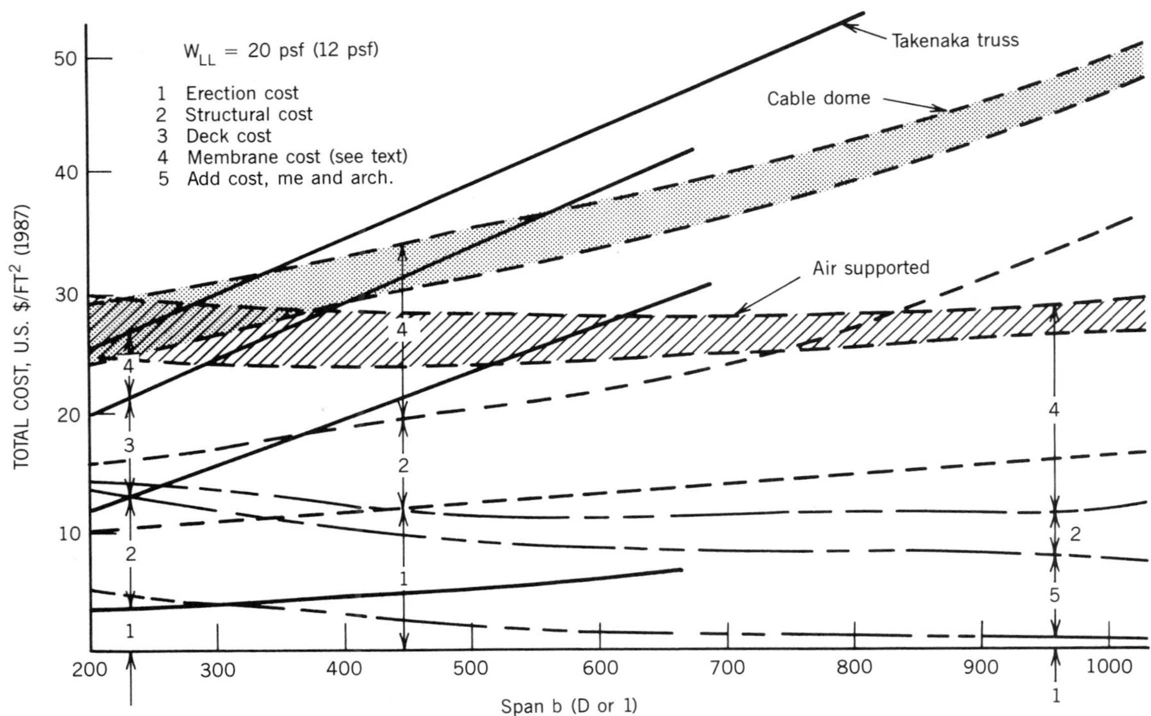

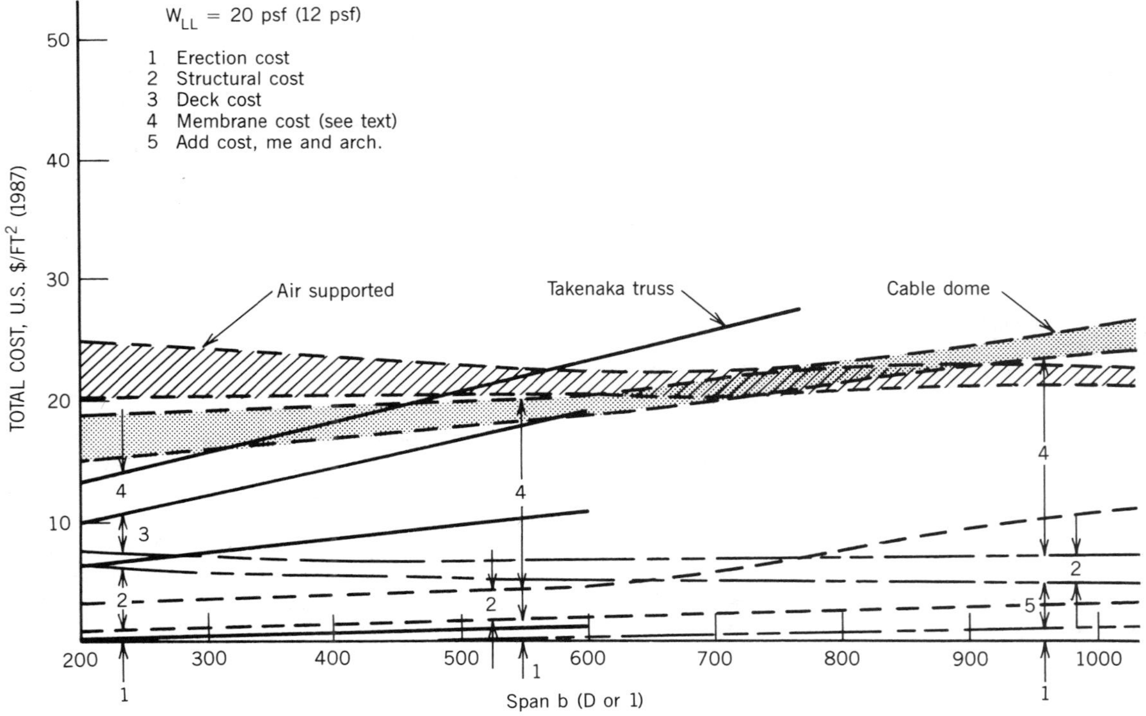

Figure 22. Cost comparison of total system.

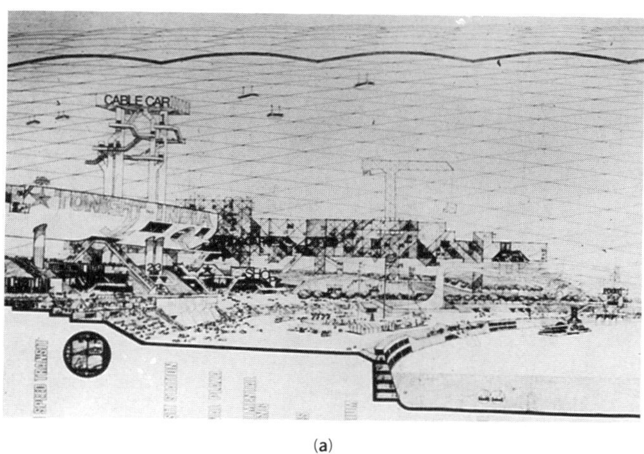

(a)

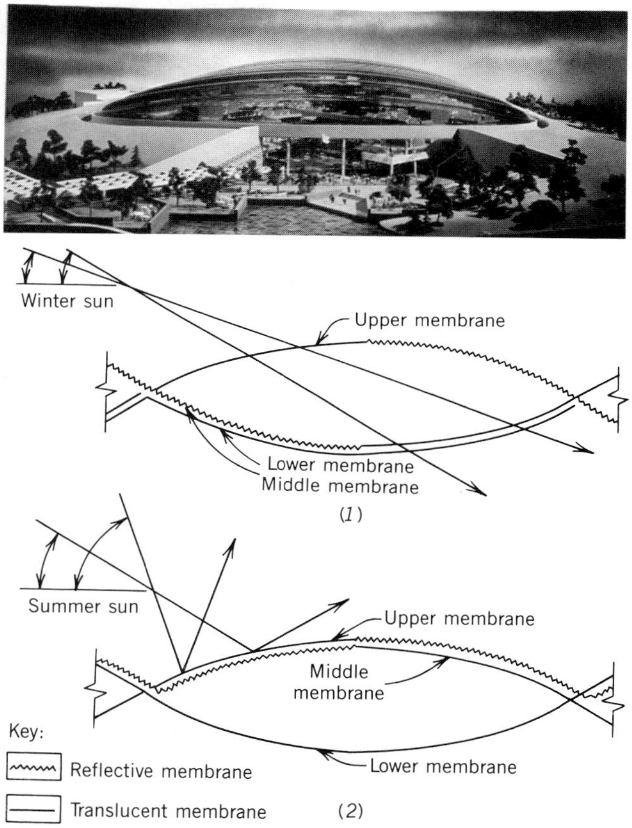

Winter sun

Upper membrane

Lower membrane
Middle membrane

(*1*)

Summer sun

Upper membrane

Middle
membrane

Key:

Reflective membrane

Lower membrane

Translucent membrane (*2*)

Cross—section of passive heating solar cell. Cell runs east—west allowing for maximum penetration of winter sun.
(*1*) Solar cell—open. (*2*) Solar cell—closed.

(b)

Figure 23. Encapsulation concepts. **(a)** Expo '76—Environmental City. **(b)** GSA Megastructure—passive-heating solar cell. **(c)** Alaska 84, a 1200-ft-diameter encapsulation. The graphs compare future needs fulfilled with the Alaska 84 encapsulation and conventional construction. Courtesy of Geiger Associates.

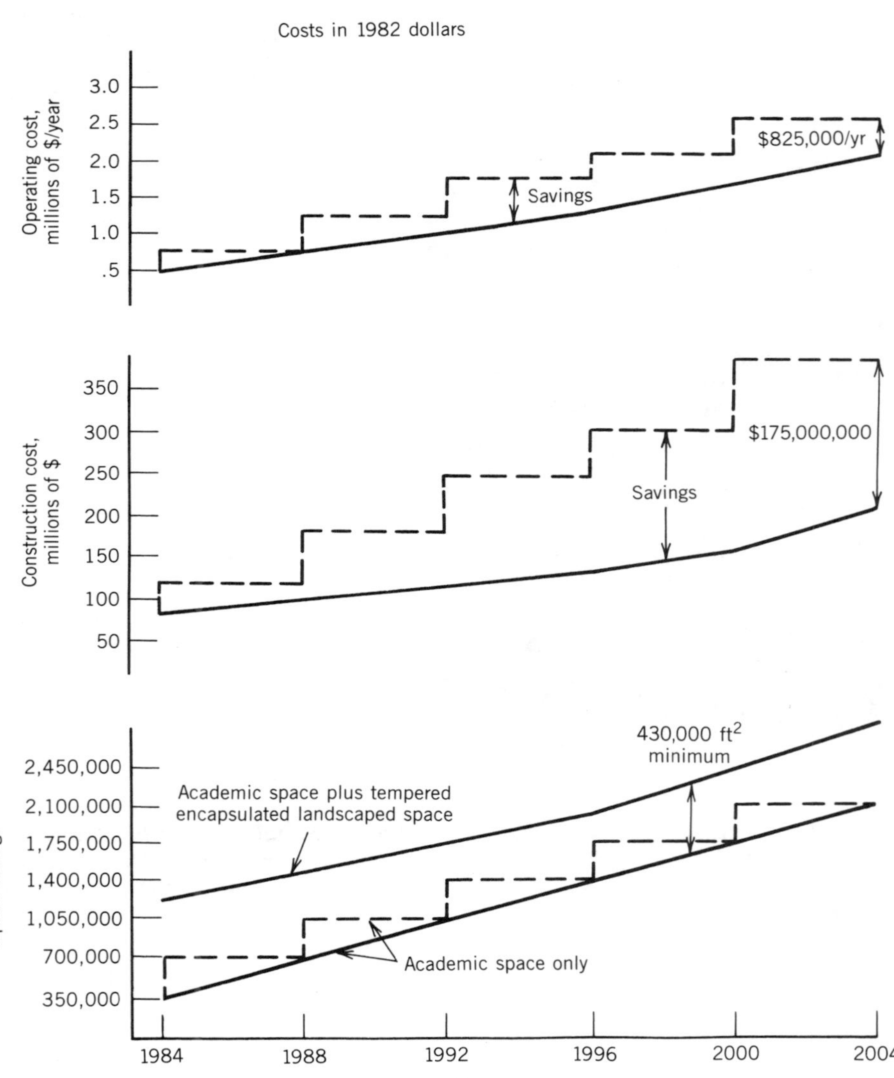
Conventional construction
Encapsulated construction
Costs in 1982 dollars
Operating cost, millions of $/year
3.0
2.5
2.0
1.5
1.0
.5
$825,000/yr
Savings
Construction cost, millions of $
350
300
250
200
150
100
50
$175,000,000
Savings
Educational gross square footage
2,450,000
2,100,000
1,750,000
1,400,000
1,050,000
700,000
350,000
430,000 ft²
minimum
Academic space plus tempered encapsulated landscaped space
Academic space only
1984
1988
1992
1996
2000
2004

(c)

roof applications (20). The results were presented in a way that easily facilitates extension to future times and any location. The computer models used in the study were compared against actual bid prices for project bids at different times in various countries. The results of the study are summarized in Figure 22. Costs are given in 1987 U.S. dollars per square foot for the United States and Korea. Korea was chosen as being representative of a developing country. Results from these curves were compared against the Takenaka Truss, a skewed chord space truss, and the cable domes designed by the author for the Korean Olympics. These three systems are compared for a live load of 20 psf for the Takenaka Truss and 60% of this value (12 psf) for the air-supported roof and cable dome. The reduction is the consequence of the load reduction permitted under the ANSI Code.

The total cost for the air-supported roof and the cable dome is presented by a band, the top part of which gives the total cost per square foot of the roof area inside the ring; the lower part gives the total cost per square foot of the roof area including the area of a 14-ft wide compression ring. The breakdown in cost is given in items 1 through 5. Whereas in the United States the air-supported roof has clearly been established as the most economical roof system, this is not the case for a developing country such as Korea. In Korea, with a labor cost equal to one-tenth that of the United States and cost of the sophisticated hardware components required the same as that in the United States, the cable dome, a much more labor intensive structural system, becomes the most economical.

It is important to note that in this cost comparison (Fig. 22) the membrane considered for the air-supported roof and cable dome is the "permanent" noncombustible Teflon-coated fiber glass, whereas for the Takenaka Truss it is a conventional membrane with a life of approximately 15 to 20 years. If for the air-supported and cable dome a single skin Tedlar-clad vinyl were considered, there would be an additional savings of \$10–12 per ft^2 when compared to the cost of the Takenaka Truss.

THE FUTURE OF MEMBRANE STRUCTURES

As the history of membrane structures from 1968 to 1978 was shaped by advances in materials, it can similarly be expected the future will be so shaped. It is clear that compression structures will be limited by considerations of buckling. Since buckling is controlled by the geometry of the cross section, the modulus of elasticity of the material and the structural configuration, advances of materials will only affect the capacity of compression structures as the modulus of elasticity is made to increase. Freudenthal (22) has shown for example that for all steel in the elastic range the modulus of elasticity is a constant, but on the other hand, the ultimate strength can be made to increase by reducing, or ideally, eliminating the imperfections of the grain boundaries. We now know that grain boundaries can be eliminated by growing metallic whiskers in a gravity-free environment as in outer space. These whiskers would have a strength thousands of times greater than materials now produced on earth. Less esoteric developments here on earth will continue to occur as has the development of Kevlar yarn and carbon filament fibers. Thus, tensile structures are the structures of the future. Similarly, it is possible to postulate one molecule thick glass, having no imperfections or brittle characteristics, that could function as an ideal transparent membrane. Although these are a few of the possibilities, it is known that the development of new materials will continue to open up new opportunities as to strength, endurance, thermal control, and the possible direct generation of electricity on the surface of the membrane.

There have been a number of studies where architectural concepts involving large-scale encapsulations have been proposed. These include the 8000-ft-diameter Expo '76—Environmental City (Fig. 23**a**) (19); the 400 × 1000 ft GSA Megastructure (Fig. 23**b**) (23) that used the roof membrane as a passive solar collector in the winter and yet rejected heat in the summer; the Jacksonville Junior College encapsulation (Fig. 24) concept that used the roof

(a)

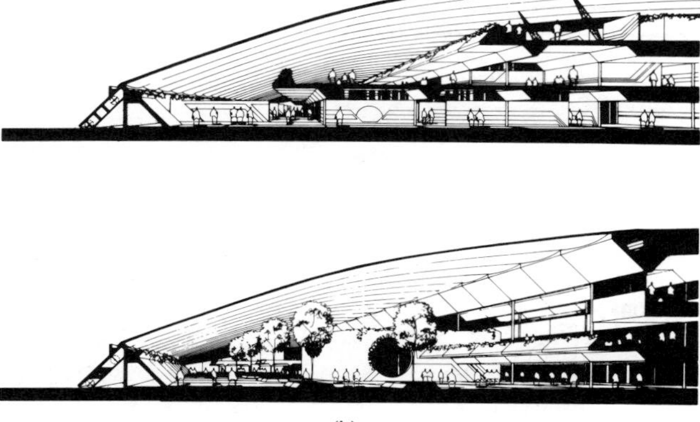
(b)

Figure 24. Jacksonville Junior College encapsulation. **(a)** Exterior. **(b)** Interior sections. **(c)** Schematic of active collector. **(a)** and **(b)** Courtesy of Geiger Associates.

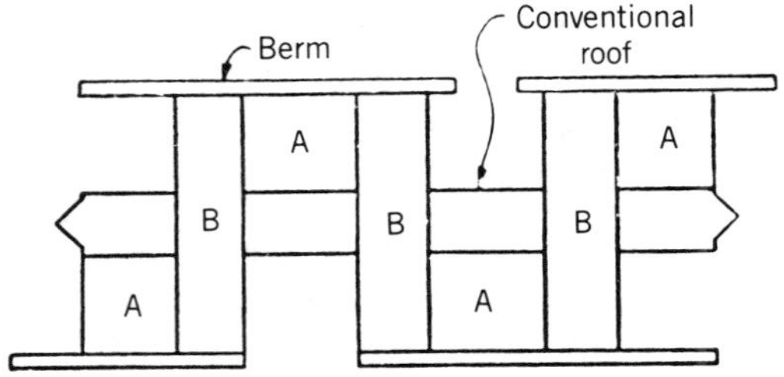

Solar cell location plan

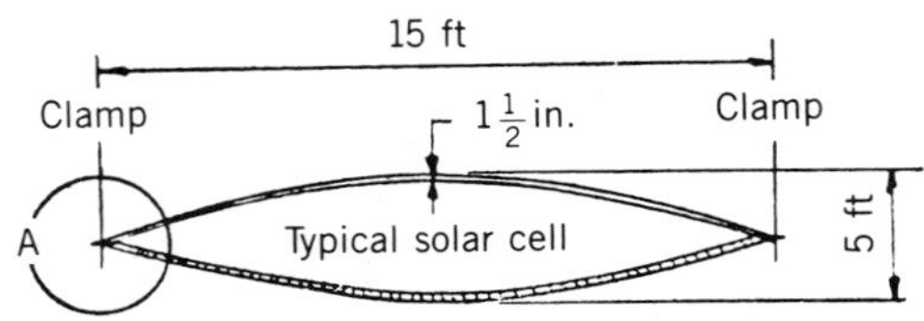

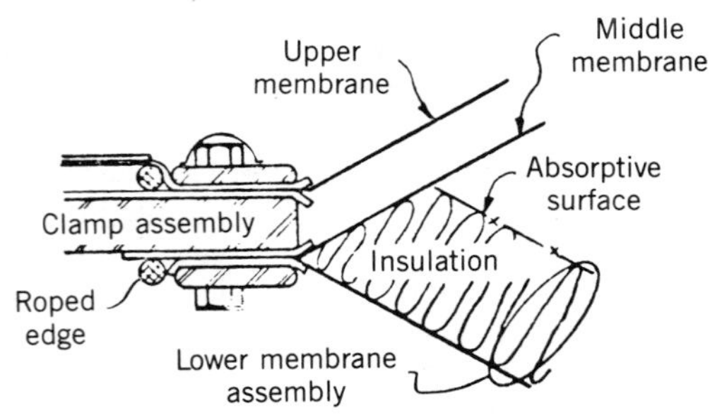

Detail A

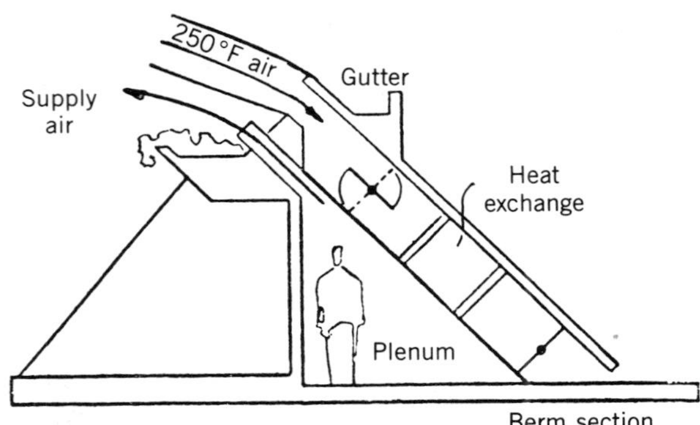

Solar cell B

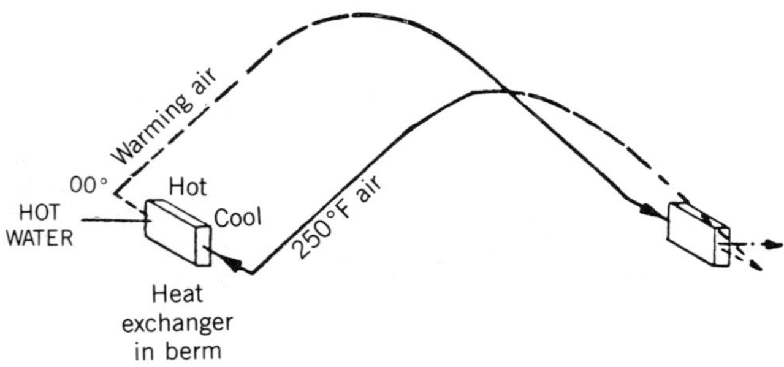

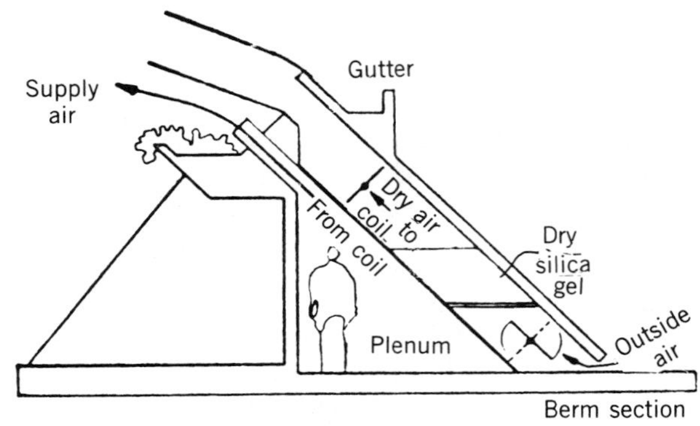

Solar cell A–humidification

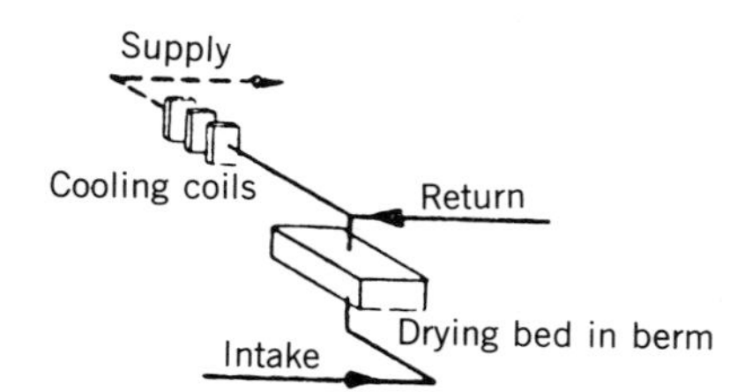

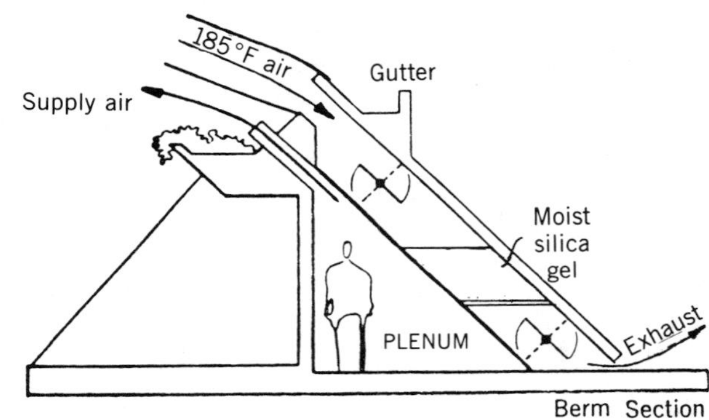

Solar cell A — Drying

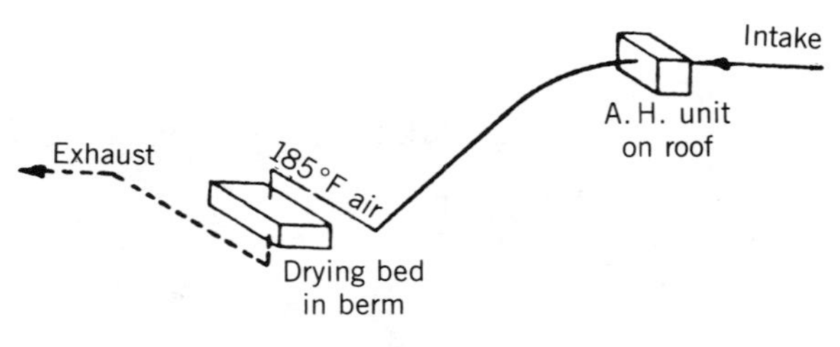

(c)

structure as an active solar collector for running absorption cooling unit (24); and the 1200-ft-diameter Alaska 84 encapsulation (Fig. 23**c**) (25).

All of the materials considered in these projects were currently off-the-shelf materials. The structural systems considered were air-supported and air-inflated (Alaska 84); the cable dome concept could be used in lieu of air support for the smaller of these structures to 1200 ft span.

Through the use of transparent membranes, there would appear to be a transparent sky seen through a cable grid—either air-supported or supported as in a cable dome. By creating a climate controlled, rain and wind protected environment below the roof, the savings in the construction cost of those structures built within the encapsulation would pay for the cost of the roof. Detailed economic analysis has shown that these savings, in addition, pay for the encapsulated recreation areas as well, areas that would not be covered if more conventional techniques of construction were used (Fig. 23**c**).

BIBLIOGRAPHY

1. W. Bird, "History of Air Structures in United States of America," *International Conference, Practical Applications for Air-Supported Structures,* Air Structures Division, Canvas Products Association International, St. Paul, Minn., 1974.
2. F. Otto, *Tensile Structures,* Vol. 1, *Pneumatic Structures,* MIT, Cambridge, Mass., 1962.
3. F. Otto, *Tensile Structures,* Vol. 2, *Cables, Nets, and Membranes,* MIT, Cambridge, Mass., 1965.
4. D. H. Geiger, "U.S. Pavilion at EXPO 70 Features Air Supported Cable Roof," *Civil Engineering—ASCE* (March 1970).
5. D. H. Geiger, "Developments in Incombustible Fabrics and Low Profile Air Structures Including Those with Thermally Active Roofs, WCOSE—1976," *Proceedings—IASS World Congress on Space Enclosures,* Concordia University, Montreal, Canada, July 1976.
6. H. J. Schek, "The Force Density Method for Form Finding and Computation of General Networks," *Computer Methods in Applied Mechanics and Engineering* (3), 115–134 (1974).
7. U.S. Pat. 4,452,848, "Composite Roof Membrane" (to D. H. Geiger).
8. "Fabric Roof Automated," *Engineering News Record* (Jan. 3, 1985).
9. U.S. Pat. 4,736,553, "Roof Structure" (to D. H. Geiger).
10. "Olympic Domes First of Their Kind," *Engineering News Record* (March 6, 1986).
11. U.S. Pat. 3,835,599 (Sept. 17, 1974) (to D. H. Geiger).
12. U.S. Pat. 3,841,038, "Roof Construction" (to D. H. Geiger).
13. K. P. Hamilton, D. M. Campbell, and D. H. Geiger, "Comparison of Air-Supported Roofs on the Vancouver, B.C. and Indianapolis Stadia."
14. "Neoprene Inserts Keep Creaks Out of 400 Foot Diameter, Cable Hung Roof," *Engineering News Record* (Nov. 1, 1973).
15. G. Beger and L. Macher, *Results of Wind Tunnel Tests on Some Pneumatic Structures,"* I.A.S.S., Stuttgart, May 1967.
16. *Building Code Requirements for Minimum Design Loads in Buildings and Other Structures (ANSI A58.1),* American National Standards Institute, Washington, D.C., 1982.
17. *Recommendations for Air Supported Structures,* IASS, Working Group nr. 7, Madrid, 1985.
18. U.S. Pat. 4,013,812, "Laminated Fabric" (to D. H. Geiger).
19. "Air Fair," Progressive Architecture, Stamford, Conn., August, 1972.
20. D. H. Geiger, "A Cost Comparison of Roof Systems for Sports Halls," Invited lecturer, *IASS Symposium,* Beijing, China, 1987; published IASS Bulletin, 1988.
21. *AISI, Manual for Structural Applications of Steel Cables for Buildings,* American Iron and Steel Institute, New York, 1973.
22. A. M. Freudenthal, *The Inelastic Behavior of Engineering Materials and Structures,* John Wiley & Sons, Inc., New York, 1950.
23. "Study Started on Air Supported Building Roof That Will Use Sun to Save Energy," *Engineering News Record* (Oct. 23, 1975).
24. D. H. Geiger and H. Berger, "Preliminary Design of Lightweight Membrane Structures Including Air Supported and Structurally Supported Systems," in R. N. White and C. G. Salmon, eds., *Building Structural Design Handbook,* John Wiley & Sons, Inc., New York, 1987.
25. "Roof Would Take to the Air Under Alaska Birthday Plan," *Engineering News Record* (April 27, 1982).

See also Suspension Cable Structures

David H. Geiger
Geiger Engineers
New York, New York

METALLIC COATINGS

Metallic coatings are used to provide pleasing decorative effects to metal or plastic, or they are used to protect a structural material against corrosive deterioration. All metallic coatings, whatever their purpose, must have a high degree of corrosion resistance in the intended environment. It is incumbent on the designer first to assess accurately the nature of the environment to which a structure will be exposed; second, to understand the limitations of the basic materials within that environment; and finally, to become familiar with those coating practices in common use for those materials and conditions. Only then can the need for protective coatings be determined and an adequate, cost-effective metallic coating type and thickness be specified that will provide the intended protection or aesthetic effect. This article briefly discusses only the most important aspects of corrosion and metallic coatings and indicates some of the available resources for specific information on corrosion and the proper use of metallic coatings.

All metallic corrosion proceeds by an electrochemical process requiring the presence of an electrolyte, usually water. In the absence of moisture, corrosion will generally not occur, provided other reactive chemicals are absent. When metal corrodes, it oxidizes, giving up its electrons, thereby forming ions. The ions go into solution and may be precipitated out as a corrosion product that may or may not inhibit further corrosion. The electrons are conducted to some other point on the metal where a substance from the environment is reduced, consuming electrons. Thus metal loss occurs at anodic sites, producing electrons, which are consumed at one or more cathode sites where reduction occurs. Reduction reactions are commonly hydrogen evolution (acids), oxygen reduction, or metal deposition. The tendency of metals to corrode is determined by their position in the electrochemical series. Metals high on the list, such as sodium, are actively corroded. Those at the bottom corrode less (copper) or not at all (gold). Thus the degree of corrosion depends on the inherent corrosion tendency of the metal, the presence of a conducting electrolyte, the rate of the respective anodic and cathodic reactions (the environment), and the degree to which corrosion products act as physical barriers to the progress of the reactions. Eight forms of corrosion that are of engineering importance have been identified (1). Of these, galvanic corrosion is of the greatest importance to the designer who is considering metallic coatings. However, the reader will benefit by referring to texts that treat the general subject of corrosion in more depth (2–5). Excellent sources of tabular information on the corrosion rates of materials and coatings in various environments for extended periods are also available (6,7). Written specifically for the architect–designer are the *Corrosion Guide* (8) and the *Paints and Coatings Handbook* (9). The former has extensive tabulations of expected corrosion rates, and the latter an excellent summary of the aspects of corrosion of particular importance to the builder.

Galvanic corrosion occurs when two dissimilar metals are coupled directly together, such as with bolting or screw fasteners. Generally, one of the metals (the more active one) will anodically corrode, the other more noble of the pair acting as the cathode. This situation is usually avoided by ensuring that dissimilar metals are positioned closely in the galvanic series or by using insulating bushings and washers. The commonly accepted progression from active to noble metals is magnesium, aluminum, zinc, iron, lead, tin–lead (terne), copper, brass, silver, graphite, carbon, platinum, and gold. More complete listings can be found in corrosion texts. The problem of galvanic corrosion is exacerbated when the anodic member is of smaller area, so that the anodic dissolution reaction is enhanced. If the fastener is the more active metal, its failure is imminent by this process, and such situations should be scrupulously avoided. An excellent resource on the proper use of fasteners is the *Building and Plant Maintenance Desk Book* (10). Nevertheless, the galvanic corrosion principle is used to provide corrosion protection with the bulk of today's metallic coatings. Zinc, cadmium, and aluminum are more active than iron and, when electrically coupled to it, will corrode instead of the iron. When zinc, cadmium, or aluminum is coated on iron by any of the various methods available, it will preserve the iron free of corrosion until the sacrificial metal coating is consumed. On the other hand, metals such as nickel, chromium, tin, lead, copper, and gold, which are more noble than iron and thus cannot sacrificially corrode when coupled to it, are also used as coatings on iron, but to a lesser extent. The use of these metals as coatings is due to their uniform corrosion at very low rates and the tenacious films of oxide that may form on them. However, in terms of tonnage used, zinc, aluminum, and zinc–aluminum alloy coatings are by far the most widely used metallic protective coatings for structural steel products. Thus metallic coatings fall into two classes, sacrificial coatings and barrier layers, with the former by far the most extensive. For architectural design and engineering of coated structures, excellent discussions of coatings are given in the *Metallic Materials Specification Handbook* (11) and the *Building Design and Construction Handbook* (12). *Metallic Coatings for Corrosion Control* (13) is an extensive overall survey text of metallic coatings.

COATING METHODS

The principal methods used to manufacture coated products are hot dipping (galvanizing), electroplating, hot powder diffusion (Sherardizing), mechanical plating, roll bonding, thermal spraying, vapor deposition in vacuum, and brush plating. Of these, hot dipping is used for pipe, strip, and fabricated structural shapes and generally those sized parts conveniently handled in molten baths. Coil coating of aluminum, zinc, and their alloys is done by hot dipping (Sendzimer process) to provide coated sheet for roofing and siding materials and a host of finished shapes that are formed from coated sheet material by drawing, punching, and bending operations. Sheet products are also electroplated with tin, copper, nickel, chromium, and cadmium as well as zinc. Electroplating and chemical bath plating are especially useful for small hardware items. Standards for these finishes have been developed by the Builder's Hardware Manufacturer's Association (BHMA), in particular Standard 1301, Section M (14). Hot processing in metal powder by the Sherardizing process for zinc and by mechanical plating for zinc, tin, tin–lead, cadmium, and tin–cadmium are processes especially appropriate for all kinds of fasteners. Mechanical plating has gained popularity because of its low cost and uniformity. Roll bonding has found use in sheet products, such as copper-clad stainless, lead-coated terne-bonded steel, and brass-clad stainless. Thermal spraying of aluminum, zinc, and their alloys has become popular, particularly in Europe, because of its low cost, versatility, and field application advantages. Vapor-deposited coating, often referred to as metallization, is limited to products that can be conveniently handled in evacuated vessels. Many decorative metallic coatings are applied to hardware, and especially to plastic items, such as lighting fixtures and louvers. Plate glass coated by metals and alloys using vacuum evaporation and sputtering techniques is used worldwide where building, thermal, and light control is achieved with striking visual effects. Cathodic arc deposition, a recently developed vacuum metallizing technique, has been used widely for tool coating. Brush plating is an electroplating technique using a fabric-coated graphite tampon flooded with electrolyte, which is hand applied to parts of varying size and geometry, generally those that are impossible to immerse in regular plating baths. Its chief application is for installing and restoring decorative coatings on outdoor structures.

Zinc-, Aluminum-, and Alloy-Coated Products

Zinc and aluminum coatings on steel are produced in enormous quantities worldwide. Zinc corrodes in neutral pH waters, including sea water, and in the atmosphere at a

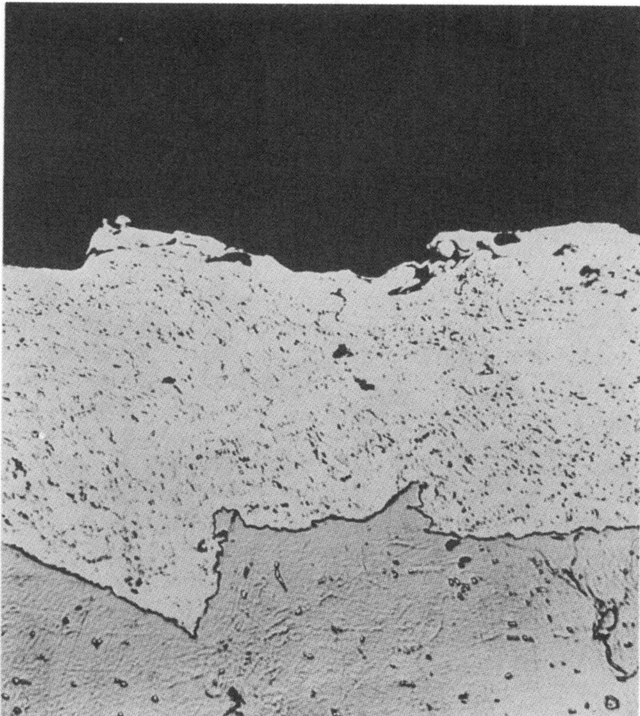

Figure 1. Cross section photomicrograph of a 100-μm thermal-sprayed zinc coating on grit-blasted steel. Up to 500 μm can be sprayed. This coating is the minimal amount required by BS 2569 and CSA G189–1966 and is ideal for organic paint sealing (15). Courtesy of the Zinc Development Association.

rate 25 times less than that of steel. It is anodic to its normal impurities as well as to iron and forms insoluble basic salts. Its coating life is directly proportional to the weight of the zinc deposited. Standard galvanized steel, grade G90, contains 275 g/m^2, and the heaviest, grade G235, about three times that. Minimal corrosion applications require at least 30 g/m^2, whereas severe corrosive applications should have 640 g/m^2, equating to a 100-μm thick coating. Figure 1 shows a cross section of a 100-μm thermal-sprayed zinc coating. This coating thickness is adequate for over 20 years protection in rural locations or 5–10 years' immersion in sea water. Thicknesses of 250 μm, applied most conveniently by spraying, may be required for industrial or coastal locations (16). Sealing of sprayed coatings with low-viscosity paints, such as vinyl, phenolic, epoxy resin, or silicone products, in most cases doubles the effective life. For most confined, relatively dry architectural applications, such extensive coating applications may not be required. An advantage of sprayed coatings for architectural applications is the fact that the thickness can be varied as required for the proper protection of local sites. Thus steel supports need only be sprayed where contact with excessive moisture is anticipated. Nevertheless, wide use for thermal sprayed zinc has been found in the protection of entire intricate exterior designs, such as that of the Centre George Pompidou in Paris. Sprayed aluminum coatings are also useful, but require thicker coatings for the same coating protection. Aluminum coatings have an advantage when immersed in sea water, where their corrosion rate of 0.02 mpy (mils per year) on a 16-year average is significantly lower than that for zinc (6). The present technology thrust is toward alloy coatings.

New alloy products produced by hot dipping include products trademarked Galvalume, or Zincalume (Australia), containing 55Al–Zn, and Galfan, a zinc-5% Al-mischmetal coating. The former (17,18) is experiencing worldwide acceptance as roofing and siding, as shown in Figure 2, because of its excellent surface and extended life, at a cost equivalent to that of G90 galvanizing. The latter is finding use in products requiring deep drawing and welding and is especially suitable for painting (19). It is more formable than the steel it protects. Aluminum-coated products should not be used with lead or copper, to avoid harmful corrosion effects.

Zinc-rich organic coatings are not ordinarily considered metallic coatings. Zinc particles in these paints are insulated by the organic paint from electrical contact with the steel and provide little if any galvanic protection. However, when these paint coatings, containing approximately 40 g/m^2 of zinc, are treated with a corona discharge, dielectric breakdown causes filamentous conduction paths to form between particles and the substrate steel. Up to 5–10 g/m^2 then becomes available for sacrificial protection of the steel. Consideration should be given to painted products processed in this manner, as well as to remedial corona treatment of previously painted structures.

Mechanical Plating and Mechanical Galvanizing

Fasteners are critical in architectural design. Coatings on fasteners are best produced by mechanical plating. Mechanical plating and mechanical galvanizing are done in barrels with powdered coating metal, water, activators, and glass beads that serve to cold-weld particles to the clean surfaces during agitation. For mechanical plating for threaded fasteners, besides being less costly than hot dipping, these methods offer the advantages of excellent uniformity and a lack of "stickers," a common problem with hot-dip parts. When stickers are separated, "holidays," or gaps in the coating, are formed, causing rust

Figure 2. Galvalume, a trademark of Bethlehem Steel Corp., building siding has excellent color, texture, and durability for exterior use (18). Courtesy of Bethlehem Steel Corp.

spots. In addition, rethreading, which often damages hot-dipped fasteners, is not necessary with mechanically galvanized parts. Quality control is enhanced, waste is reduced, and workers appreciate the ease of fit-up for bolts, nuts, and washers when they are mechanically plated. The designer should be aware that the use of galvanized fasteners with aluminum products can cause corrosion of the zinc coating and the aluminum structure. However, cadmium—tin mechanically plated fasteners have shown excellent compatibility with aluminum (20). In contrast to electroplated fastener coatings, there is no concern for hydrogen embrittlement with mechanically plated parts. Hydrogen embrittlement can cause catastrophic failure of highly stressed bolting and should be avoided by using nonembrittling coating processes.

Special Materials and Processes

New materials and processes for metallic coating are now available that deserve the attention of the designer and builder. Striking and beautiful decorative effects can be obtained with titanium nitride, which can be vapor deposited at high speed by the cathode arc process in a vacuum (21). Evaporated titanium reacts with a nitrogen residual atmosphere in the vessel to produce hard, dense, smooth, adherent, gold-colored deposits having exceptional beauty as well as wear resistance. These deposits were originally used to prolong the life of metal-cutting tools, but can be used in plumbing fixtures, appliances, knobs, bezels, electrical fixtures, fasteners, tiles, glassware, and other objects where a reflectivity exactly matching that of pure gold is desired, but at a reasonable price. Figure 3 shows the quality of such deposits on a plumbing fixture.

Brush plating is a process that has had a long history of use in the repair of electroplated components (22). The electrolyte is delivered to the surface to be plated with an absorbent cloth-covered graphite wand electrically connected to a suitable power supply. Plating is done as the tampon is moved over the surface of the object. It has been developed in recent years to repair gold leaf domes on buildings and to restore decorative statuary. Figure 4 shows the restored California capitol dome in Sacramento. After the copper base structure was cleaned, it was plated with nickel, followed by a 1.3-μm thick layer of 99.4% pure gold. Equally effective decorative coatings have been applied to stainless steel. The process can be used for first-time applications of coatings on objects of unusual size or shape or where accessibility is a problem.

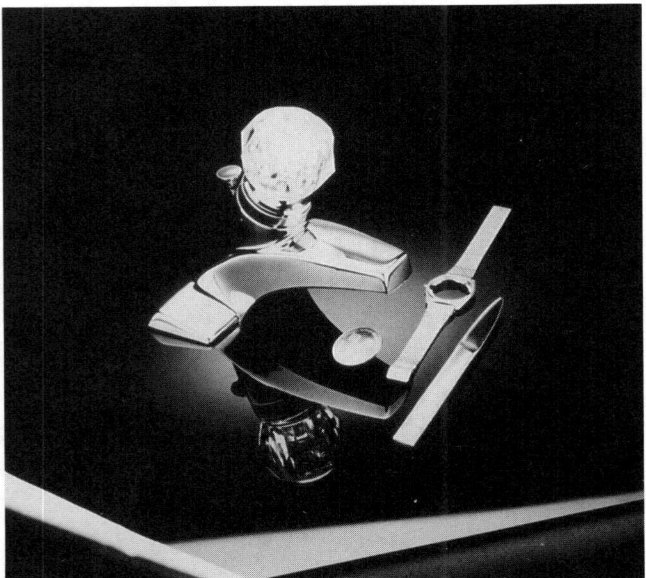

Figure 3. Plumbing fixture coated with titanium nitride illustrating the similarity of its color to that of pure gold. These coatings are very hard, adherent, and corrosion, wear, and abrasion resistant. Courtesy of Multi-Arc Vacuum Systems, Inc.

Figure 4. The Sacramento state capitol dome after refinishing with 24-karat gold over nickel by the brush-plating process (23). Courtesy of the International Nickel Company.

INFORMATION RESOURCES ON METALLIC COATINGS

Permament protection of steel is neither cheap nor easy. However, the initial cost of a correct surface preparation, followed by a proper application of a good-quality coating material, is much more economical than the cost of replacing a failed coating. It is generally more difficult to apply a corrosion protection on the second attempt than the first. When the decision has been made that a protective or decorative coating is desirable, it is advisable to seek the advice of experts in the corrosion and coating field during the planning stage. Each year the National Association of Corrosion Engineers provides a "Corrosion Engineering Buyer's Guide" in the publication *Materials Performance* (24). This volume is a guide to coating products and professional corrosion and coating consulting services. Current abstracts of worldwide literature on metallic coatings are available in the "Cleaning, Finishing, and Coating Digest" drawn from the international journal, *Metals Abstracts* (25).

BIBLIOGRAPHY

1. M. G. Fontana and N. D. Greene, *Materials Engineering,* McGraw-Hill, Inc., New York, 1978, p. 31.
2. K. Barton, transl. by J. R. Duncan, *Protection Against Atmospheric Corrosion,* Wiley-Interscience, New York, 1976.
3. L. L. Shrier, Ed., *Corrosion,* Vol. 1, and *Metal/Environmental Reactions,* Vol. 2 of *Corrosion Control,* Butterworth & Co., Ltd., Kent, UK, 1976.
4. J. T. N. Atkinson and H. VanDroffelaar, *Corrosion and its Control,* National Association of Corrosion Engineers, Houston, Tex., 1982.
5. P. A. Schweitzer, ed., *Corrosion and Corrosion Protection Handbook,* Marcel Dekker, Inc., New York, 1983.
6. F. W. Fink and W. K. Boyd, *Corrosion of Metals in Marine Environments,* Bayer & Co., Columbus, Ohio, 1970.
7. *Corrosion Tests of Flame Sprayed Coated Steel, 19 Year Report,* American Welding Society, Miami, 1974.
8. E. Rabald, *Corrosion Guide,* Elsevier, Amsterdam, the Netherlands, 1968.
9. A. Banov, *Paints and Coatings Handbook,* 2nd ed., Structures Publishing Co., Farmington, Mich., 1978.
10. R. W. Liska, *Building and Plant Maintenance Desk Book,* Prentice-Hall, Inc., Englewood Cliffs, N.J., 1980.
11. R. B. Ross, *Metallic Materials Specification Handbook,* 3rd ed., E. & F.N. Spon, London, 1980.
12. F. S. Merritt, *Building Design/Construction Handbook,* McGraw-Hill, Inc., New York, 1982.
13. V. E. Carter, *Metallic Coatings for Corrosion Control,* Newnes-Butterworths, London, 1977.
14. A. H. Brownell, *Architectural Hardware Specifications Handbook,* Chilton Book Co., Philadelphia, Pa., 1971, Appendix 5.
15. "Technical Notes on Zinc–Zinc Spraying," Zinc Development Association, London, 1976.
16. British Standards Institution, BS 5493:1977, tabulated by Kidd Creek Mines Ltd., Toronto, Ont., Canada, 1977.
17. J. B. Horton, "Aluminum–Zinc Alloys as Sacrificial Coatings," in H. Leidheiser, Jr., ed., *Corrosion Control by Coatings,* Science Press, Princeton, N.J., 1979.
18. Folder 3156C, Bethlehem Steel Corp., Bethlehem, Pa., Jan. 1979.
19. E. J. Kubel, Jr., *Material Engineering* **102,** 42 (Aug. 1985).
20. E. A. Davis, "Mechanical Plating," in *Coatings for Corrosion Prevention,* American Society for Metals, Metals Park, Ohio, 1978.
21. A. Anderson, *Metals Progress* **128**(3), 41 (1985).
22. M. Rubenstein, *Metal Finishing* **79,** (7), 21 (1981); **79,** 53 (1981).
23. "Nickel Topics," The International Nickel Co. (INCO International), New York, 1982.
24. "Corrosion Engineering Buyer's Guide," in *Materials Performance,* National Association of Corrosion Engineers, Houston, Tex.
25. *Metals Abstracts,* Institute of Metals, London, and American Society for Metals, Metals Park, Ohio.

Richard C. Krutenat
Lowell, Massachusetts

METALS. See Specific Types

MIES VAN DER ROHE, LUDWIG

Ludwig Mies was born in Aachen (Aix-la-Chapelle), Germany, to the wife of a stonemason in 1886. He attended the Cathedral School there between 1897 and 1900. In 1905 he moved to Berlin and, without formal architectural training, became an apprentice in the office of furniture designer Bruno Paul. In 1907, he built his first house as an independent architect, a wooden house in eighteenth-century style under the influence of English domestic architecture. Employed as a draftsman and designer in the office of Peter Behrens at the same time as Gropius was a senior assistant, Mies remained there until 1911. Among projects he worked on in Behrens's office were the German Embassy in St. Petersburg (1911–1912) and an early study of a house (1911) for the art collectors Anton and Hélène Kröller at the Hague in the Netherlands.

When Mies left the office of Peter Behrens, he was commissioned by Mrs. Kröller to prepare a new design for a house for the Hague, Netherlands. He worked for a year in Holland. A full-scale wood and canvas model was erected on the site, but the building was not built. (A house was eventually built to the design of H. P. Berlage.) Mies's design for the house was derived from his study of the work of Karl Friedrich Schinkel (1781–1840). The project is known from drawings and photographs of the model and the mock-up. It was about that time that Mies added his mother's family name, van der Rohe, to his surname for reason of its "sonorous" sound.

Reestablishing his practice as an independent architect in Berlin in 1912, Mies remained there until 1914, when he entered military service. After demobilization, he practiced architecture in Berlin until 1937. In 1918 he joined the Novembergruppe and served as its director of architectural exhibits until 1925. He became a member of the Zehner Ring. From 1926 to 1932, he served as first vice-president of the Deutscher Werkbund.

In 1921, a competition was held for the design of a skyscraper on the Friedrichstrasse in Berlin. Mies's scheme was forward looking, of great simplicity, in the form of three prismatic towers around a central core. The exterior was sheathed with glass. However, this project was not acceptable because the conditions of the competition could not be met with this solution.

There was no client for Mies's proposal for a glass skyscraper (1922) in the form of a thirty-story tower designed for an irregular site located near the crossing of two broad avenues. The remarkable free-form plan sheathed in glass remained a strictly aesthetic study, without a solution for its structure. The project is known from photographs of a model, drawings, and sketches.

Dating of the proposal for a concrete country house is based on evidence that it was displayed in Berlin in May 1923 and at the Weimar Bauhaus in the autumn of that year. The proposal is known from photographs of a model and a few drawings. As this project shows Mies moving to a true "modern" style, it has always been of great interest. He undertook a number of studies of concrete buildings, including office structures at this time.

The plan for a brick country house in 1924 has a remarkable resemblance to the de Stijl paintings of Theo Van Doesburg. Mies was interested in brick as a traditional material and used it in the design for this proposed country house. Walls were free standing, sliding out from beneath the roof into the landscape. The walls connected to glass enclosures produced an entirely new effect, with radical implications for living style. Mies used these concepts to good effect in the Barcelona Pavilion of 1929.

The brick monument to Karl Liebknecht and Rosa Luxemburg (1926) in Berlin commemorated the ill-fated Spartacist 1919 uprising. Mies's design was an abstract brick structure 6 m high, 12 m long, and at the widest, 4 m wide. Related to constructivist sculpture, it has also been compared to Frank Lloyd Wright's design for the Kaufmann house, "Falling Water." The five-pointed star and hammer and sickle completed the design. The Nazis ordered it destroyed in 1933. It was an exception for Mies to design a political monument, for he was normally nonpolitical. The commission came from Eduard Fuchs, president of the German Communist Party at that time. Mies was later attacked as a Communist because of this commission.

In 1927 Mies was director and designer of the Werkbund Exposition, "The Weissenhofsiedlung," overlooking Stuttgart. Sixteen architects of world renown, including Le Corbusier, Peter Behrens, Richard Docker, Hans Pelzig, Hans Scharoun, and Walter Gropius were commissioned to design and build 320 white houses. The houses were of the very latest design, using the most recently developed materials. This was the first housing project to be built in Europe using designs that were the last word in modernity—flat roofs and cubic forms. Glass and concrete were the main construction materials. The houses were built taking into consideration the latest ideas in communal living that psychologists and sociologists had devised (1).

This success was followed by Mies's appointment as Director of the German Section of the International Exposition in Barcelona, Spain. The pavilion was awarded to Mies van der Rohe in the summer of 1928 because the Weimar Republic wished to present itself as progressive. It was used as an information and reception center and was opened in the presence of the Spanish King Alfonso XIII and the royal family. Demolished in 1930, the building is known from photographs. Reconstructed in Barcelona in the 1980s, this icon of modern architecture may now be experienced in facsimile on its original site. Many feel that Mies's fame would have endured on the basis of this one building. The Barcelona chairs designed for the pavilion, originally in white leather, remain in production and have been widely used in the United States.

Mies became well known for the glass and steel, "skin and bones" clarity that the Barcelona Pavilion expressed, as well as the planar inner walls that are an outgrowth of the belief that space must be made universal and flexible.

The luxurious Tugendhat house in Brno, Czechoslovakia (1930) was the largest designed by Mies. On a sloping site, the building is a compact two-story plan, entered from the street at the upper level. The free flowing spaces of the living and dining areas give this house much of its quality. Its use of exterior terraces on both levels is comparable to Le Corbusier's Villa Stein in Garches, France, of 1927. Programmatically, the house is similar in function to large, late nineteenth-century country houses. Individual spaces could be shut off using draperies on ceiling tracks. The curved wall defining the dining room is Macassar wood, with an onyx freestanding wall defining space between living area and study. The Brno chairs designed for this house are still produced. The house suffered damage and is now owned by the city of Brno. Restoration of the house was begun in 1986.

All of Mies van der Rohe's furniture designs, with the exception of some studies, occurred in his German period. He worked for many years with the interior designer Lilly Reich (1885–1947), but the designs bearing Mies's name are considered his own. These pieces are well known because they were sold by Knoll Associates in the United States. Well-known pieces include the Barcelona chair (1929), MR chairs (1926), Tugendhat chair (1930), and Brno chair, couch, and coffee table (1930). Other pieces were simple tables based on the careful selection of materials rather than on new technology.

In 1930, Gropius recommended Mies as successor to Hannes Meyer (1889–1954) as director of the Dessau Bauhaus. During that period he was also director of the Werkbund Section, "The Dwelling," of the Berlin Building Exposition of 1931. In that year he was made a member of the Prussian Academy of Arts and Sciences. When the Dessau Bauhaus was closed by the Nazis, Mies moved it to Berlin in 1933, but again the Nazis closed the school; the faculty dispersed on August 10 of that year.

In 1937, Mies made his first trip to the United States, followed in 1938 by his immigration there. He was appointed Director of Architecture at the Armour Institute in Chicago (since 1940, the Illinois Institute of Technology). In 1944 he became a U.S. citizen.

With the establishment of a new campus for the Illinois Institute of Technology, Mies had the opportunity to plan the campus as well as several of the buildings. The first structures, started under wartime conditions, were variations on steel-framed one- to three-story buildings with brick and glass. The care in detailing intersections and corners gives the buildings distinction. The simplicity of the chapel (1952) is noteworthy, as is the last of the buildings designed by Mies for the campus, Crown Hall (1950–1956) (Fig. 1). The latter building is an enormous room, 120 × 220 ft in plan, 18 ft high without interior columns, used for the architectural school. The building is raised several feet above the ground to allow light for the below-grade School of Design. The most interesting point is the

Figure 1. S. R. Crown Hall, Illinois Institute of Technology, Chicago, Ill. Courtesy of IIT.

structural solution of exposed structural beams above the roof, making clear the method of achieving the clear-span interior. Mies ended his relationship with the school in 1958.

Dr. Edith Farnsworth commissioned a house from Mies in 1946 for weekend and vacation use, on the Fox River, Plano, Illinois. The house is a simple glass pavilion on a raised platform; the exterior columns make the roof and platform appear to float above the site. Construction started in 1949. Before completion, Dr. Farnsworth brought a lawsuit against Mies that was settled in Mies's favor. This experience may have contributed to the fact that Mies concentrated on large building types after this.

The 26-story 860–880 Lake Shore Apartments in Chicago (1948–1951) were an important advance in high-rise design. Based on a 21-ft bay, the structural cage is clearly expressed, with spaces between structural members in glass. At the ground level, service and lobby areas are set in from the columns, providing covered walk areas. For appearance, I-beams were welded to columns and mullions. This use of steel for decorative use was an aesthetic decision. White draperies against the glass gave a uniform appearance, with the possibility of interior draperies for individual selection. The buildings continue to look well, better than most buildings of their age. There has been extensive published commentary on these and other apartment towers designed by Mies.

In 1953, Mies introduced Gropius at a fete marking the latter's seventieth birthday, tracing their long association, and lauding Gropius's contributions.

The Seagram building on Park Avenue in New York City (1954–1958) (Fig.2) was set back 90 feet from Park Avenue and 35 feet from the side streets. It rises in a simple shaft to 39 stories. More space could have been built on the site under zoning laws, but the client agreed to the reduction in floor space. Lower structures behind the tower close off the center of the block. The plaza on Park Avenue, raised from the street, consists of simple

Figure 2. Seagram Building, New York City, 1957. Photograph by Ezra Stoller. Courtesy of Joseph E. Seagram & Sons, Inc.

stone paving flanked by pools. The walls are a bronze curtain wall, and the finish throughout was carefully designed by Mies. The building has landmark status.

The Toronto Dominion Centre (Fig.3) is related in concept to the Federal Center in Chicago and Westmount Square in Montreal. Mies most carefully considered the design of the Toronto project; the other two were carried out by his office under his direction. Asymmetrical groupings of towers on a plaza, the buildings have remarkable similarities despite variations in function. This prototype approach was congenial to Mies, and in Chicago it was played off with the one-story post office pavilion. The clarity of detail and care in design of the walls make these typically Miesian buildings fit their urban settings well. In the

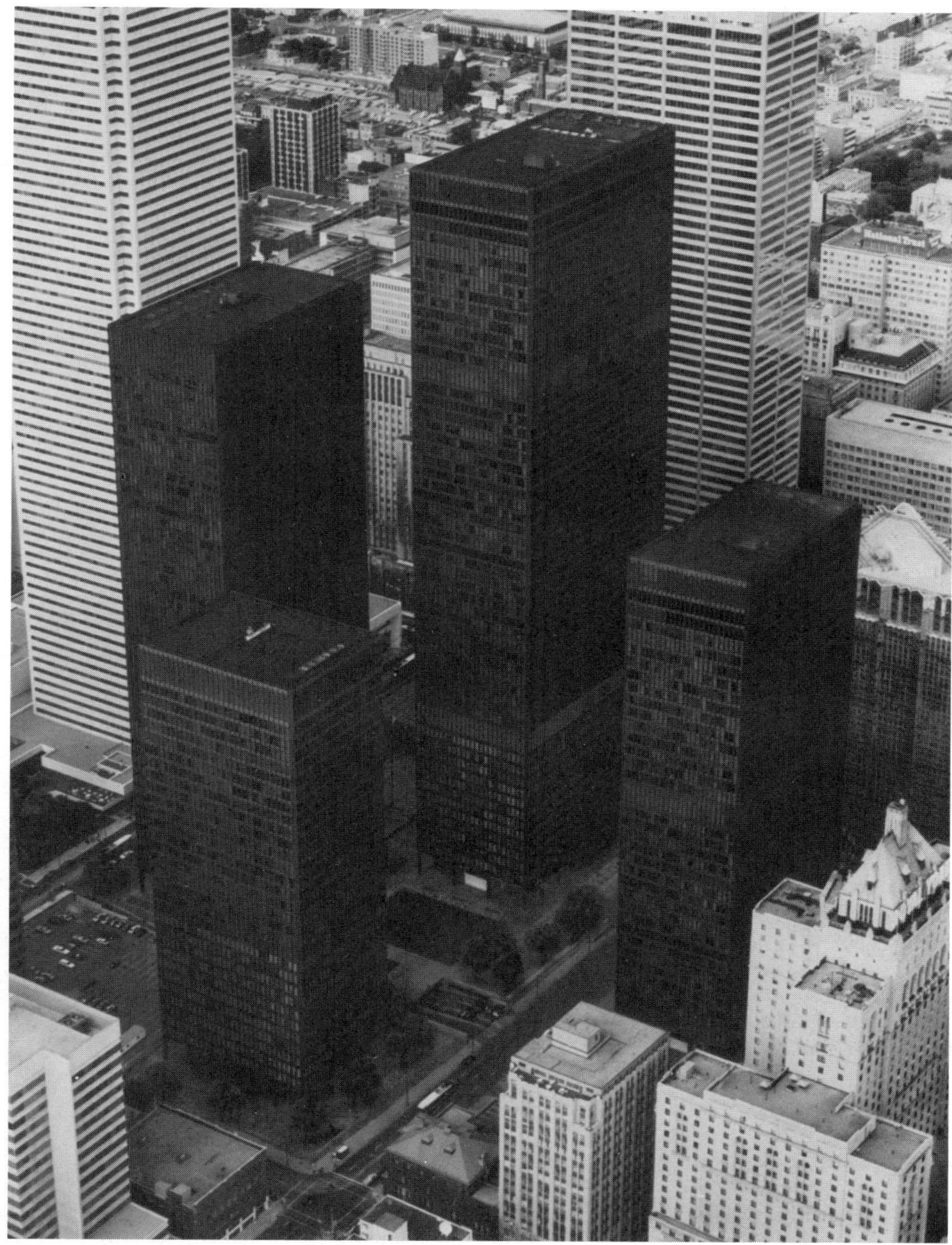

Figure 3. Toronto Dominion Centre, Toronto, Ontario, Canada. The three towers on the left were designed by Mies van der Rohe; the fourth on the right was added later. Courtesy of the Cadillac Fairview Corporation, Ltd.

Canadian projects, the underground shops, parking, and ties to transportation systems (in Montreal) were important urban considerations.

The New National Gallery for Berlin (completed 1968) was a late work, derived in concept from earlier studies for museums and the Bacardi office building project in Cuba, never built. The roof structure and supports are the essence of the building. Exterior columns were carefully designed, standing in front of an all-glass wall. The entire roof was raised in one operation, high enough for the columns to be placed on their foundations; the roof was then lowered onto pin connections. The immensity of the enclosed space has made it a difficult space for art. It is more an expression of Mies's aesthetic, and is its own exhibition.

Mies was awarded the Gold Medal of the Royal Institute of British Architects in 1959, the AIA Gold Medal in 1960, and the J. Lloyd Kimbrough Medal in 1961. He was the first architect to receive the American Presidential Medal of Freedom, in 1963. He was the recipient of prizes from the city of Munich and the German state of North Rhine-Westphalia, and from the Bund Deutscher Architekten in 1966. After a long illness, Mies van der Rohe died in Chicago on August 17, 1969, at the age of 83, only a month after the death of Walter Gropius.

One of the great masters of early twentieth-century

architecture along with Frank Lloyd Wright and Le Corbusier, Mies van der Rohe made a major impact on the look of U.S. cities. His wide acceptance by corporate America brought him more important commissions than he had received in Germany in his earlier days.

His elegant curtain walls were widely adapted by others using less expensive construction, giving rise to the glib phrase "less is a bore." He has been criticized because his buildings, although appearing machine-made, were in large part built by hand. He was accused of paying small attention to functional demands, such as ignoring excessive solar gain through glass walls. He was also described as insensitive to neighboring structures and to environmental concerns. Critics have claimed that his best work was the design of undifferentiated spaces such as lobbies, convention halls, or open office floors.

What is likely to be his lasting impact was Mies's concern with theoretical concepts, clarity of image, careful attention to detail, and rightness of proportion. These architectural concepts will survive.

BIBLIOGRAPHY

1. T. Troll, *Christ und Welt,* Stuttgart, July 18, 1969.

General References

Archival material is in the collection of the Museum of Modern Art in New York City, including models of a number of Mies's buildings.

Personal correspondence was given to the Library of Congress in Washington, D.C.

W. A. James, "Barcelona," *Progressive Architecture,* 61–67 (Aug. 1986).

P. Blake, *The Master Builders: Le Corbusier, Mies van der Rohe, Frank Lloyd Wright,* Alfred A. Knopf, Inc., New York, 1960. Reprinted with revisions by W. W. Norton & Company, New York, 1976.

P. C. Johnson, *Mies van der Rohe,* The Museum of Modern Art, New York, 1953, revised edition.

F. Schulze, in association with the Mies van der Rohe Archive of the Museum of Modern Art, *Mies van der Rohe: A Critical Biography,* University of Chicago Press, Chicago, Ill., 1986.

W. Tegethoff, *Mies van der Rohe: The Villas and Country Houses,* The Museum of Modern Art/MIT Press, Cambridge, Mass., 1986.

REGINALD R. ISAACS
Cambridge, Massachusetts

Edited by Robert T. Packard, AIA.

MITCHELL/GIURGOLA ARCHITECTS

Mitchell/Giurgola Architects was formed in Philadelphia, Pennsylvania, by Ehrman B. Mitchell and Romaldo Giurgola in 1958. Since then, the firm has been responsible for the design of a broad range of building types: places of work, places of study, places to live, and cultural institutions for the applied and performing arts. The practice is international in scope, with projects in more than 100 cities on both U.S. coasts, Australia, Jamaica, Sweden, Italy, Venezuela, Brazil, and Colombia.

APPROACH TO DESIGN

Mitchell/Giurgola is consciously committed to the search for an architecture capable of enhancing life and providing a sense of inspiration and aspiration to its inhabitants. The link between Mitchell/Giurgola projects has been the design process that created them. Each building derives its form from a specific architectural response to its programmatic intent, site, environmental conditions, and dialogue with its patrons. The firm's architecture is conceived not as a stylized container of specific activities, but rather as a place to be inhabited, a place to facilitate the course of human interaction.

Since the early 1970s, the professional staff of the firm has remained stable in terms of size and senior leadership. A tightly knit working method and design philosophy has resulted from limiting the size of the firm and having substantial participation in all projects by key principals in the firm. Mitchell and Giurgola expanded the partnership in 1975 and 1980. The partnership expanded once again in 1986.

The firm has developed and consistently embraced a design methodology that revolves around design teams formed at the outset of each project to work together from concept phase to completion. The teams provide a consistent attitude toward conceptual issues and technical matters to assure proper implementation of each project.

The firm places important emphasis on urban design as an approach to the design of individual buildings, rather than focusing on single projects as isolated elements. Conversely, Mitchell/Giurgola's approach to planning projects is to bring an overriding structural order to the fragmentary evolution of the built environment. This comprehensive approach to design has been the objective in master plans for the Massachusetts Institute of Technology (MIT), Cambridge, Massachusetts, and the Master Plan for the U.S. Capitol Grounds, Washington, D.C. (1977–1981).

In the design of large-scale campus complexes for business, industry, and educational institutions on suburban and rural sites, the purpose has been to maintain a proper relationship between the built world and the natural setting and to integrate structures into their natural surroundings. Substantial commissions of this type from private enterprise are an IBM executive education center on a landscaped rural site in Palisades, New York, an extensive office campus for IBM in Westlake, Texas, and the international headquarters for Volvo on a wooded hilltop site outside Gothenburg, Sweden.

Equally significant to Mitchell/Giurgola is a body of work that deals with small projects in the public domain, often with rather modest budgets, that require care in their conceptual development. By bringing the aspirations and dreams of its participants into sharp focus, modest

Figure 1. Tredyffrin Township Public Library. Courtesy of Mitchell/Giurgola Architects.

building programs can have a significant impact that belies their modest dimension. The Tredyffrin Township Public Library (1976) (Fig. 1), three public schools in the Friuli region of Italy devastated by earthquakes in 1976, and the Tilles Center for the Performing Arts, Long Island University, Greenvale, New York (1982), stand as examples of this commitment to the public dimension of architecture.

Considering architecture mainly as an art form, the participation of artists and craftspersons at the inception of projects has been actively pursued since 1971 with the conviction that from these joint efforts architecture acquires a more precise and comprehensive expression reflective of the cultural perspectives and values of the time. In addition, creating a link between the artist and the building tradesperson has served to raise aspirations regarding quality workmanship and the craft of building.

EARLY WORK

Early commissions for the American College in Bryn Mawr, Pennsylvania, and the National Park Service, which remain clients today, gave substance to the practice in its early years. The runner-up submission for the Boston, Massachusetts, City Hall in 1962 and the winning competition entry for the American Institute of Architects (AIA) National Headquarters in Washington, D.C. (ultimately never realized), in 1965 are seminal works of significant critical value. Participation in design competitions judged by professional juries has had a marked impact on the firm's success and includes the winning submissions for the renovations of and addition to the Louis Sullivan-designed Wainwright Building in St. Louis, Missouri, completed in 1981, and the winning submission in the international competition for the new Parliament House, Canberra, Australia (1980) (Fig. 2). More than 300 firms from around the world participated in the latter competition for one of the most important building commissions of the twentieth century.

The firm expanded to include offices in Philadelphia and New York in 1967 when Giurgola was appointed Chairman of the Division of Architecture at the Graduate School of Architecture and Planning at Columbia University, New York. Within a short period, both offices grew to include 30 architects in each location. In 1980 the office of Mitchell/Giurgola & Thorp Architects was established in Canberra to carry out the design of the new Parliament House.

Figure 2. Plan of Parliament House, Australia. Courtesy of Mitchell/Giurgola Architects.

FORMATIVE PROJECTS

Since the mid-1970s, Mitchell/Giurgola has been commissioned to design complex center-city mixed-use development projects, enlarging the scale of its project involvement from single buildings to complexes of several blocks. Significant projects have been completed in Washington, D.C., Boston, Harrisburg, Pennsylvania, and Los Angeles.

Of special concern for the firm is the design of places for education, laboratories, medical services, and manufacturing. Buildings for educational purposes have been designed for more than 24 campuses nationwide. Given the commitment to satisfy complex building programs with orderly and rigorous building design, the firm has been able to exercise its particular skills in state-of-the-art laboratory buildings completed at Columbia University and MIT for biology, chemistry, and the health sciences. A portion of the MIT building includes a health clinic to serve a population of 35,000–40,000 people. Another major outpatient care clinic has been designed for the University of California at Los Angeles. At Rensselaer Polytechnic Institute, Troy, New York, a 200,000-ft^2 industrial innovation laboratory building for robotics, microelectronics, and computer graphics has added greatly to the sophistication of that institution's facilities.

A considerable amount of study has been dedicated to the design of workplaces, which are represented by structures such as the Volvo automobile plant in Chesapeake, Virginia, and the Knoll manufacturing complex in East Greenville, Pennsylvania, and by the designs for a new assembly building for the Volvo corporation in Udevella, Sweden, and the master plan for the Torslanda plant in Gothenburg.

In June 1980 the Australian Parliament House Construction Authority announced that the joint entry of Mitchell/Giurgola Architects of New York and Richard Thorp, an Australian architect, had won first prize in the international competition for the design of the new Australian Parliament House. The parliament building complex, located in Canberra, will be a structure of approximately 2.5 million ft^2, with a construction budget of approximately $750 million. Construction began in January 1981 and was completed in 1988. The general character of its architecture is an intimate relationship with the plan of the city, the configuration of the land, and the natural setting.

COLLABORATORS

In 1984 Mitchell was obliged to withdraw from the firm because of ill health, leaving behind him a strong legacy of management for design excellence, multidisciplinary teamwork, and a highly professional approach to design. Mitchell concluded more than 10 years of active involvement in the AIA as its President in 1979–1980. During his term in office, the issues that concerned him most in the practice became his platform for the Institute.

Giurgola, in addition to his role in the firm of providing design leadership, is Ware Professor of Architecture at Columbia University and has a distinguished career in the academic world, having taught and lectured in several universities in the United States and abroad. He has written many articles in professional and academic journals. He is an advisor to the Volvo Advisory Board on Architecture and is a member of the Board of the American Academy in Rome.

The firm has evolved into two distinct partnerships, with Giurgola as a principal in both the Philadelphia and New York entities. The two partnerships, within the spirit of teamwork, carry forward and continue to develop the design tradition that has given form to all of the buildings designed by the firm over its 30-year history.

In both offices each of the principals has worked closely with Giurgola for a minimum of 10 years, and the close collaboration of the partners and staff brings to all projects a dedication to architecture that, in Giurgola's words, "depends not on a preconceived aesthetic synthesis, but on the perfect measure of the intentions, programs, technologies, and spaces which participate in a celebration of life."

Mitchell/Giurgola has received the firm award from the AIA, and Giurgola received the AIA's 1982 Gold Medal.

BIBLIOGRAPHY

General References

R. Giurgola and E. B. Mitchell, with foreword by K. Frampton, *Mitchell/Giurgola Architects,* Rizzoli, New York, 1983.

K. Ito, "Giurgola," *Space Design,* 21 (Aug. 1986).

PAUL BROCHES
Mitchell/Giurgola Architects
New York, New York

MIXED-USE BUILDINGS

There are two different, but closely related, meanings of the term mixed-use. The first pertains to a specific building or interconnected group of buildings containing at least three different types of activities, such as housing, offices, theaters, and restaurants. The second is much broader in scope, describing the diversity of facilities needed as anchors in a specific district of a city. Both are aimed at obtaining the same result: a more efficient use of urban space and, more importantly, the creation of a lively urban setting offering a richness of experiences, sights, and sounds to its human occupants.

A constant goal of mixed-use developments or districts is to draw people round-the-clock. As Eberhard H. Ziedler (of Ziedler Roberts Partnership/Architects in Toronto, Ontario, Canada) writes (1):

> Single-use structures and their districts are occupied for only part of each day or week and must stand empty and unused for the rest of the time. Multi-use structures, however, bring people together at different times.

Examples of districts that are at times virtual ghost towns are not difficult to find; most major cities in the United States have such areas. Mixed-use developments, however, can help turn around these under-used districts. As Gurney Breckenfeld recounted in *Fortune* (2):

> Downtown Houston loses both its crowds and its vitality after office hours. Streets become desolate canyons. Restaurants close early and even the two remaining movie houses may well shut their doors within a year. Yet a few miles to the west, along the freeway circling the inner core of the metropolis, The Galleria bustles with exhilarating activity from breakfast time until nearly midnight. . . . More than just a shopping center, The Galleria [designed by Hellmuth, Obata & Kassabaum] is a distinguished example of what its developer, Gerald D. Hines, calls "a whole new urban form that the American public doesn't know exists." The essence of that form and the source of its popular appeal is an intricate and compact orchestration of mixed land uses: shopping, offices, food, lodging, and entertainment.

Noted planner Edmund Bacon put it this way (3):

> Why undertake such projects? Because they intensify that richness of living, enhance people's range of experience and create easy access to a nearly inexhaustible variety of activities. Mixed-use developments are designed at a human scale and represent a positive attempt by the development community to achieve the public objective of keeping central cities alive and making cities a viable organism.

While mixed-use buildings may in themselves spur an influx of people at different times of the day and night, for long-term success these developments must also be linked closely to their specific districts. The following are examples of questions that first need to be asked. Is there a physical and aesthetic connection to the surrounding area? Are pedestrian and vehicular movements improved? Is a better use of urban space provided? Is there a framework supporting the different uses to their common benefit? Overall, it must be asked whether or not the mixed-use development responds to the emotional and political, as well as the physical, character of its surroundings.

One of the most difficult urban ills to correct is an entire district that has lost its diversity, one that has become an homogenized environment. The eminent author and urban critic Jane Jacobs put it this way (4): "The first question—and I think by far the most important question—about planning cities is this: How can cities generate enough mixture among uses—enough diversity—throughout enough of their territories, to sustain their own civilizations?" She uses New York City's Wall Street section in Lower Manhattan as an early 1960s example of an urban district in dire need of diversity, a "district suffering from extreme time unbalance among its users." At that time the Wall Street district employed some 400,000 workers, according to Jacobs, "an immense number of users for a territory sufficiently compact so that any part of it is readily accessible on foot from almost any other part." Where the district failed was in providing enough services and amenities for those workers and sufficient after-hour activities. "To see what is wrong," Jacobs suggested, "it is only necessary to drop in at any ordinary shop and observe the contrast between the mob scene at lunch and the dullness at other times. It is only necessary to observe the deathlike stillness that settles on the district after five-thirty and all day Saturday and Sunday" (4).

HISTORY OF MIXED-USE

The inclusion of mixed uses in a building, a group of buildings, or a city district is not a modern-day invention, but is a tradition steeped in history, as Zeidler suggests (5):

> "Before the industrial revolution, describing buildings as multi-use would have seemed irrelevant. Such buildings existed as a matter of course and were integrated into the fabric of European towns and cities. They have been built and used by man for centuries." He gives as an example the Greek agora, the secular center of the Greek city, an orderly arrangement of market stalls that was also the place for social and political gatherings. The Roman Baths, too, served several purposes: they were places of exercise, entertainment, and public discussions. It was not uncommon for the Baths to have libraries, theaters, and lecture and dining halls on the premises.

In medieval times, the activities of one's residential and work life most often took place in one's house, within the walls of the medieval town. When the populace grew larger than could be accommodated, the more successful inhabitants often moved outside the walls and built larger homes. While in Renaissance and baroque cities housing was still found over street-level shops, sharing a building was often the only thing in common between residential and commercial occupants.

Examples of early 1800s mixed-use structures were the Parisian and Viennese walk-ups. On the ground level were shops, restaurants, cafes, and theaters; above were four or five floors of apartments. Some buildings had continuous arcades at the ground level to provide protection from the elements. Most intriguing, as relates to the history of mixed-use structures, were the enclosed passages or gallerias, as described by Zeidler (6):

> A horizontal collection of these apartment blocks formed one long, continuous, double-sided pedestrian mall covered by a glass roof but open at each end to the street. Passages can be knit into the city fabric, incorporating existing buildings into their overall structures. Such structures were extremely lucrative largely because of the matrix of uses they contained: shops, light industrial establishments, nightclubs, restaurants, cafes, and even museums.

With the advent of the Industrial Revolution came great change. Factories were built in the heart of cities attracting workers from what were once remote villages. The resultant growth was unorderly and discordant. As Benevelo describes (7):

> Residential quarters naturally tended to be built near the place of work, so that houses and factories were often in close contact, intermingled at random and mutually inconvenient. Factory smoke permeated the houses and factory waste polluted the water, while industrial movement was generally hopelessly impeded by private traffic. The chaos was constantly

aggravated by the dynamic nature of the factories involved. Factories were transformed and expanded, houses were demolished and rebuilt, the outskirts of cities crept further into the countryside without ever finding a definite balance.

In the late eighteenth and early nineteenth centuries, in reaction to the social and environmental problems caused by industrialization, town planners and social critics known as Utopians envisioned ideal communities, built in accordance with strict land-use rules. This new planning philosophy, which included a turning away from both mixed-use buildings and diversified city districts, would ultimately have great influence on modern town planning.

Utopian communities were conceived of as isolated entities set in a benign and receptive landscape, far away from the industrial city. These communities were to be restricted to a specific physical size and number of inhabitants, since experience had shown that industrial cities suffered immensely from uncontrolled development and sharp increases in population. The Utopian strict segregation of uses can be seen in Charles Fourier's Phalanstery building that combined several activities to be laid out as follows (8):

One of the wings ought to combine all noisy workshops such as the carpenter's shop, the forge, and all hammer work. It ought also to contain all the industrial gatherings of children who are generally very noisy in industry. The other wing ought to contain the caravansary with its ballrooms and its halls appropriate to intercourse with outsiders so that these may not encumber the central portion of the palace and embarrass the domestic relations.

A much debated Utopian plan in the United States was the Garden City project by Ebenezer Howard, published in 1898. In that project Howard called for a carefully and precisely laid out community. At the center and radiating outward would be commercial and cultural activities. At the outer edges would be agricultural lands. Different functions of the city, such as schools, industries, and homes, would be in separate districts.

This strict segregation of uses was adopted by the Congres International d'Architecture Moderne (CIAM) in 1933 (five years after CIAM's founding) as a guideline to correct the urban problems of the industrial city. Through its Athens Charter, the influential CIAM called for the "aeration of the city." In 95 clauses, the charter dissected the problems of the modern city and proposed remedies. Four urban functions were identified: habitation, work, recreation, and circulation (9):

The four key functions of urbanism have called for special measures offering each function the conditions most favourable to the development of its own activity so that they may . . . bring order and classification to the usual conditions of life, work, and culture. . . . Each key function will have its own autonomy . . . each will be regarded as an entity to which land and buildings will be allocated, and all of the prodigious resources of modern techniques will be used in arranging and equipping them.

While there are notable exceptions to these rules, the CIAM town planning philosophy would remain influential until the end of the 1950s.

One of the well-known modern Utopian plans is Le Corbusier's La Ville Radieuse, a community that segregated work and living places, where the residences would be surrounded by trees and gardens far away from the grimness of industry. Although it was never realized, Le Corbusier's plan became a model of modern ideology, but to later generations it would be seen as a failed vision. "His segregation of function destroyed the symbiotic life that existed in the old city," Zeidler says. "The isolated office city created an environment of uniform consistency that lacked the variety necessary to a vibrant city. The other half of such a streamlined existence, the residential city, also failed. Both forced the totality of city life into a schizophrenic, unhealthy existence" (10).

By the 1950s, it became clear that the Athens Charter had failed to correct many of the wrongs cited in it. In fact, new problems emerged: urban congestion and a breakdown in social communications, urban decay, and abandonment. At a CIAM meeting in 1958, architect Aldo Van Eyck offered this explanation of the demise of the charter (11):

What is really wrong stems from the other enemy—the enemy of a system of analysis of 'city'—a creation of four keys, keys that don't fit the lock. We know because the lock never opened, the system never opened the lock to the human heart. This was a system, a system that may have been important at one time in order to canalize—canalize all the objections and the terrible results of chaotic cities in the 19th century. But it made an absolute. It made an absolute out of traffic and an absolute out of housing and an absolute out of reaction. But it understood nothing of what those things were really about.

Van Eyck and other architects and planners turned away from the Athens Charter to re-examine existing cities and the complex network of social relationships within them. Of particular note were studies that resulted in systems of linked buildings that were to correspond closely with the actual network of social relationships, concepts that ran counter to CIAM's doctrine of finite spaces and self-contained buildings. In the new studies, buildings were not seen as finite, fixed in program and function, but rather as generous adaptable frameworks for a variety of conditions and uses.

Perhaps the most significant predecessor to the mixed-use development, according to Zeidler, was the Berlin Free University, designed by Candilis, Josic & Woods. Here the architect's goal was "not to build flexible buildings but to establish an environment in which buildings appropriate to their function may occur, and to encourage an interaction between these buildings and their function." This project, Zeidler says, "restored the pedestrian street to its former importance and created buildings which could support a variety of uses commensurate with social needs and physical demands." While still part of the modern school, Zeidler adds, the Berlin Free University "did create a flexible building that could accept different and changing uses" (12).

MIXED-USE PROJECTS

In the United States, Rockefeller Center in New York City (architects: Reinhard & Hofmeister; Corbett, Harrison & Macmurray; and Raymond Hood, Goodley & Fouilhoux), begun in the 1930s and added to through the 1970s, was considered revolutionary in an urban design sense (Fig. 1). Here was a project that would cover 24 acres, have 21 buildings, a theater, a music hall, a sunken outdoor plaza, roof terraces, and a shopping concourse below street level. "The Rockefeller Center represented a spirited attack on the planning ideals of the Athens Charter," Zeidler says. "Like the enclosed passages and gallerias, it suggested possibilities for existing cities in large-scale multiuse projects. It demonstrated the interconnectedness of city life, the mutual dependence of different uses, and the improved urban fabric that can be achieved by recognizing this interdependence" (12).

Evolutionary changes in real estate development led to the advent of mixed-use projects in the 1960s. First came the shift to closed, climate-controlled malls starting around the mid-1950s. The buildings grew in size and freestanding fast-food outlets, office and medical buildings, and movie houses were soon constructed on parking lots on or around the periphery of shopping centers. Most often these structures were not interconnected.

In the late 1960s and early 1970s, mixed-use developments began making their way into many major urban centers. Often these projects were seen as a means to reverse urban distress. In Detroit, Mich., for example, the Renaissance Center was built at the river's edge, as a building to house many activities, such as shopping, work, entertainment, and lodging (Fig. 2). Henry Ford II, the moving force behind the project, chose John Portman as architect; Portman had demonstrated his capability in designing mixed-use projects with the Embarcadero Center in San Francisco, Calif., and Peachtree Center in Atlanta, Ga. Thereafter, 51 metropolitan area corporations formed the Renaissance Center Partnership, which was responsible for an equity investment of $137 million.

Figure 1. Rockefeller Center, New York. Courtesy of *Architecture* Magazine.

Figure 2. Renaissance Center, Detroit, Mich. Courtesy of *Architecture* Magazine.

The centerpiece of Renaissance Center is a cylinder housing a 1400-room, 73-story hotel, the tallest in the world (Fig. 3). Sheathed in a taut skin of glass and flanked by four 39-story office towers containing 2.2 million ft^2 of space, the hotel stands at the center of the 50-acre site on a four-level, 14-acre podium. The podium serves as a base for over 350,000 ft^2 of retail space and 1300 cars.

A persistent criticism of the Renaissance Center, and other similar mixed-use projects, is the physical isolation from the city at ground level. The major hindrance at RenCen is its concrete berm that appears unreasonably formidable and also forecloses any future visual link to the central business district. Perhaps more damaging is the lack of positive urban design links with the central business district; there are no connecting vistas, no discernible architectural relationships, and no integration of street patterns.

An older, and perhaps more influential, development by John Portman is Atlanta's Peachtree Center. Developed over a 15-year period beginning in the early 1960s, Peach-

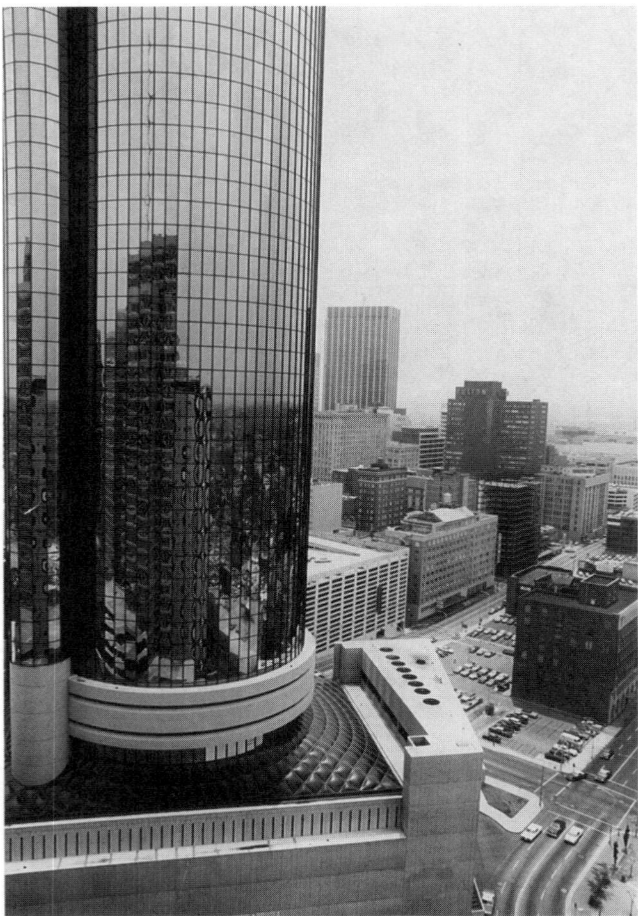

Figure 3. Renaissance Center, Detroit, Mich. Courtesy of *Architecture* Magazine.

tree Center grew as freestanding buildings spread along 2½ continuous blocks on what was then the northern edge of Atlanta's downtown. On Peachtree Street there are five office towers, two convention hotels (the Regency Hotel and the Peachtree Plaza), a merchandise mart, a building containing shops and a dinner theater, a bus station/parking garage, and an apparel mart (Figs. 4,5).

A third Portman mixed-use complex is San Francisco's Embarcadero Center, completed in 1982. The project was nicknamed the Rockefeller Center of the West, partly because David Rockefeller was one of its sponsors, and partly because it was the largest single chunk of downtown development in any U.S. city since the Rockefeller Center of the East: 8.5 acres, $375 million price tag, accommodating 18,000 people, 2.75 million ft^2 of office space, 325,000 ft^2 of retail, and underground parking for 2300 cars, all in four office buildings and one hotel. Each of the four towers is built on a three-story pedestrian gallery of shops and restaurants, and all are linked by bridges across intervening streets. Thus, Embarcadero Center houses a layered podium where people are able to walk for five blocks without encountering a vehicle.

The hotel is attached at the level of its lobby floor to the top level of the podium. The atrium lobby, one of Portman and Hyatt's most dramatic, functions as a kind of enclosed ancillary plaza to the center, and the podium functions as an extension of the hotel's public areas and facilities.

In the 1980s, the concept of mixed-use was adopted by federal, state, and even local governments. It no longer is surprising to find thriving commercial enterprises within a government complex, which was unheard of in prior times. In addition, a mixed-use development is still viewed as a viable choice in downtown development, especially where large plots of land are available.

The opening in 1983 of the renovated Old Post Office Building in Washington, D.C. heralded a new era in the use of government property. The building has 120,000 ft^2 of office space for government agencies, 60,000 ft^2 of retail space on the lower two levels, and a 10,000 ft^2 vertical national park—the building's tower. The Post Office is also connected to one of the city's metrorail stations. The Pavilion, the retail area, sits at the bottom of a 215-ft-high skylit atrium and has shops, restaurants, an "outdoor" eating area, and a stage for live entertainment set against the tower's base.

Transforming this 1899 Romanesque building, with its turrets, tower, and triumphant archways, into a mixed-use building has enlivened a part of downtown Washington very much in need of retail development (Fig. 6). It also has brought government workers out of the doldrums of a drab, isolated government office building. At the Old Post Office, the offices surround the atrium (Fig. 7). What had once been closed corridors around that atrium space now open into it through cutouts in the walls. The $10 million construction cost of the commercial Pavilion was financed privately; it was developed by the Evans Development Group of Baltimore, Md., and designed by Benjamin Thompson Associates, Cambridge, Mass. The Old Post Office renovation was designed by the Washington, D.C., architectural firm of Arthur Cotton Moore & Associates, and the Norfolk, Va., engineering firm of McGaughy, Marshall & McMillan.

Another dazzling example of a government mixed-use development is the State of Illinois Center in Chicago. Located in Chicago's North Loop area, the center houses 3000 state employees and 150,000 ft^2 of commercial space. As in the renovated Old Post Office building, the state offices surround an atrium, in this case a 17-story, 160-ft-diameter atrium. Shops, restaurants, and an auditorium are located on the first, second, and basement levels. The center is also connected to the city's elevated and subway trains.

Designed by Helmut Jahn of the Chicago architectural firm of Murphy/Jahn, and completed in 1985, the State of Illinois Center is a lively, colorful civic gathering spot. A slice is cut out of the circular atrium, where the glazed wall provides an abundance of natural light. In the atrium, exposed elevator shafts soar to the skylight. An escalator at the front entrance leads to the concourse below, and a cutout in the center of the atrium's floor allows natural light to enter the concourse. There is a steady flow of people: tourists visiting what is fast becoming the city's biggest attraction, Chicagoans there for state business or simply to cut through the building on a cold winter's day,

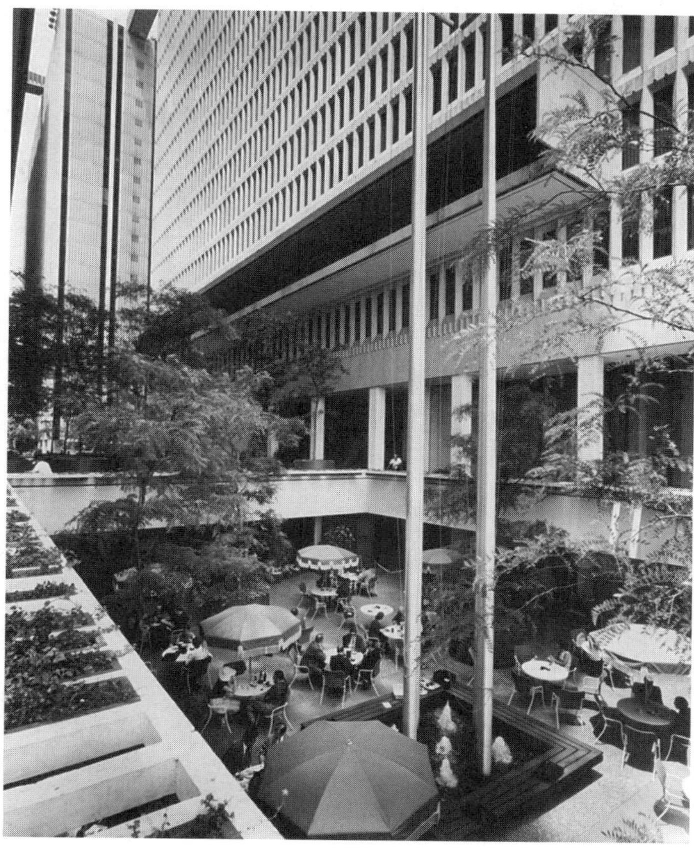

Figure 4. Peachtree Center, Atlanta, Ga. Courtesy of *Architecture* Magazine.

Figure 5. Peachtree Center, Atlanta, Ga. Courtesy of *Architecture* Magazine.

Figure 6. Renovation, Old Post Office, Washington, D.C. Courtesy of *Architecture* Magazine.

and others who browse in the shops or eat in the restaurants. The center has already established itself as a prominent focal point in the city's North Loop.

Mixed-use projects can now be found in virtually every city in the United States. In all likelihood their popularity will only increase. The following are a few examples of successful mixed-use projects:

- Allegheny Center is an office–retail–residential complex just north of downtown Pittsburgh, Pa. When

Figure 7. Old Post Office, Washington, D.C. Courtesy of *Architecture* Magazine.

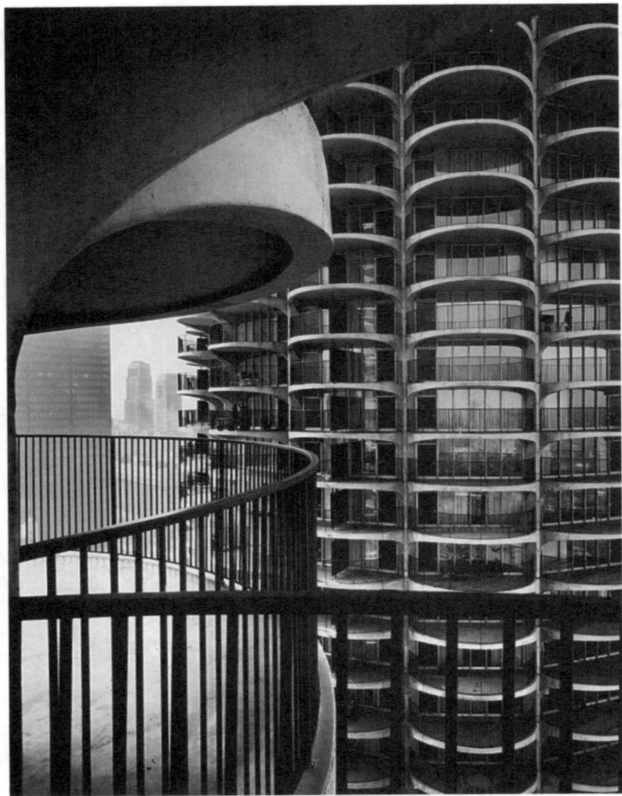

Figure 8. Marina City, Chicago, Ill. Courtesy of *Architecture* Magazine

opened, this complex consisted of two high-rise buildings, a multilevel enclosed retail mall, 50 townhouses, and 500 apartment units (Master plan; Mitchell & Ritchey).

- Butler Square is a 500,000 ft^2, turn-of-the-century warehouse in Minneapolis, Minn., that has been converted into office space, commercial facilities, and a hotel (Miller, Hanson, Westerbeck & Bell, architects). Offices and shops are arranged around a central atrium topped by a skylight.
- Charles Center is a major contributor to the rebirth of downtown Baltimore, Md. Conceived in 1957, the Center opened in the mid-1970s with 400 residential units, 1.7 million ft^2 of office space, 335,000 ft^2 of retail space, 650 hotel rooms, underground parking for 3900 cars, an 1800-seat theater, a 600-seat movie theater, and three public plazas (RTKL architects).
- The IDS Center in Minneapolis, Minn., is best known as one of the first examples of an atrium used as the building's central core. Designed by Philip Johnson and John Burgee, the complex consists of the IDS Tower, the Annex Building, the Marquette Inn and Bank Building, and the Woolworth Building. The buildings are linked by the Crystal Court, which contains shops, restaurants, service facilities, and exhibit areas.
- Marina City, in Chicago, Ill., is a mixed-use facility with a distinctive design (by Bertrand Goldberg & Associates). The complex consists of two circular towers rising from a 2-story base set on the edge of the Chicago River. Completed in 1963, the complex sits on a 3.2-acre site (Figs. 8,9).

Perhaps the most elaborate mixed-use development of the late 1980s is New York City's Battery Park City, a $1.5 billion project designed by Cesar Pelli for a 14-acre site in Manhattan's lower west side. The project, a combined effort of state and city management fueled by private investment, began in 1979 when it was saved from financial failure by the New York Urban Development Corporation. Before inviting developers' bids, a master plan was drafted that defined, among other things, exact street patterns, the general location and massing of buildings, waterfront treatment, connections and circulation, and physical and visual relationships to the surrounding neighborhood; superior design standards were set. Battery Park City includes 6 million ft^2 of commercial space, 100,000 ft^2 of retail, 150,000 ft^2 of recreation and exhibit space, and 3.5 acres of public parks and plazas.

In the case of Battery Park City, it is difficult to imagine that much land being assembled at many, if any, other locations in New York City or other downtown areas. However, the large mixed-use project may be the only feasible design method for reviving a dying area, as compared with the fragmented, one-function development.

Figure 9. Marina City, Chicago, Ill. Courtesy of *Architecture* Magazine.

MIXED-USE CHARACTERISTICS

Throughout their history, mixed-use type buildings have been built on large urban plots, and have been viewed as a means to correct urban blight and decay, as described below by the Urban Land Institute (ULI), headquartered in Washington, D.C. (13):

- By introducing residential, transient, and/or recreational activities to areas that were "dead" during nonworking hours (such as the Embarcadero Center in San Francisco, Calif., and the Watergate (Fig. 10) in Washington, D.C. designed by Italian architect Luigi Moretti).
- By maintaining and improving their own environment over time (i.e., the continuing "internal regeneration" long recognized at Rockefeller Center and now beginning to appear in mixed-use projects).
- By blending with established residential neighborhoods (e.g., Colony Square in Atlanta, Ga., designed by Jova/Daniels/Busby) where other types of high-density developments were unacceptable.
- By having a far greater catalytic effect on community development than single-purpose projects (e.g., RTKL's Charles Center in Baltimore, Md., that has triggered an extensive revitalization throughout the city's center).
- By providing a means for organizing metropolitan growth (e.g., The Galleria that serves as a focal point for a large urban center, conveniently located in suburban Houston, Tex. and known as Post Oak).

Figure 10. Watergate, Washington, D.C. Courtesy of *Architecture* Magazine.

Overall, the Urban Land Institute in *Mixed-Use Developments: New Ways of Land Use,* suggests that mixed-use projects must have these criteria: (*1*) three or more significant revenue-producing entities (retail, office, hotel, recreational, residential); (*2*) a plan that is integrated both functionally and physically with interconnecting pedestrian pathways, to which all development must conform (14). Scale and density of projects can vary tremendously, but usually are 500,000 to 30 million ft^2; are on five to 50 acres; and range from three to 10 floor-area-ratio (FAR). Other than providing a variety of reasons for people to visit a development during the day, the mix of uses should also draw people after 5:00 P.M. and during weekends. This can be accomplished by offering a variety of restaurants, movie theaters, a waterfront esplanade (where possible), museums, and recreational facilities.

Mixed-use projects usually take one of three physical configurations: megastructures, individual structures on a common platform, or freestanding structures with pedestrian connections. A megastructure is a monolithic building, usually of such considerable mass that it covers an entire city block or more. A mixed-use megastructure can take many forms: a high-rise tower with a layering of uses, such as in the John Hancock Center, Chicago, Ill.; a base structure that can begin below grade and that supports one or more high-rise towers, such as Water Tower, Ill. (Loebl, Schlossman, Bennett & Dart and C. F. Murphy, architects) and the Atlanta Center, Atlanta, Ga. (Wong & Tung and Mastin architects); and a "marble cake" mixing of uses, as in Kalamazoo Center, Kalamazoo, Mich. (Elbasani, Logan & Severin, architects). In the second type of configuration, individual buildings usually sit on a platform of two or more levels. Examples are the Houston Center and the Illinois Center.

In general, mixed-use developments pose unique planning problems, as suggested by ULI (15):

- How to accomplish superior site utilization—including incorporation of natural features and physical and functional relationships with surrounding environments.
- How to provide for an efficiently-functioning infrastructure (including parking, utilities, and effective mechanical and electrical systems) capable of servicing the differing demands of each project component.
- How to position revenue-producing uses so as to provide appropriate emphasis for each, as well as market synergy among all components.
- How to provide for easy pedestrian access among project components and to relevant adjacent areas, through positioning of components and through horizontal and vertical movement systems.
- How to offer outstanding amenities and attractions that cannot be obtained in single-purpose projects (eg, exciting "people places" capitalizing on the diversity of activities present in a mixed-use project.
- How to "mass" individual building components in the project "community" so as to create a harmonious, distinctive "sculpture" in total.

Certain design issues characterize mixed-use developments, and all are crucial to the success of a project. The first issue is the development's design relationship with the surrounding neighborhood. Over the years, solutions have ranged from a totally inward orientation to a more harmonious mix with the surrounding built environment, with the mix having the greatest long-term effects. The infrastructure needs to be carefully planned to accommodate all uses and needs; the positioning of project components can be crucial to a project's success (such as the retail stores being conveniently located to parking and street access); convenient circulation must be provided, with portions of the project closed while others remain open, perhaps around the clock.

Since the ultimate purpose of a mixed-use project is to maintain an active influx of people over a long period of time, orienting a mixed-use project for those people is of the utmost importance. As John Portman said in connection with Peachtree Center (16):

> Architecture in the traditional sense of an abstract art primarily for the benefit of the artist is no longer a viable concept. Today, architecture must reorient itself to people. It must appeal to their eternal needs to be close to nature, and to have order, variety, and spaciousness. It must eliminate, where possible, the necessity for using individual transportation modes to obtain common, everyday services. It must relate to the human scale. Most of all, it should lift the human spirit. At the same time, it must be economically feasible and be consistent with good planning.

Large atrium spaces providing natural light, room for plants, flowers, and fountains, and offering benches and/or tables are popular in mixed-use projects. These centrally located, multistoried spaces may also serve as the focal point for all interior circulation; stairs and/or escalators may connect the various levels, as well as elevators, located in or near the atrium space.

The individual success of mixed-use projects has been difficult to measure, but overall positive results have been noted. The addition of such a project in a city or suburban neighborhood almost always increases that area's vitality, usually by filling in some missing function, or functions—a hotel, theater, and/or eatery. Substantial, but less obvious, are the municipal revenues created by such a project through property taxes as well as sales taxes and other business revenues. Mixed-use developments may also act as a downtown catalyst and focal point, triggering subsequent renovation of decaying neighborhoods.

Mixed-use developments have brought diversity to urban and suburban locations. This is evidenced by the fact that such projects have consistently precipitated changes in zoning laws to allow for a more mixed environment. Says Zeidler (17):

> Modern architectural philosophy eventually influenced the bylaws and rules of most cities to such a degree that it became difficult, by law, to build a multi-use building. . . . The isolated building prototypes developed by modern architecture, such as the apartment tower, the office tower, the shopping center or the one-family house, may fulfill their internal demands;

however, thoughtlessly pushed together, they cannot create a coherent city.

Zeidler sees mixed-use projects as urban building blocks, since they contain within themselves the ability to integrate, adjust, and change within the urban fabric. In that role, mixed-use projects should adhere to 10 principles, Zeidler adds. They should (17):

- Conserve urban space—"The natural environment must be brought into balance with the needs of the built form. . . . The building could prevent the waste of urban space, such as open parking lots, unused roof areas of low structures, etc."
- Relate to and create urban activity—"The ambience of a city is determined by the urban activities that it provides and how they relate to its public spaces . . . . It is important to encourage the multi-use building not only to place its uses that relate to public activities in such a way as to maximize their accessibility and visibility, but also to encourage the introduction of such activities that help to maintain the life of the city."
- Be a link within the urban space—"Urban buildings are not sculptures within themselves, except in isolated cases, but part of a greater whole. The majority of multi-use buildings must accept their role as visual and functional links within the urban form."
- Foster social dispersion—"A by-product of growth seems to be the expulsion of unfamiliar elements. The ultimate result of this process is the ghettoization of the city and its inherent problems. . . . The multi-use building can help to maintain such a necessary fine-grained social pattern."
- Relate to the historic and cultural situation of the place—"Cities are for our life today and should not be a museum; but by totally erasing the past we may also destroy our future. The multi-use building must accept its part as a building block in such cultural continuum. It must accept the existing urban situation and at times this may even require it to fit within the shell of a historic building, or the continuation of a historic facade."
- Respect the needs of each individual function—"Any function will require a certain space to live within; however, function does not need to be taken as the only generator for the architectural expression of its form. To a degree, functions can adjust to many forms, however there are cases where a particular form can give optimum physical, psychological, or economic fulfillment to a particular function."
- Interrelate the various functions—"A restaurant close to living units is advantageous for a residential area; but the restaurant also needs working places close-by to have a noon trade. This simplistic example indicates the complexity of functional interrelation. Such joining of functions—commercial activities related to residential units, living related to work areas, etc—within close proximity, creates an urban synergetic action that multi-use buildings can achieve."
- Optimize technology—"The multi-use building must freely respond to modern technology; not as a formal expression but as a practical necessity."
- Achieve economy—"True economy is achieved if all four levels are being interrelated: capital, operating, maintenance, and adaptation costs. . . . The multi-use buildings can bring about a new level of economy in the total life cycle costs, not only within the building but also within the urban fabric."
- Respond to the human psyche—"The urban spaces created by individual buildings and their facades, as well as the interior spaces of these buildings react on the human psyche. . . . We must find expression in our buildings for a response to it, individually and as part of the urban space. The multi-use building, because it is part of architecture, must finally transcend the level of reaction and respond to the search of meaning in our life."

Overall, diversity in a single building project and within a city's neighborhoods is essential to a city's prosperity. "The physical proximity of different functions is of aid to each individual function involved," Zeidler states. "Bring people together for a night at the theater and nearby restaurants get more business. . . . Remove all residences from an office district and at five o'clock that area becomes deserted and finally dangerous. It dies without the life-giving support of other city functions" (10).

MIXED-USE URBAN DISTRICTS

Perhaps the most widely recognized proponent of diversity in the urban environment is Jane Jacobs, whose ideas, particularly as expressed in *The Death and Life of Great American Cities,* apply as much to mixed-use developments as the mixed-use urban districts:

> The district, and indeed as many of its internal parts as possible, must serve more than one primary function: preferably more than two. These must insure the presence of people who go outdoors on different schedules and are in the place for different purposes, but who are able to use facilities in common.

Primary functions were named anchors by Jacobs, specific places that predictably attract people on a regular basis, such as offices, residences, theaters, schools, and recreational facilities. "Any primary use whatever, by itself, is relatively ineffectual as a creator of city diversity," Jacobs says. "If it is combined with another primary use that brings people in and out and puts them on the street at the same time, nothing has been accomplished. In practical terms, we cannot even call these differing primary uses. However, when a primary use is combined, effectively, with another that puts people on the street at different times, then the effect can be economically stimulating: a fertile environment for secondary diversity" (19). Jacobs defines secondary diversity as enterprises that grow in response to the presence of primary uses. Secondary uses can become primary use if, say, a district of some unique type of shop develops that in itself draws significant numbers of people to those stores.

Whether or not a primary use mixture can be effective is easily tested. Do the people in the district use the same streets at different times of the day and night? If so, are these people also using some of the same facilities? An insufficient primary mixture, Jacobs suggests, is typically (20):

> [T]he principal fault in our downtowns, and often the only disastrous basic fault. Most big-city downtowns fulfill—or in the past did fulfill—all four of the necessary conditions for generating diversity. That is why they were able to become downtowns. Today, they have become too predominantly devoted to work and contain too few people after working hours. . . . In city districts that are predominantly or heavily residential, the more complexity and variety of primary uses that can be cultivated, the better, just as in downtowns. But the chief chessman that is needed in these districts is the primary use of work.

The major criticism of mixed-use (be it in a single district or a single building) concerns aesthetics. " 'Mixed uses look ugly. They cause traffic congestion. They invite ruinous uses.' These are some of the bugbears that cause cities to combat diversity," Jacobs writes. "These beliefs help shape city zoning regulations. They have helped rationalize city rebuilding into the sterile, regimented, empty thing it is. They stand in the way of planning that could deliberately encourage spontaneous diversity by providing the conditions necessary to its growth. . . . Intricate minglings of different uses in cities are not a form of chaos. On the contrary, they represent a complex and highly developed form of order" (21).

Where aesthetics, or lack of aesthetics, is rampant, Jacobs maintains, is in districts that lack exuberant diversity, such as dull residential neighborhoods dotted with a few shabby shops or low-value land uses—junk yards, used-car lots—or garish, unrelenting commercial strips. "City diversity is not innately ugly," Jacobs concludes. "That is a misconception, and a most simple-minded one. But lack of city diversity is innately either depressing on the one hand, or vulgarly chaotic on the other" (22).

Where the mixed-use concept (as either a single project or a district) will ultimately be most valuable is in the role of reshaper of the community. As Zeidler says (23): "Our most enjoyable cities are those which quietly weave together a rich and complex pattern of different uses and activities. As with any pattern or fabric, these cities need continual care and renewing—the mending and restitching of parts that run down or require change." A knowledge and understanding of mixed-use projects can therefore only lead to better environments for all.

BIBLIOGRAPHY

1. E. H. Zeidler, *Multi-Use Architecture in the Urban Context,* Van Nostrand Reinhold Co., Inc., New York, 1983, p. 298.
2. G. Breckenfield, *Fortune* (Oct. 1972).
3. R. E. Witherspoon, J. P. Abbett, and R. M. Gladstone, *Mixed-Use Developments: New Ways of Land Use,* The Urban Land Institute, Washington, D.C., 1976, p. 3.
4. J. Jacobs, *The Death and Life of Great American Cities,* Random House, New York, 1961, pp. 154–155.
5. Ref. 1, p. 11.
6. Ref. 1, p. 12.
7. L. Benevolo, *The Origins of Modern Town Planning,* The MIT Press, Cambridge, Mass., 1967, p. 10.
8. Ref. 1, p. 13.
9. *Athens Charter,* Congres International d'Architecture Moderne, 1933, p. 7.
10. Ref. 1, p. 98.
11. Ref. 1, p. 17.
12. Ref. 1, p. 16.
13. Ref. 3, p. 5.
14. Ref. 3, p. 6.
15. Ref. 3, p. 7.
16. Ref. 3, p. 57.
17. Ref. 1, p. 97.
18. Ref. 4, p. 152.
19. Ref. 4, p. 162.
20. Ref. 4, p. 174.
21. Ref. 4, p. 222.
22. Ref. 4, p. 229.
23. Ref. 1, p. 9.

General References

A. O. Dean and A. Freeman, "The Rockefeller Center of the '80s: Battery Park City's Core," *Architecture* **75,** 36–43 (Dec. 1986).

D. Canty, "Evaluation: Rockefeller Center West?" *AIA J.* **71,** 56–63 (Oct. 1982).

C. Florance, "Mixed-Use Developments," *AIA J.* **66,** 28–31 (Sept. 1977).

C. Florance, "The MXD as a Tool for Testing Blight and a Design Challenge," *AIA J.* **66,** 32–33 (Sept. 1977).

A. Freeman, "An Introverted Trio of MXDs Dominates Atlanta's New Downtown," *AIA J.* **66,** 34–37 (Sept. 1977).

L. Geller, "Hotels in the Mixed-Use Development," *J. Real Estate Development* **27,** 59–66 (Aug. 1986).

N. R. Greer, "Look What Landed in the Loop: State of Illinois Center, Chicago," *Architecture* **74,** 40–45 (Nov. 1985).

"In Progress: The Charles Center Tower, Baltimore, Md.," *Progressive Architecture* **62,** 38–43 (May 1977).

P. Lemov, "Mixed Use," *Builder* **7,** 64–73 (Nov. 1984).

R. McNeilly, "Renaissance Center," *Building Design & Construction* **18,** 38–43 (May 1977).

G. Wright, "Mixed-Use Developments Gain Momentum," *Building Design & Construction* **22,** 70–75 (Aug. 1981).

See also PLANNED COMMUNITIES (NEW TOWNS); URBAN DESIGN—ARCHITECTURE AT URBAN SCALE; URBAN DESIGN—CREATION OF LIVABLE CITIES

NORA RICHTER GREER
Architecture
Washington, D.C.

MOISTURE PROTECTION. See ROOFING MATERIALS

MORGAN, JULIA

Julia Morgan's timeline of architectural contributions places her among the foremost members of her profession. Her prolificacy in building accounted for over 800 structures in a career that spanned almost half a century. This achievement is exemplary of an established retinue of "first" accomplishments that began with her early formal training as an architect. Born in San Francisco, California, Morgan's formative years were spent in nearby Oakland, California. Indicating an early interest in architecture, she became the first woman to enroll in the engineering program at the University of California at Berkeley. There was at that time no architectural school in the western part of the United States. While at Berkeley, she worked under the tutelage of Bernard Maybeck. Maybeck encouraged her to pursue her architectural studies at his own alma mater, the Ecole des Beaux Arts in Paris, France. Upon completing her studies at Berkeley and earning the distinction of being the first woman to graduate from its program, she moved to Paris to continue her professional training. Undaunted by the fact that the Ecole had never admitted a woman, she persevered, enduring two years of intensive entrance examinations, and ultimately in 1898, she became the first woman to gain acceptance. Here, she continued to excel, winning first-merit awards in student competitions. Four years later, in 1902, she received her formal degree certification.

Following a brief work period in France and New York, she returned to her California home and went to work for the firm of John Galen Howard for two years. During this time, she earned her state certification, thus becoming the first woman architect in the State of California licensed to practice architecture. In 1904 she opened her own office, which operated continuously until 1951.

Despite her forefront efforts and achievements, Morgan favored a lifestyle of anonymity. Characterized as one of quiet discipline and total commitment to her chosen profession, she followed a working regime of 14-hour days, 6 days a week. Negating her private life, she maintained a familial-type bond with her devoted staff of long standing. Her selflessness was also imparted to the stylistic vocabulary of her work.

In the early years of practice, the majority of her work was residential. Of the numerous houses she built, the design imprint reveals more of a personal statement of the client than the architect, thus reflecting a design altruism that serves to explain why her residential work is often described as eclectic. In ably "molding each project to the emotional and budgetary needs" of a similarly eclectic clientele, Morgan's residential structures run the gamut from the simplest of buildings to the perversely ornate (1). Whether shingle style, rustic ranch, California mission, or stylized classicism, her work was reputed for its meticulous craftsmanship and detail, in which she dexterously integrated her beaux-arts training and native understanding of U.S. western architectural tradition and materials.

Balancing her early residential work in Oakland, Berkeley, and San Francisco, other commissions included the Mills College Bell Tower (1903) and its library (1905). In the aftermath of the 1906 earthquake, she was commissioned to restore the Fairmont Hotel. The merits of her success here brought her widespread attention in the northern California area, and consequently, other significant commissions came to her, including a number of churches and hospitals.

Among her clientele, Phoebe Hearst provided a steady stream of commissioned work to Morgan's office, including several family residences, and recommended Morgan to her son, newspaper magnate William Randolph Hearst. Morgan's commission to do Hearst's San Simeon estate was to become the single most publicized of her works. In its setting, Hearst's "castle" rests upon a grand hilltop overlooking the Pacific ocean. The ornate Casa Grande, as it is named, exhibits a cathedral-like presence of mixed styles and an adorned abundance, interior and exterior, of Hearst's mammoth art collection (Fig. 1). The first buildings constructed at San Simeon, three guest cottages, are stylistically as florid and unrestrained as the main residence, having undergone numerous alterations over the estate's 20-year building period. Terraced gardens, highlighted by Morgan's design of a colonnaded Neptune pool with a classic temple facade (Fig. 2), grace the estate's immediate surroundings and serve as a backdrop for the

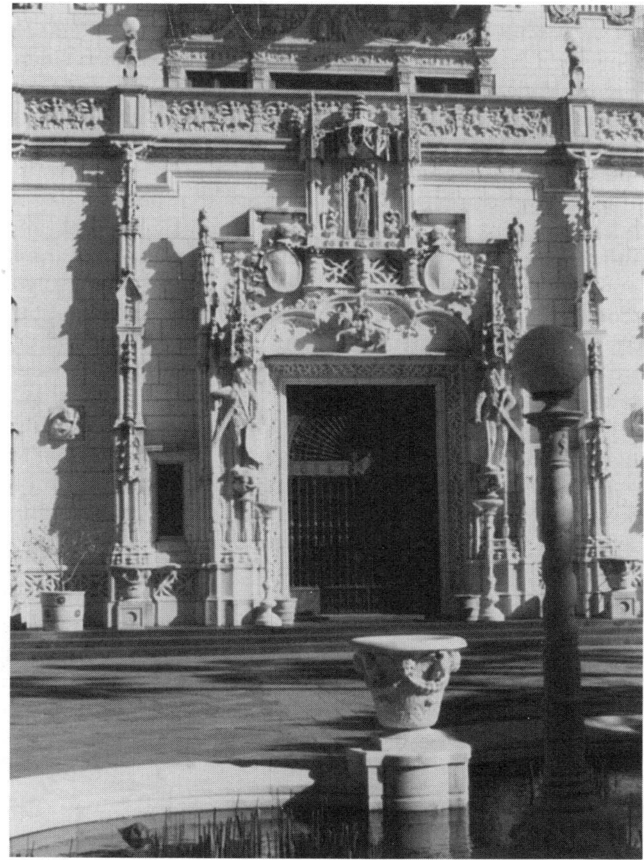

Figure 1. Front entrance detail of main residence, Casa Grande, Hearst Castle, San Simeon.

Figure 2. Neptune pool and temple facade, Hearst Castle, San Simeon.

natural landscape beyond. In stark contrast to the classical references at San Simeon, Morgan's design for Hearst's Wyntoon estate comprises a complex of cottages recalling the folk architecture of a Bavarian village, providing further example of her facility in attending disparate stylistic client preferences.

Morgan's active practice, aligned in time with the emergence of womens' organizations, correspondingly resulted in work for another principal client, the Young Women's Christian Association (YWCA). She built YWCA residential buildings and recreation centers on a number of California sites and outside the state, in Utah and Hawaii. Her YWCA Recreation Center at Asilomar, California, is today a state monument and national conference center. It is through studying these buildings that one can derive a clearer sense of Morgan's stylistic design intent and influences. As cited, her work balances the divergent influences of beaux-arts rationalism and naturalism drawn from her native landscape and reinforced by her mentor, Maybeck. Her exactitude and precision of quality and detail are a result of her engineering training and an enriched background in history and art. Morgan's institutional structures display a synthesized unity of all of these influences, which tend to modulate in balance according to their physical settings, where rural buildings accordingly weigh naturalism and urban structures bend to the beaux-arts model, although all bear the ultimate inscription of her own self-interpretation in their overall expression.

Upon the closing of her offices in 1951, she exercised her convictions on the propriety of maintaining anonymous architectural authorship. She destroyed all records of her previous work and resounded her belief that buildings should stand by themselves, remarking that "Architecture is a visual, not a verbal art" (1).

BIBLIOGRAPHY

1. S. H. Boutelle, "Julia Morgan," in *Macmillan Encyclopedia of Architects,* Vol. 3, The Free Press, New York, 1982, p. 238.

General References

Ref. 1 is a good general reference.

S. H. Boutelle, "Julia Morgan," in Susana Torre, ed., *Women in American Architecture: A Historic and Contemporary Perspective,* Whitney Library of Design, New York, 1977, pp. 79–89.

S. H. Boutelle, "Julia Morgan: A Synthesis of Tradition," *Architecture California,* 30 (Jan./Feb. 1985).

L. Olson, "A Tycoon's Home Was His Petite Architect's Castle," *Smithsonian* **16**(9), 60 (1985).

Karen J. Dominguez
Pennsylvania State University
State College, Pennsylvania

MORTAR. See Brick Masonry; Concrete Masonry

MOSQUES

Islam started in Arabia around the beginning of the seventh century. Mohammed, its prophet, introduced a monotheistic religion and his call attracted many followers. By the end of the eighth century, the Islamic empire had extended from Spain to India, and later from Anatolia to West Africa. At first, Islamic domination did not bring with it any modification to the architecture of the regions it occupied. Like any prospering civilization, however, it did create a variety of new demands that required architectural solutions. A place where the believers worshiped, a mosque, was the first building type to be introduced.

The diversity of conditions in the different Muslim regions led many researchers to question the existence of an Islamic architecture with common characteristics (1). Indeed, the Islamic empire was not a monolithic entity. It encompassed different people with different original cultures, economic systems, national heritages, physical geographies, and climatic conditions. Although there are some who would argue against the universality of Islamic architecture in general (2,3), there are few people who would disagree with the commonality of mosque architecture in particular. The mosque's function and role within the community has been amazingly consistent through time and space; it is a consistency not apparent in most other Islamic building types.

CONTEXT AND MEANING OF THE MOSQUE

As a religion, Islam is based on five pillars. These are the *Shehadat, Salat, Zakat, Siam,* and *Hajj* (4). The Shehadat is a profession required of all Muslims that there is only one God and that Mohammed is His prophet. The Salat, or prayer, is the spiritual exercise which must be performed five times daily. During prayer, the worshiper must stand facing the *Kaaba,* the holy sanctuary in Mecca. This direction called the *Qibla*, changes depending on one's geographical location. Prayer is preceded by *Woodoa,* or ablution. The Zakat is the giving of alms to the poor, the Siam is fasting during the Arab month of Ramadan, and the Hajj is the pilgrimage to Mecca, required of all who can afford it.

In the earlier days of Islam there was a need to establish a place where the *Umma,* or the community of believers, could come together and discuss matters of state and religion. This was the mosque, or the *Masjid,* meaning a place for prostration. In most of the planned settlements the mosque was centrally located, but in the settlements predating Islam and in the cases of villages, it occupied a variety of locations (Fig. 1). The importance of the mosque within the overall structure of a Muslim town was perhaps less than that of the church in a medieval European town. The absence in Islam of an institutionalized clergy explains the difference. The mosque was not an integral part of the hierarchy of institutional power; instead, it was a social and political institution that did not possess the independent source of power held by the church. Indeed, the mosque was not the source of power, but the means by which power was transmitted and shared, and the place in which the equality between ruler and ruled was manifested (9–11).

In spite of their functional importance, the early mosques were not landmarks. The location, external treatment, and physical form of early mosques indicate that they were not meant to serve as important visual symbols. Although there are exceptions, as a rule, mosques did not enjoy the visual emphasis held by the temples of other religions. The symbolic significance of the mosque is not represented in these physical qualities; rather, its importance lies in the role it plays within the community, a role that is deeply rooted in the structure of Islamic society (9,12–16).

HISTORY AND DEVELOPMENT

Early Islam did not require a specific place for prayer, for this obligation could be fulfilled anywhere, provided the times and the direction of prayer were correct. Although prayer is an individual communication with God, group prayer on Fridays (the Muslim sabbath) is considered to be an essential community obligation. The *Masjid-Jami,* or the congregational mosque, sometimes referred to as the Friday mosque, was thus established as the principal mosque for community prayer. It was usually large enough to accommodate the entire adult male population of the city; as the city expanded, neighborhood mosques were added. Many of these developed certain specialties and served social, political, and educational functions.

The first mosque ever designated as such was the Prophet's self-built mud house which was used before his death as a gathering place for the faithful. Upon its transformation to a mosque, the prophet's house became a holy place and its large courtyard was used as a prayer space. The mosques that followed were modeled after the plan of this prototype (17,18).

With the expansion of Islam into new regions, existing buildings were used as the first mosques. In the early days of Islam, the Arabs did not impose any architectural forms on the conquered countries. Instead they used existing sanctuaries to serve the simple requirements of Islam. Thus, the first mosques were churches and temples which were converted to serve the needs of the new Muslim rulers. For example, in Syria, where the direction of Qibla is due south, Byzantine churches were converted into mosques by turning the western doors into windows and piercing an entrance in the northern wall. In Persia, the Muslims converted many fire temples and existing buildings into mosques. The Friday mosque in Istakhr, for instance, had round columns with cow-like capitals resembling the double bull-headed capitals used in pre-Islamic Persia. This resemblance suggests that the mosque occupied the space of a former temple. Religious and secular buildings were also converted in Turkey. The famous Hagia Sophia, for instance, was among the earliest churches converted into a mosque by the new Ottoman rulers. Later, it became the prototype for many Ottoman mosque designs (Fig. 2).

The situation was different, however, in the cities newly founded by the Arabs, where there were no pre-existing buildings to employ. New mosques had to be built. The mosque of Kuffa, for example, one of the earliest in Iraq, was originally defined only by a ditch. Its Qibla portico was an unwalled space of reused marble columns, covered perhaps by a gabled wooden roof. Not very far away was the mosque of Basra, which was marked only by a fence of reed. In Egypt, the mosque of Amr, built in 641–642 A.D., was a small space containing a structure made of mud brick, with palm trunks as columns supporting the palm leaf mud roof. The floor was covered simply with pebbles. The situation was different in India, for by the time Muslim armies reached there in the twelfth century, Islamic building traditions were well established. The Muslims had absorbed and modified many of the building traditions of previously conquered places. The first mosques in India appear to be a result of this mature building tradition, although conversion of Hindu temples to mosques is also observed (21).

In the view of many scholars, the mosques of Black Africa and the Far East, being the most recent, are not typical examples. In Indonesia, Hinduism and Buddhism were primary sources of Mosque architecture. The mosques of Java, for instance, reflect these pre-Islamic building traditions. They have a squarish plan that recalls the Pendopo, a building erected within the ruler's compound for social gatherings and cultural activities. The forms of Masjid Angke and Masjid Banten, eg, do not resemble any other mosques within the vast regions of Islam (22,23). The mosques of West Africa, being mainly of mud brick, changed their shapes several times, making it difficult to establish their origins.

FUNCTIONS AND ELEMENTS

Although the mosque underwent many architectural changes under the influence of local styles, it always assumed the form of enclosed spaces serving the collective needs of the Muslim community. The main function served by a mosque is to provide a place for public worship, and to facilitate this function, different elements are needed. The congregational, or Friday mosque, has an open court-

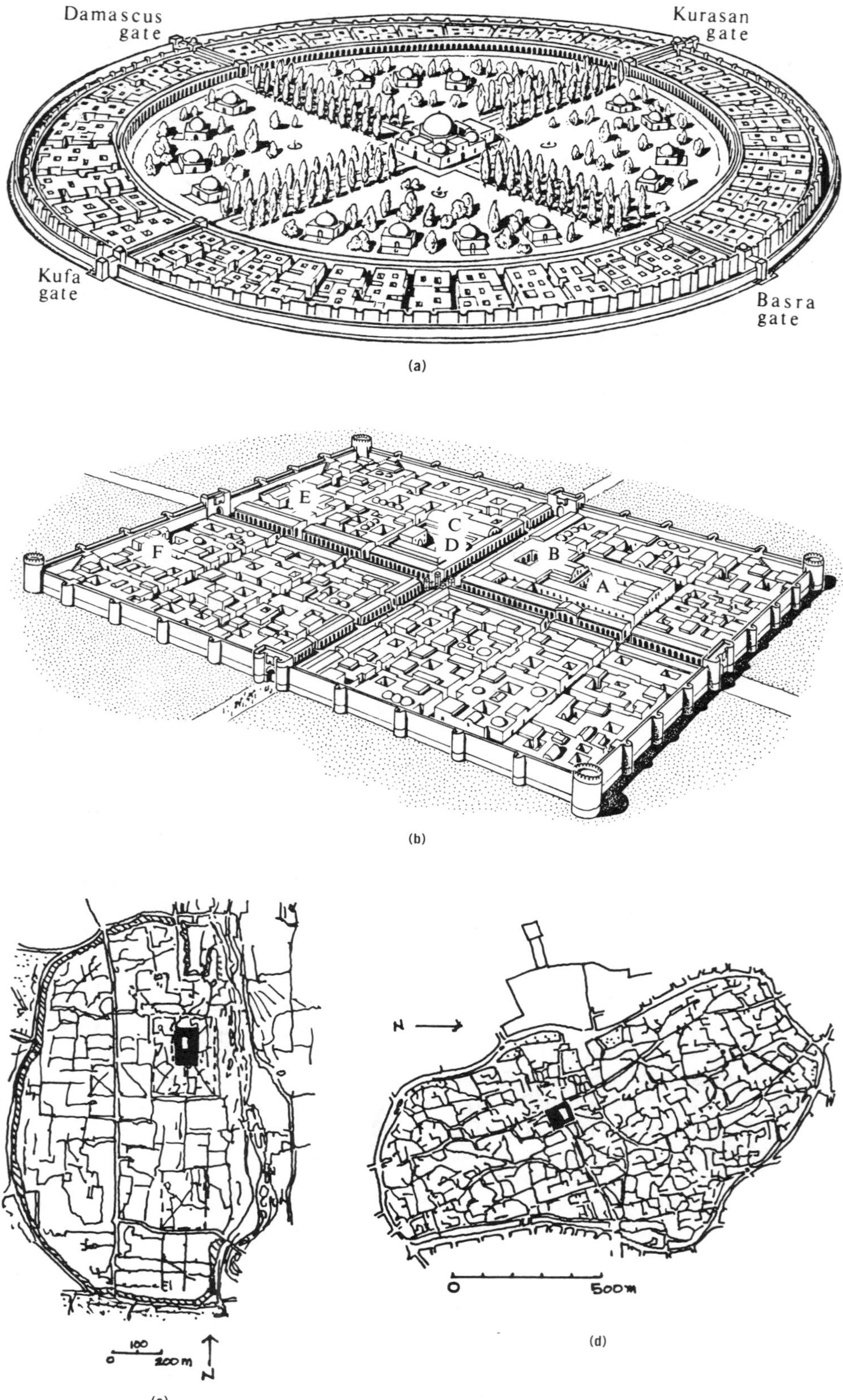

Figure 1. Location of the mosque within the city. Planned settlements: **(a)** Baghdad (16); **(b)** Anjar: A, the palace; B, mosque; C, covered market; D, lesser palace; E, F, large and small baths (*hamam*) (17). Courtesy of Hodder & Stoughton. Old settlements: **(c)** Damascus (8); **(d)** Tunis (9).

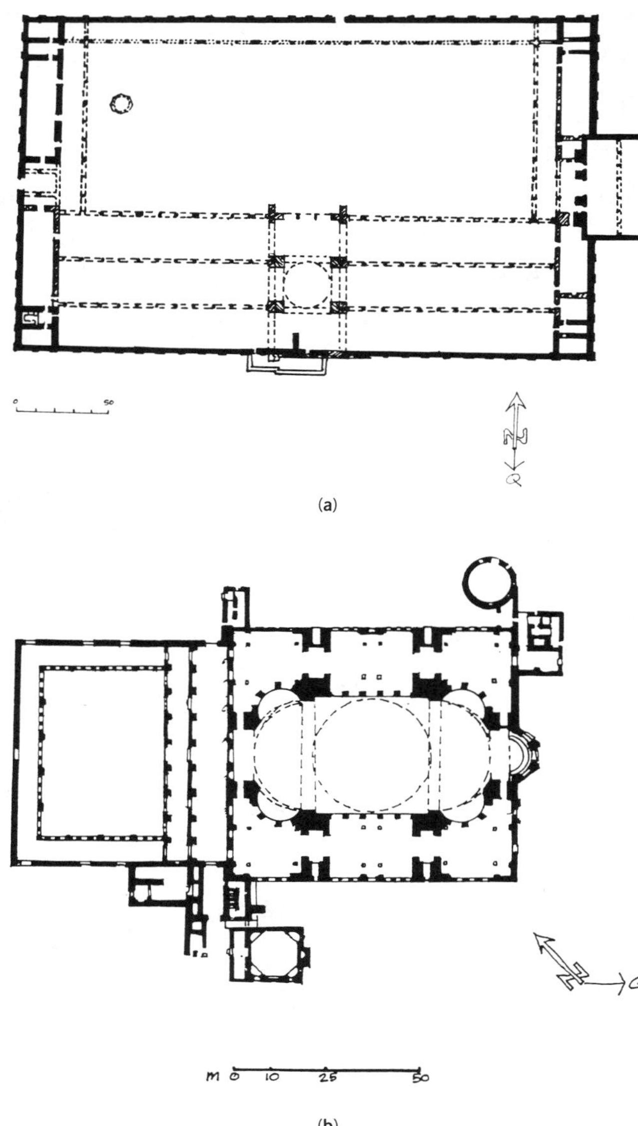

Figure 2. Churches converted into mosques. **(a)** the Ummayad Mosque, Damascus (20); **(b)** Hagia Sophia, Istanbul (21).

yard, called the *Sahn,* which in many cases contains an ablution fountain with running water. Here, worshipers cleanse themselves in preparation for prayer. The prayer ritual consists of recitations from the *Quran,* accompanied by a series of movements: standing, bowing, kneeling, and prostrating. The *Adhan,* or the call for prayer, is delivered vocally by the *Muezzin.* Although for many years the roof of the mosque was used as a place from which the call for prayer was delivered, the minaret, sometimes referred to as *Mazana* or *Manara,* was eventually introduced into the architectural scheme to facilitate this function. It stands outside the mosque, sometimes attached to it, and usually takes the form of a tower.

On the inside of the mosque, worshipers face the Qibla, which is indicated by the *Mihrab,* or a niche in the wall determining the correct orientation toward Mecca. The prayer is led by the *Imam,* the religious leader of the community. Before the prayer, the Imam sits in the *Maqsura,* an elevated pedestal or a screened enclosure, placed close to the Qibla wall. It is believed that the maqsura, also called *Dikka,* served as a seat for the Caliph during Friday prayers. Today, it is used by the Imam or the *Muqria,* a reciter of the Quran. To the right of the mihrab is the *Minbar,* which is traditionally used by the *Khatib,* the preacher who delivers the *Khutba,* the Friday sermon. The minbar is usually a wooden-frame pulpit with a few steps that elevate the Khatib to a level high enough to be seen by all worshipers (Fig. 3).

Today, small community mosques are usually furnished with a small library, a room for learning Quranic recitation, restrooms, and rooms for the mosque's caretakers. Large district mosques often contain a clinic, a nursery, and rooms for evening classes. In most countries, larger mosques have government-appointed Imams and Khatibs, who are usually religious scholars. In small mosques, the positions of Imam, Khatib, and Muezzin are filled by one individual who, in most cases, is a neighborhood elder volunteering to do the job.

PLAN FORM AND EXTERNAL APPEARANCE

Over the past 13 centuries the general requirements of the mosque have not changed significantly. Minor changes occurred in plan form, external appearance, and activity accommodated. Mosques can be classified in different ways. A classification based on differences rather than similarities would highlight the unique qualities of each regional variant.

If mosques were to be classified according to plan form or geometry, three basic types would emerge: the courtyard type, the transept type, and the type with a dominating interior space. Combinations are not uncommon. The first type basically takes the form of the Prophet's mosque, which is a simple rectangle with a sahn enclosed on most sides by *Riwaqs,* or covered porticos, of which the largest is the one facing Mecca. Examples include the mosque of Amr in Cairo and the great mosque of Kuffa. The transept type possesses a similar plan, except that the Qibla portico is cut in the middle. On the axis facing Mecca lies a transept occupying a slightly wider span lit by clerestory windows. A dome is sometimes added in the middle or at the end of the transept in order to emphasize the mihrab and accentuate the orientation toward Mecca. This type is widespread in Ummayad Syria, Spain, and parts of North Africa. Good examples of this type include Al-Hakim mosque of Cairo and the Great Mosque of Qairawan in Tunis. Chronologically, the type with a dominating interior space appeared last. The prototype for this kind seems to be Hagia Sophia. The large dome in these mosques is supported by a number of half domes, squinches, and pendentives. This solution eliminated the need for the forest of columns observed in the other types. Good examples of this type, which is widespread in Turkey, include the Sulaymaniye complex and the Blue mosque, both in Istanbul (Fig. 4). Other plans that do not fit this typology are

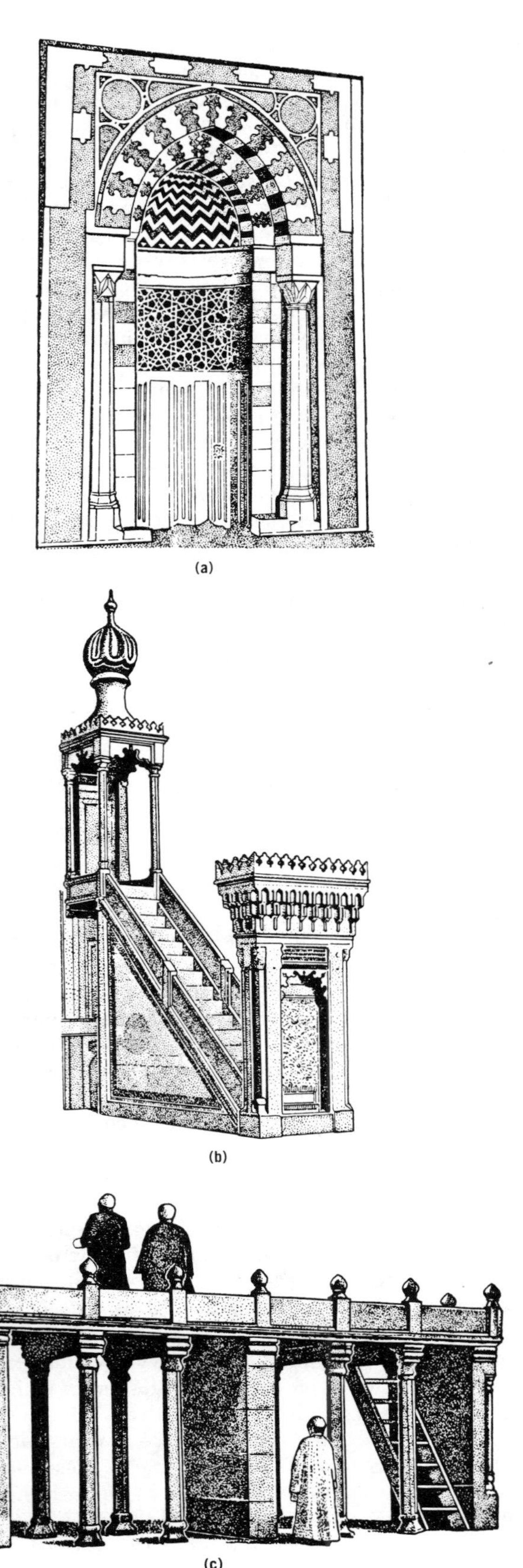

(a)

(b)

(c)

Figure 3. Internal elements of the mosque. **(a)** Mihrab; **(b)** Minbar; **(c)** Maqsura (25).

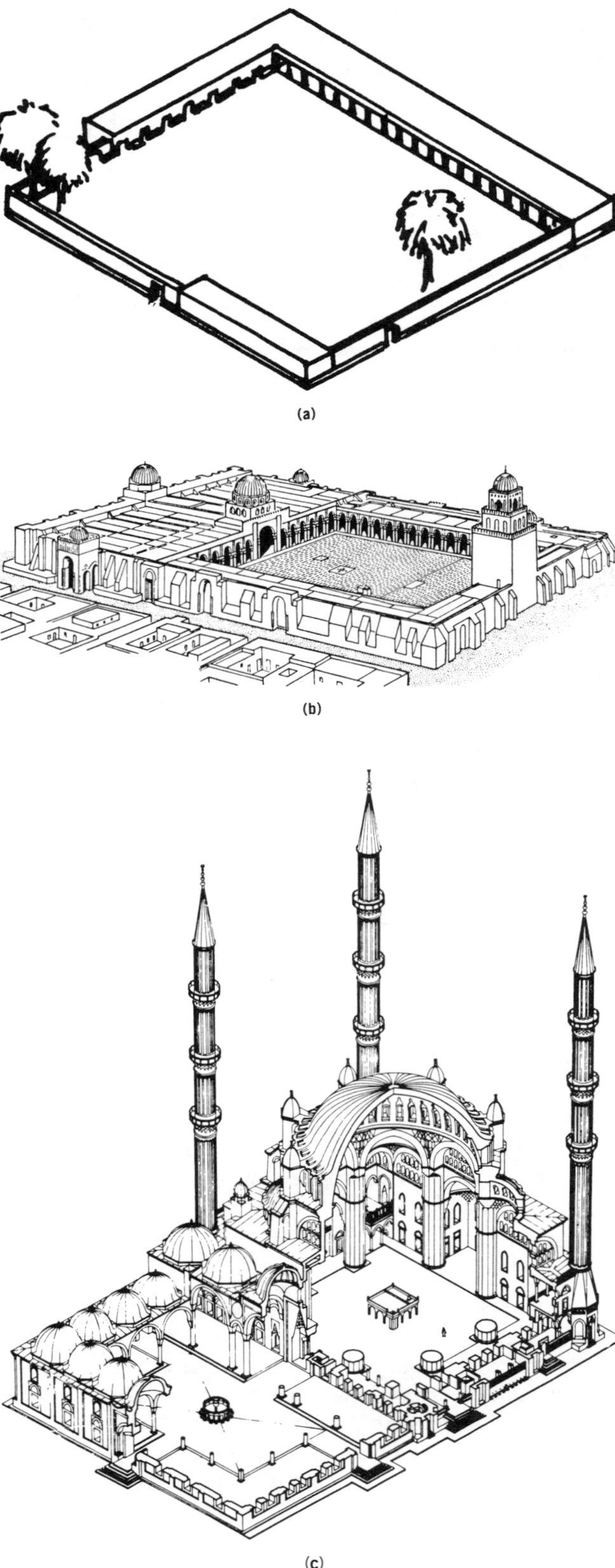

(a)

(b)

(c)

Figure 4. Plan forms. **(a)** The open courtyard type: the Prophet's house and mosque; **(b)** The transept type: The Great Mosque of Qairawan, Tunis (26); **(c)** The centralized space type: The Sulaymaniye Mosque Complex, Istanbul (27). Courtesy of Dogan Kuban, Turkey.

usually a result of a combination of the different types. The mosques of Mogul India with their onion-like domes are a combination of the courtyard type and the central interior space type. An example of this is the Pearl mosque of Agra. The Masjidi-Jami in Isfahan, with its four iwans, is a prototype of many Iranian mosques. Its plan represents a variation of the courtyard type.

A comparative survey of all major mosques indicates the existence of a definite language of Islamic visual expression (27). It possesses both a vocabulary and a grammar. On the one hand, the vocabulary deals with the aesthetic models underlying the different components of the mosque. It concerns such issues as constituent forms, surface patterns, colors, and materials employed. The grammar, on the other hand, relates the various systems of organizing these parts into a coherent whole. While this is true for most examples, scholars have debated the validity of this generalization, arguing that many aspects of this visual language exist in a multiplicity of dialects and are bound to specific cultural regions within the Muslim world (28,29). The dome, for instance, received important visual emphasis in the Persian and Turkish regions but was rather underdeveloped in Africa and the Arabian peninsula. The language of Islamic visual expression thus does not depend on elements. The absence of an element in a particular region should not nullify the existence of such language. Whether or not this language is uniquely Islamic is not the issue. What is important is that the vocabulary and grammar of mosque architecture appear to have achieved certain symbolic meanings upon which there are general societal agreements.

The minaret, for example, is an element of the vocabulary. It has been consistently used to indicate the presence of Islam. Some scholars decline to accept this and hence argue that there was no specific prescribed form for the minaret. They consider its symbolic importance as something borrowed from pre-Islamic cultures. They suggest that the minaret is only a physical sign and not a religious symbol. Its shape is only acknowledged by those who share the culture in which it was created. According to this view, the form of the minaret is defined culturally, and not religiously, and is devoid of any religious symbolism. Its significance lies not in its form but in the fact that it serves an Islamic function.

The study of Quranic quotations on minarets has proved to be instructive in studying the symbolism of the mosque. This has led some scholars to the belief that symbolic meanings and sign systems should not be sought in the architecture of the mosque but in its elements and details, such as the mihrab or the *mugarnas*. In this view the architecture of the mosque developed its own iconography. This iconography is related to the order of meanings that are inherent not in the form or the function, but mainly in the relationship among them.

Using Islamic philosophy, other scholars have introduced broader interpretations of the meaning of the different elements of the mosque, particularly the minaret, the dome, and the courtyard (30). The minaret is seen as the element connecting the sky to the earth. Its verticality represents the Muslim desire to reach the upper skies, where God is sitting. The dome is seen as an element simulating the universe. Its geometry establishes a greater contact with the earth and this symbolism serves as a reminder to the Muslim of his earthly duties. The courtyard is a large, well-defined open space, like a room without a ceiling. It plays the role of establishing the Muslim's place in space.

REGIONAL EXAMPLES

The following is a brief review of some of the most famous mosques of Islam. Although this is not a comprehensive survey, it will illustrate the tremendous variety of mosque forms and shapes in the Muslim world (31).

Arabia: Al-Haram Al-Sharief, Mecca

Before Islam, the Kaaba had been a place of pilgrimage for many Arab tribes in Arabia. After Islam, it became the most sacred site: *Al-Haram Al-Sharief.* The site was converted into a mosque by the Prophet in 630, and has seen many later additions. Today, every able-bodied Muslim is expected to make the pilgrimage at least once in his or her lifetime.

The mosque is an open courtyard containing the Kaaba, which is a large cube-shaped chamber, in its center. The ancient form of the stone-built Kaaba has been preserved in spite of several reconstructions. The entire structure has traditionally been draped with a black silk cover, which in the past was renewed annually by the reigning Caliphs (Fig. 5).

Palestine: Aqsa Mosque, Jerusalem, Ummayad Period

The Aqsa mosque was built in 715 by the Caliph Al-Walid on the site of the first Qibla before the Kaaba. It was destroyed by earthquake in 747, and reconstructed by Al-Mahdi in 780, and again by Al-Zahir in 1035. The present mosque is a result of further reconstructions and repairs, but it still maintains elements that resemble both Al-Mahdi's and Al-Zahir's plans.

In plan, the mosque is composed of seven aisles which are perpendicular to the Qibla wall. The wider central aisle is covered by a wooden truss and terminates in a dome over the mihrab. The mosque has neither an integral minaret nor a courtyard, and its most distinctive exterior element is its golden enameled dome.

Egypt: Mosque of Ibn Tulun, Cairo, Tulunid Period

This mosque was built by Ahmed Ibn Tulun, governor of Egypt, in 876–879, after the old mosque of Amr had become too small to accommodate the congregation.

The mosque consists of a square courtyard that is enclosed on three sides by two-aisled porticos. On the fourth side, facing Mecca, lies the main prayer space. It is five aisles deep and made of pointed arches carried on piers with engaged columns in the corners. In the middle of the courtyard stands an elegant, domed edifice that serves as an ablution fountain.

On the opposite side of the main prayer hall stands

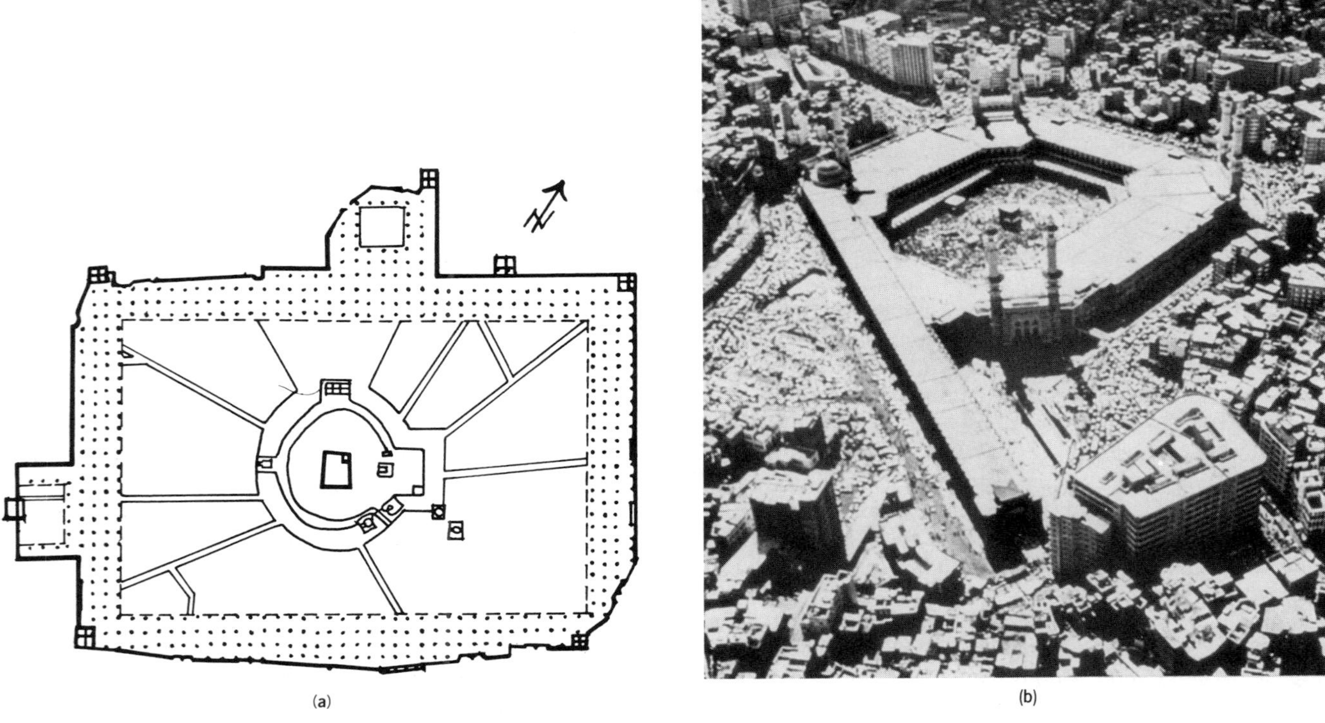

(a) (b)

Figure 5. Al-Haram Al-Sharief, Mecca (2). **(a)** Plan; **(b)** View. Courtesy of the Ministry of Information, Saudi Arabia.

the spiral minaret which was modeled after the Malwiya, the famous minaret of the Samarra mosque in Iraq. The plan changes from a square to a circle as it gets higher, and there is an outer spiral staircase. The piers that surround the courtyard have a continuous band of human-size ornamental parapeting (Fig. 6).

Tunisia: Qairawan Mosque, Aghlabid, Zirid, and Hafasid Periods

Originally founded on a Romano-Byzantine site at the time of the Arab conquest, the mosque was entirely rebuilt by Ziyadat Allah in 836.

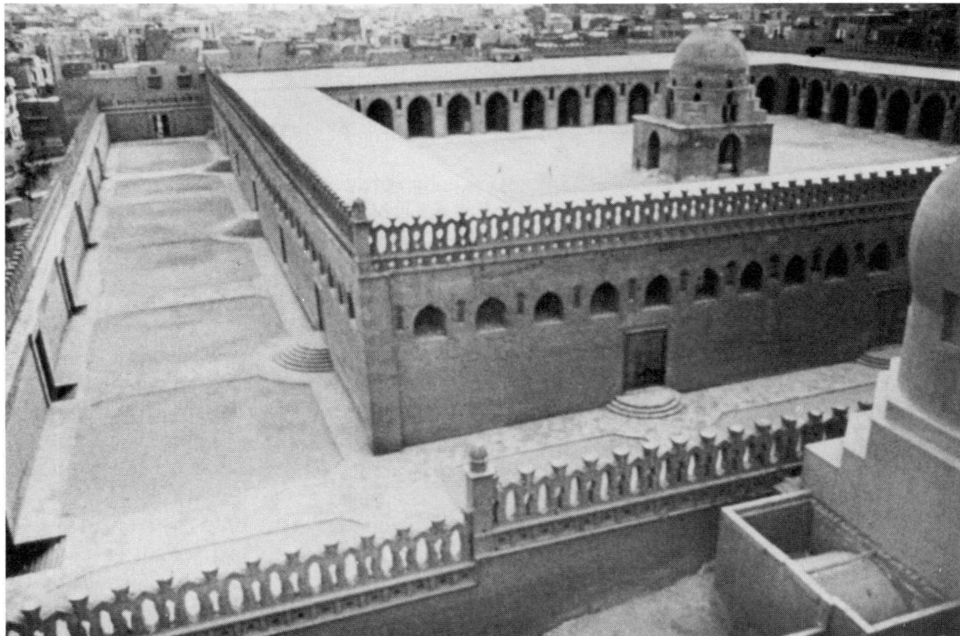

Figure 6. Ibn Tulun Mosque, Cairo.

The mosque consists of a great, oblong enclosure with its main axis pointing toward Mecca. The mosque entrances are sheltered by porches, which were later additions. The plan is of the courtyard type. It is rectangular and is surrounded by horseshoe arches braced by wooden tie-beams. The beams rest on carved stone imposts and wooden abacus blocks upon capitals of reused antique columns. The prayer hall, which stands at the end of the rectangular courtyard, is a hypostyle hall consisting of 17 aisles formed by 16 arches, and two domes, one at each end of the central aisle. The minaret is a squarish, three-story tower that is bulky and slightly tapering. It is located slightly off center, opposite the prayer hall across the courtyard.

The exterior of the mosque presents a most irregular appearance, the outline being broken by buttresses of varied spacing, size, and form. The exterior is covered with innumerable traces of whitewash.

Spain: Great Mosque of Cordoba, Ummayad Period

This mosque was originally built by Abdal-Rahman I in 785. The original plan had a prayer hall, with 11 aisles of 12 bays each, perpendicular to the Qibla wall. The mosque was considerably enlarged in 832 and 987. Years after the Christian conquest, a baroque chapel was built in its northern side.

In plan, the mosque has a long, rectangular courtyard, with a large prayer hall on its south side that is entered off center. The interior consists of 19 rows of double arcades which run perpendicular to the Qibla wall, and rest on reused antique columns. Because the columns were not tall enough to elevate the roof, each column has an additional pier on the top to support a second row of round-headed arches, with alternating stone and brick voussoirs. There are three mihrabs on the Qibla wall. The central mihrab is the original and is a deeply recessed polygonal chamber, built of marble, and decorated by floral motifs and calligraphy. In front of the Qibla wall there are three domes that have complex rib patterns, each one different.

Turkey: Sulaymaniye Mosque Complex, Istanbul, Ottoman Period

Named after Sultan Sulayman II (1520–1566), and modeled after the Hagia Sophia, this mosque was commissioned as a part of a larger complex in 1550. Sulayman abandoned the Eski Saray as his residence and gave up half its gardens to accommodate this new complex. Built by the famous Turkish architect Sinan, the complex took seven years to complete and consists of several religious, social, and educational facilities. The mosque occupies a central space within the courtyard.

In plan, the mosque consists of a rectangular courtyard with arcades on four sides, leading to the main domed prayer hall. The interior area is a square divided into 16 units, of which 4 form the central square. This central space is a cube-like space and is surmounted by a large hemisphere, creating a light, airy effect.

The exterior corresponds exactly to the interior spatial divisions and to the structural functions of an assemblage of buttresses, arches, and vaults (Fig. 7).

Iran: Masjidi-Shah, Isfahan, Safavid Period

In 1611, Shah Abbas I began the construction of his new congregational mosque. Culminating his efforts to reconstruct Isfahan, this mosque was intended to demonstrate the power of his reign. The mosque is noted for a number of important architectural innovations which have been employed in its design and its placement within the urban fabric.

The entrance iwan is located at the center of the south side of the *Maydan,* or the great square, but in order to face Mecca, the mosque itself is turned at an angle. This change of axis, which occurs within the entrance portal, was so successfully designed that it is almost imperceptible. Once past the portal, there is a rectangular courtyard containing four iwans. This traditional form is brought to a peak of perfection with the iwans and the great dome being reflected in the central pool. The prayer hall is a

(a)

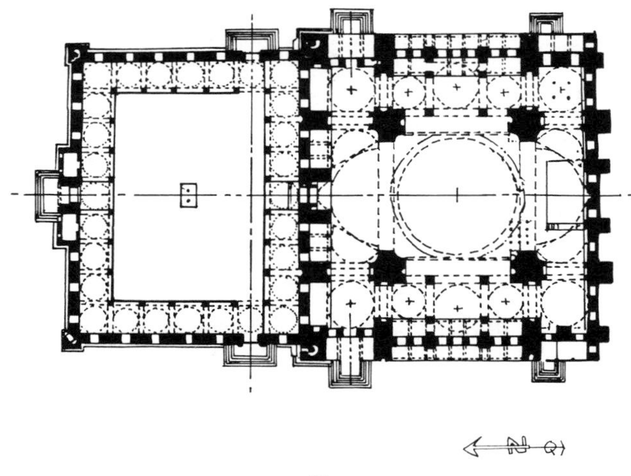

(b)

Figure 7. Sulaymaniye Mosque, Istanbul (34). **(a)** Exterior; **(b)** Plan.

(a)

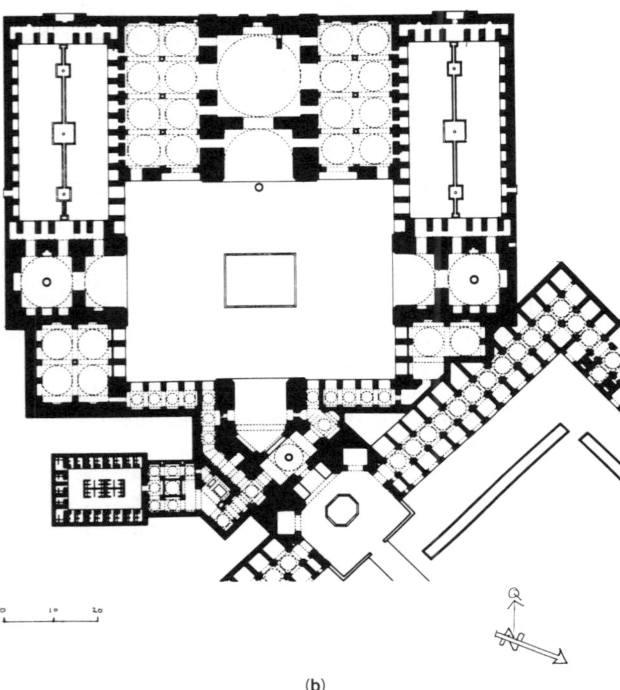

(b)

Figure 8. Masjidi Shah, Isfahan (35). **(a)** Exterior; **(b)** Plan.

small chamber with a central dome. The interior of the mosque is covered with glazed tiles of different colors, while the exterior is covered with the traditional Persian turquoise mosaic (Fig. 8).

India: Jami-Masjid, Delhi, Mogul Period

Jami-Masjid, one of the largest courtyard type mosques in India, was built for the new Shahjahanabad in 1644–1658. The entire mosque is raised on a high plinth and can be entered from large portals on three sides. On the fourth side lies the prayer hall which advances into the square courtyard, interrupting the continuation of the surrounding arcades.

From the outside, the front elevation is flanked by two four-stage minarets. There are also three drum-raised, bulbous domes made of white marble with red sandstone stripes. These domes are placed far enough behind the raised central iwan to avoid the aesthetic imbalance observed in some of the earlier mosques of India (Fig. 9).

Mali: Great Mosque of Timbuktu, Mali-Songhaia Periods

The great mosque of Timbuktu is a good example of the mud brick mosques of West Africa. This mosque, sometimes referred to as the Djinguere-Ber mosque, was founded by Mansa Musa, king of Mali, in 1325. Major reconstruction and additions to it were recorded over the following 200 years. Substantial alterations seem to have occurred between 1828 and 1853, during the period of Masina-Fulani dominance.

The entire mosque is made of mud bricks and stone rubble with clay rendering, and has a flat roof over the prayer hall, supported on arcades of mud piers. The

(a)

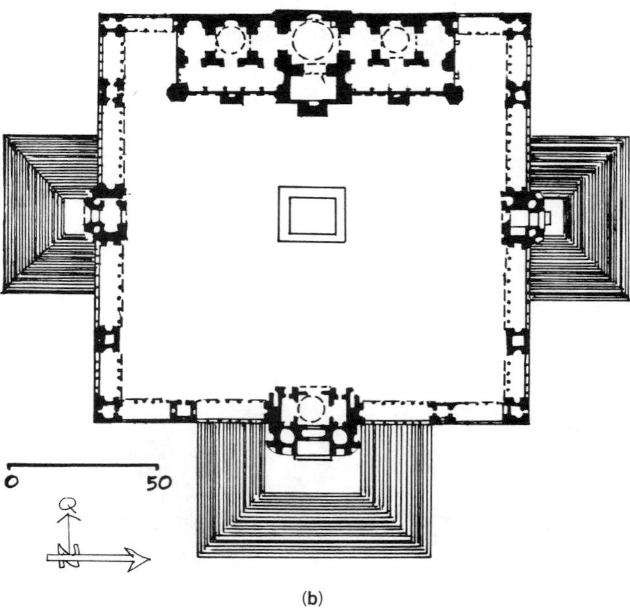

(b)

Figure 9. Jami Masjid, Delhi (36). **(a)** Interior courtyard; **(b)** Plan.

(a)

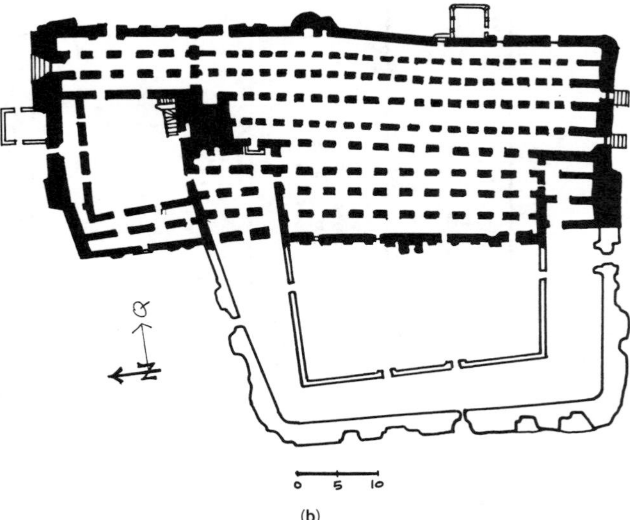

(b)

Figure 10. **(a)** Djenne Mosque, Mali; **(b)** Plan of Djinguere Ber Mosque, Timbuktu (37).

mosque is irregular in plan and consists of a small courtyard with a large prayer hall on one side. The interior arcades are regularly spaced but are irregular in size. Three of the arcades incorporate quasihorseshoe arches constructed from stone voussoirs.

From the outside, a conical tower with projecting poles rises above the mihrab and the minbar niches. The minaret is a four-sided tapering structure with an interior staircase. The pyramidal form contrasts sharply with the mihrab's exterior cone (Fig. 10).

Indonesia: Kudus Mosque, Central Java

The original form of the Indonesian mosque, especially that of Java, is a square building covered with a roof consisting of different stories, ending in an ornamental top. The majority of the Javanese mosques, which are the oldest in Indonesia, were provided with a broad front verandah under a separate roof called the *surambi.* Indonesian mosques originally had no minarets, but they consisted of multistoried roofs, a feature signifying the building's symbolic importance. In addition to the presence of storied roofs, some Javanese mosques may also be found standing in water and carried on pillars, a phenomenon not shared by any other mosques around the world.

A good example of a Javanese mosque is the Kudus mosque, built in central Java in the early part of the sixteenth century. It is made of red brick with inserted ceramic dishes, and has a squarish plan tower. Its ornamentation is restricted to stepped moldings and framed niches, imitating the form of a traditional Javanese Hindu temple. The mosque consists of two hypostyle chambers with a large square prayer hall at the end. This prayer hall consists of five aisles and five rows, with the center ones being slightly larger. The Qibla wall is flat and symmetrical, except for the niche of the mihrab (Fig. 11).

OTHER RELIGIOUS BUILDING TYPES

In addition to serving as places of public worship, mosques accommodate other religious functions. Within a few centuries of the introduction of Islam, three new categories of sacred buildings were introduced and some of these were merely attachments to the mosque. These categories were: the *Madrasa* (educational), the *khanaqah* (monastic), and the mausoleum (tomb). As the importance of these functions grew, the architecture of the mosque was modified to accommodate them (38).

Madrasa

The madrasa, or school, was introduced around the eleventh century by the Ayyubids and later the Seljuk Turks, to train theologians as defenders of orthodoxy. Later the madrasas became colleges in which teaching of all fields of human knowledge took place. Historically, madrasas played a very important cultural role in Muslim cities and were sometimes used politically by the governments in the preaching of specific ideologies.

Madrasas usually assumed a crucifix form, and were modeled after the Persian iwan-type palace, which was composed of four openings into a central court. This design spread into Egypt and was found convenient because each iwan could serve as a lecture hall for students. The four iwans have traditionally represented the four schools of Islamic thought: Hanafite, Hanbalite, Malikite, and Shafeyite. Although in many countries only one school prevailed and the teaching of the others was nonexistent, the form of the iwans was maintained, as can be observed in the later madrasa of Sheite Iran.

In many cases one of the iwans was used as a regular mosque, allowing the two building functions to merge into one common type: the madrasa mosque. Examples of these include the famous madrasa of Sultan Hassan, built in 1359 in Cairo. Its intricate plan provides a separate and distinct complex of four vaulted iwans, each entered individually from the central courtyard. The iwan facing the Qibla was slightly larger and often served as the main prayer hall. Another example is the madrasa of Sultan Qayt Bay, built in 1274 in Cairo. It conformed with the tradition of an asymmetrical exterior joining a symmetrical interior. The Madrasa of Al-Firdaus in Aleppo, built by Saladin in 1183, is one of the earliest in Syria. Its central courtyard is surrounded on three sides by an arcade of columns and on the fourth side by a vaulted iwan. In

(a)

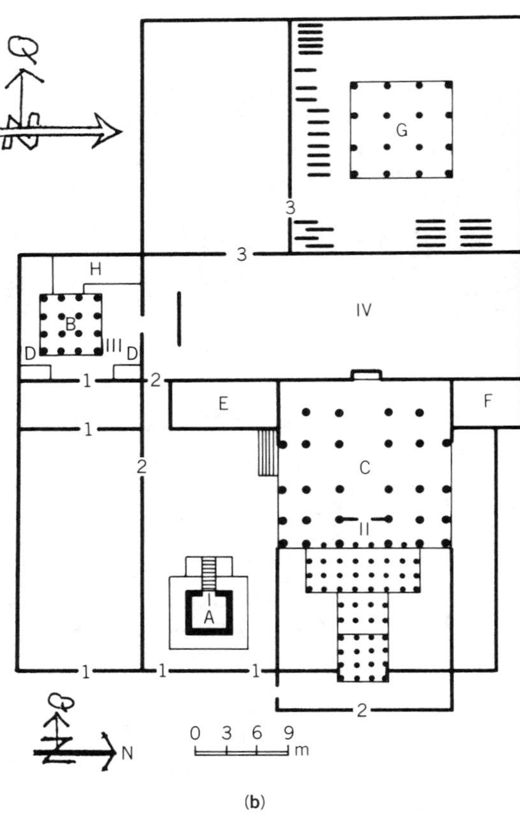

(b)

Figure 11. (a) Masjid Jami, Kota Bharu, Malaysia; **(b)** Kudus Mosque, East Java: 1, 2, 3, entrance ways; I, minaret; II, mosque; III, meeting hall; IV, graveyard; A, minaret; B, meeting hall; C, mosque; D, workshop; E, classroom; F, women's quarter; G, shrine; H, place of ablution (38).

general its plan echoes the typical crucifix form of later madrasas, in spite of its different geometry and proportions (Fig. 12). The Uluqh Beg madrasa in Samarkand, the Miri Arab madrasa in Bukhara, and the Gawhar Shah madrasa in Herat are all variations on this type.

Khanaqah

Around the twelfth century and in response to the solidification of Sufism a new building type, the khanaqah, emerged. The development of this monastic mosque cannot be considered independent of the rise of Sufi orders, which included Dervish practices. The khanaqah provided retreat cells in which the sufis and dervishes spent their time praying and studying. Sufis differ widely in their organization and rules. Like a monastery, the khanaqah required spaces to accommodate these variations.

Over the years, the number of khanaqahs diminished dramatically, as they became a prime target for secular governments intent on erasing the influence of Islam. Thus their destruction makes it difficult to discern any pattern. Most khanaqahs consist, however, of the addition to a mosque of various dependencies, such as a ceremonial hall, cells, kitchen, a refectory, a library, a guest house, and special quarters for the shaiykhs. The arrangement of the functions differs from one place to another. In Egypt, for instance, the madrasa plan is often employed, with one of the iwans serving as the ceremonial hall. This is illustrated in the khanaqah of Baybars Al-Jashinkir in Cairo, completed in 1309.

The building of Al-Naser Faraj ibn Barquq looks like a madrasa, but is a khanaqah. It has a crucifix plan but substitutes hypostyle halls for iwans. The dervishes were housed nearby in a three-story block consisting of 60 cells. During the Ottoman period, khanaqahs were combined with madrasas and mausoleums within a single building.

Mausoleum Mosques and Small Religious Buildings

Many Muslim rulers seek to be remembered by building a tomb in an existing mosque or building a madrasa complex to accompany it. It is sustained by a *Waqf,* or endowment fund. The presence of tombs in madrasas is evidence of the great esteem accorded to learning in certain Islamic societies. It also shows the high value which some rulers placed on sanctity.

The complex of Sultan Qalaun, built in Cairo in 1280, is an excellent example of a mixed-use building. It contained a madrasa mosque, a tomb, and a *Muristan,* or hospital. The tomb is separated from the madrasa mosque by a great corridor that leads to the muristan. The elegant tomb is a square chamber with four pink granite columns

(a)

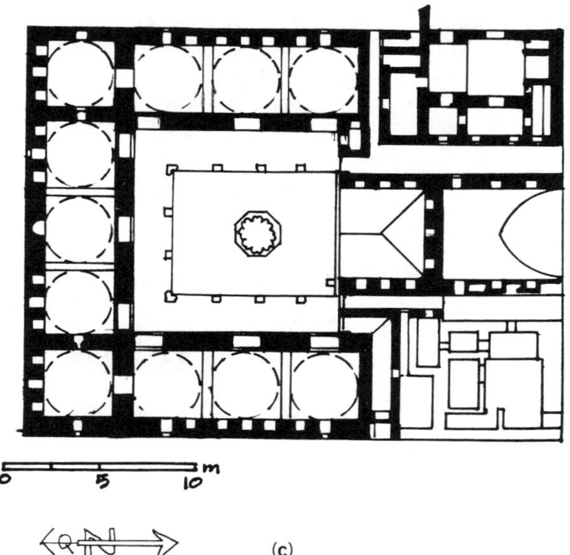

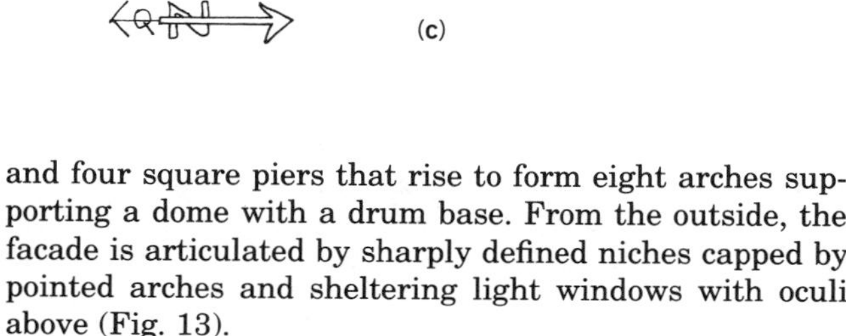

(c)

(b)

Figure 12. Madrasas and mosques. **(a)** Madrasa of Sultan Hasan, Cairo, interior courtyard; **(b)** Madrasa of Sultan Hasan Cairo (40); **(c)** Madrasa of Al Firdaus, Aleppo (41). Courtesy of Hodder & Stoughton.

and four square piers that rise to form eight arches supporting a dome with a drum base. From the outside, the facade is articulated by sharply defined niches capped by pointed arches and sheltering light windows with oculi above (Fig. 13).

The Shrine of Khwaja Abu-Nasr Parsa at Balkh in Afghanistan is another example of a tomb mosque. The structure was dedicated to a Timurid Sufi Shaykh who died in 1460. Although it is mainly a tomb, it acts as a mosque. It is considered a madrasa by the local people and a khanaqah or *Tekya* by some architectural historians. The plan shows a four-portaled structure with a square chamber, converted into an octagon by squinches. The octagon is later converted into a 16-sided polygon in which latticed windows alternate with muqarnas-filled niches. The shrine is a good example of a building that was not intended to be a mosque but acquired that title with time.

Smaller buildings for religious activity also developed everywhere in many Muslim cities. The *Zawiya* served as a prayer hall along the side streets of busy neighborhoods. The *Kutab* was a kindergarden or nursery school where children were taught the fundamentals of religion and recited the Quran. In many cases kutabs were adjoined by a *Sabil,* or water fountain.

CONSTRUCTION AND STRUCTURE

Most mosques were designed by craftspersons holding the title of *Mohandes/Banna.* The modern equivalent to this title is the architect/builder (42). The extent of specialization in the building trades varied according to the needs of the community. The craftsmen in the large urban communities were highly specialized. In many aspects of specialization high standards of perfection were reached. Most craftsmen were monitored by guild-like organizations and were loosely affiliated with one or two of their most respected members, who acted as spokespersons for the group.

Most building techniques were passed on from father

(a)

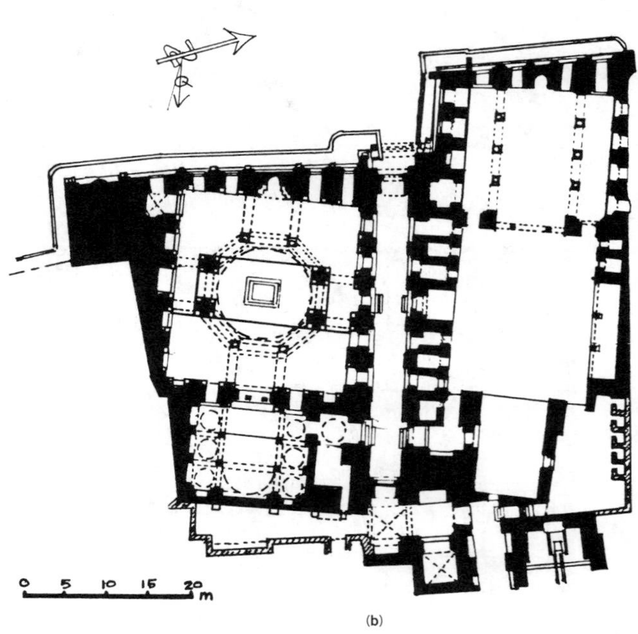

(b)

Figure 13. Sultan Qalaun tomb complex, Cairo (42). **(a)** Exterior; **(b)** Plan.

to son. Training and the organization of work varied somewhat, according to the time and place, and was rarely structured according to any fixed practice. The usual divisions were those of master, pupil, journeyman, and laborer. Craftsmen often traveled a great deal throughout the Muslim lands, undoubtedly encouraged by the active demand for new buildings.

Delicate drawing instruments found during archaeological excavations indicate that mosque builders were skilled draftsmen. Evidence also supports the view that some mosque designs were first tested with small-scale models. In contrast to the pace of construction of medieval European churches, mosques were usually built in a short period of time. This was often achieved at enormous costs and with the aid of a huge labor force (43). In terms of structure, the arch appears to be one of the primary structural elements in mosque architecture. Its use has given way to the creation of many graceful shapes. The pointed arch, which is often keel-shaped, was developed as an alternative to the semicircular arches of Rome and Byzantium. Variations of this development include the horseshoe arch, which is also frequently pointed, and was widely adopted in many parts of the Muslim world. The arches used in many mosques were enclosed in a rectangular form which balanced the movement away from the center as suggested by the pointed arch (Fig. 14). Arches were sometimes multiplied on different scales to create an overall unified pattern. Vaults were sometimes used in mosque building.

Early Islamic vaulting techniques were based on the use of fire bricks. By resting each brick on the one below, it was possible to erect an entire vault or dome without resorting to the use of a temporary timber support, as was the case in Western vaulting systems. The geometry of such systems was fairly crude, but it improved with advances in structural technology. Brick vaulting in mosques reached its highest standards in Mesopotamia and Persia. Other vertical elements of the mosque, such as the minaret, started very low and, as structural technology improved, got higher. The stability of minarets was assured by a system of superimposed stories of decreasing size, and by the inner staircase serving as the structural core. Ottoman minarets of slender appearance, using a hollow screw structural technique, reached heights of more than 70 m (Fig. 15).

The dome is another common structural element in mosque architecture. In India, it usually takes a bulbous shape and is placed on a cylindrical drum. In Iran, double domes were frequently used in order to maintain the proper scale in the interior space. In Turkey, the desire for a

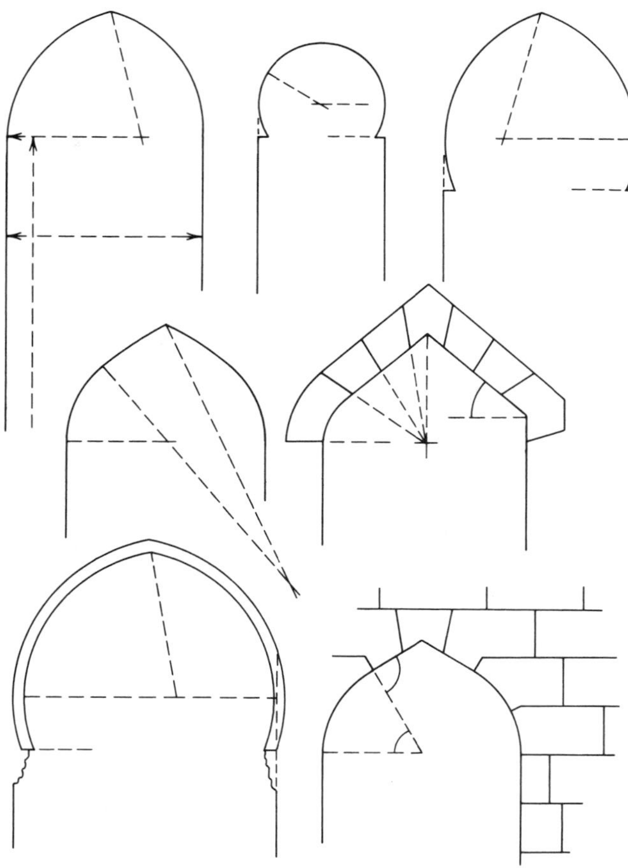

Figure 14. Arch forms.

centralized space led to the adoption of great hemispheres which dictated the size of the ground area. In Syria and Egypt, domes were low and were sometimes placed on octagonal drums.

Structural supports for the dome, which appear on the inside of mosques, also differ from place to place. The difference lies in the way the dome is joined with the square plan below. Two principal methods were employed to create a satisfying synthesis of the two forms. These were the squinch and the pendentive, which were inherited from Byzantine techniques. The former is a series of gradually projecting arches thrown across a corner, while the latter is a downward curving spherical triangle that carries the weight of each corner to the ground. A third and less common method is the use of Turkish triangles. These consist of either triangular panels whose apexes meet at a single point in each of the four corners, or a belt of triangles fitted together with their apexes upwards and downwards to form a continuous band (Fig. 16).

Through time the obsession with transforming structure into decoration led to a profound change in squinch form, resulting in the evolution of the *Muqarnas*, or stalactite. This is a very important structural and decorative element, unique to Islamic architecture. It is made of outstanding panels placed on top of one another and generally shaped as miniature quarter spheres or pointed domes, with their apexes hanging over usable space. Their shape resembles the cells of a honeycomb with each one mounting on top of the other. The muqarnas was employed in many mosques and its use spread throughout the Muslim world. The mosques of Spain contain excellent examples of muqarnases used to achieve a smooth and elegant transition between the angular walls and the spherical shape on top of them.

MATERIALS AND BUILDING TREATMENT

The diversity of Islamic architectural forms is well represented in the construction materials and building treatments employed throughout the Muslim world. Most of the important decorative features associated with mosques were introduced at an early date. The decorative use of calligraphy and the geometrical patterns on floors and walls were all well established by the tenth century A.D. (26, 27).

In Iran, the original Sassanid brick and stucco tradition was continued with the addition of enameled tile work. From the outset, brick and stucco were media for lavish ornamentation. The use of stucco complements the clarity of primary forms, rather than obscuring them. Stucco is thus used to dissolve the difference between structural and nonstructural elements. It might seem that this attempt to merge structure with surface treatment is inhibited by the use of brick, but Muslim architects were masters in using structure as decoration. The manner in which bricks were laid was such that the spaces between them were maintained, providing interesting variations of shadow densities. Brick allowed many different effects in the form of border motifs, repeat patterns, and grilles. The most outstanding examples where this medium of construction becomes its own decoration are in Bukhara: the mausoleum of Ismael Samanid, built in the tenth century, and the minaret Kalam, built in the twelfth century.

Tile was commonly used on walls and floors in the Middle East before Hellenistic times. Its use was revived in Iran by the Sassanids. Blue luster tiles, found in Mesopotamia, in addition to multicolor mosaic, were employed with such prodigality that a few centuries later they covered entire buildings, such as the Masjidi-Shah in Isfahan.

Terra cotta, or ceramic tiles, is another material commonly used as decoration on the mosques of Iran. There are three different types of ceramic tiles: (1) single colored, (2) mosaic faience, made of small tile fragments fitted into complex designs, and (3) multicolored tile. The appeal of these tiles was in their articulated implementation on walls, domes, and framing of doorways and windows. In Muslim India, much of the surface decoration of mosques was clearly derived from Hindu and Jain temples. Before and during the early days of Islam, red stone was an important building material. During Mogul times, building with red stone and decorative white marble became very common. The later days of the Mogul empire witnessed a religious orthodoxy accompanied by a change from the traditional sandstone to marble, as can be observed in the Pearl Mosque of Agra. The beauty of the marble used resides chiefly in its graining, which is frequently exposed and arranged in different patterns. Sometimes stones are

(a) (b) (c)

Figure 15. Minarets: regional variations (45). **(a)** Great Mosque, Samarra, Iraq, 847 A.D.; **(b)** Mosque of Hasan, Rabat, Morocco, 1196 A.D.; **(c)** Kadhimain Mosque, Baghdad, fifteenth century. Courtesy of Hodder & Stoughton.

perforated to form a grille, which attenuates the feeling of weight and hardness.

The Seljuk mosques in Anatolia, such as the Gok Mosque Madrasa in Sivas, were characterized by a calculated balance between plain surfaces of superb ashlar masonry and areas of rigidly controlled decoration. Later Ottoman architects in Turkey designed mosques that were more concerned with developing the concept of a unified domed space. This resulted in austere geometrical masterpieces, such as the Selimiye mosque of Edirne, in which exterior decoration played a minor role.

In Egypt, fire brick and stone were often used as principal building materials. The exterior facades, although plain, were decorated with recessed arches that broke up large expanses of wall. This can be observed in many mosques, ranging from the Fatimid mosque of Al-Hakim to the Mamluk mosque–madrasa of Sultan Hassan, both in Cairo. The use of alternating courses of lighter and darker stones characterize many of the mosques of Egypt and Syria.

Despite their grandeur, the materials used to build most mosques in Spain and North Africa were neither expensive nor substantial. The builders were successful in extracting the maximum decorative potential from these sources. Lath, plaster, and stucco were elegantly combined. Glazed-tile covered floors, and muqarnases of brick stucco pendentives decorated the interiors of many mosques, indicating an obsession with detail. In many instances, whether in the east or the west, the surface treatment of the mosque appears to have sprung more from its subju-

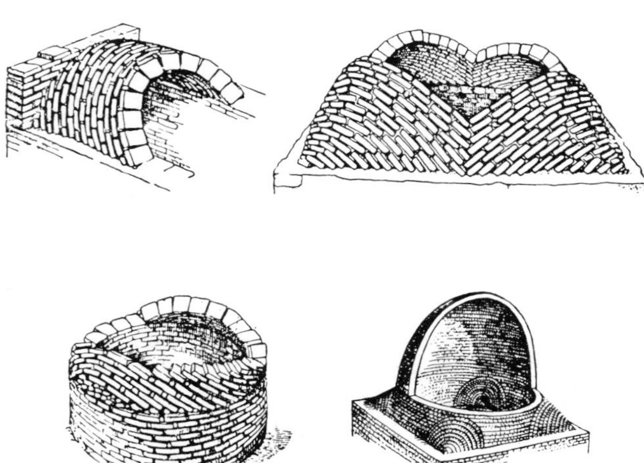

Figure 16. Vaults, domes, and squinches (46).

gation to the availability of certain building materials than its sociocultural context.

THE CONTEMPORARY MOSQUE AND ITS DESIGN STANDARDS

The mosque is the ultimate expression of a philosophy that strives for order and unity. As such, it must create an atmosphere conducive to prayer and contemplation. The design should remind the worshiper of one's place within the universe. The use of geometrical patterns creates unity, and guards against having any focal element of worship.

For a predominantly religious community, mosques play an important role in the daily life of Muslims. Their design must be given careful attention, for they serve social as well as symbolic functions. An initial objective in designing a contemporary mosque should be to establish a proper proportion between the size of the mosque and the size of the congregation. Mosques must therefore be carefully distributed within neighborhoods to maintain convenient walking distances. There are two sizes of mosques: the small neighborhood mosque, and the Friday mosque (Masjid Jami). These mosques serve different communities. The neighborhood mosque serves 1000–3000 inhabitants and is located within walking distance. The Friday mosque, or the district mosque, serves a population of 5,000–12,000. It is also used for prayer on feast days and other related religious occasions.

Although the shape of the mosque can vary, the rectangle has traditionally been favored. Closeness to the minbar and direct visual contact with the Khatib are the two central criteria in deciding the shape of the prayer hall. One of the sayings of the Prophet instructs worshipers to go early to the mosque, to pray in the first rows, and to stand shoulder to shoulder with no space between them. This promotes the solidarity of the religious community. According to these criteria, the ideal plan is one that maximizes the length of the rows and minimizes their number. A rectangular plan with the longer side facing the Qibla works well. Traditionally, proportions of 1:2 and 1:3 have been used in the prayer halls of Persian and North African mosques.

A mosque can serve anywhere from a few hundred to several thousand worshipers. For certain religious occasions, larger congregations are not uncommon. In designing neighborhood mosques, a certain percentage of the population is used as a reference to determine the size. This percentage is not always constant, varying considerably from one country to another. In most communities the adult male population is indicative of the size of the congregation.

Since the ritual is very simple, mosques require little in the way of furniture. The area requirement per person is 1 m^2 (or 10 ft^2) in the form of a rectangle 80 cm (28 in.) wide, representing the space occupied by one person sitting, and 120 cm (48 in.) long, representing the space occupied by one person kneeling. To accommodate structural elements and other space-occupying facilities, a small percentage is added. The open courtyard that usually accompanies the prayer hall has traditionally served as a natural extension of it (Fig. 17). When the number of worshipers exceeds the expected size, the courtyard is used. Segregation of men and women is essential. In many contemporary mosques this is achieved by providing a mezzanine floor with a separate outside staircase, isolated from the main prayer hall. Women worshipers should be able to view the Khatib, but their prayer hall should be screened to allow them reasonable privacy.

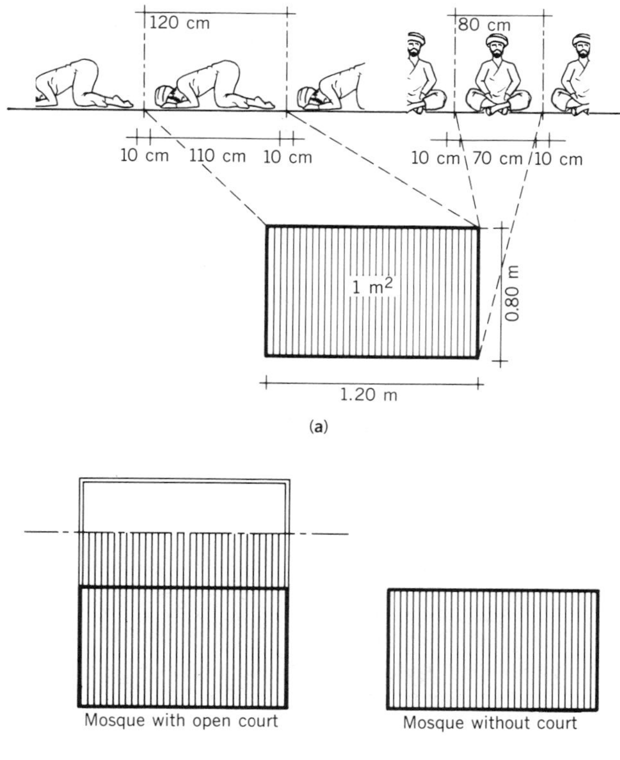

Figure 17. Mosque design standards (47). **(a)** Space requirement for a prayer in the mosque. Adding to this 20% in the case of small mosques and from 30 to 40% in the case of Jamaa mosque and 5% in the case of Eid mosque for annexes; **(b)** Efficient area of the mosque; the efficient area of the mosque with court is equal to the total of the covered area, plus half the area of the open court.

In communities that depend on vehicular transportation, parking has become important. Friday mosques should be provided with parking facilities, according to the local rate of car ownership.

The historical significance of many elements, described earlier, needs to be considered in designing a contemporary mosque. The minaret, for example, is not used today to make the call for prayer. This is done through the use of loudspeakers and, in many cases, using a recorded *Azzan*. In spite of this change in method, it is appropriate to use minarets for their acquired symbolic value, for they have become inseparable from the traditional image of the mosque.

In cultures where there was no minaret, other important elements acquired symbolic significance, and their traditional form should be considered in the design process.

This does not mean that there is no room for innovation, however. Building within contemporary societies challenges the architects to identify and create forms that are new but still familiar in the sense of conveying a specific Muslim identity. The designer of a mosque holds the ultimate responsibility of providing a building that is identifiable by a society for what it is. The design must display an understanding of the mosque's role, history, and symbolic significance. The major task of the architect is the creation of a structure that is representative of the spiritual aspirations and the social reality of Muslim society.

BIBLIOGRAPHY

1. E. Grube, "What is Islamic Architecture," in G. Michell, ed., *Architecture of The Islamic World,* William Morrow Inc., New York, 1978, pp. 10–14.
2. J. Hoag, *Islamic Architecture,* Harry Abrams Inc., New York, 1975.
3. D. Kuban, "The Geographical and Historical Basis for the Diversity of Islamic Architectural Styles," in A. German, ed., *Islamic Architecture and Urbanism,* K.F.U. Press, Dammam, Saudi Arabia, 1983, pp. 1–5.
4. In the spelling of all Arabic names in this entry, a specific transliteration system was not used. Instead the words were spelled as they are pronounced in their original languages. Throughout this article the dates of the Arabic Hijra calendar are not used. The Arabic calendar follows a lunar year and starts with Mohammed's flight to Medina in 622 A.D.
5. H. and R. Leacroft, *The Buildings of Early Islam,* Hodder & Stoughton, London, 1976.
6. Ref. 5, p. 35.
7. S. Almunjid, *Tarikh Madinat Dimashq,* Damascus, 1954.
8. A. Lezine, *Deux Villes d'Ifriqiya,* Paris, 1971.
9. A. Hourani and R. Stern, eds., *The Islamic City,* Bruno Cassirer, Oxford, England, 1970.
10. I. Lapidus, ed., *Middle Eastern Cities,* University of California Press, Berkeley, Calif., 1969.
11. C. Brown, ed., *From Madina to Metropolis,* Darwin Press, Princeton, N.J., 1973.
12. O. Grabar, *The Formation of Islamic Art,* Yale University Press, New Haven, Conn., 1973.
13. O. Grabar, "The Iconography of Islamic Architecture," in Ref. 3, pp. 6–16.
14. O. Grabar, "Symbols and Signs in Islamic Architecture," in *Architecture as Symbol and Self Identity,* Aga Khan Seminar Proceedings, Aga Khan Foundation, Geneva, 1979, pp. 1–11.
15. D. Kuban, "Symbolism in its Regional and Contemporary Context," in Ref. 14, p. 12.
16. N. Ardalan and L. Bakhtiar, *The Sense of Unity,* University of Chicago Press, Chicago, Ill., 1973.
17. K. Cresswell, *A Short Account of Early Islamic Architecture,* Penguin, London, 1958.
18. D. Kuban, *Muslim Religious Architecture,* E. J. Brill, Leiden, Netherlands, 1974.
19. Ref. 2, p. 24.
20. S. Kostof, *A History of Architecture,* Oxford University Press, New York, 1985.
21. P. Brown, *Indian Architecture—Islamic Period,* Bombay Press, Bombay, 1968.
22. M. De Graff, "The Origin of the Javanese Mosque," *Journal of South East Asian History* **14,** 1–6 (1963).
23. H. Camiwada, "L'Architecture Religieuse de L'Islam à Java," *Terra d'Islam* **7** (1935).
24. Ref. 5, p. 10.
25. Ref. 5, p. 6.
26. Ref. 15, p. 27.
27. N. Ardalan, "A Visual Language of Symbolic Forms," in Ref. 14, pp. 18–35.
28. Ref. 15, pp. 12–17.
29. Ref. 14, pp. 1–11.
30. M. Mahdi, "Islamic Philosophy and the Fine Arts," in Ref. 14, pp. 43–48.
31. "Key Monuments of Islamic Architecture," in Ref. 1, pp. 209–279.
32. Ref. 1, p. 209.
33. Ref. 1, p. 242.
34. Al Benaa, "The Mosque," *Alam El-Benaa* **1**(2) (1982).
35. Ref. 1, p. 270.
36. Ref. 1, p. 277.
37. J. Prijotoma, *Ideas and Forms of Javanese Architecture,* University of Jakarta, Jakarta, 1981.
38. J. Dickie, "Alah and Eternity: Mosques, Madrasa and Tombs," in Ref 1, pp. 15–47.
39. Ref. 5, p. 31.
40. Ref. 2, p. 220.
41. Ref. 2, p. 162.
42. L. Mayer, *Islamic Architects and their Works,* Geneva, 1956.
43. R. Lewlock, in Ref. 1, pp. 112–143.
44. Ref. 5, p. 11.
45. Ref. 5, p. 14.
46. D. Jones, "The Elements of Decoration, Surface Pattern and Light," in Ref. 1, pp. 144–175.
47. Y. Massignon, *Les Methodes de Realisation Artistiques des Peuples de l'Islam,* Paris, 1928.

General References

T. Burckhardt, *Art of Islam: Languages and Meaning,* London, 1976.

K. C. Creswell, *Early Muslim Architecture,* 2 vols., Oxford, 1932, revised 1969.

E. Esin, *Mecca the Blessed, Madinah the Radiant,* London, 1963.

E. J. Grube, *The World of Islam,* New York and Toronto, 1966.

L. Hautecour and G. Wiet, *Les Mosquees du Cairo,* 2 vols., Paris, 1932.

D. Hill and O. Grabar, *Islamic Architecture and its Decoration A.D. 800–1500,* London and Chicago, 1941.

J. Hoag, *Western Islamic Architecture,* New York, 1963.

A. Hutt, *Islamic Architecture: North Africa,* London, 1977.

A. Kuran, *The Mosque in Early Ottoman Architecture,* Chicago, 1968.

L. Prussin, *Hatumere: Islamic Design in West Africa,* Berkeley, Calif., 1986.

See also ISLAMIC ARCHITECTURE; NOMADIC ARCHITECTURE; RELIGIOUS ARCHITECTURE

NEZAR ALSAYYAD, PHD
GUITA BOOSTANI
University of California
Berkeley, California

MOTELS.

See Hotels

MOVEMENT OF PEOPLE

Human walking dates back about one million years; the ability to move habitually in a bipedal fashion separates humans from other creatures. Composed of swing and support phases, the stride that makes up walking has been described as "potentially catastrophic," a sequence of events where "a man sets out in pursuit of his center of gravity" (1). Despite its long history, human locomotion became the focus of serious scientific study relatively recently, approximately one hundred years ago with the extensive photographic analyses of Muybridge in 1884.

CULTURAL, SYMBOLIC, AND TECHNICAL IMPORTANCE

The focus of this article is on relatively mundane aspects of people's movement in and around buildings; however, it should be noted that cultural and symbolic aspects of movement are very important to building designers and others. Movement is an important cultural symbol as can be seen, for example, from ceremonial processions and their settings. Kaplan notes, "human locomotion delineates space, defines territory, creates spatial involvement. It is a form of communication, a sensory experience, environmental participation" (2). In kinesiology, the study of human movement, there is a major emphasis on human movement in dance, gymnastics, and sport. Indeed, a comprehensive text entitled, *Human Movement—A Field of Study,* makes no reference to human movement in the context of ordinary movement by individuals or crowds in and around buildings (3). In Templer's doctoral dissertation, *Stair Shape and Human Movement,* the first comprehensive historical and technical examination of this topic, he first describes the importance of stairs, especially their form, in relation to symbol and ceremony (4).

At the urban scale, the form of cities is strongly influenced by the need for human movement. Pedestrianization of entire streets is once again a basic concept in urban design. At the individual building scale, codes and safety standards, with their rules and guidelines on circulation route design (ie, means of egress), greatly influence the geometry of building spaces and some aspects of the walls, doors, etc, that define the spaces.

Despite its ubiquity, cultural significance, and importance in building safety, the movement of people in relation to building design has not been extensively studied. There have been remarkably few research programs on this topic in major building technology institutes and, in recent times, many of these programs have been terminated. Technical literature is neither complete nor well organized for designers and others concerned with people's movement in buildings. Therefore, this section can provide little more than an introduction, along with a small amount of more detailed information emphasizing certain functional issues such as movement safety and efficiency, and references containing additional information.

MOVEMENT SAFETY STATISTICS

When the safety of people using a built environment is examined, it is found that people's movement is one of the most hazardous activities. The relative extent of the hazards is not fully appreciated. By way of reference, the toll of fatalities from U.S. motor-vehicle accidents in 1984 exceeded 46,000; over 8000 of these involved pedestrians (with the proportion of pedestrian accidents especially high—over one third—in urban areas). Falls, excluding those in connection with transport vehicles, result in about 12,000 deaths annually in the United States (5). In a sample of five industrialized countries (the United States, Canada, Sweden, England and Wales, and Japan) the fall-fatality rate per 100,000 population ranged between 2.4 and 10.0 (6). The vehicle-accident fatality rate per 100,000 population in these countries ranged from 9.6 to 19.8 (7). In Sweden vehicle accidents and falls could have similar fatality rates, about 10 per 100,000 per year (6).

In the United States, the (leading) category of falls occurring on stairs has an annual fatality rate (about 2 per 100,000) just below the annual fatality rate from fires (2.9 per 100,000) (6). In countries having lower fire fatality rates (as low as 0.5 per 100,000 in Switzerland), fatal stair falls could be a relatively greater amount. In the United States some 800,000 hospital emergency department treatments annually are due to stair accidents (according to the U.S. Consumer Product Safety Commission); therefore, falls on stairs seriously injure at least 20 times more people than do fires (6).

Elderly people are especially prone to falls and vulnerable to serious injury. Relative to the general population, they are several times more likely to suffer a serious injury in a fall. The National Safety Council reports (8):

> Although the incidence of nonfatal falls is more difficult to ascertain, it has been estimated that at least one third of all elderly persons aged 60 and over suffer falls each year. A much smaller number are treated for injuries. National Health Survey data show that each year about 12 million persons in the U.S.A. are injured seriously enough in falls to require at least one day of restricted activity or medical attention. This number is unmatched by any other accident type.

DESIGN AND MANAGEMENT FOR SAFE AND EFFICIENT HUMAN MOVEMENT

Given its importance to design and use of buildings, it is surprising that there is not an up-to-date, comprehensive reference book covering the functional aspects of people's movement. The book entitled *Pedestrian Planning and Design,* based on John J. Fruin's doctoral dissertation, is currently the best single book addressing people's collective movement on walkways and stairs (9). It was out of print for several years but has recently reappeared in a slightly revised edition (10). This reference book is better known among engineers (eg, in transportation and fire protection fields) than among architectural designers. (The latter apparently refer to more general guidebooks, such as *Architectural Graphic Standards,* and the well-known national standard, *The Life Safety Code,* plus local building codes, especially in relation to means of egress.)

Key Quantitative Characteristics of People's Movement

Of the three key quantitative characteristics of people's movement, density, speed, and flow, the most important is the spatial density or, inversely, the area available to each person referred to as the "Pedestrian Area Module" by Fruin (9,10). (Density may be preferred to pedestrian area module when working in metric units, and *vice versa* when working in conventional U.S. units.) Density influences the other key characteristics: speed of movement, the distance covered in some unit of time; and flow, the number of persons passing a reference point in some unit of time. Consider, for example, a crowd of people distributed at an average density of 1.0 person/m^2 (0.09 person/ft^2). They might move along a 2.0-m (6.5-ft) wide walkway at a speed of 1.0 m/s (200 ft/min). These conditions would result in a flow of 2.0 persons/s (120 persons/min) or, stated in terms of a unit width, 1.0 person/s/m of width (18.5 persons/min/ft). The three key characteristics are mathematically related, along with path width, in the fundamental traffic equation:

$$\text{flow} = \text{speed} \times \text{density} \times \text{width} \qquad (1)$$

To use this equation correctly, a consistent set of units must be employed and speed must be measured in the horizontal plane. Dimensionally, the equation is

$$\frac{\text{person}}{\text{second}} = \frac{\text{meter}}{\text{second}} \times \frac{\text{person}}{\text{meter}^2} \times \text{meter} \qquad (2)$$

For calculations in conventional units, equation 3 (an alternative form of equation 1), may be preferred (9, 10):

$$\frac{\text{flow}}{\text{width}} = \frac{\text{speed}}{\text{area per person}} \qquad (3)$$

For example, on a walkway with 11 ft^2 (1.0 m^2) of area per person, a reasonable speed would be 210 ft/min (1.0 m/s) (9,10). Using equation 3, the flow per foot of walkway width is 19.1 persons/min (1.0 person/s). Fruin refers to the flow, expressed in persons per foot of walkway width per minute, as PFM (9,10).

Levels of Service

Using a precedent from highway engineering, the following useful classification for crowd movement has been developed: "Level of Service Design Standards" (9,10). There are six levels of service: A through F. The highest level is designated A. It has very low densities permitting individuals to move at freely-selected, independent speeds. The lowest level is F, one not recommended because it has very high crowd densities and severely restricted, slow walking speeds with major interference among people in the crowd.

Levels of service may be applied to three basic pedestrian situations: movement along level or ramped walkways, movement up or down stairs, and queuing (9,10). For example, on walkways, level of service A is described as having at least 35 ft^2 of area per person (a density of 0.31 person/m^2). Level of service F has less than 5 ft^2 of area per person (a density of 2.2 persons/m^2) resulting in very slow, shuffling speeds and a high, but variable flow of as much as 25 persons/min/ft (1.4 persons/s/m of walkway width).

The example used above, in connection with equation 3, with 11 ft^2 of area per person (1.0 person/m^2 density), falls within level of service D. It is suggested that designs consistent with this level of service represent only the most crowded public areas; however, level of service E could apply to "sports-stadium design, or rail transit facilities where there may be a large but short-term exiting of passengers from a train" (9,10).

For stairs, the respective levels of service provide somewhat less area per person and reduced speeds. For example, level of service D applies to situations with 7–10 ft^2 per person (1.5–1.1 persons/m^2 density) and accompanying stair descent speeds of 100–115 ft/min (0.50–0.58 m/s) measured horizontally. (Note that, for equations 1–3 to work properly, the horizontal component of speed must be used, rather than the speed along the slope of a stair or ramp.) This range of speeds is roughly equivalent to descending four stories of stairs per minute and the area per person allows a space approximately 3–4 treads long and 2–3 ft (0.6–0.9 m) wide. These conditions are similar to those observed in optimum-flow, evacuation exercises in office buildings (11).

Effect of Density on Speed and Flow

The relationship between density and speed is an inverse relationship; speed decreases as density increases. Figure 1 illustrates this with data for crowd movement down stairs in office-building evacuations as well as with a curve based on extrapolated data from other investigations (9,10). At very high densities—in the range of approximately 4–6 persons/m^2 (areas of 2.7–1.8 ft^2/person)—crowds become so congested that movement is no longer possible and a total blockage may ensue with serious consequences for safety. For example, the evacuation of people from a hazardous area might be critically delayed. There might also be intense psychological distress and physical crushing causing injuries and death.

Figure 2 illustrates the effect on flow of the combination of increasingly high density and decreasingly lower speed, specifically in relation to evacuation movement on stairs (11). Very few systematically collected data exist for densities exceeding 2 persons/m^2 (corresponding to an area of 5.4 ft^2/person). The available data suggest that as the densities increase, in the range of 2–4 persons/m^2 (5.4–2.7 ft^2/person), the flow drops to zero. There is an optimum density condition, around 2 persons/m^2 (5.4 ft^2/person), that permits efficient flow without seriously reducing comfort and safety. However, as noted below, unless there is an unusually large demand (by people wanting to use the circulation route) relative to its width, it is unlikely that a crowd will attain the optimum density, speed, and flow condition described here.

For example, on a stair with a nominal width (eg, wall-to-wall) of 66 in. (1.7 m), with an effective width (11,12) of 54 in. (1.4 m), it can be calculated that the optimum

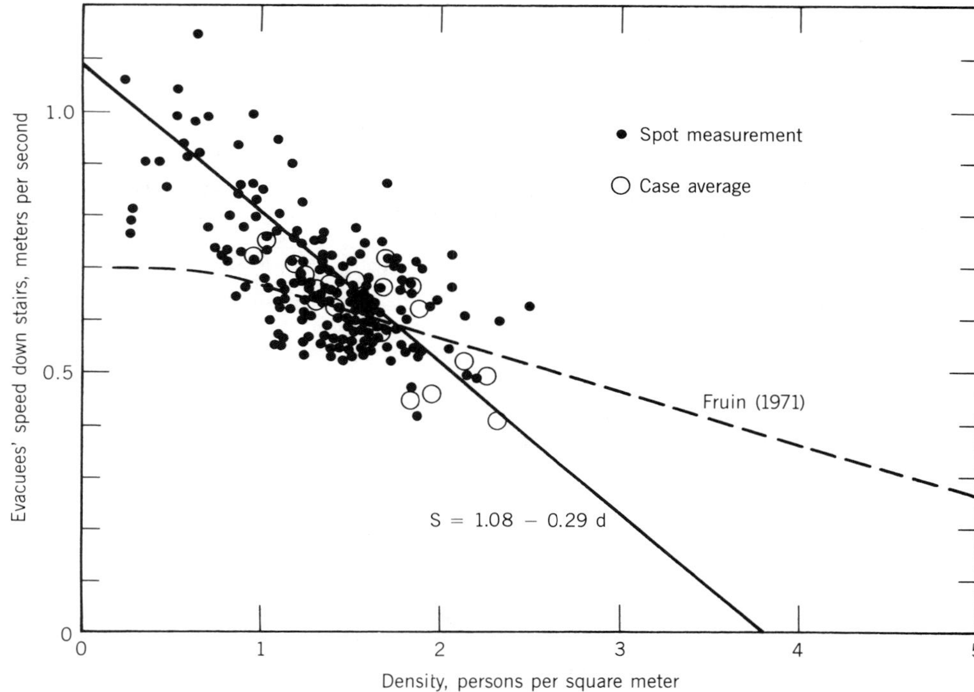

Figure 1. Relation between speed and density on stairs in office building evacuations (11).

flow is about 100 persons/min (calculated as 1.7 persons/s by multiplying the effective width of 1.4 m by the peak flow, in Fig 2, of nearly 1.2 persons/s/m of effective width). This flow condition, with about 18 persons/ft of nominal width per minute, lies on the boundary between levels of service E and F, ie, just barely acceptable for extremely busy stairs.

The concept of effective width of a circulation route, such as the stair in the preceding example, originally comes from Refs. 9 and 10, with additional empirical expansion for stairs (11,12) and for corridors (13). The effective width of stairs has also been covered in Appendix D to the 1985 edition of the *Life Safety Code* (14), which later became Chapter 2 in NFPA 101M, *Alternative Approaches to Life Safety* (15). The concept of effective width takes into account the fact that people will attempt to stay clear of boundaries of a circulation route, resulting in an edge effect. This is partly due to the lateral or side-to-side body sway that characterizes human gait, particularly at slower speeds. People must shift their upper bodies from one

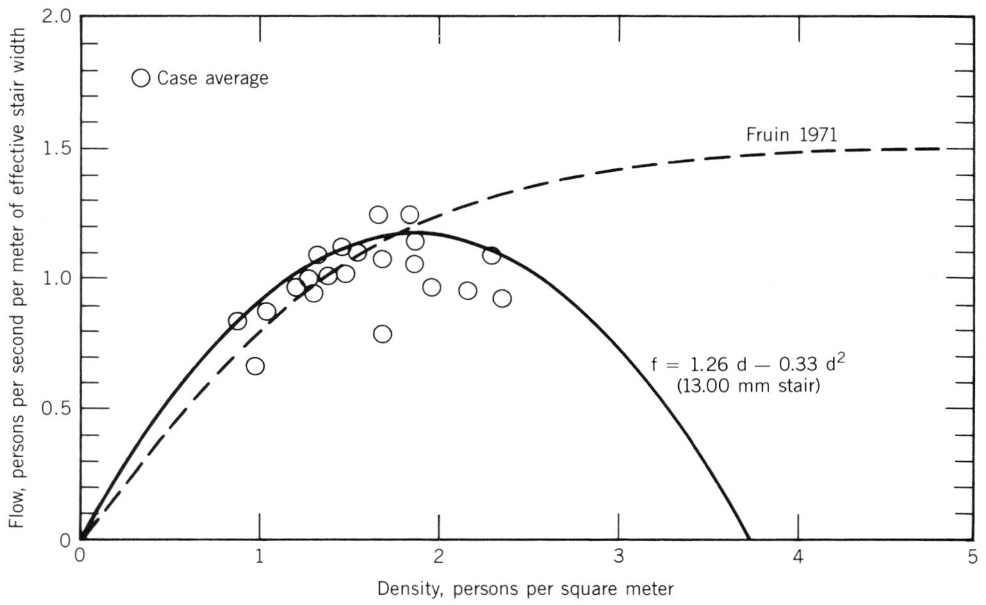

Figure 2. Relation between flow and density on stairs in office building evacuations (11).

side to another so that their center of gravity is approximately over the supporting foot on the walking surface. Body sway also influences the tendency for people not to walk shoulder-to-shoulder in regimented fashion or in regular lanes of movement.

Flow Time and Evacuation Time

Taking the preceding example (with the optimum flow calculation) further, it can be calculated that if the stair is one of three similar stairs that together serve a total population of 900 people (eg, in a theater), an optimistic prediction of the flow-time portion of the total evacuation time for the theater will be 3.0 min or 180 s. (This is easily calculated by dividing the flow of 100 persons/min, or 1.7 persons/s, into the population of 300.) Evacuation time, the factors contributing to it, and the dangers of overly optimistic predictions of flow and time are discussed at length in Ref. 16. (Ref. 17 addresses complementary safety concerns, beyond egress time efficiency, which influence width of egress stairs.)

Although this particular optimistic flow time of 3 min or 180 s is very close to the 200-s nominal flow time noted for small assembly occupancies in a new requirement for egress/evacuation capacity in the 1988 edition of the *Life Safety Code* (18), the Code is based on a more conservative calculation and does not permit this particular population and stair width condition. Taking into account the likelihood that flows would be significantly below the optimum value in the case of a small theater, the Code limits the population, using each of the three stairs, to 220 persons based on its requirement for 0.3 in. of nominal stair width per person, corresponding to level of service D with an average of about 12 persons/min/ft. Level of service D is "consistent with the more crowded public buildings and transportation terminals subjected to relatively severe peak demands" (9,10).

Only in a very large facility, such as a stadium that provides "smoke-protected assembly seating" and is protected against a range of life safety hazards, does the *Life Safety Code* (18) permit egress to occur at a lower level of service, with a large population served by relatively more-crowded egress routes and with a resulting longer flow time of about 660 s or 11 min. In this case we might expect egress flows at the optimum levels of about 18 persons/min/ft described above. Level of service E describes this condition, considered applicable only to "sports stadiums, or transit facilities where there is a large uncontrolled, short-term exodus of pedestrians" (9,10).

The above illustrates that crowd flow is influenced by the demand (the relative number of people wanting to use a circulation route) and by considerations of comfort, as perceived by members of the crowd and as reflected in the level-of-service classification. However, with increasing crowd density there comes a point where comfort and efficiency decrease drastically and where life safety is threatened. If density increases in an unchecked fashion toward the region of 0.5 person/ft^2 (5 persons/m^2), resulting in about 2 ft^2 of area per person, high flows can quickly drop to zero and crushing will begin.

CROWD-CRUSH INCIDENTS

Crowd incidents in which people are seriously injured or killed due to crushing or trampling are not restricted to emergencies such as fire or to conditions of crowd violence. Such incidents occur at sports events, religious gatherings, and rock music concerts. Fatalities and serious injuries can occur during entry, occupancy, and evacuation of a facility.

Between 1902 and 1972, there were 125 deaths and over 1000 injuries in eight crowd incidents at British football grounds. The most tragic of these, a 1971 incident at Ibrox Park, Glasgow, resulted in 66 fatalities due to a crowd crush on a stair at the conclusion of a football match.

Worldwide, the toll from crowd-crush incidents at sports events includes some 300 fatalities in Lima's National Stadium on May 24, 1964; over 95 fatalities in the National Stadium, Katmandu, Nepal, on March 12, 1988; 72 fatalities in Buenos Aires on June 23, 1968; 48 fatalities in Kayseri, Turkey, on September 17, 1967; 48 fatalities in Cairo's Zamalek Stadium on February 17, 1974; 38 fatalities in Brussels's Heysel Stadium on May 29, 1985, and 33 fatalities in Bolton, UK, on March 9, 1946. The above-mentioned Nepal National Stadium incident occurred when 30,000 spectators sought shelter from a hailstorm and encountered locked exit gates. This illustrates that spectator exuberance or fan violence at sports events, and crowd stampedes to escape fire in large buildings, are not the only causes of crowd incidents.

Rock music concerts and religious gatherings can also have crowd problems, as was seen in 1979 in the crowd crush that killed 11 people attempting to enter a concert by The Who at Cincinnati's Riverfront Coliseum; the crush that killed 21 people at a faith-healing session in Rio de Janeiro; and the crowd crush that killed six people prior to a papal mass in Brazil in October 1980. In addition, there are less-publicized incidents that have come close to being deadly, eg, crowd crushes associated with improper design or malfunction of escalators in public assembly buildings and in transit stations.

Comparing loss of life caused by fire with that caused by crowd incidents, it can be seen that crowd incidents are an equal if not greater hazard in very large buildings for public assembly. In terms of public and official concern, the crowd-crush incidents involving UK football fans—including the May 1985 crowd incident in Brussels—apparently had a greater impact in the UK than did the Bradford City football grandstand fire three weeks earlier, which killed 56 people. This is reflected in the reports of the Committee of Inquiry into Crowd Safety and Control at Sports Grounds, chaired by Mr. Justice Poppelwell (19,20) and in the *Guide to Safety at Sports Grounds* (21).

The record of crowd incidents is better in North America. In the United States, the best example of an official attempt to address crowd safety was the Task Force on Crowd Control and Safety set up by the City of Cincinnati (22) after the 1979 crowd crush at the concert by the rock group The Who. This task force addressed, in part, how to avoid the apparent problems of that event: management's failure to appreciate the seriousness of crowd conditions, failures in communication with those waiting to enter the building, and lack of coordination with police forces in the area. Facility management and event management play large roles in crowd safety.

The report by the City of Cincinnati did not fully address architectural design as a factor in crowd safety, but merely recommended a program of research on the topic at the U.S. National Bureau of Standards (NBS). The main contribution of NBS was its organization of a small-scale, one-day meeting of experts in May 1981. The report emphasized problems of ingress and included several recommendations such as the following (23):

> Strive for simplicity in all access and movement routes; this lessens the need for directional graphics and ushers. Capacity-handling channels should be continuous walking surfaces such as ramps. Stairs are satisfactory for shortening channels not subject to heavy pedestrian loads. . . . To the greatest extent possible, ingress systems should be "reversible," and usable whenever emergency egress is necessary.

To improve understanding of crowd incidents and their control, the following analysis is useful (24,25). Crowd incidents are often characterized by the following:

1. Rapid accumulation of queuing persons as the demand for a facility outstrips its supply or capacity.
2. Pedestrian densities approach about 0.67 person/ft^2 (7 persons/m^2); this critical density leaves no space between people. Shock waves, causing individuals to move involuntarily as much as 10 ft (3 m) laterally, can be seen moving through the crowds at this point.
3. Competitive rushing by a crowd away from something is termed "panic"; a competitive rush toward some objective (such as in the Cincinnati incident) is termed a "craze."

Four fundamental, interacting elements or factors are stressed (24,25): time, space, energy, and information. Design or management strategies based on control of one or more of these factors can avert or mitigate crowd incidents.

Regarding time, typically crowd incidents "occur in short periods of time when the critical capacity of a facility has been temporarily exceeded but intensive pressure to use the facility continues."

Regarding space, first, "when average densities in a crowd reach the approximate area of the human body, about 1.5 ft^2/person, individual control of movement becomes impossible." Second, the architectural layout of the space, eg, facility widths and confluence or crossing of circulation routes, can influence the likelihood of the occurrence of crowd congestion and dangerous jamming. Regarding the benefits of straightforward, unambiguous egress routes, Fruin quips, "in emergencies, 'the line-of-sight' becomes the 'line-of-flight.'"

Relative to the energy factor (24):

> The combined pressures of massed pedestrians and shock-wave effects through crowds at the critical density level produce forces which are impossible for individuals or even small groups of individuals to resist. Reports of persons being literally lifted out of their shoes and of clothes being torn off are a common result of the forces in crowd incidents. Survivors of crowd disasters report difficulty in breathing due to crowd pressures, and asphyxia is a more typical cause of death than trampling by the crowd.

It is estimated that forces were as high as 1100 lb (5.0 kN), in crowd incidents in which steel pipe railings were bent by the crush of the crowds.

Information involves both the network of people who are supervising crowds and the communication among crowd members. Crowd incidents often exhibit what can be termed a failure of front-to-back communication (and vice versa). People at the back of an unorganized or bulk queue may contribute unknowingly to the forces that can build up in the crowd. Such forces can reach crushing levels in the middle of the crowd or at the front where there is a barrier. The people being crushed are unable to communicate information about their plight to those at the back. Among the design and management solutions to this general problem is management's close observation of crowd conditions, combined with technology and an ability to communicate the condition and recommended action to people in the crowd. A potentially very effective technique, applicable to some rock music concerts and major sports events, is to utilize in-place video cameras (provided for security or for telecasting) and in-place video displays to let people know what is happening in those areas of the crowd that would not be visible otherwise. Having such potent visual information about what is happening to their peers elsewhere in the crowd should help to reduce the cumulative crowd pressure that might otherwise occur.

MOBILITY DISABILITIES

Mobility impairments to individuals can result from a variety of causes: amputation and the need to use a prosthesis or aid; muscular dystrophy; multiple sclerosis; obesity; orthopedic disorders; spina bifida; spinal cord injury (SCI) resulting in paraplegia or quadriplegia; stroke; and use of alcohol or drugs. Over the last few decades there have been special efforts in many countries to remove physical barriers to the movement of people with such disabilities. Most visible have been the special provisions made for people using wheelchairs. The U.S. National Center for Health Statistics provides an indication of the number of people using various mobility aids within the noninstitutionalized population. The statistics are expressed below as a percentage of the noninstitutionalized population in the United States (26):

0.30%	Wheelchairs
0.29%	Crutches
0.32%	Walkers
0.19%	Braces on leg or foot
0.47%	Braces elsewhere
0.10%	Artificial limb (leg or foot)

0.70%	Special shoes
1.28%	Cane or walking stick

Overall, approximately 3.0% of the noninstitutionalized population use one or more of these mobility aids. With elderly persons, having a greatly increased use of certain aids (eg, wheelchairs, walkers, and canes), this percentage rises sharply: 8.4% for people 65–74 years of age; 22.4% for people 75 years of age and over. (These increases parallel the increases in rates of fatalities from falls. For many elderly people, the need for walking aids arises from either disability after a fall or increased concern over experiencing a fall.)

Accessibility standards, such as that of the American National Standards Institute, ANSI A117.1 (27), and a wide variety of barrier-free design guides deal extensively with architectural compensations for mobility impairments, including those impairments virtually ruling out the use of stairs. Note that something on the order of 1.0% of the noninstitutionalized population cannot use stairs. However, this percentage is influenced by the greater need for walkers and wheelchairs by people over the age of 65. Therefore, the percentage of younger and middle-aged adults unable to use stairs in many work situations (such as office buildings) is on the order of 0.5%. Ramps may be helpful to some of the people who cannot use stairs; however, ramps also present mobility difficulties. Some people may, therefore, prefer stairs even though they are much more hazardous.

Generally, to assist a wide range of people with mobility disabilities (but not necessarily needing wheelchairs), much greater attention needs to be placed on three basic criteria for safe, functional circulation routes (28):

1. The walking surface(s) must be easily seen, with special attention drawn to any discontinuities such as individual, isolated steps, which should be avoided in design.
2. The geometry and finish of the walking surfaces should reduce the chance of slipping, tripping, and misstepping.
3. Effective supports such as continuous, easily reached, graspable handrails must be provided to aid in normal postural support and recovery in case of misstep.

These basic criteria are appreciated by elderly users of circulation facilities, especially stairs. However, all too often these basic easily understood criteria are ignored in the design and maintenance of these facilities.

CIRCULATION ROUTE, MODAL CHOICES, AND EXTENT OF USE

Modal choice is simply a person's selection of one of the facility options available for moving from one point to another, eg, choosing to use an escalator rather than a stair, or walking on the sidewalk instead of riding a bus. Modal choice and extent of facility use are important considerations in the design and use of urban environments and individual buildings, including homes. They influence design decisions (on the type, quality, and extent of facility provision) and operating decisions (on maintenance and other scheduling).

Modal choice at an urban scale, for example, was studied by documenting how people got to their final destinations from the New York Port Authority Bus Terminal (9,10). One third walked during the springtime period of the survey. "For up to 1000 feet from the terminal virtually all persons walked; up to one mile almost 50% walked; and two miles was the practical walking limit." Movement from curb to plane (or vice versa) in airport terminals has also been studied, and it is suggested that this takes approximately 5–7 min at some major airports (to cover 1100–1800 ft [335–550m]). Increasingly, terminals are being built either to reduce this distance or to provide alternative modes such as moving walkways, automated pedestrian movers (eg, trains), and electric carts. Additional information on urban-scale pedestrian movement and modal choices is found in a book based on extensive studies in New York City (29).

Even less studied and less well documented is people's movement inside particular kinds of buildings. In the largest of three office buildings (a 21-story, 3-tenant building with an observed peak occupancy of 3500 persons) in a 1977 study, there was an average of 3.5 uses of the exit stairs per person per day (30). Many of these uses were work related; they occurred over the entire course of the working day. Indeed the highest usage occurred in the vicinity of the fifteenth and sixteenth floors of the building: about 500 uses per day over a five-day documentation period. Stair use, which was comparable to elevator use in terms of number of trips, was favored because of time efficiency, exercise value, and other reasons (31).

As one part in a series of studies by the U.S. National Bureau of Standards (funded by the U.S. Consumer Product Safety Commission), a sample of 229 people in Milwaukee homes reported the normal home stair usage averaged nearly 20 flights per person per day (32). (Remarkably, seven people over 75 years of age reported an average of nearly 19 uses per person per day.) By using data from these and other sources, it was estimated that in 1975 in the United States there were approximately two trillion flight uses of stairs including some 31 million minor accidents and 2.66 million disabling accidents with about 540,000 requiring hospital treatment (33).

RECENT HISTORY OF RESEARCH AND PROSPECTS FOR THE TECHNOLOGY

It would have been easier in the 1970s than in the 1980s to provide a basic list of key research establishments and professional organizations concerned with people's movement in relation to the design of buildings and streets. Despite the huge social problems and opportunities presented by human movement, the 1980s brought reduced opportunities for technical advancement and sharing of knowledge. Important knowledge centers were closed or teams of experts were split up, with individual researchers often moving on to related fields of inquiry and technology transfer. Key North American examples include the termination of building use and safety studies, which had emphasized human movement in and around buildings, at the National Research Council of Canada; the termination of environmental psychology studies emphasizing stair use and safety, for example, at the U.S. National Bureau of Standards; the retirement of pedestrian movement authority John J. Fruin from the Research Department at the Port Authority of New York and New Jersey; and the end of a networking activity, PEDNET, which had been sustained through the efforts of Michael Hill at the University of Nebraska.

During the 1980s there has been reduced research activity on human movement issues, especially for nonstreet settings, within meetings of large professional organizations such as the Transportation Research Board. However, proceedings of the Environmental Design Research Association (EDRA) continue to include papers and workshop summaries covering movement topics from functional and social points of view. Complementing the broader environmental design coverage of EDRA conferences were a few smaller meetings (in 1985, 1986, 1987, and 1988) focusing on building use and safety, especially human movement issues (34,35). The 1985 and 1988 conferences dealt extensively with orientation and wayfinding, a topic pursued at the University of Montreal and the University of Wisconsin-Milwaukee that grew during the 1980s (36,37). Also related to orientation and wayfinding was research funded by the U.S. Architectural and Transportation Barriers Compliance Board (ATBCB), such as that performed at the Georgia Institute of Technology concerning the evaluation of detectable walkway surfaces with respect to the navigation capabilities of people with vision impairments (38). The related topic of people's ability to move through indoor spaces under conditions of very low-level illumination has also been addressed during the 1980s by researchers in the UK, most notably P. R. Boyce at the UK Electricity Research Council and G. M. B. Webber at the UK Building Research Establishment (39,40).

Although the growth of knowledge has slowed during the 1980s, there have been major revolutionary changes in U.S. model building codes and NFPA safety standards in relation to means of egress and stair design. These changes have been largely based on research done in the United States and Canada during the 1970s. Designers are cautioned that many rules of circulation route design, enshrined in model building codes and safety standards and accepted with little critical thought for decades, underwent significant change beginning in 1981 (41,42). One example (arising from research such as that reported in Ref. 11) is the replacement of traditional egress capacity calculation methods, based on units of exit width, with new capacity calculation methods based on smaller, per-person width increments. To achieve a cost-effective design—especially with the increasing threat of litigation and particularly following movement-related accidents—careful attention should be paid to the state of the art as represented by the latest edition of the leading life safety standard for circulation route design, the *Life Safety Code,* NFPA 101 (18), by its accompanying manual, NFPA 101M (15), and by the *Life Safety Code Handbook* (43). Attention is also drawn to the new *SFPE Handbook of Fire Protection Engineering* that contains an extensive chapter on movement of people in its fundamentals section (44) and a chapter on related applications and calculations. Even the relatively well-used design reference, *Architectural Graphics Standards,* with its more traditional collection of design advice, has recently added a page of technical guidance on a special design situation where the movement of people is very important, ie, aisle stairs in grandstands and bleachers (45). As noted in that guidance, designers of large-scale facilities for public assembly and movement should be aware of more complex, performance-based approaches to means of egress introduced into the 1988 edition of the *Life Safety Code* (18). These approaches might entail evaluations of life safety and considerations of circulation design that demand special expertise, going beyond what is gleaned from publications such as technical encyclopedias and handbooks.

BIBLIOGRAPHY

1. J. Napier, "The Antiquity of Human Walking," *Scientific American,* 56 (April 1967).
2. A. Kaplan, "Designing for Man in Motion," *AIA Journal,* 42 (Nov. 1971).
3. J. D. Brooke and H. T. A. Whiting, eds., *Human Movement—A Field of Study,* Henry Kimpton Publishers, London, 1973.
4. J. A. Templer, *Stair Shape and Human Movement,* PhD. dissertation, Columbia University, New York, 1974.
5. *Accident Facts, 1985 Edition,* National Safety Council, Chicago, Ill., 1985, pp. 8, 41.
6. J. Pauls, *Firesafety Within the Context of Building Use and Safety,* presentation to the National Fire Protection Association Annual Meeting, Atlanta, Ga., May 1986.
7. Ref. 5, p. 49.
8. Ref. 5, p. 83.
9. J. J. Fruin, *Pedestrian Planning and Design,* Metropolitan Association of Urban Designers and Environmental Planners, Inc., New York, 1971.
10. J. J. Fruin, *Pedestrian Planning and Design,* Elevator World, Educational Services Division, Mobile, Ala., 1987.
11. J. Pauls, "Building Evacuation: Research Findings and Recommendations," in D. Canter, ed., *Fires and Human Behaviour,* John Wiley & Sons, Chichester, UK, 1980, pp. 251–275.
12. J. Pauls, "The Movement of People in Buildings and Design Solutions for Means of Egress," *Fire Technology* **20**(1), 27 (1984).
13. A. T. Habicht and J. P. Braaksma, "Effective Width of Corridors," *Transportation Engineering* **110**(1), 80 (1984).
14. *Life Safety Code, NFPA 101,* National Fire Protection Association, Quincy, Mass., 1985, Appendix D.
15. *Alternative Approaches to Life Safety, NFPA 101M,* National Fire Protection Association, Quincy, Mass., 1988.
16. J. Pauls, "Calculating Evacuation Times for Tall Buildings," *Fire Safety Journal* **12,** 213 (1987).
17. J. Pauls, "Are Functional Handrails Within Our Grasp?" in *Proc. of Environmental Design Association Annual Conference, 1987,* Ottawa, Canada, pp. 121–127.
18. *Life Safety Code, NFPA 101,* National Fire Protection Association, Quincy, Mass., 1988, Chap. 8.

19. J. Poppelwell, *Interim Report,* Committee of Inquiry into Crowd Safety at Sports Grounds, Her Majesty's Stationery Office, London, UK, July 1985.
20. J. Poppelwell, *Final Report,* Committee of Inquiry into Crowd Safety at Sports Grounds, Her Majesty's Stationery Office, London, UK, January 1986.
21. Home Office/Scottish Office, *Guide to Safety at Sports Grounds,* Her Majesty's Stationery Office, London, UK, 1986.
22. *Report of the Task Force on Crowd Control and Safety,* City of Cincinnati, Cincinnati, Ohio, 1980.
23. T. F. Ventre and co-workers, *Crowd Ingress to Places of Assembly: Summary and Proceedings of an Expert's Workshop,* NBSIR 81–2361, Center for Building Technology, U.S. National Bureau of Standards, Gaithersburg, Md., 1981.
24. *Ibid.,* Appendix C.
25. J. J. Fruin, "Crowd Dynamics and Auditorium Management," *Auditorium News* **22**(5), 4, 5, 14 (1984).
26. *Vital and Health Statistics,* National Center for Health Statistics, 1977 National Health Survey, Series 10, No. 135, Tables 1 and 2.
27. *American National Standard for Buildings and Facilities—Providing Accessibility and Usability for Physically Handicapped People,* ANSI A117–1, American National Standards Institute, New York, 1986.
28. J. Pauls, "What Can We do to Improve Stair Safety?," *Building Standards* **9–12,** 42, (May–June 1984); 13, 42, (July–August 1984).
29. B. Pushkarev and J. M. Zupin, *Urban Space for Pedestrians: A Report of the Regional Plan Association,* The MIT Press, Cambridge, Mass., 1975.
30. B. M. Johnson and J. Pauls, "Study of Personnel Movement in Office Buildings," in R. J. Beck, ed., *Health Impacts of the Use, Evaluation and Design of Stairways in Office Buildings,* Health Programs Branch, Health and Welfare Canada, Ottawa, 1977, pp. 75–92.
31. R. J. Beck, ed., *Health Impacts of the Use, Evaluation and Design of Stairways in Office Buildings,* Health Programs Branch, Health and Welfare Canada, Ottawa, 1977.
32. D. H. Carson and co-workers, *Safety on Stairs,* NBS-BSS 108, Center for Building Technology, U.S. National Bureau of Standards, Gaithersburg, Md., 1978, p. 40.
33. J. C. Archea and co-workers, *Guidelines for Stair Safety,* NBS-BSS 120, Center for Building Technology, U.S. National Bureau of Standards, Gaithersburg, Md., 1979, p. 3.
34. J. Pauls, "Building Use and Safety: Conference Introduction and Summary," in *Proc. of International Conference on Building Use and Safety Technology, Los Angeles,* National Institute of Building Sciences, Washington, D.C., 1985, pp. 1–8.
35. J. D. Sime, ed., *Safety in the Built Environment,* E and F N Spon, London, 1988.
36. R. Passini, *Wayfinding in Architecture,* Van Nostrand Reinhold Co., Inc., New York, 1984.
37. G. D. Weisman, "Orientation, Pathfinding, and Architectural Legibility: a Review and Theoretical Integration," in *Proc. of International Conference on Building Use and Safety Technology, Los Angeles,* National Institute of Building Sciences, Washington, D.C., 1985, pp. 9–15.
38. J. A. Sanford, "Designing for Orientation and Safety," in *Proc. of International Conference on Building Use and Safety Technology, Los Angeles,* National Institute of Building Sciences, Washington, D.C., 1985, pp. 54–59.
39. P. R. Boyce, "Movement Under Emergency Lighting: the Effect of Illuminance," *Lighting Res. Technol.* **17**(2), 51 (1985).
40. G. M. B. Webber, "Emergency Lighting Recommendations," in *Proc. of International Conference on Building Use and Safety Technology, Los Angeles,* National Institute of Building Sciences, Washington, D.C., 1985, pp. 61–74.
41. J. Pauls, "Research Applications Related to Building Code Requirements for Means of Egress," in *Research and Design 85: General Proceedings,* American Institute of Architects, Washington, D.C., 1985, pp. 235–240.
42. J. Pauls, "Building Use and Safety: an Overview with Emphasis on Current Research Applications to Codes and Standards," in *Proc. of the Human Factors Society 28th Annual Meeting,* Vol. 2, Human Factors Society, Santa Monica, Calif., 1984, pp. 555–559.
43. J. Lathrop, ed., *Life Safety Code Handbook,* National Fire Protection Association, Quincy, Mass., 1988.
44. J. Pauls, "Movement of People," in P. DiNenno, ed., *SFPE Handbook of Fire Protection Engineering,* National Fire Protection Association, Quincy, Mass., 1988, Section 1, Chap. 15.
45. J. Pauls, "Grandstand and Bleacher Circulation Safety," in J. R. Hoke Jr., ed., *Architectural Graphic Standards,* 8th ed., John Wiley & Sons, New York, 1988, p. 675.

General References

P. DiNenno, ed., *SFPE Handbook of Fire Protection Engineering,* National Fire Protection Association, Quincy, Mass., 1988.

J. J. Fruin, *Pedestrian Planning and Design,* Elevator World, Educational Services Division, Mobile, Ala., 1987. Chapter 4 covers Levels of Service design standards for circulation facilities.

J. R. Hoke Jr., ed., *Architectural Graphic Standards,* 8th ed., John Wiley & Sons, New York, 1988. Basic information on anthropometrics and circulation space requirements is provided on pp. 2–8.

J. Lathrop, ed., *Life Safety Code Handbook,* National Fire Protection Association, Quincy, Mass., 1988. This provides the complete text of NFPA 101–1988, the *Life Safety Code,* and extensive commentaries including explanations of major changes in approaches to means of egress.

J. Panero and M. Zelnik, *Human Dimension & Interior Space: A Source Book of Design Reference Standards,* Whitney Library of Design, New York, 1979. A well-illustrated reference on anthropometrics and spatial layout.

See also American National Standards Institute (ANSI); American Society for Testing and Materials (ASTM); Architectural and Transportation Barriers Compliance Board (ATBCB); Fire Safety—Life Safety; Physical and Mental Disabilities, Design for; Zoning and Building Regulations

Jake Pauls
Hughes Associates, Inc.
Wheaton, Maryland

MOVIE THEATERS.

See Theaters and Opera Houses

MULTIFAMILY HOUSING

The term multifamily housing describes habitations in which three or more families live independently of each other in the same building. This building type includes multiple dwellings, apartments, buildings containing flats, and row houses that are on the same lot and are provided collectively with essential public services. Some very large multifamily housing developments contain all of these building types. Multifamily buildings may be owned or rented by the occupants, or the occupants may own stock in the entity that owns and operates the building. By far the most common arrangement is for the tenant to pay a monthly rent to the owner of the building. The owner may be an individual, a company, or a governmental agency.

Multifamily housing types vary widely in size and configuration. This category includes everything from a frame "three-flat" to a development such as Co-op City in the Bronx, New York, which contains 35 high-rise towers, 236 low-rise town house units, and a total population of over 60,000 people. There are three distinct structural types that are commonly used in multifamily housing: wood frame for two- or three-story buildings; masonry or concrete panel bearing wall for three- to seven-story midrise buildings; and steel or concrete frame for high-rise buildings. Each of these types is uniquely appropriate to specific urban, suburban, or rural contexts and to specific occupant groups.

There are several important reasons for the construction of multifamily habitations. The first and most important reason is a scarcity of buildable land, which may be the result of local geographic conditions or the result of the containment of many people and many functions within a rigidly imposed boundary such as a fortification. A second reason is the efficiency of the building process and the relative economy in the use of materials that is possible when three or more families are housed under the same roof and share the basic elements of building construction, the foundations, the enclosing walls, and mechanical services. The third reason is social in nature and relates to the apparent need for closeness in some societies; the desire to share living costs, child care, and food preparation; and the desire for security. These same reasons for the growth of congregate housing exist today as they have existed for centuries in the history of human communities.

EARLY EXAMPLES OF MULTIFAMILY HOUSING

The Romans were great builders and community planners. They built apartment houses six or seven stories high in the centers of their great cities, and they built high-density units of up to three stories in much smaller towns throughout the Roman Empire. There is evidence that there were apartments constructed for poor families, and there were luxury buildings as well. This pattern has persisted in multifamily housing from Roman times well into the twentieth century. The highest densities in housing seem to be the domains of the richest and the poorest elements of a society. The poorest tended to be squeezed into the least possible space, and the richest, by choice, wished to be close to each other, toward the center of the action.

There were well-planned and well-constructed apartments in some of the Roman colonies. Room sizes often exceeded those of contemporary luxury units in apartments built for prosperous Roman townspeople. Reconstructed plans of apartment houses in Ostia show living rooms that are 27 m^2, dining rooms that are 18 m^2, and bedrooms that are up to 19 m^2 in size, all quite acceptable by today's standards.

On the North American continent, over a thousand years ago, the Anasazi Indians were building what today would be called "new towns" in the desert Southwest. Their structures, typified by Pueblo Bonito in New Mexico, combined in one complex the functions of dwellings for the families of the group, the workrooms for food preparation and clothes making, and the ritual or religious functions. These structures appear to have been carefully preplanned, were well constructed of fire-resistant materials, and were richly ornamented. The cliff dwellings of the Anasazi at Mesa Verde were probably at the high point of their planning and engineering cycle. The relatively barren landscape of the region, with its scarcity of water and wood for building and cooking, required an extensive kind of infrastructure to serve these high-density sites. It was not enough to construct just the dwelling units on the mesas or against the sides of cliffs; it was also necessary to build roads and waterworks to extract from the environment the essentials of living for the occupants. These communities thrived for hundreds of years. The inhabiting tribes moved on at some point, probably because of an exhausted ecological environment, but many of their dwellings remain today as evidence of the quality of their construction.

The real growth of the multifamily type of building came in the wake of the rapid acceleration of manufacturing and commerce, known as the Industrial Revolution, that took place after the mid-eighteenth century. First in the UK, then in other European countries, and later in the United States, this movement toward urbanization brought about successive waves of migration of people from the countryside to the city and from agricultural countries to industrial countries. These people came in need of shelter, but with little money. They could afford to rent housing, but not to buy it, especially in view of the new scarcity of land near the mills and factories. The almost immediate result was gross overcrowding and a lack of sanitation that led to the spread of disease. The picture for most inhabitants of industrial cities at this point was quite bleak.

Conditions were so bad that few families with the means to live in a detached house would choose to live in an apartment building. This bias was especially strong in the United States and still exists today in many parts of the country. For most of the nineteenth century and into the first third of the twentieth century, many of the workers in the industrialized cities in the world were stacked into narrow buildings three to six stories high in the rear yards of converted town houses, with little sunlight and fresh air and with crudely fashioned common toilet facilities.

In 1833 the first building constructed for use as a tenement house was occupied in New York City. Thousands of tenement houses were constructed in the years that followed. Constructed on any available parcel of land, most had interior rooms with no windows, a single outside privy for the whole building, and a single water spigot for each of the three or four floors. In 1878 a slightly improved prototype was developed that had somewhat greater fire resistance and minimal air shafts for the ventilation of interior rooms. In 1879 the New York City Tenement Law, which regulated to a rather modest degree the construction of this type, was passed. Successive improvements in the laws were written, each resulting in somewhat more humane forms of shelter than the previous laws required. It has been a characteristic of housing construction for more than 100 years that minimum standards, once imposed, become a kind of general standard of performance. The "old-law" tenement (1879–1901) (Fig. 1) was followed by various permutations of the "new-law" tenement (1901–1929) (Fig. 2), which had larger yards at the rear, better courtyard ventilation, and running water and toilets in each apartment. Housing after 1929 was regulated by the Multiple Dwelling Law of that year, which was more comprehensive in nature and regulated housing design into the 1970s.

Most multifamily housing construction up to about 1850 was for occupancy by the working classes. Apartments for the well-to-do were constructed in Paris in the middle of the nineteenth century. Although designed to be attractive in design from the street, these early apartment types in Paris and Vienna were often jammed onto very small sites and had interior lighting and ventilating standards that were not much better than those provided for the working poor. In a relatively short period these standards

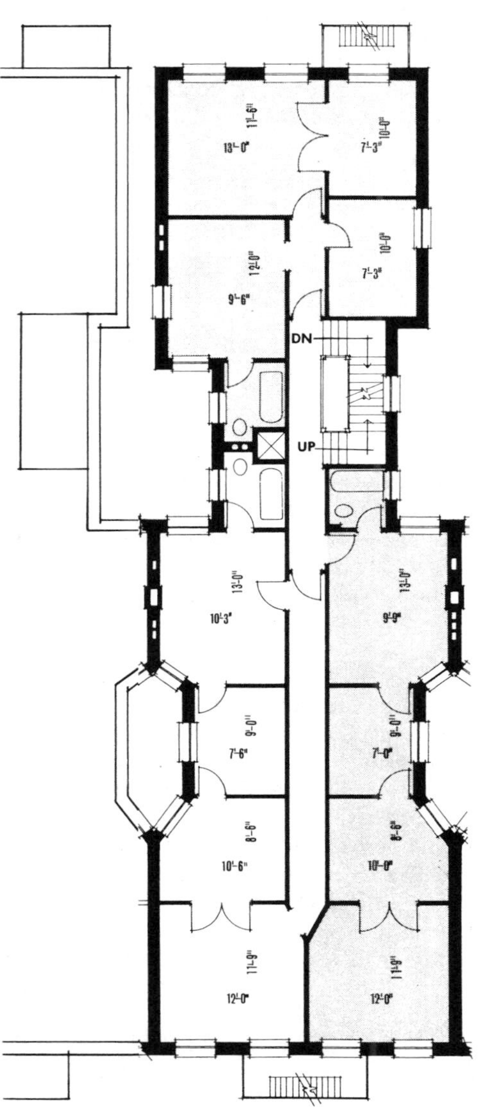

Figure 1. Plan of an old-law tenement, New York City. This type was built between 1879 and 1901. Old-law tenements have been called the worst type of legally constructed housing in the history of multifamily housing. Courtesy of the Architects' Renewal Committee in Harlem, Inc. (ARCH).

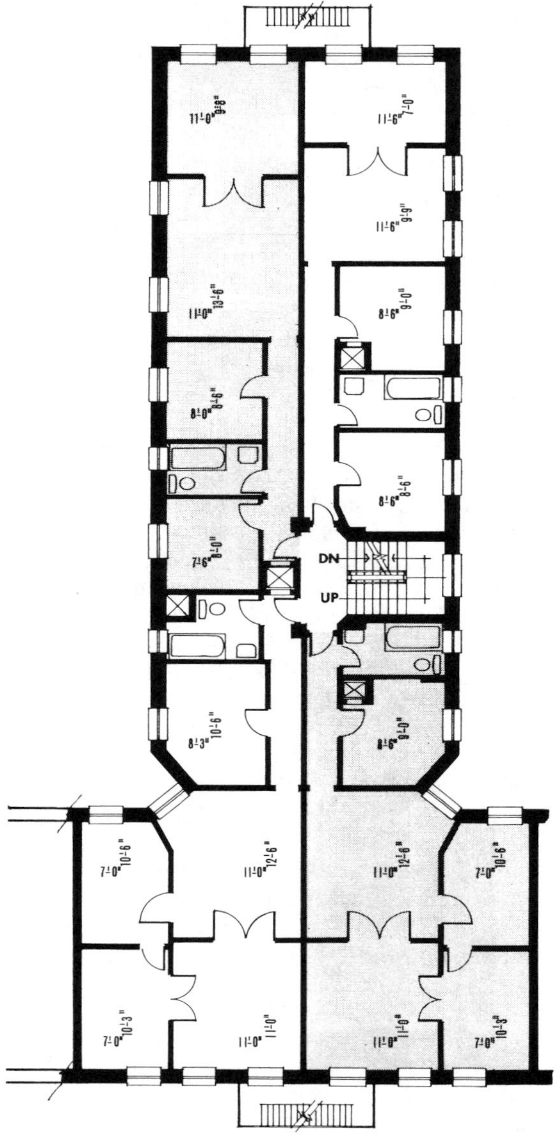

Figure 2. Plan of an early new-law tenement, New York City, constructed between 1901 and 1915. This type was an improvement over previous types, but was still marginal in lighting, ventilation, and circulation.

improved, and the idea of luxury flats spread to the UK. Advancement in the application of the electric elevator to apartment buildings made the multistory luxury home both practical and attractive to well-heeled urban dwellers. Residence in a floor-through flat on an upper floor had the advantage of privacy and distance from the sounds and smells of the street, with the potential of an attractive view from the windows as well.

The Dakota Apartments, completed in 1884, were the first luxury multiple dwellings built in New York City. The Dakota featured high ceilings, well-proportioned formal rooms that were the equal of the best townhouses of the day, four elevators, rooms for servants on the upper floors, and a fine view over Central Park. For more than 100 years it has continued to be one of the best addresses in New York City.

Multiple dwellings were not confined to cities the size of New York, Paris, or London during this period. In almost every town that had a concentration of industry, or had mills or railroads, such buildings were to be found, usually fairly small in size, but repeated many times over in a given neighborhood. In New England, the usual type was the "triple decker," a wood-framed building with porches on the front and rear, on a lot with narrow side yards.

The all-frame types were usually three stories high; in more densely developed areas the exterior walls were of masonry, and the height increased to four or five stories. It has been estimated that by the year 1930 fully half of the residents of the city of Boston lived in housing of this type.

With the Great Depression of the 1930s in the United States came a new urgency for the replacement of old and decaying housing stock. The Federal Public Housing Administration was created in 1937 and for the first time put the federal government in the business of producing housing on a large scale. The original idea was to replace run-down, substandard, slum dwellings with new sanitary units. Some of the earliest units of this type are some of the best in use today. The reasons for this are many, but it is certain that the first projects were relatively low in overall density and were well constructed because of the wide availability of skilled labor at the time. The first tenants were carefully selected and included many civil servants and schoolteachers, who were proud of their new homes.

The public housing activities of the federal government were matched in many states by similar local programs, both growing in importance in the late 1930s and again after World War II. The public housing movement went into decline in the early 1970s because of increasingly complex and difficult political impediments, usually resulting in site selection problems, excessive delays, and high costs. By this time there were other production devices and incentives for the production of housing, such as the "numbered" programs, 608, 221.d.3, and 236, which offered mortgage insurance to the developer, subsidies to the tenant, below-market interest rates, or all of these things in the interest of greater production of low- and moderate-income housing.

Public housing was and remains the best hope of the poorest families. Later programs have targeted higher-income groups. Public housing brought the concept of multifamily living to communities that had not seen it before, setting the stage for later developments in the private sector in housing. It also set a standard for the private market to follow in terms of minimum standards and basic amenities. There are many examples of public housing design that match the best private market standards 40 years after being built. There are also a few well-publicized examples of projects that did not work. The Pruitt-Igoe project in St. Louis, Missouri, was a project of enormous size that was hailed as an example of outstanding design when first built in 1955, but was taken down in 1974 because it became unmanageable, having too large a concentration of families with multiple problems. It was a high-rise misfit in a community of two-story living. Similar problem projects in other cities have been converted successfully to occupancy by older persons in good health, who enjoy and in fact prefer high-rise living.

REGULATORY PARAMETERS FOR THE DESIGN OF MULTIFAMILY HOUSING

The design of a building for occupancy by more than two families is determined to a large degree by the group of regulations in effect in the locality of the proposed project. The driving factor in the building of housing of this type by the private sector is the desire to extract the maximum economic potential from the land being developed. This maximum potential is established as public policy by the zoning resolutions and development standards of the community. These are often political in nature, rather than purely analytical. A local community may decide, for example, that it does not wish to have multifamily housing of any kind, or it may select particular areas for such use or zones for varying densities of housing. This relates to the nature and scope of local concerns about the need for housing. In the United States, for example, much of the power to regulate rests with the local city, township, or county, and occasionally with the state, but not with the federal government, except in the case of land actually owned by the federal government.

In many other countries, these decisions are made at the level of the national government. In the UK after World War II, the government, faced with a housing shortage in the built-up cities and a desire to create new subcenters away from the heart of London and other rebuilding areas, set out to build new city centers on largely undeveloped land, containing housing of varying degrees of density, the essential community services, and job centers as well. These developments were conceived and built more or less over localized interests and concerns in a manner that would likely be unacceptable in the United States today. There are many situations in which national or regional needs take precedence over local desires. The new towns of the UK and Scandinavia have been successful in this regard.

Controlling regulations for multifamily housing in most localities in the United States are as follows:

1. *Zoning regulations*. Local zoning ordinances or resolutions, as they are often called, establish the right

of the community to control the uses of the various land parcels within the boundaries of the community. Following that, they control the maximum allowable density of development. In the case of housing, the density is expressed in terms of the maximum number of families per acre or the minimum lot area per dwelling unit. The maximum height, number of stories, set-back distances from the lot perimeter lines, and required number of parking spaces per dwelling unit are also important aspects of zoning resolutions.

Since the cost of a building site is a function of the type and intensity of its permitted uses, it is common practice for the builders of housing to build to the maximum permitted density, or bulk, balanced against other requirements for on-site parking, recreational amenities, open space, or site-specific limitations such as heavy slopes, rock outcroppings, or natural features.

2. *Building codes*. Codes establish minimum requirements for life safety, structural integrity, ventilation, building systems, fire safety, and other components or functions of the building itself. In recent years building codes have been expanded to establish standards for energy conservation, accessibility to the physically handicapped, and materials that could generate toxic wastes. The building code establishes the appropriate type of construction for a building of a given size or use, and it establishes requirements for means of egress and the protection of occupants in case of fire, other emergencies, or natural disasters such as earthquakes and hurricanes.
3. *Development standards*. Where these standards are in effect, they regulate the development of the site and the infrastructures necessary for the operation of the building. These standards tend to be very local in nature and reflect concerns of the public work officials, firefighting establishments, utility companies, and similar agencies. In some localities this category includes the required approval of an architectural review board charged with the responsibility of determining the fitness of the architectural form of the proposed building. Requirements for roadway widths, on-site landscaping and screen planting, and site lighting often fall into this category, but may be a part of the local zoning resolution as well.
4. *Owners' and lenders' standards*. In some cases the owner of a property has even more stringent standards for projects that the owner expects to maintain over a period of years or sell, as the case may be. These standards are commonly expressed as requirements in the building program, but they are sometimes in code form. Perhaps the best-known standards of this type are those put forth by the U.S. Department of Housing and Urban Development (HUD) and promulgated as Minimum Property Standards (MPS) for multifamily housing. These standards have been the most commonly used reference for builders of housing. It has been generally understood that if these standards are followed, the project will be insurable by HUD and mortgageable by a local bank as well. The impact of HUD standards on the multifamily housing industry has been great over the past 20 years. Many builders of housing have learned much of what they know about the field from the MPS. Pressure from the building industry led HUD to produce an even more detailed reference manual called the *Manual of Acceptable Practices* (1), which describes in clear, prescriptive terms how to build housing acceptable to the federal government. The State of New York, in running its own housing finance agency, developed a similar set of standards, based on experience in the particular markets served in that state.
5. *Other regulations, standards, and codes*. Often there are regulations other than the usual codes and ordinances that pertain to housing design. These may vary from locality to locality and from time to time, but it is the job of the designer to determine what they are given for a project and take them into account in the design. An example of this kind of nongovernmental regulation is the practice of insurance companies of establishing insurance rates based on criteria that have little to do with the governing local codes. In such cases it may be wise to modify the building program to reduce fire areas or install sprinklers above and beyond code requirements just to make long-term savings in insurance costs.

The design process starts with a definition of the design problem in terms of the objectives of the developer and goes directly to the relevant codes and ordinances, which are, broadly taken, an expression of the housing policy of the locality. The next step is normally an analysis of the optimum number and type of housing units to be built given local housing demand matched against local housing supply. This leads to the next question, which is where the project will fit in the spectrum of housing densities.

THE SPECTRUM OF DENSITIES IN HOUSING

A convenient way of breaking down all possible housing types into categories is to group them by density of development, which is measured by the number of families or dwelling units per acre (DU/acre). A single-family house on a 100-ft^2 lot represents a density of about 4 DU/acre; a three-flat apartment building on a 50 × 100-ft lot represents a density of about 26 DU/acre. Table 1 outlines the characteristics of the main types of multifamily housing.

LOW-DENSITY HOUSING

Garden apartments of two stories are by far the most common type of low-density housing (Fig. 3). They are so named because they are normally set back some distance from the surrounding property lines, and the spaces remaining are often planted with lawns, shrubs, and flowers. The garden type contains many of the amenities of the

Table 1. Characteristics of Housing Density Groups

Characteristic	Low Density	Medium Density	High Density
Units per acre	12–36	25–75	50 and up
Story heights	2–3	3–7	7–40+
Construction types	Wood frames	Masonry wall bearing or noncombustible panel	Concrete or steel frame
Code types	5	3 and 4	1 and 2
Vertical access	Walk-up	Walk-up, elevator	Elevator
Usual location	Rural, suburban	Urban, midtown, suburban	Urban, downtown
Generic types	Row houses, garden apartments, walk-up duplexes, triplexes	Stacked flats, walk-up	High-rise, luxury units, housing for seniors
Relative cost per unit, $	10,000	14,800	16,700
Mechanical and electric costs, % total cost	17.5	24.8	24.1

single-family detached home. The duplex apartment is one in which a unit is on two floors, with the living/dining room on the first floor and bedrooms on the second floor. Duplex units require more total floor area than the traditional flat, because of the stair requirement. They are most successful when they have more than two bedrooms and the overall site density is low.

Most suburban communities in the United States allow for the development of garden apartments, but usually in a relatively low density. Parking requirements are often extensive, requiring up to one and a half parking spaces per dwelling unit in many cases, because in such localities mass transit is usually of minor impact as far as the outlying housing site is concerned.

The underlying motive for the construction of privately developed housing is usually the maximum return on invested capital, so such types are as a rule constructed up to the maximum permissible limits of the building codes and as inexpensively as possible. In most cases, this requires frame construction, entryways to a single stair serving two floors, and a maximum of eight units per entry. Where permitted, habitable basements add an effective third floor to the building mass and increase the density.

Figure 3. The exterior of a low-rise, low-density apartment building for senior citizens. The building in the foreground is the community center. Gindele and Johnson, Architects.

Basement apartments are less desirable than those above grade because they are often lacking in privacy and are susceptible to moisture problems.

A recent variant of this maximum permissible envelope is the "stacked flat," in which advantage is made of sites that have great changes in grade; entry levels are created from the grade as it changes, and no interior stair halls are required. Such stair halls, where they do exist, are a liability to an owner because they require maintenance and represent unrentable floor space.

Because of simple frame construction, light foundations, and commonly available residential building components, low-density housing units are the least expensive to construct. All of the required techniques are familiar to the typical homebuilder, and the parts are off-the-shelf. In many sections of the country, they are produced as prefabricated units, manufactured in over-the-road modules, and placed on a prepared foundation at a significant reduction in construction cost. The design of factory-prefabricated housing units is limited by the maximum size that can be carried on the public roads. Each module or building block of prefabricated construction can be no larger than 12 ft or 3.66 m wide and 60 ft or 18.3 m long. Frame construction lends itself to this kind of prefabrication.

MEDIUM-DENSITY HOUSING

Medium-density housing takes shape in many forms (Fig. 4). This is so primarily because it is most often derived from the limitations imposed by local zoning rules, which in most major cities include districts in which the maximum permissible density is too great for wood frame construction and too low for high-rise housing. These districts tend to be found in the older cities in the East and Northeast in the United States. For this reason the masonry wall bearing, three- or four-story apartment house is not often seen in the South or the West. The tenement houses of New York of the late nineteenth and early twentieth centuries and the "four-deckers" of Boston fall into this category.

Because of the generally higher construction cost, developers tend to avoid this type and density. An added deterrent to development is that land zoned to permit these medium densities tends to be either very expensive or

Figure 4. A medium-density, mid-rise building proposed as in-fill housing, Brooklyn, New York. Gindele and Johnson, Architects.

poorly located in a community. Even with the installation of elevators, the rents that can be derived from such housing are not always commensurate with the higher development and construction costs, compared with housing of low density.

An added complication is the problem of providing required or adequate parking once the density of development exceeds 30 or 40 families per acre. The normal result for medium-density situations is extensive coverage of buildings and parking lots, with little space left for landscaping, outside amenities, or sitting areas. Parking ratios are usually decreased as the density increases, but at medium densities there is insufficient revenue in most projects to permit parking in structures or under the building, and so automobile parking tends to crowd the site at this density.

On the positive side, experience seems to suggest that the masonry shells and heavy timber floors of older walk-up-type housing are durable and relatively fire safe. Thus they lend themselves to rehabilitation and upgrading from time to time, if the nature of the surrounding neighborhood warrants such investment. Even the old-law tenements of New York have sound enclosures that are today being rehabilitated and turned into luxury housing. It may be that a long-term investment in mid-density housing is more sound than investment in the two other types, representing as it does a good balance between initial cost and long-term durability. It is true too that communities zoned for medium densities generally have a well-developed infrastructure to support development, such as dependable public water and sewer service and responsive police and fire services. This is as compared with low-density housing, in which locations are often more remote and often depend on on-site water and sewage installations.

Not all housing of medium density is constructed of masonry. In some instances local codes permit medium densities in frame construction, especially when equipped with sprinkler systems for fire protection.

Structures that are adaptively reused as housing are most often occupied at medium density. In recent years it has become popular to convert former school buildings, public libraries, fire stations, or even office buildings into apartments. The construction of such buildings is normally of the fire-resistive type. The development of such housing is sometimes hindered by lack of space for on-site parking and occasionally by a lack of the community amenities that normally go along with housing.

Experiments with innovative construction techniques that will produce fire-resistive enclosures for mid-density housing have met with limited success in recent years. Operation Breakthrough, a program of the federal government in the early 1970s, stimulated research and development of new techniques in housing construction by guaranteeing a market for the actual use of selected techniques. Twenty-two demonstration projects were completed, and many of the significant breakthroughs were in mid-density units. The successful units tended to use panel systems of noncombustible elements that were cast or prepared in a factory and trucked to the site and assembled there. Much was learned about the problems of factory construction, but much of what was learned has been lost in the years since Operation Breakthrough. Housing construction is by nature localized and site-specific, and most housing, especially mid-density housing, is hard to standardize because of changes in local regulations and working conditions. Trade union rules and practices have a significant impact on the acceptability of factory-made building modules in local communities.

Medium-density housing units can be mixed with low-density units on the same site when Planned Urban Development (PUD) rules are in effect. This type of zoning category permits a site to be developed with housing types of varying configurations and densities, as long as the overall project density is within specific limitations.

HIGH-DENSITY HOUSING

The high-rise elevator building is the principal form of housing with densities of more than 50 families per acre (Fig. 5). Such housing is almost always located toward the center of major cities or in the middle of suburban subcenters. The reason for this is the desire of people to be close to the heart of things, where land is scarce and expensive.

The development and popularity of this type parallel the development of the passenger elevator, which makes all accommodations in a building equal in terms of convenience of access. Some of the most expensive housing in the world is developed in high-rise apartment houses. Even so, it is doubtful that the type will replace the single-family detached house as the dwelling of choice for most people in the United States.

Construction of high-rise housing is usually of reinforced concrete. The short floor spans that are possible and the need for economies of means make concrete flat-slab construction ideal for the type. In some locations where the concrete industry is not well developed, or where it is not competitive, buildings of steel-framed construction have been built. In center-city locations parking is provided in basement spaces or in adjacent parking structures constructed of reinforced concrete. Where the construction industry is well developed, high-rise apartment towers having up to 10 apartments per floor can be constructed at the rate of 1 floor per working week.

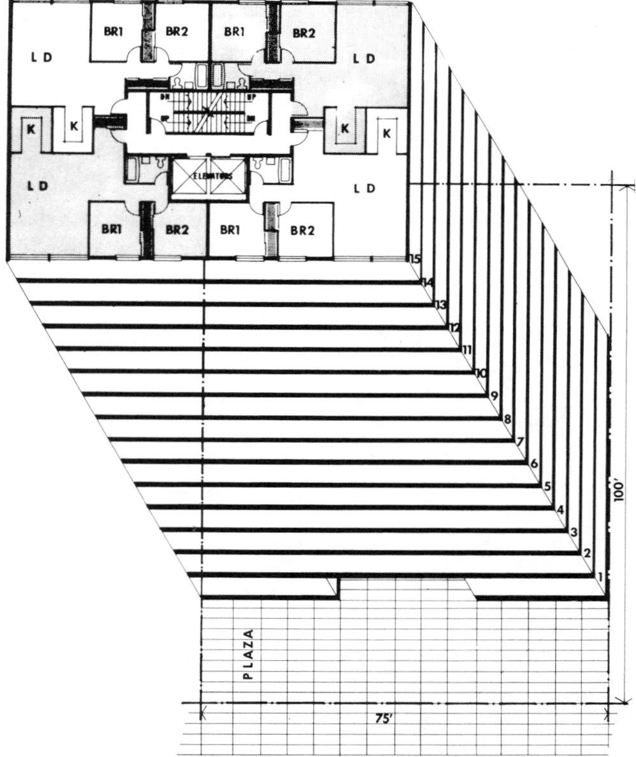

Figure 5. Conceptual plan for a 15-story building on a 7500 ft^2 site. The effective density for this plan would be 325 families per acre, and parking would have to be in the basement or off-site. Courtesy of ARCH.

Exterior walls of high-rise buildings are of brick, anchored to the concrete frame and backed by concrete block, or of precast concrete panels. All-glass exteriors, similar to those of office buildings, are rare because of the higher initial cost, long-term maintenance, and potential for excessive heat loss and heat gain. There are several recent examples of exposed poured-in-place concrete exteriors, but such construction has been found to be high in cost because of the extreme care and high skill required in the execution of the work.

During the 1950s and 1960s, the slab type of rectangularly shaped high-rise building predominated in the United States. These take as their prototype the towers envisioned by Le Corbusier in his Radiant City, the high towers of which allow for open space on the ground for landscaping and recreation, and light and fresh air in abundance. Such slab buildings commonly contained 8–12 apartments per floor and were most often constructed to heights that were appropriate to the number of elevators used. A single elevator served a building of up to 6 floors, with two elevators for 13 floors, three for 21 floors, and so on.

The shape of a high-rise tower is usually kept simple and geometrically symmetrical for reasons of economy. In extremely dense urban situations the building is built out to the limits of the zoning envelope. This explains the stepped profile of high-rise apartments of the 1960s in New York City. Cross-shaped plans increase the perimeter and allow more units per floor for a given limited length or width. In the UK and Scandinavia the "point-tower" type of square plan high-rise with a smaller number of units per floor has been used with success. Such towers are more desirable in terms of urban design than are long slabs of the same height because they tend to block less of the views in and around urban spaces and have less impact on local wind patterns.

Local housing authorities have attempted to use the high-density prototype for housing of the fully subsidized type. Aside from the obvious problems that arise from a high concentration of families with serious economic and often social problems in the same place, the high-rise type appears to work poorly where large families with young children are to be housed.

Experience suggests that high-rise housing works well where it is used exclusively for adults or for the elderly. This experience appears to be common to federal, state, and local programs in the United States and in Europe as well. Older people have the security of neighbors, complete physical access to all parts of the building, relatively high safety from fire, and an aggregate number of similar persons large enough to support common social programs and group activities in the building.

A REPRESENTATIVE EXAMPLE

Lake Street Homes, a multifamily project built in the city of Newburgh, New York, in the 1970s, illustrates several planning and design ideas in housing and is a good example of how the abstraction of numbers is developed into a completed project, providing homes at relatively modest cost to many families and a viable economic enterprise at the same time (Fig. 6).

This development was a project of the New York State Urban Development Corporation (UDC), a state agency that had the power to go into local communities that had serious housing deficiencies and construct housing. Funding of the project was through a combination of "seed money" funds advanced by the agency and a government-insured long-term mortgage. The project required the combined participation of UDC, other state agencies, HUD, and the local city government. Land costs were kept low because the project was located in an urban renewal area. Because of the nature of the occupancy, namely, families of low to moderate income only, the local government granted tax reductions. Every available device was used to reduce the ultimate cost to the users.

After lengthy consultations and deliberations between the participating agencies, the planning consultants, and the architects and their engineers, the basic numbers that established the economic structure for the project design were determined. Figures for gross floor area and coverage were developed after the first round of schematic designs. See Table 2.

It was determined, after an analysis of community needs, that there were severe shortages of housing for large families; therefore, the number of large units, four and five bedrooms, is higher than normal. Sixty-six units were planned for older persons, to be located in a nine-story mid-rise building. Approximately half of the two-bedroom units were configured as flats, and half as two-story duplex or townhouse units. The decision to locate older persons in a separate building grew from discussions with local groups and was a concession to local choice, not an abstract planning or architectural idea.

The social plan for the project was based on the need to break down the large development into subsets, or clusters, so that the residents would have a sense of neighborhood. The project was divided into 12 clusters of apartments, each cluster having the same proportional breakdown of units as the project as a whole (Fig. 7). The clusters are generally L-shaped, with the entrances fronting on the parking lot; the short leg of the L houses the laundry room. The laundry is a kind of minor social center and has a large view window so that activity in and around the parking lot can be easily observed. All of the kitchens in the duplex units face this active side of the cluster; all of the living rooms face the rear, or quiet side which has protected open spaces for play areas and a meandering walk, away from automobiles.

A long building containing two floors of apartment flats is at the center of the cluster, and it is flanked on both ends by the duplex town houses. This arrangement puts the families with the most children closer to the green areas and play areas. The mid-rise building is located in a pivotal position between the two halves of the development, positioned for the best view of the natural features of the site. Some of the clusters are other than L-shaped because of the topography, but the social organization remains the same. An old building that remained on the site was retained and refurbished as an office and recreational building for the tenants' use.

All 48 of the two-story buildings are of wood frame construction with brick veneer and plywood panel exteriors. The steeply pitched roofs, which were derived from local historic precedent, were built over prefabricated roof trusses, formed in two sections because of their height. Buildings on the lower elevations of the site have crawl-space first-floor construction; the remainder have concrete slabs on grade.

The nine-story mid-rise building was designed in a cross shape to increase the perimeter enough to allow the plan-

Figure 6. Site plan of the Lake Street Houses. The dark area in the foreground is an artificial lake. The main road skirts the clusters of buildings. Gindele and Johnson, Architects.

Table 2. Project Figures

Gross site area, acres		37.8	
Net site area, acres		31.9	
Gross building areas, ft^2 (m^2)			
low-rise		304,040 (28,245)	
mid-rise		54,200 (5,035)	
total		358,240 (33,280)	
		Unit Breakdown	
Size	*Number*	*Percentage of Total*	*Average Size, ft^2 (m^2)*
0 bedroom	49	13	560 (52.02)
1 bedroom	98	26	665 (61.78)
2 bedrooms	123	33	945 (87.79)
3 bedrooms	84	22	1200 (111.48)
4 bedrooms	12	3	1480 (137.49)
5 bedrooms	9	2	1520 (141.2)
Total	*375*		
Net density (3,707 ft^2/unit (344.38 m^2/unit)), units/net acre			11.75
Parking spaces provided			418
Parking space ratio, spaces/unit			1.1
Site coverage (buildings only), %			11.1

ning of kitchens and bathrooms with windows. This is not the usual case for mid-rise buildings. The older people interviewed in this locality did not want interior kitchens or baths, and they felt strongly enough about it to convince the development team. The structural frame is of poured-in-place reinforced concrete in a flat-slab configuration. Because of the shape and height of the building, a construction in reinforced masonry with precast concrete plank floors would have been feasible. The building contains six apartments fitted to be used by the physically handicapped, special emergency alarm systems for the elderly, an emergency generator to operate the elevators during power outages, social rooms, and other facilities for the special needs of older persons (Fig. 8).

The Lake Street Homes project has been successful in both economic and social terms. The tenancy is stable, the residents take pride in their place of residence, and an experiment that mixes families of virtually all incomes and ages in one place appears to be working. The developer, meanwhile, has been able to take advantage of tax credits and write-offs and in a few years will own the project free and clear on a relatively low ratio of actual cash equity. During the present stage of project life, the developer is strictly limited to the profit that can be taken, but the long-term arrangement is excellent. A thoughtfully de-

Figure 7. The front view of a typical cluster of apartments in the Lake Street Houses.

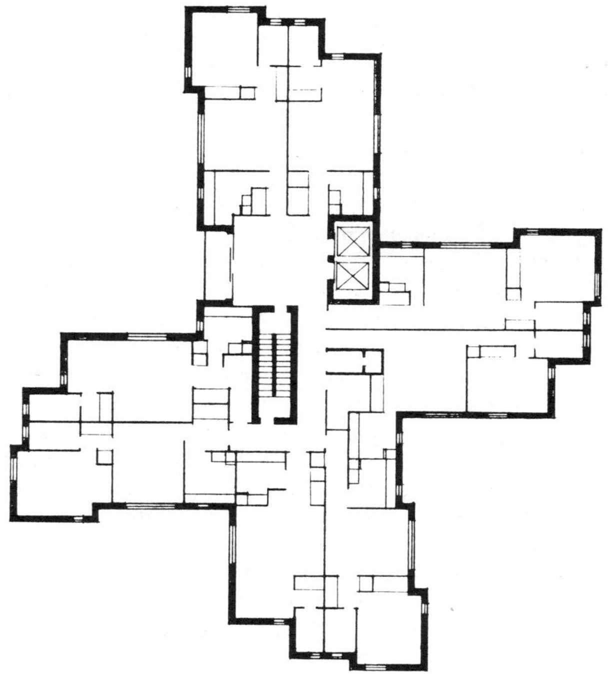

Figure 8. Plan of a typical floor of the Senior Citizens Building in the Lake Street Homes. This plan has three studio and five one-bedroom apartments per floor. It provides features that were requested by prospective tenants, including outside kitchens and bathrooms, a congregating space on each floor, corner ventilation in every unit, and a balcony for use in pleasant weather. Gindele and Johnson, Architects.

signed multifamily development has a long and productive life in both economic and social terms.

CONTEMPORARY PRACTICE

Standards for the development and construction of multifamily housing have been steadily improving over the past 100 years. Political pressures for strict regulation of housing and pressures from the marketplace for more commodious apartment living have combined to bring about almost continual change. Public concern for the provision of housing for families of low or moderate income varies in intensity with the economic climate. Private development of housing is closely tied to the availability of and interest rates on loans. Communities experience periods of oversupply and insufficient supply in recurring cycles. In the United States the production of housing directly follows changes in the income tax laws, which have until recently been favorable to developers. At the local level the existence of rent control legislation can hinder or accelerate the intensity of development, depending on its form and implementation. Of all building types, multifamily housing is probably the most sensitive to political processes and changes in the economic climate. Specific issues in contemporary practice are described here, but there are new issues each year, requiring constant upgrading of information on the part of the designer.

Energy Conservation

During the worldwide energy crises of 1973–1974 and 1979–1980, state legislatures throughout the United States enacted laws that established minimum standards for the insulation of buildings, performance standards for mechanical equipment, and design standards for building systems. To make these codes easy to follow, prescriptive standards were written, giving clear steps to follow toward acceptable energy-conscious design. Specific types and thicknesses of thermal insulation are given as alternatives in arriving at specific heat-loss goals.

In the search for more efficient heating and cooling systems, new approaches are constantly being tried. With the emergence of the condominium as a popular form of ownership of apartments, the single-unit heating/cooling plant appears to be replacing the central boiler as a source for comfort heat. Single-unit heaters have gas or electric energy sources, fit into a compact space, and are under the complete control of the occupant. The single unit allows the greatest potential for energy conservation; the unit can be run at very low temperatures if the occupant wishes, and it can be turned off entirely when the space is unused.

Attention to the issue of energy conservation will in time produce the desired result of reducing dependence on nonrenewable fuels. At the same time the cost to the occupant for heating and cooling can be moderated.

Design for Specific Occupant Groups

Apartments that are to be occupied by older persons have been produced under subsidy programs by the federal government for more than 30 years. In recent years the private sector has moved into this area of development. Housing for the elderly should be well located for access to essential services and should be two stories at most in walk-up units or in fire-resistive buildings with elevator service. Special features usually include bathrooms with ample grab bars around tubs and water closets, and doors that open outward. Alarm systems that can easily be activated by the occupant, signaling a light in the public hallway and at a central panel, are required. All spaces in a building for the elderly should be accessible by wheelchair-bound residents. The best buildings of this type have generous amounts of space for communal activities.

Provisions for apartments for occupancy by the physically handicapped are commonly required in elevator buildings and on the ground floors of other buildings. Most codes require that a number of apartments be adaptable for such use rather than completely outfitted for such use from the beginning. Special requirements include kitchen and bathroom facilities that can be used by a person using a wheelchair, reachable electric switches and elevator buttons, food and clothing storage that can be reached from a chair, and nonslip finishes throughout. As in the case of the elderly, entrance to the building, access to all public areas, and access to all areas of the apartment unit itself must be readily available to persons in wheelchairs, on crutches, or who are sight-impaired.

Acoustic Control

Few annoyances are more pervasive to the resident of a multifamily building than noise that comes from other parts of the building. For many years HUD set standards for performance that required a sound transmission class rating of 45 dB for walls between apartments and 50 dB for walls between apartments and public halls. In 1984 HUD cut back on the size and scope of its minimum property standards and at the same time placed a greater reliance on conformance to local codes. Some jurisdictions have less stringent requirements for acoustic control, and some have more rigorous requirements, including those for impact noise on the floors. Most of the problems of sound control can be solved by attention to the details of pipe and conduit penetration and by the use of carpeted floors and of walls between units that are constructed of two separate lines of framing members filled with insulating blankets.

Space Standards

The size of the rooms in an apartment is determined by local marketing strategies in the case of privately constructed housing and by agency standards in the case of publicly assisted housing. The old HUD standards as indicated in Table 3 were in place for many years and are a kind of base line against which most new units are measured. Hundreds of thousands of apartment units were built to these standards in the public and private sectors. Space limitations were increased where local market pressures or building codes required. From the designer's point of view, a much more realistic way of establishing space

Table 3. Minimum Space Sizes from 1977 HUD Minimum Property Standards

Space[a]	Minimum Area, ft^2 LU with 0 BRs	LU with 1 BR	LU with 2 BRs	LU with 3 BRs	LU with 4 BRs	Least Dimension, ft
Separate rooms						
LR		160	160	170	180	11
DR		100	100	110	120	8.33
BR (primary)[b]		120	120	120	120	9.33
BR (secondary)			80	80	80	8
Total area, BRs		120	200	280	380	
Combined spaces						
LR–DA		210	210	230	250	
LR–DA–SL	250					
LR–DA–K		270	270	300	330	
LR–SL	210					
K–DA	100	120	120	140	160	

[a] Abbreviations: LU, living unit; LR, living room; DR, dining room; DA, dining area; 0 BR, LU with no separate bedroom; K, kitchen; BR, bedroom; SL, sleeping area.
[b] Primary bedrooms shall have at least one uninterrupted wall space of at least 10 ft.

standards is to subject a proposed plan to the test of furnishability (Fig. 9). Assumptions are made about the living styles of the expected occupants, and furniture placement is indicated on the designer's schematics. Furnishability standards for HUD programs were set forth in the HUD *Manual of Acceptable Practices* (1), and even though this document is no longer the administrative standard, the principles involved are still valid. The shape and size of rooms should be such as to accommodate basic items of furniture in common use. It is interesting to note that the actual space seen in expensive housing units for sale as condominiums or cooperatives is not much greater than that seen in assisted housing. Spaces are slightly smaller in countries where more of the furniture is built in as a part of the architectural plan. The Scandinavian countries are leaders in this field. Common practice today combines living and dining spaces into a single room. Efficiency or studio (zero-bedroom) apartments work best when an alcove is provided off the main space for a bed and an additional alcove is provided for dressing (Fig. 10).

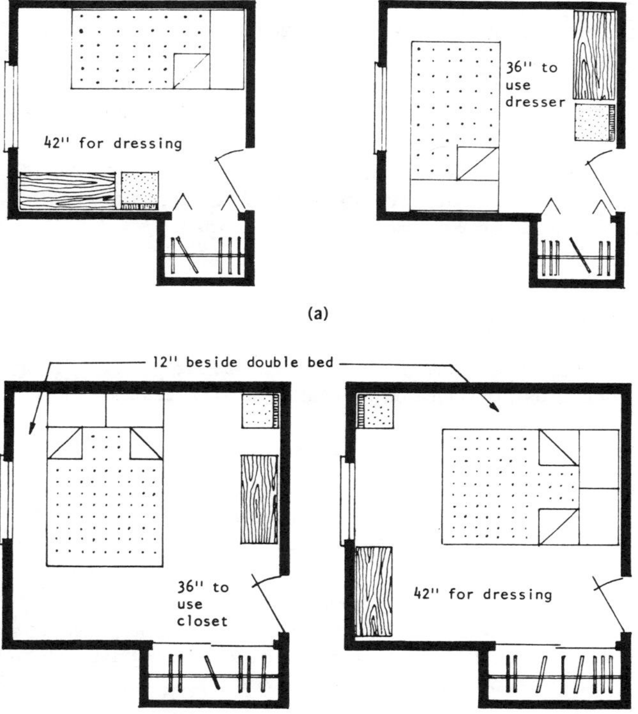

Figure 9. Furnishability diagrams from HUD's *Manual of Acceptable Practices* (1). No longer used, this manual was used as a guide by developers and builders of housing for many years. The idea of assessing the usefulness of apartment spaces is of continuing validity. (**a**) Single-occupancy bedroom; (**b**) Double-occupancy bedroom. The location of doors and windows should permit alternative furniture arrangement.

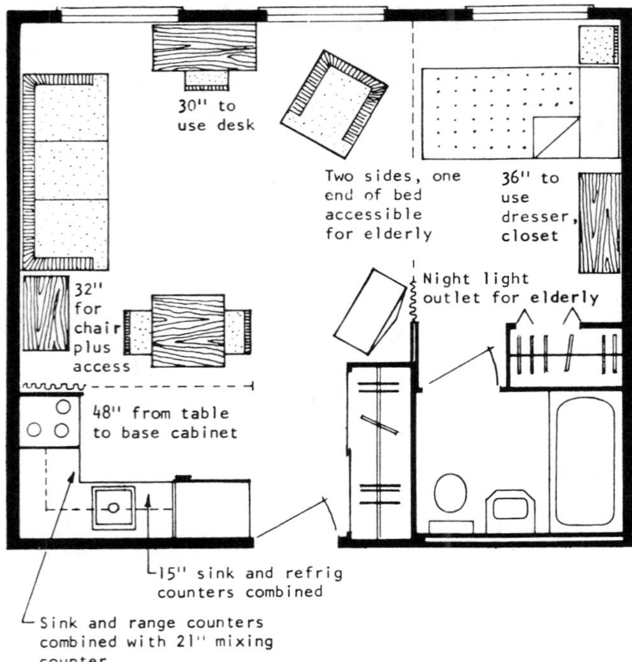

Figure 10. Plan diagram showing special planning considerations for an efficiency apartment for older persons from HUD's *Manual of Acceptable Practices* (1). Bedroom living unit with sleeping alcove; a bed alcove with natural light and ventilation and which can be screened from the living area is desirable.

The Cost of Housing

The rent paid by a tenant in an apartment building is the sum of many costs, along with the owner's profit margin. These costs are usually broken down into two categories: development costs, which represent the total expenditures necessary to put the building in place, and operating costs, which are the ongoing expenses once the building is occupied. It is important for the designer to understand the process to know where design tradeoffs can be made with elements in the overall picture. Cost elements for a typical small garden apartment development are as follows:

Development Costs	Annual Expenses
Land purchase cost	Real estate taxes
Site improvements	Insurance
"Hard costs"	Heating fuel
building construction	Utilities
off-site improvements	Maintenance
"Soft costs"	Trash and snow removal
developer's fee	
architect's/engineer's fees	Management fee
permits and inspections	Miscellaneous
interest on construction loan	
taxes during construction	

A vacancy allowance is applied to the total annual expenses based on local experience. The remaining difference between these expenses and the total projected rent is called the debt service coverage. The debt service payments on the mortgage and its interest are taken from that remainder, and what is left over represents a return to the owner on the investment in the project.

In the costs that make up the final rent, an investment in the quality of specific materials may be offset by reduced maintenance, insurance, or fuel costs. On the other hand, unwarranted costs in the design and construction result in added long-term cost burdens to the occupants. In a typical case annual expenses are about 30% of the project income after allowance for vacancies; debt service is about 63%, and the remainder represents a cushion for unexpected items or operating profit, as the case may be. The most sensitive number in the entire picture is the interest rate paid for the permanent mortgage.

The designer of multifamily housing has a great responsibility and a challenge; of all building types, this one touches most intimately the lives of families of all stations of life. Well-considered, well-developed project designs can have the direct effect of improving the quality of life for the ultimate occupants. When the best minds are put to the task of housing design, the results are striking examples of the best of environments in which the world's population could be housed. The apartment buildings at 845–860 Lake Shore Drive, Chicago, Illinois, by Mies van der Rohe are distinguished by their urbane sophistication, sensitive proportions, and careful detailing. The Unite d'Habitation of Le Corbusier at Marseilles, France, is an idea for a complete living environment on a grand scale that is applicable all over the world. The best examples of multifamily housing are developed and designed with a long-term view of the lives that are affected and the ultimate returns in social and economic terms.

In the United States about 30% of the families live in apartments. In many countries of Scandinavia and Eastern Europe, up to 80% of the population lives in multifamily housing. In the search for more efficient ways of living, and with the greater emphasis on urbanization and worldwide changes in the structure of the family, this building type is growing in importance year by year.

BIBLIOGRAPHY

1. *Manual of Accepted Practices,* U.S. Department of Housing and Urban Development, Washington, D.C., 1973.

General References

Ref. 1 is a good general reference.

C. K. Bauer, *Modern Housing,* Houghton-Mifflin Co., Boston, Mass., and New York, 1934.

C. S. Stein, *Toward New Towns for America,* The University Press of Liverpool, Liverpool, UK, 1951.

J. H. Abel, "The Apartment House," in T. Hamlin, *Forms and Functions of Twentieth Century Architecture,* Vol. III, Columbia University Press, New York, 1952.

G. H. Beyer, *Housing and Society,* 4th ed., Macmillan Co., New York, and Collier-Macmillan Ltd., London, 1967.

S. Paul, *Apartments: Their Design and Development,* Reinhold Publishing Corp., New York, 1967.

Housing in Central Harlem, Part One: The Potential for Rehabilitation and New Vest Pocket Housing, Architects' Renewal Committee in Harlem, Inc., New York, 1967.

Building The American City, Report of The National Commission on Urban Problems, Superintendent of Documents, U.S. Government Printing Office, Washington, D.C., 1968.

Minimum Property Standards for Multifamily Housing, Vol. 2, U.S. Department of Housing and Urban Development, Washington, D.C., 1977.

See also Adaptive Use; Apartment Buildings, High-rise; Construction Funding; Planned Communities—New Towns; Residential Buildings; Single-family Housing; Time-adaptive Housing

Jeh Johnson
Wappingers Falls, New York

MUMFORD, LEWIS

One of the twentieth century's preeminent urban planners, philosophers, architecture historians, and architecture critics, Lewis Mumford is a versatile author, whose writings also span the worlds of literature, the visual arts, U.S. history, and the influence of technology on Western civilization. He links these seemingly diverse subjects with the common theme that people are capable of renewing the world around them.

His espousal of the development of autonomous satellite neighborhoods (also known as "garden cities" or "greenbelt towns") around large cities led to the building of the communities of Radburn, N.J., in 1929, various U.S. greenbelt towns during the Great Depression of the 1930s, and of several "new towns" around London after World War II.

The son of a widowed Christian housekeeper and an aristocrat from a Jewish family, Lewis Mumford was born October 19, 1895, in Flushing, Long Island, New York. The boy who would grow up to become a leading authority on New York City was reared by his mother on Manhattan's Upper West Side. Frequent and long walks through the city with his maternal grandfather, Charles Graessel, awakened a fascination with its architecture. As influential as the teeming pleasures of life in the great metropolis were boyhood summers spent in the quiet farmlands of Vermont. Much of Mumford's future writings would philosophize on man's need to experience the contrasting worlds of city and country—ideally, to experience them simultaneously in garden cities on the outskirts of major metropolises.

While Mumford's prodigious literary output is amazing, it is even more admirable when one realizes that he never completed his college education and, indeed, was adamantly opposed to formally structured education. Lewis Mumford produced an opus of more than 30 books and hundreds of articles. His love for writing was manifested early at Stuyvesant High School in New York City, where he served on the editorial board of the school's magazine, and where he graduated in 1912 as valedictorian of his class.

He attended night class at the City College of New York from 1912 to 1914, working odd jobs during the day. He chose classes on the basis of their intellectual content rather than following the structured curriculum, accounting for the fact that after two full years of study he was still at the freshman level. However, he pressed on with his literary career by working on the City College yearbook and as a copyboy on the New York *Evening Telegram* newspaper. During this period he discovered the writings of Patrick Geddes of Scotland, a sociologist, biologist, and pioneer of the concept of town planning. Although Mumford did not meet Geddes until the latter's visit to New York City in 1923, an enduring correspondence between the two men began in 1914 (1).

Ill health, specifically, weak lungs and a history of tuberculosis, forced Mumford to quit his daytime studies at City College. Although he would take isolated courses there and at Columbia University in the future, this in essence marked the end of his formal education. However, the ensuing three years of informal education would prove to be the most influential ones of his youth. From 1915 on, Mumford explored New York City on foot, taking copious notes in resplendent detail, much as Geddes had done in Scotland years earlier. Mumford also read profusely on all aspects of Western culture during that period.

Despite weak health, Mumford joined the U.S. Navy during World War I, serving from April 1918 through February 1919 in Newport, Rhode Island.

Upon returning home to New York from the Navy, Mumford began his professional literary career. He became book reviewer, then assistant editor, for the biweekly magazine *The Dial.* This was significant for two reasons. First, it marked the start of a fast rise up the literary ladder. Second, he met his future wife, Sophia Wittenberg, there.

Although Mumford lost his job with *The Dial* in November 1919 owing to the sale of the paper, he had made enough contacts in the New York cultural world to allow him to earn a living as a freelance editor and writer thereafter. Significantly, the first of many articles on cities, "The Heritage of the Cities Movement in America," was published in *The Journal of the American Institute of Architects* in 1919.

In 1920, he accepted sociologist Victor Branford's invitation to work in the United Kingdom as acting editor of *The Sociological Review.* While in London, Mumford received an invitation to join Geddes in India to conduct research in that country's cities. However, Mumford declined the offer and sailed back to New York to marry Sophia.

His literary star rose quickly thereafter. He wrote his first article on architectural history for *The New Republic* (1921). He followed this with his first book, *The Story of Utopias* (1922).

Mumford became more and more active in the "regionalist" movement during the early 1920s. This movement stressed cultural and administrative decentralization versus federal involvement. He became a founding member and leader of the Regional Planning Association of America, whence came the plans for the idyllic planned communities of Sunnyside Gardens, Long Island (1925), and Radburn, New Jersey (1929). He also was active in the New

York State Housing and Regional Planning Commission, which laid the foundation for national and state planning projects, including the Tennessee Valley Authority (TVA) and "greenbelt" towns of the 1930s.

Incredible though it may seem, no general history of U.S. architecture was available until Mumford's *Sticks and Stones* (1924) was published. Concurrently, he delivered a series of lectures on the subject of architectural history at New York's New School of Social Research.

In the mid-1920s and for an interim period, Mumford turned his attention from urban planning to general U.S. culture. Indeed, he is considered one of the fathers of interdisciplinary "American studies," and his 1926 book, *The Golden Day: A Study in American Experience and Culture,* is one of Mumford's finest general works. He followed this with *Herman Melville* (1929), a major biography of the great American novelist of the nineteenth century. His next work was *The Brown Decades: A Study of the Arts in America: 1865–1895* (1931), based on a series of lectures delivered at Dartmouth College.

As important as his full-length books are his essays for *The New Yorker* magazine from 1931 to 1963, most of these in the form of a regular weekly column, "The Sky Line" alternating with "The Art Galleries." He also was a regular contributor to *Architectural Record* from 1937 to 1968, as well as to most major periodicals of the day.

Mumford was in great demand as a visiting professor and guest lecturer in colleges around the world. These included associations with Dartmouth College (from 1929 on), Columbia University (1932–1935), Stanford University (1942–1945), the University of North Carolina (1948–1952), the University of Pennsylvania (1951–1956), and the Massachusetts Institute of Technology (1957–1961).

In 1925, after their son Geddes was born, Lewis and Sophia Mumford moved from Brooklyn Heights to Sunnyside Gardens where, in 1935, their daughter Alison was born.

In 1936 the Mumfords left Sunnyside, N.Y., and settled in Amenia, N.Y., where they presently live. Mumford did most of his writing in the ensuing years, continuing, among other works, the "Renewal of Life" series. In 1942, he began a three-year visiting professorship at Stanford University. Following the Hiroshima and Nagasaki bombings at the end of World War II, he became deeply involved with the nuclear disarmament movement. This position is even more understandable when seen in the light of his belief in a technology running out of control. Similarly, his commitment to the importance of the individual versus the power of the central state led him to become an outspoken critic of Senator Joseph McCarthy's activities.

With his appointment to the University of Pennsylvania as visiting professor in 1951, Mumford had the opportunity to return to teaching city and regional planning for six years. During this time, he also gave the Bampton lectures at Columbia University, which were printed in the book *Art and Technics*.

In 1957, he became Bemis professor at MIT in Cambridge, Massachusetts, serving in that capacity for five years. In that year he also received the Gold Medal of the Royal Town Planning Institute of the United Kingdom. In 1961, Mumford received the Gold Medal from the Royal Institute of British Architects. During the MIT years he began to write his major work, *The City in History,* which was published in 1961. In 1963 he completed *The Highway and the City,* a group of essays previously published as articles in various journals.

During the following years, from 1963 to 1965, he was a distinguished scholar at Wesleyan University, Middletown, Connecticut, and was a consultant to the Urban Planning Commission at Oxford. He expressed his strong opposition to U.S. involvement in the Vietnam War during the late 1960s and early 1970s (2). The following years were very busy ones; he was extensively involved with writing once again, the latest book of which, *Sketches from Life,* was published in 1982.

At this writing, Mumford is in his 93rd year, and he still lives in Amenia, N.Y.

The largest part of Lewis Mumford's writings have been about the city and its relationship to mankind. He believes that humanity can guide its destiny and development, and that the city is a tool as well a a result of that endeavor. The following is a brief description of his most influential books.

Renewal of Life Series

Technics and Civilization (1934), along with *The Culture of Cities* (1938), *The Condition of Man* (1944), and *The Conduct of Life* (1951), form the series that he called "The Renewal of Life." They are meant to explain the major aspects of his theories on urban design and development, reinterpreting the history of human development and reassessing the role of technology and science in Western civilization. For the first time, these works place the history of science and technology within a cultural framework.

In *Technics and Civilization,* he explains his ideas on the central cultural position of technology in Western civilization. In the second work in the series, *The Culture of Cities* (1938), he explains his concepts of regional development and his idea of a balanced environment that takes advantage of the best features of rural and urban settings.

Mumford's writings of the 1950s and 1960s, his most productive period, are all linked by a theme first proposed in the Renewal of Life series, ". . . that the development of the mind and its greatest creations, language and ritual, were more important to human development than the introduction and utilization of the first primitive tools" (3). Mumford's theory is that if man fashioned himself before he created his first sophisticated tool, then he still has the capability to alter the direction of modern technology and would not be a passive victim of that technology.

Art and Technics (1952)

In this book, based on a series of lectures delivered at Columbia University in 1951, Mumford traces the relationship between two tendencies within human beings: the artistic, which is subjective, and the technical, which is objective. As he states, "Art stands for the inner and subjective side of man. . . ." He continues, "technics, on the contrary, develop mainly from the necessity to meet and master the external conditions of life. . . ." (4).

The City in History (1961)

In the book *The City in History* Mumford explored the development of urban life from the beginning of human history. He restates many of his central ideas, such as that of the need for organic growth in today's urban centers. This book, more than any other, establishes the city as a subject of scholarly concern. He begins with the origin of the village and the crystallization of the city, and continues by exploring the ancestral forms and patterns leading to the emergence of the polis. Mumford studies the city's development from Egypt and Mesopotamia through Greece, Rome, the Middle Ages, the Renaissance, and the baroque era, to the modern metropolis and suburbia. The work has been called the greatest book ever written on the city. *The New York Times* book review described the work as being more than a history but, rather, a moral philosophy of a high order and tragic poetry.

The Highway and the City (1963)

Although it was published two years later, *The Highway and the City* was written concurrently with *The City in History,* and was compiled from a series of essays written for various journals. Indeed, Mumford considered *The Highway and the City* as a seed around which a companion volume to *The City in History* could be written. In this book, Mumford treats both European and U.S. subjects. The European subjects include the Marseilles "Folly" (as he terms Le Corbusier's Unité d'Habitation), Rotterdam, the UNESCO building, and Coventry in the United Kingdom. U.S. subjects include Frank Lloyd Wright's Guggenheim Museum, modern architecture, historic Philadelphia, and, in the final chapter, the highway and the city.

The Myth of the Machine Series (1967 and 1970)

Mumford wrote a two-volume follow-up to his Renewal of Life series. The first volume—*Technics and Human Development* (1967)—and the second volume—*The Pentagon of Power* (1970)—present a reassessment of the role of technology in contemporary Western society.

Another side of Mumford's work was that of architectural critic. His writings on projects and architects appear throughout his career. He used these to illustrate his own points of view and ideas, as well as to comment on specific buildings by contemporary architects. For example, illustrating his belief in the basic failure of modern architecture to serve human needs, he says, in reference to the Unité d'Habitation in Marseilles: "Le Corbusier betrayed the human contents to produce a monumental aesthetic effect. The result is an egocentric extravagance, as imposing as an Egyptian pyramid, which was meant to give immortality to a corpse and—humanly speaking—is desolate" (5). He believes that the structure, as a living unit, is ineffective, mentioning items such as the heavy balusters that cut off the magnificent views, to emphasize his point. Mumford's bias, however, does not prevent him from acknowledging the exterior of the building as a success. He goes on to say: ". . . in Unity house it is the three-dimensional qualities of the design that strike the eye happily at every point—the pilotis, the flaring entrance louvers, the ventilators, all of which turn, under Le Corbusier's hand, into striking pieces of outdoor sculpture. Le Corbusier's originality is at its flamboyant best" (6). Mumford was one of the first to observe this stylistic enrichment of Corbusier's work after the war, even considering Ronchamp as the beginning of a return of human soul to modern architecture.

It was this admiration of plasticity, of the evidence of the hand of man to be found in a design or work, that made Mumford appreciative of the work of Frank Lloyd Wright. In his book *Art and Technics,* Mumford writes that ". . . Wright's architecture is superior to the work of Corbusier's school. In Wright's work, the subjective and symbolic elements were as important as the mechanical requirements. From his earliest prairie house onward, both the plan and elevations of Wright's buildings were informed by human ideals. . . ." (7).

It is characteristic of Mumford's opinion of the work of Wright that he wrote in *The Highway and the City,* in reference to the Guggenheim Museum, "You may go to this building to see Kandinsky or Jackson Pollock; you remain to see Frank Lloyd Wright" (8). Mumford shared with Wright the belief that technology, when used wisely, could improve the lot of the human race.

This attitude perhaps explains his criticism of much of the work of Mies Van der Rohe. He writes in *The Highway and the City* that "Mies Van der Rohe used the facilities offered by steel and glass to create elegant monuments to nothingness" (9). Mumford considered Mies's work too dry and empty, too devoid of the human touch.

Mumford has earned numerous accolades throughout his career, including the Smithsonian Association's Hodgkins Gold Medal, the National Medal for Literature, and the National Bank Award. He is an Honorary Member of planning associations in the United States, the United Kingdom, and Canada, and of the American Institute of Architects, from which he received the architectural critic's medal in 1968.

Finally, another theme found in Mumford's work that is directly influencing architectural attitudes of the post-modern era is the open questioning of the modernist formula of "Form Follows Function." This credo was never enough for Mumford, who believes that the human soul is as important an element as functionalism in determining the form of work. He states that ". . . we must not take function solely in a mechanical sense, as applying only to the physical functions of a building" (10). Technical concerns alone are not enough in determining form, for the architect ". . . has still to weigh them with other considerations that have to do with the effect of space and form on the human soul" (11). He supports his philosophy by reminding us that "So in the rebuilding of the House of Commons, Mr. Winston Churchill wisely insisted that the seating space should be considerably smaller than the actual membership, in order to preserve the closeness and intimacy of debate in the House, under normal conditions of attendance" (12). Mumford understands that a balance between the two considerations must be reached since ". . . mechanical functions, taken alone, do not fulfill all human needs, so subjective expression, if divorced from practical consideration may become willful, capricious, defiant of common sense" (13). He has always urged that the fundamental needs of society should be the basis for the enlightened application of technology, while at the same time emphasizing that the spiritual is one of those important fundamental needs. To Mumford, one cannot exist without careful consideration of the other without creating a defective whole.

In analyzing or discussing urban design projects, Mumford applied a set of constant criteria by which he judged the results. He believed that support for private and public life should be equally balanced. He also believed that the design should incorporate the best features of both country and city living. The amenities of city life, particularly of cultural and social events, should be balanced with such rural qualities as open air and space for physical activity. Mumford also believed that the designer should encourage the social needs of the individual, especially in designing the facilities required for community gatherings and encounters. He also believed very strongly that the designer of the community should consider a system that would allow for the future growth of the community, an organic growth that builds on existing features without requiring their destruction.

Mumford arrived at some of his ideas on urbanism from the work of Sir Ebenezer Howard (1850–1928). It was from Howard that he obtained his concept of organic growth and balance of urban and rural amenities.

In turn, many of Mumford's concepts are found in the community of Radburn, N.J. built by Henry Wright and Clarence Stein in 1928 (14). Neighborhoods are organized around a community center that is meant to act as its focus. The city's design also incorporates the idea of the separation of the highway from the local roads, which, in turn, are kept separate from pedestrian traffic. This formula allows for the easy accessibility found in an urban context while preserving the openness of a more rural setting.

Mumford was highly critical of the "baroque" approach to city planning; he believed that it was very unbalanced in favor of the public side of society and the state. Yet he acknowledged that ". . . there are moments when the audacity of the Baroque aesthetic, with its ruthless overriding of historic realities, provides an answer to what would be insuperable difficulties, if one sought a piecemeal solution" (15).

Mumford had a strong faith and love for cities, which made him all the more critical of what he saw as present mistakes. He writes: "If we are concerned with human values, we can no longer afford either sprawling Suburbia or the congested Metropolis: still less can we afford a congested Suburbia, whose visual openness depends upon the cellular isolation and regimentation of its component families in mass structures" (16). This criticism, however, was tempered by an understanding of how people behave and of their potential if given the right tools to develop.

When Lewis Mumford's legacy to contemporary thinking on architecture and urbanism is considered, the great influence that his writings have had must be recognized. His early studies on technology and its development and history, as well as its influence on the built environment, helped to make "urban planning," and "urban design" household words in the United States. He introduced these themes to the professional and general publics, focusing on the question of technology as a helpful tool or damaging element in daily life. Environmental and preservationist movements owe a great debt to his groundbreaking studies.

The concept and implementation of "garden cities," self-sufficient communities that would help to relieve the overcrowded central core, can be directly traced to his reevaluation and popularization of the ideas of Geddes and Howard. Mumford saw these communities as containing all the elements needed for day-to-day functioning. Besides schools and churches, they were to contain places of work, offices, commercial areas, and the like. These garden cities are not meant to be mere bedroom communities, which would only increase dependence on the automobile, but real neighborhoods. He is a believer of the neighborhood where people know each other and appreciate each other, where they can live and work together. He saw the destructive effect of highways sneaking into the heart of cities, cutting entire sections off from one another. It was, in fact, largely owing to his influence that during the 1970s city planners finally stopped these damaging intrusions into the fabric of cities.

Mumford pointed to the interpretation of those ideas in modern suburbs, which he sometimes calls "green ghetto," which are very much dependent on the automobile's technology and all its damaging effects. He believes that "the assumed right of the private motor car to go to any place in the city and park anywhere is nothing less than a license to destroy the city" (17). He has always considered the car as yet another misused technological tool, stating that "the American has sacrificed his life as a whole to the motorcar like someone who, demented with passion, wrecks his home to lavish his income on a capricious mistress who promises delights he can only occasionally enjoy" (18).

It has been a major theme of Mumford that people must be able to control technology and not let themselves be controlled by it. Over the past decades, this attitude has been introduced in the Western consciousness which no longer accepts technological advances blindly without questioning their overall implications to life and environment.

BIBLIOGRAPHY

1. L. Mumford, *Sketches from Life* (autobiography), The Dial Press, New York, 1982, p. 144.
2. L. Mumford, *The Urban Prospect,* Harcourt, Brace & World, New York, 1968, p. 240.
3. D. L. Miller, *The Lewis Mumford Reader,* Pantheon Books, New York, 1968, p. 9.
4. L. Mumford, *Art and Technics,* Columbia University Press, New York, 1952, pp. 31 and 32.
5. L. Mumford, *The Highway and the City,* Harcourt, Brace & World, New York, 1963, pp. 65 and 66.

6. *Ibid.*, pp. 56 and 57.
7. Ref. 4, p. 129.
8. Ref. 5, p. 128.
9. Ref. 5, p. 167.
10. Ref. 4, p. 124.
11. Ref. 4, p. 125.
12. Ref. 4, p. 126.
13. Ref. 4, p. 127.
14. M. D. Koenigsberg, "Urban Development: An Introduction to the Theories of Lewis Mumford," in S. F. Fava, ed., *Urbanism in World Perspective: A Reader,* T. Y. Crowell, New York, 1968, p. 575.
15. Ref. 3, p. 147.
16. L. Mumford, *The City in History,* Harcourt, Brace & World, New York, 1961, p. 511.
17. Ref. 16, p. 408.
18. Ref. 5, p. 235.

General References

J. Jacobs, *The Death and Life of Great American Cities,* Vintage Books, New York, 1961.

C. Jencks, *Modern Movements in Architecture,* Doubleday, New York, 1973.

L. Mumford, ed., *Roots of Contemporary American Architecture,* Dover, New York, 1972.

P. D. Spreiregen, *Urban Design: The Architecture of Towns and Cities,* McGraw-Hill, New York, 1965.

A. Whittick, ed. in chief, *Encyclopedia of Urban Planning,* McGraw-Hill, New York, 1974.

Charles Szoradi, AIA
Architect and Planner
Washington, D.C.

MUSEUMS

A museum, by definition, contains and maintains a collection of objects and has provisions for displaying, studying, and storing them. The collection is organized, which requires study and classification, and the objects are safeguarded and preserved. A museum must provide for the performance of these functions, as well as for the reception and information of visitors. It follows that museum building, as a type, usually includes at least (*1*) an entry and orientation area; (*2*) adjoining large halls or galleries for the principal displays, often supplemented by smaller rooms for secondary displays; (*3*) offices for the administrative staff and curators, or subject-matter specialists in charge of the collections; (*4*) rooms for the preparation, study, and storage of objects; and (*5*) spaces for the building's mechanical and maintenance functions. Most museums have various other areas for ancillary functions; these will be discussed in the section on programming.

Museums have been established to house almost every kind of object. Their collections may represent a single field or combination of fields that include, for example, the arts, archaeology, anthropology, natural history and the sciences, and histories of all sorts—of nations, regions, cities, and of many human products and activities. Museums of the fine arts are sometimes called galleries (as in the cases of the National Gallery of Art in London and in Washington, D.C.), but the terms museum and gallery should be distinguished: a museum has a permanent collection, while a gallery may be limited to changing displays of borrowed objects, owning none.

Is there a museum building type (Figs. 1 and 2)? The next section traces a formal historical type through variations that range from Renaissance prototypes to museums of the mid-twentieth century. In plan and elevation, this building type derives more from monumental public buildings and palatial residences than from the specific character of museum functions (Fig. 3). At the same time, a case can be made that most museums constructed in the past century repeatedly reveal typical and practical architectural solutions for usual functions, especially those connected with the needs of the public and with the care, handling, and display of objects. For example, sculpture is often displayed in gardens, where the gallery function takes place in the open. Almost every historic building type, from castles to barns and from churches to prisons, has been adapted for museum use. In fact, many of the smaller museums in Europe and the United States are located in adapted structures, which often make up in interest or charm what is lacking in convenience. (Two of the world's largest museums—the Louvre and the Musée d'Orsay—are in recycled buildings.) The basic functions of a museum find the clearest expression in the plans of

Figure 1. Die Glyptothek, Munich, 1815–1830, by Leo von Klenze. Early example of the traditional museum facade, with windowless walls that have central octostyle porticoes surmounted by pediments. Photograph by Wayne Andrews.

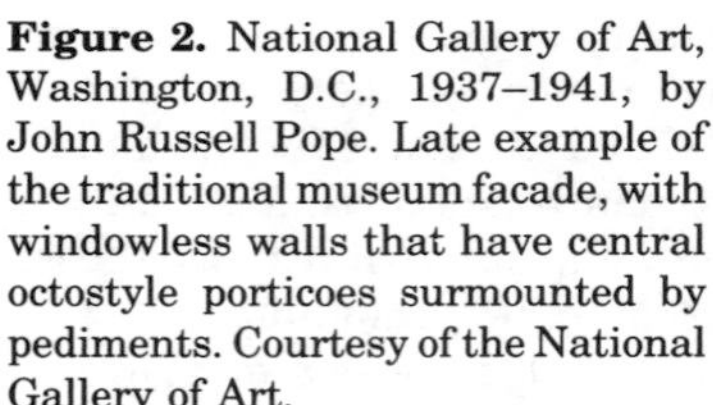

Figure 2. National Gallery of Art, Washington, D.C., 1937–1941, by John Russell Pope. Late example of the traditional museum facade, with windowless walls that have central octostyle porticoes surmounted by pediments. Courtesy of the National Gallery of Art.

buildings constructed specifically as museums, although these functions can by ingenuity be accommodated in adapted structures.

HISTORY OF THE BUILDING TYPE: EUROPEAN MUSEUMS BEFORE 1900

The origins of both systematic collections and traditional museum building types go back to Renaissance Italy. Objects from antiquity were collected and studied in the fifteenth century, and the first display of the still existing Capitoline Museum in Rome was arranged in 1471. About 1508, the architect Donato Bramante designed a court for antiquities at the Vatican, the first of several structures, including courts and loggias, planned in the sixteenth century for the display of objects. At the same time, the term museum came into usage to signify a collection. The modern concept of a public collection housed in a systematically planned museum hardly emerged before the eighteenth century, however, and developed broadly only in the nineteenth.

During the 1570s and 1580s, several long galleries for sculpture were built in Italy; thus the long hall, lit from one side, was established from the outset as a setting constructed specifically for the display of collections. Contemporary long galleries in Tudor England were built, by contrast, for exercise and then used for hanging family portraits. Other museum prototypes were established in the same period at the Uffizi in Florence. Giorgio Vasari designed the building for state offices, or *uffizi,* and Bernardo Buontalenti adapted it in the 1570s and 1580s to display art on the upper floor. In the east wing a range of rectangular rooms, with doorways in enfilade, culminates in a large octagonal *tribuna* lit from above (Fig. 4). This room, together with the Pantheon in Rome, was to influence countless museum designs over the centuries.

At the same time that prototypical gallery forms were appearing, the building of the classical type that museums were later to adopt began evolving in palaces and government structures. The Museo Nazionale in Naples was begun by Domenico Fontana in 1586 as a cavalry barrack and was adapted in 1612 to house a university, before undergoing renovation in 1790 to serve as an art museum. The basic architectural type—a rectangle of two principal stories, divided on its axis by a great central hall with monumental stairs, and flanked symmetrically by courts surrounded by ranges of rooms—persisted in gallery plans well into the twentieth century.

Although galleries for antiquities or sculpture appeared only rarely in the sixteenth century, in the seventeenth century they became common in palaces and great houses. The Earl of Arundel, who took Inigo Jones with him on his trip to Italy in 1613, returned to build a proper Italianate, side-lit long gallery for sculpture at Arundel House in London (Fig. 5). This period saw spectacular growth in collections of many kinds, including those relating to natural history, science, and curiosities in general. One natural history collection from this time formed the basis of the Old Ashmolean Museum in Oxford, a very early example of a special building erected as a museum and opened to the public, in 1683.

In Italy, the transformation of a residential palace into a series of galleries with framed paintings covering the walls and elaborately painted ceilings may be seen in Antonio del Grande's Galleria Colonna in Rome (ca 1675). It was in France, however, that the most spectacular palaces were rising, with lasting implications for the history of museums. Cardinal Mazarin's gallery, constructed by Françoise Mansard in 1645, is now part of the Bibliothèque Nationale and is the typical side-lit hall, nearly 150 ft in length. It is, of course, completely dwarfed by the 1500-ft Grande Galerie of the Louvre, built to connect the Old Louvre to the palace of the Tuileries, and substantially completed by 1610 (Fig. 6). The Grande Galerie, undoubtedly the most famous picture gallery in the world, was not constructed to display art, but contained models of French fortifications in the late seventeenth century. By that time the palace of the Louvre had become associated with art and artists, housing workshops and also, from 1692, the Academy of Painting and Sculpture. The Academy's annual exhibition took place in the Salon Carré, which adjoins the Grande Galerie on the east. The Salon Carré is a great, high ceilinged room that is rectangular in plan, despite its name. It was originally side-lit, but in the eighteenth century the Academy's paintings crowded every inch of wall, and the windows were closed over and lighting was provided from above. Proposals were also made in the course of the eighteenth century to exhibit art and create overhead lighting in the Grande Galerie, but the present skylight dates only from the 1930s. The French Revolution brought the project of a national art gallery to a head, and in 1793 the Muséum Française, displaying the former royal collections in the Salon Carré

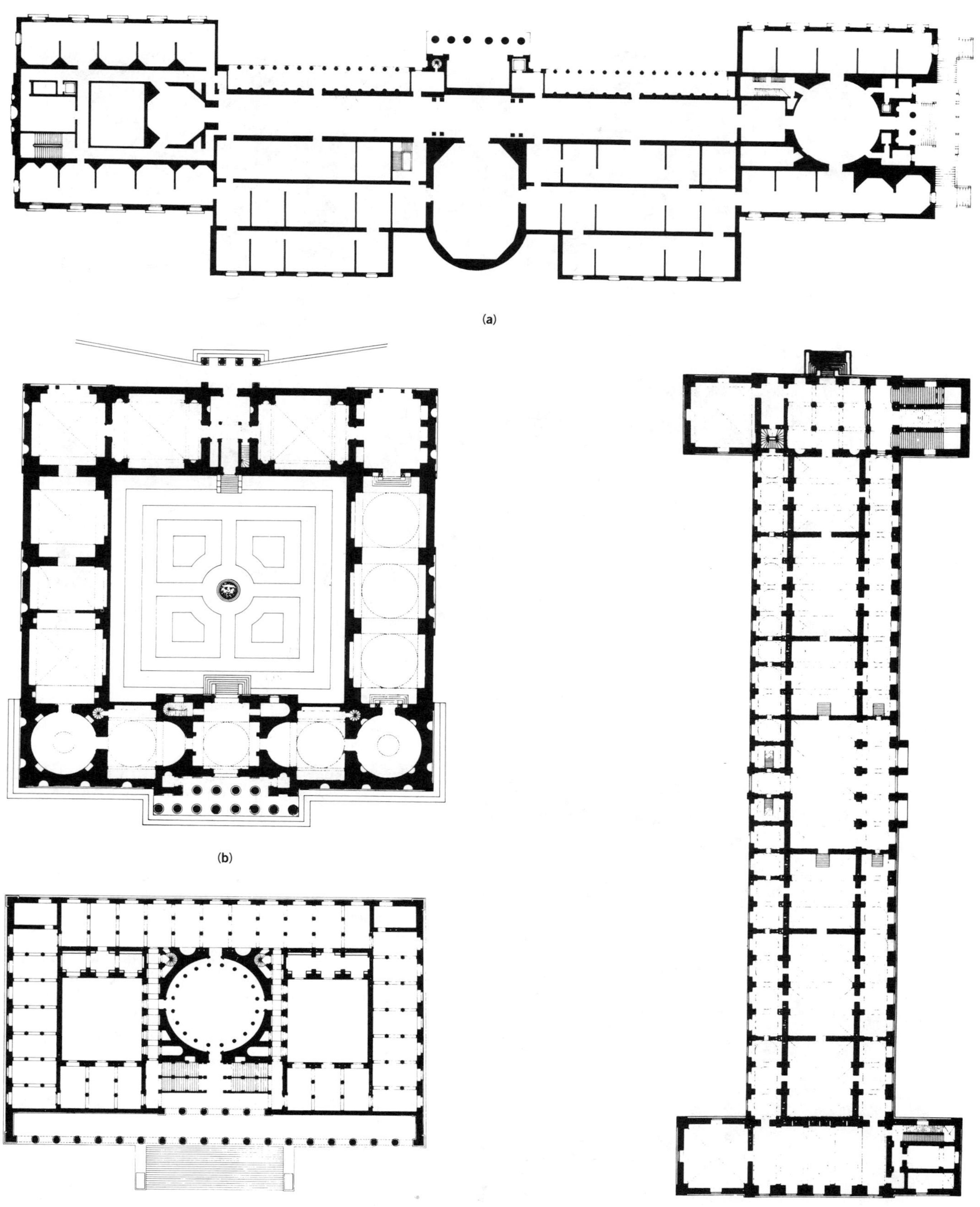

Figure 3. Comparative plans of early nineteenth-century European museums (1). (**a**) Museo del Prado, Madrid, 1784–1811, by Juan de Villanueva; (**b**) Glyptothek, Munich, 1815–1830, by Leo von Klenze; (**c**) Die Altes Museum, Berlin, 1823–1830, by Karl Friedrich Schinkel; (**d**) Alte Pinacothek, Munich, 1826–1836, by Leo von Klenze. Courtesy of M.I.T. Press.

Figure 4. The Tribuna of the Uffizi, Florence, 1574–1581, by Bernardo Buontalenti. Prototypical central-plan gallery with skylight. Courtesy of the Photographic Archives, National Gallery of Art.

Figure 5. Sculpture Gallery of the Earl of Arundel. Detail of a painting by Daniel Mytens, 1618, showing an Italianate, side-lit, long gallery in Arundel House, London. Courtesy of the National Portrait Gallery, London.

and royal apartments, was opened to the public. From this start, and growing rapidly as booty from Napoleon's excursions began to arrive, the Louvre museum extended down the Grande Galerie and then eastward into the Cour Carrée.

Other significant European museums also trace their origins to the eighteenth century. The nucleus of the British Museum collection was purchased by Parliament in 1753. Frederick the Great began Sanssouci in Potsdam in 1756. In 1737 the last of the Medici left the state of Tuscany the family collections, which 50 years later were arranged for public viewing, and eventually made up substantial parts of the collections in the Uffizi and Pitti museums. The donation to the state of the Prussian collections in 1797 led eventually to the foundation of the Berlin Museum. The Prado was designed in 1784 as a natural-history museum, but was opened in 1819 as an art gallery (Fig. 3**a**).

Along with this impetus toward public museums came a growing concern for order and a program, both in the arrangement of collections and in architectural planning. The collaboration in the 1760s of the historian J. J. Winckelmann and the collector Cardinal Albani in the arrangement of antiquities in Rome's Villa Albani is a case in point. Also carefully ordered, in a more neoclassic setting, were the collections of antiquities and objects relating to

Figure 6. Musée du Louvre, Grande Galerie, Paris, completed 1610, by Androuet Ducerceau. Converted to a picture gallery in 1796; skylight added in the 1930s. Courtesy of the Photographic Archives, National Gallery of Art.

the natural and physical sciences found in the Kassel Museum Fridericianum, a landmark example of an independent museum structure accessible to the public. Built in 1769–1777, the architect was Simon Louis du Ry. The study of classical archaeology and the rise of the neoclassical style proceeded hand in hand, and at the Vatican this partnership culminated in the 1770s in the Museo Pio-Clementino (Simonetti and Camporesi). The grand staircase, barrel vaults, and domed rotunda set the precedent for many later museums.

Projects for ideal plans for independent art-museum structures appear in the Prix de Rome competitions of the French Architectural Academy, which set the competition theme as museums five times between 1753 and 1791. Without constraints of site and with minimal concessions to program, the projects returned several times to the concept of a great square enclosing a Greek cross, with a domed gallery at the crossing. The grandest and most visionary structure of this type was designed by E. L. Boullée in 1783; the most practical and influential was published by J. N. L. Durand in his *Précis des leçons* of 1802–1809.

A frequent rationale for the extensive square plan, entrances on four sides, and inscribed cross in these grand theoretical museums was that the structure would house a multiprogrammed museum of the arts, archaeology, the physical and natural sciences, and a library. In practice, the museums that actually resulted tended to be more focused in function and plan. A series of monumental buildings in national capitals in the early nineteenth century established types for facades and plans that influenced countless succeeding buildings for a century, and to this day seem to typify the museum concept. The façades were either in a classical manner (meaning relatively Greek or Roman), or Renaissance in style. In plan, the typical building was rectangular; if there were two interior courtyards, they flanked a central hall, grand stair, or domed rotunda. The galleries were arranged in strict symmetry on either side of a monumental entrance centered on a long side. In elevation, there were usually two principal stories, the upper being either side- or top-lit.

The earliest of these prototypical buildings, the Munich Glyptothek (Leo von Klenze, 1815–1830) features a giant pedimented portico flanked by wings with aedicules containing statues (Figs. 1 and 3**b**). The facade of the Berlin Altes Museum (Karl Friederich Schinkel, 1823–1830) presents an imposing, severe colonnade behind which a monumental stairway indicates the two-storied plan of the museum (Fig. 3**c**). Its great domed rotunda—forerunner of so many domes, including Washington, D.C.'s National Gallery—is behind and not expressed externally. The British Museum in London (Sir Robert Smirke, 1823–1847) is also fronted by a colonnade, with projecting wings and a central pediment (Fig. 7). The huge domed reading room in the central court dates from the 1850s. The museum was constructed to house a library and archaeological treasures, together with scientific collections later transferred to South Kensington. Paintings were displayed in the National Gallery (William Wilkins, 1832–1838), which was constructed on an oblong plan and had a central portico leading to grand stairs (Fig. 8). The original galleries observed a strict symmetry, but major additions extended the building asymmetrically to the rear.

The Munich Glyptothek was constructed for sculpture, as its name implies. Leo von Klenze, its architect, proceeded next to design a Munich painting gallery, the Alte Pinakothek (1826–1836), in the Renaissance style (Fig. 3**d**). The ingenious and influential plan provided for a long row of great skylit galleries, flanked by smaller, windowlit rooms to the north and a connecting loggia to the south. This allowed for flexibility and differentiation of display spaces and for good circulation. Von Klenze went

Figure 7. British Museum, London, 1823–1847, by Sir Robert Smirke. Courtesy of the Photographic Archives, National Gallery of Art.

Figure 8. National Gallery, London, 1832–1838, by William Wilkins. Courtesy of the Photographic Archive, National Gallery of Art.

on to St. Petersburg to design the mammoth Hermitage, which was begun in 1859.

The second half of the nineteenth century saw a greatly accelerated growth in museums. In London, for instance, an establishment for science, art, and instruction was founded in South Kensington in 1857 in what was to expand into the labyrinthine Victoria and Albert Museum. The paintings of the British School outgrew these quarters and were moved in 1897 to the Tate gallery. Meanwhile, an enormous increase in the science collections occasioned the construction of the huge Natural History Museum, with its Romanesque facade, in the 1870s. Medieval collections and medieval stylistic touches appeared with increasing frequency from mid-century on, and Romanesque facades in particular were in vogue from the 1860s to the 1880s. Romanesque veneers, however, usually did not affect the formal and symmetrical design and plan, and it was easy to shift back in the 1890s to the beaux-arts classicism that was to prevail, at least in conservative circles, until the 1930s ("The last of the Romans"—in the classical style—was the John Russell Pope National Gallery of Art in Washington, D.C., which was designed in 1937 and opened in 1941) (Figs. 2, 9, and 10).

MUSEUMS IN THE UNITED STATES AND TWENTIETH-CENTURY DEVELOPMENTS

The history of museums in the United States must begin with the singular institution founded in Philadelphia in 1786 by the ingenious painter and natural philosopher, Charles Willson Peale. This collection of paintings, natural history, and curiosities expanded until it occupied the upper floor of the Old State House. His collection was dispersed following his death in 1827, but fortunately Peale had the foresight to document his installation in a painting. His was the first of a number of American museums combining the sciences and the arts, ranging from the Smithsonian Institution (original building by James Renwick, 1846–1855) to the Los Angeles County Museum, which spawned separate art buildings only in 1965.

Apart from Peale's pioneering venture, the United

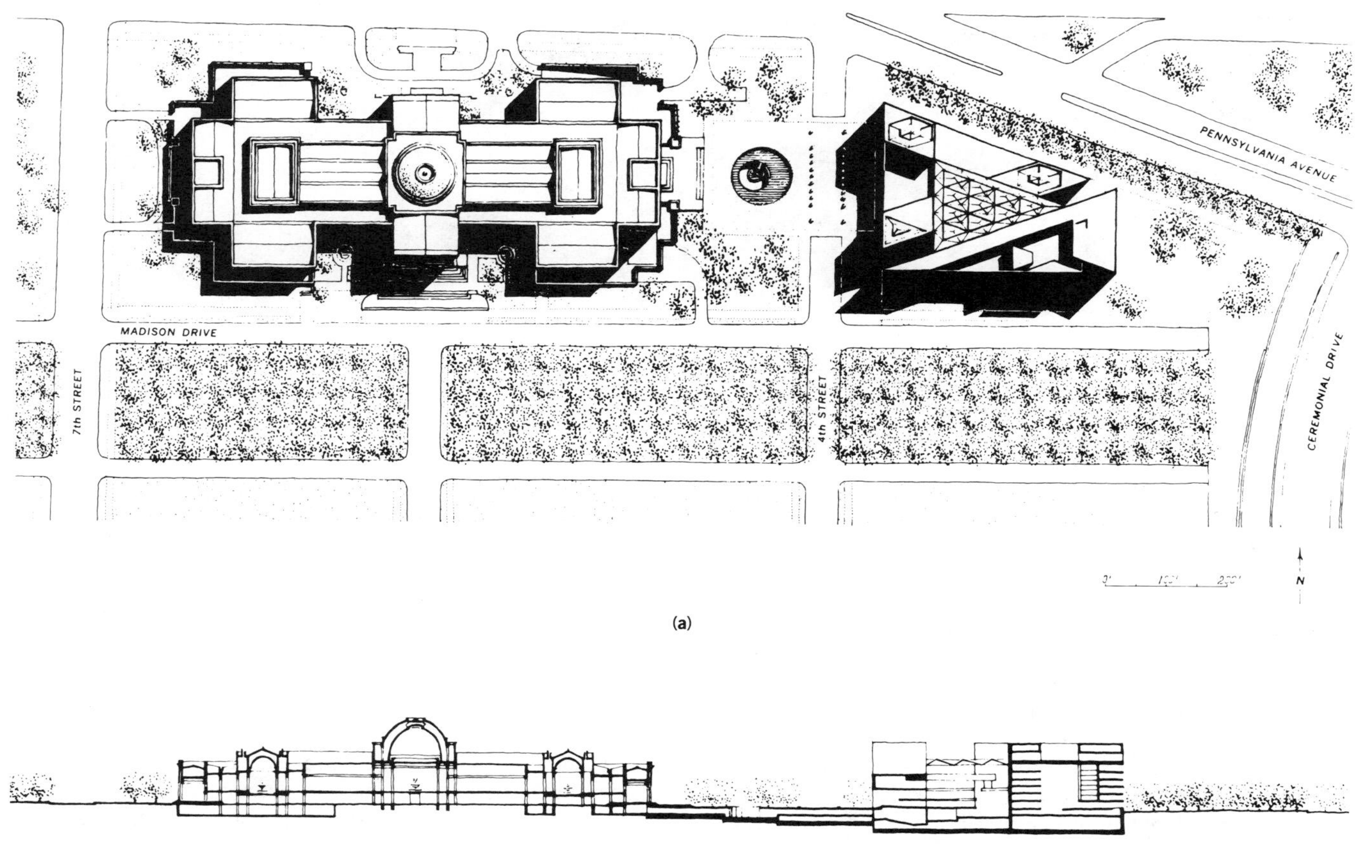

(a)

(b)

Figure 9. National Gallery of Art, Washington, D.C. **(a)** Bird's eye and **(b)** sectional drawings of museum complex showing East Building project, 1970. West Building by John Russell Pope, 1937–1941; East Building by I. M. Pei and Partners, 1971–1978. Courtesy of the Archives Office, National Gallery of Art.

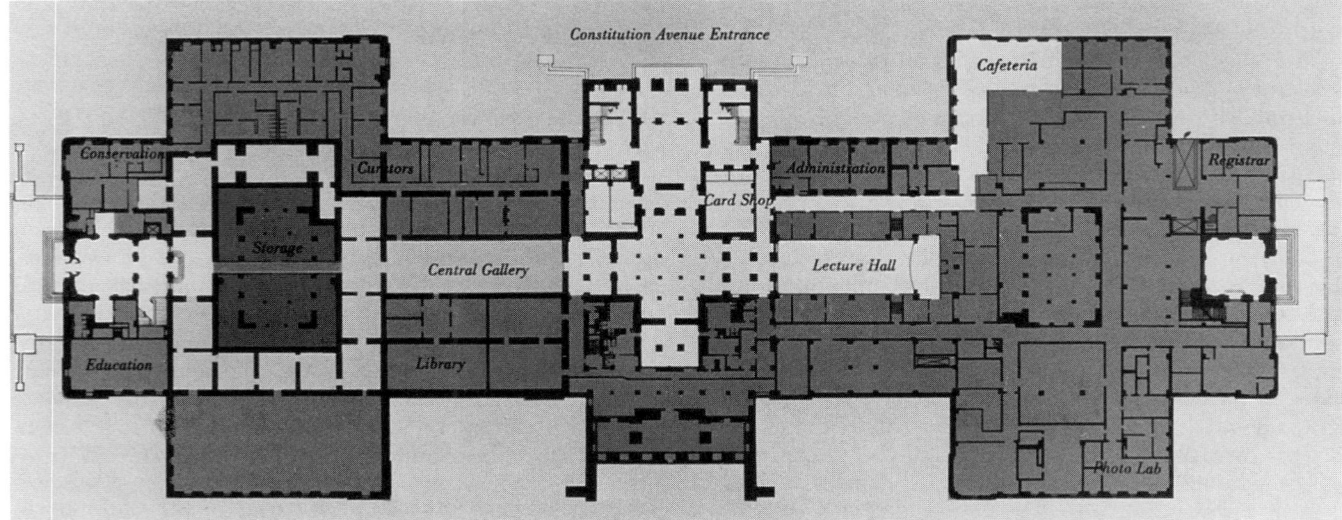

(a)

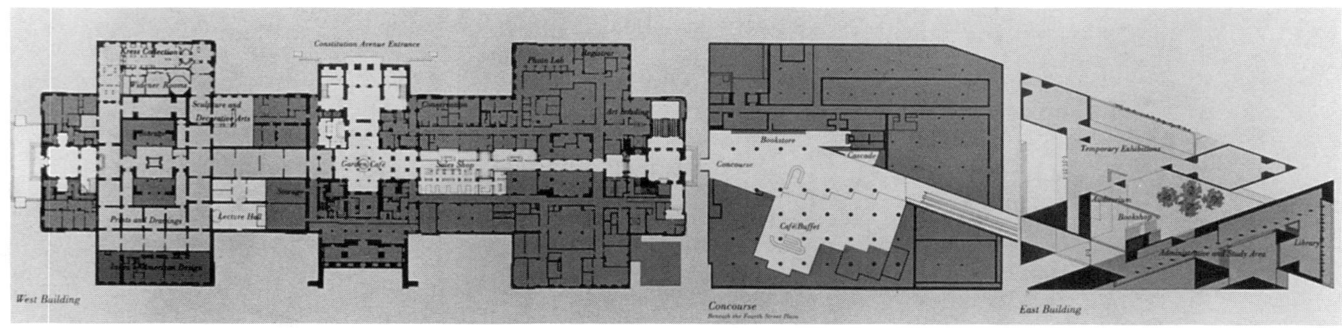

(b)

Figure 10. National Gallery of Art, Washington, D.C. **(a)** Ground floor plan of original building by John Russell Pope, 1941; and **(b)** 1984 plan showing the ground floor, West Building, after the 1976–1984 renovation by Keyes, Condon, and Florance, and the Underground Concourse and East Building ground floor, by I. M. Pei and Partners, 1971–1978. Courtesy of the Archives Office, National Gallery of Art.

States' earliest museums date only from the first half of the nineteenth century and were slow in making their appearance. Philadelphia again led the way: the first U.S. museum building, which was also the first art museum, was built for the Pennsylvania Academy of Fine Arts (John Dorsey, 1805–1806; destroyed in 1845). The modest, federal-style structure drew from the European tradition in incorporating a central domed rotunda. The next museum built in the United States, also now destroyed, was the Trumbull Gallery at Yale College in New Haven, designed by the artist Colonel John Trumbull to house his paintings (constructed 1831–1832). The galleries consisted of two large, top-lit rooms on the upper story.

The first truly monumental building in the United States to incorporate museum and gallery functions was the Old Patent Office, now shared by the Smithsonian's National Portrait Gallery and National Museum of American Art (Fig. 11). The building forms a large rectangle about a central court. The earliest wing, to the south, is 404 ft long and features a central portico copied from the facade of the Parthenon; it was designed by William Parker Elliot in 1836 and was completed by Robert Mills in 1840. Patent models and the collection of the National Institute, a precursor of the Smithsonian Institution, were displayed in the three-story building with its lofty upper gallery.

In the 1840s, architectural fashion changed abruptly, and the long reign of classical styles, descending from the early Renaissance, was challenged by the Gothic and Romanesque. Hartford, Connecticut's Atheneum (Ithiel Town and Alexander Jackson Davis, 1842–1844) was dressed out in towers and crenellations; it served as a cultural center as well as a picture gallery. Even more colorful was James Renwick's Smithsonian Building, the first Romanesque revival building in the country, constructed on the Mall in Washington, D.C. (1846–1855) (Fig. 12). The plan centered on a great hall that is 15 bays (200 ft) in length, with entrances at the central bay. To disguise this symmetry, contrasting wings extended to the east and west, and the whole was crowned by eight picturesque towers, each different. The great hall was at

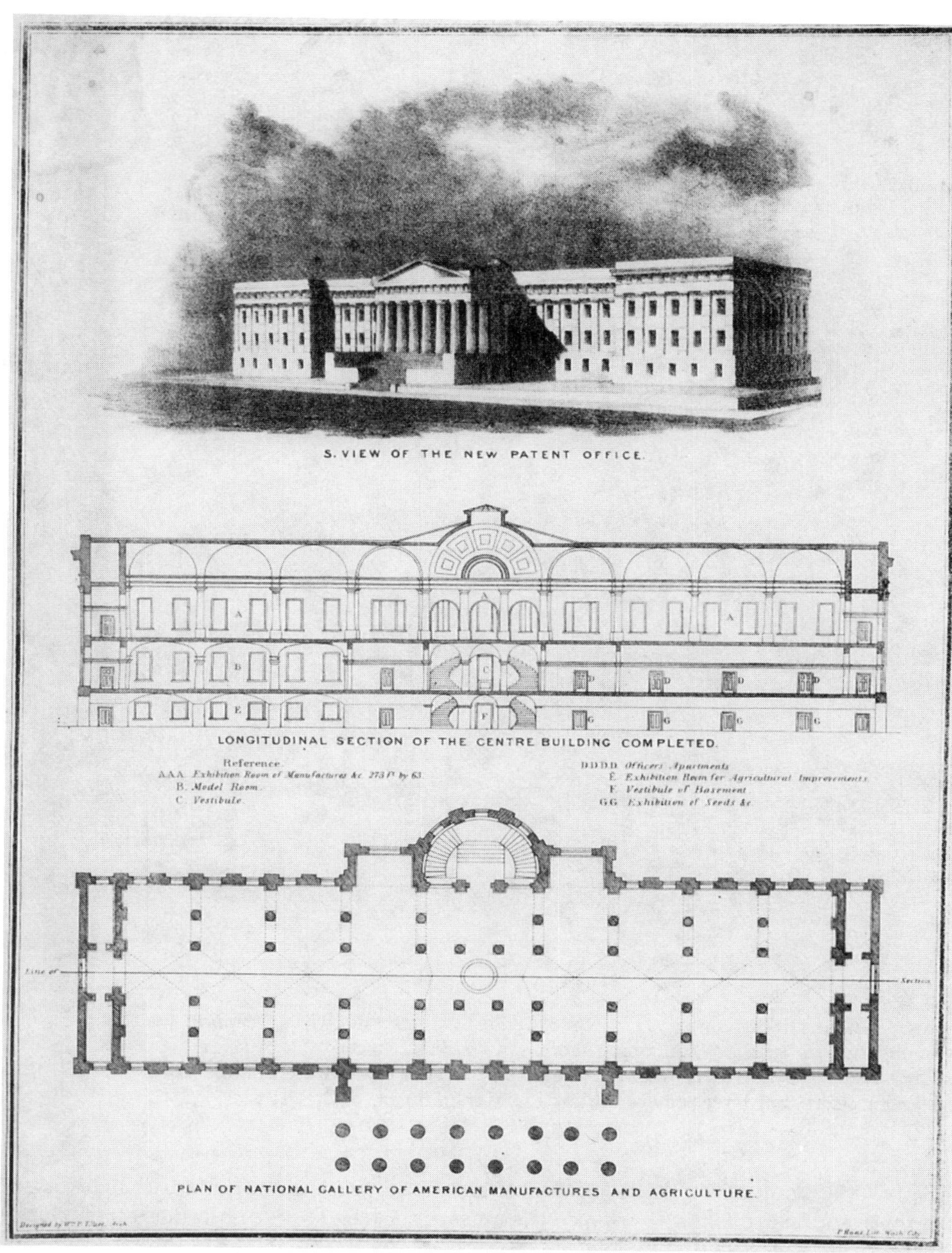

Figure 11. The Old Patent Office (south wing), Washington, D.C., 1836–1840, by Elliot and Mills. A view, section, and plan of the Patent Office (including the National Gallery of American Manufactures and Agriculture) from a lithograph, ca 1840. Courtesy of the National Archives.

ground level, an exception to the usual plan, and the stairway access to the large upper floor and its art gallery was awkward. The great hall served impressively for the display of rapidly growing natural history collections (Fig. 13), but the two halls of the eastern wing that housed paintings, sculpture, and the library were ineffectual for display. For this and various other reasons, the Smithsonian art collections soon found shelter elsewhere.

While the first half of the nineteenth century saw the founding of only a handful of museums and a break from the classical style, the second half saw the active beginning of the museum movement and, in the 1890s, a sharp swing back to beaux-arts classicism. James Renwick, again, may be considered as taking a first step in his design of Washington, D.C.'s original Corcoran Gallery, begun in 1859 as a robust, early adaptation of the Second-Empire style. The building is ornate, formal, and symmetrical, with a grand interior staircase leading to an even grander main gallery on the second floor. Although it was not completed as a museum until well after the Civil War, the building, now the Renwick Gallery, may claim to be the oldest in the United States designed solely as an art museum and serving the same function today.

Following a respite during the Civil War, U.S. museum building resumed. The Romanesque-style American Museum of Natural History in New York dates from 1869. Both the Metropolitan Museum in New York (Fig. 14) and the Museum of Fine Arts in Boston were founded in 1870. In 1876, the Boston Museum's first building was dedicated, and so were two art museums in Philadelphia. The Corcoran was finally opened the following year. From this time, museum building accelerated rapidly. Museums

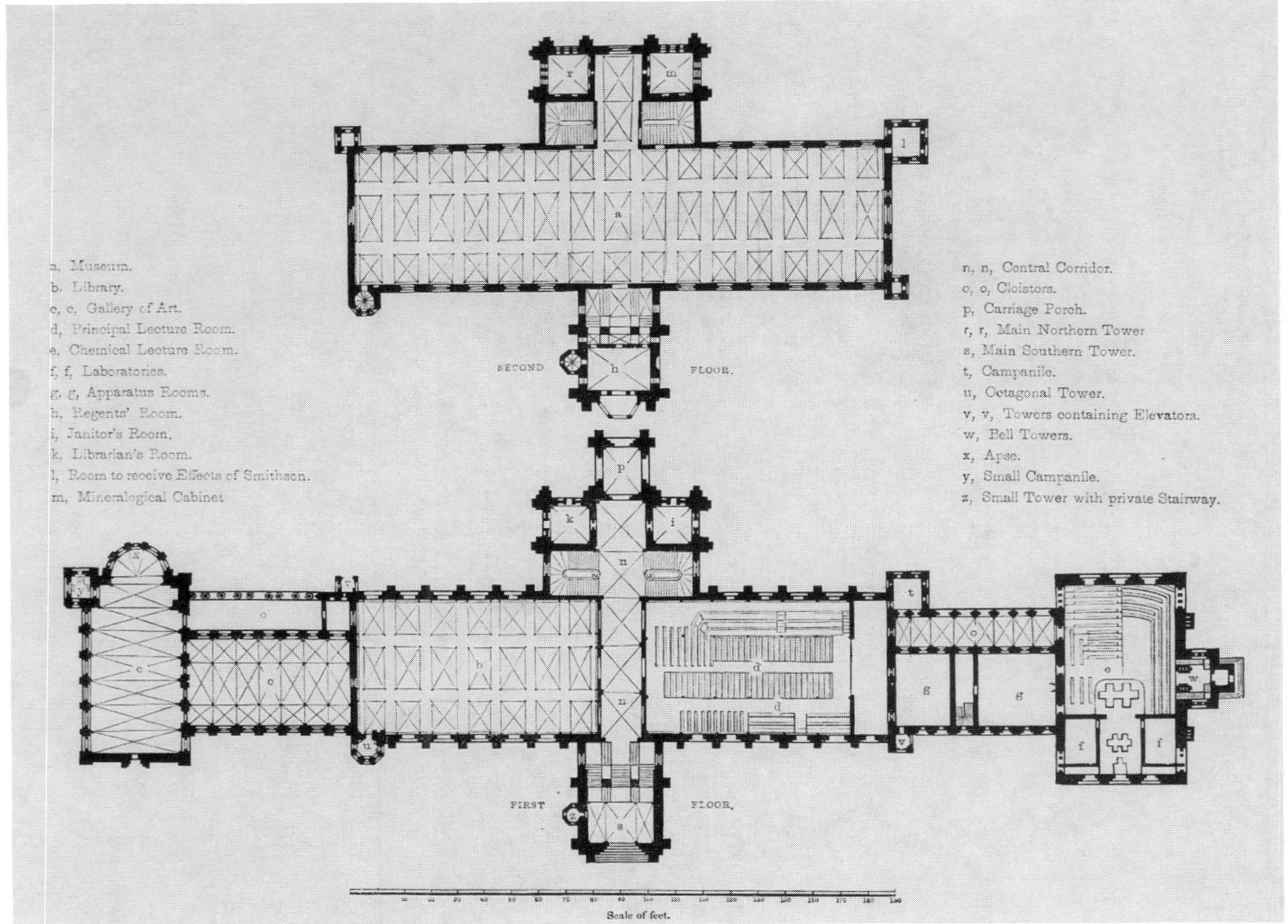

Figure 12. Smithsonian Building, Washington, D.C., 1846–1855, by James Renwick. Original plans (woodcut first published in 1849). When construction was well advanced, the museum was relocated to the first floor and the lecture room to the second. Works of art were installed on both the first and second floors, but later removed. Courtesy of the Library of Congress.

were founded in Columbus, Ohio and in Chicago in 1878 and 1879, respectively, and in Cincinnati and Detroit in 1881 and 1885. By 1898, when the American Federation of Arts issued its first annual report, it listed 42 museums.

The growth in the building of museums in the twentieth century has been astonishing. By 1921, there were 153 museums and in 1931, 235, many of them in smaller cities. After a temporary setback during the 1930s Depression and World War II, the tempo quickened again. There were 379 art museums in the United States and Canada in 1961; 597 in 1971; and 1039 in 1982. In this survey only a handful of the most important can be mentioned, and the rich diversity of this heritage can only be suggested.

An outstanding example from the 1870s, fortunately well preserved and restored, is the Pennsylvania Academy of the Fine Arts (1872–1876), an extravagant and delightful example of Frank Furness's eclectic taste (Fig. 15). The lower floor housed an art school and the upper floor has top-lit galleries that have served well to the present day (restoration by Vitetta Group, Studio Four, 1974–1977). But if fanciful eclecticism and romantic medievalism shaped the museums of the 1870s and 1880s, a new classicism characterized the 1890s. Charles Follen McKim's Walker Art Gallery (Bowdoin College, Brunswick, Maine, 1891–1893) was an early harbinger of the classical, but the country was unprepared for the spectacle that appeared almost overnight in Chicago in 1893. The World's Columbian Exposition was the occasion for the construction of the most impressively monumental complex of museums ever seen in the United States. The facades surrounding the Court of Honor borrowed freely from Greek, Roman, Renaissance, baroque and beaux-arts precedents. Their impact may be traced in almost every major museum building constructed in the next half century.

One of the first museums in the revived classical style, and one of the most restrained and dignified, was the new Corcoran Gallery in Washington, D.C. (Ernest Flagg, 1893–1895). It centers on a two-story, skylighted atrium that is open to galleries on both levels. Opposite the entrance a proper grand staircase connects the floors.

Figure 13. The Great Hall of the Smithsonian, Washington, D.C. Woodcut of the installation as a museum, first published in 1857. The material brought back by the Wilkes expedition was so extensive that two balconies were installed in the newly opened hall. Courtesy of the Library of Congress.

Between the turn of the century and World War II, art museums in traditional styles were built in most larger cities in the United States and in a host of smaller ones. Many were enlarged subsequently, but retain their original facades, often as vestigial entries. Examples include the Albright-Knox Art Gallery in Buffalo (Edward B. Green, 1900–1905); the Boston Museum of Fine Arts (Guy Lowell, 1906–1931); the Cleveland Museum of Art (Hubbell and Benes, 1916); the Detroit Institute of Arts (Paul P. Cret, 1927); and the Baltimore Museum of Art and the National Gallery of Art in Washington (both by John Russell Pope, 1929 and 1937–1941, respectively).

The fundamental plan for these examples (with many variations) was based on the concept of a two-story rectangular building entered at the center of the long side. Facing the entrance is a grand stair and/or great hall, in the form of a court, as in the second Corcoran, or flanking courts. The plan is essentially symmetrical, providing for lesser galleries and offices on the lower floor and major galleries above. A basement is used for various mechanical and support functions. Stylistically, these buildings derive largely from Greek and Roman motifs, but even when borrowing from the Georgian (the Fogg Art Museum, Cambridge, Mass., by Shepley, Rutan, and Coolidge, 1927) or Art Deco (Museum of Fine Arts, Springfield, Mass., by Tilton and Githens, 1931–1933), the formal plan and facade remain the same.

Almost all of the museums cited have been enlarged, partly to accommodate normal growth in attendance and collections, and partly because of changes in emphasis and priority in museum functions. Museums have become increasingly active on many fronts: public services and amenities; membership and fund raising; scholarships and educational programs; and collections management and conservation. Buildings have been changed or enlarged to provide for large temporary exhibitions, gift shops, cafeterias, circulation of the handicapped, school-group programs, electronic security, computer systems, conservation laboratories, climate control systems, and energy conservation.

The impact of such changes is illustrated by a comparison of the original, 1941, plan of the National Gallery of Art and the composite plan after the 1971–1978 addition by I. M. Pei and remodeling of the West Building (Figs. 9 and 10). The conservative John Russell Pope plan was indeed the last of its kind; in 1941 a revolution in museum design and concept was already under way.

In 1939, Eero and Eliel Saarinen won a competition for a Smithsonian Gallery to be constructed facing the Pope building across the Mall. Although it was never built, the gallery was conceived as an activity-center museum, in the modern idiom. The Museum of Modern Art (MOMA) (Goodwin and Stone, 1939) and the Guggenheim Museum (Frank Lloyd Wright, 1943–1959), both in New York, signaled a new era. Porticoes, pediments, columns, and cornices disappeared. Exhibits began directly at ground level. The grand stair was gone—although the Guggenheim may be regarded as the apotheosis of the domed rotunda, with

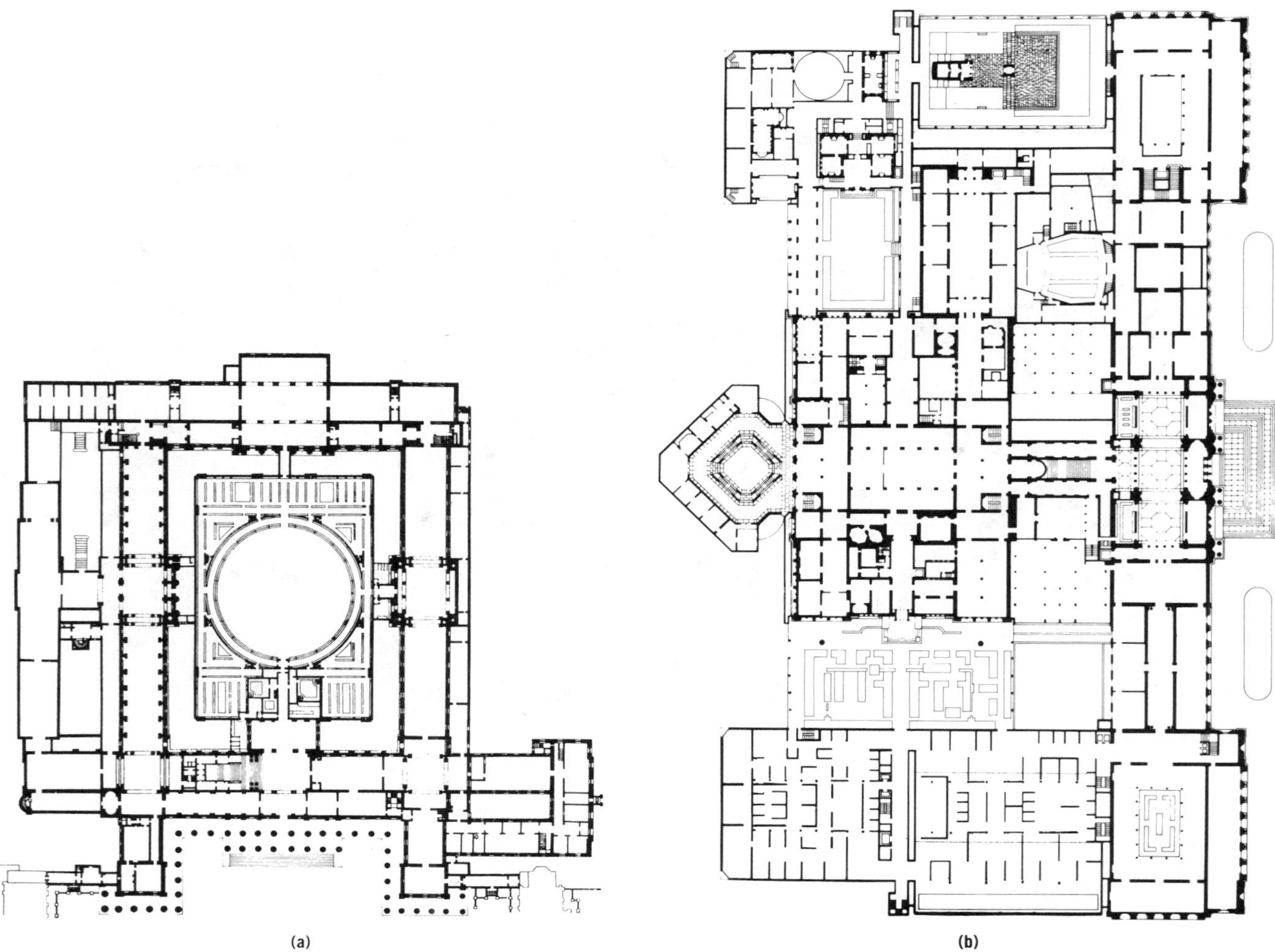

Figure 14. Comparative plans of (**a**) British Museum, London, 1823–1847, by Sir Robert Smirke; (**b**) The Metropolitan Museum of Art, New York, 1880–1979, by Vaux and Mold; Weston; McKim, Mead and White; Brown, Lawford and Forbes; Roche, Dinkeloo and Associates (1). Courtesy of M.I.T. Press.

an inverted grand stair reappearing as a descending ramp. The Guggenheim violates almost every principle of art museum design, but its combination of unusual concept and formal power contribute toward making it the most famous example of modern museum architecture in the United States (Fig. 16).

The Museum of Modern Art led the way to the widespread adoption of the International Style. Seven years before its 1939 building opened, MOMA staged an influential exhibition by Philip Johnson and Henry Russell Hitchcock entitled "The International Style: Architecture Since 1922." The 1939 museum by Goodwin and Stone introduced the concept of stacked floors with unobstructed exhibit space, which allowed for flexible arrangements of screen walls and overhead lighting. Temporary exhibitions were on the ground floor, permanent collections on the second and third levels, offices on the upper floors, and a theater for the film arts on the lower level. A sculpture garden provided a monumental focus for the entrance lobby (Fig. 17).

The 1940s saw little museum building, and construction was still relatively slow in the following decade. Eero and Eliel Saarinen's Des Moines Art Center (1948) shows the modern idiom in a warm vein, in contrast to Louis Kahn's Yale University Art Gallery (1952–1954), with its pioneering use of concrete. In 1958, Mies van der Rohe, the patron saint of the International movement, began his first addition to the Houston Museum of Fine Arts; his most spectacular gallery, an enormous clear-span area 83 × 300 ft, was added in 1973.

The golden age of modernism, evident in various museums, came in the 1960s and 1970s, a period of increased emphasis on adaptive reuse. Examples of such adaptation include, in Washington, D.C., the Old Patent Office and the Old Corcoran Gallery. The Patent Office was adapted, after use by the Civil Service Commission, to house the National Collection of Fine Arts and National Portrait Gallery in 1968 and the Corcoran was assigned, after interim use by the Court of Claims, to house the Renwick Gallery in 1965. In New York, the Carnegie Mansion became the Cooper Hewitt Museum in 1976.

The museums of the 1960s and 1970s reflect the stylistic

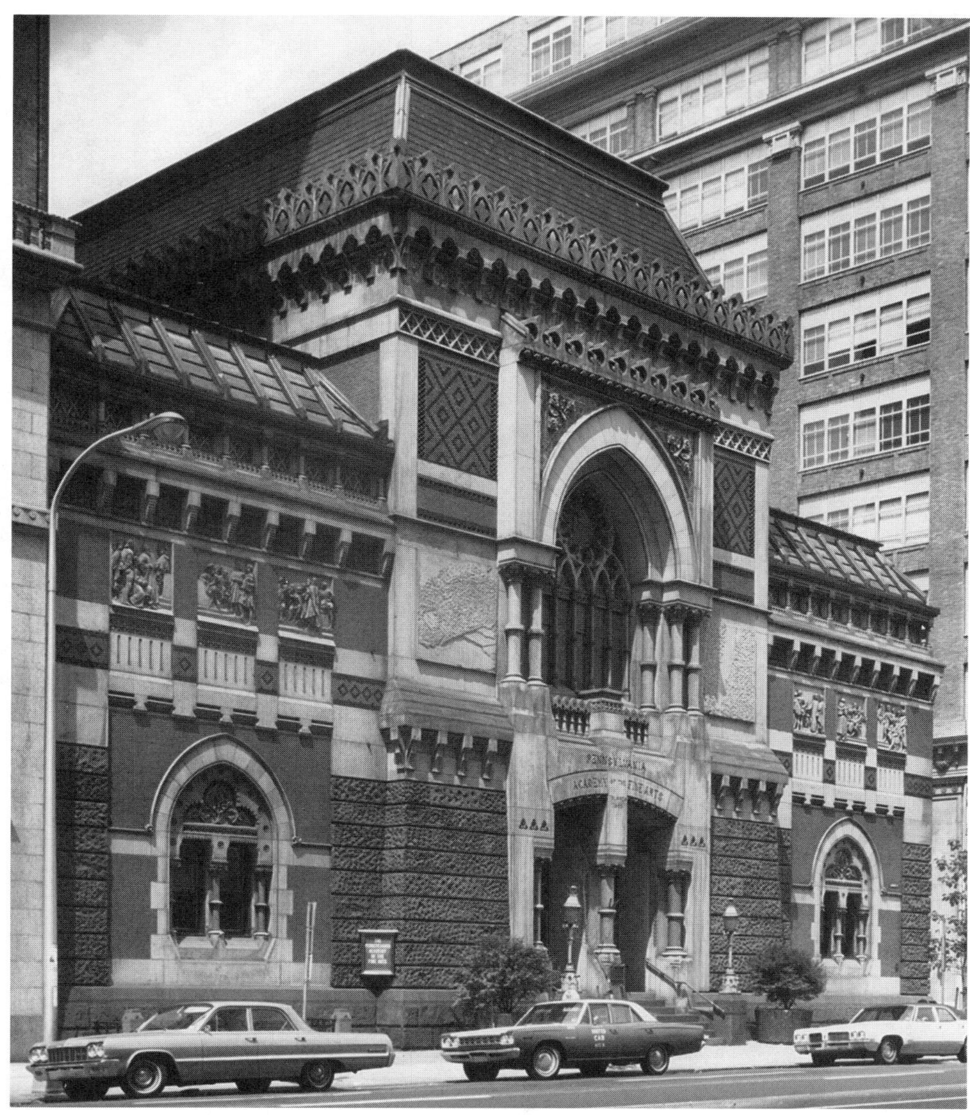

Figure 15. Pennsylvania Academy of the Fine Arts, Philadelphia, 1872–1876, by Frank Furness. Photograph by Wayne Andrews.

diversity of the modern movement. Philip Johnson's Sheldon Memorial Art Gallery at the University of Nebraska (1963) marks a turn away from his Miesian period to a formal stylistic elegance. An even greater departure from severe planarity, to a brutalism of pronounced textures and overhanging masses, occurs in Marcel Breuer's vigorous Whitney Museum of American Art in New York (1963–1966) (Fig. 18). Also highly sculptured are I. M. Pei's Everson Museum (Syracuse, New York, 1968) and Mario J. Ciampi's art museum on the campus of the University of California at Berkeley (1967–1970). At the other extreme from restrained and completely urbanized buildings like New York's Museum of Modern Art and Louis Kahn's masterly Yale Center for British Art in New Haven (1969–1977) (which incorporates commercial shops into the ground floor plan) are such garden-integrated structures as the Oakland Museum (Oakland, California, 1962–1968) by Kevin Roche, and Philip Johnson's small pavilion at Dumbarton Oaks (Washington, D.C., 1963).

Edward Larrabee Barnes's Walker Art Center (Minneapolis, 1970–1971) is a landmark example of a small, low cost, effective museum of art. In style, scale, and materials it stands in contrast to Louis Kahn's elegant Kimball Museum (Fort Worth, Texas, 1972) and I. M. Pei's East Building of the National Gallery in Washington (1971–1978). The East Building culminates the last modernist decade of museum design. The 1980s are marked by a variety of postmodern styles.

Unlike the advent of modernism in the 1930s, the advent of postmodernism has not corresponded to any marked changes in museum function or internal design, nor is modernism actually exhausted in its ability to generate vital extensions of its stylistic branches. The Dallas Museum of Fine Arts (Edward Larrabee Barnes, 1977–1983) is essentially a horizontal building in the international style, with gardens and patios on three terraced levels. The high tech aspect of this style is represented by Richard Meier's High Museum in Atlanta, Georgia (1980–1983), with its imaginative elaboration of geometrical forms and porcelain-enameled surfaces (Fig. 19). The eclectic postmodern borrowing of traditional forms and materials, such as the arch, column, cornice, gabled roof,

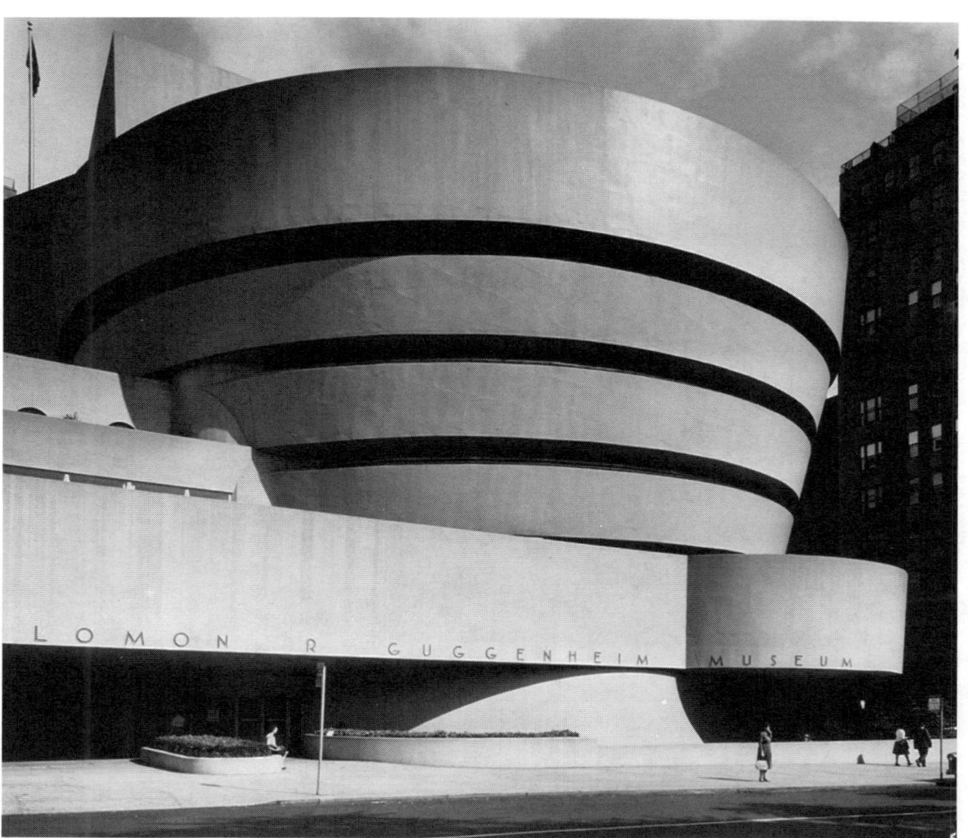

Figure 16. Guggenheim Museum, New York, 1943–1959, by Frank Lloyd Wright. Photograph by Wayne Andrews.

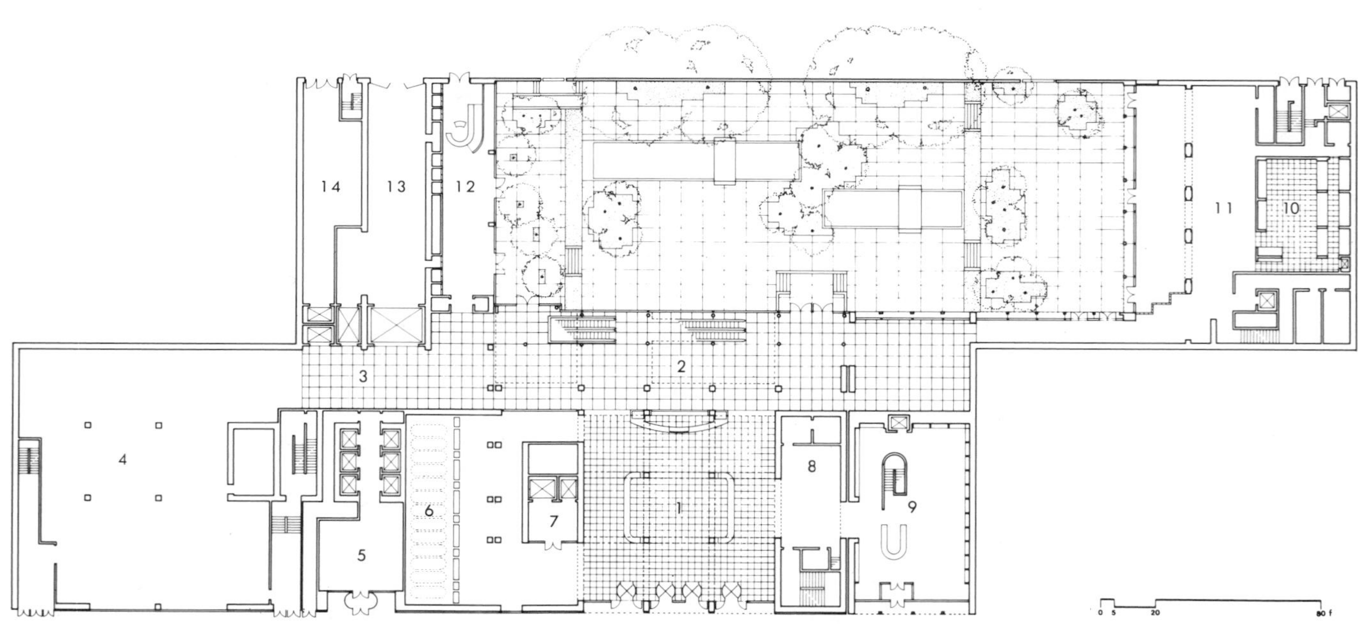

Figure 17. Museum of Modern Art, New York, Ground Floor, Goodwin and Stone, 1938–1939; Phillip Johnson, 1953 and 1964; Cesar Pelli, 1977–1983. Reception area of a major museum on a limited urban site, developed through successive remodelings. 1: Museum public lobby; 2: Garden hall; 3: Elevator lobby; 4: Temporary exhibition; 5: Tower lobby; 6: Coatroom; 7: Staff reception; 8: Membership sales; 9: Bookstore; 10: Cafeteria; 11: Public restaurant; 12: Group reception; 13: Museum service; 14: Tower service.

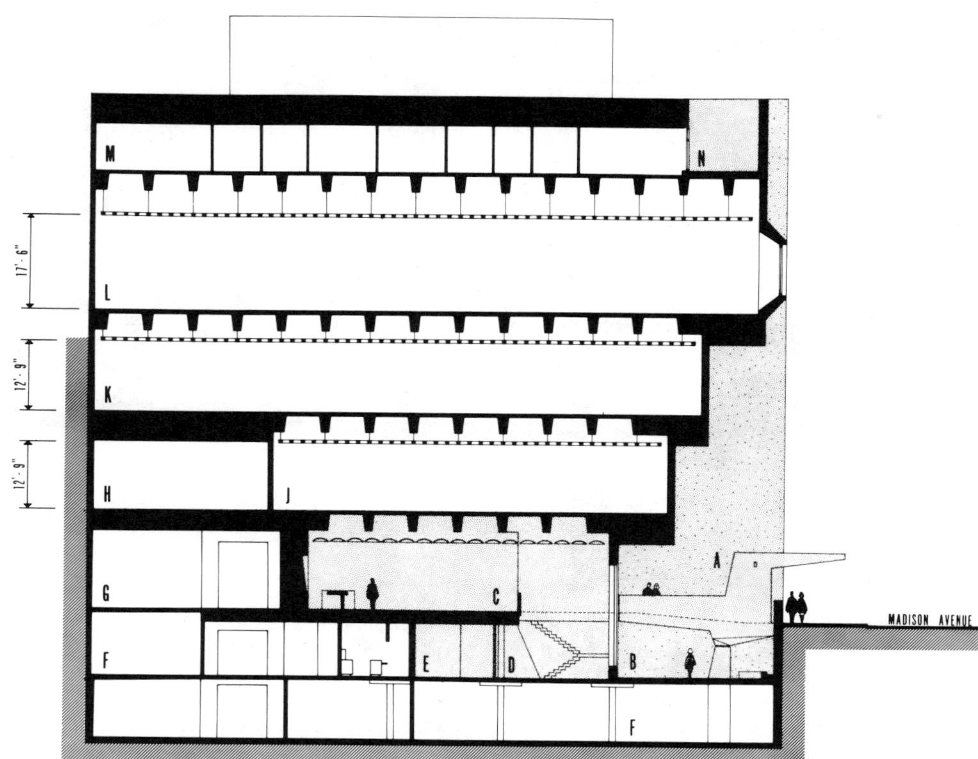

Figure 18. Whitney Museum of American Art, New York, 1963–1966, by Marcel Breuer and Hamilton Smith (Michael H. Irving, Consulting Architect). Section showing entrance bridge (A), sculpture court (B), lobby (C), cafeteria (E), art storage (F), truck dock (G), auditorium (H), galleries (J, K, L,), and offices (M). An ingenious use of lower-level space and stacked galleries helps overcome the limitations of a restricted urban site. Courtesy of Gatje, Papachristou, Smith.

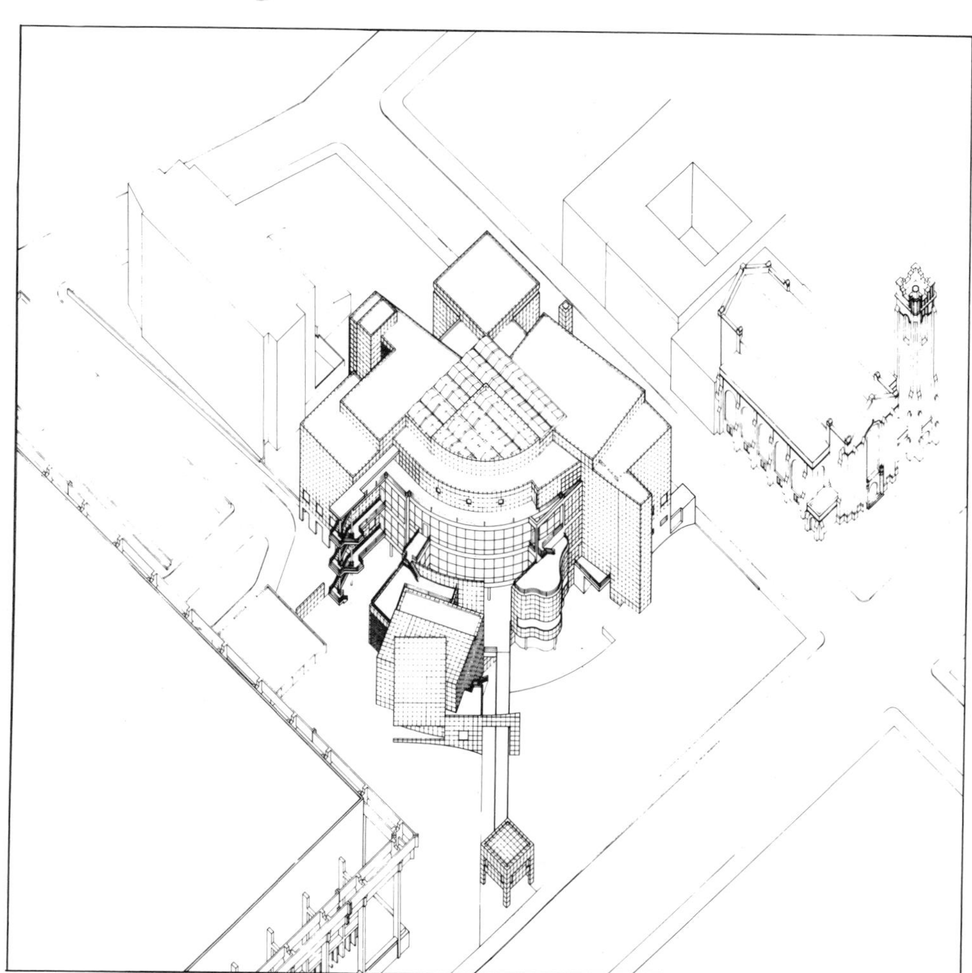

Figure 19. High Museum of Art, Atlanta, 1980–1983, by Richard Meier and Partners. Axonometric drawing. Courtesy of the architect.

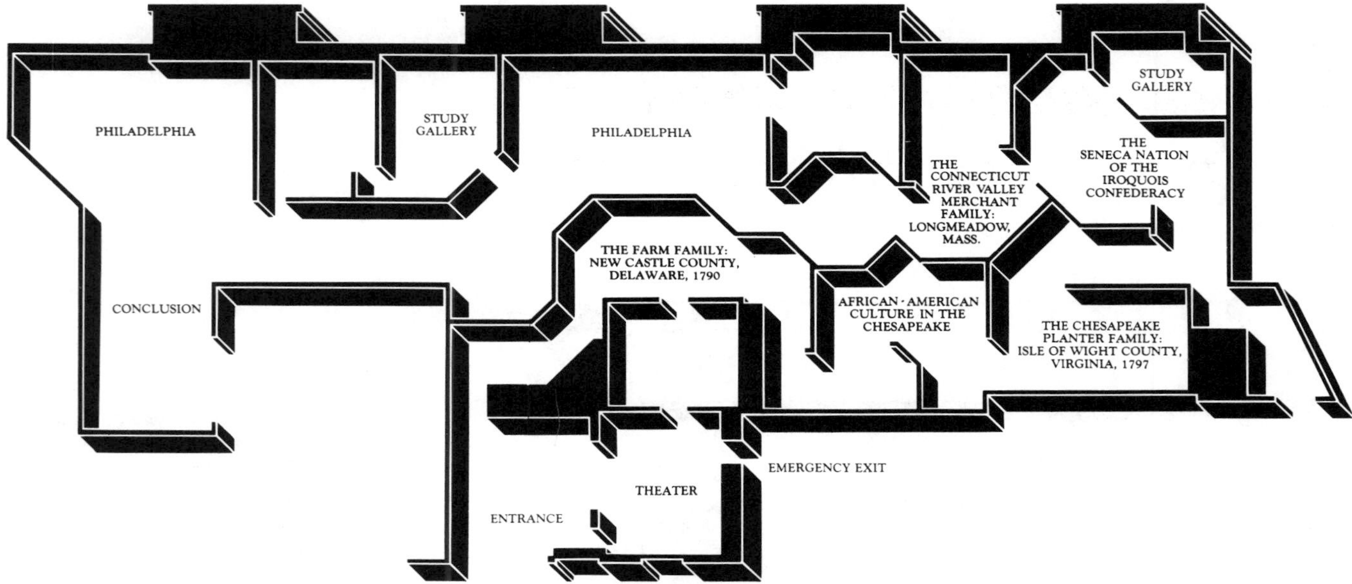

Figure 20. National Museum of American History, Smithsonian Institution, Washington, D.C. Exhibition plan for "After the Revolution—Everyday Life in America, 1780–1800" (1985), by Michael Carrigan. An example of staff reinstallation in an open plan museum. The exhibition includes, besides the theater, three audiovisual installations and a performance stage. The study galleries provide space for exhibition enrichments such as a hands-on workshop and study storage. Courtesy of the National Museum of American History.

brick, and granite, makes for contextual and harmonious relationships in the case of Charles W. Moore's Hood Museum at Dartmouth College (Hanover, New Hampshire, 1981–1983). By contrast, James Stirling's Sackler Museum (opened 1985), the satellite of Harvard's Fogg Museum, exemplifies more exotic inventiveness.

Museum expansion in the 1970s and 1980s has often come in the face of severe site limitations. Structures have gone underground, in the case of the Smithsonian's African and Oriental museums, which are behind Renwick's castle on the Mall in Washington, D.C. (Shepley-Bulfinch, 1983–1987), and Colonial Williamsburg's De Witt Wallace Gallery (opened 1985). Extensive support and service facilities were developed underground in Pei's expansion of the National Gallery of Art, and the same architect has been charged with developing a vast underground reception and support facility for the Louvre in Paris. Upward expansion, together with the construction of new revenue-producing space, is exemplified by Cesar Pelli's renovation and extension of the Museum of Modern Art in New York (1977–1984), and also in Michael Graves's postmodern design proposal for expansion of the Whitney Museum in New York.

The course of twentieth-century science-museum design in the United States parallels that of art museums, as may be seen by referring to three of the Smithsonian museums flanking the Mall in Washington, D.C. The National Museum of Natural History (Hornblower and Marshall, completed in 1911) is typical of full-blown and heavy-handed Renaissance Revival, complete with a monumental rotunda, protruding dome, and flanking interior courtyards. After World War II, the growth of the Smithsonian staff and collections necessitated the construction of the Museum of History and Technology, now the National Museum of American History, which opened in 1964. It was the final monument of McKim, Mead, and White (reincorporated as Steinmann, Cain, and White), and took its place on the Mall with an artful blend of modernism and hints at classical derivation. The three exhibition floors, while formally symmetrical, provide sufficiently open spaces to allow for the flexible presentation of changing, cross-disciplinary displays as well as continuing installations in traditional fields (Fig. 20). The third museum, devoted to the twentieth-century subjects of air and space, was designed by Gyo Obata (Hellmuth, Obata, and Kassabaum, opened in 1976). Although formally symmetrical and partly clad in marble, the structure is essentially modern in style and dramatic in its expanses of glass and steel trusswork and its huge central exhibition hall.

The great museums lining the Mall, of course, were designed under the demand that they relate to the formality and monumentality of their setting—the mile-long rectangular greensward on the axis between the Washington Monument and the west front of the Capitol. Science museums desiring the freedom to be experimental in design or revolutionary in program must be situated elsewhere, as Frank Oppenheimer's barn-like Exploration (San Francisco, founded in 1969), a place where learning about science occurs through interaction, play, and discovery, and the aesthetic is based on how one is made to feel.

MODERNISM IN EUROPE

The progression of modernism in Europe affected museum design earlier and more diversely than in the United

States. Henri Van de Velde's Folkwang Museum in Essen dates from 1902, his Rijksmuseum Kröllen Muller in Otterlo, 1937–1954, and H. P. Berlage's Gemeentemuseum at The Hague from 1935. Despite these early examples, however, the full impact of modern museum design came only after World War II, and the great museums of Le Corbusier and Mies van der Rohe (like the Guggenheim of Frank Lloyd Wright) occurred late in the architects' careers. Le Corbusier's innovative Tokyo Museum of Western Art was carried out by Japanese architects on the basis of his design in 1959. Mies's austere, imposing glass box, the Berlin National Museum, dates from 1963–1965. It is a culminating example of his style, but without concessions to the requirements of interior display (Fig. 21**a**).

In Italy several striking museums opened shortly after World War II. The installation of older paintings and sculpture, stripped of their frames and pedestals, in the Palazzo Bianco in Genoa (Franco Albini, 1950–1951), represented a revolution in display technique. Such structures as the Galleria d'Arte Moderna in Milan (I. Gardella, 1954) continued the exploration of novel design solutions. About the same time, in Denmark, an equally refreshing but very different museum of modern art was developed in close harmony with nature: the Louisiana Museum, near Copenhagen (J. Bo and V. Wohlert, 1958–1959).

Two museums dating from the 1960s may be cited to illustrate the relation of structure to nature in the broader Mediterranean tradition. The Foundation Maeght, set in a terraced garden setting on a hillside near Saint-Paul-de-Vence, is crowned by boldly sculptural light scoops (José Luís Sert, 1964). The extensive complex of the Israeli Museum in Jerusalem, opened in 1965, incorporates older structures and represents a collaborative effort (Alfred Mansfield, Dora Gad, Frederick Kiesler, Armand Bartos, and Isamu Noguchi).

The most famous modern museum in Europe, in terms of innovations in design and function, is without doubt the Centre Pompidou (Beaubourg) in Paris (Richard Rogers and Renzo Piano, 1972–1977) (Fig. 22). It serves as an information and cultural center of the broadest scope. Mechanical and circulation systems function as high tech display on the exterior, while the interior aims at maximum flexibility, with warehouse-like display areas partitioned by movable panels that frankly express their temporary nature. The result is a unique set of limitations on the effectiveness of exhibitions. The Centre Pompidou is

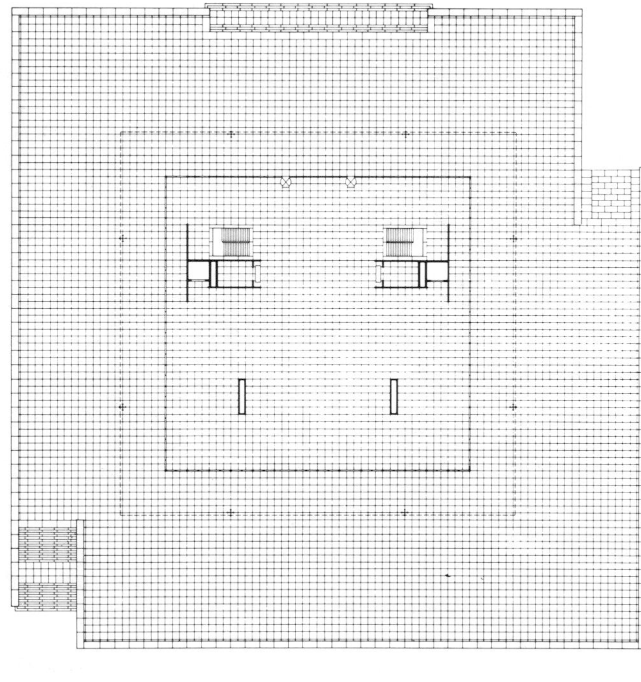

(a)

(b)

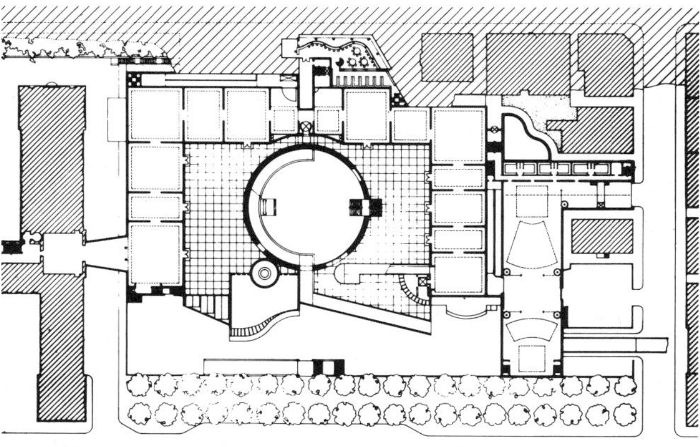

(c)

Figure 21. Comparative plans and model: (**a**) Die Neue Nationalgalerie, Berlin, 1963–1965, by Ludwig Mies van der Rohe (1). Courtesy of M.I.T. Press; (**b**) Model of Neue Staatsgalerie, Stuttgart, 1977–1984, by James Stirling. Courtesy of the Photographic Archives, National Gallery of Art; (**c**) Plan of Neue Staatsgalerie, Stuttgart (1). Courtesy of M.I.T. Press.

Figure 22. Centre Pompidou, Paris, 1972–1977, by Richard Rogers and Renzo Piano. Photograph by Wayne Andrews.

contemporaneous with the East Building of the National Gallery of Art, and the contrasting forms and philosophies of the two structures provide an instructive comparison.

The Neue Staatsgalerie in Stuttgart (1977–1984), the work of James Stirling, may be seen as a commentary on the history of museum design (Figs. 21**b,** 21**c**). On first impact, the building seems a witty and irreverent architectural parody with monumental allusions. Functionally, however, the plan succeeds in drawing on both the modern response to the needs of an active museum and on the classical heritage of providing an organized sequence of appropriately scaled galleries. It has attracted wide attention.

Buildings stirring international interest have not been confined to the United States, Europe, and Israel. The dramatic Anthropological Museum in Mexico City (Vasquez and Mijares, 1963–1965) has had broad impact. Recent Japanese architecture has been fertile in inventive forms, as evidenced by a building such as the Gunma Prefectural Museum by Arata Isozaki (1970–1974). In Japan, as well as the United States and Europe, museum building continued at full flood into the 1980s, and with the completion of Isozaki's Museum of Contemporary Art in Los Angeles (1986), an avant garde current from the East has set in.

MUSEUM PROGRAMMING

The development of a preliminary program for a museum project is complex and specialized, and as a result is too often left incomplete. The first questions that arise are most properly considered preprogramming: they concern the purpose of the museum, the governing authority, the nature of the collections, the funding, and the location.

A clear statement of the mission or goals of the museum, from which its functions derive, is the essential starting point. Endorsement of these aims and the assurance of support of the program must come from a properly constituted and recognized authority, usually the museum board. When the decision to build is made, the board often appoints a building committee, whose chairman is authorized to advise the programmer and architect on the positions taken by the committee and board. The means for developing the program is thus established and essential policy can be set about the role of the collections; the relative programs for displays; public services and research; and priorities for the use of resources toward funding, collections, space, and staff.

Funding breaks down into provisions for planning, site, construction, installation, operations, collections, purchasing, etc. Planning and construction costs may be affected by the fact that museums have many specialized, demanding functions. Plans may require many revisions and construction costs may reflect the need for special materials and finishes, and exacting standards for HVAC and lighting. Galleries, especially those with laylights and skylights above, require high ceilings and attics; the ratio of cubage to square footage is high. Finally, the installation may prove very costly, especially if special cases, mounts, vitrines, pedestals, and lighting are required. The architect may carry the project through to designing and providing installation furniture, or the museum may choose to use its own specialists, taking over the finished (or semifinished) display areas from the architects.

The question of location or site arises at an early stage

in the planning of most museums. Often, the problem is to make a choice between a downtown civic center location that is easily accessible but limited in size and parking area, and a suburban location with room for a large building "footprint," expansion, parking, and landscaping, but with inconvenient access for many potential visitors. Most museums in the United States are growing institutions and have either built additions every generation or so, or have suffered severe and chronic space problems. Successful museum programs create increasing demand for car and bus parking, offering compelling reasons for choosing a site that will permit expansion.

At this point in the preprogramming, the decisions should be firm enough so that the determining factors, the givens of the equation—the museum purpose, collection, funding, and location—should permit the first steps in conceptual programming. The relative scope, priority, and potential of the programmed activities can be derived from the givens, the implications of which, of course, remain under constant scrutiny. These factors are contextual in that they are relative to the social, cultural, and economic conditions affecting the planned museum.

The program should be developed by an experienced museum planner, director, or administrator working with the architect. When planning is to be done before the appointment of a director, a museum spokesperson with a broad background should be retained. As the program evolves, the programmer and architect should meet regularly with the chairperson of the building committee or president of the board; assumptions and decisions made in early stages often have long-term effects on the museum.

The main headings of a program are easily stated, but the detailed development may fill one or more volumes. For present purposes, the discussion organizes the principal gallery functions like a museum tour: (*1*) the reception and orientation of visitors; (*2*) exhibition and the display of the collections; (*3*) the collections' management and storage; (*4*) their study and conservation; and (*5*) administration and support services. The discussion will briefly consider (*6*) circulation and (*7*) programming for changes in existing structures.

Public Reception and Services and Education

The entrance lobby is the focal point for public reception and orientation; it also functions as a security checkpoint for visitors entering and leaving (Fig. 17). The area should be ample enough to accommodate visitor processing (ticket sales, access to the cloakroom and rest rooms, the assembly of groups, orientation through visual material and handouts, and an information desk). Add to this ready access to the galleries and to other public areas, such as a shop, an auditorium or lecture hall, a visitors' or members' lounge, a cafe or restaurant, and perhaps an audiovisual or topical display room. The space and circulation demands are heavy, all the more so because a contingency factor should be included. As the museum grows and both attendance and activities increase, the reception area must respond or give way to a major rebuilding program, as happened at the Louvre and some American museums, such as the Boston Museum of Fine Arts, the Detroit Institute of Arts, the Chicago Art Institute, the Baltimore Museum of Art, and others. Reorienting the entire museum to a new entrance location is a drastic move entailing aesthetic and functional problems, not the least of which is visitor disorientation inside and out.

In the case of museums that charge entry fees, there are obvious advantages to providing access to the restaurant facilities and sales area before the checkpoint; the cloakroom should be as close to the entry door as possible, and within sight of the guard at the door.

The program for the shop should include ready visibility for visitors entering and leaving the museum, and sufficient space to allow for growth and contingencies (many museums have found the shop a major source of revenue, and the merchandising program must be able to adapt to opportunities). Ready access to an ample stock room is helpful.

Many museums increase their attractiveness to the public by providing food services, and a cafe or lunch room for visitors (and the staff) is a desirable amenity, especially if the building is remote from public restaurants. If large enough, the dining room and auditorium may also be used for rental income. The program, however, should call attention to precautions that must be taken when the preparation and disposal of food are introduced into a museum setting: odors result; vermin are attracted; and the danger of fire is increased.

In the case of smaller museums that have only one meeting hall or auditorium, it may be necessary to make a difficult choice between a sloped floor, for the best viewing and a flat floor, for maximum flexibility. In any case, provision should be made for a wide screen and the possible use of multiple projectors. Museums present a wide variety of cultural events, and the auditorium may be called on to house not only cinema and video programs, lectures, symposia and conferences, but also occasional musical performances, dance, mime, or puppetry.

Given the range of public services that center on the main reception area, the planner should give thought to special requirements of the education department. If there are to be frequent gallery tours, and especially if volunteers are used as docents or at the information desk, a small, nearby lounge or study should be provided. If many student tours are anticipated, congestion in the lobby may be avoided by providing a separate entrance for school groups, possibly with its own provisions for coatrooms, rest rooms, an orientation–audiovisual room, and an assembly area.

Galleries and Display

The visitor proceeds from the reception–orientation area to the display area or galleries. The program for these derives from the nature of the collections and the museum's policy about the frequency of changes of installation. If there are to be frequent show changes, spaces for these should be close to the reception area, flexible, and easily serviced. It is important that ceilings be high, rooms large and capable of subdivision, and overhead lighting adaptable.

In designs for the permanent collection, the director and curators must establish the most important works and types of works to be shown, and their sequence and general arrangement: by medium (paintings, sculpture, prints), by chronology, or by subdivisions such as western, primitive, oriental. The galleries are settings meant to enhance the art and the encounter between viewer and object. The size, finishes, and general atmosphere of the galleries should relate to the objects shown; their groupings and sequences should illustrate relationships and assist in visitor orientation.

A specialist in art exhibition design should work closely with the architect as the galleries develop. Most museums have an exhibit designer or design team on staff, and the museum may wish to take over the installation design. Architects should remember that art museum customs and standards are generally quite different from those of commercial exhibits and interior decoration. The programmer should first help the museum staff and architect to formulate the broad organization of gallery sequences and sizes, leaving decisions about installation to be made with the finishing touches. A decision that should be made early on, however, is whether the museum is to plan for its own design and installation team, and if so, the team's size, it facilities, and the extent of its production support (shops for exhibition furniture, labels, silk screening, plastics, etc).

Collections Handling, Management, and Storage

Installation leads to the mention of art handlers, who may do double duty as part of the exhibit staff or may be attached to the registrar's office. Art handlers lead to the actual objects that form the collections and are put on display: the planner–programmer must consider the routes these objects take from the time they enter the museum until they end on exhibit or in storage (Fig. 23).

The truck dock for delivering art should be separated from the general delivery and trash removal dock if possible, and it should also be covered. Routes from the dock to the art-receiving area, and then on to storage and galleries, should be direct, broad, and high ceilinged. The registrar should have a record, and know the location, of every work in the museum, so he usually has an office or staff station at the art-receiving area to check on all objects entering or leaving. At the same time, because the director and chief curator call frequently for information, the registrar may also have an office near the director.

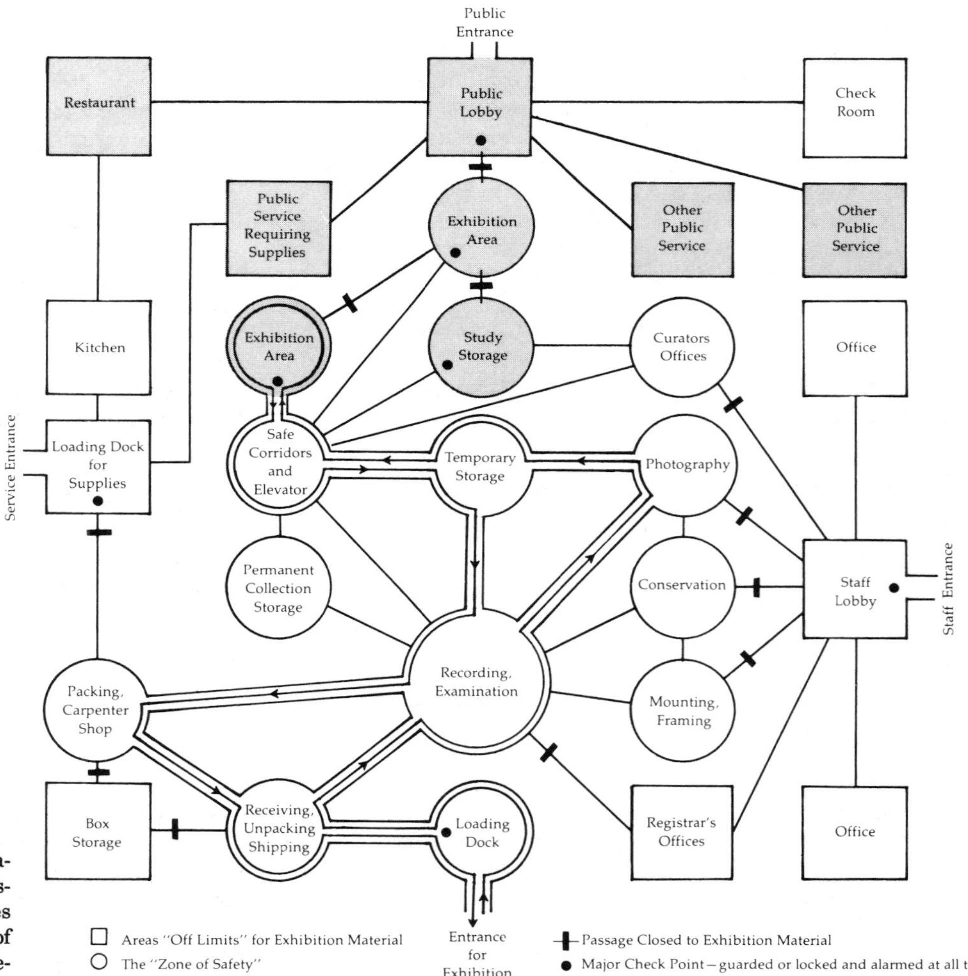

Figure 23. "Zone of Safety," diagram by David Vance of art-processing, circulation, and display zones in a large museum (2). Courtesy of the American Association of Museums.

The art-receiving area, which must be a secure zone, must be able to provide for holding crates that are to be unpacked or shipped, for unpacking, for inspection, and for holding unpacked works awaiting further disposition. There are often several rooms, one for packing, a clean room for inspecting and holding works of art, and a room for records and processing. Storage space for crates and packing materials should be nearby. Proximity of the conservator and photographer is desirable, since works are often inspected by the conservator and photographed on arrival or before departure.

Works arriving to form part of an exhibition are moved from the reception area to a staging area, where they are put on hold in storage or prepared for display. In many museums, staging takes place in a temporarily vacant gallery, but the process of exhibition preparation is more orderly if a large, secure, well-located area is permanently designated for this purpose.

Works that do not go on exhibit generally end up in storage, and this introduces another major program element. Art storage, in fact, is such a distinct discipline that it cannot be treated in depth here. Of storage in general it may be said that there is never enough room; whatever spaces are allotted are soon outgrown. Art museums collect all of the supplies and oddments of other institutions, plus many crates and a plethora of exhibit furniture, such as pedestals, cases, vitrines, benches, panels, and frames. Art storage goes beyond this, however, and its special requirements are such that it may be better to think of it as reserves maintenance. It requires ample space in well-located, large, and high ceilinged rooms, with proper equipment, good HVAC control, and special security.

Study and Conservation

The discussion now moves from the processing, display, and storage of works to their study and conservation. In the United States, the scholars who serve as specialists in the various subject areas represented by museum collections, and who are in charge of the objects corresponding to their specialty, are called curators, while the specialists in the physical preservation and restoration of the objects are called conservators. Most museums have several curators reporting through a chief curator to the director; the programmer must anticipate their needs for offices, space for assistance and researchers, and probably a library. Museum libraries usually include a photographic collection and are used for reference by visiting students and scholars. The programmer must also determine whether the museum will have one or more conservation laboratories. This usually depends on the size of the museum and perhaps on the availability of other conservation facilities in the area. A large museum may have separate laboratories for paintings, sculpture, works on paper, decorative arts, and textiles. A small museum may have only an infirmary—a room for examining and cleaning works, but without elaborate equipment or a resident conservator.

Like the conservation studio, the photographic laboratory also depends on the size of the museum. A good photography laboratory takes space, and the photographic department of a large museum runs to several supporting rooms and one or more studios. Small museums may content themselves with a darkroom, and have paintings photographed in the galleries. On-site provisions for both conservation and photography are desirable because they reduce the need to send objects away from the museum.

Administration and Support Services

Administration and support must reflect the distinctive programs of museums, as an institutional type, which derive from functions related to the public and to the objects acquired, studied, and displayed. Most museums report through a director to a governing board, which usually requires a boardroom and president's office. Depending on the size of the museum, the administrative staff expands or assumes multiple duties grouped into such broad categories as curatorial functions, development and public affairs, administrative and building management, and financial management. Larger museums may also have a legal office. A museum's need to attract visitors and donors and to supplement its regular income by fund and membership drives places special emphasis on offices devoted to information, publications, public programs and receptions, and development activities in general.

The programmer should be aware of the operational requirements characteristic of museums. Most museums are open to the public somewhere between five and eight hours a day, six or seven days a week, but the need for high security and a controlled environment is constant. Larger museums have guards on duty at all times, and elaborate monitoring systems. (Museum security is discussed below.) A guards' office and control room, perhaps a training room, guards' locker rooms, and possibly an electronics shop are necessary. Museums may have shops for the various trades and building maintenance, as well as for exhibit preparation. Given the importance of lighting for exhibitions, the electrical shop and lighting design and maintenance are especially important. Large institutions require round-the-clock engineering maintenance. Interior plants, garden courts, and the exterior landscape may necessitate a horticulturist and staff, and perhaps greenhouses. Ample truck docking facilities for deliveries and trash removal, well separated from art shipping, is important, as is garage space for museum vehicles (one or more cars or vans), if not also for staff and visitors.

These functions are only part of a museum's support system. The list continues with the mail room and message center, telephone room, supply office, storage for supplies and equipment, etc. Management of the support system falls to the building supervisor, whose office should be central to the back-of-the-house world that enables the museum to operate.

Circulation

A final program consideration, and by no means the least important, is the relationship of all of the parts, and especially the circulation of public, staff, and objects (Fig. 24). Ideally, the visitor entering the museum should sense the disposition of public services and exhibits with a minimum of help from signs and plans. Reception facilities should

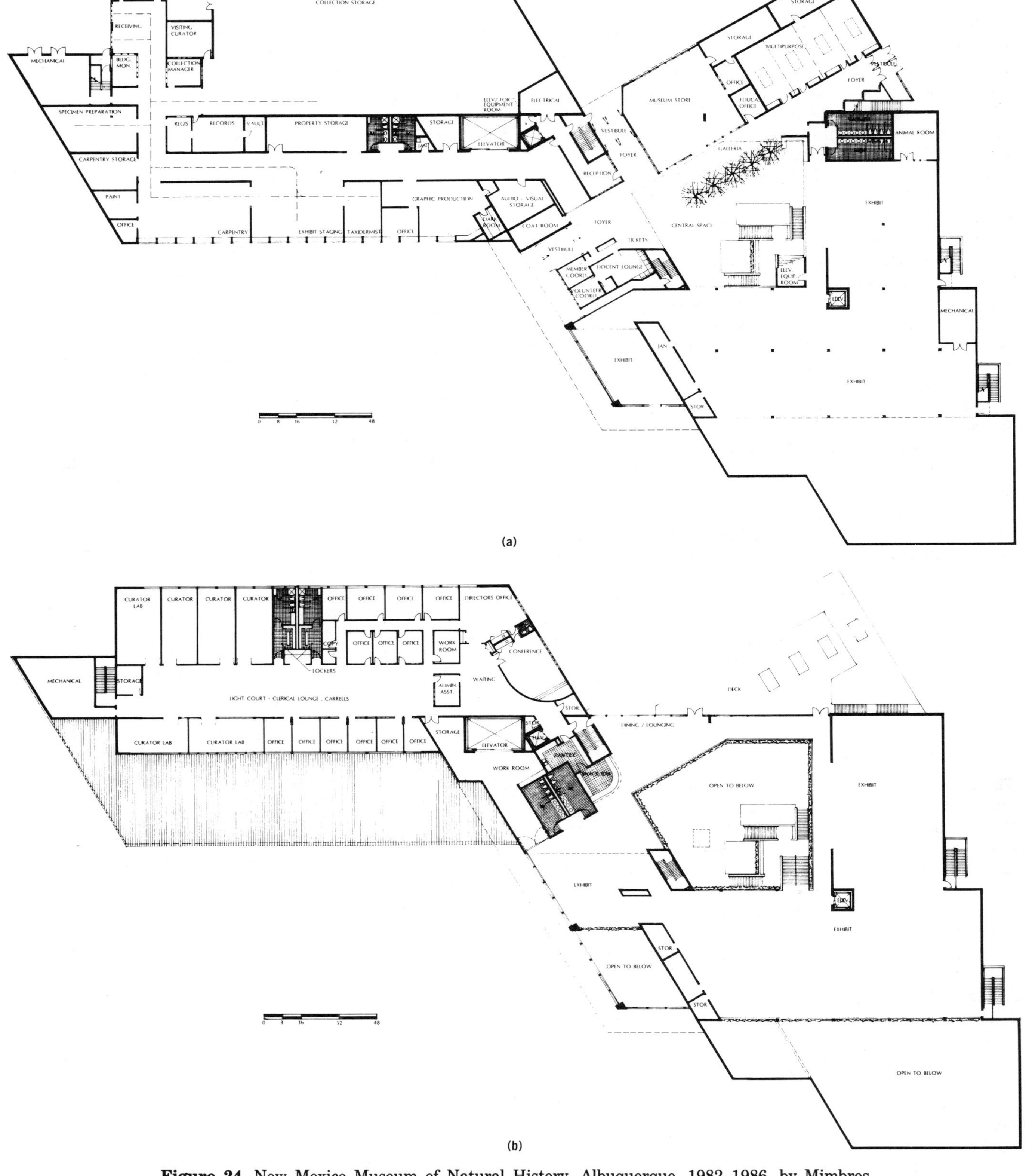

Figure 24. New Mexico Museum of Natural History, Albuquerque, 1982–1986, by Mimbres, Inc. (**a**) First and (**b**) second floors (preliminary plans). Space distribution and circulation in a moderate-sized (about 100,000 ft^2) science museum. The exhibition spaces occupy 40% of the total; public services and education, with their immediate support, occupy about 17%; the remaining curatorial, administrative, support, storage, and mechanical areas are in the remaining 43%. The New Mexico Museum of Natural History is a young institution, and specimen storage, now at 11%, is expected to expand. (In older museums, specimen storage may occupy half or more of the total area.) Museums in general vary widely in space distribution, according to their program and storage needs, but frequently the public zones occupy no more than 40% of the whole. Courtesy of Mimbres, Inc.

be visible from the entrance lobby, and then the architecture itself should lead the way. Non-exhibition areas such as the auditorium, shop, restaurant, and meeting and orientation rooms, should be conveniently close to the entrance. Since they may be used at hours when galleries are closed, these areas should be accessible from the lobby, if not directly from outside. Similarly, the changing exhibition area should be close to the entrance for reasons of visitor orientation and accessibility, and convenience for evening openings.

The main gallery plan may be designed to provide a circuit the visitor can recognize and follow easily, but that also allows for sufficient random access to permit quick visits to selected galleries. It should be possible to survey the collection either selectively or in depth, without backtracking or disorientation. In the case of large museums, a series of gallery circuits may lead from and return to a main artery. Nothing contributes to viewer restlessness and gallery fatigue more than disorientation in a nondirectional cluster of rooms.

The location of staff offices and work areas, and provisions for staff circulation require study because of the varied and specialized staff responsibilities. Considerations include whether the staff offices are to be centralized so that curatorial, administrative, and support personnel can keep in ready touch, or whether proximity to the collections and visitor areas is more important. Options should be discussed with the museum spokesperson. Frequently traveled staff routes should be made as short as possible, and behind-the-scenes passages provided for staff and service movements.

The safe and convenient circulation of museum objects is a necessity. The route from the shipping entrance to unpacking to examination and registration to processing to staging or storage should avoid public spaces (Fig. 23). The routes must also be planned to provide ample ceiling and door height (at least 10 ft) and corridor width (a minimum of 8 ft, preferably 10 ft). The turning radius at corners should not constrict the movement of long objects. Depending on the museum's anticipated needs, passage routes should be scaled to permit the movement of objects up to 10 ft high and at least 15 ft long, and freight elevators for moving works should not present a bottleneck. The freight elevators at the National Gallery of Art were designed to provide for a diagonal of 18 ft (a minimum of 12 × 14 ft or 10 × 15 ft) and a load of 9 tons. Smaller museums may find a somewhat smaller elevator adequate (10 × 12 ft or 10 ×13 ft). Science and natural history museums may need to make provisions for the movement of very large and heavy objects. The elevators at the National Museum of American History are slightly larger than 12 × 26 ft and carry 12 tons. In arriving at the final specifications, the planner should recognize that, since the maximum size and weight of objects that may be received for exhibition cannot be foreseen, generous provisions should be made. On the other hand, providing oversized and expensive routes of transit for the truly exceptional object is excessive. It is better to plan a contingency access directly into the exhibit area itself, perhaps by designing removable windows or door frames, or by allowing vertically for a hoist in a central court.

In space considerations, it is safe to assume that, whatever the nature of the museum, at least one major piece will be featured in the lobby or in sight of the entrance, and generous room should be available. In the case of temporary exhibits, a small show frequently requires 1500–3000 ft^2; a moderately sized show, 4000–6000 ft^2; a large one, 8000–10,000 ft^2; and a very large one, on occasion, 14,000 or more ft^2. The temporary exhibition area on the concourse level of the National Gallery's East Building is about 14,000 ft^2. It has a 16-ft ceiling, except for one 1200-ft^2 section that is two stories (30 ft) high. This has made possible on several occasions the effective display of very large works.

Changes in Existing Buildings

The same desiderata listed above for each museum program function obtain in planning functions in a museum expansion or adaptive reuse, but with the difference of conflicts with priorities resulting from pre-existing architectural conditions. Because the most frequent museum building programs involve additions, renovations, or adaptations of existing structures, a discussion of some of the typical problems in these changes follows.

In any modification of an existing structure, the building form is a given. It may be overlaid, or overpowered, or used as counterpoint, or in harmony, or matched. There are no rules. Only the taste, judgment, and ingenuity of the architect and client determine the route to take. In the last generation respect increased for the stylistic integrity of older buildings generally, but the battles that raged over the proposed addition to London's National Gallery, and to the Whitney and Guggenheim in New York confirm that no consensus or easy solution exists.

Any alteration to an existing structure involves stylistic design considerations and mechanical–structural problems at the outset. Programmatically, the first consideration addressed has to do with potential display areas, but this often takes such priority as to be at the expense of other functions and zones. The original entry will probably prove to be inadequate, but constructing a new entrance denigrates the exterior design of the original building and—in terms of circulation and spatial progression—disorients the interior. Adapted buildings almost never have the support space that museums require for storage and collections-related activities, including a truck dock and an object-processing area. Museums that expand piecemeal, wing by wing, seldom consider the corresponding growth in support and circulation needed because of the expansion.

The opportunity to solve such problems by building a separate gallery structure connected by an underground public and staff support area, as at the National Gallery in Washington, is rare indeed; so too are the conditions that allow an adapted museum structure to borrow truck dock and elevator space from a new, separately constructed, and adjoining office building as the National Museum of Women in the Arts did. This Washington, D.C. museum was housed in a 1907 Masonic Temple remodeled by Keyes, Condon, and Florance (1984–1987). Most museums suffer from a chronic shortage of storage and support space, and remodeling projects, for obvious reasons, tend to concentrate on galleries and public amenities.

SPECIAL CONSIDERATIONS IN MUSEUM DESIGN

The Design of Exhibit Halls and Galleries

At an early stage of museum design, the architect and client must make a choice between constructing permanent gallery rooms and providing a large open area into which exhibit settings can be fitted as installation plans develop. Permanent rooms permit the development of eloquent and architecturally related spaces with appropriate skylights and substantial finishes; open spaces permit adapting the display rooms to changing exhibitions and programs, creating environments specifically designed to enhance the objects. Both approaches can be justified. Permanent rooms are appropriate for fixed and stable collections, especially of so-called treasures, although it must be remembered that even displays of immortal works have their own life expectancy, and most museums go through periodic reinstallations. Flexible areas are more suited to programs calling for changing exhibitions, for contemporary art, and for didactic historical or scientific displays (Fig. 20). Making a choice is the more difficult because most architects want to assure that the spirit of their design concept is evident in the exhibit areas, while most curators want the same areas to serve only as settings for their objects and programs.

In any case, the design study must begin with a consideration of the collections, the number and nature of the objects to be displayed, and the intent of the display: is it primarily to set the objects off so that they may be seen to best advantage and appreciated aesthetically; is the display primarily didactic and informative; or is it some combination of these?

In theory, a gallery for the display of art should be in scale with the works to be shown; the light source should be unobtrusive, but the display areas effectively illuminated; colors, finishes, and architectural features should not distract attention from the objects; the setting should invite contemplation and the circulation should not interfere with viewing; the installation should delight, surprise, and stimulate without calling attention to itself. Among the most annoying interferences with picture viewing are corridors for through traffic, windows introduced at the level of the paintings, and architectural settings that are out of scale with the objects. All such generalizations pale before the actual experience of such a space as the Grande Galerie of the Louvre, however, which transcends such annoyances. It is fortunate that all rules for display can be broken, although there is no excuse for ignorance of principles.

Common wall finishes for painting galleries include plaster, wood, plasterboard, and fabric placed over plywood or plasterboard. Plasterboard is usually backed by plywood, so that nails may be driven in for hanging. Nail holes can be patched easily and do not cause chipping, as with plaster. Plaster walls commonly have hanging rods, moldings, or recessed channels at the top. Fabric-covered walls can give the effect of warmth or elegance, but may cause maintenance problems: they cannot be restored by a simple coat of paint or an application of spackle, and they leave marked areas whenever a picture is moved after extended hanging. Carpet-covered walls also are not without maintenance problems, and heavily textured coverings can result in a busy or even oppressive wall surface.

Gallery walls tend to be high, and with good reason. High walls can accommodate larger art works, if necessary, and high ceilings make it possible to raise the laylight or spots to an unobtrusive level. Even in a small room, a ceiling of at least 10 ft is desirable, and for middle-sized rooms, 12–15 is preferable. In galleries 25 × 40 ft or larger, laylights are often placed at 20–25 ft or more. Sheer walls of this height overwhelm most paintings, so devices such as coves, cornices, or even a painted wall division are useful in creating a field proportioned to the works to be displayed. Moldings at chair-rail height also help focus attention on the display field.

The principal circulation routes of a museum are usually hard-surfaced, consisting of terrazzo, marble, etc, which is appropriate to their function. Galleries off these routes, however, are more inviting and offer a rest to the feet if floors are made of wood or covered with a carpet. Maintenance, noisiness, and light reflection (as from a glossy wood finish) are factors to consider. Above all, the floor should be solid and perfectly level. Slate, for example, may present a beautiful muted gray surface but prove uneven enough to make sculpture installation difficult. Floor loading must be anticipated carefully. It is always possible that at some time pieces of heavy sculpture may be displayed. Provision of 150 psf is a fairly adequate safeguard; a gallery planned specifically for sculpture may require more.

The design and finish of the gallery ceiling is tied closely to the lighting. If skylights form the roof, the glass ceiling below is formed of a grid of laylights, made up of panes of shatterproof glass with (ultraviolet) filtration and sufficient diffusion to help distribute the light to the walls while preventing a direct view of the attic and skylights. If there is no skylight, the ceiling may take a variety of forms. Coffers, grids, or troughs are sometimes used so that spotlights may be pulled up within them, but such ceilings take on an assertive sculptured presence that can be more distracting than exposed fixtures. Less assertive is an arrangement of recessed track lighting in a plaster, plasterboard, or tile ceiling. The ceiling should be sufficiently high and the spotlight fixtures painted the color of the ceiling. Another ceiling solution employs a lighting cove or dropped valance to conceal fixtures a few feet out from the wall, but this limits flexibility in placing objects or panels in the room. Maximum flexibility is sometimes achieved by omitting any dropped ceiling and painting the overhead slab and all beams, ductwork, and conduits black; track and black-painted spots can then be hung where and when needed. Whatever the solution, the ceiling should not be oppressive or distracting; it should have appropriate acoustical qualities, and should allow for flexibility of installation. If it can be attractive as well, that is to be commended.

Lighting

Lighting is probably the most complex and demanding element in art-gallery design. Light is the medium through which the works of art are perceived; it also gradually destroys most of them. Inadequate light makes a painting look drab and a sculptured form weak. When it is the wrong color temperature, light distorts color values.

Directors, curators, and designers often are divided initially about whether the ideal light is natural or controlled artificial light. A balanced natural light—neither as cold as pure northern light nor as warm as direct sunlight—is the ideal combination and proportion of wavelengths for the perception of colors. A principal difficulty with natural light, however, is its extreme variation with time of day and year, and weather. Frequently, it must be supplemented during dark periods, and controlled during peak summer hours. These difficulties are in part offset by the psychological effectiveness of the living, changing quality of natural light. At the same time, providing overhead natural light may pose quite a different problem to the architect: it can be furnished to galleries on only one level, and it normally calls for a lofty attic space to condition the light between the skylight and laylight. Modern museums sometimes devise ingenious variations on the traditional skylight–laylight method of controlling natural light. José Luis Sert's Maeght Foundation gallery near Nice, the Miró museum at Barcelona (Fig. 25), Louis Kahn's Kimball Museum in Fort Worth, the Yale Center for British Art in New Haven, and Edward L. Barnes's museum in Dallas are worth studying for variations on this method.

For all of the emphasis on natural light, most modern galleries depend more on artificial light, and particularly on incandescent fixtures. Used as spots or floods on light tracks, these lights can be adjusted easily to build illumination where and in the amount needed. Unfortunately, incandescents build up heat, distort color, and require frequent bulb changes. Fluorescents are cooler, longer lasting, less wasteful of power, and are capable of producing balanced light, but their nondirectional quality makes for dull or bland illumination and they emit more uv light. Various high intensity lamps are also used in museum lighting, especially in Europe. Developments in bulbs, lamping fixtures, and track systems are taking place continually, and an experienced museum lighting consultant is an invaluable partner in any museum design project, to advise on lighting as both a science and an art.

Whatever the light source, the contribution of the light should be to make the art-viewing experience pleasant, easy, and satisfying. The ambience of the gallery should be attractive; the light sources should not glare or obtrude; the zone of the works of art should attract and hold attention. Light should strike paintings at an angle sufficient to avoid reflection from the picture surface (about 30°), and be directional enough to bring out the tactile qualities of the paint, but without exaggeration. Frame shadows should be minimized; the light on the painting's surface should be even; the wall should not show light scallops or hot spots. The light should be strong enough to bring

Figure 25. Fundació Joan Miró, Barcelona, opened 1976, by José Luis Sert. The light scoops collect light and diffuse it as they reflect it into the exhibit areas below. Photograph by F. Catalá-Roca.

out the painting's colors and the details in the darker passages, but no stronger—for reasons of preservation. The architect, of course, is seldom called on to illuminate the actual display, but he is responsible for providing the system that makes fine tuning possible, and this requires the advice of a specialist.

Education, Public Programs, and Information

At an early stage in the planning, study should be given to the variety of services that might be offered visitors and to the role of education and public programs in its entirety: from informational hand-outs and museum graphics to public-service announcements, outreach programs, performances, museum classes, and internships. Some of these will involve information systems tailored to museum needs, and facilities should provide for storing, processing, and distributing information as required.

The customary lobby information center and calendar board is replaced in some institutions by monitors that show the information sequentially. There are advantages to this system. Monitors may be placed at different entrances and at other strategic spots in the museum, and changed and updated from a central control. Special messages may be inserted at appropriate times and can be programmed to be inserted or removed in advance. A similar system, with stored museum information, can also be used interactively, allowing the visitor to question the monitor about programs, works of art, artists, etc.

More extensive information or orientation is sometimes provided in a room near the museum entrance that is set up to present films or has monitors on a counter or in cubicles. In some museums, visitors may call up introductory film programs at will.

Many museums offer visitors portable audio systems as individual tour guides to the exhibits. One system requires wiring to and broadcasting from each station. Another, more flexible and frequently preferred system operates on the principle of a continuous taped message and requires the visitor to coordinate the message segments and the viewing stations.

The public information systems of a museum are, of course, only a small part of all of the information-system requirements of a contemporary institution. Management of every museum function is becoming increasingly dependent on word processors and computers, and many offices require interconnections and access to common data bases. For instance, up-to-date exhibition and object records are needed by the registrar, exhibit designers, conservators, the education office, curators, the administrator, and the director. Museum plans should include the housing and connecting of such a system. Obviously, the management requirements museums share with other institutions—budgets, accounting, personnel, library, sales, mailing lists, membership, etc—also require information-system support.

Security

Security is of special concern in museums, of course, because of the value of the objects in the collections. In the broad sense, however, security also entails protecting the building, equipment, staff, and visitors. It involves safeguards against natural disasters, such as storms, floods, and fires, and human damage caused by riots, vandalism, theft, and careless handling. All of this necessitates a security officer, state-of-the-art security equipment, and an adequate guard force. At the planning stage, a consulting specialist in museum security is practically mandatory.

The security concerns peculiar to art galleries, and related specifically to object security, may be considered under the headings that follow.

1. *Peripheral.* The museum may be seen as a sealed box, with only limited and carefully supervised entrances and exits. Convenience and code requirements are considered, but the number of public entrances and exits is minimized—often to only one or two. Typically, two guards are stationed within sight of the entrance and checkroom, although small museums may have only one guard. Visitors must check packages, briefcases, shopping bags, and umbrellas at the entrance. Emergency exits, if required by code, call for special security provisions that, at the least, include alarms and camera surveillance.

   Staff and service entrances and exits are vulnerable points in the museum's protective system. Two-guard surveillance, plus camera monitoring by the control room, is recommended. After hours, applications for admission should be screened by both a guard at the door and a guard with a monitor in the control room.

   The peripheral security system should include all parts of the exterior that might invite penetration: windows, gratings, skylights, etc. There are many security devices available. A specialist should be consulted.
2. *Internal Circulation.* The main arteries and linkages of the building's circulation system are frequently monitored or fitted out with alarms, especially so that after-hours intrusions by unauthorized persons can be detected.
3. *Object Areas.* The areas where valuable objects are displayed or stored demand special security measures. Galleries, for example, are usually under the surveillance of guards on the scene, but also may be equipped with sensors and cameras. Usually, the main galleries of a museum are patrolled at night, but not closed individually. They may also be protected by motion detectors.

   In the planning stage, it is sensible to identify the secure areas where objects will be deposited, such as the receiving and shipping areas, exhibition-staging area, photographers' and conservators' laboratories, storage rooms, and perhaps the director's office and the boardroom. Security provisions range from door alarms to camera monitors and motion detectors. The more sophisticated card-release lock systems provide good control and records of entrances and exits.

   Dedicated storage areas may add a level of security by providing an inspection chamber (usually camera-monitored) between two sets of entry doors, supplemented by a log of entries and departures.

Object storerooms are dependent on their peripheral security in the same manner as the entire building is. Door security is not sufficient in these rooms if access is possible through ductwork or crawl spaces, or if the walls or ceilings are penetrable.

4. *Installation Security*. Objects on display in public areas are frequently protected not only by area security but also by tamper-proof devices. There are various ways to install paintings, prints, sculpture, and decorative art objects that prevent easy removal or activate alarms if the objects are approached, touched, or moved. Galleries may be equipped with an ultrasonic device that sets off an alarm whenever a vitrine, for instance, is opened; such systems should be monitored from the control room, so planning to include them should be done early.

Again, these are matters calling for the advice of a specialist, and advice should be procured in time to provide wiring and control-room capability during the construction stage.

Storage of Art Objects

In the planning and design process, storage of the collections must be differentiated totally from general storage of equipment, supplies, exhibition furniture, etc. Collections storage requires distinct criteria for access, security, and climate control, and it should be regarded as a potential object reference and study category (Fig. 26). Close consultation with museum representatives is necessary in determining the size, location, and conditions of the collections storage areas, together with storage methods and components.

Paintings customarily are stored in racks or hung on screens. If the storage area is relatively narrow or irregular, racks may allow the space to be used more efficiently than screens, but they are not as flexible and require more handling of the pictures, which can lead to damage. Racks must be specially designed to accommodate the works in the collection.

Screen storage is best in wide, high ceilinged rooms. The most convenient and efficient screens are frames with a perforated in-fill, such as a diamond-patterned, heavy-gauge wire mesh, which slide on tracks. They should be at least 10–12 ft wide and 8–10 ft high, and sturdy enough

Figure 26. National Gallery of Art, Washington, D.C., West Building painting storage room. Renovation by Keyes, Condon, and Florance, 1982. Screens suspended from overhead track. When extended, screens can be locked to opposite screens to prevent sway. Both ambient lighting and zone-controlled lighting for painting examination. Fire protection provided by Halon (sphere on far wall). Photograph by Gary Fleming, courtesy of the architect.

to resist sagging under the weight of heavy frames. The installation should be designed to prevent vibration when the frames are moved; this can be accomplished with a shock-absorbing suspension from a level ceiling track, and floor guides to prevent swaying.

For economy of space, the storage room should be planned with a wide central aisle for screen viewing and access, and with ranges of screens on either side, so that two-thirds of the room is used for storage and one-third for the central access. (A room 30 ft wide accommodates two ranges of screens 10 ft wide; a 45-ft room, 15-ft screens.) Moving screens are placed about 18 in. on center. About 2 ft of space should be provided above the frames to allow for the suspension and track systems, and for lights above the tracks to light the screens evenly when in the aisle. The design of the lighting system should be given careful study to assure good viewing conditions.

Where moving screens are not practical, fixed screens are often used. They should be placed no closer than 3 ft apart, as pictures must be carried and mounted in this space. They are clearly not as convenient for viewing or handling works as movable screens.

Works on paper are usually stored matted and mounted on a protective backing, but not framed. They are stored flat, with the smaller works (up to about 30 in.) in acid-free boxes or solander boxes, and the larger in drawers (often in shallow-drawer map cases or flat files). In planning storage areas, consideration should be given to the large, free floor space required for storing, moving, and examining large graphics (contemporary examples may measure up to 6 or 8 ft). Storage for boxes on shelves above 7 ft is inconvenient. Print storage should be adjacent to the print study room, curatorial offices, and the preparation area.

Sculpture collections embrace works of many sizes, weights, and media. The smaller objects can be accommodated on shelves or, preferably, in glass-fronted cases. These storage methods may be combined in a study room. Because some objects deteriorate under certain environmental conditions, a conservator should be consulted in connection with the design of the storage system. Large objects that require considerable space and special floor-loading provisions may be stored separately, on industrial-strength shelving, directly on the floor, or on skids.

The most diverse objects in an art museum's collections come under the category of decorative arts, and storage methods vary accordingly. Tapestries and carpets, stored in rolls, may require very long racks; furniture requires considerable cubage and a flexible shelving system. Smaller textiles may be stored in acid-free boxes, and other objects placed on shelves, drawers, trays, or in quarter cases. Open shelves leave objects exposed and custom cabinetry is expensive, so adaptable prefabricated units are desirable.

Quarter cases have long provided a practical modular system, especially for science and history museums. They are essentially boxes that are approximately 40 in. high, 29 in. wide, and 40 in. deep, fitted inside to accept shelves or trays at 2-in. intervals. The front is removable. (Half cases are twice as wide; and full cases are twice as high as half cases.) The cases are stacked two or three high, side by side and back to back, leaving aisles of about 4 ft. They are fairly adaptable to the conditions of a given space, and may be moved easily. They have presented some inconveniences, but these are overcome in currently available, comparable storage units that offer advantages in door design, glass fronts, variable depths and heights, etc.

Preservation of the Collections

At all times during the planning, design, construction, and installation of a museum there must be an ongoing review of factors affecting the safety and preservation of

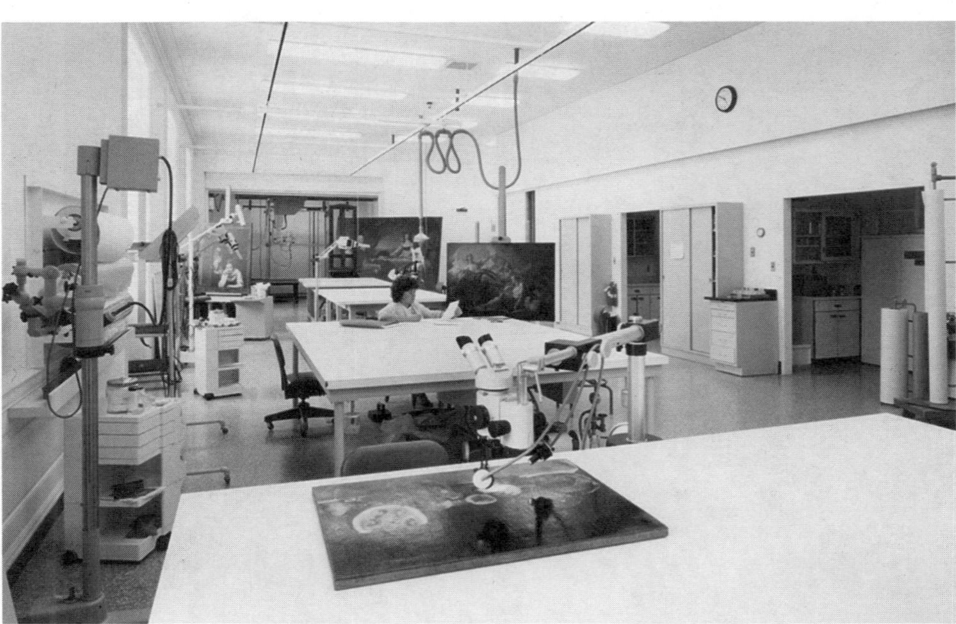

Figure 27. National Gallery of Art, Washington, D.C., West Building painting conservation laboratory. Renovation by Keyes, Condon and Florance, 1978. Remodeled from former cafeteria dining room. The X-ray room, with roll-down door, is at the far end of the laboratory. Photograph by Gary Fleming, courtesy of the architect.

the collections, wherever they are being processed, exhibited, or stored.

All light sources must be properly controlled. No shafts of direct sun should strike objects; proper uv screening should be maintained; galleries under skylights must be protected from excessively bright areas and radiant heat; and light levels should be appropriate to the objects illuminated. There is some variation in the standards set by different conservators, and the staff must advise on the museum's practices, but in general, the maximum light level prescribed for paintings is 25–40 fc; for works on paper, 5–8; and for fabrics, 5–10.

The staff must also determine the limits on temperature and humidity. Consistency is particularly important. About 70°F and 50% relative humidity, with a fluctuation of not more than ± 2–3° or ± 2–3%, is generally advisable, but a controlled seasonal variation is sometimes permitted.

Air purity is important; both fumes and particulates should be eliminated as much as possible. The contaminated air of an urban environment can be especially harmful. A 97% particulate filter is desirable, as is an air wash to dissolve atmospheric sulfides.

Other factors that may affect the preservation of objects (apart from human carelessness or maliciousness) include vibration (from gallery visitors, mechanical systems, or nearby traffic), air currents or drafts (which can cause dirt and humidity problems), and infestations (which may be aggravated by proximity to food-service areas).

Larger museums have one or more conservators on the staff who should provide advice on such matters as light control and settings for the mechanical systems, as well as on the design of their own laboratories (Fig. 27). Museums without conservators should retain consultants to make recommendations on specifications and relevant design proposals.

BIBLIOGRAPHY

1. K. Train, "Thirty Museum Plans," *Perspecta: The Yale Architectural Journal* **16,** 143–167 (1980).
2. *Museum News* **58** (4), 63 (March/April 1980).

General References

The Architectural Forum **47** (December 1927).

The Architectural Forum **56** (June 1932).

The Architectural Record **66** (December 1929).

Architecture **75** (January 1986).

R. Aloi, *Musei: Architetura, Tecnica,* Ulrico Hoepli, Milan, 1962.

M. Brawne, *The Museum Interior,* Architectural Book Publishing Company, New York, 1982.

M. Brawne, *The New Museum: Architecture and Display,* Frederick A. Praeger, New York, 1965.

J. Cantor, "Temples of the Arts: Museum Architecture in Nineteenth Century America," *The Metropolitan Museum of Art Bulletin* **28,** 351–354 (April 1970).

L. V. Coleman, *Museum Buildings,* American Association of Museums, Washington, D.C., 1950.

D. H. Dudley and I. B. Wilkinson, *Museum Registration Methods,* third ed., American Association of Museums, Washington, D.C., 1979.

L. Glaeser, *Architecture of Museums,* The Museum of Modern Art, New York, 1968.

J. D. Hilberry and S. Kalb Weinberg, "Museum Collections Storage, Part I," *Museum News* (March/April 1981).

J. D. Hilberry and S. Kalb Weinberg, "Museum Collections Storage, Part II," *Museum News* (May/June 1981).

J. D. Hilberry and S. Kalb Weinberg, "Museum Collections Storage, Part III," *Museum News* (July/August 1981).

E. V. Johnson and J. C. Horgan, *Museum Collection Storage,* United Nations Education, Scientific and Cultural Organization, Paris, 1979.

B. Lord and C. D. Lord, eds., *Planning Our Museums,* Museums Assistance Programs, National Museums of Canada, Ottawa, 1983.

Museum **26,** 3–4 (1974).

Museum **31,** 2 (1979).

Perspecta: The Yale Architectural Journal **16** (1980).

N. Pevsner, *A History of Building Types,* Princeton University Press, Princeton, N.J., 1976, Chapt. 8.

Progressive Architecture **50** (December 1969).

Progressive Architecture **56** (March 1975).

Progressive Architecture **59** (May 1978).

H. Searing, *New American Art Museums,* Whitney Museum of American Art, New York, 1982.

R. G. Tillotson, *Museum Security,* International Council of Museums, Paris, 1977.

J. M. A. Thompson, ed., *Manual of Curatorship,* The Museums Association, U.K., 1985.

G. Thomson, *The Museum Environment,* Butterworth & Co., London, 1978.

The American Association of Museums publishes an annual publications listing that includes articles on such subjects as museum management, security, conservation, storage, adaptive reuse, and energy management.

Technical publications on such subjects as museum environmental control are available from the Technical Information Service of the American Association for State and Local History, Nashville, Tenn., and the Canadian Conservation Institute, Ottawa.

See also National Building Museum

David W. Scott
Smithsonian Institution
Washington, D.C.

MUSIC HALLS

The music or concert hall is a building type within a larger category—the theater or auditorium. When examining the origins of the concert hall, one must study the theater and opera house, for its design is clearly based on these types.

The first auditoriums of record were those built by the Greeks to seat large audiences for tragedies and comedies. The great age of Greek drama was in the fifth century B.C.; unfortunately, no auditoriums from this period remain. Structures from the fourth century B.C. must be examined for visual evidence. The theaters were simple in design, taking advantage of the topography of the land for excellent seating and acoustics. An open air, semicircular seating arrangement was carved into the gently sloping hillside around a circular platform, the orchestra. The plan of the auditorium exposes the importance of the orchestra, the dancing space in the center, rather than the stage behind it. At the rear of the stage is the *skene,* or actors room, flanked on either side by secondary chambers called *parakenia.* The walls to these rooms provide a permanent architectural set, which over time became increasingly detailed.

During the first century B.C., the Roman empire engulfed the eastern Mediterranean, occupying countries with sophisticated theaters. Consequently, the Romans brought back with them the techniques necessary to construct similar structures in their cities. The earliest Roman auditoriums were constructed of wood and probably were painted. All included features resembling earlier Greek counterparts, although the orchestra was usually on a smaller scale. By the first century B.C., all Roman theaters were of stone and built on level ground in the center of the city, unlike the earlier Greek structures. The pitched seats were assembled over a series of arches, and the *skene* was built to the height of the seats, forming a completely enclosed space.

Since the earliest auditorium design, acoustics and sight line have been of prime importance. Vitruvius described theater design as "having to be built on solid foundations, on healthy sites, and designed so that everybody has a good view and is able to hear. To aid the acoustics it is recommended that bronze jars should be set in niches between the seats to give resonance, according to harmony" (1).

Smaller indoor theaters for recitation and music were built throughout the Roman empire. Larger structures often were used more for gladiator fights and circus events. The theater, used for song and dance, was usually part of an entire civic complex of governmental buildings and was given prime importance. These monumental structures were integrated into all new city plans created by the Roman empire. As with other structures in the city center, the auditorium had the formal, overpowering sense to it so often found in Roman civic architecture.

Because they were considered to be works of the devil, the early Christian Church outlawed concerts and plays, thus halting the architectural progression of the auditorium temporarily. By the tenth century A.D., part of the mass ceremony began to include short skits of biblical history, which were then transformed into short plays. Eventually, these plays became so popular that performers would conduct the religious plays in the streets of towns. Originally, small carts were pushed, carrying all necessary props, but as plays became accepted once again by the church, there was a need for audience space. Town squares became the location for the auditorium; seats were constructed of scaffolds, and the stage was elevated on a wooden platform. Seating originally encircled the stage, but time transformed the audience–stage relationship, increasingly separating actors from spectators by enlarging seating capacity.

The revival of interest in everything connected with ancient Rome that began in Italy in the late fourteenth and early fifteenth centuries and that marks the beginning of the Renaissance included the auditorium. The new theaters were based on writings by Vitruvius and ruins left by the Romans themselves. Lack of thorough information transformed many details, but a configuration similar to earlier structures was maintained.

Cesariano, basing his design on descriptions by Vitruvius, constructed a three-story semicircular building with open arches. The basic formation is correct, although lack of evidence describing seating layout caused a major design difference between his hall and earlier Roman counterparts.

Many of the auditoriums constructed during the early Renaissance were used for festivals and were thus considered temporary. They were built of relatively inexpensive materials such as wood and plaster. Private theaters were often assembled in royal court halls, allowing protection from the general public and accessibility for the nobility, the patrons of the theater. The most important theater of the Renaissance is Palladio's Teatro Olimpico at Vicenza. His goal was to create a truly Roman theater of wood, but on a much smaller scale than its prototypes. This was the last theater to employ a *scaenae frons* (architectural backdrop); after that time, all auditoriums included a picture-frame stage or movable perspective scenery for operas (2).

Scamozzi's theater at Sabionetta (1588) in Italy and Inigo Jones's work in England did not include a *scaenae frons,* but designed perspective sets behind a single arch or frame. These sets proved to be so complicated and awkward for members of the production that they were soon improved, but the frame remained and became a model for other auditoriums. The frame, known as the proscenium arch, was originally a temporary element within the theater; it eventually became an integral structural piece. Treated purely as ornament, as in Inigo Jones's masque designs, the proscenium arch was carved of wood and detailed with swags and medallions. Later, the frame was often created by a series of columns, as in the stage of the Teatre Farnese.

By the mid-seventeenth century, the present notion of the elements included in a concert hall or opera house were in existence. The horseshoe shape with boxes and galleries on various levels and a proscenium arch was common. By about 1640, every Italian court maintained a permanent private theater, many of which could seat up to three thousand people (3). Architects of the baroque period became so involved in theater design that they went beyond architecture and designed all details. Some architects not only designed the hall, but also wrote the opera, composed the music, and even created the settings, costumes, and equipment necessary for the performance.

By the mid-seventeenth century, public auditoriums were coming into existence. Capital was supplied by noble families or by a group of investors, with the clear objective of making money. This theater for profit affected the building type. Instead of elegance and ostentation and the close association of stage and auditorium, the interest was in how to accommodate as many customers as possible. Rather than one or two tiers of galleries framing the royal box with the *parterre* left void, the new halls jammed in three or four levels of galleries, divided them into boxes, and placed benches on the *parterre*.

In 1676, the first modern treatise on theater architecture was written, *Trattato Sopra la Struttural De Teatri e Scene* by Fabrizio Carini Motta (4). The author describes the contrasts between court and public auditoriums and characteristics inherent in theater design such as premium sight, acoustics, and seating capacity. He concluded that partitions between boxes should be placed perpendicular to the balustrade. Motta believed that there should be different entrances for various sections of the auditorium, revealing a clear social hierarchy among the audience. He was not interested in surface decoration, but rather in the configuration of the hall for optimum acoustics.

If the baroque period of architecture was suited for a certain building type, it would have to be the opera house. Treatment of architectural elements, material finishes, and surface details of baroque architecture enhance the spectacular ritual of attending the theater. Italy was the leader of baroque court and public theaters, and all other countries used this model for design. The auditoriums were usually horseshoe shaped, containing a large flat *parterre*, encircled by three to four tiers of boxes abutting the proscenium columns. The royal box was always distinguished by immense surface decoration and was always located on axis to the stage. Plaster molds were fabricated and employed in the production of most of the interior surface decoration. Finishes in various colored marbles, rich woods and polished and patinaed metals were exquisitely juxtaposed, developing a sumptuous glamour not found in earlier auditoriums.

By the mid-eighteenth century, the beginning of neoclassicism, there was a renewed interest in the formality and seriousness of all arts, including architecture and music. In 1755, Count Francesco Algarotti, an Italian scientist, published his *Saggio Sopera l'Opera*. In this article he advises that theaters should be of brick or stone against fire hazard, but the interior of the auditorium should be of wood, "the material from which we make musical instruments," for acoustical purposes. For optimum sight line, he believed that the ellipse was the premium shape of the auditorium, and that its ornament should be kept to a minimum (5). Concurrently, Jean Georges Moverre, in his *Observations sur la Construction d'une Nouvelle Salle de l'Opera* stated that the theater should take the place of a civic monument and should be freestanding on all four sides, easing access and reducing fire hazards. "Decoration should not be obtrusive, or the actors and scenery will be crushed by the ornament and richness" (6).

Theater design in the late eighteenth century reflected the views of Algarotti and Moverre. Numerous cities in France constructed public theaters, treating them as the focus of city planning. Metz Theatre and Lyons Theatre, typical of their era, were constructed on prominent island sites and had series of colonnades on two or all sides. The interiors included many public chambers, and a grand staircase, not only for visual attraction, but for improved circulation over earlier auditoriums. Claude-Nicholas Ledoux, planner of ideal cities, designed his theater in 1775. He found that earlier designs had made it impossible to see or hear, and considered their decoration to be vulgar and distracting. His purely functional theater was designed around three semicircular tiers of seats without boxes, receding as they rose until they reached a curving colonnade. His auditorium employed elements of classical architecture satisfying the requirements of the program, but restraining surface decoration (7).

On the other side of the Atlantic, U.S. theaters were opening up in most major cities. Two large theaters influencing those built after them were the Federal Street Theater in Boston by Charles Bulfinch and the Chestnut Street Theater in Philadelphia, both constructed in 1794. These theaters were based heavily on their neoclassical predecessors in the United Kingdom and resembled them significantly. Both auditoriums had the usual European arrangement in which the boxes, pit, and gallery each had its own entrance. This was not accepted by the equality conscious citizens of the young democratic country. The proprietors quickly made alterations that allowed all patrons to pass through a single entrance.

During the eighteenth century, the opera house became a distinct architectural type in Italy. It spread throughout the world, with its peak being the Paris Opera House of 1869. Most opera houses did not base their designs on the functional theater planning suggested by Ledoux or Gabriel, but were fashioned to develop the spectacle of attending the opera. Classicism was the architectural style used by many architects of the nineteenth century; often, restrained exteriors with porticos and ionic columns gave way to fanciful interiors. Schinkel's Neues Schauspielhaus in Berlin (1818) was the center of a town plan. Treated with a monumental scale, it has an ionic portico flanked by two wings. Gottfried Semper's Dresden Opera House of 1838 exposed the semicircle of the auditorium, the first since the middle ages. The foyers were positioned around the auditorium, so they formed demilunes, including a grand staircase at each end (8):

> Above all I have wished not to conceal the semi-cylindrical form of the auditorium, a form beautiful and varied in itself, and sanctioned moreover by theatrical tradition. I have not imprisoned it in a square cage, as most modern auditoria are.

In 1869, the Paris Opera House by Charles Garnier was completed after many years of construction. As in earlier Roman auditoriums, it was employed as a centerpiece of city planning. It was the "shrine" of opera. This edifice was Napoleon III's showplace to the world of France's power and optimism. The free standing building functions quite well in terms of seating, acoustics, and circulation, but is most notable for its grand lobby and public rooms. The opera house was conceived as an exercise in attending the theater. The richly finished rooms with balconies and galleries allow for visual contact with others attending the evening's event. Garnier's manipulation of the various interior spaces commences at the entrance, making his opera house one of the most exciting and unforgettable progressions of rooms a person can pass through before reaching the final destination. All segments of the structure are clearly expressed on the exterior, including the grand foyer with its cascading staircase, the dome auditorium, and the backstage area (9).

The German composer Richard Wagner (1813–1883) was the first to transform theater planning since the early eighteenth century. Working with architects, including Semper and Bruckwaldt, Wagner designed his ideal theater, the Bayreuth Festpielhaus. It had a fan-shaped auditorium without boxes or galleries and a sunken orchestra pit hidden from the audience. All seats were faced toward the stage, not opposing each other, for Wagner believed that the audience was not attending a social event. The stage was placed between a series of eight proscenium arches, giving the illusion of perspective, yet allowing the spectator to feel close to the event. Wagner's auditorium was employed as a model for decades after its construction, although the exterior of subsequent theaters was considered as important as the interior.

In the United States, Wagner's design theories continued to be followed, although the concert hall as a building type was manipulated. Louis Sullivan and Dankmar Adler, architect and engineer designing together, worked along with developer Ferdinand Peck to create the Auditorium theater in Chicago. Peck and other developers believed that there was a definite market for combining culture and commerce. Numerous building types, including a hotel, shopping plaza, and office tower were combined with an auditorium to create a complete center. Adler and Sullivan's theater cannot be recognized from the exterior, for it is surrounded by a hotel and topped off by an office tower. From the outside, all that can be seen is a rusticated stone base, continuing into a glass wall with iron columns of classical orders and finished with a cornice. This combination of building types proved successful and was followed in other major cities throughout North America. Auditoriums were not always within one separate structure, but were included within an entire plan for the redevelopment of city blocks. Sullivan and Adler's auditorium is considered to be a respectful combination of science and art; where Adler's efforts were spent to develop a premium shape for acoustics and sight line, Sullivan created the intricate decoration, lighting, and general mood required for a hall of this type. Presently, the complex is the home of Roosevelt University, which takes advantage of its multiple functions.

Catastrophic theater fires, causing numerous deaths in the late nineteenth century, created tremendous concern for the general safety of concert and theater goers. New, strict building codes were drawn up and enforced by governments in both Europe and North America. The new theaters were constructed of more fire-resistant materials; wood was avoided unless necessary, and iron was encased in masonry. It was now obligatory to include a fireproof curtain between the stage and the audience, to contain the flames to either zone. Architects began to provide for more entrances and exits for the theater, facilitating emergency evacuation. There was a brief period when a few concert halls were constructed partially underground, for it was thought when in a panic, people running from a fire would less likely fall over one another stepping up. Having the structure partially underground also reduces the number of steps one would have to climb to reach the seats on the uppermost balconies. There was a short period when cities did not allow an auditorium to be included with other functions, thinking it was a great fire hazard that would not only burn itself but also take with it the remaining parts of the complex (10).

Concurrent with the numerous breakthroughs in fire prevention was the general advancement in backstage services and climate control for the audience. Movable stages powered by steam began to be used in theaters across the United States, facilitating stage productions for complex operas. Hydraulic elevators became predominant in the later half of the nineteenth century and were used not only for passengers, but behind the curtain to move extremely heavy equipment and props. The most ingenious use of the new machinery was by Steel Mackaye, who installed four steam engines, perpetually in motion, supplying necessary electricity for all the house lights, ventilating the entire building, and running the elevators. As centrally supplied electricity became increasingly reliable and available, halls would no longer need to be self-powered, requiring less space for mechanical equipment.

By the late nineteenth century, classicism as the architectural style for concert halls practically vanished. A few short, but poignant architectural periods occurred before World War I, leaving showpiece buildings.

One of the great concert halls of the art nouveau style is Guimard's Humbert de Romans built in Paris in 1902. This auditorium was designed with as many sinuous, organic architectural details and as rich a spectrum of materials as any other building designed by the architect during that short period. All supporting steel was cloaked in veneers, delicately carved and polished to resemble vines and branches of trees. Unlike the traditional horseshoe shape commonly chosen by architects for the theater plan, Guimard used an elongated octagon and placed the stage so it pierced the seating area. Because the popularity of art nouveau spanned only about 20 years, just a few concert halls and opera houses were constructed; the majority of these were in Belgium, Holland, and France.

The arts and crafts movement took place at approximately the same time; a limited number of halls in this style appeared. Ernest Runz designed a series of theaters in larger British cities, all quite similar, but each unique when compared to auditoriums of other architectural periods.

World War I caused a halt to the construction of all architecture pertaining to entertainment, including concert halls. During the war, a new source of entertainment developed, the motion picture, causing a variation on the auditorium building type. By the late 1920s, hundreds of movie theaters were constructed with the style of the age, art deco. There was a tremendous interest in rebuilding what had been destroyed by World War I, leading to the construction of new concert halls in Europe.

One of the truly great halls built between the two world wars is Radio City Music Hall in New York City (1932). This immense auditorium seats up to six thousand people. Architect Peter Clark designed it around the "acoustic arches" developed previously by Adler and Sullivan in their Chicago theater. Tremendous arches, increasing in size, radiate from the stage, forming the shape of the theater, which was considered to be acoustically optimum. The fan shapes, along with all other details in the hall, are highly ornamented with surface applications of the art deco style.

Following World War II, a renewed interest in the performing arts led to the construction of many new concert halls and theaters. Now, instead of having merely one hall, a new concept of maintaining two or even three auditoriums under one roof or within a complex became prevalent in large cities throughout North America and parts of Europe. The nesting of theaters to form performing arts centers was due to the variety of backstage requirements for different productions and the number of audiences in attendance. During the postwar years, experimental productions began to surface, but usually only a tiny group would attend, creating a need for small-scale theaters. Larger audiences attending traditional operas with grand sets would require a much larger auditorium with a large backstage area. Symphony orchestras of major metropolitan areas needing a large stage but little backstage are now receiving their own halls, often located close to other auditoriums.

New York City's Lincoln Center, constructed in the early 1960s, envelops a public square purely by halls of various functions by several architects, including an opera house and an auditorium for the New York City Ballet. In Malmo, Sweden, there is a combination of two theaters within one structure, even more functional, in that the larger theater can be reduced in capacity, making it more intimate for smaller productions.

By the early 1960s, new engineering techniques, methods of construction, and materials were being discovered, and were employed by architects in their concepts of what a concert hall should be. Jorn Utzon, designer of the Sydney Opera House, repeated sail shapes to enclose a pair of auditoriums. The exterior does not reflect the interior volumes, but does make a bold statement when seen from a distance.

Recently, there has been a renewed interest in the study and reinterpretation of the architectural past. Postmodernism and its architects' fascination with details and classical planning is evident in recently built structures. Once again, concert halls are grouped with retail and office space, defraying the losses usually occurred by a metropolitan orchestra. One such design for Montreal, Canada, combines an enclosed public square, a small museum for musical instruments, an office tower, and retail space.

The theater type has existed since early in architectural history; its transformation can be traced through the ages. It seems that architects were constantly seeking the optimum form for acoustics and sight, but because of the concert hall's characteristics, there are only a few forms on which to base their design. Through almost all ages, theaters were conceived as a means of social gathering; even if they were not, as in Wagner's auditorium, they ultimately became so. Circulation and auxiliary rooms such as the foyer and lobby were as important as the auditorium for the procession of the theater-goer. Architects and city planners often employed the theater as a centerpiece of a town, giving the building monumentality. This is a building type that must be treated as a public edifice and should reflect the society's interest and involvement in the performing arts.

BIBLIOGRAPHY

1. Vitruvius, *The Ten Books on Architecture,* Book V, Chaps. III–VII, translated by M. H. Morgan, Harvard University Press, 1914; Dover Publications, N.Y., 1960.
2. S. Tidsworth, *Theatres: An Architectural and Cultural History,* Praeger, New York, 1973. pp. 46–54.
3. *Ibid.,* p. 65.
4. F. C. Motta, *Trattato Sopra la Struttural de Teatri e Scene,* 1676.
5. F. Algarotti, *Saggio Sopera l'Opera,* 1755.
6. Ref. 2, pp. 96–99.
7. Ref. 2, pp. 97–120.
8. G. Semper, "Writing for a later project, The Rio de Janeiro Opera House of 1858."
9. Ref. 2, p. 188.
10. Ref. 2, pp. 182–184.

General References

L. Benevolo, *History of Modern Architecture,* Vols. 1 and 2, The MIT Press, Cambridge, Mass., 1971.

K. V. Burian, *The Story of World Opera,* Peter Nevill Limited, London, 1961.

R. Leacroft and H. Leacroft, *Theatre and Playhouse,* Methuen, London, 1984.

H. B. Mayer and E. C. Cole, *Theatres & Auditoriums,* Reinhold, New York, 1949.

B. Moretti, *Teatri,* Ulrico Hoepedi, Milano, 1962.

A. Nicoll, *The Development of the Theatre,* George Harrap & Company, London, 1927.

P. Zucker, *Theater Und Lichtspielhauser,* Verlag Ernstwasmuth, Berlin, 1926.

See also Acoustical Design—Places of Assembly; Theaters and Opera Houses

Mitchell Benjamin
Montreal, Quebec, Canada

N

NATIONAL ARCHITECTURAL ACCREDITING BOARD (NAAB)

The National Architectural Accrediting Board (NAAB) is chartered with the responsibility to review and accredit architectural education programs throughout the United States. It was established in 1940 through a formal agreement between the American Institute of Architects (AIA), the Association of Collegiate Schools of Architecture (ACSA), and the National Council of Architectural Registration Boards (NCARB). These founding organizations were later joined by the American Institute of Architecture Students (AIAS). Together they constitute the governing body, the NAAB's Board of Directors. The Board is comprised of 11 directors. Three representatives are nominated from each of the founding professional organizations and subsequently elected by the Board. One member is appointed from the student organization, and one public–academic generalist member is nominated at large. The Board serves both as a decision-making and policy-formulating unit. In conjunction with review and accreditation activities, it engages in continuous study and evaluation of their formalized *Criteria and Procedures,* which align with the operational format of the NAAB (1). *The Criteria and Procedures* define the NAAB's organizational purpose, outline the requirements for obtaining NAAB accreditation, detail the procedural stages of the accreditation review process, and set forth its official bylaws.

The NAAB accredits only first-professional-degree programs in architecture leading to either a Bachelor of Architecture or a Master of Architecture degree. Each degree program is subject to the same review standard. In the profession of architecture, first-professional-degree education is viewed as a major step toward a career. Because accreditation is indicative of the quality of the education acquired, it serves as a basis for assessment for employment and for professional registration to practice. Given the practical experience prerequisite to examination for registration, accreditation provides an assurance that an academic program can prepare students reasonably well for internship prior to professional practice. In view of this, the NAAB sees its charge to "guarantee that graduates have competence in architectural design, that they have a grasp of technical systems and requirements, that they be able to incorporate considerations of health and safety into design, and that they understand the historical, the human, and the environmental context for architecture such that they have a sense of how architecture functions in society" (2). In its aim to satisfy these responsibilities, the NAAB further extends its objectives to include that graduates be trained to contribute to the future of the profession with a broad based representation in public and private sector practice, education and research, and those organizational entities that oversee the profession. That is to say, through accreditation, "Architecture's humanistic tradition can be made evident and vital through the first professional degree program," thereby nurturing a regeneration and continued building of this same humanistic tradition (3).

To this end, the NAAB sets forth definitive requirements for accreditation. They include the NAAB's Perspectives on Architectural Education. These perspectives are drawn from and refer to the interests of the four groups that comprise the NAAB: architectural educators, practitioners, registration-board officials, and students. In the accreditation review process, the NAAB seeks evidence that first-professional-degree programs meet the objectives of four stated perspectives. First, Education and Entry into Professional Practice aims at assuring the competence of an accredited program's graduates, such that they are trained to assume and perform their professional roles in society (4). In Education and Society, the NAAB presents an all-encompassing societal perspective, focusing on learning-awareness issues that range from developments in construction technologies and materials to professional liability, computer literacy, energy, cultural reinforcement through preservation, and adaptive use. It also looks at business management in the rendering of architectural services when the accredited programs evidence a response to the architect's evolving societal role. In Education and the Academic Environment, the NAAB holds the view that the broader academic environment houses many disciplines and therefore can, with its multiple resources and learning philosophies, serve purposefully to enhance an accredited program. Finally, Education and Individual Development speaks to the importance of education in the rounding of an architectural career, such that an accredited program should match particular interests and skills. In addition, it says that opportunities of related learning extensible to the specified NAAB criteria should be provided.

A second major requirement of the NAAB review process is the determination that a given architectural program has appropriate institutional support. This assessment is based on the conditions that the program have regional accreditation; that the general-education-breadth requirement reflect a percentage of the program curriculum; that the institution offer one or more of the four recognized first-degree programs, including a five-year Bachelor of Architecture or a Bachelor of Architecture degree for individuals with a prior degree in another field, a Master of Architecture degree requiring four years of undergraduate and two years of graduate study, or a Master of Architecture degree for individuals with an undergraduate degree from another discipline. The NAAB requires further that the program be able to verify sufficiency of resources, including human, student, faculty, staff, and physical, and informational resources, to ensure the continued accreditability of the program. Finally, architectural educational programs must provide evidence, through documentation and review, that their first-professional degree programs satisfy all Achievement-Oriented Performance Criteria (5). This last requirement includes submission of informational materials that must show the curriculum opportunity is provided, and present evidence of student achievement.

All of these NAAB requirements are addressed through formal documentation and presented for review in the form of an Architecture Program Report (APR) (6). The most extensive informational component of the APR addresses program content and student performance. The satisfaction of this requirement is identified in a school's response to 66 questions that assess achievement-oriented performance criteria. These questions are grouped into four major areas: (*1*) history, human behavior, and environmental context; (*2*) design; (*3*) technology; and (*4*) practice. The totality of the questions and their organization are intended to reflect a common-sense ordering of the design process, which progresses from the initial context for design to the design learning process itself, its technical system requirements, and ultimately to practice. The report, questions also give insight into the academic specializations of a program's teaching faculty, as well as other traditional supportive areas of strength in an architectural learning curriculum (7).

The NAAB recognizes and supports diversity among programs, and identifies the need to fulfill the broad requirements of the architectural profession. While in the process of review each program must satisfy the same criteria for program content and student performance, weighted variables in the program's review responses to the criteria questions are expected. Thus, the APR, as a collective comprehensive response to NAAB requirements, serves as a documented reference that initiates and facilitates the formal procedural accreditation review process.

The specific procedure of review begins when the school submits its APR in a specified format and context. Its contents are an Introduction, Program Mission statement, Educational Intent and NAAB Perspectives statement, Academic Context submission, Academic Program (achievement-oriented performance criteria assessment), Program Enrichment documentation, Response to Previous Visiting Team Report, Self Assessment (previous review document), and Appendix (course outlines and faculty curriculum vitae). An NAAB appointed APR reviewer, academic or practicing professional, is charged to determine that all required information has been completed with forthright responses and similarly determine whether there is need for further clarification or additional information. If the APR is complete and in order, the reviewer recommends its acceptance.

With the Board of Directors' vote to accept the APR, the next procedural step is a visit to the school of the program under review. Visitor teams are selected to reflect the composition of NAAB's member groups, one each from ACSA, AIA, NCARB, and AIAS. The team chairperson assumes full charge of the visit. Team members must be knowledgeable about the NAAB Criteria and Procedures, the Architectural Program Report, and the procedural agenda for the visit. Each school, according to the NAAB directives, develops its own review agenda for the site visit. Typically, the agenda includes an initial meeting with the program's administrator; a meeting with the institution's senior academic officer; a meeting with student representatives; a review with students, observing both their studio facilities and student projects; contact with alumni and community practitioners; and meetings with faculty. The site visit concludes with a summary oral presentation of the team's preliminary views. No indication of the visiting team's recommendations to the NAAB is shared with the school at this time. At the conclusion of the site visit, the team prepares a report that "conveys its impressions of the quality of education in terms of the NAAB's stipulated criteria, the school's educational intent, its contexts and stated academic endeavors" (8). It confirms that the program is as presented in the APR. When the team report is complete and conforms with NAAB guidelines, the report, excluding accreditation recommendation, is sent by NAAB to the School for correction of fact.

The accreditation decision is acted on at its Board of Director's regular meetings, which must occur at least twice yearly. The bylaws stipulate also that at least two-thirds of the total membership must vote in the affirmative for approval of accreditation. In formulating its judgment, the Board of course considers the school's information and the visiting team's confidential recommendation, but the decision to accreditate, state the bylaws, rests solely with the directors. Accreditation may be granted for a term of one to five years, or one to three years when a program is first accredited or when substantial changes have occurred in the program's formal curriculum. In addition to the review, the NAAB requires accreditation maintenance in the form of an annual report submitted by the school. This allows for monitoring of the implementation of team report recommendations and for updating the program's statistical information for the NAAB. A program can receive an accreditation extension of two years if it has received two consecutive terms of five-year accreditation. In cases in which accreditation is not granted, the NAAB has an appeals process. A probation rule applies to programs receiving a term of accreditation of less than five years. The rule is that a program must be granted a full five-year term at its next scheduled visit, or it will be given a two-year term of probation; if the program again fails to receive a five-year term, accreditation will be withdrawn.

A new program wishing to establish candidacy status for accreditation must observe several procedures that essentially involve an initial application, its review and approval, and thereafter, close contact and a biennial evaluation of the candidate program over a minimum of two years and a maximum of eight years. A new school of architecture cannot receive accreditation for its programs until its first professional class has graduated.

The NAAB is operationally bound to its official, published bylaws, which address the NAAB's executive structure, its organizing functions, and procedural activities. A president, president-elect, treasurer, and secretary form the executive committee. The officers are drawn from the 11 appointed members of the Board of Directors. The executive committee, in turn, is supported by two standing committees—a nominating committee, and an evaluation and training committee. At every meeting of the Board, each director is entitled to one vote; a majority quorum is required for the transaction of business.

The NAAB functions as a nonprofit organization whose financial support and budget structure is the joint concern of the AIA, the ACSA, and NCARB. Through this unified organizational and operational structure, these sponsoring organizations are committed to maintaining the continuation of the highest standards of academic practice in architectural education.

BIBLIOGRAPHY

1. *NAAB Criteria and Procedures,* The National Architectural Accrediting Board, Washington, D.C., 1984, p. 2.
2. Ref. 1, p. 7.
3. Ref. 1, p. iii.
4. Ref. 1, p. 6.
5. Ref. 1, p. 28.
6. Ref. 1, p. 26.
7. Ref. 1, p. 27.
8. Ref. 1, p. 32.

General References

Architecture Schools in North America, Petersen Guides, Princeton, N.J., 1982.

G. Brown, "Accreditation," *Inland Architect* (January/February 1985).

See also Association of Collegiate Schools of Architecture (ACSA); Education, Architectural; Intern Programs; National Council of Architectural Registration Boards (NCARB).

Karen J. Dominguez
Pennsylvania State University
State College, Pennsylvania

NATIONAL BUILDING MUSEUM

The National Building Museum (NBM) is a joint federal–private institution mandated by Congress in 1980 to celebrate the United States' past and present building accomplishments; to encourage excellence in the building arts of the United States through a national program of exhibitions, publications, and educational activities; and to collect and disseminate information concerning the built environment.

As a private, nonprofit institution, NBM raises funds from the private sector for staff and programs. The federal government provides the century-old Pension Building for the museum's home (Fig. 1) and pays for the building's maintenance, repair, and renovation. For the current renovation of the Pension Building, extensive research has been undertaken by the museum in the archives of its architect, Montgomery C. Meigs, who left extensive records on the design and construction of the building.

The museum's Board of Trustees is made up of leading figures in the building community—architects, engineers, developers, contractors, building product manufacturers, leaders in the building trade unions, and architectural historians.

The first museum galleries opened in October of 1985 with four exhibitions: "Building a National Image: Architectural Drawings for the American Democracy, 1789–1912"; "An Architectural Wonder: The U.S. Pension Building"; "America's Master Metalsmith: Samuel Yellin, 1885–1940"; and "Anatomy of a Bridge: Seven Steps in Constructing the Brooklyn Bridge." These first exhibition galleries show how the space, originally built for offices, will function when converted to museum galleries once the renovation of the building is complete in 1988 and more than justify the decision of Congress that this historic building would best be used as a museum dedicated to U.S. building.

Additional exhibitions in the first year of operation included "Built for the People of the United States of America: Fifty Years of TVA Architecture"; "Ornamental Architecture Reborn: A New Terra Cotta Vocabulary"; "Good Design in the Community: The Story of Columbus, Indiana"; and "American Decorative Window Glass: 1860–1890."

Several of the museum's early exhibitions highlighted the decorative role of material in building. This theme characterizes one aspect of the museum's role—that of clarifying for the public the important trends in current building and helping to answer the question of why designers of the moment are giving the built environment its current appearance.

The museum's first endowed gallery (dedicated in 1988), in memory of Edward F. Carlough, has been given by the Sheet Metal Workers' International Association.

In addition to its exhibitions in the Pension Building, the museum maintains a traveling exhibition program, which was begun before renovation of the galleries in the Pension Building. Circulating exhibitions have included "Speaking a New Classicism: American Architecture Now"; "Built for the People of the United States of America: Fifty Years of TVA Architecture"; "America's Master Metalsmith: Samuel Yellin, 1885–1940"; and "Ornamental Architecture Reborn: A New Terra Cotta Vocabulary."

First published in 1981, the museum's award-winning publication *Blueprints* informs readers across the country about activities in the built environment and reports on museum activities.

NBM's first book, *Building a National Image: Architectural Drawings for the American Democracy, 1789–1912* by Bates Lowry, first director of the museum, was published in conjunction with the opening exhibition by the same name.

In October 1986 the museum established the Building Hall of Fame to honor past and present U.S. citizens whose talents and labor have shaped the built environment of the United States. The first contemporary U.S. citizen chosen by the museum was J. Irwin Miller of Columbus, Indiana. The historic figures chosen in 1986 were Nicholas Biddle, James Bogardus, A. J. Downing, Fiske Kimball, Pierre Charles L'Enfant, James McMillan, Montgomery C. Meigs, Robert Mills, H. H. Richardson, J. R. Roebling, William Robert Ware, and Frank Lloyd Wright.

The educational activities of the museum include regular tours of the Pension Building as well as tours in the Washington, D.C., area and short trips to sites of architec-

(a)

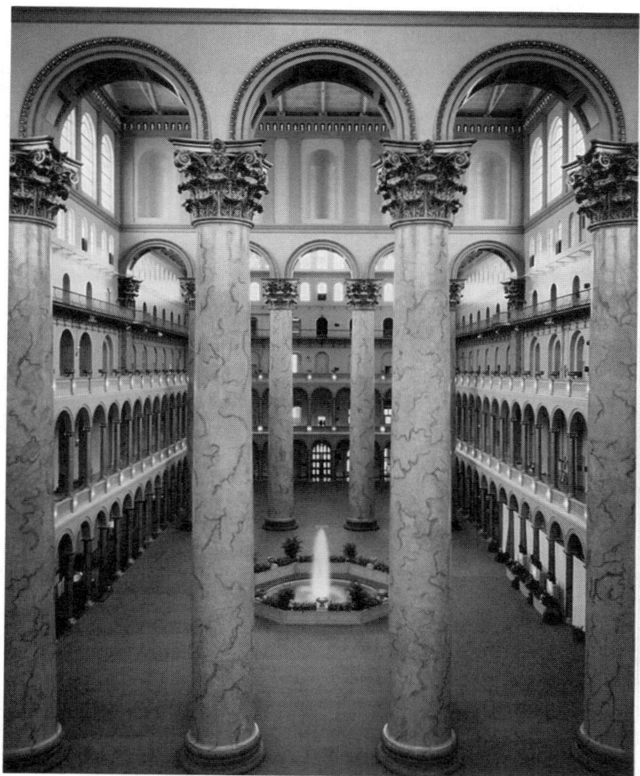

(b)

Figure 1. (**a**) Exterior and (**b**) Great Hall of the National Building Museum (old Pension Building), Washington, D.C. Courtesy of F. Harlan Hambright.

tural interest. The education department is currently developing curriculum materials and holding classes for school children in the museum in order to increase their understanding of the built environment. Films on the built environment are shown regularly at the museum.

The museum has sponsored the following design competitions: Energy Conservation in Historic Buildings (1981) and The Contemporary Terra Cotta Competition (1986).

The museum's collections are being developed, and among the first items to be received are

- The Mertes Collection, consisting of 52,000 working drawings of terra cotta facings and ornaments from the Northwestern Terra Cotta Company.
- Over 100 books of photographs detailing the construction progress of projects built by the James Stewart Company, Inc., Contractors, between 1900 and 1944.
- Films on design made by Ray and Charles Eames.
- The Wurts Brothers Collection, consisting of thousands of photographic negatives and prints taken by

Wurts Brothers Photographers, a prominent architectural photography firm, from 1894 to 1979.

- The Chalfont Archive, consisting of the complete working papers of architect William Bergen Chalfont.
- Elevator grilles that surrounded the open elevator cages in the Manhattan Building in Chicago.
- The Brothers Collection consisting of drawings, photographs, and models of the work of the Ernest L. Brothers firm of interior designers.
- Individual drawings made by nationally significant architects.
- Brooklyn Bridge models depicting in large abstract forms the engineering design of the bridge.

See also MUSEUMS

JOYCE ELLIOTT
National Building Museum
Washington, D.C.

NATIONAL BUREAU OF STANDARDS (NBS)

Measurement plays a major role in searches for new materials, new processes, and new and better technology. Providing accurate measurements is the unique mission of the National Bureau of Standards (beginning in August 1988 to be known as the National Institute of Standards and Technology). By supplying the measurement foundation for industry, science, and technology, NBS helps the nation improve product quality, achieve higher productivity, and increase competitiveness abroad.

The science of measurement affects nearly every segment of the U.S. economy, from new technologies such as advanced ceramics, automated manufacturing, superconductivity, optoelectronics, and biotechnology to more traditional fields such as weights and measures. For these and other areas of technology, NBS develops measurement techniques, reference data, test methods, and calibration services that help ensure national and international measurement capability and compatibility.

For more than 87 years, NBS research has laid the groundwork for fundamental advances in electricity, aviation, automotive engineering, construction, fire safety, and materials. It has provided essential improvements in electrical standards and developed better standards of length and new standards of light, temperature, and time. In fact, frequency measurements by NBS scientists now make it possible to tie all measurements of time and length to a single very precise standard.

As a nonregulatory agency of the U.S. Department of Commerce, NBS was established in 1901 specifically to aid manufacturing, commerce, government, and academia. Researchers from industry and universities often work in NBS laboratories with bureau experts on projects of mutual interest. For example, engineers, machinists, and computer specialists from private companies, government, and universities have joined NBS researchers to develop the quality control techniques and the computer software interface standards needed for the automated factory of the future.

To bring automated flexible manufacturing technology to small and mid-size manufacturing firms, NBS has begun a manufacturing technology centers program. The program is designed to establish regional centers that will help these companies improve their technical capabilities and competitiveness.

NBS also has some of the premier research and testing facilities in the United States, several of which are unequaled anywhere in the world. Many of these facilities are available for cooperative or proprietary research. For instance, about 300 scientists use the bureau's 20-megawatt research reactor each year for studies in environmental chemistry, biomedicine, and materials science. Among other NBS facilities are a synchrotron ultraviolet radiation facility, an automated manufacturing research facility, a large-scale structures test facility, several environmental chambers, a metals-processing laboratory, a fire research facility, and a computer and network security facility.

Two units of the National Bureau of Standards serving architects, engineers, and the construction industry are the Center for Building Technology and the Center for Fire Research.

CENTER FOR BUILDING TECHNOLOGY

More than two-thirds of the nation's fixed, reproducible wealth is invested in constructed facilities. Moreover, the construction industry is one of the nation's largest, and constructed facilities shelter and support most human activities. The quality of these facilities affects people's safety and quality of life, as well as the productivity of industry.

The NBS Center for Building Technology (CBT) increases the usefulness, safety, and economy of buildings through the advancement of building technology and its application to the improvement of building practices. CBT conducts laboratory, field, and analytical research to develop technologies for the prediction, measurement, and testing of the performance of building materials, components, systems, and practices.

Center researchers concentrate their efforts in computer-integrated construction, structural engineering, earthquake hazard reduction, building physics, building materials, and building equipment. They carry out their work in sophisticated and comprehensive laboratory facilities, which include a six-degree-of-freedom structural testing facility, a large-scale structures testing facility, environmental chambers, a guarded hot plate, and a calibrated hot box.

CBT provides technical support and information to a number of voluntary standards groups such as ASTM; the American Concrete Institute; the American Society of Heating, Refrigerating and Air Conditioning Engineers; the American Society of Civil Engineers; and building code organizations. While it contributes to the development of voluntary standards, the center does not promulgate or enforce standards or regulations. Through its work, the center helps eliminate technological market barriers of the construction industry and reduces the burdens of unnecessary or ineffective building regulations while maintaining safety.

CBT represents the United States in several international building research and standards organizations, including the International Council for Building Research, Studies, and Documentation; the International Union of Testing and Research Laboratories for Materials and Structures; and the U.S.–Japan Panel on Wind and Seismic Effects. These efforts contribute to U.S. use of foreign research accomplishments and the international competitiveness of U.S. building technology.

Much of the center's research is done in cooperation with, or for, other federal agencies, such as the Department of Energy, the General Services Administration, the Federal Emergency Management Agency, the Occupational Safety and Health Administration, and the White House. In addition, each year about 70 researchers from international and U.S. universities and industries join CBT staffers in cooperative programs.

As an impartial third party, the center is called upon to investigate the physical causes of major building and construction failures, such as the collapse of a partially constructed building in Bridgeport, Conn. in 1987 (Fig. 1), the walkway collapse in the Kansas City Hyatt Regency Hotel in 1981, and the East Chicago, Ind. ramp collapse in 1982. The results of the center's investigations are promptly and publicly reported to help preclude recurrences.

More of the center's research, however, is aimed at developing improved building practices so that such tragedies do not occur. For example, engineers at the center are working on ways to determine when poured concrete is strong enough for construction formwork to be removed. They have developed a test method for determining concrete strength and a computerized method of analysis, both of which are being considered by ASTM for adoption as voluntary standards. Important from both safety and economic standpoints, these tools will help a builder remove the formwork as soon as possible, without risking workers' safety.

Center researchers have designed and constructed a computerized facility to test how full-scale bridge and building components will perform during earthquakes (Fig. 2). In a project sponsored by the National Science Foundation, the Federal Highway Administration, and the California Department of Transportation, CBT researchers tested 30-ft-high bridge columns under conditions simulating earthquake forces (Fig. 3). They also ran tests on columns one-third and one-sixth that size. By comparing the results of both tests, the researchers will be able to determine whether the behavior of small-scale bridge columns can be used to predict that of full-scale columns. They will use this information to evaluate and refine computer models that predict how structures perform during earthquakes, enabling the building community to design safer buildings and bridges with fewer expensive physical tests.

To help the construction industry respond effectively to the opportunities and challenges offered by advanced computation and automation, CBT is investigating their application to performance prediction and measurement technology. For example, increases in computer power and reductions in computing costs will lead to "smart buildings" with integrated, automated control systems for greater usefulness, safety, and economy in operation. Center researchers are developing and verifying minute-by-minute simulations of the performance of building control systems to help owners, designers, manufacturers, and contractors set up economical and reliable automated control systems for buildings.

Computer technologies will make possible measurement advances in building diagnostics, quality assurance, and prediction of building behavior. CBT is, for example, developing modeling techniques for the microstructure of cements that will allow prediction of how cement ingredients, mixing, placement, and curing will affect the strength and durability of concrete structures.

Center researchers are formulating three-dimensional, dynamic computer simulations that will predict heat, air, moisture, and pollutant movements in buildings. These techniques will help improve energy conservation, use of solar energy and natural ventilation, and indoor air quality.

Other computer simulations are being developed and verified for dynamic tests of the thermal performance of walls. Improved test methods will provide more accurate assessments of effects of wall mass, air and moisture movements, and multidimensional heat, air, and moisture flow at junctions of building elements on thermal comfort and energy efficiency.

To provide the technical bases for substantial increases in the efficiency of innovative heat pumps and air conditioners, researchers at the center are developing and verifying computer simulations of heat transfer properties of mixed refrigerants and refrigeration cycles.

The researchers are also working with leading construction standards organizations to adapt artificial intelligence technologies to the needs of the building community and to supply the advanced performance prediction and measurement technologies that will be needed to realize the potential of expert systems for construction.

The objectives of the Center for Building Technology programs are as follows:

1. *Structural Engineering.* To increase the productivity and safety of building construction by providing technical bases for improved structural and earthquake design criteria.
2. *Building Materials Engineering.* To reduce building costs and increase building quality by providing technical bases for selecting the most cost-effective materials.
3. *Building Environment.* To reduce the cost of designing and operating buildings and increase the international competitiveness of the U.S. building industry by providing modeling, measurement, and test methods needed to use advanced computation and automation effectively in construction, improve the quality of the indoor environment, and improve the performance of building equipment.

(a)

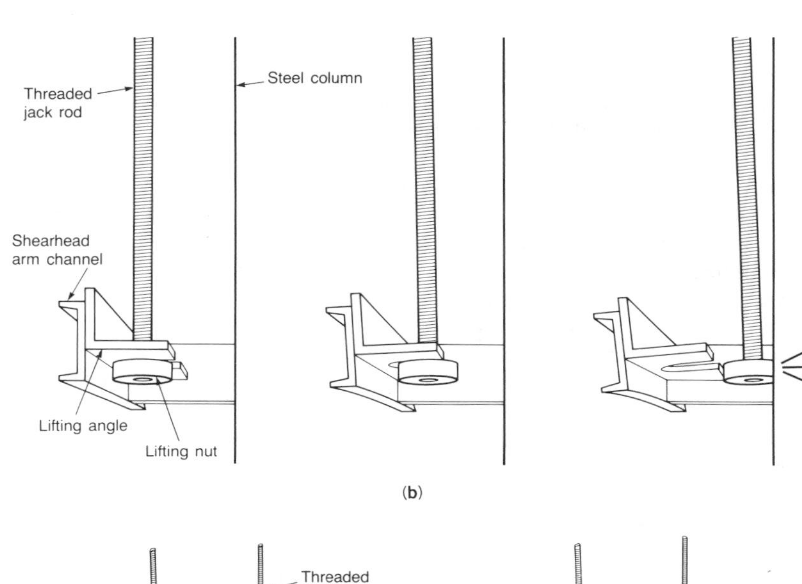

(b)

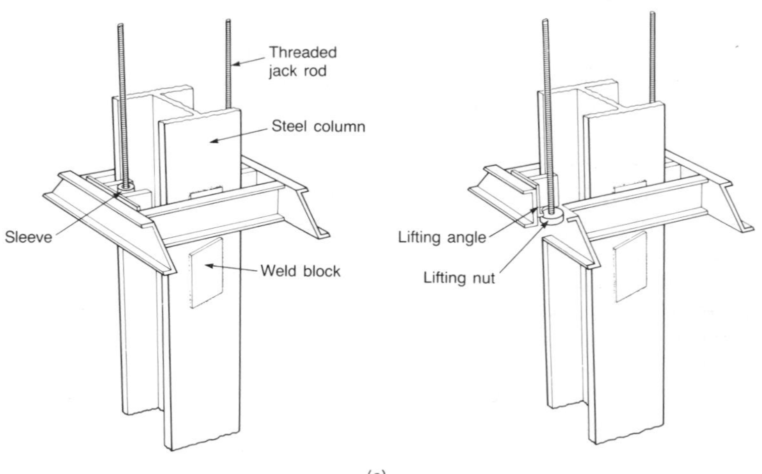

(c)

Figure 1. (a) Photograph of the L'Ambiance Plaza Building Collapse in Bridgeport, Conn. **(b)** Cutaway diagram of failure mechanism. The collapse most probably began when a jack rod supporting three concrete floor slabs slipped out of a U-shaped opening in a steel bracket, or lifting angle. **(c)** Shearhead—column assembly.

Figure 2. Tri-Directional Test Facility at the National Bureau of Standards. The Facility is a computer-controlled apparatus capable of applying cyclic loads simultaneously in three directions. It is used in examining the strength of structural components or assemblages under the application of a variety of loading phenomena such as earthquake or wind.

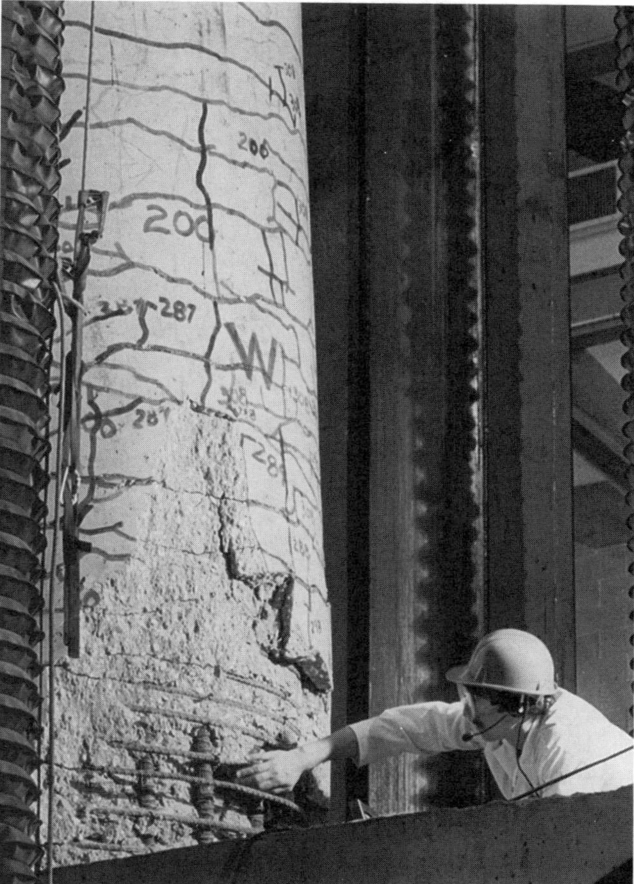

Figure 3. A researcher in the NBS Center for Building Technology studies the damage to a full-scale bridge column after being subjected to simulated seismic stresses in the NBS Large-Scale Structural Test Facility.

CENTER FOR FIRE RESEARCH

The United States has one of the worst fire loss records in the industrialized world. The NBS Center for Fire Research (CFR) is committed to providing the scientific and engineering bases needed by manufacturers and the fire protection community to reduce both these losses and the cost of fire protection.

By improving the understanding of the chemistry and physics that take place during combustion and by developing accurate computer models of fire hazards, the center provides technical information to voluntary standards organizations, engineering and design communities, building industry, fire service and fire protection organizations, and materials manufacturers. The center also helps these groups to translate the findings into new engineering practices, test methods, and proposals for improved standards or code provisions. NBS, however, does not promulgate or enforce standards or regulations.

One of the most complex and yet crucial phenomena affecting fire growth is soot formation. Incandescent soot radiates thermal energy that converts furnishings or construction materials into gaseous fuels, feeding fires. Soot also affects inhalation and obstructs vision, thus making fires less survivable. Yet the same particles form the fire "signature" that activates the now-common smoke detectors. Scientists at the center are conducting a long-term study of the fundamental chemistry and physics of soot formation. They have devised new, laser-based techniques for measuring key molecules in the chemical chain of soot growth (Fig. 4). Using multiphoton ionization measurements, researchers can detect certain organic species, such as butadiene, throughout the flame itself. They have also obtained profiles of polycyclic aromatic hydrocarbons using ultraviolet and visible fluorescence. Concurrent theoretical calculations on the "stickiness" of aromatic molecules have further clarified which chemistry is significant in building soot particles from small molecules.

Perhaps the topic of most concern in fire research today is that of fire gas toxicity. Most fire deaths are caused by the inhalation of smoke. Carbon monoxide, a combustion product of most burning materials, has been widely considered as the primary cause of these deaths. Recent laboratory tests and analyses of samples from some fire

Figure 4. The Bureau's flame chemistry research is intended to provide more information about the chemical mechanism of soot formation. This photograph illustrates a laminar hydrocarbon flame in which optical probes are being used to detect specific chemical species in the flame.

victims, however, have suggested that other toxicants or factors may contribute to some deaths. Building on a decade of leadership in measuring the lethal effects of fire-generated smoke, researchers at the center are now studying the extent to which the generation rates of a few principal toxic gases can be used to predict mortality. The results of experiments with carbon monoxide, carbon dioxide, hydrogen cyanide, hydrogen chloride, and reduced oxygen levels are helping to explain the lethality of fire gases.

Center researchers are also devising ways to predict the precise contribution of materials to a fire's severity. Their oxygen consumption technique greatly simplifies the measurement of a burning sample's rate of energy release, a key factor in the rate of fire growth. This method is now being used to measure the heat given off by furniture and wall coverings during full-sized room fires. An instrument designed by the center, the cone calorimeter, operates on the same principle and shows exceptional promise for predicting the large-scale rate of heat release using small samples.

Predicting fire growth requires a fundamental understanding of elemental fire processes, such as flame spread, and the characterization of fire-induced flows. Researchers have developed methods to correlate the speed at which flame spreads across and down a burning vertical surface with the basic thermal properties of the burning materials. Measurements of flame height and flame radiation are now providing key information in understanding upward spread of flames, a faster and therefore more critical process.

The buoyancy-driven flow of fire gases through doors and open windows and their replacement by ventilated air is also predictable. Ventilation and the rate of heat release of the burning materials are the primary factors that determine if and when a room will "flash over," a term used to describe the total involvement of all items in a room.

Information obtained in experimental work is used in mathematical models designed to predict the vulnerability of a building and its occupants to fire. These computer-based models make it possible to simulate real fire situations within a limited budget. It is far less costly to "burn" a room or building using a computer. Center researchers are now designing a true general-purpose model of fire hazard. It will include the burning behavior of a room, the movement of fire gases throughout a building, and the effect of those gases on people. By using such a model, fire professionals will be able to study "their fire" on a computer, varying each component as needed, and making quantitative decisions for improving fire safety.

Several prediction models are already available. In one model, termed ASET (available safe egress time), the computer code incorporates sound but simplified single-room fire growth. It calculates the time at which a smoke detector is activated and the time at which the room becomes uninhabitable. The difference between these two is the time that the occupants of the room have to escape.

Another model, called FAST (fire and smoke transport model), can be used to determine the smoke level and temperature in a multiroom building with a fire in one room.

The center recently set up a fire simulation laboratory, where fire protection scientists and engineers can see demonstrations and obtain hands-on experience. Researchers also use the laboratory to modify models for particular applications.

More widespread and proper use of sprinkler systems also could significantly reduce fire losses, but better operational and design criteria are needed. The center has recently produced a computer program for calculating the response time of heat-activated sprinklers. It predicts the response time based on characteristics of the fire and the location and thermal properties of the sprinkler heads. The predicted temperatures at those sites agree well with steady-state laboratory tests. Large-scale tests with growing fires are planned to establish the range of applicability of the computer code.

The Center for Fire Research also sponsors a program of grants and, to a lesser degree, contracts for fire research in support of the internal research program of the Center. Approximately 25 grants are awarded to universities and research institutes annually.

See also AMERICAN SOCIETY FOR TESTING AND MATERIALS (ASTM); ARCHITECTURE AND ENGINEERING PERFORMANCE INFORMATION CENTER

(AEPIC); Fire Resistance of Materials; Fire Safety—Life Safety; Research, Architectural; Seismic Design; Zoning and Building Regulations

National Institute of Standards and Technology
Gaithersburg, Maryland

NATIONAL COUNCIL OF ARCHITECTURAL REGISTRATION BOARDS (NCARB)

In May 1919, during an American Institute of Architects convention in Nashville, Tenn., 15 architects from 13 states came together to form an organization that would soon become the National Council of Architectural Registration Boards. Emil Lorch of Ann Arbor, Mich. and Emory S. Hall of Chicago, Ill. were elected as chairman and secretary, respectively, at this initial meeting. On May 6, 1920, Lorch was elected the first president and Hall the first secretary of the NCARB. At this meeting, registration board members were joined by officials of the American Institute of Architects and the American Association of Engineers.

The purpose of the organization, as expressed by its founding members, was to facilitate the exchange of information on examining, licensing, and regulating architects, to foster uniformity in licensing and practice laws, to facilitate reciprocal licensing, to discuss the merits of various examining methods as well as the scope and content of licensing examinations, and to strive to improve the general educational standards of the architectural profession in the United States. These goals have been modified only twice in NCARB's initial 65-year history. Today, the mission of NCARB is to work together as a council of member boards to safeguard the health, safety, and welfare of the public and to assist member boards in carrying out their duties. In response to that mission, the NCARB has charged itself to develop and recommend standards to be required of an applicant for architectural registration; to develop and recommend standards regulating the practice of architecture; to provide a process for certifying to member boards the qualifications of an architect for registration; and to represent the interests of member boards before public and private agencies.

NCARB functions as a quasi-public organization because, under the Constitution of the United States, the power to guard the health, safety, and welfare of the people is reserved to the individual state. Regulation of the profession of architecture and registering or licensing of practitioners is not accomplished nationally, but is a function of the individual state or territory of the United States.

The NCARB is a nonprofit corporation, having incorporated initially on March 26, 1921 under the Illinois nonprofit laws, and in September 1940 under the provisions of the Iowa Nonprofit Corporation Act. Its current membership consists of all legally constituted architectural registration boards of the 50 states, the District of Columbia, Guam, the Northern Mariana Islands, Puerto Rico, and the U.S. Virgin Islands. As such, these boards formulate the policies, rules, and regulations of the NCARB and elect its officers and directors. All officers and directors serve without pay.

At the turn of the century, only three states had laws regulating the practice of architecture: Illinois, the first in 1897; California; and New Jersey. By 1920, 17 more states had adopted laws regulating the practice of architecture and licensing of individuals as architects. Table 1 contains a list of states and the year in which their licensing laws were first adopted.

Table 1. Adoption of Regulations Concerning the Practice of Architecture

1897	Illinois	1921	Arizona	1937	Nebraska
1901	California	1921	Minnesota	1937	Texas
1902	New Jersey	1921	Tennessee	1939	Alaska
1909	Colorado	1921	West Virginia	1939	Arkansas
1910	Louisiana	1923	Hawaii	1941	Massachusetts
1911	Utah	1924	District of Columbia	1941	Missouri
1913	North Carolina	1925	Oklahoma	1945	Maine
1915	Florida	1925	South Dakota	1948	New Hampshire
1915	Michigan	1927	Iowa	1949	Kansas
1915	New York	1927	Puerto Rico	1949	Nevada
1917	Idaho	1928	Mississippi	1951	Vermont
1917	Montana	1929	Indiana	1951	Wyoming
1917	North Dakota	1930	Kentucky	1956	Canal Zone (dropped from rolls by Congressional action in 1978)
1917	South Carolina	1931	Alabama		
1917	Wisconsin	1931	Ohio		
1919	Georgia	1932	New Mexico		
1919	Oregon	1933	Connecticut		
1919	Pennsylvania	1933	Delaware	1960	Guam
1919	Washington	1935	Maryland	1968	Virgin Islands
1920	Virginia	1936	Rhode Island	1984	Northern Mariana Islands

ORGANIZATION

The organization, function, and processes of the NCARB are currently governed by bylaws. Originally, the NCARB had both a constitution and bylaws, which were initially adopted on November 19, 1920 at its meeting held in St. Louis, Mo. In 1958, at its meeting in Cleveland, Ohio, the NCARB adopted a new constitution and bylaws that expanded and refined its services to architectural registration boards and to members of the architectural profession. In June 1979, at its meeting in Cambridge, Mass., the NCARB streamlined its organizational and operations documents into a single bylaws document.

Initially, NCARB was directed by a president, one vice-president, and a secretary/treasurer. As the organization grew, directors were added and additional executive officers were named. Directors were elected as at-large directors. A conscious effort was made to choose officers and directors from various sections of the United States, so that no single region would be able to exercise undue influence on the work of the organization.

As the member boards began to recognize that their own interests were inseparable from many issues of registration on a national scale, groups of states began to come together to form regional conferences. The western states formed the first regional group and strongly urged the formation of other regional groups. Three other regional groups were subsequently organized and in June 1964, the NCARB agreed to create officially six regional conferences. States and territories were assigned to regions on the basis of geography as well as through existing strong professional, economic, and commercial ties. Following this development, the Board of Directors was restructured in July 1968 to include six executive officers and six directors, one director from each of the regional conferences. The officers now consist of the president, two vice-presidents, secretary, treasurer, and immediate past president. These officers also form the NCARB's Executive Committee.

To be members, NCARB's member boards are required to be members of a regional conference. Each of the six regional conferences is responsible for its own method of organization, objectives, meetings, finances, and officers. Figure 1 shows the allocation of jurisdictions to each regional conference.

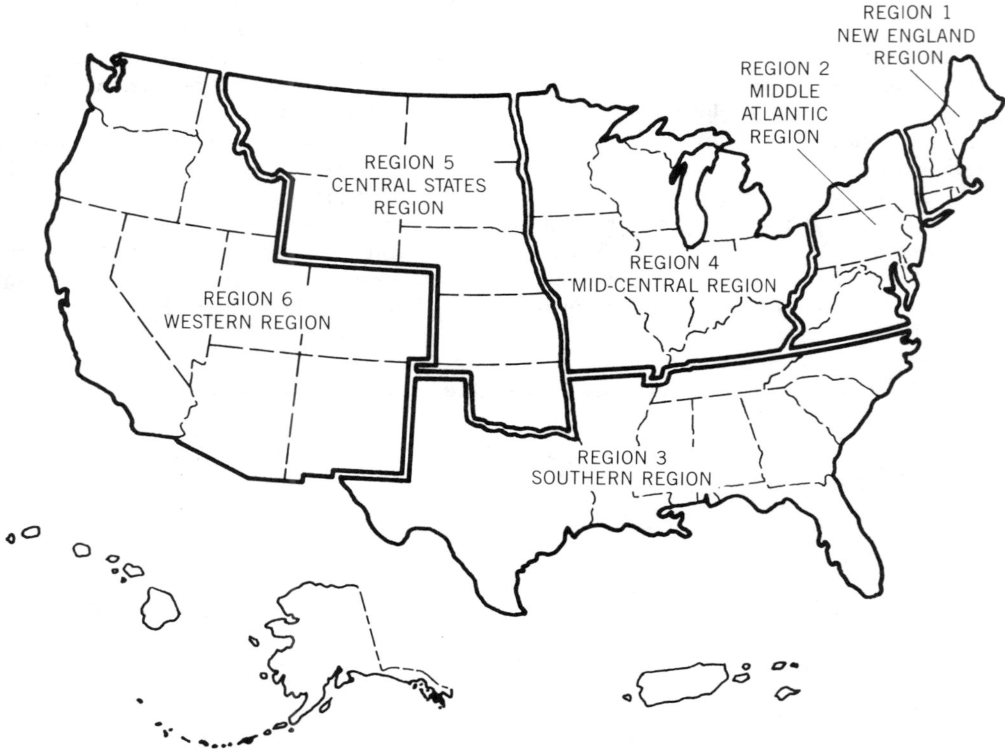

Figure 1. Allocation of jurisdictions to each regional conference. New England: Connecticut, Maine, Massachusetts, New Hampshire, Rhode Island, Vermont; Middle Atlantic: Delaware, District of Columbia, Maryland, New Jersey, New York, Pennsylvania, Virginia, West Virginia; Southern: Alabama, Arkansas, Florida, Georgia, Louisiana, Mississippi, North Carolina, Puerto Rico, South Carolina, Tennessee, Texas, Virgin Islands: Mid-Central: Illinois, Indiana, Iowa, Kentucky, Michigan, Minnesota, Missouri, Ohio, Wisconsin; Central States: Kansas, Montana, Nebraska, North Dakota, Oklahoma, South Dakota, Wyoming; Western: Alaska, Arizona, California, Colorado, Guam, Hawaii, Idaho, Nevada, New Mexico, Northern Mariana Islands, Oregon, Utah, Washington.

The first NCARB secretary/treasurer, Emory Stanford Hall, was also the prime motivator for developing an organization that would respond effectively and continually to the concerns of architectural registration boards and to the architectural profession. Hall drafted the first constitution and bylaws and saw to the proper incorporation of the NCARB as an organization not for pecuniary profit in Illinois. Under his leadership, the standards for reciprocal registration were developed and implemented, as were the guidelines and content of the NCARB examinations for registration and reciprocity. He was also responsible for organizing the effort to bring uniformity among the various state registration and practice laws. Hall was also instrumental in spearheading the development of the National Architectural Accrediting Board, whose purpose is to accredit education programs leading to professional degrees in architecture.

In its early years, NCARB's headquarters were located in the offices of Emory Hall in Chicago, Ill. Interest in NCARB grew rapidly, and the Council's office officially opened on January 3, 1921 at 1107–64 E. Van Buren Street, Chicago, Ill., with Louise E. Durham as the first executive secretary. In its first year, there were 45 transfers of individual architect qualifications for reciprocal registration. Additional staff was needed to meet the growing workload; by the Council's third year of operation, requests for reciprocity had nearly doubled.

The NCARB office remained in Chicago with Emory Hall serving continuously as the organization's secretary/treasurer until his death in 1939. William L. Perkins, having completed a year as president, assumed the secretary's position and moved NCARB's headquarters from Chicago to his office in Chariton, Iowa.

Perkins advanced the work of Hall and was instrumental in moving the NCARB examination processes forward to increase the degree of uniformity in its content and administration. The Council's office remained in Iowa until 1958, when it was moved to Oklahoma City, Okla. At this time the first executive director, Joe E. Smay, was named to manage the day-to-day affairs of the NCARB. Smay became an officer in the Council shortly thereafter, and the Board named James Sadler as the Council's executive director. Sadler served in that capacity until 1965. During his tenure, the Council office was moved again, this time from Oklahoma City to Washington, D.C. On January 3, 1962, NCARB opened its Washington office at 518 18th Street, N.W., which was staffed by Sadler and four employees who had made the transfer from Oklahoma. Two weeks later, three of those four employees left the Council and returned to Oklahoma.

The NCARB office was located near the offices of the American Institute of Architects, and this adjacency had certain benefits for NCARB during its early years in Washington. Later, after the AIA decided to construct a new headquarters building to house its operations, NCARB moved again in 1969 to 2100 M Street, N.W., and finally in 1973 occupied the top floor of the newly constructed AIA building at 1735 New York Avenue, N.W.

James Sadler resigned in 1965 and was replaced by Charles Wood. In 1967, Wood was replaced by James Rich, who filled the executive director position on a provisional basis until 1968. At that time Hayden P. Mims was named the executive director. Mims was the first non-architect to head the NCARB as executive director. In July 1979, Samuel T. Balen, FAIA, was named the NCARB executive director following the retirement of Mims.

In order to forward NCARB's interest and concern in the matters of qualification, especially in regard to architectural education, in September 1962 the NCARB created the NCARB Foundation and named the executive officers and executive director as the directors of this new foundation. The Foundation was incorporated in the District of Columbia and functioned until 1966 when its purposes and assets were transferred to the NCARB. Individuals, architectural firms, architectural construction materials suppliers, and any other persons or firms were encouraged to contribute to the Foundation in an effort to advance the uniformity in standards for registration, examinations, and regulation. The prime activities of the Foundation during its existence were providing funds to the National Architectural Accrediting Board (NAAB) and developing examination questions for use by member boards in the development of individual state examinations. This last effort was carried forward to advance uniformity in the content of registration examinations among all boards.

NCARB's operations historically were funded by dues paid by member boards. Active membership in the NCARB was reserved to legally constituted state registration boards, although associate or sustaining memberships were encouraged in the early years. Materials suppliers and architectural firms were listed as sustaining members as were individual chapters of The American Institute of Architects. After many years of serious financial constraints, NCARB began to emphasize its services in certifying the qualifications of architects and in transmitting the records of individual architects for reciprocal registration. In conjunction with these activities the NCARB began producing the examinations used by all boards. These sources of income enabled NCARB eventually to move into a more stable financial position.

NCARB's revenues come from four sources. First, individual architects pay for services that include the compilation of an NCARB record, maintaining that file in an active status by filing annual reports and paying an annual renewal fee, and transferring of the file to state registration boards for reciprocal registrations. Second, NCARB prepares the uniform examination used by all registration boards, and boards pay for each examination used. Third, an examination handbook is also prepared by NCARB and sold to individuals preparing to take the examination before their respective state boards. Finally, NCARB charges each of its member boards annual membership dues. From all these sources, the services to professionals provide 48% of NCARB's income, examinations account for 46%, publications for 4%, and member board dues, 2%. While the services to professionals account for the bulk of NCARB's financial resources, these professionals have no voice in the affairs of the Council. Conversely, the source of the smallest resource, the member board dues, has control of all aspects of the organization.

The Board of Directors and the executive director direct the affairs of the NCARB, but the ultimate control of the organization rests with the member boards. The member boards elect the officers and directors and, through the committee process, establish the standards, rules, and procedures under which the NCARB operates.

NCARB annually funds committees to study various aspects of the registration of individuals as architects and the regulation of the practice of architecture. These committees report initially to the Board of Directors, and their recommendations are brought to the membership in the form of resolutions to be acted on at the next annual meeting of the NCARB. Often, these proposals are first discussed with the membership at meetings of the regional conferences and suggestions on proposals are returned to the respective committee before a final proposal for action is offered to the membership. Individual member boards and a regional conference may also offer to the membership proposals for modifications to current procedures, standards, policies, or new proposals on these subjects.

Liaison between member boards, a regional conference, and individual boards and the NCARB Board of Directors are maintained through members of member boards serving on national committees or by direct contact between boards. Indirect contact through the mailing of reports and newsletters to each member of a member board, the member board, and officers within the regional conferences further expands the communications network and keeps the membership informed on activities, resolutions to common problems, and upcoming events. Certificate holders, members of the profession, and collateral organizations are kept abreast of NCARB activities through the publication of periodic newsletters.

Liaison between member boards occurs through regional meetings and the annual meeting. Additionally, regional directors exchange information during each meeting of the Board of Directors. NCARB assists its member boards by monitoring public and professional attitudes, positions, and needs. Through standing and special committees, the Board of Directors studies issues and recommends changes to existing standards or implementation of new standards in education, examination, licensing, internship, and professional conduct following licensing. Further, the NCARB assists member boards by developing guidelines dealing with enforcement of board rules and regulations and the procedures to be used in disciplining architects who violate them.

Relations are maintained by the Council officers, on behalf of the member boards, with other national regulatory bodies through the Interprofessional Council on Registration (ICOR). Members of ICOR consist of the National Council of Engineering Examiners (NCEE), the National Council of Landscape Architectural Registration Boards (CLARB), and the NCARB. NCARB is also a member of the Federation of Associations of Regulatory Boards, an organization whose membership consists of associations that regulate a diverse assortment of professions and occupations.

Throughout its history, NCARB has dedicated itself to improvements in state laws, rules, and regulations. Its initial thrust was to facilitate the adoption of laws regulating the practice of architecture in all U.S. jurisdictions, and to ensure the uniformity of these laws so that movement between jurisdictions by individual architects could be implemented. In the 1970s, many state legislative bodies were adopting "sunset laws" through which regulatory boards were required to demonstrate their effectiveness in protecting the public interests, as well as the need to continue the board as a regulatory agency of the state government. NCARB developed responses to these "sunset" inquiries for use by its member boards; as architectural boards were evaluated, many came away with stronger rules and regulations and commendations for the work performed, in part because of responses to sunset questions developed by NCARB committees and legal counsel.

During this period of legislative investigation, many boards were restructured in their membership so that one or more members of the boards were designated to be public members, that is, persons who were not registered in the profession regulated by the board. NCARB did not oppose this recommendation. However, it was suggested that such public members should not constitute a majority of the board, since their lack of knowledge concerning many technical and professional issues that come before the board would burden the professional members with additional work and responsibility.

NCARB has been and continues to be primarily concerned with the standards, rules, and procedures as they apply to domestic applicants for licensing and eventual NCARB certification. However, with increased ease of travel and opportunities for practice on an international scale, many foreign architects approached member boards inquiring of the processes whereby their qualifications and license from their home country might be accepted for reciprocal registration. NCARB has investigated this matter on behalf of the member boards and forwarded its recommendations to them; the recommendations have been used effectively.

Essentially, the NCARB recommended a process whereby a foreign architect's education could be assessed and given credits toward meeting the U.S. education standard. Additionally, it has studied foreign practice and has recommended that foreign architects acquire at least one year of acceptable practical experience in the offices of U.S. practicing architects before being admitted to the written examinations for licensing.

Through these investigations, NCARB was able to enter into an interrecognition agreement with the Architects Registration Council of the United Kingdom (ARCUK) and the Architects Accreditation Council of Australia (AACA). These agreements provide a procedure and process whereby architects registered in their home country may apply for recognition in the other country on the basis of the qualifications and standards required for their initial registration. The agreement with the ARCUK was enacted in 1970 and with AACA in 1973. In September 1986, the agreement with AACA was terminated; however, the agreement with ARCUK continues in full force and effect. There was no interconnection between the two agreements that would permit Australian architects to apply directly to the United Kingdom by virtue of the agreements with the NCARB, or vice versa.

ACCOMPLISHMENTS

Laws, Rules, and Regulations

NCARB's first efforts were channeled toward the development of uniform laws, rules, and regulations for use by its member boards. While some 20 boards had laws regulating the practice at the time of NCARB's founding, the work of its collective members accelerated the adoption of registration laws by the remaining 35 jurisdictions. Even though model laws were developed and definitions offered, there still existed sufficient inconsistencies among the boards to warrant constant attention to the need for uniformity of regulations, statutes, and standards.

Over the past 15 years, this topic has been addressed in great detail, culminating in the development of a model law and model regulations. These model documents do not include all enabling clauses, appointment of board members, relationships to umbrella agencies, compensation to board members, and the procedural issues normally found in the state statutes; rather they restrict themselves to issues that deal with the most crucial topics involved in the regulation of a particular profession. The model law on architecture deals with the following:

- Definitions
- Fees
- Registration qualifications
- Registration renewal
- Certificate of registration
- Seals
- Disciplinary powers
- Disciplinary procedures
- Registration evidence
- Prohibitions
- Exceptions
- Enforcement
- Penalties

The model law is contained within the NCARB document entitled *Legislative Guidelines*. The term "guidelines" is used because each existing state law contains unique language, organization, and ancillary provisions; to have attempted to introduce exact statutory language into existing statutes would have been disruptive and confusing. The guidelines set forth provisions adopted by the member boards in seven critical areas of state regulation, and the model registration statute illustrates the way in which the guideline principles fit into a statutory framework.

In the development of these guidelines, NCARB was concerned with the respective roles of statutory enactment on the one hand and board rules or regulations on the other. The board has power, by statute, to issue regulations to elucidate and further define its statutory authority. These regulations, however, may not contradict the statute. Often, statutory changes are difficult to achieve either because of timing, the mobilization to seek legislative support, or by postponement by the legislature itself. Regulations, however, may be typically adopted by a board after notice and appropriate hearings. The line of division between the content of a statute and that of a regulation lies with those questions of public policy that should be decided by the legislature. Thus, insofar as the regulations of the profession involve changing views, the rules are found in the regulations and not the statute. Consequently, NCARB developed a set of model regulations for architectural registration boards that follow the principles noted above.

In summary, the NCARB *Legislative Guidelines* leave flexibility and discretion to individual boards in bringing their statutes and regulations in line with developing national standards for architectural registration. Such flexibility is generated by placing responsibility for much of the detail of regulations with the board, while leaving the general statutory policies to the legislature.

Rules of Conduct

In July 1975, following a directive from the delegates at its annual meeting, NCARB set out to develop a set of rules on professional conduct that it could recommend to its member boards. At its meeting in 1977, the recommended rules were approved by the member boards. These rules are the latest in a series of efforts by previous committees of NCARB to address this matter. The need to deal with this issue was intensified by the challenge to the AIA Code of Ethics in the landmark Mardarosian suit against the AIA and the investigations of the U.S. Justice Department. Many boards were using the AIA Code of Ethics as the basis for their rules of conduct, and having it challenged caused NCARB to quicken its pace in the drafting of its own recommendations.

NCARB responded to the implications of this professional conduct issue in several ways. Over a two-year period it undertook a study of the conduct rules of other learned professions, held in-depth interviews with leading consumer affairs advocates, and carried out other research inquiries. These efforts led to the formation of the current NCARB rules of conduct. Their substance was drawn from the following series of considerations.

- The rules of conduct which will become the basis for the policing and disciplining of architects should be "hard-edged" rules and should not include those predatory injunctions which are often found in a list of professional obligations.
- The rules shall have as their objective the protection of the public and not the advancement of the interests of the profession of architecture.
- The architect should not be burdened unfairly with rules of conduct which are unreasonable to expect. However, the public expects to find an architect or

engineer in a leadership position on a construction project to protect its interests. Consequently, while the architect is enjoined to serve his client in a fiduciary way, he has, at the same time, a supervening duty to the public.

- The rules are intended to set out those areas of behavior for which an architect risks being disciplined by his state registration board.

As a result of these considerations, the NCARB rules of conduct as approved and recommended to its member boards who have the authority to promulgate such rules center on five general areas: competence, conflict of interest, full disclosure, compliance with laws, and professional conduct.

Seal Requirements

The sealing of architectural documents by persons other than the original preparer has long plagued registration boards. NCARB undertook the study of this issue and developed a recommendation that the sealing of construction documents prepared by or under the direction of one architect should not be sealed by a second architect after the second architect has reviewed and, perhaps, made modest modifications to the original documents. The reason for such a position is that, traditionally, state laws in nearly all U.S. jurisdictions require that documents for construction be sealed by the architect who had the production of the documents under his direct supervision. The principles underlying this tradition include the following:

1. Professional work should only be prepared by, or under the direct supervision of, architects who have demonstrated to the state board that they meet the necessary qualifications.
2. Architects should be subject to discipline by the state board for failure to adhere to minimum standards of competency and conduct in connection with their professional work.
3. Architects should be legally responsible and accountable for their professional work, with the public interest being best served by clear delineation of the scope of design responsibility.

NCARB dealt with this matter by modifying its legislative guidelines in 1986. The modification related to the existing definitions as to when a building project may be exempted from the seal of an architect or engineer. It required the preparer of "technical submissions" (for example, construction drawings, specifications, and preliminary designs), when not registered by the state as an architect or engineer, to include a statement with the documents identifying the law under which such technical submissions are exempt from the seal of an architect or engineer. NCARB has cooperated with national building code organizations to seek the incorporation of these seal requirements and exemptions, as specified in state statutes and regulations, in the building code provisions.

Examinations

Examining applicants for licensure as architects is the most intense, time-consuming, and costly aspect of any state board's activities as well as that of NCARB as an organization. From the beginning, immeasurable hours and energies have been expended by hundreds of people on determining the examination content, form of administration, consistency from year to year, scoring, and retake criteria, among many other testing aspects.

The earliest examinations were written and scored by each individual state board. Practicing architects, educators, and specialists in other disciplines were organized to prepare and score these tests. As long as each state prepared its own test specifications and test questions, and set its own passing standards, there was little chance for uniformity among the boards on examinations. With these conditions, there was no effective reciprocity system and there was no equal protection for the public across the nation.

As NCARB grew, it organized the members of its member boards into working groups during annual meetings to address the problems of uniformity in examinations. Their efforts eventually led to agreement on a syllabus of written examination subjects. Subsequently, the length of each test and the dates for administration were agreed on, and this concurrence served to achieve the goal of greater consistency in examination questions and their scoring.

A serious question persisted over how best to reconcile the varied backgrounds of applicants for NCARB certification and subsequent reciprocal registration. For architects registered without having passed a written examination, the NCARB developed a "senior classification" examination, which consisted of an oral interview and the submission of exhibits to a panel, which evaluated the architect for his conformance to the competency standards required at that time. The other test developed was called the "junior classification," which was the written examination all candidates were required to pass for certification by NCARB.

This test could be given in addition to the regular state test, or it could be given to satisfy both the state requirement for licensing and the NCARB requirement for issuance of its certification. It was quickly seen as advantageous by all jurisdictions to abandon the concept of dual written examinations and adopt for their own purposes the "junior" examinations recommended by the NCARB.

While the NCARB was working intensely to unify the examination process, groups of states began to work together to prepare a common examination for use among themselves. This development occurred initially among a number of western states; as a result of this collaboration, the Western Conference of Architectural Registration Boards came into being.

Having taken the lead, the western states were soon sharing their successes with the other states in NCARB. NCARB began to collect and disseminate test questions to all its member boards for use in individually prepared state examinations. This process worked well for about eight years.

By the late 1950s, standardized testing was making

impressive progress. Hope for a uniform examination system seemed warranted when a few states, New York in particular, converted its structural technology tests to the multiple-choice format. The NCARB examinations committees studied these latest test development techniques and methodologies and converted the Professional Administration Sub-test from the Seven-Part test syllabus to a multiple-choice format. The trial runs of this new form were judged successful, and in 1963 NCARB provided for administration of this same test in a multiple-choice format by all member boards. With this first success, NCARB was directed to convert the remaining test sections to the multiple-choice format. The only tests not converted were those requiring a graphic response, the building design and the site planning tests.

The conversion of all tests to the objective multiple-choice test format was completed and implemented by 1968, and the two graphic tests were then being developed by a national committee, including evaluation criteria for the assessment of the examinees' solutions. While the objective tests were machine-scored and passing standards were established on a national basis, the graphic examinations were evaluated by each individual board.

In an effort to generate more uniformity in the assessment of graphic solutions, states within the regional conferences began to set up a two-step procedure. All solutions from all states within the regional conference were first assessed by one of its boards. Then, following a regional review, the solutions were again assessed by the examinee's home board. This procedure was instigated to enhance reciprocity. Nonetheless, variations of opinion on the intent of evaluation criteria and their application continued to cause concern over the degree of uniformity and consistency realized in the passing standard for graphic solutions.

In 1977, an attempt to nationalize the evaluation process was undertaken when members from boards in NCARB's Western, Central, and Mid-Atlantic regions assembled in their own regions to evaluate graphic solutions. Before assuming their task, the graders were first trained in the application of the evaluation criteria and also benefited from having had the design problem requirements thoroughly discussed and understood. This regional approach was successful and the next year the regions were grouped into three grading sessions with each session having approximately the same number of solutions to evaluate. Refinements were made in the process each year and today this evaluation system is national in scope. The grading criteria and procedures have been nationally accepted and adopted. A recent refinement employs computers to record the scoring as it is being performed.

In 1968, NCARB's leadership undertook a major analysis of education, training, and examination standards, criteria, and directions. It resulted in a fundamental change in examination philosophy. Whereas the examination had previously tested for the knowledge normally acquired in school, the 1968 analysis recommended a revised examination format that emphasized the judgmental aspects of the practice of architecture. There was a strong belief by the framers of this recommendation that individuals who had graduated from accredited education programs in architecture had already demonstrated competence in certain of the technical aspects of architecture, had adequately acquired and understood the theory and principles of structure, building design, etc, and therefore needed to be tested on their ability to apply this knowledge when confronting issues of a professional nature that closely approximated day-to-day situations occurring in an architectural practice.

Individuals without the accredited architectural education would be required to demonstrate a level of knowledge, skill, and ability that normally would be acquired in accredited education programs. They would do so by passing a series of tests covering the history of architecture, technology, and design. After completing this academic examination, these examinees would proceed to take the professional examination. These two test forms became known as the Equivalency Examination and the Professional Examination.

The two-test format was finally adopted in June 1972. The first Equivalency Examination was administered in June 1973 and the first Professional Examination in December 1973. In 1976 the Equivalency Examination was renamed the Qualifying Test, to reflect more accurately how member boards were using this test.

The Equivalency Examination (Qualifying Test) was a twenty-hour examination and covered the academic subjects of architectural history and theory, as well as the technical subjects of structures, mechanical equipment, statics, and strength of materials. Also included was a single test on site planning and building design. The Professional Examination was 16 hours long and tested on the subjects of environmental analysis, building programming, design and technology, and construction.

A transition procedure was developed for examination candidates from the previously used seven-part examination. They were given credit for parts passed in that examination, similar to those in the Equivalency and Professional Examinations. The seven-part format was eventually dropped in all jurisdictions by 1978.

In the late 1970s, critics were urging that all examinations for credentializing persons' vocational qualifications should be related to the job to be performed. Many, they charged, tested candidates on unrelated and extraneous knowledge and skill, and NCARB's examinations were among them. In 1979, NCARB appointed a special committee first to assess the knowledge, skill, and ability used by professionals in the day-to-day conduct of their practices, and then to relate these aspects to the testing of examinees for minimum competency in those areas of architectural service identified as being most critical to the safeguarding of public health, safety, and welfare.

The study was completed in 1981 and the committee reported that while the NCARB examinations were reasonably related to professional practice and the public concerns, they could be improved. In 1982, another NCARB committee studied the recommendations of the earlier group and concluded that the examinations needed reorganization. It also urged that all applicants, regardless of academic background, take the same written examinations for licensure.

These recommendations were adopted, as well as an

outline for a nine-division examination. This new examination would be 32½ hours long and would be administered each June on four consecutive days. The recommendations were accepted and the examination to be given by all state registration boards was entitled the Architect Registration Examination (ARE). The first ARE was administered to candidates in June 1983. All state boards adopted both the ARE and the recommended transition procedures for candidates who were taking portions of either the Qualifying Test or the Professional Examination. The transition was accomplished in one year, and the ARE has been the only test administered since that time.

In 1986, the California Board of Architect Examiners decided that instead of administering the ARE, it would prepare its own examination. California administered its examination, the California Licensing Examination (CALE), to its candidates for the first time in July 1987.

Because the NCARB bylaws require all of its member boards to give the ARE, to further the organization's historic reciprocal registration goals, it is anticipated that those candidates who pass only the California examination will encounter serious impediments in seeking registration in other jurisdictions. In September 1987 the California Legislature passed a law restricting reciprocal licensing to architects only if their home state of registration declared the California examination and the NCARB examination equivalent. A survey of all state registration boards indicated that such a declaration was not possible. Consequently, reciprocity with California for architects does not exist and California architects registered on the basis of the California examination likewise have no reciprocity with the other 54 state registration boards.

Mediation between NCARB and the California Board was attempted but the parties could not come to any agreement. Efforts are continuing, however, to reestablish negotiations.

Internship

Before schools of architecture were established, professionals took on apprentices to teach them the rudiments and refinements of architectural practice. This was the classic mentorship method of learning architecture. As the demands on the principal architect increased, the time available for on-the-job teaching of apprentices waned. Architects urged the creation of schools expressly for the education and training of future architects. The schools grew in number and size and they filled the need for formal education. But the fledgling architect was not yet ready to become a licensed architect until a period of practical training was completed. The professional was still asked to provide the opportunities for graduates to acquire first-hand exposure to the real life complexities of practice and to learn how to apply the knowledge, skills, and abilities acquired in school. Various attempts were made over the years to structure the internship years. The registration boards usually determined the length and nature of internship. Typically, they required three years of practical training in the employ of architects before qualifying for admission to examinations and eventual registration. What constituted acceptable experience varied considerably among the member boards of NCARB for many years.

A debate over what specifically constituted acceptable experience in an internship setting lasted for decades. In 1973, during a meeting of representatives from the four collateral organizations—AIA, Association of Collegiate Schools of Architecture (ACSA), NAAB, and NCARB—the group concluded that internship was unstructured, lacked definition, and had no clear path for its successful accomplishment. It acknowledged the profession's past efforts to promote structured internship, most recently in the 1960s, when a "log book" concept for recording training experience was tried and failed.

Finally, in the mid-1970s, NCARB appointed committees in conjunction with the AIA to study this matter. They were charged with developing a definition, a process, and a program that would give architectural internship the same importance to the profession enjoyed by education, examination, and practice. In response to the charge, the assigned committees developed the Intern–Architect Development Program (IDP).

The IDP is now a program whose sponsors include not only NCARB and AIA but also the ACSA and the student organization, the American Institute of Architecture Students (AIAS). A national coordinating council for IDP now develops the policies and procedures for the program and oversees its progress. Representatives of the sponsoring organizations serve on the IDP Coordinating Council and have been influential in gaining their peers' support of the program. IDP has grown impressively as to the number of interns who satisfy its training requirements and record them on charts developed expressly for this purpose. For its part, the profession now recognizes its responsibility in making opportunities for exposure to the areas of practice identified in the IDP. Practitioners, having seen the program's benefits, are no longer hesitant to volunteer their services to become advisers (counselors) to intern–architects.

The IDP identifies 14 critical training areas of architectural practice in which an aspiring architect must acquire experience following completion of his/her education. It prescribes the amount of time to be dedicated to each of the training areas and defines the type of activity or exposure the intern should acquire in each of the training areas.

NCARB maintains the records of those interns who participate in the IDP and who have applied simultaneously for the compilation and maintenance of a "Council" record. When the intern has satisfied the requirements of the IDP, the Council forwards a complete copy of the intern's records to the registration board in the state where the intern will take the examination for registration. This record of IDP activity confirms the intern's compliance with the state's practical training requirement. After the intern has passed the examination and becomes registered in a state, this same Council record serves to substantiate the individual's qualifications for NCARB certification. Many states now stipulate that only through IDP participation and documentation can an intern comply with their required practical training.

Education

Among NCARB's original purposes was the desire to improve the general education standards of the architectural profession in the United States. In pursuit of that charge, NCARB has dedicated much energy to architectural education, primarily as it relates to the competency of an architect to provide services to the consuming public. In its early years, NCARB was as much concerned with raising the level of professionalism as it was with raising the standards of competency. But as more states enacted registration laws and as conditions of practice changed, the need for improving the quality of architectural education became apparent not only to NCARB but also to the profession as a whole.

The validation of architectural education programs was left largely to the ACSA; a particular program was likely to be deemed acceptable through the act of applying for membership in the ACSA. Practitioners and registration board officials frequently had contact with schools of architecture, either directly or through the school's graduates, but these contacts seldom guaranteed that a program was as good as it should be. A formal procedure for recognizing educational programs was needed.

The first step toward an accreditation system was taken in the late 1930s at a joint meeting of the AIA, NCARB, and ACSA. Three goals for architectural programs were enunciated at this meeting: education should satisfy the profession's needs for competency and public concern for competency, and the entry-level architect's right to a comprehensive professional education needed to be addressed.

From this meeting came the recommendation that a fourth organization be created, with the three founding organizations providing manpower and financial resources to start and subsequently maintain the new organization. At its meeting in May 1939, the NCARB unanimously passed a resolution adding its support and concurrence in the creation of the National Architectural Accrediting Board. In 1945, after delays caused by World War II and organizational groundwork, NAAB began its work in earnest.

The three founding bodies each nominate respected representatives to serve on the NAAB Board of Directors and annually contribute equal sums of money for NAAB's operation. The organization, structure, and operation of NAAB is more comprehensively discussed elsewhere in the encyclopedia; however, it is noted here in recognition of its significance to NCARB as the profession's acknowledged arbiter of accreditation procedures and criteria.

Applicants for the ARE and subsequent registration must meet certain education, training, and examination standards. Beginning in the late 1940s the education standard required applicants to hold a degree in architecture approved by the board or to have such other education and experience as the registration board deemed "equivalent." The rules, however, were framed in such a way that applicants with only a high school diploma could meet the education requirement by the substitution of practical experience for formal education. Various formulas were developed by boards to equate experience to education.

As the practice of architecture became increasingly more complex, the schools of architecture were asked to broaden their scope to encompass more architectural content and more liberal arts studies as well. To many, the old formulas that considered the high school graduate to be adequately educated were not good enough. Gradually, as the emphasis on more and better education increased, greater reliance was concentrated on the schools of architecture to prepare their students to meet the growing demands.

Inevitably, the growing complexity of both architectural practice and education triggered adjustments in the registration process, primarily in the examination content. So it was that the delegates to NCARB's 1967 annual meeting in New York City moved to establish a higher educational standard for future candidates for registration and NCARB certification. They adopted the first professional degree in architecture, accredited by NAAB, as the education standard. Just one year later, however, the delegates reversed their decision and returned to old positions, which not only recognized an accredited degree, but confused the issue by allowing practical training in many instances to count as education. However, the issue was far from settled.

In 1974, the so-called "degree requirement" was introduced once again and an NCARB committee spent another year assembling facts to be presented at the 1975 NCARB annual meeting, again in New York City. The debate on the resolution to adopt the accredited first professional degree in architecture as the standard for NCARB certification—and for registration by those boards that wished to follow the NCARB lead—was long and heated. The resolution to implement the degree requirement was defeated by a vote of 60% of the member boards in attendance.

The NCARB board of directors let the matter rest for five years. In 1980, it offered a resolution once again to raise the formal education standard for the NCARB certificate from its then-current high-school-or-equivalent requirement to a four-year baccalaureate degree in any discipline. When this proposal was placed before the delegates, an amendment was offered to change the language from a four-year bachelor degree to an accredited first professional degree in architecture. The amended resolution narrowly passed and was to take effect on July 1, 1984.

Each subsequent year, resolutions were offered to rescind the 1980 action but each failed by an increasing margin. However, a proposition was advanced for NCARB to develop a process whereby individuals who were unable to complete or even begin formal architectural studies leading to an accredited degree could nonetheless satisfy the requirement by an alternate method.

The process has since been implemented. An education standard is now established covering five areas of architectural education, specifically prescribed in content and duration in terms of semester credit hours. The areas of education prescribed include the following:

- General education, including English, mathematics, the humanities, and the social and natural sciences.
- History, human behavior and environment.

- Design.
- Technical systems: structural systems, mechanical systems for buildings, materials and methods of construction, life-safety systems, and barrier-free and handicapped design.
- Practice: process, project finance and economies, business and practice management, and laws and regulations.

By design, these areas of study parallel those set out in the NAAB accreditation standards and criteria.

The standard permits those individuals who do not pursue the accredited degree to submit whatever professional and general education they may have acquired to an independent agency for evaluation. Credit is given toward meeting the prescribed education standard, following which the candidates continue their studies in the necessary subject areas until they comply with the standard. Courses or tests may be taken at schools of architecture where the degree program has been accredited by NAAB, or at other institutions where the course content and intensity meet that offered at NAAB-accredited schools. General education courses are accepted from any institution of higher education, as is passing general education tests through the College-Level Examination Program (CLEP). Architectural design courses may be taken on or off campus at design studios or centers. However, such studios and centers must be administered and/or monitored by faculty from NAAB-accredited schools of architecture. As the individual completes course work or passes equivalency examinations, these accomplishments are recorded. When all requirements are satisfied, a final transcript is issued to registration boards and NCARB on behalf of the individual.

A process has also been designed for those architects without an accredited degree in architecture, but whose extensive professional practice of a high caliber and other education may meet the education standard for NCARB certification purposes. Such applicants must be registered architects for at least 12 years, eight of which must be as a principal. Architects intending to satisfy the education standard through this process must file applications, be recommended by their state registration board and others, and stand for an interview to demonstrate the satisfaction of any identified education deficiencies.

This recently developed program is known as the Education Evaluation Services for Architects (EESA) and is administered by a firm called Educational Credentials Evaluators (ECE) headquartered in Milwaukee, Wis. The NCARB has named this organization to administer the program on behalf of individuals seeking to satisfy the NCARB education standard. The EESA program maintains the education records of students pursuing their education in this nonmatriculated setting. With NCARB approval, ECE engages architectural educators who are highly experienced in assessing educational performance of individuals for academic credits to evaluate and advise on the acceptability of courses taken. It also maintains and provides information to students on where courses can be taken that meet the requirements of the education standards.

Candidates with foreign educational backgrounds are directed first to an organization expert in assessing foreign education before beginning the EESA process. Then they, as do domestic candidates, have their educational backgrounds assessed by the EESA educator evaluators, that is, those areas in which candidates' educations comply with or are deficient in meeting the prescribed standard are identified. They then proceed to fulfill the requirements in a manner prescribed by the program.

CONCLUSION

With the progressive adoption of registration laws over the years in each jurisdiction of the United States, the standards for registration and the regulation of architectural practice became increasingly more sophisticated and explicit. These advances have invariably been made following serious deliberation on the part of reputable men and women representing the various regulatory boards. While such generic terms as education, experience, and examination have not changed categorically as they apply to the registration process, their meaning has gained many nuances over the years.

Currently, approximately 400 people serve on state boards. Nearly every state board member is appointed by the governor. These members serve for varying terms, but as they gain an understanding of the duties of the board, each tends to serve with a growing sense of responsibility. Each learns to see registration issues and concerns from the perspectives of both the state board and the NCARB.

From these state board members comes the leadership of the Council. It is a remarkable fact that such a small reservoir of men and women has produced a succession of illustrious leaders. While their sworn duty is to their respective state boards, they strive to establish standards and procedures that are fair, uniform, and workable at the national level. Through these efforts, they have enabled NCARB to achieve the enviable goal of a reciprocity system among the states that is unequaled by any other profession in the United States.

NCARB and its member boards are always concerned about the standards for initial licensing, minimum competency, and reciprocity all directed at public health, safety, and welfare. However, they are equally concerned about the architects' professional conduct and continuing professional competence.

Legislators, through their inquiries into the necessity of the regulation of the architectural profession and the practice of architecture, have repeatedly stated their belief that the practice and the professional must be regulated on behalf of the public. Moreover, they have endorsed and commended the work of these boards.

NCARB provides a positive and effective service to the profession and the public. As an organization devoted to the public interest, NCARB must maintain a "long arm" relationship with professional associations but it can and occasionally does join in discussions with professional groups when such cooperation serves to advance the work of its member boards in their responsibilities to the public, or when it enhances the level of services NCARB provides to the profession.

BIBLIOGRAPHY

General References

NCARB Annual Meeting Reports, NCARB, Washington, D.C., 1919–1987.

NCARB Board of Directors Meeting Minutes, NCARB, Washington, D.C., 1920–1987.

NCARB Circular of Information No. 1—Organization, Services, Procedures, Records, Certifications and Examinations, NCARB, Washington, D.C., 1968–1988.

NCARB Examination Syllabus, NCARB, Washington, D.C.

NCARB Examination Handbooks, NCARB, Washington, D.C., 1973–1987.

NCARB Circular of Information No. 3—NCARB Education Standard, NCARB, Washington, D.C., 1986–1987.

NCARB White Paper, *The Practice of Architecture as It Differs from the Practice of Engineering,* NCARB, Washington, D.C., 1984; revised 1987.

NCARB White Paper, *How Architectural Registration Boards Work Together,* NCARB, Washington, D.C., 1986.

NCARB Legislative Guidelines and Model Law, NCARB, Washington, D.C., 1985, revised 1987.

NCARB Guidelines on Rules of Conduct, NCARB, Washington, D.C., 1986.

NCARB White Paper, *How NCARB Serves the Public and the Architectural Profession,* NCARB, Washington, D.C., 1986.

See also Association of Collegiate Schools of Architecture (ACSA); American Institute of Architects (AIA); Intern Programs; National Architectural Accrediting Board (NAAB); Registration Examination Process—Architects

Samuel T. Balen, FAIA
National Council of
Architectural Registration
Boards
Washington, D.C.

NATIONAL PARK SERVICE

The National Park Service (NPS), a bureau of the U.S. Department of the Interior, is a notable contributor to and continuing influence on U.S. architecture. Since its establishment in 1916, a significant number of its highest administrators have been recognized leaders in various fields of professional architecture. The fusion of the professional disciplines of natural history, landscape design, history, and architecture is represented in the NPS's dedication to the essential purpose of the agency as articulated in the language of its enabling legislation: "to conserve scenery and wildlife, and to provide for the enjoyment of natural and historic objects in such manner and means as will leave them unimpaired."

Comprehensive consideration of the responsibilities of stewardship over natural, cultural, and historical treasures of the national heritage has fostered great reliance on master planning in the management of park properties. Long a part of the NPS, its master plan goes far beyond land use delineation by incorporating into primary levels of planning detailed graphic, narrative, and statistical material useful to acquisition, zoning, circulation, security, safety, funding, infrastructure installation, development, and design. Secondary levels of master planning, such as preservation, maintenance, and interpretation, are also prepared, which contain specialized background data and detailed guidelines for use in the organization and operation of park facilities and features. For instance, an interpretive plan is prepared, dealing with park themes, visitor profiles, communication media, instruction programs, and the support services and physical facilities necessary to accomplish the park's interpretive purpose, for example, personal contact, signage, exhibits, audio-visuals, and publications. Architectural involvement can range from trailside shelters to campfire circles, amphitheaters, auditoriums, museums, visitor centers, restorations, and reconstructions.

Before the establishment of the NPS there already existed a tradition of design styles and construction materials associated with parks reflective of their natural features, historic relations, recreational or cultural patterns of use, and climatic influences. Thus, steeply pitched roofs could be found in snow country, crude timbers and undressed stones in large-scaled Western lodges, adobe construction in the Southwest, and brick buildings in Eastern parks with colonial connections. In general, however, park architecture was typified by what may be considered unobtrusive buildings, traditional in construction and restrained in design, with a character sometimes referred to as "stonesy-woodsy." This approach was consciously based on a philosophy, common among environmentalists and conservationists, that man-made forms are intrusions in natural settings and that new constructions detract from the integrity of historic places. Therefore, only absolutely essential, inconspicuous structures would be tolerated. These restrictions were addressed by various means: the primacy of landscaping, small size, subdued colors and textures, gentle profiles, horizontality, "nondirectional" buildings, harmony with natural forms, and conformance to tradition in man-made constructions—whatever would be sympathetic to the park and serve the contradiction in park purpose, that is, to conserve the resource, yet facilitate its use.

The increasing number of parks and greater diversity of themes, coupled with easier accessibility and more frequent and intensive visitation, called for more responsive and sophisticated architecture than the familiar repertoire of stonesy-woodsy shelters and eclectic administration buildings. A catalog of park building types would contain many different forms to serve many different functions: shelters (of varying kinds and sizes) and administration buildings, certainly, but also equipment and maintenance facilities, staff housing, water tanks and pump houses, comfort stations and showers, campgrounds and parking areas, sports facilities (fishing piers, docks and boathouses, ski lifts, stables, etc), markers, outdoor and indoor exhibit spaces, performing arts centers and lecture halls, sales shops and concessionaire's facilities (including lodges, hotels, laundries, food services, and transportation systems), tunnels, bridges and roads, overlooks and lookouts, rangers' stations and entrance stations, monuments and memorials, and historic structures and their adjuncts. The inventory is extensive, even without taking into account staff support requirements for larger, isolated parks where remoteness and numbers of employees create demands comparable to the urban planning programs of small cities: shopping centers, community halls, chapels, schools, libraries, and infirmaries. On the national scale there are also regional headquarters complexes and supra-regional training centers. It is no wonder successive generations of NPS architects expanded their in-house professional jargon from stonesy-woodsy to include "parkitecture."

In addition to the many types of structures necessary to operate over 40 kinds of national parks (for example, historic sites, monuments, battlefields, cemeteries, parkways, riverways, lakeshores, and seashores), the NPS has also provided extensive developments of specialized buildings for major national programs such as the Civilian Conservation Corps (CCC) during the administration of Franklin D. Roosevelt and the Job Corps during that of Lyndon B. Johnson. The CCC had a lasting effect on NPS architecture. During the decade preceding entry of the United States into World War II, funding provided through the Public Works Administration and the Emergency Relief Administration and labor provided by the hundreds of thousands of unemployed young men who constituted the Corps produced landscaping, infrastructure, buildings, trails, and recreational facilities in national, state, and local parks across the country. This program set high standards and provided excellent models for park architecture that were to last for years. It also brought to the NPS inspired and dedicated professionals who remained as expert cadres for the next great program of national park development, commencing a decade after the end of World War II.

The National Park Service's building programs benefited from the New Deal and its Civilian Conservation Corps but, like many civilian agencies, it experienced budgetary and staff cutbacks with the advent of World War II. To compound this, civilian travel, on which the parks vitally depended, almost disappeared during the war years and in the early 1950s. At the end of the Korean conflict, the NPS launched a program beginning in 1956 which, within 10 years, would rehabilitate park facilities to cope with the impact of the anticipated postwar visitation and, coincidentally, conclude in time for the NPS's fiftieth anniversary celebration in 1966. Given the appeal of the parks and mounting public demand for leisure pursuits and recreation, the billion dollar program won favor and had unquestioning support throughout its duration. Mission 66 included much more than building programs, and even the building programs included much more than structures; however, in terms of buildings alone the scope of Mission 66 is impressive. The NPS installed almost 150 visitor centers, a building type that could include lounges and toilets, information and literature counters, exhibit spaces, assembly halls, souvenir salesrooms, museum collections storage areas, administrative offices, maintenance workshops, and utility yards. Size, layout, material, and architectural expression varied widely depending on the nature of the park area, geographic location, types and numbers of visitors, and staffing. In addition to visitor centers, the Mission 66 building program also included a variety of recreational facilities for the public, training facilities for staff, and food, lodging, supplies, and transportation facilities for concessionaires (in some cases built by the concessionaires themselves, but always subject to NPS design staff review and approval). Because of the remoteness of most parks and in order to provide an additional measure of on-site security, more than 2000 staff houses were built in the parks. Subject to a congressional construction cost limitation of $20,000 per house, these were the only standardized Mission 66 building types, except for campground comfort stations. Highly capable professional design and construction staff had been recruited for Mission 66 and were given encouragement and full support by the NPS directors. The economy, effectiveness, design quality, and environmental compatibility of the Mission 66 projects were repeatedly praised in the professional press and received national design awards. Development in the parks was always based on in-depth, on-site studies by closely integrated multidiscipline teams producing comprehensive detailed, long-range, published master plans. Major structures, particularly visitor centers, were designed to lessen their impact on the sites by being nondirectional, that is, circular, spiral, polygonal, or, at least, nonorthogonal in plan. Innovation was encouraged. The Dinosaur National Monument Visitor Center (Fig. 1) at Vernal, Utah (1958), designed by the San Francisco firm of Anshen & Allen, incorporates as one of its major walls an actual cliff face where park paleontologists uncover fossils and give explanations to visitors ranged along a viewing gallery. The Mission 66 visitor center, a seminal building type, is unfortunately overlooked among the post offices, courthouses, and other more familiar categories of government buildings.

Architectural accomplishments by the NPS during Mission 66 and afterward were numerous and diverse, and they received recognition. Richard Neutra's Visitor Center at Gettysburg National Military Park, Ulrich Franzen's Interpretive Design Center at Harper's Ferry National Historical Park, and Eero Saarinen's Gateway Arch at Jefferson National Expansion Memorial National Historic Site (St. Louis) typify the scope of projects and the talent utilized in the agency's design programs, including graphics, publications, audio-visual productions, and museum exhibits. The NPS was recognized in many publications and awards programs, and was given the American Institute of Architects Citation of an Organization Award in 1970 for exceptional architectural achievement and consistent support of environmental quality. After Mission 66 the expanding national park system added to its well-established environmental concerns a new social consciousness stemming from increased involvement with urban recreation areas such as the New York City and San Francisco "gateway" complexes, "law and order" confrontations in locations as widespread as the Yosemite Valley and the National Capital Parks and, generally, population pressures affecting most of its units. These challenges de-

Figure 1. Quarry Site Visitor Center, Dinosaur National Monument, Vernal, Utah, 1958, architect Anshen & Allen. A highly functional installation, providing facilities for typical services: reception, information, visitor comfort, and administrative support. An exceptional feature is the inclusion of a fossil-bearing excavation as the main interior wall surface. Courtesy of the author.

manded new patterns of park management that called for planning new approaches to park concepts, while recognizing the increased importance of contextual regional planning, evolving economic constraints, and the pluralistic population.

Important national commemorations in recent decades have highlighted the NPS's key role in the preservation of historic architecture. Celebration of the Civil War Centennial in the mid-1970s, of the Centennial of the Statue of Liberty at Statue of Liberty National Monument (New York) in the late 1980s, and of the Bicentennial of the Constitution of the United States at Independence National Historical Park (Philadelphia) contributed to a burgeoning national preservation consciousness. With architectural conservation roots in the Antiquities Act of 1906 and the Historic Sites Act of 1935, and with the passage of the National Historic Preservation Act in 1966, the NPS was the logical leader in the federal government to demonstrate, by precepts and projects, the highest standards of architectural recording, conservation, interpretation, and use. Budgetary policy changes under Presidents Jimmy Carter and Ronald Reagan favoring maintenance and repair programs, as opposed to emphasis on new construction, have ensured consistent excellence in park architecture, proving the NPS's ability to fulfill its dual missions of conservation and use.

BIBLIOGRAPHY

General References

L. Craig and the Staff of the Federal Architecture Project, *The Federal Presence: Architecture, Politics and Symbols in U.S. Government Building,* MIT Press, Cambridge, Mass., 1978.

E. H. Zube, J. H. Crystal, and J. F. Palmer, *Visitor Center Design Evaluation,* IME Report No. R-76-5, Institute for Man and Environment, University of Massachusetts, Amherst, Mass., 1976.

A. H. Good, *Park and Recreation Structures,* U.S. Department of the Interior, National Park Service, U.S. Government Printing Office, Washington, D.C., 1938.

W. C. Everhart, *National Park Service,* Praeger Library of U.S. Departments and Agencies, Praeger Publishers, New York, 1972.

C. L. Wirth, *Parks, Politics and the People,* University of Oklahoma Press, Norman, Okla., 1980.

C. W. Short and R. Stanley-Brown, *Public Buildings: Architecture Under the Public Works Administration, 1933 to 1939,* U.S. Government Printing Office, Washington, D.C., 1939.

R. E. Koehler, "Our Park Service Serves Architecture Well," *AIA J.* **55,** 17 (1971).

R. Peck, "U.S. Property Keep Off," *Progressive Architecture* **57,** 46 (1976).

R. Robison, "Designing the Nation's Backyard," *Progressive Architecture* **54,** 70 (1973).

See also Government Buildings

J. Walter Roth, AIA
Alexandria, Virginia

NELSON, GEORGE

George Nelson (1908–1986), architect and designer, received his degrees from Yale University and the Yale School of Fine Arts. After graduation, Nelson won the Rome Prize in Architecture in 1932 and spent two years at the American Academy in Rome. His writing about new European design for *Pencil Points,* the predecessor to *Progressive Architecture* magazine, led, on his return to the United States, to his joining the staff of *Architectural Forum,* where he later became co-managing editor with Henry Wright (b. 1910). Later, he did editorial work as head of the Experimental Department for *Fortune* and Time-Life.

At the end of World War II, Nelson and Wright wrote an influential book, *Tomorrow's House* (1). Their design of the residential storage wall (1943) was a revolutionary concept, included in the book. Illustrations showed the best of the new contemporary design as shown in *Architectural Forum, Fortune,* and *Life* magazines.

Nelson was selected by the Herman Miller Company of Grand Rapids, Michigan, to be head of design for its move from traditional furniture into contemporary design. Nelson's early furniture designs (1946) also involved the publications and a new image for the company reflecting its change to a progressive force in interior design. Nelson attracted other designers to work with the firm, including Charles Eames (1907–1978).

Designs by Nelson for Herman Miller included storage wall systems, modular furniture, and office landscape furniture. Nelson maintained a design office in New York for many years, where he was involved with product design, communications, graphics, and exhibition design as well as architecture.

Nelson's limited architectural work included the pioneering house for Sherman M. Fairchild at 17 E. Sixty-fifth Street in New York (1941), which was designed with William Hamby. In this house, the living areas were grouped at the street front, and the bedrooms at the back lot line, with a central court and glazed connection containing ramps between the two sections of the house (2).

In an early exhibition of modern American furniture at the Detroit Institute of Arts, was the 1949 George Nelson design for a living room, featuring a storage wall including desk, sound equipment, books, and cupboards.

Author of many articles and books, Nelson was a design critic at Harvard's Graduate School of Design. He lectured extensively. In 1984, he was named Scholar in Residence at the Cooper–Hewitt Museum of the Smithsonian Institution in New York City. He was also a board member of the International Design Conference at Aspen (3).

He received honors and awards in architecture, industrial design, and interior design, including the Industrial Arts Medal from the American Institute of Architects (AIA), A Distinguished Award for his Contribution to the Profession of Design from the Industrial Designers Society of America (IDSA), and the Elsie de Wolfe Award from the American Society of Interior Designers (ASID).

BIBLIOGRAPHY

1. G. Nelson and H. Wright, *Tomorrow's House,* Simon & Schuster, New York, 1945.
2. N. White and E. Willensky, *AIA Guide to New York City,* Collier Books, a division of Macmillan Publishing Co., New York, 1978, p. 222.
3. P. Viladis, "George Nelson," *Progressive Architecture* **67**(5), 26 (1986).

ROBERT T. PACKARD, AIA
Reston, Virginia

NERVI, PIER LUIGI

Pier Luigi Nervi (1891–1979) was one of the key proponents of the use of concrete for modern building. His designs have been spectacular, efficient, and well suited to the qualities of the material. They fully use the sculptural capabilities of concrete instead of confining it to the post-and-lintel techniques traditionally used by such earlier proponents as Auguste Perret and François Hennebique. It was with the structures of Robert Maillart that the true potential of the material began to be explored, but Nervi helped bring the use of reinforced concrete into the twentieth century. His understanding of the way the material behaves, his ability to integrate construction methods and design fully, and his ease as a creator of forms helped him to design a number of important structures of modern architecture.

Nervi was born in Sondrio, Italy, and received his education in Bologna, obtaining his engineering diploma in 1913. He served in the Italian army during World War I and later worked in Bologna and Florence. His first significant project was a movie house in Naples (1926–1927). This was soon followed by the project that first brought him his national and international attention. The Berta Municipal Stadium in Florence (1929–1932) (Fig. 1), with its scissor structure, seating stand, roof canopy, and cantilevered stairways, was considered a success, but it was during its construction that Nervi first became aware of the limitations of wooden formwork for poured-in-place concrete (1). The stadium, like most of the Nervi projects to follow, was the result of winning a design competition.

His next major project was a series of about 12 airforce hangars built at several locations between 1935 and 1942. The Hangar at Orbetello (1941) (Fig. 2) was a cast-in-place structure with structural tile in-fill panels. It used a lamella structural system to support the required large span of 330 × 135 ft. Although beautiful in appearance and appropriate to the program, this type of hangar was difficult to build as a poured-in-place structure. For the later hangars, Nervi developed a system of precast beams that could be shop-poured and then assembled on site still using the lamella arrangement to achieve the large, clear spans.

This lamella structural configuration, consisting of a system of intercrossing beams at 45° angles to the structure's edges, creates a solid support for a thinner shell that then covers the entire structure. It provides an economical, extremely strong means of creating large, columnless spans. In fact, the spans proved so strong that when

Figure 1. Berta Municipal Stadium, Milan, under construction, (1929–1932). Drawn by F. J. Menéndez (1987).

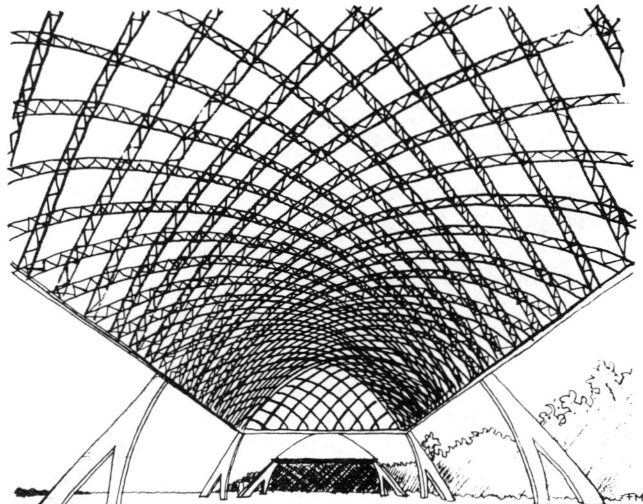

Figure 2. Concrete Hangars, Orbetello, under construction (1941). Drawn by F. J. Menéndez (1987).

the retreating Germans dynamited all of these hangars during World War II, most of the joints at the points where the beams crossed remained intact.

The hangars reveal Nervi's ability to experiment and evolve structural systems to arrive at efficient solutions (2). They also provided an opportunity for him to develop a design by using test models with which he calculated structural stresses for the forms proposed (1).

With the surge in building that took place after the war came opportunities for Nervi to create some of his most memorable forms. In 1948 he had the chance to create an exhibition hall (Salone B) at Turin, Italy (Fig. 3). The program called for a large clear-spanned hall that would be inexpensive and quick to build. Nervi's solution, using a material that he developed called ferrocement, creates what critics such as Ada Louise Huxtable have called "one of the most impressive interior spaces of the century" (1). Ferrocement is a thin, flexible and very strong structure about 2 in. thick, made out of several layers of fine ductile steel mesh embedded in a concrete shell. The exhibit hall consists of a series of precast ferrocement shapes supported on cast-in-place arches. The glazed openings in the precast shapes admit light into the hall. The repetition of the shapes creates a light, corrugated effect that spans the 312-ft width of the hall. Groups of four cast-in-place arches are then supported by fan-shaped buttresses that carry the weight to the ground. The hall is closed by an end apse, also made with the help of ferrocement. In the case of the apse, a unique system was used consisting of precast ferrocement molds made into diamond-shaped coffers facing the interior. A layer of concrete was poured over these molds to bind them together. Unfortunately, the connection between the apse and the main part of the hall was not built as originally envisioned by Nervi (1). He called for a curved glass connector that would help to unify the two parts visually. As built, the vertical, solid end wall that makes the transition between the two is rather abrupt.

The use of ferrocement, as both a precast element of the design and a precast permanent mold that forms a finished surface, helped Nervi to develop various systems of construction. These systems, with several variations, were to be used in many of his later projects such as the Beach Casino at Ostia (1950) and the Tortona Salt Warehouse (1950–1951).

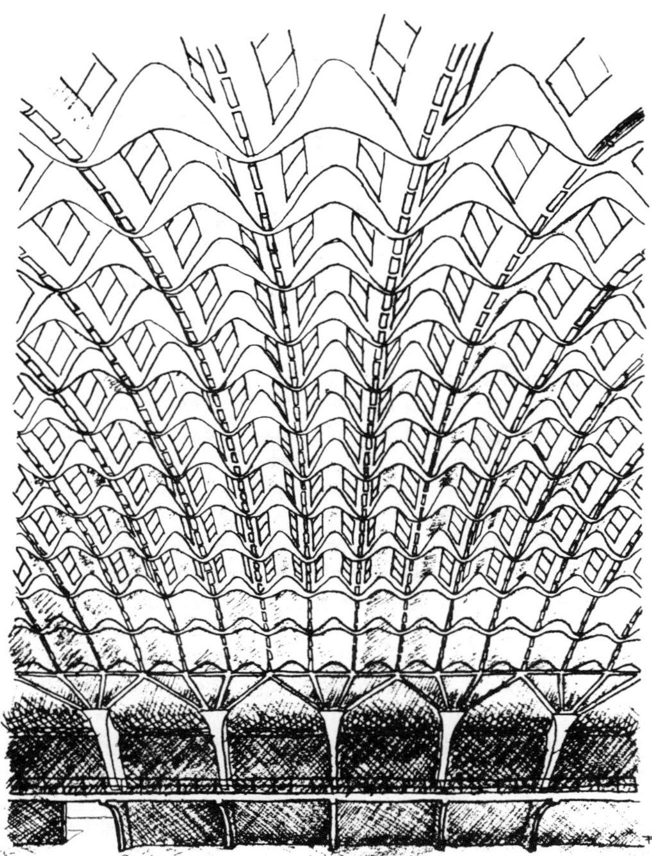

Figure 3. Exhibit Hall (Salone B), Turin (1948). Drawn by F. J. Menéndez.

One further development was the use of ferrocement as a precast reusable mold. This allowed Nervi to increase the economy of the construction as well as to reduce the time of erection. The ferrocement mold was put in place after the initial columns of the bay were constructed; the ceiling was cast one bay at a time; the molds were then lowered, moved on, placed into position at the next bay, and reused on each adjoining bay. At that time this method was economical and fast. It was first used in the Tobacco Factory at Bologna (1952), but one of the best examples can be found in the G.A.T.T.I. Wool Factory in Rome (1953).

As part of the sports complex for the 1960 Olympics in Rome, Nervi designed the Palazzetto and Palazzo dello Sporto and a stadium. The first, the Palazzetto dello Sporto (1956–1957) (Fig. 4) was designed in conjunction with Annibale Vitellozzi. It is a relatively small structure that seats 5000 spectators and has a diameter of 200 ft. Here again, prefabricated ferrocement molds were used to create a coffering of the poured-in-place concrete dome. While being true to the structural requirements of the span,

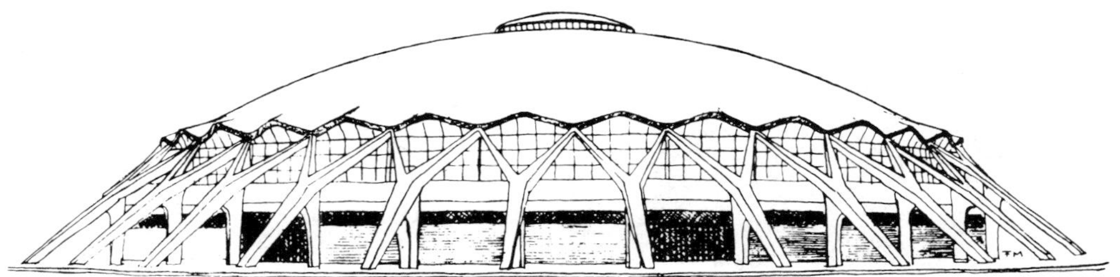

Figure 4. Palazzetto dello Sporto, Rome (1956–1957). Drawn by F. J. Menéndez.

the dome has been likened to the fan vaulting of gothic structures in its grace and beauty (2). The weight of the dome is then carried down by graceful, exposed Y-shaped buttresses all around the perimeter. This elegant building, in which each part has a clear purpose, became one of Nervi's most celebrated works.

For the Palace of Labor in Turin (1960–1961) (Fig. 5), Nervi used a beamless mushroom column system, first introduced to Europe by Robert Maillart in his Zurich warehouse of 1910 (1), to create a stately solution to the program requirements of space and light. The 16 large columns support a system of steel-ribbed canopies that remain structurally independent from each other. The separation between the 16 separate mushroom canopies allows natural light to come into the building and sets off the autonomy of each column. The perimeter glass-curtain wall with its delicate, elegant detailing forms a powerful contrast to the heroic proportions of the concrete and steel columns of the hall. Since a short construction time was a requirement, the mushroom column systems also allowed for erection of the glazing as each section was completed; it was not necessary to wait for the entire structure to be finished before work on the perimeter could begin. The work on the foundation was begun February 1, 1960, and the building was completed by December 31 of that same year.

In 1961–1962, Nervi was asked to design a bus terminal at the eastern end of the George Washington Bridge in New York City. The scheme used for his first building in the United States, based on an earlier plan of the Port of New York Authority, uses a series of triangular latticed beams to span the 187-ft width and at the same time provide the degree of natural ventilation required for the high concentration of exhaust fumes. The result of this design scheme is an interesting roof line that has been described as a concrete butterfly resting on the eastern approaches to the George Washington Bridge.

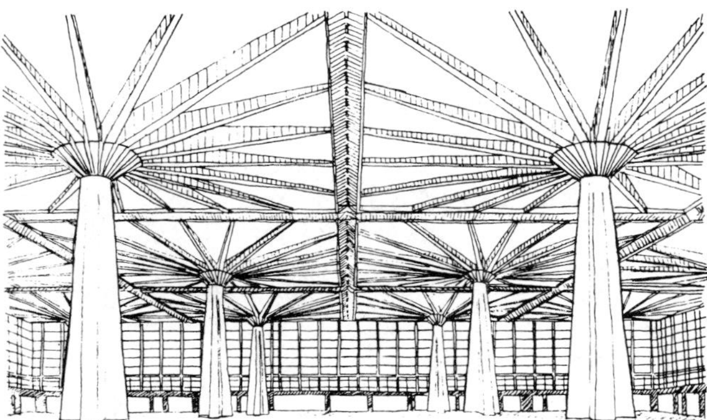

Figure 5. Palace of Labor, Turin (1960–1961). Drawn by F. J. Menéndez.

At the same time, Nervi was working on another building, one of his most beautiful designs, the Burgo Paper Mill in Mantua (1961–1963) (Fig. 6). The requirements called for a single, clear space that would house the machinery involved in the production of paper. Nervi's solution was to create a steel deck roof suspended from four steel cables which, in turn, hang from two 164-ft high towers shaped like the Greek letter lambda. In effect, the building imitates the structural configuration of a suspension bridge. The result is a space free of columns with a constant width of 98 ft and a length of 815 ft. In building the concrete towers, Nervi again called on ferrocement. The material was used to create the molds and, in this case, remained in place to make the exposed surface of the towers. Here again, a logical solution to functional requirements leads to a building of great beauty and originality.

Many of Nervi's later buildings, such as the Risorgimento Bridge in Verona (1963–1968) and the ice hockey rink at Dartmouth College in Hanover, N.H. (1975), once again exemplify his clear mastery of the material and his deep understanding of its capabilities and limitations.

Pier Luigi Nervi can be said to belong to the rational tradition of architecture (3). He strongly believed in the critical contribution that the proper, honest use of technology can make toward creating a successful, aesthetically pleasing work that fully shows its structural integrity. As he himself wrote as a Charles Eliot Norton Chair of Poetry lecturer at Harvard (1961–1962) (4):

> A technically perfect work can be aesthetically expressive, but there does not exist, either in the present or in the past, a work of art which is accepted and recognized as excellent from an aesthetic point of view, which is not excellent from a technical point of view. Good technology seems to be necessary, although not a sufficient condition for good architecture.

Nervi was not, however, content merely to satisfy structured or pragmatic requirements. He recognized and exploited the sculptural potential of concrete in many of his works. He was, as Ada Louise Huxtable says, "a form-giver" (1) who turned the newly emerging machine aesth-

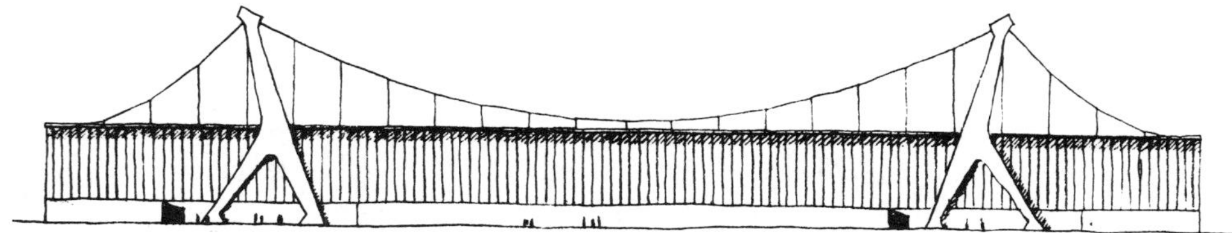

Figure 6. Burgo Paper Mill, Mantua (1961–1963). Drawn by F. J. Menéndez.

etic into a powerful and expressive personal vocabulary of forms.

BIBLIOGRAPHY

1. A. L. Huxtable, *Pier Luigi Nervi,* George Braziller, Inc., New York, 1960.
2. A. Whittick in M. Emmanuel, ed., *Contemporary Architects,* St. Martin's Press, New York, 1980.
3. C. Jenks, *Modern Movements in Architecture,* Doubleday Anchor Books, Garden City, N.Y., 1973.
4. M. Salvadori in A. K. Placze, ed., *MacMillan Encyclopedia of Architects,* The Free Press, London, 1982.

General References

L. Benevolo, *The History of Modern Architecture,* Massachusetts Institute of Technology Press, Cambridge, Mass., 1977.

V. Gregotti, *New Directions in Italian Architecture,* George Braziller, Inc., New York, 1968.

B. S. Myers, ed., *McGraw–Hill Dictionary of Art,* McGraw–Hill, Inc., New York, 1969.

P. L. Nervi, *Building, Projects, Structures: 1953–1963,* Frederick A. Praeger, New York, 1963.

N. Pevsner, *An Outline of European Architecture,* 6th ed., Penguin Books, Baltimore, Md., 1960.

B. Zevi, *The Modern Language of Architecture,* Van Nostrand Reinhold Co., Inc., New York, 1981.

FRANCISCO J. MENÉNDEZ
Washington, D.C.

NEUFERT, ERNST

HISTORY

Ernst Neufert, the younger of a German businessman's two sons, was born in 1900 in Freyburg an der Unstrut, a small village in what is today the German Democratic Republic. He attended school there until 1914, then served an apprenticeship as a bricklayer, carpenter, form setter, and concrete worker, which he finished in 1917 after taking the examination to become a journeyman. In 1918 he trained as a site supervisor at the Baugewerkschule, a technical school in the city of Weimar.

In 1919, by recommendation of the director of the Baugewerkschule, Paul Klopfer, Neufert found employment as a site supervisor in the Weimar atelier of Walter Gropius and Adolf Meyer, where he stayed until 1920. As a disciple of Gropius, he had contact with the Bauhaus in its early days; as a student he traveled to Italy and Spain, in particular to meet Antonio Gaudi in Barcelona. In 1922 he returned to the atelier of Gropius. There he was appointed project manager in 1924, after the move of the atelier along with the Bauhaus to Dessau, and the subsequent departure of Meyer. Now his contacts with the Bauhaus were as Gropius's assistant. As such, Neufert's main projects were the town theater in Jena, industrial buildings for the Fagus Werke in Alfeld an der Leine, and the Bauhaus building and Meistersiedlung in Dessau.

In 1926, Neufert, by recommendation of Hans Poelzig, was bestowed with a professorship at the Staatliche Bauhochschule in Weimar (the director of which was Otto Bartning). He was only 26 years old at the time. His responsibilities included directing a Bauatelier, an atelier for design and construction, and realizing projects with his students. With the rise of the Nazis to power in Weimar, and because of his collaboration with intellectuals accused of "cultural bolshevism," Neufert lost his post in 1930.

During the following period he taught at the private art school of Johannes Itten in Berlin (which soon was closed), worked as a free architect in Gelmeroda near Berlin, traveled, and wrote articles for the Bauwelt, a prestigious German architectural journal. His most successful enterprise of the early 1930s was the *Bauentwurfslehre* (*BEL*), a design and building guidebook. Its publication in 1936 coincided with Neufert's emigration to the United States. This "emigration" was of short duration. When he arrived he was met with the news of the enormous success of the *BEL* and of the need for a new edition. Neufert immediately returned to Germany, but not before visiting Frank Lloyd Wright in Taliesin West.

The success of the *BEL* attracted the attention of the influential Nazi architect Albert Speer (from 1937 the Generalbauinspekteur for Berlin, and later minister of the German Reich). He gave Neufert, as Speer did many other prominent architects who did not emigrate, work and responsibility in technical fields of building, and therefore the privilege of staying in Germany without being directly involved in politics or war. During this time Neufert achieved much success as an industrial architect, as the director of the sections for industrial housing of the city of Berlin and for building standards of the German industry, and through his publications. His themes were: building standardization, as in *Das Oktametersystem,* which became a pillar of the new German industrial norms; the implications of standardization on building design, as in *Bauordnungslehre;* bomb-proof housing, as in *Bomben-*

sicherer Luftschutz im Wohnungsbau, and other then-current themes.

The experience he acquired and the success he achieved during these years, without being politically compromised, gave Neufert an excellent postwar point of departure. In 1945 he moved to the territories occupied by the western military forces, which were to become the Federal Republic of Germany. He was appointed Professor für Baukunst (professor of architecture); later he was appointed Director of the Institute für Baunormung, the building standards institute at the Technische Hochschule in Darmstadt. There he opened an office and continued his work as an industrial architect and as an author. His themes were first related to the reconstruction of German cities, and later to the industrialization of building. His main clients were large industrial enterprises: the Eternit AG, the producer of asbestos; the Hoesch AG, a producer of metal elements; the Dyckerhoff AG, a cement producer; and the BASF, a chemical company. He built their plants, and they financed his research projects. The subjects of Neufert's publications were the building materials produced: *Welleternit-Handbuch, STZ Metall im Bauwesen, Stahlbeton, Styropor-Handbuch.* Due to his ability to correlate his projects, research, teaching, and publications, during this period he also became an authority in the field of industrial architecture.

In the late 1960s Neufert gradually began reducing his activities. In 1967 he left the Technische Hochschule Darmstadt. In 1980 he closed his office, and finally in 1982 he retired to Bugnaux-sur-Rolle, Switzerland. He died there in 1986.

He was married first in 1924, and a second time in 1936. He had six children; one of them became an architect.

IMPACT

The professional and personal life of Ernst Neufert are intertwined with the political and social developments of the era in which he lived. His social and economic beginnings were modest. Without family connections, fortune, or academic preparation, he relied on his enormous ambition, self-confidence, and intellect to convince the decisive personalities and authorities he met of his abilities. The path of his life ran through Germany's turbulent and dramatic twentieth-century history. He was born during the Kaiserreich, went to school and received vocational training during World War I, spent the first stage of his career in the Weimar Republic, the second in the Third Reich and during World War II, and the third in the Federal Republic of Germany.

Beginning with Paul Klopfer, who brought him to Gropius and Meyer, to Poelzig, Bartning, Itten, and others in the first stage of his career, continuing with Speer in the second stage, and finally to the large industrial enterprises in the third stage, Neufert's path was marked by the great personalities and entities with whom he worked. They appreciated and even admired his technical ability, and thus gave him the needed impetus for his ascent. In many ways Neufert became their interpreter; he translated their thoughts, their interests, and their dreams of a better architecture, whatever this meant to each, into practical solutions for everyday building problems. This role of interpreter was the foundation of his success, and it gave his work a character representative character of important developments in the German architectural scene of the time.

In the first stage of his career, Neufert's main impetus came from Walter Gropius, the personalized head of German modern architecture in its most creative and disruptive phase, that is, the Weimar Republic. The impetus was of an ideological and formal nature. Gropius must have appreciated in his young assistant Neufert's proficiency in translating, without prejudice, new architectonic ideas into appropriate constructive solutions. For his part, Neufert exploited his mentor's sense for the language of modern architecture in his own projects while leading his Bauatelier at the Weimar Bauhochschule, that is, the Abbeanum (1928) and the Studentenhaus (1929), a university institute and a students' residence in Jena, respectively. In these buildings, with their functional plans, their rational reinforced concrete skeleton construction, their clear composition of masses through the addition of simple prismatic bodies, and their extensive plastered and white painted facades, he achieved coherent and formally attractive solutions that won public acclaim.

During this period Neufert's most important achievement as a publicist was his *Bauentwurfslehre.* Conceived as a guidebook for builders, it became an international best seller in the field of construction. Its success was based on the modern concept of architectural design and on the data it offered on the functional, constructive, and typological elements of architecture requisite to make such a modern design approach practical. The *Bauentwurfslehre* constituted the contemporary functionalist version of architectural treatises like those of Vignola, with its formal basis, and of Durand, with its typological background. However, the reduction of modern architecture to standards and norms implied sacrificing its poetic dimension. This was the price paid to satisfy its function, that is, to diffuse the new possibilities of modern building design by means of employing the modern materials and structural systems, modern sanitary, electrical, mechanical, and other installations, specialized building types, and new standards and ideas of comfort in architecture, tasks it still fulfills today in many regions of the Third World.

The sacrifice of the poetic dimension of modern architecture included eliminating its ideological side, that is, reduction to the technical aspects of building. Such a separation of form from its original content signified a political neutralization welcomed by groups repelled by the originally socialist background of the modern architectural language. It made easier the integration of a technically based design, which was considered to be necessary, and of its practitioners, into the field of industrial architecture in the Third Reich. This explains the second stage of Neufert's career, that is, his easy assimilation into the system and his productive work, both as an architect and a publicist, without abandoning old positions or being compromised.

In the third phase of Neufert's career no political or social conflict existed; rather there was a great harmony between tasks awarded and expectations of him, and his

Figure 1. Dyckerhoff AG Cement Factory with silos and packing building, Amöneburg, Federal Republic of Germany (1959). Photograph by Carl Otto Rübartsch. Courtesy of Peter Neufert.

responses. This time the tasks were defined directly by industrial enterprises. His main realizations were industrial plants, and some warehouses. Prominent examples are the projects for the Dyckerhoff AG, the Eternit AG, and the Hoesch AG.

The Dyckerhoff AG plant in Amöneburg (1950s), in allusion to the cement produced by the firm, was made almost completely out of concrete. The main parts were realized with reinforced concrete cast in situ with handmade wooden forms. To exploit the specific possibilities of the concrete in this way of building, Neufert used a monolithic skeleton construction and long barrel shells, while all elements received a complex and differentiated form, in accordance with their static function (Fig. 1).

The Eternit AG plant built in Leimen (1954–1960) includes production halls, offices, and service buildings. The halls have light steel structures. The canteen and other parts have a reinforced concrete skeleton. All buildings have, of course, asbestos cement facades, which cover the supporting elements almost entirely. These facades determine, therefore, the appearance of the building, with its large vibrating corrugated surfaces, the soft round angles, and the contrast between its massive, closed character from afar and its membranous, thin effect from nearby. Here Neufert again exploited the specific formal qualities of the building material (Fig. 2).

The Hoesch AG plant in Hamm (1963 onward), includes production halls and office buildings. All of the buildings consist of prefabricated steel elements; steel profiles are used for the trusses in the wide-span halls and for the skeleton constructions of the multistory buildings, and sheet metal elements are used for the roof and wall panels. The administrative building possesses a skeleton construction on the entrance floor, and a wide-span truss over the open-plan offices of the upper floor, with sheds to evenly illuminate the internal spaces. The formal language of this fine building is based on the demonstration of the efficiency and adaptability of the metal elements, in the slimness of the stays and girders, in the airiness of the wide-span elements, in the slenderness and transparency of the enclosing parts, and in the neatness and perfection of the connecting details (Fig. 3).

The works of Neufert demonstrate a sense of quality based on the objective side of architecture, on the efficiency

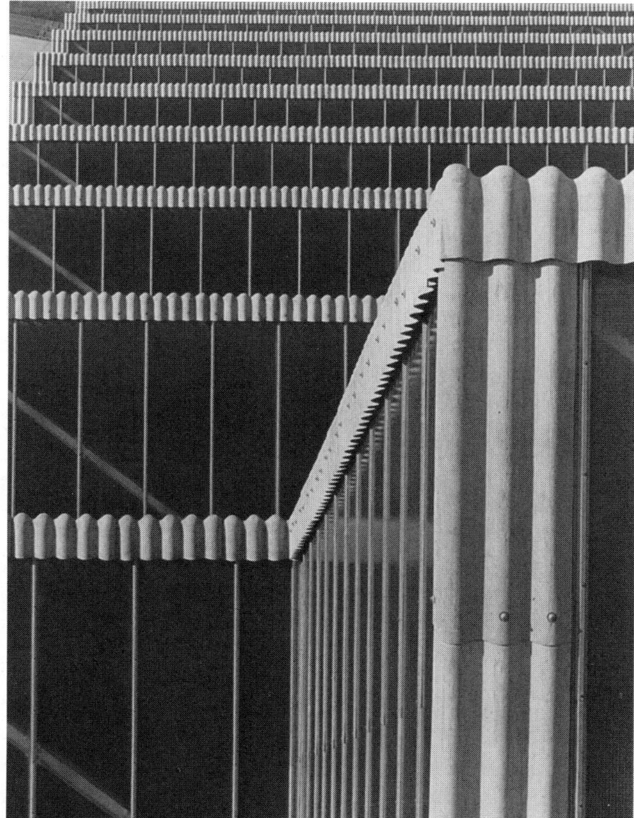

Figure 2. Eternit AG Industries, Leimen, Federal Republic of Germany (1954–1960). Photograph by Carl Otto Rübartsch. Courtesy of Peter Neufert.

Figure 3. Hoesch AG Industries Headquarters, Hamm, Federal Republic of Germany (1963 and later). Courtesy of Hoesch AG.

of the functional organization of the building, on the modern structural systems, building materials, and ways of building, and on an appearance that harmonizes all of these aspects. His formal language is, on the large scale, a synthesis of different tendencies within the international modern movement, with accents derived from Poelzig, Gropius, and Wright. On the small scale it is based on the details necessary for the specific building materials used.

Neufert did not show an interest in a new, original, and personal mode of formal expression. He became innovative solely in the field of construction, especially when the projects were related to his research programs. He renounced any dedication to less rational, more mysterious, and more human aspects of architecture. His renunciation was originally related to the conviction of the fathers of the modern movement in the poetic nature of modern architecture as an integral answer to modern life in its material aspects. For Neufert the concentration on the objective aspects of architecture constituted a necessary step away from modern architecture as an ideal approach to reality, to a real and practical answer to everyday problems. From this point of view, Neufert became a typical example of those who worked on the diffusion of modern architecture into the entire world, under changing historical conditions.

Neufert was an honorary corresponding member of the Real Academia de Ciencias y Artes, Barcelona, since 1950, an honorary corresponding member of the Royal Institute of British Architects, London, since 1953, Professor honorario of the Universidad Nacional de Ingenieria, Lima, since 1977, Dr. hc. of the Universidad Nacional de Ingenieria, Lima, since 1978, honorary member of the Instituto de Urbanismo y Planificación del Perú, Lima, since 1978, and Dr. tech. hc. of the Leopold-Franzens-Universität, Innsbruck, since 1980.

His main awards include the Plaque of Honour of the Finnish Association of Architects, the Großes Verdienstkreuz des Verdienstordens der Bundesrepublik Deutschland 1965, the Johann-Joseph-Ritter-von-Prechtel-Medaille of the Technische Hochschule Vienna 1965, the Johann-Heinrich-Merck-Ehrung of the city of Darmstadt 1970, the golden medal of honor of the city of Madrid 1975, the Stern zum Großen Verdienstkreuz 1976, and the Spanish Orden Alfonso X El Sabio 1979.

BIBLIOGRAPHY

General References

E. Neufert, *Bauentwurfslehre,* 1st ed., Bauwelt, Berlin, Germany 1936. 32nd and last German ed. during Neufert's lifetime, Vieweg, Wiesbaden, FRG, 1984.

Arte de projectar en arquitectura, 13th Spanish ed., Gustavo Gili, Barcelona, Spain 1986.

Enciclopedia pratica per progettare e costruire, 6th Italian ed., Hoepli, Milano, Italy, 1980.

Les elements des projets de construction, 6th French ed., Bordas Dunod, Paris, France, 1983.

Arte de projetar em arquitetura, 7th Portuguese ed., Gustavo Gili, Barcelona, Spain, 1981.

Architects' data, 2nd British ed., Collins, London, UK, 1981.

E. Neufert, "Das Oktametersystem," in *Der soziale Wohnungsbau in Deutschland* (13), 3–15 (1941).

E. Neufert, *Bombensicherer Luftschutz im Wohnungsbau,* Volk und Reich, Berlin, Germany, 1941.

E. Neufert, *Bauordnungslehre,* 1st ed., Volk and Reich, Berlin, Germany, 1943. 3rd ed., Ullstein, West Berlin, 1965.

E. Neufert, *Welleternit-Handbuch,* Bauverlag, Wiesbaden, FRG, 1955.

E. Neufert, *STZ Metall im Bauwesen,* Ullstein, West Berlin, 1963.

E. Neufert and W. Drechsel, *Stahlbeton,* Bauverlag, Wiesbaden, FRG, 1964.

E. Neufert, *Styropor-Handbuch,* Bauverlag, Wiesbaden, FRG, 1964.

P. Klopfer, "Ernst Neufert: Ein Architekt unserer Zeit," in *Neue Bauwelt* (11), 41–52 (1950).

F. Gotthelf, *Ernst Neufert: Ein Architekt unserer Zeit,* Ullstein, West Berlin, 1960.

J. P. Heymann-Berg, R. Netter, and H. Netter, *Ernst Neufert: Industriebauten,* Bauverlag, West Berlin, and Vincentz, Hannover, FRG, 1973.

See also BAUHAUS; GROPIUS, WALTER; MIES VAN DER ROHE, LUDWIG

MANUEL CUADRA
Technische Hochschule Darmstadt
Darmstadt, Federal Republic of Germany

NEUTRA, RICHARD

Richard Josef Neutra was one of the most prominent pioneers of the modern movement in architecture. He was an Austrian who emigrated to the United States in the early 1920s, and as a result, his architectural achievements were born of European avant-garde sensibilities and nurtured by U.S. technical developments. He was born in imperial Vienna in 1892, and as a youth he absorbed much of that city's cultural richness. After entering the Vienna Technische Hochschule in 1911 to study architecture, he joined the studio of Adolf Loos, one of the major proponents of modern architecture in Europe. Loos's rejection of the stylistic trends of the secession movement attracted young architects such as Neutra, as did his conviction that the United States was the country with the most advanced building practices and the "land of unshackled minds"—a conviction that was later to play an important role in Neutra's emigration to the United States. After completing his studies in 1918, Neutra served a brief apprenticeship in Zurich with noted landscape architect Gustav Amman, from whom he gained a knowledge of horticulture and plant ecology that would later be used in the landscape designs of his own buildings. In 1921, he became city architect of Luckenwalde, Germany, but soon left to join the office of Erich Mendelsohn in Berlin, where he was a design collaborator on several projects, including the addition to the *Berliner Tageblatt* newspaper building in Berlin in 1921–1922.

Despite his professional accomplishments within Mendelsohn's office, Neutra longed to move to the United States—the country that had so inspired his mentor Loos and that was the home of Frank Lloyd Wright, whose Wasmuth Portfolio of 1910 had introduced Neutra, as well as all of Europe, to a radically original new architecture. In 1923, with the help of fellow Austrian Rudolph Schindler, who was then working in Wright's office at Taliesin, Neutra arrived in New York eager to absorb what he could of contemporary U.S. building practice. Within a year, he joined the venerable Chicago firm of Holabird and Roche, which enabled him to gain firsthand knowledge of the U.S. building industry and to discover the architectural potentials of industrial production and prefabrication.

In 1924, he entered Frank Lloyd Wright's office at Taliesin, where he executed design studies for some of Wright's most innovative projects of the 1920s, including the Glass Skyscraper for the National Life Insurance Company. Drawn to the strong building activity and climate of California, he left Taliesin in 1925 and moved to Los Angeles, where he took up residence in Schindler's innovative house—studio complex and set out to establish his own practice. Neutra's major creative outlet during this formative period was his Rush City Reformed project, a remarkably comprehensive and elegantly drawn design of an ideal metropolis that was to serve as his continuous repository of ideas on architecture and urban planning throughout most of his practice. At the same time, his penchant for writing produced his influential first book, *Wie Baut America?* (*How America Builds*), a paean to U.S. building practice and construction published in 1927 (1). With Schindler, he entered the 1926 League of Nations Competition and produced a boldly modernist submission that was later included in a German Werkbund exhibition of noteworthy entries, along with those of Le Corbusier of France and Hannes Meyer–Hans Wittner of Switzerland. Neutra and Schindler soon associated to form the Architectural Group for Industry and Commerce (AGIC), a collaboration that produced a number of ambitious unrealized projects as well as the Jardinette Apartments in 1927, a largely Neutra-designed complex that was one of the earliest examples of the international style aesthetic in the United States.

Although his work had demonstrated an unwavering commitment to modernism and had received international attention by this time, it was with the design of the Lovell "Health" House in 1927–1929 that Neutra's reputation as a major architect of the modern movement was firmly established. Boldly perched on a spectacular hillside site in Los Angeles, this three-story house of steel, glass, and concrete displayed the tenets of the international style with great skill and poetry, and its photographic image quickly became an icon of modern architecture (Fig. 1). Neutra's interest in state-of-the-art construction technology motivated the design and production of the first completely steel-framed residence in the United States. With its steel chassis, shop-assembled units, and sprayed Gunite exterior surfaces, the house explored new building techniques within the crisp, planar modernist aesthetic. Along with Le Corbusier's Villa Stein at Garches (1927) and Mies van der Rohe's Barcelona Pavilion (1929), Neutra's Lovell "Health" House became one of the canonical buildings of the 1920s. His selection as the American delegate to the 1930 Brussels meeting of the CIAM (Congrès Internationaux d'Architecture Moderne), followed by the inclusion of his work in the New York Museum of Modern Art's epochal "Modern Architecture" exhibition in 1932, confirmed his international stature.

After extensive travel in Europe and the Far East, where he lectured extensively, he returned to Los Angeles and established an office with several young apprentices, including Gregory Ain, Harwell Hamilton Harris, and Raphael Soriano, all of whom would later contribute to the development of modern architecture in California with their own practices. The 1930s proved to be one of Neutra's most creative periods. His interest in the architecture of the low-cost house and his fascination with prefabricated building systems and components had produced earlier projects such as the Prefabricated Diatalum Dwellings scheme in 1926, with its patented adjustable metal foundations. Another project was the "One Plus Two" Prefabricated House of the same year, an ingenious expandable dwelling of lightweight floor and roof slabs suspended from a central supporting mast. For Neutra, such systems of prefabrication offered great potential for an easily replicable and anonymous house type that could be used anywhere. At the same time, his residential designs frequently displayed open floor plans, semi-outdoor living spaces, and integral landscaping, all of which contributed to a relaxed living environment directly related to a specific site and climate. His own house and office, constructed in Los Angeles in 1932 and named the V.D.I. Research House, incorporated a variety of new building materials in an elegant composition of stuccoed walls, repeated modules of indus-

Figure 1. Lovell "Health" House (1927–1929).

trial sash, and roof decks. Several houses with innovative uses of prefabricated steel elements (Beard House, 1935), plywood (Plywood Model House, 1936), and composition panels (Sciobereti House, 1939) were built in California during this period, and they collectively illustrate his continuing research into various construction systems and building technologies. For the most part, Neutra's houses of the 1930s incorporated the ribbon windows, unadorned planar surfaces and roof terraces associated with the international style.

Although the bulk of his work focused on the design of single-family residences, he also received commissions for small office buildings, schools, and housing complexes. Two noteworthy housing developments, the Landfair Apartments and the Strathmore Apartments, both constructed in Los Angeles in 1937, illustrate his efforts to express the individual housing unit and to provide generous outdoor roof decks, balconies, patios, or gardens for each dwelling space. It was in his school designs, however, that Neutra was to achieve a significant architectural milestone. His earlier Ring Plan School (1926), a radical school design developed in his Rush City Reformed project, included one-story classrooms with natural lighting from wall and roof sources and sliding glass walls that connected each classroom directly with its own outside teaching patio. In his Corona Avenue School built in 1935 in Los Angeles, these ideas were incorporated in an experimental school building that featured bilateral natural lighting and ventilation, movable furniture, and adjacent outside teaching spaces; it became an important model for future school buildings in California and other states.

Neutra's practice continued to expand during the 1940s, and he began to receive larger scale planning and architectural work. His Channel Heights Community (1942), built by the Federal Works Agency for defense workers outside of Los Angeles, housed 600 families in distinct clusters of varying redwood and stucco housing types, and its unit designs, gardens, and common spaces provided a level of amenity usually lacking in public housing. In 1943, he was asked to direct a massive planning and design effort for the postwar construction of schools, health centers, and hospitals in Puerto Rico. As chief architect, he developed a series of designs that were based on an economy of structure and a sensitivity to climatic conditions.

The Nesbitt House, built in 1942 in Los Angeles, marked a turning point in his residential designs with its use of California redwood, brick, and glass as major materials. Board-and-batten surfaces, along with brick, introduced material textures and coloration that differed greatly from the smooth, generally monochromatic austerity of his designs of the 1930s, and the use of large sliding glass walls offered a dynamic means of joining inside spaces with adjacent landscaped outside spaces. One of his most celebrated houses of the postwar 1940s was the Kaufmann House, built in 1946 on a desert site in Palm Springs, California. The design was based on a pinwheel plan organization that contrasted the solidity of its fieldstone walls with the lightness and transparency of its aluminum-framed glass walls; the house established a dramatic spatial reciprocity between inside and outside. In contrast to the Kaufmann House, the Tremaine House, built in 1948 near Santa Barbara, utilized a structural system of

Figure 2. Singleton House. Courtesy of Julius Schulman.

exposed concrete piers and beams that provided a dominant visual regularity for its stone and glass infill. With its articulated structure, the house prefigured Neutra's use of a post-and-beam system in several houses of the 1950s and 1960s.

By the end of the 1950s, Neutra's career had essentially peaked. His commissions, writings, international speaking engagements, and diverse professional activities had served his self-promotion with great effectiveness, and to some he was "second in American architecture only to the lordly Frank Lloyd Wright" (2). Still anxious to expand the scope of his practice, he formed a partnership with Robert Alexander, an architect and city planner, in 1949. The firm of Neutra and Alexander went on to secure large planning projects, including plans for the redevelopment of downtown Sacramento, California, and an extensive master plan and building program for postwar Guam. Commissions for a variety of schools, university buildings, housing complexes, and office structures in different states and countries came to the firm throughout the 1950s and 1960s. Some of their designs attempted to apply the architectural language of Neutra's earlier residential work to much larger structures, while others lapsed into the bland formalism that generally characterized much of U.S. architecture in these eras. Neutra and Alexander's most notable projects were their academic buildings for St. John's College in Annapolis, Maryland (1958), the Palos Verdes High School complex in California (1961), and the Lincoln Museum and Visitors' Center at Gettysburg, Pennsylvania (1961).

Neutra's major energies, however, still focused on the design of the single-family house, and he continued to create new possibilities for contemporary domestic architecture. His residential designs frequently possessed a more relaxed aesthetic derived from the use of natural wood, large areas of undivided plate glass, and extensions of structure in the form of cantilevered roof beams and "spider legs." Extended structural frames, projecting beams, and broad roof overhangs, in conjunction with Neutra's masterful use of the transparency of glass, produced houses that tended to dissolve the explicit boundary between inside and outside, as in the Singleton House, built in 1959 in Los Angeles. With their integral use of water and landscaping, many of these later houses evoked the minimalism and serenity of the Japanese house (Fig. 2). For Neutra, this kind of living environment engendered a positive psychological and physiological development in its occupants, and it thus reflected his concept of "biorealism." As discussed in his most well known publication, *Survival Through Design* (1954) (3), biorealism was predicated on an architecture that minimized extensive strain on the human nervous system, and it was essentially Neutra's means of ensuring that modern man could deal with the environmental stress of modern society.

By the mid-1960s, Neutra's partnership with Alexander had been dissolved, and he had completed his autobiography, *Life and Shape,* published in 1962 (4). His practice was now directed by his architect son Dion, and he established the Richard J. Neutra Institute, a nonprofit organization created to "ameliorate, by the fast advancing insights of all sciences, the human setting in which to live, to work, to rest" (5). Through a series of lectures and seminars, the Institute was dedicated to linking research in the environmental sciences with that of the planning professions, an objective that cogently summarized Neutra's own working method over a lifetime of architectural practice.

Neutra's career ended with his death in 1970. He was one of the most prolific architects of the modern movement, and his projects and executed works, most especially his numerous residential designs, eloquently demonstrate his intense personal search for a studied, yet poetic, balance between man, building, and environment.

BIBLIOGRAPHY

1. R. Neutra, *Wie Baut America?,* Julius Hoffman, Stuttgart, 1927.
2. T. S. Hines, *Richard Neutra and the Search for Modern Architecture,* Oxford University Press, New York, 1982, p. 219.
3. R. Neutra, *Survival Through Design,* Oxford University Press, New York, 1954.
4. R. Neutra, *Life and Shape,* Appleton-Century-Crofts, New York, 1962.
5. Ref. 2, p. 287.

General References

W. Boesiger, ed., *Richard Neutra 1923–50: Buildings and Projects,* Girsberger, Zurich, 1964.

W. Boesiger, ed., *Richard Neutra 1950–60: Buildings and Projects,* Girsberger, Zurich, 1964.

W. Boesiger, ed., *Richard Neutra 1961–66: Buildings and Projects,* Girsberger, Zurich, 1966.

A. Drexler and T. S. Hines, *The Architecture of Richard Neutra: From International Style to California Modern,* The Museum of Modern Art, New York, 1982. A catalog to accompany the Neutra exhibition, 1982.

T. S. Hines, *Richard Neutra and the Search for Modern Architecture,* Oxford University Press, New York, 1982. A comprehensive Neutra biography and a complete listing of all executed works.

E. McCoy, *Richard Neutra,* George Braziller, Inc., New York, 1960.

D. Neutra, *Richard Neutra: Promise and Fulfillment 1919–1932,* Southern Illinois Press, Carbondale and Edwardsville, Ill., 1986. Selections from the letters of Dione and Richard Neutra.

R. Neutra, *World and Dwelling,* Alec Tiranti, Ltd., London, 1962.

GREGORY K. HUNT
Virginia Polytechnic Institute and State University
Blacksburg, Virginia

NEW TOWNS. See PLANNED COMMUNITIES (NEW TOWNS)

NIEMEYER, OSCAR

Oscar Niemeyer Soares Filho was born in Rio de Janeiro, Brazil, in December 1907. At age 23 and already married, he began the study of architecture and civil engineering at the School of Fine Arts in Rio de Janeiro. He received his degree in architecture in 1934 and went to work for noted Brazilian architect and planner Lucio Costa, who became a major influence in his professional life. Costa was not only a leading South American modernist but, as architect of Brazil's national historical preservation organization, was also involved in restoration of some of the country's outstanding examples of baroque architectures. His work in the careful restoration of the colonial city of Ouro Prêto, a national historical landmark site, was complemented by a modern tourist hotel designed by Niemeyer in 1940. In 1936, Niemeyer had persuaded Costa to put him on a design team for the headquarters of the Ministry of Health and Education, headed by noted French architect Le Corbusier. Niemeyer's association with Le Corbusier, although brief, provided a focus and momentum for his career, which established him as South America's leading modern architect by age 40.

After his work on Le Corbusier's design team for the Ministry of Education, during which time he also worked on preliminary plans for a new national university campus, Niemeyer opened his own architectural office. His first independent project, in 1937, was Obra do Berço Day Nursery in Rio de Janeiro. In 1939, he traveled to New York with Costa to design the Brazilian Pavilion at the 1940 New York World's Fair. Meanwhile, the Ministry of Education building program had been approved and Niemeyer was named chief architect. The project firmly established his practice and his professional reputation with the Brazilian government. Juscelino Kubitschek, governor of the prosperous state of Minas Gerais, later to become president and developer of Brasília, invited Niemeyer to work on a new development, Pampulha, outside the state capital of Belo Horizonte. In 1942 and 1943, Niemeyer did a number of buildings at Pampulha including a yacht club, museum, restaurant, church, and Governor Kubitschek's own residence.

Between 1940 and 1950, Niemeyer designed office buildings, educational buildings, and housing in Rio de Janeiro and São Paulo. He was invited to serve on the advisory committee for the United Nations headquarters building in New York in 1947 and later was made an honorary member of the American Academy of Arts and Sciences.

In 1950, he produced one of his most unusual projects, the Quitandinha apartment hotel in Brazil's summer capital, Petrópolis, in the mountain area of the state of Rio de Janeiro. Soon after, he returned to Belo Horizonte to design a government complex and other buildings in Minas Gerais for Governor Kubitschek.

In the mid-1950s, he established a magazine of design, *Modulo,* which was published in Portuguese, and traveled in Europe, visiting Moscow, Warsaw, and Berlin. In 1956, Kubitschek was elected president of Brazil and announced plans for a new capital city, Brasília, to be located in the geographical center of the country as prescribed in Brazil's nineteenth-century constitution. Niemeyer was appointed adviser to the development corporation (NOVACAP) and later became its chief architect. Between 1957 and the inauguration of the new capital in 1960, Niemeyer designed the Congress buildings, the Supreme Court, the presidential offices, the cathedral and chapel, and the jewel-like Alvarado Palace (president's house). Later buildings were the Palacio dos Arcos (Foreign Ministry), the Brasília Palace Hotel, and the National Theater. After Kubitschek, his sponsor, resigned in 1960, Niemeyer completed another project, the Copán apartment building in São Paulo, and left Brazil to live abroad for the next eight years. During that time, he did designs for an urbanization project for Cesarea in Israel, the University of Ghana, and a mosque and other buildings in Algeria. A book, *My Experience in Brasília*, was published in Rio de Janeiro and reprinted in Moscow, Rome, and Paris. Among his architectural awards are the 1955 International Prize awarded by *L'Architecture d'aujourd'hui,* Paris and the 1967 Benito Juarez Prize, Mexico, for the leading contribution to art on the continent.

Returning to live in Brazil in the 1970s, Niemeyer continued his independent practice and renewed his association with Lucio Costa in a major urban development project, Rio Novo, at Barra de Tijuca, a relatively undeveloped area of beach south of Rio de Janeiro. He continues his private practice in Rio de Janeiro, maintaining his reputation as South America's leading architect.

BIBLIOGRAPHY

General References

R. Spade and Y. Futagawa, *Oscar Niemeyer,* Simon and Schuster, New York, 1971.

S. Papadaki, *The Work of Oscar Niemeyer,* Reinhold Publishing Co., New York, 1950.

H. R. Hitchcock, *Latin American Architecture Since 1945,* Museum of Modern Art, New York, 1955.

H. E. Mindlin, *Modern Architecture in Brazil,* Colibris Editora, Rio de Janeiro, 1956.

N. Evenson, *Two Brazilian Capitals: Architecture and Urbanism in Rio de Janeiro and Brasília,* Yale University Press, New Haven, Conn., 1973.

David P. Fogle
University of Maryland
College Park, Maryland

NOISE CONTROL IN BUILDINGS

That noise in buildings must be controlled is a concomitant of modern building design. The reasons are basic to human comfort and privacy. Thus, the criteria for noise control are governed by the acoustical requirements for comfort and privacy.

Knowing the criteria for acceptable noise levels in a particular space, the various sources of noise in and around the building, and the existing or proposed relation of spaces within a building, measures can be selected that will meet the desired criteria for that space. In most cases, noise control measures can be selected that do not do violence to the architecture.

There are a few elementary criteria for both comfort and privacy in occupied spaces. The problem with such criteria is that they only cover a few simple cases. In more complex situations, consideration must be given to the interaction of the noise or the speech heard with the activity of the occupants of the space.

The criteria most widely used for noise level goals in rooms are those in Table 1, which contains the design goal noise levels for each of a variety of spaces in terms of the noise criteria (NC) curves (Fig. 1). Also used is the A-weighted sound level. This is the sound level measured through an electronic circuit which approximates the sensitivity of the ear at low sound levels (Fig. 2). It has also been found to relate well to annoyance. There are, however, shortcomings in both criteria.

Some acousticians have suggested that the NC curve is not restrictive enough at low frequencies and have proposed a similar family of rating curves, the RC curves, with special tests at low frequencies (3). The actual criterion to be used for a project must consider function, the presence of tonal components in the noise, and the added cost to reduce the low frequency sounds.

Using the A-weighted sound level as a criterion can also result in excessively low frequency levels. It must be noted that none of these criteria covers the situation where discrete tone signals are present in the noise. In general, the presence of discrete tones is unacceptable until each tone is several decibels below the level of the octave band in which it occurs.

SOURCES OF NOISE

Although one can talk generally about the control of noise, a knowledge of the sources of noise that need to be controlled is critical to the development of noise control methods. The sources may be divided into three broad categories: environmental, human activity, and mechanical equipment associated with the building.

The different sources within each category require different noise control approaches because the spectra of the sounds vary widely. Typical sources within each source category are the following:

1. *Environmental Sources.*
   - *Transportation.* Air, rail, and highway systems.
   - *Industrial.* Large power plants, exhaust fans, conveying systems, plant loading and unloading equipment, off-highway vehicles, steam and gas exhausts, and process noise.
   - *Service Equipment.* Power mowers, saws, blowers, and vacuum devices.
   - *Recreational Equipment and Activity.* Snowmobiles, motorcycles, recreational vehicles, racetracks, amusement parks, marketplace activity, and public concerts.
2. *Human Activity Sources (Other than Recreational).* Speech, footfalls, household equipment including mixers, vacuum cleaners, and hair dryers, and group activities such as parties.
3. *Mechanical Equipment Sources.* Boilers, chillers, mechanical equipment rooms, cooling towers, air-cooled condensers, plumbing noise from flushing wa-

Table 1. Design Guideline Noise Criteria for Rooms[a]

Type of Space	Recommended Noise Criterion Curve, NC	Sound Level, dB(A)
Apartments and hotels	25–35	35–45
Assembly halls (with amplification)	25–30	35–40
Broadcast studios	15–25	25–30
Churches	30	37
Concert halls	20	30
Conference room (for 20 or less)	30	40
Conference and board rooms, large (for 50 or more people)	25–30	35
Courtrooms	30	40
Factories	40–64	50–75
General offices, typing and business (unoccupied)	35–45	40–50
Homes (sleeping areas)	25–35	35–45
Hospitals	30–40	40–45
Legitimate theaters (no amplification)	20–25	28–32
Libraries	30–40	35–45
Motion picture theaters	30	37
Music rooms	25	35
Restaurants	35–45	40–50
Schoolrooms	30–35	40–50
Small private offices	30–40	35–37[b]
Sports coliseums	50	60
Stores, large or supermarket and department	50	60
Stores, small	35–40	40–45

[a] Ref. 2.

[b] May be higher if sound masking is used.

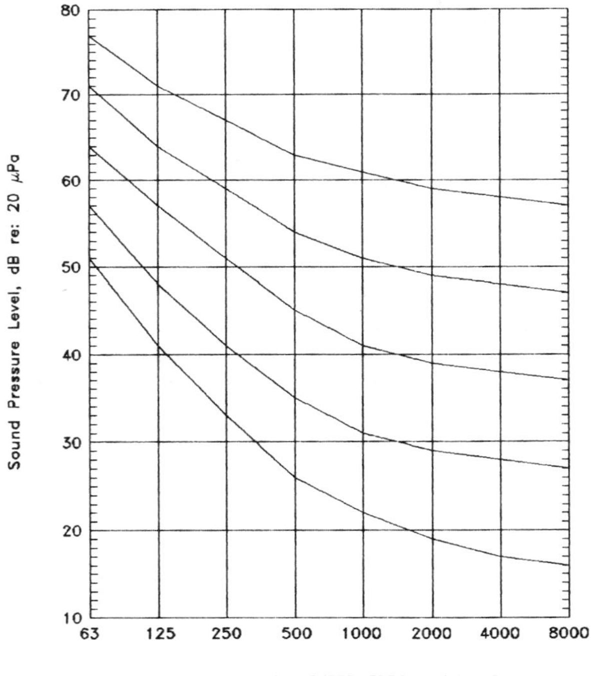

Figure 1. The noise criterion (NC) curves provide a design guide criterion for room noise without occupants, with the HVAC system operating at typical maximum settings. The room noise levels should follow the general trend of one of the curves. A room noise level which crosses one or more curves will not be found to be comfortable for the occupants, even if it has a maximum value below the value listed in Table 1.

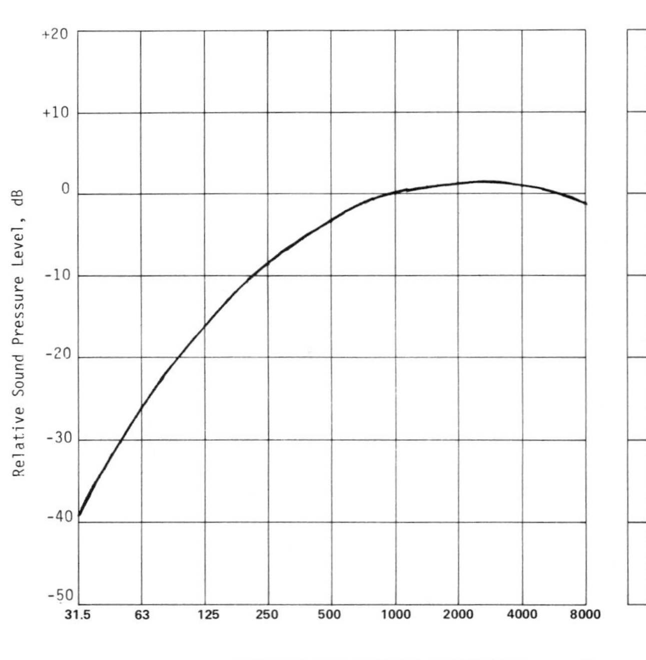

Figure 2. The A-weighting curve of the ANSI Standard S1.4. Sound levels rated using this curve may be annoying, even though they meet widely used criteria, because the curve suppresses low frequency noise, including rumble. The curve is useful for comparing changes in level of some types of room noise, such as diffuser noise and highway traffic noise.

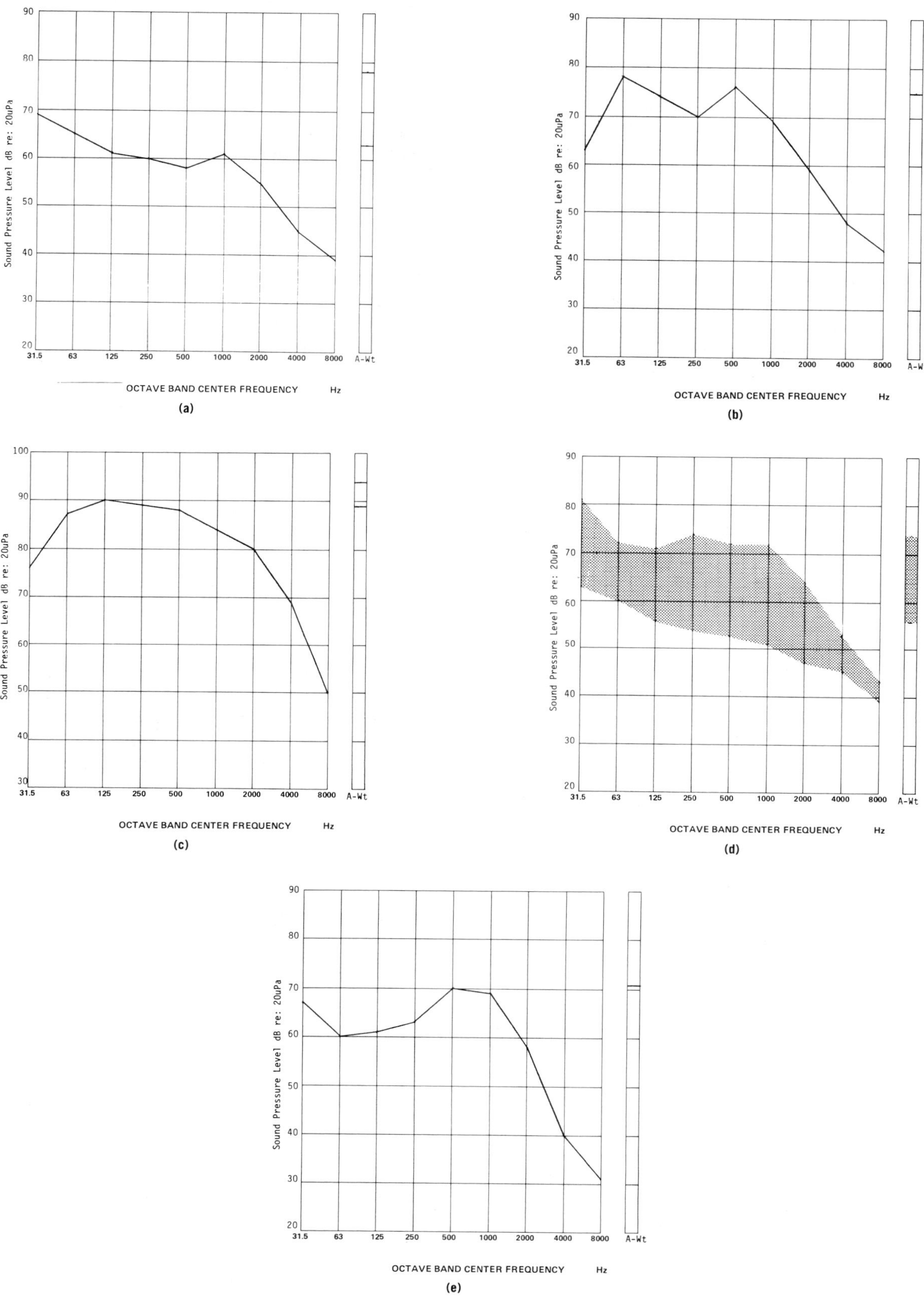

Figure 3. Spectra of typical noise sources. (**a**) Typical highway traffic at 1100 ft; (**b**) Three-cell cooling tower at 80 ft; (**c**) Jet aircraft takeoff at 1000 ft; (**d**) Range of helicopter noise spectra in a residential community; (**e**) Maximum sound levels from passby of an electric passenger train at 530 ft.

ter flow, expansion and contraction of piping, steam leaks, interior transportation, including elevators, pneumatic tubes, and mail conveying systems.

Among the properties of noise sources that need to be known, the most critical are the sound pressure level and spectrum at the receiver location. Spectra for a number of these are included in Figure 3.

It can be seen from Figure 3 that the spectra of jet aircraft, for example, are richer in low frequency energy than the spectrum of highway noise, and speech is different from music. In each case, the sound isolating method will also be different. Windows that would be adequate for an office near a highway would be inadequate near an airport. Similarly, the partitions for an office usually do not have to isolate music, but modern apartments must have floors and partitions capable of dealing with modern electronic music systems. The source spectra must be used in assessing the amount of sound isolation required to meet the criteria for various spaces.

NOISE PATHS

Sound waves travel through gases, liquids, and solids. For example, mechanical vibrations from a pump mounted on a concrete floor will result in the following:

1. The floor will vibrate, exciting the air below and within the pump room, which will cause audible sound within those spaces.
2. The connected piping will vibrate and will excite the partitions to which it is attached.
3. The fluid in the piping will contain pulsations from the pump impeller, which, in turn, will cause the piping to have a higher level of vibration than would occur from the mechanical vibrations alone. Even where a flexible section of piping is included, the fluid can transmit the pulsations so that very little reduction in vibration occurs as a result of the flexible section. (The flexible section does ensure that the piping and hangers will not be damaged from the vibration of the machine.)
4. The vibration from the pump casing and the pipe walls will cause the air adjacent to these surfaces to vibrate, thus generating sound waves which will raise the sound level within the pump room and in adjacent rooms through which the pipe passes.

In acoustics, the paths are referred to as air-, fluid-, and solid-borne noise paths. When the sound is airborne, it is sensed with the ears. However, control of noise in buildings requires attention to each path.

The noise problem can be examined by studying the following oversimplified system:

Source——————Receiver
Path

In real systems, there are a multiplicity of sources, paths, and receivers, but the simple system shown will help in examining the nature of the noise control problem.

Clearly, to achieve control of noise, one can work on any one of its elements. Many solutions become obvious from an inspection of a building site and the building's architectural, structural, and mechanical drawings. One of the most obvious solutions, control at the receiver, is not available except in industrial noise exposure situations where hearing protectors can be used by those exposed. Although some individuals do use ear plugs at home in urban environments, they cannot be considered a suitable solution to an architectural noise problem. This is actually a control on the path, since the receiver is not modified.

CONTROL OF NOISE AT THE SOURCE

Sources of noise in buildings range from exterior sources over which the designer has no control, such as aircraft and highway noise, to building-related mechanical equipment and interior public spaces, such as lounges and ballrooms, in which loud music and amplified music and speech are sources that can be heard by other occupants.

Transportation

Usually, transportation sources can only be controlled by path options. However, a few methods are available for special situations:

1. The use of plazas over rail lines or highways can reduce transportation noise for buildings located on the plaza, and reinstalling the rail lines on a track isolation system can reduce rail system vibration and noise in and above the terminal level.
2. Resurfacing a road or highway section can reduce tire–road–surface generated noise.
3. Trucking and construction firms can purchase trucks with noise control equipment to reduce their impact on the buildings served and on adjacent buildings.

Industrial Equipment

Industrial sources influence offices in the same buildings, and spaces in neighboring buildings. In industrial plant buildings, good source isolation methods can be used, but there is little incentive for the source owners to control noise, except for local regulations. At the planning and zoning level, the development of performance control regulations is critical. In some cases, source and path control can be accomplished by the industrial source owner.

Service Equipment

Service equipment, eg, power mowers, is often available in quiet versions, and quieting kits are also available. Building owners must be persuaded to buy quiet equipment or to add the quieting kit. Neighbors may need stronger persuasion, such as a visit from the health officer or code enforcement official. Some simple, effective source controls for service equipment include more effective mufflers on the engines of small, engine-driven equipment.

Recreational Equipment and Activity

There are many different categories of equipment in this source class. Engine-driven equipment can be quieted to a modest extent with mufflers.

Race tracks, amusement parks, and outdoor concert sites are usually on sites known to a builder. Cooperation can often lead to installation of barriers at critical locations by the source owner. Redirection of public address loudspeakers and use of new, highly directive horn loudspeakers can reduce noise at adjacent buildings. Also, enforcement of zoning codes and police regulations can keep the adjacent levels under control.

Human Activity Sources

Careful selection of flooring and appliances can reduce source noise levels in some areas of human activity.

Mechanical Equipment

Mechanical equipment sources can be controlled by the following measures:

1. Selection of the location to minimize the impact on building occupants.
2. Selection of a mechanical process that minimizes sound and vibration output, for example, use of a slow centrifugal fan instead of a high speed, high velocity vane-axial fan.
3. Selection of the quietest machine available of the type selected.
4. Changing or limiting the operation of the source.
5. Reducing velocities of air in ducts.
6. Changing the outlet conditions of fans and blowers.
7. Installing turning vanes in ducts.

Planning for Source Noise Control

Acoustical planning for the location of building elements is a critical part of a building's design. Included in this selection must be the location of the building with respect to exterior noise sources and the selection of the locations of the building's exterior noise-producing equipment. For instance, locating cooling towers adjacent to outdoor function spaces is obviously bad planning, but air-cooled condensers and architecturally hidden machine rooms are also noise sources to be located with care.

The location of a building's noise-producing equipment requires consideration of the location of the sleeping areas, executive offices, conference areas, and theaters and auditoriums. Some tradeoffs are inevitable, but whether locating a conference room over a railroad line or highway to accommodate a view overlooking a harbor is worth the increase in noise and the required noise control effort is a complex question involving relationships to other spaces, costs, and aesthetics. Such situations can arise, for example, in the design of college buildings and hotels. In both, noise control by orientation can be accomplished by using the noisy side for service areas. In some cases, the view can be used, since the noise does drop in level with distance, but this must be assessed by careful computation. An alternative solution is to use walls and windows with better sound isolation.

The selection of mechanical equipment for noise control involves the evaluation of the equipment sound power output, usually given as the sound power level in decibels, with the standard reference level being 10^{-12} Watt. The sound output may also be given as the sound pressure level at a specified distance. The sound levels must be given for each of the octave bands needed to assess the noise impact. This usually includes the bands having center frequencies from 63 to 4000 Hz, with the 31.5- and 8000-Hz bands included in critical cases. However, data are not always available for these two bands. Often, only the A-weighted sound level is available. Where data are not available, judicious estimates with conservative safety factors may be used. Data for a wide variety of air conditioning sources is available in the American Society of Heating, Refrigerating, and Air Conditioning Engineers (ASHRAE) Handbook (1). Other data is available from the Air Conditioning and Refrigeration Institute (4,5), whose members test their products in accordance with the appropriate standards, and some other manufacturers who test their products or predict the noise levels from their products based on tests of some models.

Using only the A-weighted sound level is similar to specifying the lighting level in footcandles, but omitting the color temperature.

The use of an alternative process is available in only certain instances, but in these instances, the payoff may be large. Typical examples include the following:

1. Using absorption refrigeration machines in place of centrifugal machines where load conditions are appropriate.
2. Dividing the cooling tower load so that several tower cells can be run at about half speed rather than shutting down cells one at a time as the cooling load drops. A drop in fan noise of 12 dB occurs for two cells at half speed versus running one of the two at full speed.

PATH NOISE CONTROL

Noise control along the path of sound transmission from its source to the building occupants is probably the most familiar area of noise control. Methods include:

1. Placing a barrier between source and receiver.
2. Enclosure of the source.
3. Enclosure of the building occupants.
4. Improved installation methods to eliminate leaks at windows, doors, and vents.
5. Installation of acoustical absorbing material in the source room and/or receiving room.
6. Control of piping and duct-transmitted sound.
7. Control of vibration from mechanical equipment.

The principles of path noise control are derivations of three elementary physical phenomena:

1. Attenuation of sound by an impervious barrier.
2. Absorption of sound energy by porous materials.
3. Reduction of the vibration forces transmitted from a vibrating machine system to radiating surfaces and structures by resilient devices.

Barriers for Noise Control

The walls of rooms are the most common barriers, but barriers erected adjacent to highways, machinery enclosures, and screens in open-plan offices are other types of barriers that also reduce noise.

Noise reduction or sound isolation in acoustics is measured in each one-third octave band in terms of the sound transmission loss (STL or TL), which is the ratio of sound energy transmitted by a partition to the energy falling on the partition, expressed in decibels. It is measured in accordance with American Society for Testing and Materials (ASTM) standard E90 (6) (Fig. 4). A single number rating, the sound transmission class (STC), is used to rate partitions for office and residential use, ASTM E413 (7). However, STC may not adequately rate exterior walls exposed to aircraft or industrial noise, or interior walls exposed to some types of music and machinery having high levels of low frequency sound energy.

The acoustical behavior of typical architectural partitions depends on the surface density and the stiffness of the partition material, but it cannot be predicted from mathematical models with very much accuracy.

The simplest model, called mass law behavior, of a partition of relatively limp material such as lead or weighted vinyl, will predict a sound transmission loss (TL) at a given frequency, F, that is determined by the surface weight, W, (lb/ft^2) of the material:

$$TL = 20 \log W + 20 \log F - 33 \text{ dB}$$

However, the bending stiffness of conventional building materials causes a degradation of transmission loss at mid-range and high frequencies, often with a deep notch in a region around the critical frequency where the speed of the bending wave in the wall or partition has the same speed as the sound in air.

A model for this behavior has been developed (7). The STC is obtained from the predicted or measured one-third octave band sound transmission loss data in accordance with ASTM E413 (7).

The models available allow the prediction of the acoustical behavior of simple partitions (Fig. 5), but as noted above, the prediction of the sound transmission loss of a stud and gypsum board partition can only be approximated. Use of the model for more complex partitions leads to results that may differ greatly from test results on full scale partitions. Measured data are available on a wide range of partition materials and systems (9). A brief listing is shown in Table 2 (from Owens-Corning Fiberglas).

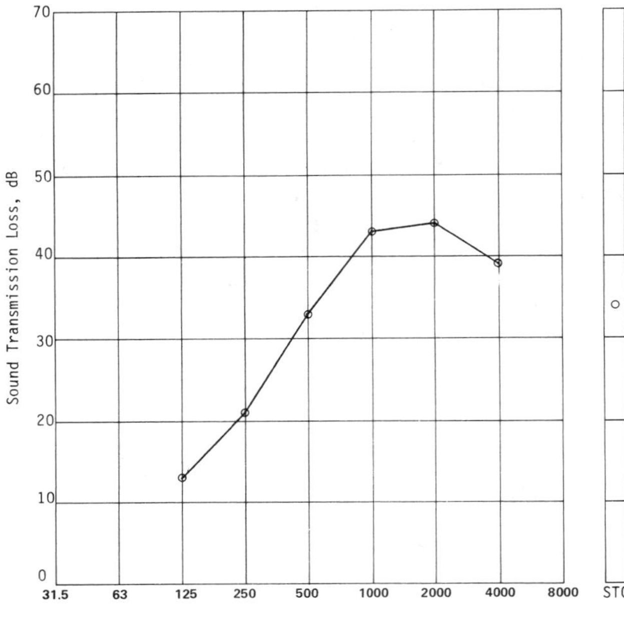

Figure 4. Test results of a gypsum drywall partition tested in accordance with ASTM E-90. Partition consisted of ½-in. gypsum board on 2½-in. steel studs, taped and spackled.

Although mathematical modeling with a computer using a widely accepted model will yield approximate answers, the requirements for aerospace test facilities and the regulation of some states and municipalities require

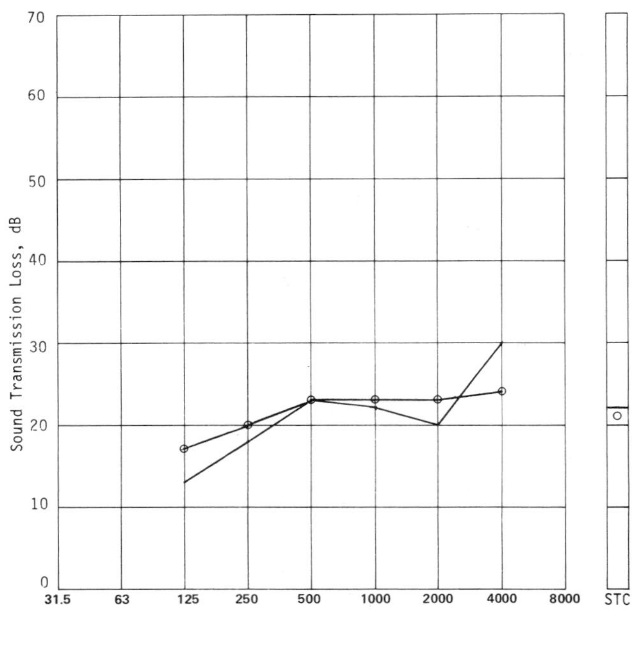

Figure 5. Plots of the sound transmission loss of ½-in. plywood as measured and as computed using the mathematical model developed by Beranek (8) and applied using a personal computer by the author. — Computed; O—O Measured.

Table 2. Sound Transmission Loss of Typical Building Materials and Assemblies

Construction Type	Octave Band Center Frequency, Hz 125	250	500	1000	2000	4000	STC
2½-in. metal studs, 24 in. o.c., ½-in. gypsum wallboard both sides	13	21	33	43	44	39	34
2½-in. metal studs, 24 in. o.c., ½-in. gypsum wallboard both sides, with R-8 glass fiber insulation	22	33	44	51	52	43	42
2½-in. metal studs, 24 in. o.c., 2 layers ½-in. gypsum wallboard both sides	23	30	45	49	52	52	45
2½-in. metal studs, 24 in. o.c., 2 layers ½-in. gypsum wallboard one side, 1 layer ½-in. gypsum wallboard other side with R-8 glass fiber insulation	30	42	51	59	62	51	50
2½-in. metal studs, 24 in. o.c., 2 layers ½-in. gypsum wallboard both sides with R-8 glass fiber insulation	36	45	54	62	65	56	54
3⅝-in. metal studs, 24 in. o.c., ½-in. gypsum wallboard both sides	16	23	37	45	46	37	36
3⅝-in. metal studs, 24 in. o.c., ½-in. gypsum wallboard both sides with R-11 glass fiber insulation	24	35	47	54	57	42	44
3⅝-in. metal studs, 24 in. o.c., 2 layers ½-in. gypsum wallboard one side, 1 layer ½-in. gypsum wallboard other side	21	29	43	50	51	42	41
3⅝-in. metal studs, 24 in. o.c., 2 layers ½-in. gypsum wallboard one side, 1 layer ½-in. gypsum wallboard other side with R-11 glass fiber insulation	33	44	52	60	63	53	52
3⅝-in. metal studs, 24 in. o.c., 2 layers ½-in. gypsum wallboard each side	30	40	49	55	58	52	50
3⅝-in. metal studs, 24 in. o.c., 2 layers ½-in. gypsum wallboard each side with R-11 glass fiber insulation	38	47	55	58	63	57	56
2 × 4 wood studs, 16 in. o.c., ½-in. gypsum wallboard both sides	15	27	36	42	47	40	35
2 × 4 wood studs, 16 in. o.c., ½-in. gypsum wallboard with R-11 glass fiber insulation	15	31	40	46	50	41	39
2 × 4 wood studs, 16 in. o.c., 2 layers ½-in. gypsum wallboard one side, 1 layer gypsum wallboard other side	17	32	40	45	50	45	38
2 × 4 wood studs, 16 in. o.c., 2 layers ½-in. gypsum wallboard both sides	15	35	43	48	53	50	39
2 × 4 wood studs, 16 in. o.c., 2 layers ½-in. gypsum wallboard both sides with R-11 glass fiber insulation	21	37	45	50	55	51	45
2 × 4 wood studs, 16 in. o.c., resilient channel one side, ½-in. gypsum wallboard both sides	15	32	40	49	52	45	39
2 × 4 wood studs, 16-in. o.c., resilient channel one side, ½-in. gypsum wallboard both sides, with R-11 glass fiber insulation	22	40	53	57	58	50	46
2 × 4 wood studs, staggered construction, 24 in. o.c., ½-in. gypsum wallboard both sides	22	23	36	46	52	41	38
2 × 4 wood studs, staggered construction, 24 in. o.c., ½-in. gypsum wallboard both sides, with R-11 glass fiber insulation	31	37	47	52	56	50	49
2 × 4 wood studs, 24 in. o.c., double stud construction, ½-in. gypsum wallboard both sides	24	32	39	48	52	39	39
2 × 4 wood studs, 24 in. o.c., double stud construction, ½-in. gypsum wallboard both sides, with R-11 glass fiber insulation	29	43	54	63	66	52	52
2 × 4 wood studs, 24 in. o.c., double stud construction, 2 layers ½-in. gypsum wallboard both sides, R-11 glass fiber insulation	37	51	64	66	71	64	61
Sheet metal, 22 gauge	16	20	24	29	35	43	29
Gypsum board, 58 in.	19	19	28	30	29	32	27
3⁄16-in. steel duct wall, 4-in. glass fiber thermal insulation, with 16-gauge sheet metal	42	44	43	50	54	60	49

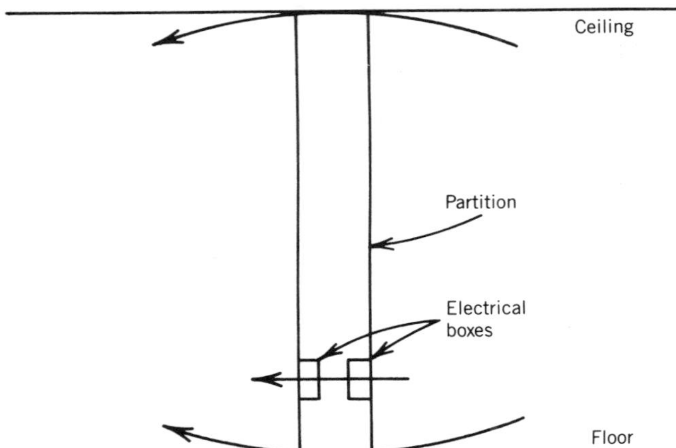

Figure 6. Typical flanking paths around a partition that can reduce the sound isolation by 20 or 30 dB.

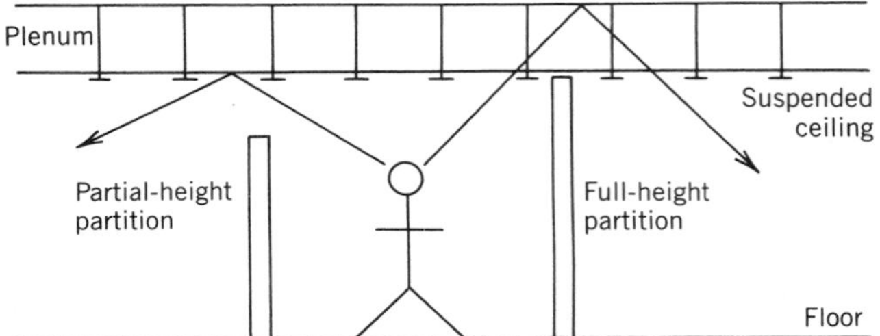

Figure 7. Flanking sound transmission in offices. The paths are not visible, but are readily detected by field testing. Even a portable radio in one room will allow observation of the paths. A stethoscope with the diaphragm removed can be used effectively to locate leaks at the perimeter and electrical boxes.

finished structures to meet specified sound transmission loss standards. The hazard of using untested partitions is obvious.

Even with a suitable partition, there may be paths around the partition which allow sound to pass in and out. These "flanking" paths can include leaks around the perimeter of the partition wherever it meets a different material (Fig. 6). Also, in modern office buildings, the office may not be fully enclosed acoustically, because the ceiling may be a visual barrier that is acoustically transparent, such as many acoustical ceiling materials. These allow sound to travel from one office to another unimpeded (Fig. 7). Some acoustical ceiling materials are specially treated to improve the sound isolation.

To avoid the transmission of sound through the flanking paths, they must be sealed. The use of two beads of acoustical sealant under floor runners and behind wall and ceiling runners will take care of these paths, although, at the floor and ceiling, a bead of caulking at the joint between the wallboard and the floor and ceiling will provide some insurance over the building's lifetime. Where the partition meets a corrugated deck at the floor above or the roof, molded neoprene filler strips are available to match commercial corrugated decking.

Electrical boxes should be spaced at least one stud width apart. For remedial situations, the back-to-back boxes must be sealed with acoustical sealant or pliable duct sealant, and the face of the box sealed to gypsum board partition with acoustical sealant. In masonry partitions without furred gypsum board, a similar approach must be used with a sealant compatible with the masonry material.

Exterior Partitions for Environmental Noise

To protect residences, office buildings, schools, and hospitals against environmental noise from aircraft and highway noise, special care must be exercised in planning the building and in the selection of materials. In residential buildings, the use of high density sheathing such as plywood, glass or mineral fiber insulation in the cavity, resilient channels (Fig. 8) to support the interior walls, and even two layers of gypsum board with the second layer laminated and nailed, help to reduce the unwanted noise. Acoustical sealant works well as adhesive. Other measures that are required include the following:

- Windows must be selected with sound transmission loss values that will not reduce that of the wall too much. When they are smaller, they do not need to

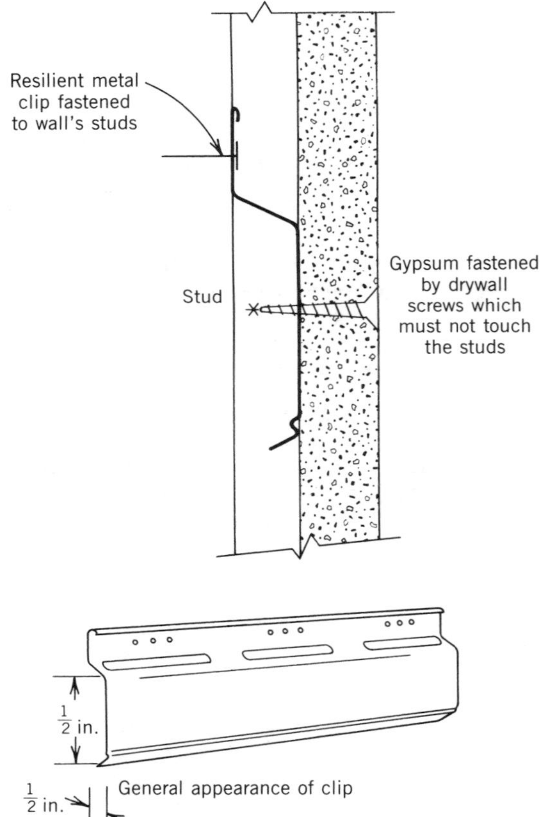

Figure 8. Resilient clips are widely used to improve transmission loss performance of gypsum board walls. By decoupling the wall face from the framing, they decrease the sound power transferred structurally from one face to the other. This is sometimes called "structural flanking."

provide quite as much sound isolation. The TL value does need to be close, if they are large.

- Windows must be sealed into the rough opening. When they are not, they will leak. A high grade of caulking, combined with the appropriate rodding, is required.
- Sound isolation is required at air inlet and exhaust ducts, which must be sealed around openings.
- The roof–ceiling system, often the largest area exposed, should provide a high level of sound isolation. Combined structures with sound isolation hangers between roof and ceiling, with a 6–12-in. thick thermal/acoustical blanket in the space, will often provide the added isolation required.

Sound Absorption

Sound energy that falls on a hard surface will impart a small portion of its energy to the surface; the rest of the energy is reflected. When a surface is porous, the sound energy is partly absorbed within the porous structure of the material and a portion of the energy is reflected (Fig. 9). If there is no impervious backing for the porous material, sound energy will also flow through the material into the adjacent space. The amount of energy absorbed and reflected is determined by the physical properties of the material, such as fiber diameter and density of the material. Porous materials that are thin absorb less sound than those that are thick. For effective absorption of speech, office, and home appliance sounds, an effective sound-absorbing material should be about 1 in. thick. Conventional absorbing materials with an air backing, such as suspended acoustical ceilings, can be effective when thinner but may not have adequate dimensional stability. Some thin, stiff, porous structures have been used in ceiling grids to provide high sound absorption.

The sound absorption of a material is stated in terms of the sound absorption coefficient, the fraction of energy falling on a material that is absorbed by the material. For architectural purposes, the sound absorption coefficient is usually measured in a reverberation room under conditions specified by the ASTM Standard Test Method C423 (7). This method calls for the testing of a 72 ft^2 specimen, usually 8 × 9 ft. However, the coefficients measured in this way are a function of the area. Patches of material may yield higher coefficients and very large areas lower coefficients. There is a large body of measured sound absorption data on architectural materials measured in accordance with the ASTM Standard. Some examples are shown in Tables 3 and 4. Again, no simple mathematical model exists that permits the prediction of a material's sound absorption with sufficient accuracy to be relied on for design or regulatory standards.

Noise Reduction by Sound Absorption

When a source of sound is located in a room, the sound energy that falls on the walls or reaches a person within the room is affected by the sound absorption in the room. Where there is no sound absorption, the multiple reflections allow the sound energy to build up within the space.

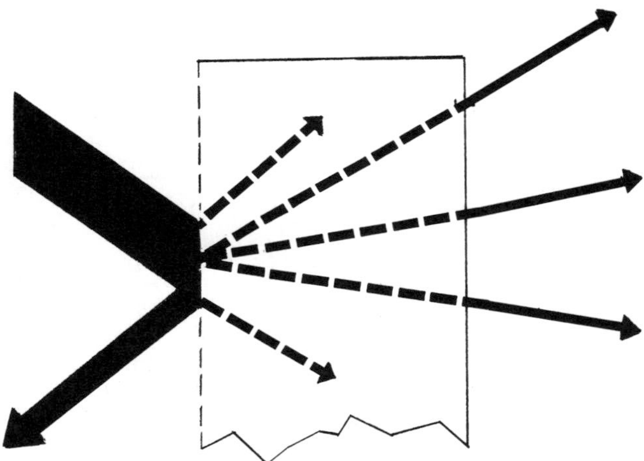

Figure 9. A schematic representation of the behavior of sound when striking a porous sound-absorbing material. The material may be film-surfaced or perforated. It passes less sound when faced on the back with an impervious material, such as aluminum foil or clay coating.

By the use of sound absorbing materials, the sound energy within the space will be reduced. This may be expressed mathematically by:

$$L_p = L_w + 10 \log_{10}\left(\frac{Q}{4\pi r^2} + \frac{4}{\alpha S}\right) \quad \text{dB}$$

Where:

L_w = the source sound power level in dB, re: $1 \cdot 10^{-12}$ W

Q = source directivity

r = distance from source in meters

α = average room absorption

S = the total room surface area in meters

As the equation shows, at any point in the space, the sound reaching the point is made up of two components, the direct component, $Q/4\pi r^2$, and the reverberant component, $4/\alpha S$. Close to the source of noise or the partition through which noise is entering, the sound level is controlled by the energy received directly from the source or partition, the first term in the equation, but in the far field, the direct energy may be lower than the reverberant field energy, the second term, and the reverberant sound's level predominates. Figure 10 shows the general nature of the sound level in a room for various amounts of sound absorption.

The amount of noise reduction (NR) that is available from the addition of sound absorption in a room can be obtained from the equation above, or at a considerable distance from the source in rooms with relatively small amount of absorbing material where $Q/4\pi r^2 \ll 4/\alpha S$, from:

$$NR = 10 \log_{10} \frac{A_2}{A_1}$$

Table 3. Sound Absorption of Typical Materials[a]

Materials	125	250	500	1000	2000	4000	NRC
	Octave Band Center Frequency, Hz						
Brick, unglazed	.03	.03	.03	.04	.05	.07	.05
Brick, unglazed, painted	.01	.01	.01	.02	.02	.03	.00
Carpet							
1/8-in. pile height	.05	.05	.10	.20	.30	.40	.15
1/4-in. pile height	.05	.10	.15	.30	.50	.55	.25
3/16-in. combined pile and foam	.05	.10	.10	.30	.40	.50	.25
5/16-in. combined pile and foam	.05	.15	.30	.40	.50	.60	.35
Concrete block, painted	.10	.05	.06	.07	.09	.08	.05
Fabrics							
Light velour, 10 oz/yd^2, hung straight, in contact with wall	.03	.04	.11	.17	.24	.35	.15
Medium velour, 14 oz/yd^2, draped to half area	.07	.31	.49	.75	.70	.60	.55
Heavy Velour, 18 oz/yd^2, draped to half area	.14	.35	.55	.72	.70	.65	.60
Floors							
Concrete or terrazzo	.01	.01	.01	.02	.02	.02	.00
Linoleum, asphalt, rubber or cork tile on concrete	.02	.03	.03	.03	.03	.02	.05
Wood	.15	.11	.10	.07	.06	.07	.10
Wood parquet in asphalt on concrete	.04	.04	.07	.06	.06	.07	.05
Glass							
1/4-in., sealed, large panes	.05	.03	.02	.02	.03	.02	.05
24 oz, operable windows (in closed condition)	.10	.05	.04	.03	.03	.03	.05
Gypsum board, 1/2-in., nailed to 2 × 4s, 16 in. o.c., painted	.10	.08	.05	.03	.03	.03	.05
Marble or glazed tile	.01	.01	.01	.01	.02	.02	.00
Plaster, gypsum or lime							
rough finish or lath	.02	.03	.04	.05	.04	.03	.05
smooth finish	.02	.02	.03	.04	.04	.03	.05
Hardwood plywood paneling, 1/4-in. thick, wood frame	.58	.22	.07	.04	.03	.07	.10
Water surface, as in a swimming pool	.01	.01	.01	.01	.02	.03	.00
Wood roof decking, tongue-and-groove cedar	.24	.19	.14	.08	.13	.10	.15
Wood panels							
1 in. thick, 6 PCF glass fiber with fabric face	.08	.34	.79	1.07	1.09	1.07	.80
2 in. thick, 6 PCF glass fiber with fabric face	.25	.99	1.2	1.14	1.06	.95	1.00

[a] Courtesy of Owens-Corning Fiberglas.

Where:

$$A = \alpha_1 S_1 + \alpha_2 S_2 + \cdots + \alpha_n S_n$$

α_n = sound absorption coefficient of nth surface

S_n = area of nth surface

Impact Isolation

There are three methods available to reduce impact noise. These are as follows:

1. A resilient pad on top of the floor, such as a carpet with underlayment.
2. A floating floor above the structural floor, supported by neoprene vibration isolation devices or springs and neoprene pads.
3. A resiliently hung ceiling below the floor on which the impacts occur. The use of resilient steel furring channels will improve the impact noise reduction in wood frame construction, but will not be nearly as effective as the other measures.

Vibration Isolation

The isolation of vibrating machinery from buildings is one of the most effective means of noise control. Installation of quiet air conditioning machines on the roof of a lightweight structure often results in high machinery noise levels heard throughout the top floor and, in some cases, lower floors as well. Frequently, the reason for this is a lack of understanding of the elementary principles of vibration control. The simplest type of vibration isolation system is a resilient device, such as a spring or elastomeric mate-

Table 4. Sound Absorption of Plain Glass Fiber Board and Baffles

Product	Mounting	Octave Band Center Frequency, Hz 125	250	500	1000	2000	4000	NRC
Plain Glass Fiber Board								
1-lb Density glass fiber board								
1 in. thick	A[a]	.12	.28	.73	.89	.92	.93	.70
2 in. thick	A	.24	.77	1.13	1.09	1.04	1.05	1.00
3 in. thick	A	.43	1.17	1.26	1.09	1.03	1.04	1.15
4 in. thick	A	.73	1.29	1.22	1.06	1.00	.97	1.15
1 in. thick	E-405[b]	.56	.85	.70	.89	.93	1.06	.85
2 in. thick	E-405	.76	1.02	.98	1.07	1.04	1.20	1.05
3-lb Density glass fiber board								
1 in. thick	A	.06	.20	.68	.91	.96	.95	.70
4 in. thick	A	.84	1.24	1.24	1.08	1.00	.97	1.15
1 in. thick	E-405	.65	.94	.76	.98	1.00	1.14	.90
6-lb Density glass fiber board								
1 in. thick	A	.08	.25	.74	.95	.97	1.00	.75
4 in. thick	A	.75	1.19	1.17	1.05	.97	.98	1.10
1 in. thick	E-405	.68	.91	.78	.97	1.05	1.18	.95
Baffles								
24 × 48 × 2, 6 PCF glass fiber, total absorption per unit Sabins		3	6	13	16.8	15	15	12

[a] Type A (formerly No. 4): Material placed against a solid backing such as a block wall.
[b] Type E-405 (formerly No. 7): Material placed over a 16-in. air space. Data includes facings exposed to sound source, if specified.

rial, placed between the vibration source and the occupied structure. This is shown schematically in Figure 11.

When the rate of vibration is low, there is no isolation. When the rate of vibration is the same as the resonance frequency of the machine-isolator-building system, the vibration is even greater than without the isolation material. Only when the rate of vibration is well above the resonance frequency will there be vibration isolation, and where the floor is not massive and stiff the isolation achieved will also depend on the dynamic characteristics of the floor.

In the elementary case, the resonance frequency is simply described by the following equation:

$$f = 3.13 \sqrt{1/d}$$

Where:

f = resonance frequency in hertz

d = static deflection of the isolator, in inches

Since the amount of isolation is greater when the resonance frequency is low with respect to the driving frequency of the source (Fig. 12), the amount of isolation achieved is controllable by the static deflection. The higher the static deflection, the better the isolation.

Where the supporting structure, often a roof, is not rigid, but has a resonance frequency close to that of the isolation system, more vibration may be transmitted than would occur without isolation.

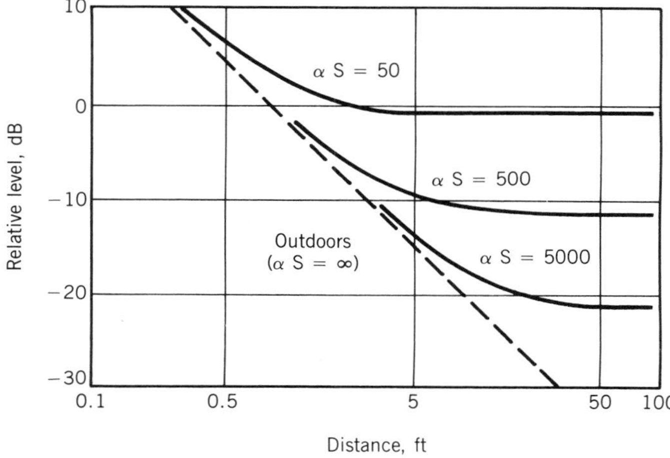

Figure 10. Sound level in a room drops as one moves away from the source until the reverberant energy is greater than that received directly from the source. Beyond that distance, the sound level remains constant.

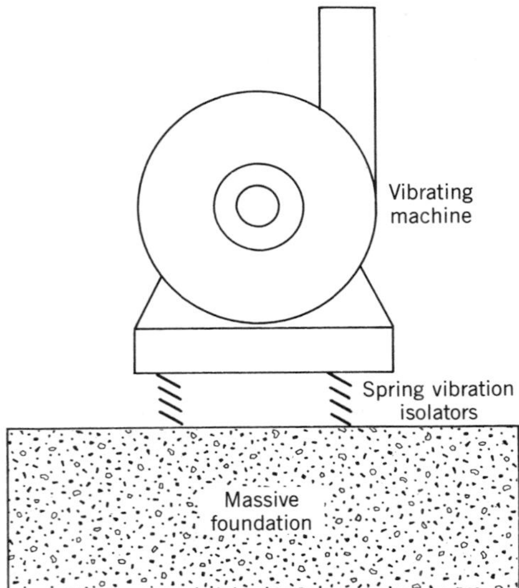

Figure 11. Isolation of a vibrating device from the building can be accomplished with a spring or elastomeric material between the source and the structure. However, the structure must have a much smaller static deflection than the spring for much isolation to be achieved.

When a machine is placed on a large, massive base, the acceleration of the base by the mechanical forces is reduced, since acceleration equals force divided by mass.

It is possible to use this method of vibration reduction in many situations, including isolation of large pumps and fans. It is almost impossible to use for large, curb-mounted air conditioning assemblies. Cooling towers have built-in mass when the sump is filled with water, and they are relatively easy to isolate using appropriate springs.

Flanking transmission paths also occur in vibration isolation systems where the piping and electrical connections can act to tie the vibrating machine to the structure. Also, even where flexible sections of piping are installed, the fluid can transmit pump pulsations across the flexible section.

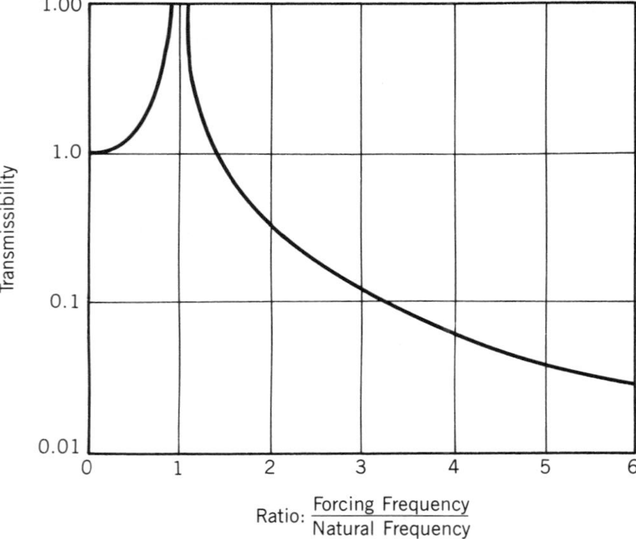

Figure 12. The relation of vibration transmission to the spring resonance frequency and the driving frequency. No vibration reduction occurs until the driving frequency is greater than 1.4 times the resonance frequency. Damping in the isolator, such as occurs in elastomeric materials, reduces the magnification at resonance, but also reduces the isolation at speeds above resonance. Selection of a good isolator is a compromise.

Reduction of Piping-transmitted Noise

Reduction of piping-transmitted noise in buildings is generally handled by providing flexible mechanical breaks between the piping and the vibrating machinery, and between the piping and the building structure (Fig. 13). Efforts to use flexible devices or mufflers to prevent the transmission of fluid-borne noise along the stream have seldom been completely successful by themselves.

Duct Noise

The control of duct-borne noise in buildings has been studied extensively and methods for predicting the noise and the reduction provided by various duct elements is available (1). The basic methods of duct noise control are as follows:

1. Providing flexible joints in the duct where it connects to a rotating machine or to a system containing a rotating machine.
2. Lining the duct with sound absorbing material for appropriate lengths, especially before and after elbows.
3. Installing mufflers, often called "silencers" or "sound traps," in the duct system to reduce the energy trans-

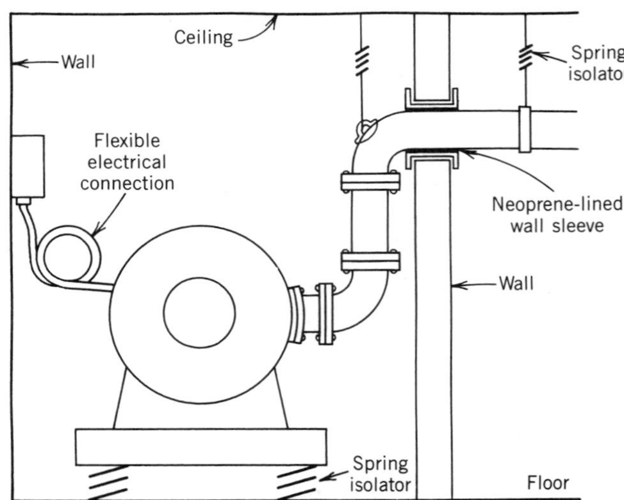

Figure 13. Vibration isolation of machinery can be vitiated by solid connection of piping and conduit to the structure. The flexible connecting methods shown will preserve the isolation.

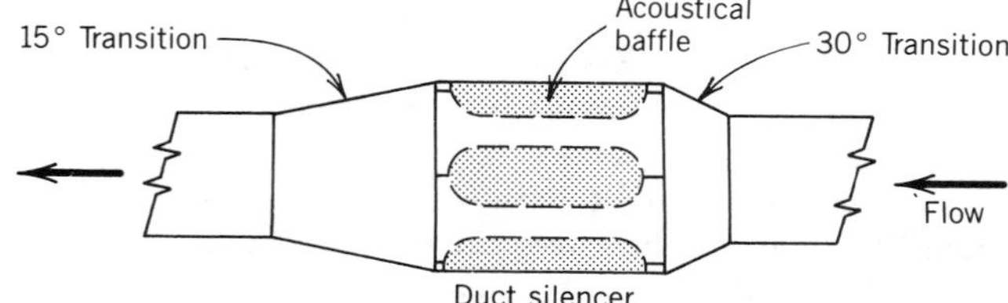

Figure 14. Schematic of a typical air conditioning duct muffler or "silencer," shown with the transitions usually required to reduce the air velocity through the unit.

cies using packaged mufflers in lengths of 3–7 ft. Also available are acoustical devices to serve as transfer ducts and louvers. Data for a variety of units are shown in Table 5.

Acoustical plenums can sometimes be fabricated by lining header ducts and small machine enclosures. The maximum noise reduction available from an acoustical plenum is the ratio of plenum surface area to exit area, expressed in decibels, typically 6–8 dB. Special plenums can be designed with internal barriers that permit noise reduction as high as 50 dB to be achieved in the mid-frequency range. Comprehensive treatment of noise control air conditioning equipment and systems is given in the literature (1,9).

Table 5. Noise Reduction Provided by Air Handling System Noise Control Devices[a]

	Octave Band Center Frequency, Hz							
	63	125	250	500	1000	2000	4000	8000
Insertion loss of 3-ft long duct muffler (flow: 1000 fpm)	7	12	16	28	35	35	28	17
Insertion loss of 3-ft long duct muffler, noise "flow" opposite air flow, 1000 fpm	7	13	17	30	36	33	26	13
Insertion loss of 5-ft long duct muffler (flow: 1000 fpm)	8	18	24	40	45	46	41	26
Insertion loss of 5-ft long duct muffler, noise "flow" opposite air flow, 1000 fpm	11	21	25	43	47	44	39	22
Insertion loss of 7-ft long duct muffler (flow: 1000 fpm)	10	20	35	45	50	43	45	34
Insertion loss of 7-ft long duct muffler, noise "flow" opposite air flow, 1000 fpm	12	23	37	46	51	48	44	30
Insertion loss of 5-ft long, low pressure drop duct muffler (flow: 2000 fpm)	6	7	13	21	29	39	20	14
Insertion loss of 5-ft long, low pressure drop duct muffler, noise "flow" opposite air flow, 2000 fpm	7	8	14	23	31	33	17	11
Noise reduction of acoustical louvers	11	13	17	18	19	20	18	15
Transfer ducts less than 10 in. in thickness, 48 in. long	23	32	35	41	51	57	58	50

[a] Courtesy of the Industrial Acoustics Company, New York.

mitted in a relatively short device. A typical duct muffler with transitions is shown in Figure 14.

4. Installing an acoustically lined plenum (possibly lining an existing plenum).

Although the mechanical break does not provide very much initial reduction, without such a break the sound will be transmitted past any duct lining or muffler, vitiating the effectiveness of the device.

The lining of ducts is most effective when the lining is at least 1/10 wavelength at the lowest frequency of interest. In past years, this was considered to be 125 Hz, and a lining thickness of 1 in. was used. At lower frequencies, there is some energy absorbed by the sheet metal duct. To obtain large amounts of absorption at low frequencies, long lengths of lining or reactive mufflers are required. During the past 30 years, the development of both the fiber-filled muffler and the "packless" muffler has resulted in the ability to control noise over a wide range of frequencies using packaged mufflers in lengths of 3–7 ft.

BIBLIOGRAPHY

1. *Systems, ASHRAE Handbook,* American Society of Heating, Refrigerating, and Air Conditioning Engineers, Inc., Atlanta, Ga., 1987, p. 52.3.
2. L. L. Beranek, "Revised Criteria for Noise in Buildings," *Noise Control Engineering* **(3)** (1), 19 (1957).
3. W. E. Blazier, "Revised Noise Criteria (RC Curves) for Application in the Acoustical Designing of HVAC Systems," *Noise Control Engineering* **16** (2) (1981).
4. *Directory of Certified Applied Air Conditioning Products,* Air Conditioning and Refrigeration Institute, Arlington, Va., Jan. 1988.
5. *Directory of Certified Unitary Air Conditioners, Air Source Heat*

Pumps, Sound Rated Outdoor Unitary Equipment, Air Conditioning and Refrigeration Institute, Arlington, Va., Jan. 1988.

6. *Standard Method for Laboratory Measurement of Airborne Sound Transmission Loss of Building Partitions, Designation E90–85, Annual Book of ASTM Standards, Construction, Section 4, Volume 4.06.* ASTM, Philadelphia, Pa., 1987, pp. 783–794.
7. *Standard Test Method for Sound Absorption and Sound Absorption Coefficients by the Reverberation Room Method, Designation C423–84a, Annual Book of ASTM Standards, Construction,* Section 4, Volume 4.06, ASTM, Philadelphia, Pa., 1987, pp. 161–171.
8. L. L. Beranek, *Noise and Vibration Control,* McGraw-Hill, New York, 1971, pp. 305–307.
9. E. M. Harris, ed., *Handbook of Noise Control,* 2nd ed., McGraw-Hill, New York, 1979.

See also Acoustical Design—Places of Assembly; Acoustical Insulation and Materials; Acoustics—General Principles; Ceilings; Sealants; Sound Reinforcement Systems

Lewis S. Goodfriend, PE
Lewis S. Goodfriend & Associates
Cedar Knolls, New Jersey

NOMADIC ARCHITECTURE

Nomadic architecture includes a broad range of building forms that have evolved in response to, or developed out of, the requirements imposed by a nomadic lifestyle. The term nomadism refers to populations (human or other) who effect periodic or cyclical displacements over time in order to obtain their economic subsistence, or to pursue religious, military, or political activity. The type of movement depends on the nature of the activity as well as on topographic and climatic factors, so that cycles of movement may vary from days to weeks, from seasons to years. Nomadic architecture therefore includes the domiciles of hunters, gatherers, pastoralists, and fishermen who follow the habits of wild or domesticated animals (whose movements are themselves dictated by climate, water resources, and topology), as well as agriculturalists who periodically move to new farm sites and itinerant tradespeople and craftspeople whose skills are in demand over a wide region. Other itinerant lifestyles include military and circus life, periodic pilgrimages, and, more recently, short-term hiking and climbing expeditions. Contemporary nomadic lifestyles are also engaged in by vacationers and retirees.

A nomadic lifestyle presumes the need for a transportable building package that is easily assembled and dismantled, is pliable, and has a weight adapted to the available means of transport—human porterage or draft animal in the case of traditional societies, mechanical in the case of contemporary societies.

Few traditional nomadic lifestyles persist in the Western world, but a survey of close to 600 non-Western cultures reveals that approximately 25% of the peoples surveyed continue to live a migrant, seminomadic, or nomadic life, often alternating between transhumance during some seasons and a sedentary existence in a fixed settlement during others (1). Recent trends in the Western world, however, indicate a marked increase in nomadism in response to economic demands, social change, and longer life spans.

Historically, nomadic architecture involving transhumant life-styles has been associated with temporary building forms, in contrast to sedentary living and permanent buildings. It should, however, be considered as permanent as any other architecture that uses natural materials, in the sense that building components are reused, reassembled, and inherited from one generation to the next, as people return to previously occupied or adjoining "permanent" living sites.

On the basis of use, two categories of nomadic building types have been distinguished: those used by rural nomads (ie, hunters, gatherers, pastoralists, and fishermen) and those used by urban dwellers (ie, princes and warriors) (2). The former include the conical-framed tents of northern Eurasia and North America, the cylindrical framed tents with conical or domed roofs of the central Asian steppes, and the stressed-skin tents of the Near and Middle East and North Africa. The latter category includes the cloth pavilions, or ridge and parasol tents, used for pragmatic military purposes and for ritual and congregation, whether political, religious, symbolic, or recreational. Available evidence suggests that in many instances these latter structures evolved out of the rural ones in the course of the growth of large-scale social structures, political institutions, and economic complexities resulting in urbanization.

Until the recent publication of several surveys (see bibliography), information on the history of nomadic architecture was available only in scattered records and accounts. Surveys of architectural history provide few, if any, references. Historic documentation consists of two kinds: the material record and published sources. The material record includes data from in situ archaeological investigations, from representation on classic finds, and from museum artifact collections. The published record includes written and graphic renderings scattered over time such as travelers' accounts and military reports.

The richest sources of information can be found in the literature of the social sciences. The ethnographic and ethnologic study of contemporary or near-contemporary nomadic societies, using folklore, ethnographic description, and oral history to record both emic and etic data, provide revealing insights into the sociocultural behaviors associated with nomadic architectures, the value systems that underlie them, and the meaning that their creators and users attach to them.

RURAL NOMADIC ARCHITECTURE

The earliest suggested evidence for nomadic architecture appears in the arctic tundra Ice Age on the Ukrainian steppes where late Mousterian and upper Paleolithic reindeer-hunting peoples roamed, approximately 40,000 B.C. Archaeological reconstruction reveals that these hunters built a low, conical framework that they covered with animal skins and restrained with mammoth bones, because forest resources and building technologies were so limited. Warming climates and the domestication of the reindeer and horse led to changes in the type of transhumant lifestyle and to the emergence of an elongated, cupolalike conical tent, the predecessor of the North American tepee.

Early Egyptian hieroglyphic texts refer to the nomadic Beja (a people who still live in the Nubian desert near the Red Sea coast) as early as 2700 B.C. Rock paintings at Tassili-n-Ajjer in the Algerian Sahara, dating from a yet-verdant environment several millenia B.C., include a number of illustrations of proto-Fulani women building their mat-frame tents. Few Assyrian, Greek, and Roman sources make reference to vernacular nomadic architecture; one exception is the *mapalia* sometimes found in genre scenes represented in North African Roman mosaics. The first description of cylindrical framed tents occurs in Marco Polo's accounts of his travels in central Asia.

The four main families of rural nomadic architecture, classified according to shape, material, and structural principles, are (*1*) skin-covered, vertically extended, conical structures; (*2*) felt-covered, cylindrical, trellis-frame structures; (*3*) textile- or skin-covered rectangular tensile structures; and (*4*) domical, ribbed arch structures covered with mats or thatch. These four main families extend in broad latitudinal bands around the globe. Conical tents are found across the cold, northern margins of Eurasia and North America, from the Scandinavian highlands to Labrador. Felt-covered trellis-type tents are spread across the plateau lands of central Asia, westward to Iran. Textile tensile structures are dispersed over the Arabian, Turkish, and Saharan plateaus, from the Mediterranean littoral to 15° latitude. The bent rib dome prevails in the upper savannah

Figure 1. The Kazak yurt *kibitka,* the American Indian tepee, and the bedouin black tent as prototypes of nomadic architecture and examples of differential building responses to climatic variation (3). Courtesy of *Scientific American.*

and Sahelian belts north and south of the Sahara Desert (Fig. 1).

Climate and vegetation vary widely in these latitudinal belts. Hunting, fishing, and pastoralist techniques also vary in response to climatic conditions and natural resources; the grasslands steppe, the sand-blown desert, the arctic tundra, the forest taiga, and the humid rain forest invoke differential human responses and varying modes of transport. Seasonal and diurnal temperature changes, wind directions and their intensity, and cyclical precipitation further contribute to the formal and stylistic variations in these main families of nomadic architecture.

The conical tent, tepee, used by nomads in Siberia, the Lapps, the Plains Indians of North America, and as a summer residence by Alaskan Eskimos, consists of a framework of inclined poles arranged in a circle, tapering toward, and secured into, a central peak around which a vellum is wrapped. In regions of high snow precipitation such as in the arctic, polar, and subpolar environments, the conical tent is particularly resistant to snowdrifts and strong winds because support poles can be adjusted to different angles. The use of a vellum derives from the pastoral technology itself; reindeer, caribou, bison, and seal require different tanning skills. The hair of the animal, when left on the skin, provides additional warmth and density; hence it is used for the sleeping section of the tepee. When hair is removed from a pelt, the skin becomes translucent and is used selectively at the entrance, to admit light. Other variations, functions of available transport facilities, changing microclimates, and cultural preference, occur in the primary support structure, the method of fastening poles, the means for supporting internal weights, the structural relationship between support poles and the enveloping vellum, and the entrance and smoke hole openings.

The trellis-frame structure, yurt or *kibitka,* is most prevalent on the central Asian steppe where minimal rainfall, strong winds, and cold winters severely limit the supply and scale of timber resources. As a consequence, the structure is composed of a multitude of small members latticed together diagonally at their intersections. The completed form consists of a two- or three-part rigid wooden armature over which a covering is extended. Resting on the ground, the armature is structurally integral and independent of its cover, its stability a function of its own weight. Hence, the self-supporting frame can be transported without dismantling. The diagonal, crisscross wall assembly, with intersections securely tied, increases resistance to multidirectional winds. A tension band applied to the upper edge of the drum after the cover has been laid further contributes to its stability.

There are two types of trellis-frame tent, distinguished by whether the roof frame that sits on the lattice drum wall is conical or uses a system of curved arched ribs tapering to a tension ring and creating a domical profile. The latter type involves more sophisticated carpentry skills, which include bentwood and joinery. Both types have felt covers. Felt making, an ancient skill among the central Asian nomads and a predecessor to weaving, presupposes the presence of domesticated sheep. Although felt has no tensile strength, its density retains heat admirably within the cylindrical form. The cylinder itself acts thermodynamically to divert winds.

The true "tent" or tensile structure prevails in the arid belt stretching from the Atlantic coast of Africa to the eastern border of Tibet, where low plains interspersed with high plateaus and mountains yield even fewer building materials. The tent depends on two critical elements: the supporting poles and the skin, or vellum, stretched taut by means of rope stays or guys. The term tent derives from *tenta,* the feminine gender of the Latin *tentus,* which in turn is derivative of the Latin verb *tendere,* to stretch. The poles are held rigid by tension created in the cords fixed to pegs anchored in the ground. When the skin is removed, the entire structure collapses. Depending on the prevailing wind intensity, the rope stays will vary in length. Differential pole pitch, variation in cover material (ie, woven textile or animal skin), and types of reinforcement combine further to resist wind and storms. The aerodynamic lines of the cover, which the position and angles of the support poles create, are often changed in response to shifting winds.

Although some nomadic groups, such as the isolated Tuareg who travel on the edge of the Sahara Desert, use leather for the tent cover, it is generally made of an assemblage of narrowly woven strips, *fliq,* of a combination of sheep, goat, and camel hair, in colors ranging from white through earthen hues to black, sewn together into a rectangle. Although a black tent absorbs more heat, it also provides more shade in the hot desert sun. Furthermore, the heat is retained and slowly radiates at night when the temperatures drop drastically. The absorbed heat can be diurnally modulated by the loose weave and the adjustable side flaps. With the rare rains, the yarns swell and expand, closing up pinholes. The natural oils of the animal hair also shed water as necessary. Sometimes a second, white lining is stretched over a section of the tent (usually in the sleeping area), to further modulate the temperature. The two building technologies critical to the success of a true tent are weaving and woodworking. Not only are floors, walls, and roofs made of textiles, but wall hangings, saddlebags, carpetbags, carpets, containers needed for the moving process, and the tent "furnishings" are also woven. The fame of Kurd, Baluchi, Turkoman, Bokhara, and Qashqai carpets had its humble beginning in the skills of the tent weaver and tent maker.

The domical, ribbed arch structure becomes a prevalent building type in areas of cultural contact between nomadic and sedentary lifestyles, in regions characterized by seminomadic living such as on the edges of the desert, in regions where nomads maintain a symbiotic relationship with their sedentary neighbors, and on occasion when sedentary agriculturalists have become nomadic. These mat-frame domes depend on the bowing action of the ribs for their stability, and they require a firm ground anchorage, obtained by using a circle of stones at the base, sometimes in combination with a tension ring. Ribs are composed of an assemblage of acacia taproots and saplings (native to the arid zones), which bend easily. Once erected, the mat-frame dome is self-sufficient, so that a variety of covering materials such as thatch, skins, woven mats, and, more recently, plastic sheeting, can be used interchangeably on the same structure.

Although the main families of nomadic architecture tend to be associated with specific cultural groups, many of these cultures utilize several different kinds of structures in the course of their cycle of transhumance through hot, dry, wet, cold, and snowy seasons. In principle, the more sedentary the lifestyle, the greater the number and size of construction materials and ground anchors. The frugal use of building resources in harsh milieus is achieved through an intimate knowledge of terrain, vegetation, and climate. Frugality also depends on an empirical knowledge of the structural properties of the available building resources so that the interface between the resources and building technology is maximized. The slenderness ratio of a conifer trunk and the bending property of an acacia root lend themselves to different tent types.

It may be easier to cut new poles or arches in regions of abundant wood, but in wood-scarce environments frames are rarely left behind when a nomadic group moves from one site to another. Frequently, the transportation process constitutes an integral link between striking and pitching a structure in which loading, transporting, and unloading techniques involve using the same structural components that make up the shelter. Armatures, poles, and vellums are converted into litters and load supports among the Tekna and Tubu camel herders in the Sahara Desert; the Inuit Eskimos turn their summer tents into winter sleds; the Siberian Koryaks wedge their sleds against building walls to provide additional resistance to the fierce arctic winds; Qashqai nomads in the Near East convert their tent poles into rafts to ford swollen rivers; the Plains Indians create travois and platforms out of their tent poles; and the northern Kenya Gabra people convert bed rails and partition screens into camel litters and palanquins (Fig. 2).

The reuse and multi-use of building components endow them with the quality of heirlooms. Long-lasting, many of them are handed down from parent to child through generations of serviceable life. Beyond physical service, these building elements acquire a symbolic, meaningful existence of their own, translated through use into rituals and metaphor. More specifically, the structural elements that are perceived to be critical to engineering success are the most highly valued, the most intricately embellished, and the best maintained in the materials repertoire. Ridge beams, support poles, tension rings, and stay fasteners are intricately carved and joined, and seams, wearing edges, and stress points are heavily embroidered. These elements are the palette of the nomadic aesthetic (Fig. 3).

In both traditional and contemporary nomadic societies, the domicile is built by women. It is they who carry responsibility for creating, pitching, maintaining, striking, and transporting it. All domestic (not real) property relating to it, including its cover, armature, furnishings, and utensils, are in their hands and of their making. The loading and unloading of the household goods is equally the women's responsibility. Even in those instances where women do not weave the tapestries or mats, no longer tan and

(a)

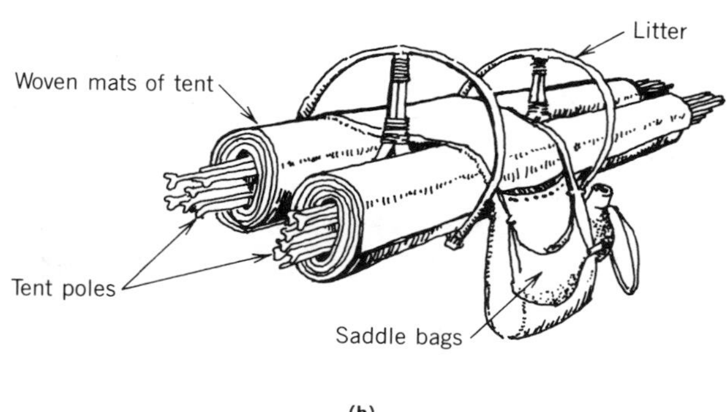

(b)

Figure 2. (**a**) Camel palanquins used by the Tekna in Mauretania and southern Morocco, 1946. Courtesy of Raymond Mauny, Phototheque IFAN, Dakar; (**b**) camel litter used by the Tubu in the central Sahara Desert (4).

decorate the vellums, and no longer work the wool into felt, it is still incumbent on a woman's family to provide these artifacts either as part of her dowry or on the birth of her first child.

In many instances, the creation of the nomadic domicile evolves directly out of behaviors associated with the marriage ritual itself. Among the Gabra of East Africa, the word for the armature tent, *min* or *man,* is directly derivative of the term for marriage, *min fuda,* "to put down a house," and echoes the building activities inherent in the four-day marriage ceremony. Among the Tuareg of West Africa, the term *ehen* is used synonymously for tent, marriage ceremony, and clan lineage. The term *ehen* carries a much broader concept than physical shelter *per se;* embedded in it is a metaphor for social support in the moral sense and a gender-discrete aesthetic.

Women builders are not professional in the sense of being casted or specially trained. Knowledge of the building process is a lore acquired by communal participation. Because the process is a recurrent one, the acquisition of skills and expertise unfolds during attendance in a lifetime atelier. While a woman can carry out the entire process alone, she more often calls on her daughters and other female relatives for help. This communal aspect is critical to learning because the knowledge is transmitted verbally, by participation, and through *in situ* observation. One of the things women do in their tents is make more tents.

Space (and the units of measure used for its definition) are often referred to anthropometrically. The span of a hand and the distance from elbow to fingertip establish the length and width of woven textile covers that in turn establish the area of a rectangular tent. The height of a person determines the length of a bed rail used to trace the radius of a circular area. Settlements of nomads are measured by the number of tents. While each structure constitutes a measure of economic viability and consumption, it is also a symbol for a married, productive female member of the group.

The absence of fixed, stationary building components in the environment appears to evoke a more tightly prescribed geometric system of spatial organization both within the volumetric spaces of the domicile and without in the settlement pattern itself (Fig. 4). The area within is divided into a cardinally oriented grid in which predictable social, ritual, and technical activities are carried out. The spatial order also follows a gender-discrete division so that the daily life of each sex unfolds in separate and segregated quarters. In the circle of a conical or domical frame structure, a hearth or a central pole establishes the line of bisection. In the rectangle, the spatial division is articulated by a pair or a row of poles that support a fabric divider, visually segregating the activities of each sex. Spaces are also divided into public and private do-

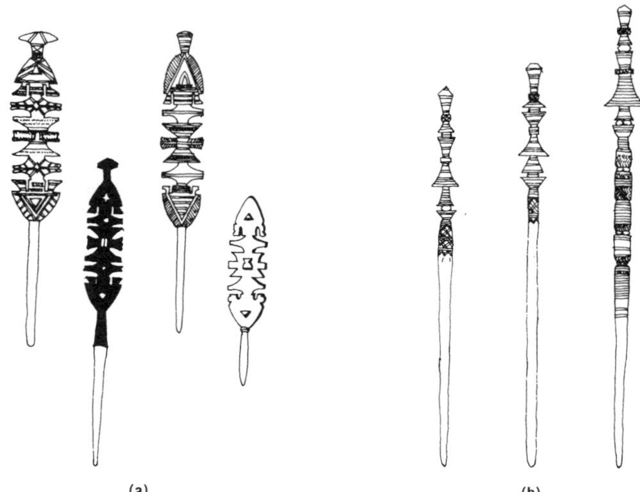

(a) (b)

Figure 3. (**a**) Cushion supports and (**b**) tent poles used by the Tuareg in the Hoggar of the Algerian Sahara (5).

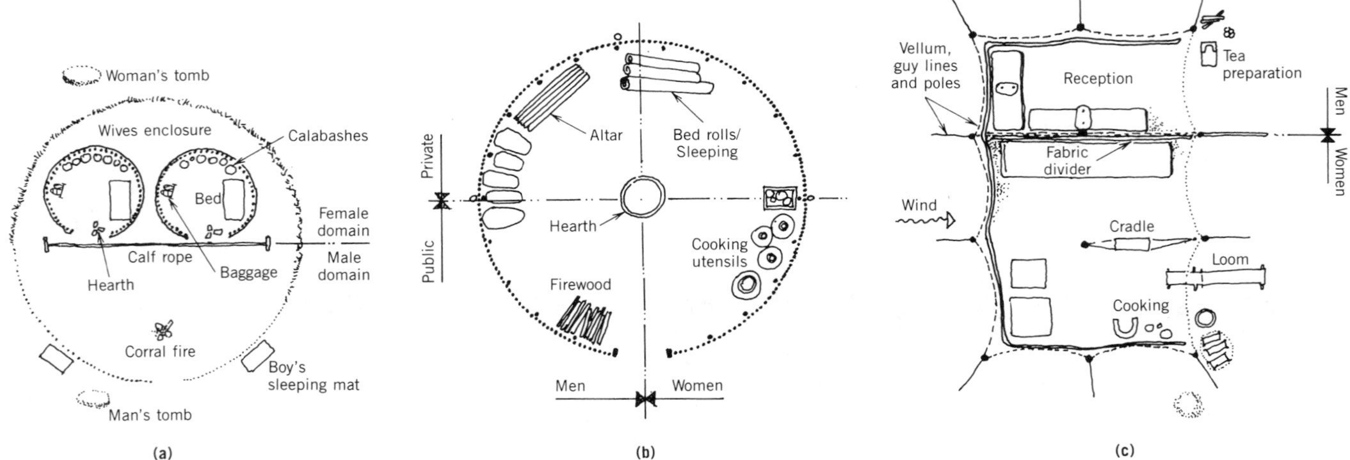

Figure 4. (**a**) Plan of a nomadic Fulani encampment, northern Nigeria; (**b**) plan of a Kirghiz or Turkestan yurt, Tartar *kibitkas* are similar; (**c**) plan of a bedouin black tent (6).

mains and into right and left sides, in association with cardinal directions. Frequently, the terms that define directions are synonymous with those used in referring to the building elements located in each of the defined areas.

The orientation of entrances (in reality a response to wind direction and velocity) is also rationalized into a cosmic myth. The Kababish in northeast Africa orient their doorways east toward Mecca whereas the Gabra face their entrances west "from whence we came." The front or "head" of the house is usually located opposite the entrance. This space, the most private and yet the most ornate, is where the most important family ritual artifacts are kept, whether these be associated with an altar, with birth, puberty, marriage, or death. In featureless environments where harshness rapidly bleaches out color, weathers exterior surfaces, and obliterates extraneous ornament and appendages, the rural nomadic architecture becomes a self-contained moving container for scenes of intense detail and color. Inside–outside space relationships are defined by this contrast rather than by fixed walls.

URBAN NOMADIC ARCHITECTURE

In the course of time, many vernacular nomadic structures that had evolved empirically were elaborated on and transformed into religious, military, and political symbols housing rituals and large congregations. The architectural imagery thus generated was incorporated into the urban environment, interwoven with the symbolism of the dome.

Innumerable references in the Old Testament refer to the nomadic, pastoral *genre de vie* of the Hebrews and to their use of tents (7). Their nomadism found quintessential ritual expression in the detailed description of the Tabernacle, a portable sanctuary set up in the center of their encampment at each stop in the wilderness. Exodus 26:4 describes how Yahweh (God) instructed Moses to make a Tabernacle, a "Tent of Meeting" with 10 sheets of fine twined linen, of purple stuffs, violet and red, and of crimson stuffs, finely brocaded with cherubs, each sheet 28 cubits long and 4 cubits wide, sewn together into two vast sections (Fig. 5). Over this fabric a second layer of woven goat hair, a third layer of ram skins dyed red, and a fourth layer of badger skins were to be laid. The supporting framework was to be made of acacia uprights and these were to be sheathed in rare metals. The detailed description suggests a close similarity with the black tents described above and still in use throughout the Near and Middle East. The space within the Tabernacle was divided into two equal parts: the Holy of Holies within which the Ark of the Covenant was located; and the sacred space for the priests, housing an altar and the candelabra, in which ritual sacrifices took place. A Great Altar was located at the entrance to the Tabernacle, in a forecourt, and the entire space was enveloped with a perimeter wall of hangings, which formed a rectangle 100 cubits long by 50 cubits wide. As a sacred, ritual center, the Tabernacle was a metaphor for the universe, a cosmic tent that subsequently was used as a spatial template for the plan of the Temple of Solomon.

In Isaiah 40:22 it is written that "It is he that sitteth upon the circle of the earth . . . that stretcheth out the heavens as a curtain, and spreadeth them out as a tent to dwell in." The metaphor finds concrete expression in the spatial organization defined by the ritual sacrifices enacted within the Tabernacle (8).

The Old Testament also contains several references to ancient Egyptian military tent encampments; how these looked is clear from the Egyptian records themselves such as the bas-reliefs at Ramesseum, Luxor, and Abu Simbel and annals and correspondence from as early as the sixth dynasty. The Assyrian record provides even clearer evidence for the proliferation of two types of tent: royal semicupola tents and domical tents framed with struts sheltering the activities of daily life in the fortified encampments. Both types are graphically illustrated on the bas-reliefs from Nineveh, Nimrud, and Kyunjik (9). The prevalent

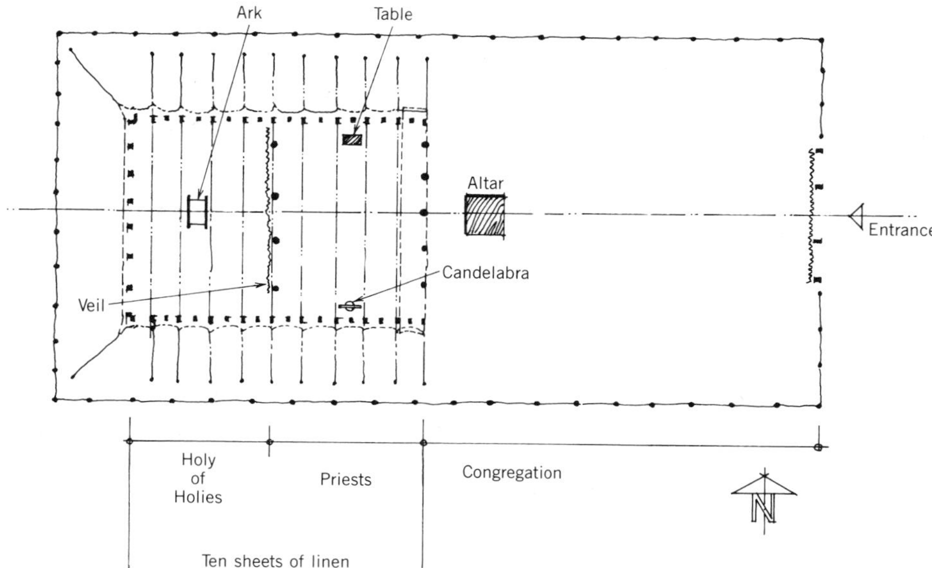

Figure 5. Plan of the Tabernacle and its fabric enclosure. Drawing based on descriptions in Exodus 25:27.

use of military and royal pavilions and service tents during the seven centuries of Assyrian conquest suggests the basis for the luxurious tent traditions characteristic of Xerxes and his successors, and in turn adaptation by the Greeks, because the few references to tents in the Greek literature (eg, Homer's *Odyssey, Iliad,* and *Aeneid*) appear to be in a Persian context (10).

The best classic documentation for military camps comes from various Roman accounts of their imperial expansion. In addition to written commentaries and archaeological monuments, Roman mosaics are an excellent source for both vernacular and military nomadic structures used in the course of time (11,12).

Three types of tent (all depicted on Trajan's column) were (*1*) the *papilio,* or butterfly tent, of the common soldier (Fig. 6); (*2*) a taller version of it with a lower gable roof used by officers; and (*3*) a marquee used by legion commanders. The vellum, composed of calfskins or goatskins stitched together in rectangular panels, was supported by a central ridgepole and kept taut with guys and triangular cross stays. Calfskin was preferred because it is more pliable and has a consistent thickness. The direction in which the skins were laid and sewn was important because skins are stronger along their horizontal dimension. The standardization and modularization into rectangles and the recurrent use of these tents coincided with the grid layout of entire camps; many features of the marching camps were adopted in the permanent forts, *limitanei,* that the Roman legions built in the far-flung provinces of their empire.

In the seventh century A.D., Islam swept across the arid belt of North Africa from its wellspring in the Arabian Peninsula and eastward to the Middle East across the steppes of western Asia, as far afield as China. A political–economic–religious phenomenon, it was instrumental in accelerating urbanization, but the sources of Islam's urban viability were the herders and pastoralists whose knowledge of caravan travel made long-distance trade and commerce possible over land masses. The black tent of the Arabs spread to the western shores of Mauretania, increasing in size and scale to accommodate the leadership of the sultanates, the sheikhdoms, and the emirates of North Africa, in whose hands the trade resided and on whom Islamic urban civilization depended. In contrast to the tepee and the yurt, the black tent can be expanded along both its rectangular axes by adding strips of woven vellum and increasing the number and size of supporting poles and crossbars. The enlarged and embellished *khaima* (Arabic) continues to be a primary part of North African panoplies during rituals, receptions, and celebrations.

The emergence of the Mongol and turkic empires during the thirteenth century contributed to the spread of the yurt and its transformation into a parasol tent as an architectural image of political and military conquest. Carried by Genghis Khan's troops on extensive campaigns, it found its way into battles waged in what is today Poland, Hungary, Bohemia, Austria, and the Balkans. By the end of

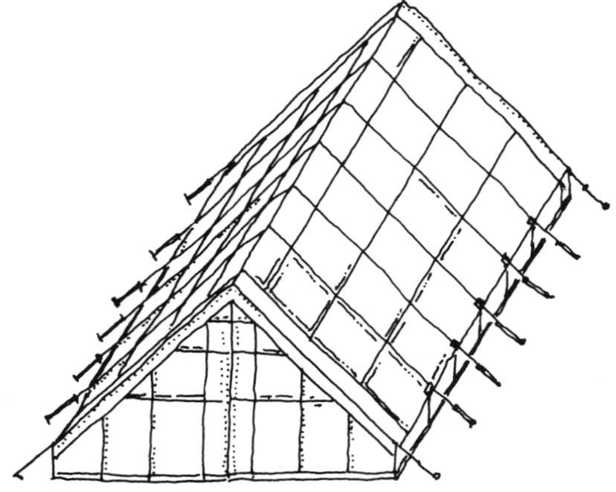

Figure 6. Roman leather tent or *papilio* (13).

his career, Genghis Khan had also conquered every nomadic tribe up to the shores of the Caspian Sea and the northern edge of Persia. He used a cavalry of nomads to rule, "anchoring his power in the self-sustaining and self-renewing vitality of the nomadic culture from which he sprang" (14). During this period of expansion, Persian historians served as high officials under Mongol sovereigns, because with the establishment of a feudal structure went the growth of institutions for conducting diplomacy and international relations. The parasol tent provided the setting.

The traditional custom of gift exchange at the conclusion of a battle helps explain the adaptation of parasol tents (and variations of them) by European powers during the Middle Ages. Accouterments of a conquered head of state were taken over and used so that the virtue, strength, and courage of the captured enemy could pass on to the conqueror. Tents were frequently exchanged as spoils of war and to cement alliances. In 1248, Louis IX received such a parasol tent from the king of Armenia; it was a sultan's pavilion from the site of a crushing defeat of Frankish forces. In turn, Louis IX gave a handsome linen tent, "made like a chapel, very costly for it was all of a fair, fine scarlet cloth" to the Khan of the Tartars (15). Confrontations among European, Mongol, Turkish, and Persian forces continued during the Crusades so that by the end of the thirteenth century the fabric pavilion was an essential part of every knight's equipment. Accounts of the Holy Grail, tales of the Crusades, and of tournaments as well as accounts of noble marriages and royal ceremonies all bear witness to the pervasive presence of tent imagery (Fig. 7).

Figure 7. Mid-fifteenth-century seignorial tent or *tref* (16).

The most splendid display of tents inherited from the age of chivalry occurred at a great festival held on the Field of the Cloth of Gold in 1520, at a summit meeting between Francis I of France and Henry VIII of Great Britain. Vying with each other for power, their entire courts were housed in hundreds of pavilions, all constructed of timber masts and canvas vellums over which were sewn great quantities of gold and silver textiles, velvets, and satins (17). The cartography of this period is rich in its use of the parasol tent as a symbol of royalty, as is amply illustrated in a "Chart of the Mediterranean Sea and Western Europe," drawn by Mateus Prunes of Majorca in 1559 (18). The location of kingdoms on maps was rendered not by palaces and castles (the more traditional symbol), but by rulers sitting in their fabric pavilions.

During this same century, Persian paintings and textiles suggest the flowering of a similar tradition in the Near and Middle East. Numerous Persian miniatures document not only the magnificent yurts and *kibitkas* in their depiction of Mongol exploits, but the presence of black tents in the genre of bedouin encampments. The scale and the sumptuous interiors of these royal tent–palaces can still be seen in the Ottoman tents preserved at Cracow, Poland, captured during the Polish–Turkish wars of the seventeenth century.

The nineteenth century witnessed a remarkable renaissance in nomadic architecture in response to new exigencies. Western imperial and colonial expansion involved major expeditions into new environments. Expeditions and explorations into little known lands followed on the awakening interest in geography and ethnography and led in turn to a renewed interest in vernacular resources. National pride and competition generated great fairs and international expositions. In 1807, Napoleon I met the defeated Tsar Alexander I aboard a barge, under a lavishly decorated parasol tent; empire style furniture designers Fontaine and Percier incorporated tentlike draperies into the design for Napoleon's bed, as well as those for men of means; Queen Victoria traveled on state visits with her personal tent; and a number of canopied bed designs exhibited at the International World's Fair of 1851, in London, received awards. The throne of Napoleon III was a close parallel to the baldachin parasol tent used by his predecessor (19).

Nineteenth-century military contingencies led to a reexamination of historical sources and a new appraisal of vernacular traditions (20). The French *tent d'abri* recalls the Roman *papilio;* the Swedish bell tent brings to mind the parasol tents of the age of chivalry; field officers were housed in ridgepole tents modeled on those used by seigniors during the Middle Ages; and a new design proposed by Godfrey Rhodes to the British army in 1858 drew its inspiration from the mat-frame structures of the Hottentots of southern Africa (Fig. 8).

Twentieth-century innovations in tensile architecture, reflecting the use of man-made materials and the social development of new nomadic lifestyles, are an extension of the continuum in the history of nomadic architecture. The same principles of transportability, the frugality of materials, ease of assembly, and resistance to harsh elements that underlay all nomadic structures led to the design of the North Face VE24 dome for high altitude climbing and trekking expeditions as a nomadic experience. The pilgrimage to Mecca, incumbent on every devout Muslim, as another kind of nomadic experience, inspired Fazlur Khan of Skidmore, Owings and Merrill to design an innovative tensile structure for the air terminal at Jid-

(a)

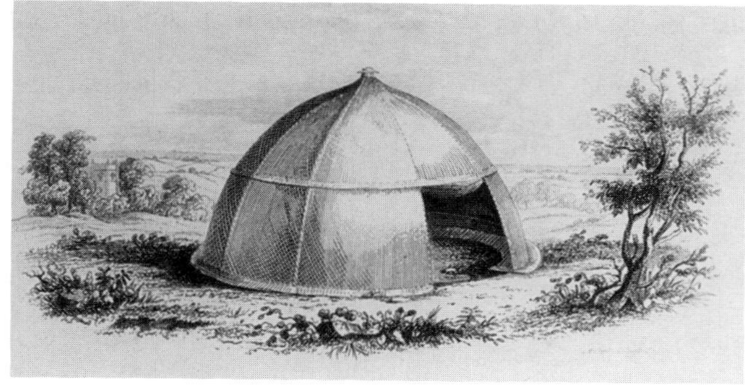

(b)

Figure 8. (**a**) Rendering of a southern African Hottentot mat-frame tent (21); (**b**) proposed design for a British military tent (22).

dah, Saudi Arabia, to accommodate the thousands of pilgrims who congregate there each year and to symbolize man's spirit of transhumance.

BIBLIOGRAPHY

1. G. P. Murdock, "World Ethnographic Sample," *American Anthropologist* **49,** 664–687 (1957).
2. P. Drew, *Tensile Architecture,* Westview Press, Boulder, Colo., 1979, p. 1.
3. J. M. Fitch and D. P. Branch, "Primitive Architecture and Climate," *Scientific American* **203,** 141 (1960).
4. Drawing after J. Chapelle, *Nomades noirs du Sahara,* Plon, Paris, 1957, p. 232.
5. Drawings after H. Lhote, *Comment campent les Touaregs,* J. Susse, Paris, 1947, Figs. 36, 37.
6. Drawing after H. R. P. Dickson, *The Arab of the Desert,* George Allen and Unwin, London, 1951, p. 75.
7. See Genesis 4:20, II Samuel 7:2, for example.
8. E. Leach, *Culture and Communication,* Cambridge University Press, Cambridge, UK, 1976, pp. 84–92.
9. Ref. 2, pp. 88–91.
10. Ref. 2, p. 72.
11. K. Dunbabin, *The Mosaics of Roman North Africa,* Clarendon Press, Oxford, UK, 1978.
12. T. Préchaur-Canonge, *La vie rurale en Afrique Romaine d'après les Mosáiques,* Presses Universitaires de France, Paris, 1962.
13. Drawing after G. Webster, *The Roman Imperial Army of the First and Second Centuries A.D.,* A. and C. Black, London, 1969, Fig. 26.
14. O. Lattimore, "Chingis Khan and the Mongol Conquests," *Scientific American* **209,** 57 (1963).
15. Ref. 2, p. 109.
16. E. E. Viollet-le-Duc, *Dictionnaire raisonné de mobilier français,* Vol. 6, V. A. Morel et Cie., Paris, 1858–1875, p. 351.
17. Ref. 2, pp. 116–121, for a detailed summary.
18. Geography and Map Division, Library of Congress.
19. E. M. Hatton, *The Tent Book,* Houghton Mifflin, Boston, 1979, pp. 30–40.
20. G. Rhodes, *Tents and Tent-Life,* Smith, Elder & Co., London, 1858.
21. Ref. 20, facing p. 114.
22. Ref. 20, facing p. 179.

General References

J. Bidault and P. Giraud, *L'Homme et la tente,* J. Susse, Paris, 1946.

T. Faegre, *Tents: Architecture of the Nomads,* Anchor Press, Garden City, N.Y., 1979.

C. G. Feilberg, *La tente noire,* Gyldendalske Boghandel, Copenhagen, 1944.

Nomads of the World, National Geographic Society, Washington, D.C., 1971.

J. Revault, ed., *Cahiers des arts et techniques d'Afrique du nord 4,* Editions Privat, Toulouse, France, 1955.

W. Creyaufmuller, *Nomadenkultur in der Westsahara,* Burgfried Verlag, H. Nowak, Hallein, Austria, 1983.

D. K. Jones, *Shepherds of the Desert,* Elm Tree Books, London, 1984.

J. Nicolaisen, *Ecology and Culture of the Pastoral Tuareg,* Grederiksholms, Copenhagen, 1963.

P. Verity, "Kababish Nomads of Northern Sudan," in P. Oliver, ed., *Shelter in Africa,* Barrie and Jenkins, London, 1971, pp. 25–35.

K. Birket-Smith, *The Eskimos,* trans. by W. E. Calvert, Methuen, London, 1959.

B. Collinder, *The Lapps,* Princeton University Press, Princeton, N.J., 1949.

A. A. Popov, *The Nganasan: The Material Culture of the Targi Samoyeds,* Indiana University Press, Bloomington, Ind., 1966.

F. Barth, *Nomads of South Persia,* Little, Brown & Co., Boston, Mass., 1968.

K. Ferdinand, "The Baluchistan Barrel-vaulted Tent," *Folk* **2,** 33–50 (1960).

S. Hallet and R. Samizay, *Traditional Architecture of Afghanistan,* Garland STPM, New York, 1980.

E. D. Phillips, *The Royal Hordes. Nomad People of the Steppes,* McGraw-Hill Inc., New York, 1966.

E. Rackow and W. Caskel, "Das Beduinenzelt," *Baessler-Archiv* **21,** 151–184 (1938).

G. Catlin, *Illustrations of the Manners, Customs and Conditions of the North American Indians,* 2 vols., George Catlin, London, 1841. Reprint 1964.

J. C. Ewers, *Murals in the Round,* Smithsonian Institution Press, Washington, D.C., 1978.

G. B. Grinnel, *The Cheyenne Indians,* 2 vols., Cooper Square Publications, New York, 1962.

R. and G. Laubin. *The Indian Tipi,* University of Oklahoma Press, Norman, Okla., 1957.

R. H. Lowie, *Indians of the Plains,* McGraw-Hill Inc., New York, 1954.

LABELLE PRUSSIN, PHD
The City College of the City University of New York
New York, New York

NOWICKI, MATTHEW

Matthew Nowicki, architect and educator, was born in 1910 in the Russian Siberian town of Chita to a well-to-do Polish family. For two years during his youth, he and his family lived in Chicago, where he learned English and became acquainted with U.S. culture. He grew up in Warsaw, graduating from the Polytechnic of Warsaw in 1936 with a Master of Architecture degree. During this period, he was influenced by the work of Le Corbusier. On graduation, he married the architect Stanislowa Sandecka, was named to the faculty of his school (1936–1943), and began practice. He received several commissions, but his office was closed at the time of the German invasion in 1939. During the war years, he worked as an instructor in the Technical School of the Municipality of Warsaw, a trade school, having learned brickwork for that purpose.

At the end of hostilities, he participated in the postwar planning for the rebuilding of Warsaw and was named Cultural Attaché to the Polish Consulate in Chicago (1945–1946), and in 1947 served as Poland's representative to the committee for the United Nations Building. Beginning in January 1948, Nowicki served as visiting critic at Pratt Institute in New York and served as a consultant to Wallace K. Harrison for the United Nations Building. When the communist government came into power in Poland, he applied for U.S. citizenship.

Nowicki was asked to be acting head of the Department of Architecture at the School of Design at North Carolina State College (now University) in Raleigh, where he served for a two-year period beginning with the fall term of 1948. His proposals for curriculum, published in the October 1949 issue of *Architectural Forum,* attracted wide support, and set the school in a new direction. At the end of World War II, the school attracted increasing numbers of students. Nowicki's kindness and devotion to hard work were an inspiration to the students, his clients, and other professionals.

Built on concepts including man, nature, and time, the curriculum was designed to include courses from related fields such as landscape architecture, architectural design, structures, descriptive drawing, humanities and history, city planning, and elective subjects. He found the opportunity during the summer of 1949 to work with Eero Saarinen at the Cranbrook Academy on a planning study for Brandeis University. In 1950, he undertook design of a number of buildings in Raleigh with William Henry Deitrick, in particular the North Carolina State Fairgrounds and the Dorton Arena (Fig. 1). In the summer of 1950, Nowicki collaborated with Clarence Stein on a proposal for Columbus Circle in New York and served as a consultant to Mayer and Whittlesey on a study for Chandigarh, India, a project that was finally awarded to Le Corbusier and Maxwell Fry. Nowicki's drawings made for Chandigarh

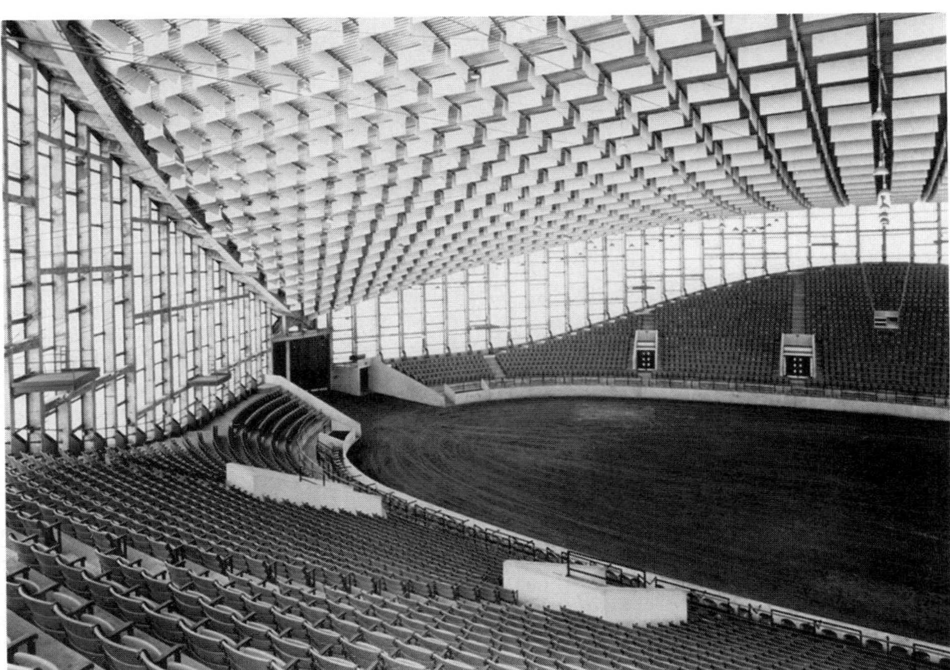

Figure 1. Dorton Arena, North Carolina State Fairgrounds, Matthew Nowicki in association with William Henley Deitrick. Photograph by Joseph Molitor. Courtesy of the American Institute of Architects Archives.

have been published, and are an interesting contrast to the work as built (1).

En route from India in August of 1950, he was killed in a plane crash in Egypt. The outpouring of articles and appreciations of Nowicki included a series of four articles written by Lewis Mumford for *Architectural Record* magazine in 1954. These were collected and published in Mumford's *Architecture as a Home for Man* in 1975 (2). Mumford emphasized Nowicki's humane approach to architectural design.

BIBLIOGRAPHY

1. B. H. Schafer, *The Writings and Sketches of Matthew Nowicki,* University Press of Virginia, Charlottesville, Va., 1973.
2. J. M. Davern, ed., *Lewis Mumford: Architecture as a Home for Man,* book 3, Architectural Record Books, New York, 1975, pp. 63–101.

Robert T. Packard, AIA
Reston, Virginia

NOYES, ELIOT

Better known for his industrial design than his architecture, Eliot Noyes (1910–1977) was one of few American architects to make significant contributions in both fields. Born in Boston, he spent his boyhood in Colorado before attending Phillips Academy in Andover, Mass. He considered becoming an artist, but at age nineteen decided on a career in architecture. Noyes entered Harvard College in 1928 and after receiving his B.A. remained in Cambridge and entered the Graduate School of Design in the fall of 1932. As the method of instruction at the GSD in the 1930s was still heavily influenced both ideologically and pedagogically by the now-stifling canons of the Ecole des Beaux Arts, Noyes turned to private study of the works of the modernist architects, in particular Le Corbusier, for his inspiration. Subsequently, Noyes discovered the Bauhaus and considered transferring to Dessau; however, in 1933 such a move was impractical. In 1935, during his third year of graduate school, seeking a new vantage point on his excessively traditionalist education, Noyes left Harvard to serve as an architect in an archaeological expedition to Iran. When he returned in 1937, the faculty at Harvard had undergone its famous transformation under Dean Hudnut. Walter Gropius and Marcel Breuer were now on the faculty. Modern architecture and the spirit of the Bauhaus permeated the new curriculum. This exposure to the Bauhaus philosophy of total design inspired Noyes's lifelong devotion to the integration of industrial design and architecture with painting and sculpture. Just as Gropius and Breuer were involved in all forms of artistic expression, so too was Noyes who became a sculptor, painter, and furniture designer as well as an architect.

On graduation from Harvard in 1938, Noyes entered the firm of Coolidge, Shepley, Bulfinch, and Abbott. He stayed there only a year before joining the office of Gropius and Breuer. In 1940, by the recommendation of Gropius, he became Director of the Department of Industrial Design at the Museum of Modern Art in New York. While at MOMA, Noyes organized the furniture competition won by Saarinen and Eames with one of the most widely copied chairs of the twentieth century—the Eames Chair.

By 1946, having decided on a career that would combine industrial design and architecture, Noyes was working as Design Director in the office of famed industrial designer Norman Bel Geddes. Two years later Noyes set up his own office in New Canaan, Conn.

A friendship with Thomas J. Watson, the future president of IBM, developed while Noyes was still at the Museum of Modern Art. This friendship blossomed into a designer–client relationship that created sleek crisp containers for delicate and intricate machinery, the most famous of which was the ubiquitous IBM electric typewriter. Their successes led to a standing relationship between Noyes and IBM. Eliot Noyes and Associates defined the corporate character of IBM by overseeing all aspects of design for the company, including that of corporate and branch offices. This unprecedented control of all design aspects of a corporation's activities created a unique environment in which both products and buildings were part of an integrated image of design.

Following Noyes's successful association with IBM, he received several commissions to redesign corporate images. As a "curator of corporate character," Noyes developed a policy in which his firm would not take on a client unless that client would "undertake to give the office regular and continuing assignments. In practice, this means architecture, interiors, display, and design tasks" (1).

Of Noyes's subsequent corporate makeovers that of the Mobil Corporation had the most impact on the American skyline. By reducing the basic enclosures of a gasoline station to a series of regular geometrical forms, Noyes created a delightfully sleek, sculptural, sheet metal-and-glass solution to the problem of providing a pleasant and clean environment for pumping gas. The bold primary colors and simple lettering were easily visible from a car traveling at 60 miles an hour. Equally sculptural were his designs for Cummins Engine Company's interiors while his design of the Vale-Marine engine was one in which all elements were reduced to simple geometric forms that, in combination, created an almost architectonic image. Similarly expressive were his design projects for Westinghouse Corporation. Most notable were his subway car studies, which seemed to capture the essence of the Machine Age vitality. These same clear, crisp lines appeared in his machinery enclosures for Perkin-Elmer.

Of course, this corporate design practice spilled over into architecture. It is no surprise to find that Noyes's buildings for corporate America were concise thin-skinned expressions of the Machine Age. In the same way that his designs for machinery clothed complex mechanical workings in simple skins, his buildings were clear statements enclosing complicated corporate personnel organizations. Noyes's house designs, in particular, were composed of simple, separate, block-like volumes in which diverse activities were meant to occur. In the interiors of his dwellings, these volumes were often separated only by the suggestion of an enclosure made through the use of wall screens or implied by wall placement. In the tradition of Wright, the division of living areas from dining areas was often denoted by a fireplace. The almost Miesian rectilinearity was tempered by his use of natural materials in their simplest forms. The choice of materials varied from region to region in the United States, signifying Noyes's belief in the necessity of regional differences in U.S. architecture, based on variations in climate and materials. This difference was expressed in the skin, not the structure or plan, of the building. At the same time he used these materials to form house components that performed double duty; stone walls began as part of the house then terminated as garden walls. It was only in the use of these natural materials that a Noyes house could be separated from a mainstream International style house.

Given Noyes's early interest in Le Corbusier it is not surprising that many of his houses followed at least a few of Corbusier's concepts, such as the incorporation of pilotis, strip windows, and open plans. Like Le Corbusier, Noyes was not afraid to experiment with new structural techniques to create a habitable environment. The urge to experiment with and create new structures was also a characteristic of his house designs. Noyes's houses built from concrete sprayed on inflatable forms was one such effort. In the final analysis Noyes and his practice was the embodiment of the principles learned while studying under Gropius and Breuer. He was a true modernist.

BIBLIOGRAPHY

1. S. Kelly, "Curator of corporate character: Eliot Noyes and Associates," *Industrial Design* **13,** 40 (June 1966).

General References

"Eliot Noyes," *Architectural Review* **121,** 361 (May 1957).

"Interiors 25: Year of Appraisal," *Interiors* **128,** 142 (Nov. 1965).

STEVEN BEDFORD
Middlebury, Connecticut

NUCLEAR FACILITIES. See POWER GENERATION—NUCLEAR

NURSING HOMES. See HEALTH CARE FACILITIES—CONTINUING CARE

O

OCCUPATIONAL SAFETY AND HEALTH ADMINISTRATION (OSHA).

See Zoning and Building Regulations

OFFICE BUILDINGS

DEFINITION, DESCRIPTION, AND HISTORY

Office buildings provide places for the collection, organization, and exchange of information. They house the leadership, management, and clerical staff of corporate organizations. The present day corporate office, be it of high-rise or low-rise construction, is a highly sophisticated environment, the product of over 150 years of refinement of a specific building type. The first office buildings as a distinctive type appeared in England in the early 1800s. They were the County Fire Office (1819) by Robert Abraham, and three insurance offices by C. R. Cockerell: the Westminster, Life and British Fire Office (London, 1831–1832); the Sun Fire Assurance Office (London, 1841–1842), and the Liverpool and London Office (Liverpool, 1855–1857). It is arguable that the sixteenth-century Town Hall of Antwerp, the seventeenth-century Town Hall of Amsterdam, and the Uffizi in Florence were office buildings.

The Uffizi, designed by Giorgio Vasari (1560–1571) for Cosimo I de Medici, housed the administrative offices of government and family commercial enterprise. The earliest banking office is documented as the Banco Mediceo (1455), a palazzo in Milan: "one must imagine negotiations taking place in any room of the palace, but some space set aside for the storing of money, and probably . . . goods, and also some space for clerks keeping the books" (1). During the early fifteenth century, double-entry bookkeeping was a highly prized skill that contributed to the growth of commerce and mercantilism throughout Europe.

In pre-industrialized times the office or counting room was a part of a merchant's dwelling, which was often adjacent to his warehouse. When manufacturing was carried out as a craft, more likely than not, the artisan's house was dwelling, shop, and office, the separate functions carried on in separate rooms or stories of the same structure. With the shift to mechanized and industrial means of production, manufacturing organizations became larger and more complex, requiring an increase in administrative and bookkeeping functions. Just as the size and complexity of the office functions attached to specific manufacturing operations increased, so, too, did the sister institutional functions of banking, financing, exchanging, and insuring.

Thus, it can be said the office building type derived its form from both the dwelling and the warehouse. Italian palazzi of the Renaissance serve as architectural models for many early office buildings (1).

Initially, these structures were of conventional masonry bearing wall facade construction; by the 1830s specialized office buildings for insurance companies were located in groups along the Strand, and on Fleet Street. Generally, these buildings were four to five stories high, the maximum distance that could be comfortably climbed by stair. In this era preceding the development of electric light, the maximum use of glass to permit natural lighting of the work area was desirable. Traditional stone construction limited window size, but the technology of cast-iron framing construction, which had been employed in warehouses and factories in England since the 1790s, allowed larger areas of glazing. While cast-iron columns had been in use for interior structure for some time and had made possible the creation of larger loft office spaces with fewer interior columns, the use of cast iron as a wall cladding material posed a dilemma of aesthetics and taste to architects and laypersons alike. Often masonry was combined with cast iron on the street facades of buildings. Despite objections from the aesthetically conservative, iron and glass facades combined with cast iron framing were developed in Britain as well as in the United States to meet the space and day lighting needs of the new loft office building type. Beginning in New York in the late 1840s, Daniel Badger and James Bogardus operated iron foundries that produced prefabricated modular building facades, and column and framing elements. Notable architectural examples were Bogardus's Laing Store (1848) and the offices of Harpers (1854).

Elisha Otis installed the first safety elevator in the Haughwout Building (New York, 1857), designed by J. P. Gaynor and Daniel Badger. With the introduction of the elevator to the metal framed building, the limits set on building height by stair and masonry construction were removed. Robert A. M. Stern summarized this development (2):

> The building of lofts quickly became the building of commercial palaces, and today the Haughwout Building endures as a perfect fusion of the American Dream—an idealized pastiche of Renaissance Italy bolted together with up to the minute Yankee ingenuity of Daniel Badger's Architectural Iron Works. Cast-iron construction established the principle of repetitive rhythms as a natural expression for prefabricated construction, as well as the idea that traditional styles could take on new life when translated into new materials rendered on a vast new scale.

The industrial growth that built factories also increased the demand for administration and bookkeeping, in turn creating a clerical industry with volumes of paperwork. Inventions of office machines to aid in these tasks included the duplicator by Gerstener in 1861 and the first practical office typewriter by E. Remington and Sons in 1868. Written communication was augmented by the development of the needle telegraph in 1837 by Cooke and Wheatstone. The Morse telegraph had its first public use in 1844, and by 1868 most American cities were connected by telegraph. In 1876 Alexander Graham Bell patented the telephone, which, in its early years, served as a means for short distance communication. In 1879 Thomas Alva Edison perfected the incandescent light bulb. Soon thereafter he set up his Pearl Street generating station, providing the first electricity to a portion of New York City. By the late nineteenth century the office had become the center of operations and communications, independently located from manufacturing, warehousing, financial, or commodity exchange functions.

In the latter half of the nineteenth century new office streets developed in London, on Victoria Street in 1871 and Shaftesbury Avenue shortly after. By the 1880s office buildings began to be concentrated in downtown Manhattan and in the Chicago loop district.

Following the catastrophic Chicago fire of 1871, land costs and investment pressures drove the design and construction of buildings to greater heights. In Chicago and New York, companies began to concentrate their office operations in taller, denser buildings, antecedents of today's urban corporate headquarters.

It was in the latter half of the nineteenth century that this predominantly American building type, the skyscraper, evolved. The architect Cesar Pelli succinctly defines this building type: "Skyscraper is a word used to describe a very tall building, and the 'very' is a comparative adverb depending on time and place" (3). Louis Sullivan's Wainwright Building (St. Louis, 1891) by Adler & Sullivan became the model of this new building type.

The skyscraper is believed to be the result of three main forces: a technological breakthrough, combined with a shortage of land, and a man-made need for a triumphant symbol. Up until about 1880 the skylines of Chicago and New York were made up of church spires or domes mixed with cupolas and towers of public and private buildings. There was a land shortage issue at this time because the two cities had definite limits to their districts. Chicago was hemmed into a small area by a railroad yard, a river, and an elevated loop railway. The Wall Street area of New York was at the tip of a small island. It is true that both cities had no great difficulty in expanding their boundaries to include other areas, but the business districts had a greater ability to attract higher rents than the nearby commercial, manufacturing, warehouse, and residential districts. The land shortage issue was one of economics rather than lack of space.

New technological developments made it feasible to build high, and the financial situations in downtown Chicago and New York made it desirable. Subsequently, the skyscraper has become a conventional vehicle for more frankly secular aspirations, which have to do with erecting permanent marks of human ingenuity and daring. Rational justifications of the basic skyscraper concept, whether found in the logic of real estate or management theory, have often obscured, but have never extinguished, the fundamental urge to create man-made landmarks. Thus, ten-story structures such as the Western Union Building by George Post (New York, 1875) or the Home Life Insurance Building by William Le Baron Jenney (Chicago, 1884) were once skyscrapers. This points to a peculiar quality of this building type: its dependence on its relationship with its surroundings. "This relative quality certainly makes it a building type of our times" (4).

Pelli perceives four main periods of skyscraper development (3). The first began with the introduction of the elevator and continued until 1909. During this phase, architects attempted to adapt existing building types, chiefly the palazzo, to new heights permitted by elevators; the Flatiron building (New York, 1903) became important during this period (Fig. 1).

The second period began with the Singer Tower (New York, 1907) by Ernest Flagg, and the Metropolitan Life Tower (New York, 1909) by Napoleon Le Brun. This phase was characterized by "exuberant explorations of the possibilities inherent in the skyscraper type" (5), namely the sculptural and symbolic possibilities. This period ended in the mid-1930s; however, it produced many memorable commercial buildings: The Chrysler Building (New York, 1930) by William Van Alen; the McGraw-Hill Building (New York, 1929) by Raymond Hood; and perhaps the most important mixed-use project, Rockefeller Center (New York, 1931) by Reinhard & Hofmeister, Corbett, Harrison & MacMurray, Hood & Fouilhoux.

The third period began after World War II and lasted until the mid-1970s. This phase was characterized by the development of high-rise buildings as a variant of the skyscraper. Buildings of this phase were influenced by the European-based theories of the International style. Some examples are: Lever House (New York, 1952) by Skidmore, Owings & Merrill (SOM) (influenced by the German Mies van der Rohe); the Seagram Building (New York, 1958) by Mies with Philip Johnson; the World Trade Center

Figure 1. The Flatiron Building, New York, 1903, D.H. Burnham & Co.

Figure 2. Citicorp Center, New York, 1975, Hugh Stubbins & Associates. Courtesy of Edward Jacobs.

(New York, 1962) by Minoru Yamasaki; the John Hancock Tower (Chicago, 1970) and the Sears Tower (Chicago, 1974) both by SOM; and the CBS Building (New York, 1965) by Eero Saarinen.

The fourth period of the last two decades of the history of modern architecture in commercial and corporate design has been one of sorting out, developing, and transforming architecture out of the rationalist vision of the international style. The international style of the past thirty years was now found to be generally energy inefficient. By the end of the 1960s, the austere glass box was not able to hold much promise of practicality. Just as it had been economics, and not aesthetics, that had won the battle of modernism after World War II, it was economics that turned clients away from the Miesian model that had filled the international landscape since the mid-1950s.

During this period the success of a few notable commercial buildings inspired clients to be more receptive to alternatives to the glass box: the Ford Foundation and the John Deere and Co. building, by Eero Saarinen & Associates; the Pennzoil Place and the IDS Building by Philip Johnson/John Burgee; the Citicorp Center by Hugh Stubbins & Associates, Peter Woytuk, Design Partner (Fig. 2); and the John Hancock Center by SOM, Bruce Graham, Design Partner.

Also during this period many corporations grew tired of the problems of urban areas and chose to move out of the city. The notable low-rise buildings of this period are: the American Can and the Weyerhaeuser Co. buildings by Skidmore, Owings & Merrill; the Johns-Mansville World Headquarters (Fig. 3) and CIGNA Headquarters (Fig. 4) by The Architects Collaborative, Inc.; and the headquarters of Union Carbide and General Foods by Kevin Roche and John Dinkeloo.

In the last half of the twentieth century, the mixed-use commercial office building began to emerge. The failure of modern planning principles, which resulted in a lack of interconnectedness of the city fabric, had led architects, social thinkers, and politicians to explore the multi-use building. This category includes all buildings that harbor more than one of three functions of human life. The multi-use commercial building promises to resurrect from the failures of the past and the confusing complexity of the present a building form that allows urban life to unfold.

The 100-story John Hancock Center by Skidmore, Owings & Merrill and Watertower Place by Lobel, Schlossman, Hackl & Dart in Chicago are two examples of com-

Figure 3. Johns-Mansville World Headquarters, Denver, Colo., 1976, The Architects Collaborative.

Figure 4. CIGNA Headquarters, Bloomfield, Conn., 1984, The Architects Collaborative, Inc. Interspace, Inc. (interiors).

mercial projects that combine office, retail, and residential space, and parking in the same structure. Each element of the complex, including office, hotel, residential, and retail, benefits from integration with a larger, more prestigious project. With its higher visibility and more ambitious overall planning concept, the impact of the entire development is far greater than the sum of its parts. In addition to its more efficient methods of land use, assembly, construction, and financing, the mixed-use commercial complex encourages innovative design, often overriding outdated zoning regulations, improving traffic circulation patterns, and initiating planning variances beneficial to both the community and developer.

One of the most successful mixed-use commercial complexes is Copley Place (Boston, 1984) by The Architects Collaborative (Fig. 5). The site was a blighted triangle of highway ramps and intersections, a gaping void in the urban fabric. Built entirely on leased air rights above railway lines and turnpike cloverleafs, the project is developed in layers, with parking at its base, retail over parking, and office buildings over retail. Twin hotels anchor the ends of the project. With the addition of 100 residential units, Copley Place became a true mixed-use project. Battery Park City (New York 1986) by Cesar Pelli is perhaps the finest mixed-use design yet produced. It includes 6 million ft^2 of office space in four towers of glass and granite, with frequent setbacks and low pyramidal and domed tops.

In the future, this commercial building type will continue to evolve from isolation to greater interconnectedness with the community, enriching the social fabric and weaving together a rich and complex pattern of different uses and activities.

TECHNOLOGICAL INNOVATIONS

Several technological developments made it possible for the office building to develop. The first was the emergence of structural engineering in the early 1800s. Laws of physics and the strength of materials along with the documentation of the laws of statics predicted the behavior of structures. For the first time, generalized laws could be applied to forms and materials without relying, as was done in the past, on the trial-and-error method that had existed throughout architectural history.

The addition of cast-iron columns to the carbon steel frame was the second factor that made it possible for the clear differentiation between the supporting skeleton of a building and the enclosing envelope, freeing structures from their height limits of load bearing construction. The virtue of the skeleton frame over the load bearing wall was an improved strength-to-weight ratio resulting in economies of foundations and speed of erection. Since floors were no longer supported on timber, fireproof construction was possible.

The third development was the invention of the safe elevator by Elisha Graves Otis of New York City in 1853. He demonstrated his elevator that year at the Crystal Palace Exposition in New York City. Mr. Otis stepped onto a platform, it was hoisted above the ground, the hoisting rope was cut, and the elevator came to a stop. He then made the historic remark: "all safe gentlemen!" The commercial architecture of office buildings, hotels, and department stores evolved rapidly as the steam powered elevator was made available. Electric drive, push-button controls, and a speed of 700 ft/min were available by the turn of the century.

Figure 5. Copley Place, Boston, Mass., 1984, The Architects Collaborative, Inc.

The fourth development had to do with lighting and air-conditioning. Although commercial buildings were not limited in height, they were limited in depth by the need for natural light and proper ventilation. The invention of the electric light by Edison in 1870 and the development of the incandescent lamp in 1907 removed some depth limitations. In 1938 fluorescent tubes were invented. This resulted in reduced energy consumption, glare, and heat buildup, and also allowed the continuous use of artificial light in very deep spaces.

All up-to-date office space had to provide for heating and natural ventilation. Heating was provided by low pressure, hot water circulation in radiators located below windows. Ventilation was provided through fresh-air inlets behind radiators. Windows were also used for direct natural ventilation.

In 1902, Willis Carrier discovered the principles of air conditioning by controlling temperature, humidity, and air movement. The Larkin Building (Buffalo, N.Y., 1904) by Frank Lloyd Wright was one of the early air-conditioned buildings; its most remarkable feature is the use of open interior space made possible by new technological innovations.

The first fully air-conditioned office structure was the Milam Building (San Antonio, Texas, 1928) by architect George Willis. The PSFS (Philadelphia Savings Fund Society) Building in Philadelphia, by Howe & Lescaze, Architects, was the first truly modern, air-conditioned office tower. After World War II the level of technology was advanced enough for air conditioning to be localized into supply and return zones. This allowed designers to subdivide building interiors into cellular rooms as required. Because of the technological services that came about, new directions in office building layouts came into being.

Building services are typically housed in a "core" that includes the vertical transportation (elevators), toilets, stairs, air-conditioning shafts, electrical closets, and fan rooms. The core usually serves the office space surrounding it. The ideal arrangement of the core usually depends on the real estate market. Typical office floor sizes today are between 20,000 and 30,000 ft^2, with a consistent dimension of about 35–45 ft from the enclosing walls to the core. Because the mechanical services and lighting are usually housed in the ceiling, space between the floor and ceiling cavity is from 4 to 5 ft.

The logical extension of the mechanical revolution led to the totally artificial environment. The technology was advanced enough by 1942 to allow the Pentagon office building to be fully air conditioned. This project had an under-floor distribution network, a pneumatic interoffice communication network, and a fire alarm system.

CAST IRON IN COMMERCIAL BUILDINGS

The use of cast iron in commercial structures became common by the mid-nineteenth century. By the end of 1830, commercial building store fronts and columns and beams were being erected in cast iron in the United States and Europe. One of the first cast-iron front buildings in the United States was the Lorillard Building (New York, 1837). The building had cast-iron columns extending through the first two stories with cast-iron beams at both levels. In Europe (c. 1843) a four-story building at No. 50 Watling Street in London incorporated cast-iron beams and columns at the upper two stories, making large windows possible. Daniel Badger produced cast-iron commercial building fronts in New York City between 1840 and 1870 for two six-story buildings. The designs were in the single-story repetitive Venetian Renaissance style with bay widths of about 6 ft. A typical multistory cast-iron front was the five-story Haughwout Building (New York, 1857).

Inventor James Bogardus was the first in the United States to develop practical methods for the construction of skeleton frames of cast iron for buildings, and to prefabricate almost every part of a building, transport the parts to the site, and erect the building in record time—sometimes in a few weeks. Whereas cast iron had been used previously, starting in the UK, for the construction of portions of building frames and bridges, Bogardus was the first to develop a system for an entire building.

Thus, Bogardus accomplished the early pioneering work that eventually led to wrought iron and, later, steel skeleton-framed buildings, and, finally, to the skyscrapers of today. His earlier buildings were not completely framed with cast iron. Eventually, Bogardus developed methods for making cast-iron fronts for buildings, another element of architecture that soon spread from New York City to other parts of the country. These cast-iron fronts might be considered the forerunners of the curtain walls of metals and other materials in use today.

In the UK, cast-iron fronts similar to those manufactured in the United States were made for export to the expanding colonies and other markets, as well as for use at home. The Jamaica Street Warehouse (Glasgow, 1855) and Oriel Chambers (Liverpool, 1864) designed by Peter Ellis, with their repetitive bay windows that foreshadowed some of the Chicago buildings of the 1880s and 1890s, are good examples. The office building at 24 Rue Reáumur in Paris, which is attributed to Georges Chedanne, uses riveted wrought-iron columns and sheet iron spandrels in a totally fresh way.

Around this time art nouveau architects, among them Victor Horta, Hector Guimard, and Frantz Jourdain, used wrought iron forged into sinuous shapes as decoration and structure, often with the acceptance of rivets as part of the decorative scheme. The Maison du Peuple (Brussels, 1896–1899) by Horta illustrates this trend. Eugene Emmanuel Viollet-le-Duc, the French architectural theorist, had advocated the use of exposed and riveted iron in his lectures.

After 1850, cast iron was used less in structural elements because of bending and other limitations of its physical properties. These limitations led to the search for a material to replace cast iron.

STEEL IN COMMERCIAL BUILDINGS

In 1854, Englishman Henry Bessemer developed a process to convert pig iron into steel by blowing air through molten iron. The air "burned" out a large portion of the carbon normally found in the pig iron, leaving behind steel. The physical properties of steel can be controlled; steel can be made highly elastic and ductile. These new properties led to the general replacement of cast iron and wrought iron.

Additional properties were discovered in the making of steel by alloying it with other material. In the second half of the nineteenth century, metallurgical science advanced at a rapid rate and many new alloys of iron were studied and developed. An example of this progress is the invention of tungsten-alloy steel in 1868, which revolutionized steel-cutting tools by providing harder, more durable cutting edges, for example, for drills and lathe bits.

Developments in metallurgy and structural theory have imposed stricter demands on the performance of iron and steel alloys, and have led to advances in structural design; special high-tensile steels are available that have a permissible tensile stress much higher than normal mild steel. These steels were used in the construction of Bailey bridge panels during World War II. Many improvements in their properties have since been made.

Stainless steel was developed accidentally in 1912. This alloy, which does not corrode, normally contains about 10–14% chromium. It is used in building products such as kitchen sinks, facing panels, bolts, and tension wires. In the 1950s, stainless exteriors were used in the Inland Steel and the Harris Trust & Savings Buildings by SOM.

Other alloys have been adopted by architects, engineers, and builders because of their special properties. Weathering steel, a copper–steel alloy, develops a tenacious oxide coating that obviates paint. Weathering steel was widely used in the 1960s for the U.S. Steel Building (Pittsburgh, 1969) by Harrison & Abramovitz, and the John Deere Building (Moline, Ill., 1962) by Eero Saarinen.

STEEL-FRAMED BUILDINGS

In the late 1880s, the multi-storied steel frame using riveted and bolted steel columns, beams, and joists was developed in Chicago. The Home Insurance Building (1884–1885), designed by William Le Baron Jenney, was the first Chicago building to use steel in its structure. In the upper six of the 10 stories, Jenney was permitted to use steel beams in place of wrought iron as originally specified. This building had originally been designed as a complete freestanding frame, but the authorities insisted that some of the loads be carried by party walls. In the Fair Building

(1891), Jenney was able to use an independent steel cage to support the entire structure, and the eight-story facade was no longer carried on heavy masonry walls.

The Auditorium Building in Chicago (1887–1889), designed by Dankmar Adler and Louis H. Sullivan, although partly of masonry construction, used iron and steel framing with impressive confidence in the creation of many of its large and elaborate volumes. The complex, containing 650,000 ft^2, included a large theater, offices, hotel rooms, and other accommodations. The Tacoma Building (1888–1889), designed by Holabird and Roche, had street elevations completely framed in iron, and all of the junctions between the structural elements were riveted, conferring extra rigidity to the structure. Baumann and Huell's Chamber of Commerce Building (1888–1889) was the first building that employed no structural masonry.

The Reliance Building (Chicago, 1891), designed by Daniel Hudson Burnham and John Wellborn Root, is an outstanding example of a freestanding steel tower with a marked vertical emphasis and a facade of steel and glass, which anticipated many twentieth-century buildings.

By the time of the 1895 depression, engineers and architects in Chicago had created many structural innovations making the framing of steel-framed buildings more reliable, efficient, and economical. These innovations included the development of bedrock caissons, fully riveted structures, and the use of wind-bracing elements integrated into the structure.

Steel framing for tall buildings began to be used tentatively in New York City before the end of the 1880s; however, New York lagged behind Chicago in structural innovation. The first application of iron framing in New York was the 11-story Tower Building at 50 Broadway (1888–1889), designed by Bradford Gilbert. The Manhattan Life Insurance Company Building (1893–1894) by Kimball and Thompson, used a completely framed structure for its 17 stories. From then on, buildings of ever increasing height were erected. By the end of the nineteenth century, a 30-story building had been built. Improvements in developing more rigid framing connections and other technical developments enabled the construction of such buildings as the 58-story Woolworth Building (1913) by Cass Gilbert (Fig. 6), and the 102-story Empire State Building (1931) designed by Shreve, Lamb, & Harmon (Fig. 7).

The modern movement, in the period after World War I, took the steel-frame structure for granted, as an indispensable instrument for achieving freedom and rationality in design. Around 1930, modern architecture began to gain ground in the United States, and following World War II the international style was applied uncompromisingly to skyscrapers. The outburst of building activity after World War II helped to perfect and spread the methods of steel-frame construction to the most diverse of building types. The need to save time, cost, and upkeep led the industry to prefabricate various versions of the curtain wall, which afforded numerous possibilities for architectural expression. Outstanding contributions in the refinement of steel structures were made by Mies van der Rohe, whose theoretical studies went back to the year 1921 with his steel and glass skyscraper near the Friedrichstrasse station in Berlin.

Figure 6. The Woolworth Building, New York, 1913, Cass Gilbert.

From the early years of this century on, many advances were made in the construction of tall, steel-framed buildings. After World War II, the use of masonry, which had been the normal external cladding, began to be superseded by the curtain wall, which had been proposed by Mies as the appropriate cladding for tall buildings as early as 1920. Examples of steel-framed structures with lightweight skin are the Alcoa Building (Pittsburgh, 1953) by Harrison and Abramovitz, with its stamped aluminum cladding panels; and Connecticut General Life Insurance (Bloomfield, Conn. 1954) by Skidmore, Owings, & Merrill (SOM). Precast concrete as a cladding material became popular in the 1960s, such as in the Pan Am Building (New York, 1960) by Gropius (TAC) and Belluschi & Roth.

Masonry cladding had contributed to the stiffness of structures, but with lighter walling systems other methods had to be found for bracing tall structures against wind and seismic loading. Elevator and service cores, which had long been used as stiffening elements, had greater

Figure 7. The Empire State Building, New York, 1931, Shreve, Lamb & Harmon.

demands placed on them. More reliable rigid connections between columns and flooring elements were also developed. Mechanical floors, carrying air conditioning and other services, were distributed at a number of levels throughout the height of the building, and these were made into rigid structural elements by the introduction of extensive diagonal bracing that would have been obstructive to windows on other floors. The use of these braced mechanical floors contributed considerably to the stiffness of the entire structure. Another form of stiffening that has become popular is the use of diagonal bracing throughout the height of the building, making the whole structure into a rigid tube. The John Hancock Building (Chicago, 1968), engineered by Fazlur Kahn of SOM, is a well-known example of this type of construction.

The Sears Tower (Chicago, 1974), which reached a height of 1460 ft, was also engineered by Fazlur Kahn of SOM as a further development of the same principle; the structure is built of nine minitubes, each 75 ft square, which reduce in number through the height of the building. These externally braced towers produce great savings in steel when compared to other types of framing for buildings of similar height.

Fireproofing steel evolved after a number of iron-framed buildings burned down in the 1830s. Prior to that time steel structures were presumed to be fireproof. The Chicago fire of 1871 was a further stimulus to the development of fireproofing techniques. Fire can weaken a structure by raising its temperature excessively. Iron and steel, although incombustible, suffer fairly rapidly by losing strength and distorting badly. Reinforced concrete can also suffer if its reinforcement is overheated. When these possibilities were recognized, they were first guarded against by means of protective layers of insulation. In the case of iron and steel this has taken various forms: lightweight, specially fabricated hollow blocks; casings of dense or lightweight concrete; and, most recently, sprayed-on insulants. In the case of reinforced concrete (and prestressed concrete) it has naturally taken the form of an adequate concrete cover to the essential reinforcement, although this cover has had to be prevented from spalling off as its temperature rises by secondary binding reinforcement in beams and columns. The most novel approach has been to protect steel columns by filling them with water to keep their temperature down. This approach has been adopted for several recent tall buildings and has entailed a return to the tubular cross section of many early cast-iron columns (which sometimes doubled as internal rainwater drains). In other cases columns have again been left bare and set some distance outside the building to reduce their exposure to the heat of a fire.

REINFORCED CONCRETE

Reinforced concrete appeared in the United States after the 1867 Exhibition in Paris. It was influenced by French research, even though there had been some independent work in France including S. T. Fowler's system for walls with reinforcement made of bolted timber grillages (patented in 1860), and Charles Williams' walls (1868) reinforced with iron straps, inspired by reinforced brickwork techniques for grain silos. Concrete and metal floor slabs made by filling in between joists over corrugated-iron plates were patented by J. Gilbert (1867). Beamless floor slabs for industrial and other buildings were first developed by C.A.P. Turner in the United States, who published an article in 1908 entitled *The Mushroom System of Construction* (6). The first commercial building to use this form of slab was the Bovey Building in Minneapolis. In the slab, the reinforcement was arranged radially near the columns, which had large capitals to help reduce the stresses around them.

The employment of reinforced concrete in large industrial complexes preceded the commercial and corporate building type. In 1915, the engineer Matte Trucco began building the Fiat-Lingotto works at Turin, with an area of over 100 acres. He adopted reinforced concrete for every type of structure, solving technical problems of great difficulty in the automobile testing track he sited on the roof of a five-story factory, and the access ramp that led up to it. It was during these years, too, that Le Corbusier, not yet thirty, was working out the premises of his architectural style. To him, reinforced concrete seemed to be the most appropriate medium. With his project for the Dom-Ino houses (1914), based on a modular grid in reinforced concrete, he set forth the theoretical preconditions for designing a free plan.

In the United States, where architecture had developed during the nineteenth century via the habitual adoption of the steel frame, the use of reinforced concrete, especially for large-scale industrial buildings, began to be accepted. A warehouse for Montgomery, Ward & Co. in Chicago, by Schmidt, Garden, and Martin, was an experiment of the early postwar years. Mies van der Rohe (with Mart Stam) prepared a scheme for the Novembergruppe Exhibition in 1922 for a reinforced concrete office block in which the stanchions are set back from the facades and supported the floors, which project out all around, by a cantilever arrangement. The external walls assume the character of a series of horizontal strips, one on top of the other.

Concrete cast in situ lends itself to the creation of forms with continuity of structure and complex special shapes. It has been used in an inventive way by many twentieth-century architects to achieve forms impossible in any other material. Frank Lloyd Wright's Johnson Wax Building (Racine, Wis., 1936–1939) employed wire-mesh reinforced concrete cantilevered mushroom roof forms, engineered by Mendel Glickman and W. W. Peters.

In the 1890s concrete began establishing itself as a common structural material. Designers such as Auguste Perret, Francois Hennebique, and Tony Garnier in France, and Robert Maillart in Switzerland, were among those who explored the potential of reinforced concrete. Perret was the first to employ the reinforced concrete skeleton in high-rise construction and to express it architecturally in his rue Franklin Apartment Building (Paris, 1903). At the same time, the 16-story Ingall Building in Cincinnati was the world's first reinforced concrete frame office building. During the first half of this century, however, concrete buildings appeared only sporadically. There was no real search for the true personality of the material; concrete systems generally imitated the steel skeleton approach. This attitude, however, changed after World War II. Sophisticated construction techniques, together with development of high quality materials, began to yield such new design concepts as the flat slab and the load-bearing facade grid wall. Both systems were challenging the traditional one-way slab and curtain wall typical for rigid frame structures. Skyscrapers, such as the 65-story Marina City Towers designed by Bertram Goldberg (Chicago, 1963), truly express the monolithic sculptural nature of concrete. Also, P. L. Nervi with Gio Ponti exploited reinforced concrete in the Pirelli Building (Milan, 1958) where the structure dramatically reduced the cross section of this very tall building.

Reinforced concrete is now common in very tall buildings; the current record holder is Watertower Place (Chicago, 1976) at 74 stories.

CURTAIN WALL

The introduction of steel and reinforced concrete frame construction resulted in a number of important changes in the methods of external wall construction. It now became possible to divide the load bearing, enclosing, and heat-insulating functions, which until then had been performed by the conventional solid wall, among separate structural components specifically designed for these purposes. The task of providing structural support is performed by the framework and thus is concentrated at a limited number of points on plan, while the actual wall consists of thin cladding units and has only enclosing and insulating functions. This separation between structural and nonstructural materials was to become one of the central features of modern architectural aesthetics. The development of the curtain wall in commercial structures was a major breakthrough in reducing the size and the weight of enclosing walls. Chicago's Monadnock Building was built in 1891 by Burnham and Root with bearing walls of masonry 6 ft thick to support the vast tonnage above. Instead of massive walls requiring months, even years, to build, a 3-in. wall that could be erected in days was adequate. Instead of a typical weight of about 100 psf for each of many feet of thickness, the wall weighs less than 10 psf. Traditional materials were initially used for the "infilling" or "cladding" of the structural frame: brick masonry faced with slabs of natural stone, or rendered externally, in conjunction with a backing of factory-made insulating slabs to provide additional thermal insulation.

Two reasons for the development of the new curtain walls are readily apparent: in a building in which the frame carries all the loads, the wall of the past has no logical place; and the new walls make use of technological advances in building materials and methods.

As currently used, the curtain wall has come to mean that which divides space, is controllable, and supports nothing but itself. Strong, flexible, light, and thin, the curtain wall logically followed the development of the skeleton frame.

The curtain wall is the end-product of a process of development that involved a number of interrelated considerations connected with technical progress, social and cultural factors, and the emergence of the modern style in architecture. The introduction and perfection of new structural techniques, making use of steel at the beginning of the nineteenth century and reinforced concrete in the second half, gave rise to the use of framed structures, for example, the Chocolate Factory (Noisiel-sur-Marne, 1871–1872) by Saulniew; second Leiter Building (Chicago, 1889–1890) by William Le Baron Jenney; and the house at Rue Franklin, (Paris, 1903) by Perret. The increased employment of this type of walling showed the importance of two characteristics in particular: slenderness, to keep the maximum floor area available for use; and lightness, so that by reducing the load on the steel frame, the house at rue Franklin might be designed with correspondingly smaller structural members.

The small dimensions of the steel frames and the progress made by the glass industry permitted an increase in window sizes, a development that was also stimulated by the demand for as much natural light as possible in industrial and commercial buildings. Between 1850 and the early years of the twentieth century the window gradually turned into the window wall, for example, Chatham Dockyard Museum, (1967); Reliance Building (Chicago) by Burnham and Root; and The Samaritaine Store (Paris, 1905) by Jourdain. Sometimes it took over the entire basic area defined by the facade, for example, Maison du Peuple (Brussels, 1896–1899) by Horta; and AEG works (Berlin, 1908–1910) by Behrens. Meanwhile, the use of large areas of glass had become widespread in greenhouses and winter gardens, pedestrian galleries, railway station roofs, and large exhibition pavilions, for example, Crystal Palace, (London, 1851) by Paxton; and Machinery Hall (Paris, 1889) by Dutert and Contamin.

The transformation of the window into the window wall and the employment of large glazed areas drew attention to a number of problems and evoked the first solutions to them. Included were questions concerning insulation; eliminating condensation; developing the secondary glazing framework, for example, Hallidie Building (San Francisco, 1918) by Polk; and countering the effects of expansion by the careful design of joints and glazing systems. Large industrial buildings and tall office blocks, conceived as endless repetitions of identical cell units, led to the use of a uniform grid for structural frames. Between the start of World War I and the start of World War II, architects of the modern movement carried out a series of experiments, each of which may be considered as perfecting some particular aspect of curtain walling by the use of modern methods of industrial production, for example, Fagus factory (Alfeld, 1911), model factory at the Werkbund Exhibition (Cologne, 1914), and Bauhaus (Dessau, 1925–1926), all by Adolf Meyer with Walter Gropius; Bijenkorf department store (Rotterdam, 1903) by Dudok; and Maison Suisse, University City (Paris, 1930), Salvation Army Hostel (Paris, 1932), and Maison Clarte (Geneva, 1932), all by Le Corbusier.

At the same time, the theoretical principles of this new means of architectural expression were being formulated via educational experiments (Bauhaus), writings (Le Corbusier), and projects (various schemes of Mies van der Rohe between 1919 and 1922; Gropius and Meyer's design for the Chicago Tribune competition, 1922). It was only after World War II, however, that the first experiments began in the real industrialization of the building trade on a vast scale. It was this period that saw the development and spread of the curtain wall in Europe and the United States, for example, UN Secretariat Building (New York, 1947–1950) by W. K. Harrison and others; and Lake Shore Drive Apartments (Chicago, 1951) and Seagram Building (New York, 1956) by Mies van der Rohe. Architects experimented with its application to different types of buildings, and discovered new possibilities of expression, with the close collaboration of manufacturers, who were always on the alert for new materials and methods.

There are many valid general possibilities for the design of the external wall. In one case, the wall design constitutes the outward expression of the structural framework, which is discernible through the cladding or is directly visible as an exposed feature of the overall architectural treatment. Some types feature three-dimensional treatment, for example, the main elevation of the Palazzo Olivetti ((Milan, 1954) by Bernasconi, Fiocchi, and Nizzoli). Others employ a flat or two-dimensional treatment, for example, the Phoenix-Rheinrohr Building (Dusseldorf, 1960) by Hentrick and Petschnigg).

Alternatively, the external wall consists purely of a skin suspended in front of the structural framework. The essential point is to give aesthetic emphasis to the nonload-bearing character of the wall. This type does not bring out the framework at all, but covers it like a sheath, for example, Lever House (New York, 1952) by Skidmore, Owings & Merrill. Some choose only the verticals, for example, Inland Steel Company Building (Chicago, 1954) by Skidmore, Owings & Merrill. Some choose only the horizontals, for example, headquarters of the Federation Nationale du Bâtiment (Paris, 1950) by Graveraux and Lopez. Yet others feature both verticals and horizontals, for example, Equitable Savings Building (Portland, Oreg., 1948) by Belluschi.

The third type differentiates between the wall unit and its frame. This is in the form of panels set in a secondary frame, which in turn is fixed to the load-bearing structure; it is common in most commercial buildings by Mies van der Rohe. Others use panels of an appropriately rigid section, which are anchored directly to the main structure, for example, Alcoa Building (Pittsburgh, 1953) by Harrison and Abramovitz.

The all-glass curtain wall in the 1960s returned to Mies's earlier notions of the primacy of surface; in this case the object is to conceal rather than reveal. Tinted glass has been widely used since the 1950s to reduce glare and heat load. Mirrored glass was first developed for the Bell Telephone Laboratories Research Center, at the prompting of Eero Saarinen and his associates Kevin Roche and John Dinkeloo. Glass can be tinted and mirrored, and both kinds are now often combined; however, it is the technique of mirroring that has brought to the glass facade a degree of abstraction that is without precedent.

When glass was first used to make the entire surface of a building—not only its windows—it was held in place by highly visible metal armatures. More recently, however, the desire to maintain perfect continuity of surface has led to the refinement of the joints, which now are made as flush as possible with the surface, often with flexible synthetics rather than metal frames. Sheets of glass can also be fastened to each other by metal clasps.

Paradoxically, the latest chapter in the curtain wall stage of commercial architecture returns to the earlier preeminence of the skin of stone and glass. One of the enduring fantasies of the 1920s and 1930s is expressed in the AT&T Building (1980) by Johnson & Burgee and the new 900 North Michigan Avenue Building (Chicago, 1988) by Kohn Pedersen Fox. Here the curtain wall employs classical forms, grand gestures, and flights of whimsy.

STRUCTURAL INNOVATIONS IN HIGH-RISE COMMERCIAL BUILDINGS

The earliest commercial buildings were basically load-bearing wall structures. This type of structural system has a great disadvantage: as the height of a building increases, the wall thickness must increase due to gravity flow, which in turn increases the weight of the building.

Early skeleton frames still carried heavy loads of masonry, although the frames were designed to carry gravity and wind loads to the foundation. Wind load was not much of a problem then, but it became one when buildings shed their heavy masonry skins, and the structures had to do all of the work.

From these beginnings, the frame was developed rapidly in the later stages of the rebuilding of Chicago following the fire of 1871. Notable achievements were the nine-story Home Insurance Building, the first building in which the frame was fully protected by fireproof casing; and the fourteen-story Reliance Building, probably the best of the steel-framed structures built toward the end of the century with all lateral stiffness provided by the frame itself, no party walls, and only light external cladding of terra cotta and glass. Reinforced-concrete frames of similar height followed early in the twentieth century. These also had beams between the columns. At the same time, reinforced-concrete frames of fewer stories, designed for heavier floor loadings, were built with beamless floors; splayed column heads were provided to collect the floor load and achieve overall rigidity.

When buildings are not very high, rigidly connected beams and columns can carry the wind. But the post-and-beam approach becomes inefficient above approximately 20 stories. Other systems that supplant post-and-beam also reach limits in efficiency as height increases.

While the reinforced-concrete frame was being developed, the steel frame was pushed to its limits, if not beyond, in a series of ever-taller skyscrapers that culminated with the Empire State Building, 85 stories high, excluding the observation tower. The need for lateral stability and the need to avoid unacceptable movements of the upper stories in the wind necessitated greatly increased amounts of steel in these buildings for bracing purposes, either in the form of diagonals or as deep portals, notwithstanding the bonus of stiffness contributed by heavy masonry claddings and additional internal walls. At heights above 20 floors, new hybrid forms that are structurally more efficient therefore have been introduced. At lower heights recent developments have concentrated on overall simplification of the frame and its design as a single entity rather than as an aggregation of individual elements. This has been facilitated by the possibility, for instance, of varying concrete strengths to achieve the required strengths of columns at different heights with little or no change in cross section, and by an architectural preference for simple, repetitive, open-floor plans. Welding and bolting, too, now have made it easier to achieve the desirable rigid joints in steelwork.

The basic structural elements of high-rise commercial structures in both steel and concrete are the following:

1. The linear elements, capable of resisting axial rotational forces, are the column and beam.
2. The surface elements are the most common load-bearing systems; these include the wall, either solid with perforations, and the slab, either solid or ribbed and supported on floor framing.
3. The spatial elements are made up of the facade and the core tied together to act as a unit.

The combination of these basic elements generates the structure of the building. The most common building types are parallel bearing walls, cores and facade-bearing walls, self-supporting boxes, cantilevered slab, flat slab, etc.

Parallel Bearing Walls

This system comprises planar vertical elements that are prestressed by their own weight, and thus efficiently absorb lateral force action. The parallel wall system is used mostly for apartment buildings where large free spaces are not needed and mechanical systems do not necessitate core structures.

Cores and Facade Bearing Walls

Planar vertical elements form exterior walls around a core structure. This allows for open interior spaces, which depend on the spanning capacities of the floor structure. The core houses mechanical and vertical transportation systems and adds to the stiffness of the building.

Self-supporting Boxes

Boxes are prefabricated three-dimensional units that resemble the bearing wall building when they are in place and joined together. The boxes are stacked like bricks in the "English pattern bond," resulting in a criss-crossed wall beam system.

Cantilevered Slab

Supporting the floor system from a central core allows for a column-free space with the strength of the slab as the limit of the building size. Large quantities of steel are required, especially with large slab projections. Slab stiffness can be increased by taking advantage of prestressing techniques. This was first adopted by Frank Lloyd Wright (1869–1959) in the Laboratory Tower for the Johnson Wax Company (Racine, Wis., 1949); the core carries all vertical loads and provides all lateral stiffness, the floors being individually cantilevered out from it. Recently, this structural system was used in the Treasury Building (Singapore, 1987) by Hugh Stubbins.

Flat Slab

This horizontal planar system generally consists of uniformly thick concrete floor slabs supported on columns. If there are no drop panels and/or capitals on top of the columns, it is referred to as a flat plat system. The system does not have deep beams in either form, allowing for a minimum story height.

Interstitial Structure

Cantilevered story-high framed structures are employed on every other floor to create usable space within and above the frame. The space within the framed floor is used for fixed operations. The totally free space above the frame can adapt to any type of activity; this type is often used in hospital or laboratory construction.

Suspension

This system offers the efficient usage of material by employing hangers instead of columns to carry the floorloads. The strength of a compression member must be reduced because of buckling, which is not the case for a tensile element, capable of utilizing its full capacity. The cables carry the gravity loads to trusses cantilevered from a central core.

A notable variation of this can be found in the Hong Kong and Shanghai Bank in Hong Kong by Foster Associates and Arup & Partners. Its suspension structure is actually several stacked one on top of the other. Suspended high-rise construction is not a new idea, although no building has used it to the extent or in the configuration of the Hong Kong Bank. Suspended construction is not the most efficient for high-rise structures, since loads must travel farther—up a hanger, along a truss, and down a column—to reach the ground. By stacking several smaller suspension structures on top of one another, the travel distance of most loads has been reduced while the benefits of suspended construction have been retained: opening up the ground level, minimizing the foundation area, and reducing the floor space devoted to structure.

Staggered Truss

Story-high trusses are arranged so that each building floor rests alternatively on the top chord of one truss and the bottom of the next. In addition to carrying the vertical loads, this truss arrangement minimizes wind bracing requirements by transferring wind loads to the base through web members and the floor slab.

Rigid Frame

Rigid joints are used between an assemblage of linear elements to form vertical and horizontal planes. The vertical planes consist of columns and girders mostly on a rectangular grid; a similar organizational grid is used for the horizontal planes consisting of beams and girders. Because the integrity of the spatial skeleton is dependent on the strength and rigidity of the individual columns and beams, story height and column spacing are controlling design considerations. The higher the building, the stiffer it must be to resist wind economically. Buildings of up to 20 stories use rigid frames to limit sway.

Rigid Frame and Core

The rigid frame responds to lateral loads primarily through flexure of the beams and columns. This type of behavior results in large lateral drift for taller buildings. However, introducing a core structure will significantly increase the lateral resistance of the building as a result of the core and frame interaction. Such core systems provide the main source of stiffness, occupying part of the total area and accommodating elevators, stairways, and other services.

Trussed Frame

Combining a rigid (or hinged) frame with vertical shear trusses provides an increase in strength and stiffness in the structure. The design of the structure may be based on using the frame for the resistance of gravity loads and the vertical truss for wind loads similar to the rigid frame and core.

One way of achieving this, first adopted on a fairly small scale for the 13-story IBM Building in Pittsburgh, and since used for the 100-story John Hancock Center in Chicago, is to depart from a pure column and beam grid in favor of a more trusslike form. In the IBM Building, an overall diagonal lattice was used, of constant mesh and cross section from top to bottom, but with different steel members according to the load to be carried. In the Hancock Center, normal beams and columns were retained, but a few very large diagonals traversing the whole facade were added. The most recent example of this system is the Citicorp Center in New York, engineered by William J. Le Messurier. It is more daring than the Hancock building; half the gravity and all wind load is brought down the trussed frame on the outside of the building and the remaining gravity load is carried by the core (Fig. 8).

Belt-Trussed Frame and Core

Belt trusses tie the facade columns to the core, thus eliminating the individual action of frame and core. The bracing is called cap trussing when it is on the top of the building and belt trussing when around lower sections. The belt trusses, working as lever arms, throw direct axial stresses into the exterior columns. When the shear truss tries to bend, the exterior rows of columns act as struts to resist this movement. These belt trusses can be used at the midsection as well as the top of the building, increasing the stiffness by 30%. This approach has been used by SOM for the 42-story First Wisconsin Center in Milwaukee.

Tube in Tube

In tube in tube construction, the exterior columns and beams are spaced so closely that the facade has the appearance of a wall with perforated window openings. The entire building acts as a hollow tube cantilevered out of the

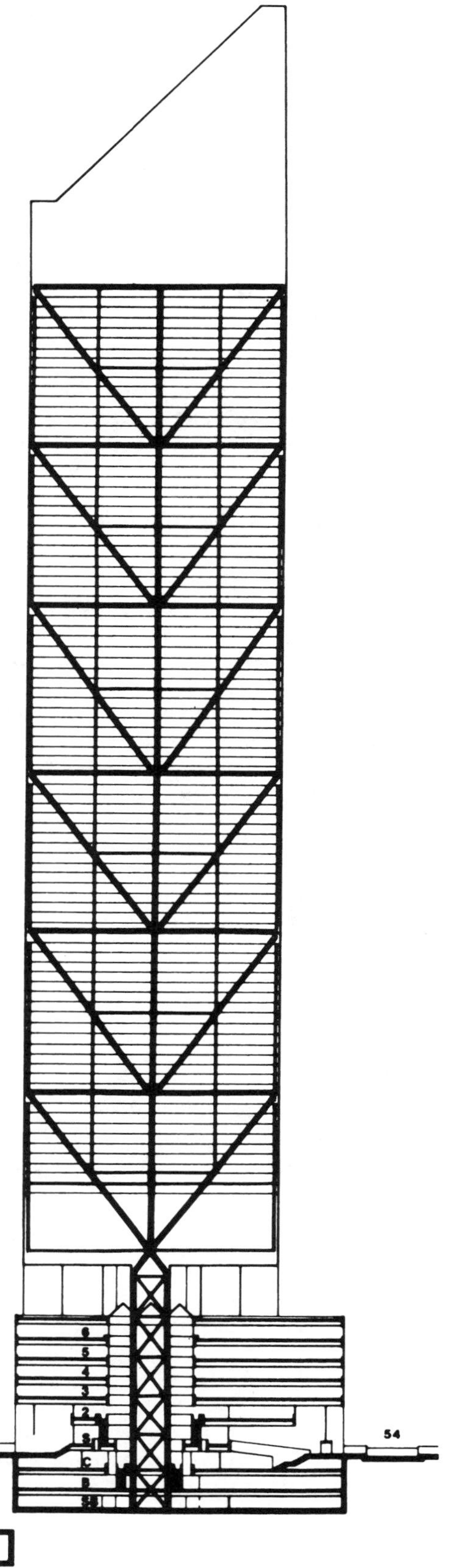

Figure 8. Citicorp Center, New York, 1985, Hugh Stubbins Associates.

ground. The interior core (tube) increases the stiffness of the building by sharing the load with the facade tube.

For buildings above 50 stories, this system has proved to be the only one capable of limiting the penalty for height to not much more than that which inevitably arises from the greater vertical loads to be carried at the base. It calls for a roughly square or circular plan, preferably identical from top to bottom or slightly reduced in area on successive floors. It is most efficient where the architectural requirement is the maximum openness of the floors between the central service core and the perimeter, allowing maximum freedom of use. Ideally, all wind loads are resisted not by bending of the individual lengths of column, but by overall tension on the windward side and overall compression on the leeward side.

In the twin towers of the 110-story World Trade Center in New York, the columns were set only 3.25 ft (1 m) apart and the beams made 4.25 ft (1.3 m) deep, coming very close to the ideal. However, response to the wind is not static since the wind force itself fluctuates. Further means may therefore be desirable to limit movement in such tall structures. In the case of the World Trade Center, dampers were incorporated in the connections of the wide spanning floor beams to the outer columns.

Bundled Tube

Perhaps the most intriguing concept to evolve in the ultrahigh skyscraper, from the standpoints of architecture and engineering, the bundled tube system can be visualized as an assemblage of individual tubes resulting in a multiple-cell tube. The increase in stiffness is apparent. The system allows for the greatest height and the most floor area. This system was pioneered by the late Fazlur Kahn, of SOM Chicago.

The bundled tube was conceived for use in the 110-story Sears Tower. The building consists of a series of framed tubes, each of which has its own structural integrity, allowing the tube bundle to be reduced as the building rises, and yielding a variety of spaces for tenant floors, which occur above the fiftieth floor. The tubes are 75 feet square, so the building is 225 × 225 ft at the base. Columns are optimally spaced 15 ft apart. At each corner of the tube is a larger column that "terminates" the tube structurally with respect to wind shear transfer. Shear lag of a bundled tube is greatly reduced, compared with an ordinary framed tube. The elevator system is divided into three zones, with two-story sky lobbies serving the double-decker elevators from the two lower zones. Sky lobbies also are served by express banks.

ZONING AND COMMERCIAL BUILDINGS

One of the most critical problems in zoning of the commercial building type is the relationship between a building and its surrounding space. This issue was once predicated on the necessity to preserve adequate light and air for interior space. Examples of adequate setback requirements to serve this purpose are rare, but the remarkable progress in the technical design of the interior environment has altered the demand for such provisions. Preservation of space for light, air, sound control, and privacy continues to be important in measuring adequate space between buildings, but its relative importance has been modified by advances in artificial illumination, sound insulation, and air conditioning. It is possible that the necessity for space in the future will derive far more from the exterior requirements than the interior demands. The amount of building floor space in relation to exterior surroundings—streets, sidewalks, parks—may become the critical factor.

Over the years there has been a constant effort to increase the distances between buildings and property lines, and to devise methods by which setbacks might compensate for increasing building heights. The ground space reserved by these provisions has never been sufficient for its purpose; the setback distances and lot coverage restrictions have been token grants of space sacrificed after the land acquired great value.

The principle of floor area ratio offers some encouragement in this direction. This is a regulation of the ratio between the area of building floor space and the area of the lot it occupies. A floor area ratio of two, for example, would permit 100% of the lot to be covered by a two-story building, or 50% of the lot to be covered by a four-story building. Recent applications of the floor area ratio (FAR) introduce the features of "bonus," or premium, space. Chicago adopted such inducements in its revised ordinance of 1957; they have also been proposed in Philadelphia. The first major overhaul of the New York City ordinance since the history-making zoning law of 1916 occurred with the revisions of 1961. The conventional "setback" requirements that produced the familiar shapes variously referred to as the ziggurat were modified by adoption of the Sky Exposure Plan for commercial zones and the Open Space Ratio for multifamily residential districts. The effect of these provisions, in combination with the inducements of increased permissible floor space in proportion to the open space reserved at the ground level, is comparable to the floor area ratio method of regulation.

This approach affords a flexibility in the shape of buildings to serve their particular functions and removes the arbitrary limitations on building heights unless such limitations may be desirable for particular purposes. As with other regulations to control the bulk of buildings on the land, the floor area ratio will be effective to the extent that it produces the required balance between enclosed floor space occupied by people and adequate ground space for vehicles and living things, be they human, animal, or plants. New York City is a typical example of a city that has evolved a flexible zoning policy to deal with commercial buildings.

New York City's pioneering 1916 zoning resolution, the first in the nation, was in large part a response to such new buildings as the Equitable Building, at 120 Broadway, which rose 540 ft straight up from its lot line without setback. To protect the streets and avenues from being turned into dark canyons, the 1916 regulations established height districts. These limited the height of a building, in proportion to the width of the street it fronted on, until it had to set back. For each foot it set back it could rise x additional feet; the ratio depended on its height district. A tower rule permitted a portion of the building, up to 25% of the lot area, to rise without setbacks provided it was a distance from the street. There were no other limitations on height or bulk.

In reaction to the "wedding cake" shape of much of New York's skyline built to the 1916 zoning envelope, and to meet other needs, zoning was completely revised in 1961. A "sky exposure plane" replaced height districts to govern setbacks. To meet the need for larger office floors, the tower that could penetrate the plane was increased from 25 to 40%. A new tool to govern bulk was introduced, the floor area ratio (FAR). The basic floor area for the largest office building was set at 15 times the lot area, FAR 15.

Another major goal of the 1961 zoning revisions was to obtain additional open space surrounding new buildings. The tower in a plaza epitomized by the elegant new Seagram Building (actually a 25% tower conforming to the 1916 regulations) was the model. A 20% floor area bonus was offered to a building with a plaza, raising the largest building to FAR 18. It was the start of incentive zoning. To meet other needs and to keep the continuity and vitality of avenues, such as Fifth and Madison, from being destroyed by plazas, the incentive system was expanded. Bonuses were offered for interior spaces and sometimes compounded, bringing FAR up to 21.6. Combined with the restrictions of the tower regulations on the smaller lots left in the core area and the increasing use of air rights, these interior bonuses put great pressure on regulations meant to protect the openness of the streets.

To return to zoning's basic principles, zoning officials, architects, and planners examined how midtown Manhattan had developed under more than fifty years of zoning. Actual development defines the public expectation of daylight and helps set the standards for new regulations. The 1916 and 1961 regulations recognized that the farther a building's mass sets back from the street the higher it can go; towers were allowed to pierce the sky exposure plane. But the regulations still tended to prescribe a fixed building envelope. The new regulations are based on an actual standard of daylight and openness for the streets of midtown, measured either against a daylight curve (first tier) or the percentage of unblocked sky (second tier). Both are derived from actual conditions resulting from midtown's historic development. They give great flexibility in building design so long as the daylight standard is achieved.

In recent years zoning and urban planning have been the subjects of intense worldwide public debate. Public concern is over the degree of rapid change occurring in commercial business districts, since this causes conflict between fostering a vital economy and retaining the urban patterns and structures that collectively form the physical urban environment. In essence, zoning and planning in the last half of the twentieth century encompass a compact mix of commercial activities, historical values, and distinctive architecture and urban forms.

BIBLIOGRAPHY

1. N. Pevsner, *A History of Building Types,* Princeton University Press, Princeton, N.J., 1976.

2. R. A. M. Stern, *Pride of Place,* Houghton-Mifflin Company, Boston, Mass., 1986, Chapt. 7.
3. C. Pelli, *Perspecta 18, The Yale Architectural Journal,* 134 (1982).
4. P. Goldberger, *The Skyscraper,* Alfred A. Knopf, New York, 1981.
5. A. L. Huxtable, *The Tall Building Artistically Reconsidered,* Pantheon Books, New York, 1982.
6. C. A. P. Turner, "The Mushroom System of Construction," *Engineering News* **61**(7), 78–81 (Feb. 18, 1908).

General References

J. Barnett, "Ford Foundation Building," *Architectural Record* **143,** 105 (Feb. 1968).

J. Barnett, *An Introduction to Urban Design,* Harper & Row, New York, 1979.

J. Barnett, *Urban Design as Public Policy,* McGraw Hill, Inc., New York, 1974.

W. Blaser, *Mies van der Rohe—Art of Structure,* Frederick Praeger, New York, 1965.

C. Condit, *American Building,* University of Chicago Press, Chicago, Ill., 1968.

C. Condit, *American Building Art: The Nineteenth Century,* Oxford University Press, New York, 1960.

C. Condit, *American Building Art: The Twentieth Century,* Oxford University Press, New York, 1961.

C. Condit, *Chicago School of Architecture,* University of Chicago Press, Chicago, 1964.

C. Condit, *The Rise of The Skyscraper,* University of Chicago Press, Chicago, 1952.

H. Ferriss, *The Metropolis of Tomorrow,* Ives-Washburn, New York, 1929.

J. M. Fitch, *American Building,* Houghton Mifflin, Boston, 1966.

C. K. Gandee, "Humana," *Architectural Record* **173,** 102 (Aug. 1985).

M. Gayle and E. V. Gillon, Jr., *Cast-Iron Architecture in New York: A Photographic Survey,* Dover, New York, 1974.

S. Giedion, *Space, Time & Architecture,* Harvard University Press, Cambridge, Mass., 1962.

M. Girouard, *Cities and People,* Yale University Press, New Haven, London, 1985.

B. P. Gould, *Planning the New Corporate Headquarters,* John Wiley & Sons, New York, 1983.

P. Guedes, *Encyclopedia of Architectural Technology,* McGraw-Hill, New York, 1979.

K. Halpern, *Downtown USA,* Whitney Library of Design, New York, 1978.

G. Hatje, *Encyclopaedia of Modern Architecture,* Thames & Hudson, London, 1963, 1971.

W. Hegemann with E. Peets, *Architektur und Stadt Baukunst,* Baugilde, Berlin, 1927.

P. Heyer, *Architects on Architecture,* Walker & Co., New York, 1966.

H.-R. Hitchcock and P. Johnson, *The International Style,* Norton, New York, 1932, 1966.

H.-R. Hitchcock, *Early Victorian Architecture in Britain,* Yale University Press, New Haven, Conn., 1954.

H.-R Hitchcock and A. Drexler, *Built in USA: Post War Architecture,* Museum of Modern Art, New York, 1952.

C. Hoyt, *Buildings for Commerce and Industry,* McGraw-Hill, Inc., New York, 1978.

Q. Hughes, "The Perils of Vision," *Architectural Forum* **123,** 48 (Nov. 1965).

W. D. Hunt, *The Contemporary Curtain Wall,* McGraw-Hill, Inc., New York, 1958.

W. D. Hunt, *Encyclopedia of American Architecture,* McGraw-Hill, Inc., New York, 1980.

W. D. Hunt, *Office Buildings,* McGraw-Hill, Inc., New York, 1961.

C. Jencks, *Sky Scrapers—Skycities,* Rizzoli, New York, 1980.

J. Joedicke, *Office Buildings,* Frederick Praeger, New York, 1962.

W. H. Jordy, *American Buildings and Their Architects,* Anchor Books, Garden City, New York, 1976.

E. Kaufmann, Jr., *The Rise of an American Architecture,* Praeger Publishers, New York, 1970.

A. Kemper, *Architectural Handbook,* John Wiley & Sons, Inc., New York, 1979.

R. Koolhaas, *Delirious New York,* Oxford University Press, New York, 1978.

C. H. Krinsky, *Rockefeller Center,* Oxford University Press, New York, 1978.

W. C. Kilham, Jr., *Raymond Hood, Architect,* Architectural Book Publishing Co., New York, 1973.

Kohn Pederson Fox, P. C., *The Architecture of Kohn Pederson Fox,* Rizzoli, New York, 1985.

I. Lambert, *New Headquarters for Hong Kong and Shanghai Banking Corp.,* Ian Lambert, Hong Kong.

A. L. Lehman, *The New York Skyscraper: A History of Its Development 1870–1939,* Ph.D. Dissertation, Yale University, New Haven, Conn., 1970.

I. McCallum, *Architecture USA,* Reinhold Publishing Corp., New York, 1959.

F. Merritt, *Building Engineering and Systems Design,* Van Nostrand Reinhold Co. Inc., New York, 1979.

H. A. Millon and A. Frazer, *Key Monuments of The History of Architecture,* Harry N. Abrams, Inc., New York, 1964.

H. Morrison, *Louis Sullivan. Prophet of Modern Architecture,* Norton & Co., New York, 1935.

F. Mujica, *History of The Skyscraper,* Da Capo Press, New York, 1929, 1930, 1977.

L. Mumford, *The Culture of Cities,* Larson Publishing Co., New York, 1938.

T. Nakamura, ed., "Cesar Pelli", *Architecture & Urbanism, Tokyo,* 35–232 (July 1985).

New York City, *Midtown Development,* Department of City Planning, New York, June 1981.

W. Pederson, *Considerations for Urban Architecture and the Tall Building,* February 1983. (*Southwest Center, The Houston Competition,* Rizzoli, New York, 1983, pp. 18–29).

W. Pehnt, *Encyclopedia of Modern Architecture,* Harry N. Abrams, Inc., New York, 1964.

C. Pelli, "Excerpts from a Conversation," *Perspecta 19, The Yale Architectural Journal* **19,** 127 (1982).

N. Pevsner, *Pioneers of Modern Design,* Faber & Faber, London, 1936.

A. K. Placzek, ed., *The Origins of Cast-Iron Architecture in America,* Da Capo Press, New York, 1970.

L. Redstone, *The New Downtowns,* McGraw-Hill Co. Inc., New York 1976.

D. M. Reynolds, *The Architecture of New York City,* Macmillan, New York, 1984.

W. Schueller, *High-Rise Building Structures,* John Wiley & Sons, New York, 1977.

M. Schuyler, *Studies in American Architecture,* Harper Bros., New York, 1892.

V. Scully, *American Architecture and Urbanism,* Praeger, New York, 1969.

Skidmore, Owings & Merrill, *Architecture of Skidmore, Owings & Merrill, 1950–1962,* Frederick Praeger, New York, 1963.

Skidmore, Owings & Merrill, *Architecture of Skidmore, Owings & Merrill, 1963–1973,* Architectural Book Publishing Co., New York, 1974.

Skidmore, Owings & Merrill, *Skidmore, Owings & Merrill: Architecture and Urbanism, 1973–1983,* Van Nostrand Reinhold Co., Inc., New York, 1983.

W. A. Starrett, *Skyscrapers and the Men Who Build Them,* Charles Scribners Sons, New York, 1928.

R. A. M. Stern, with T. Catalano and Raymond M. Hood, *Catalogue 15, IAUS,* Rizzoli, New York, 1982.

R. A. M. Stern, with G. F. Gilmartin and J. Massengale, *New York 1900,* Rizzoli, New York, 1983.

R. A. M. Stern, with G. F. Gilmartin and T. Mellins, *New York 1930,* Rizzoli, New York, 1985.

W. K. Sturges, "Cast-Iron New York," *Architectural Review* **114,** 118–121 (Oct. 1953).

E. Tafel, *Apprentice to Genius,* McGraw-Hill, New York, 1979.

J. C. Harkness, "TAC: The Heritage of Walter Gropius," *Process Architecture* (19) 11–15 (1980).

The Architects Collaborative Inc. (1945–1970), Editorial Gustano Gili, S. A. Barcelona, 1966.

W. Van Alen, "The Structure and Metal Work of the Chrysler Building," *The Architectural Forum* **53,** 493 (Oct. 1930).

W. Wagner, *Energy Efficient Buildings,* McGraw-Hill, Inc., New York, 1980.

W. Weisman, *The Architectural Significance of Rockefeller Center,* Thesis, Ohio State University, 1942.

W. Weisman, "The Anatomy and Significance of the Laing Store by James Bogardus," *Society of Architectural Historians* **31,** 221 (Oct. 1972).

W. Weisman, "Commercial Palaces of New York," *Art Bulletin* **36,** 285 (Dec. 1954).

W. Weisman, "A New View of Skyscraper History," *The Rise of an American Architecture,* Praeger, New York, 1970.

W. Weisman, "New York and the Problem of the First Skyscraper," *Society of Architectural Historians* **12,** 40 (March 1953).

See also Electrical Equipment; Electrical Systems; Envelopes, Building; Mechanical Systems; Office Facility Planning; Vertical Transportation

John P. Sheehy, AIA
Jeremy S. Wood, AIA

OFFICE FACILITY PLANNING

Offices have existed in one form or another since the money changers sat in the Temple at Jerusalem. Medieval cathedrals, the only available large enclosed space at the time, also served as offices. During the 1700s and 1800s, the private office appeared as an outgrowth of the study or library in the private home. As companies grew larger, entire residences were converted to office buildings.

In the late 1870s, the introduction of the elevator permitted office buildings to rise from three to seven or eight stories. Separate office buildings connected to a factory or warehouse also appeared around this period. However, the commercial office building as it is known today, did not become common until after World War II. Its rise was due primarily to business leaders who recognized the value of the office building in enhancing their corporate image.

The building boom of the 1950s and 1960s produced large complexes of office space containing acres of floor area. By 1981, white collar workers constituted a majority of the U.S. work force. Information processing became a significant activity for two-thirds of the work force. Thus, the office evolved from a space housing clerical functions to a support facility for information processing by people and electronic devices.

In the 1980s, it has become an accepted fact that the office environment affects productivity. Owing to its potential to deliver increased performance, the office has become a major element of corporate investment. Organizations are also finding that they must respond to a fast-changing external environment driven by economic, competitive, social, political, legal, and technological forces that present challenging opportunities for facility development.

Evolution of the office as a center for business operations has created the need for extensive facility planning and interior development services. Professionals who have specialized in the field are known as interior architects, office planners, space planners, facility planners, office design consultants, or commercial interior designers. A trend toward direct employment of facility planners by organizations began in the early 1980s, as a response to the short time frames involved in facility planning projects.

These factors affect facility planning:

1. *Competitive business climate.* All organizations, including corporations, health care, hospitality, and educational institutions seek strategic business advantages. As a result, a large number of corporations have merged, been acquired, or otherwise changed their business structure. These activities require new programs and arrangements and thus have a significant effect on office planning.
2. *Global markets.* The United States is no longer an isolated market. All organizations are forced to deal with an economy that has become truly global.
3. *Participative management.* A growing number of organizations are experimenting with participative management, encouraging communication, teamwork, lower level decision making, and self-management. These practices increase the productivity of the work force by focusing on communication and on the work to be accomplished, increasing the demand for more communication environments, team spaces, and information centers.
4. *Growing technical/professional work force.* Technical/professionals were nearly nonexistent in the traditional management structure. This group is highly educated and demands an appropriate physical environment and support tools.
5. *Increasingly sophisticated technology.* Data communications now include computer networking, inte-

grated telecommunications, and other equipment that distributes and processes information in the workplace. Hardware requires more precise installation practices and more exact specifications for cable and wiring for effective operation.

6. *Organizational change.* Organizations experience a 30% average turnover rate, as they are modified, restructured, downsized, or grow.

FACILITY PLANNING ISSUES

Office planning is the process of organizing the physical environment to support work processes and communication structures. It involves the development of planning tools, data bases, three-dimensional layouts, and specifications for materials, furnishings, equipment, and environmental services, and their integration with staffing, communication, and operational patterns. Changing organizational structures are reflected in the arrangement of the physical facility, improving communication and interaction.

Facility development usually requires a team of professionals with a variety of skills, including data collection, needs programming, operational research, interior design, architectural design, records management, telecommunications, mechanical and electrical engineering, and construction management. These professionals usually work with a facility manager familiar with the organization and its staff. Acoustics, security, lighting, and energy consultants may be retained on large projects.

Projects are usually developed as a response to strategic management planning. The results of such planning are facility performance specifications. These specifications define the elements and qualities of the facility that best support its intended functions.

Before the actual facility plan can be completed, preliminary studies of the occupants' functions and work to be performed are necessary. These studies are commonly referred to as operational research and facility programming. Collection and verification of this information is critical in allocating space, equipment, and furnishings and in projecting future changes.

Automated machinery, electronic communication systems, and data processing equipment have made the office of the 1980s extremely complex. Fast-changing technologies require that planning be not only precise, but flexible as well. Planning methods frequently make use of computers to organize and store data in a manner that facilitates quick retrieval and updating as necessary. Computer-aided design (CAD) programs to store and manipulate facility planning information will become commonplace as the need to make changes quickly increases. Many facilities have moved toward total demountable walls and office furniture, thus eliminating the need to demolish fixed walls with every change in organizational structure.

OFFICE-PLANNING CONCEPTS

Office plans fall into four categories: (*1*) conventional closed-office planning; (*2*) combination planning (closed offices with large open areas); (*3*) modified conventional planning (closed offices combined with open areas divided by partition screens); and (*4*) open planning.

Conventional closed-office planning is generally based on the assignment of private offices sized according to title and rank of the occupant. Persons of lower rank can be accommodated in semiprivate offices for two, three, or four persons. Secretaries in true conventional planning occupy a closed space adjacent to their supervisor. In combination planning, executives and managers occupy private offices, while secretaries and support staff most often work in large open areas that also serve as circulation space. Modified conventional planning is similar, except that open areas are divided into workstations by partial height partitions on two or more sides. True open planning, which has proven more acceptable in Europe than in the United States, accommodates all employees in large open areas with screens and plantings to provide the necessary acoustical and visual separation.

Each type of planning has its advantages and disadvantages. Choosing the optimum planning type requires a consideration of several factors, including construction cost, furniture cost, base building-lease costs, and the nature of the work that is performed within the organization. Acoustics, privacy, security, and staff interactions must be taken into account. Some studies have shown that more privacy supports better staff communication. The probability and cost of future moves must be taken into consideration.

If going to the open plan, there is a critical need for transition planning as an organization moves from closed offices to open planning. Midlevel managers often feel that their status in the hierarchy will be undermined owing to the move from closed to open. Most often, objections are related to the desire not to be supervised, and less to anticipated excess noise.

Work functions in offices generally fall into one of four major categories:

1. *Administrative.* Tasks are defined as paper- and computer-based, performed in support of project activities or organizational procedures and programs.
2. *Analytical.* Tasks are performed to provide analyzed data to project and programs. Research assistants and other paraprofessionals are usually included in this group.
3. *Professional/technical.* All staff who use a complementary professional expertise, such as in architecture, engineering, or the health sciences.
4. *Managerial.* This includes all levels of management.

Facility plans are increasingly based on function and less on status. There have been many attempts to simplify the work environment to eliminate the planning variations for each layer of managerial hierarchy.

Professional/technical staff, the fastest growing group in the office workplace, generally require special furnishings that do not meet most corporate standards. Thus, most organizations with stringent standards are changing criteria in order to serve the professional/technical group.

Facility Standards

Standards programs have become commonplace as facility planners attempt to minimize the number of vendors, purchase contracts, and inventories. There are two different types of facility standards: (*1*) basic building standards, which primarily relate to architectural and engineering building systems, and (*2*) functional workplace standards.

Functional workplace standards deal with factors such as floor space, office type, furnishings, lighting, allowable decoration, and finishes. While the first group is building specific, workplace standards are organization specific. Thus, they have a larger impact on productivity; for organization employees, well-developed standards programs present a more comfortable and productive environment.

Average floor space per employee is declining in the United States. However, the difference in space size between support staff and executive level is decreasing. Many organizations now recognize that administrative personnel require a larger work area to accommodate word-processing equipment and a substantial paper flow.

Many managers and executives who practice participative management are choosing a smaller floor space in their offices, to keep down obvious differences in size. They also find that a smaller office, when equipped with a conference furniture grouping, is more productive and saves on costly square footage.

Workstation Design to Support Electronic Technologies

Electronic and computer technologies have important implications for office planning. Much research has been conducted to optimize employees' comfort and productivity. One key conclusion derived from the research is that the work surface and chair must be adjustable within the correct ranges to accommodate employees' anthropometric differences. Critical measurements include work-surface height, the distance between seat and the work surface, the angle between the upper and forearms, and the wrist angle. Working at a poorly designed computer or word-processing work station can cause musculoskeletal and vision-related ailments.

References identify the optimum work-station measurement ranges, but not all are based on the computer terminal work tasks. For work stations designed to support a visual display terminal (VDT), the centerline of the screen should be 10–14 in. above the keyboard support. The most comfortable viewing range is between 18 and 24 in. in front of the screen. Adjustable chairs, with a range of 8–10 in., will correspond to the needs of the average height range of 5 ft. 2 in. to 6 ft. 3 in.

Adjustability is also desirable because people adopt a wide variety of postures when sitting in one place for a long period. A person seated at an office desk changes position on the average of once every 6 minutes. A person working at a computer terminal adjusts position as much as twice each minute.

The work surface that supports the keyboard should place it within an adjustable range of 24–28 in. Vertical and lateral adjustments can be made by using an articulated keyboard pad that moves forward, backward, up, and down. Additionally, a monitor pad placed under the terminal screen provides an additional height adjustment of 3–4 in.

In addition to the human/machine interface, the physical environment for computer terminals requires special considerations:

1. Lighting fixtures should be positioned so that they do not produce glare and veiling reflections on screens and work surfaces.
2. Heating, air conditioning, and ventilation (HVAC) capacity must be sized to offset additional heat loads generated by computers and other machines.
3. Provision must be made for data cabling connections. Cabling can be run through a number of channels, including underfloor duct, power poles, ceiling plenums, under-carpet flat cable, and raised floors.
4. Electronic equipment may have special requirements such as clean power, dedicated circuits, or isolated ground connections.
5. Floor, wall, ceiling, and work-surface finishes may require special treatment. Those finishes directly surrounding the computer terminal require the correct kV rating to minimize static electricity. Surfaces with low gloss minimize veiling reflections. Sound-absorbing surfaces aid in acoustical control where noisy printers are used.

Specialized Concerns in Office Facility Planning

Lighting. Lighting design is critical in the office environment because of its direct impact on the occupants' ability to perform tasks. Lighting levels of 40–50 footcandles (fc) are appropriate for general office tasks, whereas levels of 75–100 fc are necessary for specific tasks such as drafting or reading handwriting in pencil. Lighting levels are most effective when measured at work-surface level (generally 29 in. above the floor). Energy-saving fluorescent fixtures are typically used, often equipped with low-angle shielding lenses to prevent direct glare on CRT screens. Incandescent lighting is used for accent and more dramatic lighting at entrances and other spaces used by visitors. Dimmers are needed in conference rooms if slide or video presentations are anticipated. Natural lighting is most effective when provided from high, continuous clerestory windows or skylights, at even levels.

Task/ambient lighting is a design concept that reduces heat loads generated by light fixtures and tailors light to the specific work tasks. Low-level ambient light of about 30 fc overall is complemented by individual task lights at each workstation. Increasingly, task lights are incorporated directly into furniture or mounted under storage or shelving units. These lights, if not shielded and directed properly, will cause glare at the work surface.

Environmental Services. Cooling is nearly always the primary heating, ventilation, and air-conditioning load in offices, regardless of climate. This is due to increased building insulation and heat loads imposed by lighting, people, and equipment. Each personal computer generally injects the equivalent heat of one occupant into the environment.

Overheating can cause fatigue, which diminishes performance. Overcooling can produce restlessness. Lack of humidity in a facility increases static charge and causes general dryness of skin and eyes. Excessive humidity produces the sensation that spaces are much warmer than the temperature indicates.

Capacity must be provided not only to offset loads, but also to preserve indoor air quality. Many modern office buildings do not have operable windows; cigarette smoke and other pollutants must be removed mechanically. Variable air volume systems for office interiors, coupled with perimeter steam or hydronic terminal units, have proven to be cost-effective systems while still providing necessary comfort and control. Reheat may be necessary where large differences between loads within the same zone occur.

Sufficient temperature controls, carefully placed, prevent wide temperature variations within the office suite. Modern buildings often have large expanses of glass that can create simultaneous hot and cold areas, depending on the position of the sun. Furthermore, future changes in room partitioning may create problems when the controls become isolated from their original zones. Economizing on control systems may aggravate these problems.

The effect of air motion on comfort must be considered when designing the air-supply system. A diffusing ceiling must supply at least 25 ft per minute of air velocity in occupied spaces to avoid complaints of stuffiness and lack of air motion. Designing to a lower effective temperature can help compensate for the effects of inadequate air velocity. A steady air motion of 25–40 ft per minute is normally tolerable, but rapid variations in air motion create objectionable drafts and noises. An air velocity that may feel comfortable on the face can be too high and hence uncomfortable when felt on the neck or ankles.

Electrical Power and Cabling. A major challenge facing facility planners today is providing maximum integration, flexibility, and accessibility of the wiring system. Usually, four wiring systems are needed: electrical power wiring, communications wiring, electronics data wiring, and building automation systems wiring. Local area networks (LANS) can provide interconnections of communications, electronics, and building automation systems.

Speculative office buildings may not be equipped with sufficient power capacity to support a highly computerized office; prospective tenants should carefully compare their needs with the available capacity. Power capacity and cabling space in older buildings may also need to be increased if intensive computer and telecommunications growth is anticipated.

A minimum of 7–8 watts per square foot of electrical power is required to support a fully automated office. Most speculative buildings of the 1970s and 1980s were built with 3–4 watts, thus presenting potential lessees with inadequate supplies.

Telecommunications. Office telecommunications have imposed greater requirements in buildings to accommodate integrated telephone and data needs. A few buildings allow all tenants to share cable television, data transmission, electronic mail, and publicly available computer databases. Referred to as "intelligent buildings," these buildings incorporate cable, connections, switches, and other components directly into their structure.

Information Management. The information management system of any organization integrates paper-management procedures, records-management functions, filing systems, mail handling, and library areas. Increasing the consistency of formats, procedures, and output in each of the areas will significantly assist in creating an efficient management information system.

Paper Management. The intensity of information processing has given rise to techniques that minimize the quantity of paper generated, facilitate smooth paper flow, and provide efficient archiving. Such techniques establish procedures for copying and routing documents as well as guidelines for efficient filing, retrieval, and storage. Paper management studies are usually conducted by an operations analyst or management consultant who is an auxiliary member of the facility planning team.

Records Management. Records management addresses much more than the paper documents stored in filing cabinets. It is also concerned with tape reels, microfiche, microfilm, computer printouts, diskettes, and large-format graphics. A good management system accommodates a diversity of items. Records-management studies coinciding with an office-planning project are usually completed by a special consultant able to maximize the storage capacity of each unit of space. This consultant identifies points of document generation, flow, and use.

Filing. Filing systems within an office range from the single file drawer within an individual workstation to large mass filing rooms where miniaturized versions of documents are stored. Consistency of filing procedures is critical to maximizing office efficiency. Document storage cabinets designed to house a variety of materials in consistent formats are commercially available.

Mail Handling. Mail handling is most efficient when processed with as few steps as possible. Technologies for electronic sorting and routing of both incoming and outgoing mail are available at relatively low cost. Centralizing outgoing mail functions can prevent duplication and encourage more accurate weighing. In more mail-intensive office installations, robots that follow electronic tracks programmed to stop at predesignated mail stops are used.

Library. Library functions are an integral part of the office information-processing system. On-line document search services are increasing in popularity as an alternative to traditional cataloging systems. Large libraries of printed materials in office buildings designed only for normal structural loads can create excessive floor stresses. If floors cannot support library loads, then floors must be reinforced, or the loads must be dispersed over larger areas. Many very old buildings have loading capabilities of 100–150 lb/ft^2, whereas contemporary buildings may have as little as 50 lb/ft^2 loading capability.

Teleconferencing. Teleconferencing is increasing as organizations move toward greater communication and sophisticated data transfer. Teleconferencing facilities can be audio, audio-video, or audio-video combined with data transmission. Rooms require extra attention to soundproofing, lighting, furniture layout, and finish materials. Often, such rooms are segregated from outside noise and electronic interferences. They must also provide the comfort to enhance the conferencing activity.

Acoustics. Acoustics play an integral part in the design of offices, as noise is second only to thermal discomfort as a deterrent to employee productivity. A major aim is to prevent sound from traveling directly from one workstation to another. If this is not entirely possible, then intelligible speech should be prevented from traveling across workstation partitions. Speech privacy can be enhanced by using "white noise" machines that raise the level of background noise above the speech sound level. Good acoustical design is especially important in open offices. Although prefabricated workstation panels used in such offices are most often designed with sound-absorbing properties, consultation with an acoustical specialist may still be necessary. This is especially true in telemarketing areas or for activities requiring extreme privacy.

Vertical Transportation. Offices spanning multiple floors require efficient vertical transportation. Most common are elevators and escalators; interior stairways are primarily for first floor "monumental stairways" and fire exits. If a communicating stair is used between office floors, the surrounding structure usually requires modification to allow a cutout in the floor slab. Elevators are almost always required for handicapped access and must meet minimum size requirements. In addition, they must be sized to accommodate furniture and equipment.

Security. Security requirements can apply to information, products, and people. Office security systems include controlled card access, electronically monitored sound, and computer signal scrambling. Design of circulation corridors observable from key vantage points will discourage casual intruders.

Floor Loading. Floors must be structurally designed to support specialized functions characterized by heavy structural loads. These functions include libraries, as noted above, file rooms, medical records rooms, and other office support service areas with heavy equipment. In situations where the base building is leased, prospective tenants should confirm the design floor loads. Loading beyond the design loads must be reviewed and confirmed by a structural engineer.

Food Service. Organizations provide food service as an amenity for their employees or to encourage their staffs to remain close to the office during lunch and coffee breaks. Services range from banks of vending machines to full-service cafeterias with private dining rooms. Extensive food service usually requires consultation with a food-service specialist.

Displays and Exhibits. Displays and exhibits in corporate offices range from individual product presentations to museum-quality exhibits. These exhibits are usually part of the organization's overall marketing or public relations program and require specialized graphic and construction skills.

THE FACILITY-PLANNING PROCESS

Office facility planning includes program and budget development, site evaluation and selection, and schematic design. Establishing project goals, data collection, and projection of facility requirements are included in all phases.

Program Development

Program development or programming is the collection of information about the organization, its staffing, operations, space requirements, furniture and equipment requirements, communications, and service loads. The program defines the specific criteria to be included in the planned facility. It may be supplemented with an inventory of existing furniture and equipment that requires accommodation in the new facility.

Goals and Objectives. Good facility planning requires that the organization establish goals, determine the appropriate time frame, allocate resources, and verify any organizational constraints that will affect the physical office environment. During this process, past data are examined to estimate growth, capital budgets, and future requirements. Estimates of future revenues, anticipated market-share expansion, and changing demographics are also used to determine projections.

Support by top management will make data collection and programming more effective. A move to new or reorganized quarters presents the opportunity for changing the corporate organizational structure and/or revising procedures. Surveys to determine the quantity and flow of work output are used to uncover the need for supporting equipment for greater productivity.

Data Collection. Data are collected to determine existing conditions and to project future needs in the programming document. The necessary data include inventories of personnel, space, furnishings, communications, support services, and work-flow processes.

To establish a baseline, personnel are listed in an inventory that identifies each person to be housed by name, title, job description, department, division, and rank. A corresponding organizational chart is prepared, showing employees grouped according to unit, department, and division. The inventory of existing space is usually shown in block increments or displayed on floor plans.

Existing furnishings and equipment to be reused are listed by name, description, location, size, color, finish, manufacturer, product number, and inventory number. Each listing is supplemented with remarks relative to the condition, anticipated life span, serviceability, and specific service requirements. A separate inventory covers automated equipment, including computers, word processors, printers, and fax machines.

The communications analysis identifies the frequency of communications between individual employees, units, departments, and divisions. This analysis identifies the communication links in the organization. The strongest links indicate which departments and which persons should be in close proximity.

A support service inventory includes requirements for such functions as photocopying, telex, telefax, lounges, lunchrooms, training rooms, storage, conference, food service, and health facilities.

Projection of Facility Requirements. Data regarding existing conditions, growth requirements, and budgetary constraints are analyzed to arrive at the program for the new facility. These requirements include the following:

1. *Personnel projections.* Personnel are projected at one, two, five, ten and occasionally fifteen years, depending on the anticipated life of the lease or the building.
2. *Workstation standards.* Workstation standards are usually established for each employee classification. Standards are determined by the tasks performed, furniture to be accommodated, number and frequency of outside visitors, and intangible factors such as status and supervisory responsibility. As noted above, standards usually specify the size of the office or workstation, whether the office is private or open, required soundproofing, quality of finishes, telecommunications, data and electrical receptacles, furniture, and accessories.
3. *Total space requirements.* Floor-area standards specified for each employee type are multiplied by the personnel listings and summed by department and division. Totals are increased by a circulation factor, usually 1.25. The circulation factor will vary if the offices are open or closed, and with fire-egress requirements and any local code requirements.
4. *Adjacency requirements.* An adjacency matrix illustrated with bubble diagrams to represent ideal relationships is composed graphically from the communications analysis.
5. *Support service locations and requirements.* Shared support services are strategically located to maximize efficiency. Satellite service centers are used to combine services such as photocopying, word processing, telex, teleconferencing, and restrooms.
6. *Furnishings and equipment requirements.* Existing furnishings and equipment to be reused are subtracted from future requirements to generate a list of new items for purchase. These items should include not only individual stations, but also service equipment and public area furnishings.
7. *Base building requirements.* Base building requirements include structural, electrical, and mechanical construction; security; vertical transportation; bay size; window area; ceiling height; freight elevators; and parking. If the base building is to be leased, this information should be used to evaluate building alternatives.
8. *Anticipated service load.* Anticipated electrical and mechanical service loads can be calculated at this point to ensure that adequate building capacity is available.

Budget Development

A proposed budget is developed from the compiled program information and from past cost data. At this stage, the project budget usually includes base building costs and rent, interior construction costs, furnishings and equipment costs, professional service fees, productivity losses, miscellaneous expenses, and contingencies.

Base Building Costs and Rent. The building may be leased, purchased, or constructed. If the decision to lease, purchase, or construct has not yet been made, then the costs must be evaluated on an equal basis. Purchase or new construction options include debt service, insurance, taxes, utilities, and other expenses normally included in the rent, expressed in monthly or annual terms according to the amortization schedule. The figures also provide allowances for depreciation and sale of the building.

Interior Construction Costs. Interior construction costs include all construction not included in the base building: partitions, mechanical and electrical services, lighting, ceiling finishes, floor covering, wall finishes, and special millwork. In leased buildings, some of the interior construction cost is paid by the landlord. The amount of the cost borne by the landlord depends on the work letter prepared by the building owner at the inception of leasing. The remainder of interior construction costs are borne by the tenant. Tenants usually pay for telecommunications requirements, computer-related and other special construction, and upgrades from the standards identified in the work letter.

Furnishings and Equipment Costs. Furnishings and equipment costs are most helpful if they include costs for all new purchases, shipping, and installation.

Professional Service Fees. Professional service fees are fees paid to architectural, interior design, engineering, construction management, and other consultants required to complete the project.

Productivity Losses. The most difficult cost to estimate is the productivity loss. Any operation will suffer productivity loss from work interruptions resulting from moving. Lost hours per employee can be estimated to determine the total payroll cost, but the effects from a move also ripple through lost sales, reduced service, and staff attrition from those disenchanted with the move.

Miscellaneous Expenses. Moving costs as well as the printing of new stationery, new forms, and moving announcements are all miscellaneous expenses.

Contingencies. An additional 10–20% of the total cost is usually budgeted to cover last-minute design changes and unexpected field conditions encountered during construction.

Projection of Alternatives. Based on probable costs, the financial ramifications of alternatives (leasing, purchasing, open plan, conventional plan, etc) should be compared. Life-cycle cost analyses that incorporate first cost, operating expenses, revenue, financing, and inflation over the life of the project are often used to compare alternatives. The life over which the analyses are carried out is especially important, because short-term decisions may be different from longer term decisions.

Site and Building Selection

Site and building selection stems primarily from the program requirements. It comprises several activities, including site comparison, building analysis (if the building is existing), and lease negotiations.

Site selection begins by identifying potential locations and evaluating factors such as size, cost, utilities, transportation (both for personnel and shipping), parking, proximity to outside services used by the company, and amenities such as restaurants and parks, zoning, and surrounding neighborhoods.

If the organization is planning to lease or purchase an existing building instead of constructing a new one, then building alternatives must be evaluated. Specific criteria include the following:

1. *Lease or purchase cost.* Costs can vary much over the length of the lease, depending on the priorities of the landlord. Lease costs should be plotted for the entire length of the lease, to verify the impact of escalation clauses and other variable factors. If purchase costs for a building vary significantly in the same localized area, the condition of the building should be carefully verified.
2. *Floor area and configuration.* Different floor plans have different efficiency ratios, depending primarily on their shape and depth of bays. If the floors are small in area, an organization faces added costs as employees communicate between floors. Deep bays prevent good natural light in the interior, while shallow bays create inefficiencies in planning.
3. *Number of floors.* The number of floors in any building determines the possible number of adjacent tenants. An organization may consider the possibility of occupying more of a smaller building to gain a greater sense of identity.
4. *Column size and spacing.* The spacing between the columns will partially determine the appropriate size module for workstations. Use of a module consistent with column spacing will significantly increase the efficiency of floor-space use.
5. *Age and condition of the structure.* An old building that has been retrofitted with new systems can provide a higher quality interior environment than many newer structures. Buildings that were built in the 1960s and 1970s will have a minimum of electrical power and air-handling sized for occupancy without computers. A building in good condition structurally can be repaired cosmetically if surface finishes have been damaged.
6. *Other items.*

   Underground parking
   Condition of public areas
   Amenities such as plumbing and kitchens
   Mechanical system type and capacity
   Electrical capacity
   Window area
   Orientation
   Slab-to-slab clearances
   Fire-protection system
   Rentable and usable areas
   Elevator service
   Handicapped access
   Building standard work-letter allowances

In comparing leasing alternatives, work letters are compared to determine the quantity and quality of materials and services that each landlord will pay for in tenant buildout. Each work letter includes minimal quantities of building standard items such as partitioning, doors, lighting fixtures, cubic feet of air-handling available, number of electrical receptacles, floor covering, wall finish, and ceiling finish. Generally, if the allowances are not used by the tenant, they are forfeited. If credits are returned, dollar values are attached to each item to calculate the credit. When the final selection of the space has been made, a letter of intent is supplied to the prospective landlord.

A life safety and building cost analysis should be prepared for any space under serious consideration in order to identify code violations that require correction before occupancy. It will also identify constraints placed on office layout by codes. Code requirements govern partition construction, floor area, finishes, circulation paths, number of exits, proximity to fire exits and standpipes, energy conservation, handicapped access, alarms and fire detection, and electrical design.

Lease Negotiations. The point of departure for lease negotiations is the draft lease, which contains certain clauses open to negotiation. It includes clauses that describe conditions under which the space can be subleased and procedures for handling the profit from the sublease, options for renewing the lease and for leasing additional space, rent escalations, and build-out procedures. Other clauses, which may not be open to negotiation, should also be examined carefully, such as clauses governing the types of alterations permitted, provisions for HVAC beyond normal working hours, and the landlord's right to choose the build-out contractor.

Tenants should evaluate precisely how much usable area is actually available and how rentable floor areas are measured and calculated. The usable area is the actual square footage of a floor or office that can accommodate staff, equipment, and furniture. This is of prime interest to the tenant. The rentable area includes areas not exclusively available to the tenant such as restrooms, public corridors, and mechanical rooms. Rentable areas are used to calculate the total income-producing area of a building. The rentable area is also the basis for computation of the tenant's pro rata share of common areas on multitenant floors. These pro rata shares, sometimes known as loss, add-on, or core factors, make up the difference between the usable and rentable areas.

The Building Owners and Managers Association (BOMA) and certain large boards of realtors have developed guidelines for measuring and calculating floor areas. The following provisions are common:

1. *Single-tenancy floors*. The rentable area of a single-tenancy floor is computed by measuring to the inside finish of the permanent exterior building walls, or to the exterior glass line if at least 50% of the vertical floor-to-ceiling area is glass. Rentable area includes all area within exterior walls less stairs, elevator shafts, flues, pipe shafts, vertical ducts, HVAC rooms, janitorial closets, electrical closets, and other such rooms not available to the tenant to occupy as office space. Restrooms within and exclusively serving only that floor are included in the rentable area. No deductions are made for columns and projections necessary to the building's structure.
2. *Multiple-tenancy floors*. The rentable area of a multiple-tenancy floor is the sum of all rentable areas on that floor and is measured as described for a single-tenancy floor. To compute the rentable area for each tenant, usable area is calculated by taking dimensions to the office side of public corridors and base-building partitions and to the center of the partitions that separate adjoining tenants. The loss factor, a pro rata share of all rentable areas shared by one or more tenants, is then added to produce the rentable area.

Lease negotiations conclude with a signed lease. This may occur before the design phase or after. At the completion of this phase of planning, the tenant is assured that the base building can accommodate the facility functions satisfactorily and that the correct amount of space has been contracted for.

Schematic Layout/Conceptual Design

With commencement of the schematic design phase, the facility planning process is nearly complete. Schematic design is generally the first phase of standard architectural services, the phase in which the information collected in the planning process is illustrated graphically.

The schematic design phase often occurs during lease negotiations, since any tenant must know whether the space under consideration can accommodate all proposed functions satisfactorily. If new construction is being considered, the schematic phase represents the first actual drawings of the building and its interior spaces.

Block diagrams locate units, departments, and divisions on proposed floors, identifying the required square footage for each. Adjacencies reflect those identified in the communication survey.

Vertical relationships are diagrammed between departments and divisions to correspond with communication requirements. Vertical connections via stairway, elevator, and escalator are proposed between those entities that require close communication, but that cannot be accommodated on the same floor.

Space requirements identified in the program are sketched in the plan within the specified boundaries of each unit, department, and division. Although the design is preliminary, it is to scale and shows partitions, workstations, circulation, furniture, and equipment. Each employee is assigned to a workspace, and future staff are shown in additional spaces.

A statement of probable cost and a preliminary schedule are prepared for the entire project. Critical-path schedules show how the start of some activities depends on the completion of specific critical activities. This can speed up completion.

BIBLIOGRAPHY

General References

F. Becker, *Workspace: Creating Environments in Organizations,* Praeger Publishers, New York, 1984.

M. Brill, *Using Office Design to Increase Productivity,* Vols. 1 and 2, Workplace Design and Productivity, Buffalo, N.Y., 1984.

A. Cohen and E. Cohen, *Planning the Electronic Office,* McGraw-Hill, New York, 1983.

P. Drucker, *The New Frontiers of Management,* Dutton, New York, 1986.

E. Grandjean, ed., *The Ergonomic Aspects of VDT Terminals,* Taylor and Francis, London, 1982.

E. Grandjean, *Fitting the Task to the Man: An Ergonomic Approach,* International Publications Service, New York, 1981.

A. Kemper, *Architectural Handbook,* Wiley, New York, 1979.

W. Kleeman, Jr., *The Challenge of Interior Design,* CBI Publishers, Boston, 1981.

F. Merritt, *Building Engineering and Systems Design,* Van Nostrand Reinhold, New York, 1979.

W. Preiser, *Facility Programming,* Dowden, Hutchinson and Ross, Stroudsburg, Pa., 1978.

W. Pulgram and R. Stonis, *Designing the Automated Office,* Whitney Library of Design, New York, 1983.

M. Saphier, *Planning the New Office: From Feasibility to Move In,* McGraw-Hill, New York, 1982.

U.S. Congress, Office of Technology Assessment, *Automation of America's Offices,* Government Printing Office, Washington, D.C., 1985.

See also Ceilings; Interior Design; Lighting—Electric; Mechanical Systems; Noise Control in Buildings; Office Buildings

Maree Simmons-Forbes
The Forbes Group, Ltd.
Washington, D.C.

OLBRICH, JOSEPH M.

Joseph Maria Olbrich (1867–1908) was the Austrian architect most closely identified with the art nouveau style. Born in Troppau, he studied at the Kunstgewerbeschule (School of Applied Arts) in Vienna, and after traveling to Italy and Tunisia, he returned to work in the office of Otto Wagner from 1894 to 1898. In 1898, he designed a number of decorative villas in the art nouveau style. Demonstrating Olbrich's interest in handcrafted work and forms derived from nature, these villas include the Villa Bahr at Wien-Ober-St.-Veit, 1899–1900; Villa Stifft, Vienna; and the Berl House, Vienna. Olbrich's drawings for the interiors of these houses showed his facility with the decorative nature of art nouveau. These villas contrast with the work Olbrich did for the Vienna Secession, which was in a very different style.

In 1897, Olbrich joined Otto Wagner in the formation of the Vienna Secession, opposed to the then current historicism favored by the older generation in the city. Olbrich's most famous building is the Secession House in Vienna (1897–1898), the scene of rebel art shows under the skylighted flexible gallery space in this temple-form building. A long series of exhibitions served to promote the design of artists and architects of the secession group. The famous posters designed by Olbrich and other artists were used to publicize the exhibitions.

Although a close collaborator of Otto Wagner, Olbrich felt that each building's design should reflect the society of the time, as opposed to Wagner's objective approach to rational efficiency. The free poetic nature of Olbrich's designs were tolerated by Wagner, and Olbrich benefited from Wagner's rationalism.

In 1899, Olbrich joined a number of artists and the architect Peter Behrens in Darmstadt to form the Kunsterkolonie. At this time, there was a general turning away from art nouveau. Rivalry developed between the followers of Behrens and Olbrich, each of whom designed buildings in Darmstadt. Most of the buildings for the art colony were designed by Olbrich. The group exhibited at the 1900 Paris fair in a space designed by Olbrich, and a major exhibition and fair were held in Darmstadt in 1901, centered around Olbrich's Ernst Ludwig Haus (1899), the gallery for the colony. This gallery has been compared, by Henry-Russell Hitchcock, to the work being done at that time in Scotland by Charles Rennie Mackintosh, particularly the Glasgow School of Art (1899–1909) (1).

During the following years, Olbrich designed a number of houses at Darmstadt. He also had commissions for the Feinhals house at Cologne-Mareinburg (1908–1909) and the Tietz (now Kaufhof) department store in Dusseldorf, designed in 1906, but completed after Olbrich's death in 1908. These later works lacked the fresh quality of his earlier work and reflect the growing interest in classicism at that time. Olbrich's last works at Darmstadt were the Wedding Tower and Exhibition Gallery (1906–1908).

BIBLIOGRAPHY

1. H. R. Hitchcock, *Architecture: Nineteenth and Twentieth Centuries,* Penguin Books, Ltd, Harmondsworth, UK, 1977, p. 408.

General References

I. Latham, *Joseph Maria Olbrich,* Rizzoli, New York, 1980.

K. Varnedoe, *Vienna 1900: Art, Architecture & Design,* Museum of Modern Art, New York, 1986.

F. Russell in E. Godoli, ed., *Art Nouveau Architecture,* Rizzoli, New York, 1979, Chap. 10. This publication contains an extensive bibliography.

Robert T. Packard, AIA
Reston, Virgina

OLMSTED, FREDERICK LAW

Olmsted is best known for introducing the large rural character public park into the urban United States, for initiating the preservation of large tracts of land in their natural states, and for pioneering efforts in road systems and urban form. He made major contributions in other facets of society. He was among the first authors to use dialect in published writings, he advocated abolition of slavery on both economic and humanitarian grounds, and he pressed for proper absorption of the newly freed blacks into the economy. His writings on the prewar South are recognized by historians as authoritative. Olmsted had an awesome number of careers that overlapped in time. It is very difficult to fix the transitions from one enterprise to the next. Even though many of these ventures ended in financial failure, they usually were professionally successful or made a contribution to society.

Frederick Law Olmsted was born April 26, 1822 (d. August 28, 1903, Boston) in Hartford, Connecticut, to John and Charlotte Law (Hull) Olmsted. A year after his mother died (1826), his father married Mary Ann Bull. Within a year or so, Olmsted started attending various boarding schools in Connecticut run by stern and religious teachers (1826–1837). He then served an apprenticeship to a civil engineer (1837–1840).

After initial career attempts (one in the retail trade and another in the merchant marines, 1841–1844), he ventured into scientific agriculture, with studies at Yale University under Benjamin Silliman (1844–1845) and with direct experience while working for George Geddes in Onondaga County, New York, and running his own farm (first in Connecticut and then on Staten Island). His interest in plantings was both scientific and aesthetic, and brought him to meet and know Andrew Jackson Downing in 1847.

It was journalism that helped him to consolidate his interests in social reform, the natural environment, and education. His first book, *Walks and Talks of an American Farmer in England,* gave insight into British attitudes, especially their love of the out-of-doors. This book was based on his observations from a walking tour of the British Isles and western Europe in 1850; he was accompanied by his brother John and Charles Brace. Olmsted's comments regarding the British Birkenhead Park forecast his own park and planning career: "in a democratic America there was nothing to be thought of as comparable with this People's Garden" (1). Based on his journalistic abilities and his strong antislavery views, he was sent by the *New York Daily Times* to travel through the southern states (1852–1854). His newspaper articles on the slave states were published as a series of books and then edited into one volume, *The Cotton Kingdom* (which was very critical of slavery), to help to win British support for the North. In the United States, he urged efforts to provide educational and social opportunities to recently emancipated blacks (1861–1863). During his venture into journalism, he became part owner of a publishing firm, Dix and Edward, and editor of its *Putnam's Monthly Magazine* during 1854–1855; *Putnam's* failed financially in 1856.

By 1857, Olmsted's career focus turned to park administration with his appointment as Superintendent of Central Park, New York City, overseeing up to 4000 men. Then, in 1858, he won the design competition with Calvert Vaux for Central Park, and a month later was appointed Architect-in-Chief of the Park. In 1859, he married Mary Cleveland Perkins Olmsted, widow of his younger brother John Hull Olmsted.

During the Civil War, he was appointed Executive Secretary of the United States Sanitary Commission, which was organized to provide medical and health support for the Union armies (1861–1863). Although Olmsted took a temporary leave of absence from duties of Central Park to serve on the Commission, he made periodic visits to the park to supervise plantings and construction.

In 1863, his career changed to mining and Olmsted moved to California to become superintendent of properties for Mariposa Mining Company. This was followed by his appointment to the Yosemite Commission by Governor Low (California). Yosemite Valley and the Mariposa Grove of Big Trees were the first state parks in the United States. Olmsted was also instrumental in the Boston Park System, Niagara Falls, the Washington, D.C. parks, and many other major projects.

In his professional practice, Olmsted collaborated with a number of architects and designers, such as Calvert Vaux (Central Park; Prospect Park, Brooklyn, New York (Fig. 1); Morningside Park, New York City; Riverside, Illinois); H. H. Richardson ("Master-plan" for Staten Island; Ames Memorial Town Hall, Massachusetts; Boylston Bridge in the Boston Back Bay; Residence of Dr. John Bryant, Cohasset, Massachusetts; Thomas Crane Public Library, Quincy, Massachusetts; Mason Estate, Newport, Rhode Island); D. H. Burnham (World's Fair); and Richard Morris Hunt (Vanderbilt estate, Biltmore, North Carolina). Other collaborations included work with Horace W. S. Cleveland; Russell Sturgis; Peabody and Stearns; McKim, Mead and White; and William R. Ware. Partners in his professional practice included sons John Charles and Frederick Law, Jr. and, among others, Charles Eliot and Henry Codman. Olmsted's career was extended well into the twentieth century by the work of his sons and others such

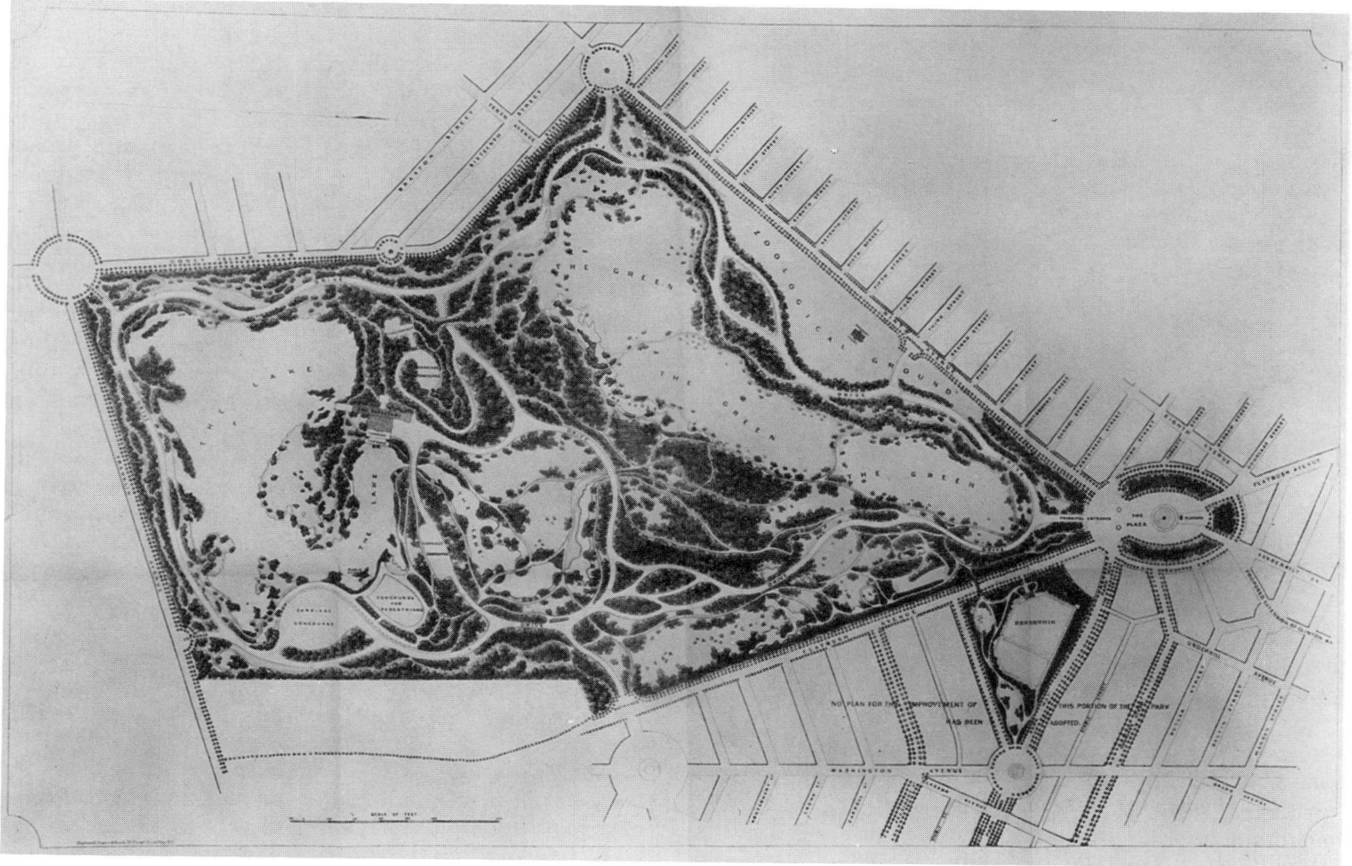

Figure 1. Design for Prospect Park, Brooklyn, New York.

as Charles Eliot II. Olmsted was given several honorary degrees including an MA from Harvard University for service to the U.S. Sanitary Commission; an MA, Amherst; and LLDs from Harvard and Yale.

BIBLIOGRAPHY

1. F. L. Olmsted, *Walks and Talks of an American Farmer in England,* c. 1852, reprint with introduction by A. L. Murray, University of Michigan Press, Ann Arbor, Mich., 1967.

General References

G. F. Chadwick, *The Park and the Town: Public Landscape in the 19th and 20th Centuries,* Frederick A. Praeger, New York, 1966.

A. Fein, ed., *Landscape into Cityscape: Frederick Law Olmsted's Plans for a Greater New York City,* Cornell University Press, Ithaca, N.Y., 1967.

A. Fein, *Frederick Law Olmsted and the American Environmental Tradition,* George Braziller, New York, 1972.

M. A. Isaacs, *Olmsted's Ecology,* unpublished manuscript, 1967.

N. T. Newton, *Design on the Land, The Development of Landscape Architecture,* The Belknap Press of Harvard University Press, Cambridge, Mass., 1971.

F. L. Olmsted, *The Slave States,* edited by Harvey Wish, Capricorn Books, New York, 1959.

F. L. Olmsted, Jr., and T. Kimball, eds., *Frederick Law Olmsted, Landscape Architect, 1822–1903,* Benjamin Blom, Inc., New York, 1970.

L. W. Roper, *A Biography of Frederick Law Olmsted,* The Johns Hopkins University Press, Baltimore, Md., 1977.

E. Stevenson, *Park Maker: A Life of Frederick Law Olmsted,* Macmillan Publishing Co., Inc., New York, 1977.

S. B. Sutton, ed., *Civilizing American Cities: A Selection of Frederick Law Olmsted's Writings on City Landscapes,* MIT Press, Cambridge, Mass., 1971.

C. Zaitzevsky, *Frederick Law Olmsted and the Boston Park System,* The Belknap Press of Harvard University Press, Cambridge, Mass., 1982.

See also LANDSCAPE ARCHITECTURE

MARK ISAACS
Alexandria, Virginia

OPERA HOUSES.

See THEATERS AND OPERA HOUSES

ORIENTAL ARCHITECTURE

CHINA

China is geographically the third largest country in the world today, slightly larger than the United States. Its topography is varied, with two-thirds of its vast land area mountainous or desert. Only one-tenth of the land is cultivated. The eastern region of China is one of the best-watered areas in the world. It is in this region that historically the population density has been the highest. The greatest amount of rain falls in the semitropical southeast, 25° N latitude, with accumulations of 50–60 in./yr. Proceeding up the eastern coast, ultimately to 45° N latitude, the climate becomes arid and harsh, with winter temperatures of 0°F being recorded. The morphology of the Chinese architectural tradition develops from indigenous geographic, climatologic, cultural, ethnic, and habitation patterns.

The written language of China, which is based on a system of pictographs still in use today, is more than 4000 years old. China, along with Sumeria, Egypt, and India, is considered to be one of the great ancient civilizations of the world. Based on known archaeologic sites and remains, the Chinese architectural tradition can be traced back at least 7000 years.

Although environmental conditions vary greatly throughout this vast land area, a specific, dominant architectural type evolved over the millennia. A system of materials, structure, organization, and orientation developed that was almost universally applied and still can be found in use today. The chronological development of the Chinese architectural tradition can be broken down into five historic stages.

During the period of the Xia (2100–1600 B.C.) China attained the highest level of development in East Asia. Because of its limited contact with other ancient civilizations, it developed an indigenous cultural form through internal exchange with its own diverse ethnic population.

In the Shang through the Zhou periods (1600–221 B.C.) the principles of wood framework construction and spatial or courtyard organization evolved.

From the Qin through the Han periods (221 B.C.–220 A.D.) these basic principles were expanded on and applied to the organization of building complexes and large urban developments. At this time, the architectural tradition had developed as an integral part of the cultural, economic, and political fabric of the Chinese people.

Buddhism entered into China from India during the Eastern Han to Northern and Southern dynasties (220–589 A.D.). It brought with it the architectural influence of India. The indigenous tradition of Chinese architecture was so well rooted that, although Buddhism made a significant impact on the theologic structure of China, it simply enriched the indigenous architectural form.

China remained a feudal society from the Sul through the Qing dynasties (589–1911 A.D.). This condition perpetuated the already institutionalized Chinese architectural system. The most significant erosion of this overwhelmingly stable architectural heritage has taken place through the influence of the Western world within the last 100 years.

The Chinese architectural tradition, which continuously evolved and matured over its 7000-year history, can be broken down into the following architectural elements:

1. *Construction System.* Rammed-earth platforms on which wood framing systems and stylized roof configurations were placed represent the elemental construction principles of the Chinese architectural tradition.

2. *Orientation.* A complex system of site and building orientation based on principles of natural observation and geomancy developed. This system, known as *feng shui* (wind and water), is one of the most significant principles applied to building organization.
3. *Courtyard.* As an outcome of cultural perceptions based on such elements as the Yin Yang (the coexistence of opposites such as positive and negative, male and female), the Chinese consider the architectural solid and the exterior spatial void to be interdependent. The development of the courtyard and its integral relationship to architectural form is recognized as a unique feature of this tradition.
4. *Garden.* Developed as an extension of the building/courtyard relationship, the garden emphasizes the integral quality of the manmade and natural world. The garden was intended to convey a sense of mystery so that from any particular vantage point the whole could not be perceived.
5. *Pagoda.* This vertical architectural element, derived from Indian prototypes, manifested the Buddhist influence in China. Sometimes integrated into the design of the Chinese garden, pagodas were often placed according to the principles of *feng-shui.*
6. *Pai-lous.* Freestanding monumental archways, with one to three bays, were often placed on a significant axis. This architectural form appears in other cultures, such as that of the Indian toranas and the Japanese torii.
7. *Wall.* A significant element in the Chinese architectural tradition, every important ensemble of buildings and spaces is defined by an enclosing wall. This element is applied to the greatest extent in the 2500-mi Great Wall of China.
8. *City.* The word *ch'eng* in Chinese has two meanings: city and wall. The assemblage of buildings in the traditional Chinese city is perhaps the finest example of urban order found in the world. It represents the summation of the totality of the architectural tradition of China.

In order to deal with the vast scale of Chinese architectural history and development, the above elements will be elaborated on as a simplification of a unique condition within the history of world civilization. This unique architectural condition represents one of the few remaining cultural artifacts in the world that has consistently maintained its essential form from its formal development 2000 years ago, in the Qin through Han dynasties, to the present day.

Construction System

The essential components of a building can be identified as the base, structure, and roof (Fig. 1). Each evolved and became highly specialized. The materials used were essentially earth for the base, wood for the structure, and various forms of tile for the roof. The ancients referred to architecture as the "work of earth and wood."

Figure 1. Buddhist Temple, Nan Yue, Hunan, China. Courtesy of C. Lundell.

Human habitation centered around the three principal rivers in China: the Yellow, Yangzi, and West. The soil condition in these areas is characteristically moist and unstable. This condition is essentially unsuitable for the construction of foundation systems that can support more than a rudimentary level of architectural development. To overcome this natural condition, the *hangtu* or rammed-earth technique developed. This involved the compacting of layer on layer of earth until a raised platform was constructed. A hierarchy evolved, where the finish material surface, be it earth, brick, or stone, and the elevation of the platform surface above the surrounding grade depicted rank and esteem within the social structure of the community.

For the most important buildings, the base is constructed in three or more levels, terraced one above the other to raise the building to a prominent position. As the base increases in height, its perimeter expands far beyond that of the building. The compacted earthen base acts as a large footing, distributing the weight of the building structure uniformly on the existing grade. The column base itself is of particular interest because of its *convetto* configuration. Constructed of stone, the round column base curves outward as it distributes the column load to the terraced base of the building. This configuration allows rainwater to flow in an unobstructed manner to the building platform, thus minimizing the penetration of water at the joint between the column base and column. The *convetto* form of the column base presents a minimum obstruction to feet and other moving objects.

Wood is the principal material from which the structure of a building is assembled. The *I Ching,* a famous historical book of Chinese wisdom, specifically considers wood and its symbolic significance. Together with fire, earth, metal, and water, wood is viewed as one of the five principal elements. Its ideogram is recognized as one of the eight oracular signs, which may also be translated into the word wind. Wood was so highly valued by the ancient Chinese that they considered it on a level with porcelain.

The structural principle most universally applied was the post and lintel system. The posts or columns were generally round in section and fabricated from pine or a type of wood called *nanmu*. The weight of the building was supported by the free-standing columns. Walls were used exclusively as spatial dividers and were not constructed to bear loads beyond their own weight as in Western architecture. Four adjacent columns, configured in square or rectangular shape within the structural system, defined a bay or *jian*. The *jian* was a standardized module from which the total floor area of a building could be determined by the number constructed.

The roof structure represents the most significant departure from the Western prototype. A complex system of brackets, *tou kung*; rectangular section beams, *nge fang*; vertical struts or short columns, *kua chu*; and purlins, *heng,* are configured at ascending elevations atop one another in a rectilinear matrix that is parallel to the ground plane. This is completely alien to the rigid triangulated truss system prevalent in the roof structure of buildings in the West.

The brackets or *tou kung* are recognized as a significant component of this system. They are equal in importance to the column capital in the West. Highly articulated, the *tou kung* function both structurally and decoratively, particularly in their placement beneath the roof eaves. This component allows the edge of the roof to project or cantilever out beyond the exterior column line.

The rectangular matrix of beams, struts, and purlins can be configured to allow the plane of the roof slope to be concave. This is one of the most characteristic elements of the traditional Chinese architectural form. Although this configuration has become stylized, its original intention was twofold. First, the concave sweep of the roof lifted the projecting edge of the eave to allow the warming winter sun to penetrate deep into the interior recesses of the structure. Second, the gentle curve slowed the flow of rainwater and projected it out beyond the perimeter of the building. On the eastern coastal areas in the southern latitudes where rainfall is abundant, the traditional curve of the roof is extreme. Proceeding north, the climate becomes arid and the curve of the roof is subtle. These regions have historically identified with the curvature of the roof indigenous to their locale. Four basic types of roof form can be found: the hip, gable, half-hip half-gable, and pyramidal. Each form can accommodate the varying degrees of roof slope curvature applicable to the different climatic regions.

The ridge atop the roof is generally heavy and bold. The ends are often embellished with sculpted fish tails or dragons. Although stylized over time, the original purpose of the ridge beam was to weigh the structure down, thereby securing its integrity. The structural system was dependent on the compressive thrust of its own weight to maintain itself. Without provision for vertical diagonal bracing, as found in Western architecture, the lateral strength of the structure was determined by surface friction between the joints, which was a result of the load imposed on them.

Originally, the surface of the roof was covered with grass or thatch. As population centers became more dense, the destructive potential of fire increased. From this threat evolved the development of fireproof ceramic roof tiles that helped to minimize the spread of fire in urban centers. Glazed tiles of specific color are used to designate function or proprietorship. Yellow tiles are reserved for the palaces of the Emperor. The roofs of the Prince's palace are covered in blue tile. Common buildings use an unglazed ceramic tile.

An integral part of the construction system was a palette of color that was applied to all or a part of every component of the system. The colors used had particular significance as to the function and location of the building. The warm colors of the spectrum, such as red and vermillion, were widely used in the northern latitudes and applied to pillars, doors, and windows. The cool colors, blues, greens, and such were applied to the architrave and other architectural elements that appear in the shadow of the roof eave. In the southern latitudes the colors are more subtle, with greater application of grays and browns and less of an overall polychrome effect.

China was one of the first countries to develop oil-based pigmented paints as a preservative for wood. The ancient Chinese believed that color has a strong association with the five basic elements: metal, wood, water, fire, and earth. The application of color in combination with the architectural form determined in part the well being of the inhabitants. The colors associated with the elements and their meaning are white with metal (peace and sorrow), blue with wood (permanency and peace), black with water (destruction), red with fire (happiness and wealth), and yellow with earth (power, wealth, and sovereignty). Red is the most predominantly applied color to architecture in China. Glazed roof tiles of yellow and blue were used exclusively on buildings occupied or acknowledged by the Emperor. Green or unglazed tile is used on most common buildings.

The ensemble of building base, structure, roof, and color palette have evolved into an intricate and highly refined system of construction. This system is a significant departure from that which developed in the West and has maintained a higher level of developmental continuity. The most significant threat to the continued development of this system has taken place in the twentieth century, with the introduction and absorption of Western cultural values and technology.

Although the traditional building technology of China has remained consistent over the past two to three thousand years, it is interesting to note that, owing to internal and external sociopolitical conflicts, few significant historical artifacts of this technology remain intact today. In the West the technologic tradition is fragmented and never developed along a single line of evolution, yet artifacts of this tradition are readily found.

Orientation

Great significance is associated with the orientation and placement of manmade artifacts in the landscape (Fig. 2). The method of placement attempts to recognize a complex system of forces, visible and invisible, that exist in the earth and to orient buildings in such a way as to be in harmony with this system. The methodology combines scientific and psychic knowledge into a form of geomancy known as *feng shui* (wind and water).

The origins of *feng shui* can be traced to early man's intimate relationship with nature during the Neolithic Age (8000–2000 B.C.). From this relationship evolved an indigenous theology based on nature worship called Taoism. Confucianism developed about the same time and is based on a system of logic and order. The basic concept of Taoism is that all things in the cosmos are vital and interrelated. The earth is thought of as being organic and to have all the characteristics of human existence. *Feng shui* is a system by which a person's existence and the earth's may be aligned for mutual benefit.

In the third century A.D., two schools of thought developed based on the basic belief system of *feng shui*. The first developed in Fujian province using astrological mapping devices. A compass was established that combined cosmic orientation with world-based knowledge, such as found in the *I Ching* (The Book of Changes). This device could be used to map out the placement and orientation of buildings. The second school of thought, developed in Jiangxi province, stressed the close scrutiny and observation of the climate and landscape and other earth-based phenomena. The shape and form of the land mass and the direction and flow of water were specific indications of internal forces within the earth that must be accommodated in the placement of buildings.

Buildings placed in harmony with these various earth forces would, it was thought, avoid natural catastrophe and promote the well being of those who inhabited them. An obvious physical manifestation of these principles can be seen in the consistent southern orientation of traditional buildings in China. Evidence of the success of *feng shui* is found in the numerous tombs uncovered throughout China whose contents, human and inanimate, have been particularly well preserved without the application of the type of preservation technology, mummification, and such found in the West.

The southern orientation of the principal building within a complex of structures disposed symmetrically about a primary north–south axis is an outcome of the application of the orientation principles of *feng shui*. The symmetric organization of the building complex itself can most probably be attributed to the ordered hierarchy of Confucian pragmatism. This type of building disposition emanates a sense of serene order that, when placed properly in the landscape, becomes one with it.

Archaeological excavations in Henan province have uncovered buildings from the Yin Dynasty (1300–1028 B.C.) that are symmetrically laid out along a north–south axis and demonstrate the application of orientation principles associated with *feng shui*. Today, *feng shui* is neither recognized nor practiced within the People's Republic of China because it is officially viewed as being nonscientifically based. In nearby Hong Kong, however, a city which more closely resembles the pace and pattern of twentieth-century Western life, geomancers professing knowledge of

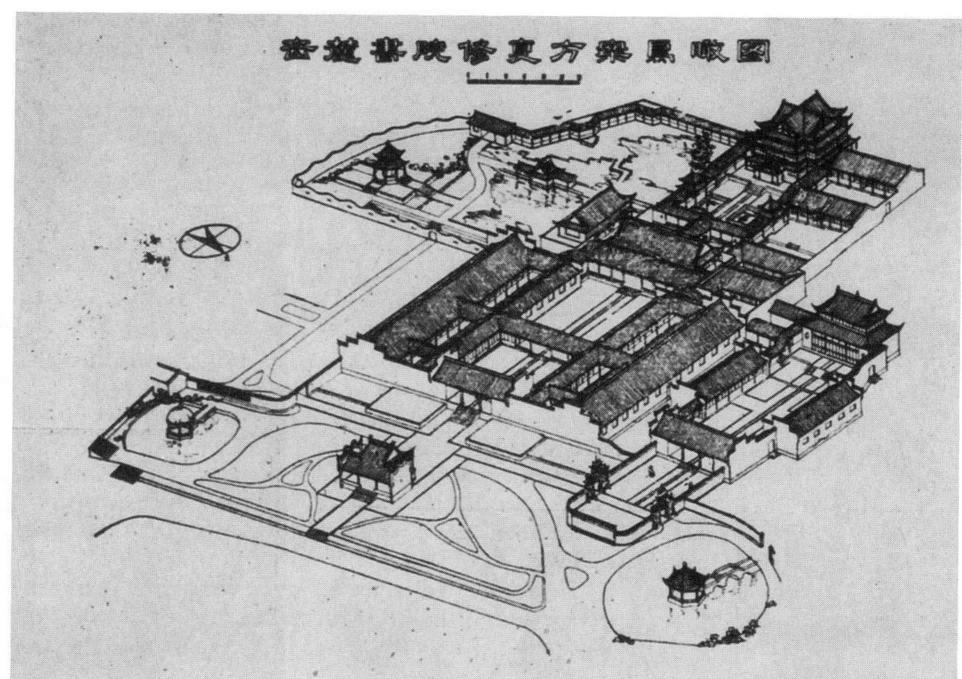

Figure 2. Aerial perspective of Yue Lu Academy, Hunan University, Chang Sha, Hunan, China. Courtesy of C. Lundell.

feng shui are consulted on the siting and orientation of modern glass and steel skyscrapers. Even with its over three-thousand-year history of application, *feng shui* remains an architectural organizing device that is mysterious and difficult to gain access to and thereby evaluate on a scientific basis.

Courtyard

Few buildings in China stand alone. Perhaps as an outcome of Taoist thought, most buildings are constructed as a part of a complex of interrelated structures (Fig. 3). To the Western eye, it is difficult to identify a Chinese building as a discrete element within its setting. In the Western architectural tradition, the recognition of the individuality of a building is more the rule than the exception.

The general organization of buildings on a site is laid out within a nine-square grid, similar to a tic-tac-toe game. The dimensions of the grid are based upon the *jian* as a modular element. The central square within the grid is left unoccupied, while the remaining eight squares are built on.

Many variations are developed from this basic scheme, but the central void is always present. The Chinese called this void or courtyard a *tien ching* (heaven well). The resultant figure/ground or solid/void relationship between building and courtyard is demonstrated in the concept of the *yin yang*. The *yin yang* professes the belief that oppositional elements, solid/void, in this case, coexist within all things.

Most courtyards are oriented on a north–south axis. The most significant building within the complex is called *zhengfang* and is established at the northern edge of the courtyard, facing south. In front of this building and to the east and west of the courtyard facing each other are subordinate buildings called *xiangfang*. At the southern end of the courtyard facing north is the *nanfang* or southern building. Beyond this building, and on the same north–south axis as the *zhengfang* and the *nanfang* facing outward is the main gate or *damen*. With the exception of the main gate, all buildings within this complex open exclusively onto the courtyard.

The function of the courtyard was varied. It served as a circulation space, device for catching water in cisterns, cooking space, light well, garden, fortified space, and ceremonial space. Great variation can be found in the size and complexity of the building/courtyard configuration. The number of buildings and courtyards was clearly determined by social status, but, in almost all cases, the north–south axis remains as the principal path of access to the *zhengfang*.

In the larger complexes, a series of symmetrically laid out courtyards and gates placed on a north–south axis must be passed through to gain access to the principal building. The bases or podiums of the buildings along this central axis are increasingly elevated as one proceeds from south to north. This articulation of mass and space heightens the grandeur of the procession and makes the visual appearance of the *zhengfang* all the more imposing.

As the Emperor was assigned the exclusive use of the color yellow, signifying his association with the earth and his position within its center, so the courtyard was the center of existence within the building complex. Invisible and intangible, it is the architectural device that brings color to the manmade environment. It was the world in a microcosm about which daily life revolved.

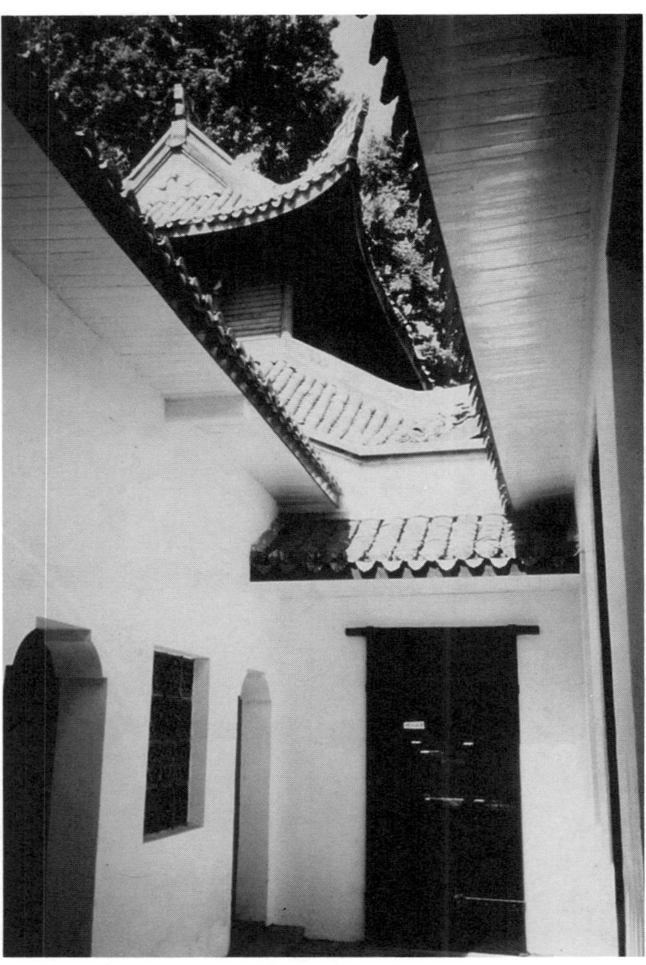

Figure 3. Interior Court at Yue Lu Academy, Hunan University, Chang Sha, Hunan, China. Courtesy of C. Lundell.

Garden

The construction of Chinese gardens (Fig. 4) can be traced back in history at least 2500 years to the Han dynasty. The garden was a rational extension of architecture and the intermediate condition between the manmade and natural world. As a realm caught between architecture, as a manifestation of mankind's comprehensible reality, and nature, as a manifestation of an incomprehensible life force, the garden provided the Chinese with a medium through which the known and unknown could be captured. The garden was the abode of the immortal.

In the design and appreciation of the garden, the concepts of *yin yang* and *feng shui* were applied in an attempt to capture the unknown through mystic knowledge. The dialectic of the garden is represented in the opposing philosophies of Confucianism and Taoism. Confucius sup-

Figure 4. Framed view of a Chinese garden, Suzhou, Jiangsu, China. Courtesy of C. Lundell.

ported a reality based on the constructed social order of the world as defined by humanity. Taosim supported all the forces of existence that live beyond humanity. The garden was the mediator between the two most significant indigenous theologies in China.

Form, shape, direction, and movement were all important elements in garden development. The geometries of the square and circle can be used to demonstrate the dialectic that exists between the order of architecture and that of the garden. The square is representative of the social structure of mankind's created reality or *li,* which is clearly manifested in the traditional order of Chinese architecture. The circle represents that reality that exists beyond mankind, or *fang-wai,* which is the condition of nature and the garden, albeit manipulated by humans in their attempt to obtain the unobtainable. The alignment of celestial bodies with various views within the garden were details that enhanced the beauty and intellectual scope of the design. Garden compositions were intended to be perceived either while moving through the landscape or by a stationary observer of a particular setting.

People were consumed by their desire to attain perfection in the construction of the garden. There is the story of the Emperor Hui-tsung of the Sung Dynasty (1082–1135) who because of his unsatiable desire to develop and expand his imperial garden wrought economic disaster on his empire through his neglect of more worldly pursuits.

The type and scale of the garden was determined basically by its ownership, private or royal. Private gardens, though often extensive, never attained the level of expansiveness of the royal garden. Garden-making became quite fashionable and, after the Sung Dynasty, 1000 A.D., the arts of poetry and landscape painting became an integral part of garden design. Gardens became more intricate and complex, ultimately reaching their zenith in the Qing Dynasty, 1800 A.D.

The private garden in general was an extension of the urban dwelling. It was a captured piece of the natural world within which the resident could take refuge from a manmade existence. Mystery and elements of concealment and revelation were an important part of the composition. Private gardens tried to evoke *xieyi* (emotion) through their ability to capture *shensi* (natural beauty). The garden design often attempted to scenographically depict the minaturized landscape. The inspiration for these compositions came from landscape paintings. Poetry was also used as a device to order the landscape. The spirit of vast natural landscapes was depicted in these small urban gardens. Mountains, forests, rivers, and lakes were translated into garden elements occupying a few square yards. Small-scale architectural structures were incorporated in the large private gardens. They were placed to provide a particular vantage point to the viewer. Windows in garden pavilions were often likened to three-dimensional pictures on a wall, the coexistence of the real and the unreal.

The principles and concepts applied to the royal gardens were similar to the private garden except that the scale in time and space was expanded. Mythologic themes were introduced. The garden was often composed of a series of smaller gardens thematically developed around a particular kind of natural scene or setting. The royal garden often incorporated into its design a significant element of the existing natural landscape such as a stream, lake, or rock outcropping. The smaller independent gardens, *zuoluo,* were often connected by a system of radial axes that unified but did not overpower the scheme of the garden. Large-scale pavilions, pagodas, and other architectural elements were introduced, which often allowed the gardens to be truly inhabited over an extended period of time. The expanded scale of the royal garden allowed humans to live in the abode of the immortal.

Pagoda

Although considered to be an architectural form indigenous to China, the pagoda (Fig. 5) can trace its origins to the Indian stupa. The world pagoda was actually first used by the Portuguese in the sixteenth century to describe the Indian stupa or temple structure. The stupa was an Indian religious structure associated with Buddhism. Its configuration was round at the base and generally hemispherical or conical in form. A mast or tower was erected at its top. The original function of the stupa was a burial tomb for the bones of Buddha.

As Buddhism expanded northward into central Asia

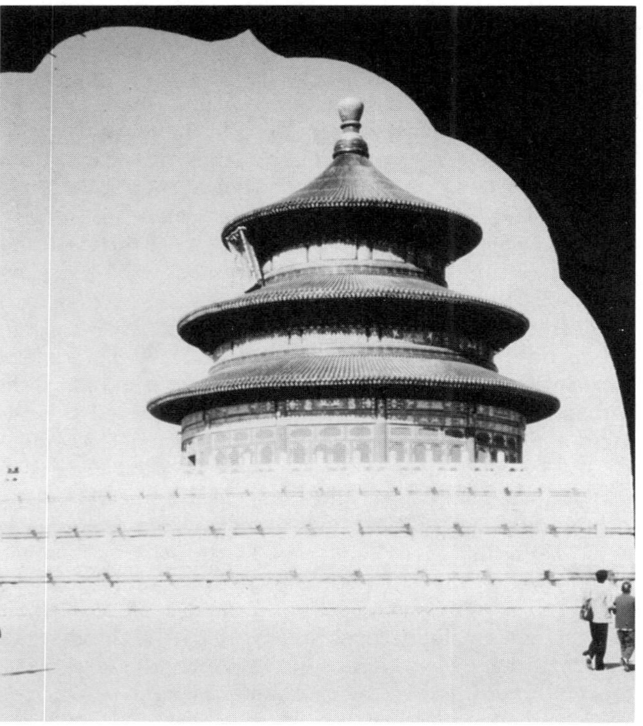

Figure 5. Hall of Prayer for Good Harvests, Temple of Heaven, Beijing, China. Courtesy of C. Lundell.

and China, it brought with it the stupa form as an architectural prototype. By the end of the Three Kingdoms period (280 A.D.) in China, the stupa form had been modified and maintained its original form only at the level of the mast or tower that was placed atop a multistoried building.

The Chinese pagoda form was distributed throughout China by the spread of Buddhism. It was generally constructed as part of a Buddhist monastery complex. The height and number of stories varies greatly, but generally the number of stories is uneven, with 13 being common among the larger structures. Access to the various levels is generally obtained through a system of internal stairs. Often, exterior balconies are located at each level.

By the time the pagoda form fully evolved, it had little resemblance to the Indian stupa. The present pagoda form is more like the ancient tower structures associated with early fortified cities. This is a clear demonstration of the absorptive ability of the architectural tradition of China.

Most of the early structures were constructed of wood and erected on an octagonal base. A traditional concave roof configuration was constructed at each level of the structure with the projecting eave supported by *tou kung*. The pagoda generally occupied the principal central space of the monastic complex and was the most significant architectural edifice. The complex would be symmetrically laid out on a north–south axis, with the principal alignment of the axis running through the centrally located pagoda.

Within the temple complex the pagoda served as a three-dimensional mandala or prayer wheel. The eight sides of the pagoda each represent the eight deities encompassing the Great Illuminator Vairocana in a Tantric Buddhist mandala. The 13 stories imply the ascending levels of knowledge or enlightenment. The notion of the pagoda serving as a stupa or burial tomb was ultimately to be left behind in India.

Wood was the principal material used for construction in the early development of the type. None of these fourth and fifth century structures remain. The oldest pagoda still standing in China is the Songyue si Pagoda, in Dengfeng, Henan Province. Constructed in the year 523 A.D., it is built of brick and mud and stands 15 stories tall (90 ft) on its octagonal base. The roofs and walls of each level are inaccessible and windowless.

As the pagoda became a part of the architectural vocabulary of China, its form was applied to secular settings and often was incorporated into a garden setting. Because of its unique ability to provide a focus or center for a composition of buildings, the principle of *feng shui* was often applied in its placement.

P'ai-lous

A ceremonial free-standing gateway, the *p'ai-lous* (Fig. 6) can be traced to the Indian *toranas*. Its form and function can be likened to the Roman triumphal arch.

Placed across a principal axis to indicate transition from one realm to another, the *p'ai-lous* generally marked the beginning of a processional axis. The importance and scale of the axis determined the number of openings or archways in the *p'ai-lous*. Often there is a single opening; a *p'ai-lous* with three openings is not unusual. In rare

Figure 6. Circular Mound Altar of Heaven, Temple of Heaven, Beijing, China. Courtesy of C. Lundell.

instances as many as five openings may be present, as seen at the principal tomb of the Ming Tombs (1550 A.D.) in Beijing.

If more than one opening is used, there is always an odd number. The central opening is always larger than the adjacent openings. Although constructed as a gate, neither the engaging wall nor the doors are present. An inscription is often placed on a lintel over the opening.

The function of a *p'ai-lous* is primarily spiritual. It manifests the act of transition and draws on the doorway or gateway form to symbolize this act. Most often these structures were constructed of stone, but in some cases they were built of wood, as demonstrated by the all-timber *p'ai-lous* located at the lake of the Summer Palace in Beijing.

The variations in size and form were great. On the more elaborate structures, a roof with glazed ceramic roof tiles was placed above the inscribed lintel stones.

Wall

In China, the wall has always served as an element of division. Sometimes this was the outcome of a need for fortification, sometimes merely demarcation. The wall served to define that which was inside and outside (Fig. 7).

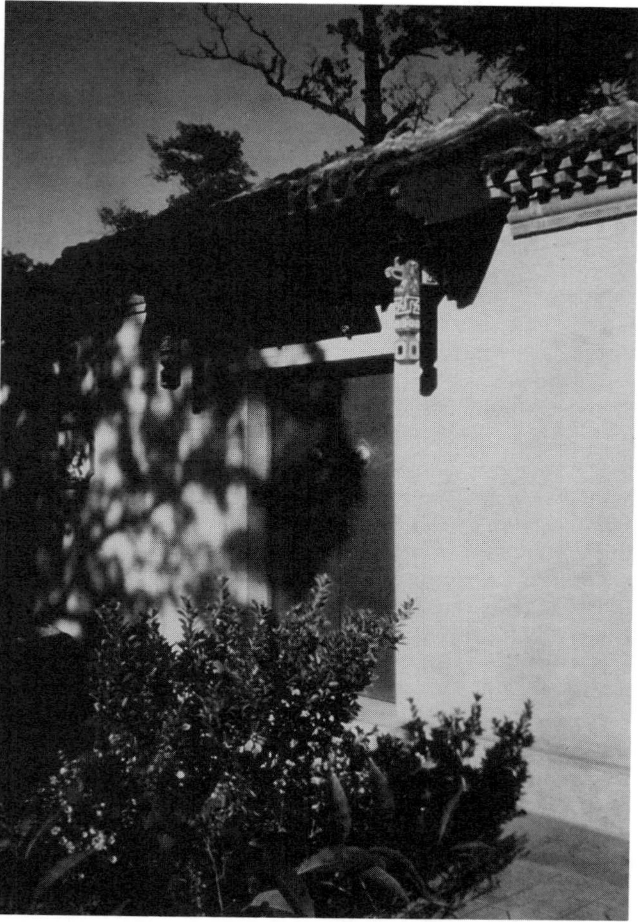

Figure 7. Garden wall and doorway, Beijing, China. Courtesy of C. Lundell.

In its application to the traditional construction system, the wall was used almost exclusively to define space. In general, it was not a part of the structural system, as is common in the West. The bearing-wall system used in Western construction is not found in the post and lintel tradition of China. In the application of the wall to interior space, the use of the term screen may be more appropriate. Interior walls or screens were often transparent, made up of intricate patterns, and highly stylized. The screens were constructed of wood and were simply used to define space rather than enclose and isolate it.

The application of the screen wall to the post and lintel construction system often led to buildings that were perceived as being open and transparent when compared to those in the West. It is only in the twentieth century that the Western architectural tradition has come to recognize the application of post and lintel screen wall construction to the technology of steel and glass or curtain-wall construction.

In its exterior application the wall becomes more substantive, very clearly defining and enclosing space. In the Chinese architectural tradition, groupings of smaller buildings each serve a particular function rather than many functions being served within a larger structure. From this more specific approach to architectural composition the Chinese have developed the spatial notions of courtyard and garden. The exterior perimeter wall served as a device to unify this ensemble of solid and void. This is clearly demonstrated by the organization of large-scale palace compounds, but it can also be found in small-scale traditional urban dwellings sometimes called courtyard houses. In the urban courtyard, house space was at a premium. Often the building structure was forced to the perimeter of the site, to allow for an internal courtyard, and was incorporated into the surrounding exterior wall.

Each ensemble of buildings and spaces is an entity unto itself, be it a small private residence or a royal palace. This entity was defined and fortified by the surrounding perimeter wall. Each building compound serves as a world unto itself, with the Western notions of public park and square being reduced and contained within the private residence as garden and courtyard. The wall defines this place and also manifests the social attitude of a world that exists inside versus a world that exists outside.

The word *ch'eng* in Chinese means both city and wall. In the way that the wall unifies and fortifies the private residence, so it is applied to the city. Surrounding its perimeter, the wall defines and fortifies the city and divides the world in terms of inside and outside. The walls surrounding the city were often massive and laid out parallel and perpendicular to the interior street grid. The integrity of the wall would be interrupted by entry gates located at the terminus of principal streets within the interior urban grid. Fortified watchtowers were often placed atop the corners of the city wall. The fortified wall usually followed the north–south, east–west alignment of the city grid.

To carry the concept of the wall to its greatest scale in application, consideration must be given to the Great

Wall of China. In Chinese the Great Wall is called "The Long Wall of Ten Thousand Li" (*Wan Li Chang Cheng*). First constructed in the fifth century B.C. by various Chinese states, the wall protected them from invasion by the northern barbarians. When the empire was unified in 221 B.C., the various segments of the wall were connected. It is said that it took 300,000 workers 10 years to complete the construction. Abandoned and reconstructed numerous times, at its greatest length the wall covered a distance of 2500 mi. The wall functioned not only as a fortification but also as an elevated roadway along which soldiers and horses could be dispatched from one location to another with great speed. The Great Wall was the only manmade artifact on earth discernible by astronauts from the moon.

Even at the vast scale of mainland China, the application of the concept of the wall used to define the world can be seen. Just as in the garden and courtyard, that which is known is inside and contained while the unknown is outside and limitless.

City

The city plan in China is clearly the outcome of the implicit order found in Confucian philosophy. It was only through the rigid order and hierarchy of this indigenous philosophy that the city plan could assume such clarity of form. The symmetric disposition of buildings about a central north–south axis became the unifying theme that was applied to the city, the neighborhood, and the house.

Written consideration of the city as a topic can be traced to the Eastern Zhou period (770–256 B.C.) in a document entitled Records of Trades (*Kaogong ji*). Han dynasty (206 B.C.–220 A.D.) scholars most probably have modified this work to accommodate their contemporary concept of the city. A portion contained therein describes the ideal capital city as being square in plan totaling 3.6 mi., 3 (*li*) at each side. This nine-square plan has three gates at each side, with nine longitudinal and nine transverse principal streets subdividing the internal plan. Each street needed to be sufficient in width to accommodate nine chariots abreast.

The city generally was enclosed within a rectangular fortified wall and contained an orthogonal street grid laid out on a north–south, east–west cross axis. The principal thoroughfare bisected the plan, running north–south. The hierarchic order of the city ran from south to north. The primary entry was in the center of the south wall, with an ascending order of buildings disposed about the principal axis as one proceeds north.

This urban design organizational prototype is most impressive, owing to the almost universal nature of its application. There is the clear implication that regardless of the social or political divisions that tore at the fabric of China over the millenia, a greater collective order transcended these internal conflicts and unified the structure of this vast land.

Despite the obvious classical rationale applied to the urban grid structure, the early configuration of this form, second century B.C., is a model of organic cellular organization. A small nuclear city was constructed within a larger city form. Both grids were surrounded by the defensive walls, and access was gained through fortified gates. This small city was of three types: palace-city (*gongcheng*), government-city (*yacheng*), or simply small-city (*zicheng*).

From 475 B.C. to 960 A.D., the city form grew and became more complex and enclosed. Neighborhoods (*fang*) or wards (*lifang*) within the city proper also became defined by enclosing walls. Ultimately, even the marketplace (*shi*) was enclosed. This compartmentalization of the city provided great security and control. Markets could be opened and closed at specific hours, curfews could be strictly enforced. These developments all took place during the heyday of military rule. These types of cities were called ward-system cities (*lifangzhi chengshi*).

During the Northern Song (eleventh century A.D.) growth and prosperity overcame the insular ward-system cities. Money was to be made, food and materials were to be traded. The walls of the ward-system cities got in the way, they restricted and impeded the ebb and flow of commercial trade. With the internal walls removed, commercial development began to take place along the major thoroughfares. The primary streets and lanes became lined with shops and markets. This new type of city form was called the street and lane system city (*jiexiangzhi chengzhi*). This is the most common city form found in China.

Twentieth-century Chinese Architecture

In the last decade of the nineteenth century, large numbers of Western architects began to arrive, particularly from England, and set up practice in the treaty ports of China. Much of the commercial architecture in the cities of Shanghai and Canton were either designed by these foreign architects or were influenced by their presence. The Western architects hired and trained local Chinese to work in their offices, thereby exposing an entire generation of Chinese to the Western architectural tradition. Many examples of buildings constructed by these firms are still intact today.

In the years 1910 to 1920, many young Chinese went to the United States and Europe to receive their formal architecture education, which essentially fell into the beaux-arts tradition. After 1945, many young students returned to China after having been exposed to Walter Gropius and the work of the International style. These influences were short lived, owing to the success of the "liberation" of China by Communism, which brought with it the architectural traditions of the Soviet Union and the return to the beaux arts.

In the period after the "cultural revolution," China began once again to embrace Western contemporary architecture. The fervor for all things Western was so great that much of the sensibility of the long building tradition of China has been overlooked, diminished by the fascination with the new and Western.

JAPAN

The Japanese archipelago covers a land area approximately the size of the state of California. It is made up of a group of four large land masses surrounded by thousands of smaller islands. The archipelago essentially runs north to south 1700 mi at approximately the same latitude as Maine to Florida, 45–20° north latitude. The average width east to west of this chain of islands is approximately 150 mi from the Pacific Ocean on the eastern shore to the Sea of Japan on the west. In general the terrain is mountainous, with a significant amount of volcanic and seismic activity. Rainfall throughout the island chain is very high, with monsoons and typhoons crossing the island shores annually. Japan is a country that is constantly threatened by the forces of nature.

Because of Japan's isolation from the land mass of Asia, its cultural evolution developed more slowly. China developed a mature architectural tradition by the end of the second century A.D. At the same time, Japan had developed only to a level equivalent to fifth century B.C. China. Much of the early influence on Japanese architecture came from the Polynesian Islands to the south. It is during this period that the most significant indigenous architectural form in Japan developed at the site of the Ise shrine.

Ise is the spiritual center of Japan's national religion, Shintoism. Shintoism is a nature-based theology/mythology propagating the origin of the Japanese people and culture.

The Jomon culture developed between 7000 and 250 B.C. It is noted for, and its name is derived from, a type of pottery created by placing cords of clay atop one another to form pots. The architecture of this period consisted of circular pit dwellings constructed of earthen mounds covered with a tentlike structure.

The Yayoi period existed between 250 B.C. and 250 A.D. The architecture of this period developed as a result of influences from the southern islands and Polynesia. Evidence of Chinese Han dynasty influence can also be found. It is probable that the first Shinto shrines can be traced to this period. These structures are houselike in form and are the prototype for the nineteenth century *Shinden-zukuri* residential style.

The Kofun period, 250–552 A.D., is identified with the development of the Haniwa. This building type is characterized by its large saddle-shaped roof, which can be found in other areas of the South Pacific. During this same period, large keyhole-shaped burial mounds developed. Small ceramic artifacts found in these mounds are referred to as *haniwa* because their form is derived from the saddle-shaped roof structure of the buildings they represent.

The Asuka period, 552–644 A.D., marks the entry of Buddhism from India through China and Korea to Japan (Fig. 8). This period represents an architectural shift from the indigenous forms of the Shinto shrine to the almost total absorption of the Chinese architectural tradition. A factor that modified Chinese architecture, in its application to Japan, was the mountainous terrain that exists throughout the island chain. This condition tended to alter the symmetric disposition of the Chinese site plan.

The Nara period, 645–783 A.D., represents the development and maturity of the Chinese architecture in Japan. The extent of this adaptation is exemplified by the Heijo capital at Nara, which is an imitation of the style and form of the Changan capital in China.

Figure 8. Great Buddha, Kamakura, Kanagawa, Japan. Courtesy of C. Lundell.

The Heian period, which lasted from 784 to 1185 A.D., marks the translation of Chinese prototypes, which up to this time were duplicated as closely as possible, to an architectural language that was more accommodating to the Japanese heritage. Temple complexes no longer followed the symmetric order of the Chinese temple plan. The residential architecture of the period followed the early Shinto-based form of the Haniwa in the development of the *Shinden-zukuri* style.

The Kamakura period lasted from 1186 to 1392 A.D. and manifests the rise of the Samurai military class and the decline of the nobility. Relations with China were reestablished and *Kara-yo,* foreign-style, architecture was introduced. This style was applied to Zen Buddhist temple construction and is exemplified by the alignment of buildings along a single axis.

The Moromachi period, 1393–1572 A.D., exemplifies a continuation and refinement of the *Kara-yo* style. The simplicity and intricate scale of the *Shindin-zukuri* residential style is combined with the *Kara-yo* to create an architectural form of more intricate dimension than that of the Kamakura period.

The Momoyama period continued from 1573 to 1614 A.D. and demonstrates a shift in emphasis from residential and temple architecture to the construction of large-scale palaces and castles. The introduction of black powder and guns to Japan by the Portuguese in 1543 greatly influenced this shift to a massive fortified building type.

The Edo period, 1615–1867 A.D., represents no significant modification of preexisting styles in Japan. The country enacted an attitude of isolation from outside world influence and did not progress internally. Decoration and ornament were lavished on contemporary buildings, but the architectural vitality of previous periods was missing.

The Meiji period, from 1868 to 1912 A.D., is represented by the opening of Japan to international trade and influence. The architecture of Western Europe became clearly evident in Japan.

During the Post World War I period, 1912–1945, much Western influence was carried to Japan by both foreign and native architects. The influences of the international style, the Bauhaus, and U.S. architecture were brought to Japan by individuals such as Antonin Raymond and Frank Lloyd Wright. Japanese architects such as Kunio Maekawa and Junzo Sakakura were greatly influenced by the work of the European modernists Walter Gropius and Le Corbusier.

During the Post World War II period, 1945–1988, Japan emerged from the destruction of World War II fully adopting the architectural language of western modernism. Of all Asian countries, Japan has been the most aggressive in embracing the architecture of modernism and postmodernism. The work of architect Kenzo Tange, strongly influenced by Le Corbusier, combined modernism with the traditional values of Japanese architecture and culture. During the 1960s, a group of young Japanese architects worked together to create an additive modular form of contemporary architecture called metabolism, which was based on an organic model that accommodates both growth and decay. In the 1970s and 1980s, Japanese architects have followed the lead of the West in confronting the work of American architect Robert Venturi and other postmodernists. Entering the latter portion of the twentieth century, Japan is poised, economically and culturally, to make significant contributions to the history of world architecture.

Much of Japanese traditional architecture is derived from China. Almost all the architectural elements indicated in the section on Chinese architecture have direct application to Japan. Those elements that differentiate the two traditions essentially appear before the introduction of Buddhism to Japan in 552 A.D. and after World War II, when Japan leaped forward economically and culturally, leaving architectural developments in China to struggle with the constraints of their own slowly evolving economic system.

The most significant developments in Japanese architecture can be characterized under the following headings:

1. *Shinto Ritual Buildings*. The indigenous architecture of Japan is based on a southern Pacific and Malaysian prototype dwelling and is associated with the native Shinto theology.
2. *Palaces and Castles*. Large residential buildings were constructed for the nobility. In some cases, these were based on the traditional dwelling style but expanded in scale; in others, the architectural type could more rightly be compared to the European medieval fortified castle.
3. *The Metabolists*. Japan was responsible for the last significant chapter of twentieth century modernism. The introduction of the Metabolist manifesto in 1960 took the machine-age international style to its final and logical conclusion.
4. *Postmodernism*. In the aftermath of modernism the emerging prosperity of Japan has allowed the luxury of cultural self-reflection. The international style has been reinterpreted in terms of both western and eastern cultural traditions.

Shinto Ritual Buildings

The ancient inhabitants of Japan were most probably a mix of aboriginals, such as the Ainu, Mongols who migrated south through Korea, and Indonesians who followed the northern flow of the Pacific Ocean currents.

Most of the significant cultural development centers around the southern islands of the Japanese archipelago. The first prototypical architectural form, pit dwellings, began to emerge between the second and first millennia B.C. Pit dwellings consist of excavated circles and rectangles varying in width from 13 to 20 ft with floor depths of 16 to 40 in. below grade. The excavated earth is deposited around the perimeter of the pit, increasing the internal height of the wall. Poles are driven into the floor of the excavation to support a ridge pole, rafters and grass, or animal skin roofing material.

Pit-dwelling structures continued in use until the second or first century B.C., when rice cultivation was introduced to Japan from Southeast Asia. At this time, elevated structures appear to have been erected primarily as grain storage facilities. The ability to store grain is associated with the emergence of the Japanese nature-based theology, Shintoism. This indigenous religion combines native mythology, ritual, and nature and ancestor worship and is closely associated with the emerging architectural prototype of the raised platform granary.

A social structure developed around the rice-based agricultural system. The aristocracy of this society became linked with the preservation of rice as a food and the preservation of the social system required to support the production of rice. The aristocracy became linked with the theology. The consequence was that the dwelling place of the priestlike aristocracy became the same as the dwelling place of the rice itself. The rice granary became the palace.

The elevated platform granary ultimately became the ritual temple. In the year 29 B.C. it is said that the Emperor Suinin removed the sacred mirror and other religious artifacts from the palace. In doing so, he created the first Shinto ritual building or temple. The raised platform granary no longer was to function as the abode of rice, nor as the abode of people, but was to become the abode of the gods.

The Shinto ritual building site at Ise-Daijingu is considered the most sacred site in Japan (Fig. 9). The two building complexes located at the site are Geku, the outer shrine, and Naiku, the inner shrine. These buildings are considered to be the prototype of indigenous architecture in Japan. Naiku was founded during the reign of Emperor Suinin, 29–70 A.D., and enshrines the god Amaterasu-Omi-Kami. The temple complex has been systematically dismantled and reconstructed every 20 years since 686 A.D. The simplicity, integrity, and purity of the complex and its setting reveal the origin and true spirit of the Japanese culture.

Figure 9. Shinto Shrine Building, Ise-Shima National Park, Mie, Japan. Courtesy of C. Lundell.

Palaces and Castles

The origin of the palace form can be traced to the Shinto ritual buildings at Ise. The character and sense of clarity of design are expressed throughout the almost 1800-year history of the development of the style. The scale of the building complex expanded as the type developed. By the year 710 A.D. the palace buildings of Japan had matured as a style and were considerably influenced by the palace complexes of China. One of the most famous complexes found in Japan today is the Imperial Palace of Kyoto, first built in 784 A.D. It has undergone numerous reconstructions in its 1200-year history, but the spirit of its design remains intact. The complex at Kyoto still maintains the restraint of ornament that recalls its origins at Ise. The palace type evolved into the fortified castle during the sixteenth century. Before this period the castle form existed at a much smaller scale and functioned primarily as a fortification.

With the introduction of the rifle by the Portuguese in 1543 A.D., great changes in the methods of warfare, fortification, and residential palace construction took place. The arrangement and planning of fortified structures was introduced to Japan by Europeans (Fig. 10). Moats were often constructed around the outside walls, as found in European castle construction. The first great castle constructed in Japan was the Azuchi castle built in 1579. Today, many of these castles are architecturally preserved, such as the Himeji castle (1581) and the Osaka castle, one of the largest in Japan. In general, the castle was surrounded by two or three moats and flanked by high stone walls. The plan was polygonal and watchtowers were placed at strategic intervals along the wall. At the center of this complex the keep was located, surrounded by the residential complex. Even though the plan configuration is clearly European in its organization, the architectural character of these structures is undeniably Japanese.

The Metabolists

Modern architecture became an important part of the redevelopment of Japan after World War II. Strongly influenced by the work of Kunio Maekawa, an advocate of the French modernist Le Corbusier, a whole generation of postwar Japanese architects embraced modernism on his terms. Most notable of these is the world-renowned architect Kenzo Tange. Tange worked in Maekawa's office for 4 years. During the war he returned to Tokyo University, where he pursued his lifelong study of urban design. It was during this period that he first began to confront the Western notion of public space as demonstrated by the Greek agora.

Historically, Japan, like its progenitor China, had confined the concept of public space to the internal function of the residential and palace courtyard. Public space as

Figure 10. Fortified castle, Kanto, Honshu, Japan. Courtesy of C. Lundell.

a function of the community as a whole was unknown in Japan. Tange felt that with the emergence of Western social, political, and economic values, the concept of public space, or as he called it "Communication Space," was a necessary component of this social evolution. By 1957, Kenzo Tange and URTEC (his firm name, derived from the term "Urbanist Architect") were preparing for the Tokyo World Design Conference to be held in 1960. This conference was to be an important point in the evolution of twentieth-century architecture in Japan.

Kenzo Tange was preparing his now famous plan for Tokyo that used large expansive bridges to span the length of Tokyo Bay with a network of housing, community, and circulation systems to accommodate the ever-growing population of the city. While he was developing this "Megastructure" proposal for presentation at the World Design Conference, five young architects were collaborating on a manuscript entitled *Metabolism 1960*. These two developments, when presented, secured the role of Japanese architects as major contributors to the development of architectural theory in the second half of the twentieth century.

The manuscript produced by the five architects was actually a compilation of five independently developed projects and manifestos, all dealing with the issue of the urban environment. The impact on architectural thought at the time was so significant that the five (Kisho Kurokawa, Kiyonori Kikutake, Fumihiko Maki, Masato Otaka, and the architectural critic Noboru Kawazoe) came to be known as the Metabolists. The central issue of the *Metabolism 1960* manuscript was the condition of change in the urban setting and the proposal for an architecture that was capable of accommodating this dynamic state. The word metabolism is derived from the biologic term for the organic process of cell growth and regeneration. These principles are applied to an architectural form that responds to the urban need for growth and regeneration in a similar fashion.

The physical application of the Metabolist theory was ultimately left to the work of Kisho Kurokawa, who was the most prolific builder of the Metabolist group. In the early 1970s, a number of buildings demonstrating his architectural approach were under construction. His Nakagin capsule building uses the concept of a central service tower accommodating additive residential units. Kurokawa was to construct a number of buildings demonstrating his Metabolic approach.

Kenzo Tange, who was not a Metabolist but acted as a mentor to the group, adopted the Metabolist approach and was responsible for its largest-scale application in his design for the Yamanashi Communications Center (Fig. 11). Tange continued to pursue the Megastructuralist approach that he developed in the Tokyo Bay Plan. The principal deterrent to the Megastructure was the large financial commitment required to accomplish such projects. Although the opportunity to apply this approach to design never became available in Japan, the rise in cost of petroleum in the 1970s provided tremendous financial reserves for the developing countries of the Middle East. It was these conditions in the Middle East that provided the fertile soil for the application of the work of Tange, Kurokawa (Fig. 12), and other architects sympathetic to the Megastructuralist approach.

By the end of the 1970s, many architects had become disenchanted with the inhumane quality of the environment often suggested by large-scale urban plans. In addition, these schemes, in most cases, were financially unapproachable. These limitations fostered the development of a more introspective and contemplative mood in the young Japanese architectural community. An architecture developed that was based on a more intimate and approachable scale.

Figure 11. Yamanashi Communications Center, Kofu City, Yamanashi, Japan. Kenzo Tange, Architect. Photography by M. Ross.

Figure 12. National Ethnological Museum, Suita City, Osaka, Japan. Kisho Kurokawa, architect. Courtesy of J. Tyner.

Postmodernism

In the last quarter of the twentieth century, many young Japanese architects are attempting to modify the architectural language of modernism to accommodate contemporary life. The culture of Japan is the result of transparent layers of influence. Indigenous Shintoism, Chinese Buddhism, Western Christianity, and twentieth-century high technology industrialism are all superimposed on a dense urban technocratic society. The contemporary architect is searching to identify an architectural language that can manifest the complex condition of his time.

Tadao Ando is a contemporary architect attempting to restore the sense of minimalism and contemplation inherent in traditional Japanese architecture. His approach attempts to deal with the reality of twentieth-century life. Reinforced concrete, steel, and glass replace the traditional materials. The language of Ando's architecture is similar to that found in the work of the American architect Louis Kahn. His residences provide a fortified refuge from the fragmented assaults of contemporary urban life. They take on an internal life that is restrained and austere. Ando is attempting to isolate a silent void within the twentieth-century city.

Ando's Ryoheki House, built in Ashiya in 1977, contains the residence between two massive, two-story, windowless reinforced concrete walls. Natural light enters the building through windows opening onto an internal courtyard and located in the ends of the concrete barrel vault roof. The building is a landmark in a sea of transience.

Arata Isozaki confronts contemporary Japanese life through the use of metaphor, poetics, and the Zen riddle. His work is often idiosyncratic and uses the structure of contemporary logic to disarm the viewer and provide a fleeting moment of insight. His poetic ability to manipulate the structure of logic comes to him through his relationship with his father, who is a famous Haiku poet.

In the West Japan General Exhibition Center, Isozaki employs a structural system that becomes a metaphor for the pylons and cables of a suspension bridge. The whole concept of the design is based on the waterfront location of the site. The roof membrane, which is supported by a tension cable structure, was intended to be reflective and transparent, recreating the visual quality of the water surface itself.

Shin Takamatsu approaches the definition of contemporary life by an intuitive and uncharted course. The materials used in his architecture are concrete, glass, and steel. This material palette is shared by a number of young architects in Japan. Although many of these architects use these materials in a minimalist way, as seen in the work of Tadao Ando, Takamatsu articulates his buildings into a literal machine metaphor. Each of his projects is approached individually. Although the aesthetic remains minimalist, the form language is specific to the site, client, and program. His designs often look like carefully crafted machine parts. Takamatsu's rich tonal renderings of plans and elevations are a trademark of his work. In his building Ark, a Nishina dentist's office in Kyoto, Takamatsu creates a form of concrete and steel that appears to be a cross between an autoclave and a steam locomotive. Takamatsu's designs represent primal intuition applied to twentieth-century technology.

Kenzo Tange believes that Japan's unique ability to assimilate outside influences can be subdivided into three developmental stages: duplication, modification, and innovation. The Japanese culture has demonstrated this process in its unique relationship with China. In the last quarter of the twentieth century, the world is being exposed to the final stage of Japan's assimilation of the cultural values and technology of Western society.

BIBLIOGRAPHY

General References

M. Bussagli, *Oriental Architecture,* Henry N. Abrams, New York, 1975.

C. Fawcett, *The New Japanese House,* Harper & Row, Scranton, Pa., 1980.

F. M. Ross, *Beyond Metabolism,* McGraw–Hill, New York, 1978.

S. Rossbach, *Feng Shui: The Chinese Art of Placement,* Dutton, New York, 1983.

S. Skinner, *The Living Earth Manual of Feng-Shui,* Routledge & Kegan Paul, Boston, 1982.

N. S. Steinhardt, *Chinese Traditional Architecture,* Chinese Institute in America, China House Gallery, New York, 1984.

Su Gin-Djih, *Chinese Architecture Past and Contemporary,* Sin Poh Amalgamated (H.K.) Limited, Hong Kong, 1964.

K. Tange and N. Kawazoe, *Ise: Prototype of Japanese Architecture,* MIT Press, Cambridge, Mass., 1965.

N. Wu, *Chinese and Indian Architecture,* George Braziller, New York, 1963.

See also Isozaki, Arata; Maekawa, Kunio; Maki, Fumihiko; Tange, Kenzo

Clark E. Lundell, AIA
Auburn University
Auburn, Alabama

ORNAMENT IN ARCHITECTURE

The definitions of ornament and decoration have remained remarkably stable over the past 350 years. Henry Cockeram's *English Dictionarie* (1623) defined decorating as "to decke, to grace, or trim" and ornament as "a garnishing." In Samuel Johnson's *Dictionary of the English Language* (1755) decoration was said to be an "embellishment; added beauty," whereas ornament was an "embellishment; decoration." *Webster's Third New International Dictionary* (1971) describes decoration as "the art of adorning, embellishing," and ornament as "something that lends grace or beauty: a decorative part or addition." Because the lexicographer's understanding reflects that of the society in which he or she works, it may be assumed that the terms ornament and decoration have been synonymous for at least the past three and a half centuries, and probably for far longer. Therefore these two terms will be used interchangeably in this article.

Embellishment, or enrichment, implies adding to what is already there. Thus, decoration or ornament exists in relation to the thing it enriches. In that sense, a statue in a museum is not an ornament but an objet d'art; when it is placed in a plaza, however, it becomes an ornament of that space. While the common assumption nowadays is that there is a qualitative difference between art and ornament (decorative art) this was not the case in some circles, even the recent past. The nineteenth-century art critic and social reformer John Ruskin said (1):

> There is no existing highest-order art but is decorative. The best sculpture yet produced has been the decoration of a temple front—the best painting, the decoration of a room. Raphael's best doing is merely the wall-colouring of a suite of apartments in the Vatican, and his cartoons were made for tapestries. Correggio's best doing is the decoration of two small church cupolas at Parma; Michael Angelo's, a ceiling in the Pope's private chapel.

As decorating has always been linked to the notion of adding beauty, architecture itself was considered a decorative art as late as the beginning of the twentieth century, "because [architecture] has to do with making that beautiful, suggestive, or attractive which might exist and do its necessary work perfectly well without the possession of any aesthetic charm" (2).

Although the terms ornament and decoration have remained interchangeable in the mind of the lay public, in some professional circles it is assumed that there is a difference between the two, ornament being more closely connected to the means of construction than decoration. Thus a pattern in marble paving would be considered ornament whereas a statue placed atop a balustrade would be a decoration. The basis for the view that subdivides types of embellishment in this way probably harks back to the Gothic revival architect A. W. N. Pugin, about whom more will be said later. Pugin himself used these two terms interchangeably, according to the convention of his time. He also said that all ornament should consist of the "enrichment of the essential construction of the building," what he called "the great principle of decorating utility" (3). That connection between structure and ornament was promoted by later nineteenth-century theorists who elaborated Pugin's thesis, arguing that ornament should somehow express the structure of a building. The "first principles of decorative art," said Sir Charles Eastlake, painter, art critic, and keeper of the National Gallery, was that the "nature of construction, so far as is possible, should always be revealed, or at least indicated, by the ornament which it bears" (4).

Differentiating between types of architectural adornments based on the relationship to structure can be confusing. Are the rich mosaics of San Vitale (Ravenna, 526–547 A.D.) ornament or decoration (Fig. 1)? They are intimately connected to the structure—contoured to the walls and vaults of that church—but they do not express or enhance that structure as Pugin and later critics felt ornament should. The mosaics hover on a shimmering gold background that blithely contradicts the solidity of the bricks and mortar behind. That a bas relief wall panel is more connected to the structure than a statue in a niche on that same wall is an arbitrary and forced distinction and one that was not made before the nineteenth century.

TYPES OF ORNAMENT

As the long-standing definitions of decoration and ornament suggest, the primary purpose of architectural embellishment over the centuries has been to beautify by addition. There are almost as many decorative styles as there are cultures of the world. A catalog of those styles would list the major civilizations of the Occident, the Orient, Africa, Oceania, and the New World, all periods of their histories, and every subgroup within those cultures that evolved an idiosyncratic way of embellishing its architecture.

Although there is a stunning variety of decorative styles, when it comes to placing that ornament on a building the choices are relatively limited. The refined Doric capitals of the Parthenon (447–432 B.C.) consisted of a blocklike abacus resting on a delicately curving, round echinus. The Great Hall of the Palace of Darius, at Persepolis (518–460 B.C.), had columns topped by twin bulls' heads surmounting four pairs of vertical double volutes. Both

Figure 1. Mosaics, San Vitale, Ravenna (A.D. 526–547). Courtesy of the author.

are examples of column capitals—the embellishment at the upper extremity of a vertical support—but they are worlds apart in conception and expression. The wide variety of decorated styles obscures the fundamental similarity in the way those styles are deployed: ornament is added to the edges of architectural forms; placed at the junctions of different materials or architectural elements; spread over flat and curving planes; and gathered to create focal points.

Edge ornaments can clarify the form they embellish or obscure it. The outer edges of the main facade of the Palazzo Farnese (Rome, 1515?–1546) are bounded by an edging of quoins. Half-timbering breaks the facades of medieval buildings into orderly, and sometimes fanciful, subdivisions, as in the Little Moreton Hall, Cheshire, UK (1550–1559). On the other hand, the trefoil and fleur-de-lis cresting of Reims Cathedral (1211–1290) does not define the roofline but feathers it into the sky.

Junctions of materials and building elements are frequently ornamented. A capital marks the point at which vertical and horizontal structure intersect. A cornice punctuates the physical juncture of the wall and the roof as well as the visual juncture of the wall and the sky. Moldings of all types occur where walls and ceilings meet and where windows and doors puncture the wall plane.

Repeating ornaments, which cover larger areas, can reinforce or contradict the two-dimensional nature of the surface. The pattern of brick joints is perhaps the most common example of a planar decoration that reinforces the solidity of the surface. The tile patterns clothing the Masjid-i-Shah Mosque, Esfahān (ca. 1610), do not imply depth and therefore reinforce the sense of surface. When a pattern implies depth it negates the plane. The more realistic the representation, the more the flatness of the surface is denied, the extreme example being a trompe l'oeil painting, which creates the illusion of three dimensions on a two-dimensional surface.

Decoration is often used to draw attention to an important architectural element, such as the entrance to the New Rathaus at Rothenburg on the Tauber, Bavaria (begun 1572) (Fig. 2). A coat of arms on the facade of the Pallazo Barbarini (Rome, 1628–1638) identifies the owner of the building and creates a visual focus for the facade. The baldachin (Bernini, 1624–1633) under the crossing of St. Peter's, marks the alleged tomb of the first Bishop of Rome and draws the eye to the spiritual and physical focus of the building.

In any discussion about the form of ornament it should be noted that the perception of what is ornament depends on one's point of view. From close up, a Gothic buttress is an architectural element that is decorated with moldings, pinnacles, and crockets. From a distance these small-

Figure 2. Entrance to the New Rathaus (right), Rothenburg on the Tauber (begun 1572). Courtesy of the author.

scale details lose their definition and become textures, while the buttress itself is seen as an embellishment of the larger structure.

PERCEPTIONS OF ORNAMENT

All ornament influences the perception of architecture. On one level, that influence depends on cultural cues. A person familiar with Western culture senses the presence of authority when standing before the columns and pediment of a classical facade, for these forms have symbolized the power of the state for over 2500 years. That same facade carries other messages as well—a reminder of the democratic ideals that are the legacy of ancient Greece, for example, an association that helped bring about a revival of Greek architecture in the United States shortly after this country was founded. Byzantine architecture conjures up the mysteries of the East; rococo recalls the extravagances of a decadent aristocracy; Gothic evokes the romance of the Middle Ages, which led nineteenth-century social reformers such as John Ruskin and William Morris to prefer the alleged spiritualism of that time to the venal commercialism of their own. The accuracy of the image is not at issue: the Greeks owned slaves and the Middle Ages was as worldly a time as any other period in history. The important point is that these evocations are an inextricable part of the experience of any architectural style, and that decoration plays a major role in triggering them.

Ornament also conveys feelings or sensations that are not circumscribed by cultural experience (5,6). This ability of the "decorative line" can make a structure seem heavy or light, airy or solid, supple and plastic or rigid and brittle, regardless of the material of which it is built. Stone can be made to appear thin and stiff (the facing of I. M. Pei's addition to the National Gallery in Washington, D.C.), or soft and malleable, as though sagging from its own weight, as in the parish church, Countisbury, North Devon, UK (Fig. 3). The ornamental line can emphasize the horizontal (Frank Lloyd Wright's raked brick joints), or the vertical (modern office towers with suppressed horizontal spandrels and raised vertical mullions). The stucco surfaces of the early modern movement were purposely smooth and unmarked, making them visually light and thin—a conscious effort to avoid the massive character of traditional masonry construction. If that stucco surface were scored, in imitation of masonry, it would appear heavier, taking on the weight of stone implied by those lines. The vertical moldings and crockets of Gothic towers and spires eat into the mass of a building and visually lighten massive stone structures such as the Cologne cathedral (1284–1880). Heavy string course moldings compromise the verticality of the Romanesque towers of the Worms cathedral, partitioning them into discrete segments that emphasize the horizontal and hence imply weight and mass (Figs. 4 and 5). While these effects sometimes depend on other elements (including massing, fenestration, and color), the most important contributors are the small-scale details—the decoration.

Figure 3. Detail of stonework at entrance to the parish church, Countisbury, North Devon, UK. Courtesy of the author.

Figure 4. Cologne cathedral (1284–1880). Courtesy of the author.

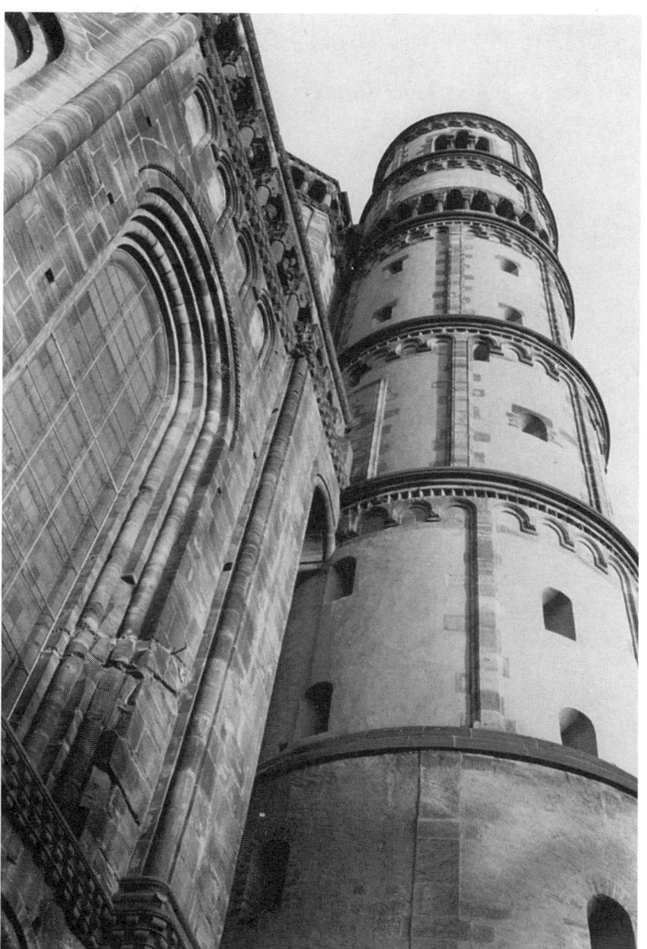

Figure 5. Worms cathedral (1110–1181). Courtesy of the author.

USES OF ORNAMENT

Fitting New with Old

When skillfully used, decoration can create a visual link between new buildings and old. Ornament is a surface effect, and part of its ability to smooth out the differences between ornamental styles lies in the fact that its placement is generally similar regardless of the style (Fig. 6). The architecture of the modern movement, on the other hand, which deprived itself of the traditional means of decorating, generally contrasts sharply with traditional styles.

The Gothic Town Hall of Bruges (1376–1420) and the neighboring Renaissance Recorder's House (1535–1537) (Fig. 7) demonstrate the remarkable ability of ornament to tie buildings of different styles into closely knit compositions. The vertical emphasis of these buildings is the key to their sympathetic relationship. One expects verticality in a Gothic building but it is surprising in the Recorder's House because the horizontal is supposed to dominate in classical architecture. In this case, however, the verticality of Gothic architecture literally overlays an otherwise typical northern Renaissance facade. Both buildings have a high proportion of window to wall, which restricts their decoration to the relatively narrow areas between the openings. The Town Hall has pairs of small sculpture platforms, with conical spires, stacked one on top of the other. Its windows are narrow and its second floor spandrels are recessed; this, and the continuous frame around both first- and second-story windows, makes them read as a single vertical unit. The turrets, elongated dormers, and cresting reinforce this verticality and feather the silhouette into the sky. The Recorder's House, on the other hand, is composed of characteristically classical forms, horizontal layers, each with a different architectural order empha-

Figure 6. Street in Haarlem, the Netherlands, with buildings from about the fourteenth century through the twentieth century, related by the use of ornamental trim. Courtesy of the author.

Figure 7. Town Hall of Bruges (1376–1420) and Recorder's House (1535–1537). Courtesy of the author.

sized by appropriate horizontal entablatures. Its window frames are contained within the height of each floor, unlike those of the Town Hall, yet its columns, with their plinths and entablatures, jut out from the facade to make a continuous vertical line from ground to cornice that overrides the classically imposed horizontality. In visual terms, the engaged columns create the same vertical feeling as the continuous window frames of the Town Hall. The facade is topped by three exuberant scroll pediments, again emphasizing the vertical, with crocket-like ornaments and crowning statues that dissolve the building's bulk as it meets the sky. A skillful manipulation of the decorative elements has overcome the fundamental antagonism between two disparate styles.

Cultural Uses

In addition to its ability to create a harmonious relationship among disparate styles, decoration has always served a concrete social need. As it beautified a building by the

Figure 8. Detail of the Panathenaic frieze. Photograph by Brent C. Brolin. Courtesy of the British Museum, London.

costliness of its materials, the refinement of its design, and quality of its craftsmanship, ornament enhanced the prestige of the individual, the state, or the god associated with that edifice (Fig. 8). Ornament has also been used to educate. The Parthenon's famous frieze reminded Athenians of the Panathenaea, the celebration of the birthday of Athena, patron goddess of the city. The caryatids of the Erectheum, on the Athenian acropolis, recalled the triumph over the people of Caryae, in the wake of which the men of that unfortunate state were slain and its women carried off into slavery, their humiliation preserved forever in the female form as architectural column (7). The Roman senate dedicated the Ara Pacis as a memorial to the safe return of Augustus from campaigns in Gaul and Spain. The "altar of peace" advised the Roman populace of Augustus's achievements, but was also a political gesture from the senate to the man who was presiding over the end of the Roman Republic (8). The use of decoration to convey religious doctrine became dogma under Pope Gregory the Great (590–604), who issued an edict forbidding decorative and artistic expression in religious buildings unless it explained the teachings of the Christian church (9):

> It is one thing to worship a picture and another to learn from the language of a picture what that is which ought to be worshiped. What those who can read learn by means of writing, that do the uneducated learn by looking at a picture . . . that, therefore, ought not to have been destroyed which had been placed in the churches, not for worship, but solely for instructing the minds of the ignorant.

TRADITIONAL GUIDELINES

For thousands of years ornament remained an unquestioned ingredient in the recipes of traditional architecture. To speak of architecture and its ornament would have been a redundancy. Architecture and ornament were a single entity. Until quite recently in the history of Western art, architectural ornament was created and arranged according to rules based on historical precedent and refined by succeeding generations of craftspeople who stated their preferences in visual terms. These were passed from generation to generation and resulted in a slow evolution of styles within a relatively restricted range of forms—the stately progress of the Greek orders through Roman, early Christian, Romanesque, Renaissance, baroque, and rococo styles. Historical precedent, and the proportional canons that defined the traditional styles, endured as the guiding standard until the end of the nineteenth century.

The only architectural treatise that has come down from Greco–Roman times, *The Ten Books on Architecture,* by Vitruvius (first century A.D.), provides an insight into the way ancient practitioners viewed ornament. The guidelines put forth by Vitruvius were not abstract but visual. The embellishments of base, capital, and entablature were predetermined by the chosen architectural order, and the size of each element was related to the others by fixed proportions (10). When he wrote about the appearance of column capitals, door jambs, and balustrades, it was in relation to other elements of the architectural composition. Thus an Ionic doorway "should be constructed with the hinge stiles one twelfth of the width of the whole aperture" (11). Nonvisual constraints were based on Roman practicality: winter dining rooms, the doors and windows of which would be closed most of the time, were not to have delicate cornice work or vaulting because those details would inevitably be "spoiled by the smoke from the fire and the constant soot from the lamps" (12). When he cited an architectural impropriety, it did not involve immorality, but an artistic solecism—a sculptor who placed statues of men pleading political causes in the gymnasium and statues of discus throwers in the forum (13). Vitruvius also objected to certain fashions in the architectural painting of his day, not for theoretical or ethical reasons but because they offended common sense, substituting reeds for columns, and "fluted appendages with curly leaves and volutes, instead of pediments . . . things [that] do not exist and cannot exist and never have existed" (14).

The rare fragments of architectural treatises that have survived from later times show that the way of thinking about ornament changed little in the thousand years after Vitruvius. Villard de Honnecourt (early thirteenth century) described his collection of notes and sketches as a how-to book, "a treatise on masonry, machinery, carpentry, and the principles of geometry" (15). Andrea Palladio (1508–1580) acknowledged his debt to Vitruvius in the first paragraph of the preface to the *Four Books on Architecture* (1570), which was written in a manner that would have been quite familiar to the Roman. Palladio did not present theories about why embellishment should be placed here or there. Also, like Vitruvius, he did not mention ornament except in connection with the architectural element it adorned—never doubting that his readers would be familiar with the ancient orders of architecture and their attendant embellishments. This description of a Tuscan-style porch is typical (16):

> The columns of the first order are Dorick, and the portico's are as broad as the said columns are long. Those above, that is, of the second order, are Ionick, one fourth part less than those of the first, under which there is a Poggio, or pedestal, two foot and three quarters high.

The visual rules of design dominated the world of architectural ornament for centuries after Palladio. *The American Builder's Companion* (1827), by "Architect and Carpenter" Asher Benjamin, is only one of a number of nineteenth-century works aimed at instructing architect–builders in the proper use of traditional architectural elements. Again, proportion dictated the shape of precedent, although Benjamin showed a flexibility that was not present among those who rigidly adhered to the proportions of the ancients. "Experience has taught me that no determinate rule for columns, in all situations, will answer; they must be proportioned according to the weight, or apparent weight they are to sustain" (17).

MODERN PRINCIPLES

Toward the middle of the nineteenth century, the traditional ways of controlling the form of decorated architecture were altered. The change was initiated by a small cadre of British designers who were disturbed by what they considered a precipitous decline in the quality of design in British architecture and decorative arts. The root cause of their dismay was the existence of a marketplace dominated by middle-class taste. The nineteenth-century art reformers were not the first to despair at this state of affairs; the problem had been noted a hundred years before. By the early eighteenth century, the wealth of Britain's new merchant class had already begun to undermine the patronage system, creating a marketplace for the arts in which supply and demand, not the taste of sophisticated patrons, was the measure of artistic success or failure. Britain was perhaps the only European country in which one could be propelled into the upper classes by the acquisition of riches. That wealth came as a result of its greatly expanded world trade and "introduced among the commercial ranks a spirit of luxury and gaming that is attended with the most fatal effects, and an emulation among merchants and traders of all kinds, to equal, or surpass the nobility and the courtiers. The plain frugal manners of men of business . . . are now disregarded for tasteless extravagance in dress and equipage, and the most expensive amusements and diversions, not only in the capital, but all over the trading towns of the kingdom" (18).

Writers were the first artists to feel the impact of the new middle class, but its influence on the taste of the marketplace soon affected all of the arts. "Once the profession of letters depended for support entirely upon the interest, good-will and purchasing habits of a broad public, it began to pay serious attention to the way in which this public experienced literary products and to raise questions about its role in the formulations of literary standards" (19). The playwright Oliver Goldsmith remarked on the disastrous effects of the public's assumption that anyone could have good taste and pretensions to great artistry (20):

> Without assigning causes for this universal presumption, we shall proceed to observe, that . . . this folly is productive of manifold evils to the community. . . . Hence, the youth of both sexes are debauched to diversion, and seduced from much more profitable occupations into idle endeavours after literary fame; and a superficial, false taste, founded on ignorance and conceit, takes possession of the public.

The invention of the category of "fine art" occurred toward the middle of the eighteenth century and rescued one select group of artists from the clutches of the marketplace. Since ancient times the arts of painting, sculpture, and architecture had been grouped with what are still known today as the decorative or manual arts. They belonged to the same family because they all required manual labor. Gentlemen were not supposed to take up painting, sculpture, or architecture because handwork was demeaning. "It is quite possible for us to take pleasure in the work [of a sculptor] and at the same time look down on the workman," said the first-century A.D. Greek biographer Plutarch, for "no young man of good breeding and high ideals feels that he must be a Pheidias or a Polycleitus" (21,22). The highborn were concerned with the intellectual arts—the liberal arts, "liberal" from the Latin *liberalis,* pertaining to freeborn men. The most familiar grouping of liberal arts comes from Martianus Capella, a fifth-century A.D. Latin writer, and included grammar, rhetoric, dialectic, geometry, arithmetic, astronomy, and music (23).

It was a French abbé, Charles Batteux, who subdivided the manual arts into three groups (24): (*1*) fine arts, concerned solely with the creation of beauty; (*2*) arts combining pleasure and utility, including architecture and eloquence; and (*3*) mechanical arts, which served only utilitarian purposes. Although the *Oxford English Dictionary on Historical Principles* traced the earliest literary use of the English term "fine art" to 1767, the newly elevated fine arts did not become the intellectual equal of the liberal arts for another 20 years. It was then that Immanuel Kant's *Critique of Judgment* (1790) provided the first theoretical foundation for the visual arts in the history of Western art. Kant declared genius to be the most important characteristic of the artist and originality to be the primary ingredient of genius. "We thus see . . . that genius is a talent for producing that for which no definite rule can be given; it is not a mere aptitude for what can be learned by a rule. Hence originality must be its first property" (25). Artists and the public quickly took Kant's dictum to heart, and within a decade of the publication of his *Critique* educated British ladies and gentlemen were fully acquainted with its lesson regarding the artist's temperament and independence from convention (26). In addition to substantially increasing the status of the artist, Kant's explanation of the nature of art suggested that it was the artist's right—even duty—to ignore the demands of the marketplace and pursue his or her personal creative impulse. Pandering to popular notions of beauty eventually came to be seen—and is still seen—as a fatal lack of the characteristic considered most essential to the artist, originality. The new view of the arts proved financially as well as psychologically beneficial to the fine-arts artist. Although the inertia of thousands of years was not halted at once, and painters and sculptors continued to be grouped with manual laborers for some decades, these artists were no longer paid like craftspeople. A wheelwright's earnings depended on whether he was an apprentice, a journeyman, or a master. The artist's earnings "cannot be defined; he is paid according to his talents, and to the celebrity which he has acquired" (27). The artist's new status had a predictably negative effect on the less fine arts, the decorative arts. Owen Jones, author of the *Grammar of Ornament* (1856), noted with dismay that the most talented artists of his time no longer deigned to try the decorative arts, choosing instead to seek fame and fortune in the more prestigious arts of painting and sculpture (28).

Nineteenth-century art reformers surveyed the marketplace and found it subject to the whims of middle-class taste. In acquiring the trappings of higher social status, the members of this wealthy new class often mistook material extravagance for cultural refinement. The noted observer of English mores Edward Bulwer-Lytton commented on this trend in his *England and the English* (1833); fashions in the marketplace changed so quickly that manufacturers could not afford to waste time with quality design or craftsmanship, finding "a meretricious and overloaded display cheaper than exquisite execution" (29). Shortly after Bulwer-Lytton made that observation, a new set of rules of design began to emerge, which did not depend on historical precedent or proportional guidelines—the two whetstones on which the ornamental arts had been honed for centuries. The new rules of design were expressed in moral terms. The Gothic revival architect Augustus Welby Northmore Pugin first articulated those principles in two small volumes published in 1841: *Contrasts: or A Parallel Between the Noble Edifices of the Middle Ages and Corresponding Buildings of the Present Day; Shewing the Present Decay of Taste* and *The True Principles of Pointed or Christian Architecture.*

- *Honest Expression of Structure:* "Pointed Architecture does *not conceal her construction, but beautifies it*" (30). "One of the chief merits of the Pointed style," Sir Charles Eastlake later wrote about Gothic architecture, is "that the origin of every decorative feature may be traced to a constructive purpose" (31). The French Gothic revival architect Viollet-le-Duc decried the dishonesty of Renaissance architects, who used piers with decorative inserts, structurally superfluous wall medallions, irrelevant objects over doorways, curved and triangular pediments, and oversized keystones—all of which he thought were improper ornaments because they were not related closely enough to structure (32).
- *Honest Expression of Function:* "It will be readily admitted, that the great test of Architectural beauty is the fitness of the design to the purpose for which it is intended, and that the style of a building should so correspond with its use that the spectator may at once perceive the purpose for which it was erected" (33). *"The external and internal appearance of an edifice should be illustrative of, and in accordance with the purpose for which it is destined. . . .* All really beautiful forms in architecture are based on the soundest principles of utility (34). As part of the general amalgam of forms-fitting-functions, decorations too had their purposes, being "emblems of [the] philosophy and mythology" of nations (35). And "the severity of Christian architecture requires a *reasonable purpose for the introduction of the smallest detail,* and daily experience proves that those who attempt this glorious style without any fixed idea of its unalterable rules, are certain to end in miserable failures" (36).
- *Honest Expression of Materials:* "Even the construction itself *should vary with the material employed,* and the designs should be adapted to the material in which they are executed. . . . Moreover, the architects of the Middle Ages were the first who *turned the natural properties of the various materials to their full account, and made their mechanism a vehicle for their art"* (33). Charles Eastlake was particularly adamant on the matter of honesty of materials; "all cast-iron ornament, except under rare conditions, is bad in style, and when employed to represent wrought work, must be detestable in the eyes of a true artist" (37).
- *Honest Expression of the Spirit of the Times:* "Acting on this principle [that the style of a building should so correspond with its use], different nations have given birth to so many various styles of Architecture, each suited to their climate, customs, and religion. . . . In new Buckingham Palace, whose marble gate cost an amount which would have erected a splendid church, there is not even a regular chapel provided for the divine office; so that both in appearance and arrangement it is utterly unsuited for a Christian residence" (33,38).

The Purpose of the Principles

The novelty of Pugin's tenets cannot be overemphasized. For millennia designers had been guided by visual criteria; within the parameters of a given style they relied on the eye to make judgments between good and bad decoration. Visual guidelines had a direct impact on the appearance of buildings—when the height of a column was increased by one diameter the consequence was immediately apparent. Pugin's abstract credo was based on an ambiguous and equivocal link between visual design and morality, and boasted no such direct connection to the appearance of things—that is clear when it is realized that for the past 150 years architects have used his principles to justify every style from Gothic revival through art nouveau, modernism, and postmodernism.

Because morally based principles of design did not exist before Pugin, it must be assumed that the artisans and builders of the preceding millennia had had no use for them. They were invented in the nineteenth century because there was a demand for them; designers needed a tool that would help them exert some control over a marketplace that exhibited the "lust of profusion which is the bane of modern design" (39). Although Pugin applied his rules to the design and decoration of buildings, they were eventually put to work for all decorative artists and served the same purpose for them that Kant's dictum had for the fine-arts artist: the principles boosted the status of the designer and gave the aesthetic judgment of the professional more authority in the marketplace than that of the general public. Challenging the taste of the public was no easy matter. "We may condemn a lady's opinion on politics," wrote Charles Eastlake, "criticise her handwriting—correct her pronunciation of Latin, and disparage her favourite author with a chance of escaping displeasure. But if we venture to question her taste—in the most ordinary sense of the word, we are sure to offend" (40). By applying a veneer of reason and morality to intuitive aesthetic judgments, Pugin had eliminated the annoying problem of taste. His principles provided a code of architectural conduct that made objections based on personal preference irrelevant. By invoking these tenets, designers' decisions appeared to be based on lofty moral judgments rather than capricious personal predilections: this is an "honest" expression of the material; that is a "dishonest" expression of function. By invoking moral doctrine to rationalize choices based on visual criteria, generations of designers have sustained the remarkable illusion that taste plays no role whatsoever in their preferences. A whole procession of advocates—of every possible aesthetic predilection including twentieth-century modernists—has zealously used Pugin's principles to explain why the style they were championing was more virtuous than any other.

Although the principles had no direct effect on the appearance of architecture, they eventually had a critical indirect consequence. Pugin had unwittingly presented designers with an alternative to the authority of the traditional styles, and for the first time in the history of Western architecture it became possible to challenge the authority of the past, which ultimately led to the rejection of traditional notions of architectural ornament.

The nineteenth-century reformers who attempted to modify the taste of the marketplace were sensitive to the realities of the economic system. They assumed that manufacturers of ornament—terra cotta, stonework, cast iron, and the like—had no choice but to accommodate consumer demand. Solving the disturbing problem of "bad taste" meant getting the marketplace to understand the principles of design and to accept the reformers' view of "good taste" in all of the decorative arts, including architecture. The process began with the founding of the British art schools; the first Normal School of Design was established in 1837 "to afford manufacturers an opportunity of acquiring a competent knowledge of the Fine Arts, as far as the same are connected with manufacturers" (42,43). The situation had improved by the time of the Great London Exhibition of 1851, a fact generally attributed to the "direct and indirect influence of the Schools of Design" (44). Yet there was still a "decided inferiority" in national taste when it came to ornamental design (45), and some reformers concluded that the only sure way to get manufacturers to produce objects of beauty was to create a demand for them within the marketplace (46). Therefore the entire British buying public—not just the manufacturers—had to be exposed to the principles of design. Only then would the public know what was beautiful and be able to demand it from architects, designers, and manufacturers. To that end, the Department of Practical Art was organized under the leadership of Henry Cole, a painter, engraver, and editor of a short-lived but important periodical, the *Journal of Design and Manufactures* (47). By the end of the 1870s nearly 1800 schools of art were instilling the principles of art into 200,000 boys and girls each year (48).

The arts and crafts movement, led by William Morris, also had as a goal the improvement of the general level of taste, but attempted to attain that end through example rather than by mass education. As part of this process Morris set about trying to raise the status of the craftsperson–ornamentist just as that of the fine-arts artist had been elevated in the previous century. To that end, he attacked the conventional view of ornament—that it was merely something to beautify—and claimed its artistic success or failure depended not on its appearance, or even on its literal or symbolic content, but on the purity and spiritual motivation of the artist. If an ornament was ugly, it was not because the designer lacked aesthetic sensibility or taste, but because the motivation behind its creation was ignoble. Anything that was fabricated for commerce or war rather than the purer pleasure of artistic creation was "dishonest" and therefore incapable of being beautiful (49). The eventual failure of all attempts to raise the level of public taste was noted by no less a person than Morris himself (50).

> The world is everywhere growing uglier and more commonplace, in spite of the conscious and very strenuous efforts of a small group of people toward the revival of art, which are so obviously out of joint with the tendency of the age that, while the uncultivated have not even heard of them, the mass of the cultivated look upon them as a joke, and even that they are now beginning to get tired of.

The "mass of the cultivated" included a phalanx of designers—the forerunners of the modern movement—who were taking the first steps toward the rejection of the decorative tradition. The deepening division between the taste of the artistic elite and that of the general public was at the heart of the final break with tradition. For the elite, "popular taste" was synonymous with "bad taste." The only reason there was good poetry in England quipped Oscar Wilde, was because the public had no interest in it (51). Famous artists and intellectuals of the time occupied themselves with the overthrow of bourgeois values, attacking middle-class truths and turning them upside down. Jacques Barzun described the battle plan of the art-elite as it was carried out in the literature of the period (52):

> Butler would take Tennyson's lines: "Tis better to have loved and lost than never to have loved at all" and recast them as "Tis better to have loved and lost than never to have lost at all." Shaw said: "The reasonable man adapts himself to the world. The unreasonable man tries to adapt the world to himself. Therefore all progress depends on the unreasonable man." In his comedies, Shaw depicted the soldier as preferring chocolate to ammunition, the womanly woman as not sweet but guileful, the marriage bond as a license to sexual indulgence, the hero as proclaiming: "Two things I hate—my duty and my mother."

The approach taken by architects and designers was guided by a similar tactic. In their frontal assault on popular taste they stood the conventional definition of beauty on its head. To the nineteenth-century art lover the historical styles and the forms of nature were the epitome of beauty; the technical forms of their age, the bridges, railroad stations, and machines, were beneath the realm of art. One of the main functions of ornament had been to cover the ugly forms of technology with beautiful ornament—"applied art." The great train sheds of his time were not even "architecture" to John Ruskin. Between 1890 and the first decade of the twentieth century, professionals transposed the conventional views of beauty and ugliness. History and nature, the wellsprings of beauty for cultured Victorian gentlemen and ladies, became synonymous with ugliness whereas industrial forms, which had been non-art at best and the epitome of ugliness at worst, were transformed into the essence of beauty.

In the course of that metamorphosis, the architectural trendsetters of the time changed the way designers perceived ornament. One sign of that change was a move toward classifying decoration by its generic characteristics rather than the historical period to which it belonged. In the late 1880s, Franz Sales Meyer published his *Handbook of Ornament, A Grammar of Industrial & Architectural Designing in All Its Branches, for Practical As Well As Theoretical Use*. The introduction to the 1894 edition of Meyer's book, written by a lecturer on applied art at the National Art-School, said, "no other book, published either in England or abroad, can compare with it, for the amount of illustration it contains, or for the order with which its contents are arranged" (53). Earlier comprehensive volumes on decoration, such as Owen Jones's *Grammar of Ornament* (28), grouped elements according to their historical period. By cataloging them according to their visual characteristics (curvilinear versus geometric forms) and the ways in which they were used (free ornaments, repeating ornaments, ornamental objects, fixed decorative panels) Meyer's *Handbook* took a step away from the notion of style defining ornament.

Walter Crane's *Line and Form* (1900) was more revolutionary in this respect, for it attempted to isolate the visual and emotional impact of ornament from its historical associations (5). Although he did not advocate the outright rejection of history or nature as sources of inspiration, his optimism about the ability of the abstract line to communicate sensations had far-reaching implications for the new attitude toward ornament. Crane concentrated on what he called the "expressive" quality of the decorative line, the ability of an abstract line to communicate feeling through association; the iron support of Otto Wagner's Karlsplatz station is rigid but appears to have sagged under its own weight (Fig. 9). No one ever doubted that decorative styles could elicit emotional responses in the onlooker, but that facet of design had almost always been linked to the character of a particular style: the sober strength of the Doric order, the austerity and power of the Romanesque, the lightness of Gothic, and the frivolity of rococo. Crane's thesis suggested that the reservoir of emotional power that had always been at the beck and call of the ornamentist working in the historical styles could be drawn upon by the simple manipulation of line and form, without having to fall back on historical overlays. The clear implication was that ornamental forms based on historical and natural precedents were no longer necessary. It was one more weapon added to the designer's arsenal in the battle against conventional taste. Like Pugin's principles, Crane's "expressive line" offered a way out, a way for designers to free themselves from the bonds of conventional taste by tapping the immense expressive power of traditional ornament without resorting to decorative vocabularies that had been vulgarized by commerce.

Figure 9. "Sagging" support, Karlsplatz station, Vienna. Otto Wagner, 1898–1899. Courtesy of the author.

TRADITIONAL ORNAMENT BANISHED

Although it may be difficult to imagine when viewing these events from an historical perspective, neither the decorative art reformers of the mid-nineteenth century nor the rebel elite of its closing decades objected to ornament in principle—only to ornament that they believed was in bad taste. Good ornamental art, according to the reformers, did not copy nature but distilled and abstracted it: "decorative art is degraded when it passes into a direct imitation of natural objects" (54).

The style called art nouveau, which flourished in the 1890s, clearly demonstrated the elite's displeasure with conventional taste and its continued interest in ornament. Art nouveau was the first truly modern style in its rejection of stylistic precedents, but it was also unabashedly and enthusiastically ornamental. If its whiplash curves were often called tendrils—implying the inspiration of nature—the cognoscenti were careful to maintain a respectful distance from that source to avoid violating the admonition against imitation. A contemporary critique of a Victor Horta design noted that the artist observed nature and was "inspired by her for this or that motif . . . [yet] his ambition has never been to do anything which might directly resemble nature" (55). While there was a conscious effort to avoid the imitative error of most historical styles, the decorative elements of art nouveau were still arranged conventionally, as column capitals, balusters, friezes, borders, architraves, and so on.

Although the attitude toward ornament was changing, virtually all of the turn-of-the-century forerunners of the modern movement were skilled ornamentists. Louis Sullivan's intricate decorations were based on natural forms and also followed traditional rules of placement, as in the Carson Pirie Scott Building, Chicago, 1899. Frank Lloyd Wright's decorative work was less conventional than Sullivan's in that it virtually excluded free-form elements, yet it too followed conventional rules of organization. The interior of Unity Temple (Oak Park, Illinois, 1906), for example, was subdivided by simplified decorative moldings (not unlike Michelangelo's Funeral Chapel for the Medici [1519–1534] in that respect), but Wright omitted the swags and garlands that were the customary accessories of such decorative schemes (Fig. 10). Leaders in European architectural circles showed a similar tendency to reject conventional forms of ornament and to create new kinds, among them Charles Rennie Mackintosh (Glasgow School of Art, Glasgow, 1906–1909), Joseph Hoffmann (Purkersdorf Sanatorium, Vienna, 1904), Joseph Maria Olbrich (Secession Building, Vienna, 1887–1898), and Otto Wagner. Wagner's work is particularly helpful in understanding the changing attitude toward ornament, for it encompassed both traditional and modern points of view. His apartment

Figure 10. Interior of Unity Temple, Oak Park, Illinois. Frank Lloyd Wright, 1906. Courtesy of the author.

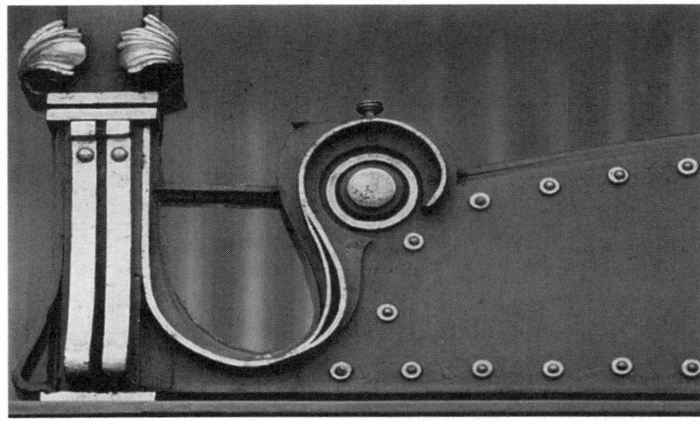

Figure 11. Detail of Karlsplatz station, Vienna. Otto Wagner, 1898–1899. Courtesy of the author.

house at Universitatstrasse 12 (Vienna, 1889) was conventional in both the type and placement of its ornament. His subway station for the Karlsplatz (Vienna, 1898–1899) used conventional and unconventional ornament, laid out in traditional ways—the floral decoration on the arch immediately above the entrance combined with the staccato pattern of rivets (Fig. 11). His Post Office Savings Bank (Vienna, 1904–1906) displayed a novel and expanded decorative vocabulary (Fig. 12). Its facade sported a grid of exposed aluminum rivets that fastened its stone cladding to its structure; a similar but more refined treatment was used for the marble of the interior. By the first decade of the twentieth century, it was already common to turn portions of mechanical or structural systems into decorative elements, and in the Post Office Savings Bank, Wagner transformed the heating outlets of the main banking room into fanciful aluminum colonettes (Fig. 13) (56).

Joseph Olbrich's "Wedding Tower" (1905), in the Darmstadt artists' colony, offered another example of a decorative hybrid that merged traditional and novel forms of ornament (Fig. 14). Its cascading tower roof was composed of conventional concentric moldings and presented an orthodox symmetry: there was a front, a back, and two sides.

Figure 12. Facade detail, Post Office Savings Bank, Vienna. Otto Wagner, 1904–1906. Courtesy of the author.

Figure 13. Heating duct, Post Office Savings Bank, Vienna. Otto Wagner, 1904–1906. Courtesy of the author.

Figure 14. "Wedding Tower" (1905), Darmstadt artists' colony. Joseph Olbrich, 1908. Courtesy of the author.

The facades themselves contradicted that reassuring familiarity. Heavy window moldings were carried around the corners, breaking through that traditional boundary of the facade in a preview of the ribbon windows, which would be made famous by modernists in the 1920s.

New Types of Ornament

Although the professional's view about what constituted proper decoration was changing, architects rationalized their new approach with the same principles that had first been proclaimed by Pugin. In explaining his art nouveau ornament, the Belgian architect Henry van de Velde relied on Pugin's terms to explain how designers should craft their ornament to arouse "a particular feeling to correspond to the function of a room" (57). Emile Gallé also harked back to Pugin in describing the need to create functional designs in the art nouveau style that took into account the nature of the material and that would not mask the construction with unnecessary ornament.

The protomodernist Adolf Loos rejected all ornament, claiming that the degree of a culture's civilization could be measured in inverse proportion to the amount of ornament it used, yet Loos too relied on Pugin's authority (59). He condemned nineteenth-century architects for having made a fetish out of ornament and attacked the current purveyors of ornamental styles—contemporaries such as Wagner, Olbrich, and Hoffmann—for having sunk to new cultural depths by assuming that a new style for the times could be created simply by inventing new types of ornament. Loos believed that such a style would emerge without any effort on the artist's part; it was already there, in fact, in the engineering works and other mechanical artifacts of the time. If architects continued to assume ornament was the essence of style, they would remain blind to this truth (60).

Ornament and the Modern Movement

After World War I, the architectural theorists who directed the progress of the modern movement also took up Pugin's principles. The century-old battle cries of functionalism, truth to materials, the expression of structure, and the expression of the spirit of the times were once again raised, this time to explain the genesis of the first style in the history of architecture that studiously avoided borrowing from the past. Modern ideology did not permit traditional ornamental elements, or the use of nontraditional ornamental elements in traditional ways. Yet despite vociferous claims to the contrary, followers of the modern movement did evolve their own rudimentary decorative palette. The choices were more limited than in the past, to be sure, but ample possibilities still existed. Because the term decoration has always been associated with the historical styles, modernists' assertions that theirs was not an ornamented style has gone largely unquestioned. To see what was decorative about it, it must be acknowledged that design choices are rarely if ever limited to ornamented or nonornamented forms. There is, instead, a decorative continuum, which extends from less ornamented to more ornamented. The rococo interior of Dominikus Zimmermann's Wies Church belongs at the more decorated end of that continuum (Bavaria, 1746–1754); the student wing of Walter Gropius's Bauhaus (Dessau, 1925–1926), its multiple balconies edged with three-tiered steel pipe railings, lies at the less ornamented end of the spectrum—but it is decorative nonetheless. While the decorative treatments of most early modern buildings were restrained, the de Stijl architect Gerrit Reitveld (1888–1964) created a rich vocabulary of forms and colors that rivaled the baroque in exuberance, as in the Schröder House, Utrecht, the Netherlands, 1924.

Some early modernists openly acknowledged the ornamental qualities of the new style. Theo Van Doesburg (1883–1931), another advocate of de Stijl, noted that one of the major differences between the historical styles and the "new style" was that the latter used "plastic form in place of imitation and decorative ornament" (61). Hans Poelzig (1869–1939) commented on the ornament of modernism when he observed that "the play of ornament, surface, and decoration in the earlier [traditional] sense is now forbidden. But has it really, totally ceased? Instead of hand-wrought, or even machine-produced ornaments, we now see the use of valuable materials: lacquer, glass, metal, stone. The interplay of these different surfaces now replaces the interplay of ornament" (62). Oddly enough, Adolf Loos produced one of the earliest examples of this modern approach to ornamenting, in the green-veined marble of the lower floors of his Goldman Salatsch House (Vienna, 1910). The marble slabs of Mies van der Rohe's Barcelona Pavilion (1929) are better-known examples of the exploitation of a material for its inherent decorative quality.

Deprived of the traditional means of embellishing buildings, generations of modernists found new ways to accomplish old effects. Instead of coats of arms or swags to create focal points, modernists turned to specific functions—stair towers, elevator shafts, utility cores, and other unique elements—for decorative emphasis. Where traditional styles had cast shadow lines with moldings that stood out from the wall, modern architects turned those moldings inside out, creating shadow lines with the incised "reveal."

Hans Poelzig called attention to other ways in which modernists created new ornament (62):

> Having been denied the use of ornament by the development of present-day architecture, [the architect] will begin to play with construction methods instead. This is an expensive game to play and the seduction of ornament was scarcely less intoxicating than that of the constructional methods placed in the hands of the present-day architect, with their seemingly limitless possibilities. In fact this new kind of "objective" practicality or realism contains just as much false romanticism, and ultimately as much unpracticality as any period which has fallen under the spell of a slogan. It is totally unpractical if I used expensive beams to span wide areas, leaving out intermediate supports which would make the construction cheaper and easier. The use of gigantic window areas without reason is no less intrinsically foolish than the previous attitude of architects who felt obliged to use heavy masses and large expanses of wall for the sake of architectural propriety.

The mullions of Mies van der Rohe's Seagram Building (New York City, 1958) represent only one of many examples of decorating with structure—or in this case pseudostructure. But structural or not, those mullions serve the same decorative purpose as the fluting of an Ionic column—they emphasize verticality. In extreme cases the penchant to play with construction, intensified by the repudiation of traditional ornamental techniques, led to dramatic elaborations of structure. Pompidou Center (Renzo Piano and Richard Rogers, Paris, 1977), demonstrates an enthusiasm for decoration that is matched by only the most flamboyant styles of the past (Fig. 15). The heroically scaled cross-bracing that scissors up the facade of the John Hancock Center in Chicago (Skidmore, Owings and Merrill, 1969) is a less splashy example of structure as ornament, but startling in its own stark way.

The extreme restrictions that modernism placed on the choice and arrangement of contemporary decoration explains why much modern ornament consisted of simple patterns. Traditional architectural designs were made up of groups of smaller elements, each of which was a finished composition in its own right; window and door openings were edged by ornamental moldings. These and other elements (pilasters, columns, quoins, string courses, cornices, surface textures, and color) were then combined in larger groupings—the individual floors of a multistory building, for example. These were assembled to create facades, which were in turn put together to form the building. Modernists' rejection of conventional techniques of composition inevitably led to an ornament that was not "finished off" or bounded, in the traditional sense of architectural design, but which appeared to be arbitrary sections cut out of patterns that could be repeated *ad infinitum* in two and sometimes three dimensions. The most familiar examples are skyscraper facades and space frames.

Modernism was only one of several new twentieth-century styles. Art deco, born almost simultaneously with the modern movement, continued the traditional philosophy and methods of architectural ornamentation. Like earlier styles, art deco borrowed from the past and from contemporary sources, adjusting the borrowed elements to

Figure 15. Structure as ornament, Pompidou Center, Paris. Renzo Piano and Richard Rogers, 1977. Courtesy of the author.

Figure 17. Art deco automotive motifs, Chicago, architect unknown, ca. 1930. Courtesy of the author.

meet its own needs. Art deco architects stylized the technological forms that modernists revered, then used them in traditional ways—in column capitals, friezes, architraves, medallions, and string courses. Its mixture of mechanistic and naturalistic motifs—all used in traditional ways—did not endear it to the architecture elite of its day, and it is rare to find this continuation of the decoration tradition mentioned in the same breath with modernism, as a style that should be practiced by "serious" architects (Figs. 16 and 17).

Figure 16. Art deco version of anthemion, Rockefeller Center. Reinhard & Hofmeister, Corbett, Harrison & MacMurray—Hood & Fouilhoux, 1931–1940. Courtesy of the author.

THE RETURN OF ORNAMENT

The profession's monolithically hostile facade toward ornament began to crack in the early 1970s, and traditional decoration gradually became an acceptable alternative to modernism. The unequivocal manner in which ornament had been banished, however, and the thoroughness with which its teaching had been eliminated from architectural education, made its reappearance awkward and embarrassing. The effects of nearly a century of professional invective against decoration had to be overcome; for generations, architects had been taught that only hacks—or worse, interior decorators—resorted to traditional forms of ornament. It was not surprising, therefore, that those with courage enough to take up that path once again did so with trepidation. Perhaps it was for that reason that many early postmodern buildings left viewers with the impression that the architects were chagrined at having partaken of the forbidden fruit. The architects of these early forays often employed traditional ornamental elements, but in tongue-in-cheek ways, as though signaling to peers that their return to ornament was going to be accomplished with originality—that is, by artists, not mere copiers.

Thus early postmodern works were characterized by the unconventional use of conventional ornament. Robert Venturi, the father of postmodernism, is a master of the use of almost traditional decorative elements almost as they had been used in the past. In his Chestnut Hill house (1962) the arc of decorative molding marking the entrance was bisected by a deep vertical split in the facade several feet wide. The same arc was then overlaid—crossed out might be a more accurate description—by a horizontal lintel (now painted over). In the main porch of the Brant

Figure 18. Main porch of the Brant House, Bermuda, 1977. Courtesy of the author.

House (Bermuda, 1977), Venturi employed cut out plywood columns with exaggerated cartoon silhouettes (Fig. 18). In Wu Hall (Princeton University, 1984), he resorted to an even odder treatment, a series of decorative elements in the shape of keystones (at least one of which was sliced through by a vertical expansion joint) that were evenly spaced along the bottom of a flat cantilever. Venturi also invoked the principles to account for the way he designed. Debunking modernists' simplistic approach to the expression of function, he explained his own love of architectural

Figure 19. Villa in New Jersey. Robert A. M. Stern, Architects, 1988. Courtesy of Robert A. M. Stern, Architects.

complexity in Pugin's terms. "The architectural complexities and distortions [of the] inside," wrote Venturi, "are reflected on the outside" (63). Other pioneers of the return to ornament distanced themselves from the tainted ornamental past by other means. Michael Graves's early works, for example, made allusions to the classical past, but these were abstracted to the point of being unidentifiable, as in the addition to the Claghorn house (1974).

As ornament has become a more familiar presence on the architectural scene, architects have become less self-conscious about employing it, resulting in a more confident and elegant handling of this traditional architectural accoutrement, as in the villa in New Jersey depicted in Figure 19 by Robert A. M. Stern, Architects (1985).

THE BORROWING TRADITION

The essence of the ornamental tradition is embodied in the word borrowing. One needs only to follow the acanthus motif through 2500 years of architectural history—and every architectural style—to realize that the hallmark of a healthy decorative tradition is its ability to be inspired by the past as well as the present. Yet within the last two centuries, the act of borrowing, in an artistic context, has come to be regarded with the greatest suspicion. The artist's dread at being considered a borrower rather than a creator grew out of the general acceptance of Kant's notion that originality is the *sine qua non* of the artist. This assumption was particularly hard on the decorative tradition. Although many famous Renaissance artists had worked in the decorative arts (Botticelli, Andrea del Sarto, Pontormo, and Uccello, to name a few) (64), the creation of decoration was turned into an inferior calling, the province of lesser mortals who lacked the magical stuff of genius. And, by making originality the first measure of art, potential ornamentists were pressured to abandon the richest sources of decorative inspiration—natural forms and the styles of the past, from Western and other cultures. If an unself-conscious ornamented architecture does return, it will be because many architects and critics believe that ornament lives because of its traditions and that invented styles, such as art nouveau and modernism, are ultimately dead ends, because the resources on which they can draw for renewal are limited. From this perspective, borrowing from the past is not a sin but a necessity in the creation and use of ornament. That was the way the great ornamental styles of the past evolved, and that is the way the ornamental styles of the future will be created.

BIBLIOGRAPHY

1. J. Ruskin in E. T. Cook and A. Wedderburn, eds., *The Works of John Ruskin,* Vol. 16, G. Allen, London, 1905, p. 320.
2. R. Sturgis, *A Dictionary of Architecture and Building,* Vol. 1, Macmillan, New York, 1902, p. 757.
3. A. W. N. Pugin, *The True Principles of Pointed or Christian Architecture,* set forth in two lectures delivered at St. Marie's, Oscott, J. Weale, London, 1841, pp. 1, 5.
4. C. Eastlake, *Hints on Household Taste,* 1868, reprint, Dover Publications, New York, 1969, p. 109.
5. W. Crane, *Line and Form,* G. Bell, London, 1900.
6. G. Scott, *The Architecture of Humanism,* 2nd ed., Charles Scribner's Sons, New York, 1969.
7. Vitruvius, *The Ten Books on Architecture,* Book 1, trans. by M. H. Morgan, 1914, reprint, Dover Publications, New York, 1960, p. 6.
8. "Ara Pacis" and "Augustus" in *Oxford Classical Dictionary,* 2nd ed., Clarendon Press, Oxford, 1970, pp. 76, 123.
9. "Iconoclasts" in *Encyclopedia Britannica,* 11th ed., The Encyclopedia Brittanica Company, New York, 1911.
10. Ref. 7, p. 155.
11. Ref. 7, p. 118.
12. Ref. 7, pp. 209–210.
13. Ref. 7, p. 212.
14. Ref. 7, p. 211.
15. F. Bucher in A. K. Placzek, ed., *Macmillan Encyclopedia of Architects,* The Free Press, New York, 1982, p. 323.
16. A. Palladio, *The Four Books of Architecture,* Book 2, trans. by I. Ware, 1570 and 1738, reprint, Dover Publications, New York, 1965, p. 42.
17. A. Benjamin, *The American Builder's Companion,* 1827, reprint, Dover Books, New York, 1969, p. 4.
18. W. Guthrie, *A New Geographical, Historical, and Commercial Grammar; and Present State of the Several Kingdoms of the World,* London. 1771, pp. 185–187.
19. L. Lowenthal and M. Fiske in M. Komarovsky, ed., *Common Frontiers of the Social Sciences,* The Free Press, Glencoe, Ill., 1957, pp. 33–96.
20. O. Goldsmith in Ref. 19, p. 313.
21. B. Radice, ed., *The Rise and Fall of Athens: Nine Greek Lives by Plutarch,* trans. by I. Scott-Kilvert, Penguin Books, Baltimore, Md., 1960, pp. 1–2.
22. R. Wittkower and M. Wittkower, *Born Under Saturn, The Character and Conduct of Artists: A Documented History from Antiquity to the French Revolution,* Norton, New York, 1963, p. 1ff.
23. "Martianus Capella" in Ref. 8, p. 653.
24. C. Batteux, *Les beaux arts réduits à une même principe,* Durrand, Paris, 1746.
25. I. Kant, *Critique of Judgment,* trans. by J. L. Bernard, Hafner Publishing Co., 1951, p. 315.
26. S. T. Coleridge, *Select Poetry, Prose, Letters: Miscellaneous Literary Criticism,* edited by S. Potter, Nonesuch Press, London, 1971, pp. 131, 311. Coleridge traveled to Germany in 1798–1799 and attended lectures for several months at the University of Göttingen.
27. *The Book of Trades, or Library of the Useful Arts,* Vol. 2., 3rd ed., Tabart & Co., London, 1806, pp. 102, 118.
28. O. Jones, *Grammar of Ornament,* 1856, reprint, Van Nostrand Reinhold, New York, 1972, p. 136.
29. E. Bulwer-Lytton, *England and the English,* 1833, reprint, University of Chicago Press, Chicago, Ill., 1970, p. 350.
30. Ref. 3, pp. 1, 3.
31. Ref. 4, p. 36.
32. E. E. Viollet-le-Duc, *Lectures on Architecture,* trans. by B. Bucknall, 1889, reprint, Grove Press, New York, 1959, p. 201.
33. A. W. N. Pugin, *Constraints: or A Parallel Between the Noble Edifices of the Middle Ages and Corresponding Buildings of the Present Day; Shewing the Present Decay of Taste,* 2nd ed., Charles Dolman, London, 1841, pp. 1–2.

34. Ref. 3, pp. 11, 18, 42.
35. Ref. 33, p. 2.
36. Ref. 3, p. 18.
37. Ref. 4, p. 46.
38. Ref. 33, p. 9.
39. Ref. 4, p. 22.
40. Ref. 4, pp. 8–9.
41. Ref. 3, p. 67.
42. Q. Bell, *The Schools of Design,* Routledge & Kegan Paul, London, 1963, pp. 72–73.
43. J. Sparkes, *The Schools of Art: Their Origin, History, Work, and Influence,* London, 1884, p. 31.
44. R. Wornum, *Art Union J.* **4,** 40 (1852).
45. R. Wornum, *The Art-Journal Illustrated Catalogue: The Industry of All Nations, 1851,* 1851, reprint, Dover Publications, New York, 1970, p. VII***.
46. H. Cole, *Introductory Address on the Science and Art Department and the South Kensington Museum,* No. 1, Chapman & Hall, London, p. 12.
47. Ref. 42, p. 253.
48. Ref. 42, pp. 257–258.
49. W. Morris, *Hopes and Fears for Art, Five Lectures Delivered in Birmingham, London, and Nottingham, 1878–1881,* 5th ed., Longman, Green, & Co., New York, 1898, p. 60.
50. W. Morris, *The Aims of Art,* Strangeways & Sons, London, 1887, p. 14.
51. O. Wilde, *Eclectic Magazine* **53,** 469 (1981).
52. J. Barzun, *The Use and Abuse of Art, Bollingen Series XXXV · 22,* Princeton University Press, Princeton, N.J., 1974, p. 50.
53. H. Stannus in F. S. Meyer, *Handbook of Ornament, A Grammar of Industrial & Architectural Designing In All Its Branches, for Practical As Well As Theoretical Use,* 8th ed., Bruno Hessling, Montreal, Canada, 1894(?).
54. Ref. 4, p. 68.
55. Thiébault-Sisson in T. Benton, C. Benton, and D. Sharp, eds., *Architecture and Design 1890–1939,* The Whitney Library of Design, New York, 1975, p. 17.
56. P. Vergo, *Art in Vienna, 1898–1918,* Phaidon, London, 1975, p. 106.
57. H. Van de Velde in Ref. 55, p. 32.
58. E. Gallé in Ref. 55, p. 30.
59. A. Loos, "Ornament et Crime," *L'Esprit nouveau,* (5) 159 (1920).
60. A Loos in Ref. 55, p. 41.
61. T. Van Doesburg in Ref. 55, p. 94.
62. H. Poelzig in Ref. 55, p. 57.
63. R. Venturi, *Complexity and Contradiction in Architecture,* Museum of Modern Art, New York, 1966, p. 119.
64. M. Wackernagel, *The World of the Florentine Renaissance Artist,* trans. by A. Luchs, Princeton University Press, Princeton, N.J., 1981, pp. 160, 195.

General References

Ref. 16 is a good general reference.

W. Crane, *The Claims of Decorative Art,* Houghton Mifflin, Boston, 1892.

W. Dyce, "Universal Infidelity in Principles of Design," *J. Design Manufactures* **6,** 1 (1852). Origins of principles of design.

W. Morris, *The Decorative Arts and Their Relation to Modern Life and Progress,* Roberts Bros., Boston, 1878. Arts and crafts ideals.

J. Ruskin, "The Nature of Gothic," in *The Stones of Venice,* Kelmscott Press, Hammersmith, 1892.

J. Ruskin, *The Seven Lamps of Architecture,* 1848, reprint, Noonday Press, New York, 1961. In particular "The Lamp of Beauty."

L. Sullivan, *A System of Architectural Ornament According with a Philosophy of Man's Powers,* Press of the American Institute of Architects, Inc., New York, 1924.

J. A. Hamilton, *Byzantine Architecture and Decoration,* 1933, reprint, Books for Libraries Press, Freeport, N.Y., 1972. Reprint of 1933 edition; poor quality illustrations; plans, some sections; good bibliography, by country.

T. G. Jackson, *Byzantine and Romanesque Architecture,* 2nd ed., Hacker Art Books, New York, 1975. Plans, sections, elevations, details; chronological tables of architectural examples.

C. A. Mango, *Byzantine Architecture,* Rizzoli, New York, 1985. Translation; plans, sections, and elevations; selected bibliography.

J. Fleming, with H. Honour and N. Pevsner, *The Penguin Dictionary of Architecture,* 2nd ed., Penguin Books, New York, 1977.

C. M. Harris, ed., *Historic Architecture Sourcebook,* McGraw-Hill Inc., New York, 1977.

J. Barzun, *The Use and Abuse of Art, Bollingen Series XXXV-22,* Princeton University Press, Princeton, N.J., 1974. Excellent for understanding why the artist's need to be "creative" signaled the end of traditional approaches to art.

B. C. Brolin, *Flight of Fancy: The Banishment and Return of Ornament,* St. Martin's Press, New York, 1985. Changing social status of artisan–artist in Western society; explanation of modernists' rejection of ornament.

B. Fletcher, *A History of Architecture on the Comparative Method,* 17th ed., Charles Scribner's Sons, New York, 1963. Extensive drawings and photographs, primarily of European styles; decorative and other comparisons among styles.

E. H. Gombrich, *The Sense of Order,* Cornell University Press, Ithaca, N.Y., 1979.

H. Pothorn, *Architectural Styles: An Historical Guide to World Design,* Facts On File, New York, ca. 1892 (*Grosse Büch der Baustile*). Survey of styles, including non-European; glossary and section titled "The Main Features That Distinguish Styles"; photographs, plans, sections, and elevations; visual comparisons among styles; explanatory and historical text.

M. Aubert, *The Art of the High Gothic Era,* trans. by P. George, Crown Publishers, New York, 1965. Some plans, sections, and elevations; many details.

L. Grodecki, *Gothic Architecture,* trans. by I. M. Paris, Rizzoli, New York, 1985. Selected bibliography; plans and sections.

J. H. Harvey, *The Gothic World, 1100–1600,* B. T. Batsford, London, 1950. Survey, by country; good background of theory, construction techniques; short bibliography.

O. Simson, *The Gothic Cathedral,* Pantheon Books, New York, 1962.

B. Allsopp, *A History of Classical Architecture: From its Origins to the Emergence of Hellenesque and Romanesque Architecture,* Sir Isaac Pitman & Sons, London, 1965. With bibliography.

F. P. Chambers, "The Aesthetics of the Ancients," *RIBA J.* **32,** 241 (1925). Classic study pointing out modern misconception of ancient ideas of "beauty"; social status of artisan–artist.

H. d'Espouy, *Fragments from Greek and Roman Architecture,* Norton, New York, 1981. Selected from original French edition of this classic work; renderings of details, some restored (Classical America edition).

A. L. Frothingham, "Greek Architects, Contractors and Building Operations," *The Architectural Record* **xxiii,** 81 (1908); **xxiv,** 321 (1908). Original sources; how Greek buildings were constructed, ornamented.

C. Roebuck, ed., *The Muses at Work: Arts, Crafts, and Professions in Ancient Greece and Rome,* MIT Press, Cambridge, Mass., 1969. See in particular: B. S. Ridgway, "Stone Carving: Sculpture," and J. V. Noble, "Pottery Manufacture." Original sources; methods of contracting for ornament for Greek buildings; status of artist–artisan in antiquity.

J. Grube and co-workers, *Architecture in the Islamic World: Its History and Social Meaning, with a Complete Survey of Key Monuments,* W. Morrow, New York, 1978. Bibliography.

J. D. Hoag, *Islamic Architecture,* Abrams, New York, 1977. Glossary, selected bibliography, synoptic tables; includes many plans, sections, elevations.

Teaching of the Decorative Arts: *Exposition Internationale des Arts Décoratifs et Industriels Modernes, 1925,* Garland, New York, 1977.

F. S. Onderdonk, *The Ferro-Concrete Style: Reinforced Concrete in Modern Architecture,* Architectural Book Publishing Co., New York, 1928.

J. Summerson, "What is Ornament and What Is Not," *Via III: Ornament. J. Graduate School Fine Arts, Univ. Penn.,* 5 (1977).

U.S. Public Buildings Administration, *Exhibition, Painting and Sculpture designed for Federal Buildings,* Section of Fine Arts, Public Buildings Administration, Federal Works Agency, Washington, D.C., 1939.

R. Nath, *History of Decorative Art in Mughal Architecture,* 1st ed., Motilal Banarsidass, Delhi, 1976.

H. Stierlin, *Iran of the Master Builders: 2500 Years of Architecture,* trans. by R. Allen and N. Ferguson, Editions Sigma, Geneva, 1971. Bibliography.

L. Benevolo, *The Architecture of the Renaissance,* trans. by J. Landry, Westview Press, Boulder, Colo., 1978.

J. Burckhardt, *The Architecture of the Renaissance,* revised and edited by P. Murray, trans. by J. Palmes, University of Chicago Press, Chicago, Ill., 1985. Bibliography; classic work on period.

P. Murray, *Renaissance Architecture,* Rizzoli International Publications, New York, 1985. Plans, sections, and elevations; selected bibliography.

M. A. Vance, *Renaissance Architecture: A Bibliography of Books in the English Language,* Vance Bibliographies, Monticello, Ill., 1982.

M. E. Blake, *Roman Construction in Italy from Nerva through the Antonines,* edited and completed by D. T. Bishop, American Philosophical Society, Philadelphia, 1973. Bibliography.

W. L. Macdonald, *The Architecture of the Roman Empire,* Yale University Press, New Haven, Conn., 1965. Bibliography.

P. Vitruvius, *On Architecture,* trans. by F. Granger, Harvard University Press, Cambridge, Mass., 1970. Only surviving antique treatise on architecture.

B. Allsopp, *Romanesque Architecture: The Romanesque Achievement,* John Day Co., New York, 1971. Bibliography.

V. I. Atroshenko, *The Origins of the Romanesque: Near Eastern Influences on European Art, 4th–12th Centuries,* Lund Humphries, London, 1985. Bibliography.

H. E. Kubach, *Romanesque Architecture,* Abrams, New York, 1975. Translation of *Architettura Romanica* in ca. 1972; many plans, sections, elevations; synoptic tables; selected bibliography.

See also Public Art

Brent C. Brolin
New York, New York

OSHA. See Regulations—Building and Zoning

OTTO, FREI

Of the post-war German architects, none has had a greater influence on world architecture than Frei Otto. Like King Arthur's sorcerer, Merlin, he seems almost to command magic powers and like Merlin he is careful to sweep away the aura of mystery with the affirmation of reason. He unites great structural insight and intuition with a passion for reason and meticulous observation and it is this which contributes to his essential ambiguity (1).

Truly a pioneer, Frei Otto is responsible for the development of modern tent structures and other variations of lightweight tensile structures. His work is at once thoroughly innovative and modern, embodying the essential principles of modern architecture; yet, it is by virtue of the tent form itself a reflection back toward tents that have been used throughout history. The dual attitudes of modern rationalism and organic romanticism naturally coexist because both attitudes strive to capture the "universal natural law." This universal law, as Le Corbusier stated, suggests that "objects tend towards a type that is determined by the evolution of forms between the ideal of maximum utility, and the satisfaction of the necessities of economical manufacture, which conform inevitably to the laws of nature." Otto would most certainly agree with Le Corbusier, with Mies van der Rohe's assertion that "questions concerning the essence of things are the only significant questions," and also with Bernard Lafaille's assertion that "to accomplish a task with the minimum use of materials is finally the only interesting problem" (2). Earlier theorists, such as futurist architect Sant'Elia, spoke of an architecture that was revolutionary, elastic, light, expendable, active, mobile, and dynamic. Of these characteristics, three were fundamental to Otto's work—lightness of weight, elasticity, and dynamism (3). Sant'Elia also spoke of an architecture that abolished the monumental and decorative, and it was into this philosophical tradition that Frei Otto began his career in 1954.

Frei Otto was born in Siegmar, Saxony, Germany on May 31, 1925. As the son and grandson of stonemasons, Otto was initiated into an art that was at once concerned with beauty and structural clarity at a very early age. From 1931 to 1943, Otto worked as a trainee stonemason at the Schadow School in Berlin.

From his youth, Otto was fascinated with airplanes; the knowledge he gained from this avocation would be directly applicable to his later tensile constructions. At the age of 15, Otto began glider flying. Through this hobby,

Otto became not only attuned to aerodynamic principles but also gained a thorough appreciation for membranes stretched over lightweight frameworks. In addition to actually flying planes, Otto also enjoyed creating and inventing model planes. This keen interest in designing through model making would become one of his primary methods for designing tensile structures throughout his professional career.

Otto joined the German Air Force as a pilot in 1943. However, in 1945, he was captured by the Allies and remained a prisoner of war for the next two years in Chartres, France. Remarkably, it was during his imprisonment that Otto had the opportunity to study structural engineering theory. Being in charge of the building and repair crews, Otto was continually presented with the problem of a design solution with the minimum use of materials. Particularly through his efforts to repair damaged bridges, Otto consistently noted that the volume of material required in a structure was inversely related to the amount of tensile members in the structure. Otto's lifelong architectural problem-solving approach of building the most possible with the least amount of material was in part shaped by his wartime experience.

After the war, in 1948, Otto commenced his architectural studies at the Technische Universitat in Charlottenburg. It soon became apparent that his approach to structural design was truly innovative in the engineering field. On a study tour to the United States from 1950 to 1951, Otto met with Eero Saarinen and civil engineer Fred Severud. In Severud's office, Otto had the opportunity to preview the drawings for Matthew Nowicki's Raleigh North Carolina State Fairgrounds Arena, the first great suspended roof structure. The project not only embodied many of Otto's ideas, but also had a significant impact on Otto's doctoral thesis, which was the first comprehensive documentation and systematic investigation of suspended roofs—then a largely unexplored field (4). Otto's thesis was published in 1954 as a book titled *Das Hängende Dach* ("The Suspended Roof").

The book caught the attention of Peter Stromeyer, a partner with the Stromeyer Company, one of the largest tent manufacturers in the world. Stromeyer contacted Otto and thereby initiated a long, fruitful collaboration that resulted in the advancement of the art of fabric tensile structures. Some of the notable tent structures designed by Otto with the Stromeyer Company include the bandstand at the 1955 Federal Garden Exhibition in Kassel, FRG, one of the first structures to have a prestressed membrane between edge cables; the entrance arch at the same exhibition in Cologne, FRG, in 1957, an arch supported-saddle structure; and the "Snow and Rocks" pavilion at the Swiss national exhibition in Lausanne in 1964, a group of five sharply peaked tents that were transitional to Otto's later cablenet structures. Some of the tents Otto designed for the Stromeyer Company were intended for mass production and many of Otto's advancements in tent construction were inspired by or derived from his theories and knowledge about structural engineering related to long-span construction bridges and suspended roofs. While the collaboration with Stromeyer was very important, Otto always regarded his work on tent structures as a testing ground for more permanent lightweight structures.

With the experience from the tent structures, Otto focused his efforts on cable network structures. These structures were similar to tent structures in that a flexible membrane, in this case a net of metal cables and not canvas, was used to stabilize tensile forces with compressive stresses concentrated in only a few masts or poles. The West German pavilion in Expo '67 in Montreal and the 1972 sports structures for the Olympic Park in Munich are his most notable works of this kind.

In 1957, in order to forge ahead with his theoretical explorations, Otto established the Development Centre for Lightweight Construction in Berlin without the assistance of any public funding. In 1964, Otto had the opportunity to incorporate the institution into the Institute for Light Surface Structures at the University of Stuttgart, where his longtime mentor, Fritz Leonhardt, was a professor. Otto was fortunate to be able to salvage and convert the West German pavilion from the Montreal exposition into the new Institute's home.

Since 1970, Otto has retired from active architectural practice and has worked as a consultant, but even more important, he has served as an advocate and stimulator of advanced architectural theories. His projects have the one criticism of failing to transform the pure rationale of structure into total architecture. However, much of this is explained by the fact that his works have usually been done in association with others, and the connections between Otto's roof structures and the surroundings have not been as sensitively managed as they could have been. Nonetheless, because Otto assumes the role of the scientist, experimenter, and inventor, and because his new solutions are without stylistic precedent, he is forced to rely on aesthetic criteria. In so doing, Otto bridges the gap between science and art (5). His concern for minimalist structures links him to the Bauhaus and international style designers while his analysis of natural forms and modern technology link him to post-World War II architects. This "ability to bridge the gap in German architectural history created by the Nazi years and to advance the frontier of structural design has made Otto one of the most important German architects working today" (5).

BIBLIOGRAPHY

1. P. Drew, *Frei Otto: Form and Structure,* Westview Press, Boulder, Colo., 1976, p. 12.
2. *Ibid.,* p. 6.
3. *Ibid.,* p. 9.
4. C. Roland, *Frei Otto: Tension Structures,* Praeger Publishers, New York, 1970, p. 1.
5. C. Pearson, "Frei Otto," in *Macmillan Encyclopedia of Architects,* Vol. 3, The Free Press, 1982, p. 332.

General References

P. Drew, "Frei Otto," in M. Emanuel, ed., *Contemporary Architects,* St. Martin's Press, New York, 1980.

F. Otto, *Das Hängende Dach: Gestalt und Struktur,* Bauwelt Verlga, Berlin, 1954.

See also MEMBRANE STRUCTURES; SUSPENSION CABLE STRUCTURES

RAVI S. WALDON, AIA
Bignell & Watkins
Annapolis, Maryland

OWNERSHIP OF BUILDINGS

In real estate the condominium is an arrangement under which a fee title to a specific part of a building or building complex can be held with an undivided interest in certain common interest elements of the building or complex (1).

Almost all plans for new cities or new neighborhoods developed in recent years include housing structures. They may include high-, medium- or low-rise apartment buildings, townhouses, and garden-type buildings. They are frequently surrounded by landscaped green areas and recreational facilities such as tennis and racquetball courts, swimming pools, sauna baths, golf courses, boating, and fishing. These various types of housing units can be condominium homes.

The condominium is a type of ownership that in residential construction occurs in a multifamily building. The purpose of a condominium is in many respects similar to cooperative housing, that is, to provide ownership to the occupant. The condominium owner owns his or her unit while the cooperative owner owns shares in a corporation that owns the building. This corporation grants to the cooperative owner right to own and use a designated portion or unit of the building.

The condominium deed conveys fee simple title to a designated unit of the building and an undivided interest in the building's common areas such as corridors, elevator, roof, and exterior site. Each condominium owner of a unit or apartment receives a recorded deed which spells out the metes and bounds as described in the Declaration. The deed also conveys to each unit owner joint ownership with other unit owners of the common elements. This joint ownership is a percentage interest in the common element to each unit owner, which usually is approximately the value of the unit related to the whole building.

The condominium owner receives most of the legal and financial benefits of a single home owner and is able to mortgage his or her unit separately from the other units in the building (2). Condominium units are also assessed and taxed separately. The legal liability of a condominium owner is similar to that of a single home owner.

The condominium unit owner is responsible for payment of his real estate taxes and his mortgage. The condominium and the cooperative unit owner both enjoy the tax benefits of the purchase and sale of real estate.

The condominium has the distinction of being the only form of real estate that has its own law. Single family homes and cooperatives operate under common and corporate law. All fifty states now have laws governing the establishment of a condominium.

The condominium has many of the advantages of an apartment unit. It allows ownership in an area or location usually not available to single family homes because of high costs of land and allows many amenities usually not affordable in a single family home, as mentioned before. The cost of the amenities can usually be afforded only when they are shared by many units.

The elimination of maintenance such as lawn care, road and walk snow-shoveling, and exterior maintenance provides condominium owners with freedom from care and responsibility and adds to their leisure time (3).

The condominium is also used extensively in the commercial and industrial fields, especially in professional buildings. Through building ownership, professionals such as accountants, architects, dentists, doctors, engineers, and lawyers may reduce some out-of-pocket expenses, invest in real estate, and obtain a sort of "hedge against inflation." Rather than contributing to the owner's profit in addition to paying his expenses in a leased building, a professional would, by owning a condominium, be able to deduct the depreciation on the condominium office from income tax. More after-tax cash earnings would be retained; retirement savings are benefited by investment in the equity of the condominium office. While there may be some disadvantages in the lack of flexibility in condominium office ownership, it retains the advantages of increased cash flow and reduced cash outflow (4).

Condominium ownership has been utilized for hotels, especially resort hotels. Hawaii was the first state to adopt condominium-enabling legislation and was the first state in which a condominium resort hotel was created. The condominium hotel concept spread rapidly throughout Hawaii. In 1971 the Securities and Exchange Commission ruled the sale of resort-hotel condominium units as a security under their purview.

Condominiums have been used in some states to legally describe "air-rights" as well as to effectively describe various ownership portions of mixed-use projects.

HISTORY

While the history of the use of the condominium form of property ownership is generally thought to be quite recent, it is not unique to the United States nor a recent creation. There is some evidence that the concept goes back to Babylonian times, about 2000 B.C. Although it was contrary to basic Roman law, the problem of shortage of land was dealt with by allowing citizens to own individual dwelling units in a multifamily building (3).

The history of ownership in multiple-occupied buildings started in the Middle Ages. During the twelfth century in Germany, buildings were divided and had different owners who also had joint ownership of the site and the common elements. The centers of cities were walled to protect them from outside attack. Limited space within these walls and the increase in population made this condominium type of ownership a reasonable solution to the problem of limited land. Some of these divided buildings were leased as well as those that had multiple owners.

There were two factors that worked against the more widespread use of the condominium during this period. First, it was contrary to basic Roman law and secondly, there was a distinct lack of clear laws or rules to regulate the maintenance and repairs of the common elements.

When the *Burgerliche Gesetzbuch,* the civil code for all Germany, was enacted, it made ownership of a part of a structure impossible (2).

The French Civil Code in 1804 granted a person the right to own a building or part of a building on land which did not belong to him. This code dealt primarily with maintenance and repair. Laws pertaining to the condominium form of ownership were used in countries such as Spain, Italy, Belgium, Germany, and France long before the United States. Such condominium laws appeared in South America in the 1940s and 1950s. These laws usually did not use the word "condominium" but referred to "horizontal property" and other terminology in an attempt to name or describe the process. The laws dealt with the allowance and protection of air space and utilized the stories of the property which divided this vertical space by horizontal planes. In 1938–1939 in the United States, new legislation improved the condominium laws by clarifying rights and obligations of unit owners, to give the right to a majority of the unit owners to make binding decisions and to appoint a management agent.

Up to World War II the majority of people living in luxury apartments occupied them under lease. During the war the government, through rent control, had kept rents low and very few apartment buildings were built. After World War II the cost of living had increased and the demand for apartments was very high.

Many owners were converting their apartment buildings to condominiums. Many developers, after the public had accepted the idea of buying their own apartments, built new condominium buildings for sale.

After the war in both France and Germany, special legislation was passed enabling condominiums, which helped in the reconstruction of cities demolished during the war. Germany also encouraged condominiums by accepting tax deductible savings for this purpose and granting mortgages to these savers.

Because of inflation, condominiums were widely used in Latin American countries as an inflation hedge and to protect equity. Home ownership was considered very important in Puerto Rico, which has strong cultural ties to Latin America. There was a scarcity of apartment sites because of the government's emphasis on agriculture and industry. Condominium apartments were successful and the need for Federal Housing Agency (FHA) financing led to the establishment of the Horizontal Property Regime of 1958.

Puerto Rico was responsible for the introduction of condominiums to the United States after receiving FHA support. At the time that the Puerto Rico Horizontal Property Act was passed, the FHA agreed to insure mortgages on the condominium units. This special treatment by the FHA was limited to Puerto Rico.

Under Section 234, the Housing Act of 1961 permitted the FHA to insure condominium mortgages in the United States and to the residents of Puerto Rico. Puerto Rico, because of the population concentration, was in serious need of high-rise and high-density housing in the urban centers. These federal loan guarantees were needed to induce financial institutions to make the required mortgage loans. The passage of Section 234 of the National Housing Act in 1961 had an extremely important role in condominium history in the United States. This act indicated the confidence of the Congress in this type of ownership and led directly to the required research to develop the safeguards required by lenders, sponsors, and purchasers. The FHA developed at this time a condominium law which was used as a model by many states. Enabling legislation for condominiums has now been enacted by every state.

While Section 234 of the 1961 Housing Act was urged by Puerto Rico for a trial testing, fortunately Congress authorized FHA insurance on a nationwide basis. While most condominium owners have not used the FHA financing, the legislation was instrumental in obtaining enabling legislation in most of the states.

The popularity of condominium ownership spurred the conversion of existing apartments in the late 1960s and early 1970s. Abuses in the process caused many states to put limitations and restrictions on this process. The condominium boom has stopped in the 1980s, as the market is largely over-built. Numerous litigations resulting from condominium development caused many developers to leave the field or curtail their operations.

The condominium, in spite of its success in the United States, is not the solution to all problems in real estate. The same sound judgment that applies to other real estate is still important. Location is of key importance. Architectural skills are needed to closely provide those amenities found in a single family house and those amenities that can be added because of the size of the condominium project. Condominiums can be expected to play an increasingly key role in solving the nation's housing needs where there is increased demand for home ownership in higher density areas of cities.

PLANNING CONCEPTS UTILIZING CONDOMINIUMS

Condominium ownership enhances the utilization of multiple or mixed-use improvements, construction over platforms, and construction on marginal or unsuitable soil by conventional methods. Creative utilization of condominium ownership is helping solve many communities' legal, financial, and community problems.

Multi-use Improvements

Because of growing needs and limited supply, it is evident to the general public that land must be used more efficiently and effectively than in the past. Because in Michigan air rights are handled legally by creating a condominium, a developer created a central downtown development project in Bay City, Michigan that united and separated four and one half city blocks into a large condominium project. These blocks were separated both vertically and horizontally into spaces required for the major uses. The major uses are parking (both underground and a ramp), a two-story, two-city-block retail shopping mall, an office tower, a hotel, a private residential condominium apartment block, and a marina and restaurant.

Each of the uses has its own ownership with certain elements such as vertical and horizontal elements and circulation held in common. While the individual residential apartments and marina berths were condominiumized, other elements, such as the hotel, office tower, and retail spaces, were not required to utilize condominium ownership. Each of the separate elements had individual ownership and would bear the obligations of separate tax assessments.

Platform Construction

Many urban communities have utilized platform construction to build over low structures such as railroad or low-rise buildings. Platform construction has also been used to construct a base for building on otherwise unbuildable sites because of rocky terrain or difficulty in providing required utilities. Because of cities' unique ability to acquire land parcels by the right of eminent domain or its implied threat and because of the high cost of parking structures relative to their financial return, many communities build and own a multilayer parking facility on top of which a private developer is enticed to erect multilevel housing and/or office or warehouse facilities. This technique allows communities to acquire the land, arrange for any moving or displacement costs, and re-offer the land at a lower cost than what the developer could produce.

Such an arrangement also provides required but expensive downtown parking in preferred locations and allows communities to be selective in terms and amenities they can require from the developer. This type of platform building is limited to larger structures on larger portions of land because of the relatively heavy legal and financial costs in relation to the size of the project.

Physical Arrangement

Condominium ownership allows almost any type of physical arrangement and still permits individual fee simple ownership of the units. Since most structures are of layer construction, it can provide the common foundation, underlying land, stairs, utility shafts, and elevators.

The potential of the site and its limitations determine the house quality and the suitability of housing type. The natural factors that have influence include water, physiography, orientation, vegetation, views, and climate. Certain manmade features include location, cultural attractions, utilities, services, buildings, and roads.

There are several basic types of contemporary cluster houses which include the row house, town house, flat, patio house, maisonette, and terrace. The origin of all of these types is the single-unit dwelling merged into a cluster, with sidewalls becoming party walls and side yards ceasing to exist. Each or all of these types described below can be included in a condominium where each individual unit has a fee title.

The row house originated in the traditional two-story house on a long narrow lot. The first floor contains the living, dining, and kitchen facilities. The bedrooms and bath are located on the second floor. In a row house, the long walls become party walls and, therefore, all views, access, daylighting and natural ventilation come from the narrow ends. Row houses can be single width, double narrow, double medium, or triple width. The townhouse is similar to the row house, with the addition of parking inside the building.

Hal Higgin, an architect and housing specialist from London, England, helped solve the rebuilding of London after World War II by a creative design which allowed the rebuilding of housing at the previous density, approximately fifty units per acre, while not exceeding the structures of surrounding blocks which were approximately 50 ft in height. This design increased the safety of children and accommodated the required parking by developing what became known as the high deck system.

The entrances to the maisonettes are depressed one half level from the street sidewalk on the two long sides of the block. Ramp entrances and exits for automobiles are at the short ends of the block. Parking for all cars is at this level 6 ft below the sidewalk. A reinforced concrete deck was poured about 6 ft above street level; apartments are entered from this elevated platform, which also provides a safe place for children to play under the supervision of the residential unit and away from street traffic.

Jack Craycroft, an architect in Dallas, Texas, utilized a similar functional distribution of parts in the condominium complex he designed and lives in. This unique condominium is built in an established neighborhood in Dallas, Texas. Each of the eight units is protected by a masonry wall which encloses a private patio. The units are clustered on two sides of an auto parking spline on the lowest level and a secured entrance level over top of it. Each of the units has a two-car garage, laundry units and storage space on the lowest level, and two floors of living space above, as illustrated in Figure 1**a.** Figure 1**b** illustrates how the parts relate in section and indicates how high density with low-rise construction can still provide many amenities.

Ralph Rapson, an architect in Minneapolis, Minnesota, designed five quality condominium units on a lot with only 100 ft of shoreline on Lake Okoboji, Iowa (Fig. 2). Rapson maximized the lake frontage and maintained excellent views of the lake to the south from each of the units by stepping the living units at an angle, also achieving privacy for each unit.

The flat is common throughout the world. This one-story dwelling has a central entrance with living facilities on one side and the sleeping facilities on the other. The flat form is extremely flexible and can assume many different configurations.

The flat is frequently stacked, as in the design developed by Arthur Danielian of Irvine, California, in Beacon Hill Vistas, in Orange County, California, shown in Figure 3. This project combines three building types including one- and two-story townhomes and stacked flats as shown in Figure 4.

Another example of the use of stacked flats in combination with garden units and townhouses is the project de-

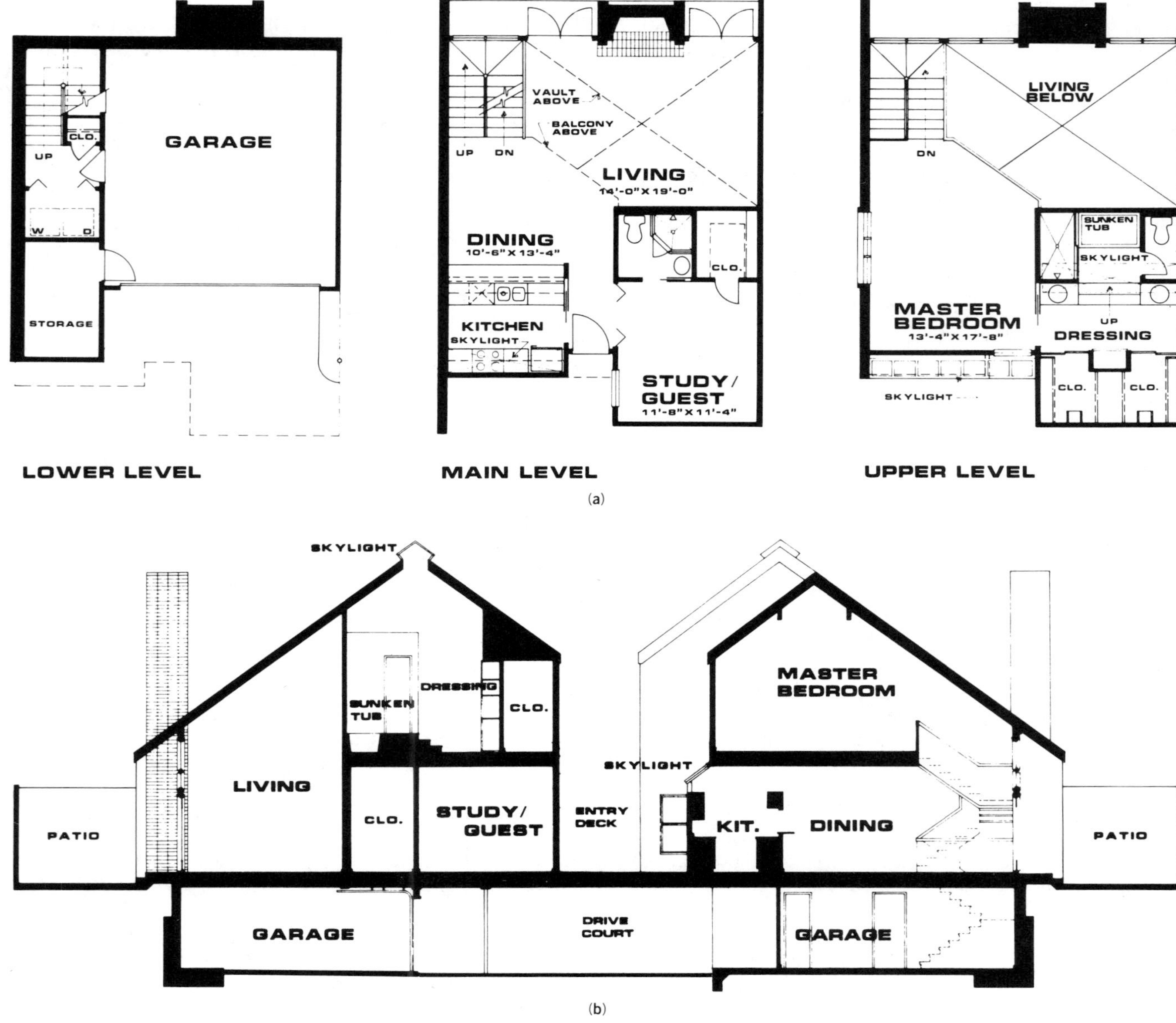

Figure 1. Condominium in Dallas, Texas. Architect: Jack Craycroft. (**a**) Unit plan; (**b**) Section. Courtesy of the architect.

signed by Paul J. Carroll and Associates of Boston, Massachusetts called the Elms at Arbor Hill in Weymouth, Mass., shown in Figure 5. Each of the two towers shown contains 105 units.

The Lakeside Condominiums in Keystone, Colorado (Fig. 6), designed by Worthington/Everett Ziegel Architects of Denver, Colorado, arrange three levels of one bedroom and efficiency along a single-loaded corridor to maximize the views of the lake and the ski slopes. The lowest level commercial space orients the pedestrian area toward the lake and away from the parking and highway.

A patio house, which is used primarily in warm dry climates, is a variation of the traditional one-story ranch house. To fit on a narrower lot, the private space is fenced in. With the elimination of the side and front yards, the form becomes a patio home.

A project called "The Mesas" located in St. George, Utah, designed by Michael Knorr and Associates, Inc. of Denver, Colorado, utilized the patio home effectively (Fig. 7). This plan type was derived from the cluster home used in this same project (Fig. 8).

The maisonette is commonly used in high-density low-rise construction. It results from stacking one two-story unit on top of another. This requires two sets of stairs from the top unit. Terrace houses result from row or patio houses being terraced up or down a hill to enhance views.

The increase in population, scarcity and increased cost of land, and the high cost of preparing marginal land and

Figure 2. Lakeside Condominium on Lake Okoboji, Iowa. Architect: Ralph Rapson. Courtesy of the architect.

land passed over in initial development combine to make the condominium an economically feasible form of home ownership.

INDUSTRIAL CONDOMINIUMS

Industrial condominiums are usually located in suburban areas throughout the United States. The demand for industrial condominiums is due to the decentralization of plants and the existence of market. Industrial condominiums are successful only in growing regions where all forms of real estate development are successful. For industrial condominiums to be purchased, as opposed to leasing space, the owner must anticipate that the value will increase shortly. The most likely candidates for an industrial condominium are usually less than 6000 ft in size. Although lack of flexibility can be a deterring factor, the buyers of these condominiums are usually local light manufacturers or sales groups. The more successful industrial condominiums are generally located in specially designed industrial parks located off major ring freeways to provide good accessibility. These types of facilities provide for locational recognition and adequate financing.

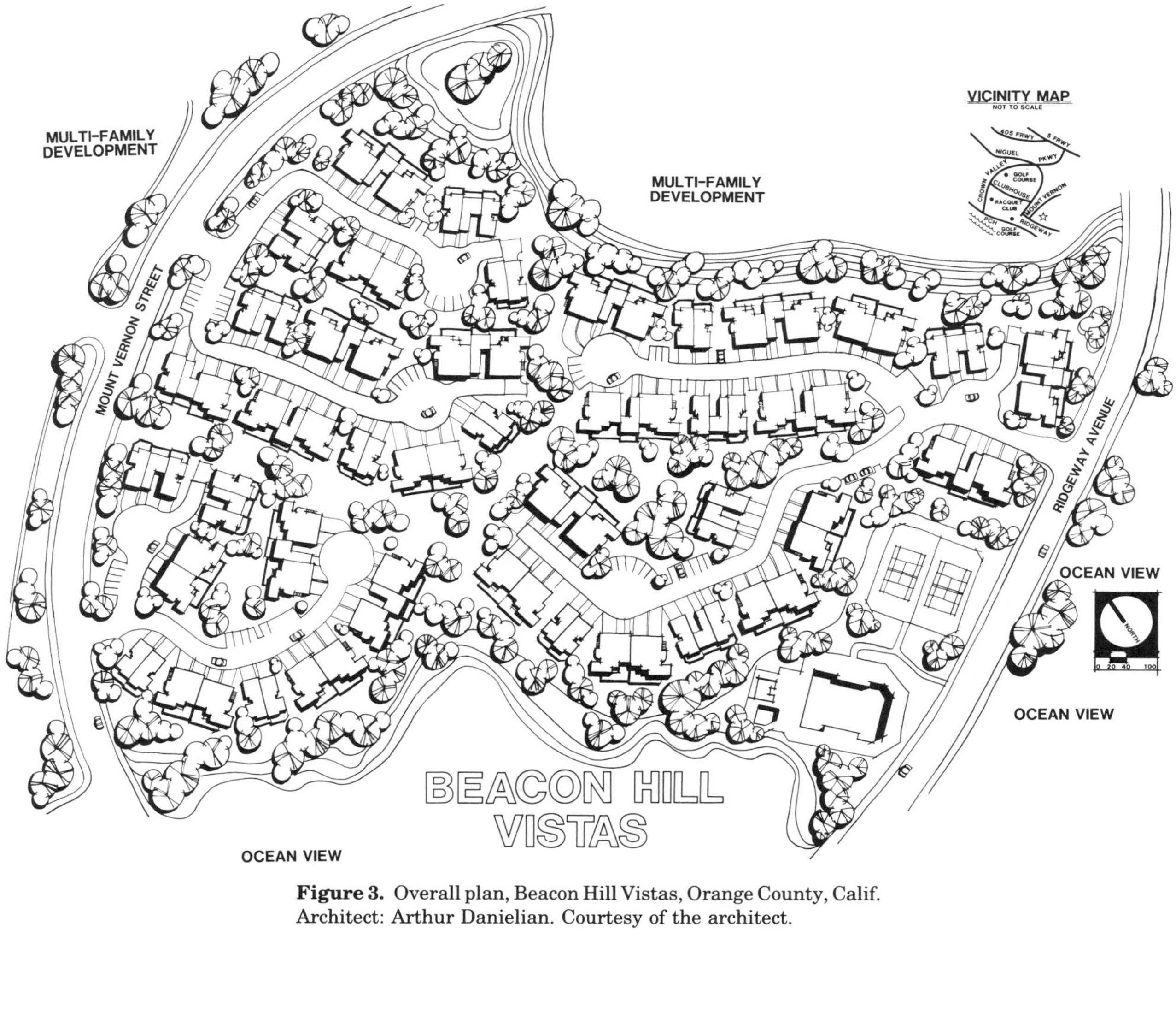

Figure 3. Overall plan, Beacon Hill Vistas, Orange County, Calif. Architect: Arthur Danielian. Courtesy of the architect.

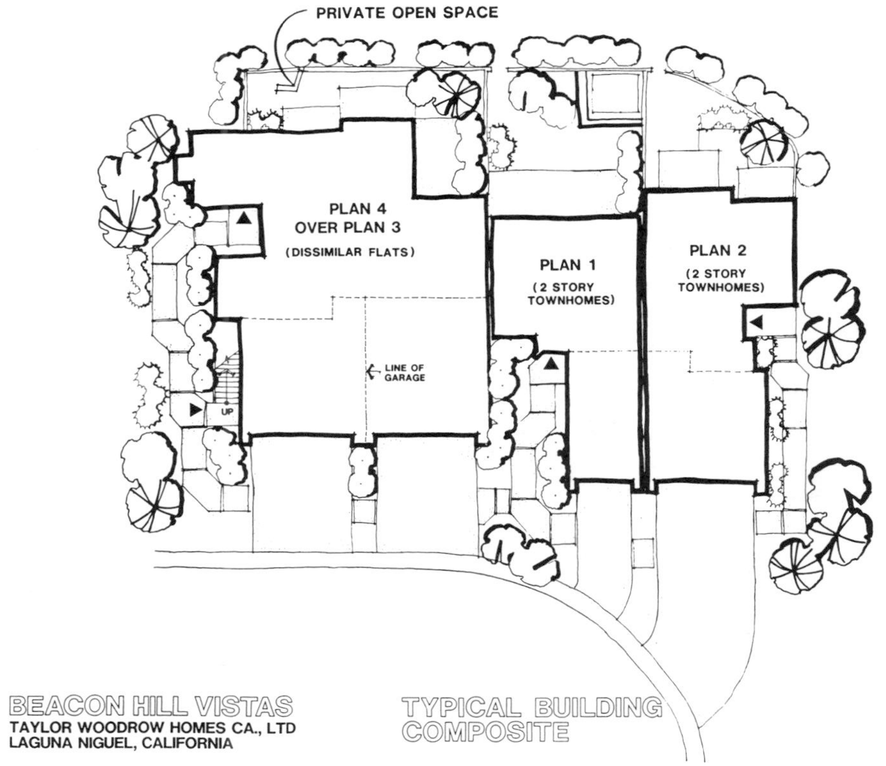

Figure 4. Typical building composite, Beacon Hill Vistas, Orange County, Calif. Courtesy of the architect.

Figure 5. The Elms at Arbor Hill in Weymouth, Mass. Architect: Paul J. Carroll and Associates. Courtesy of the architect.

Figure 6. Lakeside Condominium, Keystone, Colorado. Architect: Worthington/Everett Ziegel Architects. Courtesy of the architects.

LEGAL CONCEPTS AND BASIC DOCUMENTS

Condominium ownership makes possible the same legal and tax implications as a single-family residence. The owner can sell, rent, or occupy the unit. The condominium operates from state laws enabling condominium ownership in the state. The condominium is created by written legal documents. The most important of these documents is the Declaration, which usually contains a precise description of the land, whether fee or leased; a description of the units, common elements, and limited common elements; a statement indicating the use of the building or buildings or apartments, including restrictive uses; and a statement of other detailed legal requirements, such as service of process and provisions for amending the Declaration. The Declaration must generally be recorded with

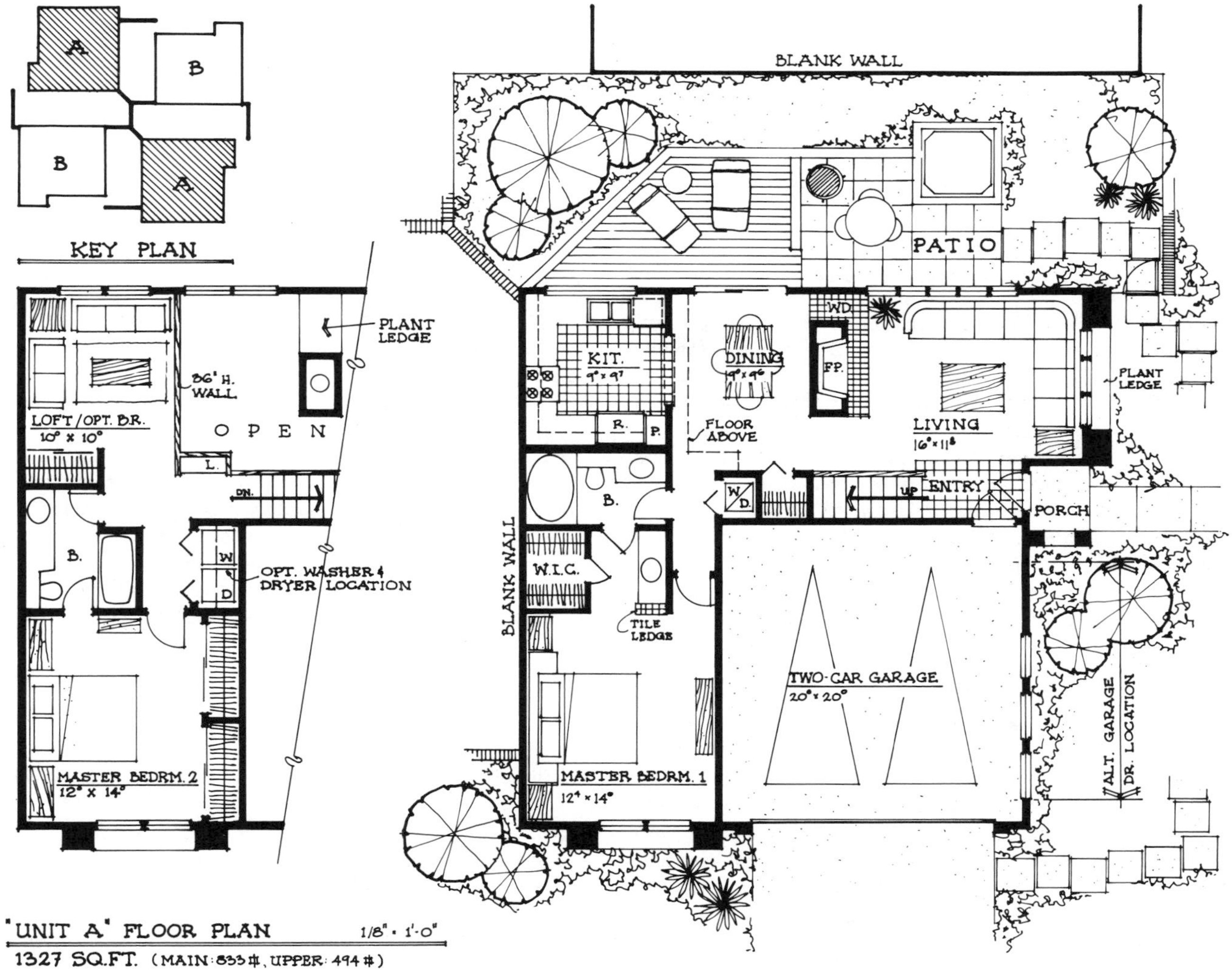

Figure 7. Patio home at The Mesas, St. George, Utah. Architect: Michael Knorr & Associates. Courtesy of the architect.

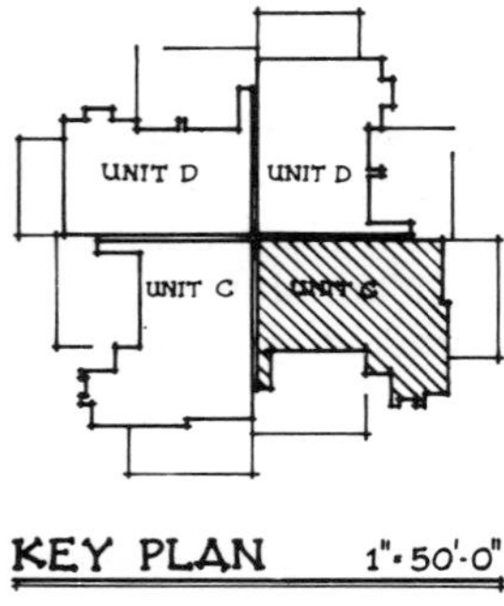

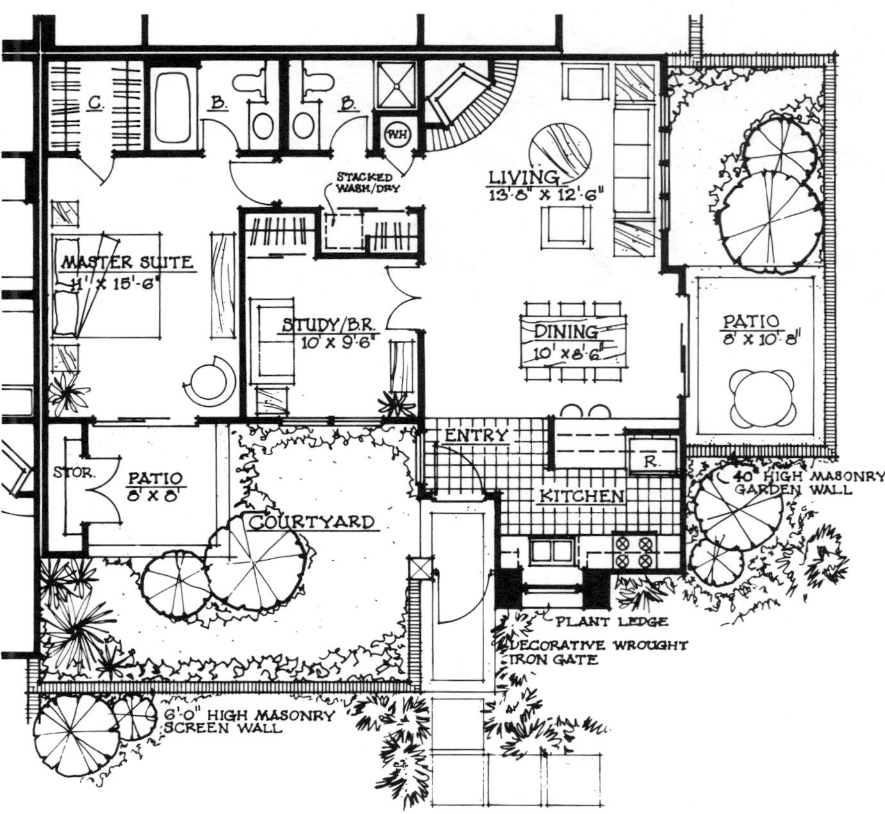

Figure 8. Cluster home at The Mesas, St. George, Utah. Architect: Michael Knorr & Associates. Courtesy of the architect.

the by-laws, articles of incorporation, and a condominium map. In most states the developer must record a master deed or lease. The Declaration also includes the legal rights and obligations of the owners. These rights include rules that determine ownership interest and voting rights.

The Declaration defines the conditions and restrictions of the condominium, and describes the nature of the improvements and the purpose intended for the property. The Declaration and the Articles of Incorporation create the condominium and give it legal powers. The Articles of Incorporation generally cover the duration, purpose, powers, membership, Board of Directors, officers, conveyances, and encumbrances, and the initial registered office and agent.

The by-laws give specific procedures for the administration of the condominium. Also included among the important legal documents is a condominium map or diagram of the total condominium community. This map, plat, or plan is usually a detailed site plan which contains the location, layout, unit numbers, and dimensions of the condominium units, and is filed at the same time as the condominium declaration. The condominium map is generally certified by an architect, land surveyor, or engineer.

Use restrictions, rules, and regulations are generally adopted by the board of directors to determine what can or cannot be done. Use restrictions are difficult to change, so some items may be included in the rules and regulations.

SECOND HOME CONDOMINIUMS

Second home condominiums are becoming more popular as the numbers of middle-aged people increase. With the increase in the length and frequency of vacations, and with the increase in efficiency of all travel, vacation locations have become more crowded and commercialized. The desire for privacy and easy access to resort-type facilities, free from crowding, has encouraged more people to seek second home condominiums. The Internal Revenue Service still allows deductions of interest and real estate taxes, which makes the carry costs more palatable.

These second home condominiums are located throughout the United States, but are generally located in a climate different from that of the primary house. Although most second homes are built to be accessible and livable throughout the year, there are many which are intended to be utilized only during certain seasons of the year.

Second homes tend to be smaller in size than principal homes because they are usually located in areas where a larger amount of outside activity is expected. Second homes can be occupied by a larger percentage of non-owners than in the case of principal residences. For this reason many second home condominiums have higher maintenance costs. A condominium whose owners contemplate short-term leasing to transients may be a less certain investment for a second home buyer.

In Hawaii and Florida, high-rise condominium homes are developed by a syndicate of investors who are given first choice of purchase. This procedure encourages speculation in units and results in increased leasing of units.

Special management problems occur in second home condominiums that are closed seasonally. In addition to the obvious security problems, there are additional costs involved, such as residential employees, that relate to operation of each extensive overhead item such as golf courses, tennis courts, and marinas. In this type of condominium it is recommended that extensive recreational facilities be organized in a separate non-profit corporation in which the condominium has a controlling interest. Second condominium homes should provide extra storage outside the unit for furniture, utensils, bedding, bicycles, etc, in anticipation of temporary leasing.

The future as well as the present supply of potable water is highly important to second home owners. Condominium ownership of second homes enables the creation of a better water supply system than could be afforded by any individual homeowner. Sites on water are more valuable and attractive if they have no limitations on swimming, boating, or ice skating. Mortgage rates on second homes generally exceed rates on one-family homes or principal residences. In general, the mortgage terms tend to be shorter. Police and fire protection are important considerations in the purchase of a second home. Because many such homes are located in remote areas, it is important that special care be given to materials use and maximization of safety.

Sea Colony at Bethany Beach, Delaware, is an ocean front high-rise for recreational second homes designed by Collins & Kronstadt Leah Hogan Collins Draper of Silver Spring, Maryland and is shown in Figure 9.

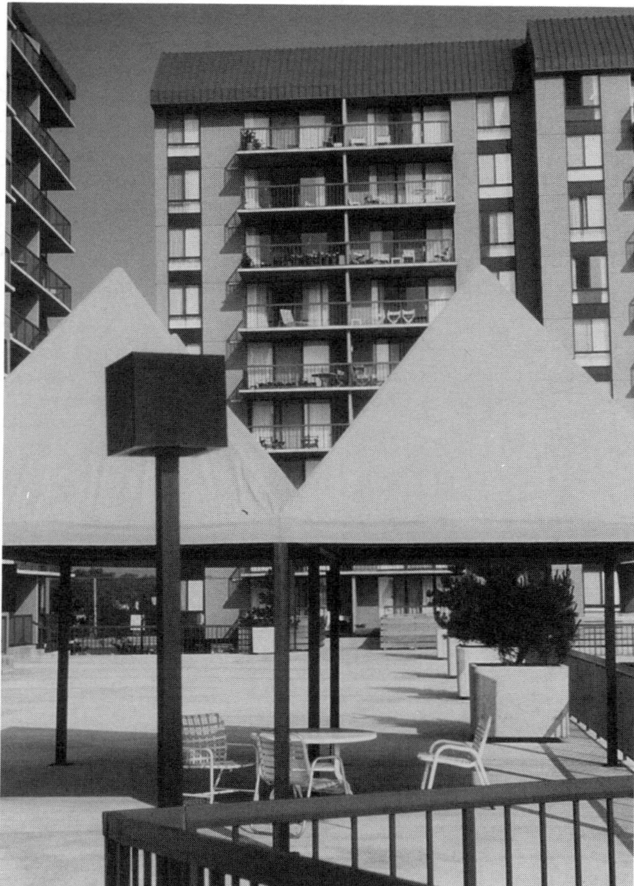

Figure 9. Sea Colony, Bethany Beach, Delaware. Architects: Collins & Kronstadt Leah Hogan Collins Draper. Courtesy of the architect.

CONDOMINIUM HOTELS

A condominium hotel is a hotel or motel in which the owner's right to use his unit is so restricted that the principal motivation for ownership is like that of a conventional hotel, that is, to make a profit on investment. The condominium hotel is designed physically so that accommodations rented to non-owners are the same as a conventional hotel. A true condominium hotel is neither an apartment hotel, which rents by the week or month, nor a second-home condominium. Multi-ownership of these properties has caused various government levels to look upon the investor as a consumer, and have sought to protect the investor or purchaser of a unit from fraud. As a result, regulatory schemes have been enacted that require the professional management to abide by both federal and state regulations, as well as the specific management agreement. Condominium hotel management is a rapidly evolving discipline in both legal and operational aspects; standardization is still taking place.

COOPERATIVE OWNERSHIP

Cooperative ownership differs in many ways from condominium ownership. In a co-op, the individual owns shares in a corporation which owns the building as opposed to a condominium where each unit is individually owned. Generally, the corporation takes out a single mortgage for the building.

In a co-op, tenants may feel more restricted in the use of their apartments than owners of condominiums. The tenant, upon re-sale, usually must obtain approval from the co-op's board of directors of the proposed purchaser. In a co-op, when the tenant or shareholder defaults on its mortgage or tax payment, the other shareholders must cover the default or risk the entire project foreclosure. The contingent liability is one of the disadvantages of co-op ownership.

BIBLIOGRAPHY

1. D. Clurman and E. L. Hebard, *Condominiums and Cooperatives,* Wiley-Interscience, New York, 1970.
2. T. J. Burke and colleagues, *Condominium, Housing for Tomorrow,* MR Management Reports, Boston, Mass., 1969.
3. J. Scavo, *The Condominium Home: A Special Marketing Challenge,* National Association of Realtors, Chicago, Ill., 1981.

4. *Owner's and Manager's Guide to Condominium Management,* Revised Edition, Institute of Real Estate Management of the National Association of Realtors, Chicago, Ill., 1984.

General References

P. M. Gunnar and J. A. Burkhart, *The Management of Hotel and Motel Condominiums,* School of Hotel Administration, Cornell University, Ithaca, N.Y., 1978.

H. E. Braun, Jr. and D. J. Page, *The Language of Real Estate in Michigan,* Real Estate Education Company, Chicago, Ill., 1979.

G. Housman, *Real Estate Review* **15,** 71–74 (Fall 1985).

R. Engstrom and M. Putnam, *Planning and Design of Townhouses and Condominiums,* The Urban Land Institute, Washington, D.C.

Executive Group, Residential Council, *Residential Development Handbook,* Urban Land Institute, Washington, D.C.

H. Hoffmann, *Row Houses and Cluster Homes,* Frederick A. Praeger, New York.

D. Mackay, *Multiple Family Housing; From Aggregation to Integration,* Architectural Book Publishing Co., New York, 1977.

R. Untermann and R. Small, *Site Planning for Cluster Housing,* Van Nostrand Reinhold Co., New York, 1977.

See also APARTMENT BUILDINGS, HIGH-RISE; HOTELS; MIXED-USE BUILDINGS; MULTIFAMILY HOUSING

LOUIS R. LUNDGREN, FAIA
The Lundgren Associates Inc.
St. Paul, Minnesota

P

PAINTS AND COATINGS

Of the many materials opposing destructive forces, paints and coatings, when selected properly and used according to recommended procedures, are among the most effective.

Usually applied in the final stages of construction, these protective, and also decorative, substances sometimes get less attention from architects and builders than they deserve. When appropriate protective material, adequate surface preparation, and suitable application techniques are demanded by knowledgeable professionals, the number of years a structure can be protected against deterioration without repainting can be multiplied. Decorative paints will also give longer service with the same attention. For those architects sufficiently interested in minimizing protective maintenance of buildings for which they are responsible, guidance information on generic materials and procedures for surface preparation and application can be obtained from such organizations as ASTM (American Society for Testing and Materials) and the Federation of Societies for Coatings Technology, both in Philadelphia; the National Paint and Coatings Association, in Washington, D.C.; Steel Structures Painting Council, Pittsburgh; and federal military and housing offices related to specifications.

Essentially, a paint or surface coating is an oil or resinous binder containing a pigment or pigments that impart color, contribute to ease of application, and either add to or detract from the light reflectivity that results in some degree of gloss or flat appearance. In addition, additives are used to improve performance of the resulting pigment–binder mixture; these may include thickening agents, antimicrobials, antiskinning agents, catalytic driers, and adhesion promoters. Pigments, binders, and additives, in almost all instances, are either suspended or dissolved in a solvent of some kind, which evaporates after the product is applied. Solvent-reduced coatings utilize petroleum distillates, and in some instances, alcohol; aqueous products are thinned with water, but must have petroleum-derived agents for film formation.

The use of paint for decoration antedated its protective function. Cave paintings in Altamira, Spain, and in France still survive after an estimated 15,000–30,000 years. The first recognizable structural protection by surface coatings was found in Egypt where arboreal gum, probably from evergreens, had been smeared over wooden ship hulls, a practice universally followed until the advent of steel bottoms in the late nineteenth century. The practice of using pitch for ship hulls goes back to Noah, whose Ark had pitch both inside and outside.

By 3000 B.C., the Egyptians had developed ways to protect and beautify their palaces, temples, and tombs. Binders were prepared from gum arabic, lime, and egg for use with available pigments, such as powdered charcoal, earth colors, chalk, and Egyptian blue, a synthetic. Molten beeswax, or encaustic, was the one weather-resistant coating used by the ancients. Early Egyptian paints, like the much earlier cave paintings, used the only solvent available—water.

Developments after this period advanced slowly. Pressed flaxseed, known as linseed oil, declined as a staple in coatings only in the middle of the twentieth century; it was first used by artists in the period that bridged the Middle Ages and the Renaissance. Two centuries passed before it was used to protect structures.

Until the early twentieth century, the major developments included the following:

1. The use of vegetable oils, mainly pressed flaxseed or linseed oil.
2. Improved modified arboreal gums, such as gum Arabic and pine rosin, which were combined as early as the eleventh century with vegetable oils and heated to form varnishes, which may be pigmented, or used in their natural translucent form.
3. Development of natural colors such as iron oxide, ochre, umber, and burnt sienna, and processed inorganic colors such as white and red lead, American- and French-process zinc oxide, lithopone, and a few synthetic colors.

Until the second decade of the twentieth century, paints were mainly composed of pigmented vegetable oil or pigmented varnish thinned with turpentine, or had binders of water-thinned casein. Surface coatings also included slaked lime, or whitewash.

Casein, a milk protein, was used by ancient Egyptians; a similar material, milk curds, was used by the ancient Hebrews to decorate their homes. Whitewash was used by pioneering Americans. For marine environments, portland cement was later added to the lime–water mix, and eventually casein and skim milk were used to aid adhesion.

Since World War II, surface protection by various kinds of coatings has advanced significantly. Trained chemists have borrowed from the discipline of biology to overcome destructive fungi and from physics to aid ease of application and speed of drying.

The distinction between paints and varnish, simply put, is in the use of pigments, including colorants and filler pigments, in paints. A pigmented varnish, as is true of pigmented vegetable oil, becomes a paint.

Varnish colored with transparent dyes or small quantities of iron oxide, but with the under-surface visible, is known as a stain. Because of air-quality considerations, some coatings firms have been offering water-reducible stains, based on clear latex, but their performance has not equaled that of traditional stains.

While oil- and varnish-based paints dry when the binder reacts with oxygen under the influence of a metal catalyst, newer surface-protective materials dry in different ways. Modern lacquer, based on nitrocellulose or its esters, was the first of these. Modern lacquers, introduced around the middle of the second decade of the twentieth century, consist mainly of nitrocellulose, cellulose acetate, or a related cellulosic, and plasticizing resins. They dry by evaporation of the solvent system in which they are applied. Since lacquers are primarily used for factory-applied finishes, they are not within the scope of this article. However, architects should require small quantities of lacquer or other materials, used on prepainted surfaces for touchup. Finished-goods suppliers often offer these in aerosol cans.

With a few exceptions, epoxy and urethane coatings, offshoots of the plastics industry and widely used for high-performance applications, dry by addition of a curing agent to the resin; since resin and curing agent must be separated until time of application, they are packaged separately and are known as two-component coatings.

Because application of two-component coatings requires more skill and because of their stronger solvents, which may be harmful, their use is usually restricted to professionals.

The water-reduced latex paints, the most commonly used paints for structural protection and decoration, have a drying process that differs from that of vegetable oil-based paint and varnish. They consist mainly of emulsions dispersed in a mixture of water and any one of several complex petroleum solvents, usually a glycol ether ester of acetic acid. These emulsion paints dry by a two-phase process somewhat related to the drying of lacquer. First the water evaporates, leaving the fine particles of latex—usually an acrylic or polyvinyl acetate copolymer—dissolved in the remaining petroleum solvent, which soon evaporates and leaves a dry film. The petroleum solvent in a latex paint is necessary to produce a homogeneous film, because the resinous binder and pigment left on the surface after evaporation of the water component would be powder-like. At the instant the water evaporates fully, the still-liquefied coating is no longer a dispersion; the solvent, a coalescing agent, takes over and keeps the solid components in solution, somewhat like a lacquer solvent, until it evaporates, leaving a dry, smooth coalesced film.

CLASSIFICATION BY ENVIRONMENT

Protective and decorative coatings can be classified according to severity of the environment in which they will function. Those used for normal residential or institutional areas are called trade sales paint, or architectural coatings. Those used for heavy duty service—in chemical environments, for marine exposure where salt spray is present, where wind-driven rain is common, or where they are subjected to frequent abrasion or high impact—are known as high performance coatings and, depending on the structure to be served, may be called industrial maintenance or institutional paints. High performance paints can be pigmented as effectively for decorative purposes as the so-called architectural paints for use on structures where longevity of protection is desired, especially for structural members that are difficult to reach for repainting. Pigments, moreover, may be of reactive types, which combine with binder or substrate to provide significant protection in troublesome environments, especially where metal is the substrate.

Both architectural and high performance paints can be further classified as to the kind of thinning agent used: solvent or water. Water-reducible paints are used far more widely in architectural applications than solvent-reduced versions; the opposite is true in high-performance coatings, but proliferating environmental regulations threaten to put strict limitations on the use of solvents, especially the strong kinds used in heavy-duty paints. Since 1970, paint companies and their raw material suppliers have succeeded in developing a considerable number of water-reducible, high-performance coatings that are approaching the performance characteristics of their solvent-borne counterparts.

Some of the replacements for older solvent-reduced paints are also solvent-borne, but with higher percentages of binder and pigment than before. Some of these products have only 10–30% solvent and are called high-solids coatings. A few use binders that, although solid, are sufficiently fluid to require no solvents. These are called 100% solids coatings.

CLASSIFICATION BY REFLECTIVITY

Both solvent-reduced and water-thinnable coatings can be formulated so they will effectively reflect light. Those that reflect the greatest amount of light are described as enamels or gloss paints; those that have dull surfaces and reflect relatively little light are described as flat paints; a paint with intermediate reflectivity is termed semigloss. Enamels or gloss paints derive their pronounced reflectivity from the high content of vehicle, or resin, in their formulation. The presence of pigments, including what are called extender pigments because they add body and reduce gloss without the higher cost of expensive hiding pigments, cuts into reflectivity. Commonly-used extender pigments are clay, calcium carbonate, talc, silica, and barium sulfate. In general, a paint formulation that has a large amount of pigment and extender will be flat; one that has relatively little pigment and extender will be an enamel; and a paint with considerable vehicle but less than an enamel of the same general type will meet the definition of a semigloss paint.

What has been said about enamels and flats pertains mainly to the appearance and performance of topcoats, but the inclusion of more or less pigment in a primer coat affects its ability to do what it is intended to do: help protect the surface and form a base for the topcoat.

Prior to the first quarter of the nineteenth century, formulating was an art rather than a blend of art and science, as it has become; paint makers could only rely on their experience to adjust the content of pigment and extenders to control the reflectivity of the resulting paint.

Now, after serious scientific chemists worked out the principles involved in formulating enamel, semigloss, and flat paints, coatings chemists can readily design products to meet the needs of their customers, both desirable performance characteristics and economic limitations. This means that good paints can be formulated for the transient apartment dweller interested only in short term service at a low price, and better paints can be provided to the homeowner seeking a product that will not require early repainting. Because it has more binder, or vehicle, a high-gloss enamel should give longer and better service than either a semigloss enamel or a flat paint, as a general rule. Longer and better service, as a practical matter, means that it will shed dirt more effectively, that it can be scrubbed without removal, that it will have greater resilience for resisting changes in temperature, and that it will reject stains and mildew more effectively. Semigloss paints, with the next largest relative amount of binder, obviously, should be more durable than a flat paint.

The problem is that a high-gloss or enamel paint, because of its high reflectivity, does not look attractive on a wide expanse of wall; it is only satisfactory as a trim or for moldings, or in a situation where sanitation is important, as in a food plant or hospital, where its smooth, hard surface can be cleaned more completely than a softer paint. A semigloss paint looks better on a large surface, but often a flat paint looks best. Some paint companies offer a so-called flat enamel, which provides the performance of an enamel but with a flatting agent to suppress the reflectivity.

Ordinary flat paints, because they have more pigment than enamels, are more buttery and are often easier to apply. Since they have relatively low percentages of binder, they penetrate less into some surfaces, such as wallboard, soft wood, and concrete, and are used for primers for these absorbent surfaces.

Understanding the formulation of high-gloss enamels, semigloss enamels, flat paints, and the flatting of an enamel will help clarify how coatings are developed and will help the architect, engineer, and student realize the care that must be exercised in selecting a product if the user is to be served conscientiously, since an uninformed choice can result in early failure and costly repainting.

Basically, formulating paints and coatings means adjusting the volume of binder and the volume of pigments to develop a product that best fulfills their purpose. The ratio of pigment to resin plus pigment is a key consideration in formulating because this determines how a coating will function. This ratio is called the Pigment Volume Concentration (hereinafter referred to as the PVC, which in this context is not relevant to poly(vinyl chloride), which also is abbreviated PVC).

PVC is established by dividing the volume of pigments (including extender pigments) by the combined volume of binder and pigments. Note that the solvent used to liquefy the mixture, whether water or a petroleum derivative, is not included. For example, if 12 gal of pigment (eg titanium dioxide, an important hiding pigment, and clay or talc, which are extender pigments) are used in a formulation with 36 gal of alkyd resin, the PVC can be derived by dividing 12 (the volume of pigment) by 48 (the volume of that pigment and the 36 gal of binder), resulting in a PVC of 25. The PVC is actually a percentage expression of the ratio that defines the term, in this case 12/48.

As the proportion of pigment is increased, the formulator increases the ratio of pigment to binder plus pigment (the PVC); the flatness of the resulting paint is also increased, because as a rule as pigment is added the dried product will diffuse less light. As the formulator increases the proportion of binder in the product, whether it be a vegetable oil or synthetic resin such as alkyd or epoxy, or a water-reducible resin, such as an acrylic or polyvinyl acetate, the PVC is decreased, and the light reflectivity is increased because the proportion of light-absorbing pigments drops as binder is added.

When a very large percentage of a paint mixture consists of pigment, available binder in the mixture does not completely surround the surface of the pigment particles. Those parts of the pigment particles that are not covered by binder interface with air trapped in the binder. Surprisingly, entrained air in the mixture plays a role in damping reflectivity of a flat paint. Air trapped in a liquid changes the diffraction and alters reflectivity. When it is desirable to eliminate some or all of the air interface, a higher percentage of binder is formulated into the mixture (ie, the ratio of pigment to a combination of pigment-plus-binder is reduced). With more binder to reflect light and less air interfaces and light-absorbing pigment to dampen it, the gloss of the resulting paint is heightened directly by the increase in binder.

The Critical Pigment Volume Concentration (CPVC) is the concentration at which all pigment particles are completely surrounded by binder. All formulations with binder in excess of the minimum needed to completely surround each pigment particle are said to be below the CPVC; all formulations with insufficient binder to completely surround each particle are said to be above the CPVC. Those that are below are either semigloss or enamel paints; those with PVCs above the CPVC have pigments partly covered by air and are described as flat paints, which adequately serve their purpose as primers or where glossy materials are not suitable for decorative or protective purposes.

This is a simple explanation of the basic determination of a gloss or flat paint. In practice, the formulating chemist must take into account the tendency of the pigments to demand binder. Some pigments and extenders, especially very fine ones (which, because they have more surface area per cubic inch than large-size particles, need more binder to completely surround them) are quite thirsty for binder. Others are less. It is logical, then, that for gloss and semigloss enamels, pigments and extenders with greater binder demand are desirable since the formulator wants to get as much binder in a given container as possible. (Note: The term binder demand is used here to avoid confusion with the term "oil absorption" used by coatings chemists, a carry-over from the days when oil paints predominated. The term oil absorption is still used when referring to pigments used in latex formulations but can be confusing and, strictly speaking, is not accurate.)

Because high gloss and semigloss enamels by definition have relatively large percentages of binder, any reputable paint company's versions are likely to be of good quality. Those persons responsible for selecting high- or semigloss enamels for structures must be careful to select a suitable primer in order to avoid faulty topcoat performance. The wrong primer can absorb binder and solvent from any freshly-applied topcoat, but is especially likely to do so with an enamel. If the pigment volume concentration of the primer is too high, the heavy content of white or color pigment and extender, even in a dry film, tends to pull binder from the topcoat, changing the latter's appearance and its ability to protect the surface; it may even cause it to lose adhesion and peel.

A primer that will not draw binder from the enamel topcoat is said to have good enamel holdout. Such a primer should be formulated just below the critical pigment volume concentration so it has all of its pigment surrounded by binder. A test for determining CPVC utilizes enamel holdout. To establish the CPVC of a combination of pigments and binders, sample primer formulations having different PVCs are made into paints, applied at a given thickness on the same substrate, and allowed to dry thoroughly. A high-gloss enamel is then painted over the dry films.

Some of the surfaces of the high-gloss topcoat will soon change appearance, losing some gloss. These are the formulations over test films with high PVCs, and the pigment in these dry films with air–pigment interfaces draws binder from the binder-rich enamel, causing it to lose some of what distinguishes it as an enamel. The critical pigment volume concentration is represented by the paint on the test substrate whose PVC is in a narrow range between that of the highest PVC that did not draw any binder and that of the paint that just barely drew some. If the test paint with a PVC of 50 drew no binder from the test enamel, and the paint with a PVC of 52 caused a slight dulling of the enamel, the CPVC could be 51.

From this it can be seen that care must be exercised in establishing a paint system of primer and topcoats, especially if the latter is an enamel or semigloss. Reputable paint companies carefully match primer to topcoat. Some companies are more conscientious about this than others. Some retail dealers offering paint may not know what goes into a system and may recommend an unsuitable combination. In any event, care should be taken to use the recommended primer for a given system, not just any primer made by the same company, because a product may be excellent for one system but not for another.

Comprehending PVC and CPVC will also help understand the need to specify, and in some cases to test for compliance, the use of high-quality architectural paints. Economic considerations cause some paint formulations to be altered in manufacture as raw material prices change. This frequently involves titanium dioxide, a white manmade substance known to be the most effective hiding pigment available to the paint maker and the most widely used pigment for opacifying a substrate. It is also quite expensive; hence, manufacturers often strive to use as little as possible and still have an opacifying film.

Replacing small amounts of titanium dioxide in an enamel usually results in relatively minor effect other than a loss of coverage per gallon, because ample binder must remain. Replacing titanium dioxide in a flat paint, however, can result in a poor product with questionable durability, because the replacement materials, in many instances, are bulkier than titanium dioxide and take up more volume, thus increasing the pigment volume concentration. Something must be taken out to make way for the added volume; usually it is binder, which means a higher PVC and a lower quality paint.

The most common replacement materials are fine-particle-size clay and calcium carbonate. To start with, the presence of these materials in excess of their useful amounts for bodying definitely increases the water-permeability while reducing dirt rejection and wear-resistance of the dry film. For example, to replace 0.5 lb or 0.75 lb of titanium dioxide requires a greater volume of these substitutes because they weigh less than TiO_2 per cubic inch and, thus, are bulkier; the PVC, then, is increased and quality drops.

Also, the removal of titanium dioxide and replacement by these fine fillers result in a condition described as poor wet hiding. This means that when the paint is applied the wet product does not hide the substrate as well as it would have if the original amount of TiO_2 were still there. So, if the original gallon of flat paint would have effectively covered 400 ft^2 of wall, the degraded product may cover only 350 ft^2 or less, because the painter must apply more wet paint to convince himself that the surface is obscured.

However, the clay and calcium carbonate, which hide poorly in a liquid such as water or solvent, actually hide about as well as titanium dioxide when paint containing them has dried. They are, therefore, said to have satisfactory dry-hide, or ability to opacify in a dry film. Titanium dioxide has the unusual ability to hide well either in a wet or dry film.

This ability of a fine filler to aid dry hiding is believed to be accomplished in high PVC paints by altering the role of air at the air–titanium dioxide interface, causing a spacing of the titanium dioxide particles by the fine fillers and changing, for some unexplained reason, the role of the air. Apparently some phenomena related to the refractive index of the binder and diffraction caused by air scarcely influences hiding when the film is wet, but effectively aids hiding when the paint dries. These fillers have no hiding function in an enamel, because air–titanium dioxide interfaces are absent.

Caution should be taken in specifying a flat paint. The top brand name of a reputable national or regional manufacturer should give satisfactory results in water-resistance, stain and dirt resistance, and scrubbability. However, most manufacturers offer more than one brand name. One of the lower-quality brands of many manufacturers is referred to almost generically as a "painters' special" and usually has less TiO_2 and binder than is desirable; it bears the name of the manufacturer but with a different identifying brand from that of the top of the line. In the interest of economy this may be acceptable, but the product is likely to be softer than the better brands, more likely to attract dirt, absorb moisture, retain stains, and rub off with scrubbing. Many national and regional manufacturers also offer a third brand for competitive reasons; bad traits cited for the "painters' special" are multiplied here. Where a top-of-the-line brand may have about 2 lb of titanium dioxide per gallon, a company's competitive brand may have 1 lb as well as far less binder. This means an extremely high PVC, poor performance, and possibly only 300 ft^2 or less of coverage, noticeably less than that of a top brand. Cost of coverage per square foot for the paint alone often is greater than that of a superior brand, not to mention the extra cost of application labor, poor appearance after a brief period, and the need for early repainting.

Therefore, the design professional must be familiar with the various brands of reputable manufacturers, regional as well as national, and limit recommendations to the products that prove to have optimum quantities of titanium dioxide and binder for the job to be done.

The design professional can obtain information from the manufacturer about components of the batch from which the paint to be used has come, or the services of a specialized testing laboratory, such as D/L Laboratories of New York City, can be used to determine quantity of components and desirable performance characteristics, such as scrubbability, stain resistance, abrasion resistance, and water permeability, among others.

TYPES OF PAINTS AND THEIR BINDERS

Solvent-reduced

Paints with vegetable oil as the binder are the oldest of the solvent-reduced paints still in use. Their importance has diminished with the advent of scientific methods in the paint and coatings field. With the exception of linseed oil produced mainly in the United States, Canada, and Australia, and tung oil, which comes from South America and China, most oils once used by the industry have lost their importance except as key components of alkyd resins, which since the late 1920s have played an important role in relatively low-priced but effective paints. Alkyd resins can actually be described as upgraded vegetable oils, since they are made by cooking a complex acid (a dicarboxylic acid such as phthalic anhydride or a related anhydride) and a fatty alcohol (usually glycerine or pentaerytritol) with a vegetable oil such as soybean, linseed, safflower, tung, castor oil, sunflower, or tall oil fatty acids, the latter a byproduct of kraft paper manufacture.

Linseed oil as a vehicle for exterior house paint is likely to maintain its importance because it is rated the best penetrant for surfaces with many layers of paint, such as older houses, and can help bind the underlying layers of paint to the surface. Linseed oil and the alkyds made with it provide tough films, but they tend to yellow because this oil contains linolenic acid, a highly unsaturated acid. Because alkyds made with soybean or tall oil fatty acids have unsaturated sites of lesser sensitivity to exposure in their oil molecules, they scarcely yellow. Those with safflower or sunflower seed oils, usually more costly, yellow not at all, but are rarely used for architectural coatings. Exterior flat architectural paints, alkyds, and linseed oil topcoats usually contain zinc oxide, which helps control mildew and color instability caused by ultraviolet rays. Use of zinc oxide has the disadvantage of water sensitivity, which under some circumstances can lead to blistering.

Except for the special use of linseed oil paints as penetrants, linseed oil and alkyd paints have been losing market share to water-reducible latex paints in both the interior and exterior architectural markets. Alkyds are still used in high-gloss enamels, but they have been supplanted to a considerable extent by new and effective acrylic-based enamels. Semigloss acrylic enamels have virtually replaced their alkyd counterparts. The move to reduce solvents for environmental reasons has been hastening the decline of these alkyd products.

Alkyds are classified by oil length, or the percentage of oil in their formulation: short oil alkyds, 33–43%; medium oil, 43–59%; and long oil, 59–85%. Short oil alkyds and most mediums are used only for factory-applied coatings. Medium oil alkyds, with oil lengths approaching those of long oil alkyds, are used in architectural coatings where hardness and durability are required, such as in floor enamels. For fast-drying paints, a medium oil alkyd with an oil length midway in the range is used for highly-pigmented alkyd flats with thickening agents to prevent excessive penetration and inconsistent sheen and color. Long oil alkyds dry more slowly and are used for gloss and semigloss enamels; they brush on easily and are extensible over wood, which permits them to expand when increased moisture content causes wood to swell. Their slower drying also permits smoother dried films and leads to less brush marks.

Varnishes resemble alkyds in several ways. They combine vegetable oils with synthetics; they dry by oxidation with the aid of metallic driers; they can be pigmented; and they are classified by oil content. Varnishes, however, have declined in importance in architectural coatings of all kinds with the advent of alkyds, and for high performance usage they have been supplanted by coatings based on state-of-the-art urethanes and epoxies. Tung oil varnishes, cooked with a phenolic, are used to some extent for porch and floor enamels where their tendency to yellow is not a consideration.

Rubber-like coatings, derived from advanced technology in the design of polymers, have been used effectively where moisture and high humidity are problems. These include chlorinated rubber, styrene acrylate, and butadiene styrene. Chlorinated rubber resists both acid and alkali and is used on concrete and, to some extent, for metal protection in moist areas because of its low permeability to water and water vapor. Coatings based on styrene acrylate are tough and water-resistant and adhere well to most surfaces. Because they are easily dissolved in low-cost mineral spirits, they are often preferred to chlorinated rubber, particularly since air quality regulations have been issued. Where cementitious surfaces must withstand wind-driven rain, texture systems consisting of styrene acrylate and perlite have been effective. Combined with aluminum pigment, styrene acrylate is also used for roof coatings. Styrene butadiene has been used successfully with silicone resins and aluminum pigments to provide protection against extremely high temperatures.

Silicone resins in coatings provide resistance to deterioration caused by oxygen. When added to such binders as alkyds, epoxies, or acrylics in air-dried coatings, weather-resistant surfaces are provided for modest increases in cost. Factory-applied versions of these produced for coil coatings used on siding are mostly proprietary formulations, but their durability is such that siding firms may guarantee them for as long as 20 years.

Epoxies provide tough maintenance coatings for exterior and interior use where impact and abrasion resistance are required. They are deficient in color retention and acid resistance, but they are notably effective in alkali environments. Formulated at low pigment levels, tile-like epoxy enamels have found widespread use in dairies and medical establishments where their smooth, hard surface permits meticulous cleanup. While epoxy paints are usually expensive, in the long run they can be economical since thick coatings, up to 40 mils, can be applied in one coat, which reduces the cost of application. Even in thinner coats, they usually outlast cheaper coatings. On the basis of cost per square foot per year of use, for example, they have been found economical as against alkyds. Since they must be cured by a second resin, epoxies usually are applied by professionals. Slow chalking, a characteristic of exterior epoxies, limits their use to industrial or other nonresidential structures, but has negligible effect on durability. Epoxies combined with coal-tar pitch are used to withstand salt or fresh water, sand, a number of chemicals, and for underground protection against moisture. Epoxy esters combine an epoxy resin with a vegetable oil for service as metal primers and for floor protection. Epoxies are also combined with polyesters to provide extremely tough, glossy films permitting maximum cleanup and service in food areas and, with the right combination of components, nuclear plants.

Urethanes, like epoxies, are somewhat costly, but their durability makes them economical on a cost per square foot per year basis. Coatings based on these binders, with some exceptions, are also two-package products and require the services of an experienced professional, one who knows to ensure adequate ventilation since the isocyanates used and the strong oxygenated solvents can be troublesome, or even toxic, in closed areas. For architectural purposes, where superior performance and color retention is important, aliphatic urethanes may be specified. These are cured with either polyesters or acrylics, resist weather degradation, and offer resistance to both acids and alkalis. They are also abrasion, impact, and stain resistant. Aliphatic urethanes are available which are air-dried to provide films equivalent in hardness and flexibility to factory-applied finishes. One usage to which they are often put is in antigraffiti paints where their hardness permits solvent removal of inks and paints without significant removal of surface. Urethane-based formulations are available to fill the most stringent practical requirements.

Single-package urethanes cure by moisture in the air but do not measure up to the two-package versions. They are used as clear coatings for redwood siding and, suitably pigmented with aluminum powder, as primers over poorly prepared metal substrates where aliphatic urethanes will be the topcoat.

Fluoropolymers are proprietary binders that combine fluorine chemicals with petroleum derivatives for extremely long service life. They are factory-applied and in wide use for aluminum windows, store fronts, siding, and roofing to assure dependable color and durability; they are especially recommended for extreme exposure conditions and where repainting is hazardous or undesirable for any reason.

Water-reducible Paints

Acrylic latex paints are among the most effective water-reducible architectural coatings for interior or exterior. The polymers on which they are based are more costly than their main competing latexes, those based on polyvinyl acetate copolymers. While versions are available for interior flat paints of various quality levels, acrylics are primarily used for exterior flats and for high gloss and semigloss enamels for inside and out. Polymers used for what are known as all-acrylic latex paints result from the reaction of methyl methacrylate, which provides hardness, and butyl acrylate, an ester of acrylic acid, which is a plasticizer or softening influence. Other acrylic latex resins result from the reaction of butyl acrylate, vinyl acetate monomer, and vinyl chloride; the result is known as an acrylic terpolymer, usually costing somewhat less than the all-acrylics. Other acrylate esters are sometimes used in place of butyl acrylate. Until recently, the all-acrylics were distinguished by wet adhesion, an ability to remain unaffected when wet soon after application, which is significant to professional painters when sudden rains occur. In recent years, the wet adhesion of acrylic terpolymers has also improved. Several hundred paint manufacturers prefer the all-acrylic; more than 100 firms prefer the terpolymer. Acrylic latex coatings are ranked first among exterior latex paints because of their colorfastness, durability, low odor, adhesion, and flexibility. As with all latex paint, those based on acrylics have low toxicity, water cleanup, nonflammability during application, and meet air quality regulations. They have excellent performance histories outdoors on cementitious surfaces of all kinds because of their alkali resistance. They resist blistering, chalking, grain-cracking, and flaking on wood, and adhere well to bare wood. In situations where solvent paints are undesirable because of odor or fire potential, acrylic paints are often used in special formulations for heavy-duty service, although they lack the durability under difficult conditions of true high-performance coatings. Because they allow the passage of water vapor, they are suited for exterior paints on porous surfaces where moisture is likely to pass from behind, as in the case of exterior walls fronting baths, kitchens, or laundry rooms. Interior flat acrylics are often formulated with higher pigment content than exterior versions because less durability is required. This permits additional modification with thixotropic agents, which thicken the paint until pressure is applied by the brush or roller; this pressure thins the material, permitting easy flow until the brushing or rolling stops and the thin coat firms and dries normally. The purpose of this is to prevent dripping over interior surfaces.

Polyvinyl acetate copolymer latexes are used more widely than acrylics, mainly because vinyl acetate monomer, the key ingredient, is easier to make and less costly than methyl methacrylate, the basic ingredient of acrylics. Both latex resins use butyl acrylate, or a similar ester, ethyl acrylate, for a plasticizing monomer. The sales volume of PVA latexes for interior flat paints far exceeds that of acrylic latexes because requirements are less demanding than for exterior paints and enamels, products dominated by acrylics.

SELECTIONS OF PAINTS AND COATINGS

The type of substrate to be painted and the particular environment in which the coating will function determine selection of the product that will give optimum service life. Usually at least two coats will be applied: a prime coat and a topcoat. For severe conditions, an intermediate coat may be used. In some few instances, a single coat may be adequate, notably in repainting, especially over old paint that has been touched up.

Under a given set of conditions, a different primer may be required for each of the three classes of substrate, wood, metal, and cementitious. However, one topcoat may be selected for any of the three kinds of primed substrate, provided it is formulated for compatibility with the primers selected. The combination of primer and topcoat, or primer, intermediate coat, and primer constitute a paint system.

Coatings for Exterior Surfaces

Prevailing conditions in the environment are key influences in selection of exterior paint. The first consideration is location, such as urban residential, rural, marine, or industrial. Exposure is also important—southern where the sun will be strong, northern where mildew may thrive because of moisture and absence of sanitizing sunlight, or under an eave, protected from the wind and rain. If the coating is to be used on or near an industrial site, selection of paint should take into account any chemicals in the air, including their relative acidity or alkalinity, as measured by pH. A marine environment requires an alkaline-resistant coating.

Meeting some of these conditions may require a high performance paint; others may demand only architectural coatings. To help in these decisions, the following discussion of paint selection is divided into three substrate types, and recommendations are based upon the circumstances of use.

Coatings for Exterior Wood. Primers for wood have special problems. They must be able to take the stresses caused by seasonal swelling of the bands forming the wood, which consist of bands formed in spring and summer which swell unevenly, especially when wet, causing stress that can cause disbondment of an inappropriate primer and resultant cracking of the system. Wood primers must also prevent penetration of moisture that would cause decay, and when used for certain woods, such as redwood and cedar, must neutralize natural dyes that would otherwise rise through the system, causing ugly stains on the surface.

Prior to 1973, when they were declared toxic and limited to 0.06% of an architectural coating, lead pigments in linseed oil or alkyd paints formed soaps that effectively blocked moisture and subdued dye stains. Since then, after much effort, resins and various proprietary compounds have been successfully used as lead-pigment replacements. The replacement materials may be obtained in alkyd or linseed oil primers, or in acrylic latex.

Some nonstaining woods cause problems, especially southern white pine, which, in spite of its desirable structural strength, tends to swell, shrink, and warp. Extensive testing has shown that an acrylic latex offered by many paint companies has successfully withstood the stresses in this wood for a more than satisfactory period.

Topcoats for wood, except that they must be flexible enough to expand and contract with the primer and substrate, are somewhat similar to those for other substrates. They include general purpose flats and enamels; trim paints, which are usually high gloss; and shake and shingle paints, which are usually semigloss; paint for new plywood and textured plywood; and heavy duty paints for industrial areas.

Trim paints for many years were almost exclusively alkyd enamels, but in recent years acrylic enamels have been gaining market acceptance because of their durability and freedom from yellowing. Shake and shingle paints of acrylic latex semigloss have been in favor longer than their high gloss enamel counterparts, and alkyd versions are still available.

New plywood should be sealed with at least two coats of a varnish-type sealer to prevent water penetration and improper service of paint or varnish topcoats. Following this, an acrylic primer and topcoat should be applied. Plywood with its ends exposed is especially vulnerable to water penetration, and these ends should be sealed with high-grade primer containing an effective pigment, such as zinc oxide and an aluminum stearate moisture-block. Neither clear coatings nor enamels are recommended for plywood because of poor results.

Textured plywood usually contains numerous end-grains, especially in grooves of the texture. Use of stains, which are really varnishes with dyes or iron oxide, is recommended because checking is likely, and staining effectively adapts to this. Attractive wood grains can be effectively protected and revealed by use of stains of various kinds.

Wood for industrial exposure may be adequately covered with a primer–topcoat system based on linseed oil or alkyd, but if chemicals and heavy abuse are to be encountered it may be necessary to use an aliphatic urethane and a suitable primer.

Where wood and metal or wood and cementitious surfaces come together, it is necessary to fill the joints with an oil-based or latex caulking compound to ensure joint stability. If slight movement is anticipated, a sealant, which permits greater stretching, is required. New caulks made of acrylic or silicone are usually adequate, but for harsh environments, those based on urethane or some other high performance material, such as polysulfide, may be necessary.

Exterior Metal Surfaces. Metal surfaces include iron, steel, galvanized metals, aluminum, bronze, and copper. Primers used on them are designed primarily to protect the substrate from the effects of water. Topcoats mainly serve to shield the primers. Some primers together with their topcoats serve only as barriers, seeking through the binder and pigmentation to block water as well as possible. Others work by having pigments that sacrifice themselves when water works through and sets up destructive electrical charges between sections of the metal.

An example of barrier primers would be those with lead or zinc oxide, which form water-repelling soaps with linseed oil or alkyd; often these also contain extender pigments, such as talc or silica, which, in some forms, help lay down barriers. For very difficult environments where moisture is heavy, primers may have zinc dust, which takes the charge instead of the steel substrate and erodes preferentially; zinc dust may be in a high performance binder such as an epoxy or urethane. These are called organic zinc-rich paints and adhere to poorly prepared surfaces. When zinc dust is contained in a silicate inorganic binder, the product is called an inorganic zinc-rich paint. It performs better than organic versions, but can be used only over carefully cleaned metal.

Red lead paints, usually in linseed oil or an alkyd, are effective where moisture exposure is mild or when conditions do not permit the kind of meticulous cleanup required by high performance primers. This includes repainting over badly damaged or worn areas where the penetrative qualities of these binders are helpful. Although it is still used effectively where regulations permit, red lead is gradually disappearing from the market; a newer product, basic silico-lead chromate, combines the anticorrosive properties of chromium and lead, with silica adding bulk. Environmentalists have been lobbying to ban the use of lead; other pigments have been favored in recent years, such as zinc oxide, and a number of proprietary products such as ferrous and zinc phosphate, barium metaphosphate, and barium metaborate, including barium salts.

While wood and cementitious substrates require careful surface preparation prior to painting, metal demands even more attention. As mentioned, linseed oil or alkyd paints function well with minimal preparation, such as hand cleaning with detergents, hard brushes, and rags, but high performance coatings, based on urethanes or epoxies, usually require some kind of power cleaning or abrasive blasting so that all residual oxidation, visible or invisible, is removed; otherwise, on iron or steel rust will be propagated upon entry of even the slightest moisture, including airborne vapor.

Power tools include needle guns for seams and corners and other irregular surfaces; wire brushes where roughness is needed; or water blasting if only loose rust or dirt is to be removed or if abrasive blasting is not possible.

Abrasive blasting utilizes compressed air, suction or centrifugal force to drive natural sand or flint, or if surfaces are delicate, ground walnut shells, corncobs, or ground slag. Abrasive blasting is especially important on steel covered with mill scale, which is an extremely tight oxidation product formed in the steel rolling process. Left on the surface, it can assure paint failure.

Typical particle sizes of abrasives are 16–40 mesh or 30–50 mesh. The finer sizes get results faster, but if deep cutting is desired, larger ones are needed. Blasting that results in too-deep roughening may cause very sharp edges over the small valleys; this may lead to extremely thin paint deposits over them and probable paint failure.

Where factory conditions can be controlled, specifiers can require for steel, iron, zinc, aluminum, copper, or brass such treatments as pickling by sulfuric or hydrochloric acid; alternatively, iron, steel, aluminum, tin, magnesium and zinc may be treated by inorganic liquids to change or modify the chemistry of the substrate so it is more resistant to moisture. Chromium or phosphate compounds are used. Specifications regulate thickness of deposit and elapsed time after depositing before painting.

Careful and specific surface preparation must be called for if metal painting is to succeed. A generalization can be made, and often is, that if the choice is between inferior paint or adequate surface preparation, the latter would be the wise choice. For specifications as to brushoff blast, commercial blast, white metal blast, or near-white metal blast, see Ref. 1.

Specifications for Metal Primers. For primer paint specifications for a mild environment or where surface conditions are bad, Federal Specifications TT-P-86, Type I-IV, call for red lead in various binders, including linseed oil, alkyds, or phenolic, a tough weather-resistant binder which requires careful surface preparation. TT-P-105 contains linseed oil and zinc oxide and requires modest surface preparation. TT-P-645 offers linseed oil and phenolic resin with basic silico lead chromate. TT-P-659 contains alkyds, with no pigment specified. TT-P-636 offers a soybean oil alkyd with no pigment specified. These all require minimal surface preparation.

TT-P-1046 uses zinc dust in a chlorinated rubber binder, with simple surface preparation. For galvanized surfaces, TT-P-641, Type I, has linseed oil with zinc dust; Types II and III have a phenolic resin with zinc dust.

In addition, various proprietary formulas are available for high performance systems, including those with epoxy polyamide resin and zinc dust; epoxy ester with basic silico-lead chromate and red iron oxide; and inorganic silicate binders with zinc dust. In some instances where two-package urethane topcoats are to be used over surfaces that cannot be carefully cleaned, certain oil-modified urethanes have served well as primers.

For rusted surfaces where circumstances prevent adequate sanding, several companies offer a rust neutralizer containing proprietary components, usually based on tannic acid or a derivative. All loose material must be brushed off, leaving only adherent rust, which, according to claims, is converted to a protective material. Extreme care is required; the material usually must stand 8–10 hours before topcoating.

Topcoats for Metal. Where exposure is in mild environments or where appearance is not significant, many of the primers described above may be used as topcoats as well. A major determinant in the selection of a topcoat to be used in a metal-coating system is the extent of the need for resistance to extremes in weather, salt spray, and water immersion. In some instances, ability to withstand abrasion and impact may enter into consideration. Often a compromise must be made. For instance, a proprietary formulation based on vinyl chloride, like most vinyl chlorides, provides outstanding salt and fresh water resistance but only fair impact resistance. A moisture-cured urethane offers better impact resistance but may not hold up as well in salt spray. The specifier has to decide which is more important under the circumstances.

Since in the section on pigment volume concentration (PVC) it was pointed out that a high percentage of resinous binder in a formulation contributes to durability, topcoats for metal, especially where service is demanding, have low PVBCs, which means that they are rich in binder. As a result, they must be carefully matched to primers that will not absorb binder and cause failure.

Specifying Topcoats for Metals.

1. *Rural Environment, Rough Substrate.* Over a linseed oil primer (TT-P-86, Type I), an alkyd-modified linseed oil topcoat may be used; an alkyd or phenolic (aluminum pigmented) topcoat may be used over an oil-modified alkyd primer. Surface preparation can be limited to hand or power tool cleaning.
2. *Rural Environment, Smooth Surface.* An alkyd topcoat over an alkyd primer is suitable for a flat finish. If a gloss is desired, an alkyd enamel, Federal Specification TT-E-489, suitable for a semigloss, or a silicone alkyd, TT-E-490, gives long wear. Surface preparation requires commercial blast cleaning.
3. *Industrial Environment with Sulfide Fumes.* A lead-free linseed oil or alkyd topcoat over a linseed oil primer (TT-P-86, Type I). Lead is avoided because of reactivity with sulfides. Surface preparation required is commercial blast cleaning.
4. *High Moisture Conditions or Fresh Water Immersion.* A topcoat based on chlorinated rubber or styrene acrylate (TT-P-95) over a phenolic primer (TT-P-86, Type IV) may be used. Surface preparation calls for commercial blast cleaning.
5. *Marine or Mild Corrosive Environment.* Same system as rural rough or smooth, except two coats of primer should be used. Surface preparation may require flame-cleaning or brush-off blasting for rough surfaces, or commercial blasting for smooth.
6. *Marine or Moderately Corrosive.* A high gloss alkyd topcoat (TTE 489), or a silicone alkyd semigloss (TTE 490) over a chlorinated rubber primer with zinc dust. Surface preparation is commercial blast cleaning.
7. *Marine, Immersion, or Highly Corrosive Atmosphere.* A vinyl chloride formulation for a primer and topcoat; urethane, epoxy, or vinyl topcoat over an inorganic zinc-rich formulation. Surface preparation is white metal or near-white metal blasting.

Exterior Cementitious Surfaces. Cementitious surfaces include concrete, concrete block, cinder block, brick, stucco, general masonry, and asbestos cement, all decidedly alkaline and porous. Most surfaces are rough, although smooth ones may be so smooth and hard that abrasive devices may be required to roughen the surface for paint. Irregularities in the surface, tiny hills and valleys, require free-flowing primers to fill them, yet not so runny that they excessively penetrate the surface. Consequently, the pigment content of paints used for moderately rough cementitious surfaces needs to be carefully considered so that penetration will be limited to just below the surface by the blocking action of the pigment; otherwise, the liquid phase would be wasted with deeper penetration and the primer would cover far too little area.

Often, thinned topcoats can be used as primers. Open-pored surfaces such as cement blocks and cinder blocks, on the other hand, require very thick fillers to block the large pores.

Other than the exposure problems already described in the discussion of wood and metal, cementitious substrates must be protected, particularly against water pressure below grade. This is accomplished by the use of rubber-like coatings containing such binders as butadiene-derived polymers with portland cement added. Coatings of this type have been tested at water pressures equal to that exerted by 100-mph winds and 70 gal of water per hour.

Specifying Topcoats for Cementitious Surfaces.

1. *Ordinary Conditions.* Acrylic emulsions used as primer and topcoat have become popular and effective. The acrylic specification TT-P-19 offers excellent abrasion and chalk resistance. Polyvinyl acetate emulsions (TT-P-55) and proprietary paints using terpolymers containing vinyl acetate and acrylate monomers have also gained acceptance. Alkyd and oil paints work well on thoroughly dry surfaces, but take several hours to dry, compared to a set-to-touch time of as little as 15 minutes for the emulsions. In considering Federal Specification paints, it must be remembered that proprietary paints often outperform them and require less dry-time.
2. *Wind-driven Rain.* Heavy texture paints are recommended for areas likely to have to withstand strong winds. The Federal Specification for coping with this problem is TT-C-555, Type II, which names no binder but requires a test with water driven by the equivalent of a 95-mph wind and a primer–filler complying with TT-P-1098. Binders of vinyl toluene acrylate have been tested successfully for topcoats, but care must be taken to assure that the proper pigment volume concentration (PVC) is used. A PVC of 55, for instance, was found superior to one of 70, which is favored by producers of low-priced versions.
3. *Chemical Environments.* To withstand weak acids or alkalis that are found near industrial areas, chlorinated rubber and styrene butadiene are preferred for enamels or semigloss, but styrene acrylate works in other types. TT-P-95 requires chlorinated rubber or styrene acrylate. Proprietary acrylic clear coatings have been found effective on concrete structures.
4. *Extensive Water Exposure.* Paints containing styrene butadiene are called for in TT-P-97 when white masonry is involved; styrene acrylate is the binder required by TT-P-1181 for tints and deep tones. For these paints, care must be taken to assure that the selected product has the proper PVC. At 45 PVC, the deposited paint is virtually impervious to moisture; at 55 PVC, permeability rises appreciably, but at a PVC of 57 it meets a necessary compromise of permeability and water resistance. Some permeability is desired because some way must be found for water that may seep in from behind or from the water table to leave as water vapor. Clear coatings for water resistance are usually selected from proprietary products based on silicone or acrylic binders.
5. *Graffiti and Stain Removal.* Proprietary formulations based on aliphatic urethanes have been successfully used to balk graffiti artists. The coatings are able to withstand solvents strong enough to re-

move the inks and paints used for the unsightly messages and art; they are capable of lasting for many years.

6. *Recoating Chalky Surfaces*. Upon removal of as much old, deteriorated paint as possible, cementitious surfaces usually have residual chalk which may be removed by sandblasting, if conditions permit. When they do not, wirebrushing and washing are necessary. A primer whose binder has wetting ability should be used on the cleaned surface to assure penetration and adhesion of the inevitable chalk that remains. A modified alkyd binder is used in TT-P-620 which was designed for this purpose. Proprietary acrylic or polyvinyl acetate emulsions, fortified with alkyds or linseed oil, have been found effective and less likely to yellow. In repainting masonry, caution must be observed to prevent wicking, a condition in which binder in the new coating migrates into the porous chalk and substrate leaving inconsistent color and gloss and a surface too rich in the pigment that remains. Efflorescence, a condition in which soluble salts leach out of concrete or masonry when water penetrates, leaves an unsightly powder which should be removed by wire brushing. Laitance, a powdery alkali that sometimes rises to the surface after concrete is poured, should also be wire brushed.

Coatings for Interior Surfaces

Interior coatings are not expected to meet the rigorous conditions likely to be encountered by exterior paints, but under some conditions high-performance coatings are required.

The purposes of interior paints and coatings can be set forth as follows:

1. They contribute notably to the living environment by improving appearance.
2. They permit more satisfactory cleanup where sanitation is a factor, such as in kitchens, bathrooms, food installations, and medical facilities.
3. They reflect light, thus aiding visibility.
4. They safeguard substrates.
5. They aid safety as markers or, with embedded abrasives, they prevent slipping.

Interior paints include general purpose and high-performance grades. To extend their decorative role, manufacturers offer, in addition to enamels, semigloss, and flat, a version known as eggshell or satin, which reflects slightly more light than a flat but has more binder and less pigment and extender; hence, it is more durable. With this advantage goes the possibility that eggshell paints, if improperly formulated, may burnish, or become undesirably glossy at places where rubbing was needed to remove stains or dirt. Burnish resistance should be specified when this type of paint is to be used. For a flat finish with maximum durability, a so-called flat enamel can be obtained; it is actually a dull-gloss enamel, with its high binder content, but with silica flatting agents added.

General purpose interior paints are based on alkyds or latex paints, with the latter dominating the market. Flat paints are divided among binders based on acrylics, polyvinyl acetate, or terpolymers that combine the best qualities of both. High-gloss enamels based on acrylic latex have been gaining market share, with alkyds stubbornly resisting penetration; semigloss interior paints have been taken over by acrylics.

High-performance coatings are mostly found in industrial establishments and institutions. Since durability, not aesthetics, is a prime concern, they are most often enamels.

Scrubbability, washability, stain resistance, and water impermeability are performance characteristics sought by knowledgeable specifiers for general purpose interior flats. Chemical resistance, water impermeability, and abrasion and impact resistance are among the characteristics sought for high-performance coatings, depending on the service to which the product will be put.

Coatings for Interior Wood. Surface preparation must be carefully executed for successful wood painting. Moisture in wood can cause swelling and cracking, and contractors hired to paint it should be required to use a moisture meter to establish dryness before using a primer or sealer. Moisture levels of 5–10% are considered safe for interior wood.

Knots, fresh sap, or natural dyes will discolor the coating unless a seal coat of phenolic resin and polyvinyl butyral is applied. Only plywood that is moisture-resistant should be used if loss of adhesion, peeling, and blistering are to be avoided when water-reduced paints are used.

Sanding is usually necessary, especially if rough spots are present. Open-pore woods, such as ash, chestnut, elm, or oak must be sealed with a compound of silica in varnish prior to painting.

Specifying Pigmented Primers for Interior Wood.

1. *Knots and Sap-moistened Areas*. Sealers meeting Federal Specification TTS 176 should be used to balk the intrusion of primer and topcoat by natural dyes in cedar, redwood, or any wood with visible problems.
2. *General Purpose Enamels and Semigloss*. An alkyd primer meeting Federal Specification TTE 543 has good enamel holdout and flexibility and is recommended for these topcoats. A faster-drying alkyd primer is to be found in TTE 545.
3. *Heavy Duty*. A pigmented gloss paint system uses a two-package epoxy primer (Federal Specification TTC 535). A pigmented moisture-curing, one-package, urethane (TTC 542) is suitable for less demanding service.

Stains consisting of varnish or clear latex with dyes or iron oxide are used to protect and reveal interesting wood grains while improving the original underlying color. Wood floors may also be stained to improve color. Porous woods, such as oak, should be pretreated with a paste or liquid filler if the surface is to be smooth.

Specifications for Interior Wood Topcoats.

1. *Clear Finishes*. To show the underlying beauty of natural wood grains, transparent finishes are desirable such as a linseed-modified urethane, Federal

Specification TT-C-540, or an alkyd spar varnish, TT-V-85, for a dull finish, or TT-V-109, also an alkyd spar varnish but glossy.

2. *Glaze Coat.* For extra protection over a primer where hard service is expected or where meticulous cleanup is required, a tile-like glaze coat is recommended; Federal Specification TTC 550 permits selection from among epoxy polyamides, epoxy polyesters, acrylics, and urethanes.
3. *Floors.* Sturdy coatings are in demand to withstand the varying degrees of grinding experienced. For household use, alkyds or phenolic floor finishes are satisfactory, but for factories or heavily-used hallways, urethanes, epoxies, coal-tar epoxies, or coal-tar urethanes should be considered.

Coatings for Interior Metal Surfaces. Interior metal topcoats are the same as those for wood and cementitious surfaces, except that they require resiliency if flexing or movement is likely. Primers, on the other hand, have the same requirements as those for exterior metal surfaces: they must be designed to protect against moisture, and they must be able to flex. Moreover, what was said about surface preparation for exterior metal finishes applies equally for interiors.

Specifications for Interior Metal Primers.

1. *Normal use.* Alkyd primers specified in Federal Specifications TT-E-485 and TT-P-645 are suitable. The former uses chrome yellow, red lead, and zinc oxide for pigmentation; the latter uses basic silico lead chromate. For surfaces that lack adequate surface preparation, a primer of moisture-cured urethane and aluminum pigment is suitable.
2. *Heavy-duty.* Epoxy primers with zinc dust or one of the new proprietary pigments are commonly used. Federal Specification TT-P-1046 calls for chlorinated rubber and zinc dust.

Coatings for Interior Cementitious Surfaces. Requirements for interior cementitious surfaces are considerably lower than those for exteriors. Except for the section treating wind-driven rain, the material on exterior cementitious surfaces is applicable here. In addition, the tile-like glaze coatings described in the section on interior wood coatings are used on cementitious surfaces in food service or medical areas where an ultra-smooth, readily-cleanable surface is required.

GLOSSARY

Airless Spray. Hydraulic pressure produces higher driving speed than is obtained in air spray. Absence of turbulence reduces overspray. Also, the greater strength of hydraulic pressure reduces the need for thinning.

Air Spray. Compressed air atomizes the paint, which is driven through an opening in a directed fog.

Brushes. A collection of natural or synthetic bristles set into a handle by a strong adhesive and protected at its base by a metal ferrule is defined as a brush, the oldest and most familiar tool for application of paint. Natural bristle, preferably made of hair from the inside of the ear of certain Chinese hogs, is used with solvent-reduced paint; synthetic bristle, made of nylon or polyester or a combination of both, is preferred for water-reduced paint. Even when spray or roller painting, the more efficient method of application, is used, brushes are often needed in border areas where no paint is needed or where a surface has a different color and overspray or over-rolling is undesirable. Brushes are also used on narrow surfaces, such as trim and molding. Aside from being slow, brushes also leave brush marks, which are not as desirable as the smooth surfaces produced by rollers, flat-pad applicators, and spray guns. For applying primer coats, brush use is preferable if tiny irregularities in a surface may be missed by rollers or spraying or if penetration is especially important.

Electrostatic Spray. Paint is driven in a manner similar to that of airless spray, but electric charges up to 80,000 volts cause the particles to move to an opposite-charged surface, usually but not necessarily metal, since even wood can be painted with chargeable materials. The major advantage of this method is that it can be used for irregular surfaces, because of a wraparound effect.

Flat-pad Applicators. Fabrics resembling those used for rollers are attached to flat metal backs affixed to a handle. They function as brushes without the brush marks associated with them.

Function. Intended function of the coating may be used to characterize it. Names used often pertain to the surface on which it will be used, such as metal, concrete, or wood, or the location, such as interior, exterior, roof, or ceiling.

Hiding Power. The ability of a given amount of paint to obscure or opacify the surface on which it is applied is its hiding power. This varies with the function of the paint and the film thickness desired for the conditions in which the product will serve. For instance, a metal coating intended to ward off frequent rain may require a film thickness of 0.014 in., or 14 mils, but an interior flat paint may need only 4 or 5 mils. While a gallon of the latter may hide 400 ft^2, the former may cover only 100 ft^2. Poorly formulated, low-cost interior flat paints may only hide 200–300 ft^2, because inadequate amounts of hiding pigments may be used.

Light Reflectance. When coatings are characterized by light reflectance, such terms as high-gloss enamel, semigloss enamel, eggshell, and flat are used to describe coatings in the descending order of light reflectance. High gloss enamels reflect more light than the others because they contain less pigment to alter light reflectance of the vehicle. Flat paints have the most pigment interfering with light reflectance.

Paint Types. Paints are characterized according to kinds of vehicles on which they are based, on the degree of light reflectance resulting from the percentage of pigments, such as hiding pigments (eg, titanium dioxide, aluminum, or zinc oxide) and filler pigments (eg, clay, talc, barium sulfate, calcium carbonate, or silica) used in the formulation, and on their function.

Powder Coatings. Application of factory-applied coatings now includes a method utilizing finely-divided powders applied by a fluidized bed, or an electrostatic process.

In the former, air-borne powders are in an enclosed area to which heated devices or parts to be coated are conveyed. A homogeneous film forms on the heated surface, which is conveyed out of the enclosure and cooled. In the more commonly-used electrostatic system, devices or parts to be coated are charged electrically and powder with an opposite charge is applied from an electrostatic spray gun similar to that described under electrostatic spray.

Rollers. These consist of a fabric, usually polyester, stretched on a cylinder, which is attached to a heavy metal wire that turns on a handle. They are more efficient than brushes for most jobs but not as efficient as spraying. They may be attached to long handles for use on hard-to-reach areas, such as ceilings. Arrangements can be made to place paint in certain specially-designed pans so that rollers can be conveniently and efficiently loaded. Definite effects can be obtained by selection of roller material. To achieve a stipple effect, carpet rollers are used; texture rollers provide a pattern and leave part of the undersurface visible. For a smooth effect, like that of spraying, mohair rollers may be used. Efficiency in roller use has been improved by use of magazine rollers, in which paint can be stored in a cylinder, and by pressure rollers, which supply paint to the roller cover through a pressurized hose.

Spray Painting. For maximum speed in application, various kinds of spray painting are best. However, care must be taken to avoid shoddy workmanship and inconsistent film build. Also, in considering whether to spray, attention must be given to time consumed in masking areas to be protected. Spray painting is of three kinds: air spray; airless spray; and electrostatic spray.

Vehicle Characterization. Vehicles commonly used in architectural finishes include alkyd resins and linseed oil, which are usually thinned with mineral spirits, or, rarely, turpentine; most architectural coatings are water-thinned and have polyvinyl acetate copolymers and acrylic latex as vehicles. High performance vehicles for finishes to be used in difficult situations include epoxies, urethanes, chlorinated rubber, styrene acrylates, and fluorinated polymers. Vehicles used for lacquers, which dry by evaporation of the strong solvents used, are mainly nitrocellulose or cellulose acetate and their derivatives. Stains contain a clear polymer, usually alkyd resin, with sufficient iron oxide or a dye to color the surface without obscuring it.

Film Application Defects

Discontinuities. If a painter leaves an edge on an area for too long before he returns to paint the adjoining area, the paint on the first surface may dry. The result will be a break in the continuity of the paint. This may also happen if the paint dries too fast. Paints are formulated to dry slowly enough to allow time for the painter to apply paint ahead and come back to the existing edge before it dries.

Holidays. Hasty work, or failure to apply paint thoroughly can cause irregular surfaces to have tiny unprotected areas. Avoiding this is especially important where the surface will be subjected to moisture and rusting or wood rot may result. Brushing, the least efficient method of application, is the best insurance against holidays because bristles can penetrate where rollers and spray guns may fail to cover.

Runs. Paint that is too thin, either because of poor formulation or because it has been excessively thinned, tends to run, leaving an unsightly buildup on the surface. When this happens, an experienced painter will paint over it until it disappears, but a novice may leave it or may fail to brush it out so the surface is smooth.

Film Failure

Alligatoring. A severe form of cracking, or crazing, resulting from the presence of several coats of paint, which through aging have lost their ability to expand and contract at the same rate as the surfaces they protect.

Blistering. When soluble substances in a coating are dissolved in water on the surface and this is repeated often enough, an osmotic cell is established beneath a thin elastic layer of the paint film. The cell increases, forming a blister, as more water is drawn in. Blisters will not form if the adhesive strength to the substrate is greater than the pressure built up in the expanding cell. The presence of soluble salts, such as those found in pigments, thickeners, or emulsifying agents, aids formation of blisters.

Chalking. Ultraviolet rays and heat erode pigmented films, especially if anatase grades of titanium dioxide are used. However, all exterior paints with titanium dioxide erode to some extent, theoretically because titanium dioxide catalyzes the gradual deterioration of the binder on exterior paint. Chalking has a favorable aspect: it helps clean exterior surfaces, but this rarely happens uniformly. Chalk also interferes with repainting old surfaces; removal is required.

Flaking. Usually when paint flakes it is near joints. Moisture entering at the joints gets under the film, causing it to peel in sheets. It may be caused by any kind of adhesion loss, such as that caused by foreign matter on the substrate when paint was applied.

Floating. The uniform coverage of the paint surface by one color of a color blend. For example, a surface appears blue because the blue component of a blend of blue and yellow rises uniformly and "floats" over the surface.

Flooding. Mottled and splotchy appearance caused by one color of a color blend floating to the surface while the paint dries.

Mildew. Caused by fungus deposited from the air, mildew can be controlled by agents included in exterior paint formulations. Purchase of a zinc oxide-containing paint with mildewcides provides greater protection than those with mildewcides alone.

Peeling. Paint may peel because water has entered behind the surface, possibly because of openings between roof and wall, and in hot weather this vaporizes and seeks to force its way through the outer wall, causing paint to disbond in the process.

Wrinkling. Two causes of wrinkling are excessive film thickness and over-use of drier in the formulation. Alternatively, mixing before painting may have caused too much drier to be present in a limited portion of the paint.

BIBLIOGRAPHY

1. *Painting Manual,* Vol. 1, Steel Structures Painting Council, Pittsburgh, Pa.

General References

A. Banov, *Paints and Coatings Handbook,* 2nd ed., McGraw-Hill, New York, 1984.

P. Nylen and E. Sunderland, *Modern Surface Coatings,* John Wiley & Sons, New York, 1965.

J. Boxall and J. A. Von Fraunhofer, *Paint Formulation,* Industrial Press, Inc., New York, 1981.

C. R. Martens, *Waterborne Coatings,* Van Nostrand Reinhold Co., New York, 1981.

W. H. Madson, ed., *Federation Series on Coatings Technology,* Units 1–23, Federation of Societies for Coatings Technology, Philadelphia, Pa., 1955–1987.

See also CORROSION; GALVANIZED COATINGS; PLASTICS; POWDER COATINGS; SEALANTS

ABEL BANOV
Greenvale, New York

PALLADIO, ANDREA

One of the most influential architects since the sixteenth century, Andrea di Pietro della Gondola, later named Andrea Palladio, was born in Padua, Italy, in 1508. His work was to become a symbol of the Italian Renaissance, widely interpreted in the western world for centuries to come. His orderly use of classical forms in symmetrical compositions have profoundly affected both British and U.S. architecture, from the eighteenth-century work of Lord Burlington in Great Britain to the postmodernism of Robert Venturi and others in the United States. His *Quatrro libri dell'archittetura* (*Four Books of Architecture*), appeared in 1570 and continues to be reproduced in several languages. His architectural practice spanned a period of 40 years and was centered in the Veneto region of northern Italy and in his adopted city of Vicenza. Arriving in Vicenza in 1524, he first worked as a stonemason in the Pedemuro works, which produced much of the city's ornamental sculpture. He acquired a patron, the wealthy, aristocratic Giangiorgio Trissino, a major influence on his career. Trissino sponsored his formal training in architecture and gave him the name Palladio. In 1541, Trissino took the young architect to Rome where Palladio developed a lasting interest in Roman classicism. He returned to Rome several times and published *The Antiquities of Rome,* a guide to the ancient sites of the city.

In addition to classical influences, Palladio was guided by the work of earlier architects of the Italian Renaissance: Bramante, Raphael, Peruzzi, Sangallo, and others. Between his first commission, the Villa Godi, Malinverni, Lonedo, c. 1537–1542, and his last, Teatro Olimpico, Vicenza, 1580, Palladio designed or received attribution for some 60 buildings, 58 of which still stand. They are now designated historic landmarks. About two dozen of these are villas, scattered about the Veneto, most privately owned and occupied. A dozen or so more are *palazzi,* city houses located, for the most part, in Vicenza, and adapted to public use. Several are church buildings, notably San Giorgio Maggiore (1564–1580) and Il Redentore (1567–1580) in Venice, and the jewellike Tempietto Barbaro (1579–1580) at Maser. Public works, in addition to the Basilica or civic building in Vicenza, include a ceremonial arch, Arco delle Scalette (1576), and a bridge, Ponte Coperto (1568–1570), in Vicenza.

Palladio's clients were the capitalist aristocrats of Venice whose great wealth was derived from trade during the fifteenth century. Competition from other European countries in the sixteenth century brought about an economic change marked by investment closer to home in industry and agriculture. Civic and religious buildings were tokens of competition among municipalities and the new country houses established the owner's presence and dominance of agricultural lands and their production.

The grandeur of ancient Rome and its symbols appealed to the rich of Venice. Palladio's interpretation in Renaissance fashion, adapting the monumental orders, columned, pedimented porticos to domestic buildings, created an ideal architect–client relationship. His plans were innovative, varying arrangements of rooms around a central axis, an

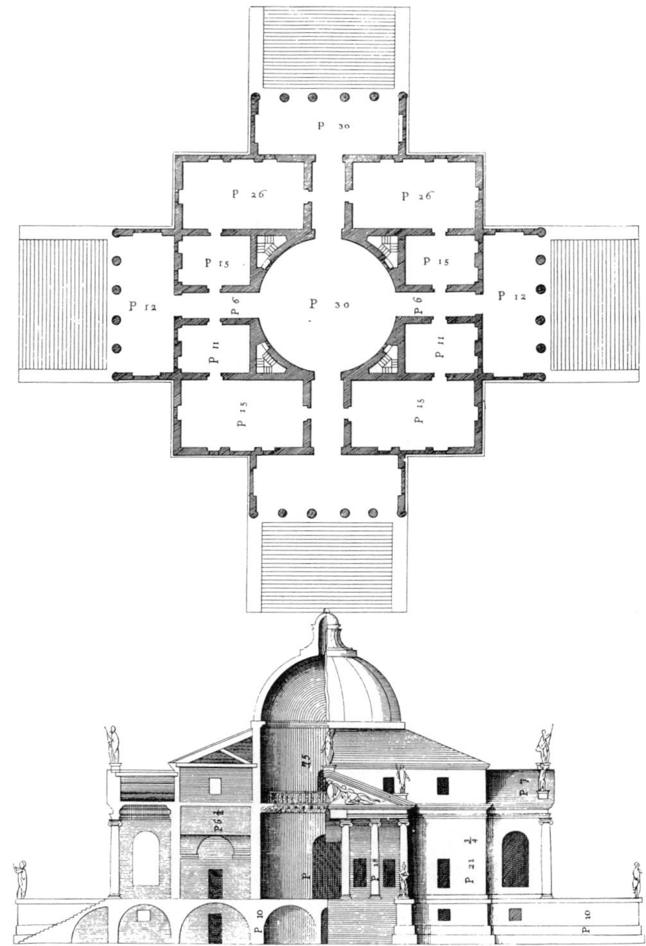

Figure 1. Drawing of La Rotunda, Villa Almerico, 1565–1569.

Figure 2. View of La Rotunda, Villa Almerico. Courtesy of the University of Maryland School of Architecture Slide Collection. Photograph by David Fogle.

axis often encompassing elements in the near and distant landscape.

Palladio's best known, and perhaps most imitated, work is La Rotunda, the Villa Almerico (1565–1569), near Vicenza (Figs. 1, 2). Designed for a papal prelate, Paulo Almerico, the building was occupied in 1569 but not completed until after Palladio's death. The plan is rectangular and symmetrical, with porticos on each of the four facades. A central great hall, the rotunda, is capped by a dome and richly ornamented with fresco paintings. It was his last, and grandest villa project. It has inspired such works as Chiswick, near London, and Jefferson's Monticello, near Charlottesville, Virginia.

The site, described by Palladio as a theater, is a hilltop with views on three sides of farm fields with the slopes of Monte Berico in the distance. The Rotunda establishes a cross-axis that gives equal importance to each elevation of the building. This is a development away from his earlier tendency to produce "frontal" buildings for which the principal elevation dominated. Villa Barbaro (c. 1549) at Maser, and Villa Emo (c. 1559) at Fanzolo, are dramatic examples.

Palladio's final design, his most imaginative, was for the Teatro Olympico, 1580, in Vicenza, a performance space for the Olympic Academy, founded in 1556 to promote the arts and sciences. Palladio was a founding member. Here is architecture of illusion, and Palladio, translating painting techniques to design, used classical forms to deceive the eye and define the varieties of spaces needed for production and audiences of the theater. In this sense he paralleled Veronese, who painted interior walls of a number of Palladian villas to create romantic scenes of elements of architecture and landscape. The theater brings into final focus the several aspects of Palladio—the classicist, the adapter of earlier forms, the creator and master of inventive design.

BIBLIOGRAPHY

General References

J. S. Ackerman, *Palladio,* Penguin Books, Harmondsworth, 1967.

R. Cevese, *Le Ville della provincia di Vicenza,* 2 vols., Rusconi, Milan, 1971.

C. Constant, *The Palladio Guide,* Princeton Architectural Press, Princeton, N.J., 1985.

A. Palladio, *The Four Books on Architecture,* 1738, trans. by Isaac Ware, Dover, New York, 1965.

L. Puppi, *Andrea Palladio,* New York Graphics Society, Boston, 1975.

R. Wittkower, *Architectural Principles in the Age of Humanism,* revised ed., Alec Tiranti, London, 1962.

G. C. Zorzi, *Le Chiese e i ponti di Andrea Palladio,* Neri Pozza, Venice, 1966.

Le Opere Pubbliche e i palazzi privati di Andrea Palladio, Nerri Pozza, Venice, 1965.

Le Ville e i Teatri de Andrea Palladio, Neri Pozza, Venice, 1968.

The Centro Internazionale di Studi di Architectura Andrea Palladio, Vicenza, Italy, has published bulletins (Bollettino) since 1960.

David P. Fogle, AICP
University of Maryland
College Park, Maryland

PARKING AND TRAFFIC CIRCULATION

A major supporting function to a building and the activities within it is the parking and traffic circulation system. Although they play a support role, parking and circulation have a profound impact on site planning and building design decisions, so they must be considered from the very outset of project planning. Employees, visitors, residents, and customers not only must be able to gain easy access to the site but must find circulation within the site safe and efficient. The traffic and parking system should contribute to and not detract from the image the building is designed to project.

This discussion of traffic circulation and parking barely scratches the surface of this large field of engineering and architectural practice. The objective is to introduce the subject, provide some basic design principles and guidelines, and direct the reader to additional sources of information where more detail can be found. Principles of parking lot and structure design are discussed first, followed by a treatment of traffic circulation concepts. The term traffic circulation is used here in a broad sense to include not only vehicular circulation but the movement of pedestrians as well.

THE PLANNING AND REGULATORY CONTEXT

Recent decades have seen processes for regulating parking and roadway design developed to a highly detailed level. The local regulatory devices most commonly used to govern parking and street design in the United States are the zoning ordinance and subdivision regulations. The zoning ordinance typically regulates the requirements for the minimum number and size of off-street parking spaces and may address other design features such as lighting and landscaping. Subdivision regulations usually govern the design of streets, driveways, and pedestrian ways.

However, the scope of authority between these two regulatory devices is not always consistent from one jurisdiction to another.

Before proceeding with project design, it is important to consult the relevant local and state regulations governing parking and circulation system design. The design objectives and principles presented here are generally accepted practices, but do not necessarily coincide with legal requirements that apply to a specific project in a particular locale. Items such as median openings and driveway locations should be discussed with state and local officials at an early stage in project development to avoid costly and time-consuming alterations in the circulation system design later in the process.

PARKING

The automobile has now become the dominant mode of transportation in many countries. One of the drawbacks of automobile use, however, is that vehicles must be stored when the trip is over. In fact, a typical motor vehicle spends more than 90% of its life in the parked position. The problem becomes particularly acute where there are many people arriving at the same destination, making it necessary to devote substantial expanses of land to vehicle storage. In countries were automobile ownership is high, it is not unusual to have more area devoted to parking than to actual floor space in the associated building. Yet the building's successful functioning often depends on the freedom of access that ample parking affords.

Definitions

Aisle. Driving area between rows of parking spaces.

Auto occupancy. The number of persons traveling in a car together. It is often cited as an average for a group of vehicles.

Clear height. Vertical clearance within a parking structure between the floor and the ceiling (including any protrusions from the ceiling).

Clear-span facility. A parking structure having no columns within the interior of a parking bay, but having its vertical supports at the outside edges of the parking bays, usually along the outside walls and at the center of the structure.

Driveway. Entrance or exit roadway between the street and the parking area.

Off-street parking. Parking in a lot or garage, off the street right-of-way.

On-street parking (curb parking). Parking that is within the street right-of-way, usually at the curbside.

Parking angle. The angle formed between the wall or curb line and a parking stall. Parking perpendicular to the wall is termed 90° parking. Parking angles as low as 30° have been used.

Parking bay. A section of a parking facility consisting of an aisle and the adjacent rows of parking spaces accessed by vehicles passing down that aisle.

Parking demand. The number of vehicles parked at or expected to be parked at a facility at a given time. Peak parking demand refers to the maximum number of vehicles that would be expected at any given time. It could be expressed as a daily peak, weekly peak, yearly peak, or peak for some other time frame.

Parking demand/supply ratio. The ratio of expected parkers to the number of available spaces. This ratio is used to gauge the adequacy of the parking supply.

Parking duration. The length of time for which a vehicle is parked at a given location. It is often calculated as an average for a given facility to indicate the characteristics of those parking there.

Parking lot. An area for parking at surface level, not in a structure.

Parking module. The width of a parking bay, measured perpendicular to the aisle.

Parking structure. Any building either above grade, below grade, or both, for purposes of parking motor vehicles.

Parking supply. The number of legal parking spaces available for use at a given location.

Parking turnover. The frequency with which a parking space is used by different parkers. Spaces used by many different parkers are said to have high turnover. Spaces used by few parkers have low turnover. Turnover is inversely related to duration, ie, parking of low duration is high in turnover.

Ramp. Any inclined portion of a parking structure. A ramp may or may not contain parking spaces.

Parking Demand Estimation

An important piece of information needed in the early stages of a development project is an estimate of the parking demand. This, in turn, indicates approximately how many parking spaces may be required. If the usable land area is limited, the amount of parking required may well be the constraining factor in the size of building that can be erected.

Even though parking demand characteristics have been extensively studied for a wide variety of land uses, demand estimation remains an inexact science. Demand has often been related to building type and size by conducting counts of vehicles parked in existing lots and garages and correlating the results with certain characteristics of the building (primarily its type and size). The resulting parking ratios or mathematical equations can then be used to estimate the parking demand characteristics of similar uses in similar settings. For example, a typical peak parking demand ratio for a suburban U.S. office building would be 2.7 cars/1000 ft^2 (2.9 cars/100 m^2) of floor space (this can vary substantially by area and building function, however). Thus a typical 100,000 ft^2 (9300 m^2) office building could be expected to have a peak demand of 270 cars. Additional spaces would normally be provided above this amount to ensure that fluctuations in demand could be accommodated.

An alternative approach is to estimate the parking demand using the following basic equation:

$$\text{Parking demand} = \frac{\text{BLDGOCC} \times \%\,\text{AUTO}}{\text{AUTOCC}}$$

where BLDGOCC = number of persons inside a building at a given time.

% AUTO = the percentage of those persons expected to ride in personal vehicles (not public transit or taxi) on their trip to that site.

AUTOCC = the auto occupancy of those vehicles expected to be parked at the site.

Although this equation oversimplifies a more complex phenomenon, it serves to illustrate the factors that drive parking demand. For office or industrial uses, these three factors can usually be estimated reasonably well, but they need to be considered by component of building occupants (eg, employees, visitors). The equation indicates that parking demand will be lower (on a per-unit basis) in areas where much of the commuting is by transit or via nonmotorized transportation modes or where there is substantial carpooling. It is not uncommon for parking demand in major downtowns to be less than half the demand for comparable buildings in the suburbs.

A typical parking demand for a suburban office building in the United States is 75 vehicles/100 employees. Local transportation departments or consulting firms should be able to provide some of the information on travel characteristics that could be used for input to the above equation. However, the amount of parking actually required may still be governed by local ordinances.

For other nonresidential use types, such as shopping centers and hotels, the market area and type of operation play a much larger role, making demand estimation more difficult. In addition, demand varies substantially over time and by season of year. For residential uses, the parking demand can be computed from the known or estimated household automobile ownership for that area.

Off-Street Parking Requirements

The number of spaces needed to accommodate demand should be set at slightly above the estimated peak demand. A general rule of thumb is that when more than 90% of the spaces are occupied, the parking facility is perceived as full, suggesting that an additional 10% above the estimated peak demand be used as a cushion. The desirability of providing this cushion decreases in denser areas where parking construction costs are higher and alternative modes of transportation are available.

The vast majority of U.S. cities have local requirements governing the minimum number of parking spaces that must be provided with buildings of various types. Although the minimum requirements are generally based on parking demand, experience has shown many of the local requirements to be inappropriate for today's conditions. It is important to analyze a building's parking needs in the context of its unique circumstances and not simply rely on the local zoning ordinance value.

Table 1 provides a suggested set of off-street parking requirements for selected land uses. The ratios apply to suburban sites in the United States and should be factored downward (based on transit use, carpooling, etc) for downtowns in major U.S. cities and for certain other countries, based on reduced levels of auto ownership. The Table 1 values are drawn from the results of several major studies on parking demand. Information on parking requirements and demand characteristics can be found in Refs. 1–5.

Table 1. Typical Off-Street Parking Requirements for Suburban U.S. Sites[a,b]

Land Use Type	Requirement
Office/Industrial	
General office	3.0–3.3 per 1000 GSF[c]
Medical office/clinic	5.0 per 1000 GSF
Industrial	0.75 per employee
Warehousing	1.0–2.0 per 1000 GSF, depending on use
Residential	
Single-family dwellings	2.0 per dwelling unit (DU)
Townhouses	2.0 per DU
Multifamily dwellings	1 per efficiency, plus 1.3 per 1 bedroom unit, plus 1.6 per 2 bedroom unit, plus 1.9 per 3+ bedroom unit
Hotels and motels	0.75 per guest room, plus 10 per 1000 SF dining/assembly room
Retail/Commercial	
Shopping centers	
Under 400,000 GLSF[c]	4.0 per 1000 GLSF
400–600,000 GLSF	4.0–5.0 per 1000 GLSF
Over 600,000 GLSF	5.0 per 1000 GLSF
Restaurants	
Fast food	18 per 1000 GSF
Sit down	15 per 1000 GSF
Cinemas	0.3 per seat
Other	
Hospitals	1.75 per bed, but individual analysis needed
Libraries	6.0 per 1000 GSF
Churches	1 per four seats

[a] Adapted from selected parking demand/supply studies and Refs. 1–5.
[b] Parking requirements in major downtown areas may be substantially lower than shown here, depending on transit ridership and other factors.
[c] GSF = gross square feet; GLSF = gross leasable square feet.

Shared Parking

The increasing trend toward mixed-use development has provided an opportunity for reductions in parking supply through the sharing of a parking facility among uses. This opportunity arises from the fact that parking demand peaks at different times of day and days of the week for different uses. For example, office-building parking demand is high during the day and low at night. Residential parking demand is high at night and low during the day. By mixing these uses, the total number of parking spaces can, at least in theory, be reduced to below what would have been required by both uses separately. Reductions of up to 20% are occasionally possible. Figure 1 illustrates the typical hourly variation in parking demand for various land-use types, from which an assessment can be made of uses that have the highest potential for shared parking.

A major report on shared parking was published by the Urban Land Institute in 1984 (7). It provides a procedure for estimating parking demand for mixed-use development and reviews several operational precautions. Shared parking must be planned carefully, and placing restrictions on how spaces are shared can render it less able to reduce parking requirements than one might have hoped. In some multifamily dwellings, for example, residents have spaces that are reserved on a 24-hour basis, and these spaces cannot be shared.

Truck Requirements

Truck loading and unloading is a vital part of building operation. Parking, docking, and maneuvering areas for trucks need to be ample enough to avoid on-site congestion and delay and allow delivery activities to take place out of the street right-of-way. Some of the most significant midday congestion problems in the downtowns of major cities can be directly attributed to inadequate loading facilities for trucks. Although loading facilities are difficult to retrofit, they can usually be planned into new facilities.

Many local zoning ordinances regulate the minimum required number of truck parking spaces, but the disparities among cities seem to be even greater than that for basic parking requirements. A recent document by the National Parking Association recommends a set of provisions governing parking for truck operations (8).

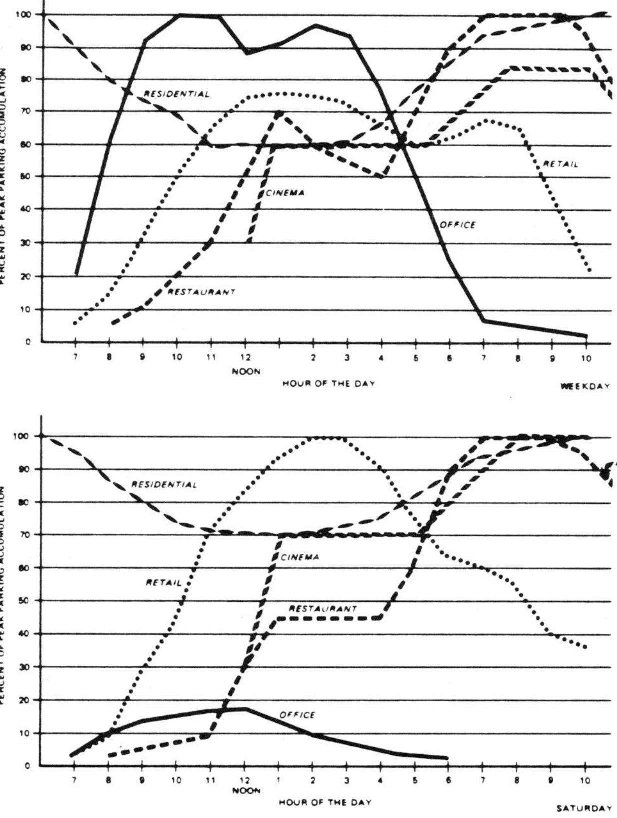

Figure 1. Hourly parking accumulation curves for individual land uses (6).

Parking Space and Aisle Dimensions

The 1970s brought about a dramatic change in the composition of the U.S. auto population. Approximately 50% of the automobiles in use today are in the compact or small-car category (3). The percentage of small cars in most other countries is substantially higher, in many cases approaching 100%. Ref. 3 provides a good overview of vehicle size classifications and their implications on space dimensions.

The Pros and Cons of Small-Car Parking. The dimensions of parking spaces for small and large cars cannot be discussed independently. There are two alternative philosophies for accommodating small and large cars. The first is to designate a separate area or row of a parking lot or garage for small car spaces, the size of which would be reduced from standard or large-car spaces. In the United States, up to 30 or 40% of the spaces could be justified for allocation to small cars. Some zoning ordinances include a variable percentage, with a higher percentage of spaces permitted in larger parking facilities. If separate small-car spaces are provided, they should be located advantageously to the building so that drivers of small cars do not fill up the full-size spaces and thereby force drivers of full-size cars to park in the remaining small-car spaces.

The second alternative is to retain only one "universal" size parking stall and allow complete intermixing of small and large cars. Because the stalls accommodate a mix of vehicle sizes, the dimensions can be slightly smaller than full-size spaces. The presence of the small vehicles makes maneuvering easier not only for the small cars, but for the larger vehicles as well. A 9-ft (2.75-m) wide space has been perhaps the most commonly used space width in the United States for many years. An 8.5-ft (2.6-m) space is acceptable in today's U.S. car fleet and is a good choice for the universal size space, given appropriate module width (see recommended dimensions in next section). This slightly smaller universal size space provides nearly the same space-saving economies as if separate small- and full-size spaces are used. In addition, it has the following advantages:

- Eliminates the operational and enforcement problems often associated with separate small-car parking.
- Eliminates confusion and misinterpretation by drivers over whether their vehicle qualifies as a small car.
- Eliminates the need for special signing and marking, and is, in general, easier to plan and administer.

Although separate spaces for small cars may be appropriate in some situations (such as in some low turnover facilities where distinct space-saving benefits can be achieved), the operational implications should be carefully considered before adopting this design. It should also be recognized that spaces that are too small are a false economy. Vehicles infringing on adjacent spaces can render a significant percentage of small-car spaces unusable. There is not complete agreement even in the parking profession as to the utility of small-car spaces. Parking facilities must be designed with the understanding of the needs of the potential users in light of the economic and physical constraints of each site.

Another design consideration in the sizing of parking spaces is the rate of parking turnover. Consideration should be given to making the high turnover spaces (such as those at a shopping center) larger; in areas with low turnover (such as spaces for employees at an office building) smaller spaces could be justified. This is a logical method of optimizing parking space sizes as long as the high- and low-turnover parkers are clearly segregated. Ref. 3 presents data on maneuvering times for various size combinations of cars and parking spaces, which may be useful in making these determinations.

Parking Space Dimensions. Tables 2 and 3 indicate recommended dimensions for full-size and small-car spaces, respectively, for parking angles between 45 and 90°. The spaces for full-size cars are classified according to approximate rates of turnover associated with various use types. Vehicle overhang [ie, where the vehicle hangs over the curb or wheel stop, usually about 2.5 ft (0.8 m)] should be included in the wall-to-wall module width. Even with a one-way aisle, some wrong-way driving can be expected and should be anticipated in the circulation system. The parking dimensions for small cars shown in Table 3 would also be generally acceptable as the basic design standard for countries in which the auto fleet was composed almost exclusively of small cars.

Table 4 indicates the relative area consumed by stalls of various sizes and angles of parking spaces in square feet (including space allocated to aisles). For most parking facilities, 90° parking is slightly more efficient than angle parking. However, restrictive dimensions of the parking area may require angle parking to be used for one or more parking bays to optimize parking facility capacity fully. Angle parking may also be desired to enforce a one-way traffic flow pattern or where ease of ingress and egress is the primary concern.

The dimensions of spaces in parking structures are complicated by the possible presence of interior columns. One could possibly justify a reduction in space size for parking structures simply on an economic basis. However, maneuvering is generally more difficult in such a structure, and a reduction is usually not practical, except perhaps for clear-span construction (no vertical supports for the width of the module). Clear-span construction has been practiced primarily for freestanding parking structures, but there are also successful examples of clear-span construction under building structures. Clear-span construction can yield approximately 10% more spaces than structures with interior columns, under conditions of comparable maneuverability. Where there are interior columns constricting movement into and out of the spaces,

Table 2. Recommended Parking Layout Dimensions for Full-Size Cars[a]

Parking Angle, °	Stall Width, ft[b]	Stall Width Parallel to Aisle, ft	Stall Depth to Wall, ft	Stall Depth to Interlock, ft[c]	Aisle Width, ft		Modules: Wall to Wall, ft		Modules: Interlock to Interlock, ft	
					2-way	1-way	2-way	1-way	2-way	1-way
90	8.25	8.25	17.5	17.5	26		61		61	
	8.50	8.50	17.5	17.5	26		61		61	
	8.75	8.75	17.5	17.5	26		61		61	
	9.00	9.00	17.5	17.5	26		61		61	
75	8.25	8.5	18.5	17.5	26	23	63	60	61	58
	8.50	8.8	18.5	17.5	26	23	63	60	61	58
	8.75	9.0	18.5	17.5	26	23	63	60	61	58
	9.00	9.3	18.5	17.5	26	23	63	60	61	58
60	8.25	9.5	18.0	16.5	26	18	62	54	59	51
	8.50	9.8	18.0	16.5	26	18	62	54	59	51
	8.75	10.1	18.0	16.5	26	18	62	54	59	51
	9.00	10.4	18.0	16.5	26	18	62	54	59	51
45	8.25	11.7	16.5	14.5	26	12	59	45	55	41
	8.50	12.0	16.5	14.5	26	12	59	45	55	41
	8.75	12.4	16.5	14.5	26	12	59	45	55	41
	9.00	12.7	16.5	14.5	26	12	59	45	55	41

[a] Adapted from material provided by Paul C. Box and Associates and James Saag.

[b] Stall widths should be selected based on expected rate of parking turnover. 9.0 = high turnover (eg, shopping center); 8.75 = moderate to high; 8.5 = low to moderate (eg, office building); 8.25 = very low (eg, industrial).

[c] Interlock = where two rows of parking meet in interlocking fashion. Depth is measured to centerline of the interlock.

Table 3. Minimum Parking Layout Dimensions for Small-Size Cars[a,b]

Parking Angle, °	Stall Width, ft	Aisle Length per Stall, ft	Depth of Stalls at Right Angle to Aisle, ft	Aisle Width, ft	Wall-to-Wall Module, ft
45	7.5	10.5	16.0	11.0	43.0
60	7.5	8.7	16.7	14.0	47.4
75	7.5	7.8	16.3	17.4	50.0
90	7.5	7.5	15.0	20.0	50.0

[a] Ref. 9.
[b] Higher turnover small-car parking spaces should be 8.0 ft wide.

the width of the stalls should usually be measured from the face of the column to assure adequate maneuverability. Thus, the center-to-center column spacing across two 90°, 8.5-ft (2.6-m) spaces would be 18.5 ft (5.3 m) for columns 1.5 ft in diameter. Spacing across three stalls would be 27 ft (8.2 m). However, there are other economic and building design issues that may need to be weighed in column spacing decisions as well.

Special-Purpose Spaces

Handicapped Parking Spaces. Several types of special-purpose spaces usually need to be accommodated in a parking facility. Spaces to accommodate vehicles with handicapped drivers or passengers should be at least 12 ft (3.7 m) wide. The quantity and design are usually regulated through local or state code. A minimum of 2% handicapped spaces is a common requirement in the United States. For very large lots, 1% may be adequate for many land-use types. Usually, a minimum lot size is required before the percentage applies (such as 20 spaces) and at least one space is required for lots in excess of that size. Some localities have developed graduated scales, with a higher percentage of handicapped spaces in smaller parking facilities, based on the probabilities of a certain number of spaces being occupied at a given time. The type of facility should be considered in establishing the number of spaces for handicapped parkers. For example, medical facilities require a higher percentage than other types of uses.

Handicapped spaces should be indicated by both a sign and pavement marking displaying a handicapped symbol and should be located closer to the building entrance than any other type of space. Careful thought should be given to curb cuts and ramping between the spaces and building entrances. Observance has generally been good, but this tends to vary with the availability of regular parking.

Table 4. Relative Area Requirements for Various Parking Layouts[a,b]

Parking Angle, °	Width of Stall, ft 8.5	Width of Stall, ft 9.0
45	270	286
60	264	281
75	264	279
90	259	275

[a] Derived from Table 2.
[b] Square feet per stall area plus one-half aisle area; does not include end-aisle circulation areas or unusable area at ends of parallel parking rows.

Requirements for Truck Parking. The size of truck parking spaces was briefly referred to in a prior section. In general, spaces for tractor trailers should be 55 ft (16.8 m) long and spaces for single-unit trucks should be 35 ft (10.7 m) long (8). Spaces for trucks should be 11 ft (3.4 m) wide with a clear height of 14 ft (4.3 m). Some facilities may require different size spaces to accommodate special needs. Perhaps more important than the size of spaces at loading docks is the maneuverability of trucks on the site. Templates are available for checking turning radii relative to the adequacy of aisles and corners. Local fire departments will be interested in this element of the design as well.

Design of Surface Parking Lots

In addition to the dimensioning of spaces, the design of surface parking lots must consider the following: drainage, overall traffic circulation patterns, turning radii, entry and exit points, pavement design, landscaping, and lighting. Factors impacting on these decisions include topography, size of parking facility, and its relationship to the buildings on the site and to the adjacent street system. Listed below are some general principles to keep in mind when laying out a parking lot (3,9,10):

- Clarity and functionality for the user is of utmost importance. Elaborate layouts that are visually attractive or symmetrical in plan view are not necessarily efficient. Rectangular layouts with straight aisles are highly preferred over curved layouts.
- Where possible, align the rows of parking so that pedestrians can walk down the aisles and not across the rows.
- Do not permit dead-end aisles, unless absolutely unavoidable. If there are dead-ends, it is imperative that

they be kept short. Drivers should be able to tell before they enter the aisle whether there are any available spaces. Turnarounds at the end of the aisle would also be highly desirable.

- The parking surface should be sloped or crowned slightly for drainage. Maximum desirable grade for the parking surface is 5%.
- Locate the parking as proximate to the building as possible to minimize walking distances. The higher turnover visitor or patron parking is normally placed closest in.
- Place pedestrian walkways out of the way of vehicle overhangs. Sidewalks should be at least 3 ft (0.9 m) from the curb.
- Plan parking bays so that vehicles can be parked on both sides of the aisles and around the perimeter of the lot. This usually results in the most efficient use of space. Parking on only one side of a bay is not an efficient use of space, but may be necessary with constricted lot dimensions.

Driveways And Aisles

- Entrance and exit driveways should not be lined with parking spaces.
- Aisle end-treatments should be rounded, to facilitate vehicular maneuverability (Fig. 2). End treatments that butt up to the entire length of the end parking stalls are not necessary. Drivers cannot see the end of the island from behind the wheel and can often be found driving over the curb where such designs exist.
- Establish access points to minimize vehicle-vehicle and vehicle-pedestrian conflict. Vehicular and pedestrian flows should be mapped in an early schematic stage as an aid to establishing overall configuration. If an entrance from the street is to be signalized, a combined entry/exit driveway is preferred. If it is not to be signalized, separate one-way entry and exit points may be preferred, with the exit usually located downstream of the entrance. There are no universal rules for making this decision, however. In either case, it is most important that entry and exit points be clear to the driver. For large facilities, multiple entry and exit points will, of course, be needed, with the number determined by a traffic analysis of the site.
- Driveways for one-way movement should be at least 12 ft (3.7 m) in width, to allow safe and expeditious movement of vehicles. The width may be reduced to 9 ft (2.75 m) at locations of entrance or exit islands on which automated access control equipment and cashier booths are placed.
- If entrance and exit driveways are combined, the combined driveway should not be less than 24 ft (7.3 m) in width.
- Turning radii at all traffic crossovers and aisle intersections should be adequate for safe circulation and orderly vehicular movement. Minimum radii of 30 ft (9.2 m) outside and 18 feet (5.5 m) inside are recommended. Areas where trucks are expected require more.

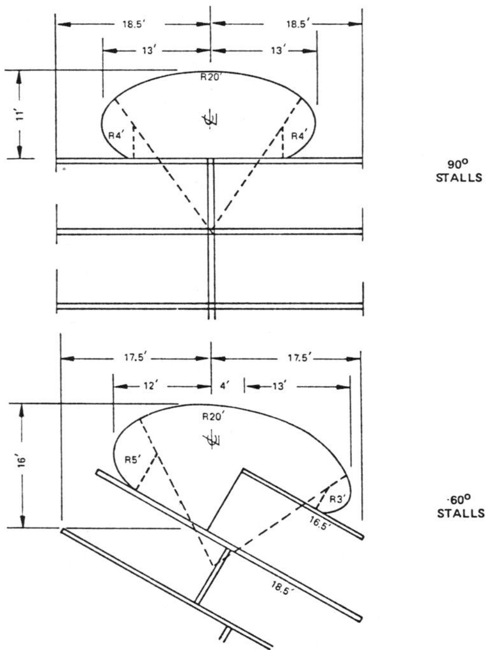

Figure 2. Examples of end-islands for 9-ft stalls (9).

- Cross aisles should be provided approximately every 30 spaces. However, the major flows of cross-aisle traffic should be directed toward the ends of the aisles where the assignment of vehicular right-of-way is more clearcut, analogous to a "Tee" type intersection. A major crossing movement at the middle of an aisle creates a series of high-conflict four-way intersections. Any cross-aisle movement should be delineated by raised islands, with the movements up and down the aisles expected to yield. A stop bar (usually a 12-in. (30-cm) white marking across pavement at the stopping location) should be used to delineate right-of-way at aisle intersections where the right-of-way is otherwise unclear.

Parking Lot Landscaping. Landscaping has become a more prevalent feature of parking lot design, and requirements are frequently being included into local ordinances. Such ordinances typically require minimum perimeter and interior landscaped areas, and functionally specify tree and shrub spacing. Substantial flexibility usually exists within those parameters. Benefits accrue both in traffic control and in the aesthetic appearance of the facility. Ref. 11 provides a good overview of parking lot landscaping principles. Approaches to landscaping range from the strategic placement of small islands to the creation of long islands of landscaping down each row. Local guidelines and authoritative references on landscape architecture should be consulted. However, it is imperative that landscaping not interfere with sight distance at the intersections of driveways and aisles.

Parking Lot Lighting. Parking lot lighting is essential for safety, security, and convenience. The recommended light level for surface parking is 1.0 to 2.0 fc at the surface of the lot. Specifications are available from manufacturers on the level of illumination provided by certain luminaires at given mounting heights and spacings. Computerized lighting packages are also available to assist in design. In parking areas near or adjacent to residential areas, luminaires should be designed to minimize annoyance to residents. Many communities have ordinances for control of lighting on parking areas adjacent to residential uses.

Design of Parking Structures

Choice of Surface or Structured Parking. Construction costs for freestanding structured parking are typically five times the cost per space for a surface lot. The cost of underground parking is often double the above-grade structured parking cost. Therefore, the question of whether to build structured parking is an important one, with potentially large cost implications. The answer is usually determined either by land costs or by limitations in size of the development site. Minimizing walking distances is another advantage of structured parking. Ref. 3 contains information that can be used in evaluating these tradeoffs.

Design Alternatives for Structured Parking. Figure 3 presents a number of alternatives for the functional design of a parking structure. Space does not permit the discussion of the pros and cons of each alternative. Further information on designing efficient parking structures can be found in Refs. 3, 9, and 12. Figure 4 shows an example plan of a major parking garage in the Washington, D.C. area.

Many of the design guidelines for parking lots also apply to parking structures. Some additional principles for structures include the following:

1. *Driveways and Aisles*
   - Separate entrances and exits are sometimes preferred for the larger structures to ease congestion problems.
   - Exit guide signing is even more important in structures than for lots, as there is a tendency for drivers to become disoriented.
2. *Ramp Slopes, Grades, and Widths*
   - Maximum slope for ramps with parking spaces on one or both sides should not exceed 5%.
   - Maximum slope for ramps without parking on either side should not exceed 12%. Curb-to-curb width of such ramps should be a minimum of 12 ft (3.7 m).
   - Curved or helical ramps should be at least 15 ft (4.6 m) in width, with a minimum outside radius of 35 ft (10.7 m).
   - Entry and exit driveways should have adequate reservoir space in keeping with the capacity of the structure. A minimum of three car lengths is usually desirable in advance of the entry or exit control points. One or two car lengths of storage should be provided after the exit control point to minimize interference with cashier operations by vehicles that have already exited.
   - Straight-line approaches to exit control points and departures from entry control points are preferred, but may not always be possible.
   - The exit area should have no visual obstructions, and vision should be unimpeded as the driver exits to the street. Blind corners should be avoided within and around the structure.
3. *Clearances*
   - The minimum vertical clearance for parking areas, aisles and driveways within the garage should be 7 ft (2.1 m) from the floor or ramp surface to the underside of any obstruction, including lighting fixtures. Parking levels to accommodate van parking should have a clear height of 8 ft (2.4 m).
   - Clearance limitation signs or headroom barriers should be installed at all vehicle entrances, with the height limit posted.
4. *Pedestrian Ingress and Egress*
   - Elevators should be located at points that are convenient for pedestrian circulation and also compatible with architectural and structural design.
   - Stairwells should be located adjacent to elevators and preferably at corners of the structure on exterior walls of the building or designed in such a manner that the least number of spaces is lost.
   - Exterior walls of elevator cabs and shafts facing the street should be glass-backed for patron security.
   - Signing should be clear for pedestrians exiting the garage to their destination as well as those returning to their vehicles. Prominently displayed color coding or symbol systems should be employed to aid drivers in recalling the level on which their vehicle was parked.
5. *Other Design Elements*
   - Minimum light intensity levels at the surface of the pavement are recommended as follows (9).

Area	Intensity, fc
Entrances/exits	50
Driving aisles/parking stalls	2–5
Stairways/security problem areas	20
Roof level	2

   - Parking structures should be made to be as aesthetically pleasing as possible within the limits of budget. Creative facade treatments can help a parking structure not just to fit in but to be an attractive part of the urban or suburban setting.

Operation of Parking Facilities

Some parking facilities require minimal attention to operational and maintenance details; others require a great deal. The line is primarily drawn between those facilities that charge for parking and those that do not. The expectation of pay parking has implications not only on equipment and personnel requirements but on design of the facility

Figure 3. Alternative functional designs for parking structures (10).

as well. Stacking or queuing areas must be examined, and the capacity of entry and exit points during the cashiering function needs to be carefully thought through.

Significant advances have been made in recent years in traffic and revenue control systems for parking facilities. Systems are available to keep track of the accumulation of vehicles in a garage, to perform accounting functions previously conducted manually, and to generally speed up the process of vehicle entry and/or exit. See Refs. 3 and 12 for treatments of these issues.

TRAFFIC AND PEDESTRIAN CIRCULATION

Whereas parking represents the holding area for vehicles, vehicular and pedestrian circulation represents the means by which vehicles and persons travel to, from, and within the site. Some aspects of circulation have already been discussed in the context of parking lot and structure design. The emphasis of this section is on overall site planning principles relating to traffic and pedestrian circulation.

Figure 4. Parking garage at the New Carrollton Metrorail Station in Prince George's County, Maryland. Courtesy of Skidmore, Owings and Merrill. Photograph by Dan Cunningham.

Definitions

Arterial street. A street or highway functioning primarily to carry through traffic movements over longer distances.

Average daily traffic volume (ADT). The average number of vehicles passing a given point on a roadway on a daily basis. For planning purposes, the average weekday traffic (AWDT) is normally used.

Collector street. A street that collects traffic from local streets, usually feeding into arterials.

Functional classification. A method of classifying streets and highways according to the primary purpose they serve. Some streets function primarily to provide access to abutting properties whereas others are designed to carry through-traffic movements. Design of the street is largely based on its function.

Level of service. A measure of the quality of traffic service on a roadway or intersection. A letter scale has been developed to rate level of service, with "A" being a high level of service and "F" being a poor level of service. Analytic methods have been developed to calculate the level of service based on traffic volume and roadway characteristics.

Local street. A street whose primary function is to provide access to abutting properties in either commercial or residential areas. These streets are usually low in traffic volume and designed for low-speed traffic.

Peak hour traffic volume. The amount of traffic passing a point on the roadway during the peak hour (usually determined as the four highest volume consecutive 15-min periods). Both the morning and evening commuting peak hours are usually of interest in traffic studies.

Tee intersection. Junction in which one roadway butts (dead-ends) into another.

Trip generation rate. The number of trips (usually referring to vehicular trips) proceeding into and out of a building site over a given period of time. Trip generation can be on a daily or hourly basis. Trip generation varies substantially by land-use type.

Traffic volume. A measure of the number of vehicles passing over a point in a given period of time.

General Principles of On-Site Traffic Circulation

This section presents general traffic circulation principles, with amplification on design elements for selected development types following in succeeding sections. On-site circulation includes all design features contributing to the safe and efficient movement of vehicles to and from peripheral roadways and within the site. The principles follow:

- The site access system should be designed to minimize travel within the site. The major entry and exit points should be located within as close proximity to the activity areas as possible. Drivers should not be made to follow a circuitous route to drop-off or parking locations.

- Three-way ("Tee") intersections are preferred to four-way for the sake of simplicity and safety for both vehicles and pedestrians. However, side streets or parking aisles should be offset by at least 125 ft (38 m) (13). Where this is not possible, four-way intersections are preferred. Cross streets or aisles carrying substantial through traffic should not be offset.
- Locate entrance and exit driveways as far from major intersections as possible, especially those intersections controlled by traffic signals. Spacing driveways too closely not only makes entry into and exit from the site difficult, but also adversely affects traffic movement and safety on the major thoroughfares. Access driveways should normally have one inbound lane 15 ft (4.6 m) wide plus two outbound lanes [left turn lane 13 ft (4.0 m) wide and right turn lane 14 ft (4.3 m) wide]. A 20–25-ft (6.1–7.6-m) curb radius and 40-ft (12.2-m) throat length are desirable (14).
- For commercial development, a consolidation of the number of access points is preferred as long as there is capacity to handle the movements at a reasonable level of service. The proliferation of driveways along arterial streets is a serious traffic efficiency and safety problem. Larger, integrated development sites with a few major entry and exit points are much preferred to traditional strip commercial development. Ref. 14 contains guidelines for driveway location.
- Control vehicular speed on local and collector streets through geometric design. Wide, straight streets encourage traffic speeds that are typically too high for roadways that primarily serve local access functions. Refs. 13 and 15 discuss philosophies of street alignment and width appropriate for various street functional classifications and land-use types. Elements of geometric design are typically controlled by state and local governments through subdivision regulations and highway design standards, which should be carefully consulted before proceeding with a traffic circulation plan.
- A median is a highly desirable design element for streets with four or more traffic lanes. Medians help to discipline traffic flow, improve the ease with which pedestrians cross the street, help to restrain vehicular speeds, and add to the aesthetics of a development. Medians should be included even if they will require that some U-turns be made to access certain sites. Typical median designs are discussed in Refs. 15 and 16.
- Intersection sight distances are an important element of vehicular and pedestrian safety. Inadequate sight distance not only contributes to safety hazards, but opens up the designer to tort liability problems. Standards for safe stopping sight distances can be found in Ref. 15. Care should be exercised to keep buildings set back from the roadway and to use only low shrubbery and nonobstructing street trees at intersections and other locations where clear sight lines must be maintained. This includes the interior of parking lots as well.
- Proper signing is an often-neglected element of a traffic circulation system. Although the circulation system should be as self-explanatory as possible, it may often need to be supplemented with signing that is clear and that meets established standards of uniformity and legibility. The *Manual on Uniform Traffic Control Devices* (MUTCD), published by the Federal Highway Administration, establishes standards for signing, markings, and other forms of traffic control (17). Conforming to these standards will produce the most effective traffic control system from a functional standpoint. Aesthetic enhancements can sometimes be added through special mountings for signs, if desired. However, the shape of the sign is an important element of the message and should not be obscured. The designer should think through the information needs from the driver's perspective.
- Roads and driveways should always intersect at right angles, not skewed.
- As a rule, traffic circles should be avoided, with the possible exception of small circles for speed control in residential areas (18) and for circulation lanes at major building drop-off points.

Traffic Circulation for Selected Development Types

To the extent that development types vary in density, spatial relationships, and function, the traffic circulation needs also vary. Low-density residential development requires a quite different arrangement of access roadways than does a high-density commercial center. The sections following indicate the most significant unique features of traffic planning for selected development types. The Urban Land Institute's *Development Handbook* series (19–22) provides additional information on several of the major use types.

Residential Development. Residential streets are a prime example of an historical trend of over-designed local streets. Many subdivisions in the 1950s and 1960s were designed with very wide residential streets under the philosophy that "wider is better." A joint effort by the American Society of Civil Engineers (ASCE), National Association of Home Builders (NAHB), and the Urban Land Institute (ULI) in 1974 resulted in a document entitled *Residential Streets: Objectives, Principles, and Design Considerations*. This document argued for reduced widths for local streets, in keeping with the low volume, low speed access function they serve. Specific street widths suggested in *Residential Streets* include:

- 36 ft (11.0 m) for collector streets (permitting parking on both sides of the street).
- 26 ft (7.0 m) for local streets with parking possible on both sides and one lane for traffic.
- 20 ft (6.1 m) for local streets with parking on one side and one lane for traffic.

These are minimum widths, and would be considered inadequate in many communities, especially those with significant snow accumulations, or on streets where there are few, if any, private driveways. This is primarily a matter of design philosophy, but is usually dictated by state and local standards already in place.

Street-width standards are still a matter of debate and are reflected differently in state and local standards within the United States and in other countries as well. Current trends in Europe and Australia are pointing toward expansion of the shared-space concept for certain local streets, in which residential street geometrics are greatly restricted and pedestrians given legal standing for shared use of the right-of-way; see Ref. 23 for discussion of the Dutch "Woonerf" and other concepts. The philosophy is reinforced with special paving, bollards, or other design features.

Residential street design should also acknowledge the role of street configuration and block length in the creation of livable residential areas. Long grid systems are no longer acceptable, having proved to be fraught with problems of through traffic and higher than desired speeds. Appleyard's *Livable Streets* (18) suggests methods for designing new streets and retrofitting old ones to make them more amenable to walking, biking, and neighborhood social life.

Shopping Centers. A great deal of attention has been paid to the development of circulation systems for shopping centers, particularly with the proliferation of regional shopping malls. The perimeter roadway has become a standard feature of most malls and has effectively reduced the pedestrian/vehicle conflicts that would otherwise occur adjacent to the buildings. A driving aisle is still needed along the building fronts for access to entrances and for general circulation.

For smaller centers, it is more acceptable to place the major traffic circulation aisle adjacent to the stores. If speed and vehicle/pedestrian conflicts become a problem, traffic controls such as stop signs or speed bumps can be employed. However, they should only be used if a problem exists and should not be applied arbitrarily. Traffic circulation should usually be designed for the counterclockwise direction to facilitate passenger loading and unloading and parcel pickup. Two-way operation will allow the greatest flexibility in patron circulation. Additional aisle width may be needed at major shopping center entrances or pickup points.

One problem at regional shopping centers is allowing for rapid exit and dispersion of traffic at the end of the day. Insofar as possible, multiple access points should be available and separate signal timing plans should be designed to handle the exiting traffic. Ways should also be sought to avoid sending traffic through signalized intersections. Special ramps for shopping center traffic may be needed.

Office and Industrial Parks. Large office and industrial parks are becoming a common suburban development type. The circulation principles applied to residential development can also generally be applied to office parks (eg, curved streets, discouraging high-speed through traffic). However, four-lane roadways may be needed on major collectors, and on-street parking may not be needed, since ample accommodations should be available in off-street facilities. Additional thought should also be given to truck movements. Turning radii at intersections will generally be greater in an office park environment.

Downtown Development. Traffic circulation for downtown development, which characteristically consists of infill development and redevelopment, is more a function of public sector action than design by the private sector. Parking is often in above-grade structures or underground. Operation of parking garages and access for delivery vehicles are usually the most important issues. Provisions for off-street loading should be designed into commercial facilities to reduce the operational problems and impacts of curbside loading.

Suburban Activity Centers and Mixed-Use Development. Major satellite activity centers, outside the downtown core, are a rapidly emerging development type in major U.S. cities. Older suburban areas are being densified and redeveloped, and major new developments are springing up in what were cornfields and cow pastures only a few years ago.

Redeveloping areas will, for the most part, be tied to the existing street system. Newly developing areas will have more design flexibility, especially if major portions of the development are being planned as a unit. A more dense, compact land-use pattern is preferred over traditional suburban low-density use. It benefits the traffic circulation system by allowing more of the short trips to be made on foot and may reduce overall reliance on the automobile.

Off-Site Traffic Considerations

Increasing congestion on the roadway network has prompted most jurisdictions in major urban areas to adopt procedures for analyzing the traffic impact of new development. The purpose of such analyses is typically to gauge the ability of the roadway network to handle the additional volumes and to identify needed road improvements. Developers are increasingly required to contribute toward road improvements needed to accommodate trips generated by the added development. Traffic forecasting procedures have been developed, ranging from simple manual techniques to complex computerized models to estimate future traffic volumes. The process of conducting a traffic impact analysis, outlined in Ref. 24, typically includes the following steps:

- Determine existing traffic volumes.
- Estimate new trips to be generated by the development, based on the composition of land uses, size of the development, and appropriate trip-generation rates.
- Forecast growth in traffic not associated with subject development (done either through computer modeling or factoring existing traffic volumes).
- Distribute the new trips onto the roadway network.
- Overlay new trips onto the future year background traffic to determine total estimated future volumes.
- Conduct an analysis to determine existing and future levels of service for appropriate roadway design alter-

natives. Future levels of service would be computed for both the unimproved and improved roadway system to quantify the added impact of the proposed development. The *1985 Highway Capacity Manual* (25) is the most current authoritative source for computing levels of service in the United States. Procedures vary for other countries.

Key to the traffic impact analysis is the trip-generation rate specified for the new development. These rates are based on historical traffic count data from existing building sites, and vary by land-use type, often significantly. Table 5 presents daily and peak hour rates typical of various types of land use. These rates generally apply to suburban development in the United States. They will tend to be lower in areas where significant transit ridership and/or carpooling exist. Local sources should be consulted for trip-generation rates appropriate to each area. The Institute of Transportation Engineers (ITE) periodically updates trip-generation data for use in traffic studies (27).

Public Transportation

Although transportation in the United States is dominated by the automobile, access for public transportation is still an important design element, particularly in the vicinity of rail transit stations. Direct walkways should be provided between bus stops or rail stations and building entrances. Benches and shelters should also be considered. Where buses are expected to enter the actual property, careful attention should be paid to standing areas, canopy height, and curb radii.

Table 5. Typical Suburban U.S. Trip-Generation Rates for Selected Land Uses[a]

		Trips in Peak Hour[b]			
		A.M.		P.M.	
Land Use	Trips Per Day[c]	In	Out	In	Out
	Office/Industrial				
General office	12/1,000 GSF	1.7	0.2	0.3	1.6
Industrial park	7.0/1,000 GSF	0.8	0.2	0.2	0.8
	Residential				
Single-family detached	10.0/DU	0.2	0.55	0.65	0.35
Apartment	6.1/DU	0.1	0.45	0.45	0.20
Hotel	8.7/GR	0.45	0.25	0.35	0.30
	Retail/Commercial				
Shopping center					
<100,000 GLSF	83/1,000 GLSF	1.5	1.35	4.9	5.1
100–500,000 GLSF	50/1,000 GLSF	0.9	0.55	2.6	2.7
>500,000 GLSF	34/1,000 GLSF	0.5	0.2	1.6	1.6
Restaurant					
Fast food	630/1,000 GSF	28	28	17	16
Sit down	96/1,000 GSF			5	2.5

[a] Adapted from Ref. 26.
[b] Rates correspond to peak hours of adjacent street traffic, typically between 7 and 9 A.M. and 4 and 6 P.M. Values typically rounded to nearest 0.05 or two significant digits.
[c] GSF = gross square feet; GLSF = gross leasable square feet; DU = dwelling unit; GR = guest room.

Pedestrian Circulation

Pedestrian circulation is another often-neglected element of site design, especially in suburban development. In downtown areas, public and private initiatives have brought about dramatic improvements in the pedestrian environment in many cities, especially in Europe (28). Refs. 29–32 provide design guidance for pedestrian facilities. The *1985 Highway Capacity Manual* provides procedures for computing pedestrian level of service, from which determinations of required sidewalk width can be made. Ref. 33 presents design guidelines for accommodations for handicapped persons.

The pedestrian circulation system (and bicycle system, if appropriate) should always be included as part of the site planning process. Suburban development is especially replete with examples of missing sidewalk (evidenced by worn footpaths) or, in some cases, the complete lack of a pedestrian network altogether. Care should be taken to examine the internal site network connecting parking lots and buildings as well as connections to adjacent streets. This analysis need not take long, but should be included in the early conceptual stages and carried through the various stages of plan development. Excellent examples exist of developments that included creative pedestrian networks and landscaping features that resulted in greatly enhanced project marketability. Several specific guidelines for the pedestrian network follow:

- Sidewalks can be justified for all arterial and collector streets and for most local streets (with the possible exception of low-density single-family residential uses). Ref. 34 contains more specific guidelines. Again, local regulations may dictate.
- Sidewalks should be at least 4 ft (1.2 m) in width and separated from the street by a planting strip, except in downtown areas. If right-of-way exists or if an easement can be obtained, sidewalks can be designed to meander, creating more interest and amenity along the path.
- Recreational pathway systems are a worthy amenity for some residential areas but must be designed with sensitivity to security and cannot be expected to serve utilitarian trips unless connections are direct.
- Pedestrians can be assisted across large parking lots by creating small landscaped islands along the most direct pedestrian path where it crosses each parking bay. Special pedestrian aisles between parking bays have typically not been worth the cost, except where that path connects major pedestrian origin and destination points (eg, a major office building near a shop-

ping center). Most parkers do not use the special path, choosing rather to walk down the driving aisle.

As stated at the beginning of this section, parking and traffic circulation must be considered as integral to one another in the site planning process and must proceed concurrently. Many references are available for amplification of the basic principles outlined here (35). As long as basic rules of safety and efficiency are followed, there is ample room for creativity in the design of parking and circulation systems responsive to the unique opportunities that arise with each development plan.

BIBLIOGRAPHY

1. *Parking Generation,* Institute of Transportation Engineers, Washington, D.C., 1985.
2. *Recommended Zoning Ordinance Provisions for Parking,* National Parking Association, Washington, D.C., 1981.
3. Urban Land Institute and National Parking Association, *The Dimensions of Parking,* Urban Land Institute, Washington, D.C. One of the better recent texts covering many aspects of the design, operation, and administration of parking.
4. *Parking Requirements for Shopping Centers: Summary Recommendations and Research Study Report,* Urban Land Institute, Washington, D.C., 1981.
5. D. K. Witherford and G. E. Kanaan, *Zoning, Parking and Traffic,* ENO Foundation for Transportation, Saugatuck, Conn., 1972.
6. Barton-Aschman Associates, Inc., "Shared Parking for Selected Land Uses," *Parking,* National Parking Association, Washington, D.C., Autumn 1983, pp. 59–66.
7. Urban Land Institute and Barton-Aschman Associates, Inc., *Shared Parking,* Urban Land Institute, Washington, D.C., 1984.
8. *Recommended Zoning Ordinance Provisions for Off-Street Loading Space,* National Parking Association, Washington, D.C., 1983.
9. *Parking Principles, Highway Research Board Special Report 125,* Highway Research Board, Washington, D.C., 1971. A major reference on all phases of parking design and operation.
10. *Transportation and Traffic Engineering Handbook,* Institute of Transportation Engineers, Washington, D.C., 1982. The primary reference document for all phases of transportation engineering.
11. M. Corwin, *Parking Lot Landscaping,* American Society of Planning Officials, Chicago, Ill., 1978.
12. *Parking Garage Planning and Operation,* ENO Foundation for Transportation, Westport, Conn., 1978. Contains most of the information needed on the design and operation of parking structures.
13. *Residential Streets; Objectives, Principles & Design Considerations,* Urban Land Institute, American Society of Civil Engineers, and National Association of Home Builders, Washington, D.C., 1974.
14. V. G. Stover and F. H. Koepke, *Transportation and Land Development,* Institute of Transportation Engineers, Prentice-Hall, Englewood Cliffs, N.J., 1987.
15. *A Policy on Geometric Design of Highways and Streets,* American Association of State Highway and Transportation Officials, Washington, D.C., 1984.
16. J. W. Flora and K. M. Keith, *Access Management for Streets and Highways,* FHWA-IP-82–3, U.S. Department of Transportation, Washington, D.C., 1982.
17. *Manual on Uniform Traffic Control Devices for Streets and Highways,* U.S. Department of Transportation, Washington, D.C., 1986.
18. D. Appleyard, *Livable Streets,* University of California Press, Berkeley, Calif., 1981.
19. J. A. Casazza and F. H. Spink, Jr., *Shopping Center Development Handbook,* 2nd ed. (Community Builders Handbook Series), Urban Land Institute, Washington, D.C., 1968.
20. D. C. Lochmoeller, et al., *Industrial Development Handbook* (Community Builders Handbook Series), Urban Land Institute, Washington, D.C., 1968.
21. W. Paul O'Mara, *Residential Development Handbook,* Community Builders Handbook Series, Urban Land Institute, Washington, D.C., 1978.
22. W. Paul O'Mara, *Office Development Handbook,* Community Builders Handbook Series, Urban Land Institute, Washington, D.C., 1982.
23. *Traffic Safety in Residential Areas,* Organization for Economic Cooperation and Development (OECD), Paris, 1979.
24. R. C. Keller and J. Mehra, *Site Impact Traffic Evaluation (S.I.T.E.) Handbook,* FHWA/PL85/004, U.S. Department of Transportation, Washington, D.C., 1985.
25. *Highway Capacity Manual, Transportation Research Board Special Report 209,* Transportation Research Board, Washington, D.C., 1985.
26. J. Mehra and C. R. Keller, *Development and Application of Trip-Generation Rates,* FHWA/PL/85/003, U.S. Department of Transportation, Washington, D.C., 1985.
27. *Trip Generation,* Institute of Transportation Engineers, Washington, D.C., 1987. A periodically updated source of trip-generation rate data.
28. *Streets for People,* Organization for Economic Cooperation and Development (OECD), Paris, France, 1974.
29. J. DeChiara and L. E. Koppelman, *Time-Saver Standards for Site Planning,* McGraw-Hill, New York, 1984. Contains a wealth of design details for parking lots, driveways, and pedestrian facilities.
30. J. J. Fruin, *Pedestrian Planning and Design,* Metropolitan Association of Urban Designers and Environmental Planners, Inc., New York, 1971.
31. S. A. Smith and co-workers, "Planning and Implementing Pedestrian Facilities in Suburban and Developing Rural Areas," *NCHRP Report 294 A and B,* Transportation Research Board, Washington, D.C., 1986.
32. R. K. Untermann, *Accommodating the Pedestrian: Adapting Towns and Neighborhoods for Walking and Bicycling,* Van Nostrand Reinhold, New York, 1984.
33. J. Templer, *The Development of a Priority Accessible Network—An Implementation Manual,* U.S. Department of Transportation, Washington, D.C., 1980.
34. R. H. Freilich and P. S. Levi, *Model Subdivision Regulations, Text and Commentary,* American Society of Planning Officials, Chicago, Ill., 1975.
35. K. Lynch and G. Hack, *Site Planning,* 3rd ed., MIT Press, Cambridge, Mass., 1984. A classic text on site planning, with sections on traffic and parking.

STEVEN A. SMITH, PE
JHK & Associates
Orlando, Florida

PATTERN-BOOK ARCHITECTURE

The term architectural pattern book refers to a tool of the early building and architectural trade in the United States that was used to communicate practical design and construction information before the advent of mass media and contemporary information storage systems. Pattern books were an important facet of the practices of carpenter–builders and architect–builders. The books were widely used before the legal distinction between an architect and a builder was defined. After the rise of the professional architect in the mid-nineteenth century, the focus of the books changed. No longer targeted to the builder, they were produced by architects for the use of the client in deciding on a particular design.

This examination of pattern books is concerned with how they reflect changes in the relationships of those in the building arts and, on a larger scale, how these changes were due to the structure of late-nineteenth-century life in the United States. The intent is to understand how the collection of pattern books of the eighteenth and early nineteenth century compare with those of the middle to late nineteenth century. Thus, the books are considered comparatively only in their outlines.

EARLY AMERICAN ARCHITECTURAL PATTERN BOOKS

Many of the pattern books used by the builders of colonial America were published in Great Britain, imported, and then republished under new titles. Some of the most popular books in the colonies during the eighteenth century included Francis Price's *The British Carpenter* and William Salmon's *Palladio Londinesis*. Both books offered American builders essential information such as geometry and arithmetic and ways of determining the size and construction of structural members. There were no plans and little decorative detail (1).

Price's *The British Carpenter* appeared in 1733 and contained a series of small, easily understood plates showing the "most approved methods of connecting timber together, for most of the various uses in building, with rules necessary to be observed therein" (2). There were also details on domes and staircases with a supplement on the Palladian orders. Salmon's *Palladio Londinesis* was published in 1734 and provided the principles of Palladian design. It also contained sections on geometry, staircases, chimneys, roofs, and the orders. With the rural, uneducated architect–builder in mind, Salmon gave directions for finding a "just proportion" by arithmetic, geometry, or the use of a table (3).

Another popular volume during this period was Batty Langley's *Builder's Jewel,* which appeared in 1741. It was, he declared, the first pocket companion for the builder "with all the useful Rules and Proportions" for orders, pediments, cupolas, and roofs, in 24 pages with 99 plates. The young carpenter was urged to study in his leisure hours, to "emulate and thereby to make himself the most useful to both himself and his country" (4).

Although these British books were popular, they often fell short in addressing problems particular to building in America. Besides geographic and climatic differences, American structures had to respond to different economic, religious, social, and political conditions than did the buildings in British pattern books. Asher Benjamin was perhaps the first architect–builder to address American building needs in book form. He relied heavily on the books of Peter Nicholson and William Chambers, two pattern-book authors popular at that time (5). His talent was in adapting their architecture into an American vernacular. Grandiose plans for country estates with extravagant decor found in the British volumes were virtually useless to the American carpenter faced with the problems of building quickly and inexpensively. In his mid-20s, Benjamin wrote *The Country Builder's Assistant* (6). This 1797 volume simplified the orders and included a great deal of technical building information. Other U.S. pattern-book authors took their cues from Benjamin's sense of the uniqueness of the art of American building. Owen Biddle's popular *Young Carpenter's Assistant* of 1805 and John Haviland's *The Builder's Assistant* of 1818 not only emulated Benjamin's work in title, but likewise provided the architect–builder with the technical knowledge he needed to make appropriate responses to local building conditions (7).

The talent of the early architect–builders was demonstrated by their ingenuity and ability to take building information and reinterpret it for the problem at hand. No canon of taste was so relentless, no rule of thumb so unyielding as to ignore a contingency in the field. The carpenter was invited, indeed expected, to apply his insights to the building problem. Because the early pattern books contained the essential elements for an American architecture and suggestions for their combination, these volumes were much like cookbooks. They offered all of the ingredients for complete buildings with enough flexibility to accommodate local tastes.

The cookbook-style pattern book was most prevalent between 1800 and 1840. It was influential in promoting the Greek revival across the expanding Western frontier and through the towns and villages of the established East and South. Here was an information source that served to transform cityscape and countryside alike, so adaptable were its contents. Some of the most popular were Edward Shaw's *Civil Architecture,* which remained in print for 47 years between 1830 and 1876 (8); Benjamin's *The Practical House Carpenter* of 1830, which appeared in several editions until 1857 (9); and two volumes by Minard Lafever, *The Modern Builder's Guide* between 1833 and 1855 (10) and *The Beauties of Modern Architecture* between 1835 and 1855 (11). These books focused on the mechanics and science of architecture and offered suggestions for stylistic treatments. Many of the new editions of Benjamin's books, for example, came about as the Greek revival developed according to national taste. Most of the technical information was refined but not greatly changed.

Although the variety of pattern books during this time was limited, those books that reached the hands of carpenters were in circulation for long periods. Of the approximately 23 volumes of the cookbook style that were published between 1797 and 1839, 22% were in print for 40 years or longer. Nearly half remained in print for 20 or more years.

CHANGES IN BUILDING

Pattern books showed the first signs of a fundamental change in their content in the early 1840s. Their audience shifted from the carpenter to the client. It was Asher Benjamin, in fact, who signaled this change 10 years earlier in his 1830 volume, *The Practical House Carpenter*. The tone of his text changed from that of an architect–builder addressing a colleague to one of a professional architect addressing a carpenter (12). This change to a "class-conscious architect" reflected other factors that were having a tremendous impact on building in the United States. The greatest social change was the growth in population. Between 1790 and 1840 the population of the country increased nearly fivefold to 17.1 million. By 1860 it had almost doubled again, reaching 34.1 million. This population boom naturally increased the demand for more buildings.

Population growth was also attended by a rapid expansion of the U.S. economy and the Western territory, both brought about in part by the industrial revolution. The growth of the factory system as a means of producing many household items was foreshadowed by the transition of the household from virtual self-sufficiency before 1810 to reliance on goods produced outside the home after the 1840s (13).

The emergence of factory production had a significant effect on building as well. Lumber was one of the first products to be adapted to factory production (14). The first steam-powered sawmill was established in New Orleans in 1803 and by 1820 the production of milled lumber was a fully mechanized activity (15). A concurrent development was the machine production of nails in the early 1830s, although a nail-manufacturing machine had been in operation as early as 1807 (16).

These two developments in building technology, milled lumber and machined nails, opened the door for balloon-frame construction, which appeared in Chicago in 1833. Balloon framing made the assembly of a building simpler and much faster, and the finished product much lighter. This breakthrough in building technology was described in Horace Greeley's *The Great Industries of the United States*. "The method of construction with wood, known as 'balloon framing'; is . . . the most important contribution to our domestic architecture which the spirit of economy, and a scientific means to ends [has] given the modern world" (17).

It was precisely at this moment in history, when the process of building was being reduced to its most elemental steps so that it could be accomplished by a laborer rather than a skilled carpenter, that the U.S. architect chose to differentiate himself from those who built. This specialization of labor contributed to the establishment of professions and professional associations. The practitioners of architectural design, who perceived their craft as something quite different from building, were among the first to establish a professional body. In 1857, under the guidance of Richard Upjohn, Richard Morris Hunt, and other leaders of the profession, the American Institute of Architects was founded. The AIA's objectives, as stated, were to "unite in fellowship the Architects of this continent, and to combine their efforts so as to promote the artistic, scientific, and practical efficiency of the profession" (18). And as the AIA code of ethics, formally adopted in 1909, stated, no architect could personally engage in building construction.

Aside from controlling the fees and professional behavior of its members, the AIA also sought to promote its members' education. It was instrumental in the establishment of the first four architecture schools in the United States and served to shape the content of their curricula. William R. Ware, an AIA member who was quite influential in the general development of architectural education, personally helped establish the country's first architectural school at the Massachusetts Institute of Technology in 1865. Other schools were established at the University of Illinois, Cornell, and Syracuse in 1867, 1871, and 1873, respectively, and all were under the direction of AIA members (19). Another facet in the professional development and regulation of architecture, licensing, was first established in Illinois in 1897.

FROM COOKBOOK TO MENU

The rise of the professional architect, architectural education, and architectural registration drastically altered the content of U.S. architectural pattern books. The authorship of these books passed into the hands of the newly established professional architect who directed them toward the consumer. Works addressed to the builder did not disappear entirely, but their number diminished significantly.

This new form of pattern book might best be described as a menu in contrast with the earlier cookbook. Menu-style books were distributed directly to the person wishing to build a new house. Inside, one could find an assortment of plans, elevations, and perspectives, plus a variety of surface and finish treatments. The architect addressed himself directly to the client and described each plan, the advantages of different stylistic treatments, and how the house might best be furnished. These books rarely contained a complete set of construction drawings and specifications. The client perused the menu, picked what he liked, and the architect would then supply the construction documents for a fee. The influence of the carpenter in home building was thus diluted. His job became one of putting together a number of predesigned and fabricated parts, where before it had offered him the opportunity to contribute to the structure's conception and execution. The professional architect, dealing directly with the client, took center stage.

The production of menu-style pattern books increased dramatically after the 1840s. By 1855, 20 such titles had appeared. After the Civil War this type of book dominated the field. When the number of cookbook-style books produced hit a low of 2 from the span 1875 to 1880, menu-style books hit an all-time high of 15 for the same period. The life span of a single menu-style volume was, however, much shorter than that of a cookbook-style. The average life span for all menus produced between 1840 and 1895 was 4.34 years, for they were concerned primarily with style, which made them obsolete after only a short time.

In the case of the menu-style books it was the author, not the particular book, that attracted readership. Thus, several noted architect–authors produced a vast number of different volumes that were in print for short periods of time, but enjoyed wide popularity. Among these were the works of Samuel Sloan, who produced 6 volumes between 1852 and 1871 (20); A. J. Bicknell, who wrote 10 different books between 1870 and 1878 (21); and Palliser, Palliser & Company, which produced 12 books between 1876 and 1893 (22).

Cookbook versus Menu

To sharpen the focus on the contrast between cookbook- and menu-style pattern books, a work of Asher Benjamin will be compared to that of Palliser, Palliser & Company, authors who best represent these respective approaches.

Benjamin's first book, *The Country Builder's Assistant* (1797), is considered to be the first manual published for use specifically by U.S. builders (23). Benjamin simplified many of the British ornaments and orders, which he said would allow the builder to produce them quickly and without "sacrificing effect." Benjamin attempted to reduce the expense of both labor and materials. In each new edition of his books, information on construction and decoration was refined and after 1814 more technical data were included (23). Benjamin published seven builder's books in all, between 1797 and 1860. *The American Builder's Companion* (1806) was first published by Etheridge & Bliss of Boston. The sixth edition, published in 1827, might be considered the most valuable for comparative purposes, having been the product of continuous refinement for over 20 years (24).

This volume shows Benjamin's concern with supplying the carpenter with practical, usable building information. In the introduction he explains what he has included in the present edition and the reasons for changes that have been made since the last. Only one sentence in the page-and-a-half introduction mentions the inclusion of entire building plans and elevations, while the greater part is concerned with architectural details.

The first section of the book is devoted to practical geometry. Benjamin explains all the elemental parts for understanding geometric constructions and forms, with corresponding illustrations. He covers basic concepts to clarify terms used in the body of the work. Next is a description of the construction of geometric figures, such as dividing a line in half by a perpendicular, constructing polygons and pentagons, and dividing angles into equal parts. There is a section on the inscription of geometric shapes, the construction of ellipses, determining the curvature of plaster and moldings, constructing columns in section and plan, and classifying different moldings and how they are constructed.

The following section is titled "The Origins of Building," and here Benjamin sketches the development of the art of building from man's first appearance on earth. He describes the Grecian orders, their ornament, and their historic development. Benjamin includes the tale of Callimachus, the Greek sculptor, coming on a monument surmounted by a basket overgrown with acanthus, which inspires him to render it in stone as a Corinthian capital. Of all the orders, Benjamin selects the Tuscan as the finest. "As this order conveys ideas of strength and rustic simplicity, it may very properly be used for rural purposes; for farm-houses, barns, sheds, stables, and greenhouses . . . and generally wherever magnificence is not required, and expense is to be avoided" (25). Benjamin then suggests the proper use of each order. "As the Doric order is, particularly in churches and temples, dedicated to male saints, so the Ionic is principally used in such as are consecrated to females of the matronal state. It is likewise employed in courts of justice, in libraries, colleges, seminaries, and other structures, having relation to arts or letters; and in private houses; and in all places dedicated to peace and tranquility" (Fig. 1). The Corinthian, of course, is used for all building "where elegance, gaiety, and magnificence are required" (26).

Benjamin includes drawings of all of the orders, showing the proportional relationships among the many parts of the column, and gives explicit instructions on how the columns should be placed in relation to each other and the overall composition of the facade (27):

> Columns, when placed within one, or one and one half diameter of each other, may be made smaller than if placed singly . . . . When more than two are wanted, the largest opening ought to be left in the centre; if more than four are wanted, place two of them about one diameter from each other, at each angle of the portico or building on which they are placed. When placed in front of a building, they ought to stand in front of the pier; never before windows and doors. When they are placed one over another, they ought to be exactly so, and the lightest on the top, as the stoutest is best calculated for support.

Throughout the book, Benjamin offers advice on columns, pilasters, moldings, pedestals, pediments, cornices, friezes, bannisters, decorative urns, architraves, front entrances, chimney pieces, ceiling decor, mantel pieces, fanlights, and windows. Benjamin includes a section on the execution of details in Grecian architecture, whose revival in the United States had been enjoying a steady growth since the late 1820s. He offers dimensions and proportions to calculate the perfect Grecian Ionic volute, and discusses at length the proportion of the Grecian Doric compared to the Roman. At the end of the book, Benjamin shifts from instruction on execution of decoration and detail to the mechanics of constructing such things as roof trusses and domes (Fig. 2). The last 10 pages of the volume offer floor plans, elevations, and a number of details for complete buildings such as town houses, country houses, meeting-houses, courthouses, and churches.

Benjamin's tone and the information that he presents contrasts dramatically with that of Palliser, Palliser & Company. The Palliser firm was founded in 1877 by George and Charles Palliser of Bridgeport, Connecticut. The Pallisers' books were popular with the public and the brothers

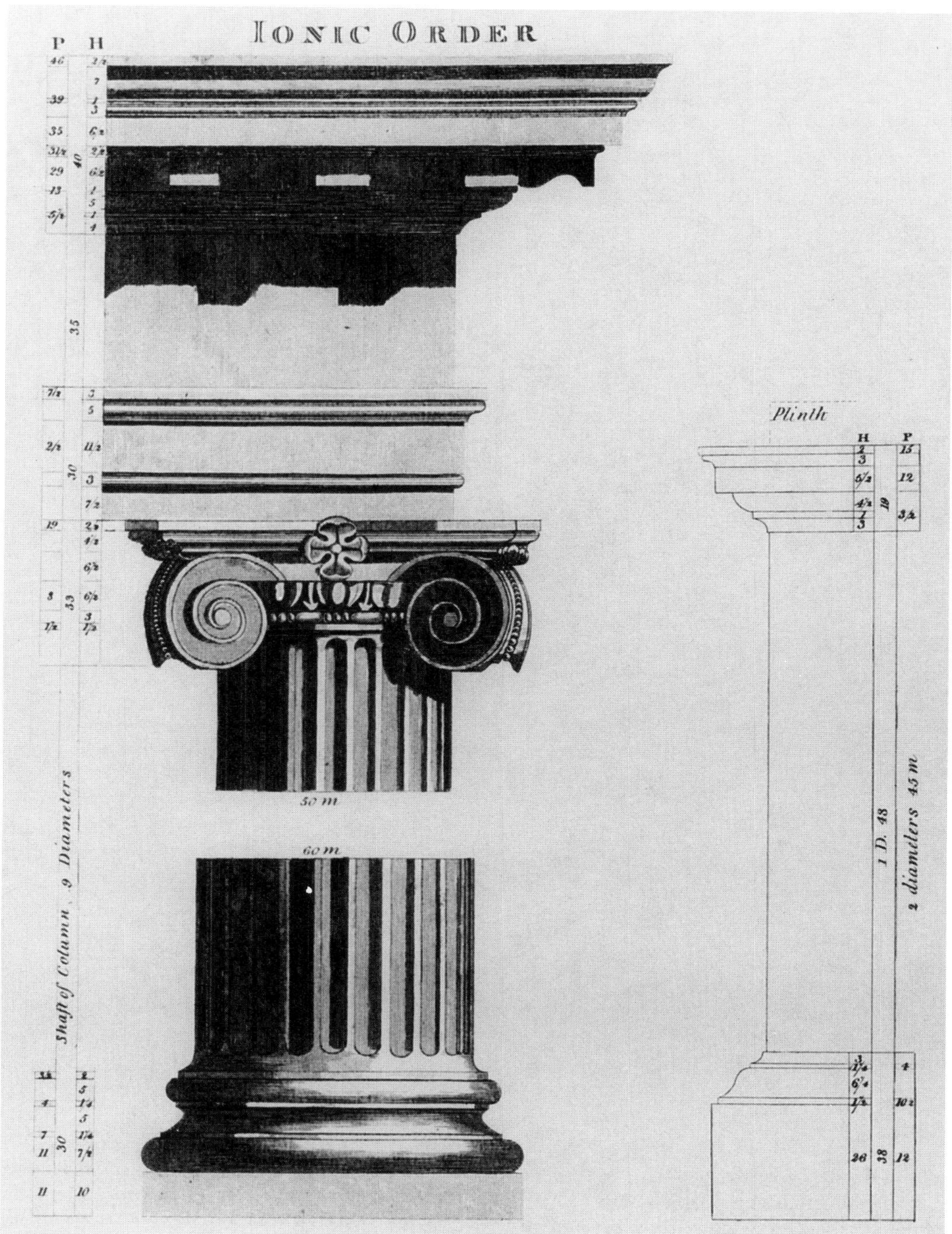

Figure 1. Proportions of Ionic order from Asher Benjamin's *The American Builder's Companion,* 1827 (25). Courtesy of Dover Publications.

made their reputation in the mail-order plan business. The Palliser designs were almost exclusively concerned with style, especially exterior treatments (28).

Palliser's New Cottage Homes and Details, published in 1887, was one of their most popular editions (Figs. 3–5). It is an example of the new pattern book, the menu, that addressed the consumer directly. The authors remark in the prefatory notes that as a result of the wide-scale sale of low cost books, now available to almost anyone, "we find in the rural districts among the buildings erected at the present day almost an entire absence of the vulgar, meaningless, square box-like or barnesque style of Architecture, sometimes pretentious and therefore jigsawed and ginger-breaded to death" (29). For this reason, another volume was produced within which could be found "a more extensive collection of designs of modern domestic Architecture of low and medium cost . . . all drawn out and explained, and with Detail Drawings illustrating the fea-

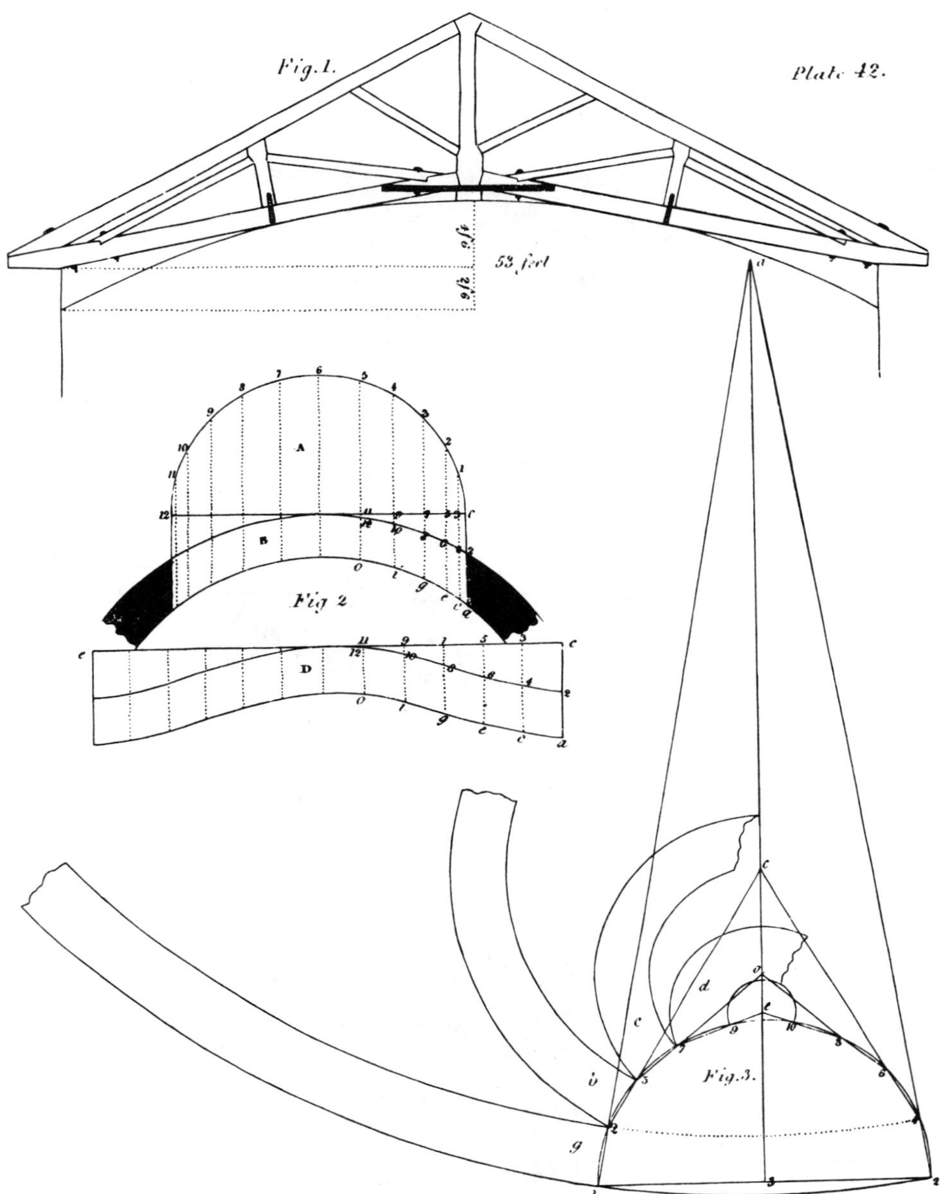

Figure 2. Diagrams for construction of trusses, window openings, and domes from Asher Benjamin's *The American Builder's Companion,* 1827 (25). Courtesy of Dover Publications.

tures which go to make up structures such as are needed to meet the wants of the American people" (29).

The authors noted that the designs they present are simple and without excessive flourish. "The ornament used . . . is of a plain, but at the same time effective order and easy of execution. Very little carved ornament is introduced, and that may be readily produced by any ordinary mechanic." The authors recount how their publications have helped to bring architectural expertise to people living in rural communities, where they would have otherwise "been obliged to plan their own houses, or copy from their neighbors." They also remind the reader that they are not in the "ready-made plan" business, but confer with each customer as to his particular needs. Many other firms, however, offered these services, and the Pallisers warned the buyer to beware (30):

> Most of them . . . put out designs that are very crude, and offer services that would apparently be of a very inferior order and clap-trap generally. Their methods are of the worst order of quackery, making deliberate calculations to mislead the public by issuing pictures, sketches of the imagination, never built, and with impossible costs of construction, given to catch the ignorant, only to prove disappointing to them when tried. Rumor has it that one of these quacks has been scheming to close up all the Architects' offices in the country so as to have a monopoly of the plan business himself, though he is not an architect, but claims to know more than them all.

The Pallisers also assure that professional architects can best serve the client's needs. They ask the client to bear in mind that it requires 7–10 years of study and application to be admitted to practice, and for this reason the architect requires a reasonable fee for his services.

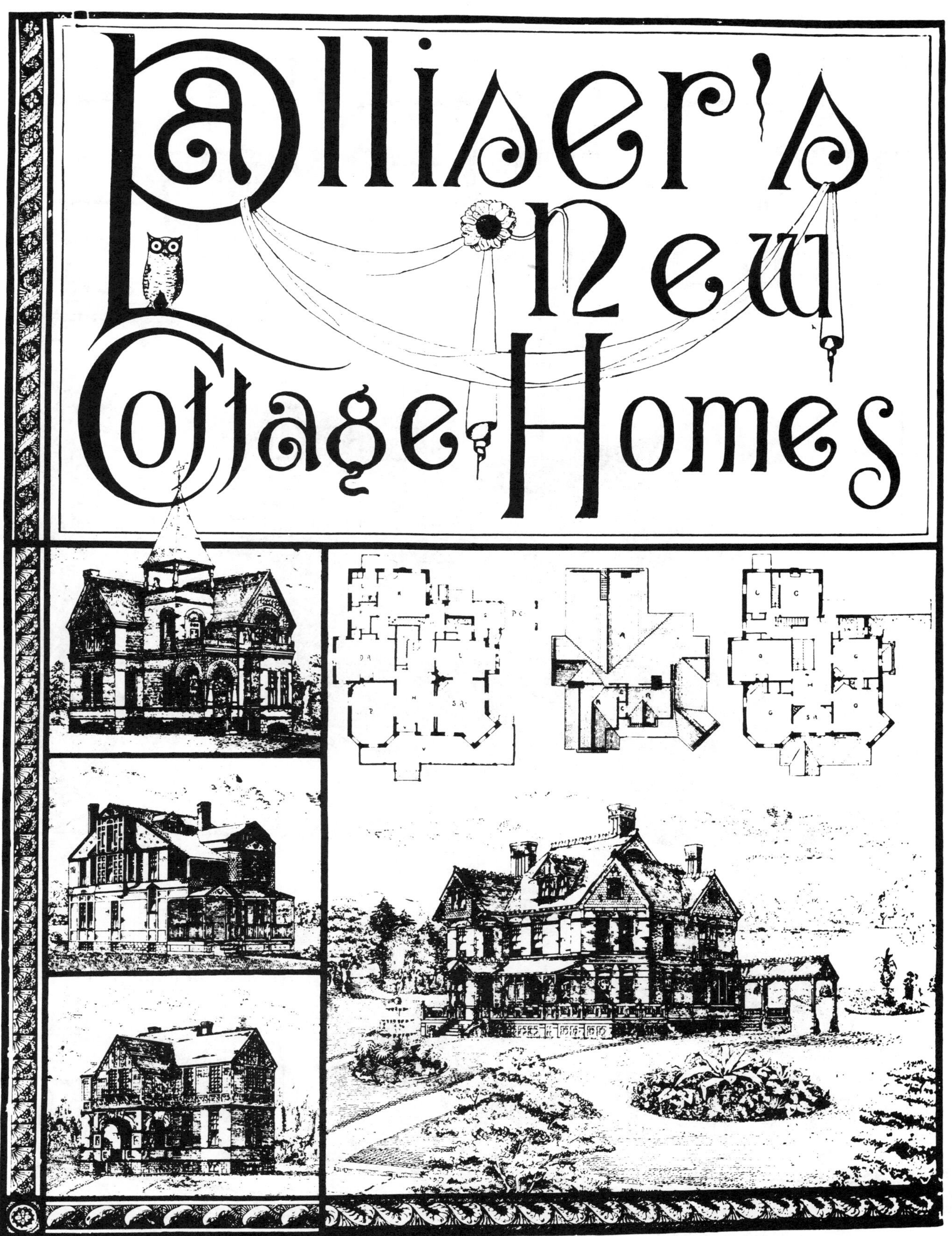

Figure 3. Typical full page showing floor plans, elevations, and perspectives from Palliser, Palliser & Company's *New Cottage Homes and Details,* 1887 (29). Courtesy of DaCapo Press.

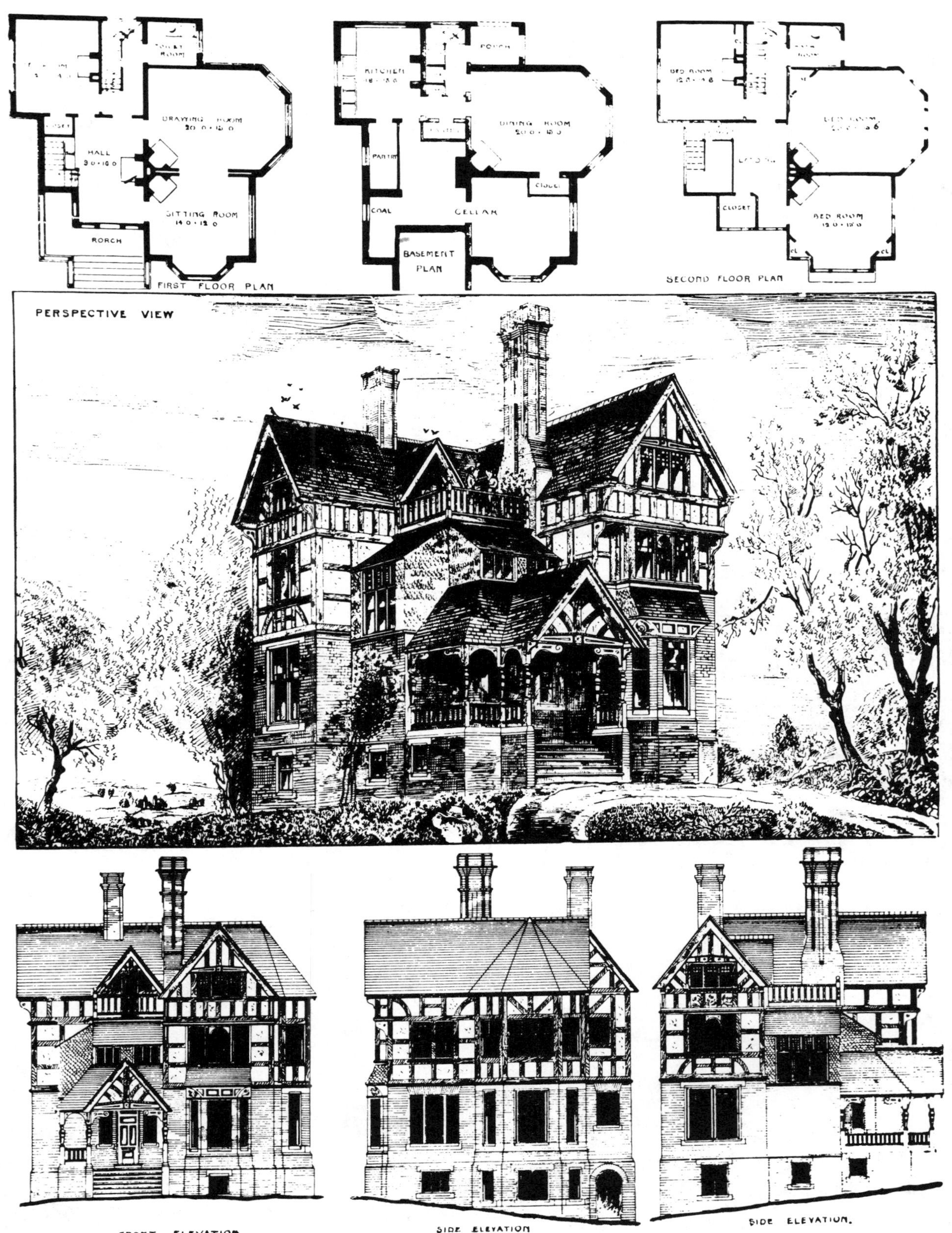

Figure 4. Typical full page showing floor plans, elevations, and perspectives from Palliser, Palliser & Company's *New Cottage Homes and Details,* 1887 (29). Courtesy of DaCapo Press.

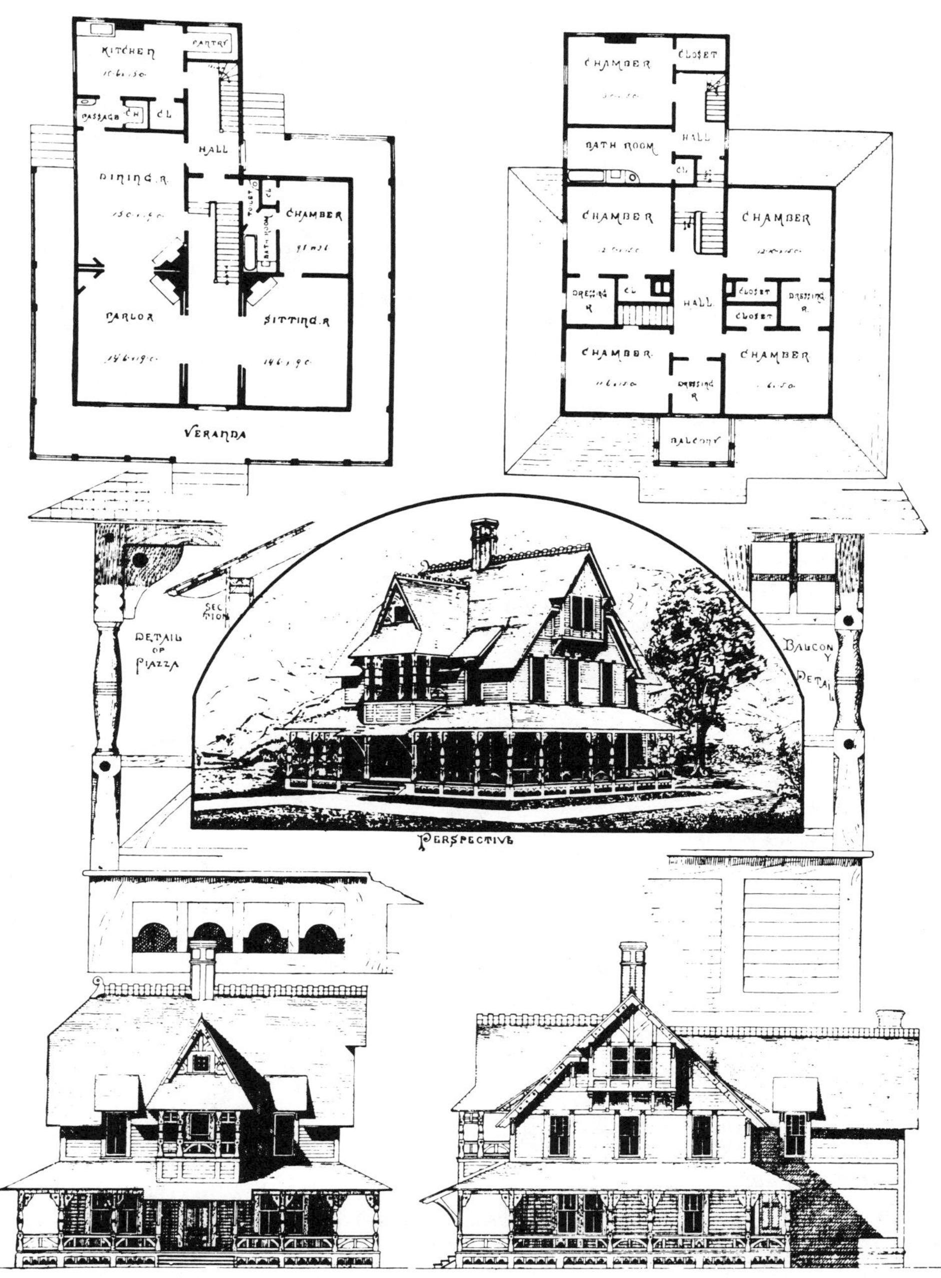

Figure 5. Typical full page showing floor plans, elevations, and perspectives from Palliser, Palliser & Company's *New Cottage Homes and Details,* 1887 (29). Courtesy of DaCapo Press.

Professional service will not be rendered if one pays less than the established fee. "Not a single building, no matter how inexpensive, should be attempted without first having a properly studied and prepared set of plans and specifications setting forth the work to be done so that after regrets may be avoided. Anyone who cannot afford this certainly cannot afford to build" (30).

After these introductory comments, 207 different designs for homes are presented, complete with plans and elevations at 1⁄16 scale, perspectives, and some interior details at 3⁄8 scale (Figs. 3–5). The houses are large and small, of masonry and wood. Each design is accompanied by a description pointing out the advantages of the particular scheme, the interior and exterior finishes, and the nature of the rooms and their arrangement. Designs #89 and #90 are specifically targeted for the U.S. businessman and others possessing considerable wealth. The authors make a particularly morbid point about the necessity of sanitary considerations during design and construction (31):

> Early last spring the elegant mansion of one of New York's wealthiest capitalists, situated on a beautiful hill in New Jersey, was turned into a house of mourning. It had been constructed on the most approved sanitary and scientific principles. Thousands of dollars had been expended in the drainage,

> plumbing, and ventilation. The surroundings were healthful, the air was pure, and yet an epidemic of diphtheria swept away a family of young and beautiful children. It was the theory of the physicians that the house was filled with malaria, which always invites diphtheria, and, skeptical as the father was, he instituted a rigid examination. Every closet, pipe, and drain was found to be perfect, and they were about to give up, baffled, when by accident they examined the furnace fresh-air box, and a few feet away from its opening, in a neighbor's lot, they discovered a mass of putrefying garbage! The mystery was explained. The malaria had found an entrance through the "fresh" air flue, and three loved ones perished because "somebody had blundered!"
>
> Life is a constant struggle for existence, and as the fittest always survives, it is the duty of every man to acquaint himself with the methods of prevention and cure of influences which would hurry him to the grave.

Throughout the book one is treated to lectures on the value of employing an architect when building a home. In one instance, a conversation is recorded between an architect and a man about to build a house, but resistant to the architect's services. The man is finally persuaded, the plans are made, and the house is built, followed by the return of the happy client. "I have learned what an architect's business is," he confesses, "and I want to say that if I ever have occasion to build again, even if it should be nothing more than a chicken-coop, I shall have my plans, specifications, etc., drawn and prepared before starting out with the work" (32).

Following the presentation of designs, there is a section on specifications. These are written as terse instructions for the tradesman. "*Door Bell*—Put a good gong bell on front door with suitable pull, etc., to match other furniture" (33). The carpenter's instructions are quite explicit throughout.

The specifications are followed by a page of instructions for the client who has selected a design and wishes to be furnished with a set of plans suited to his particular needs. The architects request how much the client can afford to spend, the local prices and quality of material and labor, a rough plan of the building lot including north arrow, a description of the surrounding buildings, sizes and uses of rooms needed, orientation of views, direction of prevailing breezes and storms, and other particulars. With this information the architect would remodel the book design to fit the client's needs, consulting with the client until a suitable design was developed. A description of charges for services follows. Finally, steps for bidding, contracting the work, and construction are outlined. The architects supply all drawings to a local builder specified by the client. A word of caution as to the nature of the architect–client relationship is included (33):

> When parties correspond with us in regard to procuring designs, we are always prompt in answering their inquiries; but oft-times people have written us simply to get our ideas and not pay for them. To all such we would say that our time is valuable, and we sincerely wish they would not trouble us. We mention this fact, because we have received scores of letters, and answered them, when the parties really never intended to employ us, but simply steal our ideas. Now our ideas are for sale, and by this means we live, and it is a pleasure as well as a livelihood, to assist people to build artistic, convenient, and comfortable homes. Perhaps if architects were rich—they seldom are—it would be sufficient compensation to them to assist people as far as possible with ideas; but as they are not, they are obliged to combine pleasure and profit in a way it is seldom done, except in architecture.

The pages that follow include contract forms and a full-page advertisement for the firm. Finally, the last 18 pages are devoted to manufacturers of standardized building materials and hardware (Fig. 6) with a note from the architects (34):

> The following pages are devoted to advertising articles of manufacture, which our experience has taught us contain much merit. It is with confidence we therefore recommend them, and we trust your patronage be extended in that direction. As a great favor to us, please mention "Palliser's New Cottage Homes," when corresponding with the parties referred to.

The image of the architect as a competent professional and businessman pervades the Palliser volume. Nowhere is found the personableness of Asher Benjamin's instruction and historic allusions.

STANDARDIZATION AND CONSOLIDATION

The books discussed above and the two works compared reveal the changes that occurred in the way that architecture was practiced in the United States during the nineteenth century. But set within a much larger context, they reflect the transformation of U.S. life as a whole, something that the practice of architecture responded to. Two words that best describe this transformation are standardization and consolidation.

Standardization and its attendant mass production had a tremendous impact on U.S. life in general and architecture in particular. While the early buildings showed personal involvement and invention, the buildings erected in the post-Civil War period were examples of an art that had become a standardized, almost anonymous, craft. Historian Henry Steele Commager writes that "the triumph of standardization over individualism was a memorial to the passing of the old America" of the early 1800s (35).

Diana Waite, architecture historian, notes that standardization brought with it a revolutionary breakthrough in building. Where before this time, building materials had been consistently worked in the same manner—by hand—industrialization brought forth standardized building materials in such profusion that they altered cityscape and countryside alike. Middle to late nineteenth-century catalogs of building elements, from the simplest roofing plate to entire building facades, offer evidence of just how comprehensive the mass production and distribution of standardized building materials had become (36). The introduction of these materials allowed the previously complicated art and craft of building to develop into a trade. Building was simplified to mere assembly (37).

But standardization did not stop with the physical elements that made up buildings. It extended into the design of buildings, and this was the factor that transformed

Figure 6. Advertisement for plumbing and door hardware from Palliser, Palliser & Company's *New Cottage Homes and Details,* 1887 (29). Courtesy of DaCapo Press.

the pattern books of the period. While the early books put little emphasis on standardized plans, such plans became the centerpiece of the books of the late nineteenth century. Exterior treatments as well were presented in a standardized fashion.

The standardization and distribution of all kinds of goods resulted in an emphasis on the material well-being of people during this time. Material progress was translated into increased comfort. Historian Jackson Lears writes that this emphasis on physical comfort and "pleasantness" was due to improvements in transportation technology, which allowed the city dweller to escape the urban chaos and retreat beyond the city's reach, to the suburbs, to a house where central heating and indoor plumbing further insulated him from environmental discomfort, a discomfort that in fact was a product of the very industrialization that allowed his escape (38).

A quality of the later pattern books in contrast to those of an earlier time is their use of perspectives, carefully crosshatched, to present the house's design. This technique gained popularity in the works of Andrew Jackson Downing, Alexander Jackson Davis, and others in the 1840s who signaled a change in the books' focus and audience. Perspective drawing set the house into its carefully landscaped context, giving it a palatial quality, which indeed communicated a feeling of restfulness and repose.

The word consolidation best describes the transformation that was taking place in the cultural world of business and industry during the last decades of the nineteenth century. By consolidating capital, industrialists were moving to consolidate their control over every aspect of the production and distribution of goods. The triumphs of business and industry also lent an air of consent to the entrepreneurial spirit, and served to cast many aspects of daily life into the marketplace.

Others consolidated control over their own form of capital: information. This period saw the advent of professionalization, the centerpiece of which was the control of information and its dispensation. The drive of the architect for consolidation of control over the building process was a counterpart to what his colleagues in other disciplines were accomplishing. Lewis Mumford writes that "by 1890 the frontier had closed, the major resources of the country were under the control of the monopolist; it became more important to consolidate gains than freshly achieve them" (39).

While captains of industry instituted monopolies on oil, steel, coal, and the railroads, practitioners of loosely cohesive crafts moved to monopolize their control as professionals. Many early professional associations were informal, found in taverns and dining clubs. Eventually these gatherings began to restrict membership to those who could show evidence of ability in a field, through experience and accomplishment recognized by the association. In this way status attached itself to professional membership. Codes of ethics were established and associations regulated fee structures and advertising of services. Thus, professional associations offered select members a guarantee of their own competence, defined and enforced rules of professional conduct, curbed or restricted the advertisement of professional services, and restricted sole remuneration for a service to a salary or fee (40). The close of the nineteenth century saw the establishment of 79 professional societies during the 1870s, 121 more during the 1880s, and 45 during the 1890s (41).

But simple proclamation of professional status was not enough. Training was needed to reflect this professional status, and for the architect it was training that would distinguish him from the builder. As architects sought to separate themselves from builders, their training was institutionalized in universities and thus made inaccessible to the public at large. It was no accident that the concept of building "design" became during this time the sole province of a professionally trained architect, something quite removed and different from construction. Sociologist Robert Gutman suggests that building design, which had never been the predominant component of the architect–builder's work, became so only after architecture was ensconced in a university setting, where design and its attendant theory served as a demarcation between the amateur and the professional. Here was the consolidation of the architect's capital: design information. For example, in the Palliser book, the arrangement of rooms according to the needs of the inhabitants and the building's placement on the site was presented as something that only a professionally trained architect could accomplish, where for centuries this had been successfully performed by builders, if not the client himself.

The role of the architect as master of design, arbiter of taste, and professional counselor in domestic matters facilitated the rise of the client–agent relationship between the market and the professional, a market that implored the professional for advice amid the dizzying change brought about by industrialization and urbanization. This role relationship is seen in the profusion of "manner books" during this time, which were used to inform the reader in the proper way in which to dress, behave, and entertain guests. There is evidence that this phenomenon was indeed a reaction to the confusion that permeated daily life as the old rules fell by the wayside (42). At the height of eclecticism in architecture, which corresponded to this time in history, the proper design of a house in a proper style to reflect the social position and aspirations of the expanding middle class could only be arrived at with the help of a professional architect trained in such matters. Through these books, the architect delineated for his client "proper manners" in architecture.

The expansion of the railroads and the nationalization of markets for every kind of mass-produced article had a "commoditizing" effect on many aspects of daily life in the late nineteenth century. The architect's role as dispenser of design transformed design into the architect's marketable commodity, over which he exerted firm control. By placing the design of the house and all its materials and hardware into the category of "marketable commodities," architecture thus became another part of the commercial market system that could ably deliver products around the country. "It matters not whether our clients reside in the States of Connecticut, Massachusetts, or New York, near to us or 3,000 miles away," wrote the Pallisers. "Distance is no obstacle—we can serve them equally as well, as upwards of two thousand of our clients residing in every state and territory in the Union, Canada, Nova Scotia, and the Brazils can testify" (43). Being a commodity also gave architecture the appearance of being just one more consumer product for the expanding middle class, as it had always been for the rich. And an architecture of quality was a marketable asset. As the Pallisers noted, "it should not be forgotten that there is a commercial value to be attached to a well arranged plan and carefully studied grouping of the exterior of the house . . . and the difference between a house of this kind and one of ordinary construction when placed on the market is at once apparent" (44).

With architecture a commodity, it should come as no surprise to find the professional architect taking on the dimension of a businessman during this time. The Pallisers, for example, presented themselves as such and presented their work as the result of many successful business ventures. "Upwards of Two Thousand public and private buildings erected in all parts of the Western World from Special Plans, etc., to meet the requirements of each case," the Pallisers boasted of their work (43). In a letter from a satisfied customer, reprinted in one of the Pallisers' house advertisements, it is stated that "their success in business may be attributed to the fact that they are thoroughly trained and practical Architects, and design the finest buildings and have them erected at the least cost, scrupulously saving every possible dollar" (43). It was this adulation and glorification of big business and the emergence of the successful businessman as hero, as Commager describes it, that marked the end of the nineteenth century with the fall of Tom Sawyer and the rise of Horatio Alger (45).

The consolidation of power was part of the industrialist's far-reaching goal of control or, more precisely, total management. Jackson Lears describes this as the "second Industrial Revolution," distinguished by the businessman's "drive for maximum profits through the adoption of the most efficient forms of organization." Lears characterizes this time as the rationalization of economic life and the marriage of technical expertise to big business (46). The United States was becoming a place where management of industrial processes for profit was more important than the processes themselves or the articles they produced.

As pattern books slowly transformed from repositories of useful information on design and building into presentations of predigested settings for homelife, the architect's attention likewise shifted from the art of building to the business of orchestrating the various processes that resulted in a completed structure. Set within a larger context, the transformation of daily artifacts from individualized visions of the world to professionally approved and successfully marketed versions of standardized, anonymous choice can be seen.

BIBLIOGRAPHY

1. H. Park, *A List of Architectural Books Available in America Before the Revolution,* Hennessey & Ingalls, Inc., Los Angeles, 1973, p. 14.
2. *Ibid.,* p. 14.
3. Ref. 1, p. 15.
4. Ref. 1, p. 18.
5. D. Upton, "Pattern Books and Professionalism," *Winterthur Portfolio* **19,** 109 (Summer/Autumn 1984).
6. J. Quinan, "Asher Benjamin and American Architecture," *Journal of the Society of Architectural Historians* **38,** 245 (Oct. 1979).
7. H. R. Hitchcock, *American Architectural Books,* DaCapo Press, New York, 1976, p. 5.
8. *Ibid.,* p. 94.
9. Ref. 7, p. 12.
10. Ref. 7, pp. 58–59.
11. Ref. 7, p. 58.
12. Ref. 5, p. 118.
13. R. M. Tryon, *Household Manufactures in the United States, 1640–1860,* Augustus M. Kelley, New York, 1966, pp. 243–247.
14. *Ibid.,* p. 259.
15. J. M. Fitch, *American Building: The Historical Forces that Shaped it,* Schocken Books, New York, 1973, p. 50.
16. *Ibid.,* p. 13.
17. H. Greeley and others, *The Great Industries of the United States,* J. B. Burr & Hyde, Hartford, Conn., 1873, p. 40.
18. H. H. Saylor, *The AIA's First Hundred Years,* The American Institute of Architects, Washington, D.C., 1957, p. 11.
19. *Ibid.,* p. 110.
20. Ref. 7, pp. 98–99.
21. Ref. 7, pp. 14–15.
22. Ref. 7, pp. 75–76.
23. Ref. 6, p. 244.
24. W. Morgan, "Introduction" in A. Benjamin, *The American Builder's Companion,* 1827, reprint, Dover Publications, New York, 1969, p. viii.
25. A. Benjamin, *The American Builder's Companion,* 1827, reprint with introduction by W. Morgan, Dover Publications, New York, 1969.
26. *Ibid.,* p. 35.
27. Ref. 25, p. 47.
28. P. Poore, *The Old House Journal* **8**(12), 190 (Dec. 1980).
29. G. Palliser and C. Palliser, *Palliser's New Cottage Homes and Details,* 1887, reprint, DaCapo Press, New York, 1975.
30. *Ibid.,* "Introductory."
31. Ref. 29, plates 31 and 32.
32. Ref. 29, plate 58.
33. Ref. 29, "Specifications."
34. Ref. 29, "A Few Words for Our Advertisers."
35. H. S. Commager, *The American Mind,* Yale University Press, New Haven, Conn., 1950, p. 21.
36. D. S. Waite, *Architectural Elements: The Technological Revolution,* Pyne Press, Princeton, N.J., 1972, p. 5.
37. *Ibid.,* p. 6.
38. J. Lears, *No Place of Grace,* Pantheon Books, New York, 1981, pp. 11–12.
39. L. Mumford, *Sticks and Stones,* W. W. Norton & Co., New York, 1934, p. 124.
40. H. M. Vollmer and D. L. Mills, *Professionalization,* Prentice-Hall, Englewood Cliffs, N.J., 1966, p. 156.
41. J. W. Ward in L. B. Holland, ed., *Who Designs America?,* Anchor Books, New York, 1966, p. 70.
42. S. Bronner, *Winterthur Portfolio* **18,** 61–62 (Winter/Spring 1984).
43. Ref. 29, "Palliser, Palliser & Co., Architects."
44. Ref. 29, "Prefatory."
45. Ref. 39, p. 40.
46. Ref. 42, p. 9.

See also ARCHITECTURAL PRESS, U.S.; LITERATURE OF ARCHITECTURE

MICHAEL J. CROSBIE, PHD
Branford, Connecticut

A version of this article appeared in *Material Culture* **17**(1)(1985).

PAVING SYSTEMS, ASPHALT

HISTORY OF ASPHALT

The modern use of asphalt as a bonding material in pavement construction began in the late 1800s. The term asphalt during these early years included a multitude of meanings. Trinidad natural asphalt, pitch, coal tar, rock asphalt, and numerous proprietary combinations were designated as asphalt. Additionally, there were numerous and varied methods of applying asphalt/aggregate paving materials. Virtually no set standards existed for any phase of the design, construction, or even material testing of asphalt pavements. However, this changed early in the twentieth century as the general knowledge of the behavior of asphalt mixes grew and as petroleum-based asphalts became available. The paving needs of the United States and the world had grown far beyond the availability of natural asphalts. Petroleum asphalts offered a consistent product that could supply the rapidly growing transportation needs of the country.

In 1902, only 18,000 metric tons of asphalt were refined from petroleum in the United States, but by 1912 the nation was consuming nearly 500,000 metric tons of petroleum asphalt. Petroleum asphalt had become the dominant source of asphalt to the virtual exclusion of all other types.

Today, the terms asphalt and petroleum asphalt are synonymous. In the United States more than 28 million metric tons of asphalt are consumed annually. This amount reaches nearly 100 million metric tons worldwide. Asphalts are used for paving, roofing systems, and hundreds of miscellaneous industrial uses. The main use of asphalt, approximately 80% of the total annual usage, is for asphalt pavement. Asphalt is used in a multitude of paving applications. These uses include airport runways, taxiways, and aprons; asphalt paving blocks; bridge deck surfacings; curbs and gutters; driveways; drainage ditches; flooring for warehouses and garages; hydraulic liners; parking lots; railroad track underlayments; sidewalks; and, the major use, for highways, roads, and streets. Worldwide, asphalt pavement is the predominant road-building material; in

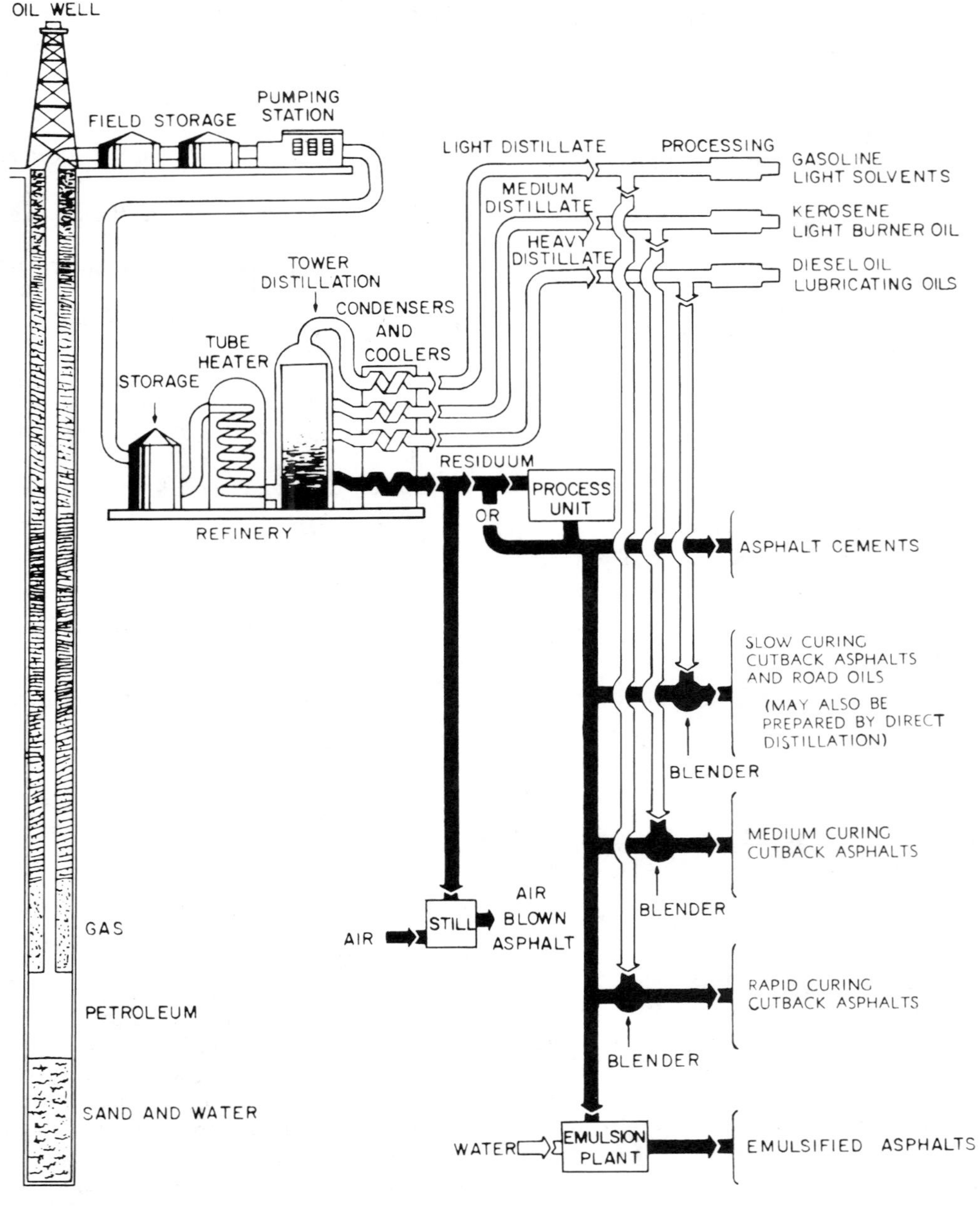

Figure 1. Petroleum asphalt flow chart. Courtesy of the Asphalt Institute.

the United States more than 90% of the highways, roads, and streets are paved with asphalt.

ASPHALT PETROLEUM REFINING

Asphalt is a black cementing material that varies widely in consistency from solid to semisolid at ambient air temperatures. When heated, asphalt softens and eventually can liquefy, which allows it to coat aggregate particles during the production of hot paving mixtures. Many persons simply refer to asphalt as bitumen, since it is composed largely of the bitumen hydrocarbons. However, the correct terminology is asphalt or asphalt cement. Asphalt is a natural constituent of most petroleums, in which it exists in solution. The crude petroleum is refined by distillation, a process in which various fractions (products) are separated out of the crude. Distillation is accomplished by raising the temperature of the crude petroleum in stages. Different fractions separate at different temperatures. The lighter fractions, such as gasoline, kerosene, and diesel fuel, are separated by simple distillation. Some heavier distillates can be separated only by a combination of heating and applying a vacuum.

Asphalt may be produced by vacuum distillation at a temperature of about 480°C. This temperature may vary somewhat, depending on the crude petroleum being refined or the grade produced.

Figure 1 is a schematic illustration of a typical refinery. It shows the flow of petroleum during the refining process. The degree of control allowed by modern refinery equipment allows the production of asphalts with specific characteristics suited to specific applications. As a result, different asphalts are produced for paving, roofing, and other special uses. To produce asphalts that meet specific requirements, refiners often blend crude petroleums of various types together before processing. Blending allows refiners to combine crudes that contain asphalts of varying characteristics in such a way that the final product will have exactly the characteristics required by the asphalt user.

ASPHALT CLASSIFICATION AND PROPERTIES

Asphalt is of particular interest to the engineer because it is a strong cement, readily adhesive, highly waterproof, and durable. It is a plastic substance that imparts controllable flexibility to paving mixtures of mineral aggregates with which it usually combines. Also, it is highly resistant to the action of most acids, alkalies, and salts. Asphalt may be readily liquefied by applying heat or by dissolving it in petroleum solvents of varying volatility or by emulsifying it.

Asphalts used for paving are classified into three general types: asphalt cement, emulsified asphalt, and cutback asphalt.

Asphalt cement is a specially prepared petroleum asphalt of a precise quality and consistency. It is used in the manufacture of asphalt pavement and provides the bonding property that holds aggregate materials together. Asphalt cements are graded according to three different systems: viscosity, viscosity after aging, and penetration. Each system contains several different grades, each of varying consistency. The asphalt viscosity system is the most widely used. Table 1, from the American Association of State Highway and Transportation Officials (AASHTO) standard specification M 226 [also the American Society

Table 1. Requirements for Asphalt Cement Graded by Viscosity[a]

Test	Viscosity Grade					
	AC-2.5	AC-5	AC-10	AC-20	AC-30	AC-40
Viscosity, 60°C, poises	250 ± 50	500 ± 100	1000 ± 200	2000 ± 400	3000 ± 600	4000 ± 800
Viscosity, 135°C, Cs-minimum	125	175	250	300	350	400
Penetration, 25°C, 100 g, 5 sec-minimum	220	140	80	60	50	40
Flash point, COC, C-minimum	162	177	219	232	232	232
Solubility in trichlorethylene, percent-minimum	99.0	99.0	99.0	99.0	99.0	99.0
Tests on residue from thin-film oven test:						
Loss on heating, percent-maximum (optional)		1.0	0.5	0.5	0.5	0.5
Viscosity, 60°C, poises-maximum	1000	2000	4000	8000	12,000	16,000
Ductility, 25°C, 5 cm/min, cm-minimum	100	100	75	50	40	25
Spot test (when and as specified) with:						
Standard naphtha solvent	Negative for all grades					
Naphtha-xylene-solvent, % xylene	Negative for all grades					
Heptane-xylene-solvent, % xylene	Negative for all grades					

[a] Courtesy of the Asphalt Institute.

for Testing and Materials (ASTM) D 3381], illustrates this system. In practice, many government agencies have modified this table to meet their specific needs. In the viscosity system, the poise is the standard unit of measurement for absolute viscosity. The higher the number of poises, the more viscous the asphalt. AC-2.5 (asphalt cement with a viscosity of 250 poises at 60°C) is referred to as a relatively "soft" asphalt. AC-40 (asphalt cement with a viscosity of 4000 poises at the same temperature) is known as a "hard" asphalt.

Less widely used is a system of grading based on the viscosity of aged asphalt samples. This system is known

Table 2. Asphalt Types and Uses[a]

	Asphalt Cements														
	Viscosity Graded Original					Viscosity Graded Residue					Penetration Graded				
Type of Construction	AC-40	AC-20	AC-10	AC-5	AC-2.5	AR-16000	AR-8000	AR-4000	AR-2000	AR-1000	40-50	60-70	85-100	120-150	200-300
															Asphalt—Aggregate Mixture
Asphalt Concrete and Hot Laid Plant Mix															
Pavement Base and Surfaces															
Highways	x	x	x	x	x[h]	x	x	x	x	x[h]	x	x	x	x	x[h]
Airports		x	x	x			x	x				x	x	x	
Parking Areas	x	x	x			x	x	x			x	x	x		
Driveways		x	x				x	x				x	x		
Curbs		x					x					x			
Industrial Floors	x	x				x	x				x	x			
Blocks	x					x					x				
Groins	x	x				x	x				x	x			
Dam Facings	x	x				x	x				x	x			
Canal and Reservoir Linings	x	x				x	x				x	x			
Cold-Laid Plant Mix[k]															
Pavement Base and Surfaces															
Open-Graded Aggregate															
Well-Graded Aggregate															
Patching, Immediate Use															
Patching, Stockpile															
Mixed-in-Place (Road Mix)[k]															
Pavement Base and Surfaces															
Open-Graded Aggregate															
Well-Graded Aggregate															
Sand					x										x
Sandy Soil					x										x
Patching, Immediate Use															
Patching, Stockpile															
Recycling															
Hot-Mix			x	x	x			x	x	x			x	x	x
Cold-Mix[k]					x					x					x
															Asphalt-Aggregate Applications
Surface Treatments															
Single Surface Treatment				x	x									x	x
Multiple Surface Treatment				x	x									x	x
Aggregate Seal				x	x				x					x	x
Sand Seal															
Slurry Seal															
															Asphalt Applications
Surface Treatment															
Fog Seal															
Prime Coat															
Tack Coat															
Dust Laying															
Mulch															
Membrane															
Canal and Reservoir Linings	x										x				
Embankment Envelopes	x	x				x	x				x	x			
Crack Filling															
Asphalt Pavements															
Portland Cement Concrete Pavements	x[e]					x[e]					x[e]				

[a] Courtesy of the Asphalt Institute.
[b] Mixed-in Prime Only.
[c] Diluted with water.
[d] Slurry mix.
[e] Rubber asphalt compounds.
[f] Diluted with water by the manufacturer.

as the AR ("aged residue" system) and is predominant in several Western states in the United States. As with viscosity-graded asphalt, the properties of these grades are set forth by AASHTO in their standard specification M 226 (or ASTM D 3381).

The third method of grading asphalt is by penetration testing. A standardized test is used that measures the depth that a special test needle sinks into an asphalt sample. The distance that the standardized needle penetrates the sample is measured in tenths of a millimeter. Each tenth of a millimeter penetration is known as a "pen." Asphalts in this system are of grades 40/50 pen being

Emulsified Asphalts[j]														Cutback-Asphalts								
Anionic								Cationic						Medium Curing (MC)[i]					Slow Curing (SC)			
RS-1	RS-2	MS-1, HFMS-1	MS-2, HFMS-2	MS-2h, HFMS-2h	HFMS-2s	SS-1	SS-1h	CRS-1	CRS-2	CMS-2	CMS-2h	CSS-1	CSS-1h	30	70	250	800	3000	70	250	800	3000
			x	x						x	x											
					x	x	x					x	x			x	x	x		x	x	x
						x	x									x	x				x	
																x	x			x	x	
			x	x						x	x											
																	x	x			x	x
					x	x	x					x	x			x	x			x	x	
					x	x	x					x	x		x	x	x					
					x	x	x					x	x			x	x					
					x	x	x					x	x			x	x				x	
																x	x			x	x	
			x	x	x	x	x			x	x	x	x									
x	x							x	x													
x	x							x	x													
x	x	x						x	x													
x	x	x						x	x													
						x	x					x	x									
		x^{f}				x^{c}	x^{c}					x^{c}	x^{c}									
			$x^{b,g}$			x^{b}	x^{b}			x^{b}		x^{b}	x^{b}	x	x	x						
x						x^{c}	x^{c}	x				x^{c}	x^{c}									
		x^{f}				x^{c}	x^{c}					x^{c}	x^{c}	x	x	x			x	x		
						x^{c}	x^{c}															
						x^{d}	x^{d}					x^{d}	x^{d}									

[g] MS-2 only.
[h] For use in cold climates.
[i] Before using MC's for spray applications (other than prime coats) check with local pollution control agency.
[j] Emulsified asphalts shown are AASHTO and ASTM grades and may not include all grades produced in all geographical areas.
[k] Evaluation of emulsified asphalt-aggregate system required to determine the proper grade of emulsified asphalt to use.

the hardest to 200/300 pen being the softest. This system was historically the first grading method for asphalts and is still used somewhat around the world. Particular properties of each grade are described in AASHTO M 20 (or ASTM D946).

Emulsified asphalts are emulsions of asphalt cement and water that contain a small amount of a chemical agent that allows these two dissimilar materials to mix. The purpose of this mixing is to allow asphalt cement to be liquefied at ambient temperatures. In this form the asphalt can be sprayed or poured without heating. Emulsified asphalts are designated as slow set (SS), medium set (MS), and rapid set (RS). Their properties are set forth in AASHTO 140 (or ASTM D977). These indicate the setting rate at which emulsified asphalt cures. Once applied, the water separates from the asphalt and evaporates into the air, thus leaving a coating of asphalt cement.

Cutback asphalts function similarly to emulsified asphalt. However, in this case, asphalt cement and a petroleum distillate are blended together. Cutbacks are designated as medium cure (MC) or slow cure (SC). Their specific properties are set forth in AASHTO M 81/82 (or ASTM D 2027/2028).

All these classes of asphalt have particular uses in asphalt paving. Table 2 summarizes these uses and the particular classes and grades of asphalt suited for these uses.

ASPHALT PAVING MIXTURES

Types

Asphalt paving mixtures can be generally divided into two main types. These types are asphalt concrete mixtures and cold mixtures.

Asphalt concrete mixtures are by far the most common paving mixtures currently in use. In the United States alone, it is estimated that more than 300,000,000 metric tons of this type of paving material are produced annually. This material is a high quality, thoroughly controlled hot mixture of asphalt cement and well-graded, high quality aggregate, adequately compacted into a uniform dense mass.

Asphalt concrete may be designed and produced from a wide range of aggregate blends, each suited to a specific use. The mixes with larger maximum size aggregates are usually used for base layers, the smaller-sized aggregate mixes for surface layers. The aggregate composition of each particular mix varies from coarse (large) size to fine (smaller) size aggregate particles. To provide a dense gradation, certain proportions of differing sized aggregates are needed. Many different compositions are specified throughout the world, the ones in any given locality generally being those that have proved adequate through long usage; in most cases, these should be used. For a general classification of mix compositions, however, consideration might be given to the mix designations shown in Table 3. This chart contains five general mix designations, ranging from the largest 37.5 mm (1½ in.) maximum size mix to a somewhat finer 9.5 mm (⅜ in.) size mix. The grading and asphalt content of these mixes agree, in general, with overall practices in many areas. The amount of asphalt required for any paving mixture should be determined by appropriate laboratory mix design testing or on the basis of past experience with similar mixtures or by a combination of both.

Another type of mix used for a special purpose is an open-graded asphalt mix. This asphalt-aggregate mixture is generally hot, but unlike the dense-graded mix, it does not contain a continuous gradation of various sized aggregates. An open-graded mix eliminates certain intermediate aggregate sizes and thus results in a final pavement that has considerably more air voids than a typical dense-graded asphalt pavement. The special purpose facilitated by this pavement is one of surface drainage. By quickly allowing rain to drain from the pavement surface, the skid resistance/traction of the pavement is maintained. These open-graded pavements are specially designed and

Table 3. Typical Composition of Hot-Mix Asphalt Concrete[a]

Sieve Size	37.5 mm	25.0 mm	19.0 mm	12.5 mm	9.5 mm
	Total Percent Passing (by Weight)				
50 mm	100				
37.5 mm	90–100	100			
25.0 mm		90–100	100		
19.0 mm	56–80		90–100	100	
12.5 mm		56–80		90–100	100
9.5 mm			56–80		90–100
4.75 mm	23–53	29–59	35–65	44–74	55–85
2.36 mm	15–41	19–45	23–49	28–58	32–67
1.18 mm					
600 μm					
300 μm	4–16	5–17	5–19	5–21	7–23
150 μm					
75 μm	0–5	1–7	2–8	2–10	2–10
Asphalt cement weight percent of total mixture	3–8	3–9	4–10	4–22	5–12

[a] Courtesy of the Asphalt Institute.

placed over dense-graded asphalt concrete pavements. Generally, open-graded surface pavements are placed in thicknesses of 20–25 mm (¾–1 in.).

A second general type of asphalt mixture is cold mix. Asphalt cold mix is a combination of unheated mineral aggregate and emulsified or cutback asphalt. There are two types of cold mixes: plant-mixed and mixed-in-place. Plant-mixed cold mixes are produced in plants that permit close control of the production process, from material proportioning through mixing. Spreading and compacting is done with conventional equipment. Mixed-in-place cold mixes, on the other hand, are produced at the paving site by means of motor graders or special in-place mixing equipment.

Cold mixes are used to a much lesser degree than hot mixes. However, they can be used on virtually all pavements as base material or for low-volume roads. They are seldom used for surface layers in urban and other heavy traffic areas.

Cold mixes have several advantages. They are versatile and economical. However, cold mix placement is limited by weather conditions and should not be done when temperatures are under 10°C.

Mixture Properties

Asphalt pavements function well because they are designed to possess certain desirable properties. A number of properties contribute to the quality of asphalt concrete pavements. These include stability, durability, impermeability, workability, flexibility, fatigue resistance, and skid resistance. Ensuring that an asphalt paving mixture has each of these properties is a major goal of a mix design.

Stability of an asphalt pavement is its ability to resist shoving and rutting under loads. A stable pavement maintains its shape and smoothness under repeated loading; an unstable pavement develops ruts (channels), ripples (washboarding or corrugation), and other signs of shifting of the mixture. In designing a mixture, stability requirements should be set high enough to handle traffic adequately, but not higher than traffic conditions require. Too high a stability value produces a pavement that is too stiff and possibly less durable than desired.

The stability of a mixture depends on internal friction and cohesion. Internal friction among the aggregate particles (interparticle friction) is related to aggregate characteristics such as shape and surface texture. Cohesion results from the bonding ability of the asphalt. A proper degree of both internal friction and cohesion in a mix prevents the aggregate particles from being moved past each other by the forces exerted by traffic. In general, the more angular the shape of the aggregate particles and the rougher their surface texture, the higher the stability of the mix will be. The binding force of cohesion increases with increasing loading (traffic) rate. Cohesion also increases as the viscosity of the asphalt increases, or as the pavement temperature decreases. Additionally, cohesion will increase with increasing asphalt content, up to a certain point. Past that point, increasing asphalt content creates too thick a film on the aggregate particles, resulting in loss of interparticle friction.

Durability of an asphalt pavement is its ability to resist weather and traffic effects such as aging-associated changes in the asphalt, disintegration of the aggregate, and stripping of the asphalt film from the aggregate. Generally, durability of a mixture can be enhanced by three methods: using maximum asphalt content, using a dense gradation of stripping-resistant aggregate, and designing and compacting the mixture for maximum impermeability.

Maximum asphalt content increases durability because thick asphalt films do not age and harden as rapidly as do thin ones. Consequently, the asphalt retains its original characteristics longer. Also, maximum asphalt content effectively seals off a greater percentage of interconnected air voids in the pavement, making it difficult for water and air to penetrate. Of course, a certain percentage of air voids must be left open in the pavement to allow for expansion of the asphalt in hot weather. A dense-graded aggregate provides closer contact among aggregate particles. This enhances the impermeability of the mixture. A sound, tough aggregate provides durability by resisting disintegration under traffic loading. Stripping-resistant aggregate resists the action of water and traffic, which tend to strip the asphalt film off aggregate particles and lead to raveling of the pavement. Under some conditions, the resistance of a mixture to stripping can be increased by the use of antistripping additives or a mineral filler such as hydrated lime.

Impermeability is the resistance of an asphalt pavement to the passage of air and water into or through it. This characteristic is related to the void content of the compacted mixture, and much of the mix design effort is directed at ensuring a proper amount of air voids. Even though this total void content is an indication of the potential for passage of air and water through a pavement, the character of these voids is also important. Size of the voids, interconnection, and the access to the surface of the pavement all enhance the degree of impermeability.

Voids must be established at a proper level in the mix design. Typically, for a dense-graded asphalt concrete the voids are set at 3–5% during the laboratory design and should not exceed 8% after the actual paving material is placed and compacted.

Workability describes the ease with which a paving mixture can be placed and compacted. Mixtures with good workability are easy to place and compact; those with poor workability are difficult to place and compact. Workability can be improved by changing mix design parameters, aggregate types, and/or gradation.

Harsh mixtures (mixtures containing a high percentage of coarse aggregate) have a tendency to segregate during handling and also may be difficult to compact. Workability is especially important where hand placement and raking (luting) around manhole covers, sharp curves, and other obstacles are required. This is also particularly critical in the placement of driveways and parking lots. It is important that mixtures used in such areas are sufficiently workable. However, a mix can be too workable. These are referred to as tender mixes. Tender mixes are too unstable to place and compact properly. They are often caused by too much medium-sized sand and smooth, rounded aggregate particles and/or too much moisture in the mix.

Although not normally a major contributor to workability problems, asphalt cement does have some effect on workability. Because the temperature of the mix affects the viscosity of the asphalt, too low a temperature will make a mix unworkable, too high a temperature may make it tender.

Flexibility is the ability of an asphalt pavement to adjust to gradual settlements and movements in the subgrade without cracking. Because virtually all subgrades either settle (under loading) or rise (from soil expansion), flexibility is a desirable characteristic for all asphalt pavements.

A somewhat more open-graded mix with high asphalt content is generally more flexible than a dense-graded, low asphalt content mix. Sometimes the need for flexibility conflicts with stability requirements, so that trade-offs have to be made.

Fatigue resistance is the pavement's resistance to repeated bending under wheel loads. Air voids, asphalt content, and asphalt viscosity have a significant effect on fatigue resistance. As the percentage of air voids in the pavement increases, either by design or lack of compaction, pavement fatigue life (the length of time during which an in-service pavement is adequately fatigue resistant) is drastically shortened. Likewise, a pavement containing asphalt that has aged and hardened significantly will have reduced resistance to fatigue.

The thickness and strength characteristics of the pavement and the supporting capability of the subgrade also have a great deal to do with determining pavement life and preventing load-associated cracking. Thicker, well-supported pavements do not bend as much under loading as do thin or poorly supported pavements. Therefore, they have longer fatigue lives.

Skid resistance is the ability of an asphalt surface to minimize skidding or slipping of vehicle tires, particularly when wet. For good skid resistance, tire treads must be able to maintain contact with the aggregate particles instead of riding on a film of water on the pavement surface.

A rough pavement surface with many little peaks and valleys will have greater skid resistance than a smooth surface. Best skid resistance is obtained with rough-textured aggregate. Special open-graded surface asphalt paving mixes also have been designed to ensure good skid resistance for high-speed traffic. Besides having a rough surface, the aggregates must resist polishing (smoothing) under traffic. Calcareous aggregates polish more easily than siliceous aggregates. Unstable mixtures that tend to rut or bleed (flush asphalt to the surface) also present serious skid-resistance problems.

Mix Design

In an asphalt paving mixture, asphalt and aggregate are blended together in precise proportions. The relative proportions of these materials determine the physical properties of the mix and ultimately how the mix will perform as a finished pavement. The most common method for determining suitable proportions of asphalt and aggregate in a mixture is the Marshall method of mix design. Aspects of the Marshall Method are generally outlined in ASTM D1559. However, details of conducting an actual test and some limiting criteria are set forth in the Asphalt Institute publication *Mix Design Methods for Asphalt Concrete* (MS-2) and will be discussed in this section.

The Marshall method uses standard test specimens 64 mm (2½ in.) high and 102 mm (4 in.) in diameter. A series of specimens, each containing the same aggregate blend but varying in asphalt content, is prepared using specific procedures to heat and mix the asphalt-aggregate mixtures. The series of mix specimens is then compacted by dropping a special compaction hammer onto the specimen a prescribed number of impacts or "blows." A density–voids analysis and a stability flow test of the compacted test specimens are two principal features of this mix design method.

The Marshall stability value is a measurement of the load under which the specimen fails. During the Marshall stability test a continuously increasing load is applied to the specimen seated in a metal frame. The load at failure is the Marshall stability value. Because Marshall stability indicates a type of mix resistance to deformation, there is a tendency to think of it as a strength measurement of the material, and that, if a certain stability value is good, a higher value would be even better. This is not correct. Thus, extremely high stability often is obtained at the expense of durability. Stability values are not the only variable to consider, but rather must be established in conjunction with the other mix variables, such as air voids, density, and flow, as well as the mix characteristics previously discussed.

Marshall flow, measured in 0.25-mm increments, represents the total deformation of the specimen (Fig. 2). A flow meter is used to determine specimen deformation that occurs during Marshall testing. The deformation is a decrease in the vertical diameter of the specimen. Mixes that have very low flow values and abnormally high Marshall stability values are considered too brittle and rigid for typical pavement use. Those with high flow values

Figure 2. Marshall mix design specimen with flow meter. Courtesy of the Asphalt Institute.

are considered too plastic and have a tendency to distort easily under traffic loads.

On completion of the stability and flow tests, a density and voids analysis (air voids and voids in mineral aggregate) is performed for each series of test specimens. The air voids are the small pockets of air between the asphalt-coated aggregate particles. The percent air voids are calculated from the bulk specific gravity of each compacted specimen and the maximum specific gravity of the paving mixture (no voids). The latter is calculated from the specific gravities of the asphalt and aggregate in the mix, with an appropriate allowance made for the amount of asphalt absorbed by the aggregate. The bulk specific gravity of compacted specimens are determined by weighing specimens in air and immersed in water. The average unit weight for each sample is determined by multiplying the bulk specific gravity of the mix by 1000 kg/m^3.

The voids in the mineral aggregate, VMA, are defined as the intergranular void space between the aggregate particles in a compacted paving mixture that includes the air voids and the effective asphalt content, expressed as a percent of the total volume. The VMA is calculated on the basis of the bulk specific gravity of the aggregate and is expressed as a percentage of the bulk volume of the compacted paving mixture. Therefore, the VMA can be calculated by subtracting the volume of the aggregate determined by its bulk specific gravity from the bulk volume of the compacted paving mixture.

To understand the characteristics of each specimen in a test series, laboratory technicians plot the Marshall test results on charts and graphs. By studying the charts, they can determine which specimen in the series best meets all the criteria for the finished pavement. The proportions of asphalt and aggregate in that specimen become the proportions used in the final mixture. Figure 3 shows five Marshall test result charts. Test values are plotted on each chart. The values are represented by dots. The first chart shows the Marshall stability values; the second the Marshall flow values; the third the unit weights (densities); the fourth the percentages of air voids; and the fifth the percentages of voids in the mineral aggregate. On each chart, the dots representing the values are connected by lines forming a smooth curve. Using the plotted data of test results, design criteria for a single optimum, best possible asphalt content can be selected. Table 4 contains some typical design criteria for the Marshall Method as suggested by the Asphalt Institute.

The foregoing discussion provides a general overview

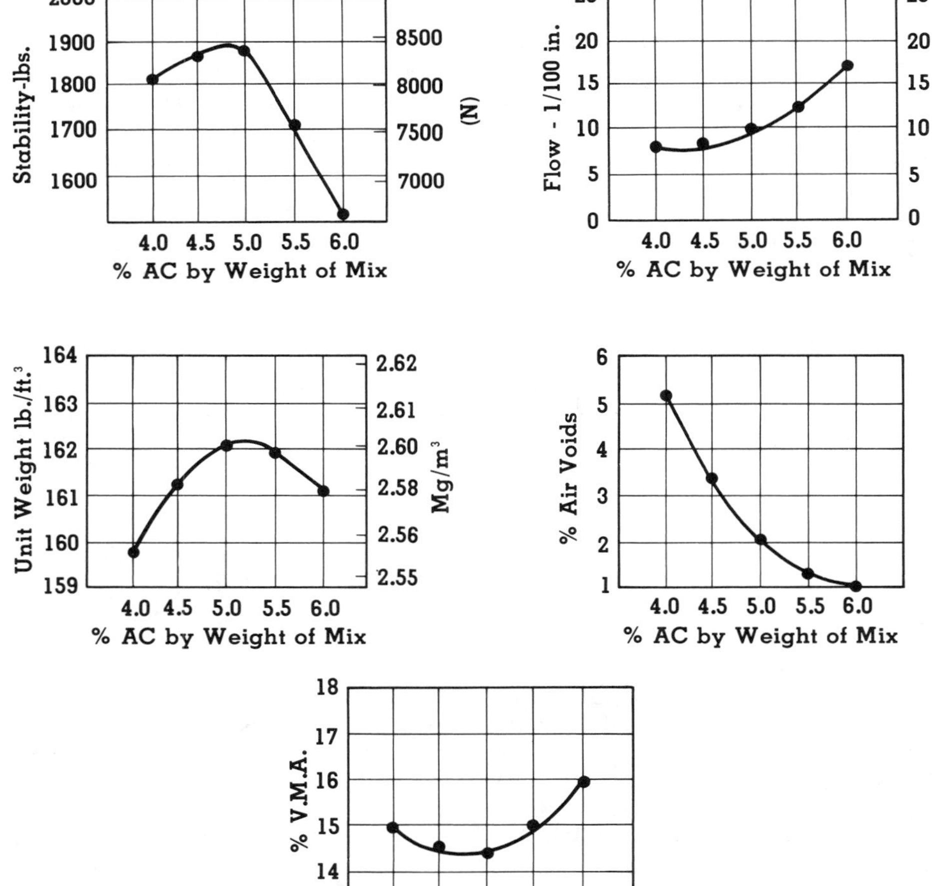

Figure 3. Example plotted curves showing test results for a series of five Marshall specimens. Courtesy of the Asphalt Institute.

Table 4. Design Criteria, Marshall Mix Design Method[a]

Marshall Method Mix Criteria	Light Traffic Surface and Base Min.	Light Traffic Surface and Base Max.	Medium Traffic Surface and Base Min.	Medium Traffic Surface and Base Max.	Heavy Traffic Surface and Base Min.	Heavy Traffic Surface and Base Max.
Compaction, number of blows each end of specimen	35		50		75	
Stability, N	3336		5338		8006	
Flow, 0.25 mm	8	18	8	16	8	14
Percent air voids	3	5	3	5	3	5
Percent air voids in mineral aggregate (VMA)	(Minimum values vary with nominal maximum particle size)					

[a] Courtesy of the Asphalt Institute.

of the Marshall method of mix design, equipment, methods, and appropriate guideline values. There are many step-by-step details for performing the Marshall test procedure and other less used mix design test methods, such as Hveem mix design method, that were not discussed here. They are more appropriate for in-depth discussion and training of technicians who actually conduct the test procedures. The material that was presented, however, should provide a better understanding of the relationship of the Marshall method of mix design to asphalt pavement performance.

ASPHALT PAVEMENT THICKNESS DESIGN

Design Considerations

The thickness design of asphalt pavements involves a consideration of soils and paving material and their behavior under loads and the determination of some thickness of pavement to carry those loads under all climatic conditions. Asphalt pavements, in addition to varying thicknesses, may also be composed of multiple layers of differing materials, such as asphalt concrete, emulsified asphalt mix, and untreated aggregate. These materials are used to construct the various pavement surface and base layers that are placed on top of the subgrade soil.

On lightly trafficked/loaded pavements, estimates are frequently made concerning the expected loads. Additionally, only estimates of soil support capabilities are used. However, more detailed information about traffic and subgrade soil conditions must be used for pavements that are subjected to heavy loads/high traffic or whose design is considered critical. Additionally, stricter material, construction standards, and controls are used. Such critical pavements are typical of major highways, airport runways, and heavy industrial loading/unloading facilities.

More asphalt paving is used for highways, roads, and streets, and in general surfaces used by trucks and automobiles than all other types combined. Because of this, this discussion will center mainly on thickness designs for these types of surfaces. However, some guidelines will also be given for the design of airfields and loading facilities.

Various methods have been used over the years for the thickness design of asphalt pavements. Designs for highways and streets in many areas of the United States are based on the empirical relationship of pavement thickness to actual traffic derived from the American Association of State Highway and Transportation Officials road test initiated in the 1950s. One much used result achieved from the experience of this early road test was the development of the so-called layer equivalency factor. Layer-equivalency factors have been used by designers to equate a unit thickness of pavement, such as 1 in. of asphalt concrete to various equivalent thicknesses of emulsified asphalt base and untreated granular bases. These methods are convenient and continue to be used. However, such fixed equivalencies have been criticized as unreliable and inadequate to meet the heavy loading needs of today's major highways.

In 1977, the Asphalt Institute initiated an effort to develop a mechanistic design procedure. Mechanistic procedures deal with the laws of mechanics as related to stresses and strains and deformation of the pavement materials. Currently, the Asphalt Institute has published mechanistic procedures for the design of highways and street pavements, as well as airports and other heavy load off-road applications. Some of these procedures will be briefly described in the following sections. In recent years, dozens of analytically based design procedures have been developed by various governments and research agencies around the world. The Asphalt Institute procedure is an example of this modern development using mechanistic pavement design procedures.

Thickness Design for Highways and Streets

In this design procedure, the pavement is regarded as a multilayered elastic system. The materials in each of the layers are characterized by a modulus of elasticity and a Poisson's ratio. The subgrade soil is characterized by a resilient modulus. Traffic is expressed in terms of repetitions of an 80-kN single-axle load applied to the pavement by dual tires. The procedure can be used to design asphalt pavements composed of various combinations of asphalt concrete surface and base, emulsified asphalt base, and untreated aggregate base.

The loads on the surface of the pavement are deemed to produce two strains, a horizontal tensile strain on the underside of the asphalt-bound layer and a vertical compressive strain at the surface of the subgrade layer. If the horizontal tensile strain is excessive, cracking of the asphalt pavement will result. If the vertical compressive strain is excessive, permanent deformation will result at the surface of the pavement from overloading and deforming the subgrade. In arriving at a design procedure, these strains are evaluated for various materials, loading conditions, and soil and environmental conditions.

A computer program is used to determine thicknesses for the asphalt pavement and subgrade strain criteria. Individual designs can be made using an analysis of this type, or, to be more readily used, graphic design charts are available that represent thickness for a wide range of variables.

Figure 4 presents a typical design chart for use in selecting pavement thicknesses. This chart represents thicknesses of full-depth asphalt concrete. This is a pavement type where asphalt concrete is used as surface and base and placed directly on the subgrade soil. This chart is to be used for a geographic area with mean average air temperature (MAAT) of 15.6°C. To use this or other such design charts, some strength value for the subgrade soil and a prediction of the number of traffic loads need to be determined. This design chart requires the user to first determine a subgrade soil resilient modulus. This can be directly determined from a laboratory test. Correlations also have been established relating such common soil values as California Bearing Ratio (CBR) to resilient modulus. The resilient modulus (M_r) may be approximated from the CBR value according to the relationship M_r (MPa) = 10.3 CBR.

The second variable to be determined is the amount of traffic loadings expected to use the pavement. Of concern are the number of weights of axle loads applied during a given design period. Typically, they range from light 9 kN automobiles to large trucks with 80–100 kN single-axle loads. The effect of various weight axle loads is represented by an equivalent 80-kN load. For example, one application of a 90-kN single-axle load is equal to about 1.5 applications of an 80 kN single-axle load. Conversely, it takes about four applications of a 60-kN single-axle load to equal one application of an 80-kN single-axle load. Knowledge is needed of the number and types of vehicles expected to use the pavement. Estimates or actual counts of the expected traffic are made for the expected design period, usually 20 years. These tabulations are then equated to equivalent 80-kN single-axle loads.

Highways and streets that carry large volumes of automobile traffic, but only a few trucks, require special attention in estimating traffic loadings. Some general guidelines can be followed for such facilities. Most parkways, residential streets, and parking lots have relatively high, almost 100%, volumes of automobile traffic. Care must be taken not to design such pavements too thin to withstand occasional heavy traffic, such as snowplows, maintenance trucks, buses, and garbage trucks. Therefore, a realistic estimate of future truck traffic on residential streets and parking lots should be attempted, and at least certain minimum thickness recommendations, as shown in Figure 4, should be maintained.

Parkways that are restricted to automobiles and buses present a different problem. Here, the total design equivalent axle loads calculated only for high volumes of exclusively light axles often is too low and results in pavements that field experience indicates are too thin. In this case, if truck traffic represents not more than 2% of the total, a reasonable estimate for total design equivalent axle loads can be obtained by multiplying 0.06 times the total traffic—automobiles, trucks, and buses.

Thickness Design for Airports

Asphalt paving is widely used around the world to accommodate aircraft-type loadings. There are a number of accepted procedures for the design of airfields. As with highways, one commonly accepted procedure for airport

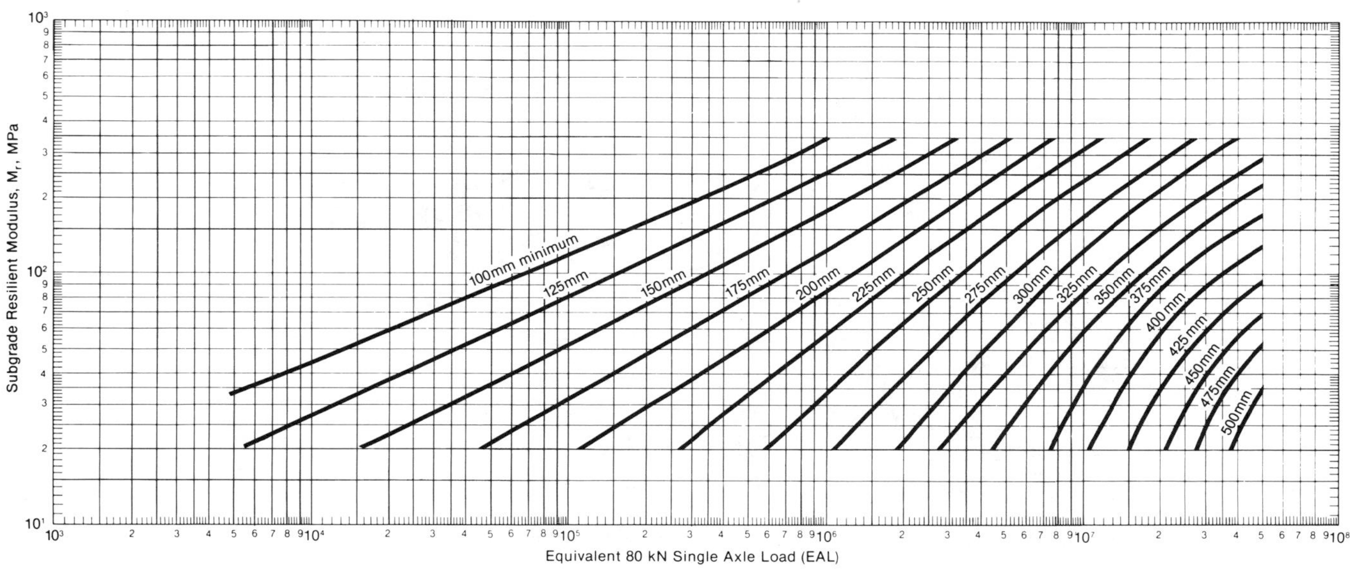

Figure 4. A typical asphalt concrete pavement thickness design chart. Courtesy of the Asphalt Institute.

pavement structure design is produced by the Asphalt Institute. As with the highway structural design system previously discussed, the airport pavement design procedure is also a mechanistic model examining the tensile strain in the asphalt layer and the subgrade soil compressive strain. Effects on the pavement of strain repetitions of a mixture of different aircraft are considered to be cumulative. Similar to highway design, aircraft traffic is summarized by equalizing the number of strain repetitions produced by the aircraft traffic mixture to a number of equivalent strain repetitions produced by an arbitrarily selected "standard" aircraft. Then, for given loading, soil, and climatic conditions, strains are analyzed and pavement thickness selected in order to ensure that selected strain criteria are not exceeded.

Because air-carrier airport pavements support extremely heavy loads, the asphalt-aggregate mixtures used must have well-defined, closely controlled mix design criteria. This is true for selection of aggregate materials as well as Marshall mix design criteria and control of material placement for the actual pavement.

ASPHALT PAVEMENT CONSTRUCTION

Asphalt Mixing Operations

An asphalt plant is an assembly of mechanical and electrical equipment where aggregates are blended, heated, dried, and finally mixed with asphalt to produce a hot, usually about 150°C, asphalt mix meeting specified requirements. Asphalt plants vary in size, with the larger plants capable of producing 175–265 metric tons/hr. Today, there are two types of plants commonly used around the world, the batch plant and the drum mix plant.

The difference between the two plant types is that batch plants (Fig. 5) dry and heat the aggregate, then, in a separate mixer called a pugmill, combine the aggregate with asphalt one batch at a time. Drum mix plants (Fig. 6), however, dry the aggregate and blend it with asphalt in a continuous process in the same piece of equipment, known as a drum mixer.

From Figure 5, the following are the steps of operation for the batch plant. Cold (unheated) aggregates stored in the cold bins (1) are proportioned by cold-feed gates (2) onto a belt conveyor or bucket elevator (3), which delivers the aggregates to the dryer (4), where they are dried and heated. Dust collectors (5) remove undesirable amounts of dust from the dryer exhaust. Remaining exhaust gases are eliminated through the plant exhaust stack (6). The dried and heated aggregates are delivered by hot elevator (7) to the screening unit (8), which separates the material into different-sized fractions and deposits them into separate hot bins (9) for temporary storage. When needed, the heated aggregates are measured in controlled amounts into the weight box (10). The aggregates are then dumped into the mixing chamber or pugmill (11), along with the proper amount of mineral filler, if needed, from mineral filler storage (12). Heated asphalt cement from the hot asphalt cement storage tank (13) is pumped into the asphalt weigh bucket (14), which weighs the asphalt cement before delivering it to the mixing chamber or pugmill, where it is combined thoroughly with the aggregates and mineral fillers if used. From the mixing chambers, the asphalt hot mix is deposited into a waiting truck or delivered into storage.

The following is a brief, general description of the sequence of processes involved in a typical drum mix plant operation (Fig. 6). Controlled gradations of aggregates are deposited in the cold feed bins (1) from which they are fed in exact proportions onto a cold-feed conveyor (2). An automatic aggregate weighing system (3) monitors the amount of aggregate flowing into the drum mixer (4). The weighing system is interlocked with the controls on the asphalt storage pump (5), which draws asphalt from a

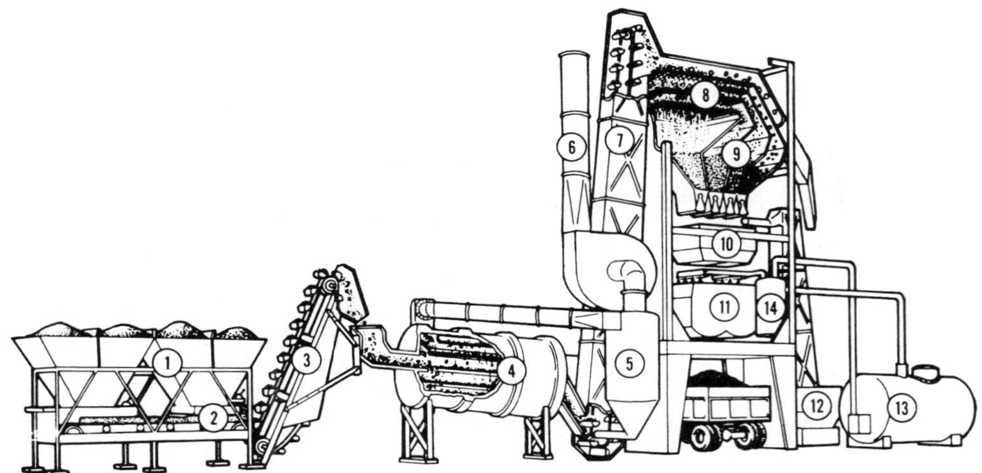

Figure 5. Asphalt batch mix plant and its components. Fourteen major parts: 1, Cold bins; 2, Cold feed gate; 3, Cold elevator; 4, Dryer; 5, Dust collector; 6, Exhaust stack; 7, Hot elevator; 8, Screening unit; 9, Hot bins; 10, Weigh box; 11, Mixing unit or pugmill; 12, Mineral filler storage; 13, Hot asphalt cement storage; 14, Asphalt weigh bucket. Courtesy of the Asphalt Institute.

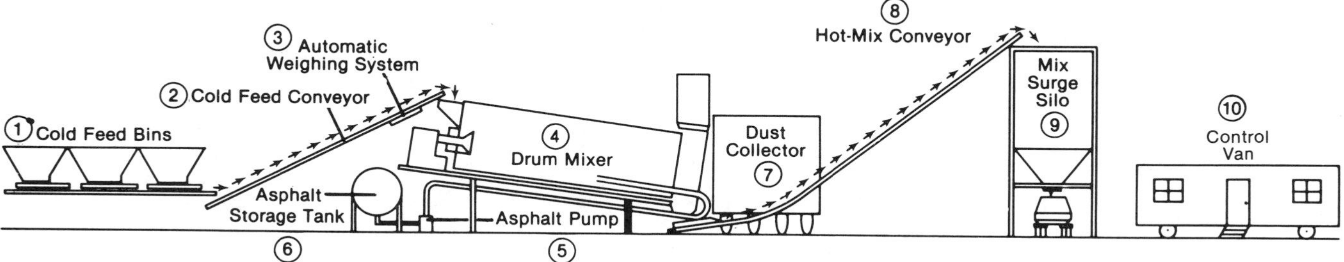

Figure 6. Asphalt drum mix plant and its components. Courtesy of the Asphalt Institute.

storage tank (6) and introduces it into the drum, where asphalt and aggregate are thoroughly blended by the drum's rotating action. A dust collection system (7) captures excess dust escaping from the drum. From the drum, the hot mix asphalt concrete is transported by hot mix conveyor (8) to a surge silo (9) from which it is loaded into trucks and hauled to the paving site. All plant operations are monitored and controlled from instruments in the control van (10).

Placing and Compacting Operations

Once produced at a mixing plant, the asphalt mixture is transported in haul trucks to the site to be paved (Fig. 7). Asphalt concrete can be placed on subgrade, granular base, asphalt cement pavement, or portland cement concrete pavement. In all cases, the surface on which the mix is to be placed must be properly graded and free of excess dust and debris before paving begins.

Asphalt concrete and portland cement concrete pavements must be repaired before being overlaid with a new asphalt layer. Before paving, the grade and alignment of the surface to be paved must be checked to be certain there is agreement with the project plans and profile.

Prime coats and tack coats, light spray applications of emulsified asphalt or cutback, are applied by a calibrated asphalt distributor at a predetermined rate and regulated by the flow of the asphalt from the tank and the distributor's forward speed. Proper spraying temperatures should be followed in all prime coating and tack coating operations. Too high a temperature will present a safety hazard or damage the materials; too low a temperature will cause difficulty in pumping and spraying. Prime and tack coating waterproofs the underlying surface and ensures a good bond between the old surface and the new pavement.

Figure 7. Placing operations showing paver, roller, and trucks with mix. Courtesy of the Asphalt Institute.

A paving machine is used to place the asphalt mix. Mix is delivered by truck to the paver's receiving hopper. The paver is capable of placing the mix at a uniform thickness and controlled smoothness and proper gradeline. The paving machine consists of two major units: a tractor unit and a screed unit. The tractor unit includes the power plant and all control systems for delivering power to systems throughout the paver. The screed unit places the hot mix layer or mat and includes the controls for regulating thickness.

Once the asphalt mixture has been placed to the proper thickness and grade, it must be compacted. Compaction is the process of compressing a given volume of asphalt mixture into a smaller volume. It is accomplished by pressing together the asphalt-coated aggregate particles, thereby eliminating most of the air voids (spaces) in the mix and increasing the density (weight to volume ratio) of the mixture. Compaction is considered successful when the finished mat reaches a certain specified content and density. This specified density should result in a pavement with some minor amount of air voids but should not exceed a maximum of about 8% air voids in the final compacted dense-graded asphalt. Compaction should be completed before the mixture cools to 85°C. Three types of rollers are commonly used, steel-wheeled rollers, consisting of steel rollers mounted on two or more tandem axles; pneumatic-tired rollers, which use rubber tires instead of steel wheels; and vibratory rollers, which employ steel drums designed to vibrate against the pavement surface.

The need for a pavement to be compacted to its required density is better understood when the effect of air, water, and traffic on an undercompacted pavement is realized. The voids in an undercompacted mix tend to be interconnected and permit the intrusion of air and water throughout the pavement. Air and water carry oxygen, which oxidizes the asphalt binder in the mix, causing it to become brittle. Consequently, the pavement itself will ultimately fail, as it can no longer withstand the repeated deflections of traffic loads. The internal presence of water at freezing temperatures can also cause an early failure in the pavement from expansion of the freezing water.

Table 5. Some Alternatives in Pavement Maintenance and Rehabilitation[a]

Problem	Possible Cause				Maintenance[b]						Rehabilitation[c]			
	Structural Failure	Mix Composition	Temp. or Moisture Changes	Const.	Patching and Routine Maintenance	Fog Seal	Surface Treatment	Slurry Seal	Surface Recycling	Thin Overlay	Open-Graded Surface	Structural Overlay	Structural Recycling	Reconstruction[d]
Alligator cracking	X				X[e]		X[f]	X[f]				X	X	X
Edge joint cracks	X		X	X	X									
Reflection cracks					X		X[f]	X[f]			X[g]	X	X	
Shrinkage cracking		X	X				X	X	X		X[g]	X	X	
Slippage cracks				X	X									
Rutting	X	X		X					X	X[h]		X	X	X
Corrugation	X	X		X					X	X[i]		X	X	X
Depressions	X			X	X								X	X
Upheaval			X		X								X	X
Potholes	X		X	X	X							X		
Raveling		X		X		X[f]	X	X	X	X				
Flushing asphalt		X		X			X		X		X			
Polished aggregate		X	X				X		X	X	X			
Loss of cover aggregate		X		X			X							

[a] Courtesy of the Asphalt Institute.
[b] Refer to *Asphalt in Pavement Maintenance* (MS-16), The Asphalt Institute, for details.
[c] When cracking exceeds 40% of the surface area of the pavement.
[d] If problem is extensive enough.
[e] Deep patch-permanent repair.
[f] Temporary repair.
[g] When accompanied by surface recycling.
[h] When rutting is minor.
[i] Over planed surface.

ASPHALT PAVEMENT MAINTENANCE AND REHABILITATION

Even the best-designed pavements eventually deteriorate. To be sure, inadequately designed and/or constructed pavements will deteriorate at an accelerated rate. Properly designed pavements deteriorate relatively slowly during the early years of their design life, but as they approach the end of their design life, this rate accelerates. Although proper maintenance lengthens the life of a pavement system, some form of rehabilitation is eventually required.

Maintenance and Rehabilitation

Pavement maintenance is the routine work performed to keep a pavement subjected to normal traffic and ordinary forces of nature as close as possible to its constructed condition. Maintenance is thought of as work primarily for the protection or rejuvenation of existing surface. It includes patching and various seal coatings and aggregate surface treatments. These are usually used to close cracks and repair failed spots in the pavement or, as with various seal coats, waterproof the entire surface.

Rehabilitation is a much more extensive procedure than is maintenance. Rehabilitation is used to restore a deteriorated pavement to its original design condition or to upgrade a pavement that experienced increased traffic demands. Rehabilitation includes thin asphalt structural overlays of 50 mm or more to correct present structural deficiencies, recycling or reuse of existing pavements for either surface or structural enhancement, and, if necessary, reconstruction, involving total replacement of an existing failed pavement. Table 5 contains a list of various pavement problems and respective maintenance and rehabilitation alternatives.

Pavement Management

To ensure long-term performance of a pavement system, timely and proper maintenance and rehabilitation procedures are vital. To this end, a program should be developed for planning and implementing pavement improvements. This is typically referred to as a PMS or pavement management system. The first step in the development of such a program is to prepare a map of the system identifying the various pavement sections. The second step is to conduct a thorough condition survey, recording the physical condition of each pavement. Next, a determination is made regarding what level of activity is needed for each pavement section. This can range from no work being required up to total reconstruction. The last step is to develop an economic analysis and a priority listing of the maintenance or rehabilitation required. This information may then be used to develop a time-based plan that takes into consideration the amount of funds available.

Although lack of budgeted funds for programs may require that certain pavement repairs be deferred, the economic consequences of such actions are undesirable. Generally, pavements suffer accelerated deterioration when defects go uncorrected, with accumulated repair costs increasing geometrically over time. The correct maintenance or rehabilitation technique instituted at the proper time will ensure that an asphalt pavement system continues to give maximum performance.

BIBLIOGRAPHY

General References

H. R. Abraham, *Asphalts and Allied Substances,* 6th ed., Van Nostrand, Princeton, N.J., 1960.

Asphalt Institute, *Thickness Design,* Manual Series No. 1 (MS-1), September 1981.

Asphalt Institute, *Mix Design Methods for Asphalt Concrete and Other Hot-Mix Types,* 5th ed., Manual Series No. 2 (MS-2), September 1986.

Asphalt Institute, *Asphalt Plant Manual,* 5th ed., Manual Series No. 3 (MS-3), January 1978.

Asphalt Institute, *Introduction to Asphalt,* 8th ed., Manual Series No. 5 (MS-5), January 1986.

Asphalt Institute, *Pocketbook of Useful Information,* 6th ed., Manual Series No. 6 (MS-6), September 1985.

Asphalt Institute, *Asphalt Paving Manual,* 5th ed., Manual Series No. 8 (MS-8), August 1983.

Asphalt Institute, *Thickness Design—Asphalt Pavements For Air Carrier Airports,* 3rd ed., Manual Series No. 11 (MS-11), October 1987.

Asphalt Institute, *Asphalt Cold Mix Manual,* 2nd ed., Manual Series No. 14 (MS-14), February 1977.

Asphalt Institute, *Asphalt in Pavement Maintenance,* 2nd ed., Manual Series No. 16 (MS-16), March 1983.

Asphalt Institute, *Asphalt Overlays for Highway and Street Rehabilitation,* 2nd ed., Manual Series No. 17 (MS-17), January 1983.

Asphalt Institute, *Asphalt Hot Mix Recycling,* 2nd ed., Manual Series No. 20 (MS-20), July 1986.

Asphalt Institute, *Principles of Construction of Hot Mix Asphalt Pavements,* Manual Series No. 22 (MS-22), January 1983.

Asphalt Institute, *Thickness Design—Asphalt Pavements For Heavy Wheel Loads,* Manual Series No. 23 (MS-23), January 1986.

Asphalt Institute, *Model Construction Specifications for Asphalt Concrete and Other Plant-Mix Types,* Specification Series No. 1 (SS-1), November 1984.

Asphalt Institute, *Specifications For Paving and Industrial Asphalts,* Specification Series No. 2 (Ss-2), February 1987.

Association of Asphalt Paving Technologists, *Annual Proceedings,* 1928–1987.

John R. Bukowski
Asphalt Institute
College Park, Maryland

PAXTON, JOSEPH

Joseph Paxton's prominence in architectural history is most directly owed to his role as the architect of one of the most significant structures in nineteenth-century architecture. The Crystal Palace, a monumental glass and iron edifice, was commissioned to house the Great London

Exhibition of 1851. Although Paxton's lifetime of professional activity embraces a number of architectural structures, many of his accomplishments were intertwined with other professional roles, which included among them landscape gardener–designer, horticulturist, author–publisher, inventor, management investor, railway executive, and Parliamentarian. Paxton was a Renaissance man whose life bridged the Victorian past and the onslaught of the industrial revolution. By one account, he was described as "one of the remarkable individuals produced by the age of *laissez faire* opportunity, self-made, self-educated, ambitious and bold" (1).

Paxton was born in England in 1803, the seventh son of a Bedfordshire farmer. At the age of 15, he became gainfully employed as a garden boy at Battlesden. He moved energetically and swiftly to positions of increasing stature, to become first the gardener at Woodhall, then to serve the Duke of Somerset at Wimbledon, and then to care for the newly opened gardens at the Horticultural Society at Chiswick. It was there that he so impressed the Duke of Devonshire with his abilities to recreate gardens and lakes, and erect fountains, cascades, arboretums, vineries, and glasshouses of exotic plants, that at the age of 23 he became the duke's head gardener at Chatsworth.

While in the duke's employ, Paxton's responsibilities expanded to include the management of the duke's six other Devonshire estates. Gradually, Paxton's role became even more far-reaching, as his service to the duke bonded a relationship of mutual trust and respect. On all affairs, both internal and external, Paxton was the duke's adviser and counsel, and the duke served as his patron, encouraging Paxton's own interests and undertakings. Such circumstance found Paxton engaged in a seemingly disparate array of activities, but all of them were logical connective outgrowths of his first work as gardener. "From building greenhouses, he had risen to building villages and bridges and reservoirs and gasworks" (2). By virtue of his land holdings, the duke had large railway interests that Paxton came to manage, and in the course of time, he became the railway director. This activity, in turn, brought him to Parliament where he was actively introducing, promoting, and, at other times, opposing the passage of railway bills. In the process, he made a personal fortune for himself in railway investments. Extending his outside interests still further, and comfortable that his internal management responsibilities were ably being handled by his wife, Sarah, he went on to publish a number of journals and magazines, among them the *Horticultural Register,* the *Magazine of Botany, Gardener's Chronicle, Paxton's Flower Garden, A Pocket Botanical Dictionary, A Calendar of Gardening Operations,* and *Treaties on the Dahlia.*

His reputation became widespread, and although he had become an established public figure, prosperous in his own right, he continued to maintain his seminal ties with horticulture in the service of the duke. This resolute connection ultimately led Paxton to the design and construction of the Crystal Palace.

Previous to this prestigious commission, Paxton had established a backlog of 20 years experience in the building of glass structures throughout the duke's properties. In the process, he also obtained design patents for his many glass building constructions, most notably among them, a ridge-and-furrow roof system that he used in a number of structures. The embryonic ideas of the Crystal Palace owe, in fact, to the design and construction of the Victoria Regia Lily House, which Paxton built at Chatsworth in 1849. It was planned to house a rare and newly discovered tropical water plant, the Victoria Regia, which originated in British Guiana. When Paxton obtained the seedling, its leaves were less than 6 in. in diameter. Paxton devised a special heated tank, stirred by waterwheels of his own design. His nurturing method proved so successful that in three months, its leaves measured 5 ft in diameter surrounding a giant center flowering bud. As it continued to grow, Paxton was moved to rehouse it. By this time, he had completed a succession of glass buildings, including a number of grander sized conservatories. Inspired by the very plant it was to house, Paxton carried into the design structural principles he observed in the plant's physical makeup, notably, that of its webbed understructure where miniature cantilevers had the capability of bearing considerable weight, which he tested out by placing his seven-year-old daughter atop the leafy construct. The Lily House emerged as an economical, light airy structure supported by hollow cast-iron columns which also served as the structure's drain spouts. Thus, the Lily House, incorporating features of Paxton's previous buildings coupled with this newly realized supporting frame, served as a prototype for the Crystal Palace.

The year following the construction of the Lily House, amid a tumultuous process of selection for the 1851 Great London Exhibition building, included a design competition yielding 245 unacceptable entries, and, as a backdrop, a feverish though ill-fated design attempt by the Commission itself to meet their own selection deadline. The Royal Commission, under these circumstances, allowed the review of Paxton's design concept for the proposed building. From an initial blotting-paper sketch, Paxton promised completion of a three-tiered glass and iron structure graced on a spatial grid totaling nearly 1 million ft^2, within six months time, in adherence with the scheduled opening-day ceremonies. Beyond its rapid construction potential, Paxton's spatially expansive design with its lightweight structure promised an exciting exhibition space that was completely demountable as well. The members of the Commission were moved to approve Paxton's expedient proposal.

The Great London Exhibition building, the Crystal Palace (Fig. 1), as it became readily known, was considered a highly successful structure. Its utilization of standardized prefabricated components accounted for its rapid and economical dry assembly construction process. Its bolted frame comprised repetitions of mass-produced structural components: 1060 iron columns, 2224 trellis girders, and 359 trusses. The building skin was similarly of glass panels. Each single-unit panel measured 10 in. wide and 49 in. long, and from it all proportioning decisions for the complete building construct were determined. Overall, 900,000 ft^2 of glazing was fixed at a rate of 63,000 ft^2 per week. This rapid fixing procedure was aided by another

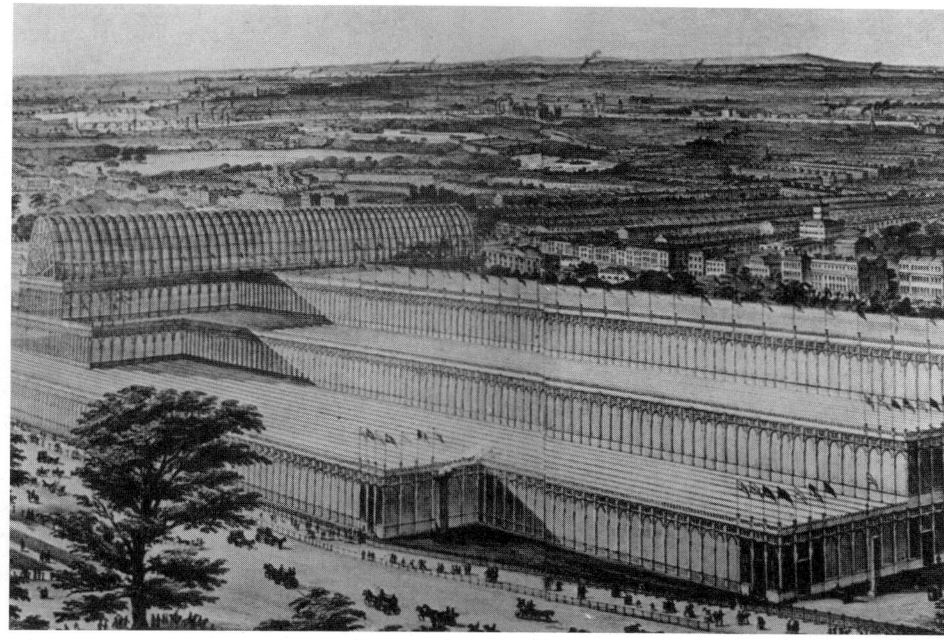

Figure 1. Lithograph of the Crystal Palace, constructed for the Great London Exhibition of 1851 (2).

Paxton invention, a roof glazing wagon that moved across the building's gutters, where two glaziers sat riding along the grooves as they slid the glass panels into place (Fig. 2).

Paxton's Crystal Palace exhibited a grandiose form. Its dimensions, 1848 ft long by 456 ft wide, covered 18 acres, although its materials of iron, wood, and glass gave it a sense of weightlessness. A central arched transept further enhanced the design, providing an aesthetic balance to the building's lengthy form. This design solution similarly addressed an interior functional requirement by accommodating a row of elm trees that the UK's Prince Consort Albert favored and wished to maintain within the building structure.

Figure 2. Roof glazing wagon used in construction of the Crystal Palace (2).

After the close of the exhibition, Paxton formed the Crystal Palace Company and obtained ownership of the structure along with other investors. Its building parts were demounted, then reassembled on an estate at Sydenham, UK. There Paxton enlarged the building and made some design alterations. Once reopened, it served as a popular public-use space until 1936. It had fallen into disrepair and was destroyed by fire that year.

Serving as an architect, Paxton continued to add other buildings to his credit, of glass and other materials; his later were in the Victorian eclectic style, but the Crystal Palace, as his greatest challenge and achievement, remains today a remarkable contribution to both the nineteenth-century age of industrialization and history's time line of architecture.

BIBLIOGRAPHY

1. E. de Mare, *London 1851, The Year of the Great Exhibition,* The Folio Society, London, 1972, Chapt. 3, p. 1.
2. C. Hobhouse, *1851 and the Crystal Palace,* John Murray, London, 1950, p. 26.

General References

Refs. 1 and 2 are good general references.

P. Beaver, *The Crystal Palace 1851–1936, A Portrait of Victorian Enterprise,* Hugh Evelyn Limited, London, 1970.

G. F. Chadwick, *The Works of Joseph Paxton 1803–1865,* Architectural Press, London, 1961.

Karen J. Dominguez
Pennsylvania State University
State College, Pennsylvania

PEI, IEOH MING

The son of a wealthy and prominent banker–economist, Ieoh Ming Pei lived in Shanghai and Hong Kong, as well as his native Canton, in the years following his birth in 1917. After attending St. John's Middle School in Shanghai, Pei came to the United States to study in 1935. As many of his father's business associates were westerners—from the UK and northern Europe—it was expected that young Pei would go abroad for his studies. Originally, he planned to attend the University of Pennsylvania to study architecture, but his own uncertainty about his drawing skills and the highly drawing-oriented program of the beaux-arts influenced program at Pennsylvania shunted Pei's interest elsewhere. He matriculated instead at MIT where he majored in architectural engineering. William Emerson, the dean at MIT, was influential in shifting Pei's interests from engineering to architecture. On graduation in 1940, it was clear that his original intention, to return to his native China to practice, was not to be. World War II and the postwar revolution in China prevented his return, and on the advice of his father he remained in the United States and became a citizen. From MIT, Pei moved to Harvard, where in 1942 he studied with Gropius and Breuer for six months. At that point, he volunteered for and served two years with the National Defense Research Committee in Princeton, New Jersey. In 1944, he returned to the Graduate School of Design (GSD) at Harvard to complete his Master's program, receiving his degree in 1946. As with others of his generation, notably Philip Johnson, Edward Larrabee Barnes, Eliot Noyes, and Paul Rudolph, he was heavily influenced by both Gropius and Breuer. Clean, flat surfaces became a trademark of the era. These and other Bauhaus ideas and ideals were most distressing to Dean Emerson, Pei's early mentor at MIT. Such notions were highly suspect in the beaux-arts atmosphere that permeated most schools of architecture in the 1940s. Despite these concerns, Pei matured and flourished under the tutelage of the Graduate School of Design's Dean Hudnut, as well as Gropius and Breuer.

He remained in Cambridge, serving as a faculty member at the GSD until 1948 when he was plucked from academe to serve as architect for developer William Zeckendorf. Known as Webb and Knapp, Zeckendorf's real estate firm was one of the most aggressive builders in the postwar period. Unlike most young architects who find their early and formative work in residences and other small scale projects, Pei was thrust immediately into the world of big buildings and big business. Among the projects undertaken by Zeckendorf, and supervised by his Director of Architecture, were the Mile High Center in Denver, Place Ville Marie in Montreal, and Kips Bay Plaza in New York City. These large-scale works all involved the kind of rigorous planning and appreciation of urban focus for which the Pei organization would be acclaimed. Not only did the years with Webb and Knapp offer Pei an extraordinary immersion into the world of corporate architecture, it also introduced him to the men who would soon become his partners, in one of the most successful U.S. architectural practices. Working with him were Henry N. Cobb, Eason H. Leonard, and later James Ingo Freed. With Cobb and Leonard as the original partners, Pei formally established his own firm, I. M. Pei and Associates (later I. M. Pei and Partners), in 1960. The end of the Zeckendorf era came amicably, something of a graduation, Pei having already begun to accept projects outside the Webb and Knapp aegis in the late 1950s. With Eason Leonard as managing partner and Henry Cobb as design partner, the firm set out to continue its large-scale planning and building efforts. In these two men Pei had two very different partners. Leonard's background included an architectural education in his native Oklahoma at Oklahoma State University in Stillwater, followed by four years in the Army Corps of Engineers. Before joining Webb and Knapp, he worked for William Lescaze, an all too often overlooked practice where the principles of modernism were first introduced to corporate America.

Cobb, by contrast, came out of a patrician Boston background with studies at Philips Exeter, Harvard College, and the Graduate School of Design at Harvard. After service in the naval reserve and a brief tenure at Hugh Stubbins's office, Cobb joined Webb and Knapp in 1950. Harry (as he is known to his associates) Cobb could certainly have had a thriving practice of his own, but he chose to be part of the firm and assume a somewhat less visible public role. At 36 he was largely responsible for the Place Ville Marie project in Montreal, an enormous undertaking in the modernist vernacular. This brainchild of Bill Zeckendorf's would largely transform the Canadian city. In the years since Webb and Knapp, Cobb has devoted part of his time to teaching, culminating in his appointment as Chairman of the Graduate School of Design at Harvard. He served in this role for five years (1980–1985) and remains on the faculty. During his tenure, Harvard's role in architectural education was given new luster and direction as Cobb sought to invigorate a somewhat stagnant program with the vitality of issues focused on urbanism and quality environment. As a sensitive observer of the city, Cobb has always imbued his work with the sense that buildings cannot stand alone, but must be a part of, and vital addition to, an urban fabric. This is exemplified in some of Cobb's best design work, notably, the John Hancock Tower in Boston (1976), the Portland (Maine) Museum of Art (1983), and Fountain Place, a mixed-use development in Dallas (1986) (Fig. 1). In each of these projects, a relatively large building or buildings has been used as the focus of an urban space and as generator of urban activity. At both Fountain Place and John Hancock a reflective glass curtain wall high-rise has been used as foil for new and established urban spaces, respectively. Hancock, sitting adjacent to H. H. Richardon's Trinity Church and McKim, Mead and White's Public Library, may be the most effective use of reflective glass in the United States.

The Portland Museum uses a much smaller project to enhance a fading downtown and establish closure and presence in an urban setting. The museum is vaguely Renaissance in feeling on the exterior with direct references to the work of Sir John Soane (Dulwich Picture Gallery) on the interior. All three projects clearly illustrate a motif in the firm's work. In almost every major project by the Pei office, an ambitious planning agenda is given life with

Figure 1. Fountain Place, Dallas, 1986. Henry N. Cobb, partner in charge.

the simple, bold geometry of a single building. In that building, a clear statement invariably renders eloquent an often complex program of disparate functions. This kind of architectural boldness is certainly within the U.S. stream of Richardson and Sullivan with whom the firm is rarely associated because the stylistic issues, at least in the early years, are so obviously drawn from the Germanic influences Pei and Cobb assimilated at the GSD, and the Miesian background of Jim Freed. While much of the firm's work may have Bauhaus aesthetic ancestry, the clarity and strength of solution is largely out of Richardson, Sullivan, and Wright. The Bauhaus never had corporate clients as did Richardson and Sullivan, and while the Pei office (like the Bauhaus) has a social agenda as evidenced by its work at Society Hill in Philadelphia, Bedford–Stuyvesant in Brooklyn, or the Denver Mall, its major efforts have been in the creation of elegant and powerful corporate and institutional icons.

After Hancock, it seemed unlikely that I. M. Pei and Partners would ever complete these corporate and institutional projects. With the glass of the Hancock Building littering the streets of Copley Square, its well-documented facade riddled with plywood, Hancock seemed like a cruel denunciation of modern architecture—buildings as sculpture, technology run amok. While most of their clients retained faith in the firm's professionalism and integrity, they were reluctant to hire Pei for fear that the firm would soon fall under the legal and financial burdens of the Hancock disaster and the incumbent lawsuits.

This came at a time when the firm seemed to be embarking on its most creative and prolific period. Having completed two of the most important poured concrete buildings in the world—the Everson Museum of Art in Syracuse (1968) (Fig. 2) and the National Center for Atmospheric Research in Boulder (1967) (Fig. 3)—the 1970s looked like the Pei decade. In both projects, the vocabulary of powerful forms of enduring beauty belied the notion that modernism meant banality. From the collaborative efforts of Pei's firm came tangible evidence that there was still a good deal of life in the modern movement. Seeing the elegant possibilities of poured concrete, the firm became the recognized expert in the postbrutalist era of architecture as almost anthropomorphic concrete art. With Hancock, the same expertise seemed to be evident in the sleek, reflective, knife-edged curtain wall. With many of its 60 stories of windows falling onto the streets of Boston, the future of I. M. Pei and Partners was very much in doubt. At first, not knowing the cause of the problem and suspecting everything, the client and architect called in a series of structural consultants to ascertain the reasons for the spectacular failure of the glass. Eventually, it was the glass itself that was recognized as the culprit; its two annealed layers were replaced by a single layer to eliminate undue movement and stress. All of the investigations and legal work took time. Many firms would have collapsed under the pressures of legal and investigative cost, and bad press. Yet, by the end of the 1970s, I. M. Pei and Partners was touted as the best architectural firm in the world. Compari-

Figure 2. The Everson Museum of Art, Syracuse, New York. I. M. Pei, partner in charge.

Figure 3. National Center for Atmospheric Research, Boulder, Colorado, 1967. I. M. Pei, partner in charge.

sons to Louis Kahn and McKim, Mead and White were not uncommon. The Hancock fiasco was stemmed largely because owner and architect never lost faith in each other. John Hancock and I. M. Pei and Partners worked as a unit to confront the problems. When the glass issue was finally resolved, Pei's East Wing of the National Gallery of Art was nearing completion and with it, the next era of the firm was taking shape.

The East Wing represents the apogee of the concrete and masonry phase of the firm's work. The building contains all of the expertise the organization acquired in the first two decades of its operation. With the East Wing, all of the precision and boldness of past work is brought into focus. From Kips Bay Plaza through the Des Moines Art Center Addition (1968); the Everson Museum; the Mellon Center for the Arts at Choate School in Wallingford, Connecticut (1972); the Atmospheric Research Center; the Christian Science Center in Boston (1973) (designed under the direction of Araldo Cossutta, who served as fourth partner from 1963–1973); the Johnson Museum of Art at Cornell University (1973); and the Oversea–Chinese Banking Corporation Centre in Singapore (1976), I. M. Pei and Partners created a series of reinforced concrete buildings of consummate clarity and power. At the East Wing, the combination of careful site design; form work produced to the tolerance of the cabinetmaker; extraordinary integration of structural, mechanical, and electrical services; and a delicacy of all elements from geometry to color represent the quintessential collaborative effort of the Pei organization. The Miesian notion of God being in the details was never more apparent than at the East Wing. The Tennessee quarry that supplied the stone for the neoclassical John Russell Pope National Gallery was reopened so that Pei could avail himself of the same material for his addition. That same stone was ground up as aggregate for the concrete of the East Wing so that the building would radiate the same pink glow of the original. Here, as with Hancock, the collaboration extends to the relationship between client and architect. As an art patron himself, Pei speaks the language of the connoisseur, a quality not lost on Paul Mellon, who financed the project, or Carter Brown, the museum's director.

In this body of reinforced concrete architecture, only the Dallas City Hall (1966–1977) stands out as an inelegant, rather ungainly sculptural form set on an arid plaza. With that noted exception, the work of this 10-year period is an incredible outpouring of sustained high quality endeavor. In retrospect, the buildings hold up very well. While much of the architectural production of the 1960s and 1970s seems dated, this group of buildings by I. M. Pei and Partners has the same power and clarity it had when it was new. This is particularly true of the museum work and the regal set of buildings at the Christian Science Center in Boston.

In 1980, Freed, Leonard Jacobsen, and Werner Wandelmaier became partners, bringing that number to six. Freed had joined Pei's office in 1956. Born in Essen, Germany, in 1930 he received his Bachelor's of Architecture from the Illinois Institute of Technology. After a time with the Army Corps of Engineers he moved to New York to work with his former teacher, Ludwig Mies van der Rohe. That Miesian influence is clearer in the work of Freed (Kips Bay Plaza, 1962, and the New York University (NYU) Towers, 1967) than in any other of the firm's work. Both projects are marked by the rigid grid translated from Miesian steel to reinforced concrete. At NYU Freed achieved an extraordinary power, playing the deeply recessed concrete grid against the blank walls of the towers. Here, and at the aluminum-clad 88 Pine Street Tower (1973) in lower Manhattan, he made his two finest contributions to that early era of the firm's development. Sitting well within the strictures of the modern movement, the work of Freed at 88 Pine Street remains pure and seductive years after its completion, another testament to the potentially enduring qualities of well-wrought modernism. The financial district of lower Manhattan experienced unparalleled growth in the 1970s and 1980s, yet 88 Pine has lost none of its power as its strength is, like so much of the firm's work, born of elegance.

Freed, like Cobb, could well be on his own. The two have remained with the firm over the decades, in part for the opportunity to work on projects of often enormous scale and almost always of great cultural significance. In addition, the resources of I. M. Pei and Partners's broad and deep expertise in such areas as high strength concrete and curtain wall construction afford designers access to ideas and solutions that would be impossible in a smaller, less prestigious organization. Like Cobb, Freed has devoted much of his energies to architectural education. From 1975 to 1978, he served as the Dean of the College of Architecture at his alma mater, the Illinois Institute of Technology.

The firm's successes, whether in the crisp concrete of the Atmospheric Research Center or the crystalline minimalism of Fountain Place, rely on the power of simple geometries that do not venture far from the original and singular ideas that Pei and his partners conceived. That raw power is tempered by careful detailing, close attention to choice of materials, and a thorough understanding of, and sensitivity to, site. The difficult site is exploited for its potential; the rich materials and details are never pretentious or precious; the geometries always make the complex look simple. When projects fail, it is usually because one of these elements has been ignored or not given its due. At the Dallas City Hall the building's sculptural qualities take precedence over site to the detriment of both. Sometimes the delay of a project results in an idea of the 1960s being drawn in the 1970s and built in the 1980s. Such was the case with Raffles City, an enormous hotel, office, convention, and shopping center in Singapore. The marvelous clarity of the nine-square grid is almost completely overwhelmed by the multiple geometries of the tower forms. The result is one of Pei's less than elegant solutions to a complex program. Such is not the case with the Louvre in Paris.

After more than two decades of successful museum building, the firm became the architects of choice of most of the world's museum directors. It was not surprising that French President Mitterrand turned to Pei to undertake the rehabilitation and addition to the Louvre, for many, the most symbolically important museum in western culture. Here, Pei has developed a most controversial

Figure 4. The Grande Louvre, Paris, 1983–1988. I. M. Pei, partner in charge.

scheme of adding space under the great courtyard, with access to that space via a glass space frame of pyramidal form (Fig. 4). Once again, the clarity of vision and seeming simplicity of execution of that vision mark the work. Undoubtedly, the critical French public will come to cherish Pei's pyramid in the same way that they grew to love Eiffel's tower.

Despite the string of triumphs, in the aftermath of John Hancock many corporate clients stayed away. Important commissions of the late 1970s went elsewhere—AT & T to Philip Johnson and John Burgee, IBM to Edward Larrabee Barnes, General Foods and Proctor and Gamble to Kohn, Pederson, Fox. By the 1980s, much of the work at I. M. Pei and Partners was overseas. While never moving headlong into the burgeoning market of the oil-rich Middle East, Pei's office did make a less than successful foray into the Shah's Iran and also experienced difficulties with projects in financially embattled Mexico. For the most part, however, the firm has concentrated on foreign markets that are stable, economically viable, and politically compatible to U.S. ideals. Thus, Pei has had an extensive presence in Singapore, helping that small nation temper its economic miracle with sound planning principles. In Hong Kong, Pei was called on by the Chinese government to design the Bank of China. This commission is particularly significant as Pei's father had, in the prerevolutionary era, served as the bank's president.

Many of the bank's officers had learned their skills from the senior Pei. In addition, and more important in the political arena, the Bank of China is Beijing's most visible presence in a place that will, in 1997, become part of the mainland. The achievement of the tallest building in Asia has been considerably overshadowed by Norman Foster's high-tech Hong Kong–Shanghai Bank building a few blocks away. Pei's tower is a highly abstracted geometrical construct of rotated and receding triangular solids, sheathed in reflective glass and cross-braced against the powerful wind loads of typhoon-prone Hong Kong. The spiraling form, despite its slenderness and height, lacks the sustaining interest and understated elegance of Hancock or 88 Pine, nor does it possess the solidarity of the Texas Commerce Bank Tower in Houston (1982). The Bank of China comes across as thin stuff more in the vein of Helmut Jahn than I. M. Pei and Partners. The project does bring to mind two other Pei buildings. Because of its highly articulated triangular structural system one is reminded of the Jacob K. Javits Convention Center in New York (1986) while its client, the Bank of China, makes comparisons to Pei's other, and first, commission for the Chinese government, the Fragrant Hill Hotel (1982), 40 km outside Beijing.

At Fragrant Hill, a 300-room hotel in a park district near the Chinese capital, Pei has attempted to bring to his native China his often-quoted "third way" of making buildings. Avoiding both an outright copying of traditional Chinese motifs (particularly the clichéd pagoda roof) as well as the modernism of the West, Pei seeks to point the way in which a third world nation may grow. By using the devices of scale, simple geometries, and close ties to the landscape, Pei has managed, at Fragrant Hill, to make one of his most eloquent statements.

Pei's long-admired traits of modesty, charm, and diplomacy have served him and his firm well. First recognized by Zeckendorf in the late 1940s, Pei has for decades used his talent and commitment to bring out the best in his colleagues and the most laudable aspirations in his clients. In a career marked by every major architectural honor including the AIA's Gold Medal (1979) and the $100,000 Pritzker Prize (1983), Pei will likely be remembered as a bastion of modernism whose appreciation for the urbane in art, planning, and architecture led him to the design of many of the world's most thoughtful projects.

BIBLIOGRAPHY

General References

J. C. Starbuck, *The Buildings of I. M. Pei and His Firm,* Vance Bibliographies, Monticello, Ill., 1978.

B. Diamonstein, *American Architecture Now,* Rizzoli, New York, 1980.

Y. Futagawa, ed., *Global Architecture,* Vol. 41, Edita, Tokyo, 1976.

ROBERT ZWIRN
Miami University
Oxford, Ohio

PERSPECTIVES, ARCHITECTURAL.

See RENDERINGS, ARCHITECTURAL

PEST CONTROL

Since man has had structures to live in, he has experienced the unwanted invasion of insects and vertebrate animals. After all, these animals occupied niches in the world long before man displaced them. Now man struggles to rid his habitats of these individuals and refers to them as pests.

As man developed his architectural concepts, his ideas were fashioned with the materials available to him. As his expertise grew and new modern building materials were developed, the structures took on various configurations. Today structures, large and small, that use building designs incorporating many of the ancient forms of architecture are built. The new materials of today make the buildings stronger, more durable, and in some cases more aesthetically pleasing than the structures of the past.

However, these structures and current technology will not stop pests such as insects, arthropods, and vertebrates from entering or using the structures for their own purposes. In fact, in many situations a place to live is offered to them.

COST

Today's populations are urbanized. According to the most current U.S. census, more than 76% of the U.S. population now lives in urban areas and this figure is increasing.

Along with this growing population is a growing population of urbanized pests. Most are annoying to the general public in their endeavors to pursue their life cycles. These should be of concern to designers and builders because some simple methods can be used to deter these pests.

The most well-documented pest situation concerns the wood-destroying organisms. These organisms include the insects (termites, beetles, and ants) as well as fungi. Their activity often results in severe damage and costly repairs. The collective term for their activity is biodeterioration. In 1977, biodeterioration of wood in construction was estimated to cost U.S. homeowners $2.7 billion. Unfortunately, subsequent surveys have not been performed on a nationwide scale. Estimates by the Structural Pest Control Industry and U.S. Forest Service for damage repair and protection of homes from termites alone come close to $1 billion annually. A survey conducted in 11 southern states during the 1970s indicated that, in private residences alone, the estimated loss caused by wood-destroying beetles was $12.9 million. In a 1984 survey in the state of Georgia, it was estimated that over $50 million were expended for termite control and repair of damage. In this same survey for 10 structural insect species, over $83 million were spent for control of the pests and repair of damage. This did not include the two major vertebrate pests, rodents and birds.

In short, there are substantial postconstruction costs experienced by homeowners and building owners throughout the United States caused by pests. Some of these costs can be eliminated with proper design and construction.

INVERTEBRATE PESTS

Built structures are almost impossible to protect against invasions or damage by pests. In the building codes and the minimum property standards of the Federal Housing Administration (now the Department of Housing and Urban Development), only preconstruction protection against termites and decay is addressed. Maintenance and rehabilitative repairs address pest control, but specifics are lacking in the codes on how to modify or alter structures to inhibit or eliminate pest invasions. Specific instructions on how to inspect and take necessary steps to eliminate pest problems have been overlooked.

There are a variety of pest problems that can arise as the structure is being built. Today, some construction includes the use of insecticide dust to deter postconstruction infestation. There are several species of cockroaches that can enter buildings in the United States. Large species such as the American (*Periplaneta americana* [Linn.]), Smokybrown (*P. fuliginosa* [Serville]), and Oriental (*Blatta orientalis* [Linn.]) live outside in warmer areas of the United States and in sewer systems in colder areas. They can access structures from the crawl areas or cracks in foundations. Sealing by caulking, or applications of pesticide dusts, can deter these insects.

The more common German cockroach (*Blattella germanica* [Linn.]) usually infests indoors and is seldom found outdoors. Once inside, cockroaches reproduce rapidly and can spread throughout a structure following "natural" openings or runways, electrical conduits, heat ducts, and pipe chases. Sealing and caulking around pipes, cracks, and crevices eliminates harborages. Use of insecticide dusts in wall voids greatly reduces the establishment of an infestation. Another cockroach similar to the German cockroach was discovered in Florida in 1986. This insect, known as the Asian cockroach (*B. asahinai*), can fly and has been reported indoors but has not been reported to establish infestations indoors.

There are many insecticide dusts on the market; it is not in the scope of this article to discuss or list these products. However, the techniques or methods should be considered.

The introduction of insecticide dust into wall voids will provide a barrier inside the structure. Infestations of fungus beetles or psocids common to new buildings could be greatly reduced or eliminated. Likewise, arthropod and insect invaders would be controlled by these applications.

It is not within the abilities of the builders to undertake these treatments. They should be contracted to licensed professional pest control operators. Such treatments have been known to be effective for up to two years after construction.

In addition, building design of multifamily or office structures provides many runways for insect and vertebrate pests. The design is such that it allows insects such as cockroaches to move freely between areas of the buildings. Designers should consider this and make provisions for sealing openings or cracks and crevices to eliminate these harborages.

Materials such as caulks or other sealants could be used to seal cracks and crevices or expansion joints to deter pest invasion or harborage. This requires careful planning and follow-through on the builder's part.

Inhibiting Wood-destroying Pests

Pest control should be undertaken in two phases, chemical and mechanical. The use of pesticides, specifically termiticides, to pretreat construction sites offers the best and most economical way to deter subterranean termite infestations. There are several chemicals registered by the Environmental Protection Agency for this use. Building codes address the subject by requiring this treatment in certain areas of the country. However, these codes do not address the methods to be used. Most are outlined on the product labels or from reference materials such as the *Approved Reference Procedures for Subterranean Termite Control* published by the National Pest Control Association. The methods are also outlined in the *United States Forest Service/Home and Garden Bulletin 64.*

The important aspect of this treatment is to make sure the proper barrier of chemical is placed around and under the structure. Once in place, termites are deterred or cannot penetrate the barrier to do damage to the structure. Mechanical controls include a variety of physical "barriers" installed to inhibit pest entry. These are most economically installed at the time of construction. To help understand the method used, some basic habits of the pests must be considered in order to effectively control them.

Insects can enter structures through extremely small openings. It would be impossible to design a building tight enough to eliminate the possibility of entrance. However, some mechanical controls have been used successfully to deter invasion. This is most evident with the wood-destroying insect, the subterranean termite. The most common subterranean species can enter through cracks as small as 0.8 mm (0.03 in.). Minimum property standards and building codes have recommended the use of termite shields of copper or other metal, placed on top of a foundation under the sill plate, to keep termites from entering the structure (Fig. 1). These have proved to be relatively useless in inhibiting invasion. However, these shields have provided inspection assistance because termites must build their shelter or exploratory tubes around a properly installed shield, thus exposing themselves and making it easier to determine if termites are present. Building codes also recommend pressure-treated or naturally durable woods. Pressure-treated woods utilize a variety of restricted use pesticides. The user of these materials must be aware of any precautions in handling or installing these wood products. These woods can be costly, but can inhibit termite invasion. However, termites have been known to penetrate pressure-treated plywoods or veneers and can tunnel over pressure-treated or naturally durable woods.

Other mechanical alterations as noted in the National Pest Control Association *Approved Reference Procedures* have been helpful in inhibiting termite invasions around more common elements of construction, such as porch or slab abutments to the structure. Because of their construc-

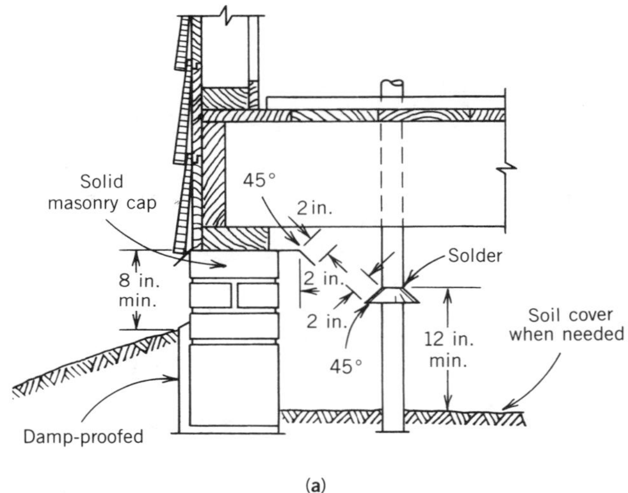

(a)

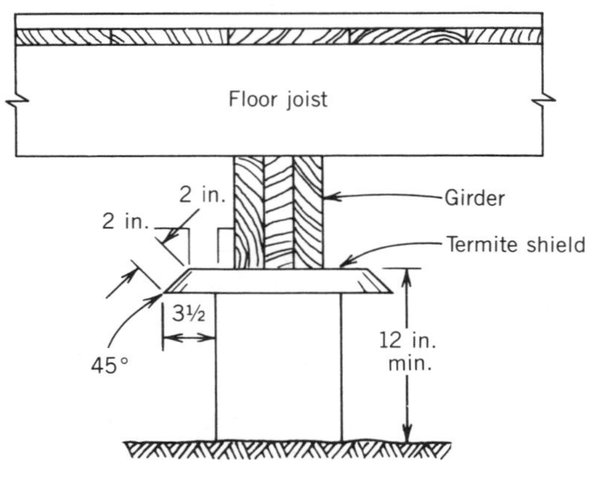

(b)

Figure 1. Diagram of termite shield placed on top of the foundation and support pier of structures. (**a**) At exterior wall; (**b**) Over interior pier. Courtesy of the U.S. Department of Agriculture.

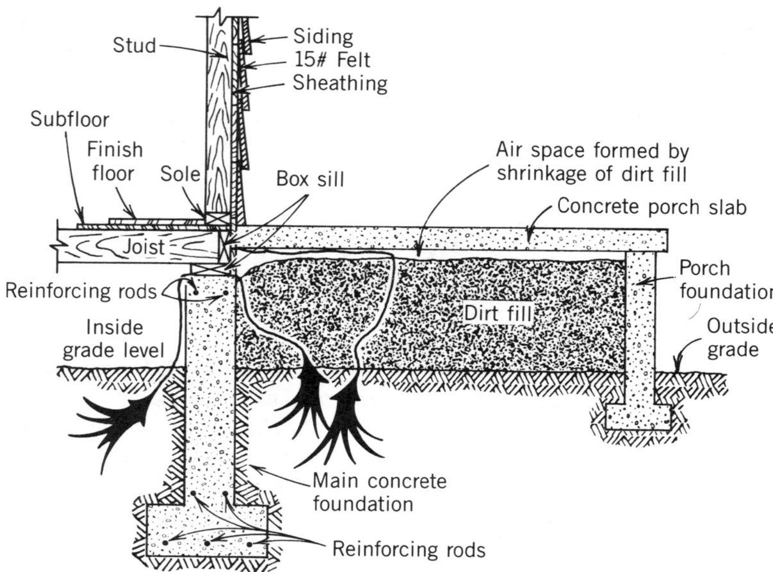

Figure 2. Back-filled porches and slab abutments to structures allow easy access for termites. Courtesy of the National Pest Control Association.

tion, back-filled porches are a primary entrance for termites into the structure (Fig. 2). Flash walls or barriers installed in these areas protect the sill plates from invasion of termites.

The wood-destroying beetle is another wood pest that is very dependent on wood moisture. There are several species that cause considerable damage to wood in structures. These beetles are usually built into the structure; that is, the wood is infested when it is placed into the structure. The circumstance that perpetuates the infestation, and thus damage from the beetles, is moisture. Moisture percentages above 10% will support active infestations of wood-destroying beetles. Proper ventilation and waterproofing can eliminate this potential problem. The National Pest Control Association recommends 1 ft^2 of ventilation for each 25 linear ft of foundation for proper ventilation of a crawl space or basement structure. Building codes and Federal Housing Administration (FHA) *Minimum Property Standards* also cite recommendations for proper ventilation.

The design and construction of log homes has been in much demand in some parts of the United States. Many of these homes are built with logs that have beetle infestations or high moisture content that attracts beetles. In many cases, the logs are not properly pretreated and may be "rushed" into construction, providing a habitat for wood-destroying beetles. Additionally, proper design and construction of these homes is critical to avoid moisture, and thus beetle or fungus problems. Properly designed drainage systems are necessary.

New Designs—New Problems

The increased emphasis on energy savings and the increased use of such construction practices as solar and plenum design have increased the possibility of pest problems. Solar designs that incorporate passive solar systems offer habitat and conditions that favor pests. Although termites are the number one concern, ants and cockroaches are a problem because most of these housing designs are in southern areas of the country.

Plenum designs offer an enclosed habitat in which pests can develop. Although plenums are dry, with little moisture to sustain most wood-infesting insects, the plenum space does offer a consistent environment for development of insect pests such as ants, cockroaches, and silverfish as well as some vertebrates such as mice and rats.

Pest problems in these structures are sometimes difficult or expensive to eliminate. Application of chemicals would not be advised because the air in these infested areas is circulated through the structure. These areas should be properly sealed to prevent entry by potential pest species.

In a series of technical releases, the National Pest Control Association discussed the problems that could arise from tightening structures to decrease energy loss. There have been increasing problems with several insects in such structures; these problems can be directly related to the slower drying out of the structures. The slow drying enables molds (fungi) to grow in wall voids and other enclosed areas. The insects that feed naturally on these fungi find a perpetuating situation that enables them to develop large populations and, to the dismay of the homeowner, an ongoing problem.

Active solar homes offer other problems. In these designs, improperly installed or leaking panels can offer a habitat for carpenter ants or formosan termites. These insects can be quite destructive, and their infestation may result in extensive damage.

VERTEBRATE PESTS

The most common vertebrate pests are rodents (rats and mice) and birds. The rats and mice of concern are called commensal rodents. This term refers to the ability of these animals to live with man. Commensal literally means "one who eats at the same table" and in some areas of the

United States this is true. These animals, especially rats, have been responsible for the transmission of more disease to man than many of the more numerous insect pests. Worldwide, the Norway rat, *Rattus norvegicus,* and the house mouse, *Mus musculus,* are common pests and the most destructive of the rodents.

Because of the rodents' habits, they often invade buildings before the structure is completed. On construction sites, human habits entice rodents to invade. Once they are established, it is a constant battle to eliminate these animals from the structure.

The physical capabilities of mice and rats cannot be underestimated when designing a structure to be rodent resistant (Table 1). Rats and especially mice can enter through small openings in the structure. Openings as small as 6 mm (¼ in.) will allow a mouse to enter, whereas a rat needs a slightly bigger opening (8 mm (½ in.)). Also, commensal rodents are very good climbers. They can climb almost any rough surface and pipes with outside diameters of 3 in. or less. One species in particular, the roof rat, *Rattus rattus,* is an excellent climber and invades structures from trees and aboveground telephone and electrical wires. These rodents have other abilities that make them particularly difficult to keep out of a structure.

Table 1. Physical Capabilities of Rats and Mice[a]

	Rats	Mice
Opening size, mm (in.)	13 (½)	6 (¼)
Reach, cm (in.)	40 (18)	30 (12)
Vertical jump, cm (in.)		
standing	60 (24)	30 (12)
running	90 (36)	30 (12)

[a] Courtesy of the National Pest Control Association.

In addition to eating and contaminating food in structures, these animals do extensive damage to electrical cables and piping by their habit of gnawing. It is estimated that rodents are responsible for 25% of the fires of unknown origin in the United States. The rodents gnaw to keep their teeth sharp and to enlarge holes or penetrate areas to nest or explore. They are capable of gnawing through many common metals, including lead, aluminum, and copper.

Rodent Exclusion

Because man often provides the means for rodent entrance, it is logical that through careful planning and design he can prevent their entrance. Exclusion is a primary control method used in rodent control. This usually means making minor changes or additions to the exterior of buildings to inhibit rodent entry. Where possible, materials that rodents do not like to gnaw on should be used, ie, 20-gauge galvanized metal to shield doors; 6-mm (¼-in.) hardware cloth to screen vents; and steel wool and concrete to seal holes. In addition, a side benefit of excluding rodents is that other vertebrates such as bats, birds, squirrels, and snakes that invade structures are also deterred.

Design

The exterior of the structure is of primary concern. Doors, windows, and vents must fit snugly and be properly screened. The area around the building should be clean and accessible to inspection. If possible, the area around the building, especially any warehouse facility, should be free of landscaping for an area of 3 ft from the outer walls.

One of the most common problems in any structure is preventing access through conduit pipe or electrical access to the structure. In many cases, holes are left in the foundations that will allow rodents to enter. A proper follow-up procedure to seal these areas after construction would prevent the entrance of rodents (Fig. 3). Other methods have been used to prevent rodents from using electrical wires to enter structures (Fig. 4). Such devices are usually installed after the rodents have been discovered entering. However, installation during construction would almost eliminate rodent entry via these avenues.

Other vertebrate pest problems are created by design and construction. The vents created to allow air circulation in attic structures or as air intakes for large commercial structures offer entrances for birds, bats, and larger animals. In some commercial buildings there are large ducts and accesses to these that have become home to feral cat populations. Covering these possible entrances with sturdy, durable screening would inhibit infestation. The material generally used for screening out bats and squirrels is ¼-in. hardware cloth (Fig. 5). For larger animals, this same material may work, but maintenance of the

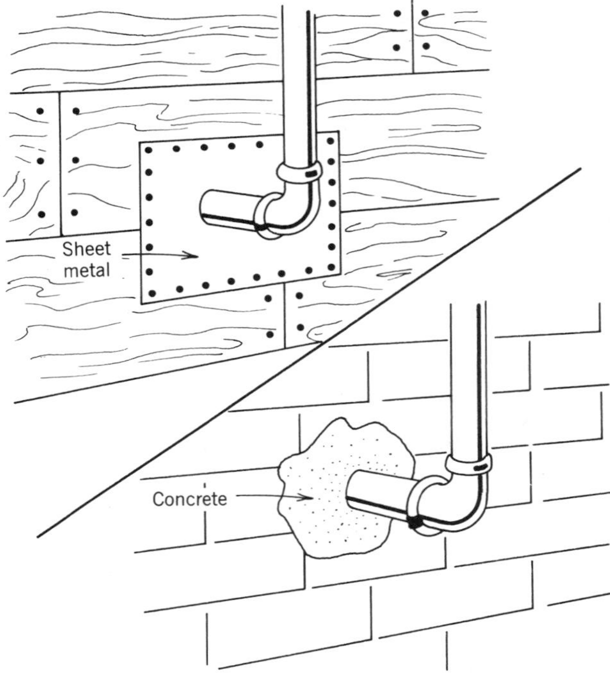

Figure 3. Concrete and sheet metal are used to seal holes around pipe or conduits that enter structures, preventing rodent entry. Courtesy of the U.S. Department of Agriculture.

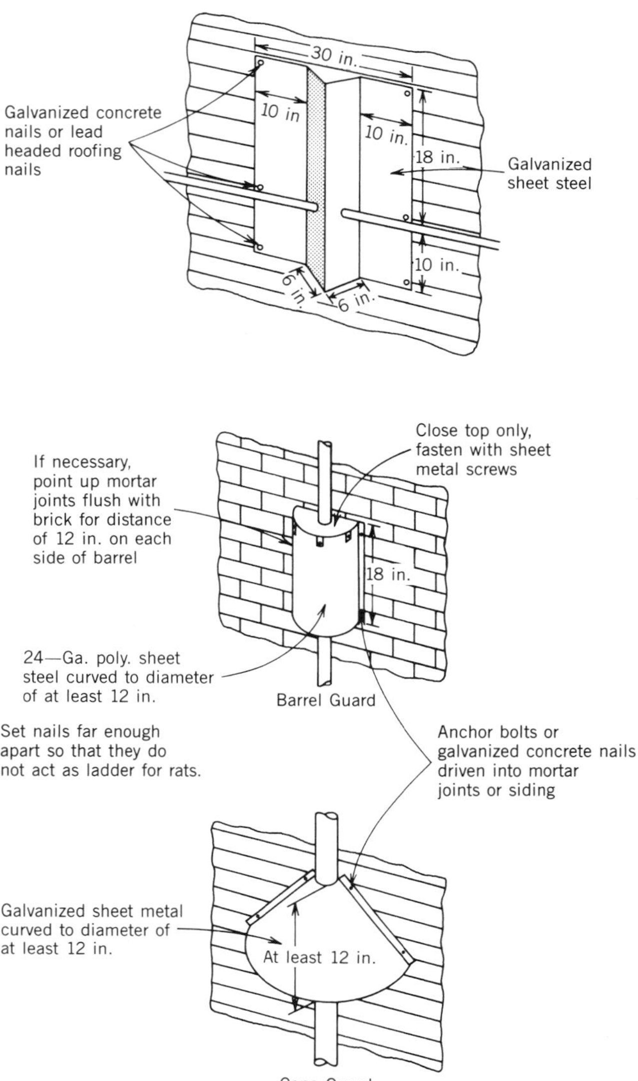

Figure 4. Metal shields around pipes and conduits can prevent rodent access to the building. Courtesy of the U.S. Department of Agriculture.

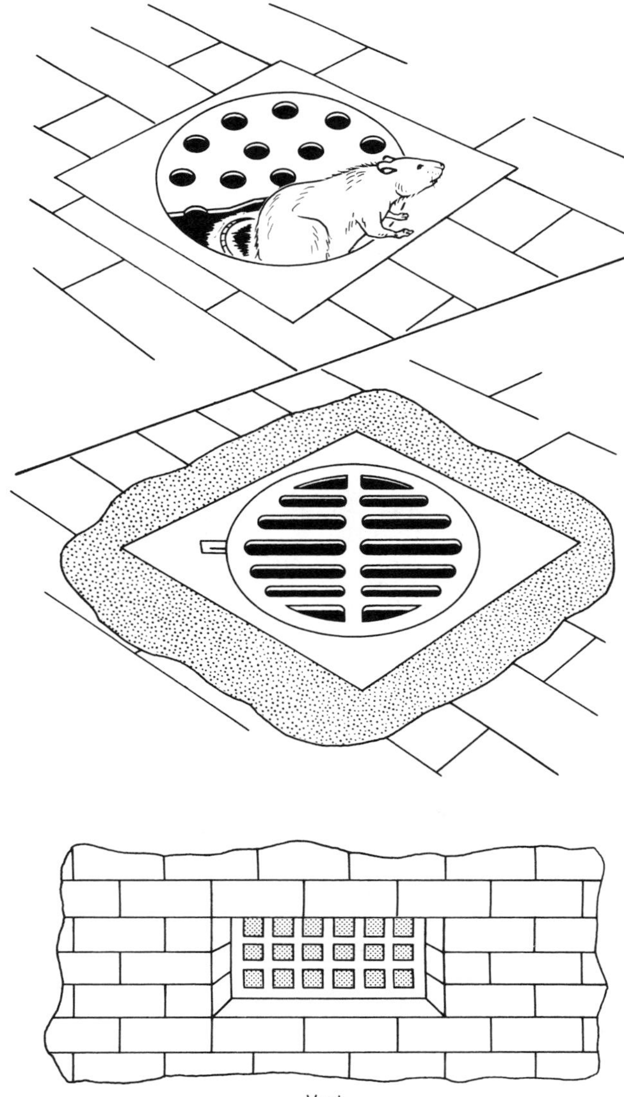

Figure 5. Screening vents and open drains inhibits rodent as well as other vertebrate entry. Courtesy of the U.S. Department of Agriculture.

structure is the key to barring such animals as raccoons, opossums, and cats from entry. Often the screening used in building residences or commercial structures is aluminum or nylon; these materials are easily dislodged, torn, or chewed through by animals such as bats, birds, squirrels, rats, mice, and raccoons.

Rats are also known for their burrowing abilities. They are capable of burrowing under a slab or wall to enter a structure. One method that has been used to deter rodent entry into a structure from burrowing is the construction of a curtain wall (Fig. 6). This is a concrete wall built next to the structure's foundation and extending as much as 2 ft below the soil surface. The wall is L-shaped so the rodent cannot burrow under it.

Bird Problems

There is no potential pest problem that is overlooked more in structural design than the potential for bird problems. There are several birds that can become nuisance pests. Sparrows, starlings, and swallows are capable of building nests in and around the exterior of structures. Sparrows (*Passer domesticus*) build large nests that are added to throughout the year. Swallows (*Petrochelidon* spp.) can attach their nests to the sides of buildings and become very difficult to discourage in some cases. European starlings (*Sturnus vulgaris*) are mostly a problem on or around buildings in the fall and winter when they group together in large flocks to roost.

Most bird species are protected in the United States.

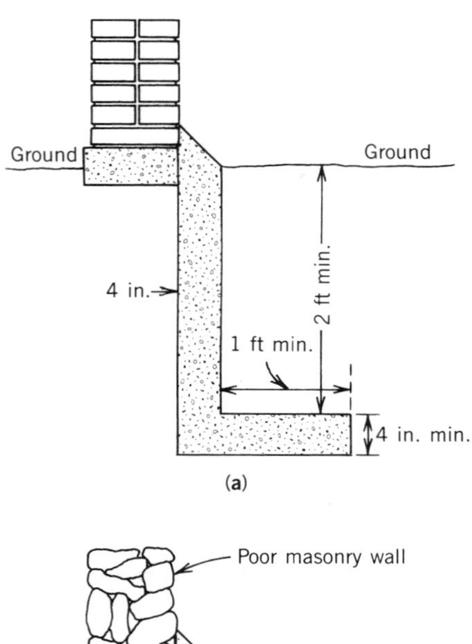

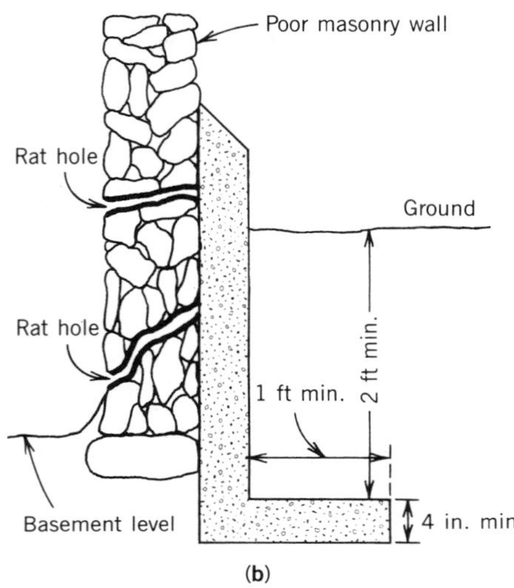

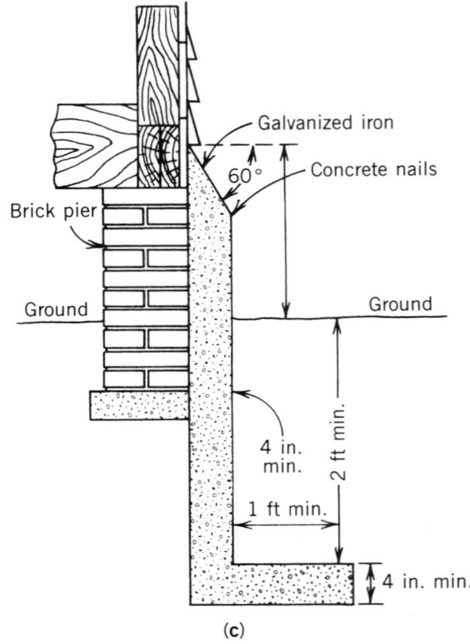

Figure 6. Curtain wall installed on slab-on-grade construction. (**a**) Foundation on ground; (**b**) Poor stone wall and foundation; (**c**) Wood sill above ground. Courtesy of the U.S. Department of Agriculture.

This means the killing of the birds becomes a problem, especially if the birds in question are migratory. Only sparrows and several species of black birds, including the starling, and the pigeon, are not protected. The pigeon, or rock dove (*Columbia livia*), is protected in Iowa.

Most bird problems can be solved by removal of nests or maintenance of the structures so that nesting sites are not offered. In the case of swallows, their nest-making activities are very persistent, and it may require several efforts to discourage them.

Pigeons are a major problem in inner cities. The pigeon is a particular problem because of its habits and the disease organisms and parasites that can be associated with this bird. Rock doves, as the name describes, nest naturally in rock cliffs and prefer high places to roost and nest.

The birds are opportunists. The problem, of course, is their nesting and roosting activities create problems for the people and the structure. Droppings from the birds will cause the deterioration or the disfigurement of structures. The pH of the droppings erodes stone and mortar and discolors or dulls surfaces of metal and glass. The droppings also offer a medium for various fungal and bacterial organisms to grow and create health problems for the humans nearby. In addition, the nesting activities attract rodent and insect problems. Bird mites can infest a structure and bite humans when the bird infestation is left unchecked.

Bird species flock in certain times of the year, but pigeons can be found in flocks most of the time. They usually have a variety of locations they visit during a given day. They feed in parks, but may roost and nest in two different areas. Also, when not feeding during the day, the flock generally has loafing sites around the feeding areas.

These birds look for protected niches that are warm in the winter and protected from heat in the summer in which to roost and nest. Manmade structures offer great opportunities for these birds. They provide columns, window ledges, and overhangs on roofs, entryways, and numerous other places for the pigeon.

After a structure is built and pigeons become a problem, the structure must be physically altered to remove the flock. Capturing the birds only makes room for more to move in later. The site is still there. Several methods have been used to discourage pigeons from invading structures. Thin metal or nylon wires stretched across roof lines or window ledges approximately 4–6 in. off the surface will

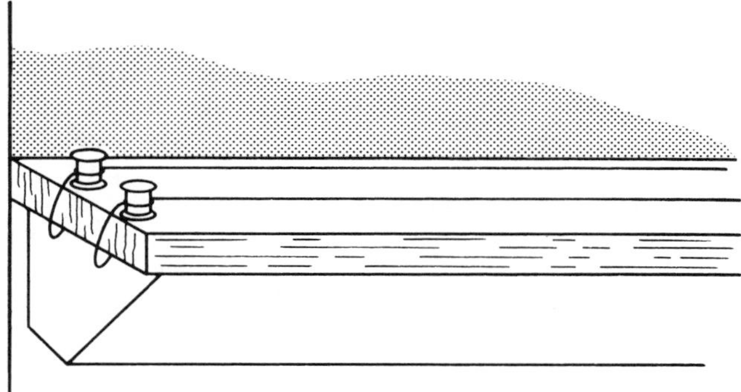

Figure 7. Thin wire across window ledges or roof lines will inhibit birds from landing. Courtesy of the National Pest Control Association.

Figure 8. The severe angle of the ledge deters birds from landing or roosting. Courtesy of the National Pest Control Association.

inhibit the landing of the bird (Fig. 7). Porcupine wire can be put in place to stop the birds from nesting or roosting on window ledges. Some buildings may require netting or screening to keep the birds out of a prime nesting or roosting area.

Some of these efforts will detract from the aesthetics of the buildings unless expensive alterations are performed. Often, however, some well-thought-out methods do not detract from the building's aesthetics and are not noticed by the public.

One such method is to construct the ledges, windows, or columns at a 45° angle (Fig. 8). The pigeon, or other bird, cannot roost or nest on these ledges and seeks other places to nest. Another method is to use acrylic plastic to cover roosting and nesting areas so not to detract from the appearance of the structure.

BIBLIOGRAPHY

General References

Economic News Notes, **XXXII**(3) (1986).

BOCA Basic Building Code/1981, Section 1317.1–4, Building Officials and Code Administrators Int., Inc., Chicago, Ill., 1981.

G. K. Douce and E. F. Saber, *Summary of Losses from Insect Damage and Costs of Control in Georgia, 1984,* Georgia Agricultural Experimental Station, University of Georgia, Athens, Ga., 1985.

"Housing and Urban Development Minimum Property Standards, Single and Multiple Family Housing," U.S. Government Printing Office, Washington, D.C., 1976.

A. P. Meehan, *Rats and Mice, Their Biology and Control,* The Rentokil Library, Brown, Knight & Truscott, Ltd., Tonbridge, Kent, 1984.

H. B. Moore, *Wood Inhabiting Insects in Houses,* Publication 133, USDA-HUD Publication, Washington, D.C., 1979.

G. W. Rambo, ed., *Approved Reference Procedures for Subterranean Termite Control,* National Pest Control Association, Dunn Loring, Va., 1985.

D. Mampe, ed., *Wood Decay in Structures,* National Pest Control Association, Dunn Loring, Va., 1976, p. 28.

W. Fitzwater, *Encyclopedia of Structural Pest Control,* Vol. 4, ESPC 041001–041913, National Pest Control Association, Dunn Loring, Va., 1976.

G. W. Rambo, ed., *Moisture Problems Technical Releases,* ESPC 053201, 053205, National Pest Control Association, Dunn Loring, Va., 1978.

L. Pinto and G. W. Rambo, eds., *Bird Management Manual,* National Pest Control Association, Dunn Loring, Va., 1982.

L. Pinto and P. Spear, *The Structural Pest Control Industry: Description and Impact on the Nation,* National Pest Control Association, Dunn Loring, Va., 1980.

W. Robinson, *Perspective in Urban Entomology, Proceedings Conference of Urban Entomology, Feb. 1986,* College Park, Md., 1986.

U.S.D.A., 1986. "Subterranean Termites, Their Prevention and Control in Building," *Forest Service Home and Garden Bulletin 64,* (1983).

W. J. Webber, *Health Hazards from Pigeons, Starlings and English Sparrows,* Thompson Publications, Fresno, Calif., 1979.

L. H. Williams and R. V. Smyth, *Estimated Losses Caused by Wood Product Insects During 1970 for Single Family Dwellings in Eleven Southern States,* Res. Pap. SO–145, U.S.D.A. Forest Service, Washington, D.C., 1979.

See also TERMITES—CONTROL BY SOIL POISONING; WOOD TREATMENT

GEORGE RAMBO, PHD
National Pest Control Association
Dunn Loring, Virginia

PEVSNER, NIKOLAUS

Sir Nikolaus Pevsner (1902–1983) was a noted historian of art and architecture. Born in Leipzig, he received his doctorate from Leipzig University in 1924. He was Assistant Keeper at the Dresden Art Gallery from 1924 to 1928 and later lecturer in the history of art and architecture at the University of Göttingen until 1933 when, with the rise of the Nazi party, he left Germany and settled in London. Early influences in Germany were described by Pevsner in 1969 (1). Many of his personal papers stored in Germany were destroyed during World War II.

Starting over again in England brought new interests and challenges. His publications revolutionized the study of British architecture, particularly the series on the buildings of England. In addition to his writing, his editorial work included membership on the editorial board of the *Architectural Review,* and he was one of the editors of the multi-volume *Pelican History of Art* (2). He wrote articles and reviewed books for newspapers and magazines, and lectured extensively. Several of his books have been translated into a number of languages.

Pevsner taught at several universities. He was Professor of Art History at Birkbeck College, University of London, and Slade Professor of Fine Art at the Universities of Cambridge (1949–1955) and Oxford (1968–1969). His honors in addition to his knighthood (1969) included the Gold Medal of the Royal Institute of British Architects (1964), and the Grand Cross of Merit from the Federal Republic of Germany (1969).

A supporter of modern architecture, Pevsner demonstrated a belief in the historic development of the arts. A critique of this approach is presented in David Watkin's *Morality and Architecture* (3).

BIBLIOGRAPHY

1. "Sir Nikolaus Pevsner" in W. B. O'Neal, ed., *Papers,* The University Press of Virginia, Charlottesville for the American Association of Architectural Bibliographers, 1970. Foreword by Sir Nikolaus Pevsner.
2. N. Pevsner, J. Nairn, eds., *The Pelican History of Art,* Penguin Books, Baltimore, approximately 50 volumes, various dates, editions.
3. "Pevsner" in D. Watkin, *Morality and Architecture,* Clarendon Press, Oxford, 1977, pp. 71–111.

General References

N. Pevsner, *Pioneers of the Modern Movement from William Morris to Walter Gropius,* Faber and Faber, London, 1936. There have been several editions of this work, the most current published by Penguin Books, Harmondsworth, 1964, and frequently republished since, under the revised title *Pioneers of Modern Design from William Morris to Walter Gropius.* Various American editions have been published by Frederick A. Stokes Co., New York (1936, 1937) and the Museum of Modern Art, New York (1949, 1957).

N. Pevsner, *An Outline of European Architecture,* Penguin Books, Harmondsworth and New York, 1942. The seventh edition of this work was published by Penguin Books, Harmondsworth with revised bibliography in 1968. The second edition was published as the first American edition by Charles Scribner's Sons, New York, 1948.

N. Pevsner, *Studies in Art, Architecture, and Design,* 2 vols., Thames and Hudson, London, 1968. Collected articles, papers, and essays.

N. Pevsner, *The Buildings of England Series,* Penguin Books, Harmondsworth, 1951 ff. Many volumes authored by Pevsner, some in association with other authors.

N. Pevsner, *A History of Building Types,* the A. W. Mellon Lectures in the Fine Arts, The National Gallery of Art, Washington, D.C., 1970. Bollingen Series XXXV.19, The Princeton University Press, Princeton, NJ, 1976.

ROBERT T. PACKARD, AIA
Reston, Virginia

PHENOLIC RESINS

Phenolic resins became a commercial reality in the early 1900s with Baekeland's commercialization of Bakelite (1). Since then, these very versatile products have expanded into many fields including the manufacture of plywood, insulation, hardboard, laminated beams, waferboard, and oriented strand board. They are, and will continue to be, a vital part of the U.S. gross national product.

Phenolic resins are widely used for the following reasons:

1. When cured, they are excellent adhesives for many different substrates.
2. When cured, they are nearly chemically inert and are not affected by water, most organic solvents, oxidation, moderately high temperatures, or reasonable mechanical stresses.
3. They are easy and safe to manufacture.
4. They are easy and safe to use.
5. They are relatively inexpensive and available.

Phenol–formaldehyde resins are by far the most important of the phenolic resins in terms of sheer volume of resin produced. Other phenols such as cresols, resorcinols, and substituted phenols are used, as are other aldehydes such as acetaldehyde, butyraldehyde, and furfural. These different phenols and aldehydes are used to make resins for highly specialized uses.

Phenolic resins are usually made as aqueous solutions in reactors by batch processes using alkaline catalysts. Phenolic resins made with enough formaldehyde to be used as received by the final processor are called resoles. Resins that are manufactured with acid catalysts and less than the required amount of formaldehyde are called novolacs, and the additional needed formaldehyde is usually added at the point of final use in the form of hexamethylenetetramine.

Phenolic resoles are ordinarily shipped in bulk as li-

Table 1. Approximate Consumption of Phenolic Resins by Industry in 1984

Industry	Weight, lb	Percent[b]
Plywood	490,000	25.5
Insulation	400,000	20.0
Hardboard	70,000	3.5
*OSB[a] and waferboard	100,000	5.0
Molded wood	25,000	1.25
Laminates	110,000	5.5
Molding compounds	350,000	17.5
Friction materials	50,000	2.5
Abrasives	55,000	2.75
Protective coatings	35,000	1.75
Foundry molds	140,000	7.0
Rubber production	25,000	1.25
Miscellaneous	150,000	7.5
Total:	*2,000,000*	*100.00*

[a] Oriented strand board.
[b] Percent figures are rounded.

quids, although some are spray dried and shipped as powders. A very small amount is shipped as rolls of dried phenolic-resin-impregnated paper.

Novolacs are manufactured by separating a hydrophobic layer of phenolic resin from the reaction mixture as a high viscosity liquid. This thick warm liquid is cooled on a Sandvik belt and flaked. The flaked resin is ground and mixed with extenders. It is then bagged and sold as a powder. Approximately 2 billion lb of phenol–formaldehyde resins were used in the United States in 1984 by the industries listed in Table 1.

STRUCTURAL WOOD COMPOSITES

Plywood

The single most important user of phenolic resin as a waterproof adhesive is the softwood-plywood industry. Softwood-plywood in the United States was first produced under the direction of Gustav A. Carlson and N. J. Bailey in early 1905 (2). These first panels were produced for an exhibit at the Portland, Oregon, World's Fair in 1905 in honor of the Lewis and Clark Expedition's centennial. Exterior plywood was first produced from a cresylic-acid–formaldehyde resin developed by James Victor Nevin (3) for Harbor Plywood Company in Aberdeen, Washington, in 1933. Phenol–formaldehyde resins soon supplanted the cresylic acid approach. Eight billion square feet of (3/8-in. basis) exterior plywood were made in the period from 1933 to 1955 (2). In 1984, approximately 20 billion ft^2 of exterior plywood was produced.

The plywood-manufacturing process consists of peeling debarked logs into veneers of appropriate thickness; drying the veneer to 3–5% moisture content in veneer dryers; spreading an adhesive mix that contains phenolic resin, extenders, and caustic soda onto the veneers; assembling the veneers, each veneer layer at right angles to the adjacent layer, to the proper panel thickness for a hot-press charge; prepressing this charge in a cold press for consolidation; feeding the prepressed panels into a hot press; pressing the charge 3–7 min at 285–330°F and 175–200 psi; and stacking the hot-pressed panels for hot-stack cure. The panels are then trimmed to the proper dimensions, graded, and banded into bundles for shipping.

Douglas fir was the primary source of softwood plywood until approximately 1955 when white fir, hemlock, and ponderosa pine began to be used. Over 70 different species can now be used for plywood (Table 2). The Pacific Northwest continued to be the primary source of softwood plywood until 1977, when southern pine plywood became dominant.

Plywood panels are used mainly in single- and multiple-dwelling construction, primarily for floors and floor underlayment, wall sheathing and decorative siding, roof sheathing and soffits, etc. One rather recent development for plywood is in all-wood foundations. Plywood is treated with a preservative and successfully competes with concrete, especially in wet or cold climates. Another large use for plywood is concrete forms. Plywood can be utilized for fire-resistant construction, wind-resistant roofs, noise-transmission control, energy conservation, box beams, plywood sandwich panels, stressed-skin panels, and specialized panel roof diaphragms.

Waferboard and Oriented Strand Board

Closely associated with plywood panels are the composition panels known as waferboard and OSB. Although only 2 billion ft^2 were made as nonveneered panels in 1983 compared to 20 billion ft^2 of plywood, it appears that these composite panels are here to stay, and they will probably supplant plywood to an appreciable extent in the future for certain of its uses because of cost and more uniform strength. See Table 3 for production breakdown by U.S. geographical area. At first glance, waferboard and OSB appear similar, but there is considerable difference in the way the two products are made. In waferboard, the flakes are usually larger, oriented randomly in the felting operation, and are bound with a powdered phenolic resin. Oriented strand board, on the other hand, normally employs liquid phenolic resins, and the flakes are somewhat smaller and are oriented in perpendicular layers (usually three to five) during mat formation. Some OSB is now being made with powdered resins. Boards made with powdered phenolic contain a maximum of 3% resin, apparently the maximum amount that can be applied. On the other hand, liquid-bonded OSB uses approximately 5% resin solids. Because OSB has oriented layers and greater resin content, it can be made much stronger than waferboard for any given thickness.

Plywood, waferboard, and OSB can be made to conform to either product or performance standards. Product Standard 1–83 (4) is the conventional standard for plywood. In the last four years, performance standards have come into play (5,6,7). Performance rated panels are recognized under the auspices of the National Evaluation Service (NES) (formerly the National Research Board) and the Federal Housing Administration (FHA) (7). The NES is sponsored jointly by Building Officials and Code Administrators International (BOCA), International Conference of Building Officials (ICBO), and the Southern Building Code Congress International (SBCCI).

Structural panels are almost universally grade marked by testing agencies such as the American Plywood Association, Timber Engineering Co., and Pittsburgh Testing Laboratories. Stamps supplied to the manufacturing mills state mill grade, span rating, thickness, exposure durability, and mill manufacturing number, and contain one or all standards (NER–108, PS 1–83, and FHA–UM–64) to which they conform. Examples of stamps in Figure 1.

Hardboard

Hardboard, as defined by the American Hardboard Association, "is a panel manufactured primarily from inter-felted ligno-cellulosic fibers, consolidated under heat and pressure in a hot press to a density of 31 pounds per cubic foot (0.5). Other materials may be added during manufacture to improve certain properties" (8). Actually, most hardboard densities are much higher than 0.5, and approach a range of 0.85–1.00 in practice. Other additives

Table 2. Classification of Species[a]

Group 1	Group 2	Group 3	Group 4	Group 5
Apitong	Cedar, Port Orford	Alder, red	Aspen	Basswood
Beech, American	Cypress	Birch, paper	bigtooth	Poplar, balsam
Birch	Douglas fir 2[b]	Cedar, Alaska	quaking	
sweet	Fir	Fir, subalpine	Cativo	
yellow	balsam	Hemlock, eastern	Cedar	
Douglas fir 1[b]	California red	Maple, bigleaf	incense	
Kapur	grand	Pine	western red	
Keruing	noble	jack	Cottonwood	
Larch, western	Pacific silver	lodgepole	eastern	
Maple, sugar	white	ponderosa	black (western poplar)	
Pine	Hemlock, western	spruce	Pine	
Caribbean	Lauan	Redwood	eastern white	
ocote	almon	Spruce	sugar	
Pine, south	bagtikan	Englemann		
loblolly	mayapis	white		
longleaf	red			
shortleaf	tangile			
slash	white			
Tanoak	Maple, black			
	Mengkulang			
	Meranti, red[c]			
	Mersawa			
	Pine			
	ponderosa			
	red			
	Virginia			
	western white			
	Spruce			
	black			
	red			
	sitka			
	Sweetgum			
	Tamarack			
	Yellow-poplar			

[a] Ref. 4. Courtesy of the American Plywood Association.

[b] Douglas fir from trees grown in the states of Washington, Oregon, California, Idaho, Montana, Wyoming, and the Canadian provinces of Alberta and British Columbia shall be classed as Douglas fir No. 1. Douglas fir from trees grown in the states of Nevada, Utah, Colorado, Arizona, and New Mexico shall be classed as Douglas fir No. 2.

[c] Red Meranti shall be limited to species having a specific gravity of 0.41 or more based on green volume and oven-dry weight.

consist almost entirely of phenolic resin added in a range of 0.5–3.0% by weight, depending on actual product.

There has been no increase in production capacity in the United States in the last 10 years, and considerable hardboard is imported from various countries. Approximately 5.7 billion ft^2 (⅛-in. basis) were made in the United States in 1984, of which 65% was used for exterior siding. Classifications are tempered, standard, service-tempered, service, and industrialite, and all can be smooth on one or two sides (Table 4).

Table 3. Structural Panel Production Summary (1984)[a]

U.S. Geographical Area	Production, million ft^2	Percent
West coast	7,700	35.0
Inland	1,870	8.5
South	10,340	47.0
North	2,090	9.5
Total	*22,000*	*100.0*

[a] Ref. 5. Courtesy of the American Plywood Association.

Classifications other than siding are used widely for many parts in the furniture business. They are also employed as substrates for grain-printed and overlayed wall paneling.

Hardboard conforms to Standards ANSI/AHA 135.4,5–1982 and 135.6–1984 (based on PS 58–73 and PS 59–73), and, where appropriate, to test method ASTM D1037. Product standard 58–73 is concerned with physical standards, whereas PS 59–73 is concerned with prefinished hardboard.

Laminated Beams

Another important structural product that employs a phenolic resin as its adhesive is the wood-laminated beam. The adhesive is actually a phenol–resorcinol–formaldehyde (PRF) resin that is very similar to a liquid novolac in that more formaldehyde must be added to it at the

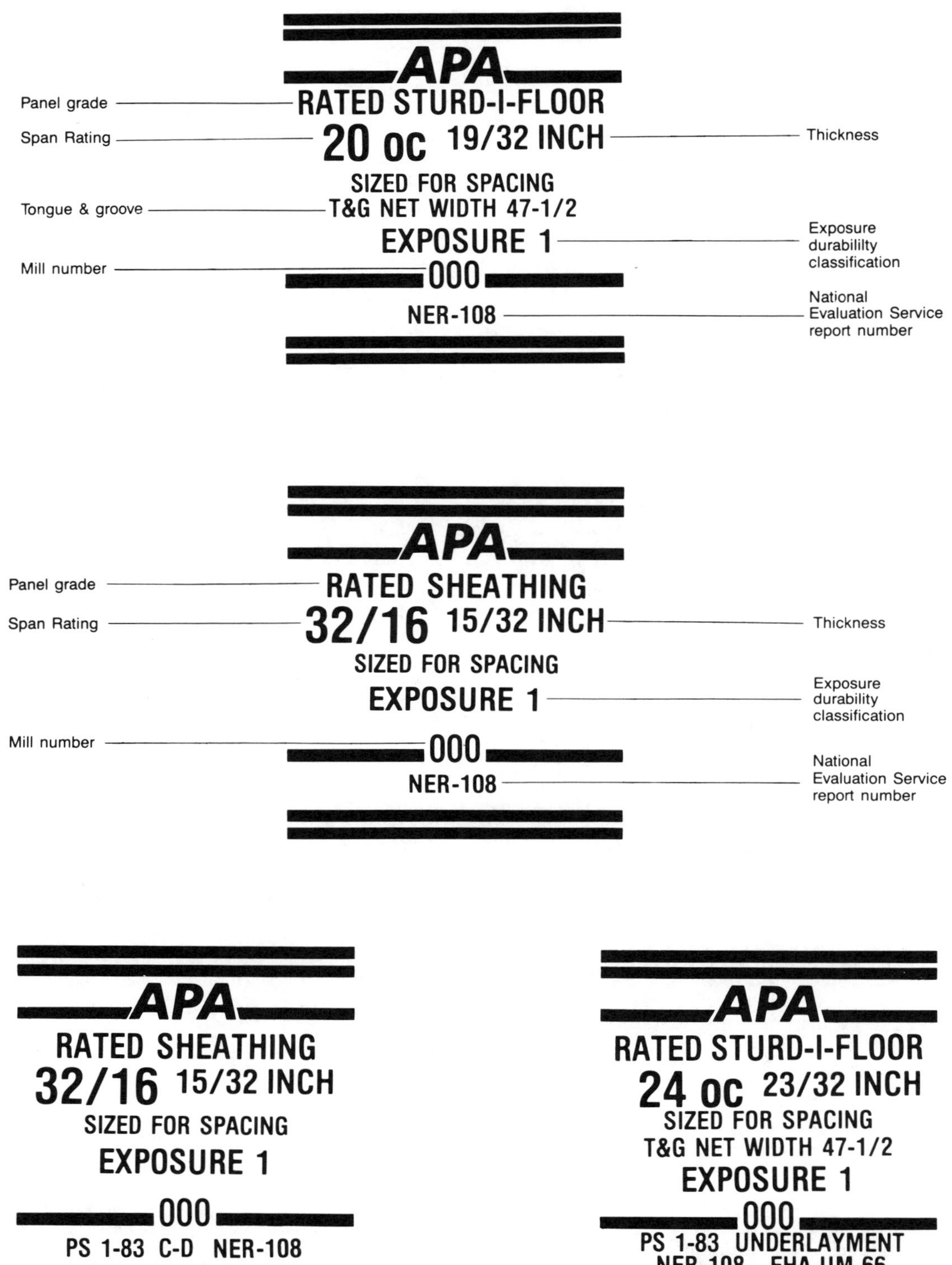

Figure 1. Plywood grade marks (7). Courtesy of the American Plywood Association.

Table 4. Classification of Hardboard by Surface Finish, Thickness, and Physical Properties[a]

Class	Nominal Thickness, in.	Water Resistance (max av per panel): Water Absorption Based on Weight, %	Water Resistance (max av per panel): Thickness swelling, %	Modulus of Rupture (min av per panel), psi	Tensile Strength (min av per panel): Parallel to Surface, psi	Tensile Strength (min av per panel): Perpendicular to Surface, psi
1. Tempered	1/12	30	25	6000	3000	130
	1/10, 1/8, 3/16	25	20			
	1/4	20	15			
	5/16	15	10			
	3/8	10	9			
2. Standard	1/12	40	30	4500	2200	90
	1/10, 1/8, 3/16	35	25			
	1/4	25	20			
	5/16	20	15			
	3/8	15	10			
3. Service-tempered	1/8	35	30	4500	2000	75
	3/16	30	30			
	1/4	30	25			
	3/8	20	15			
4. Service	1/8	45	35	3000	1500	50
	3/16	40	35			
	1/4	40	30			
	3/8	35	25			
	7/16	35	25			
	1/2	30	20			
	5/8	25	20			
	11/16	25	20			
	3/4, 13/16, 7/8, 1	20	15			
	1 1/8					
5. Industrialite	1/4	50	30	2000	1000	25
	3/8	40	25			
	7/16	40	25			
	1/2	35	25			
	5/8	30	20			
	11/16	30	20			
	3/4, 13/16, 7/8, 1, 1 1/8	25	20			

[a] Ref. 9. Courtesy of the American Hardboard Association.

time the beam is glued. The addition of resorcinol greatly increases the reactivity of the resin system, especially at temperatures of 70–90°F. It is this property that makes PRF resins ideal for laminated-beam manufacture. The resin-catalyst (paraformaldehyde and fillers) system can be designed to apply the adhesive to the laminates and still be liquid until the laminated-beam assembly is clamped and the adhesive allowed to cure in a curing chamber at slightly elevated temperature. The adhesive glue line, when properly cured, has the desired strength and water–moisture resistance needed.

Phenol–resorcinol–formaldehyde laminated beams are the load-carrying structures for roofs, bridges, towers, and marine installations. The laminates of the beams are in almost all cases finger-end jointed, then glued to the proper length needed for the desired beam. Laminated beams are known for economy, ease of installation, chemical resistance, durability, lack of thermal expansion, and safety. The safety of large laminated beams has been proven. As wood burns, it chars on the outside, but the unburned wood retains its strength (10). Steel beams rapidly lose strength above 480°F, retaining approximately 10% of

Table 5. Standards Applying to Structural Glued Laminated Timber[a]

AITC 109–81	Treating standard
AITC 110–83	Standard appearance grades
AITC 113–82	Dimension standards
AITC 117–82	Design and manufacturing standards
AITC 119–81	Hardwood specifications
AITC 200–83	Inspection manual
AITC 401–83	Manufactured lumber standard
AITC 402–83	LVL standard
AITC 403–83	End joint standard
ASTM D2016–74	Moisture content standard
ASTM D2555–81	Wood strength standard
ASTM D2559–82	Adhesive specification standard
ASTM D3024–78	Protein adhesive (dry use) standard
ASTM D3737–81	Stress standard

[a] Ref. 11. Courtesy of the American Institute of Timber Construction.

their strength at 1380°F. Most fires attain temperatures of 1290–1650°F. Softwoods commonly glued are Douglas fir, larch, hemfir, hemlock, and southern pine. Other species and laminated veneer lumber can also be used. The current voluntary product standard applying to beams is ANSI/AITC A 190.1–1983 (11), which is a revision of PS 56–73 and references the publications listed in Table 5. This standard allows for the use of adhesives other than phenol–resorcinol–formaldehyde; however, at the present time, practically all beams are made with PRF resins. Approximately 225 million board feet of structural laminated beams were manufactured in 1984.

Laminated Veneer Lumber

Laminated veneer lumber (LVL) is a relatively new product for which a significant market is developing. This product is glued with the same veneer and phenolic adhesives as those utilized in plywood, but the veneer is all glued in parallel rather than with adjacent veneer layers at right angles as in conventional plywood. Billets up to 2½ in. thick can be glued and can be made to almost any length. This length is obviously limited to the physical handling capability of the manufacturing plant. Laminated veneer lumber's strength is much more uniform than untreated lumber because the randomizing effect of gluing the veneers uniformly disperses the weaknesses and strengths of the wood. Table 6 lists design stresses of a commercially available LVL and represents acceptance by the Council of American Building Officials (NRB–12C) of the LVL as an alternative building material under that joint model building code organization.

Parallel Strand Lumber

Parallel strand lumber, a new approach to "synthetic" lumber that uses a phenolic-resin binder, is now in pilot-plant development. Very little has been said about the details of the manufacturing procedures by the manufacturer, MacMillan-Bloedel of Vancouver, British Columbia, except that 4 foot-long strands of ⅛ × ½ in. veneer and 5–10% resin solids are used. The density is approximately 0.65, and the product has ICBO approval.

INSULATION AND MOLDING COMPOUNDS

Insulation

The second largest consumer of phenolic resins is the insulation industry. By far, phenolic-resin-bonded glass-fiber insulation is the most important, followed by mineral wool and waste fiber. In the manufacture of an insulation batt, a liquid phenolic resin is sprayed on glass fibers as they are being spun, and the resin–glass combination is formed into a mat. The mat is then heated to cure the resin and drive off moisture. The batts are either shipped as made or faced with a vapor barrier such as a thin aluminum foil. Because the mats are so light in weight, they are compressed to 1/20–1/25th of their original thickness and bundled. When they are unbundled, the mats spring back to their original thickness before being used. Phenolic resins are ideal binders for insulation batts because of

Table 6. Design Stresses of LVL at Normal Load Duration[a]

					Compression Perpendicular To Grain f_c		Horizontal Shear f_v		
Thickness	Grade	Flexural Stress f_b[b]	Tension Parallel to Grain l_t	Compression Parallel to Grain f_c	Perpendicular to the Glue Line (Plank)	Parallel to the Glue Line (Joist)	Parallel to the Glue Line (Plank)	Perpendicular to the Glue Line (Joist)	Modulus of Elasticity, E
¾	2.2E	3100	2050	2850	400	500	190	285	2,200,000
to	2.0E	2800	1850	2700	400	500	190	285	2,000,000
1¾ in.	1.8E	2300	1650	2400	400	500	190	285	1,800,000
1⅞	2.2E	2650	1750	2400	400	500	160	285	2,200,000
to	2.0E	2400	1550	2300	400	500	160	285	2,000,000
2½ in.	1.8E	1950	1400	2050	400	500	160	285	1,800,000

[a] Ref. 12. Courtesy of Trus-Joist Corporation.
[b] For 12 in. depth. For other depths, multiply by the factors below. For depths less than 3.5 inches and for flat bending, use the factor for 3.5-inch depth.

Depth (in.)	3.5	5.5	7.25	9.25	12.0	16.0	20.0	24.0
Multiplier	1.15	1.09	1.06	1.03	1.00	0.97	0.94	0.93

Table 7. Insulation Specifications[a]

Typical Uses	Federal	Military	ASTM
Aircraft		MIL–B–5924B (ASB) (3)	
Air conditioning	HH–I–558B	MIL–I–22023C	C612 Class 3
Appliance	HH–I–558B	MIL–I–24244	
Boilers	HH–I–558B	MIL–I–24244	C262, C553, C612 Class 3 E136
Building	HH–I–558B		C665
Ceiling	HH–I–558B		C665
Duct lines	HH–I–558B	MIL–1–22023C	C553
Heavy density	HH–I–558B		C547
Metal building	HH–I–558B Form A and B		C553 C612 Class 3
Pipe	HH–I–558B	MIL–2781E	C547
Pipe (850°F)	HH–1–558B HH–B–100B	MIL–1–22344B	C547
Sound control			C423
Tanks	HH–I–558B	MIL–I–24244	C262, C553, C612 Class 3 E136
Water heaters	HH–I–558B	MIL–I–24244	C262,C553, C612 Class 3
Loose fill	HH–1–1030B		C764

[a] Refs. 13,14. Courtesy of Owens/Corning Fiberglas Corp. and the Manville Corp.

their excellent adherence to glass fiber and mineral wool, and their outstanding water resistance.

Phenolic-resin-bonded glass fiber is important in pipe insulation. Pipe insulation is made by wrapping a glass-fiber mat, which has been saturated with a liquid phenolic-resin mix and dried, around a mandrel. The wrapped mandrel is then placed in a heating chamber until the resin is cured. The resulting cylinder is slit and removed from the mandrel. The resin mix must be fire resistant (13,14) because there is enough organic matter from the phenolic resin to support combustion.

Approximately 10% of the phenolic-resin consumption for insulation is in acoustical padding and thermal insulation batting for automobiles. The acoustical padding employs organic waste fibers, but the insulation batting uses glass fibers. The resin is a powdered hexamethylenetetramine-cured novolac phenolic. Table 7 lists some of the specifications met by the different types of insulation.

Molding Compounds

The phenolic resin used in molding compounds can be either a novolac–hexa combination, or a dry resole resin. A typical molding compound contains 40–50% by weight of phenolic resin, and 50–60% fillers. The most common filler is wood flour, although inorganic materials such as glass fiber, clay, and talc also serve as extenders.

The electrical market is the largest consumer of phenolic molding compounds, followed by the appliance and auto industry. The electrical industry uses phenolic molding compounds for outlet boxes, receptacles, base plugs, light sockets, and similar applications. The appliance industry employs them for toasters, irons, pot handles, popcorn makers, deep-fat fryers, drip coffee makers, and electric frying pans.

LAMINATES AND COATINGS

Laminates

High density laminates are manufactured from resin-impregnated sheets of fibrous materials. The usual substrate is kraft paper, but many other substrates are used for particular purposes. Although much of the final laminate contains sheets saturated with phenolic resin, the topmost sheets are saturated with melamine resins. After saturation, the sheets are dried and cut to the proper length. The melamine sheets have the proper color and pattern desired. The combined phenolic and melamine sheets are hot pressed, usually between highly polished cauls, at temperatures up to 375°F and pressures of 2000 psi. Textured caul plates are used for other finishes.

High density laminates are made of all melamine-saturated sheets for use where exceptionally heavy abrasive conditions are expected. In recent years, fire-resistant high density laminates have been produced to meet increasingly stringent fire codes. This has been accomplished by adding fire-retardant ingredients to the phenolic-resin-saturated sheets.

Decorative laminates are made either for flat or postformable stock. Postformable sheets need plasticized phenolic and melamine resins, and the sheets are not completely cured as are the regular laminates. These postformable sheets are reheated and shaped when glued to the desired nonflat substrate. This reheating completes the cure of the resin. Decorative laminates are further differentiated by horizontal or vertical use, although, in most cases, the horizontal use is satisfactory for vertical use also.

Decorative laminates have many commercial and residential uses. Some commercial uses are restaurant and bar tables, desks, conference tables, bank teller stations, stove fixtures, bookcases, interior hallway walls, toilet compartments, movable partitions, and elevator walls. Kitchen countertops and cabinets, tables, occasional furniture, and vanity and bar tops are some of the residential uses.

High pressure laminates are expected to meet the performance standards of the International Organization of Standardization (ISO) ISO 4586–2 and National Electrical Manufacturers Association (NEMA) NEMA LD3–1980. Fire-resistant laminates are also rated by NEMA LD3–1980, but indicate a fire-rated grade such as FR–32, –50, or –87. These FR ratings are based on the laminate's performance to ASTM E84 (UL–723). For U.S. government projects, refer to Federal Specification L–P–508H (15).

Coatings

Both phenol and parasubstituted phenols are used. The phenolic resins are alkaline catalyzed, then dissolved in alcohol. These straight phenolic resins are baked on the metal surfaces for corrosion resistance and are employed for drum and can linings, milk and beer processing equipment, and water tank coatings. These coatings have excellent water (except for strong acids or alkalies), solvent, and heat resistance.

Parasubstituted phenolic resins are acid catalyzed, oil soluble, and have extensive use in protective coatings. They are allowed to react or are mixed with drying oils for paints and varnishes. These are used as finishes for all kinds of wooden floors, woodwork, and furniture. Electrical insulating varnishes and enamels also need parasubstituted phenol–formaldehyde resins.

FOUNDRY BINDERS, ABRASIVES, AND FRICTION MATERIALS

Foundry binders, abrasives, and friction materials do not play a direct role in architecture, but have a vital function in manufacturing materials for construction. For this reason, they are included here.

Foundry Binders

One important use of phenolic resins is as a foundry core binder. This is done by the hot-box, shell-molding, no-bake, or cold-box methods. The hot-box and shell-molding processes can utilize either liquid or powdered resin, but the no-bake process requires liquid resins. Shell molding is the method most extensively used and employs sand that has been precoated with phenolic resin. Therefore, no mixing or mulling must be done by the foundry. The hot-box and shell-molding processes need heat to cure the resins, but the no-bake and cold-box methods use catalysts or chemical activation for curing.

Abrasives

Abrasives can be divided into two main categories: bonded and coated abrasives. The most important use of bonded abrasives is for grinding wheels, but an enormous variety of other bonded abrasives is made, including grinding wheels, cut-off wheels, internal wheels, honing stones, dressing sticks, mounted points, abrasive cords, abrasive tapes, and tumbling stones. The most common example of a coated abrasive is sandpaper. Coated abrasives are manufactured as sheets, rolls, disks, belts, and flap wheels.

Approximately 50% of the binder used in the above products is phenolic resin, approximately 45–50 million, lb. Aluminum oxide, silicon carbide, emery, garnet, and diamond are typical examples of abrasive materials used.

Friction Materials

Phenolic resins are the principle binders for brake linings, clutch facings, and automatic transmission parts, which are the chief consumers of friction materials. Friction materials are used in many other places such as oil well drilling rigs, power derricks, and railroad cars.

BIBLIOGRAPHY

1. U.S. Pat. 939,966 (Nov. 6, 1909), L. H. Baekeland.
2. R. M. Cour, *The Plywood Age,* Binfords and Mart, Portland, Oreg., 1955.
3. U. S. Pat. 2,150,697 (Mar. 14, 1939), J. V. Nevin.
4. *U.S. Product Standard PS 1–83, Form H850,* American Plywood Association, Tacoma, Wash., Jan. 1984, p. 7.
5. *Management Bulletin No. FA–225,* American Plywood Association, Tacoma, Wash., 1984.
6. *APA Design/Construction Guide No. E30D,* American Plywood Association, Tacoma, Wash., rev. Mar. 1984/6000, p. 4.
7. *Performance Rated Panels, Form 405E,* American Plywood Association, Tacoma, Wash., Jan. 1984, pp. 3–4, 7–9.
8. *Today's Hardboard,* American Hardboard Assn., Palatine, Ill., 1988.
9. *Basic Hardboard ANSI/AHA A 135.4–1982,* American Hardboard Association, Palatine, Ill., Sept. 10, 1982, pp. 2, back page.
10. *Glulam Systems, 6.4a(d)/AM,* The American Institute of Timber Construction, Englewood, Colo., 1983, p. 9.
11. *American National Standard for Wood Products-Structural Glued Laminated Timber ANSI/AITC 190.1–1983,* American Institute of Timber Construction, Englewood, Colo., 1983, p. 1.
12. *Engineered Wood Micro-lam Laminated Veneer Lumber, 4082/7–83/15M,* Trus-Joist Corp., Boise, Idaho, 1983, back cover.
13. *Product Specification References 3–GL–4004–1,* Owens-Corning Fiberglas Corp., Toledo, Ohio, Nov. 1982, pp. 4–14.
14. *Specification Information,* Vol. 6, 74th ed., Thomas Register, 1984, pp. 4614–4654. Specification information in Manville brochures covers same specifications.
15. *Specification Information Guide* 83–020, Formica Corp., Wayne, N.J., 1983, pp. 15–16.

General References

G. L. Brode, "Phenolic Resins," in *Kirk-Othmer Encyclopedia of Chemical Technology,* Vol. 17, 3rd ed., 1982, pp. 384–446.

R. Nauth, *The Chemistry and Technology of Plastics,* Reinhold Publishing Corp., New York, 1947, pp. 15–54.

U.S. Pat. 2,631,098 (Mar. 10, 1953), D. V. Redfern.

C. G. Carll, H. E. Dickerhoot, and J. A. Youngquist, "U.S. Wood-based Panel Industry: Production Trends & Changing Markets," *Forest Products J.* **32**(6), 14 (June 1982).

C. G. Carll, H. E. Dickerhoot, and J. A. Youngquist, "U.S. Wood-base Panel Industry: Standards for Panel Products," *Forest Products J.* **32**(7), 12 (July 1982).

C. G. Carll, H. E. Dickerhoot, and J. A. Youngquist, "U.S. Wood-based Panel Industry: Research & Technological Innovations," *Forest Products J.* **32**(8), 14 (Aug. 1982).

A. M. Camarano, "Marketing Impact of All Weather Wood Foundation on Forest Products Industries," *Forest Products J.* **30**(11), 38 (Nov. 1980).

See also Glued Laminated Wood—Glulam; Plastic Laminates; Wood—Structural Panel Composites

Jerry P. Re
Eugene, Oregon

PHOTOGRAPHY, ARCHITECTURAL

HISTORY

The first photograph was that of a building. It was taken by Nicéphore Niépce in 1826 (Fig. 1). After a series of experiments with light-sensitive materials, Niépce succeeded in fixing an image on a bitumen-coated pewter plate; the subject was the view from a window of his house in Burgundy, France, showing the courtyard. The exposure time was eight hours.

Niépce and Louis Jacques Mande Daguerre later worked together to perfect the process, but not until after the death of Niépce, in 1833, did Daguerre discover a silver–iodine process which had a broad application. In 1839, when Daguerre's process was made public, Niépce's family received a token payment for his pioneering discoveries.

Eugene Atget (French), Pompeo Pozzi (Italian), and scores of others around the world developed stylistic and technical approaches to photographing architecture in the

Figure 1. "View from the Window at Gras," 1826. The world's first photograph, taken by Nicéphore Niépce. Courtesy of the Gernsheim Collection, Harry Ransom Humanities Research Center, The University of Texas at Austin.

nineteenth century. August Sander, a German, made major contributions in the early twentieth century.

Architectural photography specialists began emerging at that time—Frederick Evans (English) with his "Sea of Steps" (Fig. 2), Frances Benjamin Johnson (American), Berenice Abbott (American), Andre Kertesz (Hungarian-American), and F. S. Lincoln (American).

Ezra Stoller, a U.S. architectural photographer with architectural training, shifted and simplified contents of interiors for a more ordered look. He also made dramatic and evocative pictures of exteriors. In the mid-twentieth century his style gave rise to a neologism, "stollerize." Also in the postwar period appear Americans Hedrich-Blessing, Joseph Molitor, Julius Shulman, Phyllis Dearborn-Massar, Steve Rosenthal, Norman McGrath, Robert Lautman, Peter Aaron, Evelyn Hofer, and G. E. Kidder-Smith, and the Japanese, Yukio Futagawa, plus enough new arrivals to make expert architectural photography available to nearly all architects, engineers, designers, magazines, and product manufacturers.

There is also a growing body of architecturally oriented photographers whose work receives exposure in art galleries, more specialized photographic galleries, and in art-and-architecture oriented books and publications. This article, however, concerns the photographers who photograph for architects toward mutual goals: recording, recognition, publicity, and publication.

The American Institute of Architects's honor awards in architectural photography have been received by 17 photographers. A unique and coveted professional accolade, its very existence has elevated standards of performance in architectural photography.

APPROACHES

Architectural photographers differ in view. One school feels that since photographs are second-hand experiences compared to the multitude of impressions received as one walks through the spaces of a great building, they should be the most evocative second-hand experiences possible. A contrasting school practices non-critical documentation. Still another school feels that photographs should transcend the building and offer an insight into the vision of the architect. Most agree that the heroically dramatic photograph reached its height in the 1930s and 1940s. This approach has been replaced by a softer and more sympathetic interpretation.

Most people experience a great building through photographs; the few who are privileged to walk through great architecture will be surprised and delighted even after having seen pictures of it. There will always be a gulf between perception and interpretation, between terrain and map. Awareness that the subject is the building, not the photograph, recognizes this difference.

CONTEMPORARY ARCHITECTURAL PHOTOGRAPHY

The following photographs by some of the contemporary masters of architectural photography depict a range of opinions also expressed in the accompanying statements.

TECHNIQUE—GENERAL

The accepted standard camera is the 4 × 5 view with a series of lenses toward the wide angle (65, 75, 90 and 120mm), through the "normal" (135, 165, 180mm), and less frequently to telephoto (200, 300, 500mm and longer). Whenever slides are to be the final format, and in most architectural model work, a 35mm single-lens reflex with lenses ranging from 18, 20, 24, 28 to 35 or 50mm is chosen. Zoom lenses of top quality are relatively free of distortion above 28mm. Such a battery of lenses will permit the freedom to choose where to stand in relation to any building, interior or exterior, by providing the proper lens to fill the frame.

Standing too close while using an extremely wide-angle lens will produce bulbous exteriors and elongated and distorted interiors. Standing too far away will flatten the perspective, generally producing an unexciting effect. Details, however, especially those on upper stories, are nicely shot with a telephoto lens so they are rendered more in elevation without emphasizing too much underside. The rising and falling front of the view camera and its equivalent in the 35mm shift lens is used primarily to render verticals parallel by keeping the camera back vertical and reducing or increasing the foreground by sliding the lens up or down. Shifting the lens–film relationship horizontally can show horizontal lines as non-converging, and tilting or swinging the lens can shift the plane of focus, bringing near and far objects into focus simultaneously.

Standing in the wrong place from any distance will make near and far planes merge in the photograph, producing ambiguities and distorting spatial relationships. In recent years, "one point perspective," or the axial view, has been a useful tool, both interior and exterior. Staying far enough away will keep the building's cornice from concealing its roofline.

The missing ingredients in still photographic spatial rendition are binocular vision and motion parallax, echoes, and kinesthetic awareness. The remaining cues to space are brought into conscious use and at times exaggerated to partially make up for these losses, especially in unfamiliar spaces.

In reducing three dimensions to two, the following cues indicate space:

1. Parallel lines converging into the distance (apparent rate of convergence is set by standpoint, not lens choice).
2. Diminution of size of similar objects into the distance and diminution of texture size into the distance.
3. Overlap of objects.
4. Aerial perspective—the graying and hazing of objects in the distance.
5. Shadows cast on the ground and object upon object.
6. Loss of detail in familiar objects in the distance.

The time of day or season of the year chosen for photography has an enormous effect on the picture. The low rays of the early morning or late evening sun produce shadows and textures which delineate shapes. Very often

Figure 2. "Sea of Steps," 1903, by Frederick H. Evans. Photograph of the Steps to Charter House at Wells Cathedral. Courtesy of The Bettmann Archive.

Figure 3. Glen Gery Showroom, New York City. Courtesy of the photographer.

Architectural photography has the power to transform the ordinary into the sublime. Our job is to show the building or interior in its best possible light. The photographer's tools are composition and lighting which when skillfully used will create pictures even more dramatic than the experience of being there.

Peter Aaron
New York, N.Y.

Figure 4. Renaissance Center, Detroit, Mich. Courtesy of the photographer.

Architecture is a backdrop to explore vision, emotion and satire.

Timothy Hursley
Little Rock, Arkansas

Figure 5. Frankenmuth, Michigan. Courtesy of the photographer.

Social conscience influences much of my work. If I indulge in the now fashionable 'l'Art pour l'Art,' I apologize.

I find my interest beyond the high art of architecture, in the vast domain of man made, or destroyed environment.

In the process I still work on a few dilemmas: I am looking for an absolute formula to reduce the four dimensional experience, that architecture is, into two dimensions.

I seek to maintain a balance between language and content.

I wish to do more architecture inspired photography rather than just inspired description of architecture, and thus narrow the gulf between art/applied photography.

Finally, I try in vain to soothe the frustration of my architect friends over the fact that the public's perception of their work still largely depends on our skills.

Balthazar Korab
Troy, Michigan

Figure 6. Ruined Gardens, Eleutherian Mills, Wilmington, Del. Courtesy of the photographer.

Photographing architecture is a design task. All the disciplines of reading solid forms by flat representation apply. But this is only technical. Underlying an evocative statement is knowledge, appreciation, and strong feeling about the subject. Then it becomes possible to express the mystery of architecture without trying to explain it all.

Then it becomes possible to be swept into the aura of the building, to assist the photograph in its prime purpose to be invisible; to say 'Look,' 'see,' 'Look at *that,*' to touch the *desire to inhabit*.

Robert C. Lautman
Washington, D.C.

Figure 7. Temple of Dendur, The Metropolitan Museum of Art, New York City. Courtesy of the photographer.

The architectural photographer today has a great responsibility. Through the vehicle of photography the latest designs, new movements, unusual solutions, all manner of ideas, materials related to the architecture scene are disseminated to an increasingly large audience. Many famous structures become familiar to us only through printed media. Though sometimes the photograph can be quite literal, at other times it is not. A talented photographer can enhance the subject, focus the viewer's attention just where desired and perhaps eliminate diluting elements. Careful selection of viewpoint, patience in waiting for the right conditions, or even creating them when absent, all contribute to what may be the ideal design interpretation, but one that also is removed from reality. How often, in fact, has the reality been an anticlimax.

No two-dimensional photograph can ever be a real substitute for a true masterpiece. It may be, however, the only practical or convenient way to describe the subject. For designs which may fall short of their objectives, for whatever reasons, their passage through the lens of the architectural photographer can transform them into a result that is closer to the architect's original idea. If along the way the photograph can also achieve intrinsic artistic merit then much has been accomplished.

Norman McGrath
New York, N.Y.

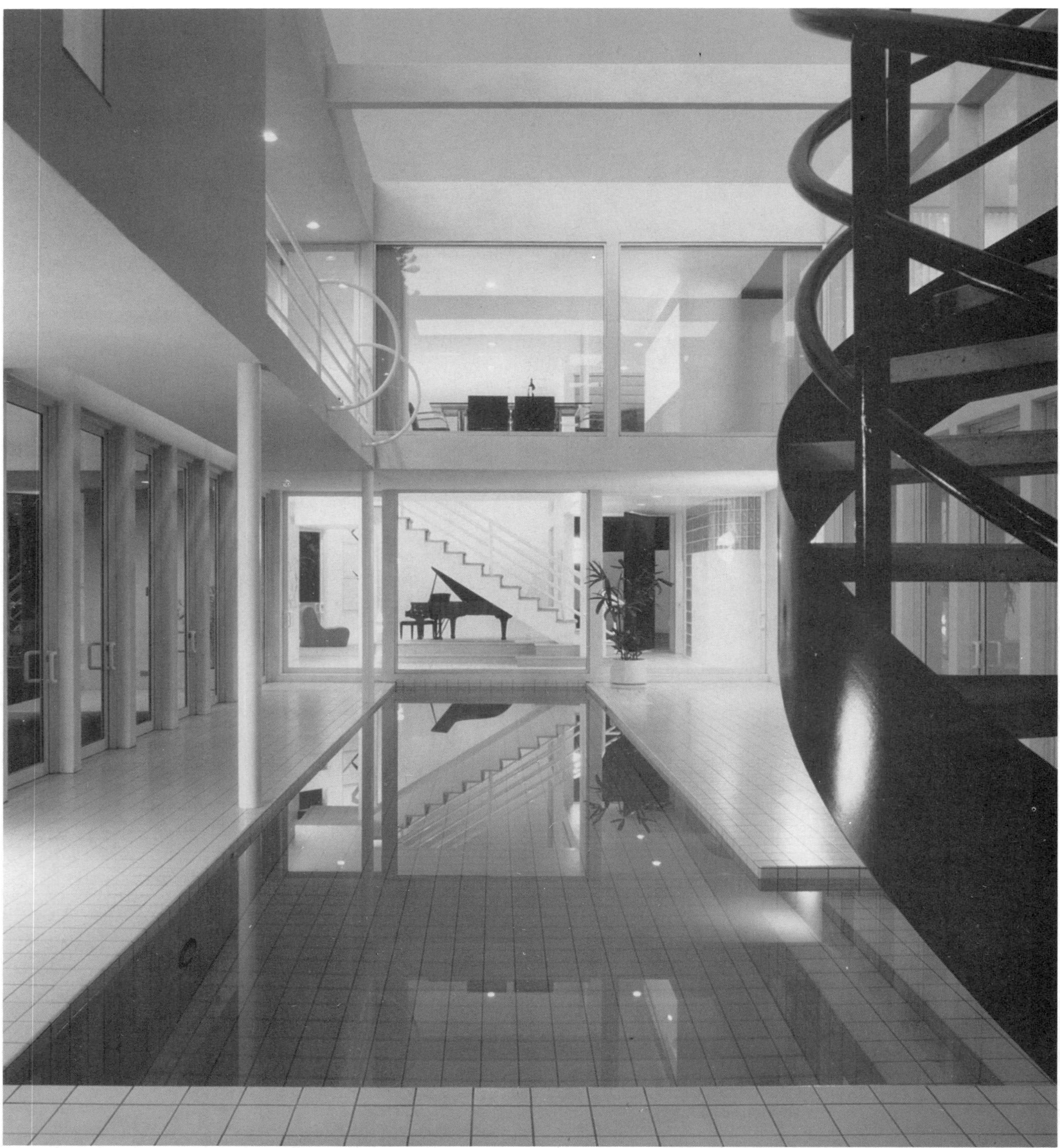

Figure 8. Photograph of a Batter/Kay design. Courtesy of the photographer.

When one faces the prospect of dramatizing a building or interior space, it is important to know what the architect/designer felt and was trying to accomplish. One must listen. Then let the building speak. What is its predominant lighting source? Is it more dramatic at night or during the day? Don't fight it. Don't take strobe lights and daylight film into it at night and destroy its incandescent lighting. Instead bring more incandescent lights of your own. Keep the camera low, not at standing level. Make sure you have foreground objects to look through—this gives the feeling of being in the space, not removed from it.

Mary E. Nichols
Los Angeles, California

Figure 9. Chrysler Building, New York City. Architect: William Van Alen. Courtesy of the photographer.

A photographer is part documentarian and part entertainer as well, for if his pictures do not interest us we will not bother to look at them. From familiarity with architecture he knows what to show; he beguiles us by his manner of showing it. Historically this manner has often taken the form of special perspectives or of juxtapositions—of people, trees, or cars to buildings or of one building to another—devices that succeed when they are fresh. But their purpose is not mere novelty for it is only through them that a photographer can make a critical or expressive statement about architecture.

Cervin Robinson

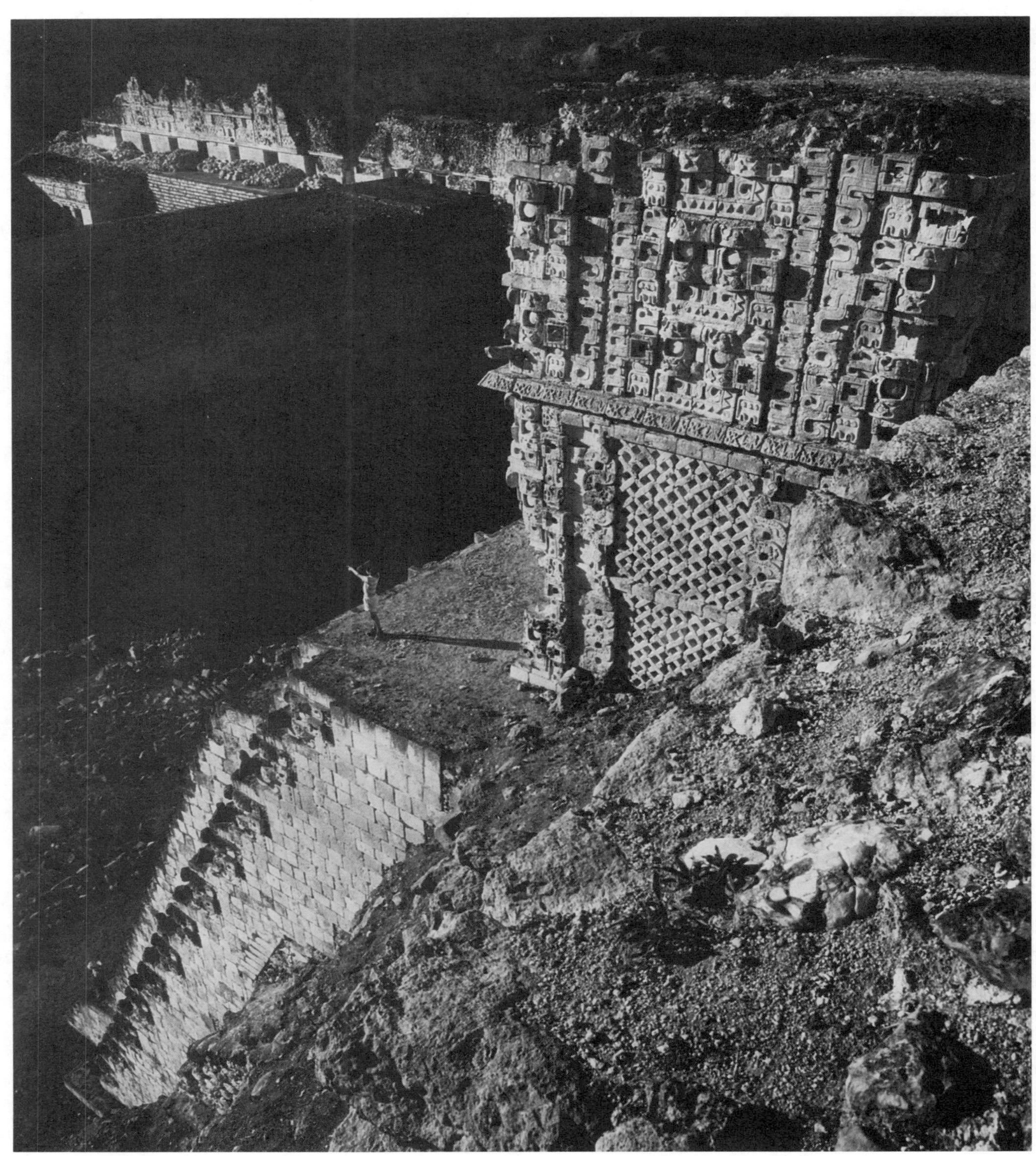

Figure 10. Pyramid of the House of the Prophet at Uxman in Yucatan. Courtesy of the photographer

Climbing up 200 steps at an incline of 60°, with a 4 × 5 camera and a bag loaded with 35mm camera and various lenses for both cameras, the rewards from this scene have been infinitely fulfilling. And to find a young Mayan child who did not see me, I came away with a strange impact—as if he were pointing to some mystical image of past centuries of his ancestors.

When asked to write a statement about views of architectural photography, my thoughts turned immediately to the directions of my feelings—what will I be producing with my camera during the next fifty years?

I have for the past decade particularly, become conscious of the values of architectural history; how the camera in reality is a catalyst in its capacity to report, evaluate, and even to edit a scene or structure. Therefore I have realized that my concern has turned toward the specific instrumentation of photography as it can demonstrate the association of architectural history with current movements towards the economic and intrinsic import of heretofore considered "useless" buildings of another era. Here in Los Angeles for example, our organization, The Los Angeles Conservancy, has created a structured body of concern for our downtown area in which exist unique buildings of the 1920s and 30s.

Photography has played monumental roles in this renaissance. It has been in a position to illustrate the essential features of an extensive period of architecture. Much of this has been published in a book, *Los Angeles Architecture,* by Paul Gleye—an architectural historian. This is a field of photography which has been sparsely explored.

Another facet of history is illustrated by my photograph of the Pyramid of the House of the Prophet at Uxmal in Yucatan. Dating from the fifth or sixth century of Mayan history, culture, and architecture, this era has been the source of extensive research on the part of historians and archeologists. This photograph has been used to illustrate the temple on the top of the pyramid. This is one of my favorite expressions wherein by the thoughtful application of camera's universal qualities, photography, architecture, and history can combine to produce an image of the qualities of our environment.

Julius Schulman
Los Angeles, California

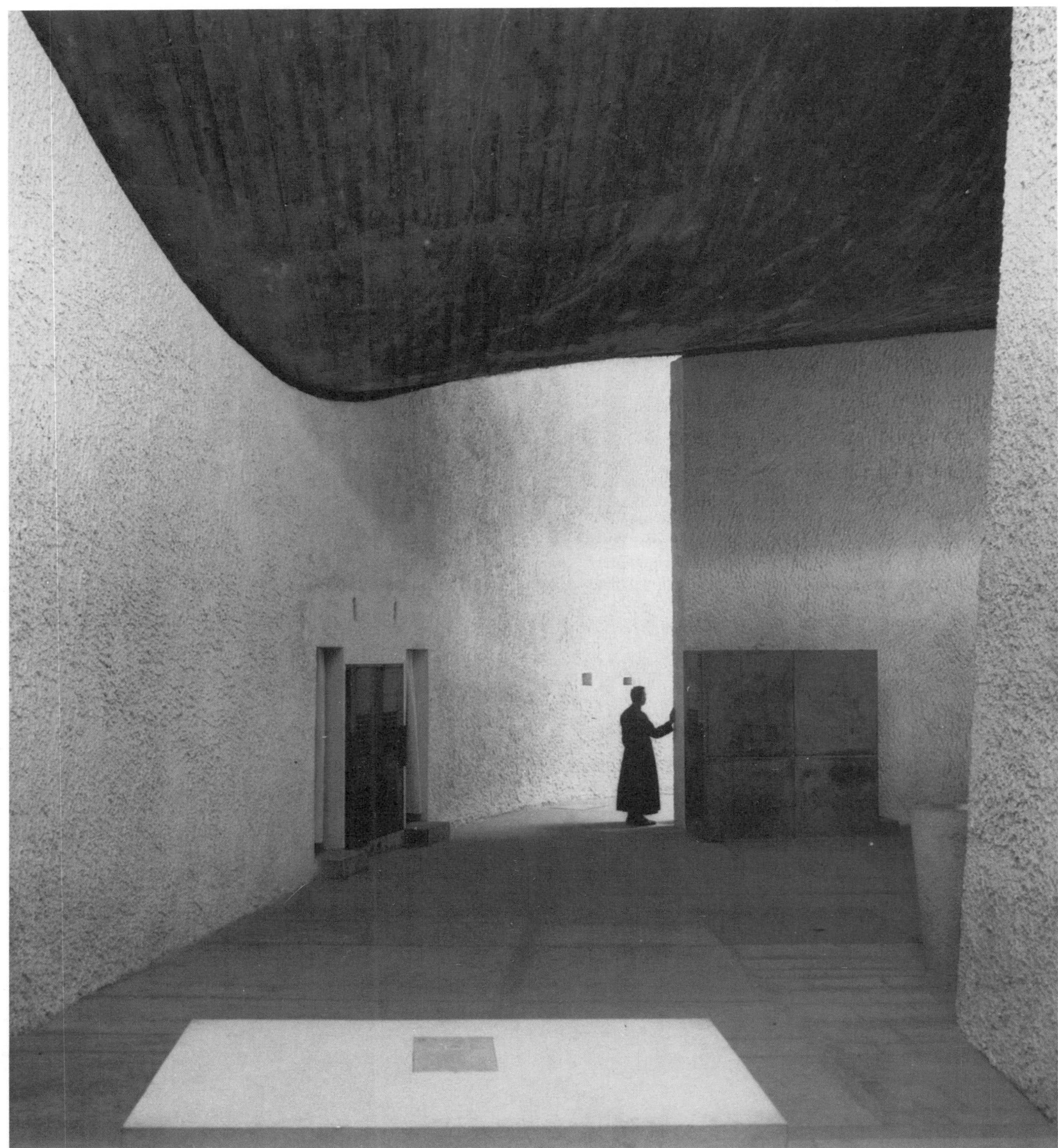

Figure 11. Church at Ronchamp, France. Architect: Le Corbusier. Courtesy of the photographer.

Architecture is many things—different to different people. As documentarians of the phenomenon we must be prepared to address the needs of all who are interested in it.

My own reaction to architecture is a sensory one and I am concerned with it and an artistic relationship of forms and spaces at human scale. As a photographer I must convey this experience on a two dimensional plane using light and a cranky piece of film. In general the more economical the means, the stronger the message conveyed.

Ezra Stoller
Mamaroneck, N.Y.

the high midday summer sun can penetrate a tall atrium to the bottom. At times, winter or early spring permits the building to be seen through tree foliage which obscures it in the summer. The "ideal" is the photograph taken on a sunny summer day with good (but not overly dramatic) clouds. However, wonderful effects can come from photographing in the snow, rain, and fog, at sunrise and sunset (especially with reflective buildings), and in the mysterious light after sunset and before sunrise. Each building requires careful assessment of the times which will best point out its uniqueness. On occasion the height of a building can be exaggerated by tipping the camera up and converging the vertical lines with a clearly deliberate tilt.

Schools without children are dull. People are often included for scale in public buildings, but not usually in living spaces because they tend to become the focus of attention and because fashions in clothing date quickly. Probably the observer of the photograph feels more invited into a residential space if no one already occupies it.

Exteriors of buildings range, as in cinematography, from long shot to medium to closeup. The change in scale permits exciting presentation or editorial layouts and provides visual contrast in slide shows.

The very long shot, showing the building in context with its surroundings, can be done from the ground, from another building, and sometimes from a helicopter or small airplane. However, aerials will sometimes reveal mechanicals on a roof that are invisible at ground level. It is best to do aerials with a fast shutter speed of 1/500 or 1/1000 of a second. When the ground drops sharply away from a building, a good picture can be gotten from a tree, a telephone pole, a rented scaffold, or a cherry-picker.

For the overall "whole-building" pictures, three major factors must be taken into consideration: standpoint, time of day, and lens choice. The standpoint is all-important. The wrong angle will not reveal the building. Too close will distort, and too far will flatten perspective. Elevations of the important facades are useful along with three-quarter views which show two elevations with one predominating.

Flat frontal illumination with the sun behind the camera is dull; sidelight moving toward backlight is increasingly dramatic. Low sun early and late in the day is exciting, but if color rendition is important, light-balancing filters should be used to cool the warm color. Conversely, warming filters are used when working in high altitudes on a very clear day, and especially when photographing in the shade on a clear day. A lens is chosen to include the building and as much of its environment as needed. If the picture necessitates using the camera's rising front it is essential to avoid lens vignetting and bellows' shadow by camera manipulation.

Pictures of thoughtful and elegant details help to complete coverage. When the details are accessible, normal lenses can be used. If the chosen detail is at a distance, longer focal lengths are necessary.

Interiors are usually best in natural light; augmentation when necessary should be inconspicuous. Daylight frequently needs to be augmented with electronic flash or blue floods to reduce harsh contrast. This must be done with delicacy to avoid an artificial and overlit feeling in the photograph. When possible, the light should appear to be coming from natural window or skylight sources.

Props—from ashtrays to books, flowers to furniture, art and sculpture—are, by tasteful choice, the objects that lend reality, giving the feeling that this is not a furniture warehouse, that real people live in or work in the space, that, possibly, someone has just left the room.

Twilight is a good time to relate the exterior to the interior by choosing a place, a time of light intensity balance, and an appropriate film and filter combination to see into, or out of, the building as well as to perceive details of the exterior. Early twilight is too flat, and late twilight produces pictures of windows in the blackness.

COLOR

Color photography is, in a sense, easier than black and white. Spatial definition is almost inherent because of likely color differences between planes.

Mixed light sources within the same scene—any combination of daylight, incandescent, fluorescents of different types—need to be corrected to match each other in most cases. When the illumination is predominantly daylight, tungsten sources can be converted with a blue gel or replaced with blue photofloods; fluorescents can be converted with magenta filters. When the illumination is mostly tungsten, windows can be converted from daylight with gels, or by photographing at twilight. Under some circumstances, mostly at night, mixed light sources can be corrected by a series of exposures on the same sheet of film, changing filters as each different light is turned on and the others off. A color temperature meter, sets of gelatin filters, and instamatic film for tests are valuable in this work. "Accurate" color rendition is not always the most evocative. As in other areas, an error in a warm direction is usually better than one which is too cool.

BLACK AND WHITE PHOTOGRAPHY

Today, black and white has the reputation of being the cheap way to go. This is unfortunate because its very abstraction makes it a strong vehicle for commentary about architecture, spatial relationships, the qualities of light, and particularly to call up memories and associations.

Black and white techniques differ from color. A pink cornice can sometimes be rendered in the same shade of gray as the blue sky. A yellow filter can delineate the difference and avoid an undefined building edge because filters, in black and white, lighten their complementary colors and darken their opposites. In this case a yellow (or pink or red or orange) filter would darken the blue sky and lighten the pink cornice.

Overly contrasting and dramatic black and whites have given way to a more gently evocative style of photographing and printing. Professionals and skilled non-professionals have precise control in print making, and there are some very proficient black and white laboratories making elegant prints.

MODEL PHOTOGRAPHY

Photographs of architectural sketch models are useful in early design phases. Usually black and white, these pictures are studied for form and mass, can be redone easily and inexpensively, even using instamatic film and enlarged photostats. When the model (and the photograph) reach final stages, a photograph can be stripped into another photograph of the site and environs, either mechanically or by computer, previsualizing the finished building in situ for clients, investors, zoning boards, and design committees. The most realistic photography is done from a precise scale model with accurate colors and scale figures, cars, and trees. A sky-blue background is used, general cool diffused lighting replicates sky light, and a spotlight is used for the sun. "Sunlight" should come from reasonable angles (not north). The edges of the model are camouflaged by shadows or hidden behind buildings. A carefully executed photograph can substitute for the actual building during construction, and can be used for publications, banks, and investors.

CHOOSING FILM AND FORMAT

The eventual use of photographs conditions the choice of camera, film, and final presentation. Architects utilize photographs differently, depending on the audience.

Many architects have printed individual sheets with photographs and specifications and can instantly construct a portfolio emphasizing special aspects of their work in response to a request from a potential client.

For magazine or book publication, 4 × 5 transparencies are usually required. There are some exceptions, however, and the publication art director's preferred format always prevails. A good photography laboratory can make reproduction-quality color duplicates, sometimes even enhancing the original. Common practice by photographers is to back these up with a set of black and white negatives so that prints, when needed, can be made from original negatives. For presentation as color prints, access can be through color negatives and a color print process such as Ektacolor. For architects who use slides in presentations to clients or in lectures, slides can be originals (sometimes multiple) from a 35mm camera, duplicates of 35mm or larger transparencies, printed from color negative materials, or direct photographs of color prints. The last takes advantage of all the color correction and manipulation that went into the print but has the disadvantage of "second-generation" image quality loss.

THE ARCHITECT–PHOTOGRAPHER CONNECTION

The architect who works in collaboration with the architectural photographer can add enormous understanding of the history of the building's conceptualization and design program. The architect–photographer relationship offers a rare potential for mutually rewarding symbiosis. The cross-stimulation which comes from a working collaboration produces memorable and exciting photographs which recall the experience of the building.

BIBLIOGRAPHY

G. Bachelard, *The Poetics of Space,* Beacon, 1958. U.S.A.

The International Center of Photography Encyclopedia of Photography, Crown, 1984.

R. M. Evans, *Eye, Film, and Camera in Color Photography,* John Wiley & Sons, Inc., New York, 1959.

C. B. Neblette, *Photography, Its Principles and Practices,* D. Van Nostrand Co., Inc., New York, 1939.

H. Gernsheim, *The History of Photography,* Oxford University Press, Oxford, UK, 1955.

R. Arnheim, *Art and Visual Perception,* University of California Press, 1954.

A. Busch, *The Photography of Architecture,* Van Nostrand Reinhold, New York, 1987.

B. Fletcher, *A History of Architecture,* 18th ed., Charles Scribners Sons, New York, 1975.

R. Barthes, *Camera Lucida,* Hill & Wang, 1981.

J. Szarkowski and M. M. Hambourg, *The Work of Atget,* 4 vols., The Museum of Modern Art, New York, 1985.

N. McGrath, *Photographing Buildings Inside and Out,* Whitney Library of Design, New York, 1987.

ROBERT C. LAUTMAN
Washington, D.C.

PHYSICAL EDUCATION. See RECREATIONAL FACILITIES

PHYSICAL AND MENTAL DISABILITIES, DESIGN FOR

The historic advent of ANSI A117.1–1961, *Specifications for Making Buildings and Facilities Accessible to and Usable by the Physically Handicapped,* the first design standard to provide special building features for people with disabilities, inaugurated a continuing debate over design details and numbers of elements to be incorporated into facilities to accommodate persons with physical disabilities. "Cost" and "need" or "benefit" issues have been at the center of this debate, with regard to the numbers of persons and types of disabilities to be accommodated, the cost of these accommodations, and justification of the cost.

Since 1961, many of the cost questions regarding new facilities have been resolved. Studies have shown that access features integrated into the early conceptual stages of the design of new facilities increase costs less than 1% on most projects (1). A 1986 study by the Bureau of the Census (2) concluded that approximately one-fifth of the population, more than 37 million people out of a population of 181 million non-institutionalized persons of age 15 or older had functional limitations; 13.5 million in this group had severe limitations. Of those with severe limitations, 55% or 7.5 million were 65 and older.

Of the 37 million people, 19.2 million had difficulty walking a quarter of a mile; 18.1 million, one tenth of the population, had difficulty walking up a flight of stairs without resting. The number of people unable to walk a quarter of a mile was 8 million and 5.2 million could not walk up a flight of stairs. Approximately 7.7 million people had difficulty hearing what was said in normal conversation and 0.5 million were completely unable to hear such a conversation. The number of people who experienced difficulty seeing words and letters in ordinary newsprint (even with corrective lenses) was 12.8 million, with 1.7 million unable to see words or letters at all.

As intriguing as these numbers are in refuting the argument that only a small minority of the population requires accessible design, they tell less than the whole story. These numbers do not include children, who benefit from many access features, parents, who often push their children around in strollers, the temporarily disabled, or the families, friends, and associates of persons with physical disabilities. At some point in time, virtually everyone will need, or benefit from, a more accommodating environment.

The extent of that need is not always evident. When the University of Michigan initiated an innovative accessible transit service five years ago, those opposed to the project said no one would use it because there were not enough disabled students or staff to make the system feasible. One year later, however, the demand was so great, and the number of riders so large, that the university considered expanding both the hours of operation and the number of vehicles. Studies showed that the "unexpected" riders, approximately half of those using the system, were students and staff who had temporary disabilities severe enough to meet the established criteria permitting use of the system (3).

Accessible design is truly a means of designing for the life span. By incorporating basic access features and universally designed products and elements in the building design, a variety of users will be assured accessibility over the life cycle of a facility and over their own life span.

The universal design concept goes beyond the access codes and standards that specify "special" features or elements. It is an approach to design that accommodates people of all ages, sizes, and abilities, and it can be applied to all buildings through the incorporation of products, features, and elements which, to the greatest extent possible, can be used by everyone (4).

The concepts of universal design and "adaptability," as incorporated in the ANSI A117.1 (1980 and 1986) (5) and the Uniform Federal Accessibility Standards (UFAS) (6), which include specifications for adaptable features in housing, are key components within the framework of designing for the life span.

The days of single-purpose buildings are gone. Increasing percentages of construction dollars are spent on retrofit and rehabilitation of existing structures to meet the needs of new users. The high costs of energy, replacement construction, and facility maintenance have created a need for life-cycle costing and value engineering. The concept of designing for the life span is consistent with these trends.

Accommodating a building's users through design can save money for organizations. Studies of hospital room mock-ups at the University of Michigan's Architecture Research Laboratory have shown that a design which allows patients to act on their own without a nurse saves money in personnel costs (7). As a result of this study, all patient-care rooms, bathrooms, and other facilities of the university's $280 million replacement hospital project were designed to be accessible. Steelcase Corporation and Coca-Cola made similar decisions about accessible design when the companies hired consultants to ensure that their new corporate headquarters was accessible from the cafeteria to the board room and executive toilet rooms. These organizations were committed to accommodating employees to reduce time away from the office due to impairment.

It is only through the application of universal design concepts that the life span will be economically and appropriately accommodated. Leon Pastalan, professor of architecture, notes (8):

> The universal design concept considers those changes that are experienced by everyone as they grow from infancy to old age. Problems related to temporary or permanent disabilities are incorporated into the concept as well. Because all groups are placed within the context of normal expectations of the human condition, trying to justify the importance of each vulnerable population group becomes unnecessary.

PHYSICAL DISABILITIES AND ENVIRONMENTAL ACCOMMODATIONS

Environmental barriers can be pervasive in their influence on the built environment, affecting the ease of movement through and use of facilities and spaces by large numbers of building users. Inappropriately designed parking spaces, walkways, entrances, elevators, telephones, drinking fountains, door hardware, toilets, and the vast majority of public transportation have precluded the use of these facilities by an increasing number of disabled and older people.

The reason that environmental barriers exist today stems from the common use of a norm which was based on the mobility, size, strength, and capabilities of an average, healthy, 30-year-old male. Most available anthropometric data commonly used in environmental design are based on this norm (9). People not fitting this norm, including men of short stature, women, children, older people, and temporarily and permanently disabled people, are required to adapt. Of this group, older people and those with temporary or permanent disabilities are at the greatest disadvantage due to the discrepancies that exist between their physical abilities and those demanded by the environment, as well as the limits on their ability to adapt.

When discussing environmental issues, the impact of functional limitations is best understood by distinguishing between the physical "condition" or source of an impairment, "disability or functional limitation," and "handicap." Physical conditions which deviate from the norm such as paralysis, hypertension, or physical size can be identified or diagnosed. A condition may result in a disability only if it interferes with a person's ability to perform one or more functions or regular activities of daily living or employment. If a disability or functional limitation is not accommodated environmentally or through the use of assistive aids or devices, the disability becomes a handicap.

Measuring the extent of functional limitation or disability among the population is imprecise due to three major problems: the nebulous contextual distinction between disability and handicap, the stigma associated with disability and handicap, and the limitations of statistical studies that have been conducted. The scarcity of empirical data on specific disabilities or functional impairments places a major limitation on the estimates which can be made (10). Most previous studies have focused on health status or conditions which deviate from the norm, focusing little on the resultant disabilities, if any. For example, a person diagnosed as having multiple sclerosis may be free of disabilities or they may have complex functional limitations involving sight, mobility, stamina, and strength. However, recent studies, while not covering all aspects of disability, have begun to gather statistics on functional limitations as they relate to the environment.

Relationship Between Age and Disabilities

A 1986 study by the Bureau of the Census provides a wealth of information relative to disability or functional limitation and age, race, sex, income levels, and a variety of other characteristics. The study gathered information on a variety of limitations relative to the environment and activities of daily living including limitations in walking up a flight of stairs or a quarter of a mile, lifting or carrying 10 pounds, getting around inside or outside the house, getting in or out of bed, seeing standard print, hearing normal conversation, and limitations in speech.

The data in Table 1 summarizes that information relative to broad age categories and severity of limitation. Individuals are considered as having a functional limitation if they have difficulty in performing one or more of the activities above. Those with severe limitations could not perform the activity without assistance from another person. The table shows much higher rates of functional limitation among persons over 65.

A closer review of the data reveals a steady increase in functional limitation relative to age (Table 2). The functional limitation rate increased from 5.2% for people of 15–24 years, to 34.2% for people of 55–64 years of age, 45.4% for those 65–69 years old, 55.3% for those 70–79 years old, and 72.5% for people of age 75 and over. The rate of severe disability increased even more sharply with age, more than doubling from 18.8%, for the 65–69 age group, to 41.2%, for those 75 years of age and older. While people over age 75 currently comprise only 5.6% of the total population, they account for over 30% of all people with severe limitations. The data in Table 3 show that this trend also applies to children. Very few people are born with a disability; more often, disabilities are acquired over the life span.

The significance of these figures becomes clearer when reviewed from the perspective of the expected growth in both numbers and percentage of the older population. It is estimated that by the year 2000, there will be more than 35 million people over age 65. By the year 2030, when the last of the baby boom generation reaches age 65, that number will have increased to 64.4 million, more than one out of every five Americans (14). Over 58% of these people will likely have one or more functional limitations. Those 75 years of age or older, who can be expected to have a functional limitation rate of 73%, will increase in numbers to almost 30 million or about 10% of the population.

Environmental Accommodations

Disabled people, like all other people, want to have free and autonomous use of the environment. Physical disabilities need not become handicaps if they can be accommodated environmentally or through the use of assistive aids. Wheelchairs and other mobility devices such as crutches, canes, and walkers are frequently used by people to accommodate their disabilities. An accommodating environment, therefore, must not only accommodate people but also the assistive aids and devices used in activities of daily living and employment situations.

Mobility Impairments. People with mobility impairments range from those who have a lack of stamina or strength and may use a cane or lower leg brace to people totally unable to walk who use power wheelchairs and who may have little use of their arms, shoulders, and hands. They use a range of mobility aids: crutches, canes, walkers, standard manual wheelchairs, power wheelchairs, and the increasingly common three-wheel scooter used by a growing number of older people who have difficulty walking long distances. People with mobility impairments need accessible routes which are stable, smooth, and firm with no abrupt changes in level greater than ¼ in. that are not beveled or ramped. Accessible pathways must extend from the entry to site, accessible parking spaces and passenger loading zones to the entry of the building. Adequate maneuvering room is needed at entry and between doors at vestibules. Steps and stairs, narrow doors, powerful door closers, and improperly located controls and hardware present barriers. People using wheelchairs need adequate turning space and clear floor area in order to approach and use bathroom fixtures, telephones, and operating controls. Controls and equipment must be easily reached and operated from a sitting position. Fixtures must be located at appropriate heights and provide adequate clearances.

Ambulatory mobility-impaired people can walk but do so with difficulty. These people may also have trouble sitting, bending, and kneeling, and may be hampered by having their hands occupied with walking aids. Many of those who use mobility aids such as walkers, canes, and crutches lack stamina or strength. They need stable, firm, slip-resistant surfaces. Grab bars in restroom facilities and handrails at steps and on ramps are critically important for this group. Street furniture and informal seating areas in buildings assist these people in moving about their environment by providing places to rest. Seating must be selected to provide safety and ease of use. Seating at public telephones and passenger pick-up areas is often

Table 1. Limitations in Specific Functional Activities of Persons of 15 Years and Over[a]

Activity	15 Years and Over[b]	15–64 Years[b]	65 Years and Over[b]
Total	180,987	154,565	26,422
With a limitation:			
number	37,304	21,889	15,465
percent	20.6	14.1	58.5
With a severe limitation:			
number	13,537	5,998	7,539
percent	7.5	3.9	28.5
Walking—¼ mi			
With a limitation:			
number	19,207	9,272	9,935
percent	10.6	6.0	37.6
With a severe limitation:			
number	7,959	3,027	4,887
percent	4.4	2.0	18.5
Using Stairs			
With a limitation:			
number	18,063	8,833	9,230
percent	10.0	5.7	34.9
With a severe limitation:			
number	5,191	1,814	3,376
percent	2.9	1.2	12.8
Lifting or Carrying			
With a limitation:			
number	18,208	9,286	8,922
percent	10.1	6.0	33.8
With a severe limitation:			
number	7,843	3,383	4,460
percent	4.3	2.2	16.9
Seeing			
With a limitation:			
number	12,802	7,061	5,742
percent	7.1	4.6	21.7
With a severe limitation:			
number	1,686	491	1,196
percent	0.9	0.3	4.5
Hearing			
With a limitation:			
number	7,694	3,677	4,017
percent	4.3	2.4	15.2
With a severe limitation:			
number	481	297	184
percent	0.3	0.2	0.7
Getting Around Outside			
With a limitation:			
number	5,998	2,038	3,960
percent	3.3	1.3	15.0
With a severe limitation:			
number	3,601	1,091	2,510
percent	2.0	0.7	9.5
Getting Around Inside			
With a limitation:			
number	2,528	867	1,661
percent	1.4	0.6	6.3
With a severe limitation:			
number	1,229	413	816
percent	0.7	0.3	3.1
Getting into and out of Bed			
With a limitation:			
number	2,057	735	1,322
percent	1.1	0.5	5.0
With a severe limitation:			
number	1,208	509	699
percent	0.7	0.3	2.6
Speech			
With a limitation:			
number	2,510	1,586	923
percent	1.4	1.0	3.5

[a] Ref. 11.

[b] Numbers are in thousands.

Table 2. Functional Limitation Status, by Age, of Persons 15 Years and Over[a]

Age, Number of Years Old	Total Number of People[b]	Total with a Functional Limitation		Total with a Severe Limitation	
		Number	Percent	Number	Percent
	180,987	37,304	20.6	13,537	7.5
15–24	39,297	2,054	5.2	346	0.9
25–34	40,464	3,049	7.5	596	1.5
35–44	30,480	4,074	13.4	890	2.9
45–54	22,264	5,110	23.0	1,431	6.4
55–64	22,060	7,552	34.2	2,734	12.4
65 and over	26,422	15,465	58.5	7,539	28.5
65–69	8,928	4,052	45.4	1,682	18.8
70–74	7,378	4,078	55.3	1,691	22.9
75 and over	10,116	7,335	72.5	4,166	41.2

[a] Ref. 12.
[b] Numbers are in thousands.

Table 3. Disability Status of Children under 18 Years of Age[a]

Age, Number of Years Old	Total Number of Children[b]	Number Disabled	Percent Disabled
0–2	10,953	136	1.2
3–5	10,522	218	2.1
6–9	12,893	443	3.4
10–14	17,275	699	4.0
15–17	10,802	420	3.9
Ability to attend school			
Does attend	62,194	1,666	2.7
Cannot attend		251	N/A

[a] Ref. 13.
[b] Numbers are in thousands.

a necessity for these people who cannot stand for long periods of time.

Communications, safety, and security issues are vitally important concerns. Fire and smoke detection systems, intercoms, electronic monitoring systems, and environmental control systems can make it possible for severely disabled people to independently monitor and control their environment. Easily operated security hardware and at least two accessible entrances are needed for safe emergency evacuation.

Visual Impairments. Visually impaired persons may be totally blind or, like many older people, may have limited vision. Those who cannot see at all use touch and hearing to move about and through the environment. Many blind people use a long cane; others rely on trained guide dogs. People with visual impairments also need accessible pathways that are stable and firm and are free of protruding objects or obstructions that are not easily detected by a cane. Overhanging signs, the underside of stairs, or tree limbs can cause serious injury as can improperly placed cantilevered drinking fountains that protrude into corridors. These same features often cause injury to sighted people as well. Furniture, planters, or low walls can be placed under obstructions to ensure safety and detectability to cane users, those with low vision, and the fully sighted. Signs and room numbers with raised letters enable blind people to read them with touch. It is very important that elevator controls and door jambs have tactile signage in order to allow independent use of this feature and the facility. Knobs or touch controls should provide feedback in audible or tactile forms. Controls for cooking and thermostats should have distinctive click positions or tactile indicators.

People with low vision range from those who may be able to perceive light and dark, to those who may see a very fuzzy image of the world with great difficulty reading standard print and street or building signage. Many older people experience this latter type of visual impairment. It becomes difficult to distinguish the edges of objects. Items on shop shelving must be examined closely, and glass display cases often keep objects at a distance where viewing is impossible. While this type of visual impairment may not be easily apparent to others, it must be environmentally accommodated through appropriately designed high contrast signage, carefully designed displays, and good lighting. Older people may need twice the lighting level to see as well as younger people with normal vision. Although glare must be avoided, brighter lighting than average at stairs or turning points along a path assists in orientation. Large high-contrast numerals and lighted switches assist people with residual vision. Contrasting surface colors and materials which are different in sound, resilience, and texture, located at level changes, alert visually impaired persons to the change.

Information desks and other sources of audible information are most useful for all visually impaired persons. Descriptive audio cassettes used in museums to provide self-guided tours are of great benefit to this population since they negate the need to read signage on exhibits and also describe significant features of objects. Similar techniques could be applied in complex buildings.

Hearing Impairments. People with hearing impairments have great difficulty communicating with others and receiving audible information. Those with partial hearing may depend on hearing aids. Others rely on sign language, writing, or lip reading. Good sight lines improve communication and allow hearing impaired individuals to see people approaching. Auditory signals such as fire alarms, class bells, and announcements on public address systems cannot be heard by deaf people. Background noise and poor acoustics confuse people with poor hearing.

Emergency signals, door bells, and telephones can be communicated with flashing lights or vibrating pagers. Information should always be provided in both visual and audible form. Redundant cuing has proven effective in older populations where individuals frequently have both hearing and visual impairments. One specially designed apartment building provides a video link from the front entry so that guests can tune in their own television set to see guests who signal their apartment for admittance to the building.

Telephones should be provided which are hearing aid compatible and have a volume controlled headset. Totally deaf and severely hearing impaired people can communicate by phone using a telecommunication device for the deaf known as TDD. These devices, which resemble small electronic typewriters, can be plugged into a headset to send typed messages that are decoded at the other end. TDDs are becoming more common in airports, transportation terminals, hotels, other places of public accommodation, and businesses. Most larger cities have TDD directories listing personal and business phone numbers which can be answered with a TDD.

Other Disabilities. People with little or no use of their arms and hands have difficulty lifting and reaching. Accessible controls and easy-to-use hardware are critically important for this group. People lacking motor coordination need these features as well as accessible pathways and building entries. People with bending, reaching, or stooping limitations may have difficulty reaching objects, outlets, or controls above their shoulders or below their knees. Access to upper or lower cabinets is generally impaired.

Among people with mental disabilities are those who are learning disabled, mentally retarded, or emotionally disturbed. Many have limitations in language or motor skills as well as comprehension and memory. Providing information signs with clear and simple language and pictures or information desks will assist this group as well as those who are illiterate or who cannot read English.

Older People. Life expectancy continues to rise as advances in medicine, sanitation, and health lower mortality rates. At the same time, chronic diseases whose incidence rises with age have become more common. While osteoarthritis, osteoporosis, hearing loss, loss of visual acuity, urinary incontinence, and dementia are common chronic health conditions (15), the physical disabilities experienced most often during the aging process generally involve mobility, strength and stamina, vision, hearing, and tactile and thermal sensitivity (16). These changes can generally be seen as a slowly progressive narrowing of capabilities, rather than a rapid decline. However, even a limited change can cause a sense of disorientation and vulnerability. Older people differ from younger disabled people in that they are more likely to have multiple impairments. Denial can be a problem that inhibits accommodation of the impairment through aids or rehabilitation (17). In addition, accidents and falls are commonplace, often resulting in injury and additional temporary impairments. Loose carpets and stairs are common causes of falls (18).

In general, older people benefit from access features developed to assist younger people with disabilities. Accessible pathways accommodate users of mobility aids and those who walk with difficulty. Carpeting must be firmly secured; environmental aids such as changes in color or tread edge-strips should be used at top and bottom of steps and when abrupt changes in level occur. Thresholds can be removed or beveled. Flooring should be slip resistant and dry to provide firm footing and prevent falls. Since mobility, strength, and stamina are often problems, environmental designers must be sure to take into consideration walking distances and provide appropriately designed seating areas adjacent to exterior walkways and interior corridors.

Spaces should be organized to provide a sense of orientation and provide stimulus due to the combination of sensory impairments often experienced, including visual impairment, hearing impairment, and reduced tactile and olfactory capabilities (19). Redundant cuing and the use of landmarks have been shown to be effective in assisting orientation and promoting appropriate responses. It is also important to avoid using colors of similar intensity on walls and floors to improve discrimination and promote depth perception. Blues and greens cause particular problems for the aging eye and patterned carpeting on stairs can cause edges to disappear.

Decreases in tactile and thermal sensitivity can cause a variety of problems in, for example, the handling of small objects and discrimination of water or room temperature. It is important to ensure that water temperature is controlled to prevent scalding, and room temperature set at a level to prevent hypothermia, a sometimes fatal problem for older people.

In accommodating people with physical disabilities, it is very important to ensure that all portions of facilities, including recreational facilities, are accessible. People with disabilities are not as limited as often presumed. People who are able-bodied today may be temporarily or permanently disabled tomorrow. Disabled people are in virtually all professions and all types of employment situations, including lawyers, architects, accountants, designers, doctors, nurses, computer specialists, clerical help, mechanics, and food service workers. McDonald's, AT&T, E.I. DuPont de Nemours, and other major corporations have established programs to retain workers with disabilities and have initiated aggressive recruiting programs. Some, like McDonalds, have also targeted programs at the older worker.

Needs and Benefits

While people with functional limitations need access features, both inside and outside buildings, and they as a group reap the greatest benefit from accessible design, many access features are beneficial to all people regardless of their functional abilities and were standard features in buildings long before access became an issue. Elevators are beneficial to everyone who must move between floors. Lever hardware and easily-grasped loop hardware are standard in Europe, and stable and firm walking surfaces and high contrast easy-to-read signage benefit most people. In fact, access requirements do not add features to buildings; they simply require different sizes or types of features to accommodate a broader variety of users.

Of course, there are those who cannot access buildings without these features and others whose access to and use of a facility would be seriously impeded. It is this group of people who "need" accessibility. While the numbers of those with functional limitations are relatively large, even greater numbers of people need more accommodating environments at least some of the time. Parents with small children in strollers benefit from curb ramps, level entries, and accessible elevators as do bicyclists, delivery personnel, and people with luggage carts. Those recovering from the temporary effects of injury or illness benefit as well. People using earphones benefit from visual cuing at elevators and children benefit from accessible drinking fountains and controls. Families, friends, and business associates of people with disabilities benefit from accessible environments as well. The disabled person is better able to act independently, without constant assistance, and social and business occasions can be scheduled without worry. The list is exhaustive. While anecdotal evidence suggests these numbers are large, such as the University of Michigan study (above) that showed that 50% of users of an accessible transit system were temporarily disabled, the extent of the benefits to the unimpaired or temporarily impaired is not known.

Access Standards and Laws

Most states have laws which require all portions of facilities which are used by the public or by employees to be accessible, with minor exceptions for certain mechanical spaces. While some states, notably Massachusetts and California, have their own detailed design standards, the majority use the 1980 or 1986 versions of ANSI A117.1, *The American National Standard for Buildings and Facilities—Providing Accessibility and Usability for Physically Handicapped People.* The three model building codes have also incorporated certain provisions of the standard or refer to it directly. ANSI A117.1 has also been incorporated with modification into the Uniform Federal Accessibility Standard (UFAS), the standard used throughout the federal government. ANSI A117.1, like other American National Standards, reflects a national consensus of those concerned, including disabled consumers, architects, designers, manufacturers, and others. People assisted by the standards provisions include ambulatory mobility-impaired persons, wheelchair users, people with visual and hearing impairments, those with coordination and reaching and manipulation limitations, and those with extremes of physical size.

ANSI A117.1 incorporates the concepts of accessible routes and accessible elements, two major concepts which together facilitate the design of facilities to accommodate the needs of physically disabled people. The basic process to follow is to design an accessible route with the appropriate clearances and features required, and then detail and specify accessible elements and fixtures. The majority of the access needs and issues raised in the previous section are addressed in ANSI.

It is important to keep in mind that ANSI A117.1 is a "minimum" standard with application to commercial building types and residential buildings. It is by necessity based on averages. In order to produce an optimum design, the standard must be sensitively applied and adapted to meet the needs of specific users in residential settings, where the user is known, and amplified to address the requirements of complex facilities. The American Hotel and Motel Association has responded to this need by developing *An Interpretation of ANSI A117.1 (1986) as Applicable to New Hotels and Motels* (20).

ANSI and all other accessibility standards have been developed by an approach of modifying the norm through the use of a few specially designed features and products to accommodate those "few" who vary from the norm. Statistics reveal the fallacy of this approach, which encourages architects and designers to simply develop a design, then modify the design by providing the requisite access details, ramps, toilet facilities, drinking fountains, and telephones. Not only is this approach more costly in both design and construction phases, it also results in facilities which have their own "functional limitations" and aesthetic problems. Access features often look tacked on or like later modifications, and disabled users of the facility must often approach and use the building differently from those who are able bodied. Accessible parking is often hidden at the back of a building and the accessible entry may be located near the loading dock. In the late 1970s and early 1980s, disabled students at major universities soon recognized that accessible parking spaces could most often be found by looking for "loading zone only" signs and following the drive to the rear of the facility. Upon recognizing the problems experienced by drivers seeking these spaces, many universities responded by developing "special" maps for handicapped students and visitors rather than integrating the information into the general campus maps passed out to everyone. The maps were then made available only upon direct request through disabled student services. Many communities also developed access guides.

Demographics and the economics of the situation call for a different approach. Edward Steinfeld, architect and gerontologist, notes (21):

> Specifying different features for different groups of people always costs more and requires massive coordination and selective judgment about who should be accommodated and where. All of these impossible issues are eliminated by the universal design concept.

UNIVERSAL DESIGN

Improved design standards, better information, new products, and lower costs have made it possible for design professionals to begin designing all buildings, interiors, and products to be usable by everyone. Instead of responding only to the minimum demands of laws which require a few special features for disabled people, it is possible to design most manufactured items and building elements to be usable by a broad range of human beings including children, elderly people, people with disabilities, and people of different sizes. This concept is called universal design. It is a concept that is now entirely possible and one that makes economic and social sense.

Development of the Concept of Universal Design

While the narrow view of human needs was originally fostered by the wide use of anthropometric data based on the average male, it was reinforced by laws created by consumer groups often working in opposition to design professionals. Faced with limited opportunities in education, employment, housing, and recreation caused by inadequately designed facilities, advocacy groups of older and disabled people have lobbied for and worked to develop design standards and building code requirements intended to force the building industry to produce accessible buildings. Since such efforts are often opposed on the basis of cost, the resulting codes were generally minimal. These "bare bones" requirements, the result of political compromises published as law, became the primary information available to an entire industry about designing for a segment of the population that numbers in the millions. While the early standards had an important purpose, they were inadequate as educational media and they reinforced the outdated, narrow view of human environmental needs by requiring a few special features for what was perceived as a few people.

Prior to the early 1980s, differences among codes and regulations for accessibility prevented designers from easily assimilating the many diverse requirements, and also deterred manufacturers from developing and marketing low cost, universally usable products. Since the codes and regulations have, until recently, differed from state to state, and between various agencies at the state and federal levels, a common approach taken by designers was to simply look up the few things the laws required while failing to realize the value of providing accessibility that goes beyond the basic items required. Manufacturers were forced to provide several models of accessible products, such as water coolers, or offer special options in order to make them marketable under the varied requirements. The result was often increased costs.

In today's society, where mass production is the method used to reduce costs, it will always cost more to build a few special and different features than to mass produce all of them to be usable by everyone. Universal design advocates the latter approach.

The Role of Uniform Standards in Promoting Universal Design

The potential of universal design was advanced significantly with the publication of revised ANSI A117.1, 1980. Since 1980, these new expanded standards have been adopted in whole or in part by over 35 states, and (with modifications) by the federal government in the *Uniform Federal Accessibility Standards* (UFAS). As a result, most states and all federal agencies were required to use the same design specifications for accessibility. An update of the ANSI standard in 1986 continued the trend toward uniformity. Some inconsistencies between ANSI and UFAS were eliminated, the language was clarified, and errors corrected. However, no major changes were made to the standard's technical provisions.

This new uniformity makes it possible for designers to learn the minimum technical requirements once and then to apply them in practice with unprecedented consistency from project to project. The improved uniformity is also making it possible for manufacturers to produce universally acceptable products that can be specified for projects throughout the country. Lower costs, better accessibility, and less design time are some benefits of the new uniformity.

Applying Universal Design Concepts

Buildings which accommodate all people through their life span can be achieved through the application of universal design principles in all phases of the environmental design process including programming, conceptual design, plan development, product specification, and design documentation. Building programs should incorporate information about the variety of building users and their abilities. Disabled and older people can be expected to be among employees, customers, and visitors to a facility. This knowledge, along with information about the functional limitations of these populations, can guide designers in making important decisions about building access in conceptual design and plan development stages, and in integrating universal design features in a sensitive manner. For example, accessible entries are needed by the 10% of the adult population that has difficulty with stairs, but they also benefit virtually everyone. While an entrance to a building can be made accessible in many ways, some are more consistent with the building form than others. Access standards permit ramps, lifts, or walks which meet the specifications set out in the standards. Ramps, which are perhaps most commonly used, are not ideal for many people, and lifts may malfunction, leaving many people unable to enter or exit. In most situations, proper siting and adjustment of footings can produce level entries. When site or design constraints conflict, level entries can be provided through the creative use of bridges to high ground, overhead walks, or exterior elevator towers which can be shared by more than one building.

Architects can also simply incorporate many of the "special features" required by the accessibility standards and make them an aesthetic benefit to everyone. The standards require accessible bathtubs to have control valves which are offset toward the outside edge of the tub. This design is required to provide an easier reach to the controls for turning on and testing the water before entering the tub. This new location is easier for all tub users to reach and requires only a shift in supply pipe location. Since the additional cost of materials can be expected to be only $15–$20 per tub, offset controls could easily become standard features in all housing (22).

With increasing frequency, architects can choose from a variety of well designed, universally usable products including hardware and electronic equipment. Today, lever hardware is a stylish item available in a range of prices from the top of the line "architectural" hardware to low-cost, durable locksets with prices which compare to door "knobs." Lever handles for doors are standard in Europe and were common in the United States during revolutionary times. They can be found in historic houses and buildings because of their simple, low-cost production and ease of use. By the time access codes began requiring easily operating hardware, levers were high-cost items used in this country primarily in medical facilities where their ease of use was considered essential for efficient, safe delivery of services. Manufacturers have responded to the increased demand for this hardware with a great variety of products at competitive costs.

Other products can and are being redesigned to make them more universal. The common pay telephone is a product that cannot be positioned at any one height suitable for everyone due to its vertical design with the coin slot at the top. Children and people in wheelchairs and those of short stature may be unable to use the phone if it is mounted too high. Tall people must stoop in an awkward position to see and use the dial if the device is located at a height appropriate for people of shorter stature. Yet, a differently designed product could easily benefit everyone. A good example is the small table-top charge card phones increasingly found in hotels. Properly located with an accessible approach and reach and adjustable volume controls, these phones can be used by everyone with a charge card.

Technological advances in modern electronics are also making universal design economically feasible. Environmental control systems can operate lighting, window shades, and electronic appliances from remote locations or at programmed intervals. New devices using computer chips can provide information to people with hearing and vision losses. Controls that provide redundant feedback through tones, light, or tactile clicks provide feedback to the user in a manner that anyone can perceive. Talking circuits allow elevator panels, vending machines, and other devices to provide audible as well as written instructions or other information in any language needed. Infrared listening systems, remote alarms, wireless devices, and computers open up unlimited design possibilities for creating truly accommodating environments and universal building products and elements at no extra cost over existing technologies. The new "Smart House" technology, while currently in the conceptual and developmental stages, offers the potential for fully integrated communications, electrical, and environmental control systems that can be used in homes or commercial facilities.

A good example of the application of universal design principles exists today in adaptable housing. "Adaptable" housing offers basic accessibility and universally designed elements and products which can easily adapt to accommodate a variety of users. Adaptable housing benefits the renter/owner as well as the developer, property management, or marketing personnel. Each individual unit can adapt as necessary either at initial occupancy or at a later point in time.

ADAPTABLE HOUSING DESIGN

Because of the wide variety of disabling conditions, it is difficult to designate one house design for all people with disabilities or functional limitations. Most housing built "for disabled people" is designed for use by those who use wheelchairs and has features that are not needed or preferred by others. Because of the special nature of such wheelchair accessible housing, requirements for construction of a minimum number of rental units have had to be legislated. In most areas of the country, the number required has been between 5% and 10% in newly constructed apartment complexes exceeding a certain size, sometimes 20 units. These minimum numbers of special wheelchair accessible units have not met the needs of disabled people, and some builders and owners have had difficulty renting them.

The small numbers produced often made it difficult for people to find an accessible unit in an appropriate neighborhood. A lack of choice in size also prevented some potential tenants from renting units. In areas where the building codes and laws did not specify the sizes of units to be made accessible, many builders made only the smaller one-bedroom units accessible. Disabled people with families or live-in attendants could not use these units. Other disabled people did not rent the accessible units because only new, more expensive apartments were made accessible and the rents were too high for those who were on fixed or limited incomes.

Non-disabled people sometimes refused to rent the accessible apartments because they did not want to be in the "handicapped" unit. They objected to the clinical appearance of bathrooms equipped with grab bars or the loss of storage space when cabinets were omitted under sinks and counters to provide knee space for wheelchair users. Some owners took losses on the units by giving rent discounts to non-disabled people who lived in them. Others modified the units, removing accessible elements or complained of continuing vacancies. Some developers/owners have appealed to code promulgating groups to eliminate all accessible housing requirements. Faced with certain setbacks in accessible housing, advocates, design researchers, and the disabled community responded by developing and promoting the concept of adaptable housing.

Adaptable housing addresses the problems of appearance and inconvenience created by some of the accessibility features. Because it provides adjustable elements that can be set to the most convenient position for each tenant, the dwelling can more appropriately fit the needs of any occupant. Adaptability eliminates the special and different appearance that made accessible units undesirable to non-disabled people by allowing some features to be temporarily hidden or omitted. Adaptable housing design is a more flexible approach to providing accessible housing and it is paving the way for larger numbers of units that are marketable to both disabled and non-disabled people.

Features of Adaptable Housing Units

An adaptable house is a wheelchair-accessible house that does not look like one, and that can accommodate a wide variety of users throughout the life of the facility. The adaptable concept includes all features normally required for full accessibility but allows some to be hidden from view by the use of removable elements, and others to be added when needed. It also requires a few key features to be adjustable in height for use by people of all sizes and abilities. This combination of fixed accessible features, adjustable features, and optional removable or added elements creates a flexible yet accessible unit that can be tailored as needed to the specific needs of the tenant.

The ANSI A117.1–1986, *American National Standard for Buildings and Facilities-Providing Accessibility and Usability for Physically Handicapped People,* and the *Uniform Federal Accessibility Standards* (UFAS) contain basic technical specifications for the fixed, accessible, adjustable, and optional features required in an adaptable dwelling. As defined in ANSI and UFAS, the features include but are not limited to those shown in Figure 1 and listed below.

1. *Fixed Accessible Features.*
   - *Wide passage doors.* Doors that provide a minimum 32 in. clear opening.
   - *An accessible route.* A clear path connecting all accessible features and spaces. This requirement means there can be no steps or stairs at the entrance to the unit and that a complete set of living facilities must be on one level unless all levels are connected by a ramp, lift, or elevator.
   - *Clear floor spaces.* Minimum floor areas around fixtures such as toilets, tubs, showers, and sinks must be clear to allow people using wheelchairs to maneuver close. The clear floor areas can be partially covered by removable elements such as cabinets, and careful design can avoid major increases in room size.
   - *Controls within easy reach and easily operated.* Light switches, thermostats, electrical receptacles, faucets, and other controls should be mounted between 9 in. and 48 to 54 in. above the floor (depending on the direction of approach) and operable with one hand. They should also not require great force or grasping to activate.
   - *Operable windows.* If operable windows are provided, they must meet requirements similar to those for controls.
   - *Visual alarms.* If warning signals are provided, such as smoke and/or fire alarms, they must be both visual and auditory, or an outlet must be provided which will connect a portable visual signal device into the alarm system.
   - *Knee spaces.* Knee spaces of particular sizes must be provided under the kitchen sink and workspace, beside wall ovens in kitchens, and under lavatories in bathrooms. These knee spaces can be temporarily concealed (see Removable Features).
   - *Tub seats.* Bathtubs must have either a seat built-in at the head end or an attachable, portable seat that fastens securely to the tub when needed. The seats are used by people who cannot step or climb over the tub rim and get down into the tub (Fig. 2).
   - *Showers.* If showers are provided, one must be a 3 × 3 ft size with a seat to allow transfer or a roll-in shower that can accommodate a person in

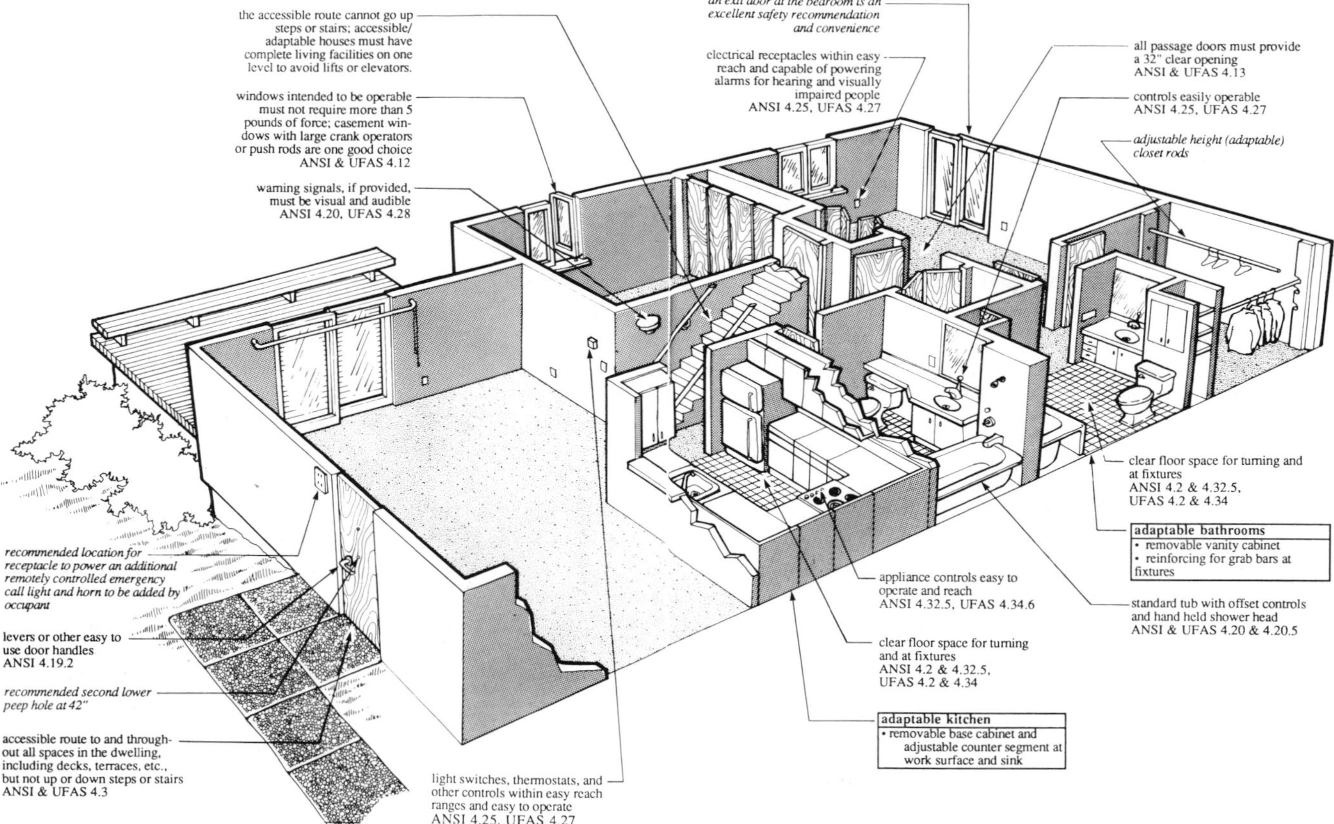

Figure 1. An accessible adaptable dwelling (23).

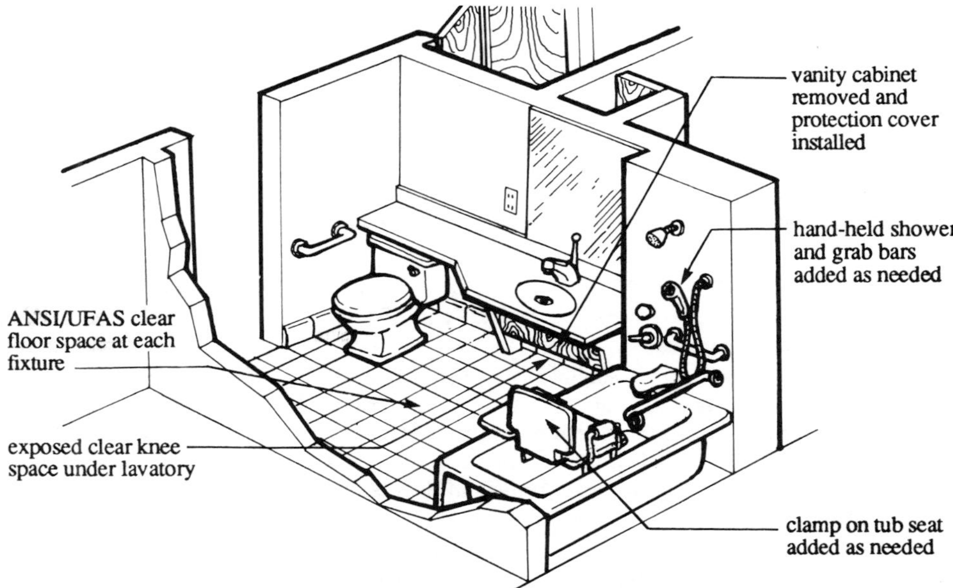

Figure 2. Small adaptable bathroom in adjusted configuration (23).

a wheelchair. If a roll-in shower is chosen, the standards do not require it to be larger than the size of a full bathtub (Fig. 3**a**). Larger sized showers may be more functional for some users (Fig. 3**b**).

- *Offset controls.* Tubs and showers must have control valves which are offset toward the outside to be easier to reach from the side of the fixture. Hand-held shower heads on flexible hoses must also be provided.
- *Reinforcing for grab bars.* Wood blocking or other reinforcing must be placed in specific locations in walls around showers, tubs and toilets to facilitate the simple addition of grab bars at a later time (Fig. 4).

2. *Adjustable Features.*
   - Segments of counter tops over knee spaces at work surfaces and sinks must be adjustable in height from a standard height of 36 in. to a low of 28 in. to allow use by people who must sit down to prepare food. The kitchen sink must be included in the adjustable counter segment and its plumbing can be connected with flexible supply pipes and removable segments or slip joints in the drain pipe. Cook tops and other appliances may also be included as adjustable features at the option of the owner, builder, or designer.
   - Adjustable height closet rods and cabinet shelves are not specifically required in ANSI or UFAS but are highly recommended to improve usability for all people.
3. *Optional Removable or Added Features.*
   - Knee spaces required under kitchen counters and bathroom lavatories can, at the builder's option, be temporarily hidden from view by removable base cabinets (Fig. 5).
   - Grab bars at tubs, showers, and toilets in bathrooms can be omitted until needed by a tenant so

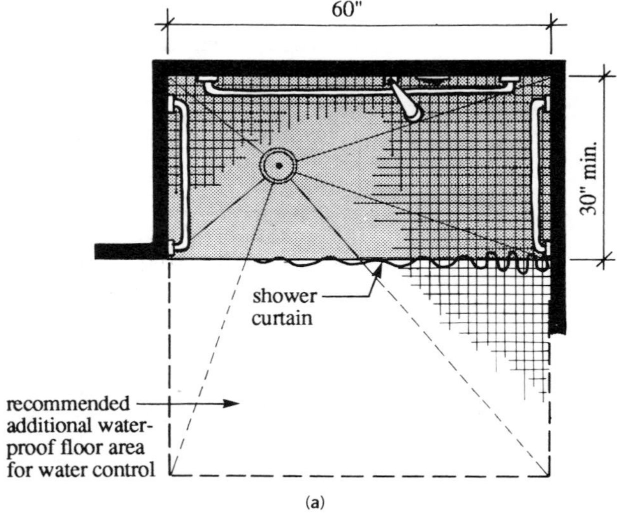

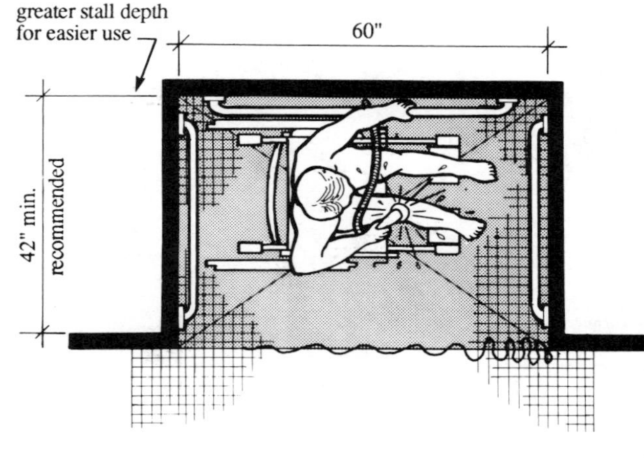

Figure 3. (a) ANSI minimum roll-in shower; **(b)** Preferred dimensions for roll-in shower (23).

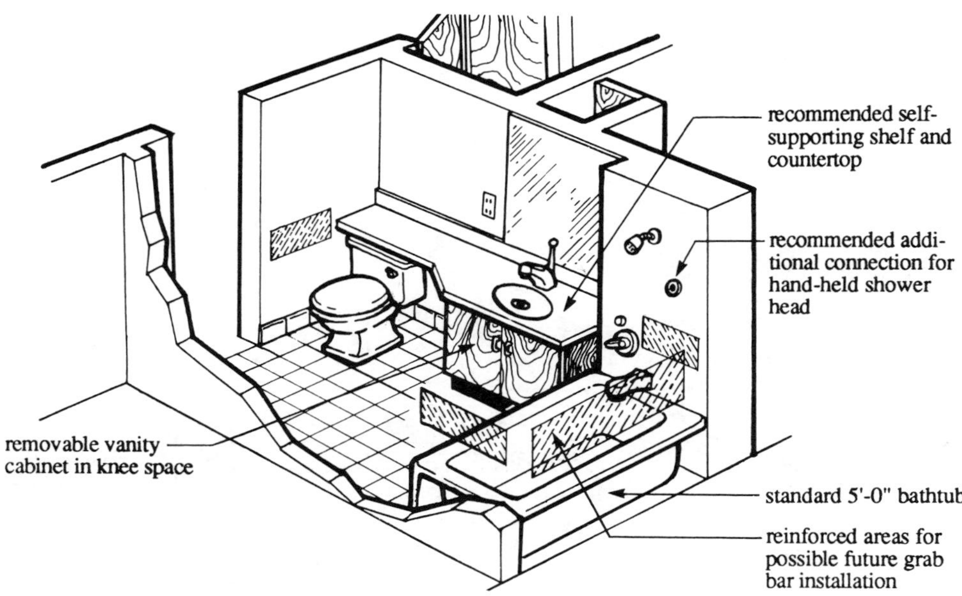

Figure 4. Small adaptable bathroom in conventional configuration (23).

long as wall reinforcing is in place that will allow the bars to be simply installed with common hardware when needed without structural modifications (Fig. 4).

- If a standard bathtub without a built-in seat is provided, a portable but securely attachable tub seat must be provided when needed.

An adaptable dwelling unit includes all accessibility features and provisions for the options at the time of construction. These truly adaptable units can be adjusted or adapted without requiring renovation because the basic access requirements, such as door widths, ground level entrances, and reachable switches and controls, are already a part of the unit. Necessary adaptations for any occupant may include removing or replacing base cabinets to reveal or conceal knee spaces under the kitchen sink, work surface, and bathroom lavatory; changing counter and sink heights; and installing or removing grab bars if necessary. These simple adjustments can be made in only a few hours and need not delay occupancy by the new tenant. Adapting a dwelling for accessibility is not the same as renovating or remodeling an inaccessible unit. Remodeling for accessibility can be an unreasonably expensive process that could require weeks or months to complete and one that may not be entirely successful in the end.

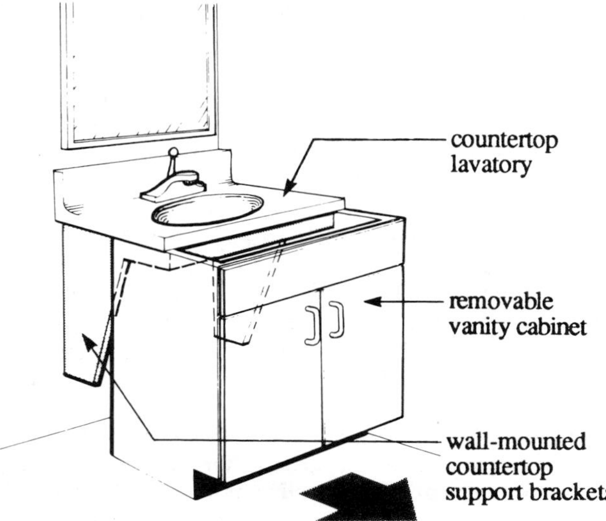

Figure 5. Removing vanity cabinet to expose knee space (23).

Relatively little information is available on the concept of adaptable housing, and there are few good examples. Literature on the topic is sparse and includes only a few early documents and the ANSI and UFAS standards. The standards contain the bare minimum specifications for adaptable features but lack advice or technical information on how to implement them. A recent publication entitled *Adaptable Housing: Marketable, Accessible Housing for Everyone* published by the Office of Policy Development and Research of the U.S. Department of Housing and Urban Development (23) provides more in-depth information on all aspects of adaptable housing, including how this exciting concept can be applied to low-income, fixed-budget housing, or more expensive upscale housing with a more generous floor plan (Fig. 6). The HUD publication, the ANSI and UFAS standards and *Adaptable Housing* by Peoples Housing of Topanga Canyon, California (24) are recommended for additional reading on the subject.

Benefits of Adaptable Housing

The adaptable housing concept benefits both those who produce and those who occupy new housing. Builders and developers of housing benefit from having accessible units that look no different from others and that can be rented as needed by disabled or non-disabled people. The access features are positive attributes that improve safety and

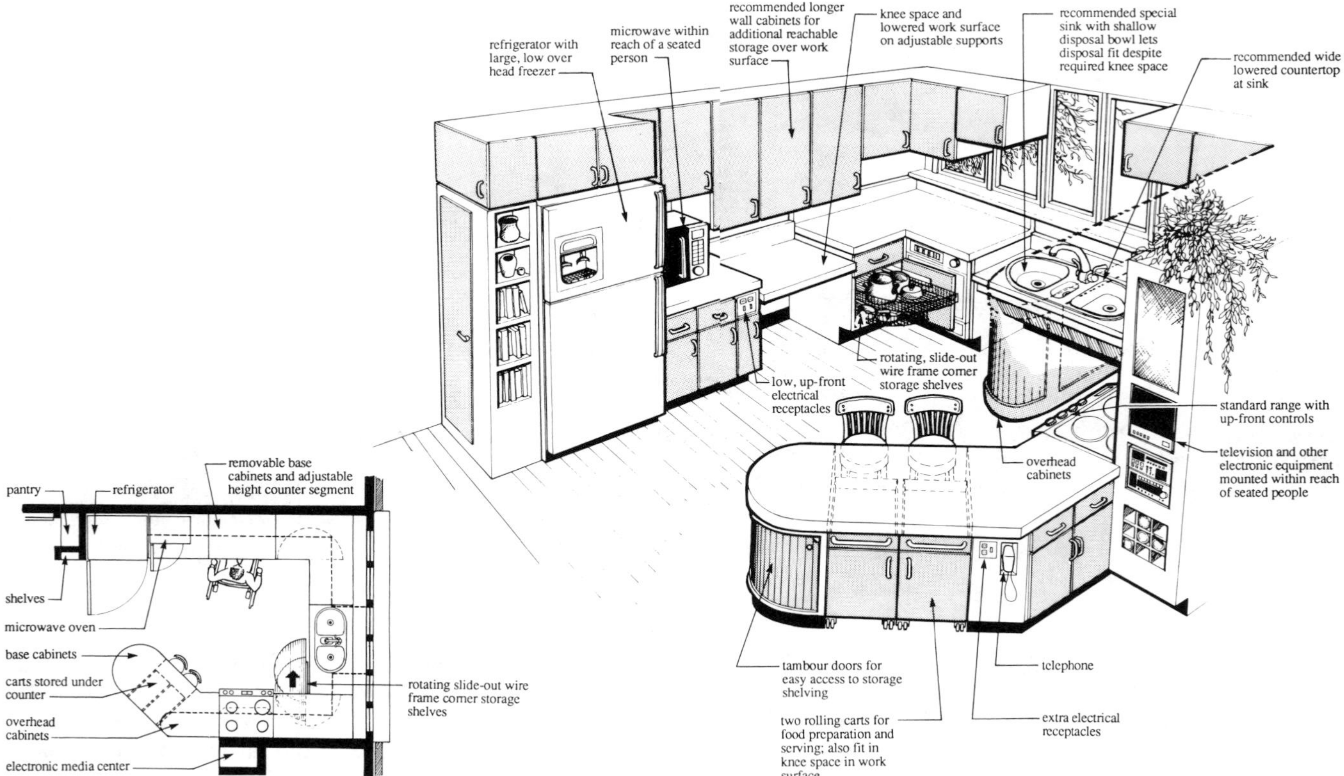

Figure 6. An elaborate kitchen with adaptable features (23).

livability for everyone. Most people like the additional clear floor space in the bathrooms for storage cabinets, shelves, or a chair in these usually cramped spaces. Wide doors and level entrances are appreciated when valuable furniture can easily and safely be moved in and dollies, strollers, and bicycles can be brought into the house without being bounced up or down stairs. Shorter, non-disabled people may appreciate adjustable countertop segments as much as those who must sit to work in their kitchens. These and other adaptability features can be made into selling points that improve the unit's marketability.

Studies of tenants conducted by Cardinal Industries, the leading manufacturer of modular adaptable housing units, show that people who find and adjust a dwelling unit to accommodate their disability will remain in the unit longer than other people. Tenant longevity is an economic benefit to owners and developers because of less frequent cleanup and reconditioning. Another type of occupant longevity can be expected; adaptable housing can change as a family's needs change over time. If a non-disabled family member becomes permanently or temporarily disabled due to aging or other causes, the house can adjust to new needs and the family need not relocate to more appropriate housing or place the individual in an institutional setting.

Increasing numbers of older people also benefit from adaptable housing since it does not look different or special. Most people, including older people, do not wish to be placed in "special" housing that separates them from others or labels them as different. Adaptability allows the dwelling to discreetly respond to the individual's changing needs throughout his or her lifespan without applying any stereotypical labels. Adaptability can allow frail older people to remain in their own homes longer than they might in non-accessible housing. If personal services become necessary for an individual, the adaptable features make it easier and less expensive to provide the services by reducing demands on the caregivers.

The friends, family, and associates of older people and those with disabilities also benefit from the ability of adaptable housing to more closely match the true needs and lifestyles of both the disabled individual and their families and service providers. Severely disabled people most often live with non-disabled spouses, friends, or personal attendants. These companions frequently do household tasks such as cooking that disabled individuals may not be able to do for themselves. In an adaptable house, the kitchen can be set for use by the non-disabled companion who uses it, while the remaining parts of the unit can be adjusted for access to the disabled occupant, a degree of flexibility not possible in fixed-access units. Friends and associates of people with disabilities benefit by having adaptable housing since they can invite disabled and non-disabled friends and family members to visit or stay in their homes.

Adaptability provides new marketing opportunities for manufacturers and fertile ground for innovation. Some existing products are being used in new ways for adaptable features. There is a growing market for innovative new products designed to be used by all people regardless of age or physical ability and capable of being specified by those who wish to produce adaptable housing. Simple cabinet work and thermostats that are easy to see and set are two such products.

Perhaps the most significant benefit to the disabled community is the potential of adaptable housing to put larger numbers of accessible units on the market. The increased marketability of the units to non-disabled people, including the growing population of older people, makes viable the idea of increased numbers of units. Several states have for some years accepted adaptable units in lieu of fixed accessible ones, but relatively few were built because products and simple methods for creating adjustable features, as well as costs, were unknown. Recently, New York and California have required percentages of adaptable units as high as 100% in some types of housing. Larger numbers of adaptable units will help create a supply of accessible houses in all price ranges, sizes, and locations and will ensure more appropriate housing for disabled people at all socioeconomic levels.

Adaptability has great potential for solving many of the problems of providing accessible, marketable housing for everyone. Attractive, flexible housing that can be tailored to the needs of a broader range of people and which does not label itself or its occupants as disabled or old is badly needed. The market for such housing is large and growing, and the concept of adaptability is receiving support from a variety of construction industry and community groups. The recognized, documented number of disabled people in the United States with significant functional limitations exceeds 37 million. Some industries that produce products for disabled people estimate their market share as being much larger, some as high as 70 million people. These figures also do not include the temporarily disabled, parents with small children, or the friends and family members of people with disabilities. The important point to remember about the numbers of people affected is that they are quite large, include people from every socioeconomic level, and represent a significant market for improved housing. If the effects of aging are included, everyone is indeed eventually affected.

OTHER HOUSING ENVIRONMENTS

A wide range of housing options and living arrangements is available for older people and those with physical disabilities. Universal design is the key to providing supportive, accommodating environments which promote independent function and control while reducing dependence on others in performing activities of daily living.

Home ownership is part of the "American Dream." It offers privacy, autonomy, and control over structure and grounds. The majority of people with disabilities and older people prefer to live in their own homes. Older people have the highest rate of home ownership among all age groups and older home owners in the suburbs are "aging in place," as are those who entered subsidized rental housing in the 1960s (25). One of the greatest obstacles to living or remaining in single-family homes is an aging environment which presents barriers to independent functioning or requires extraordinary effort to be expended in maintenance and accomplishing tasks. Since the percentage of the older population is expected to continue increasing (26), it is predicted that the demand for housing renovations to accommodate physical disabilities will continue to expand well into the twenty-first century. This accommodation can often be accomplished by the addition of an accessible bedroom and bath (where none exists on the first floor) along with other alterations to kitchen, storage, and entry to make a single level of the home accessible.

People with disabilities, older people, or their children may choose to renovate their homes to incorporate accessory apartments. Accessory apartments are created by subdividing the space in a single family home to create a separate living space, bedroom, bathroom, and kitchen. This space can be rented to tenants who agree to provide assistance to the homeowner, or the owner may choose to move into the apartment and allow the family or tenants to have the larger portion of the home (27). Local zoning ordinances have in the past precluded more than one unit on a single family lot. However, many jurisdictions have recently revised these ordinances to provide for accessory apartments when requirements are met relative to minimum lot size, parking, separate entries, above-grade windows, and other features.

Elder Cottage Housing Opportunity or ECHO housing is similar in concept to accessory apartments in that it allows disabled or older people the opportunity to live in close proximity to others who may lend assistance, while providing all parties with the privacy of separate living quarters. An ECHO unit is a small house occupied by one or two people installed in the side yard or the back yard of an existing single-family residence. ECHO housing, which is designed to the *ECHO Housing Recommended Construction and Installation Standards* developed by AARP (28), is designed to serve the individual needs of older Americans, with and without disabilities, and younger people with physical disabilities. These housing units should always be adaptable as required by the AARP standards. ECHO units, where allowed at all by zoning requirements, must meet requirements similar to accessory apartments under local zoning laws. In addition, ECHO units must also be designed to blend in with the architectural style in the existing neighborhood (Fig. 7). Occupancy permits are generally tied to the individual occupant of the unit and become void should that person move or leave the unit. The unit must then be converted to non-residential use or removed from the site. AARP has developed a range of publications on this issue including a model zoning ordinance and an ECHO Housing standard.

Other housing types include group homes, elderly apartments, congregate housing, and a range of retirement communities complete with a wide variety of activities, facilities, and services. In these special facilities, as in residential care facilities or nursing homes, the need for universal design and adaptability is critical. If society is to accommodate the life span economically, these facilities must be designed to assist the individual with declining physical abilities through a supportive environment which promotes independence in self-care and activities of daily

Figure 7. Architecturally compatible ECHO unit in a single-family neighborhood (28). Courtesy of the American Association of Retired Persons.

living while reducing dependence on personal assistance or home health care.

CONCLUSION

If design professionals can improve the quality of the built environment through universal design, the benefit to society will be significant. The benefit to the designer can also be substantial. By adopting this concept, architects will be able to offer clients a more comprehensive design service—one that serves people of all ages, physical sizes, and abilities equally well, and one that creates buildings which can grow old as gracefully as the people they shelter. This service will increase in value as the numbers of older people grow.

BIBLIOGRAPHY

1. E. Steinfeld, S. Schroeder, and coworkers, *The Estimated Cost of Accessible Buildings,* U.S. Department of Housing and Urban Development, Washington, D.C., 1979, p. 141.
2. *Disability, Functional Limitation and Health Insurance Coverage 1984/85,* Series P-70, No. 8, Bureau of the Census, Washington, D.C., 1986.
3. A. Adiv, "Public–Private Cooperation in the Provision of Special Transportation Services," *Specialized Transportation Planning and Practice* **II, III,** 185–206 (April 1986).
4. *Universal Design: Housing for the Lifespan of All People,* U.S. Department of Housing and Urban Development, Washington, D.C., 1988, p. 2.
5. *American National Standard for Buildings and Facilities—Providing Accessibility and Usability for Physically Handicapped People,* American National Standards Institute, New York, 1986.
6. *The Uniform Federal Accessibility Standards,* Department of Defense, the General Services Administration, U.S. Department of Housing and Urban Development, and the U.S. Postal Service, Washington, D.C., 1984.
7. T. Fisher, "Enabling the Disabled," *Progressive Architecture,* 122 (July 1985).
8. Ref. 4, p. 4.
9. M. J. Bednar, *Barrier Free Environments,* Dowden Hutchinson and Ross, Stroudsburg, Pa., 1977, p. 2.
10. M. P. La Plante and L. A. Grant, *Persons Who Need or Benefit from Accessible Features in the Built Environment,* U.S. Architectural and Transportation Barriers Compliance Board, Washington, D.C., Feb. 1988.
11. Ref. 2, p. 2.
12. Ref. 2, p. 4.
13. Ref. 2, p. 32.
14. *Technology and Aging in America,* Congress of the United States, Office of Technology Assessment, Washington, D.C., 1985, p. 39.
15. *Ibid.,* p. 62.
16. *Design for Aging: An Architects Guide,* The American Institute of Architects, Washington, D.C., 1985, p. 6.

17. Ref. 14, pp. 88–89.
18. H. H. Cohen, "Falls Resulting from Changes in Level With Special Reference to the Elderly," Presentation at the Annual Meeting of the Human Factors Society, October 23, 1984, unpublished.
19. L. Pastalan, "The Simulation of Age Related Sensory Losses: A New Approach to the Study of Environmental Barriers," *New Outlook for the Blind,* 356–362 (Oct. 1984).
20. *An Interpretation of ANSI A117.1 (1986) as Applicable to New Hotels and Motels,* American Hotel and Motel Association, Technology and Information Department, Washington, D.C., 1987.
21. Ref. 4, p. 14.
22. Ref. 4, p. 9.
23. *Adaptable Housing: Marketable, Accessible Housing for Everyone,* U.S. Department of Housing and Urban Development, Washington, D.C., 1987.
24. *Adaptable Housing,* Peoples Housing, Topanga Canyon, Calif., 1984.
25. Ref. 14, p. 301.
26. G. A. Christie, "The Nineties are Coming: A Briefing on the Construction Sector," *Sweet's Catalogue,* Washington, D.C., May 4, 1988.
27. Ref. 16, p. 62.
28. R. L. Mace and R. Hall-Phillips, *ECHO Housing,* American Association of Retired Persons, Washington, D.C., 1984.

General References

Refs. 7, 9, 10, 16, 23, and 28 are good general references.

Accommodation of Disabled Visitors at Historic Sites in the National Park System, U.S. Department of the Interior, Washington, D.C., 1983.

An Interpretation of ANSI A117.1 (1986), The American Hotel and Motel Association Executive Engineers Committee, New York, February 1987.

The Arts and 504: A Handbook for Making The Arts Accessible, The National Endowment for the Arts, Washington, D.C., 1985.

B. B. Raschko, *Housing Interiors for the Disabled and Elderly,* Van Nostrand Reinhold Company, New York, 1982.

Communication Systems for Disabled Users of Buildings, U.S. Department of Commerce, Washington, D.C., Dec. 1981.

A Guide to Designing Accessible Outdoor Recreation Facilities, Heritage Conservation and Recreation Service, U.S. Department of the Interior, Lake Central Regional Office, Ann Arbor, Mich., Jan. 1980.

The Guide—Making Accessibility Affordable: Facilities Evaluation and Modification Guide, a slide tape presentation, ADS Management Corporation and Barrier Free Environments, Raleigh, N.C., 1985.

Housing an Aging Population: Maximizing Choices, National Advisory Council on Aging, NACA, Government of Canada, Ottawa, May 1985.

Housing for a Maturing Population, The Urban Land Institute in cooperation with the Housing Committee, The American Institute of Architects, Washington, D.C., 1983.

Housing for the Elderly and Handicapped, U.S. Department of Housing and Urban Development, Washington, D.C., 1979.

J. J. Jordan, "Designing Buildings for Older Americans," *Aging* (Dec. 1983–Jan. 1984).

J. Majewski, *Part of Your General Public is Disabled: A Handbook for Guides in Museums, Zoos and Historic Houses,* Smithsonian Museum, Washington, D.C., 1987.

J. A. Koncelik, *Aging and the Product Environment,* Hutchinson Ross Publishing Co., Stroudsburg, Pa., 1982.

L. G. Hiatt, "Conveying the Substances of Images: Interior Design in Long-Term Care," *Contemporary Administrator* (April 1984).

L. H. Bowker, *Humanizing Institutions for the Aged,* Lexington Books, Lexington, Mass., 1982.

Orientation and Wayfinding, U.S. Architectural and Transportation Barriers Compliance Board, Washington, D.C., March 1983.

P. H. Hare and L. E. Hollis, *ECHO Housing—A Review of Zoning Issues and Other Considerations,* American Association of Retired Persons, Washington, D.C., 1983.

R. L. Mace, "Universal Design—Barrier Free Environments for Everyone," *Designers West,* 147 (Nov. 1985).

R. Hall-Lusher, "Designing for the Life Span," *Construction Specifier,* 31 (Feb. 1988).

R. Hall-Phillips and R. L. Mace, "Designing and Specifying for Accessibility: It's Getting Easier," *The Construction Specifier* **XXXVIII** (4), 46 (Apr. 1985).

See also ARCHITECTURAL AND TRANSPORTATION BARRIERS COMPLIANCE BOARD (ATBCB); HANDICAPPED ACCESS LAWS AND CODES; STAIRS AND RAMPS—SAFETY ASPECTS; ZONING AND BUILDING REGULATIONS

RUTH HALL LUSHER
Vienna, Virginia

RONALD L. MACE, FAIA
Raleigh, North Carolina

PIANO, RENZO

Renzo Piano, born in Genoa, Italy, on September 14, 1937, is usually associated with high-tech architecture, an association that is mainly due to his (and his collaborator Rogers's) provocative Centre Georges Pompidou in Paris. Although this structure signified the culmination of the architect's more rhetorical technology, his deeper interest in the whole process of developing technology in conjunction with design has always set him apart from his formalist high-tech colleagues. He does not readily fit into any trend or movement, but he clearly stands at the opposite pole to the postmodernist architect. He respects historical precedent, but rejects historical reference. Apart from what he has conveyed in personal interviews, he has refrained from theoretical pronouncements. He sees the role of the architect as the master and, if need be, the inventor of his or her tools and materials, and he upholds scientific analysis and practical experimentation together with an understanding of the human needs as the fundamental principles of architecture. Based on this belief in process over form, Piano has equated design or formal expression with the organic evolution of developing and integrating all components of a project into the final product. Recently, however, he has emphasized the formal aspect and creatively concealed the technology.

Piano's empirical craftsmanlike approach to architecture is partially anchored in his family background and training. He was born into a family of contractors and became exposed to the building process at an early age. In 1964 he graduated with an architectural degree from the Polytechnic School in Milan where he acquired his love for detail and methodical work habits from his teacher Franco Albini. He then joined his family firm and, between 1965 and 1970, took his international apprenticeships with Louis Kahn in Philadelphia, Z. S. Makowski in London, and Marco Zanuso in Milan. Although each of these masters left an imprint on Piano's work, the long friendship with Jean Prouvé seems to have exerted the strongest influence.

During this period he began to experiment with new materials, which became a lasting passion. At first he concentrated on plastics, particularly on reinforced polyester as a translucent membrane. His early structures were of a temporary nature. They were lightweight and based on geometric modules; therefore, they were capable of being extended or reduced according to need—always a "work in progress," as Piano would have it. In the model proposed for the 14th Triennale Pavilion in Milan, 1967, he turned from the repetitive symmetry of the modules to the more complex shell form. The spatial dynamics of the irregularly undulating shape of reinforced polyester and hence the irregular absorption of light in the interior pointed in new directions.

Piano's explorations into building technology became motivated by a concern for structural and spatial flexibility to accommodate changing needs. In his own office, or Building Workshop as he calls it, in the hills of Genoa (1968/now destroyed), he employed an open plan, a design feature that became one of his hallmarks. The spatial volume was enclosed by a system of structural steel pyramids with opaque and translucent panels as wall and roof membranes. In the Italian Industry Pavilion at the Osaka World Fair (1969–1970) Piano achieved an economically efficient, flexible structure. This temporary container, pinned up by a structure of prestressed steel and reinforced polyester, possessed all the qualities of a circus tent with which it also shared the rigidity that is collapsible at will. In 1971, the year of the competition for the Centre Pompidou, Piano joined Richard Rogers in London. Their office building for the B & B Italia upholstery plant in Novedrate, Como (1971–1973) is of particular interest in its anticipating aspects of the Centre Pompidou: the open-plan "box," the steel structure forming a volumetric screen on the exterior, and the rich chromatic differentiation of the systems.

Piano and Rogers's design for the Centre Georges Pompidou was selected from 681 international competition entries. The choice of an industrial-style design so antithetical to its historic setting in the heart of Paris provoked much criticism, but it presented the flexibility required by the complex needs of this multidisciplinary cultural center. When the six-story glass volume, its structural, mechanical, and circulatory systems exposed on the exterior, opened in 1977, the references ranged from a terminal monument of Archigram aesthetics and ideology (Rogers's background) to nineteenth-century ferrovitreous exhibition halls. The architects' intent behind this gigantic work of painstaking design was to create an anti-institutional "machine" or "utensil" open to everyone, ultimately to be defined by its users. The test of a decade's time has shown that the Centre Pompidou is not only the most visited monument in Paris, but has even gained an emblematic quality. Among the many reasons for its popularity is the successful communication between the structure and the plaza in front of it. A contributing feature is the escalator zigzagging diagonally across the facade—it establishes a visual link to the exterior and, by virtue of the spectacular views it offers to the user, a psychological link to the interior.

Notoriety notwithstanding, Piano turned his attention to a wide spectrum of challenges. One of these was the development of a safer, lighter, and more durable passenger vehicle for the Fiat company (1978–1980). Another was housing where adaptability and occupant participation had become determining factors in his investigations of industrialized construction systems. At first, all interior spatial divisions had been left to the occupants' decision, as was the case in the single-family houses in Cusago, Milan (1972–1974). In the Corciano estate development, Perugia (1978, Atelier Piano & Rice), a standardized outer shell containing open-plan units, Piano realized the necessity of a directive influence on the interior layout. He set up a "neighborhood workshop" to diagnose and effectively deal with the evolving needs of the community members.

The creation of the neighborhood workshop proved to become a vital instrument in Piano's urban rehabilitation projects. In 1979, UNESCO sponsored his neighborhood workshop to study the renovation of the ancient town of Otranto in southern Italy. The approach recommended was to involve the residents actively in the entire process instead of evacuating them, to upgrade the local crafts and trades, and to introduce new technologies for chemophysical and other structural analyses. The objective was to maintain the historic physical fabric and simultaneously invigorate the existing social, cultural, and economic life within it. This procedure constitutes the basis of most of Piano's other urban projects: the restructuring of the island of Burano, Venice (1980), the maintenance of the Japigia quarter in Bari (1980–1982), and the revitalization of the old Molo quarter, Genoa (1981). The last was a pilot project and, among other problems, involved a remedy for the lack of light, ventilation, and movement in the gloomy, damp buildings separated by narrow lanes. Piano combined new technologies with the traditional devices and practices of reflective panels for light, solar chimneys for ventilation, and, for movement, the placement of the social institutions on the roof tops, all of which are interconnected by gangways and pedestrian walks.

Piano's "soft-technology" approach and social concerns also distinguished his conversion of the Schlumberger Works in Montrouge, Paris (1981–1984). This early twentieth-century plant had to be converted into workshops and research facilities without arresting production. The old buildings are preserved behind the modern veneer, only one being razed to make way for the urban park incorporating a manmade hill that, in turn, houses the parking garage. This park, with all its social amenities, forms the pivot of the entire scheme and signifies an important addition in Piano's architectural vocabulary. Although he had always been very much aware of nature, especially as the inspirational force behind his technology, he now included structured nature as an active design element. Two of his more recent large-scale urban projects, the restructuring of the Lingotto industrial complex in Turin (1983) and of the old port of Genoa in preparation for the fifth Centennial of Columbus's discovery of America in 1992 (1982), feature structured parks as an essential part of their respective schemes. Piano's Genoa and Paris offices, the latter in existence since 1974, are engaged in several long-term urban projects such as the historic sector of Rhodes, Greece, and the Quai Achille Lignon, Lyons. Perhaps the strongest expression of Piano's endeavor to link the new with the old is moving his original office in 1985 from the periphery of Genoa into the historic Palazzo Doria in the very center of the old town.

Piano's buildings of this period show a similar tendency toward a synthesis of structure, function, and aesthetics. The temporary IBM Travelling Pavilion (1982–1984), for example, was a lightweight tunnel that consisted of a sophisticated combination of new and traditional materials with its structural elements inspired by floral patterns. This structure, resembling an earthworm, was erected in 20 European urban parks so that nature, the park landscape visible through the membrane, formed part of the environment for the electronic technology on display.

Projecting a sense of measured serenity, science and nature also set the parameters in the Menil Collection of Art and Historic Artifacts in Houston (1981–1986). The client's objective, which Piano had come to meet with increasing sensitivity, was a museum to fit into the unassuming suburban grid and to use natural light in the exhibition spaces. Piano (& Fitzgerald, a partnership since 1980, Houston) responded to the environmental context with a simple, clapboard-faced structure of domestic scale. The reticent, elegant character of the building's exterior and interior is countered by the subtlety of its concealed technology. Ferrocement "leaves," which are bolted into ductile iron trusses, act both as light filters and thermal screens and permit the works of art to be viewed in natural tempered light. Compared to the Centre Pompidou of 10 years before, the Menil Collection is, of course, the typological and contextual antithesis. Yet this points up Piano's approach to every design project as a unique constellation. Some of his numerous recent projects include a sports hall in Ravenna (1986), a stadium in Bari (1987), and the Synchroton in Grenoble (1987), all exhibiting a compact, powerful design, which completely integrates the technology and maintains the continuity with the environment. Noting Piano's increasing artistic self-assurance, one is tempted to recall Le Corbusier's statement that an architect can only get going seriously after he has passed fifty.

BIBLIOGRAPHY

General References

M. Dini, *Renzo Piano. Projects and Buildings 1964–1983,* Electa/Rizzoli, New York, 1984.

D. Mangin, "Piano de A à W," *Architecture d'Aujourd'hui* (246) (September 1986).

R. Piano (F. Renevier, collaborator), *Chantier ouvert au public,* Arthaud, Paris, 1985.

"Renzo Piano: architecture et technologie," *Architecture d'Aujourd'hui* (219), entire issue (February 1982).

See also ROGERS, RICHARD

BARBARA CHABROWE
Washington, D.C.

PILES, BEARING. See FOUNDATION SYSTEMS

PLANNED COMMUNITIES (NEW TOWNS)

The contemporary definition of new towns has evolved from the post-World War II English practice of satellite towns, with the following definition: a consciously planned, free standing and self-contained urban environment built in response to clearly stated objectives, as follows:

- *Economic.* Exploitation of raw materials/mining/refining, or manufacturing creates industrial new towns, located advantageously in relation to raw materials and clearly defined markets.
- *Political.* The new town's location may be symbolic of the seat of power and/or may expand or redistribute growth and development. Brasilia and Canberra are modern examples, while seventeenth-century Philadelphia represents a typical colonial new settlement.
- *Spatial.* Satellite new towns are planned within greater metropolitan regions to divert and redistribute urban growth.
- *Spatial Redistribution.* Recognizing the social costs, fragmentation, isolation and anomie, and the economic waste inherent in hyperconcentration in late industrial era cities, satellite new towns are planned.

The new towns should meet the following criteria:

1. *Social.* The new town should be planned for critical mass, based on realistic projections of population and economic growth to provide a variety of housing and employment opportunities for all incomes and stages of life, with a broad range of amenities. It should be of sufficient size for diversified social life with shopping (including secondary and neighborhood level), commercial and service activities, and educational and cultural activities self-contained on the site.
2. *Economic.* From the demand side, the new town should be located on a site large enough to provide a consumer market and labor force sufficient to support a town center and employment areas offering a variety of industrial, commercial, and service jobs.
3. *Physical.* The urban design should integrate the town functions and activities in density patterns that maximize pedestrian access and minimize the journey

to work. Planning should include environmental and land use controls designed for appropriate degrees of flexibility for long term development yet specific enough for the short term. Modern practice has abandoned the rigid Master Plan for the flexible "strategic" or "structure" plans supplemented with zoning and land-use ordinances.

NEW CAPITALS

Since the earliest Egyptian civilization, new capital cities were built for practical or symbolic reasons to govern new nation states or possessions or to transfer the seat of power to more advantageous locations. In recent times, newly independent countries started the construction of new capitals. In 1979, Dodoma, Tanzania, was constructed 300 km North of Dar es Salaam; Nigeria, more recently, began building its new capital of Obuja 500 km inland from Lagos. In 1948, the partition of India created Pakistan and divided the old Punjab state between the two countries. In India, a new Punjab state capital, Chandigarh, was created in 1954, while Pakistan initiated a new national capital, Islamabad, in 1960.

After the U.S. War of Independence, the 13 new states of the Union located Washington, D.C. on virgin land for political reasons, establishing the new capital in a geographic middle ground between the north and the south. Similarly, bypassing the rivalry between Melbourne and Sydney, Canberra, the new capital of Australia, was created in 1911. A capital may be transferred for symbolic reasons, as when Czar Peter the Great, intent on modernizing a backward Russia, created his new capital by opening a window to the west in St. Petersburg. Lenin celebrated the overthrow of the czardom by moving the revolutionary government back to Moscow. Similarly, Kemal Ataturk in 1923 created his capital in Ankara to break with the relics of the Ottoman empire in Constantinople and even changed the name of the old Byzantine capital to Istanbul.

Geopolitical considerations have dictated the transfer of capitals, to open up undeveloped areas. The location of Brasilia, officially inaugurated in 1960, was built to draw the population away from the crowded Atlantic Coast. The new capital has had a dynamic impact on the urbanization and economic development of the inland plains of Brazil.

History

The early dynastic rulers probably built the first planned new towns for reasons of prestige or strategy. Alexander the Great founded 70, of which 13 provincial capitals bear his name. The most important is Alexandria, Egypt, laid out in an extended rectilinear grid pattern covering 1300 ha.

The Greeks were perhaps the greatest new town builders, since to them the *polis* (town) was the natural political and social unit. They created cities every 25 to 30 km along the Greek and Turkish Coasts as far as the Levant. Each of the towns had a main ceremonial avenue terminating in an *agora,* or central market/meeting place, with an amphitheater at one end and temple area at the other. Residential areas were set in a grid plan while public areas were ample and often laid out in free form. However, buildings and streets were sensitively sited, conforming to topography. Population size rarely exceeded 60,000, of which 5000 were "citizens."

Pergamon, located at the western part of modern Turkey, was one of the most brilliant centers of the Hellenistic period (306–86 B.C.). Built on an ancient settlement, it was expanded in the fourth century B.C. to establish the Pergamon dynasty. The city was laid out in hierarchical fashion, respecting the topography and the land forms. The Acropolis, on high ground, was reserved for state functions with royal palaces, a library of 200,000 volumes, and splendid temples, as well as a gymnasium, marketplace, and housing for military officers and aristocrats. The middle and lower levels provided similar services for the ordinary population.

The Romans built provincial capitals on an even larger scale, extending over the continent to dominate western Europe, England, and the Near East, where they also rebuilt many Greek towns. One of the most important was Jarash, at the crossroads of traffic from Mesopotamia and Arabia in what is now modern Jordan. It is one of the best examples of a Roman provincial town; its architects designed it as a single unit in the second century A.D. with a triumphal arch, temples, amphitheater, meeting places, shops, plazas, and processional ways, with a natural spring at the center (Fig. 1).

Chinese Capitals. Many ancient Chinese capitals were planned following the book of rules of the Chou dynasty (1122–256 B.C.) which prescribed city planning principles of road layout and size in the new city with the location of the imperial palace in the middle of the central access way and with the adminitrative compound in front and the marketplace behind. A good example of this Chinese model is Changan, planned in 580 A.D., which reached 600,000 in population. It served as a model for the eighth-century Japanese capitals of Heigokyo (modern Nara) and Heiankyo (Kyoto), each 25% the size of Changan. The

Figure 1. View of Jarash, 1979.

cities were organized into residential precincts or wards of 6,000 to 10,000 population with intersecting squares.

Indian and Persian Capitals. The best known of ancient Indian capitals is Mohenjo-daro, founded in approximately 2600 B.C. on the Indus river. The city endured for about 800 years, until the seventeenth century B.C. The site was systematically laid out on a grid pattern with the principal streets running north–south to take advantage of the prevailing winds. The plan was a clear break from the traditional pattern of meandering lanes and twisting streets found in both ancient and modern cities of India and Mesopotamia. Apart from the orderly plan, the building materials were burned, not sun-dried, brick, which indicates the availability of wood from an adjacent forest now turned into a desert. Great public baths, as well as small baths in private residences, indicated that these ancient people lived more comfortably than their contemporaries in the crowded cities of India, Mesopotamia, and Egypt. The Great Mogul Akbar in 1573 A.D. built Fathepur-Sikri for his new capital; it is an outstanding urban design and architectural monument with a network of courts and open plazas. Unfortunately, site selection was poor because of an inadequate water supply, so the city was abandoned only 15 years later. In Persia the Shah Abbas moved his capital to create Ishfahan in 1598 A.D., where a fully integrated bazaar was constructed along a 2-km spine or sinew that ends at the monumental square of 8 ha (19.76 acres) enclosed by government offices, mosques, coffee houses, and a *caravanserai* or inn. It conforms to today's multiuse model of commerce, culture, and leisure activities within one complex.

Versailles. Feudal Europe, decentralized in tiny baronies and independent city states, produced no new capitals. In 1671, during the Renaissance, Louis XIV started the construction of Versailles, a palace and town complex in the baroque style. Even though only half the palace and town were completed during his lifetime, the complex had a profound effect on the later development of cities and towns throughout the world. Passing through the town on the way to the palace, the visitor does not perceive the urban landscape, being absorbed with the grandeur and the dominance of the palace. The town was built in conformity with a "building ordinance" that established heights and massing with uniform roof and eave treatments served by three main boulevards that converge at the entrance of the *cour d'honneur*. This plan influenced the design of the royal residential towns of Karlskrona Sweden (1680), Karlsruhe, Germany (1715), and the large capital cities of Washington and New Delhi.

St. Petersburg. Peter the Great (1672–1725) established St. Petersburg on the Baltic Sea coast to reinforce his commitment to modernize medieval Russia and its hinterlands by giving it a window to the west. In 1710, St. Petersburg was planned as a new capital on the Neva River. A building committee was appointed to guide and regulate all construction. Each social class was assigned a specific residential district. Peter the First recognized the need for a diversified employment base, beyond the governmental functions of the capital city, and estabished industrial, educational, and cultural institutions from the very beginning. Given the nature of the absolute monarchy, it is not surprising that amid the innovative and exemplary aspects of the town, the welfare of ordinary citizens was given low priority.

Conscripted labor, working under virtual conditions of slavery, built the town in an irreversible surge of activity. Early development of the city was rushed without regard to human or material costs and the town achieved a "critical mass" of population and economic activity well before the death of its godfather and promoter. A catalyst for growth was the Admiralty Yards, spendid baroque structures, whose naval yards and arsenals transformed the new city into the industrial center of Russia by the nineteenth century. The population, already at 200,000 by 1800, reached three million by 1900. The new capital benefited from the strong personal identification with the Czar Peter; his successor continued to grant St. Petersburg his special interest and nearly unlimited power to direct and finance the development. Thus, St. Petersburg succeeded in fulfilling Peter the Great's visionary policies and the new capital was a significant contributor to the modernization of Russia on the western model (Fig. 2).

Washington, D.C. The Congress of the United States in 1790 decided to create a new "national city" with a federal district 10 mi (16 km) square and President Washington in 1792 appointed French-born Major L'Enfant as town planner. In one year L'Enfant produced a street plan for an area of 24,000 ha (240 km^2). This grand scale was contrary to the wishes of Thomas Jefferson, who considered 500 ha (5 km^2) more than sufficient. L'Enfant's vision of a half million population was ambitious in contrast with its contemporaries—the new Russian capital of St. Petersburg had 200,000 after 80 years of forced growth, and the old prosperous city of Boston had 18,000 inhabitants. L'Enfant laid out the city over the rural hills and plains along the Potomac River. The capital was placed on the highest ground and L'Enfant accepted President Washington's suggestion to place the President's house on a ridge 1 mi to the northwest connected to the Capitol by the wide Pennsylvania Avenue. The idea of the mall undoubtedly came from Jefferson's early sketch plan for the capital. L'Enfant derived his plan from the baroque Versailles and St. Petersburg as well as the Renaissance urban design for the reconstruction of Rome under Sextus V. For some years the plan was ignored, but was then saved by the architect–planners Burnham, McKim and Olmsted in 1902 when they redefined the monumental core area of 350 ha and the development of the Potomac River edge. Today, Washington has over 660,000 population surrounded by a metropolitan area of 2.5–3 million (Fig. 3).

New Delhi. In 1910, the British transferred the capital of their Indian Raj from the commercial center of Calcutta to the old Moghul capital of Delhi. This move, announced in 1911 at the great Indian "durbar" celebrating the coronation of George V, affirmed the Empire's intention to perpetuate political dominion over this important outpost.

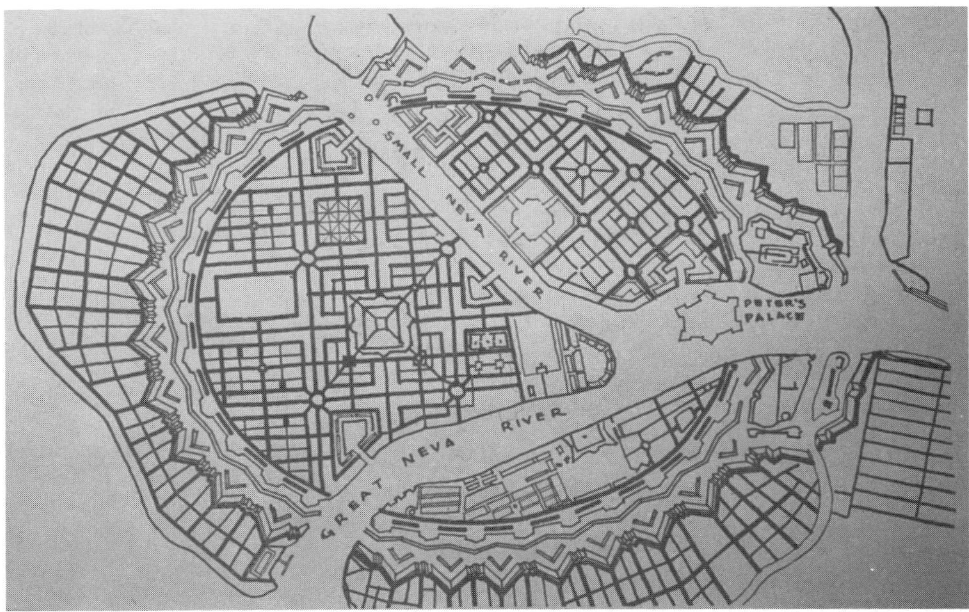

Figure 2. Plan of St. Petersburg. Courtesy of the University of Chicago Press.

Guided by a town planning committee, Sir Edward Lutyens planned New Delhi as an imperial Garden City south of Old Delhi, then a city of 250,000, a hurly burly of traditional markets and neighborhoods resembling expanded village clusters guarded by the British cantonment area to the north and the magnificent sixteenth-century Red Fort and the Jama Masjid mosque to the South. A park strip separates the old city from the new.

New Delhi is a perfect example of an extension or "add-on" new town. The New Delhi Master Plan was formally composed along a transverse boulevard, the Kingsway, 2.4 km long, with the Vice Regal Lodge or Government House at its western end. Symmetrical government office buildings set on high plinths establish a formal border. A hexagonal pattern of avenues at the eastern end were laid out for the palaces of the native princes. Kingsway serves as the base of a triangle, the north point of which is Connaught Circus, the commercial shopping and office

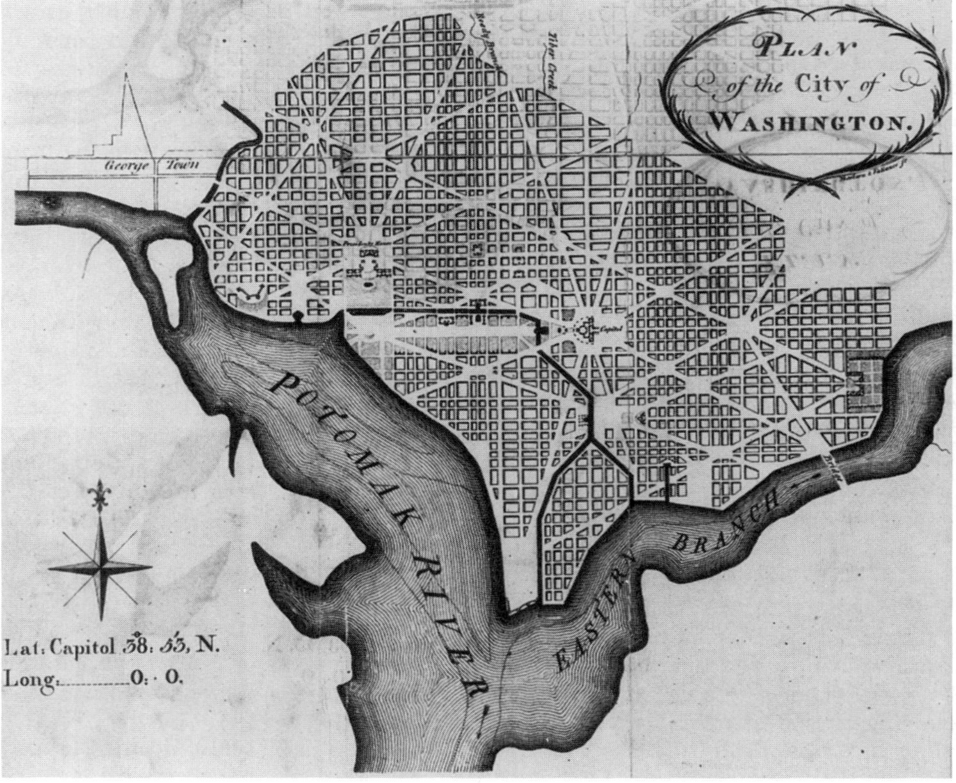

Figure 3. Plan of Washington, D.C. Courtesy of the Library of Congress.

center. Diagonal avenues extended south, serving the residential bungalows on large garden plots designed for high government officials. Lutyens was strongly influenced by L'Enfant's Plan for Washington. New Delhi was planned as a low density town for only 57,000 people in 2650 ha. It was formally inaugurated in 1929. Ten years later, the Delhi Development Committee was created to control the expansion, and in 1956 the Town Planning Organization produced an Interim General Plan intended to provide an outline for planned development while a comprehensive long range plan was prepared. By 1960 the Town Planning Organization with a consultant group headed by Albert Mayer, Gerald Breeze, and Edward Echeverria completed a draft master plan to accommodate a projected population of 4.5 million on 44,600 ha by 1981 with 850,000 growth in six satellite ring towns. These targets were surpassed before 1985. Current planning must confront the issue of diverting continuing urban immigration to new towns beyond this 200 km radius.

Figure 4. Plan of Canberra. Courtesy of the National Capital Development Commission.

Canberra. The federal capital territory came into existence in 1911 with the selection of a site of 2,537 km^2 by C. P. Scrivener, Government District Surveyor. In 1912, Walter Burly Griffin, a Chicago landscape architect, won the international competition for the design for an area of 30 km^2 along the Molonglo River for a city of 25,000 in a formal renaissance city plan. He proposed formal landscaped avenues and three artificial lakes with the main group of government buildings on three sides. The parliament triangle of 182 ha was demarcated by Kings, Commonwealth, and Constitution Avenues with the base of the triangle on the lake (Fig. 4). By 1979 the city had 220,000 population with more than 60 foreign embassies. Being a fairly homogeneous and high-income population, Canberra is free of the numerous social problems plaguing other new capitals such as Chandigarh and Washington, D.C.

Brasilia. In order to achieve a redistribution of power and wealth and open the interior of the country, Jucelieno Kubitscheck, president from 1952 to 1960, initiated the construction of Brasilia in the central plateau. In 1946 the Government of Brazil designated a Federal District of 5000 km^2 on a plateau in the inland state of Goias. The actual site was selected by the U.S. environmental geologist Donald J. Belcher in 1954; Lucio Costa won the design competition in 1957. The design is unique for its day, a formalistic nineteenth century or beaux-arts solution. Twentieth-century superblocks fitted into the curved shape of a longbow or airplane wings constitute the residential neighborhoods. They are composed on each side of an 8-lane expressway. The straight monumental north–south axis, seen as the airplane's fuselage, forms a 3.5 km-long mall ending at the "Plaza of the Three Powers" where legislative, judicial, and executive office buildings are located. The government ministries bordering the central mall are arranged like ribs along this central spinal column and are popularly called "the rack of lamb." The composition is monumental but the effect is cold and barren, since there is no landscaping to modulate the enormous scale. Pedestrian access from the adjacent areas was evidently not considered. Where the expressway system crosses the monumental axis, a four-level arrangement of over- and underpasses was required. Massive multilevel structures for retail shopping line the freeway. On one side of the mall stands the striking cathedral, designed by Oscar Niemeyer. It is isolated from the social web that purportedly supports it. To the north is a large television tower and the municipal building complex and railway station.

It is fair to say that Brasilia is the first example of a city designed around the concept of the continuous flow of traffic and a high-capacity expressway system linking a series of architectural monuments (Fig. 5). The result is a fragmented urban life. The pedestrian was virtually non-existent in the planners' minds, reflecting the elitist mentality in a country where less than 5% of the households own cars. Amenities at the pedestrian scale are provided in the interior areas of the residential superblocks, reserved for high government officials and managers in the private sector.

To accommodate the influx of migrant construction workers, the shanty town Cidade Libre or Freetown developed spontaneously as a construction camp and is now a city of 100,000. The lack of housing for low-income workers within the perimeters of the new capital area forced the

Figure 5. Brasilia Mall.

government to accelerate development of the five planned satellite towns 25–70 km from the center of Brasilia for low-income and service workers. Today they house over 450,000 population while the capital city, mainly for government employees and diplomats, has 500,000. The social stratification of Brasilia has been reinforced with the middle level civil servants and employees in row houses and walk-ups on the east side of the city and upper income administrators in elegant elevator apartments in a park-like setting on the west side, while the diplomats and the wealthy reside in villas along the shoreline of the lake. However, those fortunate enough to have obtained housing within the airplane wings, the central residential area, express great satisfaction at the convenience and high degree of amenity provided.

Chandigarh. With the partition of India, the Indian State of Punjab lost its traditional capital of Lahore, now in Pakistan. The planning of a new state capital was initially entrusted in 1950 to U.S. architect/planners Albert Mayer and Julian Whittlesey, and architect Matthew Nowicki. Mayer and Whittlesey planned a network of residential superblocks of 8000–20,000 residents each, for a first stage population of 150,000 to be expanded to 500,000. Each superblock, of 800 to 1200 m^2 or 96 hectares, was self-contained in terms of primary and secondary education, convenience shopping, small service/workshops, and recreation. Within each superblock a graduation of housing types was achieved to promote social integration of income groups including the untouchables or *harijan* caste. Pedestrian ways and greenways provided an internal network on which the community facilities were located. At the northern end of the city the capital was located in a cohesive government nucleus. However, with the tragic death of Nowicki in a plane crash in 1951, Mayer withdrew. The Government then turned to the noted Swiss architect Le Corbusier and his associate Pierre Jeanneret and the British Maxwell Frey and Jane Drew. Le Corbusier straightened the original curvilinear network into a rigid grid and applied his theory of the 7 "Vs" or road-ways, starting with V1, the national trunk road from Delhi. In this way the hierarchy of roads and pedestrian networks, implicit in the Mayer plan, became dominant in the "Corbu" plan. The town center was planned in the middle of the city, facing a large greenway which Le Corbusier called a "valley of leisure." The industrial and service areas are on the eastern edge. The Capitol complex, still at the north, consists of the Secretariat of the Ministries, the State Assembly, and the High Court. Each building is an architectural *tour de force,* but they are placed so far apart and each is so unique that they defy any spatial integration.

The residential scheme is stratified, placing the ministers and the high government officials adjacent to the capital complex, while the lowest paid clerks, at the far end of the city, have to cycle 5 km to work. However, elements of social planning within superblocks were retained from the Mayer-Nowicki plan. The city grew to 600,000 by 1980. The architectural plastic forms designed by Le Corbusier have had a profound impact on Indian architects. The same is true for the residential blocks by Jeanneret, Frey, and Drew. However, the overall planning, except for the hierarchy of circulation networks, has had little impact on contemporary Indian city planners.

Islamabad. The new capital for the new nation of Pakistan was under study from the time of the 1947 partition of India. Lahore, the traditional capital of North India, was now too close to the new border. Sir Robert Matthew was commissioned in 1959 to locate and plan an urban framework for a region much further north, along the edge of the Murgala Hills, running east–west, where ample water supply was available. Islamabad, the new administrative and cultural center of the nation, was planned to grow parallel to the existing city of Rawalpindi, which would continue as the commercial and industrial center of the region. The Islamabad/Rawalpindi metropolitan area of 25,000 ha was planned within a regional development district of 64,000 ha, allowing for ample open space reserves. C. Doxiadis and Associates prepared the master plan in a linear pattern of wide parallel zones of housing and services, starting at the city center and capital complex and extending eastward parallel to the foot hills. Doxiadis assumed that future urban growth of the old city could be contained while growth in the new city could be controlled to expand only in one direction from the center of the proposed capital complex. This concept is contrary to the natural or organic concentric expansion of central places, given an absence of physical barriers; in this case, flat open ground lies on three sides. In the Islamabad/Rawalpindi situation, natural pressures would more probably link the two centers, and further growth would be concentrated. Doxiadis, unfortunately, created an additional problem (one that Le Corbusier proposed for Chandigarh), by proposing that expansion move continually away from the government complex in only one direction, thereby lengthening the journey to work for the low-income government clerks who would live on distant, cheaper land. Vast transport corridors, with 400-m-wide rights-of-way, have accentuated the desert environment rather than creating a sense of urban containment. The residential sectors have a class hierarchy, as in Chandigarh, but are twice as large. An enclosed superblock of 324 ha serves 20,000–40,000 population, self-contained for daily needs, including services and micro-enterprises, similar to Chandigarh. The central city functions are grouped along a linear spine capable of gradual extension. Time will be the best judge of the success of this principle of a controlled unidirectional growth, a pattern that has never been achieved in urban development at any scale.

Summary of New Capital Development

The success of some of the new capital cities was due to the commitment of strong heads of state with power to exercise strong controls and divert enormous resources to their construction. This is as true of contemporary new capitals as it was of the monumental cities of the past.

Designers and planners are often imbued with the glorification of the power of the state. This judgment applies as much to the baroque creations of Peter the Great at St. Petersburg as to the modern government complexes of Brasilia and Chandigarh through the application of monumental scale and symbols and formal geometry.

However, twentieth-century planners should practice a functional analysis of the land and its resources, and fit the physical plan to a selected social and economic structure. All modern city plans have undergone engineering and economic feasibility analyses and manifest a keen appreciation for modern technology, especially the economic and cultural domination of the private automobile. However, they have failed to provide an adequate universal transportation system, reflecting the relative power relations of a small wealthy elite and the large mass of low-income citizens.

While some social planning was undertaken, notably in Chandigarh and Islamabad, none of the new capitals adequately serves the needs of its lower-income populations. Brasilia and Canberra are elite cities, while Washington is a city of gross contrasts with enclaves of the very rich and very poor. It reflects a high degree of continued racial segregation; 70% of the central city population is black, but the middle and upper income black population has spread to the close-in suburban areas. While the new appreciation of center city convenience is whitening the core, in this process real estate values rise and low-income blacks are being squeezed out.

COLONIAL NEW TOWNS

Colonization and the construction of new towns have occurred in tandem since earliest times. Documentation is available from the Chou Dynasty (1123–256 B.C.) and from the ancient Egyptian Pharaohs. The Greeks and Romans built new ports and trade centers to bind the colony to the metropolis. Although the primary purpose of colonization is the exploitation of other people and their natural resources, a secondary objective is deconcentration and migration, which permit the maintenance of certain demographic and ecological balances in the existing *polis* or towns. The Greeks believed that a town should have no more than 5000 "citizens" which generated an urban population of about 60,000 to 70,000 including slaves.

A distinction must be made between external and internal colonization. External colonization is directed by a parent state toward lands outside its boundaries. Internal colonization is the result of national policies of economic expansion to create more balanced population distribution or to make more effective use of resources within the national territory. A modern example of systematic internal colonization is the policy of Brazil to open its Amazon territories or of the Soviet Union to urbanize its Asiatic territories. Colonial towns can be grouped into five categories according to their origins: (*1*) agro-military settlements; (*2*) trade centers; (*3*) regional centers; (*4*) mining and industrial towns; and (*5*) expanded urbanization on reclaimed land.

The agro-military settlements carried the great risk of defending their borders. They often served the function of securing contested frontiers with the intention of the colonizing power to maintain a permanent presence, such as the Roman settlements in Italy and Iberia and the first wave of Hispanic conquest in the Americas. They are best represented by the Roman colonies which emerged from the prototypical military camp (*castrum*), or forts. Over time, the boundaries of the tented cohorts became solid walls and developed into permanent garrison towns. Colonial settlements were planned for about 30,000 population on a perfect grid, generally 80-m blocks or squares. Later, elaborate public buildings evolved with amenities such as aqueducts, assuring abundant water supplies, baths, fora, theaters, and stadia on a scale that surpassed present day standards.

The early Zionist kibbutzim were conceived as outposts of agricultural development, pioneers in a movement that forged a new national identity. Unfortunately today, the Israeli border kibbutz performs an agro-military function.

Hispanic New Towns

The colonization of Hispanic America was guided by a uniform policy. Starting with the plan or layout of the new towns, construction was regulated by royal ordinances which were later collected and codified by Philip the Second. The 1573 Code set the formal framework of the urbanization process which continued for three centuries with unbroken continuity. The Laws summarized the experience of half a century from the time town building started in 1493 with the first permanent settlement of Santo Domingo. The town had to be legally chartered by the King before construction could begin. A town plan had to be drawn up and a minimum number of settlers had to commit themselves to stay before the foundation act could take place. The law provided guidelines for the selection of the site and subdivision regulations controlled the size of plot or *traza,* to create a regular grid pattern staked out with the help of a measuring tape, starting from the central square. The basic plan held nine squares of about 12 hectares, consisting of a central public plaza and eight surrounding blocks. Each block was divided into 32 lots, two of which were reserved for public buildings. The more ambitious 100 *vecino* plan of Caracas consists of 25 squares. Where the town was destined to become a provincial capital, as in the case of Lima, founded in 1535 with 220 ha, exceptionally large *trazas* were planned. Open space was to be preserved by controlling the expansion of the town. A greenbelt of open space had to be reserved, three to four times larger than the built-up area. Beyond the greenbelt, farm lots were staked out for commoners and noblemen. The central square of *plaza major* was planned as the heart of the new community, around which the municipal buildings and cathedral were composed to create a civic center; the market functions were relegated to other parts of the city. The typical arrangement placed the church and episcopal palace on the east side facing the town hall. The north side was occupied by the royal houses (courts, customs house, mint, and arsenal) and the south side by the palaces of leading citizens (Fig. 6). These plazas still function today as centers for modern metropolises, as in the existing government centers of Mexico City, Bogota, and Caracas. The corner lots of the *traza* were assigned to monasteries which served as keystones to the development, as social and educational centers; they

Figure 6. Zocalo Plaza, Mexico City.

became the focus of life of their respective barrios. However, the greater part of the urbanization works of the Spanish colonial cities were completed before the 1573 statutes were codified. The symbology and logic of the colonial pattern embodied in the Law of the Indies, although of medieval origins, proved so convenient and efficient that even after the breakup of the Spanish Empire its successor states adhered to the spirit of the code in laying out further new towns.

North American Colonial Towns

New town planning in North America started a hundred years later than in Latin America. In New England in the early seventeenth century, planned villages such as Charlestown, Cambridge, New Haven, and Hartford occurred. Rectangular blocks arranged in simple grid patterns served small population clusters of 250 to 300 people, composed around the central open space or common which ranged from 3 to 7 hectares. The New Haven plan, a perfect square, is formed by three times three blocks, resembling the standard Hispano-American plan of 30 *vecinos* with the New Haven blocks twice the size of the Spanish model. A number of town sites of 50 to 100 acres were designated in Virginia and Maryland in the 1860s and 1870s. Grid patterns were drawn to accommodate 100 to 200 families on half-acre lots. The first large-scale plan for a U.S. city was prepared by the surveyor Thomas Holme for Philadelphia under the direction of William Penn. They extended a grid of 50-ft-wide streets over an area of 2 mi^2 (512 ha) divided in four quarters. The crossing of two 100-ft avenues divided the town into four quadrants with 8-acre squares located in the middle of each quadrant. A 10-acre square at the center served as a unifying focal point. Assuming one home per half acre lot, this would have generated 3,000–5,000 persons in each quadrant served by a neighborhood park. The growth of Philadelphia was rapid.

Of the numerous towns founded in New France, the little Fort of Detroit in 1701 was the simplest, a medieval *bastide,* while plans for Mobile, Alabama (1711) and New Orleans, Louisiana (1722) resembled Hispano-American models. In the eighteenth century the most innovative plan in the United States was that for Savannah, Georgia, planned by James Oglethorpe around 1733. The basic cellular unit consisted of 48 lots grouped around a public open space on each side of the square; eight lots were reserved for public buildings. The orderly expansion of town took place through the multiplication of these little neighborhoods, each serving 400 people. This remarkable concept was followed for the next 120 years because the common land, held out of construction from the beginning, was reserved to permit this expansion. Five-acre garden lots and 44-acre farms were provided within the overall road grid of 1 mi^2.

The Continental Congress in 1785 called for a land ordinance for the northwest territory, requiring a governing pattern of square subdivisions consisting of townships covering an area of 6×6 mi, each divided into 36 sections of 1 mi^2 similar to the Roman Centuriato. The adoption of the super grid for survey and distribution of the western lands effectively stretched the checker board pattern across the American continent. In California the Mexican government undertook town planning according to the Laws of the Indies until it lost the territory to the United States in 1835. However, General Vallejo, the Mexican officer who had planned Sonoma for the Mexicans, carried on, later planning the cities of Vallejo and Venezia.

Russian Internal Colonization

As early as 1587 the Russians advanced toward Siberia with the development of the first Russian colony of Tobolsk. However, it was not until the construction of the Trans-Siberian railway between 1892 and 1905 that systematic colonization of the Asian half of the Russian empire took off. The mass migration that followed reached proportions comparable to the earlier western wave of pioneers in the United States. Important towns like Novosibirsk (1893) were built along the railway and earlier foundations like Khabarovsk (1858) and Vladivostok (1880) on the Pacific shore boomed.

After the Russian Revolution, large-scale agricultural development became possible through the expropriation of the large landed estates and the later forcible collectivization of the *kulaks* or small peasant owners. New towns were founded in both the Baltic regions and in the east, e.g. Komsomolsk on the Amur River in 1932. During World War II, the relocation of vital industries resulted in a series of new towns beyond the Ural Mountains. Internal colonization through the creation of new towns is still official Soviet policy; objectives are to equalize the benefits of development throughout the vast territory, safeguard critical industries through deconcentration, and finally to take advantage of the rich pool of natural resources in Siberia. Development guidelines call for the protection and preservation of natural and human resources.

Soviet planning criteria call for town sizes ranging from 100,000 to 300,000 population based on optimal costs of construction and operation. They call for a minimum threshold of 10,000 to sustain an adequate level and variety of cultural and welfare services. However, nearly 68% of all new towns created from 1917 to 1970 still had less than 30,000 population, while another 30%, housing 16.4 million in 1970, were in the 30,000–150,000 range. Despite very strict constraints on the free movement of population and industry, designed to limit the growth of large cities and guide population and new employment into overspill towns or new settlements in the east, the policy has not succeeded and the growth of large cities far surpasses that of the smaller new towns in both rate and absolute numbers.

The basic building block is a six-story prefabricated apartment building, housing 500–1000 people. Four to fifteen large buildings form the superblock or *Kvartal*, grouping 3600 to 7500 families in an area of 9–15 ha with an average net density of 400–500 persons per hectare, over twice the densities of British new towns. Each *Kvartal* is equipped with a nine-year school (kindergarten through eighth grade), dining hall, grocery and repair shops, and athletic fields. Two to four *Kvartals* form a *micro-rayon* or neighborhood of 10,000–15,000 population in an area of 30–50 ha, for a gross density of 300 persons per hectare. The neighborhood center serves an area within 1 km with food markets, clubs, cinemas, department stores, bank, post office, polyclinic, health center, and gymnasium. The objective is a self-contained neighborhood designed to provide education, shopping, and other essential services. High residential densities permit easy and efficient access to bus and rapid rail transport. There is little provision for auto parking, and if the Soviets decide to satisfy the increasing consumer demand for private cars, there will be problems similar to those faced by the early English and Swedish new towns.

Total public ownership of urban land, together with a unified system of social, economic and spatial planning at all levels of government has produced towns and cities that have achieved a relatively high degree of conformity to social and spatial objectives. However, Soviet planners and architects are self-critical and point to a range of deficiencies in design and building techniques such as the following: rigid, overly centralized controls and design criteria that stifle creativity and produce an environment that is monotonous and too dense; inappropriate prototypes have been used, where geography and culture required different solutions; poor quality construction is widely noted; and the housing shortage will not be remedied before the end of the century. With the new Soviet policy that encourages open discussion of problems and a process of restructuring in production, one can hope for improvements in urban design and construction as well.

However, the overall achievement in building is probably unsurpassed among the nations of the world today, e.g., 100–125 new towns started in each of the three Five Year plan periods 1966–1980, culminating in 1200 new towns since the 1917 Revolution. Of these, 350 are free-standing new towns while the rest are significant expansions of existing towns or villages. Sixty-five million new housing units were built from 1957 to 1985, for an average rate surpassing 2 million units per year.

INDUSTRIAL NEW TOWNS

During the early nineteenth century a large number of industrial new towns were built at or adjacent to sites of natural resource exploitation or in the center of developing manufacturing regions. The towns in most cases were located close enough to the industries to walk to work. This in turn, had an adverse impact on the towns due to noise and smoke pollution, such as in the early mining and steel towns of the United Kingdom and the United States. With improved transportation in the last half century, cleaner living environments were created upwind from the pollution of stack and effluent, noise, and industrial traffic; however, the development goals and efficient operation of the industries generally received priority over the social objective of the town. Housing for the basic workers (direct employees), was seen as a labor control measure and was provided by the industry while the housing for the service workers was generally left unattended.

In the early 1800s, Robert Owen proposed an ideal industrial village of work and leisure for 1200 people in Scotland. However, the classic pattern of early British coal towns was not broken until 1851 when Sir Titus Salt founded a model town of Saltaire on the River Salt for about 4500 people. Set tightly against the mill, in orderly rows, three-bedroom houses for the workers were provided along with bathhouses, wash-houses, and even almshouses. Other far-sighted industrial towns followed, such as Port Sunlight Village with interior allotment gardens within each residential block. In France, under the influence of the utopian Fourier, the ironmaster Godin built a model industrial community of 1,600 people at Guise, where the workplace was integrated into the community in a single megastructure 3600 feet long.

The influence of Robert Owen was felt by the 1820s in the United States, where New England industrial towns in Manchester, New Hampshire and Lowell, Massachusetts provided an improved standard of human decency and architectural order. Robert Lowell, for whom a town was named in 1822, built the first prototype with his industrial mill town between the Merrimac River and a canal built to produce water power with the workers' housing set parallel to the mill between the canal and the road. Shops, public buildings, and private residences were provided along with innovative dormitories for female workers under the surveillance of stern house mothers. Within ten years the town reached 11,000 population.

In 1880, George M. Pullman, the inventor of the Pullman sleeping car, built a model company town for his workers, south of Chicago. By 1881 there were ample housing accommodation and community services for 8000 population on a large site of 1600 ha. The workers resented the paternalistic attitude of the company, with their shelter dependent on the employer's good will. In 1894, the workers called a labor strike that forced the company to divest itself of the town and company housing. The strike was later carried to the Pullman railway operation, which resulted in the formation of the railway unions.

In 1905, Tony Garnier designed an ideal, the *Cité Industrielle*, for 35,000 people which made a clear break with the European neoclassical model with its monumental symmetry and reestablished the principle of linear growth along a main traffic artery. A large open buffer zone separated the town from the industry, and the civic center was placed in the center of the town. The linear concept also provided for close and continued contact between the city and rural areas to their mutual benefit.

In the first flush of the Russian Revolution, the objective was to provide the backward proletariat with a decent environment for living and work, abundant fresh air and sunshine to produce healthy families, high standards of education and training to produce skilled workers, and a broad range of collective social and cultural facilities to produce the new "socialist man."

The linear concept fulfilled yet another fundamental objective of the revolution, the abolition of the invidious distinction between city and country life, transcending the "idiocy of rural life" of the prerevolutionary peasant. At the same time, it represented the rejection of the centralizing tendency of the capitalist system, with its concentration of people and activities and its deplorable slums.

Influenced by these arguments, Le Corbusier planned a *Ville Radieuse* in 1933 as his competition proposal for Moscow, a plan on a macro-grid with a raised main arterial highway down the middle, tying the civic center at one end to the industrial areas at the other, a paradigm to which he returned 20 years later in Chandigarh. This bold scheme was far too rigid and out of human scale to be practical.

The year 1931 marked the end of an exciting period of experimentation and intellectual discussion about planning, housing, and architecture by designers and theoreticians. By 1932, official Soviet policy had rejected modern architecture and stilled the debate about decentralization and linearity in urban design. The modernist tendencies were labeled "bourgeois decadence" and there was a paradoxical return to the neoclassical styles of pre-revolutionary Russia and the adoption of the hierarchical system of location of cities and towns. At the same time, a positive planning structure was instituted and clear norms and integrated procedures were adopted to guide the decade of the 1930s through an intense phase of development and construction.

With the large-scale exploitation of mineral resources for making iron and steel in the twentieth century, many industrial towns were built throughout the world; Gary, Indiana predates World War I while Bhilai, Rourkela and Durgapur (India), Ariashahr (Iran), Nova Huta (Poland), Dwnayvaros (Hungary), and Ciudad Guyana (Venezuela) were post-World War II constructions. For aluminum smelting, Kitimat (Canada) and Sabned (Guinea) were outstanding examples started in the 1960s.

The size of industrial towns varies with the level of development of the regional economy. For Kitimat, the aluminum town built in the Canadian province of British Columbia on an isolated Pacific frontier, the 4000 workers in basic industries generated almost an equivalent number of jobs in support/services. With the average family size of 3.6, and 1.5 workers from each household in a developed economy, the town grew to 18,000 population by 1980. In contrast, the new steel production towns of India generated 2.5 service workers for every basic worker, typical of Third World employment distribution. By 1980, the towns ranged in size from 100,000 to 160,000 population.

To ensure a dependable work force for new towns in the capitalist economies, the industry must bear the initial cost of construction. Housing and sufficient community facilities and amenities should be provided for the workers and their families to enjoy a fulfilling social life. However, availability is a function of the strength of the labor movement; housing is often missing in Third World installations. It is, of course, in the interest of the industry to establish a permanent work force. Nevertheless, to avoid the stigma and social/political problems of a company town, industry must plan to convey the management of the town over to the local residents, their employees. Often this is done by appointing a town manager under an elected town council. The transfer of management powers must be gradual as construction proceeds and a solid economic base is laid. Once the first stage is completed by the industry, appropriate mechanisms for municipal financing are critical. In remote areas, where there are no local governments, the state and central governments must play a role in providing guarantees for local bond issues or municipal loans for the expansion of the town in subsequent stages. It is always a dramatic moment when the industry that created the town becomes a local taxpayer for services rendered by the municipality.

Housing finance is equally important to provide flexibility and mobility. An industrial worker should be able to transfer or leave his job. He should be permitted to sell his house at a fair market value to the worker taking his place. This was carefully worked out in the town of Kitimat in 1954 through a second mortgage that was equivalent to the down payment on the house.

Ciudad Guayana

Contrasting with the Canadian experience stands the case of a Third World development effort in Ciudad Guayana, Venezuela. There a steel mill was built in 1961 along with a small company town for direct employees, at Porto Ordaz 15 km away on the west side of the Orinoco River. San Felix, a service center 25 km downstream, already existed. The Development Corporation CVG turned to MIT and Harvard University for planning assistance. Their task was to resolve the issues of regional development, as well as the detailed programming and planning of a large integrated new town for the steel and other basic industrial workers as well as service workers. However, due to the high rate of unskilled immigrants (1000 per month), ad hoc decisions were made and the seeds of fundamental problems emerged, such as differential treatment by the new town developers of direct employees and the secondary workers or job seekers attracted to the area. Moreover, there was a notable drop in the level of financial and managerial commitment required to ensure a self-sustaining economy over the long run. The initial population projections were sharply reduced, from 650,000 to 300,000. A location closer to the steel mill at Alta Vista was selected as the town center, resulting in a two-city strategy in which two-thirds of the population would be settled at Alta Vista/Porto Ordaz and one-third around San Felix, as a satellite. This meant that the unskilled workers and service population would remain on the east side around San Felix. Unfortunately, the town center at Alta Vista has not developed since private investors preferred the safer location in Porto Ordaz. A center can only be successful when the industry or promoter takes the initiative and builds the key elements of shopping, commerce, and social facilities in the first stage to set the form and architectural style so as to attract merchants and investors. While not developed as planned, the town is emerging as one of the important industrial centers in Latin America.

Poland

From 1946 to 1949, the Regional Planning Office selected three regions to be developed as the core of the industrial districts in which 40 new towns were built. One of the largest is Nova Huta (New Foundry), a new town built to house the workers of the large Lenin Iron and Steel works with an initial annual production of 1.5 million tons, which grew to three million by 1980. The steel mill located on the Vistula River provided an enormous stimulus to the economy of Cracow 10 km away. In 1949, the town planner Tadeusz Ptaszycki designed the town with strong geometric forms on a fan-shaped system of main arteries converging on the central square of the town. The urban form is reminiscent of the baroque and neoclassical periods (Fig. 7). The square, overlooking an expansive view of the Vistula Valley, is located on the periphery of the town. However, the road pattern was not very functional. Designed for 100,000 population, the housing is mainly low-rise walk-up apartments of various sizes to attempt to accommodate the range of family sizes. The social facilities were so well planned that every working mother was able to leave her child in the day nursery while she went to work. As the first large-scale new town, it had a lasting influence on all later town plans drawn up in Poland. By 1980 the town had a population of over 120,000.

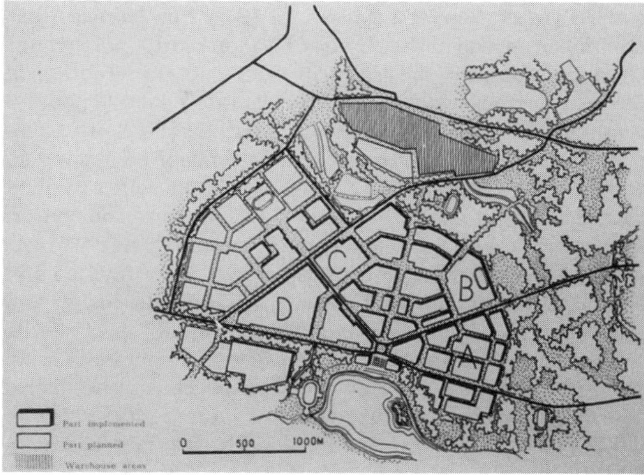

Figure 7. Nova Huta, Poland. Courtesy of Polonia Publishing House.

Soviet Experience

The Soviets have demonstrated an extraordinary ability to build hundreds of new industrial towns. In the late 1920s, Stalinsk, an iron and steel producer in the Kuznetsk Basin, Karaganda in the Kazakh coal basin, Magnitogorsk steel town in the Urals (1929), Zaporozhe at the Ukraine hydroelectric dam (1930), and Stalingrad (1929–1930) were part of the first group.

It was Miliutin's critique of Stalingrad and his alternative plan that became one of the major theoretical models of the twentieth century. The plan proposed a linear city 30 km long, in one-story construction. Miliutin had perceived that socially owned land could be treated as a free good, permitting the economy of horizontal expansion in low-cost construction, while allowing in more light and air for a healthy environment. Miliutin's critique of the competition submissions for the new steel town of Magnitogorsk allowed him another extended opportunity to articulate his ideas for a linear city.

The studies show six parallel zones: the railroad, industry and training centers, the green buffer zone with highways, the residential areas, recreation, and agriculture. The effect was to bring housing, work, and recreation into functional spatial relationships, protecting the residents from industrial pollution by interposing the greenbelt, while providing convenient and efficient access to work from the living areas.

Unfortunately, nothing came of the competition and the commission was given to the German planner Ernst May who produced a rigid plan of geometric superblocks containing serried ranks of medium-rise apartment blocks. The plan was later modified in the early 1930s. Despite its rather conventional plan, the town has been successful and represents an outstanding engineering feat since it is based on one of the greatest arched dams in the world, thrown across the Ural River. By 1980, the population was over 500,000.

DECONGESTION/OVERSPILL SATELLITE NEW TOWNS

New Towns in Britain, Scotland, and Wales

New towns are part of a century-old British tradition created by Ebenezer Howard, the father of the Garden City movement. Reacting to the grim industrial slums that housed nineteenth-century English workers, in 1898 Howard proposed that self-contained satellite new towns of about 30,000 inhabitants be built around the central city, combining the advantages of intensive urban life with the beauty and pleasures of the country." The official definition of the Garden City, adopted in 1919 by the Garden Cities and Town Planning Associations later renamed the Town and Country Planning Associations, is "a town designed for healthy living and industry: of a size that makes possible the full measure of social life but no larger, surrounded by a rural belt—all of the land being in public ownership or held in trust for the community." Howard in 1903 started his first Garden City in Letchworth and in 1919 Welwyn. Even though they were well served by rail connections, the development pace was slow due to the lack of local employment and high cost of community facilities. (Welwyn later became one of the New Towns built under the post World War II program of urban deconcentration.)

First Generation New Towns. In 1944, Sir Patrick Abercrombie proposed in the Greater London Plan, a permanent Greenbelt around the built-up area and the creation of ten new dormitory towns of approximately 30,000 population each beyond the Greenbelt. In 1945, the Reith Committee suggested that the new town concept be expanded, with increased population of 20,000–60,000, self-contained rather than satellites, located 40–50 km from the center. As a result, the British Government passed the New Towns Act in 1946 providing for a special system of finance and establishing development corporations for the design and development of each new town. A unique aspect of the legislation permitted the publicly held development corporations to acquire land at the then-current agricultural use values and to capture the full incremental value of developed land for the community which produced them, while earning a handsome return to the National Treasury which provided the initial capital investment. Thirty-three new towns were designated in the United Kingdom, of which 32 have been built, including four in Northern Ireland. The broad aim of the majority has been to relieve congestion and poor housing conditions in the large cities and metropolitan regions or conurbations. However, new towns have been successfully launched in an attempt to retain population in declining rural areas or to stimulate regional development in depressed industrial areas. Of the 14 new towns founded between 1946 and 1950, eight were designated in the southeast region of England with the expressed aim of receiving the projected overspill of one million population from London during 20 years of regional growth (Fig. 8).

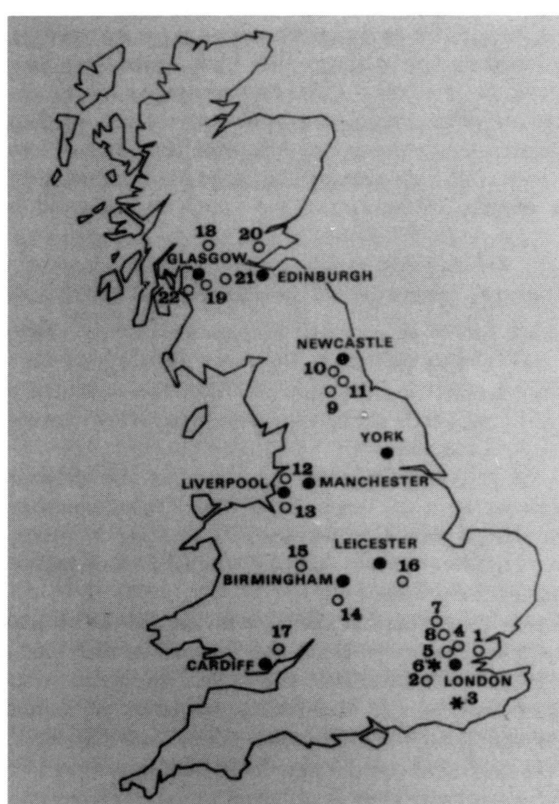

Figure 8. Distribution of New Towns in Great Britain.

The planning standards and regulations were very specific. The land area required for each new town was largely determined by the projected population. The urban area, including parks and recreation zones, was to have an overall planned density of 30 persons per hectare. The Reith Commission recommended that the designated area should include a 1200-ft-wide greenbelt surrounding the town. Thus, for a population of 60,000, the built-up area would cover 2000 ha with a greenbelt of 2400 ha for a total town area of 4400 ha. However, a modest 2500 ha were reserved for the first new towns, while populations of up to 80,000 were accommodated at Harlow and Crawley, for example. The built-up area remained at about 700 ha, producing overall densities of 100 persons per hectare.

For the site selection, the Reith Commission favored construction on virgin land to provide the widest freedom of expression to the town planners/architects and to avoid friction and disruption to an existing community since many local authorities resisted an urban invasion. However, several of the new towns benefited from the existence of a country village within their territory. Harlow, Crowley, and Hemel Hempstead, existing 5,000, 9,000, and 21,000 populations respectively, thrived and their success as new towns may be in part due to the established sense of place and local color of the original villages. Thorough technical studies of the topography, water resources, soil bearing capacity, and microclimate were factored into the site selection as well as the preservation of good farm land and access to good road and rail connections. Land ownership and tenure were also important, but not deciding factors.

The land use and zoning plans established the location of the town center, retail and commercial offices, industrial and residential neighborhoods, and the general level of amenities such as community facilities and green space. The size of the residential neighborhoods varied between 7000 and 10,000 persons. The size of the town center was calculated on the basis of 4 ha to 10,000 inhabitants, making 24 ha for a town of 60,000, located at the geometric center of the new town. Commercial shopping, town administration, and other public buildings along with a cultural center and leisure facilities formed part of the town center. Secondary centers were located in each neighborhood, with self-contained services keyed to the primary school, convenience shopping, church and community center, etc.

Industrial zones were planned for convenient walking or cycling access and were located on the outskirts, downwind from the town to avoid atmospheric pollution of the residential areas. They were located adjacent to rail and highway transportation. Incentives were provided to induce the establishment and/or relocation of industry and other large employers from the center to the new towns. The availability of a wide range of moderate cost and subsidized housing for workers was an important attraction.

Extensive planning studies of a variety of housing types and prices, including methods of subsidy, were undertaken for the residential areas to provide a broad social mix. Higher-income families initially resisted the move to the planned communities which bore a stigma as "working class" towns, but that prejudice gradually gave way to the general trend toward suburbanization and the demonstrably superior living conditions in the new towns.

The neighborhoods were generally separated by broad greenways and primary roads. Cumbernauld, Scotland, an overspill town for Glasgow founded in 1956, was an exception to these general prescriptions, planned as an experimental high-density residential estate; the first 50,000 population is housed in tightly textured rowhouses and apartments. With the growth of the town, the revised plan provided for an expansion of 20,000 in four neighborhood units on the periphery. The town center, also an experimental design, is a megastructure, standing above and separate from the community, like a moated fortress. The U.S. enclosed multilevel shopping mall was the precedent upon which it was based, but unlike the U.S. model, it was unsuccessful for several reasons. First and foremost, its market area was too small to support the original scale and secondly, its location, on an exposed wind-swept hill in the harsh Scottish climate, reverses a more desirable and conventional town layout with housing descending the slopes to the shelter of the valley as a center of activity.

The New Town Act of 1946 called for the creation of the necessary administrative and financial machinery with a development corporation for each new town. The members were nominated by the Ministry of Town and Country Planning after consultation with the Council of the locality concerned. It would not supersede the function of existing town councils, but would be in charge of new administrative districts where the new town was to be built. The financing was assured by Treasury loans, repayable over 60 years at the rate of interest prevailing for public loans at the time of issue. The British New Towns have turned into a resounding financial success. What started as a social welfare policy to provide high quality living conditions has provided substantial economies in urban management and a high return on initial investments.

The first generation of eight new towns around London had a 1980 population of over 400,000, exceeding the planned population of 383,000 set in 1946; however, Greater London, with over 10 million population today, continues to grow up to the edge of the greenbelt as well as on the other side.

The Second Phase. The second generation town plans (1950–1960) focused on higher residential densities with appropriate amenities closely integrated with the town center, in contrast to the earlier self-contained neighborhoods. The new town of Hook (never built, but influential as a prototype) was planned in 1961 as a linear urban form with the highest housing densities in the central area at 250 persons per hectare with an intermediate density of 175 pph and outer zone at 100 pph. In 1965, the National Planning Council, at the apex of a system of regional economic planning councils, concluded that cities of up to 250,000 population could stimulate economic and demographic growth more effectively than the smaller new towns typical of the immediate postwar period. As the scale of new towns proposals increased, planners became cautious about imposing rigid master plans and developed a new flexible methodology to cope with future uncertainties. The urban "structure plan" sought to create a broad framework with allowance for development in accordance with the changing market, checked and guided by the political process. Flexible planning concepts are identified within a fixed framework of long term capital budgeting for transportation and service corridors. Broad designations of land uses for various purposes are made within the development grid. Hence, the planning process is staged in its level of detail, as investment and development proceed. As a consequence, a new town in North Buckinghamshire was created to receive the overspill from the southeast region and London, as a new regional focus for urban growth. In 1967, 7,000 ha, including three existing towns, were designated as a new town called Milton Keynes, with the purpose of providing attractive residential living and work to encourage the dispersal of population from Greater London. It is located halfway between London and Birmingham near the M1 motor route and the main rail line to Manchester, Liverpool, and Glasgow. The Milton Keynes development corporation proposed a new town of 70,000 by 1981, projected to achieve 250,000 by the year 2000.

The main roads are arranged on a grid of approximately 1 km (similar to Chandigarh) with complementary, dispersed patterns of land uses throughout the city. The grid roads, originally planned with 100-m rights-of-way, were later reduced to 80 m to reflect reduced expectations in the volume and speed of traffic.

National housing policy specified a social balance of population in the new towns, with a wide variety of sizes and types of housing available for sale and rental. Renters could later convert their rental payments toward the purchase of their dwellings. Milton-Keynes's major open space resource of 1600 ha was designated as a linear park extending north/south along the axis of the city with various functions at different levels. Local parks are provided with access from adjacent housing areas along with indoor sports and recreation of all kinds (Fig. 9). Local convenience centers of 200 to 500 m^2 including community meeting halls were planned for each group of 1000 families. Located near the school, they formed the neighborhood nucleus. The district centers, at the next level of the shopping hierarchy, include large supermarkets, a multipur-

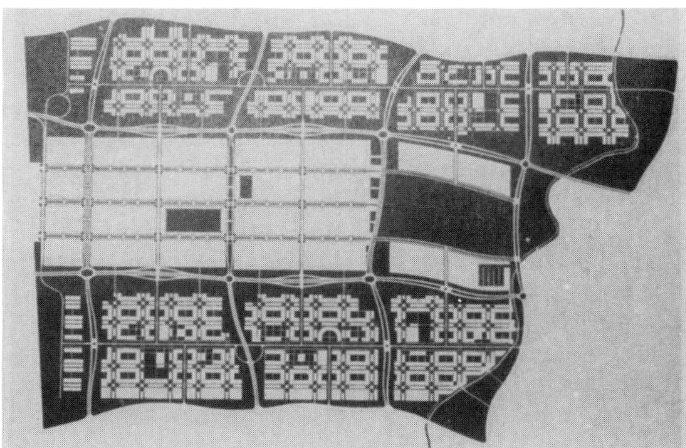

Figure 9. Milton Keynes Town Plan, 1970. Courtesy of the Milton Keynes Development Corporation.

pose shopping center with provisions for sports and community services, as well as commercial offices. The city center of Milton Keynes will provide the central place for the exchange of goods and services and will be the main social, commercial, and symbolic focus of the city, with acreage of over 290 ha, and 12,500 workers employed. The city center has been planned with high environmental standards of landscaping with wide malls, a variety of indoor leisure and entertainment activities, cinemas, restaurants, bars, nightclubs, swimming pool, etc.

In Scotland, another approach was started in 1971, with Irvine New Town, located near Glasgow. The strategy was to develop the area lying between the historic town of Irvine and its neighbor Kilwinning. A north–south development corridor was approved, extending the existing major industrial zone. The town was planned to attract and stimulate new employment in a severely depressed region. By 1986, there were a total of 17,500 jobs, of which 7,000 were in manufacturing. The planned population is 65,000 by 1990, with adequate space for industrial expansion through the turn of the century. An aggressive housing program with many open-space amenities is designed to attract new residents (Fig. 10**a**). The town center, a single structure that forms a bridge over the river, is one of many urban design features that have earned critical accolades. In addition, there is a historic district, Vennel, where young Robert Burns, Scotland's beloved poet, worked in the trade of dressing flax in 1761 (Fig. 10**b**).

In the 36 years of British new towns development, 32 have been built with a wide range of successful urban forms. They house almost two million people in a high quality urban environment and by the end of the century an estimated 3.5 million people will live in them. Unfortunately, the conservative government of the 1980s has reversed the principle of public benefit from public investment and has mandated the sale of the new towns' assets to the private sector and an abandonment of the regional development strategies which provided the context for the new towns policy.

Swedish New Towns

The Greater Stockholm Regional Plan of 1952 was developed about the same time as the Greater London Plan, based on the same philosophical foundations and similar policy objectives. Greater Stockholm, with a population of only 1.5 million in the 1980s confronted the problem of deconcentration and population growth with relatively few problems and with notable success, while it has tested a variety of solutions in both design and composition.

Faced with a severe housing shortage immediately after World War II, the Stockholm planners opted for building satellite dormitory towns of 50,000 population within a half-hour radius of the center, along a rapid transit rail line built at the same time as the new town. Blessed with a history of farsighted town fathers who had started acquiring public land for future growth as early as the seventeenth century, 70% of the city area and 50,000 hectares beyond the city boundaries are now in public ownership. Early satellite towns were planned as purely residential areas with local employment restricted to ancillary services. However, as the daily tides of commuters to and from Stockholm grew, along with a rising awareness of environmental protection and resource conservation, later policies sought a higher measure of self-containment, with housing and work opportunities to match or even exceed the resident labor force.

Vallingby, first of the satellites, consists of five large neighborhoods of 10,000 population, each with its own local center (Fig. 11). The town center, built on top of the suburban rail station, has a large pedestrian plaza and mall. It was hailed as a success from the beginning, and exceeded its planned population, achieving approximately 65,000 by 1970. Farsta, the second new town to be developed, consists of six smaller neighborhoods of 7,000 population each. Farsta and yet another new town, Skarholmen, were planned as regional service centers for surrounding areas of 170,000 to 250,000 people. This new scale was achieved by greatly increased surface parking with a perceptible interruption in the harmonious built-up texture of the towns.

The first generation satellites were distinguished by their sensitive treatment of the natural landscape and the low priority given to the automobile. The subsequent satellites, such as Taby, were more geometric in plan, with an austere, dense layout often built on a masonry plinth created by massive covered parking structures. The buildings seem to be superimposed on the land, with some violence, and reflect the rise in automobile ownership and use of the car for the journey to work, notwithstanding the excellent mass transit facilities.

Jarva, the latest of the new towns, was planned for 100,000 population and 70,000 jobs. It abandoned the neighborhood concept for the high-density linear form that underlies the Hook (English new town) plan, and proposed to divert commuting workers from Stockholm, with a job offering greatly in excess of its resident working population.

Finnish New Towns

Helsinki, the capital of Finland, has doubled in size every two decades from 1925 to 1975, when it expanded to 750,000. The planners promoted the structural dispersion of the metropolitan area with a number of planned dormitory towns in the 1950s and 1960s. Nevertheless, Helsinki's inner city area still contains 60% of the jobs. One of the most beautiful of all new towns, the Helsinki satellite Tapiola, was designed to reduce the daily flow of commuters. It was created by a private non-profit enterprise, Asuntosaatio, a housing foundation established in 1951 by six social and trade union organizations. Their aim was to create a town for everyone, in which different social groups work and live in harmony together. The Housing Foundation bought 670 ha in the rural county of Espoo, less than 10 km from the center of Helsinki, and planned, financed, and built the new town. The Tapiola planners aimed to demonstrate a new direction for Finnish town planning and housing by developing a self-contained community located on an inlet of the Gulf of Finland, with as many jobs as possible, and a versatile town center. Tapiola was designed for 5000 dwellings, with 20,000 population and

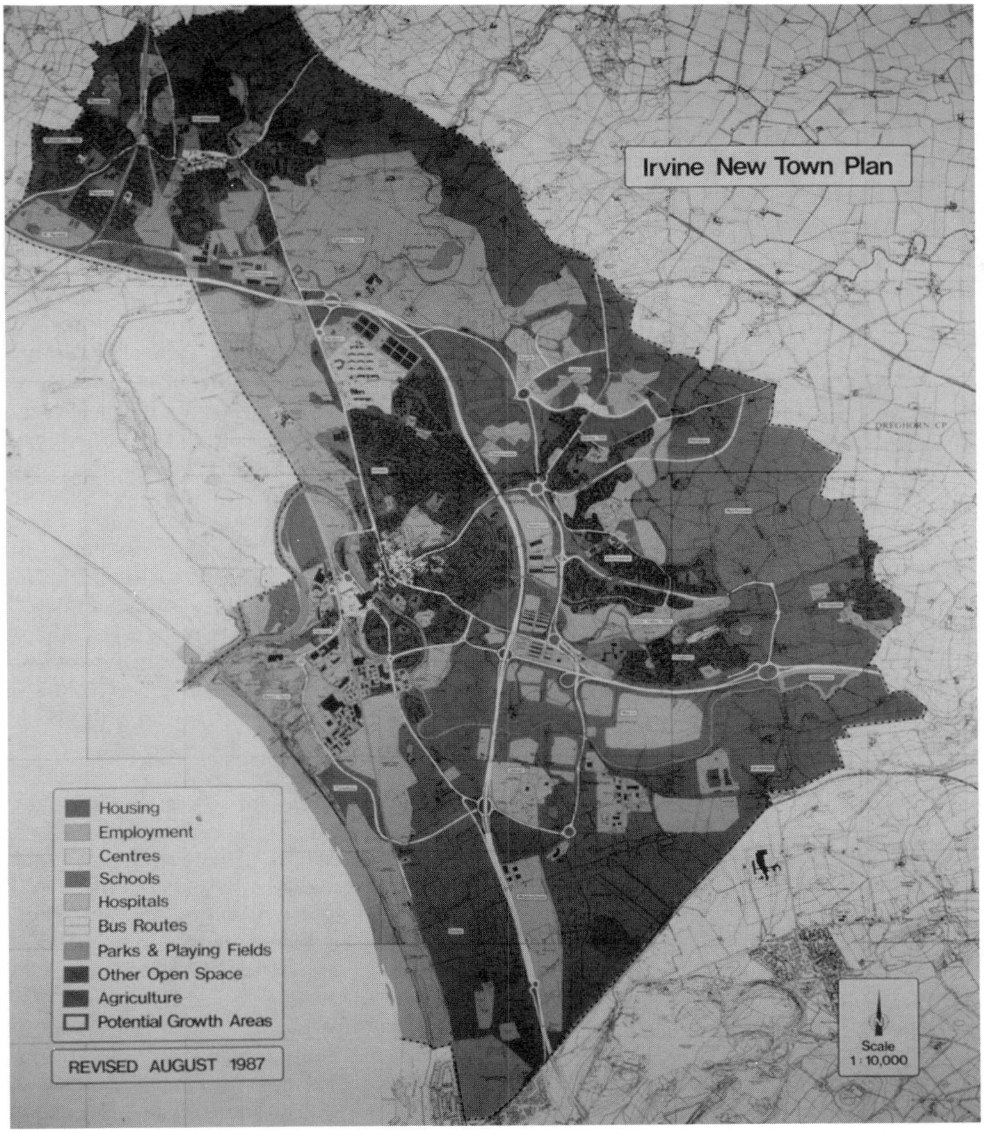

Irvine New Town Plan

Housing
Employment
Centres
Schools
Hospitals
Bus Routes
Parks & Playing Fields
Other Open Space
Agriculture
Potential Growth Areas

REVISED AUGUST 1987

Scale 1 : 10,000

(a)

(b)

Figure 10. Irvine New Town. (**a**) Plan; (**b**) view. Courtesy of the Irvine Development Corp., Scotland.

Figure 11. Vallingby New Town, 1964. Courtesy of the Stockholm Town Planning Office.

8000–10,000 jobs. The three residential neighborhoods were designed with direct linkages to interior open space with a separation of pedestrian and vehicular circulation. A primary school, movie theater, shopping center, and community center were built as part of the first neighborhood. The town center was designed to create a thriving shopping, business, administrative, and cultural center. The expansion of the center in the future will eventually serve the surrounding areas with a planned population of 80,000.

It may be that the remarkable success of the new town, its level of cultural diversity, and economic self-containment, in addition to the beauty of its design, was due to the lack of direct rail or road connection to Helsinki, despite its closeness as the crow flies. The characteristic quality of Tapiola is open green space (54%); housing and public buildings occupy 24% and 5%, respectively, while industrial and commercial lands use 6% and only 9.5% is in streets, paths, and parking. Fifty-five percent of the inhabitants are white collar and 45% blue collar; 90% of dwellings are privately owned. The imaginative and courageous approach by private development remains unmatched in Europe. Developers of new communities aspired to duplicate many of its unique features in new communities in the United States.

French New Towns

The forerunners of the French new towns in the post-World War II era were the large-scale housing estates, *grands ensembles,* of over 1000 dwellings that were built to relieve the large gap in housing construction due to the economic crisis of the 30s and the devastation of World War II. However, these large housing estates failed as new communities; they were too small, singular in purpose, and lacking in vital services. Their failures serve as lessons in how not to build. By 1958, a new legal instrument, "priority development zones" or ZUPS, were adopted and building in such designated areas within fixed urban limits proceeded at the rapid pace of 60,000 dwellings per year. The flexible and extensive financial instruments created by the government were crucial elements, the key to the speed of the new growth. They were built throughout the provinces, but they lacked amenities and planned employment, except for three large ZUPS that were to become ad hoc new towns: Herouville-St. Claire at Caen in Normandy, planned for 30,000; St. Dizier-Les Neuf, for 30,000; and Le Mirail near Toulouse for 100,000 population. The last was planned with a variety of housing types, multifunctional centers, and a full range of schools and sports facilities through the special impetus derived from its mayor's social commitment. The designers, George Candelis, A. Josic, and Shadrach Woods, proposed a high density sinew with an elevated pedestrian-way separated from vehicular traffic. The layout is based on a bold hexagonal geometry. Extending from the pedestrian walkways are low-rise apartments, one- and two-story patio dwellings, along with schools, playgrounds, and parks. The first stage of development was to consist of three self-contained districts, each with 20,000 inhabitants and a total of 11,000 dwellings. As of 1975, 5700 dwellings of all types were built with the requisite urban amenities for 25,000 population, one quarter of the planned limit. The old center of Toulouse, with its narrow streets, shops, galleries, and restaurants, remains a fascinating environment, while the overpowering mechanical urban forms of Le Mirail, although integrated in function, fall short as an aesthetic alternative.

Regional Plan for Paris. Population projections for France foresee 75 million by the year 2000, of which 80% (60 million) will be urban residents. The Paris region was expected to rise from roughly 8 million to 15 million people. Those estimates, prepared in the 1960s, were adjusted downward in recent years. In the 1965 master plan for the Paris region, Plan d'Aménagement et d'Organization Generale de la Region Parisienne (PADOG), five new self-contained towns of 500,000 each were proposed to accommodate 3 million persons, at a distance of 20–30 km from the center of the city. Two million people would be absorbed within existing suburbs. The plan as implemented was to deconcentrate population density, spreading it more widely over the region. However, the new towns are neither satellites (ie, dependent on the city center for employment) nor totally freestanding. They are linked to the center by a superb system of high-speed rapid rail and a huge expansion in highway capacity which places the center well within daily commuting range for those who choose to take or keep jobs in the city or other suburban locations. The policy objectives seek to maximize freedom of choice by offering a wide range of jobs in each of the new towns and providing the internal and external transport modes to get to them.

With the Paris Basin stretching from Le Havre/Caen on the West to the Lower Seine on the east, two main development corridors were selected. Along the northern axis, Bry-sur-Marne, Noisy Le Grand Beauchamp, and Cergy-Pontoise were planned. Along the southern axis are located Tigery-Lieusaint, Evry, Trappes-Guyancourt, and Trappes-Etany. Of the six locations, five were started simultaneously, while one site was held in reserve.

The planners aimed to create work centers and amenities for the new population and, equally important, the restructuring of existing suburbs. Cergy–Pontoise on the northern axis (30 km from the Center of Paris) has been planned for 300,000 population on a site which embraced five urban political jurisdictions (*communes*) that were persuaded to form a municipal union, approved in 1971. Served by good express rail and highway facilities, each of the sectors was planned to have a high degree of self-containment. Five residential sectors extend along the outside of the loop of the Oise River to form a horseshoe. The peninsula in the middle has been developed as a leisure park with marina facilities.

Evry, a new town on the southern axis, incorporated the existing town of Corbeil-Essonnes to form an integrated urban complex planned for 350,000 population. Well planned transport facilities of extended passenger rail service resulted in the construction of four new stations connected to feeder buses on separate lanes to link the old to the new. One hundred and fifty thousand jobs were planned; with a projected labor force of 165,000, the new town could be almost self-contained. The design of the first residential sector, Evry I, was the subject of an international competition.

The goals set for the Paris new towns and three in other metropolitan areas have been met. As of 1984, 800,000 people live in new towns, which are well served by basic transportation. Forty thousand to 50,000 people are moving into these towns each year with new types of housing and some outstanding architecture giving each area a distinctive personality. While it is too early to draw final conclusions, it is clear that the spatial planning succeeded in maintaining a unified urban region by developing new towns that are not too far apart. As a consequence, balance is achieved and self-contained employment in each new town is no longer a main issue.

Other European Planned Communities

Other remarkable achievements in planned communities are the older new towns in the Netherlands. Lelystad, the main town of the East Flevolard polder, was redesigned in 1958 for a planned population of 50,000 serving a network of agricultural settlements. The newer towns are planned for 200,000–250,000. Almere, an overspill town, is being developed on 6800 ha in the bed of Lake Lysselmeer, 4–6 m below sea level with five urban districts for 250,000 population. It is linked to Amsterdam, 25 km away, by high-speed rail. By 1984 the town had over 40,000 population. Building on reclaimed land, the Dutch were able to preserve open space for leisure and agriculture between their urban centers. Dutch town planning is admirable in its attention to well built low-rise housing, ample amenities, and the environment.

In Poland, the new town movement evolved out of the need to move 300,000 people from the industrial conurbation in the coal fields of Upper Silesia. There was a public outcry to reduce the devastating pollution from large-scale steel and iron works as well as chemical industries. The decongestion plan was greatly influenced by the British new towns. The Polish planners proposed a ring of new towns on a fast transportation corridor connected to the industrial belt. Nowe Tychy and Tarnowskil Gory are the two large towns of 100,000 each with a network of seven smaller towns, but Nowe Tychey is the most interesting.

Moscow Satellite Towns

In 1931, the Soviet capital of Moscow invited seven teams of architects and planners to produce conceptual plans for the Moscow region with the objective of developing a network of new towns. Forty percent of the existing buildings were to be demolished (64% of the houses were of wood), and the projected population of Greater Moscow was not to exceed five million. To restrain growth, new industries were to be prohibited. Ernest May, one of the three foreign teams, proposed a number of new towns of about 100,000 people in close proximity to the old city. The residential areas were to be separated from the industries (proposed and existing) by greenbelts which were narrow enough to allow the workers to walk to work (35). The plan was rejected. The adopted plan assigned new functions to the river and emphasized the capital as a political and cultural symbol. The satellite towns, some dormitory suburbs, others self-contained, are located beyond the greenbelt. Moscow, at 10 million population in 1985, has not fully succeeded in containing its growth, although central planning and strict controls on internal migration have probably slowed the rate of expansion.

The U.S. New Towns

Radburn, N.J. Based on the earlier success of Sunnyside Garden "superblock" housing development, Clarence Stein, architect, and Henry Wright, planner, started their search for a U.S. Garden City. They were impressed with the ideas of Clarence Perry, a social planner who was advocating self-contained neighborhoods of 5000 people with a community center, schools, and other institutions in the center within a four minute walk from any residence. Following the theme of Ebenezer Howard's *Garden Cities of Tomorrow,* Stein and Wright also adopted the principle of the greenbelt around new towns planned for work as well as for living. They sought solutions for a town in which people could live peacefully with the automobile or, rather, in spite of it. In 1928 they selected a 1280 acre site, 16 miles from New York City in the Borough of Fairlawn (free of predetermined official street patterns and zoning) in which to design a functional town named Radburn. The site was not large enough to establish a greenbelt, but they could create a planned community with horizontal separation of vehicular traffic from pedestrian circulation. They designed superblocks of 40–50 acres with access roads to individual dwellings, clustered cul-de-sacs, and internal pedestrian walks on the garden side joining greenways that led through pedestrian underpasses to the community center. They also reversed the conventional design of the house, placing the kitchen on the street front and the principal living areas facing interior garden and park (Figs. 12 and 13). The first families moved in May 1929. That autumn the stock market collapsed and Radburn's construction was halted. Nevertheless, the completed section conclusively demonstrated a safer and more

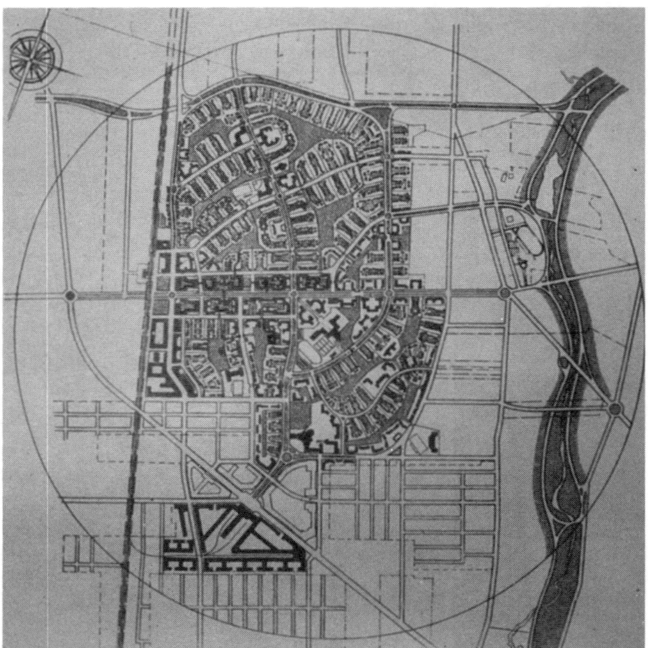

Figure 12. Radburn Plan, 1930. Courtesy of MIT Press.

orderly neighborhood. Residents were brought closer to nature. Furthermore, the superblock layout reduced the number of streets and utility runs and resulted in a more economical infrastructure.

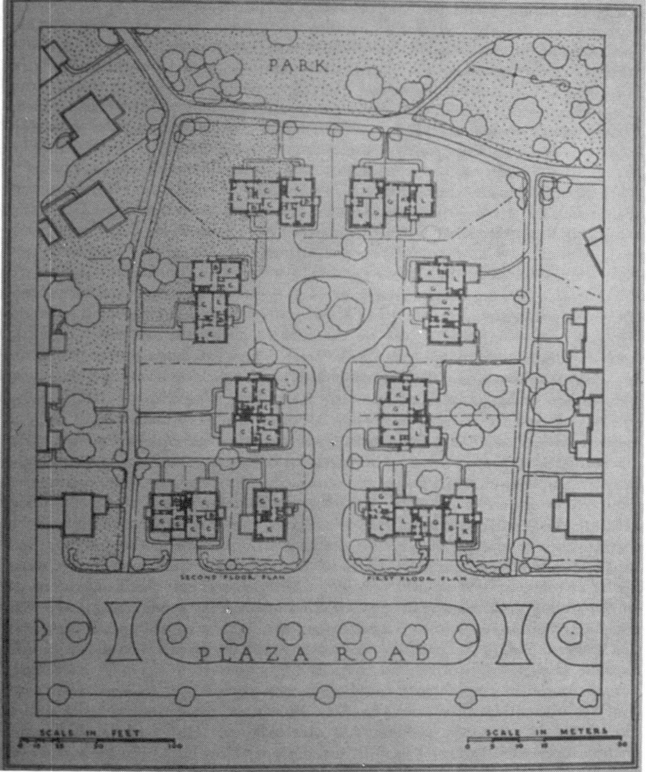

Figure 13. Radburn Cluster. Courtesy of MIT Press.

Local and federal government cooperation would have helped in the following ways: (*1*) large-scale land assembly; (*2*) financing the early phases of infrastructure; (*3*) construction of essential public buildings; and (*4*) housing assistance for low-income families. The Radburn experience became a major teaching tool in the United States. It contributed to housing policy and national legislation in the decade before the war and underlay the planning legislation and new-towns financing in the postwar period.

U.S. Greenbelt Towns. In September 1935, with 10 million or 25% of the work force unemployed in the United States, President Franklin D. Roosevelt authorized the creation of the Greenbelt towns. The Resettlement Administration was named the executing agency, responsible for their design and administration. They were the amalgamation of three basic concepts—the Garden City (from England), the Radburn concept, and the neighborhood unit. Their purpose as officially stated was: (*1*) to give useful work to men on unemployment relief; (*2*) to demonstrate in practice the soundness of planning and operating towns according to certain garden city principles; and (*3*) to provide low-rent housing in healthy surroundings, both physical and social, for low-income families. Director Rex Tugwell and his associates were deeply influenced by Ebenezer Howard's Garden City. However, due to limited funds, only three of the originally four planned new towns were built.

Plans by Douglas Ellington and R. J. Wadsworth, chief architects, and Hale Walker, town planner, for the first town, Greenbelt, Md., 13 mi from the Capital, were rushed to provide work for the unemployed workers encamped on the doorsteps of Congress. The town plan was formed by a wide inner crescent around a spacious town and community center, playfields, and playgrounds (the heart of town). The crescent was divided into residential superblocks of about 14 acres each. By late 1937, 1000 dwellings were occupied by low-income families, with some bachelor's quarters. Innovations in social policy, such as racially and economically integrated housing, community organization, and coop ownership, were achieved. Pedestrian underpasses conveniently link the residential areas to the town center and recreation areas following the Radburn model. By 1941, another 1000 dwellings were added by the federal government for workers in essential defense industries. Since Greenbelt was located adjacent to the National Agricultural Research Center at Beltsville (12,000 acres of agricultural experimental farms), it was hoped that some of the scientists and technicians would choose to live in the town. Unfortunately, less than 10% of the employees live in the town today. The land in Greenbelt was sold off to private developers in the 1960s and 50 years later the original town design has been swallowed up in speculative suburban development.

Greenhills, Ohio, is a greenbelt town located 5 mi north of Cincinnati. The initial plan was for 676 dwelling units in the first stage with a community center in the middle. Wooded ravines limit the development and tie into the surrounding greenbelt. Greendale, Wisconsin, the third Greenbelt town, was well sited with a stream that flowed through the wooded park in the center of the town.

Early in 1950, the federal government disposed of the

rental housing to private developers. Unsuccessful attempts were made to enable the consumer and housing cooperatives to own and operate the towns and their expansion area. However, with the sale of the Greenbelt properties, the Government was able to transfer the designated greenbelts to public park authorities. Even though incomplete, each of the first stage developments represented some of the best applications of the self-contained neighborhood principles.

Private Planned Communities. At the conclusion of World War II, pent-up demand for modest housing for middle- and low-income families was satisfied by a number of large-scale suburban residential communities aided by a federally funded national highway program and a program of low-cost, federally guaranteed housing finance. Notable among these are the Levittowns. A private developer, Levitt & Sons, provided much needed very inexpensive housing in single family units of good but monotonous design. All elements of the house were standardized to reduce cost. The three major Levittowns (Long Island, N.Y., New Jersey, and Pennsylvania), reached sizes of 10,000 to 12,000 dwellings. The developments provided sites for schools and churches, synagogues, and shopping areas, the latter providing an important source of revenue to the developer.

Reston, Virginia. In the 1950s, projections of rapid urban growth stimulated local and regional government entities to study conceptual plans for their development corridors. In 1961, the National Capital Planning Commission, foreseeing a doubling of population in the Washington metropolitan area which covered five counties in adjacent Maryland and Virginia, published an advisory plan for the year 2000. The plan called for low-density green wedges separating high density development corridors radiating from the capital city. New town clusters were visualized in this multilinear pattern. One such site, comprising 2870 ha straddling the Dulles Access Highway, was acquired by Robert E. Simon, Jr., who commissioned the firm of Whittlesey and Conklin to plan the new town, 17 mi from Washington, D.C. The town, planned for an ultimate population of 75,000, was structured in a linear pattern of seven "villages" lying along a high density residential "sinew" with the town center at the midpoint (Fig. 14).

The architecture of the first village center on Lake Anne was designed by the successor firm of Conklin and Rossant in 1963. In contrast to the low-density suburban pattern of the period, it featured a high-rise apartment building integrated with tight rows of town houses, and a crescent pedestrian shopping precinct with apartments in the upper stories. All of the buildings faced the lake or the quayside plaza, with its full mixture of uses and building types, and produced a highly sophisticated urban environment (Fig. 15). It was an extraordinary breakthrough; although these elements have become commonplace in the suburbs today, many have not been planned as well. The chaotic high-density mixed-use centers that punctuate the countryside in the 1980s despoil the natural environment and increase automobile congestion while blocking pedestrian movement. They are the antithesis of planned communities, a triumph of land speculation and profit-maximizing development.

In Reston, a major effort was made to encourage strong community organizations for social cohesion and ultimate town administration. The purpose was to reflect the democratic ideals and overcome the anomie of suburbia. A successful demonstration of this community spirit was the local initiative that sponsored a private commuter-bus service to supplement inadequate public transportation.

Over 20% of the total land area was preserved for major recreational use and forest parks. In addition, buildings were clustered in the residential areas, minimizing private yards in favor of the accumulation of continuous common open spaces. To maximize pedestrian access, the original plan called for the dwelling units to consist of 90% apartments and town houses, while only 10% were to be single-family detached dwellings.

The high cost of installing infrastructure long in advance of projected population growth plus a slower-than-expected absorption rate forced the original developer out. The new owners abandoned much of the innovative quality of the town plan in order to generate immediate revenue to cover the carrying costs of infrastructure, a sunk capital investment, recoverable only in the long term. The proportion of single-family units was increased dramatically and the urban "sinew" that created the pedestrian system was undermined by more conventional garden apartments and town houses.

In 1985, Reston had a population of 55,000 and approximately 8500 jobs. According to Mobil Oil, the present owner of the remaining developable tract, the town is showing a reasonable rate of return. However, the experience again demonstrated the need for long-term financing for infrastructure, including transportation and adequate subsidy programs to provide low-cost housing for the full range of workers who would be employed there. Twenty years after Reston construction was initiated, the market vindicated the "premature" higher density apartment and town house design for which the planners foresaw a need.

Columbia, Maryland. In 1962, James Rouse, a successful developer of suburban shopping malls, assembled 6,420 ha of contiguous land located halfway between Washington and Baltimore. He planned to develop a new town of 100,000 population, a market for retail shopping, and a labor force to attract industry. With a large staff of skilled professional planners, architects, and managers, financial and economic models of all of the design proposals were tested to ensure a satisfactory cash flow and return on investment through the 15-year development period. Large-scale long-term financing was secured from a private insurance company. Detailed plans for new forms of social and community organization were also prepared. The town was organized into villages of 6000–10,000 persons, with a large regional–town center designed to capture the buying power of 250,000 customers (Fig. 16). A large music pavilion and a dinner theater were added attractions. Columbia had a public commitment to develop an "open community" with a significant degree of social mix. When General Electric decided to build an assembly plant employing large numbers of unskilled workers, many of the residents were outspoken in their opposition. Nevertheless, the entry of this large-scale industry was an economic coup for the developer and has enhanced the tax base of the county and the local economy. The high level of urban amenities, including ample open spaces, were carefully planned but

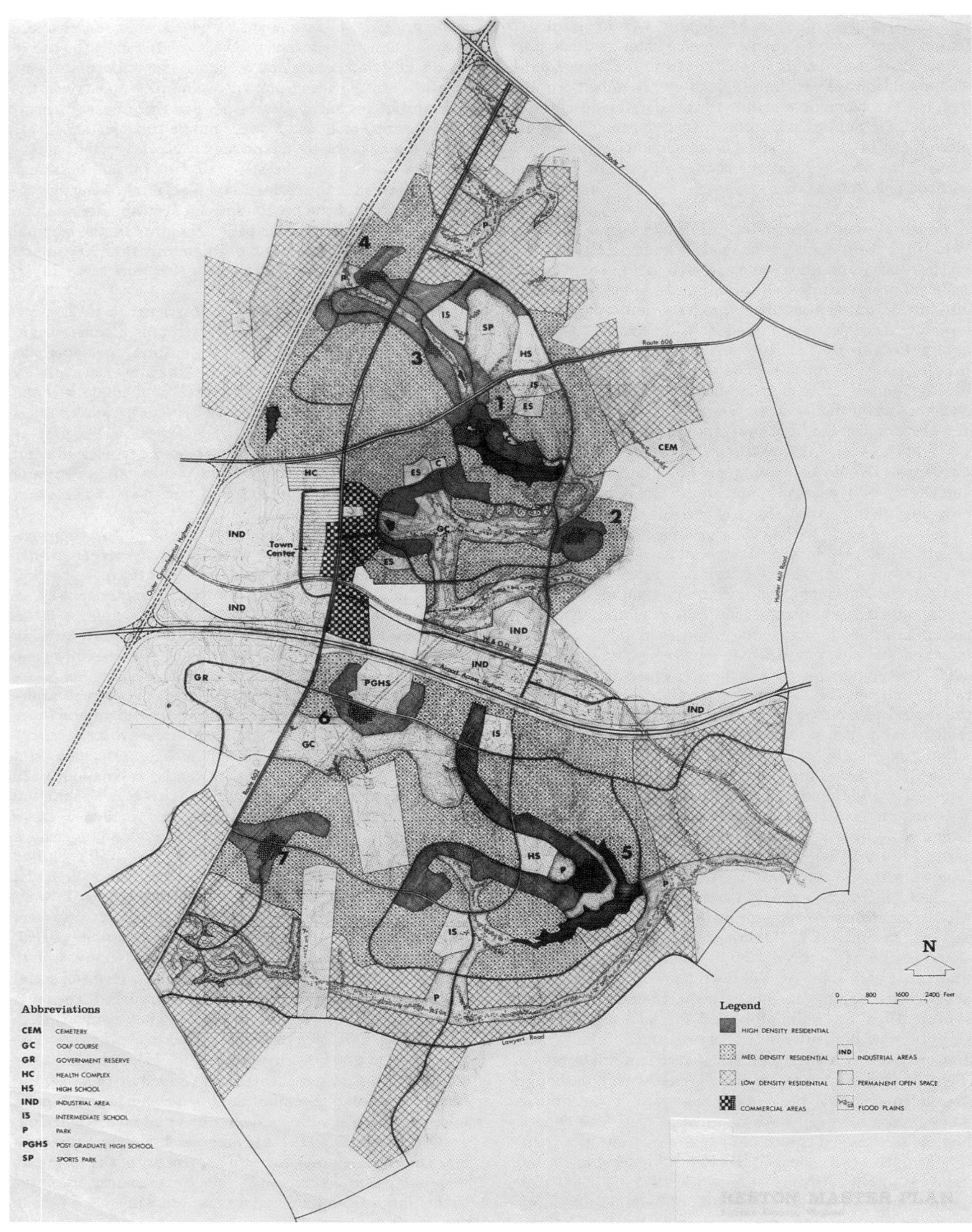
Route 7
Route 606
Hunter Mill Road
Outer Circumferential Highway
Route 602
W. & O.D. R.R.
Airport Access Highway
Lawyers Road
Town Center
CEM
HC
IND
GR
PGHS
SP
HS
IS
ES
GC
P
1
2
3
4
5
6
7
N
0 800 1600 2400 Feet
Legend
HIGH DENSITY RESIDENTIAL
MED. DENSITY RESIDENTIAL
LOW DENSITY RESIDENTIAL
COMMERCIAL AREAS
INDUSTRIAL AREAS
PERMANENT OPEN SPACE
FLOOD PLAINS
Abbreviations
CEM CEMETERY
GC GOLF COURSE
GR GOVERNMENT RESERVE
HC HEALTH COMPLEX
HS HIGH SCHOOL
IND INDUSTRIAL AREA
IS INTERMEDIATE SCHOOL
P PARK
PGHS POST GRADUATE HIGH SCHOOL
SP SPORTS PARK
RESTON MASTER PLAN

Figure 14. Reston, Va., 1963. Courtesy of Whittlesey & Conklin.

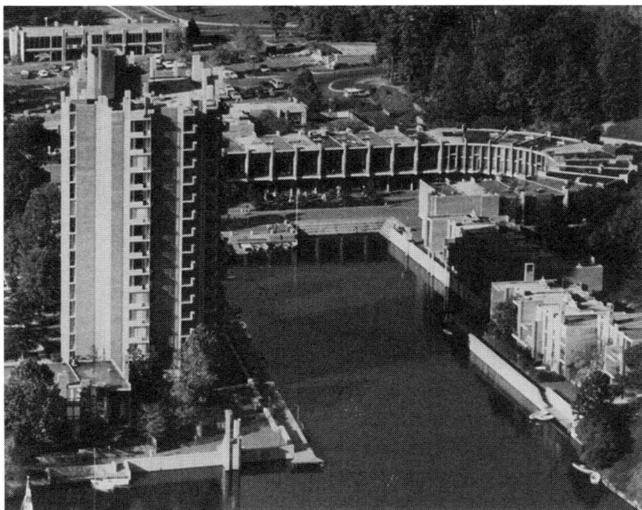

Figure 15. Reston Lake Anne Center. Courtesy of Whittlesey & Conklin.

did not result in greater efficiency. The densities are even lower than the first-generation British new towns such as Stevenage. In fact, to conform to market requirements, they replicate conventional suburban development patterns. Furthermore, there was no way to economically provide adequate bus service. This has forced most families to purchase two cars.

Irvine, California. In Irvine, a more open new town was being planned during the same period by a large development corporation. With its architect William Pereira, the incentive for the new town was the nucleus of a new campus for the University of California; the commitment from the University, forced the corporation, to plan the entire 33,200 ha holding. The present master plan envisages 500,000–750,000 people and the provision of 134,000 industrial and 150,000 white collar jobs. The first developed sector between the university and the ocean covers 14,000 ha, three times the size of Columbia, Md. Schools, shops, institutions, and leisure facilities are organized along an "environmental corridor" of continuous greenway through the villages.

The low densities of these U.S. contemporary new towns—Reston, Columbia, and Irvine—built on the primacy of the automobile and the emphasis on leisure facilities and white-collar high- and medium-income employment, are a great contrast to the higher density and broader social mix of European new towns. In addition, the private new towns of the United States shared a common problem: how to transfer the decision making responsibilities from the developer to the residents without endangering the economic goals and the timetable of the master plan. In all three cases, community associations with automatic membership for all residents were created. Many notorious battles were fought between the developers and the new residents who opposed the developer's attempts to preserve his original objectives whether concerning racial and income mixing or higher density residential construction. Although later the high price of housing made multifamily solutions common, few lower and moderate income families can find shelter in the privately sponsored new towns.

Title VII—Federal New Community Program in the United States. The relatively unplanned suburban development typical of the 1950s and 1960s and rapid growth of the metropolitan area generated public interest in creating entirely new "planned" communities in order to reduce the social and environmental cost of sprawl. In 1970 the U.S. Congress authorized the Department of Housing and Urban Development to undertake a program of new community development under Title VII of the Urban Growth and New Communities Development Act, which provided federal guarantees for loans for land acquisition and development and federal grants. The goal was to provide balanced, orderly physical development and a more desirable social environment. To be eligible for federal support, a proposed new community needed to provide an alternative to disorderly urban growth. The Act describes four types of new towns: expanded towns, self-contained new towns, satellites, and new-towns-in-town. By 1973, loan guarantees had been extended to developers for 13 new communities located in 10 states from New York to Minnesota to Texas (Cedar Riverside, Minn.; Jonathan, Minn.; Granada, N.Y.; Riverton, N.Y.; Newfields, Ohio; Park Forest South, Ill.; Maumelle, Ark.; St. Charles, Md.; Shenandoah, Ga.; Soul City, N.C.; Harbison, S.C.; Flower Mound, Texas; and The Woodlands, Texas). With the enactment of the Housing and Community Development Act of 1974, new communities became eligible for block grants to help subsidize developer's costs.

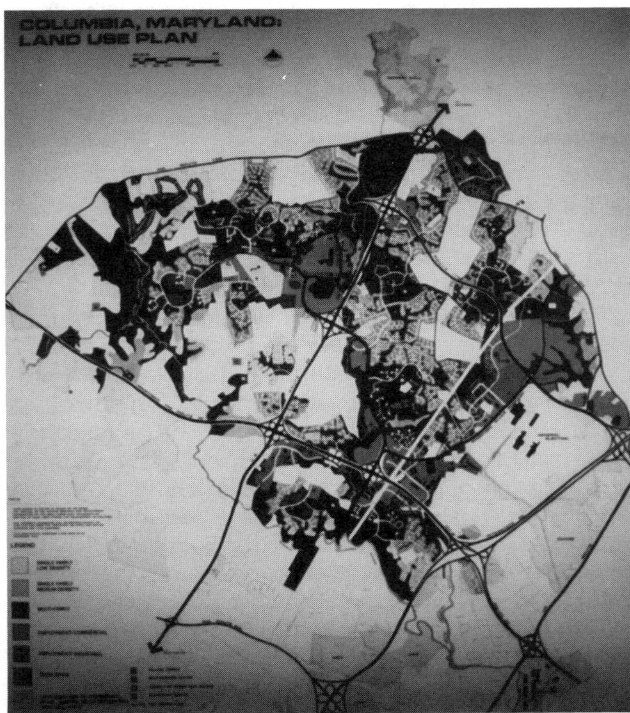

Figure 16. Columbia Town Plan, 1963. Courtesy of the Rouse Development Corporation, Columbia, Md.

The U.S. program cannot be considered a success. Only 10% of the original 20-year forecast had been achieved by 1983. Of the total 785,000 residents in 200,000 dwelling units expected by 1995, the population achieved in 1983 was 53,000 in 20,000 dwelling units. However, an amazing 3500 or 18% of these were subsidized. Thus, despite the severely reduced scale, the program did fulfill a major policy objective: a wide mixture of housing types was made available to a wide range of family incomes with a higher degree of racial integration than the standard suburban subdivision. The mix of rental and ownership units and more affordable low-priced housing was higher than the private market had produced in unplanned suburban developments. Overall, the more developed communities had a positive impact on the environmental quality and fiscal welfare of their areas, as well as on job creation. Fifteen thousand total new jobs represented 0.75 jobs per new dwelling unit, not much below the target of 0.8 jobs/d.u. However, only three communities have achieved a desirable relationship of residential and industrial land use in their developed acreage; only four communities have a relative balance of jobs and resident households. Maumelle, Arkansas designed by Edwin Crownwell and Edward Echeverria, with Albert Mayer as consulting planner, is one of the most successful of the integrated new communities, achieving 1.6 new jobs per dwelling in 1983.

The Title VII program was administered in much the same manner as a conventional federal program that disbursed funds to localities. In concept and operation the program failed to account for the financial and managerial complexities of building new towns in conjunction with the private sector. As a consequence, neither partner's needs were adequately met. By 1976, nine of the new communities had defaulted and were acquired and refinanced by HUD, three other communities defaulted but were refinanced with original owners part of the new management, and only one, Woodland, Texas, avoided default, but that project was reduced to a grandiose subdivision. In 1983, the program was terminated.

The Title VII structure suffered from basic flaws. Key among these was the requirement that interest be paid from day one, rather than awaiting the achievement of a positive cash flow—an event that might not occur for at least as long as 10 years. In addition, initial delays in processing applications added cost and confusion to the administrative process; other examples of rigidity and mismanagement are cited. Many of the developers were inexperienced, site selection was often faulty, and some applicants seem to have been approved with political rather than technical justifications. Moreover, there was no overarching federal urban development strategy against which to judge projects. A major problem was a lack of continuity and the vacillating support of the political appointees who directed the program. There were 13 administrators in the 13 years of the program, many of them unfamiliar with real estate development, working in administrations that were ideologically hostile to the concept of a federal role in urban development. On top of these internal problems were failures in the market forecast, two serious depressions, and a reduction in actual growth of population and economic activities over the optimistic forecasts of the 1960s.

There are current alternatives to new town development in the United States that are not as ambitious or extensive as those undertaken under the Title VII program. Developers and local governments in several localities across the country are currently undertaking smaller-scale projects with lower carrying costs. However, the failure of the Title VII New Communities program reflects the political climate of the country at this time.

CONCLUSION

Over the long history of the development of new towns, urban forms were designed to meet varying needs, eg the administration of expanding empires, the emergence of nation states of the baroque period, and the needs of production and environmental protection in the modern industrial era. As modern economies become overwhelmingly non-farm and urban, large and small cities face rapid expansion as the older and newly developing economies cope with the problems of housing and employing vast urban populations.

The urban growth taking place in the late twentieth century in Asia and Latin America will reach insoluble proportions if the political powers do not adopt and implement development policies that focus on the urban spatial dimension as well as the social and economic. The megalopolises of Latin America—Mexico City with 18.5 million and Sao Paulo with 17 million inhabitants—have developed gigantic problems in management and provision of services. The population projection for Mexico City by the year 2004 is about 30 million. Mexican planners are analyzing a series of studies examining alternatives: (*1*) free-standing; (*2*) satellites, or (*3*) "add-on" or linear new towns along development corridors of existing cities. The first would serve as counter-magnets to growth, provided that they are located at minimum distances, 150 to 200 km from the metropolis. The British experience has proven that with the appropriate incentives, industries can be enticed to relocate in overspill satellite new towns that provide a balance of jobs to the working population; the French experience demonstrated that large office-service centers will also move out from the city center when offered appropriate amenities and efficient transportation.

The next century will require hundreds of new towns along with major expansions of existing small and middle-sized towns to accommodate future urban growth. Governments should give serious consideration to adopting urban spatial strategies that focus on deconcentration and stimuli for constructing overspill new towns. This calls for increasing the role of governments with a will to assist in land assemblage and financing of infrastructure, adapting the successful model of the British and European implementation techniques. Although housing investment is viewed in conventional economics as a consumption expenditure, investment in infrastructure and housing can serve as a motor of economic growth, given the appropriate macroeconomic tools, including the necessary financial instruments.

The newly acquired independence of many African nations and the internal reorganization of older nations in southern Asia will no doubt result in the building of more capital cities. In Latin America, to divert the economic forces that continue to press the capital cities of Lima, Buenos Aires, and Mexico City, Peru, Argentina, and Mexico have announced planning studies to decentralize or build new capitals in the interior in the hope of reducing the dominant role that their present capital cities hold on the country. Such new capital cities would have the dual role of more even distribution of economic growth and service as government administrative centers. The case of Brasilia serves as a precedent.

New towns have produced innovative and integrated urban environments that demonstrated the viability of many types of social arrangements with varying densities, housing designs, and site arrangements. They have responded to the prevailing housing market with innovative designs, shifting from single-family detached dwellings to more densely clustered housing and multifamily units. They generally produced more livable environments at a pedestrian level, especially within the neighborhoods or local precincts. New towns have had to overcome the problem of social acceptability of new forms in pioneer locations; experience has shown that people will forego proximity to the central cities for a higher degree of amenities.

Mass tourism on an international scale has led to the development of large recreation/resort communities in Europe and in North and South America. The numbers are increasing as whole islands and coastal development areas have become second home and recreation communities. At Languedoc-Rousillon on the French Mediterranean coast, 180 km of coast were developed, starting in the late 1960s, into five resort centers varying in size and concept with a total capacity for 500,000 tourists. With the projected scale of educational needs, universities and technical and agro-training centers could become the nuclei of new year-round urban settlements.

As the sparsely settled regions of Canada, Brazil, and the USSR are developed, new industrial and service towns will appear. With further development of solar technology and tidal energies, new settlements may be established on the tundra, Sahara desert, and the sea. Artificial islands and floating communities have been on the drawing boards for years, awaiting environmental and technological breakthroughs.

Future new towns will probably be larger and certainly more integrated in terms of economic and social activities with improved education, health, communications, and public transport on development corridors similar to the Paris regional new towns. The urban spaces should adopt a more relaxed and intimate scale, a desirable departure from the monumental and rigid forms of new towns characterized by Brasilia and Le Mirail. It can be anticipated that gigantism and unbridled greed will generate their own demise just as the rush to demolition and urban renewal in the post war period produced the preservation movement and eclectic postmodernism of today. The urban design of multiple centers in future new towns will certainly strive for controlled environments. With the gradual change in family structure, housing accommodations will be smaller as the family size reduces; however, common open space and active recreation of all types will be enlarged, following the designs of Reston and Tapiola.

It has been demonstrated that it costs less to settle a given population in a new town than to resettle them through urban renewal of existing cities. Through the urbanization of new towns, quasi-public development authorities were created in the United Kingdom and France to capture the conversion or betterment value of raw land; these values were later internalized to subsidize housing and social facilities. Such profits were used in the British new towns to cross-subsidize the lower-income families. New town building acts as a stimulus to private sector initiatives. Unfortunately, new towns in the United States, where there is no national urban strategy, have a bleak short-term future with the conservative political bias of the 1970s and 1980s and reluctance to use public powers to control and guide urban growth toward a more humane living environment. For the rest of the world, new towns comprehensively planned to give equal weight to social, environmental, and economic goals offer a realistic method for balancing future population and job creation. Lastly, linear or corridor development of new towns offers a greater opportunity to integrate urban with rural environments—the town's cultural and employment opportunities within easy access to the countryside and to nature. These are all strong arguments for the adoption of new town programs as alternatives to the current trend toward urban sprawl. A strong commitment to change, to building a better society is required to reverse the prevailing patterns in the United States.

BIBLIOGRAPHY

P. Abercrombie, *Greater London Plan,* HMSO, London, 1945.

E. Akurgal, *Ancient Civilizations and Ruins of Turkey,* Haset Kitabevi, Istanbul, 1973.

G. Argan, *The Renaissance City,* George Braziller, New York, 1969.

W. Ashworth, *The Genesis of British Town Planning,* Routledge & Kegan Paul, London, 1954.

T. B. Augur, "The Challenge of a New Town," *Michigan Municipal Review* **4,** 2–3 (Feb.–Mar. 1931).

E. N. Bacon, *Design of Cities,* rev. ed., Viking Press, New York, 1973.

J. Bailey, ed., *New Towns in America, The Design and Development Process,* The American Institute of Architects, Washington D.C.

Barlow Report on the Distribution of the Industrial Population of Great Britain, London, 1940.

T. Bennett, "Crawley New Town 1958," Address to representatives of official and other organizations, Crawley CDC, March 29, 1958.

M. Bowra, et al., *Golden Ages of the Great Cities,* New York, 1952.

R. Brooks, "Social Planning in Columbia," *J. Amer. Inst. of Planners* (Nov. 1971).

K. Browne, "Test Case: Irvine New Town," *Architectural Review* (Oct. 1973).

L. Brownlow, "Radburn: A new town planned for the motor age" *International Housing and Town Planning Bulletin* (21) (Feb. 1930).

C. Buchanan & Partners, *South Hampshire Study.* A study made for the records of the Ministry of Housing and Local Government, vol. 1. "Report on the Feasibility of Major Urban

Growth"; vol. 2.1, "The Area, Its People and Activities"; vol. 2.2, "Methods and Policies", HMSO, London, 1966.

S. Buder, "The Model Town of Pullman," *J. Amer. Inst. of Planners* (Jan. 1967).

Candilis, Josic, Woods, *Une decennie d'architecture et d'urbanisme,* Ed. Eyrolles, Paris, 1968.

Candilis, G. A. Josic, S. Woods, *Toulouse Le Mirail,* Karl Kramer Verlag, Stuttgart, 1975.

Candilis, G. A. Josic, S. Woods, *Toulouse Recherches sur l'Architecture de loisirs,* Karl Kramer Verlag, Stuttgart, 1972.

F. Choay, *The Modern City: Planning in the 19th Century,* George Braziller, New York, 1969.

H. C. Chung, "Capital Cities of China," unpublished essay, Columbia University, New York, 1968.

A. Ciborowski, "L'Urbanisme polonais 1945–1965" in *City and Regional Planning in Poland,* Cornell University Press, New York, 1965.

G. R. Collins, "The Ciudad Lineal of Madrid," *J. Society of Arch. Historians* **XVIII,** 38–53 (May 1959).

G. Collins, "Linear Planning Throughout the World," *J. Soc. of Archit. Historians* **XVIII,** (Oct. 1959).

General Development Plan, Community Research and Development Corporation, Columbia, Md., Jan. 1966.

A. C. Comey and M. S. Wehrly, "Radburn, Bergen County, N.J.," Urbanism Committee, *Supplementary report, Planned Communities,* U.S. National Resources Committee, 1939.

Copenhagen Regional Plan: A Summary of the Preliminary Proposal 1948–1949, Stadsingeniorens Direktorat, Copenhagen, 1954.

10 Anos 1960–1970, Corporacion Venezolana de Guayana, Caracas, 1970.

J. Crane, "Greendale: the general plan" *Planners' Journal* **3,** 4 (July–Aug. 1937).

Doxiades Associates, "Islamabad–the Scale of the City and its Central Area", *Ekistics* **XIV** (83) (1962).

"Islamabad–Summary of Final Programme and Plan," Athens, 1962.

"Islamabad: The Creation of a New Capital," *Town Planning Review* **XXXVI** (1) (1965).

C. A. Doxiades, *Architecture in Transition,* Oxford University Press, New York, 1963.

A. C. Duff, *Britain's New Towns: An Experiment in Living,* Pall Mall Press, London, 1961.

O. D. Duncan, "Optimum Size of Cities," in P. K. Hatt and A. J. Reiss, eds., *Cities and Society,* Free Press, Glencoe, Illinois, 1967.

J. Duquesne, *Vivre a Sarcelles?,* Editions Cujas, Paris, 1966.

"Evry: Centre urbain nouveau et ville nouvelle," *Cahiers I.A.U.R.P.* **XV** (May 1969).

"Evry Councours d'amenagement urbain," *Cahiers I.A.U.R.P.* **XXXI** (1973).

G. Elmer, *Die Stadtplanung im Schwedishen Ostseereich, 1660–1715,* Svenska Bokforlaget, Sweden, 1961.

D. G. Epstein, *Brasilia: Plan and Reality,* University of California Press, Berkeley, Calif., 1973.

Evaluation of the Federal New Communities Program, HUD-PRR.934, Department of Housing and Urban Development, Washington, D.C., 1984.

N. Evenson, *Chandigarh,* University of California, Berkeley, Calif., 1966.

J. C. Fisher, *City and Regional Planning in Poland,* Cornell Univ. Press, Ithaca, N.Y., 1966.

A. Fourquier and J. Fourquier, "Planification et urbanisme en Pologne," *Cahiers I.A.U.R.P.* (Nov. 1968).

E. Y. Galantay, *New Towns—Antiquity to the Present,* George Braziller, New York, 1975.

E. Galantay, J. Perez-Canto, and H. Weber, "Evaluation of Sites for Focal Structures," CVG Staff Paper No. E-79, August 1963.

A. Garnier, *Une cite industrielle,* 2nd ed., Massin, Paris, 1929.

F. Gibberd, *Harlow New Town,* 2nd ed., Epping and Loughton, West Essex Press, August 1952.

Paul Goodman and Percival Goodman, *Communitas,* 2nd revised edition, Random House, New York, 1960.

N. Gosling, *Leningrad,* E. P. Dutton & Co., Inc., New York, 1965.

M. N. Grabania, *Tychy, miasto satelita,* Slasky Instytut, Katowice, 1966.

Final Report of the New Towns Committee, Cmd. 6876, New Towns Committee, London, 1946.

F. Gutheim, "Greenbelt revisited," *Magazine of Art* **40** (I) (Jan. 1947).

E. Gutkind, *Revolution of Environment,* London, 1946.

P. Hall, *London 2000,* Praeger, New York.

The World Cities, McGraw-Hill, New York, 1966.

G. Harding, *The Antiquities of Jordan,* Lutterworth Press, 1967.

J. E. Hardoy, "The Planning of New Capital Cities," in *UNO Planning of Metropolitan Areas and New Towns,* Uno, New York, 1967.

"La Plata, Argentina's Nineteenth-Century New Town," in *UNO Planning of Metropolitan Areas and New Towns,* New York, 1967.

Urban Planning in Pre-Columbian America, George Braziller, New York, 1968.

Harlow Development Corporation, "New Towns Population Survey 1964," *The Economist Intelligence Unit* (Jan. 1965).

D. Haskell, "Brasilia: A New Type of National City," *Architectural Forum* (Nov. 1970).

E. Howard, *Garden Cities of Tomorrow,* Faber & Faber, London, 1965.

L. Hilberseimer, *The New City: Principles of Planning,* Theobald, Chicago, 1944.

F. R. Hiorns, *Town-building in History,* Criterion Books, Inc., New York, 1958.

T. Hiraoka and K. Imai, *Chuangan and Lo-yang,* Jinbunka Gaku Kendyusho, Kyoto University, Kyoto.

W. G. Holford, "The Future of Canberra," *The Town Planning Review* **XXIX** (3) (1958).

W. G. Holford, "Green Cities of the 20th Century," *J. Town Planning Institute* (May 1947).

The Planning of a New Town (Hook), Greater London Council, London, 1965.

M. Hoppenfeld, *The Columbia Process,* Garden City Press, Ltd., Letchworth, 1970.

E. Howard, *Garden Cities of Tomorrow,* Faber and Faber, London, 1946.

C. Hussey, *The Life of Sir Edwin Lutyens,* Country Life, London, 1950.

The Irvine Company Annual Report, Newport Beach, Calif., 1973.

Irvine New Town, Irvine Development Corporation, 1971.

R. R. Isaacs, "The Neighborhood Theory," *J. Amer. Inst. of Planners* **XIV** (Spring 1948).

E. S. Kite, *L'Enfant and Washington: 1971–92,* Baltimore, 1929.

Knobelsdorf, *Tychy: Ludnosc nowego miasta satelitarnego (The Population of a New Town),* Polognia Publishing House, Warsaw, 1966.

K. F. Knyaziev, "Satellite Towns and the Development of Lárge Cities," in *Izvestiia Akademmia Stroitelsva Architektury,* 1980.

O. M. Koenigsberger, "New Towns in India," *Town Planning Review* (July 1962).

A. Korn, *History Builds the Town,* Lund Humphries, London, 1953.

M. Kosmin, *Ville Lineaire, Amenagement, Architecture,* Vincent Freal, Paris, 1952.

P. Lampl, *Cities and Planning in the Ancient Near East,* George Braziller, New York, 1968.

A. Laland, "Ville nouvelle d'Evry," *Techniques et Architecture* (5), 32.

Le Corbusier, *Concerning Town Planning,* The Architectural Press, Ltd., London, 1946.

Le Corbusier and P. Jeanneret, *Oeuvre Complete,* Les Editions d'Architecture, Zurich, 1947.

Le Corbusier, *Urbanisme,* Paris, 1925.

Development Proposals for a New City at El Tablazo, Llewelyn-Davies, Weeks, Forestier, Walker & Bor, Caracas, Feb. 1969.

L. Llewelyn-Davies, "Villes nouvelles: l'experience britannique," *Political and Parliamentary Review* (800) (June 1969).

L. Lockhart, "Shah Abbas's Isfahan," in Toynbee, *Cities of Destiny,* McGraw-Hill, New York, 1967.

The Planning of a New Town, London County Council, London, 1961.

K. Lynch, "The Form of Cities," *Scientific American* **CXC,** 20 (April 1954).

B. Malisz, *Poland Builds New Towns,* Polonia Publishing House, Warsaw, 1962.

B. Malisz, *Physical Planning for the Development of Satellite and New Towns,* Institut urbanistyki i architektury, Warsaw, 1966.

B. Malisz, *La Formation des systemes d'habitat,* Dunod, Paris, 1972.

Master Plan for Germantown, Maryland National Capital Park and Planning Commission, Rockville, Oct. 1966.

A. Mayer, *Greenbelt Towns Revisited,* HUD, Washington, D.C., 1968.

D. McFayden, *Sir Ebenezer Howard and the Town Planning Movement,* MIT Press, Cambridge, Mass., 1971.

P. Merlin, *New Towns,* Methuen & Co. Ltd., London, 1971.

N. A. Miliutin, "Sotsgorod—The Problem of Building Socialist Cities," MIT Press, Cambridge, Mass., 1974.

"Milton Keynes: A Progress Report," *Architectural Design* (June 1973).

"Milton Keynes," *Domus,* 6–18 (April 1973).

A. E. J. Morris, *History of Urban Form,* Halsted Press, New York, 1972.

L. Mumford, *The Culture of Cities,* Technics and Civilization, London, 1946.

L. Mumford, *The City in History,* Harcourt, Brace & World, Inc., New York, 1961.

L. Mumford, "The Neighborhood and the Neighborhood Unit," *The Planning Review* **XXIV** (1954).

Canberra Planning & Development, National Capital Development Commission, Canberra, 1979.

A Plan for the Year 2000: The Nation's Capital, National Capital Planning Commission, Washington, D.C., June 1961.

J. Witsen, "National Physical Planning in the Netherlands," Conference at Helsinki, Netherlands Government Physical Planning Service, November 26, 1965.

Second Report on Physical Planning in the Netherlands (condensed ed.), 2 vols., Part I, "Main Outline of National Physical Planning Policy"; Part II, "Future Pattern of Development," Netherlands Government Physical Planning Service, The Hague, 1966.

New Communities for New York, New York State Urban Development Corporation, Albany, 1970.

The New Towns of Britain, Central Office of Information, Jan. 1972.

New York State Urban Development Acts of 1968, Urban Development Corporation, Albany, 1968.

F. L. Olmsted, "Central Park," in *Forty-eight Years of Architecture,* New York, 1922–1928.

F. J. Osborn, and A. Whittick, *The New Towns: The Answer to Megalopolis,* L. Hill, London, 1963.

F. J. Osborn, "Sir Ebenezer Howard: The Evolution of His Ideas," *Town Planning Review* (Oct. 21, 1950).

E. W. Palm, "Los origines del urbanismo municipal en America," in *Contribuciones a la historia municipal de America,* Instituto Panamericano de Geografia e Historia, Mexico, 1951.

M. F. Parkins, *City Planning in Soviet Russia,* University of Chicago Press, Chicago, 1946.

D. Pass, *Vallingby & Farsta from Idea to Reality,* MIT Press, Cambridge, Mass., 1973.

C. Pawlowski, *Tony Garnier,* Centre de Recherche d'urbanisme, Paris, 1967.

C. Perry, "The Neighborhood Unit," *Regional Plan of New York and its Environs* **VII** (1929).

V. Promyslow, *Moscow in Construction,* MIR, Moscow, 1967.

B. Rowland, *The Art and Architecture of India, Buddhist, Hindu & Jain,* Penguin Books, New York, 1953.

S. E. Rasmussen, "Neighborhoods Planning," *The Planning Review* **XXVII,** 197–218 (1957).

T. A. Reiner, *The Place of the Ideal Community in Urban Planning,* University of Pennsylvania Press, Philadelphia, Pa., 1963.

J. W. Reps, *Monumental Washington,* Princeton University Press, Princeton, N.J., 1967.

J. W. Reps, *The Making of Urban America,* Princeton University Press, Princeton, N.J., 1965.

"Reston Va.," *Architectural Design* (Feb. 1973).

G. Rigotti, "I Borghi dalle 'Siedlunger' alle 'Greenbelt Towns'," *Urbanistica,* **6**(I), 3–18 (Jan.–Feb. 1973).

N. H. Richardson, "A Tale of Two Cities in North West Canada," *Plan Canada* **IV** (3), 111–125 (1963).

L. Rodwin, *Planning Urban Growth and Regional Development: The Experience of the Guayana Program,* MIT Press, Cambridge, Mass., 1969.

L. Rodwin, ed., *The Future Metropolis,* George Braziller, New York, 1961.

L. Rodwin, *Nations and Cities,* Houghton Mifflin, Boston, 1970.

H. Rosenau, *The Ideal City,* Routledge and Kegan Paul, London, 1959.

Runcorn New Town, Runcorn Development Corporation, 1967.

Senri New Town, Senboku New Town, Public Enterprise Bureau, Osaka Prefecture, 1970.

A. S. Shachar, "Israel's Development Towns," *J. Amer. Inst. of Planners* (Nov. 1971).

Shankland, Cox & Associates, *Expansion of Ipswich: Designation Proposals: Consultant's Study of the Town in its Sub-region,* HMSO, London, 1966, p. 88.

V. Shkavirov, "The Building of New Towns in the USSR," *Ekistics,* 307–320 (Nov. 1964).

V. Shkavirov and I. Smolar, "Planning of New Towns," *Arkhitektura SSSR* (7) (1966).

C. Sitte, *The Art of Building Cities,* Reinhold Publishing Corporation, New York, 1945.

E. Spiegel, *New Towns in Israel,* Karl Kramer Verlag, Stuttgart, 1966.

C. S. Stein, "Radburn and the Radburn Idea" in *Encyclopedia of Housing,* 1949–1950.

C. S. Stein, *Toward New Towns for America,* University of Liverpool, Liverpool, 1950.

F. C. Stephenson, "Greenbelt Towns in the United States," *Town and Country Planning* **10,** 40 (Winter 1942–1943).

Stockholm: Urban Environment, Vallingby Farsta, Stockholms Stadsbygnadskontor, Stockholm, 1972.

Les centres commerciaux suedois: Experiences et realisations, Stockholm Chamber of Commerce, Stockholm, 1965, p. 39.

Swedish Planning of Town Centres, Swedish Planning Institute, Stockholm, undated, p. 54.

S. Starr, "Visionary Town Planning during the Cultural Revolution," S. Fitzpatrick, ed. *Cultural Revolution in Russia,* Indiana University Press, 1928–1931.

"Thamesmead," *Architectural Forum* (July–August 1969).

R. Thomas, "London's New Towns: A Study of Self-contained and Balanced Communities," *Political and Economic Planning Publications,* 35, (April 1969).

W. Thomas, *The Lessons of the New Towns,* Scottish Housing and Town Planning Council, Aberdeen, Oct. 3, 1963, p. 10.

"New Towns Come of Age," *Town and Country Planning,* special ed., (1968).

G. T. Trewartha, "Chinese Cities: Origins and Functions," *Annals of the Association of American Geographers* **XIII** (1952).

C. Tunnard, *The City of Man,* Charles Scribner's Sons, New York, 1953.

A. Turner and J. Smulian, "New Cities in Venezuela," *Town Planning Review* **XLII** (1) (Jan. 1971).

J. Tyrwhitt, "The Size and Spacing of Urban Communities," *J. Amer. Inst. of Planners* **XV** (Summer 1949).

J. C. Underhill, *Soviet New Towns,* HUD, Washington, D.C., 1976.

J. C. Underhill, *Soviet New Towns: An Update,* unpublished, 1987.

R. Unwin, *Nothing Gained by Overcrowding,* Garden Cities and Town Planning Association, London, 1912.

Town Planning in Practice, Unwin, London, 1909.

"Villes nouvelles en Grande Bretagne," *Cahiers I.A.U.R.P.* **XXI** (1970).

"La ville nouvelle de la Vallee de la Marne," *Cahiers I.A.U.R.P.* **XXI** (1970).

H. Von Hertzen and P. Spreiregen, *Tapiola, Building a New Town,* MIT Press, Cambridge, Mass., 1971.

H. J. Walker, "Some major technical problems encountered in the planning of Greenbelt, Maryland," *Planner's Journal* **4**(2), 34–37 (Mar.–Apr. 1938).

J. B. Ward-Perkins, *Cities of Ancient Greece and Italy: Planning in Antiquity,* George Braziller, New York, 1974.

J. Wilhelm, *Brasilia 1960—Uma Interpretacao,* 2nd. ed., Acropole, Brasilia, 1960.

A. F. Wright, "Changan" in A. J. Toynbee, *Cities of Destiny,* McGraw-Hill, New York, 1967.

F. L. Wright, *Broadacre city,* Taliesin Fellowship Publication, Oct. 1940.

G. R. Collins, "Broadacre City: Wright's Utopia Re-Considered," in *Four Great Makers of Modern Architecture,* Columbia School of Architecture, New York, 1963, pp. 58–75.

H. Wright, "The Radburn Plan," *National Real Estate Journal,* 74–76 (Sept. 30, 1929).

H. Wright, *Rehousing Urban America,* Columbia University, New York, 1934.

R. E. Wycherley, *How the Greeks Built Cities,* Macmillan & Co. Ltd., London, 1962.

L. Yutan, *Imperial Peking,* Crown Publishers, Inc., New York, 1961.

B. Zevi, *Architecture as Space,* Horizon Press, New York, 1964.

Edward G. Echeverria
Paula Echeverria
Washington, D.C.

PLASTIC LAMINATES

High pressure decorative laminate sheet (plastic laminate) has become one of the most widely used materials in the construction of residential and commercial furniture, walls, doors, and many other interior surfaced areas. It combines modern color and design aesthetics with long-lasting characteristics. Its durable surface makes it ideal for applications where other materials such as wood, metal, or synthetic fabrics would fail to withstand high impact or constant traffic. With the advance of modern technology, the durability and characteristics of plastic laminate have lent themselves for use as computer floors, doors, shipboard furniture, and many other applications, which will be discussed further in this article. Plastic laminate is widely used today in banks, airports, restaurants, hotels, and homes; it is even considered an avant-garde material by designers, who have recently used it for exotic lamps, sculptures, and jewelry.

Plastic laminate is manufactured by pressing melamine-impregnated overlay and decorative pattern paper over layers of phenolic-impregnated kraft paper at pressures of approximately 1000 psi (0.7 kg/m^2) at temperatures in excess of 275°F (135°C). Table 1 lists the plastic laminate industry's standards as set by the National Electrical Manufacturers Association (NEMA). The chosen laminate should meet or exceed these standards.

The decorative pattern paper in plastic laminate consists of a high quality pigmented α-cellulose paper. This decorative paper can consist of a rainbow of solid colors or a three to four color rotagravure printing. On woodgrain patterns, modern photography and printing methods have uncannily reproduced the fine tickings and finesse of the finest wood species. A high grade α-cellulose tissue heavily saturated with melamine resin is placed over the decorative sheet. It is this melamine overlay that provides stain and abrasion resistance as well as resistance to cigarette burns, boiling water, and common household solvents.

Prior to laminating, the decorative sheet, now cut to the appropriate width and length, is laid on top of phenolic-impregnated kraft paper; the number of sheets of kraft determines the actual thickness of the plastic laminate (ie, seven sheets of kraft are used in general-purpose, 0.050-in. (1.2-mm), products). The kraft sheet is a very

TABLE 1. Performance Properties Chart[a]

Types	Grade Designation	Nominal Thickness[b]	Thickness Tolerance[b]	Wear Resistance	Scuff Resistance	Impact Resistance	Dimensional Change		Boiling-water Resistance	High Temperature Resistance	Radiant Heat Resistance	Conductive Heat Resistance	Stain Resistance		Light Resistance[c]	Appearance	Cleanability	Surface Finish	Postforming: Formability	Postforming: Blister Resistance
NEMA Test LD 3				3.01	3.02	3.03	3.04		3.05	3.06	3.07	3.08	3.09		3.10	3.11	3.12	3.13	3.14	3.15
Units		in. (mm)	in. (mm)	cycles, min.	rating,[d] min.	in. (mm), min.	% MD, max.	% CD, max.	rating,[d] min.	rating,[d] min.	min.	rating,[d] min.	reagents 1–23 rating,[d] min.	reagents 24–29 rating,[d] min.	rating,[d] min.	defects	cycles, max.		in. (mm) radius, min.	min.
General purpose	GP 50	0.050 (1.270)	±0.005 (±0.127)	400	NE	50 (1270)	0.5	0.9	NE	SL	125	NE	NE	M	SL	no ABC defects	25	see LD 3–1.04		
	GP 38	0.038 (0.965)	±0.005 (±0.127)	400	NE	35 (889)	0.6	1.0	NE	SL	100	NE	NE	M	SL		25			
	GP 28[e]	0.028 (0.711)	±0.005 (±0.127)	200	NE	20 (508)	0.7	1.2	NE	SL	80	NE	NE	M	SL		25			
	GP 20[e]	0.020 (0.508)	±0.005 (±0.127)	200	NE	15 (381)	0.8	1.3	NE	SL	60	NE	NE	M	SL		25			
Postforming	PF 42	0.042 (1.067)	±0.005 (±0.127)	400	NE	30 (762)	1.1	1.4	SL	SL	100	NE	NE	M	SL		25		⅝ (15.875)	55
	PF 30[e]	0.030 (0.762)	±0.005 (±0.127)	300	NE	20 (508)	1.1	1.4	SL	SL	80	NE	NE	M	SL		25		½ (12.700)	40
Cabinet liner	CL 20	0.020 (0.508)	±0.005 (±0.127)	50	NE	10 (254)	1.2	2.0	M	M		M	M	M	M		50			
Backer	BK 20	0.020 (0.508)	±0.005 (±0.127)																	
	BK 50	0.050 (1.270)	±0.005 (±0.127)																	
Specific purpose	SP 125	0.125 (3.175)	±0.008 (±0.203)	400	NE	75 (1905)	0.3	0.7	NE	SL	200	NE	NE	M	SL	no ABC defects	25			
	SP 62	0.062 (1.575)	±0.005 (±0.127)	400	NE	55 (1397)	0.5	0.9	NE	SL	150	NE	NE	M	SL		25			
High wear	HW 120	0.120 (3.048)	±0.008 (±0.203)	3000	NE	75 (1905)	0.3	0.7	NE	SL	200	NE	NE	M	SL		25			
	HW 80	0.080 (2.032)	±0.008 (±0.203)	3000	NE	40 (1016)	0.4	0.8	NE	SL	175	NE	NE	M	SL		25			
	HW 62	0.062 (1.575)	±0.005 (±0.127)	3000	NE	35 (889)	0.5	0.9	NE	SL	150	NE	NE	M	SL		25			
Fire rated[f]	FR 62	0.062 (1.575)	±0.005 (±0.127)	400	NE	55 (1397)	0.5	0.9	NE	SL	125		NE	M	SL		25			
	FR 50	0.050 (1.270)	±0.005 (±0.127)	400	NE	45 (1143)	0.5	0.9	NE	SL	75		NE	M	SL		25			
	FR 32	0.032 (0.813)	±0.005 (±0.127)	300	NE	20 (508)	0.7	1.2	NE	SL	50		NE	M	SL		25			

[a] NEMA Standard 12–31–1980. Courtesy of the National Electrical Manufacturers Association.

[b] See LD 3–1.07.

[c] Environmental conditions have caused certain colors to be subject to fugitive changes in appearance and the manufacturer should be consulted.

[d] Rating system: NE = no effect, SL = slight effect, M = moderate effect, X = severe effect.

[e] Not recommended for all applications; consult the manufacturer for recommended uses.

[f] Consult the manufacturer for specific flame resistance properties such as flame spread rating, fuel contribution values, and smoke generation characteristics because these NEMA standards do not specify these properties (see LD 3–1.08).

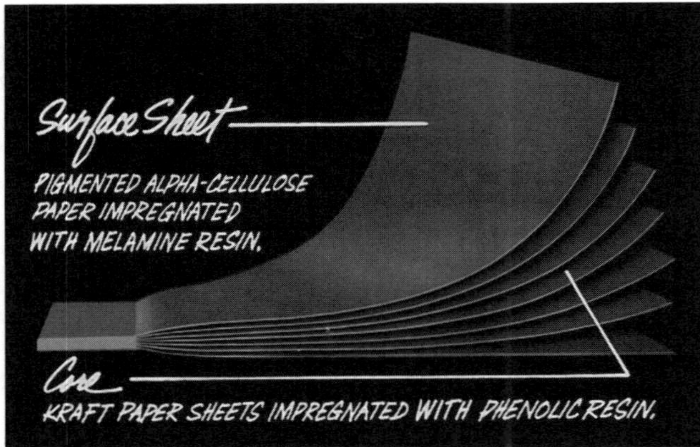

Figure 1. Cutaway cross section of plastic laminate sheet. Courtesy of NEVAMAR Corp.

tough and stable paper that provides a mechanically strong core for the plastic laminate sheet.

Each pack or assembly of sheets is then inserted into multiopening presses with about 10–12 sheets per opening. The amount of time and heat in the presses will vary with different grades and thicknesses of laminate. After this process, the backs of the sheets are sanded to provide a uniform thickness and to give a rough surface to which it is easy to adhere. The sheets are also trimmed in width and length and are usually ½–¾ in. (13–19 mm) over the required size to facilitate fabrication (Fig. 1).

HISTORIC BACKGROUND

Modern plastic laminate had its origins in the electrical insulation industry. Shellac laminates developed in Switzerland by Emil Hoefely were brought to the United States in 1908 and licensed to the electrical industry for transformer insulation. But it is Leo Baekeland's phenolic resin, which acted as a binder for the laminated plastic sheets, that is most responsible for today's plastic laminate. The properties gained by using the phenolic resins, such as dimensional stability, good dielectric strength, and resistance to moisture absorption, make it ideal for electrical insulation.

Later, C. E. Skinner of Westinghouse Corp. worked with Baekeland in his Yonkers home and basement laboratory. It was Skinner's idea to substitute Bakelite for shellac in the manufacture of Micarta. Their early tests were complete failures. The difficulty was in the technique of coating the papers to adapt to their machinery. Later, an engineer at Westinghouse Corp., Dan J. O'Connor, conceived the idea of slitting phenolic rolled tubing and pressing it flat under heat and pressure for the final curing of the phenolic resins. This was the first phenolic laminate; it was patented by Westinghouse Corp. in 1918. The Micarta Division of Westinghouse grew from O'Connor's work. O'Connor and Herb Faber, from Westinghouse Sales Division, later started the Formica Insulation Co. The name was rumored to be derived from "*for*-merly *Mica*-rta" employees. The early uses of laminated phenolic materials were primarily as gears for automobiles, insulation parts, refrigerator breaker strips, and other industrial applications. Plastic laminate manufacturing facilities played an important part in World War II. It offered very high strength products for aircraft manufacturers. The P-51 aircraft had 88 parts made of Formica laminations. Bazooka barrels, radio, radar, ships, and aircraft propellers all had laminated phenolic parts to gain extended life and wear.

After the war, plastic laminate was used in very high volume for printed-circuitry boards laminated with etched copper laminate. The use of the material came with the advent of the television. Television tuners used the printed-circuitry boards; the boards were made using copper foil. O. C. Black and Don Mackey of RCA (now part of General Electric Co.) are credited with the development of etched-circuitry boards in 1947.

Decorative laminates, as they are known and used today, were pioneered by the Formica Corp. Formica developed printed wood-grain panels for radio furniture and marble designs for soda-fountain and diner countertops. This development quickly moved to the furniture trade, which saw its practical applications in dinette tops and commercial furniture where cigarette burns and cleaning chemicals damaged widely used natural wood surfaces. An underlayer of metal foils popularized its use in the kitchen to minimize surface burns. In 1935, its widespread use in the ocean liner *Queen Mary* expanded the use of decorative laminates.

Melamine resins, one of the hardest plastics known, contributed to the growth of plastic laminate. Developed after the war, melamine did more to revolutionize plastic laminate than any other postwar development. The melamine surface in various thicknesses provides the wear resistance that makes plastic laminate practical on applications such as doors, computer-room floors, and walls. Today, there is a grade of plastic laminate for ships' bulkheads, static-dissipative plastic for clean rooms, chemically resistant sheets for laboratories, and even fade-resistant exterior grades.

Modern plastic laminate has achieved its sophistication not only in various technical grades, but more importantly, by product design. Most manufacturers today maintain hundreds of solid colors in the vogue colorations, high fidelity wood grains, geometric designs, and various textures. It is the texture that designers today point out as the next important phase for plastic laminate. Today, high gloss lacquerlike colors and grainy and three-dimensional-like surfaces are widely used.

PRODUCT TYPES

General-purpose, 0.5 ± 0.005 in. (0.5 ± 0.127 mm) thickness plastic laminate is manufactured for application to interior horizontal and vertical surfaces where a decorative and stain-resistant surface is required. Horizontal applications include surfaces of countertops, tabletops, residential and commercial furniture, vanities, case goods, store fixtures, columns, and window stools. Vertical applications include wall panels, laminated interior doors, bath enclosures, toilet partitions, elevator cab interiors, and cabinets.

General-purpose material is highly recommended anywhere where impact resistance is important as compared to the thinner grades. It is especially recommended when using glossy, high sheen finishes because the extra thickness prevents telegraphing of the substrate surface imperfections.

Vertical surface grade, 0.028 ± 0.005 in. (0.7 ± 0.127 mm), is manufactured for application to interior vertical surfaces such as wall panels, cabinet doors, case good fronts and sides, store fixtures, fascias, trim, and furniture. Vertical surfacing material has all of the wear and stain-resistant characteristics of general-purpose laminate, but it does not have the same impact resistance. It is ideal for furniture where impact resistance is not a concern, because it hides the brown seam line much better. Postforming grades are manufactured for surfaces where a directional single radius is required. It offers an attractive edge-free appearance. Suggested minimum radii are as follows:

Horizontal forming grade 0.042 in. (1.07 mm)
¼ in. (0.64 mm) inside radius
⅝ in. (15.8 mm) outside radius
Vertical forming grade 0.030 in. (0.76 mm)
¼ in. (0.64 mm) inside radius
½ in. (12.7 mm) outside radius

Recommended shop-applied heat is 313–340°F (156–171°C). Each laminate manufacturer's cure temperature varies slightly; the postformer should consult the laminate manufacturer. Postforming grades are manufactured in the same way as conventional laminates except a specially impregnated crepe paper is used that fully cures when shop heated. Postforming laminates are applied with the use of specialized heating equipment. This equipment can be a highly sophisticated postforming manufacturing line hundreds of feet long that applies the adhesive, cures it, and then heat-forms the plastic. In some areas of the United States, heat rods are used that are simple 8- or 10-ft heating elements used to soften the plastic. Recently, Pittcon Industries of Riverdale, Maryland, developed a method of chemically forming plastic laminate. This advanced technique permits bending and forming of the plastic laminate, which is not feasible in the heat process. Unusual shapes and radii are thus achieved.

Postforming laminate is most widely used in countertops, furniture tops, picture frames, and modern curved furniture (Fig. 2). Laminated floor tile (LFT) grade is manufactured specifically for floor surfacing on access flooring systems. It complies with requirements for low static generation and retention, coupled with a washable surface requiring no waxing. LFT is manufactured using a specially formulated surface sheet over a melamine-impregnated print-paper sheet. The core layer of phenolic impregnated draft papers is balanced to control dimensional stability.

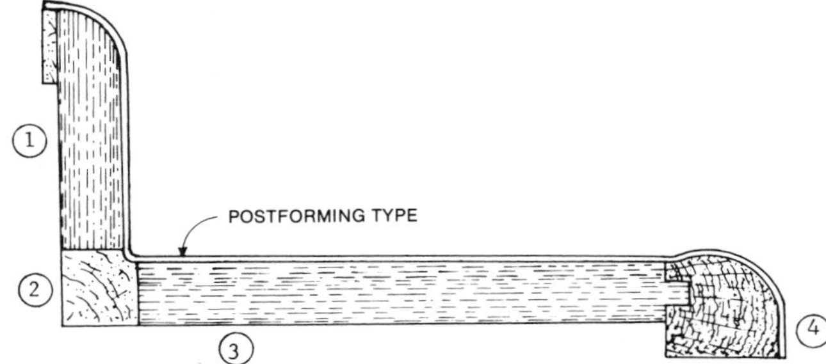

Figure 2. Typical postformed top. (1) Backsplash; (2) Cove molding; (3) Deck; (4) Bullnose molding. Courtesy of the National Electrical Manufacturers Association.

LFT is not designed for application on any subfloor stratum other than access-flooring manufacturers' steel, aluminum, wood, or particleboard components. It is not recommended for exterior use.

Thicknesses available are as follows.

FL-12 0.123 ± 0.011 in. (3.12 ± 0.28 mm)
FL-8 0.080 ± 0.008 in. (2.03 ± 0.203 mm)
FL-6 0.062 ± 0.005 in. (1.6 ± 0.13 mm)

LFT is available in full-size sheets or cut to size. Colors available for LFT are limited, so manufacturer's information must be consulted.

Fire-rated (FR) grade is manufactured for use on interior surfaces where fire-retardant decorative wear and stain-resistant surface is required. It is important to note that fire-rated plastic laminate achieves a Class 1 rating only when bonded to an approved fire-rated board or core with an approved fire-rated adhesive system. Consult the laminate manufacturer fire test results and method of construction. Underwriters Laboratory, in Chicago, maintains approved plastic laminate FR systems on file. Fire-rated plastic laminate is shipped to customers with the Underwriters Laboratory label affixed to the surface of each sheet. The fire-rated Class 1 is tested in accordance with the ASTM E84 tunnel test. Federal specifications are met by most fire-rated constructions, plus various state and local codes.

Chemical-resistant grades are manufactured for laboratory tops where the possibility of a chemical spill is such as to disqualify high pressure decorative laminate tops. These grades have a high resistance to chemical attack from organic solvents, alkalis, and acids. Specific uses are for chemistry laboratory tops and dental laboratory counters as well as in photographic and medical laboratories. Chemical-resistant grades use a special resin formulation of polyester. Contact the plastic laminate manufacturer for specifications and recommended use.

OTHER NEW DEVELOPMENTS AND PRODUCTS

Solid core laminate is a special laminate made with backing paper of the same color as the α-cellulose print sheet. Its main purpose is to hide the seam lines normally found in decorative-laminate construction. Also, in cases of excessive wear or damage, the same color appears throughout.

Abrasion-resistant print is manufactured similarly to conventional high pressure laminate except that it has a thin deposit of microscopic particles of aluminum oxide on the conventional melamine layer. This oxide layer provides superior abrasion and scuff resistance and yet does not obscure the color of the pigment in the surface sheet.

Continuous laminate is a recent outcome of the use of advanced modern equipment. The traditional method of manufacturing plastic laminate is a high pressure multiopening press as described earlier. Continuous laminate is manufactured in coil form. The very long production line starts with coils of kraft and phenolic-impregnated papers and heat and pressure are applied before the laminate is recoiled. The result, once cut, can be coil laminate or sheets.

Metal-faced laminate incorporates solid metal surfaces such as polished aluminum, brass, or copper over the kraft-paper backing. They are manufactured in the conventional multiopening press and are used similarly to standard plastic laminate.

PRODUCT USES

The list of uses for high pressure laminate has grown as technological and aesthetic improvements have been made to the product in recent years. The product's initial commercial use, and probably still the principal one, is in furniture, but new areas have emerged as listed below.

1. Walls–durable and easy to clean.
2. Access floors—antistatic, durable.
3. Ship's bulkheads—fire retardant, easy to clean.
4. Picture frames—easy to form to tight radii.
5. Doors—high impact resistance, long lasting, easy maintenance.
6. Metal core laminate—extra impact resistance.
7. Decorative ceilings.
8. Columns—formable and impact resistant.
9. Toilet partitions.
10. Soffits.

PRODUCT DESIGNS

From its early beginnings of gold sparkle and nondescript patterns, decorative laminates have come a long way (Fig. 3). Today almost every U.S. manufacturer offers between 120 and 200 modern-trend solid colors, many excellent reproduction wood grains, and abstract designs. In addition, a variety of finishes is usually available in all of the groups listed above, such as high gloss finishes, grainy textures, geometric finishes, natural slate, lineal finishes, and satin textures.

INSTALLATION

Plastic laminate should be bonded to a core material such as plywood, particleboard, flakeboard, or metal using adhesives, depending on the service for which the assembly is intended and on the bonding facilities available. In all cases, the adhesive manufacturer's instructions should be closely followed. The adhesives used will depend on the type of manufacturing equipment and procedure used by the builder of the furniture components. Generally, contact cements (solvent based) are most widely used because they provide an excellent bond while setting or curing very quickly, usually 10–12 min, and are relatively low in cost. The cure time can be accelerated by heating ovens or UV curing.

Urea adhesives provide the best bond between plastic laminate and the substrate but usually require longer cure times, up to 24 h. Widely used also is poly(vinyl acetate) (PVA) based adhesive. PVA is best known as carpenter's white glue. The components must be clamped or kept under pressure during the cure period. Thermosetting adhesives can be applied in sheet form, placed between the plastic laminate and the substrate, and then activated by heat. The builder and the adhesives manufacturer should recommend the best method and adhesive type to be used for specific construction applications.

Care should be taken to ensure that a moisture imbalance does not exist between the plastic laminate and the substrate prior to fabrication. Inside corners of cutouts should have a minimum radius of ⅛ in. (3.18 mm) with edges filed smooth to prevent stress cracking (Figs. 4 and 5).

Figure 3. Modern plastic laminate uses. Courtesy of the Decorative Laminate Products Association.

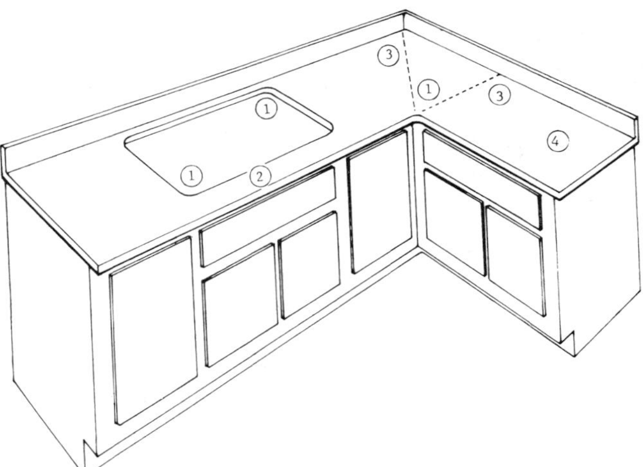

Figure 4. Proper installation guidelines. (1) Radius these corners; (2) Make this area as wide as possible; (3) Radius or seam this area as broken lines indicate; (4) Support long spans well. Courtesy of the National Electrical Manufacturers Association.

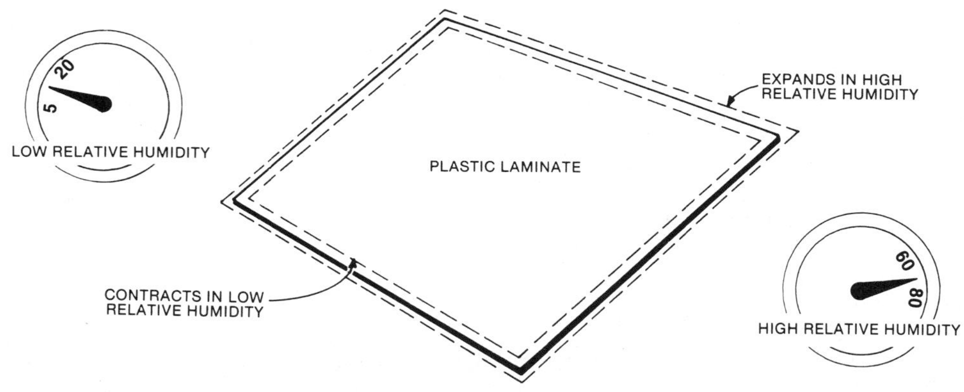

Figure 5. Effect of extreme humidity conditions on plastic laminate. Courtesy of the National Electrical Manufacturers Association.

CARE AND CLEANING

Surfaces of plastic laminate should be cleaned with a damp cloth and ordinary soap or a household ammoniated liquid detergent. Abrasive cleaners should not be used. Stubborn stains may require use of organic solvents such as alcohol, acetone, or other ketone such as methyl ethyl ketone (MEK), or lacquer thinner. Bleaching agents such as hypochlorites have also been found to be very effective. The user should be aware that organic solvents are flammable.

PRODUCT LIMITATIONS

Plastic laminate is not recommended for exterior use or direct application to plaster, gypsum, or concrete walls, or for use in areas exposed to temperatures in excess of 275°F. Thicknesses below 0.05 in. (0.5 mm) should not be used on horizontal surfaces. Fabrication should not occur at temperatures below 65°F (18°C). Both the plastic laminate and the substrate should be acclimatized in the shop for at least 48 hours prior to fabrication at room temperatures, approximately 75°F (23.9°C).

Fabrication and installation information is available by contacting the Plastic Laminate Association, National Electrical Manufacturer's Association, 2101 L Street, N.W., Washington, D.C. Also, free information and technical assistance are available by telephone or mail inquiry by contacting any of the U.S. plastic laminate manufacturers.

BIBLIOGRAPHY

General References

Installation Guide, National Electrical Manufacturers Association (NEMA), Washington, D.C.,

Plastics History—USA, Cahners Books, Boston, Mass.

Modern Plastics Encyclopedia, McGraw-Hill Inc., New York, 1976–1977.

See also ADHESIVES; AMINO RESINS; ARCHITECTURAL WOODWORK; PHENOLIC RESINS; PLASTICS

CHARLES CUSTIN
Tech-Aerofoam Products, Inc.
Miami, Florida

PLASTICS

Although plastics are relative newcomers to building, and although the total tonnage used is small compared to traditional materials such as wood, masonry, concrete, and steel, the rate of growth is large, and the number of different applications is extensive.

Plastics are synthetic organic high polymers, chemists' terminology meaning that raw materials (petroleum, natural gas, coal, cellulose, etc) are changed into new forms based on long-chain molecules or networks consisting of large numbers of repeating connected atomic clusters called monomers. Monomers are joined together or polymerized into polymers by chemical reactions promoted by combinations of heat, pressure, and catalysis. These polymers are in turn raw materials to be fabricated subsequently into final forms. In some instances, polymerization is complete during initial manufacturing and no chemical reaction occurs in final fabrication. This is particularly true of thermoplastics. In others, the thermosets, polymerization is only partial and is completed during final fabrication. All plastics are plastic at some stage, that is, they can be shaped, usually by heat, pressure, or both, but sometimes merely by casting.

As is true of wood and metals, there are many species or types of plastics, but relatively few, perhaps 20–30 principal classes, are employed significantly in building. Each class may have many variants, depending on composition and fabricating processes (1–5).

FAMILIES

Plastics are conveniently divided into two families, both important in building. Plastics in the first family consist of long entangled molecular chains whose flexibility increases with temperature. They can be softened and hardened repeatedly by heating and cooling. At high enough temperatures they are soft and may be liquid. As they cool they become progressively leathery, increasingly rigid, and finally glassy and brittle, the transition temperatures varying with the species of plastics and their formulations. These are, appropriately, called thermoplastics. Members of the second family pass through a plastic stage only once and then harden irreversibly by linking molecules together or by forming rigid networks. Heating after the linkage occurs merely makes them harder. Because heat was required to harden the first of these plastics, they were called thermosetting, and the term has persisted, even though some important types harden at ordinary temperatures. The difference in temperature-response of thermoplastics and thermosets often determines the kinds of building applications suitable for a given plastic.

Most plastics stem from a single monomer, but several monomers can be strung together on the same molecule. These are called copolymers. Properties may differ from those of the single-monomer types. Poly(vinyl chloride), for example, is hard and quite brittle at ordinary temperatures, and vinyl acetate is very soft, but the copolymer is tough and flexible, widely used as sheet and film [see Poly (vinyl chloride)]. Similarly, ABS, a copolymer of acrylonitrile, butadiene, and styrene, is tough and strong [see ABS (Acrylonitrile–butadiene–styrene)]. Copolymers, evidently, can offer an extended range of properties. Mixtures of polymers, called alloys, also broaden the range of properties.

ADDITIVES

Properties of plastics can be greatly altered by the incorporation of additives. Chief among these are plasticizers, fillers, colorants, and stabilizers.

Plasticizers

Plastics that are hard and brittle at ordinary temperatures can be made pliable and flexible by incorporating plasticizers. By acting like lubricants among the entangled molecules of thermoplastics, they have much the same softening effect as increased temperature. Plasticizers are largely ineffective in the linked structure of thermosets.

Compatibility between plastic and plasticizer is important. Some poor plasticizers, usually relatively cheap, migrate to the surface with time, leaving a greasy surface on a brittle substrate. Good plasticizers are nontoxic, do not react with and degrade the plastic, do not affect other components such as dyes and pigments, and are efficient. They may enhance or reduce resistance to weather or fire (see Durability, Fire).

Fillers

Both thermoplastics and thermosets may have fillers added to enhance performance, economics, or processability. Unmodified phenolics, for example, are hard and brittle, abrasive in molds, tend to shrink and crack during molding, and cost more than many fillers. By adding up to 50% wood flour, a good general-purpose molding material results, easier to mold and less expensive than pure phenolic. Electrical properties are enhanced by adding powdered mica. Urea formaldehyde and melamine formaldehyde are similarly modified by, for example, adding purified alpha cellulose (see Melamine; Urea Formaldehyde).

Impact modifiers are important fillers. Many plastics are hard and brittle at use temperatures. Thermoplastics may be toughened by copolymerization or by plasticizers. Both thermosets and thermoplastics can have impact resistance increased by incorporating fillers, especially fibrous, to absorb and spread high local stresses and to act as crack arresters. Many fibers, natural and synthetic, organic and inorganic, are used, usually chopped into short lengths (see Fibrous Composites, Types of Fibrous Reinforcements). Among them are cellulose such as cotton, jute, sisal, and pulp; fibrous glass; inorganics including metal and ceramic; and synthetics such as nylon, polyester, and rayon.

Colorants

Plastics range from completely clear through translucent to opaque. Acrylics and polystyrene, for example, are clear, polyamides (nylon) are limited, and others, such as phenolic molding powders, are dark, and only dark colors are possible. Dyes are suitable for transparent colors, whereas pigments result in opaque or, at best, translucent colors. Whether a plastic part is colorfast depends largely on the permanence of the dyes or pigments. Colorants should not react unfavorably with the basic resin or other constituents such as plasticizers (see Light Transmission).

Stabilizers

Some plastics are inherently resistant to deteriorating influences such as weathering and exposure to ultraviolet radiation (see Durability). The natural resistance of others may be poor but can often be greatly enhanced by the addition of stabilizers. Polyethylene, for example, deteriorates rapidly when exposed to sunlight. If approximately 2% of finely divided carbon black is added, resistance to ultraviolet is enormously increased (see Polyethylene). Similar increases are achieved with other plastics. As is true of plasticizers, good stabilizers must be compatible with the base resin.

SALIENT CHARACTERISTICS

Salient characteristics of plastics important in building are as follows:

1. *Formability*. Plastics must be formed into final shapes. The designer can choose efficient shapes, limited by fabrication (see Fabrication). One-piece construction is often feasible, eliminating joints.
2. *Light Transmission, Color*. Plastics range from highly transparent to opaque. Integral color allows fabrication without loss of color (see Colorants; Light Transmission).
3. *Corrosion and Solvent Resistance*. Plastics do not corrode as metals do and can be used in corrosive environments (see Tanks). Solvents attack plastics selectively; some resist most commonly found solvents (see Polyethylene). A few are immune to all but the most aggressive solvents (see Fluoroplastics).
4. *Ductility, Impact Resistance*. Plastics range from hard and brittle to flexible and tough (see Fillers; Toughness and Hardness).

5. *Wear Resistance.* Although plastics are soft compared to some other materials, wear resistance is often excellent (see Toughness and Hardness; Hardware).
6. *Light Weight.* Plastics are lighter than many other building materials. Structures can often be thin (see Shells; Sandwiches; Structural Shapes).
7. *Strength and Stiffness.* Strength varies from low to extremely high in composites, especially on a strength to weight basis. Stiffness, even in composites, is generally low (see Strength, Stiffness).
8. *Thermal Expansion.* Even in composites, thermal expansion is high (see Thermal Expansion and Contraction).
9. *Thermal Conductivity.* Ranges in thermal conductivity are from moderate to very low in foams (see Thermal Conductivity; Foams; Thermal Insulation).
10. *Tailorability.* Strength of composites can be tailored to meet stresses (see Fibrous Composites; Fabrication).
11. *Electrical Properties.* Plastics are insulators (see Electrical Fittings).

THERMOPLASTICS

As noted previously, thermoplastics are long-chain high polymers, the chains entangled among each other (1–3). They become more flexible with heat, allowing deformation of the mass. They become less flexible as they cool, leading to increased rigidity and hardness, ultimately to brittleness. These materials can be softened and hardened repeatedly by heating and cooling, hence the term thermoplastic.

ABS (Acrylonitrile–butadiene–styrene)

In this three-way polymer, acrylonitrile contributes aging resistance, heat stability, and chemical resistance; butadiene imparts toughness, impact strength, and low-temperature properties; and styrene adds luster and rigidity. Overall properties change by varying the ratios of the constituents, but toughness and ductility are prominent. Resistance to ultraviolet light calls for UV-absorbing additives. Flame retardance depends on halogenated additives or on alloying with polymers such as PVC [see Poly (vinyl chloride)].

Pipes and fittings, especially drain, waste, and vent, are the largest use of ABS. Refrigerator door liners and tanks are almost always ABS. Other uses include automotive, boats, power tools, faucets, shower heads, and bathtubs and surrounds (see Piping; Plumbing Fixtures).

Closely related olefin–styrene–acrylonitrile (OSA) provides weather-resistant dark-colored building components and solar-collector parts. ACS (acrylonitrile–chlorinated polyethylene–styrene) is more flame-retardant and heat-resistant. It excels in weatherability.

Acetal

Acetal is a crystalline polymer of formaldehyde. General-purpose acetals exhibit toughness at temperatures as low as −40°F (−40°C). Good wear and friction properties can be enhanced by fluorocarbon additions (see Fluoroplastics). A plumbing grade (valves, gears, bearings, tubes, etc) can be used continuously to 150°F (66°C) and in intermittent hot water up to 180°F (83°C) (see Plumbing Fixtures). Weather resistance of acetals and copolymers is enhanced by UV stabilizers and carbon black, making them usable for continuous outdoor exposure.

Acrylic (PMMA)

Acrylics comprise a family, but most building applications are based on polymethyl methacrylate (PMMA). It has excellent optical clarity, color stability, exceptional weatherability, and is lightweight. It is completely colorable with both dyes and pigments, ranging from fully transparent to opaque. Some formulations transmit, others absorb ultraviolet radiation (see Light Transmission).

Applications in building are mainly for glazing, lighting, and decorative features, especially where weather resistance, light weight, resistance to breakage, and formability are important (see Illumination). Dome-shaped skylights, for example, are vacuum-formed (see Vacuum; Thermoforming). Other uses include plumbing fixtures, spandrels, lighting fixtures of all kinds, and illuminated signs. Thin films and sheets provide protective decorative overlays for metal and other materials.

Cellulosics

Cellulosics are chemically modified cellulose, a natural high polymer derived, for example, from wood pulp or cotton linters. Plain cellulose can be made into fiber (rayon) and transparent film (cellophane), but cellulose plastics require chemical transformation. Cellulose derivatives of interest in building are cellulose nitrate (CN), cellulose acetate (CA), cellulose propionate (CP), cellulose butyrate (CB), and copolymers. Cellulose nitrate is tough and is used for lacquers, tool handles, and similar applications, as is cellulose acetate. The extreme flammability of cellulose nitrate limits its use. Cellulose acetate–propionate is used in lighting fixtures and displays. Cellulose acetate–butyrate is most widely used in building for such applications as skylights, curtain walls, small weather shelters, and, in especially weather-resistant formulations, for outdoor signs (see Illumination).

Fluoroplastics

The fluoroplastics are generally characterized by resistance to aggressive environments, including extremes of weather, and temperatures ranging from near absolute zero to 260°C (500°F). Special processes are often required to fabricate finished parts. Polytetrafluoroethylene (PTFE) is the most often used fluoroplastic. In addition to being immune to all but the most exotic organic solvents, it has extremely low frictional resistance and good antistick properties. Tough but soft, it has poor resistance to wear unless specially formulated. With fibrous and other reinforcements, it provides bearing pads such as pads for truss supports and for steam lines that expand and contract, sliding over the nonsticking surfaces. It is used as lining for piping, valves, and other components subject to extremely corrosive conditions. Other fluorocarbons employed in building include polyvinylidene fluoride (PVDF) for durable long-lived finishes for industrial buildings, and polyvinyl fluoride (PVF), used as tough, clear, flexible film possessing outstanding weather resistance, and commonly laminated to opaque or light-transmitting substrates (see Walls; Partitions). It is employed as outer glazing in solar energy collectors (see Solar Energy Collectors).

Polyamide (Nylon)

Principal properties of interest of polyamide (PA) are toughness, wear resistance, low friction, high strength, and good chemical resistance. Many variants are possible, but commercial resins come in two families and are designated, for example 6, 11, 12, and 6/6, 6/9, 6/10, and 6/12, with 6 and 6/6 most common. Moisture has a plasticizing effect, and a small percentage is necessary to maintain toughness. In extremely dry atmospheres, brittleness may develop. Long exposure to ultraviolet radiation results in degradation. This can be combatted by both colorless stabilizers and carbon black, the latter the most effective for long exposure to sunlight. Strength and stiffness are greatly enhanced by incorporating chopped glass fiber (up to 40%) and other mineral additives. Applications are generally those that take advantage of moldability, strength, toughness, wear resistance, and low friction, such as hardware parts, snap fits, parts requiring thin sections, housings, handles of power tools, and casters for furniture (see Hardware; Cabinetwork).

Polybutylene

Polybutylene is useful in building mainly as pipe for cold and hot water plumbing and for solar installations. In larger sizes it is employed to transport abrasive or corrosive materials in mines and chemical industries (see Piping; Plumbing Fixtures; Ducts).

Polycarbonate

Polycarbonate (PC) is a thermoplastic polyester based on carbonic acid. Its building uses stem primarily from a combination of high transparency, weather resistance, toughness, strength, complete colorability, and processability by a wide variety of standard fabrication methods for thermoplastics, including rotational molding for large parts (see Fabrication; Rotational Molding). It can be foamed to a broad range of densities. In building, principal uses are in glazing, including bullet-resistant laminates and explosion resistance, lighting, and decorative uses calling for transparent and opaque colors. It is widely employed as glazing for solar installations (see Solar Energy Collectors).

Polyethylene

Polyethylene (PE) is a high-volume lightweight plastic with diverse applications in many fields. Although all types of polyethylene are light in weight, four principal types are recognized, depending on density (Table 1).

Table 1. Types of Polyethylene[a]

Type	Maximum Density, g/cm^3
1	0.910–0.925
2	0.926–0.940
3	0.941–0.959
4	0.960–higher

[a] Data from the American Society for Testing and Materials.

Commercial designations include low-density polyethylene (LDPE), medium-density polyethylene (MDPE), high-density polyethylene (HDPE), linear low-density polyethylene (LLDPE), and ultrahigh-molecular-weight polyethylene (UHMWPE). Properties differ among the densities and the processes (high-pressure and low-pressure) by which they are made. Polyethylene is generally soft, waxy, flexible, and of medium strength, but hardness can vary considerably, as can toughness and other properties. Resistance to sunlight is poor except when formulated with UV stabilizers, of which carbon black is best, but colorless stabilizers can improve this property.

Although polyethylene is essentially thermoplastic, it can be cross-linked into a more rigid, less temperature-sensitive thermoset by chemical cross-linking and by high-voltage radiation. Various copolymers are available.

In building, a major use is as film for moisture barriers in building envelopes and under concrete slabs (see Moisture Barriers). Piping is widely used in irrigation and plumbing lines (see Piping). Wire and cable insulation takes advantage of good electrical properties (see Electrical Fittings).

Polyphenylene-based

Because modified polyphenylene oxide exhibits resistance to high temperatures, impact, and flame as well as good electrical properties, it is used in devices such as meters, timers, outlet and ceiling boxes, and fuse boxes. Modified polyphenylene ether resists prolonged exposure to hot water (180°F, 83°C) and is consequently used in pumps and plumbing (see Plumbing Fixtures).

Polypropylene

Polypropylene (PP), in addition to being of low density (0.90–0.91 g/cm^3), provides good chemical resistance, electrical insulation, stiffness, impact strength, heat resistance, abrasion resistance, and resistance to fatigue and stress-cracking. The plain homopolymer may be copolymerized with ethylene and others to modify its properties. Because of its temperature resistance, polypropylene is used in piping and other plumbing applications (see Plumbing Fixtures). Integral hinges are formed with lids of containers, for example, because of polypropylene's ability to withstand repeated bending or folding without cracking. Low-temperature resistance results from copolymerization with ethylene or combining with rubber. Panels and molded seats use foamed varieties.

Polystyrene

Polystyrene (PS) has long been employed in building in various forms. Crystal polystyrene is transparent and has good electrical properties but limited impact resistance. The impact grades have butadiene added to increase toughness and strength. Expandable polystyrene (EPS) has a blowing agent (usually pentane) added, which becomes gaseous at elevated temperatures and expands the polystyrene into a foam. It is as a foam that polystyrene finds its greatest use in building. It may be extruded into "logs" to be cut into slabs and blocks, or may be in the form of beads to be expanded into molded shapes, slab stock, and other forms (see Foams, Thermal Insulation).

Poly(vinyl chloride) (PVC)

Of all of the plastics employed in building, PVC finds the most widespread use, both in volume and number of applications. At the same time, construction is the largest market for PVC. Poly(vinyl chloride) is one of a family of "vinyl" polymers, including the following:

1. Poly(vinyl acetate) (PVC), used in latex paints, adhesives and surface coatings.
2. Poly(vinyl alcohol) (PVAL) for sizings and adhesives.
3. Poly(vinyl formal) (PVF) for enamels such as wire coating.
4. Poly(vinyl butyral) (PVB) for interlayers in safety glass, and in tough upholstery.
5. Poly(vinyl fluoride) (PVF), for weather-resistant outdoor films and coatings (see Fluoroplastics).
6. Poly(vinylidene chloride) (PVDC) for vapor-passage resistant film, eg, food packaging, and as corrosion-resistant lining for steel pipe.

Properties of PVC attractive for building include good strength; resistance to weather, water, and corrosion; toughness and dent resistance; hardness ranging from hard and brittle to soft and flexible; and good electrical properties. To achieve these ranges of properties, PVC is copolymerized with many of the other vinyls listed above and with various graft and block polymers and is compounded with plasticizers, many fillers, stabilizers, and impact modifiers. It may be clear or opaque, and it is compounded with organic and inorganic pigments. All fabricating processes are employed (see Fabrication). Liquid formulations are achieved with high plasticizer content (plastisols) and added organic solvents (organosols). Plastisols are foamed to form cushioning materials, eg, flooring, carpet backing, and upholstery (see Floors).

The largest single outlet is for pipe of all kinds, including pressure pipe for water supply, irrigation, and chemical processing, and nonpressure pipe for drain, waste, and vent (DWC) (see Piping). Chlorinated PVC is found in residential hot water systems. Other building uses include siding, window frames and sash, gutters and downspouts, interior molding and trim, and gaskets. Flooring sheet and tile, often foam-backed; wall coverings; upholstery; shower curtains; housewares; components of appliances; and refrigerator parts are other major applications (see Walls; Floors; Rainware; Cabinetwork; Masonry Adjuncts; Piping; Gaskets; Partitions).

Styrene–Acrylonitrile

Styrene–acrylonitrile (SAN) plastics have the gloss and clarity of polystyrene with higher heat-deflection temperature and better toughness. Among other uses are in appliances, including hardware knobs and housewares (see Hardware).

THERMOSETS

As noted previously, thermosets are cross-linked chain molecules or interlinked networks of repeating monomeric units (1–3). Until the cross-linking or interlinking is well advanced, the mass can be softened and shaped; ie, it is plastic. But when cross-linking or interlinking is complete, irreversible hardening has set in. This is called thermosetting. In the original manufacturing process, linking is stopped short of completion and is completed during final fabrication into finished objects. In some cases, called "condensation polymerization," a by-product such as water is given off during network formation and must be accommodated or disposed of, as by "breathing" presses or molds (see Fabrication).

Epoxies

Like unsaturated polyesters, epoxies (EP) are thermosetting (see Polyesters). Because of similarities, epoxies and unsaturated polyesters are often used for the same purposes, but the somewhat more complex curing and fabricating processes and higher cost of epoxies mean that they are generally employed in building when the polyesters will not do. Different formulations are employed for weatherability and for heat, flame, chemical, and electrical resistance.

Because of their brittleness, unreinforced epoxies cannot be used structurally, but when reinforced with glass fibers and other fibrous, laminar, or particulate reinforcements, they provide excellent structural materials (see Fibrous Composites). Adhesion to many materials is excellent. Consequently, among the most common building applications are reinforced plastics, laminates, crack fillers, industrial and decorative (eg, terrazzo) flooring, and adhesives for metals, masonry, and concretes. A major use is in heavy-duty protective coatings.

Melamine Formaldehyde (MF) and Urea Formaldehyde

Melamine formaldehyde (MF) and urea formaldehyde (UF) are aminoplastics possessing similar properties. Both can be colored from pure white to black. Both are formulated with alpha cellulose and other fillers for molding compounds employed in molded cases and others. In building, melamine formaldehyde is most used in decorative high-pressure laminates to provide the impregnant for the decorative sheet and the transparent protective overlay (see Laminar Composites; Doors; Cabinetwork). Urea formaldehyde has had extensive use as thermal insulating foam, but it is prohibited in many states because of formaldehyde emission. Both melamine and urea formaldehyde find high-tonnage uses as woodworking adhesives for plywood and particle board. These aminoplasts give off water as a by-product (condensation) during final fabrication.

Phenolics, Phenol-formaldehyde (PF)

One of the first resins employed in building applications, phenol-formaldehyde is sometimes called a workhorse because of its many uses. An inherently amber to dark-colored, hard, brittle, heat-resistant, low-cost, easily molded resin, phenol-formaldehyde is formulated with many different fillers and coloring agents for many different electrical, mechanical, and general-purpose uses. Wood flour, cotton flock, hydrated alumina, mica, clay, and others impart different properties, moldability, and economics. Fibrous fillers provide toughness and impact resistance. In building, many types of knobs, handles, and other molded parts are used in hardware, plumbing, and electrical components. One of the largest applications is as the backup laminate for melamine-surfaced decorative high-pressure laminates employed in countertops, furniture, doors, cabinetry, and other applications (see Laminar Composites, Cabinetwork). Large tonnages go into strong waterproof adhesives for plywood and particle board and in other engineering adhesives. Phenolics are the binders in glass and mineral-fiber thermal insulation. Foams are employed as thermal insulation in building (see Foams; Thermal Insulation). Like the aminoplasts, these "phenoplasts" give off water as a by-product (condensation) during final fabrication.

Polyester, Unsaturated

Like the epoxies, unsaturated polyesters constitute a family of thermosetting resins. In building, their major use is in reinforced plastics (see Fibrous Composites; Particulate Composites). Different formulations are classified, for example, as general-purpose, light-stabilized, surfacing, layup, chemical-resistant, heat-resistant, flame-resistant, resilient, and hard. Several grades can often be combined, eg, a hard surface on a tough substrate.

As for epoxies, the brittleness of unsaturated polyesters makes them unsuitable for building applications. They are therefore combined with fibrous or particulate reinforcements into strong, tough composites. Because of their relatively lower cost and ease of handling, they are employed much more extensively in building than are epoxies. In construction, typical applications include fascia, bathroom components, wall liners, structural shapes, molded shells, translucent panels for roofing and exterior walls, pipe, tanks, hoods, ducts, and solar-energy components.

Polyurethane

Polyurethane (PU), based on polyisocyanates and others such as polyesters, can be either thermoplastic or thermosetting. Varieties commonly used in buildings are thermosetting. Polyisocyanurates are closely related. A major use in building is as rigid insulating foams (see Foams, Thermal Insulation). Other uses include tough, hard, heavy-duty coatings, pipe, and pipe linings. Reaction injection molding (RIM) has greatly extended the applications of urethane plastics in large parts (see Reaction Injection Molding). Flexible foams are widely used in upholstery, mattresses, and automotive seating.

Silicone (SI)

Unlike other plastics, silicones are based on a silicon–oxygen linkage instead of carbon. They are either thermoplastic or thermosetting. Because of the silicon–oxygen base, they are considerably more stable than other plastics except fluorocarbons, can withstand higher temperatures, harden less rapidly at low temperatures, and resist weathering. They are nonwetting and have good moisture and chemical resistance. Among its building uses are as sealants (see Sealants).

FABRICATION

The principal raw material for the manufacture of plastics is petroleum, but coal, cellulose (wood, cotton), limestone, water, air, and others are or can be used (1–4). Heat, pressure, catalysts, and promoters are involved in the chemical processes. The resulting plastics are typically in the form of pellets or powders for molding, liquids to be mixed and catalyzed, and film or sheet.

As previously described, the long-chain molecular structure of thermoplastics allows them to be repeatedly softened by heating and hardened by cooling. Thermosets, because of their ultimate cross-linked or interlinked structure, pass through a plastic stage and then harden irrever sibly. This difference in behavior influences the fabricating processes chosen.

Which of the many fabricating processes to employ depends on the requirements of the raw materials, the final properties wanted, volume needed, and cost of the process. Some processes are specialized, others can be used with many plastics. A few of the most common processes follow. Composites have their own fabricating processes (see Composites).

High Pressure

High-pressure processes are principally compression, injection, transfer, and extrusion.

Compression Molding. In compression molding (Fig. 1), molding powder, either loose or preformed cake, is charged into a two-part mold consisting of a cavity and force whose shape, when closed, is that of the molded part. A single mold may have one to many cavities. As the heated mold

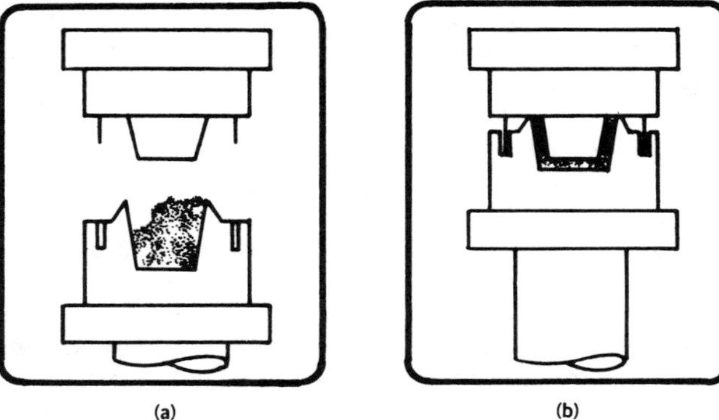

Figure 1. Compression molding. **(a)** Loose powder or preformed pellets in cavity; **(b)** Mold closed, forcing charge to take shape of mold. Courtesy of the Society of the Plastics Industry.

closes, the charge is softened and squeezed into the shape of the mold. If thermosetting, the charge first softens, then hardens and can be discharged hot. Thermoplastics are softened by heat for molding, but must be cooled and hardened in the mold before removal. In simple operations, the charging, closing, molding, and opening of the mold are done manually, but some or all steps can be automated for fast, high-volume production.

Injection Molding. The time and energy wasted in cooling compression-molded thermoplastics has led to injection molding (Fig. 2), a variant of die-casting. The mold is closed empty and kept cool. Hot thermoplastic material is forced from a heating chamber through a small channel or sprue into the cooled mold under enough pressure and at high enough velocity to fill the mold while the charge is still soft. It cools and hardens in the mold, the mold is opened, and the molded part and sprue are removed. The sprue is cut off, generally to be reground and recharged. In multiple-cavity molds, subsidiary channels or runners connect the sprue to the individual cavities.

Transfer Molding. The speed and versatility of injection molding for thermoplastics has led to its adaptation for thermosets. A measured charge of thermosetting molding powder is softened by preheating in a pot and forced by a plunger through a short channel or runners into a heated cavity or cavities where the charge hardens. The mold is opened and the molded part removed. Any excess material in channels is removed and discarded.

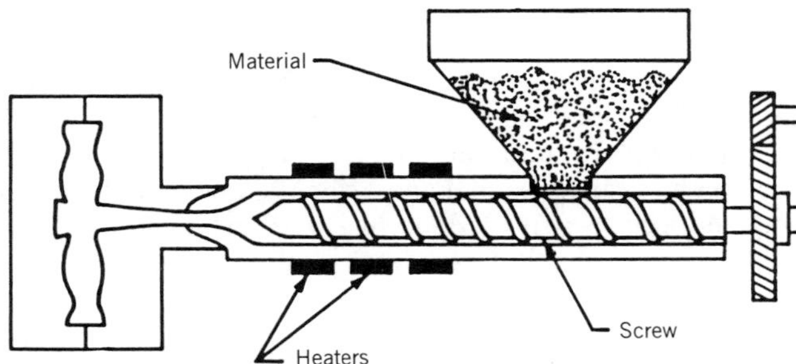

Figure 2. Injection molding. The charge is preheated in a barrel and forced into a cool, closed mold. Courtesy of the Society of the Plastics Industry.

Extrusion. In a process somewhat analogous to injection molding, continuous profiles including pipe, sheet, or such shapes as angles and channels are made by forcing a continuous stream of hot, soft plastic from a heating chamber through a die of the required profile. It is cooled as it emerges and is carried away on a moving belt to be coiled or cut into lengths. By varying the speed of the belt, the size of the cross section can be varied, but the proportions remain the same. Wire is covered by extruding the insulation over wire fed through the die. Extrusion is normally employed with thermoplastics, but it can be adapted to thermosets.

Blow Molding. In blow molding, a hollow unit called a parison is first formed and then forced by internal pneumatic pressure against a surrounding mold shaped to form a bottle or other container. Small necks, screw threads, and other features can be provided readily.

Film and Sheet Processes

The principal methods of producing thermoplastic film and sheet are calendering, casting, and extrusion plus drawing or blowing.

1. *Calendering*. Heated doughy plastic is passed between one or more pairs of rolls into continuous sheet or film. Subsequent rolls may impart texture and still others provide a printed pattern (Fig. 3).

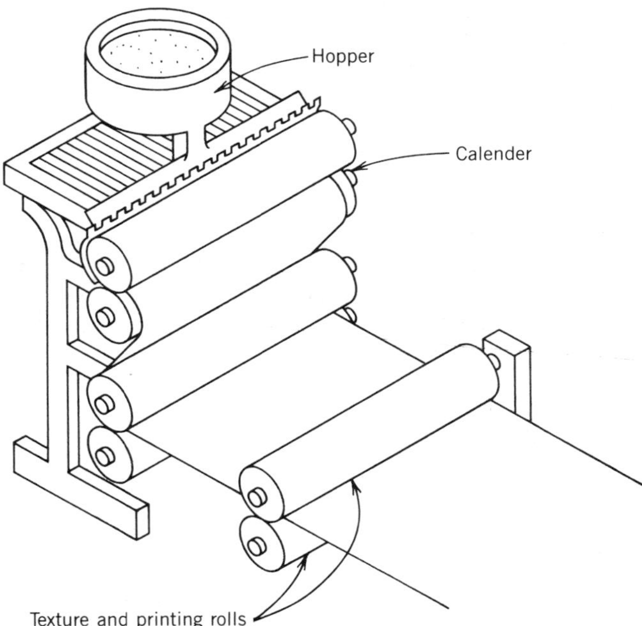

Figure 3. In calendering, a soft mass of plastic is rolled into a continuous sheet with or without backing layer. The sheet may be printed and a surface texture may be added.

2. *Casting*. Liquid molten or dissolved plastic cast on a moving belt is drawn to a predetermined thickness under a "doctor" knife, passed through a curing oven to drive off solvent if necessary, cooled, and wound into rolls or cut into lengths.
3. *Extrusion Drawing*. Extruded sheet is drawn and made thinner longitudinally or both longitudinally and transversely. In either case, orientation increases the strength and toughness.
4. *Extrusion and Blowing*. An extruded tube of plastic is immediately blown by internal air pressure to a large diameter and then cooled, slit, and flattened into wide films, eg, 30 ft (10 m) (Fig. 4).

Vacuum Forming, Thermoforming. In vacuum forming, heat-softened thermoplastic sheets are clamped over a vacuum tank with an opening that has the desired shape (domed skylight, for example). The heated sheet is drawn into the tank as the pressure is lowered; it then cools and hardens (Fig. 5).

If the plastic has a "memory," the formed sheet will flatten if heated. In "snap-back" molding, the soft, hot sheet is drawn into the tank, a mold is inserted in the drawn-down shape, the vacuum is released, and the sheet "snaps back," hugging the mold. If necessary, air pressure inside the tank can force the sheet against the mold.

Thermoforming is a variation of vacuum forming. A mold of the desired shape, such as a paneled door, is placed over a vacuum tank. Small holes in the mold, especially at low spots, lead to the tank. A sheet of plastic stretched over the tank is heated, eg, by infrared lamps, lowered over the mold, and pulled snugly against the mold by drawing a vacuum in the tank.

Casting. Thermoplastics such as acrylics and thermosets such as epoxies and unsaturated polyesters that begin as liquids can be cast and polymerized into solids. Various objects, eg, ornaments or delicate assemblages such as electronic parts, can be embedded. Large acrylic sheets are made by casting between plain or figured glass plates. Polymerization is exothermic (ie, generates heat) and must be controlled to prevent a runaway reaction.

Rotational Molding. In rotational molding, granular, powdered, or liquid plastic is introduced into a mold that is closed and rotated horizontally and vertically. The plastic is forced against the walls of the mold. If thermoplastic, the granules or powder are first softened or melted by heat and then cooled to harden. Solid thermosetting plastic is heated, melted, and hardened by heat. Liquid plastic thickens and hardens. Rotational molding can produce large parts such as containers and tanks, using plain or fine chopped-glass fiber-reinforced materials.

Figure 4. An extruded tube of plastic expanded by internal air pressure and slit into film (4). Courtesy of the MIT Press.

Reaction Injection Molding (RIM). In reaction injection molding the fast-reacting liquid ingredients of a thermosetting plastic are separately injected into a closed mold in such a way as to achieve intimate mixing. The ensuing reaction causes the mixture to harden rapidly. Large parts can be produced in a short time. The process is most suitable for large-volume production runs.

Machining

The ease of fabricating plastics, as by molding, frequently eliminates or greatly reduces the need for machining. Although it is necessary to adjust cutting angles, rakes, speed, and other factors to suit, the customary machining operations can be applied. Because thermoplastics in particular may heat, soften, and become gummy, coolants are usually necessary. If hard abrasive fillers such as glass, silica, and asbestos are present, they may require hard tools capable of holding an edge.

Influences on Properties

Fabrication can profoundly affect properties. In extrusion and injection molding, molecules are largely aligned in the direction of flow, increasing strength in that direction and decreasing at right angles. If plastic flows into an injection mold from several directions, it may not knit well at the meeting points, especially if filled, resulting in weakness. Drawing, as described above, orients the molecules of thermoplastics and increases strength and toughness.

FOAMS

Many plastics can be made into foams. Applications in building are both nonstructural and structural, such as thermal and acoustical insulation, molded cabinetry, cushioning against impact (eg, flooring materials), lightweight structural components, and cores of structural sandwiches.

Densities can be as low as ⅓ lb/ft^3 (5 kg/m^3) to that of solid plastic. Properties vary, not necessarily linearly, with density, and can be modified with reinforcing materials (see Principal Properties). Foamed plastics most commonly found in building include polystyrene, polyurethane, and urea formaldehyde. Other foamed plastics used in building are polyethylene (e.g, sealant backing), poly (vinyl chloride), cellulose acetate, and phenol formaldehyde.

Fabrication

The principal production processes in foam fabrication are extrusion, bead expansion, and liquid foaming.

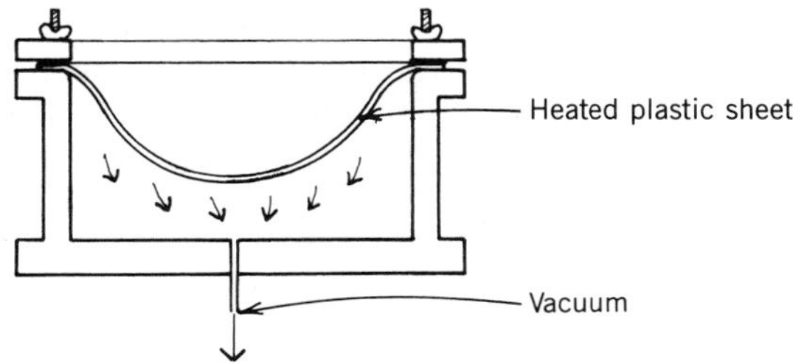

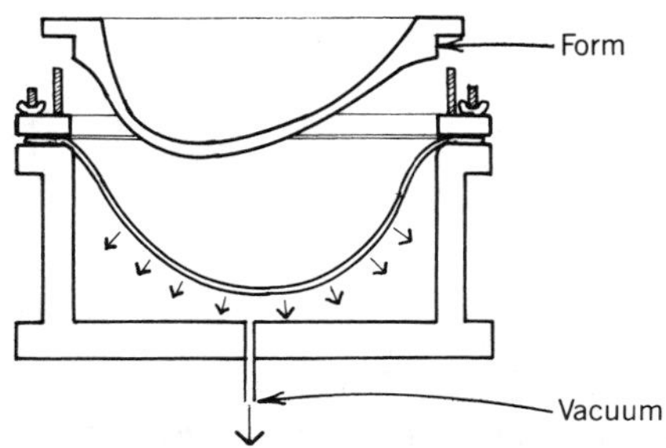

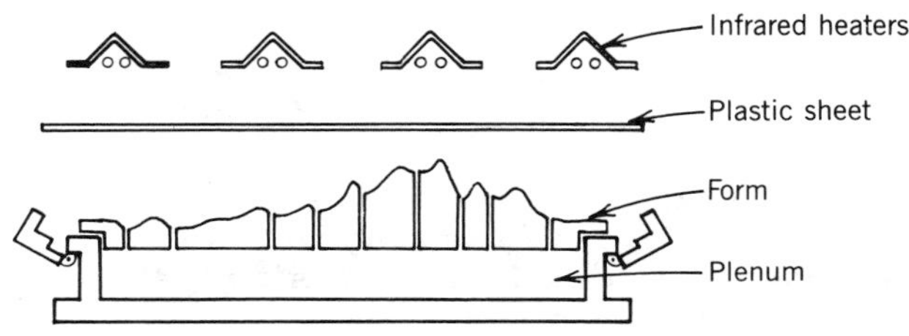

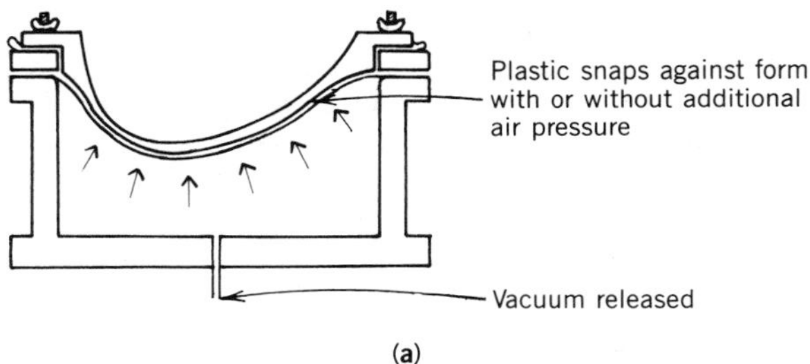

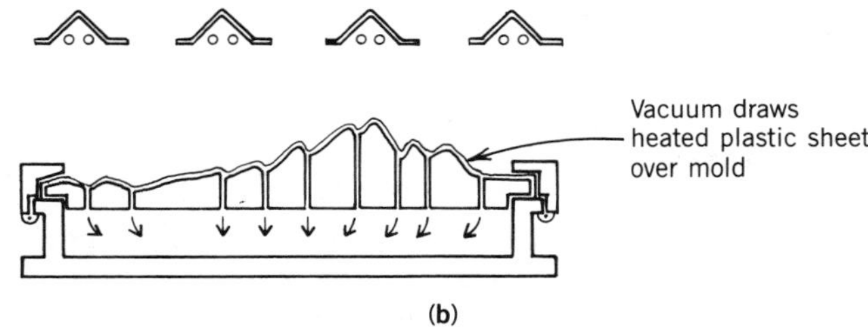

Figure 5. **(a)** Heat-softened sheet placed over the tank and drawn inward by a vacuum. The mold may be placed in space and the sheet allowed to "snap back" against it by releasing the vacuum with or without additional air pressure; **(b)** In thermoforming, a heat-softened sheet is drawn against the mold by a vacuum in a plenum under the mold (4). Courtesy of the MIT Press.

Extrusion. A thermoplastic such as polystyrene, containing a gas-forming ingredient, is introduced into the barrel of an extruder. As it leaves the die hot, the extrudate expands into a foamed "log." This is cut into blocks, slabs, or other desired shapes. Cells are "closed," ie, not interconnected.

Bead Expansion. Beads or pellets, such as polystyrene, containing a gas-forming ingredient, are introduced into a mold or cavity and heated, as by steam probe. The gas formed expands the softened beads, which fill the cavity, pressing against and welding to each other, usually leaving some porosity. The process is used to make a great variety of shapes, as well as slabs that may be cut as desired.

Liquid Foaming. Liquid components, eg, polyurethane, are mixed and immediately poured into a cavity such as a stud space. The ingredients react to form a gas, causing the mass to expand and fill the space while the plastic polymerizes and hardens. The expanding mass exerts some force, requiring the walls of the cavity to be stiff enough to resist deformation. To avoid this situation, the foam may be allowed to expand into a froth before being poured into the cavity where slight final expansion exerts no appreciable force.

Syntactic Foams and Multifoams

Syntactic foams consist of small preformed bubbles of glass, ceramic, or plastic embedded in an unblown resin matrix. In multifoams the matrix is foamed. Such reduced-weight formulations can be made into moldable materials, similar to modeling clay. Some synthetic "wood" is a mixture of small hollow glass spheres and polyester resin. Many epoxy foams are syntactic.

Reinforced Foams

Both thermoplastic and thermosetting foams, especially the denser foams, may be reinforced, commonly with-chopped glass fibers, but including others such as carbon black and metal. Usually, the reinforcement is incorporated before foaming, and reinforces the walls of the cells. Mechanical properties are increased several hundred percent with reinforcements up to 50%. Reinforcement may result in improved dimensional stability, tolerance of temperature extremes, and resistance to creep, but may result in greater weight, poorer thermal properties, more difficult processing, and increased cost.

Structural Foams

Structural foams have full-density surfaces and cellular cores, similar to bones. Consequently, they often have favorable ratios of strength and stiffness to weight while requiring reduced quantities of materials. Like other foams, structural foams may be reinforced with chopped glass fibers to increase mechanical properties (6).

Both thermoplastics and thermosets can be made into structural foams. In one process a mold, after being filled with the resin, is expanded or a core is retracted, leaving a space into which the resin can foam. In a second process, resin in a partially filled mold is allowed to expand to fill the mold, forming a solid skin or surface in contact with the mold.

COMPOSITES

For many applications in building, plain unmodified plastics are satisfactory, but for enhanced strength, stiffness, resistance to impact, and similar structural or semistructural requirements, plastics are often best combined with other materials into composites, materials whose combined properties transcend and differ from the properties of the constituents acting alone. Three common classifications of composites follow.

1. *Fibrous.* Fibers embedded in a continuous resin matrix. Lengths of fibers vary from continuous to a few hundredths of an inch (tenths of a millimeter).
2. *Laminar.* Sheets bonded together and often impregnated by a resinous binder.
3. *Particulate.* Particles embedded in a continuous resin matrix.

In each of these, the plastic acts primarily as a matrix or binder, but it may have other functions. The combined action of all constituents gives the composite its overall properties.

Fibrous Composites

Fibrous composites are often called reinforced plastics. For structural or semistructural applications, they are the most commonly employed plastics; there are many nonstructural uses as well (7–12).

An important structural attribute is that the fibers can often be arranged or tailored in the most favorable orientation to meet the stresses set up in a structural part. This is particularly true of pultrusion and filament winding (see Pultrusion; Filament Winding).

Fibers may be natural or synthetic, organic or inorganic. Among them are alpha cellulose, cotton, jute, sisal, pulp, aramid, nylon, polyester, rayon, metal (steel, aluminum, etc), boron, graphite, carbon, ceramic, and glass. Of these, glass is by far the most common in building applications.

Glass Fiber. Glass in fibrous form, usually a few ten-thousandths of an inch ($8–12 \times 10^{-4}$ mm) in diameter, is many times as strong as massive glass. Laboratory-drawn glass has exceeded 1,000,000 psi (6.9×10^6 kPa) in tensile strength, and commercial glass fibers run 400,000–700,000 psi ($2.75–4.83 \times 10^6$ kPa).

The two most-used types of glass fiber are E and C, electrical and chemical. E glass, most common in building applications, is best for general purposes, whereas C glass is best for resistance to corrosion and other chemical attack. S glass, a high-silica specialty glass, has enhanced structural properties and resistance to high temperatures.

Continuous glass filaments are drawn simultaneously in clusters or strands of 51 to 408 (usually 204) from a melt through platinum bushings. One type of staple fiber, 8–15 in. (200–380 mm) long, is formed by air jets.

Sizings are coatings to prevent damage by fibers rubbing against each other. Filaments are coated as they are drawn. Textile sizings are lubricants to prevent damage during twisting into yarns and weaving. They are later heat-cleaned or "burned" off before treatment finishes. Reinforcement sizings are compatible with later finishes.

Finishes, applied to fabrics after weaving and heat cleaning, promote good bonds between fibers and resin matrices, especially important with unsaturated polyesters (see Polyesters; Resins).

Binders hold the fibers in glass mats and preforms in position during fabrication. Binders must be compatible with the resin matrices later combined with the glass fibers.

The following is a list of types of glass fiber reinforcements.

1. *Continuous strands.* The 51 to 408 simultaneously drawn continuous filaments are gathered into rovings, ie, strands of parallel filaments (customarily 204), or yarns formed by twisting, plying, or both.
2. *Mats.* Strands are not woven but are distributed in a random pattern and held in place by binders or "needling." Reinforcing mats consist of the following: chopped strands deposited in a random pattern; continuous strands deposited in a random swirl pattern; or combined chopped and continuous strands. Surfacing mats are fine, lightweight mats generally employed to provide resin-rich smooth surfaces without protruding fibers and to promote resistance to weathering.
3. *Chopped strands.* Rovings and other continuous strands may be chopped into shorter lengths, eg,

¼–3 in. (6–76 mm), to be incorporated into chopped-strand mats, for spraying and preforming, and for incorporation into sheet and bulk molding compounds (see Fabrication).

4. *Milled Fibers.* Fibers broken into short lengths, 1⁄32–⅛ in. (0.8–3.22 mm) in a hammer mill are blended with thermoplastic and thermosetting molding compounds and with foams to enhance mechanical properties (see Reinforced Foams).
5. *Fabrics.* Many fabric patterns are obtained by different combinations of longitudinal or warp yarns and cross or fill yarns, varying markedly in weight. The principal types of yarns are as follows:
   - Continuous-filament, consisting of uninterrupted filaments. Maximum strength is achieved and fabrics are typically thin but do not drape well, ie, conform to complex shapes.
   - Staple, twisted yarns made of fibers cut to short lengths (staple). Fabrics are thicker and less strong, but drape well.
   - Rovings, heavy yarns resulting in thick heavy fabrics.

Types of Weaves. See Figure 6. The most-commonly employed weaves in fabrics for reinforced plastics follow.

1. *Plain or square.* A warp yarn passes alternately over and under fill yarns and vice versa. This is the most common weave and provides firmness and stability but does not drape well.
2. *Basket.* Two or more adjacent warp yarns pass alternately over and under two or more adjacent fill yarns and vice versa in a square pattern. Drape is better than for plain weave.
3. *Twill.* A fill yarn passes over one and then under several warp yarns to provide a diagonal pattern. Twills drape better than square weaves.
4. *Long-shaft satin.* A warp yarn passes over four or more and then under one fill yarn. Strength is high, and pliability or drape is excellent.
5. *Unidirectional.* Practically all yarns run in the longitudinal or warp direction, with just enough cross yarns to hold the fabric together. Maximum strength is achieved in the longitudinal direction.

Tapes are essentially narrow fabrics, often unidirectional. Braided sleeves and tubing are analogous. Three-dimensional shapes can be achieved by special weaving techniques.

High-Performance Fibers. Because of cost of materials and processing, high-performance fibers are largely confined to applications such as aerospace and specialties where weight saving, increased stiffness, or other attributes justify cost (8,13,14). Principal high-performance fibers are carbon, graphite, aramid, boron, beryllium, silica, and silicon carbide. Hard-drawn carbon steel, stainless steel, and chromium steel attain high strengths but at increased weight (see Composite Properties).

Resins. Although both thermoplastics and thermosetting resins are employed for reinforced plastics, the most common are thermosetting, predominantly unsaturated polyesters, followed by epoxies.

Polyester. As usually employed, the term "polyester" means unsaturated polyester, the type used for reinforced plastics. A great range of properties is possible, resulting in various classifications, of which general-purpose and specialty are two major divisions. Most applications are satisfied by general-purpose resins. Specialties include light-stable, weather-resistant, fire-resistant, resilient, hard, flexible, electrical, and many special formulations. Fillers may reduce shrinkage, lower costs, increase capacity, minimize crazing (fine cracks), and improve surface finishes. Pigments impart color. Additives include ultraviolet-light absorbers and flame retardants (see Durability, Fire).

Epoxies. Although epoxies, like polyesters, can be formulated to harden at room temperatures, they are more likely to employ at least some heat. In general, heat reduces curing time and enhances properties of both polyesters and epoxies. Post-curing by heat after a part has been

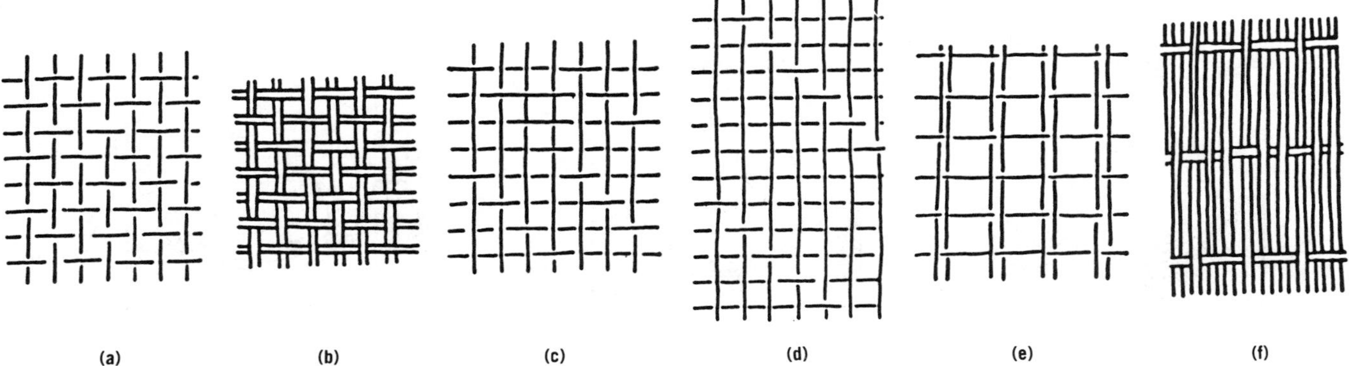

Figure 6. Types of weaves in fabrics for reinforced plastics (8): **(a)** Square or plain; **(b)** 2 × 2 basket; **(c)** twill; **(d)** long-shaft satin; **(e)** leno; **(f)** unidirectional. Courtesy of the American Society of Civil Engineers.

molded frequently improves mechanical properties still further.

High-temperature resistance of epoxies generally surpasses polyesters as does resistance to solvents and alkalies, but resistance to acids may be poorer. Dimensional stability is better and shrinkage during curing is less.

Fabrication. Some fabrication methods have been developed specifically for reinforced plastics; others are the same as or adapted from processes for plain plastics (4,8,10). Most common are hand lay-up, spray-up, vacuum-bag molding, press molding, continuous laminating, pultrusion, and filament winding.

Hand Lay-up. The oldest and often simplest process, hand lay-up, entails cutting and placing layers of mat, fabric, or both, by hand on a one-piece mold and at the same time saturating with liquid resin (Fig. 7**a**). The mold may be wood, hard plaster, concrete, sheet metal, reinforced plastic, or any other convenient material. Inserts, reinforcing ribs, or other features are incorporated at the same time. The assemblage is cured, commonly without pressure and heat, but heat accelerates and improves the cure. Pre-impregnated dry material called "prepreg" may be employed, but heat and pressure are required.

A resin-rich surfacing layer called a gel coat, incorporating a fine surfacing veil of mat or fabric, may be laid down first to obtain a smooth surface, to impart color or opacity, to enhance weather resistance, or for other purposes. A similar surface may be applied as the last layers. In any event, only the surface in contact with the mold will accurately reflect the mold's shape; the other surface will be rougher and more uneven. Evidently, quality of the final product depends strongly on the care and skill employed. Hand lay-up is practically unlimited in the sizes of parts obtainable.

Spray-up. In spray-up, rovings are fed into a chopper, chopped to a desired length, eg, ¼–3 in. (6–76 mm), and blown in a random pattern simultaneously with a spray of liquid resin onto the surface of a mold (Fig. 7**b**). Thickness can be varied as desired. Inserts, ribs, and other features can be incorporated. The mass is consolidated with serrated rollers. A first layer or gel coat and a similar final layer may be applied, as in hand lay-up. There is less waste in spray-up than in tailoring mats or fabrics for hand lay-up, and blown fibers follow contours of molds more readily. Strength of spray-up may be more variable. Quality of the product depends even more on the operator than in hand lay-up. The process can, however, be largely automated for large production runs.

Vacuum-Bag. Hand lay-up and spray-up are often called contact molding because no pressure is applied. For many uses this is sufficient, but some porosity, some resin-rich or starved areas, and unfilled sharp bends are likely to occur. Even moderate pressure may overcome such deficiencies.

Moderate pressure can be achieved by enclosing the uncured part in a flexible bag (rubber, plastic film) and drawing a vacuum inside the bag (Fig. 7**c**). This simultaneously extracts air from the bag, draws air from bubbles in the resin, and applies air pressure to the outside of the bag, commonly 10–14 psi (69–97 kPa). Still higher pressures are obtained by placing the bag-wrapped assemblage inside an autoclave or tank, drawing the vacuum inside the bag, and applying additional external air or liquid pressure.

Matched-die Molding. Contact and vacuum-bag methods achieve only moderate fiber loadings and consolidation. Only one side of the molded part is finished. Molding cycles, even with heated molds, are relatively long. Matched dies, similar to those in compression molding (see Compression Molding), permit higher pressures, although usually less than for standard molding materials. Maximum density, high fiber loadings, and shorter mold cycles are achieved, while both sides are finished. Matched dies, however, are expensive, and presses are required. Because molds and presses limit the sizes of parts, the process is employed for volume production of moderately sized parts.

Molding is expedited by several procedures:

1. *Preforms.* Chopped fibers are deposited with a binder on a screen shaped similarly to the final part. The preform is transferred to the mold, liquid resin is added, and the mold is closed and heated.
2. *Bulk molding compounds (BMC).* Chopped glass fibers are compounded with liquid resin and various fillers into a doughy mass. A weighed amount is

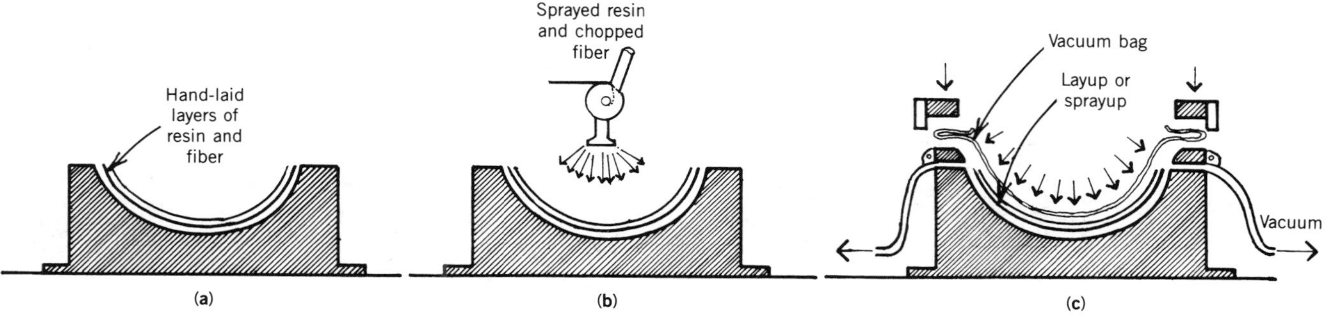

Figure 7. Types of fabrication for reinforced plastics. **(a)** Hand lay-up. Layers of mat, fabrics, or both are applied with liquid resin to mold; **(b)** Spray-up. Chopped fibers are sprayed with resin onto the mold; **(c)** Bag molding. A flexible sheet is placed over lay-up or spray-up. A vacuum is drawn under the sheet (4). Courtesy of the MIT Press.

placed in the mold and the mold is closed, forcing the compound to fill the mold where it is cured by heat.

3. *Sheet molding compound (SMC).* Random-fiber mats are compounded with polyester, fillers, and some thermoplastics into leathery sheets, tailored to proper size, and placed in a mold; the mold is then closed. Heat completes the cure.

By employing highly catalyzed resins, heating of molds can be eliminated and parts molded at ordinary temperatures, aided by the exothermal heat of the curing reaction. Alternatively, operations similar to stamping metal sheets entail heating thermoplastic reinforced sheets until soft, placing them between cool matching dies, and closing the mold to form and cool the part.

Continuous Laminating. Flat and corrugated sheets are commonly made by continuous laminating. Liquid polyester resin on a moving belt receives a random layer of chopped glass fiber, passes through squeeze rollers, remains flat or passes through corrugators, and goes into a curing oven, after which the cured sheet is cut into lengths.

Depending on formulation, fillers, pigments, and percentage of glass, such sheets may range from 85 to 90% sunlight transmittance to opaque. Weather resistance is enhanced by gel coats using weather-resistant ultraviolet-absorbing resins or by laminating thin films of highly resistant plastics such as poly(vinyl fluoride) to the surface, [See Fluoroplastics; Poly(vinyl chloride)].

Pultrusion. In extrusion, plastic is pushed through a die; in pultrusion, liquid-coated fibers are pulled through a die to form continuous profiles such as structural I, channel, angle, and box shapes. The continuous longitudinal strands, usually rovings, are combined with fabrics or mats to provide cross-directional properties.

Filament Winding. Continuous filaments, coated with resin, are wound on a rotating mandrel with the internal configuration of the finished part as its shape (Fig. 8). The orientation of the winding depends on the relative speed of rotation of the mandrel and the axial motion of the filament-dispensing mechanism. Three configurations are helical, circumferential, and polar, nearly parallel to the mandrel's axis. The configuration can be varied to match the stresses in the part in service. The combination of continuous filaments, high fiber loading, and match between stresses and orientation of fibers often results in the maximum achievable strength–weight ratios.

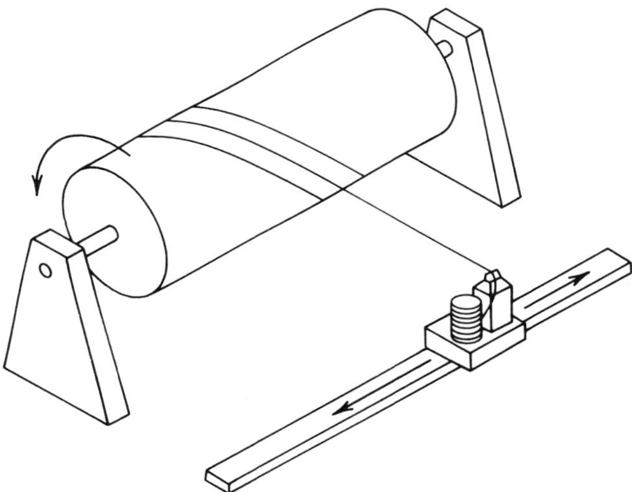

Figure 8. Filament winding. Continuous resin-coated filament is wrapped around a rotating mandrel as the feeding mechanism travels back and forth (4). Courtesy of the MIT Press.

Laminar Composites

Laminar composites consist of sheet materials bonded together and possibly impregnated by a binder of matrix. Plastics may be found in both sheet and binder, but most commonly the latter (2,4,15).

High-Pressure Laminates. In fabricating high-pressure laminates, sheet materials are impregnated with a liquid resin, dried, assembled into stacks, rolls, and bundles, and pressed and cured under pressures usually ranging from 1000 to 2000 psi (6900 to 13,800 kPA) and temperatures of 325–400°F (164–206°C) into sheet, rods, tubes, and other stock.

Decorative Laminates. In building, by far the most commonly employed laminates are decorative, for countertops, furniture parts, door and cabinet facings, and similar applications (See Doors; Cabinetwork). A base of several phenolic resin-impregnated kraft paper sheets is overlaid with a melamine–formaldehyde-impregnated decorative sheet protected by a transparent cellulose veil-reinforced melamine–formaldehyde surface (Fig. 9**a**). The decorative sheet, although usually printed paper, may be fabric, metal, wood veneer, or other sheet stock. When hot-pressed, the layers fuse into a single sheet with a matte or glossy surface finish. The surface is harder than usual varnishes and is resistant to common solvents.

Finished sheets are customarily flat, but with special resins and slight undercure, postformable sheets can be softened enough by reheating to be shaped into large-radius simple curves such as the cove backs and rounded fronts of countertops (Fig. 9**b**).

The thin sheets are customarily bonded to substrates, of which plywood and other wood products such as particleboard and waferboard are most common (Fig. 9**c**). Such a board, if faced on one side only, is unbalanced and tends to warp and twist with changes in temperature and humidity. To obtain balance, a companion sheet is bonded to the opposite face of the board. This sheet may be nondecorative phenolic-impregnated kraft paper only. Edges, such as table tops and counters, are customarily faced with strips of decorative laminate.

Utility and industrial high-pressure laminates use various papers, mats, and fabrics combined with phenolics, melamine, silicones, polyesters, and epoxies. They are made into sheets, rods, tubes, and molded shapes.

Sandwiches. As commonly employed in building, sandwiches are a special form of laminate consisting of two facings of relatively thin, hard, dense, strong materials

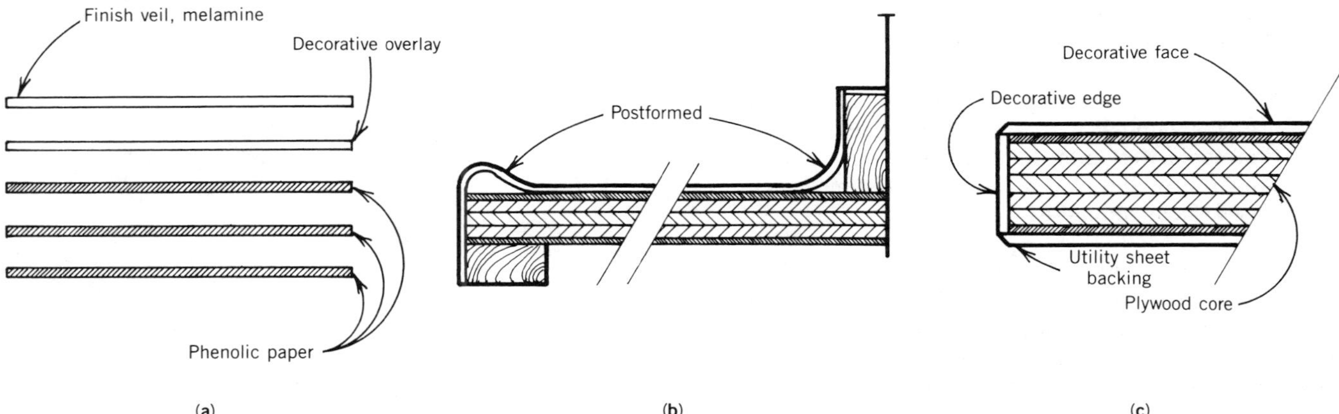

Figure 9. **(a)** Assembly of layers for high-pressure decorative laminate; **(b)** Postformed laminate for a countertop; **(c)** Laminate applied to substrate (4). Courtesy of the MIT Press.

bonded to a core of relatively thick, softer, lighter, and weaker material. The geometry, not unlike an I-beam with the facings analogous to the flanges and the core the web, provides high stiffness and bending strength (Fig. 10). The core supports the thin facings against buckling or wrinkling under compression and absorbs shear. The adhesive bond between facings and core must resist shear and tension. Facings, in addition to providing strength, must resist wear and tear, weathering, and other environmental conditions. Fire resistance, thermal insulation, and acoustical isolation depend on the properties of the materials and their configuration.

Commonly used facing materials for buildings include plywood, hardboard, and various particleboards; metal; thin concrete slabs; reinforced plastics; and high-pressure laminates. Cores use grids of wood, metal, or paper; plywood and particle board; foamed concrete; foamed glass and silicate; and foamed plastics. Adhesives, especially in demanding applications, are largely based on synthetic resins.

Particulate Composites

In particulate composites, particles are embedded in a matrix (8,16–18). The most important example in building is portland cement concrete.

Polymer Concretes. In polymerous concretes, polymers play a part in addition to, or in place of, portland cement. Three types are as follows:

1. *Polymer-impregnated concrete* (*PIC*). Cured regular concrete impregnated with a monomer subsequently polymerized in place.
2. *Polymer cement concrete* (*PCC*). Freshly mixed concrete into which a monomer or a polymer latex is mixed. The concrete cures in the usual way.
3. *Polymer concrete* (*PC*). Concrete in which a polymer replaces the portland cement. Curing is by hardening of the polymer.

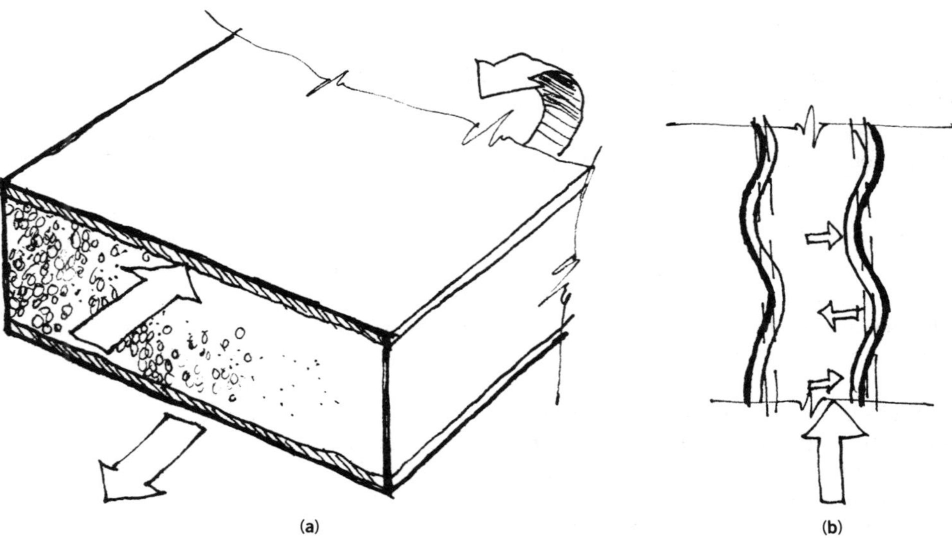

Figure 10. Principle of sandwich behavior: **(a)** in bending; **(b)** in axial compression (4). Courtesy of the MIT Press.

Polymer-Impregnated Concrete (PIC). To produce polymer-impregnated concrete, standard cured concrete is thoroughly dried and has its internal air withdrawn by vacuum. Monomer is let into the pores to saturation and is polymerized by heat, chemical means, or other suitable process. When complete saturation is not possible, as in floors or bridge decks, surface penetration to some depth may be achieved by building a temporary enclosure, introducing air hot enough to evaporate water in the concrete, cooling, flooding with monomer to achieve some penetration, eg, 1 in. (25 mm), and polymerizing the monomer.

Resin monomers employed include such thermoplastics as acrylic, styrene, and acrylonitrile, and thermosets such as polyester-styrene. Properties are frequently greatly enhanced. Mechanical properties are markedly increased as is resistance to environmental attack. Thermal properties are not greatly altered. The increases in those properties must be balanced against the costs and restrictions of the process.

Polymer Cement Concrete (PCC). To fabricate polymer cement concrete, a monomer or a polymeric latex is mixed with fresh concrete which then is cured. Monomers polymerize while the cement hardens. As compared to polymer-impregnated concrete, the mixing and deposition of polymer cement concrete is simple. It has been used extensively for resurfacing old concrete floors and deteriorated road surfaces because of its good bond to old concrete and resistance to abrasion and de-icing salts.

Polymer Concrete (PC). Polymeric binders, including polyester, epoxy, and methyl methacrylate, take the place of portland cement in otherwise standard concrete to produce polymer concrete. Curing time is generally less than a day, and can be shorter with heat. Because nothing evaporates, porosity is negligible with careful mixing. To reduce to a minimum the amount of voids to be filled by the resin, fine and coarse aggregate should be carefully graded for minimum void ratios. In a well-graded mix, the percentage is about six, similar to polymer-impregnated concrete. The process consists of mixing aggregate and catalyzed resin and immediately depositing in molds or forms where curing occurs.

Polymer concrete is employed rather extensively for building panels. A typical sandwich panel consists of facings of 1-in. (25-mm) thick glass fiber-reinforced polymer concrete, combined with a core of plastic foam (see Sandwiches). Polymer concrete is employed for quick repairs of roads, airstrips, and other installations where downtime must be minimized.

PRINCIPAL PROPERTIES, COMPARISONS

Properties of plastics and their composites of principal interest in building are strength, stiffness, toughness, hardness, thermal expansion, thermal conductivity, light transmission, durability, and resistance to fire (2,4,8). These properties must often be compared to the corresponding properties of other materials. Direct comparisons cannot often be made because of the differing characteristics of different materials. A great deal of judgment must enter into a choice, but some guidance can be afforded by comparing the expected behavior of different materials when employed in a given situation.

Tables 2–7 give data respecting various classes of plastics derived from standard tests. Some present general properties, some are more specific to structural properties, and still others relate to fire tests and durability. Such data must be used with judgment because use conditions may vary widely from test conditions. The data, however, are useful in bracketing the ranges of properties. In an actual situation, property values for specific plastics should be employed.

Strength

Strengths of plastics in tension, compression, and bending are not the same, usually least in tension. Strength (Table 2) varies from low in some soft flexible materials to high for others and may be extremely high for fibrous composites (see Fibrous Composites; Composites: Properties). Figure 11 shows approximate ranges in tension compared to other common building materials (compression for concrete, bending for wood). Some unidirectional composites are among the strongest structural materials available in the direction of the reinforcement, especially when made with the high-technology lightweight fibers (see High-Performance Fibers).

Strength of plastics, particularly thermoplastics, is affected by both time and temperature. Like wood, many plastics will sustain higher loads for a short period than for a long time. Depending on the load, deformation (creep) may increase for a time and eventually cease, or may increase, level off, and then increase at an accelerating rate to failure. Increased temperature generally reduces strength but increases deformation before failure; conversely, lowered temperature increases strength, but decreases deformation to failure and may result in brittleness.

Stiffness

By and large, stiffness of plastics as measured by modulus of elasticity is low. Plain plastics are generally much less stiff than wood parallel to the grain. Suitably modified with fibrous fillers, moduli of elasticity may rise to those of wood parallel to the grain. Even unidirectional reinforced plastics heavily loaded with glass fibers seldom exceed half the modulus of elasticity of aluminum alloys. With the high-modulus, high-strength, high-technology fibers such as graphite and aramid, moduli of elasticity of fibrous composites may exceed steel alloys at a fraction of the weight (Fig. 12).

For many building applications, if stiffness is important, advantage must be taken of the formability of plastics and composites to utilize inherently-stiff structural forms.

Toughness and Hardness

Difficult to define precisely, toughness and hardness are often measured by empirical tests. The resulting data must be used with discretion. Laboratory specimens may differ from actual products.

Table 2. Structural and Physical Properties of Representative Engineering Plastics[a,b]

Material Type / Property	ASTM Test	Thermoplastics: Acrylonitrile–Butadiene–Styrene ABS	Acrylics PMMA	Acetal	Cellulosics	Fluoroplastic PTFE	Nylon PA	Polycarbonate PC
		High Impact	Cast Sheet	Homopolymer			Type 6/6 Molding	Unfilled
Specific gravity	D792	1.01–1.05	1.17–1.20	1.42	1.22–1.40	2.14–2.20	1.13–1.15	1.20
Tensile strength, psi	D638	4400–6300	8000–12,500	9700	1900–9000	2000–5000	11,000–12,000	9500
					5–100	200–400	60–300	110
Elongation, %	D638	5–70	2–7	13–75	0.50–0.50	0.058–0.80		0.345
Tensile elastic modulus, 10^6 psi	D638	0.15–0.33	0.265–0.48	0.52	0.05–10.9	3.0	0.8–2.1	14–16
Impact strength, ft-lb/in., Izod	D256	6.0–9.3	0.3–1.4	1.2	R34–122	D50–D55	R120	M70
				2.3		(Shore)	M83	
Hardness, Rockwell	D785	R85–106	M61–100	M92–94				
Thermal conductivity, 10^{-4} cal-cm/s-cm°C	C177		0.4–4.0	5.5	4–8	6.0	5.8	4.7
Thermal expansion, 10^{-6} in./in.-°C	D696	95–110	50–90	100	100–200		80	68
Deflection temperature, °F 264 psi	D648	205–215	160–215	255–260	111–228		167	270
Deflection temperature, °F 66 psi		210–225	165–235	328–338	120–250	250	474	280
Clarity		Translucent to opaque	Transparent to opaque	Translucent to opaque		Opaque	Translucent to opaque	Translucent to opaque
Water absorption, 24 h, ⅛-in. thick, %	D570	0.20–0.45	0.2–0.4	0.25–0.40	0.8–6.5	0.01	1.0–1.3	0.15
Effect of sunlight		None to sunlight yellowing	None	Chalks slightly		None	Embrittlement	Slight discoloration and embrittlement

[a] Ref. 2. Courtesy of McGraw–Hill, Inc.

[b] Conversions: 1 psi = 6.896 kPa; 1 in. = 25.4 mm; 1 ft = 0.305 m; 1 Btu-in./h-ft²-°F = 0.144 W/m-°K; 1 ft² = 0.09 m²; 1 Btu/lbm-°F = 4184.0 J/kg-°K; 1 ft-lb/in. = 34.4 J/mm; °F = 1.8°C+32.

Toughness is commonly measured by allowing a ball to drop on and fracture a plate, or by having a pendulum strike and break off a notched or unnotched bar. The energy absorbed is an indication of toughness or resistance to impact.

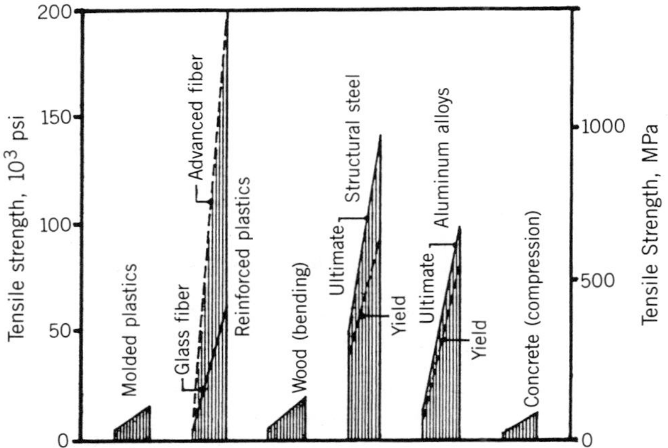

Figure 11. Strengths of plastics and other materials (8). Courtesy of the American Society of Civil Engineers.

Hardness is commonly measured by the load needed to achieve a given indentation by a hardened steel ball or a point. Other tests involve specified scratches. Wear is commonly measured by abrading a specimen under a wheel. Results of all tests are empirical.

Thermal Expansion and Contraction

All building materials expand and contract with changes in temperature, but plastics, especially plain unmodified,

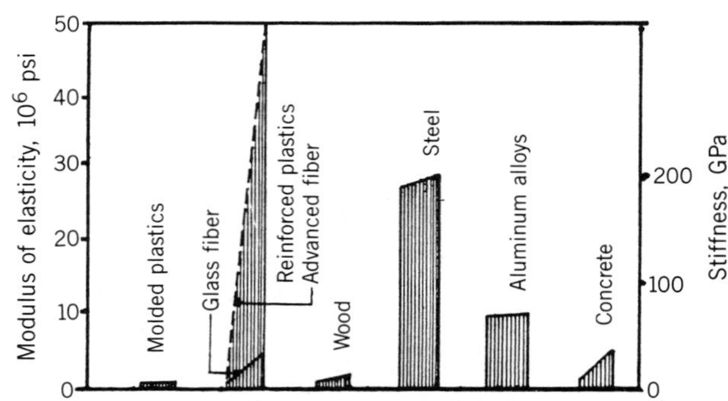

Figure 12. Stiffness of plastics and other materials (8). Courtesy of the American Society of Civil Engineers.

Table 2 ***(continued)***

				Thermosets				
Polyethylene PE	Poly-propylene PP	Polystyrene High and Medium Flow	Vinyl Polymers PVC	Polyester	Epoxy Ep	Phenolic PF	Melamine Formalde-hyde MF	Silicone SI
High Density HDPE	Homo-polymer		Rigid	Cast Rigid	Cast Unfilled	Wood-Flour Filled	Alpha-Cellulose Filled	Glass and/or Mineral Filled
0.95–0.97	0.90–0.91	1.04–1.05	1.30–1.58	1.10–1.46	1.11–1.40	1.37–1.46	1.47–1.52	1.80–2.05
3200–4500	4300–5500	5200–7500	5900–7500	6000–15,000	4000–13,000	5000–9000	5000–13,000	4000–6500
10–1200								
0.155–0.158	200–700	1.2–2.5	40–80	2	3–6	0.4–0.8	0.6–1.0	5
0.4–4.0	0.16–0.23		0.35–0.60	0.30–0.64	0.35	0.80–1.70	1.10–1.40	
D66–D73 (Shore)	0.5–2.2	0.33–0.475	0.4–22.0	0.20–0.40	0.2–1.0	0.2–0.6	0.2–0.4	0.25–8.0
	R80–R110	M60–75	D65–D85 (Shore)	50–75 Barcol	M80–M110	M100–M115	M155–M125	M80–95
11–12	0.81	3.0	3.5–5.0		4.5	4–8	6.5–10	7.18
59–110	32.2–56.7	50–83	50–100	55–100	45–65	30–45	40–45	20–50
175–196	125–140	169–202	140–170	140–400	115–550	300–370	350–390	500
	200–250	155–304	135–180					
	Transparent to opaque		Translucent to opaque	Transparent to opaque	Transparent		Translucent	Opaque
0.01	0.01–0.03	0.01–0.03	0.04–0.40	0.15–0.60	0.08–0.15	0.30–1.20	0.1–0.8	0.15–0.4
Crazes if unprotected	Crazes if unprotected		Varies with formulation	Slight Yellowing	None		Pastels yellow	None

generally change dimensions appreciably more than most, sometimes dramatically. Many fillers reduce the temperature changes markedly. Filaments such as glass reduce the overall coefficients of expansion of reinforced plastics, but even these are likely to be considerably higher than the metals and radically higher than masonry and glass. Table 2 gives ranges of values and Figure 13 compares plastics and composites with other materials.

Allowance must be made in design for the expansion and contraction of plastics. Curved or corrugated surfaces can accommodate motion. Joints and fasteners such as bolts and screws must have sufficient tolerances to permit unrestricted motion without wrinkling or cracking and tearing the plastic. Corners should have generous radii to avoid severe stress raisers (Fig. 14). Sealants must accommodate motion (see Sealants).

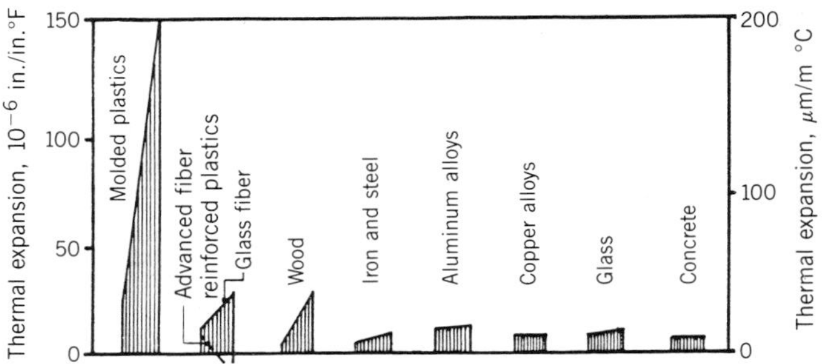

Figure 13. Thermal expansion of plastics and other materials (8). Courtesy of the American Society of Civil Engineers.

Thermal Conductivity

Plain unmodified plastics have thermal conductivities higher than wood across the grain; lower than concrete, glass, and masonry; and much lower than metals. Thermal conductivities of filled, laminated, and reinforced plastics depend on their compositions (Table 2).

Foamed plastics (Table 3) provide some of the best thermal insulators for buildings. Conductivity depends on blowing agent, density, whether open cell or closed cell, and whether expanded bead, prefoamed, or foamed in place. In general, the lower the density, the lower the conductivity unless the cell sizes become so large that appreciable convection can be set up inside them. For building insulation, densities usually range from about 0.8 to 3.0 lb/ft^3 (12.8 to 48.0 kg/m^3). Thermal conductivities, usually designated k, are in the range of 0.10–0.30 Btu/in./

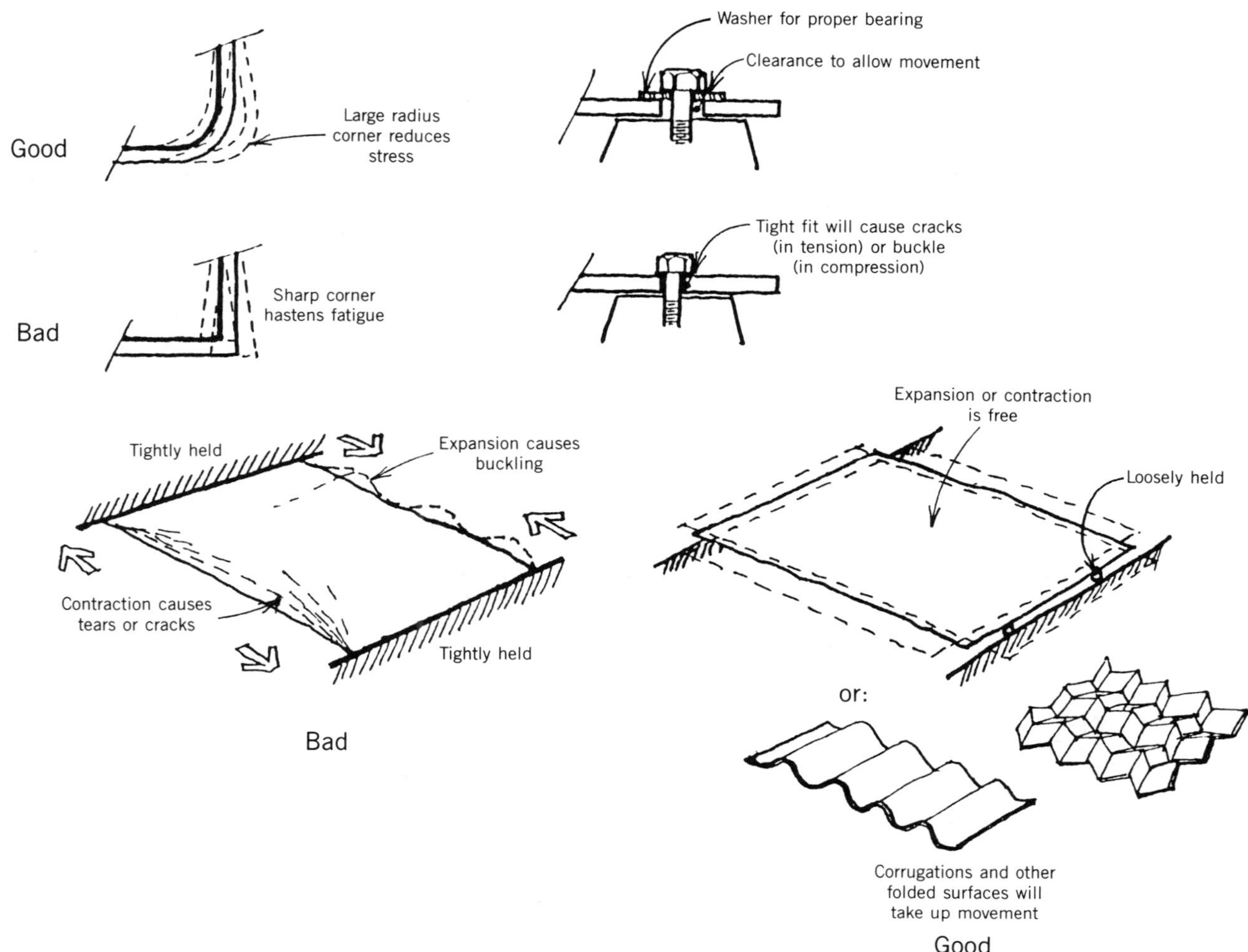

Figure 14. Good and bad practice respecting thermal expansion and contraction (4). Courtesy of the MIT Press.

h/ft^2·°F (0.014–0.042 W/m·°K). Higher densities may be needed if foams are expected to withstand appreciable stresses, as in structural sandwiches.

Service Temperatures

Thermoplastics soften as temperature rises and harden as temperature drops. Thermosets are less affected. Generally, as Table 2 shows, maximum service temperatures for plastics are above those found in buildings, even in exterior walls and roofs, but some are marginal. Conditions of use must be considered. Floor sheet and tile, for example, if warm, may be indented by the legs of furniture. Changing service temperature, unless allowed for, may cause expansion and contraction, leading to distress.

Light Transmission

Optical clarity of some plastics, such as poly(methyl methacrylate) and polycarbonate, is as high as the clearest glasses, with visible light transmission of 93% or better. Several other clear plastics, such as some types of polystyrene, poly(vinyl chloride), and cast allyl approach these values. Other transparent plastics include some polyesters, epoxies, fluorocarbons, cast phenolics, and polyolefins.

Ultraviolet and infrared transmission of different grades of acrylic, for example, may be high or low, depending on composition and wavelength. In the ultraviolet, some types transmit strongly, eg, for germ-killing, whereas others absorb strongly, eg, to prevent fading of fabrics.

Pigments reduce both clarity and transmissivity, ultimately to opacity. Dyes absorb certain wavelengths and transmit others, resulting in color change. Mixed dyes and pigments result in translucence.

Some clear plastics remain clear more or less indefinitely, others may turn yellow and become progressively darker, especially when exposed to sunlight. Crazing and blushing may occur.

The indices of refraction of most plastics are in the vicinity of 1.50, not greatly different from glass. Some are as low as 1.35, others as high as 1.60 to 1.70. Light can be "piped" around bends in clear rods provided the radii of curvature are large enough to allow total internal reflection.

Table 3. Properties of Foams[a,b]

Type	Density lb/ft^3 (ASTM D1622)	Tensile strength, psi (ASTM D1623)	Compressive stress at 10% deflection, psi (ASTM D1621)	Thermal Conductivity, k[c] Btu/ft^2/h/°F./in. (ASTM C177)	Coefficient of linear thermal expansion, 10^{-5} in./in./°F. (ASTM D696)
Cellulose acetate					
Boards and rods					
(rigid, closed cell foam)	6.0–8.0	170	125	0.31	2.5
Phenolic					
Foam-in-place	⅓–1½	3–17	2–15	0.21–0.28	
Liquid resin	2–5	20–54	22–85	0.20–0.22	0.5
Polyethylene					
Low density foam					
planks, rods	1.3–2.6	20–30	5	0.28–0.40	9.5–2.3
Polystyrene					
Shapes, boards,					
and billets	1.0	16–35	8–18	0.26–0.28	3.0–4.0
Molded from expandable					
beads	2.0	25–70	25–45	0.23–0.24[d]	3.0–4.0
	5.0	148–172	85–130	0.246	3.0–4.0
Extruded boards					
and billets	1.5–2.0	40–70	18–55	0.20–0.26	
	2.6–5.0	180–225	100–180	0.18–0.21[d]	3.0–4.0
Polyurethane					
Rigid (closed cell)	1.3–3.0	15–95	15–60	0.11–0.17[e,f]	4–8
Molded parts; boards,				0.21[g]	
blocks, slabs; pipe	4–8	90–290	70–275	0.15–0.21[e,f]	4
covering; foam-in-place;				0.21–0.29[f,g]	
pour, froth-pour.	19–25	775–1300	1200–2000	0.34–0.42[f]	4
				0.42–0.52[e,f]	
Polyvinyl chloride					
Rigid closed cell					
boards and billets	2–4	1000 and up		2.0	4.0–6.0
Urea formaldehyde					
Block, shred,					
foam-in-place	0.8–1.2	Poor	5	1.18–0.21	

[a] Ref. 2. Courtesy of McGraw-Hill, Inc.
[b] Conversions; 1 ft^3 = 0.0283 m^3; 1 psi = 6.896 kPa; 1 Btu-in./hr-ft^2-°F = 0.144 W/m-°K.
[c] Thermal resistivity R = 1/k.
[d] At 70°F.
[e] Blown with fluorocarbon.
[f] First number in each sequence is the value for unaged materials, the second number is the value after aging.
[g] Blown with CO_2.

Permeability, Water Absorption

Plastic films are employed in building for moisture barriers and as overlays for laminates and other substrates, among other purposes. Moisture barriers must display low permeability; in other applications higher permeability may be wanted. Vinylidene chloride, polyolefins (polyethylene and polypropylene), and some fluorocarbons have low permeabilities; polystyrene is intermediate; polyamides (nylon) and vinyl chlorides vary widely.

Water absorption, like permeability, varies from practically zero to several percent in standard 24-hour immersion tests (Table 2). In some instances, some moisture is beneficial. Nylon, for example, becomes brittle instead of tough if desiccated.

Temperature Dependence

Figure 15 summarizes many of the foregoing points regarding temperature effects for thermoplastics. Some properties increase, some remain unchanged, and others decrease with increasing temperature. Thermosets are affected, if at all, to a lesser extent.

Composite Properties

Fibrous. Table 4 summarizes mechanical properties of the principal types of glass and high-technology fibers. The values of specific strengths and specific elastic moduli are convenient for comparisons on a property/weight basis

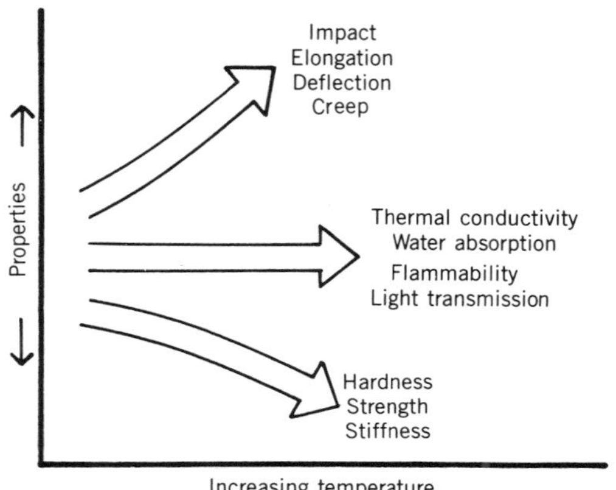

Figure 15. Temperature effects, properties of plastics (4). Courtesy of the MIT Press.

(2,8,13). Table 5 sets forth properties of glass fiber-reinforced plastics employed in high-volume production.

Particulate. Table 6 compares polymer concretes with conventional concrete. Except for insulating lightweight concrete, weights do not differ greatly, but strength-to-weight ratios show marked deviations (16,17).

Durability

Resistance to environmental factors varies widely with type of exposure, composition, form, installation, and use. Plastics, like other materials, may give a good account of themselves or may fail in a short time.

Resistance to corrosion is excellent. Resistance to rotting is similarly superior. Insects and vermin may or may not attack plastics. All plastics are resistant to a variety of solvents, but not necessarily the same ones. A few, such as PTFE, are resistant to all but the strongest reagents (see Fluorocarbons). Most plastics are resistant to solvents likely to be found in dwellings or in ordinary use. Resistance of a given plastic should be checked for a given use.

Interior Durability. The plastics discussed in this article are durable under normal indoor conditions. The temperatures, humidities, and lighting conditions usually encountered generally cause little deterioration or change. Exceptions include degradation of improperly plasticized upholstery and wall coverings, yellowing of unstabilized transparent plastics, and cracking of parts improperly fastened. Generally, properly formulated, processed, and installed plastics perform satisfactorily.

There is considerable concern over possible indoor air pollution caused by emanations from building materials, especially in air-tight construction resulting in diminished air changes. Formaldehyde, for example, may be given off by materials bonded with incompletely cured formaldehyde-containing adhesives and binders, and by improperly formulated formaldehyde-containing foams.

Exterior Durability. Exterior exposure or weathering is far more severe than is indoor use, but the more weather-resistant plastics when properly handled behave well, although plastics do not have the long histories of use of many traditional materials. Temperature and humidity extremes coupled with intense solar radiation and contaminated atmosphere may cause rapid deterioration of plastics not suited to outdoor applications. Deterioration varies with location, time of year, and duration of exposure. Plas-

Table 4. Structural and Physical Properties of Fiber Reinforcements[a,b]

Type of Fiber Reinforcement	Specific Gravity	Density, lb/in.^{3}	Tensile Strength, 10^3 psi	Specific Strength[c], 10^6 in.	Tensile Elastic Modulus, 10^6 psi	Specific Elastic Modulus[d], 10^8 in.
Glass						
E Monofilament	2.54	0.092	500	5.43	10.5	1.14
12-end roving	2.54	0.092	372	4.04	10.5	1.14
S Monofilament	2.48	0.090	665	7.39	12.4	1.38
12-end roving	2.48	0.090	550	6.17	12.4	1.38
Boron (tungsten substrate)						
4 mil or 5.6 mil	2.63	0.095	450	4.74	58	6.11
Graphite						
High strength	1.80	0.065	400	6.15	38	5.85
High modulus	1.94	0.070	300	4.29	55	7.86
Intermediate	1.74	0.063	360	5.71	27	4.29
Organic aramid[e]	1.44	0.052	400	7.69	18	3.46

[a] Ref. 8. Courtesy of the American Society of Civil Engineers.
[b] Conversions: 1 psi = 6.896 kPa; 1 in. = 25.4 mm; 1 lb/in.^{3} = 27,680 kg/m^3.
[c] Strength/density.
[d] Elastic modulus/density.
[e] Several different aramids are employed as fiber reinforcement. They have different properties, and the resulting composites also differ. The properties given here are for one type commonly used in engineering composites.

Table 5. Structural and Physical Properties of Reinforced Plastics in High-Volume Production[a,b]

Material	% Glass Fiber by Weight	Specific Gravity	Flexural Strength, 10^3 psi	Flexural Elastic Modulus, 10^6 psi	Tensile Strength at Yield, 10^3 psi	Tensile Elastic Modulus, 10^6 psi	Compressive Strength, 10^3 psi	Impact Strength, Izod ft-lb/in. of Notch	Continuous Heat Resistance, °F	Thermal Coefficient of Expansion, 10^{-6} in./in.-°F
Sheet molding compound (SMC)	15–30	1.7–2.1	18–30	1.4–2.0	8–20	1.6–2.5	15–30	8–22	300–400	8–12
Bulk molding compound (BMC)	15–35	1.8–2.1	10–20	1.4–2.0	4–10	1.6–2.5	20–30	2–10	300–400	8–12
Preform /mat (compression molded)	25–50	1.5–1.7	10–40	1.3–1.8	25–30	0.9–2.0	15–30	10–20	150–400	10–18
Chopped strand spray-up polyester	30–50	1.4–1.6	16–28	1.0–1.2	9–18	0.8–1.8	15–25	4–12	150–350	12–20
Pultruded shapes—polyester[c]										
Lengthwise		1.66–1.72	30	1.3–1.6	30–35	2.3–3.0	20–35	18–25		
Crosswise			10	0.6–0.8	5–9	0.8–1.5	10–17	4		
Pultruded sheets—polyester[d]										
Lengthwise		1.66–1.80	30–45	1.6–2.0	19–25	1.6–2.0	25–30	18–25		
Crosswise			13–18	0.9–1.5	7.5–10	0.9–1.5	18–24	5–6		
Filament wound—epoxy	30–80	1.7–2.2	100–270	5.0–7.0	80–250	4.0–9.0	45–70	40–60	500	2–6
Rod stock—polyester	40–80	1.6–2.0	100–180	4.0–6.0	60–180	4.0–6.0	30–70	45–60	150–500	3–8

[a] Ref. 8. Courtesy of the American Society of Civil Engineers.

[b] Conversions: 1 psi = 6.896 kPa; 1 ft-lb/in. = 34.4 J/mm; °F = 1.8°C + 32.

[c] Owens-Corning Fiberglas Co.

[d] Morrison Molded Fiber Glass Co.

Table 6. Comparative Physical Properties and Compressive Strengths for Concrete-Polymer Materials with PMMA[a,b]

	Polymer Loading, wt%-PMMA	Density, lb/ft^3	Specific Gravity	Compressive Strength, psi	Strength-to-Weight Ratio
Conventional concrete (control)	0.0	150	2.40	5,000	33
Polymer cement concrete (PCC)					
premix–polymer latex	1.0	150	2.40	10,000	49
Polymer impregnated concrete (PIC)					
Standard aggregate					
Undried-dipped	2.0	153	2.45	10,000	49
Dried-evacuation-filled	6.0	159	2.55	20,000	126
High-silica steam cured	8.0	159	2.55	38,000	240
Lightweight aggregate					
Structural lightweight concrete	15.0	130	2.08	25,000	193
Insulation lightweight concrete	65.0	60	0.96	5,000	84
Polymer concrete (PC)	6.0	150	2.40	20,000	133

[a] Ref. 16.
[b] Conversions: 1 lb/ft^3 = 16.02 kg/m^3; 1 psi = 6.896 kPa.

tics may do well for several years and then fail rapidly. Exposure—north, south, east, west, horizontal, vertical, angular—can markedly affect behavior. Washing by rain can make a difference. Deterioration may take many forms, serious or not, depending on the application. It may involve fading, change of color, or loss of gloss. If uniform, these may not be serious, but if nonuniform, they may be. Transparent materials may suffer loss of transparency, yellowing, color change, blooming, fogging, or crazing. Materials may become embrittled. Occasionally, slight toughening has been known to occur. Ultraviolet-stabilizers, antioxidants, retarders, and other stabilizers may markedly increase useful life, sometimes at the expense of other attributes such as transparency. Dimensional changes may result in distorted views, cracking, or buckling. Chemical or physical deterioration or both may lead ultimately to disintegration.

Deterioration may be combatted by (*1*) knowledge of the climatic conditions to be met by the building; (*2*) selection of a plastic suitable for the conditions, including inherent weather resistance, and choice of stabilizers, antioxidants, and other additives to increase weather resistance; (*3*) design to accommodate the properties of the plastic, eg, expansion and contraction; and (*4*) design for ease of replacement in case, for example, a new and experimental use fails.

Composites, Reinforced Plastics. Well-made reinforced plastic parts such as exterior panels have given a good account of themselves, but others have failed, usually because of (*1*) poor workmanship resulting in porosity and poor distribution of fiber, (*2*) fibers coming to the surface and allowing the wicking of water inward, (*3*) resins not resistant to solar and atmospheric attack, (*4*) design details leading to high local stresses as at fastenings and sharp corners, and (*5*) poor choice of dyes or pigments, leading to color change. Steps to combat these effects include (*1*) choice of inherently weather-resistant resins, (*2*) improved finishes for glass fibers to promote wetting and adhesion by the resin, (*3*) proper fabricating processes, including gel coats and, if necessary, sufficient pressure for good consolidation, (*4*) weather-resistant coatings such as baked-on finishes or applied films such as vinyl fluoride, and (*5*) renewal coatings designed to be applied to weathered surfaces.

Fire Resistance

Plastics, like other organic materials, are combustible; they can be destroyed by fire (8,19–25). Some burn readily, some with difficulty, and others do not support their own combustion. Fire is a highly complex phenomenon, and the behavior of plastics in fire is equally complex and variable. During ignition, build-up, spread, flashover, and continued burning, plastics, like organics generally, contribute to all phases, the extent depending on composition and type of use. There is intense debate concerning and research into behavior of building materials in fires. Plastics are a major consideration. The increasing use of plastics in the fabric of buildings, especially in finish items such as floors, walls, ceilings, cabinetry, and fixtures, and in concealed applications such as insulation, has led to concern respecting fire resistance. Similar strong concern exists with respect to furnishings such as furniture.

Smoke is in many ways more dangerous than flame. It not only obscures vision but contains toxic gases such as carbon monoxide and noxious debilitating gases. Smoke particles may carry aerosols such as hydrogen chloride. Whether plastics produce light or heavy smoke and toxic or noxious gases depends on composition and conditions of burning. Some plastics burn clearly in plentiful air but evolve dense smoke when smoldering, others are inherently smoke and gas producing. Much depends on conditions, but smoke can be thick, opaque, and heavy.

As is true of organics generally, the most dangerous and most prevalent gas is carbon monoxide: deadly, invisible, and odorless. Other gases, noxious or toxic or both, are generated by plastics containing chlorine, nitrogen, phosphorous, and other elements. Among the gases are hydrogen chloride, hydrogen cyanide, phosgene, acrolein, and various aldehydes. They may reach toxic levels or become unbearably nauseating before toxic levels are attained (19).

Table 7 presents flame spread and smoke developed

Table 7. Burning Characteristics of Selected Plastics Flame-spread Test[a]

Material	Flame Spread	Smoke Developed
High-Pressure Laminates[b]		
Unbonded general purpose	60	135–170
Unbonded fire resistant	5	25
Bonded to CA board		
General purpose	25–40	0–25
Fire resistant	5	5
Unbonded general purpose	115	400
Unbonded fire resistant	45–70	65
Bonded to CA board		
General purpose	70	110–160
Fire resistant	25	5
Unbonded general purpose	320–350	200–250
Unbonded fire resistant	55	85–140
Bonded to CA board		
General purpose	55–70	35–55
Fire resistant	15	10–30
Molded Plastics[b]		
Open-grid panels	25	450–over 500
Open-grid panels	130–160	Over 800
Translucent panels	10	125
Translucent panels	25	40–450
Glass Fiber Reinforced Plastics[b]		
1	15	Over 500
2	20	140–200
3	25	300–400
4	30	200
5	50	250
6	70	Over 500
7	75	Over 500
Polyester concrete[c]		
	3	55
Miscellaneous materials[d]		
Solid vinyl tile	90	
Vinyl flooring	80	
Vinyl asbestos tile	235	
Asphalt tile	82	
Louan mahogany	242	
White-pine paneling	130	
Hollow-core wood doors	325–420	
White vinyl ceiling panels	20	

[a] Ref. 8. Courtesy of the American Society of Civil Engineers.
[b] Ref. 21.
[c] Manufacturer's data.
[d] Ref. 22.

in standard flame-spread tests of representative high-pressure laminates, molded plastics, glass-fiber-reinforced plastics, polyester concrete, and miscellaneous items. The range is large, some materials showing low flame spread and smoke evolution, whereas others are high in one or both respects (see Fire Tests).

Susceptibility of plastics to fire may be decreased by (*1*) developing plastics with structures that are resistant to fire, (*2*) modifying molecular structure, and (*3*) incorporating additives. The first is difficult; the second and third are the methods commonly pursued (8).

Modification includes (*1*) decomposition products that are noncombustible or produce smothering blankets, (*2*) reduced heats of combustion, (*3*) reduced ease of ignition, (*4*) char formation, (*5*) increased specific heat or thermal conductivity to reduce hot spots, and (*6*) incombustible fillers or reinforcements.

Additives. The principal flame retardants are (*1*) alumina trihydrate, (*2*) bromine compounds, (*3*) chlorine compounds, (*4*) phosphorous compounds, and (*5*) antimony oxides (8,20). Alumina trihydrate is the most widely used. It decomposes, giving off water to dampen the flame, and has low smoke evolution. Chlorine and bromine compounds are highly efficient and versatile; both employ antimony oxides to increase efficiency. Phosphorus is a char promoter.

Flame suppressants may reduce flaming but may increase smoke evolution. Some efficient flame retardants reduce the resistance of plastics to weathering. The designer may have to choose among the various requirements of the design.

Protective Coatings. Fire-retardant coatings are introduced in an attempt to delay ignition and to reduce flame spread (8). Heat-resistant coatings can withstand elevated temperatures, eg, silicone to 650°F (340°C), zinc and aluminum pigments to 1000°F (540°C), and frits to 1400°F (760°C). Flame-retardant coatings, eg, fluorocarbons and polyimides, retard the spread of flame. Insulated coatings, called intumescents, bubble and swell in a flame to form an insulated mass of char containing carbonaceous foam, nonignitable gas in the bubbles, and heat-absorbing ingredients. Such protective coatings are not confined to plastics, but are used on wood and other materials.

Fire Tests. Many types of standard fire tests are employed (8,26–28). Most are intended for materials generally, others are specific to plastics. Among the most widely used are those of the American Society for Testing and Materials (26), Underwriters' Laboratories (27), and the National Fire Protection Association (28).

Small-scale or laboratory tests for plastics have evolved over many years. They are mainly useful in distinguishing rapidly among materials, often during research and development when only small quantities are available. Their results cannot be used to predict directly how materials will behave in actual fires, and organizations involved in fire tests emphasize this point. They are, however, convenient and commonly used as general indicators. They measure rate of burning, smoke evolution, oxygen requirements, and other attributes under laboratory conditions. They are sometimes called bench tests.

Among larger-scale tests is the widely used tunnel test for flame spread. In this test, the rate at which flame spreads along the lower surface of the test material mounted at the top of a horizontal tunnel is compared to the rate of spread on dry (6–8% moisture content) red oak, the latter arbitrarily set at 100. Smoke density evolved is measured simultaneously, with the same index of 100 for red oak (Table 7). Another large-scale test is the fire-endurance test for wall, floor, and roof assemblies. A standard fire rising in temperature at a prescribed rate (eg, 1500°F in one-half hour, 2000°F in 4 h) impinges on the test assembly, and the time required for fire or gas penetration, or rise in temperature on the unexposed side to unacceptable levels, is measured, leading to a rating in hours, eg, 1 hour, 2.5 hours. A third test is the corner test in which walls and ceiling converge at a corner, where a measured amount of fuel is set afire and the behavior of the assembly observed. These large-scale tests are for materials generally, not only plastics, and more nearly simulate actual fires than do bench tests.

Toxicity tests generally involve laboratory animals to observe the effects of smoke and toxic gases given off by burning plastics or other materials. Criteria include loss of coordination and death. Such tests remain to be standardized.

CODE REQUIREMENTS

Local municipal codes govern (8,29). There are no federal building codes, although some agencies have their own regulations. State codes are not always mandatory. Regional, national, and international organizations prepare recommended codes, and many municipalities adopt them. General provisions respecting structural safety apply to all materials. Salient provisions respecting plastics, similar in these codes, cover light-transmitting plastics and plastic foams.

Light-Transmitting Plastic Construction

Materials must meet code requirements respecting strength, durability, and sanitary and fire-resistive requirements as determined by standard tests, such as those of the American Society for Testing and Materials (26), Underwriters' Laboratories (27), and the National Fire Protection Association (28). Two combustibility classes are based on tests for burning extent and burning rate. Types of applications are glazing, wall panels, roof panels, skylights, and light-diffusing systems. Three classes of plastics are thermoplastic, thermosetting, and glass-fiber reinforced.

In a typical code provision, for example, areas of individual skylights may not be more than 100 ft^2 (9.29 m^2), curbs must be at least 4 in. (10.16 cm) high, edges must be protected by incombustible materials, aggregate areas of skylights must be not more than 25 or 33% of the total, depending on combustibility class, and skylights must be at least 4 ft (1.22 m) apart horizontally and as much as 6 ft (1.83 m) from the edge of the roof. Provisions for other applications have similar restrictions, and also cover partitions, bathroom accessories, awnings, and greenhouses.

Foams

General code requirements regarding plastic foams cover flame spread and smoke evolved. More specific requirements relate to cavities of walls, thermal barriers, thick insulation as in cold-storage rooms, foamed plastic interior trim (eg, molds, baseboards, door and window trim), and tests for exceptional installations such as cores of structural sandwiches. For example, on room side surfaces, eg, walls and ceilings, the interior side of the plastic foam must be protected by a thermal barrier having a fire rating of at least 15 min, eg, 0.5-in. (12.7-m) gypsum wallboard, installed to stay in place for at least 15 minutes. Wall cavities and other installations have similar 15-minute restrictions. Codes also regulate foam plastic for interior trim, such as picture molds, chair rails, baseboards, and door and window trim.

Life Safety Code

This National Fire Protection Association Code sets forth classes of interior finish, including plastics (30).

Federal Agencies

The Department of Housing and Urban Development in its Minimium Standards (31) regulates plastics and other materials. It issues standards for manufactured (mobile) homes. Other agencies issue similar standards, exempt from local codes.

PRINCIPAL BUILDING USES

Uses of plastics in building may be classified as nonstructural, structural, and semistructural, or auxiliary to other materials (4,5,32,33). Nonstructural uses are by far the largest in volume and in diversity of applications. Following are selected representative examples.

Nonstructural

Wall and Partition Coverings. Exterior wall coverings include sheets, strips, and extruded profiles. Sheets are commonly formed into panels of desired configurations, as by thermoforming, and applied to substrates. Strips are similarly formed. Extruded profiles include siding shaped similarly to wood and metal siding (Fig. 16), applied together with corner pieces to wood and wood-based sheathing. Interior wall coverings are mainly flexible sheets and rolls, frequently coated on paper or fabric, applied to substrates such as plasterboard and plaster (Fig. 17). Rigid sheets include decorative laminates, plastic-coated wallboards, and panels of various configurations fabricated, for example, by thermoforming. Among the most commonly employed wall coverings are acrylics, cellulose butyrate, poly(vinyl chloride), reinforced polyesters, and decorative laminates.

Windows, Toplighting. Window frames and sash, fabricated of linear extrusions, take advantage of low thermal transmission and inherent color (Fig. 18**a**), although dark colors can result in heat absorption, expansion, and distortion. Plastic overlay (Fig. 18**b**) on wood window frames and sash provides color not requiring repainting while

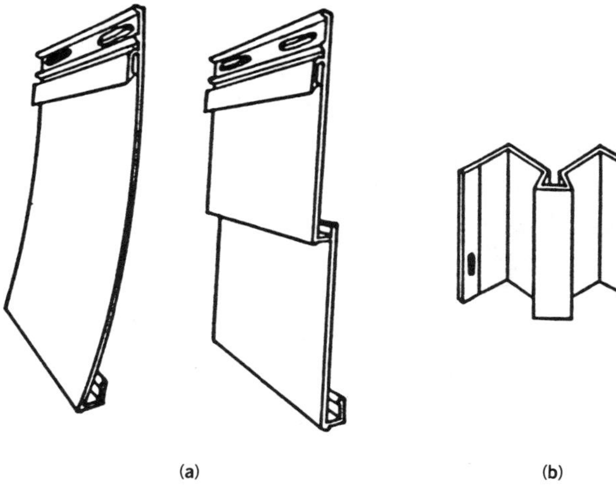

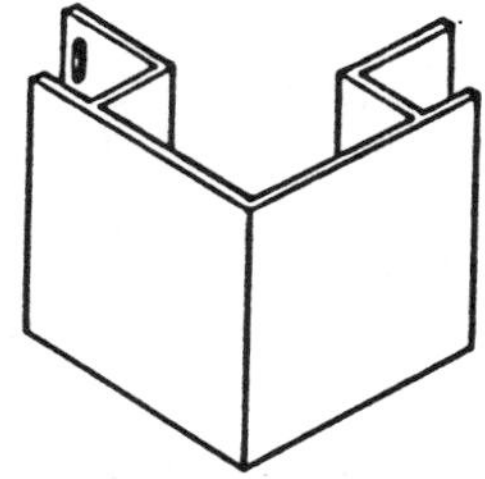

(a) (b) (c)

Figure 16. Plastic siding components (34): **(a)** Configurations; **(b)** internal corners; **(c)** external corners. Courtesy of the MIT Press.

taking advantage of wood's favorable thermal conductivity and rigidity. In metal windows, plastic thermal breaks prevent excessive heat loss and condensation. Poly(vinyl chloride) is most commonly employed.

Vacuum-formed dome-shaped skylights incorporate single or multiple lights (Fig. 19). Flat and curved sheets provide other toplighting. Allowance must be made for expansion and contraction with temperature changes. Acrylics, polycarbonate, and reinforced polyesters are most common.

Doors. High-pressure laminates, reinforced polyesters, and overlay films on wood-based or metal substrates form door facings and panels, frequently combined with cores of plastic foam, plastic-impregnated paper honeycomb or other grids, and nonplastic materials such as wood.

Figure 17. Plastic interior wall covering, floor covering, and luminous ceiling.

Thermal Insulation. Plastics provide thermal insulation mainly as (*1*) phenolic binder for glass fiber insulating batts, and (*2*) foam. Prefoamed extruded "logs" are cut into boards and applied as sheathing, roofing boards, insulation for masonry and concrete walls, perimeter insulation for concrete floor slabs, ducts, and similar purposes (Fig. 20) (see Ducts). Expandable beads, in addition to being made into boards, are placed in molds, cavities, or other spaces and heated, whereupon they expand, fill the space, and coalesce. Foamed-in-place foams consist of liquid ingredients mixed and sprayed or poured into spaces such as stud spaces and roofs, where they foam and rise to fill the space.

Moisture Barriers. Water vapor passing from warm to cool areas may condense, causing problems in building envelopes as well as reducing the efficiency of the insulation. To prevent this, barriers are interposed between the insulation and the warm side. Plastic films, mainly low-density polyethylene and poly(vinyl chloride), are employed, eg, in stud walls, above ceilings, below roofs, and below concrete slabs (Fig. 21). Open joints, tears, or other gaps must be avoided.

Floors. Calendered sheets, mainly poly(vinyl chloride), formulated with fillers, fibers, and pigments, provide flexible floor covering sheets (Fig. 22) or are cut into tiles [(see Film and Sheet Processes; Poly(vinyl Chloride)]. Sheets are commonly formulated or printed with colors and patterns, textured, and coated for moisture and stain resistance. Some have thin backings of resilient foams. Sheets and tiles are cemented to such substrates as plywood, hardboard, particleboard, and concrete. Extruded baseboards and coves accompany the flooring. Epoxy formulations with sand and small aggregate provide topping, such as terrazzo, for concrete floors.

Rainware. Poly(vinyl chloride) is the principal plastic for hanging gutters, leaders, downspouts, and appurtenances. It takes advantage of the noncorroding properties of plastics. Because of temperature extremes, allowance must be made for thermal expansion and contraction (Fig. 23).

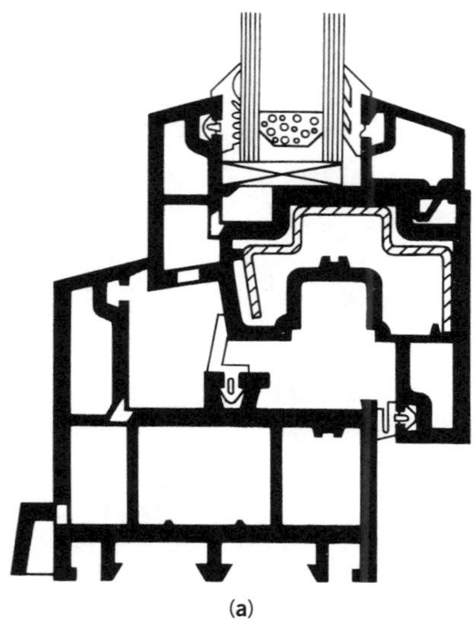

(a)

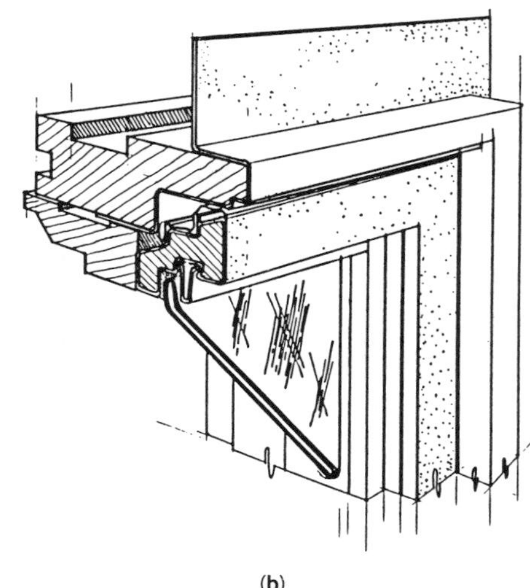

(b)

Figure 18. **(a)** Plastic window sash and frames (35). Courtesy of McGraw–Hill Information Systems Company and Dynamit Nobel. **(b)** Plastic covered wood window (34). Courtesy of the MIT Press.

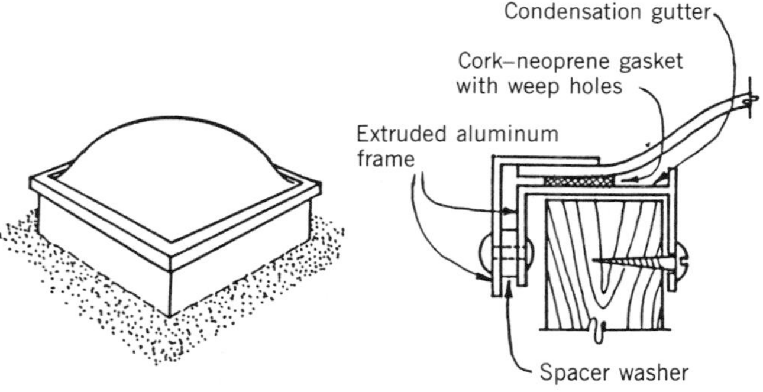

Figure 19. Dome-shaped vacuum-formed plastic skylight (34). Courtesy of the MIT Press.

Hardware. Numerous hardware parts employ a considerable range of plastics for knobs, plates, handles, hinges, sliders, runners, parts of locks and latches, rollers, cams, gears, window hardware, and many others. Nylon, phenolic, melamine and urea formaldehyde, polystyrene, ABS, cellulosics, acetal, polycarbonate, poly(vinyl chloride), and acrylics all find use (see Thermoplastics; Thermosets).

Cabinetwork, Furniture, Moldings. Counter- and table tops and doors and other cabinet parts employ high-pressure decorative laminates (see High-Pressure Laminates) (Fig. 24). Poly(vinyl chloride) and poly(vinyl butyral) are laminated to fabric for upholstery (see Poly(vinyl chloride); Poly(vinyl butyral). Building boards are faced with polyester and poly(vinyl chloride) films. Cabinet drawers are

Figure 20. Sheets of plastic insulating foam being applied to a wall (4). Courtesy of Dow Chemical.

Figure 21. Moisture barrier installed under concrete floor (4). Courtesy of Union Carbide.

Figure 22. Sheet plastic floor covering (4). Courtesy of Armstrong Industries.

molded of reinforced plastics, ABS, and others. Flexible foams provide cushioning (see Foams). Rigid foams provide moldings, chair rails, and similar items. Extrusions of poly (vinyl chloride), cellulosics, and others provide moldings (see Extrusions).

Masonry Adjuncts. Polyesters and expoxies provide decorative and wear-resistant facings for concrete blocks (see

Figure 24. Decorative laminate counter and wall covering. Luminous ceiling (4). Courtesy of Parkwood.

Polyesters; Epoxies). Epoxies and latices and copolymers of acrylics and poly(vinyl chloride) are used as additives to increase strength, toughness, and bond tenacity of stuccos. Expansion joints (Fig. 25) of preformed strips of elastomers and poly(vinyl chloride) allow relative movement of adjacent wall sections (see Gaskets).

Piping. Water, waste, drainage, and vent piping are mainly poly(vinyl chloride) and polyethylene (Fig. 26). The materials are easily cut, bent, and joined by welding, threading, and solvent cement. Hot water requires higher-

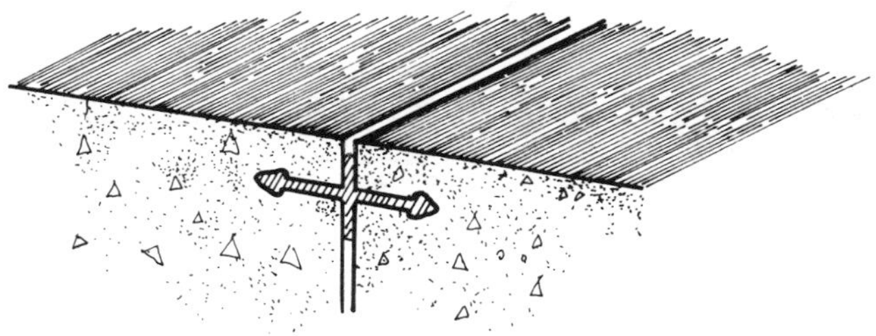

Figure 25. Expansion joint in masonry.

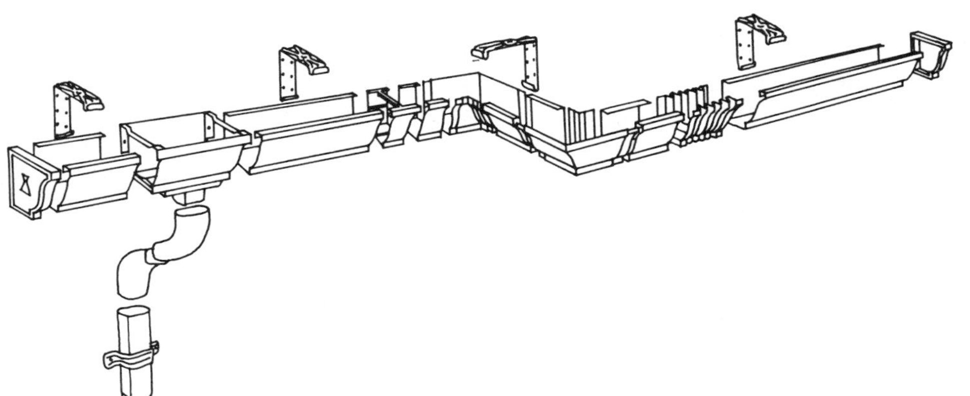

Figure 23. Gutter and downspout components (34). Courtesy of the MIT Press.

Figure 26. Plastic pipe (4). Courtesy of B. F. Goodrich Chemical.

temperature copolymers of poly(vinyl chloride), ABS, polypropylene, and others. Higher pressures may call for fiber-reinforced polyesters or epoxies. For handling chemicals, many plastics are employed as pipe or pipe linings, depending on the application.

Plumbing Fixtures. Tanks, lavatories, urinals, showers, tubs, and surrounds (Fig. 27) employ reinforced plastics, acrylics, cast epoxy compounds, and others. Finishes consist of gel coats and applied coatings. Composite fixtures may consist of thermoformed acrylics backed and stiffened by sprayed-on chopped-glass reinforced polyester (see Vacuum; Thermoforming). Among other plastics employed in plumbing fixtures are acetals and polystyrene.

Ducts. For handling air or chemical fumes, ducts may be large-diameter pipe or fabricated of sheet and structural shapes. Composition depends on the air or gas to be handled. Fans and housings may be protected by plastic coatings and overlays. Insulation is provided by blocks or slabs of foams (see Foams; Thermal Insulation). Insulation for complex shapes may be foamed in place.

Figure 27. Bathtub and surrounds. Courtesy of Owens Corning Fiberglas.

Illumination. High-percentage light transmission, clarity, colorability, light weight, formability, impact resistance, and availability as large sheets, extrusions, moldings, and thermoformed parts recommend plastics for many lighting applications, among them light transmitters, refractors, color modifiers, and filters. Allowance must be made for maximum temperatures, combustibility, possible color changes, durability outdoors, embrittlement, surface hardness (softer than glass), and thermal expansion and contraction. Uses include many kinds of fixtures, large-area illumination, eg, ceilings (Figs. 17,24), glazing resistant to breakage, street lighting resistant to vandalism, large and special shapes, and color combinations. Low-temperature light sources, eg, fluorescent, are best. High-temperature sources must be used with care. Plastics most employed are acrylics, cellulose butyrate, polycarbonate, polystyrene, and poly(vinyl chloride).

Electrical Fittings. Switch boxes, sockets, switch gear, panel boards, wall plates, circuit breakers, and many other electrical fittings employ mainly phenolic, melamine, and urea formaldehyde moldings, and high-pressure laminates. Insulation for wire and cable, easily color coded, is mainly polyethylene and poly(vinyl chloride).

Solar Energy Collectors. Cover plates for solar energy collectors employ transparent and translucent sheets that may be acrylic, polycarbonate, and glass fiber-reinforced polyesters. "Passive" storage devices include tanks for liquid storage and tiles for solid storage. Plastic piping handles both low and high temperature water or other liquids.

Structural and Semistructural

Structural and semistructural applications in building rely heavily on all kinds of composites, mainly fibrous (4,6,8). Structural applications are primary load-carrying structures; semistructural applications resist loads but transfer them to other members. Shells, sandwiches, tanks, structural shapes, tension structures, and air-supported structures are examples.

Shells. Curved shapes, simple or compound, are formed to resist applied loads with greatest structural efficiency and minimum use of materials. Synclastic and anticlastic shapes—domes, hypars—and free-form shapes can all be employed. Two examples illustrate the use of shells.

Radomes. Shelters for long-distance radars must not interfere with electromagnetic radiation, but must provide weather protection. The 150-ft (45.7-m) diameter spherical dome shown in Figure 28 consists of glass-fiber reinforced polyester panels on a network of metal bars. Smaller radomes have reinforced plastic ribs integral with the panels.

House of the Future. Four cantilevered wings projecting from a core were designed to meet Los Angeles code requirements for floor, wind, and earthquake loading plus snow loads for the northern United States (36). The glass-fiber reinforced polyester U-shaped free-form shell wings

Figure 28. Radome, 150-ft diameter. The ribs are metal, the skin is glass-fiber reinforced polyester (4). Courtesy of Lincoln Laboratories.

approximated the bending-moment curve of a uniformly loaded cantilever beam and employed the monocoque wing principle of aircraft design (Fig. 29). Floors were sandwiches with glass-fabric reinforced facings on phenolic-impregnated kraft-paper honeycomb cores. Estimated weight of the structure was about one-third that of standard house construction.

Sandwiches. Many varieties of sandwiches employing numerous materials for facings and cores are in use. Three examples illustrate the range.

Commercial Heavy Type Building Panel. Wall panels are sandwiches consisting of polymer-concrete facings 1 in. (25 mm) thick reinforced with glass roving fabric, plus 1-in. (25-mm) thick prefoamed urethane core (Fig. 30). The exterior facing is striated; the inner facing is exposed aggregate.

Translucent Panel. Highly translucent glass-fiber reinforced polyester sheets are bonded as facings to a grid core of small aluminum extrusions (Fig. 31). Panels are employed as walls and roofs for structure, enclosure, and light transmission.

Figure 29. "House of the Future," with reinforced polyester shells (4). Courtesy of Monsanto.

Figure 30. Sandwich wall panels of polymer-concrete facings on foamed urethane core.

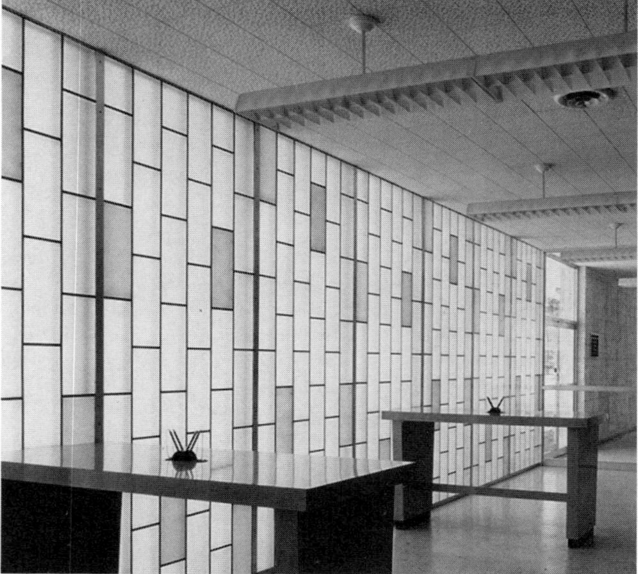

Figure 31. Translucent sandwich wall panels of glass-fiber reinforced polyester facings on aluminum grid core. Courtesy of Kalwall.

Greater London Council Flats. For a 25-story apartment building (Fig. 32**a**), the Greater London Council designed the configurations of wall panels and determined performance specifications for winds, thermal transmission, acoustical attenuation, fire penetration, and fire spread, in addition to minimum weight, thickness, and maintenance (37). The result was a composite sandwich with a mineral-loaded glass-fiber reinforced press-molded outer facing protected by a baked-on urethane coating. This was bonded with sheet foam plus epoxy to a core of foamed concrete and an inner facing of fiber-reinforced gypsum plaster bonded to the core with bitumen (Fig. 32**b**). Panels have withstood hot flames bursting outward through a window and upward on the wall.

Tanks. Tanks made of fiber-reinforced polyester or epoxy are used to hold corrosive liquids or to be buried in aggressive soils. A filament-wound glass-fiber polyester tank to hold gasoline that is to be buried is shown in Figure 33.

Structural Shapes. Pultruded shapes consisting mainly of longitudinal glass fibers, plus fabric or mat, are employed principally where corrosive or other aggressive environments would attack metal (Fig. 34). Weight saving, if critical, is achieved at increased cost by employing high-technology, high-strength, high-stiffness, low-density fibers.

Tension Structures. Cables, coated fabrics, and combinations are drawn into tension to provide large roofs and other enclosures. Two examples illustrate this.

Hadj Terminal, Jidda. Pylons 150 ft (45.7 m) high and a system of steel cables support tents 150 ft (45 m) square, consisting of glass fabric coated with polytetrafluoroethylene. The translucent fabric permits 4–18% of incident sunlight to illuminate the space below, but reflects approximately three-quarters to minimize solar heating (Fig. 35).

Munich Olympic Stadium. Steel cables drawn in tension over steel pylons support large sheets of clear polymethyl methacrylate to provide shelter and natural illumination for large areas (Fig. 36).

Air-Supported Structures. Numerous stadiums, auditoriums, warehouses, and similar spaces are enclosed by coated fabrics supported by air pressure inside the enclosure. Fabrics are commonly glass or synthetic. Coatings are generally fluorocarbon or poly(vinyl chloride). Light transmission varies with type of fabric and coating. A system of cables generally holds the fabric in place and anchors it to foundations sufficiently strong to resist the uplift brought about by the air pressure (Fig. 37).

Auxiliaries

Principal uses of plastics as auxiliaries are as (*1*) adhesives, (*2*) coatings, and (*3*) sealants and gaskets. Adhesives and coatings are discussed elsewhere in the encyclopedia.

Sealants. Sealants are viscous puttylike mastics applied in building joints by knife or gun (40). Among the plastics principally employed are acrylic, butyl, silicone, polysulfide, polymercaptan, and polyurethane. Fillers, plasticizers, and solvents or water are added to desired consistency; colors may be incorporated. Some one-part sealants, after application, attain their final cure by releasing solvent or water; others form skins by oxidation, thicken by polym erization, or retain their original consistencies; still others cure by chemical reaction with moisture in the air. Two-part sealants are mixed on the job and cure by chemical reaction of the constituents. The final product is an adherent rubbery material able to stretch or compress as the joint becomes wider or narrower, caused by contraction or expansion in the adjacent building envelope. Durability, resilience, serviceability over the expected temperature ranges, dirt pickup, and resistance to ultraviolet radiation are among the principal considerations. Tapes

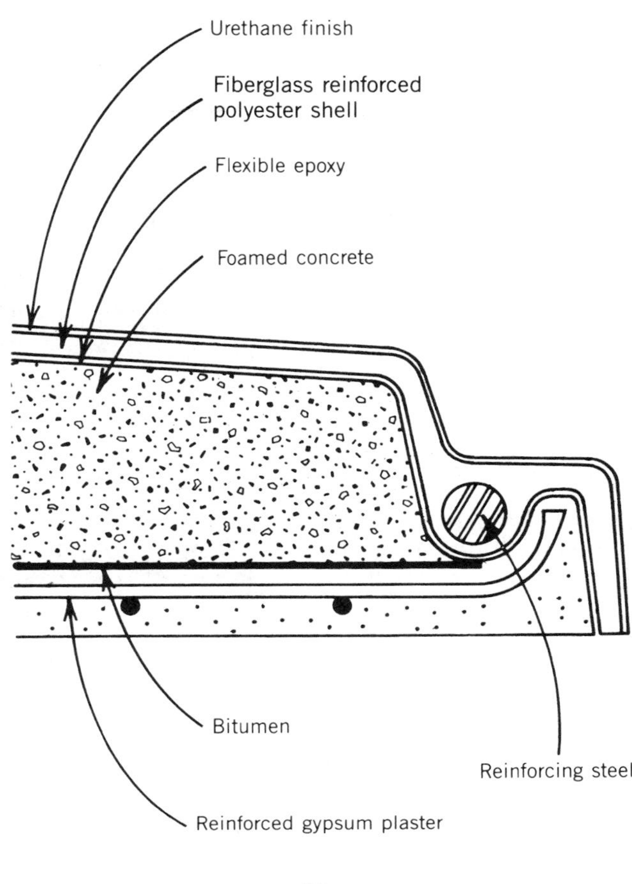

(a) (b)

Figure 32. (a) Twenty-five story apartment building; **(b)** Cross section of composite wall panel (4). Courtesy of the Greater London Council.

are solid or cellular strips pressed into joints, bonding to the adjoining surfaces.

Gaskets. Gaskets are preformed and cured strips of rubber or plastic fitted into joints to effect a seal (41). Among the principal materials are cellular and noncellular neoprene and poly(vinyl chloride). Principal requirements are similar to those for sealants. Because gaskets are not normally bonded to the adjacent surfaces, excessive compression-set becomes an important consideration.

Figure 33. Filament-wound tank. Courtesy of Owens Corning Fiberglas.

Figure 34. Pultruded structured sections. Courtesy of Morrison Molded Fiber Glass.

Figure 35. Tension roofs of glass fabric coated with polytetrafluoroethylene Hadj terminal at Jidda, Saudi Arabia. Courtesy of Civil Engineering.

Figure 36. Roof of acrylic sheets supported by steel cables, Munich Olympic Stadium.

Figure 37. Air-supported roof of the United States Pavilion at Osaka Exp '70. Courtesy of Geiger.

BIBLIOGRAPHY

1. J. Frados, ed., *Plastics Engineering Handbook of the SPI, Inc.,* 4th ed., Van Nostrand Reinhold, New York, 1976.
2. *Modern Plastics Encyclopedia, 1984–1985,* McGraw–Hill, New York, 1984.
3. C. A. Harper, ed., *Handbook of Plastics and Elastomers,* McGraw–Hill, New York, 1975.
4. A. G. H. Dietz, *Plastics for Architects and Builders,* MIT Press, Cambridge, Mass., 1969.
5. I. Skeist, ed., *Plastics in Building,* Reinhold, New York, 1966.
6. B. C. Wendle, ed., *Structural Foams,* The Society of the Plastics Industry, New York, 1985.
7. R. Nicholls, ed., *Structural Plastics Selection Manual,* Plastics Research Council, American Society of Civil Engineers, New York, 1985.
8. F. J. Heger, ed., *Structural Plastics Design Manual,* Plastics Research Council, American Society of Civil Engineers, New York, 1984.
9. M. W. Gaylord, *Reinforced Plastics Theory and Practice,* 2nd ed., Cahners, Boston, Mass., 1974.
10. J. G. Mohr et al., *SPI Handbook of Technology and Engineering of Reinforced Plastics/Composites,* 2nd ed., Van Nostrand Reinhold, New York, 1973.
11. L. J. Broutman, "Mechanical Behavior of Fiber-reinforced Plastics," in A. G. H. Dietz, ed., *Composite Engineering Laminates,* MIT Press, Cambridge, Mass., 1969, p. 125.
12. Gibbs and Cox, Inc., *Marine Design Manual for Fiberglass Reinforced Plastics,* McGraw–Hill, New York, 1960, pp. 5-2–5-39.
13. *Plastics for Aerospace Vehicles, Part I., Reinforced Plastics,* MIL-HDBK-17A, Department of Defense, Washington, D.C., 1971, pp. 2–12.
14. *Advanced Composites Design Guide,* 3rd ed., 2nd rev., Rockwell International Corporation, for Air Force Systems Command, Wright-Patterson Air Base, Ohio, Vol. I, 1973, pp. 1.1.1-4; 1.2.1-3, 4, 14-19; 1.6.6-3.
15. M. G. Young, "High-pressure Laminates," in Ref. 11, pp. 114–125.
16. *Introduction to Concrete-Polymer Materials,* FHWA-RD-75-507, Department of Transportation, Federal Highway Administration, Office of Research and Development, National Technical Information Service, Springfield, Va., 1975.
17. G. W. DePuy, "Highway Applications of Concrete Polymer Materials," in *Polymer Concrete,* Transportation Research Record 542, Transportation Research Board, National Research Council, NAS-NAE, Washington, D.C., 1975, pp. 60–66.
18. R. D. Eash and H. H. Shafer, "Reaction of Polymer Latexes with Portland Cement Concrete," in Ref. 17, pp. 1–8.
19. H. F. Mark, "Combustion of Polymers and its Retardation," *Proceedings, National Symposium on Fire Safety Aspects of Polymeric Materials,* Carnegie Institution, Washington, D.C., June 6–8, 1977.
20. V. Wigotsky, "Flame Retardants: Better "Time-buying" Compounds," *Plastics Engineering,* 23–30 (Feb. 1985).
21. *Building Materials List,* Underwriters' Laboratories, Northbrook, Ill., 1988.
22. E. L. Wilson, *Flammability and High-Temperature Characteristics of Composites,* Vol. 3, *Flame Retardance of Polymer Materials,* Dekker, New York, 1975.
23. "Fire Hazards of Materials: Plastics," in *Fire Protection Handbook,* National Fire Protection Association, Boston, Mass., 1976, pp. 3-76–3-105.
24. R. C. Anderson, *Study of the Feasibility of Regulating Products According to Smoke Potency,* AIA Codes and Standards Technology Talks Conference, Chicago, 1983.
25. *Toxic Effects Resulting From Fires in Buildings,* Symposium of 9/82 Conference, National Institute of Building Sciences, Washington, D.C., 1983.
26. *ASTM 1978 Annual Book of Standards,* Parts 18,35, American Society for Testing and Materials, Philadelphia, Pa., 1978.
27. *Underwriters' Laboratories Tests,* Underwriters' Laboratories, Inc., Chicago, Ill, 1988.
28. *Standard Methods of Fire Tests of Building Construction,* NFPA 251, National Fire Protection Association, Boston, Mass., 1972.
29. *Basic Building Code, 1975,* Building Officials and Code Administrators International, Inc., Chicago, Ill., 1975.
30. *Life Safety Code,* National Fire Protection Association, Boston, Mass., 1976.
31. HUD Minimum Property Standards, 4900.1, *One and Two-Family Dwellings;* 4910.1, *Multi-Family Housing;* 4920.1, *Care-Type Housing,* U.S. Department of Housing and Urban Development, Washington, D.C., 1973.
32. "Modern Plastics," *Materials '85,* McGraw–Hill, New York, 1985, p. 68.
33. V. Wigotsky, "Plastics in Construction—Busy Bee but Dozing Giant," *Plastics Engineering,* 17–23 (Oct. 1984).
34. A. G. H. Dietz, *Dwelling House Construction,* MIT Press, Cambridge, Mass., 1974.
35. "Doors & Windows," *Sweet's Catalog File for General Building and Renovation,* McGraw–Hill Information Systems Company, New York, 1985.
36. A. G. H. Dietz, M. E. Goody, F. J. Heger, F. J. McGarry, R. P. Whittier, "Engineering the Plastics 'House of the Future,'" Parts 1 and 2, *Modern Plastics* (June–July 1957).
37. K. J. Campbell, J. W. Davidson, A. G. H. Dietz, *Reinforced Plastics in Multi-Story Building,* Proceedings, 22nd Annual Meeting, Reinforced Plastics Division, Society of the Plastics Industry, New York, 1968.
38. F. R. Kahn, J. J. Zils, M. Salem, "Five Million Square Foot Tent Roof," *Civil Engineering,* 68–71 (Dec. 1980).
39. "Architectural Showcase," *Engineering News-Record,* (January 18, 1979).

40. J. M. Roehm, "Sealants," in J. H. Callendor (ed.), *Time-Saver Standards for Architectural Design Data,* McGraw–Hill, New York, 1982, pp. 3.108–3.117.
41. R. V. Paulus, "Gaskets," Ref. 41, pp. 3.118–3.120.

See also ACRYLICS; PHENOLIC RESINS; PLASTIC LAMINATES; PLASTICS, ABS; POLYAMIDES (NYLON); POLYESTERS; SEALANTS

ALBERT G. H. DIETZ, ScD
Winchester, Massachusetts

PLASTICS, ABS

ABS plastics are a unique family of engineering polymers composed of acrylonitrile, butadiene, and styrene. The three-monomer system can be tailored to end-product needs by varying the ratios in which they are combined. Acrylonitrile contributes heat stability, chemical resistance, and aging resistance; butadiene imparts low-temperature property retention, toughness, and impact strength; and styrene adds luster (gloss), rigidity, and processing ease.

Characteristics of interest to designers are flame retardance, high heat resistance, transparency, electroplatability, low-and-high gloss finishes, and foamability.

CHEMISTRY AND PROPERTIES

ABS is available as unpigmented pellets, specialty color-matched pellets, standard color pellets, and in powder form for alloying with other polymers such as poly(vinyl chloride) (PVC) or polycarbonate.

ABS is composed of discrete rubber particles (based on butadiene) grafted with styrene–acrylonitrile (SAN) copolymer, dispersed in a continuous matrix of SAN. Figure 1 illustrates the general dependence of key properties on rubber content. ABS properties can be varied by altering the degree of grafting, molecular weight of the free and grafted SAN, monomer ratios, heterogeneity of composition, addition of a fourth monomer (such as alpha-methyl styrene or methyl methacrylate), and by blending or alloying ABS with other polymers such as PVC or polycarbonate.

ABS plastics are viscoelastic, thermoplastic materials that are time-, temperature-, and load- (strain-) dependent. Table 1 shows the range of properties attainable with the various grades and alloys of ABS. Maximum levels of properties listed cannot be achieved simultaneously. As the content of one monomer is increased to enhance the properties associated with that monomer, properties associated with the other monomers are decreased.

In general, all standard ABS materials are light, strong, tough, and resistant to attack by most corrosive reagents. They are approved by the National Sanitation Foundation for use in potable water systems, and listed by Underwriters Laboratories for use in electrical applications. Because

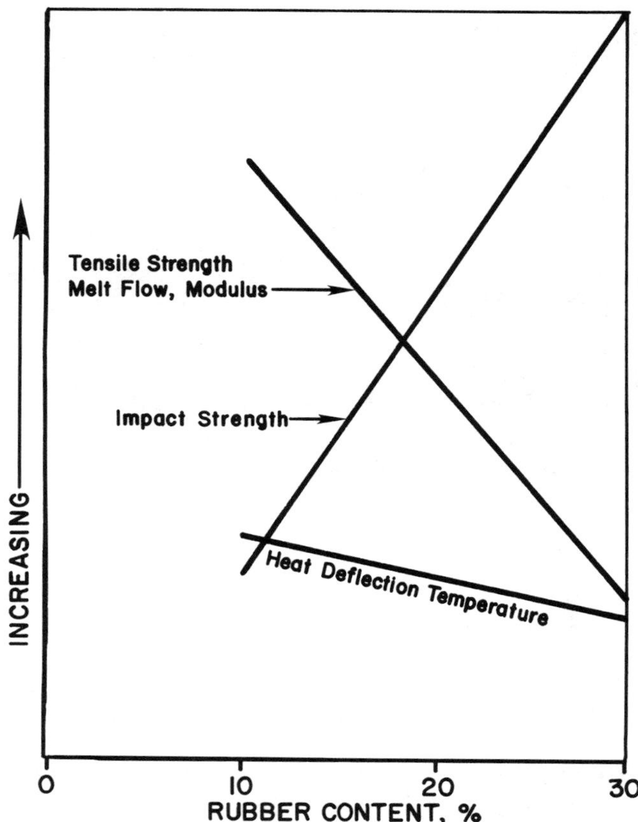

Figure 1. Property changes of ABS with rubber content.

of these and other inherent advantages, including material cost, ABS materials have a variety of uses today. Telephone, automotive, and appliance manufacturers depend on close color control, good part toughness, high-quality appearance, and ease of stain removal. Drain-waste-vent (DWV) pipe can take abuse without cracking and maintains its rigidity. Luggage, sporting goods, safety equipment, and toys depend on ABS's lightweight, flexural, and impact properties. Boats and recreational vehicles need its high strength-to-weight ratio, and its deep-draw thermoforming ability. ABS materials have relatively good electrical insulating properties, which make them suitable

Table 1. Property Extremes for Available ABS Grades

Property	Maximum	Minimum
Tensile yield strength at 73°F, 10^3 psi	8	2.3
Tensile modulus at 73°F, 10^3 psi	380	120
Flexural strength at 73°F, 10^3 psi	13	3.8
Flexural modulus at 73°F, 10^3 psi	400	130
Rockwell R hardness	117	
Shore D hardness		65
Specific gravity	1.22	0.97
Notched Izod impact, ft-lb/in.	13	2.3
Heat deflection temperature, unannealed, at 264 psi, °F.	230	145

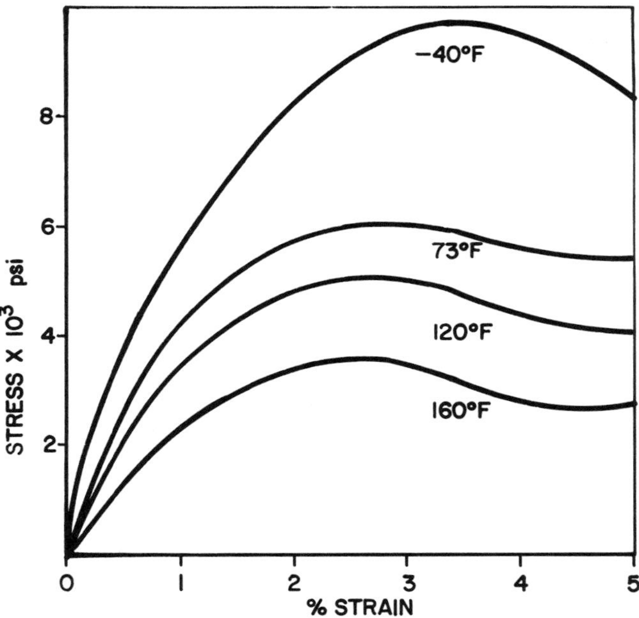

Figure 2. Stress–strain curve.

for secondary insulating applications. In portable household appliances, ABS may actually support live electrical parts. Successful part performance depends not only on correct ABS selection based on engineering properties, but also on correct part design, proper processing, and testing under simulated use conditions.

Overall chemical resistance is quite good for ABS products. They are very resistant to weak acids, as well as weak and strong bases, somewhat resistant to strong acids, and are soluble in polar solvents such as esters, ketones, and some chlorinated hydrocarbons.

Figure 2 shows the tensile stress–strain curve for a general purpose, high impact material. ABS is characterized by the capability to deform in a ductile manner at low temperatures.

Tensile strength at yield ranges from approximately 3000 to 9000 psi, depending on the specific grade. Strain at yield is typically 2–5%, while ultimate elongation varies over a wide range of values. Typical design limits are set at 0.5% strain for continuous load-bearing applications. For one-time, snap-fit designs, strain limits of 1–2% may be permissible.

METHODS OF PROCESSING

Injection molding grades of ABS can be processed on either ram- or screw-injection molding machines. Structural ABS foam parts can be molded either on standard screw-injection molding machines using an internally compounded blowing agent, or on molding machines using low-pressure nitrogen for achieving the foam structure.

Extrusion grades of ABS pellets can be converted into pipe, sheet, blow molded, or profile products using conventional single-screw or twin-screw extruders. Extruded sheet can be thermoformed by the application of heat and pressure. Extruded sheet may be embossed as desired, or may have a laminate applied as it passes through the cooling rolls. Surface lamination is widely used to impart good weatherability with color retention to achieve special decorative effects, or for improved scuff resistance. ABS is a hygroscopic material and will absorb moisture from the air, requiring drying prior to molding or extrusion.

See also PLASTICS

DON COE
Borg-Warner Chemicals
Washington, W. Virginia

PLUMBING SYSTEMS

The concern for orderly disposal of human waste can be traced to antiquity wherever large numbers of people lived together. Indeed, the term plumbing is derived from the Latin "plumbum" for lead, the early piping material. Through the years, sewage piping developed and traps or water seals evolved. However, from the late 1800s until the 1960s, formal research in this field suffered. Today, the work is much better understood and improved; factual performance tables and innovative vent systems, materials, and fastening methods are becoming widely used. In fact, more progress has been made in the plumbing engineering profession in the past decade than during the previous 50 years. Designing plumbing systems has become a science rather than an art.

Fixture Selection

The type, quantity, and spatial arrangement of plumbing fixtures is usually the prerogative of the architect. The type and quantity of fixtures to be installed in a building are predicated on the number of people to be served and the type of building occupancy. These requirements are clearly delineated in every building code. Separate facilities must be provided for male and female personnel and must be within easy access from any floor of the building. The term easy access has been interpreted to mean within one floor vertically and 75 ft horizontally.

Quality of Fixtures

Manufacturers have accepted certain standards for making plumbing fixtures. Most manufacturers adhere to these standards; therefore, fixture quality is a minor problem. The limitation of water consumption in water closets to 3.5 gallons per minute (gpm) and fixtures and designs ensuring accessibility for the handicapped now appear in many codes.

Materials used in the manufacture of fixtures are enameled cast-iron, enameled pressed steel, vitreous china, vitrified earthenware, stainless steel, plastics, aluminum, and stone compositions.

Fixture Classification

Fixtures may be classified as follows:

Water closets	Bathtubs
Urinals	Showers
Lavatories	Drinking fountains
Sinks	Bidets
Service tanks	

Water Closets. Quiet operation and economical use of water are important features. Water closets may be floor-outlet closets mounted on special closet flange connections in the floor, or wall-hung closets mounted on a combination chair carrier and fitting, which supports the watercloset without placing any stress on the wall. The wall-hung water closet permits greater ease in cleaning the floor around and below the closet. Manufacturers supply bowls with the following flushing actions: siphon jet, reverse trap, and blowout.

The siphon jet (Fig. 1) has become the most popular type in the United States. It is available in the floor-mounted or wall-hung style. It operates by action of a jet (D) of water directed through the uplet (C) of the trapway. This fills the trapway with water and the siphonic action begins immediately. It has a large water surface (A) in the bowl and a deep water seal (B). Its action is quiet, strong, and quick. The rim holes are punched at an angle producing a swirling or vortex motion of the water. This action, in conjunction with the strong jet of water in the upleg of the trapway, cleanses the bowl thoroughly and efficiently with a minimum of noise.

The reverse trap water closet (Fig. 2) is similar to the siphon jet with the following exceptions: the water surface (A) and the trapway (C) are smaller, and the water seal (B) is not as deep. Because of these differences, less water is required for its efficient operation. It could be said that the reverse trap is the economy model siphon jet.

The blowout type (Fig. 3) depends on the driving jet (D) directed into the trapway for its operation, rather than on siphonic action. It has a large water surface (A), a deep water seal (B), and a large unrestricted trapway (C). This bowl requires a higher entering water pressure to ensure adequate flushing and is noisier than siphon action bowls. This type is suitable for use in schools and commercial and office buildings where noise is not objectionable.

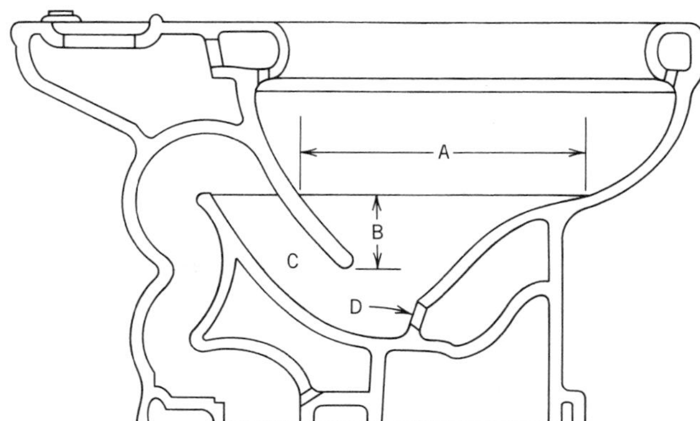

Figure 2. Reverse trap (1). Courtesy of Construction Industry Press.

All types may be obtained with an elongated rim offering a larger seat opening, which is recognized as a superior sanitary feature. The elongated bowl should be specified for all water closets intended for public use.

Seats for water closets should be of smooth, nonabsorbent material having relatively low thermal conductivity. Open-front toilet seats should be specified for water closets intended for public use.

Water Supply for Water Closets. Water for flushing water closets is supplied by means of a flush valve (flushometer) or a flush tank. Both must be capable of providing an adequate quantity of water for proper and efficient flushing. Depending on the manufacturer and type of water closet, it has been found that 3.5–7 gal of water is sufficient. Recently, a water closet requiring only one gallon for an adequate flush has been introduced into the market.

Urinals. Urinals are manufactured as floor-mounted, wall-hung, or freestanding in various sizes and shapes. Water supply for urinals must meet the same requirements as for water closets. Siphon jet and blowout urinals provide a flushing action that removes foreign matter deposited in the urinal, such as cigarette and cigar butts and candy wrappers. The washout and washdown models operate more quietly, but are intended to remove only liquid wastes.

Lavatories. Lavatories come in many shapes and sizes, providing an almost unlimited selection. They can be clas-

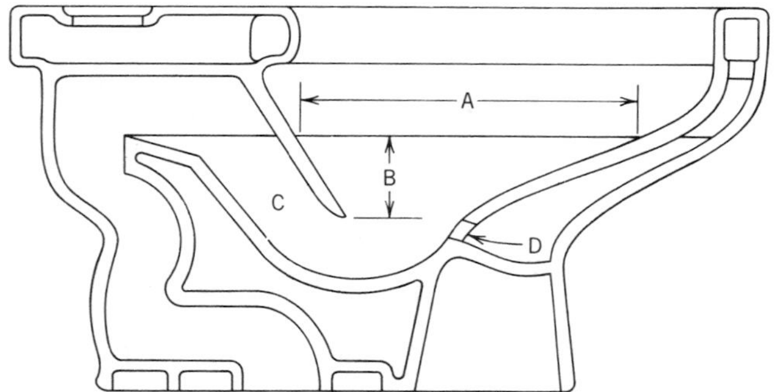

Figure 1. Siphon jet (1). Courtesy of Construction Industry Press.

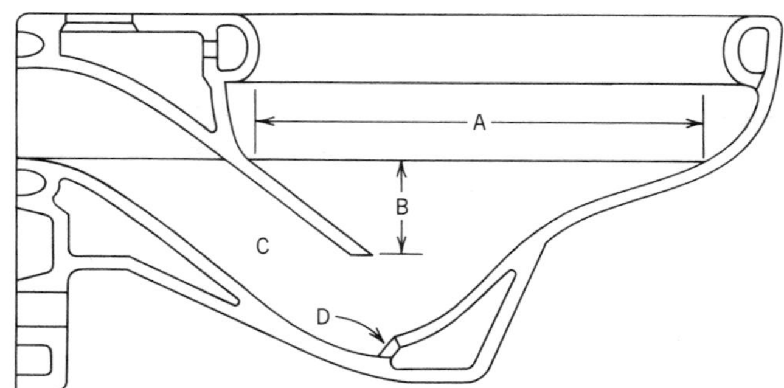

Figure 3. Blowout (1). Courtesy of Construction Industry Press.

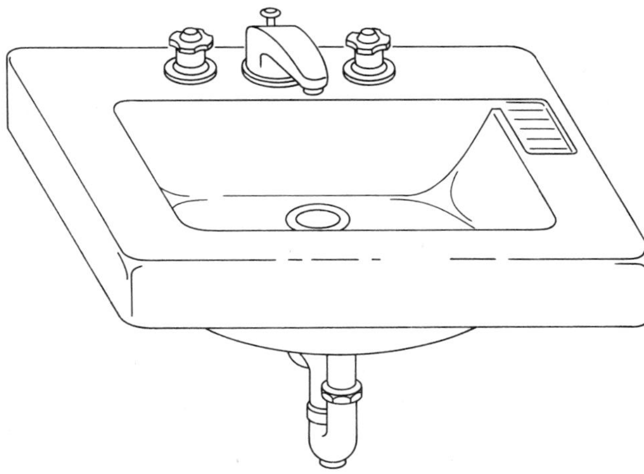

Figure 4. Slab-type lavatory (1). Courtesy of Construction Industry Press.

sified into five types as follows: slab, splash-back, shelf-back, ledge-back, and countertop. Special purpose lavatories can usually be placed within these five categories.

The slab-type lavatory comes in vitreous china and is supported by concealed or exposed arms, wall brackets, and chrome legs. The back of the fixture is usually installed 2 in. from the wall to facilitate cleaning (Fig. 4).

The splash-back lavatory has an integral back and is recommended for sanitary purposes. Splashed water remains on the fixture rather than running down the back as in the slab-type. The fixture is made of vitreous china and may be supported by wall hangers, or by concealed or exposed arms (Fig. 5).

The shelf-back lavatory reduces splashing and also provides a shelf for storage of toiletries. The fixture is made of vitreous china or enameled iron (Fig. 6).

The ledge-back lavatory offers some splash reduction

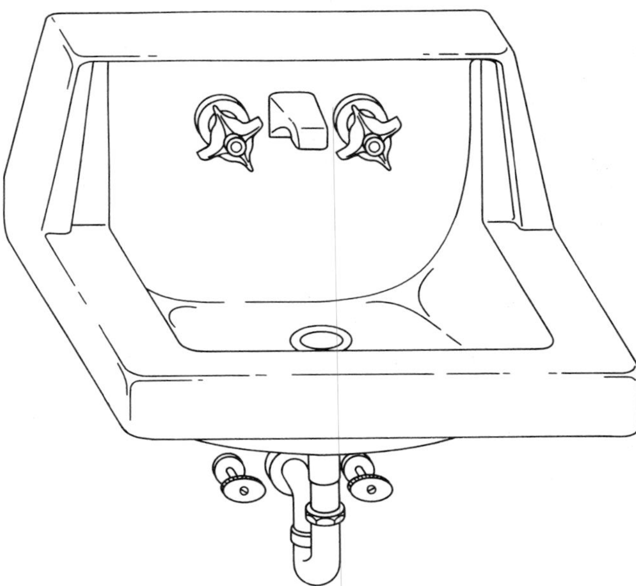

Figure 6. Shelf-back lavatory (1). Courtesy of Construction Industry Press.

and some shelf area. All four types have depressions molded into the fixture for holding bar soap, for which manufacturers offer modifications. For example, an additional hole may be provided for a liquid soap dispenser (Fig. 7).

Countertop lavatories are the most recent and probably the most diversified of any category. They come in various materials, including vitreous china, enameled cast-iron, stainless steel, plastics, fiber glass, and precast artificial marble. The popularity of countertop lavatories is because of the self-rimming feature, which does not require the use of a stainless steel rim.

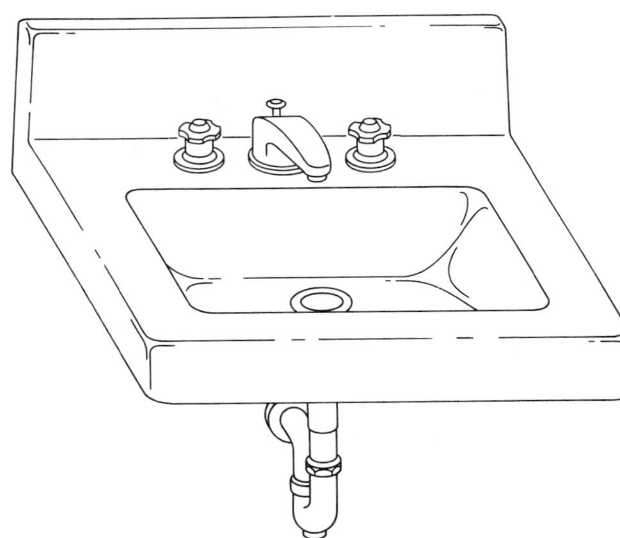

Figure 5. Splash-back lavatory (1). Courtesy of Construction Industry Press.

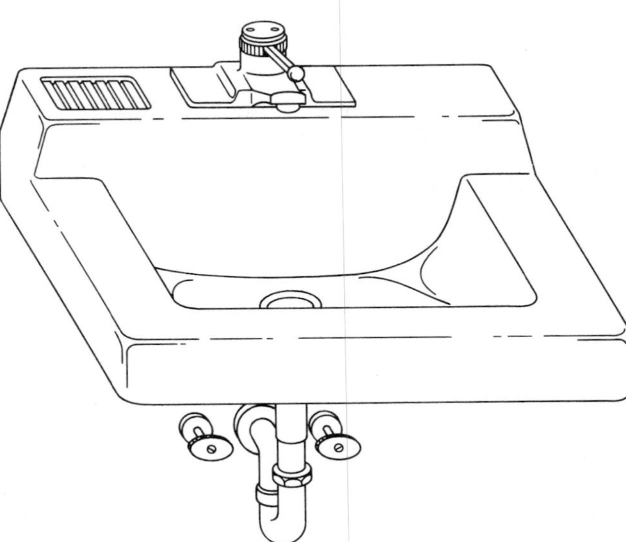

Figure 7. Ledge-back lavatory (1). Courtesy of Construction Industry Press.

The engineer should be especially aware of possible problems created when he or she specifies newer materials, and should carefully analyze the materials application to a given installation. For example, special care must be exercised regarding abrasion resistance characteristics. Abrasive cleaners tend to destroy the surface luster of newer materials much more quickly than that of traditional materials. In addition, not all newer materials are fire-resistant.

Sinks. A wide selection of sink types is available. Sinks come in single, double and triple compartment models. Two-compartment sinks, with both compartments having the same size, are the most widely used. It is recommended that one compartment be at least 15 × 18 in. for residential use to allow the acceptance of a roasting pan. The faucet spout should be high enough so that a large pot may be placed beneath it without any difficulty.

Service Sinks. The most popular service sinks have a high back, are wall-mounted and supported on a trap standard or the low-type mop basins, which are mounted on, or recessed into, the floor. Protective rim guards are recommended for both.

Bathtubs. Bathtubs are available in various sizes and shapes; however, the 5-ft bathtub has become almost standard. Recently, fiber glass and plastic models have entered the market. The plumbing engineer is strongly advised to check thoroughly with the manufacturer as to hardness of surface and resistance to abrasive cleaners.

Enameled cast-iron tubs have been preferred because of their ability to resist chipping and rusting, which happens frequently with enameled steel tubs. The thickness of enamel coating on cast iron is two to three times the coating thickness on pressed steel and has superior adherence to the base.

Showers. Shower receptors have various sizes and shapes. They are available in standard precast sizes, and custom-built models to fit any application may be obtained.

Where precast receptors are not employed, the built-up type is used. The pan for a built-up shower can be fabricated from lead, copper, or various new compositions. The pan should turn up at least 6 in. and turn over the threshold to provide a watertight installation.

Drinking Fountains. Drinking fountains (nonrefrigerated) are available as freestanding, surface-mounted, semi-recessed, pedestal, or deck type for countertops. When selecting a semi- or fully-recessed model the plumbing engineer should make certain the wall or pipe space is deep enough to accommodate the fountain and necessary piping.

Electric water coolers are available in as many variations as drinking fountains. It is extremely important to provide adequate wall thickness to accommodate the chiller unit and piping. Location of the chiller unit and grill finish should be coordinated with the architect.

Bidets. The bidet is about the same size and shape as a water closet, and could be classified as a small bath. It is used primarily for washing after using the water closet.

The hot and cold water supply and the drain fitting are very similar to those used for lavatories. However the water is introduced through a flushing rim instead of entering the bowl from a spout. The tepid water flows through the rim and while filling the bowl it warms the china hollow rim, which serves as a seat. A spray rinse is optional, and recommended, for external rinsing. Although this rinse is often called a douche it should not be construed as being designed or intended for internal use. The plumbing engineer should recommend that a soap dish and towel rack be provided within easy reach.

The foregoing has been a very brief discussion of salient features of some of the most common fixtures. The reader is referred to the catalogs of various fixture manufacturers for a complete presentation of fixtures and trim. The catalogs are an excellent source of information and give all the detailed data required.

Fixture Trap. A fixture trap is a fitting or device that provides a liquid seal, which prevents the back passage of air without materially affecting the flow of sewage or waste water through it. Figure 8 shows a typical fixture trap.

Trap Seal. The trap seal is the maximum vertical depth of liquid that a trap will retain, measured between the crown weir and the dip of the trap. A trap must provide a minimum seal of 2 in. All drainage and venting systems are designed so that pneumatic pressure variations in the system are limited to ±1 in. of water column.

Trap primers cause periodic injections of water into floor drain traps in locations where evaporation is a factor, such as boiler rooms or heavily ventilated spaces. These are demanded by plumbing codes in most jurisdictions. Where trap primers are not practical, as in residential

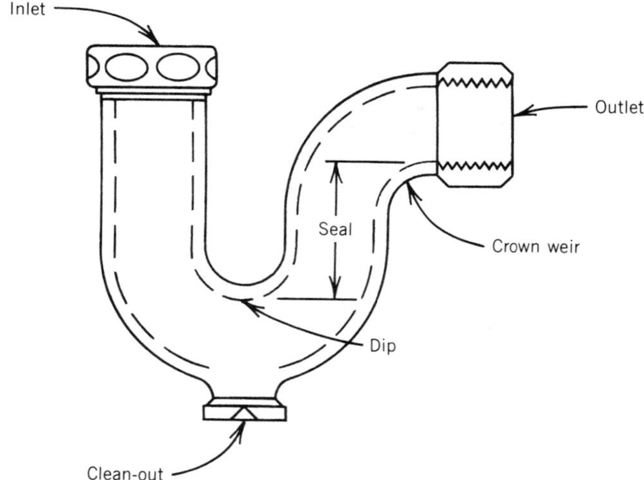

Figure 8. Typical fixture trap (1). Courtesy of Construction Industry Press.

basements, floor drains can be dangerous sources of sewer gas entry and should not be used.

Flow

Gravity Flow in Sloping Drains. When flow occurs in drain piping, it does not entirely fill the pipe under normal conditions of flow. If the pipe were to flow full, pressure fluctuations would occur that could destroy the seal of traps within the building. Gravity flow in sloping (horizontal) drain lines of a plumbing system is similar to the flow of water in open channels. Flow in open channels does not depend on pressure applied to the water, but is caused by the gravitational force induced by the slope of the drain and the height of the water in that drain.

Uniform Flow. Uniform flow is achieved in an open channel of constant shape and size and uniform slope. The slope of the water surface then matches the slope of the channel. Many formulas have been developed for determining the velocity of uniform flow in sloping drains. The one used most to solve plumbing problems is the Manning formula, proposed by Robert Manning in 1890:

$$V = \frac{1.486}{n} \times R^{2/3} \times S^{1/2}$$

where V = Velocity of flow in feet per second (fps); n = A coefficient representing roughness of pipe surface, degree of fouling, and pipe diameter; R = hydraulic radius (hydraulic mean depth of flow) in ft; and S = hydraulic slope of surface of flow in ft/ft. The quantity rate of flow is equal to the cross-sectional area of flow times the velocity of flow. This can be expressed as:

$$Q = AV$$

where Q = quantity rate of flow in cubic feet per second, (cfs); A = cross-sectional area of flow in square feet (ft^2); V = velocity of flow, fps. Substituting the value of V from Manning's Formula:

$$Q = A \times \frac{1.486}{n} \times R^{2/3} \times S^{1/2}$$

Particular note should be made of the units in the above equations. It is extremely important to convert all values to the proper units when utilizing any of the formulas.

The hydraulic mean depth of flow, R, usually called the "hydraulic radius," is the ratio of the cross-sectional area of flow to the wetted perimeter of the pipe surface (Fig. 9).

The uniform flow velocity and capacity of various size sanitary drains installed at a slope of ¼ in./ft are tabulated in Table 1 by using Manning's formula and employing the recommended values of n. Cubic feet per second has been converted to gallons per minute. For slopes of ⅛ in. and ½ in., multiply the values given in Table 1 by 0.707 and 1.414, respectively, to obtain correct figures.

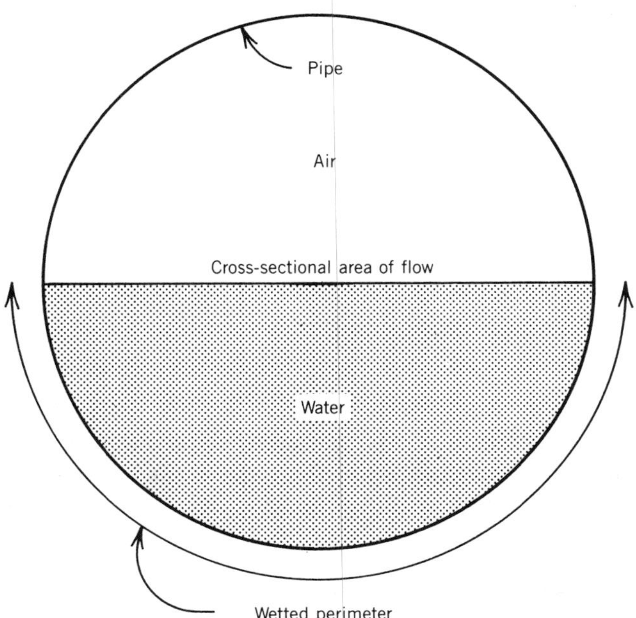

Figure 9. Half-full flow (1). Courtesy of Construction Industry Press.

Scouring Action. The minimum velocity of flow to achieve scouring action in piping is 2 fps. Sand, grit, pebbles, and other foreign matter held in suspension in the waste water will begin to deposit in the pipe when velocities fall below 2 fps. A minimum velocity of 4 fps is required to maintain greasy wastes in suspension. Minimum velocities are obtained by proper sizing and slope of pipe. An examination of Table 1 reveals that several of the pipe sizes yield velocities less than 2 fps. Because of this runs of 1.5-in. and 2-in. pipe must be held to a minimum length for entrance velocities to maintain the minimum required scouring velocity for the other short distance involved.

Surcharging. Conditions exist under which it is desirable to increase the capacity of a sewer line beyond that

Table 1. Uniform Flow Velocity and Capacity of Sanitary Drains at ¼ in. Slope

Pipe Size, in.	Full or Half-Full Flow Velocity, V, fps	Half-Full Flow Capacity, q, gpm	Full Flow Capacity, q, gpm
1½	1.85	5.85	11.7
2	1.98	9.70	19.4
2½	2.30	17.60	35.2
3	2.59	28.60	57.2
4	2.91	57.00	114.0
5	3.15	96.50	193.0
6	3.58	157.50	315.0
8	4.07	318.50	637.0
10	4.69	574.00	1148.0
12	5.31	936.00	1872.0
15	6.15	1690.00	3380.0

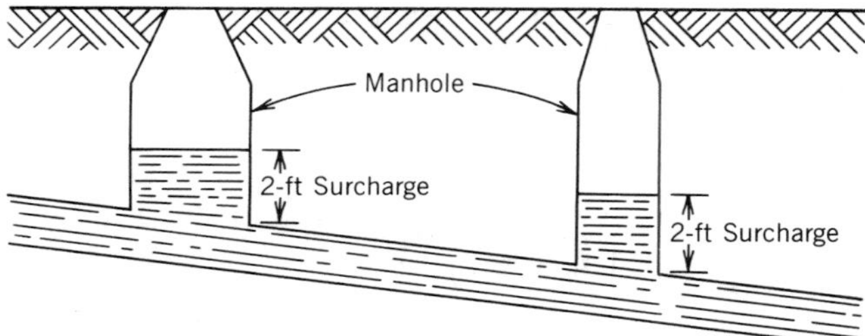

Figure 10. Illustration of sewer with a 2-ft surcharge (1). Courtesy of Construction Industry Press.

possible by gravity flow. This may occur in an existing sewer line where current demands exceed original estimates, resulting in a sewer that cannot handle peak demands. Another situation may be one of economics. It is possible to impose a pressure on a sewer line by means of surcharging, and thus increase the capacities of the sewers in relation to the amount of surcharge. It is a very simple concept, as illustrated in Figure 10. The discharge into the sewer is increased beyond its capacity of uniform flow at full flow. The water then rises in the manholes and, depending on the height of the water, imposes a pressure in excess of the gravitational force, thus increasing the velocity of flow and capacity. Surcharge is usually expressed as feet of surcharge, which is the vertical distance measured above the surface of flow. Smaller size pipe and less slope can be utilized in surcharging to obtain the same capacity as under gravity flow.

Sewer Shapes

It is important to maintain a minimum of 2 fps velocity in public sewers as well as in house drains. This presents a difficult problem where there are extremely high peak demands and long periods of relatively low flow. This is particularly true of combined sewers where large sizes are required to accommodate storm water flow, but much smaller sizes would be adequate to maintain the 2 fps velocity of the decreased sanitary flow. Engineers have overcome this problem by designing egg- or oval-shaped sewers capable of maintaining the required minimum velocities at low-flow conditions (Fig. 11). Manning's formula demonstrates how the hydraulic radius affects the velocity. In comparing the hydraulic radius for circular, egg, and oval sewers, it can be seen that by decreasing the wetted perimeter at low flow conditions, the hydraulic radius increases, consequently increasing the velocity.

Soil and Waste Stacks

"Stack" is a general term for any vertical line of soil, waste, or vent piping that collects water and wastes from fixture drains and horizontal branch drains from two or more floors of a building. This does not include vertical fixture drains and branch vents that do not pass through more than two stories before being reconnected to the soil or waste stack or vent stack. The waste water comes from

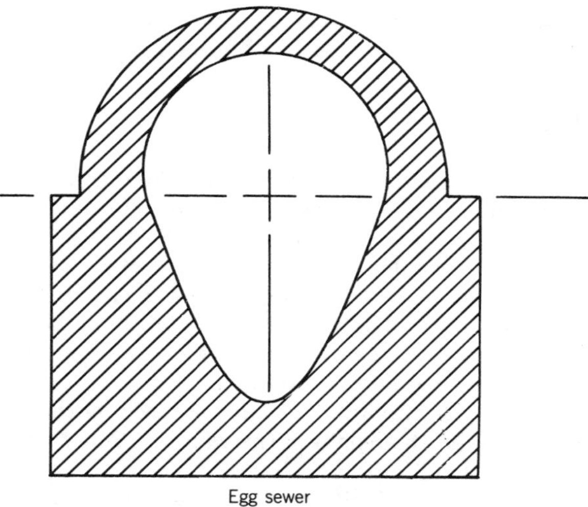

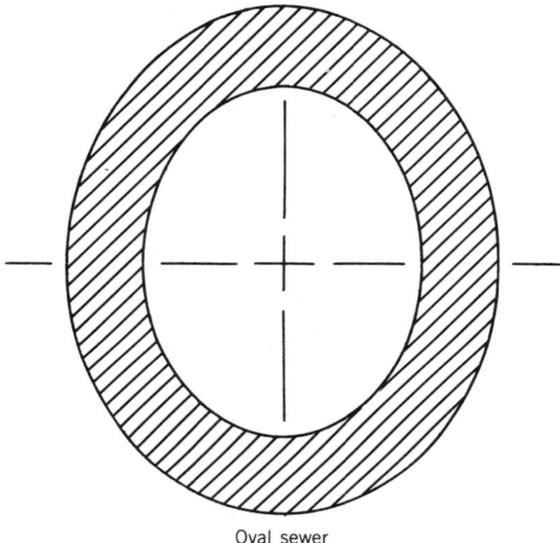

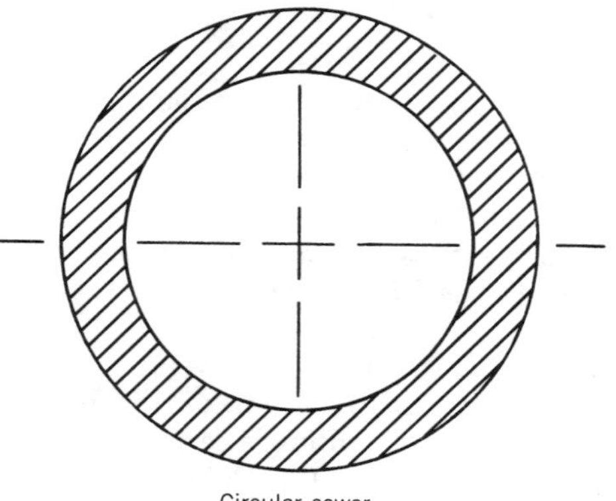

Figure 11. Sewer shapes (1). Courtesy of Construction Industry Press.

water closets, urinals, lavatories, bathtubs, showers, sinks, and various other fixtures. A soil stack collects wastes from water closets and urinals. A waste stack collects wastes that do not contain fecal matter.

Stack Connections. The horizontal branch connections to the stack are made with a sanitary tee, which is a short radius tee-wye, or with a tee-wye having a long radius. These fittings direct the waste into the stack with an initial downward velocity permitting the stack to accept an increased rate of flow at any level. The tee-wye gives the water a greater downward component than the sanitary tee. Hence the tee-wye is more advantageous for greater stack capacities, but is less favorable because it tends to create self-siphonage of the fixture traps connected to the branch. The tee-wye is often called a combination wye and one-eighth bend. It may be used in the horizontal or vertical position. The sanitary tee is used only in the vertical position.

Flow in Stacks. The characteristics of flow down a stack can best be described as follows (2):

> The character of the flow of water in partially filled vertical pipes varies with the extent to which the pipe is filled . . . For small volumes of flow, amounting to little more than a trickle, the flow is entirely on the inner wall of the stack. With the increase in volume, this adherence to the wall continues up to a point where the frictional resistance of the air causes it to diaphragm across the pipe temporarily, forming a short slug of water which descends as a slug filling the stack until the increased air pressure breaks through, the water forming the slug either being thrown against the wall or falling a short distance as separate streamlets in the center of the pipe. This diaphragming and forming slugs probably first appears in a 3″ stack when the stack is from one-fourth to one-third full. This intermittent rate partially accounts for the rapid erratic oscillations of pressure in a plumbing system.

From this it can be seen that a stack should never be designed for a capacity greater than one-third full (Fig. 12), because the pressure fluctuations in the system could greatly exceed the ±1-in. column of water pressure criterion and traps could possibly lose their seals by siphonage or blow-out.

Terminal Velocity and Length. When the plumbing engineer begins designing a system for a very tall building, he or she is invariably asked how the extremely high velocities developed at the base of the stacks will be accommodated. How will the base fitting be prevented from being blown out or broken? This is one of the oldest and most persistent myths in the plumbing profession.

Depending on the rate of flow from the branch drain into the stack, the type of stack fitting, the diameter of the stack, and the flow down the stack from upper levels, the discharge from the branch may or may not entirely fill the cross section of the stack at the point of entry. As soon as the water enters the stack, it is immediately accelerated by the force of gravity and in a very short distance it forms a sheet around the inner wall of the pipe. This sheet of water, with a core of air in the center, continues to accelerate until the frictional force exerted by the pipe wall on the falling sheet of water equals the gravitational force. From this point downward, provided no flow enters the stack as the sheet passes a fitting, the sheet of water will fall at a velocity that will remain practically unchanged. This ultimate vertical velocity is called terminal velocity and the distance in which this maximum velocity is achieved is called terminal length.

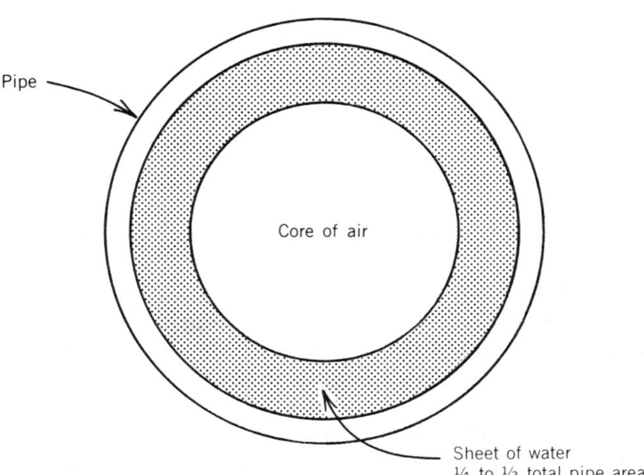

Figure 12. Cross section of stack flowing at design capacity (1). Courtesy of Construction Industry Press.

F. M. Dawson and A. A. Kalinske and R. S. Wyly and H. N. Eaton have investigated terminal velocity and derived a workable formula by treating the sheet of water as a solid hollow cylinder sliding down the inside wall of the pipe (3,4). Without showing the complicated calculus, the formulas developed for terminal velocity and terminal length are

$$V_T = 3.0\,(q/d)^{2/5}$$

$$L_T = 0.052\,V_T^2$$

where V_T = terminal velocity in stack in fps; L_T = terminal length below point of flow entry in ft; q = quantity rate of flow in gpm; and d = diameter of stack in in.

When the formulas for various pipe sizes are applied, terminal velocity is achieved at approximately 10–15 fps within 10–15 ft of fall from point of entry. This is important because it conclusively destroys the myth that water falling in a stack from a great height will destroy the fitting at the base of the stack. The velocity at the base of a 100-story stack is only slightly and insignificantly greater than the velocity at the base of a 3-story stack.

Stack Capacities. The flow capacity is the ratio of the cross-sectional area of the sheet of water to the cross-sectional area of the pipe when the flow down the stack is at terminal velocity. In entirely independent investigations, Dawson and Hunter have found that slugs of water and the resultant violent pressure fluctuations did not occur until the stack flowed ¼–⅓ full. The maximum permissible flow rates in the stack can be expressed as:

$$q = 27.8\, r^{5/3} d^{8/3}$$

where q = capacity in gpm; r = ratio of cross-sectional area of sheet of water to cross-sectional area of stack; and d = diameter of the stack in in. Values of flow rates when r = 6/24, 7/24, and 8/24 are tabulated in Table 2.

Most code authorities base their stack loading tables on a value of r = 6/24 or 7/24. The upper limit of r = 8/24 is very rarely used because of the real probability that diaphragming will occur with resultant problems.

Hydraulic Jump. At the base of a stack, flow enters the horizontal drain at a relatively high velocity as compared to the velocity of flow in a horizontal drain under uniform flow conditions. For a 3-in. stack flowing at capacity, the terminal velocity is 10.2 fps. For a 3-in. drain installed at a slope of ¼ in./ft, the velocity under uniform flow conditions at full or half-full flow is 2.59 fps. When the water reaches the bend at the bottom of the stack it is positioned at a right angle to its original flow, and for a few pipe diameters downstream it continues flowing at a relatively high velocity along the lower part of the pipe. Since the slope of the horizontal drain is not adequate for maintaining this velocity, the flow of the water slowly decreases as the depth slowly increases until critical velocity is reached. Then a sudden increase in the depth of flow occurs, which is often great enough to completely fill the cross-sectional area of the pipe. This phenomenon is called the hydraulic jump. The critical distance at which the jump may occur varies according to entrance velocity, depth of water that may already exist in the horizontal drain, and the roughness, diameter, and slope of the pipe. Therefore, it may occur at the stack fitting, or downstream up to 10 times the diameter of the stack. Less jump occurs if the horizontal drain is larger in size than the stack. Increasing the slope of the horizontal drain will also minimize the jump. After the hydraulic jump occurs and fills the drain the pipe flows full, with large bubbles of air moving with the water along the top. Surging flow conditions exist until frictional resistance retards the velocity, returning the system to uniform flow conditions.

Any offset of the stack greater than 45° may cause a hydraulic jump. Figure 13 illustrates the hydraulic jump.

Table 2. Maximum Capacities of Stacks

Pipe Size, in.	Flow in gpm r = ¼	r = 7/24	r = ⅓
2	18.5	23.5	
3	54	70	85
4	112	145	180
5	205	270	324
6	330	435	530
8	710	920	1145
10	1300	1650	2055
12	2050	2650	3365

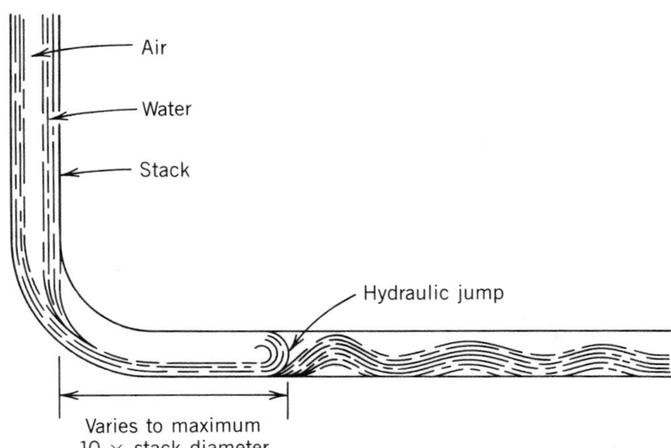

Figure 13. Hydraulic jump at offset (1). Courtesy of Construction Industry Press.

Branch Connections to Stack Offsets. Connections should not be made to the horizontal offset if at all possible. If one must be made, it should be at least 10 diameters downstream to avoid the hydraulic jump area where there is danger of excessive pressures. Connections should be made a minimum of 2 ft above and 2 ft below the offset to avoid areas subject to extreme pressure fluctuations (Fig. 14).

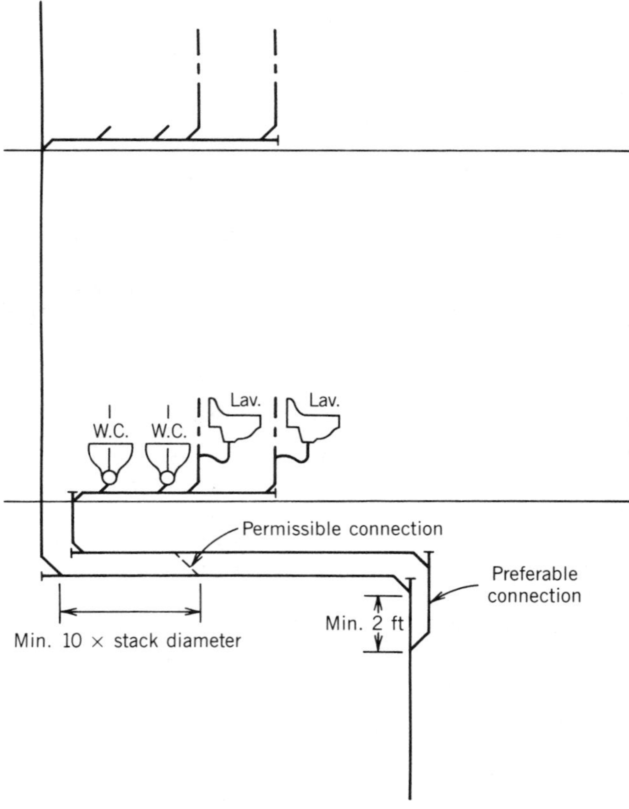

Figure 14. Piping for fixtures directly above offset (1). Courtesy of Construction Industry Press.

Piping Installation

Horizontal piping must be installed in alignment, parallel to walls and at sufficient pitch to assure a minimum velocity of flow of 2 fps. To attain this minimum velocity for scouring action, pipe 3 in. and smaller in diameter should be installed with a minimum pitch of ¼ in./ft. A pitch of ⅛ in./ft for larger pipe is satisfactory for maintaining adequate velocity.

Horizontal drainage piping should be routed so as not to pass over any equipment or fixtures where leakage from the line could cause contamination. Drainage piping must never pass over switchgear or other electrical equipment. Route piping around electrical closets. If it is impossible to avoid these areas, a pan must be installed below the pipe to collect water from leaks or condensation and a drain line run from the pan to a convenient floor drain or service sink.

Underground drainage piping should always be laid on a firm bed for its entire length with the earth scooped out at the bells to make this possible. Clean earth or screened gravel should be firmly tamped under, around, and above the pipe to a level of 1 ft above, and thereafter backfilling can be completed to grade, compacting the fill every 2 ft.

Piping above ground in the building should be securely supported by the building construction. Piping should never be hung from ductwork or other piping. Inserts, rods, hangers, piers, and anchors should be of durable material having adequate strength to perform their function. Maximum spacing between supports for various piping materials are as follows:

1. Cast-iron soil pipe.

   Horizontal: at every fitting and every joint.

   Vertical: every story.

2. Screwed piping.

   Horizontal: every 12 ft.

   Vertical: alternate floors.

3. DWV copper.

   Horizontal: every 10 ft for 2 in. and larger; every 6 ft for smaller sizes.

   Vertical: every story.

4. PVC.

   Horizontal: every 4 ft.

   Vertical: every story.

See also Table 3.

Table 3. Plumbing Pipe Materials[a]

Piping Material	Range of sizes, in.	Available Connections	Typical Systems	Critical Pressure, psi	Critical Temperature, °F
Copper: Types K, L, M, DWV	⅛–12	Brazed, soldered, compression, flared	Water for cold, hot, recirculation, sprinklers, waste and vent, air, storm drainage, gases, fuel oil	Up to 1500	Up to 400
Steel: Scheds 40 and 80	⅛–20	Screwed, flanged, welded, mechanical joint	Steam, water, gases, vents, waste, drainage		
Galvanized iron	⅛–20	Screwed, flanged, welded, mechanical joint	Water, gases, vents		
Cast iron	2–15	Mechanical, joint, lead and oakum, compression	Waste, vent, drainage, water	Up to 350	
Ductible iron	3–54				
Brass	⅛–12	Screwed, brazed, soldered	Water, air	Up to 6000	
PVC (poly vinyl chloride): Scheds 40 and 80	¼–20	Screwed, fusion, weld, cement, flanged, solvent welding			Up to 150
CPVC (chlorinated PVC): Scheds 40 and 80	½–8	Screwed, fusion, weld, cement, flanged, solvent welding			Up to 200
Asbestos cement	3–36	Grooved and gasket	Water, sewage		
Concrete w/ or w/o reinforcing	4–36 12–144	Cement, plaster	Drainage, sewer, water		
Glass	½–6	Compression, gaskets, and couplings	Chemical wastes and vent		
Lead	⅜–12	Mechanical, flange, wiping, lead burning	Waste and vent		
Vitrified clay	4–42	Compression seal	Waste, drainage		
ABS (acrylonitrile–butadiene–styrene): Scheds 40 and 80	⅛–12	Solvent welded, screwed	Sewers		Up to 160
PE (polyethylene)	½–48	Heat fusion, compression	Gas, water		Up to 140
PB (polybutylene)	¼–2	Heat fusion, flare, compression	Sprinkler, water		Up to 210

[a] Refs. 5,6.

Changes in direction of piping must be made with fittings that will not cause excessive reduction in the velocity of flow or create any other adverse effects. Short turn fittings should never be used in horizontal piping, but may be used in the vertical to transfer from the horizontal. A sanitary tee (short turn fitting) may be used in the vertical, but a double sanitary tee should never be installed. The possibility of flow crossover and the buildup of excessive pressures in the opposite inlet when one branch is discharging is an ever-present danger.

Any method of installation or use of fittings that retard flow to a greater degree than normal should not be used, ie, double hub, hub facing downstream, and tee inlet.

Cleanouts

Cleanouts are provided in piping to permit access for clearing stoppages without dismantling or breaking the piping. The size of the cleanout should be the same size as the piping, up to 4 in. For larger size piping, 4-in. cleanouts are adequate. Cleanouts should be provided at the following locations:

1. Inside the building at the point of exit. Use a wye branch or a house trap.
2. At every change of direction greater than 45°.
3. A maximum distance of 50 ft should be maintained between cleanouts for piping 4 in. and less, and 100 ft for larger piping. Underground piping larger than 10 in. in diameter should be provided with manholes at every change of direction and every 150 ft.
4. At the base of all stacks.

All cleanouts must be accessible and where necessary should be extended to the floor or wall. Adequate clearances must be provided around the cleanout for the manipulation of equipment in rodding out stoppages.

Fixtures that are readily removable without disturbing the piping are acceptable as equivalent to a cleanout.

Indirect Wastes

Waste piping that does not connect directly to the sanitary system is termed an indirect waste. The discharge from an indirect waste should be conveyed into a water-supplied, trapped, and vented receptacle or fixture. The discharge outlet should be a minimum of 1 in. above the flood level of the receptacle. The installation and sizing of indirect piping are in accordance with all rules of direct connected waste piping with one exception. Because of the low rate of flow, stoppages are more prevalent and cleanouts should be provided at every possible location.

Fixtures connected to indirect waste piping must be trapped, but it is not required that they be vented. There are no severe pneumatic effects in this piping because of the extremely low rate of flow.

Where the piping exceeds 100 ft in developed length it should be extended to the atmosphere, preferably through the roof. Ventilation is required to prevent the rapid fouling of the pipe, as absence of air promotes the formation of slime and fungi.

Special Wastes

Tank overflows, tank-emptying lines, and relief valve discharges should not connect directly to the drainage system because of the danger of contamination of the water supply. The discharge should be to an open sight drain, through an air break to an acceptable receptacle, floor drain, or onto a roof. The same method should be applied for the drains from, for example, sprinkler systems, cooling jackets, and drip pans. Steam expansion tank drains may be treated in a similar manner or by a direct connection to the house sewer, where permitted by code.

Combined Systems

A combined plumbing drainage system, or combined sewer, conveys storm and sanitary sewage in the same conduit. More communities are replacing combined sewers with separate public sanitary and storm sewers, because storm water in a combined system imposes too great a load on sewage treatments plants. This strain on the system may cause a municipality to bypass the overload around the treatment facility during heavy storms, and thus dump great quantities of raw untreated sewage into public waterways.

Sewage Disposal

Wherever public sanitary sewers or combined sewers are available for disposal of sewage from a building, the sanitary drainage system of the building must be connected to the public system. This is also the most economical method of sewage disposal. Availability of public sewers is usually defined by the municipality and can vary from 100 to 500 ft and more. Where public sewers are not available, an approved private sewage disposal system must be provided. This private system must conform to the rules and regulations of the authorities having jurisdiction in that locality. The sanitary drainage system should never discharge onto the ground or into a waterway.

The sanitary drainage system of a building should never discharge into the public storm sewer because storm water is not treated. Therefore, doing so may contaminate other water sources.

Sanitary and storm water drainage systems within a building must be independent of each other unless they discharge into a combined public sewer.

Storm Water Disposal

Every building must have adequate provisions for draining storm water from roofs, paved areas, courts, and yards. Storm water drainage systems should connect to the public storm sewer or combined sewer. When only a combined sewer is available, the storm system may be connected to the sanitary system within the building at the most convenient locations. Where a public combined sewer system exists and separate sewers are planned for future construction, the best practice is to join the sanitary and storm drains outside the building rather than within it, so that separation of those lines may be accomplished easily when separate sewers become available in the street.

The storm drain should never be connected to the public sanitary sewer where separate public storms and sanitary sewers exist. When public storm or combined sewers are not available, storm water may be run to an existing stream or into an adequate system of dry-wells.

High Temperature Wastes

Excessively high temperature wastes (above 140° F) should never discharge directly into the drainage system. High temperatures may cause excessive expansion and contraction of the piping, which in turn may cause joints to be pulled apart or loosened and solidly bedded pipe to be broken. The discharges from, for example, boiler blow-offs, steam exhaust, and condensate, must be cooled to at least 140°F before they connect to the drainage system. This may be accomplished by piping the high temperature discharge to a water supplied sump or a cooling tank. The high temperature waste may also be used to preheat the cold water supply to hot water heaters, thus accomplishing two objectives at once and conserving energy at the same time.

Drainage Systems Below Sewer Level

Where a drainage system is below the elevation of the house drain (which drains by gravity to the sewer) or the public sewer, the discharge should be conveyed to a sump or ejector, and pumped or automatically lifted up into the gravity drainage system. Sumps are used to handle clear water and need not be airtight and vented. Ejectors are used for sewage and must be airtight and vented.

Backwater Valves

There is often the danger of backflow of sewage into a building when the public sewer becomes overloaded or is surcharged. To prevent backflow and possible flooding of the building, a backwater valve should be installed in the drainage piping from all fixtures that are at an elevation below the surcharge level of the public sewer.

Rather than use a multitude of backwater valves (at each fixture), it is feasible to install a backwater valve, a manually operated gate valve, or a combination backwater and gate valve in the house drain at the point of exit inside the building and downstream from the house trap. Installation of the combination backwater and gate valve has the added advantage of not interfering with the circulation of air throughout the entire drainage system. Where there is a history of backflow, the gate valve is recommended as a positive means of protecting the building from flooding in case of a malfunction of the backwater valve. The backwater valve is nothing more than a swing check valve.

Sanitary Drainage Fixture Unit

The assigning of fixture unit values to represent their load-producing effect on the plumbing system was originally proposed in 1923. The fixture unit values were designed for application in conjunction with the probability of simultaneous use of fixtures so as to establish the maximum permissible drainage loads expressed in fixture units (FU) rather than in gallons per minute of drainage flow. Since the original proposal, various changes have been suggested and made (7). More recently, additional changes have been recommended by researchers, and further study is presently being made of fixture unit values. Table 4 gives the latest available recommended values. Again, the plumbing engineer must conform to local codes.

A fixture unit is a quantity defined in terms of the load producing effects of different kinds of plumbing fixtures on the plumbing system expressed on some arbitrarily chosen scale. Hunter conceived the idea of assigning a fixture unit value to represent the degree to which a

Table 4. Fixture Units Per Fixture or Group

Fixture Type	Fixture-Unit Value as Load Factors	
One bathroom group consisting of water closet, lavatory, and bathtub or shower stall	Tank water closet	6
	Flush-valve water closet	8
Bathtub (with or without overhead shower)[a]		2
Bidet		3
Combination sink and tray		3
Combination sink and tray with food-disposal unit		4
Dental unit or cuspidor		1
Dental lavatory		1
Dishwasher, domestic		2
Drinking fountain		½
Floor drains[b]		1
Kitchen sink, domestic		2
Kitchen sink, domestic (with food-disposal unit)		3
Lavatory, small P.O.[c]		1
Lavatory, large P.O.[c]		2
Lavatory (barber, beauty parlor, or surgeon)		2
Laundry tray (one or two compartments)		2
Shower stall, domestic		2
Showers (group) per head		3
Sinks:		
Surgeon		3
Flushing rim (with flush valve)		8
Service (trap standard)		3
Service (P trap)		2
Pot, scullery, etc		4
Urinal (pedestal, siphon jet, blowout)		8
Urinal, stall		4
Urinal, wall-hung		4
Urinal, trough (each 2-ft. section)		2
Wash sink (circular or multiple), each set of faucets		2
Water closet:		
Tank-operated		4
Valve-operated		8

[a] A shower head over a bathtub does not increase the fixture unit value.
[b] Size of floor drain shall be determined by the area of surface water to be drained.
[c] Lavatories with 1¼- or 1½-in. trap have the same load value: larger P.O. plugs have greater flow rate.

fixture loads a system when used at the maximum assumed frequency. The sole purpose of the fixture unit concept is to make possible the calculation of the design load directly on the system when the system is composed of different kinds of fixtures, with each fixture having a loading characteristic different from the others. Sizing tables in codes are given in terms of permissible fixture units for each size of pipe.

Storm Water Systems

Storm water is considered to be rain water, surface runoff, ground water, subsurface water, or similar clear liquid wastes, exclusive of sewage and industrial wastes. Design of the storm drainage system is based on the piping flowing full under uniform flow conditions. Leaders (also called conductors or downspouts) and horizontal piping can flow full as there is no need to maintain pneumatic or hydraulic pressures within any fixed limits in the system as is required in a sanitary drainage system.

When a leader or any storm drain is connected to a sanitary system, the storm piping must be trapped. The purpose of the trap is to prevent foul odors present in the sanitary piping from escaping at the roof drains or areaways. One trap may serve more than one leader. If the storm piping is run separately from the sanitary piping, one trap may serve the entire storm system before connection to the sanitary system or combined sewer. The size of leader traps shall be the same size as the horizontal runout from the leader to the house drain. A fresh air inlet is not required on the storm system for the main trap.

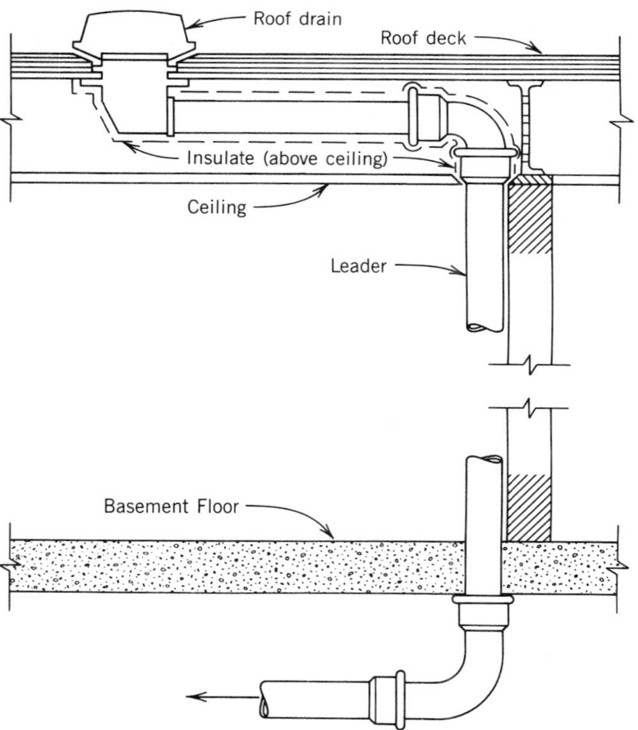

Figure 15. Provision for expansion and contraction (1). Courtesy of Construction Industry Press.

Leaders shall never be used as soil, waste, or vent pipe or vice versa. It is good practice to connect leaders at least 10 ft downstream from any soil or waste connection on the combined house drain. If the connection is any closer it tends to impede the discharge of the soil or waste when the leader is discharging and could possibly cause backups.

Because of the extremes of outside temperatures in relation to the fairly constant inside temperature, provisions should be made at the roof drains for expansion and contraction. This may be accomplished by means of an offset as illustrated in Figure 15.

When an offset connection cannot be utilized due to architectural or structural limitations, it is recommended that a roof drain with an integral expansion joint or a separate expansion joint be used. An expansion joint or offset should always be used at the connection to roof drains to prevent pipe expansion from raising the roof drain and destroying the integrity of the roof's waterproofing. Storm water piping is probably subjected to the most frequent movement of any plumbing system, although not necessarily to the maximum movement.

Low temperature liquid flow in the storm water piping will cause condensation on the outside of the piping in the building. Therefore it is advisable to insulate all storm water offsets and the bodies of all roof drains to prevent condensation from staining the ceiling (Fig. 15).

Collection Areas

Storm water should be conveyed from drainage areas at the same rate as it collects on these areas. The required rate of discharge from any collection area, depending on the size of the area and the maximum rate of rainfall per hour, is employed as the design criterion. For many regions of the United States the maximum rate of rainfall has been recorded at 4 in./h. Using this rate, it can be shown that 1 gpm will collect on 24 ft^2 of horizontal surface. Thus, 24 ft^2 of horizontal area is equivalent to 1 gpm that must be conveyed from the surface. Sizing tables in most codes are formulated on this basis. If in any locality the maximum rate of rainfall is more or less than 4 in./hour, then the area equivalent to 1 gpm may be obtained by the simple conversion of multiplying 24 by 4 and dividing by the maximum rate of rainfall in inches per hour for that particular locality.

Sizing

Sizing tables in codes generally tabulate pipe sizes in terms of drained areas based on a maximum rainfall rate of 4 in./h.

Roof Drains

Three basic components form the construction of a roof drain: strainer, flashing ring (combined with a gravel stop where required), and drain body or sump. Mushroom, or

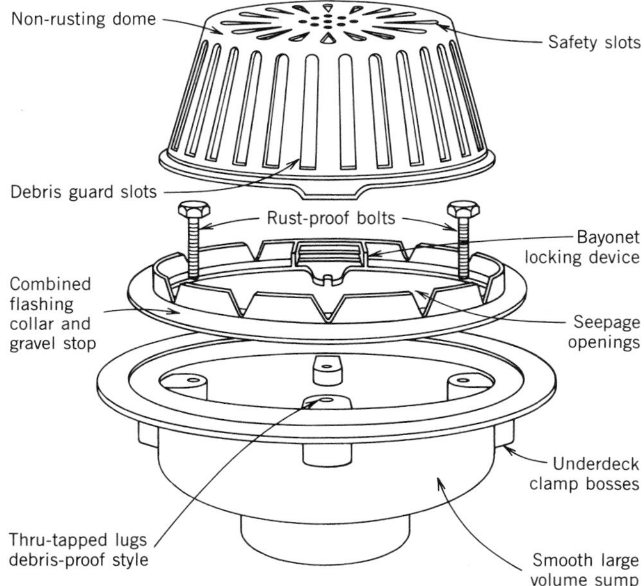

Figure 16. Typical roof drain (1). Courtesy of Construction Industry Press.

domed strainers, should be used for roofs where leaves or other debris may accumulate. An open area for drainage is still maintained even though the leaves and debris clog the lower portion of the strainer. The open area of the strainer should be 1½–2 times the area of the pipe to which it connects. Corner strainers are required when the drain is located at the corner of the roof and the parapet. Figure 16 illustrates a typical roof drain.

The connection between roofs and roof drains passing through the roof into the interior of the building should be made watertight by the use of proper flashing material. The flashing ring should clamp the flashing to the collar without puncturing the flashing. Drain bodies may be secured to metal decks and plank roofs by means of underdeck clamps. Clamps are not necessary for poured-in-place concrete roofs.

Material

Inside leaders may be cast iron, galvanized steel, galvanized ferrous alloys, brass, copper, or plastic. Underground storm drainage piping may be cast iron soil pipe, ferrous-alloy pipe, plastic, vitrified clay, concrete, bituminous fiber, or asbestos-cement depending on the requirements of the local code. Roof drains may be cast iron, copper, lead, or other acceptable corrosion-resistant material.

Flow Velocity

Although a minimum velocity of 2 fps is adequate for scouring action in sanitary piping, a greater velocity is required for storm water piping. A minimum velocity of 3 fps is required to keep the grit, sand, and debris found in storm water in suspension.

Controlled-Flow Roof Drainage

The concept of conventional roof drainage design is to drain the water from the roof as rapidly as it collects. In 1960 an alternative concept was introduced that has been extremely successful and has provided considerable benefits not obtainable by the conventional approach. It is called controlled-flow roof drainage.

Instead of attempting to drain rain water as fast as it collects, controlled-flow roof drainage drains the water at a much slower controlled rate. Excess water is permitted to accumulate on the roof under predetermined conditions and is drained off at a controlled rate after the storm. This is the same principle that is applied in the use of dams for flood control, although on a much smaller scale. The result is a marked reduction in the maximum flow rate that leaders and sewers must accommodate. Due to the reduced flow rates, pipe sizes can be drastically reduced and the loads imposed on sewage treatment plants handling the effluent of combined sewers are also greatly reduced.

Therefore, controlled-flow roof drainage not only allows more economically-sized piping to be used, but also affords a means of alleviating chronic flooding conditions prevalent when a storm occurs. Because it helps alleviate this problem, controlled-flow aids in the prevention of pollution of streams, lakes, and oceans.

The application of required data for controlled-flow design is just as sophisticated as for flood control; all factors involved must be interrelated. Fortunately, various roof drain manufacturers have investigated the engineering parameters in great detail and have waded through the involved and sophisticated mathematical calculations required to produce simplified and straightforward design procedures. Each manufacturer's procedure is slightly different due to the configuration of the end product and the method they utilize to control flow. However, the engineering principles employed are valid and can be safely followed.

By retaining water on the roof by slowing its rate of leaving, extra weight must be factored into the structural calculations. Scupper drains on the roof are used to limit the depth of water accumulated to within safe tolerances and to prevent overloading of the structure.

Pneumatic Effects in Sanitary Systems

As water flows in contact with air in vertical or horizontal piping, there is friction between the air and water. The frictional effect causes the air to be dragged along with the water at almost the same velocity. When the cross-sectional area of the water occupying the pipe is suddenly increased, such as at the hydraulic jump or where a branch discharges into the stack, the air passage is constricted. This acts as does a stoppage or a blockage to the airflow, causing a buildup of pressure, the highest pressure occurring at the constriction and diminishing upstream. This is the reason excessive pressure usually develops at the lower floors of a building and at offsets of the stack. It is important to always be aware that protection from the entry of sewer gases is afforded by the 2-in. trap seal and the design of plumbing systems must be able to maintain pressure variations within a ± 1-in. column of water.

Friction Head Loss

As air flows in a pipe a pressure loss occurs because of the friction between the air and pipe wall. This loss of pressure can be expressed by the Darcy formula:

$$h = fLV^2 = D(2g)$$

where h = friction head loss, ft of air column; f = coefficient of friction; L = length of pipe in ft; D = diameter of pipe in ft; V = velocity of air in fps; and g = gravitational acceleration, 32.2 ft/s/s.

Air Flow in Stacks

The complete venting of a sanitary drainage system is very complicated as evidenced by the variety of vents employed. There are numerous variables that produce positive and negative pneumatic pressure fluctuations; therefore, it is not feasible to prepare vent-sizing tables for each particular design. Recognizing this, authorities base the formulation of vent-sizing tables for vent stacks and horizontal branches, assuming the worst case scenario. To determine the maximum lengths and minimum diameters for vent stacks it would be valuable to review the conditions of flow in the drainage stack.

At maximum design flow, the water flows down the stack as a sheet occupying 7/24 of the cross-sectional area of the stack. The remaining 17/24 is occupied by a core of air. As the water falls down the stack, it exerts frictional drag on the core, pulling the air down with it. The air then must be replaced by an equivalent quantity so that negative pressures in excess of −1 in. of water do not develop. This is accomplished by extending the soil stack through the roof. Because of this problem, stacks must be extended full size through the roof, that is, vent stacks must not be reduced in size even though loads are less at upper portions than at lower portions of the stacks. Any decrease in size before the vent terminates at the atmosphere would cause violent pressure fluctuations.

As the water flows down the stack and enters the horizontal drain, there is severe restriction to the flow of air as the hydraulic jump occurs. The air is compressed and pressure buildup may become very high. A vent stack is located in this area to relieve the pressure by providing an avenue for airflow. Obviously, the stack must be large enough to permit the maximum quantity of air dragged down the drainage stack to discharge through it and to the atmosphere without exceeding ± 1-in. pressure fluctuation.

Permissible Length of Vent Pipe

The maximum length of vent piping, for any particular size with a pressure drop of 1 in. of water, is established by computing the pressure loss for various rates of flow in vents of various diameters. All codes tabulate the permissible length of vent pipe of various sizes for various FU loadings.

Vent Stacks

Every drainage stack should be extended full size through the roof. The pipe from the topmost drainage connection through the roof to the atmosphere is called the vent extension. The vent extension provides the air dragged down the stack and the means for the gravity circulation of air throughout the system. Vent extensions are connected with the vent stack before extending through the roof or with other vent extensions or vent stacks to a vent header. The header is then extended through the roof as a single pipe.

Every drainage stack should have an attendant vent stack. The vent stack prevents excessive pressures from developing in the lower regions of the drainage stack by simultaneously replacing the air carried down by the discharge of the drainage stack. The most effective location for the vent stack is below all drainage branch connections and preferably at the top of the horizontal drain immediately adjacent to the stack base fitting. Here pressure is at its maximum, and the danger of closure due to fouling is minimal. Figure 17 illustrates acceptable methods of vent stack connections.

The vent stack, undiminished in size, should extend through the roof or connect with the vent extension of the drainage stack at least 6 in. above the overflow of the highest fixture or connect to a vent header.

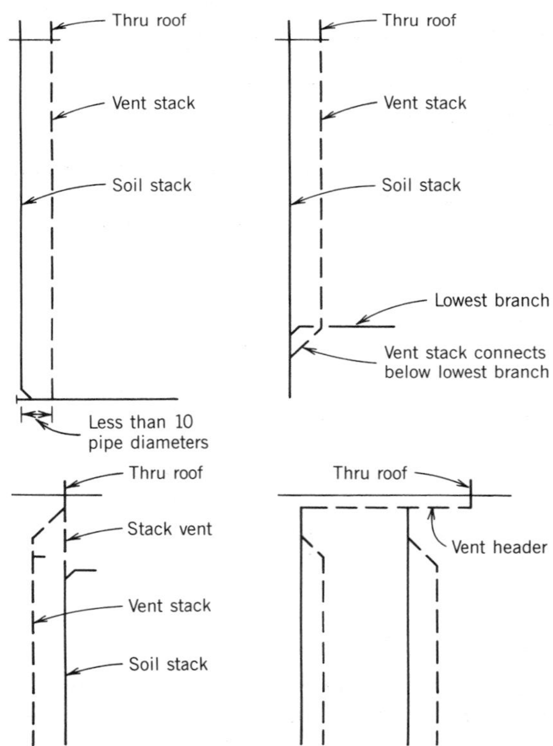

Figure 17. Various vent stack connections (1). Courtesy of Construction Industry Press.

Vent Terminals

Vent terminals should not be located within 10 ft of any door, window, or ventilation intake unless they are extended at least 2 ft above such openings. Terminals should be at least 6 in. above roof level and at least 5 ft above when the roof is used for other purposes. When it is impractical to extend the vent through the roof, it is permissible to terminate through a wall, but the terminal must be turned down and covered with a wire screen. The terminal should never be located beneath a building overhang.

Fixture Trap Vents

The water seal of all fixture traps should be protected against siphonage or blow-out by proper installation of the venting system. When drainage stacks are provided having adequate supply of air at the terminal and an adequate vent stack is provided to relieve excess pressures at the base of the drainage stack, the only additional vent protection required to prevent water seal loss in fixture traps is that necessary to prevent self-siphonage when the fixture discharges and to relieve excessive pneumatic effects in the branch drains when other fixtures discharge into the branch. Some municipalities require that every fixture trap be individually vented, but most localities permit alternate methods such as the following:

1. Wet venting.
2. Stack venting.
3. Circuit and loop venting.
4. Combination waste and vent venting.

Distance of Vent From Trap

The most comprehensive investigations of conditions under which fixture traps will be safe from self-siphonage have been conducted by the National Bureau of Standards in the United States and by the Building Research Station in the United Kingdom. The recommended maximum distances of a vent from the weir of the trap to the vent connection are tabulated in all codes.

As illustrated in Figure 18, the vent pipe opening, except for water closets and similar fixtures, must never be below the weir of the fixture trap. A fixture drain having a slope more than one pipe diameter between vent opening and trap weir has a greater tendency to self-siphon the trap seal than a fixture drain having a slope of not more than one pipe diameter.

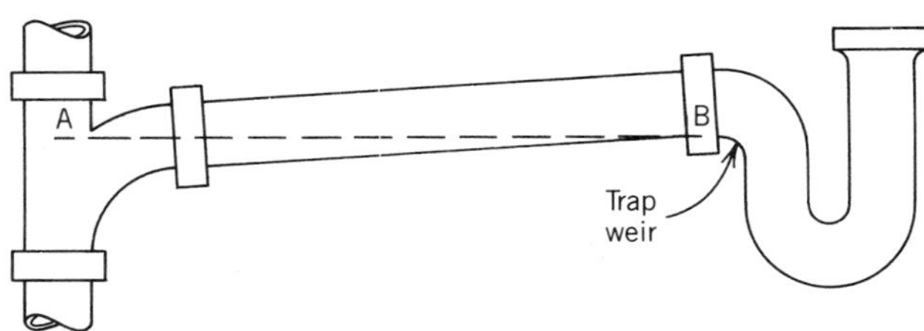

Figure 18. Vent pipe opening (1). The open vent at point A should not be lower than point B when straight level line is drawn between the two points. Courtesy of Construction Industry Press.

Relief Vents

Pressures in the drainage and vent stacks of a multistory building fluctuate constantly. The vent stack connection at the base of the drainage stack and the branch vent connections to the branch drains cannot always eliminate these fluctuations. Because the fluctuations may be caused by the simultaneous discharge of branches on various separated floors, it is extremely important that pressures throughout the drainage stack be balanced by means of relief vents located at various intervals. Drainage stacks in buildings having more than 10 branch intervals should be provided with a relief vent at each tenth interval, counting from the topmost branch down. The lower end of the relief vent should connect to the drainage stack below the drainage branch connection, and the upper end should connect to the vent stack at least 3 ft above the floor level (Fig. 19).

Relief vents are required where a drainage stack offsets at a vertical angle of more than 45°. Such offsets are subject to high pneumatic pressure increases and extreme surging flow conditions.

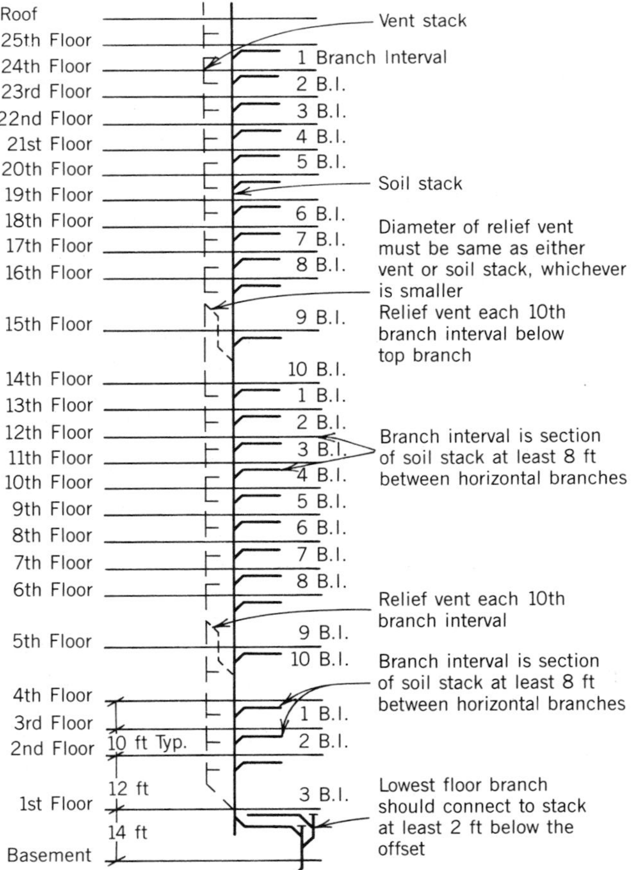

Figure 19. Venting for stacks having more than 10 branch intervals (1). Courtesy of Construction Industry Press.

Suds Pressure

The prevalent use of high-sudsing detergents in washing machines, dishwashers, laundry trays, and kitchen sinks has created serious problems in all residential buildings and especially in high-rise buildings. Until detergent manufacturers produce only nonsudsing products, the plumbing engineer must understand and deal with the dangers the presence of suds creates in the sanitary system. (In fact, suds, in and of themselves, do not enhance the cleaning ability of soaps and detergents.)

When wastes containing suds-producing ingredients flow down the stack, they are vigorously mixed with the water and air already present there. Further mixing occurs as other branch waste discharges meet this flow. These suds settle at any offsets greater than 45° in the stack and in the lower sections of the drainage system. It has been shown that when suds-producing wastes are present, sanitary and vent stacks are laden with suds; this condition has been found to exist for extended periods of time.

Liquid wastes are heavier than suds and flow easily through the suds-loaded drainage piping without carrying the suds along with the flow. For example, the difficulty of flushing the suds out of a sink is a common problem. The water simply flows through the suds and out the drain, leaving the major portion of the suds behind. The same action occurs in the lower sections of the drainage system, except for one important difference—air, as well as water, is now flowing in the piping. The air carried down with the waste discharge compresses the suds and forces them to move through any available path of relief. The relief path may be the building drain, any branches connected to the building drain, the vent stack, branch vents, individual vents, or combinations of these. A path of relief may not always be available, or could be cut off or restricted by the hydraulic jump, or may simply be inadequate because of location or size. If one or more of these conditions exists, excessively high suds pressure may develop and blow the trap seals, forcing the suds into the fixtures.

High suds pressure zones occur at every change in direction, vertically or horizontally, greater than 45°. Normal pressure relief paths are usually inadequate in size for high suds pressure. The vent pipe sizing tables in almost every code are calculated only on the basis of air flow capacity and do not take into account the more demanding flow of suds. Therefore, the pipe sizes listed in these tables do not provide adequate suds pressure relief.

Suds are much heavier than air and consequently do not flow with the same ease. They produce a much greater friction head loss for the same rate of flow. The density of old or regenerated suds varies from 2 lb/ft^3 to a high of 19 lb/ft^3, depending on the detergent. For equal rates of flow and pressure loss, the vent pipe diameter for suds relief flow must be from 20–80% greater than for air flow.

When a soil or waste stack receives suds-producing wastes from washing machines, dishwashers, laundry trays, kitchen sinks, or other fixtures, the drainage and vent piping for the lower floor fixtures or for fixtures above offsets must be arranged to avoid connection to any zone where suds pressure exists.

Suds pressure zones exist in the following areas:

1. At a soil or waste offset greater than 45°: 40 stack diameters upward and 10 stack diameters horizontally from the base fitting for the upper stack section; also at 40 stack diameters upstream from the top fitting of the lower stack section.
2. At the base of a soil or waste stack: the suds pressure zone extends 40 stack diameters upward from the base fitting.
3. In the horizontal drain from the base of a stack: the suds pressure zone extends 10 stack diameters from the base fitting and where a horizontal offset greater than 45° occurs, the pressure zones extend 40 stack diameters upstream and 10 diameters downstream from the offset fitting.
4. In a vent stack connected to a suds pressure zone: the suds pressure zone exists from the vent stack base connection upward to the level of the suds pressure zone in the soil or waste stack. Figure 20 illustrates all of the above zones.

Ejector and Sump Vents

Ejectors, other than the pneumatic type, operate at atmospheric pressure and receive drainage discharge under gravity flow conditions. An ejector is installed when the level of fixture discharge is below the level of the public sewer. It is convenient to view an ejector system as being similar to the gravity sanitary system; all of the requirements for the proper design of the sanitary system are applicable. Thus, the air required to be conveyed by the vent piping is the same as the maximum rate at which

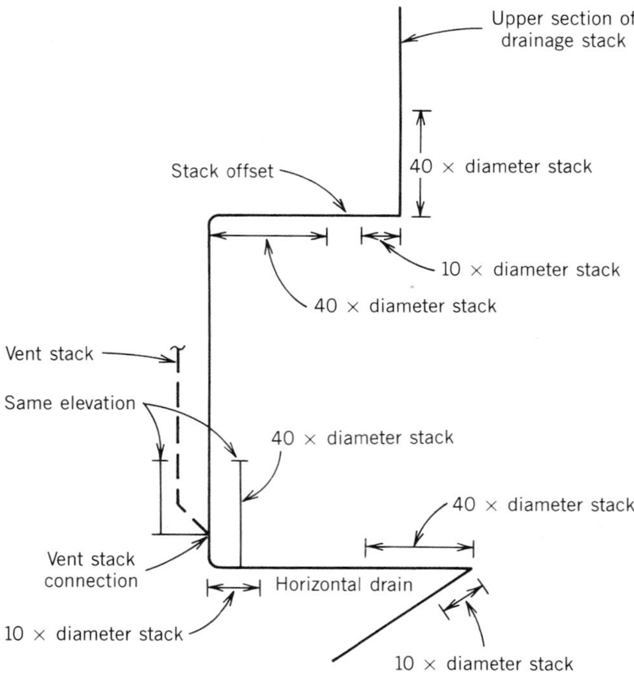

Figure 20. Suds pressure zones (1). Courtesy of Construction Industry Press.

sewage enters or is pumped out of the receiver. In practice, it has been found that 3 in. is usually adequate, except for extremely large installations.

Frost Closure

Where the danger of frost closure of vent terminals is present, the minimum size of the vent stack or vent extension through the roof should be 3 in. When a vent stack must be increased in size going through the roof, the increase should be made inside the building at least 1 ft below the roof.

The National Bureau of Standards has investigated the problem of frost closure both theoretically and experimentally. It has been demonstrated that a 3-in. vent terminal froze solidly at −30°F only over an extended period of time. The rate of closure occurs at 1½ in. for every 24 hours the temperature remains at −30°F.

Tests of Plumbing Systems

The complete storm and sanitary system should be subjected to a water test and proven watertight on completion of the rough piping installation and prior to covering or concealment. The test pressure should be a minimum of a 10-ft column of water except for the topmost 10 ft of pipe. The test pressure should never exceed a maximum of a 100-ft column of water. Greater pressure will cause lead bends to deform and blow out as well as increase the probability of blowing out the test plugs used to temporarily seal open piping in the system. If the system is higher than 100 ft, test tees may be installed at appropriate heights to test the building in sections. In practice very rarely are more than seven stories tested at one time.

If it is not possible to perform a water test, an air test is acceptable, and is performed at a pressure of 5 psi. Air tests are impractical and costly.

On completion of the sanitary system and after all fixtures are installed with traps filled with water, the system should be subjected to an additional test and proved gastight. A smoke pressure test is recommended. The smoke test is performed by introducing, at a cleanout, pungent, thick smoke by means of smoke bombs or smoke machines. When smoke appears at the roof terminals, each terminal is sealed and a smoke pressure of 1-in. column of water is maintained to prove the system gastight.

An alternative test is the peppermint vapor test. At least 2 oz of oil of peppermint are introduced into each roof terminal and vaporized by immediately pouring 10 qt of boiling water down the stack. The terminals are promptly sealed. Oil of peppermint and any person coming in contact or handling the oil must be excluded from the interior of the building for the duration of the test. Leakages will be detected by the peppermint odor at the source. However, it is very difficult to pinpoint the leak by this method.

Flow in Water Piping

Two types of water flow may exist in piping. One is known as streamline, laminar, or viscous. The other is called turbulent flow. At various viscosities (temperatures) there is a certain critical velocity for every pipe size above which turbulent flow occurs and below which laminar flow occurs. This critical velocity occurs within a range of Reynolds numbers of approximately 2100–3000. The Reynolds formula is

$$R = DV\rho/\mu$$

where R = Reynolds number, dimensionless; D = pipe diameter in ft; V = velocity of flow in fps; ρ = density of fluid in lb/ft^3; and μ = absolute viscosity in lbs/ft s.

Within the limits of accuracy required for plumbing design, it can be assumed that the critical velocity occurs at a Reynolds number of 2100. In laminar flow, the roughness of the pipe wall has a negligible effect on the flow, and the velocity of the flow of water has a significant effect. In turbulent flow, the opposite is true.

Very rarely is a velocity of less than 4 fps employed in plumbing design. The Reynolds number for a 3-in. pipe and a velocity of flow of four fps is $R = 0.25 \times 4 \times 6.5/0.0005 = 125{,}000$, well above the critical range of 2100. Almost all plumbing design deals with turbulent flow and only when very viscous liquids or extremely low velocities are encountered does the plumbing engineer deal with laminar flow. Critical velocities of ½-, 1-, and 2-in. pipe at 50°F are 0.676, 0.338, and 0.169 fps, respectively; at 140°F they are 0.247, 0.124, and 0.0617 fps, respectively.

Velocity of Flow

When the velocity of flow is measured across a section of pipe from the center to the wall, it is found that a variation exists: the greatest velocity is at the center; a minimum velocity is at the wall. The average for the entire cross section is approximately 84% of the velocity measured at the center. The plumbing engineer is concerned only with the average velocity, and all formulas are expressed in average velocity. When the term velocity is used, the average velocity of flow is employed.

Since water is incompressible within the range of pressures met in plumbing design, a definite relationship can be expressed between the quantity flowing past a given point in a given time and the velocity of flow:

$$Q = AV$$

where Q = quantity of flow in cfs; A = cross-sectional area of flow in ft^2; and V = velocity of flow in fps.

The units employed in this flow formula are inconvenient for use in plumbing design. The plumbing engineer deals in gallons per minute and inches for pipe sizes. Converting to these terms, the flow becomes

$$q = 2.448\, d^2 \mathrm{V}$$

Where q = quantity of flow in gpm; d = diameter of pipe in in.; and V = velocity of flow in fps.

Static Head

At any point below the surface of water exposed to atmospheric pressure, the pressure (head) is produced by the weight of the water above that point. The pressure is equal and effective in all directions at this point and is proportional to the depth below the surface. This pressure, called static head, static, hydrostatic head, or hydrostatic, is the measure of the potential energy. Because pressure is a function of the weight of the water, it is possible to convert the static head expressed as feet of head into pounds per square inch. To do so, multiply the height by 0.433. To convert pounds per square inch to feet of head, multiply the pounds per square inch by 2.31.

Energy Conversion

The velocity of flow at any point in a system is due to the total energy at that point. This is the sum of the potential and kinetic energy, less the friction head loss. The static head is the potential energy, some of which has been converted to kinetic energy to cause flow and some of which has been used to overcome friction. Because of this, the pressure during flow is always less than the static pressure. The pressure measured at any point during the flow of water is called the flow pressure, which is displayed on a gauge installed in the piping.

The kinetic energy of water flowing in a plumbing system is extremely small; therefore, rarely is the design velocity for water flow there greater than 8 fps. The kinetic energy (velocity head) at this velocity is $V^2/2g$ or $8^2/64.4$. This is equal to 1 ft or 0.433 psi, which is less than 0.5 $lb/in.^2$. Such an insignificant pressure may be safely ignored in all calculations.

Experiments have demonstrated that the friction head loss is inversely proportional to the diameter of the pipe, proportional to the roughness and length of the pipe, and varies approximately with the square of the velocity. Darcy expressed this relationship as:

$$h = fLV^2/D \times 2g \quad \textit{or} \quad p = wfLV^2/144D \times 2g$$

where h = friction head loss in ft; p = friction head loss in psi; w = density of fluid in lb/ft^3; f = coefficient of friction, dimensionless; L = length of pipe in ft; D = diameter of pipe in ft; V = velocity of flow in fps; and g = gravitational acceleration, 32.2 ft/s^2.

In all water flow formulas, L (length of run in feet) denotes the equivalent length of run (ELR). Every fitting and valve imposes more frictional resistance than the pipe itself. To take this additional friction head loss into account, the fitting or valve is converted to an equivalent length of pipe of the same size and imposing an equal friction loss, ie, a 4-in. elbow is equivalent to 10 ft of 4-in. pipe. Thus, if the measured length of run of 4-in. piping with one elbow is 15 ft, then the equivalent length of run is 15 + 10 = 25 ft. The length of pipe measured along the center line of pipe and fittings is the developed length. The larger the pipe size, the more significant the equivalent length of run. In the design phase of piping systems, the size of the piping is not known and the equivalent lengths cannot be accurately determined. An excellent rule of thumb is to assume the allowance for fittings and valves to be 50% of the developed length. See Table 5. Once the sizes are determined, the accuracy of the assumption can be checked.

All equipment imposes a friction head loss and must be carefully considered in the design and operation of a system. The pressure drop through, for example, meters, strainers, filters, and heaters, may be serious. The amount of pressure drop through any piece of equipment may be obtained from the manufacturer. The knowledgeable engineer is careful to specify the maximum pressure drop permitted through a piece of equipment.

Considering the energy used in any pumped system, whatever raises the flow rate or the pumping head also raises operating cost. One horsepower running one year adds $500 to electricity costs. This effect can be understood by the equation for pumping horsepower:

$$\mathrm{HP} = \frac{\mathrm{GPM} \times \text{head (in feet)}}{3960 \times \text{pump efficiency}}$$

Whenever flow is increased in a given system, head varies by the square of that change, so as the equation shows, horsepower will vary by the cube of the change.

Hydraulic Shock

Hydraulic shock is commonly and erroneously referred to as water hammer. The two terms are not synonymous. Water hammer is only one manifestation of the harmful effects created by hydraulic shock, and one symptom of a very dangerous condition. Hydraulic shock occurs when fluid flowing through a pipe is subjected to a sudden and rapid change in velocity. The kinetic energy of the fluid is converted into a dynamic pressure wave traveling at the rate of 3000 mph. This tremendous velocity produces terrific impact, rebounding back and forth in the piping until the energy is dissipated. When the piping is not adequately secured or supported, or when pipe runs are exceptionally long, these rebounding waves cause the piping to vibrate or hit against the building structure. This creates the noise commonly called "water hammer."

Noise, although a nuisance, is not inherently dangerous. Of greater importance is the hydraulic shock. It can, and does, expand and burst pipe; weaken joints, eventually leading to leaks; vibrate piping, causing pipe hangers to tear loose; wear out valves and faucets; rupture tanks and heaters; damage meters, gauges, and pressure and temperature regulators; and generally accelerate the deterioration of the entire piping system. The result is costly repair, maintenance, and replacement (Fig. 21).

Because most runs of piping within a building are relatively short and well supported, hydraulic shock may occur without any noticeable or alarming noise. Under these conditions, it can virtually destroy a system before the danger is recognized.

The most common causes of hydraulic shock are starting and stopping of pumps, improper check valves, and rapid closure of valves. The speed of valve closure time, particularly in the last 15% of movement, is directly related to the intensity of the surge pressure.

Table 5. Types of Plumbing Valves

Type	Material	Ends	Sizes, in.	Use[a]
Gate	Brass	Screwed	3 and smaller	X, W, S, G, LP
Gate	Brass	Soldered	3 and smaller	X, W, S
Gate	Iron	Flanged	3½ and larger	X, W
Globe and angle	Brass	Screwed	2½ and smaller	B, W, S, U, G, LP, A
Globe and angle	Brass	Soldered	2½ and smaller	B, W, S, U, G
Globe and angle	Iron	Flanged	3 and larger	B, W, S, U
Check	Brass	Screwed	3 and smaller	U, W, S, V
Check	Brass	Soldered	3 and smaller	U, W, S, V
Check	Iron	Flanged	3½ and larger	U, W, S, V, A
Lift check	Brass	Screwed	2 and smaller	U, A, V, G, LP
Lift check	Iron	Flanged	2½ and larger	U, A, V
Cocks	Brass	Screwed	2 and smaller	X, NG, V, W, S, A
Cocks	Iron	Flanged	2 and smaller	X, NG, V
Butterfly	Brass	Screwed	2 and smaller	B, W, S, M, C, V
Butterfly	Iron	Flanged	2½ and larger	B, W, S, M, C, V
Ball	Brass	Screwed	2 and smaller	B, W, V
Ball	Brass	Soldered	2 and smaller	B, W, V
Open screw and yoke	Brass	Screwed	2 and smaller	X, W, S, C, V
Open screw and yoke	Iron	Screwed	2½ and larger	X, W, S, C, V

[a] X = use for full open or full close.
B = can serve for balancing.
U = unidirectional.
W = useful for water.
S = useful for steam.
A = useful for air, gases.
M = available with memory stop.
C = controllable by automatic device (air, electric, bulb).
V = seat position identifiable.
G = useful for gasoline.
LP = useful for liquid petroleum gasoline.
NG = useful for natural gas (methane).

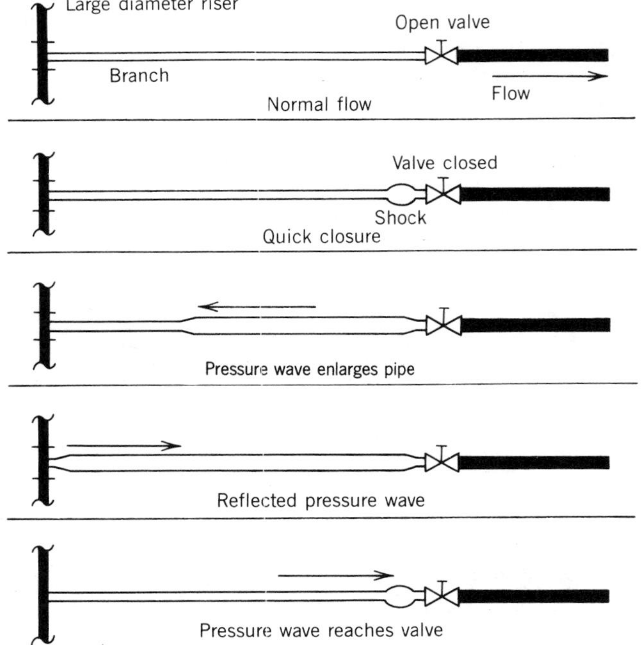

Figure 21. Illustrations of a shock wave (1). Courtesy of Construction Industry Press.

A simplified equation used to determine the magnitude of hydraulic shock is

$$P = 0.027LV/t$$

where P = psi; L = feet of pipe run; V = velocity in fps; and t = time of valve closure in s.

The following rule of thumb has given satisfactory approximations: multiply the velocity of flow by 60. This does not apply to exceptionally long runs of pipe, because, for example, if the velocity of flow is 10 fps, then the hydraulic shock would be in the range of 600 psi.

For many years, air chambers have been used to control hydraulic shock. The unit consists of a 12–15-in. long piece of capped pipe, having the same diameter as the line it serves. Air chambers have proven to be less than satisfactory and in many cases worthless. Unless they are of the correct size and contain an adequate volume of air, they are not suitable even for temporary control of shock. Although a correctly sized air chamber will temporarily control shock to within safe limits of pressure, adequate performance is effective only during the period the air chamber retains its initial charge of air. In practice, however, this initial charge of air is rapidly depleted and the chamber becomes water-logged, losing completely its ability to control shock. Recognizing this, engineers have turned to the engineered or manufactured shock absorber.

Engineered or manufactured devices utilize a cushion of inert gas or air to absorb and control hydraulic shock. The gas or air in the unit is permanently sealed. This construction provides many years of effective operation.

Swing check valves should never be used in the discharge line of pumps. When the pump stops, there is a reversal of flow and the check slams closed, causing a sudden change in velocity. Spring-loaded check valves should always be installed in lieu of swing checks. The spring-loaded check is designed to close at the exact moment water flow stops. Because there is no change in the velocity of flow when it closes, no hydraulic shock is produced.

Erosion, Noise, and Cavitation

The pressure loss of flowing fluid due to friction varies approximately with the square of the velocity. This loss is also directly related to the roughness of the pipe wall. As the velocity of flow is increased, the abrasive effect on the pipe wall increases and erosion occurs. The extent of erosion caused by velocity depends on the physical characteristics of the pipe material and the buildup of deposits on the pipe walls.

When the flow velocity is high, line noises may be produced in the form of a whistling sound. When the fluid strikes protruding high spots in the pipe wall, energy is transferred into the pipe that may cause it to move or vibrate. Generally, this vibration is dampened or absorbed by the piping. But when the piping arrangement is such that resonance develops, the vibration may gain sufficient amplitude to cause noise.

When the direction of flow is sharply changed and the velocity of flow is high, the phenomenon of "cavitation" may occur. Cavitation is always accompanied by noise, which sounds like popping balloons or gravel bouncing in the pipe. Fluids flowing around a short-radius bend at high velocity are subject to cavitation. The centrifugal force developed causes an increase of pressure at the outer bend resulting in a lowering of the pressure at the throat. In this low pressure zone, the pressure may drop below atmospheric to a pressure corresponding to the boiling point of the flowing fluid. Under this condition, the "cavity" that forms at the inside of the bend permits the fluid to flash into vapor or steam bubbles. Once these bubbles flow past the low pressure zone into the normal pressure area downstream, they collapse. The rapid volumetric changes caused by bubble formation and collapse in turn cause intense noise and stresses in the piping. Cavitation is a very serious problem in pump operation as well as in line flow, and it may literally tear a pump apart.

Most noise problems (water hammer, whistling, and cavitation) may be greatly alleviated and even eliminated by maintaining flow velocities below 10 fps in any part of the pipe system.

Flow Pressure

It is essential that the term flow pressure be thoroughly understood and not confused with static pressure. Flow pressure is the pressure that exists at any point in the system when water is flowing at that point. It is always less than the static pressure. To have flow, some of the potential energy is converted to kinetic energy and additional energy is used in overcoming friction, which results in a flow pressure that is less than the static pressure.

The minimum pressure required for the proper operation of a flush valve listed as 25 psi by the manufacturer, is the flow pressure requirement. The flush valve will not function at peak efficiency (if at all) if the engineer has erroneously designed the system so that a static pressure of less than 25 psi exists at the inlet to the flush valve.

Constant Flow

Pressures in various parts of the piping system fluctuate constantly depending on the quantity of flow. Under these conditions the rate of flow from any one outlet will vary with the change of pressure. In industrial and laboratory projects there exists equipment that must be supplied with a fixed and steady quantity of flow, regardless of line pressure fluctuations. This feature, desirable in any type of installation, is easily achieved by utilizing an automatic flow control orifice. A flow control is a simple, self-cleaning device designed to deliver a constant volume of water over a wide range of inlet pressures (Fig. 22).

The automatic controlling mechanism consists of a flexible orifice, the cross-sectional area of which varies inversely with the pressure, so that a constant flow rate is maintained under all conditions. Until the inlet pressure reaches the threshold pressure (12–15 psi), the flexible insert acts as a fixed orifice. When the threshold pressure is exceeded, the cross-sectional area of the orifice is decreased by the flexure of the insert. This causes a pressure drop equal to whatever pressure is necessary to absorb the energy not required to overcome system friction and to sustain the rated flow.

It is common for a water distribution system to experience fluctuating discharges at fixtures and equipment when other fixtures and equipment start up or shut down. Flow controls will minimize these problems because they automatically compensate for changes in the line pressure to maintain the rate of water delivery from all outlets at a preselected number of gallons per minute. A word of

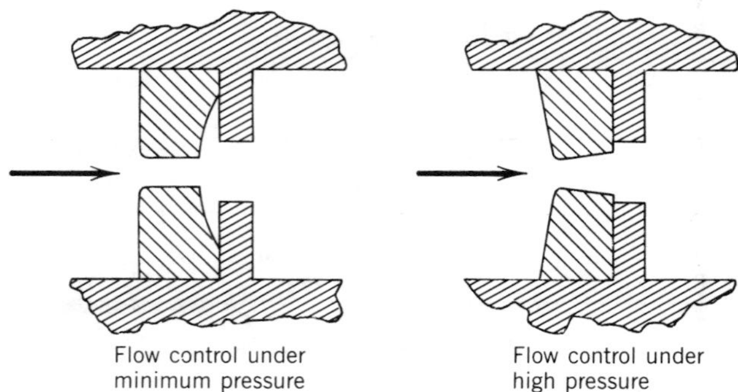

Figure 22. Flow control (1). Courtesy of Construction Industry Press.

caution: a flow control is not designed to perform the function of pressure regulation and should never be used where a pressure regulating valve is required.

Inadequate Pressure

Lack of adequate pressure is a frequent complaint and could cause serious problems. The pressure available for water distribution within a building comes from various sources. Municipalities usually maintain water pressure in their distribution mains within the range of 35–45 psi. There are localities where the pressure maintained is much less or greater. The local utility will furnish the information as to their minimum and maximum operating pressures. When utilizing only the public water main pressure for the water distribution system within a building, it is very important to determine the pressure available in the mains during summer months. Huge quantities of water are used during this period for sprinkling of lawns and for air conditioning cooling tower make-up water, which usually cause excessive pressure loss in the mains. Future growth of the area must also be analyzed. If large housing, commercial, or industrial development is anticipated, the pressure available will certainly decrease as these loads are added to the public mains. It is good practice to assume a pressure available for design purposes as 10 psi less than that quoted by the utility.

If the pressure from the public mains is inadequate for building operation, other means for increasing the pressure to an adequate level must be provided. There are three basic methods available:

1. Gravity tank system.
2. Hydropneumatic tank system.
3. Booster pump system.

Each system has advantages and disadvantages. All three should be evaluated in terms of capital expenditure, operating costs, maintenance costs, and space requirements. The system selected depends on which criteria are considered most important.

Demand Types

Some outlets impose a continuous demand on the system, and some impose an intermittent demand. Outlets such as hose bibbs, lawn irrigation, air conditioning make-up, water cooling, and similar flow requirements are considered to be continuous demands; they occur over an extended period of time. Plumbing fixtures draw water for relatively short periods of time and are considered to be intermittent demand types.

Each fixture has its own singular loading effect on the system, which is determined by the rate of water supply required, the duration of each use, and the frequency of use. The water demand is related to the number of fixtures, type of fixtures, and probable simultaneous use.

Design Loads

Arriving at a reasonably accurate estimate of the maximum probable demand is complicated because of the intermittent operation and irregular frequency of fixture use. For example: bathroom fixtures are most frequently used on arising or retiring, and, not surprisingly, during TV commercials; kitchen sinks are used heavily before and after meals; laundry trays and washing machines are most likely used in the late morning; and during the period from midnight to 6 A.M. there is very little fixture use. Luckily, fixtures are used intermittently and the total time in operation is relatively small, so it is not necessary to design for the maximum potential load. Maximum flow is therefore of no real concern to the designer. Average flow is also of no concern, because if a system were designed to meet this criterion it would not satisfy the conditions under peak flow. Therefore it is necessary to consider only the maximum probable demand (peak demand) imposed by the fixtures on a system.

Two methods have evolved in the United States for which, when used where applicable, satisfactory results have been obtained. They are the empirical method and the method of probability. The empirical method is based on arbitrary decisions arrived at from experience and judgment. It is useful only for small groups of fixtures. The method of probability is based on the theory of probability and is most accurate for large groups of fixtures.

Demand at Individual Fixtures

Certain demand rates have become generally accepted as standard. These rates are tabulated in Table 6 for the common types of fixtures and the average pressure necessary to deliver this rate of flow. The actual pressure for a specific fixture will vary with each manufacturer's design.

Although the flow rates shown in Table 6 have been accepted and are widely used by many engineers, they are outdated. Drastic changes and progress in fixture and faucet design have occurred since the establishment of these criteria: lavatories have been installed in hundreds of buildings requiring only 0.5 gpm flow; shower heads are available that deliver 3 gpm; and flow control devices are now marketed that accurately deliver any selected rate of flow under varying pressure conditions. More research is needed to determine accurately the minimum flow required at each type of fixture to satisfy the psycho-

Table 6. Demand at Individual Fixtures and Required Pressure

Fixture	Flow Pressure, psi	Flow Rate, gpm
Ordinary lavatory faucet	8	3.0
Self-closing lavatory faucet	12	2.5
Sink faucet, 3/8 in.	10	4.5
Sink faucet, 1/2 in.	5	4.5
Bathtub faucet	5	6.0
Laundry tub faucet, 1/2 in.	5	5.0
Shower head	12	5.0
Water closet flush tank	15	3.0
Water closet flush valve, 1 in.	10–25	15–45
Urinal flush valve, 3/4 in.	15	15.0
Hose bibb or sill cock, 3/4 in.	30	5.0

logical requirements of the user, and to provide the necessary sanitary requirements.

Water Supply Fixture Units

A standard method for estimating the water demand for a building has evolved through the years and has been accepted almost unanimously by plumbing designers. The system is based on categorizing fixtures according to their water supply load-producing effects on the water distribution system. The late Roy B. Hunter developed tables of load-producing characteristics (fixture unit weights) of commonly used fixtures and probability curves, which have made possible easy application of the method to actual design problems (7).

The method of probability should never be used for a small number of fixtures. Although the design load, as computed by this method, has a certain probability of not being exceeded, nevertheless, it may be exceeded on rare occasions. When a system contains only a few fixtures, the additional load imposed by only one fixture more than has been calculated by the theory of probability can very easily overload the system. When a system contains a large number of fixtures, one or several additional fixture loadings will have an insignificant effect on the system.

In developing the application of the theory of probability to determine design loads on a domestic water distribution system, Hunter assumed that the operation of the fixtures in a plumbing system could be viewed as random events. He then determined the maximum frequencies of use of the fixtures. He obtained the values of the frequencies from records collected in hotels and apartment houses during the periods of heaviest usage. He also determined characteristic values of the average rates of flow for different fixtures and the time span of a single operation of each.

If a building contains only one type of fixture, the application of the theory of probability is simple and straightforward. However, if the system is composed of a combination of various types of fixtures, the process becomes too complicated to be practical. Faced with this dilemma, Hunter devised an ingenious method to circumvent the problem, using a simple process that yields results within 0.5% accuracy of the more laborious calculations required. He conceived the idea of assigning "fixture loading factors" or "unit weights" to the different kinds of fixtures to represent the degree to which they loaded a system when used at their maximum assumed frequency. A "fixture unit weight" of 10 was arbitrarily assigned to a flush valve, and all other fixtures were assigned values based on their load-producing effect in relation to the flush value, thereby converting all fixtures to one fixture type. By using this method, the application of the theory of probability is greatly simplified.

Recently, the accuracy of Hunter's Curve has come into serious question. Results utilizing the curve have proved to be as much as 100% inflated, in some instances. The consistent "overdesign," however, should in no way be interpreted as indicating that Hunter's basic research and approach is incorrect.

Hunter's method is demonstrably accurate; however, his basic assumptions and criteria were promulgated more than 50 years ago. Many things have changed drastically since then: improvements have been made in flush-valve design, faucets, and fixtures; customs and living patterns have evolved and public water and energy conservation has been greatly emphasized. It is now necessary to alter some of his basic assumptions to bring Hunter's Curve up to date.

At present, as has been demonstrated by thousands of projects operating satisfactorily, the values obtained by use of Hunter's Curve may be safely reduced by 40%. Again it is stressed that this reduction should be applied only for systems with a large number of fixtures.

Potable Water

The physical and chemical characteristics of water to be used for human consumption are usually clearly defined by the Public Health Department of the municipality or state and by most codes. Rules and regulations have been promulgated and enforced to ensure that only potable water is distributed in public water mains. It is mandatory that building systems connect to available public mains as a positive measure for the protection of the public's health. Public water supply systems offer reliability, capacity, convenience, and above all, high quality potable water.

In areas where public water mains are not available, it is permissible to connect to an approved private source of potable water. When the source is a private utility, the utility is subject to the same criteria established for the public systems. Wells are another acceptable source of supply when public water is not available. Under no circumstances should water from any well be used until the water has been analyzed by a recognized water-testing laboratory and certified to be in conformance with the criteria established by the health authority having jurisdiction.

Potable water should be used for all drinking, food preparation, bottling, canning, washing of dishes, glasses, and kitchen utensils, and similar purposes. When a nonpotable water supply is provided in the same building as a potable supply, extreme precautions must be taken. All nonpotable water faucets and outlets and all nonpotable piping must be adequately identified by conspicuous markings, using signs, colors, or other symbols required by the authority having jurisdiction.

Whenever there is nonpotable piping in a building there is always the real danger of a cross-connection being made to the potable piping, resulting in contamination and the likelihood of disease and death.

Protection of Potable Water Supply

The following rules should be scrupulously followed in design of all water supply distribution systems:

1. No materials or chemicals that can produce toxic effects should be used.
2. There should never be a cross-connection between a private and a public water supply system.

3. Water supply piping must never be directly connected to the drainage system.
4. Water supply piping must never be directly connected to embalming, mortuary, operating, or dissection tables.
5. There must be no direct connection for pump priming.
6. There should be no direct connections to sterilizers, aspirators, or similar equipment.
7. Water used for cooling, heating, or processing must not be reintroduced to the water supply system.
8. An air gap must be provided between the overflow level of the fixture and the water supply outlet.
9. Below-the-rim water supply connections must never be made except where the configuration of the fixture makes this impossible. The connection is permitted if special precautions are taken.

Protective Methods for Below-The-Rim Supply

Where below-the-rim connections must be made, vacuum breakers located at least 6 in. above the overflow level of the fixture have given satisfactory results. When back pressure exists in the supply connection, a check valve should be installed between the fixture and the vacuum breaker.

Piping Installation

Water piping should always be installed in alignment and parallel to the walls of the building. The piping should be arranged so that it is possible to drain the entire system. There should be no sags where sediment could collect or high points where air pockets might be created.

Piping should be routed so that it does not pass over or within 2 ft of electrical switchgear, transformers, panel boards, control boards, motors, telephone equipment, etc. Where it is impossible to comply with the foregoing, a pan should be provided continuously below the piping, which is adequately supported and braced, rimmed, pitched, and drained by a ¾-in. line piped to the nearest floor drain or slop sink.

Piping should be protected where there is danger of external corrosion (such as when buried in floor fill or concrete) by applying a heavy coating of black asphaltum paint and covering the pipe with 16-gauge black iron U-covers, mitered on the corners and fastened to the floor arch. U-covers should be large enough to enclose the insulation on the piping.

Mains, risers, and branch connections to risers should be arranged to permit expansion and contraction without strain, by means of elbow swings or expansion joints.

All horizontal and vertical piping must be properly supported by means of hangers, anchors, and guides. Supports should be arranged so as to prevent excessive deflection and avoid binding stresses between supports. Anchored points should be located and constructed to permit the piping to expand and contract freely in the opposite direction from the anchored points. Guide points should be located and constructed at each side of an expansion joint or loop so that only free axial movement occurs without lateral displacement.

All screwed joints should be made with the best quality pure red lead, or another approved pipe compound, carefully applied on the male threads only. If the compound is applied to the fitting threads, it will be forced into the piping and impart a distinctive taste to the water.

All cut and threaded pipe should have the cutting burrs and sharp edges reamed out so as not to impose additional frictional losses in the system. Burrs are also a source of noise propagation as water vibrates them in passing.

All ferrous-to-nonferrous pipe connections should be made with dielectric isolating joints to prevent electrolytic action between dissimilar metals.

All copper tubing should be cut square and reamed to remove all burrs. The outside and inside of the fittings and the outside of the tubing at each end must be thoroughly cleaned with steel wool before soldering to remove all traces of oxidation, regardless of how clean the surfaces of the pipe and fittings may appear.

Unions should be provided at connections to each piece of equipment for easy dismantling and at other selected points to facilitate installation. All fittings, unions, and connections at pumps, tanks, or other major equipment 3 in. and over in size should be assembled with flanged joints and gaskets.

Underground piping entering or passing through rigid structures, such as building walls, retaining walls, and pit walls, should be sleeved to provide not less than 1-in. clearance around the pipe. The opening between the pipe and the pipe sleeve should be tightly packed with oakum and caulked with lead.

Valves

All water-control valves within the building should be constructed so they can be repacked while open and under pressure. Standard or extra heavy weight valves should be selected on the basis of the system pressure at the location of the installation.

All valves 2½ in. or smaller should be bronze with soldered, screwed, or flanged ends to match the system in which they are installed. Valves 3 in. and larger should be of cast-iron body with bronze mountings and screwed or flanged ends, as required by the system in which they are installed. Valves 3 in. and over located at pumps, tanks, and major equipment should be of the outside screw and yoke type, and flanged. Plug cocks or ball valves should be used for water balancing purposes in the hot water circulating piping system. Check valves should be of the horizontal swing type, except in the discharge piping of pumps where they should be center-guided, spring-loaded silent check type of required pressure rating.

Valve Locations

Water service lines should be equipped with a gate valve or ground-key stopcock near the curb line between the property line and the curb line. A curb box frame and cover, including extension enclosure, or box of required depth, should be provided to enclose and protect the water service valve operating mechanism. The type of valve, curb box, and location should always be coordinated with the local water company or municipal department. The curb valve and valve box should never be located under a driveway where they may be subjected to heavy concentrated loads, which could result in damage. In addition to the curb valve, a valve should be installed in the line inside the building as close to the point of entry as possible.

A riser control valve should be provided for each riser. In addition, an all-brass drain valve should be installed on each riser and located upstream of the riser control valve to provide means for draining the riser. The drain valve should be at least ¾ in. in size. Drain valves should also be provided at all low points of the piping system.

Each zone or section of the distribution system, as well as each group of fixtures or every fixture, should be provided with a shut-off valve.

Whether or not a valve should be installed in any particular location should be evaluated on the basis of ease of maintenance of the water system and maintenance costs if the valve is not installed in that particular location. Frugality in the installation of valves often results in false economy.

All valves, check valves, pressure-reducing valves, shock absorbers, tempering valves, etc, should always be easily accessible for maintenance or removal. They should always be exposed where possible and, where concealed, an access door of adequate size should be provided.

Strainers should always be provided in the inlet lines to all temperature regulating, pressure regulating, automatic modulating, or open and shut control valves. The strainers should be of the "Y" type, full pipe size, and fitted with a blow-off gate valve.

Hot Water System Design

Proper design of the domestic hot water supply system for any building is extremely important. Careful planning on the basis of available data will ensure an adequate water supply at the desired temperature to all fixtures at all times. The system must, of course, conform with all regulations of authorities having jurisdiction.

Any well-designed system should deliver the prescribed temperature at the outlet almost instantaneously to avoid the wasteful practice of running of water until the desired temperature is achieved. Hot water should be available at all times, day and night, and during low, as well as peak, demand periods.

Safety features must be built into any hot water system and they must operate automatically. Two paramount dangers to be eliminated in the design stage are excessive pressures and temperatures, which may, for example, cause hot water heaters to explode and scalding water at fixtures.

An economical heat source is of prime importance in conserving energy. Various sources include coal, gas, oil, steam, condensate, waste hot water, and electricity. Availability and cost of the above heat sources, or combinations, dictate selection. If an especially economical source does not satisfy the total demand, then it can be used to preheat the cold water supply to the heater. In some climates solar collectors have been used to great advantage as the primary or supplemental source of domestic hot water.

An economical and durable installation is achieved by judicious selection of proper materials and equipment. The piping layout also has a marked effect on this criterion and determines ease of replacement and repair.

Following installation, cost-effective operation and maintenance also depend on the proper preselection of materials and equipment. The following are some items that affect the operation and maintenance of a system: choice of instantaneous, semi-instantaneous, or storage type heaters; selection of insulation on heaters and piping; location of piping (avoiding cold, unheated areas); ease of circulation (by avoiding drops and rises in piping); bypasses around pumps and tanks; and adequate valving accessibility.

Safety Devices

Many cases have been reported in which explosion or bursting of tanks, damage to property, and scalding and injury of persons, have occurred because of hazardous pressures and temperatures. Standard plumbing equipment, including water heaters and storage tanks, is designed for a working pressure of 126 psi. Any pressure in excess of this limit is considered to be hazardous.

Water expands when heated. The increase in volume for a 100°F temperature rise is calculated to be 1.68% of its original volume. Since water is considered to be incompressible, the increased volume results in a buildup of pressure. It is absolutely necessary to provide a positive means of relieving this excess pressure. Pressure relief valves or combined temperature and pressure relief valves (T&P) satisfactorily meet this requirement.

The above-mentioned valves must have adequate capacity to prevent excessive pressure in the system when the water heating source is delivering the maximum rate of heat input.

Many contemporary pressure relief valves and the pressure elements of combined temperature and pressure relief valves are designed only for thermal expansion relief. This type of T&P valve will show only the temperature rating. Its thermal relief capacity is generally considered to be equal to or in excess of the temperature rating. In other words, it has the capacity of relieving thermal expansion in the system as long as the heat input does not exceed the rating of the valve.

The failure of hot water storage tanks and heaters was originally thought to be exclusively due to excessive pressures. The installation of pressure relief valves has therefore become a mandatory requirement of most codes. However, even where pressure relief valves were installed failures continued to occur, which indicated that more extensive protection was required for the safe operation of water-heating equipment. The opinion was advanced that overheating was the direct cause of explosions, and protection against excessive temperature as well as pressure was needed. The most extensive studies have been sponsored by the American Gas Association and the results published in their Research Reports 1151A and 1151B

(8,9). The reports supported the premise that emergency protection against excessive temperature as well as pressure is essential.

The temperature relief valve, or the temperature relief element of a combined valve, must have relieving capacity not less than the heat input operating at maximum capacity. The name plate rating on the temperature relief and combined T&P relief valves shows the temperature rating in terms of the maximum heater input on which the valves may be used.

Separate temperature and pressure relief valves may be used, but usually a combined T&P relief valve is preferred because it offers more economical and effective protection.

A relief valve on a water supply system is exposed to many elements that may affect its performance, such as corrosive water, which attacks materials, and deposits of lime, which close waterways and flow passages. Products of corrosion and lime deposits may cause the valve to become inoperative or reduce valve capacity below that of the heater. For these reasons, the minimum size of valve should be ¾ in. for inlet and outlet connections with the waterways within the valve of an area not less than the area of the inlet connection.

A relief valve must be installed so there is always free passage between the heater or tank and the relief valve. There should never be any valves or check valves installed between the relief valve and the equipment it protects.

A pressure relief valve may be installed in the cold supply to the tank, the hot supply from the tank, or directly in the heater. The temperature relief valve or combined T&P relief valve must always be installed in a position in which the hottest water in the system comes in contact with the temperature actuator or valve thermostat, respectively. If the valves are not installed as specified, they become ineffective protective devices. Wherever possible, the valves should be installed in a tapping in the tank or heater.

All valves should have a discharge pipe connected to its outlet and terminated at a point where the discharge will cause no damage to property or injury to persons. The discharge pipe size must be at least the size of the valve discharge outlet, must be as short as possible, and must run down to its terminal without sags or traps.

The pressure setting of the valve should be 25–30 lb higher than the system operating pressure to avoid false opening and dripping because of normal pressure surges in the system. The pressure setting, however, must always be less than the maximum working pressure of the material in the system.

An aquastat in the tank or heater (that will shut off the heat source when excessive temperatures develop) is an excellent added safety precaution.

Water Heaters

A brief outline of some of the more common sources of hot water supply will set forth their main characteristics and limitations.

Directly Heated Automatic Storage Heaters. In this category are placed the simple gas, propane-fired, or electrically heated storage tank heaters used universally in homes, apartments, and small institutions or establishments. Sizes range from 15- to 100-gal storage capacity. A 25–98 gph recovery rate with a temperature of 60°F is generally found. Heat input normally ranges from 10–70,000 Btus/hr.

These automatic storage heaters are highly efficient if sized properly. They are simple, inexpensive in regard to installation, piping, and controls, and exceptionally trouble-free. They serve well with all kinds of water, hard or soft, alkaline or acid. They can be drained and cleaned readily, especially if flushout hand-holes are provided. They are available with corrosion-resistant metal, glass-lined, or galvanized tanks. They are generally low-demand heaters, with low Btu input so that the heating of water is spread over several hours.

Instantaneous Heaters. The instantaneous type of water heater must have sufficient input capacity to meet all demands simultaneously. These heaters have no built-in storage volume because they are designed to supply the full load instantly and continuously. The flow of the fuel, gas or liquid, is automatically controlled by the flow of water in an on-off or a modulated-flow system. The water flow rate, temperature, and heat input are fixed at the factory. Heat input must be high in order to ensure the required flow of hot water. Because of these high flow rates and typical on-off operation, the efficiency rate is lower than the storage type.

Capacities run roughly from 1.5–10 gpm. Heat input rates run approximately 50,000 Btus/per gpm.

The instantaneous heater finds its best application where water heating demands are level and constant such as for swimming pools, certain dishwasher booster requirements, and industrial processes.

The most common form of the instantaneous heater is the U-tube, removable bundle exchanger with steam or boiler water in the shell and domestic water flowing through the tubes. Where the characteristics of the water are such as to cause rapid scale deposits, it is recommended that straight-tube floating head exchangers be used in lieu of the U-tube heater. The water is heated by conduction and the heat transfer rate increases as the water velocity increases through the tubes. A minimum velocity of 4 fps should be maintained through the tubes at full capacity conditions to minimize the rate of scale formation in the tubes.

The greatest problem with instantaneous heaters is adequately controlling the outlet water temperature to maintain acceptable limits during fluctuating demand. The best temperature control system cannot respond quickly enough to maintain satisfactory constant outlet water temperature under rapidly changing flow conditions. This undesirable fluctuation is called overshooting or undershooting.

Booster-heaters. The term "booster" is applied to describe the function or purpose of the water heater. Heaters may be the ordinary standard instantaneous types, but they serve to raise the temperature of the regular hot water supply to some higher temperature needed to perform special functions. The advantages in the use of booster heaters are as follows:

1. Only as much water need be heated to above normal system temperatures as is required for the specific job. The larger, normal uses throughout the building may be average hot water at lower temperatures.
2. Savings in investment, maintenance, and operating costs are derived from the limited use of very hot water.
3. Small boosters may be located near their job, with simple control, minimum waste, and smooth operation.

Semi-instantaneous Heaters. To overcome the shortcomings of the instantaneous heater, manufacturers have developed a limited storage-type heater known as semi-instantaneous. This type contains 10–20 s of domestic water storage according to its rated heating capacity. A 60 gpm rated heater will have approximately 20 gal of water in its shell. This small quantity of water is adequate for allowing the temperature control system to react to sudden fluctuations in water flow and for maintaining the outlet water temperature within ± 5°F. The temperature control system is almost always included with the heater.

A hot water tempering valve should always be provided for mixing cold water with the hot water from instantaneous heaters to prevent scalding water temperatures from entering the distribution system. A tempering valve should never be installed when a semi-instantaneous heater is used, as it will negate the function of its temperature control system. The semi-instantaneous heater finds its application in apartments, offices, some institutional structures, or any building in which the peak demand is spread over several hours and where the peak draws are not severe. The designer is referred to the catalogs of manufacturers for a complete and in-depth treatment of the construction and operation of the semi-instantaneous heater.

Storage Water Heaters. The primary reason for using the storage-type water heater instead of the instantaneous or semi-instantaneous is to smooth out the peak demands on heating systems where there are large volume changes in the hot water demand such as in gymnasiums (showers), laundries, kitchens, and industrial washrooms. When the correct storage capacity is combined with the correct recovery capacity and the proper size heating medium control valve is selected, a substantial reduction in the peak heat fluid demand can be realized. This results in a smaller boiler installation and less heating of medium piping.

The following example will illustrate the above point. A large high school gym class will draw 1000 gal of 140°F water in 10 minutes, none for the next 50 minutes, then another 1000 gal for 10 minutes. This is repeated throughout the school day. An ideal storage water selection for this application would have 1500 gallons storage and 1000 gallons recovery.

The larger-size storage water heater is selected since only two thirds of the stored water will be usable because it is cooled down by the entering cold water. If the heating medium is steam at 10 psi, the steam demand rate will not exceed 1000 lb/h (30 boiler HP). Based on 10 psi steam at the control valve and 100 ft of steam pipe, the correct size of pipe would be 2½ in., and the control valve size 1½ in. If an instantaneous heater is used, it must heat 1000 gal of water in 10 minutes, or at a 100 gpm instantaneous rate. This is equal to a steam demand rate of 5000 lb/h (150 boiler HP). This is five times the peak demand required by the storage heater. The steam line size would be 6 in. and the control valve 4 in., as compared to the 2½-in. line and 1½-in. valve.

Although the storage heater is more costly to install and requires more space, these requirements for 30 boiler HP compared with 150 boiler HP, plus the smaller steam supply pipe size, control system, condensate return system, fittings, etc, make the storage heater a far more economical selection for this particular application.

A conventional storage water heater generally consists of a removable U-tube, a copper tube bundle installed in the lower half of a horizontal or vertical cylindrical tank. The water to be heated enters the tank below the tube bundle and leaves at the top. The heating fluid, steam, high or medium temperature water, or other heat transfer fluid, flows through the tubes. The water is heated almost completely by convection flow across the tubes. Temperature control is accomplished by a thermostatic bulb or similar device located to sense the temperature of the water and set to shut the control valve of the heating medium when the selected temperature is reached.

Increasingly popular are modular gas-fired high efficiency water heaters piped to an insulated storage tank. Efficiency as high as 92% is achieved, with improved dependability and longer guarantees. Most systems try to establish 125°F water rather than the traditional 140°F, and make dramatic energy reductions.

Expansion and Contraction

All pipe lines subject to changes in temperature expand and contract. Piping increases (expands) and decreases (contracts) in length as the temperature increases and decreases, respectively. The unit increase in length of a material per 1°F temperature increase is called its coefficient of expansion.

The total change in length may be calculated by:

$$L_2 - L_1 = C_E L_1 (T_2 - T_1)$$

where L_1 = original pipe length in ft; L_2 = final pipe length in ft; T_1 = original temperature in °F; T_2 = final temperature in °F; and C_E = coefficient of expansion of material.

Provisions must be made for the expansion and contraction of all hot water and circulation mains, risers, and branches. If the piping is restrained from moving, it will be subjected to compressive stress on a temperature rise and to tensile stress on a temperature drop. The pipe itself is usually able to withstand these stresses, but failure frequently occurs at pipe joints and fittings when the piping cannot move freely.

The methods commonly employed to absorb pipe expansion or contraction without danger to the piping are expansion loops and offsets, and expansion joints.

It is good engineering practice to limit the total movement to be absorbed by any expansion loop or offset to a maximum of 1½ in. Thus, by anchoring at the points on the length of run that produce 1½ in. movement and placing the expansion loop or joint midway between the anchors, the maximum movement that must be accommodated is ¾ in. The loop or joint may be omitted in the majority of piping systems by taking advantage of the changes in direction normally required in the layout.

Persistent Myth

One of the most persistent myths in plumbing is that turning motion occurs at the elbows of an expansion loop. This is absolutely false. If any elbow were turned in a counterclockwise motion, the joint would be loosened and a leak would occur. A good mechanic will never "back-off" a fitting if he or she has overshot the make-up. He or she will always make another turn to center the outlet at the correct location, because backing off a fitting always results in a leak.

Movement is never accommodated by the rotating motion of the fittings; it is always absorbed by the flexure of the pipe. From this is it can be seen that the number of elbows in a loop has no bearing whatsoever on its ability to absorb movement. The developed length of pipe available for flexure is the only thing limiting the amount of expansion that can be accommodated.

In Figure 23 dashed lines indicate, in an exaggerated manner for illustrative purposes, how the pipe deforms in a 4-elbow loop. The length of leg B should be at least twice the length of A. Wherever possible, B should be larger than 2 × A.

The slip and bellows are the two types of expansion joints. The slip joint requires packing and lubrication, and thus must be placed in an accessible location for maintenance. Guides must be installed in the lines to prevent the pipes from bending and binding in the joint.

The bellows expansion joints are very satisfactory for the 1½-in. design limitation in movement usually employed in plumbing work. They should be guided or in some other way restrained to prevent collapse.

When applying pipe support, anchors, expansion loops, or joints, it is important to remember expansion occurs on any temperature rise. The greater the temperature rise, the greater the expansion. The supports, anchors, and guides are installed to restrain expansion and cause it to move in the direction desired by the designer, so that problems do not develop by negligent or improper installation. If a takeoff connection from mains or risers is located too close to floors, beams, columns, or walls, a change in temperature could cause a break in the takeoff with subsequent flooding damage.

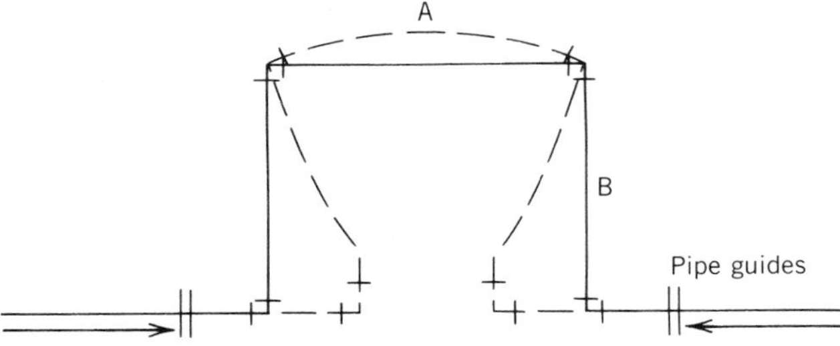

Figure 23. Pipe deformity (1). Courtesy of Construction Industry Press.

Water System Tests

All water piping in a building should be subjected to a water test to assure watertightness. Any leaks or defects discovered must be corrected. Testing of the piping should be performed before any insulation is applied to the piping and before any part of the system is covered or concealed. Potable water should be used for the test so as not to introduce any possible contaminants into the system. The test should be performed before fixtures, faucets, trim or final connections are made to equipment.

The rough piping installation should be subjected to a hydrostatic pressure of 1.5 times the working pressure of the system, and no less than 125 psi. The test should extend over a period of at least three hours and demonstrate watertightness without loss of pressure.

When the entire system has been completely installed, including all fixtures, faucets, trim, hose connections, and final connections to all equipment, it should be placed in operating condition and thoroughly checked for leaks. All valves, faucets, and trim should be operated at and adjusted for maximum performance.

Disinfection

Although utmost caution is exercised when installing pipe, there is always the danger that some form of contaminant has been introduced into the system. No water supply system may be used before it is thoroughly disinfected and the water proved safe for human consumption, regardless of cost. The following is written in the form of a specification for the disinfection of water systems.

Disinfection of Water Systems

A. General

1. Before being placed in service, all potable water piping shall be chlorinated as specified herein, in accordance with AWWA Standard C650–86 and as required by the local Building and Health Department Codes (10).
2. Chlorine may be applied by the use of chlorine gas–water mixture, direct chlorine–gas feed, or a mixture of calcium hypochlorite and water. If calcium hypochlorite is used, it shall be comparable to commercial products. The powder shall be mixed with water to form a paste thinned to a slurry and pumped or injected into the lines as specified below.
3. If direct chlorine-gas feed is used, it shall be fed

with either a solution-feed chlorinator or by a pressure-feed chlorinator with a diffuser in the pipe.

B. Procedure

1. Prior to chlorination, all dirt and foreign matter shall be removed by a thorough flushing of the potable water system. The chlorinating agent may be applied to the piping systems at any convenient point. Water shall be fed slowly into the potable water system and the chlorine applied in doses of 50 ppm of available chlorine. Retention shall be for a period of eight hours. During the chlorination process, all valves and accessories shall be operated.
2. After completion of the above requirements, the system shall be flushed until the water in the system gives chemical and bacteriological test data equal to that of the permanent potable water supply.
3. Chemical and bacteriological tests shall be conducted by a state certified laboratory and approved by the local authorities having jurisdiction. Copies of the test results shall be submitted to the architect and all governing authorities.
4. Warning signs shall be provided at all outlets while chlorinating the system.
5. If it is impossible to disinfect the potable water-storage tank as provided above, the entire interior of the tank shall be swabbed with a solution containing 200 ppm of available chlorine and the solution allowed to stand for two hours before flushing and returning to service.

BIBLIOGRAPHY

1. A. Steele, *Engineered Plumbing Design,* 2nd ed., Construction Industry Press, Elmhurst, Ill., 1982.
2. R. B. Hunter, *Report of the Subcommittee on Plumbing of the Building Code Committee,* BH13, U.S. Department of Commerce, National Bureau of Standards, Washington, D.C., 1932.
3. F. M. Dawson and A. A. Kalinske, *Report on Hydraulics and Pneumatics of Plumbing Drainage Systems,* Bulletin 10, Iowa State University Studies in Engineering, Ames, Iowa, 1937.
4. R. S. Wyly and N. N. Eaton, *Capacities of Plumbing Stacks in Building,* Building Materials and Structures Report BMS 132, National Bureau of Standards, Washington, D.C., 1952.
5. *ASPE Data Book Vol 1,* 1983–1984.
6. *ASHRAE Handbook,* American Society of Heating Refrigerating and Air Conditioning Engineers, Atlanta Ga., current edition.
7. R. B. Hunter, *Methods of Estimating Loads in Plumbing Systems,* Building Materials and Structures Report BMS 65, National Bureau of Standards, Washington, D.C., 1940.
8. Research Report 1151A, "A Study and Observation of the Effectiveness of Temperature and Pressure Relief Devices and Emergency Gas Shut-offs for Gas Water Heaters," American Gas Association, Arlington, Va., 1950.
9. Research Report 1151B, "Interindustry Investigation: Essential Characteristics and Proper Installation Procedures for Protection Devices for Domestic Storage Type Water Heaters Regardless of the Energy Used for Heating," American Gas Association, Arlington, Va., 1954.
10. AWWA Standard C–650–86, "Disinfecting Water Mains," American Water Works Association, Denver, Colo., 1986.
11. Research Report 1151B.
12. AWWA Standard code p. 87.

General References

A. Steele, *Advanced Plumbing Technology,* Construction Industry Press, Elmhurst, Ill., 1984.

ASPE Data Book, Vol. 1, Fundamentals of Plumbing Design, American Society of Plumbing Engineers, Sherman Oaks, Calif., 1983.

ASPE Data Book, Vol. 2, Special Plumbing Systems Design, American Society of Plumbing Engineers, Sherman Oaks, Calif., 1982.

L. Blenderman, *Controlled Storm Water Drainage,* Industrial Press Inc., New York, 1979.

V. T. Manas, *National Plumbing Code Handbook,* McGraw-Hill Inc., New York, 1957.

B. Stein, J. S. Reynolds, and W. J. McGuinness, *Mechanical and Electrical Equipment for Buildings,* 7th ed., John Wiley & Sons, New York, 1986.

See also Brass and Bronze; Copper; Kitchens, Residential; Mechanical Systems; Solar Design

Alfred Steele, PE
American Society of Plumbing Engineers Research Foundation
Chicago, Illinois.

Donald G. Carter, PE
Carter Engineering, Inc.
Kensington, Maryland

PLYWOOD. See Wood, Structural Panel Composites

POLYAMIDES (NYLON)

The generic term nylon identifies a set of tough, high modulus white translucent condensation polymers containing repeating amide linkages. Aliphatic polyamides such as nylon-6 and -6,6 are generally polymerized and extruded in the molten state, whereas wholly aromatic polyamides (aramids) are prepared from solution. Nylon-6 and -6,6 share the bulk of domestic and commercial sales in architectural end-use areas. Carpeting consumes most of the nylon used in homes, offices, schools, factories, and other manmade structures. Nylon-6 and -6,6 are synthesized from the same readily available petrochemical intermediates using different polymerization techniques.

Nylons are identified by a simple numeric system. The word polyamide or nylon is followed by one or more numbers. A single number indicates that the polymer is prepared from a single monomer and designates the number of carbon atoms in the linear chain of the recurring polymer unit. For example, nylon-6 is prepared by ring opening polymerization of caprolactam, which has six carbon atoms separating amine groups; nylon-11 is prepared from 11-aminoundecanoic acid, a long-chain aliphatic amino acid derived from the castor bean, which has 11 carbon atoms separating amine groups. When two numbers are used with the word nylon or polyamide, they are separated by a comma and refer to the number of carbon atoms in the individual reactants used in preparing the polymer. The first number refers to the number of carbon atoms in the diamine and the second to the number of carbons in the dibasic acid. Thus, nylon-6,6 is prepared by the reaction of hexamethylenediamine having six carbon atoms separating the amine groups and adipic acid, a six-carbon chain aliphatic dibasic acid.

Nylon was developed by Wallace H. Carothers at DuPont and commercialized in 1938 as a synthetic replacement for silk. The original manufacture of nylon intermediates from coal, air, and water has been replaced by petroleum-based routes that involve the conversion of toluene to cyclohexane and cyclohexane to adipic acid or caprolactam. Hexamethylenediamine is prepared by two commercial routes; one involves the hydrocyanation of butadiene and its subsequent reduction, and the other involves the ammoxidation of propylene to form acrylonitrile, which is then electrodimerized.

Major U.S. nylon producers now include E.I. du Pont de Nemours & Co. Inc., Monsanto Co., Allied-Signal Inc., American Enka Corp., BASF, and Courtaulds North America Inc., with combined capacity for nylon-6 and nylon-6,6 of 1.570×10^6 t in 1987. U.S. production figures for 1987 show that 214×10^3 t of nylon were used in plastic applications and 1224×10^3 t were used in fiber applications.

Manufacture

Nylon-6,6 is prepared by mixing hexamethylenediamine and adipic acid in water to form hexamethylenediammonium adipate, a water-soluble salt. The salt solution is decolorized, concentrated, and then polymerized at 275°C under 1.8 MPa pressure. The water is driven off, and the batch of nylon is extruded in ribbon form on a water-cooled casting wheel and subsequently cut into chips or flakes suitable for melt spinning fibers or extruding into shaped parts.

Nylon-6 is prepared by a water or phosphoric acid catalyzed ring opening hydrolysis at 240–280°C of caprolactam with polymerization occurring simultaneously by an addition reaction. During the reaction, unreacted caprolactam is removed and recycled while the addition polymerization, controlled by removal of water, continues to the appropriate molecular weight.

Properties

Combinations of unique properties, ie, toughness, abrasion resistance, fatigue and creep resistance, high temperature stability, oil and solvent resistance, drawability, moldability, coupled with a low coefficient of friction and excellent aesthetics have, during the 50 years of nylon's existence, resulted in a plethora of building and architectural applications. More than 719,000 t of nylon were consumed by these end uses in 1984. Commercial and residential carpeting, the major nylon end use, consumed 700,000 t in 1984. Only 224 million yd^3 of carpet, representing approximately 200,000 t of nylon, were used in 1980.

Toughness. Moisture content, composition, and degree of crystallinity determine the impact resistance of nylon. Absorbed moisture enhances toughness, but high levels of toughness are also available in the dry state if suitable plasticizers or copolymer compositions are used. If surface-coupling agents are applied properly to suitably oriented fibers, then glass-fiber reinforcement increases nylon toughness. Hand-held power tools and appliances are made more serviceable because of the superior toughness contributed by casings made of nylon.

Abrasion Resistance. Nylons offer excellent wear resistance if used within appropriate pressure velocity limits. Applications benefiting from the abrasion resistance of nylon include electric wire and cable jacketing [mainly over a poly(vinyl chloride) base], elevator guide shoes, nylon-toothed sprocket gears for unlubricated conveyor chains, and numerous other steel parts that are coatable by a fluid-bed technique.

Fatigue. Nylon's ability to resist fracture by repeated impacts at subcritical levels make it well suited for oscillating machinery parts, gears and sprockets, hammer handles, door striker plates, and shuttle looms.

Creep or Relaxation. A sustained stress lower than that required to cause immediate nonrecoverable strain causes permanent distortion or creep in plastics. Nylon's relatively higher resistance to creep improves with increasing polymer crystallinity. Gaskets and seals, furniture casters, and gears that remain under constant load take advantage of this property.

High Temperature Stability. Good form retention and oxidative-degradation resistance are facets of high-temperature stability that make nylon suitable for use in hundreds of complex moldings, such as electrical coil forms, cooking utensils, kitchen equipment, handles, housings, and baskets that contact hot metal, grease, or oil. For high-temperature applications in these end uses, glass-fiber reinforcement improves nylon stiffness.

Solubility. Polyamides are generally impervious to attack by solvents and chemicals but are soluble at room temperature in phenols, formic acid, chloral hydrate, and mineral acids. At higher temperatures, halogenated hydrocarbon–alcohol mixtures, unsaturated alcohols, nitro alcohols, and calcium chloride–methanol mixtures are solvents for aliphatic polyamides. Nylon-6,6 is soluble in methanol under pressure. Aromatic polyamides are soluble in *N,N*-dimethylacetamide (DMAC) and 1-methyl-2-pyrrolidinone (NMP). Nylons slowly absorb minor quantities of hydrocarbons and small amounts of water; the former decreases and the latter increases as the number of amide linkages in the polymer is increased.

Hydrolysis. Most nylons are unaffected by boiling water, although at higher temperatures in the molten state hydrolysis and degradation can occur. Nylons are normally stable to aqueous alkali, whereas aqueous acid rapidly degrades them. Acid hydrolysis of nylon-6,6 is slower than that of nylon-6. Hydrolytic stability and solvent resistance give nylon a competitive edge in hydraulic coupling lines, air-conditioning system hoses, rotationally molded gasoline tanks, and packages for greased machinery parts.

Drawability. Strapping for industrial packaging, monofilament bristles, strings for sports equipment, musical instruments, woven screens, and most textile applications make use of the high tensile strengths obtained by cold-drawing or otherwise orienting nylon at temperatures below its melting point.

Friction. Nylon is used extensively in sliding applications because it displays a low coefficient of friction in contact with numerous other materials, and thus is used where lubrication is not feasible. Journal bearings, bushings, slides, guides, gears, cams, and sliding guides for moving stairway handrails are typical applications.

Flame Resistance. Although nylon may be destroyed by a fire, it is actually low in flammability and in smoke and fume generation. Nylon does not contribute significantly to fire and, with suitable additives, has been employed in aircraft interiors.

Tables 1 and 2 illustrate why nylon has pioneered applications for architectural purposes such as fire hoses, tarpaulins and tents, curtains and shutters, upholstery and drapery, rope and hawsers, electrical outlets, and wire insulation.

Applications

Since its introduction in 1938, millions of metric tons of nylon have been used in upholstery, shutters, fabric structures such as radar and stadium domes, and carpets. In each of these pioneering applications, except for carpet, the tonnages consumed in these architecturally important end uses has decreased with the development of other polymers, polymer blends, and coatings. The unit value per pound of nylon in 1986 was $1.57; only polytetrafluoroethylene, polyurethane, and advanced thermoplastic engineering plastics had higher unit values.

Despite its cost, the use of nylon in carpets has increased steadily since its inception in 1947. Its use has increased because the fiber satisfies a host of performance specifications that permit the successful application of nylon carpet in offices, stores, schools, hotels, airport terminals, and train stations, as well as in less heavily trafficked areas such as bedrooms, dining and living rooms, and kitchens.

Typical construction specifications for a heavily trafficked area where the nylon carpet is intended for direct glue down installation are pile weight (minimum 22 oz./yd^2); pile density $\left(\text{minimum } 4600 = \dfrac{36 \times \text{finished pile weight oz/yd}^2}{\text{finished average pile height (in.)}}\right)$; yarn ply (minimum two ply or two ends entangled); pile yarn (filament nylon); pile surface appearance (slightly textured loop pile); construction tufted or woven of 100% synthetic materials when installed at or below grade level; coloration (multiple color tones); dye lot (minimum 2000 yd^2 with no visual difference in side and end uniformity); and dye method (yarn dyed in the singles or continuously piece-dyed).

These construction specifications should provide a carpet that satisfies the following performance specifications:

1. *Pile Fuzzing and Pilling*. Dupont TRL Method 609 with a minimum acceptable pilling rating 4.2 on a scale of 1–5.
2. *Tuft Lock. ASTM Method D1335,* "Tuft Bind of Loop Pile Floor Coverings," in which eight pulls are performed at randomly chosen points across the width of the carpet. The minimum tuft lock will be 10 lb on any single pull, with 12 lb being the average for eight pulls.
3. *Tuft Lock. ASTM Method D1335,* "Tuft Bind of Cut Pile Coverings," in which eight pulls are performed at random across the width of the test carpet and the minimum tuft lock allowed is 4 lb on any single pull with an average of 5 lb for eight pulls.
4. *Peel Strength of Secondary Backing. Federal Test Method Standard 191, Textile Test Method 5950.* The minimum acceptable average pull strength is 3.35 lb/in.
5. *Static. AATCC Test Method 134–1979* (neolite), "Electrostatic Build-up in Carpets." In this test, static discharge is not to exceed 3.5 kV.
6. *Flammability. ASTM Method 648* requires more than 0.22 W/cm^2 critical radiant flux; more stringent federal, state, or local requirements must be met if they are applicable.
7. *Dye Lightfastness. AATCC Test Method 16E-1982.* The shade change after eighty standard fading hours (Xenon Arc) shall be no less than an International Gray Scale Rating of 3.
8. *Crockfastness. AATCC Test Method 8–1981.* Minimum stain ratings on the International Gray Scale should be: Wet—4; Dry—4.
9. *Wetfastness.* "Dupont Carpet Spot Bleed Test." This test is run with both hard water and alkaline detergent (pH 9.5 test for two cycles). The stain or color change rating, on the International Gray Scale, should be no less than 3 after two cycles in either test.
10. *Atmospheric Fading. AATCC test method 129,* "Ozone"/*AATCC Test Method 23–1975,* "Burnt Gas." The minimum shade change after two cycles in each test should be no less than International Gray Scale Rating of 3.

Table 1. Physical Constants of Nylon-6 and Nylon-6,6

Property	Nylon-6	Nylon-6,6	Test Methods
Melting point, °C			
At equilibium	200–220	250–260	ASTM D789
α-Crystalline	231		
Pressure dependence	260	<270	
Density, g/cm^3			
Crystalline			
α, Monoclinic	1.24		
α, Monoclinic	1.23		
α, Monoclinic	1.21		
γ, Hexagonal	1.13		
γ, Monoclinic	1.17		
γ, Pseudohexagonal	1.155		
α, Triclinic		1.220	
α, Triclinic		1.24	
β, Triclinic		1.248	
Amorphous			
γ	1.09		
α	1.11		
Dielectric strength, (v/cm) × 10^{-4}			VDE0303, part 2[a]
Dry	150	150	
Dry at 100°C	40	40	
Humid:ca 2 wt% H_2O	80	90	
Entropy of fusion, J/(mol·K)[b]			
Crystalline	44–47.5	83–86	
Constant volume		67	
Heat of combustion, kJ/kg[b]	−31.900	−31.900	
Heat of crystallization, kJ/kg[b]	−46.5	−54	
Heat-distortion temperature, °C			ISO-R75; DIN53 461[c]
Molded, dry, at 0.46 MPa[d]	170–190	<200	
Molded, dry, at 18.5 MPa[d]	65–75	90–100	
Molded, annealed, at 0.46 MPa[d]		243	
Molded, annealed, at 18.5 MPa[d]		105	
Heat of fusion, kJ/kg[b]			
Crystalline from H_m	188		
Crystalline from H_m	191	196	
Crystalline from H_m for α-structure	230–278		
Crystalline calculated from group contribution	193	193	
Amorphous, annealed 8 h at 50°C(= 1.111)	45		
Mold shrinkage, %	0.7–1.5	0.8–1.5	
Refractive index, n_D			
α[e]		1.475	
β[e]		1.565	
γ[f]		1.58	
Moldings	1.53	01.53	
Thermal conductivity, W/(m·K)[g]			
Crystalline (wet) at 30°C	0.43	0.43	
Amorphous (wet) at 30°C	0.36	0.36	
Melt at 250°C	0.21		

[a] VDE = Verband Deutscher Elektrotechniker.
[b] To convert J to cal, divide by 4.184.
[c] DIN = Deutsches Institut fur Normung.
[d] To convert MPa to psi, multiply by 145.
[e] Calculated.
[f] Observed.
[g] To convert W/(m·K) to (Btu·in.)/(s·ft^2·°F), divide by 518.9.

The indicated test procedures are described in greater detail in federal specification DOD-C-95 "Carpets and Rugs, Wool, Nylon, Acrylic, Modacrylic, Polyester, Polypropylene," in the publication *AATCC Standard Methods of Testing Colorfastness* and in the publication *ASTM Standard Methods of Testing Pile Floor Covering*.

Fabrication

Nylon, because of its good flow characteristics, can be used in parts with molded-in threads. It can also be incorporated in structures with self-tapping screws, with snap-fit housings that hold molded parts together after pressure is

Table 2. Properties of Nylons, Dry as Molded

Property	Nylon-6	Nylon-6,6	Nylon-11	Nylon-12	Nylon-6,9	Nylon-6,12	ASTM Test Method
Specific gravity	1.13	1.14	1.04	1.02	1.09	1.07	D792
Water absorption, wt%							D570
24 h	1.6	1.5	0.3	0.25	0.5	0.5	
Equilibrium at 50% rh	2.7	2.5	0.8	0.70	1.8	1.4	
Saturation	10.5	9.5	1.9	1.5	4.5	3.0	
Melting point, °C	215	265	194	179	205	217	
Tensile yield strength, kPa[a]	8.1×10^4	8.3×10^4	5.5×10^4	5.5×10^4	5.5×10^4	5.5×10^4	D638
Elongation at break, %	50–200	40–80	200	200	125	150	D638
Flexural modulus, kPa[a]	2.7×10^6	2.8×10^6	1.2×10^6	1.1×10^6	2.0×10^6	2.0×10^6	D790
Izod impact strength, J/m of notch[b]	54	68	40	95	58	58	D256
Rockwell hardness, R scale	119	120	108	107	111	114	D785
Deflection temperature under load, °C D648							
At 455 kPa[a]	185	245	150	150	150	165	
At 1850 kPa[a]	65	75	55	55	55	82	
Dielectric strength, kV/mm							D149
Short time	17	24	16.7	18	24	16	
Step-by-step	15	11		16	20		
Dielectric constant							D150
At 60 Hz(= cs)	3.8	4.0	3.7	4.2	3.7	4.0	
At 10^3 Hz	3.7	3.9	3.7	3.8	3.6	4.0	
At 10^6 Hz	3.4	3.5	3.1	3.1	3.3	3.5	
Starting materials	Polycaprolactam	Hexamethylenediamine and adipic acid	11-Aminoundecanoic acid	Polylaurolactam	Hexamethylenediamine and azelaic acid	Hexamethylenediamine and dodecanedioic acid	

[a] To convert kPa to psi, multiply by 0.145.
[b] To convert J/m to ft·lbft/in., divide by 53.38.

applied; by press-fitting or interference fit, in which one part is inserted into another with such force that it is difficult to remove; by ultrasonic welding, in which high-frequency vibration and pressure are applied to melt the plastic at a joint and cause a weld in less than 2 s; by spin welding, in which one part is held fixed while the other spins at high speeds so that when the welder applies pressure the melted parts fuse after cooling; and by vibration welding, a form of friction welding that can be applied to large noncircular parts in which the displacement can be linear or angular and the frequency is lower than ultrasonic welding. Tables 3 and 4 list the manufacturers and trade names for polyamide plastics and polyamide carpet fibers.

Table 3. Manufacturers and Trade Names for Polyamide Plastics

Manufacturer	Nylon Type	Trade Name
United States		
Allied Corp.	6	Capron
Emser Industries	6	Grilamid
BASF	6	Ultramid
Bemis Co., Inc.	6	CRI
Celanese Corp.	6,6	Celanese
E. I. du Pont de Nemours & Co., Inc.	6,6	Zytel
	6,12	
	6,6[a]	Minlon
	6,12[a]	
Monsanto	6,6	Vydyne
	6,9	
Mobay	6	Nydur
Atochem	11	Rilsan

[a] Mineral filled.

Table 4. Manufacturers and Trade Names for Polyamide Carpet Fiber

Manufacturer	Nylon Type	Trade Name
E. I. du Pont de Nemours & Co., Inc.	6,6	Antron
		Antron Plus
		Antron XL
		Stainmaster
Allied-Signal	6,6	Anso
BASF	6	Zeftron

BIBLIOGRAPHY

General References

Designing with Capron, Allied-Signal Corp., Morristown, N.J.

Designing with Plastics, E. I. du Pont de Nemours & Co., Inc., Wilmington, Del.

M. I. Kohan, *Nylon Plastics,* John Wiley & Sons, New York, 1973.

S. Levy and J. H. Dubois, *Plastic Product Design, Engineering Handbook,* Chapman & Hall, New York, 1984.

"Resins '88 Annual Summary," *Modern Plastics,* 63–105 (Jan. 1988).

J. Preston, "Polyamides, Aromatic," in *Encyclopedia of Polymer Science and Engineering,* vol. 11, John Wiley & Sons, New York, 1988, pp. 381–409.

J. H. Saunders, "Polyamides (Fibers)," in *Encyclopedia of Chemical Technology,* vol. 18, John Wiley & Sons, New York, 1982, pp. 372–405.

P. V. Tebo, M. I. Kohan, "Nylon," in *Modern Plastics Encyclopedia,* vol. 63(10A), McGraw-Hill, New York, 1988, p. 34.

R. J. Welgos, "Polyamides, Plastics," in *Encyclopedia of Polymer Science and Engineering,* vol. 11, John Wiley & Sons, New York, 1988, pp. 445–476.

J. Zimmerman, "Polyamides," in *Encyclopedia of Polymer Science and Engineering,* vol. 11, John Wiley & Sons, New York, 1988, pp. 315–381.

Richard E. Putscher
E. I. du Pont de Nemours & Co., Inc.
Wilmington, Delaware

POLYCARBONATES

Transparent polycarbonate (PC) sheet products are available in a variety of types and grades. Because PC sheet offers much greater impact resistance than does glass, it was at first viewed largely as a glass replacement in areas where greater durability was required.

However, in the last few years the formability of PC sheet, its superior thermal insulation (up to 16% better than comparable thicknesses of glass), and its light weight have led architects and builders to use it in barrel-vaulted roofs, domes, and other curved or formed designs that are impossible or much more difficult in glass. PC sheet can be easily cold-formed on-site following appropriate manufacturer's specifications or thermoformed to gentle curves or more complex shapes, opening up a wide range of architectural design possibilities.

PC film and sheet are produced by an extrusion/calendering process. The process starts with PC pellets, which are introduced to extruders for melting and pumping through dies. The melt is then fed to a calendering stack to produce polished or textured film and sheet.

Although the initial cost of PC sheet is often above that of glass, the long-term benefits of PC sheet in maintenance and replacement make it a cost-competitive choice. For complex designs such as domes and other formed shapes, PC sheet's formability makes it a cost-effective alternative to formed glass and acrylics.

PHYSICAL CHARACTERISTICS

PC sheet, used largely as an alternative to glass and acrylics, possesses properties that make it an attractive glazing material, especially in applications that require levels of performance above that of glass or acrylic glazing. Figure 1 and Tables 1–5 provide a comparison of typical PC sheet performance with typical glass and acrylic performance.

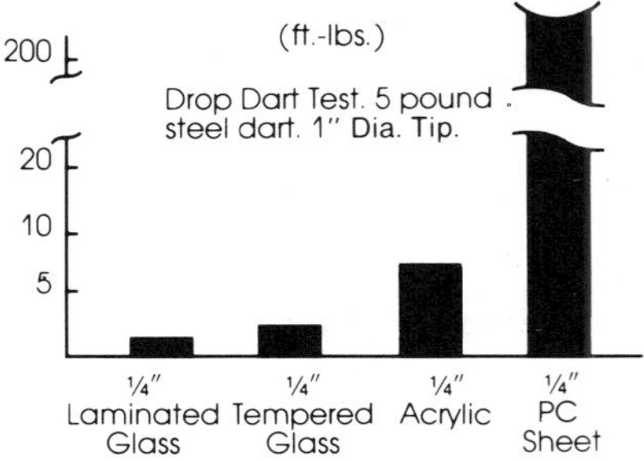

Figure 1. Impact resistance of PC sheet versus other materials.

Polycarbonate sheet exhibits up to 250 times the impact resistance of a comparable thickness of laminated glass and up to 30 times that of acrylic (Fig. 1). Tables 1 and 2 show the U-value comparison between PC sheet and glass. PC sheet provides a substantial summer heat gain and winter heat loss advantage. Coefficients of thermal expansion are listed in Table 3. The most commonly used construction materials have a coefficient within several hundred-thousandths in./in./°F. PC sheet exhibits a weight roughly one-half that of a comparable thickness of glass (Table 4), with roughly the same sound transmission properties (Table 5).

Table 1. U-value Comparison—Summer Heat Gain

Thickness, in.	U-value of PC Sheet, Btu/h·ft²·°F	U-value of Glass, Btu/h·ft²·°F	% Advantage of PC Sheet Over Glass
0.080	1.00	1.04	4
0.093	1.00	1.04	4
0.125	0.97	1.04	7
0.187	0.93	1.04	11
0.250	0.90	1.04	14
0.375	0.83	1.03	19
0.500	0.77	1.03	25
Double glazed	0.45	0.56	20

Table 2. U-value Comparison—Winter Heat Loss

Thickness, in.	U-value of PC Sheet, Btu/h·ft²·°F	U-value of Glass, Btu/h·ft²·°F	% Advantage of PC Sheet Over Glass
0.080	1.10	1.16	5
0.093	1.08	1.16	7
0.125	1.05	1.16	10
0.187	1.01	1.15	12
0.250	0.96	1.14	16
0.375	0.88	1.11	21
0.500	0.82	1.09	25
Double glazed	0.43	0.49	12

Table 3. Thermal Expansion of Construction Materials

Building Material	Coefficient of Thermal Expansion, In./In./°F
Glass	0.0000050
Aluminum	0.0000129
PC sheet	0.0000375
Acrylic	0.0000410
Steel	0.00000630

Table 4. Weight of PC Sheet vs. Glass

Thickness, in.	Weight of, PC Sheet, lb/ft²	Weight of Glass, lb/ft²
0.080	0.50	1.02
0.093	0.58	1.20
0.125	0.78	1.60
0.187	1.17	2.40
0.250	1.56	3.20
0.375	2.34	4.80
0.500	3.12	6.40

Table 5. Sound Transmission of PC Sheet vs. Float Glass

	STC Rating	
Thickness, in.	PC Sheet	Float Glass
0.125	25	23
0.187	29	
0.250	31	27
0.375	34	
0.500	34	32
1.000	39	
1.250	42	

Light and Heat Transmission

PC sheet is essentially opaque at all ultraviolet (UV) wavelengths below 385 nm, making it an excellent protective glazing for art objects or display merchandise easily damaged by UV light. Figure 2 shows the percentage of light transmitted at UV, visible, and infrared wavelengths; Table 6 gives the percentage of visible light and heat transmitted through various thicknesses of clear and tinted

Table 6. Light and Heat Transmittance of PC Sheet

	Clear		Gray/Bronze	
	% Values		% Values	
Thickness, in.	Visible Light	Solar Energy	Visible Light	Solar Energy
0.080	88	90	50	60
0.093	87	90	50	60
0.125	86	89	50	60
0.187	84	88	50	60
0.250	82	86	50	60
0.375	79	84	50	60
0.500	75	81	50	60

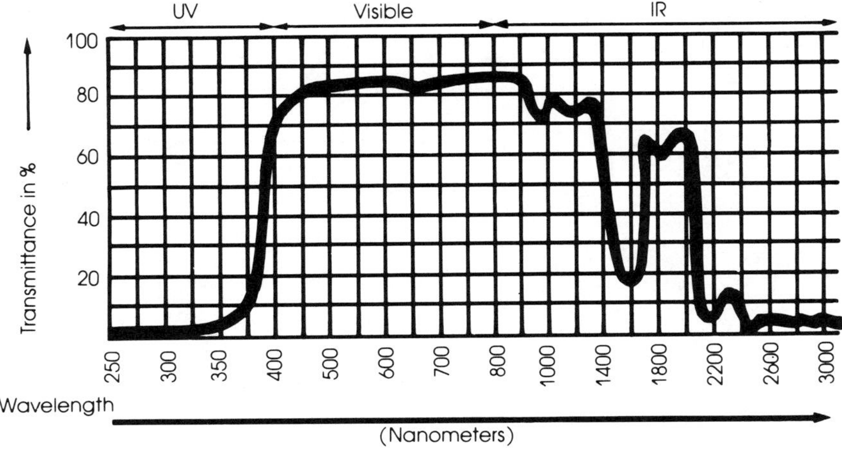

Figure 2. Ultraviolet light transmission of PC sheet.

PC sheet. The sheet provides a clarity that approaches that of glass in the visible range, but simultaneously presents an opaque screen to potentially damaging UV light.

Sizes and Types

PC sheet is available in a wide range of sizes, with standard sheets usually measuring 4 × 8 ft or 6 × 8 ft. PC sheet can easily be cut to size with common power tools. The primary considerations for choosing a specific sheet size are thickness and allowances for special-purpose sheet, such as mar-resistant or bullet-resistant sheet.

Thickness

Recommended guidelines for selecting thicknesses based on the short dimension are shown in the wind-load chart (Fig. 3). These recommendations consider deflection, wind load, and normally available rabbet and channel depths; however, they apply only to vertical glazing. Horizontal or sloped applications require thicker sheets, smaller spans, additional support consideration, or increased rigidity by forming.

PROPERTIES DESIGNED FOR SPECIFIC APPLICATIONS

New grades of PC sheet have been developed with properties designed for specific applications. The following are some of the more common commercially available types.

UV Resistance

PC sheet is available with greater UV resistance and improved weatherability for applications where the sheet will be exposed to intense, direct sunlight, such as in domes, barrel vaults, and covered walkways. Changes in PC sheet's yellowness index are visibly undetectable in freestanding glazing 36 months after installation. Figure 4 shows PC sheet's yellowness index compared to acrylic.

UV-resistant PC sheet is available in sheets as large as 96 × 142 in. and in several thicknesses. Along with clear glazing, the sheet can usually be obtained in tints such as bronze and gray. Custom coloring is also available.

Abrasion Resistance

Special coatings can improve PC sheet's abrasion resistance for flat glazing applications where marring or graffiti might be a problem, such as in schools, storefronts, entranceways, or freestanding shelters. Surface-treated sheet provides excellent chemical and impact resistance, while resisting abrasion at levels approaching glass (Table 7).

Superior Insulation

Thermal insulation can be improved up to 50% over single-layer materials by using a double-walled PC sheet. Designed for use in vertical and sloped glazing, such as skylights, space enclosures, and greenhouses, the sheet is lightweight and easily cold-formed following appropriate

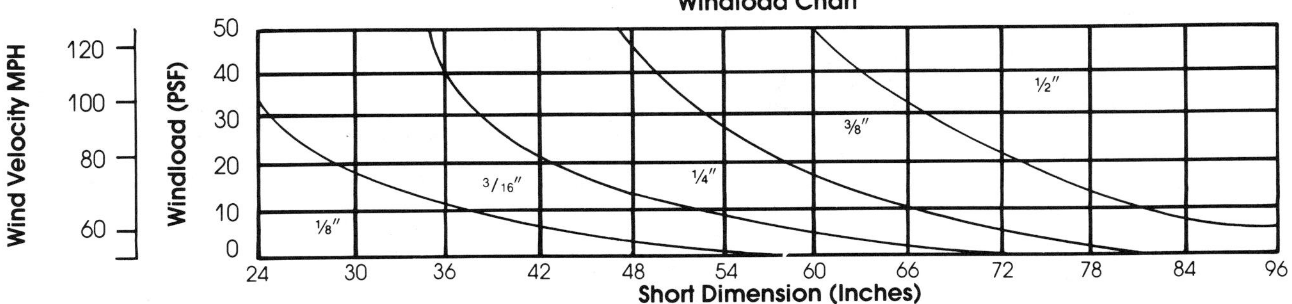

Figure 3. Wind-load chart for PC sheet.

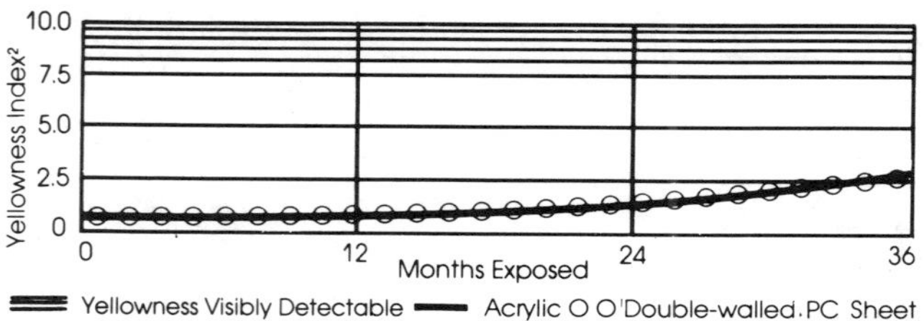

Figure 4. PC sheet yellowness index versus months exposed. Values shown are average ranges from groups of individual samples exposed concurrently at 45°, south-facing. All values are changed from original unweathered samples and do not represent absolute haze, yellowness, or light transmission. ASTM D1925 using a Gardner colorimeter.

Table 7. Abrasion Resistance Comparison Δ% Haze

	Test Method	Uncoated Polycarbonate	Coated PC Sheet	Glass
Taber abrasion 100 cycles	ASTM D1044 Z26.1	15.0	0.8	0.5
Falling silica carbide 1600 g	Z26.1	30.0	5–8	15–20
GE brush abrasion tester	1-hour harsh conditions[a]	30.0	3.0	1.0

[a] Abrasive water mixture of sandy clay screened through 100 mesh screen and continuously applied to brush water.

manufacturer specifications or thermoformed into a variety of shapes. Thickness selection should take into account deflection, wind load (uniform pressure), and standard rabbet and channel depth. Larger, double-walled PC sheet thicknesses will support correspondingly heavier loads at one-sixteenth the weight of a comparable thickness of double-walled glass (Fig. 5).

Protective Laminates

In areas where bullet resistance is needed, such as banks, kiosks, or certain specially designed guard stations, PC sheet laminates offer multishot, no-spall ballistics protection. By varying the number and thickness of layers of PC sheet, acrylic, and laminated glass, a complete family of transparent, protective laminates is available to meet a wide range of requirements. Certain of these products are designed to offer resistance to medium power handguns and to blasts from a 12-gauge shotgun or a .44-Magnum handgun. The extent of bullet resistance for any particular product should be determined from the manufacturer. On the outer layer of these laminates there is a mar-resistant coating for easier cleaning and better weather resistance.

CODE REQUIREMENTS FOR PC SHEET

PC sheet has undergone thorough industry testing to evaluate its performance and adherence to building code and government requirements for plastics used in building and construction applications.

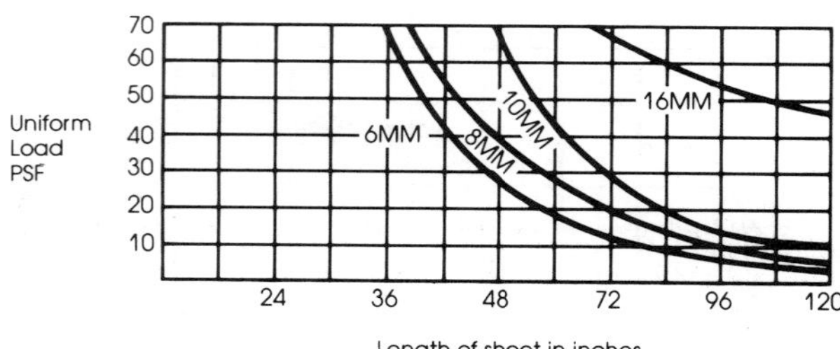

Figure 5. PC double-walled sheet maximum load capabilities, fixed 4-ft width.

Safety Standards Compliance

PC sheet glazing products (0.080-in. thickness minimum) that are properly manufactured will comply with the following requirements: Consumer Product Safety Commission's Safety Standard for Architectural Glazing Materials, 16CFR Part 1201, Category I and Category II; and the American National Standards Institute Standard Za7.1.

Model Building Code Approval

PC sheet is listed by the major Model Building Code organizations in Table 8 as an approved plastics material for light transmitting applications. PC sheet meets the following Model Building Code requirements for light-transmitting applications. (The results of laboratory fire tests reported here may not reflect the fire hazards associated with the use of these building materials.)

ASTM standard D635 measures horizontal burn rate. Plastic materials with an extent of burning of 1 in. or less are classified as CC-1. The standard also defines plastic materials with a burning rate of 2.5 in./min or less as CC-2. Properly manufactured monolithic or single-layer PC sheet has an extent of burning of less than 1 in. when tested according to ASTM D635, and sheet thicknesses of 0.125 in. or greater and double-walled sheet have been classified as CC-2 according to these requirements.

Table 8. PC Sheet Building Code Approval

Organization	Building Code	Classification[a]	Approval Number
BOCA[b]	Basic	Class CC-1 Approved Plastic	76–58
SBCC[c]	Standard	Class CC-1 Approved Plastic	7703-77
ICBO[d]	Uniform	Approved Plastic	3286

[a] This classification applies to light transmitting applications, e.g., glazing, skylights, light diffuser lenses, and sign faces. It does not apply to interior finish applications, such as ceiling tile, wainscoting, or wall panels.
[b] Building Officials and Code Administrators International, Inc.
[c] Southern Building Code Congress International, Inc.
[d] International Congress of Building Officials.

Table 9. Federal Guidelines for PC Sheet[a]

Agency	Applications	Maximum Optical Density
HEW[b]	Interior finish for hospitals and medical facilities	Average of flaming and nonflaming conditions must be less than 450
HUD[c]	Plastic bathroom tub and shower units	Less than 450 under flaming conditions
UMTA/DOT[d]	Combustible materials used in transit systems	Under both flaming and nonflaming conditions: • Less than 100 after 90 sec • Less than 200 after 4 min

[a] Results from small scale flammability tests (e.g., Numerical Flame Spread Ratings) are not intended to reflect hazards presented by this or any other material under actual fire conditions.
[b] U.S. Department of Health, Education and Welfare.
[c] U.S. Department of Housing and Urban Development.
[d] UMTA/DOT is Urban Mass Transit Association, U.S. Department of Transportation.

The typical flame-spread classification of monolithic PC sheet is 10. The rating is calculated only for that time the material remains attached to the test chamber ceiling (ASTM E-84).

Approved materials under model building codes have either a smoke density rating no greater than 450 when tested according to ASTM E-84 (tunnel test), or a smoke density rating no greater than 75 when tested according to ASTM D2843 (XP-2 smoke chamber). In the XP-2 smoke chamber, PC sheet has a typical smoke density of less than 75 under the conditions defined in ASTM D2843.

Approved materials must have a self-ignition temperature of 650°F or greater when tested according to ASTM D1929. The typical self-ignition temperature of PC is greater than 1000°F according to this test. The PC sheet manufacturer should be consulted regarding its actual PC sheet performance in these tests.

Smoke-test Compliance

Several government agencies are adopting the National Bureau of Standards smoke chamber test (NFPA 258) to measure the optical density of smoke evolved under both flaming and nonflaming conditions. PC sheet typically complies with these federal guidelines for maximum optical smoke density listed in Table 9.

USE OF PC SHEET IN CONSTRUCTION AND BUILDING

Cold-Bending PC Sheet

One of the primary advantages of PC sheet in construction is its ability to be cold-formed on site to gentle curves, allowing for easy and economical construction of domes and barrel vaults. PC sheet can be held to radius by bending the material into a curved framing or retention system.

Table 10. Recommended Radii for PC Sheet

Sheet Thickness, in.	Recommended Minimum Radius, in.
0.125	12.5
0.187	18.5
0.250	25.0
0.375	37.5
0.500	50.0

The recommended minimum radius of curvature is 100 times the thickness of the sheet. Radii less than the minimum recommendations in Table 10 may exceed the design stress limitation for PC sheet, resulting in stress crazing or failure.

Installing PC Sheet

PC sheet can be glazed with a minimum of difficulty when proper procedures are followed. When designing with PC sheet, allowance must be made for its thermal expansion and greater flexibility.

The sash where the PC sheet is to be installed is prepared by cleaning the sash surface and priming it, if necessary. The rabbet should be free of burrs. After sash openings have been carefully measured, recommended edge engagement and expansion allowance is determined by size of the sheet and wind load (Fig. 3). The sheet is then cut to the exact size required. Edges should be clean and free of notches. The sheet is glazed with sealants and tapes that have sufficient extensibility to accommodate thermal expansion without loss of adhesion to either frame or sheet.

Cutting PC Sheet

PC sheet can be cut easily and accurately with most power saws to the exact size desired. Circular-blade saws must be of triple-chip design. Failure to use this type of blade can result in uncontrollable chattering. When hand tools are used, the sheet should be clamped to a worktable to avoid undesirable vibration. Protective masking should be left in place to prevent marring.

Glazing with PC sheet should be considered a finishing operation and be scheduled as a final step in the completion of a building. Care should be taken to avoid surface marring during storage, cutting, transporting, and installation. After installation and removal of masking, PC sheet should be protected from paint, plaster, and other splashes by a polyethylene or other covering taped to framing members.

Glazing of Small Lights

PC sheet can be glazed in wood or metal sashes. Figure 6 demonstrates typical details. Nonhardening glazing compounds, including oil-based and acrylic latex caulks, can be used. However, high-grade sealants such as silicone, butyl, or polysulfide are recommended.

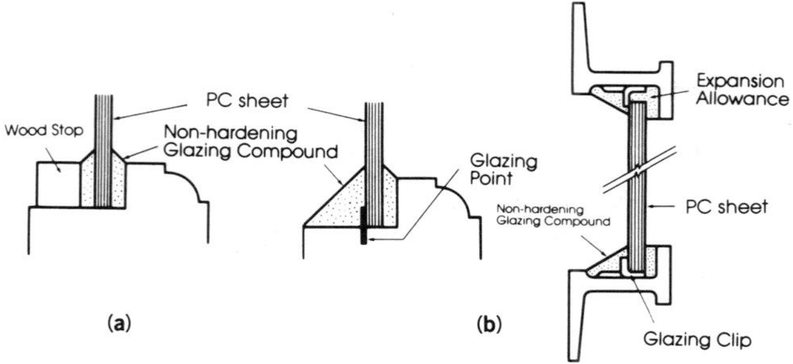

Figure 6. PC glazing in wood or metal sashes. Expansion allowances may be required in actual glazing situations. (**a**) Typical wood sashes; (**b**) Typical metal sashes.

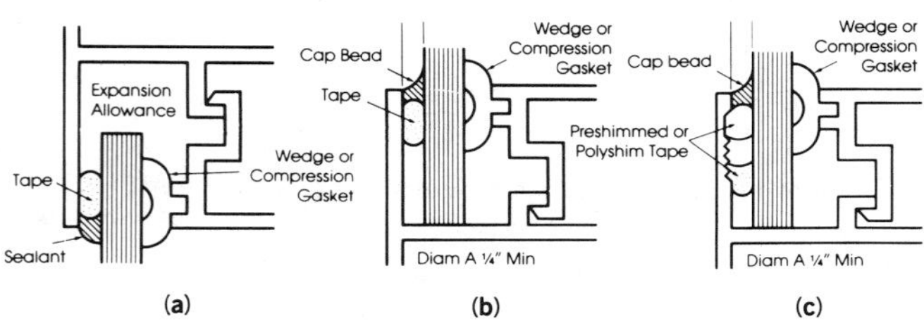

Figure 7. PC exterior glazing of intermediate and large lights. (**a**) Typical head; (**b**) Typical sill; (**c**) Serrated sash.

Glazing Intermediate and Large Lights

For openings of more than 24 × 24 in., Figures 7 and 8 show typical channel-glazed systems that have been successfully used with PC sheet. Only high-grade silicone, polysulfide, or closed-cell poly(vinyl chloride) and fully cured butyl tapes are recommended as sealants.

Dry Glazing

Dry glazing should be considered in applications where sheet expansion may exceed sealant limitations and result in failures. Neoprene or EPDM gasket manufacturers should be contacted about correct use of their products.

Double Glazing

PC sheet can be used effectively in double-glazed window systems, in double-channeled sash units (Fig. 9**a**), or for

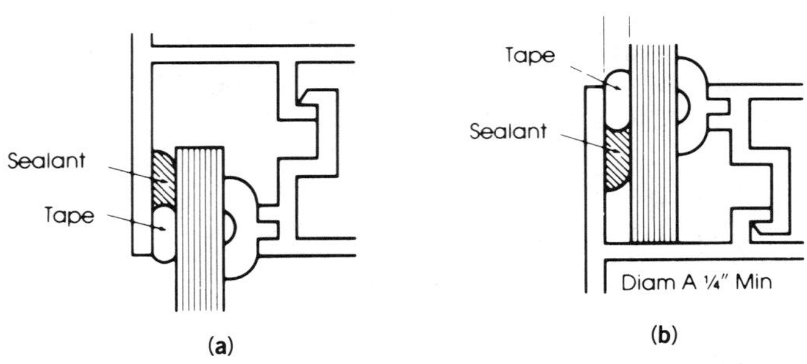

Figure 8. PC interior glazing of intermediate and large lights. (**a**) Typical head; (**b**) Typical sill.

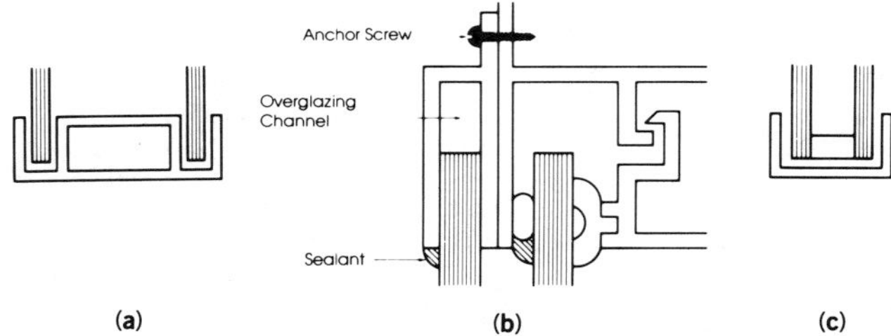

Figure 9. PC double-glazed window systems. (**a**) Double-channeled sash unit; (**b**) Overglazing and backglazing; (**c**) Sealed system.

overglazing and backglazing (Figure 9**b**). When using PC sheet in a double-glazed application, allowance must be made for its greater flexibility and expansion. Adequate separation between the two PC glazing panels will prevent PC sheet from touching during certain temperature and humidity conditions. Glazing of intermediate and large lights may require the application of small spacers between panels to maintain dead air space. When designing sealed systems with PC sheet (Figure 9**c**), certain precautionary measures should be taken to optimize performance. Individual PC manufacturers should be contacted for specific steps.

Double-Walled Sheet

When installing double-walled sheet, it is important to allow for thermal expansion to avoid bowing. Sheet should be mounted with the ribs running vertically, with the bottom edge left unsealed to assist condensed water vapor drainage (Fig. 10).

MAINTENANCE OF PC SHEET

When PC sheet is first installed, glazing compound and masking paper adhesive can be easily removed by applying naphtha or kerosene with a soft cloth, followed immediately with a thorough soap and water cleaning. Razor

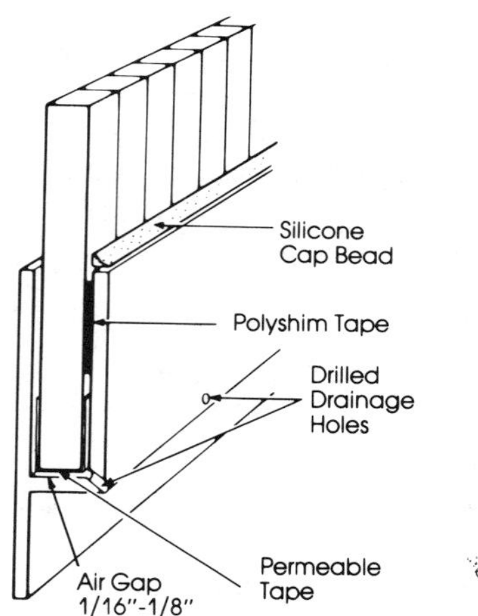

Figure 10. Vertical mounting of PC double-walled sheet.

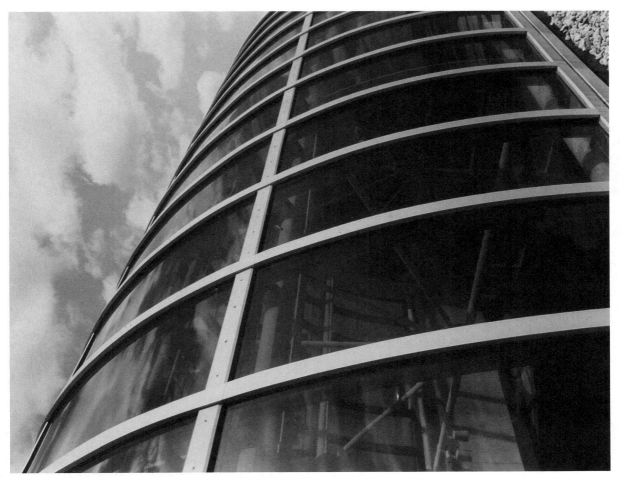

Figure 11. Polycarbonate sheet that has been surface-treated to increase its ultraviolet resistance provides durability, design flexibility, and energy efficiency. The barrel-vaulted roof of the General Electric Plastics Technology Center, Pittsfield, Mass.

Figure 12. Polycarbonate glazing with an ultraviolet surface treatment can be cold-formed on-site or thermoformed into compound shapes. This makes it an ideal material for applications such as barrel-vaulted roofs, skylights, canopies, space enclosures, and covered walkways. Pictured is the vaulted roof at General Electric Company's Technology Center, Pittsfield, Mass.

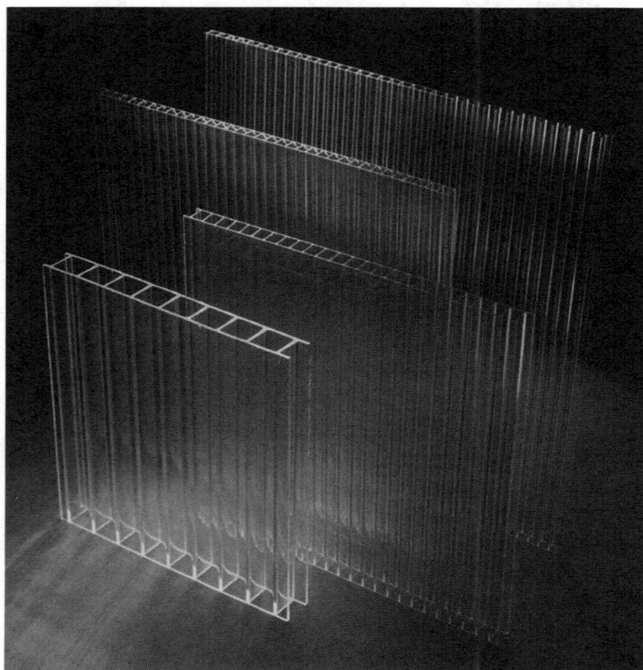

Figure 13. Double- or triple-walled polycarbonate sheet with an ultraviolet-protective outer surface has an inner dead-air space, which makes the sheet an excellent insulator. The lightweight material is easily formed on-site and offers excellent clarity and durability. It is used as primary, overglazing, sloped, and overhead glazing in skylights, greenhouses, and other curved and formed structures.

blades or other sharp instruments, such as a putty knife, should not be used to remove spots. Adherence to regular and proper cleaning procedures is recommended to preserve appearance.

Cleaning

Most common household cleaners are safe to use to clean PC sheet, although a cleaner should be tested on a sample piece. However, abrasive or highly alkaline cleaners, benzene, leaded gasoline, and acetone should not be used on PC sheet.

PC should be washed with mild soap or detergent and lukewarm water, using a clean sponge or soft cloth, and then rinsed well with clean water. It should then be thoroughly dried with a chamois or moist cellulose sponge to prevent water spots. Fresh paint splashes, grease, and smeared glazing compounds can be removed easily before drying by rubbing lightly with a good grade of naphtha, isopropyl alcohol, or butyl cellosolve. Afterward, a warm final wash should be made with mild soap and water.

Scratches

Scratches and minor abrasions can be removed or minimized by using a mild automobile polish, such as paste wax or plastic polish. A test should be made on a sample of the PC sheet before actual use.

EXAMPLES

Figures 11–13 show various uses of polycarbonates in construction.

BIBLIOGRAPHY

General References

R. Montella, *Plastics in Architecture: A Guide to Acrylic and Polycarbonate,* Marcel Dekker, New York, 1985.

"Multiwalled, ribbed polycarbonate panels are being more widely used by the construction industry with improved insulation and impact properties vs. glass," *Modern Plastics International* 36–38 (March 1987).

"New developments lead to wider use of polycarbonate," *Plastics Design Forum,* 52–60 (Feb. 1985).

"Polycarbonate glazing," *Plastics Engineering,* 116 (May 1985).

"Polycarbonate structural sheeting may be a major growth area for engineering thermoplastics in building and construction," *Plastics & Rubber Weekly,* 15–16 (May 22, 1982).

See also GLASS FILMS; GLASS IN CONSTRUCTION; SEALANTS

PETER DALRYMPLE
GE Plastics
Pittsfield, Massachusetts

All tests and comparative figures in this article are based on the use of a trademarked polycarbonate resin product of General Electric Company. Although other PC resins may also meet these requirements, these tests do not necessarily reflect the performance of those materials. The tables and figures in this article are supplied by General Electric Company. General Electric Company does not guarantee that the same results as those described herein will be obtained. Nor does General Electric Company guarantee the effectiveness or safety of any possible or suggested design for articles of manufacture as illustrated herein by any photographs, technical drawings, and the like. Each user of the material or design should make his own tests to determine the suitability of the material or design or both for his own particular use. Statements concerning possible or suggested uses of the materials or designs herein are not to be construed as constituting a license under any General Electric patent covering such use or as a recommendation for use of such materials or designs in the infringement of any patent.

POLYESTERS

Polyesters possess high impact strength, excellent electrical properties, durability, and high chemical resistance, and are suitable in a wide variety of applications. They are most commonly processed by injection molding, although other processing techniques can and are being used. In addition, polyesters can be reinforced with glass and mineral fillers.

Polyester resins find a wide variety of applications in such areas as industrial products, construction, automotive, packaging, and electrical/electronic components. Their use is also expanding into such areas as lawn and garden and material-handling industries.

TYPES OF POLYESTERS

Belonging to the crystalline family of plastics, polyesters are found in a variety of forms. Generally, they can be divided into two categories: the first is thermoset and aromatic, and the second is thermoplastic.

Thermoset

Thermoset polyesters, or unsaturated polyesters, were developed for military use during World War II. They are formed from the condensation esterification of dicarboxylic acids and dihydric alcohols capable of cross-linking with vinyl monomers to form thermoset copolymers. Today they are used in transportation, electrical, and anticorrosion applications.

Thermoplastic

Thermoplastic polyesters were developed primarily for film and packaging applications, and in the early 1970s they became important new members of the family of engineering thermoplastics as molding and extrusion compounds. Thermoplastic polyesters are distinct from thermoset polyesters in both chemical structure and properties. Formed by the polycondensation of 1,4 butanediol, or ethanediol, and dimethylterephthalate, thermoplastic polyesters are divided into two types: polybutylene terephthalate (PBT) and polyethylene terephthalate (PET) (Fig. 1).

PBT is a semicrystalline polymer with a broad range of performance characteristics that include low moisture absorption, chemical resistance, lubricity, wear resistance, stable electrical insulating properties, and high heat resistance. PBT is one of the toughest and most versatile of all engineering thermoplastics. With low melt viscosity and good flow properties that provide rapid cycle times, PBT is easily processed by injection molding, fiber and nonfilament spinning, profile extrusion, film and sheet extrusion, and nonwoven fabric formation.

PET is a condensation polymer produced through a continuous melt-phase polymerization process, followed by a solid-state process that provides a different molecular weight and yields a highly crystalline polymer. The most abundant applications of PET resins are as beverage containers and as fibers used in textiles and carpeting.

Thermoplastic polyesters are offered in both reinforced and unreinforced grades. Thirty percent glass-fiber reinforcement is the most commonly used, with ranges from 7 to 45% filler also available. Mineral and mineral–glass reinforcement can offer superior electrical performance, improved flatness and stiffness, and excellent dimensional stability.

Alloys, Blends, and Compounds. Thermoplastic polyesters can be alloyed with 10–30% nylon to facilitate glass reinforcement. In addition, moisture absorption can be reduced while mechanical properties and processability are improved when the resins are alloyed with 15–25% low-density polyethylene (LDPE).

Adding graft-containing butadiene polymers as well as thermoplastic urethane or copolyester elastomers reduces the notch sensitivity of PBT. PET–acrylic blends exhibit faster crystallization rates and improved dimensional stability. Enhanced surface gloss can be achieved when PET is blended with PBT.

Thermoplastic Elastomers. Copolyesters are a major group of thermoplastic elastomers (TPE), which have many of the properties of rubber, but do not require curing and vulcanizing. Instead, being thermoplastics, they can be easily processed by injection molding and extrusion.

Copolyester synthesis uses more than one glycol and/or more than one dibasic acid. The copolyester chain is less regular than the monopolyester chain, thus impeding crystallization tendencies. Prepared by dimethyl terephthalate, polytetramethylene, ether glycol, and 1,4 butane-

DIMETHYL TEREPHTHALATE (DMT)

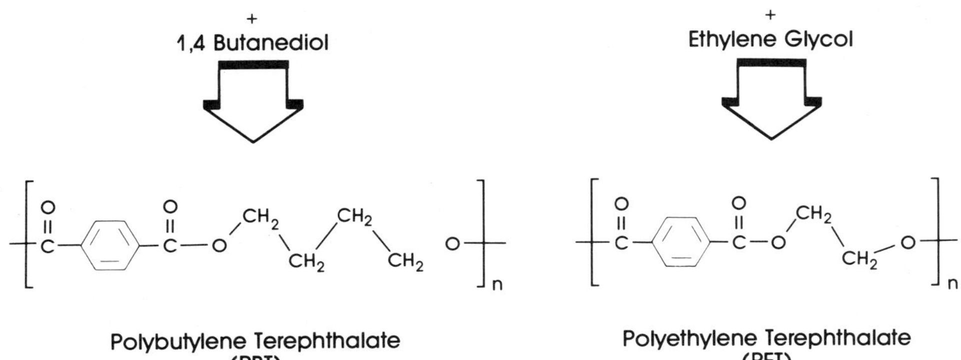

Figure 1. The structures of PBT and PET. Courtesy of General Electric Plastics.

diol, and shaped by sandwiching together hard and soft segments, copolyester thermoplastic elastomers have good chemical resistance, flame retardancy, weatherability, cold temperature flexibility, and cut-growth resistance.

Properties. Thermoplastic polyesters are strong and lightweight and exhibit stable properties over a wide range of temperatures and humidity conditions. Tensile properties of PBT range from 7500 psi for unreinforced grades to 25,000 psi for glass-reinforced grades. The corresponding flexural modulus values range from 340,000 to 1.5 × 10^6 psi. Notched Izod impact strength ranges from 1 ft-lb/in. to 17 ft-lb/in. (Table 1).

Table 1. Selected Mechanical Properties of Unmodified and Glass-filled Thermoplastic Polyesters and the Competition[a]

Material	Flexural Modulus at 73°F, psi ASTM D790	Impact Strength Notched Izod at 73°F, ft-lb/in. Notch ASTM D256
Unmodified Thermoplastic Polyester Grades vs. Competition		
PBT	340,000	1.0
PBT alloy	275,000	16.0
PBT alloy	240,000	16.0 (15 at −30°C)
PBT alloy	290,000	15.0
Acetal homopolymer	380,000–430,000	1.3–2.3
Acetal copolymer	375,000	1.4
Nylon 6/6	285,000–438,000[b]	0.7–4.3[b]
Nylon 6/6	160,000–258,000[c]	1.2–4.5[c]
Nylon 6/12	295,000[b]	1[b]
Nylon 6/12	180,000[a]	1.4[c]
Nylon 6	150,000[b]	1.5[b]
Nylon 6	108,000[c]	>1.5[c]
Glass-reinforced Thermoplastic Polyester Grades vs. Competition		
PBT alloy —10% GR	400,000	3.5
PBT alloy —30% GR	750,000	3.2
PBT —30% GR	1,000,000	2.5
Impact-modified PBT[e]	1,440,000	3.5
Acetal homopolymer	730,000	0.8
Acetal copolymer	1,100,000	1.8
Nylon 6/6 —33% GR	1,300,000[b]	2.0[b]
Nylon 6/6 —33% GR	900,000[c]	2.5[c]
Nylon 6/6 —33% GR	600,000[d]	4.0[d]
Nylon 6/12 —33% GR	1,200,000[b]	2.4[b]
Nylon 6/12 —33% GR	900,000[c]	2.5[c]
Nylon 6/12 —33% GR	800,000[d]	3.0[d]

[a] Courtesy of General Electric Plastics.
[b] DAM.
[c] 50% relative humidity.
[d] 100% relative humidity.
[e] Developmental grade.

Thermoplastic polyesters exhibit low water absorption. For instance, at 78°F, grades absorb less than 0.08% in 24 hours, and 0.38% at equilibrium. PBT polyesters absorb much less moisture than do nylons (Fig. 2).

Polyester's heat distortion temperatures (of up to 310°F at 66 psi; of up to 270°F at 264 psi for unreinforced grades), excellent chemical resistance, and low water absorption all provide long-term dimensional stability, more than 30 times better than some nylons (Fig. 3). This low deformation continues when the resin is conditioned to full moisture absorption. Both reinforced and unreinforced PBT polyesters are stable under load at elevated temperatures and for long periods of time (Fig. 4). Polyester's intrinsic lubricity and smooth surface offer both very low coefficients of friction and good abrasion resistance (Fig. 5).

A key characteristic of PBT polyesters is their outstanding chemical resistance to a variety of chemicals, including aliphatic hydrocarbons, gasoline, oils and fats, alcohols, glycols, ethers, high molecular weight esters and ketones, dilute acids and bases, detergents, and most aqueous salt solutions.

Thermoplastic polyesters also demonstrate stable property retention under ultraviolet exposure, although the resins show some discoloration when subjected to UV light. Black-pigmented, UV-stabilized grades offer the best resistance to outdoor weathering. Other colors, containing weatherability-enhancing UV-stabilizers, are also available.

Thermoplastic polyesters have outstanding electrical properties. Compared with most other engineering materials, PBT polyesters exhibit higher dielectric strength and insulating resistance, superior arc resistance, consistent dielectric constant, and low dissipation factors.

Processing, Finishing, and Assembly. Thermoplastic polyesters can be injection molded, extruded, blow molded, thermoformed, rotomolded, and pultruded. In injection molding, PBT can be processed with little property change over a broad range of mold temperatures (100–200°F). A tool temperature of 150°F usually produces optimum results. A low melt viscosity at normal processing temperatures (450–500°F) permits easy filling of long, thin-walled parts in molding. Polyesters have a number of processing advantages, including fast cycle times, excellent flow, easy release from the mold, a smooth surface out of the mold, and low tool/machine wear. These advantages combine to make thermoplastic polyester a relatively easy material with which to work.

A thermoplastic polyester part can easily be machined and assembled using a variety of techniques. These include self-tapping screws; molded inserts; ultrasonic insertion and staking; heat staking; spot, ultrasonic, and spin welding; adhesive bonding; and snap fits. Spray painting is the most widely used finishing technique; drying can be

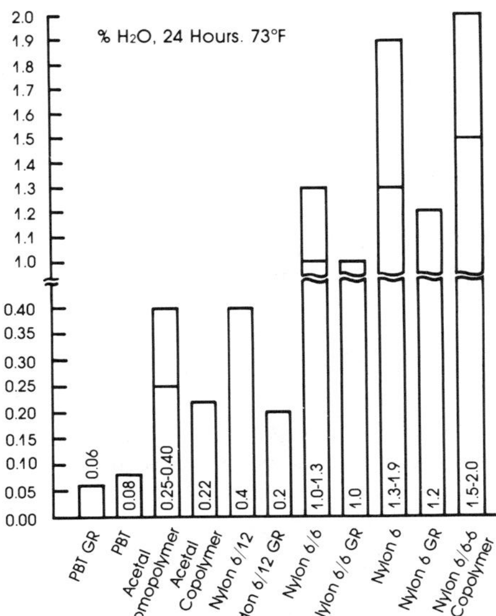

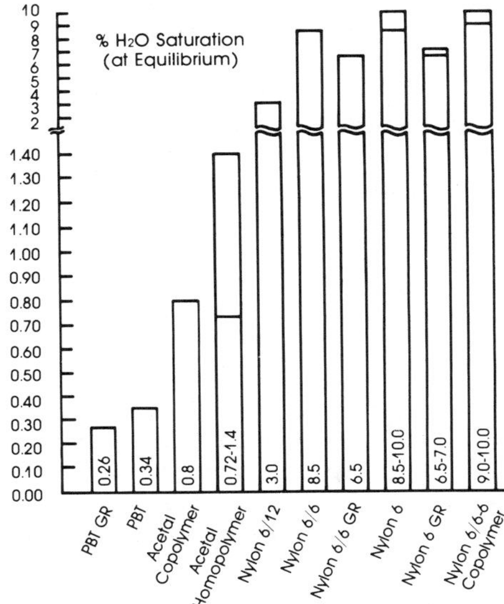

Figure 2. Water absorption at 24 hours and at equilibrium for unmodified and glass-filled thermoplastic polyesters and their competition. Data from ASTM 570. Courtesy of General Electric Plastics.

achieved by flash, air, or baking methods. Polyester can also be painted by offset and screen processes.

Applications. Because of their wide range of performance capabilities, thermoplastic polyesters are well suited for a variety of uses, including industrial/construction, housewares, parts for outdoor usage, and automotive and electrical applications.

In a construction and industrial environment, PBT is typically found in pipes, fittings and conduits, channels, roofs, plumbing, pump impellers, sprinkler bodies and levers, pipe caps, pressure vessel housings, roof anchors, cable protection, geotextiles, valve components, and heavy-duty conveyor system components such as chain links, dunnages, hangers, and gear wheels.

Uses of thermoplastic polyesters in construction include

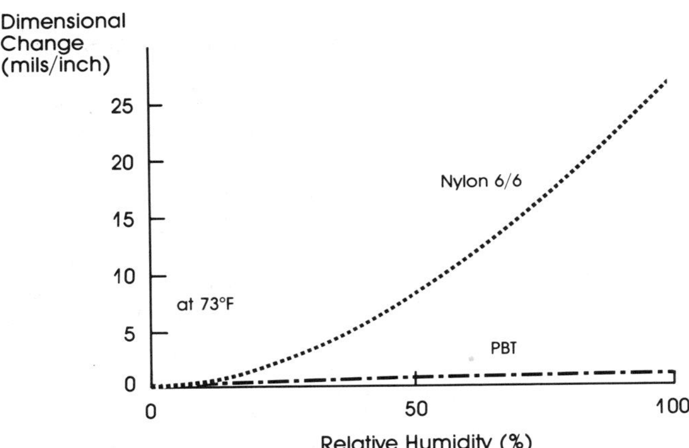

Figure 3. Dimensional stability of thermoplastic polyester versus nylon 6/6. Courtesy of General Electric Plastics.

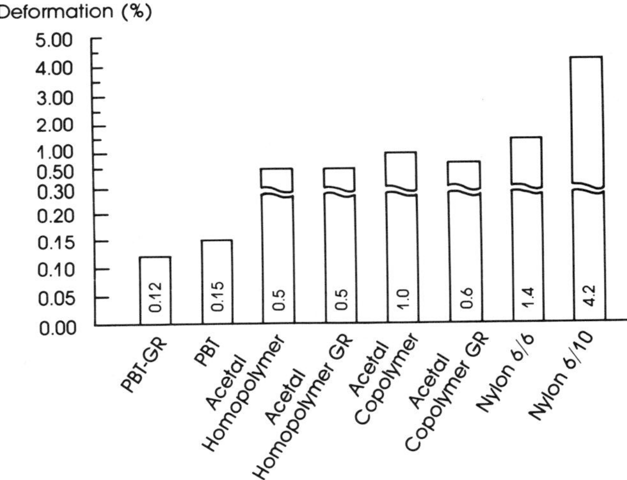

Figure 4. Deformation under load of thermoplastic polyesters versus their competition at 122°F, 2000 psi. Data from ASTM D621. Courtesy of General Electric Plastics.

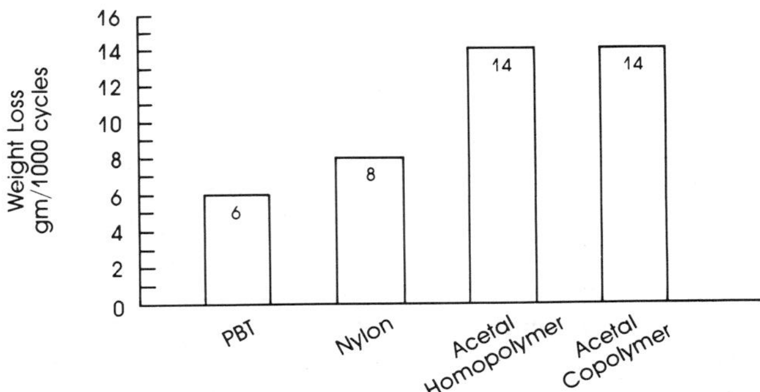

Figure 5. Taber abrasion of thermoplastic polyester versus its competition, 1000 gm load. Data from ASTM D1044. Courtesy of General Electric Plastics.

removable insulating window replacements such as corner keys, side latches, and latch release buttons on prime window master frames. The strength of these resins enables them to withstand the heavy stress associated with the corner keys that anchor the side window panels and top/bottom frames. Long-term dimensional stability helps the resins to hold close tolerances during molding and to maintain critical dimensions in order to prevent sticking. Their chemical resistance makes them impervious to alcohol and solvent-based window cleaners. These materials can also provide cost savings over nylon or acetal.

Thermoplastic polyester is replacing cast bronze, iron, and nylon in swimming pool parts such as pump brackets, volutes, and suction pots. Polyester offers chemical resistance that withstands attack from petroleum-based compounds used to seal pipes to pumps, and the resin's low water absorption provides long-term dimensional stability and low deformation under load. Furthermore, when properly designed and molded, the resin's rigidity resists the tremendous force of pumped water. Its ductility also enables it to withstand cracking when threaded pipes are tightened down.

Thermoplastic elastomers make their appearance in liner containments that prevent leakage from underground gasoline storage tanks. These containments are fabricated by extruding the elastomer in 0.03-in. thick sheets. Combining excellent chemical, abrasion, and puncture resistance with toughness, durability, and flexibility over a wide temperature range, thermoplastic elastomers are very well suited for this type of application.

Roof anchors made of PBT polyesters are being used to secure sheets of EDP without perforations, enabling an improved seal to be obtained. The resin's creep resistance, UV weatherability, low moisture absorption, and good property stability over a wide range of temperatures make it an excellent choice in such an application.

Both in and out of the house, PBT is finding use in fans, gears, furniture, frame parts and brackets, appliance housings and handles, hair-dryer nozzles, and food-processor blades. It is also used for internal support parts such as motor mounts; chair seats and backs; frying pans; toaster ovens; lawn-mower chutes; drill housings; chainsaw cases and hardware; lawn, farm, and irrigation pumps; chain links for sewage treatment plants; pipes; hangers; compressors and impellers; motor insulation and end caps; cooling fans; gears; carburetor parts; and frame components.

Many professional power-drill housings are made of thermoplastic polyester because the resin provides toughness for screw/insert retention to hold all internal parts in place. This material also has sufficient heat resistance to withstand motor operating temperatures of 250°F, and it provides necessary chemical resistance to internal lubricants and solvents commonly encountered in professional environments. Use of thermoplastic polyester in such applications eliminates the boiling operations necessary to increase the impact resistance of nylons. Also, molded-in color makes secondary painting unnecessary. Thermoplastic polyester also has an Underwriters Laboratory (UL) 94 HB listing and provides sufficient impact resistance to meet the UL drop test. This listing is not intended to reflect hazards presented by this or any other material under actual fire conditions.

Many steam irons are now being made with thermoplastic polyester because the material's heat resistance (UL rated to 140°C) makes for cool-to-the-touch housings. Additionally, the material's high impact strength allows for thinner wall designs that reduce weight in the appliance.

Automotive applications for thermoplastic polyesters include transmission components, control switches, motor end caps, window and door hardware, speedometer frames, bumpers, windshield-wiper blades, exterior body components, connectors, and other under-the-hood parts.

In electrical/electronic applications, thermoplastic polyesters are used in clampable light-fixture sockets, offering a continuous-use temperature rating of 150°C in sockets, permitting the use of bulbs of up to 75 W. The dielectric strength of thermoplastic polyester reduces shock hazard. Its ductility allows the use of snap-fit designs for easier assembly, reduced labor costs, and increased functionality. Polyester's excellent dimensional stability, low moisture absorption, and heat deflection help maintain a tight fit for bulbs in these sockets at typical temperature and humidity levels.

Because thermoplastic polyester cycles fast and can be designed in thin-walled constructions, and because of its excellent electrical properties, photoelectric-cell receptacles can be made more inexpensively and efficiently. The resin's ease of processing reduces scrap loss and eliminates secondary operations.

Finally, thermoplastic polyester is used in ballast housings because of its heat resistance (for thermoset potting operations), its chemical and creep resistance, and its stable electrical properties.

The durability, high impact strength, chemical resistance, and the excellent electrical properties of thermoplastic polyesters ensure their use in an increasingly wide variety of demanding applications at home as well as in construction and industrial settings.

BIBLIOGRAPHY

General References

Modern Plastics Encyclopedia, McGraw–Hill, New York, 1985–1986.

Material Handling: VALOX Engineering Thermoplastics; XENOY Thermoplastic Alloys; LOMOD Engineering Elastomers, GE Plastics, Pittsfield, Mass.

Plastics Properties Guide, GE Plastics, Pittsfield, Mass.

VALOX Resin Design Guide, GE Plastics, Pittsfield, Mass.

See also Acrylics; Amino Resins; Epoxy Resins; Fluoropolymers; Foamed Plastics; Phenolic Resins; Plastics; Polyamides (Nylon); Silicones; Styrene Resins

Blair Anthony
Eric Balinski
GE Plastics
Pittsfield, Massachusetts